Community Sourcebook
of
County Demographics

19th Edition

2007

ESRI

TABLE OF CONTENTS

Summary Data Section

County Maps

Introduction

ESRI provides customer and market intelligence solutions to help businesses, government agencies, and nonprofit organizations with

- Customer profiling and segmentation analysis
- Site evaluation and selection
- Market evaluation and selection
- Custom target analysis
- Direct mail campaign implementation
- Media planning
- Merchandise mix analysis
- Target marketing
- Sales forecasting

By combining demographics, consumer spending pattern intelligence, and lifestyle segmentation with innovative technology, ESRI empowers you to make better business decisions.

With annual sales of more than $660 million, ESRI has been the world leader in the geographic information system (GIS) software industry for more than 30 years. As the leader in GIS technology, ESRI offers innovative solutions that will help you create, visualize, analyze, and present information better and more clearly. Working with location information, ESRI's GIS software and solutions give you the power to solve problems you encounter every day. Organizations around the world, as well as local, state, and federal government agencies, are using ESRI GIS software to make smart and timely decisions. ESRI provides powerful GIS solutions to more than 300,000 clients in more than 200 countries. In fact, ESRI is leading the industry in providing mapping technology that meets today's global needs. ESRI offers GIS solutions to help you unlock the spatial component of your valuable data and see your organization's information from a new perspective. www.esri.com.

For more information about
ESRI's products, services, and solutions, visit www.esri.com.

ESRI
380 New York Street
Redlands, California 92373

Features of the 19th Edition

Community Sourcebook of County Demographics contains the most accurate demographic information based on ESRI's release of the 2007 updates and 2012 forecasts of key population and income data. Updated variables for population, households, families, income, race, age and spending potential for a wide variety of products and services are included in this reference tool. *Community Sourcebook of County Demographics* includes:

CBSA (Core Based Statistical Area) – the new metropolitan area definitions from the Office of Management and Budget (OMB).

U.S. County Information – more than 70 demographic variables are included in each U.S. county profile. CBSA and Designated Market Area (DMA) codes for each county are listed.

Profile Sections - demographic variables are grouped by section into profiles for Population Change, Population Composition, Households, Income and Spending Potential. Updated demographics include population, age, race, Hispanic origin, household type and household income.

Business Data - the predominant industry by county is listed in the Business Data section. This section also contains information about the total number of businesses and the total employment in each county.

Summaries - the state and national summaries provide a quick comparison of a county to state and national information.

Demographic Update Methodology - current data methodology statements explain how the population and income data are forecast from the Census 2000 base.

Explanation of Variables - definitions of the demographic variables and key terms used in the Sourcebook are included.

County Maps – individual state maps delineating county and CBSA boundaries are included as reference.

Complementary sourcebook products include the 21st edition of *Community Sourcebook of ZIP Code Demographics* and the Community Sourcebook • America with ArcReader™ CD. Bound in a handsome soft cover, the *Community Sourcebook of ZIP Code Demographics* includes 2007 demographic updates and 2012 forecasts; information about all U.S. residential ZIP Codes; business data; data from ESRI's segmentation system, Community Tapestry™; spending data; and more. Community Sourcebook • America with ArcReader contains all the data from the ZIP Code and county sourcebooks with our proprietary query, sort and report software and the ArcReader map display software.

For more information about the sourcebook products, please visit www.esri.com/sourcebooks. If you would like to speak with an account representative, please call 800-292-2224.

ESRI

Update Methodology: 2007/2012

What's Hot

If you want to follow the latest trends, find the trendsetters. To "follow the money", you may opt for areas with either the highest household income or the most rapidly growing income. To find both high income and rapid growth in income, check out these areas:

Metropolitan Statistical Area	2007 Median Household Income	2000-07 Change: Median HH Income
Bridgeport-Stamford-Norwalk, CT	$84,800	31%
Boston-Cambridge-Quincy, MA-NH	$73,000	34%
Minneapolis-St. Paul-Bloomington, MN-WI	$71,400	32%
Washington-Arlington-Alexandria, DC-VA-MD-WV	$80,100	27%
Denver-Aurora, CO	$67,500	31%

Each of these metropolitan areas, except for Bridgeport-Stamford-Norwalk, CT, has more than three million residents.[1] If you prefer to review high income in a smaller residential area, look at a micropolitan statistical area such as Los Alamos, NM that has a median income of $101,200 in 2007, up 30 percent since 2000, or a high-income county such as:

County/Metropolitan Statistical Area	2007 Median Household Income	2000-07 Change: Median HH Income
Douglas County, CO Denver-Aurora, CO	$111,300	36%
Loudoun County, VA Washington-Arlington-Alexandria, DC-VA-MD-WV	$108,100	35%
Fairfax County, VA Washington-Arlington-Alexandria, DC-VA-MD-WV	$104,500	30%
Hunterdon County, NJ New York-Northern New Jersey-Long Island, NY-NJ-PA	$103,800	31%
Somerset County, NJ New York-Northern New Jersey-Long Island, NY-NJ-PA	$100,300	31%

"To keep up with the Joneses", you want to find the areas with the best housing. Using median home value as the yardstick, a median of $400,000 or more and double-digit appreciation every year since 2000 qualifies the country's top metropolitan areas found primarily in California or Hawaii. Geographic exceptions to this pattern are the Metropolitan Statistical Areas (MSA) of New York-Northern New Jersey-Long Island, NY-NJ-PA; and Washington-Arlington-Alexandria, DC-VA-MD-WV.

Requirements at the county level are more stringent— a median home value of $600,000 or more is necessary to qualify to rank

[1] The Bridgeport-Stamford-Norwalk, CT Metropolitan Statistical Area has a 2007 population of 918,315.

among the best county markets. Double-digit appreciation in home value, 2000-2007, is typical, but not universal. The top counties are also common in California and Hawaii; notable exceptions are in counties that specialize in seasonal attractions such as Nantucket and Dukes (Martha's Vineyard) in Massachusetts and Pitkin in Colorado, better known as the site of Aspen.

Not interested in tracking the money or keeping up with the Joneses? You can simply "go with the flow" by following the population movement to the South and West. There are few changes in the list of hot spots in 2007. The fastest-growing metropolitan areas are in Florida and the Southwest. The fastest-growing counties still represent the suburban sprawl of growing metropolitan areas—Flagler County, Florida; Loudoun County, Virginia (Washington metropolitan area); Kendall County, Illinois (Chicago metropolitan area); Rockwall County, Texas (Dallas metropolitan area); Douglas County, Colorado (Denver metropolitan area); plus several counties in the Atlanta, Georgia metropolitan area.

Sustained population growth in two micropolitan areas revised their classification to *metropolitan* areas this year, Palm Coast, Florida (Flagler County) and Lake Havasu City-Kingman, Arizona (Mohave County). However, without the economic draw of a metropolitan central city, most micropolitan areas do not grow as quickly as metropolitan centers. Counties that are neither metropolitan nor micropolitan are least likely to experience rapid population growth and are most likely to lose population.

2000-07 Annual Rate	Metropolitan Counties	Micropolitan Counties	Nonmetropolitan Counties
High Growth: ≥ 2%	25%	6%	3%
Moderate Growth: 1 – 2%	29%	19%	10%
Minimal Growth: < 1%	36%	48%	44%
Loss	10%	27%	43%
Total Counties	1,092	692	1,357
Average Annual Rate	1.4%	0.6%	0.2%

Small, subcounty areas are the exception to this pattern. Because they represent a fraction of a county's population, subcounty areas can experience trends that are diametrically different from population change at the county level. For example, the population of Washington, D.C. has increased by only 3.4 percent since 2000, but Washington ZIP Code 20004 has grown by 80 percent. Although ZIP Codes can pose a challenge to time series' analysis due to administrative changes by the U.S. Postal Service in their territory, ZIP Codes remain popular geographic areas for subcounty analysis. The average annual rate of change in populated ZIP Codes from 2000 through 2007 is 1.2 percent—comparable to metropolitan counties.

ESRI's 2007 demographic data updates reflect current events such as rising inflation or interest rates and regional distinctions like the availability of jobs or affordable housing. The housing market remains central in the discussion of current trends. In 2006, the housing market was slowing, after more than a decade of upsurge.

The appreciation of home value was decelerating in most markets, and sales of existing homes were declining. Today's U.S. housing market faces various challenges. Sixty-eight percent of U.S. householders own their homes in 2007, but this represents a leveling in the rate of homeownership, which started to climb in the mid-1990s. Inventories of new and existing homes have increased; sellers are lowering their asking prices, receiving fewer offers, and experiencing longer selling periods. Home builders are reducing sales forecasts, cutting back on staff, offering buyer incentives, and experiencing rising cancellation rates. Home prices are actually declining in some markets, and new home sales are down. Existing home sales dropped 8.4 percent in March 2007, which is the largest monthly drop since 1989, according to the National Association of Realtors.[2]

What's happening? Demographics played a key role in shaping the housing market boom that began in the mid-1990s. During that period the Baby Boomers, born between 1946 and 1964, reached their peak earning years, with many in their thirties and forties. At that stage in their lives, they became first-time homebuyers or traded up to meet their changing housing needs. This contributed to a surge in housing demand that boosted the housing market.[3] Demographic change, including immigration and population growth, was not the only factor behind increasing demand. The transitory surge in demand can also be attributed to the Federal Reserve, mortgage lenders, and Wall Street investment firms.

The Fed's easy money stance contributed to the demand growth. In early 2001, the Fed began its series of rate cuts when it reduced its short-term target from 6.5 to 6 percent. The cuts continued through mid-2003 when rates plummeted to one percent. The Fed finally reversed its policy in mid-2004. Surprisingly, a Federal Reserve district bank president conceded that bad preliminary data on inflation led the bank's committee members to reduce short-term rates too low for far too long.[4] As mortgage rates fell to historic lows, lenders introduced creative mortgages and loosened credit lending standards, which benefited borrowers in the subprime market, but fueled speculative behavior. Finally, Wall Street investment firms saw an opportunity for high returns by extending credit to subprime mortgage lenders to distribute to borrowers with the greatest credit risk. All of these factors unleashed the demand for housing.

Although more householders could afford to buy homes, mortgage payments on adjustable rate loans were poised to increase. When monetary policy reversed course and the Fed began to raise short-term rates, teaser rates on risky loans increased and strained many household budgets. Borrowers who were unable to refinance into more conventional mortgages were left with few alternatives. Investment properties flooded the resale market, placing additional downward pressure on prices and eroding equity. The result has been rising delinquencies, defaults, and foreclosures. The Fed believed that defaults would not spread to the broader segment of borrowers. But it is becoming evident that borrowers who fall in the middle between subprime and prime mortgages, called "Alt-A," are starting to succumb to the same problems as subprime borrowers.

That explains how we got to this point. Now what? Demographic change continues to affect demand. Both the Baby Boomers and Generation Y can have a significant impact on the housing market in the next decade. As the Baby Boomers enter their retirement years, their housing needs are changing. Some will downsize to smaller homes with less maintenance; while others will seek second homes or vacation homes. The Generation Y cohorts, born between 1978 and 1997, are now forming new households or entering adulthood. In 2007, the median income for households headed by 25-29 year-olds is $46,600; the median income for householders younger than 25 years old is $29,800. While still in their twenties and with home prices still high, Generation Y is an important factor in the rental housing market. But as they enter their thirties in the next few years, they will be potential homebuyers.

The demand for affordable housing has not changed. In fact, housing affordability remains a key issue, particularly in large metropolitan areas such as Los Angeles or San Francisco, where median home values are more than nine times median household incomes. However, subprime mortgages with adjustable interest rates were not the best response. If the mortgage industry, or Congress, tightens credit lending practices, the market will certainly experience a drop in demand that can prolong or worsen the slump in the short term. In the long run, reducing the volume of subprime mortgages can also restore the market by bringing supply and demand back to a sustainable balance.

Because a market correction appears inevitable, what is the effect on the economy? Some analysts estimated the impact the housing contraction had on gross domestic product (GDP) growth was approximately one percentage point during the last half of 2006.[5] Other pressures such as recent productivity trends may indicate higher inflation in the future. Labor productivity, which measures the output per hour worked, has begun to weaken, which can elevate prices for goods and services. GDP is expected to grow, but at a slower pace than in 2006, and employment continues to expand. A strong labor force may serve as one explanation for the lower productivity rates. As the business cycle expansion matures and technological gains dissipate, firms may find it necessary to increase labor to expand output.

Inflation, as measured by the core personal consumption expenditure index, has risen above the Fed's upper range. Meanwhile, it has held short-term interest rates steady at 5.25 percent since mid-2006 and assumed a cautious stance on future policy adjustments. For now, the Fed believes the overall economy will exhibit "moderate growth" in 2007.

What's New in 2007
ESRI's 2007/2012 demographic data updates include more new developments uncovered by the innovative combination of spatial and demographic analysis that ESRI introduced in 2006. Collectively known as Address-Based Allocation, the techniques are designed to capture change in the distribution of the household population. To date, these techniques have uncovered not only changes in the settlement of established neighborhoods, but also new housing in previously unpopulated areas. This year, ESRI could also apply these new methods to the Gulf Coast communities impacted by the 2005 hurricane season.

Gauging the effects of Hurricanes Katrina/Rita/Wilma was complicated in 2006 by the lack of information from ESRI's usual data sources. Because the situation was "too fluid" in the impacted areas, databases that are normally updated continually were not revised right away to incorporate the loss of population and businesses. Measuring the demographic and economic consequences in 2006 proved to be a singular challenge that required the development of new methods.[6] Building from this work and incorporating data released later in 2006, ESRI was able

[2] Haggerty, James R., "House Prices Slide as Property Glut Grows", *The Wall Street Journal,* April 25, 2007, Page D1, http://online.wsj.com/article/SB117745915366081228.html
[3] Dowell Myers and Lonnie Vidaurri's article, "Real Demographics of Housing Demand in the United States," *The Lusk Review,* 1996, pp 55-61, provides a detailed discussion on how the size of an age cohort affects housing demand.
[4] Ip, Greg, "Fed Official Says Bad Data Helped Fuel Rate Cuts, Housing Speculation". *The Wall Street Journal.* November 3, 2006, Page A6.

[5] Wheeler, David C. "Housing Slump Could Lean Heavily on Economy". *The Regional Economist,* April 2007.
[6] The data sources, assumptions, and methods used to estimate the change along the Gulf Coast in 2006 are provided in a separate ESRI white paper, *Gulf Coast Update Methodology,* which is available from http://www.esri.com/data/community_data/demographic/methodology.html.

to integrate past and current changes in the distribution and characteristics of the population along the Gulf Coast.

Geography Changes
Change is inevitable with any geographic area—political or statistical. Identifying the changes in the areas for which data are tabulated and reported is critical to the analysis of trends. In the past year, there have been minor changes to metropolitan areas by the Office of Management and Budget, boundary revisions for Designated Market Areas (DMAs) by Nielsen Media Research, and changes to the boundaries of Congressional Districts in Georgia and Texas—in addition to the usual adjustment of ZIP Codes by the U.S. Postal Service.

Metropolitan changes include the latest revisions to Core Based Statistical Areas (CBSAs), released in January 2007. Changes include one new Micropolitan Statistical Area: Fredericksburg, Texas (Gillespie County) and two revisions from micropolitan to metropolitan areas: Palm Coast, Florida (Flagler County), and Lake Havasu City-Kingman, Arizona (Mohave County). There are now 939 Core Based Statistical Areas, 363 metropolitan areas, and 576 micropolitan areas.

DMAs represent the 2006-2007 markets defined by Nielsen Media Research. Most DMAs correspond to whole counties, but there are a few exceptions where counties are split into different DMAs. There are no code or name changes to DMAs; however, several counties were assigned to different DMAs. Data for Congressional Districts was updated to represent the 110th Congress, including boundary revisions to Congressional Districts in Georgia and Texas. Finally, ZIP Codes, which are defined by the U.S. Postal Service solely to expedite mail delivery, are updated to reflect its November 2006 inventory.

ESRI presents its 2007/2012 demographic forecasts, including population, age by sex, race by Hispanic origin, age by sex by race and by Hispanic origin, households and families, housing by occupancy, tenure and home value, labor force and employment by industry and occupation, and income—including household and family income distributions, household income by age of householder, and per capita income.[7] Updates of household income are also extended to provide after-tax (disposable) income and a measure of household wealth, net worth. Changes in the update base from the Census Bureau's Count Question Resolution (CQR) revisions, updated boundaries, and improvements to forecasting techniques may preclude comparison to 2006 or earlier updates.

2007 DEMOGRAPHIC UPDATE METHODOLOGY
Forecasts are prepared initially for counties and block groups (BGs). From the county database, forecasts are aggregated to CBSAs, states, or higher levels. From the block group database, forecasts can be retrieved for census tracts, places, county subdivisions, ZIP Codes, Congressional Districts for the 110th Congress, DMAs, or any user-defined site, circle, or polygon.

County Totals
The change in total population is a function of changes in household population and the population in group quarters, which are subject to different trends. The addition of a prison, for example, produces a sudden increase in the group quarters' population that is unlikely to yield an attendant change in the household population or the projected population growth of a county. A military base closing effects an immediate decrease in the household population with the reduction not only of military personnel, but also their families and civilian personnel; however, this drop is unlikely to continue. The disparity of trends in the household versus the group quarters' population is accommodated by separate projections. The group quarters' population is the Census 2000 count of group quarters, with CQR revisions and updates culled from a variety of federal, state, and local sources.

Forecasting change in the size and distribution of the household population begins at the county level with several sources of data. ESRI begins with a time series from the U.S. Census Bureau that includes county estimates through 2005.[8] Because testing has revealed improvement in accuracy by using a variety of different sources to track county population trends, ESRI also employs a time series of building permits and housing starts, plus residential postal delivery counts. Finally, local data sources that tested well against Census 2000 are reviewed.

Block Group Totals
Measuring the change in population or households at the county level is facilitated by the array of data reported for counties. Unfortunately, there is no current data reported specifically for block groups. Past trends can be calculated from previous census counts, but nothing that is current. To measure current population change by block group, ESRI models the change in households from three primary sources: the InfoBase database from Acxiom Corporation; residential delivery statistics from the U.S. Postal Service; and residential construction data from Hanley Wood Market Intelligence; in addition to several ancillary sources.

The U.S. Postal Service (USPS) publishes monthly counts of residential deliveries for every U.S. postal carrier route. This represents the most comprehensive and current information available for small, subcounty geographic areas. The USPS establishes carrier routes to enable efficient mail delivery. Carrier routes are a fluid geographic construct that is redefined continuously to incorporate real changes in the housing inventory and occupancy plus administrative changes in staffing and budgets of local post offices. These frequent changes in the carrier routes are not the only difficulty.

Converting delivery statistics from postal carrier routes to census block groups is a complex challenge. Carrier routes are defined to deliver the mail, while block groups are constructed to collect and report census data. Comparing two different areas that are defined for wholly different purposes provides one significant conversion issue. Carrier routes commonly overlap multiple block groups. In many cases, a carrier route encompasses disjointed areas that can be distant from each other, but block groups are rarely divided into multiple polygons. These overlaps require an effective method of allocating the postal delivery counts across multiple block groups.

One way to distribute delivery statistics among component block groups is to create a correspondence using boundary files. Changes in postal carrier routes can be tracked through quarterly updates of carrier route boundaries, and then delivery statistics can be assigned to block groups with 2000 census block data. Another way also employs boundary files, but assumes a uniform distribution of households within the area. Using standard geodemographic tools, it is possible to estimate the change in households from carrier route delivery statistics and to apply that change to any block group(s) in the area. But the estimated change is simply being redistributed from one summary area to another.

ESRI has developed another way to link a carrier route to the correct block group(s)-using the *actual* locations of mail deliveries. Its proprietary Address Based Allocation (ABA) solves the complex challenge of converting delivery counts from carrier routes to block groups. This allocation method uses the addresses from Acxiom's InfoBase household database. Addresses in the database are geocoded with carrier route and block group codes, using an enhanced geocoding technique and database, and serve as the foundation for the conversion. This approach is unbounded by geographic borders or arbitrary assumptions about the distribution of households or postal deliveries.

ABA results have been tested extensively. The tests include benchmarking against the 2000 Census. Manual reviews confirm

---

[7] Forecasts represent the mid-year population, July 1, unless otherwise specified.

[8] U.S. Bureau of the Census, Population Division, Table CO-EST2005-ALLDATA.

the capability of the method to identify areas with high growth. The ABA allocation method reveals sprawls and new developments across the country since Census 2000. Assessments based on other data sources verify the efficacy and precision of ABA. For the small portion of block groups where addresses are not available from the InfoBase database, delivery statistics are allocated from a correspondence file. The correspondence between census block groups and postal carrier routes is developed using quarterly updated data from Tele Atlas.

The effectiveness of the ABA relies on the precision of block group assignment to InfoBase addresses. ESRI improved the geocoding accuracy of the InfoBase file by applying ArcGIS 9.2 with the Dynamap/Address Points database from Tele Atlas, which provides coordinates that are accurate *to the building*. It offers a new development in large-scale geographic databases where addresses are represented as points rather than approximations estimated from address ranges or street segments. The database currently covers the most densely populated areas in the U.S., with continuously increasing geographic coverage. Addresses that fall outside of the coverage were geocoded with the conventional approach, based on address ranges.

Post office delivery counts or address counts provide less coverage in rural areas. Sparsely populated areas tend to have post office box ZIP Codes because there are few rural addressing systems and little comparability to urban, street delivery. The same problems characterize rural addresses in the InfoBase database. To track new housing developments, especially in previously unpopulated areas, ESRI licensed a new data source, from Hanley Wood Market Intelligence—new and planned residential construction in the top U.S. housing markets, including seven new markets added in 2006.

The new residential construction database from Hanley Wood Market Intelligence adds a unique component to ESRI's strategy for producing accurate demographic forecasts. This database identifies individual construction projects—for instance, a complex of single-family homes or townhomes, or a condominium building, with its exact location by latitude and longitude. It also pinpoints conversions of apartments into condominiums. The construction information includes:

- Total number of units planned
- Inventory of units under construction, sold and/or closed
- Type of housing—detached homes, townhomes, condominiums, etc.
- Target markets—families, seniors, empty nesters, etc.

The use of this type of information in demographic forecasts has traditionally been confined to small-scale implementation, such as producing forecasts for a specific county. ESRI partners with Hanley Wood Market Intelligence to introduce this information in a large-scale forecasting effort. The new construction database complements and corroborates the postal delivery statistics. More importantly, it tabulates planned construction to be completed in upcoming years. This information is incorporated in ESRI's five-year forecasts. Tracking residential development since 2000 with enhanced demographic and spatial analysis tools informs the 2012 forecasts more accurately than past trends.

A revised housing unit methodology applies the change in households estimated from address counts, delivery counts, and new housing construction to update household population by block group. The best techniques are derived from a combination of models and data sources. Discrepant trends are checked extensively against independent sources. Finally, totals for block groups are controlled to the county totals. The integration of demographic and spatial analysis and the addition of the Hanley Wood data for residential development represent a break from past methods and preclude comparisons to earlier updates.

Population and Household Characteristics

ESRI's population and household characteristics include the population by sex and age, race and Hispanic origin, sex by age by race and Hispanic origin, and household type. Population by sex and age include estimates by five-year age groups and by single years from less than 1 year to 84 years.

The population by age and sex is projected via a cohort survival model that calculates the components of population change separately, by age and sex. Applying survival rates specific to the cohort carries the 2000 population forward. Changes in the population by age and sex diverge at the household level. For example, an area that is losing population can age more rapidly with the loss of population in prime migrant ages, 20-34 years—unless there is a college nearby. An influx of college students can offset the loss of youthful outmigrants.

To capture these variations, ESRI's model first separated the group quarters' population from the household population and, second, keyed the calculations to the size and characteristics of the population. This stratification identified several different patterns of change by age and sex that were applied in the cohort survival model. Births were projected from area-specific, child-woman ratios. Migration was computed as a residual, the difference between the survived population and independent projections of the total population.

Accurate allocation of funds to minority groups and tracking of immigration to the U.S are two important reasons to accurately measure the growth of population by race and Hispanic origin. ESRI's database is supplemented with the Diversity Index, a measure that summarizes racial and ethnic diversity. The index shows the likelihood that two persons, chosen at random from the same area, belong to different races or ethnic groups. The index ranges from 0 (no diversity), to 100 (complete diversity).

The U.S Diversity Index currently stands at 59, an increase of one percent annually since 2000. Led primarily by Hispanic diversity, California, New Mexico, and Texas are the most diverse mainland states with diversity indices running higher than 70. The process of diversification in these states is advanced; therefore these areas are among the states with slow rates of change in diversification. Although immigration is still rising in these states, it has a smaller impact on the diversity level. Traditionally non-diverse states such as Maine, Vermont, and Connecticut are experiencing some of the highest rates of diversification. Pockets of diversity are common in less diverse states. For example, the Liberal and Garden City Micropolitan Areas in Kansas have diversity indices of more than 75.

The Hispanic population now stands at 46 million, or 15 percent of the total U.S. population. The influence of this ethnic group in American culture is on the rise, due to growth rates of 3.7 percent a year since 2000 and a projected total of 54.7 million by 2012 (approximately 17 percent of the U.S population). Although they are smaller population groups, Asian and non-Hispanic multiracial populations are following Hispanic trends closely, with growth rates of 3.8 percent and 3.1 percent respectively.

Historical trends in race and Hispanic origin play an important role in the analysis and forecasting process. Tracking intercensal population change by race was encumbered by the new reporting method in Census 2000. Race was reported as a multiple-choice item—not "one person-one race", as reported in past censuses or estimates. The Census 2000 data is not directly comparable to 1990 Census data, or to any earlier estimates or projections.

Comparisons made between single-race reporters in 2000 and 1990 underestimate the change by race. Excluding the rapid growth of the multiracial population minimizes the change by race from 1990 to 2000. Alternatively, combining single-race reporters with races reported in any combination can cut down the 63 racial groups reported in Census 2000. For example, a person who reports "White and Asian" is counted as both "White" and "Asian." This combination of single-race and multiracial reporters overcounts multiracial reporters and overestimates the change by race from 1990 to 2000. To achieve a true picture of population change by race, it is important to account for the change in multiracial reporting.

ESRI takes an innovative approach in analyzing this data to make effective use of the additional information from Census 2000.[9] The Census Bureau released most race-related data by six single-race groups and one multiple-race group. ESRI's data preserves this format and enables a comparison of 1990 and 2000 data for six single races and one multiracial group. Assuming that the probability of reporting more than one race varies by race group and geographic area as shown in Census 2000, ESRI estimates the number of likely multiple race reporters from 1990 Census data. The same approach is adopted for the population of Hispanic origin by race.

The most current source data by race and Hispanic origin is 2005 data available by county and state from the Census Bureau's estimates and its American Community Survey (ACS). Survey data is analyzed in conjunction with ESRI's estimate of change from 1990 to 2000 by race and Hispanic origin to establish county population by race and Hispanic origin. Forecasts by block group combine local changes in the distributions by race and projected change for counties. The last step controls block group distributions to county projections.

The composition of the American household continues the slow change from married-couple families to nontraditional families and single-person households. Between 1990 and 2000, the dominant share of households remained married-couple families in most states, but decreased from 55 percent of all households to 52 percent in 2000. Increased shares of single-parent and single-person units comprise the difference. The attendant change in average household size is the decline from 2.63 in 1990 to 2.59 in 2000. Through 2007, these changes continue, but even more gradually than in the 1990s.

The gradual change in household size makes it uniquely suitable to forecasting the change in households from the change in household population. Average household size is one of the most stable and predictable components of the forecasts. Household forecasts are predicated upon local patterns of change, which are controlled to the more constant trends for states and counties. Nationally, household change stabilized in the 1990s and remains at 2.59 in 2007.

Local change, however, is affected more by the singular composition of the population, and trends often vary from the national norm. Nationally, average household size decreased by less than 0.4 percent annually from 1990 to 2000. By county, the change varied from a low of –2.1 percent to a high of 1.3 percent. An increase in household size can result from higher rates of fertility locally—or from an increase in multigenerational households. Census 2000 has documented the increase in multigenerational households in areas where there is high immigration or areas with housing shortages and higher costs. From 2000 through 2007, change in household size by county ranges from –0.9 to a high of 0.6 percent.

Few block groups represent a cross-section of U.S. households. In areas that gained population from immigration in the 1990s, the trend in average household size actually reversed and increased. To distinguish local variation, ESRI's model is keyed to the characteristics of households at the block group level. This stratification identifies several different patterns of change by household type that are applied to forecast trends in the characteristics of households, both family composition and tenure. Local change is emphasized in the 2007/2012 forecasts of

households and families for counties and block groups. National and state trends are monitored with sources such as the Current Population Survey (CPS) and American Community Survey from the Census Bureau, and then applied as controls.

Use of Projections

Projections are necessarily derived from current events and past trends. The past and the present are known; the future must be extrapolated from this knowledge base. Even though projections represent the unknown, they are not uninformed. Guidelines for the development of projections also inform the use of those projections:

- The recent past provides a reasonable clue to the course of future events, especially if that information is tempered with a historical perspective.
- A stable rate of growth is easier to anticipate than rapid growth or decline.
- The risk inherent in projections is inversely related to the size of an area: the smaller the area, the greater the risk.
- The risk increases with the length of the projection interval. Any deviation of the projected trends from actual events is amplified over time.

ESRI revises its projections annually to draw upon the most recent estimates and projections of local trends. However, this data can be complemented with personal knowledge of an area to provide the qualitative, anecdotal detail that is not captured in a national database. It is incumbent upon the data user and the producers to incorporate as much information as possible when assessing local trends, especially for areas that are subject to "boom-bust" cycles.

---

[9] A more detailed discussion of ESRI's 1990-2000 race analysis is available from Sangita Vashi's paper, *Trends in the U.S. Multiracial Population 1990-2000*, presented at the 2001 Southern Demographic Association's Annual Meeting.

Spending Potential Indices
Methodology Statement

Spending potential data measure the likely expenditure for a product or service in a county, ZIP Code, or other trade area. The ESRI database includes the average expenditure per household, total expenditures and a Spending Potential Index (SPI) for over 700 products and services. The Sourcebook contains the SPIs for 20 key products or services. The SPI compares the average local expenditure for a product to the average amount spent nationally. An index of 100 is average. An SPI of 120 shows that the average spent by local consumers is 20 percent above the national average. An SPI of 85 shows that the average spent is 15 percent below the national average.

Methodology

ESRI has combined the latest Consumer Expenditure Surveys (CEX), 2002, 2003 and 2004, from the Bureau of Labor Statistics (BLS) to estimate current spending patterns. The continuing surveys include a Diary Survey for daily purchases and an Interview Survey for general purchases. The Diary Survey represents record keeping by consumer units (CU) for two consecutive weeklong periods. This component of the CEX collects data on small, daily purchases that could be overlooked by the quarterly Interview Survey. The Interview Survey collects expenditure data from consumers in five interviews conducted every three months. ESRI integrates data from both surveys to provide a comprehensive database on all consumer expenditures. To compensate for the relatively small CEX survey bases and the variability of single-year data, expenditures are combined from the 2002-2004 surveys.

Over the years, both the BLS and ESRI have updated their methods of collecting and estimating the consumer spending data. In 2004, the BLS introduced multiple imputations of income data to estimate data for missing records and in 2001, the BLS revised the Interview Survey to collect income by using ranges in addition to discrete totals. The goal is to improve the accuracy of income reporting, but the changes also affects expenditures derived directly from income data, such as Social Security deductions. Additionally, the values reported in the surveys vary for select data items due to coding and definition changes.

For example, items like investments are commonly topcoded to a select upper limit. Topcoding replaces data when the value of the reported item exceeds prescribed critical values. The critical values for each topcoded variable are estimated in accordance with Census Disclosure Review Board guidelines. The topcoded value represents the mean of the subset of all outlying observations and, therefore, is subject to large changes from year to year. Any average, including average expenditures, can be influenced by the presence of extreme values. Therefore, when the topcode is changed, the average also changes. BLS may include other coding changes.

ESRI has updated the models used to estimate consumer spending with its segmentation system, Community™ Tapestry™. The model that links the spending of consumer units in CEX surveys to all households with similar socioeconomic characteristics is a conditional probability model that integrates consumer spending with Community Tapestry, ESRI's market segmentation system. Tapestry truly differentiates consumer spending by market— especially among the smallest U.S. market areas, where distinctions can be difficult to measure, and for the largest ticket items, where consumer preferences are more pronounced. However, changes in the method of estimating consumer spending, like changes in the methods of data collection, preclude direct comparison with previous CEX databases.

Spending patterns are developed by Tapestry markets and updated to 2007 by adjusting to current levels of income. Expenditures represent 2007 annual averages and totals.

Computation of a Spending Potential Index

For any trade area, the expenditure per household for a particular product or service can be computed by linking the expenditure data to the demographic characteristics of the population. The SPI is defined as the ratio of the local average to the U.S. average expenditure. This equation shows how the index is derived:

$$SPI = \left[\frac{\text{Local Average Expenditure}}{\text{U.S. Average Expenditure}} \right] \times 100$$

How High is High?

The Spending Potential Index exhibits different value ranges for different products or services. In general, products pertaining to specific lifestyles or income levels will show a wider range of SPI values than the products or services purchased by everybody.

The SPI has an average value of 100, but the distribution of SPIs among counties varies by product. The table on the next page shows the upper range of values for select SPIs by county. This is a rough guide for determining "how high is high":

	Somewhat High	Very High	Extremely High
Medians and Percentiles of Spending Potential Indices: All U.S. Counties			
	Percentiles		
	Median	*75th*	*90th*	*95th*
Financial Services:				
Auto Loan	82	91	102	115
Home Loan	65	80	101	123
Investments	55	78	103	126
Retirement Plans	64	80	102	124
The Home:				
Home Improvements				
Home Repair	70	83	101	120
Lawn & Garden	86	95	106	119
Furnishings				
Computers and Hardware-Personal	68	81	100	118
Major Appliances	78	88	102	116
TV, Radio, Sound Equipment	73	84	99	114
Furniture	65	79	100	120
Entertainment:				
Dine Out/Carry Out	72	83	99	115
Sports Equipment	69	78	92	109
Fees & Tickets	61	78	101	121
Toys & Games	75	85	100	116
Travel	67	81	100	119
Cable TV	76	86	99	113
Personal:				
Apparel & Services	62	73	90	105
Auto Repairs	74	84	100	116
Health Insurance	84	92	102	113
Pets & Supplies	82	91	103	117

Variable Definitions

Here are definitions of the 2007 Sourcebook Spending Potential Indices:

Financial Services

Auto Loan
Reduction of principal vehicle loan, automobile finance charges, truck finance charges, motorcycle finance charges, and other vehicle finance charges. Other vehicles include motorized campers, trailer-type campers, other attachable type campers, scooters, mopeds, and boats.

Home Loan
Payments of mortgage interest and principal, property taxes, homeowners insurance, and ground rent.

Investments
Purchase price of stocks, bonds, or mutual funds.

Retirement Plans
Amount of private pension funds deducted from last pay, annualized for all consumer unit members.

The Home

Home Improvements
Home Repair
Maintenance and repair services associated with painting or papering, plumbing or water heating installation or repair, heating, air conditioning or electrical work, roofing and gutters, and other repair and maintenance work (including repair and replacement of hard surface flooring, and repair of built-in appliances such as dishwashers, garbage disposals, or range hoods). Maintenance and repair products associated with paints, wallpaper and supplies; painting and wallpapering tools and equipment; plumbing supplies and equipment; electrical supplies; heating and air conditioning; materials for hard surface flooring, roofing, gutters, downspouts, materials for plaster, panel, and siding, materials for patios, walks, fences, brick or stucco work; landscaping maintenance materials, insulation materials, materials for additions, finishing basements or attics, remodeling rooms, construction materials for jobs not started, hard surface flooring material, material for landscape maintenance.

Lawn & Garden
Gardening and lawn care services, supplies, and equipment. Expenditures for indoor plants and fresh flowers, repairs/rentals of lawn and garden equipment.

Furnishings
Computers and Hardware - Personal
Computers, computer systems, and related hardware for non-business use.

Major Appliances
Purchase of dishwashers, garbage disposals, refrigerators, freezers, washing and drying machines, cooking ovens and stoves, microwave ovens, window air conditioning units, electric floor cleaning equipment, and miscellaneous household appliances such as sewing machines, etc.

TV, Radio, Sound Equipment
Community antenna or cable TV; portion of management fees for utilities in condos or co-ops. TV and video expenditures from color TVs (console, portable, table model), VCRs, video cameras/camcorders, disc players, video cassettes, tapes, and discs, video game hardware and software, satellite dishes, rental of videos (tapes, films, and discs). Expenditures for sound equipment include sound components and component systems, CD, tape, record and video mail order clubs, records, CDs, tapes, needles, tape recorders, radios, miscellaneous equipment/accessories, musical instruments and accessories, repair and rental of musical instruments, rental and repair of TV, VCR, radio and sound equipment.

Furniture
Mattresses and box springs, other bedroom furniture, sofas, living room chairs and tables, kitchen and dining room furniture infant furniture, outdoor furniture, wall units, cabinets and other furniture.

Entertainment

Dine Out/Carry-Out
Breakfast, lunch, dinner, or snacks at fast food or full service establishments, place of employment, or vending machines.

Sports Equipment
Equipment and gear for exercise, camping, hunting, fishing and sports (water, winter, etc.), game tables, and bicycles. Also, rental or repair of miscellaneous sports equipment.

Fees and Tickets
Fees and admissions for social, recreation, or civic club memberships, sports participation, movie, theater, opera, ballet, sporting events, or recreational lessons.

Toys & Games
Toys, games, hobbies, tricycles, playground equipment, and play on arcade pinball/video games.

Travel
Transportation expenditures for airline fares, intercity trains, ships, and intercity buses. Also includes trip expenditures such as local transport, taxis and limousines, auto and truck rentals, gasoline, motor oil, parking fees, tolls, and lodging; Expenditures on food and drink on trips (alcoholic beverages and food); Entertainment-related expenses on trips for recreation, participant sports, admission to movies, sporting events, etc.

Cable TV
Community antenna service, cable, or satellite.

Personal

Apparel and Services
Men's suits, sport coats, coats and jackets, underwear, socks, nightwear, uniforms, costumes, sweaters and vests, active sportswear, shirts, pants, shorts, and accessories. Women's coats and jackets, dresses, sport coats and tailored jackets, sweaters and vests, shirts, tops, and blouses, skirts, pants, shorts, active sportswear, sleepwear, uniforms, costumes, suits, undergarments, hosiery, and accessories. Boys' and girls' coats and jackets, sweaters, shirts, underwear, sleepwear, socks and hosiery, suits, dresses and skirts, shirts and blouses, sport coats, vests, pants, shorts and shorts sets, active sportswear, uniforms, costumes, and accessories. Footwear, jewelry, and watches. Apparel products and services, such as material for making clothes, sewing patterns and notions, shoe repair and other shoe services, laundry and dry cleaning, alteration, repair and tailoring of apparel, clothing rental and storage, and watch and jewelry repair.

Auto Repairs
Expenditures for vehicle maintenance and repairs such as coolant, additives, brake and transmission fluid, tires (purchased, replaced, installed), parts, equipment, and accessories, vehicle products, miscellaneous auto repair and servicing, body work and painting, clutch, transmission, rear-end, and drive shaft repairs, brake work, steering, front end, and engine cooling system repair, motor tune up, lube, oil change, oil filters, front end alignment, wheel balance and rotation, shock absorber replacement, tire repair, air conditioning, exhaust and electrical system repair, motor repair and replacement, and auto repair service policies.

Health Insurance
Commercial health insurance coverage from traditional service health plans and preferred provider plans, health maintenance organizations, and Medicare payments. Coverage from Blue Cross/Blue Shield, which includes traditional service health plans, preferred provider plans, health maintenance organizations, commercial Medicare supplements, and other health insurance.

Pets & Supplies
Pets, pet food, pet supplies, pet services, medicine for pets, and veterinary services.

Business Data Note

ESRI business data are extracted from a comprehensive list of businesses licensed from infoUSA. The infoUSA business list contains data for nearly eleven million U.S. businesses including the business name, location, franchise code, North American Industry Classification System (NAICS) code, number of employees and sales volume. These statistics are current as of January 2007.

Data Sources
infoUSA collects and maintains its business database by referencing several sources, including directory listings (yellow pages and business white pages), annual reports, 10K's and SEC information, federal, state, and municipal government data, business magazines, newsletters and newspapers, and U.S. Postal Service information. infoUSA conducts annual telephone verifications with each business to ensure accurate and complete information.

ESRI provides reports and file extracts from the infoUSA database that include the number of businesses by NAICS code and employment size or sales volume, total employment, and total sales, where available. Industry classifications include the standard NAICS code hierarchy, plus infoUSA's proprietary industry code which expands upon the NAICS code hierarchy. Also, a special industry code for select industries is available that provides more detailed information, such as the number of rooms in hotels/motels or the number of beds in hospitals and nursing homes. Sales data are reported for business locations.

The Business Data section shows the total number of companies and employees by county for all industries. Also shown is the top industry as determined by total employment for each county. Industries are represented by three-digit NAICS industry. A complete list of NAICS definitions is included in Appendix VI.

Business Locations
infoUSA compiles an address list of businesses from its sources and telephone verification. The addresses are geocoded to assign latitude and longitude coordinates to the business site and to append a census geographic code. Most businesses are coded at the address level and assigned to a census block group. Of course, the quality of the local address system varies: address matching is better in an urban area with street-level address systems than in rural areas. Overall, 84.3 percent of the businesses are coded at the address level; 99.5 percent are assigned to a census block group. Businesses that cannot be assigned to a block group are assigned to a census tract or county.

ESRI uses the geographic codes to report business data for summary areas--states, counties, census tracts and block groups.

Explanation of Variables*

Age
Age data are reported for five-year age groups and select summary groups such as 18 years and over. These data are ESRI's 2007 projections.

Median Age
Median age is calculated from the distribution of age by five-year groups. These data are ESRI's 2007 projections. See Median.

Average Household Size
See Household.

CBSA
Core Based Statistical Areas, which include Metropolitan and Micropolitan Statistical Areas, are comprised of one or more counties and are defined by the U.S. Office of Management and Budget (OMB). Each Metropolitan Statistical Area must have at least one urbanized area of 50,000 or more inhabitants. Each Micropolitan Statistical Area must have at least one urban cluster of at least 10,000 but less than 50,000 population.

Under the standards, the county (or counties) in which at least 50 percent of the population resides within urban areas of 10,000 or more population, or that contain at least 5,000 people residing within a single urban area of 10,000 or more population, is identified as a "central county" (counties). Additional "outlying counties" are included in the CBSA if they meet specified requirements of commuting to or from the central counties.

County
Counties are the primary legal subdivisions of a state and are identified by a two-digit state FIPS code and a three-digit county FIPS code. See FIPS Code.

DMA
A Designated Market Area is a television market defined by Nielsen Media Research. DMAs are revised annually. Current definitions are from the 2006-2007 series.

Families
Households in which one or more persons in the household are related to the householder (formerly, the head of the household) by birth, marriage or adoption. The Census tabulates only one family per household. These data are Census 2000 and ESRI's 2007 projections.

FIPS Code
Federal Information Processing Standards (FIPS) for numeric codes used to identify states and counties.

Hispanic Origin
Defined by self-identification, Hispanic origin refers to ethnicity, not race. Persons of Hispanic origin may be of any race. These data are Census 2000 and ESRI's 2007 projections.

Home Value
The estimate of value is presented for total owner-occupied units. For a discussion of home value projections, see the Update Methodology. These data are ESRI's 2007 projections.

Median Home Value
This estimate divides the distribution of home value into two equal parts. Linear interpolation is used if the median home value falls below $1,000,000. If the median falls in the upper home value interval of $1,000,000+, it is represented by $1,000,001.

Home Value Base
This is the sum of the home value distribution.

Household
A household is an occupied housing unit. Household type is identified by the presence of relatives and the number of persons living in the household. Family households, with or without children, include married couples and other families--a male or female householder with no spouse present. Non-family households may be a group of unrelated persons or a single person living alone. These data are Census 2000 and ESRI's 2007 and 2012 projections.

Average Household Size
Average household size is calculated by dividing the number of persons in households by the number of households.

Household Income
See Income.

Household Income Base
This is the sum of the household income distribution.

Income
2007 Income is a forecast of income for the calendar year 2006. Income amounts are expressed in current dollars, including an adjustment for inflation or cost-of-living increases. For a discussion of income projections, see the Update Methodology. These data are ESRI 's 2007 and 2012 projections.

Median Household Income
This is the value that divides the distribution of household income into two equal parts. Pareto interpolation is used if the median falls in an income interval other than the first or last. For the lowest interval, <$10,000, linear interpolation is used. If the median falls in the upper income interval of $500,000+, it is represented by the value of $500,001.

Per Capita Income
This is the average income for all persons calculated from the aggregate income of persons 15 years and older.

Rank
Counties are ranked by 2007 median household income nationally and for each state.

Median
This is a value that divides a distribution into two equal

---

* Note: For more information about Census 2000 data, please see the 2000 Census of Population and Housing, Summary Files 1 and 3 Technical Documentation prepared by the U.S. Bureau of the Census.

parts. A median is a positional measure that is unaffected by extremely high or low values in a distribution that may affect an average.

Per Capita Income
See Income.

Population
This is the total number of residents in an area. Residence refers to the "usual place" where a person lives, which is not necessarily the legal residence. For example, college students are counted where they attend school. These data are Census 2000 and ESRI's 2007 and 2012 projections.

Race
Defined by self-identification, race detail from Census 2000 was expanded to include a multiracial component. For the first time, each individual could report up to six race categories, resulting in 63 possible race combinations. The six basic race categories are White, Black or African American, American Indian or Alaskan Native, Asian, Native Hawaiian or Other Pacific Islander, and "some other" race for persons who do not identify with one of the specified groups. ESRI forecasts race for all single and multiracial populations that are consistent with 2000 Census tabulations. Data are Census 2000 and ESRI's 2007 projections of White, Black, and Asian/ Pacific Islander populations.

Rate, Annual Percent
This is calculated as an annual compound rate of change from 2000 to 2007 for population, households, and families. For example:

$$Rate = \left[\left(\frac{P_{07}}{P_{00}} \right)^{1/7.25} - 1 \right] \times 100$$

Counties are ranked on the rate of population change within each state.

Spending Potential Index
See Spending Potential Indices Methodology.

State
States are identified by a two-digit FIPS code. The District of Columbia is included as a state-equivalent area in the ESRI database. See FIPS Code.

Summary Maps

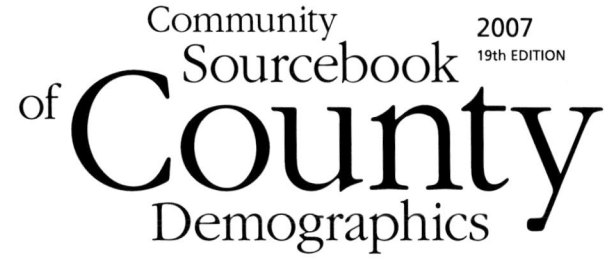

Community
Sourcebook 2007
of County 19th EDITION
Demographics

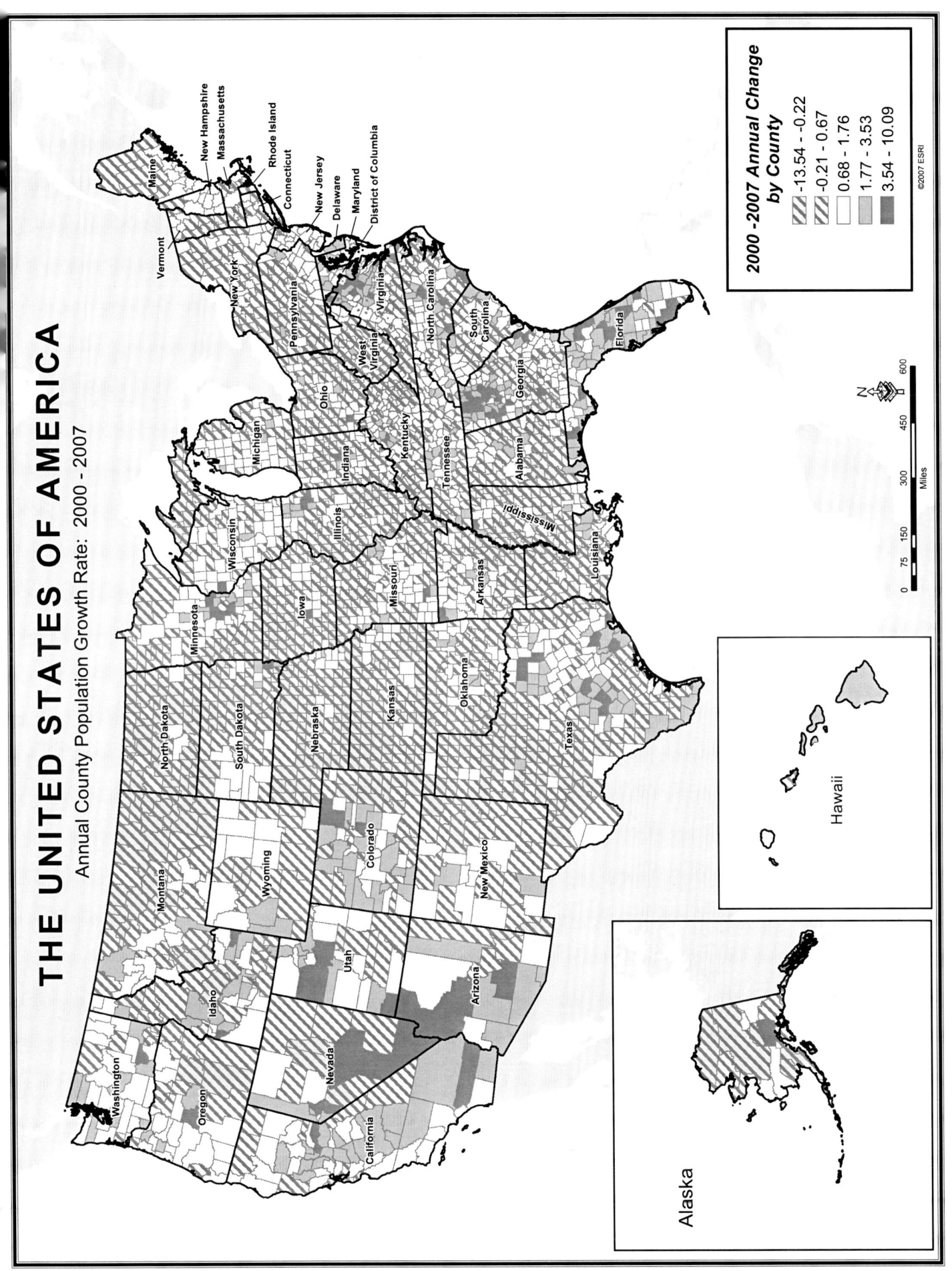

THE UNITED STATES OF AMERICA

Annual County Population Growth Rate: 2000 - 2007

2000 -2007 Annual Change by County

- -13.54 - -0.22
- -0.21 - 0.67
- 0.68 - 1.76
- 1.77 - 3.53
- 3.54 - 10.09

©2007 ESRI

Hawaii

Alaska

Maine
New Hampshire
Massachusetts
Rhode Island
Connecticut
New Jersey
Delaware
Maryland
District of Columbia
Vermont
New York
Pennsylvania
Virginia
West Virginia
North Carolina
South Carolina
Florida
Ohio
Kentucky
Georgia
Tennessee
Alabama
Michigan
Indiana
Illinois
Mississippi
Wisconsin
Missouri
Arkansas
Louisiana
Minnesota
Iowa
Kansas
Oklahoma
Texas
North Dakota
South Dakota
Nebraska
Montana
Wyoming
Colorado
New Mexico
Utah
Arizona
Idaho
Nevada
Washington
Oregon
California

N

0 75 150   300   450   600
Miles

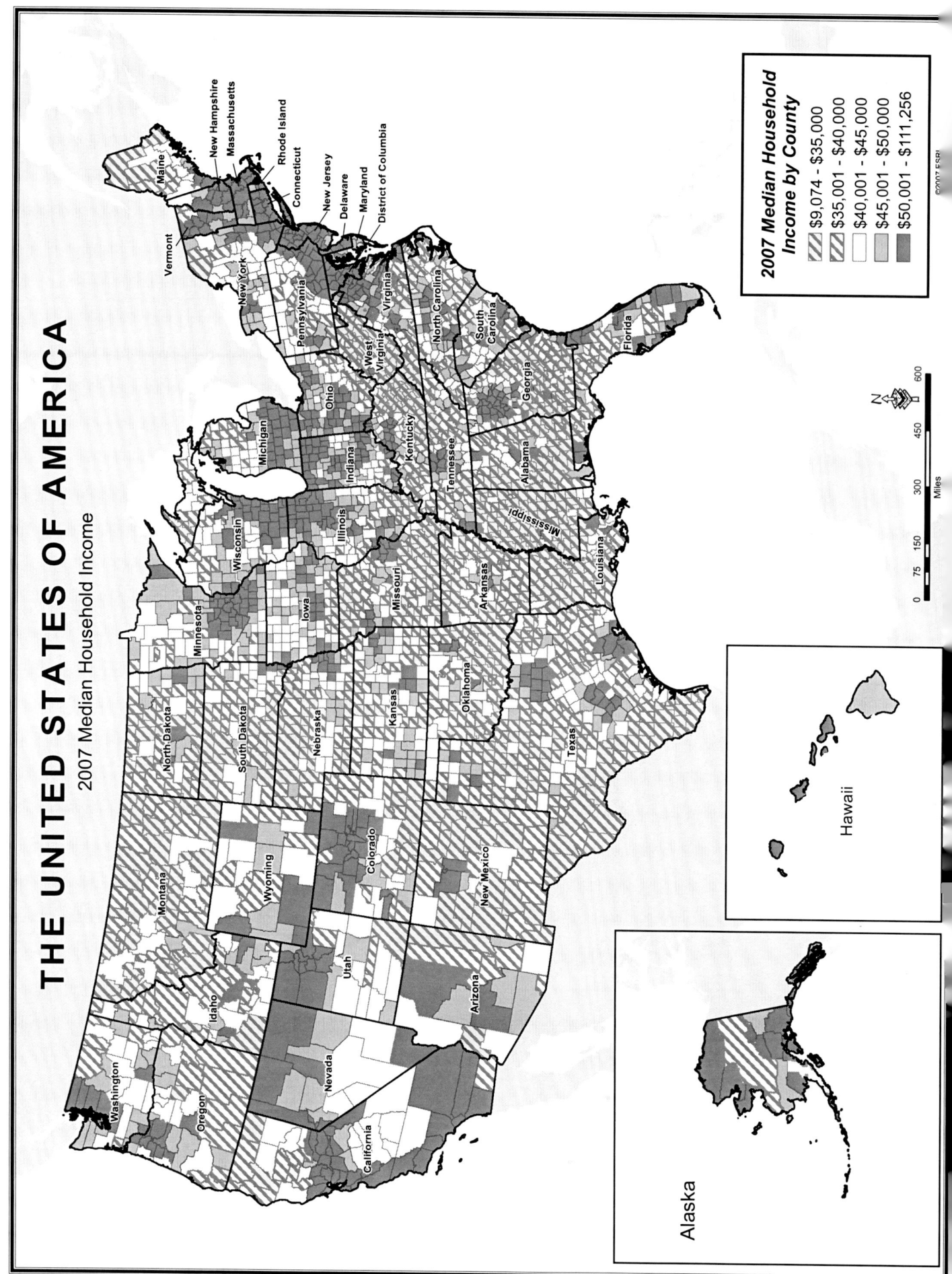

THE UNITED STATES OF AMERICA

2007 Median Household Income

2007 Median Household Income by County

- $9,074 - $35,000
- $35,001 - $40,000
- $40,001 - $45,000
- $45,001 - $50,000
- $50,001 - $111,256

©2007 ESRI

Hawaii

Alaska

0   75   150   300   450   600
Miles

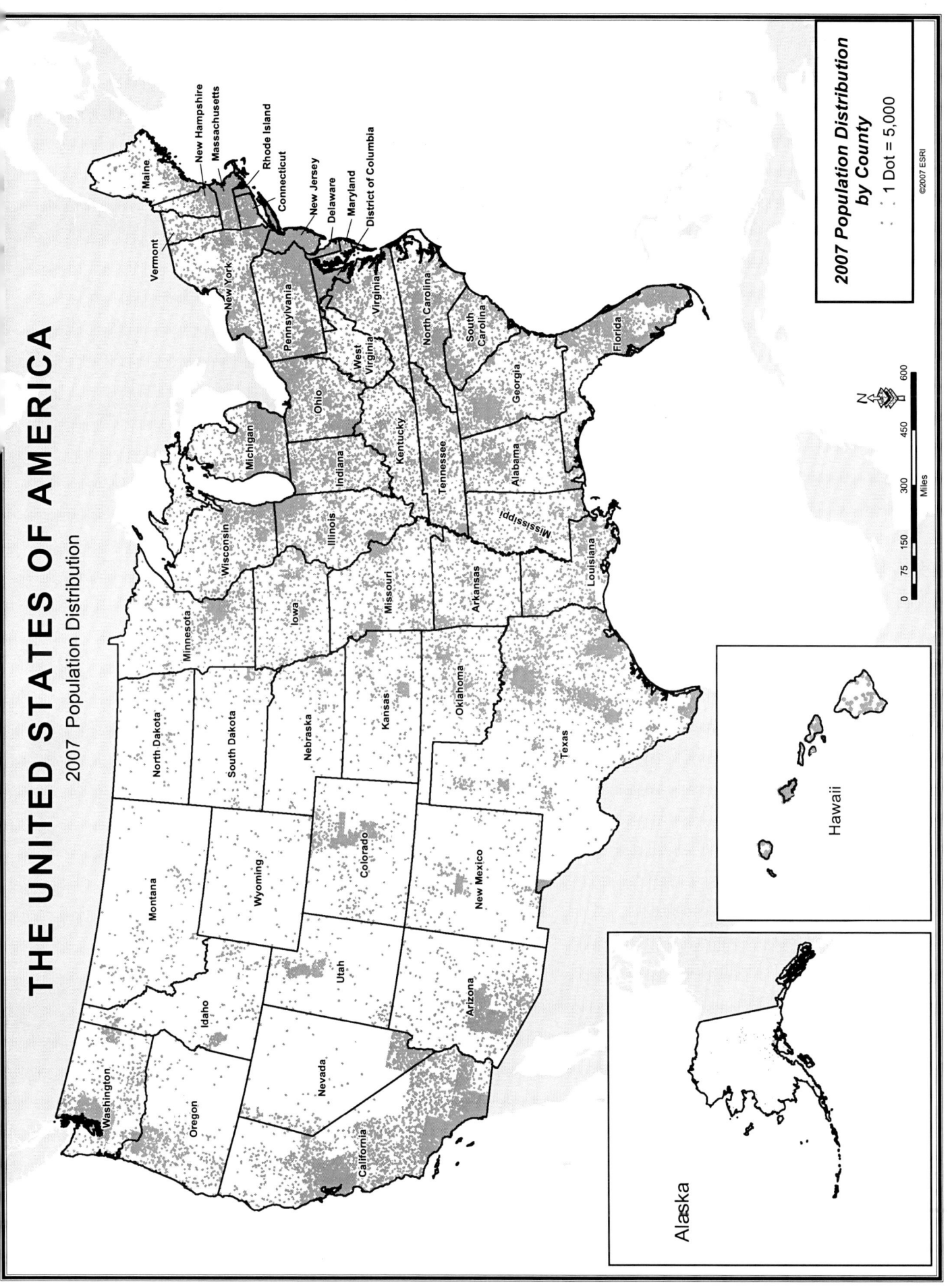

THE UNITED STATES OF AMERICA
2007 Population Distribution

2007 Population Distribution by County

1 Dot = 5,000

©2007 ESRI

Hawaii

Alaska

County Demographic Data
by State

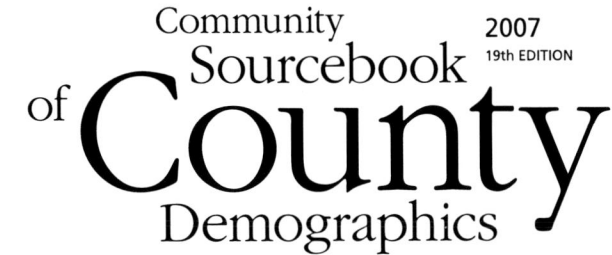

Community
Sourcebook
of County
Demographics

2007
19th EDITION

POPULATION CHANGE

COUNTY	FIPS Code	CBSA Code	DMA Code	POPULATION			2000-2007 ANNUAL RATE		RACE (%)					
									White		Black		Asian/Pacific	
				2000	2007	2012	% Rate	State Rank	2000	2007	2000	2007	2000	2007
AUTAUGA	001	33860	698	43,671	49,541	54,084	1.8	5	80.7	79.1	17.1	18.1	0.5	0.7
BALDWIN	003	19300	686	140,415	175,513	205,887	3.1	2	87.1	85.9	10.3	11.2	0.4	0.3
BARBOUR	005	21640	522	29,038	28,992	28,584	0.0	43	51.3	50.4	46.3	47.1	0.3	0.3
BIBB	007	13820	630	20,826	21,911	22,546	0.7	19	76.7	75.8	22.2	22.5	0.1	0.2
BLOUNT	009	13820	630	51,024	55,496	59,103	1.2	10	95.1	93.5	1.2	1.2	0.2	0.2
BULLOCK	011	00000	698	11,714	11,519	11,364	-0.2	53	25.3	24.3	73.1	73.7	0.2	0.3
BUTLER	013	00000	698	21,399	20,888	20,437	-0.3	59	58.4	56.3	40.8	42.7	0.2	0.2
CALHOUN	015	11500	630	112,249	112,267	112,506	0.0	43	78.9	78.3	18.5	19.0	0.6	0.6
CHAMBERS	017	46740	522	36,583	35,245	34,316	-0.5	64	60.9	58.9	38.1	39.9	0.2	0.2
CHEROKEE	019	00000	630	23,988	25,160	25,731	0.7	19	92.8	91.9	5.5	6.0	0.1	0.2
CHILTON	021	13820	630	39,593	42,696	44,706	1.0	14	86.7	85.0	10.6	11.2	0.2	0.3
CHOCTAW	023	00000	711	15,922	16,265	16,572	0.3	28	55.1	53.1	44.1	46.1	0.0	0.0
CLARKE	025	00000	686	27,867	27,255	26,762	-0.3	59	55.9	53.8	43.0	44.9	0.2	0.2
CLAY	027	00000	630	14,254	14,700	15,028	0.4	25	82.6	81.2	15.7	16.6	0.1	0.1
CLEBURNE	029	00000	524	14,123	14,527	14,791	0.4	25	94.7	94.0	3.7	4.0	0.1	0.2
COFFEE	031	21460	606	43,615	47,224	49,990	1.1	12	77.1	75.0	18.4	19.2	1.0	1.4
COLBERT	033	22520	691	54,984	55,070	55,094	0.0	43	81.5	81.0	16.6	17.1	0.3	0.3
CONECUH	035	00000	686	14,089	13,963	13,895	-0.1	49	55.4	53.3	43.6	45.4	0.2	0.2
COOSA	037	10760	630	12,202	11,937	11,652	-0.3	59	63.9	63.2	34.2	34.7	0.0	0.2
COVINGTON	039	00000	698	37,631	36,867	36,338	-0.3	59	86.2	85.0	12.4	13.2	0.2	0.3
CRENSHAW	041	00000	698	13,665	14,062	14,359	0.4	25	73.8	72.1	24.8	26.3	0.1	0.2
CULLMAN	043	18980	630	77,483	81,338	84,207	0.7	19	96.8	96.0	1.0	1.0	0.2	0.3
DALE	045	21460	606	49,129	48,419	47,914	-0.2	53	74.4	72.0	20.4	21.2	1.2	1.6
DALLAS	047	42820	698	46,365	43,469	41,574	-0.9	67	35.6	33.7	63.3	64.9	0.4	0.5
DEKALB	049	22840	691	64,452	68,200	70,797	0.8	15	92.6	90.2	1.7	1.8	0.2	0.3
ELMORE	051	33860	698	65,874	77,576	86,808	2.3	3	77.0	75.2	20.6	21.8	0.4	0.5
ESCAMBIA	053	00000	686	38,440	37,905	37,380	-0.2	53	64.4	62.2	30.8	32.2	0.3	0.4
ETOWAH	055	23460	630	103,459	103,475	103,514	0.0	43	82.9	82.4	14.7	15.1	0.5	0.5
FAYETTE	057	00000	630	18,495	18,120	17,879	-0.3	59	86.9	85.7	11.9	12.8	0.2	0.2
FRANKLIN	059	00000	691	31,223	31,527	31,751	0.1	36	89.7	86.8	4.2	4.4	0.2	0.3
GENEVA	061	20020	606	25,764	26,284	26,656	0.3	28	87.1	85.8	10.6	11.3	0.1	0.2
GREENE	063	46220	630	9,974	9,866	9,692	-0.2	53	19.1	17.8	80.3	81.5	0.1	0.1
HALE	065	46220	630	17,185	18,886	19,336	1.3	9	39.8	39.0	59.0	59.4	0.2	0.3
HENRY	067	20020	606	16,310	17,125	17,750	0.7	19	65.7	63.4	32.3	33.8	0.1	0.1
HOUSTON	069	20020	606	88,787	96,421	102,268	1.1	12	73.1	71.1	24.6	25.9	0.6	0.9
JACKSON	071	42460	691	53,926	54,579	54,858	0.2	31	91.9	90.7	3.7	4.0	0.3	0.4
JEFFERSON	073	13820	630	662,047	665,775	669,138	0.1	36	58.1	55.9	39.4	40.8	0.9	1.3
LAMAR	075	00000	673	15,904	15,616	15,413	-0.3	59	86.9	85.7	12.0	12.8	0.1	0.1
LAUDERDALE	077	22520	691	87,966	88,536	88,810	0.1	36	88.4	87.2	9.8	10.5	0.4	0.5
LAWRENCE	079	19460	691	34,803	34,646	34,456	-0.1	49	77.8	75.7	13.4	14.1	0.1	0.2
LEE	081	12220	522	115,092	130,385	141,287	1.7	6	74.1	71.9	22.7	23.7	1.7	2.3
LIMESTONE	083	26620	691	65,676	72,733	78,157	1.4	8	83.8	82.1	13.3	14.1	0.4	0.5
LOWNDES	085	33860	698	13,473	13,299	13,073	-0.2	53	25.9	24.3	73.4	74.7	0.1	0.2
MACON	087	46260	698	24,105	23,084	22,355	-0.6	65	14.0	13.0	84.6	85.3	0.4	0.5
MADISON	089	26620	691	276,700	308,174	332,579	1.5	7	72.1	69.7	22.8	23.8	1.9	2.6
MARENGO	091	00000	698	22,539	21,840	21,360	-0.4	63	47.3	45.2	51.7	53.5	0.2	0.3
MARION	093	00000	630	31,214	31,089	31,105	-0.1	49	94.8	94.0	3.6	3.9	0.2	0.3
MARSHALL	095	10700	691	82,231	88,120	92,643	1.0	14	93.4	91.2	1.5	1.5	0.3	0.4
MOBILE	097	33660	686	399,843	409,542	416,382	0.3	28	63.1	59.6	33.4	36.1	1.4	1.9
MONROE	099	00000	686	24,324	24,624	24,837	0.2	31	57.7	55.6	40.1	41.8	0.3	0.4
MONTGOMERY	101	33860	698	223,510	223,182	223,147	0.0	43	48.8	46.6	48.6	50.1	1.0	1.4
MORGAN	103	19460	691	111,064	115,430	118,521	0.5	23	85.1	83.3	11.2	11.8	0.5	0.7
PERRY	105	00000	698	11,861	11,501	11,133	-0.4	63	30.9	29.1	68.4	69.9	0.1	0.1
PICKENS	107	00000	630	20,949	20,925	21,047	0.0	43	55.9	55.1	43.0	43.8	0.1	0.1
PIKE	109	45980	698	29,605	30,062	30,617	0.2	31	60.8	58.6	36.6	38.2	0.4	0.5
RANDOLPH	111	00000	524	22,380	23,479	24,123	0.7	19	76.4	74.7	22.2	23.5	0.2	0.3
RUSSELL	113	17980	522	49,756	51,562	52,849	0.5	23	56.7	54.5	40.8	42.4	0.4	0.6
ST. CLAIR	115	13820	630	64,742	75,447	85,314	2.1	4	90.0	88.9	8.1	8.7	0.2	0.3
SHELBY	117	13820	630	143,293	183,548	219,096	3.5	1	89.8	88.4	7.4	7.9	1.0	1.5
SUMTER	119	00000	711	14,798	14,062	13,552	-0.7	66	25.9	24.4	73.2	74.5	0.1	0.2
TALLADEGA	121	45180	630	80,321	80,671	81,086	0.1	36	67.0	65.0	31.5	33.1	0.2	0.4
TALLAPOOSA	123	10760	698	41,475	41,717	41,409	0.1	36	73.5	72.7	25.4	26.1	0.2	0.2
TUSCALOOSA	125	46220	630	164,875	173,394	180,254	0.7	19	68.1	66.0	29.3	30.7	1.0	1.3
WALKER	127	13820	630	70,713	70,786	70,863	0.0	43	92.2	91.9	6.2	6.4	0.2	0.2
WASHINGTON	129	00000	686	18,097	18,251	18,375	0.1	36	65.0	62.8	26.9	28.2	0.1	0.1
WILCOX	131	00000	698	13,183	13,047	13,069	-0.1	49	27.5	26.5	71.9	73.0	0.1	0.1
WINSTON	133	00000	630	24,843	24,900	24,923	0.0	43	97.3	97.2	0.4	0.4	0.1	0.1
ALABAMA							0.7		71.1	69.8	26.0	26.6	0.7	1.0
UNITED STATES							1.2		75.1	72.7	12.3	12.6	3.8	4.5

COUNTY	% HISPANIC ORIGIN		2007 AGE DISTRIBUTION (%)										MEDIAN AGE	% 2007 Males	% 2007 Females
	2000	2007	0-4	5-9	10-14	15-19	20-24	25-44	45-64	65-84	85+	18+	2007		
AUTAUGA	1.4	2.1	7.3	6.5	7.4	7.4	6.6	28.1	25.5	10.0	1.1	74.2	36.5	48.5	51.5
BALDWIN	1.8	2.4	6.3	6.2	6.3	6.3	5.8	25.2	28.3	13.8	1.9	77.4	41.0	49.1	50.9
BARBOUR	1.6	1.7	6.4	5.9	6.4	6.6	7.7	29.0	25.3	10.8	1.9	77.2	36.9	52.5	47.5
BIBB	1.0	1.5	6.9	6.8	6.9	5.7	6.0	31.2	24.0	10.7	1.9	76.3	36.4	52.5	47.5
BLOUNT	5.3	8.1	7.1	7.1	6.5	5.9	5.2	29.0	25.7	11.8	1.6	75.6	37.8	50.4	49.6
BULLOCK	2.7	3.6	6.7	6.1	6.6	6.2	7.4	29.4	25.3	10.0	2.4	76.7	36.0	53.1	46.9
BUTLER	0.7	0.8	6.7	6.1	6.3	6.3	7.8	23.7	27.4	13.0	2.8	77.0	40.1	47.3	52.7
CALHOUN	1.6	1.6	6.2	6.0	6.1	6.2	6.5	27.0	27.5	12.7	1.8	78.3	39.2	48.1	51.9
CHAMBERS	0.8	1.0	6.9	6.5	6.6	5.6	5.9	26.7	26.4	12.9	2.6	76.6	38.9	47.8	52.2
CHEROKEE	0.9	1.3	6.1	6.1	5.9	5.2	4.6	26.7	28.3	15.2	1.9	78.6	41.6	49.7	50.3
CHILTON	2.9	4.4	7.1	7.0	6.6	6.1	5.4	29.0	25.8	11.5	1.5	75.6	37.2	49.9	50.1
CHOCTAW	0.7	0.9	7.1	7.0	5.9	6.1	5.8	24.6	28.2	13.4	1.9	76.2	40.3	47.3	52.7
CLARKE	0.6	0.8	7.8	7.4	7.0	6.1	6.5	25.6	25.6	11.9	2.0	74.1	37.3	47.6	52.4
CLAY	1.8	2.6	6.4	6.4	5.9	5.7	5.7	26.9	26.2	14.1	2.6	77.9	40.2	49.4	50.6
CLEBURNE	1.4	2.2	6.4	6.2	6.6	5.7	5.6	28.5	26.8	12.5	1.8	77.3	39.3	50.5	49.5
COFFEE	2.7	4.0	6.3	5.9	6.0	6.5	6.7	26.5	26.8	13.4	1.9	77.9	39.3	49.0	51.0
COLBERT	1.1	1.1	6.2	6.1	6.3	5.7	5.5	26.3	27.8	13.9	2.2	77.9	40.7	48.1	51.9
CONECUH	0.7	0.9	6.3	6.1	7.2	6.0	6.0	25.2	27.8	13.2	2.2	76.7	40.2	47.7	52.3
COOSA	1.3	1.3	6.5	6.4	6.3	5.5	5.3	27.6	28.2	12.6	1.6	77.8	39.9	51.1	48.9
COVINGTON	0.8	1.1	6.2	5.9	5.8	5.9	6.0	24.9	27.4	15.2	2.8	78.6	41.6	48.2	51.8
CRENSHAW	0.6	0.9	6.1	5.7	6.6	6.0	5.7	25.7	27.8	13.9	2.5	77.9	41.0	47.8	52.2
CULLMAN	2.2	3.4	6.6	6.4	6.1	5.8	5.8	27.8	26.4	13.2	1.9	77.4	39.1	49.6	50.4
DALE	3.3	4.9	7.8	6.7	6.1	6.1	7.6	28.3	24.6	11.4	1.5	75.9	35.2	49.7	50.3
DALLAS	0.6	0.7	7.8	7.2	7.0	6.8	7.5	24.3	25.6	12.0	2.0	74.1	36.4	45.8	54.2
DEKALB	5.6	8.4	7.1	6.8	6.7	5.3	5.6	29.1	25.8	11.9	1.8	76.2	37.6	49.3	50.7
ELMORE	1.2	1.8	6.8	6.4	6.6	6.5	7.0	29.7	25.8	9.9	1.4	76.3	36.6	50.6	49.4
ESCAMBIA	1.0	1.4	6.4	5.9	6.4	5.9	7.1	27.9	26.3	12.2	1.9	78.0	38.2	51.1	48.9
ETOWAH	1.7	1.7	6.5	6.3	5.9	5.9	5.6	26.6	27.0	13.8	2.3	77.6	39.8	48.2	51.8
FAYETTE	0.8	1.2	6.2	6.1	6.0	5.8	6.3	25.8	27.2	14.1	2.4	78.2	40.5	48.9	51.1
FRANKLIN	7.4	11.2	6.6	6.1	6.5	5.9	5.7	28.6	25.3	13.4	2.0	77.2	38.3	49.4	50.6
GENEVA	1.8	2.7	5.8	5.6	5.8	6.2	5.8	25.6	28.1	14.8	2.4	79.0	41.7	49.1	50.9
GREENE	0.6	0.5	7.9	7.1	7.6	5.9	8.0	22.0	27.1	12.1	2.3	73.9	37.7	47.1	52.9
HALE	0.9	1.3	8.3	7.8	7.1	6.9	6.6	26.1	24.3	10.9	2.1	72.9	35.7	47.8	52.2
HENRY	1.5	2.3	6.3	6.7	6.1	5.4	5.5	25.4	29.0	13.2	2.5	77.6	40.6	48.4	51.6
HOUSTON	1.3	1.8	6.9	6.6	6.4	6.5	6.2	26.8	26.6	12.0	2.0	76.1	38.5	47.8	52.2
JACKSON	1.1	1.7	6.3	6.4	6.3	5.7	5.4	27.9	27.4	13.0	1.6	77.4	39.4	49.2	50.8
JEFFERSON	1.6	2.2	6.5	6.3	6.5	6.7	6.5	27.8	26.3	11.3	2.1	76.8	37.5	47.5	52.5
LAMAR	1.3	2.0	6.2	5.9	5.9	5.6	5.9	27.5	26.7	13.9	2.3	78.7	40.2	48.6	51.4
LAUDERDALE	1.0	1.5	6.0	5.8	5.9	6.2	6.3	27.6	26.6	13.4	2.2	78.8	39.6	48.1	51.9
LAWRENCE	1.1	1.5	6.5	6.2	6.8	6.3	5.9	29.3	26.2	11.4	1.5	76.7	38.6	49.4	50.6
LEE	1.4	2.1	6.4	5.9	6.0	9.7	16.0	27.1	20.5	7.4	1.0	78.3	28.8	49.5	50.5
LIMESTONE	2.6	4.0	6.7	6.7	6.4	5.9	5.5	30.5	26.5	10.5	1.3	76.6	37.9	51.0	49.0
LOWNDES	0.6	0.7	7.8	7.5	6.9	7.5	7.4	24.2	26.0	11.2	1.5	73.2	36.6	46.5	53.5
MACON	0.7	0.8	6.4	6.4	6.7	10.3	10.4	22.0	23.7	12.0	2.2	76.5	33.4	46.2	53.8
MADISON	1.9	2.7	6.9	6.7	6.8	7.1	6.2	28.5	25.9	10.6	1.3	77.4	37.4	48.9	51.1
MARENGO	1.0	1.2	7.1	6.5	7.5	7.0	6.4	24.3	26.3	12.7	2.1	74.6	38.2	47.6	52.4
MARION	1.2	1.8	6.3	6.3	5.5	5.5	5.4	27.9	26.6	14.2	2.3	78.6	40.4	50.3	49.7
MARSHALL	5.7	8.6	6.9	6.6	6.6	5.7	5.6	28.1	25.9	12.8	1.8	76.4	38.7	49.0	51.0
MOBILE	1.2	1.6	7.5	6.9	7.1	7.0	6.8	27.0	25.3	10.7	1.6	74.3	35.7	48.0	52.0
MONROE	0.8	1.0	7.6	7.5	7.2	6.0	6.6	25.5	26.1	11.6	1.9	74.1	37.2	47.9	52.1
MONTGOMERY	1.2	1.6	6.8	6.6	6.7	7.6	7.8	27.8	24.4	10.4	1.8	75.7	35.0	47.8	52.2
MORGAN	3.3	4.9	6.6	6.4	6.6	6.3	5.9	28.2	26.9	11.4	1.6	76.5	38.6	49.2	50.8
PERRY	0.9	1.0	7.9	7.0	7.4	9.1	7.5	22.7	22.5	13.0	2.8	72.7	34.5	45.8	54.2
PICKENS	0.7	0.7	7.3	6.7	6.7	6.4	6.1	25.0	26.3	13.4	2.2	75.3	38.7	47.6	52.4
PIKE	1.2	1.7	6.9	6.3	6.0	7.6	9.2	27.4	23.8	10.9	1.9	77.2	33.7	47.4	52.6
RANDOLPH	1.2	1.8	6.8	6.4	6.8	6.1	6.0	26.1	26.0	13.5	2.2	76.4	39.0	48.8	51.2
RUSSELL	1.5	2.1	7.2	6.7	7.0	6.6	6.7	27.0	25.3	11.9	1.6	75.1	36.8	47.9	52.1
ST. CLAIR	1.1	1.6	6.7	6.6	6.3	6.4	5.7	28.8	27.1	11.1	1.3	76.5	38.5	50.6	49.4
SHELBY	2.0	3.1	7.3	7.7	6.8	6.2	5.4	30.6	27.2	8.1	0.8	74.6	36.5	49.0	51.0
SUMTER	1.1	1.2	7.7	6.7	7.4	7.0	8.6	25.0	24.8	10.4	2.3	74.4	33.8	46.5	53.5
TALLADEGA	1.0	1.4	6.5	6.3	6.3	6.3	6.4	27.5	27.0	11.9	1.7	77.6	38.4	49.4	50.6
TALLAPOOSA	0.6	0.6	6.2	6.1	6.3	5.8	5.6	24.8	28.7	14.0	2.5	77.9	41.4	48.2	51.8
TUSCALOOSA	1.3	1.9	6.5	6.3	6.3	7.6	9.6	27.9	24.2	10.1	1.5	77.2	33.9	48.3	51.7
WALKER	0.9	0.9	6.5	6.5	5.8	5.5	5.2	27.2	27.7	13.6	1.9	77.9	40.3	48.7	51.3
WASHINGTON	0.9	1.2	7.5	7.1	7.8	6.5	6.9	26.2	25.5	11.0	1.5	73.7	36.2	49.4	50.6
WILCOX	0.7	0.7	8.5	8.0	7.2	6.5	7.4	24.7	24.2	11.4	2.0	72.2	35.0	47.2	52.8
WINSTON	1.5	1.5	6.4	6.4	6.0	5.5	5.4	28.1	26.8	13.6	1.8	77.9	40.1	49.2	50.8
ALABAMA	1.7	2.5	6.8	6.5	6.5	6.6	6.7	27.5	26.1	11.5	1.8	76.4	37.5	48.6	51.4
UNITED STATES	12.5	15.0	6.9	6.5	6.8	7.1	7.0	27.6	25.4	10.7	1.9	75.6	36.7	49.2	50.8

COUNTY	HOUSEHOLDS					FAMILIES			MEDIAN HOUSEHOLD INCOME			
	2000	2007	2012	% Annual Rate 2000-2007	2007 Average HH Size	2000	2007	% Annual Rate 2000-2007	2007	2012	2007 National Rank	2007 State Rank
AUTAUGA	16,003	18,654	20,593	2.1	2.64	12,353	14,192	1.9	50,067	56,034	674	3
BALDWIN	55,336	71,166	84,429	3.5	2.43	40,260	50,883	3.3	46,838	51,858	922	5
BARBOUR	10,409	10,615	10,570	0.3	2.46	7,393	7,402	0.0	28,952	31,776	2962	55
BIBB	7,421	8,084	8,442	1.2	2.56	5,581	5,982	1.0	36,543	40,276	2186	25
BLOUNT	19,265	21,248	22,736	1.4	2.58	14,807	16,094	1.2	41,205	45,903	1568	10
BULLOCK	3,986	4,013	3,999	0.1	2.49	2,731	2,696	-0.2	23,587	25,933	3107	63
BUTLER	8,398	8,478	8,413	0.1	2.43	5,872	5,813	-0.1	28,282	31,169	2989	57
CALHOUN	45,307	46,768	47,441	0.4	2.35	31,300	31,675	0.2	36,712	40,427	2162	24
CHAMBERS	14,522	14,382	14,159	-0.1	2.41	10,197	9,909	-0.4	34,278	37,550	2514	36
CHEROKEE	9,719	10,512	10,888	1.1	2.36	7,202	7,664	0.9	36,088	40,256	2258	29
CHILTON	15,287	16,808	17,728	1.3	2.52	11,339	12,265	1.1	38,297	42,661	1963	17
CHOCTAW	6,363	6,786	7,017	0.9	2.38	4,573	4,790	0.6	28,192	31,033	2994	58
CLARKE	10,578	10,715	10,672	0.2	2.51	7,699	7,665	-0.1	31,949	35,170	2768	46
CLAY	5,765	6,140	6,363	0.9	2.35	4,098	4,286	0.6	32,078	35,782	2753	45
CLEBURNE	5,590	5,900	6,070	0.7	2.44	4,128	4,285	0.5	35,950	40,131	2287	30
COFFEE	17,421	19,394	20,770	1.5	2.39	12,485	13,652	1.2	38,424	42,290	1944	16
COLBERT	22,461	23,064	23,307	0.4	2.36	16,038	16,172	0.1	37,048	40,804	2121	23
CONECUH	5,792	5,956	6,014	0.4	2.33	3,941	3,971	0.1	26,267	28,813	3061	60
COOSA	4,682	4,851	4,796	0.5	2.45	3,407	3,469	0.2	34,442	37,597	2502	35
COVINGTON	15,640	15,699	15,623	0.1	2.32	10,788	10,617	-0.2	30,432	33,233	2889	52
CRENSHAW	5,577	5,892	6,081	0.8	2.36	3,891	4,032	0.5	30,325	32,894	2895	53
CULLMAN	30,706	32,435	33,749	0.8	2.48	22,487	23,352	0.5	37,872	42,192	2012	18
DALE	18,878	19,141	19,161	0.2	2.44	13,637	13,585	-0.1	37,051	40,779	2120	22
DALLAS	17,841	17,263	16,723	-0.5	2.49	12,494	11,858	-0.7	25,906	28,467	3073	61
DEKALB	25,113	26,620	27,693	0.8	2.53	18,440	19,213	0.6	35,355	39,243	2389	33
ELMORE	22,737	27,155	30,804	2.5	2.64	17,542	20,646	2.3	48,476	54,172	783	4
ESCAMBIA	14,297	14,431	14,382	0.1	2.41	10,088	9,991	-0.1	32,864	36,006	2670	41
ETOWAH	41,615	42,598	42,981	0.3	2.38	29,467	29,604	0.1	36,128	39,724	2252	28
FAYETTE	7,493	7,557	7,545	0.1	2.35	5,342	5,291	-0.1	32,968	36,726	2655	40
FRANKLIN	12,259	12,496	12,614	0.3	2.49	8,954	8,972	0.0	31,518	35,216	2796	47
GENEVA	10,477	10,932	11,185	0.6	2.38	7,457	7,639	0.3	30,571	33,476	2880	50
GREENE	3,931	4,083	4,069	0.5	2.40	2,651	2,696	0.2	22,207	24,404	3123	65
HALE	6,415	6,843	7,106	0.9	2.56	4,606	4,826	0.6	29,330	32,247	2944	54
HENRY	6,525	7,058	7,407	1.1	2.40	4,728	5,024	0.8	34,964	37,687	2434	34
HOUSTON	35,834	39,555	42,336	1.4	2.41	25,113	27,197	1.1	39,623	43,702	1763	12
JACKSON	21,615	22,510	22,892	0.6	2.40	15,830	16,207	0.3	37,339	41,615	2089	20
JEFFERSON	263,265	270,175	273,407	0.4	2.41	175,950	176,775	0.1	42,480	46,831	1401	9
LAMAR	6,468	6,529	6,517	0.1	2.36	4,715	4,679	-0.1	32,298	36,011	2732	44
LAUDERDALE	36,088	37,109	37,582	0.4	2.34	25,163	25,382	0.1	38,498	42,390	1929	15
LAWRENCE	13,538	13,901	14,003	0.4	2.48	10,197	10,303	0.1	37,168	41,474	2107	21
LEE	45,702	53,204	58,221	2.1	2.36	27,270	30,941	1.8	35,466	38,932	2372	32
LIMESTONE	24,688	27,764	30,094	1.6	2.52	18,231	20,163	1.4	43,584	48,651	1266	8
LOWNDES	4,909	5,086	5,072	0.5	2.61	3,588	3,654	0.3	26,439	29,030	3056	59
MACON	8,950	8,787	8,601	-0.3	2.35	5,543	5,311	-0.6	24,314	26,212	3101	62
MADISON	109,955	124,430	135,399	1.7	2.42	75,342	83,553	1.4	51,798	58,041	561	2
MARENGO	8,767	8,824	8,755	0.1	2.45	6,280	6,208	-0.2	30,692	33,861	2866	49
MARION	12,697	12,979	13,129	0.3	2.32	9,040	9,073	0.1	32,689	36,338	2686	42
MARSHALL	32,547	34,817	36,632	0.9	2.50	23,527	24,724	0.7	37,822	42,172	2022	19
MOBILE	150,179	154,868	158,178	0.4	2.59	106,745	108,066	0.2	38,640	42,480	1909	14
MONROE	9,383	9,874	10,106	0.7	2.47	6,774	7,002	0.5	33,471	36,643	2610	39
MONTGOMERY	86,068	88,207	89,180	0.3	2.39	56,807	56,967	0.0	40,830	44,513	1625	11
MORGAN	43,602	46,123	47,698	0.8	2.47	31,445	32,681	0.5	43,714	48,089	1249	7
PERRY	4,333	4,310	4,226	-0.1	2.53	3,046	2,974	-0.3	22,993	25,373	3114	64
PICKENS	8,086	8,276	8,406	0.3	2.50	5,790	5,818	0.1	30,465	33,324	2886	51
PIKE	11,933	12,529	12,888	0.7	2.32	7,646	7,847	0.4	28,360	31,157	2986	56
RANDOLPH	8,642	9,232	9,551	0.9	2.48	6,225	6,532	0.7	33,691	37,323	2585	38
RUSSELL	19,741	21,038	21,814	0.9	2.42	13,424	14,018	0.6	31,355	34,467	2806	48
ST. CLAIR	24,143	28,353	32,308	2.2	2.59	18,437	21,325	2.0	43,728	48,728	1248	6
SHELBY	54,631	70,926	85,283	3.7	2.56	40,617	51,873	3.4	66,467	76,773	159	1
SUMTER	5,708	5,623	5,495	-0.2	2.46	3,665	3,529	-0.5	21,324	23,444	3131	66
TALLADEGA	30,674	31,477	31,981	0.4	2.45	21,911	22,069	0.1	36,458	40,173	2202	26
TALLAPOOSA	16,656	17,102	17,170	0.4	2.37	11,807	11,903	0.1	35,699	39,373	2333	31
TUSCALOOSA	64,517	70,084	73,708	1.1	2.36	41,689	44,246	0.8	39,076	42,873	1840	13
WALKER	28,364	28,661	28,890	0.1	2.43	20,469	20,318	-0.1	33,700	36,774	2584	37
WASHINGTON	6,705	6,989	7,135	0.6	2.60	5,042	5,174	0.4	36,374	40,580	2217	27
WILCOX	4,776	4,998	5,080	0.6	2.58	3,378	3,470	0.4	19,726	21,418	3135	67
WINSTON	10,107	10,373	10,480	0.4	2.37	7,286	7,346	0.1	32,687	36,307	2687	43
ALABAMA				0.9	2.45			0.7	39,727	44,191		
UNITED STATES				1.2	2.59			1.0	53,154	62,503		

COUNTY	2007 Per Capita Income	2007 HH Income Base	2007 HOUSEHOLD INCOME DISTRIBUTION (%)					2007 Home Value Base	2007 HOME VALUE DISTRIBUTION (%)					2007 Median Home Value
			Less than $25,000	$25,000 to $49,999	$50,000 to $99,999	$100,000 to $149,999	$150,000 or More		Less than $50,000	$50,000 to $89,999	$90,000 to $174,999	$175,000 to $399,999	$400,000 or More	
AUTAUGA	22,811	18,654	23.8	26.1	35.6	11.3	3.1	15,309	19.5	17.8	39.1	21.5	2.2	111,238
BALDWIN	25,474	71,166	23.9	29.8	31.7	9.5	5.2	57,533	11.9	12.0	33.2	32.2	10.7	157,672
BARBOUR	16,633	10,615	44.6	26.0	21.3	5.5	2.5	7,953	30.7	27.5	27.2	12.4	2.3	77,504
BIBB	17,125	8,084	34.9	30.5	27.0	6.6	1.0	6,563	30.5	25.4	29.3	13.3	1.5	78,592
BLOUNT	19,629	21,248	28.7	30.9	31.2	7.2	2.0	17,917	21.2	18.2	36.8	20.4	3.3	107,387
BULLOCK	13,087	4,013	51.9	27.9	15.8	3.5	1.0	3,047	31.0	25.4	31.2	8.4	4.0	78,840
BUTLER	17,896	8,478	44.5	30.1	18.6	3.9	2.9	6,570	33.0	27.6	26.9	11.1	1.3	71,244
CALHOUN	20,733	46,768	34.8	30.4	25.3	6.6	2.8	34,638	22.2	25.1	37.6	13.0	2.0	93,342
CHAMBERS	18,096	14,382	38.2	30.3	25.4	4.3	1.7	11,079	21.7	31.8	35.0	9.7	1.7	84,122
CHEROKEE	18,642	10,512	34.5	32.6	26.1	5.3	1.6	8,718	24.8	21.7	35.0	15.1	3.3	94,473
CHILTON	18,521	16,808	31.7	31.3	29.0	6.6	1.5	13,976	21.2	20.8	37.0	18.3	2.6	103,573
CHOCTAW	17,806	6,786	45.1	26.4	20.6	5.8	2.1	5,860	37.6	24.5	26.1	9.5	2.3	69,503
CLARKE	17,764	10,715	41.1	25.6	24.4	7.3	1.7	8,796	30.1	27.2	29.8	11.3	1.5	76,418
CLAY	16,848	6,140	37.4	34.5	23.5	3.7	1.0	4,843	25.8	27.0	35.5	10.2	1.5	85,194
CLEBURNE	17,988	5,900	34.5	33.9	25.2	4.8	1.6	4,823	29.0	21.1	32.1	14.7	3.0	89,667
COFFEE	21,702	19,394	32.1	30.7	26.1	7.7	3.4	14,179	17.2	24.0	39.7	16.8	2.4	104,615
COLBERT	20,717	23,064	34.1	29.4	26.9	7.3	2.4	17,800	15.3	28.0	38.4	15.4	2.9	99,045
CONECUH	15,989	5,956	47.8	28.9	17.8	3.7	1.8	4,850	35.1	25.4	29.9	8.7	0.9	72,235
COOSA	18,063	4,851	36.4	32.5	24.8	4.5	1.7	4,138	33.1	24.3	29.3	11.0	2.3	77,727
COVINGTON	18,475	15,699	41.8	29.7	21.6	4.6	2.3	12,390	27.9	29.6	29.6	10.3	2.5	76,971
CRENSHAW	17,021	5,892	42.6	31.0	20.2	4.5	1.7	4,605	31.6	31.9	25.6	9.5	1.5	73,371
CULLMAN	19,869	32,435	32.1	32.2	26.8	6.0	2.9	25,740	17.3	18.5	38.6	21.1	4.5	117,041
DALE	18,383	19,141	34.2	31.7	26.9	5.7	1.5	12,751	21.9	27.3	38.0	10.7	2.0	90,914
DALLAS	15,895	17,263	48.8	24.0	20.6	4.8	1.9	11,675	29.1	24.8	33.2	11.1	1.8	81,140
DEKALB	18,155	26,620	35.4	31.6	26.0	4.9	2.2	21,341	23.5	25.2	35.0	13.3	3.0	91,886
ELMORE	22,053	27,155	22.5	29.2	33.8	10.3	4.2	22,382	14.8	18.0	40.2	23.3	3.7	119,733
ESCAMBIA	17,909	14,431	40.5	27.8	24.1	5.4	2.3	11,303	28.2	25.7	33.3	11.2	1.6	81,277
ETOWAH	20,072	42,598	35.3	29.7	25.8	6.5	2.7	32,320	22.8	25.4	34.6	15.1	2.1	93,488
FAYETTE	17,472	7,557	37.9	32.7	23.8	4.4	1.2	5,955	28.4	26.0	34.4	10.5	0.7	82,984
FRANKLIN	17,111	12,496	40.1	28.9	24.0	5.3	1.7	9,513	22.8	27.3	35.9	13.1	1.0	89,970
GENEVA	17,375	10,932	42.4	29.1	22.3	4.3	1.8	8,937	26.0	31.5	31.9	8.7	1.9	77,445
GREENE	15,368	4,083	54.2	25.5	15.4	2.9	2.0	3,145	38.3	26.5	27.1	7.0	1.1	64,637
HALE	14,994	6,843	43.8	28.2	22.6	4.1	1.3	5,540	36.0	23.2	26.9	12.2	1.7	72,910
HENRY	18,630	7,058	39.1	27.9	25.0	5.8	2.1	5,783	22.7	29.8	31.0	15.0	1.5	86,263
HOUSTON	22,453	39,555	32.2	28.1	27.6	8.1	3.9	28,317	15.1	23.3	40.0	18.6	2.9	107,973
JACKSON	19,545	22,510	33.0	31.3	27.5	6.2	1.9	17,861	24.2	24.8	34.3	14.4	2.3	91,633
JEFFERSON	24,886	270,173	29.5	28.1	27.6	9.3	5.6	184,056	9.7	21.9	37.3	24.8	6.3	122,313
LAMAR	17,102	6,529	38.7	31.7	24.6	3.8	1.2	5,130	30.2	30.9	28.5	9.2	1.3	73,333
LAUDERDALE	21,975	37,109	33.4	29.0	26.4	7.9	3.3	27,721	12.4	21.1	41.3	21.7	3.5	116,609
LAWRENCE	19,452	13,901	33.8	29.4	27.6	6.8	2.4	11,655	29.4	27.4	31.4	11.0	0.8	78,972
LEE	20,587	53,204	39.1	23.3	26.1	8.5	3.1	33,824	21.8	12.3	32.7	26.9	6.3	132,893
LIMESTONE	21,648	27,764	28.6	27.6	30.7	10.0	3.2	21,875	15.1	20.2	42.4	19.9	2.4	110,269
LOWNDES	15,495	5,086	47.9	25.5	20.4	3.8	2.5	4,255	40.5	23.7	23.6	9.6	2.4	63,432
MACON	16,001	8,787	50.9	26.4	16.9	3.9	2.0	6,018	21.0	27.6	39.9	10.1	1.4	91,963
MADISON	28,038	124,430	22.9	25.3	30.9	14.5	6.3	89,154	6.6	14.9	43.3	30.1	5.2	138,933
MARENGO	18,270	8,824	43.8	23.5	23.0	7.2	2.5	7,066	33.3	23.5	30.0	11.1	2.1	79,009
MARION	18,676	12,979	38.8	31.9	22.5	4.6	2.2	10,285	29.2	25.4	31.9	12.1	1.3	81,914
MARSHALL	19,898	34,817	32.5	31.1	26.5	7.1	2.9	26,631	15.3	21.1	39.2	19.3	5.1	113,336
MOBILE	19,972	154,868	33.4	28.3	27.3	7.6	3.3	109,106	13.0	21.8	43.3	18.4	3.6	112,926
MONROE	18,107	9,874	39.1	28.7	24.3	5.8	2.1	8,025	33.8	24.2	30.3	10.8	0.9	74,667
MONTGOMERY	23,320	88,207	29.9	28.8	27.1	9.6	4.7	58,091	10.5	23.3	41.1	20.4	4.7	114,930
MORGAN	22,740	46,123	28.0	28.5	30.2	9.5	3.8	34,476	14.6	24.4	40.8	18.0	2.2	103,439
PERRY	13,461	4,310	52.7	25.1	17.6	3.0	1.5	3,212	40.9	28.1	23.4	6.3	1.2	60,000
PICKENS	16,825	8,276	42.8	26.7	24.1	4.6	1.8	6,678	28.3	24.7	33.5	12.3	1.2	84,987
PIKE	17,652	12,529	44.9	28.4	20.1	4.1	2.5	8,615	28.7	24.7	28.9	14.8	2.9	83,337
RANDOLPH	17,196	9,232	37.1	32.4	24.5	4.2	1.8	7,438	27.3	23.5	34.1	12.5	2.6	88,774
RUSSELL	16,434	21,038	40.1	30.5	24.4	3.9	1.1	13,582	21.0	20.8	44.5	12.2	1.5	99,407
ST. CLAIR	21,184	28,353	26.1	30.6	31.7	8.2	3.4	23,983	20.8	18.2	33.2	23.0	4.9	113,425
SHELBY	34,792	70,926	14.5	21.0	34.5	18.1	11.9	58,310	9.8	6.7	23.6	45.8	14.1	200,214
SUMTER	13,426	5,623	55.1	24.9	16.1	2.5	1.4	4,140	43.7	22.6	25.5	6.9	1.4	60,187
TALLADEGA	18,818	31,477	36.5	29.5	25.3	6.5	2.2	24,438	25.0	24.4	33.1	14.8	2.6	90,999
TALLAPOOSA	20,544	17,102	35.6	29.6	25.0	6.8	3.1	13,296	20.8	25.7	31.1	16.7	5.6	95,885
TUSCALOOSA	22,438	70,084	33.5	26.3	27.8	8.7	3.8	45,785	13.8	12.9	37.4	30.8	5.1	141,459
WALKER	18,410	28,661	38.6	29.1	24.3	5.9	2.2	23,231	29.0	26.7	31.6	11.5	1.2	79,913
WASHINGTON	17,426	6,989	36.1	27.8	29.6	5.0	1.5	6,161	33.9	24.1	33.1	7.5	1.5	75,361
WILCOX	12,375	4,998	56.6	24.9	14.2	2.9	1.4	4,177	44.2	24.4	21.3	8.0	2.2	58,855
WINSTON	18,428	10,373	38.2	34.5	20.2	4.6	2.5	8,438	32.2	25.2	27.7	11.2	3.6	77,303
ALABAMA	21,955		32.2	28.3	27.3	8.4	3.9		17.5	21.0	36.4	20.7	4.4	110,498
UNITED STATES	27,916		21.9	25.0	32.3	12.3	8.4		7.9	10.5	27.1	35.6	19.0	192,285

SPENDING POTENTIAL INDICES

COUNTY	FINANCIAL SERVICES				THE HOME						ENTERTAINMENT						PERSONAL			
					Home Improvements		Furnishings													
	Auto Loan	Home Loan	Invest-ments	Retire-ment Plans	Home Repair	Lawn & Garden	Comput-ers & Hard-ware	Major Appli-ances	TV, Radio, Sound Equip-ment	Furni-ture	Dine out/ Carry out	Sports Equip-ment	Fees & Tickets	Toys & Games	Travel	Cable TV	Apparel & Services	Auto Repairs	Health Insur-ance	Pets & Supplies
AUTAUGA	94	86	72	84	83	91	80	87	83	82	82	79	78	86	80	84	73	84	87	90
BALDWIN	95	85	75	84	88	100	82	92	85	82	85	82	79	86	84	88	74	88	95	95
BARBOUR	72	51	33	49	54	73	52	64	60	51	59	57	45	62	51	65	51	61	70	70
BIBB	75	56	38	53	59	77	56	68	62	55	62	61	49	65	55	66	53	64	73	74
BLOUNT	88	65	42	62	69	90	64	78	70	63	70	70	56	74	63	75	60	73	83	85
BULLOCK	58	38	21	36	42	59	40	51	47	39	47	46	33	49	39	52	40	48	57	57
BUTLER	73	52	34	50	56	76	53	66	62	53	61	59	46	63	53	68	53	63	74	72
CALHOUN	76	62	56	61	64	76	65	71	69	63	68	62	60	70	64	73	60	69	77	74
CHAMBERS	73	53	39	51	56	74	55	66	63	53	62	58	48	65	54	67	53	62	73	70
CHEROKEE	77	55	33	52	60	82	54	70	61	53	61	62	46	64	54	66	52	64	75	76
CHILTON	80	58	39	55	63	84	58	72	65	57	65	64	50	69	57	70	56	67	78	79
CHOCTAW	75	49	25	46	55	78	51	67	60	49	59	61	41	63	50	66	50	62	74	75
CLARKE	78	54	32	51	59	81	55	70	63	53	63	62	46	66	54	68	53	64	76	77
CLAY	70	48	28	45	53	73	48	62	56	48	55	56	41	59	48	61	47	57	68	69
CLEBURNE	79	54	29	51	59	82	54	70	61	53	61	62	45	65	52	66	52	64	75	77
COFFEE	81	67	58	66	69	82	69	76	73	67	73	68	64	75	68	76	63	74	81	79
COLBERT	77	62	54	60	66	80	63	72	69	62	68	63	58	70	63	73	59	69	80	76
CONECUH	63	43	28	42	47	65	46	57	54	44	53	51	39	55	45	58	45	54	63	62
COOSA	76	54	31	51	59	80	54	70	62	53	61	62	46	64	54	67	52	64	75	76
COVINGTON	71	52	39	50	56	74	54	65	61	52	60	57	47	63	54	66	51	61	73	70
CRENSHAW	70	47	28	44	53	73	49	63	57	47	56	56	41	60	49	62	48	58	71	69
CULLMAN	81	63	50	61	66	84	63	74	69	62	68	66	57	71	63	73	59	70	80	79
DALE	70	57	52	57	58	67	61	64	64	59	64	58	56	66	59	66	56	64	69	67
DALLAS	61	48	43	48	49	60	50	56	57	51	56	48	47	57	50	60	49	55	62	59
DEKALB	80	58	37	55	62	82	57	71	64	57	64	64	50	68	56	69	55	66	76	78
ELMORE	96	82	67	81	83	96	79	89	83	80	83	80	75	86	79	86	72	85	92	93
ESCAMBIA	74	54	39	52	58	76	56	67	63	54	62	59	49	65	55	68	53	63	75	72
ETOWAH	73	61	57	61	64	76	62	69	68	62	67	61	59	69	63	71	59	67	76	72
FAYETTE	70	51	35	48	55	73	51	64	58	50	57	57	44	61	51	62	49	59	69	69
FRANKLIN	73	52	36	50	57	75	54	66	60	52	60	58	46	63	52	64	51	61	71	71
GENEVA	71	50	30	47	56	76	51	66	58	49	57	58	43	61	51	63	49	60	72	71
GREENE	60	41	31	40	43	59	46	53	54	45	53	47	39	54	44	58	46	53	61	58
HALE	68	45	26	43	50	69	48	60	56	46	55	55	39	57	46	61	47	57	67	67
HENRY	76	55	35	52	60	80	55	70	63	54	62	62	48	65	55	68	53	65	77	76
HOUSTON	82	73	66	72	72	81	71	77	76	72	75	68	69	77	71	78	66	75	81	80
JACKSON	80	58	41	56	63	83	59	72	66	58	65	64	51	69	58	70	56	67	78	78
JEFFERSON	84	80	86	83	79	81	83	80	85	83	84	72	82	84	82	86	76	83	84	82
LAMAR	72	49	26	46	54	75	49	64	57	48	56	57	41	60	48	61	48	59	70	71
LAUDERDALE	78	66	63	66	69	80	69	74	73	67	72	66	65	74	68	75	63	72	80	77
LAWRENCE	85	59	36	56	64	87	59	75	67	58	67	67	50	71	58	73	57	69	81	83
LEE	72	58	57	61	55	60	76	64	72	66	72	62	66	70	66	69	64	70	64	66
LIMESTONE	88	73	61	72	75	89	72	82	77	72	77	73	67	80	72	81	67	78	87	86
LOWNDES	70	47	26	44	52	74	49	63	57	48	57	56	40	59	48	63	48	59	70	70
MACON	60	45	41	46	46	58	50	54	54	49	55	47	45	56	48	60	49	54	61	58
MADISON	97	95	96	97	92	94	95	93	95	96	95	85	94	96	94	95	85	94	94	95
MARENGO	75	54	37	52	58	77	56	68	64	55	63	60	49	66	55	69	54	64	75	74
MARION	76	53	35	51	58	79	55	68	62	53	61	60	46	65	53	66	52	63	74	74
MARSHALL	82	56	49	61	67	85	64	75	70	62	69	67	57	73	63	74	60	71	81	80
MOBILE	77	68	67	69	67	74	70	71	74	70	73	63	67	74	69	76	65	72	76	74
MONROE	77	54	33	51	59	80	55	69	63	54	63	62	47	66	54	68	54	65	76	76
MONTGOMERY	80	75	80	78	73	76	78	76	81	79	80	68	78	80	77	82	72	79	79	77
MORGAN	85	74	70	74	76	86	74	80	79	74	78	72	71	81	74	81	69	78	85	84
PERRY	56	38	29	38	40	54	42	49	50	42	49	43	37	50	41	55	43	49	57	53
PICKENS	75	50	25	47	57	80	51	68	59	50	59	61	41	62	50	64	50	62	74	75
PIKE	65	50	41	50	51	62	55	59	59	53	59	53	49	60	52	62	52	59	63	62
RANDOLPH	76	52	29	49	57	79	52	68	60	52	60	60	44	64	51	65	51	62	73	74
RUSSELL	62	48	43	48	48	59	52	56	58	51	57	50	47	58	50	60	49	56	62	59
ST. CLAIR	92	73	53	70	76	94	70	84	76	71	76	75	64	80	70	81	66	79	88	90
SHELBY	133	135	119	134	128	128	123	126	120	128	121	118	124	126	123	119	109	123	120	129
SUMTER	57	37	22	35	40	57	42	50	48	39	47	46	34	49	39	51	40	48	56	55
TALLADEGA	75	59	47	57	62	78	59	69	66	59	65	61	54	68	59	71	57	66	76	74
TALLAPOOSA	82	59	42	57	65	86	62	76	70	59	68	67	53	72	61	75	59	71	83	81
TUSCALOOSA	79	68	68	70	67	74	76	73	77	72	77	67	71	76	72	77	68	75	76	75
WALKER	77	54	34	51	59	80	56	70	63	54	63	62	47	66	55	68	53	65	76	76
WASHINGTON	81	55	30	51	60	84	55	72	63	54	64	66	46	67	54	69	54	66	77	79
WILCOX	56	37	20	35	41	58	38	50	46	37	45	45	32	47	38	50	38	46	56	55
WINSTON	77	54	32	51	59	80	54	69	61	53	61	61	46	65	53	66	52	64	74	75
ALABAMA	83	70	62	70	71	83	72	77	76	71	76	69	67	77	71	79	67	76	82	81
UNITED STATES	100	100	100	100	100	100	100	100	100	100	100	100	100	100	100	100	100	100	100	100

COUNTY	FIPS Code	CBSA Code	DMA Code	POPULATION			2000-2007 ANNUAL RATE		RACE (%)					
									White		Black		Asian/Pacific	
				2000	2007	2012	% Rate	State Rank	2000	2007	2000	2007	2000	2007
ALEUTIANS EAST	013	00000	000	2,697	2,688	2,646	0.0	12	24.0	22.8	1.7	1.7	26.8	26.8
ALEUTIANS WEST	016	00000	000	5,465	5,275	5,112	-0.5	16	40.0	36.4	3.0	2.6	25.2	26.5
ANCHORAGE MUNICIPALI	020	11260	743	260,283	283,369	294,395	1.2	4	72.2	69.1	5.8	5.4	6.5	7.1
BETHEL	050	00000	000	16,006	17,427	18,411	1.2	4	12.5	11.3	0.4	0.4	1.1	1.1
BRISTOL BAY	060	00000	000	1,258	1,082	1,015	-2.1	26	52.5	48.8	0.6	0.6	0.7	0.8
DENALI	068	00000	000	1,893	1,779	1,731	-0.9	20	85.7	83.0	1.4	1.5	1.9	2.1
DILLINGHAM	070	00000	000	4,922	4,753	4,600	-0.5	16	21.6	19.4	0.4	0.4	0.6	0.7
FAIRBANKS NORTH STAR	090	21820	745	82,840	89,457	94,305	1.1	5	77.8	75.1	5.8	5.4	2.4	2.6
HAINES	100	00000	000	2,392	2,239	2,129	-0.9	20	82.5	79.7	0.1	0.1	0.8	0.9
JUNEAU CITY/BOROUGH	110	27940	747	30,711	31,592	32,114	0.4	9	74.8	71.1	0.8	0.7	5.1	5.6
KENAI PENINSULA	122	00000	743	49,691	51,595	52,812	0.5	7	86.2	83.8	0.5	0.4	1.1	1.3
KETCHIKAN GATEWAY	130	28540	000	14,070	13,315	12,773	-0.8	18	74.3	70.9	0.5	0.5	4.4	5.0
KODIAK ISLAND	150	28980	000	13,913	13,843	13,730	-0.1	14	59.7	58.2	1.0	1.0	16.8	17.3
LAKE AND PENINSULA	164	00000	000	1,823	1,587	1,473	-1.9	25	18.8	16.5	0.1	0.1	0.4	0.4
MATANUSKA-SUSITNA	170	11260	743	59,322	80,879	101,783	4.4	1	87.6	85.2	0.7	0.7	0.8	0.9
NOME	180	00000	000	9,196	9,377	9,458	0.3	10	19.3	17.3	0.4	0.4	0.7	0.7
NORTH SLOPE	185	00000	000	7,385	6,971	6,694	-0.8	18	17.1	15.2	0.7	0.6	6.8	6.9
NORTHWEST ARCTIC	188	00000	000	7,208	7,225	7,208	0.0	12	12.3	11.4	0.2	0.2	0.9	0.9
PRINCE OF WALES-OUTE	201	00000	000	6,146	5,580	5,227	-1.3	24	53.1	48.9	0.1	0.2	0.4	0.4
SITKA CITY/BOROUGH	220	00000	000	8,835	9,073	9,282	0.4	9	68.5	64.5	0.3	0.3	4.1	4.5
SKAGWAY-HOONAH-ANGOO	232	00000	000	3,436	3,150	2,959	-1.2	23	58.1	54.2	0.1	0.2	0.5	0.6
SOUTHEAST FAIRBANKS	240	00000	000	6,174	6,888	7,527	1.5	2	79.0	76.1	2.0	1.8	0.8	0.9
VALDEZ-CORDOVA	261	00000	000	10,195	10,094	9,992	-0.1	14	75.9	72.4	0.3	0.3	3.8	4.2
WADE HAMPTON	270	00000	000	7,028	7,464	7,712	0.8	6	4.7	4.2	0.1	0.1	0.1	0.1
WRANGELL-PETERSBURG	280	00000	000	6,684	6,179	5,814	-1.1	22	73.0	68.9	0.2	0.2	1.8	1.9
YAKUTAT CITY/BOROUGH	282	00000	000	808	670	607	-2.6	27	50.4	45.8	0.1	0.1	2.0	2.4
YUKON-KOYUKUK	290	00000	000	6,551	6,030	5,617	-1.1	22	24.3	21.5	0.1	0.1	0.4	0.4
ALASKA							1.1		69.3	67.2	3.5	3.2	4.5	4.8
UNITED STATES							1.2		75.1	72.7	12.3	12.6	3.8	4.5

ALASKA

B

POPULATION COMPOSITION

COUNTY	% HISPANIC ORIGIN		2007 AGE DISTRIBUTION (%)										MEDIAN AGE	% 2007 Males	% 2007 Females
	2000	2007	0-4	5-9	10-14	15-19	20-24	25-44	45-64	65-84	85+	18+	2007		
ALEUTIANS EAST	12.6	12.3	4.1	3.5	3.4	4.8	10.5	40.4	30.1	3.1	0.1	86.4	38.2	65.1	34.9
ALEUTIANS WEST	10.5	12.8	4.3	3.3	3.8	5.4	7.6	43.4	29.1	3.0	0.2	85.3	37.2	64.5	35.5
ANCHORAGE MUNICIPALI	5.7	7.3	7.5	6.8	7.5	7.7	8.0	28.8	27.0	6.1	0.6	73.5	33.8	50.3	49.7
BETHEL	0.9	1.0	10.8	8.4	9.8	11.0	8.5	26.5	19.9	4.7	0.5	64.3	26.0	53.1	46.9
BRISTOL BAY	0.6	0.6	6.7	6.9	7.3	8.3	6.0	23.4	34.9	6.3	0.2	73.2	40.4	54.5	45.5
DENALI	2.5	3.3	5.2	4.4	6.6	6.9	5.9	29.2	37.8	3.4	0.6	78.8	40.9	57.4	42.6
DILLINGHAM	2.3	2.7	9.3	8.1	8.8	9.4	8.3	23.5	24.8	7.0	0.7	67.3	30.2	51.6	48.4
FAIRBANKS NORTH STAR	4.2	5.4	7.9	6.5	6.6	8.3	11.2	29.0	24.7	5.5	0.5	74.2	30.1	51.9	48.1
HAINES	1.4	1.7	5.0	4.7	6.4	6.9	5.0	21.7	37.5	11.4	1.4	78.6	45.1	49.9	50.1
JUNEAU CITY/BOROUGH	3.4	4.3	6.1	5.5	6.8	7.6	7.6	26.2	32.1	7.1	0.9	76.6	38.4	49.7	50.3
KENAI PENINSULA	2.2	2.9	6.4	5.9	6.7	8.0	8.3	22.7	33.1	8.3	0.6	75.7	39.2	51.6	48.4
KETCHIKAN GATEWAY	2.6	3.3	6.8	6.2	7.1	7.9	8.2	24.8	29.7	8.4	1.0	75.8	37.7	50.7	49.3
KODIAK ISLAND	6.1	6.2	8.9	8.4	7.9	7.2	8.9	27.1	25.5	5.5	0.5	70.1	31.7	52.3	47.7
LAKE AND PENINSULA	1.2	1.3	8.5	6.7	9.0	9.3	10.2	22.4	26.8	6.7	0.4	70.4	29.4	51.8	48.2
MATANUSKA-SUSITNA	2.5	3.3	6.9	6.4	7.4	8.6	8.3	24.0	31.3	6.6	0.5	73.6	36.6	51.5	48.5
NOME	1.0	1.1	9.3	7.2	9.9	10.2	9.3	25.2	22.5	5.8	0.7	67.1	28.0	53.3	46.7
NORTH SLOPE	2.4	2.6	10.6	8.2	8.2	9.6	9.7	26.5	22.0	4.7	0.3	66.7	27.1	52.8	47.2
NORTHWEST ARCTIC	0.8	0.8	11.5	8.4	10.8	10.5	9.7	25.1	18.5	5.1	0.4	62.4	24.6	52.9	47.1
PRINCE OF WALES-OUTE	1.7	2.1	7.5	6.5	7.5	8.1	8.5	23.8	31.0	6.9	0.3	73.5	35.8	53.7	46.3
SITKA CITY/BOROUGH	3.3	4.1	6.2	5.3	6.3	8.4	8.9	24.7	29.6	9.5	1.0	77.0	37.6	50.7	49.3
SKAGWAY-HOONAH-ANGOO	2.8	3.3	5.4	4.4	7.3	6.7	7.3	25.9	33.8	8.7	0.6	78.7	40.9	53.1	46.9
SOUTHEAST FAIRBANKS	2.7	3.5	7.0	6.0	7.6	9.3	9.7	21.3	30.2	8.4	0.4	73.5	35.5	51.6	48.4
VALDEZ-CORDOVA	2.8	3.6	6.2	6.6	6.2	8.7	6.6	22.7	35.6	6.8	0.6	75.4	40.2	52.8	47.2
WADE HAMPTON	0.3	0.3	12.2	9.4	11.2	14.2	10.1	23.7	14.5	4.6	0.3	57.8	21.5	52.4	47.6
WRANGELL-PETERSBURG	2.0	2.5	6.5	6.4	6.4	9.0	5.8	22.8	32.6	9.1	1.3	73.8	39.5	51.7	48.3
YAKUTAT CITY/BOROUGH	0.7	0.9	4.3	4.9	8.4	6.4	7.2	27.5	35.2	6.1	0.0	77.6	41.0	60.3	39.7
YUKON-KOYUKUK	1.2	1.4	7.4	6.3	7.9	11.5	7.6	23.2	27.8	7.8	0.6	71.4	32.4	53.3	46.7
ALASKA	4.1	5.2	7.5	6.6	7.4	8.2	8.6	27.0	27.8	6.4	0.6	73.4	33.9	51.3	48.7
UNITED STATES	12.5	15.0	6.9	6.5	6.8	7.1	7.0	27.6	25.4	10.7	1.9	75.6	36.7	49.2	50.8

2-B

COUNTY	HOUSEHOLDS					FAMILIES			MEDIAN HOUSEHOLD INCOME			
	2000	2007	2012	% Annual Rate 2000-2007	2007 Average HH Size	2000	2007	% Annual Rate 2000-2007	2007	2012	2007 National Rank	2007 State Rank
ALEUTIANS EAST	526	508	499	-0.5	2.59	344	324	-0.8	56,451	65,443	346	14
ALEUTIANS WEST	1,270	1,218	1,166	-0.6	2.38	736	688	-0.9	78,444	92,182	62	2
ANCHORAGE MUNICIPALI	94,822	103,876	108,210	1.3	2.64	64,131	68,903	1.0	69,484	80,900	122	4
BETHEL	4,226	4,575	4,836	1.1	3.74	3,175	3,387	0.9	46,458	55,192	955	24
BRISTOL BAY	490	435	414	-1.6	2.49	301	261	-1.9	61,183	67,936	235	10
DENALI	785	803	792	0.3	2.14	453	452	0.0	66,686	77,811	153	6
DILLINGHAM	1,529	1,494	1,453	-0.3	3.16	1,106	1,062	-0.6	54,160	64,537	439	16
FAIRBANKS NORTH STAR	29,777	32,029	33,939	1.0	2.67	20,502	21,650	0.8	61,107	71,681	236	11
HAINES	991	952	916	-0.6	2.35	654	616	-0.8	47,812	53,804	836	21
JUNEAU CITY/BOROUGH	11,543	12,013	12,263	0.6	2.58	7,638	7,790	0.3	76,437	86,715	74	3
KENAI PENINSULA	18,438	19,598	20,275	0.8	2.56	12,716	13,270	0.6	55,731	63,470	376	15
KETCHIKAN GATEWAY	5,399	5,198	5,025	-0.5	2.51	3,634	3,430	-0.8	63,102	72,845	194	8
KODIAK ISLAND	4,424	4,433	4,389	0.0	3.08	3,257	3,214	-0.2	68,301	79,948	137	5
LAKE AND PENINSULA	588	520	486	-1.7	3.05	418	363	-1.9	44,591	50,694	1150	25
MATANUSKA-SUSITNA	20,556	28,498	36,144	4.6	2.80	15,057	20,543	4.4	62,051	70,783	210	9
NOME	2,693	2,767	2,804	0.4	3.30	1,899	1,916	0.1	51,481	60,227	580	19
NORTH SLOPE	2,109	2,004	1,923	-0.7	3.45	1,524	1,424	-0.9	80,767	95,078	50	1
NORTHWEST ARCTIC	1,780	1,807	1,810	0.2	3.83	1,405	1,409	0.0	59,086	71,096	287	12
PRINCE OF WALES-OUTE	2,262	2,110	2,001	-1.0	2.60	1,537	1,408	-1.2	47,318	52,374	883	22
SITKA CITY/BOROUGH	3,278	3,467	3,591	0.8	2.55	2,218	2,300	0.5	64,042	75,758	179	7
SKAGWAY-HOONAH-ANGOO	1,369	1,329	1,267	-0.4	2.36	867	824	-0.7	49,054	55,174	742	20
SOUTHEAST FAIRBANKS	2,098	2,400	2,657	1.9	2.74	1,506	1,694	1.6	46,978	53,467	909	23
VALDEZ-CORDOVA	3,884	3,948	3,945	0.2	2.52	2,559	2,549	-0.1	57,885	65,174	306	13
WADE HAMPTON	1,602	1,684	1,732	0.7	4.43	1,296	1,346	0.5	39,434	46,970	1791	26
WRANGELL-PETERSBURG	2,587	2,454	2,333	-0.7	2.50	1,765	1,644	-1.0	54,138	60,869	441	17
YAKUTAT CITY/BOROUGH	265	216	194	-2.8	2.51	159	127	-3.1	54,092	60,864	445	18
YUKON-KOYUKUK	2,309	2,174	2,039	-0.8	2.74	1,480	1,364	-1.1	35,578	41,590	2355	27
ALASKA				1.3	2.71			1.0	63,746	74,891		
UNITED STATES				1.2	2.59			1.0	53,154	62,503		

COUNTY	2007 Per Capita Income	2007 HH Income Base	2007 HOUSEHOLD INCOME DISTRIBUTION (%)					2007 Home Value Base	2007 HOME VALUE DISTRIBUTION (%)					2007 Median Home Value
			Less than $25,000	$25,000 to $49,999	$50,000 to $99,999	$100,000 to $149,999	$150,000 or More		Less than $50,000	$50,000 to $89,999	$90,000 to $174,999	$175,000 to $399,999	$400,000 or More	
ALEUTIANS EAST	25,223	508	18.5	26.0	30.1	14.4	11.0	316	2.5	4.7	45.9	41.5	5.4	171,988
ALEUTIANS WEST	29,777	1,218	8.0	16.9	39.0	23.7	12.3	376	3.2	10.1	42.3	33.2	11.2	164,286
ANCHORAGE MUNICIPALI	33,077	103,876	12.3	21.7	35.4	18.3	12.3	66,483	5.7	3.1	13.3	63.8	14.1	258,501
BETHEL	16,608	4,575	24.0	30.1	27.0	12.7	6.2	2,968	23.5	16.1	25.5	28.5	6.5	122,890
BRISTOL BAY	27,453	435	13.1	25.1	41.1	16.8	3.9	234	3.4	9.0	23.9	57.3	6.4	216,667
DENALI	36,082	803	14.9	21.9	34.6	21.8	6.7	556	7.0	14.7	29.0	40.6	8.6	172,872
DILLINGHAM	21,857	1,494	24.4	22.0	31.6	14.1	8.0	967	10.9	8.5	29.8	44.4	6.5	177,388
FAIRBANKS NORTH STAR	28,249	32,029	15.7	23.7	35.9	15.7	9.0	18,668	5.8	6.0	29.1	54.4	4.7	202,057
HAINES	27,476	952	23.5	28.7	31.7	11.4	4.6	696	9.8	9.3	27.9	40.1	12.9	187,209
JUNEAU CITY/BOROUGH	35,044	12,013	11.1	18.6	35.0	23.2	12.1	8,131	5.3	6.8	11.5	50.8	25.7	292,428
KENAI PENINSULA	26,763	19,598	20.3	24.6	33.4	15.5	6.1	15,068	7.6	6.6	28.2	50.5	7.1	191,072
KETCHIKAN GATEWAY	31,390	5,198	12.6	24.9	37.6	16.9	8.0	3,377	5.8	3.6	16.0	56.4	18.2	260,027
KODIAK ISLAND	28,236	4,433	12.6	21.7	34.1	19.5	12.2	2,618	4.9	4.0	22.9	53.4	14.7	238,827
LAKE AND PENINSULA	19,524	520	28.7	27.3	26.2	13.5	4.4	371	15.1	7.8	38.3	29.9	8.9	155,787
MATANUSKA-SUSITNA	26,668	28,498	17.9	22.4	35.8	16.2	7.7	23,228	5.8	6.3	20.6	59.1	8.2	218,299
NOME	20,261	2,767	23.7	24.9	30.3	14.2	6.9	1,720	15.2	14.8	35.6	31.9	2.4	132,237
NORTH SLOPE	27,804	2,004	14.0	12.9	34.0	23.7	15.5	1,055	4.5	8.1	36.0	47.2	4.2	179,531
NORTHWEST ARCTIC	19,010	1,807	19.1	24.1	32.8	15.1	8.9	1,082	7.8	10.4	38.7	37.2	5.8	158,696
PRINCE OF WALES-OUTE	21,825	2,110	23.5	29.7	35.2	8.7	3.0	1,553	26.9	8.7	23.6	31.3	9.5	148,463
SITKA CITY/BOROUGH	31,806	3,467	14.3	22.4	35.8	17.2	10.2	2,165	13.0	6.6	10.7	42.3	27.5	277,489
SKAGWAY-HOONAH-ANGOO	25,900	1,329	22.0	28.9	33.6	10.8	4.8	881	6.5	6.6	32.6	42.1	12.3	188,556
SOUTHEAST FAIRBANKS	21,609	2,400	28.4	24.1	31.5	12.0	4.0	1,743	11.0	12.0	37.3	30.6	9.0	156,994
VALDEZ-CORDOVA	29,202	3,948	20.3	23.0	32.1	16.4	8.2	2,807	17.1	9.9	21.7	42.0	9.3	179,903
WADE HAMPTON	11,180	1,684	29.1	33.6	28.9	5.9	2.5	1,169	40.6	13.3	25.4	18.6	2.0	70,962
WRANGELL-PETERSBURG	28,949	2,454	21.3	24.2	33.6	13.9	7.0	1,801	15.3	4.4	20.3	45.4	14.5	210,973
YAKUTAT CITY/BOROUGH	24,377	216	17.1	27.3	41.2	10.6	3.7	136	13.2	8.8	34.6	39.0	4.4	164,286
YUKON-KOYUKUK	17,613	2,174	37.1	25.9	26.9	7.3	2.7	1,529	23.9	18.1	36.9	19.0	2.2	110,592
ALASKA	29,430		15.5	22.7	34.8	17.1	9.9		7.5	5.6	19.9	55.6	11.4	227,284
UNITED STATES	27,916		21.9	25.0	32.3	12.3	8.4		7.9	10.5	27.1	35.6	19.0	192,285

COUNTY	FINANCIAL SERVICES				THE HOME						ENTERTAINMENT						PERSONAL			
					Home Improvements		Furnishings													
	Auto Loan	Home Loan	Invest-ments	Retire-ment Plans	Home Repair	Lawn & Garden	Comput-ers & Hard-ware	Major Appli-ances	TV, Radio, Sound Equip-ment	Furni-ture	Dine out/ Carry out	Sports Equip-ment	Fees & Tickets	Toys & Games	Travel	Cable TV	Apparel & Services	Auto Repairs	Health Insur-ance	Pets & Supplies
ALEUTIANS EAST	99	112	131	111	112	101	116	108	112	113	111	100	119	111	115	110	103	109	105	106
ALEUTIANS WEST	132	125	113	132	110	108	131	116	125	132	127	114	126	129	121	120	115	126	109	119
ANCHORAGE MUNICIPALI	123	123	123	128	116	109	127	116	121	126	122	112	126	123	122	117	112	122	110	117
BETHEL	92	84	71	80	76	78	84	84	86	86	87	78	80	84	81	85	78	88	82	82
BRISTOL BAY	93	99	101	100	101	101	87	95	87	92	87	85	92	92	92	87	79	89	92	97
DENALI	107	113	113	115	114	112	108	110	105	110	106	101	111	106	111	105	96	108	106	111
DILLINGHAM	95	99	97	97	94	88	97	95	94	97	94	90	97	93	96	91	85	97	90	92
FAIRBANKS NORTH STAR	107	103	103	107	96	92	111	100	106	108	107	97	108	108	104	102	97	106	95	100
HAINES	105	81	52	80	95	124	83	108	86	78	86	93	71	88	85	92	73	96	109	112
JUNEAU CITY/BOROUGH	123	132	136	135	127	118	128	122	123	131	124	115	132	124	128	120	113	125	117	122
KENAI PENINSULA	103	95	85	96	97	107	93	101	94	93	93	91	89	96	94	95	83	97	101	104
KETCHIKAN GATEWAY	103	114	122	114	113	104	112	108	108	112	108	101	115	109	112	106	100	108	103	107
KODIAK ISLAND	120	119	118	123	114	109	127	117	119	123	121	114	124	122	121	115	110	122	110	117
LAKE AND PENINSULA	92	89	73	87	81	85	80	84	81	83	81	77	79	83	79	81	72	83	82	86
MATANUSKA-SUSITNA	110	110	98	110	107	111	102	108	101	104	101	99	102	104	103	101	90	104	104	110
NOME	96	90	87	93	82	83	92	87	94	94	94	80	90	94	88	93	85	92	87	88
NORTH SLOPE	137	148	132	145	133	123	135	132	129	141	130	126	137	132	133	123	118	134	120	130
NORTHWEST ARCTIC	102	99	88	97	90	85	103	97	101	103	102	94	99	100	97	97	93	103	90	94
PRINCE OF WALES-OUTE	88	78	65	76	77	86	75	83	78	76	78	74	72	81	75	80	69	80	84	85
SITKA CITY/BOROUGH	108	117	124	119	113	104	116	109	111	117	112	103	119	112	115	109	103	111	104	109
SKAGWAY-HOONAH-ANGOO	93	84	72	83	83	94	82	89	83	82	83	80	78	85	82	85	74	86	90	92
SOUTHEAST FAIRBANKS	90	81	74	82	83	92	80	87	81	79	81	78	77	84	81	83	71	83	87	89
VALDEZ-CORDOVA	111	104	87	103	108	119	98	111	99	99	99	101	95	103	100	101	88	104	109	115
WADE HAMPTON	71	67	62	66	61	60	68	66	69	70	69	62	65	69	65	67	63	71	64	65
WRANGELL-PETERSBURG	112	100	86	100	103	117	95	108	98	96	98	96	92	101	97	101	86	102	109	112
YAKUTAT CITY/BOROUGH	103	91	71	88	87	98	83	93	88	86	88	83	80	90	83	90	77	89	94	97
YUKON-KOYUKUK	71	60	59	62	60	69	64	66	69	63	68	57	60	68	63	72	60	67	73	68
ALASKA	114	113	109	115	107	106	114	109	110	113	111	103	112	112	110	108	100	112	105	110
UNITED STATES	100	100	100	100	100	100	100	100	100	100	100	100	100	100	100	100	100	100	100	100

POPULATION CHANGE

COUNTY	FIPS Code	CBSA Code	DMA Code	POPULATION			2000-2007 ANNUAL RATE		RACE (%)					
									White		Black		Asian/Pacific	
				2000	2007	2012	% Rate	State Rank	2000	2007	2000	2007	2000	2007
APACHE	001	00000	790	69,423	71,642	73,313	0.4	13	19.5	18.7	0.2	0.3	0.2	0.2
COCHISE	003	43420	789	117,755	132,044	143,117	1.6	9	76.7	74.1	4.5	4.6	1.9	2.2
COCONINO	005	22380	753	116,320	128,439	136,437	1.4	10	63.1	61.2	1.0	1.1	0.9	1.0
GILA	007	37740	753	51,335	53,308	54,618	0.5	12	77.8	75.9	0.4	0.4	0.5	0.6
GRAHAM	009	40940	753	33,489	34,318	34,754	0.3	14	67.1	64.6	1.9	1.9	0.6	0.7
GREENLEE	011	40940	753	8,547	8,024	7,742	-0.9	15	74.2	71.0	0.5	0.6	0.2	0.2
LA PAZ	012	00000	753	19,715	21,108	22,107	0.9	11	74.2	72.0	0.8	0.8	0.5	0.6
MARICOPA	013	38060	753	3,072,149	3,901,548	4,623,363	3.4	4	77.4	74.4	3.7	3.9	2.3	2.7
MOHAVE	015	29420	753	155,032	202,681	245,965	3.8	2	90.1	88.6	0.5	0.6	0.9	1.1
NAVAJO	017	00000	753	97,470	113,243	126,094	2.1	7	45.9	44.3	0.9	0.9	0.4	0.5
PIMA	019	46060	789	843,746	976,521	1,082,822	2.0	8	75.1	72.1	3.0	3.1	2.2	2.5
PINAL	021	38060	753	179,727	262,209	350,734	5.3	1	70.4	67.4	2.8	2.8	0.7	0.8
SANTA CRUZ	023	35700	789	38,381	46,628	53,595	2.7	6	76.0	75.1	0.4	0.4	0.6	0.6
YAVAPAI	025	39140	753	167,517	218,514	264,859	3.7	3	91.9	90.5	0.4	0.4	0.6	0.7
YUMA	027	49740	771	160,026	193,572	223,870	2.7	6	68.3	65.3	2.2	2.2	1.1	1.2
ARIZONA							3.0		75.5	73.0	3.1	3.2	1.9	2.3
UNITED STATES							1.2		75.1	72.7	12.3	12.6	3.8	4.5

COUNTY	% HISPANIC ORIGIN		2007 AGE DISTRIBUTION (%)										MEDIAN AGE	% 2007 Males	% 2007 Females
	2000	2007	0-4	5-9	10-14	15-19	20-24	25-44	45-64	65-84	85+	18+	2007		
APACHE	4.5	5.3	9.8	8.0	9.3	10.7	9.8	22.9	20.5	8.2	0.8	66.0	26.8	49.6	50.4
COCHISE	30.7	35.8	6.8	6.0	6.1	7.5	8.0	22.4	26.7	14.8	1.7	76.8	39.4	50.1	49.9
COCONINO	10.9	13.2	7.4	6.5	7.3	8.8	11.2	27.2	23.9	7.0	0.8	74.0	30.3	49.9	50.1
GILA	16.6	20.1	6.2	5.7	6.1	6.7	6.0	18.9	29.6	18.4	2.5	77.8	45.3	49.2	50.8
GRAHAM	27.0	31.7	8.5	7.6	7.6	8.6	8.6	27.0	20.2	10.4	1.6	71.6	31.0	53.0	47.0
GREENLEE	43.1	49.1	8.6	7.6	7.5	6.9	8.0	24.5	25.6	10.2	1.1	71.6	34.7	52.3	47.7
LA PAZ	22.4	26.5	4.9	4.1	5.0	5.4	5.9	16.6	28.5	27.1	2.6	82.7	51.4	51.3	48.7
MARICOPA	24.8	29.4	8.1	7.5	7.1	6.6	6.6	29.7	22.0	10.6	1.7	73.4	34.3	50.0	50.0
MOHAVE	11.1	13.6	6.1	5.5	6.1	5.9	5.4	20.2	29.1	19.7	2.0	78.7	45.6	49.8	50.2
NAVAJO	8.2	9.8	9.2	7.8	8.4	9.5	8.0	23.0	23.2	10.1	0.9	68.6	30.9	49.6	50.4
PIMA	29.3	34.3	6.7	6.0	6.4	7.2	7.6	26.2	25.1	12.7	2.1	76.9	37.0	48.9	51.1
PINAL	29.9	34.9	7.7	7.0	6.8	6.6	6.6	26.2	23.4	14.4	1.3	74.4	36.8	52.6	47.4
SANTA CRUZ	80.8	84.2	9.1	8.6	9.0	8.2	6.1	25.7	22.7	9.5	1.1	68.0	31.9	48.2	51.8
YAVAPAI	9.8	12.1	5.1	4.8	5.2	6.0	5.8	19.2	31.3	19.9	2.8	81.3	47.8	49.0	51.0
YUMA	50.5	56.3	8.4	7.3	7.4	7.5	7.6	24.1	20.5	15.5	1.6	72.4	34.7	50.1	49.9
ARIZONA	25.3	29.6	7.7	7.0	6.9	6.9	6.9	27.6	23.3	11.9	1.8	74.3	35.4	49.9	50.1
UNITED STATES	12.5	15.0	6.9	6.5	6.8	7.1	7.0	27.6	25.4	10.7	1.9	75.6	36.7	49.2	50.8

COUNTY	HOUSEHOLDS					FAMILIES			MEDIAN HOUSEHOLD INCOME			
	2000	2007	2012	% Annual Rate 2000-2007	2007 Average HH Size	2000	2007	% Annual Rate 2000-2007	2007	2012	2007 National Rank	2007 State Rank
APACHE	19,971	20,922	21,664	0.6	3.36	15,266	15,837	0.5	28,530	32,850	2979	15
COCHISE	43,893	50,455	55,326	1.9	2.50	30,786	34,968	1.8	42,210	50,246	1424	7
COCONINO	40,448	45,500	48,831	1.6	2.75	26,946	29,907	1.4	50,358	60,373	651	2
GILA	20,140	21,065	21,663	0.6	2.49	14,090	14,560	0.5	39,955	47,181	1731	10
GRAHAM	10,116	10,489	10,686	0.5	2.96	7,614	7,817	0.4	37,443	43,430	2074	11
GREENLEE	3,117	2,962	2,874	-0.7	2.70	2,266	2,130	-0.9	47,757	54,336	841	4
LA PAZ	8,362	9,229	9,810	1.4	2.26	5,616	6,119	1.2	33,539	40,076	2605	14
MARICOPA	1,132,886	1,422,956	1,680,171	3.2	2.71	763,110	945,978	3.0	60,193	73,675	261	1
MOHAVE	62,809	81,817	99,444	3.7	2.46	43,372	55,801	3.5	40,896	48,717	1613	9
NAVAJO	30,043	35,781	40,376	2.4	3.10	23,069	27,214	2.3	35,556	41,073	2359	13
PIMA	332,350	386,116	429,352	2.1	2.47	212,092	242,839	1.9	48,329	57,567	790	3
PINAL	61,364	94,050	128,663	6.1	2.64	45,211	68,485	5.9	46,013	53,832	1002	5
SANTA CRUZ	11,809	14,511	16,775	2.9	3.20	9,511	11,595	2.8	37,187	43,336	2101	12
YAVAPAI	70,171	91,430	111,185	3.7	2.35	46,754	60,104	3.5	45,976	54,894	1006	6
YUMA	53,848	67,516	78,696	3.2	2.79	41,664	51,767	3.0	41,287	49,020	1555	8
ARIZONA				3.0	2.65			2.8	53,299	64,719		
UNITED STATES				1.2	2.59			1.0	53,154	62,503		

COUNTY	2007 Per Capita Income	2007 HH Income Base	2007 HOUSEHOLD INCOME DISTRIBUTION (%)					2007 Home Value Base	2007 HOME VALUE DISTRIBUTION (%)					2007 Median Home Value
			Less than $25,000	$25,000 to $49,999	$50,000 to $99,999	$100,000 to $149,999	$150,000 or More		Less than $50,000	$50,000 to $89,999	$90,000 to $174,999	$175,000 to $399,999	$400,000 or More	
APACHE	11,683	20,922	45.6	26.5	21.5	4.8	1.5	15,634	35.5	14.2	28.4	17.7	4.2	90,974
COCHISE	21,441	50,455	29.3	28.8	30.1	8.5	3.2	34,618	6.8	10.7	33.6	41.3	7.6	172,547
COCONINO	23,497	45,499	23.3	26.3	32.1	12.5	5.8	28,530	13.1	7.4	12.6	40.0	26.9	266,888
GILA	21,443	21,065	31.3	29.2	28.9	6.9	3.6	16,715	12.7	9.9	24.6	40.2	12.7	185,006
GRAHAM	16,039	10,489	34.1	29.0	29.0	5.8	2.1	7,792	7.9	14.2	37.1	36.7	4.2	154,807
GREENLEE	19,902	2,962	22.4	31.1	37.7	7.4	1.5	1,527	13.9	17.4	44.3	22.5	1.8	130,589
LA PAZ	19,993	9,229	36.0	34.2	22.0	5.3	2.5	7,293	22.6	15.1	33.5	24.0	4.8	119,828
MARICOPA	29,550	1,422,933	16.3	24.4	34.8	14.4	10.0	973,538	3.2	2.6	14.2	54.5	25.4	276,033
MOHAVE	21,792	81,817	27.1	33.3	28.6	7.7	3.3	61,222	5.2	9.9	35.7	42.1	7.1	173,408
NAVAJO	15,123	35,781	37.0	28.4	25.3	7.0	2.3	27,242	17.9	11.6	30.0	31.8	8.6	149,032
PIMA	26,496	386,116	23.8	28.0	30.7	11.1	6.4	252,359	5.8	5.6	25.1	49.1	14.4	207,213
PINAL	21,596	94,044	25.3	29.9	32.1	8.8	4.0	73,465	9.3	9.0	29.0	40.3	12.5	182,203
SANTA CRUZ	17,309	14,511	34.1	27.9	25.5	7.6	4.9	10,069	7.2	4.4	22.1	51.1	15.1	209,393
YAVAPAI	26,284	91,430	24.6	30.5	30.3	9.3	5.3	68,208	4.2	4.6	19.5	47.9	23.8	247,495
YUMA	19,930	67,515	27.8	31.8	28.6	8.0	3.9	49,296	10.8	8.9	38.1	37.1	5.1	159,628
ARIZONA	27,079		20.3	26.3	32.8	12.5	8.0		5.3	4.7	19.5	50.1	20.5	241,092
UNITED STATES	27,916		21.9	25.0	32.3	12.3	8.4		7.9	10.5	27.1	35.6	19.0	192,285

SPENDING POTENTIAL INDICES

COUNTY	FINANCIAL SERVICES				THE HOME						ENTERTAINMENT						PERSONAL			
					Home Improvements		Furnishings													
	Auto Loan	Home Loan	Invest-ments	Retire-ment Plans	Home Repair	Lawn & Garden	Comput-ers & Hard-ware	Major Appli-ances	TV, Radio, Sound Equip-ment	Furni-ture	Dine out/ Carry out	Sports Equip-ment	Fees & Tickets	Toys & Games	Travel	Cable TV	Apparel & Services	Auto Repairs	Health Insur-ance	Pets & Supplies
APACHE	61	52	40	49	47	54	50	55	55	53	55	48	47	53	49	56	49	56	56	54
COCHISE	80	71	67	70	71	80	73	78	76	71	75	69	69	74	73	78	66	77	82	78
COCONINO	94	86	82	88	82	85	93	88	91	90	91	82	88	90	88	89	82	92	86	89
GILA	80	69	63	68	74	89	69	81	74	68	73	69	65	71	72	78	63	77	88	81
GRAHAM	73	64	56	62	62	70	63	68	66	63	65	60	60	67	62	68	57	67	71	69
GREENLEE	86	72	56	70	72	85	70	79	75	70	74	71	65	77	69	78	64	76	83	83
LA PAZ	62	62	65	57	66	73	57	67	61	60	60	55	59	55	64	65	52	66	76	65
MARICOPA	111	113	112	113	107	104	113	108	110	114	110	102	112	109	111	107	100	113	106	107
MOHAVE	78	71	69	70	75	86	70	80	74	69	72	68	68	71	74	78	63	77	87	80
NAVAJO	74	61	47	59	61	73	60	69	65	61	65	60	55	64	60	67	57	67	72	70
PIMA	92	89	91	89	86	87	92	89	91	91	91	82	90	89	91	91	82	92	91	89
PINAL	87	79	69	76	78	88	75	84	80	77	79	73	73	77	77	82	69	82	88	84
SANTA CRUZ	83	78	64	74	71	75	73	78	76	77	76	71	71	74	73	76	68	79	77	76
YAVAPAI	89	83	83	82	87	99	81	92	85	81	84	78	80	81	87	89	73	89	99	92
YUMA	80	75	71	71	74	80	74	79	77	76	77	70	72	73	75	79	68	80	83	77
ARIZONA	102	100	98	99	96	98	100	99	99	101	99	91	99	97	99	99	89	102	100	99
UNITED STATES	100	100	100	100	100	100	100	100	100	100	100	100	100	100	100	100	100	100	100	100

| COUNTY | FIPS Code | CBSA Code | DMA Code | POPULATION | | | 2000-2007 ANNUAL RATE | | RACE (%) | | | | | |
| | | | | | | | | | White | | Black | | Asian/Pacific | |
				2000	2007	2012	% Rate	State Rank	2000	2007	2000	2007	2000	2007
ARKANSAS	001	00000	693	20,749	20,273	19,915	-0.3	61	75.2	72.9	23.4	25.4	0.4	0.5
ASHLEY	003	00000	628	24,209	23,632	23,162	-0.3	61	69.8	66.9	27.1	29.1	0.2	0.3
BAXTER	005	34260	619	38,386	41,349	43,427	1.0	20	97.8	97.4	0.1	0.1	0.4	0.5
BENTON	007	22220	670	153,406	201,997	246,293	3.9	1	90.9	88.6	0.4	0.4	1.2	1.6
BOONE	009	25460	619	33,948	36,005	37,452	0.8	27	97.6	97.1	0.1	0.1	0.3	0.5
BRADLEY	011	00000	693	12,600	12,199	11,750	-0.4	65	63.4	59.5	28.6	30.1	0.1	0.1
CALHOUN	013	15780	693	5,744	5,729	5,708	0.0	54	74.5	73.0	23.4	24.9	0.0	0.0
CARROLL	015	00000	619	25,357	28,058	30,050	1.4	8	93.6	92.0	0.1	0.1	0.5	0.6
CHICOT	017	00000	647	14,117	13,022	12,221	-1.1	75	43.2	40.3	54.0	56.2	0.4	0.5
CLARK	019	11660	693	23,546	23,745	24,043	0.1	52	74.3	71.6	22.0	23.8	0.7	0.9
CLAY	021	00000	734	17,609	16,970	16,528	-0.5	68	98.1	97.8	0.2	0.2	0.1	0.1
CLEBURNE	023	00000	693	24,046	26,068	27,355	1.1	17	98.2	97.9	0.1	0.1	0.2	0.2
CLEVELAND	025	38220	693	8,571	9,132	9,556	0.9	23	84.8	83.0	13.2	14.5	0.2	0.2
COLUMBIA	027	31620	612	25,603	25,322	24,930	-0.2	59	62.1	59.2	36.1	38.6	0.4	0.5
CONWAY	029	00000	693	20,336	20,983	21,361	0.4	45	84.3	82.4	13.1	14.3	0.3	0.4
CRAIGHEAD	031	27860	734	82,148	90,145	96,322	1.3	11	89.3	87.7	7.8	8.6	0.6	0.8
CRAWFORD	033	22900	670	53,247	58,752	62,920	1.4	8	92.2	90.6	0.9	1.0	1.2	1.6
CRITTENDEN	035	32820	640	50,866	52,811	54,191	0.5	40	50.9	47.9	47.1	49.6	0.5	0.6
CROSS	037	00000	640	19,526	19,888	20,135	0.3	48	74.8	72.4	23.7	25.8	0.3	0.4
DALLAS	039	00000	693	9,210	8,582	8,140	-1.0	73	57.0	54.0	41.0	43.5	0.2	0.3
DESHA	041	00000	693	15,341	14,459	13,871	-0.8	70	50.5	47.4	46.3	48.6	0.3	0.4
DREW	043	00000	693	18,723	19,502	19,945	0.6	34	70.3	67.6	27.2	29.3	0.4	0.6
FAULKNER	045	30780	693	86,014	102,968	114,974	2.5	4	88.3	86.7	8.5	9.3	0.8	1.0
FRANKLIN	047	22900	670	17,771	18,767	19,380	0.8	27	96.2	95.4	0.6	0.7	0.3	0.4
FULTON	049	00000	619	11,642	11,978	12,160	0.4	45	97.7	97.3	0.2	0.2	0.2	0.3
GARLAND	051	26300	693	88,068	95,740	101,427	1.2	13	88.9	87.4	7.8	8.6	0.5	0.7
GRANT	053	30780	693	16,464	17,764	18,575	1.1	17	95.5	94.8	2.5	2.7	0.2	0.2
GREENE	055	37500	734	37,331	40,331	42,539	1.1	17	97.4	97.0	0.1	0.1	0.2	0.3
HEMPSTEAD	057	26260	612	23,587	24,640	25,443	0.6	34	63.3	60.2	30.4	31.9	0.2	0.2
HOT SPRING	059	00000	693	30,353	32,070	33,093	0.8	27	87.3	85.8	10.3	11.3	0.3	0.3
HOWARD	061	00000	612	14,300	14,737	15,047	0.4	45	73.6	70.8	21.9	23.4	0.5	0.7
INDEPENDENCE	063	12900	693	34,233	35,577	36,508	0.5	40	94.9	94.0	2.0	2.3	0.7	0.9
IZARD	065	00000	734	13,249	13,924	14,411	0.7	30	96.4	95.8	1.4	1.6	0.1	0.2
JACKSON	067	00000	693	18,418	17,965	17,389	-0.3	61	80.6	78.6	17.6	19.2	0.2	0.2
JEFFERSON	069	38220	693	84,278	82,055	79,741	-0.4	65	48.5	45.5	49.6	52.2	0.7	0.9
JOHNSON	071	00000	670	22,781	25,172	26,900	1.4	8	93.7	92.2	1.4	1.5	0.3	0.4
LAFAYETTE	073	00000	612	8,559	8,229	7,915	-0.5	68	62.1	59.3	36.5	39.1	0.2	0.3
LAWRENCE	075	00000	734	17,774	17,591	17,451	-0.1	57	97.8	97.5	0.4	0.5	0.1	0.1
LEE	077	00000	640	12,580	12,215	11,973	-0.4	65	41.4	38.7	57.2	59.6	0.3	0.4
LINCOLN	079	38220	693	14,492	15,015	15,080	0.5	40	64.9	62.0	32.9	35.3	0.1	0.1
LITTLE RIVER	081	00000	612	13,628	13,677	13,708	0.0	54	74.5	73.2	21.3	22.7	0.2	0.2
LOGAN	083	00000	670	22,486	23,418	24,126	0.6	34	96.5	95.9	1.0	1.2	0.2	0.2
LONOKE	085	30780	693	52,828	66,367	78,317	3.2	3	91.0	89.8	6.4	7.1	0.5	0.6
MADISON	087	22220	670	14,243	15,452	16,352	1.1	17	95.9	95.1	0.1	0.1	0.2	0.2
MARION	089	00000	619	16,140	17,777	18,910	1.3	11	97.5	97.1	0.1	0.1	0.2	0.3
MILLER	091	45500	612	40,443	43,836	46,564	1.1	17	74.0	71.6	23.0	24.9	0.4	0.5
MISSISSIPPI	093	14180	640	51,979	48,337	45,798	-1.0	73	64.4	61.6	32.7	35.0	0.4	0.5
MONROE	095	00000	693	10,254	9,588	9,137	-0.9	71	59.4	56.6	38.8	41.4	0.2	0.2
MONTGOMERY	097	00000	693	9,245	9,586	9,831	0.5	40	95.4	94.4	0.3	0.3	0.4	0.5
NEVADA	099	26260	693	9,955	11,010	11,875	1.4	8	66.9	64.1	31.2	33.5	0.1	0.1
NEWTON	101	25460	619	8,608	8,804	8,775	0.3	48	97.4	96.9	0.1	0.2	0.2	0.2
OUACHITA	103	15780	693	28,790	27,552	26,583	-0.6	69	59.7	56.9	38.6	41.3	0.3	0.3
PERRY	105	30780	693	10,209	10,927	11,373	0.9	23	95.6	95.0	1.7	1.9	0.2	0.2
PHILLIPS	107	48340	640	26,445	24,645	23,516	-1.0	73	39.2	36.5	59.0	61.5	0.3	0.4
PIKE	109	00000	693	11,303	11,567	11,832	0.3	48	92.0	90.4	3.5	3.8	0.2	0.2
POINSETT	111	27860	640	25,614	25,834	25,972	0.1	52	91.0	89.7	7.1	7.9	0.2	0.2
POLK	113	00000	693	20,229	20,873	21,238	0.4	45	94.7	93.6	0.2	0.2	0.3	0.3
POPE	115	40780	693	54,469	58,973	61,718	1.1	17	93.7	92.6	2.6	2.9	0.7	0.9
PRAIRIE	117	00000	693	9,539	9,476	9,428	-0.1	57	84.8	83.8	13.7	14.7	0.2	0.2
PULASKI	119	30780	693	361,474	378,741	391,650	0.6	34	64.0	60.9	31.9	34.0	1.3	1.7
RANDOLPH	121	00000	734	18,195	18,919	19,422	0.5	40	97.0	96.5	1.0	1.1	0.1	0.1
ST. FRANCIS	123	22620	640	29,329	29,743	29,007	0.2	50	48.4	45.8	49.0	51.0	0.6	0.7
SALINE	125	30780	693	83,529	96,637	106,586	2.0	5	95.3	94.4	2.2	2.5	0.6	0.8
SCOTT	127	00000	670	10,996	11,635	12,108	0.8	27	93.5	91.9	0.2	0.2	1.0	1.3
SEARCY	129	00000	693	8,261	8,268	8,329	0.0	54	97.3	97.3	0.0	0.0	0.2	0.2
SEBASTIAN	131	22900	670	115,071	121,354	125,951	0.7	30	82.3	79.1	6.2	6.6	3.6	4.7
SEVIER	133	00000	612	15,757	16,762	17,515	0.9	23	79.6	75.6	4.9	5.1	0.2	0.2
SHARP	135	00000	734	17,119	18,259	19,040	0.9	23	97.1	96.7	0.5	0.5	0.1	0.2
STONE	137	00000	693	11,499	12,048	12,434	0.6	34	97.3	96.8	0.1	0.1	0.1	0.1
UNION	139	20980	628	45,629	44,302	42,974	-0.4	65	66.1	63.4	32.0	34.4	0.4	0.5
VAN BUREN	141	00000	693	16,192	16,921	17,283	0.6	34	96.8	96.2	0.3	0.3	0.3	0.4
WASHINGTON	143	22220	670	157,715	197,974	230,606	3.2	3	88.0	85.4	2.2	2.4	2.1	2.7
WHITE	145	42620	693	67,165	73,938	78,969	1.3	11	93.5	92.0	3.6	4.5	0.3	0.5
WOODRUFF	147	00000	693	8,741	8,625	8,509	-0.2	59	67.9	65.2	30.8	33.2	0.2	0.2
YELL	149	40780	693	21,139	21,905	22,439	0.5	40	86.6	83.0	1.5	1.6	0.7	0.9
ARKANSAS							1.1		80.0	78.7	15.7	15.8	0.8	1.1
UNITED STATES							1.2		75.1	72.7	12.3	12.6	3.8	4.5

POPULATION COMPOSITION

COUNTY	% HISPANIC ORIGIN		2007 AGE DISTRIBUTION (%)										MEDIAN AGE	% 2007 Males	% 2007 Females
	2000	2007	0-4	5-9	10-14	15-19	20-24	25-44	45-64	65-84	85+	18+	2007		
ARKANSAS	0.8	1.0	6.7	6.7	5.8	6.4	5.7	25.3	28.0	13.0	2.5	76.9	39.9	48.3	51.7
ASHLEY	3.2	4.2	7.1	6.6	7.3	6.1	6.1	27.1	25.8	11.9	2.0	75.2	37.7	48.8	51.2
BAXTER	1.0	1.4	4.5	4.2	4.8	5.0	5.3	19.1	30.7	22.7	3.7	83.4	50.4	48.4	51.6
BENTON	8.8	11.7	7.8	7.2	6.7	6.4	6.2	27.6	23.6	12.7	1.8	74.5	36.7	49.3	50.7
BOONE	1.1	1.5	6.3	5.8	6.2	5.8	6.3	25.1	27.0	15.0	2.5	78.2	41.2	48.6	51.4
BRADLEY	8.3	10.9	6.2	5.8	5.6	6.0	6.5	27.1	25.6	14.2	3.0	78.8	40.0	49.5	50.5
CALHOUN	1.5	1.5	5.8	5.1	6.6	6.2	6.4	24.9	28.6	14.0	2.4	78.7	41.7	48.6	51.4
CARROLL	9.7	13.0	6.6	6.6	5.6	5.5	5.8	24.9	29.0	14.1	1.9	77.8	41.5	49.5	50.5
CHICOT	2.9	3.6	7.1	6.7	6.8	6.2	7.3	25.1	25.6	12.7	2.4	75.7	37.4	49.0	51.0
CLARK	2.4	3.2	6.3	5.8	5.1	8.9	11.3	25.8	22.6	12.1	2.2	79.7	33.3	48.6	51.4
CLAY	0.8	1.1	6.3	6.0	6.1	6.0	5.5	25.3	25.9	16.0	2.8	77.9	41.3	48.9	51.1
CLEBURNE	1.2	1.6	5.4	5.0	5.3	5.5	4.9	22.0	29.8	19.8	2.5	81.0	46.3	48.8	51.2
CLEVELAND	1.6	2.2	6.9	6.4	6.6	6.0	6.0	26.9	26.2	13.4	1.7	76.4	39.4	48.9	51.1
COLUMBIA	1.1	1.4	6.4	5.8	6.1	7.6	8.1	25.6	24.7	13.2	2.6	77.9	37.6	48.2	51.8
CONWAY	1.8	2.4	6.8	6.5	6.2	5.7	5.9	25.9	26.9	13.9	2.2	77.0	40.4	49.3	50.7
CRAIGHEAD	2.1	2.9	7.1	6.4	6.0	6.8	7.7	30.7	23.8	10.0	1.6	77.1	34.3	48.7	51.3
CRAWFORD	3.3	4.4	7.7	7.1	6.9	7.0	6.4	27.7	25.7	10.2	1.3	74.1	36.4	49.7	50.3
CRITTENDEN	1.4	1.8	8.6	7.6	7.7	7.7	7.0	26.9	24.4	8.7	1.3	71.4	33.5	48.0	52.0
CROSS	0.9	1.2	7.3	6.5	7.1	6.5	6.8	26.3	26.2	11.6	1.7	75.2	37.6	48.8	51.2
DALLAS	1.9	2.5	6.2	6.5	6.9	6.6	5.9	23.9	27.8	13.1	3.0	76.4	40.5	48.5	51.5
DESHA	3.2	4.1	7.9	7.4	6.2	7.0	6.9	23.9	27.0	11.5	2.3	74.2	37.2	47.4	52.6
DREW	1.8	2.3	7.1	6.5	6.5	7.5	7.8	27.7	24.3	10.8	1.8	76.1	34.8	48.7	51.3
FAULKNER	1.8	2.4	7.2	6.2	6.1	8.5	9.5	30.8	22.1	8.3	1.3	76.7	31.7	48.8	51.2
FRANKLIN	1.7	2.4	6.9	6.4	6.5	6.3	6.5	25.8	25.8	13.3	2.5	76.4	39.1	49.8	50.2
FULTON	0.5	0.7	5.7	5.5	5.3	5.6	5.7	21.5	29.7	18.4	2.6	80.0	45.4	48.9	51.1
GARLAND	2.6	3.5	5.6	5.3	5.2	5.6	5.2	22.9	28.7	18.5	3.0	80.6	45.1	48.9	51.1
GRANT	1.1	1.6	6.5	6.6	6.1	6.9	5.8	28.1	27.2	11.2	1.6	76.6	38.8	50.1	49.9
GREENE	1.2	1.6	6.9	6.7	6.6	6.1	5.7	29.0	25.2	12.1	1.8	76.1	37.7	49.3	50.7
HEMPSTEAD	8.3	10.7	7.9	7.5	6.5	6.2	6.2	27.8	24.5	11.2	2.2	74.4	36.0	48.7	51.3
HOT SPRING	1.3	1.7	6.4	6.2	6.3	6.1	5.5	25.9	27.8	13.7	2.2	77.4	40.5	48.9	51.1
HOWARD	5.1	6.8	7.2	6.6	6.6	6.6	6.3	27.9	24.3	11.9	2.6	75.5	37.9	49.4	50.6
INDEPENDENCE	1.5	2.1	6.5	6.7	5.7	6.3	6.9	25.8	26.2	12.5	2.0	77.7	39.6	49.2	50.8
IZARD	1.0	1.4	5.2	5.0	4.8	5.2	5.0	23.9	27.4	20.2	3.4	81.9	45.7	50.9	49.1
JACKSON	1.3	1.7	5.8	5.6	5.0	6.8	9.3	25.0	26.1	13.9	2.6	80.3	39.6	47.9	52.1
JEFFERSON	1.0	1.2	7.0	6.7	6.4	7.0	7.7	26.8	25.2	11.1	2.0	76.0	36.2	49.3	50.7
JOHNSON	6.7	9.1	7.1	6.4	6.6	5.8	5.9	28.4	25.2	12.4	2.1	76.5	37.8	50.0	50.0
LAFAYETTE	1.0	1.3	6.4	5.5	6.2	6.3	6.0	23.8	28.4	14.5	2.7	77.8	41.8	48.7	51.3
LAWRENCE	0.7	0.9	6.8	6.6	5.7	6.3	6.6	25.4	25.9	14.0	2.7	77.6	39.3	48.8	51.2
LEE	2.2	2.8	6.9	5.9	6.3	6.3	9.0	28.5	23.6	11.2	2.2	77.2	35.1	52.9	47.1
LINCOLN	1.8	2.4	6.0	5.4	5.5	5.7	9.7	33.3	22.4	10.0	1.9	79.9	35.4	59.9	40.1
LITTLE RIVER	1.7	1.7	7.0	6.8	6.2	5.8	5.6	25.8	27.4	13.3	2.1	76.6	39.8	49.3	50.7
LOGAN	1.2	1.7	6.7	6.4	6.2	6.4	6.5	25.6	26.2	13.7	2.3	76.6	39.9	49.8	50.2
LONOKE	1.7	2.4	7.5	6.7	6.8	7.1	7.3	28.1	25.6	9.6	1.3	74.7	36.4	49.2	50.8
MADISON	3.1	4.2	6.7	6.2	6.4	7.1	5.9	24.7	28.2	12.8	1.9	76.3	40.1	49.8	50.2
MARION	0.8	1.0	5.3	5.0	4.9	6.1	5.7	20.3	31.1	19.1	2.5	81.1	46.7	49.5	50.5
MILLER	1.6	2.1	7.6	7.1	6.2	6.1	6.9	27.5	25.5	11.1	1.9	75.4	36.5	49.1	50.9
MISSISSIPPI	2.2	2.9	8.6	7.7	7.2	6.8	7.2	26.6	23.6	10.4	1.7	72.3	33.8	48.2	51.8
MONROE	1.3	1.6	7.3	6.6	7.3	6.1	7.4	22.0	26.2	14.2	2.8	75.2	39.7	47.0	53.0
MONTGOMERY	2.5	3.5	6.3	6.3	5.5	5.8	5.2	23.1	27.7	17.4	2.6	78.2	43.4	49.1	50.9
NEVADA	1.5	2.0	6.7	6.4	6.1	5.7	6.3	26.7	26.4	13.1	2.6	77.4	39.9	48.8	51.2
NEWTON	1.1	1.5	6.1	5.9	5.7	5.6	5.9	24.2	30.5	14.2	1.9	78.6	42.6	50.8	49.2
OUACHITA	0.7	0.9	6.4	6.0	6.2	6.6	6.9	23.8	28.1	13.4	2.6	77.4	40.6	47.8	52.2
PERRY	1.2	1.6	6.7	6.3	6.4	6.6	5.6	26.0	27.3	13.1	1.9	76.5	39.8	50.0	50.0
PHILLIPS	1.4	1.8	9.2	7.7	7.9	7.4	7.5	22.3	23.7	12.3	2.0	70.6	33.7	46.0	54.0
PIKE	3.6	4.9	6.6	6.3	5.7	6.3	5.5	25.2	26.8	14.9	2.8	77.4	41.0	49.9	50.1
POINSETT	1.4	1.9	7.0	6.6	6.4	6.6	6.1	27.0	25.8	12.7	1.9	75.9	38.2	49.3	50.7
POLK	3.5	4.8	7.1	6.8	6.1	6.0	5.9	24.8	26.2	14.7	2.3	76.3	40.0	49.5	50.5
POPE	2.1	2.8	6.8	6.1	6.3	7.8	7.3	28.1	24.6	10.9	2.0	77.0	36.1	49.4	50.6
PRAIRIE	0.8	0.8	6.3	6.2	5.4	5.9	5.2	24.8	29.6	14.0	2.6	78.4	42.3	49.6	50.4
PULASKI	2.4	3.2	7.0	6.8	6.4	6.4	6.3	28.8	26.4	10.0	1.8	75.8	36.5	48.1	51.9
RANDOLPH	0.8	1.1	6.1	5.9	5.9	6.6	5.7	25.5	26.7	15.0	2.6	78.1	41.1	49.2	50.8
ST. FRANCIS	4.9	6.2	7.7	6.4	6.6	6.3	7.5	30.7	23.6	9.5	1.6	75.3	34.4	54.2	45.8
SALINE	1.3	1.8	6.4	6.1	6.4	6.4	5.8	27.2	26.8	13.4	1.5	77.0	39.7	49.4	50.6
SCOTT	5.7	7.7	7.7	7.3	5.8	6.5	6.0	26.0	25.2	13.5	2.1	75.5	38.9	50.7	49.3
SEARCY	1.0	1.0	5.9	5.9	5.0	5.8	6.0	23.3	28.9	16.5	2.7	79.7	43.6	49.3	50.7
SEBASTIAN	6.7	8.9	7.5	6.9	6.3	6.4	6.9	27.7	25.5	10.9	2.0	75.5	37.0	49.1	50.9
SEVIER	19.7	25.4	8.2	7.9	7.7	5.7	6.1	29.0	22.6	11.1	1.7	72.8	34.8	49.9	50.1
SHARP	1.0	1.3	5.7	5.3	5.5	5.2	5.2	21.1	27.9	21.0	3.2	80.2	46.5	48.3	51.7
STONE	1.1	1.5	5.7	5.5	5.0	5.8	5.0	21.9	30.4	18.5	2.2	80.3	45.7	49.2	50.8
UNION	1.1	1.5	6.7	6.1	6.4	6.2	6.5	25.5	26.7	13.1	2.8	77.0	39.9	48.4	51.6
VAN BUREN	1.3	1.8	5.4	5.0	5.3	5.2	5.1	21.0	28.8	20.8	3.5	81.1	47.0	49.3	50.7
WASHINGTON	8.2	10.9	7.7	6.9	6.1	7.3	9.9	30.4	22.1	8.3	1.3	75.9	31.7	50.3	49.7
WHITE	1.9	2.6	6.6	6.1	6.2	7.6	8.2	27.1	24.5	11.7	2.0	77.4	36.7	48.9	51.1
WOODRUFF	0.8	1.0	7.3	7.1	6.3	6.2	6.1	23.8	27.2	13.4	2.7	75.5	40.2	47.7	52.3
YELL	12.7	16.9	6.9	6.3	6.6	6.3	6.6	27.9	24.8	12.3	2.3	76.3	37.6	50.1	49.9
ARKANSAS	3.2	4.5	7.0	6.5	6.3	6.6	6.9	27.1	25.6	12.1	2.0	76.5	37.5	49.1	50.9
UNITED STATES	12.5	15.0	6.9	6.5	6.8	7.1	7.0	27.6	25.4	10.7	1.9	75.6	36.7	49.2	50.8

COUNTY	HOUSEHOLDS					FAMILIES			MEDIAN HOUSEHOLD INCOME			
	2000	2007	2012	% Annual Rate 2000-2007	2007 Average HH Size	2000	2007	% Annual Rate 2000-2007	2007	2012	2007 National Rank	2007 State Rank
ARKANSAS	8,457	8,416	8,334	-0.1	2.37	5,967	5,765	-0.5	37,012	42,382	2126	28
ASHLEY	9,384	9,347	9,243	-0.1	2.50	6,910	6,705	-0.4	39,592	45,841	1768	17
BAXTER	17,052	18,621	19,677	1.2	2.18	11,792	12,490	0.8	37,274	44,645	2094	27
BENTON	58,212	75,894	92,373	3.7	2.63	43,474	55,277	3.4	52,181	62,645	536	2
BOONE	13,851	14,925	15,635	1.0	2.37	9,859	10,326	0.6	37,528	44,230	2054	25
BRADLEY	4,834	4,736	4,576	-0.3	2.42	3,389	3,223	-0.7	30,603	35,320	2877	67
CALHOUN	2,317	2,375	2,396	0.3	2.36	1,629	1,622	-0.1	35,159	40,210	2410	41
CARROLL	10,189	11,274	12,073	1.4	2.47	7,107	7,633	1.0	34,667	39,770	2474	43
CHICOT	5,205	4,924	4,667	-0.8	2.50	3,642	3,345	-1.2	27,253	31,484	3029	73
CLARK	8,912	9,172	9,326	0.4	2.36	5,820	5,787	-0.1	35,520	41,227	2365	39
CLAY	7,417	7,192	7,021	-0.4	2.33	5,070	4,763	-0.9	30,816	35,588	2851	64
CLEBURNE	10,190	11,197	11,820	1.3	2.30	7,405	7,919	0.9	40,112	46,861	1708	14
CLEVELAND	3,273	3,535	3,722	1.1	2.56	2,515	2,654	0.7	40,033	45,801	1724	15
COLUMBIA	9,981	10,016	9,927	0.0	2.41	6,746	6,555	-0.4	34,490	40,095	2498	47
CONWAY	7,967	8,355	8,567	0.7	2.47	5,733	5,845	0.3	38,620	45,027	1913	22
CRAIGHEAD	32,301	35,692	38,283	1.4	2.46	22,100	23,665	0.9	41,214	48,715	1566	10
CRAWFORD	19,702	21,986	23,663	1.5	2.65	15,160	16,536	1.2	41,395	48,360	1532	9
CRITTENDEN	18,471	19,606	20,319	0.8	2.66	13,373	13,808	0.4	38,642	46,127	1907	21
CROSS	7,391	7,733	7,925	0.6	2.53	5,447	5,554	0.3	36,275	41,831	2236	32
DALLAS	3,519	3,329	3,174	-0.8	2.43	2,430	2,229	-1.2	32,777	37,597	2675	56
DESHA	5,922	5,739	5,574	-0.4	2.50	4,192	3,947	-0.8	29,184	33,667	2951	68
DREW	7,337	7,808	8,077	0.9	2.40	5,092	5,257	0.4	35,793	41,634	2314	37
FAULKNER	31,882	37,998	42,773	2.5	2.57	22,454	25,990	2.0	48,752	57,286	763	5
FRANKLIN	6,882	7,361	7,644	0.9	2.48	4,965	5,167	0.6	37,502	42,963	2062	26
FULTON	4,810	5,011	5,115	0.6	2.36	3,511	3,561	0.2	31,580	36,473	2793	61
GARLAND	37,813	41,021	43,523	1.1	2.29	25,250	26,509	0.7	40,533	47,775	1656	12
GRANT	6,241	6,832	7,190	1.3	2.57	4,780	5,111	0.9	45,140	51,309	1094	6
GREENE	14,750	16,093	17,048	1.2	2.47	10,703	11,364	0.8	38,423	44,736	1945	23
HEMPSTEAD	8,959	9,353	9,654	0.6	2.61	6,378	6,471	0.2	35,563	40,882	2357	38
HOT SPRING	12,004	12,673	13,129	0.8	2.48	8,840	9,091	0.4	38,665	44,434	1902	20
HOWARD	5,471	5,726	5,887	0.6	2.51	3,920	3,991	0.2	35,270	40,421	2397	40
INDEPENDENCE	13,467	14,236	14,720	0.8	2.43	9,670	9,939	0.4	39,599	45,937	1766	16
IZARD	5,440	5,798	6,045	0.9	2.27	3,772	3,901	0.5	31,863	37,232	2774	59
JACKSON	6,971	6,738	6,551	-0.5	2.36	4,830	4,530	-0.9	31,331	36,336	2810	62
JEFFERSON	30,555	30,679	30,053	0.1	2.50	21,508	20,971	-0.3	39,110	45,691	1836	18
JOHNSON	8,738	9,595	10,252	1.3	2.55	6,235	6,657	0.9	33,903	38,799	2561	50
LAFAYETTE	3,434	3,391	3,301	-0.2	2.39	2,375	2,275	-0.6	30,777	35,600	2855	65
LAWRENCE	7,108	7,093	7,066	0.0	2.40	5,009	4,854	-0.4	32,831	37,666	2674	55
LEE	4,182	4,167	4,125	0.0	2.51	2,962	2,869	-0.4	24,859	28,360	3094	75
LINCOLN	4,265	4,374	4,434	0.3	2.58	3,129	3,125	0.0	36,067	41,300	2263	35
LITTLE RIVER	5,465	5,651	5,741	0.5	2.39	3,912	3,929	0.1	36,363	41,572	2220	31
LOGAN	8,693	9,167	9,495	0.7	2.50	6,303	6,469	0.4	34,590	39,577	2487	45
LONOKE	19,262	24,554	29,169	3.4	2.68	15,018	18,730	3.1	51,255	60,486	598	3
MADISON	5,463	5,967	6,333	1.2	2.58	4,079	4,345	0.9	34,130	39,055	2536	49
MARION	6,776	7,520	8,025	1.4	2.34	4,869	5,257	1.1	33,345	38,735	2625	52
MILLER	15,637	17,291	18,542	1.4	2.47	11,080	11,905	1.0	38,960	45,911	1859	19
MISSISSIPPI	19,349	18,263	17,410	-0.8	2.60	13,908	12,766	-1.2	34,539	40,187	2493	46
MONROE	4,105	3,895	3,734	-0.7	2.43	2,733	2,511	-1.2	27,278	31,555	3027	71
MONTGOMERY	3,785	3,960	4,076	0.6	2.39	2,749	2,799	0.2	34,817	39,815	2454	42
NEVADA	3,893	4,395	4,786	1.7	2.44	2,723	2,983	1.3	32,488	37,245	2707	57
NEWTON	3,500	3,708	3,749	0.8	2.36	2,495	2,568	0.4	30,614	35,349	2874	66
OUACHITA	11,613	11,317	11,004	-0.4	2.40	8,070	7,629	-0.8	36,108	41,494	2255	34
PERRY	3,989	4,315	4,512	1.1	2.50	2,940	3,099	0.7	37,949	43,594	2005	24
PHILLIPS	9,711	9,174	8,804	-0.8	2.65	6,767	6,203	-1.2	27,339	31,650	3025	70
PIKE	4,504	4,682	4,823	0.5	2.43	3,266	3,305	0.2	33,553	38,518	2602	51
POINSETT	10,026	10,248	10,364	0.3	2.48	7,232	7,191	-0.1	32,842	37,608	2672	54
POLK	8,047	8,345	8,508	0.5	2.48	5,796	5,846	0.1	31,165	36,009	2817	63
POPE	20,701	22,413	23,604	1.1	2.52	14,998	15,799	0.7	40,645	47,306	1650	11
PRAIRIE	3,894	3,959	3,980	0.2	2.36	2,794	2,761	-0.2	36,232	41,588	2238	33
PULASKI	147,942	156,815	163,212	0.8	2.36	95,679	97,932	0.3	49,510	59,444	710	4
RANDOLPH	7,265	7,649	7,895	0.7	2.43	5,242	5,368	0.3	34,659	39,778	2476	44
ST. FRANCIS	10,043	9,866	9,680	-0.2	2.59	7,227	6,906	-0.6	31,923	36,917	2771	58
SALINE	31,778	37,968	42,429	2.5	2.50	24,489	28,601	2.2	54,301	64,016	433	1
SCOTT	4,323	4,590	4,788	0.8	2.51	3,123	3,226	0.4	32,956	37,917	2659	53
SEARCY	3,523	3,611	3,677	0.3	2.28	2,466	2,455	-0.1	25,700	29,367	3078	74
SEBASTIAN	45,300	47,706	49,544	0.7	2.50	30,723	31,337	0.3	43,345	51,215	1296	8
SEVIER	5,708	5,993	6,225	0.7	2.77	4,226	4,323	0.3	36,527	41,903	2187	30
SHARP	7,211	7,758	8,120	1.0	2.32	5,142	5,377	0.6	31,844	37,194	2777	60
STONE	4,768	5,088	5,294	0.9	2.34	3,463	3,596	0.5	27,696	31,637	3016	69
UNION	17,989	17,700	17,262	-0.2	2.45	12,652	12,088	-0.6	36,944	43,059	2134	29
VAN BUREN	6,825	7,254	7,464	0.8	2.29	4,804	4,957	0.4	34,362	39,915	2508	48
WASHINGTON	60,151	76,922	90,171	3.5	2.49	39,483	48,805	3.0	43,752	51,104	1243	7
WHITE	25,148	28,153	30,325	1.6	2.50	18,412	20,072	1.2	40,394	46,765	1675	13
WOODRUFF	3,531	3,560	3,546	0.1	2.38	2,439	2,385	-0.3	27,268	31,473	3028	72
YELL	7,922	8,153	8,325	0.4	2.63	5,810	5,830	0.0	30,047	41,523	2207	90
ARKANSAS				1.2	2.47			0.8	41,124	48,510		
UNITED STATES				1.2	2.59			1.0	53,154	62,503		

ARKANSAS
D

INCOME

COUNTY	2007 Per Capita Income	2007 HH Income Base	2007 HOUSEHOLD INCOME DISTRIBUTION (%)					2007 Home Value Base	2007 HOME VALUE DISTRIBUTION (%)					2007 Median Home Value
			Less than $25,000	$25,000 to $49,999	$50,000 to $99,999	$100,000 to $149,999	$150,000 or More		Less than $50,000	$50,000 to $89,999	$90,000 to $174,999	$175,000 to $399,999	$400,000 or More	
ARKANSAS	20,537	8,416	34.6	29.2	28.0	5.2	3.1	5,906	29.2	30.3	31.1	8.7	0.7	76,339
ASHLEY	19,812	9,347	32.5	30.2	28.5	6.0	2.9	7,256	33.8	28.0	29.2	7.9	1.1	70,211
BAXTER	22,063	18,621	30.9	35.5	25.5	5.0	3.1	15,052	13.3	18.8	43.5	21.8	2.6	118,200
BENTON	25,412	75,894	19.2	28.0	37.1	9.1	6.7	56,250	6.6	9.5	44.9	31.4	7.6	153,721
BOONE	20,804	14,925	33.1	33.2	25.7	4.7	3.3	11,157	12.8	23.1	42.6	18.9	2.7	109,638
BRADLEY	17,705	4,736	43.6	28.0	20.9	3.8	3.8	3,505	36.6	30.0	24.8	7.2	1.4	66,022
CALHOUN	19,736	2,375	37.6	32.2	23.1	3.6	3.5	1,976	45.5	30.9	18.2	4.4	1.0	54,607
CARROLL	20,177	11,274	35.5	32.4	23.3	4.8	3.9	8,473	14.8	20.8	35.8	21.6	7.0	115,458
CHICOT	16,317	4,924	47.5	25.4	20.6	3.7	2.9	3,507	42.2	28.5	16.9	10.8	1.6	59,337
CLARK	18,743	9,172	38.3	27.3	25.7	6.4	2.3	6,200	28.1	22.0	34.5	13.4	2.1	89,863
CLAY	18,038	7,192	41.0	31.9	21.6	3.2	2.3	5,493	39.8	34.2	19.2	5.6	1.1	60,577
CLEBURNE	22,304	11,197	30.8	32.4	27.6	5.7	3.6	9,135	17.5	21.1	36.9	20.2	4.3	111,580
CLEVELAND	19,208	3,535	31.9	29.7	30.6	5.9	2.1	2,941	29.9	27.5	31.0	9.9	1.7	78,477
COLUMBIA	19,595	10,016	37.1	27.2	26.2	6.4	3.1	7,306	34.3	27.3	25.6	11.9	0.8	70,085
CONWAY	20,077	8,355	33.3	28.3	29.0	6.4	3.1	6,640	23.2	29.7	35.9	9.1	2.1	86,465
CRAIGHEAD	22,137	35,692	30.3	28.6	29.0	7.7	4.4	23,604	20.5	30.1	36.3	11.0	2.0	89,234
CRAWFORD	19,131	21,986	28.0	33.5	29.3	6.5	2.7	17,038	18.5	30.2	38.4	11.4	1.5	91,923
CRITTENDEN	18,900	19,606	33.4	27.7	28.9	6.8	3.1	12,258	24.9	31.0	33.5	9.6	1.0	83,098
CROSS	19,281	7,733	36.1	29.9	26.3	4.3	3.4	5,639	30.4	28.8	31.3	8.2	1.4	75,698
DALLAS	18,269	3,329	39.2	32.0	23.4	2.7	2.8	2,519	47.9	28.1	18.5	5.0	0.6	52,443
DESHA	17,176	5,739	43.9	27.5	20.6	4.9	3.1	3,783	37.5	33.8	24.8	3.5	0.4	63,218
DREW	20,769	7,808	36.5	27.9	26.0	5.6	4.0	5,538	34.3	25.5	26.6	12.3	1.3	74,472
FAULKNER	23,202	37,998	24.1	27.0	34.3	9.9	4.8	26,668	13.4	18.6	43.7	21.8	2.5	117,505
FRANKLIN	18,008	7,361	33.4	32.0	28.4	4.6	1.6	5,842	24.0	32.0	33.2	9.1	1.6	84,150
FULTON	18,933	5,011	39.6	33.0	21.6	3.3	2.5	4,121	24.5	28.2	30.6	13.9	2.8	85,961
GARLAND	23,151	41,021	30.6	30.5	27.5	7.6	3.8	29,952	15.1	15.9	34.0	27.5	7.5	134,650
GRANT	21,629	6,832	25.2	30.2	33.3	7.9	3.3	5,584	26.1	26.7	35.2	10.6	1.5	85,953
GREENE	19,884	16,093	32.0	31.7	28.7	4.6	2.9	11,794	16.7	30.8	37.2	13.8	1.6	93,632
HEMPSTEAD	16,939	9,353	36.5	30.7	25.9	4.9	2.0	6,661	29.6	33.3	27.0	8.6	1.5	71,710
HOT SPRING	18,609	12,673	30.7	33.3	29.7	4.8	1.5	10,044	25.7	29.4	34.4	9.6	0.9	80,940
HOWARD	19,525	5,726	35.3	30.6	25.9	4.6	3.6	4,240	30.4	27.1	29.5	10.9	2.1	77,555
INDEPENDENCE	20,543	14,236	31.4	31.3	29.7	4.6	3.0	10,839	23.4	30.8	32.7	11.5	1.6	84,478
IZARD	17,549	5,798	39.7	33.2	21.4	4.1	1.7	4,718	26.4	27.9	31.0	13.4	1.3	82,368
JACKSON	17,946	6,738	40.8	30.0	22.1	4.0	3.1	4,817	35.6	36.6	20.6	6.2	1.0	63,515
JEFFERSON	19,865	30,679	33.4	27.7	27.4	8.4	3.1	20,929	21.2	31.5	35.6	10.2	1.5	86,544
JOHNSON	17,670	9,595	37.0	31.2	25.6	4.3	2.0	7,202	22.1	33.2	32.4	10.4	2.0	84,446
LAFAYETTE	18,213	3,391	42.1	27.8	22.6	4.7	2.8	2,705	50.1	24.6	19.2	5.0	1.1	49,946
LAWRENCE	17,137	7,093	38.4	32.8	23.4	3.3	2.1	5,188	31.6	38.2	25.1	4.8	0.2	68,151
LEE	14,533	4,167	50.2	26.9	18.0	2.6	2.3	2,723	41.8	33.1	22.5	2.4	0.1	59,511
LINCOLN	15,589	4,374	35.6	31.2	25.1	5.8	2.4	3,389	33.0	26.8	29.1	9.8	1.3	73,128
LITTLE RIVER	19,910	5,651	33.9	29.8	26.9	6.7	2.6	4,418	32.1	28.7	32.1	6.7	0.3	71,882
LOGAN	17,862	9,167	36.3	33.0	24.4	3.8	2.4	7,196	25.8	32.0	31.7	8.6	1.8	79,231
LONOKE	22,397	24,554	22.0	26.5	37.3	10.6	3.6	19,055	17.9	21.2	40.9	18.5	1.4	106,309
MADISON	16,957	5,967	37.5	33.7	22.6	4.1	2.1	4,799	17.3	24.3	34.3	17.7	6.4	108,637
MARION	18,407	7,520	37.1	33.7	23.3	3.9	1.9	6,115	16.6	25.2	39.9	15.5	2.8	102,587
MILLER	20,820	17,291	34.7	26.7	27.9	7.1	3.6	12,035	26.3	30.9	33.2	8.4	1.1	81,609
MISSISSIPPI	17,762	18,263	38.2	28.1	24.5	6.6	2.7	11,082	26.4	34.5	29.6	8.9	0.7	75,965
MONROE	16,538	3,895	47.0	28.1	19.8	2.6	2.5	2,618	40.7	34.0	20.6	4.0	0.7	59,310
MONTGOMERY	18,440	3,960	35.2	35.2	23.2	4.0	2.5	3,318	36.3	21.9	29.1	10.3	2.3	75,690
NEVADA	17,457	4,395	40.0	27.3	26.7	4.2	1.8	3,367	43.2	28.0	24.2	3.9	0.6	58,716
NEWTON	16,973	3,708	41.7	34.0	20.0	2.7	1.6	3,065	29.5	26.5	30.4	11.3	2.3	79,707
OUACHITA	18,700	11,317	37.6	28.5	27.0	4.9	2.1	8,258	33.1	31.7	28.9	5.5	0.8	68,896
PERRY	19,675	4,315	31.2	32.3	27.9	6.0	2.6	3,591	27.9	30.4	31.1	7.7	2.9	79,540
PHILLIPS	15,534	9,174	47.5	27.2	19.2	3.9	2.4	5,379	38.6	30.5	23.9	6.2	0.8	64,560
PIKE	18,494	4,682	37.8	33.0	21.7	5.2	2.2	3,761	36.3	26.6	25.5	9.5	2.1	68,204
POINSETT	16,680	10,248	40.5	28.4	25.4	4.0	1.6	7,095	39.0	36.7	20.5	3.4	0.5	60,060
POLK	17,615	8,345	40.1	31.9	22.0	3.6	2.4	6,636	26.8	28.1	31.5	10.6	3.0	81,260
POPE	20,303	22,413	30.2	30.2	28.8	7.4	3.3	16,331	16.1	27.5	39.8	14.4	2.1	99,051
PRAIRIE	19,959	3,959	35.6	31.3	25.8	4.7	2.6	2,981	34.6	25.9	32.1	5.7	1.7	71,949
PULASKI	28,185	156,815	23.7	26.8	32.7	9.4	7.5	98,562	12.1	25.1	38.5	20.1	4.1	110,811
RANDOLPH	18,111	7,649	37.3	32.4	23.4	4.5	2.4	5,816	25.6	34.5	30.7	8.2	1.0	76,245
ST. FRANCIS	15,569	9,866	42.1	27.5	24.0	3.9	2.4	6,434	31.0	31.5	28.6	7.6	1.2	75,354
SALINE	25,597	37,968	17.2	27.5	40.0	11.0	4.3	31,050	16.2	20.9	39.6	20.0	3.3	112,396
SCOTT	16,790	4,590	38.3	34.3	22.0	3.8	1.5	3,479	35.0	29.8	24.5	8.4	2.3	69,871
SEARCY	15,519	3,611	49.0	31.3	16.3	2.3	1.1	2,857	30.2	33.7	26.4	7.9	1.8	69,909
SEBASTIAN	23,250	47,706	27.8	29.1	30.3	7.7	5.1	31,298	15.7	31.5	36.9	13.6	2.3	94,369
SEVIER	16,494	5,993	34.2	32.5	25.8	5.7	1.7	4,560	29.6	31.3	28.9	9.1	1.1	73,467
SHARP	18,190	7,758	37.9	36.2	20.0	3.6	2.4	6,325	22.8	37.8	27.7	10.1	1.6	78,413
STONE	17,760	5,088	46.3	30.8	17.3	3.4	2.3	4,051	24.7	27.7	33.7	11.5	2.4	85,928
UNION	20,539	17,700	34.8	28.9	26.1	6.7	3.5	13,170	33.9	29.0	26.4	8.9	1.7	70,852
VAN BUREN	20,906	7,254	36.1	33.3	23.1	4.0	3.5	5,979	27.5	26.6	32.3	11.6	2.1	84,334
WASHINGTON	22,495	76,922	27.4	28.9	31.3	7.7	4.7	47,394	8.4	11.7	45.0	27.8	7.1	144,461
WHITE	20,083	28,152	31.1	30.2	29.7	6.0	3.0	21,031	23.5	24.8	35.6	13.6	2.5	93,021
WOODRUFF	16,195	3,560	47.5	28.3	19.3	3.2	1.8	2,407	49.7	29.6	16.6	3.7	0.4	50,291
YELL	17,730	8,153	34.8	31.2	26.6	4.8	2.5	6,077	25.1	30.0	32.5	10.3	2.1	83,484
ARKANSAS	21,735		30.3	29.3	29.3	7.0	4.1		20.3	25.0	35.7	16.0	3.1	98,558
UNITED STATES	27,916		21.9	25.0	32.3	12.3	8.4		7.9	10.5	27.1	35.6	19.0	192,285

COUNTY	FINANCIAL SERVICES				THE HOME						ENTERTAINMENT						PERSONAL			
					Home Improvements		Furnishings													
	Auto Loan	Home Loan	Invest-ments	Retire-ment Plans	Home Repair	Lawn & Garden	Comput-ers & Hard-ware	Major Appli-ances	TV, Radio, Sound Equip-ment	Furni-ture	Dine out/ Carry out	Sports Equip-ment	Fees & Tickets	Toys & Games	Travel	Cable TV	Apparel & Services	Auto Repairs	Health Insur-ance	Pets & Supplies
ARKANSAS	80	60	47	58	64	82	63	73	70	60	68	64	55	72	62	74	59	70	82	78
ASHLEY	84	62	42	59	67	87	62	76	70	61	69	68	54	73	61	75	60	71	82	83
BAXTER	72	63	58	60	68	82	62	75	67	61	66	62	59	64	66	72	56	71	83	75
BENTON	101	93	84	92	92	102	90	97	92	91	92	87	87	93	91	94	81	95	99	99
BOONE	77	62	56	61	67	82	65	74	70	62	69	65	59	71	65	73	60	70	80	77
BRADLEY	71	51	42	50	56	74	56	66	64	53	62	58	48	64	55	69	53	63	76	70
CALHOUN	85	57	30	53	63	88	57	75	66	56	66	67	47	70	56	71	56	68	80	83
CARROLL	83	63	44	60	69	90	63	78	69	61	68	69	55	71	63	74	58	72	84	83
CHICOT	68	48	37	47	52	70	52	62	60	50	59	54	45	60	52	65	51	60	70	67
CLARK	74	55	46	54	59	74	62	68	66	57	65	62	53	66	59	69	57	66	74	72
CLAY	70	51	38	49	55	72	54	64	61	51	59	56	47	63	53	65	51	60	72	68
CLEBURNE	82	65	52	63	72	92	65	80	71	64	70	69	59	71	68	76	60	75	88	84
CLEVELAND	88	60	31	56	67	93	60	79	69	59	69	70	49	73	59	75	58	72	85	87
COLUMBIA	77	59	49	58	63	79	62	71	69	60	68	63	56	70	61	73	59	68	79	76
CONWAY	85	60	39	58	68	91	62	79	70	60	69	69	53	73	62	75	59	72	86	85
CRAIGHEAD	84	71	66	72	71	80	75	77	78	73	77	70	70	79	73	79	68	77	81	80
CRAWFORD	82	67	52	65	69	83	66	76	71	66	70	67	60	74	65	74	61	72	79	80
CRITTENDEN	74	65	63	66	63	69	68	68	72	68	71	60	65	72	66	74	64	70	73	70
CROSS	81	62	46	60	65	83	62	74	69	62	68	65	56	72	61	73	59	70	80	79
DALLAS	81	54	28	50	60	85	55	73	65	53	64	65	45	68	55	71	54	67	80	80
DESHA	71	50	35	49	54	73	53	64	62	52	61	56	46	62	52	67	52	62	73	70
DREW	83	63	50	62	65	81	67	75	72	64	72	67	59	74	64	76	62	72	80	79
FAULKNER	93	81	72	82	78	86	86	85	86	83	86	79	80	88	81	86	76	86	86	88
FRANKLIN	75	55	42	53	61	80	57	70	64	55	63	61	50	66	57	68	54	64	77	74
FULTON	75	55	36	52	62	83	56	72	62	54	62	62	48	64	57	68	52	65	79	77
GARLAND	79	69	68	67	74	86	70	79	75	69	73	67	66	72	72	79	64	76	87	80
GRANT	99	70	41	66	76	103	69	88	77	68	77	78	59	83	67	83	66	81	93	97
GREENE	81	61	49	60	65	82	63	74	70	61	69	65	57	73	62	74	59	70	81	78
HEMPSTEAD	72	53	41	52	57	73	56	66	64	54	62	58	49	65	55	68	54	63	73	70
HOT SPRING	77	58	43	56	62	80	59	71	65	57	64	62	52	67	59	70	55	66	78	75
HOWARD	85	60	39	57	65	88	62	76	70	60	69	67	52	73	60	75	59	71	84	83
INDEPENDENCE	84	63	47	61	68	87	64	77	71	62	70	68	57	74	63	76	60	72	84	83
IZARD	65	51	41	48	57	74	51	64	57	49	56	54	46	56	53	62	47	59	73	67
JACKSON	75	53	37	51	58	77	56	68	64	54	63	60	49	66	55	69	55	64	76	73
JEFFERSON	77	66	63	66	67	77	67	72	73	67	72	63	64	73	67	76	64	71	78	75
JOHNSON	78	55	37	53	61	82	57	71	64	55	63	62	49	67	56	69	54	65	78	76
LAFAYETTE	75	52	30	49	58	80	53	69	62	52	61	62	44	63	53	68	52	64	77	76
LAWRENCE	69	50	36	48	55	73	53	64	60	50	58	56	45	61	52	64	50	60	72	68
LEE	63	43	31	43	46	62	48	56	57	47	56	49	41	57	47	62	48	55	64	61
LINCOLN	80	55	34	52	60	82	56	71	65	55	64	63	48	68	55	71	55	66	79	78
LITTLE RIVER	81	59	39	56	65	86	59	75	67	58	66	65	51	70	59	72	56	69	81	80
LOGAN	77	54	36	52	60	80	56	70	64	54	63	61	48	67	56	69	53	65	78	75
LONOKE	95	84	66	82	82	93	79	88	83	81	83	80	75	86	79	85	73	85	89	92
MADISON	76	52	31	50	60	82	54	70	61	52	60	62	45	64	53	66	51	64	76	76
MARION	69	54	42	52	60	77	54	68	60	53	59	58	49	60	56	65	50	63	75	71
MILLER	80	64	60	65	66	79	69	74	74	67	73	65	63	75	67	75	64	73	81	77
MISSISSIPPI	73	59	50	58	60	72	60	66	66	60	65	59	56	68	59	69	57	65	72	70
MONROE	66	47	35	46	51	67	51	60	59	49	57	52	44	59	50	63	49	57	68	64
MONTGOMERY	76	54	32	52	62	84	55	72	61	53	61	62	46	64	55	66	52	65	77	77
NEVADA	74	51	30	48	58	80	53	69	61	51	60	60	44	63	52	66	51	63	76	75
NEWTON	69	49	29	46	56	77	49	65	55	47	55	56	41	58	49	60	47	59	70	70
OUACHITA	72	54	45	54	58	73	58	66	65	56	63	58	52	66	57	69	55	63	74	70
PERRY	86	61	37	58	67	91	61	78	68	60	68	69	52	73	60	74	58	71	84	85
PHILLIPS	63	48	44	49	49	62	52	57	61	52	59	49	48	59	51	65	52	58	66	60
PIKE	79	55	31	52	62	86	56	73	63	54	62	64	46	66	55	68	53	66	79	79
POINSETT	70	50	36	48	54	71	52	63	59	51	58	55	45	62	51	64	50	59	70	67
POLK	74	52	35	50	58	79	55	69	62	52	61	60	46	64	54	67	52	63	76	74
POPE	80	67	62	68	69	80	70	75	73	68	73	68	65	76	69	75	64	73	79	79
PRAIRIE	84	56	28	53	65	92	57	78	65	56	65	69	46	70	57	71	55	70	83	86
PULASKI	95	89	93	92	85	89	93	89	95	93	94	81	91	95	91	95	85	93	93	91
RANDOLPH	72	54	43	53	59	76	57	67	63	54	62	59	50	65	56	67	53	63	75	71
ST. FRANCIS	67	52	45	52	54	66	56	61	62	55	61	54	51	63	54	65	54	60	67	65
SALINE	96	91	87	88	90	97	85	92	89	87	88	81	85	89	88	92	78	90	97	94
SCOTT	71	50	36	48	56	75	54	65	59	51	59	58	45	62	52	64	50	61	72	71
SEARCY	60	42	29	41	47	64	44	55	50	42	49	48	37	52	44	54	42	51	62	59
SEBASTIAN	84	76	79	77	76	81	80	80	83	78	82	72	77	84	79	85	73	81	85	81
SEVIER	81	57	32	53	61	82	56	71	63	56	64	63	48	67	55	68	55	66	76	77
SHARP	67	54	43	51	60	76	53	66	59	52	58	56	48	58	56	64	49	62	74	69
STONE	72	50	30	47	57	78	51	67	58	49	58	59	43	61	51	63	49	61	73	73
UNION	80	63	54	63	67	82	65	74	72	64	71	65	60	73	65	76	62	71	82	78
VAN BUREN	78	61	46	57	69	91	59	77	66	59	65	65	53	66	62	72	56	71	86	81
WASHINGTON	85	72	67	74	70	77	82	77	81	77	81	73	75	81	75	80	72	80	78	80
WHITE	84	65	51	63	68	85	66	77	72	65	72	69	60	74	65	76	62	73	82	82
WOODRUFF	64	45	34	44	49	65	49	58	56	47	55	50	42	57	48	61	47	55	66	62
YELL	79	57	38	54	61	82	59	72	67	57	66	64	51	70	58	71	57	67	70	70
ARKANSAS	84	69	61	69	71	85	72	79	77	70	76	70	66	78	71	80	66	77	84	82
UNITED STATES	100	100	100	100	100	100	100	100	100	100	100	100	100	100	100	100	100	100	100	100

A

COUNTY	FIPS Code	CBSA Code	DMA Code	POPULATION 2000	POPULATION 2007	POPULATION 2012	2000-2007 ANNUAL RATE % Rate	2000-2007 ANNUAL RATE State Rank	White 2000	White 2007	Black 2000	Black 2007	Asian/Pacific 2000	Asian/Pacific 2007
ALAMEDA	001	41860	807	1,443,741	1,500,793	1,537,028	0.5	52	48.8	44.3	14.9	14.3	21.1	23.6
ALPINE	003	00000	811	1,208	1,262	1,254	0.6	49	73.7	73.8	0.6	0.6	0.4	0.4
AMADOR	005	00000	862	35,100	39,657	43,304	1.7	23	85.8	83.0	3.9	4.1	1.1	1.4
BUTTE	007	17020	868	203,171	220,904	233,944	1.2	31	84.5	80.8	1.4	1.5	3.5	4.2
CALAVERAS	009	00000	862	40,554	48,342	54,812	2.5	9	91.2	89.0	0.7	0.8	0.9	1.2
COLUSA	011	00000	862	18,804	21,886	24,734	2.1	16	64.3	59.5	0.5	0.5	1.6	1.7
CONTRA COSTA	013	41860	807	948,816	1,047,327	1,106,910	1.4	26	65.5	60.7	9.4	9.3	11.3	13.2
DEL NORTE	015	18860	802	27,507	29,547	31,053	1.0	37	78.9	76.0	4.3	4.4	2.4	2.9
EL DORADO	017	40900	862	156,299	185,347	207,643	2.4	12	89.7	87.0	0.5	0.6	2.3	2.8
FRESNO	019	23420	866	799,407	915,824	1,007,851	1.9	19	54.3	49.7	5.3	4.9	8.2	8.9
GLENN	021	00000	868	26,453	28,632	30,323	1.1	35	71.8	66.6	0.6	0.6	3.5	4.1
HUMBOLDT	023	21700	802	126,518	132,810	137,299	0.7	45	84.7	81.8	0.9	0.9	1.8	2.3
IMPERIAL	025	20940	771	142,361	170,210	193,352	2.5	9	49.4	47.1	4.0	3.5	2.1	2.1
INYO	027	13860	803	17,945	18,426	18,736	0.4	53	80.1	77.2	0.2	0.2	1.0	1.2
KERN	029	12540	800	661,645	796,111	907,690	2.6	7	61.6	56.9	6.0	5.8	3.5	3.9
KINGS	031	25260	866	129,461	150,408	166,076	2.1	16	53.7	50.3	8.3	7.4	3.3	4.0
LAKE	033	17340	807	58,309	66,564	72,989	1.8	21	86.2	83.5	2.1	2.2	1.0	1.2
LASSEN	035	45000	811	33,828	36,102	36,848	0.9	39	80.8	75.7	8.8	8.4	1.2	1.8
LOS ANGELES	037	31100	803	9,519,338	10,110,975	10,453,511	0.8	41	48.7	45.2	9.8	9.0	12.2	13.1
MADERA	039	31460	866	123,109	149,180	172,133	2.7	5	62.2	57.7	4.1	4.0	1.4	1.6
MARIN	041	41860	807	247,289	251,757	254,939	0.2	57	84.0	80.5	2.9	3.0	4.7	5.7
MARIPOSA	043	00000	866	17,130	18,680	19,854	1.2	31	88.9	86.5	0.7	0.7	0.8	1.0
MENDOCINO	045	46380	807	86,265	90,385	93,152	0.6	49	80.8	77.0	0.6	0.7	1.3	1.6
MERCED	047	32900	866	210,554	256,700	294,260	2.8	4	56.2	51.5	3.8	3.6	7.0	7.6
MODOC	049	00000	868	9,449	9,631	9,783	0.3	55	85.9	83.1	0.7	0.7	0.7	0.8
MONO	051	00000	811	12,853	13,376	13,726	0.6	49	84.2	80.8	0.5	0.5	1.2	1.4
MONTEREY	053	41500	828	401,762	425,924	437,469	0.8	41	55.9	51.8	3.7	3.4	6.5	7.1
NAPA	055	34900	807	124,279	137,087	145,262	1.4	26	80.0	75.2	1.3	1.7	3.2	3.8
NEVADA	057	46020	862	92,033	102,193	109,532	1.5	24	93.4	91.5	0.3	0.3	0.9	1.1
ORANGE	059	31100	803	2,846,289	3,081,783	3,219,175	1.1	35	64.8	59.8	1.7	1.6	13.9	15.6
PLACER	061	40900	862	248,399	339,691	410,232	4.4	1	88.6	85.7	0.8	0.9	3.1	3.8
PLUMAS	063	00000	862	20,824	22,151	23,128	0.9	39	91.8	89.9	0.6	0.7	0.6	0.8
RIVERSIDE	065	40140	803	1,545,387	2,100,707	2,553,580	4.3	2	65.6	61.2	6.2	6.0	3.9	4.4
SACRAMENTO	067	40900	862	1,223,499	1,421,408	1,561,907	2.1	16	64.0	59.1	10.0	9.9	11.6	13.5
SAN BENITO	069	41940	828	53,234	57,882	60,910	1.2	31	65.2	60.6	1.1	1.1	2.6	2.8
SAN BERNARDINO	071	40140	803	1,709,434	2,051,757	2,335,687	2.5	9	58.9	54.7	9.1	8.6	5.0	5.5
SAN DIEGO	073	41740	825	2,813,833	3,064,142	3,192,305	1.2	31	66.5	61.8	5.7	5.6	9.4	10.7
SAN FRANCISCO	075	41860	807	776,733	796,417	809,323	0.3	55	49.7	44.3	7.8	7.4	31.3	35.1
SAN JOAQUIN	077	44700	862	563,598	694,530	799,025	2.9	3	58.1	53.1	6.7	6.4	11.8	13.1
SAN LUIS OBISPO	079	42020	855	246,681	267,623	280,261	1.1	35	84.6	80.4	2.0	1.9	2.8	3.4
SAN MATEO	081	41860	807	707,161	720,611	729,531	0.3	55	59.5	54.2	3.5	3.4	21.4	23.9
SANTA BARBARA	083	42060	855	399,347	422,299	438,575	0.8	41	72.7	68.1	2.3	2.4	4.3	4.8
SANTA CLARA	085	41940	807	1,682,585	1,771,177	1,835,138	0.7	45	53.8	48.5	2.8	2.7	25.9	28.7
SANTA CRUZ	087	42100	828	255,602	264,678	270,870	0.5	52	75.1	70.2	1.0	1.0	3.6	4.2
SHASTA	089	39820	868	163,256	183,901	198,963	1.7	23	89.3	86.9	0.8	0.8	2.0	2.5
SIERRA	091	00000	862	3,555	3,521	3,474	-0.1	58	94.2	94.1	0.2	0.2	0.3	0.3
SISKIYOU	093	00000	813	44,301	46,368	47,929	0.6	49	87.1	84.4	1.3	1.4	1.3	1.6
SOLANO	095	46700	862	394,542	426,952	442,616	1.1	35	56.4	51.7	14.9	14.6	13.5	15.4
SONOMA	097	42220	807	458,614	483,728	495,810	0.7	45	81.6	77.5	1.4	1.5	3.3	3.9
STANISLAUS	099	33700	862	446,997	529,038	584,888	2.4	12	69.3	64.4	2.6	2.5	4.6	5.2
SUTTER	101	49700	862	78,930	94,937	108,456	2.6	7	67.5	62.0	1.9	1.9	11.5	13.2
TEHAMA	103	39780	868	56,039	63,673	69,817	1.8	21	84.8	81.3	0.6	0.6	0.9	1.1
TRINITY	105	00000	868	13,022	13,728	14,282	0.7	45	88.9	86.6	0.4	0.5	0.6	0.7
TULARE	107	47300	866	368,021	431,643	484,123	2.2	14	58.1	53.2	1.6	1.6	3.4	3.7
TUOLUMNE	109	38020	862	54,501	59,730	61,173	1.3	28	89.4	87.1	2.1	2.2	0.9	1.1
VENTURA	111	37100	803	753,197	827,163	874,025	1.3	28	69.9	65.0	1.9	2.0	5.6	6.3
YOLO	113	40900	862	168,660	194,942	209,797	2.0	18	67.7	62.4	2.0	2.0	10.2	11.6
YUBA	115	49700	862	60,219	71,228	81,264	2.3	13	70.6	65.4	3.2	3.2	7.7	9.1
CALIFORNIA							1.4		59.5	55.5	6.7	6.3	11.3	12.2
UNITED STATES							1.2		75.1	72.7	12.3	12.6	3.8	4.5

COUNTY	% HISPANIC ORIGIN		2007 AGE DISTRIBUTION (%)										MEDIAN AGE	% 2007 Males	% 2007 Females
	2000	2007	0-4	5-9	10-14	15-19	20-24	25-44	45-64	65-84	85+	18+	2007		
ALAMEDA	19.0	22.1	6.7	6.5	7.2	6.9	6.8	30.8	25.1	8.4	1.6	75.5	35.8	49.3	50.7
ALPINE	7.8	8.0	5.0	5.5	4.5	6.3	5.1	28.8	34.1	9.5	1.2	80.7	41.6	53.2	46.8
AMADOR	8.9	11.5	4.2	4.2	4.7	7.7	5.7	22.0	33.1	16.0	2.4	82.2	45.9	54.3	45.7
BUTTE	10.5	13.5	5.8	5.2	6.1	8.1	11.0	22.9	25.9	12.3	2.7	78.6	37.1	49.3	50.7
CALAVERAS	6.8	8.9	4.3	4.3	5.9	6.7	5.2	18.3	36.2	17.1	2.0	81.2	48.1	49.6	50.4
COLUSA	46.5	53.5	8.4	7.6	8.2	8.4	7.6	25.8	23.2	9.2	1.7	70.7	32.3	50.7	49.3
CONTRA COSTA	17.7	21.4	7.0	7.1	7.8	7.2	6.0	26.7	26.8	9.6	1.8	73.5	37.4	48.9	51.1
DEL NORTE	13.9	17.4	5.9	4.9	5.8	7.0	8.7	28.1	27.4	10.7	1.6	79.1	37.9	55.0	45.0
EL DORADO	9.3	12.0	5.8	6.0	7.5	7.3	5.5	23.7	31.8	10.8	1.5	76.0	41.4	49.9	50.1
FRESNO	44.0	49.7	9.0	7.6	8.5	8.5	8.6	27.5	20.9	8.1	1.4	69.8	30.0	50.1	49.9
GLENN	29.6	35.6	8.2	7.0	7.2	8.3	8.1	25.5	23.2	10.8	1.7	72.3	33.8	50.8	49.2
HUMBOLDT	6.5	8.3	5.6	5.1	5.8	7.4	9.2	25.9	28.5	10.5	1.9	79.4	37.5	49.5	50.5
IMPERIAL	72.2	77.0	8.2	7.1	7.9	8.8	9.1	28.1	21.0	8.8	1.1	71.3	31.1	52.0	48.0
INYO	12.6	16.0	5.3	5.1	6.0	7.1	6.6	18.9	32.8	15.3	2.8	79.0	45.6	49.0	51.0
KERN	38.4	44.6	8.8	7.4	8.4	8.4	8.5	27.7	21.8	7.9	1.2	70.4	30.6	51.3	48.7
KINGS	43.6	48.9	8.7	7.0	7.3	7.8	9.9	32.9	18.8	6.5	1.0	72.8	29.8	56.3	43.7
LAKE	11.4	14.5	5.2	4.7	6.2	7.1	5.8	19.8	32.7	15.9	2.6	79.1	45.7	49.7	50.3
LASSEN	13.8	18.9	5.0	4.5	5.5	7.2	10.3	33.5	24.7	7.9	1.2	81.0	35.4	61.7	38.3
LOS ANGELES	44.6	49.7	7.8	7.1	8.3	7.9	7.2	30.3	21.9	8.1	1.4	72.1	32.7	49.6	50.4
MADERA	44.3	50.9	8.1	6.9	8.0	7.5	7.8	27.4	23.3	9.7	1.3	72.3	33.0	48.2	51.8
MARIN	11.1	14.0	4.9	5.5	6.1	5.9	5.5	24.8	33.1	11.9	2.4	79.7	43.3	49.6	50.4
MARIPOSA	7.8	10.0	4.4	4.0	5.4	6.7	7.9	19.1	35.0	15.4	2.0	82.3	46.4	50.7	49.3
MENDOCINO	16.5	20.7	6.0	5.5	6.2	6.9	7.4	23.0	31.6	11.5	2.0	78.1	41.0	49.8	50.2
MERCED	45.3	51.2	9.5	7.7	8.8	8.9	9.0	27.0	20.0	8.0	1.2	68.4	28.9	50.2	49.8
MODOC	11.5	14.7	5.7	5.3	5.7	7.0	7.7	19.6	31.2	15.7	2.2	78.6	44.3	50.5	49.5
MONO	17.7	22.3	5.4	4.9	5.9	7.0	5.9	30.3	30.9	9.2	0.6	79.7	38.6	54.4	45.6
MONTEREY	46.8	52.8	8.1	7.1	8.0	7.8	8.0	29.8	21.9	8.0	1.4	73.2	31.9	51.8	48.2
NAPA	23.7	29.4	5.9	5.9	6.8	6.9	6.6	25.1	27.6	12.4	2.9	77.2	39.8	50.3	49.7
NEVADA	5.7	7.4	4.5	4.9	6.3	6.6	5.5	20.3	34.4	14.9	2.5	80.1	46.1	49.7	50.3
ORANGE	30.8	35.8	7.5	7.1	8.1	7.0	6.4	30.0	23.4	9.0	1.6	73.1	34.9	49.7	50.3
PLACER	9.7	12.4	7.0	7.2	7.5	7.0	6.1	25.9	27.1	10.5	1.6	73.8	38.5	49.0	51.0
PLUMAS	5.7	7.4	4.3	4.5	6.1	7.0	5.1	18.6	34.7	17.5	2.2	80.6	47.6	50.1	49.9
RIVERSIDE	36.2	42.4	8.2	7.2	8.3	8.0	7.3	26.1	22.2	10.9	1.8	71.4	33.8	49.7	50.3
SACRAMENTO	16.0	19.3	7.4	6.8	7.6	7.3	7.1	28.8	24.1	9.3	1.6	73.7	34.7	49.0	51.0
SAN BENITO	47.9	54.7	8.9	8.6	9.2	7.8	6.7	28.8	22.2	6.7	1.0	68.2	31.7	50.7	49.3
SAN BERNARDINO	39.2	45.2	8.6	7.4	8.7	8.8	8.1	27.7	22.1	7.5	1.1	69.9	30.7	50.0	50.0
SAN DIEGO	26.7	31.7	7.1	6.6	7.1	7.4	7.7	29.8	23.2	9.2	1.7	75.0	34.2	50.4	49.6
SAN FRANCISCO	14.1	16.4	4.1	3.7	3.9	4.5	5.2	40.0	25.3	11.2	2.1	85.8	38.6	50.9	49.1
SAN JOAQUIN	30.5	35.4	8.4	7.5	8.3	8.4	7.9	27.0	22.5	8.5	1.5	70.8	32.2	50.0	50.0
SAN LUIS OBISPO	16.3	20.5	5.0	4.9	5.8	8.6	10.2	23.3	27.7	12.2	2.3	80.2	39.0	50.8	49.2
SAN MATEO	21.9	25.6	6.2	6.3	6.7	6.2	5.8	29.8	26.6	10.5	2.0	77.0	38.3	49.7	50.3
SANTA BARBARA	34.2	40.6	6.7	6.0	7.0	7.9	9.1	27.5	23.0	10.6	2.2	76.1	34.3	50.3	49.7
SANTA CLARA	24.0	27.5	7.0	6.8	7.1	6.6	6.4	32.1	24.1	8.6	1.3	75.1	35.6	50.7	49.3
SANTA CRUZ	26.8	32.4	6.0	5.7	6.4	7.9	8.0	28.7	27.6	8.0	1.7	77.8	35.8	50.0	50.0
SHASTA	5.5	7.1	6.1	5.3	6.4	7.6	8.1	21.8	29.6	13.0	2.2	77.6	41.1	48.9	51.1
SIERRA	6.0	6.1	4.2	4.6	5.8	6.6	5.3	20.8	34.7	15.5	2.6	80.9	46.7	50.6	49.4
SISKIYOU	7.6	9.8	5.1	4.8	5.5	6.7	7.0	19.1	34.3	15.1	2.5	80.3	46.1	49.2	50.8
SOLANO	17.6	21.0	7.3	6.8	7.7	7.5	7.6	28.1	25.3	8.5	1.3	73.6	34.8	50.2	49.8
SONOMA	17.3	21.6	5.9	5.7	6.8	7.0	6.9	26.2	28.8	10.4	2.3	77.4	39.0	49.3	50.7
STANISLAUS	31.7	37.6	8.5	7.3	8.1	8.3	7.9	27.8	22.3	8.4	1.5	71.0	31.6	49.3	50.7
SUTTER	22.2	26.6	7.7	6.6	7.8	7.6	7.4	27.0	23.4	10.8	1.7	73.1	34.7	49.6	50.4
TEHAMA	15.8	20.0	6.7	5.5	6.7	7.3	8.3	22.5	27.4	13.5	2.1	76.4	40.0	49.5	50.5
TRINITY	4.0	5.1	4.2	4.1	5.8	6.1	6.6	17.6	37.3	16.3	1.9	81.7	48.3	50.9	49.1
TULARE	50.8	57.3	9.5	8.0	8.7	8.3	8.5	27.1	20.5	8.1	1.3	68.7	29.3	50.1	49.9
TUOLUMNE	8.2	10.6	4.2	4.1	4.7	5.6	7.7	23.2	31.7	16.2	2.5	83.8	45.3	54.3	45.7
VENTURA	33.4	39.5	7.4	7.3	8.4	7.6	6.5	27.2	25.1	8.8	1.6	72.2	35.1	49.9	50.1
YOLO	25.9	30.8	6.6	6.3	6.7	9.9	12.5	26.8	21.8	8.0	1.5	76.3	29.8	49.0	51.0
YUBA	17.4	21.2	8.4	7.3	7.9	8.1	8.6	25.7	23.2	9.6	1.3	71.5	32.2	50.3	49.7
CALIFORNIA	32.4	37.2	7.5	6.9	7.8	7.6	7.3	29.0	23.5	9.0	1.5	73.4	34.2	49.9	50.1
UNITED STATES	12.5	15.0	6.9	6.5	6.8	7.1	7.0	27.6	25.4	10.7	1.9	75.6	36.7	49.2	50.8

HOUSEHOLDS

COUNTY	HOUSEHOLDS					FAMILIES			MEDIAN HOUSEHOLD INCOME			
	2000	2007	2012	% Annual Rate 2000-2007	2007 Average HH Size	2000	2007	% Annual Rate 2000-2007	2007	2012	2007 National Rank	2007 State Rank
ALAMEDA	523,366	537,786	547,650	0.4	2.74	339,096	350,153	0.4	73,597	85,602	98	10
ALPINE	483	519	516	1.0	2.43	295	319	1.1	50,478	56,801	641	29
AMADOR	12,759	14,791	16,356	2.1	2.37	9,069	10,558	2.1	52,260	60,405	531	26
BUTTE	79,566	86,802	92,088	1.2	2.47	49,386	54,172	1.3	39,808	45,803	1750	48
CALAVERAS	16,469	19,950	22,762	2.7	2.40	11,747	14,290	2.7	50,030	57,159	680	30
COLUSA	6,097	6,957	7,819	1.8	3.09	4,576	5,240	1.9	43,034	49,536	1325	42
CONTRA COSTA	344,129	374,604	393,893	1.2	2.77	242,233	264,765	1.2	81,812	99,162	44	4
DEL NORTE	9,170	9,897	10,486	1.1	2.59	6,293	6,822	1.1	35,622	40,538	2348	55
EL DORADO	58,939	69,806	78,269	2.4	2.64	43,029	51,157	2.4	63,712	75,182	184	15
FRESNO	252,940	284,994	311,891	1.7	3.15	186,736	211,175	1.7	43,147	50,392	1312	41
GLENN	9,172	9,769	10,299	0.9	2.89	6,733	7,199	0.9	38,113	43,206	1988	51
HUMBOLDT	51,238	53,804	55,864	0.7	2.39	30,645	32,365	0.8	38,702	44,405	1894	50
IMPERIAL	39,384	47,357	54,076	2.6	3.36	31,465	37,944	2.6	39,060	44,334	1842	49
INYO	7,703	7,863	8,009	0.3	2.32	4,937	5,066	0.4	42,584	49,094	1386	43
KERN	208,652	246,047	279,857	2.3	3.10	156,401	185,081	2.3	44,072	51,397	1201	37
KINGS	34,418	39,738	44,313	2.0	3.23	26,989	31,250	2.0	44,241	50,851	1183	36
LAKE	23,974	26,728	29,260	1.5	2.45	15,370	17,221	1.6	35,779	40,785	2318	54
LASSEN	9,625	10,209	10,547	0.8	2.56	6,777	7,218	0.9	44,511	51,148	1157	35
LOS ANGELES	3,133,774	3,254,679	3,346,371	0.5	3.05	2,136,977	2,229,317	0.6	54,338	63,809	431	22
MADERA	36,155	43,353	50,046	2.5	3.24	28,610	34,406	2.6	43,883	49,949	1227	40
MARIN	100,650	102,795	104,118	0.3	2.34	60,679	62,322	0.4	93,655	112,929	13	2
MARIPOSA	6,613	7,422	7,968	1.6	2.33	4,490	5,062	1.7	41,473	47,048	1521	47
MENDOCINO	33,266	34,984	36,149	0.7	2.52	21,864	23,106	0.8	43,967	50,571	1214	39
MERCED	63,815	76,744	87,783	2.6	3.29	49,760	60,025	2.6	44,062	51,339	1204	38
MODOC	3,784	3,910	3,999	0.5	2.36	2,551	2,649	0.5	33,632	38,326	2592	58
MONO	5,137	5,522	5,700	1.0	2.38	3,145	3,400	1.1	56,259	66,230	357	20
MONTEREY	121,236	128,182	131,279	0.8	3.14	87,931	93,329	0.8	60,932	71,515	243	16
NAPA	45,402	49,884	52,768	1.3	2.64	30,694	33,878	1.4	65,907	77,532	163	14
NEVADA	36,894	41,181	44,255	1.5	2.46	25,930	29,065	1.6	56,575	65,674	342	19
ORANGE	935,287	994,232	1,031,216	0.8	3.06	667,917	712,843	0.9	75,660	88,876	83	6
PLACER	93,382	129,615	157,219	4.6	2.60	67,742	94,389	4.7	75,229	88,176	86	7
PLUMAS	9,000	9,930	10,487	1.4	2.21	6,051	6,707	1.4	44,525	51,224	1155	34
RIVERSIDE	506,218	676,427	818,403	4.1	3.05	372,386	499,445	4.1	54,283	63,471	435	23
SACRAMENTO	453,602	520,848	570,626	1.9	2.68	297,596	343,378	2.0	55,644	65,190	379	21
SAN BENITO	15,885	16,978	17,736	0.9	3.38	12,893	13,818	1.0	74,772	87,143	91	8
SAN BERNARDINO	528,594	615,724	697,584	2.1	3.25	404,327	472,538	2.2	52,779	61,911	508	25
SAN DIEGO	994,677	1,075,598	1,119,523	1.1	2.75	663,170	720,463	1.1	59,771	70,352	273	17
SAN FRANCISCO	329,700	339,843	345,588	0.4	2.28	145,186	150,828	0.5	74,447	89,884	95	9
SAN JOAQUIN	181,629	220,637	253,321	2.7	3.07	134,708	164,239	2.8	51,408	60,397	586	27
SAN LUIS OBISPO	92,739	103,357	109,080	1.5	2.44	58,654	65,711	1.6	53,233	62,361	488	24
SAN MATEO	254,103	257,484	259,594	0.2	2.76	171,249	174,338	0.2	89,546	108,079	20	3
SANTA BARBARA	136,622	145,125	150,803	0.8	2.79	89,555	95,580	0.9	58,748	68,781	291	18
SANTA CLARA	565,863	593,881	613,387	0.7	2.93	395,561	416,902	0.7	94,162	113,184	12	1
SANTA CRUZ	91,139	95,467	97,707	0.6	2.68	57,132	60,163	0.7	69,128	81,292	126	11
SHASTA	63,426	70,970	77,020	1.6	2.54	44,002	49,447	1.6	41,802	48,076	1477	46
SIERRA	1,520	1,547	1,543	0.2	2.25	986	1,009	0.3	42,174	47,190	1430	44
SISKIYOU	18,556	19,740	20,574	0.9	2.31	12,231	13,076	0.9	35,064	39,964	2423	56
SOLANO	130,403	140,259	145,300	1.0	2.93	97,375	105,109	1.1	68,894	80,596	128	12
SONOMA	172,403	181,921	186,475	0.7	2.59	112,397	119,183	0.8	67,499	79,410	143	13
STANISLAUS	145,146	168,543	185,166	2.1	3.09	109,517	127,613	2.1	49,943	58,444	686	31
SUTTER	27,033	31,962	36,302	2.3	2.93	19,946	23,670	2.4	47,731	55,712	842	32
TEHAMA	21,013	23,830	26,134	1.8	2.63	14,897	16,963	1.8	37,835	42,978	2019	52
TRINITY	5,587	5,930	6,219	0.8	2.28	3,625	3,868	0.9	33,725	38,810	2581	57
TULARE	110,385	125,594	139,995	1.8	3.39	87,061	99,390	1.8	41,879	48,099	1463	45
TUOLUMNE	21,004	22,272	22,965	0.8	2.36	14,249	15,178	0.9	47,096	54,003	898	33
VENTURA	243,234	263,529	277,874	1.1	3.09	182,959	198,910	1.2	76,319	90,005	78	5
YOLO	59,375	68,737	74,042	2.0	2.71	37,468	43,602	2.1	51,406	60,445	587	28
YUBA	20,535	24,163	27,576	2.3	2.89	14,801	17,485	2.3	36,879	41,883	2143	53
CALIFORNIA				1.2	2.92			1.3	60,268	70,268		
UNITED STATES				1.2	2.59			1.0	53,154	62,503		

COUNTY	2007 Per Capita Income	2007 HH Income Base	2007 HOUSEHOLD INCOME DISTRIBUTION (%)					2007 Home Value Base	2007 HOME VALUE DISTRIBUTION (%)					2007 Median Home Value
			Less than $25,000	$25,000 to $49,999	$50,000 to $99,999	$100,000 to $149,999	$150,000 or More		Less than $50,000	$50,000 to $89,999	$90,000 to $174,999	$175,000 to $399,999	$400,000 or More	
ALAMEDA	35,359	537,777	15.9	18.1	32.4	17.5	16.1	300,412	0.8	1.2	2.2	14.9	80.9	683,245
ALPINE	28,299	519	23.7	25.8	35.6	8.7	6.2	359	5.6	2.8	7.8	27.9	56.0	434,127
AMADOR	27,880	14,790	22.1	25.8	33.8	12.5	5.9	11,350	2.0	2.4	5.3	45.6	44.6	380,085
BUTTE	22,080	86,802	32.2	27.5	28.3	8.1	3.9	53,944	4.9	3.4	12.1	56.1	23.5	282,448
CALAVERAS	26,901	19,950	23.9	26.0	33.3	11.0	5.7	15,892	2.5	1.5	5.6	44.3	46.1	384,407
COLUSA	18,192	6,957	27.5	30.2	30.2	8.0	4.2	4,507	3.4	1.5	7.3	65.1	22.7	273,566
CONTRA COSTA	40,389	374,604	11.8	16.1	33.0	19.5	19.7	263,233	1.2	1.0	2.1	23.4	72.3	600,691
DEL NORTE	18,609	9,897	37.6	26.3	25.7	7.9	2.5	6,399	8.7	4.8	14.2	53.3	18.9	242,755
EL DORADO	32,136	69,806	14.5	23.1	35.5	15.5	11.3	52,896	2.2	1.5	2.6	30.7	63.1	466,851
FRESNO	19,002	284,988	28.7	27.7	29.0	9.2	5.4	165,222	2.3	1.7	9.2	62.4	24.5	280,067
GLENN	16,975	9,769	31.6	32.3	27.1	6.8	2.2	6,389	3.9	2.6	11.2	64.0	18.3	241,321
HUMBOLDT	21,930	53,804	33.5	28.2	27.5	7.3	3.6	31,877	4.0	2.5	7.8	55.9	29.8	313,241
IMPERIAL	16,091	47,353	33.8	26.5	27.2	8.8	3.7	28,465	8.1	5.1	18.8	61.1	6.9	209,654
INYO	23,844	7,863	31.0	26.1	29.5	9.7	3.8	5,313	14.5	6.6	9.9	35.7	33.3	300,950
KERN	19,039	246,041	28.9	26.5	29.7	10.0	4.9	155,852	3.0	2.7	12.3	64.0	18.1	260,476
KINGS	18,535	39,724	25.9	30.8	29.8	9.4	4.2	22,884	2.5	2.5	15.3	67.3	12.4	236,578
LAKE	19,860	26,728	35.8	29.2	25.0	7.3	2.8	19,301	6.1	5.4	15.8	50.2	22.5	250,777
LASSEN	20,873	10,209	28.5	26.9	32.8	8.9	2.9	7,145	5.4	4.3	14.1	57.2	19.1	249,152
LOS ANGELES	26,078	3,254,584	23.1	23.1	30.0	13.3	10.4	1,601,834	1.3	1.3	2.1	19.1	76.1	591,605
MADERA	18,101	43,353	28.6	27.9	30.5	8.3	4.6	29,145	1.5	1.6	6.7	58.2	32.0	323,278
MARIN	60,686	102,795	10.2	13.8	28.6	18.1	29.2	66,551	0.6	0.6	1.4	4.9	92.6	1,000,001
MARIPOSA	23,172	7,422	30.2	28.1	29.5	8.9	3.3	5,291	3.0	1.3	8.6	53.7	33.4	340,265
MENDOCINO	23,534	34,984	27.8	28.7	29.9	9.1	4.6	21,739	5.3	2.9	6.2	36.6	49.0	394,983
MERCED	17,606	76,744	26.9	29.1	31.1	8.7	4.2	46,308	2.2	1.5	4.3	58.7	33.4	340,095
MODOC	20,550	3,910	37.8	27.6	24.8	7.5	2.4	2,811	3.3	7.2	34.6	42.9	12.1	184,154
MONO	31,569	5,522	16.2	27.9	37.3	9.8	8.9	3,408	3.9	6.3	4.0	30.4	55.5	447,692
MONTEREY	25,661	128,179	16.5	23.7	34.5	14.8	10.5	71,841	1.7	1.2	1.9	13.6	81.6	731,032
NAPA	34,057	49,875	14.3	22.8	33.3	16.9	12.8	33,206	2.8	3.1	4.3	16.2	73.6	583,018
NEVADA	30,660	41,181	18.5	25.3	34.7	13.3	8.2	31,580	1.8	1.4	3.4	27.3	66.1	488,984
ORANGE	33,576	994,231	12.2	19.2	33.4	18.2	17.0	622,466	1.3	1.5	2.9	11.9	82.3	689,699
PLACER	37,086	129,614	12.5	18.7	35.9	17.7	15.2	96,558	1.6	0.9	2.5	23.1	71.9	532,459
PLUMAS	25,127	9,930	29.2	25.4	33.2	8.5	3.7	7,109	4.5	2.7	10.2	52.7	29.9	312,393
RIVERSIDE	23,110	676,418	21.3	24.7	33.7	13.0	7.3	473,170	3.8	2.3	6.4	41.0	46.6	382,485
SACRAMENTO	26,920	520,847	19.9	24.4	34.2	13.5	8.0	311,185	2.2	1.2	4.3	56.6	35.6	347,597
SAN BENITO	26,850	16,978	12.3	20.0	34.2	19.5	13.9	11,853	1.2	1.5	1.8	14.8	80.8	584,925
SAN BERNARDINO	20,727	615,706	22.5	24.8	33.7	12.5	6.5	403,631	3.5	2.3	5.9	49.2	39.2	352,116
SAN DIEGO	29,468	1,075,585	18.1	23.8	32.7	15.1	10.3	610,427	2.3	1.9	2.9	25.1	67.8	503,538
SAN FRANCISCO	47,627	339,843	17.9	16.6	29.4	16.5	19.7	124,839	0.7	3.1	1.6	5.4	89.2	870,997
SAN JOAQUIN	21,635	220,637	24.2	24.5	32.7	12.3	6.3	137,040	2.4	1.5	5.2	47.7	43.1	369,842
SAN LUIS OBISPO	28,635	103,354	22.2	24.8	33.2	12.0	7.8	64,965	2.0	2.0	4.4	27.2	64.4	493,665
SAN MATEO	45,936	257,483	9.8	14.3	31.3	20.9	23.7	161,000	0.8	1.1	1.5	4.8	91.8	923,909
SANTA BARBARA	29,256	145,122	18.7	23.4	33.2	13.7	11.0	83,386	1.7	1.8	3.4	26.6	66.4	630,561
SANTA CLARA	44,815	593,881	9.7	12.7	30.4	20.8	26.4	362,310	0.8	1.6	3.5	6.5	87.6	865,152
SANTA CRUZ	35,450	95,467	15.8	20.3	31.2	17.0	15.7	58,301	1.0	1.5	3.9	12.8	80.8	772,167
SHASTA	22,036	70,970	30.1	28.1	29.1	8.7	4.0	47,807	5.1	2.6	8.2	61.6	22.5	287,414
SIERRA	23,627	1,547	28.9	30.1	30.8	7.0	3.2	1,105	2.9	2.4	13.2	53.9	27.6	270,565
SISKIYOU	21,034	19,740	37.6	28.4	24.6	6.2	3.2	13,572	4.3	3.8	18.2	53.3	20.4	238,274
SOLANO	28,330	140,259	13.8	20.1	36.9	18.7	10.5	93,399	1.7	1.0	2.9	35.0	59.4	442,473
SONOMA	33,537	181,921	14.5	21.0	35.1	18.0	11.4	119,173	2.4	2.1	3.2	17.8	74.4	572,266
STANISLAUS	20,789	168,542	23.8	26.2	33.6	10.9	5.5	107,002	2.7	1.7	3.1	52.5	40.0	366,373
SUTTER	21,262	31,962	25.4	26.7	31.8	11.2	5.0	20,194	2.7	1.7	4.9	57.7	33.0	341,596
TEHAMA	19,290	23,830	32.6	30.5	27.5	6.4	3.0	16,400	4.5	3.9	15.6	59.4	16.6	238,249
TRINITY	20,520	5,930	35.9	32.5	22.8	5.8	2.9	4,320	5.9	2.2	18.0	53.4	20.5	244,938
TULARE	16,859	125,589	30.0	28.5	28.4	8.6	4.5	78,934	3.0	2.3	14.1	66.2	14.4	235,633
TUOLUMNE	25,181	22,272	24.8	28.6	32.8	9.0	4.8	16,199	4.0	2.3	5.1	51.5	37.1	351,432
VENTURA	32,144	263,527	12.6	18.1	34.0	19.3	16.0	181,195	1.4	1.6	2.8	13.0	81.1	630,182
YOLO	25,590	68,737	25.4	23.3	30.8	12.3	8.2	37,395	4.3	2.0	3.7	41.7	48.3	392,860
YUBA	16,832	24,163	33.0	32.1	26.3	6.0	2.6	13,516	5.2	2.9	9.4	62.9	19.6	252,139
CALIFORNIA	28,915		19.6	22.1	31.8	14.6	11.8		2.0	1.7	4.1	28.4	63.8	499,578
UNITED STATES	27,916		21.9	25.0	32.3	12.3	8.4		7.9	10.5	27.1	35.6	19.0	192,285

CALIFORNIA
E

SPENDING POTENTIAL INDICES

COUNTY	FINANCIAL SERVICES				THE HOME						ENTERTAINMENT						PERSONAL			
					Home Improvements		Furnishings													
	Auto Loan	Home Loan	Invest-ments	Retire-ment Plans	Home Repair	Lawn & Garden	Comput-ers & Hard-ware	Major Appli-ances	TV, Radio, Sound Equip-ment	Furni-ture	Dine out/ Carry out	Sports Equip-ment	Fees & Tickets	Toys & Games	Travel	Cable TV	Apparel & Services	Auto Repairs	Health Insur-ance	Pets & Supplies
ALAMEDA	121	135	136	136	135	116	143	130	132	139	134	134	143	129	139	126	126	136	117	127
ALPINE	105	95	80	95	103	119	90	107	91	90	91	94	86	95	94	95	80	98	106	111
AMADOR	104	91	79	91	100	119	89	106	92	88	92	92	84	91	94	97	80	99	111	109
BUTTE	77	70	71	71	71	77	78	76	76	73	76	69	73	74	75	76	68	77	78	77
CALAVERAS	97	86	76	86	95	113	84	101	87	83	86	87	80	86	89	91	75	93	104	103
COLUSA	85	77	59	71	75	81	76	83	76	76	77	78	70	77	74	75	68	82	79	82
CONTRA COSTA	141	168	172	166	168	146	159	153	149	163	151	150	168	148	163	144	141	154	140	149
DEL NORTE	71	62	58	61	66	76	64	71	66	61	65	63	59	65	64	68	57	68	74	73
EL DORADO	115	125	126	126	127	123	117	120	113	119	113	111	121	114	121	113	104	117	116	120
FRESNO	83	82	77	81	78	74	85	81	82	84	83	80	82	81	81	79	76	85	76	79
GLENN	73	65	56	62	67	74	66	72	67	64	67	66	61	69	65	68	60	70	72	73
HUMBOLDT	74	66	69	68	68	73	75	73	74	69	73	67	70	73	72	74	65	74	75	74
IMPERIAL	78	74	61	69	68	68	72	74	73	74	74	71	69	71	70	71	67	77	70	71
INYO	77	74	79	73	78	85	75	81	76	72	75	71	72	74	77	79	66	78	85	81
KERN	83	81	77	80	77	75	83	81	81	82	81	78	80	81	80	79	74	83	77	79
KINGS	86	80	71	79	75	75	84	81	81	82	82	79	79	83	79	79	74	85	77	80
LAKE	72	64	58	63	70	82	63	75	66	62	65	64	60	64	67	69	57	70	79	75
LASSEN	80	76	71	75	77	82	73	79	74	73	74	70	72	75	74	76	66	76	80	80
LOS ANGELES	101	108	103	106	106	91	118	107	108	112	111	115	114	106	112	102	104	113	94	102
MADERA	84	78	70	76	79	82	80	84	79	79	80	80	76	79	79	79	72	83	81	83
MARIN	178	216	229	218	222	189	215	201	191	212	194	206	222	186	219	182	182	205	179	196
MARIPOSA	84	69	56	68	77	96	72	86	74	68	73	75	64	74	73	78	63	80	89	89
MENDOCINO	86	79	75	79	82	91	81	87	82	78	81	78	77	81	81	83	72	84	88	88
MERCED	81	81	72	77	77	73	81	81	78	81	79	80	78	79	78	76	72	83	74	78
MODOC	77	59	47	59	67	85	64	76	67	59	66	67	55	68	63	70	57	71	80	80
MONO	102	106	101	108	109	106	109	108	100	105	101	108	106	99	109	97	92	109	100	108
MONTEREY	106	114	110	111	113	99	119	112	109	115	111	118	116	108	115	104	104	117	100	107
NAPA	115	135	138	131	138	124	129	129	121	129	122	124	134	118	133	119	113	127	120	124
NEVADA	105	106	106	106	111	118	102	111	101	102	101	99	102	99	107	104	90	107	112	111
ORANGE	130	150	150	148	149	128	150	141	137	148	139	144	152	135	149	131	131	145	126	136
PLACER	129	147	147	147	144	133	135	134	128	140	129	127	142	130	139	125	118	132	126	133
PLUMAS	82	73	69	73	79	92	73	84	76	71	75	72	70	74	77	80	65	80	89	85
RIVERSIDE	97	101	98	98	98	95	98	99	96	99	96	93	98	94	98	94	87	100	96	96
SACRAMENTO	97	102	103	102	98	91	103	97	99	103	100	93	103	99	101	96	92	100	92	96
SAN BENITO	122	143	129	135	136	117	131	131	119	133	120	132	132	121	130	111	112	130	111	124
SAN BERNARDINO	92	96	91	93	92	86	96	93	92	95	92	91	94	92	93	89	85	95	86	90
SAN DIEGO	107	112	113	113	111	100	119	109	111	116	113	110	117	110	115	107	105	115	102	107
SAN FRANCISCO	134	141	147	149	143	124	165	142	151	155	155	153	160	145	157	144	144	154	130	140
SAN JOAQUIN	90	95	91	93	92	86	93	92	90	94	91	88	93	90	92	88	83	93	86	90
SAN LUIS OBISPO	95	96	100	96	97	96	102	98	97	97	98	93	99	95	100	96	88	100	97	98
SAN MATEO	155	187	191	186	190	159	189	176	167	184	171	184	192	163	189	158	161	180	154	169
SANTA BARBARA	106	114	116	113	115	103	122	112	111	116	113	114	120	109	118	107	105	117	103	109
SANTA CLARA	166	193	192	193	192	162	197	182	175	191	178	191	197	172	194	164	167	188	158	175
SANTA CRUZ	121	138	140	138	138	119	144	133	128	137	130	138	142	124	140	120	121	138	117	128
SHASTA	80	74	75	74	77	83	77	80	78	74	77	72	74	77	77	79	68	79	83	81
SIERRA	86	67	45	66	77	101	68	88	72	65	71	76	59	73	70	77	61	79	90	92
SISKIYOU	74	60	53	60	67	83	65	75	67	60	66	65	57	67	65	71	57	70	80	77
SOLANO	109	124	124	122	121	108	119	114	113	120	114	110	123	114	119	110	106	115	106	112
SONOMA	114	128	130	126	128	117	125	122	117	124	118	118	127	115	126	114	109	123	115	120
STANISLAUS	89	92	87	89	88	84	90	89	87	90	88	86	89	87	89	85	80	90	84	87
SUTTER	86	87	83	85	85	84	87	87	85	86	85	82	85	85	85	84	78	87	84	86
TEHAMA	76	64	56	63	69	81	67	76	70	65	69	67	62	69	67	72	61	73	78	78
TRINITY	71	60	53	59	66	81	61	73	64	59	63	62	56	63	63	67	54	68	77	74
TULARE	81	79	71	76	75	74	79	79	78	79	78	77	76	78	77	76	71	81	75	77
TUOLUMNE	88	81	79	81	88	100	80	92	83	79	82	79	78	80	85	87	72	87	97	93
VENTURA	126	151	150	146	150	128	143	139	132	144	133	139	148	131	145	126	125	139	124	133
YOLO	94	91	92	92	89	84	106	93	98	97	99	93	99	96	97	93	91	99	87	92
YUBA	71	62	57	62	61	66	68	68	68	65	68	63	63	68	65	67	60	69	68	68
CALIFORNIA	111	119	116	117	117	105	123	116	115	120	116	117	121	113	120	110	108	120	106	112
UNITED STATES	100	100	100	100	100	100	100	100	100	100	100	100	100	100	100	100	100	100	100	100

COUNTY	FIPS Code	CBSA Code	DMA Code	POPULATION			2000-2007 ANNUAL RATE		RACE (%)					
									White		Black		Asian/Pacific	
				2000	2007	2012	% Rate	State Rank	2000	2007	2000	2007	2000	2007
ADAMS	001	19740	751	347,983	423,639	477,080	2.8	6	76.9	74.4	3.1	3.1	3.3	3.8
ALAMOSA	003	00000	751	14,966	15,688	16,212	0.7	36	71.2	68.4	1.0	1.0	1.0	1.2
ARAPAHOE	005	19740	751	487,967	552,801	596,361	1.7	21	79.9	77.8	7.7	8.0	4.1	4.9
ARCHULETA	007	00000	751	9,898	12,174	14,000	2.9	4	88.3	86.7	0.4	0.4	0.3	0.4
BACA	009	00000	752	4,517	4,178	3,939	-1.1	64	93.7	92.7	0.0	0.1	0.2	0.3
BENT	011	00000	752	5,998	5,947	5,999	-0.1	53	79.5	79.1	3.7	3.8	0.6	0.6
BOULDER	013	14500	751	269,794	285,787	293,516	0.8	32	88.4	86.6	0.9	0.9	3.1	3.7
BROOMFIELD	014	19740	751	39,232	48,974	55,303	3.1	3	88.8	87.0	0.9	1.0	4.1	5.0
CHAFFEE	015	00000	751	16,242	17,435	18,245	1.0	28	90.9	89.7	1.6	1.7	0.5	0.6
CHEYENNE	017	00000	751	2,231	2,148	2,094	-0.5	58	92.9	92.6	0.5	0.5	0.1	0.1
CLEAR CREEK	019	19740	751	9,322	9,400	9,407	0.1	49	96.4	96.3	0.3	0.3	0.4	0.4
CONEJOS	021	00000	751	8,400	8,808	9,074	0.7	36	72.8	70.8	0.2	0.2	0.2	0.2
COSTILLA	023	00000	751	3,663	3,573	3,448	-0.3	54	60.9	60.3	0.8	0.8	1.1	1.2
CROWLEY	025	00000	752	5,518	5,579	5,714	0.2	45	82.9	82.6	7.0	7.3	0.8	0.8
CUSTER	027	00000	752	3,503	4,169	4,531	2.4	11	95.9	95.5	0.4	0.4	0.3	0.4
DELTA	029	00000	751	27,834	30,888	32,711	1.4	24	92.3	91.2	0.5	0.6	0.3	0.4
DENVER	031	19740	751	554,636	578,062	591,337	0.6	39	65.3	62.7	11.1	11.1	2.9	3.4
DOLORES	033	00000	751	1,844	1,857	1,860	0.1	49	95.3	95.3	0.1	0.1	0.4	0.4
DOUGLAS	035	19740	751	175,766	276,640	360,913	6.5	1	92.8	91.7	1.0	1.0	2.6	3.2
EAGLE	037	20780	751	41,659	50,121	55,951	2.6	8	85.4	83.2	0.3	0.4	0.9	1.1
ELBERT	039	19740	751	19,872	23,823	25,912	2.5	10	95.2	94.6	0.6	0.7	0.5	0.6
EL PASO	041	17820	752	516,929	593,415	651,072	1.9	19	81.2	79.2	6.5	6.8	2.8	3.4
FREMONT	043	15860	752	46,145	48,890	50,224	0.8	32	89.5	88.8	5.3	5.6	0.6	0.7
GARFIELD	045	00000	751	43,791	53,303	60,435	2.7	7	90.0	88.4	0.4	0.5	0.5	0.6
GILPIN	047	19740	751	4,757	5,112	5,277	1.0	28	94.4	93.7	0.5	0.6	0.9	1.1
GRAND	049	00000	751	12,442	14,313	15,753	2.0	16	95.2	94.4	0.5	0.5	0.8	1.0
GUNNISON	051	00000	751	13,956	14,728	15,085	0.7	36	95.1	94.4	0.5	0.6	0.6	0.7
HINSDALE	053	00000	751	790	789	786	0.0	52	97.3	97.3	0.0	0.0	0.3	0.3
HUERFANO	055	00000	752	7,862	7,886	7,848	0.0	52	81.0	80.6	2.7	2.8	0.5	0.5
JACKSON	057	00000	751	1,577	1,509	1,432	-0.6	60	96.2	96.0	0.3	0.3	0.1	0.1
JEFFERSON	059	19740	751	525,330	534,512	538,620	0.2	45	90.6	89.2	0.9	1.0	2.4	2.9
KIOWA	061	00000	752	1,622	1,531	1,471	-0.8	63	96.1	95.9	0.5	0.5	0.1	0.1
KIT CARSON	063	00000	751	8,011	7,722	7,405	-0.5	58	87.3	85.2	1.7	1.8	0.4	0.4
LAKE	065	20780	751	7,812	7,946	8,026	0.2	45	77.6	74.8	0.2	0.2	0.4	0.5
LA PLATA	067	20420	790	43,941	50,436	55,038	1.9	19	87.3	86.1	0.3	0.3	0.5	0.6
LARIMER	069	22660	751	251,494	288,955	308,656	1.9	19	91.4	90.1	0.7	0.7	1.6	2.0
LAS ANIMAS	071	00000	752	15,207	15,804	16,190	0.5	41	82.6	81.2	0.4	0.4	0.6	0.7
LINCOLN	073	00000	751	6,087	5,794	5,604	-0.7	61	86.3	84.5	5.0	5.2	0.6	0.8
LOGAN	075	44540	751	20,504	20,736	20,732	0.2	45	91.7	89.9	2.0	2.0	0.5	0.6
MESA	077	24300	773	116,255	137,377	154,280	2.3	13	92.3	91.2	0.5	0.6	0.6	0.8
MINERAL	079	00000	751	831	960	1,041	2.0	16	96.9	96.9	0.0	0.0	0.0	0.0
MOFFAT	081	00000	751	13,184	13,684	14,058	0.5	41	93.6	92.7	0.2	0.2	0.4	0.5
MONTEZUMA	083	00000	790	23,830	25,363	26,494	0.9	30	81.7	80.4	0.1	0.1	0.3	0.3
MONTROSE	085	33940	773	33,432	39,952	44,908	2.5	10	90.0	88.5	0.3	0.3	0.5	0.6
MORGAN	087	22820	751	27,171	28,637	29,626	0.7	36	79.7	76.9	0.3	0.4	0.3	0.4
OTERO	089	00000	752	20,311	19,545	19,057	-0.5	58	79.0	76.7	0.8	0.8	0.8	0.9
OURAY	091	00000	751	3,742	4,556	5,144	2.8	6	96.3	96.0	0.1	0.1	0.4	0.5
PARK	093	19740	751	14,523	16,966	18,761	2.2	14	95.1	94.5	0.5	0.5	0.4	0.5
PHILLIPS	095	00000	751	4,480	4,719	4,860	0.7	36	93.0	91.9	0.2	0.2	0.4	0.5
PITKIN	097	00000	751	14,872	15,861	16,594	0.9	30	94.3	93.4	0.5	0.6	1.2	1.4
PROWERS	099	00000	751	14,483	13,965	13,480	-0.5	58	78.6	75.8	0.3	0.3	0.4	0.5
PUEBLO	101	39380	752	141,472	154,712	163,229	1.2	26	79.5	77.5	1.9	1.9	0.7	0.8
RIO BLANCO	103	00000	751	5,986	6,077	6,152	0.2	45	95.0	94.9	0.2	0.2	0.3	0.3
RIO GRANDE	105	00000	751	12,413	13,065	13,415	0.7	36	73.9	71.0	0.3	0.4	0.2	0.3
ROUTT	107	00000	751	19,690	22,648	24,104	1.9	19	96.9	96.5	0.1	0.1	0.5	0.6
SAGUACHE	109	00000	751	5,917	6,967	7,627	2.3	13	71.3	68.6	0.1	0.2	0.5	0.5
SAN JUAN	111	00000	751	558	575	588	0.4	42	97.1	97.2	0.0	0.0	0.5	0.5
SAN MIGUEL	113	00000	773	6,594	7,391	7,911	1.6	23	93.6	92.6	0.3	0.4	0.8	1.0
SEDGWICK	115	00000	751	2,747	2,593	2,489	-0.8	63	90.5	88.7	0.5	0.6	0.8	1.1
SUMMIT	117	43540	751	23,548	25,715	27,082	1.2	26	91.8	90.6	0.7	0.7	0.9	1.2
TELLER	119	17820	752	20,555	23,017	24,715	1.6	23	94.9	94.3	0.5	0.6	0.7	0.8
WASHINGTON	121	00000	751	4,926	4,796	4,692	-0.4	55	96.4	95.8	0.0	0.0	0.1	0.1
WELD	123	24540	751	180,798	249,299	306,249	4.5	2	81.7	79.2	0.6	0.6	0.9	1.1
YUMA	125	00000	751	9,841	9,901	9,923	0.1	49	94.2	94.0	0.1	0.1	0.1	0.1
COLORADO							1.8		82.8	81.1	3.8	3.8	2.3	2.8
UNITED STATES							1.2		75.1	72.7	12.3	12.6	3.8	4.5

POPULATION COMPOSITION

COUNTY	% HISPANIC ORIGIN		2007 AGE DISTRIBUTION (%)										MEDIAN AGE	% 2007 Males	% 2007 Females
	2000	2007	0-4	5-9	10-14	15-19	20-24	25-44	45-64	65-84	85+	18+	2007		
ADAMS	29.0	33.1	8.4	7.8	7.4	6.8	6.7	31.7	22.9	7.4	0.9	72.4	33.0	50.8	49.2
ALAMOSA	41.4	46.3	7.1	6.3	7.0	9.5	10.2	26.2	23.8	8.2	1.6	75.0	31.0	50.1	49.9
ARAPAHOE	11.8	14.0	6.7	6.9	7.3	7.3	6.3	28.7	27.5	8.1	1.2	74.5	36.5	49.2	50.8
ARCHULETA	16.8	19.8	5.1	5.8	7.0	6.9	3.7	22.8	36.8	11.1	0.9	77.4	44.2	50.8	49.2
BACA	7.0	8.5	6.4	6.5	5.2	5.6	7.3	19.3	29.0	16.8	3.8	78.5	44.7	50.1	49.9
BENT	30.2	30.9	6.4	6.0	5.0	5.9	7.8	27.7	25.5	13.5	2.1	78.7	38.4	55.4	44.6
BOULDER	10.7	12.7	5.9	6.0	6.0	7.9	9.2	30.3	26.5	7.0	1.2	78.4	34.9	50.5	49.5
BROOMFIELD	9.0	10.7	8.0	8.3	7.8	6.8	5.8	32.3	24.7	5.7	0.7	71.7	34.9	49.8	50.2
CHAFFEE	8.6	10.3	4.3	4.3	4.7	5.3	7.3	23.3	34.5	14.4	2.0	83.4	45.5	53.1	46.9
CHEYENNE	8.1	8.4	6.7	6.4	6.1	8.9	5.9	23.6	26.9	12.3	3.2	74.8	40.2	50.5	49.5
CLEAR CREEK	3.9	4.0	5.3	6.1	5.2	5.6	5.1	26.1	38.0	8.0	0.7	79.7	43.1	51.9	48.1
CONEJOS	58.9	63.7	8.5	7.6	7.4	7.6	7.5	22.5	24.3	12.7	2.0	71.7	35.6	49.5	50.5
COSTILLA	67.6	68.1	5.8	6.1	5.5	6.2	6.6	20.5	30.4	16.7	2.1	78.8	44.3	50.5	49.5
CROWLEY	22.5	23.0	4.9	4.2	4.6	4.9	9.5	38.0	24.1	8.2	1.7	83.3	37.3	66.8	33.2
CUSTER	2.5	3.0	4.8	5.5	5.5	5.0	4.6	17.2	40.4	16.2	0.8	80.9	49.1	51.1	48.9
DELTA	11.4	13.6	5.8	5.4	5.6	6.2	6.7	19.8	31.8	15.8	2.8	79.1	45.3	50.3	49.7
DENVER	31.7	35.9	6.8	6.4	5.9	5.8	6.6	35.2	22.8	8.8	1.8	77.7	34.6	50.7	49.3
DOLORES	3.9	3.9	5.0	4.6	5.3	5.9	5.8	23.3	32.8	15.0	2.4	81.7	45.1	51.3	48.7
DOUGLAS	5.1	6.1	8.6	10.0	9.5	6.6	4.0	29.8	26.2	4.9	0.3	67.4	35.9	49.8	50.2
EAGLE	23.2	27.1	6.8	6.0	5.6	5.6	6.7	41.0	24.0	4.1	0.3	78.3	32.9	54.5	45.5
ELBERT	3.9	4.7	6.4	7.4	8.1	8.2	4.8	26.5	32.1	6.0	0.6	72.6	39.6	50.1	49.9
EL PASO	11.3	13.4	7.7	7.1	7.0	7.6	7.7	29.0	25.0	7.8	1.1	73.8	34.3	50.1	49.9
FREMONT	10.3	12.4	4.9	4.6	4.9	6.2	7.7	29.3	27.6	12.6	2.3	81.7	40.4	56.9	43.1
GARFIELD	16.7	19.8	7.4	6.8	6.6	7.0	7.6	28.5	27.3	7.8	1.1	74.9	35.4	51.2	48.8
GILPIN	4.2	5.2	5.5	5.0	5.3	5.5	4.1	33.0	35.8	5.5	0.4	80.4	40.7	53.3	46.7
GRAND	4.4	5.3	5.6	5.4	5.0	5.5	6.1	31.5	32.5	7.7	0.7	80.5	39.3	52.8	47.2
GUNNISON	5.0	6.1	4.4	4.2	4.4	8.8	13.6	32.2	24.9	6.7	0.9	84.0	32.3	54.4	45.6
HINSDALE	1.5	1.5	5.7	6.1	4.3	4.4	2.3	19.4	44.2	12.4	1.1	81.0	48.0	51.3	48.7
HUERFANO	35.1	35.8	4.5	3.9	4.9	6.5	6.7	23.1	32.9	14.7	2.7	82.3	45.2	53.9	46.1
JACKSON	6.5	6.8	5.6	5.4	6.5	5.5	5.5	22.7	36.1	11.5	1.2	78.5	44.2	50.0	50.0
JEFFERSON	10.0	11.9	6.0	6.3	6.7	7.0	6.1	27.4	29.7	9.5	1.5	76.6	39.1	49.7	50.3
KIOWA	3.1	3.3	6.6	5.7	6.4	5.4	7.0	23.4	28.1	13.9	3.5	77.9	42.1	50.2	49.8
KIT CARSON	13.7	16.3	6.8	5.8	6.0	6.5	7.9	26.1	26.9	11.6	2.3	77.1	39.2	53.1	46.9
LAKE	36.1	41.1	8.0	6.7	6.3	7.1	9.3	30.8	23.7	7.2	0.9	75.1	31.7	53.4	46.6
LA PLATA	10.4	12.3	4.9	5.0	6.0	8.0	10.1	25.8	30.1	9.0	1.1	80.2	37.8	51.0	49.0
LARIMER	8.3	9.9	6.1	5.8	5.9	7.8	8.8	29.0	26.8	8.4	1.3	78.3	34.8	50.0	50.0
LAS ANIMAS	41.5	46.3	5.7	5.1	6.1	6.9	7.3	21.5	29.9	14.6	3.0	79.2	43.1	49.0	51.0
LINCOLN	8.5	10.3	5.2	5.0	5.9	6.6	7.8	29.0	26.2	11.6	2.7	79.9	39.3	57.2	42.8
LOGAN	11.9	14.6	6.9	6.3	6.2	7.4	8.1	25.9	25.1	11.9	2.3	76.9	36.7	51.3	48.7
MESA	10.0	12.0	6.3	5.8	6.1	7.2	7.0	23.9	28.1	13.2	2.4	77.6	40.2	49.0	51.0
MINERAL	2.0	2.3	4.3	4.1	5.5	6.3	3.2	20.0	37.6	17.4	1.7	82.1	48.6	51.3	48.7
MOFFAT	9.5	11.4	6.8	6.5	6.1	7.9	7.5	25.4	30.4	8.0	1.3	75.4	37.2	51.7	48.3
MONTEZUMA	9.5	11.3	7.0	6.4	6.6	7.0	6.6	22.6	30.1	12.0	1.8	75.4	40.3	49.4	50.6
MONTROSE	14.9	17.6	6.9	6.4	6.7	6.1	7.1	22.1	29.3	13.2	2.3	76.0	40.8	49.3	50.7
MORGAN	31.2	35.8	8.9	8.1	7.6	6.7	7.0	25.8	23.4	10.4	2.1	71.2	34.4	50.6	49.4
OTERO	37.6	42.5	6.9	5.9	6.7	7.2	7.7	23.0	25.6	14.3	2.8	76.2	39.0	49.1	50.9
OURAY	4.1	5.0	4.4	4.9	6.1	5.8	3.5	21.0	40.5	12.7	1.1	80.9	47.2	50.6	49.4
PARK	4.3	5.2	5.4	6.0	6.6	5.5	3.4	27.0	38.1	7.6	0.4	78.3	43.0	51.8	48.2
PHILLIPS	11.8	14.1	7.4	6.6	6.8	6.4	5.0	22.6	27.2	14.0	4.0	75.1	41.5	48.3	51.7
PITKIN	6.5	8.0	3.7	3.2	4.2	5.8	7.2	32.7	34.1	8.6	0.6	85.2	40.5	52.9	47.1
PROWERS	32.9	37.6	8.3	7.2	7.4	7.7	7.5	26.4	23.5	9.9	2.1	72.5	33.2	50.5	49.5
PUEBLO	38.0	42.8	6.9	6.4	6.7	6.7	6.9	26.0	25.8	12.3	2.2	76.0	37.6	49.0	51.0
RIO BLANCO	4.9	5.1	5.8	5.4	4.9	8.6	9.2	22.4	30.9	11.4	1.3	79.0	40.4	50.2	49.8
RIO GRANDE	41.7	46.8	7.0	6.3	6.5	6.8	6.7	22.8	28.8	12.9	2.2	75.8	40.5	49.2	50.8
ROUTT	3.2	3.9	5.0	5.1	5.4	6.3	5.7	32.8	33.4	5.9	0.5	80.7	37.9	53.7	46.3
SAGUACHE	45.3	50.3	7.2	6.3	6.9	6.8	8.3	22.9	31.0	9.5	1.1	75.6	39.2	50.7	49.3
SAN JUAN	7.3	7.5	4.5	4.0	4.9	6.4	2.4	23.8	46.6	7.3	0.0	81.7	46.6	52.9	47.1
SAN MIGUEL	6.7	8.1	4.2	3.3	4.7	3.9	5.8	43.1	29.8	5.1	0.1	85.4	36.1	54.3	45.7
SEDGWICK	11.4	13.7	5.8	5.7	6.1	5.0	5.6	22.0	27.8	18.0	4.0	79.1	44.8	50.3	49.7
SUMMIT	9.8	11.7	5.0	4.0	3.8	4.5	8.7	46.6	22.7	4.5	0.1	84.6	32.1	58.5	41.5
TELLER	3.5	4.2	5.5	6.0	6.8	6.6	5.6	24.5	35.9	8.6	0.5	77.5	42.5	50.6	49.4
WASHINGTON	6.3	7.6	6.7	6.3	5.8	6.4	6.3	21.8	29.3	15.1	2.4	77.1	42.7	51.2	48.8
WELD	27.1	31.3	8.0	7.5	7.0	7.8	7.6	29.2	23.8	7.9	1.1	73.3	32.8	50.2	49.8
YUMA	12.9	13.3	7.0	6.8	6.4	6.8	7.0	23.8	26.7	12.5	3.0	75.4	39.1	49.0	51.0
COLORADO	17.1	19.6	6.9	6.8	6.7	7.0	7.0	29.5	26.3	8.5	1.3	75.5	35.8	50.3	49.7
UNITED STATES	12.5	15.0	6.9	6.5	6.8	7.1	7.0	27.6	25.4	10.7	1.9	75.6	36.7	49.2	50.8

COUNTY	HOUSEHOLDS					FAMILIES			MEDIAN HOUSEHOLD INCOME			
	2000	2007	2012	% Annual Rate 2000-2007	2007 Average HH Size	2000	2007	% Annual Rate 2000-2007	2007	2012	2007 National Rank	2007 State Rank
ADAMS	122,808	150,173	168,970	2.8	2.80	87,762	105,111	2.5	60,097	72,015	266	17
ALAMOSA	5,467	5,812	6,055	0.8	2.53	3,654	3,792	0.5	36,405	42,219	2211	53
ARAPAHOE	190,909	215,628	232,481	1.7	2.54	125,791	138,479	1.3	69,154	81,760	125	9
ARCHULETA	3,980	4,985	5,793	3.2	2.43	2,872	3,526	2.9	45,288	49,743	1078	29
BACA	1,905	1,770	1,672	-1.0	2.31	1,269	1,151	-1.3	33,948	38,084	2554	59
BENT	2,003	2,041	2,061	0.3	2.52	1,388	1,383	0.0	34,164	39,072	2534	58
BOULDER	106,542	113,472	116,564	0.9	2.44	63,070	65,209	0.5	71,929	85,147	111	8
BROOMFIELD	14,179	17,659	19,959	3.1	2.77	10,540	12,883	2.8	85,557	104,900	28	2
CHAFFEE	6,584	7,187	7,597	1.2	2.24	4,362	4,648	0.9	41,597	46,595	1505	36
CHEYENNE	880	855	838	-0.4	2.48	603	574	-0.7	42,951	46,557	1335	32
CLEAR CREEK	4,019	4,089	4,113	0.2	2.29	2,608	2,588	-0.1	63,426	73,215	189	11
CONEJOS	2,980	3,211	3,345	1.0	2.73	2,211	2,340	0.8	28,160	30,848	2996	63
COSTILLA	1,503	1,496	1,460	-0.1	2.39	1,030	1,002	-0.4	22,998	26,299	3113	64
CROWLEY	1,358	1,370	1,416	0.1	2.62	958	947	-0.2	32,336	36,329	2727	60
CUSTER	1,480	1,787	1,958	2.6	2.32	1,078	1,276	2.4	41,153	45,180	1581	38
DELTA	11,058	12,327	13,085	1.5	2.43	7,940	8,673	1.2	39,373	44,121	1803	44
DENVER	239,235	248,070	252,623	0.5	2.28	119,300	118,909	0.0	52,548	63,810	520	22
DOLORES	785	808	820	0.4	2.30	542	545	0.1	38,431	43,193	1942	47
DOUGLAS	60,924	96,389	125,921	6.5	2.87	49,850	77,828	6.3	111,256	136,947	1	1
EAGLE	15,148	18,024	20,013	2.4	2.76	9,020	10,425	2.0	83,721	102,728	35	3
ELBERT	6,770	8,058	8,730	2.4	2.95	5,655	6,651	2.3	77,875	87,802	67	4
EL PASO	192,409	222,540	244,722	2.0	2.60	133,829	151,397	1.7	60,261	72,296	259	16
FREMONT	15,232	16,334	16,876	1.0	2.43	10,501	11,009	0.7	41,871	48,288	1467	35
GARFIELD	16,229	19,705	22,322	2.7	2.66	11,286	13,404	2.4	59,547	69,589	277	19
GILPIN	2,043	2,201	2,276	1.0	2.31	1,264	1,325	0.7	63,275	72,751	190	12
GRAND	5,075	5,929	6,583	2.2	2.35	3,217	3,660	1.8	57,502	64,600	319	20
GUNNISON	5,649	6,040	6,227	0.9	2.28	2,968	3,066	0.4	46,832	54,947	923	27
HINSDALE	359	358	357	0.0	2.20	247	241	-0.3	44,746	48,998	1133	30
HUERFANO	3,082	3,138	3,148	0.2	2.22	1,920	1,902	-0.1	31,725	36,269	2785	61
JACKSON	661	641	612	-0.4	2.34	443	419	-0.8	37,469	41,102	2068	50
JEFFERSON	205,424	211,362	214,015	0.4	2.49	139,974	140,727	0.1	73,113	84,768	100	6
KIOWA	665	634	612	-0.7	2.38	452	421	-1.0	37,218	42,225	2099	51
KIT CARSON	2,990	2,882	2,760	-0.5	2.50	2,081	1,963	-0.8	39,970	44,869	1728	41
LAKE	2,977	3,004	3,022	0.1	2.61	1,915	1,883	-0.2	49,112	58,657	741	26
LA PLATA	17,342	20,236	22,293	2.2	2.40	10,892	12,372	1.8	49,685	56,936	697	25
LARIMER	97,164	112,365	120,416	2.0	2.51	63,197	71,257	1.7	61,770	72,705	217	15
LAS ANIMAS	6,173	6,468	6,656	0.6	2.38	4,095	4,186	0.3	34,767	39,798	2461	57
LINCOLN	2,058	1,939	1,861	-0.8	2.44	1,389	1,277	-1.2	40,018	45,324	1726	40
LOGAN	7,551	7,623	7,623	0.1	2.46	5,064	4,997	-0.2	39,927	45,315	1738	42
MESA	45,823	54,334	61,297	2.4	2.47	31,563	36,579	2.1	44,190	50,956	1191	31
MINERAL	377	438	477	2.1	2.19	251	285	1.8	40,839	44,480	1623	39
MOFFAT	4,983	5,220	5,393	0.6	2.56	3,576	3,671	0.4	51,684	59,881	569	23
MONTEZUMA	9,201	9,971	10,523	1.1	2.50	6,518	6,915	0.8	38,698	43,484	1896	46
MONTROSE	13,043	15,706	17,720	2.6	2.51	9,311	10,981	2.3	42,207	47,422	1425	33
MORGAN	9,539	9,911	10,180	0.5	2.84	6,969	7,101	0.3	42,166	48,267	1431	34
OTERO	7,920	7,682	7,523	-0.4	2.47	5,473	5,188	-0.7	36,389	42,164	2213	54
OURAY	1,576	1,929	2,186	2.8	2.35	1,123	1,346	2.5	50,604	55,987	633	24
PARK	5,894	6,983	7,780	2.4	2.42	4,223	4,902	2.1	62,744	70,323	197	13
PHILLIPS	1,781	1,867	1,918	0.7	2.48	1,239	1,270	0.3	39,334	43,422	1814	45
PITKIN	6,807	7,268	7,610	0.9	2.14	3,185	3,272	0.4	77,529	90,335	72	5
PROWERS	5,307	5,100	4,911	-0.5	2.68	3,728	3,505	-0.8	36,753	42,386	2158	52
PUEBLO	54,579	59,956	63,444	1.3	2.51	37,332	40,084	1.0	41,283	48,218	1556	37
RIO BLANCO	2,306	2,378	2,429	0.4	2.46	1,646	1,662	0.1	45,865	52,184	1018	28
RIO GRANDE	4,701	4,998	5,161	0.8	2.56	3,417	3,563	0.6	38,104	42,827	1989	49
ROUTT	7,953	9,245	9,895	2.1	2.42	4,778	5,396	1.7	66,276	77,677	161	10
SAGUACHE	2,300	2,761	3,054	2.6	2.51	1,556	1,824	2.2	30,568	34,213	2881	62
SAN JUAN	269	290	301	1.0	1.97	158	165	0.6	35,708	38,440	2328	55
SAN MIGUEL	3,015	3,457	3,749	1.9	2.13	1,424	1,572	1.4	62,612	75,557	200	14
SEDGWICK	1,165	1,097	1,053	-0.8	2.31	803	740	-1.1	34,906	39,885	2445	56
SUMMIT	9,120	9,988	10,519	1.3	2.48	4,768	5,047	0.8	73,095	86,485	101	7
TELLER	7,993	9,009	9,711	1.7	2.54	5,925	6,556	1.4	60,074	68,073	267	18
WASHINGTON	1,989	1,943	1,904	-0.3	2.45	1,408	1,346	-0.6	38,303	42,257	1962	48
WELD	63,197	86,974	106,734	4.5	2.81	45,206	60,934	4.2	53,167	62,656	492	21
YUMA	3,800	3,820	3,827	0.1	2.56	2,644	2,600	-0.2	39,690	43,709	1756	43
COLORADO				1.8	2.54			1.5	60,976	72,859		
UNITED STATES				1.2	2.59			1.0	53,154	62,503		

COUNTY	2007 Per Capita Income	2007 HH Income Base	2007 HOUSEHOLD INCOME DISTRIBUTION (%)					2007 Home Value Base	2007 HOME VALUE DISTRIBUTION (%)					2007 Median Home Value
			Less than $25,000	$25,000 to $49,999	$50,000 to $99,999	$100,000 to $149,999	$150,000 or More		Less than $50,000	$50,000 to $89,999	$90,000 to $174,999	$175,000 to $399,999	$400,000 or More	
ADAMS	25,813	150,173	14.0	25.1	40.2	14.0	6.6	108,457	7.2	3.5	21.5	61.6	6.2	208,178
ALAMOSA	19,110	5,812	34.9	28.8	26.6	6.9	2.8	3,898	12.3	15.6	43.8	24.4	3.8	124,309
ARAPAHOE	36,078	215,628	11.5	21.4	37.8	15.8	13.5	151,858	1.4	1.5	17.2	63.1	16.7	240,397
ARCHULETA	25,846	4,985	23.7	32.3	31.0	8.2	4.8	3,964	6.6	6.8	22.2	42.4	22.1	232,347
BACA	18,579	1,770	38.5	32.4	23.1	3.9	2.1	1,387	32.2	23.6	33.7	8.2	2.3	78,967
BENT	18,126	2,041	35.4	32.7	25.6	4.2	2.1	1,457	23.3	25.3	40.4	7.2	3.8	92,204
BOULDER	39,633	113,471	14.6	18.9	32.5	17.6	16.4	76,189	4.0	1.0	6.3	52.6	36.2	328,233
BROOMFIELD	36,942	17,657	7.1	15.1	37.1	23.7	17.0	14,004	4.4	3.9	5.1	70.1	16.5	270,071
CHAFFEE	24,460	7,187	27.9	32.0	28.3	7.8	4.0	5,472	8.4	5.3	21.2	48.1	17.0	219,393
CHEYENNE	21,013	855	29.7	28.8	31.8	6.5	3.2	660	19.4	25.3	41.4	12.9	1.1	100,000
CLEAR CREEK	37,411	4,089	13.5	22.5	36.0	17.2	10.7	3,217	5.9	3.5	12.6	51.9	26.0	277,088
CONEJOS	14,053	3,211	45.1	29.3	19.9	4.2	1.4	2,597	25.8	26.3	36.0	10.5	1.5	87,101
COSTILLA	13,403	1,496	53.7	29.3	14.0	1.9	1.1	1,204	25.0	26.4	32.6	13.5	2.5	88,172
CROWLEY	17,418	1,370	37.2	35.0	21.5	3.6	2.6	1,032	17.2	26.1	40.1	14.1	2.6	100,909
CUSTER	24,350	1,787	28.4	29.5	29.5	7.4	5.1	1,456	8.4	8.4	22.7	37.6	22.9	224,658
DELTA	20,911	12,327	30.0	31.6	29.4	6.4	2.6	9,820	6.5	6.9	37.4	39.8	9.4	172,855
DENVER	31,931	248,067	21.3	26.1	32.5	10.8	9.3	137,134	0.7	2.2	25.9	57.0	14.2	223,333
DOLORES	21,479	808	33.9	29.0	30.0	4.8	2.4	640	15.0	20.3	40.0	22.5	2.2	112,963
DOUGLAS	49,976	96,389	4.1	8.2	30.5	26.5	30.9	85,732	0.3	0.2	1.5	55.9	42.1	372,097
EAGLE	40,379	18,024	7.2	15.9	37.1	21.0	18.8	11,906	5.5	5.0	6.0	25.7	57.7	461,898
ELBERT	31,471	8,058	7.8	18.3	40.4	21.5	12.0	7,307	2.2	1.7	7.2	50.9	38.0	354,373
EL PASO	29,351	222,540	15.0	24.6	37.2	14.4	8.9	150,921	3.4	2.0	23.1	59.3	12.3	222,229
FREMONT	20,628	16,333	28.1	30.1	32.1	7.6	2.1	12,739	7.4	9.3	46.3	32.8	4.2	147,595
GARFIELD	27,462	19,705	14.0	26.6	38.5	14.5	6.5	13,435	6.4	6.9	13.5	45.7	27.5	275,945
GILPIN	32,831	2,201	13.4	22.1	41.6	16.6	6.3	1,770	1.6	1.3	12.1	64.2	20.8	275,078
GRAND	31,408	5,929	14.8	26.1	39.7	12.3	7.1	4,240	5.8	2.2	12.6	47.7	31.7	295,463
GUNNISON	27,755	6,040	23.3	29.7	32.3	8.6	6.1	3,693	5.1	5.2	12.0	49.3	28.4	267,962
HINSDALE	30,862	358	19.6	37.2	31.8	3.6	7.8	242	3.7	4.1	15.7	41.3	35.1	321,739
HUERFANO	19,853	3,138	39.1	30.7	23.2	4.2	2.8	2,309	9.2	19.9	39.8	23.9	7.3	120,222
JACKSON	20,872	641	29.0	35.6	27.5	5.5	2.5	451	18.0	14.4	35.9	24.4	7.3	127,757
JEFFERSON	36,744	211,362	10.7	19.5	38.2	18.6	13.0	158,215	1.1	0.9	11.8	68.7	17.5	260,522
KIOWA	21,026	634	33.9	31.4	24.8	5.4	4.6	470	28.5	26.6	37.4	6.0	1.5	82,727
KIT CARSON	21,136	2,882	29.7	29.6	30.6	6.7	3.4	2,155	17.6	16.9	43.1	19.2	3.2	116,098
LAKE	23,822	3,004	20.5	30.6	37.3	7.2	4.5	2,100	14.0	10.4	35.5	35.4	4.7	148,583
LA PLATA	27,775	20,236	23.5	26.7	32.6	10.2	6.9	14,385	9.3	4.2	13.4	48.8	24.2	265,049
LARIMER	30,936	112,365	16.6	22.4	36.8	15.1	9.2	79,279	4.6	2.3	14.1	63.5	15.5	237,981
LAS ANIMAS	19,685	6,468	37.1	30.2	25.2	4.7	2.7	4,732	11.6	14.1	46.2	23.0	5.1	130,175
LINCOLN	20,543	1,939	27.1	34.3	28.7	7.3	2.6	1,398	14.7	17.9	44.0	19.3	4.1	116,837
LOGAN	20,982	7,623	31.2	28.5	30.8	6.4	3.1	5,549	9.9	17.0	41.3	28.8	2.9	127,399
MESA	23,585	54,334	25.2	31.2	31.3	8.2	4.1	40,755	5.1	3.3	26.2	52.8	12.6	211,597
MINERAL	24,926	438	26.3	35.2	28.3	7.1	3.2	338	12.1	7.7	28.7	32.5	18.9	183,333
MOFFAT	22,251	5,217	20.3	27.1	41.4	9.6	1.6	3,895	9.4	12.8	41.8	31.9	4.2	142,448
MONTEZUMA	20,734	9,971	29.8	32.6	28.3	6.2	3.2	7,697	10.8	9.5	36.4	34.9	8.5	152,920
MONTROSE	20,730	15,706	27.4	31.3	31.6	7.4	2.3	12,161	10.7	7.4	33.5	39.6	8.7	170,670
MORGAN	18,578	9,911	25.0	34.0	31.8	6.6	2.7	7,089	8.9	8.5	48.6	30.2	3.8	139,457
OTERO	18,877	7,682	35.7	28.8	27.5	5.6	2.3	5,530	12.3	26.1	46.7	14.1	0.8	104,602
OURAY	30,149	1,929	20.5	28.8	33.4	9.8	7.5	1,478	7.6	2.9	8.7	37.5	43.3	364,130
PARK	30,814	6,983	12.7	24.5	41.3	14.9	6.6	6,208	3.2	3.1	13.0	63.6	17.1	260,738
PHILLIPS	20,532	1,867	31.3	32.4	28.3	3.9	4.1	1,461	10.1	19.0	46.1	23.4	1.4	124,943
PITKIN	53,621	7,268	9.9	17.7	37.3	16.2	18.8	4,500	1.1	1.8	11.8	20.0	65.3	694,554
PROWERS	17,520	5,100	32.3	33.7	26.6	5.2	2.3	3,533	22.0	19.2	43.0	14.5	1.4	101,575
PUEBLO	21,656	59,952	29.8	28.8	29.7	8.0	3.7	43,740	6.4	13.6	53.1	24.6	2.3	129,571
RIO BLANCO	21,961	2,378	24.1	30.2	36.2	7.4	2.0	1,758	8.4	11.0	46.1	28.8	5.6	139,507
RIO GRANDE	19,983	4,998	31.4	31.6	29.0	4.1	3.9	3,682	12.4	16.2	42.0	23.7	5.7	121,274
ROUTT	34,822	9,245	13.8	19.3	40.5	15.8	10.6	6,666	6.6	3.4	14.0	31.0	45.0	360,752
SAGUACHE	15,894	2,761	41.8	32.2	20.1	4.1	1.8	2,002	21.5	19.5	35.2	16.2	7.6	105,858
SAN JUAN	21,517	290	35.9	34.8	24.1	2.1	3.1	204	2.9	2.9	28.9	53.9	11.3	199,219
SAN MIGUEL	46,298	3,457	16.7	21.2	34.1	15.3	12.8	1,900	2.9	2.0	8.9	34.9	51.3	416,327
SEDGWICK	19,919	1,097	33.6	37.6	22.1	3.8	2.9	831	23.3	23.9	40.8	10.5	1.4	93,750
SUMMIT	37,753	9,988	9.4	19.8	38.2	19.1	13.6	6,184	3.6	1.4	8.9	35.4	50.7	405,022
TELLER	29,225	9,009	12.7	25.9	39.9	14.8	6.8	7,479	3.3	2.2	16.9	61.8	15.8	249,149
WASHINGTON	21,662	1,943	28.3	36.1	25.7	6.4	3.4	1,486	15.3	20.0	42.3	18.5	3.8	114,938
WELD	23,852	86,971	21.0	25.2	35.6	12.3	5.9	62,362	5.6	4.3	26.9	50.5	12.6	200,187
YUMA	19,654	3,820	30.1	32.6	28.6	5.8	2.9	2,830	10.0	19.4	45.7	20.8	4.1	120,194
COLORADO	31,684		16.6	23.3	35.2	14.4	10.6		4.0	3.5	20.1	55.0	17.5	234,884
UNITED STATES	27,916		21.9	25.0	32.3	12.3	8.4		7.9	10.5	27.1	35.6	19.0	192,285

COUNTY	FINANCIAL SERVICES				THE HOME						ENTERTAINMENT						PERSONAL			
					Home Improvements		Furnishings													
	Auto Loan	Home Loan	Invest- ments	Retire- ment Plans	Home Repair	Lawn & Garden	Comput- ers & Hard- ware	Major Appli- ances	TV, Radio, Sound Equip- ment	Furni- ture	Dine out/ Carry out	Sports Equip- ment	Fees & Tickets	Toys & Games	Travel	Cable TV	Apparel & Services	Auto Repairs	Health Insur- ance	Pets & Supplies
ADAMS	102	103	99	103	96	92	102	98	99	103	100	93	102	101	99	96	91	101	92	97
ALAMOSA	72	62	59	63	61	67	69	67	68	65	68	62	63	69	65	68	60	68	68	69
ARAPAHOE	124	130	134	134	125	116	131	122	125	132	126	116	133	126	128	122	116	126	116	122
ARCHULETA	102	79	51	78	92	121	80	105	84	76	84	90	69	86	83	89	72	93	106	109
BACA	73	49	31	48	58	80	54	69	60	50	59	61	44	64	53	65	50	63	77	74
BENT	75	53	39	51	60	81	58	71	65	53	64	62	49	68	57	70	54	66	82	75
BOULDER	131	136	140	141	131	121	146	129	134	141	136	127	144	134	138	128	125	136	120	130
BROOMFIELD	139	160	155	161	150	134	144	139	136	152	137	133	153	141	145	130	126	138	127	138
CHAFFEE	84	71	64	72	79	96	74	86	77	70	75	74	68	75	76	80	65	81	91	88
CHEYENNE	94	60	26	57	74	106	63	89	70	60	71	79	49	77	62	75	59	78	93	98
CLEAR CREEK	117	124	124	125	129	132	116	125	114	118	114	113	119	114	122	115	103	119	122	126
CONEJOS	68	45	21	42	52	74	46	62	53	44	53	56	37	56	45	58	45	56	67	69
COSTILLA	54	38	24	37	44	60	40	51	44	38	44	44	33	46	40	48	37	46	56	55
CROWLEY	76	52	34	50	60	83	56	72	63	52	62	63	46	67	56	68	52	65	80	77
CUSTER	92	71	46	70	83	109	72	94	76	69	75	82	62	77	75	81	65	84	95	99
DELTA	79	63	52	62	71	90	66	80	70	63	69	69	59	70	68	75	59	74	86	83
DENVER	98	92	96	96	89	85	106	94	102	102	104	94	101	100	99	100	95	102	92	94
DOLORES	82	61	40	59	69	91	62	78	67	60	67	69	53	70	62	72	58	72	82	84
DOUGLAS	193	234	228	238	222	193	202	196	185	218	188	190	220	195	207	176	176	192	172	195
EAGLE	154	157	145	163	145	133	165	147	151	162	155	152	161	154	155	143	142	156	133	147
ELBERT	129	147	139	147	146	137	126	133	121	135	122	124	135	129	131	119	112	126	122	135
EL PASO	106	109	112	112	103	98	110	102	105	110	106	97	110	107	107	102	96	106	99	103
FREMONT	75	68	71	69	70	78	70	74	72	67	71	65	67	71	71	74	62	72	80	75
GARFIELD	103	102	97	104	100	100	104	102	100	103	100	97	101	101	102	98	91	103	97	103
GILPIN	102	113	122	116	113	107	105	105	101	108	102	96	111	103	109	100	93	103	101	106
GRAND	117	99	77	100	102	120	99	112	101	98	102	101	92	104	99	104	89	107	111	116
GUNNISON	94	78	75	83	77	85	97	87	91	87	92	83	86	91	87	89	82	92	85	90
HINSDALE	110	86	55	84	100	131	87	113	91	83	91	98	75	93	90	97	77	101	115	118
HUERFANO	69	53	46	53	60	77	59	69	63	54	61	60	51	63	59	67	52	64	76	71
JACKSON	87	58	28	55	69	97	60	82	66	57	67	72	48	71	59	72	56	72	86	90
JEFFERSON	122	135	143	138	132	121	130	124	124	133	125	116	135	125	131	121	115	125	118	123
KIOWA	83	58	41	56	66	90	63	79	71	58	69	69	53	74	63	77	59	72	89	84
KIT CARSON	91	63	39	61	72	97	67	85	74	63	74	75	56	78	66	79	62	78	92	91
LAKE	89	78	82	81	75	78	90	83	89	84	88	78	84	88	84	87	78	85	85	83
LA PLATA	99	89	85	91	88	95	96	94	94	91	94	87	90	94	91	93	84	95	94	97
LARIMER	108	109	110	112	105	103	113	106	107	111	108	100	111	108	109	104	98	108	101	106
LAS ANIMAS	70	57	58	57	62	75	63	69	67	58	65	60	56	66	62	70	56	67	77	71
LINCOLN	82	62	53	62	68	86	68	79	73	63	71	69	59	75	67	76	61	74	87	82
LOGAN	80	66	63	66	70	82	70	77	73	67	72	68	64	75	69	76	63	74	82	79
MESA	83	79	82	80	79	84	80	82	81	79	80	73	79	80	80	82	71	81	85	82
MINERAL	88	69	44	68	80	105	70	91	73	66	73	79	60	75	72	78	62	81	92	95
MOFFAT	84	78	77	78	76	81	78	80	79	77	79	72	76	81	77	80	70	80	82	82
MONTEZUMA	81	66	53	65	71	87	69	80	71	66	71	70	61	73	68	74	61	75	82	82
MONTROSE	81	67	57	66	71	86	69	79	72	66	71	69	63	73	69	75	62	74	83	82
MORGAN	81	68	60	67	70	81	70	77	73	68	73	69	65	75	69	75	64	75	81	79
OTERO	70	59	57	58	62	72	62	67	66	59	65	59	57	67	62	69	56	65	75	69
OURAY	114	90	61	89	104	136	91	118	95	87	95	101	79	96	94	101	81	105	120	122
PARK	108	112	102	112	114	117	100	111	98	104	99	100	102	103	104	99	89	104	105	113
PHILLIPS	88	61	35	59	72	98	63	84	69	61	70	74	52	76	62	73	59	75	88	92
PITKIN	148	159	168	167	161	145	169	153	157	166	160	155	170	154	166	151	148	159	142	153
PROWERS	71	59	54	59	60	69	62	66	67	61	66	59	57	68	61	69	58	65	72	68
PUEBLO	76	73	80	74	73	76	74	75	77	74	75	66	74	76	75	78	67	75	80	75
RIO BLANCO	84	73	62	72	76	89	71	81	74	71	74	72	67	78	72	77	64	77	84	85
RIO GRANDE	83	63	47	61	70	89	67	80	71	63	70	71	57	73	66	75	60	75	85	84
ROUTT	119	122	116	124	120	118	118	118	113	120	115	113	119	116	118	111	104	118	112	120
SAGUACHE	65	51	32	48	54	68	51	63	54	50	55	56	44	56	51	56	47	59	63	65
SAN JUAN	69	53	34	52	62	81	54	71	56	52	56	61	47	58	56	60	48	63	71	74
SAN MIGUEL	131	130	126	137	134	129	142	133	134	138	137	134	139	133	139	130	126	137	125	135
SEDGWICK	77	53	37	52	61	83	58	73	66	54	64	64	48	68	58	70	54	67	82	77
SUMMIT	138	118	110	130	107	108	140	119	134	136	137	119	130	137	125	129	124	133	113	123
TELLER	106	110	104	110	112	114	100	109	99	103	99	99	103	102	104	99	89	103	104	110
WASHINGTON	94	61	32	58	74	104	65	88	72	61	73	78	52	79	64	78	61	79	95	97
WELD	97	96	90	95	91	91	94	93	92	94	92	87	93	94	92	90	83	94	90	94
YUMA	86	59	36	57	69	95	63	82	69	59	69	72	51	74	62	74	58	74	88	89
COLORADO	112	113	113	115	110	107	115	110	111	114	112	104	114	112	112	109	101	112	106	110
UNITED STATES	100	100	100	100	100	100	100	100	100	100	100	100	100	100	100	100	100	100	100	100

POPULATION CHANGE

COUNTY	FIPS Code	CBSA Code	DMA Code	POPULATION			2000-2007 ANNUAL RATE		RACE (%)					
									White		Black		Asian/Pacific	
				2000	2007	2012	% Rate	State Rank	2000	2007	2000	2007	2000	2007
FAIRFIELD	001	14860	501	882,567	918,315	943,125	0.5	7	79.3	76.1	10.0	10.6	3.3	4.7
HARTFORD	003	25540	533	857,183	887,101	909,037	0.5	7	76.9	73.4	11.7	12.4	2.5	3.5
LITCHFIELD	005	45860	533	182,193	193,083	201,037	0.8	4	95.8	94.7	1.1	1.2	1.2	1.8
MIDDLESEX	007	25540	533	155,071	166,150	173,700	1.0	3	91.3	89.2	4.4	5.1	1.6	2.3
NEW HAVEN	009	35300	533	824,008	852,576	870,874	0.5	7	79.4	76.3	11.3	12.1	2.4	3.4
NEW LONDON	011	35980	533	259,088	271,317	279,062	0.6	5	87.0	84.4	5.3	5.9	2.0	3.0
TOLLAND	013	25540	533	136,364	150,104	158,016	1.3	1	92.3	90.4	2.7	2.9	2.3	3.6
WINDHAM	015	48740	533	109,091	118,229	124,990	1.1	2	91.3	89.4	1.9	2.0	0.9	1.3
CONNECTICUT							0.6		81.6	78.8	9.1	9.7	2.5	3.5
UNITED STATES							1.2		75.1	72.7	12.3	12.6	3.8	4.5

COUNTY	% HISPANIC ORIGIN		2007 AGE DISTRIBUTION (%)										MEDIAN AGE	% 2007 Males	% 2007 Females
	2000	2007	0-4	5-9	10-14	15-19	20-24	25-44	45-64	65-84	85+	18+	2007		
FAIRFIELD	11.9	14.4	6.9	7.7	7.8	7.1	5.2	26.3	26.1	10.8	2.2	73.2	38.5	48.6	51.4
HARTFORD	11.5	14.0	6.2	6.2	6.8	7.3	6.3	25.2	27.1	12.2	2.7	76.4	39.9	48.3	51.7
LITCHFIELD	2.1	2.7	5.6	5.8	6.8	7.2	5.1	23.5	31.2	12.2	2.6	77.2	42.6	49.0	51.0
MIDDLESEX	3.0	4.0	5.8	6.2	6.7	6.9	5.8	25.1	29.3	11.7	2.6	77.4	41.2	49.0	51.0
NEW HAVEN	10.1	12.3	6.2	6.2	6.8	7.7	6.6	25.7	26.4	11.5	2.8	76.3	38.9	48.2	51.8
NEW LONDON	5.1	6.4	6.1	6.0	6.6	7.6	6.9	25.9	27.4	11.5	2.2	77.0	39.3	49.4	50.6
TOLLAND	2.8	3.5	5.5	5.9	6.1	10.0	10.0	24.3	27.2	9.4	1.6	78.2	37.0	49.6	50.4
WINDHAM	7.1	8.9	6.1	5.8	6.7	7.8	7.1	26.8	27.3	10.3	2.2	77.2	38.7	49.5	50.5
CONNECTICUT	9.4	11.4	6.3	6.5	7.0	7.5	6.2	25.6	27.0	11.4	2.5	75.8	39.3	48.6	51.4
UNITED STATES	12.5	15.0	6.9	6.5	6.8	7.1	7.0	27.6	25.4	10.7	1.9	75.6	36.7	49.2	50.8

COUNTY	HOUSEHOLDS					FAMILIES			MEDIAN HOUSEHOLD INCOME			
	2000	2007	2012	% Annual Rate 2000-2007	2007 Average HH Size	2000	2007	% Annual Rate 2000-2007	2007	2012	2007 National Rank	2007 State Rank
FAIRFIELD	324,232	335,228	344,121	0.5	2.68	228,399	234,506	0.4	84,825	102,263	30	1
HARTFORD	335,098	347,577	357,335	0.5	2.47	222,356	228,812	0.4	63,791	75,808	182	5
LITCHFIELD	71,551	76,102	79,519	0.9	2.50	49,598	52,372	0.8	72,253	85,842	109	4
MIDDLESEX	61,341	66,238	69,657	1.1	2.41	40,580	43,477	1.0	76,079	90,094	79	2
NEW HAVEN	319,040	330,851	338,989	0.5	2.49	210,687	216,763	0.4	61,558	72,642	223	7
NEW LONDON	99,835	106,266	110,320	0.9	2.43	67,193	70,975	0.8	63,477	75,445	187	6
TOLLAND	49,431	53,779	57,140	1.2	2.53	34,134	36,867	1.1	75,678	88,601	81	3
WINDHAM	41,142	44,533	47,295	1.1	2.56	28,223	30,330	1.0	55,549	64,599	382	8
CONNECTICUT				0.6	2.53			0.5	68,430	81,316		
UNITED STATES				1.2	2.59			1.0	53,154	62,503		

COUNTY	2007 Per Capita Income	2007 HH Income Base	2007 HOUSEHOLD INCOME DISTRIBUTION (%)					2007 Home Value Base	2007 HOME VALUE DISTRIBUTION (%)					2007 Median Home Value
			Less than $25,000	$25,000 to $49,999	$50,000 to $99,999	$100,000 to $149,999	$150,000 or More		Less than $50,000	$50,000 to $89,999	$90,000 to $174,999	$175,000 to $399,999	$400,000 or More	
FAIRFIELD	49,464	335,228	13.0	16.3	27.1	18.9	24.6	240,892	0.9	1.4	5.3	30.6	61.8	492,672
HARTFORD	34,312	347,576	18.3	21.2	32.1	16.3	12.1	233,961	0.9	1.5	15.9	63.9	17.8	254,682
LITCHFIELD	36,903	76,102	13.3	19.6	34.3	19.2	13.6	59,173	0.4	1.2	12.1	58.9	27.3	288,111
MIDDLESEX	38,695	66,238	12.4	18.1	33.8	20.9	14.9	49,552	0.9	1.6	10.4	62.4	24.7	294,580
NEW HAVEN	32,277	330,850	19.2	21.9	32.0	15.9	11.0	219,317	0.9	1.5	12.1	61.1	24.5	283,854
NEW LONDON	32,251	106,262	15.8	22.5	35.9	16.1	9.7	74,227	2.0	1.6	9.8	64.1	22.5	279,094
TOLLAND	34,010	53,779	12.2	18.4	36.0	19.8	13.7	40,873	0.9	1.6	9.6	69.8	18.1	273,901
WINDHAM	26,298	44,533	19.9	24.8	35.7	14.2	5.4	31,432	2.1	1.7	19.9	68.1	8.2	222,498
CONNECTICUT	37,645		16.3	20.0	31.6	17.3	14.8		1.0	1.5	11.2	54.8	31.5	297,091
UNITED STATES	27,916		21.9	25.0	32.3	12.3	8.4		7.9	10.5	27.1	35.6	19.0	192,285

SPENDING POTENTIAL INDICES

COUNTY	FINANCIAL SERVICES				THE HOME						ENTERTAINMENT						PERSONAL			
					Home Improvements		Furnishings													
	Auto Loan	Home Loan	Invest-ments	Retire-ment Plans	Home Repair	Lawn & Garden	Comput-ers & Hard-ware	Major Appli-ances	TV, Radio, Sound Equip-ment	Furni-ture	Dine out/ Carry out	Sports Equip-ment	Fees & Tickets	Toys & Games	Travel	Cable TV	Apparel & Services	Auto Repairs	Health Insur-ance	Pets & Supplies
FAIRFIELD	160	198	215	195	205	174	189	181	179	193	182	174	205	176	196	176	173	179	169	176
HARTFORD	108	120	136	122	122	112	120	114	118	121	119	105	126	116	122	118	110	116	114	113
LITCHFIELD	117	139	156	139	142	129	129	129	125	132	124	117	138	124	135	124	115	125	125	127
MIDDLESEX	122	141	154	142	141	129	133	130	128	136	129	120	141	128	137	127	119	129	126	129
NEW HAVEN	101	115	129	115	116	105	114	109	112	115	112	101	120	110	116	111	105	110	107	107
NEW LONDON	104	114	130	116	114	107	112	108	110	113	110	99	117	110	114	109	101	109	107	108
TOLLAND	118	134	146	136	133	121	128	123	123	130	123	115	135	124	130	120	114	123	117	123
WINDHAM	88	97	111	98	98	92	94	93	94	96	93	84	99	94	97	94	86	92	92	92
CONNECTICUT	120	139	155	139	141	127	135	130	132	137	132	121	144	130	139	131	123	130	127	128
UNITED STATES	100	100	100	100	100	100	100	100	100	100	100	100	100	100	100	100	100	100	100	100

COUNTY	FIPS Code	CBSA Code	DMA Code	POPULATION			2000-2007 ANNUAL RATE		RACE (%)					
									White		Black		Asian/Pacific	
				2000	2007	2012	% Rate	State Rank	2000	2007	2000	2007	2000	2007
KENT	001	20100	504	126,697	152,757	177,094	2.6	2	73.5	70.3	20.7	22.4	1.7	2.6
NEW CASTLE	003	37980	504	500,265	536,016	559,251	1.0	3	73.1	69.6	20.2	21.7	2.6	3.9
SUSSEX	005	42580	576	156,638	191,685	219,226	2.8	1	80.3	77.7	14.9	16.3	0.8	1.2
DELAWARE							1.6		74.6	71.5	19.2	20.7	2.1	3.1
UNITED STATES							1.2		75.1	72.7	12.3	12.6	3.8	4.5

DELAWARE

B

POPULATION COMPOSITION

COUNTY	% HISPANIC ORIGIN		2007 AGE DISTRIBUTION (%)										MEDIAN AGE	% 2007 Males	% 2007 Females
	2000	2007	0-4	5-9	10-14	15-19	20-24	25-44	45-64	65-84	85+	18+	2007		
KENT	3.2	4.1	7.3	6.6	6.9	7.9	7.1	27.1	24.7	10.8	1.5	74.9	36.1	48.3	51.7
NEW CASTLE	5.3	6.7	6.6	6.4	6.9	7.3	7.2	28.4	25.0	10.3	1.8	76.0	36.6	48.6	51.4
SUSSEX	4.4	5.8	5.8	5.5	5.7	5.5	5.2	23.4	29.1	17.7	2.2	79.6	44.3	49.0	51.0
DELAWARE	4.8	6.1	6.5	6.3	6.7	7.1	6.7	27.1	25.9	12.0	1.8	76.6	38.1	48.6	51.4
UNITED STATES	12.5	15.0	6.9	6.5	6.8	7.1	7.0	27.6	25.4	10.7	1.9	75.6	36.7	49.2	50.8

8-B

COUNTY	HOUSEHOLDS					FAMILIES			MEDIAN HOUSEHOLD INCOME			
	2000	2007	2012	% Annual Rate 2000-2007	2007 Average HH Size	2000	2007	% Annual Rate 2000-2007	2007	2012	2007 National Rank	2007 State Rank
KENT	47,224	57,574	67,264	2.8	2.59	33,615	39,963	2.4	50,818	59,477	622	2
NEW CASTLE	188,935	200,942	210,228	0.9	2.58	127,106	131,449	0.5	67,164	80,144	148	1
SUSSEX	62,577	77,504	89,265	3.0	2.43	43,869	52,956	2.6	50,067	59,690	674	3
DELAWARE				1.6	2.55			1.3	60,094	69,601		
UNITED STATES				1.2	2.59			1.0	53,154	62,503		

DELAWARE
D

INCOME

COUNTY	2007 Per Capita Income	2007 HH Income Base	2007 HOUSEHOLD INCOME DISTRIBUTION (%)					2007 Home Value Base	2007 HOME VALUE DISTRIBUTION (%)					2007 Median Home Value
			Less than $25,000	$25,000 to $49,999	$50,000 to $99,999	$100,000 to $149,999	$150,000 or More		Less than $50,000	$50,000 to $89,999	$90,000 to $174,999	$175,000 to $399,999	$400,000 or More	
KENT	23,600	57,574	22.1	26.9	36.3	10.4	4.4	41,664	9.3	4.6	21.0	56.8	8.4	209,137
NEW CASTLE	32,931	200,942	14.5	20.6	35.3	18.1	11.5	145,113	2.4	1.9	13.3	63.3	19.2	266,433
SUSSEX	26,088	77,504	22.4	27.5	35.4	9.1	5.6	63,729	9.2	6.3	21.4	47.7	15.4	210,761
DELAWARE	29,822		17.6	23.2	35.5	14.7	8.9		5.3	3.5	16.6	58.2	16.4	244,022
UNITED STATES	27,916		21.9	25.0	32.3	12.3	8.4		7.9	10.5	27.1	35.6	19.0	192,285

COUNTY	FINANCIAL SERVICES				THE HOME						ENTERTAINMENT						PERSONAL			
					Home Improvements		Furnishings													
	Auto Loan	Home Loan	Invest-ments	Retire-ment Plans	Home Repair	Lawn & Garden	Comput-ers & Hard-ware	Major Appli-ances	TV, Radio, Sound Equip-ment	Furni-ture	Dine out/ Carry out	Sports Equip-ment	Fees & Tickets	Toys & Games	Travel	Cable TV	Apparel & Services	Auto Repairs	Health Insur-ance	Pets & Supplies
KENT	90	85	82	85	83	87	84	86	85	84	85	78	83	87	83	86	76	85	87	88
NEW CASTLE	112	124	133	125	122	113	121	115	118	123	119	106	126	118	122	117	110	116	113	115
SUSSEX	96	85	77	83	90	106	82	96	87	82	86	83	79	86	86	92	75	91	102	98
DELAWARE	106	108	110	108	108	108	105	106	105	106	105	96	107	105	107	106	95	106	107	107
UNITED STATES	100	100	100	100	100	100	100	100	100	100	100	100	100	100	100	100	100	100	100	100

POPULATION CHANGE

A

COUNTY	FIPS Code	CBSA Code	DMA Code	POPULATION			2000-2007 ANNUAL RATE		RACE (%)					
									White		Black		Asian/Pacific	
				2000	2007	2012	% Rate	State Rank	2000	2007	2000	2007	2000	2007
DISTRICT OF COLUMBIA	001	47900	511	572,059	591,318	606,595	0.5	1	30.8	33.1	60.0	56.5	2.7	3.1

DISTRICT OF COLUMBIA UNITED STATES														
DISTRICT OF COLUMBIA							0.5		30.8	33.1	60.0	56.5	2.7	3.1
UNITED STATES							1.2		75.1	72.7	12.3	12.6	3.8	4.5

9-A

COUNTY	% HISPANIC ORIGIN		2007 AGE DISTRIBUTION (%)									MEDIAN AGE	% 2007 Males	% 2007 Females
	2000	2007	0-4	5-9	10-14	15-19	20-24	25-44	45-64	65-84	85+	18+	2007		
DISTRICT OF COLUMBIA	7.9	8.8	5.6	5.4	5.9	7.0	7.4	32.2	24.3	10.4	1.9	79.9	35.9	47.2	52.8
DISTRICT OF COLUMBIA	7.9	8.8	5.6	5.4	5.9	7.0	7.4	32.2	24.3	10.4	1.9	79.9	35.9	47.2	52.8
UNITED STATES	12.5	15.0	6.9	6.5	6.8	7.1	7.0	27.6	25.4	10.7	1.9	75.6	36.7	49.2	50.8

COUNTY	HOUSEHOLDS					FAMILIES			MEDIAN HOUSEHOLD INCOME			
	2000	2007	2012	% Annual Rate 2000-2007	2007 Average HH Size	2000	2007	% Annual Rate 2000-2007	2007	2012	2007 National Rank	2007 State Rank
DISTRICT OF COLUMBIA	248,338	260,635	269,548	0.7	2.13	114,166	115,517	0.2	50,151	58,997	668	1
DISTRICT OF COLUMBIA				0.7	2.13			0.2	50,151	58,997		
UNITED STATES				1.2	2.59			1.0	53,154	62,503		

COUNTY	2007 Per Capita Income	2007 HH Income Base	2007 HOUSEHOLD INCOME DISTRIBUTION (%)					2007 Home Value Base	2007 HOME VALUE DISTRIBUTION (%)					2007 Median Home Value
			Less than $25,000	$25,000 to $49,999	$50,000 to $99,999	$100,000 to $149,999	$150,000 or More		Less than $50,000	$50,000 to $89,999	$90,000 to $174,999	$175,000 to $399,999	$400,000 or More	
DISTRICT OF COLUMBIA	37,402	260,626	26.1	23.8	26.5	11.5	12.0	112,895	0.3	0.4	3.3	42.1	53.9	429,220
DISTRICT OF COLUMBIA	37,402		26.1	23.8	26.5	11.5	12.0		0.3	0.4	3.3	42.1	53.9	429,220
UNITED STATES	27,916		21.9	25.0	32.3	12.3	8.4		7.9	10.5	27.1	35.6	19.0	192,285

COUNTY	FINANCIAL SERVICES				THE HOME						ENTERTAINMENT						PERSONAL			
					Home Improvements		Furnishings													
	Auto Loan	Home Loan	Invest-ments	Retire-ment Plans	Home Repair	Lawn & Garden	Comput-ers & Hard-ware	Major Appli-ances	TV, Radio, Sound Equip-ment	Furni-ture	Dine out/ Carry out	Sports Equip-ment	Fees & Tickets	Toys & Games	Travel	Cable TV	Apparel & Services	Auto Repairs	Health Insur-ance	Pets & Supplies
DISTRICT OF COLUMBIA	101	96	104	102	97	92	117	100	119	113	122	97	115	114	111	120	114	109	103	102
DISTRICT OF COLUMBIA	101	96	104	102	97	92	117	100	119	113	122	97	115	114	111	120	114	109	103	102
UNITED STATES	100	100	100	100	100	100	100	100	100	100	100	100	100	100	100	100	100	100	100	100

COUNTY	FIPS Code	CBSA Code	DMA Code	POPULATION			2000-2007 ANNUAL RATE		RACE (%)					
									White		Black		Asian/Pacific	
				2000	2007	2012	% Rate	State Rank	2000	2007	2000	2007	2000	2007
ALACHUA	001	23540	592	217,955	244,351	261,319	1.6	46	73.5	69.0	19.3	21.9	3.6	4.7
BAKER	003	27260	561	22,259	26,351	29,600	2.4	26	84.0	81.0	13.9	16.5	0.4	0.6
BAY	005	37460	656	148,217	170,892	188,982	2.0	37	84.2	80.9	10.6	12.6	1.8	2.5
BRADFORD	007	00000	561	26,088	29,254	31,192	1.6	46	76.3	72.2	20.8	24.1	0.7	0.9
BREVARD	009	37340	534	476,230	557,320	623,285	2.2	31	86.8	84.0	8.4	9.9	1.6	2.1
BROWARD	011	33100	528	1,623,018	1,801,370	1,912,070	1.4	50	70.6	67.1	20.5	22.2	2.3	2.9
CALHOUN	013	00000	656	13,017	14,276	15,258	1.3	53	79.9	76.3	15.8	18.4	0.6	0.8
CHARLOTTE	015	39460	571	141,627	167,237	184,721	2.3	28	92.6	90.7	4.4	5.3	0.9	1.2
CITRUS	017	26140	539	118,085	142,431	164,661	2.6	21	95.0	93.8	2.4	2.9	0.8	1.1
CLAY	019	27260	561	140,814	186,285	228,565	3.9	12	87.4	84.5	6.7	7.9	2.1	2.8
COLLIER	021	34940	571	251,377	337,239	405,519	4.1	10	86.1	82.7	4.5	5.1	0.7	0.9
COLUMBIA	023	29380	561	56,513	65,939	73,786	2.2	31	79.7	76.1	17.0	19.9	0.7	0.9
DESOTO	027	11580	571	32,209	34,935	36,965	1.1	57	73.3	68.7	12.7	13.6	0.4	0.5
DIXIE	029	00000	592	13,827	15,879	17,290	1.9	41	88.8	86.4	9.0	10.7	0.3	0.4
DUVAL	031	27260	561	778,879	897,561	993,055	2.0	37	65.8	60.8	27.8	31.3	2.8	3.6
ESCAMBIA	033	37860	686	294,410	311,624	323,870	0.8	61	72.4	67.8	21.4	24.5	2.3	3.1
FLAGLER	035	37380	534	49,832	100,050	171,946	10.1	1	87.3	84.6	8.8	10.4	1.2	1.6
FRANKLIN	037	00000	656	11,057	11,670	12,956	0.7	63	81.2	76.1	16.3	18.7	0.2	0.4
GADSDEN	039	45220	530	45,087	48,360	50,228	1.0	58	38.7	34.4	57.1	60.5	0.3	0.3
GILCHRIST	041	23540	592	14,437	17,216	19,577	2.5	24	90.5	88.4	7.0	8.4	0.2	0.2
GLADES	043	00000	571	10,576	11,065	11,333	0.6	65	77.0	73.1	10.5	11.7	0.3	0.5
GULF	045	00000	656	13,332	15,817	17,541	2.4	26	79.9	76.4	16.9	19.1	0.4	0.7
HAMILTON	047	00000	530	13,327	14,763	15,436	1.4	50	58.8	54.1	37.7	41.6	0.2	0.3
HARDEE	049	48100	539	26,938	28,677	29,349	0.9	59	70.7	65.5	8.3	8.6	0.4	0.4
HENDRY	051	17500	571	36,210	39,613	42,449	1.2	55	66.1	62.4	14.7	14.7	0.5	0.6
HERNANDO	053	45300	539	130,802	165,587	203,494	3.3	15	92.9	91.1	4.1	4.9	0.7	0.9
HIGHLANDS	055	42700	539	87,366	100,654	111,339	2.0	37	83.5	79.9	9.3	10.6	1.1	1.4
HILLSBOROUGH	057	45300	539	998,948	1,202,714	1,365,553	2.6	21	75.2	71.3	15.0	16.3	2.3	2.8
HOLMES	059	00000	656	18,564	19,675	20,458	0.8	61	89.8	87.6	6.5	7.8	0.4	0.6
INDIAN RIVER	061	42680	548	112,947	141,440	166,391	3.2	16	87.4	84.6	8.2	9.6	0.8	1.0
JACKSON	063	00000	656	46,755	50,534	52,534	1.1	57	70.2	65.6	26.6	30.4	0.4	0.5
JEFFERSON	065	45220	530	12,902	14,900	15,694	2.0	37	59.3	54.1	38.3	43.0	0.3	0.4
LAFAYETTE	067	00000	530	7,022	8,089	8,435	2.0	37	79.3	75.1	14.4	16.5	0.1	0.2
LAKE	069	36740	534	210,528	292,691	359,915	4.6	7	87.5	84.6	9.3	9.8	0.8	1.1
LEE	071	15980	571	440,888	634,375	831,457	5.1	6	87.7	84.7	6.6	7.7	0.8	1.1
LEON	073	45220	530	239,452	268,888	289,723	1.6	46	66.4	61.5	29.1	32.8	1.9	2.5
LEVY	075	00000	592	34,450	40,218	44,874	2.2	31	85.9	83.1	11.0	12.9	0.4	0.5
LIBERTY	077	00000	656	7,021	8,104	8,757	2.0	37	76.4	72.3	18.4	21.3	0.1	0.2
MADISON	079	00000	530	18,733	19,687	20,104	0.7	63	57.5	52.6	40.3	44.8	0.3	0.4
MANATEE	081	42260	539	264,002	325,067	376,957	2.9	19	86.4	83.3	8.2	9.5	0.9	1.3
MARION	083	36100	534	258,916	328,656	389,684	3.3	15	84.2	81.0	11.5	13.5	0.7	1.0
MARTIN	085	38940	548	126,731	145,777	158,042	1.9	41	89.9	87.2	5.3	6.2	0.7	0.9
MIAMI-DADE	086	33100	528	2,253,362	2,474,342	2,621,085	1.3	53	69.7	70.5	20.3	18.8	1.4	1.5
MONROE	087	28580	528	79,589	79,765	78,627	0.0	67	90.7	88.9	4.8	5.4	0.9	1.1
NASSAU	089	27260	561	57,663	70,951	82,288	2.9	19	90.0	87.9	7.7	9.3	0.5	0.7
OKALOOSA	091	23020	686	170,498	193,913	210,241	1.8	43	83.4	79.9	9.1	10.6	2.6	3.5
OKEECHOBEE	093	36380	548	35,910	39,610	42,262	1.4	50	79.3	74.4	7.9	8.8	0.7	0.9
ORANGE	095	36740	534	896,344	1,109,263	1,289,485	3.0	17	68.6	64.2	18.2	19.5	3.4	4.3
OSCEOLA	097	36740	534	172,493	270,882	372,785	6.4	3	77.2	73.2	7.4	7.9	2.3	2.8
PALM BEACH	099	33100	548	1,131,184	1,331,326	1,485,464	2.3	28	79.1	75.4	13.8	15.5	1.6	2.0
PASCO	101	45300	539	344,765	454,148	555,126	3.9	12	93.7	91.9	2.1	2.5	1.0	1.3
PINELLAS	103	45300	539	921,482	943,079	952,685	0.3	66	85.9	82.8	9.0	10.5	2.1	2.9
POLK	105	29460	539	483,924	581,653	664,210	2.6	21	79.6	75.5	13.5	15.4	1.0	1.3
PUTNAM	107	37260	561	70,423	76,969	82,104	1.2	55	77.9	73.7	17.0	19.6	0.5	0.6
ST. JOHNS	109	27260	561	123,135	178,025	224,335	5.2	4	90.9	88.8	6.3	7.5	1.0	1.4
ST. LUCIE	111	38940	548	192,695	276,684	362,920	5.1	6	79.1	75.4	15.4	17.6	1.0	1.3
SANTA ROSA	113	37860	686	117,743	150,523	180,381	3.4	13	90.7	88.6	4.2	5.1	1.4	1.9
SARASOTA	115	42260	539	325,957	391,032	445,786	2.5	24	92.6	90.8	4.2	5.0	0.8	1.1
SEMINOLE	117	36740	534	365,196	425,266	468,105	2.1	33	82.4	78.8	9.5	10.8	2.5	3.3
SUMTER	119	45540	534	53,345	86,433	121,740	6.9	2	82.6	79.3	13.8	16.0	0.5	0.6
SUWANNEE	121	00000	530	34,844	39,714	43,791	1.8	43	84.5	81.5	12.1	14.2	0.6	0.7
TAYLOR	123	00000	530	19,256	20,220	20,614	0.7	63	77.8	74.0	19.0	22.3	0.5	0.6
UNION	125	00000	561	13,442	15,282	15,693	1.8	43	73.6	69.3	22.8	26.3	0.3	0.5
VOLUSIA	127	19660	534	443,343	517,851	577,794	2.2	31	86.1	83.1	9.3	10.9	1.0	1.4
WAKULLA	129	45220	530	22,863	30,654	37,151	4.1	10	86.1	83.4	11.5	13.7	0.3	0.4
WALTON	131	00000	656	40,601	55,788	68,165	4.5	8	88.4	86.0	7.0	8.3	0.5	0.7
WASHINGTON	133	00000	656	20,973	23,209	24,719	1.4	50	81.7	78.4	13.7	16.1	0.4	0.6
FLORIDA							2.3		78.0	75.4	14.6	15.6	1.7	2.2
UNITED STATES							1.2		75.1	72.7	12.3	12.6	3.8	4.5

POPULATION COMPOSITION

COUNTY	% HISPANIC ORIGIN 2000	2007	2007 AGE DISTRIBUTION (%) 0-4	5-9	10-14	15-19	20-24	25-44	45-64	65-84	85+	18+	MEDIAN AGE 2007	% 2007 Males	% 2007 Females
ALACHUA	5.7	7.9	5.1	4.5	5.1	10.0	16.6	25.7	22.8	8.8	1.5	81.9	29.7	48.9	51.1
BAKER	1.9	2.7	7.6	6.6	6.1	7.5	9.0	28.8	24.4	9.1	1.0	75.2	34.4	52.2	47.8
BAY	2.4	3.5	6.1	5.6	6.1	6.0	6.2	27.6	27.7	13.0	1.5	78.5	40.2	49.6	50.4
BRADFORD	2.4	3.4	5.8	5.3	5.3	5.1	7.6	31.2	26.4	11.6	1.7	80.6	38.3	56.6	43.4
BREVARD	4.6	6.6	5.3	4.9	5.8	6.3	6.0	22.2	28.2	18.4	2.9	80.2	44.7	48.7	51.3
BROWARD	16.7	22.1	6.4	6.2	6.6	6.4	5.8	27.1	25.9	12.2	3.4	76.8	39.9	48.2	51.8
CALHOUN	3.8	5.4	6.3	6.2	5.0	5.7	7.1	30.2	25.1	12.4	2.0	79.0	37.7	54.0	46.0
CHARLOTTE	3.3	4.8	3.6	3.4	3.9	4.3	3.8	15.4	29.3	31.2	5.1	86.4	56.9	47.5	52.5
CITRUS	2.7	3.9	3.8	3.4	4.1	5.0	4.4	15.5	30.6	29.0	4.3	85.6	55.3	48.1	51.9
CLAY	4.3	6.2	6.9	6.3	7.0	7.3	7.1	27.0	27.8	9.6	1.1	75.3	37.7	49.1	50.9
COLLIER	19.6	26.6	5.4	5.1	5.2	4.8	4.8	21.7	26.8	23.2	3.0	81.3	47.3	49.7	50.3
COLUMBIA	2.7	3.9	6.7	6.2	6.1	6.5	7.4	25.4	26.6	13.3	1.7	77.1	38.8	50.6	49.4
DESOTO	24.9	32.4	6.3	5.4	5.7	6.5	8.1	27.3	22.2	16.4	2.1	78.8	37.4	56.0	44.0
DIXIE	1.8	2.6	5.8	5.3	5.2	5.0	6.2	25.7	28.2	17.1	1.6	80.5	42.8	53.8	46.2
DUVAL	4.1	5.6	7.2	6.6	6.7	7.2	7.3	29.1	25.2	9.1	1.5	75.2	35.5	48.5	51.5
ESCAMBIA	2.7	3.8	6.2	5.7	5.9	7.8	8.0	27.4	25.0	12.1	1.8	78.4	36.7	49.7	50.3
FLAGLER	5.1	7.3	4.4	4.3	4.5	4.9	4.2	17.8	30.3	26.9	2.7	83.6	52.1	47.7	52.3
FRANKLIN	2.4	3.1	5.1	5.2	4.1	5.3	5.3	26.1	30.5	16.3	2.1	82.4	44.3	53.2	46.8
GADSDEN	6.2	8.0	6.8	6.5	6.7	6.5	7.7	27.5	25.9	10.7	1.6	76.1	36.4	47.8	52.2
GILCHRIST	2.8	4.1	6.1	5.5	5.9	7.2	11.3	22.6	26.1	13.6	1.7	78.5	38.1	52.2	47.8
GLADES	15.1	20.5	6.2	5.5	5.9	5.3	6.7	25.3	25.4	18.0	1.7	79.2	41.2	54.9	45.1
GULF	2.0	4.3	5.1	4.7	5.8	5.7	6.1	24.1	30.1	16.5	1.9	81.0	44.0	51.9	48.1
HAMILTON	6.4	8.5	6.2	6.2	5.4	6.3	8.2	31.3	25.1	9.8	1.5	78.5	36.4	58.4	41.6
HARDEE	35.7	44.8	8.2	7.5	6.5	6.4	7.4	30.5	20.7	11.5	1.4	74.2	33.3	54.9	45.1
HENDRY	39.6	48.3	8.4	7.1	7.5	8.6	9.4	28.9	19.7	9.3	1.0	71.9	30.4	55.0	45.0
HERNANDO	5.0	7.3	4.6	4.2	4.7	5.3	4.9	17.5	28.8	26.0	4.0	83.2	51.4	47.5	52.5
HIGHLANDS	12.1	16.8	5.1	4.5	4.8	5.2	5.3	18.1	25.9	26.5	4.6	82.4	50.7	48.9	51.1
HILLSBOROUGH	18.0	23.9	6.9	6.5	6.8	7.0	7.0	28.8	24.8	10.5	1.7	75.7	36.5	49.0	51.0
HOLMES	1.9	2.8	5.8	5.4	5.8	5.9	6.8	28.6	26.0	13.6	2.1	79.4	39.4	53.3	46.7
INDIAN RIVER	6.5	9.4	4.9	4.6	5.1	5.4	5.3	19.3	27.5	23.2	4.7	82.2	48.7	48.3	51.7
JACKSON	2.9	4.1	5.7	5.2	5.5	5.8	7.1	29.5	26.6	12.6	2.1	80.1	39.3	53.0	47.0
JEFFERSON	2.2	3.1	5.0	4.8	5.0	5.6	6.3	28.9	30.2	12.1	2.2	81.6	41.5	53.7	46.3
LAFAYETTE	9.1	12.8	5.5	5.4	5.6	4.5	8.4	36.4	20.9	11.9	1.5	81.0	35.9	62.1	37.9
LAKE	5.6	8.1	5.7	5.3	5.5	5.4	4.8	22.0	25.8	22.5	3.1	80.3	46.0	48.4	51.6
LEE	9.5	13.5	5.4	5.0	5.2	5.3	5.0	20.9	27.5	22.4	3.3	81.2	47.4	48.8	51.2
LEON	3.5	4.8	5.6	5.2	5.4	9.6	15.2	26.6	23.7	7.4	1.3	80.3	30.6	47.8	52.2
LEVY	3.9	5.6	5.9	5.4	5.7	6.0	6.2	21.8	30.6	16.7	1.8	79.4	44.3	48.7	51.3
LIBERTY	4.5	6.3	5.8	5.0	5.2	5.7	6.3	36.2	24.4	10.2	1.0	80.3	36.5	60.0	40.0
MADISON	3.2	4.3	5.9	5.6	5.8	6.8	7.1	28.0	25.1	13.3	2.3	78.3	38.1	52.4	47.6
MANATEE	9.3	13.1	5.5	5.4	5.3	5.6	5.1	20.8	27.4	21.1	3.9	80.4	46.7	48.3	51.7
MARION	6.0	8.6	5.2	4.7	5.1	5.8	5.6	20.2	27.0	23.2	3.1	81.4	47.3	48.2	51.8
MARTIN	7.5	10.8	4.3	4.1	5.1	5.4	4.5	18.4	30.3	23.3	4.5	83.0	50.4	49.0	51.0
MIAMI-DADE	57.3	64.4	6.7	6.3	6.8	7.1	6.9	29.3	23.4	11.5	1.9	75.9	36.5	48.5	51.5
MONROE	15.8	21.8	4.2	4.1	4.5	4.8	4.7	25.9	36.6	13.7	1.6	84.4	46.0	53.0	47.0
NASSAU	1.5	2.2	6.1	5.9	5.9	6.7	5.8	25.4	29.5	13.4	1.4	77.9	41.3	49.1	50.9
OKALOOSA	4.3	6.1	6.5	5.6	5.9	6.4	7.7	27.8	25.8	12.9	1.3	78.2	38.3	50.0	50.0
OKEECHOBEE	18.6	25.2	6.7	5.9	6.1	7.2	7.3	26.6	23.9	14.6	1.7	77.0	37.5	53.9	46.1
ORANGE	18.8	24.6	6.9	6.2	6.7	7.2	7.8	31.5	23.7	8.6	1.3	76.1	34.5	49.5	50.5
OSCEOLA	29.4	37.7	7.0	6.3	7.2	7.5	7.6	28.0	25.0	10.0	1.3	74.8	35.7	49.3	50.7
PALM BEACH	12.4	17.0	5.5	5.5	5.8	5.9	5.0	23.0	26.1	18.6	4.6	79.6	44.5	48.0	52.0
PASCO	5.7	8.3	5.6	5.4	5.3	5.6	5.1	22.0	27.5	19.6	3.9	80.2	45.7	48.2	51.8
PINELLAS	4.6	6.7	4.8	4.6	5.3	5.5	5.3	22.8	29.5	18.0	4.4	82.0	46.2	47.7	52.3
POLK	9.5	13.2	6.6	6.2	6.3	6.5	6.0	24.7	25.6	15.7	2.3	76.9	40.4	49.1	50.9
PUTNAM	5.9	8.3	6.4	5.7	6.1	6.3	6.0	22.2	28.6	16.7	1.9	78.0	42.8	49.6	50.4
ST. JOHNS	2.6	3.9	5.5	5.7	6.2	6.9	6.0	23.2	31.3	13.3	2.0	78.4	42.9	48.8	51.2
ST. LUCIE	8.2	11.4	5.7	5.3	6.0	6.3	5.5	21.7	25.9	20.5	3.1	79.2	44.7	48.5	51.5
SANTA ROSA	2.5	3.7	6.6	6.4	6.2	7.0	6.5	26.8	27.9	11.5	1.1	76.4	39.6	49.9	50.1
SARASOTA	4.3	6.3	4.0	3.9	4.6	4.8	4.1	18.6	28.6	25.9	5.3	84.5	52.3	47.4	52.6
SEMINOLE	11.2	15.5	6.3	6.0	6.6	6.9	6.3	28.3	28.1	10.0	1.5	76.8	38.3	49.0	51.0
SUMTER	6.3	8.9	3.9	3.6	3.9	4.0	4.7	20.7	26.1	30.9	2.3	86.2	53.1	52.6	47.4
SUWANNEE	4.9	7.0	6.4	6.1	6.1	5.2	6.0	24.7	27.3	15.9	2.2	78.3	41.7	48.8	51.2
TAYLOR	1.5	2.2	6.0	5.6	5.8	6.2	6.6	27.4	27.9	13.0	1.6	78.9	40.0	51.9	48.1
UNION	3.5	5.0	5.7	4.9	4.6	6.1	8.2	39.2	23.9	6.7	0.7	81.2	36.2	66.2	33.8
VOLUSIA	6.6	9.4	4.9	4.7	5.2	6.3	6.0	22.3	28.5	18.7	3.4	81.6	45.4	48.5	51.5
WAKULLA	1.9	2.8	6.1	5.7	5.8	6.4	6.9	27.8	29.8	10.4	1.0	78.4	39.7	52.1	47.9
WALTON	2.2	3.2	5.2	4.9	5.4	5.1	4.9	25.2	31.3	16.5	1.6	81.3	44.6	51.1	48.9
WASHINGTON	2.3	3.3	6.3	5.9	5.8	5.5	6.1	26.6	28.0	13.5	2.4	78.5	40.8	51.9	48.1
FLORIDA	16.8	20.5	6.0	5.6	6.0	6.4	6.4	25.5	26.2	15.2	2.7	78.5	41.0	48.8	51.2
UNITED STATES	12.5	15.0	6.9	6.5	6.8	7.1	7.0	27.6	25.4	10.7	1.9	75.6	36.7	49.2	50.8

COUNTY	HOUSEHOLDS					FAMILIES			MEDIAN HOUSEHOLD INCOME			
	2000	2007	2012	% Annual Rate 2000-2007	2007 Average HH Size	2000	2007	% Annual Rate 2000-2007	2007	2012	2007 National Rank	2007 State Rank
ALACHUA	87,509	100,848	108,894	2.0	2.29	47,819	53,705	1.6	38,512	44,486	1925	43
BAKER	7,043	8,539	9,762	2.7	2.82	5,599	6,710	2.5	47,677	53,974	846	21
BAY	59,597	70,576	78,859	2.4	2.37	40,480	47,065	2.1	44,008	50,490	1207	30
BRADFORD	8,497	9,580	10,404	1.7	2.55	6,196	6,878	1.5	39,786	45,183	1752	38
BREVARD	198,195	233,013	261,850	2.3	2.35	132,480	152,836	2.0	50,329	59,311	655	17
BROWARD	654,445	709,373	747,674	1.1	2.51	411,403	436,625	0.8	53,418	63,756	478	9
CALHOUN	4,468	5,033	5,462	1.7	2.49	3,130	3,466	1.4	31,345	35,233	2807	64
CHARLOTTE	63,864	75,891	84,219	2.4	2.17	44,123	51,516	2.2	45,033	52,291	1108	28
CITRUS	52,634	63,326	73,423	2.6	2.22	36,339	42,962	2.3	38,156	43,950	1981	44
CLAY	50,243	67,301	83,086	4.1	2.74	39,389	52,115	3.9	60,328	69,111	256	4
COLLIER	102,973	137,076	165,065	4.0	2.43	71,264	93,209	3.8	61,221	72,378	234	3
COLUMBIA	20,925	24,751	28,031	2.3	2.53	14,919	17,359	2.1	36,891	41,820	2141	49
DESOTO	10,746	11,655	12,341	1.1	2.73	7,676	8,188	0.9	36,906	41,824	2139	48
DIXIE	5,205	6,016	6,650	2.0	2.41	3,660	4,159	1.8	30,694	34,402	2865	66
DUVAL	303,747	355,652	395,413	2.2	2.48	201,678	231,662	1.9	50,508	59,545	639	16
ESCAMBIA	111,049	121,155	127,438	1.2	2.39	74,163	79,399	0.9	43,433	50,483	1280	32
FLAGLER	21,294	43,360	75,121	10.3	2.29	15,683	31,459	10.1	49,298	56,977	722	18
FRANKLIN	4,096	4,980	5,606	2.7	2.24	2,727	3,254	2.5	32,452	37,009	2717	62
GADSDEN	15,867	17,228	18,148	1.1	2.62	11,429	12,213	0.9	37,812	43,011	2024	45
GILCHRIST	5,021	6,122	7,047	2.8	2.60	3,715	4,464	2.6	35,660	39,715	2335	52
GLADES	3,852	4,053	4,175	0.7	2.49	2,764	2,863	0.5	37,451	42,881	2073	46
GULF	4,931	5,928	6,712	2.6	2.38	3,537	4,185	2.3	37,000	41,837	2129	47
HAMILTON	4,161	4,642	4,965	1.5	2.54	2,995	3,288	1.3	29,949	33,577	2914	67
HARDEE	8,166	8,470	8,636	0.5	3.10	6,253	6,400	0.3	35,499	39,558	2367	54
HENDRY	10,850	11,894	12,741	1.3	3.12	8,141	8,798	1.1	40,217	45,694	1697	37
HERNANDO	55,425	70,306	86,695	3.3	2.33	40,019	49,961	3.1	40,267	46,410	1693	36
HIGHLANDS	37,471	42,620	47,075	1.8	2.33	25,794	28,827	1.5	36,597	42,015	2181	51
HILLSBOROUGH	391,357	473,925	539,603	2.7	2.49	255,222	302,993	2.4	51,096	60,404	604	14
HOLMES	6,921	7,478	7,865	1.1	2.39	4,893	5,199	0.8	32,266	36,069	2739	63
INDIAN RIVER	49,137	62,728	74,447	3.4	2.22	32,708	40,969	3.2	49,144	57,838	738	19
JACKSON	16,620	18,096	19,065	1.2	2.40	11,607	12,418	0.9	35,131	39,176	2413	57
JEFFERSON	4,695	5,276	5,682	1.6	2.45	3,307	3,654	1.4	39,225	43,969	1828	40
LAFAYETTE	2,142	2,375	2,518	1.4	2.63	1,591	1,738	1.2	35,595	39,236	2351	53
LAKE	88,413	122,780	151,295	4.6	2.35	62,468	85,301	4.4	45,699	53,137	1031	25
LEE	188,599	274,210	361,253	5.3	2.29	127,611	182,156	5.0	50,569	59,663	636	15
LEON	96,521	112,082	122,091	2.1	2.29	54,305	61,511	1.7	46,739	54,667	932	22
LEVY	13,867	16,409	18,431	2.3	2.41	9,674	11,254	2.1	32,660	37,083	2691	61
LIBERTY	2,222	2,606	2,903	2.2	2.45	1,554	1,792	2.0	34,012	38,126	2547	58
MADISON	6,629	7,098	7,343	0.9	2.51	4,683	4,931	0.7	30,983	34,816	2833	65
MANATEE	112,460	139,652	162,398	3.0	2.29	73,726	89,785	2.8	48,487	56,822	782	20
MARION	106,755	137,142	164,005	3.5	2.34	74,637	94,251	3.3	39,452	45,435	1789	39
MARTIN	55,288	63,423	68,932	1.9	2.24	36,194	40,710	1.6	53,870	63,676	458	7
MIAMI-DADE	776,774	852,579	901,594	1.3	2.85	548,493	592,021	1.1	45,328	52,871	1075	27
MONROE	35,086	35,348	34,872	0.1	2.22	20,387	20,056	-0.2	53,014	62,303	500	10
NASSAU	21,980	27,433	32,034	3.1	2.56	16,532	20,345	2.9	54,990	63,347	405	6
OKALOOSA	66,269	77,209	84,443	2.1	2.45	46,499	53,266	1.9	51,932	61,156	552	12
OKEECHOBEE	12,593	13,979	15,030	1.5	2.66	9,022	9,852	1.2	36,780	41,670	2153	50
ORANGE	336,286	418,149	486,941	3.1	2.60	220,258	268,553	2.8	51,958	61,357	551	11
OSCEOLA	60,977	95,948	131,908	6.5	2.80	45,077	69,880	6.2	46,661	53,419	940	24
PALM BEACH	474,175	550,873	613,678	2.1	2.38	303,772	345,769	1.8	56,863	67,023	332	5
PASCO	147,566	188,803	229,879	3.5	2.38	99,073	124,409	3.2	41,282	47,875	1557	35
PINELLAS	414,968	425,659	430,497	0.4	2.16	243,339	243,813	0.0	46,725	54,568	933	23
POLK	187,233	227,336	260,744	2.7	2.50	132,305	157,978	2.5	43,899	50,379	1223	31
PUTNAM	27,839	30,238	32,299	1.1	2.50	19,464	20,785	0.9	33,812	38,277	2573	59
ST. JOHNS	49,614	71,311	89,977	5.1	2.46	34,103	48,153	4.9	63,436	75,293	188	1
ST. LUCIE	76,933	111,066	146,368	5.2	2.47	54,258	77,030	5.0	45,572	52,950	1044	26
SANTA ROSA	43,793	54,979	66,026	3.2	2.69	33,321	41,265	3.0	51,451	59,615	582	13
SARASOTA	149,937	180,069	205,905	2.6	2.14	94,528	111,163	2.3	53,515	63,014	475	8
SEMINOLE	139,572	164,178	181,509	2.3	2.57	97,249	112,375	2.0	62,628	73,999	199	2
SUMTER	20,779	35,168	51,841	7.5	2.20	15,035	25,048	7.3	38,609	43,852	1916	42
SUWANNEE	13,460	15,533	17,233	2.0	2.51	9,687	11,000	1.8	35,250	39,241	2401	56
TAYLOR	7,176	7,611	7,841	0.8	2.46	5,129	5,349	0.6	35,424	39,444	2380	55
UNION	3,367	3,719	3,904	1.4	2.71	2,606	2,843	1.2	41,388	46,914	1534	34
VOLUSIA	184,723	215,195	240,739	2.1	2.34	120,064	137,113	1.8	44,066	51,205	1202	29
WAKULLA	8,450	11,429	14,102	4.3	2.53	6,237	8,310	4.0	42,915	47,618	1341	33
WALTON	16,548	23,261	28,783	4.8	2.31	11,119	15,338	4.5	39,019	44,372	1850	41
WASHINGTON	7,931	8,860	9,536	1.5	2.43	5,648	6,206	1.3	32,933	37,030	2666	60
FLORIDA				2.4	2.46			2.1	48,591	56,912		
UNITED STATES				1.2	2.59			1.0	53,154	62,503		

COUNTY	2007 Per Capita Income	2007 HH Income Base	2007 HOUSEHOLD INCOME DISTRIBUTION (%)					2007 Home Value Base	2007 HOME VALUE DISTRIBUTION (%)					2007 Median Home Value
			Less than $25,000	$25,000 to $49,999	$50,000 to $99,999	$100,000 to $149,999	$150,000 or More		Less than $50,000	$50,000 to $89,999	$90,000 to $174,999	$175,000 to $399,999	$400,000 or More	
ALACHUA	24,351	100,844	34.4	25.9	25.1	9.2	5.4	58,303	5.1	8.4	30.0	46.2	10.4	191,393
BAKER	19,419	8,539	24.5	27.7	37.7	7.7	2.3	7,075	9.2	17.3	35.4	33.8	4.3	148,567
BAY	23,809	70,576	26.6	29.6	31.4	8.5	3.9	50,419	5.7	8.7	29.3	45.8	10.4	189,059
BRADFORD	18,813	9,580	29.2	32.4	30.3	6.0	2.1	7,760	8.4	12.2	35.6	36.8	7.0	160,333
BREVARD	27,380	233,013	21.0	28.7	33.7	11.0	5.7	179,022	3.1	3.3	22.6	54.2	16.9	226,720
BROWARD	29,540	709,373	21.6	25.2	31.5	12.7	9.1	508,574	2.6	4.4	15.3	49.3	28.4	275,752
CALHOUN	16,407	5,033	39.7	31.2	23.1	4.5	1.5	4,135	13.7	19.2	35.3	28.8	3.1	128,675
CHARLOTTE	27,401	75,891	23.4	32.1	31.9	8.3	4.3	64,567	1.5	4.4	28.6	50.8	14.7	216,084
CITRUS	23,008	63,326	29.2	34.3	27.0	6.7	2.9	55,017	4.4	10.5	33.9	42.8	8.4	178,181
CLAY	26,643	67,301	14.0	25.6	39.3	14.8	6.3	53,987	2.0	5.8	22.3	58.7	11.3	221,898
COLLIER	38,689	137,076	15.0	24.9	32.3	14.2	13.6	106,893	1.7	1.7	5.3	36.6	54.7	434,526
COLUMBIA	18,699	24,751	32.7	31.8	27.0	6.3	2.2	19,572	7.7	12.5	35.6	38.3	5.8	161,329
DESOTO	17,597	11,655	32.1	33.4	26.9	5.0	2.5	8,997	9.2	17.4	38.0	28.5	6.9	138,220
DIXIE	17,534	6,016	41.6	30.3	21.1	4.7	2.2	5,258	14.8	23.1	34.1	22.8	5.2	114,526
DUVAL	26,433	355,651	21.7	27.7	33.7	10.8	6.1	234,422	3.6	6.7	34.0	45.9	9.8	189,386
ESCAMBIA	23,448	121,155	26.6	30.2	30.4	8.7	4.1	84,875	6.1	12.2	40.4	36.0	5.2	156,335
FLAGLER	27,795	43,360	19.7	31.1	34.7	9.4	5.1	37,137	1.9	1.8	10.2	60.2	25.9	292,772
FRANKLIN	20,015	4,980	37.8	30.8	24.2	4.9	2.3	4,061	8.2	14.9	27.5	31.6	17.8	172,888
GADSDEN	18,096	17,228	32.9	30.5	28.4	5.8	2.4	13,714	11.8	21.9	38.4	24.1	3.7	122,135
GILCHRIST	17,696	6,122	33.1	33.9	26.5	4.3	2.2	5,345	10.2	17.3	35.3	32.9	4.2	142,207
GLADES	19,566	4,053	33.0	30.9	25.6	7.9	2.7	3,378	7.5	12.8	40.7	33.6	5.3	150,716
GULF	19,430	5,928	32.9	31.6	28.2	5.0	2.3	4,913	5.5	14.8	31.7	38.5	9.5	169,503
HAMILTON	15,497	4,642	42.6	28.5	24.5	3.3	1.1	3,686	11.4	25.5	34.5	25.5	3.1	115,992
HARDEE	15,706	8,470	33.5	33.1	25.2	5.5	2.7	6,459	9.3	18.6	38.9	27.9	5.3	133,992
HENDRY	16,419	11,894	30.8	30.7	28.8	7.1	2.6	8,899	10.1	15.0	39.3	30.3	5.3	142,507
HERNANDO	22,518	70,306	26.0	35.4	29.7	5.9	3.0	61,520	2.9	7.2	30.5	51.3	8.2	197,562
HIGHLANDS	20,941	42,620	32.3	34.3	24.5	6.0	2.9	34,718	7.7	13.0	37.8	35.8	5.7	157,622
HILLSBOROUGH	28,170	473,916	21.2	27.7	31.6	12.0	7.5	317,885	3.8	4.8	22.4	53.3	15.8	221,772
HOLMES	17,792	7,478	39.5	30.9	23.4	4.1	2.1	6,228	13.3	16.8	36.8	27.1	5.9	132,448
INDIAN RIVER	33,987	62,728	22.3	28.5	30.7	9.7	8.8	50,075	4.7	5.7	24.3	45.3	20.0	219,148
JACKSON	18,674	18,096	35.7	32.0	23.9	6.3	2.1	14,459	9.1	16.3	35.5	34.3	4.8	148,090
JEFFERSON	20,907	5,276	33.5	27.8	27.0	8.4	3.3	4,359	9.0	19.7	35.8	27.5	7.9	141,578
LAFAYETTE	17,787	2,375	33.3	33.6	26.1	3.9	3.1	1,962	8.3	19.0	33.1	33.6	6.0	151,285
LAKE	25,186	122,780	23.8	30.8	32.0	8.8	4.5	102,160	6.2	8.5	25.0	47.8	12.6	204,660
LEE	30,666	274,203	19.6	29.7	33.6	9.5	7.5	215,742	2.8	3.7	17.4	49.3	26.7	266,762
LEON	27,618	112,080	28.1	24.5	29.6	11.1	6.7	67,380	4.2	6.8	28.7	49.8	10.6	198,021
LEVY	18,221	16,409	37.1	33.0	23.0	5.0	1.9	13,947	8.6	16.1	38.8	30.6	5.9	139,380
LIBERTY	19,198	2,606	36.5	30.3	24.5	5.6	3.0	2,176	19.1	17.1	28.9	29.3	5.7	123,399
MADISON	16,700	7,098	41.8	28.8	23.6	3.6	2.3	5,696	11.4	21.4	35.8	25.8	5.6	129,369
MANATEE	28,418	139,652	22.4	29.1	32.3	10.1	6.1	106,410	6.8	6.2	18.5	47.7	20.8	235,636
MARION	22,112	137,142	29.6	33.2	27.3	6.6	3.3	112,057	6.1	9.7	30.5	44.6	9.1	184,543
MARTIN	36,495	63,423	18.8	27.4	30.8	11.9	11.0	51,815	3.5	3.7	18.0	41.0	33.9	275,098
MIAMI-DADE	23,299	852,561	28.7	25.5	28.6	9.6	7.6	517,726	1.3	1.9	8.3	52.7	35.8	330,382
MONROE	33,374	35,344	20.9	26.0	32.8	12.0	8.3	23,349	6.1	3.6	5.9	27.5	56.9	454,037
NASSAU	28,080	27,433	19.6	24.9	36.7	12.0	6.8	22,618	4.7	7.8	24.0	44.9	18.5	214,854
OKALOOSA	26,635	77,209	17.7	30.0	35.7	11.2	5.4	53,438	3.3	4.7	22.3	55.0	14.7	223,155
OKEECHOBEE	18,371	13,979	31.3	33.3	26.8	6.0	2.6	10,821	6.7	11.8	38.5	36.7	6.3	162,341
ORANGE	26,874	418,591	19.5	28.3	33.1	12.0	7.0	266,597	2.9	3.0	16.9	59.3	17.8	240,038
OSCEOLA	20,718	95,948	21.6	32.0	34.1	8.8	3.4	67,548	4.7	3.6	16.4	63.4	11.8	233,012
PALM BEACH	35,765	550,872	18.8	25.2	31.8	12.4	11.8	423,092	2.9	4.3	15.4	45.6	31.8	288,274
PASCO	22,373	188,803	27.4	32.9	29.3	7.1	3.3	158,466	5.2	8.1	38.1	40.4	8.3	171,756
PINELLAS	29,875	425,657	24.3	28.8	30.8	9.5	6.5	311,478	6.6	6.2	26.9	46.6	13.7	200,869
POLK	22,923	227,238	25.6	30.8	30.9	8.5	4.1	172,462	7.1	11.7	36.3	39.0	5.9	163,037
PUTNAM	18,848	30,238	36.4	31.0	24.2	5.6	2.8	24,688	8.5	17.6	39.4	29.4	5.1	135,719
ST. JOHNS	37,499	71,311	16.7	22.6	32.0	14.6	14.0	56,271	2.2	4.2	14.8	46.5	32.4	301,771
ST. LUCIE	23,882	111,066	24.0	31.0	32.6	8.0	4.4	88,911	4.4	4.7	19.9	57.9	13.1	227,958
SANTA ROSA	24,566	54,979	20.1	28.1	35.0	11.1	5.7	45,316	5.6	9.7	30.1	45.4	9.3	184,987
SARASOTA	35,849	180,069	18.7	27.5	34.0	10.6	9.1	145,827	2.3	3.2	14.6	53.3	26.6	265,584
SEMINOLE	32,444	164,178	14.2	23.6	35.6	16.1	10.5	118,387	1.6	2.0	13.4	60.7	22.2	269,326
SUMTER	21,564	35,168	29.7	35.2	26.6	6.2	2.4	30,832	6.3	10.1	24.6	45.4	13.5	205,497
SUWANNEE	17,823	15,533	35.8	30.9	26.4	5.0	1.9	12,877	7.8	16.6	38.0	30.1	7.4	145,435
TAYLOR	18,479	7,610	35.3	30.9	24.8	6.9	2.1	6,205	14.0	18.3	32.5	31.2	4.0	132,848
UNION	17,678	3,719	27.1	33.0	31.6	5.5	2.7	2,875	11.8	17.0	36.2	31.4	3.5	142,980
VOLUSIA	24,844	215,195	25.6	30.8	31.0	8.0	4.7	166,602	4.3	4.0	24.7	55.2	11.8	213,747
WAKULLA	20,876	11,429	24.0	33.4	31.7	8.1	2.8	9,791	7.8	13.5	33.0	39.7	5.9	164,555
WALTON	22,973	23,261	30.4	31.9	27.3	6.4	4.0	18,911	8.8	12.6	25.4	33.3	19.9	187,623
WASHINGTON	18,547	8,860	38.3	29.9	23.7	5.6	2.5	7,401	8.7	14.4	32.9	37.8	6.1	161,270
FLORIDA	27,311		23.3	28.0	31.3	10.4	7.0		3.9	5.6	21.7	48.5	20.2	231,576
UNITED STATES	27,916		21.9	25.0	32.3	12.3	8.4		7.9	10.5	27.1	35.6	19.0	192,285

COUNTY	FINANCIAL SERVICES				THE HOME						ENTERTAINMENT						PERSONAL			
					Home Improvements		Furnishings													
	Auto Loan	Home Loan	Invest-ments	Retire-ment Plans	Home Repair	Lawn & Garden	Comput-ers & Hard-ware	Major Appli-ances	TV, Radio, Sound Equip-ment	Furni-ture	Dine out/ Carry out	Sports Equip-ment	Fees & Tickets	Toys & Games	Travel	Cable TV	Apparel & Services	Auto Repairs	Health Insur-ance	Pets & Supplies
ALACHUA	81	65	68	70	63	68	88	73	83	76	83	70	77	80	76	79	75	80	73	75
BAKER	86	78	66	76	74	80	74	79	77	75	77	71	72	79	74	78	68	78	80	81
BAY	82	75	74	76	75	82	78	80	79	76	78	71	75	79	77	80	69	79	83	81
BRADFORD	79	64	51	62	68	83	63	75	68	62	68	66	58	70	64	72	59	71	80	79
BREVARD	86	90	103	90	91	92	87	89	89	89	88	77	91	86	92	91	79	89	95	88
BROWARD	98	103	112	104	101	98	103	99	102	104	102	91	105	99	104	102	93	103	102	99
CALHOUN	71	50	31	48	56	75	51	65	57	49	57	57	43	60	50	62	48	60	70	70
CHARLOTTE	80	81	92	78	89	99	76	88	81	78	79	72	79	73	86	87	69	85	101	87
CITRUS	72	69	69	66	75	88	64	78	69	66	68	64	65	63	72	75	58	75	89	78
CLAY	107	109	101	109	104	103	100	103	99	104	99	94	102	102	101	98	89	101	99	104
COLLIER	127	132	142	130	137	145	124	136	127	128	126	117	129	117	136	132	112	134	146	133
COLUMBIA	74	62	55	61	62	74	63	69	67	61	66	61	58	67	62	70	57	67	74	72
DESOTO	74	62	55	60	66	79	62	73	67	62	66	62	59	66	64	71	57	70	79	74
DIXIE	69	53	37	50	59	78	53	68	59	52	58	58	47	58	55	63	49	63	74	71
DUVAL	93	88	90	91	83	84	93	87	92	92	92	80	90	93	89	92	83	91	88	88
ESCAMBIA	81	76	81	77	75	79	78	78	81	77	80	69	77	80	78	82	71	79	83	79
FLAGLER	92	88	87	87	94	108	81	96	86	84	85	80	82	81	90	91	74	91	104	96
FRANKLIN	73	57	42	55	64	83	56	72	62	55	61	61	50	62	58	67	52	66	78	76
GADSDEN	74	62	53	61	62	73	62	69	67	62	67	61	58	69	62	70	58	67	73	72
GILCHRIST	78	60	39	57	64	82	58	72	63	58	64	64	52	67	58	67	55	67	75	77
GLADES	76	66	56	63	69	81	63	75	69	64	67	64	60	66	67	72	58	72	81	76
GULF	71	62	55	60	67	81	60	72	65	59	64	61	57	64	64	69	55	68	79	74
HAMILTON	68	46	25	43	51	71	47	61	56	46	55	55	39	57	46	61	47	57	68	68
HARDEE	82	61	40	57	64	84	61	75	68	60	68	66	53	70	60	73	58	70	81	80
HENDRY	78	69	58	67	66	74	68	73	71	69	71	66	64	72	67	72	63	73	74	74
HERNANDO	73	71	74	67	77	88	67	79	72	68	70	64	68	66	74	77	61	75	89	78
HIGHLANDS	69	64	65	61	69	81	62	73	67	63	66	60	61	61	68	72	57	71	83	73
HILLSBOROUGH	98	96	98	98	92	91	99	94	98	99	98	88	98	98	97	97	89	98	94	95
HOLMES	74	52	31	49	59	82	53	70	59	51	59	61	44	62	53	64	50	63	74	75
INDIAN RIVER	104	106	114	103	111	119	98	109	103	102	102	92	102	97	108	108	90	107	120	108
JACKSON	75	57	41	55	62	80	58	71	64	56	63	62	51	65	58	68	55	66	76	76
JEFFERSON	89	65	44	63	72	95	67	83	74	64	73	73	58	77	66	79	62	77	90	89
LAFAYETTE	85	58	31	55	67	94	59	79	66	57	66	69	48	70	59	72	56	71	85	87
LAKE	84	83	82	80	85	94	78	87	81	80	80	74	78	78	83	84	70	85	94	87
LEE	95	98	107	96	102	106	93	100	96	96	95	86	96	90	100	99	84	99	108	99
LEON	89	80	84	85	76	77	99	83	92	89	93	80	90	90	88	88	84	90	81	84
LEVY	68	57	47	54	62	76	56	68	61	55	59	58	52	59	59	65	51	64	74	70
LIBERTY	87	59	32	56	67	93	60	79	69	58	68	70	50	73	59	75	58	72	85	87
MADISON	71	50	32	48	56	76	52	66	59	51	59	57	44	61	51	64	50	61	71	71
MANATEE	89	89	97	88	93	99	87	93	89	88	88	80	88	84	92	93	78	92	101	92
MARION	75	70	68	67	74	85	67	78	71	68	70	65	66	68	72	75	61	75	86	78
MARTIN	112	115	126	114	121	130	109	121	112	111	110	103	112	104	119	117	97	117	131	119
MIAMI-DADE	88	88	89	88	85	80	94	88	92	93	93	86	92	90	91	91	86	93	86	86
MONROE	108	99	89	99	104	115	101	110	101	99	101	101	97	100	103	103	90	107	110	111
NASSAU	109	102	92	100	100	109	95	103	98	97	98	92	94	100	97	101	87	100	106	107
OKALOOSA	93	89	92	91	87	88	93	89	91	91	91	82	91	92	91	91	82	91	90	90
OKEECHOBEE	74	67	59	64	68	77	65	73	68	65	67	64	62	66	67	70	58	71	77	73
ORANGE	99	95	94	98	88	87	101	92	98	99	98	88	97	98	95	96	89	98	91	93
OSCEOLA	84	79	74	79	75	77	81	80	80	80	80	75	78	80	78	79	72	82	78	80
PALM BEACH	112	121	135	120	123	121	116	118	116	119	116	104	121	110	122	118	104	119	124	116
PASCO	76	73	73	71	76	84	70	78	73	71	72	67	70	70	74	76	63	76	85	78
PINELLAS	86	87	101	88	90	93	88	89	91	88	89	77	90	86	92	93	80	90	98	89
POLK	84	77	76	76	78	87	77	83	80	76	79	72	75	78	79	83	69	81	89	83
PUTNAM	73	60	52	57	64	79	61	72	66	59	65	62	55	64	62	70	56	68	79	74
ST. JOHNS	129	135	138	136	135	137	125	131	126	129	125	117	130	125	131	127	112	128	133	132
ST. LUCIE	78	83	94	82	85	87	78	83	81	81	80	70	82	77	84	83	71	81	89	82
SANTA ROSA	99	96	86	94	94	100	88	96	90	91	90	86	88	93	90	92	80	92	96	98
SARASOTA	101	109	125	106	114	118	101	109	105	105	103	92	107	96	112	109	91	108	121	107
SEMINOLE	114	120	124	123	115	109	118	112	114	119	114	105	120	115	117	111	104	114	108	112
SUMTER	71	65	63	60	73	88	60	76	66	62	65	61	60	61	68	72	55	72	87	77
SUWANNEE	76	56	36	53	62	83	56	71	62	55	61	62	48	64	56	66	52	65	76	77
TAYLOR	75	57	44	55	62	80	58	70	64	57	63	61	52	65	58	69	55	66	77	75
UNION	80	69	56	67	67	77	67	74	70	67	70	66	63	72	67	72	61	72	76	77
VOLUSIA	80	79	88	79	82	87	78	82	81	78	80	71	79	77	82	84	71	81	90	82
WAKULLA	88	72	50	69	74	92	68	83	73	68	73	73	62	75	69	77	63	77	85	87
WALTON	85	70	55	68	76	95	68	83	73	68	73	72	63	73	71	78	63	77	89	87
WASHINGTON	75	57	40	55	63	82	57	72	63	56	62	63	50	65	58	67	53	66	77	76
FLORIDA	93	92	96	92	92	95	92	93	93	93	93	84	92	91	94	95	83	95	97	93
UNITED STATES	100	100	100	100	100	100	100	100	100	100	100	100	100	100	100	100	100	100	100	100

COUNTY	FIPS Code	CBSA Code	DMA Code	POPULATION			2000-2007 ANNUAL RATE		RACE (%)					
									White		Black		Asian/Pacific	
				2000	2007	2012	% Rate	State Rank	2000	2007	2000	2007	2000	2007
APPLING	001	00000	507	17,419	17,928	18,344	0.4	113	76.8	72.6	19.6	22.4	0.3	0.4
ATKINSON	003	20060	525	7,609	8,144	8,515	0.9	89	66.8	60.5	19.6	21.1	0.1	0.2
BACON	005	00000	507	10,103	10,452	10,622	0.5	108	81.5	78.0	15.7	18.1	0.3	0.4
BAKER	007	10500	525	4,074	4,007	3,947	-0.2	142	47.4	45.0	50.4	52.8	0.0	0.0
BALDWIN	009	33300	503	44,700	47,473	49,219	0.8	97	54.2	49.2	43.4	47.8	1.0	1.2
BANKS	011	00000	524	14,422	17,100	18,999	2.4	40	93.2	91.1	3.2	3.8	0.7	0.9
BARROW	013	12060	524	46,144	68,815	91,522	5.7	6	84.8	81.4	9.7	11.3	2.2	2.9
BARTOW	015	12060	524	76,019	95,795	109,955	3.2	28	87.8	85.0	8.7	10.2	0.5	0.7
BEN HILL	017	22340	525	17,484	17,478	17,498	0.0	134	63.3	61.0	32.6	34.9	0.3	0.3
BERRIEN	019	00000	525	16,235	17,227	17,829	0.8	97	85.5	82.4	11.4	13.4	0.4	0.5
BIBB	021	31420	503	153,887	155,181	155,730	0.1	130	50.1	45.2	47.3	51.7	1.1	1.3
BLECKLEY	023	00000	503	11,666	12,462	12,892	0.9	89	73.2	69.0	24.6	28.2	1.0	1.2
BRANTLEY	025	15260	561	14,629	16,271	17,528	1.5	61	94.4	93.0	4.0	4.8	0.1	0.1
BROOKS	027	46660	530	16,450	16,789	17,078	0.3	119	57.4	52.3	39.3	43.4	0.3	0.4
BRYAN	029	42340	507	23,417	31,504	38,499	4.2	14	82.8	79.6	14.1	16.4	0.8	1.1
BULLOCH	031	44340	507	55,983	65,115	71,854	2.1	45	68.7	64.2	28.8	32.5	0.9	1.1
BURKE	033	12260	520	22,243	23,598	24,596	0.8	97	46.9	42.0	51.0	55.4	0.3	0.3
BUTTS	035	12060	524	19,522	21,934	25,046	1.6	56	69.2	64.8	28.8	32.8	0.3	0.3
CALHOUN	037	00000	525	6,320	6,138	6,097	-0.4	147	38.3	33.9	60.6	64.7	0.1	0.1
CAMDEN	039	41220	561	43,664	49,616	54,932	1.8	50	75.0	70.8	20.1	22.9	1.1	1.4
CANDLER	043	00000	507	9,577	10,577	11,164	1.4	67	65.4	60.0	27.1	29.8	0.3	0.4
CARROLL	045	12060	524	87,268	114,060	133,324	3.8	17	80.5	76.9	16.3	18.9	0.6	0.8
CATOOSA	047	16860	575	53,282	63,372	70,966	2.4	40	96.4	95.3	1.3	1.5	0.7	1.0
CHARLTON	049	00000	561	10,282	10,867	11,128	0.8	97	68.6	64.1	29.3	33.2	0.4	0.5
CHATHAM	051	42340	507	232,048	251,527	264,380	1.1	82	55.3	50.2	40.5	44.5	1.8	2.2
CHATTAHOOCHEE	053	17980	522	14,882	14,351	14,004	-0.5	152	58.1	52.5	29.9	32.2	2.3	2.7
CHATTOOGA	055	44900	524	25,470	26,703	27,383	0.7	104	86.7	84.0	11.2	13.2	0.1	0.2
CHEROKEE	057	12060	524	141,903	213,490	280,620	5.8	5	92.4	90.0	2.5	2.9	0.8	1.1
CLARKE	059	12020	524	101,489	113,528	119,523	1.6	56	64.9	59.8	27.3	30.1	3.2	3.9
CLAY	061	00000	522	3,357	3,210	3,066	-0.6	156	38.4	33.9	60.5	64.8	0.3	0.4
CLAYTON	063	12060	524	236,517	287,882	320,323	2.7	32	37.9	33.4	51.6	53.8	4.6	5.3
CLINCH	065	00000	530	6,878	7,016	7,118	0.3	119	68.9	64.5	29.5	33.5	0.1	0.2
COBB	067	12060	524	607,751	693,135	744,791	1.8	50	72.4	67.5	18.8	21.0	3.1	3.9
COFFEE	069	20060	525	37,413	40,809	42,944	1.2	76	68.2	63.2	25.9	28.8	0.6	0.7
COLQUITT	071	34220	525	42,053	44,175	45,624	0.7	104	67.8	62.2	23.5	25.8	0.3	0.4
COLUMBIA	073	12260	520	89,288	112,770	132,145	3.3	26	82.7	79.1	11.2	13.0	3.4	4.5
COOK	075	00000	525	15,771	16,824	17,570	0.9	89	67.9	63.3	29.1	32.8	0.5	0.6
COWETA	077	12060	524	89,215	121,069	147,257	4.3	11	78.9	75.1	18.0	20.7	0.7	0.9
CRAWFORD	079	31420	503	12,495	14,289	15,123	1.9	47	72.9	68.4	23.8	27.1	0.2	0.2
CRISP	081	18380	525	21,996	22,353	22,479	0.2	125	54.1	49.0	43.4	47.7	0.7	0.9
DADE	083	16860	575	15,154	16,269	17,007	1.0	85	97.5	96.8	0.6	0.8	0.4	0.6
DAWSON	085	12060	524	15,999	21,469	25,500	4.1	15	97.2	96.3	0.4	0.4	0.4	0.5
DECATUR	087	12460	530	28,240	29,981	31,172	0.8	97	57.1	52.1	39.9	44.0	0.4	0.5
DEKALB	089	12060	524	665,865	726,977	756,859	1.2	76	35.8	31.6	54.2	56.3	4.1	4.7
DODGE	091	00000	503	19,171	19,631	19,682	0.3	119	69.0	64.5	29.4	33.4	0.2	0.3
DOOLY	093	00000	503	11,525	11,656	11,628	0.2	125	46.0	40.9	49.5	53.2	0.5	0.6
DOUGHERTY	095	10500	525	96,065	95,553	94,879	-0.1	139	37.8	33.3	60.1	64.2	0.6	0.7
DOUGLAS	097	12060	524	92,174	124,827	154,979	4.3	11	77.3	73.3	18.5	21.2	1.2	1.5
EARLY	099	00000	606	12,354	12,219	12,075	-0.2	142	50.3	45.4	48.1	52.7	0.2	0.3
ECHOLS	101	46660	530	3,754	4,506	5,145	2.6	34	77.1	70.9	6.9	7.5	0.1	0.1
EFFINGHAM	103	42340	507	37,535	50,502	62,836	4.2	14	84.7	81.7	13.0	15.2	0.5	0.6
ELBERT	105	00000	567	20,511	21,171	21,577	0.4	113	66.9	62.3	30.9	34.8	0.3	0.3
EMANUEL	107	00000	520	21,837	22,719	23,508	0.5	108	63.7	58.8	33.3	37.1	0.2	0.3
EVANS	109	00000	507	10,495	11,450	12,107	1.2	76	61.7	56.3	33.0	36.4	0.3	0.4
FANNIN	111	00000	524	19,798	26,888	32,311	4.3	11	98.0	97.4	0.1	0.1	0.2	0.3
FAYETTE	113	12060	524	91,263	109,534	122,557	2.5	37	83.9	80.6	11.5	13.3	2.4	3.2
FLOYD	115	40660	524	90,565	96,522	100,003	0.9	89	81.3	77.4	13.3	15.3	1.0	1.3
FORSYTH	117	12060	524	98,407	158,051	216,067	6.8	3	95.0	93.2	0.7	0.8	0.8	1.1
FRANKLIN	119	00000	567	20,285	22,128	23,353	1.2	76	89.5	87.3	8.8	10.5	0.3	0.4
FULTON	121	12060	524	816,006	957,637	1,062,254	2.2	43	48.1	43.2	44.6	47.7	3.1	3.7
GILMER	123	00000	524	23,456	30,732	35,605	3.8	17	93.6	91.0	0.3	0.3	0.5	0.7
GLASCOCK	125	00000	520	2,556	2,747	2,841	1.0	85	90.6	88.6	8.3	9.9	0.0	0.0
GLYNN	127	15260	561	67,568	75,027	80,577	1.5	61	70.7	66.3	26.5	29.9	0.7	0.8
GORDON	129	15660	524	44,104	53,264	60,294	2.6	34	89.7	86.2	3.5	4.0	0.6	0.8
GRADY	131	00000	530	23,659	24,999	25,709	0.8	97	64.6	59.5	30.1	33.5	0.3	0.4
GREENE	133	00000	524	14,406	16,396	17,653	1.8	50	53.0	48.0	44.4	48.7	0.3	0.4
GWINNETT	135	12060	524	588,448	800,680	964,588	4.3	11	72.7	67.5	13.3	14.6	7.2	8.9
HABERSHAM	137	18460	524	35,902	42,852	48,743	2.5	37	88.9	85.7	4.5	5.2	2.0	2.6
HALL	139	23580	524	139,277	176,932	204,351	3.4	25	80.8	75.8	7.3	8.0	1.5	1.9
HANCOCK	141	33300	503	10,076	9,859	9,769	-0.3	144	21.5	18.4	77.8	80.7	0.1	0.1
HARALSON	143	12060	524	25,690	28,925	31,026	1.6	56	93.0	91.4	5.4	6.5	0.3	0.5
HARRIS	145	17980	522	23,695	29,794	35,097	3.2	28	78.4	74.8	19.5	22.5	0.5	0.7
HART	147	00000	567	22,997	24,916	26,250	1.1	82	79.1	75.5	19.4	22.5	0.5	0.7
HEARD	149	12060	524	11,012	11,982	12,456	1.2	76	87.5	85.0	10.8	12.8	0.2	0.2
HENRY	151	12060	524	119,341	196,080	262,017	7.1	2	81.4	77.9	14.7	17.0	1.8	2.3
HOUSTON	153	47580	503	110,765	135,930	154,482	2.9	30	70.6	66.1	24.8	28.0	1.7	2.1
IRWIN	155	22340	525	9,931	10,161	10,162	0.3	119	72.0	67.6	25.9	29.5	0.3	0.4
GEORGIA							2.3		65.1	62.1	28.7	29.8	2.2	2.7
UNITED STATES							1.2		75.1	72.7	12.3	12.6	3.8	4.5

COUNTY	% HISPANIC ORIGIN		2007 AGE DISTRIBUTION (%)										MEDIAN AGE	% 2007 Males	% 2007 Females
	2000	2007	0-4	5-9	10-14	15-19	20-24	25-44	45-64	65-84	85+	18+	2007		
APPLING	4.5	6.2	7.7	7.3	6.6	6.0	6.9	27.3	26.1	10.5	1.5	74.7	36.3	49.7	50.3
ATKINSON	17.0	22.4	10.1	9.8	7.2	5.9	6.7	29.4	21.5	8.3	1.1	69.5	31.8	49.8	50.2
BACON	3.4	4.6	7.6	7.9	6.1	5.5	6.1	29.0	24.3	11.8	1.8	75.1	36.6	49.1	50.9
BAKER	2.7	2.8	7.6	7.1	6.7	6.6	5.4	28.2	25.4	11.5	1.6	74.8	36.8	46.3	53.7
BALDWIN	1.4	1.7	5.2	4.7	5.4	8.1	9.3	30.8	24.7	10.3	1.4	80.7	35.9	54.1	45.9
BANKS	3.4	4.9	7.6	7.9	6.6	5.8	5.3	29.8	26.2	9.7	1.1	74.5	36.7	50.6	49.4
BARROW	3.2	4.4	8.4	7.6	7.3	6.5	5.7	33.2	22.6	7.6	1.1	72.5	34.2	50.0	50.0
BARTOW	3.3	4.6	7.9	7.4	7.2	6.7	5.9	30.6	24.7	8.6	1.1	73.4	35.4	49.5	50.5
BEN HILL	4.6	4.6	7.4	6.9	6.7	6.8	6.5	26.6	25.5	11.6	2.0	74.8	36.3	48.3	51.7
BERRIEN	2.4	3.3	7.3	7.2	6.5	6.8	6.0	27.9	25.5	11.2	1.6	74.8	36.8	49.1	50.9
BIBB	1.3	1.6	7.2	6.9	7.0	7.5	6.7	26.3	25.1	11.2	2.0	74.6	36.1	46.3	53.7
BLECKLEY	0.9	1.2	6.6	6.3	6.9	9.9	6.6	25.9	23.6	12.1	2.0	75.3	36.6	48.7	51.3
BRANTLEY	1.0	1.4	7.6	7.0	6.6	7.2	6.8	28.2	25.7	10.0	1.0	74.4	36.2	50.3	49.7
BROOKS	3.1	4.0	7.1	6.6	6.6	6.4	6.7	25.4	26.2	12.6	2.4	75.8	38.1	47.9	52.1
BRYAN	2.0	2.6	7.6	7.2	6.8	8.0	9.1	26.4	26.5	7.5	0.9	73.5	34.6	49.5	50.5
BULLOCH	1.9	2.5	6.0	5.1	5.4	12.7	16.6	25.0	19.8	8.2	1.3	80.2	27.5	48.9	51.1
BURKE	1.4	1.8	8.2	7.6	7.9	7.4	7.5	25.0	25.5	9.5	1.5	71.6	34.3	47.4	52.6
BUTTS	1.4	1.8	7.0	6.8	6.5	6.5	6.1	27.8	27.4	10.5	1.3	75.8	37.8	48.8	51.2
CALHOUN	3.0	3.2	6.2	6.0	5.0	5.0	8.4	33.1	24.2	10.1	1.9	79.8	36.8	57.7	42.3
CAMDEN	3.6	4.8	9.2	7.4	7.5	8.1	8.2	33.4	20.4	5.2	0.5	70.8	30.1	50.7	49.3
CANDLER	9.2	12.3	7.4	7.3	6.2	6.8	6.6	26.4	24.6	12.2	2.6	75.0	36.7	50.5	49.5
CARROLL	2.6	3.5	7.3	6.8	6.7	7.9	8.0	29.2	23.7	9.2	1.3	75.3	34.1	49.0	51.0
CATOOSA	1.2	1.6	6.8	6.3	6.7	6.3	5.5	28.9	26.4	11.6	1.5	76.3	38.2	48.5	51.5
CHARLTON	0.8	1.0	6.9	6.2	6.0	8.3	8.7	28.9	23.7	9.9	1.3	76.2	35.2	53.8	46.2
CHATHAM	2.3	2.9	6.7	6.1	6.6	7.1	7.6	28.0	24.7	11.5	1.9	76.7	35.9	48.5	51.5
CHATTAHOOCHEE	10.4	13.3	8.6	8.2	7.4	10.6	21.9	34.9	6.2	2.0	0.1	72.6	23.5	63.8	36.2
CHATTOOGA	2.1	2.9	6.7	6.9	5.6	5.4	6.6	29.2	25.3	12.4	1.9	77.7	37.8	51.8	48.2
CHEROKEE	5.4	7.6	7.9	8.2	7.2	6.5	5.0	31.5	26.1	6.8	0.8	72.7	36.0	50.0	50.0
CLARKE	6.3	8.3	5.2	4.7	4.2	10.8	21.4	27.6	17.5	7.4	1.3	83.1	26.7	48.9	51.1
CLAY	1.0	1.1	7.4	6.4	6.5	5.4	6.9	19.3	29.2	15.8	3.0	76.4	42.7	45.2	54.8
CLAYTON	7.5	9.2	8.2	7.1	7.7	7.9	8.5	31.7	22.2	6.2	0.6	72.3	31.5	48.6	51.4
CLINCH	0.8	1.0	7.5	7.3	6.8	6.4	5.8	28.0	25.5	11.2	1.4	74.0	36.4	50.0	50.0
COBB	7.7	10.1	7.1	7.0	7.0	6.8	6.2	33.3	25.1	6.5	0.9	74.7	35.0	49.8	50.2
COFFEE	6.8	9.1	7.9	7.5	7.0	6.8	7.5	30.3	22.8	8.8	1.4	73.7	33.5	50.2	49.8
COLQUITT	10.8	14.5	7.9	7.6	6.6	6.5	7.0	28.8	23.2	10.5	1.8	74.1	34.7	50.1	49.9
COLUMBIA	2.6	3.4	7.0	6.8	7.6	7.5	6.8	27.2	28.5	7.6	1.0	73.7	36.9	49.0	51.0
COOK	3.1	4.1	8.0	7.8	6.6	7.2	5.5	28.0	23.2	11.9	1.8	73.2	35.7	48.2	51.8
COWETA	3.1	4.2	8.2	7.8	7.5	6.7	5.8	30.5	24.6	8.0	1.0	72.5	35.4	49.6	50.4
CRAWFORD	2.4	3.4	6.8	6.5	6.9	7.0	5.7	28.7	28.0	9.6	0.9	75.6	38.0	50.2	49.8
CRISP	1.7	2.3	8.0	7.2	7.2	6.5	7.0	25.6	25.0	11.5	2.0	73.7	36.1	47.3	52.7
DADE	0.9	1.3	5.9	5.9	6.4	7.6	7.5	26.4	27.7	11.3	1.3	78.2	37.6	49.8	50.2
DAWSON	1.6	2.3	7.0	7.0	6.9	5.6	4.1	29.8	28.6	10.3	0.8	75.7	39.3	50.3	49.7
DECATUR	3.2	4.2	7.8	7.5	6.9	6.7	6.5	26.8	24.8	11.1	2.0	73.7	36.2	48.2	51.8
DEKALB	7.9	9.6	6.9	6.6	6.6	6.7	7.3	34.2	23.2	7.4	1.2	76.1	34.1	48.8	51.2
DODGE	1.3	1.7	6.3	5.9	6.4	7.7	6.3	28.5	25.1	11.7	1.9	76.1	37.5	52.3	47.7
DOOLY	4.7	6.0	7.1	6.6	5.9	6.0	7.2	30.5	25.2	9.9	1.6	76.9	36.1	53.4	46.6
DOUGHERTY	1.3	1.6	7.6	7.1	7.0	8.1	7.8	26.6	23.6	10.6	1.7	73.9	33.8	46.8	53.2
DOUGLAS	2.9	3.8	7.2	6.6	6.8	6.8	7.1	30.0	26.6	7.9	0.9	75.3	36.0	49.1	50.9
EARLY	1.2	1.5	7.4	6.9	7.2	7.0	6.3	23.7	25.8	12.8	2.8	74.0	38.5	47.1	52.9
ECHOLS	19.7	26.3	8.9	7.4	6.2	6.6	9.9	33.5	19.4	7.5	0.7	73.9	30.2	54.5	45.5
EFFINGHAM	1.4	1.9	8.0	7.4	7.1	6.9	6.7	29.9	25.6	7.6	0.8	73.3	34.9	49.6	50.4
ELBERT	2.4	3.1	6.6	6.4	6.2	6.3	5.9	26.5	26.8	13.2	2.0	76.8	39.0	48.3	51.7
EMANUEL	3.4	4.6	7.2	6.6	6.1	7.1	6.9	26.9	25.9	11.3	1.9	75.5	36.6	48.5	51.5
EVANS	6.0	8.0	7.2	6.7	6.6	7.0	7.2	29.0	23.7	10.7	1.9	75.2	35.5	49.0	51.0
FANNIN	0.7	0.9	5.4	5.6	4.8	5.2	4.4	24.0	30.9	17.5	2.2	80.9	45.4	48.5	51.5
FAYETTE	2.8	3.7	5.8	6.5	8.3	7.9	5.1	24.2	32.7	8.4	1.1	74.1	40.6	49.0	51.0
FLOYD	5.5	7.5	6.6	6.3	6.3	7.1	6.8	27.5	25.0	12.4	2.1	77.0	37.4	48.7	51.3
FORSYTH	5.6	7.7	9.2	9.9	7.5	5.5	4.2	32.8	23.6	6.5	0.7	69.9	35.6	50.8	49.2
FRANKLIN	0.9	1.3	6.5	6.1	6.5	6.2	6.0	26.3	27.0	13.4	2.0	77.5	39.6	49.1	50.9
FULTON	5.9	7.4	6.8	6.6	6.7	7.0	7.2	33.0	23.9	7.6	1.3	76.1	34.2	49.4	50.6
GILMER	7.7	10.8	7.2	7.5	6.2	5.1	4.6	28.3	26.8	12.9	1.3	75.9	38.9	50.9	49.1
GLASCOCK	0.5	0.7	6.8	7.0	6.0	4.6	5.6	24.8	27.5	14.7	3.1	77.5	41.4	48.3	51.7
GLYNN	3.0	3.8	6.5	6.2	6.3	7.2	6.6	24.2	27.8	12.9	2.2	76.6	39.7	48.0	52.0
GORDON	7.4	10.5	7.3	7.1	6.6	5.9	5.7	31.5	24.6	10.0	1.2	75.3	36.2	50.0	50.0
GRADY	5.2	6.9	7.3	7.2	6.5	6.1	6.3	27.1	26.4	11.3	1.8	75.2	37.3	47.8	52.2
GREENE	2.9	3.7	6.7	6.4	5.8	5.7	5.6	22.9	32.4	12.7	1.7	77.7	42.6	48.6	51.4
GWINNETT	10.9	14.0	7.9	7.7	7.5	6.9	6.7	32.7	24.7	5.4	0.6	72.6	34.1	50.2	49.8
HABERSHAM	7.7	10.4	6.3	6.2	5.9	6.7	6.5	27.2	26.7	12.6	1.8	77.9	38.7	51.2	48.8
HALL	19.6	25.4	8.3	8.1	6.7	6.2	6.2	32.2	22.6	8.6	1.1	73.2	33.6	51.1	48.9
HANCOCK	0.5	0.6	6.0	5.4	5.9	6.1	7.5	29.6	26.3	11.6	1.7	79.0	38.0	53.3	46.7
HARALSON	0.6	0.8	7.1	6.9	6.8	6.4	5.7	28.5	25.3	11.8	1.6	75.3	37.8	49.2	50.8
HARRIS	1.1	1.4	5.8	5.9	7.3	6.0	5.4	25.2	32.0	10.8	1.4	77.1	41.5	49.8	50.2
HART	0.9	1.1	6.3	6.3	5.9	5.9	5.1	26.1	27.6	14.9	2.0	78.0	41.3	49.7	50.3
HEARD	1.1	1.4	8.0	7.8	7.9	6.5	5.4	28.1	25.0	9.7	1.4	72.1	36.0	49.4	50.6
HENRY	2.3	3.0	8.1	7.7	7.5	7.0	5.8	30.8	24.9	7.4	0.8	72.3	35.4	49.3	50.7
HOUSTON	3.0	3.9	7.4	6.4	7.2	7.7	8.4	28.3	24.9	8.5	1.0	74.3	34.5	49.1	50.9
IRWIN	2.0	2.8	7.1	7.0	6.5	9.4	6.8	28.2	20.4	11.7	2.3	72.9	35.6	50.0	50.0
GEORGIA	5.3	6.9	7.3	7.0	6.9	7.0	7.1	30.3	24.6	8.7	1.3	74.8	35.0	49.4	50.6
UNITED STATES	12.5	15.0	6.9	6.5	6.8	7.1	7.0	27.6	25.4	10.7	1.9	75.6	36.7	49.2	50.8

COUNTY	HOUSEHOLDS					FAMILIES			MEDIAN HOUSEHOLD INCOME			
	2000	2007	2012	% Annual Rate 2000-2007	2007 Average HH Size	2000	2007	% Annual Rate 2000-2007	2007	2012	2007 National Rank	2007 State Rank
APPLING	6,606	6,864	7,058	0.5	2.57	4,856	4,901	0.1	36,004	40,817	2275	98
ATKINSON	2,717	2,926	3,065	1.0	2.77	1,981	2,071	0.6	31,501	35,128	2799	139
BACON	3,833	4,001	4,105	0.6	2.54	2,815	2,854	0.2	31,857	36,215	2775	136
BAKER	1,514	1,510	1,496	0.0	2.65	1,094	1,058	-0.5	36,111	40,952	2254	97
BALDWIN	14,758	16,036	16,913	1.2	2.45	9,843	10,312	0.6	42,935	49,545	1337	56
BANKS	5,364	6,390	7,120	2.4	2.67	4,160	4,835	2.1	45,884	51,300	1016	43
BARROW	16,354	24,401	32,469	5.7	2.80	12,542	18,237	5.3	55,803	64,892	371	23
BARTOW	27,176	34,446	39,613	3.3	2.75	21,028	25,998	3.0	54,086	63,135	447	26
BEN HILL	6,673	6,771	6,823	0.2	2.53	4,629	4,545	-0.3	33,409	38,416	2615	120
BERRIEN	6,261	6,769	7,062	1.1	2.52	4,541	4,762	0.7	35,884	40,583	2298	100
BIBB	59,667	60,389	60,847	0.2	2.48	39,824	38,865	-0.3	43,433	50,850	1280	53
BLECKLEY	4,372	4,693	4,898	1.0	2.48	3,122	3,248	0.5	39,646	45,134	1760	72
BRANTLEY	5,436	6,227	6,799	1.9	2.60	4,153	4,633	1.5	35,751	40,027	2324	103
BROOKS	6,155	6,430	6,615	0.6	2.55	4,371	4,423	0.2	32,513	36,760	2704	130
BRYAN	8,089	11,072	13,651	4.4	2.83	6,510	8,720	4.1	60,219	69,496	260	16
BULLOCH	20,743	24,502	27,403	2.3	2.49	12,341	13,942	1.7	36,690	42,642	2169	94
BURKE	7,934	8,554	8,987	1.0	2.72	5,803	6,075	0.6	32,833	37,343	2673	127
BUTTS	6,455	8,125	9,371	3.2	2.68	4,867	5,961	2.8	47,498	53,613	863	39
CALHOUN	1,962	1,930	1,936	-0.2	2.49	1,347	1,280	-0.7	29,345	33,570	2940	151
CAMDEN	14,705	17,255	19,195	2.2	2.82	11,375	13,017	1.9	51,880	60,687	557	30
CANDLER	3,375	3,691	3,889	1.2	2.74	2,426	2,572	0.8	30,082	34,009	2905	146
CARROLL	31,568	41,563	48,908	3.9	2.66	23,026	29,427	3.4	47,385	53,676	874	41
CATOOSA	20,425	24,539	27,665	2.6	2.55	15,391	17,995	2.2	49,191	56,652	733	32
CHARLTON	3,342	3,546	3,673	0.8	2.69	2,499	2,580	0.4	33,313	37,821	2628	121
CHATHAM	89,865	98,364	104,312	1.3	2.45	59,431	62,718	0.7	47,952	56,393	822	38
CHATTAHOOCHEE	2,932	2,853	2,782	-0.4	3.32	2,623	2,523	-0.5	45,470	51,654	1055	44
CHATTOOGA	9,577	10,256	10,617	0.9	2.44	6,836	7,094	0.5	37,112	42,171	2113	91
CHEROKEE	49,495	75,028	98,906	5.9	2.83	39,194	58,060	5.6	78,587	91,646	61	4
CLARKE	39,706	45,129	47,950	1.8	2.31	19,678	21,178	1.0	35,571	41,466	2356	105
CLAY	1,347	1,333	1,291	-0.1	2.36	928	888	-0.6	26,173	30,162	3064	159
CLAYTON	82,243	97,592	107,980	2.4	2.91	59,190	68,107	2.0	54,324	63,961	432	25
CLINCH	2,512	2,636	2,706	0.7	2.53	1,823	1,855	0.2	31,961	36,307	2766	135
COBB	227,487	256,333	274,818	1.7	2.66	156,579	170,492	1.2	76,420	91,267	77	5
COFFEE	13,354	14,548	15,409	1.2	2.67	9,791	10,357	0.8	36,607	41,386	2180	95
COLQUITT	15,495	16,433	17,056	0.8	2.61	11,066	11,371	0.4	33,993	38,574	2551	117
COLUMBIA	31,120	40,451	47,873	3.7	2.77	25,348	32,280	3.4	72,932	84,643	104	6
COOK	5,882	6,351	6,675	1.1	2.61	4,280	4,487	0.7	32,716	37,083	2681	128
COWETA	31,442	42,772	52,098	4.3	2.81	24,699	32,810	4.0	66,291	77,568	160	11
CRAWFORD	4,461	5,177	5,513	2.1	2.74	3,457	3,914	1.7	44,600	50,197	1147	47
CRISP	8,337	8,585	8,693	0.4	2.54	5,872	5,853	0.0	32,336	37,147	2727	133
DADE	5,633	6,171	6,523	1.3	2.50	4,264	4,548	0.9	41,409	46,483	1531	63
DAWSON	6,069	8,320	9,996	4.4	2.56	4,687	6,266	4.1	57,763	64,924	311	19
DECATUR	10,380	11,170	11,704	1.0	2.61	7,543	7,877	0.6	35,199	40,420	2404	109
DEKALB	249,339	275,348	286,624	1.4	2.59	156,670	166,124	0.8	64,671	77,415	172	12
DODGE	7,062	7,245	7,326	0.4	2.43	4,885	4,845	-0.1	33,769	38,002	2576	118
DOOLY	3,909	3,973	3,990	0.2	2.58	2,767	2,723	-0.2	33,294	37,788	2630	122
DOUGHERTY	35,552	36,368	36,478	0.3	2.51	24,293	23,998	-0.2	38,574	44,624	1921	82
DOUGLAS	32,822	45,343	56,806	4.6	2.73	24,912	33,513	4.2	62,532	73,255	201	14
EARLY	4,695	4,749	4,737	0.2	2.52	3,294	3,225	-0.3	30,935	35,027	2838	142
ECHOLS	1,264	1,496	1,697	2.4	3.01	937	1,078	2.0	30,637	33,339	2870	145
EFFINGHAM	13,151	17,946	22,474	4.4	2.80	10,490	14,000	4.1	56,917	66,321	331	21
ELBERT	8,004	8,382	8,595	0.6	2.49	5,768	5,858	0.2	35,186	39,787	2406	110
EMANUEL	8,045	8,577	8,945	0.9	2.57	5,749	5,941	0.5	29,686	33,375	2925	148
EVANS	3,778	4,147	4,412	1.3	2.60	2,680	2,849	0.8	30,774	34,850	2856	144
FANNIN	8,369	11,648	14,158	4.7	2.29	6,011	8,109	4.2	36,796	41,717	2151	93
FAYETTE	31,524	38,149	42,870	2.7	2.86	25,990	30,846	2.4	91,656	112,189	15	1
FLOYD	34,028	36,334	37,719	0.9	2.54	24,214	25,051	0.5	43,951	51,303	1215	49
FORSYTH	34,565	55,028	74,996	6.6	2.86	28,106	43,830	6.3	90,724	110,717	16	2
FRANKLIN	7,888	8,717	9,253	1.4	2.47	5,696	6,105	1.0	38,993	44,337	1854	78
FULTON	321,242	376,607	418,703	2.2	2.46	185,721	207,926	1.6	63,123	77,423	193	13
GILMER	9,071	11,943	13,884	3.9	2.55	6,692	8,561	3.5	41,554	46,710	1510	61
GLASCOCK	1,004	1,101	1,151	1.3	2.39	716	761	0.8	35,822	40,961	2309	102
GLYNN	27,208	30,110	32,488	1.4	2.44	18,401	19,653	0.9	48,566	56,383	775	33
GORDON	16,173	19,642	22,288	2.7	2.69	12,261	14,497	2.3	46,869	52,901	920	42
GRADY	8,797	9,405	9,715	0.9	2.63	6,508	6,760	0.5	34,565	39,137	2490	113
GREENE	5,477	6,464	7,067	2.3	2.51	4,040	4,631	1.9	41,901	48,327	1459	59
GWINNETT	202,317	270,943	324,544	4.1	2.93	152,296	198,467	3.7	79,730	96,794	55	3
HABERSHAM	13,259	16,160	18,499	2.8	2.55	9,854	11,675	2.4	43,435	49,510	1278	52
HALL	47,381	58,958	67,705	3.1	2.96	36,021	43,654	2.7	56,358	65,625	351	22
HANCOCK	3,237	3,330	3,343	0.4	2.57	2,311	2,304	0.0	26,252	30,191	3062	157
HARALSON	9,826	11,159	12,022	1.8	2.56	7,196	7,934	1.4	38,452	43,365	1939	83
HARRIS	8,822	11,209	13,281	3.4	2.63	6,986	8,676	3.0	58,096	66,173	304	18
HART	9,106	10,009	10,651	1.3	2.42	6,615	7,058	0.9	39,327	44,261	1817	76
HEARD	4,043	4,440	4,633	1.3	2.67	3,042	3,250	0.9	40,037	44,901	1722	70
HENRY	41,373	68,211	91,399	7.1	2.86	33,323	53,771	6.8	72,290	83,312	108	7
HOUSTON	40,911	50,948	58,338	3.1	2.61	30,221	36,567	2.7	55,427	64,957	386	24
IRWIN	3,644	3,704	3,725	0.2	2.59	2,698	2,663	-0.2	36,198	41,045	2243	96
GEORGIA				2.3	2.65			2.0	55,102	65,884		
UNITED STATES				1.2	2.59			1.0	53,154	62,503		

COUNTY	2007 Per Capita Income	2007 HH Income Base	2007 HOUSEHOLD INCOME DISTRIBUTION (%)					2007 Home Value Base	2007 HOME VALUE DISTRIBUTION (%)					2007 Median Home Value
			Less than $25,000	$25,000 to $49,999	$50,000 to $99,999	$100,000 to $149,999	$150,000 or More		Less than $50,000	$50,000 to $89,999	$90,000 to $174,999	$175,000 to $399,999	$400,000 or More	
APPLING	18,677	6,864	36.6	27.3	26.7	6.9	2.5	5,465	30.8	28.4	30.1	9.6	1.1	76,107
ATKINSON	14,892	2,926	42.1	28.8	22.6	4.5	1.9	2,209	50.2	25.6	16.7	6.7	0.8	49,778
BACON	17,346	4,001	41.1	28.3	24.5	3.4	2.6	3,040	32.5	30.9	27.6	7.4	1.5	68,921
BAKER	18,913	1,510	36.2	28.8	26.2	6.2	2.6	1,184	37.1	26.1	31.0	5.7	0.2	69,667
BALDWIN	22,356	16,036	28.4	27.9	30.1	8.2	5.4	10,776	18.9	22.2	38.5	17.2	3.2	103,545
BANKS	20,683	6,390	25.2	29.8	34.6	6.9	3.6	5,213	14.1	19.5	37.1	23.9	5.4	118,561
BARROW	22,991	24,401	18.7	24.2	41.8	10.8	4.5	18,685	6.4	9.5	51.0	29.3	3.8	147,549
BARTOW	23,459	34,446	18.0	26.9	40.0	10.2	4.9	26,221	9.7	15.7	45.9	25.2	3.6	130,284
BEN HILL	17,875	6,771	39.6	26.1	24.9	7.2	2.3	4,597	29.0	30.6	30.3	9.1	0.9	77,670
BERRIEN	19,123	6,769	34.6	32.6	25.7	4.5	2.6	5,162	31.3	25.1	32.5	9.5	1.6	76,839
BIBB	24,226	60,389	30.8	24.2	29.4	9.9	5.6	36,207	12.8	25.6	41.3	16.8	3.4	106,199
BLECKLEY	20,025	4,693	32.8	27.6	29.5	7.7	2.5	3,615	26.4	24.0	37.7	10.6	1.3	89,320
BRANTLEY	16,951	6,227	32.9	33.9	27.4	4.3	1.6	5,384	35.6	27.5	24.1	10.9	2.0	70,332
BROOKS	17,228	6,430	39.2	28.9	25.1	4.7	2.2	4,978	23.7	24.0	32.0	16.9	3.4	94,440
BRYAN	25,773	11,072	20.4	22.7	34.4	14.6	7.9	8,649	10.9	10.2	27.6	40.9	10.4	178,367
BULLOCH	20,456	24,502	35.7	26.8	25.6	7.8	4.1	14,509	19.2	16.7	38.2	22.1	3.7	115,037
BURKE	16,209	8,554	41.4	25.3	25.3	5.9	2.1	6,504	28.3	28.9	32.3	8.9	1.6	80,412
BUTTS	21,343	8,124	23.7	28.6	35.7	8.2	3.8	6,283	8.5	13.9	51.9	21.7	4.1	129,818
CALHOUN	15,513	1,930	43.1	28.9	22.2	4.0	1.8	1,409	38.7	29.7	25.0	6.2	0.5	66,313
CAMDEN	21,228	17,255	19.9	27.3	39.7	9.5	3.6	11,050	14.0	16.0	48.5	18.8	2.9	118,255
CANDLER	14,979	3,691	42.9	27.7	22.8	5.2	1.3	2,744	31.8	30.1	24.7	11.2	2.3	71,344
CARROLL	22,171	41,563	26.5	26.0	33.7	9.3	4.4	29,700	11.2	16.9	44.2	23.4	4.2	124,501
CATOOSA	22,391	24,539	23.1	27.6	36.8	9.3	3.1	19,086	9.2	16.4	48.1	23.2	3.0	125,919
CHARLTON	16,008	3,546	38.0	29.4	25.8	5.1	1.7	2,879	34.6	24.8	29.2	10.5	0.9	74,414
CHATHAM	27,336	98,364	26.4	25.1	30.6	10.3	7.5	60,483	6.1	10.0	37.6	33.4	12.8	166,186
CHATTAHOOCHEE	15,499	2,853	17.7	37.6	36.5	6.7	1.6	811	24.7	30.0	35.1	7.3	3.0	85,787
CHATTOOGA	18,209	10,256	33.0	31.3	29.3	4.9	1.5	7,823	24.1	28.7	34.0	11.4	1.9	85,883
CHEROKEE	34,152	75,028	9.5	17.1	39.0	20.3	14.2	63,283	3.2	3.2	24.9	56.8	11.9	212,174
CLARKE	22,403	45,129	38.4	24.6	24.6	6.9	5.4	19,440	11.3	10.3	40.7	31.8	5.8	143,234
CLAY	19,325	1,333	48.7	26.0	18.2	3.0	4.1	1,005	42.8	26.3	21.7	6.6	2.7	59,797
CLAYTON	22,250	97,589	15.6	29.3	39.5	11.1	4.5	59,876	4.6	8.8	62.9	22.2	1.3	132,135
CLINCH	16,122	2,636	42.5	29.1	22.8	3.4	2.3	1,945	36.5	30.3	25.9	4.6	2.6	65,980
COBB	37,199	256,333	10.1	18.4	36.7	18.7	16.1	176,323	2.5	2.4	30.1	52.6	12.4	212,592
COFFEE	18,631	14,548	33.4	31.6	26.1	5.7	3.3	10,962	33.3	27.6	28.6	9.2	1.4	73,426
COLQUITT	17,609	16,433	37.5	28.8	26.0	5.0	2.7	11,188	28.1	27.3	31.4	11.0	2.2	81,179
COLUMBIA	31,975	40,451	11.3	19.3	39.5	18.1	11.8	33,517	5.7	7.2	40.4	39.0	7.7	167,069
COOK	16,225	6,351	37.9	31.9	23.6	5.2	1.4	4,793	26.4	31.5	30.5	10.2	1.3	78,955
COWETA	28,554	42,772	14.6	19.9	39.7	16.7	9.0	33,639	5.2	6.3	36.8	45.1	6.6	178,606
CRAWFORD	19,224	5,177	27.9	28.2	34.2	7.1	2.6	4,387	22.0	24.4	43.2	9.8	0.7	95,661
CRISP	18,112	8,585	41.6	24.9	23.5	7.3	2.7	5,323	23.8	25.5	34.3	13.5	2.8	91,106
DADE	20,383	6,171	28.9	31.1	31.0	6.2	2.9	5,002	20.7	20.6	38.9	17.5	2.5	103,497
DAWSON	27,414	8,320	17.6	25.4	37.6	13.1	6.2	6,848	6.4	8.1	29.1	39.0	17.5	196,429
DECATUR	18,479	11,170	36.8	28.3	26.1	5.8	3.1	8,187	21.4	28.1	34.5	13.6	2.4	90,735
DEKALB	33,100	275,348	14.2	21.9	37.5	14.0	12.4	162,977	1.2	4.1	40.2	41.8	12.8	186,676
DODGE	18,767	7,245	38.9	30.1	21.7	6.4	2.9	5,398	37.1	28.5	24.2	8.5	1.6	67,622
DOOLY	17,906	3,973	39.0	27.3	26.1	4.4	3.3	2,880	26.7	32.1	30.6	9.6	1.0	76,458
DOUGHERTY	21,508	36,368	35.1	25.7	26.9	7.5	4.7	19,988	15.5	31.9	38.4	12.1	2.1	93,123
DOUGLAS	27,456	45,343	14.2	23.0	39.8	15.9	7.1	34,222	5.9	6.3	51.1	32.2	4.5	146,585
EARLY	17,774	4,749	44.4	25.8	20.4	6.5	2.8	3,488	34.2	30.2	27.6	6.8	1.3	70,171
ECHOLS	16,270	1,496	41.0	29.5	22.5	3.5	3.5	1,142	25.4	24.4	31.6	18.6	0.0	90,323
EFFINGHAM	23,962	17,946	17.5	24.5	40.9	11.6	5.5	14,940	9.6	13.4	32.5	38.3	6.2	159,119
ELBERT	17,755	8,382	37.6	30.2	25.5	4.9	1.8	6,416	24.5	27.8	33.5	12.1	2.0	85,280
EMANUEL	16,571	8,577	44.9	26.4	20.7	5.5	2.5	6,170	30.1	33.8	26.7	8.3	1.1	70,984
EVANS	15,420	4,147	42.8	30.7	21.2	3.7	1.7	3,020	32.9	24.6	30.6	10.1	1.8	76,188
FANNIN	20,422	11,648	33.9	32.1	26.4	5.4	2.2	9,666	13.9	18.5	38.0	24.0	5.6	119,680
FAYETTE	41,578	38,149	6.9	12.6	35.4	22.0	23.1	33,139	4.0	1.4	14.7	62.0	17.9	248,649
FLOYD	22,251	36,334	27.4	28.0	32.0	8.2	4.3	24,734	11.2	22.5	43.1	19.2	4.0	113,788
FORSYTH	41,852	55,028	9.4	13.2	32.5	21.8	23.2	48,521	4.1	3.7	15.0	53.1	24.1	270,433
FRANKLIN	19,777	8,717	31.9	30.1	30.5	4.7	2.8	6,950	17.5	24.2	36.9	15.6	5.8	104,303
FULTON	41,376	376,600	20.8	19.9	27.6	13.4	18.4	199,793	2.1	8.2	27.5	33.9	28.2	235,108
GILMER	20,498	11,943	28.3	31.8	30.4	6.2	3.2	9,450	16.2	18.6	34.4	26.6	4.2	125,726
GLASCOCK	18,055	1,101	37.8	29.7	24.8	6.1	1.6	885	31.0	32.1	26.7	8.0	2.3	75,000
GLYNN	27,241	30,110	26.0	25.1	30.3	12.0	6.8	20,116	8.8	14.5	30.4	29.1	17.3	161,096
GORDON	21,575	19,642	24.8	28.1	35.4	8.2	3.5	14,354	13.0	15.2	46.3	21.3	4.2	120,756
GRADY	17,298	9,405	38.1	28.7	25.0	5.8	2.4	6,987	22.3	27.0	32.8	14.5	3.4	91,177
GREENE	29,276	6,464	32.6	24.5	25.1	8.1	9.7	4,991	21.8	19.3	23.1	11.0	24.7	108,666
GWINNETT	33,348	270,943	8.0	17.0	38.4	21.4	15.2	198,624	2.8	1.3	24.2	62.8	8.8	214,063
HABERSHAM	21,553	16,160	27.4	29.4	32.4	7.1	3.7	12,472	11.8	16.0	39.2	27.5	5.5	133,027
HALL	24,324	58,958	18.8	24.4	36.8	12.8	7.3	42,405	8.1	8.1	36.0	36.4	11.4	169,135
HANCOCK	14,501	3,330	48.0	28.6	18.3	3.8	1.3	2,541	35.4	32.2	24.8	6.8	0.8	66,949
HARALSON	19,161	11,159	32.5	30.1	29.1	5.9	2.4	8,510	16.8	25.7	41.9	13.1	2.5	101,190
HARRIS	26,894	11,209	19.7	21.6	36.8	15.1	6.8	9,690	9.1	13.1	35.2	38.7	9.6	168,750
HART	20,777	10,009	31.8	28.4	30.2	6.6	3.0	8,117	13.7	22.9	35.4	21.7	6.3	110,987
HEARD	18,215	4,440	31.2	29.7	31.9	5.3	1.8	3,483	23.4	24.5	39.3	11.6	1.2	93,519
HENRY	29,382	68,211	8.8	10.7	40.0	10.9	9.1	55,104	4.2	5.7	34.8	49.6	5.7	185,407
HOUSTON	25,119	50,948	17.7	26.7	37.9	12.3	5.4	35,444	8.8	21.9	50.4	17.6	1.3	113,720
IRWIN	18,249	3,704	34.1	30.9	26.2	5.8	3.1	2,875	28.9	35.2	23.9	10.7	1.4	73,399
GEORGIA	28,047		21.3	23.7	33.4	12.5	9.2		9.8	12.6	35.8	33.1	8.8	148,827
UNITED STATES	27,916		21.9	25.0	32.3	12.3	8.4		7.9	10.5	27.1	35.6	19.0	192,285

SPENDING POTENTIAL INDICES

COUNTY	FINANCIAL SERVICES				THE HOME						ENTERTAINMENT						PERSONAL			
					Home Improvements		Furnishings													
	Auto Loan	Home Loan	Invest-ments	Retire-ment Plans	Home Repair	Lawn & Garden	Comput-ers & Hard-ware	Major Appli-ances	TV, Radio, Sound Equip-ment	Furni-ture	Dine out/ Carry out	Sports Equip-ment	Fees & Tickets	Toys & Games	Travel	Cable TV	Apparel & Services	Auto Repairs	Health Insur-ance	Pets & Supplies
APPLING	81	61	42	59	64	81	61	73	67	60	67	65	54	71	60	71	58	69	77	78
ATKINSON	72	51	30	48	54	72	51	64	58	50	57	58	44	61	50	62	49	60	68	70
BACON	79	53	29	50	58	81	54	69	62	53	62	62	45	66	53	67	53	64	75	77
BAKER	90	58	27	54	65	93	60	80	71	58	70	72	48	75	58	78	59	73	87	89
BALDWIN	87	74	72	75	74	83	81	81	84	78	83	73	76	83	78	86	74	82	85	84
BANKS	98	70	40	65	74	101	68	86	76	67	77	77	58	82	66	82	65	79	92	95
BARROW	98	93	80	91	87	92	87	91	88	89	88	84	86	91	86	89	78	90	90	93
BARTOW	99	91	78	89	87	95	87	92	89	88	89	83	84	92	86	91	79	90	93	95
BEN HILL	72	54	46	54	58	72	58	66	65	56	64	59	52	66	57	69	55	64	74	70
BERRIEN	81	61	42	58	64	82	61	74	68	60	67	66	54	70	60	72	58	69	79	79
BIBB	84	79	87	82	77	80	83	79	86	83	86	70	82	85	82	88	77	83	85	81
BLECKLEY	86	64	43	61	68	88	63	77	71	63	71	69	56	74	63	76	61	72	84	84
BRANTLEY	73	57	39	54	58	72	56	67	61	56	61	60	50	64	55	64	53	63	69	71
BROOKS	75	54	34	51	57	75	55	67	63	54	62	60	47	64	54	67	53	63	73	73
BRYAN	105	106	99	107	99	96	102	100	100	104	100	94	103	103	100	98	90	101	95	101
BULLOCH	78	61	56	63	60	69	77	70	75	68	75	66	67	74	68	74	66	74	72	73
BURKE	70	54	43	54	56	69	56	63	63	56	62	56	51	64	55	66	55	62	69	68
BUTTS	93	74	59	72	77	94	74	85	79	73	79	76	67	82	73	84	69	81	90	91
CALHOUN	71	45	20	42	51	74	47	63	56	46	56	58	37	59	46	62	47	58	70	71
CAMDEN	93	86	71	85	80	84	83	85	82	84	83	79	80	86	80	82	73	84	82	87
CANDLER	70	51	32	48	55	72	51	64	58	50	57	57	44	60	50	62	49	59	68	69
CARROLL	91	78	70	78	77	87	81	84	84	79	83	76	76	85	78	85	73	83	87	87
CATOOSA	87	79	72	78	78	86	76	82	80	76	79	73	74	81	76	82	69	80	85	84
CHARLTON	79	52	26	48	58	81	53	69	61	52	61	63	43	65	51	67	52	64	75	77
CHATHAM	96	89	93	92	87	91	94	91	96	93	96	82	92	95	92	97	86	94	95	92
CHATTAHOOCHEE	85	57	47	62	48	53	87	67	80	72	81	71	71	85	69	74	72	78	62	67
CHATTOOGA	78	55	35	52	59	80	56	70	64	54	63	62	48	67	55	68	54	65	76	76
CHEROKEE	138	151	140	151	141	134	134	135	129	141	130	127	139	135	135	125	118	132	125	136
CLARKE	75	58	61	63	54	58	86	66	79	72	80	65	73	76	71	75	72	76	66	68
CLAY	82	53	24	49	59	85	55	73	66	53	65	66	44	68	54	72	55	67	81	81
CLAYTON	94	87	83	90	79	78	94	84	91	92	91	81	89	92	87	88	83	91	82	85
CLINCH	74	48	22	44	53	77	49	65	58	48	58	59	39	61	48	64	49	60	72	73
COBB	139	142	139	148	132	124	143	131	136	145	138	126	143	140	137	131	126	137	123	132
COFFEE	83	65	47	62	66	82	64	75	70	64	70	67	58	73	63	74	61	72	79	80
COLQUITT	75	57	46	56	60	75	59	68	65	58	65	60	53	67	58	69	56	65	74	72
COLUMBIA	127	138	129	137	130	124	122	124	118	129	119	115	127	123	124	116	108	121	117	124
COOK	70	53	39	51	54	69	54	62	60	53	59	55	48	62	53	64	51	60	67	67
COWETA	117	119	110	118	112	112	110	111	109	114	110	102	111	113	110	109	99	110	109	113
CRAWFORD	89	70	47	67	71	89	66	80	73	67	73	72	60	76	66	77	63	75	83	86
CRISP	72	55	47	55	57	71	60	66	67	58	65	58	54	67	58	70	57	65	73	69
DADE	90	66	41	63	70	92	64	80	71	64	72	72	56	76	63	76	61	74	85	88
DAWSON	108	100	85	99	102	114	92	105	95	94	95	93	90	99	95	97	84	99	105	109
DECATUR	79	59	46	58	63	80	62	72	69	60	68	64	55	71	61	73	59	69	79	77
DEKALB	119	115	116	120	108	104	124	111	120	123	121	108	121	120	117	117	111	120	108	113
DODGE	80	55	36	53	60	82	58	72	67	56	66	64	49	69	57	72	56	67	80	78
DOOLY	84	56	30	52	61	86	58	74	68	56	67	67	47	71	56	74	57	69	82	82
DOUGHERTY	77	68	74	71	67	72	74	72	79	74	78	63	72	77	72	80	70	75	78	73
DOUGLAS	109	110	103	110	102	100	105	103	102	107	103	96	105	105	103	101	93	104	99	103
EARLY	79	52	28	49	58	82	54	71	64	53	63	64	44	66	53	70	54	65	78	78
ECHOLS	74	69	59	67	63	66	67	69	68	67	68	62	65	70	66	68	60	69	68	70
EFFINGHAM	106	98	78	95	92	100	89	97	91	93	92	88	87	95	88	93	81	94	95	100
ELBERT	75	54	37	52	58	77	55	67	63	54	62	59	48	65	54	68	53	63	74	73
EMANUEL	72	50	32	48	54	74	53	65	61	51	60	58	45	63	52	66	52	62	72	71
EVANS	69	50	31	47	53	71	50	63	57	49	56	56	43	59	49	61	48	58	67	68
FANNIN	79	58	37	55	66	88	59	76	64	56	64	66	50	67	59	69	55	68	81	81
FAYETTE	157	190	197	192	186	167	165	166	156	175	157	154	180	160	173	152	145	160	153	165
FLOYD	85	74	72	75	76	85	77	81	81	75	80	72	73	81	76	84	70	80	87	83
FORSYTH	169	193	177	193	177	161	168	166	158	180	160	158	177	168	169	151	146	163	149	165
FRANKLIN	83	60	41	57	66	88	62	77	69	59	68	68	53	72	61	74	58	71	84	82
FULTON	140	133	141	143	128	125	148	131	145	146	147	126	145	144	140	143	135	142	131	134
GILMER	91	66	40	63	72	97	65	83	72	64	72	74	56	76	64	77	62	76	87	90
GLASCOCK	74	52	36	50	58	78	55	68	62	52	60	59	46	64	54	67	51	62	76	73
GLYNN	95	91	94	92	90	94	91	92	93	91	92	82	90	92	91	95	83	93	96	93
GORDON	96	75	56	73	77	96	75	82	81	74	80	78	67	84	73	85	70	82	91	93
GRADY	76	56	40	54	60	78	57	69	64	56	63	60	50	66	56	69	55	65	75	74
GREENE	119	92	70	89	101	131	91	114	103	91	101	99	82	102	95	111	87	106	125	121
GWINNETT	140	148	136	150	134	124	140	131	132	145	134	127	142	138	135	126	122	135	120	132
HABERSHAM	91	71	54	69	76	96	71	85	77	70	77	75	64	80	71	82	66	79	90	91
HALL	106	101	93	100	97	100	99	101	99	100	99	95	97	101	97	98	89	101	99	102
HANCOCK	62	43	30	42	46	63	46	55	54	45	53	48	40	54	45	59	46	53	63	60
HARALSON	86	61	38	57	65	88	61	76	69	60	68	67	52	73	60	74	58	70	82	83
HARRIS	107	100	92	100	105	116	92	106	96	95	95	94	92	100	96	99	85	99	107	110
HART	84	62	44	60	69	91	64	79	70	61	70	70	55	73	64	75	60	73	85	85
HEARD	86	61	35	57	65	88	60	76	68	59	68	68	51	72	59	73	58	70	81	84
HENRY	121	128	118	128	119	114	117	116	113	122	114	109	120	118	116	110	103	116	109	117
HOUSTON	96	94	90	95	87	87	92	89	91	94	91	82	91	90	90	90	82	91	88	90
IRWIN	83	58	37	55	63	86	59	74	67	58	67	65	50	71	58	73	57	69	81	81
GEORGIA	111	102	94	103	98	104	103	103	104	103	104	96	100	106	100	104	93	104	104	106
UNITED STATES	100	100	100	100	100	100	100	100	100	100	100	100	100	100	100	100	100	100	100	100

COUNTY	FIPS Code	CBSA Code	DMA Code	POPULATION			2000-2007 ANNUAL RATE		RACE (%)					
									White		Black		Asian/Pacific	
				2000	2007	2012	% Rate	State Rank	2000	2007	2000	2007	2000	2007
JACKSON	157	00000	524	41,589	58,167	73,943	4.7	8	89.0	86.5	7.8	9.1	1.0	1.3
JASPER	159	12060	524	11,426	14,384	16,681	3.2	28	71.0	66.7	27.3	31.0	0.2	0.2
JEFF DAVIS	161	00000	507	12,684	13,042	13,275	0.4	113	81.2	77.5	15.1	17.4	0.5	0.6
JEFFERSON	163	00000	520	17,266	16,822	16,482	-0.4	147	42.1	37.3	56.3	60.6	0.2	0.2
JENKINS	165	00000	520	8,575	8,788	8,887	0.3	119	56.3	51.2	40.5	44.6	0.3	0.4
JOHNSON	167	20140	503	8,560	9,503	9,463	1.5	61	62.4	57.8	37.0	41.5	0.1	0.2
JONES	169	31420	503	23,639	28,075	31,005	2.4	40	75.0	71.1	23.3	26.8	0.6	0.7
LAMAR	171	12060	524	15,912	17,575	18,758	1.4	67	67.8	63.3	30.4	34.4	0.4	0.5
LANIER	173	46660	530	7,241	7,676	8,134	0.8	97	71.6	67.3	25.6	29.2	0.4	0.5
LAURENS	175	20140	503	44,874	47,575	49,286	0.8	97	63.4	58.7	34.5	38.7	0.8	1.0
LEE	177	10500	525	24,757	32,185	38,589	3.7	20	82.2	79.0	15.5	18.1	0.9	1.1
LIBERTY	179	25980	507	61,610	63,846	65,255	0.5	108	46.6	41.5	42.8	45.5	2.2	2.6
LINCOLN	181	00000	520	8,348	8,541	8,682	0.3	119	64.3	59.6	34.4	38.7	0.2	0.3
LONG	183	25980	507	10,304	11,348	12,007	1.3	72	68.4	63.6	24.3	26.8	0.8	1.0
LOWNDES	185	46660	530	92,115	102,189	109,893	1.4	67	62.0	57.1	34.0	37.8	1.2	1.5
LUMPKIN	187	00000	524	21,016	27,128	32,029	3.6	22	94.0	92.2	1.5	1.7	0.5	0.6
MCDUFFIE	189	12260	520	21,231	21,837	22,186	0.4	113	60.8	56.0	37.5	41.9	0.4	0.4
MCINTOSH	191	15260	507	10,847	11,973	12,865	1.4	67	61.3	56.6	36.8	41.2	0.3	0.4
MACON	193	00000	503	14,074	13,718	13,529	-0.4	147	37.4	32.8	59.5	63.2	0.7	0.8
MADISON	195	12020	524	25,730	28,682	30,564	1.5	61	89.0	86.6	8.5	10.0	0.3	0.4
MARION	197	17980	522	7,144	7,527	7,796	0.7	104	60.8	55.9	34.1	37.5	0.3	0.4
MERIWETHER	199	12060	524	22,534	24,278	25,389	1.0	85	56.1	51.2	42.2	46.8	0.3	0.4
MILLER	201	00000	530	6,383	6,147	5,983	-0.5	152	70.3	66.0	28.9	33.0	0.1	0.2
MITCHELL	205	00000	525	23,932	23,797	23,696	-0.1	139	49.6	44.6	47.9	52.2	0.3	0.4
MONROE	207	31420	503	21,757	25,214	27,561	2.1	45	70.4	66.1	27.9	31.8	0.4	0.5
MONTGOMERY	209	47080	507	8,270	9,143	9,708	1.4	67	69.7	65.0	27.2	30.8	0.2	0.3
MORGAN	211	00000	524	15,457	18,714	21,392	2.7	32	69.7	65.3	28.5	32.4	0.3	0.4
MURRAY	213	19140	575	36,506	41,928	45,416	1.9	47	95.3	93.4	0.6	0.7	0.3	0.4
MUSCOGEE	215	17980	522	186,291	188,107	189,113	0.1	130	50.4	45.4	43.7	47.3	1.7	2.0
NEWTON	217	12060	524	62,001	99,060	135,020	6.7	4	75.3	71.3	22.2	25.5	0.7	1.0
OCONEE	219	12020	524	26,225	33,600	39,386	3.5	24	89.6	87.0	6.4	7.5	1.5	2.0
OGLETHORPE	221	12020	524	12,635	14,326	15,346	1.7	52	78.3	74.6	19.8	22.8	0.3	0.4
PAULDING	223	12060	524	81,678	133,863	183,475	7.1	2	90.6	88.5	7.0	8.2	0.4	0.6
PEACH	225	22980	503	23,668	25,803	27,316	1.2	76	51.3	46.4	45.4	49.3	0.4	0.4
PICKENS	227	12060	524	22,983	29,934	35,173	3.7	20	96.2	95.0	1.3	1.5	0.3	0.3
PIERCE	229	48180	561	15,636	17,578	19,104	1.6	56	86.9	84.2	10.9	12.8	0.2	0.3
PIKE	231	12060	524	13,688	17,914	21,121	3.8	17	83.6	80.6	14.8	17.3	0.4	0.5
POLK	233	16340	524	38,127	42,356	45,093	1.5	61	80.5	76.2	13.3	15.2	0.4	0.5
PULASKI	235	00000	503	9,588	9,742	9,803	0.2	125	63.0	58.3	34.3	38.3	0.5	0.6
PUTNAM	237	00000	524	18,812	21,148	22,633	1.6	56	67.5	62.9	29.9	33.7	0.7	0.9
QUITMAN	239	21640	522	2,598	2,511	2,453	-0.5	152	52.1	49.5	46.9	49.5	0.0	0.0
RABUN	241	00000	524	15,050	17,647	19,385	2.2	43	94.9	92.9	0.8	0.9	0.4	0.5
RANDOLPH	243	00000	522	7,791	7,456	7,246	-0.6	156	38.9	34.4	59.5	63.7	0.3	0.3
RICHMOND	245	12260	520	199,775	200,679	199,671	0.1	130	45.6	40.7	49.8	53.6	1.6	2.0
ROCKDALE	247	12060	524	70,111	84,111	94,429	2.5	37	75.7	71.4	18.2	20.6	2.0	2.5
SCHLEY	249	11140	522	3,766	4,173	4,480	1.4	67	65.8	61.0	31.3	35.2	0.2	0.3
SCREVEN	251	00000	507	15,374	15,762	15,862	0.3	119	53.6	48.7	45.3	49.9	0.3	0.4
SEMINOLE	253	00000	530	9,369	9,491	9,644	0.2	125	61.7	56.6	34.7	38.5	0.2	0.2
SPALDING	255	12060	524	58,417	63,874	67,860	1.2	76	66.5	61.8	31.1	35.0	0.7	0.9
STEPHENS	257	45740	567	25,435	25,575	25,275	0.1	130	85.7	83.0	12.0	14.1	0.7	0.9
STEWART	259	00000	522	5,252	4,880	4,664	-1.0	159	37.1	32.7	61.5	65.7	0.2	0.2
SUMTER	261	11140	522	33,200	33,267	32,866	0.0	134	48.2	45.7	49.0	51.6	0.6	0.6
TALBOT	263	00000	522	6,498	6,838	7,117	0.7	104	36.8	32.4	61.6	65.7	0.3	0.4
TALIAFERRO	265	00000	520	2,077	1,939	1,831	-0.9	158	38.2	33.6	60.3	64.6	0.0	0.1
TATTNALL	267	00000	507	22,305	23,630	24,652	0.8	97	60.5	54.6	31.4	34.3	0.4	0.5
TAYLOR	269	00000	522	8,815	8,951	9,001	0.2	125	55.4	50.4	42.6	47.0	0.2	0.2
TELFAIR	271	00000	503	11,794	13,207	13,067	1.6	56	59.7	54.8	38.4	42.8	0.2	0.2
TERRELL	273	10500	525	10,970	10,958	10,777	0.0	134	37.9	35.6	60.7	63.0	0.4	0.4
THOMAS	275	45620	530	42,737	46,229	48,668	1.1	82	59.0	54.1	38.9	43.2	0.5	0.6
TIFT	277	45700	525	38,407	40,831	42,633	0.8	97	65.3	60.1	28.0	30.9	1.0	1.2
TOOMBS	279	47080	507	26,067	27,476	28,557	0.7	104	69.2	64.0	24.2	26.8	0.5	0.6
TOWNS	281	00000	524	9,319	11,150	12,502	2.5	37	98.8	98.4	0.1	0.2	0.3	0.4
TREUTLEN	283	00000	503	6,854	6,654	6,497	-0.4	147	65.7	61.1	33.1	37.3	0.3	0.3
TROUP	285	29300	524	58,779	64,554	68,411	1.3	72	65.8	61.1	31.9	35.9	0.6	0.8
TURNER	287	00000	525	9,504	9,521	9,488	0.0	134	56.4	53.9	41.0	43.5	0.3	0.3
TWIGGS	289	31420	503	10,590	10,534	10,318	-0.1	139	54.9	52.3	43.7	46.2	0.1	0.1
UNION	291	00000	524	17,289	22,143	25,536	3.5	24	97.9	97.3	0.6	0.7	0.2	0.3
UPSON	293	45580	524	27,597	28,409	28,926	0.4	113	70.6	66.3	27.9	31.8	0.4	0.5
WALKER	295	16860	575	61,053	65,287	68,224	0.9	89	94.4	93.1	3.8	4.5	0.3	0.4
WALTON	297	12060	524	60,687	85,580	107,374	4.9	7	83.0	79.8	14.4	16.8	0.7	0.9
WARE	299	48180	561	35,483	34,288	34,170	-0.5	152	69.7	65.2	28.0	31.8	0.5	0.7
WARREN	301	00000	520	6,336	6,051	5,869	-0.6	156	39.5	34.9	59.5	63.8	0.1	0.2
WASHINGTON	303	00000	503	21,176	20,562	20,662	-0.4	147	45.7	40.9	53.2	57.8	0.3	0.4
WAYNE	305	27700	507	20,505	29,000	01,225	1.4	67	76.7	72.8	20.3	23.2	0.5	0.6
WEBSTER	307	00000	522	2,390	2,292	2,191	-0.6	156	50.5	48.0	47.0	49.4	0.0	0.0
WHEELER	309	00000	503	6,179	6,689	6,722	1.1	82	64.6	59.9	33.2	37.1	0.1	0.1
WHITE	311	00000	524	19,944	25,778	20,001	3.6	22	95.2	93.8	2.2	2.6	0.7	0.9
GEORGIA							2.3		65.1	62.1	28.7	29.8	2.2	2.7
UNITED STATES							1.2		75.1	72.7	12.3	12.6	3.8	4.5

POPULATION COMPOSITION

COUNTY	% HISPANIC ORIGIN		2007 AGE DISTRIBUTION (%)										MEDIAN AGE	% 2007 Males	% 2007 Females
	2000	2007	0-4	5-9	10-14	15-19	20-24	25-44	45-64	65-84	85+	18+	2007		
JACKSON	3.0	4.1	7.5	7.1	7.2	6.0	5.5	30.6	25.2	9.6	1.3	74.5	36.6	50.4	49.6
JASPER	2.1	2.7	7.0	6.7	6.9	6.5	5.6	26.6	27.6	11.6	1.5	75.4	38.8	49.3	50.7
JEFF DAVIS	5.1	6.9	7.9	7.8	6.4	6.5	6.3	27.1	25.3	11.4	1.3	74.0	36.3	49.7	50.3
JEFFERSON	1.5	1.9	7.4	7.1	6.9	7.1	6.2	27.2	24.9	11.1	2.2	74.3	36.8	47.7	52.3
JENKINS	3.3	4.3	7.4	7.1	7.0	6.6	6.8	26.0	25.6	11.5	2.0	74.5	37.3	48.8	51.2
JOHNSON	0.9	1.1	6.5	6.7	6.7	16.0	4.9	21.0	22.0	13.1	3.0	67.5	33.7	53.2	46.8
JONES	0.7	0.9	6.6	6.3	6.9	6.5	6.9	26.5	28.4	10.4	1.5	76.5	39.0	49.1	50.9
LAMAR	1.1	1.3	6.3	6.0	6.9	7.9	6.1	27.5	26.3	11.6	1.4	76.8	37.8	48.1	51.9
LANIER	1.7	2.3	7.8	6.7	7.3	6.0	7.6	29.3	24.7	9.3	1.3	74.4	34.7	50.7	49.3
LAURENS	1.2	1.5	7.0	6.8	6.9	6.2	6.2	26.8	26.2	11.8	2.0	75.6	37.8	48.5	51.5
LEE	1.2	1.6	7.5	7.1	7.2	7.4	7.8	29.4	26.8	6.1	0.6	73.6	34.9	50.5	49.5
LIBERTY	8.2	10.3	10.8	8.4	7.1	8.5	13.2	32.4	15.2	4.0	0.4	69.4	25.8	52.6	47.4
LINCOLN	1.0	1.2	5.3	5.5	6.7	5.9	5.6	25.1	30.4	14.2	1.3	78.7	42.2	48.9	51.1
LONG	8.4	10.9	11.6	9.8	8.1	6.0	7.6	34.0	17.0	5.4	0.5	66.9	27.9	50.9	49.1
LOWNDES	2.7	3.4	7.3	6.7	6.5	8.0	10.1	30.8	21.2	8.3	1.1	75.5	31.1	49.9	50.1
LUMPKIN	3.5	4.9	6.7	6.2	6.1	8.6	8.4	28.8	24.8	9.4	1.2	77.3	34.7	49.3	50.7
MCDUFFIE	1.3	1.7	7.3	6.8	6.7	7.4	7.0	26.3	26.3	10.7	1.6	74.7	36.9	47.7	52.3
MCINTOSH	0.9	1.1	6.3	6.6	7.2	7.1	5.1	23.8	30.1	12.8	1.2	75.2	40.5	49.7	50.3
MACON	2.6	3.3	7.3	6.8	6.7	6.3	6.7	26.8	26.6	11.0	1.9	75.3	37.3	49.7	50.3
MADISON	2.0	2.8	7.0	6.8	6.9	6.3	5.4	29.3	26.7	10.2	1.4	75.3	37.8	49.4	50.6
MARION	5.8	7.5	6.5	5.8	8.0	7.3	6.5	27.0	27.5	9.8	1.5	75.0	37.3	49.6	50.4
MERIWETHER	0.8	1.0	6.9	6.6	6.7	6.9	6.2	26.1	26.7	11.8	2.1	75.8	38.4	48.4	51.6
MILLER	0.7	0.9	6.4	5.7	6.3	6.6	6.4	24.5	26.9	14.1	3.1	77.5	41.0	47.8	52.2
MITCHELL	2.1	2.7	7.4	7.2	7.2	6.3	7.3	29.0	23.5	10.5	1.7	74.4	34.9	51.0	49.0
MONROE	1.3	1.6	6.3	6.2	6.8	6.8	6.5	26.8	29.0	10.3	1.4	77.0	38.8	50.1	49.9
MONTGOMERY	3.3	4.5	6.9	6.6	6.3	7.1	8.4	28.7	24.0	10.7	1.4	76.8	35.3	52.0	48.0
MORGAN	1.6	2.0	6.6	6.3	7.6	6.1	5.2	27.1	27.6	11.6	1.8	75.7	39.1	49.0	51.0
MURRAY	5.5	7.7	8.2	8.0	7.0	6.3	5.7	31.8	24.1	8.2	0.7	72.9	34.7	50.3	49.7
MUSCOGEE	4.5	5.6	7.4	6.6	6.7	7.8	8.6	27.8	23.2	10.3	1.7	75.2	33.7	48.9	51.1
NEWTON	1.9	2.4	8.1	7.8	7.1	7.2	5.4	31.2	23.3	8.8	1.1	72.7	35.0	48.9	51.1
OCONEE	3.2	4.4	6.7	6.6	8.1	8.0	5.8	25.1	30.1	8.4	1.2	73.2	38.2	49.5	50.5
OGLETHORPE	1.4	1.8	7.1	6.8	6.7	6.0	5.0	27.7	27.7	11.3	1.6	75.6	39.2	48.9	51.1
PAULDING	1.7	2.3	9.4	8.6	7.8	6.7	5.1	35.0	21.0	5.8	0.6	69.9	33.2	49.8	50.2
PEACH	4.2	5.3	6.6	6.2	6.8	8.0	9.5	27.9	24.0	9.8	1.1	76.4	33.8	48.5	51.5
PICKENS	2.0	2.9	6.3	6.3	5.7	5.8	4.9	27.2	28.1	14.5	1.4	78.3	41.1	49.2	50.8
PIERCE	2.3	3.2	7.0	6.6	6.5	7.0	6.7	27.3	26.6	11.0	1.4	75.8	37.7	49.8	50.2
PIKE	1.2	1.6	7.1	7.1	6.6	7.4	5.7	27.9	26.6	10.3	1.3	74.6	37.8	50.0	50.0
POLK	7.7	10.5	7.4	7.3	6.1	6.3	6.2	28.7	24.4	11.7	1.8	75.3	36.5	50.3	49.7
PULASKI	2.8	3.6	6.4	6.4	5.7	5.3	6.7	29.9	26.1	11.6	2.0	78.4	37.9	43.3	56.7
PUTNAM	2.2	2.8	6.1	6.3	5.2	5.6	5.2	24.9	30.3	15.1	1.3	79.0	42.6	49.3	50.7
QUITMAN	0.5	0.5	6.5	6.1	6.6	5.6	5.3	21.7	29.2	16.6	2.5	77.5	43.6	47.7	52.3
RABUN	4.5	6.5	5.6	5.8	5.7	5.6	4.4	24.2	30.1	16.4	2.1	79.3	44.0	50.0	50.0
RANDOLPH	1.2	1.4	7.3	6.7	6.7	7.9	7.4	22.6	26.1	12.4	2.8	75.5	38.2	47.0	53.0
RICHMOND	2.8	3.4	7.2	6.6	6.9	7.8	8.3	28.1	23.8	9.9	1.4	75.1	33.7	48.3	51.7
ROCKDALE	6.0	7.9	6.4	5.9	6.9	7.3	7.1	27.4	28.6	9.2	1.1	76.2	37.7	49.7	50.3
SCHLEY	2.4	3.2	8.7	9.0	6.6	7.0	5.9	27.5	24.2	9.9	1.2	71.0	35.8	48.2	51.8
SCREVEN	1.0	1.1	6.6	6.1	7.1	7.6	6.1	25.3	27.2	11.9	2.1	75.6	38.6	48.2	51.8
SEMINOLE	3.7	5.0	7.6	7.2	6.3	5.9	5.9	24.1	26.8	14.2	2.1	75.3	39.6	48.4	51.6
SPALDING	1.6	2.1	7.5	7.0	7.1	6.8	6.5	27.7	25.0	10.6	1.6	74.2	35.9	48.7	51.3
STEPHENS	1.0	1.3	6.2	6.0	6.1	6.8	6.6	25.6	26.7	13.7	2.4	78.2	39.4	48.4	51.6
STEWART	1.5	1.8	6.1	6.7	7.2	5.1	5.5	24.4	28.0	13.6	3.4	77.0	41.1	48.1	51.9
SUMTER	2.7	2.6	7.8	7.3	7.0	7.5	8.0	27.0	23.1	9.9	2.5	73.9	33.6	47.4	52.6
TALBOT	1.3	1.4	5.8	5.7	6.6	6.0	4.9	24.2	31.6	13.5	1.7	78.4	42.7	47.0	53.0
TALIAFERRO	0.9	1.2	6.6	7.2	4.0	6.8	5.4	24.4	26.5	16.3	2.8	77.9	42.1	49.0	51.0
TATTNALL	8.4	11.4	6.4	6.1	5.2	6.2	8.4	34.4	22.2	9.5	1.5	78.8	34.4	56.8	43.2
TAYLOR	1.8	2.4	7.2	6.9	7.3	6.1	5.7	27.2	26.0	11.3	2.2	74.7	37.7	49.5	50.5
TELFAIR	1.8	2.4	5.4	5.5	4.6	5.1	8.9	34.1	23.8	10.4	2.1	81.5	36.7	58.7	41.3
TERRELL	1.2	1.3	7.8	7.5	7.0	6.6	6.9	24.4	25.6	12.1	2.1	73.7	37.3	47.8	52.2
THOMAS	1.7	2.2	7.0	6.4	6.7	7.0	7.1	25.6	26.4	11.6	2.2	75.5	38.3	47.3	52.7
TIFT	7.7	10.2	7.9	7.2	6.8	7.2	7.5	27.3	24.1	10.5	1.6	74.3	34.3	48.9	51.1
TOOMBS	8.9	11.8	8.1	7.4	6.6	7.3	7.8	26.4	23.9	10.8	1.8	73.5	34.8	48.3	51.7
TOWNS	0.7	1.0	4.4	4.4	4.2	6.5	4.3	18.9	30.4	23.9	3.1	84.5	50.6	47.8	52.2
TREUTLEN	1.2	1.4	7.5	7.6	6.1	6.9	7.1	26.3	25.2	11.5	1.8	75.1	35.6	49.8	50.2
TROUP	1.7	2.2	7.2	6.9	7.3	7.2	6.7	27.1	25.5	10.2	1.8	74.1	36.0	48.1	51.9
TURNER	2.6	2.6	8.2	7.0	7.1	7.3	6.6	26.4	24.6	10.9	2.0	73.5	35.3	48.7	51.3
TWIGGS	1.1	1.1	7.0	6.8	6.7	6.4	6.1	27.4	27.2	11.2	1.2	75.6	37.9	47.9	52.1
UNION	0.9	1.2	5.0	4.9	5.1	5.2	4.6	22.3	31.0	19.5	2.5	81.9	47.0	49.5	50.5
UPSON	1.2	1.5	6.6	6.2	6.7	6.7	5.6	27.3	25.9	12.6	2.4	76.5	39.1	48.1	51.9
WALKER	0.9	1.3	6.6	6.5	6.3	5.8	5.5	28.2	26.9	12.5	1.8	77.0	39.0	49.1	50.9
WALTON	1.9	2.6	8.3	8.0	7.0	6.4	5.6	30.6	24.5	8.4	1.2	72.8	35.7	48.9	51.1
WARE	1.9	2.6	6.7	6.5	6.3	6.4	6.2	26.6	25.9	13.0	2.4	76.5	38.4	49.0	51.0
WARREN	0.8	1.0	6.8	6.9	6.4	5.9	5.7	25.0	27.8	12.8	2.8	76.4	40.1	46.8	53.2
WASHINGTON	0.6	0.8	6.8	6.5	7.4	6.7	6.7	26.7	26.8	10.5	1.8	75.2	37.9	46.0	54.0
WAYNE	3.8	5.0	6.8	6.2	6.4	6.6	6.7	30.1	25.5	10.4	1.3	76.5	36.8	52.6	47.4
WEBSTER	2.8	2.9	7.0	7.1	6.5	5.0	5.9	25.6	28.2	12.6	2.1	76.4	40.0	51.0	49.0
WHEELER	3.5	4.6	5.7	5.7	4.7	5.3	8.1	34.2	24.9	9.4	2.0	80.7	36.9	59.1	40.9
WHITE	1.6	2.2	6.3	6.3	6.0	6.7	5.0	26.9	27.9	13.2	1.5	77.6	40.2	49.8	50.2
GEORGIA	5.3	6.9	7.3	7.0	6.9	7.0	7.1	30.3	24.6	8.7	1.3	74.8	35.0	49.4	50.6
UNITED STATES	12.5	15.0	6.9	6.5	6.8	7.1	7.0	27.6	25.4	10.7	1.9	75.6	36.7	49.2	50.8

COUNTY	HOUSEHOLDS					FAMILIES			MEDIAN HOUSEHOLD INCOME			
	2000	2007	2012	% Annual Rate 2000-2007	2007 Average HH Size	2000	2007	% Annual Rate 2000-2007	2007	2012	2007 National Rank	2007 State Rank
JACKSON	15,057	21,209	27,110	4.8	2.69	11,488	15,766	4.5	48,556	54,918	777	34
JASPER	4,175	5,309	6,180	3.4	2.70	3,122	3,860	3.0	48,289	55,288	793	37
JEFF DAVIS	4,828	5,062	5,196	0.7	2.56	3,591	3,660	0.3	32,307	36,576	2730	134
JEFFERSON	6,339	6,286	6,207	-0.1	2.60	4,548	4,371	-0.5	31,208	35,392	2815	140
JENKINS	3,214	3,353	3,418	0.6	2.58	2,270	2,294	0.1	28,937	32,765	2964	152
JOHNSON	3,130	3,190	3,209	0.3	2.47	2,240	2,213	-0.2	28,378	32,584	2984	156
JONES	8,659	10,446	11,639	2.6	2.64	6,665	7,838	2.3	52,029	59,797	545	29
LAMAR	5,712	6,522	7,017	1.8	2.60	4,286	4,761	1.5	45,055	51,084	1106	45
LANIER	2,593	2,810	3,001	1.1	2.65	1,932	2,036	0.7	35,091	39,854	2417	112
LAURENS	17,083	18,438	19,268	1.1	2.51	12,177	12,731	0.6	38,781	44,106	1880	79
LEE	8,229	10,888	13,181	3.9	2.88	6,796	8,821	3.7	61,487	72,030	225	15
LIBERTY	19,383	20,388	20,953	0.7	2.90	15,145	15,551	0.4	41,437	47,699	1527	62
LINCOLN	3,251	3,429	3,527	0.7	2.48	2,379	2,436	0.3	37,872	42,671	2012	87
LONG	3,574	3,896	4,101	1.2	2.91	2,678	2,840	0.8	35,424	38,811	2380	107
LOWNDES	32,654	37,527	40,928	1.9	2.54	22,242	24,684	1.4	40,606	46,874	1653	67
LUMPKIN	7,537	9,926	11,878	3.9	2.58	5,363	6,843	3.4	47,393	53,792	872	40
MCDUFFIE	7,970	8,317	8,511	0.6	2.58	5,857	5,934	0.2	38,671	43,545	1900	80
MCINTOSH	4,202	4,769	5,180	1.8	2.48	3,014	3,315	1.3	35,837	40,632	2307	101
MACON	4,834	4,854	4,841	0.1	2.64	3,483	3,392	-0.4	28,775	32,829	2970	153
MADISON	9,800	11,063	11,863	1.7	2.57	7,332	8,050	1.3	43,390	48,720	1287	54
MARION	2,668	2,878	3,011	1.1	2.59	1,912	1,999	0.6	34,266	38,368	2517	114
MERIWETHER	8,248	9,089	9,617	1.3	2.62	6,012	6,428	0.9	38,661	43,968	1903	81
MILLER	2,487	2,437	2,391	-0.3	2.46	1,766	1,677	-0.7	32,374	36,627	2723	131
MITCHELL	8,063	8,276	8,340	0.4	2.65	5,937	5,923	0.0	32,369	36,629	2724	132
MONROE	7,719	9,075	9,997	2.3	2.71	6,009	6,894	1.9	53,878	61,786	457	27
MONTGOMERY	2,919	3,290	3,539	1.7	2.53	2,063	2,251	1.2	36,939	41,910	2135	92
MORGAN	5,558	6,858	7,913	2.9	2.70	4,302	5,180	2.6	48,532	54,786	780	35
MURRAY	13,286	15,385	16,718	2.0	2.71	10,261	11,588	1.7	43,689	48,585	1255	51
MUSCOGEE	69,819	71,511	72,296	0.3	2.50	47,678	47,167	-0.1	43,706	51,659	1250	50
NEWTON	21,997	35,563	48,819	6.9	2.75	17,113	26,997	6.5	57,198	68,181	324	20
OCONEE	9,051	11,587	13,580	3.5	2.88	7,326	9,181	3.2	67,533	78,874	142	8
OGLETHORPE	4,849	5,601	6,049	2.0	2.54	3,541	3,970	1.6	42,423	47,644	1406	58
PAULDING	28,089	46,496	63,881	7.2	2.86	22,893	37,129	6.9	66,499	78,922	157	10
PEACH	8,436	9,363	10,007	1.4	2.63	6,002	6,455	1.0	41,303	46,949	1553	64
PICKENS	8,960	11,874	14,062	4.0	2.50	6,795	8,769	3.6	51,260	60,017	597	31
PIERCE	5,958	6,839	7,508	1.9	2.55	4,439	4,953	1.5	35,162	39,211	2408	111
PIKE	4,755	6,307	7,481	4.0	2.79	3,785	4,909	3.7	53,504	61,336	476	28
POLK	14,012	15,654	16,698	1.5	2.65	10,338	11,222	1.1	39,637	44,994	1762	73
PULASKI	3,407	3,506	3,551	0.4	2.46	2,339	2,326	-0.1	38,202	43,499	1974	84
PUTNAM	7,402	8,565	9,255	2.0	2.45	5,474	6,156	1.6	44,343	49,908	1176	48
QUITMAN	1,047	1,027	1,009	-0.3	2.44	756	719	-0.7	30,789	34,827	2852	143
RABUN	6,279	7,506	8,329	2.5	2.31	4,353	5,031	2.0	41,632	47,367	1501	60
RANDOLPH	2,909	2,832	2,775	-0.4	2.52	1,971	1,852	-0.9	26,246	30,266	3063	158
RICHMOND	73,920	75,866	75,870	0.4	2.51	49,509	49,003	-0.1	41,063	47,594	1588	65
ROCKDALE	24,052	29,366	33,159	2.8	2.82	18,883	22,519	2.5	67,068	77,786	149	9
SCHLEY	1,435	1,615	1,746	1.6	2.58	1,042	1,138	1.2	37,974	42,657	1999	86
SCREVEN	5,797	5,967	6,044	0.4	2.56	4,103	4,091	0.0	35,372	40,150	2386	108
SEMINOLE	3,573	3,703	3,799	0.5	2.48	2,597	2,612	0.1	33,112	37,972	2644	125
SPALDING	21,519	23,831	25,478	1.4	2.64	15,783	16,972	1.0	44,994	52,029	1112	46
STEPHENS	9,951	10,135	10,062	0.3	2.43	7,070	6,974	-0.2	35,933	41,168	2291	99
STEWART	2,007	1,934	1,871	-0.5	2.38	1,349	1,255	-1.0	29,500	33,469	2930	149
SUMTER	12,025	12,063	11,992	0.0	2.59	8,498	8,252	-0.4	37,465	42,801	2069	90
TALBOT	2,538	2,750	2,901	1.1	2.48	1,824	1,916	0.7	31,711	36,009	2786	138
TALIAFERRO	870	843	807	-0.4	2.27	559	521	-1.0	28,739	32,900	2971	154
TATTNALL	7,057	7,643	8,042	1.1	2.60	4,874	5,103	0.6	34,217	38,867	2526	116
TAYLOR	3,281	3,400	3,454	0.5	2.50	2,285	2,289	0.0	30,053	34,051	2908	147
TELFAIR	4,140	4,140	4,127	0.0	2.41	2,872	2,778	-0.5	31,846	35,973	2776	137
TERRELL	4,002	4,011	3,972	0.0	2.64	2,912	2,833	-0.4	33,195	37,640	2639	124
THOMAS	16,309	17,920	19,044	1.3	2.50	11,466	12,195	0.9	37,828	42,943	2021	88
TIFT	13,919	15,039	15,822	1.1	2.61	10,105	10,591	0.7	40,286	45,944	1690	68
TOOMBS	9,877	10,576	11,066	0.9	2.55	6,825	7,063	0.5	32,933	37,403	2666	126
TOWNS	3,998	4,888	5,533	2.8	2.18	2,825	3,344	2.4	40,727	47,553	1638	66
TREUTLEN	2,531	2,515	2,480	-0.1	2.49	1,825	1,759	-0.5	29,423	33,723	2935	150
TROUP	21,920	24,247	25,847	1.4	2.59	15,615	16,734	1.0	43,355	50,047	1292	55
TURNER	3,435	3,498	3,507	0.3	2.68	2,538	2,510	-0.2	31,073	34,986	2826	141
TWIGGS	3,832	3,919	3,882	0.3	2.66	2,861	2,845	-0.1	37,740	42,578	2029	89
UNION	7,159	9,419	11,000	3.9	2.30	5,209	6,652	3.4	39,398	44,849	1796	74
UPSON	10,722	11,156	11,420	0.5	2.50	7,690	7,757	0.1	38,050	43,338	1994	85
WALKER	23,605	25,572	26,930	1.1	2.50	17,472	18,391	0.7	40,138	45,508	1703	69
WALTON	21,307	29,927	37,639	4.8	2.83	16,995	23,343	4.5	58,354	67,420	300	17
WARE	13,475	13,642	13,703	0.2	2.42	9,299	9,097	-0.3	35,471	40,728	2371	106
WARREN	2,435	2,402	2,363	-0.2	2.47	1,692	1,616	-0.6	32,702	37,151	2683	129
WASHINGTON	7,435	7,624	7,725	0.3	2.60	5,384	5,358	-0.1	35,707	40,511	2330	104
WAYNE	9,324	10,448	11,271	1.6	2.57	6,937	7,559	1.2	39,376	44,253	1801	75
WEBSTER	811	808	870	0.2	2.55	675	647	-0.6	33,540	38,050	2604	119
WHEELER	2,011	2,079	2,113	0.5	2.48	1,395	1,394	0.0	28,646	32,541	2973	155
WHITE	7,731	10,135	11,821	3.8	2.49	5,784	7,376	3.4	42,870	48,244	1345	57
GEORGIA			2.3	2.65			2.0	55,102	65,884		
UNITED STATES			1.2	2.59			1.0	53,154	62,503		

COUNTY	2007 Per Capita Income	2007 HH Income Base	2007 HOUSEHOLD INCOME DISTRIBUTION (%)					2007 Home Value Base	2007 HOME VALUE DISTRIBUTION (%)					2007 Median Home Value
			Less than $25,000	$25,000 to $49,999	$50,000 to $99,999	$100,000 to $149,999	$150,000 or More		Less than $50,000	$50,000 to $89,999	$90,000 to $174,999	$175,000 to $399,999	$400,000 or More	
JACKSON	22,241	21,209	25.7	25.6	34.7	9.8	4.3	16,167	12.2	14.6	37.6	28.2	7.4	135,728
JASPER	22,188	5,309	24.2	27.8	36.7	7.5	3.7	4,240	12.8	15.3	43.6	24.0	4.4	119,966
JEFF DAVIS	17,172	5,062	38.3	31.8	22.8	4.5	2.6	3,945	35.7	28.0	28.9	6.7	0.7	70,523
JEFFERSON	16,665	6,286	42.7	27.7	23.5	3.4	2.8	4,592	37.3	26.2	27.9	7.3	1.2	66,420
JENKINS	16,428	3,353	45.1	24.8	22.0	6.5	1.7	2,496	36.0	29.5	24.0	8.3	2.2	65,969
JOHNSON	16,120	3,190	44.9	24.7	23.4	5.3	1.8	2,557	40.8	30.8	22.4	5.6	0.4	57,391
JONES	23,588	10,446	21.8	25.5	37.2	10.9	4.7	8,977	19.9	22.2	39.6	17.0	1.4	103,103
LAMAR	21,061	6,522	25.0	30.0	33.9	7.7	3.4	4,802	11.4	20.7	45.6	17.8	4.6	114,007
LANIER	16,705	2,810	33.5	34.1	26.0	4.9	1.5	2,161	26.0	25.7	34.1	12.2	2.1	86,456
LAURENS	20,698	18,438	33.4	27.6	28.3	7.1	3.6	13,331	23.2	27.0	35.5	12.5	1.8	89,693
LEE	25,996	10,888	15.1	22.2	39.7	15.2	7.8	8,660	13.8	12.8	47.1	24.3	1.9	127,761
LIBERTY	17,226	20,388	25.5	34.9	31.0	6.2	2.4	10,475	13.7	18.2	53.5	13.4	1.1	110,529
LINCOLN	19,296	3,429	33.4	29.4	28.6	6.9	1.7	2,819	24.5	25.0	28.2	17.6	4.6	90,793
LONG	14,492	3,896	33.7	36.7	24.9	3.7	1.0	2,647	30.0	26.9	35.9	6.3	0.8	81,544
LOWNDES	21,054	37,522	31.5	26.5	30.3	7.5	4.2	23,176	11.6	15.4	36.9	30.6	5.5	140,994
LUMPKIN	22,235	9,926	26.1	26.0	34.8	8.6	4.5	7,309	10.4	11.8	35.6	33.2	9.0	152,488
MCDUFFIE	20,481	8,317	33.8	27.9	27.6	7.2	3.5	6,006	17.3	27.6	35.6	16.7	2.9	97,045
MCINTOSH	17,925	4,769	35.0	32.3	26.0	5.0	1.7	3,990	29.6	20.3	25.7	16.5	8.0	90,244
MACON	15,348	4,854	43.3	25.8	24.3	4.8	1.8	3,574	32.6	32.2	28.1	6.1	1.1	71,122
MADISON	20,410	11,063	26.9	29.8	33.5	7.7	2.1	8,962	17.5	20.8	41.7	16.4	3.5	109,279
MARION	16,866	2,878	38.0	28.9	25.5	6.3	1.4	2,268	28.0	22.1	35.6	10.4	4.0	89,853
MERIWETHER	19,368	9,089	33.2	28.0	28.4	7.6	2.8	6,820	21.5	25.2	36.2	14.3	2.8	94,837
MILLER	18,825	2,437	39.6	29.8	21.5	5.6	3.5	1,900	31.3	31.2	26.4	9.6	1.5	71,986
MITCHELL	16,995	8,276	40.6	27.5	23.2	5.7	3.0	6,003	26.3	30.0	31.0	11.2	1.5	81,177
MONROE	24,273	9,075	21.3	24.6	36.1	12.7	5.3	7,294	14.9	18.8	35.2	27.3	3.8	115,829
MONTGOMERY	18,470	3,290	34.3	29.1	27.2	6.7	2.6	2,582	38.3	21.2	28.4	10.2	1.9	72,809
MORGAN	23,814	6,858	24.2	27.0	33.5	10.0	5.3	5,398	10.6	15.2	35.3	26.7	12.2	137,280
MURRAY	19,476	15,385	26.3	30.6	34.3	6.5	2.4	11,549	23.8	19.8	39.1	15.2	2.1	101,508
MUSCOGEE	23,386	71,511	27.5	28.0	30.7	8.5	5.3	41,376	6.0	19.0	49.5	22.0	3.5	122,607
NEWTON	25,075	35,563	16.6	24.8	40.7	11.9	6.0	27,787	5.7	9.2	47.2	32.6	5.3	149,606
OCONEE	31,673	11,587	12.9	21.2	35.5	17.6	12.8	9,408	6.5	5.6	25.5	46.0	16.4	216,428
OGLETHORPE	21,449	5,601	28.1	30.5	30.5	7.1	3.7	4,652	18.4	18.6	38.8	20.2	4.0	111,743
PAULDING	26,191	46,496	11.5	20.2	45.8	17.2	5.4	40,394	4.8	5.9	48.1	37.8	3.3	160,195
PEACH	20,212	9,363	31.6	25.6	29.2	10.1	3.5	6,516	18.4	22.3	41.4	16.6	1.3	102,065
PICKENS	25,517	11,874	21.0	27.5	37.0	8.9	5.7	9,807	11.6	13.8	36.9	27.8	9.9	136,183
PIERCE	17,128	6,839	36.6	30.5	25.5	6.1	1.3	5,534	31.7	27.5	28.0	11.3	1.4	77,354
PIKE	22,800	6,307	20.7	24.9	39.6	9.4	5.4	5,189	10.0	13.5	36.6	33.9	6.0	146,013
POLK	18,984	15,654	30.6	31.3	29.4	6.2	2.6	11,330	12.8	24.8	44.7	15.4	2.3	107,424
PULASKI	21,529	3,506	34.3	27.6	27.2	6.2	4.7	2,613	20.2	24.1	37.9	15.8	2.0	99,638
PUTNAM	25,521	8,565	27.6	27.6	29.9	9.3	5.5	6,844	15.9	20.9	33.1	20.0	10.1	116,769
QUITMAN	17,521	1,027	39.5	33.8	20.4	4.4	1.9	834	35.6	33.8	24.0	6.6	0.0	66,491
RABUN	25,274	7,506	25.6	33.6	29.1	6.5	5.2	6,021	12.8	13.8	35.1	26.5	11.8	139,817
RANDOLPH	15,234	2,832	48.3	25.1	20.0	4.7	1.9	1,984	43.1	29.1	20.8	6.0	1.0	59,648
RICHMOND	21,748	75,866	30.2	28.8	28.9	7.9	4.2	44,777	10.9	22.7	50.2	13.7	2.5	109,833
ROCKDALE	28,861	29,366	13.7	21.8	37.4	17.5	9.6	22,118	3.9	4.9	43.9	41.1	6.3	167,631
SCHLEY	18,392	1,615	34.9	29.9	26.6	6.1	2.5	1,253	28.9	32.4	27.3	9.1	2.3	73,598
SCREVEN	17,521	5,967	35.8	31.6	26.4	3.9	2.3	4,676	30.8	28.4	29.9	9.8	1.0	74,505
SEMINOLE	18,790	3,703	38.3	27.9	25.0	6.0	2.8	2,994	27.0	31.7	31.7	8.9	0.8	77,891
SPALDING	21,318	23,831	26.7	27.6	33.0	8.7	4.0	15,317	9.3	18.9	49.1	19.3	3.4	117,402
STEPHENS	19,737	10,135	33.3	32.3	25.6	5.9	2.8	7,462	15.3	24.6	41.6	15.6	2.8	105,903
STEWART	19,388	1,934	42.9	31.1	19.3	3.8	2.9	1,432	43.7	26.6	22.5	5.0	2.2	56,081
SUMTER	19,131	12,063	32.8	31.1	26.1	6.7	3.3	7,835	20.0	31.7	33.7	12.9	1.5	87,565
TALBOT	17,595	2,750	42.2	23.8	26.6	5.6	1.8	2,272	36.6	25.9	27.3	9.2	0.9	66,241
TALIAFERRO	19,200	843	43.5	29.8	18.6	4.9	3.2	654	35.8	31.5	26.5	6.3	0.0	64,894
TATTNALL	16,716	7,643	38.3	27.3	27.4	4.9	2.1	5,502	31.4	27.0	31.3	9.6	0.8	77,359
TAYLOR	16,335	3,400	42.8	27.7	22.3	5.3	2.0	2,645	31.9	29.6	29.4	8.0	1.0	73,103
TELFAIR	17,372	4,140	41.5	28.3	21.7	5.5	2.9	3,264	40.4	31.2	22.2	5.2	1.0	59,752
TERRELL	17,526	4,011	40.1	28.4	24.1	3.9	3.4	2,707	25.3	32.5	32.6	8.0	1.7	80,210
THOMAS	20,156	17,920	34.3	27.5	28.0	6.8	3.5	12,747	20.4	25.4	34.7	16.3	3.2	97,232
TIFT	21,151	15,039	31.9	27.2	28.1	8.7	4.1	10,233	25.0	21.4	33.6	16.5	3.5	96,558
TOOMBS	17,864	10,576	39.8	26.2	25.2	6.4	2.4	7,045	29.9	25.8	32.4	10.6	1.3	78,786
TOWNS	24,300	4,888	30.2	29.9	28.0	6.9	4.9	4,176	14.6	10.2	29.5	34.0	11.7	154,978
TREUTLEN	16,253	2,515	43.4	27.9	22.9	3.4	2.4	1,903	46.0	21.5	24.0	7.6	0.8	58,678
TROUP	22,358	24,247	29.5	26.6	30.4	8.3	5.2	15,927	11.7	20.6	43.0	20.9	3.9	118,132
TURNER	16,363	3,498	42.4	26.9	22.3	6.4	2.0	2,530	34.0	31.0	25.7	8.0	1.3	71,813
TWIGGS	18,068	3,919	34.5	27.0	28.9	7.6	2.0	3,239	37.9	30.1	26.6	4.3	1.2	66,446
UNION	23,027	9,419	30.0	30.5	29.8	6.7	3.0	7,801	7.4	11.4	36.1	35.1	9.9	160,269
UPSON	20,143	11,156	32.6	27.9	28.3	6.5	2.9	7,910	16.1	30.7	39.3	12.5	1.5	93,756
WALKER	19,776	25,572	29.3	31.3	31.6	5.5	2.2	19,873	15.9	26.3	42.5	12.9	2.4	98,714
WALTON	24,557	29,927	17.9	24.7	38.3	13.1	6.1	23,247	7.0	9.1	39.7	36.5	7.8	161,043
WARE	18,921	13,642	36.5	29.4	26.4	5.4	2.3	9,728	30.2	29.8	30.4	8.1	1.5	78,637
WARREN	17,941	2,402	41.6	28.1	24.5	3.0	2.7	1,866	34.5	29.7	27.3	7.2	1.3	69,732
WASHINGTON	18,380	7,624	37.4	25.3	27.2	7.4	2.7	5,692	29.9	26.2	28.7	13.4	1.8	79,945
WAYNE	19,532	10,448	33.0	27.2	29.2	7.5	3.1	8,061	28.8	26.3	30.7	12.2	2.0	81,697
WEBSTER	18,306	898	37.3	30.4	25.1	3.6	3.7	734	44.1	24.4	24.3	5.7	1.5	60,606
WHEELER	16,261	2,079	44.4	27.9	20.4	4.8	2.5	1,628	37.0	26.8	28.3	6.5	1.3	68,609
WHITE	21,079	10,135	24.8	32.3	33.5	6.1	2.5	8,112	8.4	11.0	36.5	37.4	6.7	157,095
GEORGIA	28,047		21.3	23.7	33.4	12.5	9.2		9.8	12.6	35.8	33.1	8.8	148,827
UNITED STATES	27,916		21.9	25.0	32.3	12.3	8.4		7.9	10.5	27.1	35.6	19.0	192,285

12-D

COUNTY	FINANCIAL SERVICES				THE HOME						ENTERTAINMENT						PERSONAL			
					Home Improvements		Furnishings													
	Auto Loan	Home Loan	Invest-ments	Retire-ment Plans	Home Repair	Lawn & Garden	Comput-ers & Hard-ware	Major Appli-ances	TV, Radio, Sound Equip-ment	Furni-ture	Dine out/ Carry out	Sports Equip-ment	Fees & Tickets	Toys & Games	Travel	Cable TV	Apparel & Services	Auto Repairs	Health Insur-ance	Pets & Supplies
JACKSON	98	83	63	80	81	95	78	88	83	79	83	79	73	86	77	87	72	85	92	93
JASPER	99	77	57	74	83	104	75	91	83	75	82	81	68	87	76	89	71	84	98	98
JEFF DAVIS	75	54	36	52	57	74	55	67	62	54	62	60	48	65	54	66	53	63	72	72
JEFFERSON	74	51	32	49	55	75	53	66	62	52	61	59	45	64	52	67	52	62	73	72
JENKINS	75	50	26	46	55	78	51	67	60	50	60	61	42	63	50	66	50	62	74	74
JOHNSON	74	47	21	44	53	77	49	65	58	47	57	59	39	61	48	64	49	60	72	73
JONES	101	86	68	84	87	101	81	93	86	82	86	84	77	90	81	90	75	88	96	98
LAMAR	89	72	59	71	74	89	71	81	78	71	77	71	66	80	71	82	67	78	87	86
LANIER	73	57	42	55	58	72	57	66	63	56	62	59	51	65	56	66	54	63	70	70
LAURENS	84	66	54	65	69	84	67	76	74	67	73	67	61	75	66	78	64	74	82	81
LEE	118	112	90	109	106	114	100	109	102	105	103	100	99	107	100	104	91	105	107	113
LIBERTY	77	61	53	64	55	59	75	66	73	69	73	65	67	75	66	70	65	73	64	67
LINCOLN	83	59	34	55	66	91	58	77	66	57	66	67	49	69	59	71	56	70	83	84
LONG	65	58	49	57	55	58	57	60	59	57	58	54	54	61	56	59	51	60	59	61
LOWNDES	80	69	67	71	66	71	77	73	78	74	77	67	72	77	72	77	69	76	75	74
LUMPKIN	92	81	68	80	79	89	77	84	80	78	80	76	74	82	77	83	71	82	86	88
MCDUFFIE	86	67	52	66	68	84	68	77	75	67	74	68	62	77	67	79	65	75	84	82
MCINTOSH	77	54	30	51	60	82	55	71	62	53	62	63	46	65	55	67	53	65	76	77
MACON	69	47	29	45	51	71	49	62	59	48	58	55	42	59	48	64	49	59	69	68
MADISON	90	70	47	67	71	90	66	80	72	67	72	71	60	76	66	77	63	75	83	86
MARION	76	54	31	51	58	77	54	68	61	53	61	61	46	65	53	65	52	63	72	74
MERIWETHER	87	61	40	58	66	89	63	78	72	61	71	69	54	75	62	78	61	73	86	85
MILLER	82	55	28	52	63	89	56	76	65	55	65	67	46	68	56	71	55	68	82	83
MITCHELL	74	55	43	55	57	73	58	66	65	57	64	58	52	67	57	69	56	65	73	71
MONROE	102	95	81	93	93	102	87	96	90	89	90	86	86	93	88	93	80	92	97	100
MONTGOMERY	80	59	39	56	63	83	60	74	67	58	66	66	52	69	59	72	57	69	80	80
MORGAN	105	87	65	84	90	109	82	98	88	83	88	87	76	93	83	93	77	91	101	104
MURRAY	90	69	47	65	71	89	67	80	73	67	73	72	60	78	66	77	63	76	83	86
MUSCOGEE	82	79	87	82	76	76	82	77	84	82	83	70	82	84	81	84	75	81	81	78
NEWTON	98	99	98	99	97	97	95	96	95	96	95	87	96	98	95	95	85	95	96	97
OCONEE	128	138	141	140	138	135	123	130	121	129	122	117	130	125	129	122	111	124	125	131
OGLETHORPE	93	71	47	68	74	95	68	84	75	68	75	75	61	78	68	80	65	78	88	90
PAULDING	113	116	98	114	104	103	103	105	101	109	102	98	104	106	102	99	91	104	99	106
PEACH	84	70	60	69	70	82	69	76	76	70	75	67	66	76	69	80	66	75	82	80
PICKENS	102	86	71	84	88	106	82	95	88	83	87	84	78	89	84	92	76	90	101	100
PIERCE	73	56	39	54	58	73	55	66	61	55	61	59	49	64	54	64	52	63	70	71
PIKE	104	88	68	86	88	103	82	95	87	84	87	85	78	91	83	91	76	90	97	100
POLK	84	62	48	60	66	85	65	76	72	62	71	67	57	75	63	76	61	71	83	81
PULASKI	90	67	52	66	73	95	69	83	78	68	77	72	62	80	69	84	66	78	93	89
PUTNAM	102	79	54	77	88	113	80	100	86	77	85	87	70	88	81	91	73	92	104	105
QUITMAN	77	49	21	45	55	80	51	68	61	49	60	62	40	64	50	67	51	63	75	77
RABUN	97	74	51	72	82	108	74	93	80	72	80	82	65	83	75	86	68	85	98	99
RANDOLPH	66	44	26	42	48	68	47	59	56	45	54	53	39	57	46	61	46	55	67	65
RICHMOND	79	71	74	74	67	71	76	72	79	75	78	65	74	78	73	80	70	77	77	74
ROCKDALE	115	120	119	121	115	112	112	112	111	116	112	103	116	115	114	110	101	112	109	114
SCHLEY	85	59	32	55	64	88	58	75	65	57	66	67	48	71	56	71	56	68	80	83
SCREVEN	79	54	30	50	59	81	55	70	64	54	63	63	46	67	54	69	54	65	77	77
SEMINOLE	81	56	32	52	63	86	57	75	66	55	65	66	48	68	57	72	55	69	83	81
SPALDING	82	74	74	74	73	80	76	78	80	75	79	68	74	81	75	82	70	77	83	80
STEPHENS	78	59	49	58	64	81	62	73	69	59	67	64	55	71	62	73	58	69	80	77
STEWART	85	54	23	50	61	88	56	75	67	54	66	68	44	70	54	73	56	69	83	84
SUMTER	77	61	56	62	62	74	68	71	72	65	71	63	62	73	65	75	63	71	76	74
TALBOT	79	50	22	46	56	81	52	70	62	50	61	63	41	65	51	68	52	64	77	78
TALIAFERRO	79	50	22	46	57	82	52	70	62	50	62	64	41	65	51	68	52	64	77	78
TATTNALL	74	57	41	54	59	74	57	67	63	56	62	60	51	65	56	66	54	64	72	72
TAYLOR	73	48	23	45	55	78	49	66	58	48	57	59	40	60	49	63	48	60	72	74
TELFAIR	78	51	27	48	58	81	54	70	64	52	63	63	44	66	53	70	53	65	79	77
TERRELL	76	55	40	54	58	76	58	68	67	57	66	61	51	68	57	72	57	66	76	74
THOMAS	79	66	57	65	67	78	66	73	71	66	71	64	62	72	66	75	62	71	78	76
TIFT	84	71	66	71	70	80	75	77	80	74	79	69	70	80	73	82	70	78	82	81
TOOMBS	68	58	56	58	58	65	61	64	65	60	64	57	58	66	60	67	57	64	68	66
TOWNS	82	71	60	68	79	97	68	86	73	68	72	72	64	69	74	78	62	79	92	87
TREUTLEN	74	47	20	43	53	76	48	65	58	47	57	59	39	61	47	64	49	60	72	73
TROUP	87	75	71	76	76	85	78	81	83	77	82	72	74	84	76	85	72	81	86	84
TURNER	72	52	39	51	57	75	56	67	62	53	61	59	48	63	54	66	53	63	73	72
TWIGGS	85	57	29	53	63	87	58	76	68	57	67	69	48	71	57	74	57	70	82	84
UNION	87	67	44	65	77	102	68	88	72	65	72	76	59	73	70	77	61	79	91	92
UPSON	81	63	52	61	66	82	65	74	72	63	71	65	59	74	64	77	61	71	82	78
WALKER	81	63	50	61	67	84	63	75	70	62	69	66	57	73	63	74	60	70	81	79
WALTON	105	102	90	101	98	103	93	99	95	97	95	91	93	99	94	95	85	96	98	102
WARE	73	57	48	56	60	74	59	67	66	57	65	59	54	67	59	71	56	65	76	71
WARREN	80	52	24	48	58	83	53	71	63	52	62	64	43	66	52	69	53	65	78	79
WASHINGTON	81	58	38	55	62	83	59	73	69	58	68	65	51	70	58	75	58	69	81	79
WAYNE	81	67	56	65	69	82	67	76	72	66	71	67	62	73	66	75	62	73	80	79
WEBSTER	84	54	23	49	60	87	55	75	66	54	66	68	44	69	54	73	55	68	82	84
WHEELER	75	49	24	46	55	79	50	66	59	49	59	60	41	62	49	65	50	61	73	75
WHITE	85	72	54	70	73	87	69	80	72	69	72	71	64	74	69	75	63	76	81	84
GEORGIA	111	102	94	103	98	104	103	103	104	103	104	96	100	106	100	104	93	104	104	106
UNITED STATES	100	100	100	100	100	100	100	100	100	100	100	100	100	100	100	100	100	100	100	100

POPULATION CHANGE

COUNTY	FIPS Code	CBSA Code	DMA Code	POPULATION			2000-2007 ANNUAL RATE		RACE (%)					
									White		Black		Asian/Pacific	
				2000	2007	2012	% Rate	State Rank	2000	2007	2000	2007	2000	2007
WHITFIELD	313	19140	575	83,525	95,837	104,340	1.9	47	80.9	75.2	3.8	4.2	1.0	1.2
WILCOX	315	00000	503	8,577	8,541	8,371	-0.1	139	62.6	60.2	36.2	38.6	0.2	0.2
WILKES	317	00000	520	10,687	10,486	10,227	-0.3	144	55.1	50.3	43.1	47.4	0.3	0.3
WILKINSON	319	00000	503	10,220	10,542	10,756	0.4	113	58.0	53.1	40.7	45.3	0.1	0.1
WORTH	321	10500	525	21,967	22,006	22,018	0.0	134	68.7	66.5	29.6	31.8	0.2	0.2
GEORGIA							2.3		65.1	62.1	28.7	29.8	2.2	2.7
UNITED STATES							1.2		75.1	72.7	12.3	12.6	3.8	4.5

COUNTY	% HISPANIC ORIGIN		2007 AGE DISTRIBUTION (%)										MEDIAN AGE	% 2007 Males	% 2007 Females
	2000	2007	0-4	5-9	10-14	15-19	20-24	25-44	45-64	65-84	85+	18+	2007		
WHITFIELD	22.1	28.8	8.2	7.9	6.8	6.0	6.1	30.5	23.3	9.7	1.4	73.4	34.7	50.6	49.4
WILCOX	1.6	1.6	6.1	6.6	5.2	5.1	7.1	30.7	26.5	10.7	2.0	79.2	37.8	56.6	43.4
WILKES	2.0	2.5	6.3	5.7	6.1	5.5	6.4	25.6	27.3	14.5	2.7	78.7	41.4	48.3	51.7
WILKINSON	1.0	1.3	7.5	7.7	5.6	6.5	6.0	26.8	26.4	11.9	1.6	75.2	38.1	48.1	51.9
WORTH	1.1	1.1	7.3	6.8	6.8	7.2	7.2	25.1	27.1	11.0	1.5	74.6	37.5	48.0	52.0
GEORGIA	5.3	6.9	7.3	7.0	6.9	7.0	7.1	30.3	24.6	8.7	1.3	74.8	35.0	49.4	50.6
UNITED STATES	12.5	15.0	6.9	6.5	6.8	7.1	7.0	27.6	25.4	10.7	1.9	75.6	36.7	49.2	50.8

COUNTY	HOUSEHOLDS					FAMILIES			MEDIAN HOUSEHOLD INCOME			
	2000	2007	2012	% Annual Rate 2000-2007	2007 Average HH Size	2000	2007	% Annual Rate 2000-2007	2007	2012	2007 National Rank	2007 State Rank
WHITFIELD	29,385	32,947	35,631	1.6	2.87	22,149	24,169	1.2	48,449	56,038	784	36
WILCOX	2,785	2,756	2,714	-0.1	2.49	1,976	1,893	-0.6	33,266	37,722	2634	123
WILKES	4,314	4,333	4,270	0.1	2.39	2,970	2,883	-0.4	34,242	39,162	2520	115
WILKINSON	3,827	4,025	4,148	0.7	2.59	2,806	2,866	0.3	39,847	44,643	1746	71
WORTH	8,106	8,297	8,381	0.3	2.63	6,124	6,102	0.0	39,001	43,983	1852	77
GEORGIA				2.3	2.65			2.0	55,102	65,884		
UNITED STATES				1.2	2.59			1.0	53,154	62,503		

COUNTY	2007 Per Capita Income	2007 HH Income Base	2007 HOUSEHOLD INCOME DISTRIBUTION (%)					2007 Home Value Base	2007 HOME VALUE DISTRIBUTION (%)					2007 Median Home Value
			Less than $25,000	$25,000 to $49,999	$50,000 to $99,999	$100,000 to $149,999	$150,000 or More		Less than $50,000	$50,000 to $89,999	$90,000 to $174,999	$175,000 to $399,999	$400,000 or More	
WHITFIELD	22,384	32,947	22.2	29.0	33.7	9.1	6.0	22,637	11.7	15.1	44.4	22.9	5.8	127,410
WILCOX	17,575	2,756	38.4	28.4	25.3	5.3	2.6	2,215	38.7	29.8	24.7	6.8	0.0	65,187
WILKES	18,952	4,333	37.3	27.8	26.9	6.0	2.1	3,311	24.4	29.2	31.0	13.0	2.3	86,056
WILKINSON	18,154	4,025	33.8	27.7	31.1	5.7	1.7	3,326	29.3	29.5	32.1	7.8	1.4	77,955
WORTH	19,293	8,297	33.4	27.7	29.8	5.8	3.2	6,371	24.1	32.2	34.2	8.4	1.1	81,312
GEORGIA	28,047		21.3	23.7	33.4	12.5	9.2		9.8	12.6	35.8	33.1	8.8	148,827
UNITED STATES	27,916		21.9	25.0	32.3	12.3	8.4		7.9	10.5	27.1	35.6	19.0	192,285

SPENDING POTENTIAL INDICES

COUNTY	FINANCIAL SERVICES				THE HOME						ENTERTAINMENT						PERSONAL			
					Home Improvements		Furnishings													
	Auto Loan	Home Loan	Invest-ments	Retire-ment Plans	Home Repair	Lawn & Garden	Comput-ers & Hard-ware	Major Appli-ances	TV, Radio, Sound Equip-ment	Furni-ture	Dine out/ Carry out	Sports Equip-ment	Fees & Tickets	Toys & Games	Travel	Cable TV	Apparel & Services	Auto Repairs	Health Insur-ance	Pets & Supplies
WHITFIELD	99	85	72	84	85	96	86	92	89	86	90	85	80	92	84	91	80	91	93	95
WILCOX	82	54	25	50	61	87	55	74	65	53	64	66	44	68	54	71	54	67	81	82
WILKES	76	55	37	52	61	81	56	70	64	54	63	62	48	66	56	70	54	65	78	76
WILKINSON	82	57	32	53	62	86	58	74	66	56	66	66	48	69	57	72	56	68	81	81
WORTH	85	63	45	61	67	86	64	76	71	63	71	68	56	74	63	76	61	72	82	83
GEORGIA	111	102	94	103	98	104	103	103	104	103	104	96	100	106	100	104	93	104	104	106
UNITED STATES	100	100	100	100	100	100	100	100	100	100	100	100	100	100	100	100	100	100	100	100

COUNTY	FIPS Code	CBSA Code	DMA Code	POPULATION			2000-2007 ANNUAL RATE		RACE (%)					
									White		Black		Asian/Pacific	
				2000	2007	2012	% Rate	State Rank	2000	2007	2000	2007	2000	2007
HAWAII	001	25900	744	148,677	178,585	203,810	2.6	1	31.5	31.9	0.5	0.6	38.0	37.1
HONOLULU	003	26180	744	876,156	911,056	934,955	0.5	4	21.3	21.4	2.4	2.9	54.9	54.0
KALAWAO	005	00000	744	147	121	111	-2.6	5	25.9	26.4	0.0	0.0	65.3	62.8
KAUAI	007	28180	744	58,463	62,999	66,288	1.0	3	29.5	29.8	0.3	0.4	45.1	44.4
MAUI	009	27980	744	128,094	146,794	159,119	1.9	2	33.9	34.3	0.4	0.5	41.7	40.9
HAWAII							1.0		24.3	24.7	1.8	2.2	51.0	49.7
UNITED STATES							1.2		75.1	72.7	12.3	12.6	3.8	4.5

POPULATION COMPOSITION

COUNTY	% HISPANIC ORIGIN		2007 AGE DISTRIBUTION (%)										MEDIAN AGE	% 2007 Males	% 2007 Females
	2000	2007	0-4	5-9	10-14	15-19	20-24	25-44	45-64	65-84	85+	18+	2007		
HAWAII	9.5	10.5	6.0	5.8	6.9	7.1	6.8	23.1	30.8	11.6	1.8	76.8	40.5	50.1	49.9
HONOLULU	6.7	7.4	6.6	6.0	6.5	6.4	7.4	28.9	24.7	11.4	2.0	77.1	36.7	50.2	49.8
KALAWAO	4.1	5.0	1.7	0.0	0.0	1.7	0.0	9.9	43.0	43.0	0.8	97.5	63.0	46.3	53.7
KAUAI	8.2	9.1	6.1	5.7	7.4	7.6	7.1	23.4	29.2	11.4	2.1	75.9	39.5	49.8	50.2
MAUI	7.8	8.9	6.5	6.2	6.7	7.0	7.2	25.9	28.9	9.9	1.7	76.2	38.1	49.9	50.1
HAWAII	7.2	8.1	6.5	6.0	6.6	6.6	7.3	27.5	26.3	11.2	1.9	76.9	37.4	50.1	49.9
UNITED STATES	12.5	15.0	6.9	6.5	6.8	7.1	7.0	27.6	25.4	10.7	1.9	75.6	36.7	49.2	50.8

COUNTY	HOUSEHOLDS					FAMILIES			MEDIAN HOUSEHOLD INCOME			
	2000	2007	2012	% Annual Rate 2000-2007	2007 Average HH Size	2000	2007	% Annual Rate 2000-2007	2007	2012	2007 National Rank	2007 State Rank
HAWAII	52,985	64,744	74,503	2.8	2.71	36,903	44,513	2.6	48,166	54,678	802	4
HONOLULU	286,450	303,237	313,155	0.8	2.90	205,672	215,138	0.6	62,824	72,139	196	1
KALAWAO	115	98	91	-2.2	1.23	22	18	-2.7	9,074	9,681	3141	5
KAUAI	20,183	22,598	24,137	1.6	2.76	14,572	16,125	1.4	54,112	61,841	444	3
MAUI	43,507	50,840	55,462	2.2	2.86	29,899	34,482	2.0	58,456	65,953	298	2
HAWAII				1.3	2.86			1.1	59,776	67,554		
UNITED STATES				1.2	2.59			1.0	53,154	62,503		

COUNTY	2007 Per Capita Income	2007 HH Income Base	2007 HOUSEHOLD INCOME DISTRIBUTION (%)					2007 Home Value Base	2007 HOME VALUE DISTRIBUTION (%)					2007 Median Home Value
			Less than $25,000	$25,000 to $49,999	$50,000 to $99,999	$100,000 to $149,999	$150,000 or More		Less than $50,000	$50,000 to $89,999	$90,000 to $174,999	$175,000 to $399,999	$400,000 or More	
HAWAII	23,511	64,744	25.7	25.9	30.6	12.2	5.6	42,870	1.3	1.6	6.5	42.0	48.5	392,597
HONOLULU	28,096	303,227	16.9	22.1	33.3	17.5	10.2	173,032	0.6	0.8	2.2	19.0	77.5	654,067
KALAWAO	12,645	98	67.3	32.7	0.0	0.0	0.0	0	0.0	0.0	0.0	0.0	0.0	0
KAUAI	25,768	22,598	20.9	24.6	33.3	14.7	6.5	14,263	0.4	0.3	1.6	21.2	76.5	564,428
MAUI	27,238	50,840	18.5	23.4	34.3	15.1	8.8	30,541	0.5	0.6	1.5	18.9	78.5	635,826
HAWAII	27,254		18.6	23.0	33.0	16.3	9.1		0.7	0.9	2.8	22.9	72.8	603,121
UNITED STATES	27,916		21.9	25.0	32.3	12.3	8.4		7.9	10.5	27.1	35.6	19.0	192,285

COUNTY	FINANCIAL SERVICES				THE HOME						ENTERTAINMENT						PERSONAL			
					Home Improvements		Furnishings													
	Auto Loan	Home Loan	Invest- ments	Retire- ment Plans	Home Repair	Lawn & Garden	Comput- ers & Hard- ware	Major Appli- ances	TV, Radio, Sound Equip- ment	Furni- ture	Dine out/ Carry out	Sports Equip- ment	Fees & Tickets	Toys & Games	Travel	Cable TV	Apparel & Services	Auto Repairs	Health Insur- ance	Pets & Supplies
HAWAII	88	89	88	88	93	96	87	93	86	86	86	84	87	86	90	87	77	89	92	93
HONOLULU	104	117	117	116	115	100	122	112	110	117	112	114	121	109	119	105	104	116	101	108
KALAWAO	18	13	20	15	14	16	22	18	23	19	23	17	19	20	20	25	21	21	24	18
KAUAI	89	108	107	103	110	97	100	101	94	101	95	98	105	93	105	92	88	99	93	98
MAUI	100	113	112	112	111	99	115	108	104	111	105	110	113	102	113	99	97	111	98	106
HAWAII	100	112	112	111	111	99	115	108	105	111	106	108	114	104	113	101	98	111	99	106
UNITED STATES	100	100	100	100	100	100	100	100	100	100	100	100	100	100	100	100	100	100	100	100

POPULATION CHANGE

COUNTY	FIPS Code	CBSA Code	DMA Code	POPULATION			2000-2007 ANNUAL RATE		RACE (%)					
									White		Black		Asian/Pacific	
				2000	2007	2012	% Rate	State Rank	2000	2007	2000	2007	2000	2007
ADA	001	14260	757	300,904	370,738	428,133	2.9	5	92.9	92.0	0.6	0.8	1.9	2.2
ADAMS	003	00000	757	3,476	4,020	4,473	2.0	12	96.3	96.0	0.1	0.1	0.2	0.2
BANNOCK	005	38540	758	75,565	79,225	81,893	0.7	27	91.3	90.4	0.6	0.7	1.2	1.4
BEAR LAKE	007	00000	770	6,411	6,384	6,287	-0.1	39	97.7	97.6	0.1	0.1	0.1	0.1
BENEWAH	009	00000	881	9,171	9,295	9,390	0.2	35	88.7	88.1	0.1	0.1	0.2	0.2
BINGHAM	011	13940	758	41,735	44,513	46,563	0.9	25	82.4	80.6	0.2	0.2	0.6	0.7
BLAINE	013	00000	760	18,991	22,518	24,815	2.4	9	90.7	89.4	0.1	0.2	0.8	0.9
BOISE	015	14260	757	6,670	8,022	9,030	2.6	6	95.2	94.8	0.1	0.1	0.4	0.5
BONNER	017	00000	881	36,835	40,259	42,832	1.2	21	96.6	96.3	0.1	0.1	0.3	0.4
BONNEVILLE	019	26820	758	82,522	96,473	107,973	2.2	11	92.8	91.7	0.5	0.6	0.9	1.1
BOUNDARY	021	00000	881	9,871	10,868	11,640	1.3	20	95.2	94.8	0.2	0.2	0.6	0.8
BUTTE	023	00000	758	2,899	2,769	2,685	-0.6	44	94.7	94.0	0.3	0.3	0.2	0.3
CAMAS	025	00000	757	991	1,100	1,178	1.4	18	95.2	94.5	0.2	0.2	0.2	0.3
CANYON	027	14260	757	131,441	179,835	217,636	4.4	3	83.1	80.8	0.3	0.4	0.9	1.1
CARIBOU	029	00000	758	7,304	7,160	7,026	-0.3	41	96.1	95.6	0.1	0.1	0.2	0.2
CASSIA	031	15420	760	21,416	21,694	21,794	0.2	35	84.7	82.4	0.2	0.2	0.4	0.5
CLARK	033	00000	758	1,022	1,104	1,127	1.1	22	74.2	74.3	0.1	0.1	0.3	0.3
CLEARWATER	035	00000	881	8,930	8,955	8,835	0.0	38	94.8	94.7	0.1	0.1	0.4	0.4
CUSTER	037	00000	758	4,342	4,227	4,078	-0.4	42	97.3	96.9	0.0	0.0	0.0	0.0
ELMORE	039	34300	757	29,130	30,270	30,992	0.5	30	85.4	83.5	3.2	3.9	1.9	2.2
FRANKLIN	041	30860	770	11,329	12,887	14,106	1.8	13	95.1	94.3	0.1	0.1	0.2	0.2
FREMONT	043	39940	758	11,819	12,584	13,020	0.9	25	91.4	90.1	0.2	0.2	0.4	0.5
GEM	045	14260	757	15,181	17,190	18,721	1.7	15	93.8	93.0	0.1	0.1	0.4	0.5
GOODING	047	00000	760	14,155	15,195	15,836	1.0	23	87.6	85.9	0.2	0.3	0.3	0.3
IDAHO	049	00000	881	15,511	15,865	15,959	0.3	33	94.1	93.7	0.1	0.1	0.3	0.3
JEFFERSON	051	26820	758	19,155	22,926	26,383	2.5	7	90.9	89.4	0.3	0.4	0.3	0.4
JEROME	053	46300	760	18,342	20,169	21,585	1.3	20	87.0	85.1	0.2	0.3	0.3	0.4
KOOTENAI	055	17660	881	108,685	137,096	164,992	3.3	4	95.8	95.5	0.2	0.2	0.6	0.7
LATAH	057	34140	881	34,935	36,632	37,622	0.7	27	93.9	93.2	0.6	0.7	2.2	2.6
LEMHI	059	00000	758	7,806	8,162	8,358	0.6	29	96.6	96.4	0.1	0.1	0.2	0.3
LEWIS	061	00000	881	3,747	3,794	3,829	0.2	35	92.2	92.0	0.3	0.3	0.5	0.5
LINCOLN	063	00000	760	4,044	4,752	5,338	2.3	10	86.5	84.6	0.5	0.7	0.5	0.6
MADISON	065	39940	758	27,467	37,616	48,227	4.4	3	95.5	94.8	0.2	0.3	0.7	0.9
MINIDOKA	067	15420	760	20,174	19,501	18,930	-0.5	43	78.1	75.1	0.3	0.3	0.4	0.5
NEZ PERCE	069	30300	881	37,410	38,401	39,104	0.4	32	91.6	91.0	0.3	0.3	0.7	0.9
ONEIDA	071	00000	770	4,125	4,258	4,344	0.4	32	97.5	97.2	0.1	0.1	0.2	0.2
OWYHEE	073	14260	757	10,644	11,741	12,543	1.4	18	76.9	74.1	0.2	0.2	0.5	0.6
PAYETTE	075	36620	757	20,578	23,106	25,066	1.6	16	90.3	89.0	0.1	0.1	0.9	1.0
POWER	077	38540	758	7,538	7,594	7,639	0.1	37	83.8	83.6	0.1	0.1	0.4	0.4
SHOSHONE	079	00000	881	13,771	13,447	13,225	-0.3	41	95.8	95.6	0.1	0.1	0.3	0.4
TETON	081	27220	758	5,999	9,041	11,128	5.8	1	91.3	89.9	0.2	0.2	0.4	0.5
TWIN FALLS	083	46300	760	64,284	72,799	79,609	1.7	15	92.5	91.5	0.2	0.2	0.8	1.0
VALLEY	085	00000	757	7,651	9,094	10,335	2.4	9	96.4	96.1	0.0	0.1	0.3	0.4
WASHINGTON	087	00000	757	9,977	10,429	10,769	0.6	29	87.6	85.9	0.1	0.1	1.1	1.3
IDAHO							2.2		91.0	89.9	0.4	0.5	1.0	1.2
UNITED STATES							1.2		75.1	72.7	12.3	12.6	3.8	4.5

15-A

COUNTY	% HISPANIC ORIGIN		2007 AGE DISTRIBUTION (%)									MEDIAN AGE	% 2007 Males	% 2007 Females
	2000	2007	0-4	5-9	10-14	15-19	20-24	25-44	45-64	65-84	85+	18+	2007		
ADA	4.5	5.1	7.9	7.3	7.1	6.7	7.3	30.4	24.6	7.4	1.4	73.7	33.9	50.1	49.9
ADAMS	1.6	1.8	4.0	4.1	5.6	7.5	7.4	17.4	35.8	16.2	2.0	81.6	47.4	52.1	47.9
BANNOCK	4.7	5.3	8.4	7.2	6.7	7.5	9.5	28.2	22.5	8.5	1.5	73.7	30.3	49.5	50.5
BEAR LAKE	2.4	2.4	8.1	6.6	6.5	8.1	9.5	20.0	26.0	12.6	2.5	73.6	36.4	49.6	50.4
BENEWAH	1.5	1.7	6.6	6.4	6.4	6.5	6.2	22.8	30.0	13.2	1.8	76.3	41.5	51.1	48.9
BINGHAM	13.3	15.1	9.8	8.1	7.8	7.9	9.0	24.5	22.8	8.8	1.3	69.3	30.1	50.0	50.0
BLAINE	10.7	12.3	5.4	5.6	5.9	6.8	5.9	27.5	32.9	9.1	0.8	78.9	40.1	51.6	48.4
BOISE	3.4	3.9	6.1	6.9	6.4	6.5	5.2	20.9	36.5	10.6	1.0	75.9	43.7	51.2	48.8
BONNER	1.6	1.9	5.6	5.7	6.3	7.0	5.8	21.5	34.5	11.9	1.6	77.8	43.6	50.1	49.9
BONNEVILLE	6.9	8.0	8.9	7.9	7.5	7.8	8.1	25.8	23.9	8.8	1.3	70.7	31.9	49.8	50.2
BOUNDARY	3.4	3.8	6.8	6.8	6.5	6.9	8.2	20.6	30.7	12.1	1.5	75.4	40.0	50.3	49.7
BUTTE	4.1	4.8	6.5	5.8	7.3	6.6	8.3	19.5	29.7	14.5	1.9	76.3	41.4	49.4	50.6
CAMAS	5.5	6.5	4.3	4.9	8.4	7.6	4.5	25.0	32.1	11.4	1.9	77.0	42.1	51.6	48.4
CANYON	18.6	21.2	9.6	8.6	7.8	7.1	6.8	29.4	21.0	8.1	1.6	69.8	31.1	49.8	50.2
CARIBOU	4.0	4.6	8.1	7.4	7.1	7.0	7.8	23.2	26.3	11.2	1.9	73.1	35.9	49.8	50.2
CASSIA	18.7	21.3	9.6	8.1	8.0	7.4	8.4	23.9	22.8	9.8	2.0	69.7	31.3	50.4	49.6
CLARK	34.2	34.2	9.7	8.3	9.6	6.5	8.3	25.3	22.6	9.0	0.7	68.5	31.4	52.4	47.6
CLEARWATER	1.8	1.9	5.0	4.6	5.4	5.6	7.1	22.4	32.5	15.4	2.0	81.5	44.9	53.7	46.3
CUSTER	4.2	4.8	5.4	5.2	5.4	7.2	6.1	20.5	35.4	13.3	1.5	79.0	45.1	50.7	49.3
ELMORE	12.0	13.5	8.7	7.1	5.7	6.7	12.3	33.7	17.7	7.0	1.0	74.8	29.7	54.7	45.3
FRANKLIN	5.2	6.1	11.1	9.4	8.5	8.2	7.3	24.9	20.0	8.8	1.8	65.7	28.6	50.2	49.8
FREMONT	10.6	12.2	9.2	8.4	6.8	7.9	7.6	24.7	23.6	10.4	1.6	70.6	32.6	51.8	48.2
GEM	6.9	7.9	7.5	7.0	7.0	6.5	6.6	23.8	26.3	12.8	2.5	74.4	38.5	49.4	50.6
GOODING	17.1	19.3	8.5	7.6	7.3	6.4	6.4	25.7	24.1	11.7	2.3	72.9	35.7	51.3	48.7
IDAHO	1.6	1.8	5.4	5.0	5.4	6.6	8.3	18.4	33.2	15.2	2.6	80.1	45.6	50.9	49.1
JEFFERSON	10.0	11.6	9.9	8.2	8.5	8.2	9.0	24.3	22.4	8.3	1.1	68.2	29.2	50.6	49.2
JEROME	17.2	19.5	8.9	7.7	7.7	6.7	7.9	25.9	23.9	9.7	1.6	71.5	33.3	50.8	49.2
KOOTENAI	2.3	2.6	7.0	6.4	7.0	6.9	6.7	26.2	27.5	10.6	1.7	75.4	37.6	49.5	50.5
LATAH	2.1	2.4	5.4	4.5	4.9	11.2	16.8	25.8	21.8	7.7	1.8	82.0	28.7	51.9	48.1
LEMHI	2.2	2.5	5.2	5.0	6.1	6.9	6.1	19.1	34.9	14.5	2.2	79.2	46.0	50.1	49.9
LEWIS	1.9	1.9	5.3	4.4	6.5	7.0	6.5	19.3	30.8	17.9	2.3	79.2	45.5	51.1	48.9
LINCOLN	13.4	15.5	8.1	7.3	7.3	7.2	6.3	26.5	24.7	11.0	1.8	72.9	35.3	52.0	48.0
MADISON	3.9	4.6	7.4	6.1	6.8	22.8	21.5	15.1	14.2	5.3	0.9	74.6	21.6	48.1	51.9
MINIDOKA	25.5	28.7	9.0	7.8	7.5	6.6	7.9	24.3	24.5	10.8	1.7	71.7	33.8	50.3	49.7
NEZ PERCE	1.9	2.2	6.2	5.4	6.0	6.3	7.2	25.6	27.0	13.6	2.8	78.9	39.6	49.0	51.0
ONEIDA	2.3	2.7	8.9	6.8	6.2	6.6	10.5	20.3	25.5	13.0	2.3	74.2	36.3	50.8	49.2
OWYHEE	23.1	26.1	8.5	7.4	8.2	7.3	6.6	26.2	23.8	10.5	1.5	71.1	34.2	52.5	47.5
PAYETTE	11.9	13.5	8.2	7.2	7.7	7.3	7.2	24.6	24.8	11.2	1.8	72.3	35.4	49.5	50.5
POWER	21.7	21.8	9.1	7.7	8.0	8.1	8.3	24.3	23.9	9.2	1.3	69.6	32.1	50.6	49.4
SHOSHONE	1.9	2.2	5.6	5.1	5.8	5.8	6.5	21.7	30.7	16.2	2.5	79.8	44.6	49.8	50.2
TETON	11.8	13.5	8.7	8.4	7.8	6.9	7.0	31.7	23.2	5.5	0.8	70.5	32.3	52.5	47.5
TWIN FALLS	9.4	10.7	7.9	6.9	6.6	6.7	8.1	25.9	24.6	11.0	2.5	74.7	35.0	49.2	50.8
VALLEY	2.0	2.3	4.2	4.7	6.1	7.1	4.3	20.8	37.0	14.4	1.4	79.5	46.3	51.9	48.1
WASHINGTON	13.8	15.7	7.1	6.7	7.2	6.4	6.9	21.9	26.7	14.5	2.6	75.1	40.4	49.5	50.5
IDAHO	7.9	9.0	8.0	7.1	7.0	7.5	8.1	26.8	24.7	9.3	1.6	73.6	33.9	50.1	49.9
UNITED STATES	12.5	15.0	6.9	6.5	6.8	7.1	7.0	27.6	25.4	10.7	1.9	75.6	36.7	49.2	50.8

COUNTY	HOUSEHOLDS					FAMILIES			MEDIAN HOUSEHOLD INCOME			
	2000	2007	2012	% Annual Rate 2000-2007	2007 Average HH Size	2000	2007	% Annual Rate 2000-2007	2007	2012	2007 National Rank	2007 State Rank
ADA	113,408	142,723	165,855	3.2	2.54	77,361	96,055	3.0	62,235	76,528	207	2
ADAMS	1,421	1,702	1,921	2.5	2.34	1,031	1,220	2.3	34,251	38,734	2518	44
BANNOCK	27,192	29,247	30,473	1.0	2.63	19,213	20,410	0.8	47,783	58,130	839	5
BEAR LAKE	2,259	2,325	2,318	0.4	2.72	1,710	1,743	0.3	39,857	45,531	1743	28
BENEWAH	3,580	3,720	3,791	0.5	2.46	2,537	2,604	0.4	37,958	42,881	2003	36
BINGHAM	13,317	14,556	15,356	1.2	3.03	10,713	11,612	1.1	45,034	52,129	1107	12
BLAINE	7,780	9,392	10,402	2.6	2.36	4,841	5,751	2.4	68,466	85,118	133	1
BOISE	2,616	3,213	3,641	2.9	2.47	1,899	2,305	2.7	46,043	51,989	997	9
BONNER	14,693	16,437	17,624	1.6	2.43	10,264	11,340	1.4	40,391	45,666	1678	27
BONNEVILLE	28,753	34,587	39,084	2.6	2.76	21,463	25,539	2.4	54,784	66,223	411	4
BOUNDARY	3,707	4,221	4,582	1.8	2.52	2,698	3,039	1.7	37,877	42,718	2009	37
BUTTE	1,089	1,080	1,062	-0.1	2.54	803	788	-0.3	36,479	41,033	2198	42
CAMAS	396	453	491	1.9	2.42	287	324	1.7	42,175	47,365	1429	21
CANYON	45,018	62,219	75,453	4.6	2.84	33,954	46,441	4.4	46,117	55,217	986	8
CARIBOU	2,560	2,603	2,592	0.2	2.73	1,978	1,992	0.1	45,460	51,625	1057	11
CASSIA	7,060	7,271	7,336	0.4	2.94	5,489	5,600	0.3	41,335	47,168	1545	22
CLARK	340	354	359	0.6	3.12	257	265	0.4	38,564	43,421	1922	35
CLEARWATER	3,456	3,528	3,505	0.3	2.35	2,483	2,505	0.1	39,459	44,523	1788	30
CUSTER	1,770	1,791	1,752	0.2	2.32	1,197	1,194	0.0	39,063	43,988	1841	33
ELMORE	9,092	9,672	9,983	0.9	2.71	6,848	7,209	0.7	43,808	51,083	1235	15
FRANKLIN	3,476	4,006	4,397	2.0	3.20	2,873	3,288	1.9	44,779	51,241	1132	13
FREMONT	3,885	4,230	4,426	1.2	2.88	3,029	3,268	1.1	40,481	46,128	1661	26
GEM	5,539	6,290	6,847	1.8	2.70	4,175	4,690	1.6	42,707	49,604	1364	19
GOODING	5,046	5,373	5,570	0.9	2.79	3,719	3,915	0.7	39,519	45,138	1778	29
IDAHO	6,084	6,324	6,420	0.5	2.40	4,294	4,407	0.4	36,671	42,305	2172	41
JEFFERSON	5,901	7,253	8,427	2.9	3.15	4,880	5,954	2.8	45,723	52,098	1030	10
JEROME	6,298	6,911	7,376	1.3	2.90	4,806	5,221	1.1	43,119	50,146	1315	17
KOOTENAI	41,308	52,210	62,912	3.3	2.60	29,668	37,054	3.1	47,146	54,758	894	6
LATAH	13,059	13,910	14,426	0.9	2.33	7,764	8,129	0.6	42,726	51,235	1362	18
LEMHI	3,275	3,508	3,622	1.0	2.32	2,217	2,342	0.8	37,003	42,206	2127	39
LEWIS	1,554	1,617	1,647	0.5	2.33	1,050	1,078	0.4	38,880	45,026	1871	34
LINCOLN	1,447	1,715	1,928	2.4	2.75	1,050	1,230	2.2	39,386	43,864	1798	31
MADISON	7,129	10,260	13,366	5.2	3.56	4,855	6,893	5.0	40,652	46,332	1648	24
MINIDOKA	6,973	6,883	6,725	-0.2	2.81	5,360	5,238	-0.3	39,094	44,693	1839	32
NEZ PERCE	15,286	15,912	16,264	0.6	2.37	10,151	10,419	0.4	46,663	55,625	939	7
ONEIDA	1,430	1,513	1,557	0.8	2.78	1,093	1,145	0.6	42,244	48,077	1421	20
OWYHEE	3,710	4,133	4,420	1.5	2.82	2,756	3,038	1.4	34,324	38,988	2511	43
PAYETTE	7,371	8,279	8,965	1.6	2.78	5,576	6,199	1.5	40,494	46,189	1660	25
POWER	2,560	2,621	2,648	0.3	2.88	1,968	1,996	0.2	40,676	47,001	1645	23
SHOSHONE	5,906	5,927	5,886	0.0	2.24	3,858	3,814	-0.2	36,990	43,436	2130	40
TETON	2,078	3,228	4,017	6.3	2.79	1,465	2,247	6.1	54,940	66,041	408	3
TWIN FALLS	23,853	27,475	30,185	2.0	2.60	16,967	19,305	1.8	43,603	51,143	1261	16
VALLEY	3,208	3,941	4,537	2.9	2.29	2,251	2,731	2.7	44,367	50,225	1171	14
WASHINGTON	3,762	3,965	4,096	0.7	2.59	2,737	2,851	0.6	37,161	42,270	2108	38
IDAHO				2.4	2.65			2.3	48,501	58,059		
UNITED STATES				1.2	2.59			1.0	53,154	62,503		

COUNTY	2007 Per Capita Income	2007 HH Income Base	2007 HOUSEHOLD INCOME DISTRIBUTION (%)					2007 Home Value Base	2007 HOME VALUE DISTRIBUTION (%)					2007 Median Home Value
			Less than $25,000	$25,000 to $49,999	$50,000 to $99,999	$100,000 to $149,999	$150,000 or More		Less than $50,000	$50,000 to $89,999	$90,000 to $174,999	$175,000 to $399,999	$400,000 or More	
ADA	30,892	142,723	14.6	24.2	37.5	14.7	8.9	103,263	3.9	3.1	19.5	60.2	13.2	224,748
ADAMS	18,425	1,702	33.3	37.7	22.7	5.1	1.2	1,373	8.7	11.4	39.1	29.6	11.2	154,056
BANNOCK	22,842	29,247	25.0	27.1	33.0	10.2	4.7	21,044	7.6	10.9	58.2	21.6	1.6	130,923
BEAR LAKE	17,560	2,325	26.0	36.0	31.4	5.9	0.8	1,951	5.7	13.4	60.3	17.7	2.8	129,566
BENEWAH	19,066	3,720	30.9	33.1	28.8	5.6	1.5	2,982	16.7	13.9	39.2	24.3	5.8	129,088
BINGHAM	18,112	14,556	23.6	32.7	33.0	8.1	2.7	11,712	7.8	9.7	54.7	25.1	2.7	142,216
BLAINE	42,397	9,392	12.8	22.6	34.5	14.8	15.3	6,651	3.7	1.9	5.7	29.2	59.4	477,222
BOISE	23,279	3,213	26.6	27.5	32.6	9.7	3.4	2,715	9.1	10.8	28.8	38.0	13.3	178,665
BONNER	20,635	16,437	30.8	30.5	29.7	6.7	2.3	13,032	6.5	8.1	37.3	36.7	11.4	171,267
BONNEVILLE	24,663	34,587	19.4	25.5	36.9	12.3	6.0	26,316	5.4	9.4	54.0	28.0	3.2	142,303
BOUNDARY	19,095	4,221	31.2	33.5	29.1	4.0	2.2	3,363	9.0	5.0	41.7	35.9	8.5	165,449
BUTTE	18,595	1,080	32.7	31.0	28.2	6.1	1.9	852	10.2	21.2	50.8	15.6	2.1	117,037
CAMAS	23,831	453	27.2	31.8	30.5	6.6	4.0	359	2.5	16.4	45.1	26.5	9.5	150,721
CANYON	19,849	62,219	22.4	31.6	34.7	8.1	3.1	46,684	5.7	6.3	42.4	40.6	5.0	168,843
CARIBOU	19,724	2,603	25.5	29.7	34.5	8.5	1.8	2,103	9.9	12.9	52.7	21.2	3.3	132,295
CASSIA	17,362	7,271	28.3	32.7	30.3	6.3	2.4	5,417	9.6	9.3	56.7	19.8	4.6	138,209
CLARK	12,772	354	31.4	41.5	24.0	2.5	0.6	246	21.1	18.7	52.8	6.1	1.2	107,609
CLEARWATER	19,754	3,528	30.0	34.8	29.0	4.8	1.4	2,811	15.4	15.8	41.6	23.5	3.7	127,054
CUSTER	20,294	1,791	32.9	30.5	28.9	6.1	1.7	1,379	10.5	9.6	47.0	24.4	8.5	145,135
ELMORE	18,823	9,672	22.4	37.2	31.5	7.1	1.8	5,799	10.0	9.3	45.8	32.7	2.2	151,759
FRANKLIN	17,381	4,006	19.7	37.8	32.9	6.9	2.7	3,282	4.1	10.5	64.4	19.7	1.4	131,444
FREMONT	17,239	4,230	27.0	36.5	28.5	5.8	2.2	3,593	11.3	14.0	48.9	22.4	3.4	133,325
GEM	19,069	6,290	28.8	30.5	29.9	8.7	2.2	5,087	5.2	5.1	40.7	42.4	6.5	173,466
GOODING	17,800	5,373	28.1	34.6	29.3	5.1	2.8	4,001	7.1	11.5	48.4	25.6	7.3	143,190
IDAHO	18,305	6,324	33.3	34.9	25.4	5.0	1.4	4,982	10.6	9.9	43.8	27.5	8.2	146,203
JEFFERSON	17,643	7,253	23.3	32.4	33.6	8.2	2.5	6,208	9.2	11.1	54.1	22.5	3.2	138,032
JEROME	18,513	6,911	25.0	34.3	30.3	7.6	2.8	4,990	6.8	10.5	49.0	28.0	5.7	144,215
KOOTENAI	22,694	52,210	22.6	30.7	33.6	9.4	3.7	39,754	6.3	5.6	19.6	53.5	15.0	222,478
LATAH	22,974	13,910	29.7	27.2	30.3	9.4	3.5	8,391	13.6	6.3	25.6	46.8	7.7	188,269
LEMHI	20,065	3,508	35.7	32.6	23.7	5.8	2.3	2,737	9.0	10.3	45.7	28.1	6.8	149,001
LEWIS	20,440	1,617	33.3	31.4	26.8	6.7	1.8	1,233	8.2	12.8	54.8	21.6	2.6	135,547
LINCOLN	17,619	1,715	28.2	35.0	29.6	5.7	1.6	1,318	6.4	11.6	57.4	21.5	3.0	135,734
MADISON	14,673	10,256	29.1	32.2	30.0	5.8	3.0	6,236	9.1	6.8	34.9	43.0	6.2	173,677
MINIDOKA	17,722	6,883	30.9	32.5	29.2	4.7	2.7	5,395	8.1	13.0	57.8	18.9	2.2	128,172
NEZ PERCE	24,193	15,912	24.5	28.8	34.3	9.2	3.2	11,220	5.9	4.1	25.9	55.8	8.3	210,278
ONEIDA	17,509	1,513	25.7	36.1	32.9	3.7	1.6	1,263	7.6	8.3	50.7	29.9	3.5	150,411
OWYHEE	16,573	4,133	33.6	36.1	22.3	5.4	2.7	2,974	11.5	10.9	43.6	24.4	9.6	141,588
PAYETTE	18,553	8,279	29.3	32.4	30.6	4.4	3.3	6,289	6.0	8.4	50.9	30.5	4.2	155,631
POWER	18,993	2,621	28.2	34.6	26.4	7.3	3.5	2,006	12.5	17.1	51.2	16.8	2.3	123,653
SHOSHONE	20,350	5,927	34.0	31.2	28.2	5.0	1.6	4,395	12.1	18.0	54.6	14.1	1.3	119,299
TETON	23,617	3,228	15.3	27.8	44.0	9.0	4.0	2,420	10.0	5.5	18.0	49.5	16.9	229,571
TWIN FALLS	21,363	27,475	26.2	32.3	31.0	7.0	3.6	19,332	6.6	7.1	47.5	33.3	5.5	157,173
VALLEY	24,123	3,941	24.3	32.6	32.9	7.5	2.7	3,174	4.9	4.2	31.2	43.1	16.7	205,099
WASHINGTON	19,110	3,965	32.1	33.8	26.1	4.6	3.4	3,003	5.3	8.5	48.4	32.0	5.7	157,021
IDAHO	23,464		22.4	29.2	33.6	9.9	4.9		6.5	7.0	36.2	41.2	9.1	175,701
UNITED STATES	27,916		21.9	25.0	32.3	12.3	8.4		7.9	10.5	27.1	35.6	19.0	192,285

SPENDING POTENTIAL INDICES

COUNTY	FINANCIAL SERVICES				THE HOME						ENTERTAINMENT						PERSONAL			
					Home Improvements		Furnishings													
	Auto Loan	Home Loan	Investments	Retirement Plans	Home Repair	Lawn & Garden	Computers & Hardware	Major Appliances	TV, Radio, Sound Equipment	Furniture	Dine out/ Carry out	Sports Equipment	Fees & Tickets	Toys & Games	Travel	Cable TV	Apparel & Services	Auto Repairs	Health Insurance	Pets & Supplies
ADA	111	115	113	117	107	102	113	106	108	114	108	101	113	110	110	105	98	109	102	107
ADAMS	72	54	32	52	62	83	54	71	58	52	58	62	46	61	55	62	50	64	73	76
BANNOCK	86	80	84	82	78	80	87	82	85	82	84	75	83	86	83	84	75	84	83	83
BEAR LAKE	79	59	42	57	67	87	60	76	66	58	65	66	52	69	61	71	56	69	82	80
BENEWAH	79	58	38	56	66	87	58	75	64	57	64	65	51	67	59	69	55	68	80	80
BINGHAM	87	73	60	71	75	88	71	81	76	71	75	72	67	79	71	79	66	77	85	85
BLAINE	136	147	145	149	147	139	143	141	134	143	135	138	145	135	144	130	124	141	132	142
BOISE	92	75	55	74	85	106	74	93	77	72	77	81	67	80	76	82	67	84	94	97
BONNER	80	64	49	63	70	88	65	79	68	63	68	69	58	70	66	72	59	73	81	82
BONNEVILLE	96	97	100	98	94	93	94	93	94	95	93	85	95	96	94	93	84	93	93	94
BOUNDARY	79	61	45	59	66	85	62	75	66	60	66	66	54	69	61	70	57	69	79	80
BUTTE	84	56	28	53	67	94	58	79	64	55	65	69	47	69	57	69	54	70	83	86
CAMAS	94	73	47	72	85	111	74	96	77	70	77	83	64	79	76	82	66	86	97	100
CANYON	85	79	72	78	75	80	77	79	78	78	78	72	75	80	76	78	69	79	79	81
CARIBOU	90	68	46	66	75	97	68	85	73	66	73	75	59	78	68	78	63	78	89	91
CASSIA	84	64	46	62	68	86	65	78	71	64	71	69	57	74	64	74	61	73	82	82
CLARK	71	49	28	46	54	74	49	63	55	48	55	56	41	59	48	59	47	58	67	69
CLEARWATER	78	58	37	56	67	89	59	76	64	57	64	66	50	66	60	69	54	69	81	81
CUSTER	81	57	32	55	68	93	59	79	63	56	64	69	48	67	59	68	54	70	82	85
ELMORE	79	67	60	68	64	70	73	71	73	69	73	66	67	75	68	72	64	73	72	73
FRANKLIN	89	71	57	70	78	97	71	85	76	70	76	75	65	81	72	80	66	79	90	91
FREMONT	84	61	40	59	69	90	62	79	68	61	68	69	54	72	62	72	58	72	83	85
GEM	82	65	54	64	71	87	66	78	72	64	71	68	60	75	66	76	61	72	84	82
GOODING	83	61	42	59	68	88	63	78	69	60	68	69	54	72	63	73	58	72	84	83
IDAHO	70	55	41	53	62	80	56	70	60	54	60	60	49	61	57	65	51	64	75	73
JEFFERSON	88	76	61	74	78	90	72	83	76	73	76	74	68	79	72	79	66	78	85	87
JEROME	84	71	61	70	73	85	71	79	74	70	74	70	66	78	70	77	64	75	82	82
KOOTENAI	88	82	77	82	80	87	80	84	81	80	81	76	78	82	80	82	72	82	85	86
LATAH	79	64	65	67	64	70	85	73	80	73	80	70	74	78	74	77	71	78	73	75
LEMHI	76	58	40	56	67	87	59	76	63	56	63	66	51	65	60	67	54	68	79	80
LEWIS	79	56	38	54	64	87	60	76	67	56	66	66	50	70	60	72	55	69	84	80
LINCOLN	85	60	33	57	68	92	60	79	65	58	66	70	50	71	59	70	56	71	82	86
MADISON	77	59	55	62	57	65	82	68	75	69	77	67	69	74	69	72	68	74	67	71
MINIDOKA	84	60	41	58	68	89	63	78	69	60	69	69	54	73	62	74	59	72	84	84
NEZ PERCE	82	74	81	76	76	83	80	81	81	75	80	71	76	81	79	83	70	80	86	81
ONEIDA	79	61	46	58	71	90	60	77	66	60	66	67	54	70	62	71	57	70	83	83
OWYHEE	82	55	32	53	63	87	58	75	65	56	65	66	48	70	57	69	55	68	80	82
PAYETTE	84	66	49	64	71	89	66	79	71	65	71	69	59	75	65	75	61	74	83	84
POWER	88	73	55	71	75	89	71	83	75	71	75	74	66	79	71	77	65	78	84	87
SHOSHONE	69	55	54	54	60	74	60	67	65	56	63	58	54	64	60	69	54	64	77	69
TETON	103	99	77	96	91	97	89	95	89	93	89	88	87	94	88	89	79	92	91	98
TWIN FALLS	82	73	72	73	74	83	75	79	78	73	77	70	72	80	74	80	68	77	84	81
VALLEY	90	70	45	69	81	106	71	92	74	67	74	80	61	76	73	79	63	82	93	96
WASHINGTON	81	62	45	60	69	88	63	77	69	61	68	68	55	72	63	73	59	71	82	82
IDAHO	93	85	78	85	84	91	86	89	86	84	86	81	82	88	84	87	76	87	90	91
UNITED STATES	100	100	100	100	100	100	100	100	100	100	100	100	100	100	100	100	100	100	100	100

COUNTY	FIPS Code	CBSA Code	DMA Code	POPULATION			2000-2007 ANNUAL RATE		RACE (%)					
									White		Black		Asian/Pacific	
				2000	2007	2012	% Rate	State Rank	2000	2007	2000	2007	2000	2007
ADAMS	001	39500	717	68,277	67,795	67,256	-0.1	70	95.1	94.2	3.1	3.5	0.4	0.5
ALEXANDER	003	16020	632	9,590	8,621	8,055	-1.5	102	63.0	59.6	34.9	37.8	0.4	0.5
BOND	005	41180	609	17,633	18,562	19,252	0.7	20	90.7	89.4	7.4	8.4	0.3	0.4
BOONE	007	40420	610	41,786	53,347	64,516	3.4	4	90.1	87.6	0.9	1.0	0.5	0.7
BROWN	009	00000	717	6,950	6,900	6,850	-0.1	70	80.3	79.2	18.2	19.3	0.2	0.2
BUREAU	011	36860	682	35,503	35,625	35,660	0.0	56	96.8	96.0	0.3	0.4	0.5	0.7
CALHOUN	013	41180	609	5,084	5,271	5,411	0.5	27	98.8	98.6	0.0	0.0	0.2	0.2
CARROLL	015	00000	682	16,674	16,535	16,363	-0.1	70	96.9	96.2	0.5	0.6	0.4	0.6
CASS	017	00000	648	13,695	14,181	14,570	0.5	27	94.9	93.6	0.4	0.5	0.3	0.4
CHAMPAIGN	019	16580	648	179,669	191,869	199,575	0.9	15	78.8	75.1	11.2	12.3	6.5	8.3
CHRISTIAN	021	45380	648	35,372	35,283	35,215	0.0	56	96.3	96.1	2.1	2.3	0.4	0.4
CLARK	023	00000	581	17,008	16,848	16,678	-0.1	70	98.8	98.5	0.2	0.2	0.2	0.2
CLAY	025	00000	609	14,560	14,396	14,279	-0.2	80	98.5	98.2	0.1	0.1	0.5	0.7
CLINTON	027	41180	609	35,535	37,510	39,010	0.7	20	94.2	93.2	3.9	4.4	0.4	0.5
COLES	029	16660	648	53,196	51,742	51,092	-0.4	96	95.4	92.8	2.3	3.6	0.8	1.5
COOK	031	16980	602	5,376,741	5,407,427	5,407,147	0.1	47	56.3	52.7	26.1	26.6	4.9	5.8
CRAWFORD	033	00000	581	20,452	19,840	19,424	-0.4	96	93.6	92.5	4.5	5.1	0.4	0.5
CUMBERLAND	035	16660	648	11,253	11,500	11,452	0.3	37	98.8	98.6	0.1	0.1	0.2	0.2
DEKALB	037	16980	602	88,969	104,383	116,630	2.2	8	88.5	86.2	4.6	5.1	2.4	3.1
DE WITT	039	00000	648	16,798	16,731	16,695	-0.1	70	97.8	97.7	0.5	0.5	0.3	0.3
DOUGLAS	041	00000	648	19,922	20,217	20,451	0.2	41	97.3	96.5	0.3	0.3	0.3	0.3
DUPAGE	043	16980	602	904,161	951,514	983,762	0.7	20	84.0	80.6	3.1	3.3	7.9	9.9
EDGAR	045	00000	648	19,704	19,303	19,058	-0.3	88	97.1	96.6	1.8	2.1	0.2	0.2
EDWARDS	047	00000	649	6,971	6,914	6,886	-0.1	70	98.9	98.9	0.1	0.1	0.4	0.4
EFFINGHAM	049	20820	648	34,264	34,851	35,209	0.2	41	98.7	98.3	0.2	0.2	0.3	0.4
FAYETTE	051	00000	609	21,802	22,016	22,234	0.1	47	94.0	93.1	4.9	5.5	0.2	0.2
FORD	053	16580	648	14,241	14,274	14,301	0.0	56	98.2	98.1	0.2	0.3	0.3	0.3
FRANKLIN	055	00000	632	39,018	39,426	40,503	0.1	47	98.6	98.1	0.2	0.2	0.2	0.4
FULTON	057	15900	675	38,250	38,212	38,221	0.0	56	95.1	94.6	3.6	3.4	0.3	0.7
GALLATIN	059	00000	632	6,445	6,383	6,356	-0.1	70	98.4	98.3	0.3	0.3	0.1	0.1
GREENE	061	00000	609	14,761	14,365	14,111	-0.4	96	98.1	97.7	0.7	0.8	0.1	0.1
GRUNDY	063	16980	602	37,535	47,174	57,943	3.2	6	97.1	96.3	0.2	0.2	0.3	0.4
HAMILTON	065	34500	632	8,621	8,511	8,469	-0.2	80	98.2	97.9	0.7	0.8	0.1	0.2
HANCOCK	067	00000	717	20,121	19,716	19,473	-0.3	88	98.7	98.4	0.2	0.2	0.3	0.3
HARDIN	069	00000	632	4,800	4,590	4,475	-0.6	101	95.4	94.5	2.8	3.1	0.6	0.8
HENDERSON	071	15460	682	8,213	8,271	8,180	0.1	47	98.5	98.4	0.3	0.3	0.1	0.1
HENRY	073	19340	682	51,020	51,025	51,063	0.0	56	96.2	96.0	1.1	1.2	0.3	0.3
IROQUOIS	075	00000	648	31,334	31,322	31,334	0.0	56	95.9	95.7	0.7	0.8	0.3	0.3
JACKSON	077	16060	632	59,612	58,310	57,934	-0.3	88	80.8	77.4	13.0	14.2	3.1	4.4
JASPER	079	00000	581	10,117	9,824	9,632	-0.4	96	99.1	99.0	0.1	0.1	0.2	0.3
JEFFERSON	081	34500	632	40,045	40,482	40,800	0.1	47	89.9	88.3	7.8	8.8	0.5	0.6
JERSEY	083	41180	609	21,668	23,299	24,517	1.0	13	98.1	97.7	0.5	0.6	0.3	0.4
JO DAVIESS	085	00000	682	22,289	22,823	23,197	0.3	37	98.7	98.3	0.2	0.2	0.2	0.2
JOHNSON	087	00000	632	12,878	13,412	14,081	0.6	23	83.5	81.4	14.2	15.8	0.2	0.2
KANE	089	16980	602	404,119	513,390	591,602	3.4	4	79.3	75.9	5.8	6.0	1.8	2.2
KANKAKEE	091	28100	602	103,833	110,495	115,350	0.9	15	79.9	77.2	15.5	17.0	0.7	0.9
KENDALL	093	16980	602	54,544	91,652	136,000	7.4	1	92.9	91.1	1.3	1.5	0.9	1.2
KNOX	095	23660	682	55,836	53,914	52,637	-0.5	99	89.9	88.1	6.3	7.0	0.7	0.9
LAKE	097	16980	602	644,356	725,913	786,499	1.7	9	80.1	76.6	6.9	7.5	3.9	4.9
LA SALLE	099	36860	602	111,509	114,573	117,003	0.4	32	95.0	93.8	1.5	1.7	0.6	0.7
LAWRENCE	101	00000	581	15,452	15,795	15,466	0.3	37	98.0	97.5	0.8	0.9	0.1	0.2
LEE	103	19940	610	36,062	36,020	36,244	0.0	56	92.7	92.2	4.9	5.3	0.6	0.6
LIVINGSTON	105	38700	675	39,678	39,517	39,657	-0.1	70	92.3	91.0	5.2	5.8	0.3	0.4
LOGAN	107	30660	648	31,183	30,852	30,580	-0.1	70	91.7	90.4	6.6	7.4	0.6	0.7
MCDONOUGH	109	31380	717	32,913	33,231	32,967	0.1	47	92.9	90.3	3.5	4.8	2.1	2.7
MCHENRY	111	16980	602	260,077	328,096	381,435	3.3	5	93.9	92.3	0.6	0.7	1.5	1.9
MCLEAN	113	14060	675	150,433	166,785	178,759	1.4	10	89.2	87.2	6.2	6.9	2.1	2.7
MACON	115	19500	648	114,706	111,415	109,039	-0.4	96	83.5	81.3	14.1	15.7	0.6	0.8
MACOUPIN	117	41180	609	49,019	48,985	48,919	0.0	56	98.0	97.9	0.8	0.9	0.2	0.2
MADISON	119	41180	609	258,941	267,380	273,529	0.4	32	90.2	88.7	7.3	8.2	0.6	0.8
MARION	121	16460	609	41,691	40,916	40,412	-0.3	88	94.0	93.0	3.8	4.3	0.6	0.8
MARSHALL	123	37900	675	13,180	13,378	13,568	0.2	41	98.2	97.8	0.3	0.4	0.3	0.3
MASON	125	00000	675	16,038	15,899	15,809	-0.1	70	98.8	98.6	0.1	0.1	0.2	0.3
MASSAC	127	37140	632	15,161	15,467	15,701	0.3	37	92.6	91.4	5.5	6.2	0.3	0.3
MENARD	129	44180	648	12,486	13,146	13,622	0.7	20	98.6	98.3	0.4	0.4	0.2	0.2
MERCER	131	19340	682	16,957	17,397	17,477	0.4	32	98.4	98.0	0.3	0.3	0.2	0.2
MONROE	133	41180	609	27,619	32,681	36,658	2.3	7	98.8	98.5	0.1	0.1	0.3	0.4
MONTGOMERY	135	00000	609	30,652	30,448	30,350	-0.1	70	94.9	93.8	3.7	3.8	0.3	0.9
MORGAN	137	27300	648	36,616	36,264	36,059	-0.1	70	92.3	91.0	5.4	5.8	0.5	0.9
MOULTRIE	139	00000	648	14,287	14,818	15,213	0.5	27	98.9	98.7	0.2	0.2	0.1	0.2
OGLE	141	40300	610	51,032	55,369	58,629	1.1	12	95.3	94.1	0.4	0.5	0.5	0.6
PEORIA	143	37900	675	183,433	184,934	185,850	0.1	47	79.4	76.6	16.1	17.8	1.7	2.2
PERRY	145	00000	632	20,004	22,979	22,925	-0.1	70	89.6	87.9	8.0	9.0	0.3	0.4
PIATT	147	16580	648	16,365	17,251	17,917	0.7	20	98.8	98.6	0.2	0.3	0.1	0.2
PIKE	149	00000	717	17,384	17,074	16,897	-0.2	80	97.4	96.9	1.5	1.7	0.3	0.3
POPE	151	00000	632	4,413	4,147	4,262	-0.2	80	93.3	93.0	3.8	4.0	0.3	0.3
PULASKI	153	00000	632	7,348	7,058	6,866	-0.6	101	66.5	63.2	31.0	33.7	0.9	1.2
ILLINOIS							0.8		73.5	71.2	15.1	15.3	3.4	4.2
UNITED STATES							1.2		75.1	72.7	12.3	12.6	3.8	4.5

POPULATION COMPOSITION

COUNTY	% HISPANIC ORIGIN		2007 AGE DISTRIBUTION (%)										MEDIAN AGE	% 2007 Males	% 2007 Females
	2000	2007	0-4	5-9	10-14	15-19	20-24	25-44	45-64	65-84	85+	18+	2007		
ADAMS	0.8	1.1	6.5	5.8	6.2	6.8	7.2	24.4	25.9	13.8	3.3	77.6	40.0	48.4	51.6
ALEXANDER	1.4	1.8	6.4	6.3	6.0	6.2	6.5	25.8	26.3	13.8	2.7	77.4	39.5	49.8	50.2
BOND	1.4	1.9	5.8	5.6	5.7	6.5	7.8	28.7	25.6	12.1	2.2	79.7	37.9	53.9	46.1
BOONE	12.5	16.1	7.9	7.3	8.0	7.4	6.1	27.3	25.6	8.9	1.3	72.0	36.2	50.2	49.8
BROWN	3.9	4.1	4.3	3.9	5.0	4.9	10.4	36.9	22.5	10.0	2.2	84.2	36.0	64.1	35.9
BUREAU	4.9	6.5	6.2	5.6	6.2	6.1	7.1	23.7	27.4	14.3	3.3	78.2	41.4	49.0	51.0
CALHOUN	0.6	0.8	5.9	5.2	5.5	5.5	6.1	25.1	27.8	16.2	2.8	80.2	42.9	50.1	49.9
CARROLL	2.0	2.7	5.9	5.4	5.7	6.2	6.4	22.8	29.0	15.6	3.1	79.2	43.4	49.7	50.3
CASS	8.5	11.1	7.1	6.7	6.2	5.7	5.8	27.5	25.8	12.8	2.4	76.4	38.8	49.9	50.1
CHAMPAIGN	2.9	3.8	5.7	5.4	5.6	11.0	15.7	25.8	21.0	8.1	1.6	79.8	29.4	50.5	49.5
CHRISTIAN	1.0	1.0	6.2	5.7	6.2	6.4	6.1	25.6	26.9	13.7	3.2	77.9	40.8	50.4	49.6
CLARK	0.3	0.4	6.3	5.8	6.8	6.0	6.2	24.4	27.3	14.1	3.1	77.6	41.4	48.6	51.4
CLAY	0.6	0.8	6.3	5.5	6.5	5.9	5.9	25.5	26.5	14.2	3.8	78.1	41.2	48.5	51.5
CLINTON	1.6	2.1	6.4	5.9	6.4	6.2	6.6	28.7	25.5	12.1	2.1	77.5	38.6	51.6	48.4
COLES	1.4	2.4	5.6	5.2	5.1	7.7	14.6	25.0	23.5	11.2	2.2	80.9	33.4	48.8	51.2
COOK	19.9	23.8	7.2	6.8	7.4	6.9	6.6	29.9	23.2	10.1	1.9	74.4	34.7	48.6	51.4
CRAWFORD	1.7	2.3	5.8	5.3	5.3	6.0	7.2	27.1	26.8	13.9	2.6	80.0	40.5	52.2	47.8
CUMBERLAND	0.6	0.8	7.0	6.2	6.3	6.2	6.6	25.9	26.8	12.3	2.7	76.6	39.2	49.3	50.7
DEKALB	6.6	8.6	6.6	5.9	6.0	9.1	14.8	26.1	21.6	8.2	1.7	77.6	30.2	49.8	50.2
DE WITT	1.3	1.3	6.4	6.2	6.1	6.0	6.2	25.9	27.6	12.9	2.6	77.6	40.3	48.9	51.1
DOUGLAS	3.5	4.6	7.4	7.1	5.9	6.8	6.4	25.2	25.7	13.2	2.4	75.5	38.7	48.8	51.2
DUPAGE	9.0	11.4	7.0	7.4	7.4	6.7	5.9	28.7	26.3	8.9	1.7	74.0	36.8	49.3	50.7
EDGAR	0.8	1.0	6.1	5.4	5.9	6.0	6.6	25.3	27.4	14.1	3.3	79.0	41.2	49.1	50.9
EDWARDS	0.5	0.5	5.8	5.7	6.2	5.5	4.9	25.5	28.4	15.0	3.1	79.0	42.2	48.6	51.4
EFFINGHAM	0.7	1.0	7.6	6.8	7.2	7.0	7.1	25.3	25.7	11.2	2.2	74.2	37.2	50.1	49.9
FAYETTE	0.8	1.1	6.4	6.2	5.5	6.3	6.9	27.7	25.7	12.8	2.5	78.3	39.0	52.3	47.7
FORD	1.2	1.3	6.9	6.3	5.9	6.9	6.3	23.3	26.2	14.1	3.9	76.4	41.0	48.5	51.5
FRANKLIN	0.6	0.9	6.0	5.6	5.7	5.9	5.6	25.3	27.9	14.9	3.1	79.2	41.9	48.5	51.5
FULTON	1.2	1.4	5.7	5.4	5.4	6.8	6.9	26.1	26.0	14.4	3.2	80.1	40.5	50.3	49.7
GALLATIN	0.9	0.9	5.5	5.3	6.2	5.0	6.0	25.1	28.6	15.1	3.1	80.2	42.8	49.0	51.0
GREENE	0.5	0.7	6.5	6.0	6.1	6.7	6.7	24.9	26.2	13.8	3.0	77.4	40.0	49.4	50.6
GRUNDY	4.1	5.5	7.1	6.6	6.7	6.8	7.0	27.3	26.6	10.2	1.8	75.5	37.4	49.9	50.1
HAMILTON	0.6	0.8	6.3	5.9	6.0	5.2	6.0	24.3	27.6	15.3	3.3	78.5	42.2	48.8	51.2
HANCOCK	0.5	0.7	5.9	5.4	6.3	5.9	6.4	23.4	29.0	14.4	3.1	78.8	42.4	48.9	51.1
HARDIN	1.1	1.4	5.6	5.6	4.7	4.2	6.5	24.4	30.7	15.8	2.5	81.7	44.3	50.1	49.9
HENDERSON	0.9	0.9	6.1	5.8	5.5	5.2	5.6	23.7	31.0	14.9	2.4	79.6	43.8	49.7	50.3
HENRY	2.9	3.0	6.2	5.9	6.2	6.5	6.6	24.0	28.5	13.1	3.0	77.7	41.3	49.2	50.8
IROQUOIS	3.9	4.1	6.5	6.1	6.2	6.5	5.8	23.7	27.7	14.4	3.3	77.2	41.9	49.6	50.4
JACKSON	2.4	3.7	5.4	4.8	4.9	8.0	16.9	27.5	21.3	9.3	1.9	81.8	30.1	51.2	48.8
JASPER	0.5	0.6	6.1	5.6	6.0	6.5	6.5	26.1	27.3	13.0	2.7	78.2	40.7	49.7	50.3
JEFFERSON	1.3	1.7	5.9	5.6	6.1	6.7	6.5	26.9	27.1	12.6	2.6	78.5	39.5	51.2	48.8
JERSEY	0.7	1.0	6.2	5.9	6.1	7.2	7.5	24.8	27.2	12.7	2.2	77.6	40.0	49.0	51.0
JO DAVIESS	1.5	2.1	5.7	5.5	5.8	5.6	5.9	22.8	30.2	16.1	2.5	79.6	44.2	50.1	49.9
JOHNSON	2.9	3.7	5.0	4.7	4.7	5.4	8.3	30.8	26.2	13.2	1.8	82.9	39.1	58.7	41.3
KANE	23.7	29.1	8.5	8.5	8.1	7.0	6.0	29.0	23.9	7.7	1.3	70.4	33.8	50.2	49.8
KANKAKEE	4.8	6.2	7.2	6.5	7.2	7.3	7.0	26.5	25.3	11.0	2.0	74.9	36.3	49.0	51.0
KENDALL	7.5	9.8	8.2	8.1	7.6	6.2	5.4	30.5	25.2	7.7	1.0	72.1	35.7	49.8	50.2
KNOX	3.4	4.5	5.8	5.5	5.6	6.5	7.4	25.0	26.7	14.2	3.3	79.6	40.7	50.0	50.0
LAKE	14.4	18.0	8.0	8.3	8.4	7.6	6.0	27.5	25.4	7.8	1.2	71.0	35.0	50.3	49.7
LA SALLE	5.2	6.9	6.7	6.1	6.2	6.5	6.9	25.5	26.4	12.9	2.8	77.0	39.8	49.6	50.4
LAWRENCE	0.9	1.2	5.7	4.9	5.8	5.4	5.6	23.0	26.9	16.9	5.8	80.4	44.8	47.0	53.0
LEE	3.2	3.3	5.8	5.3	6.0	7.1	7.0	27.0	27.3	12.1	2.5	78.7	40.0	51.0	49.0
LIVINGSTON	2.7	3.5	6.4	5.7	6.1	6.7	7.5	26.4	26.3	12.0	2.8	77.8	38.7	49.5	50.5
LOGAN	1.6	2.1	5.5	5.2	5.5	7.4	8.1	28.2	25.4	12.0	2.7	80.3	37.9	50.2	49.8
MCDONOUGH	1.5	2.4	4.5	4.5	4.7	10.0	17.5	22.6	22.1	11.3	2.8	83.0	31.7	49.6	50.4
MCHENRY	7.5	9.9	8.3	8.1	7.9	6.9	5.4	29.0	26.0	7.3	1.1	71.3	35.8	50.2	49.8
MCLEAN	2.5	3.3	6.5	6.3	6.4	9.3	12.4	27.4	22.4	7.9	1.6	77.1	31.6	48.5	51.5
MACON	1.0	1.3	6.2	5.9	6.3	7.2	7.3	23.7	27.8	13.2	2.4	77.6	39.9	47.8	52.2
MACOUPIN	0.6	0.6	6.0	5.5	6.1	6.6	7.0	24.7	27.3	13.6	3.2	78.6	40.9	49.1	50.9
MADISON	1.5	2.0	6.4	5.9	6.3	6.9	6.8	26.8	26.6	12.2	2.1	77.5	38.6	48.5	51.5
MARION	0.9	1.2	6.7	6.2	6.5	6.4	6.5	25.0	26.6	13.2	2.9	76.7	39.9	48.6	51.4
MARSHALL	1.0	1.4	5.7	5.2	6.8	5.6	5.2	23.6	29.2	15.1	3.5	78.9	43.3	49.5	50.5
MASON	0.5	0.7	6.0	5.6	6.3	6.0	5.7	24.8	27.9	14.7	2.9	78.3	41.8	49.4	50.6
MASSAC	0.8	1.1	6.4	6.1	6.3	5.0	6.1	25.6	26.7	14.6	3.0	78.2	41.2	48.1	51.9
MENARD	0.8	1.0	6.2	5.7	7.2	6.4	6.9	25.2	28.2	12.1	2.2	77.1	41.0	49.4	50.6
MERCER	1.3	1.7	6.1	5.6	6.0	6.4	6.4	24.6	28.9	13.3	2.7	78.4	41.8	49.6	50.4
MONROE	0.7	1.0	6.8	6.7	6.5	6.7	5.7	25.6	27.8	12.0	2.1	75.8	40.2	49.2	50.8
MONTGOMERY	1.1	1.9	6.1	5.7	5.8	7.2	7.8	25.5	25.6	13.1	3.1	78.8	39.3	50.1	49.9
MORGAN	1.4	1.9	5.7	5.3	5.8	8.3	8.3	24.9	26.2	12.9	2.8	79.4	39.3	49.4	50.6
MOULTRIE	0.5	0.6	6.8	6.2	6.5	6.0	6.1	24.3	26.9	13.8	3.5	76.8	40.9	49.0	51.0
OGLE	6.0	7.9	6.6	6.1	7.2	7.2	7.1	24.7	27.7	11.4	2.1	75.6	39.1	49.7	50.3
PEORIA	2.1	2.7	6.8	6.3	6.5	7.1	7.5	25.3	26.2	11.8	2.4	76.4	37.4	48.3	51.7
PERRY	1.8	2.3	5.5	5.1	5.5	6.2	7.4	28.8	26.1	12.9	2.6	80.4	39.2	53.7	46.3
PIATT	0.6	0.8	6.3	6.2	6.4	6.0	6.4	23.3	29.4	13.5	2.5	77.4	42.0	49.0	51.0
PIKE	0.5	0.7	6.1	5.6	6.2	6.0	6.2	24.3	27.0	14.7	3.9	78.5	41.6	49.9	50.1
POPE	0.9	0.9	4.9	4.8	4.6	8.8	7.0	22.3	28.4	16.6	2.7	80.9	43.4	51.1	48.9
PULASKI	1.5	1.8	6.6	6.2	6.5	7.1	7.1	23.5	26.3	14.2	2.6	76.4	39.9	48.4	51.6
ILLINOIS	12.3	14.9	7.1	6.9	7.1	7.0	6.8	28.3	24.7	10.2	1.9	74.8	35.9	49.1	50.9
UNITED STATES	12.5	15.0	6.9	6.5	6.8	7.1	7.0	27.6	25.4	10.7	1.9	75.6	36.7	49.2	50.8

COUNTY	HOUSEHOLDS					FAMILIES			MEDIAN HOUSEHOLD INCOME			
	2000	2007	2012	% Annual Rate 2000-2007	2007 Average HH Size	2000	2007	% Annual Rate 2000-2007	2007	2012	2007 National Rank	2007 State Rank
ADAMS	26,860	26,995	26,891	0.1	2.41	18,003	17,551	-0.4	42,596	48,862	1384	62
ALEXANDER	3,808	3,456	3,234	-1.3	2.33	2,475	2,175	-1.8	29,197	31,441	2949	101
BOND	6,155	6,593	6,901	1.0	2.45	4,348	4,533	0.6	46,284	52,362	974	47
BOONE	14,597	18,550	22,389	3.4	2.86	11,260	14,010	3.1	65,040	76,121	169	8
BROWN	2,108	2,117	2,108	0.1	2.33	1,380	1,342	-0.4	40,702	44,826	1640	70
BUREAU	14,182	14,411	14,504	0.2	2.44	9,890	9,771	-0.2	49,909	57,845	687	32
CALHOUN	2,046	2,155	2,228	0.7	2.42	1,439	1,475	0.3	38,736	42,604	1890	78
CARROLL	6,794	6,816	6,778	0.0	2.39	4,681	4,561	-0.4	45,178	51,256	1087	51
CASS	5,347	5,550	5,707	0.5	2.52	3,692	3,724	0.1	41,714	47,080	1488	66
CHAMPAIGN	70,597	76,598	80,504	1.1	2.30	39,308	40,944	0.6	46,974	54,045	910	44
CHRISTIAN	13,921	14,054	14,099	0.1	2.38	9,477	9,290	-0.3	43,700	49,597	1252	56
CLARK	6,971	6,960	6,912	0.0	2.39	4,808	4,664	-0.4	43,236	49,504	1308	60
CLAY	5,839	5,828	5,803	0.0	2.39	4,003	3,881	-0.4	35,640	39,906	2342	90
CLINTON	12,754	13,800	14,523	1.1	2.55	9,226	9,731	0.7	54,604	62,042	415	19
COLES	21,043	21,096	20,957	0.0	2.28	12,071	11,632	-0.5	38,889	44,286	1870	77
COOK	1,974,181	1,982,616	1,981,874	0.1	2.68	1,269,592	1,233,623	-0.4	58,245	67,777	302	12
CRAWFORD	7,842	7,650	7,501	-0.3	2.39	5,447	5,165	-0.7	38,417	42,935	1947	80
CUMBERLAND	4,368	4,524	4,530	0.5	2.51	3,085	3,111	0.1	43,388	49,139	1288	58
DEKALB	31,674	37,386	42,153	2.3	2.57	19,964	22,782	1.8	56,963	64,896	329	13
DE WITT	6,770	6,814	6,829	0.1	2.42	4,683	4,581	-0.3	51,744	60,227	566	22
DOUGLAS	7,574	7,767	7,893	0.3	2.56	5,476	5,475	0.0	48,779	56,334	762	38
DUPAGE	325,601	342,683	354,745	0.7	2.73	234,354	240,306	0.3	84,141	101,158	33	1
EDGAR	7,874	7,770	7,693	-0.2	2.38	5,326	5,099	-0.6	41,209	46,477	1567	68
EDWARDS	2,905	2,912	2,913	0.0	2.35	2,027	1,974	-0.4	37,359	41,806	2086	85
EFFINGHAM	13,001	13,459	13,704	0.5	2.55	9,182	9,250	0.1	48,091	54,564	809	42
FAYETTE	8,146	8,338	8,468	0.3	2.43	5,657	5,630	-0.1	37,401	41,928	2081	84
FORD	5,639	5,686	5,710	0.1	2.44	3,903	3,825	-0.3	46,698	53,084	936	45
FRANKLIN	16,408	16,739	17,274	0.3	2.32	10,971	10,852	-0.2	32,680	36,264	2689	97
FULTON	14,877	15,000	15,064	0.1	2.38	10,252	10,045	-0.3	40,099	45,135	1712	73
GALLATIN	2,726	2,736	2,741	0.1	2.31	1,838	1,790	-0.4	29,887	32,223	2916	99
GREENE	5,757	5,639	5,556	-0.3	2.49	4,078	3,889	-0.7	36,379	40,687	2215	87
GRUNDY	14,293	18,187	22,469	3.4	2.57	10,278	12,743	3.0	64,142	75,191	178	9
HAMILTON	3,462	3,412	3,392	-0.2	2.43	2,436	2,337	-0.6	34,685	38,050	2470	93
HANCOCK	8,069	7,966	7,892	-0.2	2.43	5,606	5,377	-0.6	44,390	50,256	1168	53
HARDIN	1,987	1,950	1,916	-0.3	2.25	1,367	1,303	-0.7	30,738	33,572	2857	98
HENDERSON	3,365	3,428	3,407	0.3	2.39	2,377	2,356	-0.1	42,540	47,259	1393	63
HENRY	20,056	20,287	20,402	0.2	2.49	14,309	14,094	-0.2	48,285	54,929	795	41
IROQUOIS	12,220	12,320	12,369	0.1	2.49	8,712	8,553	-0.3	45,997	52,129	1004	48
JACKSON	24,215	24,427	24,422	0.1	2.17	12,653	12,226	-0.5	29,453	33,363	2934	100
JASPER	3,930	3,872	3,821	-0.2	2.52	2,850	2,738	-0.6	40,687	45,399	1641	71
JEFFERSON	15,374	15,732	15,937	0.3	2.41	10,559	10,496	-0.1	39,832	44,762	1749	74
JERSEY	8,096	8,867	9,413	1.3	2.53	5,861	6,254	0.9	50,989	57,936	617	26
JO DAVIESS	9,218	9,701	9,983	0.7	2.33	6,287	6,423	0.3	48,627	54,786	773	39
JOHNSON	4,183	4,582	4,877	1.3	2.41	3,052	3,259	0.9	38,354	42,044	1955	81
KANE	133,901	166,775	191,410	3.1	3.04	101,454	123,538	2.8	73,982	86,077	96	6
KANKAKEE	38,182	40,924	42,949	1.0	2.59	26,759	27,896	0.6	51,539	59,985	578	24
KENDALL	18,798	31,354	46,611	7.3	2.92	14,969	24,497	7.0	79,398	91,127	56	4
KNOX	22,056	21,558	21,128	-0.3	2.30	14,429	13,660	-0.8	43,277	49,638	1304	59
LAKE	216,297	242,240	262,108	1.6	2.92	163,978	179,522	1.3	83,072	100,074	38	2
LA SALLE	43,417	45,113	46,229	0.5	2.47	29,840	30,120	0.1	50,049	57,938	678	31
LAWRENCE	6,309	6,185	6,075	-0.3	2.33	4,254	4,046	-0.7	35,490	39,631	2370	92
LEE	13,253	13,544	13,716	0.3	2.46	9,138	9,075	-0.1	51,073	59,211	609	25
LIVINGSTON	14,374	14,618	14,745	0.2	2.48	9,948	9,833	-0.2	50,575	57,172	635	27
LOGAN	11,113	11,063	10,998	-0.1	2.40	7,583	7,328	-0.5	48,863	56,555	758	37
MCDONOUGH	12,360	12,501	12,452	0.2	2.25	7,096	6,902	-0.4	37,544	41,794	2052	83
MCHENRY	89,403	112,466	130,729	3.2	2.90	69,303	85,379	2.9	80,151	95,462	51	3
MCLEAN	56,746	63,145	68,184	1.5	2.45	35,470	38,121	1.0	58,489	67,433	297	11
MACON	46,561	46,101	45,442	-0.1	2.34	30,960	29,719	-0.6	46,526	52,931	951	46
MACOUPIN	19,253	19,437	19,508	0.1	2.46	13,629	13,394	-0.2	44,194	50,537	1190	55
MADISON	101,953	107,297	110,646	0.7	2.44	70,070	71,633	0.3	51,664	60,119	570	23
MARION	16,619	16,461	16,321	-0.1	2.43	11,487	11,059	-0.5	42,364	48,558	1409	64
MARSHALL	5,225	5,382	5,495	0.4	2.43	3,718	3,728	0.0	50,227	56,849	662	29
MASON	6,389	6,395	6,384	0.0	2.45	4,563	4,447	-0.4	43,646	49,596	1257	57
MASSAC	6,261	6,464	6,596	0.4	2.34	4,318	4,330	0.0	37,602	42,411	2044	82
MENARD	4,873	5,202	5,423	0.9	2.49	3,550	3,695	0.6	56,538	64,792	344	14
MERCER	6,624	6,869	6,932	0.5	2.50	4,914	4,973	0.2	49,637	56,390	700	33
MONROE	10,275	12,278	13,834	2.5	2.63	7,780	9,089	2.2	66,997	78,366	150	7
MONTGOMERY	11,507	11,577	11,603	0.1	2.41	7,927	7,752	-0.3	39,168	43,545	1834	75
MORGAN	14,039	14,086	14,070	0.0	2.34	9,251	8,995	-0.4	45,173	51,253	1090	52
MOULTRIE	5,405	5,658	5,833	0.6	2.54	3,976	4,063	0.3	48,929	55,384	753	36
OGLE	19,278	21,056	22,361	1.2	2.60	14,168	15,099	0.9	56,044	64,418	362	17
PEORIA	72,733	74,418	75,205	0.3	2.39	47,133	46,679	-0.1	49,577	57,407	706	34
PERRY	8,504	8,590	8,630	0.1	2.39	5,843	5,734	-0.3	38,936	43,460	1861	76
PIATT	6,475	6,913	7,221	0.9	2.47	4,727	4,922	0.6	56,130	64,177	360	16
PIKE	6,876	6,807	6,755	-0.1	2.40	4,780	4,601	-0.5	35,955	09,504	2200	88
POPE	1,769	1,751	1,728	-0.1	2.29	1,220	1,173	-0.5	33,861	37,135	2566	94
PULASKI	2,893	2,810	2,746	-0.4	2.41	1,942	1,830	-0.8	28,549	30,792	2978	102
ILLINOIS				0.7	2.64			0.4	58,985	68,478		
UNITED STATES				1.2	2.59			1.0	53,154	62,503		

COUNTY	2007 Per Capita Income	2007 HH Income Base	2007 HOUSEHOLD INCOME DISTRIBUTION (%)					2007 Home Value Base	2007 HOME VALUE DISTRIBUTION (%)					2007 Median Home Value
			Less than $25,000	$25,000 to $49,999	$50,000 to $99,999	$100,000 to $149,999	$150,000 or More		Less than $50,000	$50,000 to $89,999	$90,000 to $174,999	$175,000 to $399,999	$400,000 or More	
ADAMS	22,338	26,995	26.9	31.2	31.9	6.5	3.5	20,438	11.4	17.6	46.2	22.1	2.7	124,101
ALEXANDER	18,510	3,456	44.4	30.5	19.4	3.2	2.5	2,551	45.0	26.0	22.5	5.4	1.2	55,140
BOND	21,783	6,593	25.2	29.6	32.9	9.7	2.6	5,351	14.9	20.1	42.1	20.9	2.0	114,211
BOONE	28,179	18,550	14.3	21.8	39.3	16.2	8.4	14,916	6.2	3.4	39.6	44.3	6.5	176,711
BROWN	18,944	2,117	30.8	31.6	31.0	4.6	2.0	1,611	22.9	28.5	35.5	11.4	1.7	88,109
BUREAU	24,614	14,411	21.9	28.2	36.5	10.0	3.4	11,260	6.3	15.7	50.3	24.7	3.0	134,007
CALHOUN	19,732	2,155	30.6	29.8	32.9	5.3	1.4	1,770	13.1	19.9	46.2	18.9	2.0	114,430
CARROLL	23,216	6,816	24.8	30.5	34.3	7.4	3.0	5,366	11.1	19.4	44.8	19.1	5.6	121,344
CASS	19,598	5,550	27.6	31.4	33.2	6.5	1.3	4,268	18.6	28.4	41.0	11.2	0.9	94,871
CHAMPAIGN	26,047	76,595	27.3	25.4	32.0	10.0	5.4	44,792	7.9	12.8	47.7	28.4	3.2	136,637
CHRISTIAN	21,995	14,054	25.9	31.4	33.0	7.2	2.5	10,963	12.8	26.1	45.8	14.1	1.2	105,622
CLARK	21,729	6,960	27.7	30.6	32.5	6.9	2.2	5,514	17.2	21.1	44.3	16.4	1.0	109,339
CLAY	18,997	5,828	32.6	36.0	24.7	4.8	1.9	4,737	24.3	27.4	36.6	10.4	1.3	87,484
CLINTON	24,110	13,800	19.9	24.9	39.7	11.3	4.0	11,295	11.2	15.7	46.7	24.3	2.1	130,066
COLES	22,382	21,096	33.5	27.1	28.5	7.6	3.2	13,585	10.5	19.1	47.5	19.9	3.0	121,012
COOK	29,578	1,982,539	20.4	22.4	33.1	13.8	10.3	1,194,224	1.6	1.9	21.0	54.9	20.6	249,349
CRAWFORD	20,333	7,650	30.2	32.0	29.2	6.2	2.5	6,253	17.2	30.5	40.7	10.2	1.4	93,148
CUMBERLAND	20,379	4,524	25.1	32.4	35.1	5.5	2.0	3,781	13.6	19.4	46.1	19.6	1.3	116,804
DEKALB	25,050	37,384	21.2	22.6	37.5	13.6	5.1	23,382	2.8	1.6	16.4	69.4	9.8	231,623
DE WITT	26,324	6,814	21.8	26.3	35.6	11.3	5.0	5,252	8.7	17.2	50.4	20.2	3.4	126,885
DOUGLAS	22,953	7,767	19.1	32.3	36.1	9.6	2.9	6,146	10.6	18.3	48.9	20.5	1.6	121,177
DUPAGE	40,690	342,683	8.1	15.6	35.5	22.8	18.0	267,580	0.4	0.4	7.9	60.2	31.1	319,235
EDGAR	21,562	7,770	27.3	34.1	30.5	5.3	3.0	5,947	16.6	28.8	38.5	14.5	1.6	96,256
EDWARDS	19,721	2,912	30.0	36.1	27.5	3.9	2.4	2,405	30.8	24.6	35.1	8.1	1.4	80,547
EFFINGHAM	23,125	13,459	22.9	29.2	36.0	7.9	4.0	10,477	9.2	11.6	46.1	29.0	4.0	140,440
FAYETTE	18,869	8,336	31.5	32.9	28.8	5.1	1.7	6,786	18.5	24.0	42.0	14.2	1.4	101,018
FORD	22,745	5,686	22.4	31.5	33.8	10.2	2.1	4,447	10.0	18.9	55.6	15.1	0.5	114,164
FRANKLIN	18,405	16,739	37.8	32.1	23.6	5.0	1.6	13,263	26.5	30.7	33.1	8.8	0.8	80,179
FULTON	21,033	15,000	28.4	32.6	30.1	6.7	2.3	11,709	15.9	27.1	43.6	12.3	1.1	99,982
GALLATIN	18,171	2,736	42.6	29.7	22.0	3.1	2.6	2,248	36.6	23.1	30.8	8.9	0.7	74,552
GREENE	18,428	5,639	31.1	34.8	27.3	5.1	1.7	4,394	24.0	28.8	35.1	9.7	2.4	86,125
GRUNDY	28,813	18,187	15.1	21.1	39.2	18.7	5.9	13,628	5.0	2.2	20.5	62.1	10.2	223,595
HAMILTON	18,415	3,412	35.4	32.5	25.2	4.9	2.0	2,823	31.3	22.4	34.4	11.2	0.7	83,853
HANCOCK	21,294	7,966	24.6	31.3	36.0	6.2	1.9	6,525	18.1	23.7	43.6	13.0	1.7	100,470
HARDIN	18,263	1,950	40.5	33.2	20.5	4.6	1.3	1,594	28.6	30.3	31.5	9.1	0.5	72,353
HENDERSON	20,978	3,428	24.6	35.2	32.4	6.2	1.6	2,771	21.3	26.8	36.8	14.1	1.0	92,488
HENRY	23,402	20,287	22.7	29.1	34.5	10.3	3.4	16,318	14.1	24.4	43.0	17.0	1.5	108,134
IROQUOIS	22,473	12,320	24.1	30.0	35.9	7.1	3.0	9,698	8.0	14.8	50.3	24.3	2.6	134,041
JACKSON	20,277	24,427	43.4	25.2	22.7	5.8	2.9	13,639	20.6	20.1	38.7	17.8	2.8	107,515
JASPER	19,744	3,872	27.8	30.6	34.0	6.0	1.7	3,266	15.5	21.5	43.5	18.0	1.5	112,020
JEFFERSON	20,668	15,732	30.5	30.6	29.7	6.7	2.5	12,040	21.2	20.8	40.2	16.1	1.8	101,908
JERSEY	24,511	8,867	23.5	25.3	36.2	10.4	4.6	7,069	6.7	14.6	49.1	25.5	4.1	133,114
JO DAVIESS	26,067	9,701	21.4	30.0	36.4	7.7	4.5	7,695	5.7	12.1	40.7	33.2	8.3	154,612
JOHNSON	20,150	4,582	32.5	30.8	27.8	6.1	2.8	3,920	19.3	19.9	40.3	18.2	2.3	109,521
KANE	30,894	166,775	11.1	18.7	37.4	19.2	13.6	129,699	0.7	0.9	13.6	61.3	23.5	270,452
KANKAKEE	23,808	40,924	22.3	26.1	36.1	11.0	4.5	29,434	8.0	10.1	47.3	31.9	2.7	145,452
KENDALL	31,657	31,354	7.9	16.0	42.2	22.2	11.7	26,875	0.3	0.5	5.5	72.0	21.6	285,031
KNOX	22,830	21,558	25.6	31.4	33.0	7.3	2.6	15,879	11.3	25.4	46.8	14.5	2.0	108,834
LAKE	40,393	242,240	10.0	16.1	33.0	20.2	20.6	192,516	2.0	0.9	14.3	51.2	31.6	282,359
LA SALLE	24,017	45,113	23.0	26.9	36.2	10.3	3.5	34,804	5.6	12.1	47.8	31.3	3.2	145,689
LAWRENCE	19,755	6,185	34.3	32.3	26.2	4.6	2.5	4,861	26.0	31.5	34.3	7.1	1.2	78,127
LEE	24,307	13,544	20.2	28.4	37.0	10.5	3.8	10,325	5.9	9.9	54.5	25.8	3.9	141,602
LIVINGSTON	23,304	14,618	21.5	27.7	37.4	10.2	3.2	11,155	9.7	13.2	50.8	24.4	1.9	133,503
LOGAN	23,049	11,063	22.2	28.9	36.5	9.4	3.0	8,179	8.4	14.4	55.9	19.6	1.6	128,785
MCDONOUGH	20,456	12,501	35.2	28.4	27.4	6.5	2.4	8,154	17.3	23.9	40.2	16.4	2.1	103,500
MCHENRY	34,029	112,466	8.8	15.7	39.2	22.3	13.9	95,147	0.4	0.4	7.2	67.3	24.6	290,731
MCLEAN	28,789	63,145	19.1	23.0	36.2	13.9	7.8	43,357	7.8	9.8	47.4	32.1	2.9	145,968
MACON	25,173	46,101	25.5	28.3	32.3	9.8	4.1	33,923	19.6	28.4	39.2	11.5	1.2	92,408
MACOUPIN	21,541	19,437	25.8	31.3	32.6	7.7	2.5	15,656	12.8	23.0	44.4	18.3	1.5	111,976
MADISON	25,986	107,297	22.1	26.2	35.6	11.1	5.0	81,247	8.2	19.5	47.0	23.0	2.3	122,559
MARION	21,446	16,461	28.5	30.1	32.0	6.9	2.6	12,890	22.0	25.9	39.1	11.8	1.2	92,652
MARSHALL	23,515	5,382	19.8	30.0	39.3	8.6	2.3	4,400	9.7	22.2	49.8	17.0	1.3	114,791
MASON	21,374	6,395	25.4	31.6	34.4	6.2	2.4	5,045	16.3	24.5	47.4	10.7	1.1	102,230
MASSAC	19,731	6,464	34.6	29.3	27.8	7.0	1.4	5,167	18.4	24.1	40.4	15.8	1.2	103,412
MENARD	26,796	5,202	18.0	24.8	40.3	12.1	4.7	4,201	9.0	19.0	46.8	24.8	0.5	121,720
MERCER	22,930	6,869	21.7	28.7	38.2	9.1	2.4	5,593	14.0	26.3	39.9	17.1	2.7	104,661
MONROE	29,342	12,278	12.6	20.8	41.4	18.5	6.8	10,123	2.0	3.7	34.9	53.6	5.9	200,772
MONTGOMERY	19,934	11,577	30.7	31.0	30.2	6.1	2.0	9,264	19.9	26.6	37.5	14.6	1.4	95,222
MORGAN	23,217	14,086	24.9	30.6	33.0	8.3	3.2	10,243	9.9	17.2	48.5	21.9	2.5	125,262
MOULTRIE	22,744	5,658	20.4	30.6	36.6	9.1	3.3	4,549	9.3	16.3	51.3	21.7	1.4	125,384
OGLE	25,795	21,056	18.1	25.5	38.2	12.9	5.2	16,177	4.2	5.1	43.1	42.8	4.8	171,118
PEORIA	26,553	74,418	24.0	26.3	32.9	11.0	5.7	52,030	10.9	20.4	44.9	20.8	3.0	118,312
PERRY	19,556	8,590	30.7	32.5	29.4	5.7	1.7	6,888	19.9	26.9	40.7	11.5	1.0	94,048
PIATT	26,787	6,913	17.0	26.1	41.4	11.0	4.5	5,663	7.6	14.9	48.4	27.3	1.7	129,097
PIKE	18,485	6,807	34.6	30.4	29.7	3.8	1.4	5,384	21.6	25.5	38.8	12.1	2.0	94,078
POPE	18,932	1,751	35.1	33.6	25.6	3.9	1.8	1,463	21.6	22.1	38.1	15.0	3.2	101,052
PULASKI	15,500	2,810	45.2	28.2	21.5	4.4	0.6	2,170	42.6	27.9	23.5	5.3	0.6	59,091
ILLINOIS	29,497		19.3	22.8	34.2	14.1	9.6		5.2	7.9	27.4	44.0	15.4	208,761
UNITED STATES	27,916		21.9	25.0	32.3	12.3	8.4		7.9	10.5	27.1	35.6	19.0	192,285

COUNTY	FINANCIAL SERVICES				THE HOME						ENTERTAINMENT						PERSONAL			
					Home Improvements		Furnishings													
	Auto Loan	Home Loan	Invest-ments	Retire-ment Plans	Home Repair	Lawn & Garden	Comput-ers & Hard-ware	Major Appli-ances	TV, Radio, Sound Equip-ment	Furni-ture	Dine out/ Carry out	Sports Equip-ment	Fees & Tickets	Toys & Games	Travel	Cable TV	Apparel & Services	Auto Repairs	Health Insur-ance	Pets & Supplies
ADAMS	78	72	73	72	74	81	72	76	76	72	75	67	71	78	73	79	67	74	83	78
ALEXANDER	71	50	36	49	55	74	54	65	63	52	61	56	46	63	53	68	53	62	73	70
BOND	88	70	60	69	76	93	72	83	78	69	76	73	65	81	72	82	66	78	90	88
BOONE	118	116	109	116	114	117	109	114	109	112	109	105	110	114	110	109	98	112	113	116
BROWN	76	55	43	53	62	82	60	72	67	55	65	63	51	68	59	72	55	67	82	77
BUREAU	86	81	86	81	86	94	79	87	83	79	82	74	79	86	82	86	73	82	93	88
CALHOUN	80	56	38	54	65	88	60	76	67	56	66	66	50	70	60	73	56	69	85	81
CARROLL	88	70	59	69	78	96	71	85	78	69	76	74	65	81	72	82	66	78	92	89
CASS	78	61	53	60	65	80	64	73	71	61	69	64	58	73	64	75	59	69	82	76
CHAMPAIGN	86	76	81	80	73	75	93	80	88	85	89	76	86	87	84	86	80	86	80	81
CHRISTIAN	79	67	67	67	72	84	69	77	75	67	73	67	66	76	71	79	64	73	86	79
CLARK	81	65	59	64	70	85	68	77	74	65	72	67	62	75	68	77	62	72	85	80
CLAY	74	55	44	54	61	78	58	70	65	55	63	61	51	66	58	69	54	65	78	73
CLINTON	92	86	86	86	90	98	82	91	87	83	85	79	82	90	85	89	76	86	96	93
COLES	73	63	71	66	64	69	76	69	75	68	74	63	70	74	71	75	66	72	74	70
COOK	101	106	112	107	105	96	112	103	110	111	112	100	114	108	110	109	104	108	101	102
CRAWFORD	78	61	52	60	67	84	63	75	70	60	68	65	57	72	64	75	59	69	84	78
CUMBERLAND	85	65	47	63	72	92	64	80	71	63	70	70	57	75	65	75	61	73	85	85
DEKALB	89	88	94	90	86	83	99	88	93	92	94	83	95	92	93	89	85	91	84	88
DE WITT	94	85	88	86	89	98	85	91	90	84	88	79	83	93	86	92	77	87	98	94
DOUGLAS	93	77	66	76	83	99	76	89	82	75	81	78	71	86	77	86	70	82	94	93
DUPAGE	145	170	175	171	167	147	158	152	149	164	151	144	169	152	161	145	141	151	140	150
EDGAR	80	63	58	63	69	84	68	77	74	64	72	67	62	76	68	78	62	73	86	79
EDWARDS	76	56	42	54	63	82	59	72	66	56	64	63	51	68	59	70	55	66	80	76
EFFINGHAM	88	77	78	78	81	91	79	86	83	77	81	76	75	85	79	85	72	82	91	88
FAYETTE	75	57	44	56	64	81	59	71	65	57	64	62	52	68	59	70	55	66	79	76
FORD	84	72	69	72	78	90	73	82	78	71	77	71	69	81	74	82	67	78	91	85
FRANKLIN	67	51	45	50	56	71	55	64	62	51	60	56	49	62	55	66	51	60	73	66
FULTON	76	63	63	63	68	81	67	74	72	64	70	64	62	73	67	76	61	70	83	76
GALLATIN	68	48	38	47	54	72	54	64	61	49	59	56	46	62	53	66	50	60	75	67
GREENE	74	55	44	54	60	78	59	70	66	55	64	61	52	67	59	70	55	65	79	73
GRUNDY	101	108	113	107	107	104	101	103	101	104	101	93	105	104	104	101	92	101	102	104
HAMILTON	75	53	36	51	61	82	56	71	63	53	62	62	47	66	56	68	53	65	79	76
HANCOCK	85	64	49	63	72	92	66	81	72	63	71	71	58	76	66	76	61	74	87	86
HARDIN	65	50	41	48	55	71	53	63	59	49	57	54	46	59	53	64	48	59	73	66
HENDERSON	87	61	36	58	70	96	62	81	69	60	69	71	52	73	62	74	58	73	87	88
HENRY	85	78	78	77	82	91	76	84	82	76	80	73	75	84	79	85	70	80	92	86
IROQUOIS	90	72	58	70	80	99	71	87	77	70	77	76	65	81	73	82	66	79	93	92
JACKSON	64	49	53	52	49	56	70	58	66	58	66	56	59	64	60	65	59	63	62	60
JASPER	82	60	45	59	69	89	62	78	69	60	68	68	55	73	63	74	58	71	86	83
JEFFERSON	78	64	57	63	68	82	65	74	71	64	70	64	61	72	66	75	61	71	82	77
JERSEY	95	82	76	82	88	102	82	93	88	80	86	81	78	90	84	91	75	87	100	96
JO DAVIESS	91	79	76	79	86	101	79	90	85	77	83	78	76	86	82	89	73	85	99	93
JOHNSON	82	63	48	60	70	91	64	80	70	62	69	69	56	71	65	75	59	73	87	84
KANE	126	143	142	142	136	122	133	129	126	137	127	124	138	128	133	122	118	129	119	126
KANKAKEE	88	86	90	87	85	88	84	85	87	86	86	76	85	88	85	88	77	85	89	87
KENDALL	129	147	141	146	139	128	127	129	122	136	123	121	136	129	131	118	112	125	118	129
KNOX	77	68	72	69	72	81	71	76	77	69	75	66	69	77	72	80	66	74	85	77
LAKE	158	183	187	184	178	159	168	163	158	175	160	156	179	162	171	153	149	163	150	161
LA SALLE	84	82	90	82	84	88	80	84	84	80	82	73	81	85	82	86	73	81	90	84
LAWRENCE	73	57	51	56	63	78	61	70	67	57	65	61	54	67	61	71	56	66	79	73
LEE	88	83	87	84	86	94	81	87	85	82	84	75	81	89	83	87	74	84	93	89
LIVINGSTON	90	76	74	77	81	94	78	87	83	76	82	76	74	86	79	86	71	83	94	90
LOGAN	83	76	81	76	81	89	77	83	81	75	80	71	75	83	79	85	70	79	91	84
MCDONOUGH	70	53	55	55	57	67	71	66	70	60	69	61	60	68	64	70	60	68	71	68
MCHENRY	133	156	155	156	149	134	138	136	131	146	132	129	138	136	141	127	122	134	125	136
MCLEAN	101	98	102	102	94	93	106	97	101	102	102	91	102	103	100	99	92	100	95	98
MACON	82	78	87	79	79	84	80	81	84	79	83	71	80	84	81	86	74	81	88	82
MACOUPIN	80	68	64	67	73	86	69	78	75	67	73	68	65	77	70	79	64	74	87	81
MADISON	87	87	100	89	88	88	87	87	89	87	88	76	89	90	89	91	79	86	92	87
MARION	79	67	64	66	70	82	68	75	75	67	73	65	65	76	69	78	64	72	84	77
MARSHALL	87	74	69	73	82	96	74	86	80	72	79	74	70	82	76	85	69	80	95	89
MASON	82	67	58	66	73	90	67	79	73	65	72	69	62	77	68	78	62	74	87	83
MASSAC	72	58	53	57	61	74	60	68	66	58	65	59	55	67	60	70	56	65	76	70
MENARD	100	92	90	92	95	104	89	97	92	89	91	86	87	95	91	94	81	93	101	100
MERCER	89	75	66	74	81	97	74	86	80	73	79	75	69	84	75	84	68	80	94	91
MONROE	105	119	127	119	120	114	103	109	103	110	103	96	113	108	110	104	94	103	107	110
MONTGOMERY	76	61	55	60	66	80	63	73	70	61	68	63	58	71	64	73	58	68	81	75
MORGAN	80	72	78	73	76	84	75	79	79	73	77	69	73	79	76	81	68	77	86	81
MOULTRIE	91	75	65	74	82	98	74	88	81	73	80	77	70	85	76	85	69	81	95	92
OGLE	96	93	95	93	96	101	90	96	92	90	92	86	90	95	92	94	82	92	99	98
PEORIA	87	85	98	88	85	87	88	86	91	88	89	76	89	90	89	92	80	87	92	86
PERRY	76	58	47	56	64	81	61	72	68	58	66	63	54	70	61	73	57	67	81	76
PIATT	96	92	95	92	96	104	87	96	91	88	90	83	88	94	91	93	80	91	101	98
PIKE	73	54	38	52	62	81	56	70	62	53	61	61	48	65	56	67	52	64	78	75
POPE	74	53	34	50	60	81	55	70	61	52	60	61	46	64	55	58	51	64	77	75
PULASKI	61	43	31	42	47	64	46	56	54	44	52	49	40	54	46	58	45	53	64	60
ILLINOIS	105	108	112	109	108	104	109	106	109	109	109	99	110	109	109	108	100	107	106	106
UNITED STATES	100	100	100	100	100	100	100	100	100	100	100	100	100	100	100	100	100	100	100	100

A

POPULATION CHANGE

COUNTY	FIPS Code	CBSA Code	DMA Code	POPULATION			2000-2007 ANNUAL RATE		RACE (%)					
									White		Black		Asian/Pacific	
				2000	2007	2012	% Rate	State Rank	2000	2007	2000	2007	2000	2007
PUTNAM	155	36860	675	6,086	6,327	6,494	0.5	27	97.6	97.1	0.6	0.7	0.3	0.3
RANDOLPH	157	00000	609	33,893	33,264	33,047	-0.3	88	88.7	89.0	9.3	7.8	0.3	1.1
RICHLAND	159	00000	581	16,149	15,779	15,522	-0.3	88	98.2	97.7	0.3	0.3	0.6	0.8
ROCK ISLAND	161	19340	682	149,374	147,972	147,079	-0.1	70	85.5	82.9	7.5	8.2	1.1	1.5
ST. CLAIR	163	41180	609	256,082	266,149	273,649	0.5	27	67.9	64.7	28.8	31.3	1.0	1.2
SALINE	165	25380	632	26,733	26,491	26,308	-0.1	70	94.1	93.2	4.1	4.6	0.2	0.3
SANGAMON	167	44100	648	188,951	194,928	199,213	0.4	32	87.4	85.5	9.7	10.8	1.1	1.5
SCHUYLER	169	00000	717	7,189	7,186	7,210	0.0	56	98.8	98.8	0.2	0.2	0.1	0.1
SCOTT	171	27300	717	5,537	5,535	5,540	0.0	56	99.5	99.5	0.0	0.0	0.1	0.1
SHELBY	173	00000	648	22,893	22,932	22,734	0.0	56	98.9	98.9	0.2	0.2	0.2	0.2
STARK	175	37900	675	6,332	6,215	6,137	-0.3	88	98.6	98.4	0.1	0.1	0.2	0.2
STEPHENSON	177	23300	610	48,979	48,331	47,920	-0.2	80	89.3	87.6	7.7	8.6	0.7	1.0
TAZEWELL	179	37900	675	128,485	132,353	135,405	0.4	32	97.4	96.8	0.9	1.0	0.5	0.7
UNION	181	00000	632	18,293	18,734	19,050	0.3	37	96.3	95.4	0.8	0.9	0.3	0.4
VERMILION	183	19180	648	83,919	82,265	81,249	-0.3	88	85.8	83.7	10.6	11.8	0.6	0.8
WABASH	185	00000	649	12,937	12,650	12,450	-0.3	88	97.9	97.4	0.4	0.4	0.5	0.7
WARREN	187	23660	682	18,735	18,311	18,022	-0.3	88	95.6	94.6	1.6	1.8	0.4	0.6
WASHINGTON	189	00000	609	15,148	15,659	16,034	0.5	27	98.6	98.3	0.3	0.4	0.2	0.3
WAYNE	191	00000	649	17,151	16,675	16,299	-0.4	96	98.7	98.4	0.2	0.2	0.3	0.5
WHITE	193	00000	649	15,371	15,448	15,525	0.1	47	98.2	98.1	0.3	0.3	0.2	0.2
WHITESIDE	195	44580	682	60,653	60,175	59,848	-0.1	70	92.8	91.0	1.0	1.1	0.4	0.5
WILL	197	16980	602	502,266	700,923	884,787	4.7	2	81.8	79.0	10.5	11.4	2.2	2.8
WILLIAMSON	199	32060	632	61,296	64,375	66,587	0.7	20	95.3	94.5	2.5	2.8	0.5	0.7
WINNEBAGO	201	40420	610	278,418	296,738	310,396	0.9	15	82.5	79.7	10.5	11.5	1.8	2.2
WOODFORD	203	37900	675	35,469	38,792	41,267	1.2	11	98.5	98.1	0.3	0.3	0.3	0.4
ILLINOIS							0.8		73.5	71.2	15.1	15.3	3.4	4.2
UNITED STATES							1.2		75.1	72.7	12.3	12.6	3.8	4.5

COUNTY	% HISPANIC ORIGIN		2007 AGE DISTRIBUTION (%)										MEDIAN AGE	% 2007 Males	% 2007 Females
	2000	2007	0-4	5-9	10-14	15-19	20-24	25-44	45-64	65-84	85+	18+	2007		
PUTNAM	2.8	3.7	6.2	6.1	5.8	6.5	5.8	24.2	29.6	13.6	2.1	78.0	42.1	49.7	50.3
RANDOLPH	1.5	2.2	5.9	5.6	5.4	7.3	7.9	27.1	25.9	12.1	2.9	79.6	38.7	51.0	49.0
RICHLAND	0.8	1.0	6.5	5.9	5.5	6.5	6.7	24.9	26.2	15.0	2.7	78.2	41.0	48.7	51.3
ROCK ISLAND	8.6	11.0	6.4	5.9	5.7	6.9	7.2	25.3	27.1	12.8	2.6	78.2	39.2	48.5	51.5
ST. CLAIR	2.2	2.8	7.0	6.5	7.1	7.3	7.0	26.4	25.8	10.8	2.1	74.9	36.9	47.9	52.1
SALINE	1.0	1.3	6.0	5.6	5.4	7.8	6.0	23.2	27.2	15.5	3.4	78.2	42.2	48.4	51.6
SANGAMON	1.1	1.4	6.3	6.2	6.7	6.5	6.4	26.5	27.9	11.3	2.2	76.8	39.3	48.1	51.9
SCHUYLER	0.5	0.6	6.0	6.0	5.6	5.3	5.3	24.8	28.9	14.9	3.2	79.2	42.9	50.4	49.6
SCOTT	0.2	0.2	6.9	6.3	6.0	5.7	6.2	25.0	27.3	13.6	2.9	77.2	41.1	48.6	51.4
SHELBY	0.5	0.5	6.3	5.8	6.7	6.2	6.0	24.5	26.9	14.6	2.9	77.4	41.2	49.5	50.5
STARK	0.9	1.1	6.4	6.3	6.5	5.7	5.9	24.0	27.3	14.2	3.7	77.2	41.7	48.5	51.5
STEPHENSON	1.5	2.0	6.4	5.6	6.3	6.6	7.0	24.4	27.3	13.5	2.8	77.7	40.7	48.3	51.7
TAZEWELL	1.0	1.4	6.3	6.1	6.3	6.1	6.0	26.5	27.5	13.0	2.3	77.6	40.1	49.1	50.9
UNION	2.6	3.5	5.5	4.9	5.8	6.1	5.9	25.0	28.7	15.0	3.0	80.0	42.8	48.9	51.1
VERMILION	3.0	3.9	6.8	6.2	6.3	6.1	6.6	25.4	26.5	13.7	2.4	77.0	39.6	49.4	50.6
WABASH	0.7	1.0	6.4	5.8	5.9	5.8	7.2	25.0	28.5	12.8	2.8	78.6	40.7	49.2	50.8
WARREN	2.7	3.6	5.8	5.6	5.4	8.2	9.0	23.0	26.7	13.4	2.9	79.6	39.6	48.6	51.4
WASHINGTON	0.7	1.0	6.1	5.7	6.1	6.9	6.4	25.1	27.5	13.5	2.7	77.9	41.1	49.7	50.3
WAYNE	0.6	0.8	6.3	6.2	5.4	6.2	5.7	24.9	26.7	15.4	3.1	78.3	41.6	48.8	51.2
WHITE	0.7	0.7	5.5	5.2	5.1	5.5	5.7	23.9	28.9	16.2	4.0	80.7	44.4	48.1	51.9
WHITESIDE	8.8	11.5	6.6	6.1	6.1	6.5	6.9	24.6	27.2	13.4	2.7	77.5	40.2	49.1	50.9
WILL	8.7	11.1	8.7	8.6	8.2	6.9	5.6	30.1	23.9	7.2	1.0	70.3	34.6	49.9	50.1
WILLIAMSON	1.2	1.7	6.1	5.7	5.7	5.9	6.0	26.5	27.2	14.2	2.8	79.0	40.9	48.5	51.5
WINNEBAGO	6.9	8.9	7.1	6.7	6.8	7.0	6.5	26.9	26.3	10.8	1.9	75.1	37.5	49.0	51.0
WOODFORD	0.7	0.9	6.6	6.7	7.0	7.2	6.0	23.5	28.1	11.8	3.0	75.3	39.8	49.1	50.9
ILLINOIS	12.3	14.9	7.1	6.9	7.1	7.0	6.8	28.3	24.7	10.2	1.9	74.8	35.9	49.1	50.9
UNITED STATES	12.5	15.0	6.9	6.5	6.8	7.1	7.0	27.6	25.4	10.7	1.9	75.6	36.7	49.2	50.8

HOUSEHOLDS

COUNTY	HOUSEHOLDS					FAMILIES			MEDIAN HOUSEHOLD INCOME			
	2000	2007	2012	% Annual Rate 2000-2007	2007 Average HH Size	2000	2007	% Annual Rate 2000-2007	2007	2012	2007 National Rank	2007 State Rank
PUTNAM	2,415	2,543	2,624	0.7	2.48	1,749	1,794	0.4	55,195	63,805	396	18
RANDOLPH	12,084	12,159	12,151	0.1	2.43	8,363	8,180	-0.3	45,428	51,599	1061	50
RICHLAND	6,660	6,598	6,530	-0.1	2.37	4,534	4,362	-0.5	37,273	42,146	2095	86
ROCK ISLAND	60,712	60,400	60,198	-0.1	2.37	39,162	37,700	-0.5	47,784	55,135	837	43
ST. CLAIR	96,810	102,471	106,208	0.8	2.55	67,323	69,277	0.4	48,430	54,893	786	40
SALINE	10,992	10,966	10,919	0.0	2.31	7,229	6,988	-0.5	33,060	36,658	2650	96
SANGAMON	78,722	81,875	84,055	0.5	2.34	49,898	50,166	0.1	53,303	61,887	484	21
SCHUYLER	2,975	3,011	3,038	0.2	2.35	2,070	2,039	-0.2	40,248	44,006	1694	72
SCOTT	2,222	2,250	2,264	0.2	2.44	1,562	1,539	-0.2	43,121	48,261	1314	61
SHELBY	9,056	9,182	9,149	0.2	2.47	6,502	6,422	-0.2	45,664	51,982	1033	49
STARK	2,525	2,512	2,495	-0.1	2.43	1,765	1,708	-0.5	42,064	46,907	1440	65
STEPHENSON	19,785	19,735	19,657	0.0	2.41	13,471	13,043	-0.4	49,218	55,822	731	35
TAZEWELL	50,327	53,004	54,672	0.7	2.44	35,859	36,769	0.3	56,498	64,986	345	15
UNION	7,290	7,534	7,692	0.5	2.37	4,973	4,992	0.1	35,704	39,214	2332	89
VERMILION	33,406	33,112	32,863	-0.1	2.39	22,313	21,441	-0.5	40,780	45,962	1633	69
WABASH	5,192	5,154	5,106	-0.1	2.42	3,588	3,462	-0.5	41,449	46,700	1523	67
WARREN	7,166	7,035	6,936	-0.3	2.43	4,968	4,740	-0.6	44,387	50,614	1169	54
WASHINGTON	5,848	6,093	6,260	0.6	2.53	4,242	4,310	0.2	50,115	56,383	669	30
WAYNE	7,143	7,040	6,921	-0.2	2.34	4,973	4,767	-0.6	35,557	39,733	2358	91
WHITE	6,534	6,647	6,716	0.2	2.26	4,376	4,319	-0.2	33,680	36,848	2588	95
WHITESIDE	23,684	23,825	23,838	0.1	2.47	16,759	16,408	-0.3	50,539	58,355	637	28
WILL	167,542	230,753	291,810	4.5	3.00	130,972	176,760	4.2	77,661	91,536	68	5
WILLIAMSON	25,358	26,989	28,103	0.9	2.32	16,969	17,516	0.4	38,615	43,537	1914	79
WINNEBAGO	107,980	114,774	120,171	0.8	2.54	73,666	76,033	0.4	54,395	62,897	427	20
WOODFORD	12,797	14,210	15,233	1.5	2.65	9,807	10,657	1.2	62,389	71,233	204	10
ILLINOIS				0.7	2.64			0.4	58,985	68,478		
UNITED STATES				1.2	2.59			1.0	53,154	62,503		

COUNTY	2007 Per Capita Income	2007 HH Income Base	2007 HOUSEHOLD INCOME DISTRIBUTION (%)					2007 Home Value Base	2007 HOME VALUE DISTRIBUTION (%)					2007 Median Home Value
			Less than $25,000	$25,000 to $49,999	$50,000 to $99,999	$100,000 to $149,999	$150,000 or More		Less than $50,000	$50,000 to $89,999	$90,000 to $174,999	$175,000 to $399,999	$400,000 or More	
PUTNAM	24,882	2,543	16.4	27.0	43.1	10.4	3.0	2,139	7.0	10.8	48.4	32.1	1.8	149,418
RANDOLPH	21,416	12,159	25.8	29.8	35.6	6.4	2.5	9,857	15.0	22.8	43.8	17.0	1.5	109,320
RICHLAND	20,341	6,598	32.8	29.6	29.6	5.9	2.1	5,180	17.9	23.0	39.3	17.3	2.6	105,400
ROCK ISLAND	24,971	60,400	24.0	28.0	33.7	10.2	4.2	43,489	10.2	24.1	48.6	15.8	1.3	108,452
ST. CLAIR	23,879	102,471	24.7	26.7	33.4	10.3	4.9	71,323	12.9	19.5	42.9	22.2	2.5	118,990
SALINE	18,756	10,966	37.1	31.8	24.2	5.1	1.8	8,557	27.9	27.5	33.4	9.7	1.5	81,430
SANGAMON	28,922	81,875	20.2	26.3	35.4	11.8	6.3	59,059	10.9	21.1	45.5	20.3	2.3	116,051
SCHUYLER	20,534	3,011	30.0	32.8	30.3	4.3	2.7	2,422	25.1	23.7	37.3	12.4	1.4	92,177
SCOTT	20,381	2,250	28.7	29.7	33.8	6.0	1.9	1,788	19.0	25.6	38.4	14.9	2.1	97,293
SHELBY	21,739	9,182	23.6	31.1	35.5	7.4	2.4	7,577	13.9	21.6	45.4	16.8	2.3	115,311
STARK	20,538	2,512	26.2	33.5	32.3	6.1	1.9	1,988	15.4	31.4	40.7	11.0	1.4	93,523
STEPHENSON	24,267	19,735	22.6	28.2	36.0	10.3	2.9	15,123	10.0	13.5	47.1	26.7	2.6	135,936
TAZEWELL	27,523	53,004	18.1	25.5	37.9	13.0	5.6	41,405	5.8	16.7	52.8	23.3	1.4	125,607
UNION	19,277	7,534	35.1	31.1	26.2	5.5	2.1	5,833	18.4	23.8	38.0	18.0	1.8	102,358
VERMILION	20,914	33,112	28.7	31.2	30.8	7.2	2.1	24,422	23.6	30.8	34.9	10.0	0.6	83,335
WABASH	20,943	5,154	29.0	30.4	31.7	6.4	2.5	3,984	22.1	29.6	33.0	14.0	1.3	87,527
WARREN	21,413	7,035	25.9	29.9	33.9	7.9	2.3	5,378	15.9	26.5	41.8	13.9	1.9	101,986
WASHINGTON	23,397	6,093	21.7	28.1	37.9	9.2	3.0	5,033	10.7	20.7	46.1	19.9	2.7	125,710
WAYNE	18,932	7,040	33.6	32.4	28.2	4.4	1.5	5,701	28.5	26.8	34.7	8.8	1.2	82,071
WHITE	19,317	6,647	37.0	32.3	24.5	4.6	1.6	5,293	30.5	28.6	31.2	9.0	0.7	75,094
WHITESIDE	24,108	23,825	20.6	28.7	38.5	8.6	3.6	18,226	4.3	15.3	56.2	22.5	1.7	129,943
WILL	31,379	230,753	10.3	16.6	38.7	21.3	13.2	194,600	1.0	1.5	16.2	61.4	19.9	264,863
WILLIAMSON	21,734	26,989	32.5	29.1	28.7	6.6	3.0	20,360	17.4	24.0	39.4	16.7	2.5	105,642
WINNEBAGO	26,612	114,774	20.2	25.3	35.7	13.2	5.7	82,789	5.0	13.5	55.7	24.2	1.6	133,060
WOODFORD	27,582	14,210	13.8	22.4	43.0	14.2	6.6	11,979	5.7	10.9	48.4	31.9	3.1	144,193
ILLINOIS	29,497		19.3	22.8	34.2	14.1	9.6		5.2	7.9	27.4	44.0	15.4	208,761
UNITED STATES	27,916		21.9	25.0	32.3	12.3	8.4		7.9	10.5	27.1	35.6	19.0	192,285

SPENDING POTENTIAL INDICES

COUNTY	FINANCIAL SERVICES				THE HOME						ENTERTAINMENT						PERSONAL			
					Home Improvements		Furnishings													
	Auto Loan	Home Loan	Invest- ments	Retire- ment Plans	Home Repair	Lawn & Garden	Comput- ers & Hard- ware	Major Appli- ances	TV, Radio, Sound Equip- ment	Furni- ture	Dine out/ Carry out	Sports Equip- ment	Fees & Tickets	Toys & Games	Travel	Cable TV	Apparel & Services	Auto Repairs	Health Insur- ance	Pets & Supplies
PUTNAM	98	81	67	80	89	108	79	95	84	78	84	83	74	89	81	89	73	87	99	100
RANDOLPH	83	69	61	68	74	89	69	80	75	68	74	69	65	77	70	80	64	75	87	83
RICHLAND	75	61	53	59	66	80	62	72	68	60	67	63	57	70	63	72	58	67	80	75
ROCK ISLAND	80	80	95	81	82	83	81	81	84	81	83	70	83	84	83	86	74	80	88	81
ST. CLAIR	85	83	90	84	81	83	83	82	86	83	85	72	83	86	83	88	76	83	88	83
SALINE	68	52	47	51	56	71	57	65	63	53	61	56	50	63	56	67	52	61	74	67
SANGAMON	93	93	103	96	92	91	94	91	95	94	94	82	95	95	94	95	85	93	95	92
SCHUYLER	80	57	41	55	65	86	61	76	69	57	67	66	52	71	61	74	57	69	85	80
SCOTT	83	59	43	57	67	89	63	77	70	59	69	68	53	73	62	76	58	71	87	82
SHELBY	84	69	61	68	75	90	69	81	75	67	74	70	65	78	70	79	64	75	88	84
STARK	82	60	44	59	69	90	63	78	70	60	69	69	54	74	63	75	59	72	86	84
STEPHENSON	84	77	80	78	81	89	78	83	82	77	81	73	76	83	79	84	72	81	89	85
TAZEWELL	92	95	108	97	97	97	91	94	94	93	92	81	95	95	95	95	83	91	99	94
UNION	73	56	45	54	62	79	58	70	65	55	64	61	52	66	59	70	54	65	79	74
VERMILION	74	63	65	63	66	76	67	71	73	64	70	62	63	73	67	76	62	69	81	73
WABASH	78	65	59	65	69	82	66	75	71	65	70	65	62	74	66	75	61	71	81	78
WARREN	79	67	66	67	71	83	70	76	75	67	73	66	66	76	70	78	64	73	84	79
WASHINGTON	95	76	62	75	84	103	76	91	82	74	81	80	69	87	77	86	70	84	97	96
WAYNE	73	53	40	51	59	77	56	68	63	53	62	59	49	65	56	68	52	63	77	72
WHITE	71	52	41	51	58	76	56	67	63	52	61	58	48	64	56	67	52	62	76	70
WHITESIDE	85	80	86	81	84	90	79	84	84	80	82	73	80	86	82	86	73	81	91	86
WILL	128	146	146	147	139	127	132	129	126	139	127	121	140	131	134	123	117	128	121	128
WILLIAMSON	76	63	63	64	66	77	68	73	73	64	71	64	63	73	68	76	61	71	81	74
WINNEBAGO	92	93	103	95	91	90	94	91	95	94	94	81	95	96	94	95	85	92	94	91
WOODFORD	106	106	106	106	110	115	97	107	100	100	99	94	100	104	102	102	89	101	109	109
ILLINOIS	105	108	112	109	108	104	109	106	109	109	109	99	110	109	109	108	100	107	106	106
UNITED STATES	100	100	100	100	100	100	100	100	100	100	100	100	100	100	100	100	100	100	100	100

COUNTY	FIPS Code	CBSA Code	DMA Code	POPULATION 2000	POPULATION 2007	POPULATION 2012	2000-2007 ANNUAL RATE % Rate	2000-2007 ANNUAL RATE State Rank	RACE (%) White 2000	White 2007	Black 2000	Black 2007	Asian/Pacific 2000	Asian/Pacific 2007
ADAMS	001	19540	509	33,625	34,027	34,293	0.2	61	97.3	96.5	0.1	0.2	0.2	0.3
ALLEN	003	23060	509	331,849	350,645	364,345	0.8	28	83.1	80.6	11.3	12.3	1.4	2.0
BARTHOLOMEW	005	18020	527	71,435	74,435	76,658	0.6	34	94.2	92.8	1.8	2.0	1.9	2.7
BENTON	007	29140	582	9,421	9,237	9,112	-0.3	86	96.9	96.1	0.2	0.2	0.1	0.1
BLACKFORD	009	00000	527	14,048	13,883	13,746	-0.2	81	98.4	98.1	0.1	0.1	0.2	0.2
BOONE	011	26900	527	46,107	54,194	60,774	2.3	4	97.9	97.4	0.4	0.4	0.5	0.7
BROWN	013	26900	527	14,957	15,931	16,681	0.9	24	98.2	97.8	0.2	0.2	0.2	0.3
CARROLL	015	29140	527	20,165	20,835	21,353	0.5	42	97.6	97.0	0.2	0.2	0.1	0.1
CASS	017	30900	527	40,930	40,241	39,704	-0.2	81	93.7	92.1	1.3	1.4	0.6	0.8
CLARK	019	31140	529	96,472	106,185	113,593	1.3	12	90.3	88.9	6.6	7.4	0.6	0.9
CLAY	021	45460	581	26,556	27,265	27,592	0.4	47	98.4	98.1	0.3	0.4	0.1	0.2
CLINTON	023	23140	527	33,866	33,996	33,996	0.1	67	94.4	92.7	0.3	0.3	0.2	0.3
CRAWFORD	025	00000	529	10,743	11,197	11,566	0.6	34	98.3	97.9	0.2	0.2	0.3	0.4
DAVIESS	027	47780	581	29,820	30,223	30,520	0.2	61	97.5	96.9	0.4	0.5	0.3	0.4
DEARBORN	029	17140	515	46,109	50,357	53,568	1.2	14	98.1	97.7	0.6	0.7	0.3	0.4
DECATUR	031	24700	527	24,555	25,393	25,953	0.5	42	98.5	98.1	0.0	0.1	0.7	1.0
DEKALB	033	12140	509	40,285	42,120	43,391	0.6	34	97.8	97.2	0.3	0.3	0.4	0.5
DELAWARE	035	34620	527	118,769	117,432	115,386	-0.2	81	90.7	89.4	6.7	7.5	0.7	1.0
DUBOIS	037	27540	649	39,674	42,351	44,358	0.9	24	97.5	96.8	0.1	0.2	0.2	0.3
ELKHART	039	21140	588	182,791	200,091	213,376	1.3	12	86.4	83.6	5.2	5.7	1.0	1.3
FAYETTE	041	18220	527	25,588	24,983	24,563	-0.3	86	97.2	96.7	1.7	1.9	0.3	0.4
FLOYD	043	31140	529	70,823	73,414	75,176	0.5	42	93.2	92.2	4.4	4.9	0.5	0.7
FOUNTAIN	045	00000	527	17,954	17,681	17,503	-0.2	81	98.7	98.4	0.1	0.1	0.2	0.3
FRANKLIN	047	17140	515	22,151	23,555	24,461	0.9	24	99.0	98.8	0.0	0.0	0.2	0.3
FULTON	049	00000	588	20,511	20,997	21,340	0.3	54	96.2	95.4	0.8	0.9	0.4	0.6
GIBSON	051	21780	649	32,500	33,103	33,572	0.3	54	96.5	95.8	1.9	2.2	0.5	0.7
GRANT	053	31980	527	73,403	70,626	68,431	-0.5	91	89.2	87.7	7.2	8.0	0.6	0.8
GREENE	055	14020	581	33,157	33,971	34,564	0.3	54	98.6	98.3	0.1	0.1	0.2	0.3
HAMILTON	057	26900	527	182,740	262,276	332,747	5.1	1	94.4	92.9	1.5	1.7	2.5	3.5
HANCOCK	059	26900	527	55,391	67,944	78,500	2.9	3	98.4	98.1	0.1	0.2	0.4	0.6
HARRISON	061	31140	529	34,325	37,365	39,560	1.2	14	98.4	98.1	0.4	0.4	0.2	0.3
HENDRICKS	063	26900	527	104,093	137,860	163,239	4.0	2	96.7	96.0	1.1	1.3	0.7	1.0
HENRY	065	35220	527	48,508	47,216	46,063	-0.4	88	98.0	97.6	0.9	1.0	0.2	0.3
HOWARD	067	29020	527	84,964	85,213	85,371	0.0	72	89.7	88.1	6.5	7.3	1.0	1.4
HUNTINGTON	069	26540	509	38,075	38,175	38,200	0.0	72	98.2	98.1	0.2	0.2	0.3	0.3
JACKSON	071	42980	529	41,335	42,309	42,906	0.3	54	96.1	95.1	0.5	0.6	0.8	1.2
JASPER	073	16980	602	30,043	33,239	35,505	1.4	9	98.0	97.5	0.3	0.4	0.2	0.3
JAY	075	00000	509	21,806	21,945	22,050	0.1	67	97.6	97.0	0.3	0.3	0.4	0.5
JEFFERSON	077	31500	529	31,705	32,671	33,432	0.4	47	96.2	95.5	1.5	1.6	0.6	0.9
JENNINGS	079	35860	529	27,554	28,684	29,416	0.6	34	97.5	97.0	0.7	0.8	0.3	0.4
JOHNSON	081	26900	527	115,209	134,724	149,961	2.2	5	97.0	96.3	0.8	0.9	0.9	1.2
KNOX	083	47180	581	39,256	37,871	37,044	-0.5	91	96.4	95.7	1.9	2.1	0.6	0.8
KOSCIUSKO	085	47700	588	74,057	78,293	81,246	0.8	28	94.6	93.0	0.6	0.7	0.6	0.8
LAGRANGE	087	00000	588	34,909	37,442	39,250	1.0	20	96.7	95.8	0.2	0.2	0.3	0.4
LAKE	089	16980	602	484,564	501,095	513,309	0.5	42	66.7	63.7	25.3	26.5	0.9	1.1
LAPORTE	091	33140	602	110,106	112,068	113,572	0.2	61	86.3	84.3	10.1	11.1	0.5	0.9
LAWRENCE	093	13260	527	45,922	45,435	44,979	-0.1	76	97.9	97.5	0.4	0.4	0.3	0.4
MADISON	095	11300	527	133,358	131,896	131,035	-0.2	81	89.9	88.5	7.9	8.7	0.4	0.6
MARION	097	26900	527	860,454	875,030	884,516	0.2	61	70.5	67.4	24.2	26.0	1.5	2.0
MARSHALL	099	38500	588	45,128	47,032	48,448	0.6	34	95.5	94.3	0.3	0.3	0.3	0.5
MARTIN	101	00000	581	10,369	10,268	10,185	-0.1	76	98.9	98.8	0.2	0.2	0.2	0.2
MIAMI	103	37940	527	36,082	35,092	34,271	-0.4	88	93.7	92.8	3.0	3.4	0.3	0.5
MONROE	105	14020	527	120,563	127,754	133,628	0.8	28	90.8	88.8	3.0	3.3	3.4	4.8
MONTGOMERY	107	18820	527	37,629	38,547	39,154	0.3	54	96.8	96.0	0.8	0.9	0.5	0.6
MORGAN	109	26900	527	66,689	72,092	75,710	1.1	17	98.6	98.3	0.1	0.1	0.3	0.4
NEWTON	111	16980	602	14,566	15,007	15,306	0.4	47	97.3	96.7	0.2	0.2	0.3	0.4
NOBLE	113	28340	509	46,275	48,387	49,611	0.6	34	94.0	92.0	0.4	0.4	0.4	0.8
OHIO	115	17140	515	5,623	6,062	6,342	1.0	20	98.7	98.5	0.5	0.5	0.2	0.2
ORANGE	117	00000	529	19,306	19,650	19,930	0.2	61	97.9	97.6	0.6	0.7	0.2	0.3
OWEN	119	14020	527	21,786	23,775	25,071	1.2	14	98.2	97.9	0.3	0.3	0.2	0.3
PARKE	121	00000	581	17,241	17,698	17,985	0.4	47	96.4	95.9	2.1	2.4	0.2	0.3
PERRY	123	00000	649	18,899	18,592	18,182	-0.2	81	97.6	97.3	1.4	1.6	0.1	0.2
PIKE	125	27540	649	12,837	13,239	13,468	0.4	47	99.1	98.9	0.1	0.1	0.2	0.3
PORTER	127	16980	602	146,798	162,410	174,440	1.4	9	95.3	94.2	0.9	1.0	0.9	1.3
POSEY	129	21780	649	27,061	27,271	27,410	0.1	67	98.0	97.7	0.9	1.0	0.2	0.2
PULASKI	131	00000	588	13,755	14,314	14,695	0.6	34	97.5	97.1	0.9	1.0	0.2	0.3
PUTNAM	133	26900	527	36,019	37,582	38,660	0.6	34	94.9	94.0	2.9	3.3	0.6	0.8
RANDOLPH	135	00000	527	27,401	26,517	25,888	-0.5	91	98.1	97.6	0.3	0.3	0.3	0.4
RIPLEY	137	00000	515	26,523	29,362	31,066	1.4	9	98.3	97.9	0.0	0.1	0.4	0.5
RUSH	139	00000	527	18,261	18,265	18,312	0.0	72	97.7	97.7	0.6	0.6	0.5	0.5
ST. JOSEPH	141	43780	588	265,559	269,077	270,840	0.2	61	82.4	79.6	11.5	12.6	1.4	1.9
SCOTT	143	42500	529	22,960	23,775	24,283	0.5	42	98.6	98.3	0.0	0.1	0.2	0.3
SHELBY	145	26900	527	43,445	44,237	44,785	0.2	61	97.3	96.6	0.8	0.9	0.6	0.9
SPENCER	147	00000	649	20,391	21,083	22,002	0.0	24	97.7	97.2	0.6	0.7	0.2	0.3
STARKE	149	00000	588	23,556	24,061	24,561	0.3	54	97.5	96.9	0.2	0.3	0.2	0.3
STEUBEN	151	11420	509	33,214	35,377	36,996	0.9	24	97.2	96.5	0.4	0.4	0.4	0.6
SULLIVAN	153	45460	581	21,751	21,920	22,040	0.1	67	94.1	93.0	4.3	4.8	0.2	0.2
INDIANA							0.7		87.5	86.0	8.4	8.8	1.0	1.4
UNITED STATES							1.2		75.1	72.7	12.3	12.6	3.8	4.5

POPULATION COMPOSITION

COUNTY	% HISPANIC ORIGIN		2007 AGE DISTRIBUTION (%)										MEDIAN AGE	% 2007 Males	% 2007 Females
	2000	2007	0-4	5-9	10-14	15-19	20-24	25-44	45-64	65-84	85+	18+	2007		
ADAMS	3.3	4.5	8.6	7.6	8.3	7.3	6.6	25.8	23.0	10.3	2.6	71.0	33.9	49.8	50.2
ALLEN	4.2	5.5	7.6	7.2	7.3	7.0	6.7	27.3	25.6	9.5	1.7	73.6	35.4	49.0	51.0
BARTHOLOMEW	2.2	3.0	7.2	7.1	6.9	6.6	5.5	26.7	26.8	11.5	1.7	74.7	38.0	49.4	50.6
BENTON	2.6	3.5	7.1	6.6	6.7	7.2	6.3	25.2	25.9	12.0	3.0	75.0	38.6	50.1	49.9
BLACKFORD	0.6	0.8	6.5	6.4	6.1	6.5	5.7	25.7	27.6	13.2	2.2	77.1	40.1	49.7	50.3
BOONE	1.2	1.6	7.1	7.2	8.0	7.2	5.9	24.5	28.4	9.8	1.9	73.1	38.8	49.1	50.9
BROWN	0.9	1.2	5.1	5.3	5.8	5.5	5.2	23.4	35.3	12.7	1.6	80.2	44.7	50.3	49.7
CARROLL	2.9	4.0	7.0	6.8	6.6	6.4	5.6	25.8	27.8	12.0	2.0	75.7	39.4	50.2	49.8
CASS	7.1	9.4	7.2	6.6	6.0	6.8	6.4	26.6	26.4	11.9	2.2	75.9	38.1	50.5	49.5
CLARK	1.9	2.5	6.6	6.5	6.1	5.9	6.0	28.5	27.5	11.3	1.7	77.3	38.6	48.9	51.1
CLAY	0.6	0.8	6.8	6.4	6.4	6.1	6.2	26.3	27.1	12.4	2.3	76.7	39.2	48.9	51.1
CLINTON	7.3	9.7	7.3	6.6	6.8	6.7	6.5	27.2	24.6	11.8	2.7	75.4	37.2	49.7	50.3
CRAWFORD	0.9	1.3	6.4	6.3	6.4	6.6	5.5	27.1	28.3	11.9	1.4	76.8	39.6	50.7	49.3
DAVIESS	2.1	2.8	7.9	7.2	7.1	6.7	6.6	25.3	24.7	12.0	2.4	73.6	36.6	49.7	50.3
DEARBORN	0.6	0.8	6.9	6.6	6.7	7.1	6.5	26.7	27.7	10.2	1.4	75.4	38.4	49.6	50.4
DECATUR	0.5	0.7	7.6	7.3	6.4	6.1	5.6	28.2	25.2	11.6	2.0	75.0	37.3	49.7	50.3
DEKALB	1.7	2.3	7.7	7.3	7.2	6.8	5.8	27.8	26.4	9.3	1.7	73.5	36.3	50.2	49.8
DELAWARE	1.1	1.5	5.8	5.4	5.5	9.1	12.2	24.0	23.9	12.1	2.1	79.8	34.9	48.2	51.8
DUBOIS	2.8	3.8	7.2	7.1	6.8	6.7	6.3	26.6	26.7	10.7	2.0	74.8	38.2	49.7	50.3
ELKHART	8.9	11.7	8.1	7.6	7.2	7.3	6.2	28.5	24.2	9.3	1.7	72.6	34.6	49.8	50.2
FAYETTE	0.5	0.7	6.5	6.1	6.6	5.5	6.0	26.4	27.3	13.2	2.4	77.3	39.6	48.8	51.2
FLOYD	1.1	1.5	6.6	6.0	6.6	6.5	6.3	27.0	28.5	10.8	1.8	76.8	39.0	48.3	51.7
FOUNTAIN	1.1	1.4	6.9	6.6	6.8	6.4	6.0	25.5	26.0	13.6	2.2	75.8	39.4	50.2	49.8
FRANKLIN	0.5	0.6	7.2	6.9	7.7	6.6	5.7	26.9	26.5	11.0	1.6	74.2	37.9	50.3	49.7
FULTON	2.3	3.1	6.9	6.3	7.0	6.1	6.2	25.6	26.9	13.0	2.2	76.1	39.7	49.8	50.2
GIBSON	0.7	1.0	6.6	6.2	6.4	5.8	6.9	25.4	27.3	12.9	2.4	77.2	40.0	49.2	50.8
GRANT	2.4	3.2	6.0	5.5	6.3	7.9	8.6	23.7	26.5	13.3	2.2	78.6	38.9	48.4	51.6
GREENE	0.8	1.1	6.3	6.1	6.0	6.2	5.6	26.5	27.7	13.1	2.3	77.7	40.6	49.4	50.6
HAMILTON	1.6	2.1	9.1	9.5	8.8	6.6	4.7	29.9	24.3	6.3	0.8	68.2	34.9	49.1	50.9
HANCOCK	0.9	1.3	6.7	6.7	6.8	6.6	5.8	25.8	29.3	10.9	1.4	75.7	40.0	49.5	50.5
HARRISON	1.0	1.3	6.7	6.4	6.2	6.0	6.2	27.9	28.8	10.3	1.4	77.0	39.5	49.9	50.1
HENDRICKS	1.1	1.5	7.4	7.1	7.5	7.2	6.2	27.6	26.7	9.2	1.2	73.5	37.2	49.8	50.2
HENRY	0.8	1.1	6.3	6.1	6.2	6.1	5.6	26.2	27.5	13.8	2.3	77.6	40.8	48.5	51.5
HOWARD	2.0	2.7	7.0	6.7	6.4	6.5	6.2	26.0	27.3	12.1	1.9	75.9	38.6	48.5	51.5
HUNTINGTON	1.0	1.0	6.9	6.4	6.4	7.3	6.9	26.3	26.0	11.1	2.7	76.1	37.6	49.1	50.9
JACKSON	2.7	3.6	7.3	6.9	6.8	5.8	5.7	29.1	25.6	11.0	1.9	75.4	37.2	50.0	50.0
JASPER	2.4	3.3	7.1	6.7	6.9	7.4	7.1	26.1	25.7	11.1	1.8	75.0	36.7	49.8	50.2
JAY	1.8	2.4	7.5	6.7	7.4	6.2	5.9	25.5	25.9	12.9	2.1	74.6	38.4	49.3	50.7
JEFFERSON	1.0	1.4	6.4	5.9	6.4	7.3	7.4	26.0	27.1	11.7	1.7	77.5	38.5	49.4	50.6
JENNINGS	0.7	0.9	7.6	6.9	7.7	6.4	5.7	28.6	25.9	10.1	1.2	73.8	36.7	49.8	50.2
JOHNSON	1.4	1.9	7.5	7.0	7.1	7.3	6.7	27.8	24.9	9.9	1.6	73.9	36.0	49.0	51.0
KNOX	0.8	1.1	6.0	5.5	5.5	8.6	9.2	23.7	26.2	12.8	2.6	79.3	38.6	49.8	50.2
KOSCIUSKO	5.0	6.7	7.6	7.3	6.9	6.6	6.1	27.2	26.0	10.6	1.8	74.2	36.6	50.2	49.8
LAGRANGE	3.1	4.3	10.4	10.1	7.8	7.1	6.2	27.1	20.8	9.3	1.2	67.3	30.6	51.0	49.0
LAKE	12.2	15.4	7.1	6.8	7.1	6.5	6.6	25.9	26.5	11.6	1.9	75.1	37.3	48.2	51.8
LAPORTE	3.1	4.1	6.5	6.1	6.3	6.3	7.0	27.0	27.2	11.8	1.9	77.5	38.7	50.9	49.1
LAWRENCE	0.9	1.2	6.4	6.5	6.3	5.7	5.3	26.5	27.7	13.4	2.1	77.3	40.5	49.0	51.0
MADISON	1.5	2.0	6.4	6.1	6.2	6.5	6.5	26.8	26.3	12.8	2.2	77.5	39.0	49.4	50.6
MARION	3.9	5.0	7.3	6.7	6.7	7.1	7.2	29.9	24.1	9.4	1.6	75.1	34.8	48.6	51.4
MARSHALL	5.9	7.9	7.5	7.1	7.0	6.6	6.4	26.7	26.0	10.7	1.9	74.2	37.0	50.2	49.8
MARTIN	0.4	0.6	6.2	6.4	5.9	6.2	6.1	25.4	29.2	12.8	1.8	77.7	40.6	50.8	49.2
MIAMI	1.3	1.8	6.5	5.9	6.6	6.7	6.8	27.3	27.1	11.5	1.7	77.0	38.6	50.8	49.2
MONROE	1.9	2.5	5.1	4.7	4.5	11.0	18.2	26.0	20.8	8.3	1.3	82.8	28.8	49.3	50.7
MONTGOMERY	1.6	2.2	6.8	6.2	7.0	7.3	6.5	25.7	26.1	12.3	2.1	75.9	38.7	50.1	49.9
MORGAN	0.7	1.0	7.3	7.2	6.8	6.4	6.0	27.3	27.6	10.1	1.2	74.7	38.1	50.0	50.0
NEWTON	2.9	3.9	6.3	6.1	6.8	5.9	6.6	26.5	27.7	12.0	2.0	77.1	39.9	50.0	50.0
NOBLE	7.1	9.5	8.2	7.7	7.3	6.8	6.3	28.6	24.7	8.9	1.5	72.8	34.8	50.6	49.4
OHIO	0.4	0.6	6.0	5.7	5.7	7.6	5.9	25.8	27.8	13.7	1.8	77.8	40.8	50.0	50.0
ORANGE	0.6	0.7	7.0	6.6	6.4	6.5	5.6	25.9	27.4	12.7	2.0	76.0	39.4	49.3	50.7
OWEN	0.8	1.0	6.4	6.3	6.4	6.9	6.6	25.5	28.4	12.1	1.5	76.7	40.1	49.7	50.3
PARKE	0.6	0.8	5.7	5.3	5.8	6.5	6.6	26.4	28.6	13.3	1.8	79.2	41.1	48.0	52.0
PERRY	0.7	0.9	5.6	5.2	5.5	5.6	7.7	28.4	27.4	12.4	2.2	80.5	40.1	52.6	47.4
PIKE	0.6	0.8	6.2	6.2	6.3	5.7	5.7	26.1	27.7	14.0	2.1	77.8	41.1	50.4	49.6
PORTER	4.8	6.4	6.4	6.4	6.4	7.1	7.1	25.9	29.2	10.0	1.5	76.7	38.2	49.2	50.8
POSEY	0.4	0.6	6.5	6.2	6.6	7.3	6.2	25.0	29.5	11.0	1.7	76.0	40.1	49.9	50.1
PULASKI	1.4	1.9	6.4	5.9	7.0	6.7	6.6	24.7	27.8	12.6	2.3	76.5	40.1	50.8	49.2
PUTNAM	1.1	1.5	6.3	6.1	5.8	8.2	9.4	26.5	24.5	11.3	1.7	78.0	36.8	51.9	48.1
RANDOLPH	1.2	1.6	6.9	6.6	6.2	6.3	5.8	25.6	27.1	13.4	2.2	76.4	39.8	49.4	50.6
RIPLEY	0.9	1.3	7.7	7.2	7.3	6.5	5.8	26.7	25.7	11.2	1.9	73.7	37.6	49.5	50.5
RUSH	0.5	0.5	7.0	6.5	7.1	6.8	5.6	26.3	26.2	12.3	2.2	75.2	38.8	49.5	50.5
ST. JOSEPH	4.7	6.2	7.0	6.6	6.6	8.0	8.2	25.9	24.7	10.8	2.2	75.5	35.7	48.7	51.3
SCOTT	1.0	1.3	7.5	7.4	6.1	6.4	6.0	29.5	25.6	10.3	1.2	75.2	36.7	49.8	50.2
SHELBY	1.1	1.6	7.0	6.7	6.6	6.7	6.2	27.1	27.3	10.7	1.8	75.7	38.4	49.9	50.1
SPENCER	1.5	2.0	6.5	6.2	6.7	6.4	5.6	26.6	28.4	11.9	1.7	76.5	40.1	50.5	49.5
STARKE	2.2	2.9	6.6	6.2	7.2	6.6	6.1	25.9	26.7	13.0	1.7	75.9	38.8	49.9	50.1
STEUBEN	2.1	2.8	6.8	6.3	6.7	7.1	6.8	27.2	27.0	10.5	1.5	76.3	37.3	50.7	49.3
SULLIVAN	0.8	1.1	5.9	5.4	5.5	5.3	7.3	29.1	27.1	12.3	2.1	80.0	39.2	53.9	46.1
INDIANA	3.5	4.6	7.0	6.7	6.7	7.1	7.2	27.2	25.7	10.6	1.8	75.6	36.6	49.3	50.7
UNITED STATES	12.5	15.0	6.9	6.5	6.8	7.1	7.0	27.6	25.4	10.7	1.9	75.6	36.7	49.2	50.8

COUNTY	HOUSEHOLDS					FAMILIES			MEDIAN HOUSEHOLD INCOME			
	2000	2007	2012	% Annual Rate 2000-2007	2007 Average HH Size	2000	2007	% Annual Rate 2000-2007	2007	2012	2007 National Rank	2007 State Rank
ADAMS	11,818	12,236	12,433	0.5	2.74	8,668	8,682	0.0	50,395	58,617	649	44
ALLEN	128,745	137,969	144,246	1.0	2.50	86,235	88,696	0.4	54,575	64,324	418	17
BARTHOLOMEW	27,936	29,289	30,278	0.7	2.51	20,067	20,317	0.2	54,845	63,956	410	15
BENTON	3,558	3,546	3,514	0.0	2.55	2,549	2,451	-0.5	50,066	58,187	675	46
BLACKFORD	5,690	5,763	5,762	0.2	2.37	4,029	3,934	-0.3	42,918	49,269	1339	80
BOONE	17,081	20,425	23,026	2.5	2.61	12,810	14,846	2.1	62,460	73,040	202	6
BROWN	5,897	6,426	6,782	1.2	2.46	4,435	4,685	0.8	51,548	57,961	577	33
CARROLL	7,718	8,103	8,342	0.7	2.55	5,686	5,777	0.2	52,120	59,924	541	28
CASS	15,715	15,667	15,492	0.0	2.50	10,928	10,492	-0.6	48,815	56,947	760	53
CLARK	38,751	44,037	47,686	1.8	2.38	26,541	29,007	1.2	50,398	58,650	648	43
CLAY	10,216	10,631	10,793	0.6	2.54	7,435	7,481	0.1	45,102	50,949	1100	68
CLINTON	12,545	12,708	12,738	0.2	2.60	9,059	8,867	-0.3	50,765	57,981	624	39
CRAWFORD	4,181	4,483	4,680	1.0	2.48	3,057	3,170	0.5	38,419	42,242	1946	91
DAVIESS	10,894	11,179	11,311	0.4	2.66	7,823	7,749	-0.1	41,747	47,224	1485	86
DEARBORN	16,832	18,808	20,171	1.5	2.65	12,768	13,845	1.1	60,316	68,123	257	8
DECATUR	9,389	10,036	10,392	0.9	2.50	6,878	7,111	0.5	50,151	58,367	668	45
DEKALB	15,134	16,219	16,856	1.0	2.57	10,915	11,298	0.5	55,335	63,752	392	14
DELAWARE	47,131	47,270	46,769	0.0	2.31	29,686	28,447	-0.6	43,604	50,723	1260	77
DUBOIS	14,813	16,236	17,172	1.3	2.56	10,743	11,378	0.8	54,427	62,182	425	18
ELKHART	66,154	72,969	77,893	1.4	2.70	47,659	50,768	0.9	54,586	63,240	417	16
FAYETTE	10,199	10,211	10,129	0.0	2.40	7,151	6,898	-0.5	47,954	55,524	821	55
FLOYD	27,511	28,914	29,797	0.7	2.50	19,707	19,993	0.2	55,405	64,835	387	13
FOUNTAIN	7,041	7,043	7,000	0.0	2.48	5,038	4,863	-0.5	46,393	53,103	960	60
FRANKLIN	7,868	8,593	9,010	1.2	2.70	6,130	6,515	0.8	51,716	58,200	568	30
FULTON	8,082	8,381	8,542	0.5	2.49	5,739	5,740	0.0	46,365	52,522	962	61
GIBSON	12,847	13,361	13,643	0.5	2.43	9,092	9,118	0.0	46,282	52,602	975	63
GRANT	28,319	27,876	27,224	-0.2	2.36	19,578	18,547	-0.7	45,611	52,871	1041	65
GREENE	13,372	13,995	14,340	0.6	2.39	9,366	9,447	0.1	41,478	47,471	1520	88
HAMILTON	65,933	95,551	121,686	5.3	2.73	50,849	71,615	4.8	90,527	110,781	18	1
HANCOCK	20,718	26,234	30,689	3.3	2.57	16,156	19,902	2.9	69,003	79,720	127	3
HARRISON	12,917	14,496	15,531	1.6	2.55	9,712	10,566	1.2	51,730	58,148	567	29
HENDRICKS	37,275	51,058	61,213	4.4	2.63	29,084	38,760	4.0	69,641	81,128	121	2
HENRY	19,486	19,387	19,048	-0.1	2.40	13,975	13,423	-0.6	47,603	55,317	855	57
HOWARD	34,800	35,088	35,325	0.1	2.40	23,572	22,834	-0.4	55,772	64,769	372	11
HUNTINGTON	14,242	14,620	14,749	0.4	2.51	10,280	10,193	-0.1	51,640	60,403	573	31
JACKSON	16,052	16,869	17,264	0.7	2.48	11,573	11,748	0.2	48,965	55,613	751	51
JASPER	10,686	12,106	13,039	1.7	2.66	8,213	9,037	1.3	53,128	60,982	496	25
JAY	8,405	8,584	8,658	0.3	2.53	6,016	5,932	-0.2	44,373	50,739	1170	70
JEFFERSON	12,148	12,899	13,330	0.8	2.40	8,435	8,623	0.3	47,629	55,378	853	56
JENNINGS	10,134	10,768	11,117	0.8	2.61	7,604	7,830	0.4	47,453	54,093	866	58
JOHNSON	42,434	51,188	57,561	2.6	2.56	31,600	36,928	2.2	67,366	78,570	146	5
KNOX	15,552	15,384	15,137	-0.1	2.31	10,136	9,604	-0.7	38,977	44,636	1857	90
KOSCIUSKO	27,283	29,852	31,237	1.2	2.58	19,997	21,161	0.8	53,160	60,998	494	24
LAGRANGE	11,225	12,246	12,900	1.2	3.04	8,856	9,411	0.8	50,956	57,218	618	38
LAKE	181,633	190,262	196,179	0.6	2.60	127,036	128,197	0.1	53,867	63,480	459	20
LAPORTE	41,050	42,637	43,555	0.5	2.48	28,597	28,605	0.0	51,588	60,402	576	32
LAWRENCE	18,535	18,900	18,930	0.3	2.36	13,139	12,925	-0.2	44,875	51,206	1123	69
MADISON	53,052	53,117	53,078	0.0	2.38	36,211	34,847	-0.5	48,921	57,028	754	52
MARION	352,164	365,212	371,333	0.5	2.34	213,454	210,837	-0.2	51,333	60,933	589	34
MARSHALL	16,519	17,540	18,156	0.8	2.65	12,188	12,523	0.4	52,456	61,259	523	26
MARTIN	4,183	4,283	4,306	0.3	2.37	2,876	2,832	-0.2	44,257	50,690	1182	72
MIAMI	13,716	13,726	13,542	0.0	2.45	9,803	9,468	-0.5	48,191	54,839	799	54
MONROE	46,898	51,080	54,107	1.2	2.23	24,737	25,424	0.4	41,704	48,208	1489	87
MONTGOMERY	14,595	15,142	15,423	0.5	2.47	10,246	10,241	0.0	50,687	57,967	630	41
MORGAN	24,437	26,814	28,358	1.3	2.66	19,025	20,308	0.9	58,907	66,519	288	9
NEWTON	5,340	5,611	5,758	0.7	2.64	4,000	4,074	0.3	49,624	56,003	701	48
NOBLE	16,696	17,735	18,262	0.8	2.69	12,294	12,637	0.4	52,335	60,122	528	27
OHIO	2,201	2,436	2,573	1.4	2.47	1,588	1,700	0.9	51,296	60,018	595	36
ORANGE	7,621	7,961	8,151	0.6	2.43	5,340	5,374	0.1	37,968	42,291	2001	92
OWEN	8,282	9,237	9,811	1.5	2.54	6,192	6,693	1.1	43,667	48,934	1256	75
PARKE	6,415	6,700	6,844	0.6	2.47	4,627	4,671	0.1	43,205	49,050	1310	78
PERRY	7,270	7,319	7,250	0.1	2.36	5,071	4,917	-0.4	43,851	49,711	1230	74
PIKE	5,119	5,365	5,482	0.6	2.44	3,682	3,727	0.2	41,985	47,610	1450	84
PORTER	54,649	61,948	67,279	1.7	2.56	39,709	43,509	1.3	67,375	78,758	145	4
POSEY	10,205	10,494	10,615	0.4	2.57	7,613	7,585	-0.1	54,187	61,866	438	19
PULASKI	5,170	5,483	5,663	0.8	2.54	3,780	3,876	0.3	42,518	48,117	1395	82
PUTNAM	12,374	13,224	13,727	0.9	2.51	9,121	9,435	0.5	46,955	53,253	911	59
RANDOLPH	10,937	10,829	10,650	-0.1	2.42	7,798	7,449	-0.6	42,820	49,806	1350	81
RIPLEY	9,842	11,163	11,911	1.8	2.60	7,272	7,982	1.3	50,760	57,638	626	40
RUSH	6,923	7,094	7,174	0.3	2.53	5,047	4,997	-0.1	46,234	52,631	981	64
ST. JOSEPH	100,743	103,636	104,755	0.4	2.47	66,802	65,908	-0.2	51,329	60,898	590	35
SCOTT	8,832	9,422	9,733	0.9	2.50	6,495	6,703	0.4	42,075	47,577	1438	83
SHELBY	16,561	17,289	17,656	0.6	2.52	12,057	12,165	0.1	53,806	61,671	463	21
SPENCER	7,569	8,214	8,643	1.1	2.60	5,755	6,063	0.7	50,429	56,489	646	42
STARKE	8,740	9,123	9,381	0.6	2.60	6,447	6,513	0.1	45,175	51,120	1080	67
STEUBEN	12,738	13,875	14,623	1.2	2.48	8,911	9,350	0.7	53,215	61,100	490	23
SULLIVAN	7,819	8,023	8,114	0.4	2.45	5,573	5,518	-0.1	40,415	45,646	1672	89
INDIANA				1.0	2.49			0.5	52,632	61,929		
UNITED STATES				1.2	2.59			1.0	53,154	62,503		

COUNTY	2007 Per Capita Income	2007 HH Income Base	2007 HOUSEHOLD INCOME DISTRIBUTION (%)					2007 Home Value Base	2007 HOME VALUE DISTRIBUTION (%)					2007 Median Home Value
			Less than $25,000	$25,000 to $49,999	$50,000 to $99,999	$100,000 to $149,999	$150,000 or More		Less than $50,000	$50,000 to $89,999	$90,000 to $174,999	$175,000 to $399,999	$400,000 or More	
ADAMS	21,655	12,236	19.5	30.0	36.5	10.7	3.4	9,538	9.6	22.7	49.0	17.3	1.4	110,695
ALLEN	27,250	137,969	19.0	26.2	36.6	12.2	6.0	99,143	11.7	25.4	43.1	17.1	2.7	107,786
BARTHOLOMEW	26,738	29,289	19.2	25.6	36.2	13.7	5.3	22,028	12.2	10.7	48.7	25.6	2.8	128,100
BENTON	22,182	3,546	19.5	30.4	38.5	9.6	2.0	2,730	13.5	35.3	45.0	6.0	0.1	91,127
BLACKFORD	20,993	5,763	25.0	33.4	34.1	6.1	1.4	4,567	19.9	39.9	33.3	6.2	0.8	80,377
BOONE	32,428	20,425	16.3	23.2	35.7	13.4	11.5	16,277	5.4	6.9	42.2	32.9	12.5	163,752
BROWN	25,093	6,426	21.1	26.9	37.3	11.1	3.6	5,492	6.9	9.5	44.9	34.7	4.0	152,151
CARROLL	23,610	8,103	19.8	27.2	39.3	10.7	2.9	6,529	11.2	25.2	46.1	16.2	1.2	105,209
CASS	23,563	15,667	20.3	30.8	34.4	10.9	3.6	11,685	13.7	33.4	41.8	10.2	0.9	93,494
CLARK	25,668	44,037	20.6	28.9	35.8	10.7	3.9	31,325	9.6	16.5	52.2	19.5	2.2	118,864
CLAY	20,877	10,631	25.3	31.2	33.5	7.8	2.1	8,483	18.3	29.6	41.2	10.2	0.7	92,918
CLINTON	22,282	12,708	22.3	26.8	38.0	10.2	2.8	9,414	7.9	23.0	53.2	14.5	1.4	109,111
CRAWFORD	18,830	4,483	33.9	30.7	27.5	6.4	1.5	3,741	24.6	30.9	35.2	7.3	2.0	83,117
DAVIESS	19,896	11,179	28.5	30.3	31.8	6.4	2.9	8,841	17.3	30.5	39.4	11.7	1.2	93,359
DEARBORN	26,188	18,808	15.8	24.1	41.0	13.9	5.2	14,963	4.9	10.4	42.0	38.8	3.9	160,153
DECATUR	23,764	10,036	18.9	30.9	37.1	10.4	2.8	7,494	8.4	17.5	52.4	19.5	2.2	117,139
DEKALB	25,117	16,219	17.2	26.7	40.7	11.8	3.7	13,302	13.0	20.5	46.9	17.7	1.9	110,607
DELAWARE	24,052	47,270	28.6	27.5	30.1	9.7	4.2	32,172	17.3	33.3	39.2	9.2	1.0	89,346
DUBOIS	25,286	16,236	17.5	27.6	40.3	10.5	4.1	12,798	8.8	18.6	48.1	22.1	2.3	119,804
ELKHART	24,934	72,969	17.6	26.9	39.7	10.5	5.4	53,471	10.0	17.2	50.7	19.7	2.5	121,566
FAYETTE	24,083	10,211	23.5	28.4	35.3	9.3	3.6	7,418	10.2	28.2	46.7	13.6	1.3	103,744
FLOYD	27,884	28,914	19.3	24.5	36.0	13.6	6.7	21,284	3.9	14.0	50.4	28.9	2.7	137,118
FOUNTAIN	22,171	7,043	23.2	31.1	35.9	7.6	2.2	5,550	18.5	34.0	39.4	7.4	0.7	87,253
FRANKLIN	22,886	8,593	20.8	27.3	38.0	10.2	3.7	7,078	10.1	15.9	42.2	27.2	4.6	133,637
FULTON	22,230	8,381	22.8	30.8	35.7	8.4	2.2	6,646	14.2	27.9	43.0	12.9	2.0	99,258
GIBSON	22,492	13,361	25.5	28.5	34.7	9.0	2.3	10,512	20.1	29.2	37.1	12.8	0.7	91,201
GRANT	23,454	27,876	26.0	28.6	32.3	9.8	3.3	20,718	17.4	34.0	39.4	8.5	0.7	88,439
GREENE	21,144	13,995	29.7	29.7	30.5	8.5	1.7	11,296	22.5	26.8	37.8	12.2	0.7	91,236
HAMILTON	44,511	95,551	7.6	12.9	35.4	22.2	21.8	78,289	2.5	2.5	28.4	52.3	14.3	214,288
HANCOCK	32,089	26,234	11.6	22.5	38.8	18.7	8.4	21,575	3.2	6.3	45.4	41.0	4.1	166,555
HARRISON	24,068	14,496	20.0	27.5	38.2	10.8	3.4	12,236	11.7	16.7	45.1	24.2	2.2	122,981
HENDRICKS	30,177	51,058	11.4	20.4	41.5	18.5	8.3	42,603	5.4	3.7	41.9	45.5	3.5	173,191
HENRY	24,316	19,387	23.3	29.3	33.7	10.2	3.5	15,081	10.8	24.3	48.5	14.8	1.6	109,608
HOWARD	28,168	35,088	20.2	24.5	35.5	13.9	5.9	25,498	11.2	33.5	41.4	12.7	1.1	96,237
HUNTINGTON	24,094	14,620	18.6	29.3	39.1	9.6	3.4	11,401	10.8	28.3	44.8	15.0	1.1	103,325
JACKSON	23,430	16,869	21.1	30.0	37.6	8.1	3.2	12,759	16.2	19.1	47.8	15.1	1.8	110,469
JASPER	23,511	12,106	19.0	27.2	38.9	11.6	3.3	9,528	5.2	10.7	46.8	34.0	3.2	152,840
JAY	20,437	8,584	23.9	33.7	34.2	6.4	1.7	6,738	19.6	34.0	35.9	8.8	1.6	86,335
JEFFERSON	23,042	12,899	22.9	29.5	35.0	10.1	2.6	9,742	12.4	21.4	46.9	17.1	2.2	111,463
JENNINGS	21,190	10,768	21.2	32.6	35.6	8.0	2.5	8,602	18.7	23.1	45.9	10.7	1.7	101,825
JOHNSON	30,490	51,188	13.3	21.6	39.9	16.6	8.6	39,465	6.8	5.1	50.1	34.5	3.5	151,677
KNOX	20,949	15,384	33.5	27.7	29.5	6.7	2.7	10,767	22.4	34.5	31.0	10.6	1.6	80,559
KOSCIUSKO	24,984	29,852	18.0	27.7	39.5	10.2	4.7	23,828	13.6	17.5	44.9	20.8	3.2	118,424
LAGRANGE	19,977	12,246	17.3	31.3	38.7	9.4	3.3	10,089	7.0	13.8	44.6	29.9	4.6	137,811
LAKE	25,149	190,253	22.6	23.5	35.8	12.6	5.4	133,349	7.5	17.1	45.8	26.9	2.7	131,116
LAPORTE	24,340	42,637	21.0	27.3	36.7	11.4	3.6	32,395	6.9	13.7	50.6	26.0	2.8	130,340
LAWRENCE	22,579	18,900	26.1	29.7	33.4	8.7	2.1	15,043	18.0	27.5	40.9	12.7	0.8	96,374
MADISON	25,280	53,117	21.7	29.3	33.6	11.1	4.3	39,924	14.2	32.7	42.9	9.2	1.0	93,835
MARION	28,098	365,182	21.2	27.4	34.0	11.3	6.1	221,038	8.6	22.7	48.6	17.6	2.5	117,463
MARSHALL	23,579	17,540	18.5	28.0	38.8	10.8	3.9	13,654	7.8	18.8	51.8	18.8	2.7	117,894
MARTIN	21,999	4,283	26.6	29.5	35.1	6.2	2.5	3,500	26.2	31.8	31.1	9.6	1.3	79,560
MIAMI	22,782	13,725	22.9	29.2	36.4	8.9	2.5	10,561	19.5	30.8	38.6	10.1	1.1	89,699
MONROE	24,387	51,079	31.5	25.8	28.3	9.5	5.0	28,279	9.8	7.7	46.2	31.6	4.7	145,958
MONTGOMERY	23,810	15,142	21.1	28.0	38.5	9.4	3.1	11,294	8.6	19.7	54.0	16.2	1.6	116,264
MORGAN	25,500	26,814	17.8	23.8	40.5	13.3	4.5	21,635	8.9	8.8	49.5	28.8	3.9	140,302
NEWTON	21,622	5,611	20.5	29.9	38.9	8.3	2.5	4,542	6.5	19.7	51.0	21.3	1.6	123,533
NOBLE	22,596	17,735	17.7	29.5	39.6	10.1	3.0	13,985	10.5	17.9	48.8	20.9	2.0	117,616
OHIO	24,174	2,436	21.0	27.6	36.5	12.6	2.3	1,906	9.5	9.1	44.1	32.2	5.1	140,302
ORANGE	20,061	7,961	31.7	32.6	28.0	4.9	2.8	6,349	25.4	30.0	34.1	9.7	0.9	83,024
OWEN	21,111	9,237	24.0	33.2	32.4	7.8	2.5	7,614	14.3	20.3	42.5	20.5	2.3	115,988
PARKE	21,195	6,700	26.0	31.3	31.8	8.5	2.4	5,414	24.5	29.1	34.3	9.9	2.2	84,717
PERRY	21,703	7,319	26.9	30.0	33.7	7.2	2.2	5,846	14.5	31.6	42.6	10.2	1.1	94,669
PIKE	20,250	5,365	26.7	32.4	32.7	7.2	1.0	4,450	29.7	31.6	32.4	6.0	0.3	76,070
PORTER	30,641	61,948	14.7	19.9	40.7	17.0	7.7	48,052	7.7	4.0	41.5	40.8	6.0	168,844
POSEY	24,260	10,494	21.1	25.1	37.6	12.9	3.4	8,652	13.4	22.1	47.0	16.5	1.1	109,903
PULASKI	21,217	5,483	25.0	34.3	30.2	7.1	3.4	4,464	17.4	27.6	40.3	13.0	1.7	96,173
PUTNAM	21,507	13,224	22.9	30.1	34.3	9.1	3.5	10,488	9.2	16.9	48.1	23.4	2.4	120,954
RANDOLPH	21,488	10,829	26.6	31.3	33.6	6.6	1.9	8,331	18.6	34.2	37.5	8.5	1.2	86,739
RIPLEY	22,381	11,163	21.3	27.5	38.7	9.4	3.0	8,708	8.4	15.9	47.1	25.3	3.3	129,600
RUSH	21,783	7,094	23.8	31.0	33.6	8.9	2.7	5,346	7.9	23.9	50.1	14.8	3.4	112,193
ST. JOSEPH	25,647	103,636	21.5	27.0	34.9	11.2	5.4	75,003	8.0	26.5	45.6	17.9	1.9	110,820
SCOTT	20,508	9,422	28.1	32.1	30.1	7.5	2.2	7,220	18.2	29.8	41.2	10.2	0.6	92,802
SHELBY	25,906	17,289	18.7	27.1	37.2	12.6	4.4	12,901	5.7	18.9	52.8	20.3	2.3	120,660
SPENCER	22,339	8,214	20.9	28.6	37.7	10.2	2.6	6,904	13.7	22.9	44.6	16.4	2.5	110,858
STARKE	20,695	9,123	26.0	29.5	34.6	7.6	2.3	7,439	11.8	23.5	52.1	11.3	1.4	106,281
STEUBEN	25,466	13,875	17.2	28.5	40.1	10.1	4.1	10,947	11.9	15.5	43.3	23.8	5.4	124,409
SULLIVAN	19,604	8,023	29.5	32.2	29.2	6.7	2.5	6,460	23.5	35.3	33.3	7.1	0.7	78,343
INDIANA	26,366		20.8	26.3	35.6	11.7	5.6		10.4	20.0	44.7	21.9	3.0	119,366
UNITED STATES	27,916		21.9	25.0	32.3	12.3	8.4		7.9	10.5	27.1	35.6	19.0	192,285

COUNTY	FINANCIAL SERVICES				THE HOME						ENTERTAINMENT						PERSONAL			
					Home Improvements		Furnishings													
	Auto Loan	Home Loan	Invest-ments	Retire-ment Plans	Home Repair	Lawn & Garden	Comput-ers & Hard-ware	Major Appli-ances	TV, Radio, Sound Equip-ment	Furni-ture	Dine out/ Carry out	Sports Equip-ment	Fees & Tickets	Toys & Games	Travel	Cable TV	Apparel & Services	Auto Repairs	Health Insur-ance	Pets & Supplies
ADAMS	90	78	75	78	83	96	78	87	83	77	82	76	75	87	79	87	72	82	94	90
ALLEN	95	94	101	97	91	91	95	92	96	95	95	83	95	98	94	95	86	93	94	93
BARTHOLOMEW	97	92	94	93	93	98	91	94	94	91	78	73	71	84	75	82	68	79	90	88
BENTON	87	75	70	75	80	93	74	84	79	74	78	73	71	84	75	82	61	69	81	76
BLACKFORD	78	63	57	62	67	81	65	73	72	63	70	63	60	74	65	75	61	69	81	76
BOONE	120	124	128	126	125	124	116	120	116	119	115	108	120	120	119	115	104	116	119	121
BROWN	98	81	64	80	90	110	79	97	84	78	83	85	73	87	82	88	72	88	100	102
CARROLL	94	79	69	78	86	103	77	91	83	77	82	79	73	88	79	87	72	84	95	96
CASS	88	77	79	78	80	91	79	85	84	77	82	74	76	87	80	87	73	82	92	87
CLARK	86	83	90	84	82	86	84	84	86	83	85	75	83	87	84	87	76	84	88	85
CLAY	82	68	60	67	73	88	68	79	74	67	73	69	64	77	69	78	64	74	86	83
CLINTON	86	78	77	78	81	90	77	83	82	77	81	73	76	85	78	84	72	80	89	86
CRAWFORD	84	57	30	53	63	87	57	74	65	56	65	66	47	69	55	70	55	68	80	82
DAVIESS	83	66	60	66	72	87	69	79	75	67	74	69	63	77	69	79	64	74	86	83
DEARBORN	100	99	101	100	99	102	94	98	96	96	95	88	95	99	96	96	85	95	100	100
DECATUR	89	80	78	80	84	94	79	86	83	79	82	76	77	87	80	85	72	82	91	89
DEKALB	97	88	85	89	91	100	85	94	89	86	88	82	84	94	87	91	78	89	97	97
DELAWARE	80	72	79	74	72	77	81	77	83	76	82	68	77	82	78	83	73	79	83	78
DUBOIS	96	88	90	89	92	100	87	94	90	87	89	83	85	94	88	92	79	90	98	96
ELKHART	98	91	91	92	92	98	91	95	94	91	93	85	90	97	91	96	83	93	98	97
FAYETTE	85	75	78	75	78	88	77	82	83	75	81	72	74	84	78	85	71	80	90	85
FLOYD	98	97	105	99	96	97	97	96	98	97	96	86	97	99	97	98	87	96	99	96
FOUNTAIN	89	70	58	69	75	93	70	83	78	69	76	72	64	82	71	82	66	77	90	88
FRANKLIN	98	85	71	83	89	104	79	93	85	81	85	82	76	90	81	89	74	86	96	98
FULTON	89	71	59	69	77	95	71	84	77	70	76	73	65	81	71	81	66	78	90	89
GIBSON	84	71	66	70	75	88	72	80	78	70	76	71	67	80	72	81	66	76	88	83
GRANT	83	75	79	76	77	85	76	80	81	75	79	69	74	83	77	84	70	78	88	82
GREENE	80	65	55	63	69	84	65	76	72	63	70	64	60	73	66	76	61	71	84	79
HAMILTON	169	193	186	196	181	164	171	167	161	182	162	159	182	169	173	154	149	165	152	166
HANCOCK	114	123	132	125	123	119	112	115	112	117	111	103	119	116	117	111	101	112	114	116
HARRISON	97	82	70	80	86	101	80	92	85	79	84	81	75	88	80	89	74	86	96	96
HENDRICKS	114	121	118	120	116	113	110	112	108	115	109	103	114	112	112	107	98	110	108	113
HENRY	86	77	79	77	81	91	77	84	83	77	81	72	76	85	79	86	71	80	91	86
HOWARD	94	91	102	93	92	95	93	93	96	92	94	81	93	97	94	97	84	92	99	93
HUNTINGTON	90	83	84	84	85	93	82	87	86	82	85	76	81	89	83	88	75	84	93	89
JACKSON	90	78	71	78	81	92	76	85	81	77	80	74	73	85	77	83	70	81	89	88
JASPER	96	87	82	87	90	101	83	92	87	84	86	81	82	91	85	90	76	87	96	96
JAY	81	65	58	64	70	85	67	76	74	65	72	66	62	76	67	78	62	72	85	80
JEFFERSON	85	73	72	73	75	86	76	81	80	73	78	71	71	81	76	83	68	79	88	83
JENNINGS	88	74	63	73	76	89	72	82	78	73	77	72	68	81	72	81	67	78	86	85
JOHNSON	112	114	114	116	108	105	111	107	108	113	108	99	112	111	109	106	98	109	105	108
KNOX	73	60	62	61	63	74	68	70	71	63	69	62	62	71	66	74	61	69	78	72
KOSCIUSKO	100	87	79	86	90	103	85	95	89	85	89	84	81	93	86	93	78	90	99	99
LAGRANGE	98	82	64	79	87	104	77	92	83	78	83	82	72	88	78	87	73	85	95	98
LAKE	88	91	102	93	90	88	89	87	92	91	91	77	93	92	91	93	83	88	91	88
LAPORTE	87	84	90	85	85	90	83	86	86	83	85	75	83	88	85	88	76	84	91	87
LAWRENCE	85	68	59	66	72	89	69	80	76	67	74	70	63	78	69	80	64	75	88	84
MADISON	86	82	90	83	84	90	82	85	87	82	85	74	82	88	84	89	75	83	93	86
MARION	92	86	92	90	82	83	94	86	94	92	94	79	91	94	89	94	85	91	89	87
MARSHALL	92	84	85	85	89	98	82	90	87	83	86	79	81	91	84	90	76	86	96	93
MARTIN	86	64	48	62	70	91	66	80	74	63	73	70	58	77	66	80	62	74	90	85
MIAMI	88	73	65	72	77	92	74	83	80	73	79	73	69	83	74	83	69	79	90	87
MONROE	80	67	72	71	66	70	90	74	83	77	84	71	79	81	78	80	75	81	74	76
MONTGOMERY	86	79	82	79	83	91	79	85	83	78	82	74	78	86	80	86	73	81	90	87
MORGAN	98	97	99	98	99	103	91	97	93	93	92	86	93	97	94	94	83	93	99	99
NEWTON	90	76	65	75	82	97	73	86	79	73	80	76	70	83	75	83	68	80	91	90
NOBLE	93	82	75	82	85	95	80	89	84	81	84	79	77	88	81	87	74	85	92	92
OHIO	87	80	86	81	81	88	81	84	84	79	82	74	79	85	81	86	73	82	90	86
ORANGE	83	59	41	57	65	86	62	76	69	60	68	66	53	72	60	74	58	70	82	81
OWEN	89	72	54	69	75	91	68	81	74	69	74	72	63	78	68	78	64	76	85	87
PARKE	86	67	55	65	74	93	68	82	75	66	74	71	61	77	69	80	64	76	89	87
PERRY	86	65	51	63	70	90	67	80	75	64	73	70	59	77	66	80	63	74	88	85
PIKE	85	60	38	57	66	89	61	77	70	59	69	68	52	73	61	75	58	71	85	84
PORTER	109	116	122	117	114	110	109	109	108	112	108	99	113	110	112	107	98	108	101	110
POSEY	94	86	82	86	89	99	82	91	86	83	85	80	81	90	84	89	75	86	95	94
PULASKI	91	68	48	65	76	99	68	85	75	66	75	75	60	80	68	81	64	78	92	92
PUTNAM	87	74	68	73	79	93	74	84	79	73	78	74	70	82	74	82	68	79	89	88
RANDOLPH	81	66	60	66	71	85	67	77	74	66	72	67	63	77	68	78	63	72	85	80
RIPLEY	91	77	68	76	82	96	76	87	81	75	80	76	72	85	77	84	70	81	92	91
RUSH	86	71	66	71	77	91	72	82	78	71	76	72	67	81	73	81	67	77	88	86
ST. JOSEPH	88	87	98	90	87	87	89	87	91	89	90	77	90	91	89	91	81	88	91	87
SCOTT	81	65	57	65	66	79	67	74	73	66	72	65	62	75	66	76	63	72	80	77
SHELBY	96	89	92	90	92	99	88	93	91	88	90	82	87	95	89	93	80	90	97	96
SPENCER	94	78	63	76	85	102	73	89	79	75	79	79	70	85	76	84	69	81	93	95
STARKE	87	70	58	68	75	91	69	81	75	68	75	71	64	79	70	80	65	76	87	85
STEUBEN	99	85	75	84	89	103	84	94	88	83	88	84	79	92	84	91	77	90	98	99
SULLIVAN	80	62	40	60	68	87	63	76	70	61	69	66	56	72	63	75	59	71	84	81
INDIANA	95	89	91	91	89	94	90	92	93	90	92	82	89	95	90	94	82	91	95	93
UNITED STATES	100	100	100	100	100	100	100	100	100	100	100	100	100	100	100	100	100	100	100	100

POPULATION CHANGE

COUNTY	FIPS Code	CBSA Code	DMA Code	POPULATION			2000-2007 ANNUAL RATE		RACE (%)					
									White		Black		Asian/Pacific	
				2000	2007	2012	% Rate	State Rank	2000	2007	2000	2007	2000	2007
SWITZERLAND	155	00000	515	9,065	10,110	10,878	1.5	6	98.8	98.5	0.2	0.3	0.1	0.1
TIPPECANOE	157	29140	582	148,955	160,816	169,079	1.1	17	88.9	85.4	2.5	3.5	4.5	6.1
TIPTON	159	29020	527	16,577	16,424	16,247	-0.1	76	98.3	97.9	0.1	0.2	0.3	0.5
UNION	161	00000	515	7,349	7,515	7,644	0.3	54	98.7	98.5	0.2	0.3	0.2	0.3
VANDERBURGH	163	21780	649	171,922	173,302	174,083	0.1	67	89.3	87.8	8.2	9.1	0.8	1.1
VERMILLION	165	45460	581	16,788	16,790	16,826	0.0	72	98.4	98.4	0.3	0.3	0.1	0.1
VIGO	167	45460	581	105,848	105,020	104,058	-0.1	76	90.7	89.2	6.0	6.7	1.3	1.8
WABASH	169	47340	509	34,960	33,858	32,870	-0.4	88	97.4	96.9	0.4	0.5	0.4	0.6
WARREN	171	00000	582	8,419	8,980	9,330	0.9	24	99.1	98.9	0.1	0.1	0.2	0.3
WARRICK	173	21780	649	52,383	57,977	62,329	1.4	9	97.5	96.9	1.0	1.1	0.7	1.0
WASHINGTON	175	31140	529	27,223	28,405	29,173	0.6	34	98.8	98.5	0.1	0.1	0.2	0.2
WAYNE	177	39980	542	71,097	70,123	69,503	-0.2	81	92.0	90.8	5.1	5.7	0.5	0.8
WELLS	179	23060	509	27,600	28,555	29,048	0.5	42	98.3	97.9	0.2	0.2	0.2	0.3
WHITE	181	00000	527	25,267	25,909	26,304	0.3	54	95.2	93.8	0.2	0.2	0.3	0.4
WHITLEY	183	23060	509	30,707	33,181	35,048	1.1	17	98.4	98.1	0.2	0.2	0.2	0.3
INDIANA							0.7		87.5	86.0	8.4	8.8	1.0	1.4
UNITED STATES							1.2		75.1	72.7	12.3	12.6	3.8	4.5

19-A

COUNTY	% HISPANIC ORIGIN		2007 AGE DISTRIBUTION (%)										MEDIAN AGE	% 2007 Males	% 2007 Females
	2000	2007	0-4	5-9	10-14	15-19	20-24	25-44	45-64	65-84	85+	18+	2007		
SWITZERLAND	0.9	1.2	6.5	6.1	7.0	6.5	5.5	27.5	26.9	12.4	1.5	76.3	38.9	51.1	48.9
TIPPECANOE	5.3	6.9	5.9	5.4	5.5	10.3	16.2	27.5	20.1	7.8	1.4	80.1	28.6	51.6	48.4
TIPTON	1.2	1.6	6.3	6.1	6.1	6.2	6.3	25.8	28.6	12.2	2.4	77.7	40.4	49.6	50.4
UNION	0.3	0.4	7.4	7.3	6.7	6.2	6.3	26.8	25.7	11.9	1.7	74.5	38.2	50.0	50.0
VANDERBURGH	1.0	1.3	6.3	5.9	5.9	7.0	7.6	26.6	25.8	12.5	2.6	78.3	38.1	47.7	52.3
VERMILLION	0.6	0.7	6.3	6.3	5.8	5.8	5.8	26.0	28.7	12.8	2.4	78.1	40.8	49.4	50.6
VIGO	1.2	1.6	6.1	5.6	5.7	7.7	9.6	26.6	24.9	11.5	2.3	79.0	36.2	50.0	50.0
WABASH	1.2	1.6	6.1	5.7	5.9	7.6	7.3	25.3	26.5	12.7	2.8	78.1	39.0	48.8	51.2
WARREN	0.4	0.6	6.0	6.0	6.7	7.2	5.3	25.3	28.1	13.6	1.7	76.6	40.8	50.9	49.1
WARRICK	0.6	0.9	6.5	6.3	7.0	6.6	6.2	25.7	29.8	10.5	1.5	76.0	39.8	49.2	50.8
WASHINGTON	0.7	1.0	6.9	6.6	6.7	6.4	5.9	28.2	26.9	10.7	1.6	75.9	37.7	50.3	49.7
WAYNE	1.4	1.8	6.3	5.9	5.9	7.0	7.1	25.6	26.4	13.3	2.3	77.8	39.5	48.3	51.7
WELLS	1.4	1.9	6.8	6.4	6.8	6.8	6.6	25.3	27.4	11.6	2.3	75.9	39.0	49.6	50.4
WHITE	5.3	7.2	6.6	6.2	6.6	6.1	6.1	26.3	27.3	12.8	2.0	76.8	39.6	49.6	50.4
WHITLEY	0.9	1.2	6.9	6.8	6.5	6.8	6.0	26.3	28.0	10.8	1.9	75.6	38.5	49.8	50.2
INDIANA	3.5	4.6	7.0	6.7	6.7	7.1	7.2	27.2	25.7	10.6	1.8	75.6	36.6	49.3	50.7
UNITED STATES	12.5	15.0	6.9	6.5	6.8	7.1	7.0	27.6	25.4	10.7	1.9	75.6	36.7	49.2	50.8

COUNTY	HOUSEHOLDS					FAMILIES			MEDIAN HOUSEHOLD INCOME			
	2000	2007	2012	% Annual Rate 2000-2007	2007 Average HH Size	2000	2007	% Annual Rate 2000-2007	2007	2012	2007 National Rank	2007 State Rank
SWITZERLAND	3,435	3,912	4,238	1.8	2.56	2,540	2,802	1.4	44,364	49,712	1174	71
TIPPECANOE	55,226	62,018	66,013	1.6	2.36	32,403	34,572	0.9	49,375	57,330	716	49
TIPTON	6,469	6,566	6,550	0.2	2.47	4,750	4,665	-0.2	58,590	66,603	294	10
UNION	2,793	2,910	2,977	0.6	2.56	2,072	2,090	0.1	45,183	51,764	1085	66
VANDERBURGH	70,623	72,266	73,031	0.3	2.30	44,442	43,436	-0.3	46,333	54,113	966	62
VERMILLION	6,762	6,878	6,927	0.2	2.40	4,715	4,617	-0.3	43,031	49,355	1328	79
VIGO	40,998	41,338	41,188	0.1	2.33	26,058	25,118	-0.5	41,910	49,150	1457	85
WABASH	13,215	13,117	12,833	-0.1	2.43	9,393	8,992	-0.6	50,053	58,166	677	47
WARREN	3,219	3,514	3,681	1.2	2.52	2,423	2,566	0.8	51,173	58,331	602	37
WARRICK	19,438	22,151	24,073	1.8	2.59	15,176	16,829	1.4	61,041	71,034	239	7
WASHINGTON	10,264	10,938	11,311	0.9	2.57	7,582	7,820	0.4	43,622	48,740	1259	76
WAYNE	28,469	28,272	28,143	-0.1	2.40	19,308	18,422	-0.6	43,926	51,002	1217	73
WELLS	10,402	10,997	11,270	0.8	2.55	7,625	7,797	0.3	53,755	61,529	464	22
WHITE	9,727	10,089	10,267	0.5	2.54	7,093	7,109	0.0	49,292	56,026	724	50
WHITLEY	11,711	13,014	13,891	1.5	2.51	8,605	9,250	1.0	55,680	63,225	378	12
INDIANA				1.0	2.49			0.5	52,632	61,929		
UNITED STATES				1.2	2.59			1.0	53,154	62,503		

COUNTY	2007 Per Capita Income	2007 HH Income Base	2007 HOUSEHOLD INCOME DISTRIBUTION (%)					2007 Home Value Base	2007 HOME VALUE DISTRIBUTION (%)					2007 Median Home Value
			Less than $25,000	$25,000 to $49,999	$50,000 to $99,999	$100,000 to $149,999	$150,000 or More		Less than $50,000	$50,000 to $89,999	$90,000 to $174,999	$175,000 to $399,999	$400,000 or More	
SWITZERLAND	21,155	3,912	27.8	29.4	33.9	6.4	2.5	3,080	11.4	21.9	43.8	19.7	3.2	112,866
TIPPECANOE	25,857	62,012	24.7	25.9	32.5	11.2	5.9	35,593	6.9	15.3	54.0	21.2	2.6	124,732
TIPTON	27,184	6,566	18.4	22.6	39.0	15.7	4.3	5,313	12.0	29.8	45.3	12.3	0.7	98,042
UNION	22,219	2,910	22.0	34.4	32.1	8.6	2.9	2,234	12.0	23.7	44.0	16.9	3.4	108,840
VANDERBURGH	26,148	72,264	25.5	28.1	32.3	9.2	4.9	48,988	12.0	28.4	41.2	16.1	2.3	102,124
VERMILLION	23,066	6,878	27.1	30.4	31.8	7.2	3.5	5,508	24.7	35.7	32.0	7.4	0.3	77,037
VIGO	22,755	41,337	29.8	27.9	30.6	7.7	4.0	28,268	17.9	30.4	38.1	12.3	1.3	92,158
WABASH	23,642	13,117	20.1	29.8	37.5	9.8	2.7	10,078	12.2	28.0	44.4	14.3	1.1	102,667
WARREN	23,061	3,514	20.4	28.0	39.5	9.5	2.6	2,875	14.2	27.5	41.2	14.0	3.1	99,464
WARRICK	28,405	22,151	15.1	23.9	39.3	15.2	6.5	18,560	8.6	18.0	43.2	27.1	3.1	127,613
WASHINGTON	20,481	10,938	27.3	29.8	34.0	6.6	2.2	8,940	15.6	24.2	42.7	15.6	1.9	104,958
WAYNE	22,511	28,272	26.9	29.2	32.9	8.0	3.0	19,752	12.7	26.2	46.5	13.4	1.2	105,076
WELLS	24,185	10,997	17.1	28.6	40.3	10.9	3.1	8,968	12.4	25.3	46.6	14.8	0.8	104,734
WHITE	22,494	10,089	20.3	30.5	38.8	7.7	2.7	7,842	10.6	19.0	49.7	18.0	2.7	113,070
WHITLEY	25,840	13,014	17.3	27.1	39.7	12.2	3.7	10,866	10.7	19.4	48.4	19.8	1.5	114,583
INDIANA	26,366		20.8	26.3	35.6	11.7	5.6		10.4	20.0	44.7	21.9	3.0	119,366
UNITED STATES	27,916		21.9	25.0	32.3	12.3	8.4		7.9	10.5	27.1	35.6	19.0	192,285

SPENDING POTENTIAL INDICES

COUNTY	FINANCIAL SERVICES				THE HOME						ENTERTAINMENT						PERSONAL			
					Home Improvements		Furnishings													
	Auto Loan	Home Loan	Invest- ments	Retire- ment Plans	Home Repair	Lawn & Garden	Comput- ers & Hard- ware	Major Appli- ances	TV, Radio, Sound Equip- ment	Furni- ture	Dine out/ Carry out	Sports Equip- ment	Fees & Tickets	Toys & Games	Travel	Cable TV	Apparel & Services	Auto Repairs	Health Insur- ance	Pets & Supplies
SWITZERLAND	90	67	50	65	73	95	69	84	75	67	75	74	60	78	68	81	65	78	90	90
TIPPECANOE	90	80	84	84	77	79	96	83	91	87	91	79	88	91	87	88	82	89	83	85
TIPTON	104	91	81	90	96	111	87	100	93	88	92	88	84	98	89	97	81	93	106	104
UNION	89	75	66	75	80	95	74	85	79	73	78	75	70	83	75	82	68	80	91	89
VANDERBURGH	84	80	92	83	80	81	85	81	87	83	85	73	84	87	84	88	77	83	87	82
VERMILLION	88	69	59	68	75	93	71	83	79	69	77	72	65	82	72	84	67	78	92	87
VIGO	77	69	77	72	70	76	76	74	79	73	77	66	73	78	74	80	68	75	81	76
WABASH	89	76	74	76	80	93	77	85	83	76	82	74	73	86	78	87	71	81	94	88
WARREN	92	75	64	74	83	101	74	89	81	73	80	77	69	86	76	86	70	81	96	93
WARRICK	108	107	101	107	106	110	99	105	100	102	100	95	100	105	101	101	90	101	105	107
WASHINGTON	90	67	46	64	71	92	66	81	73	65	73	72	58	77	65	78	63	75	86	87
WAYNE	78	70	77	71	72	79	74	76	78	72	76	66	72	79	74	80	67	75	83	77
WELLS	93	85	82	85	88	97	82	90	86	82	85	79	80	89	83	88	75	85	94	93
WHITE	89	75	68	75	81	95	74	85	79	74	78	75	70	83	75	83	69	80	90	89
WHITLEY	97	89	89	89	92	100	87	94	90	87	89	83	85	94	88	93	79	90	98	97
INDIANA	95	89	91	91	89	94	90	92	93	90	92	82	89	95	90	94	82	91	95	93
UNITED STATES	100	100	100	100	100	100	100	100	100	100	100	100	100	100	100	100	100	100	100	100

COUNTY	FIPS Code	CBSA Code	DMA Code	POPULATION			2000-2007 ANNUAL RATE		RACE (%)					
									White		Black		Asian/Pacific	
				2000	2007	2012	% Rate	State Rank	2000	2007	2000	2007	2000	2007
ADAIR	001	00000	679	8,243	8,055	7,907	-0.3	71	98.9	98.6	0.1	0.1	0.2	0.3
ADAMS	003	00000	679	4,482	4,264	4,106	-0.7	95	98.9	98.6	0.1	0.1	0.2	0.3
ALLAMAKEE	005	00000	637	14,675	15,073	15,354	0.4	22	95.9	94.6	0.1	0.2	0.3	0.4
APPANOOSE	007	00000	679	13,721	13,583	13,509	-0.1	54	98.2	97.8	0.4	0.5	0.3	0.4
AUDUBON	009	00000	679	6,830	6,639	6,501	-0.4	80	99.2	99.0	0.1	0.2	0.2	0.3
BENTON	011	16300	637	25,308	27,325	28,838	1.1	6	98.8	98.6	0.2	0.2	0.2	0.3
BLACK HAWK	013	47940	637	128,012	127,631	128,027	0.0	47	88.4	86.5	8.0	8.9	1.0	1.5
BOONE	015	14340	679	26,224	26,892	27,409	0.3	27	98.5	98.1	0.4	0.4	0.2	0.3
BREMER	017	47940	637	23,325	24,704	25,654	0.8	10	98.2	97.8	0.5	0.6	0.5	0.8
BUCHANAN	019	00000	637	21,093	21,384	21,665	0.2	34	98.4	98.0	0.3	0.3	0.4	0.6
BUENA VISTA	021	44740	624	20,411	20,442	20,514	0.0	47	88.0	88.0	0.4	0.4	4.3	4.3
BUTLER	023	00000	637	15,305	15,337	15,400	0.0	47	99.0	99.0	0.1	0.1	0.2	0.2
CALHOUN	025	00000	679	11,115	10,651	10,317	-0.6	91	98.1	97.7	0.7	0.8	0.2	0.3
CARROLL	027	00000	679	21,421	21,099	20,894	-0.2	62	98.9	98.5	0.2	0.2	0.3	0.5
CASS	029	00000	652	14,684	14,583	14,521	-0.1	54	98.8	98.6	0.2	0.2	0.2	0.3
CEDAR	031	00000	637	18,187	18,745	19,146	0.4	22	98.5	98.1	0.2	0.2	0.3	0.5
CERRO GORDO	033	32380	611	46,447	45,388	44,785	-0.3	71	96.3	95.3	0.8	0.9	0.7	1.1
CHEROKEE	035	00000	624	13,035	12,254	11,756	-0.8	98	98.3	97.9	0.3	0.3	0.4	0.7
CHICKASAW	037	00000	637	13,095	12,822	12,691	-0.3	71	98.7	98.4	0.1	0.1	0.3	0.4
CLARKE	039	00000	679	9,133	9,387	9,551	0.4	22	96.6	95.6	0.1	0.1	0.4	0.6
CLAY	041	43980	624	17,372	17,069	16,877	-0.2	62	98.1	97.5	0.2	0.2	0.8	1.3
CLAYTON	043	00000	637	18,678	18,931	19,145	0.2	34	98.9	98.7	0.1	0.2	0.1	0.2
CLINTON	045	17540	682	50,149	49,537	49,177	-0.2	62	95.9	95.1	1.9	2.2	0.6	0.9
CRAWFORD	047	00000	652	16,942	16,999	17,054	0.0	47	93.1	93.0	0.8	0.8	0.5	0.5
DALLAS	049	19780	679	40,750	56,285	71,514	4.6	1	94.7	93.2	0.7	0.8	0.7	1.1
DAVIS	051	00000	631	8,541	8,715	8,832	0.3	27	98.3	98.0	0.2	0.2	0.2	0.4
DECATUR	053	00000	679	8,689	8,589	8,517	-0.2	62	96.5	96.4	1.0	1.0	0.7	0.8
DELAWARE	055	00000	637	18,404	18,433	18,429	0.0	47	99.3	99.3	0.1	0.1	0.2	0.2
DES MOINES	057	15460	682	42,351	40,586	39,459	-0.6	91	93.7	92.5	3.6	4.1	0.6	1.0
DICKINSON	059	44020	624	16,424	17,069	17,559	0.5	19	98.9	98.7	0.2	0.2	0.2	0.3
DUBUQUE	061	20220	637	89,143	92,767	95,199	0.6	16	97.1	96.3	0.9	1.0	0.7	1.0
EMMET	063	00000	624	11,027	10,659	10,425	-0.5	87	97.4	96.6	0.2	0.3	0.3	0.5
FAYETTE	065	00000	637	22,008	21,362	20,919	-0.4	80	97.7	97.1	0.5	0.6	0.4	0.7
FLOYD	067	00000	611	16,900	16,775	16,754	-0.1	54	98.1	97.6	0.2	0.3	0.5	0.8
FRANKLIN	069	00000	679	10,704	10,597	10,534	-0.1	54	94.9	93.2	0.1	0.1	0.2	0.3
FREMONT	071	00000	652	8,010	7,798	7,645	-0.4	80	98.0	97.4	0.0	0.1	0.2	0.4
GREENE	073	00000	679	10,366	10,221	10,157	-0.2	62	98.2	97.7	0.1	0.2	0.3	0.4
GRUNDY	075	47940	637	12,369	12,681	12,926	0.3	27	99.0	98.7	0.1	0.1	0.3	0.4
GUTHRIE	077	19780	679	11,353	11,845	12,252	0.6	16	98.6	98.3	0.1	0.1	0.2	0.3
HAMILTON	079	00000	679	16,438	16,567	16,673	0.1	41	96.7	95.6	0.2	0.3	1.5	2.3
HANCOCK	081	00000	611	12,100	11,936	11,818	-0.2	62	97.7	96.9	0.1	0.1	0.3	0.5
HARDIN	083	00000	679	18,812	18,390	18,091	-0.3	71	97.1	96.4	0.6	0.7	0.4	0.5
HARRISON	085	36540	652	15,666	16,056	16,310	0.3	27	98.7	98.4	0.1	0.1	0.2	0.3
HENRY	087	00000	682	20,336	20,638	20,829	0.2	34	94.8	93.3	1.5	1.7	1.9	2.9
HOWARD	089	00000	611	9,932	9,747	9,627	-0.3	71	99.1	98.9	0.1	0.1	0.2	0.3
HUMBOLDT	091	00000	679	10,381	10,233	10,123	-0.2	62	98.6	98.2	0.1	0.1	0.3	0.5
IDA	093	00000	624	7,837	7,444	7,174	-0.7	95	99.0	98.8	0.1	0.1	0.2	0.4
IOWA	095	00000	637	15,671	16,609	17,282	0.8	10	98.7	98.3	0.2	0.2	0.3	0.5
JACKSON	097	00000	682	20,296	20,446	20,574	0.1	41	99.0	98.7	0.1	0.1	0.2	0.3
JASPER	099	35500	679	37,213	37,379	37,444	0.1	41	97.6	97.0	0.8	0.9	0.5	0.7
JEFFERSON	101	00000	631	16,181	15,877	15,676	-0.3	71	96.0	94.8	0.6	0.7	1.7	2.7
JOHNSON	103	26980	637	111,006	124,240	133,403	1.6	3	90.1	87.1	2.9	3.3	4.2	6.3
JONES	105	16300	637	20,221	20,580	20,814	0.2	34	96.7	96.1	1.8	2.1	0.2	0.3
KEOKUK	107	00000	637	11,400	11,264	11,181	-0.2	62	99.0	98.7	0.1	0.1	0.2	0.4
KOSSUTH	109	00000	679	17,163	16,261	15,696	-0.7	95	98.8	98.4	0.1	0.1	0.4	0.5
LEE	111	22800	717	38,052	36,951	36,121	-0.4	80	94.2	93.0	2.8	3.2	0.5	0.8
LINN	113	16300	637	191,701	206,024	216,512	1.0	7	93.9	92.5	2.6	2.9	1.4	2.2
LOUISA	115	34700	682	12,183	11,980	11,809	-0.2	62	93.9	92.1	0.3	0.3	0.2	0.3
LUCAS	117	00000	679	9,422	9,496	9,543	0.1	41	98.4	98.4	0.1	0.1	0.3	0.3
LYON	119	00000	725	11,763	11,681	11,630	-0.1	54	99.1	99.1	0.1	0.1	0.2	0.2
MADISON	121	19780	679	14,019	15,689	17,084	1.6	3	98.6	98.3	0.1	0.1	0.2	0.3
MAHASKA	123	36820	679	22,335	22,411	22,463	0.0	47	97.2	97.2	0.6	0.6	0.9	0.9
MARION	125	37800	679	32,052	33,874	35,003	0.8	10	97.5	96.6	0.4	0.5	1.1	1.6
MARSHALL	127	32260	679	39,311	39,967	40,453	0.2	34	90.4	87.7	0.9	1.0	0.8	1.2
MILLS	129	36540	652	14,547	15,324	15,913	0.7	13	98.0	97.5	0.3	0.5	0.3	0.5
MITCHELL	131	00000	611	10,874	10,936	10,979	0.1	41	99.3	99.3	0.2	0.2	0.2	0.2
MONONA	133	00000	624	10,020	9,705	9,446	-0.4	80	98.3	97.3	0.1	0.5	0.2	0.6
MONROE	135	00000	679	8,016	7,825	7,696	-0.3	71	98.4	98.0	0.2	0.2	0.4	0.6
MONTGOMERY	137	00000	652	11,771	11,295	10,989	-0.6	91	98.2	97.7	0.1	0.1	0.3	0.4
MUSCATINE	139	34700	682	41,722	43,771	45,385	0.7	13	90.7	88.0	0.7	0.8	0.8	1.2
O'BRIEN	141	00000	624	15,102	14,718	14,464	-0.4	80	98.0	97.5	0.3	0.4	0.5	0.8
OSCEOLA	143	00000	725	7,003	6,758	6,573	-0.5	87	98.0	97.5	0.1	0.1	0.2	0.3
PAGE	145	00000	652	16,976	16,005	15,950	-0.5	87	96.1	95.3	1.7	1.9	0.5	0.7
PALO ALTO	147	00000	624	10,147	9,846	9,650	-0.4	80	98.6	97.9	0.1	0.6	0.3	0.5
PLYMOUTH	149	00000	624	24,849	25,414	25,772	0.3	27	98.2	97.7	0.3	0.3	0.3	0.5
POCAHONTAS	151	00000	679	8,662	7,061	7,571	-1.2	99	98.5	98.2	0.2	0.3	0.2	0.3
POLK	153	19780	679	374,601	411,995	440,666	1.3	5	88.3	85.6	4.8	5.4	2.7	4.0
IOWA							0.5		93.9	92.4	2.1	2.4	1.3	2.0
UNITED STATES							1.2		75.1	72.7	12.3	12.6	3.8	4.5

POPULATION COMPOSITION

COUNTY	% HISPANIC ORIGIN		2007 AGE DISTRIBUTION (%)										MEDIAN AGE	% 2007 Males	% 2007 Females
	2000	2007	0-4	5-9	10-14	15-19	20-24	25-44	45-64	65-84	85+	18+	2007		
ADAIR	0.7	0.9	6.1	5.4	5.6	6.1	6.5	22.0	27.8	15.5	4.9	79.0	43.8	49.0	51.0
ADAMS	0.6	0.8	5.9	5.6	5.9	6.6	5.2	22.7	27.6	16.5	3.9	78.0	43.7	50.4	49.6
ALLAMAKEE	3.5	4.8	6.3	6.3	6.0	6.6	5.7	24.3	27.4	14.2	3.3	77.4	41.6	50.4	49.6
APPANOOSE	1.0	1.3	6.1	5.3	5.9	6.3	6.3	24.0	27.3	15.2	3.5	78.8	42.2	48.0	52.0
AUDUBON	0.5	0.7	6.5	5.2	6.5	6.7	6.6	19.6	26.3	17.4	5.1	77.6	44.2	48.2	51.8
BENTON	0.6	0.8	7.0	6.1	7.0	6.9	6.1	25.8	26.8	11.6	2.6	75.5	40.0	50.7	49.3
BLACK HAWK	1.8	2.5	6.2	5.7	6.1	7.6	10.6	25.0	25.0	11.4	2.4	78.5	35.4	48.2	51.8
BOONE	0.8	1.1	6.2	5.8	6.1	6.8	6.5	25.2	27.5	12.6	3.1	77.6	40.2	49.0	51.0
BREMER	0.6	0.7	5.7	5.3	6.4	8.2	8.9	21.9	26.8	13.5	3.2	78.7	40.0	48.8	51.2
BUCHANAN	0.6	0.8	7.4	6.8	6.8	7.1	6.7	24.9	26.0	11.9	2.5	74.5	38.0	50.2	49.8
BUENA VISTA	12.5	12.7	6.1	6.0	6.6	8.0	8.9	23.7	25.3	12.3	3.1	77.2	37.8	50.3	49.7
BUTLER	0.6	0.6	5.8	5.6	6.1	6.2	6.4	22.7	28.7	14.9	3.7	78.6	43.0	49.3	50.7
CALHOUN	0.9	1.2	5.5	5.2	5.4	6.0	7.3	21.7	28.0	16.1	4.6	80.7	44.0	50.4	49.6
CARROLL	0.5	0.7	6.5	5.7	6.5	6.9	7.5	22.8	26.5	14.0	3.7	77.3	40.9	49.2	50.8
CASS	0.7	0.9	5.7	5.3	5.8	6.0	6.6	21.7	28.2	16.6	4.2	79.5	44.2	49.1	50.9
CEDAR	0.9	1.2	6.4	5.9	6.4	6.1	6.4	24.3	29.2	12.3	3.1	77.5	41.5	49.7	50.3
CERRO GORDO	2.8	3.7	6.0	5.8	5.9	6.8	7.2	24.0	27.5	13.7	3.1	78.4	40.9	48.4	51.6
CHEROKEE	1.0	1.2	5.7	5.5	5.8	6.8	6.7	21.2	29.1	15.6	3.6	78.6	43.7	49.5	50.5
CHICKASAW	0.6	0.9	6.2	6.1	6.4	6.4	6.8	22.9	27.6	14.4	3.1	77.1	41.7	50.2	49.8
CLARKE	4.0	5.4	6.8	6.3	5.9	6.9	6.7	23.6	27.5	13.2	3.1	76.8	40.6	49.5	50.5
CLAY	1.1	1.5	6.3	5.9	6.2	6.1	6.3	25.3	28.2	12.9	3.0	78.0	40.7	48.5	51.5
CLAYTON	0.8	1.0	6.2	5.7	6.1	6.4	6.5	22.3	29.1	14.3	3.4	77.9	42.7	49.8	50.2
CLINTON	1.3	1.7	6.7	6.3	6.1	6.9	6.8	24.5	27.1	12.8	2.8	76.7	40.0	48.9	51.1
CRAWFORD	8.7	8.9	6.9	6.4	6.1	7.4	6.8	23.8	26.9	12.7	3.1	76.1	39.9	50.8	49.2
DALLAS	5.4	7.2	8.6	8.3	7.1	5.7	6.2	28.8	25.5	8.3	1.5	72.4	35.8	49.6	50.4
DAVIS	0.7	1.0	7.5	7.0	6.0	6.3	6.0	23.3	27.1	13.4	3.4	75.6	40.3	50.1	49.9
DECATUR	1.7	1.7	5.9	5.1	6.4	9.5	11.3	19.8	24.6	14.1	3.4	78.9	37.6	49.2	50.8
DELAWARE	0.7	0.7	7.0	6.0	7.0	7.2	7.0	24.4	26.5	12.3	2.5	75.3	39.5	49.7	50.3
DES MOINES	1.7	2.3	6.5	5.8	6.2	5.9	7.1	24.8	27.4	13.5	2.7	77.9	40.5	48.6	51.4
DICKINSON	0.7	0.9	5.2	5.3	5.2	5.8	5.4	22.0	31.2	16.5	3.4	80.7	45.8	48.9	51.1
DUBUQUE	1.2	1.6	6.7	6.4	6.7	7.2	7.6	24.7	25.7	12.3	2.7	76.3	38.2	48.6	51.4
EMMET	4.3	5.7	5.8	5.3	5.9	7.3	6.8	23.6	26.2	14.9	4.1	78.7	41.1	49.1	50.9
FAYETTE	1.5	2.0	6.4	5.7	6.3	6.6	7.8	22.5	26.6	14.6	3.6	78.0	41.2	50.0	50.0
FLOYD	1.3	1.8	6.5	6.0	6.4	6.1	6.6	23.0	26.9	14.9	3.7	77.3	41.6	48.8	51.2
FRANKLIN	6.0	8.0	6.3	5.5	6.0	5.6	7.5	22.0	28.0	15.2	4.0	79.0	42.7	49.7	50.3
FREMONT	2.2	2.9	5.8	5.4	6.2	6.7	6.3	21.9	28.8	15.7	3.3	78.5	43.5	49.5	50.5
GREENE	1.7	2.2	6.4	5.6	6.1	6.4	7.6	20.8	26.8	15.8	4.5	78.0	43.0	49.1	50.9
GRUNDY	0.6	0.8	5.8	5.3	6.3	6.8	6.1	22.5	28.2	15.1	3.8	78.2	43.0	49.3	50.7
GUTHRIE	1.1	1.4	5.9	5.5	5.9	5.7	5.7	22.6	28.9	16.5	3.3	79.0	44.2	50.1	49.9
HAMILTON	1.4	1.9	6.8	6.4	6.1	6.6	6.3	24.3	26.8	13.6	3.1	76.6	40.6	50.0	50.0
HANCOCK	2.5	3.4	6.7	6.0	5.9	6.5	7.5	22.3	28.1	13.8	3.3	77.2	42.0	49.8	50.2
HARDIN	2.4	3.2	6.1	5.7	5.7	8.0	7.3	20.9	26.8	15.2	4.3	77.5	42.0	49.2	50.8
HARRISON	0.7	1.0	6.4	5.8	6.6	7.1	6.4	24.1	27.0	13.5	3.1	76.6	41.0	49.6	50.4
HENRY	1.3	1.7	6.3	5.7	6.2	7.1	8.1	26.9	26.0	11.0	2.8	77.6	38.4	51.1	48.9
HOWARD	0.6	0.7	6.8	5.8	6.5	6.2	6.4	23.5	26.2	14.2	4.3	76.9	41.4	49.5	50.5
HUMBOLDT	1.0	1.3	6.2	5.4	5.4	6.9	7.7	21.1	28.0	15.5	3.9	78.8	43.2	49.6	50.4
IDA	0.5	0.6	6.0	5.5	5.6	6.9	6.8	20.8	28.4	15.7	4.3	78.4	43.7	48.7	51.3
IOWA	1.0	1.3	6.5	6.0	7.1	7.1	6.1	23.4	27.1	13.2	3.4	75.8	41.2	48.9	51.1
JACKSON	0.6	0.8	6.3	5.7	6.6	6.7	6.3	24.0	27.7	13.9	2.8	77.2	41.5	49.8	50.2
JASPER	1.0	1.3	6.3	5.9	6.6	6.2	6.3	25.7	26.9	13.4	2.7	77.2	40.4	50.7	49.3
JEFFERSON	1.8	2.4	5.1	5.2	5.4	6.9	7.8	21.2	35.6	10.3	2.6	80.0	43.7	49.6	50.4
JOHNSON	2.5	3.3	5.8	5.3	5.2	9.4	15.4	29.8	21.6	6.4	1.2	80.5	29.4	49.9	50.1
JONES	1.1	1.4	5.9	5.3	6.2	6.3	7.1	26.5	27.1	12.9	2.5	78.6	40.4	52.6	47.4
KEOKUK	0.5	0.7	6.6	5.6	6.7	5.9	6.7	22.7	27.8	14.3	3.7	77.5	41.9	49.0	51.0
KOSSUTH	0.8	1.1	6.1	5.2	5.8	6.4	8.3	20.0	28.4	16.1	3.6	78.9	43.6	49.1	50.9
LEE	2.4	3.2	6.1	5.5	5.9	6.6	6.7	24.3	28.6	13.4	2.9	78.8	41.4	49.8	50.2
LINN	1.4	1.9	7.0	6.7	6.9	6.6	7.0	28.2	25.2	10.3	2.0	75.6	36.4	49.2	50.8
LOUISA	12.6	16.3	7.5	7.5	7.0	6.9	6.1	27.1	24.5	11.2	2.2	73.6	36.8	49.9	50.1
LUCAS	0.9	0.9	6.5	5.8	6.6	6.6	6.3	22.9	26.7	14.9	3.7	76.9	41.7	48.9	51.1
LYON	0.4	0.4	7.0	6.7	7.0	7.0	6.3	23.5	25.6	13.6	3.4	74.8	39.5	50.1	49.9
MADISON	0.7	1.0	7.0	7.0	6.6	6.6	6.7	24.2	27.5	11.7	2.7	75.1	39.3	49.6	50.4
MAHASKA	0.9	0.9	6.8	6.1	6.3	6.7	7.6	25.0	25.9	12.9	2.8	76.9	38.9	50.0	50.0
MARION	0.8	1.1	6.3	6.1	6.4	8.5	8.0	23.6	25.6	12.7	2.8	78.0	38.4	50.0	50.0
MARSHALL	9.0	11.8	6.7	5.9	6.5	6.2	7.4	24.0	27.4	13.3	2.7	77.2	40.0	50.1	49.9
MILLS	1.2	1.6	6.5	5.9	7.1	6.8	7.6	23.7	29.2	11.3	1.9	76.3	40.3	50.1	49.9
MITCHELL	0.6	0.6	6.7	5.5	6.6	7.0	6.6	20.7	26.9	15.4	4.5	76.7	42.9	49.1	50.9
MONONA	0.7	0.9	5.6	5.1	6.0	6.1	6.5	20.7	28.0	16.9	5.1	79.8	45.0	48.8	51.2
MONROE	0.5	0.7	6.8	6.4	6.3	5.9	6.5	23.2	26.3	15.0	3.6	76.8	41.1	49.2	50.8
MONTGOMERY	1.3	1.7	6.3	5.9	6.2	6.7	6.5	22.5	27.8	14.2	4.0	77.5	42.0	47.6	52.4
MUSCATINE	11.9	15.5	7.2	6.5	7.0	6.5	6.7	27.0	26.7	10.3	2.0	75.2	37.3	49.6	50.4
O'BRIEN	1.8	2.4	6.2	5.7	5.7	6.5	7.6	22.0	26.3	15.5	4.4	78.3	42.1	49.3	50.7
OSCEOLA	1.8	2.4	6.5	6.3	5.8	6.8	6.3	22.5	28.5	13.7	3.5	77.0	41.9	49.2	50.8
PAGE	1.6	2.1	5.7	5.3	5.3	6.9	7.2	24.6	26.6	14.7	3.8	79.1	41.4	51.1	48.9
PALO ALTO	0.8	1.0	6.1	4.9	5.6	6.5	8.1	21.6	26.9	16.3	3.9	80.3	42.6	49.0	51.0
PLYMOUTH	1.3	1.8	6.9	6.5	7.0	6.8	7.8	22.9	27.9	11.5	2.7	75.4	39.2	50.1	49.9
POCAHONTAS	0.9	1.2	5.5	4.7	5.5	7.6	7.0	19.3	29.6	16.8	4.0	79.4	45.2	49.6	50.4
POLK	4.4	5.8	7.4	7.1	6.8	6.7	6.8	29.3	24.9	9.3	1.7	74.7	35.7	48.8	51.2
IOWA	2.8	3.7	6.6	6.2	6.4	7.1	7.9	25.5	26.0	11.7	2.6	76.9	37.9	49.3	50.7
UNITED STATES	12.5	15.0	6.9	6.5	6.8	7.1	7.0	27.6	25.4	10.7	1.9	75.6	36.7	49.2	50.8

COUNTY	HOUSEHOLDS					FAMILIES			MEDIAN HOUSEHOLD INCOME			
	2000	2007	2012	% Annual Rate 2000-2007	2007 Average HH Size	2000	2007	% Annual Rate 2000-2007	2007	2012	2007 National Rank	2007 State Rank
ADAIR	3,398	3,369	3,318	-0.1	2.33	2,324	2,262	-0.4	43,348	50,081	1294	64
ADAMS	1,867	1,798	1,736	-0.5	2.30	1,236	1,167	-0.8	37,142	42,440	2111	95
ALLAMAKEE	5,722	5,980	6,127	0.6	2.45	3,929	4,033	0.4	40,826	46,142	1627	83
APPANOOSE	5,779	5,842	5,847	0.1	2.29	3,803	3,768	-0.1	35,344	40,787	2393	98
AUDUBON	2,773	2,725	2,675	-0.2	2.37	1,926	1,859	-0.5	40,036	45,930	1723	88
BENTON	9,746	10,665	11,293	1.3	2.53	7,053	7,597	1.0	51,481	59,151	580	9
BLACK HAWK	49,683	51,162	51,646	0.4	2.39	31,963	32,236	0.1	46,877	54,419	918	32
BOONE	10,374	10,810	11,052	0.6	2.41	7,135	7,302	0.3	51,311	60,178	592	10
BREMER	8,860	9,558	10,015	1.1	2.42	6,324	6,710	0.8	50,281	58,671	656	16
BUCHANAN	7,933	8,238	8,411	0.5	2.55	5,675	5,797	0.3	45,840	51,653	1019	44
BUENA VISTA	7,499	7,529	7,550	0.1	2.53	5,125	5,051	-0.2	43,069	49,576	1320	65
BUTLER	6,175	6,357	6,443	0.4	2.37	4,470	4,531	0.2	44,723	51,225	1136	52
CALHOUN	4,513	4,360	4,233	-0.5	2.28	3,015	2,857	-0.7	41,162	47,801	1580	79
CARROLL	8,486	8,606	8,622	0.2	2.39	5,669	5,640	-0.1	45,466	52,731	1056	46
CASS	6,120	6,188	6,195	0.2	2.28	4,094	4,061	-0.1	40,628	46,512	1652	85
CEDAR	7,147	7,492	7,695	0.7	2.46	5,136	5,295	0.4	50,723	57,966	627	14
CERRO GORDO	19,374	19,312	19,140	0.0	2.28	12,398	12,100	-0.3	45,906	54,266	1012	43
CHEROKEE	5,378	5,200	5,031	-0.5	2.29	3,598	3,411	-0.7	43,465	50,008	1276	62
CHICKASAW	5,192	5,222	5,212	0.1	2.42	3,646	3,602	-0.2	46,238	53,374	980	40
CLARKE	3,584	3,684	3,743	0.4	2.51	2,498	2,523	0.1	42,320	48,756	1415	68
CLAY	7,259	7,311	7,284	0.1	2.30	4,774	4,715	-0.2	43,773	50,398	1242	59
CLAYTON	7,375	7,684	7,847	0.6	2.41	5,134	5,256	0.3	41,056	46,903	1589	80
CLINTON	20,105	20,289	20,285	0.1	2.39	13,676	13,546	-0.1	46,623	53,831	943	34
CRAWFORD	6,441	6,527	6,558	0.2	2.51	4,488	4,468	-0.1	41,222	47,034	1564	78
DALLAS	15,584	21,842	27,864	4.8	2.56	11,166	15,396	4.5	61,266	71,515	232	1
DAVIS	3,207	3,310	3,364	0.4	2.58	2,286	2,319	0.2	39,324	43,896	1818	91
DECATUR	3,337	3,316	3,290	-0.1	2.35	2,150	2,093	-0.4	33,482	38,297	2609	99
DELAWARE	6,834	7,009	7,071	0.3	2.59	5,030	5,082	0.1	44,652	50,288	1141	54
DES MOINES	17,270	16,922	16,554	-0.3	2.35	11,535	11,085	-0.5	46,056	53,539	996	41
DICKINSON	7,103	7,532	7,802	0.8	2.23	4,760	4,950	0.5	47,351	53,901	879	30
DUBUQUE	33,690	36,006	37,442	0.9	2.44	23,111	24,251	0.7	49,138	56,995	739	20
EMMET	4,450	4,417	4,359	-0.1	2.30	2,909	2,831	-0.4	41,341	47,760	1544	76
FAYETTE	8,778	8,696	8,570	-0.1	2.36	5,952	5,787	-0.4	40,396	46,518	1674	87
FLOYD	6,828	6,919	6,947	0.2	2.36	4,708	4,687	-0.1	43,506	50,094	1274	61
FRANKLIN	4,356	4,352	4,338	0.0	2.38	2,985	2,929	-0.3	44,676	51,425	1140	53
FREMONT	3,199	3,167	3,118	-0.1	2.41	2,243	2,182	-0.4	46,301	52,360	970	38
GREENE	4,205	4,156	4,124	-0.2	2.40	2,859	2,772	-0.4	41,886	48,225	1461	69
GRUNDY	4,984	5,188	5,306	0.6	2.42	3,584	3,669	0.3	48,015	54,651	814	25
GUTHRIE	4,641	4,932	5,122	0.8	2.36	3,251	3,394	0.6	45,115	51,188	1098	49
HAMILTON	6,692	6,862	6,943	0.3	2.38	4,600	4,635	0.1	48,233	55,627	796	23
HANCOCK	4,795	4,819	4,799	0.1	2.44	3,376	3,334	-0.2	46,041	52,272	998	42
HARDIN	7,628	7,542	7,438	-0.2	2.32	5,085	4,932	-0.4	43,698	50,265	1253	60
HARRISON	6,115	6,364	6,491	0.6	2.48	4,305	4,402	0.3	46,493	53,470	952	35
HENRY	7,626	7,852	7,966	0.4	2.42	5,268	5,329	0.2	47,783	55,127	839	27
HOWARD	3,974	3,961	3,928	0.0	2.39	2,650	2,590	-0.3	41,850	47,172	1470	70
HUMBOLDT	4,295	4,309	4,285	0.0	2.34	2,884	2,840	-0.2	47,106	54,078	897	31
IDA	3,213	3,138	3,055	-0.3	2.32	2,186	2,095	-0.6	43,381	50,515	1290	63
IOWA	6,163	6,602	6,888	1.0	2.47	4,300	4,527	0.7	50,536	57,310	638	15
JACKSON	8,078	8,369	8,509	0.5	2.41	5,587	5,683	0.2	41,390	46,769	1533	74
JASPER	14,689	15,033	15,163	0.3	2.37	10,265	10,321	0.1	51,298	60,053	594	11
JEFFERSON	6,649	6,650	6,606	0.0	2.29	4,279	4,194	-0.3	41,541	47,447	1513	72
JOHNSON	44,080	51,256	55,741	2.1	2.26	23,578	26,691	1.7	49,829	58,459	690	18
JONES	7,560	7,881	8,056	0.6	2.41	5,301	5,429	0.3	46,815	54,018	925	33
KEOKUK	4,586	4,613	4,600	0.1	2.41	3,153	3,115	-0.2	41,797	48,231	1478	71
KOSSUTH	6,974	6,785	6,605	-0.4	2.36	4,792	4,575	-0.6	41,373	47,204	1538	75
LEE	15,161	14,949	14,699	-0.2	2.36	10,248	9,916	-0.5	45,081	51,833	1102	50
LINN	76,753	84,568	89,648	1.3	2.38	50,335	54,358	1.1	58,795	68,442	289	4
LOUISA	4,519	4,471	4,408	-0.1	2.64	3,319	3,233	-0.4	47,836	55,083	832	26
LUCAS	3,811	3,839	3,849	0.1	2.42	2,561	2,532	-0.2	38,409	44,674	1948	93
LYON	4,428	4,508	4,531	0.2	2.55	3,264	3,270	0.0	44,810	50,897	1129	51
MADISON	5,326	6,074	6,634	1.8	2.55	3,923	4,407	1.6	50,790	58,027	623	13
MAHASKA	8,880	9,044	9,111	0.3	2.41	6,147	6,148	0.0	45,756	52,784	1027	45
MARION	12,017	12,861	13,374	0.9	2.47	8,527	8,972	0.7	52,080	60,934	542	7
MARSHALL	15,338	15,726	15,933	0.3	2.46	10,456	10,523	0.1	47,682	55,465	844	28
MILLS	5,324	5,715	5,971	1.0	2.56	3,938	4,163	0.8	51,836	60,533	558	8
MITCHELL	4,294	4,361	4,389	0.2	2.44	2,984	2,977	0.0	42,493	48,406	1399	66
MONONA	4,211	4,144	4,054	-0.2	2.27	2,738	2,639	-0.5	41,241	47,845	1562	77
MONROE	3,228	3,204	3,165	-0.1	2.39	2,210	2,153	-0.4	42,389	48,828	1407	67
MONTGOMERY	4,886	4,738	4,617	-0.4	2.33	3,259	3,100	-0.7	40,403	46,160	1673	86
MUSCATINE	15,847	16,939	17,665	0.9	2.54	11,290	11,867	0.7	52,491	62,181	521	6
O'BRIEN	6,001	5,955	5,883	-0.1	2.37	4,125	4,019	-0.4	44,477	51,437	1161	55
OSCEOLA	2,778	2,731	2,669	-0.2	2.44	1,942	1,876	-0.5	41,411	47,600	1530	73
PAGE	6,708	6,666	6,422	-0.3	2.27	4,459	4,279	-0.6	43,893	50,470	1224	58
PALO ALTO	4,119	4,085	4,035	-0.1	2.31	2,874	2,697	-0.4	40,973	47,409	1603	81
PLYMOUTH	9,372	9,785	9,989	0.6	2.56	6,806	6,994	0.4	50,276	57,282	657	17
POCAHONTAS	3,017	3,388	3,242	-0.9	2.30	2,431	2,234	-1.2	40,827	46,586	1626	82
POLK	149,112	167,215	179,654	1.6	2.41	96,001	106,131	1.3	59,092	69,847	286	3
IOWA				0.8	2.41			0.5	49,331	57,806		
UNITED STATES				1.2	2.59			1.0	53,154	62,503		

COUNTY	2007 Per Capita Income	2007 HH Income Base	2007 HOUSEHOLD INCOME DISTRIBUTION (%)					2007 Home Value Base	2007 HOME VALUE DISTRIBUTION (%)					2007 Median Home Value
			Less than $25,000	$25,000 to $49,999	$50,000 to $99,999	$100,000 to $149,999	$150,000 or More		Less than $50,000	$50,000 to $89,999	$90,000 to $174,999	$175,000 to $399,999	$400,000 or More	
ADAIR	21,656	3,369	25.1	32.5	35.3	5.3	1.8	2,592	21.2	29.6	38.6	8.9	1.7	88,840
ADAMS	19,464	1,798	29.8	33.9	30.1	5.2	1.0	1,382	29.5	28.2	29.3	10.6	2.4	76,437
ALLAMAKEE	20,122	5,980	26.5	35.4	30.2	5.9	2.1	4,687	18.8	25.9	39.4	13.5	2.5	96,743
APPANOOSE	18,721	5,842	35.1	33.7	25.8	4.0	1.5	4,408	34.1	29.4	27.0	8.7	0.7	68,589
AUDUBON	21,775	2,725	28.7	34.0	29.0	5.2	3.2	2,194	24.9	31.7	31.7	8.7	3.0	80,136
BENTON	23,154	10,665	19.5	28.6	39.4	10.7	1.8	8,644	11.9	20.6	44.6	20.6	2.3	113,957
BLACK HAWK	24,757	51,162	24.0	29.3	32.9	9.3	4.6	36,249	14.1	23.4	42.6	17.8	2.0	107,944
BOONE	25,074	10,810	19.9	28.4	39.2	8.6	3.9	8,375	14.8	24.9	40.1	17.9	2.2	105,403
BREMER	24,254	9,558	18.9	30.8	37.4	9.2	3.8	7,629	5.5	14.6	48.2	27.5	4.2	138,072
BUCHANAN	22,410	8,238	23.5	31.1	35.0	7.2	3.2	6,598	15.8	22.6	44.2	14.0	3.5	105,535
BUENA VISTA	20,462	7,529	24.9	33.9	31.9	6.1	3.1	5,487	20.6	28.0	36.4	12.2	2.8	91,796
BUTLER	21,817	6,357	24.6	32.7	33.8	7.0	1.8	5,191	18.9	29.0	38.8	11.1	2.1	92,661
CALHOUN	21,745	4,360	27.4	32.5	31.8	5.8	2.4	3,441	25.3	33.0	32.7	7.3	1.7	79,134
CARROLL	23,517	8,606	24.2	30.2	35.2	6.9	3.5	6,567	12.9	23.5	46.1	14.7	2.8	107,480
CASS	21,391	6,188	27.0	35.3	29.4	6.1	2.1	4,738	19.1	30.3	38.4	10.8	1.4	90,638
CEDAR	23,300	7,492	19.3	29.7	39.8	9.4	1.9	5,905	10.3	16.3	48.9	21.1	3.3	121,875
CERRO GORDO	24,895	19,312	25.3	28.7	34.7	7.4	4.0	14,164	11.1	24.7	44.9	16.6	2.6	106,319
CHEROKEE	22,543	5,200	25.1	33.6	32.0	6.7	2.6	3,935	20.4	34.0	33.3	10.3	1.9	84,761
CHICKASAW	21,963	5,222	22.2	32.5	36.7	6.5	2.2	4,260	15.6	24.4	44.1	14.5	1.4	101,818
CLARKE	20,357	3,684	26.0	31.8	33.6	6.4	2.2	2,747	16.7	27.9	38.6	15.3	1.6	98,204
CLAY	23,784	7,311	25.5	32.6	32.3	6.3	3.3	5,221	14.4	23.9	44.2	14.7	2.9	104,992
CLAYTON	20,679	7,684	26.4	34.9	31.2	5.5	2.1	6,026	15.7	25.8	42.0	13.2	3.3	99,445
CLINTON	22,630	20,289	24.9	28.7	35.8	8.4	2.2	15,166	15.8	25.5	44.2	12.7	1.8	100,946
CRAWFORD	19,538	6,527	26.6	35.2	31.0	5.4	1.8	4,910	24.1	29.6	35.6	9.6	1.1	84,873
DALLAS	29,665	21,842	14.5	25.3	37.4	14.4	8.3	17,067	8.4	10.9	34.2	36.5	10.0	164,456
DAVIS	18,254	3,310	30.7	29.9	33.4	4.8	1.1	2,690	26.1	27.3	33.0	11.7	1.9	85,864
DECATUR	18,375	3,316	36.2	33.8	23.8	3.6	2.7	2,415	35.9	24.9	28.4	9.6	1.3	71,071
DELAWARE	21,145	7,009	24.3	31.6	34.0	7.4	2.7	5,586	10.9	18.5	46.4	18.5	5.7	116,706
DES MOINES	24,330	16,922	24.9	29.4	34.1	8.1	3.4	12,849	16.2	30.1	38.9	13.1	1.7	95,389
DICKINSON	27,084	7,532	21.0	31.9	34.3	8.0	4.8	5,996	10.7	15.2	39.1	27.1	8.0	132,754
DUBUQUE	24,717	36,006	20.7	30.2	36.2	8.8	4.0	27,142	7.6	13.4	51.3	24.3	3.5	130,655
EMMET	21,848	4,417	25.1	35.2	30.2	7.2	2.2	3,390	25.1	33.5	33.1	7.1	1.2	78,810
FAYETTE	20,896	8,696	28.9	33.1	30.9	4.9	2.3	6,724	21.6	31.0	34.6	10.5	2.3	86,493
FLOYD	21,528	6,919	26.6	31.0	34.9	5.6	2.0	5,270	15.0	29.2	42.3	12.2	1.3	96,674
FRANKLIN	22,651	4,352	24.6	31.4	33.8	7.9	2.3	3,339	22.9	32.2	33.3	9.4	2.2	82,938
FREMONT	22,401	3,167	26.3	27.4	37.0	6.3	3.0	2,427	20.4	26.2	38.8	12.5	2.1	94,588
GREENE	20,702	4,156	27.4	32.0	32.8	5.8	1.9	3,215	29.0	31.9	30.7	6.2	2.3	76,044
GRUNDY	23,436	5,188	19.5	32.9	36.4	8.9	2.3	4,226	12.0	23.8	43.9	17.9	2.4	110,635
GUTHRIE	24,305	4,932	24.8	30.6	33.4	7.5	3.7	3,993	20.8	27.0	32.6	15.3	4.4	93,315
HAMILTON	23,893	6,862	22.1	29.8	37.4	8.1	2.6	5,138	14.3	27.2	44.4	11.8	2.2	99,954
HANCOCK	22,074	4,819	20.5	34.7	36.4	6.1	2.3	3,850	23.7	28.7	35.6	10.6	1.4	86,009
HARDIN	22,016	7,542	24.6	33.9	32.9	6.4	2.2	5,763	22.7	34.2	32.6	9.0	1.5	81,855
HARRISON	22,115	6,364	23.6	30.3	35.5	8.1	2.4	4,981	15.7	23.2	40.9	18.3	1.9	105,807
HENRY	22,046	7,852	24.1	28.3	37.0	7.7	2.9	5,908	16.9	21.2	45.4	15.1	1.4	105,420
HOWARD	21,225	3,961	26.7	32.7	32.7	5.6	2.3	3,193	19.4	30.7	34.7	12.9	2.3	89,912
HUMBOLDT	23,393	4,309	23.5	29.8	36.8	7.0	3.0	3,355	19.9	24.6	39.5	13.5	2.5	98,608
IDA	23,072	3,138	26.2	31.4	33.2	6.2	3.0	2,364	22.5	33.0	31.6	10.2	2.6	81,081
IOWA	22,657	6,602	19.1	30.0	41.0	7.8	2.0	5,255	10.7	18.5	44.9	22.9	3.0	124,362
JACKSON	20,687	8,369	27.6	32.2	32.4	5.9	1.9	6,523	14.6	19.8	43.7	18.4	3.5	110,713
JASPER	24,616	15,033	19.9	28.4	39.4	9.2	3.2	11,663	8.9	18.5	50.0	20.9	1.8	116,571
JEFFERSON	24,641	6,650	26.5	32.3	28.1	8.5	4.6	4,655	20.5	22.0	38.1	16.0	3.4	99,680
JOHNSON	29,856	51,256	24.7	25.4	29.4	12.4	8.0	30,100	10.3	5.7	35.7	40.6	7.7	171,756
JONES	21,970	7,881	22.7	30.9	36.0	8.2	2.2	6,137	13.7	24.6	44.2	15.0	2.5	105,670
KEOKUK	21,047	4,613	28.4	30.3	33.7	5.5	2.2	3,694	27.9	32.1	31.0	7.0	2.1	77,238
KOSSUTH	21,225	6,785	27.5	33.0	31.0	6.3	2.2	5,384	28.7	29.3	29.9	10.6	1.5	78,550
LEE	23,100	14,949	25.0	30.9	33.8	7.0	3.3	11,518	23.7	30.5	34.1	10.6	1.2	84,776
LINN	29,765	84,568	15.8	25.3	39.1	13.1	6.7	62,994	8.6	13.0	52.6	23.2	2.6	124,850
LOUISA	21,154	4,471	20.1	32.1	36.9	8.6	2.3	3,536	22.5	26.0	39.3	10.7	1.6	92,171
LUCAS	19,045	3,839	32.1	31.3	30.8	4.2	1.7	3,049	29.4	25.5	32.7	10.6	1.8	80,353
LYON	20,271	4,508	23.0	33.2	34.5	8.0	1.3	3,736	17.6	28.4	39.6	12.4	2.0	95,298
MADISON	23,812	6,074	20.3	28.7	37.8	8.8	4.3	4,840	9.1	16.3	41.7	27.1	5.8	137,011
MAHASKA	22,427	9,044	24.3	31.1	35.1	6.7	2.8	6,619	17.1	27.1	39.8	14.1	2.0	96,573
MARION	23,730	12,861	20.6	26.7	39.2	10.5	3.0	9,964	13.0	18.5	42.9	22.8	2.9	121,273
MARSHALL	23,126	15,726	22.2	30.3	35.0	9.1	3.4	11,851	15.5	27.7	42.0	13.8	1.0	98,486
MILLS	23,715	5,715	19.3	28.5	36.9	11.7	3.6	4,615	10.0	16.9	41.8	27.9	3.5	130,758
MITCHELL	20,596	4,361	25.0	35.1	32.1	6.5	1.4	3,602	16.4	27.7	40.7	13.1	2.1	97,634
MONONA	21,998	4,144	28.0	32.6	31.4	5.6	2.4	3,221	27.9	32.3	30.5	7.6	1.6	77,124
MONROE	21,277	3,204	28.0	31.6	31.8	6.6	2.0	2,562	26.6	29.7	33.7	8.8	1.1	81,000
MONTGOMERY	20,726	4,738	28.0	34.1	30.3	6.1	1.5	3,560	26.9	29.2	34.0	8.3	1.6	80,400
MUSCATINE	24,801	16,939	20.0	27.0	37.0	11.8	4.2	13,076	13.6	19.7	43.8	20.7	2.2	114,121
O'BRIEN	21,671	5,955	23.4	33.9	34.7	6.1	1.9	4,669	22.1	32.7	34.3	9.6	1.3	83,328
OSCEOLA	20,742	2,731	28.7	30.5	31.2	6.8	2.7	2,162	27.7	32.1	33.5	6.1	0.7	76,770
PAGE	21,877	6,566	27.9	29.9	33.0	7.1	2.2	4,829	23.1	30.0	36.9	9.3	0.7	85,207
PALO ALTO	22,539	4,085	27.4	32.4	32.0	5.2	2.9	3,105	25.1	33.4	32.8	7.2	1.5	78,230
PLYMOUTH	24,395	9,785	20.6	29.1	36.5	9.1	4.7	7,749	7.8	16.5	48.8	22.3	4.6	127,173
POCAHONTAS	22,044	3,388	28.0	33.6	30.3	5.1	2.9	2,731	37.7	33.4	23.6	4.0	1.3	60,082
POLK	31,165	167,215	16.1	25.5	36.3	14.1	7.9	118,207	6.3	14.0	46.0	29.9	3.8	140,890
IOWA	25,252		21.8	28.9	35.0	9.8	4.5		13.7	20.9	42.4	20.1	2.9	113,209
UNITED STATES	27,916		21.9	25.0	32.3	12.3	8.4		7.9	10.5	27.1	35.6	19.0	192,285

COUNTY	Auto Loan	Home Loan	Invest-ments	Retire-ment Plans	Home Repair	Lawn & Garden	Comput-ers & Hard-ware	Major Appli-ances	TV, Radio, Sound Equip-ment	Furni-ture	Dine out/ Carry out	Sports Equip-ment	Fees & Tickets	Toys & Games	Travel	Cable TV	Apparel & Services	Auto Repairs	Health Insur-ance	Pets & Supplies
ADAIR	84	60	43	58	68	91	65	80	72	60	71	70	55	75	64	77	60	74	90	85
ADAMS	74	54	40	52	63	82	57	71	63	54	62	62	49	66	57	68	53	65	79	76
ALLAMAKEE	85	59	37	56	68	92	62	80	69	58	69	70	52	73	62	75	58	72	88	86
APPANOOSE	68	49	43	49	55	72	56	65	62	51	60	57	48	63	55	66	51	61	74	68
AUDUBON	88	60	40	58	70	95	66	83	74	61	72	73	54	77	65	79	61	76	93	89
BENTON	89	79	72	78	84	95	77	87	81	77	80	76	74	85	78	84	71	82	92	90
BLACK HAWK	82	79	90	81	79	82	84	81	85	81	84	72	83	85	83	86	75	82	87	81
BOONE	87	82	90	84	84	90	83	87	86	81	84	76	82	87	85	87	74	84	92	87
BREMER	88	81	83	81	86	96	79	88	84	79	82	76	78	86	82	87	72	83	95	90
BUCHANAN	91	74	62	72	82	100	73	88	79	72	79	77	68	83	75	84	68	81	94	93
BUENA VISTA	85	66	56	66	71	88	69	79	75	66	73	70	62	78	69	78	63	75	87	84
BUTLER	82	64	54	63	71	89	66	79	73	63	72	69	60	76	67	78	62	73	89	83
CALHOUN	81	60	49	59	68	88	65	78	73	60	71	68	56	74	65	78	60	72	90	82
CARROLL	87	70	65	70	77	94	74	85	80	70	78	74	68	81	75	84	68	80	94	88
CASS	79	60	50	59	67	85	63	75	70	60	68	66	56	72	64	74	59	70	84	79
CEDAR	89	76	68	75	81	95	75	86	80	74	79	75	71	83	76	83	69	80	92	90
CERRO GORDO	81	74	83	76	77	83	78	80	81	76	79	70	76	82	79	83	70	79	87	81
CHEROKEE	83	62	51	61	70	89	67	80	75	63	72	69	59	76	67	79	62	74	90	83
CHICKASAW	84	66	55	64	74	93	68	82	75	65	73	71	61	78	69	80	63	75	91	86
CLARKE	82	62	53	62	68	86	67	78	73	62	71	68	59	74	66	77	61	73	86	81
CLAY	84	68	64	68	74	88	73	81	77	69	76	72	66	80	72	80	66	78	88	85
CLAYTON	84	59	40	57	69	93	63	80	70	59	69	70	53	73	63	75	58	73	88	86
CLINTON	79	73	73	71	73	82	72	77	77	71	76	67	70	79	73	80	66	75	85	79
CRAWFORD	82	59	44	58	67	87	63	77	70	60	69	67	54	73	63	74	59	71	85	81
DALLAS	111	110	102	111	106	108	105	106	103	107	104	98	105	108	104	102	93	104	103	108
DAVIS	81	56	34	54	66	89	59	76	65	56	65	67	49	70	58	70	55	69	82	83
DECATUR	72	50	38	50	56	75	60	68	63	53	63	61	49	65	56	66	53	65	74	72
DELAWARE	90	70	53	68	78	98	70	86	75	69	75	75	63	81	70	79	65	78	91	92
DES MOINES	81	76	84	77	79	85	77	80	81	76	80	69	77	83	78	84	71	78	87	81
DICKINSON	93	78	69	77	84	102	79	92	84	76	83	80	73	84	81	88	72	87	99	95
DUBUQUE	86	84	90	85	86	90	83	86	86	83	85	75	83	87	85	88	76	84	91	88
EMMET	81	61	53	61	67	84	67	76	73	63	71	67	59	76	66	77	61	72	86	79
FAYETTE	81	60	47	59	67	86	64	76	71	61	69	67	56	74	64	75	59	71	85	81
FLOYD	80	64	56	63	70	87	66	78	72	63	71	68	60	75	67	76	61	72	86	81
FRANKLIN	87	66	54	66	73	92	70	82	76	67	75	72	62	80	70	80	64	78	90	87
FREMONT	90	65	47	64	75	99	69	86	76	65	75	76	59	80	69	81	64	79	94	92
GREENE	82	59	44	58	67	88	64	78	71	59	69	69	54	74	64	76	59	72	87	83
GRUNDY	89	73	63	71	81	98	72	87	79	71	78	75	67	82	74	83	67	80	94	91
GUTHRIE	95	69	50	67	79	104	73	91	81	69	79	79	62	85	73	86	67	83	100	97
HAMILTON	90	72	63	72	78	94	75	86	80	72	79	75	68	84	74	83	68	81	92	90
HANCOCK	89	66	49	63	74	96	68	84	76	65	75	74	59	79	68	81	64	77	93	90
HARDIN	81	63	56	62	70	88	67	79	74	64	72	68	60	76	68	78	62	74	88	82
HARRISON	86	69	62	69	75	91	72	82	78	69	76	72	66	81	72	81	66	77	90	86
HENRY	84	72	67	72	76	88	73	81	77	71	76	71	69	80	73	79	66	77	86	84
HOWARD	87	60	40	59	70	94	64	82	71	61	71	72	54	76	64	76	60	74	89	88
HUMBOLDT	85	69	62	68	77	93	71	83	76	69	75	72	65	79	72	80	65	78	91	87
IDA	87	64	51	62	72	94	69	83	77	64	75	72	60	79	69	83	64	77	95	87
IOWA	87	73	66	73	79	93	73	84	78	72	77	74	69	82	74	81	67	79	90	88
JACKSON	79	63	54	62	70	86	64	76	70	62	69	66	58	73	65	73	60	70	82	80
JASPER	87	80	82	80	84	92	79	86	83	78	82	75	78	86	81	85	72	82	91	88
JEFFERSON	86	74	72	74	79	91	77	84	80	74	79	75	72	82	77	83	69	81	90	88
JOHNSON	99	86	88	92	82	83	107	90	100	97	101	88	97	99	95	95	91	99	88	92
JONES	83	72	66	71	76	88	71	81	76	70	75	70	68	80	72	79	65	76	87	84
KEOKUK	85	59	40	57	68	92	64	80	72	59	71	71	53	75	63	78	59	74	91	86
KOSSUTH	82	60	46	59	69	89	64	79	70	60	69	69	55	73	64	75	59	72	86	84
LEE	82	71	72	71	75	85	73	79	79	71	77	69	70	80	74	82	68	76	88	81
LINN	98	100	107	102	98	96	99	97	99	100	98	87	101	100	99	99	89	98	98	97
LOUISA	91	73	58	71	78	94	72	84	77	72	77	75	66	83	72	81	67	79	89	90
LUCAS	74	54	45	52	60	79	60	71	67	55	65	62	51	67	59	71	55	66	81	74
LYON	87	61	41	60	71	96	65	83	72	62	71	73	55	77	65	77	60	75	90	89
MADISON	93	81	76	81	85	97	81	90	84	79	83	80	77	87	82	87	73	85	95	93
MAHASKA	83	67	65	68	73	87	73	80	77	69	76	71	66	79	72	80	66	77	88	83
MARION	88	80	83	81	84	92	80	87	84	79	82	76	78	86	82	87	73	83	93	88
MARSHALL	82	76	80	76	78	85	77	80	81	76	80	70	76	83	78	83	71	79	87	82
MILLS	92	82	80	83	85	94	84	89	86	81	85	80	80	88	84	88	75	86	94	92
MITCHELL	85	59	42	58	69	92	64	80	72	60	70	70	54	75	64	77	59	73	90	85
MONONA	82	59	47	58	68	88	64	78	72	60	70	68	55	74	64	78	60	72	89	82
MONROE	83	63	50	61	69	88	65	78	73	62	71	68	58	75	65	78	61	72	88	82
MONTGOMERY	75	60	54	59	65	79	63	72	70	61	68	62	58	71	63	73	59	68	81	74
MUSCATINE	90	87	94	88	88	91	85	88	89	86	87	77	86	91	87	90	78	86	93	89
O'BRIEN	83	62	53	62	69	87	67	79	75	63	73	69	59	77	67	80	62	74	90	82
OSCEOLA	83	61	45	59	70	91	64	79	71	61	70	69	55	74	64	75	60	73	87	85
PAGE	78	63	62	63	69	83	68	76	73	64	72	66	62	75	68	77	62	72	84	78
PALO ALTO	86	62	48	60	70	92	68	82	76	62	73	72	58	78	67	81	62	76	93	86
PLYMOUTH	94	83	80	83	89	101	83	92	87	82	86	82	79	90	84	90	75	87	97	96
POCAHONTAS	87	59	38	57	69	94	64	82	72	59	71	72	53	76	63	77	59	74	91	88
POLK	104	105	112	108	101	98	107	101	105	107	105	90	107	107	105	104	95	104	101	101
IOWA	90	81	80	82	83	92	84	88	87	81	85	78	80	88	83	88	76	86	93	90
UNITED STATES	100	100	100	100	100	100	100	100	100	100	100	100	100	100	100	100	100	100	100	100

POPULATION CHANGE

COUNTY	FIPS Code	CBSA Code	DMA Code	POPULATION			2000-2007 ANNUAL RATE		RACE (%)					
									White		Black		Asian/Pacific	
				2000	2007	2012	% Rate	State Rank	2000	2007	2000	2007	2000	2007
POTTAWATTAMIE	155	36540	652	87,704	91,882	94,735	0.6	16	96.0	95.0	0.8	0.9	0.5	0.8
POWESHIEK	157	00000	679	18,815	19,316	19,595	0.4	22	96.7	95.8	0.5	0.6	1.1	1.7
RINGGOLD	159	00000	679	5,469	5,460	5,410	0.0	47	99.1	99.1	0.1	0.1	0.2	0.2
SAC	161	00000	624	11,529	10,888	10,498	-0.8	98	98.5	98.2	0.3	0.3	0.2	0.3
SCOTT	163	19340	682	158,668	163,609	167,278	0.4	22	88.5	86.3	6.1	6.9	1.6	2.4
SHELBY	165	00000	652	13,173	12,789	12,485	-0.4	80	98.7	98.4	0.1	0.1	0.3	0.4
SIOUX	167	00000	624	31,589	32,714	33,325	0.5	19	97.3	96.5	0.2	0.2	0.6	0.9
STORY	169	11180	679	79,981	85,539	88,147	0.9	8	91.1	88.1	1.8	2.1	5.1	7.7
TAMA	171	00000	637	18,103	18,339	18,539	0.2	34	90.4	88.8	0.3	0.3	0.2	0.3
TAYLOR	173	00000	679	6,958	6,684	6,512	-0.6	91	97.7	97.0	0.0	0.0	0.4	0.5
UNION	175	00000	679	12,309	11,994	11,788	-0.4	80	98.4	97.8	0.2	0.3	0.3	0.6
VAN BUREN	177	00000	631	7,809	7,930	8,029	0.2	34	98.6	98.3	0.1	0.1	0.3	0.5
WAPELLO	179	36900	631	36,051	36,371	36,704	0.1	41	96.3	95.3	0.9	1.1	0.7	1.0
WARREN	181	19780	679	40,671	44,583	47,646	1.3	5	98.1	97.6	0.3	0.3	0.4	0.7
WASHINGTON	183	26980	637	20,670	21,676	22,469	0.7	13	97.0	96.2	0.3	0.3	0.3	0.4
WAYNE	185	00000	679	6,730	6,479	6,320	-0.5	87	98.8	98.5	0.1	0.1	0.2	0.3
WEBSTER	187	22700	679	40,235	39,493	38,581	-0.3	71	93.4	92.0	3.4	3.8	0.7	1.2
WINNEBAGO	189	00000	611	11,723	11,477	11,380	-0.3	71	97.4	96.5	0.2	0.2	0.7	1.1
WINNESHIEK	191	00000	637	21,310	21,638	21,858	0.2	34	97.9	96.6	0.5	1.0	0.8	1.3
WOODBURY	193	43580	624	103,877	102,941	102,228	-0.1	54	87.5	84.4	2.0	2.2	2.4	3.6
WORTH	195	32380	611	7,909	7,781	7,695	-0.2	62	98.4	98.0	0.3	0.3	0.2	0.2
WRIGHT	197	00000	679	14,334	13,708	13,325	-0.6	91	95.9	94.7	0.2	0.2	0.2	0.3
IOWA							0.5		93.9	92.4	2.1	2.4	1.3	2.0
UNITED STATES							1.2		75.1	72.7	12.3	12.6	3.8	4.5

COUNTY	% HISPANIC ORIGIN		2007 AGE DISTRIBUTION (%)										MEDIAN AGE	% 2007 Males	% 2007 Females
	2000	2007	0-4	5-9	10-14	15-19	20-24	25-44	45-64	65-84	85+	18+	2007		
POTTAWATTAMIE	3.3	4.4	6.8	6.1	6.6	7.0	7.3	26.1	26.6	11.6	1.9	76.4	38.1	49.1	50.9
POWESHIEK	1.2	1.6	5.6	5.1	5.6	8.7	9.7	21.4	26.3	13.9	3.7	79.8	40.3	48.3	51.7
RINGGOLD	0.2	0.2	6.5	5.8	5.8	5.2	6.7	20.9	27.0	17.6	4.5	78.4	44.3	49.0	51.0
SAC	1.0	1.3	6.0	5.5	5.4	6.2	6.8	21.0	28.2	16.3	4.5	79.1	44.2	49.2	50.8
SCOTT	4.1	5.3	7.0	6.7	6.7	7.2	6.9	26.9	27.0	9.9	1.8	75.5	36.9	49.2	50.8
SHELBY	0.7	0.9	6.4	5.4	6.6	6.7	7.1	20.5	27.6	15.8	3.9	77.6	43.2	48.8	51.2
SIOUX	2.6	3.4	7.1	6.5	6.6	10.1	10.3	22.4	23.0	11.3	2.7	75.3	33.2	49.2	50.8
STORY	1.5	2.0	5.2	4.6	4.8	10.7	20.6	23.8	20.3	8.0	1.9	82.2	27.5	51.2	48.8
TAMA	3.8	5.0	7.3	6.7	6.4	6.7	6.7	22.2	26.2	14.3	3.6	75.3	40.1	49.1	50.9
TAYLOR	3.8	5.1	6.2	5.5	5.7	5.9	6.8	22.4	27.5	15.5	4.5	79.1	43.0	48.9	51.1
UNION	1.0	1.4	6.2	5.9	5.8	6.2	7.5	23.5	27.5	14.1	3.3	79.0	41.3	48.3	51.7
VAN BUREN	0.8	1.0	5.9	5.4	5.9	6.6	6.3	22.6	28.2	15.7	3.4	78.7	43.0	49.7	50.3
WAPELLO	2.2	3.0	6.1	5.7	6.0	6.8	6.4	24.7	27.4	13.9	3.0	78.4	40.7	48.9	51.1
WARREN	1.1	1.4	6.9	6.7	6.7	7.6	7.2	24.9	27.3	10.9	1.9	75.5	38.3	48.6	51.4
WASHINGTON	2.7	3.7	7.0	6.8	6.5	6.4	5.6	24.6	27.1	12.6	3.5	75.7	40.4	48.7	51.3
WAYNE	0.7	1.0	5.7	5.1	5.6	6.3	6.9	20.4	28.3	17.3	4.4	79.5	45.0	47.7	52.3
WEBSTER	2.3	3.1	6.5	6.0	5.7	7.6	8.5	23.4	25.5	13.3	3.4	78.3	38.7	49.4	50.6
WINNEBAGO	2.0	2.7	5.8	5.5	5.5	7.8	7.8	22.0	28.3	13.5	3.9	79.3	41.6	49.3	50.7
WINNESHIEK	0.8	1.2	5.6	4.9	5.5	9.1	11.5	22.4	25.6	12.0	3.3	80.7	37.8	49.4	50.6
WOODBURY	9.1	11.8	7.8	7.0	7.3	7.1	7.2	27.1	24.0	10.3	2.2	73.9	34.8	49.3	50.7
WORTH	1.6	2.1	6.0	5.5	7.3	5.3	5.6	24.1	28.6	14.1	3.5	77.8	42.6	50.1	49.9
WRIGHT	4.9	6.6	6.0	5.3	6.3	6.1	6.7	21.9	28.3	14.9	4.3	78.4	43.3	49.4	50.6
IOWA	2.8	3.7	6.6	6.2	6.4	7.1	7.9	25.5	26.0	11.7	2.6	76.9	37.9	49.3	50.7
UNITED STATES	12.5	15.0	6.9	6.5	6.8	7.1	7.0	27.6	25.4	10.7	1.9	75.6	36.7	49.2	50.8

COUNTY	HOUSEHOLDS					FAMILIES			MEDIAN HOUSEHOLD INCOME			
	2000	2007	2012	% Annual Rate 2000-2007	2007 Average HH Size	2000	2007	% Annual Rate 2000-2007	2007	2012	2007 National Rank	2007 State Rank
POTTAWATTAMIE	33,844	36,029	37,356	0.9	2.50	23,619	24,702	0.6	50,919	60,619	619	12
POWESHIEK	7,398	7,756	7,960	0.7	2.29	4,880	5,015	0.4	46,395	53,513	959	37
RINGGOLD	2,245	2,268	2,250	0.1	2.35	1,537	1,524	-0.1	35,348	40,245	2391	97
SAC	4,746	4,587	4,452	-0.5	2.32	3,199	3,034	-0.7	40,653	46,814	1647	84
SCOTT	62,334	65,194	67,077	0.6	2.46	41,895	42,985	0.4	53,693	63,397	466	5
SHELBY	5,173	5,167	5,078	0.0	2.42	3,705	3,645	-0.2	45,446	51,800	1059	47
SIOUX	10,693	11,225	11,534	0.7	2.65	8,064	8,345	0.5	48,288	54,517	794	22
STORY	29,383	32,682	34,020	1.5	2.33	17,056	18,515	1.1	49,757	57,791	693	19
TAMA	7,018	7,188	7,277	0.3	2.49	4,971	5,006	0.1	46,465	53,481	954	36
TAYLOR	2,824	2,747	2,682	-0.4	2.37	1,913	1,826	-0.6	38,640	44,894	1909	92
UNION	5,242	5,242	5,200	0.0	2.23	3,354	3,282	-0.3	39,794	46,300	1751	90
VAN BUREN	3,181	3,283	3,341	0.4	2.38	2,164	2,193	0.2	37,314	42,085	2091	94
WAPELLO	14,784	15,146	15,342	0.3	2.34	9,797	9,840	0.1	39,879	46,088	1740	89
WARREN	14,708	16,542	17,852	1.6	2.59	11,214	12,434	1.4	61,067	69,290	238	2
WASHINGTON	8,056	8,607	8,965	0.9	2.47	5,628	5,906	0.7	47,452	53,949	867	29
WAYNE	2,821	2,754	2,690	-0.3	2.32	1,919	1,839	-0.6	36,182	41,919	2244	96
WEBSTER	15,878	15,716	15,410	-0.1	2.34	10,300	9,987	-0.4	44,475	51,530	1162	56
WINNEBAGO	4,749	4,770	4,759	0.1	2.31	3,182	3,136	-0.2	48,183	56,929	800	24
WINNESHIEK	7,734	8,071	8,240	0.6	2.40	5,188	5,311	0.3	46,268	52,054	978	39
WOODBURY	39,151	39,158	38,935	0.0	2.56	26,432	25,938	-0.3	49,013	58,234	745	21
WORTH	3,278	3,279	3,257	0.0	2.34	2,264	2,223	-0.3	43,950	49,952	1216	57
WRIGHT	5,940	5,743	5,588	-0.5	2.34	3,939	3,736	-0.7	45,251	52,463	1081	48
IOWA				0.8	2.41			0.5	49,331	57,806		
UNITED STATES				1.2	2.59			1.0	53,154	62,503		

COUNTY	2007 Per Capita Income	2007 HH Income Base	2007 HOUSEHOLD INCOME DISTRIBUTION (%)					2007 Home Value Base	2007 HOME VALUE DISTRIBUTION (%)					2007 Median Home Value
			Less than $25,000	$25,000 to $49,999	$50,000 to $99,999	$100,000 to $149,999	$150,000 or More		Less than $50,000	$50,000 to $89,999	$90,000 to $174,999	$175,000 to $399,999	$400,000 or More	
POTTAWATTAMIE	24,547	36,029	20.3	28.5	36.7	10.2	4.2	26,383	9.5	23.3	46.4	18.9	1.9	110,815
POWESHIEK	23,784	7,756	22.7	31.5	34.5	7.8	3.5	5,725	13.0	21.7	42.6	20.2	2.6	113,204
RINGGOLD	18,627	2,268	33.7	34.5	26.1	4.5	1.2	1,759	33.3	28.1	24.2	12.3	2.1	69,370
SAC	21,235	4,587	28.6	33.9	29.3	6.1	2.0	3,598	28.1	32.6	31.0	6.6	1.7	75,907
SCOTT	27,027	65,194	20.2	26.0	35.5	12.4	5.8	47,283	8.0	19.2	46.4	23.5	2.9	120,422
SHELBY	21,962	5,167	22.8	32.6	35.1	7.6	1.9	4,074	12.0	26.3	43.0	16.0	2.7	106,012
SIOUX	20,593	11,225	20.7	31.4	37.5	7.6	2.8	9,176	9.5	19.7	49.1	19.7	2.0	119,334
STORY	25,941	32,682	23.6	26.6	33.0	11.2	5.5	19,775	9.6	8.1	43.7	35.0	3.7	150,921
TAMA	21,190	7,188	22.7	31.5	36.8	6.7	2.3	5,687	17.9	26.6	42.0	10.9	2.6	95,718
TAYLOR	19,469	2,747	30.8	33.3	30.2	4.0	1.7	2,142	37.9	32.8	23.2	5.2	1.0	60,819
UNION	21,712	5,242	29.0	32.8	30.6	5.8	1.9	3,887	25.8	29.7	34.7	8.6	1.3	81,296
VAN BUREN	19,059	3,283	30.7	36.6	27.4	3.8	1.5	2,664	37.5	28.0	26.2	8.0	0.4	65,849
WAPELLO	20,952	15,146	29.4	33.5	28.8	5.7	2.5	11,686	30.4	30.7	28.3	9.1	1.4	71,639
WARREN	26,387	16,542	15.2	23.6	42.5	14.1	4.6	13,505	7.6	8.1	50.5	31.1	2.7	145,048
WASHINGTON	22,085	8,607	21.8	31.5	37.3	7.3	2.1	6,666	11.0	18.5	47.3	21.1	2.0	118,697
WAYNE	19,379	2,754	34.0	33.1	25.4	5.4	2.1	2,218	42.4	27.5	21.6	6.6	1.9	58,622
WEBSTER	23,178	15,716	25.3	31.2	32.5	7.8	3.3	11,497	18.2	29.8	39.2	11.1	1.7	92,383
WINNEBAGO	23,946	4,770	20.8	30.9	38.0	8.0	2.4	3,706	20.9	29.3	39.2	9.6	1.1	89,758
WINNESHIEK	22,200	8,071	23.0	31.2	34.8	8.1	2.9	6,106	9.2	18.2	45.0	23.3	4.3	124,727
WOODBURY	23,718	39,158	21.9	29.0	35.4	9.6	4.1	27,674	16.3	31.0	39.6	12.0	1.0	92,786
WORTH	21,156	3,279	24.5	34.4	33.7	6.2	1.2	2,641	19.9	33.9	34.7	9.4	2.0	84,601
WRIGHT	23,203	5,743	24.6	30.8	35.6	6.5	2.5	4,373	26.3	33.8	31.3	7.3	1.3	76,113
IOWA	25,252		21.8	28.9	35.0	9.8	4.5		13.7	20.9	42.4	20.1	2.9	113,209
UNITED STATES	27,916		21.9	25.0	32.3	12.3	8.4		7.9	10.5	27.1	35.6	19.0	192,285

SPENDING POTENTIAL INDICES

COUNTY	FINANCIAL SERVICES				THE HOME						ENTERTAINMENT						PERSONAL			
					Home Improvements		Furnishings													
	Auto Loan	Home Loan	Invest-ments	Retire-ment Plans	Home Repair	Lawn & Garden	Comput-ers & Hard-ware	Major Appli-ances	TV, Radio, Sound Equip-ment	Furni-ture	Dine out/ Carry out	Sports Equip-ment	Fees & Tickets	Toys & Games	Travel	Cable TV	Apparel & Services	Auto Repairs	Health Insur-ance	Pets & Supplies
POTTAWATTAMIE	86	84	92	86	85	88	84	85	87	84	85	75	84	88	85	88	76	84	90	86
POWESHIEK	85	71	70	71	76	89	76	83	80	71	78	73	70	80	75	83	68	79	90	85
RINGGOLD	73	52	36	50	60	80	56	70	62	52	61	61	47	64	56	67	51	64	78	74
SAC	81	58	43	56	66	88	63	78	71	58	69	68	53	73	63	76	58	72	88	82
SCOTT	91	92	101	94	92	91	93	91	93	93	92	82	94	94	93	93	83	91	93	91
SHELBY	84	68	57	66	76	94	68	82	73	67	73	71	62	77	69	78	63	76	89	87
SIOUX	92	70	55	69	78	99	73	88	78	69	78	78	64	83	73	83	67	81	94	93
STORY	89	77	84	81	75	79	99	83	92	86	92	80	88	90	88	89	83	90	84	85
TAMA	83	67	58	65	72	88	69	80	75	66	73	69	63	77	69	79	63	75	88	83
TAYLOR	76	54	42	52	61	81	59	71	67	54	65	62	50	69	59	72	55	66	83	75
UNION	73	62	61	62	66	76	64	70	70	62	68	61	60	71	65	73	59	68	79	73
VAN BUREN	78	53	33	51	62	85	57	73	63	53	63	64	47	67	56	68	53	66	80	79
WAPELLO	72	63	65	63	66	75	65	70	71	63	69	61	63	71	66	74	60	68	79	72
WARREN	98	102	106	102	102	102	94	98	94	97	94	88	98	97	97	95	85	95	98	99
WASHINGTON	87	70	58	68	76	94	70	84	76	69	75	73	64	80	71	80	65	78	91	88
WAYNE	75	52	38	50	60	80	57	70	64	52	63	62	48	67	55	69	53	65	80	75
WEBSTER	82	70	72	70	73	84	75	79	80	71	78	69	70	81	74	83	68	77	89	81
WINNEBAGO	85	71	70	72	76	89	75	83	79	71	77	72	70	81	75	82	67	79	91	85
WINNESHIEK	88	70	59	69	78	95	73	85	76	70	76	76	65	80	73	80	66	80	90	91
WOODBURY	86	81	88	83	81	85	84	83	87	83	85	74	83	88	83	88	76	84	89	84
WORTH	83	60	42	59	69	91	62	79	69	60	68	69	53	74	62	73	58	72	85	85
WRIGHT	87	66	55	65	73	92	70	83	78	66	76	72	62	81	70	82	65	77	93	87
IOWA	90	81	80	82	83	92	84	88	87	81	85	78	80	88	83	88	76	86	93	90
UNITED STATES	100	100	100	100	100	100	100	100	100	100	100	100	100	100	100	100	100	100	100	100

COUNTY	FIPS Code	CBSA Code	DMA Code	POPULATION 2000	POPULATION 2007	POPULATION 2012	2000-2007 ANNUAL RATE % Rate	2000-2007 ANNUAL RATE State Rank	RACE (%) White 2000	White 2007	Black 2000	Black 2007	Asian/Pacific 2000	Asian/Pacific 2007
ALLEN	001	00000	603	14,385	13,975	13,692	-0.4	61	94.8	94.0	1.6	1.7	0.3	0.4
ANDERSON	003	00000	616	8,110	8,201	8,268	0.2	27	97.4	97.3	0.3	0.3	0.2	0.2
ATCHISON	005	11860	616	16,774	16,708	16,658	-0.1	38	91.6	91.3	5.3	5.5	0.4	0.4
BARBER	007	00000	678	5,307	5,048	4,873	-0.7	78	97.1	96.5	0.4	0.5	0.1	0.1
BARTON	009	24460	678	28,205	27,963	27,819	-0.1	38	93.0	91.3	1.1	1.2	0.2	0.3
BOURBON	011	00000	603	15,379	15,021	14,764	-0.3	51	94.1	93.4	3.1	3.3	0.4	0.6
BROWN	013	00000	605	10,724	10,457	10,277	-0.3	51	86.9	85.9	1.6	1.7	0.2	0.3
BUTLER	015	48620	678	59,482	64,478	68,142	1.1	8	94.9	94.2	1.4	1.5	0.4	0.6
CHASE	017	21380	678	3,030	3,058	3,085	0.1	32	96.9	96.8	1.0	1.1	0.1	0.1
CHAUTAUQUA	019	00000	671	4,359	4,295	4,237	-0.2	42	93.8	93.7	0.3	0.3	0.1	0.1
CHEROKEE	021	00000	603	22,605	21,890	21,383	-0.4	61	92.3	91.5	0.6	0.7	0.3	0.4
CHEYENNE	023	00000	678	3,165	3,090	3,041	-0.3	51	97.9	97.9	0.1	0.1	0.3	0.4
CLARK	025	00000	678	2,390	2,335	2,291	-0.3	51	95.8	95.6	0.3	0.3	0.1	0.1
CLAY	027	00000	605	8,822	8,600	8,456	-0.4	61	97.7	97.4	0.6	0.6	0.1	0.2
CLOUD	029	00000	605	10,268	9,785	9,476	-0.7	78	98.3	98.0	0.3	0.4	0.3	0.4
COFFEY	031	00000	605	8,865	8,968	9,046	0.2	27	97.0	96.4	0.2	0.2	0.3	0.5
COMANCHE	033	00000	678	1,967	1,885	1,839	-0.6	72	98.0	97.9	0.1	0.1	0.3	0.3
COWLEY	035	49060	678	36,291	35,590	34,802	-0.3	51	90.1	88.5	2.7	2.9	1.5	2.1
CRAWFORD	037	38260	603	38,242	38,542	38,774	0.1	32	93.3	92.1	1.8	2.0	1.2	1.7
DECATUR	039	00000	678	3,472	3,154	2,941	-1.3	103	97.9	97.5	0.5	0.6	0.3	0.3
DICKINSON	041	00000	678	19,344	19,653	19,877	0.2	27	96.4	95.8	0.6	0.7	0.3	0.4
DONIPHAN	043	41140	638	8,249	8,057	7,823	-0.3	51	94.8	94.2	2.0	2.2	0.3	0.3
DOUGLAS	045	29940	616	99,962	107,920	112,759	1.1	8	86.1	83.9	4.2	4.5	3.2	4.4
EDWARDS	047	00000	678	3,449	3,321	3,245	-0.5	68	92.5	90.2	0.3	0.4	0.3	0.5
ELK	049	00000	678	3,261	3,141	3,054	-0.5	68	95.1	94.2	0.2	0.2	0.2	0.4
ELLIS	051	25700	678	27,507	27,111	26,776	-0.2	42	96.1	95.1	0.7	0.7	0.8	1.2
ELLSWORTH	053	00000	678	6,525	6,537	6,552	0.0	35	93.7	93.4	3.6	3.7	0.3	0.3
FINNEY	055	23780	678	40,523	40,042	39,407	-0.2	42	69.1	64.2	1.3	1.2	2.9	3.5
FORD	057	19980	678	32,458	34,434	35,910	0.8	11	74.9	70.5	1.6	1.6	2.2	2.6
FRANKLIN	059	28140	616	24,784	26,616	27,856	1.0	10	95.0	94.3	1.2	1.3	0.3	0.4
GEARY	061	31740	605	27,947	26,034	24,792	-1.0	95	64.1	60.9	22.0	22.5	3.6	4.7
GOVE	063	00000	678	3,068	2,906	2,799	-0.7	78	97.9	97.6	0.1	0.1	0.1	0.1
GRAHAM	065	00000	678	2,946	2,717	2,588	-1.1	99	94.9	94.2	3.2	3.5	0.3	0.4
GRANT	067	00000	678	7,909	7,683	7,449	-0.4	61	77.0	72.2	0.2	0.2	0.4	0.5
GRAY	069	00000	678	5,904	6,090	6,221	0.4	20	92.3	90.1	0.2	0.2	0.2	0.3
GREELEY	071	00000	678	1,534	1,416	1,331	-1.1	99	93.1	91.0	0.2	0.2	0.2	0.3
GREENWOOD	073	00000	678	7,673	7,295	7,036	-0.7	78	96.5	95.9	0.1	0.2	0.1	0.1
HAMILTON	075	00000	678	2,670	2,679	2,682	0.0	35	81.6	80.7	0.5	0.5	0.6	0.6
HARPER	077	00000	678	6,536	6,119	5,809	-0.9	89	97.2	96.8	0.2	0.2	0.2	0.2
HARVEY	079	48620	678	32,869	34,248	35,005	0.6	14	91.0	88.9	1.6	1.7	0.6	0.8
HASKELL	081	00000	678	4,307	4,337	4,365	0.1	32	85.1	84.4	0.2	0.2	0.6	0.6
HODGEMAN	083	00000	678	2,085	2,121	2,152	0.2	27	97.3	97.3	0.9	0.9	0.0	0.0
JACKSON	085	45820	605	12,657	13,782	14,652	1.2	6	90.2	89.5	0.5	0.6	0.2	0.3
JEFFERSON	087	45820	605	18,426	19,964	21,076	1.1	8	96.7	96.2	0.4	0.4	0.2	0.2
JEWELL	089	00000	722	3,791	3,406	3,187	-1.5	105	98.8	98.6	0.0	0.0	0.1	0.1
JOHNSON	091	28140	616	451,086	529,857	588,984	2.2	1	91.1	89.2	2.6	2.8	2.9	3.9
KEARNY	093	00000	678	4,531	4,646	4,725	0.3	23	80.3	75.8	0.6	0.6	0.4	0.5
KINGMAN	095	00000	678	8,673	8,403	8,179	-0.4	61	97.5	97.0	0.2	0.2	0.3	0.4
KIOWA	097	00000	678	3,278	3,129	3,037	-0.6	72	97.2	96.6	0.2	0.2	0.4	0.4
LABETTE	099	37660	603	22,835	22,423	22,189	-0.3	51	89.3	88.1	4.7	5.0	0.3	0.5
LANE	101	00000	678	2,155	1,986	1,891	-1.1	99	97.7	97.2	0.0	0.0	0.1	0.2
LEAVENWORTH	103	28140	616	68,691	75,756	80,796	1.4	3	84.2	82.5	10.4	11.0	1.2	1.6
LINCOLN	105	00000	678	3,578	3,483	3,415	-0.4	61	98.3	98.2	0.1	0.1	0.1	0.1
LINN	107	28140	616	9,570	10,535	11,305	1.3	5	97.5	97.2	0.6	0.7	0.2	0.2
LOGAN	109	00000	678	3,046	2,852	2,723	-0.9	89	96.7	96.1	0.6	0.6	0.2	0.3
LYON	111	21380	605	35,935	36,384	36,739	0.2	27	83.3	79.4	2.3	2.3	2.0	2.7
MCPHERSON	113	32700	678	29,554	30,656	31,464	0.5	17	96.5	95.9	0.8	0.9	0.4	0.5
MARION	115	00000	678	13,361	13,206	13,059	-0.2	42	97.1	96.5	0.5	0.5	0.2	0.3
MARSHALL	117	00000	605	10,965	10,649	10,448	-0.4	61	98.1	97.8	0.2	0.2	0.2	0.3
MEADE	119	00000	678	4,631	4,692	4,737	0.2	27	91.1	90.7	0.4	0.4	0.2	0.2
MIAMI	121	28140	616	28,351	31,866	34,627	1.6	2	96.0	95.4	1.5	1.7	0.2	0.3
MITCHELL	123	00000	678	6,932	6,486	6,172	-0.9	89	97.6	97.2	0.6	0.3	0.5	0.5
MONTGOMERY	125	17700	671	36,252	34,564	33,488	-0.7	78	85.8	84.3	6.1	6.5	0.5	0.7
MORRIS	127	00000	605	6,104	6,003	5,933	-0.2	42	97.5	97.0	0.3	0.4	0.2	0.3
MORTON	129	00000	678	3,496	3,402	3,298	-0.4	61	88.4	87.8	0.2	0.2	1.1	1.1
NEMAHA	131	00000	605	10,717	10,493	10,342	-0.3	51	98.3	98.1	0.5	0.5	0.2	0.2
NEOSHO	133	00000	603	16,997	16,584	16,283	-0.3	51	94.9	94.0	0.9	0.9	0.3	0.5
NESS	135	00000	678	3,454	3,126	2,921	-1.4	104	98.2	97.9	0.1	0.1	0.1	0.1
NORTON	137	00000	678	5,953	5,715	5,552	-0.6	72	93.3	92.4	4.0	4.3	0.4	0.6
OSAGE	139	45820	605	16,712	17,403	17,781	0.6	14	97.3	96.8	0.2	0.2	0.3	0.4
OSBORNE	141	00000	678	4,452	4,082	3,853	-1.2	102	98.6	98.3	0.1	0.1	0.2	0.3
OTTAWA	143	41460	678	6,163	6,398	6,567	0.5	17	97.5	97.1	0.5	0.6	0.1	0.2
PAWNEE	145	00000	678	7,233	6,810	6,530	-0.8	84	91.0	89.7	5.0	5.3	0.6	0.8
PHILLIPS	147	00000	722	6,001	5,599	5,331	-1.0	95	98.3	97.9	0.2	0.0	0.4	0.6
POTTAWATOMIE	149	31740	605	18,209	19,904	21,372	1.3	5	96.3	95.7	0.7	0.7	0.3	0.5
PRATT	151	00000	678	9,647	9,655	9,669	0.0	35	95.3	95.1	1.0	1.0	0.6	0.6
RAWLINS	153	00000	678	2,966	2,736	2,585	-1.1	99	98.5	98.3	0.3	0.3	0.1	0.1
KANSAS							0.6		86.1	84.2	5.7	5.8	1.8	2.5
UNITED STATES							1.2		75.1	72.7	12.3	12.6	3.8	4.5

KANSAS

B

POPULATION COMPOSITION

COUNTY	% HISPANIC ORIGIN		2007 AGE DISTRIBUTION (%)										MEDIAN AGE	% 2007 Males	% 2007 Females
	2000	2007	0-4	5-9	10-14	15-19	20-24	25-44	45-64	65-84	85+	18+	2007		
ALLEN	1.9	2.6	6.4	5.3	5.6	6.9	8.5	23.2	27.1	13.7	3.2	78.8	40.6	49.1	50.9
ANDERSON	1.1	1.1	7.2	5.9	6.3	6.4	6.9	22.6	25.9	15.3	3.6	76.7	41.7	49.6	50.4
ATCHISON	1.9	2.1	6.9	6.1	6.4	8.6	8.3	23.2	24.5	13.0	3.0	76.1	37.1	48.4	51.6
BARBER	2.0	2.8	5.6	5.0	5.4	6.8	7.3	19.4	30.2	16.6	3.6	79.7	45.2	49.2	50.8
BARTON	8.3	11.1	6.7	6.2	6.2	7.6	7.3	22.3	26.5	14.0	3.2	76.7	40.4	48.6	51.4
BOURBON	1.3	1.8	6.8	5.3	6.5	6.4	8.5	23.5	26.2	13.2	3.5	77.9	39.5	48.7	51.3
BROWN	2.3	3.0	7.0	6.3	5.9	6.3	7.6	21.5	27.4	13.9	4.1	77.0	41.1	48.8	51.2
BUTLER	2.2	3.1	7.2	6.6	6.8	7.7	7.9	25.0	26.9	10.0	1.9	74.7	37.1	50.2	49.8
CHASE	1.7	1.8	6.4	6.2	5.3	6.1	6.4	23.7	28.4	13.9	3.5	78.4	42.6	51.1	48.9
CHAUTAUQUA	1.4	1.4	5.4	4.2	5.5	6.8	7.9	18.8	26.2	20.1	5.2	80.9	46.0	48.4	51.6
CHEROKEE	1.3	1.8	7.2	6.8	6.4	6.4	6.4	25.9	25.9	12.6	2.4	75.6	38.7	49.0	51.0
CHEYENNE	2.6	2.7	5.2	4.5	6.0	6.6	7.3	18.4	29.7	17.2	5.0	80.3	46.0	49.7	50.3
CLARK	4.0	4.2	6.6	6.2	6.8	5.6	7.9	19.0	27.8	16.4	3.8	76.4	43.5	50.1	49.9
CLAY	0.8	1.1	5.6	5.2	5.9	6.9	6.7	22.2	28.4	14.8	4.3	79.0	43.1	50.0	50.0
CLOUD	0.6	0.8	5.3	4.7	5.5	8.4	7.5	21.1	25.0	16.8	5.7	80.3	43.1	47.7	52.3
COFFEY	1.5	2.1	6.2	5.8	6.3	6.2	7.5	23.3	29.3	12.3	2.9	77.6	41.6	49.3	50.7
COMANCHE	1.8	1.9	5.8	5.7	5.3	6.0	5.1	17.9	28.6	19.6	6.0	79.0	48.0	49.1	50.9
COWLEY	3.6	4.8	6.8	5.9	6.4	7.5	8.0	24.1	25.8	12.6	2.9	76.8	38.5	49.1	50.9
CRAWFORD	2.4	3.2	6.7	5.5	5.3	7.6	11.6	24.7	23.3	11.9	3.3	79.1	34.7	49.0	51.0
DECATUR	1.0	1.3	5.0	4.4	5.4	7.1	7.0	17.4	30.3	17.9	5.5	80.6	46.9	49.7	50.3
DICKINSON	2.3	3.1	6.1	5.4	6.1	6.7	7.2	22.3	28.4	14.4	3.4	78.1	42.5	49.3	50.7
DONIPHAN	1.2	1.6	6.6	6.2	5.9	8.8	7.4	22.8	27.2	12.5	2.5	77.5	38.2	50.0	50.0
DOUGLAS	3.3	4.4	5.6	5.0	5.0	10.2	17.5	28.6	20.1	6.7	1.2	81.0	28.1	49.9	50.1
EDWARDS	9.7	12.9	6.7	6.0	5.3	6.1	7.3	21.2	27.3	16.0	4.0	78.3	42.9	49.7	50.3
ELK	2.2	2.9	4.8	4.0	5.1	6.9	7.0	19.2	27.8	20.0	5.2	81.5	47.3	48.2	51.8
ELLIS	2.4	3.2	5.9	5.0	5.1	9.1	13.1	24.9	22.7	11.5	2.6	80.0	33.3	49.0	51.0
ELLSWORTH	3.6	3.8	4.6	4.0	4.7	6.4	9.1	22.7	28.8	15.6	4.1	82.8	43.9	52.9	47.1
FINNEY	43.3	50.8	10.6	9.2	8.6	8.1	8.1	28.7	19.6	6.1	0.9	66.9	28.5	51.1	48.9
FORD	37.7	45.2	9.7	8.3	7.7	7.3	7.9	28.7	20.0	8.5	1.9	70.0	30.3	51.7	48.3
FRANKLIN	2.6	3.6	7.2	6.2	6.4	7.7	7.4	25.4	25.9	11.4	2.5	75.7	37.6	50.0	50.0
GEARY	8.5	11.0	9.7	7.4	6.7	6.8	9.9	29.4	20.4	8.3	1.2	72.2	29.4	49.6	50.4
GOVE	1.2	1.7	6.4	6.0	6.7	6.1	7.0	18.1	28.6	16.9	4.2	77.0	44.8	49.2	50.8
GRAHAM	0.8	1.1	4.9	4.3	4.9	5.5	7.6	20.0	28.4	20.8	3.6	82.4	46.7	48.1	51.9
GRANT	34.7	42.4	9.1	8.5	7.1	7.6	8.6	26.3	23.4	8.0	1.2	70.7	32.2	50.3	49.7
GRAY	9.8	13.0	8.5	7.4	7.8	7.0	6.7	26.8	24.7	8.5	2.6	71.7	34.6	49.6	50.4
GREELEY	11.5	15.3	7.8	6.0	7.4	6.8	5.0	24.6	26.3	13.1	3.0	74.2	41.5	50.2	49.8
GREENWOOD	1.7	2.4	5.9	5.5	5.1	6.2	6.8	21.2	27.8	17.3	4.2	79.5	44.6	49.3	50.7
HAMILTON	20.6	21.7	7.5	7.1	6.2	7.0	5.8	24.8	24.9	13.5	3.2	74.5	39.3	50.0	50.0
HARPER	1.1	1.5	6.1	5.6	5.4	6.8	6.9	20.0	27.0	17.5	4.6	78.5	44.3	48.6	51.4
HARVEY	8.0	10.7	6.7	6.3	6.5	7.9	7.1	23.8	25.8	12.6	3.2	75.9	38.8	48.8	51.2
HASKELL	23.6	24.7	9.6	8.9	7.4	6.8	6.1	26.8	24.4	8.7	1.4	69.7	32.7	51.3	48.7
HODGEMAN	2.7	2.8	5.8	5.7	7.5	7.1	7.9	21.6	26.4	14.3	3.7	76.1	41.8	49.3	50.7
JACKSON	1.5	2.0	7.3	6.9	6.3	7.1	7.1	23.3	27.1	12.5	2.4	75.1	39.8	49.3	50.7
JEFFERSON	1.3	1.8	6.7	6.4	6.5	6.6	6.7	24.6	29.4	11.4	1.7	76.3	40.8	50.9	49.1
JEWELL	0.7	1.0	5.0	4.6	4.9	5.8	7.2	17.5	30.7	19.6	4.7	81.7	48.1	49.8	50.2
JOHNSON	4.0	5.4	7.5	7.9	7.3	6.8	5.5	29.1	26.2	8.2	1.6	73.0	36.5	49.1	50.9
KEARNY	26.6	33.4	9.4	8.2	8.1	8.4	6.7	25.2	23.1	9.2	1.7	68.7	33.3	51.7	48.3
KINGMAN	1.4	2.0	6.9	5.9	6.2	7.4	7.2	19.9	27.2	15.6	3.7	76.3	42.4	49.4	50.6
KIOWA	2.0	2.7	5.9	5.3	6.0	6.6	6.4	21.0	29.1	16.4	3.3	78.8	43.9	49.7	50.3
LABETTE	3.1	4.1	6.6	5.7	6.0	7.3	8.5	23.7	26.1	12.6	3.4	77.5	39.7	49.4	50.6
LANE	1.4	2.1	5.7	5.1	6.1	5.8	7.1	21.6	29.2	15.5	3.8	78.8	44.0	50.2	49.8
LEAVENWORTH	3.8	5.1	7.1	7.1	6.1	6.5	7.8	28.9	26.2	9.1	1.3	75.8	36.7	53.0	47.0
LINCOLN	1.0	1.1	5.3	5.1	4.8	6.4	5.9	19.5	31.2	17.1	4.7	80.8	46.7	49.6	50.4
LINN	0.9	1.3	6.5	6.7	5.7	5.9	6.0	22.4	29.3	15.0	2.6	77.4	42.9	50.3	49.7
LOGAN	1.6	2.2	7.3	5.6	5.2	7.0	7.5	20.6	27.3	15.7	3.8	77.5	42.3	48.4	51.6
LYON	16.7	21.6	7.2	6.1	6.1	8.4	12.0	25.9	23.2	8.9	2.3	76.8	31.5	49.4	50.6
MCPHERSON	1.9	2.7	6.2	5.4	5.8	8.3	9.1	21.9	26.7	12.9	3.6	78.0	39.8	49.0	51.0
MARION	1.9	2.6	5.9	5.6	6.2	7.2	6.8	20.6	27.3	15.7	4.6	77.9	43.3	49.2	50.8
MARSHALL	0.8	1.0	5.6	4.9	4.9	7.1	7.4	21.4	28.6	15.8	4.3	80.0	44.2	49.7	50.3
MEADE	10.9	11.5	8.4	7.7	7.5	6.6	5.8	23.4	24.0	13.4	3.2	72.0	37.4	50.1	49.9
MIAMI	1.6	2.2	7.1	6.8	6.6	7.3	7.0	25.4	28.1	10.0	1.7	75.1	38.9	49.8	50.2
MITCHELL	0.9	1.2	5.3	4.9	5.4	8.9	6.7	20.6	28.3	15.2	4.6	79.6	43.7	49.7	50.3
MONTGOMERY	3.1	4.1	6.6	5.6	6.1	6.8	7.8	23.3	26.6	14.0	3.2	77.9	40.4	48.5	51.5
MORRIS	2.2	3.0	6.0	5.6	5.7	6.9	7.6	19.8	29.2	15.4	3.8	78.3	43.9	49.3	50.7
MORTON	14.1	14.9	9.1	7.9	6.9	6.5	6.9	22.9	25.5	12.1	2.0	72.1	36.2	48.4	51.6
NEMAHA	0.7	1.0	8.2	6.8	6.7	6.6	7.3	20.6	24.1	14.7	5.0	74.1	40.6	49.5	50.5
NEOSHO	2.9	4.0	6.6	5.6	6.0	7.3	7.7	23.5	26.1	14.0	3.2	77.7	40.1	48.7	51.3
NESS	1.5	2.0	5.9	5.2	5.5	4.9	7.4	19.6	29.0	17.5	5.0	79.9	45.8	50.4	49.6
NORTON	2.4	3.2	5.2	4.6	5.3	6.0	8.8	25.0	27.1	13.6	4.3	80.6	41.6	55.7	44.3
OSAGE	1.5	2.1	6.6	6.4	6.6	7.1	6.4	23.1	28.0	13.2	2.7	75.8	41.3	49.3	50.7
OSBORNE	0.4	0.5	5.2	4.6	5.3	7.3	6.9	19.2	28.9	16.8	5.9	80.1	45.9	49.0	51.0
OTTAWA	1.3	1.8	6.0	5.5	5.9	6.3	7.4	22.4	29.3	13.6	3.6	78.6	42.9	50.2	49.8
PAWNEE	4.2	5.6	5.8	5.8	4.9	8.0	7.2	23.1	27.5	14.0	3.8	78.4	41.7	53.3	46.7
PHILLIPS	0.7	0.9	5.8	5.6	5.2	6.7	6.4	21.1	28.0	16.2	4.8	78.8	44.3	49.5	50.5
POTTAWATOMIE	2.3	3.1	7.8	7.4	6.8	7.2	6.6	25.3	26.6	10.3	2.1	73.5	37.1	49.7	50.3
PRATT	3.1	3.3	6.2	5.8	5.4	7.3	8.2	20.6	27.7	14.9	3.8	78.6	42.2	48.9	51.1
RAWLINS	0.8	1.1	4.8	4.5	5.3	6.2	9.7	16.1	30.2	18.3	4.9	81.2	46.9	51.0	49.0
KANSAS	7.0	8.9	7.2	6.7	6.6	7.3	8.0	26.2	25.3	10.5	2.2	75.3	36.1	49.6	50.4
UNITED STATES	12.5	15.0	6.9	6.5	6.8	7.1	7.0	27.6	25.4	10.7	1.9	75.6	36.7	49.2	50.8

COUNTY	HOUSEHOLDS					FAMILIES			MEDIAN HOUSEHOLD INCOME			
	2000	2007	2012	% Annual Rate 2000-2007	2007 Average HH Size	2000	2007	% Annual Rate 2000-2007	2007	2012	2007 National Rank	2007 State Rank
ALLEN	5,775	5,680	5,591	-0.2	2.40	3,895	3,780	-0.4	38,574	43,961	1921	74
ANDERSON	3,221	3,279	3,312	0.2	2.46	2,265	2,277	0.1	40,146	45,188	1700	59
ATCHISON	6,275	6,319	6,326	0.1	2.48	4,278	4,250	-0.1	41,850	47,830	1470	46
BARBER	2,235	2,160	2,099	-0.5	2.31	1,511	1,442	-0.6	39,734	44,728	1754	63
BARTON	11,393	11,410	11,408	0.0	2.38	7,530	7,436	-0.2	39,645	45,187	1761	64
BOURBON	6,161	6,051	5,955	-0.2	2.43	4,126	3,996	-0.4	37,771	43,007	2027	79
BROWN	4,318	4,259	4,204	-0.2	2.41	2,949	2,870	-0.4	38,772	44,178	1881	71
BUTLER	21,527	23,536	24,958	1.2	2.65	16,049	17,360	1.1	56,067	64,267	361	4
CHASE	1,246	1,279	1,300	0.4	2.30	817	828	0.2	39,418	44,297	1794	67
CHAUTAUQUA	1,796	1,768	1,742	-0.2	2.34	1,235	1,200	-0.4	34,554	38,714	2491	101
CHEROKEE	8,875	8,621	8,422	-0.4	2.50	6,242	5,985	-0.6	36,805	41,625	2150	85
CHEYENNE	1,360	1,334	1,314	-0.3	2.28	920	890	-0.5	36,345	41,057	2223	89
CLARK	979	952	931	-0.4	2.40	676	649	-0.6	40,424	45,371	1669	56
CLAY	3,617	3,563	3,516	-0.2	2.37	2,516	2,447	-0.4	40,891	46,072	1615	52
CLOUD	4,163	3,996	3,875	-0.6	2.28	2,698	2,552	-0.8	38,636	43,960	1910	73
COFFEY	3,489	3,540	3,572	0.2	2.49	2,477	2,483	0.0	44,871	50,213	1124	32
COMANCHE	872	857	844	-0.2	2.12	541	523	-0.5	34,450	38,798	2500	102
COWLEY	14,039	13,883	13,605	-0.2	2.43	9,616	9,381	-0.3	42,240	48,288	1422	44
CRAWFORD	15,504	15,652	15,750	0.1	2.35	9,436	9,372	-0.1	36,137	41,468	2250	93
DECATUR	1,494	1,378	1,292	-1.1	2.20	982	893	-1.3	36,031	40,788	2272	94
DICKINSON	7,903	8,120	8,247	0.4	2.38	5,424	5,500	0.2	43,818	50,232	1233	33
DONIPHAN	3,173	3,142	3,064	-0.1	2.44	2,184	2,136	-0.3	39,414	44,472	1795	68
DOUGLAS	38,486	42,851	45,196	1.5	2.32	21,159	23,117	1.2	47,778	55,724	840	21
EDWARDS	1,455	1,405	1,374	-0.5	2.32	956	910	-0.7	36,143	40,432	2248	92
ELK	1,412	1,364	1,326	-0.5	2.24	924	880	-0.7	32,237	36,061	2741	104
ELLIS	11,193	11,250	11,200	0.1	2.30	6,773	6,695	-0.2	42,084	49,597	1437	45
ELLSWORTH	2,481	2,515	2,533	0.2	2.27	1,639	1,639	0.0	43,405	49,723	1284	37
FINNEY	12,948	12,726	12,484	-0.2	3.10	9,750	9,483	-0.4	49,287	58,165	726	14
FORD	10,852	11,220	11,622	0.5	3.00	7,856	8,028	0.3	47,966	56,447	819	19
FRANKLIN	9,452	10,190	10,697	1.0	2.54	6,722	7,158	0.9	48,163	55,645	803	17
GEARY	10,458	9,884	9,464	-0.8	2.57	7,578	7,082	-0.9	40,857	47,876	1619	53
GOVE	1,245	1,192	1,153	-0.6	2.39	861	814	-0.8	40,058	44,970	1719	62
GRAHAM	1,263	1,192	1,146	-0.8	2.22	848	789	-1.0	37,051	41,330	2120	81
GRANT	2,742	2,705	2,638	-0.2	2.81	2,099	2,051	-0.3	49,307	56,655	721	13
GRAY	2,045	2,106	2,148	0.4	2.82	1,556	1,586	0.3	47,280	52,644	886	24
GREELEY	602	568	538	-0.8	2.45	414	386	-1.0	41,038	45,985	1593	50
GREENWOOD	3,234	3,088	2,980	-0.6	2.30	2,153	2,028	-0.8	36,326	41,101	2226	90
HAMILTON	1,054	1,040	1,033	-0.2	2.53	716	697	-0.4	38,897	43,726	1867	70
HARPER	2,773	2,609	2,479	-0.8	2.28	1,807	1,676	-1.0	35,338	39,449	2394	97
HARVEY	12,581	13,250	13,597	0.7	2.48	8,930	9,293	0.6	51,086	59,569	607	9
HASKELL	1,481	1,483	1,487	0.0	2.90	1,154	1,146	-0.1	45,475	51,364	1054	27
HODGEMAN	796	814	827	0.3	2.56	581	587	0.1	42,662	48,426	1373	41
JACKSON	4,727	5,197	5,546	1.3	2.61	3,506	3,813	1.2	48,392	54,589	787	16
JEFFERSON	6,830	7,453	7,887	1.2	2.64	5,194	5,611	1.1	52,761	59,316	509	6
JEWELL	1,695	1,555	1,468	-1.2	2.16	1,098	993	-1.4	36,480	41,159	2196	88
JOHNSON	174,570	205,192	228,458	2.3	2.56	121,618	141,111	2.1	78,730	93,541	60	1
KEARNY	1,542	1,583	1,610	0.4	2.91	1,200	1,220	0.2	46,854	52,301	921	25
KINGMAN	3,371	3,292	3,211	-0.3	2.49	2,421	2,336	-0.5	45,445	51,278	1060	28
KIOWA	1,365	1,318	1,285	-0.5	2.29	924	880	-0.7	38,279	43,089	1964	76
LABETTE	9,194	9,120	9,057	-0.1	2.36	6,118	5,987	-0.3	37,646	42,960	2041	80
LANE	910	848	811	-1.0	2.31	613	564	-1.1	42,638	48,228	1377	42
LEAVENWORTH	23,071	26,022	28,111	1.7	2.65	17,206	19,199	1.5	59,599	68,541	275	2
LINCOLN	1,529	1,503	1,478	-0.2	2.27	1,040	1,009	-0.4	36,857	41,271	2148	84
LINN	3,807	4,229	4,554	1.5	2.46	2,747	3,017	1.3	43,094	48,752	1318	38
LOGAN	1,243	1,178	1,129	-0.7	2.37	857	802	-0.9	38,303	42,582	1962	75
LYON	13,691	13,922	14,072	0.2	2.50	8,642	8,652	0.0	41,204	48,099	1569	49
MCPHERSON	11,205	11,723	12,072	0.6	2.48	7,968	8,235	0.5	51,229	59,734	600	8
MARION	5,114	5,042	4,975	-0.2	2.47	3,689	3,595	-0.4	41,457	46,732	1522	48
MARSHALL	4,458	4,360	4,287	-0.3	2.39	3,027	2,921	-0.5	38,656	42,981	1904	72
MEADE	1,728	1,726	1,731	0.0	2.65	1,252	1,236	-0.2	43,469	49,160	1275	36
MIAMI	10,365	11,738	12,792	1.7	2.65	7,798	8,742	1.6	57,244	65,673	323	3
MITCHELL	2,850	2,704	2,585	-0.7	2.27	1,863	1,742	-0.9	40,892	45,966	1614	51
MONTGOMERY	14,903	14,343	13,940	-0.5	2.35	9,954	9,449	-0.7	37,964	43,364	2002	78
MORRIS	2,539	2,519	2,497	-0.1	2.35	1,777	1,743	-0.3	39,428	44,354	1793	66
MORTON	1,306	1,277	1,240	-0.3	2.62	961	929	-0.5	45,028	51,437	1109	31
NEMAHA	3,959	3,891	3,836	-0.2	2.57	2,765	2,684	-0.4	40,683	45,871	1644	55
NEOSHO	6,739	6,595	6,475	-0.3	2.44	4,684	4,524	-0.5	40,273	46,289	1692	58
NESS	1,516	1,404	1,324	-1.1	2.17	978	892	-1.3	39,461	44,399	1786	65
NORTON	2,266	2,180	2,114	-0.5	2.26	1,471	1,395	-0.7	36,682	40,958	2170	87
OSAGE	6,490	6,813	6,980	0.7	2.52	4,737	4,916	0.5	45,343	51,092	1071	29
OSBORNE	1,940	1,799	1,704	-1.0	2.20	1,208	1,103	-1.2	34,979	39,344	2432	100
OTTAWA	2,430	2,525	2,591	0.5	2.46	1,717	1,762	0.4	45,198	50,442	1084	30
PAWNEE	2,739	2,578	2,463	-0.8	2.29	1,787	1,658	-1.0	42,271	47,645	1420	43
PHILLIPS	2,406	2,344	2,235	-0.9	2.33	1,723	1,596	-1.1	41,687	47,079	1495	47
POTTAWATOMIE	6,771	7,481	8,018	1.4	2.63	4,931	5,387	1.2	48,965	55,531	751	15
PRATT	3,963	4,007	4,028	0.2	2.33	2,641	2,632	0.0	43,571	50,504	1269	35
RAWLINS	1,269	1,201	1,147	0.8	2.23	847	790	-1.0	38,143	42,953	1984	77
KANSAS				0.7	2.50			0.5	51,343	60,554		
UNITED STATES				1.2	2.59			1.0	53,154	62,503		

COUNTY	2007 Per Capita Income	2007 HH Income Base	2007 HOUSEHOLD INCOME DISTRIBUTION (%)					2007 Home Value Base	2007 HOME VALUE DISTRIBUTION (%)					2007 Median Home Value
			Less than $25,000	$25,000 to $49,999	$50,000 to $99,999	$100,000 to $149,999	$150,000 or More		Less than $50,000	$50,000 to $89,999	$90,000 to $174,999	$175,000 to $399,999	$400,000 or More	
ALLEN	19,235	5,680	30.9	34.2	28.9	4.1	1.9	4,319	37.8	32.6	23.9	4.9	0.8	61,063
ANDERSON	19,265	3,279	27.5	35.2	31.0	4.7	1.6	2,654	27.4	26.6	33.3	11.9	0.9	83,540
ATCHISON	19,489	6,319	27.0	33.7	31.9	5.7	1.7	4,719	23.9	33.4	32.7	9.5	0.6	79,030
BARBER	20,925	2,160	27.2	36.9	28.8	4.7	2.4	1,663	53.3	23.3	19.8	2.6	1.0	45,902
BARTON	20,949	11,410	29.6	32.6	29.7	6.0	2.1	8,396	28.7	31.3	33.1	6.3	0.5	75,335
BOURBON	19,796	6,051	31.1	32.7	29.4	3.9	2.8	4,544	34.2	31.5	27.1	6.2	1.0	68,579
BROWN	18,801	4,259	32.5	30.9	30.3	5.4	0.9	3,123	31.6	28.1	33.3	6.3	0.6	75,591
BUTLER	25,119	23,536	17.6	26.5	38.3	12.5	5.1	18,603	15.1	26.7	41.2	15.7	1.2	103,468
CHASE	20,661	1,279	28.8	33.6	29.5	6.3	1.9	961	35.6	26.8	27.2	9.7	0.7	69,754
CHAUTAUQUA	19,131	1,768	34.8	37.3	21.5	4.0	2.4	1,460	52.4	25.1	16.8	4.2	1.6	47,348
CHEROKEE	17,892	8,621	33.3	31.8	29.1	4.2	1.6	6,677	35.6	28.6	29.1	6.4	0.3	67,030
CHEYENNE	20,697	1,334	29.9	40.0	22.1	5.8	2.2	1,047	32.8	28.8	28.7	8.0	1.6	71,357
CLARK	22,349	952	27.3	33.4	30.3	4.9	4.1	743	38.6	31.0	23.7	5.8	0.9	62,348
CLAY	20,551	3,563	26.9	33.2	32.8	5.7	1.4	2,774	28.3	30.2	31.7	9.6	0.2	75,951
CLOUD	21,844	3,996	29.9	34.3	28.4	4.4	3.0	3,019	38.7	31.4	26.3	3.6	0.1	64,018
COFFEY	21,675	3,540	25.3	30.7	33.0	8.6	2.5	2,823	23.4	27.6	36.9	11.1	1.0	88,767
COMANCHE	21,951	857	32.6	37.0	24.9	2.8	2.8	645	55.7	24.0	16.9	3.4	0.0	45,000
COWLEY	21,223	13,883	28.9	29.1	32.6	6.7	2.8	10,081	27.3	32.2	31.4	8.3	0.8	77,263
CRAWFORD	20,181	15,652	34.5	29.6	27.6	5.5	2.8	10,343	29.7	29.8	29.1	10.3	1.0	74,815
DECATUR	19,220	1,378	30.6	39.1	25.7	3.9	0.7	1,067	40.3	28.9	26.9	3.0	0.9	63,281
DICKINSON	21,586	8,120	24.9	32.3	34.5	6.5	1.8	6,191	19.0	29.8	39.1	11.2	1.0	91,880
DONIPHAN	18,880	3,142	30.3	33.5	30.2	4.2	1.8	2,391	30.2	31.5	29.6	7.9	0.8	74,761
DOUGLAS	26,697	42,851	25.2	27.0	31.9	9.6	6.3	23,071	7.2	6.3	43.1	37.6	5.7	163,767
EDWARDS	20,980	1,405	32.1	34.5	26.9	4.1	2.4	1,107	45.9	32.7	17.3	2.5	1.6	54,691
ELK	19,000	1,364	37.2	32.9	23.9	4.3	1.6	1,113	54.4	19.0	19.9	3.6	3.0	44,677
ELLIS	24,316	11,250	28.9	28.4	31.3	7.1	4.3	7,290	13.5	16.4	50.4	18.1	1.6	118,372
ELLSWORTH	21,283	2,515	27.6	30.3	33.2	7.7	1.1	2,023	38.2	31.6	24.9	5.1	0.2	63,629
FINNEY	19,688	12,726	19.7	31.0	37.1	7.9	4.3	8,489	18.8	17.4	47.4	15.0	1.3	107,734
FORD	19,464	11,220	21.9	30.3	36.1	7.5	4.2	7,484	21.7	27.7	38.8	10.9	0.8	90,854
FRANKLIN	21,781	10,190	21.6	30.3	38.4	7.2	2.4	7,645	15.5	21.6	44.7	17.1	1.0	109,058
GEARY	20,899	9,884	24.7	35.7	29.4	6.8	3.3	5,238	17.5	31.1	40.9	10.1	0.3	91,837
GOVE	21,038	1,192	27.2	34.3	30.4	5.6	2.5	966	34.7	28.7	29.9	6.3	0.4	70,000
GRAHAM	21,626	1,192	32.6	34.1	25.8	4.8	2.7	957	40.3	34.1	23.0	2.4	0.2	61,823
GRANT	21,676	2,705	18.4	32.4	36.5	9.6	3.1	2,070	24.1	19.4	38.5	17.5	0.5	96,888
GRAY	22,045	2,106	18.6	34.4	34.9	7.4	4.7	1,578	20.7	23.1	43.9	11.8	0.6	99,703
GREELEY	25,509	568	25.0	34.5	27.3	8.1	5.1	434	27.9	30.4	31.6	9.7	0.5	78,929
GREENWOOD	19,665	3,088	32.3	34.0	27.8	3.6	2.4	2,367	46.9	24.5	19.4	7.8	1.3	53,125
HAMILTON	19,683	1,040	27.7	36.8	26.5	5.6	3.4	738	23.4	34.7	34.7	6.9	0.3	81,429
HARPER	20,079	2,609	35.0	31.6	26.9	4.6	1.9	1,972	34.0	34.5	25.1	5.8	0.7	66,043
HARVEY	23,875	13,250	19.3	29.3	38.8	9.6	2.9	9,738	15.1	29.7	43.1	11.7	0.4	96,224
HASKELL	20,651	1,483	19.4	36.0	32.6	7.8	4.2	1,104	23.1	28.0	35.1	12.9	0.9	88,000
HODGEMAN	19,675	814	26.8	34.5	30.8	5.4	2.5	647	33.4	31.4	29.7	4.5	1.1	69,151
JACKSON	21,596	5,197	20.8	31.0	37.8	8.0	2.4	4,238	14.4	21.3	42.6	20.3	1.3	112,240
JEFFERSON	22,742	7,453	18.7	26.7	43.5	8.0	3.1	6,387	12.2	17.3	44.9	23.2	2.4	124,936
JEWELL	20,833	1,555	33.4	37.2	23.0	4.0	2.3	1,249	58.4	22.1	15.6	2.9	1.0	39,590
JOHNSON	40,266	205,191	8.3	18.3	37.4	19.0	16.9	151,630	1.2	1.3	29.9	55.9	11.7	214,657
KEARNY	19,151	1,583	21.7	32.7	35.4	7.0	3.2	1,195	27.1	23.0	38.3	10.7	0.8	89,766
KINGMAN	22,301	3,292	24.2	31.3	33.8	7.8	2.9	2,604	24.5	29.6	32.7	11.9	1.3	83,515
KIOWA	20,972	1,318	29.2	33.5	29.5	5.7	2.1	970	41.1	30.4	24.0	3.9	0.5	61,915
LABETTE	19,326	9,120	31.2	33.8	28.5	5.1	1.4	6,776	40.6	28.6	23.8	6.1	0.9	61,142
LANE	23,262	848	24.8	34.9	31.1	5.7	3.5	666	31.5	38.9	24.6	4.8	0.2	68,382
LEAVENWORTH	25,137	26,022	14.5	26.2	41.0	13.4	4.8	17,923	6.8	15.4	44.9	30.5	2.4	142,204
LINCOLN	19,617	1,503	30.8	36.3	26.7	4.7	1.5	1,192	42.5	30.8	21.7	4.2	0.8	58,812
LINN	20,478	4,229	27.2	31.2	34.8	5.2	1.6	3,533	26.8	23.0	32.7	15.0	2.4	90,322
LOGAN	21,331	1,178	26.7	36.7	26.8	6.9	2.9	911	31.9	29.0	32.7	6.4	0.0	74,167
LYON	20,246	13,922	27.5	31.4	31.0	7.7	2.3	8,741	22.0	25.2	40.6	11.3	0.9	93,976
MCPHERSON	24,033	11,723	19.2	29.0	39.6	8.8	3.4	8,842	10.8	20.4	49.8	17.7	1.3	117,337
MARION	19,911	5,042	26.9	33.9	32.3	4.9	2.1	4,080	25.1	30.6	33.5	9.9	0.8	80,127
MARSHALL	20,706	4,360	29.3	34.1	28.1	5.5	3.0	3,504	36.9	26.6	27.9	7.5	1.1	69,005
MEADE	20,120	1,726	24.3	34.9	30.2	8.2	2.3	1,311	27.4	31.4	33.0	6.9	1.3	77,557
MIAMI	26,328	11,738	16.6	25.6	38.9	13.0	5.9	9,389	10.4	14.1	33.9	35.7	6.0	150,728
MITCHELL	22,654	2,704	28.1	33.1	30.0	6.0	2.8	2,064	31.3	27.7	29.5	10.3	1.2	76,259
MONTGOMERY	20,120	14,343	32.4	32.2	27.9	5.6	1.8	10,481	35.1	31.7	26.1	6.6	0.6	65,832
MORRIS	21,764	2,519	29.3	34.1	28.8	5.1	2.8	1,988	32.9	28.0	28.9	9.2	1.0	71,017
MORTON	21,818	1,277	22.3	33.8	32.5	8.2	3.1	936	21.7	28.3	42.1	7.7	0.2	90,000
NEMAHA	19,566	3,891	28.5	33.6	30.8	4.2	2.9	3,168	24.5	29.5	32.8	12.0	1.3	85,099
NEOSHO	20,628	6,595	27.9	34.8	29.2	5.4	2.8	5,006	35.1	30.6	27.4	6.3	0.6	66,018
NESS	22,431	1,404	29.2	33.8	28.4	6.5	2.1	1,088	42.9	30.7	21.6	4.3	0.5	59,506
NORTON	19,570	2,180	30.7	36.5	27.1	3.0	2.8	1,717	35.1	29.4	31.1	4.0	0.4	67,958
OSAGE	20,877	6,813	23.5	32.1	36.0	6.9	1.6	5,515	15.7	25.7	43.0	14.3	1.4	103,128
OSBORNE	19,845	1,799	32.9	38.1	22.5	4.7	1.8	1,435	49.8	26.9	17.9	4.1	1.3	50,221
OTTAWA	21,522	2,525	23.0	32.5	36.2	5.5	2.7	2,090	22.9	31.0	33.0	12.1	1.1	84,296
PAWNEE	22,842	2,578	24.4	33.9	31.5	6.2	4.0	1,953	29.1	38.4	26.3	5.9	0.4	70,143
PHILLIPS	21,639	2,344	28.0	31.8	34.4	3.5	2.3	1,856	36.8	25.8	32.7	4.0	0.6	70,348
POTTAWATOMIE	21,576	7,481	21.1	30.0	37.7	9.0	2.3	5,980	18.7	17.1	45.7	16.7	1.8	111,924
PRATT	22,623	4,007	25.5	32.1	32.2	7.1	3.1	3,006	26.6	31.2	30.8	10.5	0.8	80,885
RAWLINS	21,068	1,201	31.2	32.1	27.9	6.7	2.0	937	44.4	25.9	24.3	5.2	0.1	58,203
KANSAS	26,438		20.9	27.6	34.5	10.6	6.4		16.9	21.4	36.0	22.2	3.5	112,948
UNITED STATES	27,916		21.9	25.0	32.3	12.3	8.4		7.9	10.5	27.1	35.6	19.0	192,285

COUNTY	FINANCIAL SERVICES				THE HOME						ENTERTAINMENT						PERSONAL			
					Home Improvements		Furnishings													
	Auto Loan	Home Loan	Invest-ments	Retire-ment Plans	Home Repair	Lawn & Garden	Comput-ers & Hard-ware	Major Appli-ances	TV, Radio, Sound Equip-ment	Furni-ture	Dine out/ Carry out	Sports Equip-ment	Fees & Tickets	Toys & Games	Travel	Cable TV	Apparel & Services	Auto Repairs	Health Insur-ance	Pets & Supplies
ALLEN	73	55	49	55	60	76	61	69	66	57	65	61	53	68	60	70	55	66	77	72
ANDERSON	79	56	39	54	65	87	60	75	66	56	66	66	50	70	60	71	56	69	84	81
ATCHISON	74	61	59	61	66	78	65	71	70	62	68	62	60	72	64	73	59	68	79	74
BARBER	86	56	28	53	67	95	60	81	66	56	66	72	47	72	58	71	56	72	86	89
BARTON	76	62	59	62	66	79	66	73	71	63	70	64	61	72	66	75	60	70	82	75
BOURBON	75	58	53	58	63	78	63	71	69	60	67	62	57	71	62	73	58	68	79	74
BROWN	73	54	43	53	61	79	58	70	64	54	63	61	50	67	58	68	53	65	79	74
BUTLER	98	95	95	96	94	99	91	95	93	92	92	85	91	96	92	94	82	92	97	97
CHASE	82	56	35	54	65	90	60	77	67	56	66	68	49	71	59	72	56	70	85	84
CHAUTAUQUA	74	53	39	51	60	80	57	70	65	53	63	61	49	66	57	70	53	65	80	74
CHEROKEE	73	55	44	54	60	76	57	68	64	55	62	59	51	66	57	68	53	63	75	71
CHEYENNE	81	54	33	52	64	89	59	77	66	55	65	68	48	70	58	71	55	69	84	83
CLARK	98	62	27	59	76	110	66	92	72	62	74	82	51	80	64	78	62	81	96	102
CLAY	77	59	51	58	65	82	63	74	69	59	68	65	56	70	63	73	58	69	83	77
CLOUD	79	61	57	61	67	83	67	76	73	62	71	66	60	74	67	77	61	72	87	79
COFFEY	89	68	51	66	76	96	69	84	75	66	74	74	61	79	69	79	64	77	91	90
COMANCHE	76	54	44	53	61	80	60	72	68	55	66	63	51	70	60	73	55	67	84	75
COWLEY	80	66	63	66	70	83	69	76	75	66	73	66	64	76	69	78	63	73	85	79
CRAWFORD	71	57	58	58	59	69	67	67	70	61	68	60	60	69	63	71	59	67	73	69
DECATUR	72	49	32	47	57	79	54	68	60	50	59	60	44	63	53	65	50	62	76	73
DICKINSON	81	64	55	63	70	87	66	78	73	64	71	68	60	75	67	77	61	73	86	82
DONIPHAN	77	56	40	55	62	81	59	72	65	56	64	64	51	68	59	69	55	67	79	77
DOUGLAS	89	77	84	82	73	75	100	82	93	88	93	79	90	91	88	88	83	90	81	83
EDWARDS	81	56	40	55	65	88	62	77	70	57	68	68	51	72	61	75	57	71	87	82
ELK	69	50	39	48	56	74	55	66	62	50	60	57	46	63	54	66	50	61	76	69
ELLIS	80	71	76	74	71	75	83	76	81	76	80	70	77	80	77	80	72	79	79	78
ELLSWORTH	79	61	52	60	68	86	65	77	71	61	70	67	58	73	65	76	60	72	86	80
FINNEY	89	84	78	83	79	80	86	84	85	85	85	79	82	86	82	83	76	87	83	84
FORD	86	79	70	76	76	80	80	83	81	80	81	77	76	82	78	81	73	84	82	82
FRANKLIN	83	73	73	74	76	86	74	80	78	73	77	70	72	81	75	80	68	77	85	83
GEARY	78	66	69	68	64	69	77	72	78	72	77	66	71	79	72	77	68	75	75	72
GOVE	92	58	25	55	72	103	62	86	68	58	69	77	48	75	60	73	58	76	90	96
GRAHAM	80	56	41	54	64	86	62	75	69	56	67	66	51	72	61	74	57	70	86	80
GRANT	93	85	78	85	85	94	80	88	84	82	83	78	79	88	82	86	74	85	90	91
GRAY	109	78	45	75	87	116	78	101	85	77	86	90	66	91	77	90	73	92	105	110
GREELEY	114	72	31	69	89	128	77	107	84	73	86	95	59	93	75	91	72	94	112	119
GREENWOOD	74	54	41	52	61	80	58	71	65	54	63	61	50	66	58	70	53	66	81	74
HAMILTON	91	58	25	55	71	102	61	85	67	58	68	76	47	74	60	72	57	75	89	95
HARPER	74	53	43	52	60	78	59	70	67	54	64	61	50	68	59	72	54	65	82	73
HARVEY	88	79	82	80	81	89	80	84	84	79	83	74	78	86	81	87	73	83	92	86
HASKELL	106	73	38	70	84	115	74	98	81	72	82	88	61	88	73	86	69	89	103	108
HODGEMAN	85	58	39	56	68	92	64	80	72	59	70	71	52	75	63	77	59	73	90	86
JACKSON	91	71	58	70	79	98	73	87	78	70	77	77	66	82	73	82	67	80	92	92
JEFFERSON	96	82	65	80	88	105	77	93	81	78	81	82	73	86	79	85	71	85	95	98
JEWELL	76	52	34	50	61	83	57	72	64	52	62	63	47	67	56	68	53	66	81	77
JOHNSON	140	154	159	158	148	136	146	139	139	151	140	131	152	142	146	135	128	141	132	139
KEARNY	95	73	47	70	77	98	70	87	76	70	76	78	62	80	70	80	65	80	90	94
KINGMAN	91	69	53	67	78	99	71	87	78	68	77	77	63	82	72	83	66	80	95	92
KIOWA	81	56	40	54	64	87	62	76	69	56	67	67	51	72	61	74	57	70	87	81
LABETTE	69	56	57	57	59	70	61	65	67	58	65	57	57	67	61	70	56	64	75	67
LANE	94	62	36	60	74	103	67	88	75	63	74	78	54	80	66	81	62	79	96	96
LEAVENWORTH	96	95	102	98	94	93	96	94	96	95	95	85	97	98	96	95	86	94	95	94
LINCOLN	75	51	34	50	60	82	56	71	63	52	62	62	46	66	56	68	52	65	80	76
LINN	86	62	39	60	71	95	63	81	69	61	69	71	54	73	63	75	59	73	87	87
LOGAN	81	58	48	57	66	86	66	77	74	59	71	67	56	75	65	80	60	72	91	80
LYON	74	62	64	64	63	70	73	70	73	67	72	64	66	73	68	73	64	72	73	72
MCPHERSON	90	79	80	80	82	93	81	87	85	79	83	76	78	87	82	88	73	84	94	89
MARION	81	61	46	59	69	89	63	78	69	60	68	68	55	72	64	74	58	72	85	83
MARSHALL	82	58	43	57	67	88	63	78	71	58	69	68	53	73	63	76	58	71	88	82
MEADE	91	62	39	60	73	100	67	86	75	62	74	76	55	80	66	81	62	78	96	93
MIAMI	101	101	103	102	101	103	95	99	97	97	95	88	97	100	98	97	85	96	101	101
MITCHELL	87	62	43	60	72	97	66	83	73	62	72	73	55	77	66	78	61	76	92	90
MONTGOMERY	71	58	57	59	62	73	63	68	69	59	66	59	58	69	63	72	58	66	78	70
MORRIS	84	60	45	59	68	90	66	80	73	61	71	70	56	75	65	78	60	74	90	85
MORTON	92	74	60	73	77	94	75	86	79	73	79	77	68	82	75	83	68	82	91	91
NEMAHA	84	58	42	57	67	90	65	79	73	59	71	70	54	75	64	78	59	73	91	84
NEOSHO	78	63	59	63	68	81	66	74	72	64	70	64	61	75	66	76	61	71	83	77
NESS	85	56	32	54	67	94	61	80	68	57	67	71	49	73	60	73	57	72	88	88
NORTON	75	53	40	52	60	80	59	71	66	53	64	62	49	68	58	71	54	66	82	75
OSAGE	83	68	59	67	73	89	68	79	74	66	72	70	63	77	69	78	63	74	86	83
OSBORNE	74	51	34	49	59	81	55	70	62	51	61	62	46	65	55	67	51	64	79	75
OTTAWA	89	64	44	62	74	98	67	85	74	63	73	75	57	79	67	80	62	77	93	91
PAWNEE	90	65	49	63	73	97	71	86	78	65	76	75	60	81	70	84	65	79	96	90
PHILLIPS	83	61	46	59	70	91	64	80	71	61	70	69	55	74	64	76	59	73	88	85
POTTAWATOMIE	89	79	66	78	80	91	74	84	78	75	78	76	71	82	75	00	00	00	88	88
PRATT	81	67	64	66	73	86	70	79	75	66	73	69	65	76	71	79	63	75	88	81
RAWLINS	79	54	37	53	63	86	60	75	67	55	65	66	49	70	59	72	55	68	84	80
KANSAS	97	89	88	90	89	95	92	93	93	90	93	84	88	95	90	94	82	93	97	95
UNITED STATES	100	100	100	100	100	100	100	100	100	100	100	100	100	100	100	100	100	100	100	100

POPULATION CHANGE

COUNTY	FIPS Code	CBSA Code	DMA Code	POPULATION 2000	POPULATION 2007	POPULATION 2012	2000-2007 ANNUAL RATE % Rate	2000-2007 ANNUAL RATE State Rank	White 2000	White 2007	Black 2000	Black 2007	Asian/Pacific 2000	Asian/Pacific 2007
RENO	155	26740	678	64,790	63,819	63,163	-0.2	42	91.6	90.0	2.9	3.1	0.5	0.7
REPUBLIC	157	00000	722	5,835	5,404	5,048	-1.1	99	98.6	98.3	0.3	0.3	0.2	0.3
RICE	159	00000	678	10,761	10,557	10,431	-0.3	51	94.7	93.6	1.2	1.2	0.4	0.5
RILEY	161	31740	605	62,843	64,919	66,390	0.4	20	84.8	82.3	6.9	7.2	3.4	4.6
ROOKS	163	00000	678	5,685	5,354	5,142	-0.8	84	97.1	96.7	1.1	1.2	0.2	0.3
RUSH	165	00000	678	3,551	3,441	3,379	-0.4	61	98.5	98.2	0.3	0.3	0.1	0.2
RUSSELL	167	00000	678	7,370	6,982	6,735	-0.7	78	97.6	97.2	0.5	0.5	0.3	0.5
SALINE	169	41460	678	53,597	54,941	55,898	0.3	23	89.2	86.9	3.1	3.3	1.7	2.4
SCOTT	171	00000	678	5,120	4,812	4,607	-0.9	89	95.5	94.1	0.1	0.1	0.1	0.2
SEDGWICK	173	48620	678	452,869	475,703	492,170	0.7	12	79.4	76.3	9.1	9.4	3.4	4.5
SEWARD	175	30580	678	22,510	23,443	24,066	0.6	14	65.4	60.6	3.8	3.5	2.9	3.5
SHAWNEE	177	45820	605	169,871	174,971	178,563	0.4	20	82.9	80.6	9.0	9.5	1.0	1.3
SHERIDAN	179	00000	678	2,813	2,709	2,643	-0.5	68	98.6	98.3	0.1	0.1	0.2	0.3
SHERMAN	181	00000	678	6,760	6,354	6,071	-0.9	89	93.8	92.1	0.4	0.4	0.4	0.5
SMITH	183	00000	722	4,536	4,212	3,939	-1.0	95	98.8	98.6	0.1	0.1	0.2	0.2
STAFFORD	185	00000	678	4,789	4,445	4,196	-1.0	95	95.0	93.5	0.1	0.2	0.1	0.2
STANTON	187	00000	678	2,406	2,280	2,191	-0.7	78	84.4	80.7	0.6	0.7	0.2	0.2
STEVENS	189	00000	678	5,463	5,492	5,469	0.1	32	83.0	82.2	0.9	0.9	0.3	0.3
SUMNER	191	48620	678	25,946	25,530	25,073	-0.2	42	94.6	93.7	0.7	0.8	0.3	0.4
THOMAS	193	00000	678	8,180	7,724	7,410	-0.8	84	97.1	96.5	0.4	0.5	0.3	0.4
TREGO	195	00000	678	3,319	3,098	2,956	-0.9	89	97.8	97.3	0.2	0.2	0.5	0.7
WABAUNSEE	197	45820	605	6,885	7,158	7,367	0.5	17	97.2	96.8	0.5	0.5	0.2	0.3
WALLACE	199	00000	678	1,749	1,637	1,563	-0.9	89	94.6	93.3	0.6	0.7	0.2	0.2
WASHINGTON	201	00000	605	6,483	6,178	5,982	-0.7	78	98.9	98.8	0.1	0.1	0.0	0.1
WICHITA	203	00000	678	2,531	2,408	2,327	-0.7	78	86.3	82.5	0.1	0.1	0.1	0.2
WILSON	205	00000	603	10,332	10,023	9,827	-0.4	61	96.8	96.2	0.4	0.4	0.3	0.4
WOODSON	207	00000	603	3,788	3,617	3,507	-0.6	72	97.0	96.5	0.8	0.9	0.1	0.1
WYANDOTTE	209	28140	616	157,882	153,668	150,803	-0.4	61	58.2	55.4	28.3	28.1	1.7	2.1
KANSAS							0.6		86.1	84.2	5.7	5.8	1.8	2.5
UNITED STATES							1.2		75.1	72.7	12.3	12.6	3.8	4.5

23-A

COUNTY	% HISPANIC ORIGIN		2007 AGE DISTRIBUTION (%)										MEDIAN AGE	% 2007 Males	% 2007 Females
	2000	2007	0-4	5-9	10-14	15-19	20-24	25-44	45-64	65-84	85+	18+	2007		
RENO	5.7	7.6	6.6	6.3	5.8	6.4	7.7	25.0	26.4	12.8	3.1	77.6	39.3	50.6	49.4
REPUBLIC	0.9	1.3	4.9	4.9	4.2	6.5	6.9	17.7	30.6	18.7	5.6	81.9	47.8	48.7	51.3
RICE	5.6	7.6	6.1	5.5	6.0	8.8	10.6	20.6	24.9	14.3	3.2	78.4	38.3	48.6	51.4
RILEY	4.6	6.1	5.8	4.8	4.2	11.7	24.3	25.6	15.6	6.5	1.6	82.2	24.9	53.4	46.6
ROOKS	1.1	1.5	6.4	5.5	5.8	6.9	7.3	22.4	25.7	15.9	4.0	77.9	42.1	50.1	49.9
RUSH	1.0	1.4	5.2	4.9	5.3	6.1	6.1	20.0	28.9	18.3	5.2	80.9	46.5	49.1	50.9
RUSSELL	0.9	1.2	5.6	5.1	5.5	5.4	7.3	20.6	28.0	18.0	4.6	80.5	45.3	48.7	51.3
SALINE	6.0	8.1	7.0	6.4	6.7	7.2	7.6	25.6	25.7	11.6	2.2	75.7	37.3	49.6	50.4
SCOTT	6.3	8.5	6.3	5.9	6.0	7.1	7.3	22.3	28.7	12.9	3.6	77.5	41.8	49.1	50.9
SEDGWICK	8.0	10.6	8.0	7.4	7.4	7.0	6.9	27.6	24.9	9.2	1.6	73.0	34.6	49.5	50.5
SEWARD	42.1	49.6	9.9	8.7	7.8	7.7	8.8	28.9	19.7	7.1	1.4	69.2	29.2	51.2	48.8
SHAWNEE	7.3	9.6	6.7	6.3	6.3	6.7	7.0	25.6	27.3	11.8	2.2	76.7	38.6	48.5	51.5
SHERIDAN	1.5	2.0	5.4	5.4	5.7	7.6	5.5	21.3	29.1	16.7	3.4	78.7	44.4	51.2	48.8
SHERMAN	8.4	11.3	6.4	6.2	5.7	6.6	8.4	24.6	25.6	13.6	3.0	78.4	38.3	51.8	48.2
SMITH	0.7	1.0	4.7	4.5	4.7	6.1	7.1	18.3	28.6	20.0	6.0	81.8	47.7	49.1	50.9
STAFFORD	5.4	7.3	6.1	5.6	5.6	7.6	7.2	20.4	27.8	15.1	4.5	77.6	43.4	49.7	50.3
STANTON	23.7	30.1	8.8	7.6	6.8	6.4	5.4	28.2	24.1	11.0	1.8	72.7	35.9	51.6	48.4
STEVENS	21.7	22.8	9.1	7.9	7.6	6.7	7.2	25.4	24.1	9.8	2.3	71.2	34.1	49.9	50.1
SUMNER	3.6	4.9	7.1	6.2	6.6	7.3	7.7	22.3	28.0	12.1	2.7	75.4	39.4	49.1	50.9
THOMAS	1.8	2.5	7.0	6.2	6.2	8.4	8.7	23.5	25.3	12.2	2.5	76.9	36.1	48.4	51.6
TREGO	0.8	1.0	5.6	5.2	5.2	5.5	8.2	18.1	29.4	17.9	4.9	80.4	46.0	47.9	52.1
WABAUNSEE	1.9	2.5	6.7	6.3	5.8	6.6	6.9	22.5	30.0	13.0	2.3	77.3	42.0	50.8	49.2
WALLACE	4.8	6.5	6.8	5.1	7.9	5.9	9.5	19.9	28.0	13.8	3.2	76.7	41.6	49.9	50.1
WASHINGTON	0.6	0.9	6.3	6.3	5.3	5.9	6.0	20.1	27.2	17.5	5.3	78.1	45.0	51.0	49.0
WICHITA	18.4	23.8	8.3	8.8	7.3	5.0	5.4	23.6	26.2	12.6	2.9	72.3	37.8	51.5	48.5
WILSON	1.7	2.3	6.0	5.5	6.3	7.2	6.5	22.3	27.5	14.9	3.7	77.7	42.1	48.6	51.4
WOODSON	1.4	1.9	5.3	5.4	3.6	6.2	7.4	21.0	30.3	16.5	4.3	81.8	45.7	49.2	50.8
WYANDOTTE	16.0	20.3	8.3	7.2	7.2	7.1	7.7	27.8	23.4	9.6	1.6	73.1	33.3	48.9	51.1
KANSAS	7.0	8.9	7.2	6.7	6.6	7.3	8.0	26.2	25.3	10.5	2.2	75.3	36.1	49.6	50.4
UNITED STATES	12.5	15.0	6.9	6.5	6.8	7.1	7.0	27.6	25.4	10.7	1.9	75.6	36.7	49.2	50.8

COUNTY	HOUSEHOLDS					FAMILIES			MEDIAN HOUSEHOLD INCOME			
	2000	2007	2012	% Annual Rate 2000-2007	2007 Average HH Size	2000	2007	% Annual Rate 2000-2007	2007	2012	2007 National Rank	2007 State Rank
RENO	25,498	25,338	25,151	-0.1	2.39	17,309	16,970	-0.3	43,693	50,664	1254	34
REPUBLIC	2,557	2,386	2,232	-1.0	2.21	1,685	1,550	-1.1	36,780	41,476	2153	86
RICE	4,050	3,977	3,925	-0.3	2.43	2,832	2,745	-0.4	43,033	49,339	1327	39
RILEY	22,137	23,514	24,395	0.8	2.36	12,262	12,690	0.5	40,391	46,676	1678	57
ROOKS	2,362	2,253	2,173	-0.6	2.29	1,556	1,463	-0.8	35,988	40,282	2278	95
RUSH	1,548	1,516	1,494	-0.3	2.21	1,014	979	-0.5	36,962	41,447	2132	83
RUSSELL	3,207	3,064	2,963	-0.6	2.21	2,021	1,900	-0.8	35,000	39,169	2429	99
SALINE	21,436	22,098	22,520	0.4	2.42	14,211	14,447	0.2	47,314	55,110	884	23
SCOTT	2,045	1,956	1,885	-0.6	2.42	1,435	1,356	-0.8	50,447	57,882	643	10
SEDGWICK	176,444	185,734	192,352	0.7	2.53	117,770	122,250	0.5	53,814	63,375	461	5
SEWARD	7,419	7,575	7,720	0.3	3.04	5,503	5,557	0.1	47,412	55,903	871	22
SHAWNEE	68,920	72,552	74,531	0.7	2.34	44,685	46,347	0.5	51,302	59,855	593	7
SHERIDAN	1,124	1,101	1,081	-0.3	2.42	796	770	-0.5	40,076	45,031	1714	61
SHERMAN	2,758	2,624	2,517	-0.7	2.37	1,783	1,672	-0.9	40,108	45,513	1710	60
SMITH	1,953	1,819	1,700	-1.0	2.26	1,323	1,216	-1.2	33,934	38,203	2557	103
STAFFORD	2,010	1,875	1,771	-1.0	2.33	1,295	1,190	-1.2	37,014	41,408	2124	82
STANTON	858	818	788	-0.7	2.72	638	602	-0.8	47,954	54,080	821	20
STEVENS	1,988	1,987	1,972	0.0	2.73	1,457	1,440	-0.2	50,422	57,399	647	11
SUMNER	9,888	9,808	9,657	-0.1	2.56	7,092	6,951	-0.3	47,966	54,587	819	19
THOMAS	3,226	3,096	2,988	-0.6	2.40	2,126	2,011	-0.8	45,801	53,305	1024	26
TREGO	1,412	1,355	1,307	-0.6	2.21	936	886	-0.8	35,935	40,624	2290	96
WABAUNSEE	2,633	2,765	2,856	0.7	2.55	1,958	2,034	0.5	49,363	54,740	718	12
WALLACE	674	640	615	-0.7	2.52	477	447	-0.9	39,334	44,211	1814	69
WASHINGTON	2,673	2,577	2,506	-0.5	2.32	1,781	1,694	-0.7	35,116	39,684	2415	98
WICHITA	967	939	915	-0.4	2.54	723	696	-0.5	40,756	45,729	1635	54
WILSON	4,203	4,092	4,014	-0.4	2.39	2,848	2,737	-0.5	36,310	41,121	2229	91
WOODSON	1,642	1,593	1,555	-0.4	2.20	1,052	1,006	-0.6	30,827	35,439	2850	105
WYANDOTTE	59,700	57,965	56,821	-0.4	2.62	39,174	37,484	-0.6	42,874	50,501	1344	40
KANSAS				0.7	2.50			0.5	51,343	60,554		
UNITED STATES				1.2	2.59			1.0	53,154	62,503		

INCOME

COUNTY	2007 Per Capita Income	2007 HH Income Base	2007 HOUSEHOLD INCOME DISTRIBUTION (%)					2007 Home Value Base	2007 HOME VALUE DISTRIBUTION (%)					2007 Median Home Value
			Less than $25,000	$25,000 to $49,999	$50,000 to $99,999	$100,000 to $149,999	$150,000 or More		Less than $50,000	$50,000 to $89,999	$90,000 to $174,999	$175,000 to $399,999	$400,000 or More	
RENO	22,989	25,338	24.6	32.3	32.7	6.9	3.4	18,332	20.1	29.0	38.7	11.0	1.3	91,385
REPUBLIC	21,153	2,386	31.9	35.0	26.4	4.1	2.6	1,912	47.3	26.7	20.2	5.0	0.8	54,561
RICE	20,404	3,977	27.1	32.1	32.6	6.1	2.0	3,095	39.6	29.4	23.9	6.6	0.5	62,233
RILEY	21,808	23,514	31.6	27.9	27.8	8.4	4.3	11,468	11.4	13.8	48.7	23.2	2.9	126,466
ROOKS	19,049	2,253	30.4	38.3	26.9	3.1	1.5	1,761	43.3	32.3	19.6	3.8	0.9	57,993
RUSH	21,536	1,516	32.3	32.8	27.8	5.1	1.9	1,250	53.4	25.3	16.6	4.2	0.4	47,296
RUSSELL	21,097	3,064	35.4	30.8	24.4	6.9	2.5	2,344	41.9	29.2	23.6	4.9	0.4	61,881
SALINE	24,045	22,098	21.7	31.4	35.7	7.5	3.8	15,602	9.3	22.2	46.2	20.4	1.9	116,772
SCOTT	27,025	1,956	24.4	25.1	35.1	9.3	6.2	1,487	18.4	28.9	41.5	9.1	2.2	94,939
SEDGWICK	26,374	185,734	19.1	26.7	36.9	11.4	5.8	126,205	14.0	28.9	40.4	14.9	1.9	100,652
SEWARD	18,980	7,575	22.1	30.5	35.2	8.3	3.9	4,984	24.3	27.3	36.1	11.0	1.3	88,137
SHAWNEE	27,021	72,552	20.3	28.2	35.7	11.1	4.7	50,180	13.3	25.0	43.7	16.6	1.4	108,170
SHERIDAN	20,387	1,101	28.2	37.2	27.3	4.3	2.9	915	32.1	24.3	36.4	6.3	0.9	79,914
SHERMAN	21,027	2,624	27.8	34.3	29.2	7.0	1.7	1,855	20.4	31.3	37.5	9.4	1.3	88,409
SMITH	18,446	1,819	32.9	34.2	28.2	4.3	0.4	1,464	43.0	28.2	23.8	4.1	0.9	56,867
STAFFORD	19,570	1,875	30.4	36.3	27.8	4.0	1.5	1,477	46.6	27.6	21.5	3.7	0.6	53,613
STANTON	23,067	818	22.7	29.5	35.2	7.5	5.1	567	25.6	23.8	39.0	11.6	0.0	90,875
STEVENS	22,488	1,987	18.5	31.1	38.6	8.2	3.7	1,533	20.1	22.4	37.8	17.7	2.0	98,191
SUMNER	21,870	9,808	23.1	29.3	36.0	9.1	2.5	7,638	24.4	30.0	36.5	8.5	0.6	84,214
THOMAS	24,230	3,096	23.0	30.9	32.1	9.9	4.1	2,194	14.1	22.2	48.5	13.8	1.5	107,403
TREGO	20,546	1,355	33.7	29.8	30.1	4.8	1.6	1,111	36.8	26.3	31.7	4.3	0.9	68,038
WABAUNSEE	21,626	2,765	20.1	30.6	40.6	6.8	1.8	2,321	17.4	26.3	39.3	16.4	0.6	99,702
WALLACE	21,437	640	29.5	32.5	27.0	6.6	4.4	505	38.6	32.3	25.3	3.2	0.6	62,411
WASHINGTON	18,642	2,577	31.6	38.3	25.0	3.6	1.6	2,074	46.8	27.7	21.2	3.6	0.7	53,545
WICHITA	20,940	939	27.6	32.3	29.7	6.8	3.6	715	35.4	26.0	31.9	5.9	0.8	72,451
WILSON	18,407	4,092	34.0	32.4	27.8	4.1	1.7	3,228	41.2	30.5	23.3	4.5	0.5	58,304
WOODSON	18,103	1,593	38.4	35.6	20.1	4.6	1.3	1,308	44.7	27.2	22.2	4.9	0.9	58,961
WYANDOTTE	20,078	57,957	27.2	30.4	31.6	8.0	2.7	37,262	26.8	36.5	30.4	5.6	0.7	73,849
KANSAS	26,438		20.9	27.6	34.5	10.6	6.4		16.9	21.4	36.0	22.2	3.5	112,948
UNITED STATES	27,916		21.9	25.0	32.3	12.3	8.4		7.9	10.5	27.1	35.6	19.0	192,285

SPENDING POTENTIAL INDICES

COUNTY	FINANCIAL SERVICES				THE HOME						ENTERTAINMENT						PERSONAL			
					Home Improvements		Furnishings													
	Auto Loan	Home Loan	Invest-ments	Retire-ment Plans	Home Repair	Lawn & Garden	Comput-ers & Hard-ware	Major Appli-ances	TV, Radio, Sound Equip-ment	Furni-ture	Dine out/ Carry out	Sports Equip-ment	Fees & Tickets	Toys & Games	Travel	Cable TV	Apparel & Services	Auto Repairs	Health Insur-ance	Pets & Supplies
RENO	81	73	74	74	76	84	75	79	78	73	77	69	72	80	75	81	68	77	85	81
REPUBLIC	78	56	40	54	65	86	59	74	65	56	65	65	50	69	59	70	55	68	82	80
RICE	81	61	50	60	69	88	65	78	72	61	70	68	57	74	65	77	60	72	88	82
RILEY	77	58	61	63	55	61	88	68	80	72	81	68	73	78	72	75	72	77	68	70
ROOKS	72	51	38	49	58	77	56	68	63	51	61	60	47	65	55	68	52	63	78	72
RUSH	79	55	40	54	63	85	61	75	69	56	67	66	51	71	60	74	56	69	86	79
RUSSELL	77	54	41	53	62	82	60	73	68	55	65	64	50	70	59	73	55	67	84	77
SALINE	82	79	87	81	78	80	81	80	83	80	81	71	81	84	81	83	73	80	84	80
SCOTT	105	82	67	81	91	113	86	102	91	81	90	90	76	94	86	95	77	94	109	107
SEDGWICK	94	91	96	93	88	88	93	89	94	93	93	81	92	95	91	93	84	91	92	90
SEWARD	85	77	70	76	73	75	80	79	80	79	81	76	76	81	77	79	72	82	78	78
SHAWNEE	87	87	97	89	86	86	88	86	90	88	88	77	89	90	89	90	80	87	90	86
SHERIDAN	90	57	25	54	70	101	60	84	66	57	68	75	47	74	59	72	56	74	88	94
SHERMAN	79	60	52	60	65	81	66	75	71	61	70	66	58	73	65	75	60	71	83	78
SMITH	70	48	32	47	56	76	53	66	59	49	58	59	52	62	63	70	49	61	75	71
STAFFORD	76	53	38	51	61	82	58	72	65	53	63	63	48	68	57	70	54	66	82	76
STANTON	114	73	31	69	89	129	77	107	85	73	86	96	59	94	75	92	72	95	113	119
STEVENS	101	77	57	75	84	107	79	95	85	76	85	84	69	90	78	90	73	88	102	101
SUMNER	85	72	69	72	77	89	74	82	80	71	77	72	69	82	75	83	67	78	91	85
THOMAS	93	72	63	73	78	96	79	89	82	74	81	79	70	85	77	85	70	85	94	93
TREGO	75	55	40	53	64	84	57	72	63	55	63	63	49	67	58	68	53	66	80	78
WABAUNSEE	91	70	51	69	78	99	70	87	76	68	75	77	62	80	70	80	65	79	92	93
WALLACE	98	62	27	59	77	110	66	92	73	63	74	82	51	81	65	79	62	81	97	102
WASHINGTON	75	50	29	48	59	83	54	71	60	50	60	63	44	64	53	65	50	64	78	77
WICHITA	95	62	29	59	75	107	65	89	72	62	73	79	51	78	64	78	61	79	94	99
WILSON	71	52	43	51	58	75	57	67	63	53	61	59	49	65	56	67	53	63	75	71
WOODSON	64	48	38	46	54	70	51	62	57	48	55	54	44	57	52	61	47	58	71	65
WYANDOTTE	73	67	75	69	64	67	73	68	76	71	75	60	71	76	70	77	67	72	74	69
KANSAS	97	89	88	90	89	95	92	93	93	90	93	84	88	95	90	94	82	93	97	95
UNITED STATES	100	100	100	100	100	100	100	100	100	100	100	100	100	100	100	100	100	100	100	100

COUNTY	FIPS Code	CBSA Code	DMA Code	POPULATION			2000-2007 ANNUAL RATE		RACE (%)					
									White		Black		Asian/Pacific	
				2000	2007	2012	% Rate	State Rank	2000	2007	2000	2007	2000	2007
ADAIR	001	00000	529	17,244	17,294	17,292	0.0	94	96.0	95.9	2.6	2.6	0.3	0.3
ALLEN	003	00000	659	17,800	18,626	19,171	0.6	44	97.6	97.2	1.1	1.1	0.1	0.2
ANDERSON	005	23180	541	19,111	21,507	23,170	1.6	14	96.5	96.2	2.3	2.5	0.1	0.2
BALLARD	007	37140	632	8,286	8,453	8,558	0.3	70	95.3	94.8	2.9	3.0	0.2	0.3
BARREN	009	23980	736	38,033	39,904	40,999	0.7	37	94.3	93.6	4.1	4.3	0.4	0.6
BATH	011	34660	541	11,085	11,782	12,221	0.8	31	96.9	96.5	1.8	2.0	0.0	0.0
BELL	013	33180	557	30,060	29,530	29,183	-0.2	108	96.0	95.5	2.4	2.5	0.4	0.6
BOONE	015	17140	515	85,991	115,147	141,000	4.1	2	95.2	94.0	1.5	1.6	1.3	1.9
BOURBON	017	30460	541	19,360	19,906	20,283	0.4	61	90.4	89.3	6.9	7.2	0.1	0.2
BOYD	019	26580	564	49,752	48,448	47,404	-0.4	116	96.0	95.5	2.5	2.7	0.3	0.4
BOYLE	021	19220	541	27,697	28,594	29,250	0.4	61	87.8	86.7	9.7	10.1	0.6	0.8
BRACKEN	023	17140	515	8,279	8,773	9,093	0.8	31	98.5	98.2	0.6	0.6	0.1	0.1
BREATHITT	025	00000	541	16,100	16,051	16,006	0.0	94	98.7	98.7	0.4	0.4	0.3	0.3
BRECKINRIDGE	027	00000	529	18,648	19,284	19,692	0.5	51	95.8	95.4	2.9	3.0	0.1	0.1
BULLITT	029	31140	529	61,236	72,968	82,273	2.4	7	98.1	97.7	0.4	0.4	0.3	0.4
BUTLER	031	00000	736	13,010	13,646	14,086	0.7	37	97.9	97.4	0.5	0.5	0.2	0.2
CALDWELL	033	00000	632	13,060	12,797	12,584	-0.3	112	93.9	93.3	4.8	5.1	0.2	0.2
CALLOWAY	035	34660	632	34,177	35,186	35,897	0.4	61	93.5	92.4	3.6	3.7	1.4	2.0
CAMPBELL	037	17140	515	88,616	88,004	86,850	-0.1	102	96.6	96.1	1.6	1.7	0.6	0.8
CARLISLE	039	00000	632	5,351	5,290	5,244	-0.2	108	97.8	97.7	1.0	1.0	0.1	0.1
CARROLL	041	00000	529	10,155	10,456	10,616	0.4	61	95.2	94.1	1.9	2.0	0.2	0.3
CARTER	043	00000	564	26,889	27,639	28,136	0.4	61	99.0	98.8	0.1	0.1	0.1	0.2
CASEY	045	00000	541	15,447	16,189	16,705	0.6	44	98.3	97.9	0.3	0.3	0.1	0.2
CHRISTIAN	047	17300	659	72,265	71,880	71,145	-0.1	102	69.9	67.8	23.7	24.1	1.2	1.7
CLARK	049	30460	541	33,144	36,015	38,048	1.2	20	93.6	92.9	4.8	5.0	0.2	0.3
CLAY	051	00000	541	24,556	24,598	24,453	0.0	94	93.9	93.8	4.8	4.9	0.1	0.1
CLINTON	053	00000	659	9,634	9,687	9,654	0.1	85	99.1	99.1	0.1	0.1	0.2	0.2
CRITTENDEN	055	00000	632	9,384	9,044	8,743	-0.5	117	98.2	98.0	0.7	0.7	0.1	0.1
CUMBERLAND	057	00000	659	7,147	7,161	7,161	0.0	94	95.3	95.2	3.4	3.5	0.1	0.1
DAVIESS	059	36980	649	91,545	94,206	95,440	0.4	61	93.7	93.0	4.3	4.6	0.4	0.6
EDMONSON	061	14540	736	11,644	11,858	11,983	0.3	70	98.4	98.2	0.6	0.6	0.1	0.1
ELLIOTT	063	00000	564	6,748	6,853	6,926	0.2	78	99.0	98.9	0.0	0.0	0.0	0.0
ESTILL	065	00000	541	15,307	15,012	14,752	-0.3	112	99.1	98.9	0.1	0.1	0.0	0.1
FAYETTE	067	30460	541	260,512	280,854	293,566	1.0	25	81.0	79.0	13.5	13.8	2.5	3.5
FLEMING	069	00000	541	13,792	14,575	15,046	0.8	31	97.3	97.0	1.4	1.5	0.2	0.2
FLOYD	071	00000	564	42,441	42,226	41,926	-0.1	102	97.7	97.4	1.3	1.4	0.3	0.5
FRANKLIN	073	23180	541	47,687	48,310	48,613	0.2	78	88.0	86.9	9.4	9.8	0.7	1.1
FULTON	075	46460	632	7,752	7,038	6,576	-1.3	120	75.1	73.9	23.2	24.1	0.3	0.4
GALLATIN	077	17140	515	7,870	8,572	9,069	1.2	20	96.7	96.2	1.6	1.7	0.2	0.3
GARRARD	079	00000	541	14,792	16,388	17,563	1.4	16	95.7	95.3	3.1	3.2	0.0	0.1
GRANT	081	17140	515	22,384	25,384	27,606	1.7	12	98.3	97.9	0.3	0.3	0.3	0.5
GRAVES	083	32460	632	37,028	36,564	36,167	-0.2	108	92.7	91.6	4.4	4.6	0.2	0.3
GRAYSON	085	00000	529	24,053	25,034	25,720	0.6	44	98.3	97.9	0.5	0.5	0.1	0.2
GREEN	087	00000	529	11,518	11,519	11,435	0.0	94	96.2	96.1	2.6	2.7	0.1	0.1
GREENUP	089	26580	564	36,891	37,373	37,726	0.2	78	98.1	97.7	0.6	0.6	0.4	0.6
HANCOCK	091	36980	649	8,392	8,689	8,911	0.5	51	98.0	97.7	0.8	0.9	0.2	0.2
HARDIN	093	21060	529	94,174	99,743	103,829	0.8	31	82.0	79.9	11.9	12.2	2.0	2.9
HARLAN	095	00000	557	33,202	31,710	30,798	-0.6	119	95.6	95.1	2.6	2.8	0.3	0.4
HARRISON	097	00000	541	17,983	18,683	19,029	0.5	51	95.6	95.0	2.5	2.6	0.2	0.2
HART	099	00000	736	17,445	18,920	19,891	1.1	22	92.6	92.0	6.2	6.5	0.1	0.2
HENDERSON	101	21780	649	44,829	45,757	46,419	0.3	70	91.2	90.4	7.1	7.4	0.3	0.5
HENRY	103	31140	529	15,060	16,308	17,106	1.1	22	94.0	92.9	3.3	3.4	0.4	0.5
HICKMAN	105	00000	632	5,262	5,031	4,849	-0.6	119	88.4	87.5	9.9	10.4	0.1	0.1
HOPKINS	107	31580	649	46,519	46,186	45,958	-0.1	102	92.0	91.3	6.2	6.5	0.4	0.5
JACKSON	109	00000	541	13,495	14,031	14,327	0.5	51	99.2	99.0	0.1	0.1	0.0	0.0
JEFFERSON	111	31140	529	693,604	715,196	730,287	0.4	61	77.4	75.7	18.9	19.5	1.4	2.0
JESSAMINE	113	30460	541	39,041	46,661	53,002	2.5	6	94.4	93.6	3.1	3.3	0.6	0.9
JOHNSON	115	00000	564	23,445	23,767	24,028	0.2	78	98.6	98.4	0.3	0.3	0.3	0.4
KENTON	117	17140	515	151,464	155,991	159,179	0.4	61	94.0	93.2	3.8	4.0	0.6	0.9
KNOTT	119	00000	541	17,649	17,609	17,536	0.0	94	98.3	98.3	0.7	0.7	0.2	0.2
KNOX	121	00000	541	31,795	32,909	33,661	0.5	51	97.8	97.5	0.8	0.9	0.2	0.3
LARUE	123	21060	529	13,373	13,906	14,263	0.5	51	94.6	94.1	3.5	3.7	0.2	0.3
LAUREL	125	30940	541	52,715	56,455	59,228	0.9	28	97.7	97.3	0.6	0.7	0.4	0.5
LAWRENCE	127	00000	564	15,569	16,203	16,499	0.6	44	98.9	98.8	0.1	0.1	0.1	0.1
LEE	129	00000	541	7,916	7,832	7,691	-0.1	102	95.1	95.0	3.8	3.9	0.1	0.1
LESLIE	131	00000	531	12,401	12,060	11,856	-0.4	116	99.2	99.0	0.1	0.1	0.1	0.2
LETCHER	133	00000	531	25,277	24,847	24,508	-0.2	108	98.7	98.5	0.5	0.5	0.3	0.4
LEWIS	135	32500	564	14,092	14,135	14,157	0.0	94	98.9	98.9	0.2	0.2	0.0	0.0
LINCOLN	137	19220	541	23,361	25,653	27,121	1.3	18	96.1	95.6	2.5	2.7	0.1	0.1
LIVINGSTON	139	37140	632	9,804	9,771	9,743	0.0	94	98.5	98.5	0.1	0.1	0.0	0.0
LOGAN	141	00000	659	26,573	26,840	27,025	0.1	85	90.7	89.9	7.6	8.0	0.2	0.3
LYON	143	00000	632	8,080	8,371	8,566	0.5	51	91.9	91.1	6.7	7.0	0.2	0.3
MCCRACKEN	145	37140	632	65,514	63,880	62,791	-0.3	112	86.8	85.7	10.9	11.3	0.6	0.8
MCCREARY	147	00000	557	17,080	19,382	19,767	1.8	10	98.0	97.7	0.6	0.7	0.0	0.0
MCLEAN	149	36980	649	9,938	10,046	10,118	0.1	85	98.6	98.3	0.4	0.4	0.1	0.1
MADISON	151	40080	541	70,872	79,996	87,170	1.7	12	93.0	92.1	4.4	4.7	0.7	1.1
MAGOFFIN	153	00000	541	13,332	13,580	13,707	0.3	70	99.3	99.2	0.2	0.2	0.1	0.1
KENTUCKY							0.7		90.1	89.2	7.3	7.5	0.8	1.1
UNITED STATES							1.2		75.1	72.7	12.3	12.6	3.8	4.5

POPULATION COMPOSITION

COUNTY	% HISPANIC ORIGIN 2000	% HISPANIC ORIGIN 2007	2007 AGE DISTRIBUTION (%) 0-4	5-9	10-14	15-19	20-24	25-44	45-64	65-84	85+	18+	MEDIAN AGE 2007	% 2007 Males	% 2007 Females
ADAIR	0.8	0.8	6.3	6.1	5.9	6.9	7.1	26.8	25.8	13.2	1.9	78.2	38.7	48.7	51.3
ALLEN	0.8	1.2	7.0	6.5	6.8	5.9	6.0	28.2	25.6	12.2	1.7	76.1	37.8	49.4	50.6
ANDERSON	0.8	1.2	7.5	7.6	7.4	6.1	4.4	30.6	25.7	9.2	1.4	73.5	37.1	49.2	50.8
BALLARD	0.6	0.9	6.0	6.3	5.3	5.7	4.8	26.0	29.7	13.7	2.5	78.9	42.1	49.8	50.2
BARREN	0.9	1.4	6.6	6.3	6.3	5.5	6.1	26.6	27.3	13.1	2.2	77.5	40.0	48.6	51.4
BATH	0.8	1.2	6.8	6.8	6.3	5.4	4.8	28.2	27.6	12.2	2.1	76.9	39.6	49.4	50.6
BELL	0.6	1.0	6.2	6.1	5.7	6.2	6.0	27.6	28.0	12.5	1.8	78.2	39.8	48.2	51.8
BOONE	2.0	2.9	8.2	7.7	7.9	6.6	6.4	30.5	24.5	7.3	0.8	72.1	34.4	49.3	50.7
BOURBON	2.6	3.8	6.5	6.1	6.4	6.5	6.0	27.1	27.0	12.4	2.0	77.0	39.8	48.8	51.2
BOYD	1.1	1.7	5.4	5.2	5.4	5.3	5.8	27.0	29.0	14.8	2.0	80.7	42.0	49.4	50.6
BOYLE	1.4	2.1	5.4	5.3	6.5	6.9	8.1	25.9	27.3	12.4	2.1	79.2	39.1	49.7	50.3
BRACKEN	0.5	0.7	6.8	6.9	6.2	6.2	5.6	28.1	26.6	11.9	1.6	76.4	38.5	49.9	50.1
BREATHITT	0.7	0.7	5.9	6.3	6.6	6.6	6.4	27.5	28.3	11.1	1.5	77.2	38.8	49.6	50.4
BRECKINRIDGE	0.7	1.0	6.3	6.5	5.8	6.1	6.0	25.8	28.4	13.5	1.6	77.7	40.7	49.6	50.4
BULLITT	0.6	0.9	7.3	7.2	7.1	6.2	5.5	30.0	27.6	8.6	0.6	74.7	37.2	49.8	50.2
BUTLER	1.0	1.5	6.6	6.4	5.8	6.5	6.2	29.1	26.4	11.4	1.6	77.2	38.1	49.8	50.2
CALDWELL	0.6	0.9	5.6	5.4	5.8	5.4	5.4	24.2	29.8	15.6	2.8	79.9	43.7	48.4	51.6
CALLOWAY	1.4	2.0	5.0	4.7	4.5	8.2	13.1	24.6	24.3	13.2	2.4	83.0	36.4	48.4	51.6
CAMPBELL	0.9	1.3	7.0	6.5	6.1	7.2	7.0	28.3	25.0	11.1	1.8	76.4	36.7	48.4	51.6
CARLISLE	0.8	0.8	6.2	6.4	5.7	5.3	7.0	25.7	26.5	14.6	2.6	78.6	40.5	48.4	51.6
CARROLL	3.2	4.8	7.0	6.4	6.5	5.6	6.7	29.0	26.4	11.0	1.4	76.6	37.6	50.4	49.6
CARTER	0.6	0.9	6.6	6.2	6.8	5.8	6.1	28.5	26.8	11.7	1.6	77.1	38.1	49.3	50.7
CASEY	1.3	1.9	6.5	6.4	6.2	5.9	5.5	26.8	27.4	13.4	1.8	77.4	40.0	49.4	50.6
CHRISTIAN	4.8	6.8	10.2	7.9	6.4	6.4	11.8	29.5	17.7	8.6	1.5	72.9	28.5	51.8	48.2
CLARK	1.2	1.8	6.6	6.1	6.4	6.3	5.9	28.3	27.9	11.2	1.5	76.9	38.9	48.5	51.5
CLAY	1.4	1.4	5.7	5.6	7.0	6.4	5.6	31.9	26.4	10.2	1.2	77.6	37.6	52.9	47.1
CLINTON	1.2	1.2	6.6	6.5	5.8	4.8	4.4	27.3	28.3	14.4	1.9	78.3	41.3	48.5	51.5
CRITTENDEN	0.5	0.8	5.7	5.3	5.7	5.9	5.7	25.2	29.4	14.6	2.5	79.6	42.6	48.4	51.6
CUMBERLAND	0.6	0.6	6.1	5.7	6.0	5.5	6.0	25.1	27.5	15.6	2.4	78.8	42.2	48.7	51.3
DAVIESS	0.9	1.4	6.9	6.5	6.3	6.7	6.9	26.2	26.4	12.0	2.1	76.3	38.2	48.3	51.7
EDMONSON	0.6	0.8	6.3	6.0	5.6	5.8	5.4	27.9	28.0	13.2	1.8	78.5	40.4	49.6	50.4
ELLIOTT	0.6	0.9	6.7	6.3	6.2	5.9	5.4	27.0	28.1	12.4	2.1	77.3	39.7	49.3	50.7
ESTILL	0.5	0.8	6.3	5.9	6.6	5.3	5.6	29.8	26.4	12.3	1.7	78.0	39.2	48.8	51.2
FAYETTE	3.3	4.8	6.1	6.0	5.7	6.8	8.4	32.8	24.1	8.8	1.4	79.0	34.5	49.2	50.8
FLEMING	0.7	1.1	6.8	6.7	6.8	5.7	5.8	28.3	26.9	11.3	1.7	76.2	38.1	49.6	50.4
FLOYD	0.6	0.9	5.9	6.0	5.7	5.5	6.0	29.1	29.0	11.2	1.5	78.9	39.5	49.5	50.5
FRANKLIN	1.1	1.6	5.9	5.8	5.8	6.5	6.6	28.1	28.4	11.4	1.6	79.0	39.3	48.6	51.4
FULTON	0.7	1.0	6.8	6.5	5.6	6.3	7.7	24.6	26.2	13.7	2.7	77.3	39.5	47.4	52.6
GALLATIN	1.0	1.5	7.6	7.2	8.0	6.8	5.4	28.3	26.2	9.1	1.4	73.0	36.6	49.9	50.1
GARRARD	1.3	2.0	6.2	6.3	6.5	6.0	5.3	28.9	27.6	11.7	1.6	77.5	39.8	49.5	50.5
GRANT	1.0	1.5	8.4	7.9	7.0	6.7	6.4	30.4	23.8	8.3	1.1	72.5	34.1	49.7	50.3
GRAVES	2.4	3.6	6.8	6.7	6.1	6.0	5.8	26.5	26.6	12.9	2.6	76.7	39.7	49.2	50.8
GRAYSON	0.8	1.2	6.5	6.1	6.6	5.7	5.8	27.5	27.4	12.9	1.6	77.5	39.1	49.7	50.3
GREEN	0.9	1.0	5.5	5.2	5.6	5.8	5.4	26.5	28.8	14.6	2.6	80.0	42.5	49.6	50.4
GREENUP	0.6	0.8	5.8	5.7	6.1	5.6	5.5	25.8	29.3	14.6	1.7	78.9	41.8	48.3	51.7
HANCOCK	0.8	1.2	7.4	7.0	6.9	6.6	5.1	28.3	26.8	10.6	1.2	74.7	37.4	49.3	50.7
HARDIN	3.4	4.8	7.2	6.7	6.6	7.5	8.3	28.2	24.8	9.5	1.2	75.2	35.0	50.5	49.5
HARLAN	0.7	1.0	6.1	6.1	6.3	5.9	6.1	25.5	29.7	12.3	1.9	77.9	40.7	48.1	51.9
HARRISON	1.2	1.7	6.4	6.2	6.6	5.7	5.9	27.8	28.1	11.2	2.1	77.4	39.3	49.1	50.9
HART	0.9	1.3	6.9	6.5	6.5	5.9	6.0	27.5	26.5	12.4	1.7	76.4	38.9	49.7	50.3
HENDERSON	1.0	1.4	6.4	6.3	6.2	6.0	6.7	27.2	28.2	11.3	1.7	77.5	39.2	48.8	51.2
HENRY	2.3	3.3	7.0	6.8	6.5	6.1	5.5	27.1	28.3	11.2	1.7	76.1	39.2	50.1	49.9
HICKMAN	1.0	1.5	5.5	5.6	5.5	5.4	5.1	25.5	27.8	16.3	3.3	80.0	43.2	47.9	52.1
HOPKINS	0.9	1.4	6.1	6.0	6.1	6.2	5.6	26.3	28.6	12.9	2.4	78.1	40.3	47.9	52.1
JACKSON	0.5	0.8	6.8	6.6	6.5	6.1	5.5	29.8	25.9	11.4	1.4	76.3	37.5	49.7	50.3
JEFFERSON	1.8	2.6	6.6	6.5	6.6	6.3	6.1	27.5	26.8	11.6	2.0	76.6	38.5	48.0	52.0
JESSAMINE	1.3	2.0	7.3	6.8	7.0	7.8	7.9	28.2	24.8	8.8	1.2	74.4	34.1	49.3	50.7
JOHNSON	0.6	0.9	6.1	6.4	5.5	5.5	5.8	27.3	29.7	12.3	1.5	78.7	40.4	48.4	51.6
KENTON	1.1	1.6	7.4	6.8	6.5	6.6	6.4	29.5	25.6	9.7	1.5	75.3	36.1	49.3	50.7
KNOTT	0.6	0.6	6.1	5.8	6.4	6.4	6.7	27.1	29.4	10.5	1.5	78.3	39.4	49.9	50.1
KNOX	0.6	0.8	7.2	6.9	6.7	6.1	5.9	27.4	26.4	11.5	1.9	75.7	37.8	48.8	51.2
LARUE	1.0	1.6	6.6	6.3	5.9	6.1	5.9	26.4	27.7	13.0	2.1	77.4	40.5	48.8	51.2
LAUREL	0.6	0.8	7.2	7.2	6.4	5.6	5.4	29.4	27.0	10.6	1.3	75.9	37.6	49.2	50.8
LAWRENCE	0.4	0.6	6.0	5.3	6.4	5.8	6.3	27.9	28.9	12.1	1.4	78.7	39.6	49.7	50.3
LEE	0.4	0.4	5.3	5.0	5.0	6.4	7.4	28.8	27.1	12.9	1.9	80.8	39.9	51.9	48.1
LESLIE	0.6	0.9	6.1	6.3	5.7	5.7	5.2	28.9	29.0	11.8	1.4	78.4	40.2	49.1	50.9
LETCHER	0.4	0.7	5.7	5.9	6.0	5.9	6.3	27.1	30.0	11.6	1.6	78.9	40.6	49.3	50.7
LEWIS	0.4	0.4	6.7	6.2	6.7	5.6	5.7	29.4	26.7	11.4	1.6	77.1	38.4	49.9	50.1
LINCOLN	0.9	1.3	6.9	6.7	6.5	6.3	5.7	28.9	25.4	12.0	1.5	75.9	38.0	49.2	50.8
LIVINGSTON	0.8	0.8	5.4	5.3	5.6	5.3	4.7	27.1	30.5	14.1	2.1	80.5	42.9	49.6	50.4
LOGAN	1.1	1.6	7.2	6.9	6.7	5.6	6.0	28.0	26.1	11.5	1.9	75.7	38.2	48.7	51.3
LYON	0.7	1.1	3.9	3.5	4.3	4.0	5.5	29.9	29.4	16.9	2.6	85.9	44.3	56.8	43.2
MCCRACKEN	1.1	1.6	6.0	5.8	6.4	5.8	5.5	25.7	29.0	13.2	2.6	78.3	41.5	47.8	52.2
MCCREARY	0.6	0.9	6.2	6.2	6.0	7.1	6.6	31.4	25.6	9.9	1.0	77.1	36.4	53.5	46.5
MCLEAN	0.8	1.3	6.6	6.7	5.7	5.4	5.4	26.9	28.4	12.9	2.0	77.8	40.4	49.5	50.6
MADISON	1.0	1.4	6.5	5.9	5.7	8.0	9.6	31.6	22.8	8.7	1.2	78.8	32.4	48.8	51.2
MAGOFFIN	0.4	0.6	7.3	6.9	6.0	5.7	5.9	30.0	26.6	10.1	1.5	76.4	37.7	49.4	50.6
KENTUCKY	1.5	2.2	6.6	6.4	6.3	6.4	6.6	28.3	26.5	11.1	1.7	77.0	37.7	49.2	50.8
UNITED STATES	12.5	15.0	6.9	6.5	6.8	7.1	7.0	27.6	25.4	10.7	1.9	75.6	36.7	49.2	50.8

COUNTY	HOUSEHOLDS					FAMILIES			MEDIAN HOUSEHOLD INCOME			
	2000	2007	2012	% Annual Rate 2000-2007	2007 Average HH Size	2000	2007	% Annual Rate 2000-2007	2007	2012	2007 National Rank	2007 State Rank
ADAIR	6,747	6,961	7,030	0.4	2.38	4,801	4,786	0.0	29,771	34,299	2923	87
ALLEN	6,910	7,353	7,601	0.9	2.51	5,110	5,272	0.4	37,682	43,339	2035	58
ANDERSON	7,320	8,405	9,110	1.9	2.54	5,526	6,161	1.5	55,128	63,938	404	8
BALLARD	3,395	3,527	3,588	0.5	2.35	2,415	2,423	0.0	39,521	45,531	1776	48
BARREN	15,346	16,516	17,117	1.0	2.38	10,939	11,374	0.5	38,800	45,361	1878	51
BATH	4,445	4,872	5,112	1.3	2.39	3,194	3,383	0.8	31,371	35,780	2805	81
BELL	12,004	12,307	12,337	0.3	2.34	8,522	8,437	-0.1	23,621	27,001	3105	109
BOONE	31,258	42,792	52,844	4.4	2.68	23,435	31,132	4.0	72,465	87,163	106	2
BOURBON	7,681	8,130	8,371	0.8	2.42	5,448	5,567	0.3	43,390	50,796	1287	34
BOYD	20,010	19,877	19,610	-0.1	2.32	14,111	13,531	-0.6	41,517	48,574	1516	39
BOYLE	10,574	11,245	11,635	0.9	2.32	7,345	7,529	0.3	44,322	51,734	1178	29
BRACKEN	3,228	3,517	3,681	1.2	2.48	2,346	2,474	0.7	42,046	47,973	1444	38
BREATHITT	6,170	6,403	6,478	0.5	2.44	4,541	4,566	0.1	23,299	26,272	3110	110
BRECKINRIDGE	7,324	7,783	8,024	0.8	2.44	5,307	5,457	0.4	37,321	43,041	2090	61
BULLITT	22,171	27,254	31,146	2.9	2.67	17,745	21,296	2.5	54,482	61,981	423	9
BUTLER	5,059	5,449	5,678	1.0	2.46	3,709	3,868	0.6	36,361	41,959	2221	65
CALDWELL	5,431	5,454	5,406	0.1	2.30	3,801	3,682	-0.4	35,361	41,219	2387	70
CALLOWAY	13,862	14,671	15,122	0.8	2.19	8,594	8,691	0.2	37,925	45,000	2006	57
CAMPBELL	34,742	35,560	35,508	0.3	2.42	23,093	22,702	-0.2	54,368	64,787	429	10
CARLISLE	2,208	2,234	2,231	0.2	2.34	1,575	1,540	-0.3	36,866	42,958	2146	62
CARROLL	3,940	4,156	4,254	0.7	2.46	2,723	2,767	0.2	45,403	52,923	1064	23
CARTER	10,342	11,040	11,408	0.9	2.45	7,741	8,016	0.5	32,293	36,690	2733	79
CASEY	6,260	6,776	7,078	1.1	2.36	4,421	4,621	0.6	26,396	30,152	3058	100
CHRISTIAN	24,857	25,429	25,317	0.3	2.59	18,350	18,190	-0.1	39,341	45,997	1811	50
CLARK	13,015	14,590	15,595	1.6	2.44	9,548	10,363	1.1	50,175	57,979	664	15
CLAY	8,556	8,992	9,064	0.7	2.49	6,440	6,569	0.3	19,622	21,922	3136	119
CLINTON	4,086	4,257	4,301	0.6	2.26	2,811	2,822	0.1	23,810	27,411	3103	108
CRITTENDEN	3,829	3,760	3,654	-0.3	2.37	2,706	2,564	-0.7	35,819	41,079	2310	68
CUMBERLAND	2,976	3,058	3,085	0.4	2.31	2,040	2,019	-0.1	26,783	30,799	3044	97
DAVIESS	36,033	38,399	39,306	0.9	2.39	24,828	25,489	0.4	46,793	54,889	927	20
EDMONSON	4,648	4,895	5,011	0.7	2.39	3,461	3,534	0.3	30,928	35,356	2839	83
ELLIOTT	2,638	2,791	2,862	0.8	2.43	1,926	1,973	0.3	24,740	28,008	3096	105
ESTILL	6,108	6,229	6,210	0.3	2.39	4,432	4,372	-0.2	28,406	32,781	2983	90
FAYETTE	108,288	119,608	126,214	1.4	2.24	62,955	66,149	0.7	52,190	62,563	535	11
FLEMING	5,367	5,795	6,022	1.1	2.49	3,965	4,150	0.6	34,645	39,937	2479	72
FLOYD	16,881	17,637	17,765	0.6	2.34	12,267	12,403	0.2	25,615	29,357	3081	102
FRANKLIN	19,907	20,793	21,161	0.6	2.24	12,839	12,854	0.0	51,008	60,295	616	14
FULTON	3,237	3,004	2,824	-1.0	2.26	2,115	1,883	-1.6	30,867	36,325	2846	85
GALLATIN	2,902	3,230	3,441	1.5	2.62	2,136	2,304	1.0	44,089	50,243	1197	30
GARRARD	5,741	6,456	6,943	1.6	2.52	4,336	4,734	1.2	42,558	49,144	1389	37
GRANT	8,175	9,453	10,340	2.0	2.67	6,219	6,988	1.6	47,949	55,338	823	16
GRAVES	14,841	14,862	14,743	0.0	2.41	10,562	10,215	-0.5	38,317	44,861	1960	55
GRAYSON	9,596	10,283	10,678	1.0	2.40	6,966	7,224	0.5	34,241	39,350	2522	75
GREEN	4,706	4,811	4,809	0.3	2.36	3,379	3,340	-0.2	31,401	36,272	2804	80
GREENUP	14,536	15,272	15,640	0.7	2.42	11,026	11,249	0.3	40,943	47,919	1609	41
HANCOCK	3,215	3,450	3,588	1.0	2.50	2,436	2,539	0.6	44,972	50,978	1113	26
HARDIN	34,497	37,960	40,073	1.3	2.52	25,347	27,013	0.9	47,503	55,484	862	18
HARLAN	13,291	13,266	13,068	0.0	2.36	9,446	9,107	-0.5	22,758	26,318	3119	114
HARRISON	7,012	7,454	7,648	0.8	2.47	5,065	5,209	0.4	44,619	51,312	1143	27
HART	6,769	7,471	7,892	1.4	2.50	4,811	5,128	0.9	30,964	35,949	2835	82
HENDERSON	18,095	19,015	19,496	0.7	2.36	12,570	12,731	0.2	44,501	51,914	1159	28
HENRY	5,844	6,432	6,774	1.3	2.53	4,333	4,624	0.9	46,106	52,124	988	22
HICKMAN	2,188	2,153	2,096	-0.2	2.27	1,542	1,464	-0.7	38,700	44,724	1895	52
HOPKINS	18,820	19,217	19,315	0.3	2.36	13,400	13,215	-0.2	38,364	44,861	1953	54
JACKSON	5,307	5,717	5,918	1.0	2.43	3,953	4,130	0.6	24,408	27,422	3100	106
JEFFERSON	287,012	300,710	309,278	0.6	2.34	182,971	183,565	0.0	51,621	61,928	575	13
JESSAMINE	13,867	17,059	19,597	2.9	2.63	10,657	12,751	2.5	51,631	61,177	574	12
JOHNSON	9,103	9,559	9,798	0.7	2.43	6,867	7,003	0.3	30,257	34,360	2897	86
KENTON	59,444	62,632	64,538	0.7	2.46	39,444	39,917	0.2	57,848	69,124	307	5
KNOTT	6,717	7,042	7,115	0.7	2.42	4,992	5,074	0.2	24,249	27,464	3102	107
KNOX	12,416	13,350	13,862	1.0	2.42	8,936	9,290	0.5	22,400	25,989	3121	116
LARUE	5,275	5,599	5,779	0.8	2.45	3,866	3,973	0.4	40,060	45,976	1717	46
LAUREL	20,353	22,603	24,058	1.5	2.47	15,364	16,563	1.0	33,348	38,386	2624	77
LAWRENCE	5,954	6,411	6,614	1.0	2.50	4,478	4,680	0.6	25,807	29,472	3076	101
LEE	2,985	3,076	3,059	0.4	2.31	2,122	2,113	-0.1	22,767	26,157	3118	113
LESLIE	4,885	5,013	5,000	0.4	2.38	3,668	3,653	-0.1	21,568	24,407	3129	118
LETCHER	10,085	10,371	10,378	0.4	2.37	7,461	7,434	0.0	25,247	28,605	3089	103
LEWIS	5,422	5,623	5,704	0.5	2.48	4,049	4,075	0.1	26,761	30,489	3047	98
LINCOLN	9,206	10,445	11,180	1.8	2.43	6,732	7,395	1.3	32,358	37,072	2725	78
LIVINGSTON	3,996	4,067	4,082	0.2	2.37	2,893	2,849	-0.2	38,227	43,374	1972	56
LOGAN	10,506	10,871	11,034	0.5	2.44	7,577	7,583	0.0	39,898	45,773	1739	47
LYON	2,898	3,085	3,190	0.9	2.21	2,043	2,098	0.4	40,123	46,695	1705	45
MCCRACKEN	27,736	27,721	27,474	0.0	2.26	18,457	17,724	-0.6	42,671	50,459	1371	36
MCCREARY	6,520	7,015	7,277	1.0	2.45	4,756	4,951	0.6	22,771	25,739	3117	112
MCLEAN	3,984	4,139	4,209	0.5	2.40	2,801	2,890	0.1	38,064	40,807	2265	66
MADISON	27,152	31,283	34,528	2.0	2.39	18,218	20,176	1.4	41,330	48,376	1546	40
MAGOFFIN	5,024	5,355	5,517	0.9	2.50	3,857	3,998	0.5	22,927	26,072	3115	111
KENTUCKY				1.1	2.41			0.6	42,861	50,528		
UNITED STATES				1.2	2.59			1.0	53,154	62,503		

COUNTY	2007 Per Capita Income	2007 HH Income Base	2007 HOUSEHOLD INCOME DISTRIBUTION (%)					2007 Home Value Base	2007 HOME VALUE DISTRIBUTION (%)					2007 Median Home Value
			Less than $25,000	$25,000 to $49,999	$50,000 to $99,999	$100,000 to $149,999	$150,000 or More		Less than $50,000	$50,000 to $89,999	$90,000 to $174,999	$175,000 to $399,999	$400,000 or More	
ADAIR	19,160	6,961	43.2	27.4	22.7	3.3	3.5	5,597	30.4	28.3	31.7	8.2	1.4	79,670
ALLEN	18,431	7,353	33.6	30.4	29.8	4.1	2.1	5,861	24.7	25.4	34.8	13.7	1.4	89,866
ANDERSON	24,054	8,405	17.2	26.5	43.9	10.0	2.5	6,748	6.0	12.6	52.3	27.3	1.9	133,773
BALLARD	21,723	3,527	30.8	28.6	29.3	9.0	2.4	2,904	31.4	25.2	31.1	10.5	1.8	77,667
BARREN	21,297	16,516	32.7	29.3	28.7	6.3	3.0	12,086	15.6	25.5	43.1	13.4	2.3	102,887
BATH	18,440	4,872	41.4	29.2	21.6	5.4	2.4	3,912	33.7	27.3	27.1	10.8	1.0	75,292
BELL	14,853	12,307	52.1	27.7	16.2	2.6	1.4	8,461	43.7	28.8	21.9	5.1	0.5	58,146
BOONE	33,335	42,792	12.3	19.3	38.3	18.3	11.8	32,132	6.1	5.6	38.7	43.1	6.5	174,118
BOURBON	23,685	8,130	29.0	27.8	28.8	10.2	4.2	5,427	9.5	17.3	47.2	19.3	6.8	120,755
BOYD	23,283	19,877	30.6	27.9	28.8	8.6	4.2	14,622	19.2	29.6	38.8	11.1	1.3	91,474
BOYLE	24,842	11,245	28.5	26.9	29.9	9.7	4.9	7,900	10.4	17.7	46.1	22.5	3.3	117,661
BRACKEN	20,164	3,517	27.1	33.3	30.2	7.9	1.6	2,736	23.8	26.0	35.1	13.3	1.8	90,278
BREATHITT	13,684	6,403	52.3	26.6	16.9	3.2	1.0	4,942	54.4	20.7	20.3	4.0	0.7	44,571
BRECKINRIDGE	19,522	7,783	33.7	31.5	26.9	5.5	2.4	6,389	25.6	27.6	35.2	9.9	1.8	86,139
BULLITT	23,599	27,254	17.0	27.8	39.8	12.0	3.4	22,931	9.1	9.1	49.0	30.9	1.9	141,329
BUTLER	18,193	5,449	35.0	31.3	28.1	4.0	1.7	4,352	32.6	27.3	31.4	8.0	0.6	76,692
CALDWELL	20,393	5,454	35.7	30.2	26.4	5.1	2.6	4,260	29.8	29.8	30.9	8.9	0.7	75,345
CALLOWAY	22,162	14,671	31.7	32.0	25.4	7.5	3.4	10,078	18.7	19.3	42.4	17.3	2.4	106,383
CAMPBELL	28,114	35,560	20.0	25.6	34.8	13.3	6.2	24,686	6.7	16.7	49.5	24.1	3.0	125,862
CARLISLE	20,412	2,234	30.4	37.5	24.1	5.6	2.4	1,871	32.3	32.1	28.5	6.5	0.6	68,766
CARROLL	21,495	4,156	30.6	23.8	33.9	9.4	2.3	2,799	20.1	19.1	41.9	16.3	2.6	103,857
CARTER	16,892	11,040	40.9	29.0	24.2	4.6	1.3	8,981	39.1	29.1	25.2	6.0	0.6	62,330
CASEY	16,117	6,776	47.5	30.3	17.3	2.9	2.1	5,507	40.0	28.7	24.7	6.1	0.5	62,521
CHRISTIAN	18,458	25,429	28.5	35.3	27.5	6.5	2.3	14,296	15.9	22.3	44.8	14.5	2.5	102,922
CLARK	25,045	14,590	24.4	25.4	35.3	10.5	4.4	10,173	12.3	15.2	42.5	26.2	3.8	129,471
CLAY	12,312	8,992	59.5	21.7	14.9	3.0	0.9	6,785	51.6	25.2	19.1	3.7	0.4	48,522
CLINTON	15,977	4,257	51.7	28.3	15.8	2.9	1.3	3,314	43.3	28.9	20.2	6.5	1.0	58,277
CRITTENDEN	19,249	3,760	35.3	30.2	26.7	6.0	1.8	3,041	31.1	35.4	25.4	7.6	0.5	67,756
CUMBERLAND	15,872	3,058	46.9	32.4	15.1	4.1	1.4	2,392	33.2	30.1	29.1	6.9	0.7	70,743
DAVIESS	24,364	38,399	26.2	27.2	33.0	9.7	4.0	27,270	12.2	30.2	41.8	14.5	1.3	98,415
EDMONSON	17,315	4,895	41.2	31.4	22.2	3.8	1.4	4,186	28.6	33.0	30.5	7.5	0.4	75,128
ELLIOTT	14,909	2,791	50.4	26.3	17.1	4.7	1.4	2,297	42.4	32.0	19.6	5.5	0.5	59,641
ESTILL	15,964	6,229	43.8	31.3	19.2	4.2	1.4	4,666	38.3	31.6	22.6	7.4	0.0	62,396
FAYETTE	31,731	119,608	22.2	25.9	31.2	11.9	8.8	67,466	3.4	7.5	47.8	34.3	7.0	154,741
FLEMING	17,858	5,795	37.5	30.8	23.8	6.0	1.9	4,609	24.3	32.0	30.0	11.7	1.9	82,389
FLOYD	15,995	17,637	49.1	26.7	18.5	4.0	1.7	13,555	41.9	28.5	22.0	7.3	0.3	60,164
FRANKLIN	28,500	20,793	22.1	27.0	32.6	12.5	5.8	13,678	10.6	12.2	51.0	23.6	2.6	126,262
FULTON	18,944	3,004	41.0	29.0	23.2	4.7	2.1	1,963	36.4	36.5	20.8	5.5	0.8	58,946
GALLATIN	20,271	3,230	28.2	28.2	32.5	8.4	2.7	2,516	16.9	19.5	42.8	18.1	2.7	105,543
GARRARD	21,416	6,456	28.8	28.3	33.1	6.9	2.9	4,990	10.9	19.4	47.9	20.8	1.1	113,833
GRANT	21,487	9,453	20.8	31.5	35.8	9.2	2.7	7,120	22.5	16.3	40.4	19.2	1.6	108,883
GRAVES	20,680	14,862	34.9	27.4	27.7	7.0	3.0	11,599	24.3	27.7	36.4	10.8	0.9	87,058
GRAYSON	18,552	10,283	34.6	34.2	23.7	5.5	1.9	8,007	23.1	28.0	37.6	10.3	1.1	88,202
GREEN	19,073	4,811	41.2	29.8	21.6	5.0	2.3	3,789	27.4	32.4	31.6	7.9	0.7	76,767
GREENUP	22,031	15,272	30.4	28.4	29.3	8.3	3.6	12,494	25.3	28.5	34.6	10.2	1.4	85,087
HANCOCK	21,193	3,450	26.7	28.2	33.8	9.5	1.8	2,851	30.6	27.0	30.9	11.3	0.3	78,580
HARDIN	22,811	37,960	21.3	31.3	34.4	9.4	3.5	25,785	11.9	12.1	47.3	24.7	4.1	137,119
HARLAN	14,541	13,266	53.4	27.2	15.3	2.5	1.6	9,831	46.8	31.1	18.6	3.3	0.2	53,473
HARRISON	22,217	7,454	24.9	31.2	31.9	9.5	2.6	5,364	11.9	19.5	44.8	20.9	2.8	114,210
HART	17,111	7,471	40.0	32.0	21.6	4.8	1.6	5,832	24.4	32.3	33.0	9.2	1.1	83,023
HENDERSON	23,992	19,015	27.2	28.1	32.1	8.8	3.7	12,973	21.7	26.6	37.7	12.9	1.0	92,025
HENRY	22,792	6,432	26.6	26.8	33.3	9.7	3.6	5,038	15.7	19.9	41.3	19.5	3.6	110,153
HICKMAN	21,319	2,153	35.2	29.4	25.2	7.6	2.6	1,762	36.2	30.0	26.6	5.8	1.4	67,395
HOPKINS	21,606	19,217	31.7	31.3	27.7	5.9	3.4	14,465	30.9	30.7	29.5	8.0	1.0	72,928
JACKSON	12,855	5,717	50.8	32.2	14.5	1.9	0.7	4,603	40.4	28.3	26.7	4.5	0.1	61,003
JEFFERSON	30,058	300,706	22.3	26.2	31.7	12.0	7.8	197,770	5.4	13.8	48.1	27.6	5.1	136,869
JESSAMINE	25,329	17,059	18.9	29.4	33.0	12.1	6.7	11,566	7.1	10.3	45.9	30.5	6.2	141,229
JOHNSON	17,631	9,559	42.7	29.4	21.1	4.3	2.5	7,375	35.9	25.5	30.4	6.9	1.3	69,862
KENTON	29,981	62,632	18.1	24.8	36.1	13.0	8.1	42,083	5.4	13.4	49.6	27.9	3.8	138,559
KNOTT	14,326	7,042	51.2	26.4	17.7	3.7	1.0	5,621	49.0	26.9	19.6	4.1	0.3	51,170
KNOX	13,539	13,350	54.1	27.5	13.6	3.6	1.1	9,657	42.7	23.7	25.7	7.0	1.0	58,934
LARUE	20,488	5,599	30.6	31.5	27.9	7.6	2.4	4,515	14.5	23.2	39.2	19.3	3.8	113,956
LAUREL	18,159	22,603	38.0	32.2	22.0	5.2	2.5	17,558	26.4	24.1	35.7	12.2	1.5	89,066
LAWRENCE	15,041	6,411	48.8	27.2	18.3	4.1	1.6	5,031	41.9	29.0	22.7	5.0	1.3	59,345
LEE	15,279	3,076	53.1	27.4	13.8	3.6	2.1	2,361	45.9	25.1	24.7	3.8	0.5	54,898
LESLIE	12,950	5,013	55.5	25.8	15.2	3.1	0.5	4,123	57.2	25.9	15.0	1.6	0.3	43,561
LETCHER	15,029	10,371	49.5	27.0	19.2	3.0	1.2	8,403	49.5	27.7	19.4	2.8	0.5	50,585
LEWIS	14,671	5,623	46.5	29.4	19.7	3.5	0.9	4,585	44.4	29.1	21.3	4.4	0.8	55,298
LINCOLN	17,292	10,445	39.7	30.3	24.1	4.1	1.8	8,267	26.5	25.6	37.4	9.4	1.1	86,721
LIVINGSTON	20,719	4,067	29.3	32.5	30.2	6.0	1.9	3,472	28.3	30.0	31.3	8.0	2.3	79,530
LOGAN	20,107	10,871	30.6	31.1	30.2	5.7	2.4	8,282	21.0	26.8	36.8	13.6	1.8	92,361
LYON	20,717	3,085	30.5	30.1	29.6	7.4	2.4	2,533	19.3	23.8	34.5	19.8	2.6	98,738
MCCRACKEN	25,627	27,721	29.9	27.1	28.7	9.6	4.8	19,277	20.0	21.7	35.6	20.0	2.7	105,383
MCCREARY	12,349	7,015	54.4	31.3	11.7	1.8	0.9	5,356	47.7	29.9	19.3	2.7	0.4	52,556
MCLEAN	19,418	4,139	35.4	31.1	26.9	4.3	2.3	3,343	37.8	29.6	25.5	6.1	0.9	66,403
MADISON	21,783	31,283	29.7	29.6	29.0	8.4	3.2	19,036	15.6	17.9	42.5	22.7	1.3	116,552
MAGOFFIN	13,277	5,355	52.8	26.1	16.7	2.9	1.4	4,390	49.3	24.5	20.6	5.1	0.5	50,917
KENTUCKY	23,912		29.2	27.7	29.0	9.1	4.9		18.5	19.6	39.0	19.8	3.1	109,419
UNITED STATES	27,916		21.9	25.0	32.3	12.3	8.4		7.9	10.5	27.1	35.6	19.0	192,285

SPENDING POTENTIAL INDICES

KENTUCKY

E

COUNTY	FINANCIAL SERVICES				THE HOME						ENTERTAINMENT						PERSONAL			
					Home Improvements		Furnishings													
	Auto Loan	Home Loan	Invest-ments	Retire-ment Plans	Home Repair	Lawn & Garden	Comput-ers & Hard-ware	Major Appli-ances	TV, Radio, Sound Equip-ment	Furni-ture	Dine out/ Carry out	Sports Equip-ment	Fees & Tickets	Toys & Games	Travel	Cable TV	Apparel & Services	Auto Repairs	Health Insur-ance	Pets & Supplies
ADAIR	79	56	37	53	62	83	58	72	65	55	64	64	49	68	57	70	55	67	79	78
ALLEN	81	57	35	54	63	85	57	73	64	56	64	64	49	69	56	69	55	67	78	79
ANDERSON	94	84	76	83	87	98	80	90	84	81	84	80	78	89	81	87	74	85	93	93
BALLARD	87	63	39	60	72	97	64	83	71	61	71	72	54	74	64	77	60	75	89	89
BARREN	80	64	56	62	68	84	66	76	72	64	71	66	60	74	66	76	61	71	82	80
BATH	78	53	29	50	59	82	54	70	62	52	61	63	45	65	53	67	52	64	77	77
BELL	59	40	26	39	44	60	43	53	50	41	49	48	36	51	42	54	42	50	60	58
BOONE	128	135	126	136	124	117	126	122	121	131	121	116	128	126	124	116	110	123	114	122
BOURBON	84	74	78	75	78	87	78	82	81	75	80	72	74	83	77	83	70	79	88	85
BOYD	82	70	69	69	74	86	73	80	79	70	77	70	68	78	73	83	67	77	89	82
BOYLE	89	78	79	78	81	92	81	87	86	78	84	77	77	86	81	89	73	84	94	89
BRACKEN	88	61	36	58	67	92	62	79	70	60	69	70	52	74	60	75	59	72	85	86
BREATHITT	60	39	18	36	44	63	40	54	48	39	47	48	32	50	39	52	40	49	59	60
BRECKINRIDGE	82	58	37	56	65	88	59	76	67	57	66	67	50	70	59	72	56	69	82	82
BULLITT	95	89	82	89	89	96	83	91	86	85	86	81	83	90	85	87	76	87	92	94
BUTLER	77	55	37	53	59	79	56	69	64	55	63	61	49	67	55	68	54	64	75	74
CALDWELL	76	58	46	56	65	83	60	73	67	57	65	63	53	68	61	72	56	67	82	77
CALLOWAY	78	59	54	60	63	77	72	73	73	64	72	66	62	72	66	74	63	72	77	76
CAMPBELL	93	92	104	95	91	91	96	92	97	94	95	83	96	97	95	97	86	93	97	92
CARLISLE	83	58	38	55	63	85	60	74	68	57	67	66	51	71	59	73	57	69	82	80
CARROLL	84	69	60	68	70	83	70	77	75	68	74	68	65	77	69	79	64	75	84	81
CARTER	73	51	28	48	55	76	51	66	58	50	58	59	43	61	50	63	49	60	71	72
CASEY	67	46	25	43	51	71	46	60	54	45	53	54	38	56	46	58	45	55	66	66
CHRISTIAN	76	58	54	60	58	67	69	67	71	64	71	62	62	73	64	72	62	70	70	69
CLARK	90	82	83	82	81	88	83	85	87	82	85	76	81	87	82	88	75	84	91	87
CLAY	55	36	18	33	40	57	37	49	44	36	43	44	30	46	36	48	37	45	54	55
CLINTON	64	43	22	40	48	68	44	58	51	42	50	51	36	53	43	55	43	53	63	64
CRITTENDEN	77	56	38	53	62	82	57	71	65	55	64	63	49	67	57	70	54	66	79	77
CUMBERLAND	62	44	28	42	49	67	46	58	52	44	51	50	39	54	45	56	43	53	63	62
DAVIESS	83	79	86	80	80	84	79	81	83	79	81	71	79	83	80	84	73	80	87	82
EDMONSON	74	50	26	47	56	78	50	66	58	49	58	59	42	61	50	63	49	60	71	73
ELLIOTT	65	42	19	39	48	68	43	58	51	42	51	53	35	54	43	56	43	53	64	65
ESTILL	67	45	27	43	50	68	47	59	54	45	53	53	39	57	46	59	45	55	65	65
FAYETTE	102	95	101	100	90	90	107	95	103	102	103	90	102	103	100	101	93	101	95	96
FLEMING	79	55	33	52	60	81	55	70	62	54	62	62	47	66	54	67	53	64	75	76
FLOYD	65	45	26	42	49	68	46	59	53	45	52	53	38	55	45	58	45	54	65	64
FRANKLIN	91	86	93	87	86	90	90	89	91	87	90	80	88	91	89	92	81	90	94	90
FULTON	67	52	48	52	54	66	56	61	63	54	61	53	51	63	55	67	53	60	70	63
GALLATIN	91	71	48	68	72	91	67	81	73	68	74	72	61	77	67	78	64	76	84	87
GARRARD	83	72	67	71	76	88	70	80	74	70	74	70	67	77	72	78	65	75	85	83
GRANT	92	78	62	76	77	89	75	84	79	76	79	75	71	82	74	82	69	81	86	88
GRAVES	81	61	50	60	66	84	65	76	71	62	70	67	57	73	64	75	60	71	83	80
GRAYSON	76	55	38	53	59	78	56	69	63	55	62	61	48	66	55	67	53	64	75	74
GREEN	77	55	35	52	61	82	56	71	63	54	63	62	48	66	56	68	53	65	78	77
GREENUP	84	68	59	66	74	90	68	80	75	66	74	70	63	77	69	82	64	75	89	84
HANCOCK	90	68	46	65	71	92	67	81	74	66	74	72	59	78	66	79	63	75	86	87
HARDIN	88	78	73	79	76	83	81	82	82	79	81	75	77	84	78	82	72	82	83	84
HARLAN	59	40	24	37	44	61	42	53	49	40	48	48	35	51	41	54	41	50	60	58
HARRISON	89	71	58	69	76	93	70	83	77	70	76	73	65	81	71	82	66	77	89	88
HART	75	52	31	49	58	78	53	68	60	51	60	60	44	63	52	65	51	62	73	74
HENDERSON	84	74	76	75	75	84	77	80	81	75	79	71	74	82	76	83	70	79	86	82
HENRY	96	74	55	72	78	97	73	87	80	72	80	77	66	84	73	85	69	81	93	93
HICKMAN	85	59	34	56	66	92	60	78	68	58	68	69	50	72	59	74	57	71	85	85
HOPKINS	81	64	56	64	68	82	67	75	73	65	71	66	61	75	66	77	62	72	83	79
JACKSON	56	37	18	34	41	59	38	50	44	37	44	45	31	46	37	48	37	46	54	56
JEFFERSON	95	96	109	99	94	93	98	94	99	98	98	84	100	98	98	99	89	96	98	94
JESSAMINE	96	93	95	96	89	90	96	92	94	94	94	85	94	96	93	93	84	94	92	93
JOHNSON	75	51	29	48	57	79	53	68	61	51	60	61	44	63	52	66	51	63	74	75
KENTON	101	102	111	104	99	97	103	99	104	103	103	90	104	104	102	103	93	101	101	99
KNOTT	63	40	17	37	45	65	41	56	50	40	49	51	33	52	40	55	41	51	61	62
KNOX	56	38	24	36	42	58	41	51	47	39	46	46	34	48	39	51	39	47	56	56
LARUE	84	63	46	61	69	88	64	77	70	62	70	68	57	74	63	75	60	72	83	82
LAUREL	76	56	39	54	60	78	57	69	63	55	62	61	50	66	56	67	54	64	74	74
LAWRENCE	64	45	28	42	49	67	47	59	54	45	53	53	39	55	46	58	45	55	65	64
LEE	62	41	25	39	46	64	45	56	52	42	51	51	36	53	43	57	44	53	63	62
LESLIE	56	35	15	33	40	58	37	49	44	36	43	45	29	46	36	48	37	45	54	55
LETCHER	63	41	20	38	46	66	43	57	51	41	50	51	35	53	42	56	42	52	63	63
LEWIS	65	44	22	41	49	69	44	58	51	43	51	52	36	54	43	57	43	53	63	65
LINCOLN	72	51	34	49	55	74	53	65	59	51	59	58	45	62	51	63	50	60	70	71
LIVINGSTON	85	61	34	57	69	95	61	80	67	59	67	70	51	71	61	73	57	72	85	87
LOGAN	83	62	43	60	66	86	62	75	69	61	68	67	54	73	61	73	59	70	81	81
LYON	83	62	42	60	71	94	64	81	70	60	69	70	55	71	65	75	59	74	87	86
MCCRACKEN	84	76	81	77	77	85	78	81	83	77	81	71	76	82	79	85	72	80	89	83
MCCREARY	55	35	15	32	39	57	36	49	44	35	43	44	29	46	35	48	36	45	54	55
MCLEAN	81	56	32	53	63	88	57	75	65	55	65	66	47	68	57	71	55	68	80	80
MADISON	81	67	63	68	66	75	75	74	76	71	76	68	68	77	70	77	67	75	77	77
MAGOFFIN	60	38	17	35	43	62	40	53	47	38	47	48	32	50	39	52	40	49	58	60
KENTUCKY	89	76	68	75	77	89	78	84	82	76	81	75	73	84	77	84	71	82	88	87
UNITED STATES	100	100	100	100	100	100	100	100	100	100	100	100	100	100	100	100	100	100	100	100

POPULATION CHANGE

COUNTY	FIPS Code	CBSA Code	DMA Code	POPULATION			2000-2007 ANNUAL RATE		RACE (%)					
									White		Black		Asian/Pacific	
				2000	2007	2012	% Rate	State Rank	2000	2007	2000	2007	2000	2007
MARION	155	00000	529	18,212	18,571	18,960	0.3	70	89.2	88.3	9.1	9.5	0.4	0.6
MARSHALL	157	00000	632	30,125	30,984	31,557	0.4	61	98.6	98.2	0.1	0.1	0.2	0.2
MARTIN	159	00000	564	12,578	14,177	14,086	1.7	12	99.3	99.1	0.0	0.0	0.1	0.2
MASON	161	32500	515	16,800	16,681	16,606	-0.1	102	90.9	90.0	7.2	7.5	0.4	0.6
MEADE	163	31140	529	26,349	28,381	29,851	1.0	25	92.4	91.3	4.1	4.3	0.7	0.9
MENIFEE	165	34460	541	6,556	6,890	7,097	0.7	37	97.6	97.3	1.4	1.5	0.0	0.1
MERCER	167	00000	541	20,817	21,776	22,431	0.6	44	94.0	93.2	3.7	3.9	0.5	0.7
METCALFE	169	23980	736	10,037	10,329	10,520	0.4	61	97.3	97.0	1.6	1.7	0.1	0.1
MONROE	171	00000	659	11,756	11,514	11,318	-0.3	112	95.6	94.9	2.8	2.9	0.0	0.1
MONTGOMERY	173	34460	541	22,554	24,816	26,514	1.3	18	95.1	94.6	3.5	3.6	0.1	0.2
MORGAN	175	00000	541	13,948	14,686	15,067	0.7	37	94.6	94.1	4.4	4.6	0.2	0.3
MUHLENBERG	177	16420	649	31,839	31,627	31,343	-0.1	102	94.2	93.7	4.6	4.9	0.1	0.2
NELSON	179	31140	529	37,477	43,254	47,558	2.0	8	92.8	92.0	5.5	5.8	0.5	0.8
NICHOLAS	181	00000	541	6,813	6,845	6,877	0.1	85	98.3	98.3	0.8	0.9	0.1	0.1
OHIO	183	00000	649	22,916	23,852	24,464	0.6	44	97.7	97.2	0.7	0.8	0.2	0.3
OLDHAM	185	31140	529	46,178	58,610	68,570	3.3	4	93.6	92.7	4.2	4.5	0.4	0.7
OWEN	187	00000	515	10,547	11,432	12,050	1.1	22	97.0	96.4	1.1	1.2	0.2	0.4
OWSLEY	189	00000	541	4,858	4,907	4,886	0.1	85	99.2	99.2	0.1	0.1	0.1	0.1
PENDLETON	191	17140	515	14,390	15,202	15,757	0.8	31	98.4	98.1	0.5	0.5	0.1	0.2
PERRY	193	00000	541	29,390	29,492	29,588	0.0	94	97.3	97.3	1.6	1.7	0.5	0.5
PIKE	195	00000	564	68,736	68,741	68,914	0.0	94	98.3	98.3	0.5	0.5	0.4	0.4
POWELL	197	00000	541	13,237	13,647	13,912	0.4	61	98.6	98.4	0.6	0.6	0.1	0.1
PULASKI	199	43700	541	56,217	59,274	61,390	0.7	37	97.5	97.0	1.1	1.1	0.4	0.6
ROBERTSON	201	00000	515	2,266	2,304	2,326	0.2	78	98.6	98.7	0.0	0.0	0.0	0.0
ROCKCASTLE	203	40080	541	16,582	16,815	16,935	0.2	78	98.8	98.6	0.1	0.1	0.1	0.2
ROWAN	205	00000	541	22,094	22,335	22,472	0.1	85	96.0	93.6	1.6	3.3	0.9	1.2
RUSSELL	207	00000	541	16,315	16,897	17,286	0.5	51	98.3	98.0	0.6	0.6	0.2	0.2
SCOTT	209	30460	541	33,061	41,842	49,641	3.3	4	91.9	90.9	5.4	5.6	0.5	0.7
SHELBY	211	31140	529	33,337	40,999	47,280	2.9	5	86.6	84.8	8.8	9.1	0.5	0.7
SIMPSON	213	00000	659	16,405	16,924	17,186	0.4	61	87.8	86.9	10.2	10.7	0.6	0.9
SPENCER	215	31140	529	11,766	16,868	21,154	5.1	1	97.5	97.1	1.1	1.2	0.1	0.1
TAYLOR	217	15820	529	22,927	23,241	23,460	0.2	78	93.6	93.1	5.1	5.3	0.2	0.3
TODD	219	00000	659	11,971	12,176	12,280	0.2	78	89.3	88.3	8.8	9.1	0.2	0.3
TRIGG	221	17300	659	12,597	13,521	14,116	1.0	25	88.3	87.5	9.8	10.2	0.3	0.4
TRIMBLE	223	31140	529	8,125	9,243	9,811	1.8	10	97.9	97.4	0.3	0.3	0.1	0.1
UNION	225	00000	649	15,637	15,341	15,152	-0.3	112	85.0	84.0	12.9	13.4	0.1	0.2
WARREN	227	14540	736	92,522	102,880	110,930	1.5	15	87.0	85.3	8.6	8.8	1.4	2.0
WASHINGTON	229	00000	529	10,916	11,485	11,848	0.7	37	90.6	89.8	7.5	7.8	0.3	0.4
WAYNE	231	00000	541	19,923	20,391	20,677	0.3	70	97.0	96.5	1.5	1.6	0.1	0.2
WEBSTER	233	21780	649	14,120	14,251	14,367	0.1	85	93.6	92.8	4.7	4.9	0.1	0.2
WHITLEY	235	18340	541	35,865	37,845	39,270	0.7	37	98.4	98.1	0.3	0.4	0.2	0.3
WOLFE	237	00000	541	7,065	7,243	7,325	0.3	70	99.2	99.1	0.2	0.2	0.1	0.1
WOODFORD	239	30460	541	23,208	24,827	25,961	0.9	28	92.1	91.1	5.4	5.6	0.3	0.5
KENTUCKY							0.7		90.1	89.2	7.3	7.5	0.8	1.1
UNITED STATES							1.2		75.1	72.7	12.3	12.6	3.8	4.5

COUNTY	% HISPANIC ORIGIN		2007 AGE DISTRIBUTION (%)									MEDIAN AGE		
	2000	2007	0-4	5-9	10-14	15-19	20-24	25-44	45-64	65-84	85+	18+	2007	% 2007 Males	% 2007 Females
MARION	0.8	1.2	6.9	6.5	6.6	5.4	6.5	29.7	25.8	10.6	2.0	76.7	37.4	50.9	49.1
MARSHALL	0.8	1.1	5.2	4.9	5.6	5.6	5.0	25.7	29.2	16.1	2.7	80.9	43.7	49.1	50.9
MARTIN	0.6	0.9	6.2	6.5	6.3	5.5	7.1	32.8	26.2	8.5	0.8	77.4	36.0	55.3	44.7
MASON	1.0	1.4	6.3	6.0	5.7	6.4	5.7	26.1	28.6	13.0	2.2	78.1	40.5	48.7	51.3
MEADE	2.2	3.2	8.9	7.3	6.5	6.3	7.7	29.4	24.7	8.4	0.8	73.5	33.8	50.2	49.8
MENIFEE	1.1	1.6	6.1	5.7	5.9	7.1	6.6	26.9	27.9	12.4	1.4	78.2	39.2	50.7	49.3
MERCER	1.3	1.9	6.5	6.2	7.1	5.6	5.0	26.9	28.1	12.7	2.0	76.7	40.4	48.8	51.2
METCALFE	0.5	0.8	6.6	6.4	6.7	5.8	5.1	27.4	26.6	13.5	2.0	76.8	39.5	49.1	50.9
MONROE	1.4	2.2	6.7	6.3	6.5	5.0	5.6	27.3	26.7	13.8	2.1	77.5	39.9	48.8	51.2
MONTGOMERY	1.1	1.7	6.9	7.0	6.4	5.8	5.2	29.2	26.7	10.9	1.8	76.0	37.8	49.1	50.9
MORGAN	0.6	0.9	5.6	5.5	6.0	5.4	7.6	32.0	26.0	10.3	1.6	79.6	37.3	55.5	44.5
MUHLENBERG	0.7	1.1	6.1	6.3	5.5	5.8	5.5	27.4	27.7	13.4	2.3	78.7	40.6	50.0	50.0
NELSON	1.1	1.6	7.5	6.9	6.8	6.7	7.0	27.8	26.2	9.8	1.3	74.7	36.6	49.2	50.8
NICHOLAS	0.5	0.5	6.3	6.7	6.2	5.3	5.0	28.7	26.3	13.1	2.6	77.7	39.9	48.8	51.2
OHIO	1.0	1.5	6.6	6.1	6.0	6.0	5.9	27.3	27.2	12.6	2.2	77.6	39.5	49.4	50.6
OLDHAM	1.3	1.9	6.3	7.0	7.4	7.0	5.7	26.8	31.3	7.6	0.9	74.8	39.4	52.3	47.7
OWEN	1.0	1.5	6.3	6.3	6.7	5.9	5.3	27.2	28.0	12.4	1.9	77.1	39.7	49.8	50.2
OWSLEY	0.7	0.7	5.5	5.6	5.9	6.1	5.6	26.1	29.3	13.3	2.6	79.2	41.4	49.9	50.1
PENDLETON	0.7	1.0	7.1	6.3	7.9	7.2	6.0	29.0	25.7	9.7	1.2	74.2	36.5	50.5	49.5
PERRY	0.5	0.5	5.8	6.1	6.5	6.1	5.8	28.9	29.1	10.4	1.3	78.2	38.8	49.0	51.0
PIKE	0.7	0.7	6.0	6.2	5.9	5.6	5.3	28.4	29.7	11.6	1.3	78.5	39.9	49.1	50.9
POWELL	0.7	1.0	6.9	7.2	6.5	5.9	6.1	29.9	25.8	10.7	1.1	75.8	36.8	50.1	49.9
PULASKI	0.8	1.2	5.9	5.9	5.9	5.9	5.5	27.3	27.7	14.0	1.8	78.6	40.9	49.0	51.0
ROBERTSON	0.9	0.9	5.6	5.2	7.6	5.3	5.0	26.4	27.7	14.6	2.7	78.5	42.2	49.4	50.6
ROCKCASTLE	0.6	0.9	6.1	6.2	6.5	6.1	5.1	30.1	26.0	12.2	1.8	77.3	38.8	49.9	50.1
ROWAN	1.1	1.7	6.0	5.2	5.4	9.6	12.5	27.7	21.5	10.6	1.4	79.3	31.5	48.9	51.1
RUSSELL	0.9	1.3	5.7	5.7	5.7	5.3	5.3	26.2	28.8	15.2	2.1	79.7	42.4	48.7	51.3
SCOTT	1.6	2.4	7.8	7.4	7.0	6.9	7.4	31.6	23.4	7.4	1.1	74.0	33.5	49.4	50.6
SHELBY	4.5	6.6	6.8	6.8	6.4	6.6	5.7	28.9	27.4	10.0	1.4	76.0	38.2	49.4	50.6
SIMPSON	0.9	1.3	7.5	7.6	6.3	6.3	5.4	28.3	25.4	11.2	2.0	74.7	37.5	48.7	51.3
SPENCER	1.1	1.7	7.2	7.1	7.4	5.9	5.1	30.0	27.4	9.0	1.0	74.7	38.1	50.5	49.5
TAYLOR	0.8	1.2	6.2	5.8	5.9	6.7	6.7	25.4	27.4	14.1	1.9	78.6	40.7	48.5	51.5
TODD	1.7	2.5	7.7	7.7	6.8	5.9	5.2	28.2	25.4	11.2	1.9	74.2	37.1	49.7	50.3
TRIGG	0.9	1.3	5.9	6.1	5.9	6.0	4.2	25.8	28.4	15.8	1.8	78.3	42.4	49.3	50.7
TRIMBLE	1.4	2.0	6.8	6.7	6.8	6.7	5.3	28.9	27.1	10.2	1.5	75.6	37.9	49.4	50.6
UNION	1.6	2.2	6.4	6.1	5.4	10.3	8.7	24.6	25.6	11.2	1.7	76.9	35.6	50.7	49.3
WARREN	2.7	3.9	6.5	6.1	6.0	7.6	9.0	29.7	24.1	9.6	1.5	78.2	33.8	49.2	50.8
WASHINGTON	1.6	2.4	6.0	6.1	6.7	7.1	5.6	26.7	26.7	13.0	2.1	76.9	39.5	49.5	50.5
WAYNE	1.5	2.2	6.9	7.1	6.0	6.1	5.5	27.9	26.7	12.2	1.7	76.2	38.2	49.6	50.4
WEBSTER	1.9	2.8	6.3	5.7	6.5	5.3	6.0	27.3	28.1	12.7	2.0	78.2	39.6	49.7	50.3
WHITLEY	0.7	1.0	6.5	6.2	6.7	7.1	6.9	26.8	26.2	11.7	1.9	76.6	37.7	48.6	51.4
WOLFE	0.5	0.8	6.6	7.0	7.1	5.3	5.0	28.1	27.8	11.0	1.9	75.9	39.1	49.7	50.3
WOODFORD	3.0	4.4	6.0	6.1	6.4	6.9	5.6	26.6	31.0	9.9	1.3	77.3	40.3	48.4	51.6
KENTUCKY	1.5	2.2	6.6	6.4	6.3	6.4	6.6	28.3	26.5	11.1	1.7	77.0	37.7	49.2	50.8
UNITED STATES	12.5	15.0	6.9	6.5	6.8	7.1	7.0	27.6	25.4	10.7	1.9	75.6	36.7	49.2	50.8

HOUSEHOLDS

COUNTY	HOUSEHOLDS					FAMILIES			MEDIAN HOUSEHOLD INCOME			
	2000	2007	2012	% Annual Rate 2000-2007	2007 Average HH Size	2000	2007	% Annual Rate 2000-2007	2007	2012	2007 National Rank	2007 State Rank
MARION	6,613	6,986	7,237	0.8	2.49	4,755	4,858	0.3	37,621	43,761	2042	59
MARSHALL	12,412	13,092	13,450	0.7	2.32	8,993	9,176	0.3	43,925	50,572	1218	32
MARTIN	4,776	4,955	4,990	0.5	2.50	3,621	3,650	0.1	21,628	24,453	3128	117
MASON	6,847	6,983	7,017	0.3	2.34	4,698	4,612	-0.3	37,346	43,708	2087	60
MEADE	9,470	10,567	11,269	1.5	2.68	7,393	8,034	1.2	45,327	51,414	1076	24
MENIFEE	2,537	2,767	2,893	1.2	2.40	1,900	2,012	0.8	27,045	30,962	3036	95
MERCER	8,423	9,043	9,400	1.0	2.39	6,039	6,267	0.5	43,977	50,848	1213	31
METCALFE	4,016	4,239	4,355	0.7	2.41	2,883	2,942	0.3	28,818	33,271	2968	89
MONROE	4,741	4,725	4,666	0.0	2.41	3,380	3,254	-0.5	27,905	32,372	3006	92
MONTGOMERY	8,902	10,114	10,940	1.8	2.41	6,435	7,070	1.3	39,469	46,251	1784	49
MORGAN	4,752	5,224	5,455	1.3	2.46	3,570	3,810	0.9	26,924	30,690	3041	96
MUHLENBERG	12,357	12,683	12,723	0.4	2.37	9,056	8,999	-0.1	34,509	39,575	2496	74
NELSON	13,953	16,652	18,548	2.5	2.56	10,267	11,869	2.0	47,651	54,632	849	17
NICHOLAS	2,710	2,776	2,805	0.3	2.43	1,952	1,933	-0.1	36,452	41,903	2205	64
OHIO	8,899	9,522	9,863	0.9	2.47	6,587	6,831	0.5	36,044	41,330	2270	67
OLDHAM	14,856	19,350	22,973	3.7	2.83	12,199	15,551	3.4	83,972	102,944	34	1
OWEN	4,086	4,514	4,785	1.4	2.51	2,996	3,208	0.9	40,480	46,571	1662	43
OWSLEY	1,894	1,973	1,986	0.6	2.44	1,388	1,399	0.1	18,726	20,972	3139	120
PENDLETON	5,170	5,530	5,745	0.9	2.72	3,971	4,131	0.5	47,084	53,703	900	19
PERRY	11,460	12,046	12,263	0.7	2.42	8,493	8,651	0.3	26,679	30,588	3049	99
PIKE	27,612	28,913	29,411	0.6	2.34	20,364	20,660	0.2	29,027	33,214	2957	88
POWELL	5,044	5,422	5,609	1.0	2.50	3,784	3,948	0.6	30,920	35,279	2842	84
PULASKI	22,719	24,719	25,908	1.2	2.35	16,339	17,189	0.7	34,097	39,142	2541	76
ROBERTSON	866	895	907	0.5	2.50	622	621	0.0	36,454	41,324	2203	63
ROCKCASTLE	6,544	6,877	7,024	0.7	2.40	4,763	4,843	0.2	28,116	32,126	2998	91
ROWAN	7,927	8,224	8,350	0.5	2.33	5,216	5,190	-0.1	34,520	40,293	2495	73
RUSSELL	6,941	7,423	7,687	0.9	2.25	4,796	4,939	0.4	27,108	30,976	3034	94
SCOTT	12,110	15,807	18,984	3.7	2.55	8,990	11,376	3.3	61,716	74,690	218	4
SHELBY	12,104	15,204	17,660	3.2	2.60	9,121	11,119	2.8	57,617	67,118	316	6
SIMPSON	6,415	6,758	6,906	0.7	2.47	4,637	4,724	0.3	45,012	51,853	1110	25
SPENCER	4,251	6,187	7,786	5.3	2.71	3,357	4,763	4.9	57,011	64,757	328	7
TAYLOR	9,233	9,611	9,792	0.6	2.35	6,559	6,594	0.1	35,096	40,180	2416	71
TODD	4,569	4,730	4,793	0.5	2.55	3,369	3,377	0.0	35,634	40,268	2346	69
TRIGG	5,215	5,736	6,038	1.3	2.34	3,767	4,007	0.9	40,861	46,796	1618	42
TRIMBLE	3,137	3,662	3,922	2.2	2.51	2,297	2,596	1.7	43,376	49,397	1291	35
UNION	5,710	5,769	5,758	0.1	2.42	4,081	3,986	-0.3	43,910	51,130	1219	33
WARREN	35,365	40,691	44,343	2.0	2.39	23,427	25,890	1.4	46,279	54,324	976	21
WASHINGTON	4,121	4,496	4,705	1.2	2.48	3,020	3,191	0.8	40,354	46,151	1684	44
WAYNE	7,913	8,363	8,584	0.8	2.42	5,812	5,949	0.3	25,184	28,697	3091	104
WEBSTER	5,560	5,724	5,805	0.4	2.44	4,054	4,041	0.0	38,501	44,371	1928	53
WHITLEY	13,780	14,992	15,738	1.2	2.44	9,888	10,398	0.7	27,781	31,904	3012	93
WOLFE	2,816	2,989	3,063	0.8	2.37	1,977	2,025	0.3	22,404	25,422	3120	115
WOODFORD	8,893	9,808	10,374	1.4	2.49	6,641	7,105	0.9	61,961	73,707	213	3
KENTUCKY				1.1	2.41			0.6	42,861	50,528		
UNITED STATES				1.2	2.59			1.0	53,154	62,503		

COUNTY	2007 Per Capita Income	2007 HH Income Base	2007 HOUSEHOLD INCOME DISTRIBUTION (%)					2007 Home Value Base	2007 HOME VALUE DISTRIBUTION (%)					2007 Median Home Value
			Less than $25,000	$25,000 to $49,999	$50,000 to $99,999	$100,000 to $149,999	$150,000 or More		Less than $50,000	$50,000 to $89,999	$90,000 to $174,999	$175,000 to $399,999	$400,000 or More	
MARION	19,203	6,986	33.3	31.0	27.3	5.9	2.6	5,480	18.1	23.7	43.8	12.9	1.5	98,262
MARSHALL	23,400	13,092	27.3	29.1	31.6	8.8	3.2	10,834	17.0	21.3	39.4	20.4	1.8	107,204
MARTIN	12,585	4,955	55.6	24.7	15.9	2.7	1.1	3,946	43.8	23.5	23.7	8.0	1.1	59,179
MASON	21,902	6,983	33.4	30.4	25.7	6.8	3.6	4,791	19.2	23.3	39.1	16.2	2.2	98,337
MEADE	20,183	10,567	22.4	32.9	34.1	8.2	2.3	7,852	17.5	23.8	39.4	18.2	1.1	102,169
MENIFEE	14,655	2,767	46.8	30.9	18.4	3.1	0.8	2,259	36.4	29.4	29.4	4.5	0.3	67,775
MERCER	22,880	9,043	26.5	29.2	33.1	8.6	2.6	6,825	8.1	20.8	46.7	21.2	3.2	119,623
METCALFE	16,944	4,239	42.4	30.3	21.5	3.8	2.1	3,388	34.1	28.3	29.6	7.8	0.3	71,942
MONROE	17,411	4,725	44.6	30.4	20.0	2.7	2.3	3,596	33.2	24.4	31.6	9.5	1.3	75,856
MONTGOMERY	21,496	10,114	29.5	30.8	29.0	7.3	3.4	7,335	18.2	19.8	41.8	17.9	2.4	105,143
MORGAN	15,363	5,224	46.8	30.3	17.3	3.7	1.9	4,187	40.1	28.0	23.3	7.8	0.9	65,239
MUHLENBERG	18,862	12,683	37.0	30.2	24.9	5.9	2.1	10,520	32.5	30.1	28.8	7.7	1.0	72,321
NELSON	22,901	16,652	23.9	28.4	34.2	9.3	4.1	13,001	10.0	18.1	45.6	23.3	3.0	120,198
NICHOLAS	19,803	2,776	35.7	31.9	22.0	7.9	2.4	2,103	26.3	28.7	36.9	7.3	0.8	82,641
OHIO	18,912	9,522	34.5	30.7	27.1	5.6	2.0	7,695	33.3	30.0	29.8	6.6	0.3	72,795
OLDHAM	36,050	19,350	9.4	16.5	33.2	22.8	18.1	16,890	2.8	3.2	27.1	53.6	13.4	221,114
OWEN	19,836	4,514	30.2	29.1	30.9	7.7	2.1	3,568	21.6	23.0	36.4	15.5	3.5	98,977
OWSLEY	12,152	1,973	61.3	22.7	13.1	1.6	1.3	1,544	50.6	30.3	16.4	2.3	0.3	49,454
PENDLETON	19,831	5,530	25.4	27.4	35.9	9.2	2.0	4,348	14.7	24.1	42.7	18.0	0.6	104,132
PERRY	15,520	12,046	47.5	27.3	19.9	3.6	1.7	9,351	43.7	28.3	22.1	5.2	0.6	57,561
PIKE	17,783	28,913	44.1	27.6	21.9	4.3	2.2	22,831	36.9	26.3	29.0	6.5	1.3	67,294
POWELL	16,765	5,422	40.9	31.1	21.9	4.1	2.1	4,072	33.2	28.4	31.0	6.6	0.8	75,060
PULASKI	19,228	24,719	37.1	31.9	23.5	5.0	2.6	18,922	24.9	25.3	36.2	12.1	1.6	89,834
ROBERTSON	16,952	895	36.3	29.8	28.4	5.0	0.4	707	29.8	22.8	36.9	10.0	0.4	84,861
ROCKCASTLE	15,518	6,877	45.0	28.9	21.8	3.2	1.1	5,498	39.1	28.2	26.1	6.0	0.7	61,951
ROWAN	18,760	8,224	37.4	28.8	25.2	5.7	2.8	5,800	27.4	23.1	33.6	13.7	2.1	89,258
RUSSELL	16,418	7,423	46.5	31.8	16.0	4.1	1.6	5,942	31.3	28.0	30.6	8.4	1.7	75,324
SCOTT	29,655	15,807	18.0	22.1	35.2	15.5	9.1	11,213	9.5	9.4	41.7	33.7	5.7	153,485
SHELBY	26,576	15,204	18.7	24.2	35.2	15.6	6.2	11,174	2.5	8.9	39.0	39.1	10.5	173,884
SIMPSON	21,474	6,758	25.4	30.3	34.0	8.0	2.3	4,940	11.1	18.8	48.9	19.0	2.3	113,587
SPENCER	23,910	6,187	19.3	24.0	39.3	14.1	3.3	5,134	11.8	9.7	32.6	40.3	5.6	163,248
TAYLOR	19,366	9,611	37.5	31.2	23.7	5.2	2.4	7,032	14.9	26.0	46.4	11.0	1.7	98,666
TODD	18,049	4,730	35.8	30.9	26.5	4.9	1.9	3,671	25.9	30.9	30.8	10.5	1.9	80,688
TRIGG	21,659	5,736	30.4	30.8	29.8	6.5	2.5	4,697	16.6	22.1	39.4	19.1	2.8	106,509
TRIMBLE	20,614	3,662	26.7	31.0	32.6	7.6	2.1	2,981	22.5	22.7	37.9	14.6	2.2	98,051
UNION	22,300	5,769	27.4	28.9	32.4	7.9	3.4	4,527	29.5	28.5	32.5	8.7	0.7	77,914
WARREN	24,950	40,683	26.6	26.6	31.5	10.0	5.2	26,416	11.8	11.3	45.8	27.3	3.8	132,544
WASHINGTON	20,702	4,496	30.1	31.8	28.8	6.1	3.2	3,619	15.9	25.6	38.9	16.4	3.2	102,645
WAYNE	15,891	8,363	49.7	28.3	17.0	2.3	2.7	6,450	41.8	25.8	23.4	8.1	0.9	59,653
WEBSTER	19,379	5,724	32.1	30.3	29.4	6.5	1.7	4,505	42.5	28.4	24.7	3.5	0.9	58,882
WHITLEY	16,483	14,992	45.4	29.7	18.4	4.2	2.3	10,989	37.8	27.2	26.8	7.0	1.2	68,271
WOLFE	13,013	2,989	53.7	28.5	15.2	1.6	1.0	2,238	47.1	26.4	21.0	4.5	1.1	53,041
WOODFORD	30,711	9,808	15.8	24.2	34.2	18.6	7.3	7,249	3.2	6.1	42.9	40.5	7.3	170,599
KENTUCKY	23,912		29.2	27.7	29.0	9.1	4.9		18.5	19.6	39.0	19.8	3.1	109,419
UNITED STATES	27,916		21.9	25.0	32.3	12.3	8.4		7.9	10.5	27.1	35.6	19.0	192,285

SPENDING POTENTIAL INDICES

| COUNTY | FINANCIAL SERVICES | | | | THE HOME | | | | | | ENTERTAINMENT | | | | | | PERSONAL | | | |
| | | | | | Home Improvements | | Furnishings | | | | | | | | | | | | | |
	Auto Loan	Home Loan	Invest-ments	Retire-ment Plans	Home Repair	Lawn & Garden	Comput-ers & Hard-ware	Major Appli-ances	TV, Radio, Sound Equip-ment	Furni-ture	Dine out/ Carry out	Sports Equip-ment	Fees & Tickets	Toys & Games	Travel	Cable TV	Apparel & Services	Auto Repairs	Health Insur-ance	Pets & Supplies
MARION	82	60	46	58	65	84	62	74	70	60	69	65	55	73	61	74	59	69	81	79
MARSHALL	86	70	58	69	77	95	70	84	76	68	75	73	64	78	72	80	65	78	90	88
MARTIN	57	37	16	34	41	60	38	51	45	37	45	46	30	47	37	50	38	47	56	57
MASON	82	63	55	62	68	85	68	77	73	64	72	68	60	75	66	77	62	73	84	81
MEADE	88	70	55	69	69	81	72	77	76	71	76	71	66	79	69	78	66	76	80	81
MENIFEE	64	42	21	39	47	66	43	56	50	42	50	51	35	53	42	54	42	52	61	63
MERCER	82	72	70	72	76	87	72	80	77	71	75	70	69	78	74	80	66	76	86	82
METCALFE	72	50	29	47	55	76	50	65	57	49	57	57	42	61	49	61	48	59	70	71
MONROE	73	50	31	48	56	76	52	66	59	50	59	59	43	63	51	64	50	61	73	72
MONTGOMERY	82	68	59	67	71	84	68	77	73	67	72	68	64	76	68	76	63	73	82	81
MORGAN	69	47	26	44	52	71	48	62	55	46	55	55	40	58	47	60	46	57	67	68
MUHLENBERG	77	56	37	53	62	82	56	71	64	55	63	63	49	67	56	69	54	65	78	77
NELSON	93	77	66	77	77	90	79	85	82	77	82	77	73	85	76	84	72	83	88	89
NICHOLAS	84	58	36	55	65	88	60	76	68	57	67	67	50	71	59	74	57	70	83	83
OHIO	81	58	37	55	63	85	58	73	66	56	65	65	50	69	57	71	56	67	80	79
OLDHAM	146	169	170	169	165	153	146	149	140	155	141	138	158	145	153	139	130	144	140	150
OWEN	83	62	44	60	68	89	63	77	70	61	69	68	55	73	63	75	59	71	84	83
OWSLEY	51	34	20	32	37	52	36	45	43	35	42	40	30	42	35	47	36	43	51	50
PENDLETON	90	70	51	67	72	90	69	81	76	68	75	72	62	79	68	80	65	76	87	86
PERRY	65	43	24	41	48	68	46	59	54	44	53	53	37	56	45	58	45	55	65	65
PIKE	73	50	29	47	55	75	51	65	59	50	59	59	43	61	50	64	50	61	71	72
POWELL	74	51	29	48	55	76	51	65	59	51	58	59	43	62	50	63	50	60	70	72
PULASKI	74	56	45	54	60	77	58	69	64	56	63	61	51	66	57	68	54	65	76	73
ROBERTSON	74	52	28	49	60	83	52	70	58	51	58	61	43	61	52	63	49	63	75	76
ROCKCASTLE	67	44	21	41	49	70	45	59	53	44	52	54	36	56	44	57	44	54	65	66
ROWAN	74	58	47	57	59	72	63	68	66	59	65	61	56	67	60	68	57	66	71	71
RUSSELL	63	45	28	43	51	69	46	59	51	44	51	52	39	53	46	56	43	54	64	64
SCOTT	112	112	107	113	104	104	108	106	106	110	106	99	107	110	106	104	95	107	104	107
SHELBY	98	98	102	99	100	101	95	98	97	97	96	88	97	99	97	97	87	96	99	100
SIMPSON	82	71	65	70	74	86	69	78	74	69	73	68	66	77	70	77	64	74	83	81
SPENCER	97	93	88	93	92	97	86	92	89	88	88	83	87	92	88	90	78	89	94	95
TAYLOR	72	57	50	56	62	77	59	69	65	57	64	60	53	66	59	69	55	65	75	72
TODD	83	56	30	53	63	87	56	74	63	55	64	66	46	69	55	69	54	67	79	82
TRIGG	85	64	42	61	70	91	64	80	70	62	70	70	55	73	64	75	60	73	85	85
TRIMBLE	89	67	43	64	71	92	64	80	71	65	71	71	57	76	64	76	61	74	84	87
UNION	88	74	64	72	77	92	72	83	79	72	78	73	68	82	73	83	68	79	91	87
WARREN	88	81	82	83	79	83	86	83	86	84	86	77	83	87	83	86	77	85	85	85
WASHINGTON	87	65	46	62	71	93	65	80	73	63	72	71	57	77	65	78	62	74	88	86
WAYNE	67	46	27	43	50	69	47	60	54	46	54	54	39	57	46	59	46	56	66	66
WEBSTER	81	59	39	57	64	84	59	74	67	58	66	65	52	70	59	71	57	68	79	80
WHITLEY	67	48	36	47	52	69	52	62	58	49	57	55	44	59	50	62	49	58	68	66
WOLFE	56	36	16	33	40	58	37	49	44	36	43	45	29	46	36	48	37	45	54	55
WOODFORD	114	112	106	112	110	115	103	111	105	106	104	100	104	108	106	106	93	107	110	113
KENTUCKY	89	76	68	75	77	89	78	84	82	76	81	75	73	84	77	84	71	82	88	87
UNITED STATES	100	100	100	100	100	100	100	100	100	100	100	100	100	100	100	100	100	100	100	100

COUNTY	FIPS Code	CBSA Code	DMA Code	POPULATION			2000-2007 ANNUAL RATE		RACE (%)					
									White		Black		Asian/Pacific	
				2000	2007	2012	% Rate	State Rank	2000	2007	2000	2007	2000	2007
ACADIA	001	18940	642	58,861	60,192	61,085	0.3	31	80.7	77.8	18.2	20.9	0.2	0.2
ALLEN	003	00000	643	25,440	25,633	25,993	0.1	39	71.9	68.2	24.6	27.6	0.6	0.8
ASCENSION	005	12940	716	76,627	96,146	110,734	3.2	2	77.4	74.0	20.3	23.1	0.4	0.5
ASSUMPTION	007	38200	716	23,388	23,850	24,184	0.3	31	67.2	63.1	31.5	35.2	0.2	0.3
AVOYELLES	009	00000	644	41,481	42,787	43,708	0.4	24	68.5	64.5	29.5	33.1	0.2	0.2
BEAUREGARD	011	19760	643	32,986	34,672	36,319	0.7	15	84.2	81.5	12.9	14.9	0.6	0.9
BIENVILLE	013	00000	612	15,752	15,704	15,588	0.0	45	54.9	52.2	43.8	46.5	0.2	0.2
BOSSIER	015	43340	612	98,310	110,186	118,928	1.6	6	74.7	70.9	20.8	23.5	1.3	1.9
CADDO	017	43340	612	252,161	257,276	261,364	0.3	31	52.9	48.4	44.6	48.6	0.7	1.0
CALCASIEU	019	29340	643	183,577	191,448	197,057	0.6	17	73.6	66.4	24.0	30.6	0.7	1.0
CALDWELL	021	00000	628	10,560	10,558	10,553	0.0	45	80.4	78.7	17.9	19.6	0.1	0.2
CAMERON	023	29340	643	9,991	8,526	8,338	-2.2	62	93.7	94.9	3.9	2.3	0.5	1.0
CATAHOULA	025	00000	628	10,920	10,569	10,214	-0.4	53	71.8	68.1	27.1	30.6	0.1	0.2
CLAIBORNE	027	00000	612	16,851	16,473	16,142	-0.3	50	51.8	47.4	47.4	51.6	0.1	0.2
CONCORDIA	029	35020	628	20,247	19,551	19,065	-0.5	57	60.7	56.5	37.7	41.7	0.2	0.3
DE SOTO	031	43340	612	25,494	26,392	27,089	0.5	20	56.0	51.6	42.2	46.2	0.2	0.2
EAST BATON ROUGE	033	12940	716	412,852	425,099	434,419	0.4	24	56.2	51.5	40.1	43.7	2.1	2.9
EAST CARROLL	035	00000	628	9,421	8,884	8,517	-0.8	59	31.6	28.0	67.3	70.7	0.3	0.4
EAST FELICIANA	037	12940	716	21,360	21,572	21,873	0.1	39	51.8	47.4	47.1	51.3	0.2	0.3
EVANGELINE	039	00000	642	35,434	36,265	36,791	0.3	31	70.4	66.6	28.6	32.1	0.2	0.2
FRANKLIN	041	00000	628	21,263	20,729	20,159	-0.4	53	67.2	63.1	31.6	35.4	0.2	0.3
GRANT	043	10780	644	18,698	21,104	21,757	1.7	5	85.4	83.0	11.9	13.7	0.2	0.2
IBERIA	045	35340	642	73,266	75,691	77,506	0.5	20	65.1	60.6	30.8	34.1	2.0	2.7
IBERVILLE	047	12940	716	33,320	33,077	32,711	-0.1	47	49.3	44.9	49.7	53.9	0.3	0.4
JACKSON	049	40820	628	15,397	15,519	15,589	0.1	39	71.0	67.2	27.9	31.4	0.2	0.3
JEFFERSON	051	35380	622	455,466	437,195	424,201	-0.6	58	69.8	61.3	22.9	29.1	3.1	4.6
JEFFERSON DAVIS	053	27660	642	31,435	31,622	31,728	0.1	39	80.6	77.6	17.8	20.4	0.2	0.3
LAFAYETTE	055	29180	642	190,503	204,326	214,773	1.0	10	73.4	69.5	23.8	26.8	1.1	1.6
LAFOURCHE	057	26380	622	89,974	95,375	99,515	0.8	13	82.9	78.9	12.6	15.6	0.7	1.1
LA SALLE	059	00000	628	14,282	14,381	14,463	0.1	39	86.1	84.8	12.2	13.4	0.2	0.2
LINCOLN	061	40820	628	42,509	43,834	44,922	0.4	24	57.4	55.4	39.8	41.1	1.3	1.8
LIVINGSTON	063	12940	716	91,814	115,734	136,667	3.2	2	94.3	92.9	4.2	5.4	0.2	0.2
MADISON	065	45260	628	13,728	12,561	12,149	-1.2	61	37.9	33.9	60.3	64.1	0.2	0.2
MOREHOUSE	067	12820	628	31,021	30,188	29,171	-0.4	53	55.8	51.4	43.4	47.6	0.2	0.3
NATCHITOCHES	069	35060	612	39,080	39,993	41,140	0.3	31	57.9	53.4	38.4	42.2	0.5	0.6
ORLEANS	071	35380	622	484,674	264,969	285,769	-8.0	63	28.1	36.6	67.3	57.8	2.3	2.7
OUACHITA	073	33740	628	147,250	150,993	154,270	0.3	31	64.5	60.2	33.6	37.4	0.7	0.9
PLAQUEMINES	075	35380	622	26,757	28,966	30,627	1.1	9	69.8	75.3	23.4	19.7	2.6	1.1
POINTE COUPEE	077	12940	716	22,763	22,817	22,826	0.0	45	60.9	58.3	37.8	40.4	0.3	0.3
RAPIDES	079	10780	644	126,337	130,534	133,854	0.5	20	66.5	62.3	30.4	33.9	0.9	1.2
RED RIVER	081	00000	612	9,622	9,716	9,801	0.1	39	57.9	55.2	40.9	43.6	0.1	0.1
RICHLAND	083	00000	628	20,981	21,099	21,178	0.1	39	61.0	56.7	38.0	42.1	0.2	0.2
SABINE	085	00000	612	23,459	23,902	24,242	0.3	31	72.7	68.9	16.9	19.0	0.2	0.2
ST. BERNARD	087	35380	622	67,229	23,420	25,649	-14.0	64	88.3	66.3	7.6	30.0	1.3	1.3
ST. CHARLES	089	35380	622	48,072	53,008	56,827	1.4	7	72.4	67.2	25.2	30.2	0.6	0.5
ST. HELENA	091	12940	716	10,525	10,382	10,262	-0.2	48	46.5	42.2	52.4	56.6	0.1	0.1
ST. JAMES	093	00000	622	21,216	21,622	21,926	0.3	31	50.0	45.6	49.4	53.7	0.0	0.1
ST. JOHN THE BAPTIST	095	35380	622	43,044	46,973	49,929	1.2	8	52.6	48.2	44.8	48.6	0.6	0.8
ST. LANDRY	097	36660	642	87,700	91,014	93,378	0.5	20	56.5	52.1	42.1	46.3	0.2	0.3
ST. MARTIN	099	29180	642	48,583	51,767	54,079	0.9	12	65.9	61.7	32.0	35.6	0.9	1.3
ST. MARY	101	34020	716	53,500	52,369	51,143	-0.3	50	62.8	58.3	31.8	35.1	1.7	2.3
ST. TAMMANY	103	35380	622	191,268	229,541	261,220	2.5	3	87.0	83.8	9.9	12.4	0.8	1.0
TANGIPAHOA	105	25220	622	100,588	117,017	130,337	2.1	4	69.8	63.4	28.4	34.5	0.4	0.3
TENSAS	107	00000	628	6,618	6,151	5,799	-1.0	60	43.4	39.2	55.4	59.4	0.1	0.2
TERREBONNE	109	26380	622	104,503	111,664	117,038	0.9	12	74.1	70.3	17.8	20.1	0.8	1.2
UNION	111	33740	628	22,803	23,304	23,647	0.3	31	69.8	65.9	27.9	31.4	0.3	0.4
VERMILION	113	10020	642	53,807	56,659	58,905	0.7	15	82.7	78.1	14.2	17.4	1.8	2.9
VERNON	115	22860	644	52,531	51,199	50,316	-0.4	53	73.7	69.6	17.1	19.1	1.9	2.6
WASHINGTON	117	14220	622	43,926	45,009	45,854	0.3	31	67.4	63.4	31.5	35.3	0.2	0.2
WEBSTER	119	33380	612	41,831	41,775	41,785	0.0	45	65.5	63.0	32.8	35.3	0.2	0.2
WEST BATON ROUGE	121	12940	716	21,601	22,486	22,524	0.6	17	62.8	58.5	35.5	39.4	0.2	0.3
WEST CARROLL	123	00000	628	12,314	11,961	11,564	-0.4	53	79.9	76.9	18.9	21.6	0.1	0.2
WEST FELICIANA	125	12940	716	15,111	15,592	16,222	0.4	24	48.6	44.3	50.5	54.7	0.2	0.3
WINN	127	00000	628	16,894	16,260	15,862	-0.5	57	66.3	62.2	32.0	35.8	0.2	0.3
LOUISIANA							-0.3		63.9	62.2	32.5	33.5	1.3	1.6
UNITED STATES							1.2		75.1	72.7	12.3	12.6	3.8	4.5

POPULATION COMPOSITION

COUNTY	% HISPANIC ORIGIN		2007 AGE DISTRIBUTION (%)										MEDIAN AGE	% 2007 Males	% 2007 Females
	2000	2007	0-4	5-9	10-14	15-19	20-24	25-44	45-64	65-84	85+	18+	2007		
ACADIA	0.9	1.0	8.2	7.7	7.0	7.0	7.1	26.2	24.5	10.6	1.7	72.9	35.3	48.9	51.1
ALLEN	4.5	5.0	6.7	6.2	6.4	6.1	7.2	32.2	23.0	10.7	1.6	77.1	35.9	55.8	44.2
ASCENSION	2.5	2.9	8.5	7.7	7.3	6.7	6.9	30.6	24.4	6.9	0.9	72.4	33.9	49.3	50.7
ASSUMPTION	1.2	1.3	7.3	6.7	7.2	6.5	6.8	28.0	26.5	9.7	1.4	74.9	36.5	48.6	51.4
AVOYELLES	1.0	1.1	7.2	6.8	6.5	6.0	7.2	27.8	24.8	11.5	2.2	75.8	36.9	49.5	50.5
BEAUREGARD	1.4	1.7	7.2	6.8	7.1	6.6	7.1	26.7	25.8	11.4	1.4	75.0	36.9	50.3	49.7
BIENVILLE	0.9	1.0	7.1	6.3	6.6	6.2	7.1	24.0	25.5	13.9	3.2	76.2	39.9	48.1	51.9
BOSSIER	3.1	3.6	7.7	7.2	6.7	7.1	7.3	28.2	24.4	10.2	1.2	74.2	35.1	49.1	50.9
CADDO	1.5	1.6	7.0	6.6	6.6	7.2	7.4	26.0	25.4	11.6	2.2	75.5	36.3	47.6	52.4
CALCASIEU	1.3	1.6	7.4	6.8	6.8	6.8	7.5	27.3	25.3	10.6	1.5	75.0	35.6	48.8	51.2
CALDWELL	1.5	1.5	6.2	5.9	6.3	6.2	6.5	27.5	26.5	12.9	1.9	77.8	39.1	51.1	48.9
CAMERON	2.2	2.0	7.1	6.9	6.6	7.0	6.1	28.4	26.5	10.5	1.0	74.8	36.9	50.5	49.5
CATAHOULA	0.9	1.0	6.8	6.4	6.3	5.7	7.0	25.9	26.9	13.1	1.9	77.1	38.8	50.5	49.5
CLAIBORNE	0.8	0.8	6.3	5.8	6.2	6.6	7.1	25.1	26.3	13.9	2.8	77.7	40.0	50.2	49.8
CONCORDIA	1.5	1.6	7.4	7.0	6.6	6.5	7.2	23.6	27.3	12.6	1.9	75.1	38.7	49.5	50.5
DE SOTO	1.6	1.7	7.3	6.8	6.7	7.1	6.6	24.5	27.5	11.5	2.0	74.9	38.2	48.2	51.8
EAST BATON ROUGE	1.8	1.9	7.0	6.6	6.6	8.1	9.7	27.4	24.1	9.0	1.4	75.8	32.7	48.0	52.0
EAST CARROLL	1.2	1.2	8.1	7.1	8.0	7.7	8.5	26.9	21.1	10.6	1.9	72.2	31.9	51.5	48.5
EAST FELICIANA	0.7	0.8	6.7	6.7	6.3	5.9	7.1	28.8	26.9	10.5	1.3	76.7	37.4	53.4	46.6
EVANGELINE	1.0	1.1	8.4	7.7	7.1	6.8	7.3	26.2	23.6	10.9	2.0	72.7	35.3	49.9	50.1
FRANKLIN	0.8	0.8	7.6	7.1	6.3	6.9	6.5	25.0	24.7	13.4	2.4	74.8	37.8	48.3	51.7
GRANT	1.1	1.3	7.1	6.7	6.8	6.2	6.7	28.8	25.5	10.6	1.5	75.4	36.7	52.5	47.5
IBERIA	1.5	1.7	8.3	7.8	7.1	7.2	6.8	27.0	24.4	9.8	1.6	72.4	34.7	48.3	51.7
IBERVILLE	1.0	1.1	6.7	6.2	6.7	6.3	7.8	29.9	25.3	9.7	1.3	76.6	36.0	50.1	49.9
JACKSON	0.6	0.7	6.8	6.6	5.6	5.9	6.1	26.1	26.4	13.8	2.7	77.4	39.9	47.9	52.1
JEFFERSON	7.1	7.9	6.6	6.4	6.6	6.5	6.6	27.8	26.7	11.2	1.6	76.4	37.7	48.0	52.0
JEFFERSON DAVIS	1.0	1.1	8.0	7.3	7.4	6.6	6.8	25.7	24.9	11.7	1.7	73.3	36.1	48.5	51.5
LAFAYETTE	1.7	2.0	7.5	6.8	6.5	7.2	8.4	29.0	24.5	8.9	1.2	75.1	33.6	48.6	51.4
LAFOURCHE	1.4	1.8	7.3	6.6	6.6	6.8	7.0	29.0	25.2	10.2	1.3	75.6	36.4	48.9	51.1
LA SALLE	0.8	0.8	6.4	6.1	6.5	7.3	6.8	26.2	26.0	12.6	2.1	76.2	38.1	50.2	49.8
LINCOLN	1.2	1.3	6.4	5.6	5.3	10.4	15.5	24.2	21.0	9.8	1.9	79.5	29.1	49.2	50.8
LIVINGSTON	1.1	1.4	7.9	7.1	7.2	6.9	7.3	29.8	24.9	8.1	0.8	73.5	34.6	49.7	50.3
MADISON	2.1	2.3	8.9	8.0	7.6	9.1	8.5	24.4	22.2	9.6	1.8	69.5	30.9	50.0	50.0
MOREHOUSE	0.7	0.8	7.4	6.8	6.9	6.3	7.1	25.8	25.1	12.4	2.2	75.1	37.0	48.0	52.0
NATCHITOCHES	1.4	1.6	7.5	6.8	6.0	9.4	10.6	25.2	22.7	10.1	1.8	76.0	31.2	47.9	52.1
ORLEANS	3.1	4.6	6.6	6.2	6.5	7.6	8.8	28.1	24.5	9.8	1.7	76.7	34.4	47.5	52.5
OUACHITA	1.2	1.3	7.5	7.0	7.0	7.6	7.6	27.7	23.3	10.7	1.6	74.2	33.7	47.4	52.6
PLAQUEMINES	1.6	2.2	8.4	7.5	7.6	6.5	6.9	29.4	23.7	9.1	0.8	72.3	34.1	50.0	50.0
POINTE COUPEE	1.1	1.1	7.1	6.7	6.8	5.8	7.1	25.1	27.7	11.8	1.9	75.9	39.0	48.6	51.4
RAPIDES	1.4	1.5	7.3	6.8	6.8	6.6	7.1	26.4	25.2	11.9	1.8	75.0	37.1	47.9	52.1
RED RIVER	1.0	1.1	8.3	7.3	7.6	6.9	7.1	24.8	24.2	11.7	2.1	72.6	35.5	47.5	52.5
RICHLAND	1.1	1.2	7.8	7.3	6.6	5.8	7.0	25.9	25.0	12.3	2.3	74.9	37.0	47.2	52.8
SABINE	2.7	3.1	6.9	6.4	5.9	6.2	6.3	24.0	27.2	14.9	2.2	77.0	40.9	49.0	51.0
ST. BERNARD	5.1	4.8	6.5	5.7	6.1	6.4	6.8	27.3	26.9	12.8	1.5	77.8	39.1	48.4	51.6
ST. CHARLES	2.8	3.3	7.5	7.2	7.5	7.3	6.8	27.5	26.6	8.7	1.0	73.2	36.5	48.7	51.3
ST. HELENA	1.0	1.1	7.7	7.4	6.7	6.5	6.3	25.0	26.4	11.9	1.6	74.4	37.6	48.7	51.3
ST. JAMES	0.6	0.7	7.4	6.8	7.3	6.7	7.0	26.8	25.7	10.9	1.4	74.4	36.6	48.3	51.7
ST. JOHN THE BAPTIST	2.9	3.2	8.2	7.4	7.5	7.3	7.5	27.2	26.2	7.8	0.9	72.4	34.3	48.5	51.5
ST. LANDRY	0.9	1.0	8.3	7.6	6.8	6.7	7.3	25.3	24.6	11.6	1.8	73.1	35.9	48.0	52.0
ST. MARTIN	0.8	0.9	8.0	7.7	7.0	6.8	6.9	27.3	25.8	9.2	1.2	73.1	35.0	49.3	50.7
ST. MARY	2.2	2.4	7.8	7.1	7.5	7.0	7.1	26.3	25.3	10.6	1.3	73.2	36.0	48.9	51.1
ST. TAMMANY	2.5	3.0	7.2	7.0	7.2	6.9	6.6	25.6	29.1	9.3	1.1	74.2	38.1	48.8	51.2
TANGIPAHOA	1.5	1.8	7.5	6.9	6.8	7.2	8.5	27.4	25.1	9.4	1.3	75.0	33.9	48.5	51.5
TENSAS	1.3	1.4	6.8	6.6	5.4	6.9	8.9	23.0	28.3	11.6	2.4	77.4	38.9	50.4	49.6
TERREBONNE	1.6	1.8	7.9	7.0	6.9	6.9	7.8	28.5	24.6	9.3	1.1	74.0	34.6	49.0	51.0
UNION	2.0	2.3	7.2	6.9	6.0	5.5	5.9	26.2	26.7	13.6	2.0	76.5	39.1	48.9	51.1
VERMILION	1.4	1.7	7.6	6.9	6.7	6.4	6.8	27.3	25.1	11.3	2.0	74.9	36.9	48.7	51.3
VERNON	5.9	6.8	9.6	7.3	6.2	6.6	11.9	30.2	19.1	8.1	0.9	73.4	29.1	52.4	47.6
WASHINGTON	0.8	0.8	7.3	7.1	6.6	6.0	6.8	25.5	26.5	12.4	1.9	75.4	37.7	49.0	51.0
WEBSTER	0.9	0.9	6.8	6.4	5.8	6.6	6.5	25.0	26.5	14.0	2.4	77.0	40.1	48.3	51.7
WEST BATON ROUGE	1.4	1.6	7.3	6.8	6.8	6.8	7.6	28.7	25.7	9.3	1.1	75.0	35.7	49.2	50.8
WEST CARROLL	1.3	1.5	6.6	5.9	6.3	5.9	7.8	25.9	25.9	13.4	2.5	77.8	39.2	51.0	49.0
WEST FELICIANA	1.0	1.1	4.7	4.3	4.9	5.3	8.6	36.8	28.0	6.6	0.8	82.7	37.6	65.4	34.6
WINN	0.9	1.0	6.5	6.3	5.8	6.1	7.4	28.6	25.5	11.7	2.1	77.9	37.7	52.8	47.2
LOUISIANA	2.4	2.7	7.3	6.8	6.7	7.0	7.7	27.4	25.2	10.3	1.5	75.1	35.5	48.7	51.3
UNITED STATES	12.5	15.0	6.9	6.5	6.8	7.1	7.0	27.6	25.4	10.7	1.9	75.6	36.7	49.2	50.8

COUNTY	HOUSEHOLDS					FAMILIES			MEDIAN HOUSEHOLD INCOME			
	2000	2007	2012	% Annual Rate 2000-2007	2007 Average HH Size	2000	2007	% Annual Rate 2000-2007	2007	2012	2007 National Rank	2007 State Rank
ACADIA	21,142	22,055	22,565	0.6	2.68	15,676	15,991	0.3	29,915	32,391	2915	43
ALLEN	8,102	8,454	8,689	0.6	2.56	5,927	6,043	0.3	30,423	32,711	2890	41
ASCENSION	26,691	34,583	40,261	3.6	2.76	20,789	26,415	3.4	51,038	56,226	615	3
ASSUMPTION	8,239	8,678	8,924	0.7	2.73	6,312	6,512	0.4	34,861	38,054	2446	22
AVOYELLES	14,736	15,635	16,170	0.8	2.54	10,584	10,960	0.5	25,983	27,828	3071	56
BEAUREGARD	12,104	13,071	13,858	1.1	2.56	9,080	9,593	0.8	36,355	39,973	2222	18
BIENVILLE	6,108	6,227	6,236	0.3	2.46	4,216	4,182	-0.1	26,571	28,693	3051	53
BOSSIER	36,628	42,107	45,879	1.9	2.57	26,627	29,880	1.6	44,596	48,710	1148	4
CADDO	97,974	101,081	103,304	0.4	2.48	64,980	65,095	0.0	35,251	38,208	2400	21
CALCASIEU	68,613	73,635	76,602	1.0	2.54	49,034	51,322	0.6	39,303	42,830	1820	14
CALDWELL	3,941	4,055	4,102	0.4	2.43	2,819	2,828	0.0	30,200	31,802	2899	42
CAMERON	3,592	3,135	3,096	-1.9	2.70	2,703	2,309	-2.1	37,469	40,543	2068	17
CATAHOULA	4,082	4,076	3,989	0.0	2.47	2,994	2,919	-0.3	25,338	27,064	3086	59
CLAIBORNE	6,270	6,259	6,181	0.0	2.45	4,336	4,212	-0.4	28,276	30,752	2990	47
CONCORDIA	7,521	7,470	7,369	-0.1	2.53	5,433	5,266	-0.4	25,172	27,154	3092	60
DE SOTO	9,691	10,283	10,665	0.8	2.54	6,969	7,214	0.5	30,604	32,849	2876	40
EAST BATON ROUGE	156,365	164,788	169,890	0.7	2.49	102,581	104,895	0.3	41,624	44,943	1503	10
EAST CARROLL	2,969	2,851	2,747	-0.6	2.75	2,140	2,005	-0.9	22,395	24,090	3122	63
EAST FELICIANA	6,699	7,128	7,347	0.9	2.66	5,032	5,239	0.6	35,642	38,636	2338	20
EVANGELINE	12,736	13,335	13,658	0.6	2.59	9,151	9,347	0.3	22,907	24,723	3116	62
FRANKLIN	7,754	7,755	7,617	0.0	2.57	5,705	5,574	-0.3	25,714	27,490	3077	57
GRANT	7,073	7,588	7,922	1.0	2.55	5,274	5,533	0.7	32,066	34,499	2754	32
IBERIA	25,381	26,455	27,249	0.6	2.80	19,165	19,552	0.3	34,571	37,691	2488	24
IBERVILLE	10,674	10,867	10,839	0.2	2.74	8,012	7,982	-0.1	32,128	35,108	2747	31
JACKSON	6,086	6,302	6,403	0.5	2.42	4,300	4,338	0.1	31,641	34,520	2791	35
JEFFERSON	176,234	168,894	164,294	-0.6	2.56	120,183	112,011	-1.0	42,816	46,590	1352	8
JEFFERSON DAVIS	11,480	11,808	11,956	0.4	2.64	8,525	8,570	0.1	30,889	33,605	2845	39
LAFAYETTE	72,372	79,110	83,820	1.2	2.52	48,839	51,888	0.8	41,226	45,002	1563	11
LAFOURCHE	32,057	34,217	35,931	0.9	2.74	24,296	25,387	0.6	38,665	41,656	1902	16
LA SALLE	5,291	5,438	5,515	0.4	2.47	3,798	3,810	0.0	31,484	34,208	2801	37
LINCOLN	15,235	16,139	16,747	0.8	2.39	9,686	9,939	0.4	29,860	32,340	2918	44
LIVINGSTON	32,630	42,119	50,236	3.6	2.73	25,545	32,351	3.3	43,729	47,684	1247	6
MADISON	4,469	4,303	4,184	-0.5	2.69	3,140	2,946	-0.9	23,223	25,074	3111	61
MOREHOUSE	11,382	11,406	11,152	0.0	2.56	8,319	8,143	-0.3	28,271	30,734	2991	48
NATCHITOCHES	14,263	15,164	15,780	0.8	2.50	9,503	9,812	0.4	28,611	31,030	2975	46
ORLEANS	188,251	101,403	109,851	-8.2	2.49	112,977	58,765	-8.6	32,959	36,261	2658	28
OUACHITA	55,216	57,340	58,960	0.5	2.56	38,319	38,741	0.2	35,967	39,160	2281	19
PLAQUEMINES	9,021	10,020	10,710	1.5	2.82	6,999	7,623	1.2	42,734	46,587	1359	9
POINTE COUPEE	8,397	8,674	8,789	0.4	2.59	6,171	6,227	0.1	34,196	37,012	2527	26
RAPIDES	47,120	49,854	51,679	0.8	2.51	33,133	34,157	0.4	32,950	35,985	2661	29
RED RIVER	3,414	3,483	3,525	0.3	2.71	2,527	2,520	0.0	26,290	28,444	3060	54
RICHLAND	7,490	7,751	7,876	0.5	2.57	5,481	5,540	0.1	26,054	28,140	3068	55
SABINE	9,221	9,627	9,864	0.6	2.44	6,596	6,717	0.3	29,332	31,747	2943	45
ST. BERNARD	25,123	8,962	9,898	-13.0	2.61	18,301	6,379	-14.0	33,087	36,706	2649	27
ST. CHARLES	16,422	18,290	19,671	1.5	2.87	13,094	14,325	1.2	51,086	55,759	607	2
ST. HELENA	3,873	3,949	3,959	0.3	2.61	2,784	2,769	-0.1	27,843	30,259	3007	49
ST. JAMES	6,992	7,347	7,546	0.7	2.91	5,550	5,726	0.4	39,273	42,824	1824	15
ST. JOHN THE BAPTIST	14,283	15,942	17,105	1.5	2.92	11,314	12,401	1.3	43,627	47,044	1258	7
ST. LANDRY	32,328	34,077	35,301	0.7	2.63	23,205	23,864	0.4	25,586	27,462	3082	58
ST. MARTIN	17,164	18,818	19,902	1.3	2.71	12,983	13,934	1.0	34,241	37,341	2522	25
ST. MARY	19,317	19,482	19,267	0.1	2.66	14,090	13,874	-0.2	31,556	34,442	2795	36
ST. TAMMANY	69,253	83,601	95,606	2.6	2.72	52,727	62,329	2.3	55,764	62,361	374	1
TANGIPAHOA	36,558	43,239	48,599	2.3	2.63	25,768	29,696	2.0	32,052	34,526	2756	33
TENSAS	2,416	2,310	2,198	-0.6	2.45	1,635	1,521	-1.0	21,861	23,486	3126	64
TERREBONNE	35,997	39,507	41,852	1.3	2.79	27,409	29,458	1.0	39,747	43,207	1753	13
UNION	8,857	9,317	9,572	0.7	2.45	6,412	6,583	0.4	32,518	35,473	2703	30
VERMILION	19,832	21,306	22,335	1.0	2.62	14,453	15,158	0.7	32,041	34,581	2757	34
VERNON	18,260	18,219	18,081	0.0	2.62	13,706	13,381	-0.3	34,835	37,573	2452	23
WASHINGTON	16,467	17,331	17,835	0.7	2.50	11,646	11,947	0.4	26,581	28,746	3050	52
WEBSTER	16,501	16,833	16,984	0.3	2.43	11,559	11,486	-0.1	31,042	33,390	2828	38
WEST BATON ROUGE	7,663	8,188	8,288	0.9	2.68	5,736	5,996	0.6	41,220	44,325	1565	12
WEST CARROLL	4,458	4,419	4,302	-0.1	2.53	3,250	3,148	-0.4	26,988	28,703	3037	51
WEST FELICIANA	3,645	3,901	4,171	0.9	2.68	2,705	2,830	0.6	44,075	47,781	1200	5
WINN	5,930	5,846	5,741	-0.2	2.49	4,235	4,071	-0.5	27,830	30,196	3010	50
LOUISIANA				-0.1	2.59			-0.3	37,186	40,783		
UNITED STATES				1.2	2.59			1.0	53,154	62,503		

26-C

LOUISIANA
D

INCOME

COUNTY	2007 Per Capita Income	2007 HH Income Base	2007 HOUSEHOLD INCOME DISTRIBUTION (%)					2007 Home Value Base	2007 HOME VALUE DISTRIBUTION (%)					2007 Median Home Value
			Less than $25,000	$25,000 to $49,999	$50,000 to $99,999	$100,000 to $149,999	$150,000 or More		Less than $50,000	$50,000 to $89,999	$90,000 to $174,999	$175,000 to $399,999	$400,000 or More	
ACADIA	15,730	22,055	43.1	28.2	22.2	4.2	2.3	15,816	27.1	26.5	33.9	11.1	1.4	84,335
ALLEN	15,588	8,454	42.4	28.4	22.3	5.1	1.7	6,367	27.2	27.3	34.6	9.9	0.9	81,676
ASCENSION	21,624	34,583	23.8	25.1	36.1	11.8	3.1	28,170	16.5	16.7	34.6	28.9	3.2	126,433
ASSUMPTION	16,668	8,678	38.0	27.1	27.1	5.9	1.9	7,212	31.1	19.6	32.8	14.9	1.5	88,479
AVOYELLES	14,292	15,635	48.3	27.4	19.6	3.1	1.6	11,525	27.2	27.1	35.8	9.0	0.9	83,260
BEAUREGARD	18,502	13,071	33.9	30.6	26.1	7.1	2.3	10,353	28.2	23.8	33.7	12.7	1.6	86,157
BIENVILLE	14,499	6,227	47.5	28.8	19.3	3.1	1.3	4,805	38.8	26.3	25.8	7.8	1.3	65,185
BOSSIER	21,735	42,107	26.8	28.4	32.5	8.7	3.6	29,047	16.9	19.6	40.0	20.7	2.8	112,797
CADDO	20,659	101,076	36.4	28.7	23.9	7.0	4.0	63,713	20.3	25.1	36.3	15.7	2.6	98,329
CALCASIEU	20,814	73,634	32.3	28.4	27.9	7.9	3.5	52,172	20.0	25.2	37.0	15.7	2.0	97,999
CALDWELL	16,318	4,055	43.2	28.3	23.3	3.5	1.8	3,182	33.0	26.2	29.7	10.2	0.8	73,122
CAMERON	17,943	3,135	33.5	29.4	29.4	5.4	2.3	2,646	35.4	26.3	26.7	10.3	1.3	72,143
CATAHOULA	14,683	4,076	49.3	29.0	15.8	4.4	1.5	3,358	41.6	24.4	25.9	7.1	0.9	60,931
CLAIBORNE	16,126	6,259	45.3	28.9	19.3	4.5	2.0	4,714	31.2	27.5	28.4	11.0	1.9	74,762
CONCORDIA	14,038	7,470	49.7	27.4	18.6	2.9	1.3	5,601	32.4	27.4	30.5	8.6	1.1	75,417
DE SOTO	15,834	10,283	42.2	27.8	24.4	4.3	1.3	7,801	28.8	27.0	31.4	11.8	1.1	80,631
EAST BATON ROUGE	23,434	164,782	30.9	26.5	27.5	9.6	5.5	100,258	7.9	15.4	42.0	29.2	5.4	137,751
EAST CARROLL	11,798	2,851	53.9	30.6	11.7	2.6	1.3	1,749	37.2	32.3	25.8	3.8	0.9	60,051
EAST FELICIANA	17,520	7,128	37.5	26.7	26.0	7.5	2.3	5,826	26.7	22.0	29.8	17.8	3.7	92,702
EVANGELINE	13,400	13,335	52.6	24.4	17.8	3.9	1.3	9,186	28.1	29.7	31.8	9.8	0.7	76,657
FRANKLIN	14,135	7,755	48.5	31.7	15.4	2.7	1.6	5,858	35.8	28.8	27.0	7.8	0.5	68,722
GRANT	16,258	7,588	40.0	30.2	22.8	5.4	1.6	6,147	33.3	26.3	28.0	11.5	0.9	74,650
IBERIA	16,400	26,450	38.2	28.3	25.1	5.9	2.6	19,268	21.8	22.3	38.9	15.0	2.1	100,462
IBERVILLE	16,160	10,867	40.3	27.1	23.7	6.1	2.7	8,294	25.7	22.6	33.6	16.1	2.0	92,811
JACKSON	17,304	6,302	40.3	29.3	23.1	5.6	1.7	4,826	29.1	27.8	30.1	11.2	1.9	77,895
JEFFERSON	22,982	168,887	27.3	29.7	29.0	9.5	4.5	106,982	3.1	7.8	42.9	38.1	8.1	166,314
JEFFERSON DAVIS	15,557	11,808	41.9	28.8	22.9	4.8	1.6	8,782	23.1	26.7	38.8	10.3	1.1	90,253
LAFAYETTE	22,707	79,110	30.9	27.4	27.6	9.4	4.7	51,697	15.8	15.5	37.8	26.5	4.4	126,539
LAFOURCHE	18,049	34,217	32.6	29.8	28.9	6.0	2.6	26,454	19.2	21.4	39.2	18.1	2.1	105,961
LA SALLE	16,247	5,438	40.6	30.4	22.9	4.6	1.6	4,478	36.6	25.3	28.7	8.7	0.7	69,418
LINCOLN	17,478	16,136	43.2	25.3	24.0	4.9	2.6	9,487	20.5	19.4	37.3	19.2	3.6	108,854
LIVINGSTON	19,436	42,119	25.9	30.3	33.1	8.5	2.2	34,984	18.9	19.0	37.6	23.0	1.5	112,947
MADISON	12,003	4,303	52.7	30.1	14.0	2.4	0.8	2,628	34.9	26.8	28.9	8.2	1.1	71,046
MOREHOUSE	15,603	11,406	45.4	27.4	21.4	4.1	1.8	8,076	30.4	29.8	29.8	9.2	0.9	73,333
NATCHITOCHES	16,357	15,164	44.9	28.6	19.2	4.8	2.5	9,674	26.3	20.7	36.0	14.5	2.5	94,948
ORLEANS	18,901	101,397	39.0	29.0	23.1	5.4	3.5	46,753	9.1	30.5	32.7	19.8	8.0	107,328
OUACHITA	19,861	57,340	35.6	28.0	25.2	7.6	3.5	36,418	21.8	23.2	36.7	16.0	2.2	98,339
PLAQUEMINES	19,434	10,019	29.7	28.6	28.7	9.5	3.5	7,797	27.7	16.0	24.1	26.5	5.8	107,728
POINTE COUPEE	17,739	8,674	38.1	28.4	24.9	6.2	2.2	6,676	22.6	23.0	32.3	19.2	2.9	97,670
RAPIDES	18,776	49,854	38.1	29.5	23.4	6.0	3.1	33,724	21.3	24.1	37.6	14.8	2.1	95,837
RED RIVER	13,812	3,483	47.7	28.6	18.9	3.1	1.7	2,629	32.6	28.9	30.4	6.9	1.1	72,098
RICHLAND	14,859	7,751	48.4	25.8	20.2	3.7	1.9	5,561	28.1	27.8	30.9	12.6	0.7	80,045
SABINE	17,030	9,627	42.2	30.6	20.5	4.5	2.2	7,721	35.4	22.4	29.8	11.0	1.3	74,021
ST. BERNARD	18,325	8,954	38.7	29.5	23.5	5.0	3.3	6,633	13.8	31.1	45.8	8.6	0.7	95,061
ST. CHARLES	22,031	18,290	23.5	25.2	33.8	12.6	4.8	14,778	7.3	11.1	38.6	36.6	6.4	158,872
ST. HELENA	14,910	3,949	45.8	26.8	21.1	4.8	1.4	3,311	33.5	22.2	29.1	11.7	3.5	76,159
ST. JAMES	17,289	7,347	33.9	25.2	29.1	10.1	1.7	6,216	23.1	20.1	37.0	18.8	1.0	102,630
ST. JOHN THE BAPTIST	18,280	15,942	28.6	27.1	31.9	10.1	2.3	12,767	11.7	11.9	49.3	24.8	2.2	133,441
ST. LANDRY	13,805	34,077	49.1	26.9	18.8	3.8	1.4	23,858	26.4	28.2	32.6	11.5	1.3	82,816
ST. MARTIN	15,962	18,818	38.7	28.8	25.8	5.0	1.7	15,196	26.7	25.6	33.3	13.3	1.2	86,426
ST. MARY	15,621	19,482	41.2	28.4	23.7	5.3	1.4	14,259	26.1	19.9	40.2	12.0	1.8	98,181
ST. TAMMANY	27,593	83,601	21.7	23.1	31.6	15.0	8.6	67,004	7.2	7.2	30.5	43.7	11.4	188,186
TANGIPAHOA	16,565	43,239	39.9	28.4	23.9	5.9	2.0	31,360	21.4	17.7	36.0	21.1	3.8	111,119
TENSAS	15,053	2,310	54.4	27.1	11.7	4.4	2.4	1,579	37.0	27.2	20.0	11.9	3.9	66,919
TERREBONNE	18,931	39,507	32.6	28.0	28.4	7.7	3.3	29,587	17.5	20.5	42.7	16.6	2.7	109,271
UNION	17,139	9,317	38.2	31.8	23.5	5.3	1.3	7,510	33.2	26.9	29.2	9.3	1.4	74,803
VERMILION	16,406	21,306	40.6	27.9	24.3	5.5	1.8	16,324	24.8	24.6	34.8	13.8	2.0	91,025
VERNON	16,223	18,213	32.8	36.6	24.7	4.4	1.5	10,217	29.2	22.8	36.5	9.8	1.7	86,503
WASHINGTON	14,777	17,331	47.2	29.0	18.9	3.5	1.4	13,091	28.4	25.6	32.3	11.8	1.9	83,779
WEBSTER	17,646	16,833	40.6	30.9	21.7	4.8	2.1	12,408	27.7	28.8	31.6	10.2	1.7	79,829
WEST BATON ROUGE	19,116	8,188	29.8	29.6	29.6	8.6	2.4	6,399	22.6	18.8	38.1	19.2	1.3	105,002
WEST CARROLL	14,762	4,419	46.7	28.8	19.3	3.9	1.4	3,474	35.6	29.2	26.3	7.9	1.1	68,099
WEST FELICIANA	18,525	3,901	30.4	25.6	29.6	9.9	4.5	2,901	21.7	14.6	30.8	22.6	10.3	118,561
WINN	14,614	5,846	44.8	32.1	17.4	4.3	1.4	4,316	41.3	27.0	23.5	7.0	1.2	59,895
LOUISIANA	19,796		34.5	28.1	26.2	7.6	3.6		18.1	19.9	36.5	21.5	3.9	112,331
UNITED STATES	27,916		21.9	25.0	32.3	12.3	8.4		7.9	10.5	27.1	35.6	19.0	192,285

COUNTY	FINANCIAL SERVICES				THE HOME						ENTERTAINMENT						PERSONAL			
					Home Improvements		Furnishings													
	Auto Loan	Home Loan	Invest-ments	Retire-ment Plans	Home Repair	Lawn & Garden	Comput-ers & Hard-ware	Major Appli-ances	TV, Radio, Sound Equip-ment	Furni-ture	Dine out/ Carry out	Sports Equip-ment	Fees & Tickets	Toys & Games	Travel	Cable TV	Apparel & Services	Auto Repairs	Health Insur-ance	Pets & Supplies
ACADIA	69	52	39	51	54	70	53	62	60	53	59	55	48	62	53	64	51	60	69	67
ALLEN	68	50	37	48	54	70	52	62	59	51	58	55	46	61	51	64	50	59	70	67
ASCENSION	93	85	70	83	79	87	79	85	82	82	82	77	77	85	78	84	73	83	85	88
ASSUMPTION	78	57	36	54	61	80	56	70	64	56	63	63	49	67	55	68	54	65	75	76
AVOYELLES	61	43	30	42	47	63	45	55	52	44	52	49	39	53	45	57	44	53	62	60
BEAUREGARD	79	61	46	59	64	80	61	72	67	60	66	64	55	70	60	71	57	68	77	77
BIENVILLE	61	42	25	40	46	64	43	55	51	43	50	49	36	52	43	56	43	52	61	61
BOSSIER	82	76	74	77	74	77	77	77	78	77	78	70	75	80	75	79	70	78	79	78
CADDO	73	66	70	68	64	69	70	68	74	70	73	61	68	73	69	76	65	71	74	70
CALCASIEU	78	70	70	71	69	75	72	73	75	71	74	65	70	75	71	77	66	74	78	75
CALDWELL	69	48	28	46	53	74	49	63	57	48	56	55	41	58	49	62	48	58	69	69
CAMERON	83	62	38	59	66	87	60	76	67	60	67	67	53	70	60	71	57	70	80	82
CATAHOULA	65	43	21	40	49	69	44	59	51	43	51	53	36	54	43	56	43	54	64	65
CLAIBORNE	67	48	32	46	53	71	49	62	57	48	56	54	43	58	49	62	48	58	69	67
CONCORDIA	57	42	33	42	45	59	44	52	51	44	50	45	39	51	44	55	43	50	59	56
DE SOTO	67	49	34	47	52	68	50	60	57	49	56	53	44	58	49	61	49	57	66	65
EAST BATON ROUGE	82	76	82	80	74	75	84	77	84	82	84	71	81	83	80	83	76	82	79	79
EAST CARROLL	50	36	31	36	38	49	40	45	48	40	46	39	36	46	39	52	40	45	53	48
EAST FELICIANA	83	61	39	58	65	85	60	75	68	60	67	67	53	70	60	73	58	70	80	82
EVANGELINE	58	41	29	40	44	58	43	52	50	42	49	46	38	51	42	54	42	50	58	56
FRANKLIN	62	43	28	41	47	63	45	56	52	44	51	49	38	53	44	57	44	52	62	60
GRANT	72	53	33	50	57	75	52	66	59	52	59	58	45	61	52	64	50	61	71	71
IBERIA	72	59	52	58	60	71	60	66	65	59	64	58	56	66	59	68	56	64	71	70
IBERVILLE	74	55	41	54	57	74	57	67	65	56	64	59	51	66	56	70	55	65	74	72
JACKSON	69	51	37	49	55	72	52	64	60	51	59	56	46	61	52	64	50	60	71	68
JEFFERSON	80	79	87	81	78	78	82	78	82	82	82	71	82	82	81	83	74	81	81	79
JEFFERSON DAVIS	68	50	37	49	54	70	52	62	58	50	57	55	45	60	51	63	49	59	69	67
LAFAYETTE	83	77	77	79	73	76	81	77	81	80	81	71	78	81	78	81	72	80	78	79
LAFOURCHE	81	64	49	62	66	81	64	74	69	63	69	66	58	72	63	73	60	70	78	78
LA SALLE	70	49	31	47	54	74	50	64	57	49	57	56	43	60	50	62	48	59	70	69
LINCOLN	63	50	52	53	49	56	64	57	63	57	63	53	56	62	57	63	56	61	60	59
LIVINGSTON	85	74	59	72	72	81	70	77	73	71	73	70	67	76	69	75	64	75	78	81
MADISON	50	36	31	36	37	49	41	45	48	40	46	39	36	47	40	51	40	45	52	48
MOREHOUSE	66	47	36	46	51	66	51	59	58	49	57	52	44	58	49	62	49	57	66	64
NATCHITOCHES	66	48	39	48	50	64	55	60	60	51	59	54	47	60	52	62	51	59	65	64
ORLEANS	63	58	66	62	57	57	67	60	69	65	69	55	65	66	64	69	63	65	63	61
OUACHITA	75	66	66	67	64	70	70	69	73	69	72	62	67	72	68	74	64	71	73	71
PLAQUEMINES	86	73	59	71	73	83	74	80	77	73	77	74	69	80	72	78	68	78	81	84
POINTE COUPEE	76	56	41	55	60	78	58	69	66	56	64	61	51	66	58	70	55	66	77	74
RAPIDES	71	62	59	63	62	70	63	67	68	63	67	59	61	67	63	70	59	66	72	69
RED RIVER	65	43	24	42	48	67	46	58	53	45	53	52	38	55	44	57	45	54	63	64
RICHLAND	65	45	30	44	50	67	48	59	55	46	54	52	41	56	47	59	46	55	66	64
SABINE	69	51	36	49	56	74	52	65	58	51	58	56	46	59	52	63	49	60	71	69
ST. BERNARD	70	64	63	63	64	70	64	68	67	63	66	60	62	67	64	69	58	66	73	69
ST. CHARLES	92	92	89	92	90	92	85	89	86	88	86	80	87	89	87	87	78	87	89	91
ST. HELENA	70	45	21	42	51	73	47	63	55	45	54	56	37	58	46	60	46	57	68	70
ST. JAMES	85	63	42	60	68	89	62	78	70	62	70	69	55	74	62	76	60	72	83	85
ST. JOHN THE BAPTIST	80	74	66	73	72	79	71	75	74	72	74	68	69	76	70	76	65	74	78	79
ST. LANDRY	58	43	34	43	45	58	46	52	52	45	51	46	41	53	45	56	45	51	59	56
ST. MARTIN	74	54	35	51	56	74	54	66	61	54	61	59	47	64	53	65	52	62	71	71
ST. MARY	66	52	42	51	53	66	53	60	59	53	58	53	48	60	52	63	51	58	66	64
ST. TAMMANY	109	113	106	113	108	108	102	106	101	107	101	97	105	104	104	101	91	103	103	107
TANGIPAHOA	70	55	46	55	55	67	58	63	62	56	62	57	53	63	56	64	54	62	67	66
TENSAS	61	43	32	43	46	62	46	55	54	46	53	48	41	53	46	59	46	54	62	59
TERREBONNE	82	70	61	69	70	80	70	76	74	70	73	68	66	76	69	77	65	74	80	79
UNION	74	51	28	48	56	78	52	67	59	50	59	60	43	62	51	64	50	61	73	74
VERMILION	72	54	38	52	57	74	54	65	60	54	60	58	48	62	54	64	52	62	71	70
VERNON	69	50	40	51	50	61	61	61	62	55	62	57	52	64	55	62	54	62	62	63
WASHINGTON	61	44	32	43	48	63	46	56	53	45	52	49	40	54	46	58	45	53	63	60
WEBSTER	68	53	44	52	56	70	55	63	61	54	60	55	50	62	54	65	52	61	70	67
WEST BATON ROUGE	77	72	68	72	69	75	68	72	72	70	71	64	68	73	69	73	63	71	75	74
WEST CARROLL	66	45	25	43	52	72	46	61	52	44	52	53	38	55	46	57	44	55	66	67
WEST FELICIANA	94	76	60	74	77	93	75	86	81	74	80	77	69	83	75	85	69	82	91	91
WINN	62	43	30	42	47	63	46	56	53	45	52	49	40	54	45	58	45	53	62	60
LOUISIANA	77	67	62	67	67	75	69	72	73	68	72	65	66	73	68	75	64	72	76	75
UNITED STATES	100	100	100	100	100	100	100	100	100	100	100	100	100	100	100	100	100	100	100	100

COUNTY	FIPS Code	CBSA Code	DMA Code	POPULATION			2000-2007 ANNUAL RATE		RACE (%)					
									White		Black		Asian/Pacific	
				2000	2007	2012	% Rate	State Rank	2000	2007	2000	2007	2000	2007
ANDROSCOGGIN	001	30340	500	103,793	109,926	114,593	0.8	9	97.0	96.5	0.7	0.8	0.6	0.8
AROOSTOOK	003	00000	552	73,938	73,496	73,449	-0.1	16	96.8	96.3	0.4	0.5	0.5	0.7
CUMBERLAND	005	38860	500	265,612	283,903	293,659	0.9	7	95.7	94.8	1.1	1.3	1.4	2.0
FRANKLIN	007	00000	500	29,467	30,293	30,578	0.4	13	98.0	97.6	0.2	0.3	0.4	0.6
HANCOCK	009	00000	537	51,791	56,956	60,336	1.3	2	97.6	97.3	0.3	0.3	0.4	0.6
KENNEBEC	011	12300	500	117,114	123,172	127,809	0.7	10	97.5	97.0	0.3	0.4	0.6	0.9
KNOX	013	40500	500	39,618	42,289	43,904	0.9	7	98.3	98.0	0.2	0.3	0.4	0.5
LINCOLN	015	00000	500	33,616	36,225	38,022	1.0	4	98.5	98.2	0.2	0.2	0.4	0.5
OXFORD	017	00000	500	54,755	58,455	61,076	0.9	7	98.3	98.0	0.2	0.2	0.4	0.5
PENOBSCOT	019	12620	537	144,919	149,947	153,534	0.5	11	96.6	96.0	0.5	0.6	0.7	1.0
PISCATAQUIS	021	00000	537	17,235	17,687	17,990	0.4	13	97.8	97.6	0.2	0.3	0.3	0.4
SAGADAHOC	023	38860	500	35,214	37,589	39,132	0.9	7	96.5	95.9	0.9	1.1	0.7	1.0
SOMERSET	025	00000	537	50,888	51,683	52,279	0.2	14	98.0	97.7	0.2	0.2	0.4	0.5
WALDO	027	00000	537	36,280	39,419	41,583	1.2	3	97.9	97.7	0.2	0.2	0.2	0.3
WASHINGTON	029	00000	537	33,941	33,702	33,537	-0.1	16	93.5	92.7	0.3	0.3	0.3	0.4
YORK	031	38860	500	186,742	207,794	222,913	1.5	1	97.6	97.1	0.4	0.5	0.8	1.1
MAINE							0.8		96.9	96.4	0.5	0.6	0.7	1.0
UNITED STATES							1.2		75.1	72.7	12.3	12.6	3.8	4.5

POPULATION COMPOSITION

B

COUNTY	% HISPANIC ORIGIN		2007 AGE DISTRIBUTION (%)										MEDIAN AGE	% 2007 Males	% 2007 Females
	2000	2007	0-4	5-9	10-14	15-19	20-24	25-44	45-64	65-84	85+	18+	2007	2007	2007
ANDROSCOGGIN	1.0	1.3	5.9	5.6	5.9	7.2	7.0	26.4	27.5	12.1	2.5	78.5	40.1	48.7	51.3
AROOSTOOK	0.6	0.8	5.0	4.9	5.4	6.8	6.7	23.2	30.5	15.0	2.5	80.7	43.6	48.9	51.1
CUMBERLAND	1.0	1.3	5.6	5.4	6.0	7.5	7.0	26.1	28.9	11.2	2.3	78.7	40.3	48.6	51.4
FRANKLIN	0.5	0.8	5.1	4.8	5.4	8.9	9.0	22.6	29.6	12.5	2.1	80.4	40.9	48.5	51.5
HANCOCK	0.6	0.9	4.8	4.7	5.4	6.5	6.1	23.8	33.4	12.8	2.3	81.1	44.1	49.2	50.8
KENNEBEC	0.7	1.0	5.5	5.3	5.9	7.3	7.1	24.5	30.2	12.1	2.1	79.0	41.4	48.6	51.4
KNOX	0.6	0.8	5.2	5.0	5.3	6.1	6.1	23.5	32.4	13.5	2.8	80.5	44.1	49.3	50.7
LINCOLN	0.5	0.6	4.8	4.7	5.6	6.2	5.3	21.6	34.9	14.4	2.5	80.7	46.1	48.9	51.1
OXFORD	0.5	0.7	5.4	5.2	5.9	6.8	5.8	23.5	31.4	13.8	2.2	79.0	43.4	48.9	51.1
PENOBSCOT	0.6	0.8	5.3	4.9	5.5	7.8	8.7	25.5	28.8	11.7	1.8	80.2	39.9	49.1	50.9
PISCATAQUIS	0.5	0.7	4.8	4.6	5.0	6.8	7.0	20.9	33.4	14.9	2.6	81.1	45.5	49.4	50.6
SAGADAHOC	1.1	1.5	6.0	5.6	6.0	7.1	6.9	24.6	30.9	11.0	1.9	77.9	41.1	49.1	50.9
SOMERSET	0.5	0.6	5.7	5.6	5.8	6.6	6.3	24.9	30.6	12.6	1.9	78.6	41.7	49.2	50.8
WALDO	0.6	0.8	5.6	5.6	5.7	6.5	5.7	24.9	32.3	12.0	1.7	79.1	42.3	49.5	50.5
WASHINGTON	0.8	1.1	5.3	4.8	5.8	6.2	6.3	24.1	30.4	14.4	2.6	80.4	43.2	49.1	50.9
YORK	0.7	1.0	5.7	5.6	6.5	7.1	5.9	25.1	30.1	11.9	2.1	77.7	41.5	48.7	51.3
MAINE	0.7	1.0	5.5	5.3	5.9	7.1	6.8	24.9	30.1	12.3	2.2	79.1	41.5	48.9	51.1
UNITED STATES	12.5	15.0	6.9	6.5	6.8	7.1	7.0	27.6	25.4	10.7	1.9	75.6	36.7	49.2	50.8

Copyright © 2007 ESRI. All rights reserved. Reproduction by any method is prohibited.

COUNTY	HOUSEHOLDS					FAMILIES			MEDIAN HOUSEHOLD INCOME			
	2000	2007	2012	% Annual Rate 2000-2007	2007 Average HH Size	2000	2007	% Annual Rate 2000-2007	2007	2012	2007 National Rank	2007 State Rank
ANDROSCOGGIN	42,028	45,205	47,584	1.0	2.35	27,183	28,619	0.7	42,855	49,152	1346	8
AROOSTOOK	30,356	31,270	31,707	0.4	2.28	20,436	20,642	0.1	34,124	38,411	2538	14
CUMBERLAND	107,989	117,486	122,707	1.2	2.33	67,699	72,009	0.9	55,140	63,993	403	1
FRANKLIN	11,806	12,407	12,694	0.7	2.33	7,748	7,976	0.4	37,732	43,273	2031	12
HANCOCK	21,864	24,754	26,573	1.7	2.25	14,238	15,781	1.4	43,587	50,595	1264	6
KENNEBEC	47,683	51,608	54,193	1.1	2.32	31,328	33,212	0.8	43,285	49,124	1302	7
KNOX	16,608	18,068	18,977	1.2	2.25	10,728	11,425	0.9	45,120	52,099	1096	5
LINCOLN	14,158	15,689	16,670	1.4	2.28	9,545	10,370	1.2	47,082	54,373	901	4
OXFORD	22,314	24,482	25,886	1.3	2.35	15,180	16,336	1.0	40,119	45,568	1707	11
PENOBSCOT	58,096	62,033	64,405	0.9	2.31	37,813	39,535	0.6	40,964	46,587	1604	9
PISCATAQUIS	7,278	7,718	7,967	0.8	2.26	4,858	5,049	0.5	33,683	38,143	2586	15
SAGADAHOC	14,117	15,428	16,232	1.2	2.41	9,636	10,331	1.0	51,089	58,357	605	3
SOMERSET	20,496	21,498	22,053	0.7	2.36	14,117	14,533	0.4	36,496	41,422	2190	13
WALDO	14,726	16,491	17,639	1.6	2.36	10,053	11,045	1.3	40,574	46,032	1654	10
WASHINGTON	14,118	14,476	14,614	0.3	2.26	9,304	9,347	0.1	31,037	35,294	2829	16
YORK	74,563	83,889	90,809	1.6	2.44	50,819	56,079	1.4	53,329	62,050	482	2
MAINE				1.1	2.34			0.9	45,463	52,125		
UNITED STATES				1.2	2.59			1.0	53,154	62,503		

COUNTY	2007 Per Capita Income	2007 HH Income Base	2007 HOUSEHOLD INCOME DISTRIBUTION (%)					2007 Home Value Base	2007 HOME VALUE DISTRIBUTION (%)					2007 Median Home Value
			Less than $25,000	$25,000 to $49,999	$50,000 to $99,999	$100,000 to $149,999	$150,000 or More		Less than $50,000	$50,000 to $89,999	$90,000 to $174,999	$175,000 to $399,999	$400,000 or More	
ANDROSCOGGIN	22,583	45,205	27.5	30.1	31.7	7.7	2.9	29,195	5.8	6.9	45.5	38.7	3.1	164,790
AROOSTOOK	18,808	31,270	36.7	31.8	25.6	4.3	1.6	22,964	11.4	22.0	49.2	16.4	1.0	114,701
CUMBERLAND	30,923	117,486	18.9	25.6	35.2	12.4	7.9	79,296	2.9	2.4	14.1	62.1	18.6	253,939
FRANKLIN	20,118	12,407	31.9	31.8	28.2	6.1	1.9	9,492	6.9	12.9	46.6	29.5	4.1	147,416
HANCOCK	24,755	24,754	26.0	30.8	31.0	8.2	4.0	18,949	5.0	7.4	28.4	43.9	15.3	195,637
KENNEBEC	22,765	51,608	27.3	29.7	32.8	7.3	2.9	37,051	5.5	7.9	44.1	38.4	4.2	164,006
KNOX	25,360	18,068	24.8	30.8	31.9	7.9	4.6	13,491	2.7	4.8	29.9	46.4	16.2	205,493
LINCOLN	25,892	15,688	22.7	30.2	33.8	9.1	4.3	13,086	5.3	5.0	23.9	48.4	17.4	217,779
OXFORD	20,975	24,482	29.0	32.0	30.7	6.2	2.1	18,959	7.0	11.7	43.0	33.6	4.6	155,306
PENOBSCOT	22,280	62,030	29.9	29.7	29.6	7.9	3.0	43,633	8.8	13.4	46.8	28.4	2.6	143,960
PISCATAQUIS	18,359	7,718	37.3	32.5	24.5	4.4	1.2	6,145	8.4	20.5	47.5	21.1	2.4	122,839
SAGADAHOC	25,427	15,428	20.7	27.9	37.1	10.7	3.6	11,210	2.7	4.6	25.5	56.6	10.6	211,968
SOMERSET	19,320	21,498	32.3	32.7	27.7	5.7	1.6	16,833	9.7	16.5	49.7	21.7	2.4	129,927
WALDO	21,625	16,491	29.8	30.5	29.2	8.0	2.6	13,229	8.3	11.9	36.7	36.9	6.2	161,041
WASHINGTON	17,689	14,476	41.0	30.8	22.4	4.5	1.3	11,305	11.3	17.4	46.4	21.5	3.5	127,275
YORK	26,630	83,889	19.9	26.4	37.7	10.9	5.2	61,644	2.5	3.4	20.5	58.8	14.7	231,999
MAINE	24,625		25.8	28.9	32.3	8.8	4.2		5.6	8.4	33.1	43.3	9.6	181,780
UNITED STATES	27,916		21.9	25.0	32.3	12.3	8.4		7.9	10.5	27.1	35.6	19.0	192,285

SPENDING POTENTIAL INDICES

COUNTY	FINANCIAL SERVICES				THE HOME						ENTERTAINMENT						PERSONAL			
					Home Improvements		Furnishings													
	Auto Loan	Home Loan	Invest-ments	Retire-ment Plans	Home Repair	Lawn & Garden	Comput-ers & Hard-ware	Major Appli-ances	TV, Radio, Sound Equip-ment	Furni-ture	Dine out/ Carry out	Sports Equip-ment	Fees & Tickets	Toys & Games	Travel	Cable TV	Apparel & Services	Auto Repairs	Health Insur-ance	Pets & Supplies
ANDROSCOGGIN	76	70	77	72	72	77	73	75	76	72	75	66	72	76	73	77	66	74	79	76
AROOSTOOK	67	52	47	52	57	72	57	65	62	53	60	57	50	62	56	65	52	61	72	68
CUMBERLAND	99	101	109	104	102	101	103	101	101	102	101	93	104	100	103	100	92	101	100	102
FRANKLIN	74	61	54	61	65	78	64	72	66	60	66	63	58	68	63	69	57	68	75	74
HANCOCK	88	72	57	72	80	100	73	89	76	70	76	77	66	78	75	80	66	82	92	92
KENNEBEC	78	70	72	70	72	81	72	77	75	70	74	68	69	75	72	77	65	75	82	78
KNOX	89	75	66	75	81	98	77	89	80	74	79	78	71	81	78	84	69	83	93	92
LINCOLN	94	78	59	77	86	107	76	94	80	75	80	82	70	81	79	84	69	86	97	98
OXFORD	76	63	57	63	70	84	65	76	69	62	68	66	60	70	66	72	59	70	81	78
PENOBSCOT	78	67	66	68	69	78	72	75	74	68	73	67	67	74	70	76	64	74	79	77
PISCATAQUIS	66	50	42	50	56	71	54	64	60	50	58	55	48	60	54	63	49	59	72	66
SAGADAHOC	90	82	81	84	84	91	84	88	85	82	84	79	81	87	84	86	75	86	90	90
SOMERSET	74	58	46	56	63	79	59	70	64	57	63	61	53	66	59	68	55	65	76	74
WALDO	83	65	47	63	72	91	65	80	70	64	70	70	58	72	66	74	60	74	84	85
WASHINGTON	66	49	36	47	55	72	51	63	56	49	56	55	44	58	51	60	48	58	69	67
YORK	91	92	95	93	93	96	89	92	89	89	89	83	90	90	91	90	80	90	93	94
MAINE	85	77	75	77	80	90	79	84	81	77	80	75	75	81	79	83	71	82	88	87
UNITED STATES	100	100	100	100	100	100	100	100	100	100	100	100	100	100	100	100	100	100	100	100

COUNTY	FIPS Code	CBSA Code	DMA Code	POPULATION			2000-2007 ANNUAL RATE		RACE (%)					
									White		Black		Asian/Pacific	
				2000	2007	2012	% Rate	State Rank	2000	2007	2000	2007	2000	2007
ALLEGANY	001	19060	511	74,930	74,067	73,225	-0.2	23	93.0	91.1	5.3	6.7	0.5	0.8
ANNE ARUNDEL	003	12580	512	489,656	526,533	550,405	1.0	17	81.2	76.8	13.6	16.3	2.4	3.2
BALTIMORE	005	12580	512	754,292	797,364	825,836	0.8	20	74.4	69.0	20.1	23.7	3.2	4.2
CALVERT	009	47900	511	74,563	91,373	103,496	2.8	1	83.9	80.1	13.1	15.9	0.9	1.2
CAROLINE	011	00000	512	29,772	33,168	35,861	1.5	13	81.7	77.4	14.8	17.8	0.6	0.8
CARROLL	013	12580	512	150,897	173,937	190,301	2.0	7	95.7	94.3	2.3	2.9	0.8	1.1
CECIL	015	37980	512	85,951	101,988	114,611	2.4	4	93.4	91.4	3.9	4.9	0.7	1.0
CHARLES	017	47900	511	120,546	144,577	163,329	2.5	2	68.5	62.8	26.1	30.3	1.9	2.4
DORCHESTER	019	15700	576	30,674	32,577	34,011	0.8	20	69.4	63.9	28.4	33.3	0.7	0.9
FREDERICK	021	47900	511	195,277	230,323	255,284	2.3	6	89.3	86.3	6.4	7.8	1.7	2.3
GARRETT	023	00000	508	29,846	31,639	32,974	0.8	20	98.8	98.4	0.4	0.5	0.2	0.3
HARFORD	025	12580	512	218,590	248,322	271,377	1.8	9	86.8	83.3	9.3	11.3	1.6	2.2
HOWARD	027	12580	512	247,842	277,901	295,753	1.6	11	74.3	68.5	14.4	16.8	7.7	10.1
KENT	029	00000	512	19,197	20,862	21,700	1.2	16	79.6	75.1	17.4	20.8	0.6	0.8
MONTGOMERY	031	47900	511	873,341	949,347	996,106	1.2	16	64.8	58.1	15.1	16.6	11.3	13.9
PRINCE GEORGE'S	033	47900	511	801,515	856,679	891,685	0.9	18	27.0	23.1	62.7	64.7	3.9	4.5
QUEEN ANNE'S	035	12580	512	40,563	47,682	52,644	2.3	6	89.0	86.2	8.8	10.8	0.6	0.8
ST. MARY'S	037	30500	511	86,211	102,578	115,929	2.4	4	81.6	77.2	13.9	16.8	1.9	2.5
SOMERSET	039	41540	576	24,747	26,103	26,810	0.7	22	56.4	50.2	41.1	46.6	0.5	0.6
TALBOT	041	20660	512	33,812	38,575	42,443	1.8	9	82.0	77.8	15.4	18.6	0.9	1.3
WASHINGTON	043	25180	511	131,923	146,581	158,321	1.5	13	89.7	86.9	7.8	9.6	0.8	1.2
WICOMICO	045	41540	576	84,644	95,555	104,194	1.7	10	72.6	67.2	23.3	27.4	1.8	2.3
WORCESTER	047	36180	576	46,543	51,713	54,551	1.5	13	81.2	77.0	16.7	20.1	0.6	0.8
BALTIMORE CITY	510	12580	512	651,154	627,932	612,354	-0.5	24	31.6	26.7	64.3	68.6	1.6	1.9
MARYLAND							1.1		64.0	60.1	27.9	29.6	4.0	5.0
UNITED STATES							1.2		75.1	72.7	12.3	12.6	3.8	4.5

POPULATION COMPOSITION

COUNTY	% HISPANIC ORIGIN		2007 AGE DISTRIBUTION (%)										MEDIAN AGE	% 2007 Males	% 2007 Females
	2000	2007	0-4	5-9	10-14	15-19	20-24	25-44	45-64	65-84	85+	18+	2007		
ALLEGANY	0.8	1.2	5.1	4.8	5.1	7.2	8.3	25.6	25.8	15.1	3.0	81.4	40.5	50.3	49.7
ANNE ARUNDEL	2.6	3.9	6.5	6.7	6.8	6.9	5.9	28.5	27.4	10.0	1.3	75.8	38.3	49.7	50.3
BALTIMORE	1.8	2.6	5.8	5.7	6.3	7.4	6.7	25.8	27.0	12.8	2.6	77.9	39.9	47.5	52.5
CALVERT	1.5	2.3	6.8	6.5	8.1	7.7	6.4	26.4	28.4	8.4	1.3	73.5	38.4	49.0	51.0
CAROLINE	2.7	3.9	6.3	5.6	7.1	7.3	6.2	26.1	27.7	11.8	1.8	76.4	39.5	49.1	50.9
CARROLL	1.0	1.5	6.5	6.5	7.7	7.8	5.9	25.0	29.1	9.7	1.7	74.4	39.8	49.4	50.6
CECIL	1.5	2.3	6.9	6.5	7.2	7.3	5.7	27.9	27.4	9.9	1.2	74.6	37.8	49.5	50.5
CHARLES	2.3	3.2	7.2	6.8	7.5	7.2	6.2	29.2	26.5	8.4	1.0	73.8	37.1	48.9	51.1
DORCHESTER	1.3	1.8	5.5	5.2	6.2	6.5	5.7	24.1	29.2	15.2	2.4	78.8	42.9	47.6	52.4
FREDERICK	2.4	3.6	7.0	7.1	7.7	7.6	5.8	27.3	27.2	8.7	1.5	73.5	37.8	49.2	50.8
GARRETT	0.4	0.7	6.3	5.7	6.6	6.0	5.8	25.3	28.7	13.5	2.1	77.8	41.2	49.5	50.5
HARFORD	1.9	2.8	7.1	7.0	7.5	7.1	5.9	26.3	27.8	10.1	1.3	74.0	38.5	48.9	51.1
HOWARD	3.0	4.3	6.9	7.4	8.4	7.2	5.2	27.9	27.8	8.0	1.2	72.4	37.8	49.2	50.8
KENT	2.8	4.2	4.7	4.5	5.5	8.2	7.5	21.3	29.4	15.8	3.2	81.3	43.9	48.2	51.8
MONTGOMERY	11.5	15.5	6.4	7.3	7.4	6.9	5.2	27.8	27.1	10.0	2.0	74.4	38.4	48.1	51.9
PRINCE GEORGE'S	7.1	8.9	6.9	6.7	7.6	7.9	7.3	29.0	25.4	8.2	1.0	74.3	35.1	47.8	52.2
QUEEN ANNE'S	1.1	1.7	6.3	6.5	6.6	6.6	5.2	24.2	30.1	12.9	1.7	76.5	42.0	49.6	50.4
ST. MARY'S	2.0	2.9	7.2	7.0	7.4	7.7	6.7	28.7	25.1	9.0	1.2	73.8	36.1	50.3	49.7
SOMERSET	1.3	1.8	4.7	4.5	4.7	7.9	10.6	28.3	25.0	12.6	1.8	83.2	37.6	53.7	46.3
TALBOT	1.8	2.7	5.0	4.9	5.7	6.0	5.1	21.2	31.2	17.8	3.1	80.5	46.4	47.8	52.2
WASHINGTON	1.2	1.8	6.2	5.9	6.1	6.4	6.5	27.9	26.4	12.5	2.2	77.8	39.5	51.0	49.0
WICOMICO	2.2	3.1	6.2	6.0	6.3	7.9	7.7	25.6	27.1	11.4	1.8	77.4	38.1	47.7	52.3
WORCESTER	1.3	1.9	4.7	4.6	5.2	5.4	4.5	22.8	30.3	20.0	2.4	82.1	46.7	48.9	51.1
BALTIMORE CITY	1.7	2.1	6.3	5.9	7.0	8.0	7.9	27.0	24.8	11.2	2.0	76.5	36.4	46.8	53.2
MARYLAND	4.3	5.8	6.5	6.5	7.1	7.3	6.4	27.3	26.8	10.4	1.7	75.5	38.0	48.4	51.6
UNITED STATES	12.5	15.0	6.9	6.5	6.8	7.1	7.0	27.6	25.4	10.7	1.9	75.6	36.7	49.2	50.8

28-B

COUNTY	HOUSEHOLDS					FAMILIES			MEDIAN HOUSEHOLD INCOME			
	2000	2007	2012	% Annual Rate 2000-2007	2007 Average HH Size	2000	2007	% Annual Rate 2000-2007	2007	2012	2007 National Rank	2007 State Rank
ALLEGANY	29,322	29,388	29,220	0.0	2.30	18,896	18,230	-0.5	37,464	42,741	2070	22
ANNE ARUNDEL	178,670	194,799	205,112	1.2	2.62	129,193	136,724	0.8	77,574	89,818	70	5
BALTIMORE	299,877	316,565	328,704	0.7	2.46	198,605	202,212	0.2	61,891	71,069	216	12
CALVERT	25,447	31,646	36,083	3.1	2.87	20,149	24,497	2.7	81,804	96,128	45	3
CAROLINE	11,097	12,452	13,497	1.6	2.63	8,156	8,896	1.2	45,351	50,027	1068	19
CARROLL	52,503	61,047	67,116	2.1	2.79	41,094	46,674	1.8	75,391	84,922	84	7
CECIL	31,223	37,268	42,120	2.5	2.70	23,290	27,047	2.1	60,548	68,406	251	13
CHARLES	41,668	50,882	58,036	2.8	2.81	32,277	38,471	2.5	77,953	90,258	65	4
DORCHESTER	12,706	13,714	14,430	1.1	2.32	8,506	8,861	0.6	40,444	44,832	1666	20
FREDERICK	70,060	83,547	93,131	2.5	2.70	51,949	60,245	2.1	75,676	86,274	82	6
GARRETT	11,476	12,516	13,210	1.2	2.48	8,356	8,850	0.8	37,528	41,753	2054	21
HARFORD	79,667	91,478	100,545	1.9	2.70	60,403	67,574	1.6	71,424	82,487	113	8
HOWARD	90,043	100,774	107,293	1.6	2.72	65,790	71,527	1.2	96,131	113,919	10	1
KENT	7,666	8,517	8,989	1.5	2.27	5,136	5,507	1.0	47,234	53,177	889	17
MONTGOMERY	324,565	351,930	369,137	1.1	2.67	224,225	235,186	0.7	90,063	106,197	19	2
PRINCE GEORGE'S	286,610	304,333	317,133	0.8	2.76	198,066	203,435	0.4	67,216	77,151	147	10
QUEEN ANNE'S	15,315	18,272	20,298	2.5	2.58	11,542	13,409	2.1	68,844	78,897	129	9
ST. MARY'S	30,642	37,495	42,972	2.8	2.65	22,306	26,512	2.4	66,622	76,737	155	11
SOMERSET	8,361	8,927	9,304	0.9	2.33	5,444	5,598	0.4	34,002	37,492	2549	24
TALBOT	14,307	16,550	18,319	2.0	2.29	9,630	10,757	1.5	52,946	60,259	504	14
WASHINGTON	49,726	56,500	61,654	1.8	2.43	34,092	37,450	1.3	48,878	54,622	757	15
WICOMICO	32,218	37,083	40,690	2.0	2.49	21,781	24,211	1.5	46,574	52,046	946	18
WORCESTER	19,694	22,339	23,773	1.8	2.28	13,278	14,545	1.3	48,710	54,450	764	16
BALTIMORE CITY	257,996	245,619	239,872	-0.7	2.45	147,154	133,814	-1.3	35,911	40,461	2294	23
MARYLAND				1.1	2.61			0.7	65,627	76,746		
UNITED STATES				1.2	2.59			1.0	53,154	62,503		

MARYLAND

D

INCOME

COUNTY	2007 Per Capita Income	2007 HH Income Base	2007 HOUSEHOLD INCOME DISTRIBUTION (%)					2007 Home Value Base	2007 HOME VALUE DISTRIBUTION (%)					2007 Median Home Value
			Less than $25,000	$25,000 to $49,999	$50,000 to $99,999	$100,000 to $149,999	$150,000 or More		Less than $50,000	$50,000 to $89,999	$90,000 to $174,999	$175,000 to $399,999	$400,000 or More	
ALLEGANY	20,499	29,388	33.4	30.0	28.1	6.4	2.2	20,950	5.5	11.5	37.8	41.2	4.0	165,472
ANNE ARUNDEL	36,758	194,791	9.8	17.8	37.2	20.6	14.5	149,135	1.6	0.8	2.8	56.1	38.8	361,904
BALTIMORE	32,807	316,559	15.3	23.7	36.3	15.1	9.6	217,912	0.7	0.5	7.2	69.4	22.2	283,872
CALVERT	33,478	31,646	8.4	14.9	38.6	24.2	13.9	27,211	1.1	0.7	1.3	36.8	60.1	455,681
CAROLINE	20,592	12,452	24.5	31.0	33.6	8.3	2.6	9,412	3.4	3.3	14.5	65.5	13.3	238,664
CARROLL	31,120	61,041	10.8	18.4	38.8	21.2	10.8	50,584	0.9	0.3	1.4	55.0	42.4	377,710
CECIL	26,479	37,268	15.8	23.9	39.7	14.7	6.0	28,422	4.4	2.5	10.5	67.6	15.0	262,368
CHARLES	32,006	50,882	9.4	17.4	38.3	23.1	11.9	40,370	1.0	0.5	2.4	43.6	52.5	411,115
DORCHESTER	22,959	13,714	31.0	28.6	29.8	7.3	3.4	9,812	4.9	5.5	24.4	51.5	13.7	209,456
FREDERICK	33,250	83,547	10.9	18.7	37.6	20.8	12.0	64,340	0.7	0.2	2.0	53.2	43.8	378,516
GARRETT	19,831	12,516	32.0	31.8	27.5	6.0	2.7	9,900	4.7	7.8	25.8	50.8	10.9	203,440
HARFORD	31,604	91,478	10.9	20.3	39.1	19.7	10.0	72,282	1.8	1.1	4.9	59.9	32.4	333,332
HOWARD	45,121	100,774	6.7	13.1	32.0	24.0	24.2	75,615	1.3	1.1	2.9	36.8	57.9	451,679
KENT	27,455	8,517	24.8	28.2	32.4	9.2	5.4	6,140	1.5	1.9	12.6	58.6	25.4	265,456
MONTGOMERY	46,679	351,930	8.5	14.6	31.7	21.4	23.7	246,399	0.5	0.4	3.0	33.6	62.6	485,420
PRINCE GEORGE'S	29,497	304,333	12.0	21.9	38.2	18.3	9.6	192,313	0.4	0.7	3.6	52.9	42.5	378,272
QUEEN ANNE'S	33,565	18,272	14.5	18.6	37.4	19.0	10.4	15,376	1.5	1.7	5.3	49.9	41.6	363,731
ST. MARY'S	29,163	37,495	13.1	21.1	40.1	18.1	7.6	27,470	2.4	0.9	3.9	56.6	36.1	354,282
SOMERSET	19,785	8,927	37.2	30.0	24.6	5.1	3.1	6,322	11.7	15.6	47.4	22.3	3.1	130,696
TALBOT	35,271	16,550	21.4	25.3	31.7	11.2	10.4	12,094	0.8	2.1	7.4	50.5	39.3	342,945
WASHINGTON	24,193	56,500	23.1	28.0	35.3	9.7	4.0	38,085	2.3	1.8	13.3	69.8	12.8	248,873
WICOMICO	23,801	37,083	25.0	28.5	32.5	9.6	4.3	25,256	5.1	9.2	45.4	35.5	4.8	157,924
WORCESTER	27,647	22,339	22.3	29.0	33.9	9.4	5.4	16,996	1.9	3.6	14.4	57.5	22.6	259,705
BALTIMORE CITY	20,813	245,592	36.6	27.8	24.5	7.3	3.8	127,234	3.9	7.9	44.7	38.1	5.4	164,504
MARYLAND	33,153		15.6	21.1	34.4	17.0	12.0		1.5	1.8	9.6	50.5	36.6	341,459
UNITED STATES	27,916		21.9	25.0	32.3	12.3	8.4		7.9	10.5	27.1	35.6	19.0	192,285

COUNTY	FINANCIAL SERVICES				THE HOME						ENTERTAINMENT						PERSONAL			
					Home Improvements		Furnishings													
	Auto Loan	Home Loan	Invest-ments	Retire-ment Plans	Home Repair	Lawn & Garden	Comput-ers & Hard-ware	Major Appli-ances	TV, Radio, Sound Equip-ment	Furni-ture	Dine out/ Carry out	Sports Equip-ment	Fees & Tickets	Toys & Games	Travel	Cable TV	Apparel & Services	Auto Repairs	Health Insur-ance	Pets & Supplies
ALLEGANY	67	60	69	60	63	70	64	66	69	61	67	57	62	67	65	72	59	65	76	67
ANNE ARUNDEL	129	147	154	148	144	132	136	133	131	141	132	124	145	133	140	128	121	132	126	133
BALTIMORE	106	115	129	117	114	107	114	109	111	115	112	99	118	110	115	111	102	111	109	108
CALVERT	127	156	154	153	150	132	133	134	126	142	127	125	146	131	139	123	118	129	122	132
CAROLINE	80	74	71	74	77	85	72	79	74	72	74	70	71	77	73	76	66	75	81	81
CARROLL	115	136	142	135	134	122	121	121	116	126	116	112	130	118	126	114	108	118	115	121
CECIL	100	105	104	104	103	102	98	100	97	100	97	92	100	100	100	97	88	98	97	102
CHARLES	120	140	141	139	136	122	126	124	120	132	121	116	134	123	129	117	112	122	116	124
DORCHESTER	78	70	70	70	73	83	71	77	75	70	74	67	68	75	72	77	65	74	82	79
FREDERICK	119	138	142	138	135	121	127	124	121	132	122	116	135	124	129	118	113	122	115	123
GARRETT	79	62	48	61	69	87	63	77	68	61	67	67	56	70	64	72	58	71	81	81
HARFORD	115	130	134	130	125	116	118	117	114	123	115	108	125	117	121	112	105	116	111	116
HOWARD	165	189	191	194	183	162	175	166	163	183	166	160	186	169	176	158	154	167	151	166
KENT	96	82	73	82	91	108	84	97	88	81	87	85	78	88	86	92	76	91	102	100
MONTGOMERY	156	186	195	186	188	163	177	168	166	182	169	162	190	166	181	162	159	168	156	165
PRINCE GEORGE'S	106	114	117	114	112	101	116	108	112	116	114	103	119	112	114	110	106	111	102	107
QUEEN ANNE'S	121	131	131	131	132	130	117	124	116	122	116	112	123	119	123	116	105	119	120	126
ST. MARY'S	108	115	114	116	112	107	109	108	105	112	106	101	112	108	110	103	97	107	102	108
SOMERSET	76	56	45	55	62	79	62	72	66	58	66	64	53	67	60	70	57	69	77	76
TALBOT	112	111	118	111	117	126	109	118	111	109	110	103	109	107	115	114	98	114	124	118
WASHINGTON	82	81	89	82	83	84	82	82	83	81	82	74	82	84	83	84	74	81	85	83
WICOMICO	84	80	84	82	81	85	82	82	83	81	83	74	81	84	82	84	74	82	85	84
WORCESTER	91	83	83	83	89	103	83	94	87	82	86	81	80	84	87	91	75	90	101	95
BALTIMORE CITY	63	64	70	64	64	62	70	64	74	69	74	57	71	70	69	76	69	67	69	65
MARYLAND	114	125	131	125	124	115	121	117	119	124	120	109	127	119	123	118	110	118	114	117
UNITED STATES	100	100	100	100	100	100	100	100	100	100	100	100	100	100	100	100	100	100	100	100

POPULATION CHANGE

COUNTY	FIPS Code	CBSA Code	DMA Code	POPULATION			2000-2007 ANNUAL RATE		RACE (%)					
									White		Black		Asian/Pacific	
				2000	2007	2012	% Rate	State Rank	2000	2007	2000	2007	2000	2007
BARNSTABLE	001	12700	506	222,230	230,069	235,166	0.5	7	94.2	93.2	1.8	2.1	0.7	0.9
BERKSHIRE	003	38340	532	134,953	134,073	133,550	-0.1	13	95.0	93.9	2.0	2.3	1.0	1.4
BRISTOL	005	39300	521	534,678	553,975	565,183	0.5	7	91.0	89.2	2.0	2.4	1.3	1.8
DUKES	007	00000	506	14,987	15,743	16,205	0.7	4	90.7	89.4	2.4	2.8	0.5	0.7
ESSEX	009	14460	506	723,419	754,115	775,658	0.6	5	86.4	83.1	2.6	3.0	2.4	3.2
FRANKLIN	011	44140	543	71,535	73,377	74,754	0.4	8	95.4	94.3	0.9	1.1	1.1	1.5
HAMPDEN	013	44140	543	456,228	464,758	469,863	0.3	10	79.1	75.1	8.1	9.0	1.4	1.8
HAMPSHIRE	015	44140	543	152,251	155,745	158,554	0.3	10	91.1	88.8	2.0	2.3	3.5	4.8
MIDDLESEX	017	14460	506	1,465,396	1,483,460	1,494,498	0.2	12	85.9	82.4	3.4	3.8	6.3	8.5
NANTUCKET	019	00000	506	9,520	10,513	10,968	1.4	1	87.8	85.7	8.3	9.6	0.7	1.0
NORFOLK	021	14460	506	650,308	665,207	674,769	0.3	10	89.0	86.1	3.2	3.7	5.5	7.6
PLYMOUTH	023	14460	506	472,822	505,547	530,439	0.9	3	88.7	86.8	4.6	5.3	0.9	1.3
SUFFOLK	025	14460	506	689,807	677,582	667,912	-0.2	14	57.8	52.9	22.2	23.6	7.1	8.9
WORCESTER	027	49340	506	750,963	806,147	848,423	1.0	2	89.6	87.1	2.7	3.1	2.7	3.7
MASSACHUSETTS							0.4		84.5	81.7	5.4	5.9	3.8	5.0
UNITED STATES							1.2		75.1	72.7	12.3	12.6	3.8	4.5

COUNTY	% HISPANIC ORIGIN		2007 AGE DISTRIBUTION (%)										MEDIAN AGE	% 2007 Males	% 2007 Females
	2000	2007	0-4	5-9	10-14	15-19	20-24	25-44	45-64	65-84	85+	18+	2007		
BARNSTABLE	1.3	1.8	4.5	4.5	5.4	6.1	5.0	19.6	32.0	19.0	3.8	81.6	47.9	47.4	52.6
BERKSHIRE	1.7	2.2	5.1	4.9	5.9	7.7	7.2	22.3	29.0	14.6	3.4	79.9	43.0	47.9	52.1
BRISTOL	3.6	4.7	6.4	6.2	6.9	7.3	6.3	27.3	26.1	11.2	2.4	76.3	38.5	48.3	51.7
DUKES	1.0	1.3	5.0	5.3	5.3	7.1	6.5	23.2	35.0	10.9	1.9	79.7	43.6	49.3	50.7
ESSEX	11.0	14.0	6.4	6.6	7.3	7.5	6.2	25.3	27.1	11.1	2.5	75.1	39.2	48.2	51.8
FRANKLIN	2.0	2.6	5.1	4.8	5.8	6.9	7.3	24.1	32.1	11.2	2.6	80.3	42.1	48.6	51.4
HAMPDEN	15.2	18.9	6.5	6.1	6.9	7.9	7.1	25.0	26.0	11.7	2.6	75.8	38.3	48.1	51.9
HAMPSHIRE	3.4	4.4	4.4	4.5	5.3	10.9	12.5	23.7	26.8	9.7	2.3	82.1	36.4	46.8	53.2
MIDDLESEX	4.6	5.8	6.0	6.4	6.6	7.1	6.0	29.9	25.6	10.3	2.1	77.1	37.8	48.7	51.3
NANTUCKET	2.2	2.9	5.4	5.8	5.0	5.1	5.3	35.3	27.8	8.8	1.4	80.5	38.8	51.8	48.2
NORFOLK	1.8	2.4	6.1	6.6	6.8	6.7	5.2	27.5	26.8	11.6	2.6	76.3	39.7	48.0	52.0
PLYMOUTH	2.4	3.2	6.8	7.1	7.5	7.4	5.8	25.6	27.6	10.3	2.0	74.1	38.8	48.9	51.1
SUFFOLK	15.5	18.3	5.6	5.2	5.7	7.9	9.4	35.4	20.5	8.6	1.8	79.8	33.1	48.5	51.5
WORCESTER	6.8	8.7	6.5	6.5	7.2	7.7	6.5	26.4	26.5	10.4	2.3	75.3	38.3	49.0	51.0
MASSACHUSETTS	6.8	8.4	6.1	6.2	6.7	7.4	6.6	27.6	26.1	10.9	2.3	76.8	38.3	48.4	51.6
UNITED STATES	12.5	15.0	6.9	6.5	6.8	7.1	7.0	27.6	25.4	10.7	1.9	75.6	36.7	49.2	50.8

COUNTY	HOUSEHOLDS					FAMILIES			MEDIAN HOUSEHOLD INCOME			
	2000	2007	2012	% Annual Rate 2000-2007	2007 Average HH Size	2000	2007	% Annual Rate 2000-2007	2007	2012	2007 National Rank	2007 State Rank
BARNSTABLE	94,822	100,125	103,035	0.8	2.24	61,041	63,664	0.6	61,707	75,067	219	6
BERKSHIRE	56,006	56,373	56,598	0.1	2.27	35,110	34,889	-0.1	49,287	57,957	726	14
BRISTOL	205,411	214,509	219,883	0.6	2.52	140,610	145,244	0.4	55,371	65,098	391	10
DUKES	6,421	6,759	6,962	0.7	2.30	3,791	3,932	0.5	60,109	72,347	264	9
ESSEX	275,419	286,347	294,802	0.5	2.58	185,094	190,272	0.4	67,821	81,332	140	5
FRANKLIN	29,466	30,708	31,520	0.6	2.34	18,415	18,944	0.4	51,250	60,473	599	12
HAMPDEN	175,288	179,921	182,650	0.4	2.50	115,773	117,446	0.2	49,467	57,133	712	13
HAMPSHIRE	55,991	58,791	60,530	0.7	2.35	33,819	35,024	0.5	60,311	70,985	258	8
MIDDLESEX	561,220	571,335	577,724	0.2	2.50	361,076	363,208	0.1	81,743	101,479	46	2
NANTUCKET	3,699	4,067	4,232	1.3	2.40	2,106	2,284	1.1	78,253	99,823	63	3
NORFOLK	248,827	256,512	261,334	0.4	2.53	165,858	169,017	0.3	85,114	105,107	29	1
PLYMOUTH	168,361	180,708	190,349	1.0	2.74	122,421	130,154	0.8	73,061	87,564	102	4
SUFFOLK	278,722	277,721	274,554	0.0	2.32	139,159	136,298	-0.3	51,964	62,469	549	11
WORCESTER	283,927	303,106	320,146	0.9	2.58	192,423	203,148	0.8	61,627	72,804	220	7
MASSACHUSETTS				0.5	2.50			0.3	66,046	79,243		
UNITED STATES				1.2	2.59			1.0	53,154	62,503		

COUNTY	2007 Per Capita Income	2007 HH Income Base	2007 HOUSEHOLD INCOME DISTRIBUTION (%)					2007 Home Value Base	2007 HOME VALUE DISTRIBUTION (%)					2007 Median Home Value
			Less than $25,000	$25,000 to $49,999	$50,000 to $99,999	$100,000 to $149,999	$150,000 or More		Less than $50,000	$50,000 to $89,999	$90,000 to $174,999	$175,000 to $399,999	$400,000 or More	
BARNSTABLE	35,135	100,125	17.0	22.8	35.2	15.2	9.9	79,250	0.3	0.3	1.8	48.0	49.6	398,289
BERKSHIRE	28,348	56,373	24.9	25.8	31.9	11.1	6.4	38,815	2.1	2.7	30.1	51.4	13.7	208,627
BRISTOL	27,509	214,509	23.6	21.9	32.3	15.0	7.3	136,806	0.5	0.7	4.7	65.1	29.0	334,137
DUKES	35,260	6,759	16.8	24.4	35.4	13.1	10.3	4,935	0.1	0.1	0.2	20.7	78.8	622,018
ESSEX	35,481	286,347	18.2	18.8	31.4	16.9	14.7	187,362	0.4	0.8	6.2	47.9	44.7	375,690
FRANKLIN	27,328	30,708	23.1	25.5	33.0	12.9	5.4	21,153	1.4	1.4	22.9	63.7	10.7	225,431
HAMPDEN	24,970	179,921	25.9	24.5	32.0	12.1	5.5	114,808	0.9	1.9	27.5	61.5	8.1	210,747
HAMPSHIRE	30,263	58,781	18.4	23.3	34.6	14.6	9.1	39,277	0.4	1.4	10.2	71.1	16.9	267,984
MIDDLESEX	43,877	571,333	13.0	15.7	30.9	20.6	19.7	363,889	0.5	0.6	4.3	40.0	54.7	425,305
NANTUCKET	45,887	4,067	10.4	18.1	33.1	18.6	19.8	2,632	0.0	0.4	0.6	1.3	97.6	1,000,001
NORFOLK	45,708	256,512	11.7	15.6	30.4	21.3	20.9	183,041	0.6	0.4	2.1	41.2	55.8	435,568
PLYMOUTH	33,380	180,700	15.0	17.8	34.1	19.7	13.3	139,071	0.5	0.9	5.9	57.1	35.6	338,179
SUFFOLK	31,026	277,721	26.7	21.4	29.1	13.3	9.5	99,284	0.8	0.7	4.2	47.7	46.5	385,701
WORCESTER	30,413	303,105	19.9	21.1	32.2	16.7	10.2	200,822	0.6	0.9	12.8	66.2	19.6	264,757
MASSACHUSETTS	35,397		18.4	19.5	31.6	17.1	13.3		0.6	0.8	8.0	51.5	39.0	348,621
UNITED STATES	27,916		21.9	25.0	32.3	12.3	8.4		7.9	10.5	27.1	35.6	19.0	192,285

SPENDING POTENTIAL INDICES

COUNTY	FINANCIAL SERVICES				THE HOME						ENTERTAINMENT						PERSONAL			
					Home Improvements		Furnishings													
	Auto Loan	Home Loan	Invest-ments	Retire-ment Plans	Home Repair	Lawn & Garden	Comput-ers & Hard-ware	Major Appli-ances	TV, Radio, Sound Equip-ment	Furni-ture	Dine out/ Carry out	Sports Equip-ment	Fees & Tickets	Toys & Games	Travel	Cable TV	Apparel & Services	Auto Repairs	Health Insur-ance	Pets & Supplies
BARNSTABLE	107	113	118	112	120	125	105	116	107	108	106	101	110	102	115	111	95	111	121	115
BERKSHIRE	86	89	105	91	92	92	89	90	91	89	90	79	92	89	93	93	81	89	95	90
BRISTOL	86	100	109	98	101	90	97	94	96	99	96	87	103	95	100	95	90	93	91	92
DUKES	113	115	105	115	122	126	114	122	108	111	108	115	110	108	116	107	98	117	115	123
ESSEX	110	134	144	130	138	119	129	124	124	131	126	119	139	122	133	123	119	124	118	121
FRANKLIN	85	89	103	91	90	88	90	88	89	89	88	79	92	89	91	89	80	88	89	88
HAMPDEN	80	86	99	87	86	82	88	84	88	87	88	76	90	87	88	88	81	85	86	83
HAMPSHIRE	98	105	118	108	105	99	108	101	104	106	104	94	110	103	108	102	95	103	100	101
MIDDLESEX	133	164	173	161	169	143	159	150	150	160	153	147	171	148	163	148	146	150	140	147
NANTUCKET	148	177	175	177	177	156	170	164	150	169	152	166	172	148	173	143	140	165	146	161
NORFOLK	138	178	191	172	185	156	163	159	156	169	158	150	181	154	172	155	151	155	149	155
PLYMOUTH	112	141	151	137	144	125	128	127	123	133	124	118	140	123	134	122	117	123	120	124
SUFFOLK	87	86	90	89	87	79	107	90	106	100	109	91	104	100	100	105	102	97	89	90
WORCESTER	100	115	128	114	115	104	111	107	108	112	109	99	117	108	114	107	101	107	104	106
MASSACHUSETTS	110	128	138	126	131	116	126	120	122	127	124	114	133	120	129	122	116	120	116	118
UNITED STATES	100	100	100	100	100	100	100	100	100	100	100	100	100	100	100	100	100	100	100	100

COUNTY	FIPS Code	CBSA Code	DMA Code	POPULATION			2000-2007 ANNUAL RATE		RACE (%)					
									White		Black		Asian/Pacific	
				2000	2007	2012	% Rate	State Rank	2000	2007	2000	2007	2000	2007
ALCONA	001	00000	583	11,719	11,941	12,188	0.3	59	98.0	97.8	0.2	0.2	0.2	0.3
ALGER	003	00000	553	9,862	10,188	10,433	0.4	53	87.8	86.7	6.1	6.7	0.4	0.5
ALLEGAN	005	10880	563	105,665	116,417	123,841	1.3	12	93.5	92.2	1.3	1.4	0.6	0.8
ALPENA	007	10980	583	31,314	30,120	29,298	-0.5	82	98.2	97.9	0.2	0.3	0.3	0.5
ANTRIM	009	00000	540	23,110	25,435	26,722	1.3	12	97.0	96.6	0.2	0.2	0.2	0.4
ARENAC	011	00000	513	17,269	17,912	18,380	0.5	46	95.4	94.8	1.8	2.0	0.3	0.4
BARAGA	013	00000	553	8,746	8,760	8,708	0.0	74	78.6	78.3	5.0	5.3	0.3	0.3
BARRY	015	24340	563	56,755	60,956	63,522	1.0	23	97.4	96.9	0.2	0.3	0.3	0.4
BAY	017	13020	513	110,157	109,920	109,629	0.0	74	94.9	94.0	1.3	1.4	0.5	0.7
BENZIE	019	45900	540	15,998	18,565	20,271	2.1	2	96.4	96.0	0.3	0.3	0.2	0.2
BERRIEN	021	35660	588	162,453	164,065	165,329	0.1	68	79.7	77.5	15.9	17.2	1.2	1.7
BRANCH	023	17740	563	45,787	47,632	48,382	0.5	46	93.4	91.8	2.6	3.4	0.4	0.6
CALHOUN	025	12980	563	137,985	139,466	140,147	0.1	68	83.9	81.9	10.9	11.8	1.1	1.6
CASS	027	43780	588	51,104	52,594	53,360	0.4	53	89.2	87.8	6.1	6.7	0.5	0.8
CHARLEVOIX	029	00000	540	26,090	28,167	29,561	1.1	18	96.3	95.8	0.2	0.2	0.3	0.5
CHEBOYGAN	031	00000	540	26,448	27,868	28,710	0.7	35	94.8	94.3	0.2	0.3	0.2	0.3
CHIPPEWA	033	42300	540	38,543	39,841	40,876	0.5	46	75.9	74.4	5.5	6.0	0.5	0.8
CLARE	035	00000	540	31,252	32,417	33,118	0.5	46	97.4	97.0	0.3	0.4	0.3	0.4
CLINTON	037	29620	551	64,753	73,695	79,229	1.8	4	96.4	95.7	0.6	0.7	0.6	0.8
CRAWFORD	039	00000	540	14,273	15,444	16,071	1.1	18	96.4	95.9	1.5	1.7	0.3	0.4
DELTA	041	21540	553	38,520	38,863	39,120	0.1	68	95.8	95.4	0.1	0.1	0.3	0.5
DICKINSON	043	27020	553	27,472	27,846	28,146	0.2	62	98.0	97.6	0.1	0.1	0.4	0.6
EATON	045	29620	551	103,655	110,042	114,239	0.8	31	90.3	88.7	5.3	5.8	1.2	1.7
EMMET	047	00000	540	31,437	34,862	37,095	1.4	8	94.3	93.8	0.5	0.5	0.5	0.7
GENESEE	049	22420	513	436,141	448,530	457,013	0.4	53	75.3	72.9	20.4	21.9	0.8	1.2
GLADWIN	051	00000	513	26,023	27,632	28,459	0.8	31	97.6	97.3	0.1	0.1	0.3	0.4
GOGEBIC	053	00000	676	17,370	17,057	16,455	-0.3	79	94.2	93.6	1.8	1.9	0.2	0.3
GRAND TRAVERSE	055	45900	540	77,654	88,138	95,018	1.8	4	96.5	95.9	0.4	0.4	0.5	0.8
GRATIOT	057	10940	513	42,285	42,503	42,688	0.1	68	92.0	90.8	3.7	4.1	0.4	0.5
HILLSDALE	059	00000	551	46,527	48,435	48,926	0.6	39	97.6	97.1	0.4	0.5	0.3	0.5
HOUGHTON	061	26340	553	36,016	36,791	37,373	0.3	59	95.5	94.4	0.9	1.1	1.8	2.7
HURON	063	00000	513	36,079	35,535	35,083	-0.2	78	98.0	97.6	0.2	0.2	0.4	0.5
INGHAM	065	29620	551	279,320	285,541	290,191	0.3	59	79.5	76.2	10.9	11.8	3.7	5.2
IONIA	067	24340	563	61,518	66,112	68,710	1.0	23	92.0	90.8	4.6	5.0	0.3	0.6
IOSCO	069	00000	513	27,339	27,170	27,063	-0.1	76	96.9	96.4	0.4	0.4	0.5	0.8
IRON	071	00000	553	13,138	12,750	12,592	-0.4	81	96.3	95.8	1.1	1.2	0.2	0.3
ISABELLA	073	34380	513	63,351	70,671	74,284	1.5	6	91.5	90.2	1.9	2.1	1.4	2.1
JACKSON	075	27100	551	158,422	166,133	170,591	0.7	35	88.5	87.1	7.9	8.7	0.6	0.8
KALAMAZOO	077	28020	563	238,603	247,947	254,585	0.5	46	84.6	82.4	9.7	10.6	1.9	2.7
KALKASKA	079	45900	540	16,571	17,879	18,567	1.1	18	97.5	97.2	0.2	0.2	0.3	0.4
KENT	081	24340	563	574,335	610,444	632,764	0.8	31	83.1	80.7	8.9	9.6	1.9	2.7
KEWEENAW	083	26340	553	2,301	2,324	2,385	0.1	68	95.0	94.7	3.5	3.7	0.1	0.1
LAKE	085	00000	540	11,333	12,437	13,186	1.3	12	84.7	83.1	11.2	12.2	0.2	0.3
LAPEER	087	19820	505	87,904	95,682	101,148	1.2	15	96.2	95.5	0.8	0.9	0.4	0.6
LEELANAU	089	45900	540	21,119	23,320	24,923	1.4	8	93.5	92.9	0.2	0.3	0.3	0.4
LENAWEE	091	10300	547	98,890	103,377	106,648	0.6	39	92.5	91.2	2.1	2.3	0.5	0.7
LIVINGSTON	093	19820	505	156,951	193,121	219,760	2.9	1	97.1	96.5	0.5	0.5	0.6	0.9
LUCE	095	00000	540	7,024	7,159	7,261	0.3	59	82.8	81.1	7.5	8.1	0.4	1.0
MACKINAC	097	00000	540	11,943	12,031	12,323	0.1	68	80.1	80.0	0.2	0.2	0.3	0.3
MACOMB	099	19820	505	788,149	852,992	900,183	1.1	18	92.7	91.1	2.7	3.0	2.2	3.1
MANISTEE	101	00000	540	24,527	26,020	26,865	0.8	31	94.2	93.3	1.6	1.8	0.4	0.5
MARQUETTE	103	32100	553	64,634	64,904	64,934	0.1	68	95.1	94.4	1.3	1.4	0.5	0.8
MASON	105	00000	540	28,274	29,454	30,385	0.6	39	95.8	95.2	0.7	0.8	0.3	0.4
MECOSTA	107	13660	540	40,553	43,403	45,633	0.9	27	92.7	90.6	3.6	4.8	0.9	1.3
MENOMINEE	109	31940	658	25,326	25,498	25,616	0.1	68	96.2	95.9	0.1	0.1	0.2	0.3
MIDLAND	111	33220	513	82,874	85,240	86,837	0.4	53	95.5	94.4	1.0	1.2	1.5	2.2
MISSAUKEE	113	15620	540	14,478	15,548	16,140	1.0	23	97.5	97.1	0.2	0.2	0.3	0.4
MONROE	115	33780	505	145,945	156,822	163,765	1.0	23	95.4	94.6	1.9	2.1	0.5	0.7
MONTCALM	117	00000	563	61,266	65,579	68,523	0.9	27	94.8	94.0	2.2	2.4	0.3	0.5
MONTMORENCY	119	00000	540	10,315	10,713	10,915	0.5	46	98.4	98.1	0.2	0.3	0.1	0.1
MUSKEGON	121	34740	563	170,200	177,180	181,580	0.6	39	81.3	79.3	14.2	15.4	0.4	0.6
NEWAYGO	123	24340	563	47,874	51,305	53,380	1.0	23	94.8	93.9	1.1	1.2	0.3	0.5
OAKLAND	125	19820	505	1,194,156	1,235,774	1,255,681	0.5	46	82.8	79.9	10.1	10.8	4.2	5.9
OCEANA	127	00000	563	26,873	29,174	30,780	1.1	18	90.4	88.6	0.3	0.3	0.3	0.4
OGEMAW	129	00000	513	21,645	22,284	22,738	0.4	53	97.5	97.0	0.1	0.1	0.4	0.6
ONTONAGON	131	00000	553	7,818	7,444	7,217	-0.7	83	97.2	96.8	0.0	0.0	0.2	0.3
OSCEOLA	133	00000	540	23,197	24,183	24,749	0.6	39	97.5	97.1	0.3	0.4	0.2	0.3
OSCODA	135	00000	540	9,418	9,471	9,579	0.1	68	97.8	97.8	0.1	0.1	0.1	0.1
OTSEGO	137	00000	540	23,301	25,573	27,045	1.3	12	97.5	97.1	0.2	0.2	0.4	0.6
OTTAWA	139	26100	563	238,314	267,058	282,621	1.6	5	91.5	89.5	1.0	1.1	2.1	3.0
PRESQUE ISLE	141	00000	540	14,411	14,507	14,542	0.1	68	98.1	98.0	0.3	0.3	0.2	0.2
ROSCOMMON	143	00000	540	25,469	26,745	27,626	0.7	35	98.0	97.7	0.3	0.4	0.2	0.3
SAGINAW	145	40980	513	210,039	208,714	206,568	-0.1	76	75.3	72.9	18.6	19.9	0.8	1.1
ST. CLAIR	147	19820	505	164,235	174,977	181,631	0.9	27	95.0	94.2	2.1	2.3	0.4	0.6
ST. JOSEPH	149	44780	563	62,422	64,176	65,489	0.4	53	93.5	92.4	2.6	2.8	0.6	0.9
SANILAC	151	00000	505	44,547	45,692	46,307	0.4	53	96.9	96.3	0.3	0.3	0.3	0.4
SCHOOLCRAFT	153	00000	553	8,903	8,781	8,704	-0.2	70	88.7	87.7	1.6	1.8	0.4	0.6
MICHIGAN							0.5		80.2	78.6	14.2	14.5	1.8	2.6
UNITED STATES							1.2		75.1	72.7	12.3	12.6	3.8	4.5

POPULATION COMPOSITION

COUNTY	% HISPANIC ORIGIN 2000	% HISPANIC ORIGIN 2007	0-4	5-9	10-14	15-19	20-24	25-44	45-64	65-84	85+	18+	MEDIAN AGE 2007	% 2007 Males	% 2007 Females
ALCONA	0.7	0.9	4.3	4.1	4.9	4.7	5.0	17.3	33.0	23.8	3.0	83.6	51.7	50.9	49.1
ALGER	1.0	1.2	4.6	4.5	4.7	5.5	7.2	24.4	32.4	14.0	2.5	82.6	44.2	53.9	46.1
ALLEGAN	5.7	7.1	7.5	6.9	7.1	7.2	6.6	26.7	26.8	9.5	1.6	74.2	37.0	50.0	50.0
ALPENA	0.6	0.7	5.8	5.2	5.3	6.5	7.0	22.7	30.0	14.9	2.6	79.8	43.2	48.9	51.1
ANTRIM	1.2	1.5	5.9	5.6	6.0	6.5	5.3	22.5	30.5	15.8	2.0	78.3	43.8	50.3	49.7
ARENAC	1.4	1.7	5.7	5.0	5.7	5.8	6.4	24.0	29.8	15.7	1.9	80.1	43.2	51.7	48.3
BARAGA	0.9	0.9	5.3	5.4	5.7	6.3	6.6	26.7	27.7	13.1	3.2	79.8	40.7	52.9	47.1
BARRY	1.5	1.8	6.8	6.5	7.0	6.6	5.9	25.9	28.7	11.1	1.5	75.6	39.5	50.0	50.0
BAY	3.9	4.9	6.2	5.9	6.3	6.3	6.0	25.6	28.6	12.8	2.4	77.8	40.6	48.8	51.2
BENZIE	1.5	1.8	6.0	5.7	5.9	5.8	5.0	23.5	30.3	15.6	2.1	78.7	43.7	49.5	50.5
BERRIEN	3.0	3.7	6.6	6.0	6.7	7.1	7.2	24.3	27.7	12.3	2.2	76.4	39.5	48.7	51.3
BRANCH	3.0	3.7	6.6	5.9	6.1	6.6	7.0	28.2	26.3	11.5	1.8	77.6	38.1	51.1	48.9
CALHOUN	3.2	3.9	6.5	6.0	6.7	7.4	7.1	25.9	26.6	11.7	2.1	76.3	38.1	48.7	51.3
CASS	2.4	3.0	6.1	5.9	6.3	6.7	6.3	24.6	29.7	12.8	1.6	77.6	41.1	50.2	49.8
CHARLEVOIX	1.0	1.3	6.6	6.5	6.3	6.7	5.6	23.6	29.7	13.0	2.0	76.3	41.4	49.5	50.5
CHEBOYGAN	0.8	0.9	6.1	5.8	5.7	5.7	5.7	22.5	30.7	15.6	2.2	78.7	43.8	49.7	50.3
CHIPPEWA	1.6	1.9	5.5	5.0	4.9	7.9	9.5	29.0	25.6	10.9	1.7	81.3	36.9	54.6	45.4
CLARE	1.1	1.4	6.0	5.3	6.1	6.3	6.3	22.1	28.9	17.1	1.8	78.7	43.3	49.5	50.5
CLINTON	2.6	3.3	6.8	6.6	7.4	6.7	6.0	25.1	28.9	11.0	1.6	74.9	39.7	49.6	50.4
CRAWFORD	1.0	1.3	5.6	4.8	5.4	7.3	7.1	22.1	29.9	15.8	2.0	79.6	43.4	51.5	48.5
DELTA	0.5	0.6	5.7	5.3	5.5	6.3	6.7	23.2	30.4	14.2	2.7	79.6	43.0	49.5	50.5
DICKINSON	0.7	0.9	5.7	5.2	6.7	6.9	6.8	22.6	29.6	13.3	3.1	77.8	42.4	49.7	50.3
EATON	3.2	4.0	6.4	6.0	6.2	7.2	7.2	26.0	29.0	10.4	1.7	77.1	38.5	48.6	51.4
EMMET	0.9	1.1	6.2	6.2	6.3	6.2	5.8	24.2	31.2	11.9	2.1	77.3	41.5	49.5	50.5
GENESEE	2.3	2.8	7.1	6.8	7.6	6.9	6.2	26.7	26.4	10.8	1.5	74.3	37.0	48.2	51.8
GLADWIN	1.0	1.2	5.7	5.4	5.5	6.0	5.3	22.0	29.6	18.4	2.0	79.5	45.0	49.7	50.3
GOGEBIC	0.9	1.1	4.7	4.2	4.5	6.8	8.5	22.0	27.8	16.7	4.9	82.9	44.5	51.2	48.8
GRAND TRAVERSE	1.5	1.9	6.1	5.8	6.1	6.8	7.0	25.5	29.3	11.1	2.2	77.7	39.8	48.8	51.2
GRATIOT	4.4	5.5	6.1	5.7	5.9	7.5	8.2	28.3	24.8	11.1	2.4	78.4	36.9	52.2	47.8
HILLSDALE	1.2	1.5	6.5	6.3	6.3	7.7	6.9	24.8	27.6	12.1	1.8	76.6	38.7	49.9	50.1
HOUGHTON	0.7	0.9	5.6	5.1	5.1	9.5	13.5	22.0	24.2	12.0	3.0	80.5	34.4	53.5	46.5
HURON	1.6	2.1	5.8	5.4	5.7	6.2	6.2	22.3	29.4	15.9	3.0	79.0	43.8	50.0	50.0
INGHAM	5.8	7.0	6.2	5.7	6.1	9.1	12.7	26.6	24.1	8.0	1.5	78.3	31.9	48.6	51.4
IONIA	2.8	3.4	7.1	6.6	6.5	7.7	9.6	28.4	24.3	8.4	1.4	75.8	33.9	53.6	46.4
IOSCO	1.0	1.2	5.0	4.3	5.6	6.1	6.1	19.0	31.5	19.6	2.7	81.1	47.2	49.3	50.7
IRON	0.6	0.8	4.5	4.0	4.9	5.9	7.3	19.3	31.6	17.9	4.5	82.9	47.6	49.8	50.2
ISABELLA	2.2	2.7	5.3	4.6	4.9	13.2	19.8	22.3	20.3	8.2	1.3	81.9	26.5	47.9	52.1
JACKSON	2.2	2.7	6.6	6.2	6.6	7.0	6.4	27.2	27.0	11.0	2.0	76.3	38.5	51.2	48.8
KALAMAZOO	2.6	3.2	6.3	6.1	6.3	8.6	10.6	25.6	24.9	9.8	1.9	77.3	34.4	48.4	51.6
KALKASKA	0.9	1.1	6.7	5.9	6.6	6.3	6.2	25.3	28.3	13.0	1.5	76.7	40.4	50.2	49.8
KENT	7.0	8.5	7.8	7.2	7.3	7.5	7.2	28.8	24.1	8.6	1.7	73.3	34.0	49.4	50.6
KEWEENAW	0.8	0.8	4.1	5.1	5.3	7.3	3.8	18.8	34.2	18.0	3.4	80.6	48.7	52.0	48.0
LAKE	1.7	2.1	5.3	5.1	4.9	9.0	5.8	19.0	29.9	18.9	2.1	80.0	45.5	52.9	47.1
LAPEER	3.1	3.9	6.8	6.5	7.4	6.9	6.2	26.8	28.8	9.4	1.1	74.9	38.5	50.7	49.3
LEELANAU	3.3	4.1	4.9	5.1	6.4	6.6	5.1	19.9	34.7	15.4	2.0	79.4	46.2	50.1	49.9
LENAWEE	7.0	8.6	6.3	6.1	6.6	7.2	6.7	26.3	27.8	11.0	1.9	76.7	38.5	50.0	50.0
LIVINGSTON	1.2	1.6	7.0	7.5	7.8	7.3	5.3	26.5	29.2	8.4	1.0	72.9	38.5	50.4	49.6
LUCE	1.8	2.1	5.0	5.1	5.3	8.3	9.4	25.3	26.3	13.2	2.1	81.5	38.4	53.5	46.5
MACKINAC	0.9	0.9	4.6	4.6	5.3	6.6	5.8	21.4	32.0	17.4	2.3	81.5	46.2	50.2	49.8
MACOMB	1.6	2.0	6.6	6.5	6.6	6.1	5.2	28.8	26.4	11.7	2.1	76.5	38.8	49.1	50.9
MANISTEE	2.6	3.2	5.3	5.3	5.4	6.0	6.8	22.7	30.0	15.8	2.7	80.3	43.9	50.9	49.1
MARQUETTE	0.7	1.0	5.1	4.7	5.1	8.2	9.8	24.9	28.3	11.6	2.3	81.6	38.8	50.1	49.9
MASON	3.0	3.8	5.6	5.2	5.9	6.7	6.6	22.7	30.6	14.2	2.5	79.4	43.1	49.5	50.5
MECOSTA	1.3	1.8	6.1	5.6	5.5	8.5	12.0	23.9	24.1	12.7	1.6	79.2	34.8	51.1	48.9
MENOMINEE	0.8	0.9	6.0	5.9	5.6	6.1	6.6	23.2	30.2	13.9	2.6	78.8	42.7	49.9	50.1
MIDLAND	1.6	1.9	6.4	6.0	7.3	7.5	7.1	25.4	27.6	11.0	1.9	75.9	38.8	49.1	50.9
MISSAUKEE	1.2	1.5	6.9	6.2	6.4	6.6	6.6	24.0	27.8	13.6	1.8	76.4	40.5	50.3	49.7
MONROE	2.1	2.7	6.6	6.4	7.0	7.4	6.3	26.4	28.0	10.4	1.5	75.3	38.3	49.7	50.3
MONTCALM	2.3	2.8	6.9	6.2	7.0	7.1	6.9	27.9	25.7	10.8	1.5	75.8	37.1	51.4	48.6
MONTMORENCY	0.6	0.8	4.5	4.3	4.6	5.2	6.1	17.9	32.9	21.9	2.6	83.3	49.7	49.5	50.5
MUSKEGON	3.5	4.3	7.0	6.4	7.0	7.1	6.8	26.6	26.2	10.8	2.0	75.1	37.1	49.6	50.4
NEWAYGO	3.9	4.8	7.2	6.6	7.2	7.7	6.8	24.4	26.8	11.7	1.6	74.1	38.2	50.0	50.0
OAKLAND	2.4	2.9	6.4	6.8	7.1	6.5	5.3	27.8	28.1	10.1	1.8	75.6	38.8	49.0	51.0
OCEANA	11.6	14.2	6.8	6.1	6.4	7.1	7.4	23.9	27.7	12.7	1.9	76.0	39.8	50.6	49.4
OGEMAW	1.2	1.5	5.4	4.8	5.7	6.2	6.4	20.9	34.0	17.9	2.3	80.1	45.3	49.6	50.4
ONTONAGON	0.7	0.9	4.4	4.3	4.3	5.9	5.9	18.3	33.6	20.0	3.4	83.2	49.1	50.8	49.2
OSCEOLA	1.0	1.2	6.5	5.8	6.5	7.3	7.0	24.5	27.3	13.4	1.7	76.5	39.8	49.4	50.6
OSCODA	0.9	1.0	5.4	4.8	5.5	6.1	6.4	18.1	32.5	19.0	2.2	80.5	47.2	49.3	50.7
OTSEGO	0.8	0.9	6.3	6.0	7.1	6.8	5.9	25.1	28.4	12.8	1.5	76.0	40.4	49.8	50.2
OTTAWA	7.0	8.6	7.8	7.2	7.1	8.5	8.3	27.3	23.4	8.7	1.7	73.5	33.2	49.2	50.8
PRESQUE ISLE	0.5	0.6	5.0	4.9	4.9	5.1	6.5	20.3	31.6	18.9	2.8	82.1	47.2	49.8	50.2
ROSCOMMON	0.8	1.0	4.5	4.3	5.5	5.3	5.3	17.8	33.2	21.6	2.5	82.4	49.5	49.6	50.4
SAGINAW	6.7	8.1	6.7	6.4	7.0	7.0	6.6	25.5	26.7	11.7	2.3	75.7	38.0	48.2	51.8
ST. CLAIR	2.2	2.7	6.8	6.4	6.9	6.8	6.3	26.6	27.7	10.7	1.8	75.7	38.8	49.4	50.6
ST. JOSEPH	4.0	4.9	7.5	6.8	6.6	6.6	6.7	26.9	25.9	11.2	1.9	74.9	37.2	49.5	50.5
SANILAC	2.8	3.5	6.8	6.6	6.4	6.8	6.0	24.9	27.3	13.0	2.2	75.8	40.0	49.9	50.1
SCHOOLCRAFT	0.9	1.1	5.8	5.3	5.7	5.5	6.8	22.0	30.1	16.2	2.6	79.8	44.2	50.2	49.8
MICHIGAN	3.3	3.9	6.7	6.5	7.0	7.2	6.8	26.8	26.5	10.7	1.8	75.6	37.4	49.2	50.8
UNITED STATES	12.5	15.0	6.9	6.5	6.8	7.1	7.0	27.6	25.4	10.7	1.9	75.6	36.7	49.2	50.8

COUNTY	HOUSEHOLDS					FAMILIES			MEDIAN HOUSEHOLD INCOME			
	2000	2007	2012	% Annual Rate 2000-2007	2007 Average HH Size	2000	2007	% Annual Rate 2000-2007	2007	2012	2007 National Rank	2007 State Rank
ALCONA	5,132	5,359	5,522	0.6	2.19	3,568	3,625	0.2	38,260	43,511	1966	67
ALGER	3,785	4,054	4,218	1.0	2.27	2,587	2,693	0.6	41,972	46,558	1452	50
ALLEGAN	38,165	43,145	46,276	1.7	2.65	28,405	31,390	1.4	54,007	60,814	453	15
ALPENA	12,818	12,692	12,488	-0.1	2.33	8,694	8,366	-0.5	41,349	46,469	1541	56
ANTRIM	9,222	10,383	11,000	1.6	2.42	6,712	7,376	1.3	45,251	50,488	1081	40
ARENAC	6,710	7,166	7,445	0.9	2.39	4,719	4,906	0.5	38,981	43,726	1856	66
BARAGA	3,353	3,409	3,422	0.2	2.31	2,223	2,192	-0.2	39,518	43,630	1779	63
BARRY	21,035	23,065	24,214	1.3	2.62	15,994	17,166	1.0	54,086	60,892	447	14
BAY	43,930	44,967	45,327	0.3	2.41	30,039	29,900	-0.1	46,925	53,479	915	33
BENZIE	6,500	7,729	8,517	2.4	2.37	4,593	5,320	2.0	46,073	53,045	994	39
BERRIEN	63,569	65,467	66,511	0.4	2.44	43,336	43,383	0.0	46,790	53,296	929	35
BRANCH	16,349	17,113	17,491	0.6	2.57	11,570	11,801	0.3	46,450	52,438	956	37
CALHOUN	54,100	55,299	55,873	0.3	2.44	36,249	35,981	-0.1	47,369	54,052	877	30
CASS	19,676	20,785	21,301	0.8	2.49	14,298	14,738	0.4	48,301	54,026	792	25
CHARLEVOIX	10,400	11,490	12,163	1.4	2.43	7,306	7,861	1.0	47,109	52,670	896	32
CHEBOYGAN	10,835	11,784	12,299	1.2	2.33	7,579	8,028	0.8	39,000	43,203	1853	65
CHIPPEWA	13,474	14,432	15,030	1.0	2.35	8,962	9,316	0.5	41,699	47,577	1492	53
CLARE	12,686	13,484	13,904	0.8	2.37	8,749	9,048	0.5	35,072	40,096	2421	77
CLINTON	23,653	27,863	30,303	2.3	2.62	17,976	20,728	2.0	62,996	69,923	195	6
CRAWFORD	5,625	6,178	6,519	1.3	2.38	4,037	4,325	1.0	40,142	44,869	1702	61
DELTA	15,836	16,486	16,809	0.6	2.32	10,684	10,804	0.2	41,891	46,494	1460	51
DICKINSON	11,386	11,831	12,072	0.5	2.31	7,579	7,647	0.1	41,874	47,014	1465	52
EATON	40,167	43,569	45,681	1.1	2.49	28,251	29,846	0.8	59,973	67,116	271	9
EMMET	12,577	14,412	15,511	1.9	2.38	8,527	9,496	1.5	47,681	54,240	845	28
GENESEE	169,825	177,451	182,064	0.6	2.50	115,956	117,789	0.2	51,660	60,284	571	19
GLADWIN	10,561	11,560	12,053	1.3	2.36	7,616	8,131	0.9	38,219	42,896	1973	68
GOGEBIC	7,425	7,183	6,973	-0.5	2.15	4,581	4,284	-0.9	31,810	35,560	2780	83
GRAND TRAVERSE	30,396	35,216	38,429	2.1	2.42	20,726	23,344	1.7	52,179	60,067	537	17
GRATIOT	14,501	14,926	15,128	0.4	2.51	10,401	10,442	0.1	44,953	50,682	1114	41
HILLSDALE	17,335	18,477	18,807	0.9	2.55	12,544	13,041	0.5	47,203	52,762	891	31
HOUGHTON	13,793	14,315	14,634	0.5	2.35	8,143	8,152	0.0	33,831	37,700	2571	81
HURON	14,597	14,821	14,812	0.2	2.35	10,141	10,019	-0.2	42,199	47,416	1426	47
INGHAM	108,593	111,867	114,452	0.4	2.40	63,767	63,339	-0.1	50,069	58,259	672	24
IONIA	20,606	22,532	23,691	1.2	2.65	15,151	16,181	0.9	51,065	57,117	612	20
IOSCO	11,727	12,116	12,244	0.5	2.21	7,855	7,881	0.0	37,819	42,431	2023	69
IRON	5,748	5,689	5,659	-0.1	2.14	3,614	3,462	-0.6	34,081	38,115	2543	80
ISABELLA	22,425	25,800	27,604	2.0	2.48	13,014	14,427	1.4	40,959	45,941	1605	58
JACKSON	58,168	61,604	63,659	0.8	2.52	40,840	42,123	0.4	51,755	59,393	564	18
KALAMAZOO	93,479	99,791	103,542	0.9	2.38	57,936	59,809	0.4	51,039	58,483	614	21
KALKASKA	6,428	7,143	7,506	1.5	2.48	4,636	5,024	1.1	42,790	47,991	1355	46
KENT	212,890	229,814	239,389	1.1	2.60	144,123	151,174	0.7	56,444	64,618	347	10
KEWEENAW	998	1,066	1,102	0.9	2.09	605	625	0.4	34,711	39,107	2464	78
LAKE	4,704	5,218	5,605	1.4	2.23	3,055	3,285	1.0	32,442	37,186	2719	82
LAPEER	30,729	34,693	37,174	1.7	2.70	23,889	26,438	1.4	61,441	67,629	228	8
LEELANAU	8,436	9,574	10,344	1.8	2.41	6,216	6,890	1.4	55,374	62,073	390	12
LENAWEE	35,930	38,363	39,972	0.9	2.57	26,052	27,137	0.6	53,995	60,737	455	16
LIVINGSTON	55,384	70,365	80,935	3.4	2.72	43,506	54,226	3.1	82,870	96,959	39	1
LUCE	2,481	2,618	2,694	0.7	2.33	1,740	1,787	0.4	36,759	40,406	2156	72
MACKINAC	5,067	5,269	5,469	0.5	2.25	3,408	3,441	0.1	41,320	47,619	1549	57
MACOMB	309,203	336,980	357,987	1.2	2.51	210,867	223,400	0.8	64,553	75,369	173	3
MANISTEE	9,860	10,644	11,080	1.1	2.32	6,715	7,045	0.7	40,802	45,802	1629	59
MARQUETTE	25,767	26,899	27,306	0.6	2.26	16,480	16,662	0.2	42,984	48,431	1332	45
MASON	11,406	12,174	12,647	0.9	2.39	7,878	8,180	0.5	41,350	46,386	1540	55
MECOSTA	14,915	16,586	17,725	1.5	2.42	9,893	10,676	1.1	40,420	45,295	1671	60
MENOMINEE	10,529	10,911	11,089	0.5	2.30	7,006	7,049	0.1	39,297	43,472	1822	64
MIDLAND	31,769	33,680	34,631	0.8	2.49	22,691	23,452	0.5	54,780	62,426	412	13
MISSAUKEE	5,450	5,993	6,277	1.3	2.56	4,046	4,348	1.0	41,523	46,125	1515	54
MONROE	53,772	59,505	62,846	1.4	2.61	39,933	43,187	1.1	61,591	69,577	221	7
MONTCALM	22,079	24,213	25,522	1.3	2.60	16,176	17,323	0.9	43,537	48,492	1272	44
MONTMORENCY	4,455	4,775	4,928	1.0	2.22	3,047	3,175	0.6	36,318	41,357	2228	74
MUSKEGON	63,330	66,890	68,963	0.8	2.56	44,298	45,553	0.4	46,321	52,661	967	38
NEWAYGO	17,599	19,172	20,052	1.2	2.64	12,941	13,768	0.9	44,230	49,330	1186	42
OAKLAND	471,115	496,018	507,715	0.7	2.46	315,392	322,452	0.3	77,651	89,377	69	2
OCEANA	9,778	10,829	11,508	1.4	2.62	7,265	7,864	1.1	42,180	47,415	1428	48
OGEMAW	8,842	9,368	9,670	0.8	2.35	6,189	6,386	0.4	36,301	40,871	2230	75
ONTONAGON	3,456	3,401	3,341	-0.2	2.14	2,225	2,119	-0.7	34,643	38,580	2480	79
OSCEOLA	8,861	9,477	9,794	0.9	2.51	6,413	6,690	0.6	40,111	44,420	1709	62
OSCODA	3,921	4,011	4,079	0.3	2.35	2,719	2,707	-0.1	35,460	40,476	2373	76
OTSEGO	8,995	10,153	10,857	1.7	2.50	6,539	7,203	1.3	47,896	53,819	828	26
OTTAWA	81,662	93,491	99,853	1.9	2.75	61,360	68,707	1.6	64,285	73,214	175	4
PRESQUE ISLE	6,155	6,444	6,554	0.6	2.22	4,201	4,277	0.2	37,339	41,445	2089	70
ROSCOMMON	11,250	12,041	12,520	0.9	2.19	7,619	7,924	0.5	37,000	42,402	2129	71
SAGINAW	80,430	80,729	80,429	0.1	2.51	55,790	54,494	-0.3	46,913	53,507	917	34
ST. CLAIR	62,072	67,818	71,014	1.2	2.56	44,631	47,553	0.9	55,763	63,315	375	11
ST. JOSEPH	23,381	24,455	25,097	0.6	2.58	16,803	16,921	0.0	47,816	53,732	831	27
SANILAC	16,871	17,684	18,064	0.7	2.54	12,169	12,445	0.3	43,542	48,475	1271	43
SCHOOLCRAFT	3,606	3,649	3,653	0.2	2.30	2,498	2,461	-0.2	36,438	40,503	2208	73
MICHIGAN				0.7	2.52			0.4	54,480	62,717		
UNITED STATES				1.2	2.59			1.0	53,154	62,503		

INCOME

COUNTY	2007 Per Capita Income	2007 HH Income Base	2007 HOUSEHOLD INCOME DISTRIBUTION (%)					2007 Home Value Base	2007 HOME VALUE DISTRIBUTION (%)					2007 Median Home Value
			Less than $25,000	$25,000 to $49,999	$50,000 to $99,999	$100,000 to $149,999	$150,000 or More		Less than $50,000	$50,000 to $89,999	$90,000 to $174,999	$175,000 to $399,999	$400,000 or More	
ALCONA	21,775	5,359	30.3	35.9	26.0	5.2	2.5	4,805	9.3	19.3	44.9	22.0	4.6	118,445
ALGER	21,185	4,054	27.8	32.3	32.3	5.6	1.9	3,367	13.3	24.1	44.2	15.7	2.8	108,503
ALLEGAN	24,218	43,145	18.0	27.3	39.2	11.3	4.3	35,973	9.2	8.6	45.5	32.6	4.2	150,545
ALPENA	21,712	12,692	29.3	30.1	32.1	6.2	2.3	10,101	8.0	22.3	51.1	16.9	1.7	110,596
ANTRIM	23,573	10,383	23.8	32.9	32.0	7.9	3.5	8,838	7.5	13.1	40.8	26.5	12.1	145,896
ARENAC	20,479	7,166	31.8	30.5	28.0	7.4	2.3	6,071	14.0	22.4	44.3	16.4	2.9	107,858
BARAGA	19,493	3,409	31.6	30.7	30.6	5.8	1.3	2,675	19.2	26.2	42.6	11.0	1.0	96,073
BARRY	24,868	23,065	16.6	28.4	39.4	11.1	4.5	19,861	4.8	8.2	47.6	34.2	5.3	154,327
BAY	24,640	44,967	25.1	28.0	31.3	11.6	4.0	35,848	9.9	19.2	49.2	19.8	2.0	116,602
BENZIE	23,828	7,729	22.0	33.0	34.7	6.9	3.3	6,644	6.2	11.7	44.1	30.9	7.2	148,235
BERRIEN	24,818	65,467	26.4	26.9	31.7	10.2	4.9	47,864	9.0	12.9	43.4	28.9	5.8	140,536
BRANCH	20,992	17,113	22.5	31.7	35.1	8.6	2.1	13,622	10.5	19.5	46.8	20.3	2.9	116,528
CALHOUN	23,913	55,297	24.6	28.2	33.2	10.2	3.8	40,660	12.0	22.4	42.5	20.9	2.2	113,989
CASS	23,799	20,785	22.7	29.4	34.5	9.8	3.6	17,127	9.3	15.1	45.2	25.1	5.2	132,350
CHARLEVOIX	24,502	11,490	22.5	30.9	33.7	9.1	3.8	9,395	6.7	10.6	41.6	30.7	10.5	155,074
CHEBOYGAN	22,160	11,784	29.2	35.5	26.5	5.3	3.5	9,780	9.1	17.1	44.1	24.0	5.8	127,244
CHIPPEWA	19,920	14,432	30.0	29.7	31.8	6.4	2.0	10,780	14.1	22.9	44.9	16.4	1.7	108,103
CLARE	19,684	13,484	34.9	32.6	24.7	5.4	2.3	11,121	19.2	23.5	41.0	15.3	1.1	100,515
CLINTON	28,478	27,863	13.8	23.8	40.3	16.1	6.1	23,876	6.2	5.4	39.6	44.1	4.7	172,672
CRAWFORD	21,090	6,178	25.6	37.5	28.4	5.9	2.7	5,118	10.9	23.1	47.1	16.7	2.2	111,264
DELTA	22,401	16,486	28.9	29.3	31.7	7.7	2.4	13,187	10.5	24.1	45.3	18.1	1.9	108,961
DICKINSON	22,384	11,831	28.7	30.9	30.5	7.4	2.6	9,539	15.4	31.5	35.5	15.7	2.0	93,676
EATON	27,991	43,569	15.3	25.1	39.2	15.4	5.0	32,705	5.3	7.2	46.5	38.1	2.8	158,379
EMMET	26,379	14,412	22.3	30.9	31.9	9.8	5.1	11,046	5.8	8.0	37.6	37.6	11.1	171,461
GENESEE	26,160	177,451	23.3	25.1	33.1	12.6	5.9	130,934	15.5	18.3	40.3	23.6	2.3	119,414
GLADWIN	20,739	11,560	29.8	34.5	26.7	6.6	2.4	9,924	14.3	18.7	41.9	23.1	2.0	117,694
GOGEBIC	19,530	7,183	38.9	32.3	22.2	4.4	2.2	5,653	39.6	28.6	22.3	8.0	1.5	61,044
GRAND TRAVERSE	28,106	35,216	17.1	30.1	36.0	10.4	6.3	27,508	5.8	6.4	39.3	39.5	9.0	172,196
GRATIOT	20,706	14,926	25.1	31.1	32.9	8.5	2.3	11,710	12.3	23.7	46.9	16.0	1.1	108,186
HILLSDALE	21,820	18,477	23.0	30.8	35.0	8.3	2.8	14,886	10.2	17.4	44.7	24.8	2.9	122,396
HOUGHTON	18,620	14,315	37.4	30.5	24.6	5.6	1.9	10,254	25.5	28.8	32.5	11.5	1.6	83,485
HURON	22,118	14,821	27.1	32.0	31.6	6.7	2.5	12,404	10.5	21.9	45.5	18.5	3.6	112,068
INGHAM	26,937	111,866	23.9	26.0	32.2	11.3	6.6	69,067	6.8	13.0	44.7	31.4	4.1	140,169
IONIA	21,710	22,532	21.6	27.1	38.4	10.1	2.9	18,196	8.2	12.3	50.2	26.6	2.7	134,792
IOSCO	21,509	12,116	30.5	34.9	27.3	5.2	2.1	9,968	8.9	24.7	45.1	18.8	2.4	110,500
IRON	19,677	5,689	36.1	33.2	25.2	4.1	1.4	4,688	29.1	29.7	29.7	9.7	1.7	74,298
ISABELLA	20,758	25,800	30.2	29.8	28.7	8.1	3.2	16,478	10.1	14.8	49.1	23.5	2.5	125,323
JACKSON	24,513	61,603	21.6	26.6	36.3	11.1	4.4	47,564	10.1	15.4	44.3	27.4	2.8	128,479
KALAMAZOO	27,688	99,798	22.6	26.2	32.8	12.1	6.3	66,409	7.1	11.5	45.8	31.3	4.4	146,163
KALKASKA	20,156	7,143	25.1	34.4	32.4	6.4	1.6	6,089	10.9	19.5	49.9	17.3	2.5	115,986
KENT	27,298	229,814	18.1	25.7	36.8	12.5	6.9	162,919	6.2	8.7	47.9	32.4	4.8	151,166
KEWEENAW	21,949	1,066	32.0	38.6	21.9	5.2	2.4	951	34.1	24.3	24.3	12.4	4.9	69,810
LAKE	18,566	5,218	38.0	33.2	22.6	4.4	1.8	4,356	25.5	25.6	34.3	12.6	2.0	88,352
LAPEER	26,806	34,693	14.9	24.1	38.6	16.9	5.5	29,545	4.9	6.1	36.9	46.1	6.1	180,284
LEELANAU	29,798	9,574	16.1	27.6	38.9	11.0	6.3	8,159	1.9	3.7	28.3	43.8	22.4	229,118
LENAWEE	24,870	38,363	18.4	27.3	37.8	12.2	4.4	30,305	6.7	10.6	47.0	33.0	2.7	146,209
LIVINGSTON	37,354	70,365	8.3	16.0	35.9	24.9	14.9	62,045	2.8	3.3	16.9	62.4	14.6	246,346
LUCE	18,474	2,618	31.2	37.2	26.1	4.2	1.4	2,114	19.6	24.2	43.8	10.9	1.5	98,966
MACKINAC	22,598	5,269	27.3	33.8	30.4	6.0	2.4	4,210	10.3	16.1	46.1	22.3	5.2	125,804
MACOMB	30,936	336,980	14.8	22.7	35.8	18.4	8.3	266,979	4.5	5.5	39.8	45.8	4.4	175,373
MANISTEE	21,607	10,644	29.2	31.9	30.6	5.8	2.6	8,676	10.3	24.4	42.3	19.6	3.3	113,442
MARQUETTE	23,147	26,899	27.6	29.6	32.5	7.4	2.9	18,956	12.5	23.5	47.8	14.7	1.5	107,893
MASON	21,819	12,174	28.6	31.2	30.0	7.6	2.6	9,612	10.1	19.5	45.8	21.4	3.3	116,645
MECOSTA	20,865	16,586	30.3	31.4	28.2	7.0	3.1	12,311	11.5	17.4	44.0	24.5	2.5	122,641
MENOMINEE	20,520	10,911	30.3	32.2	30.6	5.3	1.6	8,718	19.4	26.8	41.2	11.6	1.1	95,308
MIDLAND	29,929	33,680	20.4	25.8	31.6	13.0	9.2	26,602	8.5	15.0	45.6	26.9	4.0	129,500
MISSAUKEE	19,564	5,993	26.3	35.6	30.5	5.5	2.2	5,045	12.7	21.2	45.8	17.8	2.4	111,394
MONROE	27,860	59,504	16.8	22.6	37.9	16.4	6.2	48,494	7.9	7.2	37.1	43.1	4.6	170,209
MONTCALM	19,541	24,213	25.1	32.5	34.0	6.7	1.7	19,863	11.0	18.4	49.8	19.1	1.7	118,393
MONTMORENCY	20,936	4,775	31.4	36.3	25.4	4.6	2.3	4,112	11.2	23.8	43.2	19.2	2.6	109,188
MUSKEGON	21,945	66,890	25.5	28.8	34.0	8.5	3.2	52,230	12.8	19.9	48.3	17.0	2.0	113,158
NEWAYGO	19,904	19,172	26.4	31.2	32.7	7.7	2.1	16,228	12.3	17.2	46.9	21.7	1.9	120,321
OAKLAND	42,223	496,017	12.0	18.7	32.4	19.8	17.1	374,236	3.8	4.4	24.4	51.2	16.2	225,417
OCEANA	19,490	10,829	27.3	32.2	31.5	6.6	2.4	9,014	12.8	20.3	43.8	19.4	3.7	113,065
OGEMAW	19,606	9,368	33.1	33.2	26.5	5.5	1.7	7,917	14.3	22.4	43.1	18.6	1.7	109,173
ONTONAGON	20,737	3,401	34.3	33.7	25.4	4.6	2.0	2,885	37.6	30.5	24.3	6.6	1.0	64,637
OSCEOLA	19,368	9,477	28.6	33.7	30.2	5.6	2.0	7,758	14.8	24.3	44.7	14.2	2.0	104,087
OSCODA	18,984	4,011	34.3	35.7	23.3	5.2	1.5	3,447	15.1	27.2	39.4	16.2	2.1	101,616
OTSEGO	24,117	10,153	21.1	31.7	33.8	9.7	3.8	8,355	5.3	10.6	49.7	30.2	4.2	145,002
OTTAWA	27,633	93,491	12.8	22.7	42.1	15.4	7.1	75,934	5.8	4.8	42.4	41.9	5.1	169,924
PRESQUE ISLE	21,056	6,444	31.4	35.9	25.6	5.3	1.9	5,507	12.2	22.8	43.7	18.8	2.4	110,713
ROSCOMMON	22,090	12,041	31.0	34.5	26.5	5.4	2.5	10,359	11.2	24.0	42.3	19.1	3.3	109,571
SAGINAW	23,977	80,729	25.4	27.7	30.7	11.9	4.3	60,077	16.4	19.8	43.3	19.1	1.4	111,223
ST. CLAIR	26,535	67,818	19.5	25.0	37.1	13.1	5.3	54,307	7.0	9.4	41.0	37.9	4.7	158,130
ST. JOSEPH	22,056	24,455	23.3	29.3	35.9	8.2	3.3	18,993	8.8	18.7	51.2	19.0	2.4	118,417
SANILAC	20,549	17,684	26.5	32.1	31.8	7.2	2.4	14,573	8.4	14.8	49.9	23.5	3.3	127,711
SCHOOLCRAFT	20,499	3,649	34.4	30.7	26.5	6.2	2.2	2,985	20.3	25.5	35.6	16.4	2.1	95,853
MICHIGAN	27,982		20.7	25.1	33.5	13.3	7.4		9.3	13.4	39.3	32.1	5.8	145,372
UNITED STATES	27,916		21.9	25.0	32.3	12.3	8.4		7.9	10.5	27.1	35.6	19.0	192,285

COUNTY	FINANCIAL SERVICES				THE HOME						ENTERTAINMENT						PERSONAL			
					Home Improvements		Furnishings													
	Auto Loan	Home Loan	Invest-ments	Retire-ment Plans	Home Repair	Lawn & Garden	Comput-ers & Hard-ware	Major Appli-ances	TV, Radio, Sound Equip-ment	Furni-ture	Dine out/ Carry out	Sports Equip-ment	Fees & Tickets	Toys & Games	Travel	Cable TV	Apparel & Services	Auto Repairs	Health Insur-ance	Pets & Supplies
ALCONA	75	62	49	59	70	89	60	77	65	60	64	64	55	63	64	70	55	71	83	79
ALGER	82	62	43	61	71	93	63	81	68	61	68	70	55	71	65	73	58	73	85	85
ALLEGAN	99	91	80	90	91	100	86	94	88	87	88	84	84	92	87	90	78	90	95	97
ALPENA	77	65	62	65	70	83	67	76	71	65	70	66	63	72	68	74	61	71	81	78
ANTRIM	94	72	49	71	82	106	73	92	78	70	77	80	64	81	74	83	67	84	96	97
ARENAC	80	61	45	59	69	90	63	79	68	60	68	68	55	69	64	73	58	72	85	83
BARAGA	74	56	46	55	63	80	59	71	67	56	64	62	53	67	60	72	55	66	82	74
BARRY	98	91	85	91	95	105	85	96	89	87	88	85	85	93	88	91	78	90	98	100
BAY	81	82	92	82	84	87	79	83	83	80	81	71	82	83	83	85	73	80	89	83
BENZIE	88	76	62	75	81	97	73	88	77	73	76	76	69	77	76	80	66	82	91	90
BERRIEN	87	81	85	82	83	89	82	85	86	82	84	75	81	87	83	88	75	84	91	87
BRANCH	85	73	67	73	78	90	72	82	77	72	76	71	69	81	73	80	67	77	87	85
CALHOUN	83	78	85	80	79	83	80	81	83	80	82	71	80	85	80	85	74	80	86	82
CASS	92	79	70	78	85	100	77	89	82	77	82	78	73	86	79	86	72	83	94	93
CHARLEVOIX	92	79	69	79	84	99	78	90	82	77	81	79	74	84	80	85	70	84	95	93
CHEBOYGAN	83	64	48	63	72	93	67	82	72	63	71	71	58	73	68	76	61	75	87	86
CHIPPEWA	73	64	64	65	66	75	67	71	69	65	68	62	64	70	67	71	60	69	75	73
CLARE	73	58	48	56	64	81	60	72	65	57	64	62	54	64	61	70	55	68	80	75
CLINTON	105	111	114	111	111	110	100	106	101	105	100	94	105	105	105	101	91	101	105	107
CRAWFORD	79	64	55	63	71	88	67	79	71	63	70	68	60	71	68	75	60	73	84	82
DELTA	77	68	66	67	73	84	68	77	73	67	72	67	65	74	70	76	63	73	83	79
DICKINSON	76	68	70	68	72	81	68	75	73	67	71	65	67	74	71	76	63	72	83	76
EATON	97	100	105	102	99	98	96	96	95	98	95	87	99	98	98	95	86	95	96	98
EMMET	93	86	81	86	90	101	84	94	86	83	85	82	81	86	87	88	75	89	96	96
GENESEE	90	90	98	92	88	89	89	88	92	91	91	78	91	92	90	93	82	89	92	89
GLADWIN	79	61	45	59	69	89	62	78	68	60	67	67	55	69	64	73	57	71	85	82
GOGEBIC	65	50	50	50	55	69	58	64	63	52	61	55	50	62	57	67	52	61	75	65
GRAND TRAVERSE	99	98	97	98	97	100	94	98	94	95	94	88	94	95	96	95	84	96	98	99
GRATIOT	82	72	70	72	75	86	71	79	76	71	75	69	69	79	72	78	66	75	84	81
HILLSDALE	88	73	64	72	79	94	73	84	77	72	77	74	68	81	74	81	67	79	88	88
HOUGHTON	67	51	52	52	55	66	63	64	66	55	64	57	55	64	59	68	55	63	72	65
HURON	83	66	53	64	73	92	66	81	73	64	71	70	60	74	68	77	61	75	89	85
INGHAM	91	85	95	89	82	83	97	86	95	92	94	80	93	94	91	93	85	91	88	88
IONIA	91	82	77	82	85	95	78	87	82	79	82	77	77	86	80	85	72	82	90	90
IOSCO	73	60	52	59	66	82	62	74	67	59	65	63	56	65	64	71	56	69	81	75
IRON	65	52	47	51	57	72	56	65	61	52	59	56	50	59	57	65	50	61	74	66
ISABELLA	78	62	60	64	61	70	81	71	77	70	77	68	70	76	71	75	69	76	72	74
JACKSON	89	88	94	89	89	92	85	88	88	87	87	78	87	90	88	89	78	86	92	90
KALAMAZOO	92	87	97	91	86	87	97	89	95	92	95	82	94	95	93	93	85	92	90	90
KALKASKA	80	66	51	64	69	84	64	76	69	64	68	66	59	71	65	72	59	71	80	80
KENT	98	98	103	101	95	93	100	96	99	100	99	88	101	101	98	98	90	98	95	96
KEWEENAW	70	57	56	56	62	76	60	68	67	57	64	58	56	65	63	72	55	65	82	69
LAKE	66	54	43	51	59	75	53	66	58	52	57	56	48	57	55	63	49	61	73	68
LAPEER	103	107	108	107	107	108	98	103	98	102	98	94	102	102	102	99	89	100	101	105
LEELANAU	110	99	83	98	108	127	93	113	96	93	96	98	89	98	99	101	84	104	114	116
LENAWEE	94	90	92	91	93	98	87	93	90	88	89	82	87	93	89	91	79	89	95	95
LIVINGSTON	137	160	163	162	156	143	141	142	134	149	135	132	152	139	146	131	125	137	131	142
LUCE	73	54	41	52	61	80	58	70	64	53	62	61	49	65	58	69	53	65	79	74
MACKINAC	78	66	57	64	72	88	67	79	70	64	69	68	61	68	69	74	59	74	84	81
MACOMB	102	113	125	114	112	105	107	105	106	110	106	94	113	107	110	106	97	105	106	105
MANISTEE	79	64	57	63	70	86	67	78	71	64	70	67	61	72	68	76	61	73	84	80
MARQUETTE	76	68	73	69	69	76	75	74	76	70	75	66	71	75	73	77	66	74	79	75
MASON	80	66	60	66	72	87	69	79	73	66	72	68	63	74	69	76	62	74	84	82
MECOSTA	80	64	54	64	67	81	71	75	73	66	73	68	63	72	68	74	63	74	79	79
MENOMINEE	74	59	52	58	64	79	61	71	67	59	65	62	56	68	61	71	57	67	78	74
MIDLAND	107	106	107	106	106	110	101	105	103	103	102	95	102	105	103	104	92	103	107	107
MISSAUKEE	84	63	42	60	71	93	62	80	69	61	69	69	54	72	63	74	59	73	86	86
MONROE	99	107	114	107	107	104	98	101	99	102	99	91	104	101	103	99	90	99	101	102
MONTCALM	82	67	56	66	72	85	66	77	71	66	71	68	62	74	67	75	62	72	81	81
MONTMORENCY	71	59	49	57	66	82	59	73	64	57	63	62	54	62	63	69	54	68	81	74
MUSKEGON	81	77	79	78	77	83	76	79	79	77	78	69	76	81	77	81	70	78	83	81
NEWAYGO	86	69	52	67	72	90	67	80	73	67	72	71	61	76	67	77	63	75	85	85
OAKLAND	137	154	166	157	152	139	146	141	141	151	142	131	154	142	149	139	131	141	136	141
OCEANA	85	66	48	64	72	92	65	80	71	64	70	70	58	74	66	76	61	74	85	85
OGEMAW	72	57	47	56	64	80	60	72	64	57	63	62	53	64	61	68	54	67	78	74
ONTONAGON	69	54	46	53	60	76	57	68	64	54	61	58	51	63	59	68	52	64	78	70
OSCEOLA	80	61	47	59	66	85	62	75	68	60	67	66	55	70	61	72	58	69	80	80
OSCODA	68	57	49	55	63	78	56	70	62	55	60	58	52	59	60	66	51	65	77	71
OTSEGO	92	81	72	81	85	99	80	91	82	78	82	80	76	85	81	85	71	85	93	93
OTTAWA	109	115	114	115	110	107	107	107	105	110	105	98	110	108	108	103	95	106	104	107
PRESQUE ISLE	76	57	42	56	64	84	60	74	66	56	64	64	52	66	61	70	55	68	81	77
ROSCOMMON	73	63	54	60	69	85	62	76	67	61	65	64	58	64	66	72	56	71	84	77
SAGINAW	84	82	90	83	82	86	81	83	85	82	84	72	83	85	83	87	76	82	89	84
ST. CLAIR	93	97	105	98	97	97	92	94	93	94	92	83	95	95	95	94	84	92	96	95
ST. JOSEPH	87	74	69	74	79	92	75	84	80	74	79	70	71	00	75	83	62	79	89	87
SANILAC	84	67	53	65	74	92	67	81	72	65	72	71	61	76	68	76	62	75	86	86
SCHOOLCRAFT	74	57	50	56	64	82	63	74	68	58	66	64	55	67	63	72	57	69	81	76
MICHIGAN	99	98	103	100	98	100	97	98	99	98	98	88	98	100	98	100	89	98	101	99
UNITED STATES	100	100	100	100	100	100	100	100	100	100	100	100	100	100	100	100	100	100	100	100

POPULATION CHANGE

COUNTY	FIPS Code	CBSA Code	DMA Code	POPULATION			2000-2007 ANNUAL RATE		RACE (%)					
									White		Black		Asian/Pacific	
				2000	2007	2012	% Rate	State Rank	2000	2007	2000	2007	2000	2007
SHIAWASSEE	155	37020	513	71,687	74,431	76,408	0.5	46	97.4	96.9	0.2	0.2	0.3	0.4
TUSCOLA	157	00000	513	58,266	59,092	59,786	0.2	62	96.0	94.8	1.1	1.7	0.3	0.5
VAN BUREN	159	28020	563	76,263	80,926	84,175	0.8	31	87.9	86.3	5.2	5.7	0.3	0.4
WASHTENAW	161	11460	505	322,895	354,947	374,037	1.3	12	77.4	73.7	12.3	13.0	6.3	8.9
WAYNE	163	19820	505	2,061,162	2,008,976	1,962,754	-0.4	81	51.7	48.7	42.2	44.0	1.7	2.4
WEXFORD	165	15620	540	30,484	33,359	35,385	1.3	12	97.3	96.8	0.2	0.2	0.4	0.7
MICHIGAN							0.5		80.2	78.6	14.2	14.5	1.8	2.6
UNITED STATES							1.2		75.1	72.7	12.3	12.6	3.8	4.5

31-A

COUNTY	% HISPANIC ORIGIN		2007 AGE DISTRIBUTION (%)									MEDIAN AGE	% 2007 Males	% 2007 Females
	2000	2007	0-4	5-9	10-14	15-19	20-24	25-44	45-64	65-84	85+	18+	2007		
SHIAWASSEE	1.8	2.3	6.8	6.5	7.0	6.7	6.0	26.7	27.8	10.9	1.6	75.6	38.7	49.4	50.6
TUSCOLA	2.3	2.9	6.3	5.9	6.6	7.0	6.6	25.9	28.3	11.5	1.9	76.9	39.4	49.9	50.1
VAN BUREN	7.4	9.1	7.0	6.6	6.9	7.2	7.0	24.9	28.1	10.6	1.7	75.0	38.3	49.7	50.3
WASHTENAW	2.7	3.3	6.1	5.8	5.9	8.5	11.6	29.2	24.4	7.4	1.3	78.7	33.0	50.2	49.8
WAYNE	3.7	4.4	7.3	7.0	8.2	7.3	5.7	27.5	24.9	10.2	1.8	72.9	35.9	48.1	51.9
WEXFORD	1.0	1.3	6.7	6.0	6.5	6.8	7.4	24.9	27.6	12.2	2.0	76.5	39.7	49.8	50.2
MICHIGAN	3.3	3.9	6.7	6.5	7.0	7.2	6.8	26.8	26.5	10.7	1.8	75.6	37.4	49.2	50.8
UNITED STATES	12.5	15.0	6.9	6.5	6.8	7.1	7.0	27.6	25.4	10.7	1.9	75.6	36.7	49.2	50.8

COUNTY	HOUSEHOLDS					FAMILIES			MEDIAN HOUSEHOLD INCOME			
	2000	2007	2012	% Annual Rate 2000-2007	2007 Average HH Size	2000	2007	% Annual Rate 2000-2007	2007	2012	2007 National Rank	2007 State Rank
SHIAWASSEE	26,896	28,657	29,715	0.9	2.57	19,862	20,676	0.6	50,208	56,596	663	23
TUSCOLA	21,454	22,410	22,905	0.6	2.58	15,981	16,314	0.3	47,666	53,222	847	29
VAN BUREN	27,982	30,273	31,697	1.1	2.61	20,327	21,463	0.8	46,632	52,528	942	36
WASHTENAW	125,327	139,351	148,001	1.5	2.39	73,690	79,042	1.0	64,207	75,077	176	5
WAYNE	768,440	749,284	732,433	-0.3	2.64	511,717	484,340	-0.8	50,586	58,919	634	22
WEXFORD	11,824	13,202	14,104	1.5	2.50	8,386	9,124	1.2	42,108	47,350	1435	49
MICHIGAN				0.7	2.52			0.4	54,480	62,717		
UNITED STATES				1.2	2.59			1.0	53,154	62,503		

COUNTY	2007 Per Capita Income	2007 HH Income Base	2007 HOUSEHOLD INCOME DISTRIBUTION (%)					2007 Home Value Base	2007 HOME VALUE DISTRIBUTION (%)					2007 Median Home Value
			Less than $25,000	$25,000 to $49,999	$50,000 to $99,999	$100,000 to $149,999	$150,000 or More		Less than $50,000	$50,000 to $89,999	$90,000 to $174,999	$175,000 to $399,999	$400,000 or More	
SHIAWASSEE	23,866	28,657	20.6	29.1	35.8	10.9	3.6	23,164	7.3	10.9	52.5	27.0	2.4	137,027
TUSCOLA	22,033	22,410	22.0	30.5	34.9	9.7	2.8	18,904	9.8	16.5	50.1	22.4	1.2	123,873
VAN BUREN	21,478	30,273	24.6	29.0	34.0	9.7	2.6	24,299	11.4	15.8	46.1	24.1	2.6	124,884
WASHTENAW	34,830	139,351	17.8	21.3	32.0	16.3	12.5	84,790	4.1	4.5	20.0	53.9	17.5	235,557
WAYNE	24,901	749,249	25.2	24.2	31.7	12.2	6.7	505,578	15.7	23.2	39.5	18.6	3.1	107,240
WEXFORD	21,203	13,202	26.2	34.0	29.5	7.4	2.8	10,527	14.2	20.3	42.8	20.0	2.7	113,298
MICHIGAN	27,982		20.7	25.1	33.5	13.3	7.4		9.3	13.4	39.3	32.1	5.8	145,372
UNITED STATES	27,916		21.9	25.0	32.3	12.3	8.4		7.9	10.5	27.1	35.6	19.0	192,285

SPENDING POTENTIAL INDICES

COUNTY	FINANCIAL SERVICES				THE HOME						ENTERTAINMENT						PERSONAL			
					Home Improvements		Furnishings													
	Auto Loan	Home Loan	Invest-ments	Retire-ment Plans	Home Repair	Lawn & Garden	Comput-ers & Hard-ware	Major Appli-ances	TV, Radio, Sound Equip-ment	Furni-ture	Dine out/ Carry out	Sports Equip-ment	Fees & Tickets	Toys & Games	Travel	Cable TV	Apparel & Services	Auto Repairs	Health Insur-ance	Pets & Supplies
SHIAWASSEE	90	86	86	86	88	94	81	88	84	83	84	77	82	88	84	86	75	84	91	90
TUSCOLA	88	76	69	76	81	95	74	85	79	74	78	74	71	83	76	82	69	79	90	89
VAN BUREN	88	75	66	74	78	91	73	83	78	73	78	73	70	82	74	81	68	79	87	87
WASHTENAW	117	114	121	120	110	106	128	112	120	122	122	109	124	120	120	116	111	119	108	113
WAYNE	88	89	100	91	87	87	89	86	93	91	92	76	92	92	90	95	84	89	92	87
WEXFORD	82	69	64	69	72	84	70	78	74	68	73	68	66	76	70	77	64	74	83	80
MICHIGAN	99	98	103	100	98	100	97	98	99	98	98	88	98	100	98	100	89	98	101	99
UNITED STATES	100	100	100	100	100	100	100	100	100	100	100	100	100	100	100	100	100	100	100	100

| COUNTY | FIPS Code | CBSA Code | DMA Code | POPULATION | | | 2000-2007 ANNUAL RATE | | RACE (%) | | | | | |
| | | | | | | | | | White | | Black | | Asian/Pacific | |
				2000	2007	2012	% Rate	State Rank	2000	2007	2000	2007	2000	2007
AITKIN	001	00000	613	15,301	16,758	17,883	1.3	24	96.4	96.0	0.2	0.3	0.2	0.3
ANOKA	003	33460	613	298,084	339,272	371,125	1.8	14	93.6	92.1	1.6	2.0	1.7	2.3
BECKER	005	00000	724	30,000	32,481	33,749	1.1	30	89.4	88.5	0.2	0.2	0.4	0.5
BELTRAMI	007	13420	613	39,650	43,575	46,001	1.3	24	76.7	75.7	0.4	0.5	0.6	0.8
BENTON	009	41060	613	34,226	39,637	43,143	2.0	10	96.2	95.4	0.8	0.8	1.2	1.6
BIG STONE	011	00000	613	5,820	5,527	5,327	-0.7	83	98.4	98.1	0.2	0.2	0.4	0.6
BLUE EARTH	013	31860	737	55,941	61,505	65,167	1.3	24	95.0	93.6	1.2	1.5	1.9	2.5
BROWN	015	35580	737	26,911	26,699	26,201	-0.1	60	97.8	96.3	0.1	0.8	0.4	0.6
CARLTON	017	20260	676	31,671	34,588	36,319	1.2	28	91.7	90.9	1.0	1.2	0.4	0.5
CARVER	019	33460	613	70,205	93,309	114,167	4.0	4	95.9	94.9	0.6	0.6	1.6	2.1
CASS	021	14660	613	27,150	29,824	31,550	1.3	24	86.5	85.8	0.1	0.1	0.3	0.4
CHIPPEWA	023	00000	613	13,088	12,841	12,680	-0.3	71	96.8	95.7	0.2	0.3	0.3	0.7
CHISAGO	025	33460	613	41,101	53,065	61,189	3.6	6	97.2	96.7	0.5	0.5	0.7	1.0
CLAY	027	22020	724	51,229	56,295	60,218	1.3	24	94.0	92.6	0.5	0.7	0.9	1.2
CLEARWATER	029	00000	724	8,423	8,600	8,742	0.3	47	89.3	88.5	0.2	0.2	0.3	0.3
COOK	031	00000	676	5,168	5,749	6,113	1.5	19	89.5	88.6	0.3	0.4	0.4	0.5
COTTONWOOD	033	00000	613	12,167	11,975	11,835	-0.2	65	95.2	93.8	0.3	0.4	1.7	2.3
CROW WING	035	14660	613	55,099	62,837	67,407	1.8	14	97.6	97.3	0.3	0.3	0.3	0.4
DAKOTA	037	33460	613	355,904	410,244	453,446	2.0	10	91.4	89.1	2.3	2.8	2.9	3.9
DODGE	039	40340	611	17,731	20,375	22,101	1.9	12	96.6	95.5	0.2	0.2	0.4	0.6
DOUGLAS	041	10820	613	32,821	37,177	40,280	1.7	17	98.5	98.1	0.2	0.2	0.4	0.6
FARIBAULT	043	00000	613	16,181	15,635	15,275	-0.5	77	97.1	96.3	0.2	0.3	0.4	0.5
FILLMORE	045	00000	611	21,122	22,208	22,877	0.7	36	98.9	98.6	0.2	0.2	0.1	0.2
FREEBORN	047	10660	611	32,584	32,194	31,886	-0.2	65	95.2	93.8	0.2	0.3	0.6	0.8
GOODHUE	049	39860	613	44,127	47,578	50,131	1.0	33	96.6	95.8	0.6	0.8	0.6	0.8
GRANT	051	00000	613	6,289	6,203	6,124	-0.2	65	98.3	98.2	0.2	0.2	0.2	0.2
HENNEPIN	053	33460	613	1,116,200	1,155,253	1,176,156	0.5	39	80.5	76.3	9.0	10.8	4.8	6.2
HOUSTON	055	29100	702	19,718	20,289	20,582	0.4	43	98.5	98.1	0.3	0.4	0.4	0.5
HUBBARD	057	00000	613	18,376	19,100	19,617	0.5	39	96.3	95.9	0.2	0.2	0.3	0.4
ISANTI	059	33460	613	31,287	40,756	48,642	3.7	5	97.6	97.2	0.3	0.3	0.4	0.6
ITASCA	061	00000	676	43,992	45,109	45,892	0.3	47	94.6	94.1	0.2	0.2	0.3	0.4
JACKSON	063	00000	613	11,268	11,127	11,032	-0.2	65	97.1	96.2	0.1	0.1	1.4	1.9
KANABEC	065	00000	613	14,996	16,805	18,093	1.6	18	97.3	96.7	0.2	0.2	0.5	0.6
KANDIYOHI	067	48820	613	41,203	42,170	42,840	0.3	47	93.6	91.7	0.5	0.6	0.4	0.6
KITTSON	069	00000	724	5,285	4,959	4,745	-0.9	86	98.1	97.6	0.2	0.2	0.2	0.3
KOOCHICHING	071	00000	676	14,355	13,876	13,581	-0.5	77	96.1	95.7	0.2	0.2	0.2	0.3
LAC QUI PARLE	073	00000	613	8,067	7,534	7,188	-0.9	86	98.8	98.6	0.2	0.2	0.3	0.4
LAKE	075	00000	676	11,058	11,324	11,563	0.3	47	98.0	97.6	0.1	0.1	0.2	0.3
LAKE OF THE WOODS	077	00000	724	4,522	4,546	4,568	0.1	56	97.2	97.1	0.3	0.3	0.2	0.3
LE SUEUR	079	00000	613	25,426	28,223	30,367	1.4	20	96.6	95.5	0.1	0.2	0.3	0.5
LINCOLN	081	00000	725	6,429	6,149	5,967	-0.6	80	98.8	98.5	0.0	0.1	0.2	0.3
LYON	083	32140	613	25,425	25,650	25,934	0.1	56	93.6	91.8	1.5	1.9	1.7	2.3
MCLEOD	085	26780	613	34,898	37,927	40,255	1.2	28	96.6	95.6	0.2	0.3	0.6	0.8
MAHNOMEN	087	00000	724	5,190	5,115	5,057	-0.2	65	62.9	62.4	0.1	0.1	0.1	0.1
MARSHALL	089	00000	724	10,155	9,946	9,836	-0.3	71	97.2	96.5	0.1	0.1	0.2	0.2
MARTIN	091	21860	737	21,802	21,421	21,169	-0.2	65	97.2	96.3	0.3	0.3	0.4	0.6
MEEKER	093	00000	613	22,644	24,350	25,364	1.0	33	97.3	96.5	0.2	0.2	0.4	0.5
MILLE LACS	095	00000	613	22,330	26,670	30,123	2.5	7	93.6	93.1	0.3	0.3	0.2	0.3
MORRISON	097	00000	613	31,712	33,915	35,161	0.9	35	98.5	98.1	0.2	0.3	0.3	0.4
MOWER	099	12380	611	38,603	39,251	39,686	0.2	53	94.7	93.1	0.6	0.7	1.5	2.0
MURRAY	101	00000	725	9,165	8,914	8,729	-0.4	74	98.3	97.9	0.1	0.1	0.2	0.3
NICOLLET	103	31860	613	29,771	32,315	34,043	1.1	30	96.4	95.4	0.8	1.0	1.2	1.6
NOBLES	105	49380	725	20,832	20,695	20,587	-0.1	60	86.5	82.8	1.1	1.3	4.1	5.2
NORMAN	107	00000	724	7,442	7,049	6,786	-0.7	83	95.3	94.5	0.1	0.1	0.3	0.4
OLMSTED	109	40340	611	124,277	143,833	156,563	2.0	10	90.3	87.7	2.7	3.3	4.3	5.7
OTTER TAIL	111	22260	724	57,159	58,492	59,365	0.3	47	97.1	96.4	0.3	0.4	0.5	0.7
PENNINGTON	113	00000	724	13,584	13,684	13,760	0.1	56	97.0	96.9	0.2	0.2	0.6	0.7
PINE	115	00000	613	26,530	28,759	30,142	1.1	30	94.4	93.6	1.3	1.6	0.3	0.4
PIPESTONE	117	00000	725	9,895	9,506	9,227	-0.6	80	96.7	96.1	0.2	0.2	0.5	0.7
POLK	119	24220	724	31,369	31,280	31,258	0.0	58	94.2	94.0	0.3	0.3	0.3	0.3
POPE	121	00000	613	11,236	11,679	11,993	0.5	39	98.9	98.6	0.2	0.3	0.1	0.1
RAMSEY	123	33460	613	511,035	518,321	522,637	0.2	53	77.4	72.5	7.6	9.0	8.8	11.2
RED LAKE	125	00000	724	4,299	4,354	4,407	0.2	53	97.4	97.4	0.2	0.2	0.1	0.1
REDWOOD	127	00000	613	16,815	16,183	15,685	-0.5	77	95.0	94.4	0.1	0.2	0.4	0.5
RENVILLE	129	00000	613	17,154	16,951	16,760	-0.2	65	95.7	94.5	0.1	0.1	0.2	0.3
RICE	131	22060	613	56,665	64,563	69,228	1.8	14	93.6	91.9	1.3	1.6	1.5	2.0
ROCK	133	00000	725	9,721	9,456	9,256	-0.4	74	97.3	96.6	0.5	0.7	0.6	0.9
ROSEAU	135	00000	724	16,338	16,823	17,186	0.4	43	95.9	95.1	0.1	0.2	1.8	2.4
ST. LOUIS	137	20260	676	200,528	199,416	196,912	-0.1	60	94.9	94.0	0.8	1.1	0.7	0.9
SCOTT	139	33460	613	89,498	131,802	168,464	5.5	1	93.6	92.3	0.9	0.9	2.2	2.9
SHERBURNE	141	33460	613	64,417	91,109	110,344	4.9	2	96.7	96.2	0.9	1.3	0.6	0.8
SIBLEY	143	00000	613	15,356	15,926	16,341	0.5	39	95.6	94.2	0.1	0.2	0.3	0.4
STEARNS	145	41060	613	133,166	150,538	164,560	1.7	17	96.0	95.0	0.8	1.6	1.6	2.2
STEELE	147	36940	613	33,680	37,113	39,722	1.3	24	95.2	93.8	1.1	1.3	0.9	1.2
STEVENS	149	00000	613	10,053	9,810	9,613	-0.3	71	96.1	94.8	0.9	1.3	0.9	1.4
SWIFT	151	00000	613	11,956	11,460	11,023	-0.6	80	90.7	88.3	2.7	3.4	3.0	3.8
TODD	153	00000	613	24,426	25,251	25,757	0.5	30	97.5	97.0	0.1	0.1	0.3	0.4
MINNESOTA							1.2		89.4	87.5	3.5	4.1	2.9	3.7
UNITED STATES							1.2		75.1	72.7	12.3	12.6	3.8	4.5

POPULATION COMPOSITION

COUNTY	% HISPANIC ORIGIN		2007 AGE DISTRIBUTION (%)										MEDIAN AGE	% 2007 Males	% 2007 Females
	2000	2007	0-4	5-9	10-14	15-19	20-24	25-44	45-64	65-84	85+	18+	2007		
AITKIN	0.6	0.8	4.8	4.0	5.4	4.9	6.6	17.8	32.1	21.1	3.3	82.9	49.1	50.4	49.6
ANOKA	1.7	2.3	7.7	7.5	7.6	7.0	6.0	30.7	25.2	7.4	0.9	72.8	35.4	50.2	49.8
BECKER	0.8	1.0	6.6	6.2	5.7	6.8	7.0	22.1	29.7	13.5	2.5	77.2	41.9	50.1	49.9
BELTRAMI	1.0	1.2	7.4	6.4	6.8	9.0	10.6	24.0	23.9	9.9	1.9	74.6	32.1	49.3	50.7
BENTON	0.9	1.2	7.7	6.6	6.2	6.7	8.4	31.1	23.1	8.0	2.1	75.6	33.1	50.1	49.9
BIG STONE	0.3	0.5	5.3	4.6	5.5	7.1	7.5	18.1	28.4	18.7	4.9	80.2	46.1	48.5	51.5
BLUE EARTH	1.8	2.4	5.8	5.0	4.9	9.5	14.8	26.2	22.1	9.3	2.4	81.0	30.2	50.0	50.0
BROWN	2.0	3.0	5.8	5.3	5.8	8.3	8.3	23.0	27.2	13.1	3.3	78.6	40.4	49.7	50.3
CARLTON	0.8	1.1	6.1	5.7	6.0	6.6	7.7	24.5	28.3	12.5	2.6	78.2	40.6	50.8	49.2
CARVER	2.6	3.5	8.8	8.8	8.6	7.3	5.7	29.3	24.4	6.1	1.0	69.2	35.2	49.9	50.1
CASS	0.8	1.0	5.3	4.7	6.2	6.8	6.5	20.3	30.5	17.4	2.2	79.3	45.1	50.5	49.5
CHIPPEWA	1.9	2.6	6.2	5.8	6.3	6.4	7.5	21.4	28.5	13.9	3.9	78.1	42.2	49.2	50.8
CHISAGO	1.2	1.6	7.8	7.2	7.6	7.5	6.7	28.5	24.7	8.2	1.7	72.5	35.9	50.9	49.1
CLAY	3.7	5.0	6.4	6.0	6.1	10.2	12.1	23.1	23.2	10.4	2.3	77.2	33.2	48.3	51.7
CLEARWATER	0.8	1.0	6.4	5.8	5.5	6.6	7.3	22.5	27.9	14.9	3.3	78.3	42.1	50.3	49.7
COOK	0.8	1.0	4.2	4.3	4.5	5.3	5.0	20.0	39.2	14.5	2.9	83.5	48.1	49.8	50.2
COTTONWOOD	2.2	3.0	6.1	6.1	6.0	6.3	6.5	21.2	27.4	15.4	4.9	77.7	43.2	49.2	50.8
CROW WING	0.7	1.0	6.3	5.6	6.2	6.4	6.8	23.1	28.4	14.7	2.5	78.3	41.9	49.5	50.5
DAKOTA	2.9	4.0	7.8	7.6	7.6	7.3	5.8	30.9	25.1	6.9	1.0	72.2	35.2	49.4	50.6
DODGE	3.0	4.1	8.1	7.4	7.4	6.7	7.3	26.1	25.4	9.6	2.1	72.8	36.3	49.5	50.5
DOUGLAS	0.6	0.8	5.9	5.2	5.4	6.0	7.7	23.4	28.3	14.7	3.5	80.1	42.3	49.7	50.3
FARIBAULT	3.5	4.8	5.8	5.0	5.6	6.4	7.5	19.9	29.2	16.1	4.5	79.6	44.9	50.1	49.9
FILLMORE	0.5	0.7	6.3	6.0	6.2	6.5	6.7	22.7	27.6	14.1	3.8	77.2	41.7	49.6	50.4
FREEBORN	6.3	8.5	6.2	5.6	5.5	6.0	7.0	23.2	27.8	15.3	3.5	79.1	42.6	49.3	50.7
GOODHUE	1.1	1.5	6.4	6.0	6.2	6.9	7.8	24.0	28.2	11.7	2.8	77.0	40.4	49.7	50.3
GRANT	0.5	0.5	5.7	5.0	5.3	6.6	6.7	21.5	27.5	17.1	4.7	79.9	44.5	48.9	51.1
HENNEPIN	4.1	5.3	6.4	6.4	6.5	6.8	6.7	30.5	25.4	9.2	2.0	76.8	36.6	49.3	50.7
HOUSTON	0.6	0.8	6.0	5.4	6.6	7.6	7.1	23.0	29.3	12.0	3.0	76.8	41.0	49.8	50.2
HUBBARD	0.7	0.9	5.7	5.3	5.7	6.5	6.7	20.7	30.5	16.5	2.4	79.2	44.5	49.7	50.3
ISANTI	0.8	1.1	7.3	6.4	6.8	7.6	8.2	26.3	26.1	9.4	1.9	74.7	36.9	50.2	49.8
ITASCA	0.6	0.8	5.5	5.0	5.5	6.3	7.5	21.5	31.7	14.4	2.6	80.1	44.0	49.9	50.1
JACKSON	1.9	2.6	5.8	5.1	5.5	6.4	7.5	22.1	28.7	14.5	4.3	79.7	43.1	50.4	49.6
KANABEC	0.9	1.3	6.5	6.0	6.4	6.8	7.8	23.6	28.1	12.6	2.1	76.9	40.1	50.6	49.4
KANDIYOHI	8.0	10.8	6.8	5.8	6.4	6.7	8.4	24.5	27.3	11.4	2.7	77.0	38.1	49.7	50.3
KITTSON	1.3	1.8	6.7	6.7	5.5	6.8	5.3	19.7	29.3	15.3	4.7	76.8	44.4	49.7	50.3
KOOCHICHING	0.6	0.8	5.5	5.2	6.3	6.2	6.7	21.1	31.0	15.1	2.9	79.2	44.3	49.7	50.3
LAC QUI PARLE	0.3	0.3	5.5	5.3	5.2	6.8	8.1	18.2	29.8	16.1	5.0	79.7	45.5	49.6	50.4
LAKE	0.6	0.8	5.3	5.0	4.8	6.3	6.2	20.3	32.0	17.2	2.8	80.9	46.2	49.8	50.2
LAKE OF THE WOODS	0.6	0.7	4.3	3.4	6.3	7.7	6.8	20.7	32.3	15.4	3.0	81.0	45.4	50.2	49.8
LE SUEUR	3.9	5.4	6.7	6.2	6.7	6.9	6.7	25.7	27.5	11.3	2.2	76.0	39.4	50.2	49.8
LINCOLN	0.9	1.2	5.9	5.8	5.4	5.6	5.1	23.2	25.1	18.2	5.5	79.0	44.3	49.4	50.6
LYON	4.0	5.4	6.9	6.1	6.2	7.8	10.8	24.1	24.2	10.6	3.2	77.2	35.2	49.2	50.8
MCLEOD	3.6	5.0	7.3	6.8	6.4	7.7	7.0	26.9	24.9	10.5	2.4	74.5	36.8	49.8	50.2
MAHNOMEN	0.9	0.9	7.8	6.7	7.4	6.6	7.0	21.2	26.9	13.6	2.7	73.9	40.0	51.0	49.0
MARSHALL	2.9	4.0	6.1	5.9	5.4	6.3	7.0	22.5	29.0	14.8	3.2	78.7	43.0	50.7	49.3
MARTIN	1.9	2.7	5.9	5.1	5.9	6.5	7.8	20.2	29.8	14.7	4.1	79.1	43.9	49.0	51.0
MEEKER	2.2	2.9	6.8	6.4	6.2	6.7	6.8	23.7	27.7	12.6	3.1	76.5	40.5	50.7	49.3
MILLE LACS	1.0	1.3	6.7	6.1	6.1	7.5	6.7	24.6	27.0	12.6	2.8	76.5	40.2	49.5	50.5
MORRISON	0.6	0.9	7.2	6.6	6.2	7.2	7.1	24.8	26.2	12.1	2.6	75.4	38.8	50.5	49.5
MOWER	4.3	5.8	6.7	5.7	6.2	6.2	7.3	24.4	25.5	14.1	3.9	77.6	40.6	49.5	50.5
MURRAY	1.5	2.1	5.8	5.1	5.9	6.4	6.8	20.8	28.9	16.4	3.9	79.2	44.4	49.6	50.4
NICOLLET	1.8	2.4	6.2	5.6	5.8	9.4	12.0	25.2	24.6	9.4	1.8	78.9	33.6	49.7	50.3
NOBLES	11.2	14.6	7.4	6.8	6.3	6.0	7.4	24.2	25.9	12.8	3.3	75.8	38.7	50.3	49.7
NORMAN	3.1	4.2	6.7	5.9	5.7	6.7	6.4	21.8	27.1	15.5	4.2	77.2	43.1	49.6	50.4
OLMSTED	2.4	3.2	7.3	6.9	6.6	7.1	7.1	27.8	26.0	9.4	1.8	74.7	36.5	49.3	50.7
OTTER TAIL	1.7	2.3	5.9	5.2	5.6	6.5	7.5	20.7	29.7	15.4	3.4	79.3	43.9	50.4	49.6
PENNINGTON	1.2	1.3	6.6	5.4	5.3	6.2	9.3	24.2	27.5	12.1	3.4	79.3	39.1	49.7	50.3
PINE	1.8	2.4	5.9	5.4	6.3	7.2	6.5	25.3	28.3	13.1	2.0	77.8	40.7	52.2	47.8
PIPESTONE	0.7	0.9	6.6	5.8	5.9	6.3	8.2	22.2	25.6	15.1	4.3	77.8	41.6	48.4	51.6
POLK	4.8	5.0	6.2	5.8	6.1	7.8	8.4	21.8	26.5	13.8	3.6	77.4	40.4	49.5	50.5
POPE	0.5	0.7	5.5	4.6	5.6	6.8	7.4	20.9	29.1	15.6	4.5	79.9	44.4	49.8	50.2
RAMSEY	5.3	6.8	6.9	6.1	6.6	7.6	7.9	28.6	24.5	9.6	2.2	76.3	34.8	48.3	51.7
RED LAKE	0.3	0.3	6.5	5.9	4.9	6.1	8.3	21.5	28.3	15.0	3.5	78.8	42.3	50.1	49.9
REDWOOD	1.1	1.6	6.6	6.1	5.8	6.5	7.3	22.5	26.6	14.3	4.4	77.2	41.6	50.2	49.8
RENVILLE	5.1	6.9	6.5	6.3	6.1	6.6	7.2	22.3	27.1	13.9	4.0	76.7	41.3	49.9	50.1
RICE	5.5	7.4	6.3	6.0	6.4	9.8	11.0	24.5	24.5	9.5	2.1	76.8	34.5	49.5	50.5
ROCK	1.3	1.8	6.4	5.6	6.7	6.4	6.4	22.6	26.4	15.2	4.3	77.1	42.1	49.4	50.6
ROSEAU	0.4	0.6	7.8	7.0	6.7	7.9	7.4	25.8	25.7	9.6	2.2	73.6	37.2	51.4	48.6
ST. LOUIS	0.8	1.1	5.2	4.9	5.5	7.6	8.9	23.1	28.7	12.9	3.2	80.7	41.2	49.4	50.6
SCOTT	2.7	3.6	9.5	9.3	8.1	6.5	4.8	33.6	22.0	5.4	0.8	68.9	33.9	50.2	49.8
SHERBURNE	1.1	1.5	8.8	7.8	7.7	7.6	7.9	30.3	22.6	6.1	1.1	71.2	32.8	50.5	49.5
SIBLEY	5.4	7.4	7.1	6.7	6.9	7.0	5.8	25.8	25.1	12.7	3.0	75.0	39.3	51.0	49.0
STEARNS	1.4	1.9	6.8	6.3	6.2	8.6	11.4	27.0	22.9	9.1	1.6	76.4	32.7	50.2	49.8
STEELE	3.8	5.1	7.1	6.3	6.6	7.6	7.2	26.3	25.5	11.0	2.4	75.2	37.6	49.5	50.5
STEVENS	0.9	1.3	5.5	4.7	4.6	11.2	15.1	19.7	23.4	12.2	3.4	82.2	34.1	48.8	51.2
SWIFT	2.7	3.6	5.7	5.2	5.9	5.5	7.1	28.2	25.7	12.8	3.8	79.6	40.1	56.1	43.9
TODD	1.9	2.5	6.7	5.5	6.3	6.5	9.1	21.9	27.6	14.0	2.5	77.7	40.9	50.4	49.6
MINNESOTA	2.9	3.8	6.9	6.5	6.6	7.2	7.4	27.6	25.7	9.9	2.1	75.7	36.8	49.6	50.4
UNITED STATES	12.5	15.0	6.9	6.5	6.8	7.1	7.0	27.6	25.4	10.7	1.9	75.6	36.7	49.2	50.8

COUNTY	HOUSEHOLDS					FAMILIES			MEDIAN HOUSEHOLD INCOME			
	2000	2007	2012	% Annual Rate 2000-2007	2007 Average HH Size	2000	2007	% Annual Rate 2000-2007	2007	2012	2007 National Rank	2007 State Rank
AITKIN	6,644	7,451	8,029	1.6	2.23	4,457	4,849	1.2	39,579	46,414	1769	74
ANOKA	106,428	123,497	136,367	2.1	2.72	79,413	89,993	1.7	75,185	89,825	88	5
BECKER	11,844	13,142	13,790	1.4	2.43	8,190	8,832	1.0	43,267	50,248	1306	62
BELTRAMI	14,337	16,039	17,105	1.6	2.58	9,752	10,592	1.1	41,599	48,215	1504	71
BENTON	13,065	15,393	16,908	2.3	2.53	8,518	9,715	1.8	52,893	62,108	506	21
BIG STONE	2,377	2,286	2,211	-0.5	2.34	1,611	1,504	-0.9	36,164	40,249	2247	86
BLUE EARTH	21,062	23,811	25,574	1.7	2.40	12,621	13,749	1.2	48,907	57,654	756	31
BROWN	10,598	10,705	10,585	0.1	2.38	7,164	7,026	-0.3	49,460	57,417	713	30
CARLTON	12,064	13,445	14,276	1.5	2.45	8,406	9,106	1.1	50,268	59,447	658	27
CARVER	24,356	33,052	40,618	4.3	2.79	18,774	24,937	4.0	85,980	106,078	26	3
CASS	10,893	12,238	13,057	1.6	2.40	7,730	8,453	1.2	42,616	49,577	1380	67
CHIPPEWA	5,361	5,359	5,328	0.0	2.34	3,599	3,490	-0.4	44,924	53,148	1117	55
CHISAGO	14,454	18,691	21,719	3.6	2.76	11,082	14,021	3.3	65,747	78,345	164	10
CLAY	18,670	21,065	22,840	1.7	2.47	12,347	13,496	1.2	48,199	56,998	798	34
CLEARWATER	3,330	3,479	3,574	0.6	2.42	2,288	2,320	0.2	36,488	41,186	2193	84
COOK	2,350	2,696	2,903	1.9	2.11	1,438	1,591	1.4	45,970	53,360	1007	48
COTTONWOOD	4,917	4,905	4,867	0.0	2.36	3,341	3,234	-0.4	39,108	44,805	1837	77
CROW WING	22,250	26,112	28,264	2.2	2.37	15,183	17,301	1.8	47,379	55,069	876	38
DAKOTA	131,151	154,272	171,707	2.3	2.64	94,011	107,720	1.9	79,359	98,163	57	4
DODGE	6,420	7,542	8,237	2.2	2.68	4,853	5,573	1.9	59,521	67,992	279	14
DOUGLAS	13,276	15,449	16,930	2.1	2.36	9,030	10,203	1.7	46,681	54,358	938	42
FARIBAULT	6,652	6,532	6,419	-0.3	2.32	4,477	4,265	-0.7	41,526	46,875	1514	72
FILLMORE	8,228	8,820	9,152	1.0	2.46	5,721	5,961	0.6	45,731	52,780	1028	50
FREEBORN	13,356	13,448	13,413	0.1	2.35	9,013	8,804	-0.3	46,033	53,526	999	46
GOODHUE	16,983	18,620	19,749	1.3	2.49	11,900	12,685	0.9	59,218	68,080	284	15
GRANT	2,534	2,537	2,517	0.0	2.37	1,741	1,693	-0.4	40,350	45,580	1685	73
HENNEPIN	456,129	479,915	490,398	0.7	2.35	267,303	270,656	0.2	68,364	83,240	136	8
HOUSTON	7,633	8,034	8,223	0.7	2.48	5,408	5,540	0.3	51,139	59,419	603	25
HUBBARD	7,435	7,890	8,169	0.8	2.40	5,347	5,527	0.5	44,079	50,954	1199	59
ISANTI	11,236	14,999	18,080	4.1	2.69	8,420	10,983	3.7	61,271	70,435	231	11
ITASCA	17,789	18,780	19,339	0.8	2.36	12,385	12,710	0.4	45,135	52,156	1095	53
JACKSON	4,556	4,591	4,588	0.1	2.36	3,117	3,048	-0.3	45,208	52,065	1083	52
KANABEC	5,759	6,577	7,132	1.8	2.54	4,146	4,614	1.5	47,080	54,266	902	40
KANDIYOHI	15,936	16,648	17,048	0.6	2.48	10,972	11,137	0.2	50,005	59,000	682	29
KITTSON	2,167	2,069	1,992	-0.6	2.33	1,448	1,340	-1.1	39,007	43,940	1851	78
KOOCHICHING	6,040	6,024	5,979	0.0	2.26	3,962	3,827	-0.5	44,347	51,298	1175	58
LAC QUI PARLE	3,316	3,190	3,068	-0.5	2.29	2,225	2,075	-1.0	38,730	43,667	1893	81
LAKE	4,646	4,841	4,981	0.6	2.28	3,141	3,177	0.2	51,887	61,269	555	24
LAKE OF THE WOODS	1,903	1,979	2,017	0.5	2.27	1,267	1,277	0.1	42,965	51,069	1334	65
LE SUEUR	9,630	10,908	11,829	1.7	2.56	6,922	7,637	1.4	56,363	64,864	350	19
LINCOLN	2,653	2,595	2,540	-0.3	2.29	1,786	1,696	-0.7	37,514	42,199	2060	82
LYON	9,715	10,017	10,194	0.4	2.45	6,331	6,320	0.0	48,210	55,587	797	33
MCLEOD	13,449	14,945	16,004	1.5	2.51	9,433	10,194	1.1	57,699	66,086	314	18
MAHNOMEN	1,969	1,990	1,987	0.1	2.53	1,367	1,342	-0.3	35,543	40,052	2360	87
MARSHALL	4,101	4,121	4,118	0.1	2.38	2,836	2,768	-0.3	42,541	49,518	1392	68
MARTIN	9,067	9,100	9,067	0.1	2.30	6,045	5,882	-0.4	43,054	50,073	1323	64
MEEKER	8,590	9,427	9,896	1.3	2.53	6,132	6,553	0.9	50,251	58,404	660	28
MILLE LACS	8,638	10,522	11,999	2.8	2.49	6,006	7,112	2.4	46,093	53,127	990	45
MORRISON	11,816	12,983	13,610	1.3	2.57	8,461	9,056	0.9	45,318	52,387	1077	51
MOWER	15,582	15,988	16,201	0.4	2.40	10,318	10,260	-0.1	46,286	54,516	973	44
MURRAY	3,722	3,696	3,648	-0.1	2.37	2,602	2,514	-0.5	42,623	48,831	1379	66
NICOLLET	10,642	11,881	12,688	1.5	2.50	7,309	7,925	1.1	58,746	67,759	292	16
NOBLES	7,939	7,912	7,865	0.0	2.57	5,520	5,346	-0.4	45,109	52,477	1099	54
NORMAN	3,010	2,894	2,800	-0.5	2.37	2,008	1,872	-1.0	38,933	43,988	1862	79
OLMSTED	47,807	56,256	61,636	2.3	2.50	32,308	36,893	1.8	66,787	80,122	152	9
OTTER TAIL	22,671	23,604	24,101	0.6	2.42	15,768	15,954	0.2	43,583	50,683	1268	61
PENNINGTON	5,525	5,700	5,791	0.4	2.32	3,555	3,548	0.0	43,229	50,859	1309	63
PINE	9,939	11,005	11,650	1.4	2.48	6,918	7,448	1.0	46,873	53,923	919	41
PIPESTONE	4,069	4,005	3,924	-0.2	2.32	2,727	2,602	-0.6	39,216	44,944	1830	76
POLK	12,070	12,356	12,468	0.3	2.42	8,045	7,986	-0.1	43,738	50,796	1245	60
POPE	4,513	4,803	4,979	0.9	2.37	3,064	3,164	0.4	44,863	52,215	1126	56
RAMSEY	201,236	206,668	209,007	0.4	2.42	120,016	118,734	-0.1	60,181	71,109	262	13
RED LAKE	1,727	1,805	1,852	0.6	2.32	1,132	1,146	0.2	38,731	43,938	1892	80
REDWOOD	6,674	6,563	6,411	-0.2	2.39	4,526	4,319	-0.6	45,977	52,456	1005	47
RENVILLE	6,779	6,806	6,764	0.1	2.44	4,622	4,504	-0.4	45,953	52,444	1009	49
RICE	18,888	21,969	23,792	2.1	2.62	13,347	15,105	1.7	61,015	70,131	241	12
ROCK	3,843	3,813	3,759	-0.1	2.42	2,707	2,614	-0.5	47,818	55,202	835	37
ROSEAU	6,190	6,527	6,732	0.7	2.54	4,439	4,558	0.4	47,829	54,299	833	36
ST. LOUIS	82,619	83,956	83,670	0.2	2.24	51,374	50,415	-0.3	46,562	54,821	949	43
SCOTT	30,692	45,878	58,983	5.7	2.85	23,977	35,115	5.4	87,262	107,544	22	1
SHERBURNE	21,581	31,191	38,099	5.2	2.86	16,743	23,697	4.9	73,779	86,248	97	6
SIBLEY	5,772	6,076	6,266	0.7	2.57	4,089	4,188	0.3	50,332	56,929	654	26
STEARNS	47,604	55,817	62,006	2.2	2.56	32,129	36,550	1.8	53,393	62,022	479	20
STEELE	12,846	14,349	15,453	1.5	2.54	9,077	9,868	1.2	57,807	66,379	309	17
STEVENS	3,751	3,732	3,687	-0.1	2.36	2,307	2,277	0.5	47,160	54,743	893	39
SWIFT	4,353	4,171	4,009	-0.6	2.35	2,882	2,676	-1.0	42,009	47,511	1446	69
TODD	9,342	9,863	10,143	0.8	2.53	6,510	6,680	0.4	39,576	45,285	1770	75
MINNESOTA				1.4	2.49			1.1	61,307	73,160		
UNITED STATES				1.2	2.59			1.0	53,154	62,503		

COUNTY	2007 Per Capita Income	2007 HH Income Base	2007 HOUSEHOLD INCOME DISTRIBUTION (%)					2007 Home Value Base	2007 HOME VALUE DISTRIBUTION (%)					2007 Median Home Value
			Less than $25,000	$25,000 to $49,999	$50,000 to $99,999	$100,000 to $149,999	$150,000 or More		Less than $50,000	$50,000 to $89,999	$90,000 to $174,999	$175,000 to $399,999	$400,000 or More	
AITKIN	23,242	7,451	29.8	31.8	29.6	5.8	3.1	6,405	8.8	15.7	39.1	31.8	4.7	146,054
ANOKA	31,576	123,497	9.2	18.0	43.7	19.7	9.4	104,022	3.7	2.0	17.5	68.7	8.1	228,353
BECKER	22,219	13,142	28.0	29.5	31.4	7.9	3.2	10,728	10.3	16.1	39.2	28.5	5.9	142,200
BELTRAMI	19,905	16,039	29.4	30.0	30.7	7.0	3.0	12,146	15.0	18.5	40.0	23.3	3.2	127,855
BENTON	24,317	15,393	18.6	28.1	40.1	9.6	3.7	10,640	8.2	6.9	40.6	40.6	3.7	165,685
BIG STONE	18,711	2,286	33.2	35.8	25.7	3.8	1.6	1,950	25.6	31.0	29.8	11.0	2.6	80,857
BLUE EARTH	24,606	23,811	21.5	29.8	35.8	8.6	4.3	16,235	8.8	8.0	39.2	38.8	5.2	165,091
BROWN	24,868	10,705	21.4	29.2	37.5	8.3	3.6	8,715	8.0	13.6	45.6	29.3	3.4	147,382
CARLTON	23,311	13,445	23.2	26.5	37.0	10.6	2.7	11,189	6.5	11.5	44.2	35.6	2.2	154,077
CARVER	39,805	33,052	8.4	15.2	35.1	22.0	19.3	28,052	3.9	1.0	8.1	56.7	30.4	299,620
CASS	21,905	12,238	27.7	30.8	31.9	6.7	3.0	10,580	8.7	14.1	34.3	31.7	11.1	157,745
CHIPPEWA	22,634	5,359	23.8	31.6	35.1	7.1	2.4	4,178	11.0	23.8	42.8	19.7	2.7	116,172
CHISAGO	27,690	18,691	12.8	20.9	42.6	16.6	7.1	16,376	6.4	3.1	17.8	61.4	11.3	232,970
CLAY	23,554	21,065	23.9	27.9	34.0	9.9	4.3	15,399	6.9	12.4	55.6	23.9	1.2	133,733
CLEARWATER	19,248	3,479	35.5	28.1	28.5	6.0	2.0	2,880	18.4	22.7	40.9	16.4	1.7	108,121
COOK	27,495	2,696	22.1	32.0	33.3	8.4	4.1	2,156	6.8	9.3	33.9	36.3	13.7	175,000
COTTONWOOD	20,854	4,905	28.6	34.4	29.8	4.7	2.5	3,985	19.4	28.4	36.5	13.0	2.7	95,085
CROW WING	24,673	26,112	24.5	28.2	34.9	8.5	3.9	21,084	5.5	9.9	34.9	40.3	9.5	174,434
DAKOTA	36,659	154,272	8.0	17.6	39.3	20.6	14.6	122,527	3.3	1.5	10.9	67.5	16.7	262,627
DODGE	25,166	7,542	15.5	25.7	41.6	12.7	4.4	6,428	7.4	11.2	45.7	31.7	3.9	146,372
DOUGLAS	24,394	15,449	25.0	28.3	34.8	8.0	3.9	12,129	5.4	8.2	37.1	42.6	6.6	173,556
FARIBAULT	21,310	6,532	26.8	34.3	31.1	5.9	1.9	5,340	19.2	29.2	36.7	12.6	2.3	93,333
FILLMORE	22,046	8,820	23.7	31.1	35.7	6.7	2.8	7,219	8.0	14.1	43.7	28.1	6.1	143,278
FREEBORN	23,557	13,448	23.3	31.6	34.9	7.4	3.0	10,736	8.0	19.4	45.8	23.1	3.7	128,289
GOODHUE	28,410	18,620	17.1	23.7	40.3	12.6	6.3	14,943	5.3	4.5	30.2	49.5	10.4	200,901
GRANT	21,057	2,537	28.5	32.8	30.9	5.5	2.3	2,105	17.1	25.9	40.0	14.0	3.0	103,355
HENNEPIN	39,037	479,915	13.9	21.4	34.0	16.9	13.8	326,218	0.7	2.0	20.4	59.9	17.1	239,657
HOUSTON	24,555	8,034	20.0	28.6	38.4	9.4	3.7	6,594	7.7	15.7	45.9	26.5	4.2	136,807
HUBBARD	22,785	7,890	26.0	31.3	32.0	7.4	3.2	6,631	8.7	15.1	35.9	33.3	6.9	149,891
ISANTI	26,228	14,999	14.2	24.8	42.2	13.5	5.3	12,889	3.0	3.9	27.5	57.8	7.8	208,124
ITASCA	22,782	18,780	25.9	29.0	34.6	7.9	2.5	15,740	10.2	17.7	42.5	25.4	4.2	134,984
JACKSON	21,759	4,591	23.0	33.4	35.8	6.0	1.8	3,693	15.3	22.9	41.6	16.4	3.8	109,643
KANABEC	22,033	6,577	22.7	30.5	36.6	7.7	2.5	5,606	9.5	12.5	38.9	36.0	3.2	154,861
KANDIYOHI	25,061	16,648	20.6	29.4	35.8	9.7	4.5	12,800	5.7	8.1	46.8	33.0	6.4	157,083
KITTSON	20,293	2,069	29.1	34.7	30.2	4.0	1.9	1,732	31.2	29.4	32.6	6.1	0.8	74,483
KOOCHICHING	23,857	6,024	28.6	27.9	33.7	6.7	3.0	4,921	16.1	22.6	43.4	16.5	1.4	111,128
LAC QUI PARLE	21,206	3,190	29.9	33.6	29.0	5.2	2.3	2,614	24.6	25.9	33.1	13.4	3.0	89,172
LAKE	25,827	4,841	20.9	26.8	39.8	9.6	2.9	4,101	6.1	23.1	43.8	23.0	4.0	130,179
LAKE OF THE WOODS	23,355	1,979	26.9	33.1	30.0	6.8	3.1	1,694	14.2	28.7	39.1	16.1	1.9	107,527
LE SUEUR	25,853	10,908	17.8	25.1	40.5	12.1	4.4	9,215	4.4	6.8	35.9	44.6	8.3	182,972
LINCOLN	19,372	2,595	30.9	36.9	26.8	4.3	1.2	2,112	19.7	32.4	32.7	13.4	1.8	87,644
LYON	22,885	10,017	23.8	28.3	36.6	8.2	3.1	7,052	9.6	14.6	45.1	28.0	2.7	141,628
MCLEOD	26,034	14,945	16.1	26.4	42.1	11.5	3.8	11,866	4.5	5.1	37.1	46.8	6.6	182,210
MAHNOMEN	17,000	1,990	32.4	34.5	27.6	4.9	0.6	1,571	17.3	23.5	39.6	15.1	4.5	106,587
MARSHALL	20,752	4,121	27.3	31.4	34.2	5.5	1.6	3,480	23.4	25.0	39.8	10.5	1.4	92,872
MARTIN	23,391	9,100	26.4	31.1	33.8	5.8	2.9	7,160	13.1	25.5	40.9	17.3	3.2	110,480
MEEKER	23,622	9,427	20.8	28.9	37.4	9.1	3.8	7,802	5.8	11.3	41.0	35.2	6.6	160,471
MILLE LACS	22,363	10,522	25.3	29.4	34.8	7.4	3.1	8,562	6.2	9.7	40.4	39.9	3.7	164,115
MORRISON	20,900	12,983	26.1	29.2	34.8	7.0	2.9	10,758	5.9	13.9	44.4	31.8	4.0	150,194
MOWER	24,499	15,988	23.0	31.1	33.9	8.0	3.9	12,697	6.9	19.1	49.0	21.6	3.4	128,104
MURRAY	21,388	3,696	25.6	34.8	32.7	4.8	2.2	3,139	19.8	25.4	36.4	15.2	3.2	100,710
NICOLLET	27,024	11,881	14.7	26.8	40.4	12.3	5.9	9,179	5.4	5.5	32.9	49.2	7.1	189,284
NOBLES	21,413	7,912	25.2	29.9	34.5	7.0	3.4	6,060	14.2	25.2	39.9	18.1	2.5	110,938
NORMAN	19,546	2,894	30.2	33.6	29.4	5.1	1.7	2,376	25.2	27.9	36.3	8.8	1.8	85,614
OLMSTED	34,173	56,256	13.5	21.8	38.1	15.3	11.4	43,466	4.7	6.0	45.3	38.2	5.7	163,019
OTTER TAIL	22,493	23,604	26.2	31.4	32.3	6.8	3.3	19,150	8.4	14.9	42.6	29.7	4.5	142,843
PENNINGTON	22,785	5,700	27.6	29.7	33.6	6.1	3.0	4,319	17.8	21.6	44.6	15.0	1.0	107,857
PINE	21,911	11,005	23.9	29.2	36.7	7.5	2.7	9,304	8.7	13.7	41.0	32.7	3.8	150,296
PIPESTONE	20,751	4,005	29.0	33.7	30.4	4.8	2.0	3,167	17.3	32.8	35.4	12.3	2.3	89,916
POLK	22,406	12,356	27.0	29.9	32.5	7.2	3.4	9,318	16.1	21.2	42.9	18.4	1.3	116,178
POPE	23,803	4,803	25.5	30.8	33.9	6.2	3.6	3,934	7.7	17.5	42.9	27.5	4.4	136,655
RAMSEY	31,572	206,668	17.0	24.6	35.4	13.3	9.7	134,992	2.4	3.4	30.6	54.7	9.0	206,745
RED LAKE	19,116	1,805	30.9	33.1	30.4	4.5	1.2	1,468	24.4	28.3	37.1	9.5	0.7	86,061
REDWOOD	23,241	6,563	23.1	32.0	34.4	7.5	2.9	5,311	18.2	23.6	39.0	16.8	2.4	107,874
RENVILLE	22,239	6,806	22.1	33.3	35.2	6.9	2.4	5,591	14.9	24.3	43.1	14.0	3.7	108,135
RICE	25,632	21,969	15.8	23.9	41.2	13.4	5.7	17,429	4.9	3.4	24.6	55.5	11.6	215,095
ROCK	22,592	3,813	23.8	28.5	37.6	7.1	2.9	3,034	8.9	18.8	48.8	20.5	3.0	126,771
ROSEAU	21,472	6,527	19.7	32.9	39.1	6.2	2.1	5,540	18.0	16.7	44.7	19.6	1.1	122,826
ST. LOUIS	24,973	83,956	26.4	27.0	34.0	8.6	4.0	63,852	7.7	20.8	45.7	22.6	4.2	127,674
SCOTT	36,420	45,878	7.2	13.7	37.9	25.4	15.9	40,050	1.9	1.4	6.3	65.5	24.9	295,070
SHERBURNE	28,788	31,191	9.5	17.9	45.9	19.0	7.8	26,504	1.7	1.5	14.3	70.7	11.7	256,273
SIBLEY	22,685	6,076	21.5	28.1	39.8	7.6	3.1	5,002	5.5	13.8	44.1	29.0	7.6	149,964
STEARNS	25,458	55,816	19.2	27.0	37.6	10.6	5.6	42,030	4.0	6.9	42.9	41.1	5.0	168,759
STEELE	26,093	14,349	15.3	26.3	42.5	11.3	4.6	11,661	3.2	4.7	38.8	47.8	5.6	181,397
STEVENS	23,101	3,732	28.9	24.6	35.6	6.9	4.0	2,684	9.4	23.2	41.3	23.0	3.2	122,040
SWIFT	20,298	4,171	26.5	32.6	33.7	5.2	2.0	3,287	13.7	24.4	44.2	14.6	3.0	109,812
TODD	19,376	9,863	30.2	32.2	29.5	5.9	2.2	8,266	11.9	20.8	43.2	21.4	2.6	122,550
MINNESOTA	31,101		16.5	23.5	36.5	14.2	9.3		5.0	7.2	28.0	48.9	11.0	201,524
UNITED STATES	27,916		21.9	25.0	32.3	12.3	8.4		7.9	10.5	27.1	35.6	19.0	192,285

COUNTY	FINANCIAL SERVICES				THE HOME						ENTERTAINMENT						PERSONAL			
					Home Improvements		Furnishings													
	Auto Loan	Home Loan	Invest-ments	Retire-ment Plans	Home Repair	Lawn & Garden	Comput-ers & Hard-ware	Major Appli-ances	TV, Radio, Sound Equip-ment	Furni-ture	Dine out/ Carry out	Sports Equip-ment	Fees & Tickets	Toys & Games	Travel	Cable TV	Apparel & Services	Auto Repairs	Health Insur-ance	Pets & Supplies
AITKIN	80	65	54	64	73	92	67	82	71	64	70	70	60	70	69	76	60	76	87	84
ANOKA	117	132	133	132	125	114	120	117	116	126	116	110	127	120	122	113	107	117	110	117
BECKER	86	68	56	67	76	95	71	85	75	67	74	74	63	77	71	79	64	78	89	89
BELTRAMI	78	67	63	68	67	75	72	73	73	69	73	66	67	74	69	74	64	73	76	76
BENTON	89	81	83	84	79	82	87	83	87	85	86	77	83	89	83	86	77	86	85	85
BIG STONE	72	51	38	50	58	78	56	69	64	51	61	60	47	65	56	68	52	63	79	72
BLUE EARTH	87	76	79	79	77	82	89	83	86	82	87	76	82	87	83	85	77	85	84	85
BROWN	89	82	82	82	86	95	79	87	83	80	82	76	78	86	82	86	73	83	93	90
CARLTON	84	80	83	80	84	90	77	84	80	77	79	73	77	83	80	83	70	80	88	86
CARVER	152	179	174	180	170	151	157	154	147	167	148	147	168	155	159	141	137	151	138	154
CASS	83	68	53	67	75	93	68	83	72	66	71	72	62	73	70	76	62	77	87	86
CHIPPEWA	83	65	60	65	71	87	71	80	75	66	74	70	63	77	70	79	63	76	88	83
CHISAGO	109	117	113	117	112	109	106	108	104	111	104	99	110	108	108	102	94	106	104	109
CLAY	85	79	82	81	78	82	86	82	84	82	84	75	82	85	82	84	75	83	84	83
CLEARWATER	78	56	38	54	64	86	59	74	66	55	64	65	50	68	59	71	55	68	82	79
COOK	92	73	55	73	83	106	76	94	79	72	78	82	67	80	78	83	67	86	97	97
COTTONWOOD	80	58	49	58	66	86	64	76	70	60	69	67	55	73	63	75	59	71	85	81
CROW WING	87	76	73	77	81	93	79	87	81	76	80	77	74	81	80	84	70	83	91	89
DAKOTA	131	146	147	148	139	126	137	131	130	142	132	124	143	134	137	126	121	132	122	131
DODGE	99	99	95	99	98	101	90	96	91	94	91	86	92	96	93	92	82	92	96	98
DOUGLAS	86	74	72	75	80	93	77	86	81	74	79	76	72	81	78	84	69	82	92	88
FARIBAULT	83	58	42	57	67	90	63	78	71	59	69	69	53	74	63	76	59	72	88	84
FILLMORE	88	67	54	66	75	94	71	84	76	67	75	75	62	79	71	80	64	79	91	89
FREEBORN	82	72	70	72	78	88	72	80	77	72	77	70	70	80	74	81	68	77	87	84
GOODHUE	102	99	101	100	102	106	97	102	98	97	97	91	97	100	99	100	87	99	104	104
GRANT	85	58	38	56	68	93	63	80	71	59	70	71	52	75	62	76	59	73	90	86
HENNEPIN	121	128	140	132	125	117	132	122	128	132	129	115	135	127	130	125	118	126	120	122
HOUSTON	92	81	75	81	87	99	81	91	84	79	83	81	77	88	82	86	73	86	95	95
HUBBARD	85	70	58	69	76	94	72	85	75	69	74	74	65	76	73	79	64	79	88	88
ISANTI	99	101	105	103	100	100	97	99	96	98	96	89	99	99	99	96	86	97	98	99
ITASCA	81	70	65	69	76	90	71	81	75	68	74	71	66	76	72	79	64	76	88	84
JACKSON	84	63	49	62	71	92	66	80	72	63	71	70	58	76	66	77	61	74	88	85
KANABEC	87	74	64	73	78	92	73	84	77	72	76	74	69	79	74	80	67	79	88	87
KANDIYOHI	92	81	79	82	85	95	85	90	87	82	86	81	80	89	84	89	76	88	94	93
KITTSON	83	55	31	53	65	91	59	78	66	55	66	69	47	71	58	71	55	70	85	85
KOOCHICHING	83	69	62	68	76	91	69	81	76	68	74	70	65	78	71	80	65	76	89	85
LAC QUI PARLE	83	57	37	55	66	90	62	78	69	57	68	69	51	73	61	74	57	71	88	84
LAKE	85	79	81	78	86	97	78	88	82	77	81	75	76	82	82	86	71	83	95	89
LAKE OF THE WOODS	83	66	57	66	73	90	70	82	74	66	73	71	63	75	71	78	62	77	87	85
LE SUEUR	96	94	94	95	98	103	88	97	90	90	89	86	89	94	92	92	80	91	98	99
LINCOLN	75	52	36	50	60	81	57	71	64	52	62	62	47	66	56	68	52	65	80	75
LYON	86	71	66	72	75	86	78	82	80	74	80	74	71	82	75	82	70	80	86	85
MCLEOD	92	92	92	92	93	95	90	92	89	90	89	84	90	92	90	90	81	90	91	94
MAHNOMEN	73	50	32	48	58	80	54	69	60	50	60	61	44	64	53	65	50	63	77	74
MARSHALL	83	60	40	58	70	92	62	80	68	59	68	70	53	72	62	73	58	72	86	86
MARTIN	84	67	61	66	73	89	71	81	77	67	75	71	64	78	71	81	65	76	90	84
MEEKER	91	79	76	79	85	98	79	89	83	78	82	79	75	86	81	86	72	84	94	93
MILLE LACS	84	74	70	74	78	90	75	83	77	72	76	73	71	79	76	80	67	79	87	85
MORRISON	83	69	63	69	75	90	71	81	75	68	74	72	65	77	71	78	64	76	86	85
MOWER	85	78	82	79	82	90	78	84	83	78	82	73	77	84	80	86	72	81	92	86
MURRAY	85	60	41	58	70	94	64	81	71	60	70	71	54	75	64	76	59	74	90	87
NICOLLET	99	100	102	101	99	99	97	98	96	98	96	90	98	98	98	95	87	97	96	99
NOBLES	84	70	64	69	76	90	72	82	77	70	76	72	67	79	72	80	66	78	88	85
NORMAN	80	54	33	52	63	87	58	75	65	54	64	67	47	69	58	70	54	68	83	81
OLMSTED	118	124	130	127	120	114	121	116	118	123	118	108	124	120	120	116	107	118	114	117
OTTER TAIL	85	68	58	68	76	94	72	85	76	68	75	74	64	77	72	79	65	79	90	88
PENNINGTON	79	68	71	68	70	79	73	76	76	69	74	67	68	76	72	78	65	75	82	77
PINE	86	71	59	71	79	96	73	86	76	70	75	75	66	78	74	79	65	80	89	89
PIPESTONE	78	57	47	56	64	82	63	74	69	58	67	65	54	71	62	73	57	69	83	78
POLK	84	67	64	68	72	86	74	80	78	69	77	71	67	79	72	81	67	78	87	83
POPE	91	70	57	69	78	98	74	88	79	70	78	77	65	82	74	83	67	82	95	92
RAMSEY	101	105	117	108	103	97	110	102	108	109	108	95	111	107	108	107	99	106	102	102
RED LAKE	74	53	38	52	61	81	57	70	63	53	62	62	48	66	56	68	53	64	79	75
REDWOOD	91	67	53	66	76	99	70	88	78	68	77	77	62	82	72	83	66	81	96	93
RENVILLE	89	66	51	64	75	97	69	85	77	66	75	74	60	80	69	82	64	78	95	90
RICE	98	102	106	103	102	100	97	99	96	99	96	90	100	99	99	96	87	97	97	100
ROCK	86	70	61	68	79	96	70	85	75	69	75	74	65	79	72	79	65	78	91	90
ROSEAU	90	73	55	71	76	92	70	83	75	71	75	74	65	79	70	78	65	78	86	88
ST. LOUIS	79	76	85	77	79	82	78	79	81	77	79	70	78	80	79	82	71	78	85	80
SCOTT	143	167	159	167	156	139	146	143	137	156	139	137	156	145	148	132	128	141	129	142
SHERBURNE	117	129	120	129	118	109	118	114	112	123	113	108	121	116	116	107	102	114	104	114
SIBLEY	92	76	66	75	83	100	76	89	81	74	80	79	71	85	77	85	70	82	95	93
STEARNS	95	90	90	92	90	94	94	92	92	91	93	85	91	95	91	92	83	92	92	94
STEELE	93	95	98	95	95	95	91	93	91	92	91	84	93	94	92	91	82	91	94	94
STEVENS	87	68	60	68	75	92	77	84	80	72	80	76	68	81	74	82	69	82	90	00
SWIFT	83	60	45	58	69	91	64	79	71	60	69	69	55	74	64	76	59	72	88	84
TODD	79	59	47	58	66	86	63	76	69	59	68	67	55	72	63	73	58	70	84	80
MINNESOTA	109	109	110	111	109	110	109	108	107	109	108	100	109	109	108	107	97	108	108	110
UNITED STATES	100	100	100	100	100	100	100	100	100	100	100	100	100	100	100	100	100	100	100	100

COUNTY	FIPS Code	CBSA Code	DMA Code	POPULATION			2000-2007 ANNUAL RATE		RACE (%)					
									White		Black		Asian/Pacific	
				2000	2007	2012	% Rate	State Rank	2000	2007	2000	2007	2000	2007
TRAVERSE	155	00000	613	4,134	3,828	3,641	-1.1	87	96.4	96.1	0.0	0.0	0.3	0.5
WABASHA	157	40340	613	21,610	23,092	24,080	0.9	35	98.0	97.4	0.2	0.3	0.4	0.6
WADENA	159	00000	613	13,713	13,951	14,112	0.2	53	97.9	97.5	0.5	0.6	0.2	0.3
WASECA	161	00000	613	19,526	19,953	20,254	0.3	47	94.7	93.2	2.3	2.8	0.5	0.8
WASHINGTON	163	33460	613	201,130	235,241	261,088	2.2	8	93.6	91.9	1.8	2.3	2.2	2.9
WATONWAN	165	00000	737	11,876	11,283	10,879	-0.7	83	88.5	85.3	0.4	0.4	0.9	1.1
WILKIN	167	47420	724	7,138	6,999	6,897	-0.3	71	97.8	97.3	0.2	0.2	0.2	0.2
WINONA	169	49100	702	49,985	51,163	51,739	0.3	47	95.8	94.6	0.8	1.0	1.9	2.6
WRIGHT	171	33460	613	89,986	121,489	147,579	4.2	3	97.9	97.3	0.3	0.4	0.4	0.6
YELLOW MEDICINE	173	00000	613	11,080	10,681	10,417	-0.5	77	96.1	95.4	0.1	0.1	0.2	0.2
MINNESOTA							1.2		89.4	87.5	3.5	4.1	2.9	3.7
UNITED STATES							1.2		75.1	72.7	12.3	12.6	3.8	4.5

COUNTY	% HISPANIC ORIGIN		2007 AGE DISTRIBUTION (%)										MEDIAN AGE	% 2007 Males	% 2007 Females
	2000	2007	0-4	5-9	10-14	15-19	20-24	25-44	45-64	65-84	85+	18+	2007		
TRAVERSE	1.2	1.7	6.3	5.1	5.1	7.1	8.2	18.6	25.5	18.6	5.5	79.1	44.7	49.1	50.9
WABASHA	1.7	2.3	6.2	5.4	6.6	7.2	7.1	24.9	27.7	12.3	2.7	77.2	40.4	50.0	50.0
WADENA	0.9	1.3	6.8	6.1	6.1	6.6	6.9	22.0	26.1	15.8	3.7	77.0	41.7	49.4	50.6
WASECA	2.9	4.0	7.0	7.0	5.6	6.5	6.7	28.5	25.7	10.5	2.6	76.5	37.1	52.1	47.9
WASHINGTON	1.9	2.6	7.5	7.8	7.9	7.1	5.9	28.0	27.4	7.4	1.0	72.1	36.9	49.6	50.4
WATONWAN	15.2	19.9	7.8	6.9	6.5	6.5	7.2	21.9	25.5	14.3	3.4	74.8	39.0	49.1	50.9
WILKIN	1.5	2.1	7.2	6.2	6.3	7.2	6.9	23.1	27.8	12.1	3.1	75.3	40.4	49.3	50.7
WINONA	1.4	1.9	5.7	5.2	5.3	9.8	13.2	23.9	23.8	10.5	2.6	80.1	33.3	48.6	51.4
WRIGHT	1.1	1.5	8.7	8.0	7.6	7.5	6.6	29.1	23.6	7.6	1.2	71.0	34.6	50.3	49.7
YELLOW MEDICINE	1.8	2.4	6.7	5.6	5.6	6.1	7.9	21.6	27.0	15.2	4.3	78.5	42.6	50.0	50.0
MINNESOTA	2.9	3.8	6.9	6.5	6.6	7.2	7.4	27.6	25.7	9.9	2.1	75.7	36.8	49.6	50.4
UNITED STATES	12.5	15.0	6.9	6.5	6.8	7.1	7.0	27.6	25.4	10.7	1.9	75.6	36.7	49.2	50.8

COUNTY	HOUSEHOLDS					FAMILIES			MEDIAN HOUSEHOLD INCOME			
	2000	2007	2012	% Annual Rate 2000-2007	2007 Average HH Size	2000	2007	% Annual Rate 2000-2007	2007	2012	2007 National Rank	2007 State Rank
TRAVERSE	1,717	1,618	1,549	-0.8	2.30	1,129	1,031	-1.2	36,332	40,320	2225	85
WABASHA	8,277	9,034	9,499	1.2	2.52	5,878	6,247	0.8	52,370	60,851	527	22
WADENA	5,426	5,647	5,764	0.6	2.39	3,609	3,642	0.1	37,499	42,904	2063	83
WASECA	7,059	7,357	7,521	0.6	2.52	4,990	5,062	0.2	51,966	60,382	548	23
WASHINGTON	71,462	85,527	95,898	2.5	2.71	54,665	64,007	2.2	86,505	106,573	25	2
WATONWAN	4,627	4,425	4,270	-0.6	2.51	3,143	2,919	-1.0	44,849	52,325	1127	57
WILKIN	2,752	2,757	2,735	0.0	2.49	1,927	1,878	-0.4	48,024	56,529	813	35
WINONA	18,744	19,414	19,822	0.5	2.42	11,704	11,711	0.0	48,683	57,389	767	32
WRIGHT	31,465	43,969	53,981	4.7	2.74	23,923	32,692	4.4	68,463	80,856	134	7
YELLOW MEDICINE	4,439	4,336	4,246	-0.3	2.39	2,974	2,817	-0.7	41,718	47,774	1487	70
MINNESOTA				1.4	2.49			1.1	61,307	73,160		
UNITED STATES				1.2	2.59			1.0	53,154	62,503		

COUNTY	2007 Per Capita Income	2007 HH Income Base	2007 HOUSEHOLD INCOME DISTRIBUTION (%)					2007 Home Value Base	2007 HOME VALUE DISTRIBUTION (%)					2007 Median Home Value
			Less than $25,000	$25,000 to $49,999	$50,000 to $99,999	$100,000 to $149,999	$150,000 or More		Less than $50,000	$50,000 to $89,999	$90,000 to $174,999	$175,000 to $399,999	$400,000 or More	
TRAVERSE	20,972	1,618	34.2	31.3	26.8	4.4	3.3	1,319	33.6	25.9	29.3	9.4	1.7	69,938
WABASHA	24,706	9,034	18.4	28.6	39.6	9.5	3.9	7,545	8.2	12.3	45.3	30.0	4.2	142,682
WADENA	19,479	5,647	34.6	29.6	28.7	5.0	2.2	4,456	13.8	24.0	41.6	19.1	1.5	112,844
WASECA	23,364	7,357	17.4	30.4	40.2	8.6	3.5	6,008	4.8	9.1	49.0	33.1	4.0	154,545
WASHINGTON	39,601	85,527	6.7	15.0	37.0	23.1	18.3	74,061	2.2	0.8	10.2	63.9	22.8	273,832
WATONWAN	20,824	4,425	22.8	33.6	35.2	6.2	2.1	3,473	15.3	27.9	39.8	14.3	2.8	105,837
WILKIN	22,353	2,757	23.1	29.1	37.5	7.7	2.6	2,258	15.8	21.3	43.3	18.2	1.4	112,298
WINONA	23,772	19,414	23.1	28.2	35.6	9.2	4.0	14,102	6.3	7.1	42.6	38.4	5.5	164,325
WRIGHT	29,295	43,969	11.6	20.6	43.5	16.5	7.8	37,485	5.2	3.5	14.7	63.7	12.9	238,455
YELLOW MEDICINE	20,982	4,336	28.1	31.9	32.5	5.1	2.4	3,506	16.6	26.0	39.4	15.5	2.5	105,428
MINNESOTA	31,101		16.5	23.5	36.5	14.2	9.3		5.0	7.2	28.0	48.9	11.0	201,524
UNITED STATES	27,916		21.9	25.0	32.3	12.3	8.4		7.9	10.5	27.1	35.6	19.0	192,285

SPENDING POTENTIAL INDICES

COUNTY	FINANCIAL SERVICES				THE HOME						ENTERTAINMENT						PERSONAL			
					Home Improvements		Furnishings													
	Auto Loan	Home Loan	Invest-ments	Retire-ment Plans	Home Repair	Lawn & Garden	Comput-ers & Hard-ware	Major Appli-ances	TV, Radio, Sound Equip-ment	Furni-ture	Dine out/ Carry out	Sports Equip-ment	Fees & Tickets	Toys & Games	Travel	Cable TV	Apparel & Services	Auto Repairs	Health Insur-ance	Pets & Supplies
TRAVERSE	80	56	42	55	64	86	62	76	70	57	68	66	52	72	61	75	57	70	87	80
WABASHA	97	84	73	83	88	102	82	93	86	81	85	82	78	89	83	89	74	88	97	97
WADENA	74	56	49	55	63	79	61	71	67	57	65	62	54	67	61	71	56	67	80	74
WASECA	93	82	75	82	87	99	79	90	83	79	83	80	76	87	81	86	73	84	94	94
WASHINGTON	145	172	172	174	164	146	151	148	142	161	144	140	164	148	155	137	133	146	135	148
WATONWAN	82	65	58	65	71	86	68	78	74	65	73	68	62	77	68	78	63	74	86	82
WILKIN	91	69	54	69	77	98	72	87	77	69	77	76	63	82	72	81	66	80	93	93
WINONA	84	78	84	80	79	83	83	82	84	80	83	73	81	84	82	84	74	82	86	83
WRIGHT	113	122	119	122	116	110	111	112	108	116	109	104	116	112	113	106	99	110	106	112
YELLOW MEDICINE	83	60	44	58	70	92	64	80	71	60	70	70	55	74	64	76	59	73	89	85
MINNESOTA	109	109	110	111	109	110	109	108	107	109	108	100	109	109	108	107	97	108	108	110
UNITED STATES	100	100	100	100	100	100	100	100	100	100	100	100	100	100	100	100	100	100	100	100

COUNTY	FIPS Code	CBSA Code	DMA Code	POPULATION 2000	POPULATION 2007	POPULATION 2012	2000-2007 ANNUAL RATE % Rate	2000-2007 ANNUAL RATE State Rank	RACE (%) White 2000	White 2007	Black 2000	Black 2007	Asian/Pacific 2000	Asian/Pacific 2007
ADAMS	001	35020	718	34,340	32,631	31,507	-0.7	77	46.0	43.8	52.8	54.6	0.3	0.4
ALCORN	003	18420	640	34,558	35,497	36,142	0.4	33	87.4	86.1	11.1	11.9	0.3	0.4
AMITE	005	32620	716	13,599	14,067	14,358	0.5	28	56.4	54.2	42.7	44.6	0.1	0.1
ATTALA	007	00000	718	19,661	19,455	19,281	-0.1	63	58.3	56.0	40.0	41.8	0.3	0.4
BENTON	009	00000	640	8,026	7,986	8,032	-0.1	63	61.7	60.9	36.8	37.6	0.1	0.1
BOLIVAR	011	17380	647	40,633	40,208	39,946	-0.1	63	33.2	31.8	65.1	66.2	0.5	0.7
CALHOUN	013	00000	673	15,069	15,010	15,007	-0.1	63	69.4	68.7	28.7	29.4	0.1	0.1
CARROLL	015	24900	647	10,769	10,874	10,829	0.1	52	62.7	60.6	36.6	38.5	0.2	0.2
CHICKASAW	017	00000	673	19,440	19,600	19,740	0.1	52	56.9	54.6	41.3	43.0	0.2	0.3
CHOCTAW	019	00000	673	9,758	9,681	9,631	-0.1	63	68.0	67.2	30.7	31.5	0.1	0.2
CLAIBORNE	021	00000	718	11,831	11,804	11,994	0.0	57	15.2	14.7	84.1	84.6	0.1	0.1
CLARKE	023	32940	711	17,955	18,287	18,551	0.3	40	64.5	62.4	34.8	36.7	0.1	0.2
CLAY	025	48500	673	21,979	21,431	21,018	-0.3	71	42.8	40.7	56.3	58.2	0.2	0.2
COAHOMA	027	17260	640	30,622	28,919	27,785	-0.8	80	29.3	27.5	69.2	70.6	0.5	0.7
COPIAH	029	27140	718	28,757	29,937	30,782	0.6	22	47.8	45.6	51.0	52.8	0.2	0.2
COVINGTON	031	00000	710	19,407	20,404	21,077	0.7	18	63.4	61.3	35.6	37.5	0.1	0.2
DESOTO	033	32820	640	107,199	151,362	191,484	4.9	1	85.8	84.1	11.4	12.1	0.7	0.9
FORREST	035	25620	710	72,604	76,263	78,929	0.7	18	64.3	62.1	33.6	35.2	0.8	1.0
FRANKLIN	037	00000	718	8,448	8,614	8,748	0.3	40	62.8	60.7	36.3	38.2	0.1	0.1
GEORGE	039	37700	746	19,144	20,847	21,650	1.2	10	89.4	88.1	8.8	9.5	0.2	0.2
GREENE	041	00000	686	13,299	13,493	13,391	0.2	47	72.8	70.9	26.2	27.8	0.1	0.1
GRENADA	043	24980	647	23,263	23,603	23,899	0.2	47	57.9	55.7	40.9	42.9	0.4	0.5
HANCOCK	045	25060	622	42,967	33,978	31,961	-3.2	82	90.2	92.0	6.8	5.2	0.9	0.5
HARRISON	047	25060	746	189,601	181,413	174,723	-0.6	74	73.1	69.4	21.1	23.5	2.7	3.4
HINDS	049	27140	718	250,800	251,503	252,576	0.0	57	37.3	35.2	61.1	62.8	0.6	0.8
HOLMES	051	00000	718	21,609	21,946	21,995	0.2	47	20.5	19.1	78.7	79.8	0.2	0.2
HUMPHREYS	053	00000	718	11,206	10,634	10,214	-0.7	77	27.2	25.5	71.5	72.8	0.3	0.4
ISSAQUENA	055	00000	718	2,274	1,982	1,788	-1.9	81	36.3	34.3	62.8	64.6	0.0	0.0
ITAWAMBA	057	46180	673	22,770	23,864	24,494	0.6	22	92.5	91.6	6.5	7.0	0.2	0.3
JACKSON	059	37700	746	131,420	139,330	145,182	0.8	14	75.4	73.2	20.9	22.0	1.6	2.2
JASPER	061	29860	710	18,149	18,676	18,991	0.4	33	46.5	44.3	52.9	54.9	0.1	0.1
JEFFERSON	063	00000	718	9,740	9,587	9,339	-0.2	69	13.1	12.1	86.5	87.3	0.1	0.1
JEFFERSON DAVIS	065	00000	718	13,962	13,624	13,250	-0.3	71	41.7	39.5	57.4	59.3	0.2	0.2
JONES	067	29860	710	64,958	67,543	69,500	0.5	28	71.1	68.9	26.3	27.8	0.3	0.4
KEMPER	069	32940	711	10,453	10,406	9,953	-0.1	63	39.0	38.2	58.1	59.0	0.1	0.1
LAFAYETTE	071	37060	640	38,744	43,019	46,261	1.5	8	71.9	69.5	25.0	26.4	1.7	2.4
LAMAR	073	25620	710	39,070	45,339	50,377	2.1	5	85.3	83.9	12.9	13.8	0.7	0.9
LAUDERDALE	075	32940	711	78,161	77,842	77,592	-0.1	63	60.1	57.9	38.2	39.9	0.5	0.7
LAWRENCE	077	00000	718	13,258	13,754	14,120	0.5	28	66.9	64.9	32.1	33.8	0.3	0.4
LEAKE	079	00000	718	20,940	22,643	23,347	1.1	11	56.1	53.5	37.4	38.7	0.2	0.2
LEE	081	46180	673	75,755	78,999	81,256	0.6	22	73.7	71.7	24.5	25.9	0.5	0.7
LEFLORE	083	24900	647	37,947	37,347	36,954	-0.2	69	30.0	28.1	67.7	68.9	0.7	0.9
LINCOLN	085	15020	718	33,166	34,106	34,673	0.4	33	69.4	67.4	29.7	31.4	0.3	0.4
LOWNDES	087	18060	673	61,586	61,334	61,274	-0.1	63	56.5	54.1	41.6	43.3	0.6	0.8
MADISON	089	27140	718	74,674	91,779	106,313	2.9	2	60.3	57.9	37.5	39.1	1.3	1.8
MARION	091	00000	710	25,595	25,913	26,178	0.2	47	67.0	64.9	31.9	33.6	0.2	0.3
MARSHALL	093	32820	640	34,993	37,134	38,665	0.8	14	48.4	46.2	50.4	52.2	0.1	0.2
MONROE	095	00000	673	38,014	38,052	38,039	0.0	57	68.4	67.6	30.8	31.6	0.2	0.2
MONTGOMERY	097	00000	673	12,189	12,243	12,267	0.1	52	54.3	53.3	45.0	45.8	0.3	0.3
NESHOBA	099	00000	711	28,684	29,785	30,512	0.5	28	65.5	62.4	19.3	20.0	0.2	0.3
NEWTON	101	00000	711	21,838	22,371	22,751	0.3	40	65.0	62.6	30.4	31.8	0.2	0.3
NOXUBEE	103	00000	673	12,548	12,516	12,345	0.0	57	29.5	28.7	69.3	70.1	0.1	0.1
OKTIBBEHA	105	44260	673	42,902	44,023	44,774	0.4	33	58.7	56.0	37.4	38.8	2.6	3.5
PANOLA	107	00000	640	34,274	35,399	36,174	0.4	33	50.5	48.2	48.4	50.3	0.2	0.3
PEARL RIVER	109	38100	622	48,621	54,522	58,319	1.6	7	85.6	84.1	12.2	13.0	0.3	0.4
PERRY	111	25620	710	12,138	12,196	12,214	0.1	52	76.2	75.5	22.6	23.2	0.2	0.2
PIKE	113	32620	718	38,940	39,816	40,452	0.3	40	51.2	49.0	47.5	49.4	0.3	0.5
PONTOTOC	115	46180	673	26,726	28,633	29,978	1.0	12	84.4	82.9	14.0	14.9	0.1	0.1
PRENTISS	117	00000	673	25,556	26,089	26,558	0.3	40	85.9	84.6	12.9	13.9	0.2	0.2
QUITMAN	119	00000	640	10,117	9,711	9,335	-0.6	74	30.5	28.6	68.6	70.2	0.2	0.2
RANKIN	121	27140	718	115,327	137,744	155,857	2.5	3	81.0	79.3	17.1	18.2	0.7	1.0
SCOTT	123	00000	718	28,423	29,796	30,773	0.7	18	57.2	54.9	38.9	40.0	0.2	0.3
SHARKEY	125	00000	718	6,580	6,204	5,958	-0.8	80	29.4	27.6	69.3	70.8	0.3	0.4
SIMPSON	127	27140	718	27,639	28,761	29,557	0.6	22	64.4	62.2	34.3	36.1	0.2	0.2
SMITH	129	00000	718	16,182	16,288	16,327	0.1	52	76.1	74.4	23.1	24.6	0.1	0.2
STONE	131	25060	746	13,622	15,244	16,281	1.6	7	79.4	77.8	19.2	20.4	0.2	0.3
SUNFLOWER	133	26940	647	34,369	33,407	32,760	-0.4	72	28.9	27.1	69.9	71.2	0.4	0.5
TALLAHATCHIE	135	00000	647	14,903	14,303	13,886	-0.6	74	39.6	37.6	59.4	61.2	0.4	0.5
TATE	137	32820	640	25,370	28,107	29,830	1.4	9	67.8	65.8	31.0	32.7	0.1	0.2
TIPPAH	139	00000	640	20,826	21,655	22,232	0.5	28	81.8	80.1	15.9	16.9	0.1	0.2
TISHOMINGO	141	00000	673	19,163	19,634	19,998	0.3	40	94.9	94.0	3.1	3.4	0.1	0.1
TUNICA	143	32820	640	9,227	10,977	12,022	2.4	4	27.5	25.9	70.2	71.2	0.5	0.6
UNION	145	00000	673	25,362	26,840	27,847	0.8	14	83.4	81.9	14.9	16.0	0.2	0.3
WALTHALL	147	00000	718	15,156	15,821	16,290	0.6	22	54.6	52.4	44.1	46.0	0.3	0.4
WARREN	149	46980	718	49,644	49,269	49,059	-0.1	63	55.0	52.7	43.2	45.0	0.6	0.9
WASHINGTON	151	24740	647	62,977	59,903	57,927	-0.7	77	34.0	32.0	64.6	66.1	0.5	0.7
WAYNE	153	00000	710	21,216	21,697	22,003	0.3	40	61.3	59.1	38.0	40.0	0.2	0.2
MISSISSIPPI							0.6		61.4	60.1	36.3	37.0	0.7	0.9
UNITED STATES							1.2		75.1	72.7	12.3	12.6	3.8	4.5

POPULATION COMPOSITION

COUNTY	% HISPANIC ORIGIN		2007 AGE DISTRIBUTION (%)										MEDIAN AGE			
	2000	2007	0-4	5-9	10-14	15-19	20-24	25-44	45-64	65-84	85+	18+	2007	% 2007 Males	% 2007 Females
ADAMS	0.8	0.9	6.9	6.3	6.7	6.3	7.1	22.6	27.8	14.1	2.2	76.3	40.3	46.4	53.6
ALCORN	1.3	1.7	6.6	6.6	6.1	5.5	5.4	28.0	26.7	12.9	2.2	77.4	39.1	49.0	51.0
AMITE	0.8	1.0	6.3	5.8	6.2	6.0	7.0	24.6	28.7	13.6	1.8	78.2	40.5	49.0	51.0
ATTALA	1.4	1.9	6.9	6.2	6.5	6.3	6.2	25.5	25.6	14.1	2.7	76.6	39.0	48.6	51.4
BENTON	1.0	1.1	7.9	7.2	6.6	5.6	5.4	27.5	24.5	13.1	2.0	74.8	36.9	48.3	51.7
BOLIVAR	1.2	2.7	7.8	7.4	7.1	8.6	9.6	26.0	22.6	9.2	1.7	73.2	31.4	47.0	53.0
CALHOUN	2.1	2.1	7.0	6.7	6.1	5.7	6.7	26.2	26.0	12.9	2.7	76.7	38.5	48.1	51.9
CARROLL	0.7	0.9	5.7	5.4	5.9	6.5	6.9	25.7	29.4	12.7	1.8	79.4	40.8	50.6	49.4
CHICKASAW	2.3	3.0	8.0	7.6	7.6	6.6	6.0	27.3	23.7	11.2	2.1	72.8	35.5	49.0	51.0
CHOCTAW	0.8	0.8	6.9	6.9	6.5	7.1	6.6	24.7	26.4	12.7	2.2	75.1	38.6	48.3	51.7
CLAIBORNE	0.8	0.8	7.1	7.1	6.8	10.3	13.3	22.9	22.0	8.5	2.0	75.1	28.7	46.5	53.5
CLARKE	0.7	0.8	7.0	6.6	7.1	5.8	6.0	25.6	26.8	12.8	2.2	75.7	39.1	48.0	52.0
CLAY	0.9	1.1	7.8	7.4	7.5	6.7	7.1	26.0	25.2	10.5	1.8	73.4	34.5	47.8	52.2
COAHOMA	0.9	1.1	9.4	8.4	7.9	8.0	8.1	23.7	22.6	9.8	2.0	69.4	31.5	46.2	53.8
COPIAH	1.2	1.4	6.9	6.7	6.4	8.6	7.6	25.7	25.8	10.8	1.6	75.8	35.5	48.5	51.5
COVINGTON	0.8	1.0	7.9	7.4	7.8	6.3	6.3	26.8	24.4	11.4	1.7	73.1	35.7	48.5	51.5
DESOTO	2.3	3.2	7.8	7.4	7.2	6.9	5.5	30.4	25.1	9.0	0.8	73.4	35.7	49.5	50.5
FORREST	1.3	1.6	7.2	5.9	6.2	7.8	12.7	27.3	21.6	9.5	1.7	77.2	30.9	47.4	52.6
FRANKLIN	0.5	0.7	7.2	6.6	5.4	6.5	7.3	23.9	27.9	13.0	2.1	76.9	39.6	48.4	51.6
GEORGE	1.6	2.2	8.2	7.5	7.8	6.7	6.3	28.8	23.2	10.0	1.5	72.3	34.1	50.3	49.7
GREENE	0.8	1.0	7.1	7.0	5.8	6.0	9.0	32.9	22.0	8.9	1.3	76.8	33.3	57.3	42.7
GRENADA	0.6	0.8	7.0	6.7	7.0	7.0	5.7	27.1	25.3	12.0	2.2	75.0	37.5	47.2	52.8
HANCOCK	1.8	2.3	6.4	6.0	6.0	6.7	5.9	24.6	28.7	14.2	1.5	77.5	41.3	49.7	50.3
HARRISON	2.6	3.1	7.3	6.6	6.7	7.3	7.8	28.2	24.4	10.5	1.2	75.5	35.1	49.9	50.1
HINDS	0.8	0.9	7.5	7.1	7.2	7.8	8.0	27.6	23.9	9.3	1.6	73.9	33.4	47.3	52.7
HOLMES	0.9	0.9	8.4	7.7	8.3	9.0	8.8	23.9	21.7	10.2	2.0	71.1	31.0	46.7	53.3
HUMPHREYS	1.5	1.8	8.7	7.3	8.3	7.4	8.9	25.9	22.2	9.5	1.8	71.2	31.8	47.3	52.7
ISSAQUENA	0.4	0.6	6.4	4.9	6.6	7.9	9.9	29.5	22.4	11.0	1.4	77.3	35.1	53.6	46.4
ITAWAMBA	1.0	1.3	6.4	6.0	6.9	7.4	6.3	27.7	24.8	12.5	1.9	77.0	37.4	48.9	51.1
JACKSON	2.1	2.5	7.3	6.7	7.1	6.8	6.8	28.0	25.7	10.5	1.1	74.7	36.3	49.5	50.5
JASPER	0.6	0.8	7.4	6.8	7.5	6.0	6.3	26.5	25.7	11.7	2.1	74.6	37.1	48.0	52.0
JEFFERSON	0.7	0.7	7.5	7.2	6.5	6.9	8.0	27.8	25.2	9.0	1.8	74.8	34.0	50.2	49.8
JEFFERSON DAVIS	0.8	0.9	7.7	7.1	7.0	6.1	6.5	25.6	26.4	11.4	2.1	74.4	36.7	48.0	52.0
JONES	2.0	2.6	7.3	7.1	6.2	6.3	6.3	27.3	25.3	12.4	1.8	76.0	37.1	48.8	51.2
KEMPER	0.7	0.7	6.8	6.5	6.3	8.2	7.6	24.8	25.0	12.1	2.9	76.7	36.5	48.2	51.8
LAFAYETTE	1.1	1.4	5.6	4.9	4.6	9.9	17.3	28.0	19.4	8.8	1.6	82.1	28.4	49.6	50.4
LAMAR	1.1	1.5	7.7	6.9	7.0	6.5	7.9	29.5	24.0	9.3	1.2	74.6	34.1	48.1	51.9
LAUDERDALE	1.1	1.5	7.2	6.7	6.8	7.0	7.0	26.8	24.4	11.6	2.5	75.4	36.4	48.0	52.0
LAWRENCE	0.7	0.8	7.0	6.8	6.7	6.1	6.8	25.9	26.3	12.8	1.7	75.9	38.1	48.2	51.8
LEAKE	2.1	2.7	7.3	7.1	6.4	5.8	6.7	28.2	24.4	11.8	2.2	75.7	36.1	50.7	49.3
LEE	1.2	1.5	7.6	7.2	7.1	6.7	6.2	28.2	24.9	10.3	1.7	73.9	36.3	48.4	51.6
LEFLORE	1.9	2.3	8.3	7.7	7.4	8.0	9.6	26.6	21.2	9.3	2.0	72.3	31.0	48.3	51.7
LINCOLN	0.7	0.9	7.3	7.1	6.9	5.8	6.4	27.1	25.8	11.6	1.9	75.1	37.0	48.2	51.8
LOWNDES	1.1	1.4	7.9	7.3	7.2	7.1	7.5	27.9	23.7	9.7	1.7	73.4	34.2	47.7	52.3
MADISON	1.0	1.3	7.7	8.1	7.5	7.1	6.2	29.3	24.6	7.9	1.5	72.3	35.0	47.6	52.4
MARION	0.6	0.8	7.2	6.8	7.4	6.4	6.8	26.4	25.3	11.6	2.1	74.6	36.6	48.9	51.1
MARSHALL	1.2	1.5	7.2	7.0	6.5	6.8	7.6	27.5	26.0	10.2	1.2	75.4	35.6	49.6	50.4
MONROE	0.7	0.7	7.0	6.5	7.2	6.3	6.5	26.8	25.4	12.2	2.1	75.4	37.5	47.8	52.2
MONTGOMERY	0.8	0.8	7.0	6.4	6.7	6.2	6.8	24.7	26.4	13.7	2.4	76.1	39.1	46.9	53.1
NESHOBA	1.2	1.5	8.1	7.7	7.4	6.1	6.6	26.4	24.1	11.5	2.1	73.0	35.5	47.9	52.1
NEWTON	0.9	1.2	7.4	7.0	6.6	7.1	6.2	26.3	24.9	12.4	2.0	75.4	36.7	48.8	51.2
NOXUBEE	1.1	1.1	8.6	8.0	7.3	6.7	7.3	25.5	24.4	10.2	2.0	72.1	34.0	48.1	51.9
OKTIBBEHA	1.1	1.4	6.3	5.2	5.0	9.7	20.6	25.2	19.1	7.7	1.1	80.4	26.7	50.4	49.6
PANOLA	1.1	1.4	8.1	7.9	7.0	7.1	6.5	27.3	24.0	10.4	1.7	72.7	34.3	48.2	51.8
PEARL RIVER	1.4	1.9	7.2	7.0	6.7	6.5	6.2	26.2	26.4	12.3	1.4	75.3	37.9	48.8	51.2
PERRY	1.0	1.0	8.1	7.2	7.6	5.8	7.1	27.4	25.0	10.5	1.2	73.3	34.8	48.9	51.1
PIKE	0.7	0.9	7.7	7.2	7.2	6.1	7.2	25.1	25.4	11.9	2.1	74.4	36.5	47.2	52.8
PONTOTOC	1.8	2.4	7.6	7.1	6.9	6.6	6.3	28.5	24.6	10.6	1.8	74.4	36.5	49.0	51.0
PRENTISS	0.7	0.9	7.2	6.8	6.4	7.2	6.8	27.5	24.4	11.9	1.9	76.0	36.4	49.0	51.0
QUITMAN	0.5	0.6	8.5	7.8	8.4	8.2	6.6	24.9	22.7	10.9	2.2	70.2	33.2	46.5	53.5
RANKIN	1.3	1.8	7.2	6.9	6.2	6.3	6.9	30.5	25.6	9.3	1.0	75.9	36.1	49.0	51.0
SCOTT	5.8	7.6	7.8	7.3	7.2	6.6	6.0	27.8	24.9	10.8	1.8	73.7	35.9	49.0	51.0
SHARKEY	1.3	1.5	8.9	8.4	8.5	7.1	7.8	24.1	24.5	8.9	1.8	69.9	31.6	47.5	52.5
SIMPSON	1.2	1.5	7.3	6.9	7.4	6.6	5.8	27.2	25.5	11.4	1.8	74.2	36.4	48.8	51.2
SMITH	0.6	0.8	7.5	7.0	6.9	6.6	6.4	26.7	24.7	12.5	1.8	74.6	36.7	49.2	50.8
STONE	1.2	1.6	7.0	6.9	6.8	8.6	7.9	26.4	24.8	10.2	1.4	75.4	34.5	49.8	50.2
SUNFLOWER	1.3	1.6	7.6	6.9	7.2	7.9	10.0	30.5	20.8	7.6	1.6	74.1	30.9	53.9	46.1
TALLAHATCHIE	0.9	1.0	7.5	6.2	8.1	7.3	6.6	26.1	25.1	11.2	2.0	73.8	35.8	47.2	52.8
TATE	0.9	1.1	7.1	6.9	6.8	8.5	7.6	26.7	25.0	10.0	1.5	75.0	35.1	48.8	51.2
TIPPAH	2.1	2.8	6.7	6.3	6.3	6.3	6.5	28.8	24.8	12.1	2.2	77.0	37.4	49.0	51.0
TISHOMINGO	1.8	2.5	6.1	5.8	6.5	5.4	5.4	27.2	26.5	14.8	2.4	78.3	40.9	48.8	51.2
TUNICA	2.5	3.0	8.6	8.0	7.8	8.2	7.0	27.6	23.4	8.2	1.2	70.4	31.1	48.0	52.0
UNION	1.6	2.2	7.7	7.5	6.6	5.8	5.5	29.1	24.5	11.5	1.8	74.7	36.5	49.1	50.9
WALTHALL	1.3	1.6	7.6	7.1	7.0	6.3	6.3	26.2	25.4	12.0	2.2	74.6	36.4	48.2	51.8
WARREN	1.0	1.3	7.7	7.0	7.4	6.6	7.0	25.6	26.7	10.1	1.8	73.8	36.0	47.1	52.9
WASHINGTON	0.8	1.0	8.7	7.9	8.1	7.1	7.9	25.1	23.7	9.7	1.8	71.0	32.6	47.3	52.7
WAYNE	0.6	0.8	8.2	7.6	7.6	6.0	6.8	26.4	25.0	10.9	1.5	73.0	35.2	47.7	52.3
MISSISSIPPI	1.4	1.8	7.4	7.0	6.9	7.0	7.5	27.4	24.6	10.5	1.7	74.8	35.2	48.6	51.4
UNITED STATES	12.5	15.0	6.9	6.5	6.8	7.1	7.0	27.6	25.4	10.7	1.9	75.6	36.7	49.2	50.8

COUNTY	HOUSEHOLDS					FAMILIES			MEDIAN HOUSEHOLD INCOME			
	2000	2007	2012	% Annual Rate 2000-2007	2007 Average HH Size	2000	2007	% Annual Rate 2000-2007	2007	2012	2007 National Rank	2007 State Rank
ADAMS	13,677	13,377	13,061	-0.3	2.41	9,403	8,969	-0.6	28,617	31,138	2974	56
ALCORN	14,224	14,977	15,404	0.7	2.33	9,921	10,201	0.4	32,745	35,709	2679	24
AMITE	5,271	5,590	5,778	0.8	2.50	3,878	4,028	0.5	29,457	31,883	2933	53
ATTALA	7,567	7,633	7,614	0.1	2.50	5,383	5,307	-0.2	27,659	29,579	3017	64
BENTON	2,999	3,075	3,132	0.3	2.56	2,216	2,224	0.0	27,841	30,300	3008	62
BOLIVAR	13,776	14,094	14,192	0.3	2.70	9,719	9,714	0.0	26,948	29,391	3038	67
CALHOUN	6,019	6,150	6,211	0.3	2.40	4,258	4,250	0.0	30,658	33,251	2868	45
CARROLL	4,071	4,215	4,248	0.5	2.50	3,068	3,115	0.2	32,628	35,605	2693	27
CHICKASAW	7,253	7,477	7,594	0.4	2.59	5,289	5,335	0.1	30,697	33,183	2864	44
CHOCTAW	3,686	3,780	3,809	0.3	2.48	2,668	2,676	0.0	30,611	32,997	2875	46
CLAIBORNE	3,685	3,850	3,949	0.6	2.67	2,532	2,580	0.3	26,106	28,511	3067	70
CLARKE	6,978	7,308	7,498	0.6	2.48	5,025	5,148	0.3	30,441	33,113	2888	48
CLAY	8,152	8,227	8,167	0.1	2.56	5,888	5,813	-0.2	31,673	34,511	2788	37
COAHOMA	10,553	10,149	9,810	-0.5	2.77	7,479	7,026	-0.9	25,292	27,039	3087	75
COPIAH	10,142	10,797	11,204	0.9	2.65	7,498	7,819	0.6	30,163	32,649	2902	50
COVINGTON	7,126	7,708	8,053	1.1	2.61	5,281	5,596	0.8	30,280	32,768	2896	49
DESOTO	38,792	55,806	71,258	5.1	2.70	30,112	42,555	4.9	55,995	62,272	364	2
FORREST	27,183	29,175	30,449	1.0	2.43	17,305	18,042	0.6	30,923	32,963	2841	42
FRANKLIN	3,211	3,339	3,414	0.5	2.55	2,337	2,379	0.2	28,365	30,836	2985	58
GEORGE	6,742	7,385	7,724	1.3	2.73	5,308	5,715	1.0	40,094	43,799	1713	8
GREENE	4,148	4,287	4,309	0.5	2.58	3,152	3,196	0.2	32,206	35,178	2744	31
GRENADA	8,820	9,232	9,464	0.6	2.50	6,301	6,446	0.3	31,667	34,611	2790	39
HANCOCK	16,897	13,634	12,928	-2.9	2.46	11,822	9,314	-3.2	36,526	38,795	2188	14
HARRISON	71,538	70,143	68,012	-0.3	2.48	48,605	46,457	-0.6	39,312	41,497	1819	10
HINDS	91,030	93,583	94,507	0.4	2.59	62,315	62,473	0.0	38,597	41,573	1918	11
HOLMES	7,314	7,481	7,553	0.3	2.81	5,231	5,230	0.0	19,498	21,580	3137	82
HUMPHREYS	3,765	3,649	3,531	-0.4	2.89	2,697	2,555	-0.7	23,613	25,627	3106	77
ISSAQUENA	726	644	580	-1.6	2.67	510	441	-2.0	22,078	24,167	3125	79
ITAWAMBA	8,773	9,331	9,649	0.9	2.46	6,501	6,773	0.6	35,524	38,707	2363	16
JACKSON	47,676	51,556	54,124	1.1	2.67	35,724	37,861	0.8	42,811	45,527	1353	5
JASPER	6,708	7,106	7,312	0.8	2.61	4,956	5,143	0.5	27,972	30,543	3003	60
JEFFERSON	3,308	3,389	3,343	0.3	2.63	2,339	2,340	0.0	20,316	22,486	3132	81
JEFFERSON DAVIS	5,177	5,233	5,162	0.1	2.58	3,770	3,729	-0.2	25,393	27,470	3085	74
JONES	24,275	25,724	26,655	0.8	2.56	17,555	18,197	0.5	32,693	35,721	2685	25
KEMPER	3,909	3,919	3,787	0.0	2.49	2,786	2,731	-0.3	27,555	30,094	3019	65
LAFAYETTE	14,373	16,502	18,063	1.9	2.31	8,318	9,239	1.5	31,669	33,848	2789	38
LAMAR	14,396	17,075	19,130	2.4	2.63	10,721	12,458	2.1	43,815	48,500	1234	4
LAUDERDALE	29,990	30,516	30,652	0.2	2.43	20,569	20,416	-0.1	34,038	36,605	2546	21
LAWRENCE	5,040	5,358	5,552	0.8	2.55	3,751	3,907	0.6	32,483	35,546	2709	28
LEAKE	7,611	8,078	8,377	0.8	2.62	5,566	5,781	0.5	30,736	33,418	2858	43
LEE	29,200	30,455	31,424	0.6	2.55	20,810	21,211	0.3	41,564	45,619	1508	6
LEFLORE	12,956	13,039	12,996	0.1	2.64	8,890	8,724	-0.3	24,487	26,545	3098	76
LINCOLN	12,538	13,152	13,468	0.7	2.54	9,191	9,439	0.4	31,496	34,332	2800	40
LOWNDES	22,849	23,234	23,373	0.2	2.56	16,405	16,311	-0.1	36,375	39,864	2216	15
MADISON	27,219	34,381	40,210	3.3	2.61	19,332	23,859	2.9	57,080	65,470	327	1
MARION	9,336	9,654	9,835	0.5	2.58	6,882	6,968	0.2	27,932	30,422	3004	61
MARSHALL	12,163	13,339	14,092	1.3	2.65	9,115	9,798	1.0	32,936	35,893	2664	23
MONROE	14,603	14,991	15,136	0.4	2.51	10,667	10,721	0.1	34,645	37,758	2479	19
MONTGOMERY	4,690	4,831	4,887	0.4	2.50	3,369	3,393	0.1	28,991	31,449	2960	55
NESHOBA	10,694	11,391	11,789	0.9	2.56	7,746	8,072	0.6	32,078	35,078	2753	32
NEWTON	8,221	8,626	8,849	0.7	2.51	6,004	6,166	0.4	32,646	35,614	2692	26
NOXUBEE	4,470	4,627	4,629	0.5	2.66	3,225	3,265	0.2	26,053	28,234	3069	71
OKTIBBEHA	15,945	17,193	17,726	1.0	2.34	9,265	9,668	0.6	27,725	29,586	3014	63
PANOLA	12,232	12,978	13,405	0.8	2.68	9,019	9,372	0.5	30,520	33,230	2883	47
PEARL RIVER	18,078	20,806	22,474	2.0	2.58	13,583	15,327	1.7	35,016	37,944	2425	18
PERRY	4,420	4,547	4,593	0.4	2.66	3,333	3,361	0.1	31,751	34,600	2783	36
PIKE	14,792	15,486	15,880	0.6	2.51	10,502	10,740	0.3	27,418	29,936	3022	66
PONTOTOC	10,097	10,933	11,480	1.1	2.59	7,563	8,030	0.8	37,217	40,719	2100	12
PRENTISS	9,821	10,324	10,604	0.7	2.46	7,166	7,372	0.4	32,274	35,237	2738	29
QUITMAN	3,565	3,494	3,390	-0.3	2.73	2,507	2,399	-0.6	23,001	25,000	3112	78
RANKIN	42,089	51,518	59,161	2.8	2.57	31,136	37,330	2.5	52,208	57,831	533	3
SCOTT	10,183	10,838	11,247	0.9	2.72	7,534	7,853	0.6	30,989	33,627	2832	41
SHARKEY	2,163	2,134	2,078	-0.2	2.86	1,589	1,534	-0.5	25,456	27,668	3083	73
SIMPSON	10,076	10,748	11,160	0.9	2.58	7,381	7,707	0.6	31,878	34,804	2773	35
SMITH	6,046	6,229	6,300	0.4	2.59	4,556	4,602	0.1	35,413	38,538	2383	17
STONE	4,747	5,316	5,721	1.6	2.69	3,628	3,988	1.3	34,539	37,662	2493	20
SUNFLOWER	9,637	9,476	9,290	-0.2	2.97	7,312	7,051	-0.5	28,576	31,084	2976	57
TALLAHATCHIE	5,263	5,203	5,112	-0.2	2.73	3,828	3,705	-0.4	25,951	28,031	3072	72
TATE	8,850	10,120	10,898	1.9	2.66	6,714	7,532	1.6	41,150	45,092	1583	7
TIPPAH	8,108	8,662	9,001	0.9	2.45	5,907	6,175	0.6	33,322	36,206	2627	22
TISHOMINGO	7,917	8,293	8,514	0.6	2.34	5,575	5,706	0.3	31,966	34,943	2765	33
TUNICA	3,258	4,088	4,548	3.2	2.65	2,192	2,680	2.8	26,557	28,906	3053	69
UNION	9,786	10,520	10,970	1.0	2.53	7,245	7,630	0.7	36,864	40,299	2147	13
WALTHALL	5,571	5,994	6,253	1.0	2.61	4,114	4,334	0.7	26,839	29,192	3043	68
WARREN	18,756	19,012	19,076	0.2	2.58	13,220	13,092	0.1	30,833	43,435	1748	9
WASHINGTON	22,158	21,663	21,171	-0.3	2.73	15,937	15,232	-0.6	29,417	31,774	2936	54
WAYNE	7,857	8,255	8,463	0.7	2.60	5,857	6,031	0.4	29,779	32,030	2922	52
MISSISSIPPI				0.9	2.57			0.6	35,903	39,445		
UNITED STATES				1.2	2.59			1.0	53,154	62,503		

COUNTY	2007 Per Capita Income	2007 HH Income Base	2007 HOUSEHOLD INCOME DISTRIBUTION (%) Less than $25,000	$25,000 to $49,999	$50,000 to $99,999	$100,000 to $149,999	$150,000 or More	2007 Home Value Base	2007 HOME VALUE DISTRIBUTION (%) Less than $50,000	$50,000 to $89,999	$90,000 to $174,999	$175,000 to $399,999	$400,000 or More	2007 Median Home Value
ADAMS	18,240	13,377	44.2	29.4	19.0	4.6	3.0	9,419	21.6	34.6	31.0	9.9	2.9	81,383
ALCORN	18,366	14,977	39.2	30.5	23.9	4.8	1.7	11,069	24.8	30.5	32.2	10.5	2.0	83,670
AMITE	15,920	5,590	43.3	31.9	19.3	3.9	1.6	4,779	34.3	27.9	25.6	8.9	3.3	70,422
ATTALA	15,568	7,633	45.5	28.8	20.2	3.9	1.6	5,916	32.7	34.3	25.3	6.7	1.1	68,539
BENTON	14,132	3,075	45.9	31.1	18.6	3.8	0.6	2,578	26.4	36.5	31.5	5.2	0.4	74,818
BOLIVAR	14,373	14,094	46.8	28.7	18.4	4.0	2.2	8,686	29.4	32.7	28.0	9.0	1.0	71,881
CALHOUN	16,916	6,150	42.6	28.6	23.1	4.0	1.8	4,724	31.3	36.1	25.3	6.6	0.6	67,639
CARROLL	18,673	4,215	39.1	29.3	24.2	4.1	3.2	3,560	31.3	30.8	24.6	11.7	1.5	71,623
CHICKASAW	15,291	7,477	42.0	31.0	22.1	3.6	1.4	5,831	33.9	33.9	25.2	5.8	1.1	67,968
CHOCTAW	16,145	3,780	42.3	32.9	18.9	3.8	2.1	3,055	26.9	33.5	29.7	8.3	1.5	76,622
CLAIBORNE	13,764	3,850	48.5	27.5	16.7	5.4	2.0	3,073	37.3	33.4	22.4	5.8	1.2	61,400
CLARKE	16,537	7,308	41.5	29.9	22.9	4.1	1.5	6,130	35.3	30.5	28.1	5.6	0.5	68,167
CLAY	17,405	8,227	40.4	28.1	23.4	5.7	2.5	6,037	19.8	35.5	33.6	9.4	1.7	84,704
COAHOMA	14,207	10,149	49.5	25.0	18.6	4.5	2.4	5,855	30.8	34.4	27.2	6.1	1.5	68,595
COPIAH	14,922	10,797	42.3	29.5	21.7	5.1	1.3	8,581	32.2	30.6	27.7	8.1	1.4	72,258
COVINGTON	17,202	7,708	41.5	31.3	20.6	3.9	2.7	6,500	34.8	28.2	28.3	7.5	1.2	69,421
DESOTO	24,855	55,806	16.6	26.5	40.1	12.5	4.3	44,338	4.9	14.0	49.1	29.3	2.7	134,089
FORREST	17,298	29,174	41.7	29.9	21.3	4.8	2.4	17,621	20.9	28.6	35.4	13.8	1.3	90,860
FRANKLIN	15,418	3,339	44.5	28.6	22.5	2.7	1.7	2,855	39.3	29.7	23.6	6.9	0.5	62,279
GEORGE	17,181	7,385	31.3	31.2	29.8	5.8	1.9	6,335	19.7	18.7	32.9	24.6	4.1	112,465
GREENE	14,935	4,287	40.3	31.8	22.3	4.0	1.5	3,709	33.8	29.5	27.8	7.8	1.1	70,910
GRENADA	16,703	9,232	39.0	32.0	22.7	4.6	1.7	6,422	19.0	29.8	38.0	11.8	1.4	91,535
HANCOCK	19,949	13,634	34.4	30.8	25.8	5.9	3.1	10,855	19.1	20.7	36.0	20.9	3.3	109,221
HARRISON	20,372	70,142	30.9	31.5	27.9	6.6	3.2	44,443	10.5	18.0	44.4	22.6	4.5	125,274
HINDS	20,825	93,583	32.6	29.8	26.4	7.1	4.2	59,847	14.8	31.7	37.3	13.5	2.6	94,645
HOLMES	11,794	7,481	57.6	24.9	13.1	2.6	1.8	5,446	43.4	31.1	20.7	3.7	1.1	57,317
HUMPHREYS	12,047	3,649	51.8	28.0	16.3	2.6	1.3	2,272	35.0	33.2	26.1	5.5	0.2	66,216
ISSAQUENA	12,781	644	54.8	23.8	16.5	2.6	2.3	434	44.5	23.0	21.2	8.3	3.0	57,059
ITAWAMBA	18,121	9,331	34.4	32.9	25.2	5.5	2.0	7,690	24.5	34.5	31.4	8.7	0.9	81,107
JACKSON	20,237	51,556	27.3	30.8	31.0	7.7	3.2	38,618	7.6	12.6	40.8	33.4	5.6	149,671
JASPER	14,710	7,106	44.7	30.4	19.9	3.5	1.5	6,106	35.3	31.3	25.2	6.4	1.8	67,016
JEFFERSON	11,430	3,389	56.7	25.5	14.6	2.6	0.6	2,728	39.1	34.0	21.2	3.4	2.3	61,674
JEFFERSON DAVIS	14,352	5,233	49.3	28.4	17.2	3.3	1.8	4,392	35.8	33.6	25.6	4.5	0.5	65,404
JONES	17,508	25,724	36.5	34.0	22.1	4.9	2.4	19,759	29.6	30.8	28.2	9.8	1.6	75,472
KEMPER	14,420	3,919	45.7	31.7	17.7	3.5	1.3	3,252	31.8	37.0	25.1	5.2	0.9	67,934
LAFAYETTE	18,837	16,502	41.4	25.4	25.3	5.1	2.8	9,954	20.2	20.1	31.4	23.1	5.2	109,774
LAMAR	22,946	17,075	26.8	29.7	30.0	8.2	5.3	12,912	16.3	17.4	35.9	24.3	6.1	124,323
LAUDERDALE	18,631	30,516	38.7	28.1	25.0	5.7	2.6	20,709	22.9	29.5	32.8	12.6	2.3	86,445
LAWRENCE	16,858	5,358	40.1	25.7	27.2	5.6	1.4	4,488	27.3	35.2	29.7	6.4	1.4	73,808
LEAKE	15,157	8,078	40.9	32.1	20.7	4.7	1.6	6,583	32.2	32.7	25.4	7.9	1.7	71,316
LEE	21,457	30,455	28.8	30.8	29.5	7.0	3.9	21,271	15.2	21.6	41.5	18.2	3.4	110,650
LEFLORE	14,379	13,039	50.6	25.5	16.9	4.5	2.5	7,046	22.9	38.6	27.7	9.2	1.5	76,099
LINCOLN	16,643	13,152	39.7	30.3	22.2	5.9	1.8	10,235	26.8	30.4	31.0	10.4	1.4	80,739
LOWNDES	19,116	23,234	35.1	29.3	25.6	6.9	3.1	15,572	16.0	26.6	39.8	15.7	1.9	100,831
MADISON	29,755	34,381	20.7	23.6	31.9	13.4	10.4	24,413	11.4	13.3	34.4	32.6	8.3	149,898
MARION	14,645	9,654	45.6	29.9	19.5	3.4	1.7	7,743	28.3	32.8	29.3	8.4	1.2	74,216
MARSHALL	16,703	13,339	38.1	30.8	24.3	4.3	2.6	10,689	27.4	32.0	30.4	9.2	1.0	78,241
MONROE	16,887	14,991	36.3	32.2	25.9	4.2	1.4	11,812	26.1	28.9	32.6	10.8	1.5	82,669
MONTGOMERY	15,819	4,831	44.6	30.2	19.1	4.0	2.1	3,716	28.7	37.5	27.4	5.4	1.0	71,796
NESHOBA	17,070	11,391	39.7	30.2	23.4	4.5	2.3	9,004	26.5	33.7	28.3	9.3	2.3	77,580
NEWTON	16,789	8,626	38.2	31.1	24.9	4.1	1.7	7,048	31.8	33.1	28.5	5.8	0.9	71,590
NOXUBEE	14,381	4,627	48.3	28.5	17.2	3.9	2.1	3,660	40.4	31.5	20.1	5.8	2.2	59,385
OKTIBBEHA	17,354	17,193	45.9	25.2	20.0	6.5	2.4	9,513	23.7	21.3	33.0	18.6	3.4	100,138
PANOLA	15,546	12,978	41.7	29.7	22.0	4.7	2.0	10,092	35.2	29.9	27.3	6.6	1.0	68,302
PEARL RIVER	17,939	20,806	35.4	31.4	25.4	5.5	2.4	16,640	20.6	25.2	35.3	16.4	2.5	96,920
PERRY	14,764	4,547	40.7	30.6	24.3	3.5	0.9	3,822	34.0	30.4	28.2	6.6	0.8	70,330
PIKE	16,421	15,486	46.0	28.3	19.3	3.8	2.6	11,479	27.5	32.7	27.5	10.4	1.8	75,261
PONTOTOC	18,318	10,933	32.4	32.2	28.3	4.7	2.4	8,549	20.5	31.2	37.6	9.3	1.3	88,004
PRENTISS	16,720	10,324	38.5	32.9	22.4	4.9	1.3	8,055	24.9	35.7	30.3	8.3	0.8	77,172
QUITMAN	12,314	3,494	52.6	27.2	16.2	2.7	1.3	2,383	47.5	33.4	16.4	2.1	0.5	52,088
RANKIN	24,816	51,518	19.7	27.8	35.8	11.8	4.9	39,781	15.4	17.2	41.6	23.3	2.6	120,404
SCOTT	15,955	10,838	40.7	30.6	22.9	3.5	2.3	8,500	39.4	31.7	22.4	5.1	1.4	61,766
SHARKEY	13,263	2,134	49.3	25.9	19.8	3.6	1.5	1,410	36.9	35.2	24.7	3.0	0.1	64,671
SIMPSON	16,079	10,748	39.8	30.9	23.2	4.2	1.9	8,673	33.6	28.9	28.9	7.7	0.8	70,751
SMITH	17,529	6,229	35.5	30.3	27.8	4.3	2.2	5,375	33.3	27.0	29.9	8.2	1.6	75,160
STONE	17,217	5,316	37.5	27.9	25.9	5.7	3.0	4,304	21.5	19.0	35.5	18.5	5.5	108,517
SUNFLOWER	13,309	9,476	44.4	28.0	21.5	3.8	2.3	5,909	24.9	40.8	28.2	5.2	0.9	71,944
TALLAHATCHIE	12,698	5,203	48.1	30.5	17.5	2.8	1.1	3,946	45.2	31.9	18.6	4.0	0.3	55,013
TATE	19,274	10,120	29.6	29.7	31.1	7.1	2.5	7,934	20.1	24.7	38.6	15.7	0.9	95,156
TIPPAH	16,693	8,662	37.5	33.5	24.0	3.6	1.3	6,791	27.3	33.3	28.8	9.3	1.4	76,851
TISHOMINGO	18,201	8,293	38.8	33.7	21.1	4.1	2.3	6,559	24.6	34.3	31.7	8.5	1.0	78,958
TUNICA	14,513	4,088	47.6	27.8	19.2	3.9	1.5	2,123	36.1	33.3	23.9	5.3	1.4	68,194
UNION	18,418	10,520	33.3	30.6	30.1	4.2	1.9	8,196	21.5	30.9	35.7	10.4	1.4	86,934
WALTHALL	14,973	5,994	47.1	28.3	19.5	3.2	2.0	4,962	29.1	28.1	31.3	9.0	2.6	78,389
WARREN	20,619	19,012	31.9	28.9	26.9	8.9	3.4	13,024	23.6	22.2	35.6	16.4	2.2	96,997
WASHINGTON	15,679	21,663	43.7	28.0	21.1	4.4	2.7	13,028	26.9	35.1	27.9	8.2	1.8	73,923
WAYNE	15,359	8,255	43.4	31.6	18.6	4.5	1.9	6,972	42.2	27.4	22.7	6.9	0.7	59,097
MISSISSIPPI	18,800		35.6	29.5	25.6	6.3	3.0		22.0	26.4	34.0	15.1	2.5	92,555
UNITED STATES	27,916		21.9	25.0	32.3	12.3	8.4		7.9	10.5	27.1	35.6	19.0	192,285

COUNTY	FINANCIAL SERVICES				THE HOME						ENTERTAINMENT						PERSONAL			
					Home Improvements		Furnishings													
	Auto Loan	Home Loan	Invest-ments	Retire-ment Plans	Home Repair	Lawn & Garden	Comput-ers & Hard-ware	Major Appli-ances	TV, Radio, Sound Equip-ment	Furni-ture	Dine out/ Carry out	Sports Equip-ment	Fees & Tickets	Toys & Games	Travel	Cable TV	Apparel & Services	Auto Repairs	Health Insur-ance	Pets & Supplies
ADAMS	67	54	50	54	56	68	57	62	63	56	62	54	53	63	56	67	54	62	70	66
ALCORN	71	53	41	51	57	73	54	65	61	53	60	57	48	63	54	65	52	61	71	69
AMITE	71	47	24	44	53	75	48	64	56	47	55	57	39	59	47	61	47	58	70	71
ATTALA	65	46	33	45	51	68	49	60	56	47	55	52	42	57	48	60	47	56	66	64
BENTON	65	43	20	39	47	68	43	58	51	42	51	52	35	54	42	56	43	53	63	65
BOLIVAR	61	47	42	47	48	59	51	55	57	50	56	48	46	56	50	61	49	55	62	58
CALHOUN	73	49	25	45	54	76	49	65	57	48	57	58	40	61	48	63	48	59	71	72
CARROLL	84	56	28	52	64	90	57	76	66	55	66	68	46	69	56	72	56	69	83	84
CHICKASAW	70	47	26	45	52	72	48	62	56	47	56	56	40	59	47	61	47	57	68	68
CHOCTAW	69	48	33	46	53	71	51	62	57	48	57	56	43	60	49	62	49	58	68	68
CLAIBORNE	66	45	26	43	49	68	46	59	55	46	54	53	39	56	46	60	46	55	65	65
CLARKE	72	49	26	45	54	76	50	65	58	48	57	58	41	61	49	63	49	60	72	72
CLAY	73	54	42	53	57	73	57	65	64	56	63	57	51	66	55	68	55	63	72	70
COAHOMA	58	47	48	49	47	55	51	52	58	52	57	45	49	57	50	61	51	54	60	55
COPIAH	68	48	33	46	51	69	50	60	58	49	57	53	43	59	49	62	48	57	68	66
COVINGTON	79	54	30	50	59	82	55	71	64	54	63	63	46	67	54	69	54	65	77	78
DESOTO	98	99	94	100	94	95	92	94	91	95	91	86	93	95	92	90	82	92	91	95
FORREST	63	52	52	54	51	57	62	58	63	57	62	53	56	62	57	63	55	61	61	59
FRANKLIN	70	46	22	43	52	75	47	64	55	46	55	57	38	58	47	61	47	58	69	71
GEORGE	82	61	39	58	63	82	59	73	66	59	66	65	52	70	58	70	57	68	77	79
GREENE	74	50	28	47	55	76	51	65	58	50	58	58	42	62	50	63	49	60	71	72
GRENADA	69	51	39	50	53	68	53	62	60	52	59	54	47	61	52	64	51	60	68	66
HANCOCK	74	66	61	65	68	78	65	73	68	64	67	63	62	68	67	71	59	70	77	74
HARRISON	75	68	69	69	66	70	71	70	73	70	72	63	69	73	69	73	64	72	73	72
HINDS	78	71	74	74	68	72	74	72	78	75	77	64	73	77	73	79	69	75	76	74
HOLMES	55	37	26	37	40	55	41	49	49	40	48	43	35	49	40	53	41	48	56	53
HUMPHREYS	56	41	33	41	43	55	44	50	51	44	49	44	39	51	43	54	43	49	56	54
ISSAQUENA	58	41	29	40	44	59	43	52	51	43	50	45	38	51	43	56	43	51	59	57
ITAWAMBA	80	56	34	53	61	82	56	71	63	55	63	63	48	67	55	68	54	65	76	78
JACKSON	80	75	73	75	74	79	72	76	75	74	75	67	72	76	73	77	66	75	79	78
JASPER	69	45	21	41	50	71	46	61	55	45	54	55	37	57	45	60	46	56	67	68
JEFFERSON	50	35	24	34	37	50	37	44	45	37	44	39	32	44	36	49	37	43	51	49
JEFFERSON DAVIS	66	43	20	40	48	69	44	59	53	43	52	54	36	55	43	58	44	54	65	66
JONES	75	55	41	54	59	77	57	68	64	56	63	60	50	66	56	69	54	64	75	73
KEMPER	64	42	23	40	47	66	44	57	53	43	52	51	36	54	43	58	44	53	64	63
LAFAYETTE	69	52	50	55	52	60	70	62	67	60	67	59	60	66	61	66	59	66	63	64
LAMAR	92	82	70	82	80	87	83	85	84	82	84	79	79	86	80	84	75	85	85	88
LAUDERDALE	70	58	55	58	58	67	61	64	66	60	65	56	57	66	60	69	58	64	70	67
LAWRENCE	75	51	29	48	57	79	53	68	61	50	60	61	43	64	52	66	51	62	75	74
LEAKE	71	47	27	45	52	72	50	63	58	48	57	56	41	60	49	63	49	59	70	69
LEE	85	72	65	72	73	84	73	79	77	72	77	70	69	79	72	80	68	77	83	83
LEFLORE	57	46	47	48	46	53	51	51	57	51	56	44	48	56	49	60	50	54	58	54
LINCOLN	69	53	42	51	55	70	54	63	60	53	60	55	48	62	53	64	52	60	69	67
LOWNDES	75	64	60	65	64	73	66	69	70	66	69	61	63	71	65	72	61	69	74	72
MADISON	114	110	103	114	105	106	109	106	108	112	109	99	108	111	106	107	98	108	103	109
MARION	65	46	29	43	50	68	47	59	54	46	54	52	40	56	46	59	46	55	66	65
MARSHALL	78	54	32	52	58	79	55	69	64	55	63	62	47	67	54	69	54	65	76	76
MONROE	71	52	38	51	56	72	53	64	60	53	60	56	47	63	52	64	51	60	70	69
MONTGOMERY	68	47	30	45	51	69	49	61	57	48	56	54	42	59	48	62	48	57	68	66
NESHOBA	72	54	42	53	57	72	56	65	62	55	62	57	50	64	55	66	53	62	71	70
NEWTON	74	51	30	48	57	78	52	67	60	51	59	59	44	63	52	65	51	62	73	73
NOXUBEE	67	44	24	42	49	69	46	59	55	45	54	53	38	57	45	60	46	56	66	66
OKTIBBEHA	62	45	44	48	45	53	66	55	63	54	63	54	54	61	56	61	55	60	57	58
PANOLA	71	50	33	48	54	73	52	64	60	51	59	57	44	62	51	64	50	60	71	70
PEARL RIVER	76	60	46	58	64	79	59	71	65	58	64	62	54	67	59	69	56	66	76	75
PERRY	67	49	31	46	52	67	49	60	55	48	55	54	43	58	48	59	47	57	65	65
PIKE	67	50	39	49	53	67	52	61	60	52	59	54	47	60	52	64	51	59	68	65
PONTOTOC	83	59	37	56	63	85	59	74	67	58	66	66	51	71	58	72	57	68	80	80
PRENTISS	70	50	36	48	55	72	52	63	59	50	58	56	45	61	51	63	50	59	70	70
QUITMAN	53	39	34	39	40	51	42	47	50	42	48	40	38	48	41	53	42	47	54	50
RANKIN	97	93	85	93	89	92	89	91	90	90	89	83	88	92	88	90	80	90	90	93
SCOTT	77	52	27	48	57	79	53	68	62	52	61	62	44	65	52	67	52	63	75	76
SHARKEY	63	44	32	43	47	63	47	56	55	46	54	49	41	56	46	60	47	54	64	61
SIMPSON	71	50	34	48	54	72	52	64	60	51	59	57	45	62	51	65	51	60	71	69
SMITH	81	55	31	52	60	83	56	72	64	54	64	64	47	68	55	69	54	66	78	79
STONE	77	62	49	61	62	75	62	70	67	61	66	62	57	69	61	70	57	67	74	73
SUNFLOWER	63	51	47	52	51	61	54	57	60	54	59	50	50	60	53	63	52	58	64	61
TALLAHATCHIE	59	40	25	38	43	60	42	52	50	41	49	46	35	51	41	55	42	50	59	57
TATE	86	67	52	66	69	86	67	78	73	67	73	69	61	76	66	77	63	74	83	83
TIPPAH	72	50	31	47	54	74	51	64	58	50	58	57	43	61	50	63	49	59	70	70
TISHOMINGO	74	52	34	49	57	77	53	66	60	51	59	59	45	63	52	65	51	61	73	72
TUNICA	57	48	49	49	46	52	52	52	56	51	55	46	49	55	50	57	49	54	56	54
UNION	80	58	39	55	62	82	58	71	66	57	65	63	50	70	57	70	56	67	78	78
WALTHALL	69	46	24	43	51	72	47	62	56	46	55	55	39	58	47	61	47	57	68	68
WARREN	79	69	67	70	68	76	71	73	75	70	74	65	68	75	70	70	60	74	78	76
WASHINGTON	63	53	54	55	53	61	56	58	62	56	61	50	54	61	55	65	54	59	65	60
WAYNE	71	47	25	44	52	74	49	63	57	47	56	57	40	60	47	62	48	58	69	70
MISSISSIPPI	77	62	52	62	63	76	64	70	69	63	69	63	59	71	63	72	60	69	75	74
UNITED STATES	100	100	100	100	100	100	100	100	100	100	100	100	100	100	100	100	100	100	100	100

POPULATION CHANGE

COUNTY	FIPS Code	CBSA Code	DMA Code	POPULATION			2000-2007 ANNUAL RATE		RACE (%)					
									White		Black		Asian/Pacific	
				2000	2007	2012	% Rate	State Rank	2000	2007	2000	2007	2000	2007
WEBSTER	155	00000	673	10,294	10,495	10,453	0.3	40	77.6	75.8	20.9	22.2	0.2	0.3
WILKINSON	157	00000	716	10,312	10,350	10,239	0.1	52	31.2	30.4	68.2	69.0	0.0	0.0
WINSTON	159	00000	673	20,160	20,531	20,778	0.3	40	55.3	53.1	43.2	45.1	0.1	0.1
YALOBUSHA	161	00000	673	13,051	13,573	13,933	0.5	28	60.5	58.4	38.7	40.6	0.2	0.2
YAZOO	163	49540	718	28,149	29,683	29,588	0.7	18	44.7	43.3	54.0	55.1	0.4	0.5
MISSISSIPPI							0.6		61.4	60.1	36.3	37.0	0.7	0.9
UNITED STATES							1.2		75.1	72.7	12.3	12.6	3.8	4.5

COUNTY	% HISPANIC ORIGIN		2007 AGE DISTRIBUTION (%)										MEDIAN AGE	% 2007 Males	% 2007 Females
	2000	2007	0-4	5-9	10-14	15-19	20-24	25-44	45-64	65-84	85+	18+	2007		
WEBSTER	1.7	2.2	7.4	6.8	6.3	6.0	7.1	24.7	25.8	13.2	2.6	76.0	38.9	48.7	51.3
WILKINSON	0.4	0.4	6.0	5.8	6.4	6.2	9.6	27.7	25.0	10.7	2.6	78.1	36.4	52.9	47.1
WINSTON	1.2	1.5	7.0	6.5	6.6	6.5	7.2	25.3	25.8	12.8	2.3	75.9	37.9	49.2	50.8
YALOBUSHA	1.0	1.2	6.7	6.3	6.8	5.6	6.0	25.6	27.2	13.5	2.3	76.8	39.6	48.6	51.4
YAZOO	4.4	5.6	7.5	6.7	6.9	6.2	6.8	30.6	24.0	9.7	1.7	75.1	34.9	54.0	46.0
MISSISSIPPI	1.4	1.8	7.4	7.0	6.9	7.0	7.5	27.4	24.6	10.5	1.7	74.8	35.2	48.6	51.4
UNITED STATES	12.5	15.0	6.9	6.5	6.8	7.1	7.0	27.6	25.4	10.7	1.9	75.6	36.7	49.2	50.8

COUNTY	HOUSEHOLDS					FAMILIES			MEDIAN HOUSEHOLD INCOME			
	2000	2007	2012	% Annual Rate 2000-2007	2007 Average HH Size	2000	2007	% Annual Rate 2000-2007	2007	2012	2007 National Rank	2007 State Rank
WEBSTER	3,905	4,033	4,032	0.4	2.55	2,877	2,910	0.2	32,219	35,131	2742	30
WILKINSON	3,578	3,672	3,680	0.4	2.49	2,510	2,515	0.0	21,837	23,872	3127	80
WINSTON	7,578	7,919	8,097	0.6	2.52	5,473	5,594	0.3	31,933	34,940	2770	34
YALOBUSHA	5,260	5,607	5,812	0.9	2.40	3,599	3,741	0.5	29,864	32,479	2917	51
YAZOO	9,178	9,264	9,264	0.1	2.77	6,644	6,558	-0.2	28,222	30,813	2993	59
MISSISSIPPI				0.9	2.57			0.6	35,903	39,445		
UNITED STATES				1.2	2.59			1.0	53,154	62,503		

COUNTY	2007 Per Capita Income	2007 HH Income Base	2007 HOUSEHOLD INCOME DISTRIBUTION (%)					2007 Home Value Base	2007 HOME VALUE DISTRIBUTION (%)					2007 Median Home Value
			Less than $25,000	$25,000 to $49,999	$50,000 to $99,999	$100,000 to $149,999	$150,000 or More		Less than $50,000	$50,000 to $89,999	$90,000 to $174,999	$175,000 to $399,999	$400,000 or More	
WEBSTER	16,144	4,033	39.8	32.0	23.0	3.7	1.5	3,151	28.0	33.7	30.6	7.0	0.8	73,946
WILKINSON	14,191	3,672	54.1	25.8	15.4	2.4	2.3	3,031	44.0	29.6	19.4	5.2	1.8	57,062
WINSTON	16,841	7,919	39.4	31.3	23.1	4.2	1.9	6,276	25.6	31.4	32.3	8.6	2.0	81,314
YALOBUSHA	17,068	5,607	41.3	31.4	21.8	4.0	1.6	4,435	32.7	34.9	22.4	8.6	1.5	68,033
YAZOO	13,906	9,264	45.5	27.8	20.4	4.4	1.8	6,382	32.1	31.6	27.8	8.1	0.4	71,102
MISSISSIPPI	18,800		35.6	29.5	25.6	6.3	3.0		22.0	26.4	34.0	15.1	2.5	92,555
UNITED STATES	27,916		21.9	25.0	32.3	12.3	8.4		7.9	10.5	27.1	35.6	19.0	192,285

SPENDING POTENTIAL INDICES

COUNTY	FINANCIAL SERVICES				THE HOME						ENTERTAINMENT						PERSONAL			
					Home Improvements		Furnishings													
	Auto Loan	Home Loan	Invest-ments	Retire-ment Plans	Home Repair	Lawn & Garden	Comput-ers & Hard-ware	Major Appli-ances	TV, Radio, Sound Equip-ment	Furni-ture	Dine out/ Carry out	Sports Equip-ment	Fees & Tickets	Toys & Games	Travel	Cable TV	Apparel & Services	Auto Repairs	Health Insur-ance	Pets & Supplies
WEBSTER	71	49	32	46	54	73	52	64	59	49	58	57	43	61	50	64	50	60	70	70
WILKINSON	65	42	21	40	47	67	44	58	53	43	52	52	36	54	43	58	44	54	64	64
WINSTON	71	51	36	49	55	73	54	65	62	52	60	57	46	63	53	66	52	61	72	70
YALOBUSHA	72	49	27	45	54	76	50	65	58	48	57	58	41	60	49	63	49	60	72	72
YAZOO	65	48	38	48	50	65	51	58	58	50	57	51	45	58	50	62	50	57	65	63
MISSISSIPPI	77	62	52	62	63	76	64	70	69	63	69	63	59	71	63	72	60	69	75	74
UNITED STATES	100	100	100	100	100	100	100	100	100	100	100	100	100	100	100	100	100	100	100	100

COUNTY	FIPS Code	CBSA Code	DMA Code	POPULATION			2000-2007 ANNUAL RATE		RACE (%)					
									White		Black		Asian/Pacific	
				2000	2007	2012	% Rate	State Rank	2000	2007	2000	2007	2000	2007
ADAIR	001	28860	631	24,977	24,648	24,297	-0.2	102	95.8	93.0	1.2	3.2	1.4	2.0
ANDREW	003	41140	638	16,492	17,136	17,590	0.5	52	98.4	98.1	0.4	0.5	0.2	0.3
ATCHISON	005	00000	652	6,430	6,060	5,827	-0.8	115	97.0	96.6	2.1	2.3	0.1	0.2
AUDRAIN	007	33020	604	25,853	25,525	25,088	-0.2	102	91.1	89.9	7.2	8.1	0.4	0.5
BARRY	009	00000	619	34,010	36,298	37,768	0.9	28	94.1	92.9	0.1	0.1	0.3	0.4
BARTON	011	00000	603	12,541	13,100	13,507	0.6	45	96.9	96.5	0.3	0.3	0.4	0.5
BATES	013	28140	616	16,653	17,072	17,377	0.3	62	97.3	96.9	0.6	0.7	0.2	0.2
BENTON	015	00000	619	17,180	19,119	20,646	1.5	14	98.0	97.7	0.1	0.2	0.1	0.2
BOLLINGER	017	16020	632	12,029	12,291	12,427	0.3	62	97.8	97.5	0.2	0.2	0.2	0.3
BOONE	019	17860	604	135,454	150,922	160,089	1.5	14	85.4	82.7	8.5	9.7	3.0	4.2
BUCHANAN	021	41140	638	85,998	86,100	86,175	0.0	91	92.7	91.6	4.4	4.9	0.5	0.7
BUTLER	023	38740	632	40,867	40,921	40,977	0.0	91	92.2	91.8	5.2	5.6	0.4	0.5
CALDWELL	025	28140	616	8,969	9,166	9,257	0.3	62	98.6	98.4	0.1	0.2	0.1	0.2
CALLAWAY	027	27620	604	40,766	43,388	45,616	0.9	28	91.8	90.4	5.7	6.3	0.5	0.9
CAMDEN	029	00000	619	37,051	40,749	43,358	1.3	17	97.7	97.3	0.3	0.3	0.3	0.5
CAPE GIRARDEAU	031	16020	632	68,693	71,726	73,925	0.6	45	92.1	90.3	5.3	6.5	0.8	1.1
CARROLL	033	00000	616	10,285	10,196	10,129	-0.1	97	96.9	96.8	1.7	1.9	0.1	0.1
CARTER	035	00000	632	5,941	6,226	6,248	0.6	45	96.6	96.2	0.1	0.1	0.1	0.2
CASS	037	28140	616	82,092	99,191	113,378	2.6	5	95.6	94.9	1.4	1.6	0.5	0.7
CEDAR	039	00000	619	13,733	14,220	14,571	0.5	52	96.6	96.0	0.3	0.4	0.5	0.7
CHARITON	041	00000	604	8,438	8,055	7,810	-0.6	111	96.0	95.5	3.2	3.6	0.1	0.2
CHRISTIAN	043	44180	619	54,285	72,466	89,266	4.1	1	97.3	96.8	0.3	0.3	0.3	0.5
CLARK	045	22800	717	7,416	7,418	7,412	0.0	91	98.8	98.8	0.1	0.1	0.1	0.1
CLAY	047	28140	616	184,006	206,419	224,112	1.6	11	92.5	91.0	2.7	3.0	1.4	2.0
CLINTON	049	28140	616	18,979	21,263	22,915	1.6	11	96.6	96.1	1.5	1.7	0.2	0.2
COLE	051	27620	604	71,397	74,498	76,600	0.6	45	87.1	85.2	9.9	11.0	0.9	1.4
COOPER	053	00000	604	16,670	17,617	18,285	0.8	36	89.0	87.7	9.0	10.0	0.3	0.4
CRAWFORD	055	00000	609	22,804	24,128	25,107	0.8	36	98.3	98.0	0.1	0.2	0.2	0.3
DADE	057	00000	619	7,923	8,056	8,161	0.2	74	97.5	97.1	0.3	0.3	0.2	0.3
DALLAS	059	44180	619	15,661	16,677	17,258	0.9	28	97.5	97.1	0.1	0.1	0.1	0.1
DAVIESS	061	00000	616	8,016	8,201	8,355	0.3	62	98.7	98.5	0.0	0.0	0.3	0.4
DEKALB	063	41140	638	11,597	12,661	12,886	1.2	20	89.1	85.2	8.9	12.0	0.2	0.5
DENT	065	00000	619	14,927	15,111	15,201	0.2	74	97.1	96.6	0.4	0.4	0.2	0.3
DOUGLAS	067	00000	619	13,084	13,668	14,067	0.6	45	96.9	96.4	0.1	0.1	0.2	0.3
DUNKLIN	069	28380	632	33,155	32,491	31,999	-0.3	105	88.6	87.1	8.7	9.7	0.4	0.4
FRANKLIN	071	41180	609	93,807	102,632	109,395	1.2	20	97.5	97.1	0.9	1.1	0.3	0.4
GASCONADE	073	00000	609	15,342	16,179	16,822	0.7	40	98.7	98.5	0.1	0.1	0.2	0.2
GENTRY	075	00000	616	6,861	6,673	6,564	-0.4	107	98.6	98.3	0.1	0.1	0.3	0.5
GREENE	077	44180	619	240,391	259,829	274,565	1.1	23	93.5	92.4	2.3	2.5	1.2	1.7
GRUNDY	079	00000	616	10,432	10,485	10,533	0.1	83	97.6	97.6	0.4	0.4	0.2	0.2
HARRISON	081	00000	616	8,850	8,906	8,967	0.1	83	98.3	98.3	0.1	0.1	0.2	0.2
HENRY	083	00000	616	21,997	22,457	22,728	0.3	62	96.6	96.1	1.0	1.2	0.3	0.4
HICKORY	085	00000	619	8,940	9,483	9,805	0.8	36	97.5	96.9	0.1	0.4	0.1	0.1
HOLT	087	00000	616	5,351	5,107	4,945	-0.6	111	98.5	98.3	0.1	0.1	0.2	0.2
HOWARD	089	17860	604	10,212	10,189	10,166	0.0	91	91.1	90.6	6.8	7.3	0.2	0.2
HOWELL	091	48460	619	37,238	38,957	40,184	0.6	45	96.4	95.9	0.3	0.3	0.4	0.6
IRON	093	00000	609	10,697	10,725	10,732	0.0	91	96.7	96.6	1.6	1.7	0.1	0.1
JACKSON	095	28140	616	654,880	673,880	687,627	0.4	56	70.1	67.0	23.3	25.1	1.5	2.0
JASPER	097	27900	603	104,686	112,096	117,624	0.9	28	92.6	91.3	1.5	1.7	0.8	1.1
JEFFERSON	099	41180	609	198,099	220,843	237,867	1.5	14	97.5	97.0	0.7	0.8	0.4	0.5
JOHNSON	101	47660	616	48,258	51,650	53,893	0.9	28	90.1	88.4	4.3	4.8	1.6	2.2
KNOX	103	00000	717	4,361	4,225	4,123	-0.4	107	98.5	98.3	0.1	0.1	0.1	0.2
LACLEDE	105	30060	619	32,513	35,266	37,341	1.1	23	97.0	96.5	0.4	0.5	0.3	0.5
LAFAYETTE	107	28140	616	32,960	33,479	33,815	0.2	74	95.5	94.8	2.3	2.6	0.3	0.4
LAWRENCE	109	00000	619	35,204	37,303	38,845	0.8	36	95.7	94.9	0.3	0.3	0.4	0.4
LEWIS	111	39500	717	10,494	10,531	10,567	0.0	91	95.9	95.7	2.5	2.7	0.2	0.2
LINCOLN	113	41180	609	38,944	49,727	60,395	3.4	2	96.1	95.5	1.7	2.0	0.2	0.3
LINN	115	00000	616	13,754	13,173	12,736	-0.6	111	98.0	97.7	0.6	0.7	0.1	0.2
LIVINGSTON	117	00000	616	14,558	14,391	14,255	-0.2	102	95.9	95.3	2.3	2.6	0.3	0.4
MCDONALD	119	22220	603	21,681	23,037	23,753	0.8	36	89.7	88.2	0.2	0.2	0.3	0.4
MACON	121	00000	631	15,762	15,758	15,784	0.0	91	96.2	96.0	2.2	2.4	0.2	0.2
MADISON	123	00000	632	11,800	11,992	12,114	0.2	74	98.3	98.0	0.1	0.1	0.3	0.4
MARIES	125	00000	604	8,903	9,331	9,680	0.6	45	97.4	97.0	0.3	0.4	0.1	0.2
MARION	127	25300	717	28,289	28,659	28,916	0.2	74	93.3	92.3	4.6	5.2	0.4	0.5
MERCER	129	00000	616	3,757	3,593	3,479	-0.6	111	98.7	98.6	0.2	0.2	0.1	0.1
MILLER	131	00000	604	23,564	25,022	25,812	0.8	36	98.0	97.7	0.3	0.3	0.1	0.2
MISSISSIPPI	133	00000	632	13,427	13,584	13,313	0.2	74	77.9	75.6	20.5	22.7	0.1	0.2
MONITEAU	135	27620	604	14,827	15,351	15,848	0.5	52	92.7	91.6	3.8	4.2	0.3	0.5
MONROE	137	00000	717	9,311	9,505	9,632	0.3	62	94.7	94.0	3.8	4.3	0.2	0.2
MONTGOMERY	139	00000	604	12,136	12,573	12,862	0.5	52	96.0	95.4	2.0	2.3	0.1	0.4
MORGAN	141	00000	604	19,309	21,754	23,708	1.7	9	97.3	97.0	0.5	0.6	0.1	0.2
NEW MADRID	143	00000	632	19,760	18,993	18,482	-0.5	108	83.2	81.3	15.4	17.1	0.1	0.2
NEWTON	145	27900	603	52,636	56,067	58,601	0.9	28	93.3	92.3	0.6	0.7	0.6	0.8
NODAWAY	147	32340	616	21,912	22,000	22,106	0.1	83	96.6	95.8	1.3	1.5	0.9	1.3
OREGON	149	00000	619	10,344	10,491	10,593	0.2	74	94.6	94.1	0.1	0.1	0.1	0.2
OSAGE	151	27620	604	13,062	13,688	14,184	0.6	45	98.6	98.4	0.2	0.2	0.1	0.1
OZARK	153	00000	619	9,542	9,720	9,840	0.3	62	97.6	97.2	0.1	0.2	0.1	0.1
MISSOURI							0.8		84.9	83.7	11.2	11.7	1.2	1.6
UNITED STATES							1.2		75.1	72.7	12.3	12.6	3.8	4.5

POPULATION COMPOSITION

COUNTY	% HISPANIC ORIGIN		2007 AGE DISTRIBUTION (%)										MEDIAN AGE	% 2007 Males	% 2007 Females
	2000	2007	0-4	5-9	10-14	15-19	20-24	25-44	45-64	65-84	85+	18+	2007		
ADAIR	1.3	1.5	5.4	4.7	4.5	10.4	16.9	24.0	21.7	10.1	2.3	82.2	30.5	48.0	52.0
ANDREW	0.8	1.1	6.5	6.3	6.8	6.4	6.0	25.4	28.8	11.4	2.4	76.4	40.2	48.8	51.2
ATCHISON	0.7	0.8	4.8	4.1	6.5	7.7	6.6	21.7	29.6	15.0	4.0	79.8	43.9	50.2	49.8
AUDRAIN	0.7	0.9	6.6	6.0	6.1	6.1	6.4	27.3	25.4	13.0	3.1	77.5	39.3	45.5	54.5
BARRY	5.0	6.3	7.0	6.5	6.9	6.3	6.2	24.6	26.1	14.3	2.1	75.8	39.9	49.8	50.2
BARTON	0.9	1.2	8.1	7.6	6.9	6.6	6.5	24.4	25.8	12.5	2.5	73.9	38.2	49.2	50.8
BATES	1.1	1.4	6.7	6.0	6.3	6.5	6.9	24.5	26.3	13.7	3.0	77.0	40.5	48.8	51.2
BENTON	0.9	1.1	4.6	4.5	4.5	5.6	5.2	18.0	32.4	22.8	2.5	82.9	50.3	49.7	50.3
BOLLINGER	0.6	0.7	6.4	5.8	6.5	6.8	6.6	25.5	26.9	13.7	1.7	77.1	39.8	49.7	50.3
BOONE	1.8	2.2	6.2	5.5	5.8	9.7	13.4	28.6	22.0	7.4	1.4	78.7	30.1	48.5	51.5
BUCHANAN	2.4	3.0	6.5	5.8	6.1	7.4	7.7	27.7	24.4	12.0	2.6	77.7	37.3	49.5	50.5
BUTLER	1.0	1.0	6.6	6.1	5.8	6.0	6.2	25.5	27.0	14.5	2.3	77.9	40.4	48.1	51.9
CALDWELL	0.7	0.9	6.6	6.2	6.7	7.4	6.0	23.6	27.0	13.6	2.8	75.7	40.6	49.5	50.5
CALLAWAY	0.9	1.2	6.4	5.9	6.7	8.2	8.6	27.4	25.4	9.9	1.6	77.1	36.4	50.3	49.7
CAMDEN	0.9	1.2	4.6	4.4	4.7	5.2	4.8	20.0	34.6	20.0	1.6	82.9	48.8	50.2	49.8
CAPE GIRARDEAU	0.9	1.2	6.0	5.5	6.0	7.5	8.7	26.7	25.6	11.5	2.4	78.6	37.2	48.9	51.1
CARROLL	0.7	0.7	6.9	6.5	5.8	6.1	5.6	23.5	27.1	15.2	3.3	77.3	41.8	48.9	51.1
CARTER	1.2	1.5	6.4	6.3	6.0	6.3	5.4	24.9	28.3	14.4	2.0	77.6	41.5	48.9	51.1
CASS	2.2	2.8	7.5	7.1	7.0	7.2	6.2	26.4	26.2	10.5	1.9	73.8	37.6	49.1	50.9
CEDAR	1.1	1.4	5.8	5.6	5.7	7.5	5.7	20.7	28.5	17.6	2.9	78.0	44.3	49.4	50.6
CHARITON	0.6	0.7	5.9	5.1	5.1	5.7	7.3	20.9	29.0	16.7	4.3	80.3	45.0	48.3	51.7
CHRISTIAN	1.3	1.7	7.9	7.3	6.9	6.8	6.6	28.7	25.2	9.2	1.3	73.8	35.2	48.6	51.4
CLARK	0.7	0.7	6.5	6.0	6.3	5.9	5.6	25.3	27.7	13.8	2.8	77.5	41.3	49.8	50.2
CLAY	3.6	4.5	7.5	6.9	6.6	6.7	6.6	29.6	25.4	9.3	1.4	74.9	36.0	48.7	51.3
CLINTON	1.1	1.4	6.9	6.5	6.0	6.8	7.2	24.4	27.6	11.9	2.6	76.1	40.0	49.1	50.9
COLE	1.3	1.6	6.5	6.2	6.0	7.0	7.5	28.5	26.6	9.8	1.9	77.4	37.0	50.4	49.6
COOPER	0.9	1.1	5.9	5.7	5.9	7.1	10.7	24.7	25.3	11.8	2.8	78.8	36.7	54.0	46.0
CRAWFORD	0.8	1.0	6.9	6.4	6.4	6.3	6.3	25.1	26.4	14.0	2.2	76.3	39.9	49.3	50.7
DADE	0.8	1.1	6.5	6.1	5.3	6.2	6.2	21.6	28.3	16.4	3.4	78.5	43.6	49.0	51.0
DALLAS	0.9	1.2	7.0	6.9	6.3	7.0	6.3	23.8	27.8	12.9	2.0	75.2	39.6	49.7	50.3
DAVIESS	0.7	0.9	7.6	7.0	6.3	6.4	5.3	23.3	27.2	14.3	2.6	75.1	40.3	48.3	51.7
DEKALB	1.1	1.4	5.4	4.7	4.8	7.5	8.5	32.4	23.9	10.8	2.0	82.0	37.7	59.3	40.7
DENT	0.8	0.9	6.8	6.5	6.0	5.7	5.8	23.6	27.2	15.5	2.9	77.2	41.9	48.6	51.4
DOUGLAS	0.8	1.1	6.2	5.6	5.7	6.3	7.5	21.4	28.7	16.1	2.4	78.5	42.8	49.4	50.6
DUNKLIN	2.5	3.1	7.4	6.9	6.4	6.1	5.7	25.1	25.6	13.9	2.8	75.5	39.2	47.8	52.2
FRANKLIN	0.7	0.9	7.2	6.7	7.0	6.6	6.4	27.3	26.6	10.6	1.6	75.2	38.0	50.0	50.0
GASCONADE	0.4	0.5	6.3	5.9	5.8	6.6	6.1	23.3	27.7	15.1	3.3	77.8	42.4	49.1	50.9
GENTRY	0.6	0.8	6.8	6.1	6.4	6.3	6.6	23.0	24.3	16.0	4.4	76.6	41.5	49.3	50.7
GREENE	1.8	2.3	6.2	5.8	5.7	7.2	9.0	27.6	25.2	11.1	2.2	78.8	36.4	48.8	51.2
GRUNDY	1.6	1.6	6.3	5.7	5.8	6.8	6.3	21.6	27.2	16.4	4.0	78.6	43.1	47.6	52.4
HARRISON	1.0	1.0	7.1	6.6	5.2	5.6	5.5	22.6	26.1	17.0	4.2	77.7	42.8	49.1	50.9
HENRY	0.9	1.1	6.1	5.4	5.7	6.3	5.9	24.4	27.5	15.5	3.1	78.9	42.4	49.2	50.8
HICKORY	0.8	0.9	4.5	4.0	4.8	5.8	5.8	16.2	32.1	24.0	2.9	84.0	51.9	49.3	50.7
HOLT	0.4	0.5	5.3	4.6	5.8	6.4	6.1	23.4	28.7	15.5	4.1	80.3	44.0	50.1	49.9
HOWARD	0.9	0.9	6.2	5.4	5.9	7.8	9.9	23.8	26.1	11.9	3.0	78.8	37.8	48.4	51.6
HOWELL	1.2	1.5	7.0	6.3	6.0	6.5	7.1	23.8	26.0	14.7	2.6	76.7	40.1	48.6	51.4
IRON	0.6	0.6	6.2	5.7	6.0	5.8	6.2	23.5	28.6	15.1	2.8	78.4	42.4	48.4	51.6
JACKSON	5.4	6.5	7.1	6.6	6.6	6.8	6.8	28.4	25.4	10.6	1.9	75.7	36.6	48.3	51.7
JASPER	3.5	4.3	7.4	6.6	6.6	6.8	7.2	27.3	24.8	11.1	2.0	75.5	35.8	48.8	51.2
JEFFERSON	1.0	1.3	7.3	6.8	6.8	6.8	6.5	28.8	26.9	9.0	1.1	74.9	36.9	49.8	50.2
JOHNSON	2.9	3.6	6.9	5.9	6.1	9.4	14.3	26.6	21.0	8.4	1.4	77.4	29.4	50.6	49.4
KNOX	0.6	0.8	6.7	6.2	5.9	5.9	5.9	21.9	27.0	17.0	3.5	77.4	43.5	48.2	51.8
LACLEDE	1.2	1.6	7.3	6.7	6.4	6.3	6.7	26.6	25.7	12.3	1.9	75.7	38.2	49.2	50.8
LAFAYETTE	1.2	1.5	6.5	5.8	6.6	6.8	6.7	25.4	26.9	12.6	2.6	76.8	40.0	49.0	51.0
LAWRENCE	3.4	4.3	7.6	7.0	6.9	6.4	6.2	25.4	25.0	13.0	2.4	74.5	38.1	49.8	50.2
LEWIS	0.7	0.8	7.4	6.9	5.8	7.7	8.7	23.3	23.8	13.2	3.1	76.2	37.3	49.5	50.5
LINCOLN	1.1	1.4	7.8	6.6	7.5	7.8	7.2	26.8	25.8	9.1	1.4	73.1	36.2	49.5	50.5
LINN	0.8	0.9	6.8	5.9	6.1	6.1	7.4	22.3	26.0	15.5	3.9	77.4	41.4	47.5	52.5
LIVINGSTON	0.6	0.8	6.6	5.9	5.9	5.5	7.8	23.5	26.8	14.3	3.7	78.2	41.1	46.4	53.6
MCDONALD	9.4	11.6	8.0	7.6	7.5	6.9	6.1	27.9	24.1	10.5	1.3	72.7	35.8	51.0	49.0
MACON	0.8	0.8	6.8	6.2	6.2	5.4	6.3	23.5	27.2	14.8	3.7	77.5	41.7	49.2	50.8
MADISON	0.6	0.7	6.2	5.8	5.7	6.4	6.4	24.8	27.5	14.5	2.8	78.4	41.4	48.3	51.7
MARIES	1.2	1.5	7.0	6.5	6.2	6.5	5.7	24.9	27.3	14.2	1.8	76.5	40.7	51.1	48.9
MARION	0.9	1.1	6.9	6.3	6.5	7.3	7.5	24.4	25.4	12.7	3.1	76.0	38.6	47.4	52.6
MERCER	0.3	0.3	6.1	5.7	5.4	5.0	6.6	21.2	29.0	17.4	3.7	80.0	45.1	49.0	51.0
MILLER	1.0	1.2	7.2	6.8	6.4	6.1	6.4	25.9	26.3	12.7	2.1	75.8	38.8	49.5	50.5
MISSISSIPPI	1.0	1.2	7.3	7.0	5.5	6.5	6.3	25.5	24.8	13.7	3.4	76.1	39.3	46.8	53.2
MONITEAU	2.9	3.7	7.1	6.6	6.6	6.1	7.0	29.2	24.5	10.5	2.3	75.9	36.6	53.1	46.9
MONROE	0.6	0.7	7.0	6.7	5.7	6.3	6.6	23.1	26.6	14.9	3.1	76.7	41.3	49.7	50.3
MONTGOMERY	0.8	1.0	6.0	5.4	6.2	6.8	6.8	23.7	28.5	13.1	3.4	78.2	41.7	49.9	50.1
MORGAN	0.8	1.0	6.1	5.9	5.8	5.6	5.1	20.7	28.8	19.5	2.4	78.7	45.6	49.2	50.8
NEW MADRID	0.9	1.1	7.1	6.2	7.0	5.7	6.5	25.5	26.9	12.8	2.3	76.2	38.9	48.3	51.7
NEWTON	2.2	2.7	7.2	6.9	6.6	6.4	6.5	25.6	26.6	12.2	2.0	75.4	38.4	49.1	50.9
NODAWAY	0.7	0.9	4.8	4.5	4.8	11.0	17.7	21.8	21.4	11.1	2.9	82.7	31.0	50.1	49.9
OREGON	1.1	1.4	6.2	5.6	5.7	5.9	5.9	22.6	29.1	15.9	2.9	78.9	43.5	49.1	50.9
OSAGE	0.6	0.7	7.1	6.6	6.5	5.9	5.9	28.6	24.9	12.3	2.2	76.3	38.3	51.0	49.0
OZARK	0.9	1.2	5.6	5.4	5.1	5.1	5.7	21.0	30.3	19.5	2.2	80.8	46.3	49.6	50.4
MISSOURI	2.1	2.6	6.8	6.3	6.5	7.0	7.2	26.7	26.0	11.5	2.1	76.4	37.7	48.8	51.2
UNITED STATES	12.5	15.0	6.9	6.5	6.8	7.1	7.0	27.6	25.4	10.7	1.9	75.6	36.7	49.2	50.8

COUNTY	HOUSEHOLDS					FAMILIES			MEDIAN HOUSEHOLD INCOME			
	2000	2007	2012	% Annual Rate 2000-2007	2007 Average HH Size	2000	2007	% Annual Rate 2000-2007	2007	2012	2007 National Rank	2007 State Rank
ADAIR	9,669	9,649	9,537	0.0	2.27	5,343	5,121	-0.6	33,101	38,531	2648	84
ANDREW	6,273	6,601	6,806	0.7	2.56	4,636	4,764	0.4	49,583	56,608	705	14
ATCHISON	2,722	2,607	2,521	-0.6	2.21	1,778	1,650	-1.0	36,478	40,583	2200	61
AUDRAIN	9,844	9,738	9,607	-0.1	2.39	6,758	6,498	-0.5	39,343	44,504	1809	37
BARRY	13,398	14,364	14,953	1.0	2.50	9,584	10,012	0.6	34,705	39,100	2465	72
BARTON	4,895	5,093	5,238	0.5	2.54	3,440	3,485	0.2	34,979	39,333	2432	70
BATES	6,511	6,686	6,804	0.4	2.51	4,556	4,554	0.0	36,721	41,405	2161	56
BENTON	7,420	8,416	9,160	1.8	2.24	5,176	5,711	1.4	33,998	39,405	2550	77
BOLLINGER	4,576	4,735	4,809	0.5	2.56	3,463	3,504	0.2	36,134	40,751	2251	65
BOONE	53,094	61,033	65,315	1.9	2.33	31,391	34,769	1.4	47,079	54,845	903	18
BUCHANAN	33,557	34,030	34,222	0.2	2.39	21,928	21,545	-0.2	43,197	49,963	1311	27
BUTLER	16,718	17,034	17,175	0.3	2.35	11,313	11,192	-0.1	33,602	38,932	2595	81
CALDWELL	3,523	3,633	3,679	0.4	2.49	2,503	2,514	0.1	36,705	41,351	2165	59
CALLAWAY	14,416	15,918	16,883	1.4	2.53	10,338	11,123	1.0	48,560	55,977	776	15
CAMDEN	15,779	17,710	19,004	1.6	2.27	11,298	12,356	1.2	44,638	51,975	1142	23
CAPE GIRARDEAU	26,980	28,824	29,939	0.9	2.37	17,941	18,591	0.5	44,927	51,963	1116	21
CARROLL	4,169	4,164	4,144	0.0	2.40	2,879	2,795	-0.4	36,363	40,906	2220	63
CARTER	2,378	2,540	2,569	0.9	2.42	1,673	1,740	0.5	27,103	30,650	3035	111
CASS	30,168	36,861	42,349	2.8	2.66	22,978	27,470	2.5	62,362	72,789	206	4
CEDAR	5,685	5,930	6,088	0.6	2.34	3,892	3,944	0.2	32,472	37,261	2710	87
CHARITON	3,469	3,370	3,289	-0.4	2.33	2,344	2,211	-0.8	37,801	42,127	2025	51
CHRISTIAN	20,425	27,650	34,278	4.3	2.60	15,652	20,741	4.0	48,040	56,072	812	16
CLARK	2,966	3,040	3,068	0.3	2.40	2,079	2,072	0.0	34,641	38,729	2481	74
CLAY	72,558	81,546	88,785	1.6	2.50	50,120	54,762	1.2	62,048	72,608	211	5
CLINTON	7,152	8,141	8,829	1.8	2.56	5,301	5,893	1.5	50,762	58,272	625	11
COLE	27,040	29,014	30,083	1.0	2.39	17,940	18,669	0.6	53,638	62,365	468	7
COOPER	5,932	6,403	6,714	1.1	2.43	4,139	4,346	0.7	42,606	48,664	1382	28
CRAWFORD	8,858	9,500	9,936	1.0	2.50	6,354	6,639	0.6	36,708	41,391	2163	57
DADE	3,202	3,269	3,313	0.3	2.43	2,276	2,263	-0.1	34,111	37,833	2539	76
DALLAS	6,030	6,437	6,663	0.9	2.57	4,381	4,563	0.6	32,462	36,949	2713	88
DAVIESS	3,178	3,290	3,365	0.5	2.48	2,265	2,283	0.1	36,167	40,175	2245	64
DEKALB	3,528	3,686	3,791	0.6	2.48	2,472	2,512	0.2	38,005	43,651	1997	49
DENT	5,982	6,157	6,233	0.4	2.41	4,278	4,290	0.0	32,090	36,323	2750	92
DOUGLAS	5,201	5,516	5,709	0.8	2.46	3,672	3,792	0.4	30,581	34,704	2878	102
DUNKLIN	13,411	13,308	13,163	-0.1	2.39	9,166	8,836	-0.5	30,160	34,204	2903	105
FRANKLIN	34,945	38,757	41,586	1.4	2.62	25,689	27,804	1.1	52,992	60,882	503	9
GASCONADE	6,171	6,584	6,875	0.9	2.41	4,291	4,451	0.5	41,642	47,126	1498	32
GENTRY	2,747	2,673	2,627	-0.4	2.42	1,884	1,781	-0.8	33,602	37,527	2595	81
GREENE	97,859	108,798	116,168	1.5	2.28	61,837	66,481	1.0	42,545	49,701	1391	30
GRUNDY	4,382	4,469	4,514	0.3	2.27	2,888	2,855	-0.2	32,543	36,910	2699	86
HARRISON	3,658	3,677	3,697	0.1	2.36	2,489	2,432	-0.3	33,553	37,450	2602	82
HENRY	9,133	9,422	9,568	0.4	2.35	6,245	6,261	0.0	37,159	42,541	2109	54
HICKORY	3,911	4,178	4,328	0.9	2.24	2,737	2,844	0.5	31,340	36,566	2808	96
HOLT	2,237	2,166	2,108	-0.4	2.31	1,503	1,412	-0.9	34,525	38,376	2494	75
HOWARD	3,836	3,865	3,867	0.1	2.43	2,633	2,577	-0.3	38,461	44,169	1936	46
HOWELL	14,762	15,624	16,183	0.8	2.44	10,611	10,947	0.4	30,855	35,149	2849	98
IRON	4,197	4,299	4,340	0.3	2.41	2,962	2,953	0.0	30,406	34,066	2892	104
JACKSON	266,294	277,308	284,169	0.6	2.39	166,143	167,200	0.1	49,741	59,089	694	13
JASPER	41,412	44,280	46,452	0.9	2.47	27,943	29,004	0.5	38,964	45,347	1858	40
JEFFERSON	71,499	80,977	87,877	1.7	2.70	54,528	60,424	1.4	58,703	67,551	293	6
JOHNSON	17,410	18,797	19,712	1.1	2.56	11,814	12,387	0.7	43,525	50,325	1273	25
KNOX	1,791	1,746	1,706	-0.4	2.37	1,217	1,152	-0.8	31,816	35,592	2778	95
LACLEDE	12,760	13,994	14,874	1.3	2.49	9,190	9,823	0.9	36,085	41,247	2260	66
LAFAYETTE	12,569	12,885	13,046	0.3	2.53	9,095	9,090	0.0	46,696	53,402	937	19
LAWRENCE	13,568	14,425	15,023	0.8	2.54	9,735	10,086	0.5	37,524	42,399	2059	53
LEWIS	3,956	4,005	4,030	0.2	2.44	2,710	2,665	-0.2	36,511	41,242	2189	60
LINCOLN	13,851	17,821	21,697	3.5	2.76	10,555	13,285	3.2	53,360	62,088	480	8
LINN	5,697	5,480	5,299	-0.5	2.36	3,761	3,508	-1.0	33,825	38,285	2572	78
LIVINGSTON	5,736	5,749	5,721	0.0	2.34	3,800	3,693	-0.4	39,052	44,972	1846	39
MCDONALD	8,113	8,619	8,878	0.8	2.65	5,867	6,078	0.5	32,394	36,710	2721	89
MACON	6,501	6,588	6,632	0.2	2.34	4,384	4,313	-0.2	35,855	40,376	2303	68
MADISON	4,711	4,858	4,943	0.4	2.42	3,333	3,345	0.0	30,421	34,646	2891	103
MARIES	3,519	3,755	3,924	0.9	2.46	2,502	2,599	0.5	37,578	42,407	2048	52
MARION	11,066	11,363	11,522	0.4	2.41	7,523	7,505	0.0	39,869	46,290	1741	34
MERCER	1,600	1,538	1,490	-0.5	2.30	1,089	1,017	-0.9	34,793	38,210	2457	71
MILLER	9,284	10,009	10,384	1.0	2.46	6,443	6,758	0.7	37,157	42,197	2110	55
MISSISSIPPI	5,383	5,344	5,294	-0.1	2.37	3,673	3,542	-0.5	27,832	31,885	3009	110
MONITEAU	5,259	5,564	5,774	0.8	2.54	3,731	3,845	0.4	44,898	51,018	1122	22
MONROE	3,656	3,787	3,858	0.5	2.46	2,567	2,588	0.1	36,705	41,311	2165	59
MONTGOMERY	4,775	5,024	5,170	0.7	2.44	3,336	3,414	0.3	39,851	45,121	1745	35
MORGAN	7,850	8,921	9,749	1.8	2.41	5,547	6,138	1.4	37,895	44,038	2008	50
NEW MADRID	7,824	7,716	7,589	-0.2	2.42	5,505	5,283	-0.6	32,241	36,563	2740	90
NEWTON	20,140	21,654	22,701	1.0	2.54	14,733	15,456	0.7	42,557	48,600	1390	29
NODAWAY	8,138	8,411	8,561	0.5	2.28	4,818	4,799	-0.1	38,892	44,620	1868	42
OREGON	4,263	4,364	4,418	0.3	2.38	3,010	3,000	0.0	26,110	29,352	3066	114
OSAGE	4,922	5,296	5,550	1.0	2.55	3,580	3,756	0.7	46,275	51,847	977	20
OZARK	3,950	4,068	4,135	0.4	2.37	2,857	2,869	0.1	30,730	34,898	2861	100
MISSOURI				0.9	2.45			0.5	47,568	55,657		
UNITED STATES				1.2	2.59			1.0	53,154	62,503		

COUNTY	2007 Per Capita Income	2007 HH Income Base	2007 HOUSEHOLD INCOME DISTRIBUTION (%)					2007 Home Value Base	2007 HOME VALUE DISTRIBUTION (%)					2007 Median Home Value
			Less than $25,000	$25,000 to $49,999	$50,000 to $99,999	$100,000 to $149,999	$150,000 or More		Less than $50,000	$50,000 to $89,999	$90,000 to $174,999	$175,000 to $399,999	$400,000 or More	
ADAIR	20,550	9,644	39.2	29.0	22.4	5.6	3.8	5,984	17.5	21.6	37.0	20.3	3.6	110,736
ANDREW	24,346	6,601	21.3	29.2	35.1	9.6	4.8	5,372	15.7	15.2	44.9	21.3	2.9	118,898
ATCHISON	21,108	2,607	33.5	33.5	25.0	5.8	2.1	1,856	27.6	30.0	34.3	7.0	1.1	78,403
AUDRAIN	20,128	9,738	29.0	32.5	29.5	6.8	2.2	7,363	18.8	24.5	37.4	17.0	2.3	100,489
BARRY	18,428	14,364	34.3	35.4	23.9	4.1	2.4	11,120	16.0	24.0	38.3	17.9	3.8	104,775
BARTON	17,106	5,093	35.0	32.8	26.5	4.3	1.5	3,831	22.2	28.4	34.8	13.2	1.5	89,005
BATES	18,347	6,686	31.9	34.6	26.5	5.1	1.9	5,122	21.5	26.4	33.0	16.2	2.9	94,059
BENTON	19,867	8,416	36.3	33.2	24.3	4.0	2.2	6,995	18.8	22.5	39.5	17.3	1.9	104,099
BOLLINGER	16,729	4,735	33.4	34.9	26.3	3.8	1.6	3,898	23.4	24.0	34.7	16.0	1.9	94,139
BOONE	26,188	61,033	24.9	27.8	30.5	11.6	5.2	36,243	10.7	10.2	40.9	32.5	5.6	145,346
BUCHANAN	22,391	34,030	27.8	29.3	32.2	7.4	3.3	23,564	15.8	26.6	40.3	15.6	1.7	99,744
BUTLER	19,891	17,034	38.0	31.0	23.0	4.9	3.1	12,083	24.3	26.7	34.0	12.1	2.9	88,065
CALDWELL	18,722	3,633	32.1	33.5	26.9	5.4	2.1	2,862	25.0	24.5	30.2	17.6	2.7	90,980
CALLAWAY	22,080	15,918	21.2	30.1	36.8	8.9	2.9	12,435	15.6	18.3	43.6	19.3	3.2	115,904
CAMDEN	26,246	17,710	23.6	32.7	30.9	8.6	4.3	14,757	10.6	11.8	32.4	35.3	9.9	160,693
CAPE GIRARDEAU	24,030	28,824	26.1	29.0	32.2	8.1	4.5	20,246	11.2	12.9	40.2	30.9	4.9	141,006
CARROLL	19,316	4,164	32.7	36.8	23.3	4.5	2.7	3,152	26.5	26.8	34.2	9.8	2.7	82,482
CARTER	16,242	2,540	46.3	30.8	17.3	3.1	2.5	1,992	30.1	27.7	30.6	9.4	2.1	77,440
CASS	27,020	36,861	14.0	23.3	42.0	14.7	5.9	29,819	8.0	10.5	42.3	35.0	4.3	150,004
CEDAR	17,486	5,930	37.4	34.9	23.0	3.3	1.5	4,722	21.3	26.9	33.4	16.7	1.7	92,943
CHARITON	19,039	3,370	34.2	33.4	26.7	3.7	1.9	2,748	30.7	25.1	31.5	11.6	1.0	78,966
CHRISTIAN	23,498	27,650	20.8	31.1	34.2	9.7	4.2	21,329	8.9	9.6	46.2	31.3	4.0	142,673
CLARK	18,859	3,040	33.7	33.5	26.3	5.1	1.5	2,426	29.2	27.0	31.1	10.4	2.3	79,058
CLAY	29,677	81,546	12.7	25.5	40.4	14.6	6.8	59,043	4.0	7.1	51.9	34.0	3.0	149,707
CLINTON	24,009	8,141	20.6	28.6	35.9	11.0	4.0	6,535	7.0	17.7	45.2	26.5	3.6	129,968
COLE	26,350	29,014	19.5	26.9	37.2	11.5	4.8	20,242	6.2	10.6	51.7	28.4	3.1	137,500
COOPER	19,327	6,403	26.4	33.3	33.5	5.4	1.5	4,870	12.2	20.4	40.5	23.7	3.1	117,515
CRAWFORD	18,468	9,500	34.7	31.5	27.5	4.4	2.0	7,425	14.7	23.6	39.2	18.7	3.8	109,907
DADE	17,188	3,269	35.1	37.7	22.7	2.9	1.6	2,606	19.8	26.1	36.1	15.0	3.0	96,772
DALLAS	17,186	6,437	38.5	31.5	24.5	3.0	2.5	5,169	21.1	22.9	37.7	15.4	3.0	101,677
DAVIESS	18,864	3,290	32.2	36.4	24.3	4.7	2.4	2,568	23.5	22.7	33.5	18.5	1.7	97,519
DEKALB	16,868	3,686	31.4	33.0	28.7	5.6	1.2	2,770	21.6	20.9	37.8	16.9	2.7	100,413
DENT	16,859	6,157	38.3	33.6	22.8	3.8	1.4	4,673	19.6	26.7	38.3	13.7	1.7	95,525
DOUGLAS	16,540	5,516	39.2	37.0	18.9	2.8	2.1	4,413	19.5	24.0	35.5	17.9	3.1	100,877
DUNKLIN	16,750	13,308	43.5	28.4	22.4	4.1	1.6	9,103	30.1	33.2	30.3	5.5	0.9	69,670
FRANKLIN	24,191	38,757	18.8	27.6	38.6	11.2	3.8	30,848	10.6	12.5	39.4	32.0	5.5	145,543
GASCONADE	20,739	6,584	26.9	33.6	31.6	5.9	2.1	5,369	14.2	19.9	41.8	18.8	5.2	117,133
GENTRY	18,735	2,673	34.3	34.8	24.5	4.0	2.4	2,056	31.9	22.5	32.7	10.9	2.0	79,907
GREENE	25,215	108,795	26.5	31.7	29.0	7.8	5.0	71,395	7.4	15.6	49.9	23.2	3.9	125,817
GRUNDY	18,952	4,469	36.5	33.5	24.2	3.5	2.4	3,283	35.1	25.2	27.0	10.8	2.0	71,540
HARRISON	17,072	3,677	36.4	36.7	22.7	3.3	1.1	2,810	32.7	24.4	32.0	9.6	1.4	75,202
HENRY	20,403	9,442	32.6	32.6	26.6	5.8	2.4	7,022	19.4	24.7	37.0	16.8	2.2	99,567
HICKORY	17,400	4,178	37.8	37.6	19.7	3.6	1.2	3,566	20.4	27.4	35.2	14.9	2.2	93,540
HOLT	19,307	2,166	35.6	33.6	24.3	4.6	1.9	1,654	30.8	27.0	31.6	8.9	1.8	76,607
HOWARD	18,863	3,865	31.3	30.9	29.5	6.8	1.4	2,962	22.1	24.0	34.4	15.5	4.0	97,697
HOWELL	17,052	15,624	40.5	33.4	20.6	3.4	1.9	11,756	19.2	22.8	39.2	15.7	3.1	102,034
IRON	16,721	4,299	40.1	32.5	22.4	3.6	1.3	3,338	24.4	31.3	32.3	10.2	1.8	81,403
JACKSON	26,675	277,301	22.6	27.7	33.0	11.2	5.6	179,555	9.4	20.3	45.8	21.3	3.2	119,006
JASPER	20,143	44,280	30.3	32.5	28.3	6.3	2.5	30,521	17.1	30.9	39.9	10.8	1.3	92,551
JEFFERSON	24,873	80,977	15.3	26.3	40.0	13.8	4.5	68,168	13.6	8.6	41.3	33.4	3.1	147,691
JOHNSON	20,607	18,797	26.4	30.5	32.2	8.0	3.0	11,937	11.8	15.2	41.6	27.9	3.5	135,481
KNOX	15,880	1,746	38.4	37.1	20.5	3.4	0.6	1,377	32.7	24.5	26.3	13.1	3.3	75,211
LACLEDE	19,328	13,994	32.9	33.0	25.6	5.8	2.6	10,419	20.0	20.3	38.5	17.6	3.6	107,597
LAFAYETTE	22,575	12,885	23.4	30.0	34.5	9.0	3.2	9,910	16.4	21.0	40.8	19.0	2.8	109,089
LAWRENCE	18,611	14,425	32.2	33.7	26.7	5.3	2.1	10,972	16.6	22.8	41.0	17.1	2.4	105,574
LEWIS	18,782	4,005	33.5	33.6	26.2	4.5	2.2	3,117	31.7	24.4	31.8	9.7	2.4	78,764
LINCOLN	21,700	17,821	19.2	26.9	40.4	10.8	2.6	14,552	12.4	11.4	36.2	33.5	6.5	147,880
LINN	18,371	5,480	35.9	33.3	24.8	4.3	1.6	4,274	34.2	26.9	28.2	9.6	1.1	69,753
LIVINGSTON	21,104	5,749	32.5	30.3	28.1	5.7	3.4	4,166	24.1	23.1	35.3	14.7	2.7	95,529
MCDONALD	15,978	8,619	37.9	35.2	21.9	3.1	1.9	6,356	21.6	24.7	34.3	15.7	3.7	95,683
MACON	19,274	6,588	32.6	35.9	24.9	4.8	1.7	5,111	24.7	23.7	37.8	11.9	1.9	92,713
MADISON	15,825	4,858	41.1	33.0	21.7	3.1	1.1	3,760	22.2	31.6	34.7	10.3	1.3	83,333
MARIES	18,673	3,755	31.7	31.9	29.9	5.7	0.9	3,101	18.4	21.7	36.7	19.0	4.1	107,219
MARION	20,681	11,363	30.8	28.9	31.4	6.4	2.6	8,190	18.3	24.4	37.5	17.8	1.9	102,604
MERCER	18,251	1,538	35.4	33.8	25.0	4.1	1.7	1,204	41.3	25.0	22.4	7.8	3.5	61,358
MILLER	19,177	10,009	32.3	33.3	27.0	5.1	2.3	7,667	18.1	22.3	37.6	18.7	3.3	105,712
MISSISSIPPI	16,772	5,344	45.2	28.5	19.5	4.2	2.6	3,503	33.2	30.0	28.1	7.7	1.0	68,593
MONITEAU	20,268	5,564	25.4	31.6	34.0	6.7	2.3	4,397	17.3	23.4	40.0	16.9	2.4	103,831
MONROE	17,765	3,787	30.4	37.4	27.9	2.8	1.5	3,022	20.4	26.2	33.8	16.6	3.0	95,787
MONTGOMERY	18,650	5,024	30.9	33.0	29.7	5.3	1.1	4,000	18.8	24.6	34.0	17.9	4.8	101,515
MORGAN	20,625	8,921	31.3	34.1	26.2	5.2	3.1	7,461	17.6	19.1	36.5	23.9	2.9	116,042
NEW MADRID	17,391	7,716	39.6	31.3	22.7	4.8	1.7	5,290	35.5	29.8	28.2	6.2	0.2	67,667
NEWTON	21,788	21,654	25.6	32.3	30.7	6.7	3.6	16,934	19.1	24.4	38.1	15.5	2.9	99,590
NODAWAY	20,141	8,411	31.5	30.7	29.8	5.4	2.6	5,489	20.7	18.9	35.0	22.6	2.8	111,010
OREGON	15,043	4,364	47.5	33.5	14.7	2.7	1.6	3,476	30.9	24.2	31.4	11.3	2.2	80,000
OSAGE	20,571	5,296	23.8	31.0	36.2	7.5	1.5	4,444	12.9	20.2	42.7	21.5	2.7	117,430
OZARK	17,105	4,068	40.4	34.8	20.3	2.6	2.0	3,359	23.5	23.7	32.4	16.1	4.3	94,947
MISSOURI	25,475		24.2	28.2	31.9	10.2	5.6		11.5	16.8	39.7	26.8	5.2	130,140
UNITED STATES	27,916		21.9	25.0	32.3	12.3	8.4		7.9	10.5	27.1	35.6	19.0	192,285

COUNTY	FINANCIAL SERVICES				THE HOME						ENTERTAINMENT						PERSONAL			
					Home Improvements		Furnishings													
	Auto Loan	Home Loan	Invest-ments	Retire-ment Plans	Home Repair	Lawn & Garden	Comput-ers & Hard-ware	Major Appli-ances	TV, Radio, Sound Equip-ment	Furni-ture	Dine out/ Carry out	Sports Equip-ment	Fees & Tickets	Toys & Games	Travel	Cable TV	Apparel & Services	Auto Repairs	Health Insur-ance	Pets & Supplies
ADAIR	72	55	56	57	57	67	73	67	71	62	70	62	62	70	65	70	61	69	71	69
ANDREW	99	83	68	81	88	105	80	95	86	80	85	83	75	89	82	90	74	88	100	100
ATCHISON	77	55	45	54	62	81	61	72	69	55	66	63	52	70	61	74	56	68	85	76
AUDRAIN	78	60	54	60	66	82	65	74	72	61	69	65	58	73	64	76	60	70	84	77
BARRY	77	58	41	55	62	81	58	71	64	57	64	63	51	67	58	69	55	66	77	76
BARTON	73	52	37	51	58	76	55	67	62	53	61	59	47	65	54	65	52	62	74	72
BATES	74	56	46	54	62	79	60	71	66	56	64	62	52	67	59	70	55	66	79	74
BENTON	67	57	52	55	63	76	57	69	62	56	60	58	53	59	61	67	52	65	78	69
BOLLINGER	74	52	33	50	57	77	53	67	60	52	60	59	45	64	52	65	51	62	73	73
BOONE	89	78	81	82	74	77	94	82	89	86	90	78	86	89	85	87	81	88	81	83
BUCHANAN	76	71	80	73	71	76	75	74	78	73	76	65	73	79	74	80	68	74	81	75
BUTLER	73	59	54	59	61	73	62	68	67	60	66	59	57	68	61	70	57	66	75	70
CALDWELL	76	57	42	55	63	82	60	73	66	56	64	63	52	67	60	71	55	67	81	76
CALLAWAY	88	78	71	77	77	86	77	82	80	76	79	73	74	82	76	83	70	80	86	85
CAMDEN	91	79	69	78	86	105	76	93	81	76	80	79	73	79	82	86	69	86	99	95
CAPE GIRARDEAU	83	76	81	78	77	82	82	80	82	78	81	72	78	82	79	82	72	80	83	82
CARROLL	78	54	37	53	62	84	59	73	66	55	65	65	49	69	58	71	55	67	82	79
CARTER	68	46	27	44	53	73	48	63	55	46	55	55	40	58	48	60	46	57	69	68
CASS	104	106	105	106	103	104	98	102	98	101	98	91	100	101	100	98	87	99	101	103
CEDAR	65	51	41	49	56	72	52	64	58	50	56	55	47	57	53	62	48	59	71	66
CHARITON	76	52	33	50	61	83	56	72	63	52	62	63	46	66	55	67	52	65	80	77
CHRISTIAN	93	86	75	86	81	86	84	86	84	84	84	79	81	87	82	84	75	85	85	88
CLARK	77	54	36	52	62	83	57	72	64	54	63	63	48	67	56	68	53	66	79	77
CLAY	103	107	111	109	101	97	105	100	103	106	102	92	106	105	104	101	92	102	99	100
CLINTON	92	84	82	84	87	97	82	90	86	82	84	79	80	89	84	88	75	85	94	92
COLE	91	90	94	92	89	89	90	89	90	90	90	81	90	91	90	90	81	90	90	90
COOPER	76	63	57	63	68	82	63	73	68	62	67	64	59	70	65	71	58	69	79	76
CRAWFORD	77	57	41	55	62	81	59	71	65	57	64	63	51	68	58	69	55	66	77	76
DADE	71	49	32	47	57	77	52	67	59	49	58	59	43	62	52	63	49	61	74	72
DALLAS	74	53	37	51	59	80	56	69	62	53	61	61	47	65	55	66	52	64	76	74
DAVIESS	78	54	37	53	63	85	59	74	66	55	65	65	49	69	59	71	54	68	83	79
DEKALB	73	55	47	54	61	77	59	69	64	56	63	61	52	66	59	68	54	65	76	73
DENT	67	48	36	47	54	72	52	63	58	48	56	55	44	59	51	62	48	59	71	67
DOUGLAS	68	48	34	47	54	73	51	63	57	49	56	56	43	59	50	61	48	59	69	68
DUNKLIN	64	48	39	47	52	66	51	59	58	49	56	52	46	59	51	62	49	57	67	63
FRANKLIN	97	87	80	87	89	100	83	93	88	84	87	82	81	92	85	91	77	88	96	96
GASCONADE	83	62	47	61	69	89	64	77	70	61	69	68	56	73	64	75	59	72	85	83
GENTRY	76	53	39	51	60	81	58	71	66	53	64	63	49	68	57	70	54	66	82	76
GREENE	83	76	81	78	75	79	83	79	83	79	82	72	79	83	80	83	73	81	83	80
GRUNDY	69	51	44	50	56	72	56	65	63	52	61	57	49	63	56	67	52	61	74	68
HARRISON	68	47	32	45	54	74	51	64	57	47	56	56	42	60	50	62	47	59	72	69
HENRY	74	59	52	58	64	78	62	71	69	60	67	62	57	69	63	73	58	68	80	74
HICKORY	61	51	41	48	56	70	49	62	53	49	52	52	46	51	52	57	45	58	68	63
HOLT	78	52	29	50	62	86	56	73	62	52	62	65	45	66	55	67	52	66	80	80
HOWARD	76	57	47	56	61	77	61	70	67	58	66	62	54	69	60	71	56	67	79	74
HOWELL	68	51	41	50	55	70	54	63	59	51	58	55	47	61	53	63	50	60	70	67
IRON	69	48	31	46	55	75	50	65	57	48	56	56	42	59	50	62	47	59	71	69
JACKSON	88	85	94	88	82	82	89	84	91	89	90	76	89	90	87	91	81	87	88	85
JASPER	74	64	66	65	65	72	68	70	72	66	70	61	65	73	67	74	62	69	76	71
JEFFERSON	101	97	89	96	94	98	90	96	92	93	92	86	90	95	91	93	82	93	96	98
JOHNSON	81	66	62	68	65	73	79	73	77	72	78	69	71	79	72	76	69	76	74	76
KNOX	65	43	25	42	52	72	47	61	52	44	52	54	38	56	46	56	44	55	67	67
LACLEDE	78	60	49	59	63	79	62	71	68	61	67	63	56	70	61	72	58	68	78	76
LAFAYETTE	89	74	67	73	77	91	76	85	82	73	80	75	70	83	76	85	69	81	92	88
LAWRENCE	78	59	46	58	64	81	61	72	67	59	66	63	54	70	60	71	57	67	79	76
LEWIS	76	56	45	55	62	80	60	71	67	57	65	62	53	69	60	71	56	67	79	75
LINCOLN	94	82	70	81	81	91	80	87	83	80	83	78	76	86	79	85	73	84	89	90
LINN	69	52	45	51	58	73	56	66	62	53	61	57	50	64	56	66	52	62	74	69
LIVINGSTON	77	62	60	61	67	81	66	74	73	63	70	65	61	73	67	77	61	71	84	77
MCDONALD	73	53	35	50	57	74	53	66	59	52	59	58	46	63	52	63	50	61	70	71
MACON	74	55	43	54	61	78	58	70	64	55	63	61	51	66	58	69	54	65	77	74
MADISON	62	46	36	44	51	66	49	59	54	46	53	51	42	55	48	58	46	55	65	62
MARIES	74	58	45	57	64	80	59	71	64	57	63	61	53	67	59	68	55	65	76	74
MARION	74	65	69	66	67	75	68	71	72	66	70	62	65	73	68	75	62	70	79	72
MERCER	72	49	31	47	57	79	52	68	59	49	58	59	43	62	52	63	49	61	75	73
MILLER	76	59	47	57	63	80	61	72	67	59	66	63	54	68	61	70	57	68	78	76
MISSISSIPPI	64	46	38	46	49	63	52	58	59	50	58	51	46	60	50	63	50	57	66	61
MONITEAU	86	67	53	65	70	87	68	79	76	66	74	70	61	77	68	80	63	75	88	83
MONROE	73	52	37	51	59	78	56	68	62	52	61	60	47	65	55	66	52	63	76	73
MONTGOMERY	72	57	48	56	62	77	59	69	65	57	63	60	53	67	59	69	55	64	76	72
MORGAN	77	63	55	61	70	87	63	77	69	62	68	65	58	67	66	74	58	72	85	79
NEW MADRID	69	51	38	49	55	71	53	63	60	51	59	56	47	62	53	65	51	60	71	68
NEWTON	89	72	60	71	76	93	72	83	77	71	77	74	66	81	72	81	67	78	89	88
NODAWAY	73	55	51	56	58	70	70	68	70	61	70	63	59	69	63	70	61	69	72	71
OREGON	60	43	29	41	49	66	45	57	50	42	49	49	38	52	45	54	42	52	63	61
OSAGE	85	67	52	65	74	93	66	81	73	65	72	71	60	77	67	77	62	74	87	86
OZARK	60	50	33	48	57	76	50	65	56	49	55	56	43	57	51	60	47	60	71	69
MISSOURI	92	84	84	85	84	91	86	88	88	85	88	79	83	89	85	90	78	87	92	90
UNITED STATES	100	100	100	100	100	100	100	100	100	100	100	100	100	100	100	100	100	100	100	100

A

COUNTY	FIPS Code	CBSA Code	DMA Code	POPULATION			2000-2007 ANNUAL RATE		RACE (%)					
									White		Black		Asian/Pacific	
				2000	2007	2012	% Rate	State Rank	2000	2007	2000	2007	2000	2007
PEMISCOT	155	00000	640	20,047	18,901	18,111	-0.8	115	71.8	69.0	26.2	28.7	0.3	0.4
PERRY	157	00000	632	18,132	18,778	19,253	0.5	52	98.2	97.8	0.2	0.2	0.7	1.0
PETTIS	159	42740	616	39,403	40,094	40,576	0.2	74	92.1	90.7	3.0	3.4	0.4	0.6
PHELPS	161	40620	609	39,825	42,118	43,422	0.8	36	93.2	91.7	1.5	1.7	2.4	3.5
PIKE	163	00000	609	18,351	18,685	19,000	0.2	74	88.4	86.9	9.2	10.2	0.2	0.3
PLATTE	165	28140	616	73,781	83,960	91,204	1.8	7	91.5	89.9	3.5	3.9	1.7	2.4
POLK	167	44180	619	26,992	29,641	31,587	1.3	17	97.3	96.8	0.5	0.5	0.2	0.3
PULASKI	169	22780	619	41,165	44,803	45,616	1.2	20	78.4	75.5	12.0	13.0	2.6	3.6
PUTNAM	171	00000	631	5,223	5,248	5,253	0.1	83	99.1	99.1	0.1	0.1	0.1	0.1
RALLS	173	25300	717	9,626	9,956	10,166	0.5	52	97.9	97.7	1.1	1.3	0.1	0.1
RANDOLPH	175	33620	604	24,663	24,866	25,079	0.1	83	90.6	89.3	7.0	7.9	0.4	0.6
RAY	177	28140	616	23,354	24,839	25,842	0.9	28	96.5	96.0	1.5	1.7	0.2	0.3
REYNOLDS	179	00000	609	6,689	6,814	6,935	0.3	62	95.6	95.1	0.5	0.6	0.2	0.3
RIPLEY	181	00000	734	13,509	13,757	13,937	0.3	62	97.2	96.8	0.0	0.0	0.2	0.4
ST. CHARLES	183	41180	609	283,883	355,587	414,517	3.2	3	94.7	93.7	2.7	3.0	0.9	1.3
ST. CLAIR	185	00000	619	9,652	9,796	9,891	0.2	74	97.4	97.0	0.2	0.3	0.2	0.2
STE. GENEVIEVE	186	00000	609	17,842	18,194	18,387	0.3	62	98.0	97.7	0.7	0.8	0.2	0.2
ST. FRANCOIS	187	22100	609	55,641	61,770	64,829	1.5	14	96.1	95.5	2.0	2.3	0.3	0.5
ST. LOUIS	189	41180	609	1,016,315	1,006,003	998,392	-0.1	97	76.8	73.9	19.0	20.8	2.2	3.2
SALINE	195	32180	616	23,756	23,320	23,056	-0.3	105	90.0	88.5	5.4	6.0	0.6	0.8
SCHUYLER	197	28860	631	4,170	4,419	4,614	0.8	36	98.4	98.2	0.0	0.0	0.2	0.3
SCOTLAND	199	00000	631	4,983	4,923	4,885	-0.2	102	98.8	98.8	0.2	0.2	0.1	0.1
SCOTT	201	43460	632	40,422	41,156	41,679	0.2	74	87.7	86.1	10.5	11.7	0.2	0.3
SHANNON	203	00000	619	8,324	8,628	8,847	0.5	52	95.1	94.5	0.2	0.2	0.1	0.1
SHELBY	205	00000	717	6,799	6,808	6,823	0.0	91	97.9	97.8	1.0	1.0	0.1	0.1
STODDARD	207	00000	632	29,705	30,148	30,479	0.2	74	97.3	97.0	0.9	1.0	0.1	0.1
STONE	209	14700	619	28,658	31,265	33,044	1.2	20	97.6	97.3	0.1	0.1	0.2	0.3
SULLIVAN	211	00000	631	7,219	7,168	7,062	-0.1	97	95.0	94.9	0.1	0.2	0.2	0.2
TANEY	213	14700	619	39,703	45,153	49,455	1.8	7	96.2	95.6	0.3	0.4	0.4	0.6
TEXAS	215	00000	619	23,003	24,527	24,756	0.9	28	96.5	96.0	0.2	0.2	0.4	0.5
VERNON	217	00000	603	20,454	20,357	20,302	-0.1	97	97.0	96.9	0.6	0.7	0.3	0.4
WARREN	219	41180	609	24,525	30,436	35,441	3.0	4	95.9	95.3	1.9	2.2	0.3	0.4
WASHINGTON	221	41180	609	23,344	23,928	24,284	0.3	62	95.5	94.9	2.5	2.8	0.2	0.2
WAYNE	223	00000	632	13,259	13,375	13,452	0.1	83	97.7	97.4	0.2	0.2	0.1	0.2
WEBSTER	225	44180	619	31,045	35,097	38,266	1.7	9	96.2	95.6	1.2	1.3	0.3	0.4
WORTH	227	00000	616	2,382	2,263	2,184	-0.7	113	99.0	98.9	0.2	0.2	0.1	0.2
WRIGHT	229	00000	619	17,955	18,104	18,166	0.1	83	97.6	97.3	0.3	0.3	0.1	0.2
ST. LOUIS CITY	510	41180	609	348,189	344,683	343,846	-0.1	97	43.8	40.5	51.2	53.6	2.0	2.7
MISSOURI							0.8		84.9	83.7	11.2	11.7	1.2	1.6
UNITED STATES							1.2		75.1	72.7	12.3	12.6	3.8	4.5

B

COUNTY	% HISPANIC ORIGIN		2007 AGE DISTRIBUTION (%)										MEDIAN AGE	% 2007 Males	% 2007 Females
	2000	2007	0-4	5-9	10-14	15-19	20-24	25-44	45-64	65-84	85+	18+	2007		
PEMISCOT	1.6	1.9	8.5	7.1	7.9	6.7	6.8	24.9	24.1	11.7	2.3	72.4	35.5	47.3	52.7
PERRY	0.5	0.6	7.0	6.8	6.1	6.4	5.5	27.7	25.6	12.2	2.7	76.1	38.8	49.8	50.2
PETTIS	3.9	4.8	7.5	6.7	6.2	6.5	6.8	26.9	25.0	12.2	2.3	75.7	37.5	48.9	51.1
PHELPS	1.2	1.5	5.8	5.4	5.6	8.5	9.4	25.5	25.4	12.3	2.1	79.1	36.6	50.9	49.1
PIKE	1.6	2.0	5.7	5.1	6.1	6.4	7.8	27.9	26.3	12.3	2.4	79.3	39.1	54.2	45.8
PLATTE	3.0	3.7	6.8	6.6	6.7	6.4	6.5	28.8	28.4	8.5	1.4	76.0	37.5	49.4	50.6
POLK	1.3	1.6	7.0	6.4	6.2	8.4	9.5	23.5	23.5	13.3	2.3	76.2	36.4	48.6	51.4
PULASKI	5.8	7.1	7.4	6.5	5.8	12.2	14.1	27.3	18.6	7.2	0.9	76.3	27.5	54.1	45.9
PUTNAM	0.6	0.6	6.8	5.8	5.3	6.6	5.3	22.6	25.9	18.1	3.4	78.0	43.4	49.7	50.3
RALLS	0.4	0.6	5.9	5.6	6.1	6.3	6.2	24.6	30.4	12.9	1.9	78.4	42.0	50.3	49.7
RANDOLPH	1.1	1.4	6.6	5.9	6.1	6.1	7.2	28.1	25.6	12.0	2.4	77.8	38.2	51.9	48.1
RAY	1.1	1.4	6.9	6.3	6.6	7.3	7.1	24.9	27.4	11.9	1.7	75.8	39.2	50.2	49.8
REYNOLDS	0.8	1.0	6.0	6.0	5.9	5.7	6.1	23.1	29.4	16.1	1.8	78.3	42.9	50.9	49.1
RIPLEY	1.0	1.2	6.4	6.0	6.1	6.2	5.9	24.7	26.6	15.9	2.3	77.9	41.5	48.6	51.4
ST. CHARLES	1.5	1.8	7.9	7.5	7.4	7.2	6.3	28.7	25.7	8.3	1.0	72.6	35.7	49.2	50.8
ST. CLAIR	1.0	1.2	5.7	5.4	5.4	6.1	5.4	20.2	29.8	18.4	3.4	79.5	46.1	50.1	49.9
STE. GENEVIEVE	0.7	0.9	6.4	5.8	6.6	6.7	6.7	25.4	27.7	12.7	2.0	77.1	40.5	50.3	49.7
ST. FRANCOIS	0.8	1.0	6.1	5.5	5.6	6.2	7.3	28.5	25.5	12.9	2.5	79.2	39.0	51.9	48.1
ST. LOUIS	1.4	1.7	6.1	6.2	6.9	7.0	6.3	25.5	27.2	12.3	2.4	76.6	39.5	47.5	52.5
SALINE	4.4	5.5	6.5	5.9	5.7	7.8	8.3	24.6	25.7	12.6	3.0	77.9	38.2	49.5	50.5
SCHUYLER	0.6	0.8	6.6	5.8	6.2	5.7	5.7	22.4	27.3	17.1	3.2	77.9	43.3	48.8	51.2
SCOTLAND	0.8	0.9	8.0	7.3	6.5	6.4	6.1	24.3	23.2	14.7	3.6	74.1	39.2	48.7	51.3
SCOTT	1.1	1.4	7.2	6.5	7.0	6.8	6.4	26.5	25.9	11.7	2.0	75.1	37.7	48.4	51.6
SHANNON	0.9	1.1	6.6	6.0	6.4	6.4	6.8	22.9	28.3	14.6	1.9	77.1	41.2	49.2	50.8
SHELBY	0.6	0.6	6.3	5.6	6.4	6.4	6.7	22.5	27.8	14.3	4.0	77.5	42.2	47.8	52.2
STODDARD	0.8	1.0	6.0	5.5	5.8	6.7	6.1	25.9	26.7	14.7	2.7	78.7	41.2	48.5	51.5
STONE	1.0	1.3	5.5	5.3	5.5	4.9	4.6	21.2	31.3	19.9	1.8	80.7	47.0	49.2	50.8
SULLIVAN	8.8	8.9	7.5	7.4	6.1	5.9	5.3	24.3	26.3	13.7	3.5	75.2	39.6	50.6	49.4
TANEY	2.4	3.0	6.2	5.9	5.6	6.5	6.7	24.9	27.3	15.0	2.0	78.9	40.8	48.4	51.6
TEXAS	1.0	1.2	5.9	5.3	5.7	5.8	6.6	21.7	27.6	16.9	4.5	79.6	44.3	47.7	52.3
VERNON	0.8	0.9	6.8	6.3	6.3	8.5	6.2	23.8	26.5	13.0	2.6	75.7	39.0	48.4	51.6
WARREN	1.3	1.6	6.9	6.5	6.3	7.1	5.6	25.9	27.8	12.6	1.3	75.8	40.0	50.0	50.0
WASHINGTON	0.7	0.9	6.9	6.4	6.0	6.5	7.4	28.6	25.3	11.6	1.4	76.8	36.9	51.6	48.4
WAYNE	0.5	0.6	5.8	5.2	5.2	5.9	6.5	21.5	28.6	18.9	2.4	80.2	45.0	49.7	50.3
WEBSTER	1.3	1.6	7.8	7.2	7.2	7.0	6.5	27.6	24.7	10.5	1.5	73.5	36.4	50.4	49.6
WORTH	0.3	0.4	6.0	5.8	5.6	5.2	7.7	21.8	25.8	18.0	4.2	79.5	43.8	49.4	50.6
WRIGHT	0.8	1.0	7.4	6.7	6.1	6.7	7.3	23.1	25.6	14.8	2.2	75.7	39.1	48.8	51.2
ST. LOUIS CITY	2.0	2.3	6.8	6.0	7.2	7.5	7.7	28.3	24.1	10.1	2.3	75.6	35.3	47.6	52.4
MISSOURI	2.1	2.6	6.8	6.3	6.5	7.0	7.2	26.7	26.0	11.5	2.1	76.4	37.7	48.8	51.2
UNITED STATES	12.5	15.0	6.9	6.5	6.8	7.1	7.0	27.6	25.4	10.7	1.9	75.6	36.7	49.2	50.8

COUNTY	HOUSEHOLDS					FAMILIES			MEDIAN HOUSEHOLD INCOME			
	2000	2007	2012	% Annual Rate 2000-2007	2007 Average HH Size	2000	2007	% Annual Rate 2000-2007	2007	2012	2007 National Rank	2007 State Rank
PEMISCOT	7,855	7,543	7,279	-0.6	2.47	5,317	4,959	-1.0	26,389	30,291	3059	113
PERRY	6,904	7,280	7,518	0.7	2.53	4,955	5,093	0.4	43,313	48,946	1301	26
PETTIS	15,568	15,941	16,155	0.3	2.47	10,568	10,507	-0.1	39,334	45,737	1814	38
PHELPS	15,683	16,901	17,561	1.0	2.35	10,235	10,687	0.6	36,466	42,314	2201	62
PIKE	6,451	6,716	6,882	0.6	2.46	4,477	4,531	0.2	38,511	43,581	1926	44
PLATTE	29,278	33,871	37,052	2.0	2.45	20,222	22,742	1.6	69,963	81,920	118	2
POLK	9,917	10,984	11,742	1.4	2.55	7,140	7,705	1.1	35,953	41,050	2284	67
PULASKI	13,433	14,174	14,636	0.7	2.61	9,949	10,251	0.4	41,776	48,305	1482	31
PUTNAM	2,228	2,245	2,246	0.1	2.31	1,517	1,485	-0.3	30,730	34,490	2861	100
RALLS	3,736	3,912	4,012	0.6	2.52	2,784	2,847	0.3	44,197	49,936	1189	24
RANDOLPH	9,199	9,455	9,597	0.4	2.40	6,234	6,223	0.0	38,480	44,205	1933	45
RAY	8,743	9,445	9,886	1.1	2.60	6,540	6,904	0.7	51,059	58,456	613	10
REYNOLDS	2,721	2,854	2,942	0.7	2.33	1,915	1,956	0.3	30,635	34,738	2871	101
RIPLEY	5,416	5,602	5,709	0.5	2.43	3,848	3,874	0.1	26,740	30,180	3048	112
ST. CHARLES	101,663	129,922	152,563	3.4	2.71	77,104	96,383	3.1	73,167	86,102	99	1
ST. CLAIR	4,040	4,132	4,181	0.3	2.33	2,790	2,775	-0.1	29,986	34,281	2912	106
STE. GENEVIEVE	6,586	6,847	6,973	0.5	2.61	4,926	5,002	0.2	47,176	53,906	892	17
ST. FRANCOIS	20,793	22,842	24,278	1.3	2.44	14,669	15,688	0.9	38,339	43,973	1957	48
ST. LOUIS	404,312	406,493	406,092	0.1	2.43	270,810	264,158	-0.3	63,775	75,119	183	3
SALINE	9,015	8,881	8,782	-0.2	2.44	6,017	5,750	-0.6	40,985	47,374	1601	33
SCHUYLER	1,725	1,846	1,934	0.9	2.36	1,193	1,241	0.5	33,427	36,981	2613	83
SCOTLAND	1,902	1,845	1,816	-0.4	2.60	1,302	1,227	-0.8	32,682	36,609	2688	85
SCOTT	15,626	16,171	16,480	0.5	2.51	11,223	11,317	0.1	38,527	44,317	1924	43
SHANNON	3,319	3,500	3,613	0.7	2.45	2,358	2,423	0.4	24,480	27,365	3099	115
SHELBY	2,745	2,766	2,776	0.1	2.37	1,848	1,807	-0.3	34,673	38,332	2473	73
STODDARD	12,064	12,454	12,676	0.4	2.36	8,481	8,523	0.1	32,134	36,462	2746	91
STONE	11,822	12,957	13,702	1.3	2.39	8,843	9,470	0.9	39,384	45,234	1799	36
SULLIVAN	2,925	2,881	2,826	-0.2	2.44	1,961	1,874	-0.6	31,098	35,392	2825	97
TANEY	16,158	18,538	20,370	1.9	2.36	11,053	12,317	1.5	38,400	44,632	1951	47
TEXAS	9,378	9,679	9,850	0.4	2.37	6,647	6,680	0.1	29,008	32,930	2958	108
VERNON	7,966	7,992	7,989	0.0	2.41	5,436	5,298	-0.4	35,802	40,386	2311	69
WARREN	9,185	11,610	13,622	3.3	2.60	6,892	8,515	3.0	50,061	57,188	676	12
WASHINGTON	8,406	8,848	9,096	0.7	2.56	6,237	6,409	0.4	32,001	36,266	2764	94
WAYNE	5,551	5,710	5,789	0.4	2.32	3,839	3,840	0.0	28,333	32,369	2988	109
WEBSTER	11,073	12,673	13,876	1.9	2.70	8,437	9,447	1.6	38,905	44,719	1866	41
WORTH	1,009	958	923	-0.7	2.31	677	624	-1.1	32,024	36,002	2758	93
WRIGHT	7,081	7,213	7,261	0.3	2.48	5,023	4,982	-0.1	29,819	33,926	2919	107
ST. LOUIS CITY	147,076	143,160	142,851	-0.4	2.33	76,976	71,756	-1.0	33,654	39,003	2590	79
MISSOURI				0.9	2.45			0.5	47,568	55,657		
UNITED STATES				1.2	2.59			1.0	53,154	62,503		

COUNTY	2007 Per Capita Income	2007 HH Income Base	2007 HOUSEHOLD INCOME DISTRIBUTION (%)					2007 Home Value Base	2007 HOME VALUE DISTRIBUTION (%)					2007 Median Home Value
			Less than $25,000	$25,000 to $49,999	$50,000 to $99,999	$100,000 to $149,999	$150,000 or More		Less than $50,000	$50,000 to $89,999	$90,000 to $174,999	$175,000 to $399,999	$400,000 or More	
PEMISCOT	15,638	7,543	48.1	28.3	17.4	4.4	1.8	4,594	35.8	33.5	24.1	6.2	0.4	64,468
PERRY	20,118	7,280	25.9	32.8	33.9	5.3	2.1	5,919	13.0	18.7	44.8	22.0	1.6	123,314
PETTIS	20,090	15,941	27.8	35.0	29.3	5.6	2.4	11,793	15.6	25.1	40.7	16.3	2.4	103,065
PHELPS	20,361	16,901	34.3	30.1	26.6	6.0	3.0	11,459	17.1	19.5	40.4	20.3	2.7	111,595
PIKE	18,531	6,716	31.8	31.0	29.5	5.8	1.8	5,083	21.0	23.9	33.9	18.0	3.2	99,756
PLATTE	34,706	33,871	11.6	20.6	39.5	17.3	11.0	23,570	2.0	3.3	39.8	46.4	8.4	185,829
POLK	17,022	10,984	33.5	34.0	26.0	4.8	1.7	8,137	15.2	22.3	39.2	19.9	3.4	113,243
PULASKI	17,936	14,172	23.2	37.5	32.1	5.5	1.7	8,562	19.3	20.4	41.5	17.5	1.2	107,405
PUTNAM	17,087	2,245	40.4	34.5	21.1	2.8	1.2	1,763	29.1	32.2	29.3	7.4	2.0	73,105
RALLS	20,404	3,912	24.2	32.9	34.5	7.2	1.2	3,258	17.8	23.6	34.9	19.2	4.4	104,303
RANDOLPH	19,354	9,455	30.4	32.5	29.2	6.0	1.9	6,957	28.5	28.1	29.1	12.1	2.1	77,737
RAY	23,098	9,445	20.9	27.9	36.6	11.8	2.8	7,615	10.4	18.2	47.0	22.5	1.9	119,262
REYNOLDS	15,938	2,854	41.7	33.6	20.7	3.2	0.8	2,259	29.0	27.5	30.9	11.1	1.5	79,413
RIPLEY	15,124	5,602	46.8	31.8	17.3	2.6	1.5	4,443	34.9	27.2	27.3	8.7	1.9	71,475
ST. CHARLES	31,499	129,921	9.3	19.7	42.3	18.3	10.3	107,737	4.3	3.0	30.7	55.1	6.9	197,752
ST. CLAIR	17,015	4,132	39.3	34.2	21.9	3.4	1.2	3,330	29.5	21.6	33.9	13.2	1.7	87,643
STE. GENEVIEVE	21,155	6,847	22.5	31.3	36.0	8.2	2.0	5,712	12.3	15.5	42.0	27.4	2.9	128,653
ST. FRANCOIS	18,997	22,842	32.2	31.8	28.0	6.1	1.9	17,059	16.6	23.9	39.5	17.3	2.5	104,829
ST. LOUIS	36,043	406,493	15.1	23.3	34.2	15.7	11.8	306,425	1.5	11.8	37.5	36.6	12.7	172,848
SALINE	20,561	8,881	28.6	32.4	29.7	6.3	3.0	6,305	22.1	24.7	35.6	15.2	2.4	95,276
SCHUYLER	18,114	1,846	38.9	31.9	24.4	2.7	2.1	1,425	32.1	24.3	28.4	11.6	3.7	77,961
SCOTLAND	17,126	1,845	38.8	33.5	20.1	4.2	3.4	1,439	33.4	23.8	31.5	10.5	0.8	73,642
SCOTT	19,360	16,171	32.2	29.9	29.0	6.8	2.1	11,527	21.4	25.8	35.7	15.1	1.9	94,961
SHANNON	13,274	3,500	50.9	31.5	14.6	2.3	0.7	2,821	33.3	28.3	26.9	9.1	2.3	71,791
SHELBY	18,157	2,766	36.0	34.7	22.7	5.0	1.5	2,112	31.3	26.9	27.5	11.9	2.4	75,345
STODDARD	18,102	12,454	38.4	32.7	22.4	4.6	2.0	9,236	25.3	26.7	34.4	11.9	1.7	86,698
STONE	21,763	12,957	28.4	35.5	26.6	6.0	3.5	10,687	12.7	14.6	36.7	29.8	6.3	137,552
SULLIVAN	16,419	2,881	39.7	31.6	24.2	3.0	1.5	2,115	35.4	25.7	27.4	9.2	2.3	71,167
TANEY	21,230	18,538	27.5	36.6	26.9	6.0	2.9	13,167	15.1	17.3	40.0	23.1	4.4	124,373
TEXAS	16,360	9,679	43.7	32.1	19.1	3.2	1.9	7,561	25.4	22.5	34.5	14.7	2.8	93,679
VERNON	18,630	7,992	35.2	31.2	26.3	5.1	2.2	5,899	22.0	25.7	34.5	15.5	2.3	93,518
WARREN	24,251	11,610	19.9	30.0	34.0	11.9	4.2	9,760	11.9	8.6	35.3	37.3	6.8	162,130
WASHINGTON	16,095	8,848	40.4	30.6	24.0	3.7	1.4	7,158	32.4	23.3	31.8	11.1	1.4	78,933
WAYNE	16,643	5,710	44.0	31.8	19.5	3.2	1.5	4,545	35.8	27.0	27.3	8.7	1.2	65,563
WEBSTER	17,916	12,673	28.7	34.4	29.0	6.0	2.0	10,049	13.6	19.2	43.7	20.8	2.7	116,173
WORTH	17,655	958	38.1	35.4	22.1	3.2	1.1	748	46.5	24.2	21.1	6.3	1.9	53,768
WRIGHT	16,270	7,213	42.4	33.0	18.7	3.5	2.4	5,383	22.7	24.1	33.0	16.4	3.8	96,372
ST. LOUIS CITY	19,711	143,153	38.5	28.5	24.4	5.7	2.9	70,060	12.3	30.6	42.9	12.0	2.2	98,631
MISSOURI	25,475		24.2	28.2	31.9	10.2	5.6		11.5	16.8	39.7	26.8	5.2	130,140
UNITED STATES	27,916		21.9	25.0	32.3	12.3	8.4		7.9	10.5	27.1	35.6	19.0	192,285

SPENDING POTENTIAL INDICES

COUNTY	FINANCIAL SERVICES				THE HOME						ENTERTAINMENT						PERSONAL			
					Home Improvements		Furnishings													
	Auto Loan	Home Loan	Invest-ments	Retire-ment Plans	Home Repair	Lawn & Garden	Comput-ers & Hard-ware	Major Appli-ances	TV, Radio, Sound Equip-ment	Furni-ture	Dine out/ Carry out	Sports Equip-ment	Fees & Tickets	Toys & Games	Travel	Cable TV	Apparel & Services	Auto Repairs	Health Insur-ance	Pets & Supplies
PEMISCOT	62	45	36	45	47	60	49	55	56	48	55	48	43	57	47	60	48	54	62	59
PERRY	82	65	53	63	71	87	65	77	72	64	71	68	60	75	66	76	61	72	85	82
PETTIS	75	63	62	64	65	75	66	71	71	65	70	62	63	73	66	74	61	69	78	72
PHELPS	72	61	61	61	64	74	67	70	69	62	68	62	61	69	65	71	59	68	76	72
PIKE	76	57	47	56	63	81	61	72	67	57	66	63	53	69	60	72	56	67	80	76
PLATTE	119	125	124	128	119	113	120	116	116	123	117	109	123	119	119	113	106	117	110	116
POLK	69	53	45	53	56	69	60	65	63	55	62	58	52	63	57	65	53	63	69	68
PULASKI	78	60	52	61	60	70	70	70	71	64	70	65	62	73	64	71	62	71	72	72
PUTNAM	67	46	30	45	54	73	49	63	55	46	55	56	41	58	49	60	46	58	70	68
RALLS	87	65	44	63	72	93	65	81	71	64	71	72	57	75	65	75	61	74	85	87
RANDOLPH	72	60	60	60	63	73	64	68	68	61	67	60	59	69	63	71	58	66	76	70
RAY	91	80	77	80	84	96	79	88	84	78	82	77	76	88	80	86	72	83	93	91
REYNOLDS	64	46	28	44	52	70	46	60	51	45	51	52	39	53	46	55	43	55	64	65
RIPLEY	63	44	27	41	49	67	45	58	52	43	51	51	38	54	45	56	43	53	64	63
ST. CHARLES	119	131	128	131	123	115	119	118	115	125	115	110	124	119	120	112	105	117	111	118
ST. CLAIR	64	48	37	47	54	71	50	62	56	48	54	54	44	56	51	60	46	58	70	65
STE. GENEVIEVE	86	75	67	74	79	92	72	83	76	72	76	72	69	80	73	80	66	77	87	86
ST. FRANCOIS	74	60	54	59	63	77	63	70	68	60	62	62	57	69	62	71	58	67	77	73
ST. LOUIS	116	127	143	130	126	119	122	118	121	125	120	106	129	121	125	120	110	119	119	118
SALINE	78	63	62	64	67	79	69	74	74	65	72	65	63	75	68	77	62	72	83	76
SCHUYLER	73	50	31	48	58	80	54	69	60	50	59	61	44	63	53	65	50	63	76	75
SCOTLAND	75	52	34	50	60	82	56	71	63	52	62	63	46	66	56	68	52	65	80	76
SCOTT	74	62	58	62	64	75	64	70	69	63	68	61	60	70	63	72	60	68	75	73
SHANNON	57	39	21	36	44	61	40	52	45	38	45	46	33	47	39	49	38	47	57	57
SHELBY	72	50	36	49	58	78	55	68	62	51	60	60	46	64	54	67	51	63	77	72
STODDARD	69	51	42	50	56	73	55	65	61	52	60	57	48	63	54	65	51	61	73	68
STONE	84	67	48	64	75	96	66	84	71	64	70	72	59	71	68	76	60	76	89	87
SULLIVAN	67	48	34	47	53	70	51	62	57	49	56	54	44	59	50	61	48	58	68	66
TANEY	76	65	62	64	68	80	68	75	71	65	69	65	63	70	68	74	60	72	81	76
TEXAS	66	47	33	45	53	71	50	62	55	47	54	54	42	57	49	59	46	57	68	66
VERNON	72	56	47	55	61	76	60	68	65	57	64	60	53	66	59	68	55	65	74	72
WARREN	98	87	76	86	90	102	83	94	86	84	86	83	80	89	84	89	75	89	96	97
WASHINGTON	71	50	33	47	55	74	52	65	59	50	58	58	44	61	51	63	50	60	70	70
WAYNE	63	47	34	45	52	69	48	61	54	46	53	52	42	55	49	59	45	56	68	64
WEBSTER	80	62	47	60	65	81	62	73	68	61	67	65	56	71	62	72	58	69	78	77
WORTH	70	47	30	46	55	76	51	66	57	48	57	58	42	61	51	62	48	60	73	71
WRIGHT	65	48	39	47	53	68	52	61	57	49	56	54	45	59	51	61	48	58	68	65
ST. LOUIS CITY	62	54	64	58	53	56	65	58	68	62	67	52	62	66	61	69	61	63	64	59
MISSOURI	92	84	84	85	84	91	86	88	88	85	88	79	83	89	85	90	78	87	92	90
UNITED STATES	100	100	100	100	100	100	100	100	100	100	100	100	100	100	100	100	100	100	100	100

COUNTY	FIPS Code	CBSA Code	DMA Code	POPULATION			2000-2007 ANNUAL RATE		RACE (%)					
									White		Black		Asian/Pacific	
				2000	2007	2012	% Rate	State Rank	2000	2007	2000	2007	2000	2007
BEAVERHEAD	001	00000	754	9,202	8,971	8,820	-0.4	37	95.9	95.2	0.2	0.2	0.2	0.3
BIG HORN	003	00000	756	12,671	12,882	13,027	0.2	20	36.6	33.8	0.0	0.1	0.2	0.3
BLAINE	005	00000	755	7,009	6,915	6,864	-0.2	28	52.6	50.5	0.2	0.2	0.1	0.1
BROADWATER	007	00000	766	4,385	4,623	4,777	0.7	13	97.0	96.6	0.3	0.3	0.2	0.2
CARBON	009	13740	756	9,552	10,258	10,792	1.0	9	97.1	96.6	0.3	0.3	0.4	0.4
CARTER	011	00000	764	1,360	1,334	1,318	-0.3	31	98.6	98.6	0.1	0.1	0.1	0.1
CASCADE	013	24500	755	80,357	80,456	80,578	0.0	25	90.7	90.3	1.1	1.2	0.9	0.9
CHOUTEAU	015	00000	755	5,970	5,848	5,783	-0.3	31	84.0	82.0	0.1	0.1	0.3	0.4
CUSTER	017	00000	756	11,696	11,333	11,113	-0.4	37	97.0	96.7	0.1	0.1	0.3	0.4
DANIELS	019	00000	687	2,017	1,872	1,783	-1.0	52	96.0	95.4	0.0	0.0	0.3	0.5
DAWSON	021	00000	798	9,059	8,612	8,346	-0.7	45	97.4	97.1	0.3	0.3	0.1	0.2
DEER LODGE	023	00000	754	9,417	8,969	8,660	-0.7	45	95.9	95.5	0.2	0.2	0.4	0.5
FALLON	025	00000	687	2,837	2,746	2,663	-0.4	37	98.6	98.5	0.1	0.1	0.4	0.4
FERGUS	027	00000	755	11,893	11,581	11,400	-0.4	37	97.1	96.7	0.1	0.1	0.2	0.2
FLATHEAD	029	28060	762	74,471	86,440	98,259	2.1	2	96.3	95.8	0.2	0.2	0.5	0.7
GALLATIN	031	14580	754	67,831	84,457	99,081	3.1	1	96.2	95.6	0.2	0.3	1.0	1.2
GARFIELD	033	00000	756	1,279	1,196	1,137	-0.9	49	99.1	99.1	0.1	0.1	0.2	0.2
GLACIER	035	00000	755	13,247	13,436	13,576	0.2	20	35.4	32.4	0.1	0.1	0.1	0.1
GOLDEN VALLEY	037	00000	756	1,042	1,146	1,229	1.3	5	99.1	99.0	0.0	0.0	0.1	0.1
GRANITE	039	00000	762	2,830	2,928	2,996	0.5	17	96.3	96.1	0.0	0.0	0.2	0.2
HILL	041	25660	755	16,673	16,194	15,915	-0.4	37	79.5	77.3	0.1	0.1	0.4	0.5
JEFFERSON	043	25740	754	10,049	11,195	12,224	1.5	4	96.1	95.5	0.1	0.2	0.5	0.6
JUDITH BASIN	045	00000	755	2,329	2,255	2,191	-0.4	37	98.6	98.6	0.0	0.0	0.1	0.1
LAKE	047	00000	762	26,507	28,334	29,699	0.9	11	71.4	68.7	0.1	0.1	0.3	0.4
LEWIS AND CLARK	049	25740	766	55,716	59,835	62,963	1.0	9	95.2	94.6	0.2	0.2	0.6	0.7
LIBERTY	051	00000	755	2,158	2,091	2,045	-0.4	37	99.2	99.2	0.0	0.0	0.3	0.3
LINCOLN	053	00000	881	18,837	19,170	19,432	0.2	20	96.1	95.6	0.1	0.1	0.4	0.4
MCCONE	055	00000	687	1,977	1,842	1,757	-1.0	52	97.0	96.6	0.3	0.3	0.3	0.4
MADISON	057	00000	754	6,851	7,131	7,407	0.6	15	97.0	96.6	0.0	0.0	0.3	0.3
MEAGHER	059	00000	756	1,932	1,947	1,956	0.1	23	97.2	97.1	0.0	0.0	0.2	0.2
MINERAL	061	00000	762	3,884	4,080	4,228	0.7	13	94.6	94.0	0.2	0.2	0.5	0.7
MISSOULA	063	33540	762	95,802	104,711	111,447	1.2	7	94.0	93.2	0.3	0.3	1.1	1.4
MUSSELSHELL	065	00000	756	4,497	4,491	4,496	0.0	25	96.9	96.8	0.1	0.1	0.2	0.2
PARK	067	00000	756	15,694	15,965	16,176	0.2	20	96.6	96.1	0.4	0.5	0.4	0.5
PETROLEUM	069	00000	756	493	495	498	0.1	23	99.2	99.2	0.0	0.0	0.0	0.0
PHILLIPS	071	00000	755	4,601	4,416	4,311	-0.6	42	89.4	88.1	0.2	0.2	0.3	0.4
PONDERA	073	00000	755	6,424	6,163	5,982	-0.6	42	83.7	81.7	0.1	0.1	0.2	0.2
POWDER RIVER	075	00000	756	1,858	1,739	1,642	-0.9	49	97.4	97.0	0.0	0.0	0.1	0.2
POWELL	077	00000	754	7,180	7,159	7,167	0.0	25	92.5	92.2	0.5	0.5	0.4	0.4
PRAIRIE	079	00000	798	1,199	1,105	1,047	-1.1	55	98.0	97.8	0.0	0.0	0.2	0.2
RAVALLI	081	00000	762	36,070	40,518	43,917	1.6	3	96.7	96.2	0.1	0.2	0.4	0.5
RICHLAND	083	00000	687	9,667	9,125	8,788	-0.8	46	96.6	96.0	0.1	0.1	0.2	0.2
ROOSEVELT	085	00000	687	10,620	10,372	10,213	-0.3	31	40.9	37.7	0.0	0.0	0.5	0.5
ROSEBUD	087	00000	756	9,383	9,243	9,185	-0.2	28	64.4	61.4	0.2	0.3	0.3	0.3
SANDERS	089	00000	762	10,227	10,972	11,526	1.0	9	91.9	90.9	0.1	0.1	0.3	0.4
SHERIDAN	091	00000	687	4,105	3,557	3,215	-2.0	56	97.0	96.5	0.1	0.1	0.3	0.4
SILVER BOW	093	15580	754	34,606	33,148	32,205	-0.6	42	95.4	94.7	0.2	0.2	0.5	0.6
STILLWATER	095	00000	756	8,195	8,575	8,826	0.6	15	96.8	96.3	0.1	0.2	0.2	0.3
SWEET GRASS	097	00000	756	3,609	3,754	3,849	0.5	17	97.0	96.5	0.1	0.1	0.4	0.5
TETON	099	00000	755	6,445	6,371	6,289	-0.2	28	96.3	96.2	0.2	0.2	0.1	0.1
TOOLE	101	00000	755	5,267	5,113	4,959	-0.4	37	93.9	93.1	0.2	0.2	0.3	0.4
TREASURE	103	00000	756	861	794	754	-1.1	55	96.4	96.1	0.1	0.1	0.3	0.4
VALLEY	105	00000	755	7,675	7,184	6,860	-0.9	49	88.1	86.6	0.1	0.2	0.3	0.3
WHEATLAND	107	00000	756	2,259	2,111	2,018	-0.9	49	97.0	96.6	0.1	0.2	0.4	0.5
WIBAUX	109	00000	687	1,068	991	936	-1.0	52	98.0	97.9	0.2	0.2	0.2	0.2
YELLOWSTONE	111	13740	756	129,352	141,022	150,082	1.2	7	92.8	91.8	0.4	0.5	0.6	0.7
MONTANA							0.8		90.6	89.9	0.3	0.3	0.6	0.7
UNITED STATES							1.2		75.1	72.7	12.3	12.6	3.8	4.5

POPULATION COMPOSITION

COUNTY	% HISPANIC ORIGIN		2007 AGE DISTRIBUTION (%)										MEDIAN AGE	% 2007 Males	% 2007 Females
	2000	2007	0-4	5-9	10-14	15-19	20-24	25-44	45-64	65-84	85+	18+	2007		
BEAVERHEAD	2.7	3.3	5.8	5.5	5.4	9.5	7.8	22.9	28.8	12.0	2.3	78.2	39.5	51.1	48.9
BIG HORN	3.7	3.8	9.8	8.4	8.1	8.7	7.4	24.1	24.5	7.9	1.2	67.9	30.8	49.3	50.7
BLAINE	1.0	1.0	8.8	8.0	7.8	7.6	8.9	21.9	24.6	10.6	1.8	70.5	33.7	48.9	51.1
BROADWATER	1.3	1.6	5.5	5.4	6.4	6.1	5.0	21.3	33.4	14.4	2.4	78.3	45.1	51.2	48.8
CARBON	1.8	2.2	5.1	4.8	5.6	6.5	6.6	19.8	35.3	13.8	2.5	80.4	45.8	50.1	49.9
CARTER	0.6	0.6	4.3	4.1	4.2	9.1	9.7	19.6	31.0	14.5	3.6	80.1	44.4	47.8	52.2
CASCADE	2.4	2.5	6.9	5.9	6.1	7.0	8.2	25.0	26.4	12.2	2.2	76.9	38.0	49.5	50.5
CHOUTEAU	0.7	0.8	7.3	5.8	6.2	6.8	8.9	19.9	29.0	12.8	3.3	76.4	40.9	50.2	49.8
CUSTER	1.5	1.9	6.2	5.4	6.3	6.5	7.2	23.0	28.2	14.1	3.1	78.3	41.7	49.0	51.0
DANIELS	1.6	2.0	5.0	4.3	5.3	5.1	7.4	17.3	31.9	18.6	4.9	82.1	48.7	48.9	51.1
DAWSON	0.9	1.1	5.2	4.6	5.1	7.5	8.3	20.9	30.8	14.7	2.8	81.0	43.6	49.5	50.5
DEER LODGE	1.6	2.0	4.7	4.5	4.8	8.0	8.4	19.4	31.7	15.2	3.3	81.3	45.1	50.1	49.9
FALLON	0.4	0.4	4.9	4.4	5.6	6.5	9.0	19.4	31.0	16.2	2.9	80.7	45.1	50.8	49.2
FERGUS	0.8	1.0	5.5	4.8	5.7	6.1	7.9	19.3	30.7	16.4	3.6	79.7	45.4	48.8	51.2
FLATHEAD	1.4	1.8	5.8	5.7	6.5	6.7	7.2	22.7	32.0	11.6	1.9	77.8	41.7	49.5	50.5
GALLATIN	1.5	1.9	5.9	5.3	5.2	7.8	12.5	29.5	25.3	7.3	1.2	80.0	31.6	52.1	47.9
GARFIELD	0.4	0.4	7.0	7.6	4.8	5.1	5.9	22.5	29.8	13.8	3.6	77.3	43.0	51.6	48.4
GLACIER	1.2	1.1	8.8	7.2	7.6	9.4	9.7	22.3	25.0	8.7	1.1	70.2	31.1	49.4	50.6
GOLDEN VALLEY	1.2	1.6	5.1	5.7	4.8	6.9	7.6	18.2	34.9	15.4	1.6	79.7	45.9	51.7	48.3
GRANITE	1.3	1.3	4.9	4.7	4.6	7.5	6.0	19.9	34.6	15.9	1.9	80.7	46.5	51.0	49.0
HILL	1.2	1.4	7.6	6.6	6.2	7.8	8.7	24.4	26.6	10.3	2.0	75.2	34.4	50.0	50.0
JEFFERSON	1.5	1.8	5.2	5.4	6.9	8.3	6.2	20.5	36.4	9.7	1.4	76.9	43.5	50.5	49.5
JUDITH BASIN	0.6	0.6	5.1	5.0	6.1	6.7	7.4	19.3	33.3	14.7	2.3	79.8	45.2	52.8	47.2
LAKE	2.5	2.8	6.8	6.2	6.3	7.8	8.0	21.2	29.6	12.2	1.9	75.7	40.0	49.1	50.9
LEWIS AND CLARK	1.5	1.9	6.0	5.6	6.1	7.4	7.9	23.6	31.1	10.5	1.9	77.8	40.5	49.2	50.8
LIBERTY	0.2	0.2	5.8	5.1	4.5	6.3	10.0	19.2	30.1	15.4	3.6	80.3	44.3	49.1	50.9
LINCOLN	1.4	1.8	5.0	4.7	5.7	7.3	6.3	19.3	34.8	15.2	1.8	79.8	46.0	50.5	49.5
MCCONE	1.0	1.1	5.2	5.4	5.9	7.8	5.5	19.3	32.3	16.6	2.2	78.9	45.5	49.7	50.3
MADISON	1.9	2.4	4.6	4.4	4.9	5.4	6.7	19.8	36.6	15.4	2.2	82.4	47.3	50.8	49.2
MEAGHER	1.5	1.5	5.7	4.5	7.1	5.7	6.7	18.8	32.1	16.4	2.8	79.2	45.7	50.5	49.5
MINERAL	1.6	1.9	5.0	4.8	5.9	6.2	6.3	21.8	33.3	15.0	1.7	80.2	45.1	51.2	48.8
MISSOULA	1.6	2.0	5.7	5.1	5.5	7.5	11.2	28.4	26.3	8.6	1.6	80.0	34.0	49.9	50.1
MUSSELSHELL	1.6	1.6	5.0	5.0	5.5	5.2	8.6	18.2	35.2	14.3	3.0	81.3	46.4	48.6	51.4
PARK	1.8	2.3	5.5	5.2	5.4	6.6	6.8	22.7	34.0	11.6	2.2	79.7	43.5	49.8	50.2
PETROLEUM	1.2	1.2	7.1	7.3	6.9	5.3	5.1	23.2	28.1	15.6	1.6	75.4	41.9	53.1	46.9
PHILLIPS	1.2	1.5	5.4	4.6	6.8	7.2	8.0	19.4	31.4	13.9	3.4	78.1	44.2	50.2	49.8
PONDERA	0.8	1.0	7.2	5.8	6.0	8.5	9.9	19.4	27.7	12.9	2.7	75.5	39.9	48.7	51.3
POWDER RIVER	0.6	0.7	6.1	6.8	6.4	6.6	4.9	18.6	31.3	16.2	3.0	76.3	45.3	48.9	51.1
POWELL	1.9	2.0	4.4	4.6	4.7	7.3	8.8	26.3	28.3	13.2	2.3	81.8	41.4	59.7	40.3
PRAIRIE	0.7	0.7	3.7	4.1	4.6	3.8	6.1	15.2	41.5	16.8	4.2	84.8	52.2	52.3	47.7
RAVALLI	1.9	2.3	5.6	5.7	6.2	7.2	6.1	20.6	32.5	13.8	2.3	77.9	44.0	49.5	50.5
RICHLAND	2.2	2.7	6.3	5.5	6.2	7.6	8.2	20.7	30.5	12.4	2.6	77.2	41.6	50.1	49.9
ROOSEVELT	1.2	1.1	8.6	6.8	9.1	8.8	9.1	21.5	24.8	9.3	2.1	69.6	32.1	49.2	50.8
ROSEBUD	2.3	2.5	8.3	7.6	7.5	8.7	8.4	20.8	28.8	8.7	1.1	71.0	34.9	49.4	50.6
SANDERS	1.6	1.9	4.6	4.5	4.8	7.3	6.5	17.6	36.9	15.9	1.9	81.3	48.1	50.7	49.3
SHERIDAN	1.1	1.3	4.9	4.6	4.8	5.8	8.3	16.0	33.3	18.0	4.4	81.8	47.9	50.9	49.1
SILVER BOW	2.7	3.4	5.9	5.4	6.1	6.8	6.7	24.6	28.5	13.1	2.9	78.7	40.9	49.5	50.5
STILLWATER	2.0	2.4	5.5	5.3	6.7	6.5	5.8	21.7	34.1	12.5	1.9	78.1	43.9	50.9	49.1
SWEET GRASS	1.5	1.9	6.2	5.5	6.2	7.2	5.4	21.4	32.2	12.9	3.1	77.5	43.6	50.0	50.0
TETON	1.1	1.2	6.6	6.0	6.0	6.5	8.3	20.1	28.8	14.6	3.0	77.3	42.6	49.6	50.4
TOOLE	1.2	1.4	5.7	4.7	5.7	6.7	9.0	24.4	28.5	12.4	2.9	79.7	41.2	52.3	47.7
TREASURE	1.5	1.6	6.4	5.4	4.8	8.7	7.3	17.1	33.0	15.0	2.3	78.2	45.1	51.4	48.6
VALLEY	0.8	0.9	5.8	5.2	6.2	6.1	7.7	19.6	29.8	16.3	3.2	79.0	44.5	49.2	50.8
WHEATLAND	1.1	1.3	6.3	6.0	6.8	6.6	6.2	19.8	30.3	14.8	3.2	76.4	43.1	49.4	50.6
WIBAUX	0.4	0.4	5.7	5.0	5.1	7.0	8.0	19.4	30.0	15.7	4.1	80.2	44.9	47.4	52.6
YELLOWSTONE	3.7	4.5	6.6	6.3	6.5	6.9	6.5	25.9	28.1	11.1	2.2	76.5	38.7	49.0	51.0
MONTANA	2.0	2.4	6.2	5.7	6.1	7.2	8.2	24.0	29.1	11.4	2.1	77.8	39.5	49.9	50.1
UNITED STATES	12.5	15.0	6.9	6.5	6.8	7.1	7.0	27.6	25.4	10.7	1.9	75.6	36.7	49.2	50.8

COUNTY	HOUSEHOLDS					FAMILIES			MEDIAN HOUSEHOLD INCOME			
	2000	2007	2012	% Annual Rate 2000-2007	2007 Average HH Size	2000	2007	% Annual Rate 2000-2007	2007	2012	2007 National Rank	2007 State Rank
BEAVERHEAD	3,684	3,657	3,624	-0.1	2.32	2,355	2,263	-0.5	33,968	38,059	2553	30
BIG HORN	3,924	4,020	4,081	0.3	3.15	3,033	3,046	0.1	32,454	35,993	2716	40
BLAINE	2,501	2,460	2,440	-0.2	2.78	1,794	1,722	-0.6	30,059	34,088	2907	49
BROADWATER	1,752	1,871	1,945	0.9	2.44	1,270	1,323	0.6	37,420	41,069	2078	13
CARBON	4,065	4,440	4,709	1.2	2.29	2,706	2,870	0.8	37,667	41,459	2039	11
CARTER	543	535	530	-0.2	2.46	383	368	-0.5	29,411	31,591	2937	52
CASCADE	32,547	32,860	33,091	0.1	2.38	21,450	21,010	-0.3	40,238	46,233	1695	9
CHOUTEAU	2,226	2,170	2,142	-0.4	2.60	1,614	1,535	-0.7	33,592	36,993	2596	31
CUSTER	4,768	4,660	4,587	-0.3	2.34	3,092	2,930	-0.7	35,522	40,152	2364	22
DANIELS	892	850	819	-0.7	2.16	561	517	-1.1	31,136	33,539	2820	44
DAWSON	3,625	3,514	3,435	-0.4	2.31	2,477	2,333	-0.8	36,690	40,873	2169	16
DEER LODGE	3,995	3,826	3,702	-0.6	2.25	2,526	2,342	-1.0	32,470	36,928	2711	39
FALLON	1,140	1,130	1,108	-0.1	2.39	804	777	-0.5	34,662	38,699	2475	26
FERGUS	4,860	4,825	4,792	-0.1	2.28	3,197	3,081	-0.5	35,507	39,472	2366	23
FLATHEAD	29,588	33,560	38,237	1.8	2.54	20,425	22,544	1.4	40,511	45,489	1659	8
GALLATIN	26,323	33,029	39,002	3.2	2.46	16,196	19,641	2.7	46,248	53,745	979	2
GARFIELD	532	519	500	-0.3	2.28	366	347	-0.7	28,845	30,854	2967	54
GLACIER	4,304	4,361	4,406	0.2	3.04	3,246	3,216	-0.1	32,607	36,159	2695	38
GOLDEN VALLEY	365	410	445	1.6	2.40	263	288	1.3	30,710	32,594	2862	47
GRANITE	1,200	1,254	1,289	0.6	2.31	785	795	0.2	32,622	35,969	2694	37
HILL	6,457	6,354	6,282	-0.2	2.49	4,255	4,061	-0.6	36,583	41,369	2183	18
JEFFERSON	3,747	4,210	4,618	1.6	2.61	2,846	3,131	1.3	48,549	53,688	778	1
JUDITH BASIN	951	918	891	-0.5	2.46	662	622	-0.9	31,811	33,650	2779	42
LAKE	10,192	11,020	11,617	1.1	2.52	7,217	7,605	0.7	33,107	36,450	2645	34
LEWIS AND CLARK	22,850	24,866	26,338	1.2	2.36	14,958	15,783	0.7	44,743	50,773	1134	3
LIBERTY	833	813	797	-0.3	2.49	584	554	-0.7	34,949	38,516	2437	25
LINCOLN	7,764	8,109	8,322	0.6	2.34	5,335	5,417	0.2	30,786	32,907	2854	46
MCCONE	810	775	749	-0.6	2.38	597	558	-0.9	34,231	37,507	2524	29
MADISON	2,956	3,136	3,287	0.8	2.25	1,921	1,976	0.4	34,274	37,117	2515	28
MEAGHER	803	811	816	0.1	2.37	529	518	-0.3	32,707	35,302	2682	36
MINERAL	1,584	1,694	1,771	0.9	2.37	1,068	1,109	0.5	30,919	32,920	2843	45
MISSOULA	38,439	42,476	45,485	1.4	2.38	23,145	24,689	0.9	41,804	48,103	1475	7
MUSSELSHELL	1,878	1,895	1,906	0.1	2.31	1,235	1,209	-0.3	29,799	32,738	2921	50
PARK	6,828	7,130	7,314	0.6	2.21	4,223	4,262	0.1	37,234	41,567	2097	14
PETROLEUM	211	216	219	0.3	2.29	137	136	-0.1	27,435	29,806	3021	56
PHILLIPS	1,848	1,806	1,777	-0.3	2.40	1,241	1,177	-0.7	33,232	36,427	2636	32
PONDERA	2,410	2,309	2,240	-0.6	2.64	1,739	1,623	-0.9	35,396	38,550	2384	24
POWDER RIVER	737	695	659	-0.8	2.45	525	483	-1.1	31,735	33,817	2784	43
POWELL	2,422	2,432	2,444	0.1	2.37	1,634	1,595	-0.3	36,165	40,242	2246	19
PRAIRIE	537	509	489	-0.7	2.12	355	326	-1.2	29,196	32,051	2950	53
RAVALLI	14,289	16,178	17,606	1.7	2.47	10,182	11,234	1.4	37,026	40,785	2123	15
RICHLAND	3,878	3,757	3,662	-0.4	2.40	2,653	2,497	-0.8	37,561	41,931	2051	12
ROOSEVELT	3,581	3,511	3,464	-0.3	2.88	2,615	2,501	-0.6	29,487	32,641	2931	51
ROSEBUD	3,307	3,320	3,328	0.1	2.76	2,417	2,369	-0.3	41,931	47,108	1455	6
SANDERS	4,273	4,702	5,000	1.3	2.29	2,897	3,098	0.9	30,444	32,855	2887	48
SHERIDAN	1,741	1,533	1,393	-1.7	2.24	1,140	972	-2.2	33,222	35,914	2637	33
SILVER BOW	14,432	13,934	13,584	-0.5	2.30	8,931	8,338	-0.9	36,669	42,149	2173	17
STILLWATER	3,234	3,420	3,538	0.8	2.46	2,348	2,422	0.4	43,796	47,750	1237	5
SWEET GRASS	1,476	1,539	1,579	0.6	2.40	987	998	0.2	37,861	41,129	2014	10
TETON	2,538	2,516	2,487	-0.1	2.51	1,762	1,699	-0.5	34,653	38,057	2477	27
TOOLE	1,962	1,859	1,795	-0.7	2.47	1,309	1,204	-1.1	35,764	39,841	2321	21
TREASURE	357	336	323	-0.8	2.36	242	221	-1.2	32,127	34,083	2748	41
VALLEY	3,150	2,986	2,867	-0.7	2.34	2,128	1,961	-1.1	36,041	39,984	2271	20
WHEATLAND	853	798	760	-0.9	2.20	541	490	-1.4	28,180	30,849	2995	55
WIBAUX	421	394	373	-0.9	2.42	287	261	-1.3	32,747	36,157	2678	35
YELLOWSTONE	52,084	57,305	61,292	1.3	2.41	34,219	36,521	0.9	44,257	50,828	1182	4
MONTANA				1.0	2.43			0.5	39,634	45,166		
UNITED STATES				1.2	2.59			1.0	53,154	62,503		

COUNTY	2007 Per Capita Income	2007 HH Income Base	2007 HOUSEHOLD INCOME DISTRIBUTION (%)					2007 Home Value Base	2007 HOME VALUE DISTRIBUTION (%)					2007 Median Home Value
			Less than $25,000	$25,000 to $49,999	$50,000 to $99,999	$100,000 to $149,999	$150,000 or More		Less than $50,000	$50,000 to $89,999	$90,000 to $174,999	$175,000 to $399,999	$400,000 or More	
BEAVERHEAD	18,874	3,657	38.0	27.6	27.6	4.9	1.8	2,353	12.8	8.5	37.2	33.6	7.9	155,399
BIG HORN	12,856	4,020	37.5	33.2	24.3	3.9	1.1	2,606	21.8	17.7	42.8	11.7	6.0	109,846
BLAINE	14,445	2,460	41.5	29.9	22.4	5.1	1.1	1,513	18.2	23.5	39.5	16.1	2.8	101,828
BROADWATER	19,748	1,871	28.6	37.8	26.2	4.6	2.7	1,481	10.9	7.7	41.9	28.8	10.7	152,529
CARBON	20,424	4,440	31.4	32.6	28.2	6.2	1.6	3,315	9.6	9.6	31.7	35.2	13.9	172,770
CARTER	14,731	535	44.3	32.1	19.6	3.0	0.9	403	36.7	15.4	16.4	8.9	22.6	82,917
CASCADE	21,572	32,860	29.6	32.0	29.4	5.7	3.3	21,347	7.4	8.7	41.5	38.0	4.5	163,981
CHOUTEAU	16,733	2,163	35.2	35.2	23.5	3.8	2.2	1,496	13.9	16.8	42.4	20.1	6.8	127,875
CUSTER	19,262	4,660	34.1	32.4	26.4	5.7	1.4	3,278	16.9	18.8	44.3	15.4	4.6	116,397
DANIELS	18,685	850	40.7	33.8	19.2	4.7	1.6	666	27.2	23.4	33.9	12.6	2.9	89,091
DAWSON	18,827	3,514	35.8	30.6	26.7	5.3	1.7	2,600	17.0	22.7	45.3	13.7	1.4	106,536
DEER LODGE	18,997	3,826	37.2	32.4	25.4	3.2	1.8	2,809	10.5	19.3	44.2	24.1	2.0	129,199
FALLON	18,641	1,130	35.8	30.8	27.8	3.7	1.9	871	22.2	23.3	35.8	11.3	7.5	97,453
FERGUS	19,284	4,825	34.9	33.0	24.9	5.3	1.9	3,550	13.2	15.9	43.2	20.5	7.2	129,515
FLATHEAD	20,762	33,560	29.0	33.0	28.4	6.2	3.4	24,668	8.0	4.8	21.3	49.5	16.4	215,934
GALLATIN	23,724	33,029	23.3	30.7	32.9	8.8	4.3	20,651	8.4	3.7	11.3	52.6	24.1	266,664
GARFIELD	15,775	519	43.5	31.2	22.0	2.3	1.0	386	29.0	21.5	24.1	7.8	17.6	88,750
GLACIER	13,812	4,361	38.5	32.4	22.3	5.0	1.8	2,738	18.4	17.5	47.7	14.1	2.3	113,452
GOLDEN VALLEY	15,759	410	43.2	31.5	20.2	3.4	1.7	318	8.2	30.5	35.5	16.4	9.4	103,030
GRANITE	19,802	1,254	38.0	32.0	22.7	4.5	2.8	938	13.3	13.5	32.8	28.5	11.8	143,000
HILL	18,570	6,353	34.7	30.6	27.3	5.2	2.3	4,106	13.0	14.1	43.1	27.6	2.2	133,817
JEFFERSON	21,917	4,210	24.1	27.3	36.0	9.4	3.3	3,503	8.1	6.1	25.9	43.8	16.1	221,107
JUDITH BASIN	16,431	918	40.3	35.5	18.5	3.5	2.2	710	21.7	18.2	35.2	15.6	9.3	111,111
LAKE	17,934	11,019	36.8	33.2	23.2	4.3	2.5	7,924	9.3	5.8	25.9	39.1	19.9	214,709
LEWIS AND CLARK	23,317	24,866	24.4	31.5	33.0	8.4	2.7	17,448	8.8	5.1	23.9	53.7	8.5	198,172
LIBERTY	17,862	813	35.7	31.0	27.1	4.3	2.0	584	17.3	18.3	40.8	20.0	3.6	112,647
LINCOLN	16,102	8,109	41.2	34.0	20.6	3.5	0.6	6,231	12.9	11.9	38.9	29.7	6.6	142,769
MCCONE	18,476	775	34.6	35.5	24.6	3.2	2.1	604	25.2	27.3	34.1	8.8	4.6	86,250
MADISON	19,585	3,136	34.3	35.4	23.9	4.2	2.1	2,207	5.9	6.4	28.5	39.3	19.9	202,567
MEAGHER	16,327	811	38.3	36.4	20.6	3.7	1.0	597	13.6	17.9	41.2	22.1	5.2	127,730
MINERAL	17,563	1,694	40.7	33.1	20.0	4.2	2.0	1,258	11.4	10.6	35.9	33.1	9.1	156,716
MISSOULA	22,318	42,476	29.2	29.4	30.4	7.6	3.4	26,336	9.3	4.7	12.7	58.1	15.1	239,902
MUSSELSHELL	17,682	1,895	41.8	32.7	20.6	2.9	2.0	1,457	18.7	16.7	36.4	22.0	6.1	118,078
PARK	21,659	7,130	32.9	32.9	26.3	4.8	3.1	4,775	11.0	4.9	32.4	37.3	14.5	179,959
PETROLEUM	18,419	216	45.8	32.9	14.8	2.8	3.7	162	24.7	22.2	37.0	12.3	3.7	94,545
PHILLIPS	17,538	1,806	38.8	29.5	27.1	3.2	1.5	1,286	21.2	23.0	40.4	13.8	1.6	100,577
PONDERA	17,001	2,309	36.6	29.9	26.1	5.5	1.9	1,635	11.6	16.9	45.7	20.4	5.4	130,598
POWDER RIVER	17,403	695	37.0	37.0	21.9	2.2	2.0	517	18.0	22.8	31.9	15.5	11.8	107,237
POWELL	17,270	2,432	32.2	38.4	23.6	4.3	1.5	1,745	10.1	16.9	39.4	22.8	10.8	138,088
PRAIRIE	17,015	509	42.0	37.3	16.5	3.7	0.4	396	30.8	28.3	30.6	6.6	3.8	76,471
RAVALLI	20,559	16,178	31.0	34.7	25.5	5.6	3.3	12,282	6.8	4.0	17.6	51.3	20.3	246,445
RICHLAND	19,332	3,757	31.1	34.1	28.9	4.0	1.9	2,727	16.9	19.3	47.6	15.0	1.2	110,794
ROOSEVELT	13,621	3,511	43.4	30.0	20.5	4.5	1.5	2,294	22.1	27.2	41.2	7.7	1.9	91,024
ROSEBUD	18,328	3,320	31.0	27.2	33.0	7.0	1.9	2,247	23.7	19.1	41.4	11.9	3.9	103,886
SANDERS	17,511	4,702	40.7	33.1	20.9	3.6	1.7	3,616	9.6	13.4	32.9	31.2	12.9	160,921
SHERIDAN	18,527	1,533	35.1	38.4	20.1	4.6	1.8	1,226	28.1	24.6	34.8	11.8	0.7	83,774
SILVER BOW	20,992	13,934	33.7	30.8	27.1	5.6	2.7	9,789	9.6	17.0	43.5	26.1	3.8	132,465
STILLWATER	20,997	3,420	25.6	30.8	35.4	6.2	2.0	2,623	10.8	8.0	26.8	39.9	14.5	186,589
SWEET GRASS	20,677	1,539	31.1	34.9	25.7	5.1	3.2	1,146	7.7	7.7	26.9	38.5	19.3	193,238
TETON	17,376	2,516	34.4	34.7	25.2	4.5	1.3	1,900	8.2	13.9	46.4	24.9	6.6	142,376
TOOLE	17,530	1,858	35.2	32.4	27.2	3.2	2.0	1,321	16.0	18.6	47.1	15.2	3.1	112,102
TREASURE	16,211	336	38.7	38.1	18.8	3.3	1.2	243	28.0	25.5	26.7	14.4	5.3	84,333
VALLEY	19,592	2,986	34.3	32.2	26.8	4.2	2.5	2,264	17.6	21.2	44.3	14.7	2.3	109,683
WHEATLAND	15,078	798	44.0	34.3	18.4	2.8	0.5	583	11.3	28.8	45.3	11.3	3.3	102,995
WIBAUX	18,341	394	36.8	32.7	24.1	4.3	2.0	290	26.9	22.8	32.4	12.4	5.5	91,111
YELLOWSTONE	23,801	57,305	26.8	29.2	31.7	7.8	4.4	39,606	7.8	7.5	43.8	36.2	4.7	160,800
MONTANA	20,909		30.5	31.5	28.6	6.4	3.0		10.3	9.3	31.2	38.7	10.6	173,301
UNITED STATES	27,916		21.9	25.0	32.3	12.3	8.4		7.9	10.5	27.1	35.6	19.0	192,285

COUNTY	FINANCIAL SERVICES				THE HOME						ENTERTAINMENT						PERSONAL			
					Home Improvements		Furnishings													
	Auto Loan	Home Loan	Invest-ments	Retire-ment Plans	Home Repair	Lawn & Garden	Comput-ers & Hard-ware	Major Appli-ances	TV, Radio, Sound Equip-ment	Furni-ture	Dine out/ Carry out	Sports Equip-ment	Fees & Tickets	Toys & Games	Travel	Cable TV	Apparel & Services	Auto Repairs	Health Insur-ance	Pets & Supplies
BEAVERHEAD	70	54	47	54	60	75	59	69	62	55	61	61	52	63	58	65	53	65	73	72
BIG HORN	63	50	44	50	51	61	54	58	58	52	57	52	49	59	52	59	50	58	62	61
BLAINE	62	47	44	48	50	63	53	58	58	50	57	51	47	59	51	61	49	57	65	61
BROADWATER	79	57	41	56	66	88	62	77	68	57	67	67	52	70	62	73	56	70	85	81
CARBON	75	58	45	57	65	83	61	74	65	57	64	64	53	66	61	68	55	68	78	77
CARTER	66	42	18	40	51	74	44	62	49	42	50	55	34	54	43	53	41	55	65	69
CASCADE	74	66	73	67	67	73	72	72	74	68	72	64	69	74	71	75	64	72	77	72
CHOUTEAU	75	50	30	49	58	80	56	70	61	52	61	63	45	65	54	65	52	65	76	76
CUSTER	68	56	58	56	61	72	61	67	65	57	63	58	56	65	61	68	55	64	75	69
DANIELS	70	46	26	45	55	77	50	66	56	47	56	59	40	60	49	60	47	59	72	72
DAWSON	71	54	45	53	59	75	58	68	63	54	62	59	51	65	58	67	53	64	75	70
DEER LODGE	61	54	60	53	58	66	58	62	63	54	60	53	55	61	59	66	53	60	72	62
FALLON	73	52	39	50	59	78	57	69	65	52	62	61	48	66	57	69	53	64	80	73
FERGUS	73	53	42	52	60	78	58	69	64	53	62	61	50	66	58	68	53	65	78	73
FLATHEAD	79	71	66	71	73	83	71	78	73	70	72	69	68	74	72	75	64	75	80	80
GALLATIN	87	76	75	79	75	80	86	81	83	80	84	76	80	84	80	82	75	84	81	83
GARFIELD	65	42	18	39	51	73	44	61	48	42	49	55	34	54	43	52	41	54	64	68
GLACIER	64	53	49	54	54	64	55	60	59	55	59	52	52	60	55	62	51	59	64	63
GOLDEN VALLEY	72	46	20	43	56	81	48	67	53	46	54	60	37	59	47	57	45	60	71	75
GRANITE	76	54	37	53	63	85	58	74	64	54	63	65	49	66	58	68	53	67	80	78
HILL	68	59	63	60	60	67	64	65	66	61	65	58	60	67	62	68	57	65	70	67
JEFFERSON	88	81	69	80	84	94	76	87	77	77	77	77	74	80	78	80	69	81	86	90
JUDITH BASIN	73	46	20	44	57	82	49	68	54	47	55	61	38	60	48	58	46	61	72	76
LAKE	71	58	49	58	62	75	60	69	63	58	62	61	55	64	60	65	54	65	72	71
LEWIS AND CLARK	79	75	75	76	75	80	76	78	76	75	76	70	74	77	76	77	68	77	79	79
LIBERTY	76	52	34	50	61	83	57	72	63	52	62	63	46	67	56	68	52	65	80	77
LINCOLN	62	46	33	45	53	69	48	60	52	45	51	52	41	53	49	56	44	55	65	64
MCCONE	75	50	32	49	59	82	55	70	61	51	61	62	45	65	54	66	51	64	78	78
MADISON	73	55	34	53	64	85	56	73	59	53	59	64	47	61	57	64	50	66	76	78
MEAGHER	67	45	26	43	53	74	48	63	54	45	53	56	39	58	48	58	45	57	69	69
MINERAL	70	52	31	50	60	81	52	69	56	50	56	60	44	59	53	61	48	62	72	74
MISSOULA	76	69	72	71	68	71	79	73	76	73	76	68	73	75	74	75	68	75	73	74
MUSSELSHELL	69	48	33	46	55	75	52	65	58	48	57	57	43	61	51	63	48	60	73	69
PARK	73	60	56	61	64	77	65	72	67	61	66	63	59	67	64	70	57	69	76	74
PETROLEUM	76	49	21	46	60	86	51	72	56	49	58	64	40	63	50	61	48	63	75	80
PHILLIPS	72	49	31	47	57	79	53	68	59	49	58	60	43	63	52	64	49	62	75	73
PONDERA	73	54	43	54	60	77	58	69	63	55	62	61	50	65	57	67	53	65	75	73
POWDER RIVER	78	49	21	47	61	88	52	73	58	50	59	65	40	64	51	62	49	65	77	81
POWELL	69	55	48	54	61	75	58	68	63	54	61	59	52	64	59	67	52	63	75	70
PRAIRIE	58	46	34	44	52	67	45	59	49	45	49	50	41	49	48	53	41	54	64	61
RAVALLI	78	65	57	65	72	88	67	79	70	64	69	69	61	70	69	73	60	73	82	82
RICHLAND	74	56	47	56	63	79	61	71	65	57	64	62	53	68	60	69	55	67	78	75
ROOSEVELT	62	47	40	47	50	62	51	57	56	49	55	50	45	58	50	59	48	56	63	61
ROSEBUD	79	66	56	66	66	78	67	73	71	66	70	65	62	73	66	73	61	72	77	77
SANDERS	65	51	35	50	58	75	51	66	55	49	54	57	45	55	53	58	46	60	69	68
SHERIDAN	73	48	28	47	58	80	52	69	58	49	58	61	42	62	51	63	49	62	75	75
SILVER BOW	68	63	73	63	65	70	67	68	70	64	68	59	65	69	67	72	60	67	76	68
STILLWATER	85	68	48	66	75	94	66	82	70	65	70	72	59	74	67	74	61	75	85	87
SWEET GRASS	84	60	40	59	70	93	64	81	68	60	68	71	53	72	63	73	58	73	85	87
TETON	74	51	34	50	60	81	55	70	60	52	60	62	46	64	54	64	51	64	76	76
TOOLE	71	53	47	52	59	75	59	68	64	54	63	60	51	66	58	68	54	64	77	71
TREASURE	69	44	19	42	54	78	47	65	51	44	52	58	36	57	46	55	44	57	68	72
VALLEY	74	56	47	55	64	81	59	71	65	57	64	62	52	67	60	69	55	66	78	75
WHEATLAND	60	40	25	39	48	66	44	57	49	41	48	50	35	52	43	53	41	51	62	61
WIBAUX	74	52	38	50	59	80	57	70	65	52	63	62	48	67	57	69	53	65	80	74
YELLOWSTONE	81	78	84	79	77	80	80	79	81	78	80	71	79	80	79	82	72	80	82	80
MONTANA	76	66	63	66	68	78	70	74	72	67	71	66	65	72	69	74	62	72	78	76
UNITED STATES	100	100	100	100	100	100	100	100	100	100	100	100	100	100	100	100	100	100	100	100

NEBRASKA

POPULATION CHANGE

A

COUNTY	FIPS Code	CBSA Code	DMA Code	POPULATION 2000	2007	2012	2000-2007 ANNUAL RATE % Rate	State Rank	RACE (%) White 2000	White 2007	Black 2000	Black 2007	Asian/Pacific 2000	Asian/Pacific 2007
ADAMS	001	25580	722	31,151	32,061	32,578	0.4	20	94.5	92.9	0.6	0.7	1.6	2.4
ANTELOPE	003	00000	722	7,452	7,135	6,925	-0.6	63	98.8	98.6	0.1	0.1	0.1	0.1
ARTHUR	005	00000	751	444	406	387	-1.2	89	96.4	96.1	0.0	0.0	0.9	1.0
BANNER	007	42420	751	819	789	769	-0.5	58	95.8	95.7	0.1	0.1	0.1	0.1
BLAINE	009	00000	722	583	531	488	-1.3	91	99.0	98.9	0.0	0.0	0.0	0.0
BOONE	011	00000	722	6,259	5,906	5,676	-0.8	75	99.2	99.1	0.0	0.1	0.1	0.1
BOX BUTTE	013	00000	751	12,158	11,205	10,617	-1.1	87	90.8	88.8	0.4	0.4	0.5	0.8
BOYD	015	00000	722	2,438	2,323	2,253	-0.7	70	98.9	98.8	0.0	0.0	0.2	0.2
BROWN	017	00000	722	3,525	3,301	3,148	-0.9	79	98.6	98.3	0.0	0.0	0.3	0.4
BUFFALO	019	28260	722	42,259	45,684	48,306	1.1	6	95.2	93.9	0.5	0.6	0.7	1.1
BURT	021	00000	652	7,791	7,401	7,115	-0.7	70	97.6	97.2	0.2	0.2	0.2	0.3
BUTLER	023	00000	722	8,767	8,772	8,720	0.0	30	98.4	98.4	0.1	0.1	0.2	0.2
CASS	025	36540	652	24,334	26,515	28,172	1.2	4	97.9	97.5	0.2	0.2	0.4	0.5
CEDAR	027	00000	624	9,615	9,200	8,900	-0.6	63	99.1	98.9	0.1	0.1	0.1	0.1
CHASE	029	00000	722	4,068	3,842	3,692	-0.8	75	97.8	97.2	0.2	0.2	0.2	0.3
CHERRY	031	00000	751	6,148	6,064	6,021	-0.2	36	94.2	94.1	0.1	0.1	0.4	0.4
CHEYENNE	033	00000	751	9,830	10,144	10,362	0.4	20	96.3	95.3	0.1	0.2	0.4	0.6
CLAY	035	25580	722	7,039	7,070	7,030	0.1	27	97.6	97.5	0.2	0.2	0.3	0.3
COLFAX	037	00000	652	10,441	10,784	11,012	0.4	20	81.7	77.1	0.1	0.1	0.3	0.4
CUMING	039	00000	652	10,203	9,907	9,638	-0.4	49	95.9	94.6	0.1	0.2	0.2	0.3
CUSTER	041	00000	722	11,793	11,436	11,204	-0.4	49	98.6	98.4	0.1	0.1	0.2	0.2
DAKOTA	043	43580	624	20,253	20,781	21,114	0.4	20	78.8	74.0	0.6	0.7	3.1	4.3
DAWES	045	00000	751	9,060	8,537	8,243	-0.8	75	93.3	92.3	0.8	0.9	0.4	0.5
DAWSON	047	30420	722	24,365	24,986	25,423	0.3	23	82.3	77.9	0.3	0.4	0.7	0.9
DEUEL	049	00000	751	2,098	2,034	1,992	-0.4	49	97.3	97.2	0.0	0.0	0.4	0.4
DIXON	051	43580	624	6,339	6,307	6,296	-0.1	32	94.6	94.6	0.0	0.0	0.3	0.3
DODGE	053	23340	652	36,160	36,729	37,194	0.2	25	95.9	94.7	0.4	0.5	0.6	0.9
DOUGLAS	055	36540	652	463,585	500,075	527,660	1.1	6	81.0	78.4	11.5	12.0	1.8	2.5
DUNDY	057	00000	678	2,292	2,192	2,132	-0.6	63	96.9	96.8	0.0	0.0	0.5	0.5
FILLMORE	059	00000	722	6,634	6,485	6,385	-0.3	41	97.8	97.3	0.2	0.2	0.1	0.1
FRANKLIN	061	00000	722	3,574	3,444	3,369	-0.5	58	99.2	99.1	0.0	0.0	0.1	0.1
FRONTIER	063	00000	722	3,099	2,900	2,774	-0.9	79	98.3	97.9	0.1	0.1	0.3	0.4
FURNAS	065	00000	722	5,324	5,163	5,067	-0.4	49	98.2	97.9	0.1	0.1	0.2	0.3
GAGE	067	13100	722	22,993	23,631	24,052	0.4	20	97.7	97.3	0.3	0.4	0.3	0.5
GARDEN	069	00000	751	2,292	2,096	1,927	-1.2	89	98.3	97.8	0.1	0.2	0.3	0.4
GARFIELD	071	00000	722	1,902	1,782	1,703	-0.9	79	98.8	98.6	0.0	0.0	0.1	0.2
GOSPER	073	30420	722	2,143	2,048	1,978	-0.6	63	98.8	98.7	0.0	0.0	0.2	0.2
GRANT	075	00000	751	747	680	660	-1.3	91	98.8	98.7	0.0	0.0	0.3	0.3
GREELEY	077	00000	722	2,714	2,609	2,545	-0.5	58	97.9	97.5	0.7	0.7	0.1	0.1
HALL	079	24260	722	53,534	55,640	57,231	0.5	15	88.7	85.4	0.4	0.4	1.2	1.7
HAMILTON	081	00000	722	9,403	9,704	9,924	0.4	20	98.4	98.0	0.2	0.2	0.2	0.3
HARLAN	083	00000	722	3,786	3,532	3,317	-1.0	83	98.9	98.7	0.1	0.1	0.1	0.1
HAYES	085	00000	722	1,068	1,054	1,035	-0.2	36	97.2	97.2	0.2	0.2	0.3	0.3
HITCHCOCK	087	00000	722	3,111	3,000	2,938	-0.5	58	98.4	98.1	0.1	0.1	0.1	0.2
HOLT	089	00000	722	11,551	10,711	10,138	-1.0	83	98.9	98.6	0.0	0.0	0.2	0.3
HOOKER	091	00000	751	783	760	749	-0.4	49	98.7	98.7	0.0	0.0	0.1	0.1
HOWARD	093	24260	722	6,567	6,909	7,119	0.7	10	98.7	98.4	0.3	0.3	0.1	0.2
JEFFERSON	095	00000	722	8,333	7,901	7,614	-0.7	70	98.4	98.0	0.1	0.1	0.2	0.3
JOHNSON	097	00000	652	4,488	4,770	4,799	0.8	9	93.5	91.5	0.1	0.1	2.7	4.0
KEARNEY	099	28260	722	6,882	6,788	6,705	-0.2	36	97.8	97.8	0.2	0.2	0.2	0.3
KEITH	101	00000	751	8,875	8,590	8,234	-0.4	49	96.8	95.9	0.1	0.1	0.2	0.2
KEYA PAHA	103	00000	722	983	951	918	-0.5	58	99.4	99.4	0.0	0.0	0.0	0.0
KIMBALL	105	00000	751	4,089	3,881	3,712	-0.7	70	97.0	96.5	0.2	0.2	0.1	0.2
KNOX	107	00000	624	9,374	9,182	9,059	-0.3	41	91.6	90.6	0.1	0.1	0.2	0.3
LANCASTER	109	30700	722	250,291	274,677	292,999	1.3	2	90.1	87.8	2.8	3.0	2.9	4.3
LINCOLN	111	35820	740	34,632	36,117	37,202	0.6	12	94.7	93.3	0.5	0.6	0.4	0.6
LOGAN	113	35820	740	774	735	714	-0.7	70	98.6	98.5	0.1	0.1	0.0	0.0
LOUP	115	00000	722	712	722	711	0.2	25	98.9	98.9	0.0	0.0	0.1	0.1
MCPHERSON	117	35820	740	533	516	504	-0.4	49	97.9	97.9	0.0	0.0	0.4	0.4
MADISON	119	35740	624	35,226	35,501	35,374	0.1	27	91.4	89.1	0.9	1.0	0.4	0.6
MERRICK	121	24260	722	8,204	8,108	8,056	-0.2	36	98.3	98.3	0.2	0.2	0.2	0.2
MORRILL	123	00000	764	5,440	5,237	5,064	-0.5	58	93.7	91.9	0.1	0.1	0.2	0.3
NANCE	125	00000	722	4,038	3,750	3,540	-1.0	83	98.4	98.1	0.0	0.0	0.0	0.1
NEMAHA	127	00000	652	7,576	7,181	6,903	-0.7	70	97.6	97.0	0.4	0.4	0.6	0.9
NUCKOLLS	129	00000	722	5,057	4,705	4,472	-1.0	83	98.9	98.6	0.0	0.0	0.2	0.2
OTOE	131	00000	652	15,396	16,264	16,891	0.8	9	97.4	96.7	0.3	0.3	0.3	0.4
PAWNEE	133	00000	722	3,087	2,942	2,850	-0.7	70	98.9	98.6	0.0	0.0	0.3	0.4
PERKINS	135	00000	722	3,200	3,127	3,087	-0.3	41	97.7	97.6	0.0	0.0	0.2	0.2
PHELPS	137	00000	722	9,747	9,485	9,260	-0.4	49	97.8	97.2	0.1	0.1	0.3	0.4
PIERCE	139	35740	624	7,857	7,799	7,745	-0.1	32	98.7	98.6	0.1	0.1	0.2	0.2
PLATTE	141	18100	652	31,662	31,806	31,881	0.1	27	94.3	92.6	0.4	0.4	0.4	0.6
POLK	143	00000	722	5,639	5,651	5,669	0.0	30	98.9	98.9	0.0	0.0	0.1	0.1
RED WILLOW	145	00000	722	11,448	11,105	10,838	-0.4	49	97.5	97.0	0.2	0.2	0.2	0.3
RICHARDSON	147	00000	652	9,531	9,045	8,697	-0.7	70	95.6	95.1	0.2	0.2	0.1	0.2
ROCK	149	00000	722	1,756	1,621	1,574	-1.1	87	99.0	98.8	0.0	0.0	0.2	0.2
SALINE	151	00000	722	13,843	14,359	14,658	0.5	15	93.0	90.8	0.4	0.4	1.7	2.5
SARPY	153	36540	652	122,595	151,197	175,662	2.9	1	89.2	87.2	4.4	4.6	2.0	2.9
NEBRASKA							0.8		89.6	87.5	4.0	4.3	1.3	2.0
UNITED STATES							1.2		75.1	72.7	12.3	12.6	3.8	4.5

COUNTY	% HISPANIC ORIGIN		2007 AGE DISTRIBUTION (%)										MEDIAN AGE	% 2007 Males	% 2007 Females
	2000	2007	0-4	5-9	10-14	15-19	20-24	25-44	45-64	65-84	85+	18+	2007		
ADAMS	4.6	6.1	6.4	5.7	5.9	8.3	8.3	24.6	25.1	12.4	3.3	77.9	37.7	49.2	50.8
ANTELOPE	0.7	0.9	6.9	6.3	5.5	7.0	7.2	20.4	28.4	14.8	3.6	76.7	42.8	49.2	50.8
ARTHUR	1.4	1.5	5.9	5.9	4.4	6.4	5.7	23.6	27.6	18.2	2.2	80.3	43.7	48.8	51.2
BANNER	5.6	5.8	5.2	4.2	5.2	11.0	7.2	20.8	29.5	15.6	1.3	78.8	43.4	52.6	47.4
BLAINE	0.2	0.2	5.6	5.3	6.8	5.5	8.3	23.7	26.0	16.8	2.1	79.3	42.7	50.7	49.3
BOONE	0.9	1.2	6.6	5.9	6.4	8.0	7.1	19.9	27.6	14.6	3.8	75.3	42.2	50.1	49.9
BOX BUTTE	7.6	10.1	6.8	5.9	6.2	6.8	9.5	20.6	30.4	10.9	2.9	76.7	39.1	50.1	49.9
BOYD	0.1	0.1	6.0	5.2	5.5	6.0	7.8	17.3	30.5	16.8	4.9	79.6	46.1	48.7	51.3
BROWN	0.8	1.1	5.9	5.6	5.1	6.6	6.1	21.0	28.9	16.5	4.3	78.5	44.8	49.7	50.3
BUFFALO	4.7	6.3	6.7	6.0	6.4	9.5	11.7	25.8	22.7	9.0	2.2	76.5	31.7	49.2	50.8
BURT	1.3	1.7	6.2	5.7	6.1	6.3	7.1	19.3	28.8	16.6	3.8	77.9	44.4	49.3	50.7
BUTLER	1.7	1.7	7.2	7.1	6.0	6.8	6.6	22.7	27.5	13.3	2.8	75.4	40.7	51.6	48.4
CASS	1.5	2.0	7.0	6.7	7.0	6.6	6.3	25.0	28.7	10.8	1.9	75.2	39.8	49.4	50.6
CEDAR	0.4	0.6	7.0	5.8	6.7	8.0	8.2	19.8	26.6	13.8	4.1	75.3	40.3	51.0	49.0
CHASE	3.4	4.6	6.0	5.8	4.9	6.4	6.2	20.9	30.1	15.2	4.3	79.1	44.7	48.9	51.1
CHERRY	0.9	0.9	6.5	6.1	5.9	7.1	6.5	22.5	28.4	14.0	3.0	76.9	41.3	49.4	50.6
CHEYENNE	4.5	6.0	6.8	6.3	5.2	6.5	8.5	22.9	27.6	13.4	2.7	77.6	40.5	49.6	50.4
CLAY	3.5	3.5	6.6	5.9	6.4	6.6	7.1	21.7	28.9	14.1	2.9	76.9	42.3	49.4	50.6
COLFAX	26.2	32.8	7.8	7.4	7.7	6.0	6.6	27.7	23.5	10.7	2.6	73.2	35.8	52.3	47.7
CUMING	5.5	7.4	7.3	6.6	5.8	6.7	6.7	22.5	26.3	14.3	3.9	75.9	41.0	51.2	48.8
CUSTER	0.9	1.2	6.1	5.6	6.5	7.1	6.0	20.9	27.8	15.9	4.1	77.3	43.5	49.7	50.3
DAKOTA	22.6	28.2	8.9	7.9	7.7	7.1	7.5	27.8	22.9	8.6	1.5	71.0	32.2	49.7	50.3
DAWES	2.4	3.2	5.0	4.4	5.2	12.3	14.8	20.5	22.6	12.4	2.8	80.7	31.6	49.0	51.0
DAWSON	25.4	31.8	8.7	8.2	7.2	6.6	6.6	25.7	24.3	10.2	2.4	71.9	35.0	50.7	49.3
DEUEL	2.7	2.8	5.2	4.4	4.1	6.7	8.3	18.8	31.2	17.3	4.1	82.2	46.1	48.9	51.1
DIXON	5.5	5.6	7.0	6.5	5.8	7.5	6.7	22.4	27.7	13.1	3.3	76.2	40.3	50.2	49.8
DODGE	3.9	5.3	6.5	5.7	5.9	6.9	7.6	24.7	25.4	13.9	3.4	78.2	39.9	48.4	51.6
DOUGLAS	6.7	8.8	7.5	7.4	7.1	6.9	6.6	29.4	24.4	9.1	1.6	73.9	34.7	49.0	51.0
DUNDY	3.2	3.4	5.3	5.5	5.4	5.0	7.7	19.2	31.7	15.6	4.6	80.5	46.1	49.9	50.1
FILLMORE	1.7	2.3	6.2	5.9	6.1	7.5	5.9	20.4	28.0	15.6	4.4	76.4	43.6	49.3	50.7
FRANKLIN	0.6	0.9	5.8	5.2	5.9	6.2	5.6	20.2	27.0	19.1	5.0	78.8	45.7	49.0	51.0
FRONTIER	1.0	1.3	5.9	5.6	5.6	9.4	9.2	18.9	27.8	14.7	2.9	78.3	41.2	50.4	49.6
FURNAS	1.1	1.6	5.9	5.8	6.5	5.5	6.0	19.0	29.0	17.1	5.2	78.2	45.7	48.6	51.4
GAGE	0.9	1.2	6.3	5.8	5.7	6.4	7.3	23.6	27.1	14.3	3.7	78.5	41.6	48.9	51.1
GARDEN	1.4	2.1	4.1	3.1	4.6	7.4	7.7	18.6	29.0	20.4	5.1	83.2	47.7	49.2	50.8
GARFIELD	1.0	1.3	5.7	4.5	5.8	6.8	8.8	15.1	29.3	18.3	5.6	79.8	47.1	47.6	52.4
GOSPER	1.3	1.3	5.8	5.2	5.5	6.1	5.4	21.3	29.1	17.5	4.1	79.3	45.4	49.8	50.2
GRANT	1.3	1.5	5.1	4.6	4.9	6.9	12.6	18.1	31.5	15.0	1.3	81.9	43.7	53.1	46.9
GREELEY	0.8	1.1	6.5	5.4	7.4	6.6	6.4	20.8	26.2	16.3	4.4	76.1	42.8	50.3	49.7
HALL	14.0	18.2	7.7	7.2	6.9	6.4	6.7	26.2	25.4	11.3	2.3	74.3	36.7	49.7	50.3
HAMILTON	1.1	1.5	6.9	6.4	7.7	6.8	7.9	22.0	27.5	12.1	2.7	74.6	40.2	50.2	49.8
HARLAN	0.8	1.0	5.4	4.7	6.1	6.7	6.1	18.2	30.9	18.1	4.0	79.5	46.7	49.8	50.2
HAYES	2.5	2.6	4.5	4.1	6.9	7.5	7.9	16.6	32.0	17.6	3.0	80.2	46.4	50.8	49.2
HITCHCOCK	1.4	1.9	4.9	4.3	5.5	5.5	8.7	19.3	30.1	17.6	4.2	82.1	46.0	49.7	50.3
HOLT	0.7	1.0	6.5	5.9	6.0	7.0	7.5	20.1	28.8	14.3	3.9	77.1	43.0	49.3	50.7
HOOKER	1.0	1.1	5.0	4.1	4.7	8.3	8.0	15.1	30.0	18.2	6.6	80.9	47.4	46.6	53.4
HOWARD	1.0	1.4	6.8	5.7	6.4	7.3	7.2	23.3	27.1	13.6	2.6	76.5	40.6	50.5	49.5
JEFFERSON	1.3	1.8	5.6	5.4	5.0	6.5	6.0	21.1	29.8	15.8	4.7	79.9	44.3	49.4	50.6
JOHNSON	2.9	3.8	5.5	4.9	5.5	5.9	6.2	19.8	27.7	16.8	7.6	80.4	46.2	47.2	52.8
KEARNEY	2.3	2.4	6.5	6.1	6.5	6.3	6.2	23.9	28.8	12.3	3.3	76.5	41.3	50.4	49.6
KEITH	4.2	5.7	6.3	5.4	5.5	6.6	8.4	19.8	29.5	15.9	2.5	78.6	43.5	49.2	50.8
KEYA PAHA	3.9	4.0	6.5	6.1	6.9	5.8	3.4	23.4	28.0	16.8	3.0	76.7	43.4	50.9	49.1
KIMBALL	3.3	4.5	5.9	5.2	6.0	6.8	6.9	19.7	28.3	17.7	3.6	78.7	44.7	48.6	51.4
KNOX	0.9	1.2	6.2	5.9	5.5	6.9	6.5	19.0	28.2	17.3	4.5	77.6	45.0	49.3	50.7
LANCASTER	3.4	4.5	6.7	6.2	6.0	7.7	9.0	30.6	23.7	8.5	1.6	77.5	32.9	49.9	50.1
LINCOLN	5.4	7.3	6.8	6.0	6.6	6.5	7.9	23.6	28.0	12.2	2.4	76.0	39.1	49.4	50.6
LOGAN	0.9	1.0	5.4	5.2	4.9	5.9	8.7	17.4	35.0	15.1	2.4	81.2	46.2	49.5	50.5
LOUP	1.7	1.7	6.5	6.9	4.6	8.6	5.7	19.0	29.8	16.1	2.9	76.9	44.2	51.7	48.3
MCPHERSON	1.5	1.6	8.3	8.3	4.5	5.8	8.3	18.2	30.2	13.2	3.1	75.4	41.3	49.4	50.6
MADISON	8.6	11.5	7.2	6.3	6.5	7.6	8.7	25.3	24.6	11.0	2.8	76.1	35.8	50.0	50.0
MERRICK	2.0	2.1	6.6	6.4	7.1	6.8	6.6	22.9	26.6	14.1	2.8	75.2	41.1	49.0	51.0
MORRILL	10.1	13.3	6.2	5.8	5.7	8.0	6.5	21.5	29.0	14.3	2.9	77.1	42.1	49.9	50.1
NANCE	1.1	1.5	6.6	6.0	6.1	6.8	6.7	21.1	28.7	15.1	3.0	76.9	42.7	50.8	49.2
NEMAHA	1.0	1.3	5.0	4.5	5.8	8.2	10.5	20.2	29.1	12.8	3.8	80.4	41.9	48.8	51.2
NUCKOLLS	1.0	1.4	5.8	5.1	4.7	6.1	7.8	18.2	29.9	18.1	4.3	80.5	46.2	48.9	51.1
OTOE	2.4	3.4	6.9	6.3	6.2	6.5	6.2	22.5	27.8	14.1	3.4	76.5	41.7	49.5	50.5
PAWNEE	0.7	0.9	5.7	4.9	6.3	5.8	6.1	17.9	29.2	18.6	5.5	79.5	46.9	48.9	51.1
PERKINS	2.3	2.4	5.8	5.1	6.1	6.4	7.4	21.7	28.6	14.7	4.1	79.0	43.2	50.2	49.8
PHELPS	2.3	3.1	6.5	6.2	6.6	6.4	7.0	22.8	27.3	13.5	3.7	76.6	41.4	49.5	50.5
PIERCE	0.7	0.7	6.9	6.3	6.5	7.0	8.0	23.2	27.0	11.6	3.5	75.7	40.0	50.2	49.8
PLATTE	6.5	8.8	7.6	7.0	6.8	7.4	7.7	24.5	26.1	10.8	2.1	74.1	36.7	50.0	50.0
POLK	1.1	1.1	6.1	5.7	6.6	5.2	6.9	20.8	28.9	15.5	4.3	78.5	43.9	50.4	49.6
RED WILLOW	2.5	3.3	6.6	5.8	6.2	6.2	7.2	22.2	27.1	15.6	3.2	78.1	41.6	48.5	51.5
RICHARDSON	1.0	1.4	5.8	4.9	6.3	6.9	7.6	20.7	27.6	16.0	4.2	78.5	43.6	48.7	51.3
ROCK	0.5	0.7	5.8	6.0	4.0	6.1	6.7	20.1	31.0	15.7	4.5	80.4	45.7	48.2	51.8
SALINE	6.6	8.7	6.8	6.0	6.2	7.9	8.7	24.4	24.9	11.5	3.7	77.0	37.4	50.0	50.0
SARPY	4.4	5.8	8.4	7.9	7.4	7.1	7.0	31.1	23.3	7.0	0.7	71.8	33.1	49.6	50.4
NEBRASKA	5.5	7.2	7.1	6.6	6.6	7.2	7.6	26.7	25.3	10.7	2.2	75.6	36.3	49.4	50.6
UNITED STATES	12.5	15.0	6.9	6.5	6.8	7.1	7.0	27.6	25.4	10.7	1.9	75.6	36.7	49.2	50.8

COUNTY	HOUSEHOLDS					FAMILIES			MEDIAN HOUSEHOLD INCOME			
	2000	2007	2012	% Annual Rate 2000-2007	2007 Average HH Size	2000	2007	% Annual Rate 2000-2007	2007	2012	2007 National Rank	2007 State Rank
ADAMS	12,141	12,450	12,662	0.3	2.43	7,969	8,066	0.2	46,919	55,358	916	12
ANTELOPE	2,953	2,876	2,810	-0.4	2.44	2,072	1,993	-0.5	34,974	38,384	2433	64
ARTHUR	185	172	165	-1.0	2.36	138	127	-1.1	32,302	35,784	2731	82
BANNER	311	307	302	-0.2	2.57	238	233	-0.3	37,508	41,964	2061	51
BLAINE	238	220	203	-1.1	2.41	169	155	-1.2	29,522	32,514	2929	92
BOONE	2,454	2,341	2,257	-0.6	2.48	1,700	1,603	-0.8	36,494	40,355	2192	55
BOX BUTTE	4,780	4,504	4,305	-0.8	2.44	3,299	3,072	-1.0	49,295	57,701	723	8
BOYD	1,014	977	952	-0.5	2.33	670	637	-0.7	30,615	33,507	2873	89
BROWN	1,530	1,466	1,411	-0.6	2.22	996	942	-0.8	33,132	36,509	2642	75
BUFFALO	15,930	17,513	18,662	1.3	2.45	10,222	11,084	1.1	45,180	51,603	1086	17
BURT	3,155	3,013	2,898	-0.6	2.42	2,241	2,117	-0.8	39,348	43,738	1808	42
BUTLER	3,426	3,474	3,470	0.2	2.50	2,351	2,356	0.0	42,368	46,962	1408	27
CASS	9,161	10,125	10,817	1.4	2.59	6,806	7,450	1.3	56,568	64,549	343	3
CEDAR	3,623	3,528	3,437	-0.4	2.55	2,564	2,469	-0.5	39,302	43,291	1821	43
CHASE	1,662	1,603	1,554	-0.5	2.33	1,164	1,110	-0.7	37,856	41,869	2015	49
CHERRY	2,508	2,532	2,539	0.1	2.36	1,711	1,707	0.0	34,770	39,129	2460	67
CHEYENNE	4,071	4,253	4,364	0.6	2.36	2,685	2,770	0.4	40,769	46,753	1634	31
CLAY	2,756	2,791	2,781	0.2	2.50	1,981	1,984	0.0	39,988	44,247	1727	37
COLFAX	3,682	3,671	3,720	0.0	2.90	2,593	2,556	-0.2	42,327	47,421	1414	28
CUMING	3,945	3,864	3,768	-0.3	2.50	2,757	2,670	-0.4	39,234	43,906	1826	44
CUSTER	4,826	4,720	4,636	-0.3	2.37	3,320	3,208	-0.5	35,642	39,365	2338	60
DAKOTA	7,095	7,237	7,327	0.3	2.83	5,089	5,136	0.1	49,202	58,572	732	9
DAWES	3,512	3,405	3,308	-0.4	2.22	2,085	1,991	-0.6	36,007	40,969	2274	56
DAWSON	8,824	8,842	8,930	0.0	2.77	6,275	6,218	-0.1	44,006	50,336	1208	21
DEUEL	908	900	890	-0.1	2.23	601	588	-0.3	38,769	43,135	1882	46
DIXON	2,413	2,411	2,407	0.0	2.57	1,706	1,687	-0.2	39,950	44,392	1732	38
DODGE	14,433	14,872	15,132	0.4	2.39	9,750	9,923	0.2	45,729	52,204	1029	15
DOUGLAS	182,194	197,614	209,279	1.1	2.47	115,083	123,074	0.9	55,154	65,343	401	4
DUNDY	961	925	901	-0.5	2.28	637	606	-0.7	31,904	35,621	2772	84
FILLMORE	2,689	2,651	2,619	-0.2	2.34	1,802	1,754	-0.4	40,685	45,084	1642	32
FRANKLIN	1,485	1,432	1,400	-0.5	2.33	1,021	973	-0.7	33,976	37,438	2552	70
FRONTIER	1,192	1,124	1,077	-0.8	2.45	829	773	-1.0	37,490	41,317	2065	52
FURNAS	2,278	2,219	2,178	-0.4	2.27	1,490	1,432	-0.5	35,442	39,010	2375	61
GAGE	9,316	9,696	9,915	0.6	2.33	6,208	6,381	0.4	42,048	47,638	1443	29
GARDEN	1,020	951	880	-1.0	2.14	659	607	-1.1	30,858	34,641	2847	87
GARFIELD	813	778	749	-0.6	2.22	529	500	-0.8	31,683	35,742	2787	85
GOSPER	863	831	804	-0.5	2.40	655	625	-0.6	42,630	47,211	1378	26
GRANT	292	266	258	-1.3	2.56	226	204	-1.4	40,292	44,462	1689	34
GREELEY	1,077	1,057	1,039	-0.3	2.41	734	712	-0.4	33,377	36,809	2620	74
HALL	20,356	21,236	21,852	0.6	2.56	14,085	14,522	0.4	46,342	53,590	965	13
HAMILTON	3,503	3,648	3,741	0.6	2.62	2,677	2,764	0.4	47,857	53,758	830	11
HARLAN	1,597	1,502	1,413	-0.8	2.31	1,050	975	-1.0	35,429	38,925	2378	62
HAYES	430	430	424	0.0	2.45	312	309	-0.1	31,057	34,226	2827	86
HITCHCOCK	1,287	1,266	1,250	-0.2	2.32	900	875	-0.4	33,102	36,559	2646	76
HOLT	4,608	4,376	4,182	-0.7	2.40	3,171	2,977	-0.9	35,952	39,689	2286	57
HOOKER	335	328	324	-0.3	2.24	220	213	-0.4	32,486	35,909	2708	80
HOWARD	2,546	2,701	2,790	0.8	2.54	1,798	1,885	0.7	40,299	45,152	1688	33
JEFFERSON	3,527	3,385	3,275	-0.6	2.29	2,354	2,232	-0.7	37,225	41,205	2098	53
JOHNSON	1,887	1,915	1,931	0.2	2.33	1,255	1,257	0.0	37,898	42,124	2007	47
KEARNEY	2,643	2,629	2,602	-0.1	2.48	1,902	1,872	-0.2	45,839	50,823	1020	14
KEITH	3,707	3,658	3,533	-0.2	2.32	2,535	2,472	-0.3	40,038	45,481	1721	36
KEYA PAHA	409	400	388	-0.3	2.38	292	282	-0.5	28,343	31,031	2987	93
KIMBALL	1,727	1,672	1,612	-0.4	2.29	1,136	1,086	-0.6	35,763	39,577	2322	59
KNOX	3,811	3,770	3,731	-0.1	2.37	2,594	2,535	-0.3	32,015	35,438	2760	83
LANCASTER	99,187	110,581	118,755	1.5	2.37	60,702	66,681	1.3	53,058	62,368	498	5
LINCOLN	14,076	14,989	15,575	0.9	2.36	9,445	9,936	0.7	44,693	51,200	1139	19
LOGAN	316	313	308	-0.1	2.35	229	224	-0.3	37,873	41,451	2010	48
LOUP	289	295	291	0.3	2.45	207	209	0.1	30,379	33,326	2893	90
MCPHERSON	202	195	190	-0.5	2.65	158	151	-0.6	30,786	33,872	2854	88
MADISON	13,436	13,685	13,684	0.3	2.50	8,895	8,945	0.1	43,730	50,185	1246	23
MERRICK	3,209	3,208	3,200	0.0	2.49	2,308	2,283	-0.2	41,320	46,213	1549	30
MORRILL	2,138	2,082	2,020	-0.4	2.46	1,494	1,438	-0.5	35,251	38,743	2400	63
NANCE	1,577	1,486	1,409	-0.8	2.45	1,107	1,031	-1.0	36,886	40,868	2142	54
NEMAHA	3,047	2,966	2,864	-0.4	2.28	1,981	1,904	-0.5	39,523	44,925	1775	41
NUCKOLLS	2,218	2,115	2,030	-0.7	2.20	1,445	1,360	-0.8	33,560	36,934	2599	73
OTOE	6,060	6,419	6,671	0.8	2.48	4,232	4,433	0.6	45,171	50,978	1091	18
PAWNEE	1,339	1,290	1,254	-0.5	2.24	850	808	-0.7	33,733	37,077	2578	72
PERKINS	1,275	1,270	1,264	-0.1	2.42	894	880	-0.2	40,127	44,526	1704	35
PHELPS	3,844	3,777	3,697	-0.2	2.44	2,682	2,604	-0.4	45,575	51,997	1043	16
PIERCE	2,979	2,982	2,969	0.0	2.57	2,142	2,121	-0.1	37,678	41,825	2037	50
PLATTE	12,076	12,340	12,453	0.3	2.55	8,461	8,546	0.1	48,070	54,900	810	10
POLK	2,259	2,292	2,310	0.2	2.40	1,569	1,574	0.0	43,807	48,432	1236	22
RED WILLOW	4,710	4,622	4,530	-0.3	2.34	3,190	3,091	-0.4	39,097	43,739	1838	45
RICHARDSON	3,993	3,811	3,667	-0.6	2.32	2,568	2,417	-0.8	34,800	38,170	2455	66
ROCK	763	732	720	-0.6	2.17	501	474	-0.8	30,164	33,592	2901	91
SALINE	5,188	5,392	5,501	0.5	2.50	3,507	3,600	0.4	43,270	49,019	1305	24
SARPY	43,426	55,212	64,990	3.4	2.71	33,238	41,880	3.2	67,481	79,713	144	1
NEBRASKA				0.9	2.47			0.7	49,064	57,487		
UNITED STATES				1.2	2.59			1.0	53,154	62,503		

COUNTY	2007 Per Capita Income	2007 HH Income Base	2007 HOUSEHOLD INCOME DISTRIBUTION (%)					2007 Home Value Base	2007 HOME VALUE DISTRIBUTION (%)					2007 Median Home Value
			Less than $25,000	$25,000 to $49,999	$50,000 to $99,999	$100,000 to $149,999	$150,000 or More		Less than $50,000	$50,000 to $89,999	$90,000 to $174,999	$175,000 to $399,999	$400,000 or More	
ADAMS	23,210	12,450	22.6	30.8	35.0	8.1	3.4	8,692	13.8	26.7	43.4	14.6	1.5	102,389
ANTELOPE	17,094	2,876	34.8	36.5	23.4	4.2	1.1	2,265	39.2	27.5	22.2	9.2	1.9	64,810
ARTHUR	18,594	172	35.5	34.9	22.1	3.5	4.1	113	46.0	20.4	21.2	10.6	1.8	59,000
BANNER	19,018	307	29.6	31.9	30.9	4.2	3.3	207	17.4	34.3	31.4	16.9	0.0	87,083
BLAINE	14,524	220	39.5	40.5	16.8	3.2	0.0	150	60.0	20.7	6.0	4.0	9.3	34,444
BOONE	18,625	2,341	30.8	36.2	26.3	4.4	2.2	1,818	31.2	28.5	26.2	11.5	2.6	74,435
BOX BUTTE	23,888	4,504	24.3	26.4	36.7	9.3	3.3	3,294	19.1	30.4	39.1	10.6	0.9	90,599
BOYD	16,458	977	42.7	34.4	18.1	3.7	1.1	802	60.8	19.8	14.3	3.6	1.4	36,528
BROWN	18,996	1,466	37.1	37.2	20.3	3.7	1.7	1,129	37.9	32.5	23.4	5.2	1.0	63,775
BUFFALO	22,053	17,513	24.0	31.3	33.5	8.1	3.2	11,695	15.7	16.1	45.2	21.1	1.9	116,869
BURT	19,874	3,013	28.9	34.7	29.3	5.0	2.1	2,355	23.7	31.8	31.7	10.7	2.2	81,443
BUTLER	19,902	3,474	24.9	34.5	33.3	5.6	1.7	2,716	25.3	28.3	34.4	10.2	1.8	84,310
CASS	25,362	10,125	15.8	27.1	41.9	11.3	4.0	8,256	11.5	16.9	41.3	26.4	3.8	121,641
CEDAR	18,356	3,528	27.6	38.2	28.3	3.7	2.1	2,897	29.0	31.0	29.8	9.1	1.0	76,084
CHASE	21,111	1,603	29.1	35.4	26.6	6.1	2.8	1,273	29.5	31.8	30.2	7.1	1.5	74,031
CHERRY	19,191	2,532	34.0	33.0	25.7	5.5	1.8	1,650	27.2	26.0	30.3	10.2	6.3	85,268
CHEYENNE	21,732	4,253	26.5	34.2	30.4	6.0	2.9	3,202	24.3	37.3	28.0	8.5	1.9	76,566
CLAY	19,981	2,791	27.9	35.2	29.2	5.4	2.4	2,235	34.3	31.0	28.0	6.4	0.4	68,764
COLFAX	17,391	3,671	24.8	35.1	32.1	6.1	1.9	2,857	27.0	31.6	33.3	7.6	0.5	78,312
CUMING	19,401	3,864	26.1	38.8	28.5	4.1	2.5	2,876	17.4	29.3	38.4	12.0	3.0	94,267
CUSTER	19,048	4,720	31.8	36.2	26.1	4.2	1.7	3,581	36.5	28.3	24.2	7.8	3.2	67,287
DAKOTA	20,558	7,237	22.2	28.5	35.8	10.4	3.1	5,092	21.0	26.6	41.1	11.0	0.3	92,563
DAWES	20,704	3,405	35.5	28.7	25.3	7.1	3.4	2,208	31.9	29.0	29.0	8.3	1.8	73,333
DAWSON	19,423	8,842	25.4	31.5	33.9	5.9	3.3	6,396	19.3	34.5	36.5	8.8	0.9	85,694
DEUEL	21,433	900	29.0	33.9	29.9	5.2	2.0	722	32.4	34.1	24.5	8.0	1.0	67,722
DIXON	18,207	2,411	27.9	34.3	32.1	4.2	1.5	1,896	27.3	33.0	31.3	7.9	0.6	79,669
DODGE	22,462	14,872	24.1	30.9	35.0	7.2	2.7	10,519	12.8	21.9	48.0	15.9	1.4	110,534
DOUGLAS	29,259	197,614	19.0	26.2	33.8	13.1	7.9	130,718	7.9	16.5	45.7	25.0	4.9	133,109
DUNDY	18,385	925	37.9	31.1	23.9	4.9	2.2	699	53.4	23.0	16.2	4.6	2.9	46,987
FILLMORE	20,615	2,651	25.9	37.7	29.0	5.6	1.8	2,046	31.1	32.3	26.7	8.4	1.5	71,173
FRANKLIN	18,559	1,432	34.3	38.3	21.6	3.6	2.2	1,187	49.8	26.0	17.7	5.0	1.5	50,333
FRONTIER	20,080	1,124	28.4	38.5	25.4	4.6	3.1	847	27.9	29.8	31.6	8.3	2.5	79,304
FURNAS	20,073	2,219	31.9	37.1	24.2	4.2	2.5	1,746	48.3	26.5	19.2	4.8	1.1	52,231
GAGE	21,324	9,696	25.9	33.8	32.1	6.1	2.2	7,161	18.4	28.3	37.9	14.5	0.9	94,866
GARDEN	18,487	951	37.6	35.6	22.0	3.5	1.3	695	38.0	30.8	27.3	3.3	0.6	64,435
GARFIELD	17,262	778	40.6	32.4	22.1	4.2	0.6	585	41.2	23.4	26.8	6.8	1.7	62,333
GOSPER	22,050	831	24.3	36.0	30.7	5.3	3.7	652	22.2	24.7	36.5	13.3	3.2	93,509
GRANT	16,938	266	28.6	38.3	29.3	2.3	1.5	190	57.9	22.1	16.8	2.6	0.5	39,750
GREELEY	16,424	1,057	36.1	36.7	22.5	3.7	0.9	853	46.8	28.6	16.2	5.6	2.8	53,819
HALL	21,977	21,236	24.7	29.5	34.9	7.1	3.8	14,663	9.2	23.2	51.0	15.3	1.4	110,717
HAMILTON	21,688	3,648	19.4	33.4	36.8	7.6	2.9	2,836	17.9	20.6	45.8	13.5	2.2	103,947
HARLAN	18,832	1,502	32.0	37.2	25.5	3.0	2.3	1,235	40.2	28.3	23.7	6.7	1.1	63,207
HAYES	16,708	430	38.8	36.5	19.1	4.0	1.6	323	45.2	23.5	18.6	8.7	4.0	57,381
HITCHCOCK	18,283	1,266	37.1	34.1	22.5	4.6	1.7	1,017	43.6	34.2	16.9	4.0	1.3	56,753
HOLT	18,631	4,376	34.5	33.6	25.9	4.1	1.9	3,349	30.4	25.0	34.2	7.4	3.0	81,158
HOOKER	18,905	328	36.6	40.2	18.6	2.4	2.1	253	44.3	30.0	19.4	2.0	4.3	57,632
HOWARD	18,741	2,701	28.8	34.0	30.4	4.9	1.9	2,133	20.7	26.5	34.5	15.3	3.0	94,048
JEFFERSON	20,923	3,385	32.2	32.3	29.0	4.0	2.6	2,654	40.8	28.2	22.9	6.6	1.5	59,608
JOHNSON	19,439	1,915	32.2	32.0	29.1	4.7	2.1	1,490	28.7	32.2	29.5	8.5	1.1	74,809
KEARNEY	21,267	2,629	22.6	32.7	36.4	6.5	1.8	2,025	15.3	26.9	42.1	13.8	1.9	101,968
KEITH	21,244	3,658	26.8	36.0	29.7	5.7	1.9	2,764	20.0	32.1	37.8	8.2	1.9	87,121
KEYA PAHA	13,816	400	44.0	42.5	10.3	2.0	1.3	301	53.8	15.0	14.0	5.0	12.3	45,741
KIMBALL	20,883	1,672	31.9	35.2	25.7	4.8	2.4	1,308	35.8	32.1	25.8	6.0	0.3	64,466
KNOX	16,658	3,770	38.2	35.3	22.1	3.1	1.2	2,923	40.6	30.7	20.9	7.1	0.7	61,748
LANCASTER	27,713	110,579	19.2	27.4	35.9	11.5	6.1	70,349	3.7	9.1	54.6	29.2	3.4	140,936
LINCOLN	23,240	14,989	26.3	29.5	32.6	8.5	3.2	10,813	16.9	24.5	42.2	14.5	1.9	101,734
LOGAN	19,058	313	25.9	41.2	27.2	4.8	1.0	234	25.6	30.3	32.1	7.7	4.3	77,500
LOUP	14,926	295	40.3	38.0	18.0	2.7	1.0	237	47.3	19.0	13.9	12.2	7.6	54,643
MCPHERSON	14,932	195	39.5	32.3	22.1	6.2	0.0	136	45.6	29.4	11.8	8.8	4.4	60,000
MADISON	20,876	13,685	26.0	30.3	33.1	8.5	2.1	9,428	13.9	25.4	44.8	14.8	1.1	103,975
MERRICK	19,396	3,208	25.4	38.5	30.1	4.6	1.4	2,462	26.4	28.6	33.9	8.7	2.5	82,278
MORRILL	17,475	2,082	34.3	33.3	26.9	4.0	1.4	1,548	37.5	30.6	23.3	7.1	1.5	66,136
NANCE	18,866	1,486	32.6	35.5	25.6	4.3	2.1	1,146	34.6	33.1	23.8	6.3	2.2	67,838
NEMAHA	21,679	2,966	28.9	30.8	30.4	7.7	2.1	2,225	25.9	31.0	31.2	10.2	1.7	79,114
NUCKOLLS	18,909	2,115	34.4	40.4	20.5	2.9	1.8	1,726	52.5	23.6	18.9	4.5	0.4	47,943
OTOE	21,759	6,419	24.0	32.1	33.8	7.3	2.8	4,927	16.9	23.6	37.1	19.3	3.0	104,711
PAWNEE	19,138	1,290	35.1	37.2	21.9	4.0	1.8	1,061	49.4	26.8	17.7	5.4	0.8	50,903
PERKINS	20,730	1,270	28.1	32.9	29.7	6.7	2.6	992	31.8	29.4	29.6	6.8	2.4	72,639
PHELPS	23,146	3,777	23.5	32.0	33.6	7.4	3.5	2,875	14.1	32.6	41.0	10.4	1.9	94,207
PIERCE	19,158	2,982	30.5	32.6	29.0	5.1	2.7	2,383	24.1	30.1	33.2	11.4	1.3	83,781
PLATTE	22,590	12,340	21.4	30.2	36.8	8.5	3.1	9,376	10.5	23.1	49.3	15.5	1.7	107,166
POLK	21,382	2,292	24.6	33.3	35.2	4.6	2.3	1,819	27.9	28.0	33.5	8.3	2.3	81,731
RED WILLOW	19,812	4,622	30.2	34.3	28.5	5.4	1.6	3,399	27.6	32.3	32.8	7.2	0.1	77,114
RICHARDSON	18,491	3,811	34.8	33.0	26.6	4.3	1.3	2,942	43.0	30.9	19.6	5.2	1.2	57,279
ROCK	17,654	732	40.3	35.7	19.4	3.3	1.4	550	45.0	28.8	10.0	5.1	2.2	56,111
SALINE	20,100	5,392	26.4	30.6	34.9	6.1	2.0	3,973	20.0	26.1	40.9	11.0	2.2	94,760
SARPY	29,046	55,212	9.3	21.8	44.8	16.9	7.2	39,844	2.2	4.4	54.8	35.2	3.4	159,063
NEBRASKA	25,004		21.9	29.0	34.0	10.1	5.0		14.0	19.3	43.3	20.4	3.0	115,851
UNITED STATES	27,916		21.9	25.0	32.3	12.3	8.4		7.9	10.5	27.1	35.6	19.0	192,285

SPENDING POTENTIAL INDICES

COUNTY	FINANCIAL SERVICES				THE HOME						ENTERTAINMENT						PERSONAL			
					Home Improvements		Furnishings													
	Auto Loan	Home Loan	Invest-ments	Retire-ment Plans	Home Repair	Lawn & Garden	Comput-ers & Hard-ware	Major Appli-ances	TV, Radio, Sound Equip-ment	Furni-ture	Dine out/ Carry out	Sports Equip-ment	Fees & Tickets	Toys & Games	Travel	Cable TV	Apparel & Services	Auto Repairs	Health Insur-ance	Pets & Supplies
ADAMS	81	76	86	78	78	82	79	80	81	77	80	70	78	82	80	83	71	79	86	81
ANTELOPE	74	48	24	46	58	83	52	70	57	49	58	62	41	62	51	62	48	62	75	77
ARTHUR	79	50	22	48	62	89	53	74	59	51	60	66	41	65	52	64	50	66	78	83
BANNER	88	56	24	53	69	99	59	83	65	56	67	74	46	73	58	71	56	73	87	92
BLAINE	63	40	17	38	50	71	43	59	47	40	48	53	33	52	42	51	40	53	62	66
BOONE	81	53	30	51	64	89	58	76	64	54	64	67	46	69	57	69	54	68	83	83
BOX BUTTE	88	77	75	77	79	90	78	85	82	77	81	74	75	85	79	84	71	82	91	87
BOYD	70	44	19	42	55	78	47	65	52	44	53	58	36	57	46	56	44	58	69	73
BROWN	77	49	21	46	60	86	52	72	57	49	58	64	40	63	50	61	48	64	75	80
BUFFALO	81	72	71	74	72	78	78	77	78	74	77	71	73	79	75	78	69	78	79	79
BURT	83	56	33	54	66	91	60	78	67	56	67	69	49	72	59	72	56	71	86	85
BUTLER	86	57	35	55	68	94	62	81	69	58	69	71	50	74	61	75	58	73	89	88
CASS	100	91	84	91	95	106	86	97	90	88	90	86	85	95	88	92	79	92	100	101
CEDAR	80	54	35	53	64	87	59	76	66	55	65	67	48	70	58	71	55	69	84	81
CHASE	89	58	27	55	70	100	61	84	67	58	68	74	48	73	60	73	57	74	88	93
CHERRY	76	53	38	52	61	82	58	72	64	54	63	64	49	67	57	68	53	66	79	77
CHEYENNE	80	64	56	64	70	85	67	77	72	64	71	68	61	75	67	75	61	73	84	81
CLAY	89	58	29	55	70	99	62	84	68	58	69	74	49	74	61	74	58	75	89	92
COLFAX	86	62	39	60	70	92	63	81	69	62	70	72	54	74	63	74	59	74	85	87
CUMING	84	57	35	56	67	92	61	79	67	58	67	70	50	73	60	72	57	72	85	86
CUSTER	79	52	29	50	63	88	56	75	63	53	63	66	45	68	55	68	52	67	81	82
DAKOTA	87	78	72	78	77	83	80	83	81	79	81	75	76	83	78	82	72	82	84	84
DAWES	72	52	52	54	55	67	73	67	71	60	71	62	60	70	64	71	62	69	72	69
DAWSON	87	69	53	66	74	90	70	82	75	68	75	74	63	78	69	78	65	78	87	86
DEUEL	87	55	24	53	68	98	59	82	64	56	66	73	45	71	57	70	55	72	86	91
DIXON	83	54	29	52	65	92	58	78	64	55	65	69	46	70	57	70	54	70	84	85
DODGE	79	71	73	72	73	81	72	76	77	72	75	67	71	78	73	79	67	75	83	78
DOUGLAS	100	99	107	103	95	93	103	96	102	103	102	88	103	103	100	101	92	100	98	96
DUNDY	73	49	29	47	58	80	53	69	59	49	58	61	43	63	52	64	49	62	76	75
FILLMORE	87	57	29	54	68	96	61	82	67	57	67	72	48	73	60	73	56	73	88	89
FRANKLIN	77	50	27	48	61	85	54	72	60	51	60	64	43	65	53	65	50	65	78	79
FRONTIER	86	58	35	56	68	95	63	81	70	58	69	72	51	75	62	75	58	74	90	88
FURNAS	77	53	36	51	61	84	58	73	65	53	64	64	48	68	57	70	54	67	82	78
GAGE	78	62	58	62	68	82	66	75	72	63	70	65	61	74	66	75	61	71	83	78
GARDEN	65	46	36	45	52	69	51	62	58	47	56	54	43	59	51	62	47	57	71	65
GARFIELD	63	44	35	43	50	67	49	59	56	45	54	52	42	57	49	60	45	55	69	62
GOSPER	97	62	27	59	76	109	65	91	72	62	73	81	50	80	64	78	61	80	95	101
GRANT	78	50	21	47	61	88	53	73	58	50	59	66	41	64	52	63	49	65	77	82
GREELEY	72	46	20	44	56	81	48	68	53	46	54	60	37	59	47	58	45	60	71	75
HALL	80	76	82	78	76	79	78	78	79	77	78	70	77	80	78	80	70	78	81	79
HAMILTON	93	73	56	72	80	100	73	89	78	72	78	79	66	83	73	81	67	82	93	95
HARLAN	76	52	27	50	63	87	54	74	59	52	59	65	44	63	54	63	50	66	76	80
HAYES	74	47	20	45	58	83	50	69	55	47	56	62	38	61	49	59	47	61	73	77
HITCHCOCK	74	50	28	48	59	82	53	70	59	50	59	62	43	63	52	63	49	63	76	76
HOLT	80	52	25	49	63	90	55	75	61	52	61	67	43	67	54	66	51	67	80	83
HOOKER	77	49	21	47	61	87	52	73	57	49	58	65	40	64	51	62	49	64	76	81
HOWARD	80	56	39	55	65	86	61	76	66	57	66	67	51	70	60	70	55	70	83	81
JEFFERSON	82	56	36	54	65	90	60	77	68	56	67	68	50	71	60	73	56	70	86	83
JOHNSON	81	53	30	51	64	89	58	76	64	54	64	67	46	69	57	69	54	69	83	83
KEARNEY	91	64	41	62	75	101	67	86	74	63	74	76	56	79	67	80	62	78	94	93
KEITH	78	61	52	61	68	84	65	76	69	62	68	66	58	71	65	72	58	71	81	79
KEYA PAHA	59	38	16	36	46	67	40	56	44	38	45	50	31	49	39	48	37	49	58	62
KIMBALL	78	55	44	54	62	82	62	73	70	56	67	64	52	71	61	75	57	68	86	77
KNOX	69	46	27	44	54	76	49	65	55	46	55	57	40	59	49	59	46	58	71	70
LANCASTER	92	90	97	94	86	85	97	88	94	94	94	82	95	95	93	92	85	93	89	89
LINCOLN	82	73	73	73	75	83	74	79	78	73	76	70	71	80	74	79	67	77	84	81
LOGAN	81	51	22	49	63	91	54	76	60	52	61	68	42	66	53	65	51	67	80	84
LOUP	66	42	18	40	52	74	44	62	49	42	50	55	34	54	44	53	42	55	65	69
MCPHERSON	71	45	20	43	56	80	48	67	53	46	54	60	37	59	47	57	45	59	70	75
MADISON	78	69	69	70	70	77	72	74	75	70	74	66	69	76	71	76	65	73	79	76
MERRICK	80	58	42	57	67	87	61	76	68	58	67	67	52	72	61	72	57	70	84	82
MORRILL	73	50	34	49	58	79	55	69	61	50	60	60	45	64	54	66	51	63	77	73
NANCE	79	54	35	52	63	86	59	74	66	54	65	66	48	69	58	71	54	68	83	80
NEMAHA	81	60	51	60	67	85	66	77	73	61	70	68	58	74	66	77	60	73	87	81
NUCKOLLS	70	48	32	47	56	76	53	66	59	49	58	59	43	62	52	63	49	61	75	71
OTOE	85	70	61	69	77	93	70	82	75	69	74	72	65	79	71	79	65	76	88	87
PAWNEE	74	50	31	48	58	81	54	69	60	50	60	61	44	64	53	65	50	63	77	75
PERKINS	88	58	33	56	69	96	63	82	70	59	70	73	50	75	62	75	58	74	90	90
PHELPS	93	71	56	70	79	100	73	89	79	71	78	77	65	84	73	83	67	82	95	94
PIERCE	83	61	42	59	69	90	62	78	68	60	68	69	54	73	62	73	58	71	84	84
PLATTE	85	78	78	78	81	90	76	83	80	77	79	73	75	83	78	82	70	80	88	86
POLK	91	60	32	57	72	100	64	85	71	60	71	76	51	77	63	77	60	77	92	93
RED WILLOW	73	57	50	56	63	78	60	70	67	57	65	61	54	68	61	71	56	66	80	73
RICHARDSON	70	50	39	49	57	75	55	66	62	50	60	58	47	64	55	67	51	62	77	70
ROCK	64	44	32	43	51	69	49	61	55	45	54	53	41	57	48	59	45	56	69	64
SALINE	81	65	56	64	70	85	68	78	72	64	71	69	61	75	68	75	61	73	84	81
SARPY	112	117	114	119	108	102	112	106	108	115	108	100	114	112	110	104	98	108	101	106
NEBRASKA	92	82	79	83	83	91	85	88	87	84	87	80	81	89	84	88	77	87	92	91
UNITED STATES	100	100	100	100	100	100	100	100	100	100	100	100	100	100	100	100	100	100	100	100

COUNTY	FIPS Code	CBSA Code	DMA Code	POPULATION			2000-2007 ANNUAL RATE		RACE (%)					
									White		Black		Asian/Pacific	
				2000	2007	2012	% Rate	State Rank	2000	2007	2000	2007	2000	2007
SAUNDERS	155	36540	652	19,830	21,207	22,057	0.9	7	98.5	98.2	0.1	0.1	0.2	0.3
SCOTTS BLUFF	157	42420	759	36,951	36,716	36,613	-0.1	32	87.6	84.6	0.3	0.3	0.6	0.9
SEWARD	159	30700	722	16,496	17,227	17,703	0.6	12	98.0	97.6	0.3	0.3	0.3	0.5
SHERIDAN	161	00000	751	6,198	5,796	5,537	-0.9	79	88.1	86.8	0.1	0.1	0.2	0.2
SHERMAN	163	00000	722	3,318	3,232	3,184	-0.4	49	98.5	98.5	0.1	0.1	0.3	0.3
SIOUX	165	00000	759	1,475	1,450	1,439	-0.2	36	97.6	97.6	0.0	0.0	0.2	0.2
STANTON	167	35740	624	6,455	6,676	6,843	0.5	15	96.7	96.0	0.4	0.4	0.1	0.2
THAYER	169	00000	722	6,055	5,615	5,249	-1.0	83	98.7	98.4	0.0	0.0	0.1	0.2
THOMAS	171	00000	740	729	635	581	-1.9	93	99.5	99.4	0.0	0.0	0.0	0.0
THURSTON	173	00000	624	7,171	7,438	7,649	0.5	15	45.8	43.0	0.2	0.2	0.1	0.1
VALLEY	175	00000	722	4,647	4,506	4,379	-0.4	49	98.1	97.6	0.2	0.2	0.2	0.2
WASHINGTON	177	36540	652	18,780	20,459	21,690	1.2	4	98.1	97.7	0.3	0.4	0.4	0.6
WAYNE	179	00000	624	9,851	9,640	9,622	-0.3	41	96.8	96.1	0.9	1.0	0.4	0.5
WEBSTER	181	00000	722	4,061	3,880	3,765	-0.6	63	98.1	97.7	0.1	0.2	0.5	0.8
WHEELER	183	00000	722	886	808	785	-1.3	91	99.1	99.0	0.0	0.0	0.0	0.0
YORK	185	00000	722	14,598	14,306	14,055	-0.3	41	96.8	96.1	1.0	1.0	0.6	0.8
NEBRASKA							0.8		89.6	87.5	4.0	4.3	1.3	2.0
UNITED STATES							1.2		75.1	72.7	12.3	12.6	3.8	4.5

POPULATION COMPOSITION

COUNTY	% HISPANIC ORIGIN		2007 AGE DISTRIBUTION (%)										MEDIAN AGE	% 2007 Males	% 2007 Females
	2000	2007	0-4	5-9	10-14	15-19	20-24	25-44	45-64	65-84	85+	18+	2007		
SAUNDERS	1.0	1.4	6.7	6.0	6.9	7.2	6.8	23.7	28.0	12.3	2.4	75.8	40.8	49.9	50.1
SCOTTS BLUFF	17.2	22.0	6.7	6.0	6.4	6.5	7.7	23.1	27.2	13.4	3.0	76.9	39.8	47.9	52.1
SEWARD	1.1	1.5	5.8	5.1	5.9	9.2	10.3	23.1	25.5	12.1	2.9	79.0	37.0	50.8	49.2
SHERIDAN	1.5	1.9	6.3	5.8	6.0	6.1	7.4	19.5	29.3	15.5	4.2	78.0	44.0	49.1	50.9
SHERMAN	1.0	1.1	5.9	5.1	5.5	6.6	7.1	19.2	29.3	17.2	4.2	79.4	45.4	49.3	50.7
SIOUX	2.3	2.3	5.5	5.4	5.7	5.5	6.0	21.8	31.7	16.9	1.6	80.3	45.1	53.0	47.0
STANTON	2.3	3.1	7.2	6.9	6.4	7.5	7.6	23.9	26.9	11.3	2.4	74.8	38.1	49.7	50.3
THAYER	1.0	1.4	6.3	5.8	5.8	5.5	7.1	18.9	28.3	17.4	4.9	78.6	45.4	49.1	50.9
THOMAS	0.8	0.9	5.8	6.8	4.4	3.3	8.5	19.5	35.9	12.8	3.0	81.3	46.0	51.8	48.2
THURSTON	2.4	2.8	10.5	8.9	9.6	8.8	7.8	22.6	19.5	10.5	1.9	65.4	29.0	49.2	50.8
VALLEY	1.6	2.2	6.3	5.5	6.0	6.3	7.1	19.6	27.6	17.1	4.3	78.1	44.3	48.0	52.0
WASHINGTON	1.1	1.5	6.5	6.1	7.1	7.5	7.6	23.8	28.4	11.0	2.0	75.9	39.4	49.8	50.2
WAYNE	1.5	2.0	5.8	4.7	5.5	11.6	14.8	23.2	20.9	11.1	2.4	80.2	29.2	48.1	51.9
WEBSTER	0.5	0.7	5.7	5.1	6.0	6.5	5.7	19.3	28.5	18.3	5.0	78.8	46.0	48.8	51.2
WHEELER	0.6	0.6	8.5	8.0	6.7	5.3	7.1	18.3	28.8	15.5	1.7	73.6	41.4	49.6	50.4
YORK	1.4	1.9	5.8	5.6	6.2	7.6	7.7	22.8	27.4	13.5	3.5	78.0	41.0	47.9	52.1
NEBRASKA	5.5	7.2	7.1	6.6	6.6	7.2	7.6	26.7	25.3	10.7	2.2	75.6	36.3	49.4	50.6
UNITED STATES	12.5	15.0	6.9	6.5	6.8	7.1	7.0	27.6	25.4	10.7	1.9	75.6	36.7	49.2	50.8

COUNTY	HOUSEHOLDS					FAMILIES			MEDIAN HOUSEHOLD INCOME			
	2000	2007	2012	% Annual Rate 2000-2007	2007 Average HH Size	2000	2007	% Annual Rate 2000-2007	2007	2012	2007 National Rank	2007 State Rank
SAUNDERS	7,498	8,104	8,459	1.1	2.59	5,443	5,822	0.9	50,432	57,581	645	7
SCOTTS BLUFF	14,887	15,021	15,068	0.1	2.40	10,170	10,139	0.0	39,658	45,645	1758	40
SEWARD	6,013	6,379	6,619	0.8	2.48	4,215	4,421	0.7	52,162	60,250	540	6
SHERIDAN	2,549	2,438	2,351	-0.6	2.32	1,729	1,634	-0.8	34,316	37,853	2512	69
SHERMAN	1,394	1,403	1,402	0.1	2.26	935	929	-0.1	33,101	36,585	2648	77
SIOUX	605	605	605	0.0	2.40	444	440	-0.1	34,636	38,183	2484	68
STANTON	2,297	2,414	2,491	0.7	2.72	1,784	1,858	0.6	42,690	47,192	1367	25
THAYER	2,541	2,391	2,245	-0.8	2.27	1,691	1,570	-1.0	35,786	39,494	2316	58
THOMAS	325	301	279	-1.1	2.11	216	198	-1.2	32,887	36,604	2668	78
THURSTON	2,255	2,308	2,358	0.3	3.18	1,724	1,750	0.2	33,920	38,555	2559	71
VALLEY	1,965	1,926	1,879	-0.3	2.30	1,299	1,257	-0.5	32,449	35,943	2718	81
WASHINGTON	6,940	7,675	8,180	1.4	2.60	5,149	5,637	1.3	59,435	67,119	280	2
WAYNE	3,437	3,443	3,443	0.0	2.49	2,205	2,179	-0.2	39,852	45,949	1744	39
WEBSTER	1,708	1,652	1,609	-0.5	2.25	1,119	1,068	-0.6	34,914	38,366	2443	65
WHEELER	352	330	325	-0.9	2.45	244	226	-1.1	32,498	35,979	2706	79
YORK	5,722	5,691	5,628	-0.1	2.38	3,933	3,865	-0.2	44,594	50,478	1149	20
NEBRASKA				0.9	2.47			0.7	49,064	57,487		
UNITED STATES				1.2	2.59			1.0	53,154	62,503		

INCOME

COUNTY	2007 Per Capita Income	2007 HH Income Base	2007 HOUSEHOLD INCOME DISTRIBUTION (%)					2007 Home Value Base	2007 HOME VALUE DISTRIBUTION (%)					2007 Median Home Value
			Less than $25,000	$25,000 to $49,999	$50,000 to $99,999	$100,000 to $149,999	$150,000 or More		Less than $50,000	$50,000 to $89,999	$90,000 to $174,999	$175,000 to $399,999	$400,000 or More	
SAUNDERS	22,277	8,104	20.2	29.2	38.8	9.3	2.5	6,619	9.3	18.2	44.0	25.0	3.4	124,321
SCOTTS BLUFF	21,499	15,021	29.8	32.3	27.5	7.4	3.0	10,395	18.2	29.5	38.5	12.5	1.2	92,855
SEWARD	23,467	6,379	20.6	26.5	39.7	9.3	3.8	4,762	10.5	17.8	47.0	22.1	2.6	120,239
SHERIDAN	18,128	2,438	35.4	35.8	23.5	3.8	1.5	1,788	39.1	29.5	23.9	5.1	2.3	63,103
SHERMAN	17,323	1,403	34.9	40.6	20.8	2.3	1.5	1,145	42.4	31.2	18.4	5.8	2.2	59,611
SIOUX	20,636	605	30.9	38.2	22.8	4.6	3.5	419	33.7	25.5	21.5	10.7	8.6	73,167
STANTON	18,594	2,414	21.9	38.4	32.4	5.2	2.2	1,978	17.3	25.5	44.1	11.2	2.0	96,272
THAYER	19,513	2,391	31.2	36.2	26.1	4.9	1.6	1,954	44.2	29.1	21.2	4.0	1.6	57,755
THOMAS	19,012	301	38.9	32.9	23.3	5.0	0.0	229	51.5	21.0	18.3	7.9	1.3	48,542
THURSTON	13,068	2,308	35.3	34.3	25.4	3.9	1.0	1,490	34.3	29.3	28.5	7.1	0.9	68,865
VALLEY	17,952	1,926	35.6	35.6	24.1	2.9	1.8	1,503	41.4	28.8	23.6	5.3	0.9	61,723
WASHINGTON	26,138	7,675	16.7	24.9	39.5	14.0	5.0	6,106	6.9	8.9	40.2	36.4	7.6	159,715
WAYNE	19,075	3,443	28.5	31.8	31.1	6.7	1.9	2,329	11.3	26.0	47.1	14.9	0.8	105,788
WEBSTER	18,875	1,652	32.9	38.0	23.9	3.6	1.6	1,328	42.6	29.5	21.9	5.2	0.8	58,909
WHEELER	16,999	330	38.8	37.3	17.6	4.2	2.1	237	46.0	25.3	19.8	3.0	5.9	55,938
YORK	21,998	5,691	22.6	34.2	34.6	6.0	2.7	4,122	15.9	26.8	40.9	14.3	2.1	98,979
NEBRASKA	25,004		21.9	29.0	34.0	10.1	5.0		14.0	19.3	43.3	20.4	3.0	115,851
UNITED STATES	27,916		21.9	25.0	32.3	12.3	8.4		7.9	10.5	27.1	35.6	19.0	192,285

COUNTY	FINANCIAL SERVICES				THE HOME						ENTERTAINMENT						PERSONAL			
					Home Improvements		Furnishings													
	Auto Loan	Home Loan	Invest-ments	Retire-ment Plans	Home Repair	Lawn & Garden	Comput-ers & Hard-ware	Major Appli-ances	TV, Radio, Sound Equip-ment	Furni-ture	Dine out/ Carry out	Sports Equip-ment	Fees & Tickets	Toys & Games	Travel	Cable TV	Apparel & Services	Auto Repairs	Health Insur-ance	Pets & Supplies
SAUNDERS	92	76	63	75	82	99	74	88	79	74	79	78	69	84	75	83	69	81	93	93
SCOTTS BLUFF	75	66	69	66	69	77	70	73	74	67	72	64	66	74	70	76	64	72	80	75
SEWARD	91	78	77	80	83	95	82	89	84	78	83	80	77	86	82	86	72	86	94	92
SHERIDAN	71	49	32	47	57	78	53	67	60	49	59	59	44	63	52	64	49	61	75	72
SHERMAN	67	45	28	44	53	74	49	63	55	46	54	56	40	58	49	59	46	58	70	68
SIOUX	89	57	24	54	70	101	60	84	66	57	67	75	46	73	59	72	56	74	88	93
STANTON	85	64	44	62	70	90	64	79	70	62	70	70	56	74	64	74	60	73	84	85
THAYER	77	52	31	50	61	85	56	73	63	52	62	64	45	67	55	67	52	66	80	79
THOMAS	72	46	20	44	57	82	49	68	54	46	55	61	38	60	48	58	46	60	71	76
THURSTON	64	50	45	51	54	66	53	60	59	52	58	52	49	61	53	62	50	58	67	64
VALLEY	71	48	29	46	56	78	52	67	58	48	57	59	42	61	51	62	48	61	74	72
WASHINGTON	99	97	98	98	100	105	93	99	93	93	93	88	93	98	95	94	83	94	99	101
WAYNE	78	56	49	58	62	78	70	74	71	61	70	67	58	72	65	72	60	72	78	77
WEBSTER	73	50	32	48	58	80	54	69	61	50	60	61	44	64	53	65	50	63	77	74
WHEELER	75	48	21	46	59	85	51	71	56	48	57	63	39	62	50	60	47	62	74	79
YORK	85	65	56	65	73	90	70	81	75	66	74	72	62	78	69	78	64	76	88	86
NEBRASKA	92	82	79	83	83	91	85	88	87	84	87	80	81	89	84	88	77	87	92	91
UNITED STATES	100	100	100	100	100	100	100	100	100	100	100	100	100	100	100	100	100	100	100	100

COUNTY	FIPS Code	CBSA Code	DMA Code	POPULATION			2000-2007 ANNUAL RATE		RACE (%)					
									White		Black		Asian/Pacific	
				2000	2007	2012	% Rate	State Rank	2000	2007	2000	2007	2000	2007
CHURCHILL	001	21980	811	23,982	25,517	26,611	0.9	9	84.2	82.8	1.6	1.7	2.9	3.0
CLARK	003	29820	839	1,375,765	1,893,507	2,308,978	4.5	2	71.6	69.4	9.1	9.3	5.7	5.6
DOUGLAS	005	23820	811	41,259	51,304	59,550	3.1	5	91.9	90.8	0.3	0.3	1.4	1.4
ELKO	007	21220	770	45,291	47,118	48,296	0.5	11	82.0	80.0	0.6	0.6	0.8	0.8
ESMERALDA	009	00000	811	971	979	917	0.1	13	82.0	81.9	0.1	0.1	0.2	0.2
EUREKA	011	21220	770	1,651	1,512	1,438	-1.2	17	89.3	87.3	0.4	0.5	0.8	0.9
HUMBOLDT	013	00000	811	16,106	17,367	18,345	1.0	8	83.2	81.1	0.5	0.5	0.6	0.6
LANDER	015	00000	811	5,794	5,395	5,365	-1.0	16	84.4	82.3	0.2	0.2	0.4	0.4
LINCOLN	017	00000	839	4,165	4,342	4,466	0.6	10	91.5	90.5	1.8	1.9	0.4	0.4
LYON	019	22280	811	34,501	52,742	73,370	6.0	1	88.6	87.0	0.7	0.7	0.7	0.8
MINERAL	021	00000	811	5,071	4,899	4,804	-0.5	15	73.9	72.7	4.8	5.1	0.9	0.9
NYE	023	37220	839	32,485	42,728	52,061	3.9	3	89.6	88.3	1.2	1.3	1.1	1.1
PERSHING	027	00000	811	6,693	6,689	6,600	0.0	14	77.7	77.7	5.3	5.2	0.9	0.9
STOREY	029	39900	811	3,399	4,359	5,501	3.5	4	93.0	92.1	0.3	0.3	1.1	1.2
WASHOE	031	39900	811	339,486	420,930	487,526	3.0	6	80.4	78.2	2.1	2.2	4.7	4.7
WHITE PINE	033	00000	770	9,181	9,248	9,309	0.1	13	86.4	86.4	4.1	4.0	1.0	1.0
CARSON CITY	510	16180	811	52,457	56,641	58,574	1.1	7	85.3	83.4	1.8	1.9	1.9	1.9
NEVADA							3.9		75.2	72.7	6.8	7.1	4.9	4.9
UNITED STATES							1.2		75.1	72.7	12.3	12.6	3.8	4.5

COUNTY	% HISPANIC ORIGIN		2007 AGE DISTRIBUTION (%)									MEDIAN AGE	% 2007 Males	% 2007 Females
	2000	2007	0-4	5-9	10-14	15-19	20-24	25-44	45-64	65-84	85+	18+	2007		
CHURCHILL	8.7	10.7	8.4	7.1	6.9	7.3	7.9	25.4	24.9	10.6	1.5	73.2	35.4	49.9	50.1
CLARK	22.0	26.0	7.4	6.7	6.9	6.4	6.1	30.0	24.5	10.8	1.1	75.0	36.3	50.4	49.6
DOUGLAS	7.4	9.2	4.9	5.2	6.2	7.2	5.8	20.4	32.4	16.2	1.6	79.2	45.2	50.1	49.9
ELKO	19.7	23.8	8.9	7.6	7.7	7.9	8.4	28.0	24.2	6.5	0.6	70.9	31.6	51.5	48.5
ESMERALDA	10.2	10.1	4.3	3.8	5.2	4.6	6.0	19.7	32.8	22.3	1.3	83.9	49.1	55.8	44.2
EUREKA	9.6	11.8	6.5	5.5	6.7	8.0	8.1	23.3	28.7	12.2	1.0	76.1	40.4	50.7	49.3
HUMBOLDT	18.9	22.8	8.2	7.4	7.4	7.7	7.7	25.7	27.3	7.6	0.9	71.9	35.0	52.2	47.8
LANDER	18.5	22.5	7.7	6.0	8.5	8.5	9.1	22.0	29.7	7.7	0.9	72.0	35.3	50.8	49.2
LINCOLN	5.3	6.6	6.6	6.5	6.2	10.0	8.9	17.5	27.6	15.2	1.5	73.6	39.6	51.8	48.2
LYON	11.0	13.5	6.7	6.5	6.9	7.4	5.8	24.2	28.5	12.7	1.3	75.1	40.2	50.2	49.8
MINERAL	8.4	10.3	5.5	5.0	5.7	7.6	6.9	19.1	30.2	17.6	2.6	78.8	45.3	50.1	49.9
NYE	8.4	10.3	5.8	5.2	5.9	6.8	5.7	18.5	31.3	19.2	1.3	78.7	46.2	51.2	48.8
PERSHING	19.3	19.2	6.7	6.2	5.9	7.2	9.3	31.0	24.5	7.9	1.3	77.0	35.4	61.2	38.8
STOREY	5.1	6.4	4.2	4.1	5.8	5.7	3.0	22.9	39.1	13.9	1.4	82.1	47.0	51.9	48.1
WASHOE	16.6	20.1	7.0	6.6	6.6	7.0	6.8	28.2	26.8	9.8	1.3	75.8	36.8	50.3	49.7
WHITE PINE	11.0	10.9	6.0	5.5	5.6	6.5	9.2	26.5	26.4	12.4	1.8	78.7	38.3	55.7	44.3
CARSON CITY	14.2	17.4	6.3	5.6	6.3	6.3	7.0	25.6	27.1	13.5	2.4	78.0	40.0	51.3	48.7
NEVADA	19.7	23.7	7.3	6.6	6.9	6.6	6.3	29.0	25.3	10.9	1.1	75.3	36.7	50.5	49.5
UNITED STATES	12.5	15.0	6.9	6.5	6.8	7.1	7.0	27.6	25.4	10.7	1.9	75.6	36.7	49.2	50.8

HOUSEHOLDS

COUNTY	HOUSEHOLDS					FAMILIES			MEDIAN HOUSEHOLD INCOME			
	2000	2007	2012	% Annual Rate 2000-2007	2007 Average HH Size	2000	2007	% Annual Rate 2000-2007	2007	2012	2007 National Rank	2007 State Rank
CHURCHILL	8,912	9,509	9,914	0.9	2.65	6,465	6,831	0.8	49,176	55,419	736	9
CLARK	512,253	704,837	857,673	4.5	2.66	339,693	461,939	4.3	56,432	66,146	348	6
DOUGLAS	16,401	20,714	24,207	3.3	2.47	11,894	14,877	3.1	66,474	77,881	158	1
ELKO	15,638	16,209	16,582	0.5	2.86	11,493	11,803	0.4	61,529	71,210	224	2
ESMERALDA	455	471	446	0.5	2.07	260	265	0.3	41,438	48,341	1525	15
EUREKA	666	613	584	-1.1	2.45	440	400	-1.3	47,447	52,157	868	11
HUMBOLDT	5,733	6,194	6,546	1.1	2.77	4,136	4,426	0.9	57,268	65,460	321	5
LANDER	2,093	1,973	1,973	-0.8	2.69	1,523	1,421	-1.0	55,306	64,385	393	7
LINCOLN	1,540	1,648	1,717	0.9	2.42	1,011	1,069	0.8	41,273	48,153	1558	16
LYON	13,007	19,945	27,784	6.1	2.62	9,449	14,351	5.9	47,265	52,739	887	12
MINERAL	2,197	2,199	2,187	0.0	2.18	1,380	1,363	-0.2	41,049	47,945	1590	17
NYE	13,309	17,754	21,766	4.1	2.39	9,068	11,961	3.9	44,702	51,740	1138	14
PERSHING	1,962	1,955	1,918	0.0	2.70	1,383	1,364	-0.2	48,347	53,844	789	10
STOREY	1,462	1,911	2,432	3.8	2.28	969	1,252	3.6	57,418	64,002	320	4
WASHOE	132,084	163,427	188,860	3.0	2.54	83,752	102,314	2.8	58,789	69,322	290	3
WHITE PINE	3,282	3,393	3,457	0.5	2.36	2,161	2,207	0.3	45,064	51,439	1105	13
CARSON CITY	20,171	21,773	22,500	1.1	2.45	13,256	14,140	0.9	52,926	62,195	505	8
NEVADA				3.9	2.63			3.8	56,308	65,921		
UNITED STATES				1.2	2.59			1.0	53,154	62,503		

COUNTY	2007 Per Capita Income	2007 HH Income Base	2007 HOUSEHOLD INCOME DISTRIBUTION (%)					2007 Home Value Base	2007 HOME VALUE DISTRIBUTION (%)					2007 Median Home Value
			Less than $25,000	$25,000 to $49,999	$50,000 to $99,999	$100,000 to $149,999	$150,000 or More		Less than $50,000	$50,000 to $89,999	$90,000 to $174,999	$175,000 to $399,999	$400,000 or More	
CHURCHILL	23,220	9,509	20.6	30.2	36.7	8.0	4.5	6,436	8.0	4.6	13.4	63.2	10.9	231,374
CLARK	27,543	704,831	17.8	25.6	36.1	12.7	7.9	429,462	2.8	1.9	6.6	64.9	23.9	302,825
DOUGLAS	34,531	20,714	14.0	20.7	40.0	14.4	10.9	15,734	1.7	2.0	4.8	44.9	46.6	386,702
ELKO	23,865	16,209	16.2	22.5	43.9	13.2	4.2	11,663	11.0	4.5	17.8	58.4	8.3	227,940
ESMERALDA	24,080	471	28.7	28.7	33.5	8.7	0.4	321	18.1	16.8	42.4	22.7	0.0	120,833
EUREKA	22,448	613	30.8	21.7	36.5	8.3	2.6	464	15.3	9.7	37.9	31.3	5.8	149,554
HUMBOLDT	24,142	6,194	17.9	23.1	43.3	11.3	4.3	4,606	6.8	7.1	23.0	55.5	7.6	203,754
LANDER	21,926	1,973	19.8	23.0	45.6	10.2	1.5	1,547	15.7	10.5	33.7	38.2	1.9	155,421
LINCOLN	20,237	1,648	36.1	21.4	34.7	6.0	1.8	1,267	11.4	10.4	30.8	42.0	5.4	168,842
LYON	22,089	19,944	21.8	31.8	36.6	6.1	3.6	15,432	4.4	2.7	20.0	61.2	11.8	233,532
MINERAL	22,365	2,191	31.0	29.0	32.5	6.5	1.0	1,631	12.1	14.5	43.0	29.4	1.0	137,270
NYE	22,791	17,754	26.3	29.9	31.9	8.7	3.1	13,794	6.3	3.9	21.7	60.3	7.8	216,409
PERSHING	21,555	1,955	26.4	25.3	38.9	7.0	2.4	1,398	10.7	8.8	29.5	46.2	4.7	177,167
STOREY	29,353	1,911	13.8	29.7	40.4	11.2	4.9	1,547	3.5	2.5	5.9	69.7	18.3	265,427
WASHOE	30,441	163,427	17.3	24.2	36.6	13.0	8.9	99,860	4.4	2.2	8.1	54.8	30.4	323,503
WHITE PINE	23,370	3,393	27.1	28.0	35.7	6.4	2.8	2,620	6.0	12.7	41.9	32.5	6.9	154,079
CARSON CITY	27,145	21,773	20.0	26.7	36.6	10.6	6.1	14,151	6.8	3.6	9.8	58.6	21.2	282,575
NEVADA	27,752		18.0	25.5	36.4	12.5	7.7		3.6	2.3	8.4	61.8	24.0	297,001
UNITED STATES	27,916		21.9	25.0	32.3	12.3	8.4		7.9	10.5	27.1	35.6	19.0	192,285

COUNTY	FINANCIAL SERVICES				THE HOME						ENTERTAINMENT						PERSONAL			
					Home Improvements		Furnishings													
	Auto Loan	Home Loan	Invest-ments	Retire-ment Plans	Home Repair	Lawn & Garden	Comput-ers & Hard-ware	Major Appli-ances	TV, Radio, Sound Equip-ment	Furni-ture	Dine out/ Carry out	Sports Equip-ment	Fees & Tickets	Toys & Games	Travel	Cable TV	Apparel & Services	Auto Repairs	Health Insur-ance	Pets & Supplies
CHURCHILL	91	83	78	84	82	88	84	86	84	83	85	79	81	87	82	85	75	86	86	88
CLARK	102	100	99	102	96	94	103	98	100	103	101	94	102	100	100	98	92	102	96	98
DOUGLAS	113	127	138	128	127	122	115	119	114	120	113	106	123	112	123	114	103	116	118	118
ELKO	100	101	90	99	92	92	94	95	93	97	93	88	94	96	93	91	83	95	91	95
ESMERALDA	79	64	48	60	71	91	62	79	68	61	67	67	56	66	65	73	57	73	86	82
EUREKA	88	78	61	75	74	84	71	80	75	73	75	72	69	77	71	78	66	77	81	83
HUMBOLDT	99	94	84	93	91	97	90	95	91	91	91	86	88	94	90	92	81	93	94	97
LANDER	89	85	73	83	79	83	79	83	80	81	80	75	78	82	79	81	71	83	82	84
LINCOLN	73	64	53	62	68	82	61	74	65	61	64	63	58	62	65	68	55	70	79	75
LYON	90	80	68	78	80	92	75	85	79	76	78	76	72	81	77	81	69	81	87	89
MINERAL	68	64	68	63	68	77	63	71	68	62	66	59	63	66	67	72	57	68	80	70
NYE	80	72	69	70	76	88	71	82	75	70	73	69	69	71	75	79	63	79	90	82
PERSHING	84	76	66	74	72	80	73	78	76	73	75	70	70	77	73	77	66	76	80	80
STOREY	105	86	62	84	98	125	85	109	90	83	89	93	76	89	90	96	76	99	113	113
WASHOE	106	107	109	110	101	97	111	102	106	110	107	98	110	106	107	104	98	107	99	103
WHITE PINE	80	68	70	69	71	81	73	78	77	68	74	68	68	77	73	80	64	75	86	78
CARSON CITY	89	93	100	94	92	90	93	91	91	93	91	83	94	90	94	91	82	92	92	90
NEVADA	101	100	99	102	96	95	103	98	100	102	100	93	101	100	100	98	91	102	96	98
UNITED STATES	100	100	100	100	100	100	100	100	100	100	100	100	100	100	100	100	100	100	100	100

COUNTY	FIPS Code	CBSA Code	DMA Code	POPULATION			2000-2007 ANNUAL RATE		RACE (%)					
									White		Black		Asian/Pacific	
				2000	2007	2012	% Rate	State Rank	2000	2007	2000	2007	2000	2007
BELKNAP	001	29060	506	56,325	63,373	68,788	1.6	1	97.6	97.2	0.3	0.3	0.6	0.8
CARROLL	003	00000	500	43,666	48,602	52,030	1.5	3	98.2	97.9	0.2	0.2	0.4	0.6
CHESHIRE	005	28300	506	73,825	79,350	83,368	1.0	9	97.8	97.4	0.4	0.5	0.5	0.7
COOS	007	13620	500	33,111	33,714	33,927	0.2	10	98.1	97.8	0.1	0.1	0.4	0.6
GRAFTON	009	30100	523	81,743	88,695	93,741	1.1	7	95.8	94.7	0.5	0.6	1.8	2.6
HILLSBOROUGH	011	31700	506	380,841	414,036	437,419	1.2	6	93.9	92.4	1.3	1.5	2.0	2.9
MERRIMACK	013	18180	506	136,225	151,780	163,113	1.5	3	97.1	96.5	0.5	0.6	0.9	1.3
ROCKINGHAM	015	14460	506	277,359	305,354	325,028	1.3	5	96.8	96.0	0.6	0.7	1.1	1.7
STRAFFORD	017	14460	506	112,233	124,514	132,329	1.4	4	96.3	95.4	0.6	0.7	1.4	2.1
SULLIVAN	019	17200	523	40,458	43,394	45,647	1.0	9	98.0	97.7	0.2	0.3	0.4	0.6
NEW HAMPSHIRE							1.3		96.0	95.1	0.7	0.8	1.3	1.9
UNITED STATES							1.2		75.1	72.7	12.3	12.6	3.8	4.5

POPULATION COMPOSITION

COUNTY	% HISPANIC ORIGIN		2007 AGE DISTRIBUTION (%)										MEDIAN AGE	% 2007 Males	% 2007 Females
	2000	2007	0-4	5-9	10-14	15-19	20-24	25-44	45-64	65-84	85+	18+	2007		
BELKNAP	0.7	1.0	5.3	5.2	6.3	6.2	5.9	23.9	32.2	12.8	2.2	79.3	43.2	49.3	50.7
CARROLL	0.5	0.6	4.7	4.6	5.4	6.5	5.5	20.9	35.4	14.9	2.2	81.1	46.3	49.3	50.7
CHESHIRE	0.7	0.9	5.1	5.0	5.8	8.9	8.7	23.4	28.9	12.0	2.2	79.8	40.3	48.8	51.2
COOS	0.6	0.8	5.0	4.7	5.6	6.3	6.2	22.3	31.4	15.1	3.4	80.7	44.9	49.1	50.9
GRAFTON	1.1	1.5	4.9	4.8	5.7	9.1	10.2	22.7	28.8	11.6	2.1	80.4	39.3	49.4	50.6
HILLSBOROUGH	3.2	4.1	6.5	6.4	7.3	7.6	6.3	27.1	27.4	9.6	1.8	75.2	38.3	49.4	50.6
MERRIMACK	1.0	1.3	5.7	5.6	6.6	7.8	7.1	24.7	29.8	10.5	2.2	77.5	40.5	49.4	50.6
ROCKINGHAM	1.2	1.6	6.2	6.3	7.4	7.2	5.6	26.0	30.1	9.7	1.5	75.4	40.3	49.4	50.6
STRAFFORD	1.0	1.3	5.9	5.5	6.1	8.7	9.9	26.4	26.1	9.7	1.6	78.4	36.5	48.7	51.3
SULLIVAN	0.5	0.7	5.5	5.3	6.1	6.8	5.7	24.1	30.8	13.5	2.3	78.8	42.8	49.6	50.4
NEW HAMPSHIRE	1.7	2.1	5.9	5.8	6.7	7.6	6.9	25.4	29.1	10.6	1.9	77.1	39.9	49.3	50.7
UNITED STATES	12.5	15.0	6.9	6.5	6.8	7.1	7.0	27.6	25.4	10.7	1.9	75.6	36.7	49.2	50.8

COUNTY	HOUSEHOLDS					FAMILIES			MEDIAN HOUSEHOLD INCOME			
	2000	2007	2012	% Annual Rate 2000-2007	2007 Average HH Size	2000	2007	% Annual Rate 2000-2007	2007	2012	2007 National Rank	2007 State Rank
BELKNAP	22,459	25,823	28,290	1.9	2.41	15,501	17,566	1.7	53,336	61,863	481	5
CARROLL	18,351	20,763	22,406	1.7	2.31	12,312	13,715	1.5	48,918	56,674	755	9
CHESHIRE	28,299	30,735	32,552	1.1	2.44	18,784	20,080	0.9	52,624	61,202	515	7
COOS	13,961	14,396	14,643	0.4	2.27	9,164	9,299	0.2	41,069	46,678	1587	10
GRAFTON	31,598	34,680	37,048	1.3	2.36	20,266	21,867	1.1	52,748	62,382	510	6
HILLSBOROUGH	144,455	156,368	165,451	1.1	2.60	98,855	105,429	0.9	68,835	81,086	130	2
MERRIMACK	51,843	57,937	62,615	1.5	2.51	35,473	39,060	1.3	61,465	71,148	226	3
ROCKINGHAM	104,529	116,634	124,941	1.5	2.60	74,358	81,845	1.3	75,264	87,708	85	1
STRAFFORD	42,581	47,956	51,360	1.7	2.48	27,759	30,750	1.4	56,011	65,153	363	4
SULLIVAN	16,530	18,131	19,270	1.3	2.36	11,179	12,077	1.1	49,668	56,703	698	8
NEW HAMPSHIRE				1.4	2.51			1.2	62,216	72,795		
UNITED STATES				1.2	2.59			1.0	53,154	62,503		

COUNTY	2007 Per Capita Income	2007 HH Income Base	2007 HOUSEHOLD INCOME DISTRIBUTION (%)					2007 Home Value Base	2007 HOME VALUE DISTRIBUTION (%)					2007 Median Home Value
			Less than $25,000	$25,000 to $49,999	$50,000 to $99,999	$100,000 to $149,999	$150,000 or More		Less than $50,000	$50,000 to $89,999	$90,000 to $174,999	$175,000 to $399,999	$400,000 or More	
BELKNAP	28,455	25,823	17.7	28.4	37.1	11.0	5.8	19,644	4.7	4.8	25.3	53.9	11.5	204,013
CARROLL	28,106	20,763	21.5	29.6	33.6	9.2	6.1	16,498	3.5	4.3	22.2	50.2	19.8	226,533
CHESHIRE	26,480	30,735	18.5	28.5	37.2	10.5	5.3	22,400	4.3	4.3	26.2	55.6	9.6	202,858
COOS	21,455	14,396	29.5	31.2	31.6	5.7	2.0	10,537	7.8	13.6	50.5	25.1	3.0	137,013
GRAFTON	28,532	34,680	20.0	26.7	36.2	9.9	7.1	24,416	4.3	5.7	28.9	46.8	14.3	201,357
HILLSBOROUGH	33,184	156,368	13.6	20.4	37.5	16.7	11.8	105,164	1.4	2.1	12.0	67.3	17.2	267,164
MERRIMACK	29,528	57,937	15.0	23.9	39.3	13.9	7.9	41,452	4.7	4.0	21.4	58.2	11.7	219,278
ROCKINGHAM	35,793	116,634	11.0	18.6	38.1	18.6	13.7	90,205	2.0	3.3	10.0	58.5	26.2	297,897
STRAFFORD	27,051	47,956	17.5	25.6	39.3	12.1	5.6	31,887	6.1	5.6	23.6	55.1	9.6	206,492
SULLIVAN	26,489	18,131	20.8	29.6	36.2	8.8	4.6	13,432	4.6	6.4	39.3	40.9	8.8	174,546
NEW HAMPSHIRE	31,189		15.5	23.1	37.5	14.4	9.5		3.2	3.9	18.7	57.5	16.6	245,115
UNITED STATES	27,916		21.9	25.0	32.3	12.3	8.4		7.9	10.5	27.1	35.6	19.0	192,285

COUNTY	FINANCIAL SERVICES				THE HOME						ENTERTAINMENT						PERSONAL			
					Home Improvements		Furnishings													
	Auto Loan	Home Loan	Invest-ments	Retire-ment Plans	Home Repair	Lawn & Garden	Comput-ers & Hard-ware	Major Appli-ances	TV, Radio, Sound Equip-ment	Furni-ture	Dine out/ Carry out	Sports Equip-ment	Fees & Tickets	Toys & Games	Travel	Cable TV	Apparel & Services	Auto Repairs	Health Insur-ance	Pets & Supplies
BELKNAP	100	95	92	95	100	109	92	102	94	92	93	90	91	95	95	96	83	96	103	104
CARROLL	101	84	65	83	94	118	85	104	88	81	87	90	76	88	88	93	75	95	107	108
CHESHIRE	93	90	93	91	93	98	90	94	91	89	90	84	89	92	91	92	81	91	95	95
COOS	75	61	57	61	67	81	65	73	69	61	68	64	59	69	65	73	59	69	80	76
GRAFTON	100	90	89	92	95	105	97	101	96	92	96	91	91	96	96	98	85	99	103	103
HILLSBOROUGH	113	126	135	128	123	113	122	116	118	124	119	109	127	119	123	115	110	118	111	116
MERRIMACK	102	107	114	109	108	105	105	105	103	105	102	96	107	103	106	102	93	103	103	105
ROCKINGHAM	123	142	146	142	140	128	129	129	124	134	125	120	138	126	133	122	115	126	121	128
STRAFFORD	94	92	97	94	90	91	97	92	95	94	95	86	95	95	94	94	86	94	92	93
SULLIVAN	92	84	85	84	89	99	83	91	87	82	86	80	81	89	85	90	76	87	96	94
NEW HAMPSHIRE	108	112	116	114	113	111	110	110	108	110	108	101	112	109	111	107	98	109	108	111
UNITED STATES	100	100	100	100	100	100	100	100	100	100	100	100	100	100	100	100	100	100	100	100

POPULATION CHANGE

COUNTY	FIPS Code	CBSA Code	DMA Code	POPULATION			2000-2007 ANNUAL RATE		RACE (%)					
									White		Black		Asian/Pacific	
				2000	2007	2012	% Rate	State Rank	2000	2007	2000	2007	2000	2007
ATLANTIC	001	12100	504	252,552	280,554	302,352	1.5	3	68.4	63.8	17.6	18.5	5.1	6.6
BERGEN	003	35620	501	884,118	912,024	931,274	0.4	19	78.4	73.6	5.3	5.5	10.7	13.9
BURLINGTON	005	37980	504	423,394	457,939	480,455	1.1	8	78.4	75.1	15.1	16.5	2.7	3.7
CAMDEN	007	37980	504	508,932	522,763	533,057	0.4	19	70.9	66.6	18.1	19.3	3.8	5.0
CAPE MAY	009	36140	504	102,326	105,752	108,398	0.5	16	91.6	89.9	5.1	5.7	0.7	1.0
CUMBERLAND	011	47220	504	146,438	154,911	160,663	0.8	12	65.9	62.7	20.2	20.0	1.0	1.7
ESSEX	013	35620	501	793,633	808,222	818,183	0.3	21	44.5	41.3	41.2	41.6	3.8	4.7
GLOUCESTER	015	37980	504	254,673	286,627	311,894	1.6	2	87.1	84.8	9.1	10.1	1.5	2.1
HUDSON	017	35620	501	608,975	621,735	630,867	0.3	21	55.6	52.2	13.5	12.8	9.4	11.0
HUNTERDON	019	35620	501	121,989	133,860	142,520	1.3	6	93.9	92.3	2.2	2.5	2.0	2.7
MERCER	021	45940	504	350,761	371,660	385,426	0.8	12	68.5	64.0	19.8	21.2	5.0	6.6
MIDDLESEX	023	35620	501	750,162	803,610	843,310	1.0	9	68.4	62.8	9.1	9.3	13.9	17.6
MONMOUTH	025	35620	501	615,301	646,801	664,272	0.7	14	84.4	81.3	8.1	8.8	4.0	5.4
MORRIS	027	35620	501	470,212	500,527	521,334	0.9	10	87.2	83.7	2.8	3.2	6.3	8.5
OCEAN	029	35620	501	510,916	571,226	610,398	1.6	2	93.0	91.4	3.0	3.4	1.3	1.8
PASSAIC	031	35620	501	489,049	507,598	519,311	0.5	16	62.3	57.6	13.2	13.3	3.7	4.6
SALEM	033	37980	504	64,285	67,536	69,985	0.7	14	81.2	78.5	14.8	16.3	0.6	0.9
SOMERSET	035	35620	501	297,490	327,727	348,863	1.3	6	79.3	75.1	7.5	8.0	8.4	11.1
SUSSEX	037	35620	501	144,166	158,040	168,270	1.3	6	95.7	94.5	1.0	1.2	1.2	1.7
UNION	039	35620	501	522,541	540,294	553,396	0.5	16	65.5	62.0	20.8	21.2	3.9	4.9
WARREN	041	10900	501	102,437	112,205	118,460	1.3	6	94.5	92.7	1.9	2.6	1.2	1.7
NEW JERSEY							0.8		72.6	69.2	13.6	13.9	5.7	7.4
UNITED STATES							1.2		75.1	72.7	12.3	12.6	3.8	4.5

B

COUNTY	% HISPANIC ORIGIN		2007 AGE DISTRIBUTION (%)										MEDIAN AGE	% 2007 Males	% 2007 Females
	2000	2007	0-4	5-9	10-14	15-19	20-24	25-44	45-64	65-84	85+	18+	2007		
ATLANTIC	12.2	15.4	6.4	6.0	7.4	7.4	6.5	25.7	26.6	11.9	2.0	75.6	38.8	48.4	51.6
BERGEN	10.3	13.2	6.0	6.7	7.1	6.4	5.0	26.6	27.4	12.4	2.5	76.1	40.4	48.3	51.7
BURLINGTON	4.2	5.5	6.3	6.5	6.9	6.7	6.0	26.7	27.1	11.9	1.9	76.2	39.6	49.3	50.7
CAMDEN	9.7	12.4	6.7	6.4	7.1	7.4	6.5	26.9	26.1	10.9	2.1	75.1	37.7	48.4	51.6
CAPE MAY	3.3	4.5	5.1	4.7	5.9	6.5	5.5	21.4	29.5	18.0	3.4	80.2	45.5	48.2	51.8
CUMBERLAND	19.0	23.6	6.4	5.6	6.7	7.4	7.7	28.6	24.5	11.0	2.0	77.1	36.5	50.5	49.5
ESSEX	15.4	18.8	7.2	7.3	7.7	7.4	6.2	28.6	23.7	10.0	1.9	73.3	35.5	47.8	52.2
GLOUCESTER	2.6	3.5	6.5	6.7	7.2	7.4	6.3	27.0	26.6	10.5	1.7	75.1	38.0	48.5	51.5
HUDSON	39.8	45.4	6.5	5.8	6.4	6.9	7.1	34.8	22.0	8.9	1.6	77.2	34.4	49.4	50.6
HUNTERDON	2.8	3.8	5.9	7.4	8.0	6.9	4.6	23.9	32.2	9.7	1.5	74.2	41.4	49.3	50.7
MERCER	9.7	12.4	6.2	6.4	7.1	7.7	6.7	27.3	26.1	10.5	2.0	76.1	37.6	48.8	51.2
MIDDLESEX	13.6	16.8	6.4	6.5	6.8	7.1	6.6	29.1	24.9	10.7	1.9	76.2	37.3	49.2	50.8
MONMOUTH	6.2	8.2	6.5	7.1	7.8	7.2	5.1	25.1	28.2	11.0	2.1	74.1	39.9	48.7	51.3
MORRIS	7.8	10.3	6.5	7.6	7.6	6.7	4.6	26.7	28.0	10.6	1.8	74.2	39.7	49.2	50.8
OCEAN	5.0	6.8	6.3	5.7	6.2	6.0	5.1	22.4	25.5	18.6	4.2	77.9	43.8	47.5	52.5
PASSAIC	30.0	36.0	7.4	7.2	7.7	7.3	6.4	28.7	23.5	9.8	2.0	73.4	35.4	48.6	51.4
SALEM	3.9	5.2	6.2	6.0	6.8	6.7	6.2	25.0	28.3	12.4	2.4	76.8	40.3	48.4	51.6
SOMERSET	8.7	11.2	6.9	8.1	8.3	6.4	4.2	27.6	27.1	9.5	1.8	72.3	38.8	49.0	51.0
SUSSEX	3.3	4.6	6.4	6.7	7.9	7.4	5.2	25.1	30.8	9.1	1.4	74.2	40.0	49.3	50.7
UNION	19.7	24.4	6.9	7.1	7.4	7.0	5.7	28.0	24.9	10.7	2.3	74.2	37.5	48.4	51.6
WARREN	3.7	5.0	6.6	6.6	7.2	6.7	5.7	25.7	28.5	10.9	2.1	75.4	40.1	48.8	51.2
NEW JERSEY	13.3	16.1	6.5	6.7	7.2	7.0	5.9	27.4	26.0	11.3	2.1	75.3	38.3	48.7	51.3
UNITED STATES	12.5	15.0	6.9	6.5	6.8	7.1	7.0	27.6	25.4	10.7	1.9	75.6	36.7	49.2	50.8

HOUSEHOLDS

COUNTY	HOUSEHOLDS					FAMILIES			MEDIAN HOUSEHOLD INCOME			
	2000	2007	2012	% Annual Rate 2000-2007	2007 Average HH Size	2000	2007	% Annual Rate 2000-2007	2007	2012	2007 National Rank	2007 State Rank
ATLANTIC	95,024	105,219	113,377	1.4	2.60	63,151	69,751	1.4	54,266	62,974	436	18
BERGEN	330,817	339,129	346,157	0.3	2.66	235,070	240,469	0.3	82,528	99,407	41	4
BURLINGTON	154,371	168,891	178,486	1.2	2.63	111,581	121,822	1.2	74,551	86,460	94	8
CAMDEN	185,744	192,372	197,020	0.5	2.66	129,844	134,170	0.5	60,103	69,586	265	14
CAPE MAY	42,148	44,465	45,904	0.7	2.32	27,372	28,806	0.7	52,423	61,946	526	19
CUMBERLAND	49,143	51,587	53,694	0.7	2.75	35,185	36,853	0.6	47,946	55,440	824	21
ESSEX	283,736	289,570	293,291	0.3	2.72	193,498	197,001	0.2	55,144	63,795	402	17
GLOUCESTER	90,717	102,980	112,734	1.8	2.73	67,197	76,124	1.7	68,404	79,760	135	12
HUDSON	230,546	235,712	239,397	0.3	2.60	143,532	146,327	0.3	50,670	58,981	631	20
HUNTERDON	43,678	48,048	51,329	1.3	2.70	32,837	36,055	1.3	103,777	124,615	4	1
MERCER	125,807	133,327	138,697	0.8	2.63	86,288	91,233	0.8	72,155	83,763	110	9
MIDDLESEX	265,815	279,868	292,946	0.7	2.80	190,930	200,585	0.7	77,559	91,007	71	7
MONMOUTH	224,236	236,085	242,895	0.7	2.70	160,233	168,335	0.7	81,626	98,042	48	5
MORRIS	169,711	179,908	187,631	0.8	2.73	124,907	132,175	0.8	100,583	119,287	6	2
OCEAN	200,402	224,586	240,440	1.6	2.51	137,803	154,061	1.6	58,406	68,160	299	15
PASSAIC	163,856	167,393	170,509	0.3	2.96	119,689	122,028	0.3	61,026	70,538	240	13
SALEM	24,295	25,575	26,588	0.7	2.59	17,371	18,247	0.7	56,939	65,791	330	16
SOMERSET	108,984	118,857	126,350	1.2	2.72	78,409	85,333	1.2	100,258	119,744	8	3
SUSSEX	50,831	56,553	60,614	1.5	2.76	38,805	43,096	1.5	81,411	97,531	49	6
UNION	186,124	188,912	192,568	0.2	2.82	133,352	135,064	0.2	70,021	81,534	117	11
WARREN	38,660	43,032	45,651	1.5	2.57	27,485	30,634	1.5	70,919	82,402	116	10
NEW JERSEY				0.7	2.69			0.7	69,831	81,268		
UNITED STATES				1.2	2.59			1.0	53,154	62,503		

COUNTY	2007 Per Capita Income	2007 HH Income Base	2007 HOUSEHOLD INCOME DISTRIBUTION (%)					2007 Home Value Base	2007 HOME VALUE DISTRIBUTION (%)					2007 Median Home Value
			Less than $25,000	$25,000 to $49,999	$50,000 to $99,999	$100,000 to $149,999	$150,000 or More		Less than $50,000	$50,000 to $89,999	$90,000 to $174,999	$175,000 to $399,999	$400,000 or More	
ATLANTIC	26,034	105,219	20.2	25.2	36.0	12.2	6.4	72,400	1.6	1.9	11.4	65.1	19.9	280,182
BERGEN	43,503	339,126	12.1	16.3	31.2	19.3	21.1	237,424	0.5	0.8	1.9	20.8	76.0	545,930
BURLINGTON	34,894	168,890	10.9	19.2	37.4	18.6	13.9	133,922	0.8	1.1	9.9	67.0	21.3	282,085
CAMDEN	28,878	192,370	19.2	22.5	34.9	13.8	9.6	139,365	1.7	4.5	16.6	66.4	10.8	236,437
CAPE MAY	31,409	44,465	21.8	25.7	31.6	12.6	8.3	34,081	1.0	1.1	8.2	50.7	38.9	344,537
CUMBERLAND	21,637	51,587	25.8	26.0	33.3	10.2	4.7	36,424	3.4	5.5	32.8	54.1	4.2	189,055
ESSEX	31,402	289,550	25.5	20.6	28.0	12.9	13.0	142,014	0.7	0.8	5.1	47.6	45.8	381,528
GLOUCESTER	29,690	102,980	14.1	20.2	37.5	18.2	9.9	84,053	1.3	1.0	11.1	74.3	12.3	253,536
HUDSON	27,379	235,711	26.0	23.3	29.7	11.8	9.2	79,932	0.6	1.1	6.8	56.4	35.1	350,511
HUNTERDON	51,632	48,048	7.6	11.2	29.1	20.2	32.0	41,035	0.2	0.2	1.8	30.0	67.7	516,739
MERCER	37,002	133,326	16.2	18.3	31.9	17.3	16.2	92,919	0.6	2.2	16.1	50.2	30.9	300,676
MIDDLESEX	34,656	279,854	12.2	17.2	34.8	19.6	16.1	194,684	0.7	0.8	3.6	53.9	41.0	372,641
MONMOUTH	42,075	236,084	13.0	16.6	31.0	17.8	21.6	181,543	0.7	0.8	3.9	38.9	55.7	435,952
MORRIS	50,784	179,908	7.5	12.4	29.7	20.8	29.6	140,998	0.2	0.5	2.0	27.6	69.6	531,796
OCEAN	29,768	224,586	18.9	23.7	34.2	14.4	8.8	189,914	1.7	3.0	12.5	61.3	21.6	285,122
PASSAIC	27,147	167,391	19.5	21.8	31.2	16.3	11.3	98,430	0.5	0.4	1.9	46.8	50.4	402,205
SALEM	26,047	25,575	20.0	23.6	36.7	14.0	5.7	19,296	3.0	4.6	25.3	58.9	8.2	208,871
SOMERSET	52,258	118,853	7.9	11.8	30.2	19.0	31.1	94,008	0.3	0.3	2.3	34.8	62.4	485,454
SUSSEX	36,398	56,553	10.1	15.6	36.6	21.6	16.2	47,704	0.4	0.4	3.9	65.2	30.2	334,986
UNION	34,081	188,912	16.6	19.3	31.5	16.9	15.7	121,965	0.5	0.5	2.7	51.4	44.9	381,473
WARREN	33,629	43,032	14.7	18.0	37.0	18.2	12.2	32,680	0.6	0.7	11.1	62.1	25.5	301,208
NEW JERSEY	35,359		16.3	19.2	32.4	16.6	15.6		0.9	1.4	7.2	49.0	41.6	362,535
UNITED STATES	27,916		21.9	25.0	32.3	12.3	8.4		7.9	10.5	27.1	35.6	19.0	192,285

COUNTY	FINANCIAL SERVICES				THE HOME						ENTERTAINMENT						PERSONAL			
					Home Improvements		Furnishings													
	Auto Loan	Home Loan	Invest-ments	Retire-ment Plans	Home Repair	Lawn & Garden	Comput-ers & Hard-ware	Major Appli-ances	TV, Radio, Sound Equip-ment	Furni-ture	Dine out/ Carry out	Sports Equip-ment	Fees & Tickets	Toys & Games	Travel	Cable TV	Apparel & Services	Auto Repairs	Health Insur-ance	Pets & Supplies
ATLANTIC	88	94	102	95	93	88	95	91	94	95	94	84	98	93	95	94	87	92	90	90
BERGEN	131	175	186	166	185	152	160	157	154	166	158	149	181	151	171	155	152	152	147	152
BURLINGTON	120	139	151	139	138	126	129	126	125	134	125	116	138	126	134	124	116	125	122	125
CAMDEN	99	111	122	110	110	102	106	103	106	109	106	93	113	105	109	106	98	104	104	103
CAPE MAY	97	103	118	103	107	109	98	103	100	100	99	89	103	96	105	104	89	101	111	102
CUMBERLAND	82	81	89	81	82	84	82	83	85	82	84	73	83	85	83	86	76	82	86	83
ESSEX	99	112	119	110	116	101	119	109	121	118	123	105	125	116	120	122	118	112	108	108
GLOUCESTER	106	123	133	123	121	112	112	112	110	117	110	101	121	112	117	109	101	110	109	111
HUDSON	84	86	86	86	87	77	102	89	101	97	104	92	101	97	97	100	99	95	86	87
HUNTERDON	174	231	248	229	236	199	197	197	183	210	186	184	224	186	212	180	177	187	178	193
MERCER	124	144	158	144	146	130	139	133	136	142	137	124	149	135	143	136	128	133	130	132
MIDDLESEX	121	145	150	140	147	127	138	133	131	141	133	127	147	131	141	129	126	132	124	129
MONMOUTH	138	175	189	170	179	154	159	156	152	165	153	145	175	151	167	150	145	152	148	153
MORRIS	167	221	233	214	228	189	196	193	183	205	186	185	220	183	208	179	178	187	174	188
OCEAN	95	111	124	106	116	111	99	106	100	105	100	91	108	95	109	103	91	103	111	103
PASSAIC	95	113	114	107	116	98	113	107	110	113	113	106	120	108	114	110	108	108	100	103
SALEM	90	96	108	96	97	96	91	93	94	93	93	82	96	94	95	95	84	91	97	93
SOMERSET	177	222	230	220	223	190	201	194	188	210	191	186	221	191	209	184	181	190	177	191
SUSSEX	127	161	168	158	160	138	140	140	133	148	134	130	155	136	147	130	126	135	128	138
UNION	112	139	145	132	144	121	135	130	130	136	133	126	145	128	139	129	127	128	121	125
WARREN	111	131	145	131	131	119	120	119	117	124	117	108	129	118	125	116	108	116	115	118
NEW JERSEY	117	139	148	136	142	125	133	129	130	136	132	121	143	128	138	130	124	128	124	126
UNITED STATES	100	100	100	100	100	100	100	100	100	100	100	100	100	100	100	100	100	100	100	100

COUNTY	FIPS Code	CBSA Code	DMA Code	POPULATION			2000-2007 ANNUAL RATE		RACE (%)					
									White		Black		Asian/Pacific	
				2000	2007	2012	% Rate	State Rank	2000	2007	2000	2007	2000	2007
BERNALILLO	001	10740	790	556,678	628,408	685,028	1.7	3	70.8	69.3	2.8	2.9	2.0	2.4
CATRON	003	00000	790	3,543	3,753	3,885	0.8	13	87.8	86.8	0.3	0.3	0.7	0.9
CHAVES	005	40740	790	61,382	61,924	62,073	0.1	25	72.0	70.7	2.0	2.1	0.6	0.7
CIBOLA	006	24380	790	25,595	27,815	28,633	1.2	9	39.6	37.5	1.0	1.0	0.4	0.5
COLFAX	007	00000	790	14,189	14,319	14,437	0.1	25	81.5	80.8	0.3	0.3	0.3	0.4
CURRY	009	17580	634	45,044	46,740	48,094	0.5	15	72.4	70.8	6.9	7.2	1.9	2.3
DE BACA	011	00000	790	2,240	2,214	2,197	-0.2	29	84.0	83.8	0.0	0.0	0.2	0.2
DONA ANA	013	29740	765	174,682	202,485	224,870	2.1	2	67.8	67.1	1.6	1.6	0.8	1.0
EDDY	015	16100	790	51,658	51,269	51,128	-0.1	28	76.3	75.2	1.6	1.7	0.5	0.6
GRANT	017	43500	790	31,002	30,883	30,777	-0.1	28	75.7	74.8	0.5	0.6	0.3	0.4
GUADALUPE	019	00000	790	4,680	4,714	4,708	0.1	25	54.1	53.9	1.3	1.3	0.6	0.6
HARDING	021	00000	790	810	820	798	0.2	22	84.3	84.3	0.4	0.4	0.0	0.0
HIDALGO	023	00000	790	5,932	5,448	5,156	-1.2	33	83.8	83.2	0.4	0.5	0.3	0.4
LEA	025	26020	790	55,511	56,428	57,162	0.2	22	67.1	65.6	4.4	4.6	0.4	0.5
LINCOLN	027	40760	790	19,411	21,318	22,754	1.3	7	83.6	82.5	0.4	0.4	0.3	0.4
LOS ALAMOS	028	31060	790	18,343	19,680	20,759	1.0	11	90.3	89.0	0.4	0.4	3.8	4.6
LUNA	029	19700	790	25,016	26,909	28,272	1.0	11	74.3	73.6	0.9	1.0	0.3	0.4
MCKINLEY	031	23700	790	74,798	76,285	77,196	0.3	18	16.4	14.9	0.4	0.4	0.5	0.5
MORA	033	00000	790	5,180	5,303	5,359	0.3	18	58.9	58.6	0.1	0.1	0.1	0.2
OTERO	035	10460	790	62,298	64,998	66,623	0.6	14	73.7	72.2	3.9	4.1	1.3	1.5
QUAY	037	00000	634	10,155	9,395	9,175	-1.1	32	82.1	81.1	0.8	0.9	0.9	1.1
RIO ARRIBA	039	21580	790	41,190	42,104	42,637	0.3	18	56.6	56.1	0.3	0.4	0.3	0.3
ROOSEVELT	041	38780	634	18,018	18,408	18,540	0.3	18	74.1	72.6	1.7	1.8	0.7	0.8
SANDOVAL	043	10740	790	89,908	113,590	137,531	3.3	1	65.1	62.9	1.7	1.8	1.1	1.3
SAN JUAN	045	22140	790	113,801	125,916	135,300	1.4	6	52.8	49.7	0.4	0.5	0.3	0.4
SAN MIGUEL	047	29780	790	30,126	29,084	28,404	-0.5	30	56.2	55.8	0.8	0.6	0.6	0.7
SANTA FE	049	42140	790	129,292	144,001	154,484	1.5	4	73.5	72.5	0.6	0.7	0.9	1.1
SIERRA	051	00000	790	13,270	13,368	13,419	0.1	25	87.0	86.9	0.5	0.5	0.3	0.3
SOCORRO	053	00000	790	18,078	18,540	18,799	0.3	18	62.9	61.4	0.6	0.7	1.2	1.4
TAOS	055	45340	790	29,979	31,750	32,630	0.8	13	63.8	62.7	0.4	0.4	0.5	0.6
TORRANCE	057	10740	790	16,911	18,441	19,157	1.2	9	73.9	72.6	1.7	1.8	0.4	0.5
UNION	059	00000	634	4,174	3,990	3,868	-0.6	31	80.4	79.3	0.0	0.0	0.5	0.5
VALENCIA	061	10740	790	66,152	73,195	77,251	1.4	6	66.5	65.5	1.3	1.3	0.4	0.5
NEW MEXICO							1.3		66.8	65.4	1.9	2.0	1.1	1.4
UNITED STATES							1.2		75.1	72.7	12.3	12.6	3.8	4.5

POPULATION COMPOSITION

COUNTY	% HISPANIC ORIGIN		2007 AGE DISTRIBUTION (%)									MEDIAN AGE	% 2007 Males	% 2007 Females
	2000	2007	0-4	5-9	10-14	15-19	20-24	25-44	45-64	65-84	85+	18+	2007		
BERNALILLO	42.0	43.8	7.2	6.8	6.5	6.8	7.3	28.6	25.5	9.8	1.6	75.6	35.7	48.9	51.1
CATRON	19.2	20.6	3.7	3.7	4.8	5.6	6.7	13.9	39.6	20.5	1.5	84.3	52.1	51.4	48.6
CHAVES	43.8	46.1	7.5	6.6	7.0	7.8	8.1	24.0	24.2	12.4	2.4	74.2	35.7	49.4	50.6
CIBOLA	33.4	33.3	8.0	6.8	7.4	7.5	8.3	27.1	24.1	9.8	1.1	73.2	33.5	50.7	49.3
COLFAX	47.5	49.9	5.6	5.1	6.3	7.9	6.0	20.5	31.3	14.7	2.7	78.0	43.9	50.5	49.5
CURRY	30.4	32.1	9.0	7.1	7.0	7.7	10.1	26.3	21.2	9.8	1.8	72.5	31.6	49.7	50.3
DE BACA	35.3	35.5	6.0	5.7	5.2	5.1	7.0	20.9	24.8	21.0	4.4	80.1	45.1	49.1	50.9
DONA ANA	63.4	65.3	8.1	7.1	7.4	8.7	9.6	26.2	22.0	9.7	1.2	72.7	31.0	49.1	50.9
EDDY	38.8	41.0	7.7	6.9	6.9	6.9	8.3	22.6	26.5	11.9	2.3	74.3	37.1	48.7	51.3
GRANT	48.8	51.1	7.1	6.6	5.9	6.7	7.0	22.1	27.9	14.5	2.2	76.3	40.3	48.7	51.3
GUADALUPE	81.2	81.3	5.8	5.0	5.4	6.6	8.6	28.0	26.5	12.7	1.4	79.6	39.6	54.7	45.3
HARDING	44.9	45.0	3.3	2.9	5.1	4.5	9.0	17.2	31.6	22.3	4.0	86.1	50.9	51.3	48.7
HIDALGO	56.0	58.4	8.1	7.2	7.9	8.1	7.2	22.9	25.4	11.4	1.7	71.7	36.0	49.8	50.2
LEA	39.6	41.7	8.3	7.2	7.0	7.6	8.5	25.9	23.5	10.7	1.4	73.1	33.4	50.1	49.9
LINCOLN	25.6	27.4	5.2	4.7	5.5	6.5	5.7	19.4	33.8	17.6	1.6	80.7	46.8	48.7	51.3
LOS ALAMOS	11.7	12.7	5.3	5.8	7.4	6.9	5.2	21.8	33.6	12.2	1.9	77.0	43.5	49.9	50.1
LUNA	57.7	60.0	8.5	7.4	7.4	7.1	6.8	21.7	23.1	15.9	2.2	72.2	37.3	48.4	51.6
MCKINLEY	12.4	11.8	9.7	8.0	9.5	10.2	9.3	25.1	20.6	6.7	0.8	66.4	27.4	48.4	51.6
MORA	81.6	82.9	6.6	6.3	5.5	6.5	7.8	21.2	30.2	14.5	1.5	77.6	42.3	50.2	49.8
OTERO	32.2	33.8	7.7	6.7	7.1	8.0	8.5	25.8	23.8	11.3	1.2	73.7	34.8	49.9	50.1
QUAY	38.0	40.2	5.8	4.8	6.0	6.6	7.3	20.4	30.0	16.1	2.9	79.2	44.2	48.8	51.2
RIO ARRIBA	72.9	73.3	7.2	6.4	6.9	7.9	7.2	27.0	26.5	9.7	1.2	74.6	35.6	49.4	50.6
ROOSEVELT	33.3	35.3	7.8	6.6	7.2	9.3	10.3	26.3	20.8	9.9	1.7	74.2	29.8	49.1	50.9
SANDOVAL	29.4	30.5	7.7	7.1	7.4	7.6	7.0	26.6	26.1	9.1	1.5	73.1	35.7	48.6	51.4
SAN JUAN	15.0	15.3	8.6	7.3	7.8	8.2	9.2	25.7	23.9	8.4	1.0	71.4	31.3	49.7	50.3
SAN MIGUEL	78.0	79.3	6.9	6.0	6.8	8.6	8.2	25.0	26.5	10.5	1.6	75.7	36.2	49.3	50.7
SANTA FE	49.0	51.2	6.0	5.8	5.9	6.8	7.1	26.1	30.6	10.3	1.4	78.2	39.8	48.9	51.1
SIERRA	26.3	26.4	4.8	4.3	5.0	5.9	5.6	15.9	32.4	22.8	3.3	82.1	50.9	50.2	49.8
SOCORRO	48.7	50.2	7.2	6.7	6.7	9.7	9.2	24.4	24.6	9.9	1.4	74.4	32.7	51.0	49.0
TAOS	57.9	59.6	5.5	5.5	5.7	6.3	5.9	24.6	33.0	11.9	1.5	79.2	42.8	49.4	50.6
TORRANCE	37.2	39.2	6.9	6.1	7.2	8.2	7.8	27.1	26.9	8.8	1.0	74.6	36.0	53.3	46.7
UNION	35.1	37.3	6.8	5.7	6.5	6.5	8.7	20.2	27.9	14.9	2.6	76.5	41.3	49.5	50.5
VALENCIA	55.0	57.0	7.9	6.9	7.2	7.9	7.5	26.8	25.0	9.6	1.2	73.2	35.3	50.2	49.8
NEW MEXICO	42.1	43.7	7.5	6.7	6.9	7.5	7.9	26.3	25.4	10.3	1.5	74.5	35.3	49.2	50.8
UNITED STATES	12.5	15.0	6.9	6.5	6.8	7.1	7.0	27.6	25.4	10.7	1.9	75.6	36.7	49.2	50.8

COUNTY	HOUSEHOLDS					FAMILIES			MEDIAN HOUSEHOLD INCOME			
	2000	2007	2012	% Annual Rate 2000-2007	2007 Average HH Size	2000	2007	% Annual Rate 2000-2007	2007	2012	2007 National Rank	2007 State Rank
BERNALILLO	220,936	257,483	283,291	2.1	2.40	141,237	158,783	1.6	49,953	59,144	685	4
CATRON	1,584	1,775	1,865	1.6	2.11	1,041	1,127	1.1	28,720	32,814	2972	30
CHAVES	22,561	23,066	23,273	0.3	2.60	16,077	15,970	-0.1	34,444	39,176	2501	17
CIBOLA	8,327	9,039	9,459	1.1	2.83	6,281	6,650	0.8	33,276	37,941	2633	18
COLFAX	5,821	6,130	6,263	0.7	2.28	3,977	4,057	0.3	37,053	42,234	2118	10
CURRY	16,766	17,894	18,587	0.9	2.54	11,869	12,302	0.5	35,932	41,517	2292	14
DE BACA	922	932	930	0.1	2.30	615	601	-0.3	29,181	32,849	2953	25
DONA ANA	59,556	71,122	79,720	2.5	2.77	42,912	49,833	2.1	36,916	43,236	2138	11
EDDY	19,379	19,802	19,930	0.3	2.55	14,060	13,975	-0.1	38,802	44,732	1877	8
GRANT	12,146	12,694	12,835	0.6	2.38	8,511	8,629	0.2	35,381	40,692	2385	16
GUADALUPE	1,655	1,721	1,743	0.5	2.41	1,145	1,154	0.1	27,920	31,218	3005	32
HARDING	371	398	393	1.0	2.06	232	240	0.5	30,486	33,507	2885	24
HIDALGO	2,152	2,051	1,966	-0.7	2.61	1,543	1,428	-1.1	28,991	32,265	2960	27
LEA	19,699	20,629	21,113	0.6	2.64	14,714	15,022	0.3	36,206	41,636	2241	13
LINCOLN	8,202	9,328	10,079	1.8	2.26	5,631	6,207	1.4	41,313	47,522	1551	7
LOS ALAMOS	7,497	8,239	8,749	1.3	2.38	5,341	5,701	0.9	101,199	118,770	5	1
LUNA	9,397	10,256	10,798	1.2	2.60	6,592	6,984	0.8	24,841	27,758	3095	33
MCKINLEY	21,476	22,263	22,700	0.5	3.39	16,679	16,904	0.2	30,574	35,477	2879	23
MORA	2,017	2,162	2,217	1.0	2.43	1,398	1,452	0.5	28,030	31,176	3001	31
OTERO	22,984	24,497	25,354	0.9	2.58	16,802	17,436	0.5	37,843	43,566	2017	9
QUAY	4,201	4,022	3,976	-0.6	2.29	2,845	2,637	-1.0	29,155	32,562	2954	26
RIO ARRIBA	15,044	16,083	16,528	0.9	2.59	10,815	11,241	0.5	35,792	41,180	2315	15
ROOSEVELT	6,639	6,789	6,845	0.3	2.57	4,544	4,502	-0.1	32,082	36,704	2751	22
SANDOVAL	31,411	41,129	50,463	3.8	2.74	23,632	30,183	3.4	58,055	69,574	305	2
SAN JUAN	37,711	43,195	46,981	1.9	2.89	28,930	32,369	1.6	42,426	49,327	1405	5
SAN MIGUEL	11,134	11,255	11,141	0.1	2.47	7,533	7,374	-0.3	32,535	37,550	2701	19
SANTA FE	52,482	57,945	62,402	1.4	2.43	32,787	34,861	0.8	54,453	64,838	424	3
SIERRA	6,113	6,282	6,334	0.4	2.09	3,617	3,569	-0.2	28,947	32,948	2963	29
SOCORRO	6,675	7,018	7,190	0.7	2.54	4,491	4,571	0.2	28,965	33,677	2961	28
TAOS	12,675	14,167	14,776	1.5	2.22	7,755	8,341	1.0	32,420	37,010	2720	21
TORRANCE	6,024	6,482	6,797	1.0	2.66	4,392	4,598	0.6	36,384	41,354	2214	12
UNION	1,733	1,708	1,673	-0.2	2.33	1,177	1,123	-0.6	32,468	36,691	2712	20
VALENCIA	22,681	25,636	27,228	1.7	2.78	17,340	19,144	1.4	41,791	47,926	1479	6
NEW MEXICO				1.8	2.56			1.2	43,379	51,081		
UNITED STATES				1.2	2.59			1.0	53,154	62,503		

COUNTY	2007 Per Capita Income	2007 HH Income Base	2007 HOUSEHOLD INCOME DISTRIBUTION (%)					2007 Home Value Base	2007 HOME VALUE DISTRIBUTION (%)					2007 Median Home Value
			Less than $25,000	$25,000 to $49,999	$50,000 to $99,999	$100,000 to $149,999	$150,000 or More		Less than $50,000	$50,000 to $89,999	$90,000 to $174,999	$175,000 to $399,999	$400,000 or More	
BERNALILLO	27,590	257,479	23.0	27.0	32.0	11.2	6.7	164,893	5.9	4.1	26.1	54.1	9.9	208,475
CATRON	18,267	1,775	44.7	28.9	20.8	4.5	1.1	1,437	18.9	15.0	33.4	22.0	10.7	129,567
CHAVES	18,220	23,066	36.1	30.5	24.7	6.0	2.6	16,464	17.8	28.1	37.6	14.1	2.4	96,883
CIBOLA	14,898	9,030	37.7	32.5	23.6	4.7	1.5	6,937	22.0	24.6	41.2	10.0	2.1	96,457
COLFAX	21,435	6,130	31.5	32.9	27.9	4.9	2.7	4,485	10.7	17.4	44.2	19.4	8.4	123,882
CURRY	18,802	17,894	33.7	32.7	25.4	5.0	3.2	10,755	11.9	25.7	46.8	13.8	1.9	107,390
DE BACA	16,802	932	43.6	30.6	20.6	4.4	0.9	727	27.1	25.3	31.2	12.7	3.7	86,111
DONA ANA	17,975	71,121	35.3	27.9	26.1	7.7	3.1	48,233	17.9	15.6	39.4	23.1	4.0	122,015
EDDY	19,663	19,802	33.4	29.0	28.1	6.8	2.7	14,761	13.6	24.4	45.4	14.5	2.2	106,349
GRANT	19,226	12,694	35.2	31.3	26.3	4.8	2.4	9,502	12.9	13.9	41.4	26.7	5.2	137,029
GUADALUPE	14,256	1,721	45.4	32.7	18.5	2.6	0.8	1,279	25.5	24.2	36.9	11.2	2.3	90,523
HARDING	20,021	398	42.0	29.4	23.4	2.8	2.5	302	43.4	22.8	18.2	10.6	5.0	56,897
HIDALGO	15,545	2,051	45.2	28.3	20.1	4.3	2.0	1,401	21.3	27.1	41.8	8.1	1.6	92,443
LEA	17,928	20,629	34.5	30.3	27.0	5.9	2.3	15,008	23.8	29.9	35.6	9.7	1.0	84,716
LINCOLN	24,760	9,328	29.8	29.1	28.2	8.9	4.0	7,262	10.0	13.2	37.7	29.4	9.8	148,563
LOS ALAMOS	48,744	8,239	7.2	10.5	31.4	27.0	23.9	6,515	3.9	1.7	8.6	43.0	42.8	366,102
LUNA	13,888	10,256	50.3	27.1	18.6	2.4	1.6	7,710	21.6	27.1	40.9	9.2	1.3	92,794
MCKINLEY	12,596	22,260	43.3	27.0	22.5	5.0	2.2	16,093	39.6	16.5	28.0	13.5	2.4	71,826
MORA	15,771	2,162	44.7	30.8	18.5	4.3	1.7	1,784	21.2	19.2	31.6	20.5	7.5	114,005
OTERO	17,757	24,497	30.9	33.7	28.2	5.6	1.6	16,550	14.3	18.6	44.8	19.8	2.5	116,896
QUAY	18,060	4,022	43.8	28.8	21.2	4.3	1.9	2,866	24.6	25.2	35.1	12.1	3.0	90,313
RIO ARRIBA	18,196	16,083	34.6	29.6	27.1	6.3	2.4	13,090	17.3	13.3	31.9	28.5	8.9	142,302
ROOSEVELT	17,201	6,789	41.2	27.6	24.0	4.8	2.5	4,275	17.5	27.7	40.7	12.8	1.3	97,677
SANDOVAL	25,661	41,129	16.6	24.6	39.9	13.0	5.9	34,259	6.3	4.1	31.4	47.4	10.9	192,936
SAN JUAN	18,294	43,193	29.9	28.4	30.6	8.0	3.1	32,617	19.8	13.7	34.6	27.9	4.0	132,292
SAN MIGUEL	17,546	11,255	38.9	29.4	24.7	5.0	2.0	8,231	17.8	14.5	38.4	25.0	4.4	133,893
SANTA FE	30,522	57,944	20.2	25.8	32.3	12.9	8.9	39,915	7.6	5.0	10.5	42.5	34.3	308,299
SIERRA	18,986	6,282	43.7	30.4	20.2	3.6	2.2	4,734	16.2	23.7	41.6	15.9	2.6	106,036
SOCORRO	17,025	7,018	43.8	25.2	21.2	7.4	2.3	4,984	19.8	16.7	38.7	20.9	3.9	114,892
TAOS	21,230	14,167	40.3	29.3	22.2	5.0	3.2	10,768	13.8	9.4	22.7	35.2	18.9	190,793
TORRANCE	17,281	6,482	33.1	33.7	25.6	5.9	1.6	5,426	13.0	16.0	45.2	22.2	3.5	129,690
UNION	18,204	1,708	37.7	32.7	23.5	4.3	1.9	1,254	19.9	27.4	38.8	10.4	3.6	93,953
VALENCIA	18,398	25,636	27.3	32.8	29.6	7.9	2.4	21,401	8.3	11.1	43.7	32.5	4.4	151,533
NEW MEXICO	22,579		28.7	28.0	29.3	9.0	4.9		12.5	11.8	31.7	34.9	9.1	159,748
UNITED STATES	27,916		21.9	25.0	32.3	12.3	8.4		7.9	10.5	27.1	35.6	19.0	192,285

COUNTY	FINANCIAL SERVICES				THE HOME						ENTERTAINMENT						PERSONAL			
					Home Improvements		Furnishings													
	Auto Loan	Home Loan	Invest-ments	Retire-ment Plans	Home Repair	Lawn & Garden	Comput-ers & Hard-ware	Major Appli-ances	TV, Radio, Sound Equip-ment	Furni-ture	Dine out/ Carry out	Sports Equip-ment	Fees & Tickets	Toys & Games	Travel	Cable TV	Apparel & Services	Auto Repairs	Health Insur-ance	Pets & Supplies
BERNALILLO	92	91	93	92	87	85	94	89	92	93	92	83	92	91	91	91	84	93	88	88
CATRON	58	50	41	49	56	70	49	62	52	48	51	52	46	50	53	55	44	57	66	62
CHAVES	71	62	59	61	63	71	62	68	67	62	66	59	60	67	63	70	58	66	74	68
CIBOLA	67	53	43	52	55	67	55	62	60	54	59	55	50	61	54	63	51	60	67	66
COLFAX	78	60	49	59	67	85	63	76	69	60	68	66	56	70	64	74	58	70	83	79
CURRY	70	61	62	62	59	63	67	65	69	65	68	59	63	69	64	69	60	67	68	65
DE BACA	64	45	32	43	51	69	49	61	55	45	54	53	41	57	49	60	45	56	69	64
DONA ANA	74	66	61	65	62	66	69	68	71	68	70	62	65	69	66	70	63	70	69	68
EDDY	76	66	60	65	62	75	66	72	71	66	70	63	63	71	66	73	61	70	77	73
GRANT	70	60	54	59	62	72	60	68	64	59	63	59	57	64	61	67	55	65	72	69
GUADALUPE	58	40	26	38	45	61	43	53	49	40	48	47	36	50	42	53	41	49	61	57
HARDING	75	47	20	45	58	84	50	70	55	48	56	62	39	61	49	60	47	62	73	78
HIDALGO	65	49	37	47	51	64	52	59	58	51	58	52	46	59	50	62	50	57	65	62
LEA	73	63	54	60	61	68	62	67	67	63	67	60	59	67	62	69	59	67	71	68
LINCOLN	91	71	50	70	80	103	72	90	76	69	76	78	63	78	74	81	65	82	93	94
LOS ALAMOS	145	182	196	182	184	160	162	160	152	169	153	150	178	153	171	149	144	156	148	158
LUNA	59	44	32	42	47	61	46	55	51	44	50	48	39	51	45	54	43	52	60	58
MCKINLEY	65	57	46	54	52	58	55	59	60	58	60	53	52	59	54	61	53	60	61	59
MORA	67	46	24	43	53	74	46	62	53	45	53	55	38	56	46	58	45	56	67	68
OTERO	70	60	53	60	60	67	62	65	64	61	64	59	58	65	61	66	56	65	68	67
QUAY	65	50	41	48	54	70	53	63	59	51	57	54	47	58	53	63	49	60	71	65
RIO ARRIBA	74	64	52	62	63	71	62	69	65	63	65	62	59	66	62	66	57	67	70	71
ROOSEVELT	68	53	47	53	53	63	62	63	64	57	63	57	54	64	57	64	55	64	66	64
SANDOVAL	101	106	99	104	99	97	97	98	95	101	95	91	98	96	97	94	86	98	95	98
SAN JUAN	80	73	64	71	69	74	71	74	73	72	73	67	68	74	70	74	65	74	75	75
SAN MIGUEL	66	57	52	55	56	63	59	62	62	57	61	55	54	61	58	63	53	62	65	63
SANTA FE	102	106	106	106	104	100	105	103	102	105	102	98	105	101	105	100	93	105	100	103
SIERRA	56	52	54	50	56	65	52	60	55	51	53	49	50	50	56	58	46	58	67	59
SOCORRO	68	54	45	54	54	64	60	62	61	56	61	57	53	62	56	62	53	63	64	64
TAOS	76	59	44	58	65	84	61	74	65	58	64	65	53	66	61	69	55	69	78	78
TORRANCE	75	62	47	60	62	75	60	69	64	60	64	62	55	66	60	67	55	66	72	73
UNION	69	49	37	48	55	74	54	65	61	49	59	57	46	63	53	66	50	61	76	69
VALENCIA	78	71	63	70	69	75	68	73	71	69	71	66	67	73	69	72	62	72	75	75
NEW MEXICO	85	78	74	78	76	81	79	81	81	79	80	74	77	80	78	81	72	81	82	81
UNITED STATES	100	100	100	100	100	100	100	100	100	100	100	100	100	100	100	100	100	100	100	100

POPULATION CHANGE

COUNTY	FIPS Code	CBSA Code	DMA Code	POPULATION			2000-2007 ANNUAL RATE		RACE (%)					
									White		Black		Asian/Pacific	
				2000	2007	2012	% Rate	State Rank	2000	2007	2000	2007	2000	2007
ALBANY	001	10580	532	294,565	300,502	303,989	0.3	32	83.2	80.6	11.1	12.3	2.8	3.5
ALLEGANY	003	00000	514	49,927	50,646	50,517	0.2	38	97.0	96.4	0.7	0.8	0.7	0.9
BRONX	005	35620	501	1,332,650	1,383,835	1,418,603	0.5	23	29.9	29.0	35.6	35.0	3.1	3.5
BROOME	007	13780	502	200,536	197,472	194,735	-0.2	59	91.3	89.6	3.3	3.6	2.8	3.6
CATTARAUGUS	009	36460	514	83,955	83,121	82,485	-0.1	54	94.6	93.5	1.1	1.5	0.5	0.6
CAYUGA	011	12180	555	81,963	81,764	81,958	0.0	48	93.3	92.3	4.0	4.5	0.4	0.6
CHAUTAUQUA	013	27460	514	139,750	137,116	134,796	-0.3	61	94.0	92.9	2.2	2.6	0.4	0.5
CHEMUNG	015	21300	565	91,070	89,603	88,351	-0.2	59	91.0	89.0	5.8	6.7	0.8	1.1
CHENANGO	017	00000	502	51,401	52,528	53,334	0.3	32	97.6	97.2	0.8	0.9	0.3	0.4
CLINTON	019	38460	523	79,894	84,129	87,517	0.7	15	93.3	92.3	3.6	4.0	0.7	0.9
COLUMBIA	021	26460	532	63,094	65,674	67,753	0.6	19	92.1	90.8	4.5	5.0	0.8	1.1
CORTLAND	023	18660	555	48,599	48,665	48,574	0.0	48	96.9	96.3	0.9	1.2	0.4	0.5
DELAWARE	025	00000	502	48,055	48,425	49,919	0.1	43	96.4	95.8	1.2	1.3	0.5	0.7
DUTCHESS	027	39100	501	280,150	302,282	315,921	1.1	5	83.7	81.3	9.3	10.2	2.5	3.3
ERIE	029	15380	514	950,265	934,432	920,797	-0.2	59	82.2	79.9	13.0	14.3	1.5	1.9
ESSEX	031	00000	523	38,851	40,348	41,326	0.5	23	94.8	94.0	2.8	3.1	0.5	0.6
FRANKLIN	033	31660	523	51,134	51,592	52,048	0.1	43	84.0	82.4	6.6	7.3	0.4	0.5
FULTON	035	24100	532	55,073	56,311	57,310	0.3	32	96.0	95.1	1.8	2.0	0.5	0.9
GENESEE	037	12860	514	60,370	59,755	59,162	-0.1	54	94.7	93.8	2.1	2.4	0.5	0.7
GREENE	039	00000	532	48,195	51,202	53,511	0.8	10	90.8	89.2	5.5	6.1	0.6	1.0
HAMILTON	041	00000	532	5,379	5,213	5,105	-0.4	62	97.7	97.3	0.4	0.5	0.2	0.3
HERKIMER	043	46540	526	64,427	64,038	63,637	-0.1	54	97.8	97.4	0.5	0.6	0.4	0.5
JEFFERSON	045	48060	549	111,738	117,433	121,521	0.7	15	88.7	87.0	5.8	6.5	1.1	1.3
KINGS	047	35620	501	2,465,326	2,547,018	2,606,302	0.5	23	41.2	38.2	36.4	37.0	7.6	8.9
LEWIS	049	00000	549	26,944	27,397	27,691	0.2	38	98.2	97.8	0.4	0.4	0.3	0.4
LIVINGSTON	051	40380	538	64,328	66,170	67,316	0.4	28	94.0	92.5	3.0	3.5	0.8	1.3
MADISON	053	45060	555	69,441	70,879	71,369	0.3	32	96.5	95.9	1.3	1.5	0.6	0.7
MONROE	055	40380	538	735,343	743,039	747,131	0.1	43	79.1	76.5	13.7	15.0	2.5	3.1
MONTGOMERY	057	11220	532	49,708	49,397	49,264	-0.1	54	94.9	94.0	1.2	1.3	0.5	0.7
NASSAU	059	35620	501	1,334,544	1,337,642	1,338,171	0.0	48	79.3	76.5	10.1	10.9	4.8	5.9
NEW YORK	061	35620	501	1,537,195	1,630,965	1,699,498	0.8	10	54.4	50.8	17.4	17.7	9.5	11.2
NIAGARA	063	15380	514	219,846	217,711	215,672	-0.1	54	90.7	89.4	6.1	6.9	0.6	0.8
ONEIDA	065	46540	526	235,469	235,086	235,525	0.0	48	90.2	88.6	5.7	6.3	1.2	1.7
ONONDAGA	067	45060	555	458,336	459,031	459,621	0.0	48	84.8	82.6	9.4	10.3	2.1	2.7
ONTARIO	069	40380	538	100,224	106,743	111,605	0.9	7	95.0	94.1	2.1	2.3	0.7	0.9
ORANGE	071	39100	501	341,367	382,014	410,038	1.6	1	83.7	81.6	8.1	8.8	1.5	1.9
ORLEANS	073	40380	514	44,171	43,604	43,651	-0.2	59	89.1	86.6	7.3	7.8	0.3	1.4
OSWEGO	075	45060	555	122,377	124,054	124,711	0.2	38	97.2	96.6	0.6	0.7	0.4	0.6
OTSEGO	077	36580	526	61,676	65,081	65,936	0.7	15	95.8	94.0	1.7	2.6	0.7	1.0
PUTNAM	079	35620	501	95,745	101,697	105,179	0.8	10	93.9	92.7	1.6	1.8	1.3	1.6
QUEENS	081	35620	501	2,229,379	2,279,689	2,316,306	0.3	32	44.1	40.7	20.0	19.8	17.6	20.3
RENSSELAER	083	10580	532	152,538	157,681	161,658	0.5	23	91.1	89.4	4.7	5.5	1.7	2.1
RICHMOND	085	35620	501	443,728	482,225	511,069	1.2	3	77.6	74.6	9.7	10.3	5.7	7.1
ROCKLAND	087	35620	501	286,753	297,869	304,468	0.5	23	76.9	73.7	11.0	11.9	5.6	6.9
ST. LAWRENCE	089	36300	549	111,931	112,878	113,515	0.1	43	94.5	93.5	2.4	2.8	0.7	1.0
SARATOGA	091	10580	532	200,635	220,758	236,170	1.3	2	96.0	94.9	1.4	1.7	1.1	1.5
SCHENECTADY	093	10580	532	146,555	149,887	152,451	0.3	32	87.8	85.7	6.8	7.6	2.0	2.5
SCHOHARIE	095	10580	532	31,582	32,318	33,048	0.3	32	96.6	96.0	1.3	1.4	0.4	0.5
SCHUYLER	097	00000	565	19,224	19,735	20,104	0.4	28	96.5	95.9	1.5	1.6	0.3	0.4
SENECA	099	42900	555	33,342	35,034	35,313	0.7	15	95.0	94.1	2.3	2.5	0.7	0.9
STEUBEN	101	18500	565	98,726	99,898	100,626	0.2	38	96.4	95.7	1.4	1.5	0.9	1.2
SUFFOLK	103	35620	501	1,419,369	1,506,021	1,561,288	0.8	10	84.6	82.4	6.9	7.6	2.5	3.1
SULLIVAN	105	00000	501	73,966	80,096	85,073	1.1	5	85.3	83.4	8.5	9.3	1.2	1.5
TIOGA	107	13780	502	51,784	51,833	51,898	0.0	48	97.5	97.4	0.5	0.6	0.6	0.6
TOMPKINS	109	27060	555	96,501	101,681	104,248	0.7	15	85.5	81.7	3.6	5.3	7.2	8.5
ULSTER	111	28740	501	177,749	188,788	196,874	0.8	10	88.9	87.2	5.4	6.0	1.3	1.7
WARREN	113	24020	532	63,303	67,837	71,273	1.0	6	97.5	96.9	0.6	0.7	0.6	0.7
WASHINGTON	115	24020	532	61,042	63,858	65,900	0.6	19	95.0	94.2	2.9	3.3	0.3	0.4
WAYNE	117	40380	538	93,765	94,820	95,531	0.2	38	93.8	92.8	3.2	3.6	0.5	0.6
WESTCHESTER	119	35620	501	923,459	956,514	977,840	0.5	23	71.3	68.4	14.2	15.0	4.5	5.6
WYOMING	121	00000	514	43,424	43,354	43,404	0.0	48	91.8	92.2	5.5	4.9	0.4	0.6
YATES	123	00000	538	24,621	25,484	26,151	0.5	23	97.9	97.5	0.6	0.6	0.3	0.4
NEW YORK							0.4		67.9	65.5	15.9	16.4	5.6	6.6
UNITED STATES							1.2		75.1	72.7	12.3	12.6	3.8	4.5

COUNTY	% HISPANIC ORIGIN 2000	2007	2007 AGE DISTRIBUTION (%) 0-4	5-9	10-14	15-19	20-24	25-44	45-64	65-84	85+	18+	MEDIAN AGE 2007	% 2007 Males	% 2007 Females
ALBANY	3.1	3.6	5.5	5.3	6.1	8.1	7.9	25.8	26.6	12.0	2.7	79.1	38.8	48.0	52.0
ALLEGANY	0.9	1.1	5.7	5.4	5.8	11.1	10.9	21.9	25.2	11.9	2.2	78.9	35.9	50.0	50.0
BRONX	48.4	50.0	8.4	7.5	9.0	7.9	7.2	29.3	20.6	8.6	1.5	70.4	31.9	46.8	53.2
BROOME	2.0	2.4	5.6	5.2	6.0	8.2	8.2	23.6	26.6	13.7	3.0	79.3	40.2	48.4	51.6
CATTARAUGUS	0.9	1.3	6.2	6.0	6.3	8.3	7.6	23.5	27.6	12.4	2.2	76.9	39.3	49.2	50.8
CAYUGA	2.0	2.3	6.1	5.6	6.2	7.0	7.4	26.1	27.4	11.9	2.4	77.9	39.6	50.6	49.4
CHAUTAUQUA	4.2	5.0	5.9	5.4	6.2	7.8	8.6	23.2	27.1	13.0	2.8	78.3	39.8	49.1	50.9
CHEMUNG	1.8	2.4	6.0	5.7	6.2	7.2	7.6	25.0	27.1	12.9	2.5	78.2	39.7	49.8	50.2
CHENANGO	1.1	1.3	6.1	5.6	6.4	6.9	7.0	23.8	28.8	13.0	2.3	77.5	41.2	49.5	50.5
CLINTON	2.5	2.9	5.3	5.2	6.1	7.8	8.9	28.3	25.6	11.1	1.6	79.3	37.5	51.3	48.7
COLUMBIA	2.5	3.0	5.3	4.9	6.3	7.4	5.8	23.0	31.5	13.3	2.6	78.7	43.3	49.9	50.1
CORTLAND	1.2	1.3	5.9	5.4	6.1	9.7	10.9	24.1	24.9	11.0	2.0	78.7	35.8	48.6	51.4
DELAWARE	2.0	2.4	5.2	4.9	5.6	7.9	6.1	21.6	30.0	15.7	2.9	79.9	44.0	49.4	50.6
DUTCHESS	6.4	7.4	6.1	6.0	7.1	8.4	7.2	25.6	26.9	10.8	1.8	76.3	38.4	49.8	50.2
ERIE	3.3	3.8	6.0	5.8	6.5	7.2	6.6	25.0	26.9	13.4	2.7	77.6	40.1	47.9	52.1
ESSEX	2.2	2.6	5.2	4.7	5.3	6.8	6.8	26.0	29.6	13.3	2.4	80.5	42.0	52.0	48.0
FRANKLIN	4.0	4.6	5.2	4.7	6.0	7.0	8.1	29.8	26.4	10.8	1.9	80.0	38.4	55.0	45.0
FULTON	1.6	1.9	5.8	5.2	6.4	7.2	6.6	24.8	28.5	12.7	2.7	77.9	41.1	49.5	50.5
GENESEE	1.5	1.8	6.3	5.7	6.7	7.0	7.2	25.5	27.3	12.0	2.3	76.9	39.7	49.5	50.5
GREENE	4.3	5.0	5.4	5.0	5.7	8.4	7.9	22.7	29.6	12.9	2.3	79.8	41.4	50.7	49.3
HAMILTON	1.1	1.2	4.5	4.4	4.7	4.5	6.2	20.4	36.7	16.4	2.3	83.3	48.0	50.4	49.6
HERKIMER	0.9	1.1	5.8	5.2	6.3	6.7	7.3	24.3	28.2	13.3	2.9	79.0	41.3	48.7	51.3
JEFFERSON	4.2	4.9	7.5	6.1	6.5	7.0	10.1	28.5	23.0	9.5	1.7	75.9	33.7	51.9	48.1
KINGS	19.8	21.0	7.6	6.7	7.6	7.4	7.4	29.8	22.2	9.7	1.6	73.7	33.4	47.2	52.8
LEWIS	0.6	0.8	6.5	5.9	6.4	7.2	6.8	25.6	27.9	11.7	1.9	76.5	39.5	50.0	50.0
LIVINGSTON	2.3	2.6	5.5	5.4	5.8	10.3	11.4	23.8	26.1	10.0	1.8	79.4	36.4	49.4	50.6
MADISON	1.1	1.3	5.9	5.8	6.2	9.7	8.4	23.6	27.6	10.9	1.9	77.7	38.5	49.2	50.8
MONROE	5.3	6.1	6.2	6.1	6.9	7.9	7.2	25.6	26.6	11.0	2.4	76.3	38.2	48.3	51.7
MONTGOMERY	6.9	8.2	6.2	5.5	6.1	6.5	6.4	24.0	27.8	13.8	3.7	78.0	41.7	48.0	52.0
NASSAU	10.0	11.4	6.3	7.0	7.7	6.8	4.8	25.7	26.7	12.6	2.4	74.8	40.0	48.4	51.6
NEW YORK	27.2	29.2	4.9	4.4	4.6	5.5	6.6	36.9	24.9	10.4	1.8	83.2	37.3	47.7	52.3
NIAGARA	1.3	1.6	6.1	5.6	6.4	7.1	6.6	24.9	27.9	12.8	2.5	77.8	40.6	48.5	51.5
ONEIDA	3.2	3.7	5.7	5.3	6.3	7.6	7.5	24.7	26.4	13.4	3.0	78.7	40.1	49.4	50.6
ONONDAGA	2.4	2.9	6.4	6.2	6.9	7.9	7.7	24.8	26.2	11.7	2.3	76.2	38.2	48.0	52.0
ONTARIO	2.1	2.6	5.9	5.8	6.9	7.5	6.6	24.3	29.4	11.4	2.1	77.2	40.5	49.1	50.9
ORANGE	11.6	13.4	7.6	7.0	7.8	8.3	7.0	25.6	26.0	9.1	1.6	72.5	36.2	50.1	49.9
ORLEANS	3.9	4.9	6.3	5.7	5.9	9.6	9.9	25.5	25.2	10.0	1.9	78.6	35.6	50.5	49.5
OSWEGO	1.3	1.6	6.3	5.7	6.9	8.4	8.6	26.1	26.4	9.9	1.6	76.7	36.9	49.4	50.6
OTSEGO	1.9	2.5	4.8	4.8	5.8	9.3	10.4	21.8	28.2	12.5	2.4	80.2	39.8	48.8	51.2
PUTNAM	6.2	7.4	6.4	7.2	8.1	6.9	4.8	26.5	29.3	9.4	1.4	73.8	39.9	49.8	50.2
QUEENS	25.0	26.1	6.5	6.0	6.7	6.3	6.1	31.8	24.1	10.6	1.9	77.0	36.5	48.3	51.7
RENSSELAER	2.1	2.6	6.0	5.7	6.3	7.6	7.4	25.8	27.4	11.6	2.2	77.8	39.1	48.9	51.1
RICHMOND	12.1	13.7	6.7	6.6	7.7	7.4	6.1	28.3	25.9	9.6	1.7	74.4	36.7	48.4	51.6
ROCKLAND	10.2	11.5	7.6	7.7	7.9	7.5	5.8	24.9	25.2	11.7	1.8	72.1	37.2	48.8	51.2
ST. LAWRENCE	1.8	2.2	5.5	5.2	5.9	9.0	10.1	24.8	26.2	11.5	1.8	79.5	37.3	51.0	49.0
SARATOGA	1.4	1.8	6.3	6.3	6.7	6.9	6.0	27.1	28.7	10.4	1.7	76.7	39.6	49.3	50.7
SCHENECTADY	3.2	3.8	6.0	5.8	6.7	7.2	6.1	24.4	27.4	13.3	3.2	77.2	41.1	48.5	51.5
SCHOHARIE	1.9	2.2	5.5	5.3	6.0	9.0	7.4	22.9	29.1	12.6	2.2	79.2	40.6	49.8	50.2
SCHUYLER	1.2	1.4	5.8	5.4	6.4	7.1	7.0	23.2	30.1	12.7	2.3	78.1	41.7	50.3	49.7
SENECA	2.0	2.3	5.5	4.9	6.2	6.8	7.6	25.7	28.0	12.9	2.5	79.1	40.2	50.8	49.2
STEUBEN	0.8	1.0	6.3	5.8	6.5	6.9	6.9	24.2	28.1	13.0	2.3	77.1	40.6	49.1	50.9
SUFFOLK	10.5	12.2	6.9	7.2	7.9	7.1	5.0	27.2	26.2	10.7	1.8	73.7	38.4	49.1	50.9
SULLIVAN	9.2	10.7	6.0	5.4	6.1	7.7	6.5	24.1	29.7	12.7	1.8	77.6	41.2	51.0	49.0
TIOGA	1.0	1.0	6.4	6.1	6.5	7.3	6.8	23.7	29.4	12.2	1.7	76.5	40.7	49.5	50.5
TOMPKINS	3.1	4.0	4.4	4.1	5.0	10.8	16.9	25.5	23.3	8.3	1.7	82.9	30.9	50.2	49.8
ULSTER	6.2	7.2	5.4	5.3	6.4	7.6	7.3	25.4	29.0	11.6	2.0	78.6	40.4	49.8	50.2
WARREN	1.0	1.3	5.4	4.9	6.3	7.2	5.9	24.4	30.4	13.3	2.2	79.1	42.4	48.7	51.3
WASHINGTON	2.0	2.4	5.7	5.3	6.1	7.4	6.8	26.6	28.1	12.0	2.0	78.3	40.0	51.5	48.5
WAYNE	2.4	2.9	6.7	6.3	7.0	7.3	6.8	25.8	28.2	10.3	1.7	75.3	39.0	49.7	50.3
WESTCHESTER	15.6	17.4	6.6	7.4	7.9	7.2	5.2	26.3	25.9	11.3	2.3	73.7	38.6	48.1	51.9
WYOMING	2.9	2.7	5.5	5.2	6.1	7.6	8.1	28.6	26.7	10.3	1.9	79.4	38.2	53.1	46.9
YATES	0.9	1.1	6.7	6.4	6.9	7.9	7.3	21.5	27.8	13.3	2.2	75.6	40.2	49.2	50.8
NEW YORK	15.1	16.4	6.5	6.2	7.0	7.2	6.7	28.1	25.3	10.9	2.0	76.0	37.2	48.4	51.6
UNITED STATES	12.5	15.0	6.9	6.5	6.8	7.1	7.0	27.6	25.4	10.7	1.9	75.6	36.7	49.2	50.8

HOUSEHOLDS

COUNTY	HOUSEHOLDS					FAMILIES			MEDIAN HOUSEHOLD INCOME			
	2000	2007	2012	% Annual Rate 2000-2007	2007 Average HH Size	2000	2007	% Annual Rate 2000-2007	2007	2012	2007 National Rank	2007 State Rank
ALBANY	120,512	123,678	125,827	0.4	2.29	70,973	72,123	0.2	55,573	65,530	381	14
ALLEGANY	18,009	18,285	18,395	0.2	2.48	12,189	12,279	0.1	40,121	46,162	1706	58
BRONX	463,212	478,822	490,238	0.5	2.79	315,090	323,208	0.4	35,419	42,014	2381	62
BROOME	80,749	80,784	80,348	0.0	2.32	50,231	49,802	-0.1	44,547	51,830	1153	40
CATTARAUGUS	32,023	32,450	32,502	0.2	2.46	21,662	21,780	0.1	40,997	46,650	1599	54
CAYUGA	30,558	31,163	31,512	0.3	2.48	20,829	21,079	0.2	46,171	53,226	983	32
CHAUTAUQUA	54,515	54,527	53,966	0.0	2.40	35,966	35,681	-0.1	41,546	48,144	1511	50
CHEMUNG	35,049	35,104	34,854	0.0	2.40	23,280	23,129	-0.1	45,627	52,682	1038	36
CHENANGO	19,926	20,736	21,243	0.6	2.47	13,546	13,986	0.4	41,172	46,751	1579	53
CLINTON	29,423	31,857	33,625	1.1	2.42	19,261	20,680	1.0	45,904	52,609	1013	35
COLUMBIA	24,796	26,412	27,510	0.9	2.39	16,580	17,519	0.8	52,040	60,409	544	19
CORTLAND	18,210	18,511	18,642	0.2	2.45	11,619	11,708	0.1	42,119	48,404	1434	48
DELAWARE	19,270	19,830	20,694	0.4	2.33	12,735	12,998	0.3	40,211	45,849	1698	57
DUTCHESS	99,536	107,562	112,785	1.1	2.64	69,201	74,236	1.0	69,383	82,335	123	7
ERIE	380,873	380,927	377,800	0.0	2.37	243,359	241,295	-0.1	49,234	58,170	730	25
ESSEX	15,028	15,947	16,515	0.8	2.34	9,832	10,348	0.7	43,318	49,820	1300	44
FRANKLIN	17,931	18,546	18,907	0.5	2.41	11,805	12,108	0.4	38,802	44,373	1877	60
FULTON	21,884	22,806	23,383	0.6	2.39	14,520	15,012	0.5	41,882	48,184	1462	49
GENESEE	22,770	22,917	22,864	0.1	2.54	15,823	15,812	0.0	49,708	57,383	695	22
GREENE	18,256	19,793	20,906	1.1	2.39	12,073	12,982	1.0	44,916	51,694	1120	38
HAMILTON	2,362	2,346	2,324	-0.1	2.18	1,558	1,536	-0.2	38,688	43,612	1897	61
HERKIMER	25,734	26,029	26,073	0.2	2.42	17,101	17,158	0.0	40,663	46,822	1646	55
JEFFERSON	40,068	42,891	44,896	0.9	2.54	28,142	29,912	0.8	42,332	48,608	1413	47
KINGS	880,727	904,633	924,568	0.4	2.77	584,120	595,126	0.3	42,491	50,565	1400	46
LEWIS	10,040	10,458	10,693	0.6	2.59	7,307	7,563	0.5	41,245	46,377	1561	52
LIVINGSTON	22,150	23,131	23,687	0.6	2.57	15,346	15,912	0.5	51,921	60,407	553	21
MADISON	25,368	26,463	26,938	0.6	2.49	17,577	18,204	0.5	49,283	57,143	727	24
MONROE	286,512	291,720	294,674	0.2	2.45	184,479	186,244	0.1	57,828	68,225	308	11
MONTGOMERY	20,038	20,217	20,293	0.1	2.39	13,111	13,121	0.0	40,386	46,478	1679	56
NASSAU	447,387	447,009	447,088	0.0	2.94	347,026	344,829	-0.1	95,477	116,506	11	2
NEW YORK	738,644	771,489	803,348	0.6	2.03	301,970	310,940	0.4	67,911	87,538	139	8
NIAGARA	87,846	87,784	87,422	0.0	2.43	58,582	58,080	-0.1	48,113	56,476	806	28
ONEIDA	90,496	92,416	93,387	0.3	2.38	59,170	59,931	0.2	45,260	52,334	1079	37
ONONDAGA	181,153	185,408	187,031	0.3	2.40	115,320	117,005	0.2	51,976	61,591	547	20
ONTARIO	38,370	41,677	43,955	1.1	2.49	26,354	28,408	1.0	55,767	64,804	373	13
ORANGE	114,788	127,382	137,085	1.4	2.89	84,457	93,124	1.4	66,828	79,800	151	9
ORLEANS	15,363	15,553	15,658	0.2	2.62	10,839	10,894	0.1	47,053	54,483	907	30
OSWEGO	45,522	46,917	47,640	0.4	2.54	31,233	31,947	0.3	44,390	50,467	1168	41
OTSEGO	23,291	24,879	25,435	0.9	2.39	15,120	16,017	0.8	41,257	47,215	1560	51
PUTNAM	32,703	35,052	36,430	1.0	2.84	25,179	26,833	0.9	96,239	117,452	9	1
QUEENS	782,664	789,214	796,250	0.1	2.86	537,991	538,432	0.0	55,921	66,917	365	12
RENSSELAER	59,894	62,387	64,323	0.6	2.45	39,028	40,312	0.4	54,043	63,499	450	17
RICHMOND	156,341	170,420	181,190	1.2	2.78	114,052	123,510	1.1	71,712	86,582	112	6
ROCKLAND	92,675	95,368	97,500	0.4	3.04	70,944	72,591	0.3	90,586	111,273	17	3
ST. LAWRENCE	40,506	41,181	41,742	0.2	2.47	26,939	27,163	0.1	39,948	46,034	1734	59
SARATOGA	78,165	87,432	94,398	1.6	2.48	53,738	59,659	1.5	62,665	73,401	198	10
SCHENECTADY	59,684	61,164	62,407	0.3	2.37	38,037	38,648	0.2	53,138	62,870	495	18
SCHOHARIE	11,991	12,488	12,907	0.6	2.44	8,175	8,451	0.5	44,827	51,536	1128	39
SCHUYLER	7,374	7,718	7,934	0.6	2.48	5,189	5,391	0.5	43,400	49,227	1285	43
SENECA	12,630	12,988	13,205	0.4	2.47	8,632	8,811	0.3	46,107	53,267	987	33
STEUBEN	39,071	39,962	40,502	0.3	2.46	26,212	26,599	0.2	44,013	50,544	1206	42
SUFFOLK	469,299	496,315	515,476	0.8	2.97	360,422	379,056	0.7	83,592	103,583	37	5
SULLIVAN	27,661	30,682	32,927	1.4	2.46	18,324	20,163	1.3	45,917	52,864	1010	34
TIOGA	19,725	20,136	20,349	0.3	2.55	14,326	14,528	0.2	49,361	56,768	719	23
TOMPKINS	36,420	38,381	39,699	0.7	2.31	19,120	19,917	0.6	47,929	56,469	825	29
ULSTER	67,499	72,188	75,832	0.9	2.45	43,563	46,192	0.8	54,240	63,845	437	15
WARREN	25,726	28,017	29,711	1.2	2.38	17,068	18,439	1.1	48,636	56,151	772	27
WASHINGTON	22,458	24,120	25,229	1.0	2.49	15,798	16,849	0.9	46,305	52,427	969	31
WAYNE	34,908	36,020	36,572	0.4	2.59	25,066	25,689	0.3	54,085	62,384	448	16
WESTCHESTER	337,142	344,819	351,735	0.3	2.70	235,201	238,815	0.2	84,463	104,596	31	4
WYOMING	14,906	15,235	15,404	0.3	2.56	10,713	10,876	0.2	48,676	55,963	769	26
YATES	9,029	9,412	9,692	0.6	2.58	6,284	6,502	0.5	42,561	48,772	1388	45
NEW YORK				0.4	2.61			0.3	56,704	67,544		
UNITED STATES				1.2	2.59			1.0	53,154	62,503		

COUNTY	2007 Per Capita Income	2007 HH Income Base	2007 HOUSEHOLD INCOME DISTRIBUTION (%)					2007 Home Value Base	2007 HOME VALUE DISTRIBUTION (%)					2007 Median Home Value
			Less than $25,000	$25,000 to $49,999	$50,000 to $99,999	$100,000 to $149,999	$150,000 or More		Less than $50,000	$50,000 to $89,999	$90,000 to $174,999	$175,000 to $399,999	$400,000 or More	
ALBANY	31,433	123,678	20.1	25.1	32.7	13.1	9.0	75,512	1.2	0.9	17.0	73.3	7.6	231,479
ALLEGANY	19,342	18,285	30.6	31.4	29.6	6.1	2.3	13,925	10.4	21.4	41.2	25.8	1.1	130,356
BRONX	17,682	478,795	38.2	25.7	25.1	7.1	4.0	104,327	9.5	2.9	7.3	33.8	46.5	381,710
BROOME	24,944	80,784	27.2	28.2	30.6	9.0	5.1	54,864	5.5	11.2	54.5	26.8	2.1	143,716
CATTARAUGUS	20,309	32,450	28.1	33.0	30.1	6.6	2.1	24,885	8.3	15.1	41.3	33.1	2.2	148,346
CAYUGA	22,395	31,162	23.8	30.5	34.2	8.2	3.3	23,252	4.4	6.6	42.9	42.6	3.6	169,349
CHAUTAUQUA	21,743	54,527	27.9	31.4	30.3	7.2	3.1	39,207	6.2	14.5	44.2	32.1	3.1	150,216
CHEMUNG	23,585	35,104	25.4	30.0	31.9	8.4	4.3	25,101	11.1	29.3	40.8	17.4	1.4	104,560
CHENANGO	20,641	20,736	28.4	32.4	29.5	7.2	2.6	16,075	10.3	15.6	39.3	32.6	2.1	146,671
CLINTON	22,565	31,857	27.3	27.4	33.2	8.8	3.3	22,742	6.2	7.5	31.7	50.4	4.1	181,768
COLUMBIA	28,811	26,412	19.9	28.0	34.3	10.4	7.4	19,390	3.1	2.6	15.8	65.6	12.8	238,375
CORTLAND	21,221	18,511	28.9	29.5	31.1	7.1	3.3	12,462	4.1	5.7	45.8	41.9	2.6	168,495
DELAWARE	21,971	19,830	28.0	33.1	29.2	6.7	3.0	15,449	6.1	7.7	35.8	44.9	5.5	175,592
DUTCHESS	31,964	107,558	14.6	20.4	34.8	17.8	12.4	77,127	1.3	1.3	4.5	68.7	24.2	326,362
ERIE	26,780	380,904	25.4	25.3	32.4	10.9	6.1	260,053	4.5	10.1	49.0	34.0	2.5	149,454
ESSEX	22,478	15,947	26.8	30.5	32.3	7.1	3.2	12,151	4.3	6.6	38.2	43.3	7.7	176,733
FRANKLIN	19,503	18,546	30.7	31.4	29.9	5.9	2.1	13,562	7.7	14.7	40.2	34.4	3.0	153,136
FULTON	21,419	22,806	28.1	31.4	31.1	6.8	2.7	16,990	5.3	13.5	41.6	36.8	2.9	156,615
GENESEE	23,201	22,917	18.8	31.5	37.5	8.9	3.3	17,283	2.7	2.7	40.5	51.9	2.1	180,027
GREENE	23,883	19,793	26.0	29.1	31.9	8.7	4.3	14,836	2.9	2.9	24.9	63.0	6.4	201,684
HAMILTON	23,754	2,346	28.9	35.0	26.2	6.5	3.3	1,911	2.3	5.5	29.1	55.1	8.0	195,056
HERKIMER	20,207	26,029	30.2	30.6	31.0	6.2	2.0	19,209	10.2	18.8	46.2	23.2	1.6	127,797
JEFFERSON	20,124	42,891	27.9	31.6	31.0	6.7	2.7	26,979	5.7	10.6	42.1	38.1	3.5	160,871
KINGS	21,956	904,589	33.3	23.1	27.3	9.4	6.9	269,916	2.3	1.7	4.0	29.5	62.6	464,962
LEWIS	18,794	10,458	28.9	32.1	31.8	5.4	1.7	8,311	6.2	13.0	45.4	32.6	2.8	152,550
LIVINGSTON	23,184	23,129	20.1	27.8	37.8	10.4	3.9	17,791	9.5	13.8	49.5	25.9	1.3	134,494
MADISON	25,099	26,463	21.3	29.4	33.9	9.8	5.5	20,467	7.4	13.1	43.6	33.6	2.3	145,919
MONROE	30,253	291,718	20.1	23.3	33.2	14.3	9.2	197,859	2.0	9.1	48.7	36.7	3.4	158,138
MONTGOMERY	21,490	20,217	29.9	30.2	30.3	6.5	3.1	14,172	5.5	12.6	45.4	34.0	2.5	151,956
NASSAU	43,664	447,007	9.8	12.5	29.8	21.5	26.4	366,946	0.2	0.3	1.0	23.1	75.5	514,232
NEW YORK	58,659	771,478	22.5	16.7	25.2	13.6	21.9	170,012	3.6	0.8	2.7	26.5	66.3	634,846
NIAGARA	24,587	87,784	24.7	27.0	33.2	10.4	4.8	63,627	6.0	15.4	49.0	28.6	0.9	137,314
ONEIDA	23,798	92,416	26.4	28.3	32.3	8.5	4.5	64,740	6.5	12.9	51.0	27.8	1.7	143,098
ONONDAGA	28,152	185,408	22.9	25.2	32.9	11.7	7.2	124,900	2.1	7.3	53.3	34.4	2.9	153,534
ONTARIO	27,876	41,677	17.7	25.8	37.5	12.6	6.5	31,668	7.4	9.7	42.6	34.8	5.6	154,452
ORANGE	28,437	127,381	15.5	20.5	35.2	17.6	11.2	89,324	1.3	1.0	6.5	71.4	19.8	304,685
ORLEANS	21,245	15,553	21.5	31.8	36.0	7.6	3.1	12,072	13.2	25.3	46.9	14.2	0.4	104,895
OSWEGO	21,301	46,917	25.9	29.8	32.3	9.3	2.7	35,237	10.8	17.5	48.3	22.5	0.9	127,212
OTSEGO	21,975	24,879	28.1	31.3	30.1	6.8	3.6	18,737	5.8	7.1	37.0	44.7	5.3	175,064
PUTNAM	42,937	35,052	7.6	12.2	32.1	23.7	24.4	29,466	0.3	0.4	1.0	43.3	55.0	422,617
QUEENS	25,225	789,192	21.3	23.4	33.6	13.3	8.5	362,339	1.2	1.9	7.9	35.7	53.3	417,867
RENSSELAER	27,070	62,387	20.1	26.1	35.5	12.1	6.2	42,365	2.1	2.4	23.0	67.2	5.2	210,759
RICHMOND	32,305	170,417	16.4	17.8	33.7	18.4	13.7	113,182	0.3	0.3	1.3	39.1	58.9	441,593
ROCKLAND	38,813	95,366	11.5	14.4	28.3	21.2	24.6	70,749	0.7	0.9	1.9	30.6	65.8	479,154
ST. LAWRENCE	19,794	41,176	30.8	30.6	29.6	6.5	2.6	30,126	8.4	16.2	40.3	32.8	2.3	147,186
SARATOGA	31,391	87,432	14.4	23.5	38.4	14.2	9.4	65,317	4.9	2.5	15.8	68.3	8.6	236,268
SCHENECTADY	28,301	61,164	21.1	26.0	34.1	12.3	6.5	41,794	0.8	2.2	32.1	60.9	4.1	194,513
SCHOHARIE	22,617	12,488	24.0	31.6	32.7	8.4	3.3	9,687	5.0	5.1	35.7	50.2	3.9	181,354
SCHUYLER	21,275	7,718	25.2	33.1	32.5	6.4	2.8	6,120	7.4	11.4	38.6	39.4	3.2	162,188
SENECA	22,466	12,988	23.2	31.1	32.6	10.0	3.1	9,894	4.5	8.7	40.5	42.8	3.5	169,088
STEUBEN	22,979	39,962	26.7	30.4	31.0	7.7	4.2	30,170	7.9	12.6	41.2	34.5	3.8	155,582
SUFFOLK	36,351	496,303	10.2	15.8	33.7	20.4	19.9	405,498	0.4	0.4	1.6	53.0	44.6	384,349
SULLIVAN	23,887	30,682	26.8	27.5	31.2	9.5	5.1	21,765	3.6	3.7	26.3	59.8	6.6	199,983
TIOGA	23,703	20,136	20.7	29.9	35.1	10.2	4.0	16,084	9.8	12.0	48.0	28.7	1.4	144,678
TOMPKINS	26,997	38,376	26.2	25.5	31.2	9.2	7.9	21,831	5.1	3.8	31.8	52.2	7.1	193,100
ULSTER	27,280	72,188	20.5	25.4	35.1	12.3	6.7	51,164	1.7	1.7	10.8	70.9	14.9	268,049
WARREN	26,476	28,017	21.2	30.2	33.8	9.7	5.1	20,371	1.8	1.9	13.1	69.0	14.1	241,385
WASHINGTON	22,442	24,120	23.1	31.4	33.9	8.6	3.0	18,543	1.9	2.7	24.8	64.1	6.5	207,837
WAYNE	24,553	36,020	18.7	27.4	37.8	11.9	4.2	28,730	10.1	15.0	49.8	24.2	0.9	131,091
WESTCHESTER	48,006	344,811	14.0	16.2	26.4	17.9	25.5	218,551	0.3	1.0	5.3	24.1	69.4	576,218
WYOMING	21,421	15,235	20.3	31.2	38.5	7.6	2.5	12,040	2.9	6.1	41.0	47.6	2.4	175,026
YATES	20,863	9,412	25.5	32.5	32.2	7.0	2.8	7,425	4.0	7.2	37.7	42.2	8.9	176,845
NEW YORK	31,110		22.5	22.2	30.6	13.1	11.7		2.9	4.7	19.9	38.6	33.8	296,301
UNITED STATES	27,916		21.9	25.0	32.3	12.3	8.4		7.9	10.5	27.1	35.6	19.0	192,285

COUNTY	FINANCIAL SERVICES				THE HOME						ENTERTAINMENT						PERSONAL			
					Home Improvements		Furnishings													
	Auto Loan	Home Loan	Invest-ments	Retire-ment Plans	Home Repair	Lawn & Garden	Comput-ers & Hard-ware	Major Appli-ances	TV, Radio, Sound Equip-ment	Furni-ture	Dine out/ Carry out	Sports Equip-ment	Fees & Tickets	Toys & Games	Travel	Cable TV	Apparel & Services	Auto Repairs	Health Insur-ance	Pets & Supplies
ALBANY	95	99	115	102	100	96	104	97	103	103	103	89	106	101	104	103	94	100	100	98
ALLEGANY	76	61	55	60	66	81	65	74	70	61	68	64	58	71	65	73	59	70	81	76
BRONX	48	49	50	50	52	47	66	55	76	63	78	50	66	68	64	80	76	59	61	55
BROOME	80	77	89	78	78	81	81	80	83	79	82	70	80	82	81	85	74	80	86	80
CATTARAUGUS	77	65	60	64	69	81	66	74	71	64	70	65	62	72	66	74	61	70	80	77
CAYUGA	81	75	78	76	78	85	76	80	78	75	78	71	74	80	77	81	69	78	85	82
CHAUTAUQUA	75	68	70	69	72	80	70	75	74	69	73	65	68	75	71	77	65	73	81	77
CHEMUNG	80	75	84	76	78	83	78	79	82	76	80	69	77	81	79	84	72	78	87	80
CHENANGO	82	64	53	63	70	87	66	78	71	64	71	68	60	73	66	75	61	73	83	82
CLINTON	82	75	75	75	76	83	76	79	78	75	78	71	74	79	76	80	69	78	82	81
COLUMBIA	100	93	91	93	100	111	94	104	96	92	95	91	91	96	97	99	84	98	107	106
CORTLAND	75	69	73	70	69	74	74	72	75	71	74	65	71	75	72	75	66	73	76	74
DELAWARE	81	64	53	64	72	90	68	81	72	64	71	70	60	73	68	76	61	75	86	84
DUTCHESS	109	128	138	126	129	116	121	118	118	124	118	109	129	118	125	117	110	117	114	117
ERIE	84	87	103	89	88	87	87	86	90	88	89	74	91	89	90	92	81	86	92	86
ESSEX	82	68	61	68	75	90	71	82	75	68	74	71	65	75	72	79	64	77	88	84
FRANKLIN	76	60	51	59	66	81	64	74	68	61	67	65	57	69	64	71	58	70	79	77
FULTON	75	67	69	67	70	80	69	74	73	67	71	65	66	73	70	75	63	72	80	76
GENESEE	83	81	88	82	84	88	80	84	82	80	81	73	81	84	82	84	73	81	87	85
GREENE	88	76	67	76	83	99	78	90	80	75	80	78	72	81	79	84	70	84	93	93
HAMILTON	85	66	42	65	76	100	67	87	70	63	70	75	57	71	69	74	59	78	88	91
HERKIMER	72	62	63	62	66	77	65	71	69	62	68	62	61	70	65	72	59	68	78	73
JEFFERSON	77	65	63	66	65	74	72	73	73	68	73	66	67	74	69	74	64	73	76	74
KINGS	65	68	70	69	71	64	84	72	89	80	92	70	85	82	82	92	88	76	75	72
LEWIS	79	62	48	60	68	86	62	75	67	61	67	66	56	70	62	71	58	69	80	80
LIVINGSTON	90	84	84	85	87	94	83	88	86	83	85	78	82	88	84	87	76	85	91	91
MADISON	95	86	84	86	90	101	85	94	89	84	88	82	83	91	87	92	78	89	98	96
MONROE	99	103	118	106	102	99	105	99	105	105	104	89	107	104	105	105	95	102	103	100
MONTGOMERY	75	64	69	64	68	78	69	74	74	65	72	64	65	73	69	77	63	71	82	75
NASSAU	145	208	221	193	220	178	177	180	169	189	172	167	206	168	195	170	167	169	166	173
NEW YORK	140	135	145	148	140	127	175	144	177	167	184	147	172	166	166	177	174	158	145	146
NIAGARA	80	82	95	83	83	84	81	81	84	82	83	70	84	84	83	86	75	81	87	82
ONEIDA	78	77	89	78	80	83	78	79	81	78	80	69	79	81	80	84	72	78	86	80
ONONDAGA	90	92	107	95	92	90	95	91	96	95	95	81	97	95	95	96	86	92	94	91
ONTARIO	99	97	101	98	99	103	95	99	96	95	95	88	95	97	97	98	86	96	101	100
ORANGE	106	123	131	121	123	110	116	114	113	119	113	106	123	114	119	112	106	112	108	112
ORLEANS	82	75	81	76	77	84	76	79	80	75	78	69	75	82	77	82	69	77	86	81
OSWEGO	83	72	69	71	72	81	74	78	77	72	76	69	70	78	72	79	67	76	82	80
OTSEGO	83	67	59	67	73	88	73	81	75	68	75	72	65	76	72	78	65	77	85	84
PUTNAM	144	202	210	190	209	171	169	172	160	181	163	160	196	163	184	159	157	161	155	167
QUEENS	80	92	95	89	96	83	100	91	102	98	104	89	104	96	101	104	99	93	91	89
RENSSELAER	88	92	106	93	92	90	94	90	93	92	93	81	95	93	94	93	84	91	92	90
RICHMOND	100	132	136	122	138	115	122	119	123	127	126	111	138	120	130	126	122	115	115	116
ROCKLAND	139	184	194	175	192	159	166	164	158	173	161	156	186	157	176	157	154	158	151	158
ST. LAWRENCE	76	62	57	62	67	80	67	74	70	63	69	65	61	71	66	73	60	71	79	77
SARATOGA	108	113	117	114	111	110	108	108	106	110	106	99	111	108	110	106	96	107	107	109
SCHENECTADY	87	93	112	95	94	91	94	91	95	94	94	80	97	93	96	96	85	91	96	90
SCHOHARIE	86	73	66	73	79	93	74	84	77	72	77	74	69	79	75	81	67	79	89	87
SCHUYLER	83	68	57	67	75	91	69	81	73	67	72	71	63	75	70	77	63	75	86	85
SENECA	83	75	76	75	79	89	76	83	80	74	78	72	73	81	78	83	69	79	89	85
STEUBEN	84	74	72	73	78	89	75	82	79	73	78	72	71	80	76	82	69	79	88	85
SUFFOLK	130	174	179	162	179	151	150	154	143	158	145	143	169	143	162	142	138	146	141	148
SULLIVAN	87	77	73	77	82	95	81	89	83	77	82	79	75	83	81	86	72	85	92	91
TIOGA	91	82	78	81	85	95	79	88	84	80	83	77	77	86	81	87	73	84	93	91
TOMPKINS	91	80	87	85	79	83	100	86	95	90	95	83	91	92	91	92	86	92	87	88
ULSTER	92	95	103	95	98	97	95	96	94	94	94	86	96	94	97	95	85	94	97	96
WARREN	91	85	84	85	89	99	84	92	87	83	86	81	82	87	87	90	76	88	97	94
WASHINGTON	86	74	70	74	80	93	75	84	79	73	78	74	71	82	76	82	68	79	90	88
WAYNE	95	88	85	88	90	98	84	92	88	86	87	81	83	92	86	90	77	88	95	95
WESTCHESTER	150	191	206	186	201	169	182	175	177	187	181	166	201	171	192	178	173	172	167	171
WYOMING	82	78	78	78	82	90	74	82	78	75	77	72	74	81	77	80	68	77	86	85
YATES	84	68	60	67	74	92	72	83	76	68	75	73	64	76	72	79	64	78	89	86
NEW YORK	99	107	114	107	111	103	113	107	115	112	117	100	117	111	114	117	110	108	109	107
UNITED STATES	100	100	100	100	100	100	100	100	100	100	100	100	100	100	100	100	100	100	100	100

POPULATION CHANGE

COUNTY	FIPS Code	CBSA Code	DMA Code	POPULATION			2000-2007 ANNUAL RATE		RACE (%)					
									White		Black		Asian/Pacific	
				2000	2007	2012	% Rate	State Rank	2000	2007	2000	2007	2000	2007
ALAMANCE	001	15500	518	130,800	144,506	154,475	1.4	31	75.6	73.5	18.8	18.9	0.9	1.2
ALEXANDER	003	25860	517	33,603	37,076	39,054	1.4	31	92.0	90.7	4.6	4.7	1.0	1.4
ALLEGHANY	005	00000	518	10,677	11,275	11,686	0.8	58	95.7	94.5	1.2	1.2	0.2	0.3
ANSON	007	16740	517	25,275	26,040	26,089	0.4	83	49.5	48.3	48.6	49.4	0.6	0.8
ASHE	009	00000	517	24,384	26,624	28,100	1.2	37	97.2	96.4	0.7	0.7	0.2	0.3
AVERY	011	00000	517	17,167	18,224	18,724	0.8	58	94.0	93.0	3.5	3.6	0.2	0.3
BEAUFORT	013	47820	545	44,958	47,055	48,574	0.6	69	68.4	67.1	29.0	29.5	0.2	0.3
BERTIE	015	00000	545	19,773	19,562	19,419	-0.1	94	36.3	35.2	62.3	63.1	0.1	0.1
BLADEN	017	00000	550	32,278	33,626	34,347	0.6	69	57.2	55.7	37.9	38.3	0.1	0.2
BRUNSWICK	019	48900	550	73,143	99,227	123,847	4.3	4	82.3	81.0	14.4	14.7	0.3	0.4
BUNCOMBE	021	11700	567	206,330	225,601	239,170	1.2	37	89.1	87.8	7.5	7.7	0.7	0.9
BURKE	023	25860	517	89,148	91,576	93,151	0.4	83	86.0	83.6	6.7	6.8	3.7	4.9
CABARRUS	025	16740	517	131,063	159,612	181,772	2.8	11	83.3	81.5	12.2	12.4	0.9	1.2
CALDWELL	027	25860	517	77,415	80,695	82,290	0.6	69	91.7	90.6	5.5	5.6	0.4	0.6
CAMDEN	029	21020	544	6,885	9,707	12,682	4.9	2	80.6	79.6	17.3	17.8	0.6	0.8
CARTERET	031	33980	545	59,383	64,704	68,637	1.2	37	90.3	89.3	7.0	7.2	0.6	0.8
CASWELL	033	00000	518	23,501	24,264	24,691	0.4	83	61.1	59.7	36.5	37.2	0.2	0.2
CATAWBA	035	25860	517	141,685	155,050	163,647	1.3	34	85.0	82.7	8.4	8.4	3.0	3.9
CHATHAM	037	20500	560	49,329	59,765	67,919	2.7	13	74.9	72.1	17.1	17.0	0.6	0.8
CHEROKEE	039	00000	575	24,298	27,204	29,462	1.6	28	94.8	94.0	1.6	1.6	0.3	0.4
CHOWAN	041	00000	544	14,526	14,769	15,251	0.2	90	60.5	58.8	37.5	38.4	0.4	0.4
CLAY	043	00000	524	8,775	10,303	11,509	2.2	17	98.0	97.7	0.8	0.8	0.2	0.2
CLEVELAND	045	43140	517	96,287	99,965	102,293	0.5	77	76.8	75.6	20.9	21.4	0.7	0.9
COLUMBUS	047	00000	550	54,749	55,205	55,432	0.1	92	63.4	61.9	30.9	31.4	0.3	0.3
CRAVEN	049	35100	545	91,436	94,746	97,591	0.5	77	69.9	68.1	25.1	25.4	1.1	1.4
CUMBERLAND	051	22180	560	302,963	309,872	313,420	0.3	87	55.2	52.9	34.9	34.6	2.2	2.8
CURRITUCK	053	47260	544	18,190	25,089	31,817	4.5	3	90.4	89.6	7.2	7.5	0.4	0.6
DARE	055	28620	544	29,967	36,789	42,277	2.9	9	94.7	93.9	2.7	2.7	0.4	0.6
DAVIDSON	057	45640	518	147,246	159,144	167,235	1.1	42	87.1	85.6	9.1	9.3	0.8	1.1
DAVIE	059	49180	518	34,835	40,627	45,059	2.1	18	90.4	89.3	6.8	7.0	0.4	0.4
DUPLIN	061	00000	545	49,063	53,063	55,945	1.1	42	58.7	55.0	28.9	28.0	0.2	0.3
DURHAM	063	20500	560	223,314	254,733	274,815	1.8	25	50.9	48.6	39.5	38.8	3.3	4.3
EDGECOMBE	065	40580	560	55,606	54,130	52,915	-0.4	100	40.1	39.0	57.5	57.6	0.1	0.2
FORSYTH	067	49180	518	306,067	338,409	363,124	1.4	31	68.5	66.3	25.6	25.7	1.1	1.4
FRANKLIN	069	39580	560	47,260	56,188	62,667	2.4	15	66.0	64.3	30.0	30.3	0.3	0.4
GASTON	071	16740	517	190,365	198,673	204,095	0.6	69	83.0	81.7	13.9	14.2	1.0	1.3
GATES	073	00000	544	10,516	11,547	12,349	1.3	34	59.1	58.0	39.2	40.0	0.3	0.3
GRAHAM	075	00000	567	7,993	8,275	8,466	0.5	77	91.9	91.0	0.2	0.2	0.2	0.2
GRANVILLE	077	00000	560	48,498	56,182	60,189	2.0	20	60.7	59.1	34.9	35.2	0.4	0.5
GREENE	079	24780	545	18,974	20,326	21,133	1.0	48	51.8	49.6	41.2	40.8	0.1	0.1
GUILFORD	081	24660	518	421,048	458,085	484,766	1.2	37	64.5	62.5	29.3	29.4	2.5	3.3
HALIFAX	083	40260	560	57,370	56,656	56,098	-0.2	96	42.6	41.3	52.6	53.1	0.6	0.7
HARNETT	085	20380	560	91,025	108,100	121,935	2.4	15	71.1	69.0	22.5	22.6	0.7	0.9
HAYWOOD	087	11700	567	54,033	57,966	60,393	1.0	48	96.8	96.3	1.3	1.3	0.2	0.3
HENDERSON	089	11700	567	89,173	102,665	113,241	2.0	20	92.5	90.1	3.1	3.9	0.6	0.8
HERTFORD	091	00000	544	22,601	24,253	24,343	1.0	48	37.4	36.9	59.6	59.4	0.3	0.5
HOKE	093	22180	560	33,646	43,778	54,052	3.7	5	44.5	42.6	37.6	37.1	1.0	1.2
HYDE	095	00000	545	5,826	5,754	5,712	-0.2	96	62.7	62.3	35.1	35.4	0.4	0.4
IREDELL	097	44380	517	122,660	149,877	171,561	2.8	11	82.2	80.5	13.7	13.9	1.3	1.7
JACKSON	099	00000	567	33,121	37,982	40,510	1.9	23	85.7	84.1	1.7	1.7	0.5	0.7
JOHNSTON	101	39580	560	121,965	155,954	184,180	3.4	7	78.1	75.7	15.7	15.7	0.3	0.5
JONES	103	35100	545	10,381	10,341	10,299	-0.1	94	61.0	60.6	35.9	36.2	0.2	0.2
LEE	105	41820	560	49,040	56,213	62,122	1.9	23	70.0	66.9	20.5	20.1	0.7	0.9
LENOIR	107	28820	545	59,648	58,919	58,112	-0.2	96	56.5	54.9	40.4	40.9	0.4	0.5
LINCOLN	109	30740	517	63,780	73,688	80,786	2.0	20	90.2	88.9	6.4	6.6	0.3	0.4
MCDOWELL	111	00000	567	42,151	44,641	46,142	0.8	58	92.2	90.8	4.2	4.3	0.9	1.2
MACON	113	00000	567	29,811	33,292	35,959	1.5	29	97.2	96.7	1.2	1.2	0.4	0.6
MADISON	115	11700	567	19,635	21,042	21,966	1.0	48	97.6	97.1	0.8	0.9	0.2	0.3
MARTIN	117	00000	545	25,593	25,092	24,704	-0.3	98	52.5	51.2	45.4	46.1	0.3	0.4
MECKLENBURG	119	16740	517	695,454	855,127	985,683	2.9	9	64.0	61.6	27.9	27.7	3.2	4.2
MITCHELL	121	00000	567	15,687	16,313	16,578	0.5	77	97.9	97.3	0.2	0.2	0.2	0.3
MONTGOMERY	123	00000	518	26,822	27,971	28,873	0.6	69	69.1	66.1	21.8	21.6	1.7	2.1
MOORE	125	43860	560	74,769	84,923	92,724	1.8	25	80.2	78.6	15.5	15.8	0.5	0.7
NASH	127	40580	560	87,420	94,608	99,277	1.1	42	61.9	60.2	33.9	34.3	0.6	0.8
NEW HANOVER	129	48900	550	160,307	190,471	218,258	2.4	15	79.9	78.6	17.0	17.4	0.9	1.2
NORTHAMPTON	131	40260	544	22,086	22,344	22,589	0.2	90	39.1	38.0	59.4	60.2	0.1	0.2
ONSLOW	133	27340	545	150,355	163,334	167,545	1.1	42	72.1	69.4	18.5	18.4	1.9	2.4
ORANGE	135	20500	560	118,227	124,599	128,266	0.7	62	78.0	75.5	13.8	13.6	4.1	5.5
PAMLICO	137	35100	545	12,934	13,490	13,963	0.6	69	73.2	72.0	24.6	25.2	0.4	0.5
PASQUOTANK	139	21020	544	34,897	39,353	42,702	1.7	27	56.9	55.6	40.0	40.7	0.9	1.2
PENDER	141	48900	550	41,082	50,208	57,982	2.8	11	72.7	71.1	23.6	24.0	0.2	0.3
PERQUIMANS	143	21020	544	11,368	12,322	13,048	1.1	42	70.8	69.8	28.0	28.7	0.2	0.3
PERSON	145	20500	560	35,623	38,022	39,408	0.9	53	68.8	67.4	28.2	28.8	0.2	0.2
PITT	147	24780	545	133,798	151,342	165,179	1.7	27	62.1	60.4	33.6	34.0	1.1	1.5
POLK	149	00000	567	18,324	19,908	20,606	1.1	42	92.3	91.5	5.9	6.1	0.3	0.4
RANDOLPH	151	24660	518	130,454	140,578	147,532	1.0	48	89.2	87.3	5.6	5.7	0.7	0.9
RICHMOND	153	40460	517	46,564	47,685	48,261	0.3	87	64.8	63.3	30.5	31.0	0.7	0.9
NORTH CAROLINA							1.7		72.1	70.4	21.6	21.5	1.5	2.0
UNITED STATES							1.2		75.1	72.7	12.3	12.6	3.8	4.5

NORTH CAROLINA

POPULATION COMPOSITION

B

COUNTY	% HISPANIC ORIGIN		2007 AGE DISTRIBUTION (%)										MEDIAN AGE	% 2007 Males	% 2007 Females
	2000	2007	0-4	5-9	10-14	15-19	20-24	25-44	45-64	65-84	85+	18+	2007		
ALAMANCE	6.8	8.8	6.4	6.3	6.2	7.4	6.1	27.9	25.9	11.9	2.0	77.1	38.2	48.4	51.6
ALEXANDER	2.5	3.3	6.8	7.2	6.4	5.3	4.8	29.5	26.8	11.6	1.6	76.4	38.9	50.1	49.9
ALLEGHANY	5.0	6.4	5.1	5.4	5.1	4.2	4.4	25.4	30.9	17.2	2.3	81.9	45.2	50.1	49.9
ANSON	0.8	1.0	6.6	6.1	6.7	5.8	6.1	28.6	26.4	11.4	2.3	77.0	38.2	50.2	49.8
ASHE	2.4	3.2	5.3	5.6	4.9	4.5	4.5	26.3	30.5	16.0	2.4	81.4	44.3	49.9	50.1
AVERY	2.4	3.2	4.7	4.8	5.3	5.9	5.8	30.6	27.6	13.4	1.9	82.2	40.1	53.5	46.5
BEAUFORT	3.2	4.2	6.0	5.8	5.9	5.7	5.2	24.5	30.4	14.4	2.1	78.8	42.6	48.2	51.8
BERTIE	1.0	1.2	6.4	6.2	6.3	6.5	6.0	23.6	28.9	13.8	2.2	77.5	41.4	47.5	52.5
BLADEN	3.7	4.9	6.5	6.6	6.5	5.4	5.6	26.1	28.4	13.0	1.9	77.1	40.2	48.7	51.3
BRUNSWICK	2.7	3.5	5.3	5.2	5.3	5.5	4.7	23.5	31.2	17.9	1.4	80.9	45.3	49.3	50.7
BUNCOMBE	2.8	3.6	5.5	5.5	5.7	6.3	5.6	27.2	28.6	13.3	2.4	79.6	41.2	48.3	51.7
BURKE	3.6	4.8	6.1	6.1	6.2	7.2	5.5	28.2	26.6	12.2	1.7	77.4	39.0	50.6	49.4
CABARRUS	5.1	6.6	7.1	6.7	7.0	6.3	5.7	29.5	26.4	9.7	1.5	75.3	37.4	49.6	50.4
CALDWELL	2.5	3.4	6.4	6.5	6.3	6.7	4.7	29.0	27.3	12.5	1.7	77.4	39.6	49.7	50.3
CAMDEN	0.7	0.9	5.7	5.9	6.1	6.8	4.6	26.7	29.9	12.9	1.4	78.0	41.7	49.6	50.4
CARTERET	1.7	2.2	4.9	4.9	5.1	5.4	4.8	24.0	32.7	16.2	1.9	81.7	45.4	49.3	50.7
CASWELL	1.8	2.4	5.6	5.6	6.2	6.0	5.7	28.0	29.1	12.1	1.6	78.8	40.5	51.1	48.9
CATAWBA	5.6	7.1	6.4	6.3	6.6	6.2	5.3	29.5	26.9	11.2	1.6	77.2	38.3	49.7	50.3
CHATHAM	9.6	12.7	6.1	6.4	5.8	5.5	4.4	28.3	28.7	12.5	2.4	78.2	40.9	49.4	50.6
CHEROKEE	1.2	1.6	5.5	5.7	5.1	4.6	4.6	23.0	31.2	17.7	2.6	80.9	46.0	49.2	50.8
CHOWAN	1.5	2.2	5.8	5.8	6.1	7.2	6.0	21.9	28.9	15.6	2.7	78.3	43.0	47.4	52.6
CLAY	0.8	1.0	4.2	4.2	4.8	4.3	4.2	20.6	36.1	18.1	3.4	84.2	49.6	48.9	51.1
CLEVELAND	1.5	1.9	6.6	6.5	6.9	6.8	5.4	27.6	26.4	11.8	1.9	75.9	38.5	48.6	51.4
COLUMBUS	2.3	3.1	6.8	6.6	6.3	5.8	6.1	26.8	27.2	12.6	1.7	76.7	39.3	48.4	51.6
CRAVEN	4.0	5.2	7.2	6.1	6.1	6.3	8.9	25.9	24.9	13.2	1.5	77.5	36.6	50.3	49.7
CUMBERLAND	6.9	8.7	8.2	7.1	6.7	7.8	10.0	31.0	20.7	7.8	0.8	73.9	30.8	50.8	49.2
CURRITUCK	1.4	1.8	6.2	5.8	6.0	6.8	5.7	25.7	31.2	11.3	1.4	77.9	41.4	49.8	50.2
DARE	2.2	2.9	5.0	5.5	5.5	5.4	4.2	27.2	32.3	13.5	1.3	80.5	43.3	50.5	49.5
DAVIDSON	3.2	4.3	6.5	6.4	6.5	5.9	5.1	28.9	27.6	11.6	1.6	77.0	39.5	49.2	50.8
DAVIE	3.5	4.5	6.3	6.4	6.7	5.8	4.8	26.8	28.9	12.6	1.7	77.0	40.7	49.6	50.4
DUPLIN	15.1	20.0	7.5	7.2	6.5	6.0	5.6	29.7	24.5	11.4	1.6	75.1	36.3	50.3	49.7
DURHAM	7.6	9.8	6.6	6.4	6.1	7.2	7.5	33.3	23.2	8.1	1.5	77.2	34.3	48.6	51.4
EDGECOMBE	2.8	3.7	6.6	6.4	7.2	6.9	6.3	25.9	27.2	11.6	1.8	75.5	38.2	46.8	53.2
FORSYTH	6.4	8.3	6.4	6.5	6.6	6.9	6.1	28.1	26.0	11.6	1.8	76.6	38.1	48.1	51.9
FRANKLIN	4.4	5.8	6.9	7.0	6.4	6.4	5.4	29.8	26.8	9.8	1.4	75.9	38.2	49.6	50.4
GASTON	3.0	3.8	6.6	6.4	6.6	6.4	5.4	29.0	26.6	11.3	1.6	76.5	38.2	48.7	51.3
GATES	0.8	0.9	6.0	5.4	6.9	7.6	6.1	25.4	28.0	12.7	1.9	77.1	41.2	49.2	50.8
GRAHAM	0.8	0.9	5.9	6.0	5.6	5.0	4.3	25.2	29.2	16.5	2.3	79.5	43.6	49.3	50.7
GRANVILLE	4.0	5.3	6.1	6.0	6.6	6.7	6.0	30.9	26.1	10.2	1.4	77.2	37.8	53.4	46.6
GREENE	8.0	10.8	7.0	7.2	6.1	5.8	6.5	29.7	25.5	10.5	1.7	76.1	36.5	51.8	48.2
GUILFORD	3.8	4.9	6.4	6.3	6.4	7.4	6.6	29.5	25.4	10.4	1.7	77.1	36.7	48.1	51.9
HALIFAX	1.0	1.3	6.4	5.8	7.0	6.8	6.4	25.7	27.2	12.8	2.0	76.6	39.5	48.1	51.9
HARNETT	5.9	7.7	7.7	7.1	7.0	7.0	6.4	31.5	22.9	9.2	1.2	74.2	34.4	49.7	50.3
HAYWOOD	1.4	1.8	5.3	5.2	5.4	5.3	4.2	24.9	30.1	17.0	2.5	80.8	44.8	48.5	51.5
HENDERSON	5.5	7.2	5.6	5.7	5.4	5.1	4.3	24.3	28.3	17.9	3.2	80.1	44.6	48.7	51.3
HERTFORD	1.6	2.0	5.3	4.9	6.1	6.9	7.9	25.5	28.4	13.0	2.1	79.7	40.5	49.0	51.0
HOKE	7.2	9.1	9.3	8.5	7.4	6.7	6.8	32.8	20.6	7.1	0.8	70.7	31.8	50.7	49.3
HYDE	2.2	2.3	4.5	4.3	6.0	4.7	7.1	27.1	29.9	13.7	2.7	82.0	42.4	53.1	46.9
IREDELL	3.4	4.5	6.9	6.7	7.2	6.4	4.9	28.8	26.6	11.0	1.5	75.2	38.4	49.5	50.5
JACKSON	1.7	2.2	4.8	5.0	4.6	9.2	10.2	23.9	27.8	12.7	1.8	82.6	38.5	49.1	50.9
JOHNSTON	7.7	10.3	7.9	7.8	6.9	5.7	4.9	33.2	23.9	8.6	1.1	74.2	35.8	49.9	50.1
JONES	2.7	2.7	5.9	5.9	6.5	6.9	5.3	24.6	29.3	13.6	2.0	77.0	41.8	48.5	51.5
LEE	11.7	15.3	7.0	6.5	6.4	6.4	6.4	27.9	26.3	11.5	1.6	76.3	37.9	49.6	50.4
LENOIR	3.2	4.2	6.5	6.3	6.7	6.3	5.8	25.3	27.5	13.7	1.9	76.5	40.1	47.8	52.2
LINCOLN	5.7	7.3	6.4	6.3	6.8	6.1	5.0	29.6	27.7	10.8	1.4	76.7	39.0	50.0	50.0
MCDOWELL	2.9	3.9	6.1	6.3	5.8	5.6	5.1	29.0	27.3	13.0	1.7	78.4	39.5	50.2	49.8
MACON	1.5	1.9	5.1	4.9	5.1	5.6	4.6	20.9	32.4	18.6	2.9	81.4	47.4	48.2	51.8
MADISON	1.4	1.8	5.6	6.0	5.6	7.0	5.6	25.7	28.3	13.8	2.4	79.4	41.0	49.5	50.5
MARTIN	2.1	2.7	6.3	6.1	6.6	6.2	5.8	24.3	28.7	13.9	2.1	77.2	41.2	46.7	53.3
MECKLENBURG	6.5	8.3	7.2	7.1	6.9	6.9	6.6	33.0	23.9	7.3	1.1	74.8	34.8	49.3	50.7
MITCHELL	2.0	2.6	5.0	5.2	5.3	5.5	4.8	25.4	29.9	16.5	2.4	81.0	44.1	49.3	50.7
MONTGOMERY	10.4	13.6	7.0	6.9	6.6	5.3	5.3	27.9	27.4	11.9	1.8	76.3	38.1	50.9	49.1
MOORE	4.0	5.3	5.6	5.4	5.7	5.8	5.0	22.8	26.6	19.6	3.5	79.7	44.8	48.1	51.9
NASH	3.4	4.5	6.4	6.4	6.8	6.7	5.8	27.6	27.4	11.2	1.7	76.5	38.7	48.6	51.4
NEW HANOVER	2.0	2.6	5.6	5.6	5.5	6.4	7.1	29.1	27.0	12.1	1.7	80.2	38.6	48.4	51.6
NORTHAMPTON	0.7	1.0	5.9	5.5	6.1	6.4	6.1	23.0	29.6	15.1	2.3	78.5	42.9	48.4	51.6
ONSLOW	7.2	9.4	8.6	6.5	5.4	9.1	18.1	29.4	16.2	6.2	0.5	76.3	26.0	57.1	42.9
ORANGE	4.5	5.8	4.8	5.0	5.9	9.7	11.6	29.0	24.9	7.9	1.3	80.0	33.2	48.0	52.0
PAMLICO	1.3	1.7	5.0	4.9	4.9	5.3	5.2	22.5	31.8	18.1	2.3	82.2	46.4	50.6	49.4
PASQUOTANK	1.2	1.5	6.3	5.8	5.9	7.9	8.3	26.0	25.9	11.8	2.2	77.8	37.9	48.9	51.1
PENDER	3.6	4.8	5.7	5.8	5.9	5.8	5.1	26.1	30.2	14.0	1.4	78.9	42.2	50.4	49.6
PERQUIMANS	0.6	0.7	5.4	5.2	5.2	6.6	6.3	22.1	30.2	16.5	2.5	80.0	44.4	48.0	52.0
PERSON	2.1	2.8	6.3	6.1	6.4	6.2	4.9	27.4	29.0	12.0	1.8	77.4	40.5	48.7	51.3
PITT	3.2	4.2	6.6	6.0	6.0	8.3	11.2	29.4	22.7	8.5	1.3	78.2	32.1	47.7	52.3
POLK	3.0	3.7	5.0	5.4	5.4	5.1	4.1	22.5	30.6	17.3	4.7	80.9	46.8	47.9	52.1
RANDOLPH	6.6	8.7	6.8	6.8	6.4	6.2	5.1	29.5	27.0	10.7	1.5	76.2	38.3	49.8	50.2
RICHMOND	2.8	3.6	6.8	6.5	6.8	7.2	6.7	26.7	25.3	12.2	1.8	76.0	37.3	49.8	50.2
NORTH CAROLINA	4.7	6.2	6.7	6.5	6.4	6.7	6.5	29.2	25.8	10.7	1.6	76.6	37.2	49.3	50.7
UNITED STATES	12.5	15.0	6.9	6.5	6.8	7.1	7.0	27.6	25.4	10.7	1.9	75.6	36.7	49.2	50.8

COUNTY	HOUSEHOLDS					FAMILIES			MEDIAN HOUSEHOLD INCOME			
	2000	2007	2012	% Annual Rate 2000-2007	2007 Average HH Size	2000	2007	% Annual Rate 2000-2007	2007	2012	2007 National Rank	2007 State Rank
ALAMANCE	51,584	57,274	61,387	1.5	2.45	35,526	38,424	1.1	48,368	55,980	788	22
ALEXANDER	13,137	14,598	15,505	1.5	2.49	9,744	10,593	1.2	45,999	51,324	1003	33
ALLEGHANY	4,593	4,976	5,215	1.1	2.22	3,169	3,344	0.7	35,857	41,092	2302	82
ANSON	9,204	9,469	9,569	0.4	2.53	6,667	6,700	0.1	35,939	40,708	2288	80
ASHE	10,411	11,740	12,556	1.7	2.24	7,422	8,169	1.3	34,858	39,377	2447	85
AVERY	6,532	7,093	7,411	1.1	2.27	4,546	4,808	0.8	36,738	41,500	2159	76
BEAUFORT	18,319	19,742	20,625	1.0	2.35	12,954	13,618	0.7	38,231	43,663	1971	66
BERTIE	7,743	7,943	7,999	0.4	2.44	5,424	5,426	0.0	30,164	33,888	2901	100
BLADEN	12,897	13,823	14,297	1.0	2.38	8,935	9,328	0.6	32,278	35,966	2736	96
BRUNSWICK	30,438	42,899	54,253	4.8	2.30	22,028	30,330	4.5	45,604	53,066	1042	35
BUNCOMBE	85,776	96,093	102,744	1.6	2.27	55,661	60,540	1.2	46,121	53,210	985	30
BURKE	34,528	35,643	36,356	0.4	2.47	24,331	24,502	0.1	42,974	48,581	1333	46
CABARRUS	49,519	60,727	69,288	2.9	2.59	36,526	43,809	2.5	58,493	67,446	296	4
CALDWELL	30,768	32,796	33,708	0.9	2.42	22,399	23,332	0.6	43,004	48,595	1331	45
CAMDEN	2,662	3,835	5,051	5.2	2.53	2,024	2,857	4.9	46,575	52,185	945	29
CARTERET	25,204	28,101	30,114	1.5	2.26	17,376	18,872	1.1	48,161	55,647	804	24
CASWELL	8,670	9,156	9,411	0.8	2.50	6,401	6,611	0.4	41,557	46,164	1509	55
CATAWBA	55,533	61,247	64,868	1.4	2.49	39,111	42,071	1.0	49,596	56,322	703	16
CHATHAM	19,741	24,263	27,702	2.9	2.44	13,855	16,605	2.5	53,182	61,689	491	9
CHEROKEE	10,336	11,963	13,135	2.0	2.25	7,373	8,330	1.7	34,094	38,695	2542	91
CHOWAN	5,580	5,973	6,223	0.9	2.42	4,007	4,187	0.6	38,092	43,528	1992	70
CLAY	3,847	4,686	5,318	2.8	2.17	2,727	3,241	2.4	38,192	43,603	1976	67
CLEVELAND	37,046	38,911	40,011	0.7	2.50	27,001	27,721	0.4	42,642	48,186	1376	48
COLUMBUS	21,308	22,059	22,388	0.5	2.44	15,048	15,196	0.1	32,455	36,769	2715	94
CRAVEN	34,582	37,457	39,084	1.1	2.41	25,060	26,512	0.8	45,177	52,128	1088	39
CUMBERLAND	107,358	113,879	116,524	0.8	2.54	77,656	80,474	0.5	47,694	56,163	843	25
CURRITUCK	6,902	9,706	12,386	4.8	2.57	5,203	7,165	4.5	49,541	56,395	708	17
DARE	12,690	15,864	18,352	3.1	2.30	8,451	10,270	2.7	53,014	61,631	500	10
DAVIDSON	58,156	63,215	66,670	1.2	2.49	42,535	45,197	0.8	46,714	52,797	934	28
DAVIE	13,750	16,289	18,156	2.4	2.47	10,261	11,897	2.1	49,524	56,726	709	18
DUPLIN	18,267	19,907	21,037	1.2	2.61	13,067	13,898	0.9	35,885	40,610	2297	81
DURHAM	89,015	103,282	111,921	2.1	2.37	54,045	60,669	1.6	55,861	66,113	367	5
EDGECOMBE	20,392	20,111	19,762	-0.2	2.63	14,812	14,295	-0.5	38,184	43,638	1978	68
FORSYTH	123,851	139,264	150,061	1.6	2.36	81,693	89,259	1.2	53,587	63,105	472	8
FRANKLIN	17,843	21,547	24,160	2.6	2.55	12,875	15,186	2.3	47,512	53,886	861	27
GASTON	73,936	78,291	80,968	0.8	2.50	53,327	55,156	0.5	49,483	57,071	711	19
GATES	3,901	4,367	4,706	1.6	2.61	2,933	3,216	1.3	42,219	46,994	1423	51
GRAHAM	3,354	3,616	3,755	1.0	2.26	2,411	2,538	0.7	31,512	35,088	2797	98
GRANVILLE	16,654	19,577	21,312	2.3	2.53	12,048	13,834	1.9	49,186	56,621	734	20
GREENE	6,696	7,304	7,653	1.2	2.61	4,958	5,292	0.9	37,840	42,683	2018	72
GUILFORD	168,667	185,748	197,359	1.3	2.39	109,819	117,435	0.9	54,979	64,663	407	6
HALIFAX	22,122	22,409	22,417	0.2	2.45	15,302	15,104	-0.2	32,288	36,773	2735	95
HARNETT	33,800	40,145	45,391	2.4	2.62	24,107	27,947	2.1	43,904	50,785	1221	42
HAYWOOD	23,100	25,367	26,672	1.3	2.25	16,043	17,171	0.9	41,633	47,555	1500	54
HENDERSON	37,414	43,703	48,465	2.2	2.31	26,357	30,024	1.8	47,634	55,090	851	26
HERTFORD	8,953	9,234	9,386	0.4	2.40	6,237	6,271	0.1	32,502	36,711	2705	93
HOKE	11,373	15,115	18,842	4.0	2.82	8,746	11,398	3.7	42,657	50,447	1374	47
HYDE	2,185	2,244	2,259	0.4	2.28	1,434	1,431	0.0	33,579	37,492	2597	92
IREDELL	47,360	58,487	67,222	3.0	2.53	34,658	41,842	2.6	52,663	61,292	513	11
JACKSON	13,191	15,432	16,765	2.2	2.23	8,586	9,756	1.8	41,187	47,597	1573	57
JOHNSTON	46,595	58,827	69,346	3.3	2.62	33,692	41,562	2.9	51,896	61,205	554	12
JONES	4,061	4,166	4,198	0.4	2.46	2,938	2,943	0.0	36,202	40,407	2242	79
LEE	18,466	21,228	23,478	1.9	2.61	13,361	15,007	1.6	48,307	54,918	791	23
LENOIR	23,862	24,170	24,034	0.2	2.37	16,182	15,952	-0.2	37,974	43,317	1999	71
LINCOLN	24,041	28,120	30,960	2.2	2.59	18,181	20,831	1.9	49,819	55,718	691	15
MCDOWELL	16,604	18,024	18,803	1.1	2.40	11,962	12,679	0.8	39,524	44,464	1774	61
MACON	12,828	14,577	15,843	1.8	2.25	8,908	9,861	1.4	39,340	44,901	1812	63
MADISON	8,000	8,802	9,306	1.3	2.28	5,595	6,003	1.0	37,284	42,117	2093	74
MARTIN	10,020	10,098	10,042	0.1	2.46	7,198	7,083	-0.2	34,730	39,297	2462	88
MECKLENBURG	273,416	341,708	395,670	3.1	2.46	175,063	212,258	2.7	65,741	78,572	165	2
MITCHELL	6,551	6,968	7,142	0.9	2.31	4,737	4,922	0.5	36,566	41,497	2184	78
MONTGOMERY	9,848	10,537	10,949	0.9	2.57	7,187	7,515	0.6	39,341	43,685	1811	62
MOORE	30,713	35,023	38,390	1.8	2.37	21,950	24,437	1.5	51,658	60,100	572	13
NASH	33,644	36,978	39,039	1.3	2.50	23,931	25,667	1.0	45,565	52,003	1046	37
NEW HANOVER	68,183	83,856	97,536	2.9	2.22	41,599	49,509	2.4	50,869	60,303	620	14
NORTHAMPTON	8,691	9,132	9,366	0.7	2.36	5,952	6,090	0.3	32,098	36,387	2749	97
ONSLOW	48,122	51,936	54,077	1.1	2.62	36,594	38,700	0.8	43,055	50,537	1322	44
ORANGE	45,863	50,931	52,854	1.5	2.24	26,126	28,813	1.4	54,157	63,851	440	7
PAMLICO	5,178	5,537	5,790	0.9	2.32	3,718	3,883	0.6	42,472	49,111	1402	50
PASQUOTANK	12,907	14,867	16,361	2.0	2.46	9,094	10,215	1.6	37,179	42,515	2106	75
PENDER	16,054	20,057	23,383	3.1	2.44	11,712	14,304	2.8	44,364	51,249	1174	41
PERQUIMANS	4,645	5,190	5,564	1.5	2.35	3,378	3,688	1.2	36,701	42,276	2167	77
PERSON	14,085	15,373	16,071	1.2	2.45	10,115	10,780	0.9	45,211	50,975	1082	38
PITT	52,539	61,404	67,845	2.2	2.36	32,237	36,480	1.7	41,872	48,473	1466	52
POLK	7,000	8,670	9,114	1.3	2.24	5,339	5,700	0.9	45,566	52,645	1045	36
RANDOLPH	50,659	54,425	57,169	1.0	2.56	37,348	39,239	0.7	46,080	52,138	992	31
RICHMOND	17,873	18,556	18,910	0.5	2.46	12,574	12,733	0.2	34,788	39,478	2458	87
NORTH CAROLINA				1.9	2.45			1.5	49,687	58,375		
UNITED STATES				1.2	2.59			1.0	53,154	62,503		

INCOME

COUNTY	2007 Per Capita Income	2007 HH Income Base	2007 HOUSEHOLD INCOME DISTRIBUTION (%)					2007 Home Value Base	2007 HOME VALUE DISTRIBUTION (%)					2007 Median Home Value
			Less than $25,000	$25,000 to $49,999	$50,000 to $99,999	$100,000 to $149,999	$150,000 or More		Less than $50,000	$50,000 to $89,999	$90,000 to $174,999	$175,000 to $399,999	$400,000 or More	
ALAMANCE	24,308	57,274	23.6	28.0	34.9	9.0	4.6	40,918	15.9	15.3	42.4	23.5	2.9	116,907
ALEXANDER	21,990	14,598	23.5	30.6	36.2	7.1	2.7	11,884	17.7	20.2	42.3	17.6	2.2	109,148
ALLEGHANY	21,879	4,976	34.8	31.1	25.0	5.5	3.5	3,972	10.6	15.6	41.9	23.4	8.5	126,811
ANSON	18,208	9,469	35.4	29.4	28.1	4.7	2.5	7,268	23.8	28.1	35.8	10.3	2.0	87,491
ASHE	20,526	11,740	36.7	31.4	25.2	4.1	2.5	9,591	14.2	15.1	40.6	25.3	4.7	129,240
AVERY	19,745	7,093	34.9	31.0	27.4	4.1	2.5	5,785	17.4	16.9	37.6	22.5	5.5	116,567
BEAUFORT	21,263	19,742	34.3	27.8	27.2	7.7	3.1	15,017	19.3	22.1	36.4	17.8	4.4	104,713
BERTIE	17,341	7,943	42.6	28.5	22.2	4.4	2.3	6,034	25.5	31.5	35.5	6.9	0.7	83,787
BLADEN	18,367	13,823	40.0	28.4	24.5	4.6	2.5	10,881	24.1	28.1	37.5	9.2	1.1	87,080
BRUNSWICK	25,605	42,899	25.6	29.0	32.9	7.7	4.8	35,537	8.8	10.2	28.8	38.5	13.7	181,389
BUNCOMBE	25,973	96,093	24.6	29.5	32.9	8.2	4.8	68,719	11.6	9.2	29.2	39.2	10.8	174,951
BURKE	21,250	35,643	26.4	31.6	33.1	6.0	2.9	26,892	18.5	21.1	46.1	12.9	1.4	102,266
CABARRUS	27,320	60,727	17.1	24.7	38.5	13.1	6.7	46,003	9.3	11.1	39.3	36.1	4.8	146,013
CALDWELL	21,257	32,796	27.3	30.7	32.9	6.9	2.2	24,985	15.8	22.5	45.8	14.3	1.6	105,694
CAMDEN	22,288	3,835	23.2	30.4	32.1	11.7	2.6	3,224	10.3	8.7	42.3	35.6	3.0	144,783
CARTERET	26,857	28,101	25.1	26.8	34.0	9.3	4.9	21,864	12.6	11.1	32.1	33.5	10.6	154,280
CASWELL	19,582	9,156	29.9	29.2	32.5	6.4	1.9	7,351	12.7	20.4	48.5	16.6	1.9	112,707
CATAWBA	25,094	61,247	20.6	29.8	35.5	9.2	4.9	45,155	10.0	15.1	46.5	24.2	4.2	123,562
CHATHAM	28,802	24,263	21.8	25.1	34.4	11.8	6.9	18,995	14.5	11.0	31.8	31.5	11.2	146,197
CHEROKEE	19,983	11,963	36.9	31.8	24.6	4.7	2.1	9,895	16.4	19.0	40.8	21.1	2.7	114,078
CHOWAN	19,591	5,973	33.0	30.5	28.1	6.8	1.5	4,370	15.4	19.9	39.7	20.9	4.1	113,957
CLAY	22,836	4,686	32.8	31.1	25.3	7.8	3.0	3,977	7.2	15.1	41.7	26.2	9.9	138,159
CLEVELAND	21,410	38,951	28.9	29.0	32.1	6.9	3.2	28,906	15.2	17.2	45.5	19.5	2.7	116,000
COLUMBUS	18,002	22,059	40.4	27.4	25.4	4.7	2.2	17,060	22.4	23.5	38.3	14.7	1.2	96,222
CRAVEN	23,096	37,457	26.0	28.8	33.4	8.1	3.8	25,566	12.9	13.9	42.6	26.3	4.3	128,550
CUMBERLAND	22,558	113,879	23.1	29.7	34.6	8.6	4.1	69,440	8.9	14.7	57.3	17.5	1.7	118,181
CURRITUCK	23,958	9,706	22.5	28.0	36.8	8.7	4.0	8,002	6.7	8.1	18.0	51.8	15.4	225,163
DARE	30,326	15,864	18.2	28.1	36.4	10.8	6.6	12,065	5.9	4.2	30.9	46.1	13.0	198,793
DAVIDSON	22,684	63,215	24.7	28.4	35.5	8.4	3.0	47,731	12.7	13.7	42.9	27.7	3.0	132,297
DAVIE	26,839	16,289	21.7	28.8	32.4	10.3	6.8	13,648	16.1	14.1	35.7	27.3	6.8	128,988
DUPLIN	17,955	19,907	35.6	30.3	26.6	4.7	2.7	15,171	25.3	19.9	41.2	12.6	1.0	97,521
DURHAM	30,245	103,282	20.5	24.2	34.1	12.3	8.8	57,491	2.4	6.0	37.8	47.4	6.5	183,277
EDGECOMBE	18,057	20,111	34.2	29.9	27.8	5.7	2.4	13,235	24.6	33.0	36.4	5.4	0.6	80,395
FORSYTH	30,035	139,264	20.8	25.6	34.1	11.4	8.1	92,933	6.9	12.8	45.7	30.0	4.6	140,529
FRANKLIN	21,686	21,547	25.7	26.8	35.8	9.0	2.7	17,012	18.9	18.0	40.3	20.8	2.0	113,403
GASTON	24,112	78,291	23.3	27.2	35.5	9.7	4.2	54,987	9.8	19.1	48.2	20.7	2.2	117,938
GATES	19,495	4,367	31.3	27.5	31.5	7.3	2.3	3,613	22.2	21.5	39.1	15.8	1.4	100,388
GRAHAM	17,831	3,616	42.4	29.0	22.5	4.5	1.6	3,011	21.9	23.9	36.7	15.4	2.1	97,893
GRANVILLE	22,353	19,577	25.4	25.3	35.9	9.6	3.8	14,944	12.7	14.5	42.0	27.5	3.3	132,152
GREENE	17,296	7,304	34.1	30.5	28.5	5.2	1.8	5,555	23.2	27.5	41.7	6.7	0.9	89,198
GUILFORD	30,608	185,748	19.5	25.4	34.7	11.6	8.9	118,890	5.1	13.5	45.6	30.3	5.5	138,336
HALIFAX	17,650	22,409	41.1	27.4	24.0	5.4	2.1	15,379	22.6	26.1	38.8	10.7	1.8	91,885
HARNETT	20,420	40,145	28.6	27.8	33.0	7.4	3.1	28,825	17.3	14.3	43.7	22.0	2.7	121,199
HAYWOOD	23,164	25,367	29.0	30.6	31.0	6.8	2.6	19,880	12.3	11.4	33.1	35.3	7.9	157,192
HENDERSON	26,575	43,703	22.6	30.1	33.7	8.6	5.0	34,798	9.8	7.7	24.4	45.9	12.3	199,712
HERTFORD	18,579	9,234	39.5	30.1	22.2	5.4	2.8	6,569	26.4	28.0	36.3	8.7	0.7	84,076
HOKE	18,030	15,115	27.4	32.2	31.5	6.3	2.5	11,531	19.3	20.1	46.9	12.3	1.5	105,315
HYDE	17,473	2,244	36.6	34.8	22.6	4.5	1.4	1,779	26.4	24.7	30.4	15.8	2.7	88,010
IREDELL	26,399	58,487	20.2	26.7	36.7	10.3	6.0	44,762	7.8	9.7	38.7	33.5	10.4	155,742
JACKSON	22,947	15,432	30.4	29.6	29.3	6.7	4.0	11,346	13.3	16.0	34.1	27.6	9.0	135,969
JOHNSTON	23,373	58,827	22.9	25.3	37.2	10.5	4.1	44,092	13.9	13.4	45.2	25.2	2.2	130,964
JONES	19,478	4,166	35.1	32.3	25.5	4.5	2.6	3,362	22.2	22.6	40.3	12.8	2.1	98,627
LEE	23,471	21,228	24.4	27.3	32.7	11.3	4.3	15,470	11.4	13.5	43.0	28.5	3.6	135,625
LENOIR	20,965	24,170	33.8	28.8	28.2	6.2	3.0	16,559	19.4	22.2	41.7	14.8	1.8	103,754
LINCOLN	23,106	28,120	21.1	29.1	36.7	9.0	4.0	22,386	11.6	14.0	41.2	27.5	5.7	134,440
MCDOWELL	19,928	18,024	29.8	33.4	29.5	5.1	2.3	14,102	20.1	23.3	42.0	13.0	1.6	100,441
MACON	22,800	14,577	31.5	31.6	27.6	6.1	3.1	11,942	7.6	11.6	41.1	31.8	8.0	144,305
MADISON	20,049	8,802	34.5	30.3	27.9	5.2	2.1	6,848	17.6	15.0	30.3	29.2	8.0	139,892
MARTIN	18,593	10,098	36.9	28.5	26.5	5.9	2.2	7,413	21.1	25.3	42.3	10.1	1.1	94,485
MECKLENBURG	36,594	341,708	14.0	22.2	35.8	14.8	13.2	217,126	2.1	5.5	33.2	45.9	13.2	196,635
MITCHELL	19,882	6,968	33.8	31.7	27.6	4.6	2.3	5,686	18.0	21.4	41.6	17.8	1.4	105,527
MONTGOMERY	20,323	10,537	33.0	28.9	29.0	5.6	3.6	8,215	19.0	22.1	38.8	15.9	4.2	104,034
MOORE	28,989	35,023	21.5	26.7	34.8	9.5	7.5	27,796	12.6	11.5	29.5	35.3	11.0	160,056
NASH	23,427	36,978	27.9	26.5	31.6	9.3	4.7	25,700	19.0	19.1	42.3	16.7	2.9	107,702
NEW HANOVER	30,167	83,856	23.5	25.6	33.1	10.9	6.9	55,429	5.0	3.2	16.6	55.2	20.1	240,202
NORTHAMPTON	18,408	9,132	41.4	26.5	24.3	5.5	2.3	7,107	25.9	30.2	32.2	9.5	2.2	81,740
ONSLOW	18,845	51,936	24.7	33.5	32.9	6.4	2.4	31,045	8.8	8.2	27.5	47.9	7.6	186,113
ORANGE	35,229	50,931	23.3	23.1	28.7	12.4	12.6	30,891	9.2	5.2	24.2	41.8	19.6	216,958
PAMLICO	23,228	5,537	29.4	27.6	31.9	7.7	3.3	4,588	19.2	18.9	36.7	19.4	5.9	110,884
PASQUOTANK	19,199	14,867	35.0	28.0	27.7	6.6	2.7	10,011	13.2	16.2	48.4	19.8	2.4	119,250
PENDER	22,868	20,057	28.6	27.3	32.1	8.4	3.6	16,675	11.6	10.2	32.1	34.7	11.3	165,158
PERQUIMANS	19,381	5,190	35.5	30.7	26.2	6.1	1.5	4,117	18.0	20.8	38.7	18.0	4.4	106,905
PERSON	22,165	15,373	27.1	28.3	35.2	7.0	2.5	11,649	8.6	16.4	48.7	23.4	2.8	122,414
PITT	23,285	61,404	32.1	25.7	29.1	8.6	4.5	36,397	15.2	20.7	43.3	18.4	2.3	108,802
POLK	25,704	8,679	23.5	31.2	33.2	7.9	4.2	6,906	10.6	13.5	34.1	32.5	9.4	146,455
RANDOLPH	21,862	54,425	23.7	30.6	35.3	7.4	2.9	42,231	16.3	18.7	46.0	17.3	1.6	110,358
RICHMOND	18,173	18,556	37.1	29.4	26.2	5.2	2.1	13,557	24.7	29.4	36.4	8.7	1.0	84,423
NORTH CAROLINA	26,409		23.6	26.7	33.2	10.0	6.5		11.3	13.3	38.1	30.6	6.7	139,312
UNITED STATES	27,916		21.9	25.0	32.3	12.3	8.4		7.9	10.5	27.1	35.6	19.0	192,285

COUNTY	FINANCIAL SERVICES				THE HOME						ENTERTAINMENT						PERSONAL			
					Home Improvements		Furnishings													
	Auto Loan	Home Loan	Invest-ments	Retire-ment Plans	Home Repair	Lawn & Garden	Comput-ers & Hard-ware	Major Appli-ances	TV, Radio, Sound Equip-ment	Furni-ture	Dine out/ Carry out	Sports Equip-ment	Fees & Tickets	Toys & Games	Travel	Cable TV	Apparel & Services	Auto Repairs	Health Insur-ance	Pets & Supplies
ALAMANCE	89	80	78	81	81	88	81	85	84	80	83	76	79	85	81	86	74	83	89	87
ALEXANDER	95	71	45	67	75	98	69	86	76	69	76	76	60	81	68	81	65	79	90	93
ALLEGHANY	82	59	38	57	67	91	61	79	68	58	67	68	52	71	61	73	57	71	85	84
ANSON	81	55	34	53	60	83	58	73	68	56	66	65	49	70	57	73	56	68	81	79
ASHE	79	56	35	54	64	86	57	74	64	55	63	64	48	67	57	69	54	67	79	80
AVERY	80	57	33	55	66	90	58	77	63	56	64	67	48	67	58	69	54	69	81	83
BEAUFORT	79	64	53	62	68	83	64	75	70	63	69	66	59	71	65	74	60	71	81	79
BERTIE	74	49	26	46	55	77	51	67	60	49	59	60	42	63	50	66	50	62	74	74
BLADEN	76	53	31	50	58	80	54	69	62	52	61	61	45	64	53	67	52	63	75	75
BRUNSWICK	90	80	68	77	83	98	76	89	80	76	79	77	73	79	79	84	69	85	94	91
BUNCOMBE	87	79	80	80	80	88	81	84	84	79	83	75	78	83	81	86	73	83	89	86
BURKE	88	67	50	65	71	91	68	81	74	66	74	72	60	78	67	79	63	76	87	86
CABARRUS	103	100	98	101	97	100	97	99	99	98	98	90	97	101	97	99	87	98	100	100
CALDWELL	86	65	50	63	70	88	66	78	72	65	72	69	59	76	65	77	62	73	84	84
CAMDEN	91	74	55	72	82	101	71	88	76	71	76	77	66	80	73	81	66	80	91	93
CARTERET	94	80	69	79	86	103	79	93	84	78	83	81	74	84	82	88	72	88	99	96
CASWELL	88	61	35	58	67	92	61	79	69	60	69	70	52	74	60	75	59	72	84	86
CATAWBA	97	83	73	83	85	98	83	91	87	82	87	82	79	90	83	90	77	88	95	95
CHATHAM	106	97	89	95	100	112	92	103	96	93	96	92	90	98	95	100	85	98	107	107
CHEROKEE	75	55	36	53	63	84	56	73	62	54	62	63	48	64	57	67	52	66	78	77
CHOWAN	75	57	47	56	63	80	62	72	68	58	66	63	54	68	61	72	57	68	79	76
CLAY	79	63	46	62	72	92	64	81	68	61	67	69	56	68	66	72	57	73	85	84
CLEVELAND	87	69	56	68	73	90	69	80	76	68	75	71	63	79	69	80	65	76	87	85
COLUMBUS	75	53	34	51	58	79	55	69	62	53	61	61	46	64	54	67	53	64	75	75
CRAVEN	85	74	71	74	75	84	76	80	79	75	79	72	73	80	76	81	69	79	85	82
CUMBERLAND	87	78	74	80	72	76	83	79	83	81	83	73	79	84	78	82	74	82	80	80
CURRITUCK	98	84	66	82	87	103	79	93	84	80	84	82	75	86	81	88	73	88	96	98
DARE	108	93	74	91	101	122	91	109	94	89	94	95	84	95	94	99	82	101	112	113
DAVIDSON	88	75	67	75	78	90	74	82	79	74	78	73	70	82	74	82	69	78	87	86
DAVIE	106	89	74	87	93	111	85	100	91	86	91	88	81	95	87	96	79	93	105	105
DUPLIN	82	58	35	55	62	84	58	73	66	57	66	65	50	70	57	71	56	68	79	80
DURHAM	102	94	98	100	89	90	105	94	103	102	103	89	101	103	99	101	94	101	94	96
EDGECOMBE	75	59	51	59	61	75	61	68	68	61	67	60	56	69	60	72	58	67	75	73
FORSYTH	99	97	103	100	95	95	100	96	100	99	100	88	100	100	98	100	90	99	98	97
FRANKLIN	92	75	52	71	75	92	71	84	77	72	77	76	65	80	71	81	66	79	87	89
GASTON	89	80	80	81	81	88	81	84	85	81	84	75	79	87	81	87	75	83	90	87
GATES	88	64	37	60	69	93	63	81	70	62	70	72	54	74	62	76	60	74	86	88
GRAHAM	71	49	25	46	55	77	49	66	56	48	56	58	40	59	49	61	47	59	70	72
GRANVILLE	93	82	69	80	81	93	77	86	82	79	82	77	74	85	78	85	72	83	90	90
GREENE	81	56	32	52	60	83	56	72	64	55	64	64	47	68	55	69	54	66	77	79
GUILFORD	103	100	105	104	96	97	104	99	104	104	104	91	103	105	101	103	94	102	100	100
HALIFAX	71	52	39	51	56	72	54	65	63	53	61	57	48	63	54	67	53	62	73	69
HARNETT	85	71	59	70	70	81	72	78	75	71	75	70	67	77	70	77	65	76	81	81
HAYWOOD	84	66	51	64	73	92	67	82	72	64	71	71	60	74	68	77	61	75	87	86
HENDERSON	94	81	73	79	86	102	80	92	85	79	84	80	76	85	83	90	73	88	100	95
HERTFORD	74	54	42	53	58	75	58	68	66	56	64	61	51	66	57	70	56	65	76	73
HOKE	80	72	58	69	68	75	68	74	71	69	70	67	65	73	67	72	62	72	74	76
HYDE	72	48	24	45	55	78	50	66	57	48	57	59	40	60	49	63	48	60	72	73
IREDELL	101	93	86	93	93	101	90	96	92	91	92	86	88	95	90	94	82	93	98	99
JACKSON	83	66	56	66	72	89	72	81	74	67	74	71	63	74	71	77	64	77	85	84
JOHNSTON	96	86	71	84	83	92	82	89	85	83	84	81	78	88	81	86	74	86	90	91
JONES	85	58	30	54	65	91	58	77	66	57	66	68	48	70	57	72	56	70	83	85
LEE	90	83	81	83	82	89	82	86	86	83	85	76	81	87	82	88	76	85	90	87
LENOIR	78	63	55	62	65	78	65	72	71	64	70	63	60	71	64	75	61	70	79	76
LINCOLN	98	80	62	78	83	100	77	90	83	77	82	80	71	86	77	87	72	85	94	96
MCDOWELL	83	59	38	56	64	86	60	75	68	58	67	66	51	72	59	73	57	69	82	81
MACON	80	66	52	65	73	92	67	82	70	64	69	70	60	70	69	74	60	75	86	84
MADISON	78	58	40	55	63	83	58	72	64	57	64	64	51	67	58	69	55	67	78	78
MARTIN	77	56	37	53	60	80	57	70	65	56	64	63	49	67	56	70	55	66	77	76
MECKLENBURG	126	125	126	131	117	113	130	119	125	130	126	113	128	127	124	122	115	125	114	120
MITCHELL	80	56	33	53	63	86	57	74	64	55	64	65	48	67	56	69	54	67	80	80
MONTGOMERY	91	65	41	62	72	97	65	83	73	64	73	74	56	77	65	78	62	76	89	91
MOORE	103	94	90	93	96	110	90	101	96	91	95	87	89	93	94	100	83	97	109	103
NASH	91	78	69	78	80	92	77	85	82	78	82	76	74	84	77	85	72	82	89	89
NEW HANOVER	94	91	96	93	90	92	95	92	94	93	94	84	93	93	94	94	84	94	93	93
NORTHAMPTON	76	51	29	48	57	79	53	69	62	52	61	61	44	64	53	68	52	64	76	75
ONSLOW	79	68	61	69	63	68	74	71	74	71	74	67	69	76	69	73	65	74	71	72
ORANGE	118	107	106	112	104	107	121	110	117	115	118	106	114	117	113	114	106	116	108	113
PAMLICO	90	70	50	67	77	100	68	87	75	68	75	75	61	76	71	81	64	80	93	92
PASQUOTANK	74	61	56	61	62	73	64	69	68	62	67	60	59	69	63	71	59	68	75	72
PENDER	90	74	57	72	78	96	72	86	77	72	77	76	66	78	74	81	66	81	91	91
PERQUIMANS	71	58	49	56	62	78	58	70	64	57	62	60	53	62	60	68	54	66	77	72
PERSON	87	70	58	69	73	88	71	81	76	69	75	72	65	78	70	80	65	77	86	85
PITT	84	68	62	71	65	73	80	75	80	75	80	70	72	80	73	79	71	79	76	78
POLK	00	76	61	73	82	101	73	80	70	73	70	76	60	78	77	85	68	83	06	92
RANDOLPH	91	73	58	71	76	93	72	83	78	71	78	74	66	82	71	82	68	79	88	89
RICHMOND	73	56	44	54	59	74	57	66	65	56	63	59	52	66	57	69	55	64	73	71
NORTH CAROLINA	99	87	79	87	87	97	89	93	91	88	91	84	84	93	87	93	81	92	96	96
UNITED STATES	100	100	100	100	100	100	100	100	100	100	100	100	100	100	100	100	100	100	100	100

POPULATION CHANGE

COUNTY	FIPS Code	CBSA Code	DMA Code	POPULATION			2000-2007 ANNUAL RATE		RACE (%)					
									White		Black		Asian/Pacific	
				2000	2007	2012	% Rate	State Rank	2000	2007	2000	2007	2000	2007
ROBESON	155	31300	570	123,339	128,885	131,737	0.6	69	32.8	31.0	25.1	24.5	0.4	0.5
ROCKINGHAM	157	24660	518	91,928	93,208	93,971	0.2	90	77.3	75.9	19.6	20.0	0.3	0.4
ROWAN	159	41580	517	130,340	136,558	140,092	0.6	69	80.0	78.3	15.8	16.0	0.9	1.2
RUTHERFORD	161	22580	567	62,899	65,027	66,255	0.5	77	86.8	85.9	11.2	11.6	0.4	0.5
SAMPSON	163	00000	560	60,161	64,426	67,061	0.9	53	59.8	56.9	29.9	29.5	0.4	0.5
SCOTLAND	165	29900	570	35,998	37,540	37,902	0.6	69	51.5	49.9	37.3	37.7	0.5	0.7
STANLY	167	10620	517	58,100	60,470	61,823	0.6	69	84.7	83.2	11.5	11.7	1.8	2.4
STOKES	169	49180	518	44,711	47,267	48,784	0.8	58	93.4	92.6	4.7	4.8	0.2	0.3
SURRY	171	34340	518	71,219	73,922	75,735	0.5	77	90.4	88.3	4.2	4.2	0.6	0.8
SWAIN	173	00000	567	12,968	13,902	14,564	1.0	48	66.3	63.9	1.7	1.7	0.2	0.2
TRANSYLVANIA	175	14820	567	29,334	30,960	32,170	0.7	62	93.7	93.0	4.2	4.4	0.4	0.5
TYRRELL	177	00000	545	4,149	4,268	4,218	0.4	83	56.5	54.7	39.4	39.7	0.7	1.0
UNION	179	16740	517	123,677	178,366	235,046	5.2	1	82.8	81.0	12.5	12.7	0.6	0.8
VANCE	181	25780	560	42,954	43,762	44,102	0.3	87	48.2	46.8	48.3	48.5	0.4	0.5
WAKE	183	39580	560	627,846	811,478	975,327	3.6	6	72.4	69.9	19.7	19.7	3.4	4.5
WARREN	185	00000	560	19,972	20,716	21,242	0.5	77	38.9	37.7	54.5	54.9	0.2	0.2
WASHINGTON	187	00000	545	13,723	13,344	13,085	-0.4	100	48.3	46.8	48.9	49.4	0.4	0.5
WATAUGA	189	14380	517	42,695	45,576	46,157	0.9	53	96.5	93.7	1.6	3.4	0.6	0.8
WAYNE	191	24140	560	113,329	116,891	119,812	0.4	83	61.3	59.2	33.0	33.1	1.0	1.3
WILKES	193	35900	518	65,632	69,182	71,759	0.7	62	93.0	91.8	4.2	4.3	0.4	0.5
WILSON	195	48980	560	73,814	78,746	81,964	0.9	53	55.8	54.0	39.3	39.4	0.4	0.6
YADKIN	197	49180	518	36,348	38,535	39,831	0.8	58	92.5	90.9	3.4	3.5	0.2	0.3
YANCEY	199	00000	567	17,774	18,853	19,632	0.8	58	98.0	97.6	0.6	0.6	0.1	0.2
NORTH CAROLINA							1.7		72.1	70.4	21.6	21.5	1.5	2.0
UNITED STATES							1.2		75.1	72.7	12.3	12.6	3.8	4.5

COUNTY	% HISPANIC ORIGIN		2007 AGE DISTRIBUTION (%)										MEDIAN AGE	% 2007 Males	% 2007 Females
	2000	2007	0-4	5-9	10-14	15-19	20-24	25-44	45-64	65-84	85+	18+	2007		
ROBESON	4.9	6.1	8.1	7.4	7.2	7.1	7.0	28.9	23.9	9.1	1.2	73.2	33.6	49.1	50.9
ROCKINGHAM	3.1	4.1	6.1	6.1	6.2	5.9	5.0	27.4	28.3	13.1	2.0	78.0	40.6	48.6	51.4
ROWAN	4.1	5.4	6.7	6.4	6.4	6.6	6.0	28.3	26.0	11.5	2.1	76.6	38.2	49.6	50.4
RUTHERFORD	1.8	2.3	6.2	6.1	6.7	5.8	5.0	27.5	26.8	13.6	2.3	77.4	40.0	48.8	51.2
SAMPSON	10.8	14.2	7.4	7.3	6.6	5.8	5.4	29.8	24.8	11.2	1.7	75.1	36.6	50.1	49.9
SCOTLAND	1.2	1.5	7.1	6.7	7.2	7.9	7.1	25.6	25.9	10.6	2.0	74.6	36.3	47.3	52.7
STANLY	2.1	2.8	6.4	6.1	6.5	6.8	5.6	27.9	26.4	12.3	2.0	77.0	39.1	49.9	50.1
STOKES	1.9	2.5	6.4	6.6	6.4	5.9	4.9	28.6	28.3	11.3	1.6	76.9	39.8	49.4	50.6
SURRY	6.5	8.7	6.3	6.3	6.4	5.8	5.0	28.1	26.5	13.4	2.2	77.4	39.8	49.4	50.6
SWAIN	1.5	1.8	6.1	6.2	6.5	6.5	5.4	25.1	28.8	13.6	2.0	77.5	41.0	49.2	50.8
TRANSYLVANIA	1.0	1.3	4.9	4.9	4.9	6.3	5.0	21.4	29.9	19.6	3.0	81.7	46.7	48.2	51.8
TYRRELL	3.6	4.9	5.0	4.6	4.9	5.8	7.8	29.7	27.0	13.0	2.0	81.7	40.2	55.1	44.9
UNION	6.2	8.0	8.3	8.3	7.5	6.6	5.0	31.0	24.3	7.9	0.9	71.8	35.5	50.1	49.9
VANCE	4.6	5.8	7.0	6.4	7.7	7.5	6.0	27.2	25.4	11.2	1.6	74.4	36.6	47.9	52.1
WAKE	5.4	7.0	7.2	7.1	7.0	7.0	6.9	33.0	24.3	6.6	0.9	74.6	34.6	49.6	50.4
WARREN	1.6	2.0	5.4	5.2	5.6	6.3	6.0	24.3	29.4	15.6	2.2	79.9	43.2	49.6	50.4
WASHINGTON	2.3	3.1	6.6	6.3	6.3	5.8	6.3	23.1	29.8	13.5	2.2	77.1	41.0	47.7	52.3
WATAUGA	1.5	2.1	4.3	4.1	4.5	8.8	13.5	25.8	26.8	10.6	1.5	83.3	36.1	50.2	49.8
WAYNE	4.9	6.6	7.1	6.5	6.5	6.7	7.0	28.8	24.8	11.2	1.3	75.9	36.3	49.5	50.5
WILKES	3.4	4.6	6.1	6.4	5.9	5.2	4.8	28.5	28.2	13.0	1.8	78.3	40.6	49.7	50.3
WILSON	6.0	7.9	6.7	6.7	6.7	6.4	6.0	26.6	27.1	12.1	1.6	76.2	38.4	48.2	51.8
YADKIN	6.5	8.5	6.7	6.8	6.6	5.8	4.5	28.4	26.9	12.5	1.8	76.3	39.6	49.7	50.3
YANCEY	2.7	3.3	5.5	5.7	5.6	5.0	4.4	25.4	30.6	15.5	2.5	80.2	43.9	49.5	50.5
NORTH CAROLINA	4.7	6.2	6.7	6.5	6.4	6.7	6.5	29.2	25.8	10.7	1.6	76.6	37.2	49.3	50.7
UNITED STATES	12.5	15.0	6.9	6.5	6.8	7.1	7.0	27.6	25.4	10.7	1.9	75.6	36.7	49.2	50.8

COUNTY	HOUSEHOLDS					FAMILIES			MEDIAN HOUSEHOLD INCOME			
	2000	2007	2012	% Annual Rate 2000-2007	2007 Average HH Size	2000	2007	% Annual Rate 2000-2007	2007	2012	2007 National Rank	2007 State Rank
ROBESON	43,677	46,147	47,466	0.8	2.71	32,015	33,068	0.4	34,692	39,909	2469	89
ROCKINGHAM	36,989	37,724	38,195	0.3	2.44	26,194	26,067	-0.1	41,696	47,594	1494	53
ROWAN	49,940	52,875	54,357	0.8	2.49	35,495	36,678	0.5	45,881	52,254	1017	34
RUTHERFORD	25,191	26,589	27,305	0.7	2.39	17,938	18,480	0.4	37,456	42,268	2071	73
SAMPSON	22,273	24,147	25,222	1.1	2.61	16,222	17,186	0.8	38,439	43,250	1941	64
SCOTLAND	13,399	13,951	14,238	0.6	2.55	9,673	9,837	0.2	38,153	43,616	1983	69
STANLY	22,223	23,362	23,980	0.7	2.50	16,156	16,598	0.4	44,575	50,403	1152	40
STOKES	17,579	18,976	19,740	1.1	2.46	13,035	13,768	0.8	46,059	51,772	995	32
SURRY	28,408	29,508	30,290	0.5	2.46	20,484	20,783	0.2	40,319	45,348	1686	60
SWAIN	5,137	5,640	5,967	1.3	2.39	3,631	3,887	0.9	34,848	39,655	2449	86
TRANSYLVANIA	12,320	13,434	14,140	1.2	2.23	8,666	9,213	0.8	48,589	55,850	774	21
TYRRELL	1,537	1,568	1,569	0.3	2.33	1,056	1,048	-0.1	30,707	33,947	2863	99
UNION	43,390	62,873	83,098	5.2	2.81	34,280	48,801	5.0	64,184	76,387	177	3
VANCE	16,199	16,825	17,070	0.5	2.55	11,643	11,810	0.2	38,269	43,663	1965	65
WAKE	242,040	314,505	378,717	3.7	2.52	158,765	200,403	3.3	72,665	86,553	105	1
WARREN	7,708	8,274	8,613	1.0	2.40	5,448	5,704	0.6	34,315	38,868	2513	90
WASHINGTON	5,367	5,392	5,358	0.1	2.44	3,906	3,835	-0.3	35,084	39,611	2419	84
WATAUGA	16,540	18,267	18,707	1.4	2.20	9,410	10,021	0.9	40,571	46,240	1655	59
WAYNE	42,612	45,170	46,688	0.8	2.49	30,244	31,282	0.5	42,495	49,206	1398	49
WILKES	26,650	28,424	29,683	0.9	2.40	19,311	20,123	0.6	40,943	46,032	1609	58
WILSON	28,613	30,694	32,049	1.0	2.51	19,782	20,672	0.6	41,326	47,159	1547	56
YADKIN	14,505	15,537	16,099	1.0	2.45	10,593	11,090	0.6	43,544	48,599	1270	43
YANCEY	7,472	8,135	8,558	1.2	2.30	5,373	5,713	0.8	35,734	40,504	2327	83
NORTH CAROLINA				1.9	2.45			1.5	49,687	58,375		
UNITED STATES				1.2	2.59			1.0	53,154	62,503		

COUNTY	2007 Per Capita Income	2007 HH Income Base	2007 HOUSEHOLD INCOME DISTRIBUTION (%)					2007 Home Value Base	2007 HOME VALUE DISTRIBUTION (%)					2007 Median Home Value
			Less than $25,000	$25,000 to $49,999	$50,000 to $99,999	$100,000 to $149,999	$150,000 or More		Less than $50,000	$50,000 to $89,999	$90,000 to $174,999	$175,000 to $399,999	$400,000 or More	
ROBESON	16,507	46,147	37.7	28.7	26.1	5.4	2.1	34,052	28.2	26.8	35.6	8.3	1.1	82,168
ROCKINGHAM	21,291	37,724	30.2	29.2	30.5	7.3	2.8	28,222	16.3	23.6	43.7	15.1	1.3	104,312
ROWAN	22,214	52,875	25.3	29.1	33.8	8.7	3.1	39,446	11.5	14.7	46.0	24.3	3.4	127,726
RUTHERFORD	19,932	26,589	33.2	30.6	28.3	5.5	2.4	20,145	17.8	22.4	40.2	16.9	2.6	105,603
SAMPSON	18,641	24,147	34.1	29.2	28.3	5.3	3.2	18,088	18.9	22.2	43.3	14.2	1.4	102,818
SCOTLAND	19,876	13,951	34.7	25.2	29.7	6.9	3.5	9,840	18.9	26.1	38.5	14.9	1.5	96,005
STANLY	21,798	23,362	27.6	28.2	33.8	7.3	3.2	18,088	11.1	16.5	44.8	24.2	3.5	125,729
STOKES	22,078	18,976	24.7	29.4	35.7	7.8	2.4	15,690	18.9	17.0	46.0	16.6	1.4	108,742
SURRY	21,018	29,508	30.6	31.6	28.4	6.2	3.2	22,809	16.2	18.0	41.2	21.7	2.9	116,323
SWAIN	18,793	5,640	36.0	31.0	25.8	5.1	2.2	4,405	16.8	19.3	37.5	20.5	5.9	117,084
TRANSYLVANIA	26,218	13,434	24.0	27.4	35.0	9.7	3.9	10,761	11.3	12.2	33.0	35.2	8.4	155,849
TYRRELL	17,752	1,568	42.1	29.0	21.9	4.8	2.2	1,194	28.9	30.6	30.6	8.5	1.5	77,636
UNION	28,179	62,873	14.3	21.6	40.8	14.1	9.2	51,210	5.8	6.4	35.3	41.2	11.4	181,968
VANCE	19,775	16,825	33.7	30.0	26.9	6.3	3.1	11,404	19.0	20.1	40.4	17.4	3.1	106,522
WAKE	36,635	314,502	12.3	20.2	35.3	16.7	15.4	211,565	4.8	3.2	25.9	53.2	12.9	215,260
WARREN	18,674	8,274	38.0	29.9	24.8	4.5	2.9	6,490	22.8	24.2	32.9	16.1	4.0	96,080
WASHINGTON	18,895	5,392	38.7	28.0	24.3	6.1	2.9	4,024	19.6	25.4	43.3	10.3	1.4	97,256
WATAUGA	22,924	18,267	31.8	28.2	29.0	7.7	3.3	11,686	9.1	8.7	28.8	40.6	12.8	187,373
WAYNE	21,395	45,170	27.4	30.9	31.1	7.2	3.4	30,278	18.6	19.7	45.0	15.1	1.6	106,582
WILKES	21,389	28,424	30.2	31.2	29.8	5.8	3.1	22,454	16.9	16.3	40.2	23.0	3.6	118,827
WILSON	21,427	30,694	32.2	26.8	29.8	7.3	3.9	19,378	12.0	16.3	48.4	20.6	2.7	119,799
YADKIN	22,069	15,537	27.1	29.6	32.8	7.7	2.9	12,598	19.3	19.0	41.9	18.1	1.8	106,145
YANCEY	19,915	8,135	34.4	32.3	27.0	4.3	2.0	6,597	15.5	18.8	38.4	24.8	2.6	118,353
NORTH CAROLINA	26,409		23.6	26.7	33.2	10.0	6.5		11.3	13.3	38.1	30.6	6.7	139,312
UNITED STATES	27,916		21.9	25.0	32.3	12.3	8.4		7.9	10.5	27.1	35.6	19.0	192,285

COUNTY	FINANCIAL SERVICES				THE HOME						ENTERTAINMENT						PERSONAL			
					Home Improvements		Furnishings													
	Auto Loan	Home Loan	Invest-ments	Retire-ment Plans	Home Repair	Lawn & Garden	Comput-ers & Hard-ware	Major Appli-ances	TV, Radio, Sound Equip-ment	Furni-ture	Dine out/ Carry out	Sports Equip-ment	Fees & Tickets	Toys & Games	Travel	Cable TV	Apparel & Services	Auto Repairs	Health Insur-ance	Pets & Supplies
ROBESON	72	57	44	55	58	71	58	66	64	57	63	59	53	65	57	67	55	64	70	70
ROCKINGHAM	83	66	56	64	69	85	67	77	74	66	73	67	61	76	67	78	63	73	84	81
ROWAN	87	73	66	73	75	87	74	81	79	73	78	71	70	81	73	82	68	78	86	84
RUTHERFORD	81	59	42	57	64	83	60	73	67	59	67	65	53	70	59	72	57	68	79	79
SAMPSON	84	61	40	58	65	86	61	75	68	60	68	67	53	71	60	73	58	70	81	82
SCOTLAND	80	66	59	66	67	78	68	73	73	67	72	65	63	73	67	76	63	72	79	77
STANLY	87	72	61	70	77	92	71	82	77	70	76	72	66	80	71	81	66	77	88	87
STOKES	91	71	51	68	74	93	69	83	75	69	75	74	62	79	69	79	65	77	87	89
SURRY	85	65	52	63	69	88	67	78	73	64	72	69	59	75	66	77	62	74	85	83
SWAIN	76	56	35	54	63	83	57	72	62	55	62	63	48	65	57	67	53	66	77	78
TRANSYLVANIA	92	76	65	74	83	103	76	91	82	74	81	78	70	81	79	87	70	85	99	95
TYRRELL	77	50	23	46	57	81	52	69	61	60	60	63	41	64	51	67	51	63	76	77
UNION	117	119	106	118	114	114	108	112	107	113	107	104	110	112	108	106	97	109	107	114
VANCE	78	65	58	64	65	76	66	72	72	66	71	64	62	72	65	75	62	71	78	75
WAKE	131	135	130	138	125	119	134	124	128	136	129	120	134	131	129	123	117	129	117	125
WARREN	79	54	29	51	61	85	55	73	63	53	63	65	46	65	55	69	53	66	79	80
WASHINGTON	77	56	38	54	60	80	57	70	66	56	65	62	50	68	57	71	56	66	77	76
WATAUGA	81	61	53	62	64	79	78	76	76	67	76	70	65	75	70	76	66	77	78	80
WAYNE	82	71	65	71	70	78	72	75	76	72	75	68	69	77	71	78	67	75	79	78
WILKES	87	65	46	62	71	91	64	79	71	64	71	70	57	76	64	76	61	73	85	86
WILSON	82	68	63	69	70	82	71	76	77	70	76	68	67	77	70	80	67	75	83	80
YADKIN	93	68	46	65	74	97	68	84	75	67	75	74	59	80	67	81	64	77	90	91
YANCEY	78	56	35	53	63	86	57	73	64	55	63	64	48	67	57	69	54	67	80	79
NORTH CAROLINA	99	87	79	87	87	97	89	93	91	88	91	84	84	93	87	93	81	92	96	96
UNITED STATES	100	100	100	100	100	100	100	100	100	100	100	100	100	100	100	100	100	100	100	100

COUNTY	FIPS Code	CBSA Code	DMA Code	POPULATION			2000-2007 ANNUAL RATE		RACE (%)					
									White		Black		Asian/Pacific	
				2000	2007	2012	% Rate	State Rank	2000	2007	2000	2007	2000	2007
ADAMS	001	00000	687	2,593	2,483	2,421	-0.6	31	98.5	98.1	0.5	0.6	0.2	0.3
BARNES	003	00000	724	11,775	11,396	11,169	-0.5	26	97.9	97.5	0.5	0.5	0.2	0.3
BENSON	005	00000	724	6,964	7,034	7,098	0.1	9	50.8	48.3	0.1	0.1	0.0	0.0
BILLINGS	007	19860	687	888	808	771	-1.3	51	98.8	98.6	0.0	0.0	0.1	0.1
BOTTINEAU	009	00000	687	7,149	6,861	6,717	-0.6	31	97.2	96.6	0.2	0.3	0.2	0.3
BOWMAN	011	00000	687	3,242	3,169	3,126	-0.3	17	99.0	99.0	0.0	0.0	0.0	0.0
BURKE	013	00000	687	2,242	2,105	2,029	-0.9	45	99.2	98.9	0.1	0.2	0.1	0.3
BURLEIGH	015	13900	687	69,416	76,890	82,497	1.4	2	95.0	93.9	0.3	0.3	0.4	0.7
CASS	017	22020	724	123,138	137,913	148,720	1.6	1	95.1	93.8	0.8	0.9	1.3	2.0
CAVALIER	019	00000	724	4,831	4,339	4,131	-1.5	53	98.1	97.7	0.1	0.2	0.1	0.2
DICKEY	021	00000	724	5,757	5,561	5,414	-0.5	26	97.8	97.2	0.1	0.1	0.5	0.8
DIVIDE	023	00000	687	2,283	2,192	2,145	-0.6	31	99.0	99.0	0.0	0.0	0.5	0.5
DUNN	025	00000	687	3,600	3,526	3,488	-0.3	17	86.6	85.4	0.0	0.0	0.1	0.1
EDDY	027	00000	724	2,757	2,618	2,556	-0.7	35	96.4	95.6	0.1	0.1	0.2	0.3
EMMONS	029	00000	687	4,331	4,082	3,960	-0.8	40	99.1	98.8	0.0	0.0	0.3	0.5
FOSTER	031	00000	724	3,759	3,612	3,533	-0.5	26	99.0	98.9	0.1	0.2	0.0	0.0
GOLDEN VALLEY	033	00000	687	1,924	1,808	1,734	-0.9	45	97.8	97.3	0.0	0.0	0.1	0.2
GRAND FORKS	035	24220	724	66,109	67,691	67,454	0.3	7	93.0	91.4	1.4	1.6	1.0	1.6
GRANT	037	00000	687	2,841	2,684	2,638	-0.8	40	96.9	96.2	0.0	0.0	0.4	0.5
GRIGGS	039	00000	724	2,754	2,600	2,514	-0.8	40	99.3	99.1	0.0	0.0	0.1	0.3
HETTINGER	041	00000	687	2,715	2,625	2,540	-0.5	26	98.9	98.9	0.1	0.2	0.1	0.2
KIDDER	043	00000	687	2,753	2,607	2,551	-0.7	35	99.5	99.4	0.2	0.2	0.1	0.1
LAMOURE	045	00000	724	4,701	4,576	4,504	-0.4	21	99.2	99.0	0.0	0.0	0.1	0.2
LOGAN	047	00000	687	2,308	2,146	2,050	-1.0	47	99.2	98.9	0.1	0.1	0.2	0.3
MCHENRY	049	33500	687	5,987	5,799	5,688	-0.4	21	98.7	98.5	0.1	0.1	0.0	0.1
MCINTOSH	051	00000	687	3,390	3,215	3,121	-0.7	35	98.9	98.6	0.0	0.0	0.3	0.5
MCKENZIE	053	00000	687	5,737	5,711	5,729	-0.1	13	77.4	75.6	0.1	0.1	0.1	0.1
MCLEAN	055	00000	687	9,311	8,958	8,747	-0.5	26	92.5	91.0	0.0	0.0	0.1	0.2
MERCER	057	00000	687	8,644	8,560	8,521	-0.1	13	96.0	95.8	0.0	0.0	0.6	0.7
MORTON	059	13900	687	25,303	26,887	28,115	0.8	3	95.8	94.9	0.2	0.2	0.3	0.5
MOUNTRAIL	061	00000	687	6,631	6,634	6,656	0.0	11	66.0	63.8	0.1	0.1	0.3	0.3
NELSON	063	00000	724	3,715	3,514	3,408	-0.8	40	98.6	98.2	0.1	0.1	0.3	0.4
OLIVER	065	00000	687	2,065	1,896	1,798	-1.2	49	97.6	97.1	0.1	0.2	0.1	0.2
PEMBINA	067	00000	724	8,585	8,263	8,079	-0.5	26	95.5	94.5	0.2	0.2	0.2	0.3
PIERCE	069	00000	687	4,675	4,249	4,004	-1.3	51	98.5	98.0	0.1	0.1	0.3	0.4
RAMSEY	071	00000	724	12,066	11,362	10,900	-0.8	40	92.3	90.7	0.2	0.2	0.3	0.4
RANSOM	073	00000	724	5,890	6,102	6,261	0.5	4	97.9	97.4	0.2	0.2	0.3	0.4
RENVILLE	075	33500	687	2,610	2,530	2,489	-0.4	21	97.7	97.6	0.2	0.2	0.5	0.5
RICHLAND	077	47420	724	17,998	17,528	17,312	-0.4	21	96.8	96.1	0.3	0.4	0.3	0.4
ROLETTE	079	00000	687	13,674	14,002	14,250	0.3	7	25.1	21.1	0.1	0.1	0.1	0.1
SARGENT	081	00000	724	4,366	4,310	4,278	-0.2	14	98.2	98.2	0.0	0.0	0.0	0.0
SHERIDAN	083	00000	687	1,710	1,550	1,484	-1.3	51	99.2	99.2	0.1	0.1	0.0	0.0
SIOUX	085	00000	687	4,044	4,164	4,256	0.4	5	14.3	11.8	0.0	0.0	0.1	0.1
SLOPE	087	00000	687	767	726	699	-0.8	40	99.7	99.7	0.0	0.0	0.0	0.0
STARK	089	19860	687	22,636	22,789	22,900	0.1	9	97.5	97.0	0.2	0.3	0.3	0.4
STEELE	091	00000	724	2,258	2,133	2,068	-0.8	40	98.3	98.0	0.0	0.0	0.0	0.1
STUTSMAN	093	27420	724	21,908	21,107	20,527	-0.5	26	97.5	96.9	0.3	0.3	0.4	0.6
TOWNER	095	00000	724	2,876	2,703	2,603	-0.9	45	97.3	96.7	0.1	0.1	0.1	0.1
TRAILL	097	00000	724	8,477	8,476	8,459	0.0	11	97.3	97.2	0.1	0.1	0.2	0.2
WALSH	099	00000	724	12,389	11,785	11,422	-0.7	35	94.9	93.5	0.3	0.4	0.2	0.3
WARD	101	33500	687	58,795	57,548	56,925	-0.3	17	92.4	90.8	2.2	2.6	0.9	1.3
WELLS	103	00000	687	5,102	4,695	4,486	-1.1	48	99.1	98.9	0.1	0.1	0.2	0.4
WILLIAMS	105	48780	687	19,761	19,294	19,000	-0.3	17	92.9	91.6	0.1	0.1	0.2	0.3
NORTH DAKOTA							0.3		92.4	91.2	0.6	0.7	0.6	0.9
UNITED STATES							1.2		75.1	72.7	12.3	12.6	3.8	4.5

POPULATION COMPOSITION

COUNTY	% HISPANIC ORIGIN		2007 AGE DISTRIBUTION (%)										MEDIAN AGE	% 2007 Males	% 2007 Females
	2000	2007	0-4	5-9	10-14	15-19	20-24	25-44	45-64	65-84	85+	18+	2007		
ADAMS	0.3	0.4	4.8	4.3	4.8	6.9	7.6	17.4	30.4	18.7	5.1	81.6	47.6	48.3	51.7
BARNES	0.5	0.8	5.5	4.8	5.4	7.6	8.9	20.6	27.9	15.0	4.3	80.7	42.8	49.4	50.6
BENSON	0.8	0.8	10.2	8.0	8.1	8.8	8.8	21.2	21.5	11.2	2.2	68.3	30.9	49.9	50.1
BILLINGS	0.3	0.4	3.8	3.1	4.6	6.3	8.9	18.3	38.7	13.9	2.4	85.0	46.9	53.3	46.7
BOTTINEAU	0.5	0.7	4.3	3.8	5.9	7.6	7.9	18.7	32.3	15.6	4.0	82.1	46.0	50.8	49.2
BOWMAN	0.7	0.7	5.0	4.4	5.2	6.7	7.9	18.9	31.8	15.9	4.2	81.0	45.9	48.8	51.2
BURKE	0.4	0.6	4.3	3.5	5.9	4.7	7.9	16.8	33.2	20.0	3.8	83.6	48.8	50.3	49.7
BURLEIGH	0.7	0.9	6.4	6.0	6.4	7.3	7.7	27.6	26.4	10.2	2.1	77.2	36.9	49.0	51.0
CASS	1.2	1.7	6.8	5.9	6.1	7.6	10.8	30.8	22.9	7.6	1.6	77.7	31.7	50.2	49.8
CAVALIER	0.6	0.9	4.5	4.0	5.1	7.5	7.6	15.9	30.7	20.0	4.7	81.5	48.2	49.9	50.1
DICKEY	1.4	1.9	6.0	5.5	6.1	6.9	7.3	21.8	26.5	14.8	5.2	78.6	41.5	49.8	50.2
DIVIDE	0.6	0.6	3.5	2.9	4.7	6.3	7.9	15.6	30.7	21.6	7.0	84.8	50.7	50.8	49.2
DUNN	0.8	0.8	6.3	5.4	5.8	6.9	8.0	19.4	30.8	14.1	3.2	77.9	43.7	51.0	49.0
EDDY	0.6	0.8	5.5	4.5	6.5	5.8	6.8	19.2	29.2	17.4	5.0	80.0	45.9	49.0	51.0
EMMONS	1.2	1.6	6.2	5.1	6.5	6.3	6.8	17.5	26.8	20.4	4.3	77.7	45.9	50.1	49.9
FOSTER	0.2	0.2	6.2	4.8	6.5	7.2	7.5	20.7	26.7	16.5	4.0	78.0	43.1	50.0	50.0
GOLDEN VALLEY	1.0	1.4	6.2	5.2	7.9	8.4	6.9	17.5	28.4	14.7	4.9	74.4	43.2	48.0	52.0
GRAND FORKS	2.1	2.8	6.4	5.4	5.4	10.1	13.9	28.7	20.6	7.6	1.8	79.0	29.0	51.2	48.8
GRANT	0.6	0.8	4.8	4.4	5.4	6.6	7.5	16.7	30.8	18.9	4.9	80.8	47.9	51.2	48.8
GRIGGS	0.4	0.6	5.2	5.6	4.5	5.2	9.0	17.0	31.1	17.0	5.3	81.7	47.2	50.1	49.9
HETTINGER	0.2	0.2	4.8	4.5	4.5	6.6	7.3	15.8	30.3	20.0	6.3	81.9	49.0	49.9	50.1
KIDDER	0.6	0.8	5.5	5.4	4.6	5.7	7.5	18.5	30.6	18.3	3.9	81.1	46.5	51.4	48.6
LAMOURE	0.6	0.8	5.5	4.1	5.4	6.1	8.9	18.0	29.9	18.2	3.9	80.9	46.0	50.4	49.6
LOGAN	0.7	1.0	6.2	5.9	5.0	6.0	5.5	18.3	26.8	21.2	5.1	78.7	46.9	49.3	50.7
MCHENRY	0.4	0.6	5.3	5.1	4.7	6.4	7.3	20.2	30.0	17.0	3.8	80.8	45.5	51.1	48.9
MCINTOSH	0.8	1.2	5.3	4.3	4.0	5.3	7.7	14.7	25.6	25.1	8.0	83.3	50.3	47.8	52.2
MCKENZIE	1.0	1.0	7.0	5.9	6.2	8.4	10.1	16.8	30.5	12.1	3.1	75.7	41.5	49.7	50.3
MCLEAN	0.9	1.1	5.0	4.8	5.3	5.9	8.3	17.8	33.7	15.4	3.9	81.1	46.7	49.5	50.5
MERCER	0.4	0.4	4.9	4.6	7.5	8.6	9.3	19.2	32.3	11.0	2.6	77.2	42.6	50.4	49.6
MORTON	0.6	0.9	6.7	6.0	6.6	6.8	7.6	24.1	28.2	11.8	2.2	76.3	39.7	49.8	50.2
MOUNTRAIL	1.3	1.3	6.9	6.6	6.9	7.1	7.6	20.1	28.0	13.1	3.6	75.0	40.3	49.3	50.7
NELSON	0.2	0.2	4.2	3.6	4.6	6.6	7.1	16.7	30.1	21.3	5.9	82.8	49.2	49.2	50.8
OLIVER	0.6	0.9	4.7	4.2	5.4	6.9	10.2	16.7	38.0	12.1	1.7	81.5	46.0	52.5	47.5
PEMBINA	3.1	4.2	5.5	4.9	5.2	6.7	7.9	20.7	31.1	14.2	3.6	80.2	44.2	50.4	49.6
PIERCE	0.6	0.9	5.7	5.1	5.3	5.9	8.7	20.1	26.3	17.7	5.0	80.1	44.4	49.5	50.5
RAMSEY	0.5	0.7	6.0	5.4	6.2	7.9	8.3	21.4	27.1	13.7	3.9	77.8	41.5	49.4	50.6
RANSOM	0.8	1.1	6.4	5.7	6.0	6.0	6.3	22.7	27.8	15.2	3.9	77.8	42.9	51.6	48.4
RENVILLE	0.7	0.8	5.0	4.3	5.5	5.5	10.5	18.3	29.4	17.2	4.3	81.7	45.5	49.5	50.5
RICHLAND	0.7	1.0	6.3	5.8	5.7	10.0	10.1	22.8	25.1	11.4	2.9	78.2	36.9	52.1	47.9
ROLETTE	0.8	0.7	9.8	8.0	8.6	9.6	8.9	24.1	20.9	8.8	1.3	67.4	28.6	48.8	51.2
SARGENT	0.7	0.7	5.9	5.5	7.3	6.8	5.1	23.0	29.6	14.5	2.3	77.1	42.6	52.9	47.1
SHERIDAN	0.4	0.5	3.5	3.0	5.0	6.6	7.4	15.4	33.7	21.7	3.7	84.5	49.8	51.2	48.8
SIOUX	1.6	1.6	11.4	9.7	10.5	8.9	8.7	26.4	18.3	5.5	0.5	63.0	25.5	50.3	49.7
SLOPE	0.1	0.1	5.0	4.5	4.5	5.0	8.8	17.9	34.8	17.1	2.3	83.1	46.9	53.6	46.4
STARK	1.0	1.5	5.9	5.5	6.8	8.6	8.4	23.0	26.3	12.3	3.1	77.1	38.7	49.4	50.6
STEELE	0.2	0.2	6.5	5.7	5.6	6.7	8.1	19.4	29.0	16.7	2.3	78.2	43.7	50.3	49.7
STUTSMAN	0.9	1.3	5.4	5.1	5.7	8.1	8.5	22.4	27.9	13.7	3.3	79.6	41.5	49.5	50.5
TOWNER	0.2	0.3	5.0	5.1	4.0	7.5	8.4	17.5	32.1	15.4	5.0	80.7	46.2	49.5	50.5
TRAILL	2.2	2.2	6.4	5.9	5.5	7.8	8.7	21.1	26.6	13.7	4.3	78.3	41.3	50.0	50.0
WALSH	5.7	7.7	6.1	5.7	5.6	6.4	7.5	21.9	28.8	14.1	3.8	78.4	42.8	49.9	50.1
WARD	1.9	2.6	7.6	6.5	6.0	7.3	9.5	28.0	22.5	10.3	2.4	76.1	33.0	49.9	50.1
WELLS	0.3	0.4	5.3	4.4	4.7	6.6	7.5	17.9	29.3	19.4	5.0	81.3	46.9	50.2	49.8
WILLIAMS	0.9	1.3	6.2	5.1	5.6	6.9	11.1	19.7	29.3	12.9	3.1	78.8	41.1	48.8	51.2
NORTH DAKOTA	1.2	1.6	6.4	5.7	6.0	7.7	9.5	25.1	25.6	11.3	2.7	77.8	36.8	50.0	50.0
UNITED STATES	12.5	15.0	6.9	6.5	6.8	7.1	7.0	27.6	25.4	10.7	1.9	75.6	36.7	49.2	50.8

COUNTY	HOUSEHOLDS					FAMILIES			MEDIAN HOUSEHOLD INCOME			
	2000	2007	2012	% Annual Rate 2000-2007	2007 Average HH Size	2000	2007	% Annual Rate 2000-2007	2007	2012	2007 National Rank	2007 State Rank
ADAMS	1,121	1,113	1,100	-0.1	2.16	725	690	-0.7	34,628	39,678	2485	38
BARNES	4,884	4,850	4,792	-0.1	2.24	3,118	2,963	-0.7	38,761	45,095	1886	23
BENSON	2,328	2,374	2,399	0.3	2.94	1,701	1,677	-0.2	34,409	40,763	2505	39
BILLINGS	366	354	343	-0.5	2.28	256	239	-0.9	38,845	44,156	1873	22
BOTTINEAU	2,962	2,947	2,919	-0.1	2.23	1,954	1,867	-0.6	35,704	40,958	2332	30
BOWMAN	1,358	1,371	1,369	0.1	2.25	891	863	-0.4	38,601	43,687	1917	24
BURKE	1,013	985	963	-0.4	2.14	681	637	-0.9	30,690	34,950	2867	48
BURLEIGH	27,670	31,463	34,210	1.8	2.35	18,198	19,860	1.2	54,545	66,233	420	1
CASS	51,315	59,648	65,269	2.1	2.23	29,825	32,977	1.4	50,455	60,248	642	3
CAVALIER	2,017	1,869	1,802	-1.0	2.26	1,361	1,213	-1.6	38,188	43,318	1977	26
DICKEY	2,283	2,239	2,194	-0.3	2.30	1,500	1,411	-0.8	35,014	40,181	2427	36
DIVIDE	1,005	996	987	-0.1	2.11	649	616	-0.7	35,952	41,101	2286	29
DUNN	1,378	1,396	1,399	0.2	2.49	987	966	-0.3	36,064	41,497	2265	28
EDDY	1,164	1,131	1,112	-0.4	2.25	744	691	-1.0	33,860	38,795	2567	40
EMMONS	1,786	1,744	1,716	-0.3	2.29	1,241	1,168	-0.8	31,568	36,087	2794	46
FOSTER	1,540	1,521	1,503	-0.2	2.32	1,032	980	-0.7	38,890	44,065	1869	21
GOLDEN VALLEY	761	732	707	-0.5	2.31	507	469	-1.1	35,583	40,898	2353	33
GRAND FORKS	25,435	26,311	26,542	0.5	2.32	15,623	15,428	-0.2	46,175	54,466	982	6
GRANT	1,195	1,177	1,173	-0.2	2.20	801	758	-0.8	28,021	31,991	3002	53
GRIGGS	1,178	1,157	1,134	-0.2	2.20	781	737	-0.8	35,253	40,468	2398	35
HETTINGER	1,152	1,128	1,105	-0.3	2.21	779	734	-0.8	35,415	40,506	2382	34
KIDDER	1,158	1,151	1,142	-0.1	2.23	788	754	-0.6	30,654	35,000	2869	49
LAMOURE	1,942	1,953	1,946	0.1	2.30	1,308	1,265	-0.5	35,638	40,766	2344	31
LOGAN	963	928	898	-0.5	2.23	660	612	-1.0	33,453	38,279	2611	42
MCHENRY	2,526	2,537	2,525	0.1	2.26	1,701	1,643	-0.5	33,163	37,925	2641	43
MCINTOSH	1,467	1,424	1,393	-0.4	2.14	975	909	-1.0	31,466	35,901	2803	47
MCKENZIE	2,151	2,194	2,220	0.3	2.58	1,549	1,529	-0.2	35,608	41,280	2349	32
MCLEAN	3,815	3,809	3,772	0.0	2.31	2,711	2,615	-0.5	39,441	44,710	1790	19
MERCER	3,346	3,422	3,450	0.3	2.47	2,445	2,422	-0.1	53,822	63,005	460	2
MORTON	9,889	10,867	11,517	1.3	2.43	6,931	7,348	0.8	47,062	54,736	904	4
MOUNTRAIL	2,560	2,628	2,660	0.4	2.46	1,753	1,733	-0.2	32,849	38,198	2671	45
NELSON	1,628	1,582	1,549	-0.4	2.12	1,005	933	-1.0	34,909	40,021	2444	37
OLIVER	791	763	734	-0.5	2.48	604	566	-0.9	45,067	51,335	1104	11
PEMBINA	3,535	3,513	3,477	-0.1	2.30	2,365	2,259	-0.6	44,923	51,202	1118	12
PIERCE	1,964	1,833	1,742	-0.9	2.24	1,277	1,142	-1.5	33,518	39,670	2606	41
RAMSEY	4,957	4,768	4,604	-0.5	2.29	3,187	2,938	-1.1	45,636	52,891	1036	8
RANSOM	2,350	2,491	2,577	0.8	2.34	1,560	1,588	0.2	45,372	51,145	1066	10
RENVILLE	1,085	1,092	1,090	0.1	2.26	749	726	-0.4	36,583	41,703	2183	27
RICHLAND	6,885	6,921	6,897	0.1	2.36	4,427	4,264	-0.5	45,964	53,397	1008	7
ROLETTE	4,556	4,754	4,865	0.6	2.91	3,367	3,403	0.1	32,870	39,028	2669	44
SARGENT	1,786	1,810	1,814	0.2	2.37	1,243	1,215	-0.3	45,417	51,585	1062	9
SHERIDAN	731	684	663	-0.9	2.24	515	465	-1.4	30,000	34,186	2910	50
SIOUX	1,095	1,144	1,174	0.6	3.58	872	889	0.3	28,265	32,929	2992	52
SLOPE	313	310	303	-0.1	2.34	223	213	-0.6	29,628	33,760	2927	51
STARK	8,932	9,284	9,459	0.5	2.35	5,874	5,860	0.0	40,997	48,137	1599	17
STEELE	923	880	854	-0.7	2.42	635	584	-1.1	43,346	49,397	1295	14
STUTSMAN	8,954	8,858	8,706	-0.1	2.20	5,648	5,346	-0.8	42,066	49,043	1439	15
TOWNER	1,218	1,181	1,151	-0.4	2.23	786	730	-1.0	39,140	44,230	1835	20
TRAILL	3,341	3,408	3,426	0.3	2.36	2,232	2,188	-0.3	46,562	52,656	949	5
WALSH	5,029	4,940	4,847	-0.2	2.31	3,321	3,131	-0.8	41,385	47,757	1535	16
WARD	23,041	23,177	23,147	0.1	2.39	15,370	14,855	-0.5	43,353	51,393	1293	13
WELLS	2,215	2,096	2,023	-0.8	2.18	1,454	1,320	-1.3	38,485	43,733	1932	25
WILLIAMS	8,095	8,185	8,175	0.2	2.30	5,261	5,099	-0.4	39,459	46,541	1788	18
NORTH DAKOTA				0.7	2.33			0.1	44,455	52,373		
UNITED STATES				1.2	2.59			1.0	53,154	62,503		

COUNTY	2007 Per Capita Income	2007 HH Income Base	2007 HOUSEHOLD INCOME DISTRIBUTION (%)					2007 Home Value Base	2007 HOME VALUE DISTRIBUTION (%)					2007 Median Home Value
			Less than $25,000	$25,000 to $49,999	$50,000 to $99,999	$100,000 to $149,999	$150,000 or More		Less than $50,000	$50,000 to $89,999	$90,000 to $174,999	$175,000 to $399,999	$400,000 or More	
ADAMS	22,315	1,113	35.8	34.9	21.7	4.4	3.2	808	43.3	26.9	25.0	3.6	1.2	59,818
BARNES	21,423	4,850	32.0	29.9	30.2	5.3	2.6	3,491	28.5	24.9	36.3	9.7	0.7	85,041
BENSON	14,697	2,374	36.9	29.0	27.5	5.2	1.3	1,653	50.0	25.3	19.3	4.5	0.8	49,965
BILLINGS	22,497	354	33.1	28.0	29.9	5.4	3.7	276	42.8	15.2	26.1	10.1	5.8	73,571
BOTTINEAU	20,312	2,947	31.9	34.8	25.7	6.0	1.6	2,374	36.5	27.9	27.7	7.0	1.0	70,052
BOWMAN	22,334	1,371	30.4	34.0	27.3	5.5	2.8	1,098	29.2	29.1	34.0	6.7	1.0	78,837
BURKE	17,880	985	42.0	31.6	22.1	3.8	0.5	834	56.4	21.6	18.7	2.4	1.0	44,479
BURLEIGH	27,690	31,463	19.6	25.7	37.9	11.3	5.5	21,728	13.0	7.8	46.8	29.9	2.5	142,168
CASS	28,600	59,648	21.4	28.0	34.5	10.0	6.0	33,288	7.2	10.6	46.0	33.1	3.0	147,126
CAVALIER	19,923	1,869	29.3	35.5	28.3	5.5	1.6	1,531	39.6	25.9	29.1	5.2	0.3	64,873
DICKEY	19,445	2,239	35.0	33.9	23.7	4.9	2.5	1,636	33.7	25.7	33.1	6.5	1.0	75,948
DIVIDE	19,925	996	36.0	30.9	25.8	5.9	1.3	818	51.1	27.8	18.6	2.2	0.4	48,714
DUNN	19,147	1,396	36.0	31.2	25.5	4.3	3.0	1,125	37.6	27.8	25.7	6.0	2.8	66,039
EDDY	20,857	1,130	35.4	32.0	24.4	4.2	4.0	861	45.1	30.0	19.5	3.5	2.0	55,903
EMMONS	18,232	1,744	39.6	31.9	21.6	4.6	2.2	1,456	44.4	23.8	22.1	6.5	3.2	60,000
FOSTER	21,276	1,521	29.1	32.3	30.1	6.6	1.9	1,146	29.3	24.4	35.6	9.2	1.4	85,000
GOLDEN VALLEY	18,394	732	32.5	35.5	26.0	5.1	1.0	577	36.2	33.8	26.3	2.6	1.0	66,354
GRAND FORKS	23,573	26,311	23.1	30.4	34.2	8.3	4.0	14,450	9.2	14.0	47.1	27.6	2.2	135,552
GRANT	17,713	1,177	44.2	31.6	19.1	3.1	2.0	942	55.4	21.3	16.7	4.5	2.1	43,929
GRIGGS	20,593	1,157	31.8	34.6	26.4	4.9	2.3	915	42.2	26.2	24.3	5.6	1.7	58,720
HETTINGER	20,064	1,128	35.2	34.0	23.5	5.1	2.2	947	47.8	28.6	19.6	3.9	0.0	52,050
KIDDER	18,288	1,151	41.4	32.1	19.9	5.2	1.5	944	43.6	22.0	24.4	7.0	3.0	60,444
LAMOURE	20,768	1,953	32.7	32.5	26.9	5.1	2.8	1,582	41.1	29.8	23.1	4.0	2.0	59,338
LOGAN	21,316	928	37.7	31.5	21.7	5.5	3.7	797	49.2	30.0	14.3	4.6	1.9	51,102
MCHENRY	18,898	2,537	36.4	32.8	24.3	4.7	1.9	2,073	42.8	27.0	21.8	6.7	1.7	57,706
MCINTOSH	19,680	1,424	40.3	33.4	20.2	3.1	3.0	1,182	53.7	26.7	15.8	3.1	0.6	45,963
MCKENZIE	18,304	2,194	32.4	34.7	25.3	4.7	2.8	1,645	35.9	27.2	30.3	5.5	1.1	72,926
MCLEAN	20,369	3,809	30.7	31.6	29.9	6.4	1.4	3,149	27.7	29.8	33.6	7.9	1.1	78,492
MERCER	23,939	3,422	24.2	22.0	39.7	11.5	2.6	2,893	19.9	27.5	43.7	7.8	1.1	93,670
MORTON	22,889	10,867	24.9	28.4	35.6	7.5	3.6	8,290	24.0	20.0	39.8	14.1	2.1	99,613
MOUNTRAIL	17,140	2,628	35.7	36.4	22.1	4.1	1.7	1,931	39.0	29.6	26.6	4.0	0.8	63,519
NELSON	20,105	1,582	34.5	34.2	24.6	5.4	1.3	1,277	45.3	27.3	23.5	2.8	1.1	56,263
OLIVER	21,121	763	26.3	28.0	33.9	10.1	1.6	655	23.2	25.3	38.2	12.4	0.9	92,065
PEMBINA	23,518	3,513	23.1	32.3	34.0	7.6	3.0	2,779	27.0	28.6	35.9	8.0	0.6	82,302
PIERCE	18,782	1,833	34.0	39.4	20.9	3.8	1.9	1,355	31.7	24.0	35.0	8.1	1.3	79,682
RAMSEY	23,412	4,767	27.2	28.3	34.6	6.6	3.2	3,159	27.1	22.8	37.9	11.3	0.9	90,061
RANSOM	22,236	2,491	26.0	29.5	34.7	6.9	2.9	1,899	24.1	25.9	38.2	10.8	1.1	90,038
RENVILLE	20,862	1,092	29.9	37.7	25.8	4.5	2.1	859	32.7	29.0	29.2	8.6	0.5	73,258
RICHLAND	21,619	6,919	25.4	29.5	35.5	7.2	2.4	4,869	22.5	23.2	39.4	13.9	1.0	96,651
ROLETTE	14,451	4,754	39.8	27.6	26.0	4.8	1.7	3,247	32.5	29.8	31.7	5.8	0.3	71,474
SARGENT	23,031	1,810	24.3	31.6	33.6	8.0	2.5	1,460	38.5	25.3	28.4	7.1	0.8	68,391
SHERIDAN	17,204	684	41.7	33.5	18.7	4.8	1.3	580	58.3	19.1	13.1	7.6	1.9	42,500
SIOUX	10,322	1,144	42.8	32.0	21.4	3.1	0.7	543	45.5	19.5	29.1	3.7	2.2	55,568
SLOPE	19,291	310	40.3	29.7	24.8	0.6	4.5	269	59.1	16.7	20.4	3.3	0.4	40,926
STARK	20,834	9,284	29.9	30.1	30.7	6.8	2.5	6,583	14.2	21.1	52.0	11.7	1.0	106,716
STEELE	22,277	880	22.3	36.0	32.2	6.1	3.4	690	42.0	28.4	24.9	4.3	0.3	61,154
STUTSMAN	22,475	8,858	28.9	29.5	32.6	6.4	2.7	6,057	20.7	23.5	44.3	10.3	1.3	96,546
TOWNER	23,210	1,181	31.4	32.9	27.3	4.6	3.9	891	42.2	28.7	24.9	3.5	0.7	62,273
TRAILL	22,418	3,408	24.0	29.8	35.4	8.8	2.0	2,519	20.1	26.8	43.5	9.1	0.5	93,491
WALSH	21,383	4,940	27.6	32.7	32.2	5.0	2.6	3,834	28.5	29.7	33.4	7.6	0.9	78,407
WARD	22,329	23,177	24.8	32.3	32.1	7.5	3.3	14,716	16.6	17.4	47.2	17.4	1.4	112,452
WELLS	22,444	2,096	33.8	31.0	27.1	5.3	2.8	1,622	41.2	28.6	21.5	7.1	1.6	62,642
WILLIAMS	22,202	8,185	29.8	32.4	28.2	6.6	2.9	5,887	25.5	29.6	37.5	7.0	0.3	82,998
NORTH DAKOTA	23,628		26.1	29.8	32.3	7.9	3.8		21.5	19.2	39.8	17.7	1.8	105,753
UNITED STATES	27,916		21.9	25.0	32.3	12.3	8.4		7.9	10.5	27.1	35.6	19.0	192,285

COUNTY	FINANCIAL SERVICES				THE HOME						ENTERTAINMENT						PERSONAL			
					Home Improvements		Furnishings													
	Auto Loan	Home Loan	Invest-ments	Retire-ment Plans	Home Repair	Lawn & Garden	Comput-ers & Hard-ware	Major Appli-ances	TV, Radio, Sound Equip-ment	Furni-ture	Dine out/ Carry out	Sports Equip-ment	Fees & Tickets	Toys & Games	Travel	Cable TV	Apparel & Services	Auto Repairs	Health Insur-ance	Pets & Supplies
ADAMS	82	56	40	55	65	88	62	77	70	57	68	68	52	73	61	75	57	71	88	82
BARNES	76	58	52	58	65	81	65	73	69	60	69	65	57	70	63	73	59	70	81	77
BENSON	71	51	35	50	62	72	56	66	61	53	60	59	47	64	54	64	52	63	70	71
BILLINGS	93	59	25	56	73	104	62	87	69	59	70	78	48	76	61	74	58	77	91	97
BOTTINEAU	78	54	36	52	63	85	58	74	65	54	64	65	48	68	58	70	54	68	82	79
BOWMAN	89	59	33	56	70	98	63	83	70	59	70	74	51	76	62	76	59	75	91	91
BURKE	69	44	19	42	54	78	46	65	51	44	52	58	36	57	45	55	43	57	68	72
BURLEIGH	93	91	96	93	88	88	93	90	93	92	92	83	92	93	92	92	83	92	91	91
CASS	93	83	84	87	78	80	96	85	92	91	93	81	89	93	88	90	83	91	84	86
CAVALIER	80	53	29	50	63	88	57	75	63	53	63	66	45	68	56	68	53	67	81	82
DICKEY	79	54	35	52	63	86	58	74	65	54	64	65	48	69	58	70	54	68	83	80
DIVIDE	70	49	38	48	56	75	55	66	62	50	60	58	46	64	54	66	50	62	77	70
DUNN	85	56	27	54	67	94	59	80	65	56	66	71	47	71	58	70	55	71	84	88
EDDY	77	55	44	54	62	81	61	73	69	56	66	63	52	70	61	74	56	68	85	76
EMMONS	72	49	30	47	57	79	53	68	59	49	58	60	43	63	52	63	49	62	75	74
FOSTER	82	57	43	56	66	88	64	78	72	58	69	68	53	74	63	77	59	72	89	82
GOLDEN VALLEY	76	51	30	49	60	83	55	71	61	51	61	63	44	65	54	66	51	64	78	77
GRAND FORKS	83	69	74	74	67	71	86	75	84	78	84	72	78	84	78	82	75	82	78	77
GRANT	69	46	26	44	54	76	49	65	55	46	55	57	40	59	48	59	46	58	71	70
GRIGGS	80	53	29	51	63	88	57	75	63	53	63	67	45	68	56	68	53	68	82	82
HETTINGER	82	52	23	50	64	93	55	77	61	53	62	69	43	68	54	66	52	68	81	86
KIDDER	71	47	27	45	56	78	51	67	57	48	57	59	41	61	50	61	47	60	73	73
LAMOURE	82	55	35	54	65	90	60	78	68	56	67	68	49	72	60	73	56	70	86	84
LOGAN	88	56	24	53	69	99	59	82	65	56	66	74	46	72	58	70	55	73	87	92
MCHENRY	73	49	33	48	58	79	54	68	60	50	59	60	44	64	53	65	50	62	77	73
MCINTOSH	71	50	37	49	57	76	55	67	62	50	60	59	46	64	54	67	51	62	77	71
MCKENZIE	79	56	37	54	63	85	60	74	66	56	66	66	50	70	59	71	56	69	82	80
MCLEAN	80	57	39	56	66	88	59	76	65	57	65	67	51	70	59	70	55	69	82	81
MERCER	95	79	62	77	80	96	78	89	82	77	82	80	71	85	77	85	71	85	93	93
MORTON	84	74	71	74	75	84	75	80	79	73	77	71	72	80	75	81	68	78	86	82
MOUNTRAIL	69	50	40	50	55	71	55	64	61	52	60	56	47	63	54	64	51	61	71	68
NELSON	75	50	31	48	59	82	55	70	61	51	60	62	44	65	54	66	51	64	78	76
OLIVER	93	62	29	58	74	105	64	88	71	61	72	78	51	77	63	77	60	78	93	97
PEMBINA	89	66	50	65	75	96	70	85	77	66	75	75	61	80	70	82	64	79	94	90
PIERCE	68	51	44	51	57	72	56	65	60	52	59	58	49	62	56	63	50	62	72	68
RAMSEY	81	67	70	68	71	83	75	79	78	69	76	71	68	78	73	80	66	78	85	81
RANSOM	88	61	45	60	71	95	68	83	77	62	74	73	57	79	67	82	63	77	95	88
RENVILLE	82	55	32	53	65	91	60	78	66	55	66	69	48	71	59	72	55	70	85	84
RICHLAND	85	64	51	64	68	84	71	79	74	67	74	71	62	78	68	76	64	76	83	83
ROLETTE	64	51	48	52	52	61	56	59	61	54	59	52	51	61	54	63	52	59	64	62
SARGENT	97	65	33	62	77	107	67	91	73	65	75	81	54	81	66	79	63	81	95	100
SHERIDAN	70	45	19	42	55	79	47	66	52	45	53	59	36	57	46	56	44	58	69	73
SIOUX	56	46	42	48	45	54	48	50	52	49	52	44	45	54	46	54	46	51	54	54
SLOPE	82	52	22	49	64	92	55	77	60	52	62	68	42	67	54	65	51	68	80	85
STARK	74	63	64	64	65	73	69	71	71	65	70	64	64	71	67	72	61	70	75	73
STEELE	98	62	27	59	76	110	66	92	72	62	74	82	51	80	64	78	61	81	96	102
STUTSMAN	79	63	61	63	67	80	70	75	74	65	72	67	63	74	68	76	63	73	83	78
TOWNER	95	60	26	58	74	107	64	89	70	61	72	80	49	78	63	76	60	79	99	99
TRAILL	87	65	53	63	73	94	70	84	77	65	75	73	61	80	70	83	64	78	95	88
WALSH	82	59	45	58	67	88	64	78	71	60	69	69	55	74	64	75	59	72	87	83
WARD	78	68	71	70	67	72	77	74	77	72	77	68	72	78	73	77	68	76	77	75
WELLS	84	57	37	55	67	92	62	80	70	58	69	70	51	74	61	75	58	72	89	86
WILLIAMS	78	63	60	63	66	78	70	74	74	65	72	67	63	75	68	76	63	73	81	76
NORTH DAKOTA	85	70	65	71	72	83	78	80	79	73	79	73	70	81	74	81	69	80	84	83
UNITED STATES	100	100	100	100	100	100	100	100	100	100	100	100	100	100	100	100	100	100	100	100

OHIO
A

POPULATION CHANGE

COUNTY	FIPS Code	CBSA Code	DMA Code	POPULATION 2000	POPULATION 2007	POPULATION 2012	2000-2007 ANNUAL RATE % Rate	2000-2007 ANNUAL RATE State Rank	White 2000	White 2007	Black 2000	Black 2007	Asian/Pacific 2000	Asian/Pacific 2007
ADAMS	001	00000	515	27,330	27,901	28,284	0.3	43	97.8	97.4	0.2	0.2	0.2	0.2
ALLEN	003	30620	558	108,473	106,239	105,781	-0.3	81	84.9	83.2	12.2	13.4	0.6	0.8
ASHLAND	005	11740	510	52,523	54,553	55,706	0.5	27	97.5	97.0	0.8	0.9	0.6	0.9
ASHTABULA	007	11780	510	102,728	104,283	105,168	0.2	51	94.1	93.2	3.2	3.5	0.4	0.5
ATHENS	009	11900	535	62,223	62,134	62,384	0.0	64	93.5	93.3	2.4	2.5	1.9	2.0
AUGLAIZE	011	47540	542	46,611	47,298	47,782	0.2	51	98.1	97.7	0.2	0.3	0.4	0.7
BELMONT	013	48540	554	70,226	69,022	68,165	-0.2	76	95.0	94.3	3.6	4.1	0.3	0.5
BROWN	015	17140	515	42,285	46,288	48,922	1.3	9	98.1	97.8	0.9	1.0	0.1	0.2
BUTLER	017	17140	515	332,807	362,849	384,592	1.2	11	91.2	89.4	5.3	6.0	1.6	2.4
CARROLL	019	15940	510	28,836	29,424	29,856	0.3	43	98.2	97.9	0.5	0.6	0.1	0.2
CHAMPAIGN	021	46500	542	38,890	39,934	40,350	0.4	35	95.7	95.1	2.3	2.6	0.3	0.4
CLARK	023	44220	542	144,742	141,426	139,720	-0.3	81	88.1	86.6	8.9	9.9	0.5	0.8
CLERMONT	025	17140	515	177,977	195,739	208,902	1.3	9	97.1	96.5	0.9	1.0	0.7	1.0
CLINTON	027	48940	515	40,543	42,997	44,709	0.8	17	96.0	95.3	2.2	2.4	0.4	0.6
COLUMBIANA	029	20620	536	112,075	110,904	110,062	-0.1	71	96.4	95.9	2.2	2.5	0.3	0.4
COSHOCTON	031	18740	535	36,655	36,535	36,460	0.0	64	97.4	95.7	1.1	2.3	0.3	0.5
CRAWFORD	033	15340	535	46,966	45,792	44,979	-0.3	81	98.0	97.6	0.6	0.7	0.3	0.5
CUYAHOGA	035	17460	510	1,393,978	1,341,405	1,306,534	-0.5	86	67.4	64.3	27.4	29.3	1.8	2.7
DARKE	037	24820	542	53,309	53,277	53,262	0.0	64	98.1	98.0	0.4	0.4	0.3	0.3
DEFIANCE	039	19580	547	39,500	39,047	38,720	-0.2	76	92.6	91.4	1.8	1.9	0.4	0.6
DELAWARE	041	18140	535	109,989	163,164	210,702	5.6	1	94.2	93.0	2.5	2.8	1.6	2.4
ERIE	043	41780	510	79,551	79,773	79,947	0.0	64	88.6	87.2	8.6	9.5	0.4	0.6
FAIRFIELD	045	18140	535	122,759	143,976	161,346	2.2	4	95.1	94.2	2.7	3.0	0.7	1.1
FAYETTE	047	47860	535	28,433	29,272	29,902	0.4	35	95.6	94.9	2.1	2.3	0.5	0.7
FRANKLIN	049	18140	535	1,068,978	1,130,253	1,173,805	0.8	17	75.5	72.3	17.9	19.2	3.1	4.6
FULTON	051	45780	547	42,084	43,410	44,268	0.4	35	95.7	94.8	0.2	0.3	0.5	0.7
GALLIA	053	38580	564	31,069	30,806	30,676	-0.1	71	95.3	94.6	2.7	3.0	0.4	0.5
GEAUGA	055	17460	510	90,895	96,678	100,624	0.9	13	97.4	96.9	1.2	1.4	0.4	0.7
GREENE	057	19380	542	147,886	156,653	161,491	0.8	17	89.2	87.3	6.4	7.0	2.1	3.1
GUERNSEY	059	15740	535	40,792	41,419	41,801	0.2	51	96.3	95.7	1.5	1.7	0.3	0.5
HAMILTON	061	17140	515	845,303	807,987	782,259	-0.6	87	72.9	70.1	23.4	25.3	1.6	2.4
HANCOCK	063	22300	547	71,295	75,565	78,464	0.8	17	95.1	94.0	1.1	1.2	1.2	1.9
HARDIN	065	00000	535	31,945	32,178	32,121	0.1	57	97.5	97.0	0.7	0.8	0.4	0.7
HARRISON	067	00000	554	15,856	15,893	15,937	0.0	64	96.5	96.4	2.2	2.3	0.1	0.1
HENRY	069	00000	547	29,210	29,623	29,909	0.2	51	95.3	94.4	0.6	0.6	0.4	0.6
HIGHLAND	071	00000	515	40,875	42,994	44,298	0.7	22	96.9	96.4	1.5	1.7	0.4	0.5
HOCKING	073	00000	535	28,241	29,040	29,619	0.4	35	97.5	97.2	0.9	1.0	0.1	0.1
HOLMES	075	00000	510	38,943	41,363	43,114	0.8	17	99.0	98.9	0.3	0.4	0.1	0.1
HURON	077	35940	510	59,487	60,889	61,936	0.3	43	96.0	95.3	1.0	1.1	0.3	0.4
JACKSON	079	00000	564	32,641	33,920	34,798	0.5	27	97.9	97.5	0.6	0.7	0.2	0.3
JEFFERSON	081	48260	554	73,894	70,434	67,758	-0.7	88	92.5	90.8	5.7	7.0	0.4	0.6
KNOX	083	34540	535	54,500	60,216	64,113	1.4	7	97.7	96.5	0.7	1.5	0.4	0.5
LAKE	085	17460	510	227,511	234,632	239,827	0.4	35	95.4	94.4	2.0	2.2	0.9	1.4
LAWRENCE	087	26580	564	62,319	62,490	62,612	0.0	64	96.6	96.0	2.1	2.3	0.2	0.3
LICKING	089	18140	535	145,491	161,833	173,717	1.5	6	95.6	94.4	2.1	2.8	0.6	0.9
LOGAN	091	13340	542	46,005	47,990	49,280	0.6	23	96.1	95.5	1.7	1.9	0.4	0.6
LORAIN	093	17460	510	284,664	303,635	318,164	0.9	13	85.5	83.7	8.5	9.2	0.6	0.9
LUCAS	095	45780	547	455,054	454,043	452,671	0.0	64	77.5	74.9	17.0	18.5	1.2	1.8
MADISON	097	18140	535	40,213	42,757	44,588	0.8	17	91.8	90.4	6.2	6.8	0.5	0.9
MAHONING	099	49660	536	257,555	252,459	244,745	-0.3	81	81.0	79.0	15.9	17.3	0.5	0.7
MARION	101	32020	535	66,217	66,661	66,866	0.1	57	92.1	91.0	5.7	6.3	0.5	0.9
MEDINA	103	17460	510	151,095	173,779	189,829	1.9	5	97.3	96.6	0.9	1.0	0.7	1.0
MEIGS	105	00000	564	23,072	23,129	23,141	0.0	64	97.7	97.7	0.7	0.7	0.1	0.1
MERCER	107	16380	542	40,924	41,758	42,385	0.3	43	98.4	98.1	0.1	0.1	0.3	0.5
MIAMI	109	19380	542	98,868	101,415	103,239	0.4	35	95.8	94.9	2.0	2.2	0.8	1.2
MONROE	111	00000	554	15,180	15,094	15,023	-0.1	71	98.7	98.7	0.3	0.3	0.1	0.1
MONTGOMERY	113	19380	542	559,062	548,035	540,895	-0.3	81	76.6	74.0	19.9	21.5	1.3	2.0
MORGAN	115	00000	535	14,897	15,261	15,526	0.3	43	93.7	92.9	3.4	3.8	0.1	0.1
MORROW	117	18140	535	31,628	34,707	37,034	1.3	9	98.4	98.1	0.3	0.3	0.1	0.2
MUSKINGUM	119	49780	596	84,585	85,989	87,051	0.2	51	93.9	93.1	4.0	4.5	0.3	0.4
NOBLE	121	00000	554	14,058	14,468	14,595	0.4	35	92.5	91.7	6.7	7.4	0.1	0.1
OTTAWA	123	45780	547	40,985	41,654	42,112	0.2	51	96.6	95.9	0.6	0.7	0.3	0.4
PAULDING	125	00000	509	20,293	20,096	19,866	-0.1	71	95.9	95.2	1.0	1.1	0.2	0.2
PERRY	127	00000	535	34,078	35,448	36,478	0.5	27	98.5	98.3	0.2	0.2	0.1	0.2
PICKAWAY	129	18140	535	52,727	54,332	56,917	0.4	35	91.9	90.9	6.4	7.1	0.3	0.4
PIKE	131	00000	535	27,695	28,718	29,207	0.5	27	96.7	96.2	0.9	1.0	0.2	0.3
PORTAGE	133	10420	510	152,061	159,919	165,288	0.7	22	94.4	93.4	3.2	3.5	0.8	1.3
PREBLE	135	19380	542	42,337	42,658	42,836	0.1	57	98.5	98.2	0.3	0.4	0.3	0.4
PUTNAM	137	00000	558	34,726	35,187	35,525	0.2	51	96.3	95.5	0.2	0.2	0.2	0.3
RICHLAND	139	31900	510	128,852	128,920	128,891	0.0	64	88.2	88.0	9.4	9.5	0.5	0.6
ROSS	141	17060	535	73,345	75,420	76,678	0.4	35	91.7	90.7	6.2	6.9	0.4	0.6
SANDUSKY	143	23380	547	61,792	61,321	60,990	-0.1	71	92.2	91.0	2.7	2.9	0.3	0.4
SCIOTO	145	39020	564	79,195	76,854	75,510	-0.4	85	94.9	94.2	2.7	3.0	0.3	0.4
SENECA	147	45660	547	58,683	57,830	57,246	-0.2	76	95.0	94.2	1.8	2.0	0.4	0.6
SHELBY	149	43380	542	47,910	49,114	49,973	0.3	43	96.0	95.1	1.5	1.7	1.0	1.5
STARK	151	15940	510	378,098	382,325	385,535	0.2	51	90.3	89.0	7.2	8.0	0.6	0.8
SUMMIT	153	10420	510	542,899	547,763	550,038	0.1	57	83.5	81.4	13.2	14.4	1.4	2.1
OHIO							0.3		85.0	83.5	11.5	12.0	1.2	1.8
UNITED STATES							1.2		75.1	72.7	12.3	12.6	3.8	4.5

COUNTY	% HISPANIC ORIGIN		2007 AGE DISTRIBUTION (%)										MEDIAN AGE	% 2007 Males	% 2007 Females
	2000	2007	0-4	5-9	10-14	15-19	20-24	25-44	45-64	65-84	85+	18+	2007		
ADAMS	0.6	0.8	6.8	6.3	6.8	6.3	5.7	27.6	26.7	12.1	1.8	76.2	38.3	48.9	51.1
ALLEN	1.4	1.7	6.8	6.3	6.5	7.3	7.4	25.1	26.5	12.0	2.2	76.4	37.9	49.8	50.2
ASHLAND	0.6	0.8	6.8	6.4	6.3	7.7	7.7	24.5	26.4	11.9	2.3	76.5	37.7	49.5	50.5
ASHTABULA	2.2	2.7	6.7	6.2	6.5	6.7	6.5	25.1	27.6	12.4	2.3	76.5	39.6	48.8	51.2
ATHENS	1.0	1.0	4.9	4.4	4.6	11.9	20.7	23.0	20.7	8.5	1.4	83.4	27.4	49.1	50.9
AUGLAIZE	0.7	0.8	7.1	6.5	7.0	6.8	6.9	25.4	26.7	11.2	2.5	75.3	38.3	49.3	50.7
BELMONT	0.4	0.5	5.0	5.0	5.3	5.9	6.5	24.6	29.6	14.9	3.2	81.0	43.3	49.6	50.4
BROWN	0.4	0.5	7.3	6.8	7.0	6.8	6.2	27.9	25.9	10.7	1.4	74.7	37.3	49.2	50.8
BUTLER	1.4	1.7	7.1	6.7	6.7	7.7	8.5	27.2	25.1	9.6	1.4	75.6	35.3	48.8	51.2
CARROLL	0.5	0.7	6.1	6.0	6.2	6.2	5.6	25.3	29.6	13.1	1.9	77.8	41.3	49.6	50.4
CHAMPAIGN	0.7	0.8	6.7	6.3	6.8	6.6	6.6	25.8	28.2	11.2	1.9	76.3	39.0	49.3	50.7
CLARK	1.2	1.4	6.5	6.2	6.3	6.9	7.1	24.3	26.9	13.3	2.4	77.0	39.5	48.1	51.9
CLERMONT	0.9	1.1	7.6	7.1	7.0	6.6	6.6	27.9	26.9	9.0	1.2	74.2	36.6	49.0	51.0
CLINTON	0.7	0.8	7.2	6.6	6.4	7.3	7.2	26.7	26.3	10.5	1.7	76.0	37.0	49.3	50.7
COLUMBIANA	1.2	1.4	5.9	5.7	6.0	6.4	6.2	26.1	28.6	12.8	2.2	78.5	40.5	50.0	50.0
COSHOCTON	0.6	0.7	6.7	6.3	6.4	6.6	6.7	24.9	27.2	13.2	2.1	76.8	39.6	49.0	51.0
CRAWFORD	0.8	0.9	6.8	6.3	6.0	6.4	6.7	25.1	27.1	13.4	2.4	77.2	39.7	48.6	51.4
CUYAHOGA	3.4	3.9	6.4	6.2	6.9	7.0	6.1	25.5	26.3	12.9	2.7	76.2	39.3	47.5	52.5
DARKE	0.9	0.9	6.9	6.4	6.6	6.4	6.0	25.7	26.6	12.6	2.8	76.2	39.6	49.1	50.9
DEFIANCE	7.2	8.6	7.1	6.7	6.2	6.5	7.3	25.2	27.8	11.4	1.8	76.3	37.8	49.6	50.4
DELAWARE	1.0	1.2	7.8	8.3	8.1	6.9	5.4	28.1	27.0	7.5	0.9	71.5	36.8	49.6	50.4
ERIE	2.1	2.5	6.0	5.7	6.3	6.5	6.4	23.4	29.1	14.4	2.4	78.0	42.0	48.9	51.1
FAIRFIELD	0.8	1.0	7.0	7.0	6.9	6.7	5.8	27.7	27.3	10.2	1.5	75.3	38.0	49.9	50.1
FAYETTE	1.2	1.5	6.7	6.3	6.4	6.2	6.1	26.4	27.2	12.6	2.0	76.6	39.2	49.3	50.7
FRANKLIN	2.3	2.6	7.2	6.7	6.7	7.2	8.3	30.4	23.5	8.7	1.4	75.6	34.0	48.7	51.3
FULTON	5.8	6.9	7.3	7.1	6.9	6.7	6.3	25.5	27.7	10.6	2.0	74.6	38.1	49.4	50.6
GALLIA	0.6	0.7	6.5	6.1	6.3	6.5	7.0	25.8	27.5	12.3	1.8	77.4	39.3	49.0	51.0
GEAUGA	0.6	0.7	6.5	7.0	7.7	7.5	5.1	21.3	31.0	12.0	1.8	74.0	41.4	49.3	50.7
GREENE	1.2	1.5	5.8	5.6	6.1	9.0	9.2	24.5	26.9	11.2	1.6	78.5	37.0	48.8	51.2
GUERNSEY	0.6	0.8	6.9	6.5	6.4	6.5	6.6	24.8	27.4	13.0	2.0	76.2	39.6	48.8	51.2
HAMILTON	1.1	1.3	6.6	6.3	6.5	7.6	7.5	26.4	25.4	11.4	2.3	76.2	37.1	47.9	52.1
HANCOCK	3.1	3.7	6.8	6.4	6.7	7.1	6.8	26.3	26.5	11.0	2.4	76.1	37.7	48.6	51.4
HARDIN	0.8	0.9	6.5	5.9	6.0	9.1	11.0	25.0	23.8	10.8	1.9	77.9	34.0	49.2	50.8
HARRISON	0.4	0.4	5.7	5.8	5.6	5.8	5.2	23.9	30.5	14.8	2.9	79.4	43.7	49.0	51.0
HENRY	5.4	6.5	6.9	6.5	7.0	6.7	6.3	25.6	27.0	11.5	2.3	75.2	38.4	49.9	50.1
HIGHLAND	0.5	0.6	7.4	6.8	6.7	6.6	5.8	26.8	25.7	12.2	1.9	75.0	37.8	48.9	51.1
HOCKING	0.4	0.5	6.8	6.6	6.1	5.9	6.0	25.8	28.5	12.7	1.6	77.0	40.1	50.1	49.9
HOLMES	0.7	0.9	10.9	9.8	8.6	8.0	7.1	26.5	19.0	8.6	1.4	65.7	28.5	50.3	49.7
HURON	3.6	4.3	7.6	7.0	7.1	7.1	6.3	26.8	25.8	10.5	1.7	74.0	36.4	49.2	50.8
JACKSON	0.6	0.7	6.7	6.6	6.1	6.6	5.9	27.4	26.9	11.9	1.8	76.5	38.2	48.5	51.5
JEFFERSON	0.6	0.7	5.1	5.0	5.3	5.9	6.4	23.3	29.7	16.2	2.9	81.2	44.2	48.5	51.5
KNOX	0.7	0.8	6.3	5.9	6.6	8.0	8.3	23.5	26.9	12.4	2.0	77.7	38.6	49.0	51.0
LAKE	1.7	2.1	6.0	6.0	6.4	6.4	5.5	25.7	28.9	12.9	2.2	77.6	41.1	48.6	51.4
LAWRENCE	0.6	0.7	6.3	6.0	6.2	5.8	5.9	26.9	27.4	13.5	1.8	77.9	39.9	48.2	51.8
LICKING	0.8	0.9	6.9	6.8	6.5	6.8	6.6	26.3	27.8	10.9	1.5	76.0	38.6	49.3	50.7
LOGAN	0.7	0.9	7.1	6.4	6.9	6.3	6.3	25.6	27.4	12.1	2.0	75.8	39.0	49.3	50.7
LORAIN	6.9	8.1	6.9	6.7	6.9	6.9	6.4	25.8	27.2	11.3	1.8	75.4	38.4	49.0	51.0
LUCAS	4.5	5.3	6.8	6.3	6.9	7.5	6.9	26.7	25.6	10.9	2.2	75.6	38.4	48.3	51.7
MADISON	0.7	1.0	6.3	5.7	6.3	7.5	8.1	28.3	25.6	10.4	1.8	77.7	37.3	52.5	47.5
MAHONING	3.0	3.5	5.8	5.6	6.2	6.4	6.0	24.4	27.6	14.6	3.4	78.7	41.7	48.3	51.7
MARION	1.1	1.3	6.2	5.7	6.1	6.9	7.3	27.4	26.7	11.8	2.0	78.1	38.5	51.4	48.6
MEDINA	0.9	1.1	6.9	7.0	7.2	6.6	5.6	26.2	28.8	10.2	1.5	74.7	39.2	49.2	50.8
MEIGS	0.6	0.6	5.8	5.5	5.7	6.0	6.1	26.6	29.1	13.3	1.9	79.4	41.4	48.9	51.1
MERCER	1.1	1.4	7.7	7.1	7.5	7.1	6.9	24.3	25.9	11.4	2.1	73.3	36.8	50.4	49.6
MIAMI	0.7	0.9	6.5	6.0	6.5	6.8	7.0	24.9	28.2	12.2	1.9	76.8	39.7	49.2	50.8
MONROE	0.4	0.4	5.5	5.2	5.6	6.2	6.0	23.6	30.3	15.5	2.3	80.0	43.5	49.4	50.6
MONTGOMERY	1.3	1.5	6.5	6.1	6.3	6.9	7.5	25.8	26.3	12.4	2.1	77.1	38.3	48.1	51.9
MORGAN	0.4	0.5	6.3	5.8	6.3	6.1	6.2	24.5	27.9	14.7	2.3	77.9	41.5	49.2	50.8
MORROW	0.6	0.7	6.6	6.2	6.9	6.8	6.0	26.4	28.2	11.4	1.4	76.0	39.2	49.9	50.1
MUSKINGUM	0.5	0.6	6.9	6.2	6.7	7.0	7.0	25.8	26.0	12.3	2.2	76.3	38.2	48.2	51.8
NOBLE	0.4	0.5	5.4	4.9	5.4	6.1	10.3	30.3	24.1	11.6	1.8	81.1	36.8	57.0	43.0
OTTAWA	3.7	4.5	5.3	5.0	5.7	6.1	6.0	22.9	32.1	14.5	2.3	80.1	44.3	49.6	50.4
PAULDING	3.0	3.6	6.9	6.6	6.6	6.4	6.3	27.0	27.4	11.2	1.7	76.1	38.3	49.1	50.9
PERRY	0.4	0.5	7.6	7.2	7.3	6.4	6.5	26.7	26.5	10.3	1.5	73.9	36.9	50.0	50.0
PICKAWAY	0.6	0.8	6.2	5.9	6.5	7.0	6.8	28.9	26.6	10.7	1.3	77.0	37.9	53.4	46.6
PIKE	0.6	0.7	7.4	6.8	6.7	6.4	6.5	27.6	24.7	11.8	2.1	75.2	36.9	48.9	51.1
PORTAGE	0.7	0.9	6.1	6.0	6.1	8.4	9.7	26.4	26.0	10.0	1.4	78.1	35.7	48.9	51.1
PREBLE	0.4	0.5	6.5	6.2	6.3	6.3	6.0	26.3	28.1	12.5	1.8	77.1	40.0	50.0	50.0
PUTNAM	4.4	5.3	7.7	7.4	7.1	7.2	6.1	25.8	25.6	10.9	2.1	73.2	36.8	49.9	50.1
RICHLAND	0.9	1.0	6.4	6.2	6.2	6.7	6.7	25.7	27.0	13.0	2.1	77.2	39.2	50.2	49.8
ROSS	0.6	0.7	6.3	5.9	6.0	6.1	6.8	29.0	27.2	11.2	1.7	78.2	38.7	52.2	47.8
SANDUSKY	7.0	8.3	6.7	6.2	6.4	6.6	6.6	25.5	27.4	12.2	2.3	76.6	39.2	49.3	50.7
SCIOTO	0.6	0.7	6.5	6.2	5.8	6.2	6.5	27.4	25.9	13.4	2.1	77.8	38.5	49.2	50.8
SENECA	3.4	4.0	6.4	6.0	6.5	7.4	7.4	25.6	27.3	11.6	2.0	77.0	38.0	49.8	50.2
SHELBY	0.8	1.0	7.7	7.5	7.5	6.6	6.1	27.1	25.5	9.9	2.0	73.1	36.5	49.9	50.1
STARK	0.9	1.1	6.3	6.1	6.4	6.8	6.1	24.7	28.1	13.1	2.4	77.2	40.4	48.3	51.7
SUMMIT	0.9	1.0	6.5	6.4	6.9	6.7	6.1	26.0	27.1	12.1	2.2	76.2	39.2	48.3	51.7
OHIO	1.9	2.2	6.7	6.4	6.6	7.0	7.0	26.3	26.4	11.5	2.0	76.3	38.0	48.7	51.3
UNITED STATES	12.5	15.0	6.9	6.5	6.8	7.1	7.0	27.6	25.4	10.7	1.9	75.6	36.7	49.2	50.8

COUNTY	HOUSEHOLDS					FAMILIES			MEDIAN HOUSEHOLD INCOME			
	2000	2007	2012	% Annual Rate 2000-2007	2007 Average HH Size	2000	2007	% Annual Rate 2000-2007	2007	2012	2007 National Rank	2007 State Rank
ADAMS	10,501	10,996	11,263	0.6	2.51	7,616	7,761	0.3	35,348	40,024	2391	82
ALLEN	40,646	41,130	41,296	0.2	2.47	28,213	27,690	-0.3	45,412	51,616	1063	57
ASHLAND	19,524	20,527	21,120	0.7	2.53	14,015	14,329	0.3	47,433	53,664	869	49
ASHTABULA	39,397	40,761	41,433	0.5	2.51	27,768	27,900	0.1	43,457	49,852	1277	61
ATHENS	22,501	23,204	23,535	0.4	2.34	12,710	12,555	-0.2	32,991	37,166	2654	87
AUGLAIZE	17,376	18,054	18,415	0.5	2.56	12,776	12,929	0.2	53,250	61,833	486	22
BELMONT	28,309	28,243	28,106	0.0	2.32	19,263	18,621	-0.5	35,868	41,021	2301	81
BROWN	15,555	17,360	18,485	1.5	2.64	11,785	12,842	1.2	46,424	52,522	958	53
BUTLER	123,082	136,137	145,207	1.4	2.64	87,892	94,488	1.0	60,164	70,355	263	8
CARROLL	11,126	11,627	11,913	0.6	2.50	8,156	8,299	0.2	42,818	48,844	1351	64
CHAMPAIGN	14,952	15,647	15,946	0.6	2.50	10,868	11,068	0.3	53,163	61,239	493	24
CLARK	56,648	56,216	55,866	-0.1	2.46	39,383	37,915	-0.5	49,382	56,862	715	39
CLERMONT	66,013	74,285	80,067	1.6	2.62	49,077	53,833	1.3	60,868	71,227	246	6
CLINTON	15,416	16,658	17,448	1.1	2.52	11,075	11,635	0.7	49,568	55,959	707	38
COLUMBIANA	42,973	42,952	42,861	0.0	2.49	30,688	29,814	-0.4	41,437	47,184	1527	71
COSHOCTON	14,356	14,547	14,604	0.2	2.48	10,168	10,008	-0.2	42,156	48,228	1432	67
CRAWFORD	18,957	18,915	18,752	0.0	2.39	13,173	12,754	-0.4	44,121	50,869	1194	60
CUYAHOGA	571,457	557,675	546,075	-0.3	2.35	354,615	333,336	-0.8	47,992	55,331	816	45
DARKE	20,419	20,908	21,110	0.3	2.50	14,898	14,849	0.0	47,475	53,690	864	48
DEFIANCE	15,138	15,380	15,427	0.2	2.50	11,016	10,896	-0.2	54,898	63,479	409	13
DELAWARE	39,674	59,529	77,364	5.8	2.70	30,658	44,974	5.4	87,083	106,788	23	1
ERIE	31,727	32,774	33,241	0.4	2.38	21,750	21,774	0.0	52,277	60,543	530	28
FAIRFIELD	45,425	53,772	60,629	2.4	2.63	34,149	39,442	2.0	60,058	70,005	269	9
FAYETTE	11,054	11,643	12,005	0.7	2.46	7,841	8,025	0.3	45,011	51,914	1111	59
FRANKLIN	438,778	469,558	490,639	0.9	2.36	263,601	271,180	0.4	52,804	61,219	507	25
FULTON	15,480	16,332	16,806	0.7	2.63	11,693	12,040	0.4	53,492	60,878	477	21
GALLIA	12,060	12,267	12,329	0.2	2.44	8,592	8,491	-0.2	36,324	41,524	2227	79
GEAUGA	31,630	34,242	35,931	1.1	2.79	24,997	26,504	0.8	74,751	87,103	92	3
GREENE	55,312	60,650	63,436	1.3	2.44	39,159	41,713	0.9	60,363	70,644	255	7
GUERNSEY	16,094	16,583	16,821	0.4	2.47	11,234	11,233	0.0	36,278	41,391	2235	80
HAMILTON	346,790	338,017	329,806	-0.4	2.33	212,459	199,313	-0.9	50,444	58,391	644	33
HANCOCK	27,898	30,322	31,809	1.2	2.43	19,127	20,151	0.7	53,221	60,547	489	23
HARDIN	11,963	12,140	12,199	0.2	2.47	8,129	7,993	-0.2	41,991	47,917	1448	68
HARRISON	6,398	6,585	6,675	0.4	2.37	4,517	4,515	0.0	36,673	41,999	2171	78
HENRY	10,935	11,340	11,553	0.5	2.56	7,966	8,040	0.1	51,285	58,126	596	31
HIGHLAND	15,587	16,658	17,261	0.9	2.56	11,395	11,855	0.5	42,509	48,571	1397	66
HOCKING	10,843	11,394	11,732	0.7	2.48	7,824	7,999	0.3	41,760	47,533	1483	70
HOLMES	11,337	12,215	12,797	1.0	3.31	9,190	9,718	0.8	45,662	52,520	1034	56
HURON	22,307	23,306	23,897	0.6	2.59	16,225	16,495	0.2	49,666	56,921	699	36
JACKSON	12,619	13,375	13,827	0.8	2.50	9,130	9,416	0.4	36,723	41,605	2160	77
JEFFERSON	30,417	30,000	29,187	-0.2	2.28	20,596	19,673	-0.6	37,180	42,195	2105	75
KNOX	19,975	22,350	23,936	1.6	2.53	14,364	15,634	1.2	47,550	53,884	858	46
LAKE	89,700	94,443	97,447	0.7	2.45	62,564	63,922	0.3	59,680	68,382	274	10
LAWRENCE	24,732	25,526	25,885	0.4	2.42	17,809	17,874	0.1	34,679	39,258	2471	85
LICKING	55,609	62,663	67,717	1.7	2.53	40,126	43,988	1.3	54,636	63,484	414	14
LOGAN	17,956	19,079	19,729	0.8	2.48	12,731	13,142	0.4	50,345	57,044	652	34
LORAIN	105,836	115,580	122,390	1.2	2.56	76,192	80,923	0.8	55,718	64,785	377	12
LUCAS	182,847	183,802	184,353	0.1	2.41	116,330	112,810	-0.4	46,639	53,809	941	52
MADISON	13,672	14,922	15,769	1.2	2.56	10,034	10,669	0.8	54,137	62,606	442	19
MAHONING	102,587	101,058	98,845	-0.2	2.36	68,865	65,669	-0.7	42,663	48,840	1372	65
MARION	24,578	25,098	25,375	0.3	2.46	17,252	17,107	-0.1	47,088	54,030	899	50
MEDINA	54,542	63,633	70,061	2.1	2.71	42,202	48,140	1.8	69,954	81,777	119	4
MEIGS	9,234	9,500	9,607	0.4	2.41	6,572	6,571	0.0	32,459	36,530	2714	88
MERCER	14,756	15,457	15,860	0.6	2.67	11,017	11,254	0.3	52,444	60,604	524	27
MIAMI	38,437	39,735	40,687	0.5	2.52	27,943	28,112	0.1	54,296	63,168	434	18
MONROE	6,021	6,155	6,197	0.3	2.43	4,411	4,391	-0.1	36,876	41,897	2144	76
MONTGOMERY	229,229	228,912	227,688	0.0	2.33	146,843	141,510	-0.5	49,178	55,708	735	41
MORGAN	5,890	6,229	6,424	0.8	2.42	4,178	4,293	0.4	35,066	39,982	2422	84
MORROW	11,499	12,910	13,905	1.6	2.66	8,852	9,711	1.3	49,595	56,023	704	37
MUSKINGUM	32,518	33,228	33,766	0.3	2.51	22,873	22,692	-0.1	42,832	49,027	1347	63
NOBLE	4,546	4,738	4,821	0.6	2.56	3,318	3,366	0.2	40,359	45,781	1683	73
OTTAWA	16,474	17,195	17,577	0.6	2.39	11,733	11,901	0.2	53,809	61,299	462	20
PAULDING	7,773	7,948	7,964	0.3	2.51	5,693	5,668	-0.1	49,052	56,001	743	42
PERRY	12,500	13,203	13,660	0.8	2.66	9,352	9,630	0.4	41,777	47,753	1481	69
PICKAWAY	17,599	19,236	20,372	1.2	2.58	13,287	14,171	0.9	51,958	58,932	551	29
PIKE	10,444	11,039	11,308	0.8	2.56	7,667	7,892	0.4	38,456	43,777	1938	74
PORTAGE	56,449	60,516	63,245	1.0	2.51	39,201	40,771	0.5	54,346	62,641	430	17
PREBLE	16,001	16,536	16,777	0.5	2.55	12,138	12,247	0.1	51,439	58,248	583	30
PUTNAM	12,200	12,739	13,025	0.6	2.73	9,303	9,489	0.3	56,299	63,795	354	11
RICHLAND	49,534	51,047	51,500	0.4	2.40	34,297	34,285	0.0	45,793	52,693	1025	55
ROSS	27,136	28,414	29,167	0.6	2.45	19,174	19,503	0.2	45,330	51,515	1074	58
SANDUSKY	23,717	24,136	24,252	0.2	2.50	16,960	16,772	-0.2	49,790	57,631	692	35
SCIOTO	30,871	30,778	30,506	0.0	2.39	21,372	20,670	-0.5	33,923	38,261	2558	86
SENECA	22,292	22,510	22,515	0.1	2.49	15,741	15,439	-0.3	46,028	52,149	1000	54
SHELBY	17,636	18,527	19,041	0.7	2.62	13,083	13,398	0.3	54,501	62,998	422	15
STARK	148,316	151,232	153,217	0.3	2.47	102,739	101,608	-0.2	48,655	55,870	771	43
SUMMIT	217,788	221,870	223,925	0.3	2.43	144,601	142,483	-0.2	52,658	61,140	514	26
OHIO				0.5	2.45			0.1	50,660	58,568		
UNITED STATES				1.2	2.59			1.0	53,154	62,503		

COUNTY	2007 Per Capita Income	2007 HH Income Base	2007 HOUSEHOLD INCOME DISTRIBUTION (%)					2007 Home Value Base	2007 HOME VALUE DISTRIBUTION (%)					2007 Median Home Value
			Less than $25,000	$25,000 to $49,999	$50,000 to $99,999	$100,000 to $149,999	$150,000 or More		Less than $50,000	$50,000 to $89,999	$90,000 to $174,999	$175,000 to $399,999	$400,000 or More	
ADAMS	18,008	10,996	35.9	30.1	26.6	5.4	2.0	8,448	22.1	30.9	34.4	11.4	1.3	86,622
ALLEN	22,613	41,130	25.5	29.4	32.2	9.2	3.7	30,724	13.4	25.5	43.0	16.4	1.7	107,190
ASHLAND	22,356	20,527	21.8	31.1	34.3	9.5	3.3	16,020	7.8	15.3	49.4	24.5	3.0	131,043
ASHTABULA	21,272	40,761	25.7	30.7	32.9	8.0	2.7	31,228	12.1	24.6	45.9	16.1	1.2	108,078
ATHENS	19,202	23,204	39.8	27.4	23.0	6.7	3.2	14,749	23.9	23.4	35.2	15.3	2.2	95,723
AUGLAIZE	25,467	18,054	17.0	28.8	37.1	12.6	4.5	14,518	6.8	22.7	49.6	19.0	1.9	116,158
BELMONT	20,058	28,243	35.0	30.7	26.4	5.9	2.0	21,841	20.5	30.7	36.2	11.4	1.3	88,420
BROWN	21,538	17,360	22.7	31.2	34.7	8.0	3.3	14,192	14.1	17.0	48.4	18.5	1.9	115,577
BUTLER	28,628	136,831	16.7	24.4	34.9	16.0	7.9	100,873	5.7	10.6	42.0	38.0	3.7	156,547
CARROLL	21,009	11,627	26.6	31.6	33.0	5.9	2.8	9,555	14.8	23.6	42.1	17.8	1.7	108,494
CHAMPAIGN	24,649	15,647	19.2	27.4	38.5	11.3	3.6	12,286	9.0	15.2	50.4	23.1	2.4	126,329
CLARK	24,688	56,216	22.1	28.4	34.2	10.9	4.4	41,724	10.6	25.1	48.0	15.2	1.1	108,417
CLERMONT	29,344	74,285	15.4	24.4	35.9	15.6	8.6	57,304	8.5	7.2	44.3	34.8	5.3	154,606
CLINTON	23,383	16,658	20.9	29.5	36.0	10.6	3.0	12,036	7.8	14.7	51.4	23.3	2.8	126,608
COLUMBIANA	20,567	42,952	27.4	32.5	30.4	7.2	2.5	33,625	17.8	27.0	41.4	12.8	1.1	97,308
COSHOCTON	20,863	14,547	25.8	33.0	31.3	7.9	2.0	11,399	18.6	24.9	39.5	15.4	1.7	100,571
CRAWFORD	22,103	18,915	25.0	31.5	33.3	7.8	2.3	14,231	12.7	29.0	46.3	11.0	1.0	99,428
CUYAHOGA	28,120	557,667	25.1	26.7	30.3	11.0	6.9	369,446	4.1	16.3	49.1	26.3	4.1	133,360
DARKE	23,427	20,908	22.2	30.5	34.7	9.0	3.6	16,511	7.3	17.9	50.8	21.4	2.7	123,063
DEFIANCE	25,487	15,380	17.2	26.8	39.3	13.3	3.4	12,532	11.1	20.2	50.1	17.4	1.1	113,054
DELAWARE	43,379	59,529	9.0	16.1	32.0	21.3	21.7	49,171	3.2	2.6	17.2	55.4	21.6	264,477
ERIE	27,369	32,774	19.8	27.8	35.3	11.8	5.4	24,555	6.2	12.3	44.2	32.8	4.5	147,458
FAIRFIELD	28,182	53,772	15.1	25.9	35.9	15.3	7.8	42,439	3.5	7.3	40.4	44.5	4.2	172,186
FAYETTE	22,647	11,643	23.2	32.1	34.3	6.7	3.7	8,186	7.0	19.4	54.2	17.0	2.4	116,914
FRANKLIN	29,366	469,555	20.5	26.9	33.2	12.3	7.1	282,768	3.3	13.2	46.9	32.0	4.7	145,880
FULTON	24,129	16,332	15.7	30.4	38.6	11.8	3.6	13,431	9.3	11.7	50.3	27.4	1.4	131,518
GALLIA	19,266	12,267	35.1	30.9	24.7	7.2	2.1	9,496	25.5	25.1	36.7	11.5	1.2	89,306
GEAUGA	37,248	34,242	10.8	19.8	35.6	17.1	16.7	30,304	4.2	2.5	24.2	54.0	15.1	225,825
GREENE	30,446	60,645	17.5	23.2	34.4	15.9	9.0	43,961	2.7	11.1	47.4	34.7	4.0	151,672
GUERNSEY	18,813	16,583	32.5	33.8	26.6	5.2	1.9	12,582	21.0	32.4	34.7	10.7	1.2	86,043
HAMILTON	30,827	338,014	23.5	26.1	30.4	11.5	8.6	213,458	2.8	11.3	51.9	27.5	6.5	142,873
HANCOCK	26,892	30,322	18.1	28.2	36.7	11.9	5.1	22,945	9.1	14.2	47.5	26.3	2.8	129,452
HARDIN	20,454	12,140	28.0	30.9	31.8	7.1	2.3	9,143	16.2	28.3	43.6	10.8	1.1	97,397
HARRISON	20,765	6,585	31.5	33.9	26.8	5.3	2.5	5,258	22.9	38.0	30.3	7.8	1.0	78,303
HENRY	23,709	11,340	18.0	30.3	38.4	10.1	3.1	9,364	11.0	19.4	50.6	17.4	1.6	112,500
HIGHLAND	20,651	16,658	26.9	32.1	30.6	7.8	2.6	12,981	12.7	22.5	45.5	16.8	2.5	110,252
HOCKING	20,346	11,394	27.7	31.6	31.9	6.1	2.7	8,912	16.2	21.2	44.9	15.4	2.2	108,825
HOLMES	18,313	12,215	20.8	35.5	32.2	6.6	4.9	9,634	8.0	12.9	40.4	31.2	7.6	149,808
HURON	22,605	23,306	19.9	30.4	37.6	9.2	2.9	17,482	9.9	13.7	51.3	23.1	2.0	124,914
JACKSON	17,943	13,375	33.9	31.4	27.6	5.6	1.4	10,235	22.8	30.3	34.9	11.0	1.0	85,318
JEFFERSON	20,950	30,000	33.1	30.3	28.0	6.5	2.2	23,031	22.9	32.8	36.0	7.6	0.8	82,923
KNOX	22,593	22,350	23.1	29.5	34.4	9.1	3.9	17,460	6.7	15.9	50.6	24.2	2.5	125,591
LAKE	29,381	94,443	14.7	25.7	38.4	14.8	6.4	75,181	3.2	5.0	50.6	37.9	3.3	160,084
LAWRENCE	18,395	25,526	36.7	30.7	25.4	5.4	1.8	19,717	18.9	30.4	40.4	9.5	0.8	90,925
LICKING	26,470	62,663	18.4	26.7	35.9	13.4	5.7	48,290	6.9	12.1	45.8	31.2	3.9	144,628
LOGAN	24,251	19,079	21.0	28.6	35.7	11.1	3.6	14,889	10.6	21.5	45.9	19.4	2.6	114,675
LORAIN	27,269	115,580	18.5	25.6	35.4	13.8	6.8	88,676	4.4	10.9	51.1	30.8	2.9	142,287
LUCAS	25,798	183,801	26.1	26.8	30.8	10.6	5.7	125,333	13.3	22.8	41.2	19.9	2.8	110,719
MADISON	24,570	14,922	18.4	26.9	36.7	13.2	4.8	11,234	11.3	9.4	47.3	28.2	3.8	133,528
MAHONING	23,321	101,057	28.7	28.4	29.8	9.5	3.6	76,019	18.2	26.2	39.2	15.0	1.4	99,073
MARION	22,604	25,098	22.5	30.3	35.3	9.0	2.9	18,923	11.3	28.7	44.5	14.0	1.5	102,547
MEDINA	30,776	63,633	11.3	21.3	39.0	18.9	9.5	52,870	1.5	3.1	38.8	51.0	5.6	186,414
MEIGS	17,357	9,500	38.3	31.6	24.5	4.1	1.4	7,718	33.2	30.6	30.0	5.9	0.4	74,099
MERCER	23,189	15,457	18.1	28.7	39.3	10.0	3.9	12,696	8.7	15.4	48.8	24.1	3.0	123,037
MIAMI	27,262	39,735	17.7	27.4	36.3	12.5	6.1	29,855	3.1	11.4	53.3	29.5	2.7	138,591
MONROE	18,569	6,155	31.8	34.0	28.8	4.1	1.2	5,096	26.2	31.8	33.7	7.7	0.6	81,497
MONTGOMERY	27,403	228,912	22.9	27.8	32.1	11.3	5.9	155,100	6.4	21.3	50.6	19.5	2.2	116,449
MORGAN	17,684	6,229	36.1	31.5	27.1	4.3	0.9	5,013	23.0	28.4	38.0	9.5	1.1	88,135
MORROW	22,325	12,910	18.6	31.8	37.7	8.7	3.2	10,860	8.1	13.5	49.4	26.7	2.3	136,214
MUSKINGUM	21,714	33,228	27.0	30.9	31.6	7.1	3.4	25,225	15.6	23.6	43.5	15.9	1.4	106,459
NOBLE	18,048	4,738	29.4	33.6	30.3	5.0	1.8	3,885	25.9	26.0	35.3	11.5	1.2	87,261
OTTAWA	27,528	17,195	17.4	28.6	35.8	13.4	4.8	14,209	6.6	10.5	47.6	30.9	4.5	143,936
PAULDING	23,122	7,948	19.5	31.5	37.6	8.5	2.9	6,781	16.3	29.8	43.4	9.8	0.6	95,500
PERRY	19,170	13,203	26.2	32.2	33.0	6.5	2.1	10,757	20.7	27.0	37.4	12.8	2.1	93,734
PICKAWAY	23,140	19,236	20.3	27.6	36.2	12.3	3.7	14,892	13.9	10.5	42.4	30.5	2.6	138,044
PIKE	19,169	11,039	33.1	30.2	26.8	7.8	2.1	8,121	24.7	24.7	37.2	12.7	0.7	90,949
PORTAGE	26,254	60,516	19.1	26.5	36.3	12.4	5.8	44,733	9.6	7.9	45.7	33.3	3.6	151,950
PREBLE	23,344	16,536	17.7	30.6	39.0	10.3	2.4	13,443	6.5	14.6	53.7	23.0	2.2	126,338
PUTNAM	23,864	12,739	17.4	26.1	40.4	12.2	3.9	10,936	9.9	16.7	50.2	22.2	1.0	121,191
RICHLAND	23,727	51,047	24.5	29.7	32.4	9.4	4.0	37,910	11.5	21.6	47.4	18.2	1.3	111,998
ROSS	22,201	28,414	25.9	29.5	32.1	9.0	3.5	21,639	17.9	19.4	43.9	17.3	1.4	107,374
SANDUSKY	24,568	24,136	19.8	30.5	35.0	10.9	3.9	18,777	7.5	20.1	52.2	18.9	1.3	117,411
SCIOTO	19,055	30,778	37.5	29.9	24.2	5.9	2.4	22,473	25.4	33.3	30.9	9.5	0.8	78,398
SENECA	21,789	22,510	22.4	32.4	35.1	7.8	2.4	17,468	11.8	26.2	45.4	15.4	1.1	106,481
SHELBY	25,185	18,527	17.2	27.4	37.7	13.1	4.6	14,301	0.0	12.3	59.2	26.1	2.5	130,526
STARK	25,417	151,232	22.2	29.1	33.4	10.1	5.2	113,505	7.9	19.4	49.1	21.5	2.2	121,424
SUMMIT	28,918	221,870	20.9	26.4	32.4	13.1	7.2	161,742	4.9	18.0	45.1	28.2	3.9	131,678
OHIO	26,868		22.0	27.3	32.9	11.6	6.2		8.1	16.4	45.5	26.3	3.7	129,643
UNITED STATES	27,916		21.9	25.0	32.3	12.3	8.4		7.9	10.5	27.1	35.6	19.0	192,285

SPENDING POTENTIAL INDICES

| COUNTY | FINANCIAL SERVICES | | | | THE HOME | | | | | | ENTERTAINMENT | | | | | | PERSONAL | | | |
| | | | | | Home Improvements | | Furnishings | | | | | | | | | | | | | |
	Auto Loan	Home Loan	Invest-ments	Retire-ment Plans	Home Repair	Lawn & Garden	Comput-ers & Hard-ware	Major Appli-ances	TV, Radio, Sound Equip-ment	Furni-ture	Dine out/ Carry out	Sports Equip-ment	Fees & Tickets	Toys & Games	Travel	Cable TV	Apparel & Services	Auto Repairs	Health Insur-ance	Pets & Supplies
ADAMS	78	54	33	52	60	83	56	71	64	54	63	63	47	67	55	69	53	65	78	77
ALLEN	79	75	83	77	78	82	76	78	80	76	78	68	76	81	78	82	70	77	85	79
ASHLAND	85	77	76	77	80	90	76	83	80	76	79	73	74	83	77	83	70	79	88	85
ASHTABULA	78	71	72	71	74	82	71	76	75	70	74	66	69	77	72	78	65	73	83	78
ATHENS	70	54	51	56	54	64	70	64	68	60	68	60	60	67	62	67	60	66	67	66
AUGLAIZE	93	93	100	94	96	100	87	93	90	90	89	81	90	94	91	92	80	89	98	95
BELMONT	70	59	58	58	63	75	61	69	68	59	66	59	58	68	63	72	57	65	79	70
BROWN	91	77	62	75	78	91	74	84	79	74	78	75	69	82	74	82	68	80	88	88
BUTLER	103	106	112	108	102	99	105	101	104	106	103	92	107	105	104	102	94	102	100	101
CARROLL	85	68	54	66	75	92	66	81	73	66	72	71	61	77	68	77	63	74	86	86
CHAMPAIGN	92	84	83	85	88	97	82	90	85	82	85	79	81	90	84	88	75	85	93	93
CLARK	83	84	96	85	85	86	82	83	86	83	84	72	85	86	85	87	76	82	89	83
CLERMONT	110	111	107	112	107	106	106	106	105	108	105	98	107	108	106	104	95	106	104	108
CLINTON	88	80	80	81	82	89	80	85	82	79	82	75	78	85	80	84	72	82	88	87
COLUMBIANA	78	64	64	66	71	82	68	75	73	66	72	65	64	75	68	76	63	72	82	78
COSHOCTON	79	67	62	67	71	83	67	75	73	67	72	66	64	75	68	76	63	72	82	79
CRAWFORD	76	70	75	71	72	79	71	74	75	70	73	64	70	77	72	77	65	72	81	76
CUYAHOGA	87	89	105	92	90	88	91	87	94	92	93	77	94	92	93	95	85	90	93	88
DARKE	88	78	76	78	83	95	77	86	82	77	81	75	75	85	79	85	71	81	92	89
DEFIANCE	96	86	83	86	90	100	84	92	89	84	88	81	82	93	86	92	78	88	98	96
DELAWARE	161	185	185	188	178	162	165	163	156	174	157	154	176	162	169	151	145	159	150	163
ERIE	89	92	103	93	94	94	88	90	91	90	90	79	92	92	92	92	81	88	95	91
FAIRFIELD	105	109	111	109	108	108	101	105	102	104	101	94	104	105	104	102	91	102	105	106
FAYETTE	84	73	72	73	77	87	74	81	79	73	77	70	71	82	75	82	68	77	88	83
FRANKLIN	96	91	97	96	87	86	100	90	98	98	99	85	98	98	95	96	89	96	91	91
FULTON	96	89	84	89	92	101	84	93	87	85	86	82	83	91	86	89	77	87	95	96
GALLIA	76	59	48	57	63	79	61	71	67	59	66	63	54	68	60	71	57	67	78	75
GEAUGA	139	162	173	164	164	153	142	148	138	149	138	135	154	140	152	137	127	141	141	148
GREENE	103	107	119	110	106	102	108	102	105	107	105	94	110	106	108	104	96	104	102	103
GUERNSEY	72	58	53	57	61	74	61	68	66	59	65	59	56	67	61	69	56	65	75	70
HAMILTON	96	96	111	100	95	93	102	95	102	101	102	86	103	101	100	102	92	99	99	95
HANCOCK	93	90	94	91	92	96	90	92	91	89	90	82	90	94	91	92	81	90	95	94
HARDIN	79	64	60	64	67	80	70	74	73	66	72	66	63	75	67	76	63	72	80	78
HARRISON	81	59	44	57	66	88	63	77	70	59	69	67	54	72	62	76	58	71	87	81
HENRY	93	83	76	82	88	100	79	90	84	80	83	79	77	89	81	87	74	84	95	94
HIGHLAND	84	67	58	66	72	88	68	79	74	67	73	69	63	77	68	78	63	74	85	83
HOCKING	81	65	54	63	69	85	65	76	71	64	70	67	60	74	65	75	61	71	82	80
HOLMES	97	80	59	76	83	96	80	92	83	79	84	88	72	87	78	84	74	88	91	94
HURON	85	78	80	79	81	89	78	83	82	78	81	73	77	84	79	84	72	80	88	86
JACKSON	74	55	43	54	59	76	57	68	64	55	63	60	51	66	57	68	54	64	74	72
JEFFERSON	70	61	62	60	66	76	62	69	68	61	67	59	60	68	64	72	58	66	79	71
KNOX	86	79	81	79	82	91	78	84	81	77	80	74	76	83	79	84	71	81	89	87
LAKE	95	105	119	106	106	101	98	99	99	101	98	88	105	99	103	99	89	97	101	99
LAWRENCE	70	55	48	54	60	74	57	66	63	55	62	58	52	64	57	67	54	63	74	70
LICKING	94	95	101	96	95	97	92	94	93	92	92	84	93	95	94	94	83	92	97	95
LOGAN	89	81	80	81	84	94	80	87	84	80	83	77	78	87	82	87	73	84	92	90
LORAIN	93	101	114	102	102	98	96	96	97	99	96	85	101	98	99	97	87	95	98	96
LUCAS	84	83	96	86	82	82	87	83	89	86	88	73	87	88	86	89	79	85	88	83
MADISON	91	94	100	94	94	95	89	92	91	91	90	81	92	93	92	92	81	89	94	93
MAHONING	76	76	86	77	77	80	75	76	79	76	78	66	77	78	78	82	70	76	84	77
MARION	81	76	82	77	78	83	76	79	81	76	79	69	76	82	78	83	70	78	86	80
MEDINA	114	126	131	128	124	116	115	116	112	120	112	106	122	115	119	110	102	113	111	116
MEIGS	70	50	34	48	56	75	53	65	59	50	58	57	45	61	52	63	50	61	71	70
MERCER	92	85	82	85	90	99	81	91	85	82	85	80	80	89	83	88	75	85	94	94
MIAMI	95	97	105	98	98	99	94	95	95	95	94	84	96	98	96	96	85	93	98	96
MONROE	73	57	44	54	63	81	56	70	63	55	62	60	51	65	58	67	53	64	77	74
MONTGOMERY	87	86	99	89	86	86	89	85	91	89	90	76	90	89	89	92	81	87	91	86
MORGAN	71	52	38	51	58	76	54	67	60	52	59	58	47	63	54	65	51	61	73	71
MORROW	95	79	65	77	85	102	76	90	82	76	81	79	72	87	77	86	71	83	95	95
MUSKINGUM	82	71	71	72	74	84	73	78	78	72	76	69	70	79	73	81	67	76	85	81
NOBLE	82	60	40	57	67	88	60	76	67	58	67	67	52	71	60	72	57	69	82	82
OTTAWA	97	90	84	90	97	110	86	99	90	86	89	86	84	92	90	93	79	92	102	102
PAULDING	94	76	62	75	82	100	74	88	80	74	80	77	69	86	75	85	69	81	94	94
PERRY	83	66	51	64	69	86	65	77	71	64	71	68	59	75	65	75	61	72	82	81
PICKAWAY	89	86	88	87	87	92	83	88	86	84	84	77	83	88	85	87	75	85	91	89
PIKE	81	62	47	59	67	85	62	75	68	61	68	66	55	71	62	73	59	70	81	80
PORTAGE	97	92	93	93	91	94	94	93	93	92	93	85	92	95	92	93	84	93	93	95
PREBLE	90	82	77	81	87	98	77	88	82	78	81	77	76	86	80	85	72	82	92	92
PUTNAM	101	90	79	88	97	112	83	98	88	85	88	86	82	95	86	92	78	90	102	104
RICHLAND	81	78	84	79	80	85	78	81	81	78	80	70	78	82	79	83	72	79	86	82
ROSS	86	74	68	73	75	87	74	81	78	73	78	71	70	81	74	81	68	78	86	84
SANDUSKY	89	84	88	84	87	94	82	88	86	82	84	76	82	89	84	88	75	84	93	90
SCIOTO	71	57	52	57	61	74	60	67	65	58	64	59	55	66	60	69	56	65	74	70
SENECA	81	72	73	73	76	85	72	79	77	72	75	68	71	80	74	79	67	75	85	81
SHELBY	95	92	95	93	95	101	88	94	91	89	90	82	89	95	91	93	80	90	98	96
STARK	86	87	97	88	89	91	85	87	88	86	87	76	87	89	88	90	78	85	93	88
SUMMIT	93	98	112	100	98	95	97	94	98	98	97	84	101	98	99	99	88	95	98	95
OHIO	92	90	97	92	91	93	91	91	93	91	92	81	91	93	91	94	83	91	95	92
UNITED STATES	100	100	100	100	100	100	100	100	100	100	100	100	100	100	100	100	100	100	100	100

COUNTY	FIPS Code	CBSA Code	DMA Code	POPULATION			2000-2007 ANNUAL RATE		RACE (%)					
									White		Black		Asian/Pacific	
				2000	2007	2012	% Rate	State Rank	2000	2007	2000	2007	2000	2007
TRUMBULL	155	49660	536	225,116	218,225	213,508	-0.4	85	90.2	89.0	7.9	8.7	0.5	0.7
TUSCARAWAS	157	35420	510	90,914	92,808	94,040	0.3	43	97.9	97.1	0.7	1.2	0.3	0.5
UNION	159	18140	535	40,909	49,559	55,895	2.7	3	95.2	94.5	2.8	3.1	0.6	0.8
VAN WERT	161	46780	509	29,659	28,970	28,517	-0.3	81	97.4	97.0	0.7	0.8	0.2	0.3
VINTON	163	00000	564	12,806	13,313	13,592	0.5	27	98.1	97.8	0.4	0.4	0.1	0.1
WARREN	165	17140	515	158,383	208,670	251,710	3.9	2	94.7	93.7	2.7	2.8	1.3	2.0
WASHINGTON	167	37620	597	63,251	62,307	61,512	-0.2	76	97.3	96.8	0.9	1.0	0.5	0.7
WAYNE	169	49300	510	111,564	116,057	119,030	0.5	27	96.5	95.8	1.6	1.7	0.7	1.0
WILLIAMS	171	00000	547	39,188	39,582	39,820	0.1	57	96.5	95.8	0.7	0.8	0.5	0.8
WOOD	173	45780	547	121,065	128,253	133,382	0.8	17	94.8	93.7	1.3	1.4	1.0	1.6
WYANDOT	175	00000	547	22,908	23,501	23,896	0.4	35	97.9	97.4	0.1	0.2	0.5	0.8
OHIO							0.3		85.0	83.5	11.5	12.0	1.2	1.8
UNITED STATES							1.2		75.1	72.7	12.3	12.6	3.8	4.5

POPULATION COMPOSITION

COUNTY	% HISPANIC ORIGIN		2007 AGE DISTRIBUTION (%)										MEDIAN AGE	% 2007 Males	% 2007 Females
	2000	2007	0-4	5-9	10-14	15-19	20-24	25-44	45-64	65-84	85+	18+	2007		
TRUMBULL	0.8	0.9	6.1	5.8	6.2	6.3	6.0	24.8	28.4	13.9	2.5	78.0	41.2	48.7	51.3
TUSCARAWAS	0.7	0.9	6.7	6.5	6.2	6.3	6.2	25.6	27.7	12.4	2.3	76.8	39.6	49.2	50.8
UNION	0.8	0.9	7.7	7.5	7.4	6.7	5.5	30.3	25.3	8.2	1.3	73.2	36.2	48.1	51.9
VAN WERT	1.6	1.9	6.7	6.0	6.9	6.6	6.4	25.5	27.1	12.5	2.3	76.4	39.1	49.5	50.5
VINTON	0.5	0.6	7.3	7.2	7.0	6.5	5.9	27.5	26.4	10.8	1.3	74.5	36.7	50.0	50.0
WARREN	1.0	1.2	8.0	8.0	7.4	6.5	6.1	28.8	25.2	8.6	1.2	72.5	36.3	50.0	50.0
WASHINGTON	0.5	0.6	5.8	5.7	6.1	6.4	6.7	24.2	29.1	13.7	2.2	78.8	41.5	48.7	51.3
WAYNE	0.8	0.9	7.1	6.8	6.9	7.6	7.1	25.4	26.4	10.9	1.8	74.9	36.9	49.6	50.4
WILLIAMS	2.7	3.2	6.6	6.1	6.5	6.6	6.9	26.0	27.4	11.4	2.3	76.7	38.6	49.8	50.2
WOOD	3.3	4.0	5.9	5.6	6.0	9.4	12.1	24.4	25.2	9.7	1.8	78.7	34.0	48.7	51.3
WYANDOT	1.5	1.8	6.8	6.3	6.3	6.5	6.4	26.2	26.7	12.7	2.3	76.6	39.0	49.2	50.8
OHIO	1.9	2.2	6.7	6.4	6.6	7.0	7.0	26.3	26.4	11.5	2.0	76.3	38.0	48.7	51.3
UNITED STATES	12.5	15.0	6.9	6.5	6.8	7.1	7.0	27.6	25.4	10.7	1.9	75.6	36.7	49.2	50.8

COUNTY	HOUSEHOLDS					FAMILIES			MEDIAN HOUSEHOLD INCOME			
	2000	2007	2012	% Annual Rate 2000-2007	2007 Average HH Size	2000	2007	% Annual Rate 2000-2007	2007	2012	2007 National Rank	2007 State Rank
TRUMBULL	89,020	88,398	87,312	-0.1	2.42	61,648	59,373	-0.5	46,746	53,219	931	51
TUSCARAWAS	35,653	36,488	37,084	0.3	2.51	25,315	25,173	-0.1	43,108	49,292	1317	62
UNION	14,346	17,663	20,087	2.9	2.67	10,884	13,080	2.6	64,771	76,809	170	5
VAN WERT	11,587	11,600	11,532	0.0	2.46	8,358	8,139	-0.4	47,995	55,210	815	44
VINTON	4,892	5,192	5,344	0.8	2.54	3,552	3,667	0.4	35,317	40,333	2396	83
WARREN	55,966	74,300	90,236	4.0	2.72	43,261	56,147	3.7	75,099	90,384	89	2
WASHINGTON	25,137	25,273	25,164	0.1	2.39	17,683	17,260	-0.3	41,201	47,064	1571	72
WAYNE	40,445	42,992	44,423	0.8	2.62	29,488	30,507	0.5	50,700	58,221	629	32
WILLIAMS	15,105	15,609	15,848	0.5	2.47	10,666	10,705	0.1	49,364	55,574	717	40
WOOD	45,172	49,232	51,851	1.2	2.44	29,695	31,284	0.7	54,423	62,868	426	16
WYANDOT	8,882	9,342	9,596	0.7	2.47	6,269	6,403	0.3	47,523	54,476	860	47
OHIO				0.5	2.45			0.1	50,660	58,568		
UNITED STATES				1.2	2.59			1.0	53,154	62,503		

COUNTY	2007 Per Capita Income	2007 HH Income Base	2007 HOUSEHOLD INCOME DISTRIBUTION (%)					2007 Home Value Base	2007 HOME VALUE DISTRIBUTION (%)					2007 Median Home Value
			Less than $25,000	$25,000 to $49,999	$50,000 to $99,999	$100,000 to $149,999	$150,000 or More		Less than $50,000	$50,000 to $89,999	$90,000 to $174,999	$175,000 to $399,999	$400,000 or More	
TRUMBULL	24,311	88,398	23.9	29.8	32.1	10.2	4.0	67,831	12.0	25.5	46.1	15.2	1.1	106,257
TUSCARAWAS	21,262	36,488	24.4	34.3	31.4	7.0	2.8	28,280	12.2	20.7	46.9	18.6	1.6	113,180
UNION	27,079	17,663	13.8	21.7	40.8	17.4	6.2	14,150	6.8	5.9	37.5	44.6	5.1	174,320
VAN WERT	23,451	11,600	18.3	33.8	36.2	9.1	2.5	9,669	13.8	29.7	43.7	11.8	1.0	98,661
VINTON	17,307	5,192	33.2	34.1	26.3	4.4	2.0	4,164	25.4	32.7	33.6	7.7	0.6	80,535
WARREN	34,136	74,300	10.7	18.7	36.6	19.5	14.5	60,035	2.3	3.0	36.8	48.1	9.8	193,778
WASHINGTON	22,546	25,273	27.8	30.9	29.9	8.4	3.0	19,833	16.9	25.6	41.3	14.6	1.5	101,261
WAYNE	23,228	42,992	19.0	30.1	36.7	10.2	3.9	32,710	9.4	9.4	49.6	28.6	2.9	140,742
WILLIAMS	23,317	15,609	19.2	31.6	38.0	8.7	2.6	12,353	10.7	21.3	50.8	16.0	1.2	111,434
WOOD	27,399	49,232	19.5	25.9	34.8	13.4	6.4	36,116	12.9	10.4	42.5	30.6	3.6	140,716
WYANDOT	22,424	9,342	18.8	34.1	37.1	8.0	2.0	7,239	11.4	22.5	49.8	14.4	2.0	110,211
OHIO	26,868		22.0	27.3	32.9	11.6	6.2		8.1	16.4	45.5	26.3	3.7	129,643
UNITED STATES	27,916		21.9	25.0	32.3	12.3	8.4		7.9	10.5	27.1	35.6	19.0	192,285

COUNTY	FINANCIAL SERVICES				THE HOME						ENTERTAINMENT						PERSONAL			
					Home Improvements		Furnishings													
	Auto Loan	Home Loan	Invest- ments	Retire- ment Plans	Home Repair	Lawn & Garden	Comput- ers & Hard- ware	Major Appli- ances	TV, Radio, Sound Equip- ment	Furni- ture	Dine out/ Carry out	Sports Equip- ment	Fees & Tickets	Toys & Games	Travel	Cable TV	Apparel & Services	Auto Repairs	Health Insur- ance	Pets & Supplies
TRUMBULL	83	80	87	80	82	88	79	83	83	79	81	72	79	84	81	86	73	80	90	84
TUSCARAWAS	80	71	69	70	74	84	70	77	75	70	74	68	68	77	71	78	65	74	83	80
UNION	105	110	108	110	109	108	100	105	100	104	100	95	104	104	103	99	90	101	102	106
VAN WERT	87	78	75	77	82	93	75	84	80	76	79	73	74	84	77	83	70	79	90	88
VINTON	77	54	33	51	59	79	54	68	61	53	61	61	46	65	53	66	52	63	74	75
WARREN	131	144	142	146	138	129	131	130	127	138	127	121	138	132	133	124	116	128	123	130
WASHINGTON	81	71	71	71	75	85	72	79	76	70	75	69	69	77	73	79	66	75	86	81
WAYNE	90	83	82	83	87	94	82	88	85	82	84	79	80	88	83	87	75	85	92	91
WILLIAMS	88	77	72	77	81	93	76	85	80	76	80	75	73	84	77	83	70	80	90	89
WOOD	97	94	97	96	93	95	97	94	96	95	96	86	96	97	95	95	86	95	95	96
WYANDOT	84	74	72	74	78	89	72	81	77	73	76	70	70	81	74	80	67	76	87	84
OHIO	92	90	97	92	91	93	91	91	93	91	92	81	91	93	91	94	83	91	95	92
UNITED STATES	100	100	100	100	100	100	100	100	100	100	100	100	100	100	100	100	100	100	100	100

COUNTY	FIPS Code	CBSA Code	DMA Code	POPULATION 2000	POPULATION 2007	POPULATION 2012	2000-2007 ANNUAL RATE % Rate	2000-2007 ANNUAL RATE State Rank	RACE (%) White 2000	White 2007	Black 2000	Black 2007	Asian/Pacific 2000	Asian/Pacific 2007
ADAIR	001	00000	671	21,038	22,005	22,704	0.6	25	48.5	46.4	0.2	0.2	0.1	0.2
ALFALFA	003	00000	650	6,105	5,894	5,774	-0.5	70	89.4	87.9	4.2	4.5	0.2	0.2
ATOKA	005	00000	657	13,879	14,734	15,339	0.8	17	75.9	73.5	5.9	6.2	0.2	0.3
BEAVER	007	00000	634	5,857	5,784	5,740	-0.2	62	92.7	92.6	0.3	0.3	0.1	0.1
BECKHAM	009	21120	650	19,799	19,139	19,776	-0.5	70	87.1	85.3	5.5	5.9	0.4	0.6
BLAINE	011	00000	650	11,976	12,859	12,804	1.0	12	76.3	73.7	6.7	6.9	1.5	2.0
BRYAN	013	20460	657	36,534	38,549	40,124	0.7	21	80.0	77.9	1.4	1.5	0.5	0.6
CADDO	015	00000	650	30,150	30,553	30,779	0.2	39	65.5	63.4	2.9	3.1	0.2	0.3
CANADIAN	017	36420	650	87,697	102,856	115,751	2.2	3	87.0	84.8	2.2	2.3	2.5	3.4
CARTER	019	11620	657	45,621	47,653	49,056	0.6	25	77.9	75.6	7.6	8.0	0.6	0.9
CHEROKEE	021	45140	671	42,521	46,332	48,980	1.2	9	56.4	53.9	1.2	1.2	0.3	0.4
CHOCTAW	023	00000	657	15,342	15,576	15,756	0.2	39	68.6	66.3	10.9	11.5	0.2	0.3
CIMARRON	025	00000	634	3,148	2,988	2,885	-0.7	73	85.8	82.5	0.6	0.6	0.2	0.2
CLEVELAND	027	36420	650	208,016	236,705	258,206	1.8	5	83.6	80.9	3.6	3.7	2.9	3.9
COAL	029	00000	657	6,031	5,953	5,830	-0.2	62	75.2	75.0	0.4	0.4	0.3	0.3
COMANCHE	031	30020	627	114,996	115,386	115,017	0.0	52	65.2	62.2	19.0	19.4	2.5	3.3
COTTON	033	00000	627	6,614	6,627	6,640	0.0	52	84.7	84.6	2.9	2.9	0.2	0.2
CRAIG	035	00000	671	14,950	15,131	15,267	0.2	39	68.5	65.1	3.1	3.2	0.2	0.3
CREEK	037	46140	671	67,367	70,393	72,448	0.6	25	82.3	80.2	2.6	2.7	0.3	0.4
CUSTER	039	00000	650	26,142	26,249	26,256	0.1	46	81.4	78.5	2.9	3.0	0.9	1.2
DELAWARE	041	00000	671	37,077	39,841	41,381	1.0	12	70.2	67.9	0.1	0.1	0.2	0.3
DEWEY	043	00000	650	4,743	4,643	4,594	-0.3	66	92.2	92.0	0.1	0.1	0.1	0.1
ELLIS	045	00000	650	4,075	4,066	4,079	0.0	52	96.3	96.3	0.0	0.0	0.1	0.1
GARFIELD	047	21420	650	57,813	57,775	57,789	0.0	52	88.7	88.5	3.3	3.3	1.3	1.4
GARVIN	049	00000	650	27,210	27,521	27,694	0.2	39	84.9	83.1	2.6	2.7	0.3	0.4
GRADY	051	36420	650	45,516	50,272	53,884	1.4	7	87.3	85.6	3.1	3.2	0.4	0.5
GRANT	053	00000	650	5,144	4,996	4,907	-0.4	68	95.3	94.6	0.1	0.1	0.2	0.2
GREER	055	00000	650	6,061	6,027	5,929	-0.1	57	81.5	81.2	8.8	8.9	0.3	0.3
HARMON	057	00000	650	3,283	3,080	2,956	-0.9	77	72.6	68.8	9.8	9.9	0.2	0.3
HARPER	059	00000	650	3,562	3,378	3,258	-0.7	73	95.9	94.9	0.0	0.0	0.1	0.2
HASKELL	061	00000	671	11,792	12,158	12,345	0.4	32	78.2	76.1	0.6	0.6	0.3	0.4
HUGHES	063	00000	650	14,154	14,068	13,880	-0.1	57	72.8	72.6	4.5	4.6	0.2	0.2
JACKSON	065	11060	627	28,439	26,987	25,829	-0.7	73	76.1	72.6	8.0	8.2	1.3	1.7
JEFFERSON	067	00000	627	6,818	6,572	6,409	-0.5	70	87.1	85.0	0.7	0.7	1.2	1.6
JOHNSTON	069	00000	657	10,513	10,620	10,680	0.1	46	76.1	73.8	1.7	1.7	0.3	0.4
KAY	071	38620	650	48,080	47,299	46,524	-0.2	62	84.2	82.1	1.8	1.9	0.6	0.7
KINGFISHER	073	00000	650	13,926	14,482	14,899	0.5	29	88.1	85.9	1.6	1.7	0.2	0.3
KIOWA	075	00000	650	10,227	9,991	9,844	-0.3	66	83.5	81.7	4.7	4.9	0.4	0.5
LATIMER	077	00000	671	10,692	10,619	10,559	-0.1	57	73.0	72.9	1.0	1.0	0.2	0.2
LE FLORE	079	22900	670	48,109	50,473	52,211	0.7	21	80.4	78.2	2.2	2.3	0.2	0.3
LINCOLN	081	36420	650	32,080	32,576	32,846	0.2	39	86.4	84.8	2.5	2.6	0.3	0.4
LOGAN	083	36420	650	33,924	37,914	40,521	1.5	6	81.6	79.6	11.0	11.6	0.4	0.5
LOVE	085	11620	657	8,831	9,359	9,744	0.8	17	84.1	82.0	2.2	2.3	0.3	0.4
MCCLAIN	087	36420	650	27,740	32,243	36,373	2.1	4	87.3	85.3	0.7	0.7	0.3	0.4
MCCURTAIN	089	00000	612	34,402	34,472	34,508	0.0	52	70.5	70.3	9.3	9.4	0.2	0.2
MCINTOSH	091	00000	671	19,456	19,725	19,863	0.2	39	72.6	70.2	4.1	4.3	0.2	0.2
MAJOR	093	00000	650	7,545	7,453	7,393	-0.2	62	95.0	94.9	0.2	0.2	0.1	0.1
MARSHALL	095	00000	657	13,184	14,499	15,523	1.3	8	78.0	74.9	1.8	1.9	0.2	0.3
MAYES	097	00000	671	38,369	40,631	42,289	0.8	17	72.1	69.6	0.3	0.3	0.3	0.4
MURRAY	099	00000	650	12,623	12,792	12,881	0.2	39	80.8	78.8	1.9	2.0	0.4	0.5
MUSKOGEE	101	34780	671	69,451	72,111	73,916	0.5	29	63.7	61.1	13.2	13.7	0.6	0.8
NOBLE	103	00000	650	11,411	11,367	11,281	-0.1	57	86.4	86.3	1.6	1.6	0.4	0.4
NOWATA	105	00000	671	10,569	10,989	11,278	0.5	29	72.4	69.9	2.5	2.6	0.1	0.2
OKFUSKEE	107	00000	671	11,814	11,493	11,167	-0.4	68	65.5	63.2	10.4	10.9	0.1	0.1
OKLAHOMA	109	36420	650	660,448	705,548	739,059	0.9	14	70.4	67.2	15.0	15.4	2.9	3.8
OKMULGEE	111	46140	671	39,685	40,796	41,600	0.4	32	69.7	67.2	10.2	10.6	0.2	0.3
OSAGE	113	46140	671	44,437	46,476	47,709	0.6	25	67.0	64.4	10.8	11.3	0.3	0.4
OTTAWA	115	33060	603	33,194	34,013	34,446	0.3	33	74.1	71.6	0.6	0.6	0.4	0.6
PAWNEE	117	46140	671	16,612	16,785	16,892	0.1	46	82.3	80.5	0.7	0.7	0.3	0.3
PAYNE	119	44660	650	68,190	73,622	76,714	1.1	10	84.3	81.8	3.6	3.8	3.0	4.2
PITTSBURG	121	32540	671	43,953	44,675	45,104	0.2	39	77.2	75.0	4.0	4.2	0.3	0.4
PONTOTOC	123	10220	657	35,143	35,750	36,229	0.2	39	75.8	73.6	2.1	2.2	0.5	0.6
POTTAWATOMIE	125	43060	650	65,521	69,495	72,159	0.8	17	79.9	77.8	2.9	3.0	0.7	1.0
PUSHMATAHA	127	00000	657	11,667	11,606	11,534	-0.1	57	78.0	77.9	0.8	0.8	0.2	0.2
ROGER MILLS	129	00000	650	3,436	3,395	3,387	-0.2	62	91.8	91.7	0.3	0.3	0.1	0.1
ROGERS	131	46140	671	70,641	84,745	96,388	2.5	1	79.9	77.6	0.7	0.8	0.4	0.5
SEMINOLE	133	00000	650	24,894	25,021	25,125	0.1	46	70.7	68.5	5.6	5.9	0.3	0.4
SEQUOYAH	135	22900	670	38,972	41,479	43,273	0.9	14	68.1	65.3	1.9	1.9	0.3	0.3
STEPHENS	137	20340	627	43,182	43,740	44,181	0.2	39	88.4	86.8	2.2	2.3	0.3	0.5
TEXAS	139	25100	634	20,107	21,157	21,743	0.7	21	76.7	72.5	0.7	0.7	0.7	0.8
TILLMAN	141	00000	627	9,287	8,716	8,307	-0.9	77	74.2	70.8	9.0	9.1	0.4	0.5
TULSA	143	46140	671	563,299	592,004	610,541	0.7	21	75.0	72.2	10.9	11.3	1.7	2.2
WAGONER	145	46140	671	57,491	68,499	77,120	2.4	2	80.1	77.8	3.8	4.0	0.5	0.7
WASHINGTON	147	12780	671	48,996	49,237	49,267	0.1	46	81.2	78.7	2.5	2.6	0.8	1.0
WASHITA	149	00000	650	11,508	11,517	11,538	0.0	52	92.3	92.2	0.4	0.4	0.3	0.3
WOODS	151	00000	650	9,089	8,579	8,295	-0.8	75	93.4	92.4	2.4	2.6	0.6	0.8
WOODWARD	153	49260	650	18,486	19,304	19,645	0.6	25	92.2	90.7	1.1	1.2	0.5	0.7
OKLAHOMA							0.8		76.2	73.7	7.6	7.8	1.4	1.9
UNITED STATES							1.2		75.1	72.7	12.3	12.6	3.8	4.5

COUNTY	% HISPANIC ORIGIN		2007 AGE DISTRIBUTION (%)										MEDIAN AGE	% 2007 Males	% 2007 Females
	2000	2007	0-4	5-9	10-14	15-19	20-24	25-44	45-64	65-84	85+	18+	2007	2007	2007
ADAIR	3.1	3.7	8.0	7.3	8.1	7.1	6.7	27.2	23.5	10.5	1.6	72.1	34.4	49.9	50.1
ALFALFA	2.9	3.8	5.0	4.8	4.1	5.1	6.4	27.8	27.0	16.1	3.7	82.8	43.2	57.2	42.8
ATOKA	1.4	1.8	6.2	5.6	5.6	5.7	6.5	28.4	26.9	13.0	2.1	79.2	39.9	54.2	45.8
BEAVER	10.8	11.0	6.5	5.2	7.2	6.4	7.6	23.4	27.9	13.0	2.8	77.2	41.3	50.9	49.1
BECKHAM	5.4	7.0	7.2	6.3	6.1	6.1	7.2	25.6	26.6	12.2	2.7	76.7	38.6	49.1	50.9
BLAINE	6.6	8.4	5.8	4.9	4.9	6.4	9.1	29.8	24.0	11.8	3.3	80.5	37.5	58.0	42.0
BRYAN	2.6	3.4	6.7	6.0	6.0	6.8	7.5	26.4	25.3	12.9	2.4	77.5	37.3	48.9	51.1
CADDO	6.3	7.6	7.2	6.2	6.9	7.5	7.9	24.7	25.1	12.1	2.3	74.9	37.2	50.1	49.9
CANADIAN	3.9	5.0	6.9	6.3	6.5	7.0	7.7	26.4	28.5	9.4	1.2	76.0	37.5	49.6	50.4
CARTER	2.8	3.5	6.9	6.7	6.2	6.3	6.4	24.3	27.2	13.6	2.4	76.3	39.9	48.4	51.6
CHEROKEE	4.1	5.1	7.2	6.3	6.3	8.3	9.9	25.5	23.7	11.2	1.7	76.1	33.4	49.2	50.8
CHOCTAW	1.6	2.0	6.7	5.8	6.1	6.6	6.5	24.1	26.4	14.9	2.9	77.4	40.8	47.7	52.3
CIMARRON	15.4	19.4	7.2	6.8	5.9	7.3	6.2	22.5	25.7	14.8	3.5	75.4	40.8	49.9	50.1
CLEVELAND	4.0	5.1	6.5	5.7	5.8	7.7	10.5	29.4	25.1	8.2	1.0	78.2	33.3	50.0	50.0
COAL	2.1	2.2	7.0	6.1	7.1	6.5	6.0	24.0	26.2	14.6	2.5	75.9	39.8	49.3	50.7
COMANCHE	8.4	10.4	8.2	7.1	6.6	8.1	10.1	28.8	21.1	8.8	1.2	74.0	30.8	51.8	48.2
COTTON	4.9	4.9	7.0	6.5	6.9	5.6	6.2	25.0	25.8	13.8	3.1	76.2	39.8	50.6	49.4
CRAIG	1.2	1.9	6.3	5.9	5.6	5.7	6.2	26.0	28.0	13.9	2.3	78.7	41.4	50.8	49.2
CREEK	1.9	2.4	7.0	6.7	6.9	6.7	7.1	24.9	27.3	11.8	1.6	75.3	38.3	49.1	50.9
CUSTER	9.0	11.4	6.4	5.6	5.7	9.2	13.5	23.2	22.8	11.0	2.5	78.1	33.0	49.0	51.0
DELAWARE	1.8	2.2	6.3	6.0	5.8	5.9	5.7	21.9	29.3	16.9	2.2	78.1	43.7	49.2	50.8
DEWEY	2.7	2.7	5.8	4.7	5.3	5.4	7.7	20.5	30.4	15.8	4.5	80.9	45.3	49.3	50.7
ELLIS	2.6	2.7	4.9	4.7	5.3	5.1	6.4	20.6	31.1	18.0	3.9	81.9	47.2	49.7	50.3
GARFIELD	4.1	4.2	7.0	6.2	5.9	6.0	6.9	25.9	26.2	13.3	2.6	77.2	39.0	48.8	51.2
GARVIN	3.4	4.4	7.0	6.4	5.9	5.6	7.0	24.3	26.4	14.6	2.9	77.4	40.4	48.4	51.6
GRADY	2.9	3.7	7.2	6.6	6.1	6.8	7.3	25.5	27.1	11.6	1.9	76.3	38.3	49.0	51.0
GRANT	1.8	2.4	5.9	4.8	6.5	5.7	7.9	21.2	27.7	16.6	3.6	79.2	43.6	49.0	51.0
GREER	7.4	7.6	5.0	4.4	4.2	5.7	8.2	29.8	24.1	15.0	3.5	83.0	40.0	56.5	43.5
HARMON	22.8	28.0	7.0	6.1	5.6	6.2	7.9	22.1	25.9	14.6	4.5	77.2	40.7	49.4	50.6
HARPER	5.6	7.4	5.1	4.7	5.0	6.0	7.0	21.1	30.6	17.3	3.2	81.6	45.7	49.7	50.3
HASKELL	1.5	1.9	7.6	6.8	6.7	5.6	6.2	24.1	26.1	14.4	2.6	75.5	39.2	49.1	50.9
HUGHES	2.5	2.6	6.0	5.4	5.9	5.7	6.7	26.2	26.2	14.8	3.0	79.3	40.9	52.0	48.0
JACKSON	15.6	19.4	8.6	7.4	6.8	7.1	7.9	27.4	22.8	10.0	1.9	73.0	33.4	50.2	49.8
JEFFERSON	7.0	9.0	6.7	6.1	6.3	5.3	6.6	23.6	26.1	15.9	3.4	77.5	41.1	48.7	51.3
JOHNSTON	2.5	3.1	6.7	6.4	6.3	6.6	6.6	23.8	27.8	13.5	2.3	77.0	40.3	49.2	50.8
KAY	4.3	5.4	7.3	6.3	6.4	6.7	7.6	22.9	26.2	13.7	2.8	76.0	39.3	48.8	51.2
KINGFISHER	6.9	8.9	7.0	6.0	6.6	6.1	7.3	24.3	27.6	12.7	2.3	76.4	40.0	48.9	51.1
KIOWA	6.7	8.6	6.3	5.4	5.4	6.3	7.5	22.4	27.5	15.7	3.5	79.0	42.8	49.8	50.2
LATIMER	1.5	1.6	7.2	6.1	5.8	7.7	7.9	23.3	24.8	14.9	2.2	77.3	39.1	49.7	50.3
LE FLORE	3.8	4.9	7.2	6.7	6.3	6.3	6.8	27.0	25.6	12.4	1.8	76.2	37.5	50.0	50.0
LINCOLN	1.5	1.9	6.9	6.4	6.6	6.6	6.8	24.3	27.8	12.7	1.9	76.0	39.9	49.6	50.4
LOGAN	2.9	3.8	6.1	6.3	6.0	8.7	9.2	24.2	26.9	10.8	1.9	77.3	37.2	49.7	50.3
LOVE	7.0	9.0	6.3	6.1	6.3	6.2	6.4	23.9	27.5	14.8	2.4	77.3	41.2	49.7	50.3
MCCLAIN	4.9	6.3	7.0	6.7	6.2	6.3	7.1	26.1	27.9	11.4	1.3	76.3	39.0	49.7	50.3
MCCURTAIN	3.1	3.1	7.6	7.0	6.7	6.6	6.5	25.0	26.1	12.5	1.8	74.6	37.8	48.4	51.6
MCINTOSH	1.3	1.6	5.6	5.1	4.9	5.9	6.4	19.9	29.4	20.2	2.6	80.9	46.6	48.1	51.9
MAJOR	4.0	4.1	6.1	5.9	5.3	6.2	6.7	20.8	29.7	15.8	3.5	79.0	44.3	49.3	50.7
MARSHALL	8.6	10.8	6.5	6.4	5.4	5.4	6.0	22.0	28.1	17.8	2.5	78.5	43.7	49.4	50.6
MAYES	1.9	2.3	7.1	6.5	6.5	6.8	6.4	25.6	26.1	13.2	1.9	75.8	38.4	49.6	50.4
MURRAY	3.1	4.0	7.0	6.7	5.6	5.0	6.4	24.3	26.9	15.4	2.7	77.6	41.3	49.8	50.2
MUSKOGEE	2.7	3.3	7.2	6.6	6.4	6.3	7.1	25.5	25.8	12.5	2.5	76.1	37.8	48.6	51.4
NOBLE	1.8	1.8	6.7	6.3	6.1	6.2	6.4	25.2	28.0	12.9	2.2	77.1	40.1	49.6	50.4
NOWATA	1.2	1.5	6.8	6.5	6.6	6.3	6.5	23.3	27.2	14.3	2.5	76.3	40.7	49.4	50.6
OKFUSKEE	1.6	2.0	6.7	6.0	5.4	5.8	7.1	26.3	25.9	14.3	2.5	78.4	40.3	51.8	48.2
OKLAHOMA	8.7	10.8	7.4	6.8	6.5	6.5	7.5	28.6	24.6	10.3	1.7	75.5	34.9	48.8	51.2
OKMULGEE	1.9	2.4	7.2	6.2	6.5	7.3	7.6	23.6	26.3	13.0	2.2	76.0	38.3	49.0	51.0
OSAGE	2.1	2.6	6.3	5.9	6.3	6.7	7.3	24.0	29.4	12.4	1.6	77.4	40.5	50.6	49.4
OTTAWA	3.2	4.1	6.8	6.3	6.4	7.6	6.9	23.8	25.5	14.3	2.5	76.4	38.9	48.9	51.1
PAWNEE	1.2	1.5	6.6	5.9	6.5	6.7	6.7	23.6	28.6	13.1	2.2	76.9	40.4	49.4	50.6
PAYNE	2.1	2.7	5.5	4.6	4.5	9.7	18.9	26.3	19.9	8.6	1.9	82.4	28.4	51.1	48.9
PITTSBURG	2.1	2.7	5.7	5.3	5.8	5.9	7.2	24.9	27.8	14.9	2.6	79.6	41.7	50.9	49.1
PONTOTOC	2.3	2.9	6.6	5.6	6.0	6.9	9.0	25.5	24.7	13.1	2.4	78.1	37.2	48.4	51.6
POTTAWATOMIE	2.4	3.0	7.0	6.3	6.3	7.2	7.8	26.2	25.2	12.1	1.9	76.6	36.8	48.8	51.2
PUSHMATAHA	1.6	1.7	6.7	6.2	5.8	6.8	6.6	22.2	26.8	16.3	2.6	77.3	41.9	48.4	51.6
ROGER MILLS	2.6	2.7	6.0	6.5	5.2	5.4	6.2	22.0	30.0	15.5	3.2	78.8	44.1	50.2	49.8
ROGERS	1.8	2.3	7.2	6.9	7.3	7.1	6.7	25.4	27.1	11.1	1.2	74.2	38.2	49.3	50.7
SEMINOLE	2.2	2.8	7.1	6.4	6.1	6.4	7.3	23.6	26.3	14.4	2.5	76.6	39.6	48.5	51.5
SEQUOYAH	2.0	2.5	7.3	6.8	6.7	6.6	6.1	26.3	26.1	12.4	1.6	75.1	38.1	49.7	50.3
STEPHENS	4.0	5.1	6.5	6.3	5.6	5.9	6.7	22.7	28.1	15.3	2.9	78.1	42.3	48.6	51.4
TEXAS	29.9	36.0	8.8	7.8	6.7	7.0	9.0	28.8	21.8	8.8	1.3	72.8	31.6	51.7	48.3
TILLMAN	17.7	21.9	6.7	6.3	6.0	7.1	7.0	23.7	24.0	15.5	3.7	76.2	40.4	49.9	50.1
TULSA	6.0	7.6	7.4	6.8	6.7	6.9	7.7	27.7	25.0	10.0	1.7	75.1	35.3	48.7	51.3
WAGONER	2.5	3.2	7.3	6.9	7.2	6.6	7.1	25.9	27.6	10.4	1.0	74.6	37.7	49.4	50.6
WASHINGTON	2.6	3.4	6.1	5.6	6.0	6.8	7.6	21.7	27.9	15.5	2.9	78.2	41.8	48.3	51.7
WASHITA	4.5	4.6	6.9	6.0	5.8	6.1	7.5	23.7	26.8	13.9	3.3	77.6	41.0	48.9	51.1
WOODS	2.4	3.2	4.7	4.0	4.8	7.5	12.1	23.9	23.7	15.2	4.2	83.4	39.1	51.4	48.6
WOODWARD	4.8	6.3	6.9	6.3	5.3	6.6	8.1	25.4	26.7	12.2	2.4	77.6	38.6	50.6	49.4
OKLAHOMA	5.2	6.5	7.1	6.4	6.3	6.9	7.9	26.5	25.6	11.4	1.9	76.3	36.6	49.4	50.6
UNITED STATES	12.5	15.0	6.9	6.5	6.8	7.1	7.0	27.6	25.4	10.7	1.9	75.6	36.7	49.2	50.8

COUNTY	HOUSEHOLDS					FAMILIES			MEDIAN HOUSEHOLD INCOME			
	2000	2007	2012	% Annual Rate 2000-2007	2007 Average HH Size	2000	2007	% Annual Rate 2000-2007	2007	2012	2007 National Rank	2007 State Rank
ADAIR	7,471	7,950	8,257	0.9	2.72	5,567	5,826	0.6	31,335	36,651	2809	62
ALFALFA	2,199	2,132	2,086	-0.4	2.27	1,482	1,407	-0.7	35,991	40,664	2277	34
ATOKA	4,964	5,391	5,690	1.1	2.43	3,503	3,735	0.9	29,309	33,324	2945	69
BEAVER	2,245	2,227	2,211	-0.1	2.55	1,706	1,666	-0.3	43,835	49,437	1231	11
BECKHAM	7,356	7,822	8,136	0.9	2.40	5,002	5,209	0.6	33,796	38,757	2575	49
BLAINE	4,159	4,160	4,150	0.0	2.47	2,867	2,811	-0.3	34,247	38,763	2519	47
BRYAN	14,422	15,401	16,079	0.9	2.45	9,943	10,405	0.6	34,127	39,131	2537	48
CADDO	10,957	11,185	11,310	0.3	2.59	7,961	7,986	0.0	32,999	37,434	2653	58
CANADIAN	31,484	37,544	42,567	2.5	2.68	24,432	28,718	2.3	57,748	66,781	312	1
CARTER	17,992	19,048	19,702	0.8	2.44	12,642	13,131	0.5	35,847	41,091	2306	37
CHEROKEE	16,175	17,816	18,976	1.3	2.49	11,077	11,955	1.1	33,170	38,149	2640	57
CHOCTAW	6,220	6,438	6,561	0.5	2.38	4,286	4,349	0.2	27,349	31,359	3024	75
CIMARRON	1,257	1,206	1,168	-0.6	2.44	868	816	-0.8	36,404	41,211	2212	32
CLEVELAND	79,186	92,969	102,523	2.2	2.45	53,833	61,919	1.9	53,311	63,033	483	3
COAL	2,373	2,354	2,305	-0.1	2.50	1,654	1,609	-0.4	28,136	32,295	2997	73
COMANCHE	39,808	41,264	41,433	0.5	2.57	28,858	29,393	0.3	42,354	49,019	1410	14
COTTON	2,614	2,649	2,664	0.2	2.44	1,840	1,830	-0.1	33,682	38,790	2587	52
CRAIG	5,620	5,713	5,768	0.2	2.45	3,948	3,939	0.0	37,078	41,946	2117	30
CREEK	25,289	26,521	27,357	0.7	2.63	19,024	19,635	0.4	41,686	48,288	1496	15
CUSTER	10,136	10,329	10,410	0.3	2.41	6,581	6,559	0.0	35,735	41,614	2326	38
DELAWARE	14,838	16,161	16,863	1.2	2.43	10,767	11,521	0.9	35,160	40,863	2409	42
DEWEY	1,962	1,960	1,955	0.0	2.30	1,336	1,308	-0.3	33,551	38,140	2603	55
ELLIS	1,769	1,815	1,843	0.4	2.21	1,219	1,225	0.1	33,729	38,104	2580	50
GARFIELD	23,175	23,365	23,437	0.1	2.40	15,799	15,608	-0.2	40,980	47,408	1602	18
GARVIN	10,865	11,087	11,183	0.3	2.43	7,608	7,615	0.0	34,348	39,345	2509	46
GRADY	17,341	19,434	20,958	1.6	2.54	12,799	14,105	1.3	40,459	46,664	1665	20
GRANT	2,089	2,034	1,996	-0.4	2.41	1,455	1,388	-0.6	34,920	39,401	2442	44
GREER	2,237	2,169	2,125	-0.4	2.27	1,442	1,366	-0.7	30,924	35,181	2840	64
HARMON	1,266	1,186	1,135	-0.9	2.47	863	792	-1.2	26,873	31,000	3042	76
HARPER	1,509	1,456	1,414	-0.5	2.29	1,030	974	-0.8	40,816	46,310	1628	19
HASKELL	4,624	4,788	4,862	0.5	2.51	3,379	3,440	0.2	29,218	33,384	2948	70
HUGHES	5,319	5,311	5,243	0.0	2.40	3,677	3,600	-0.3	27,623	31,684	3018	74
JACKSON	10,590	10,164	9,749	-0.6	2.58	7,666	7,227	-0.8	38,674	45,144	1898	25
JEFFERSON	2,716	2,633	2,568	-0.4	2.37	1,864	1,772	-0.7	28,568	32,573	2977	72
JOHNSTON	4,057	4,147	4,180	0.3	2.51	2,899	2,912	0.1	29,817	33,858	2920	66
KAY	19,157	19,001	18,715	-0.1	2.43	13,136	12,772	-0.4	37,727	43,468	2033	28
KINGFISHER	5,247	5,516	5,694	0.7	2.58	3,894	4,027	0.5	45,615	52,020	1040	7
KIOWA	4,208	4,177	4,139	-0.1	2.31	2,814	2,734	-0.4	31,613	35,938	2792	60
LATIMER	3,951	3,991	3,996	0.1	2.49	2,869	2,847	-0.1	28,868	32,997	2966	71
LE FLORE	17,861	18,964	19,700	0.8	2.58	13,201	13,783	0.6	33,506	38,508	2608	56
LINCOLN	12,178	12,562	12,739	0.4	2.56	9,122	9,258	0.2	37,731	43,169	2032	27
LOGAN	12,389	13,903	15,018	1.6	2.53	8,994	9,917	1.4	45,511	52,620	1049	8
LOVE	3,442	3,688	3,854	1.0	2.51	2,556	2,693	0.7	40,142	46,029	1702	21
MCCLAIN	10,331	12,161	13,779	2.3	2.63	8,042	9,333	2.1	46,292	53,712	971	6
MCCURTAIN	13,216	13,538	13,673	0.3	2.51	9,536	9,596	0.1	29,383	34,018	2938	67
MCINTOSH	8,085	8,314	8,414	0.4	2.33	5,685	5,735	0.1	31,510	35,982	2798	61
MAJOR	3,046	3,069	3,068	0.1	2.39	2,209	2,186	-0.1	37,737	42,894	2030	26
MARSHALL	5,371	5,958	6,395	1.4	2.39	3,800	4,137	1.2	32,010	36,344	2763	59
MAYES	14,823	15,916	16,647	1.0	2.52	10,818	11,416	0.7	38,879	45,383	1872	24
MURRAY	5,003	5,129	5,183	0.3	2.42	3,589	3,614	0.1	36,989	42,604	2131	31
MUSKOGEE	26,458	27,805	28,689	0.7	2.47	18,463	19,028	0.4	35,347	40,648	2392	40
NOBLE	4,504	4,557	4,547	0.2	2.43	3,213	3,191	-0.1	41,481	47,448	1519	16
NOWATA	4,147	4,308	4,416	0.5	2.50	2,991	3,051	0.3	36,142	41,496	2249	33
OKFUSKEE	4,270	4,203	4,093	-0.2	2.48	2,972	2,870	-0.5	29,379	33,357	2939	68
OKLAHOMA	266,834	287,913	303,092	1.1	2.39	170,663	179,960	0.7	43,773	51,215	1242	12
OKMULGEE	15,300	15,859	16,181	0.5	2.52	10,701	10,881	0.2	33,711	38,736	2582	51
OSAGE	16,617	17,609	18,162	0.8	2.55	12,214	12,725	0.6	43,108	49,994	1317	13
OTTAWA	12,984	13,202	13,340	0.2	2.49	9,121	9,102	0.0	33,573	38,466	2598	54
PAWNEE	6,383	6,483	6,528	0.2	2.56	4,747	4,743	0.0	39,053	45,059	1844	22
PAYNE	26,680	28,124	29,489	0.7	2.32	15,316	15,711	0.4	35,868	41,730	2301	36
PITTSBURG	17,157	17,611	17,857	0.4	2.37	11,944	12,022	0.1	34,930	40,076	2441	43
PONTOTOC	13,978	14,366	14,602	0.4	2.41	9,426	9,487	0.1	33,674	38,678	2589	53
POTTAWATOMIE	24,540	26,165	27,296	0.9	2.53	17,730	18,565	0.6	38,906	44,875	1865	23
PUSHMATAHA	4,739	4,777	4,769	0.1	2.39	3,290	3,252	-0.2	26,765	30,323	3046	77
ROGER MILLS	1,428	1,460	1,478	0.3	2.30	988	991	0.0	35,935	40,562	2290	35
ROGERS	25,724	30,580	34,831	2.4	2.74	20,091	23,551	2.2	55,804	64,526	370	2
SEMINOLE	9,575	9,715	9,782	0.2	2.52	6,793	6,767	-0.1	31,004	35,266	2830	63
SEQUOYAH	14,761	16,010	16,828	1.1	2.56	10,989	11,726	0.9	34,487	39,547	2499	45
STEPHENS	17,463	17,917	18,177	0.4	2.41	12,591	12,688	0.1	37,442	43,082	2076	29
TEXAS	7,153	7,411	7,562	0.5	2.80	5,248	5,345	0.3	43,873	50,159	1228	10
TILLMAN	3,594	3,419	3,274	-0.7	2.43	2,486	2,318	-1.0	30,086	34,253	2904	65
TULSA	226,892	239,598	247,371	0.8	2.42	147,316	152,110	0.4	48,540	57,685	779	5
WAGONER	21,010	25,456	28,841	2.7	2.68	16,698	19,969	2.5	52,163	61,132	539	4
WASHINGTON	20,179	20,590	20,715	0.3	2.36	14,031	14,042	0.0	44,898	51,965	1122	9
WASHITA	4,506	4,553	4,574	0.1	2.48	3,265	3,241	-0.1	35,434	40,057	2377	39
WOODS	3,684	3,542	3,429	-0.5	2.16	2,243	2,103	-0.9	35,188	40,311	2405	41
WOODWARD	7,141	7,448	7,640	0.6	2.43	5,078	5,196	0.3	41,384	47,415	1537	17
OKLAHOMA				0.9	2.46			0.7	41,984	48,966		
UNITED STATES				1.2	2.59			1.0	53,154	62,503		

COUNTY	2007 Per Capita Income	2007 HH Income Base	2007 HOUSEHOLD INCOME DISTRIBUTION (%)					2007 Home Value Base	2007 HOME VALUE DISTRIBUTION (%)					2007 Median Home Value
			Less than $25,000	$25,000 to $49,999	$50,000 to $99,999	$100,000 to $149,999	$150,000 or More		Less than $50,000	$50,000 to $89,999	$90,000 to $174,999	$175,000 to $399,999	$400,000 or More	
ADAIR	14,509	7,950	40.2	32.0	23.1	3.4	1.3	5,860	30.8	35.9	23.0	7.9	2.5	67,586
ALFALFA	19,024	2,132	33.9	35.4	24.2	3.9	2.5	1,736	55.3	24.3	16.0	4.3	0.1	45,306
ATOKA	16,001	5,391	43.6	30.3	20.7	3.8	1.7	4,120	33.9	30.3	27.2	7.5	1.1	70,815
BEAVER	20,995	2,227	25.1	31.5	33.3	7.2	2.9	1,763	33.1	23.6	32.3	9.4	1.6	78,333
BECKHAM	19,179	7,822	36.9	31.9	23.0	5.2	2.9	5,561	36.1	24.7	27.6	10.2	1.3	71,576
BLAINE	17,048	4,160	35.6	32.6	25.0	5.2	1.6	3,196	42.1	28.0	24.6	5.1	0.2	58,869
BRYAN	17,994	15,401	37.2	31.9	24.0	5.0	2.0	10,740	31.0	27.5	31.1	9.4	0.9	75,970
CADDO	16,424	11,185	37.6	32.1	24.5	4.3	1.5	8,232	37.7	30.6	26.4	4.7	0.6	63,722
CANADIAN	25,098	37,544	16.4	25.8	39.7	12.9	5.2	29,706	8.6	17.0	53.1	19.7	1.6	121,248
CARTER	19,512	19,048	34.4	29.8	27.2	6.3	2.2	13,644	29.1	28.0	30.1	11.0	1.7	79,083
CHEROKEE	17,412	17,816	38.5	30.4	24.2	5.0	1.9	11,929	21.5	27.8	36.6	12.3	1.8	90,997
CHOCTAW	15,280	6,438	46.4	29.0	20.7	3.0	0.9	4,591	37.3	33.5	22.9	5.6	0.7	63,013
CIMARRON	19,317	1,206	34.7	33.1	24.4	4.9	2.9	879	43.6	28.0	21.2	5.9	1.4	56,726
CLEVELAND	26,679	92,969	21.1	25.8	35.2	11.9	6.0	62,403	7.0	17.9	50.4	22.1	2.5	124,516
COAL	14,986	2,354	44.4	31.8	19.6	3.0	1.2	1,765	42.9	29.4	20.5	4.9	2.3	57,155
COMANCHE	19,747	41,264	28.5	30.4	31.0	7.4	2.7	25,004	7.2	15.3	47.0	27.3	3.2	138,393
COTTON	18,579	2,649	38.1	27.5	25.7	6.8	1.9	2,030	33.3	30.4	28.9	6.9	0.3	71,296
CRAIG	19,330	5,713	31.9	35.0	25.7	4.5	2.9	4,306	28.6	26.7	30.1	12.1	2.5	79,773
CREEK	20,022	26,521	29.0	30.8	30.2	7.0	3.0	20,702	27.3	28.5	32.6	10.6	1.0	81,584
CUSTER	19,743	10,329	34.4	30.8	26.2	5.8	2.8	6,586	27.0	21.6	37.9	12.0	1.4	92,057
DELAWARE	19,891	16,161	34.3	32.4	25.0	5.2	3.2	12,810	25.0	23.1	31.1	15.7	5.1	93,769
DEWEY	19,818	1,960	37.0	31.3	24.0	4.8	2.9	1,550	43.3	25.7	25.1	5.0	0.9	59,455
ELLIS	20,681	1,815	34.5	34.9	22.8	5.7	2.1	1,461	47.0	27.9	20.5	3.2	1.4	53,398
GARFIELD	21,515	23,365	28.6	32.8	28.8	6.5	3.2	16,481	26.7	30.2	31.4	10.4	1.3	79,965
GARVIN	18,534	11,087	36.9	31.0	25.2	4.5	2.4	8,181	32.4	34.4	24.3	8.1	0.9	68,670
GRADY	20,058	19,434	29.5	30.3	30.5	7.1	2.6	14,710	23.2	27.4	34.5	13.8	1.1	88,921
GRANT	19,277	2,034	33.6	34.2	25.1	4.8	2.4	1,601	44.0	26.9	22.9	5.7	0.6	56,655
GREER	16,898	2,169	41.7	31.8	20.0	4.9	1.7	1,628	51.1	29.1	15.4	3.8	0.6	49,193
HARMON	15,757	1,186	46.4	28.9	19.3	3.4	2.0	911	58.2	21.1	16.9	3.8	0.0	43,992
HARPER	21,812	1,456	28.2	33.7	28.7	6.9	2.5	1,151	42.6	28.8	21.9	5.6	1.1	57,844
HASKELL	16,913	4,788	42.6	31.6	20.1	3.1	2.7	3,715	35.6	30.6	24.9	7.0	1.9	66,566
HUGHES	15,886	5,311	45.9	29.3	19.1	4.3	1.4	4,031	46.3	25.3	20.7	6.8	0.9	54,284
JACKSON	19,424	10,164	31.1	30.6	29.2	6.3	2.8	6,161	25.4	30.0	32.6	10.3	1.7	81,745
JEFFERSON	16,140	2,633	45.1	29.2	20.2	4.1	1.4	1,961	49.9	28.6	14.8	5.2	1.5	50,137
JOHNSTON	16,426	4,147	42.9	31.2	19.6	4.2	2.0	3,073	38.4	30.5	23.9	6.1	1.1	62,149
KAY	20,957	19,001	32.0	30.0	27.1	6.8	3.5	13,650	29.4	30.1	30.0	9.3	1.2	75,625
KINGFISHER	22,755	5,516	23.9	31.4	31.1	10.1	3.5	4,334	25.9	24.7	34.4	14.2	0.9	89,201
KIOWA	17,958	4,177	41.2	29.7	22.3	4.9	2.0	3,143	46.8	31.5	16.5	4.4	0.7	53,618
LATIMER	16,302	3,991	43.6	29.6	20.9	3.7	2.2	2,991	33.3	32.7	27.5	4.9	1.6	69,382
LE FLORE	16,971	18,964	37.3	31.1	25.2	4.6	2.0	14,315	31.6	30.2	29.9	6.9	1.4	73,714
LINCOLN	18,572	12,562	31.4	34.2	26.4	6.0	2.0	10,043	25.5	31.0	32.0	10.5	1.1	80,717
LOGAN	22,447	13,903	25.6	28.8	32.5	9.2	3.9	10,907	20.8	26.5	33.4	17.1	2.1	94,824
LOVE	20,332	3,688	30.5	30.2	30.4	5.9	3.0	3,004	28.3	31.2	28.2	10.3	2.1	73,935
MCCLAIN	22,723	12,161	23.2	30.7	32.5	9.7	3.9	9,898	18.8	22.8	37.0	17.7	3.8	103,118
MCCURTAIN	16,869	13,538	43.1	28.6	20.9	5.2	2.1	9,944	36.9	30.0	24.0	7.5	1.7	64,768
MCINTOSH	20,418	8,314	40.8	28.9	21.7	5.4	3.3	6,576	30.7	26.8	31.1	10.0	1.5	76,913
MAJOR	20,395	3,069	31.1	32.1	29.6	5.1	2.2	2,485	31.0	29.6	30.4	7.6	1.4	74,950
MARSHALL	18,366	5,958	39.1	31.9	22.3	4.4	2.3	4,724	30.9	30.7	29.5	7.6	1.3	72,123
MAYES	19,639	15,916	30.6	31.2	29.1	6.5	2.6	12,280	21.3	28.7	35.2	12.8	2.0	89,979
MURRAY	19,395	5,129	32.1	32.8	27.7	5.6	1.8	3,818	31.1	30.9	29.0	8.0	1.0	73,864
MUSKOGEE	19,081	27,805	36.1	29.8	25.8	5.4	2.9	19,378	26.4	29.8	33.5	9.2	1.2	81,674
NOBLE	21,221	4,557	28.2	32.3	29.0	8.0	2.5	3,444	29.0	30.3	29.6	10.2	1.0	77,133
NOWATA	17,982	4,308	34.8	32.3	26.5	4.4	2.0	3,352	36.2	27.7	24.9	8.9	2.4	67,160
OKFUSKEE	15,596	4,203	43.6	31.4	19.5	3.9	1.6	3,206	39.8	27.3	24.6	7.3	1.0	62,768
OKLAHOMA	24,969	287,905	26.4	30.0	29.1	9.3	5.2	174,253	13.4	27.4	38.9	17.1	3.2	105,977
OKMULGEE	17,568	15,859	37.7	30.1	24.5	5.8	1.8	11,501	34.2	30.5	26.6	7.7	1.0	66,323
OSAGE	20,837	17,609	28.2	29.8	30.6	8.2	3.2	14,167	32.9	25.0	30.1	10.3	1.6	77,334
OTTAWA	17,323	13,202	35.8	34.0	24.6	3.6	2.0	9,745	31.6	30.2	28.0	8.9	1.3	71,716
PAWNEE	19,247	6,483	29.0	34.2	28.2	6.3	2.3	5,187	34.5	28.3	28.3	7.9	1.0	68,581
PAYNE	20,559	28,124	37.3	27.1	24.4	7.5	3.7	15,797	22.2	20.8	36.3	18.2	2.5	103,569
PITTSBURG	18,852	17,611	37.0	30.2	25.3	5.3	2.2	13,373	30.8	30.6	27.8	9.4	1.4	73,341
PONTOTOC	18,903	14,366	37.3	30.3	24.9	4.9	2.6	9,661	27.4	27.3	32.7	10.7	1.9	82,189
POTTAWATOMIE	19,755	26,165	31.1	31.1	28.6	6.3	3.0	18,957	23.3	32.2	34.2	9.5	0.8	80,997
PUSHMATAHA	16,044	4,777	46.5	30.7	17.8	3.3	1.7	3,721	37.2	31.7	23.2	6.1	1.8	63,278
ROGER MILLS	21,322	1,460	34.4	32.7	24.0	5.5	3.4	1,149	38.2	24.1	26.4	9.5	1.8	71,731
ROGERS	23,693	30,580	19.3	25.3	39.2	11.5	4.7	24,828	14.0	17.8	45.5	20.0	2.6	118,124
SEMINOLE	16,626	9,715	41.0	32.0	20.9	4.3	1.7	7,066	42.3	28.8	22.0	6.0	0.9	58,736
SEQUOYAH	17,101	16,010	37.5	30.2	25.8	4.4	2.0	12,059	26.8	31.9	31.6	8.4	1.4	77,892
STEPHENS	20,542	17,917	32.5	31.8	26.4	6.4	2.9	13,548	26.6	30.0	33.0	9.1	1.2	77,789
TEXAS	19,238	7,411	26.1	31.5	31.8	8.0	2.7	5,007	24.3	27.0	35.9	10.6	2.1	88,370
TILLMAN	17,915	3,419	43.0	29.7	19.9	4.6	2.8	2,638	53.9	23.0	17.9	4.1	1.1	45,612
TULSA	27,225	239,598	23.4	28.0	31.3	10.6	6.8	148,708	11.1	23.2	43.9	18.2	3.6	111,222
WAGONER	23,584	25,456	20.9	26.8	36.6	11.1	4.6	20,615	17.6	20.9	42.9	16.7	1.9	109,118
WASHINGTON	26,456	20,590	27.7	27.6	28.9	9.5	6.3	15,271	23.3	26.3	35.5	12.8	2.1	90,467
WASHITA	18,909	4,553	33.5	34.0	24.8	5.2	2.5	3,401	40.3	31.0	22.7	5.9	0.1	61,034
WOODS	21,642	3,542	35.5	31.0	25.2	4.8	3.5	2,469	37.0	29.5	26.0	6.3	1.2	67,380
WOODWARD	20,711	7,448	28.7	32.5	28.9	7.5	2.5	5,385	24.7	30.1	36.5	7.6	1.0	84,043
OKLAHOMA	22,509		28.9	29.5	29.2	8.2	4.2		20.6	25.7	36.9	14.4	2.3	95,826
UNITED STATES	27,916		21.9	25.0	32.3	12.3	8.4		7.9	10.5	27.1	35.6	19.0	192,285

SPENDING POTENTIAL INDICES

COUNTY	FINANCIAL SERVICES				THE HOME						ENTERTAINMENT						PERSONAL			
					Home Improvements		Furnishings													
	Auto Loan	Home Loan	Invest-ments	Retire-ment Plans	Home Repair	Lawn & Garden	Comput-ers & Hard-ware	Major Appli-ances	TV, Radio, Sound Equip-ment	Furni-ture	Dine out/ Carry out	Sports Equip-ment	Fees & Tickets	Toys & Games	Travel	Cable TV	Apparel & Services	Auto Repairs	Health Insur-ance	Pets & Supplies
ADAIR	68	47	31	46	51	68	49	60	56	48	55	53	42	59	48	60	47	56	66	65
ALFALFA	81	54	30	51	64	89	57	76	64	54	64	67	46	69	57	69	53	68	82	83
ATOKA	66	47	33	45	54	72	50	63	56	47	55	55	42	57	50	60	47	58	69	67
BEAVER	94	64	35	61	75	103	67	88	74	64	74	79	54	80	66	79	62	80	94	97
BECKHAM	72	56	49	56	59	73	61	67	67	57	65	59	54	68	60	70	56	65	76	70
BLAINE	74	52	38	51	59	79	57	70	64	53	62	61	48	66	56	68	53	65	78	74
BRYAN	69	54	47	54	57	70	59	65	63	55	62	57	52	64	57	66	54	63	71	67
CADDO	69	52	41	51	57	73	55	65	61	53	60	56	48	63	55	65	52	61	73	69
CANADIAN	98	99	97	99	96	97	92	95	93	95	92	85	94	96	93	93	83	93	95	96
CARTER	74	61	56	60	63	75	63	69	69	61	67	61	58	69	63	72	58	67	77	72
CHEROKEE	67	53	48	53	55	67	60	63	62	56	62	57	53	62	57	64	54	62	67	66
CHOCTAW	59	43	33	42	48	63	46	56	52	43	51	48	40	53	46	56	43	52	63	59
CIMARRON	82	55	31	52	65	91	59	77	66	55	65	69	47	70	58	71	55	70	85	84
CLEVELAND	95	91	89	93	84	85	96	89	93	93	93	83	92	93	91	90	83	92	87	90
COAL	60	44	35	42	49	65	48	58	53	45	52	51	41	54	47	56	44	54	64	61
COMANCHE	76	67	67	69	64	68	73	70	74	71	74	64	69	75	69	74	66	72	73	71
COTTON	75	53	39	52	60	80	58	71	65	53	63	62	49	67	57	70	54	65	81	75
CRAIG	81	57	40	55	65	87	61	76	69	57	67	67	51	71	61	75	57	70	86	81
CREEK	84	69	57	67	71	84	68	78	74	67	73	69	63	76	68	78	63	74	83	81
CUSTER	70	58	62	60	60	68	69	67	70	62	69	60	62	69	65	71	60	67	72	68
DELAWARE	78	61	47	59	67	86	61	76	67	60	66	65	55	67	63	72	57	70	82	79
DEWEY	78	53	33	51	62	86	58	74	64	53	64	65	47	68	57	69	53	67	82	80
ELLIS	79	53	32	51	62	86	57	74	64	53	63	66	46	68	56	69	53	67	82	80
GARFIELD	76	66	69	68	69	78	70	74	74	68	72	64	67	75	67	77	63	72	81	75
GARVIN	72	53	45	53	59	75	59	68	65	54	63	59	51	66	58	70	54	64	78	71
GRADY	79	65	60	65	68	81	67	75	73	65	71	65	62	74	67	76	62	72	82	77
GRANT	81	54	30	52	64	90	58	77	64	54	64	68	46	69	57	69	54	69	83	84
GREER	66	47	36	46	53	70	52	62	58	47	56	55	44	60	51	63	48	58	72	66
HARMON	63	45	36	44	51	67	50	60	57	46	55	52	43	58	50	61	46	56	70	63
HARPER	86	58	36	56	68	94	63	81	70	58	69	71	51	74	62	75	58	73	90	87
HASKELL	71	51	35	49	57	77	53	67	60	50	59	58	45	62	53	64	50	61	74	71
HUGHES	64	46	34	44	51	68	49	60	56	46	54	52	42	57	49	60	46	56	68	63
JACKSON	76	61	60	63	61	70	70	70	74	65	72	63	64	74	67	75	63	71	76	71
JEFFERSON	63	45	34	44	51	68	49	60	55	45	54	52	42	57	49	60	45	55	69	63
JOHNSTON	68	49	35	47	54	73	52	64	59	49	58	56	44	60	51	63	49	59	71	68
KAY	76	64	65	65	67	78	68	73	74	65	71	64	64	74	68	77	62	71	82	75
KINGFISHER	95	77	61	74	83	102	74	90	81	75	81	79	69	85	76	86	70	83	96	96
KIOWA	68	49	39	48	54	71	54	64	61	49	58	56	46	62	53	65	50	61	74	67
LATIMER	69	49	34	47	55	73	52	64	58	49	57	56	44	60	51	63	49	59	71	68
LE FLORE	73	53	38	52	58	76	56	67	63	53	61	59	48	65	55	67	53	63	75	72
LINCOLN	80	58	40	55	64	85	60	74	67	57	66	65	51	69	60	72	56	68	83	79
LOGAN	89	79	73	79	81	92	78	85	81	77	80	76	74	83	78	84	71	82	89	88
LOVE	87	63	42	60	69	93	64	80	72	62	71	70	55	75	63	77	60	73	87	86
MCCLAIN	94	81	68	80	82	95	78	88	83	78	82	78	74	86	79	86	72	84	92	92
MCCURTAIN	71	50	35	49	55	73	53	65	60	51	59	57	46	62	52	65	51	61	71	70
MCINTOSH	75	60	49	57	66	84	61	75	67	59	65	63	55	65	63	71	56	70	83	77
MAJOR	81	59	41	56	68	90	61	78	68	58	67	68	52	72	61	73	57	71	86	84
MARSHALL	70	55	43	53	60	77	56	68	62	54	60	58	50	61	57	66	52	64	76	71
MAYES	81	63	48	61	66	84	63	75	70	62	69	66	57	72	63	74	59	70	81	79
MURRAY	77	56	43	55	63	83	61	73	68	57	66	64	52	69	60	72	56	68	82	77
MUSKOGEE	71	60	60	60	62	72	63	68	69	61	67	59	60	68	63	71	59	66	75	70
NOBLE	84	65	51	64	70	87	67	78	73	65	72	69	60	76	66	78	62	74	85	82
NOWATA	76	54	37	51	60	82	57	71	64	54	63	62	48	66	56	69	53	65	78	76
OKFUSKEE	65	47	34	45	52	69	50	61	56	47	55	53	43	58	49	60	47	56	68	65
OKLAHOMA	84	78	84	81	75	77	85	79	86	82	85	73	82	85	81	85	76	83	83	80
OKMULGEE	69	54	48	54	59	80	58	64	64	55	62	56	52	64	57	68	54	62	72	67
OSAGE	84	69	60	68	73	87	70	80	76	68	74	70	65	77	70	80	64	76	87	83
OTTAWA	67	53	48	52	57	70	57	64	63	54	61	55	51	63	56	66	53	61	72	66
PAWNEE	82	61	44	59	66	85	63	76	70	60	69	67	55	72	62	74	59	71	83	80
PAYNE	72	58	59	61	57	64	76	66	73	66	73	62	66	71	67	71	64	70	69	68
PITTSBURG	70	56	52	55	61	75	60	68	65	56	63	59	54	64	60	69	54	65	76	70
PONTOTOC	70	55	54	56	58	70	62	66	66	58	64	58	56	66	60	69	56	65	73	68
POTTAWATOMIE	78	65	59	65	67	79	67	74	72	65	71	65	62	73	67	75	62	71	80	76
PUSHMATAHA	64	46	31	44	52	70	48	61	54	45	53	53	41	56	48	59	45	55	68	65
ROGER MILLS	85	57	34	55	67	93	61	80	68	57	68	71	50	73	60	74	57	72	88	87
ROGERS	97	93	87	93	92	98	87	93	89	89	89	83	87	92	88	91	79	90	94	96
SEMINOLE	68	50	40	49	54	70	54	63	60	51	59	55	47	62	53	64	50	60	71	66
SEQUOYAH	73	53	39	52	58	76	56	67	62	54	61	59	48	64	55	66	52	63	73	72
STEPHENS	76	62	56	61	66	81	64	73	71	61	69	64	59	71	65	75	59	70	83	76
TEXAS	86	69	55	68	71	85	73	80	75	70	75	73	65	78	70	77	65	78	83	84
TILLMAN	73	51	38	50	58	77	56	68	63	52	62	60	47	65	55	68	52	63	78	72
TULSA	93	89	93	92	85	85	93	88	93	92	93	80	92	94	90	93	84	91	90	88
WAGONER	94	88	82	88	88	95	85	91	87	86	86	81	83	90	85	88	77	88	92	93
WASHINGTON	90	83	89	84	85	93	84	88	89	82	86	77	83	88	86	92	76	86	97	89
WASHITA	78	55	39	54	63	84	61	74	66	56	65	65	50	70	59	70	55	68	81	79
WOODS	76	57	52	57	62	77	67	72	71	60	69	64	58	71	64	74	59	70	81	75
WOODWARD	83	64	51	63	68	84	67	77	73	60	72	68	60	76	64	77	62	73	85	81
OKLAHOMA	84	72	69	73	73	82	76	79	79	74	78	71	72	80	74	81	69	78	84	81
UNITED STATES	100	100	100	100	100	100	100	100	100	100	100	100	100	100	100	100	100	100	100	100

COUNTY	FIPS Code	CBSA Code	DMA Code	POPULATION			2000-2007 ANNUAL RATE		RACE (%)					
									White		Black		Asian/Pacific	
				2000	2007	2012	% Rate	State Rank	2000	2007	2000	2007	2000	2007
BAKER	001	00000	820	16,741	16,798	16,792	0.0	31	95.7	95.6	0.2	0.2	0.4	0.4
BENTON	003	18700	801	78,153	82,483	85,965	0.7	22	89.2	87.2	0.8	0.9	4.7	5.8
CLACKAMAS	005	38900	820	338,391	375,391	403,090	1.4	11	91.3	89.6	0.7	0.7	2.6	3.3
CLATSOP	007	11820	820	35,630	37,028	38,069	0.5	25	93.1	91.9	0.5	0.6	1.4	1.7
COLUMBIA	009	38900	820	43,560	48,853	53,258	1.6	8	94.4	93.7	0.2	0.3	0.7	0.9
COOS	011	18300	801	62,779	64,076	66,023	0.3	27	92.0	91.1	0.3	0.3	1.1	1.3
CROOK	013	39260	820	19,182	22,842	25,820	2.4	2	93.0	91.4	0.0	0.1	0.5	0.6
CURRY	015	15060	813	21,137	22,664	23,814	1.0	15	92.9	92.1	0.2	0.2	0.8	1.0
DESCHUTES	017	13460	821	115,367	156,004	194,015	4.3	1	94.8	93.9	0.2	0.2	0.8	1.0
DOUGLAS	019	40700	801	100,399	105,822	109,884	0.7	22	93.9	93.1	0.2	0.2	0.7	0.9
GILLIAM	021	00000	820	1,915	1,907	1,882	-0.1	33	96.8	96.7	0.2	0.2	0.2	0.2
GRANT	023	00000	820	7,935	7,752	7,576	-0.3	35	95.7	95.2	0.1	0.1	0.2	0.3
HARNEY	025	00000	820	7,609	7,380	7,218	-0.4	36	91.9	91.2	0.1	0.1	0.6	0.7
HOOD RIVER	027	26220	820	20,411	22,527	23,898	1.4	11	78.9	74.4	0.6	0.7	1.6	1.9
JACKSON	029	32780	813	181,269	204,464	220,869	1.7	6	91.6	90.1	0.4	0.4	1.1	1.3
JEFFERSON	031	00000	820	19,009	21,476	23,111	1.7	6	69.0	66.0	0.3	0.3	0.5	0.6
JOSEPHINE	033	24420	813	75,726	83,038	88,563	1.3	13	93.9	93.0	0.3	0.3	0.7	0.9
KLAMATH	035	28900	813	63,775	67,237	69,486	0.7	22	87.3	85.7	0.6	0.7	0.9	1.1
LAKE	037	00000	813	7,422	7,315	7,217	-0.2	34	91.0	89.4	0.1	0.2	0.8	1.1
LANE	039	21660	801	322,959	342,781	357,477	0.8	18	90.6	89.1	0.8	0.8	2.2	2.7
LINCOLN	041	00000	820	44,479	46,860	48,679	0.7	22	90.6	89.4	0.3	0.3	1.1	1.3
LINN	043	10540	820	103,069	111,474	117,958	1.1	14	93.2	92.1	0.3	0.4	0.9	1.1
MALHEUR	045	36620	757	31,615	31,639	31,408	0.0	31	75.8	75.4	1.2	1.3	2.0	2.0
MARION	047	41420	820	284,834	312,257	330,736	1.3	13	81.6	77.8	0.9	0.9	2.1	2.5
MORROW	049	37820	810	10,995	12,224	12,926	1.5	9	76.3	71.0	0.1	0.1	0.5	0.6
MULTNOMAH	051	38900	820	660,486	694,967	717,684	0.7	22	79.2	76.1	5.7	6.0	6.0	7.3
POLK	053	41420	820	62,380	71,544	78,602	1.9	4	89.2	87.2	0.4	0.5	1.3	1.6
SHERMAN	055	00000	820	1,934	2,029	2,089	0.7	22	93.6	93.6	0.2	0.2	0.5	0.4
TILLAMOOK	057	00000	820	24,262	25,833	26,976	0.9	16	93.9	92.8	0.2	0.3	0.9	1.0
UMATILLA	059	37820	810	70,548	74,834	76,672	0.8	18	82.0	78.5	0.8	0.9	0.9	1.1
UNION	061	29260	820	24,530	25,066	25,492	0.3	27	94.3	93.4	0.5	0.6	1.5	1.8
WALLOWA	063	00000	881	7,226	7,218	7,174	0.0	31	96.5	96.5	0.0	0.0	0.3	0.3
WASCO	065	17180	820	23,791	24,098	24,289	0.2	28	86.6	84.2	0.3	0.3	1.3	1.6
WASHINGTON	067	38900	820	445,342	517,996	575,388	2.1	3	82.2	78.7	1.1	1.2	7.0	8.4
WHEELER	069	00000	820	1,547	1,561	1,570	0.1	29	93.3	93.3	0.1	0.1	0.3	0.3
YAMHILL	071	38900	820	84,992	95,296	103,126	1.6	8	89.0	86.8	0.8	0.9	1.2	1.4
OREGON							1.3		86.6	84.4	1.6	1.7	3.2	3.9
UNITED STATES							1.2		75.1	72.7	12.3	12.6	3.8	4.5

OREGON

B

POPULATION COMPOSITION

COUNTY	% HISPANIC ORIGIN		2007 AGE DISTRIBUTION (%)										MEDIAN AGE	% 2007 Males	% 2007 Females
	2000	2007	0-4	5-9	10-14	15-19	20-24	25-44	45-64	65-84	85+	18+	2007		
BAKER	2.3	2.4	5.5	5.1	5.3	6.9	7.4	19.6	30.9	16.2	3.1	79.7	45.1	49.9	50.1
BENTON	4.7	6.2	5.1	5.0	5.4	9.0	13.3	26.4	25.5	8.5	1.7	80.4	32.4	50.0	50.0
CLACKAMAS	4.9	6.7	6.3	6.3	6.9	6.8	6.4	25.1	30.6	9.8	1.8	76.2	39.4	49.4	50.6
CLATSOP	4.5	6.1	5.5	5.3	5.6	7.4	7.5	21.9	31.5	13.0	2.4	79.3	42.6	49.5	50.5
COLUMBIA	2.5	3.4	6.5	5.9	6.7	7.4	7.1	24.0	30.4	10.5	1.6	76.2	40.0	49.9	50.1
COOS	3.4	4.6	4.8	4.6	4.9	6.5	7.0	20.4	32.2	16.7	2.8	81.8	46.1	48.9	51.1
CROOK	5.6	7.6	6.5	5.8	6.4	7.3	5.6	22.7	30.1	14.0	1.7	77.0	41.5	49.8	50.2
CURRY	3.6	4.8	4.1	3.8	4.5	5.7	5.1	15.9	35.1	22.5	3.2	83.8	51.8	49.2	50.8
DESCHUTES	3.7	5.1	6.1	5.8	6.3	6.9	6.4	25.0	30.1	11.7	1.7	77.5	40.5	49.5	50.5
DOUGLAS	3.3	4.4	5.7	5.3	5.6	6.5	6.6	21.8	30.8	15.4	2.4	79.4	43.8	49.2	50.8
GILLIAM	1.8	1.8	4.6	4.4	5.7	6.0	5.4	20.9	32.9	17.7	2.4	80.9	46.4	51.2	48.8
GRANT	2.1	2.8	6.0	5.4	6.2	6.1	7.8	19.5	31.1	14.9	3.0	78.3	44.2	49.4	50.6
HARNEY	4.2	5.6	5.7	5.4	6.6	8.0	5.0	22.5	30.5	14.3	2.0	77.2	42.9	51.2	48.8
HOOD RIVER	25.0	31.5	7.5	7.1	6.8	7.2	6.9	26.2	26.7	9.4	2.2	74.0	36.3	49.8	50.2
JACKSON	6.7	9.0	6.1	5.6	6.3	6.9	6.5	23.8	29.8	12.5	2.5	77.8	41.0	48.8	51.2
JEFFERSON	17.7	22.8	7.9	7.2	7.5	7.9	6.2	25.1	24.9	11.9	1.4	72.3	36.3	50.2	49.8
JOSEPHINE	4.3	5.8	5.4	4.9	5.7	6.6	6.3	20.0	32.3	16.0	2.8	79.9	45.8	48.6	51.4
KLAMATH	7.8	10.3	6.4	5.8	6.4	7.4	6.8	23.7	28.9	12.7	2.0	77.0	40.0	50.2	49.8
LAKE	5.4	7.4	5.1	4.7	5.8	6.9	6.9	19.7	32.4	16.3	2.2	79.7	45.5	50.3	49.7
LANE	4.6	6.2	5.7	5.3	5.8	7.1	9.1	25.4	28.1	11.3	2.2	79.5	38.3	49.2	50.8
LINCOLN	4.8	6.4	4.7	4.6	4.7	6.0	5.8	19.8	34.7	17.0	2.6	82.2	47.8	48.7	51.3
LINN	4.4	5.9	7.0	6.4	6.4	6.6	6.8	24.9	27.5	11.9	2.4	76.1	38.7	49.4	50.6
MALHEUR	25.6	25.9	8.0	7.0	6.6	6.7	8.6	27.2	22.7	10.8	2.3	74.5	33.9	53.9	46.1
MARION	17.1	22.1	7.7	7.0	6.9	7.3	7.6	27.2	24.1	10.1	2.1	74.1	33.9	50.3	49.7
MORROW	24.4	30.9	8.8	8.0	7.6	6.5	8.2	24.5	25.6	9.6	1.1	71.7	34.4	51.5	48.5
MULTNOMAH	7.5	9.9	6.2	5.9	5.8	6.3	6.9	31.6	26.7	8.7	2.0	78.5	32.9	49.7	50.3
POLK	8.8	11.7	6.1	5.8	6.2	7.9	8.8	23.0	27.2	11.8	2.2	77.6	36.5	48.5	51.5
SHERMAN	4.9	4.9	5.2	5.1	4.9	8.4	6.7	19.3	32.9	15.4	3.1	79.9	38.2	50.4	49.6
TILLAMOOK	5.1	6.9	4.9	4.7	5.6	6.1	5.5	20.7	33.3	16.8	2.2	80.9	45.3	50.6	49.4
UMATILLA	16.1	21.0	7.7	6.9	7.1	6.4	8.1	27.0	24.8	10.2	1.9	74.5	46.5	51.6	48.4
UNION	2.4	3.3	6.0	5.6	5.5	7.7	8.7	23.0	28.9	11.8	2.8	78.7	35.1	48.8	51.2
WALLOWA	1.7	1.7	4.9	4.9	5.3	7.2	6.3	17.7	34.9	16.0	2.9	80.0	39.2	50.1	49.9
WASCO	9.3	12.4	6.6	6.0	6.0	6.7	7.1	21.5	29.4	14.0	2.6	77.1	47.3	49.4	50.6
WASHINGTON	11.2	14.5	7.8	7.5	7.3	6.4	6.6	31.4	24.4	7.2	1.4	73.5	41.7	49.8	50.2
WHEELER	5.1	5.2	4.5	4.5	3.7	6.5	10.4	13.8	33.4	20.9	2.2	82.1	34.3	51.8	48.2
YAMHILL	10.6	14.0	7.1	6.5	6.7	7.9	7.8	26.7	25.9	9.6	1.9	75.4	50.6	50.4	49.6
													35.6		
OREGON	8.0	10.5	6.5	6.1	6.3	6.8	7.2	26.7	27.7	10.6	2.0	77.1	37.8	49.7	50.3
UNITED STATES	12.5	15.0	6.9	6.5	6.8	7.1	7.0	27.6	25.4	10.7	1.9	75.6	36.7	49.2	50.8

52-B

COUNTY	HOUSEHOLDS					FAMILIES			MEDIAN HOUSEHOLD INCOME			
	2000	2007	2012	% Annual Rate 2000-2007	2007 Average HH Size	2000	2007	% Annual Rate 2000-2007	2007	2012	2007 National Rank	2007 State Rank
BAKER	6,883	6,933	6,962	0.1	2.35	4,681	4,672	0.0	36,775	41,883	2154	33
BENTON	30,145	32,556	34,140	1.1	2.39	18,244	19,486	0.9	52,607	61,831	516	7
CLACKAMAS	128,201	140,217	150,705	1.2	2.66	91,670	99,461	1.1	66,646	78,857	154	1
CLATSOP	14,703	15,432	15,952	0.7	2.33	9,450	9,820	0.5	45,804	53,188	1023	15
COLUMBIA	16,375	18,414	20,115	1.6	2.64	12,034	13,431	1.5	56,816	66,001	335	3
COOS	26,213	27,115	28,137	0.5	2.31	17,448	17,877	0.3	39,477	45,199	1782	27
CROOK	7,354	8,737	9,878	2.4	2.58	5,425	6,400	2.3	43,282	50,000	1303	19
CURRY	9,543	10,395	11,010	1.2	2.15	6,180	6,665	1.0	36,550	41,672	2185	34
DESCHUTES	45,595	62,836	78,564	4.5	2.46	31,953	43,669	4.4	52,074	61,423	543	8
DOUGLAS	39,821	42,528	44,464	0.9	2.45	28,218	29,889	0.8	40,879	46,974	1616	24
GILLIAM	819	831	828	0.2	2.26	544	547	0.1	41,341	47,242	1544	23
GRANT	3,246	3,210	3,156	-0.2	2.36	2,233	2,189	-0.3	39,945	45,109	1735	26
HARNEY	3,036	2,968	2,915	-0.3	2.43	2,094	2,029	-0.4	37,489	42,632	2066	31
HOOD RIVER	7,248	7,893	8,332	1.2	2.74	5,175	5,590	1.1	47,588	55,333	856	10
JACKSON	71,532	81,008	87,723	1.7	2.48	48,423	54,343	1.6	45,911	53,299	1011	14
JEFFERSON	6,727	7,622	8,219	1.7	2.80	5,166	5,815	1.6	44,460	51,115	1163	18
JOSEPHINE	31,000	34,220	36,626	1.4	2.40	21,364	23,377	1.2	38,750	44,435	1888	29
KLAMATH	25,205	26,224	27,158	0.5	2.51	17,293	17,828	0.4	38,626	44,349	1912	30
LAKE	3,084	3,104	3,094	0.1	2.34	2,152	2,147	0.0	35,634	40,673	2346	35
LANE	130,453	139,621	146,278	0.9	2.40	82,180	87,043	0.8	46,448	53,851	957	12
LINCOLN	19,296	20,486	21,374	0.8	2.26	12,244	12,867	0.7	40,852	46,859	1620	25
LINN	39,541	42,852	45,409	1.1	2.58	28,232	30,350	1.0	46,778	54,066	930	11
MALHEUR	10,221	10,076	9,955	-0.2	2.80	7,346	7,184	-0.3	37,095	42,518	2116	32
MARION	101,641	110,069	116,255	1.1	2.73	70,458	75,644	1.0	50,335	59,241	653	9
MORROW	3,776	4,084	4,286	1.1	2.98	2,920	3,139	1.0	46,386	53,634	961	13
MULTNOMAH	272,098	287,698	297,307	0.8	2.36	152,232	158,983	0.6	53,566	63,984	473	5
POLK	23,058	26,068	28,711	1.7	2.65	16,130	18,081	1.6	53,112	62,138	497	6
SHERMAN	797	836	861	0.7	2.43	546	568	0.5	42,193	47,538	1427	21
TILLAMOOK	10,200	10,912	11,437	0.9	2.32	6,798	7,203	0.8	42,310	48,752	1416	20
UMATILLA	25,195	26,314	26,926	0.6	2.68	17,846	18,480	0.5	45,070	51,785	1103	16
UNION	9,740	10,068	10,298	0.5	2.42	6,514	6,672	0.3	41,987	48,314	1449	22
WALLOWA	3,029	3,059	3,058	0.1	2.32	2,084	2,086	0.0	39,428	44,854	1793	28
WASCO	9,401	9,509	9,588	0.2	2.48	6,503	6,519	0.0	44,503	51,690	1158	17
WASHINGTON	169,162	193,957	215,002	1.9	2.65	114,074	129,596	1.8	66,565	78,682	156	2
WHEELER	653	662	668	0.2	2.31	445	447	0.1	34,778	39,204	2459	36
YAMHILL	28,732	32,554	35,379	1.7	2.77	21,372	24,041	1.6	54,980	64,110	406	4
OREGON				1.3	2.51			1.2	51,735	60,975		
UNITED STATES				1.2	2.59			1.0	53,154	62,503		

COUNTY	2007 Per Capita Income	2007 HH Income Base	2007 HOUSEHOLD INCOME DISTRIBUTION (%)					2007 Home Value Base	2007 HOME VALUE DISTRIBUTION (%)					2007 Median Home Value
			Less than $25,000	$25,000 to $49,999	$50,000 to $99,999	$100,000 to $149,999	$150,000 or More		Less than $50,000	$50,000 to $89,999	$90,000 to $174,999	$175,000 to $399,999	$400,000 or More	
BAKER	19,566	6,933	31.7	35.9	25.6	5.0	1.8	5,026	5.4	9.7	40.7	32.4	11.9	162,917
BENTON	28,721	32,556	23.2	24.6	31.7	12.8	7.8	19,496	4.2	2.4	9.5	63.7	20.2	270,123
CLACKAMAS	33,419	140,217	12.9	21.7	36.5	16.5	12.4	102,650	3.8	2.8	5.9	46.5	40.9	360,422
CLATSOP	24,804	15,432	25.5	28.4	34.1	8.0	4.0	10,319	5.0	3.1	14.7	57.5	19.7	252,221
COLUMBIA	25,337	18,414	18.9	24.0	40.4	11.7	5.0	14,327	5.6	2.6	15.4	58.6	17.8	263,158
COOS	21,678	27,115	32.2	29.8	29.5	5.8	2.9	19,133	7.0	6.3	36.7	42.2	7.8	175,041
CROOK	20,509	8,737	26.7	30.7	34.2	6.2	2.3	6,659	7.0	5.3	29.0	46.1	12.5	190,297
CURRY	22,748	10,395	32.2	32.9	26.9	4.8	3.2	7,833	12.4	6.1	19.8	43.1	18.6	218,271
DESCHUTES	28,214	62,836	18.8	28.9	34.9	10.6	6.8	46,698	2.5	2.6	8.6	48.4	38.0	340,652
DOUGLAS	20,895	42,528	28.3	32.3	30.6	6.1	2.7	31,470	6.5	5.7	34.4	44.3	9.1	182,253
GILLIAM	22,240	831	28.5	31.4	30.7	7.2	2.2	599	5.5	17.0	41.9	30.9	4.7	147,083
GRANT	20,686	3,210	27.9	36.3	27.7	5.8	2.3	2,440	11.3	9.8	40.7	28.9	9.4	150,680
HARNEY	20,496	2,968	28.3	36.4	25.4	6.9	3.0	2,225	10.4	14.9	40.4	24.3	10.1	144,325
HOOD RIVER	22,113	7,893	20.7	31.9	34.7	7.5	5.2	5,327	6.2	2.0	10.4	55.8	25.6	280,726
JACKSON	24,807	81,008	24.7	29.6	31.5	8.8	5.4	55,831	6.6	3.9	10.7	53.6	25.2	276,904
JEFFERSON	19,256	7,622	21.7	36.1	32.2	7.3	2.7	5,618	7.0	4.3	31.2	48.8	8.7	189,185
JOSEPHINE	21,088	34,220	31.7	32.4	26.6	6.2	3.2	24,800	5.5	4.0	23.0	54.8	12.7	219,721
KLAMATH	20,217	26,224	31.2	30.9	28.9	5.9	3.2	18,433	6.0	10.3	40.7	36.5	6.5	161,137
LAKE	19,925	3,104	34.5	31.2	27.2	4.7	2.4	2,225	12.4	15.1	42.6	23.3	6.7	130,880
LANE	25,123	139,620	25.4	28.4	32.5	8.7	5.1	90,410	5.0	3.2	15.0	62.3	14.6	241,143
LINCOLN	23,663	20,486	28.5	31.5	30.1	6.7	3.3	13,857	5.6	3.2	19.6	52.0	19.6	248,715
LINN	22,252	42,852	23.6	29.7	34.6	8.6	3.5	30,114	5.0	4.0	19.0	58.6	13.4	228,161
MALHEUR	17,524	10,076	31.7	33.2	26.9	5.8	2.3	6,677	7.3	10.3	39.8	35.7	6.8	160,475
MARION	22,854	110,069	20.3	29.3	35.8	10.0	4.6	71,805	4.4	3.8	24.2	56.9	10.7	212,817
MORROW	19,000	4,084	20.6	33.1	36.3	7.0	3.0	3,062	14.0	9.7	35.9	35.3	5.1	154,696
MULTNOMAH	29,741	287,698	20.0	26.2	34.8	11.2	7.8	170,035	2.2	1.2	7.7	66.7	22.2	284,003
POLK	24,420	26,068	20.2	26.8	36.4	11.0	5.6	18,418	3.9	4.0	17.9	59.7	14.4	235,008
SHERMAN	21,461	836	28.6	30.6	31.6	5.7	3.5	605	8.8	14.0	45.8	26.6	4.8	141,168
TILLAMOOK	23,406	10,912	26.6	32.6	31.7	5.6	3.5	8,115	5.3	2.5	18.7	52.9	20.5	239,057
UMATILLA	20,415	26,314	25.3	30.4	33.4	7.9	3.0	17,769	8.4	6.3	35.6	42.9	6.8	174,465
UNION	21,520	10,068	30.0	29.6	30.1	7.0	3.3	6,924	6.5	7.2	36.0	41.0	9.4	175,739
WALLOWA	21,709	3,059	31.1	32.1	27.3	6.2	3.3	2,277	3.4	6.0	29.5	44.0	17.0	201,798
WASCO	22,022	9,509	26.1	30.0	32.5	8.2	3.2	6,725	5.6	5.4	32.1	48.7	8.3	187,049
WASHINGTON	32,332	193,957	12.3	22.6	37.4	16.4	11.3	122,780	2.6	1.8	5.1	57.1	33.5	345,100
WHEELER	19,850	662	32.5	37.2	23.9	3.3	3.2	489	5.5	16.4	40.5	22.3	15.3	149,423
YAMHILL	24,049	32,554	17.4	27.2	38.7	10.7	6.0	23,396	3.5	4.5	13.7	54.8	23.4	264,940
OREGON	26,912		20.9	27.2	34.2	10.9	6.8		4.3	3.4	15.0	55.1	22.2	267,166
UNITED STATES	27,916		21.9	25.0	32.3	12.3	8.4		7.9	10.5	27.1	35.6	19.0	192,285

COUNTY	FINANCIAL SERVICES				THE HOME						ENTERTAINMENT						PERSONAL			
					Home Improvements		Furnishings													
	Auto Loan	Home Loan	Investments	Retirement Plans	Home Repair	Lawn & Garden	Computers & Hardware	Major Appliances	TV, Radio, Sound Equipment	Furniture	Dine out/ Carry out	Sports Equipment	Fees & Tickets	Toys & Games	Travel	Cable TV	Apparel & Services	Auto Repairs	Health Insurance	Pets & Supplies
BAKER	73	56	47	56	62	79	60	71	65	56	63	62	53	65	60	69	54	66	78	73
BENTON	96	92	97	96	89	88	105	92	98	98	99	88	100	97	97	95	90	98	90	93
CLACKAMAS	119	130	136	133	130	122	124	122	119	127	120	114	129	121	126	118	110	121	117	123
CLATSOP	84	76	75	77	79	89	79	84	80	76	80	74	75	80	80	83	70	82	88	86
COLUMBIA	97	94	91	94	95	100	90	96	91	91	91	87	90	94	92	92	82	92	95	98
COOS	73	64	64	64	68	79	67	74	70	64	69	64	63	69	69	73	60	71	81	75
CROOK	83	67	56	66	73	90	69	81	74	67	73	70	63	75	70	78	63	76	87	84
CURRY	72	65	60	63	71	84	63	76	67	63	65	64	61	63	68	71	56	72	82	76
DESCHUTES	100	97	93	98	97	102	95	99	95	95	95	90	94	95	96	96	84	98	99	101
DOUGLAS	78	66	60	65	71	84	67	77	71	65	70	67	63	71	69	75	61	73	83	79
GILLIAM	91	58	25	55	71	103	61	86	68	58	69	76	47	75	60	73	57	76	90	95
GRANT	83	62	40	60	68	89	62	77	67	60	67	68	54	70	61	71	57	71	81	83
HARNEY	82	60	45	59	68	89	63	78	70	60	69	68	55	73	63	75	59	71	86	83
HOOD RIVER	93	80	71	80	81	92	83	88	84	81	84	81	77	86	81	85	74	87	90	91
JACKSON	87	82	83	83	85	91	84	88	85	82	84	79	82	84	85	86	75	86	90	89
JEFFERSON	86	71	54	70	73	88	70	81	74	69	74	71	64	77	70	77	64	77	83	85
JOSEPHINE	76	64	58	64	70	85	67	77	70	64	69	67	61	69	69	73	59	73	82	79
KLAMATH	76	65	62	65	68	78	68	74	71	66	70	65	64	71	68	74	62	72	79	75
LAKE	76	57	43	55	64	83	59	73	65	56	64	63	52	67	59	70	55	67	80	77
LANE	84	80	84	82	80	83	86	83	85	82	84	76	83	84	84	84	76	84	84	84
LINCOLN	81	69	61	68	75	91	70	82	73	68	72	71	65	72	72	77	63	77	86	84
LINN	83	77	76	77	79	85	77	82	79	76	79	73	75	80	78	81	70	80	85	84
MALHEUR	77	60	49	59	64	78	65	73	69	62	68	66	57	70	63	71	60	70	77	76
MARION	87	84	87	85	83	83	88	86	87	86	87	80	86	86	86	86	78	88	86	86
MORROW	90	75	57	73	75	88	75	84	78	74	78	77	69	81	74	79	68	82	85	87
MULTNOMAH	91	94	104	97	93	87	102	92	98	99	99	89	101	97	99	96	91	97	91	92
POLK	91	90	92	90	90	92	92	91	90	89	90	83	90	90	91	90	81	91	91	92
SHERMAN	92	62	31	58	73	103	63	87	70	61	71	76	51	76	63	76	60	77	92	95
TILLAMOOK	86	69	53	68	78	99	70	87	74	68	73	75	63	75	72	78	63	80	91	91
UMATILLA	82	72	69	72	73	82	75	79	77	73	76	70	71	78	74	78	67	77	82	81
UNION	79	65	61	66	69	81	72	76	73	67	73	68	65	73	70	75	64	74	80	79
WALLOWA	82	63	45	61	72	93	64	81	69	62	69	71	56	72	65	73	59	74	85	86
WASCO	78	72	77	72	74	82	74	78	77	72	75	68	72	76	75	79	66	76	84	79
WASHINGTON	119	122	122	126	115	109	122	114	117	124	118	109	123	119	119	113	108	118	110	115
WHEELER	66	62	59	59	67	79	58	71	63	59	61	58	58	56	65	67	52	68	79	70
YAMHILL	94	96	99	96	96	96	93	95	92	93	92	86	94	94	94	92	83	93	94	96
OREGON	95	92	93	93	92	95	95	94	94	93	94	87	93	94	94	94	84	95	95	95
UNITED STATES	100	100	100	100	100	100	100	100	100	100	100	100	100	100	100	100	100	100	100	100

POPULATION CHANGE

COUNTY	FIPS Code	CBSA Code	DMA Code	POPULATION 2000	POPULATION 2007	POPULATION 2012	2000-2007 ANNUAL RATE % Rate	2000-2007 ANNUAL RATE State Rank	RACE (%) White 2000	White 2007	Black 2000	Black 2007	Asian/Pacific 2000	Asian/Pacific 2007
ADAMS	001	23900	566	91,292	102,417	110,924	1.6	5	95.4	94.4	1.2	1.4	0.5	0.7
ALLEGHENY	003	38300	508	1,281,666	1,240,864	1,210,673	-0.4	62	84.3	81.8	12.4	14.1	1.7	2.4
ARMSTRONG	005	38300	508	72,392	71,321	70,249	-0.2	55	98.3	98.0	0.8	1.0	0.1	0.2
BEAVER	007	38300	508	181,412	178,124	175,983	-0.3	58	92.5	91.3	6.0	6.9	0.3	0.4
BEDFORD	009	00000	574	49,984	50,657	51,130	0.2	36	98.5	98.2	0.4	0.4	0.3	0.4
BERKS	011	39740	504	373,638	406,222	430,127	1.2	9	88.2	85.9	3.7	4.1	1.0	1.5
BLAIR	013	11020	574	129,144	126,760	124,568	-0.3	58	97.6	97.1	1.2	1.4	0.4	0.5
BRADFORD	015	42380	577	62,761	63,798	64,552	0.2	36	97.9	97.5	0.4	0.5	0.5	0.7
BUCKS	017	37980	504	597,635	638,174	667,760	0.9	18	92.5	90.7	3.3	3.7	2.3	3.3
BUTLER	019	38300	508	174,083	187,301	196,770	1.0	14	97.8	97.3	0.8	0.9	0.6	0.9
CAMBRIA	021	27780	574	152,598	147,230	143,255	-0.5	65	95.8	95.0	2.8	3.3	0.4	0.6
CAMERON	023	00000	574	5,974	5,641	5,453	-0.8	67	98.8	98.6	0.4	0.4	0.2	0.2
CARBON	025	10900	577	58,802	62,436	65,136	0.8	20	97.8	97.4	0.6	0.7	0.3	0.5
CENTRE	027	44300	574	135,758	145,418	150,743	1.0	14	91.4	89.1	2.6	3.0	4.0	5.7
CHESTER	029	37980	504	433,501	491,334	535,668	1.7	4	89.2	87.1	6.2	7.1	2.0	2.8
CLARION	031	00000	508	41,765	41,866	42,313	0.0	47	98.2	97.8	0.8	0.9	0.3	0.5
CLEARFIELD	033	20180	574	83,382	84,517	84,545	0.2	36	97.4	96.9	1.5	1.7	0.3	0.4
CLINTON	035	30820	577	37,914	38,263	38,547	0.1	40	98.3	97.9	0.5	0.6	0.4	0.6
COLUMBIA	037	14100	577	64,151	66,262	67,438	0.4	28	97.6	97.0	0.8	0.9	0.6	0.8
CRAWFORD	039	32740	516	90,366	90,956	90,540	0.1	40	97.0	96.4	1.6	1.9	0.3	0.4
CUMBERLAND	041	25420	566	213,674	229,813	241,656	1.0	14	94.4	93.1	2.4	2.7	1.7	2.5
DAUPHIN	043	25420	566	251,798	259,807	265,816	0.4	28	77.1	73.8	16.9	18.9	2.0	2.8
DELAWARE	045	37980	504	550,864	562,286	569,010	0.3	33	80.3	76.9	14.5	16.3	3.3	4.6
ELK	047	41260	574	35,112	33,700	32,606	-0.6	66	99.0	98.7	0.1	0.2	0.4	0.6
ERIE	049	21500	516	280,843	283,041	284,981	0.1	40	90.9	89.1	6.1	7.3	0.7	1.0
FAYETTE	051	38300	508	148,644	147,657	145,418	-0.1	52	95.3	94.5	3.5	4.1	0.2	0.3
FOREST	053	00000	508	4,946	5,706	5,610	2.0	3	95.9	95.2	2.2	2.6	0.1	0.2
FRANKLIN	055	16540	566	129,313	142,664	153,170	1.4	8	95.3	94.4	2.3	2.7	0.6	0.8
FULTON	057	00000	511	14,261	15,125	15,727	0.8	20	98.3	97.9	0.7	0.8	0.1	0.2
GREENE	059	00000	508	40,672	39,936	39,057	-0.3	58	95.1	94.1	3.9	4.3	0.2	0.4
HUNTINGDON	061	26500	574	45,586	46,971	47,764	0.4	28	93.3	92.2	5.1	6.0	0.2	0.3
INDIANA	063	26860	508	89,605	89,830	89,754	0.0	47	96.9	96.1	1.6	1.8	0.8	1.1
JEFFERSON	065	00000	574	45,932	46,041	46,017	0.0	47	99.0	98.7	0.1	0.1	0.2	0.3
JUNIATA	067	00000	566	22,821	24,097	24,919	0.8	20	98.1	97.6	0.4	0.4	0.4	0.6
LACKAWANNA	069	42540	577	213,295	212,195	211,281	-0.1	52	96.7	95.9	1.3	1.5	0.8	1.1
LANCASTER	071	29540	566	470,658	503,871	527,947	0.9	18	91.5	89.4	2.8	3.3	1.5	2.1
LAWRENCE	073	35260	508	94,643	92,154	90,363	-0.4	62	95.0	94.1	3.6	4.2	0.3	0.4
LEBANON	075	30140	566	120,327	129,684	136,703	1.0	14	94.5	93.2	1.3	1.4	0.9	1.3
LEHIGH	077	10900	504	312,090	336,831	355,733	1.1	10	87.0	84.4	3.6	3.9	2.1	3.0
LUZERNE	079	42540	577	319,250	315,626	312,521	-0.2	55	96.6	95.9	1.7	2.0	0.6	0.9
LYCOMING	081	48700	577	120,044	119,726	119,979	0.0	47	93.9	92.4	4.3	5.4	0.4	0.6
MCKEAN	083	14620	514	45,936	44,532	43,342	-0.4	62	96.5	95.8	1.9	2.2	0.3	0.5
MERCER	085	49660	536	120,293	120,203	120,144	0.0	47	93.1	92.7	5.3	5.7	0.4	0.4
MIFFLIN	087	30380	566	46,486	46,850	47,104	0.1	40	98.5	98.2	0.5	0.6	0.3	0.4
MONROE	089	20700	577	138,687	171,850	199,550	3.0	2	88.2	86.2	6.0	6.8	1.1	1.6
MONTGOMERY	091	37980	504	750,097	789,528	817,818	0.7	22	86.5	83.4	7.5	8.6	4.1	5.7
MONTOUR	093	14100	577	18,236	18,652	18,929	0.3	33	96.7	95.8	1.0	1.2	1.3	1.9
NORTHAMPTON	095	10900	504	267,066	296,679	319,742	1.5	6	91.2	89.4	2.8	3.1	1.4	2.0
NORTHUMBERLAND	097	44980	577	94,556	93,303	92,363	-0.2	55	97.1	96.5	1.5	1.8	0.2	0.3
PERRY	099	25420	566	43,602	45,608	47,023	0.6	23	98.5	98.2	0.4	0.5	0.2	0.2
PHILADELPHIA	101	37980	504	1,517,550	1,475,892	1,447,465	-0.4	62	45.0	40.8	43.2	45.3	4.5	5.9
PIKE	103	35620	501	46,302	58,748	69,513	3.3	1	93.1	91.8	3.3	3.7	0.6	0.9
POTTER	105	00000	514	18,080	18,704	19,093	0.5	24	98.1	97.6	0.3	0.3	0.5	0.8
SCHUYLKILL	107	39060	577	150,336	149,951	149,176	0.0	47	96.6	95.8	2.1	2.4	0.4	0.7
SNYDER	109	42780	577	37,546	38,602	39,379	0.4	28	97.9	97.5	0.8	0.9	0.4	0.6
SOMERSET	111	43740	574	80,023	79,989	79,276	0.0	47	97.4	97.2	1.6	1.7	0.2	0.3
SULLIVAN	113	00000	577	6,556	6,609	6,687	0.1	40	95.6	95.4	2.2	2.4	0.2	0.2
SUSQUEHANNA	115	00000	577	42,238	43,429	44,320	0.4	28	98.5	98.2	0.3	0.4	0.2	0.3
TIOGA	117	00000	565	41,373	42,112	42,627	0.2	36	98.1	97.7	0.6	0.7	0.3	0.4
UNION	119	30260	577	41,624	44,602	45,897	1.0	14	90.1	88.4	6.9	7.8	1.1	1.6
VENANGO	121	36340	508	57,565	56,728	56,205	-0.2	55	97.6	97.2	1.1	1.3	0.2	0.4
WARREN	123	47620	516	43,863	42,239	41,106	-0.5	65	98.7	98.4	0.2	0.2	0.3	0.4
WASHINGTON	125	38300	508	202,897	208,353	212,373	0.4	28	95.3	94.4	3.3	3.8	0.4	0.5
WAYNE	127	00000	577	47,722	51,361	53,772	1.0	14	96.7	96.1	1.6	1.8	0.4	0.6
WESTMORELAND	129	38300	508	369,993	370,570	370,926	0.0	47	96.6	95.7	2.0	2.5	0.5	0.8
WYOMING	131	42540	577	28,080	28,991	29,508	0.4	28	98.3	97.9	0.5	0.6	0.3	0.4
YORK	133	49620	566	381,751	422,449	453,855	1.4	8	92.8	91.3	3.7	4.2	0.9	1.3
PENNSYLVANIA							0.4		85.4	83.7	10.0	10.5	1.8	2.5
UNITED STATES							1.2		75.1	72.7	12.3	12.6	3.8	4.5

COUNTY	% HISPANIC ORIGIN		2007 AGE DISTRIBUTION (%)										MEDIAN AGE	% 2007 Males	% 2007 Females
	2000	2007	0-4	5-9	10-14	15-19	20-24	25-44	45-64	65-84	85+	18+	2007		
ADAMS	3.6	4.5	6.0	5.7	6.6	7.5	6.9	26.0	27.4	11.8	2.1	77.5	39.5	49.1	50.9
ALLEGHENY	0.9	1.1	5.4	5.4	5.9	6.8	6.4	24.6	28.0	14.6	3.1	79.5	41.9	47.6	52.4
ARMSTRONG	0.4	0.5	5.6	5.2	5.9	5.9	5.8	24.5	29.7	14.6	2.7	79.6	43.0	49.0	51.0
BEAVER	0.7	0.9	5.4	5.2	6.0	6.4	5.9	23.5	28.9	15.8	2.9	79.5	43.4	48.0	52.0
BEDFORD	0.5	0.7	6.2	6.1	5.8	6.0	5.1	25.7	28.3	14.6	2.2	78.2	41.6	49.6	50.4
BERKS	9.7	11.8	6.2	5.8	6.7	7.4	6.3	25.8	26.9	12.4	2.5	77.2	39.8	49.1	50.9
BLAIR	0.5	0.6	5.7	5.4	5.8	6.4	6.3	25.1	28.0	14.4	2.9	79.7	41.7	48.3	51.7
BRADFORD	0.6	0.8	6.2	5.9	6.3	6.6	6.2	24.1	28.5	13.7	2.4	77.4	41.3	49.1	50.9
BUCKS	2.3	2.9	6.3	6.6	7.0	6.8	5.3	26.2	28.4	11.4	1.9	75.7	40.2	49.0	51.0
BUTLER	0.6	0.7	6.4	6.4	6.5	6.9	6.4	25.6	27.4	11.8	2.5	76.7	39.7	49.0	51.0
CAMBRIA	0.9	1.1	5.0	4.8	5.3	6.5	6.5	24.1	28.7	15.6	3.4	81.3	43.3	48.9	51.1
CAMERON	0.6	0.7	5.1	4.3	6.2	6.5	7.8	21.7	29.3	16.0	3.0	80.1	43.8	49.1	50.9
CARBON	1.5	1.8	5.4	5.1	5.5	6.2	5.4	25.3	29.5	14.8	2.8	80.0	43.2	49.0	51.0
CENTRE	1.7	2.0	4.6	4.3	4.7	10.2	19.4	25.3	20.9	9.2	1.5	83.5	29.3	51.5	48.5
CHESTER	3.7	4.6	6.5	7.0	7.4	7.5	6.0	25.4	28.0	10.4	1.8	74.4	38.9	49.2	50.8
CLARION	0.4	0.5	5.5	5.4	5.4	7.8	9.5	24.5	26.4	13.4	2.2	80.4	38.7	48.5	51.5
CLEARFIELD	0.6	0.7	5.6	5.3	5.7	6.1	6.0	27.1	27.9	13.7	2.6	79.7	41.3	50.8	49.2
CLINTON	0.5	0.7	5.5	5.0	5.4	8.0	9.1	23.5	26.6	14.5	2.6	80.5	40.0	48.7	51.3
COLUMBIA	0.9	1.2	4.9	4.7	5.2	8.7	10.2	23.3	27.1	13.3	2.6	81.9	39.8	47.8	52.2
CRAWFORD	0.6	0.7	6.0	5.7	6.3	7.5	7.0	24.3	27.8	13.0	2.5	78.0	40.2	48.9	51.1
CUMBERLAND	1.3	1.7	5.3	5.3	5.8	7.6	7.5	24.9	27.9	13.3	2.5	79.8	40.7	48.9	51.1
DAUPHIN	4.1	4.9	6.0	5.7	6.6	6.7	6.2	25.9	28.4	12.3	2.2	77.5	40.2	48.0	52.0
DELAWARE	1.5	1.8	6.1	6.1	6.8	8.0	6.5	25.0	25.9	12.6	2.8	76.4	39.2	47.9	52.1
ELK	0.4	0.5	5.9	5.7	5.8	6.3	6.0	25.3	27.7	14.5	2.7	78.5	41.7	49.8	50.2
ERIE	2.2	2.7	6.2	5.8	6.6	7.8	8.2	25.0	26.4	11.7	2.4	77.2	37.8	49.1	50.9
FAYETTE	0.4	0.5	5.7	5.5	5.8	5.7	5.4	25.2	28.8	14.6	3.2	79.5	42.5	48.2	51.8
FOREST	1.2	1.5	3.3	2.7	4.3	20.1	5.1	16.5	25.4	19.6	3.0	75.4	43.3	57.2	42.8
FRANKLIN	1.8	2.2	6.3	6.1	6.2	6.4	5.4	26.0	27.1	14.0	2.6	77.5	40.7	48.6	51.4
FULTON	0.4	0.4	6.4	6.3	6.0	6.3	5.0	26.7	27.8	13.7	1.9	77.4	40.4	50.0	50.0
GREENE	0.9	1.3	5.2	4.9	5.8	6.9	7.1	27.0	28.8	11.9	2.4	80.9	39.8	51.4	48.6
HUNTINGDON	1.1	1.4	5.4	5.5	5.0	7.0	7.5	27.5	27.0	13.0	2.1	80.3	39.7	52.9	47.1
INDIANA	0.5	0.6	5.0	4.8	5.2	8.3	12.1	22.7	27.0	12.5	2.4	81.7	38.3	48.7	51.3
JEFFERSON	0.4	0.5	5.7	5.4	5.7	6.2	6.4	24.6	28.5	14.6	2.9	79.4	42.1	49.2	50.8
JUNIATA	1.6	2.0	6.7	6.6	6.3	6.0	4.9	26.9	26.9	13.5	2.3	76.6	40.0	49.8	50.2
LACKAWANNA	1.4	1.7	5.3	5.0	5.7	6.9	6.4	24.3	27.4	15.5	3.6	80.2	42.5	47.5	52.5
LANCASTER	5.7	7.0	6.9	6.7	7.1	7.3	6.3	25.7	25.9	11.7	2.5	75.1	37.9	49.1	50.9
LAWRENCE	0.6	0.7	5.6	5.5	6.0	6.7	6.3	23.0	28.2	15.4	3.4	79.0	42.6	47.9	52.1
LEBANON	5.0	6.1	6.1	5.9	6.1	6.5	5.8	25.3	27.9	13.5	2.8	78.1	41.1	49.0	51.0
LEHIGH	10.2	12.3	5.9	5.8	6.6	7.2	6.1	25.0	27.6	13.1	2.9	77.4	40.8	48.4	51.6
LUZERNE	1.2	1.4	5.0	4.7	5.4	6.5	6.1	25.1	27.9	15.7	3.6	81.2	43.1	48.6	51.4
LYCOMING	0.7	0.9	5.6	5.2	5.9	7.5	7.6	24.9	27.5	13.3	2.5	79.3	40.3	49.0	51.0
MCKEAN	1.1	1.3	5.9	5.5	6.1	6.6	6.5	26.0	27.3	13.5	2.7	78.5	40.3	50.5	49.5
MERCER	0.7	0.7	5.7	5.6	5.8	7.4	7.0	23.0	27.6	14.9	3.1	78.7	41.6	48.9	51.1
MIFFLIN	0.6	0.7	6.5	6.2	6.2	6.4	5.4	25.8	26.7	14.1	2.6	77.0	40.7	48.8	51.2
MONROE	6.6	8.1	6.0	5.8	7.1	8.0	6.7	24.5	29.0	11.3	1.5	76.3	40.2	49.5	50.5
MONTGOMERY	2.0	2.5	6.1	6.5	6.7	6.8	5.4	26.2	27.1	12.6	2.7	76.4	40.2	48.5	51.5
MONTOUR	0.9	1.1	5.6	5.4	6.3	7.3	5.6	23.5	28.8	14.4	3.0	77.9	42.5	47.7	52.3
NORTHAMPTON	6.7	8.2	5.6	5.4	6.3	7.6	6.9	24.3	28.4	12.8	2.7	78.4	41.0	48.9	51.1
NORTHUMBERLAND	1.1	1.4	5.2	4.9	5.1	6.4	6.5	24.9	28.2	15.6	3.2	80.7	42.9	49.6	50.4
PERRY	0.7	0.9	6.1	5.8	6.4	6.7	5.8	26.6	29.8	11.3	1.5	77.4	40.3	49.6	50.4
PHILADELPHIA	8.5	9.5	6.5	6.1	7.1	8.0	7.6	27.5	23.3	11.3	2.4	75.9	35.4	46.6	53.4
PIKE	5.0	6.2	6.0	5.6	7.3	7.6	5.3	22.0	30.4	14.5	1.3	76.3	42.7	50.0	50.0
POTTER	0.6	0.7	6.4	6.0	6.4	6.7	6.1	23.5	28.4	13.9	2.5	77.0	41.3	49.5	50.5
SCHUYLKILL	1.1	1.5	5.0	4.7	5.4	6.0	6.0	26.1	28.1	15.5	3.3	81.5	42.8	50.2	49.8
SNYDER	1.0	1.2	5.8	5.6	5.8	8.3	7.8	25.2	26.9	12.6	2.0	78.7	39.2	49.2	50.8
SOMERSET	0.7	0.7	5.4	5.1	5.4	6.1	6.0	25.6	28.5	14.8	3.0	80.5	42.4	50.0	50.0
SULLIVAN	1.1	1.1	4.6	4.4	4.2	8.9	5.8	20.6	29.7	18.3	3.6	81.5	45.9	50.7	49.3
SUSQUEHANNA	0.7	0.8	5.9	5.5	6.3	6.6	6.1	23.4	30.3	13.6	2.4	78.3	42.5	49.9	50.1
TIOGA	0.5	0.6	5.7	5.3	5.7	7.4	8.4	23.1	27.8	14.2	2.4	79.4	40.9	49.0	51.0
UNION	3.9	4.7	4.7	4.7	4.9	8.3	9.6	29.3	24.5	11.5	2.4	82.2	37.4	56.3	43.7
VENANGO	0.5	0.6	5.8	5.4	5.7	7.1	6.2	23.1	29.9	14.5	2.3	78.6	42.6	49.0	51.0
WARREN	0.3	0.4	5.7	5.6	5.8	6.5	6.4	22.9	30.0	14.5	2.5	78.8	42.9	49.2	50.8
WASHINGTON	0.6	0.7	5.4	5.5	6.0	6.4	5.9	23.5	29.4	14.9	2.9	79.3	43.1	48.3	51.7
WAYNE	1.7	2.1	5.6	5.3	6.0	6.0	5.6	23.6	31.0	14.4	2.4	79.2	43.5	50.9	49.1
WESTMORELAND	0.5	0.6	5.1	5.1	5.9	6.2	5.4	23.7	30.2	15.5	2.9	80.2	44.1	48.4	51.6
WYOMING	0.7	0.8	5.9	5.8	6.8	7.1	6.2	25.3	29.4	11.6	1.9	77.2	40.2	50.1	49.9
YORK	3.0	3.7	6.0	5.8	6.6	6.9	6.1	26.0	28.5	11.9	2.1	77.4	40.5	49.3	50.7
PENNSYLVANIA	3.2	3.9	5.9	5.8	6.4	7.2	6.6	25.4	27.2	13.0	2.6	77.9	40.2	48.5	51.5
UNITED STATES	12.5	15.0	6.9	6.5	6.8	7.1	7.0	27.6	25.4	10.7	1.9	75.6	36.7	49.2	50.8

COUNTY	HOUSEHOLDS					FAMILIES			MEDIAN HOUSEHOLD INCOME			
	2000	2007	2012	% Annual Rate 2000-2007	2007 Average HH Size	2000	2007	% Annual Rate 2000-2007	2007	2012	2007 National Rank	2007 State Rank
ADAMS	33,652	38,081	41,530	1.7	2.59	24,777	27,362	1.4	52,459	60,532	522	15
ALLEGHENY	537,150	527,664	517,870	-0.2	2.28	332,237	315,039	-0.7	50,158	59,839	666	19
ARMSTRONG	29,005	29,229	29,016	0.1	2.40	20,548	20,153	-0.3	39,217	45,291	1829	56
BEAVER	72,576	72,642	72,297	0.0	2.39	50,521	49,159	-0.4	47,239	55,340	888	25
BEDFORD	19,768	20,426	20,794	0.5	2.46	14,493	14,608	0.1	40,031	45,478	1725	50
BERKS	141,570	153,215	162,509	1.1	2.56	98,463	103,595	0.7	56,332	65,591	352	11
BLAIR	51,518	51,636	51,133	0.0	2.38	34,895	33,945	-0.4	41,586	49,198	1506	43
BRADFORD	24,453	25,387	25,929	0.5	2.47	17,308	17,483	0.1	42,680	49,308	1368	35
BUCKS	218,725	236,126	248,543	1.1	2.66	160,946	169,538	0.7	78,883	95,624	59	3
BUTLER	65,862	72,180	76,487	1.3	2.50	46,839	49,968	0.9	54,038	63,606	452	13
CAMBRIA	60,531	59,743	58,690	-0.2	2.31	40,615	38,878	-0.6	38,634	45,780	1911	59
CAMERON	2,465	2,348	2,278	-0.7	2.37	1,624	1,499	-1.1	39,608	45,689	1764	52
CARBON	23,701	25,613	26,932	1.1	2.40	16,416	17,244	0.7	44,137	51,557	1193	30
CENTRE	49,323	53,581	56,183	1.1	2.41	28,501	29,778	0.6	45,494	53,697	1052	27
CHESTER	157,905	180,176	197,619	1.8	2.64	113,303	125,934	1.5	85,956	104,946	27	1
CLARION	16,052	16,619	16,951	0.5	2.41	10,735	10,782	0.1	37,572	42,918	2049	63
CLEARFIELD	32,785	33,561	33,889	0.3	2.39	22,926	22,820	-0.1	38,911	44,941	1864	58
CLINTON	14,773	15,218	15,460	0.4	2.37	9,934	9,927	0.0	38,456	44,398	1938	60
COLUMBIA	24,915	26,023	26,712	0.6	2.38	16,564	16,769	0.2	42,292	48,896	1418	37
CRAWFORD	34,678	35,540	35,635	0.3	2.45	23,871	23,763	-0.1	41,186	47,172	1574	45
CUMBERLAND	83,015	90,969	96,625	1.3	2.37	56,077	59,628	0.9	59,921	71,162	272	5
DAUPHIN	102,670	106,590	109,450	0.5	2.38	66,132	66,430	0.1	53,545	62,967	474	14
DELAWARE	206,320	210,595	213,795	0.3	2.56	139,453	138,124	-0.1	65,392	78,355	166	4
ELK	14,124	13,889	13,582	-0.2	2.39	9,748	9,311	-0.6	47,419	54,712	870	22
ERIE	106,507	107,926	109,152	0.2	2.49	71,039	69,796	-0.2	46,023	53,980	1001	26
FAYETTE	59,969	60,168	59,749	0.0	2.38	41,170	40,129	-0.4	34,955	40,624	2436	66
FOREST	2,000	1,981	1,954	-0.1	2.24	1,328	1,275	-0.6	34,425	40,239	2503	67
FRANKLIN	50,633	56,790	61,445	1.6	2.46	36,410	39,781	1.2	50,162	57,579	665	18
FULTON	5,660	6,154	6,471	1.2	2.44	4,097	4,343	0.8	41,353	46,597	1539	44
GREENE	15,060	15,097	14,862	0.0	2.44	10,588	10,327	-0.3	37,725	43,620	2034	62
HUNTINGDON	16,759	17,566	18,059	0.7	2.39	11,798	12,035	0.3	41,008	46,724	1597	47
INDIANA	34,123	34,986	35,343	0.3	2.41	22,517	22,371	-0.1	37,525	43,413	2057	64
JEFFERSON	18,375	18,763	18,905	0.3	2.40	12,861	12,772	-0.1	39,595	45,605	1767	53
JUNIATA	8,584	9,165	9,524	0.9	2.58	6,467	6,748	0.6	41,628	46,918	1502	42
LACKAWANNA	86,218	87,003	87,285	0.1	2.34	55,758	54,439	-0.3	44,524	52,678	1156	29
LANCASTER	172,560	187,870	198,135	1.2	2.61	124,129	131,668	0.8	57,258	66,128	322	8
LAWRENCE	37,091	36,521	36,006	-0.2	2.44	25,886	24,779	-0.6	41,979	49,757	1451	38
LEBANON	46,551	50,862	54,018	1.2	2.46	32,761	34,825	0.8	50,703	58,303	628	17
LEHIGH	121,906	131,982	139,812	1.1	2.47	82,106	86,239	0.7	56,725	67,589	339	10
LUZERNE	130,687	131,765	131,632	0.1	2.29	84,304	82,250	-0.3	43,590	51,670	1263	33
LYCOMING	47,003	48,427	49,003	0.4	2.37	31,703	31,691	0.0	42,441	49,650	1404	36
MCKEAN	18,024	17,667	17,294	-0.3	2.36	12,098	11,503	-0.7	41,802	48,917	1477	40
MERCER	46,712	47,346	47,647	0.2	2.40	32,387	31,908	-0.2	43,584	51,059	1266	34
MIFFLIN	18,413	18,827	19,048	0.3	2.45	12,905	12,834	-0.1	39,683	45,787	1757	51
MONROE	49,454	61,119	71,022	3.0	2.75	36,459	43,969	2.6	57,768	66,377	310	7
MONTGOMERY	286,098	301,802	313,306	0.7	2.54	197,640	202,662	0.3	79,785	96,770	54	2
MONTOUR	7,085	7,388	7,550	0.6	2.40	4,817	4,875	0.2	47,298	54,598	885	24
NORTHAMPTON	101,541	113,394	122,938	1.5	2.52	71,074	77,194	1.1	58,306	68,957	301	6
NORTHUMBERLAND	38,835	39,067	39,001	0.1	2.29	25,589	24,941	-0.4	39,535	46,192	1773	55
PERRY	16,695	17,833	18,560	0.9	2.53	12,320	12,844	0.6	50,853	57,196	621	16
PHILADELPHIA	590,071	578,811	570,005	-0.3	2.45	352,331	332,968	-0.8	39,541	46,456	1772	54
PIKE	17,433	22,165	26,247	3.4	2.63	13,026	16,175	3.0	55,638	64,091	380	12
POTTER	7,005	7,355	7,557	0.7	2.50	4,999	5,110	0.3	40,200	45,781	1699	49
SCHUYLKILL	60,530	61,497	61,672	0.2	2.31	40,116	39,494	-0.2	41,907	49,686	1458	39
SNYDER	13,654	14,322	14,740	0.7	2.54	9,979	10,209	0.3	43,884	50,164	1226	31
SOMERSET	31,222	31,786	31,845	0.2	2.38	22,044	21,839	-0.1	38,259	44,240	1967	61
SULLIVAN	2,660	2,733	2,803	0.4	2.24	1,754	1,746	-0.1	37,442	42,775	2076	65
SUSQUEHANNA	16,529	17,379	17,913	0.7	2.47	11,777	12,057	0.3	40,630	46,310	1651	48
TIOGA	15,925	16,573	16,931	0.6	2.43	11,191	11,329	0.2	39,171	44,634	1833	57
UNION	13,178	14,167	14,832	1.0	2.45	9,205	9,623	0.6	49,988	57,091	684	20
VENANGO	22,747	22,836	22,808	0.1	2.40	15,926	15,544	-0.3	41,028	47,878	1595	46
WARREN	17,696	17,357	17,018	-0.3	2.37	12,122	11,544	-0.7	44,601	51,362	1146	28
WASHINGTON	81,130	84,631	86,900	0.6	2.40	56,052	56,819	0.2	48,684	57,950	766	21
WAYNE	18,350	20,057	21,246	1.2	2.44	12,942	13,764	0.9	41,787	47,680	1480	41
WESTMORELAND	149,813	152,593	153,924	0.3	2.37	104,597	103,594	-0.1	47,325	55,545	882	23
WYOMING	10,762	11,371	11,706	0.8	2.48	7,704	7,928	0.4	43,783	50,000	1239	32
YORK	148,219	165,835	179,207	1.6	2.50	105,486	114,902	1.2	56,775	65,367	337	9
PENNSYLVANIA				0.5	2.45			0.2	51,375	60,635		
UNITED STATES				1.2	2.59			1.0	53,154	62,503		

COUNTY	2007 Per Capita Income	2007 HH Income Base	2007 HOUSEHOLD INCOME DISTRIBUTION (%)					2007 Home Value Base	2007 HOME VALUE DISTRIBUTION (%)					2007 Median Home Value
			Less than $25,000	$25,000 to $49,999	$50,000 to $99,999	$100,000 to $149,999	$150,000 or More		Less than $50,000	$50,000 to $89,999	$90,000 to $174,999	$175,000 to $399,999	$400,000 or More	
ADAMS	23,476	38,081	18.6	28.5	38.9	10.6	3.4	29,521	3.7	3.1	27.3	58.3	7.5	203,490
ALLEGHENY	29,961	527,664	24.7	25.2	31.3	11.3	7.5	356,829	9.1	18.9	45.3	22.7	4.0	125,453
ARMSTRONG	20,195	29,229	31.4	31.2	28.8	6.3	2.3	22,677	16.5	25.5	41.9	15.3	0.9	100,748
BEAVER	24,253	72,642	24.1	28.6	33.2	10.4	3.7	54,819	10.3	17.9	48.3	22.1	1.3	125,574
BEDFORD	20,178	20,426	28.6	34.6	29.0	5.8	2.0	16,460	10.6	11.0	44.0	30.1	4.3	150,250
BERKS	26,756	153,215	19.2	24.9	36.3	13.5	6.2	114,150	4.0	8.3	32.6	48.9	6.2	186,788
BLAIR	21,665	51,636	28.9	30.0	31.4	7.0	2.7	37,936	13.8	21.9	44.8	17.7	1.8	111,345
BRADFORD	21,764	25,387	26.3	32.4	30.8	7.3	3.2	19,350	9.9	12.2	47.5	26.3	4.0	142,846
BUCKS	37,687	236,126	10.6	17.8	34.8	20.6	16.2	184,197	1.5	1.1	4.2	61.9	31.3	323,242
BUTLER	27,121	72,180	20.6	25.5	34.7	12.2	7.0	56,535	10.1	8.2	39.3	36.1	6.2	158,938
CAMBRIA	21,262	59,743	30.9	31.6	28.3	6.4	2.8	44,916	18.4	24.8	40.5	14.6	1.6	100,191
CAMERON	20,137	2,348	28.2	34.9	30.3	5.1	1.5	1,763	10.6	21.3	51.0	16.1	1.1	116,706
CARBON	22,013	25,613	25.9	30.8	33.3	7.8	2.3	20,126	5.0	10.7	40.3	40.9	3.0	164,282
CENTRE	23,833	53,576	27.5	26.7	30.5	10.1	5.3	32,660	7.5	5.8	36.0	43.5	7.2	176,988
CHESTER	43,177	180,176	9.8	16.3	31.2	22.3	20.4	138,543	1.8	1.2	6.2	49.7	41.1	359,837
CLARION	19,590	16,619	32.4	31.6	27.9	5.9	2.2	12,120	11.7	15.9	45.6	24.6	2.2	132,720
CLEARFIELD	20,129	33,561	31.4	31.4	28.7	6.3	2.2	26,646	13.3	21.3	44.5	19.3	1.6	116,636
CLINTON	20,169	15,218	32.3	31.9	27.1	6.2	2.5	11,164	10.1	12.0	49.7	25.7	2.6	146,502
COLUMBIA	21,780	26,023	28.0	30.9	30.0	8.0	3.0	18,958	7.8	7.7	46.3	34.0	4.2	159,533
CRAWFORD	21,319	35,540	28.1	31.6	30.0	7.4	3.0	27,024	11.1	15.2	44.7	26.0	2.9	137,201
CUMBERLAND	30,529	90,969	15.7	25.0	37.5	13.9	7.9	67,004	5.2	3.3	36.4	49.7	5.4	185,912
DAUPHIN	28,820	106,590	19.8	26.7	34.4	12.7	6.5	70,525	5.2	9.9	42.5	37.5	5.0	162,137
DELAWARE	33,393	210,595	16.2	21.9	33.7	16.3	12.0	152,680	1.3	3.2	22.7	54.7	18.2	248,780
ELK	23,265	13,889	23.7	29.1	36.1	9.1	2.1	11,093	6.3	14.4	48.0	28.8	2.4	149,278
ERIE	22,957	107,926	25.4	28.7	32.8	9.1	4.0	75,336	12.3	20.3	45.7	19.6	2.0	114,504
FAYETTE	19,475	60,168	36.5	29.8	25.0	6.2	2.5	44,280	23.7	24.9	38.4	11.6	1.4	92,120
FOREST	17,910	1,981	34.9	31.9	27.4	4.4	1.4	1,636	10.1	24.0	49.4	14.4	2.0	116,667
FRANKLIN	24,460	56,790	20.3	29.5	36.1	10.6	3.5	42,454	5.5	4.2	37.5	48.0	4.9	180,040
FULTON	20,050	6,154	26.4	35.1	30.9	6.0	1.6	4,882	10.1	9.4	42.9	33.8	3.8	157,193
GREENE	19,490	15,097	33.6	29.3	27.5	7.4	2.2	11,281	17.6	23.1	38.9	18.3	2.1	109,472
HUNTINGDON	20,001	17,566	28.8	31.8	30.9	6.8	1.8	13,685	10.2	15.0	45.0	26.7	3.1	139,563
INDIANA	19,779	34,986	33.7	30.0	26.7	6.9	2.6	25,233	13.7	16.3	42.9	24.2	3.0	134,287
JEFFERSON	20,253	18,763	29.5	35.0	27.6	5.5	2.4	14,521	10.5	23.1	46.5	18.4	1.6	117,003
JUNIATA	19,850	9,165	24.6	36.3	30.6	6.4	2.1	7,202	5.5	9.8	42.3	37.8	4.7	164,952
LACKAWANNA	24,732	87,003	28.4	27.2	30.2	9.5	4.8	59,714	3.8	9.6	50.4	32.5	3.7	149,244
LANCASTER	26,610	187,870	16.2	26.1	39.1	12.7	5.9	134,471	3.2	2.7	32.2	54.6	7.3	201,884
LAWRENCE	21,755	36,521	29.5	29.1	30.3	7.7	3.4	28,338	10.7	17.7	41.0	27.3	3.2	137,723
LEBANON	25,023	50,862	19.7	29.5	35.4	11.2	4.2	37,361	4.6	7.8	43.3	40.0	4.3	165,752
LEHIGH	29,181	131,982	19.6	24.5	34.2	13.7	7.9	91,632	2.3	3.1	26.5	56.8	11.4	219,770
LUZERNE	24,171	131,765	28.5	28.0	30.6	8.9	4.1	93,602	6.5	14.8	49.0	26.9	2.7	138,039
LYCOMING	22,430	48,427	27.0	32.1	29.9	7.6	3.4	34,044	6.7	11.3	52.8	26.6	2.6	140,763
MCKEAN	21,299	17,667	28.2	30.8	31.8	6.7	2.4	13,308	13.3	27.2	44.3	14.0	1.1	105,578
MERCER	22,735	47,346	25.7	31.3	31.8	7.8	3.4	36,300	18.2	23.6	41.8	15.2	1.3	101,101
MIFFLIN	19,583	18,827	30.8	32.2	29.3	5.7	2.0	14,080	7.7	15.0	49.3	25.5	2.5	140,314
MONROE	25,034	61,119	18.5	24.4	36.1	15.4	5.5	48,280	2.1	2.1	21.1	65.3	9.4	232,813
MONTGOMERY	41,542	301,799	10.5	17.9	34.6	19.7	17.3	223,842	0.6	0.6	7.1	62.0	29.8	318,887
MONTOUR	25,787	7,388	22.0	31.0	32.4	9.0	5.6	5,445	5.2	7.2	40.3	40.9	6.5	171,151
NORTHAMPTON	28,198	113,394	18.4	24.2	35.7	14.6	7.1	83,892	1.5	2.4	22.1	63.4	10.6	234,647
NORTHUMBERLAND	21,068	39,067	31.2	30.9	29.8	6.0	2.0	28,839	14.1	17.2	39.9	26.1	2.8	136,857
PERRY	23,415	17,833	20.7	28.2	37.8	10.4	2.9	14,289	8.4	9.0	44.3	34.8	3.5	155,835
PHILADELPHIA	21,425	578,797	34.4	26.1	27.4	7.9	4.2	344,639	9.9	17.7	45.0	24.4	3.1	130,707
PIKE	25,566	22,165	18.5	25.7	37.5	13.3	5.0	18,837	1.4	1.8	15.6	67.1	14.2	250,244
POTTER	20,133	7,355	28.9	32.9	30.0	5.7	2.5	5,734	10.8	16.6	41.2	27.5	3.9	136,200
SCHUYLKILL	22,340	61,497	28.6	30.2	31.6	6.5	3.0	47,997	11.8	22.4	38.6	24.7	2.6	125,451
SNYDER	21,326	14,322	24.8	32.9	32.3	6.8	3.2	11,047	5.3	6.5	45.5	38.2	4.6	165,939
SOMERSET	19,660	31,784	31.3	33.0	28.7	5.1	1.9	24,933	13.0	17.8	44.6	21.7	2.9	126,635
SULLIVAN	21,369	2,733	31.6	32.3	26.3	7.5	2.3	2,211	6.6	13.6	41.2	31.5	7.1	154,652
SUSQUEHANNA	20,707	17,379	28.9	31.5	30.2	7.0	2.4	13,906	7.2	9.8	42.1	35.6	5.3	160,768
TIOGA	19,956	16,573	30.2	31.3	28.9	6.0	2.3	12,723	11.0	14.1	44.4	27.1	3.3	140,651
UNION	22,949	14,167	23.2	26.8	34.6	10.7	4.7	10,504	4.6	4.4	37.1	46.3	7.6	182,500
VENANGO	20,870	22,836	30.0	30.3	30.4	6.8	2.6	17,539	14.8	24.7	43.4	15.5	1.6	109,023
WARREN	22,814	17,357	25.0	31.3	33.1	7.9	2.7	13,647	10.5	20.9	47.9	19.0	1.7	122,162
WASHINGTON	26,434	84,631	24.3	26.9	32.2	10.7	5.8	65,552	12.6	17.1	38.8	26.5	5.0	130,384
WAYNE	21,418	20,057	27.9	31.9	30.4	6.8	3.0	16,175	4.5	4.5	34.1	48.4	8.5	192,132
WESTMORELAND	25,984	152,593	24.0	28.6	31.8	10.5	5.2	119,724	10.1	15.1	44.9	26.5	3.4	132,138
WYOMING	22,055	11,371	26.7	29.9	31.3	8.9	3.3	9,054	8.2	9.0	45.7	34.0	3.2	151,834
YORK	27,112	165,835	16.6	26.5	39.4	12.2	5.3	126,928	4.1	3.7	31.3	54.2	6.7	197,227
PENNSYLVANIA	27,602		22.8	25.8	32.4	11.8	7.1		7.0	10.9	34.4	38.2	9.5	169,830
UNITED STATES	27,916		21.9	25.0	32.3	12.3	8.4		7.9	10.5	27.1	35.6	19.0	192,285

SPENDING POTENTIAL INDICES

COUNTY	FINANCIAL SERVICES				THE HOME						ENTERTAINMENT						PERSONAL			
					Home Improvements		Furnishings													
	Auto Loan	Home Loan	Invest-ments	Retire-ment Plans	Home Repair	Lawn & Garden	Comput-ers & Hard-ware	Major Appli-ances	TV, Radio, Sound Equip-ment	Furni-ture	Dine out/ Carry out	Sports Equip-ment	Fees & Tickets	Toys & Games	Travel	Cable TV	Apparel & Services	Auto Repairs	Health Insur-ance	Pets & Supplies
ADAMS	89	86	86	86	89	95	82	89	84	83	84	79	82	87	84	86	75	84	91	91
ALLEGHENY	90	93	111	95	94	94	95	92	98	94	96	81	97	95	97	99	87	93	100	92
ARMSTRONG	74	61	56	60	67	81	63	72	69	61	67	62	58	70	64	73	59	68	80	75
BEAVER	80	80	90	80	83	87	77	81	82	78	80	70	80	82	81	85	72	79	89	82
BEDFORD	79	64	52	62	70	87	63	76	69	62	68	66	58	72	64	73	59	70	81	80
BERKS	95	97	106	98	99	99	94	96	96	96	95	85	97	97	97	98	86	94	100	97
BLAIR	74	68	73	68	72	78	69	73	73	68	72	63	68	74	70	76	64	71	81	74
BRADFORD	85	69	60	68	76	92	69	82	75	68	74	71	64	78	71	79	64	76	88	86
BUCKS	129	156	167	155	156	139	140	139	134	147	135	128	152	136	147	132	126	135	132	138
BUTLER	99	97	98	97	98	102	93	98	95	94	94	87	94	97	95	96	84	94	100	99
CAMBRIA	71	65	70	64	69	78	66	71	72	64	70	61	64	71	68	76	61	69	82	72
CAMERON	73	58	56	58	64	78	63	71	68	59	66	62	57	69	62	72	58	67	79	74
CARBON	77	70	72	70	75	85	69	77	74	69	73	66	68	75	72	78	64	73	84	79
CENTRE	85	75	78	78	76	81	90	81	86	81	87	76	83	85	83	84	78	84	82	83
CHESTER	150	177	190	179	177	159	163	160	154	169	155	149	175	156	169	151	144	157	150	159
CLARION	77	57	45	56	63	81	63	72	68	59	67	64	55	70	61	71	58	69	79	76
CLEARFIELD	77	61	54	60	67	82	63	73	69	61	68	64	58	70	64	73	58	69	81	77
CLINTON	73	61	60	60	65	78	64	71	69	61	68	62	60	70	64	73	59	68	78	73
COLUMBIA	79	67	66	68	71	82	72	76	75	68	74	68	67	77	71	78	65	74	82	79
CRAWFORD	82	67	61	66	73	88	69	79	74	67	73	69	64	76	69	78	64	74	85	82
CUMBERLAND	101	105	116	106	107	107	102	103	103	103	102	92	105	103	105	104	92	102	107	104
DAUPHIN	93	94	104	95	94	94	95	93	97	95	96	83	96	96	96	98	87	94	97	94
DELAWARE	107	129	144	126	132	118	119	118	119	124	119	106	131	117	126	120	111	115	118	116
ELK	83	74	74	73	80	91	72	82	78	72	76	70	71	80	75	82	67	76	89	84
ERIE	81	78	86	79	79	82	79	80	82	79	81	70	79	82	80	84	73	79	85	81
FAYETTE	71	57	53	56	62	75	60	68	67	58	65	59	55	67	61	71	57	65	78	71
FOREST	69	52	41	50	58	76	55	67	62	52	60	58	48	62	56	66	51	62	76	70
FRANKLIN	87	83	85	82	86	93	80	87	84	81	83	76	80	85	83	86	74	83	91	89
FULTON	82	61	43	58	68	88	61	76	68	60	68	67	54	71	61	72	58	70	82	83
GREENE	76	61	53	59	66	81	63	73	69	60	68	64	57	70	63	73	58	69	81	77
HUNTINGDON	78	63	55	61	69	85	64	75	69	62	68	66	58	72	64	73	59	70	81	79
INDIANA	74	59	53	59	63	77	67	71	69	61	68	63	59	70	64	71	60	69	77	74
JEFFERSON	76	61	54	60	66	82	63	73	69	61	68	64	58	71	64	73	59	69	81	76
JUNIATA	82	68	56	66	74	90	65	78	70	65	70	69	61	75	67	74	61	72	82	83
LACKAWANNA	78	80	95	80	83	85	79	81	83	79	81	69	81	81	82	85	73	79	89	81
LANCASTER	97	98	103	99	99	100	96	98	96	96	96	88	97	98	97	97	87	96	99	99
LAWRENCE	76	71	74	70	75	84	70	77	75	70	74	66	70	75	73	79	65	73	85	78
LEBANON	89	84	88	85	88	95	83	89	87	83	86	77	83	89	85	89	77	85	94	91
LEHIGH	96	102	117	104	102	99	101	99	101	102	100	88	105	101	103	102	92	99	101	98
LUZERNE	77	74	86	74	78	83	75	78	80	74	78	68	75	79	78	83	69	76	88	79
LYCOMING	77	71	75	72	74	81	72	76	76	71	75	66	71	77	73	78	66	74	82	77
MCKEAN	78	66	62	64	70	84	66	76	73	65	71	65	62	74	67	77	62	71	84	79
MERCER	80	73	78	73	78	86	73	79	78	73	77	68	72	79	75	82	68	76	88	81
MIFFLIN	75	61	54	60	66	80	62	72	68	60	67	63	57	70	62	71	58	67	79	75
MONROE	99	101	100	101	102	105	93	99	93	96	93	89	96	96	96	94	84	95	98	101
MONTGOMERY	135	162	178	161	163	145	149	146	143	155	144	135	162	143	156	142	134	144	141	145
MONTOUR	91	84	91	84	88	97	85	91	88	82	87	80	83	89	86	91	77	87	98	92
NORTHAMPTON	95	103	117	104	104	101	98	99	99	100	99	88	103	100	102	100	90	97	102	99
NORTHUMBERLAND	71	62	65	62	65	75	65	69	70	62	68	61	62	70	65	73	60	67	78	71
PERRY	91	79	73	79	83	96	78	88	82	77	81	77	75	85	79	85	71	83	92	91
PHILADELPHIA	65	70	75	67	71	67	71	67	76	72	76	59	75	73	72	79	72	69	72	68
PIKE	99	96	86	96	101	110	89	102	90	91	90	90	89	92	93	92	80	95	100	104
POTTER	83	62	46	61	69	90	64	79	70	61	69	69	56	73	65	75	59	73	86	84
SCHUYLKILL	76	68	73	67	72	81	69	75	75	67	73	65	67	75	71	79	64	72	85	76
SNYDER	85	72	65	71	78	91	72	82	77	71	76	72	68	80	73	80	67	77	88	86
SOMERSET	75	59	52	58	65	81	61	72	67	59	66	63	56	69	62	71	57	67	80	75
SULLIVAN	77	62	51	60	69	87	63	77	68	61	67	66	57	68	65	72	58	71	82	80
SUSQUEHANNA	82	65	53	64	73	91	65	79	71	64	70	69	60	74	67	75	61	73	85	84
TIOGA	79	61	48	60	67	85	63	75	69	61	68	66	56	71	63	73	59	70	81	80
UNION	92	85	85	85	90	99	83	91	87	83	86	80	82	89	85	90	77	87	96	94
VENANGO	77	64	59	63	69	83	66	75	72	64	70	65	61	73	66	76	61	71	83	77
WARREN	84	71	65	69	76	90	70	81	76	69	75	70	66	79	72	80	66	76	88	85
WASHINGTON	88	87	97	87	91	95	86	90	90	85	88	78	87	90	89	92	79	87	97	90
WAYNE	84	69	53	67	76	95	69	84	73	66	72	73	62	74	70	77	62	77	88	88
WESTMORELAND	86	86	94	85	90	95	82	88	86	83	84	74	86	86	86	89	76	84	95	89
WYOMING	88	73	61	71	79	96	70	84	76	70	75	74	66	80	72	80	66	77	89	89
YORK	95	95	101	96	97	99	92	95	94	93	93	84	94	96	94	95	84	93	98	97
PENNSYLVANIA	93	94	102	94	97	99	93	95	96	93	95	84	95	95	95	98	86	93	100	96
UNITED STATES	100	100	100	100	100	100	100	100	100	100	100	100	100	100	100	100	100	100	100	100

COUNTY	FIPS Code	CBSA Code	DMA Code	POPULATION			2000-2007 ANNUAL RATE		RACE (%)					
									White		Black		Asian/Pacific	
				2000	2007	2012	% Rate	State Rank	2000	2007	2000	2007	2000	2007
BRISTOL	001	39300	521	50,648	52,683	52,732	0.5	3	96.8	96.0	0.7	0.8	1.0	1.4
KENT	003	39300	521	167,090	172,366	175,915	0.4	4	95.5	94.5	0.9	1.1	1.4	1.9
NEWPORT	005	39300	521	85,433	85,074	84,242	-0.1	5	91.5	89.7	3.7	4.3	1.3	1.7
PROVIDENCE	007	39300	521	621,602	645,977	659,529	0.5	3	78.4	74.5	6.5	7.2	3.0	3.8
WASHINGTON	009	39300	521	123,546	129,785	132,778	0.7	1	94.8	93.6	0.9	1.1	1.5	2.1
RHODE ISLAND							0.5		85.0	82.2	4.5	4.9	2.3	3.0
UNITED STATES							1.2		75.1	72.7	12.3	12.6	3.8	4.5

B

COUNTY	% HISPANIC ORIGIN		2007 AGE DISTRIBUTION (%)										MEDIAN AGE	% 2007 Males	% 2007 Females
	2000	2007	0-4	5-9	10-14	15-19	20-24	25-44	45-64	65-84	85+	18+	2007		
BRISTOL	1.1	1.6	5.1	5.3	6.6	9.4	7.7	22.3	26.7	13.8	3.1	78.9	40.8	48.4	51.6
KENT	1.7	2.3	5.7	5.7	6.3	6.5	5.1	26.2	28.8	12.9	2.6	78.1	41.6	48.1	51.9
NEWPORT	2.8	3.8	5.6	5.5	6.1	7.1	6.5	25.8	28.9	12.1	2.5	78.9	40.9	48.8	51.2
PROVIDENCE	13.4	17.1	6.3	5.8	6.6	8.1	8.0	27.0	24.3	11.2	2.7	77.1	36.8	48.2	51.8
WASHINGTON	1.4	2.0	5.6	5.9	6.6	8.0	7.3	24.4	29.1	11.1	2.1	78.0	40.1	48.6	51.4
RHODE ISLAND	8.7	11.2	6.0	5.7	6.5	7.8	7.3	26.3	26.0	11.7	2.6	77.6	38.5	48.3	51.7
UNITED STATES	12.5	15.0	6.9	6.5	6.8	7.1	7.0	27.6	25.4	10.7	1.9	75.6	36.7	49.2	50.8

54-B

COUNTY	HOUSEHOLDS					FAMILIES			MEDIAN HOUSEHOLD INCOME			
	2000	2007	2012	% Annual Rate 2000-2007	2007 Average HH Size	2000	2007	% Annual Rate 2000-2007	2007	2012	2007 National Rank	2007 State Rank
BRISTOL	19,033	19,404	19,568	0.3	2.48	13,359	13,363	0.0	65,291	78,311	167	2
KENT	67,320	69,984	71,799	0.5	2.44	44,964	45,764	0.2	60,565	70,149	250	4
NEWPORT	35,228	35,161	35,043	0.0	2.34	22,232	21,678	-0.3	65,102	77,942	168	3
PROVIDENCE	239,936	245,764	251,415	0.3	2.51	152,823	152,962	0.0	46,146	53,676	984	5
WASHINGTON	46,907	50,179	51,744	0.9	2.48	32,020	33,568	0.7	69,210	81,830	124	1
RHODE ISLAND				0.4	2.48			0.1	53,334	62,664		
UNITED STATES				1.2	2.59			1.0	53,154	62,503		

COUNTY	2007 Per Capita Income	2007 HH Income Base	2007 HOUSEHOLD INCOME DISTRIBUTION (%)					2007 Home Value Base	2007 HOME VALUE DISTRIBUTION (%)					2007 Median Home Value
			Less than $25,000	$25,000 to $49,999	$50,000 to $99,999	$100,000 to $149,999	$150,000 or More		Less than $50,000	$50,000 to $89,999	$90,000 to $174,999	$175,000 to $399,999	$400,000 or More	
BRISTOL	34,886	19,404	18.2	19.9	31.9	15.4	14.6	13,837	0.2	0.2	1.6	56.2	41.9	375,763
KENT	30,545	69,984	18.1	21.8	38.7	13.5	7.9	50,093	0.7	1.1	6.1	75.0	17.1	269,731
NEWPORT	35,500	35,161	16.8	20.6	36.3	13.8	12.6	21,797	0.9	1.3	2.0	53.5	42.4	375,000
PROVIDENCE	23,981	245,764	29.0	24.4	30.4	10.5	5.6	131,115	0.6	0.6	6.0	75.5	17.3	280,741
WASHINGTON	33,794	50,179	15.1	19.7	36.3	16.6	12.4	36,705	1.0	0.6	2.0	56.9	39.5	367,442
RHODE ISLAND	27,627		24.0	22.9	33.1	12.2	7.8		0.7	0.7	4.9	69.8	24.0	301,595
UNITED STATES	27,916		21.9	25.0	32.3	12.3	8.4		7.9	10.5	27.1	35.6	19.0	192,285

COUNTY	FINANCIAL SERVICES				THE HOME						ENTERTAINMENT						PERSONAL			
					Home Improvements		Furnishings													
	Auto Loan	Home Loan	Invest-ments	Retire-ment Plans	Home Repair	Lawn & Garden	Comput-ers & Hard-ware	Major Appli-ances	TV, Radio, Sound Equip-ment	Furni-ture	Dine out/ Carry out	Sports Equip-ment	Fees & Tickets	Toys & Games	Travel	Cable TV	Apparel & Services	Auto Repairs	Health Insur-ance	Pets & Supplies
BRISTOL	108	138	155	133	144	124	126	125	123	131	124	115	141	121	135	124	117	121	122	122
KENT	92	110	128	109	112	101	103	102	101	106	101	91	111	101	108	101	94	100	101	100
NEWPORT	106	122	134	122	124	111	120	115	114	120	115	110	126	113	123	113	107	116	110	113
PROVIDENCE	77	82	92	81	82	76	87	81	86	85	86	77	88	84	86	85	80	83	81	79
WASHINGTON	112	130	136	129	131	121	119	120	115	123	115	111	127	115	124	114	107	117	115	119
RHODE ISLAND	87	97	109	97	98	90	98	93	96	98	97	88	102	95	99	96	90	95	92	92
UNITED STATES	100	100	100	100	100	100	100	100	100	100	100	100	100	100	100	100	100	100	100	100

A

COUNTY	FIPS Code	CBSA Code	DMA Code	POPULATION			2000-2007 ANNUAL RATE		RACE (%)					
									White		Black		Asian/Pacific	
				2000	2007	2012	% Rate	State Rank	2000	2007	2000	2007	2000	2007
ABBEVILLE	001	00000	567	26,167	26,632	26,841	0.2	37	68.3	67.2	30.3	31.1	0.3	0.3
AIKEN	003	12260	520	142,552	155,874	165,960	1.2	14	71.4	70.0	25.6	26.0	0.7	0.9
ALLENDALE	005	00000	520	11,211	10,945	10,736	-0.3	44	27.4	26.5	71.0	71.4	0.2	0.3
ANDERSON	007	11340	567	165,740	180,513	191,510	1.2	14	81.6	80.5	16.6	17.1	0.4	0.6
BAMBERG	009	00000	520	16,658	15,870	15,312	-0.7	46	36.5	35.4	62.5	63.3	0.2	0.3
BARNWELL	011	00000	520	23,478	23,252	23,039	-0.1	40	55.2	53.8	42.6	43.2	0.4	0.6
BEAUFORT	013	25940	507	120,937	154,876	181,530	3.5	1	70.7	68.8	24.0	24.0	0.8	1.1
BERKELEY	015	16700	519	142,651	161,486	177,368	1.7	7	68.0	66.1	26.6	26.9	2.0	2.6
CALHOUN	017	17900	546	15,185	15,965	16,373	0.7	22	50.0	48.9	48.7	49.5	0.2	0.2
CHARLESTON	019	16700	519	309,969	345,500	367,737	1.5	9	61.9	60.4	34.5	34.9	1.2	1.6
CHEROKEE	021	23500	567	52,537	53,632	54,176	0.3	33	76.9	75.6	20.6	21.0	0.3	0.4
CHESTER	023	16900	517	34,068	33,153	32,137	-0.4	45	59.9	58.7	38.7	39.5	0.3	0.4
CHESTERFIELD	025	00000	517	42,768	44,564	45,640	0.6	24	64.3	63.0	33.2	33.8	0.3	0.4
CLARENDON	027	00000	546	32,502	34,769	36,215	0.9	18	44.9	43.7	53.1	53.8	0.3	0.4
COLLETON	029	47500	519	38,264	40,272	41,407	0.7	22	55.5	54.2	42.2	42.9	0.3	0.4
DARLINGTON	031	22500	570	67,394	68,271	68,757	0.2	37	57.0	55.8	41.7	42.5	0.2	0.3
DILLON	033	19900	570	30,722	30,810	30,541	0.0	39	50.4	49.9	45.3	45.9	0.4	0.4
DORCHESTER	035	16700	519	96,413	121,201	146,436	3.2	2	71.0	69.5	25.1	25.5	1.2	1.6
EDGEFIELD	037	12260	520	24,595	26,500	27,236	1.0	17	56.8	55.6	41.5	42.2	0.3	0.4
FAIRFIELD	039	17900	546	23,454	24,175	24,665	0.4	30	39.6	38.5	59.1	59.8	0.2	0.3
FLORENCE	041	22500	570	125,761	132,047	136,732	0.7	22	58.7	57.3	39.3	40.1	0.7	1.0
GEORGETOWN	043	23860	519	55,797	64,246	70,987	2.0	5	59.7	58.4	38.6	39.3	0.3	0.4
GREENVILLE	045	24860	567	379,616	420,579	451,398	1.4	12	77.5	75.9	18.3	18.5	1.4	1.9
GREENWOOD	047	24940	567	66,271	68,726	70,120	0.5	26	65.6	64.2	31.7	32.2	0.7	1.0
HAMPTON	049	00000	507	21,386	21,093	20,980	-0.2	42	42.9	41.9	55.7	56.2	0.2	0.2
HORRY	051	34820	570	196,629	243,477	288,859	3.0	4	81.0	79.6	15.5	15.8	0.8	1.1
JASPER	053	25940	507	20,678	22,836	24,459	1.4	12	42.4	40.9	52.7	52.4	0.5	0.6
KERSHAW	055	17900	546	52,647	58,705	63,368	1.5	9	71.6	70.4	26.3	26.9	0.3	0.5
LANCASTER	057	29580	517	61,351	65,179	67,795	0.8	19	71.0	69.7	26.9	27.5	0.3	0.4
LAURENS	059	24860	567	69,567	70,895	71,495	0.3	33	71.6	69.7	26.2	27.3	0.2	0.3
LEE	061	00000	546	20,119	20,366	20,396	0.2	37	35.0	34.0	63.6	64.1	0.2	0.3
LEXINGTON	063	17900	546	216,014	244,352	266,281	1.7	7	84.2	82.9	12.6	12.9	1.1	1.5
MCCORMICK	065	00000	520	9,958	10,297	10,485	0.5	26	44.8	43.6	53.9	54.7	0.3	0.4
MARION	067	00000	570	35,466	34,892	34,437	-0.2	42	41.7	40.5	56.3	56.9	0.3	0.4
MARLBORO	069	13500	570	28,818	29,275	28,317	0.2	37	44.5	43.0	50.7	51.2	0.2	0.3
NEWBERRY	071	35140	546	36,108	37,411	38,147	0.5	26	64.0	62.7	33.1	33.5	0.4	0.5
OCONEE	073	42860	567	66,215	72,013	76,280	1.2	14	89.1	88.0	8.4	8.6	0.4	0.5
ORANGEBURG	075	36700	546	91,582	93,514	92,455	0.3	33	37.2	36.1	60.9	61.5	0.4	0.6
PICKENS	077	24860	567	110,757	116,838	120,662	0.7	22	90.3	89.1	6.8	7.0	1.2	1.6
RICHLAND	079	17900	546	320,677	356,842	383,801	1.5	9	50.3	48.7	45.2	45.4	1.8	2.4
SALUDA	081	17900	546	19,181	19,771	20,216	0.4	30	65.8	64.1	30.0	30.0	0.0	0.1
SPARTANBURG	083	43900	567	253,791	275,235	291,145	1.1	16	75.1	73.4	20.8	21.1	1.5	2.0
SUMTER	085	44940	546	104,646	107,718	109,972	0.4	30	50.1	48.7	46.7	47.2	1.0	1.3
UNION	087	46420	567	29,881	29,135	28,517	-0.3	44	67.8	66.7	31.0	31.9	0.2	0.3
WILLIAMSBURG	089	00000	519	37,217	38,246	37,243	0.4	30	32.7	31.8	66.3	67.0	0.2	0.3
YORK	091	16740	517	164,614	203,817	236,493	3.0	4	77.2	75.8	19.2	19.5	0.9	1.2
SOUTH CAROLINA							1.4		67.2	66.1	29.5	29.5	0.9	1.3
UNITED STATES							1.2		75.1	72.7	12.3	12.6	3.8	4.5

COUNTY	% HISPANIC ORIGIN		2007 AGE DISTRIBUTION (%)										MEDIAN AGE	% 2007 Males	% 2007 Females
	2000	2007	0-4	5-9	10-14	15-19	20-24	25-44	45-64	65-84	85+	18+	2007		
ABBEVILLE	0.8	1.1	6.7	6.7	6.3	7.1	6.1	25.6	26.9	12.4	2.0	76.3	38.5	48.3	51.7
AIKEN	2.1	2.8	6.7	6.4	6.8	6.6	6.2	26.5	27.4	11.7	1.6	76.1	38.7	48.4	51.6
ALLENDALE	1.6	2.2	6.9	6.5	6.7	6.2	7.7	27.8	26.0	10.3	2.0	76.2	36.5	53.6	46.4
ANDERSON	1.1	1.5	6.7	6.5	6.4	6.2	5.3	27.2	27.6	12.3	1.8	76.7	39.4	48.7	51.3
BAMBERG	0.7	0.8	6.2	6.3	6.4	8.7	8.3	23.6	26.4	12.2	1.9	76.8	37.2	47.4	52.6
BARNWELL	1.4	1.9	7.2	7.0	6.8	7.4	6.2	26.8	26.8	10.2	1.7	74.4	36.9	48.8	51.2
BEAUFORT	6.8	9.0	6.5	5.8	5.5	6.7	7.4	24.2	24.5	17.5	1.8	78.8	39.9	50.0	50.0
BERKELEY	2.8	3.7	7.4	6.5	6.5	8.1	8.3	29.0	25.3	8.2	0.8	75.2	33.8	50.5	49.5
CALHOUN	1.4	1.7	6.1	6.2	6.3	6.2	5.3	24.8	30.9	12.5	1.8	77.5	41.6	47.7	52.3
CHARLESTON	2.4	3.2	6.4	6.1	6.0	7.4	7.7	28.9	25.0	10.7	1.7	77.6	36.1	48.5	51.5
CHEROKEE	2.1	2.9	7.2	7.1	6.7	6.6	5.6	28.9	25.7	10.6	1.6	75.1	37.0	48.9	51.1
CHESTER	0.7	0.9	6.8	6.5	6.8	7.0	6.2	26.9	27.0	11.4	1.5	75.6	38.0	48.7	51.3
CHESTERFIELD	2.3	3.0	6.8	6.5	7.0	6.8	5.6	27.8	27.2	10.7	1.5	75.4	38.1	48.8	51.2
CLARENDON	1.7	2.3	6.1	5.6	5.9	7.2	7.8	23.1	28.6	14.2	1.7	78.4	40.3	49.5	50.5
COLLETON	1.4	1.9	7.0	6.8	6.9	6.7	6.6	24.9	27.5	12.0	1.6	75.2	38.5	48.2	51.8
DARLINGTON	1.0	1.3	6.8	6.6	7.3	6.4	5.7	26.7	27.5	11.2	1.7	75.4	37.9	47.7	52.3
DILLON	1.8	1.8	7.6	7.1	7.2	7.0	6.7	27.1	25.6	10.3	1.6	73.7	35.6	47.0	53.0
DORCHESTER	1.8	2.4	6.8	6.0	7.3	7.7	7.3	28.2	26.6	9.0	1.1	75.1	36.8	49.1	50.9
EDGEFIELD	2.0	2.7	6.0	6.0	5.8	6.7	7.9	29.5	27.5	9.3	1.4	78.7	37.4	54.2	45.8
FAIRFIELD	1.1	1.4	6.8	6.7	6.6	6.3	5.4	26.3	29.0	11.0	1.9	76.0	39.3	47.7	52.3
FLORENCE	1.1	1.4	6.5	6.3	6.7	7.0	6.5	27.6	27.0	10.7	1.7	76.3	37.6	47.3	52.7
GEORGETOWN	1.6	2.2	6.1	6.0	6.2	6.3	5.0	23.7	30.1	14.9	1.7	77.7	42.5	48.0	52.0
GREENVILLE	3.8	5.0	6.7	6.6	6.5	6.8	6.5	28.8	26.1	10.4	1.6	76.3	37.2	48.9	51.1
GREENWOOD	2.9	3.8	6.9	6.4	6.7	7.3	6.9	26.9	25.0	11.8	2.0	75.7	36.7	47.3	52.7
HAMPTON	2.6	3.2	6.9	6.7	6.8	6.9	6.6	27.7	26.4	10.5	1.6	75.3	36.5	51.1	48.9
HORRY	2.6	3.5	5.9	5.4	5.6	5.7	5.7	28.8	26.6	15.0	1.3	79.8	40.3	49.1	50.9
JASPER	5.8	7.8	7.5	6.9	7.0	6.8	7.0	30.0	24.0	9.4	1.3	74.6	34.6	52.9	47.1
KERSHAW	1.7	2.2	6.6	6.5	6.6	6.5	6.0	25.9	28.4	11.8	1.6	76.1	39.5	48.5	51.5
LANCASTER	1.6	2.2	6.6	6.4	6.8	6.3	6.1	28.6	26.6	11.2	1.5	76.4	38.0	50.2	49.8
LAURENS	1.9	2.7	6.6	6.5	6.3	6.9	6.0	27.3	26.4	11.9	2.0	76.5	38.5	48.8	51.2
LEE	1.3	1.7	6.4	6.3	6.7	5.8	7.3	27.9	27.4	10.4	1.8	77.1	37.3	51.1	48.9
LEXINGTON	1.9	2.6	6.8	6.4	6.8	6.6	6.4	28.0	27.9	9.6	1.4	75.9	37.9	48.8	51.2
MCCORMICK	0.9	1.1	4.2	4.0	5.0	5.5	6.1	26.2	29.2	17.6	2.1	83.4	44.3	53.4	46.6
MARION	1.8	2.3	7.1	6.5	7.0	6.5	6.9	26.2	27.6	10.6	1.6	75.5	36.8	47.0	53.0
MARLBORO	0.7	0.9	6.3	6.1	6.2	6.3	7.2	30.2	26.3	10.0	1.5	77.6	36.7	52.4	47.6
NEWBERRY	4.2	5.6	6.6	6.4	5.9	6.6	6.5	27.0	27.1	11.7	2.2	77.5	39.0	48.9	51.1
OCONEE	2.4	3.2	6.0	6.0	5.9	5.4	4.7	26.3	28.1	15.7	1.7	78.7	41.7	49.5	50.5
ORANGEBURG	1.0	1.2	6.5	6.2	6.4	8.1	8.5	25.0	25.4	11.9	2.0	77.1	36.8	46.8	53.2
PICKENS	1.7	2.3	6.0	6.0	5.7	8.8	11.0	26.5	23.9	10.4	1.7	78.7	34.5	50.2	49.8
RICHLAND	2.7	3.5	6.3	6.1	6.4	8.7	9.1	29.1	24.2	8.7	1.3	76.9	34.0	48.4	51.6
SALUDA	7.3	9.7	6.8	6.7	6.5	5.3	6.3	26.9	27.0	12.4	2.0	76.8	38.9	50.0	50.0
SPARTANBURG	2.8	3.8	6.6	6.5	6.6	6.6	5.8	28.4	26.6	11.2	1.7	76.6	38.1	49.0	51.0
SUMTER	1.8	2.4	7.6	7.0	6.8	7.2	8.0	27.2	24.4	10.3	1.6	74.4	35.1	48.7	51.3
UNION	0.7	0.9	6.4	6.5	6.5	5.7	5.0	26.8	27.4	13.6	2.1	77.1	40.4	47.4	52.6
WILLIAMSBURG	0.7	0.9	6.8	6.4	6.6	6.7	7.0	26.1	27.5	11.3	1.6	76.4	37.5	49.3	50.7
YORK	2.0	2.6	6.8	6.4	6.9	7.4	6.4	28.2	26.9	9.7	1.3	75.4	37.3	48.7	51.3
SOUTH CAROLINA	2.4	3.2	6.6	6.3	6.4	7.0	6.9	27.7	26.3	11.2	1.6	76.7	37.4	48.9	51.1
UNITED STATES	12.5	15.0	6.9	6.5	6.8	7.1	7.0	27.6	25.4	10.7	1.9	75.6	36.7	49.2	50.8

COUNTY	HOUSEHOLDS					FAMILIES			MEDIAN HOUSEHOLD INCOME			
	2000	2007	2012	% Annual Rate 2000-2007	2007 Average HH Size	2000	2007	% Annual Rate 2000-2007	2007	2012	2007 National Rank	2007 State Rank
ABBEVILLE	10,131	10,561	10,752	0.6	2.45	7,288	7,348	0.1	40,377	46,424	1681	27
AIKEN	55,587	62,400	67,128	1.6	2.46	39,434	42,767	1.1	47,331	55,191	881	10
ALLENDALE	3,915	3,936	3,907	0.1	2.46	2,617	2,531	-0.5	25,227	28,842	3090	46
ANDERSON	65,649	72,467	77,416	1.4	2.45	47,276	50,474	0.9	44,921	51,456	1119	15
BAMBERG	6,123	6,086	5,943	-0.1	2.43	4,253	4,077	-0.6	29,278	33,281	2946	45
BARNWELL	9,021	9,295	9,344	0.4	2.47	6,433	6,405	-0.1	35,355	40,565	2389	38
BEAUFORT	45,532	60,791	72,214	4.1	2.45	33,060	42,727	3.6	60,417	70,810	253	1
BERKELEY	49,922	58,060	64,646	2.1	2.70	37,696	42,578	1.7	50,037	58,767	679	7
CALHOUN	5,917	6,504	6,769	1.3	2.43	4,270	4,540	0.8	40,862	47,003	1617	25
CHARLESTON	123,326	142,120	153,658	2.0	2.34	77,416	85,372	1.4	47,866	56,057	829	8
CHEROKEE	20,495	21,517	21,974	0.7	2.46	14,614	14,829	0.2	41,173	47,334	1577	24
CHESTER	12,880	12,937	12,694	0.1	2.54	9,343	9,083	-0.4	39,602	45,596	1765	28
CHESTERFIELD	16,557	17,827	18,495	1.0	2.46	11,703	12,169	0.5	36,212	41,612	2240	36
CLARENDON	11,812	13,246	14,028	1.6	2.50	8,598	9,083	1.1	33,864	38,909	2564	39
COLLETON	14,470	15,786	16,468	1.2	2.53	10,494	11,079	0.8	36,485	41,896	2194	34
DARLINGTON	25,793	26,201	26,554	0.2	2.56	18,444	18,108	-0.3	38,733	44,921	1891	31
DILLON	11,199	11,628	11,685	0.5	2.61	8,065	8,098	0.1	32,767	37,058	2676	41
DORCHESTER	34,709	44,315	54,097	3.4	2.68	26,293	32,618	3.0	54,588	64,092	416	4
EDGEFIELD	8,270	9,029	9,420	1.2	2.58	6,214	6,587	0.8	43,034	49,401	1325	18
FAIRFIELD	8,774	9,467	9,804	1.1	2.51	6,387	6,672	0.6	37,240	42,908	2096	33
FLORENCE	47,147	50,670	53,068	1.0	2.53	33,798	35,120	0.5	42,886	49,205	1343	19
GEORGETOWN	21,659	26,103	29,290	2.6	2.44	15,844	18,498	2.2	44,209	51,490	1188	17
GREENVILLE	149,556	168,202	181,795	1.6	2.44	102,012	110,497	1.1	51,794	61,128	562	5
GREENWOOD	25,729	26,847	27,518	0.6	2.47	17,754	17,857	0.1	42,442	48,710	1403	21
HAMPTON	7,444	7,686	7,754	0.4	2.55	5,312	5,302	0.0	35,852	41,109	2304	37
HORRY	81,800	105,211	126,543	3.5	2.29	54,515	67,396	3.0	45,374	52,622	1065	12
JASPER	7,042	8,017	8,701	1.8	2.68	5,092	5,611	1.3	38,232	44,135	1970	32
KERSHAW	20,188	23,195	25,325	1.9	2.51	14,918	16,616	1.5	47,467	54,547	865	9
LANCASTER	23,178	25,436	26,821	1.3	2.48	16,840	17,890	0.8	42,703	48,984	1365	20
LAURENS	26,290	27,250	27,713	0.5	2.50	18,870	18,915	0.0	41,514	47,555	1517	22
LEE	6,886	7,261	7,379	0.7	2.55	4,916	5,010	0.3	33,385	38,414	2619	40
LEXINGTON	83,240	96,115	105,734	2.0	2.51	59,830	66,822	1.5	56,247	65,937	358	2
MCCORMICK	3,558	3,891	4,032	1.2	2.27	2,604	2,758	0.8	39,190	45,370	1831	29
MARION	13,301	13,564	13,581	0.3	2.55	9,511	9,375	-0.2	32,543	36,923	2699	42
MARLBORO	10,478	10,405	10,168	-0.1	2.50	7,338	7,032	-0.6	32,310	36,898	2729	43
NEWBERRY	14,026	14,947	15,400	0.9	2.43	9,809	10,088	0.4	40,790	46,901	1631	26
OCONEE	27,283	30,277	32,380	1.4	2.36	19,589	21,023	1.0	45,347	52,532	1069	13
ORANGEBURG	34,118	35,529	35,617	0.6	2.48	23,876	23,997	0.1	36,265	41,231	2237	35
PICKENS	41,306	45,137	47,066	1.2	2.43	28,453	29,968	0.7	45,119	51,384	1097	14
RICHLAND	120,101	137,859	150,629	1.9	2.37	76,378	83,974	1.3	50,255	59,314	659	6
SALUDA	7,127	7,513	7,741	0.7	2.60	5,295	5,413	0.3	44,263	50,623	1180	16
SPARTANBURG	97,735	107,643	114,718	1.3	2.49	69,299	73,725	0.9	46,792	54,405	928	11
SUMTER	37,728	40,175	41,608	0.9	2.60	27,611	28,482	0.4	41,185	47,251	1575	23
UNION	12,087	12,217	12,129	0.1	2.35	8,495	8,288	-0.3	39,052	45,095	1846	30
WILLIAMSBURG	13,714	14,177	13,987	0.5	2.56	10,050	10,068	0.0	29,471	34,117	2932	44
YORK	61,051	77,676	91,065	3.4	2.57	44,915	55,375	2.9	55,229	64,676	395	3
SOUTH CAROLINA				1.7	2.47			1.2	46,513	54,235		
UNITED STATES				1.2	2.59			1.0	53,154	62,503		

COUNTY	2007 Per Capita Income	2007 HH Income Base	2007 HOUSEHOLD INCOME DISTRIBUTION (%)					2007 Home Value Base	2007 HOME VALUE DISTRIBUTION (%)					2007 Median Home Value
			Less than $25,000	$25,000 to $49,999	$50,000 to $99,999	$100,000 to $149,999	$150,000 or More		Less than $50,000	$50,000 to $89,999	$90,000 to $174,999	$175,000 to $399,999	$400,000 or More	
ABBEVILLE	19,439	10,561	31.0	29.8	31.2	5.9	2.1	8,593	20.1	24.7	38.1	15.4	1.7	97,798
AIKEN	24,478	62,400	26.2	26.2	31.7	10.8	5.1	48,101	15.7	18.8	41.7	20.1	3.7	115,260
ALLENDALE	14,897	3,936	49.7	26.7	17.7	3.9	2.1	2,902	27.8	38.6	26.1	7.0	0.6	70,111
ANDERSON	23,011	72,467	26.6	28.9	31.6	9.3	3.6	56,271	16.1	22.3	39.6	19.4	2.6	107,671
BAMBERG	16,247	6,086	44.8	27.0	21.6	4.6	2.0	4,612	30.2	26.8	33.3	8.9	0.8	78,505
BARNWELL	19,632	9,295	37.9	25.3	26.7	7.4	2.7	7,160	30.5	25.4	33.8	9.4	0.8	79,384
BEAUFORT	33,949	60,791	16.6	24.0	34.3	13.5	11.5	45,354	7.3	7.2	21.9	32.8	30.7	244,466
BERKELEY	21,754	58,060	21.1	28.8	35.7	10.7	3.7	43,911	13.2	11.6	36.8	33.4	5.0	151,046
CALHOUN	22,102	6,504	31.9	27.5	28.9	7.7	4.0	5,527	21.6	28.4	33.3	14.8	2.0	90,015
CHARLESTON	28,265	142,120	26.1	25.8	30.3	10.3	7.5	89,788	6.8	7.5	26.9	38.7	20.1	207,821
CHEROKEE	20,758	21,517	30.0	29.5	30.6	7.2	2.6	16,229	18.5	23.8	42.0	14.5	1.2	100,565
CHESTER	18,868	12,937	31.1	30.6	29.7	7.0	1.5	10,273	20.8	26.5	38.9	12.6	1.2	93,601
CHESTERFIELD	18,201	17,827	35.6	29.6	27.1	6.0	1.7	13,840	26.4	26.4	35.4	10.5	1.3	85,938
CLARENDON	18,184	13,246	38.5	28.1	24.8	6.0	2.5	10,616	25.0	22.2	37.3	13.5	2.0	93,820
COLLETON	18,628	15,786	35.4	28.5	28.2	5.3	2.6	12,805	20.6	25.6	36.1	13.9	3.8	95,967
DARLINGTON	20,195	26,201	34.3	27.4	27.3	7.0	3.9	20,494	26.8	26.4	33.8	11.8	1.2	85,210
DILLON	16,507	11,628	39.9	29.1	24.1	5.0	2.0	8,559	30.2	28.6	33.1	7.4	0.6	77,926
DORCHESTER	24,394	44,315	18.9	26.2	36.9	13.2	4.8	33,972	10.0	9.4	30.4	42.1	8.2	175,664
EDGEFIELD	19,932	9,029	29.6	27.2	31.4	8.5	3.3	7,352	16.9	22.7	38.2	19.4	2.9	107,405
FAIRFIELD	19,677	9,467	35.7	27.1	26.8	7.3	3.2	7,407	20.5	26.9	36.3	13.4	2.9	93,845
FLORENCE	22,483	50,670	29.2	28.2	29.5	8.7	4.4	37,719	20.7	24.7	36.9	15.0	2.7	96,486
GEORGETOWN	25,758	26,103	28.1	27.0	30.0	8.7	6.2	21,467	19.3	15.8	30.5	23.1	11.3	125,906
GREENVILLE	28,128	168,202	21.9	26.2	32.8	11.6	7.6	117,807	9.9	15.0	42.2	27.8	5.0	134,519
GREENWOOD	21,949	26,847	29.3	28.9	30.2	7.8	3.8	19,007	12.7	22.4	42.1	19.8	3.1	114,309
HAMPTON	17,817	7,686	36.1	29.0	26.7	5.6	2.6	6,093	27.5	29.4	32.7	9.1	1.2	79,959
HORRY	25,516	105,211	22.9	32.1	32.4	8.1	4.5	78,189	10.1	9.9	28.9	41.5	9.7	178,232
JASPER	18,634	8,017	33.5	29.5	27.2	6.5	3.3	6,317	24.3	19.2	38.0	14.3	4.2	99,086
KERSHAW	23,196	23,195	24.1	28.8	34.4	9.4	3.3	19,250	15.4	19.9	42.4	19.5	2.8	113,339
LANCASTER	20,772	25,436	27.2	30.5	32.1	7.8	2.3	19,491	13.8	21.8	43.9	18.8	1.8	111,443
LAURENS	19,872	27,250	29.6	30.5	30.7	7.0	2.2	21,407	22.1	26.1	39.0	11.5	1.3	92,186
LEE	17,876	7,261	39.5	28.9	22.9	5.9	2.7	5,819	29.3	32.0	30.3	8.0	0.5	76,101
LEXINGTON	27,387	96,115	18.1	25.9	35.6	14.5	5.9	75,510	11.8	13.0	43.9	26.5	4.8	133,903
MCCORMICK	20,843	3,891	36.0	25.8	28.1	6.5	3.8	3,185	25.2	28.3	24.5	14.7	7.3	84,838
MARION	17,410	13,564	40.2	27.6	24.7	5.4	2.1	10,139	25.7	27.0	36.2	10.0	1.2	86,386
MARLBORO	16,550	10,405	40.2	29.1	24.0	4.9	1.7	7,555	25.8	34.9	33.4	5.4	0.4	78,070
NEWBERRY	20,539	14,947	30.4	29.8	29.1	7.9	2.7	11,660	19.3	23.6	36.4	17.8	2.9	102,737
OCONEE	24,373	30,277	25.8	29.4	32.0	8.6	4.2	24,174	16.7	17.2	35.9	22.7	7.4	121,058
ORANGEBURG	19,108	35,529	36.8	27.4	26.4	6.6	2.8	27,286	23.1	25.3	37.7	12.1	1.8	92,279
PICKENS	22,231	45,137	27.0	29.0	32.2	8.2	3.6	33,773	17.3	20.1	41.9	18.6	2.2	108,394
RICHLAND	27,339	137,849	23.1	26.6	32.3	10.8	7.2	87,472	5.1	13.2	47.5	27.2	7.1	139,303
SALUDA	20,675	7,513	28.0	28.6	32.8	7.7	2.9	6,144	17.8	25.0	38.1	16.7	2.4	99,866
SPARTANBURG	23,727	107,640	25.1	27.9	32.9	9.5	4.6	79,373	15.1	23.0	42.7	16.7	2.4	106,742
SUMTER	19,986	40,175	30.5	29.4	29.7	7.2	3.2	28,644	18.2	24.4	40.9	14.8	1.6	100,734
UNION	20,202	12,217	31.6	31.5	29.1	5.9	1.9	9,511	25.8	26.1	37.9	9.1	1.2	87,060
WILLIAMSBURG	16,299	14,177	43.8	26.8	22.5	4.6	2.3	11,504	31.5	27.6	30.5	9.7	0.7	75,838
YORK	26,561	77,676	19.8	25.3	36.1	12.5	6.3	58,109	9.9	12.6	38.4	32.6	6.4	145,558
SOUTH CAROLINA	24,375		25.8	27.6	31.7	9.7	5.2		14.4	17.5	37.6	24.2	6.4	123,378
UNITED STATES	27,916		21.9	25.0	32.3	12.3	8.4		7.9	10.5	27.1	35.6	19.0	192,285

COUNTY	FINANCIAL SERVICES				THE HOME						ENTERTAINMENT						PERSONAL			
					Home Improvements		Furnishings													
	Auto Loan	Home Loan	Invest-ments	Retire-ment Plans	Home Repair	Lawn & Garden	Comput-ers & Hard-ware	Major Appli-ances	TV, Radio, Sound Equip-ment	Furni-ture	Dine out/ Carry out	Sports Equip-ment	Fees & Tickets	Toys & Games	Travel	Cable TV	Apparel & Services	Auto Repairs	Health Insur-ance	Pets & Supplies
ABBEVILLE	81	59	41	57	64	84	61	74	68	59	67	66	52	70	60	72	57	69	80	80
AIKEN	92	82	75	81	82	92	80	87	84	80	84	78	77	86	80	87	74	84	91	90
ALLENDALE	63	44	31	43	46	63	47	56	56	46	54	49	41	55	46	60	47	54	64	61
ANDERSON	88	74	66	74	77	90	74	83	80	74	79	73	70	82	74	83	69	79	88	86
BAMBERG	67	47	34	46	51	69	50	60	58	49	57	53	43	58	49	63	49	58	69	65
BARNWELL	84	60	37	57	63	84	60	75	69	60	68	67	52	72	59	74	58	70	81	82
BEAUFORT	123	115	113	116	115	126	115	121	117	115	116	107	113	113	118	120	103	120	127	122
BERKELEY	92	82	69	81	78	86	81	84	83	81	82	78	77	86	78	83	73	84	85	87
CALHOUN	94	66	38	63	73	98	66	85	75	65	75	76	56	79	65	81	64	78	91	93
CHARLESTON	95	90	92	92	88	90	95	91	95	93	94	84	93	94	92	94	85	94	92	92
CHEROKEE	83	65	51	63	67	83	66	75	72	65	72	67	60	75	65	76	62	72	81	80
CHESTER	80	60	45	59	63	80	61	71	68	60	67	63	54	70	60	72	58	68	77	76
CHESTERFIELD	77	55	36	52	59	78	56	68	64	55	63	61	48	66	55	69	54	64	75	74
CLARENDON	78	56	37	53	61	82	57	72	66	56	64	63	49	66	57	71	55	67	80	77
COLLETON	77	60	44	57	62	78	60	71	67	59	66	63	54	68	60	70	57	68	76	76
DARLINGTON	84	66	52	64	68	84	66	77	73	66	72	68	60	75	66	78	63	74	83	82
DILLON	71	52	38	51	55	71	54	64	62	54	61	57	48	63	53	66	53	62	71	69
DORCHESTER	100	93	82	92	90	96	89	94	91	90	91	86	87	94	88	92	80	92	94	97
EDGEFIELD	88	71	56	69	73	90	70	81	76	70	76	72	64	79	70	80	66	77	86	86
FAIRFIELD	83	58	38	56	63	85	62	75	71	60	70	66	53	73	60	76	60	71	83	82
FLORENCE	88	76	67	75	76	87	76	82	81	76	80	73	72	82	75	84	71	81	87	86
GEORGETOWN	101	80	62	78	87	110	79	97	87	79	86	84	72	87	82	94	75	91	105	102
GREENVILLE	101	94	92	96	92	97	95	95	97	95	96	87	93	98	93	98	86	96	98	97
GREENWOOD	83	69	66	70	71	82	74	78	78	71	77	69	69	79	72	81	68	77	83	80
HAMPTON	82	55	31	52	61	84	57	73	66	55	66	66	47	69	56	72	56	68	80	81
HORRY	88	77	72	77	77	87	79	84	81	78	81	74	75	80	79	84	71	83	88	86
JASPER	84	66	47	63	67	82	66	76	72	65	71	68	59	75	64	75	62	73	80	81
KERSHAW	93	78	64	76	81	96	75	87	81	75	80	77	71	84	76	84	70	82	91	92
LANCASTER	85	67	53	65	70	86	67	77	73	66	73	68	61	76	66	78	63	74	83	82
LAURENS	82	63	50	62	66	82	65	75	72	64	71	66	58	74	64	76	61	72	81	79
LEE	82	55	32	53	61	84	57	73	68	56	67	65	48	69	56	74	57	69	81	81
LEXINGTON	101	99	94	99	95	97	95	97	95	96	95	88	94	97	95	95	85	96	96	98
MCCORMICK	84	63	46	61	69	91	62	78	72	63	71	68	56	71	64	78	61	74	87	84
MARION	74	53	37	51	56	73	56	66	64	55	63	59	48	65	54	68	54	64	72	72
MARLBORO	73	51	33	49	55	75	53	66	62	52	61	59	45	64	52	67	52	62	73	72
NEWBERRY	82	62	47	61	67	85	65	76	71	63	70	68	57	74	64	75	61	72	82	81
OCONEE	95	74	56	71	79	100	73	88	80	72	79	78	66	82	74	85	68	82	95	94
ORANGEBURG	78	60	47	58	63	79	62	72	69	61	68	64	56	70	61	73	59	69	78	77
PICKENS	88	71	59	70	72	85	76	80	79	72	78	73	68	81	72	81	69	79	84	84
RICHLAND	96	92	95	95	86	87	97	90	96	96	96	83	95	96	93	95	86	94	91	91
SALUDA	94	66	39	62	73	100	66	86	75	65	75	76	56	79	66	81	64	78	92	93
SPARTANBURG	92	78	70	78	80	92	79	86	84	78	83	76	75	86	78	87	73	83	91	90
SUMTER	81	68	59	68	68	79	69	75	74	69	73	67	65	76	68	76	65	74	79	78
UNION	81	57	39	55	62	83	59	72	68	58	67	64	51	70	58	73	57	68	81	79
WILLIAMSBURG	73	50	31	47	55	75	52	65	61	50	60	59	44	62	51	66	51	61	73	72
YORK	101	96	93	96	94	99	93	96	95	94	95	87	92	97	93	97	84	95	99	99
SOUTH CAROLINA	93	80	72	80	81	92	81	87	85	81	85	78	77	87	80	88	75	86	91	90
UNITED STATES	100	100	100	100	100	100	100	100	100	100	100	100	100	100	100	100	100	100	100	100

COUNTY	FIPS Code	CBSA Code	DMA Code	POPULATION			2000-2007 ANNUAL RATE		RACE (%)					
									White		Black		Asian/Pacific	
				2000	2007	2012	% Rate	State Rank	2000	2007	2000	2007	2000	2007
AURORA	003	00000	725	3,058	2,989	2,936	-0.3	45	95.7	95.4	0.3	0.3	0.1	0.1
BEADLE	005	26700	725	17,023	15,827	15,037	-1.0	58	96.9	96.2	0.7	0.9	0.3	0.5
BENNETT	007	00000	764	3,574	3,605	3,630	0.1	32	40.9	38.4	0.3	0.3	0.2	0.2
BON HOMME	009	00000	725	7,260	7,252	7,158	0.0	37	95.5	95.1	0.6	0.6	0.1	0.1
BROOKINGS	011	15100	725	28,220	29,853	30,717	0.8	15	96.4	95.2	0.3	0.4	1.4	2.1
BROWN	013	10100	725	35,460	35,144	35,086	-0.1	42	95.5	94.4	0.3	0.4	0.5	0.7
BRULE	015	00000	725	5,364	5,197	5,084	-0.4	47	89.9	87.7	0.3	0.3	0.5	0.7
BUFFALO	017	00000	725	2,032	2,089	2,131	0.4	20	16.3	14.8	0.1	0.1	0.0	0.0
BUTTE	019	00000	764	9,094	9,661	10,090	0.8	15	95.5	94.5	0.1	0.1	0.2	0.4
CAMPBELL	021	00000	687	1,782	1,571	1,425	-1.7	66	99.3	99.1	0.0	0.0	0.1	0.1
CHARLES MIX	023	00000	725	9,350	9,479	9,593	0.2	28	69.6	65.0	0.1	0.2	0.1	0.1
CLARK	025	00000	725	4,143	3,874	3,669	-0.9	55	98.6	98.3	0.1	0.1	0.1	0.2
CLAY	027	46820	725	13,537	13,243	12,927	-0.3	45	92.8	90.7	1.0	1.2	2.0	3.0
CODINGTON	029	47980	725	25,897	26,356	26,688	0.2	28	96.7	95.9	0.1	0.2	0.3	0.4
CORSON	031	00000	687	4,181	4,310	4,394	0.4	20	37.2	32.3	0.1	0.1	0.0	0.1
CUSTER	033	00000	764	7,275	8,063	8,534	1.4	5	94.2	93.0	0.3	0.3	0.2	0.3
DAVISON	035	33580	725	18,741	19,294	19,682	0.4	20	96.2	95.3	0.3	0.3	0.4	0.7
DAY	037	00000	725	6,267	5,949	5,744	-0.7	52	91.3	89.4	0.1	0.2	0.1	0.2
DEUEL	039	00000	725	4,498	4,518	4,535	0.1	32	98.5	98.5	0.1	0.1	0.2	0.2
DEWEY	041	00000	725	5,972	6,090	6,153	0.3	24	24.1	20.4	0.0	0.0	0.2	0.2
DOUGLAS	043	00000	725	3,458	3,318	3,228	-0.6	50	98.1	97.7	0.1	0.1	0.1	0.2
EDMUNDS	045	10100	725	4,367	4,228	4,122	-0.4	47	99.2	99.0	0.1	0.1	0.1	0.2
FALL RIVER	047	00000	764	7,453	7,622	7,741	0.3	24	90.5	88.6	0.3	0.4	0.3	0.4
FAULK	049	00000	725	2,640	2,626	2,620	-0.1	42	99.5	99.5	0.1	0.1	0.0	0.0
GRANT	051	00000	725	7,847	7,520	7,266	-0.6	50	98.6	98.3	0.0	0.0	0.2	0.3
GREGORY	053	00000	725	4,792	4,468	4,254	-1.0	58	93.2	91.8	0.0	0.1	0.2	0.3
HAAKON	055	00000	764	2,196	2,012	1,888	-1.2	62	96.4	95.7	0.0	0.0	0.1	0.1
HAMLIN	057	47980	725	5,540	5,940	6,250	1.0	11	98.5	98.1	0.1	0.2	0.2	0.3
HAND	059	00000	725	3,741	3,373	3,136	-1.4	65	99.3	99.2	0.0	0.0	0.1	0.1
HANSON	061	33580	725	3,139	3,615	4,004	2.0	2	99.5	99.4	0.0	0.0	0.2	0.2
HARDING	063	00000	764	1,353	1,242	1,197	-1.2	62	97.6	97.0	0.3	0.4	0.6	0.9
HUGHES	065	38180	725	16,481	16,912	17,098	0.4	20	88.9	86.6	0.2	0.2	0.4	0.6
HUTCHINSON	067	00000	725	8,075	7,999	7,953	-0.1	42	98.8	98.7	0.1	0.1	0.1	0.1
HYDE	069	00000	725	1,671	1,686	1,700	0.1	32	91.1	90.3	0.1	0.1	0.1	0.1
JACKSON	071	00000	764	2,930	2,931	2,939	0.0	37	50.1	47.2	0.0	0.0	0.1	0.1
JERAULD	073	00000	725	2,295	2,274	2,271	-0.1	42	99.0	98.9	0.0	0.0	0.1	0.1
JONES	075	00000	764	1,193	1,103	1,039	-1.1	60	95.8	95.4	0.0	0.0	0.1	0.1
KINGSBURY	077	00000	725	5,815	5,804	5,798	0.0	37	98.5	98.5	0.1	0.1	0.3	0.3
LAKE	079	00000	725	11,276	11,260	11,290	0.0	37	97.8	97.7	0.2	0.2	0.5	0.6
LAWRENCE	081	43940	764	21,802	23,572	24,901	1.1	9	95.8	94.8	0.2	0.3	0.4	0.6
LINCOLN	083	43620	725	24,131	36,903	49,882	6.0	1	97.5	97.0	0.3	0.3	0.5	0.7
LYMAN	085	00000	725	3,895	3,891	3,881	0.0	37	64.7	62.1	0.1	0.1	0.2	0.2
MCCOOK	087	43620	725	5,832	6,226	6,525	0.9	12	98.9	98.6	0.1	0.1	0.2	0.3
MCPHERSON	089	00000	725	2,904	2,742	2,675	-0.8	53	99.3	99.2	0.0	0.0	0.1	0.3
MARSHALL	091	00000	725	4,576	4,614	4,648	0.1	32	92.6	91.9	0.1	0.1	0.1	0.1
MEADE	093	39660	764	24,253	26,303	27,600	1.1	9	92.7	91.0	1.5	1.8	0.7	1.0
MELLETTE	095	00000	725	2,083	2,101	2,117	0.1	32	44.7	42.0	0.0	0.0	0.1	0.1
MINER	097	00000	725	2,884	2,682	2,557	-1.0	58	98.8	98.5	0.5	0.7	0.1	0.1
MINNEHAHA	099	43620	725	148,281	169,362	185,798	1.9	3	93.0	91.2	1.5	1.9	1.1	1.6
MOODY	101	00000	725	6,595	6,694	6,763	0.2	28	84.9	83.7	0.3	0.3	0.6	0.6
PENNINGTON	103	39660	764	88,565	97,456	104,263	1.3	6	86.7	84.0	0.9	1.0	0.9	1.4
PERKINS	105	00000	764	3,363	3,050	2,807	-1.3	63	96.6	95.9	0.1	0.2	0.2	0.3
POTTER	107	00000	725	2,693	2,437	2,279	-1.4	65	98.1	97.7	0.0	0.0	0.2	0.3
ROBERTS	109	00000	725	10,016	10,224	10,399	0.3	24	68.3	63.5	0.1	0.1	0.2	0.3
SANBORN	111	00000	725	2,675	2,600	2,545	-0.4	47	98.9	98.8	0.0	0.0	0.4	0.4
SHANNON	113	00000	764	12,466	13,234	13,641	0.8	15	4.5	3.7	0.1	0.1	0.1	0.1
SPINK	115	00000	725	7,454	6,999	6,705	-0.9	55	97.6	96.9	0.2	0.3	0.1	0.3
STANLEY	117	38180	725	2,772	3,020	3,182	1.2	7	93.0	91.6	0.2	0.2	0.3	0.4
SULLY	119	00000	725	1,556	1,617	1,662	0.5	17	97.8	97.7	0.0	0.0	0.1	0.1
TODD	121	00000	725	9,050	9,773	10,329	1.1	9	12.6	10.4	0.1	0.1	0.1	0.2
TRIPP	123	00000	725	6,430	6,124	5,912	-0.7	52	87.5	85.0	0.0	0.1	0.1	0.1
TURNER	125	43620	725	8,849	8,975	9,060	0.2	28	98.9	98.6	0.1	0.2	0.2	0.3
UNION	127	43580	624	12,584	14,332	15,694	1.8	4	96.8	95.8	0.3	0.4	1.3	2.0
WALWORTH	129	00000	725	5,974	5,605	5,352	-0.9	55	86.6	83.9	0.0	0.1	0.2	0.3
YANKTON	135	49460	725	21,652	22,061	22,064	0.3	24	95.1	93.9	1.2	1.5	0.4	0.7
ZIEBACH	137	00000	764	2,519	2,668	2,780	0.8	15	26.4	22.4	0.0	0.0	0.1	0.1
SOUTH DAKOTA							0.9		88.7	87.2	0.6	0.8	0.6	0.9
UNITED STATES							1.2		75.1	72.7	12.3	12.6	3.8	4.5

POPULATION COMPOSITION

COUNTY	% HISPANIC ORIGIN		2007 AGE DISTRIBUTION (%)										MEDIAN AGE	% 2007 Males	% 2007 Females
	2000	2007	0-4	5-9	10-14	15-19	20-24	25-44	45-64	65-84	85+	18+	2007		
AURORA	2.1	2.1	6.6	5.6	6.8	8.2	6.3	20.0	25.3	16.9	4.3	75.1	42.4	51.8	48.2
BEADLE	0.9	1.2	6.0	5.3	5.7	6.8	6.5	23.2	28.0	14.7	3.7	78.9	42.4	49.2	50.8
BENNETT	2.0	2.0	9.4	9.0	10.2	8.8	7.2	22.9	21.1	9.6	1.7	65.6	29.2	49.8	50.2
BON HOMME	0.6	0.6	5.3	4.9	5.3	7.0	8.8	24.2	26.1	14.1	4.3	79.8	41.4	56.4	43.6
BROOKINGS	0.9	1.1	5.7	5.0	4.8	10.8	18.3	24.8	20.3	8.2	2.1	81.5	27.8	50.3	49.7
BROWN	0.7	0.9	6.5	6.1	5.7	7.0	7.7	25.7	25.9	12.6	2.9	78.1	38.4	48.4	51.6
BRULE	0.5	0.6	6.3	6.4	7.9	8.3	8.7	20.8	25.2	13.1	3.2	73.8	38.4	48.6	51.4
BUFFALO	0.9	0.9	12.6	9.2	9.5	8.9	11.0	21.7	18.5	8.2	0.5	63.2	24.5	50.0	50.0
BUTTE	2.9	3.8	6.6	5.4	6.6	8.3	7.9	22.8	27.3	13.0	2.1	75.8	40.1	49.2	50.8
CAMPBELL	0.2	0.3	6.0	5.0	6.2	6.6	7.8	19.4	27.1	18.7	3.3	77.7	44.5	51.4	48.6
CHARLES MIX	1.9	2.1	9.0	7.2	7.6	7.6	7.3	21.2	23.7	13.1	3.3	71.0	35.8	48.9	51.1
CLARK	0.5	0.6	6.2	5.4	5.7	6.6	7.2	20.3	26.9	16.1	4.4	78.4	43.3	49.7	50.3
CLAY	0.9	1.1	5.4	4.6	4.4	12.3	22.4	22.7	18.1	8.2	2.0	82.6	25.5	48.6	51.4
CODINGTON	1.1	1.4	7.5	6.5	6.3	6.1	8.3	26.3	25.3	11.1	2.6	76.1	36.4	49.7	50.3
CORSON	2.1	2.2	9.7	9.0	10.3	9.1	7.5	23.2	20.7	9.6	0.9	65.1	28.4	50.4	49.6
CUSTER	1.5	1.9	4.7	4.6	5.5	7.9	5.8	18.5	35.6	15.2	2.2	79.6	46.6	51.2	48.8
DAVISON	0.7	0.9	6.8	6.0	6.4	7.7	8.7	25.3	23.8	12.0	3.2	76.7	36.1	49.0	51.0
DAY	0.4	0.5	6.1	5.6	5.3	7.2	7.1	18.9	28.8	16.9	4.2	78.3	44.9	49.2	50.8
DEUEL	0.8	0.8	6.4	5.4	5.7	6.8	6.8	21.8	27.9	15.6	3.6	78.5	42.9	50.3	49.7
DEWEY	0.9	0.9	10.5	8.7	9.6	9.4	9.7	24.0	20.0	7.4	0.8	65.1	27.0	47.8	52.2
DOUGLAS	0.4	0.5	6.9	5.6	5.3	7.2	9.3	17.2	28.1	15.4	4.9	77.6	43.6	49.2	50.8
EDMUNDS	0.5	0.6	6.4	5.3	7.0	6.9	6.9	20.2	26.2	16.7	4.4	76.6	43.4	49.2	50.8
FALL RIVER	1.7	2.2	4.8	4.6	5.5	6.5	7.1	16.4	33.1	18.8	3.2	80.9	48.2	52.7	47.3
FAULK	0.2	0.2	6.4	5.6	5.3	7.4	7.7	20.2	25.9	18.6	2.9	78.0	43.5	50.6	49.4
GRANT	0.5	0.7	6.4	5.7	6.0	6.4	7.9	20.6	28.8	14.4	3.8	77.5	43.0	49.8	50.2
GREGORY	0.9	1.1	5.4	5.0	5.1	6.7	8.4	17.8	28.7	18.0	4.8	80.2	45.9	49.2	50.8
HAAKON	0.6	0.8	6.2	5.2	5.6	4.6	9.8	19.1	31.5	14.3	3.8	80.3	44.6	49.8	50.2
HAMLIN	0.6	0.8	7.8	6.3	6.6	6.6	7.1	22.9	25.6	13.4	3.6	74.7	40.1	50.0	50.0
HAND	0.3	0.4	5.8	5.2	5.3	6.6	7.5	18.4	28.0	19.0	4.2	79.6	45.8	49.2	50.8
HANSON	0.1	0.1	7.9	7.4	7.3	6.6	5.4	24.9	26.4	12.3	1.8	73.3	38.0	50.4	49.6
HARDING	1.6	2.2	4.2	7.3	9.4	11.7	2.8	22.1	28.6	11.8	2.2	69.2	40.2	51.3	48.7
HUGHES	1.2	1.5	6.6	6.4	7.3	7.1	8.0	22.6	28.0	11.1	2.9	75.2	39.4	48.0	52.0
HUTCHINSON	0.5	0.5	6.4	5.9	5.6	6.5	6.3	19.8	25.5	18.2	5.8	77.7	44.6	48.7	51.3
HYDE	0.5	0.5	7.9	8.2	4.7	6.4	6.2	18.8	25.7	17.7	4.4	75.2	43.2	50.7	49.3
JACKSON	0.4	0.4	9.2	7.8	7.4	9.0	10.8	20.2	23.1	10.4	1.9	69.6	31.0	50.1	49.9
JERAULD	0.3	0.3	3.8	4.0	4.0	5.3	6.4	20.8	29.6	20.3	5.8	85.0	49.6	50.6	49.4
JONES	0.3	0.4	5.7	4.9	4.8	6.3	8.1	19.9	33.2	14.9	2.2	81.0	45.1	50.1	49.9
KINGSBURY	0.7	0.7	5.8	5.0	5.3	6.8	6.8	20.1	28.1	17.2	4.8	79.4	45.1	49.2	50.8
LAKE	0.8	0.8	5.8	5.4	5.8	9.5	9.3	22.4	26.2	12.8	2.9	78.8	38.4	50.2	49.8
LAWRENCE	1.8	2.4	5.1	4.6	5.6	9.3	8.8	24.7	28.1	11.2	2.6	80.0	38.5	49.1	50.9
LINCOLN	0.7	0.9	8.0	7.5	7.2	6.9	6.5	28.1	26.2	7.8	1.7	74.3	35.2	49.8	50.2
LYMAN	0.5	0.5	9.5	8.2	7.9	6.9	6.5	22.5	25.6	11.0	1.9	69.8	35.3	51.2	48.8
MCCOOK	0.8	1.0	7.4	6.4	7.5	7.2	6.5	21.9	26.2	12.9	4.1	74.2	40.5	50.1	49.9
MCPHERSON	0.2	0.3	6.2	6.3	5.3	5.1	5.3	17.5	24.9	23.9	5.4	79.1	47.8	47.8	52.2
MARSHALL	0.8	0.8	6.5	5.2	7.2	6.7	7.7	19.1	27.9	15.4	4.4	76.7	43.3	50.6	49.4
MEADE	2.1	2.7	7.6	6.3	6.3	7.4	9.6	25.2	26.7	9.4	1.6	75.3	35.5	50.3	49.7
MELLETTE	1.7	1.7	9.5	9.4	9.6	8.0	5.6	21.8	23.1	10.9	2.1	66.3	33.0	50.2	49.8
MINER	0.6	0.8	6.0	5.2	5.6	6.7	7.7	20.4	27.7	16.2	4.5	79.1	44.0	49.5	50.5
MINNEHAHA	2.1	2.8	7.5	6.9	6.7	7.1	7.7	30.0	24.0	8.5	1.8	75.6	34.4	49.6	50.4
MOODY	0.8	0.8	6.9	6.1	6.1	7.7	9.1	22.5	27.6	11.4	2.6	76.0	38.3	50.4	49.6
PENNINGTON	2.6	3.3	7.2	6.4	6.1	7.5	8.4	26.2	26.4	10.3	1.7	76.1	35.6	49.6	50.4
PERKINS	0.7	1.0	6.3	6.0	5.6	5.7	7.1	19.0	30.0	16.1	4.1	78.8	45.1	49.0	51.0
POTTER	0.2	0.2	5.0	4.3	5.5	6.3	8.5	17.0	29.6	18.9	4.9	80.9	47.0	49.8	50.2
ROBERTS	0.6	0.7	7.5	6.0	8.0	6.8	7.8	21.5	25.8	13.6	3.0	74.4	38.9	49.4	50.6
SANBORN	1.0	1.0	6.5	6.2	5.5	5.5	7.1	21.7	29.7	15.2	2.7	78.4	43.2	52.8	47.2
SHANNON	1.4	1.3	12.2	9.8	11.8	11.8	10.1	23.9	15.5	4.6	0.3	58.4	22.2	49.1	50.9
SPINK	0.4	0.5	5.9	5.4	5.7	6.9	10.7	20.8	27.0	14.6	2.9	79.8	41.1	50.5	49.5
STANLEY	0.4	0.6	6.0	5.3	7.1	6.4	8.5	25.2	30.0	10.5	1.1	77.4	39.8	50.4	49.6
SULLY	0.8	0.7	6.7	5.6	5.6	6.1	6.6	23.1	28.8	15.3	2.3	78.6	43.0	51.9	48.1
TODD	1.5	1.4	12.8	11.0	11.6	10.0	8.2	23.0	17.6	5.4	0.3	58.1	22.8	48.8	51.2
TRIPP	0.9	1.0	7.3	5.9	6.9	6.7	7.6	21.6	26.2	14.3	3.6	75.5	41.3	49.3	50.7
TURNER	0.4	0.5	6.0	5.6	5.9	7.1	6.3	22.5	28.1	14.5	4.0	77.7	42.8	49.7	50.3
UNION	1.3	1.6	6.9	6.3	7.2	6.2	6.7	24.8	28.2	11.5	2.1	75.8	39.3	49.6	50.4
WALWORTH	0.6	0.7	6.4	6.3	5.7	5.8	6.9	19.9	27.2	18.4	3.6	78.1	44.4	48.7	51.3
YANKTON	1.8	2.4	6.5	5.9	6.7	6.7	7.3	26.1	27.0	11.1	2.7	77.0	38.5	51.2	48.8
ZIEBACH	1.0	0.9	13.3	8.7	8.2	8.6	9.6	22.9	21.1	6.8	0.7	64.7	25.9	48.3	51.7
SOUTH DAKOTA	1.4	1.8	7.1	6.4	6.5	7.5	8.5	25.1	25.4	11.1	2.4	75.9	36.4	49.7	50.3
UNITED STATES	12.5	15.0	6.9	6.5	6.8	7.1	7.0	27.6	25.4	10.7	1.9	75.6	36.7	49.2	50.8

COUNTY	HOUSEHOLDS					FAMILIES			MEDIAN HOUSEHOLD INCOME			
	2000	2007	2012	% Annual Rate 2000-2007	2007 Average HH Size	2000	2007	% Annual Rate 2000-2007	2007	2012	2007 National Rank	2007 State Rank
AURORA	1,165	1,163	1,149	0.0	2.40	817	809	-0.1	36,113	41,162	2253	36
BEADLE	7,210	6,888	6,604	-0.6	2.23	4,532	4,286	-0.8	37,746	43,665	2028	30
BENNETT	1,123	1,135	1,142	0.1	3.13	819	823	0.1	29,669	33,304	2926	56
BON HOMME	2,635	2,627	2,603	0.0	2.33	1,786	1,765	-0.2	36,452	41,379	2205	33
BROOKINGS	10,665	11,430	11,903	1.0	2.32	6,219	6,590	0.8	44,948	52,873	1115	8
BROWN	14,638	15,015	15,150	0.4	2.26	9,322	9,469	0.2	44,320	52,601	1179	12
BRULE	1,998	1,975	1,943	-0.2	2.44	1,328	1,301	-0.3	41,439	49,131	1524	18
BUFFALO	526	549	562	0.6	3.78	422	438	0.5	14,674	16,163	3140	66
BUTTE	3,516	3,788	3,968	1.0	2.52	2,467	2,637	0.9	35,445	40,670	2374	44
CAMPBELL	725	654	598	-1.4	2.37	508	455	-1.5	34,716	40,161	2463	47
CHARLES MIX	3,343	3,430	3,479	0.4	2.71	2,328	2,369	0.2	31,181	35,368	2816	54
CLARK	1,598	1,513	1,435	-0.8	2.51	1,111	1,043	-0.9	36,279	41,590	2234	35
CLAY	4,878	4,833	4,728	-0.1	2.27	2,720	2,664	-0.3	34,640	41,104	2482	48
CODINGTON	10,357	10,787	11,004	0.6	2.40	6,872	7,091	0.4	46,618	55,221	944	7
CORSON	1,271	1,315	1,339	0.5	3.28	950	976	0.4	25,261	28,847	3088	63
CUSTER	2,970	3,402	3,660	1.9	2.27	2,068	2,349	1.8	43,264	48,988	1307	15
DAVISON	7,585	7,952	8,162	0.7	2.34	4,773	4,951	0.5	44,089	53,142	1197	13
DAY	2,586	2,526	2,464	-0.3	2.29	1,688	1,633	-0.5	36,087	40,956	2259	37
DEUEL	1,843	1,902	1,928	0.4	2.34	1,259	1,289	0.3	38,338	43,686	1958	28
DEWEY	1,863	1,934	1,963	0.5	3.09	1,387	1,429	0.4	28,808	33,149	2969	57
DOUGLAS	1,321	1,306	1,284	-0.2	2.46	947	930	-0.2	33,842	38,678	2570	51
EDMUNDS	1,681	1,646	1,607	-0.3	2.49	1,211	1,177	-0.4	38,768	44,045	1883	26
FALL RIVER	3,127	3,300	3,386	0.7	2.17	1,976	2,065	0.6	35,993	41,150	2276	39
FAULK	1,014	1,018	1,017	0.1	2.53	709	706	-0.1	35,880	40,814	2299	41
GRANT	3,116	3,078	3,006	-0.2	2.37	2,156	2,112	-0.3	40,306	45,769	1687	24
GREGORY	2,022	1,944	1,871	-0.5	2.25	1,290	1,227	-0.7	27,701	31,591	3015	59
HAAKON	870	837	796	-0.5	2.35	620	591	-0.7	35,606	40,409	2350	43
HAMLIN	2,048	2,216	2,334	1.1	2.60	1,452	1,558	1.0	41,312	46,643	1552	19
HAND	1,543	1,436	1,350	-1.0	2.30	1,051	970	-1.1	39,034	43,803	1848	25
HANSON	1,115	1,294	1,434	2.1	2.79	848	978	2.0	40,784	46,529	1632	21
HARDING	525	502	490	-0.6	2.39	353	335	-0.7	30,000	34,453	2910	55
HUGHES	6,512	6,819	6,960	0.6	2.35	4,310	4,471	0.5	53,240	63,296	487	4
HUTCHINSON	3,190	3,212	3,206	0.1	2.39	2,193	2,190	0.0	35,783	40,548	2317	42
HYDE	679	695	703	0.3	2.37	456	463	0.2	37,971	43,405	2000	29
JACKSON	945	957	962	0.2	3.04	676	680	0.1	28,453	32,313	2981	58
JERAULD	987	1,014	1,027	0.4	2.20	651	663	0.3	36,057	40,811	2266	38
JONES	509	489	468	-0.6	2.26	328	312	-0.7	36,622	42,357	2179	32
KINGSBURY	2,406	2,461	2,478	0.3	2.29	1,592	1,614	0.2	37,652	42,522	2040	31
LAKE	4,372	4,497	4,543	0.4	2.36	2,830	2,882	0.3	43,009	50,429	1330	16
LAWRENCE	8,881	9,946	10,668	1.6	2.25	5,560	6,163	1.4	41,009	48,397	1596	20
LINCOLN	8,782	13,713	18,659	6.3	2.67	6,669	10,346	6.2	63,674	77,319	185	1
LYMAN	1,400	1,430	1,437	0.3	2.71	1,010	1,024	0.2	34,386	39,046	2506	49
MCCOOK	2,204	2,380	2,499	1.1	2.55	1,559	1,670	1.0	42,647	48,094	1375	17
MCPHERSON	1,227	1,181	1,158	-0.5	2.26	822	783	-0.7	27,233	31,138	3031	61
MARSHALL	1,844	1,895	1,920	0.4	2.39	1,252	1,275	0.3	36,451	41,291	2206	34
MEADE	8,805	9,964	10,625	1.7	2.55	6,700	7,532	1.6	44,439	50,837	1164	10
MELLETTE	694	718	730	0.5	2.86	499	512	0.4	27,326	31,443	3026	60
MINER	1,212	1,164	1,123	-0.6	2.26	789	750	-0.7	34,936	39,576	2438	45
MINNEHAHA	57,996	67,836	74,999	2.2	2.41	37,573	43,526	2.0	56,215	68,236	359	3
MOODY	2,526	2,626	2,673	0.5	2.52	1,762	1,817	0.4	44,702	52,194	1138	9
PENNINGTON	34,641	39,187	42,397	1.7	2.42	23,271	26,093	1.6	48,812	59,249	761	6
PERKINS	1,429	1,332	1,237	-1.0	2.24	937	866	-1.1	32,667	37,153	2690	53
POTTER	1,145	1,075	1,018	-0.9	2.20	767	714	-1.0	35,900	40,636	2296	40
ROBERTS	3,683	3,810	3,886	0.5	2.63	2,619	2,688	0.4	34,219	38,870	2525	50
SANBORN	1,043	1,038	1,024	-0.1	2.47	732	723	-0.2	40,440	45,806	1667	22
SHANNON	2,785	3,012	3,121	1.1	4.29	2,354	2,535	1.0	25,884	30,364	3074	62
SPINK	2,847	2,714	2,606	-0.7	2.40	1,933	1,827	-0.8	38,757	43,933	1887	27
STANLEY	1,111	1,253	1,337	1.7	2.40	775	867	1.6	49,876	56,207	688	5
SULLY	630	670	694	0.9	2.41	443	467	0.7	40,382	45,670	1680	23
TODD	2,462	2,720	2,896	1.4	3.55	1,917	2,105	1.3	23,707	26,968	3104	64
TRIPP	2,550	2,507	2,448	-0.2	2.40	1,720	1,676	-0.4	34,838	39,518	2451	46
TURNER	3,510	3,624	3,676	0.4	2.42	2,478	2,539	0.3	43,344	49,678	1298	14
UNION	4,927	5,740	6,332	2.1	2.48	3,520	4,070	2.0	56,377	65,918	349	2
WALWORTH	2,506	2,408	2,316	-0.5	2.25	1,643	1,565	-0.7	33,729	38,386	2580	52
YANKTON	8,187	8,394	8,449	0.3	2.38	5,407	5,494	0.2	44,412	51,824	1165	11
ZIEBACH	741	803	842	1.1	3.32	594	640	1.0	21,524	24,273	3130	65
SOUTH DAKOTA				1.2	2.45			1.1	45,336	54,010		
UNITED STATES				1.2	2.59			1.0	53,154	62,503		

COUNTY

COUNTY	2007 Per Capita Income	2007 HH Income Base	2007 HOUSEHOLD INCOME DISTRIBUTION (%)					2007 Home Value Base	2007 HOME VALUE DISTRIBUTION (%)					2007 Median Home Value
			Less than $25,000	$25,000 to $49,999	$50,000 to $99,999	$100,000 to $149,999	$150,000 or More		Less than $50,000	$50,000 to $89,999	$90,000 to $174,999	$175,000 to $399,999	$400,000 or More	
AURORA	17,530	1,163	33.0	33.5	28.5	4.4	0.5	905	45.6	27.1	22.8	3.2	1.3	57,054
BEADLE	21,922	6,888	32.4	30.1	29.1	6.0	2.4	4,776	24.0	30.6	35.4	9.0	1.0	84,525
BENNETT	11,949	1,134	41.1	33.1	20.9	4.3	0.6	686	42.9	28.0	23.3	5.1	0.7	60,345
BON HOMME	17,363	2,627	31.9	36.2	27.1	3.9	0.9	2,021	30.0	29.7	31.5	8.5	0.3	78,838
BROOKINGS	22,779	11,430	27.2	27.6	33.1	8.6	3.5	6,811	14.9	15.2	43.7	23.8	2.4	127,106
BROWN	24,269	15,015	26.4	29.0	34.4	7.0	3.2	10,180	18.6	22.1	42.2	15.5	1.6	104,943
BRULE	19,848	1,975	27.8	34.0	30.3	5.6	2.3	1,427	25.9	24.2	37.1	9.5	3.3	89,943
BUFFALO	6,280	549	63.9	24.8	10.0	0.5	0.7	242	57.0	16.5	16.9	7.0	2.5	43,200
BUTTE	17,533	3,788	34.6	33.4	25.4	5.1	1.6	2,826	32.2	25.0	28.7	11.6	2.5	75,991
CAMPBELL	17,558	654	35.0	32.9	26.5	4.9	0.8	542	53.1	28.2	12.2	5.0	1.5	46,047
CHARLES MIX	14,273	3,430	39.9	31.6	24.1	3.5	0.9	2,390	32.0	25.4	31.1	8.1	3.4	78,803
CLARK	18,002	1,513	33.1	33.4	28.0	3.9	1.6	1,225	40.8	28.0	24.1	4.5	2.6	62,463
CLAY	19,848	4,833	37.4	25.2	27.7	6.4	3.3	2,679	20.9	17.3	41.0	18.1	2.7	108,106
CODINGTON	23,479	10,787	24.6	29.1	35.1	7.1	4.1	7,695	12.5	19.1	46.1	20.2	2.2	118,817
CORSON	10,587	1,315	49.4	28.3	18.8	2.7	0.8	805	61.4	20.6	13.0	5.0	0.0	33,750
CUSTER	22,141	3,402	27.0	30.5	33.7	6.8	2.0	2,667	19.3	17.1	33.9	22.8	6.9	116,679
DAVISON	23,951	7,952	26.8	29.6	31.9	7.8	4.0	5,049	15.4	24.0	42.1	16.6	1.9	105,631
DAY	19,091	2,526	33.8	32.7	27.9	4.2	1.3	1,948	47.6	23.9	20.9	6.4	1.1	53,966
DEUEL	19,565	1,902	30.8	33.6	29.9	4.0	1.7	1,536	32.4	25.7	29.0	11.6	1.4	76,022
DEWEY	11,625	1,931	42.6	35.1	18.2	3.1	1.1	1,091	48.8	25.5	20.1	3.8	1.9	51,392
DOUGLAS	17,541	1,306	33.4	38.1	23.3	3.4	1.8	1,061	38.1	28.6	26.3	6.2	0.8	62,434
EDMUNDS	18,907	1,646	31.7	31.5	29.0	5.7	2.1	1,355	42.8	22.8	24.4	7.8	2.1	63,681
FALL RIVER	21,118	3,300	33.0	32.7	25.8	6.2	2.3	2,356	37.1	20.7	31.2	7.3	3.6	75,950
FAULK	17,744	1,018	33.7	33.6	26.2	5.0	1.5	837	50.1	23.7	20.7	3.6	2.0	49,934
GRANT	21,169	3,078	28.3	33.6	29.5	6.0	2.6	2,416	25.5	25.7	36.5	11.3	1.1	88,121
GREGORY	16,750	1,944	45.6	30.5	19.2	3.5	1.2	1,480	49.1	24.4	20.2	5.2	1.1	51,733
HAAKON	21,613	837	28.6	38.2	24.0	5.3	3.9	655	34.8	29.3	25.8	5.8	4.3	70,804
HAMLIN	19,972	2,216	26.6	34.4	31.3	4.8	2.9	1,832	26.9	31.1	32.3	8.7	1.0	78,678
HAND	23,103	1,436	32.1	32.3	26.5	5.3	3.8	1,078	36.8	30.1	25.0	6.1	1.9	69,846
HANSON	18,212	1,294	28.9	31.2	31.8	5.6	2.5	1,037	28.4	29.4	32.2	8.8	1.3	77,440
HARDING	16,589	502	42.6	31.3	20.7	3.4	2.0	378	33.3	33.6	20.1	2.9	10.1	71,579
HUGHES	27,315	6,819	19.2	26.7	39.4	9.8	4.9	4,633	13.6	14.2	46.9	24.6	0.7	131,874
HUTCHINSON	18,791	3,212	33.5	34.3	26.2	4.2	1.9	2,551	35.9	26.8	26.7	9.7	0.9	69,747
HYDE	20,606	695	31.8	31.5	26.3	8.3	2.0	508	47.2	23.6	22.8	3.5	2.8	55,600
JACKSON	12,987	957	42.5	34.6	17.9	3.2	1.8	627	53.0	21.1	16.1	4.8	5.1	45,978
JERAULD	20,274	1,014	36.9	30.9	25.9	3.9	2.4	747	34.5	32.9	29.7	2.5	0.3	68,623
JONES	19,967	489	36.6	30.9	24.7	5.7	2.0	364	45.1	24.2	22.3	7.4	1.1	56,667
KINGSBURY	20,448	2,461	31.1	32.8	29.0	5.1	2.0	1,890	35.9	26.9	26.9	8.6	1.7	69,385
LAKE	21,941	4,497	25.3	33.3	33.0	5.7	2.7	3,219	12.8	23.3	44.5	17.9	1.6	110,386
LAWRENCE	23,433	9,946	30.1	30.7	29.4	5.9	3.9	6,584	18.7	18.5	36.8	21.9	4.2	118,758
LINCOLN	29,560	13,713	12.3	23.5	43.0	13.1	8.1	11,007	5.6	10.7	43.8	32.3	7.7	152,412
LYMAN	17,700	1,430	36.4	30.6	26.3	4.4	2.4	1,016	34.4	31.3	26.0	6.8	1.6	65,500
MCCOOK	19,772	2,380	26.7	32.1	33.9	5.3	2.0	1,894	23.3	27.6	35.9	12.7	0.5	88,522
MCPHERSON	15,971	1,181	46.1	30.9	18.5	2.7	1.8	983	58.2	20.8	14.8	3.6	2.7	38,841
MARSHALL	18,711	1,895	33.2	32.7	28.4	4.4	1.2	1,490	36.6	28.9	26.7	6.4	1.3	67,876
MEADE	21,766	9,964	21.8	35.8	31.9	7.5	2.9	6,971	15.6	15.0	42.6	21.2	5.6	129,353
MELLETTE	13,089	718	45.8	27.3	20.6	5.7	0.6	476	55.9	20.8	15.8	4.8	2.7	43,000
MINER	19,061	1,164	34.8	33.9	26.0	4.0	1.3	904	52.4	22.9	17.3	6.3	1.1	47,708
MINNEHAHA	28,257	67,836	16.2	27.0	38.6	11.9	6.3	44,860	7.9	11.5	50.7	27.3	2.6	137,974
MOODY	21,491	2,626	24.0	32.4	33.7	6.9	3.0	1,942	17.7	31.3	37.8	11.6	1.6	91,544
PENNINGTON	25,414	39,187	20.8	30.2	34.8	9.3	4.9	26,464	13.5	10.8	43.1	28.1	4.5	136,095
PERKINS	19,699	1,332	37.7	32.2	23.9	3.0	3.2	1,033	48.7	25.7	12.7	6.4	6.6	51,552
POTTER	21,540	1,075	32.4	34.5	25.2	5.2	2.7	860	38.8	30.7	25.6	4.8	0.1	65,690
ROBERTS	16,494	3,810	36.6	31.9	25.0	4.8	1.7	2,700	35.1	29.0	24.2	10.0	1.7	69,037
SANBORN	21,459	1,038	31.3	33.4	26.4	5.1	3.8	819	46.0	22.8	23.8	6.6	0.7	55,159
SHANNON	8,183	3,012	48.3	27.3	19.5	4.4	0.5	1,559	63.4	14.6	16.8	3.1	2.1	35,457
SPINK	19,545	2,714	29.8	35.5	25.3	7.1	2.2	2,030	46.3	27.4	20.5	4.9	0.8	54,839
STANLEY	25,737	1,253	21.1	29.0	37.7	7.9	4.2	977	21.4	20.5	35.3	18.6	4.2	106,307
SULLY	21,251	670	25.2	38.4	28.2	5.2	3.0	518	29.2	26.1	33.8	6.0	5.0	78,205
TODD	9,622	2,720	51.9	27.3	15.4	4.3	1.1	1,289	55.2	17.5	21.4	2.4	3.5	40,217
TRIPP	18,197	2,507	38.1	30.4	25.7	3.1	2.7	1,905	37.5	27.4	24.6	8.5	2.0	66,890
TURNER	21,680	3,624	25.7	33.1	32.6	5.8	2.8	2,841	22.4	31.6	34.6	10.5	0.8	85,402
UNION	30,264	5,740	17.2	26.1	37.5	11.7	7.5	4,329	17.6	19.0	36.5	20.0	6.8	110,070
WALWORTH	19,056	2,408	37.1	31.5	24.8	5.5	1.0	1,744	39.7	29.5	23.1	6.4	1.3	60,859
YANKTON	22,204	8,394	25.1	31.5	33.5	6.2	3.6	5,932	15.3	20.7	45.1	16.3	2.7	110,537
ZIEBACH	9,362	803	55.0	29.5	12.2	2.1	1.1	490	36.5	30.6	22.2	6.1	4.5	64,898
SOUTH DAKOTA	23,161		25.2	29.7	32.9	8.1	4.1		20.2	18.5	39.3	19.0	3.0	111,328
UNITED STATES	27,916		21.9	25.0	32.3	12.3	8.4		7.9	10.5	27.1	35.6	19.0	192,285

COUNTY	FINANCIAL SERVICES				THE HOME						ENTERTAINMENT						PERSONAL			
					Home Improvements		Furnishings													
	Auto Loan	Home Loan	Invest-ments	Retire-ment Plans	Home Repair	Lawn & Garden	Comput-ers & Hard-ware	Major Appli-ances	TV, Radio, Sound Equip-ment	Furni-ture	Dine out/ Carry out	Sports Equip-ment	Fees & Tickets	Toys & Games	Travel	Cable TV	Apparel & Services	Auto Repairs	Health Insur-ance	Pets & Supplies
AURORA	75	50	28	48	59	83	54	71	60	50	59	63	43	64	53	64	50	64	77	77
BEADLE	75	60	58	59	66	80	65	73	71	61	69	64	59	71	65	75	59	70	83	76
BENNETT	61	43	32	42	48	64	48	57	54	44	53	50	40	55	47	58	45	54	64	60
BON HOMME	73	50	33	48	58	80	54	69	61	50	60	61	45	64	54	66	50	63	77	74
BROOKINGS	84	65	62	68	66	76	85	77	81	73	81	72	73	80	75	80	72	80	78	80
BROWN	81	71	75	73	73	82	76	79	79	73	77	70	72	80	75	80	68	77	84	81
BRULE	79	59	53	59	66	83	67	76	70	61	69	68	57	72	65	74	59	72	83	80
BUFFALO	34	24	24	26	24	30	31	30	36	30	35	25	28	34	28	38	31	33	35	32
BUTTE	72	55	41	53	59	74	57	67	62	55	61	60	50	64	56	65	53	63	73	71
CAMPBELL	76	48	21	46	59	85	51	71	56	48	57	63	39	62	50	61	48	63	75	79
CHARLES MIX	62	45	39	44	50	64	51	58	56	46	54	51	43	57	49	59	46	55	66	61
CLARK	80	52	28	50	63	89	56	75	62	53	62	67	45	68	55	67	52	67	81	82
CLAY	72	52	52	55	53	63	78	65	73	63	73	63	63	71	65	71	64	71	68	68
CODINGTON	82	74	79	75	76	83	77	80	80	75	78	71	74	81	77	81	69	79	85	82
CORSON	54	42	36	43	43	54	45	49	49	45	49	43	41	51	43	51	43	49	53	53
CUSTER	83	64	44	63	74	96	66	84	70	62	69	73	57	71	68	74	59	76	87	88
DAVISON	81	71	80	73	73	80	79	78	82	75	80	69	75	82	77	83	70	79	85	79
DAY	75	51	32	49	60	82	56	71	62	51	61	63	45	66	55	67	51	65	79	77
DEUEL	79	53	32	51	63	87	57	75	64	53	63	66	46	68	56	69	53	68	82	81
DEWEY	58	44	35	44	46	57	46	52	51	46	50	46	41	52	45	53	44	51	56	56
DOUGLAS	74	50	33	49	59	80	55	69	62	51	60	61	45	65	54	66	51	63	78	75
EDMUNDS	83	55	30	53	66	92	59	78	66	55	66	69	47	71	58	71	55	70	85	85
FALL RIVER	75	56	47	55	63	82	61	73	67	56	65	63	53	67	62	72	55	68	82	76
FAULK	77	52	33	50	61	84	57	73	63	52	62	64	46	67	56	68	52	66	81	78
GRANT	81	62	50	60	69	89	65	79	71	61	70	68	57	74	65	76	60	73	87	83
GREGORY	63	44	31	42	51	68	48	60	54	44	53	53	40	56	47	58	44	55	68	64
HAAKON	91	61	30	58	72	102	63	86	69	60	70	75	50	75	62	75	59	76	90	94
HAMLIN	94	62	30	59	74	105	64	88	71	61	72	78	51	77	63	77	60	78	93	97
HAND	89	62	44	60	71	96	68	84	77	62	75	74	57	79	67	82	63	77	96	89
HANSON	92	59	25	56	72	103	62	86	68	59	69	77	48	76	61	74	58	76	91	96
HARDING	73	46	20	44	57	82	49	68	54	46	55	61	38	60	48	58	46	60	71	76
HUGHES	95	91	91	92	90	95	90	92	91	90	91	83	89	92	90	93	81	91	95	94
HUTCHINSON	76	53	37	51	61	82	58	72	65	53	63	63	48	68	57	70	53	66	82	77
HYDE	80	58	45	56	65	85	63	76	71	58	69	67	54	73	63	76	58	71	86	80
JACKSON	64	47	36	47	51	66	51	59	56	48	55	52	44	58	49	59	47	56	66	63
JERAULD	75	52	36	50	60	82	57	71	64	52	62	63	47	67	56	69	53	65	80	76
JONES	81	52	22	49	64	92	55	76	60	52	61	68	42	67	54	65	51	68	80	85
KINGSBURY	80	55	37	53	64	86	60	75	67	55	66	66	49	70	59	72	55	69	84	82
LAKE	82	64	60	64	70	86	72	80	75	66	74	70	63	76	70	79	64	76	87	82
LAWRENCE	80	67	64	68	70	81	74	78	76	70	75	69	68	76	72	78	66	77	82	80
LINCOLN	113	115	110	115	113	113	108	111	107	111	107	102	110	111	109	107	97	109	109	113
LYMAN	82	57	35	56	65	88	60	76	66	58	66	67	50	70	59	70	57	70	81	83
MCCOOK	85	59	41	57	68	92	65	80	73	59	71	71	53	75	64	78	60	74	91	85
MCPHERSON	62	42	27	41	49	67	46	58	51	42	50	51	38	54	45	55	42	53	65	62
MARSHALL	76	52	34	50	61	83	57	72	63	52	62	63	46	67	56	68	52	65	80	77
MEADE	90	73	59	72	74	88	75	83	79	72	78	75	68	81	73	81	68	80	87	87
MELLETTE	62	45	33	45	49	63	48	56	52	47	52	49	42	55	46	55	45	54	60	61
MINER	74	50	32	48	59	80	54	69	61	50	60	61	44	64	54	66	50	63	77	75
MINNEHAHA	98	95	99	98	90	90	98	93	97	97	96	86	97	98	95	95	87	96	93	94
MOODY	89	64	50	64	73	95	71	85	76	65	75	75	60	79	70	80	64	79	93	90
PENNINGTON	88	83	87	85	81	84	88	85	87	85	87	78	85	88	85	87	77	87	87	86
PERKINS	75	51	34	50	60	82	56	71	63	52	62	62	46	66	55	68	52	65	79	76
POTTER	80	55	38	54	64	87	61	76	68	56	67	67	50	71	60	73	56	70	86	81
ROBERTS	74	50	33	48	59	80	55	70	61	51	60	62	45	64	54	66	51	64	77	75
SANBORN	92	61	36	59	73	101	66	87	74	62	73	77	54	79	65	80	62	78	95	94
SHANNON	50	44	46	47	41	44	46	44	50	48	50	38	45	51	45	51	45	48	48	47
SPINK	80	55	41	54	64	87	62	76	68	57	67	67	51	71	60	73	57	70	85	82
STANLEY	102	85	61	82	85	101	80	93	84	81	85	83	74	88	79	88	74	88	95	98
SULLY	93	59	25	56	73	104	62	87	69	59	70	78	48	76	61	74	58	77	91	97
TODD	50	40	41	44	39	45	45	44	49	46	49	38	43	50	43	51	44	47	48	47
TRIPP	75	51	31	49	60	83	55	71	61	51	61	63	45	65	54	66	51	64	78	77
TURNER	90	61	39	59	72	99	67	85	74	62	73	75	54	79	66	80	62	77	95	92
UNION	111	101	94	101	105	115	101	109	104	99	103	98	97	106	102	106	91	105	113	112
WALWORTH	70	50	41	49	57	75	56	67	62	51	61	59	47	63	55	66	51	63	75	71
YANKTON	84	72	69	73	74	84	75	80	78	73	77	71	70	79	74	80	67	78	84	83
ZIEBACH	51	34	23	35	38	51	40	46	44	38	44	41	33	46	37	46	38	45	49	50
SOUTH DAKOTA	87	74	68	74	76	87	79	83	81	75	80	75	72	83	76	83	70	81	87	86
UNITED STATES	100	100	100	100	100	100	100	100	100	100	100	100	100	100	100	100	100	100	100	100

COUNTY	FIPS Code	CBSA Code	DMA Code	POPULATION			2000-2007 ANNUAL RATE		RACE (%)					
									White		Black		Asian/Pacific	
				2000	2007	2012	% Rate	State Rank	2000	2007	2000	2007	2000	2007
ANDERSON	001	28940	557	71,330	73,776	75,593	0.5	65	93.4	92.3	3.9	4.2	0.8	1.2
BEDFORD	003	43180	659	37,586	44,354	49,972	2.3	9	86.8	84.9	8.5	9.0	0.5	0.7
BENTON	005	00000	659	16,537	16,973	17,215	0.4	72	96.4	95.9	2.1	2.3	0.2	0.3
BLEDSOE	007	00000	575	12,367	12,921	13,174	0.6	59	94.4	93.7	3.7	4.0	0.1	0.2
BLOUNT	009	28940	557	105,823	118,621	128,494	1.6	18	94.7	93.8	2.9	3.2	0.7	1.0
BRADLEY	011	17420	575	87,965	95,360	101,067	1.1	34	93.0	91.8	4.0	4.3	0.6	0.8
CAMPBELL	013	29220	557	39,854	41,284	42,067	0.5	65	98.1	97.8	0.3	0.3	0.2	0.3
CANNON	015	34980	659	12,826	13,602	14,088	0.8	47	96.9	96.3	1.5	1.6	0.1	0.2
CARROLL	017	00000	639	29,475	29,704	29,554	0.1	89	87.7	86.3	10.3	11.2	0.2	0.2
CARTER	019	27740	531	56,742	59,560	60,287	0.7	54	97.5	97.0	1.0	1.1	0.3	0.4
CHEATHAM	021	34980	659	35,912	40,700	44,434	1.7	16	96.9	96.3	1.5	1.6	0.2	0.3
CHESTER	023	27180	639	15,540	16,479	17,217	0.8	47	88.1	86.9	10.0	10.9	0.2	0.3
CLAIBORNE	025	00000	557	29,862	32,860	34,923	1.3	25	97.8	97.4	0.8	0.8	0.3	0.4
CLAY	027	00000	659	7,976	8,259	8,466	0.5	65	96.8	96.2	1.4	1.6	0.3	0.4
COCKE	029	35460	557	33,565	35,508	36,920	0.8	47	96.2	95.6	2.0	2.2	0.2	0.2
COFFEE	031	46100	659	48,014	52,028	54,954	1.1	34	93.4	92.2	3.6	3.9	0.8	1.1
CROCKETT	033	00000	640	14,532	14,869	15,099	0.3	80	82.0	79.8	14.4	15.2	0.1	0.1
CUMBERLAND	035	18900	557	46,802	52,915	57,709	1.7	16	98.1	97.6	0.1	0.1	0.3	0.4
DAVIDSON	037	34980	659	569,891	599,512	620,455	0.7	54	67.0	64.0	25.9	27.0	2.4	3.2
DECATUR	039	00000	659	11,731	12,061	12,257	0.4	72	94.1	93.1	3.5	3.8	0.2	0.3
DEKALB	041	00000	659	17,423	18,436	19,186	0.8	47	95.6	94.5	1.4	1.6	0.2	0.2
DICKSON	043	34980	659	43,156	48,306	51,577	1.6	18	93.3	92.3	4.6	5.0	0.3	0.4
DYER	045	20540	640	37,279	38,315	38,807	0.4	72	85.4	83.9	12.9	13.9	0.4	0.5
FAYETTE	047	32820	640	28,806	35,782	41,894	3.0	3	62.5	60.1	35.9	38.0	0.2	0.3
FENTRESS	049	00000	557	16,625	17,687	18,454	0.9	43	99.2	99.1	0.1	0.1	0.1	0.1
FRANKLIN	051	46100	659	39,270	42,561	44,522	1.1	34	92.2	91.1	5.5	6.0	0.4	0.6
GIBSON	053	26480	639	48,152	48,759	49,145	0.2	86	78.7	76.8	19.7	21.2	0.2	0.2
GILES	055	00000	659	29,447	29,932	30,138	0.2	86	86.4	85.1	11.8	12.8	0.4	0.5
GRAINGER	057	34100	557	20,659	22,374	23,670	1.1	34	98.4	98.0	0.3	0.4	0.1	0.2
GREENE	059	24620	531	62,909	67,385	70,602	1.0	39	96.4	95.8	2.1	2.3	0.3	0.4
GRUNDY	061	00000	575	14,332	14,368	14,381	0.0	92	98.3	98.3	0.1	0.1	0.2	0.2
HAMBLEN	063	34100	557	58,128	61,091	63,179	0.7	54	90.7	88.7	4.1	4.4	0.6	0.9
HAMILTON	065	16860	575	307,896	320,956	329,764	0.6	59	76.3	74.0	20.1	21.5	1.3	1.8
HANCOCK	067	00000	557	6,786	6,781	6,779	0.0	92	97.9	97.9	0.5	0.5	0.1	0.1
HARDEMAN	069	00000	640	28,105	28,683	29,001	0.3	80	57.3	54.9	41.0	43.1	0.3	0.4
HARDIN	071	00000	639	25,578	26,202	26,609	0.3	80	94.9	94.2	3.7	4.0	0.2	0.3
HAWKINS	073	28700	531	53,563	57,765	60,858	1.0	39	97.2	96.8	1.5	1.7	0.2	0.3
HAYWOOD	075	15140	640	19,797	19,881	19,924	0.1	89	46.7	45.6	51.0	52.2	0.1	0.1
HENDERSON	077	00000	639	25,522	26,874	27,849	0.7	54	90.5	89.4	8.0	8.7	0.1	0.2
HENRY	079	37540	659	31,115	32,134	32,685	0.4	72	89.2	88.0	9.0	9.7	0.3	0.4
HICKMAN	081	34980	659	22,295	24,309	25,710	1.2	29	93.7	92.9	4.5	4.9	0.1	0.1
HOUSTON	083	00000	659	8,088	8,313	8,480	0.4	72	94.6	93.7	3.3	3.6	0.2	0.3
HUMPHREYS	085	00000	659	17,929	18,776	19,385	0.6	59	95.5	94.9	2.9	3.2	0.3	0.4
JACKSON	087	18260	659	10,984	11,346	11,582	0.4	72	98.6	98.4	0.1	0.2	0.1	0.1
JEFFERSON	089	34100	557	44,294	50,709	55,495	1.9	14	95.7	94.9	2.3	2.5	0.3	0.4
JOHNSON	091	00000	531	17,499	18,767	19,349	1.0	39	96.4	95.9	2.4	2.6	0.1	0.2
KNOX	093	28940	557	382,032	418,446	446,529	1.3	25	88.1	86.5	8.6	9.3	1.3	1.8
LAKE	095	00000	632	7,954	7,551	7,175	-0.7	95	66.6	64.2	31.2	33.1	0.1	0.2
LAUDERDALE	097	00000	640	27,101	27,743	28,160	0.3	80	63.8	61.4	34.1	36.1	0.2	0.2
LAWRENCE	099	29980	659	39,926	41,688	43,026	0.6	59	96.8	96.2	1.5	1.6	0.3	0.4
LEWIS	101	00000	659	11,367	11,698	11,848	0.4	72	97.1	96.6	1.5	1.6	0.2	0.3
LINCOLN	103	00000	691	31,340	32,597	33,367	0.5	65	90.3	89.1	7.4	8.0	0.4	0.5
LOUDON	105	28940	557	39,086	45,288	50,228	2.1	13	95.9	94.9	1.1	1.2	0.2	0.3
MCMINN	107	11940	575	49,015	51,868	53,642	0.8	47	92.7	91.5	4.5	4.9	0.7	1.0
MCNAIRY	109	00000	640	24,653	25,844	26,731	0.7	54	92.2	91.3	6.2	6.8	0.1	0.2
MACON	111	34980	659	20,386	22,124	23,244	1.1	34	97.9	97.3	0.2	0.2	0.3	0.4
MADISON	113	27180	639	91,837	98,674	102,887	1.0	39	65.2	62.8	32.5	34.3	0.6	0.9
MARION	115	16860	575	27,776	29,622	30,658	0.9	43	94.3	93.6	4.1	4.5	0.2	0.3
MARSHALL	117	30280	659	26,767	29,683	31,595	1.4	22	89.4	87.9	7.8	8.4	0.3	0.4
MAURY	119	17940	659	69,498	81,118	90,584	2.2	11	82.4	80.4	14.3	15.2	0.4	0.5
MEIGS	121	00000	575	11,086	12,145	12,947	1.3	25	97.7	97.3	1.2	1.4	0.2	0.3
MONROE	123	00000	557	38,961	43,561	47,248	1.6	18	94.9	93.9	2.3	2.5	0.4	0.5
MONTGOMERY	125	17300	659	134,768	159,529	180,047	2.4	6	73.2	70.4	19.2	20.1	2.0	2.7
MOORE	127	46100	659	5,740	6,287	6,684	1.3	25	95.8	95.2	2.7	3.0	0.1	0.2
MORGAN	129	00000	557	19,757	20,237	20,564	0.3	80	96.7	96.3	2.2	2.4	0.1	0.2
OBION	131	46460	632	32,450	32,316	32,051	-0.1	94	88.2	86.8	9.8	10.7	0.2	0.3
OVERTON	133	18260	659	20,118	20,859	21,382	0.5	65	98.6	98.3	0.3	0.3	0.1	0.2
PERRY	135	00000	659	7,631	7,807	7,941	0.3	80	96.6	96.0	1.7	1.9	0.2	0.3
PICKETT	137	00000	659	4,945	4,979	4,929	0.1	89	99.2	99.2	0.1	0.1	0.0	0.0
POLK	139	17420	575	16,050	16,286	16,411	0.2	86	98.3	98.0	0.1	0.2	0.1	0.2
PUTNAM	141	18260	659	62,315	69,504	74,922	1.5	20	94.5	93.1	1.7	1.8	1.0	1.4
RHEA	143	00000	575	28,400	30,823	32,577	1.1	34	95.4	94.5	2.0	2.2	0.3	0.5
ROANE	145	25340	557	51,910	53,976	55,538	0.5	65	95.2	94.5	2.7	3.0	0.4	0.6
ROBERTSON	147	34980	659	54,433	64,363	71,896	2.3	9	89.1	87.8	8.6	9.3	0.3	0.5
RUTHERFORD	149	34980	659	182,023	244,295	299,111	4.1	1	85.7	83.6	9.5	10.2	1.9	2.7
SCOTT	151	00000	557	21,127	22,425	23,357	0.8	47	98.5	98.2	0.1	0.1	0.1	0.2
SEQUATCHIE	153	16860	575	11,370	13,203	14,682	2.1	13	98.7	98.4	0.2	0.2	0.2	0.2
TENNESSEE							1.2		80.2	78.9	16.4	16.8	1.0	1.4
UNITED STATES							1.2		75.1	72.7	12.3	12.6	3.8	4.5

COUNTY	% HISPANIC ORIGIN		2007 AGE DISTRIBUTION (%)										MEDIAN AGE	% 2007 Males	% 2007 Females
	2000	2007	0-4	5-9	10-14	15-19	20-24	25-44	45-64	65-84	85+	18+	2007		
ANDERSON	1.1	1.6	5.5	5.4	6.1	6.0	5.8	24.9	29.2	14.5	2.6	79.2	42.4	47.9	52.1
BEDFORD	7.5	10.3	7.7	7.2	6.5	5.7	5.5	30.2	24.8	10.8	1.6	75.0	36.2	49.9	50.1
BENTON	0.9	1.4	5.3	5.0	6.2	5.4	5.1	24.5	29.7	16.5	2.4	80.3	44.0	48.8	51.2
BLEDSOE	1.1	1.6	5.9	6.0	5.9	6.7	5.0	30.1	27.7	11.7	1.1	78.0	39.0	54.8	45.2
BLOUNT	1.1	1.5	5.7	5.7	6.0	6.1	5.5	27.2	28.8	12.9	2.0	78.9	41.0	48.6	51.4
BRADLEY	2.1	2.9	6.6	6.3	6.1	6.2	6.0	29.8	26.1	11.4	1.4	77.5	37.7	49.1	50.9
CAMPBELL	0.7	1.0	6.0	5.8	5.9	5.7	5.2	28.1	27.2	14.3	1.9	78.8	40.5	48.6	51.4
CANNON	1.2	1.7	6.9	6.6	6.7	6.0	6.0	27.6	26.1	12.3	1.9	76.1	38.7	49.2	50.8
CARROLL	1.3	1.8	6.1	5.7	6.0	6.2	6.2	26.3	26.0	14.6	3.0	78.5	40.6	48.3	51.7
CARTER	0.9	1.3	5.5	5.4	5.1	6.0	5.9	28.5	27.5	13.7	2.3	80.7	40.6	49.0	51.0
CHEATHAM	1.2	1.7	7.2	7.0	6.9	6.7	6.0	29.9	26.9	8.3	1.0	74.6	37.4	50.3	49.7
CHESTER	1.0	1.3	6.9	6.7	6.1	8.1	8.2	26.3	24.0	11.7	2.0	76.6	35.4	49.0	51.0
CLAIBORNE	0.6	0.9	5.7	5.6	6.3	6.4	5.5	28.2	27.8	12.9	1.6	78.5	39.8	48.4	51.6
CLAY	1.4	1.9	5.3	5.0	5.7	5.5	5.3	28.0	27.9	15.3	2.1	80.8	42.4	48.9	51.1
COCKE	1.1	1.5	6.0	5.9	5.8	5.4	5.2	27.9	29.1	13.2	1.5	79.1	40.8	48.8	51.2
COFFEE	2.2	3.1	6.8	6.4	6.6	6.2	6.2	26.6	25.9	13.4	1.9	76.5	39.2	49.0	51.0
CROCKETT	5.5	7.6	6.9	6.3	6.6	5.8	6.0	27.5	25.5	12.5	2.7	76.7	39.3	48.7	51.3
CUMBERLAND	1.2	1.8	5.5	5.2	5.4	5.3	4.9	23.2	27.2	21.2	2.1	80.6	45.4	48.4	51.6
DAVIDSON	4.6	6.2	6.4	6.1	5.8	6.8	7.7	31.3	24.4	9.8	1.7	78.3	35.6	48.7	51.3
DECATUR	2.0	2.8	5.9	5.8	5.8	5.0	4.8	26.3	27.4	16.4	2.7	79.6	42.5	48.9	51.1
DEKALB	3.6	5.2	6.2	6.4	5.6	5.5	5.2	29.8	26.9	12.5	1.8	78.5	40.0	49.8	50.2
DICKSON	1.1	1.6	7.1	6.6	6.9	6.6	6.0	28.2	26.5	10.6	1.5	75.3	37.6	49.5	50.5
DYER	1.2	1.6	6.8	6.3	7.1	6.0	6.0	27.9	26.5	11.4	2.0	76.1	38.2	48.3	51.7
FAYETTE	1.0	1.4	6.6	7.0	6.0	6.5	5.1	25.5	29.3	12.3	1.5	76.2	40.3	49.5	50.5
FENTRESS	0.5	0.8	6.3	6.2	6.1	5.6	5.7	26.7	28.5	13.0	1.8	78.0	40.4	49.6	50.4
FRANKLIN	1.6	2.2	6.0	6.1	5.6	6.8	7.3	25.3	27.5	13.4	1.9	78.8	40.1	48.9	51.1
GIBSON	1.1	1.5	6.5	6.1	6.4	5.9	5.6	26.6	26.1	14.0	2.8	77.4	40.4	47.8	52.2
GILES	0.9	1.2	6.4	6.2	6.1	6.1	6.1	26.5	27.7	12.8	2.1	77.7	40.2	49.3	50.7
GRAINGER	1.1	1.6	6.1	6.3	6.2	5.1	5.1	29.3	28.0	12.5	1.3	78.2	39.7	50.3	49.7
GREENE	1.0	1.5	5.7	5.7	5.9	5.8	5.0	27.9	27.8	14.2	1.9	79.1	41.0	49.1	50.9
GRUNDY	1.0	1.0	7.1	6.9	6.5	5.6	5.2	28.3	26.0	12.5	2.0	76.0	38.3	49.4	50.6
HAMBLEN	5.7	7.9	6.6	6.5	6.1	5.2	5.4	29.1	26.6	12.9	1.6	77.7	38.9	49.7	50.3
HAMILTON	1.8	2.4	5.9	5.9	6.0	6.5	6.1	27.3	27.8	12.4	2.1	78.5	39.6	48.1	51.9
HANCOCK	0.4	0.4	5.6	5.3	5.4	5.7	5.8	26.1	29.8	14.3	2.0	80.3	42.0	49.1	50.9
HARDEMAN	1.0	1.3	6.1	5.9	6.0	6.1	7.1	30.7	25.6	10.7	1.8	78.2	37.3	53.8	46.2
HARDIN	1.0	1.5	5.9	5.7	6.2	5.4	5.1	26.3	28.5	14.8	2.1	78.8	41.6	49.6	50.4
HAWKINS	0.8	1.1	6.2	6.3	6.0	5.5	5.1	28.7	27.8	12.6	1.7	78.0	39.9	48.9	51.1
HAYWOOD	2.6	2.6	7.2	6.9	7.9	6.0	5.8	27.1	26.1	10.8	2.1	74.3	36.7	47.2	52.8
HENDERSON	1.0	1.4	6.6	6.7	6.4	5.7	5.4	28.7	26.8	12.0	1.8	76.7	38.9	48.6	51.4
HENRY	1.0	1.4	5.7	5.6	5.4	5.5	5.1	24.8	29.1	16.1	2.6	79.9	43.4	49.1	50.9
HICKMAN	1.0	1.4	6.5	6.7	6.2	6.4	5.8	29.3	26.3	11.3	1.6	76.7	38.1	53.2	46.8
HOUSTON	1.2	1.8	6.5	6.8	6.2	6.0	4.5	25.0	27.3	15.2	2.5	76.6	41.0	49.5	50.5
HUMPHREYS	0.8	1.2	6.0	6.0	6.3	6.0	5.3	26.3	28.4	14.0	1.8	77.9	40.8	49.7	50.3
JACKSON	0.8	1.2	5.9	5.8	5.9	5.1	5.1	26.6	29.4	14.3	1.9	79.4	41.9	49.7	50.3
JEFFERSON	1.3	1.9	6.2	6.1	6.1	6.6	6.2	27.9	26.5	12.8	1.6	78.0	39.1	49.7	50.3
JOHNSON	0.9	1.2	5.0	4.9	4.7	5.0	4.8	30.2	29.3	14.1	2.0	82.3	42.1	54.1	45.9
KNOX	1.3	1.7	6.0	6.0	5.9	6.9	7.5	28.0	26.7	11.4	1.8	78.7	38.2	48.6	51.4
LAKE	1.4	1.8	4.7	4.9	4.2	5.6	10.3	33.9	22.6	11.8	1.9	83.3	36.3	62.6	37.4
LAUDERDALE	1.2	1.5	6.9	6.5	6.5	5.7	7.3	30.8	24.7	9.9	1.8	76.8	36.1	52.6	47.4
LAWRENCE	1.0	1.4	7.0	6.6	6.9	6.4	5.7	28.1	24.9	12.5	1.9	75.7	38.0	49.1	50.9
LEWIS	1.2	1.7	6.7	6.5	6.8	6.3	6.4	26.6	26.9	12.2	1.6	75.9	38.8	49.8	50.2
LINCOLN	1.0	1.4	6.2	6.2	5.7	6.0	5.5	26.6	27.6	14.0	2.2	78.2	41.1	49.0	51.0
LOUDON	2.3	3.3	5.6	5.6	5.5	5.4	4.4	24.0	29.7	18.0	1.9	80.1	44.7	49.1	50.9
MCMINN	1.8	2.5	6.4	6.2	6.5	5.8	5.5	27.1	27.6	13.1	1.9	77.5	39.9	48.7	51.3
MCNAIRY	0.9	1.3	6.3	6.3	6.6	5.4	5.0	26.8	27.2	14.2	2.2	77.4	40.6	48.7	51.3
MACON	1.7	2.4	7.2	7.2	6.5	5.9	5.5	29.3	25.6	11.0	1.8	75.4	37.5	49.6	50.4
MADISON	1.7	2.3	6.9	6.6	6.8	7.3	7.0	28.0	25.6	10.0	1.8	75.7	36.0	48.6	51.4
MARION	0.7	1.0	6.0	6.1	5.8	6.0	5.1	27.9	29.5	12.3	1.4	78.5	40.5	49.5	50.5
MARSHALL	2.9	4.0	6.7	6.2	6.7	5.9	6.2	28.2	28.0	10.5	1.7	76.8	38.4	49.1	50.9
MAURY	3.3	4.5	6.9	6.7	6.2	7.0	6.0	26.7	28.7	10.3	1.6	75.8	38.3	49.0	51.0
MEIGS	0.6	0.8	6.9	7.3	6.3	5.6	5.2	29.3	26.9	11.3	1.2	75.9	38.2	50.6	49.4
MONROE	1.8	2.5	6.5	6.3	6.7	6.4	5.2	28.3	26.7	12.1	1.7	76.6	38.5	49.6	50.4
MONTGOMERY	5.2	6.9	8.8	7.8	7.1	7.1	7.4	33.9	20.1	6.9	0.8	72.1	31.3	50.4	49.6
MOORE	0.8	1.1	6.0	5.8	5.7	6.0	4.8	25.6	29.9	14.1	2.0	78.8	41.9	50.1	49.9
MORGAN	0.6	0.9	5.9	6.0	6.2	5.6	5.9	31.4	27.0	10.7	1.4	78.4	38.4	53.3	46.7
OBION	1.9	2.7	6.5	6.5	6.2	5.2	5.4	26.9	27.9	13.2	2.4	77.6	40.0	48.8	51.2
OVERTON	0.7	1.0	6.3	6.4	5.8	5.3	5.3	27.4	27.3	14.2	1.9	78.2	40.2	49.1	50.9
PERRY	0.8	1.1	6.0	6.0	6.1	6.2	5.1	24.9	27.8	15.7	2.2	77.9	41.7	49.6	50.4
PICKETT	0.8	0.8	6.1	6.3	4.1	5.3	5.0	24.8	28.5	17.7	2.2	80.4	43.7	49.5	50.5
POLK	0.7	1.0	6.5	6.8	5.6	5.4	4.2	28.7	27.7	13.4	1.7	77.7	40.2	49.9	50.1
PUTNAM	3.0	4.3	6.1	5.7	5.7	7.4	9.4	27.4	24.7	11.9	1.8	79.2	36.4	49.9	50.1
RHEA	1.7	2.4	6.3	6.3	6.0	6.4	6.0	27.1	27.5	12.5	1.9	77.7	39.1	48.8	51.2
ROANE	0.7	1.0	5.8	6.0	5.5	5.5	5.2	25.3	29.6	15.0	2.0	79.3	42.6	48.9	51.1
ROBERTSON	2.7	3.7	6.9	6.6	6.8	6.7	5.8	29.5	26.3	10.1	1.3	75.6	37.6	49.8	50.2
RUTHERFORD	2.8	3.9	7.8	7.1	6.8	7.1	8.3	32.9	22.5	6.7	0.8	74.6	32.5	49.0	50.2
SCOTT	0.6	0.8	7.1	7.3	6.6	5.7	5.6	30.2	25.8	10.4	1.3	75.6	36.7	50.4	50.4
SEQUATCHIE	0.8	1.2	7.0	7.1	6.7	5.6	4.7	29.5	26.4	11.6	1.4	75.8	37.9	49.8	50.2
TENNESSEE	2.2	3.0	6.6	6.4	6.4	6.5	6.4	28.4	26.4	11.2	1.7	76.8	37.8	49.0	51.0
UNITED STATES	12.5	15.0	6.9	6.5	6.8	7.1	7.0	27.6	25.4	10.7	1.9	75.6	36.7	49.2	50.8

COUNTY	HOUSEHOLDS					FAMILIES			MEDIAN HOUSEHOLD INCOME			
	2000	2007	2012	% Annual Rate 2000-2007	2007 Average HH Size	2000	2007	% Annual Rate 2000-2007	2007	2012	2007 National Rank	2007 State Rank
ANDERSON	29,780	31,303	32,306	0.7	2.33	20,513	20,975	0.3	44,613	51,953	1144	21
BEDFORD	13,905	16,345	18,373	2.3	2.68	10,350	11,893	1.9	45,622	52,737	1039	20
BENTON	6,863	7,177	7,334	0.6	2.33	4,888	4,984	0.3	33,947	38,784	2555	72
BLEDSOE	4,430	4,746	4,887	1.0	2.48	3,312	3,471	0.6	34,931	39,867	2440	70
BLOUNT	42,667	48,087	52,333	1.7	2.42	30,642	33,684	1.3	47,006	54,717	908	18
BRADLEY	34,281	37,989	40,617	1.4	2.46	24,660	26,655	1.1	43,703	50,942	1251	26
CAMPBELL	16,125	17,248	17,820	0.9	2.36	11,575	12,075	0.6	30,346	34,785	2894	87
CANNON	4,998	5,380	5,603	1.0	2.50	3,644	3,827	0.7	40,426	46,567	1668	39
CARROLL	11,779	11,971	11,981	0.2	2.39	8,394	8,316	-0.1	36,660	41,977	2174	56
CARTER	23,486	24,593	25,153	0.6	2.30	16,351	16,669	0.3	32,963	37,721	2656	81
CHEATHAM	12,878	14,801	16,245	1.9	2.72	10,162	11,462	1.7	56,584	65,999	341	5
CHESTER	5,660	6,159	6,472	1.2	2.52	4,198	4,465	0.9	42,602	49,152	1383	30
CLAIBORNE	11,799	13,377	14,403	1.7	2.41	8,680	9,613	1.4	30,950	35,515	2837	85
CLAY	3,379	3,603	3,739	0.9	2.27	2,333	2,421	0.5	28,065	32,095	3000	90
COCKE	13,762	14,967	15,746	1.2	2.35	9,720	10,300	0.8	30,630	35,191	2872	86
COFFEE	18,885	20,789	22,094	1.3	2.46	13,589	14,592	1.0	43,872	51,180	1229	24
CROCKETT	5,632	5,794	5,889	0.4	2.51	4,065	4,079	0.0	35,850	40,917	2305	64
CUMBERLAND	19,508	22,733	25,120	2.1	2.30	14,518	16,539	1.8	38,763	45,433	1885	45
DAVIDSON	237,405	253,981	264,677	0.9	2.26	138,106	142,408	0.4	51,811	62,024	560	9
DECATUR	4,908	5,151	5,279	0.7	2.30	3,415	3,489	0.3	33,710	38,602	2583	75
DEKALB	6,984	7,485	7,827	1.0	2.42	4,989	5,212	0.6	36,445	41,694	2207	58
DICKSON	16,473	18,713	20,091	1.8	2.55	12,175	13,516	1.5	48,693	56,485	765	14
DYER	14,751	15,318	15,565	0.5	2.46	10,459	10,587	0.2	41,436	48,442	1528	34
FAYETTE	10,467	13,503	16,067	3.6	2.62	8,020	10,133	3.3	48,678	55,895	768	15
FENTRESS	6,693	7,331	7,745	1.3	2.39	4,819	5,150	0.9	27,749	31,736	3013	91
FRANKLIN	15,003	16,602	17,563	1.4	2.45	11,160	12,072	1.1	44,184	50,760	1192	22
GIBSON	19,518	20,060	20,332	0.4	2.38	13,578	13,582	0.0	38,340	44,602	1956	48
GILES	11,713	12,153	12,336	0.5	2.42	8,360	8,457	0.2	42,733	49,345	1360	29
GRAINGER	8,270	9,208	9,857	1.5	2.41	6,158	6,704	1.2	33,409	38,253	2615	77
GREENE	25,756	28,066	29,689	1.2	2.34	18,130	19,246	0.8	37,365	43,379	2084	51
GRUNDY	5,562	5,754	5,837	0.5	2.46	4,056	4,096	0.1	27,244	31,152	3030	93
HAMBLEN	23,211	24,833	25,865	0.9	2.43	16,604	17,322	0.6	41,045	47,928	1591	36
HAMILTON	124,444	131,881	136,491	0.8	2.37	83,692	86,163	0.4	49,703	59,051	696	12
HANCOCK	2,769	2,877	2,918	0.5	2.30	1,938	1,961	0.2	23,319	25,795	3109	95
HARDEMAN	9,412	9,901	10,137	0.7	2.50	6,764	6,937	0.3	34,673	39,428	2473	71
HARDIN	10,426	10,962	11,255	0.7	2.35	7,442	7,626	0.3	33,506	38,370	2608	76
HAWKINS	21,936	24,293	25,883	1.4	2.36	15,932	17,224	1.1	38,797	45,079	1879	44
HAYWOOD	7,558	7,781	7,879	0.4	2.52	5,418	5,440	0.1	33,286	38,095	2631	78
HENDERSON	10,306	11,055	11,542	1.0	2.40	7,451	7,797	0.6	39,477	45,607	1782	42
HENRY	13,019	13,649	13,962	0.7	2.32	9,006	9,188	0.3	36,705	42,490	2165	55
HICKMAN	8,081	8,962	9,542	1.4	2.56	5,952	6,449	1.1	37,036	42,433	2122	52
HOUSTON	3,216	3,367	3,460	0.6	2.41	2,300	2,348	0.3	35,801	40,841	2312	65
HUMPHREYS	7,238	7,747	8,070	0.9	2.39	5,145	5,366	0.6	43,785	50,470	1238	25
JACKSON	4,466	4,696	4,828	0.7	2.39	3,141	3,216	0.3	31,469	36,135	2802	83
JEFFERSON	17,155	20,027	22,086	2.2	2.45	12,612	14,383	1.8	40,957	47,060	1606	38
JOHNSON	6,827	7,466	7,815	1.2	2.28	4,754	5,060	0.9	27,528	31,134	3020	92
KNOX	157,872	174,912	187,834	1.4	2.32	100,726	108,089	1.0	48,142	57,117	805	16
LAKE	2,410	2,225	2,083	-1.1	2.30	1,615	1,448	-1.5	26,481	30,426	3054	94
LAUDERDALE	9,567	10,010	10,269	0.6	2.50	6,816	6,951	0.3	36,410	42,232	2210	59
LAWRENCE	15,480	16,396	17,013	0.8	2.52	11,369	11,761	0.5	36,931	42,677	2137	53
LEWIS	4,381	4,554	4,627	0.5	2.52	3,216	3,265	0.2	36,871	42,310	2145	54
LINCOLN	12,503	13,247	13,661	0.8	2.43	9,083	9,393	0.5	41,152	47,346	1582	35
LOUDON	15,944	18,900	21,165	2.4	2.37	11,802	13,671	2.0	51,354	60,096	588	10
MCMINN	19,721	21,274	22,178	1.1	2.40	14,318	15,078	0.7	39,473	45,751	1783	43
MCNAIRY	9,980	10,661	11,113	0.9	2.37	7,133	7,428	0.6	35,983	41,115	2279	62
MACON	7,916	8,663	9,123	1.3	2.53	5,806	6,206	0.9	35,957	41,158	2282	63
MADISON	35,552	38,586	40,471	1.1	2.46	24,652	26,038	0.8	46,711	54,768	935	19
MARION	11,037	12,115	12,693	1.3	2.42	8,131	8,719	1.0	38,153	43,823	1983	49
MARSHALL	10,307	11,511	12,274	1.5	2.55	7,475	8,148	1.2	47,990	55,573	817	17
MAURY	26,444	31,293	35,123	2.3	2.55	19,274	22,265	2.0	52,207	61,290	534	7
MEIGS	4,304	4,802	5,157	1.5	2.51	3,264	3,564	1.2	35,089	40,189	2418	69
MONROE	15,329	17,523	19,199	1.9	2.45	11,243	12,552	1.5	36,336	41,543	2224	60
MONTGOMERY	48,330	58,257	66,149	2.6	2.66	35,964	42,377	2.3	49,607	58,672	702	13
MOORE	2,211	2,492	2,683	1.7	2.48	1,687	1,862	1.4	44,082	50,264	1198	23
MORGAN	6,990	7,371	7,581	0.7	2.52	5,237	5,403	0.4	33,048	37,851	2651	80
OBION	13,182	13,388	13,382	0.2	2.37	9,404	9,309	-0.1	40,987	47,320	1600	37
OVERTON	8,110	8,602	8,901	0.8	2.40	5,924	6,134	0.5	32,201	36,801	2745	82
PERRY	3,023	3,149	3,226	0.6	2.43	2,163	2,197	0.2	33,858	38,833	2568	73
PICKETT	2,091	2,170	2,176	0.5	2.26	1,461	1,476	0.1	29,271	33,879	2947	88
POLK	6,448	6,749	6,892	0.6	2.38	4,750	4,856	0.3	35,641	40,821	2340	66
PUTNAM	24,865	27,841	30,174	1.6	2.39	16,417	17,832	1.1	38,354	44,426	1955	47
RHEA	11,184	12,370	13,202	1.4	2.41	8,104	8,747	1.1	36,478	41,647	2200	57
ROANE	21,200	22,523	23,383	0.8	2.37	15,242	15,797	0.5	41,491	47,885	1518	33
ROBERTSON	19,906	23,880	26,821	2.5	2.67	15,442	18,159	2.3	53,638	62,517	468	6
RUTHERFORD	66,443	92,105	113,840	4.6	2.59	47,457	64,141	4.2	59,379	69,716	282	3
SCOTT	8,203	9,011	9,526	1.3	2.47	6,016	6,454	1.0	28,408	32,562	2982	89
SEQUATCHIE	4,463	5,319	5,982	2.4	2.46	3,311	3,857	2.1	37,525	43,072	2057	50
TENNESSEE				1.4	2.45			1.0	46,151	54,180		
UNITED STATES				1.2	2.59			1.0	53,154	62,503		

COUNTY	2007 Per Capita Income	2007 HH Income Base	2007 HOUSEHOLD INCOME DISTRIBUTION (%)					2007 Home Value Base	2007 HOME VALUE DISTRIBUTION (%)					2007 Median Home Value
			Less than $25,000	$25,000 to $49,999	$50,000 to $99,999	$100,000 to $149,999	$150,000 or More		Less than $50,000	$50,000 to $89,999	$90,000 to $174,999	$175,000 to $399,999	$400,000 or More	
ANDERSON	24,113	31,303	27.4	28.5	31.1	8.9	4.1	23,030	10.9	18.2	44.2	23.2	3.5	120,103
BEDFORD	20,469	16,345	26.2	29.1	34.0	8.0	2.7	12,209	9.9	19.1	47.9	18.8	4.2	116,778
BENTON	18,149	7,177	35.7	33.9	24.2	5.1	1.1	5,827	22.7	26.0	36.8	12.6	1.9	91,824
BLEDSOE	17,673	4,746	36.3	30.8	26.0	4.8	2.1	3,907	23.0	25.7	32.8	15.3	3.1	91,935
BLOUNT	24,203	48,087	24.2	28.9	33.9	8.7	4.4	36,982	11.1	11.2	40.6	31.9	5.1	144,043
BRADLEY	22,850	37,989	28.0	28.7	31.1	8.1	4.0	26,585	8.2	14.6	46.2	26.2	4.8	135,247
CAMPBELL	16,778	17,248	43.1	30.9	20.6	3.8	1.6	12,844	25.2	28.5	35.0	9.8	1.5	84,680
CANNON	19,808	5,380	31.8	28.7	31.3	6.1	2.1	4,258	13.9	18.7	45.5	20.0	1.9	117,188
CARROLL	20,095	11,971	34.5	30.7	26.7	5.5	2.6	9,521	23.0	29.9	35.1	10.7	1.3	85,593
CARTER	18,201	24,593	37.9	32.7	23.1	4.6	1.6	18,657	17.5	23.0	42.3	15.4	1.8	103,724
CHEATHAM	23,797	14,801	16.1	26.5	42.5	10.9	3.9	12,464	5.6	9.0	45.1	36.8	3.5	154,389
CHESTER	19,573	6,159	29.9	27.7	33.1	7.8	1.5	4,798	21.8	28.6	38.6	10.1	0.8	89,443
CLAIBORNE	16,649	13,377	41.8	29.8	23.0	3.8	1.5	10,606	25.1	22.1	39.7	11.1	2.0	93,921
CLAY	16,904	3,603	44.8	32.6	17.3	3.0	2.3	2,912	33.8	27.0	29.1	8.6	1.6	76,524
COCKE	17,274	14,967	42.6	30.8	21.2	3.6	1.8	11,442	25.0	22.8	38.4	12.0	1.9	92,846
COFFEE	22,544	20,789	28.5	27.8	32.0	8.0	3.6	15,092	13.1	19.6	43.9	20.1	3.2	115,035
CROCKETT	18,254	5,794	35.2	29.7	27.8	5.3	2.0	4,411	17.2	29.0	40.7	12.6	0.5	94,679
CUMBERLAND	21,456	22,733	31.2	33.0	26.8	6.1	2.8	18,425	12.9	19.4	38.6	25.0	4.0	119,165
DAVIDSON	30,129	253,979	21.3	26.7	34.0	10.7	7.3	143,235	2.8	7.6	45.2	35.3	9.2	162,600
DECATUR	20,145	5,151	36.9	31.8	24.4	3.9	3.0	4,153	25.5	29.6	33.5	9.8	1.7	83,264
DEKALB	20,361	7,485	35.3	29.1	27.3	5.2	3.1	5,709	9.2	19.4	47.2	19.6	4.6	120,096
DICKSON	22,416	18,713	24.0	27.4	36.2	9.3	3.0	14,400	7.9	13.4	46.9	27.6	4.2	135,690
DYER	20,783	15,318	31.2	28.4	30.7	6.7	2.9	10,309	11.4	26.5	44.2	16.1	1.9	105,832
FAYETTE	23,108	13,503	26.3	25.1	34.1	9.9	4.6	10,967	11.7	22.4	32.6	26.6	6.7	120,053
FENTRESS	15,724	7,331	46.0	29.4	19.5	3.4	1.7	5,841	31.8	27.0	29.4	10.7	1.1	75,608
FRANKLIN	21,756	16,602	28.5	27.9	32.7	7.4	3.4	13,174	14.0	18.8	42.9	19.5	4.8	115,495
GIBSON	20,117	20,060	31.3	30.8	29.5	6.5	1.9	14,693	16.8	29.1	39.9	12.8	1.4	95,493
GILES	21,953	12,153	28.3	29.9	31.0	8.0	2.8	9,304	11.4	23.1	46.6	15.9	3.0	109,748
GRAINGER	18,144	9,208	38.0	31.0	25.2	3.4	2.4	7,744	20.4	24.4	36.1	16.0	3.1	98,860
GREENE	20,214	28,066	32.8	31.9	27.7	5.3	2.3	21,764	16.0	20.4	44.5	16.1	3.1	108,062
GRUNDY	14,743	5,754	45.8	30.4	19.6	3.2	1.0	4,749	31.5	31.8	28.2	7.1	1.4	72,191
HAMBLEN	22,121	24,833	29.7	30.6	29.5	6.6	3.7	18,293	9.0	15.9	50.3	21.2	3.5	124,083
HAMILTON	27,854	131,881	24.2	26.1	32.6	10.2	6.9	88,598	7.5	14.5	46.3	25.6	6.1	133,453
HANCOCK	14,455	2,877	52.4	27.5	16.5	2.6	1.0	2,290	33.8	27.4	29.2	8.1	1.5	70,093
HARDEMAN	16,880	9,901	38.0	30.4	25.4	4.4	1.8	7,449	21.5	32.1	35.1	10.4	0.9	86,346
HARDIN	19,165	10,962	37.9	31.7	21.9	6.4	2.1	8,570	24.1	25.7	34.4	13.6	2.2	90,359
HAWKINS	20,212	24,293	32.4	31.0	28.9	5.6	2.1	19,318	17.4	22.1	43.2	15.3	1.9	107,721
HAYWOOD	18,233	7,781	38.6	27.7	26.0	5.5	2.2	5,251	12.9	30.1	41.4	13.9	1.6	98,024
HENDERSON	20,476	11,055	32.0	30.3	29.6	5.7	2.5	8,837	21.1	24.1	37.8	15.4	1.6	96,257
HENRY	19,730	13,649	33.1	32.7	27.1	5.4	1.7	10,654	17.1	25.0	38.7	16.4	2.7	100,246
HICKMAN	17,696	8,962	33.3	31.8	28.5	4.6	1.8	7,248	15.4	20.9	45.3	16.5	2.0	111,292
HOUSTON	19,040	3,367	36.4	29.1	26.0	6.7	1.9	2,625	21.0	27.8	38.1	12.2	1.0	91,618
HUMPHREYS	22,201	7,747	27.5	29.0	34.0	6.9	2.6	6,114	15.1	21.6	42.1	18.8	2.4	109,018
JACKSON	18,203	4,696	39.8	32.0	22.3	3.1	2.8	3,820	19.2	26.5	38.9	13.2	2.2	95,563
JEFFERSON	20,619	20,027	30.5	30.5	30.3	5.8	2.9	15,746	15.7	16.5	41.0	21.6	5.2	121,680
JOHNSON	16,826	7,466	45.5	30.6	19.0	2.8	2.2	6,007	27.0	22.5	37.0	11.8	1.8	90,694
KNOX	28,175	174,909	26.0	25.6	30.5	10.8	7.1	118,527	7.0	13.1	44.5	29.2	6.1	142,393
LAKE	15,041	2,225	47.2	26.4	22.1	3.1	1.2	1,372	23.7	40.2	28.7	5.4	2.0	77,034
LAUDERDALE	17,771	10,010	35.2	28.7	30.1	3.3	2.6	6,665	18.4	33.5	37.3	9.2	1.7	88,029
LAWRENCE	19,426	16,396	32.8	32.7	27.2	4.7	2.6	12,776	14.4	23.2	45.5	15.3	1.7	106,367
LEWIS	17,800	4,554	34.4	30.4	28.9	5.2	1.0	3,649	21.3	27.4	36.9	13.5	0.8	91,527
LINCOLN	22,317	13,247	30.5	28.9	28.5	8.3	3.7	10,252	16.1	23.2	38.6	19.3	2.8	105,943
LOUDON	27,335	18,900	22.4	25.9	35.3	10.7	5.7	15,094	8.0	15.2	39.6	24.8	12.5	138,894
MCMINN	20,626	21,274	31.3	30.0	29.3	7.1	2.3	16,296	13.8	21.4	43.3	17.9	3.6	110,127
MCNAIRY	19,550	10,661	35.1	31.3	26.8	4.6	2.2	8,605	25.7	28.7	33.4	10.7	1.4	83,921
MACON	18,539	8,663	34.6	29.5	28.6	5.1	2.1	6,888	21.9	24.0	38.7	13.0	2.4	96,461
MADISON	25,246	38,586	25.9	27.6	31.2	9.7	5.6	26,214	14.1	24.5	43.5	15.3	2.6	104,213
MARION	20,330	12,115	31.4	32.8	26.7	6.2	2.8	9,855	22.9	23.2	38.5	13.4	2.0	94,632
MARSHALL	22,149	11,511	25.0	26.8	35.6	9.7	2.9	8,555	9.0	17.1	49.5	20.2	4.3	125,600
MAURY	24,749	31,293	22.6	24.8	36.1	11.6	4.9	23,130	7.2	13.1	43.8	31.3	4.7	143,276
MEIGS	17,835	4,802	34.2	31.8	27.7	4.5	1.7	3,965	22.5	20.2	33.2	19.5	4.5	103,229
MONROE	18,711	17,523	33.4	32.6	27.0	5.0	2.1	13,878	20.1	20.6	40.1	16.2	3.1	105,286
MONTGOMERY	22,230	58,257	20.0	30.4	36.6	9.2	3.8	37,717	5.3	12.8	59.4	20.0	2.4	127,142
MOORE	23,212	2,492	25.5	31.2	30.7	7.9	4.6	2,098	9.0	18.7	38.5	26.9	6.9	127,703
MORGAN	16,108	7,371	35.9	34.1	24.9	3.8	1.2	6,143	24.3	30.6	36.3	7.6	1.2	83,021
OBION	21,830	13,388	30.6	29.5	30.1	6.6	3.2	9,748	15.6	29.6	39.7	13.2	1.9	95,602
OVERTON	16,593	8,602	38.7	32.1	25.7	2.5	1.0	7,008	23.5	21.0	39.7	13.7	2.2	98,866
PERRY	19,233	3,149	36.6	31.6	23.7	5.8	2.4	2,709	27.7	29.6	30.0	12.0	0.7	79,775
PICKETT	18,506	2,170	40.9	32.2	21.5	3.0	2.5	1,834	19.6	26.6	35.0	15.5	3.3	96,931
POLK	20,121	6,749	33.8	31.4	26.7	5.6	2.6	5,501	22.1	24.7	37.0	13.4	2.7	94,580
PUTNAM	20,946	27,841	32.8	29.9	27.3	6.9	3.2	18,653	8.2	14.3	47.2	25.0	5.3	133,797
RHEA	19,452	12,370	34.6	30.4	26.3	6.2	2.4	9,493	19.8	21.7	40.8	15.8	2.0	100,683
ROANE	23,071	22,523	30.3	28.3	29.3	8.4	3.7	17,639	16.5	19.5	39.8	20.4	3.7	113,277
ROBERTSON	23,782	23,880	19.9	25.8	38.8	11.8	3.7	18,513	5.1	9.3	45.8	35.5	4.2	155,333
RUTHERFORD	25,585	82,105	17.6	23.5	38.8	13.7	6.4	66,261	4.8	4.2	43.7	43.1	4.3	171,253
SCOTT	16,126	9,011	44.2	31.5	20.1	2.6	1.7	6,984	31.6	26.7	31.1	8.9	1.6	75,298
SEQUATCHIE	19,636	5,319	33.7	32.0	25.8	6.1	2.4	4,135	19.0	18.5	40.9	16.9	4.7	109,279
TENNESSEE	24,928		26.4	27.4	31.5	9.3	5.4		10.8	17.5	40.9	25.4	5.4	127,358
UNITED STATES	27,916		21.9	25.0	32.3	12.3	8.4		7.9	10.5	27.1	35.6	19.0	192,285

TENNESSEE
E

SPENDING POTENTIAL INDICES

COUNTY	FINANCIAL SERVICES				THE HOME						ENTERTAINMENT						PERSONAL			
					Home Improvements		Furnishings													
	Auto Loan	Home Loan	Invest-ments	Retire-ment Plans	Home Repair	Lawn & Garden	Computers & Hard-ware	Major Appli-ances	TV, Radio, Sound Equip-ment	Furni-ture	Dine out/ Carry out	Sports Equip-ment	Fees & Tickets	Toys & Games	Travel	Cable TV	Apparel & Services	Auto Repairs	Health Insur-ance	Pets & Supplies
ANDERSON	84	74	73	73	77	87	74	81	79	73	78	71	71	79	75	82	68	78	88	84
BEDFORD	87	71	60	70	74	88	71	80	77	71	76	71	66	81	71	81	67	77	86	85
BENTON	72	52	34	49	58	78	53	67	59	51	58	58	45	61	53	64	50	61	74	72
BLEDSOE	80	55	33	52	60	82	55	71	63	54	63	63	47	67	54	68	53	65	76	77
BLOUNT	90	79	72	78	82	93	78	86	82	77	81	76	75	84	79	85	71	82	90	89
BRADLEY	86	73	68	73	76	87	75	81	79	73	78	73	71	81	74	82	69	79	87	85
CAMPBELL	67	47	33	45	52	70	50	61	56	47	56	54	42	58	49	61	47	57	68	66
CANNON	84	61	44	58	66	87	63	76	70	60	69	68	54	73	61	75	59	71	83	82
CARROLL	81	60	45	58	64	84	61	74	69	59	68	65	54	72	61	74	58	69	81	79
CARTER	70	52	37	50	56	73	54	65	60	52	59	57	47	62	53	64	51	61	71	69
CHEATHAM	101	95	80	93	90	96	86	93	88	90	88	84	86	92	87	90	78	90	92	96
CHESTER	83	63	49	61	65	83	65	75	71	63	70	67	57	74	63	75	61	71	81	80
CLAIBORNE	69	49	32	46	54	72	50	63	56	49	56	56	42	59	49	60	48	58	68	68
CLAY	67	47	28	44	51	70	47	60	54	46	53	53	40	57	47	58	45	55	66	66
COCKE	69	49	33	47	54	72	51	63	57	49	57	55	43	60	50	62	48	58	69	68
COFFEE	86	72	67	71	74	87	74	80	79	72	78	71	69	80	73	82	68	78	87	84
CROCKETT	79	56	36	53	62	83	57	72	65	56	64	64	49	68	56	70	55	66	79	78
CUMBERLAND	78	62	52	59	68	87	63	76	69	61	68	66	57	68	65	74	58	72	85	80
DAVIDSON	96	88	96	93	84	85	99	90	99	96	99	83	96	98	94	98	89	96	92	91
DECATUR	81	56	34	53	61	84	57	73	62	55	65	65	48	69	57	71	55	67	81	79
DEKALB	86	61	37	58	67	91	61	78	69	59	68	69	52	73	61	74	58	72	85	85
DICKSON	89	77	66	76	77	88	75	83	80	75	79	74	72	82	75	83	70	80	86	86
DYER	80	65	59	65	67	80	68	74	73	66	72	65	63	75	66	76	63	72	79	78
FAYETTE	100	80	58	77	85	105	76	93	83	77	83	83	70	87	77	88	72	86	97	100
FENTRESS	65	45	27	42	50	69	46	59	53	45	52	53	38	55	45	57	45	55	64	65
FRANKLIN	89	69	52	67	75	95	69	83	76	67	75	73	62	79	69	81	65	77	90	89
GIBSON	77	59	50	58	63	79	62	71	69	60	67	62	55	71	61	73	58	68	79	75
GILES	91	66	45	64	73	96	67	83	75	65	74	73	58	79	66	80	63	76	90	89
GRAINGER	79	54	29	50	59	82	53	69	61	53	61	62	44	65	52	66	52	63	74	77
GREENE	79	59	44	57	64	82	60	73	67	59	66	64	53	70	60	71	57	68	79	78
GRUNDY	65	43	23	40	48	67	44	58	51	43	51	52	36	54	43	56	43	53	63	64
HAMBLEN	83	69	64	69	72	85	71	78	76	69	75	69	66	79	70	79	66	75	84	82
HAMILTON	92	90	99	92	90	92	91	90	93	91	92	80	92	93	92	95	83	91	95	92
HANCOCK	60	39	18	36	44	63	40	54	47	39	47	48	32	49	39	51	39	49	59	60
HARDEMAN	75	53	34	50	57	77	54	67	62	53	62	60	46	64	53	67	53	63	74	73
HARDIN	76	56	40	54	61	79	57	70	64	55	63	61	50	66	57	68	54	65	76	74
HAWKINS	81	60	42	57	64	84	60	73	67	59	66	65	52	70	59	71	57	68	79	79
HAYWOOD	75	56	44	55	59	76	59	68	66	57	65	60	52	68	57	70	56	65	74	73
HENDERSON	85	61	41	58	66	87	62	76	69	61	69	68	53	73	60	74	59	70	81	83
HENRY	74	56	45	55	62	79	58	70	65	56	64	61	52	66	59	69	55	66	77	74
HICKMAN	79	57	37	54	62	83	57	72	65	56	64	63	49	68	57	69	54	66	78	77
HOUSTON	79	56	37	53	62	83	57	72	65	55	64	63	49	67	57	71	55	67	80	77
HUMPHREYS	90	67	47	64	73	95	67	82	74	66	74	73	59	78	66	79	63	76	88	89
JACKSON	76	53	32	50	58	80	54	68	61	52	60	61	45	64	53	66	51	63	75	75
JEFFERSON	85	65	48	63	68	87	66	77	71	64	71	69	58	74	65	75	61	73	82	83
JOHNSON	69	47	27	44	53	74	48	63	55	46	54	56	40	57	48	60	46	57	69	69
KNOX	93	87	92	89	86	90	93	90	93	90	93	82	90	93	91	94	83	92	93	91
LAKE	59	43	38	42	46	60	49	55	55	45	53	49	42	54	47	58	46	53	63	58
LAUDERDALE	77	55	38	53	58	77	58	69	66	56	65	62	50	68	56	70	56	65	75	75
LAWRENCE	83	61	43	58	65	86	62	75	69	60	68	66	54	73	60	74	59	70	81	81
LEWIS	77	55	37	53	59	79	56	69	64	55	63	61	48	67	55	68	54	64	76	74
LINCOLN	90	68	51	66	75	96	68	83	76	67	75	73	61	79	68	81	65	77	90	89
LOUDON	99	86	80	85	92	107	84	97	90	84	89	84	81	91	87	94	78	91	103	100
MCMINN	80	62	51	61	67	83	64	74	70	62	69	65	58	73	63	75	60	70	81	79
MCNAIRY	82	57	34	54	63	86	57	74	65	56	65	65	48	69	56	71	55	67	80	80
MACON	83	57	34	54	62	86	58	74	66	56	65	66	48	70	56	71	56	68	80	81
MADISON	91	83	83	85	82	88	86	86	89	85	88	78	83	89	84	91	79	87	91	89
MARION	86	61	37	58	67	90	61	77	69	60	68	69	52	73	60	74	58	71	84	84
MARSHALL	88	75	66	74	77	89	74	82	79	74	78	72	70	82	74	83	69	78	87	85
MAURY	93	87	86	87	87	93	85	89	88	85	87	80	84	90	86	90	78	87	93	92
MEIGS	80	55	31	52	60	83	55	71	62	54	62	63	46	67	53	67	53	65	75	78
MONROE	80	56	36	54	61	83	57	72	64	56	64	64	48	68	56	69	55	66	78	78
MONTGOMERY	89	80	74	82	75	78	85	81	84	83	84	76	80	86	80	82	75	84	80	82
MOORE	95	74	55	71	83	105	72	91	80	71	79	79	65	84	74	85	68	82	97	96
MORGAN	73	51	27	47	56	77	50	66	57	50	57	59	42	61	49	62	49	60	70	72
OBION	84	64	53	63	69	87	67	78	74	65	73	68	60	76	66	79	63	73	86	82
OVERTON	69	49	32	46	53	72	50	62	56	48	55	55	42	59	49	61	47	57	68	82
PERRY	81	57	35	54	64	87	58	75	66	56	65	65	49	69	58	71	55	68	81	81
PICKETT	70	51	33	49	58	78	53	67	58	50	58	58	45	60	53	63	49	61	73	72
POLK	85	59	35	56	65	89	59	76	67	58	67	67	50	71	58	72	57	69	82	83
PUTNAM	80	62	54	62	64	78	70	73	72	64	72	67	62	73	66	74	63	72	78	77
RHEA	82	58	38	55	64	86	59	74	66	57	66	65	50	69	58	71	56	68	80	80
ROANE	86	70	61	69	74	90	71	81	77	69	76	71	65	79	71	81	66	77	88	85
ROBERTSON	97	88	78	87	88	98	84	92	88	85	87	83	82	91	85	90	77	88	94	95
RUTHERFORD	100	97	90	98	89	89	98	93	95	98	95	88	95	97	93	92	86	96	89	94
SCOTT	71	48	25	45	53	73	48	63	56	47	55	56	40	59	47	61	47	58	69	70
SEQUATCHIE	87	60	33	56	65	90	59	76	67	58	67	68	50	72	58	72	57	70	81	84
TENNESSEE	93	80	75	81	81	92	83	87	86	81	86	78	78	88	81	88	76	86	91	90
UNITED STATES	100	100	100	100	100	100	100	100	100	100	100	100	100	100	100	100	100	100	100	100

COUNTY	FIPS Code	CBSA Code	DMA Code	POPULATION			2000-2007 ANNUAL RATE		RACE (%)					
									White		Black		Asian/Pacific	
				2000	2007	2012	% Rate	State Rank	2000	2007	2000	2007	2000	2007
SEVIER	155	42940	557	71,170	84,552	95,383	2.4	6	97.3	96.6	0.6	0.6	0.6	0.8
SHELBY	157	32820	640	897,472	930,815	948,051	0.5	65	47.3	44.7	48.6	50.1	1.7	2.2
SMITH	159	34980	659	17,712	19,311	20,497	1.2	29	95.4	94.7	2.5	2.8	0.2	0.2
STEWART	161	17300	659	12,370	13,296	13,852	1.0	39	95.3	94.2	1.3	1.4	1.5	2.1
SULLIVAN	163	28700	531	153,048	154,803	156,064	0.2	86	96.6	96.0	1.9	2.1	0.4	0.6
SUMNER	165	34980	659	130,449	152,235	169,746	2.2	11	91.5	90.2	5.8	6.3	0.7	1.0
TIPTON	167	32820	640	51,271	60,711	67,802	2.4	6	77.9	75.9	19.9	21.3	0.4	0.6
TROUSDALE	169	34980	659	7,259	7,903	8,392	1.2	29	86.6	85.0	11.4	12.3	0.1	0.2
UNICOI	171	27740	531	17,667	18,109	18,380	0.3	80	98.0	97.3	0.1	0.1	0.2	0.2
UNION	173	28940	557	17,808	19,667	20,982	1.4	22	98.5	98.1	0.1	0.1	0.2	0.2
VAN BUREN	175	00000	659	5,508	5,811	6,044	0.7	54	99.0	98.8	0.1	0.1	0.1	0.1
WARREN	177	32660	659	38,276	39,926	41,034	0.6	59	91.7	89.5	3.2	3.4	0.5	0.6
WASHINGTON	179	27740	531	107,198	116,727	124,106	1.2	29	93.7	92.7	3.8	4.1	0.7	1.0
WAYNE	181	00000	659	16,842	17,250	17,439	0.3	80	91.9	91.0	6.8	7.4	0.3	0.4
WEAKLEY	183	32280	632	34,895	34,550	34,645	-0.1	94	90.3	88.8	6.9	7.5	1.3	1.9
WHITE	185	00000	659	23,102	24,546	25,580	0.8	47	96.6	96.0	1.6	1.8	0.3	0.4
WILLIAMSON	187	34980	659	126,638	164,410	197,204	3.7	2	91.6	90.1	5.2	5.6	1.3	1.8
WILSON	189	34980	659	88,809	106,391	120,711	2.5	4	91.5	90.4	6.3	6.8	0.5	0.7
TENNESSEE							1.2		80.2	78.9	16.4	16.8	1.0	1.4
UNITED STATES							1.2		75.1	72.7	12.3	12.6	3.8	4.5

B

COUNTY	% HISPANIC ORIGIN		2007 AGE DISTRIBUTION (%)										MEDIAN AGE	% 2007 Males	% 2007 Females
	2000	2007	0-4	5-9	10-14	15-19	20-24	25-44	45-64	65-84	85+	18+	2007		
SEVIER	1.2	1.8	5.9	5.9	5.9	5.6	4.9	28.4	29.3	12.6	1.4	78.8	40.8	49.2	50.8
SHELBY	2.6	3.4	7.4	7.1	7.6	7.4	7.0	28.0	25.1	9.0	1.5	73.4	34.7	47.9	52.1
SMITH	1.1	1.6	6.8	6.7	5.9	6.1	6.3	28.3	27.0	10.9	1.9	76.8	39.0	49.8	50.2
STEWART	1.0	1.4	6.0	5.8	6.2	5.8	5.5	26.4	28.5	14.2	1.7	78.4	41.6	50.0	50.0
SULLIVAN	0.7	1.0	5.5	5.6	5.7	5.8	4.9	26.1	29.2	15.1	2.2	79.7	42.6	48.5	51.5
SUMNER	1.8	2.5	6.8	6.9	6.4	6.3	6.3	27.5	28.1	10.4	1.4	76.0	38.7	49.1	50.9
TIPTON	1.2	1.7	7.4	6.5	7.3	7.4	7.1	27.9	25.9	9.4	1.1	74.3	36.2	49.3	50.7
TROUSDALE	1.5	2.2	6.1	6.0	6.8	5.5	5.5	27.2	28.3	12.6	2.0	77.8	40.3	49.6	50.4
UNICOI	1.9	2.8	5.6	5.8	4.9	4.9	4.8	26.0	29.4	15.9	2.7	80.7	43.5	49.1	50.9
UNION	0.8	1.1	6.9	6.7	5.9	6.4	5.8	29.2	26.7	11.1	1.1	76.5	38.3	49.9	50.1
VAN BUREN	0.3	0.5	6.0	6.1	6.2	5.2	5.5	27.9	28.4	13.1	1.6	78.7	40.3	50.3	49.7
WARREN	4.9	6.9	6.7	6.5	6.1	5.9	5.7	28.8	26.3	12.3	1.8	77.2	38.4	49.6	50.4
WASHINGTON	1.4	2.0	5.9	5.7	5.6	6.0	6.3	28.8	27.2	12.4	2.0	79.6	39.3	48.9	51.1
WAYNE	0.8	1.2	5.2	4.9	5.6	5.6	6.5	32.0	25.5	12.8	1.9	80.9	38.9	55.2	44.8
WEAKLEY	1.2	1.6	6.2	5.7	5.6	7.2	9.6	26.9	24.5	12.1	2.2	79.5	36.4	49.0	51.0
WHITE	1.0	1.5	6.1	6.2	5.8	5.9	5.5	26.9	27.5	14.1	1.8	78.2	40.6	49.4	50.6
WILLIAMSON	2.5	3.6	7.2	8.0	8.3	7.3	5.3	26.4	29.5	7.2	0.9	71.9	37.4	49.3	50.7
WILSON	1.3	1.8	6.7	6.7	6.7	6.7	5.6	27.8	28.8	9.7	1.3	75.8	39.0	49.4	50.6
TENNESSEE	2.2	3.0	6.6	6.4	6.4	6.5	6.4	28.4	26.4	11.2	1.7	76.8	37.8	49.0	51.0
UNITED STATES	12.5	15.0	6.9	6.5	6.8	7.1	7.0	27.6	25.4	10.7	1.9	75.6	36.7	49.2	50.8

COUNTY	HOUSEHOLDS					FAMILIES			MEDIAN HOUSEHOLD INCOME			
	2000	2007	2012	% Annual Rate 2000-2007	2007 Average HH Size	2000	2007	% Annual Rate 2000-2007	2007	2012	2007 National Rank	2007 State Rank
SEVIER	28,467	34,231	38,865	2.6	2.45	20,836	24,468	2.2	43,033	50,126	1327	28
SHELBY	338,366	356,008	364,229	0.7	2.56	228,644	233,758	0.3	51,078	60,997	608	11
SMITH	6,878	7,600	8,107	1.4	2.52	5,070	5,474	1.1	43,424	50,089	1281	27
STEWART	4,930	5,356	5,600	1.1	2.46	3,652	3,877	0.8	39,949	45,610	1733	41
SULLIVAN	63,556	66,569	67,867	0.6	2.29	44,802	45,714	0.3	41,756	48,176	1484	32
SUMNER	48,941	58,500	65,884	2.5	2.58	37,054	43,344	2.2	57,588	67,704	317	4
TIPTON	18,106	21,813	24,531	2.6	2.74	14,173	16,748	2.3	51,980	60,727	546	8
TROUSDALE	2,780	3,052	3,249	1.3	2.54	2,036	2,183	1.0	40,053	45,804	1720	40
UNICOI	7,516	7,913	8,123	0.7	2.25	5,222	5,352	0.3	35,582	40,520	2354	67
UNION	6,742	7,613	8,197	1.7	2.57	5,194	5,745	1.4	33,198	38,451	2638	79
VAN BUREN	2,180	2,373	2,502	1.2	2.42	1,620	1,724	0.9	33,811	38,729	2574	74
WARREN	15,181	16,136	16,710	0.8	2.43	10,821	11,210	0.5	38,407	44,786	1949	46
WASHINGTON	44,195	48,690	52,166	1.3	2.32	29,466	31,520	0.9	41,807	48,897	1474	31
WAYNE	5,936	6,218	6,372	0.6	2.40	4,324	4,423	0.3	31,254	35,903	2814	84
WEAKLEY	13,599	13,905	14,036	0.3	2.34	9,125	9,063	-0.1	36,215	41,395	2239	61
WHITE	9,229	10,000	10,505	1.1	2.42	6,771	7,164	0.8	35,149	40,111	2411	68
WILLIAMSON	44,725	58,965	71,128	3.9	2.77	35,758	46,309	3.6	88,854	108,684	21	1
WILSON	32,798	40,120	45,948	2.8	2.62	25,595	30,701	2.5	61,919	72,421	215	2
TENNESSEE				1.4	2.45			1.0	46,151	54,180		
UNITED STATES				1.2	2.59			1.0	53,154	62,503		

COUNTY	2007 Per Capita Income	2007 HH Income Base	2007 HOUSEHOLD INCOME DISTRIBUTION (%)					2007 Home Value Base	2007 HOME VALUE DISTRIBUTION (%)					2007 Median Home Value
			Less than $25,000	$25,000 to $49,999	$50,000 to $99,999	$100,000 to $149,999	$150,000 or More		Less than $50,000	$50,000 to $89,999	$90,000 to $174,999	$175,000 to $399,999	$400,000 or More	
SEVIER	22,012	34,231	25.8	32.4	32.0	6.7	3.0	25,618	13.0	11.8	37.5	32.3	5.5	145,478
SHELBY	27,318	356,007	23.8	25.1	31.7	11.5	7.9	227,792	7.4	27.5	36.0	24.0	5.1	114,145
SMITH	20,837	7,600	27.9	30.4	32.6	6.3	2.9	6,055	10.4	17.4	43.0	24.8	4.4	129,243
STEWART	19,907	5,355	29.5	31.7	31.9	3.9	3.0	4,293	17.4	21.1	43.2	17.1	1.1	107,146
SULLIVAN	24,257	66,569	29.6	29.2	29.2	7.9	4.1	50,984	14.2	18.5	42.6	21.3	3.4	118,276
SUMNER	27,265	58,500	17.7	24.8	38.4	12.8	6.3	44,744	5.3	7.1	37.5	42.4	7.8	175,380
TIPTON	22,118	21,813	23.2	24.1	38.4	10.6	3.6	16,845	12.1	18.7	50.0	18.2	1.0	111,991
TROUSDALE	19,513	3,052	31.2	30.3	30.3	6.0	2.1	2,366	10.6	20.5	48.6	17.2	3.0	115,667
UNICOI	19,583	7,913	34.5	32.0	26.7	5.0	1.8	6,127	15.7	20.1	42.0	20.0	2.2	113,897
UNION	17,011	7,613	38.9	30.4	24.0	4.7	2.0	6,210	23.0	21.5	39.7	13.3	2.4	97,086
VAN BUREN	19,498	2,373	36.3	31.9	27.3	2.5	2.0	2,029	26.1	31.6	33.3	7.8	1.3	79,837
WARREN	19,919	16,136	33.4	28.6	29.6	5.8	2.6	11,882	12.2	24.3	43.8	17.2	2.5	107,369
WASHINGTON	23,940	48,690	30.4	28.1	29.5	7.5	4.5	33,731	8.6	13.0	44.5	28.5	5.4	141,802
WAYNE	16,840	6,218	38.7	35.5	21.5	2.4	2.0	5,167	31.2	28.9	30.8	8.0	1.0	76,097
WEAKLEY	19,495	13,905	35.0	29.3	28.9	4.8	2.0	9,779	18.0	26.3	41.3	12.9	1.5	97,400
WHITE	18,622	10,000	34.9	32.4	25.6	5.2	1.9	8,048	15.1	21.5	45.0	15.7	2.6	106,877
WILLIAMSON	44,942	58,965	9.1	14.5	32.1	21.0	23.3	48,596	1.7	2.2	12.0	50.6	33.4	321,130
WILSON	28,217	40,120	15.9	22.0	39.9	15.6	6.6	32,905	5.3	6.1	30.3	50.8	7.5	197,556
TENNESSEE	24,928		26.4	27.4	31.5	9.3	5.4		10.8	17.5	40.9	25.4	5.4	127,358
UNITED STATES	27,916		21.9	25.0	32.3	12.3	8.4		7.9	10.5	27.1	35.6	19.0	192,285

COUNTY	FINANCIAL SERVICES				THE HOME							ENTERTAINMENT						PERSONAL			
					Home Improvements		Furnishings														
	Auto Loan	Home Loan	Invest-ments	Retire-ment Plans	Home Repair	Lawn & Garden	Comput-ers & Hard-ware	Major Appli-ances	TV, Radio, Sound Equip-ment	Furni-ture	Dine out/ Carry out	Sports Equip-ment	Fees & Tickets	Toys & Games	Travel	Cable TV	Apparel & Services	Auto Repairs	Health Insur-ance	Pets & Supplies
SEVIER	84	72	62	71	75	88	71	81	74	70	74	71	67	76	72	77	64	76	84	84
SHELBY	98	94	99	98	89	90	98	92	99	99	99	83	97	99	95	99	90	97	94	93
SMITH	90	67	44	64	71	93	66	81	73	65	73	72	58	78	65	78	63	75	87	88
STEWART	85	61	37	58	67	91	61	78	68	59	68	68	52	71	60	73	58	71	84	85
SULLIVAN	83	72	71	71	76	88	73	81	79	71	77	71	70	79	74	82	67	77	89	83
SUMNER	101	100	99	101	99	102	95	99	96	97	96	89	96	99	97	97	86	97	100	101
TIPTON	96	84	69	82	82	94	80	88	84	81	84	79	76	87	79	87	74	85	91	92
TROUSDALE	85	61	40	58	67	89	62	77	70	60	69	68	53	74	61	75	59	71	84	84
UNICOI	73	55	41	53	59	76	56	67	63	54	62	59	49	65	56	67	53	63	75	71
UNION	75	55	35	52	59	77	55	67	61	54	60	60	47	64	54	65	52	63	72	73
VAN BUREN	85	59	32	55	64	88	58	75	65	57	66	67	48	70	56	71	56	68	80	83
WARREN	78	60	49	59	64	79	63	72	68	61	68	64	56	71	61	72	59	69	77	76
WASHINGTON	84	71	71	72	73	83	77	80	80	73	78	71	71	80	75	82	69	79	85	82
WAYNE	74	50	30	47	56	77	52	66	59	50	59	59	43	62	51	64	50	61	73	72
WEAKLEY	76	56	45	55	60	76	62	69	66	58	66	62	53	68	59	69	57	66	75	74
WHITE	78	55	36	53	61	81	56	70	63	55	63	62	48	67	55	68	54	65	76	76
WILLIAMSON	171	198	194	201	191	173	174	173	164	185	166	164	187	172	178	158	153	168	157	173
WILSON	107	108	106	109	107	109	100	105	101	103	101	95	102	105	102	101	90	102	104	107
TENNESSEE	93	80	75	81	81	92	83	87	86	81	86	78	78	88	81	88	76	86	91	90
UNITED STATES	100	100	100	100	100	100	100	100	100	100	100	100	100	100	100	100	100	100	100	100

TEXAS

POPULATION CHANGE

COUNTY	FIPS Code	CBSA Code	DMA Code	POPULATION			2000-2007 ANNUAL RATE		RACE (%)					
									White		Black		Asian/Pacific	
				2000	2007	2012	% Rate	State Rank	2000	2007	2000	2007	2000	2007
ANDERSON	001	37300	623	55,109	56,842	57,977	0.4	128	66.4	62.8	23.5	24.6	0.5	0.6
ANDREWS	003	11380	633	13,004	12,717	12,543	-0.3	202	77.1	73.4	1.6	1.6	0.7	0.8
ANGELINA	005	31260	709	80,130	83,452	85,732	0.6	105	75.1	71.8	14.7	15.5	0.7	0.8
ARANSAS	007	18580	600	22,497	25,423	27,670	1.7	47	87.4	85.0	1.4	1.5	2.8	3.4
ARCHER	009	48660	627	8,854	9,136	9,306	0.4	128	95.5	94.4	0.1	0.1	0.2	0.2
ARMSTRONG	011	11100	634	2,148	2,202	2,241	0.3	139	95.4	95.3	0.3	0.3	0.0	0.0
ATASCOSA	013	41700	641	38,628	43,910	47,395	1.8	43	73.2	70.1	0.6	0.6	0.4	0.4
AUSTIN	015	26420	618	23,590	26,928	29,447	1.8	43	80.2	77.4	10.6	11.2	0.3	0.4
BAILEY	017	00000	651	6,594	6,588	6,603	0.0	170	66.7	65.8	1.3	1.3	0.1	0.1
BANDERA	019	41700	641	17,645	20,444	22,292	2.1	33	94.0	92.7	0.3	0.4	0.3	0.4
BASTROP	021	12420	635	57,733	72,555	82,885	3.2	17	80.2	77.6	8.8	9.1	0.5	0.6
BAYLOR	023	00000	627	4,093	3,883	3,735	-0.7	229	91.0	89.2	3.3	3.7	0.6	0.8
BEE	025	13300	600	32,359	32,997	32,671	0.3	139	67.9	65.7	9.9	9.3	0.5	0.6
BELL	027	28660	625	237,974	277,582	309,682	2.1	33	63.4	59.6	20.4	21.1	3.0	3.6
BEXAR	029	41700	641	1,392,931	1,588,786	1,736,397	1.8	43	68.9	66.5	7.2	6.8	1.7	1.9
BLANCO	031	00000	635	8,418	9,607	10,278	1.8	43	91.0	88.9	0.7	0.8	0.2	0.2
BORDEN	033	00000	651	729	741	748	0.2	148	90.5	90.3	0.1	0.1	0.0	0.0
BOSQUE	035	00000	623	17,204	18,686	19,699	1.1	69	90.8	88.7	1.9	2.1	0.1	0.2
BOWIE	037	45500	612	89,306	92,914	95,011	0.5	117	73.3	70.8	23.4	25.2	0.5	0.6
BRAZORIA	039	26420	618	241,767	295,743	339,784	2.8	19	77.1	73.8	8.5	8.7	2.0	2.4
BRAZOS	041	17780	625	152,415	169,288	177,530	1.5	54	74.5	70.8	10.7	11.1	4.1	4.9
BREWSTER	043	00000	633	8,866	9,060	9,159	0.3	139	81.1	78.3	1.2	1.2	0.4	0.5
BRISCOE	045	00000	634	1,790	1,736	1,706	-0.4	211	83.4	82.7	2.3	2.4	0.1	0.1
BROOKS	047	00000	600	7,976	7,733	7,579	-0.4	211	75.8	75.0	0.2	0.2	0.2	0.2
BROWN	049	15220	662	37,674	38,531	39,028	0.3	139	87.4	84.9	4.0	4.3	0.4	0.5
BURLESON	051	17780	625	16,470	17,743	18,575	1.0	75	74.1	70.6	15.1	15.9	0.2	0.2
BURNET	053	00000	635	34,147	43,414	50,968	3.4	14	89.6	87.3	1.5	1.6	0.3	0.4
CALDWELL	055	12420	635	32,194	36,883	39,428	1.9	39	70.1	66.8	8.5	8.3	0.4	0.4
CALHOUN	057	47020	618	20,647	20,794	20,862	0.1	159	78.0	75.0	2.6	2.6	3.3	3.8
CALLAHAN	059	10180	662	12,905	13,826	14,515	1.0	75	94.8	93.4	0.2	0.3	0.3	0.4
CAMERON	061	15180	636	335,227	395,867	440,440	2.3	27	80.3	79.4	0.5	0.5	0.5	0.5
CAMP	063	00000	709	11,549	12,522	13,133	1.1	69	69.5	65.9	19.2	20.1	0.2	0.3
CARSON	065	11100	634	6,516	6,626	6,716	0.2	148	93.8	92.3	0.6	0.6	0.2	0.2
CASS	067	00000	612	30,438	30,641	30,811	0.1	159	78.2	75.9	19.5	21.2	0.2	0.2
CASTRO	069	00000	634	8,285	7,696	7,333	-1.0	242	75.4	72.2	2.3	2.2	0.0	0.0
CHAMBERS	071	26420	618	26,031	33,827	40,628	3.7	11	81.9	78.4	9.8	11.8	0.7	0.5
CHEROKEE	073	27380	709	46,659	49,376	51,041	0.8	87	74.3	71.1	16.0	16.8	0.5	0.6
CHILDRESS	075	00000	634	7,688	7,756	7,684	0.1	159	67.7	66.8	14.1	14.3	0.4	0.3
CLAY	077	48660	627	11,006	11,412	11,709	0.5	117	95.3	94.3	0.4	0.5	0.1	0.1
COCHRAN	079	00000	651	3,730	3,366	3,151	-1.4	251	64.5	59.5	4.5	4.4	0.3	0.3
COKE	081	00000	661	3,864	3,902	3,878	0.1	159	88.8	88.5	1.9	2.0	0.1	0.1
COLEMAN	083	00000	662	9,235	8,724	8,495	-0.8	234	88.5	86.0	2.2	2.3	0.2	0.3
COLLIN	085	19100	623	491,675	720,059	918,111	5.4	2	81.4	77.9	4.8	5.1	7.0	8.6
COLLINGSWORTH	087	00000	634	3,206	3,035	2,897	-0.8	234	79.8	76.3	5.3	5.6	0.2	0.2
COLORADO	089	00000	618	20,390	20,960	21,265	0.4	128	72.8	69.3	14.8	15.4	0.2	0.3
COMAL	091	41700	641	78,021	105,664	131,754	4.3	8	89.1	86.7	0.9	1.0	0.5	0.6
COMANCHE	093	00000	623	14,026	13,937	13,983	-0.1	178	87.3	86.8	0.4	0.5	0.1	0.1
CONCHO	095	00000	661	3,966	3,868	3,826	-0.3	202	88.2	87.9	1.0	1.0	0.2	0.2
COOKE	097	23620	623	36,363	39,158	40,678	1.0	75	88.8	86.5	3.1	3.3	0.3	0.4
CORYELL	099	28660	625	74,978	77,356	79,161	0.4	128	65.3	61.7	21.8	22.8	2.2	2.7
COTTLE	101	00000	634	1,904	1,749	1,664	-1.2	248	81.5	78.8	9.9	10.4	0.0	0.0
CRANE	103	00000	633	3,996	3,985	4,003	0.0	170	73.7	73.0	2.9	2.9	0.4	0.4
CROCKETT	105	00000	661	4,099	3,978	3,914	-0.4	211	76.3	73.2	0.7	0.7	0.3	0.3
CROSBY	107	31180	651	7,072	6,795	6,610	-0.5	219	63.8	59.0	3.9	3.8	0.1	0.1
CULBERSON	109	00000	765	2,975	2,710	2,536	-1.3	250	68.9	66.5	0.7	0.8	0.6	0.6
DALLAM	111	00000	634	6,222	6,125	6,056	-0.2	190	82.6	82.0	1.6	1.7	0.2	0.2
DALLAS	113	19100	623	2,218,899	2,378,203	2,487,978	1.0	75	58.4	55.1	20.3	20.0	4.0	4.6
DAWSON	115	29500	651	14,985	14,300	13,871	-0.6	225	72.5	70.0	8.7	8.3	0.2	0.3
DEAF SMITH	117	25820	634	18,561	18,629	18,706	0.1	159	72.3	71.8	1.5	1.5	0.4	0.4
DELTA	119	19100	623	5,327	5,384	5,420	0.1	159	87.9	87.6	8.3	8.5	0.2	0.1
DENTON	121	19100	623	432,976	604,608	755,462	4.7	6	81.7	78.5	5.9	6.2	4.1	5.0
DEWITT	123	00000	641	20,013	20,630	21,088	0.4	128	76.4	73.6	11.0	11.3	0.2	0.3
DICKENS	125	00000	651	2,762	2,713	2,687	-0.2	190	77.6	76.9	8.2	8.3	0.4	0.4
DIMMIT	127	00000	641	10,248	10,019	9,841	-0.3	202	77.0	76.0	0.9	0.8	0.7	0.8
DONLEY	129	00000	634	3,828	3,879	3,792	0.2	148	91.4	91.1	3.9	4.0	0.1	0.1
DUVAL	131	00000	600	13,120	12,945	12,730	-0.2	190	80.2	79.4	0.5	0.5	0.1	0.2
EASTLAND	133	00000	662	18,297	18,541	18,704	0.2	148	91.0	89.0	2.2	2.4	0.2	0.3
ECTOR	135	36220	633	121,123	126,294	128,880	0.6	105	73.7	70.2	4.6	4.5	0.7	0.8
EDWARDS	137	00000	641	2,162	2,036	1,957	-0.8	234	83.3	80.6	0.8	0.9	0.1	0.1
ELLIS	139	19100	623	111,360	142,282	167,952	3.4	14	80.6	77.7	8.6	9.1	0.4	0.5
EL PASO	141	21340	765	679,622	751,891	804,703	1.4	57	73.9	73.0	3.1	2.8	1.1	1.1
ERATH	143	44500	623	33,001	34,968	36,151	0.8	87	89.7	87.2	0.8	0.9	0.4	0.5
FALLS	145	00000	625	18,576	18,003	17,529	-0.4	211	61.5	58.1	27.5	28.4	0.1	0.2
FANNIN	147	14300	623	31,242	34,311	36,550	1.3	61	86.6	84.5	8.0	8.7	0.3	0.4
FAYETTE	149	00000	635	21,804	22,909	23,658	0.7	94	84.6	81.8	7.0	7.5	0.3	0.4
FISHER	151	00000	662	4,344	4,230	4,174	-0.4	211	83.7	80.4	2.8	2.9	0.1	0.2
FLOYD	153	00000	651	7,771	7,253	6,849	-0.9	238	74.2	70.6	3.4	3.3	0.2	0.2
TEXAS							2.0		71.0	68.4	11.5	11.4	2.8	3.3
UNITED STATES							1.2		75.1	72.7	12.3	12.6	3.8	4.5

 59-A

TEXAS

B

COUNTY	% HISPANIC ORIGIN		2007 AGE DISTRIBUTION (%)										MEDIAN AGE	% 2007 Males	% 2007 Females
	2000	2007	0-4	5-9	10-14	15-19	20-24	25-44	45-64	65-84	85+	18+	2007		
ANDERSON	12.2	15.3	5.7	5.4	4.8	5.3	8.1	36.1	23.0	9.8	1.8	80.9	36.2	60.8	39.2
ANDREWS	40.0	47.1	8.0	7.0	6.7	8.2	9.2	23.8	24.7	11.1	1.3	73.2	35.0	49.5	50.5
ANGELINA	14.3	18.1	8.0	7.2	6.7	6.7	7.1	27.5	24.1	10.8	1.8	74.0	35.1	49.2	50.8
ARANSAS	20.3	25.2	5.7	5.1	5.6	6.1	6.7	19.5	30.5	18.6	2.2	79.9	45.8	50.0	50.0
ARCHER	4.9	6.4	6.8	6.2	7.3	7.0	6.5	23.8	28.6	12.4	1.6	75.3	40.6	50.0	50.0
ARMSTRONG	5.4	5.7	5.6	5.6	5.9	7.2	5.7	21.8	28.9	15.5	3.7	78.1	43.5	49.6	50.4
ATASCOSA	58.6	65.4	8.7	8.0	7.6	8.1	7.6	26.1	23.4	9.2	1.3	70.6	32.9	49.4	50.6
AUSTIN	16.1	20.3	6.9	6.4	6.6	6.4	7.0	24.2	28.3	11.7	2.4	76.1	39.3	49.6	50.4
BAILEY	47.3	48.9	8.7	7.9	7.2	7.0	7.4	23.4	24.0	12.4	2.2	72.0	35.4	49.1	50.9
BANDERA	13.5	17.3	5.6	5.6	5.7	7.1	5.7	21.2	32.5	15.1	1.6	78.5	44.4	49.6	50.4
BASTROP	24.0	29.4	7.5	7.2	6.9	6.9	6.9	26.4	27.6	9.3	1.3	74.1	37.0	51.2	48.8
BAYLOR	9.3	12.1	5.4	4.0	5.3	7.9	7.4	18.5	28.5	18.8	4.2	80.2	46.0	47.1	52.9
BEE	53.9	60.4	6.1	5.5	5.4	6.9	11.1	35.4	19.7	8.6	1.3	79.4	31.5	60.9	39.1
BELL	16.7	20.5	9.2	7.7	6.9	7.3	9.4	31.1	19.8	7.4	1.2	72.2	29.9	50.2	49.8
BEXAR	54.3	60.7	8.0	7.4	7.2	7.5	7.8	28.8	23.2	8.8	1.4	73.1	33.2	48.8	51.2
BLANCO	15.3	19.5	6.2	6.1	5.6	5.9	5.7	21.5	33.4	12.7	2.8	78.5	44.2	49.6	50.4
BORDEN	11.9	12.6	4.6	3.4	4.7	6.6	8.0	22.5	30.9	18.1	1.2	83.5	45.1	50.6	49.4
BOSQUE	12.2	15.7	6.3	5.5	5.5	6.3	5.9	21.2	30.0	15.7	3.7	78.8	44.5	49.4	50.6
BOWIE	4.5	5.7	6.6	6.0	6.4	6.1	7.3	28.1	26.1	11.3	2.1	77.3	37.7	50.5	49.5
BRAZORIA	22.8	27.9	8.2	7.6	7.2	7.0	7.2	29.0	25.1	7.9	0.9	72.8	34.7	51.3	48.7
BRAZOS	17.9	22.1	6.5	5.3	5.2	11.4	22.3	26.6	16.0	5.6	1.0	79.4	24.8	50.8	49.2
BREWSTER	43.6	50.8	5.7	5.0	5.5	7.3	8.0	26.5	26.9	13.3	1.7	80.3	36.6	50.1	49.9
BRISCOE	22.7	23.9	7.3	6.7	6.1	6.7	6.6	22.2	26.1	15.7	2.5	75.9	41.5	49.4	50.6
BROOKS	91.6	93.5	8.6	7.5	7.9	7.8	7.0	22.0	24.4	12.9	1.9	71.1	35.9	48.6	51.4
BROWN	15.4	19.5	6.4	5.9	5.9	8.6	7.7	22.8	26.1	13.9	2.6	76.8	39.2	49.7	50.3
BURLESON	14.6	18.4	7.2	6.4	5.9	6.7	7.1	23.5	27.0	13.9	2.2	76.5	39.6	49.0	51.0
BURNET	14.8	18.8	6.7	6.6	5.6	6.1	6.1	22.9	28.2	15.6	2.3	77.5	42.2	48.7	51.3
CALDWELL	40.4	47.2	7.7	6.8	6.8	7.4	7.6	27.7	24.0	10.1	2.0	73.9	35.3	49.8	50.2
CALHOUN	40.9	47.6	8.3	7.5	7.5	6.6	5.9	25.5	25.1	12.2	1.3	72.8	36.7	50.5	49.5
CALLAHAN	6.3	8.3	5.9	5.3	5.5	7.1	7.4	22.5	28.1	15.7	2.4	78.8	42.6	48.4	51.6
CAMERON	84.3	87.7	10.1	8.9	8.5	8.2	7.6	26.7	19.4	9.4	1.2	67.6	29.6	48.2	51.8
CAMP	14.8	18.5	7.7	7.1	6.6	6.2	5.7	25.7	24.7	13.9	2.3	74.8	38.4	49.1	50.9
CARSON	7.0	9.2	6.5	5.9	6.4	6.9	7.5	21.7	28.0	14.4	2.6	76.7	41.7	49.4	50.6
CASS	1.7	2.3	6.3	5.8	6.0	5.7	6.7	23.2	28.7	14.7	2.9	78.5	42.2	48.5	51.5
CASTRO	51.6	58.8	9.0	8.0	8.5	8.1	6.8	22.5	24.6	10.9	1.5	69.2	33.5	49.8	50.2
CHAMBERS	10.8	13.6	6.9	6.4	7.0	6.6	8.0	25.7	29.6	8.8	1.0	75.5	37.4	49.9	50.1
CHEROKEE	13.2	16.7	7.3	6.5	6.6	6.6	6.7	26.9	24.7	12.3	2.3	75.8	37.2	50.6	49.4
CHILDRESS	20.5	21.4	6.0	5.4	5.0	7.0	11.0	29.5	21.8	11.8	2.4	79.7	36.2	60.2	39.8
CLAY	3.7	4.9	6.1	5.7	5.8	6.3	6.2	23.1	30.2	14.5	2.0	78.5	43.1	48.6	51.4
COCHRAN	44.1	51.3	7.5	6.9	7.3	8.8	7.8	24.3	21.7	13.8	1.9	72.4	36.3	48.2	51.8
COKE	16.9	17.9	5.0	4.0	5.8	10.2	7.4	17.8	26.1	19.6	4.1	79.0	44.8	50.3	49.7
COLEMAN	14.0	17.9	6.4	5.8	5.2	6.3	6.6	20.6	26.6	18.2	4.3	78.7	44.3	48.2	51.8
COLLIN	10.3	13.0	8.7	9.1	8.2	6.6	5.4	32.5	23.9	5.1	0.5	69.8	34.3	49.9	50.1
COLLINGSWORTH	20.4	25.4	6.6	5.6	5.7	7.0	8.6	20.9	25.5	15.9	4.2	77.9	42.2	48.8	51.2
COLORADO	19.7	24.5	6.4	5.8	5.8	7.5	7.9	20.9	27.5	15.1	3.2	77.9	41.6	49.0	51.0
COMAL	22.6	28.1	6.3	6.3	6.2	7.1	5.6	24.0	29.6	12.8	2.1	76.7	41.3	49.1	50.9
COMANCHE	20.9	22.0	6.9	6.4	5.9	6.7	5.6	23.4	24.6	16.9	3.6	76.7	41.3	49.1	50.9
CONCHO	41.3	43.1	4.2	3.9	3.7	4.2	10.1	37.6	22.9	11.1	2.4	85.8	36.3	64.7	35.3
COOKE	10.0	12.9	7.0	6.2	6.4	7.9	6.9	24.1	26.1	13.1	2.2	75.6	38.5	49.7	50.3
CORYELL	12.6	15.7	8.2	7.4	6.2	7.6	12.9	35.7	15.8	5.5	0.7	74.7	28.4	51.2	48.8
COTTLE	18.9	23.6	5.5	5.3	5.5	7.3	5.5	21.0	26.5	18.7	4.6	78.7	44.8	47.9	52.1
CRANE	43.9	45.5	8.0	7.4	7.5	7.3	9.7	22.3	25.3	10.7	1.8	72.5	36.2	49.2	50.8
CROCKETT	54.7	61.8	7.0	6.5	6.4	7.7	8.3	21.6	28.6	11.5	2.2	75.1	38.9	49.5	50.5
CROSBY	48.9	56.2	8.8	7.2	7.2	7.5	6.7	23.3	24.1	12.3	2.9	71.8	35.1	47.7	52.3
CULBERSON	72.2	77.2	7.9	7.0	7.9	7.7	9.9	23.9	22.5	12.0	1.0	72.5	34.0	50.5	49.5
DALLAM	28.4	29.8	9.0	7.9	8.6	7.6	7.1	28.7	21.5	8.5	1.0	69.5	32.4	50.6	49.4
DALLAS	29.9	35.2	8.1	7.6	7.3	7.1	7.5	31.7	22.1	7.4	1.1	72.7	32.5	50.0	50.0
DAWSON	48.2	55.0	6.8	5.9	5.8	6.7	8.7	30.1	22.5	11.2	2.3	77.4	35.8	55.9	44.1
DEAF SMITH	57.4	59.1	9.4	8.7	8.1	8.0	7.3	25.0	20.7	11.0	1.9	68.9	31.2	48.8	51.2
DELTA	3.1	3.3	6.5	5.3	6.8	6.4	7.2	25.3	26.4	13.0	3.0	77.5	40.5	49.0	51.0
DENTON	12.2	15.4	8.3	8.1	7.2	6.9	7.6	33.2	23.1	4.9	0.6	72.4	32.7	49.9	50.1
DEWITT	27.2	33.0	5.9	5.2	5.7	5.9	6.0	26.4	27.0	14.5	3.2	79.3	41.8	51.7	48.3
DICKENS	23.9	25.1	4.4	4.5	4.1	5.3	9.2	29.6	23.8	15.2	4.0	83.5	40.4	57.4	42.6
DIMMIT	85.0	88.0	8.8	7.5	8.6	9.0	7.6	23.1	23.3	10.5	1.7	69.4	32.3	48.6	51.4
DONLEY	6.3	6.7	4.8	4.3	5.9	9.7	7.4	18.2	27.2	18.9	3.5	80.2	44.7	49.0	51.0
DUVAL	88.0	90.6	7.9	7.1	7.0	8.3	7.8	26.0	22.3	11.7	1.8	72.7	34.1	50.3	49.7
EASTLAND	10.8	14.0	6.3	5.7	5.3	7.4	7.9	20.0	27.0	16.9	3.4	79.0	42.7	48.7	51.3
ECTOR	42.4	49.3	8.4	7.1	7.4	7.8	9.3	25.8	23.2	9.7	1.3	72.5	31.9	49.0	51.0
EDWARDS	45.1	52.3	6.4	4.6	7.8	8.9	8.0	18.5	27.8	16.6	1.5	75.4	42.1	50.9	49.1
ELLIS	18.4	23.0	7.8	7.1	6.9	7.9	8.2	26.6	25.9	8.3	1.2	73.4	34.4	49.7	50.3
EL PASO	78.2	82.3	9.2	8.1	8.4	7.9	8.3	28.0	20.7	8.4	1.0	69.5	30.3	48.5	51.5
ERATH	15.0	19.2	6.7	6.0	5.9	8.7	9.7	27.8	22.4	10.4	2.4	77.7	32.4	49.8	50.2
FALLS	15.8	19.6	6.4	5.6	6.8	8.8	7.3	24.8	24.3	13.2	2.8	75.3	37.6	46.3	53.7
FANNIN	5.6	7.3	6.2	5.6	5.9	6.2	7.6	26.9	25.7	13.6	2.5	78.9	39.7	53.1	46.9
FAYETTE	12.8	16.4	5.8	5.3	5.8	5.7	6.3	21.8	28.9	16.0	4.4	79.6	44.5	49.0	51.0
FISHER	21.4	26.7	6.4	5.7	5.3	6.4	5.9	20.5	27.6	18.4	3.8	78.9	44.8	48.5	51.5
FLOYD	45.9	53.1	8.6	8.1	8.2	7.6	6.1	23.0	22.6	12.8	3.0	70.2	35.7	48.6	51.4
TEXAS	32.0	36.4	8.0	7.4	7.2	7.3	7.8	28.9	23.5	8.6	1.3	73.1	33.4	49.7	50.3
UNITED STATES	12.5	15.0	6.9	6.5	6.8	7.1	7.0	27.6	25.4	10.7	1.9	75.6	36.7	49.2	50.8

COUNTY	HOUSEHOLDS					FAMILIES			MEDIAN HOUSEHOLD INCOME			
	2000	2007	2012	% Annual Rate 2000-2007	2007 Average HH Size	2000	2007	% Annual Rate 2000-2007	2007	2012	2007 National Rank	2007 State Rank
ANDERSON	15,678	16,491	17,029	0.7	2.55	11,343	11,818	0.6	38,497	43,832	1930	119
ANDREWS	4,601	4,602	4,583	0.0	2.75	3,519	3,489	-0.1	40,525	46,242	1658	89
ANGELINA	28,685	30,175	31,111	0.7	2.68	21,263	22,161	0.6	41,131	47,371	1584	80
ARANSAS	9,132	10,462	11,481	1.9	2.40	6,397	7,251	1.7	38,806	45,412	1875	111
ARCHER	3,345	3,470	3,545	0.5	2.61	2,517	2,588	0.4	45,807	52,275	1022	42
ARMSTRONG	802	819	833	0.3	2.59	613	622	0.2	45,343	51,343	1071	48
ATASCOSA	12,816	14,655	15,866	1.9	2.97	10,016	11,364	1.8	39,965	45,450	1729	94
AUSTIN	8,747	9,917	10,825	1.7	2.68	6,479	7,279	1.6	46,075	52,407	993	40
BAILEY	2,348	2,368	2,384	0.1	2.76	1,778	1,778	0.0	34,185	38,639	2530	191
BANDERA	7,010	8,096	8,819	2.0	2.50	5,060	5,786	1.9	46,930	52,378	914	35
BASTROP	20,097	25,423	29,136	3.3	2.77	14,776	18,517	3.2	52,709	58,996	511	25
BAYLOR	1,791	1,695	1,630	-0.8	2.26	1,157	1,080	-0.9	30,203	35,250	2898	237
BEE	9,061	9,144	9,087	0.1	2.70	6,580	6,574	0.0	34,817	39,346	2454	181
BELL	85,507	101,384	113,843	2.4	2.64	61,971	72,748	2.2	46,098	53,620	989	39
BEXAR	488,942	556,250	609,175	1.8	2.79	345,717	389,208	1.6	48,672	56,620	770	30
BLANCO	3,303	3,759	4,021	1.8	2.51	2,390	2,693	1.7	46,949	52,945	912	33
BORDEN	292	305	312	0.6	2.43	217	225	0.5	34,850	38,779	2448	179
BOSQUE	6,726	7,318	7,717	1.2	2.48	4,854	5,230	1.0	41,541	48,233	1513	77
BOWIE	33,058	35,170	36,290	0.9	2.45	23,426	24,658	0.7	40,527	46,904	1657	88
BRAZORIA	81,954	101,390	117,286	3.0	2.81	63,128	77,458	2.9	60,911	71,714	245	9
BRAZOS	55,202	62,663	65,999	1.8	2.50	30,390	33,952	1.5	36,938	43,598	2136	145
BREWSTER	3,669	3,800	3,876	0.5	2.27	2,216	2,263	0.3	33,279	38,211	2632	208
BRISCOE	724	704	693	-0.4	2.47	511	492	-0.5	35,077	38,623	2420	175
BROOKS	2,711	2,668	2,632	-0.2	2.87	2,080	2,030	-0.3	22,202	25,513	3124	252
BROWN	14,306	14,716	14,948	0.4	2.47	10,013	10,189	0.2	37,871	43,697	2013	131
BURLESON	6,363	6,864	7,194	1.1	2.57	4,572	4,882	0.9	40,103	46,182	1711	92
BURNET	13,133	16,565	19,446	3.3	2.55	9,661	12,071	3.1	45,499	52,476	1051	46
CALDWELL	10,816	12,488	13,395	2.0	2.82	8,075	9,239	1.9	44,063	50,429	1203	57
CALHOUN	7,442	7,519	7,559	0.1	2.74	5,572	5,579	0.0	42,513	48,479	1396	67
CALLAHAN	5,061	5,455	5,745	1.0	2.51	3,752	4,007	0.9	38,592	43,828	1919	116
CAMERON	97,267	115,756	129,335	2.4	3.38	79,944	94,531	2.3	31,956	36,654	2767	220
CAMP	4,336	4,689	4,912	1.1	2.63	3,158	3,381	0.9	37,123	42,023	2112	141
CARSON	2,470	2,547	2,597	0.4	2.56	1,884	1,926	0.3	47,613	53,967	854	31
CASS	12,190	12,538	12,728	0.4	2.41	8,658	8,813	0.2	34,330	39,027	2510	188
CASTRO	2,761	2,612	2,507	-0.8	2.93	2,160	2,025	-0.9	36,019	40,513	2273	159
CHAMBERS	9,139	11,981	14,459	3.8	2.80	7,216	9,389	3.7	57,560	66,467	318	12
CHEROKEE	16,651	17,636	18,238	0.8	2.64	12,098	12,688	0.7	34,844	39,508	2450	180
CHILDRESS	2,474	2,436	2,406	-0.2	2.40	1,651	1,606	-0.4	34,798	39,824	2456	182
CLAY	4,323	4,532	4,674	0.7	2.50	3,181	3,302	0.5	42,592	48,540	1385	65
COCHRAN	1,309	1,204	1,137	-1.1	2.73	1,017	929	-1.2	32,736	36,806	2680	213
COKE	1,544	1,579	1,578	0.3	2.28	1,068	1,080	0.2	35,639	40,911	2343	166
COLEMAN	3,889	3,685	3,592	-0.7	2.32	2,608	2,443	-0.9	31,303	36,033	2812	223
COLLIN	181,970	264,298	337,714	5.3	2.71	132,268	190,207	5.1	93,175	115,892	14	1
COLLINGSWORTH	1,294	1,218	1,161	-0.8	2.44	916	854	-1.0	30,856	35,543	2848	233
COLORADO	7,641	7,846	7,971	0.4	2.55	5,406	5,492	0.2	39,960	45,518	1730	95
COMAL	29,066	39,026	48,686	4.1	2.68	21,881	29,117	4.0	56,284	64,385	355	13
COMANCHE	5,522	5,466	5,476	-0.1	2.49	3,925	3,844	-0.3	34,099	38,502	2540	194
CONCHO	1,058	1,027	1,013	-0.4	2.43	758	728	-0.6	37,677	42,500	2038	134
COOKE	13,643	14,692	15,276	1.0	2.60	10,004	10,668	0.9	45,447	51,875	1058	47
CORYELL	19,950	20,895	21,568	0.6	2.89	15,782	16,407	0.5	44,578	51,886	1151	51
COTTLE	820	770	738	-0.9	2.23	550	509	-1.1	31,127	35,561	2822	226
CRANE	1,360	1,365	1,378	0.1	2.87	1,083	1,079	-0.1	38,834	43,751	1874	110
CROCKETT	1,524	1,494	1,479	-0.3	2.62	1,114	1,081	-0.4	34,422	38,513	2504	186
CROSBY	2,512	2,437	2,381	-0.4	2.75	1,866	1,792	-0.6	30,961	35,514	2836	231
CULBERSON	1,052	994	943	-0.8	2.72	797	747	-0.9	30,896	34,949	2844	232
DALLAM	2,317	2,246	2,205	-0.4	2.72	1,628	1,562	-0.6	34,064	39,199	2544	195
DALLAS	807,621	847,325	880,576	0.7	2.76	533,613	553,069	0.5	55,842	66,099	368	15
DAWSON	4,726	4,542	4,408	-0.5	2.65	3,503	3,335	-0.7	34,039	38,504	2545	196
DEAF SMITH	6,180	6,275	6,334	0.2	2.93	4,834	4,870	0.1	35,037	39,735	2424	176
DELTA	2,094	2,118	2,131	0.2	2.49	1,462	1,463	0.0	36,098	41,330	2256	156
DENTON	158,903	216,618	269,835	4.4	2.74	111,324	150,134	4.2	75,743	90,210	80	5
DEWITT	7,207	7,474	7,667	0.5	2.52	5,132	5,269	0.4	34,637	39,197	2483	185
DICKENS	980	970	964	-0.1	2.26	639	625	-0.3	31,148	35,548	2819	225
DIMMIT	3,308	3,339	3,327	0.1	2.96	2,645	2,651	0.0	26,775	30,748	3045	246
DONLEY	1,578	1,567	1,532	-0.1	2.29	1,057	1,037	-0.3	35,707	40,597	2330	163
DUVAL	4,350	4,355	4,327	0.0	2.81	3,268	3,246	-0.1	26,940	30,316	3039	244
EASTLAND	7,321	7,396	7,463	0.1	2.39	5,036	5,031	0.0	33,131	38,223	2643	210
ECTOR	43,846	45,823	46,904	0.6	2.71	31,716	32,821	0.5	38,767	45,368	1884	112
EDWARDS	801	771	748	-0.5	2.60	586	559	-0.6	31,162	35,744	2818	224
ELLIS	37,020	47,078	55,585	3.4	2.98	29,660	37,451	3.3	61,939	71,108	214	7
EL PASO	210,022	235,442	253,403	1.6	3.14	166,226	184,953	1.5	38,488	44,472	1931	120
ERATH	12,568	13,142	13,579	0.6	2.50	8,108	8,372	0.4	37,110	42,177	2114	142
FALLS	6,496	6,291	6,102	-0.4	2.54	4,410	4,220	-0.6	32,533	37,253	2702	215
FANNIN	11,105	12,228	13,093	1.3	2.52	7,990	8,711	1.2	41,384	47,369	1537	78
FAYETTE	8,722	9,171	9,476	0.7	2.44	6,047	6,286	0.5	41,579	47,620	1507	76
FISHER	1,785	1,771	1,762	-0.1	2.35	1,245	1,222	-0.3	33,889	38,418	2563	200
FLOYD	2,730	2,548	2,405	-0.9	2.79	2,111	1,954	-1.1	32,944	37,701	2662	211
TEXAS				1.9	2.76			1.8	51,090	60,298		
UNITED STATES				1.2	2.59			1.0	53,154	62,503		

COUNTY	2007 Per Capita Income	2007 HH Income Base	2007 HOUSEHOLD INCOME DISTRIBUTION (%)					2007 Home Value Base	2007 HOME VALUE DISTRIBUTION (%)					2007 Median Home Value
			Less than $25,000	$25,000 to $49,999	$50,000 to $99,999	$100,000 to $149,999	$150,000 or More		Less than $50,000	$50,000 to $89,999	$90,000 to $174,999	$175,000 to $399,999	$400,000 or More	
ANDERSON	18,054	16,491	31.7	30.9	28.4	6.1	2.9	12,408	27.5	30.4	29.2	10.9	1.9	79,280
ANDREWS	18,938	4,602	28.0	33.9	30.0	5.5	2.6	3,692	42.4	31.0	20.9	5.4	0.3	56,409
ANGELINA	19,599	30,175	29.3	30.2	30.0	7.4	3.1	22,234	27.5	30.1	31.5	9.6	1.3	80,440
ARANSAS	23,079	10,462	32.0	29.1	25.9	8.9	4.1	8,028	27.0	20.9	30.8	16.2	5.1	94,507
ARCHER	23,207	3,470	24.6	29.3	32.9	9.1	4.1	2,857	30.2	25.9	31.0	11.3	1.5	78,173
ARMSTRONG	20,666	819	25.6	29.5	33.1	9.3	2.4	658	25.7	26.7	31.8	13.4	2.4	85,556
ATASCOSA	17,084	14,655	32.5	28.6	29.4	6.9	2.6	11,616	32.9	28.0	28.2	9.0	2.0	72,335
AUSTIN	22,032	9,917	24.6	29.4	31.6	10.1	4.4	7,805	16.2	18.2	34.2	24.4	7.1	119,040
BAILEY	16,020	2,368	36.0	32.7	24.2	4.8	2.3	1,731	47.6	27.0	20.6	4.5	0.3	53,609
BANDERA	23,765	8,096	25.4	26.9	33.7	9.9	4.0	6,787	14.3	18.2	33.9	29.0	4.7	127,160
BASTROP	22,567	25,423	21.2	25.7	37.2	11.6	4.3	20,686	15.2	18.5	38.9	24.1	3.3	122,847
BAYLOR	18,281	1,695	41.2	31.0	21.8	4.2	1.7	1,250	47.0	27.4	20.3	4.8	0.5	53,455
BEE	15,591	9,144	36.7	29.4	27.4	5.1	1.4	6,185	31.9	36.0	24.4	6.4	1.3	69,375
BELL	22,062	101,384	21.1	33.2	32.8	8.7	4.1	58,760	13.9	24.6	46.3	13.4	1.8	102,966
BEXAR	23,134	556,235	23.8	27.2	32.2	10.5	6.2	351,079	12.4	27.2	38.4	18.2	3.8	105,637
BLANCO	23,926	3,759	25.9	27.0	32.5	10.0	4.5	3,014	8.3	17.7	36.1	26.6	11.2	143,794
BORDEN	22,530	305	33.1	28.5	25.2	9.2	3.9	231	38.1	28.1	22.5	7.8	3.5	69,167
BOSQUE	21,528	7,318	29.4	29.6	30.2	7.4	3.4	5,779	27.0	26.0	30.5	13.1	3.4	85,274
BOWIE	21,654	35,170	31.7	27.3	29.3	8.1	3.6	25,439	27.5	28.1	32.9	9.7	1.7	80,468
BRAZORIA	26,132	101,390	17.1	23.1	35.8	16.3	7.7	76,635	15.4	18.9	39.9	23.8	1.9	116,653
BRAZOS	21,806	62,663	37.5	22.8	25.4	8.7	5.6	29,725	16.5	16.2	38.2	25.0	4.0	124,051
BREWSTER	19,475	3,800	37.0	31.0	23.7	5.5	2.8	2,356	30.1	22.1	30.1	13.4	4.4	86,408
BRISCOE	17,236	704	36.1	32.7	25.1	5.1	1.0	553	52.1	28.0	16.8	2.0	1.1	47,946
BROOKS	12,319	2,668	54.2	24.4	17.2	2.6	1.6	1,977	53.4	27.0	16.6	2.7	0.3	45,439
BROWN	19,547	14,716	33.5	28.8	28.7	6.3	2.7	10,844	35.3	30.5	24.6	8.4	1.2	68,137
BURLESON	20,098	6,864	30.7	30.4	28.6	7.7	2.7	5,536	31.3	28.2	26.6	12.0	1.9	75,436
BURNET	23,519	16,565	24.6	29.3	31.8	9.3	5.0	13,170	15.3	19.2	32.2	24.7	8.6	121,083
CALDWELL	19,005	12,488	24.9	31.1	33.0	8.4	2.6	8,941	21.1	25.6	36.4	13.6	3.3	94,517
CALHOUN	20,025	7,519	28.7	28.7	30.7	8.6	3.4	5,602	30.9	31.0	28.4	9.1	0.5	73,832
CALLAHAN	18,686	5,455	31.4	33.3	27.8	5.7	1.7	4,457	33.1	30.5	27.4	7.8	1.1	73,186
CAMERON	13,293	115,756	39.8	29.1	22.7	5.7	2.7	80,004	35.1	32.0	24.0	7.8	1.1	66,456
CAMP	18,971	4,689	35.1	30.1	24.9	7.0	2.9	3,568	23.6	32.4	30.3	11.5	2.2	81,634
CARSON	23,103	2,547	21.0	31.8	34.4	9.6	3.3	2,154	32.6	30.3	29.2	7.1	0.9	71,265
CASS	19,129	12,538	36.4	30.6	25.1	5.6	2.4	9,980	32.3	31.3	28.5	6.8	1.0	70,661
CASTRO	16,575	2,612	32.4	34.1	24.3	6.2	3.1	1,898	35.9	30.2	24.6	7.4	1.9	70,179
CHAMBERS	24,699	11,981	20.1	21.4	36.5	16.7	5.3	10,106	27.5	20.2	32.2	17.9	2.2	95,054
CHEROKEE	17,557	17,636	34.6	32.5	25.2	5.2	2.6	13,289	32.1	29.2	27.0	10.0	1.6	73,090
CHILDRESS	17,467	2,436	36.3	30.0	28.4	3.4	1.9	1,755	39.7	29.6	25.7	3.8	1.2	63,442
CLAY	20,402	4,532	26.5	31.8	32.2	7.3	2.2	3,792	33.2	28.3	28.5	8.7	1.3	70,731
COCHRAN	16,543	1,204	37.5	32.6	22.2	4.9	2.8	907	61.0	23.3	11.8	3.3	0.7	39,657
COKE	21,209	1,579	35.2	29.0	25.4	7.3	3.1	1,260	36.5	31.2	25.5	5.0	1.8	67,238
COLEMAN	18,525	3,685	39.9	34.6	20.9	4.6	2.9	2,779	48.5	25.2	16.2	7.2	2.8	51,680
COLLIN	46,033	264,294	7.1	14.1	32.3	22.0	24.4	187,187	3.1	4.2	24.5	55.2	13.0	216,028
COLLINGSWORTH	18,342	1,218	38.8	32.3	19.9	6.2	2.9	967	47.8	27.4	20.4	3.8	0.6	52,945
COLORADO	21,259	7,846	32.5	26.5	29.8	6.7	4.5	6,109	29.0	25.9	26.8	14.9	3.3	82,586
COMAL	26,995	39,026	17.3	25.8	36.8	12.7	7.4	30,709	9.0	14.5	32.7	35.1	8.7	156,652
COMANCHE	17,504	5,466	38.2	29.6	25.5	5.0	1.7	4,234	36.3	26.1	25.6	8.5	3.4	68,127
CONCHO	19,613	1,027	32.9	29.6	27.7	5.1	4.8	785	39.0	28.5	20.0	8.2	4.3	66,846
COOKE	21,926	14,692	26.2	28.5	31.9	10.0	3.4	10,846	18.3	25.5	34.0	18.0	4.2	100,702
CORYELL	17,754	20,895	20.5	35.6	34.1	7.2	2.7	11,892	14.7	32.7	43.2	8.3	1.1	92,658
COTTLE	18,452	770	40.6	31.0	22.3	4.0	1.9	564	60.8	21.6	13.3	4.3	0.0	41,757
CRANE	17,443	1,365	31.0	31.6	27.4	8.4	1.5	1,161	44.3	36.7	16.1	2.2	0.7	54,290
CROCKETT	17,404	1,494	34.9	27.8	30.1	5.3	2.0	1,090	37.8	27.2	25.6	7.9	1.6	66,500
CROSBY	17,101	2,437	40.7	30.1	21.0	5.0	3.2	1,734	50.6	30.2	16.8	2.1	0.4	49,482
CULBERSON	14,053	994	41.8	31.6	22.9	2.4	1.3	715	54.3	28.1	13.0	2.8	1.8	46,789
DALLAM	16,461	2,246	34.0	34.6	25.2	3.7	2.6	1,461	32.9	41.8	19.5	4.2	1.6	65,780
DALLAS	28,577	847,314	18.1	26.2	32.9	12.9	10.0	462,643	8.8	22.3	42.5	20.1	6.3	116,192
DAWSON	18,278	4,542	35.3	32.8	22.8	4.9	4.2	3,402	43.9	29.2	20.1	6.5	0.3	57,647
DEAF SMITH	15,870	6,275	33.9	34.1	24.6	5.1	2.2	4,344	34.7	32.0	26.0	6.4	1.0	67,031
DELTA	18,938	2,118	36.0	28.2	27.5	6.1	2.2	1,658	40.3	33.4	21.8	4.2	0.4	56,880
DENTON	35,857	216,618	11.2	18.8	33.8	20.3	15.9	144,221	5.3	6.6	37.4	42.6	8.2	176,700
DEWITT	18,331	7,474	35.3	31.5	24.2	6.5	2.6	5,822	34.1	29.5	25.0	9.1	2.2	69,564
DICKENS	17,128	970	41.8	30.4	22.6	3.8	1.4	763	60.9	23.6	13.0	2.5	0.0	39,670
DIMMIT	11,716	3,339	47.3	29.4	19.8	3.0	0.5	2,492	58.5	24.4	13.9	2.7	0.5	42,664
DONLEY	19,842	1,567	35.0	31.3	25.3	6.3	2.2	1,194	38.9	27.3	24.5	7.5	1.8	64,458
DUVAL	14,034	4,355	46.6	27.1	21.0	3.4	2.0	3,569	59.5	22.7	13.8	3.8	0.3	41,642
EASTLAND	18,773	7,396	36.6	33.8	21.9	4.7	3.0	5,740	48.8	26.1	17.8	6.0	1.3	51,607
ECTOR	18,833	45,823	31.1	31.4	27.7	6.6	3.2	31,960	32.6	32.2	27.1	7.4	0.7	70,421
EDWARDS	16,165	771	41.9	27.9	23.1	5.6	1.6	620	41.0	24.2	17.6	10.5	6.8	62,245
ELLIS	25,154	47,078	16.1	22.5	38.7	15.8	6.9	36,540	11.5	20.5	42.8	21.8	3.5	117,115
EL PASO	16,921	235,442	31.7	29.6	27.2	7.8	3.7	153,782	8.2	22.5	54.0	13.2	2.0	111,776
ERATH	20,143	13,142	32.9	31.6	24.0	8.0	3.4	8,567	23.9	24.2	33.2	15.2	3.6	93,615
FALLS	17,407	6,291	40.0	28.6	23.8	5.4	2.2	4,593	41.7	30.3	19.1	7.1	1.7	58,993
FANNIN	20,027	12,228	30.0	28.7	30.9	7.4	2.9	9,311	26.9	28.6	31.0	12.0	1.5	80,770
FAYETTE	22,366	9,171	29.9	28.3	29.8	8.1	3.9	7,282	17.0	24.6	33.2	18.9	5.6	104,374
FISHER	18,842	1,771	37.7	29.7	26.3	4.2	2.1	1,380	53.5	23.7	15.9	5.9	1.1	47,333
FLOYD	17,315	2,548	36.3	30.7	22.2	7.7	3.1	1,911	47.5	26.8	20.0	5.2	0.4	53,467
TEXAS	25,413		22.9	25.9	31.0	12.0	8.1		16.4	21.8	36.0	21.0	4.7	110,551
UNITED STATES	27,916		21.9	25.0	32.3	12.3	8.4		7.9	10.5	27.1	35.6	19.0	192,285

COUNTY	FINANCIAL SERVICES				THE HOME						ENTERTAINMENT						PERSONAL			
					Home Improvements		Furnishings													
	Auto Loan	Home Loan	Invest-ments	Retire-ment Plans	Home Repair	Lawn & Garden	Comput-ers & Hard-ware	Major Appli-ances	TV, Radio, Sound Equip-ment	Furni-ture	Dine out/ Carry out	Sports Equip-ment	Fees & Tickets	Toys & Games	Travel	Cable TV	Apparel & Services	Auto Repairs	Health Insur-ance	Pets & Supplies
ANDERSON	78	63	55	62	66	80	65	74	71	64	70	64	60	71	65	74	61	71	80	77
ANDREWS	79	69	62	67	68	77	67	74	73	69	73	65	65	74	68	75	64	73	78	74
ANGELINA	82	69	60	68	69	79	70	76	74	69	74	68	66	76	69	77	65	74	80	78
ARANSAS	85	71	60	69	77	95	72	86	77	70	75	74	66	75	74	81	65	81	92	88
ARCHER	98	80	61	78	87	105	78	94	82	77	82	84	71	87	79	86	72	87	97	100
ARMSTRONG	88	68	51	65	79	100	67	86	73	66	74	75	60	78	69	78	63	78	92	92
ATASCOSA	81	69	51	65	64	74	65	73	71	68	71	65	61	71	64	73	62	72	74	74
AUSTIN	94	79	66	78	82	97	77	89	82	77	81	79	72	85	78	85	71	84	92	93
BAILEY	74	53	35	50	57	75	55	68	62	54	62	60	47	64	54	66	53	64	75	71
BANDERA	96	79	58	77	85	104	77	93	81	75	81	82	70	84	78	85	70	86	96	98
BASTROP	98	88	74	85	85	96	83	91	87	84	87	82	80	89	83	90	76	89	94	94
BAYLOR	66	48	41	47	53	68	54	62	61	49	58	54	46	61	53	65	49	58	72	64
BEE	68	56	47	54	56	67	57	64	62	57	61	56	52	62	56	64	54	62	68	65
BELL	87	77	73	79	71	74	85	78	83	81	83	74	79	85	79	82	74	83	78	79
BEXAR	94	89	84	89	81	82	90	86	91	92	91	80	88	90	87	90	82	91	86	86
BLANCO	97	78	55	76	86	108	78	96	82	75	82	84	69	84	79	87	70	88	99	100
BORDEN	99	63	27	60	77	111	67	93	73	63	75	83	51	81	65	79	62	82	97	103
BOSQUE	86	66	50	65	75	97	69	86	75	65	73	74	60	76	71	80	63	79	92	89
BOWIE	83	69	64	69	70	82	72	77	77	70	76	68	67	78	71	81	67	76	84	80
BRAZORIA	110	108	99	107	102	103	102	104	102	105	102	96	102	105	101	101	91	104	102	105
BRAZOS	79	62	63	66	58	61	91	70	83	76	84	70	77	79	75	77	75	80	68	71
BREWSTER	68	55	50	55	56	67	62	65	64	57	63	57	55	63	59	65	55	64	68	66
BRISCOE	77	49	21	46	60	86	52	72	57	49	58	64	40	63	51	62	48	64	76	80
BROOKS	58	45	29	41	42	52	43	51	50	47	50	45	39	48	43	52	44	51	53	51
BROWN	76	61	55	60	65	80	64	73	70	61	68	63	58	70	64	73	59	69	80	75
BURLESON	85	64	46	61	69	90	65	79	73	63	71	69	57	74	65	78	61	74	87	84
BURNET	96	78	63	76	84	103	78	93	84	76	83	81	71	84	80	89	72	87	99	97
CALDWELL	84	73	61	71	70	80	72	77	76	72	75	69	68	77	71	78	66	76	81	79
CALHOUN	88	70	54	68	74	91	70	82	77	70	76	73	64	79	70	80	66	78	87	86
CALLAHAN	79	58	39	55	64	85	59	74	65	56	65	64	51	68	59	70	55	68	81	79
CAMERON	69	59	47	55	54	60	58	62	63	61	64	56	54	60	57	64	57	64	63	60
CAMP	83	60	42	58	66	88	63	77	71	61	70	67	54	73	62	76	60	72	85	82
CARSON	93	80	65	77	88	104	75	92	80	76	81	80	72	85	78	84	71	84	95	97
CASS	76	56	41	54	62	81	58	71	65	56	64	62	50	67	58	70	55	66	79	76
CASTRO	82	60	35	55	60	78	60	73	68	62	68	64	51	68	58	71	59	71	76	75
CHAMBERS	111	97	73	94	94	108	91	102	95	93	95	93	86	99	90	98	83	98	103	107
CHEROKEE	77	59	44	57	62	79	60	71	66	58	65	62	53	68	59	70	56	67	76	75
CHILDRESS	72	52	44	52	57	74	59	67	66	54	63	59	51	67	57	70	54	64	78	70
CLAY	84	62	44	60	71	94	64	81	70	62	70	71	55	73	65	75	59	74	88	87
COCHRAN	80	54	27	51	61	85	55	74	62	55	63	65	45	66	54	66	53	67	77	80
COKE	79	60	48	59	67	87	65	77	71	59	69	67	56	71	65	76	58	71	87	80
COLEMAN	69	50	42	50	56	72	56	65	62	52	61	57	48	63	55	66	52	61	74	68
COLLIN	176	191	180	195	177	163	177	168	167	186	169	163	183	174	174	160	155	170	154	169
COLLINGSWORTH	74	52	40	51	58	77	58	69	64	54	63	60	49	67	56	68	53	64	77	73
COLORADO	90	67	48	64	74	97	70	86	77	67	76	75	60	79	70	82	65	80	94	90
COMAL	103	104	104	104	105	109	97	104	98	99	98	93	99	99	101	100	88	100	105	105
COMANCHE	74	51	33	49	58	80	55	69	61	52	61	61	45	64	54	66	51	64	77	74
CONCHO	94	64	43	62	75	103	70	89	79	65	77	79	58	83	69	85	65	81	100	96
COOKE	87	76	72	75	78	88	76	82	81	75	79	72	73	82	76	84	70	80	89	85
CORYELL	85	67	56	69	63	72	79	74	78	73	78	71	70	81	71	77	69	78	75	77
COTTLE	67	47	37	46	54	71	53	64	60	48	58	56	45	61	52	64	49	59	74	67
CRANE	78	68	54	63	66	76	63	72	70	67	70	63	60	69	64	72	62	71	75	73
CROCKETT	78	57	32	52	58	76	56	70	63	58	64	62	48	65	55	67	55	67	73	73
CROSBY	78	55	38	53	60	80	59	72	68	57	66	63	50	69	58	72	56	68	81	76
CULBERSON	62	50	33	44	44	52	47	53	54	52	55	47	43	51	46	56	48	55	55	52
DALLAM	68	55	52	55	56	65	60	64	64	58	63	55	55	66	58	66	55	62	68	64
DALLAS	112	103	101	106	96	95	113	103	111	111	112	100	108	110	106	108	102	111	100	103
DAWSON	80	65	51	60	66	80	64	75	72	65	71	64	59	71	64	75	62	72	81	76
DEAF SMITH	73	61	46	57	58	67	59	66	65	62	65	59	55	64	59	67	58	67	69	66
DELTA	77	57	42	55	62	82	60	73	68	57	66	63	52	69	60	72	56	68	81	77
DENTON	143	143	132	146	131	126	143	132	135	144	137	127	140	140	135	130	124	137	124	134
DEWITT	82	56	33	53	63	88	58	75	66	56	66	66	48	70	58	72	56	69	83	82
DICKENS	68	47	34	46	54	73	52	64	58	47	57	56	43	60	51	62	48	59	74	68
DIMMIT	54	47	35	43	41	44	45	48	49	48	49	43	42	47	43	49	44	50	48	46
DONLEY	76	55	41	54	63	83	60	73	66	55	64	64	51	67	60	70	54	69	82	77
DUVAL	64	51	34	46	45	53	49	55	56	54	57	48	44	53	48	58	50	57	57	53
EASTLAND	71	54	46	53	59	76	59	69	66	54	63	59	51	66	59	70	54	65	79	71
ECTOR	75	68	63	67	63	68	70	69	72	70	72	63	67	72	68	72	64	72	71	69
EDWARDS	67	54	39	50	53	65	52	62	59	55	59	54	48	56	53	61	51	62	66	62
ELLIS	110	110	103	109	104	105	103	105	103	106	103	96	103	106	103	103	92	104	103	106
EL PASO	78	72	64	70	65	66	72	71	74	75	75	67	69	72	70	73	67	75	70	69
ERATH	79	63	57	63	65	77	71	74	73	66	72	67	63	74	67	74	63	73	77	77
FALLS	73	53	42	52	58	77	57	68	66	54	64	59	50	66	57	71	54	65	78	72
FANNIN	84	64	52	63	70	88	67	79	74	64	73	69	59	76	67	79	62	74	87	83
FAYETTE	92	66	45	63	75	100	69	87	77	65	76	77	58	80	69	82	64	80	95	93
FISHER	74	51	35	50	59	80	56	70	63	52	62	62	46	66	55	68	52	64	79	75
FLOYD	77	62	47	57	61	73	61	71	68	63	68	62	56	67	61	71	60	69	75	71
TEXAS	104	95	88	96	90	94	98	96	99	98	99	90	94	99	94	98	89	99	96	97
UNITED STATES	100	100	100	100	100	100	100	100	100	100	100	100	100	100	100	100	100	100	100	100

POPULATION CHANGE

COUNTY	FIPS Code	CBSA Code	DMA Code	POPULATION			2000-2007 ANNUAL RATE		RACE (%)					
									White		Black		Asian/Pacific	
				2000	2007	2012	% Rate	State Rank	2000	2007	2000	2007	2000	2007
FOARD	155	00000	627	1,622	1,562	1,537	-0.5	219	84.2	83.4	3.3	3.4	0.2	0.2
FORT BEND	157	26420	618	354,452	501,974	640,521	4.9	4	57.0	53.3	19.8	19.7	11.2	13.0
FRANKLIN	159	00000	709	9,458	10,561	11,420	1.5	54	89.2	86.9	3.9	4.3	0.2	0.3
FREESTONE	161	00000	623	17,867	19,178	19,842	1.0	75	75.6	72.8	18.9	20.2	0.3	0.4
FRIO	163	00000	641	16,252	16,576	16,800	0.3	139	71.9	70.7	4.9	4.4	0.4	0.5
GAINES	165	00000	651	14,467	14,750	14,958	0.3	139	80.3	76.9	2.3	2.3	0.2	0.2
GALVESTON	167	26420	618	250,158	291,355	324,503	2.1	33	72.7	69.9	15.4	16.0	2.1	2.4
GARZA	169	00000	651	4,872	5,577	5,537	1.9	39	74.8	71.0	4.8	4.8	0.1	0.1
GILLESPIE	171	23240	635	20,814	23,921	26,387	1.9	39	92.8	91.0	0.2	0.2	0.2	0.3
GLASSCOCK	173	00000	633	1,406	1,341	1,290	-0.7	229	77.5	76.4	0.5	0.5	0.2	0.2
GOLIAD	175	47020	641	6,928	7,119	7,230	0.4	128	82.6	80.2	4.8	4.9	0.2	0.3
GONZALES	177	00000	641	18,628	19,541	20,043	0.7	94	72.2	69.0	8.4	8.3	0.3	0.4
GRAY	179	37420	634	22,744	21,041	19,947	-1.1	245	82.2	78.9	5.8	6.2	0.4	0.5
GRAYSON	181	43300	657	110,595	120,067	126,941	1.1	69	87.2	85.1	5.9	6.4	0.6	0.8
GREGG	183	30980	709	111,379	116,670	119,782	0.6	105	72.9	69.9	19.9	21.1	0.7	0.9
GRIMES	185	00000	618	23,552	25,919	27,822	1.3	61	71.8	69.1	20.0	20.8	0.3	0.4
GUADALUPE	187	41700	641	89,023	112,552	132,141	3.3	15	77.6	74.4	5.0	5.0	1.0	1.1
HALE	189	38380	651	36,602	35,925	35,421	-0.3	202	66.8	62.9	5.8	5.6	0.3	0.4
HALL	191	00000	634	3,782	3,639	3,527	-0.5	219	72.0	67.5	8.2	8.4	0.2	0.2
HAMILTON	193	00000	623	8,229	8,407	8,553	0.3	139	93.8	92.1	0.1	0.2	0.2	0.3
HANSFORD	195	00000	634	5,369	5,253	5,191	-0.3	202	79.9	75.7	0.0	0.0	0.2	0.3
HARDEMAN	197	00000	627	4,724	4,405	4,155	-1.0	242	85.4	82.6	4.8	5.2	0.3	0.4
HARDIN	199	13140	692	48,073	52,255	54,532	1.2	65	90.9	89.6	6.9	7.6	0.2	0.3
HARRIS	201	26420	618	3,400,578	3,919,764	4,239,461	2.0	36	58.7	55.6	18.5	18.1	5.2	5.9
HARRISON	203	32220	612	62,110	64,971	67,027	0.6	105	71.3	68.5	24.0	25.8	0.3	0.4
HARTLEY	205	00000	634	5,537	5,414	5,330	-0.3	202	81.1	77.7	8.1	8.7	0.3	0.4
HASKELL	207	00000	662	6,093	5,659	5,419	-1.0	242	82.8	79.1	2.8	3.0	0.2	0.2
HAYS	209	12420	635	97,589	135,596	166,524	4.6	7	78.9	75.0	3.7	4.2	0.9	1.0
HEMPHILL	211	00000	634	3,351	3,310	3,304	-0.2	190	87.6	87.1	1.6	1.6	0.3	0.3
HENDERSON	213	11980	623	73,277	82,205	88,927	1.6	50	88.5	86.6	6.6	7.2	0.3	0.4
HIDALGO	215	32580	636	569,463	732,166	865,301	3.5	12	77.7	76.9	0.5	0.5	0.6	0.6
HILL	217	00000	623	32,321	35,572	37,535	1.3	61	84.2	81.5	7.4	7.9	0.3	0.3
HOCKLEY	219	30220	651	22,716	22,608	22,572	-0.1	178	74.4	70.3	3.7	3.7	0.2	0.2
HOOD	221	24180	623	41,100	49,330	55,512	2.5	23	94.8	93.5	0.3	0.4	0.4	0.4
HOPKINS	223	44860	623	31,960	33,737	34,657	0.7	94	85.1	82.7	8.0	8.6	0.3	0.4
HOUSTON	225	00000	709	23,185	23,297	23,329	0.1	159	68.6	66.0	27.9	29.6	0.3	0.4
HOWARD	227	13700	633	33,627	33,449	32,563	-0.1	178	80.1	77.3	4.1	4.1	0.6	0.7
HUDSPETH	229	00000	765	3,344	3,481	3,595	0.6	105	87.2	86.5	0.3	0.3	0.2	0.2
HUNT	231	19100	623	76,596	84,205	88,552	1.3	61	83.6	81.1	9.5	10.2	0.6	0.8
HUTCHINSON	233	14420	634	23,857	22,379	21,426	-0.9	238	87.0	84.3	2.4	2.6	0.4	0.5
IRION	235	41660	661	1,771	1,778	1,785	0.1	159	90.7	90.4	0.4	0.4	0.0	0.0
JACK	237	00000	623	8,763	9,146	9,419	0.6	105	88.7	86.6	5.5	6.0	0.3	0.4
JACKSON	239	00000	618	14,391	14,378	14,354	0.0	170	76.5	75.8	7.6	7.7	0.4	0.4
JASPER	241	00000	692	35,604	35,826	36,012	0.1	159	78.2	75.7	17.8	19.3	0.3	0.4
JEFF DAVIS	243	00000	633	2,207	2,442	2,629	1.4	57	90.5	88.8	0.9	1.0	0.1	0.1
JEFFERSON	245	13140	692	252,051	254,759	255,870	0.1	159	57.2	53.7	33.7	35.6	2.9	3.3
JIM HOGG	247	00000	600	5,281	5,200	5,102	-0.2	190	80.4	80.5	0.5	0.5	0.2	0.2
JIM WELLS	249	10860	600	39,326	41,199	42,280	0.6	105	77.9	76.4	0.6	0.6	0.5	0.6
JOHNSON	251	19100	623	126,811	151,478	169,682	2.5	23	90.0	87.9	2.5	2.7	0.7	0.9
JONES	253	10180	662	20,785	20,343	20,114	-0.3	202	78.8	76.1	11.5	9.6	1.1	1.1
KARNES	255	00000	641	15,446	15,279	15,307	-0.1	178	68.5	66.0	10.8	10.4	0.5	0.5
KAUFMAN	257	19100	623	71,313	96,259	119,692	4.2	10	81.1	78.3	10.5	11.2	0.5	0.6
KENDALL	259	41700	641	23,743	32,013	39,780	4.2	10	92.9	91.2	0.3	0.4	0.3	0.4
KENEDY	261	28780	600	414	409	404	-0.2	190	64.5	64.1	0.7	0.7	0.5	0.5
KENT	263	00000	651	859	784	737	-1.3	250	95.5	95.0	0.2	0.3	0.0	0.0
KERR	265	28500	641	43,653	47,529	50,217	1.2	65	88.9	86.5	1.8	1.9	0.6	0.7
KIMBLE	267	00000	661	4,468	4,611	4,696	0.4	128	90.3	87.9	0.1	0.1	0.5	0.6
KING	269	00000	627	356	318	301	-1.5	253	94.1	93.4	0.0	0.0	0.0	0.0
KINNEY	271	00000	641	3,379	3,329	3,278	-0.2	190	75.8	75.3	1.7	1.7	0.1	0.1
KLEBERG	273	28780	600	31,549	31,031	30,800	-0.2	190	71.9	70.0	3.7	3.4	1.6	1.7
KNOX	275	00000	662	4,253	4,000	3,885	-0.8	234	74.3	70.0	6.9	7.1	0.3	0.4
LAMAR	277	37580	623	48,499	50,020	50,995	0.4	128	82.5	80.4	13.5	14.7	0.4	0.5
LAMB	279	00000	651	14,709	14,598	14,486	-0.1	178	76.1	73.0	4.3	4.2	0.1	0.1
LAMPASAS	281	28660	625	17,762	19,841	21,420	1.5	54	86.8	84.0	3.1	3.3	0.8	1.0
LA SALLE	283	00000	641	5,866	6,094	6,265	0.5	117	81.5	80.8	3.5	3.2	0.3	0.3
LAVACA	285	00000	641	19,210	19,106	19,026	-0.1	178	86.9	84.6	6.8	7.3	0.2	0.2
LEE	287	00000	635	15,657	16,537	17,072	0.8	87	76.6	73.4	12.1	12.6	0.3	0.3
LEON	289	00000	625	15,335	16,383	17,172	0.9	82	83.5	81.0	10.4	11.2	0.2	0.2
LIBERTY	291	26420	618	70,154	77,363	82,647	1.4	57	78.9	76.0	12.8	13.7	0.4	0.4
LIMESTONE	293	00000	625	22,051	23,201	24,014	0.7	94	70.8	67.2	19.1	20.1	0.1	0.2
LIPSCOMB	295	00000	634	3,057	3,178	3,271	0.5	117	82.9	78.8	0.5	0.6	0.1	0.1
LIVE OAK	297	00000	600	12,309	12,136	12,031	-0.2	190	87.3	85.4	2.4	2.5	0.2	0.3
LLANO	299	00000	635	17,044	19,508	20,870	1.9	39	96.3	95.3	0.3	0.3	0.4	0.5
LOVING	001	00000	633	67	65	65	-0.4	211	89.6	89.2	0.0	0.0	0.0	0.0
LUBBOCK	303	31180	651	242,628	261,085	271,248	1.0	75	74.3	70.4	7.7	7.8	1.3	1.6
LYNN	305	00000	651	6,550	6,333	6,202	-0.5	219	75.5	72.1	2.8	2.8	0.2	0.2
MCCULLOCH	307	00000	661	8,205	8,024	7,933	-0.3	202	84.6	81.5	1.6	1.6	0.2	0.2
TEXAS							2.0		71.0	68.4	11.5	11.4	2.8	3.3
UNITED STATES							1.2		75.1	72.7	12.3	12.6	3.8	4.5

POPULATION COMPOSITION

COUNTY	% HISPANIC ORIGIN		2007 AGE DISTRIBUTION (%)										MEDIAN AGE	% 2007 Males	% 2007 Females
	2000	2007	0-4	5-9	10-14	15-19	20-24	25-44	45-64	65-84	85+	18+	2007		
FOARD	16.3	17.3	6.5	5.4	7.4	6.1	6.9	21.1	25.0	17.0	4.5	77.0	42.4	47.1	52.9
FORT BEND	21.1	25.1	8.0	8.3	8.3	7.9	6.7	27.6	27.3	5.5	0.6	70.3	34.6	49.5	50.5
FRANKLIN	8.9	11.6	6.0	5.5	5.9	5.9	6.3	23.4	27.8	16.7	2.5	79.1	42.9	48.7	51.3
FREESTONE	8.2	10.5	5.9	5.6	5.5	6.3	7.9	26.1	26.7	13.4	2.6	79.4	39.8	52.7	47.3
FRIO	73.8	78.5	8.1	7.5	7.7	6.9	9.0	29.6	21.0	8.9	1.4	72.6	31.4	54.9	45.1
GAINES	35.8	42.7	9.4	8.3	7.3	9.4	8.7	25.2	21.5	9.0	1.3	69.0	30.1	49.2	50.8
GALVESTON	18.0	22.4	7.0	6.7	6.9	6.9	7.0	26.4	27.7	10.0	1.4	75.2	37.4	48.9	51.1
GARZA	37.2	44.0	5.8	5.2	6.2	8.3	8.3	32.0	21.4	10.9	1.9	77.2	34.7	58.7	41.3
GILLESPIE	15.9	20.2	5.3	5.0	5.4	5.4	5.5	18.8	30.2	19.8	4.4	80.9	48.1	47.4	52.6
GLASSCOCK	29.9	31.4	9.5	7.4	7.8	6.3	8.7	22.5	26.6	10.2	0.9	71.6	36.8	52.1	47.9
GOLIAD	35.2	41.9	6.0	5.6	6.2	6.0	7.0	22.1	30.1	14.8	2.2	78.5	43.1	50.0	50.0
GONZALES	39.6	46.4	7.7	6.9	6.3	7.1	6.8	25.1	24.9	12.6	2.6	74.6	37.2	50.2	49.8
GRAY	13.0	16.6	6.2	5.4	6.2	6.3	8.2	24.6	25.2	14.9	3.1	78.6	39.9	51.7	48.3
GRAYSON	6.8	8.8	6.7	5.8	6.3	6.9	7.5	25.0	27.0	12.5	2.3	77.3	39.1	48.7	51.3
GREGG	9.1	11.6	7.2	6.5	6.8	7.0	7.7	26.2	25.3	11.3	2.0	75.5	36.0	48.7	51.3
GRIMES	16.1	20.0	6.6	6.1	5.9	6.1	6.2	27.6	28.1	11.5	1.9	77.7	39.5	53.7	46.3
GUADALUPE	33.2	39.7	7.5	7.0	6.9	7.5	7.8	25.9	26.3	9.8	1.4	74.3	36.4	49.2	50.8
HALE	47.9	54.9	8.9	7.7	7.5	8.2	8.5	25.6	20.8	10.7	2.0	71.5	32.0	50.7	49.3
HALL	27.5	33.5	8.1	6.9	7.6	6.1	6.1	21.4	23.2	16.9	3.7	73.4	40.2	48.6	51.4
HAMILTON	7.4	9.7	6.0	5.3	5.8	6.5	6.0	20.8	27.0	17.9	4.7	78.7	44.7	48.6	51.4
HANSFORD	31.5	38.2	7.5	6.3	7.4	6.2	7.6	23.4	26.7	12.7	2.3	74.9	38.9	49.2	50.8
HARDEMAN	14.5	18.5	7.0	6.9	4.9	6.4	7.4	22.2	25.9	15.2	4.1	77.0	41.0	48.0	52.0
HARDIN	2.5	3.4	7.2	6.9	6.8	6.5	7.0	26.3	27.1	10.9	1.4	75.2	37.6	49.5	50.5
HARRIS	32.9	38.4	8.2	7.7	7.7	7.3	7.3	30.5	23.5	6.9	0.9	72.0	32.5	49.8	50.2
HARRISON	5.3	6.9	6.7	6.3	6.4	7.4	8.1	24.8	27.3	11.2	1.8	76.5	37.9	48.8	51.2
HARTLEY	13.7	17.5	5.7	6.0	4.7	5.1	3.8	34.1	28.5	10.1	2.0	80.1	40.4	61.0	39.0
HASKELL	20.5	25.7	5.7	5.0	5.5	6.2	7.4	19.1	24.2	18.1	4.4	79.8	45.7	47.7	52.3
HAYS	29.6	35.9	6.7	6.2	6.1	8.8	14.5	27.0	22.8	6.9	1.0	76.5	30.0	50.9	49.1
HEMPHILL	15.6	16.5	5.9	5.7	5.7	8.9	6.6	21.5	30.3	12.9	2.6	76.3	42.0	50.9	49.1
HENDERSON	6.9	9.0	6.5	6.2	5.8	6.2	5.7	22.6	28.4	16.4	2.2	77.8	42.7	49.5	50.5
HIDALGO	88.3	90.9	10.8	9.6	9.1	8.2	7.6	28.2	17.6	8.0	1.0	65.6	28.0	48.7	51.3
HILL	13.5	17.2	7.2	6.7	6.0	6.3	6.7	23.4	26.6	14.4	2.6	76.4	40.2	49.5	50.5
HOCKLEY	37.2	44.2	8.0	6.8	7.0	8.1	9.3	24.6	23.6	10.7	1.8	73.9	33.3	49.3	50.7
HOOD	7.2	9.5	5.7	5.6	5.7	6.1	6.0	21.5	29.1	18.2	2.1	79.2	44.5	48.9	51.1
HOPKINS	9.3	12.0	6.9	6.3	6.3	6.4	6.9	26.0	26.4	12.5	2.4	76.7	38.5	49.3	50.7
HOUSTON	7.5	9.5	5.6	4.9	5.7	6.1	6.5	26.6	27.1	14.7	2.7	80.0	41.7	53.5	46.5
HOWARD	37.5	44.3	6.1	5.2	5.5	6.3	8.9	30.2	23.5	12.3	2.0	79.6	36.7	56.0	44.0
HUDSPETH	75.0	79.8	9.7	7.9	8.7	7.9	9.7	24.8	20.5	10.2	0.6	69.2	30.7	51.1	48.9
HUNT	8.3	10.7	6.9	6.3	6.3	7.7	8.2	25.7	25.7	11.5	1.8	76.1	36.9	49.8	50.2
HUTCHINSON	14.7	18.7	7.1	6.6	6.4	6.7	8.5	22.0	27.7	12.8	2.3	75.9	38.5	49.1	50.9
IRION	24.6	25.9	5.8	5.9	5.0	7.5	6.6	22.3	31.4	13.3	2.1	78.8	43.4	49.6	50.4
JACK	7.9	10.2	6.0	5.7	5.2	7.1	8.4	27.3	25.0	13.1	2.2	79.1	38.8	54.4	45.6
JACKSON	24.7	25.9	7.5	7.2	6.1	5.9	7.5	24.6	26.1	12.6	2.5	75.6	38.7	49.8	50.2
JASPER	3.9	5.1	7.2	6.7	6.4	6.1	7.0	25.0	26.1	13.7	1.9	76.0	39.3	48.8	51.2
JEFF DAVIS	35.5	42.4	4.0	4.7	5.4	7.9	5.8	20.9	33.9	15.4	2.0	80.3	45.9	51.1	48.9
JEFFERSON	10.5	13.1	6.9	6.2	6.6	6.7	7.7	27.4	25.0	11.4	2.1	76.4	36.3	50.3	49.7
JIM HOGG	90.0	90.6	8.6	7.7	7.3	8.5	7.9	23.9	21.7	12.1	2.3	70.8	34.2	49.6	50.4
JIM WELLS	75.7	80.5	8.8	8.0	7.4	7.7	8.0	25.1	22.6	10.6	1.6	70.9	32.9	49.0	51.0
JOHNSON	12.1	15.6	7.7	7.0	6.8	7.3	7.7	27.0	25.9	9.4	1.2	74.2	35.7	50.0	50.0
JONES	20.9	25.0	5.6	4.6	5.2	10.2	12.7	26.3	22.0	11.1	2.4	80.8	34.5	54.9	45.1
KARNES	47.4	54.1	5.9	5.1	5.1	6.0	10.7	33.0	20.6	11.2	2.4	80.5	34.2	59.7	40.3
KAUFMAN	11.1	14.2	7.4	6.8	7.2	7.5	7.7	26.0	26.5	9.6	1.3	74.0	36.2	49.4	50.6
KENDALL	17.9	22.6	6.1	6.3	7.0	7.7	5.6	21.4	31.0	12.7	2.2	75.7	42.4	48.9	51.1
KENEDY	79.0	80.2	10.0	7.8	8.6	3.9	10.3	23.0	21.5	14.4	0.5	71.1	35.3	53.3	46.7
KENT	9.1	9.9	3.8	4.2	5.0	6.4	5.1	17.3	30.7	21.4	6.0	83.3	50.2	47.2	52.8
KERR	19.1	24.0	5.5	5.0	5.3	6.7	6.8	18.9	27.5	20.3	4.0	79.9	46.2	48.1	51.9
KIMBLE	20.7	26.0	6.1	6.2	5.2	5.9	6.3	20.6	29.6	17.6	2.7	79.0	44.9	48.3	51.7
KING	9.6	10.7	6.9	5.7	8.8	11.0	3.5	21.7	30.8	11.3	0.3	69.5	40.7	48.7	51.3
KINNEY	50.5	52.2	6.4	5.3	6.5	6.5	8.0	17.4	25.7	21.5	2.7	77.7	44.9	50.6	49.4
KLEBERG	65.4	71.1	8.1	6.9	6.2	8.2	10.5	28.9	20.5	9.4	1.3	74.7	30.1	50.6	49.4
KNOX	25.1	30.8	7.4	6.4	5.9	8.0	7.1	20.3	23.9	16.8	4.2	74.7	41.2	46.8	53.2
LAMAR	3.3	4.3	7.4	6.7	6.3	6.7	6.4	25.6	25.3	13.0	2.8	75.8	38.4	47.9	52.1
LAMB	43.5	50.5	8.3	7.5	6.5	6.7	7.8	23.2	23.4	13.6	2.9	73.2	36.7	49.3	50.7
LAMPASAS	15.1	19.1	7.2	6.5	6.5	6.9	7.3	24.9	26.6	12.0	2.1	75.6	38.4	49.3	50.7
LA SALLE	77.1	81.5	7.5	6.9	7.2	8.9	8.1	27.0	22.8	10.2	1.4	72.8	33.8	53.1	46.9
LAVACA	11.4	14.6	6.3	6.1	5.5	6.0	6.5	22.2	27.4	15.9	4.3	78.5	43.2	48.8	51.2
LEE	18.2	22.7	7.5	6.4	6.1	9.8	7.3	23.9	25.4	11.5	2.2	74.2	36.4	50.6	49.4
LEON	7.9	10.2	6.0	5.3	5.4	6.2	7.2	20.8	28.9	17.8	2.3	79.4	44.3	49.7	50.3
LIBERTY	10.9	13.9	7.4	6.6	6.9	7.1	7.6	29.2	25.0	9.0	1.2	74.8	35.0	49.1	50.9
LIMESTONE	13.0	16.4	6.7	6.2	6.1	7.0	6.6	25.8	26.0	13.1	2.6	76.6	38.5	50.9	49.1
LIPSCOMB	20.7	26.0	6.8	6.5	6.2	6.0	9.0	21.2	25.9	15.3	3.1	76.6	41.3	49.6	50.4
LIVE OAK	38.0	45.0	5.0	4.6	5.3	5.9	10.1	24.2	28.7	14.1	2.2	81.4	41.7	55.6	44.4
LLANO	5.1	6.8	3.6	3.5	3.5	4.4	4.2	14.6	33.8	28.2	3.9	86.6	56.2	48.8	51.2
LOVING	10.4	10.8	3.1	3.1	3.1	7.7	3.1	10.8	55.4	13.8	0.0	83.1	51.4	52.3	47.7
LUBBOCK	27.5	33.3	7.4	6.6	6.2	8.1	10.7	28.4	21.8	9.3	1.5	76.0	31.0	49.1	50.9
LYNN	44.6	51.8	8.1	7.0	6.8	8.2	8.0	23.2	24.8	12.2	1.7	72.9	36.7	49.7	50.3
MCCULLOCH	27.0	33.2	7.2	6.8	5.9	7.1	7.1	20.2	27.4	15.3	3.0	76.0	41.1	47.5	52.5
TEXAS	32.0	36.4	8.0	7.4	7.2	7.3	7.8	28.9	23.5	8.6	1.3	73.1	33.4	49.7	50.3
UNITED STATES	12.5	15.0	6.9	6.5	6.8	7.1	7.0	27.6	25.4	10.7	1.9	75.6	36.7	49.2	50.8

COUNTY	HOUSEHOLDS					FAMILIES			MEDIAN HOUSEHOLD INCOME			
	2000	2007	2012	% Annual Rate 2000-2007	2007 Average HH Size	2000	2007	% Annual Rate 2000-2007	2007	2012	2007 National Rank	2007 State Rank
FOARD	664	645	635	-0.4	2.38	438	420	-0.6	31,125	35,813	2823	227
FORT BEND	110,915	151,731	193,189	4.4	3.27	93,040	126,536	4.3	82,719	99,599	40	2
FRANKLIN	3,754	4,237	4,606	1.7	2.45	2,733	3,055	1.5	39,232	44,626	1827	105
FREESTONE	6,588	7,182	7,482	1.2	2.46	4,664	5,033	1.1	38,122	43,348	1986	126
FRIO	4,743	4,977	5,111	0.7	2.90	3,643	3,792	0.6	29,337	32,955	2942	241
GAINES	4,681	4,800	4,882	0.3	3.05	3,756	3,824	0.2	35,928	40,236	2293	160
GALVESTON	94,782	110,673	123,631	2.2	2.59	66,156	76,418	2.0	54,132	63,384	443	19
GARZA	1,663	1,671	1,668	0.1	2.61	1,218	1,212	-0.1	33,338	37,781	2626	207
GILLESPIE	8,521	9,932	11,043	2.1	2.35	6,081	7,015	2.0	45,897	52,231	1014	41
GLASSCOCK	483	474	462	-0.3	2.83	355	345	-0.4	42,043	47,780	1445	70
GOLIAD	2,644	2,761	2,822	0.6	2.54	1,975	2,044	0.5	40,800	46,421	1630	84
GONZALES	6,782	7,148	7,342	0.7	2.69	4,873	5,083	0.6	33,901	38,415	2562	199
GRAY	8,793	8,193	7,775	-1.0	2.36	6,052	5,575	-1.1	39,262	45,857	1825	104
GRAYSON	42,849	45,857	48,448	0.9	2.55	30,191	31,973	0.8	45,778	52,565	1026	43
GREGG	42,687	44,584	45,817	0.6	2.54	29,677	30,655	0.4	42,777	49,692	1356	64
GRIMES	7,753	8,716	9,447	1.6	2.67	5,630	6,267	1.5	39,519	44,598	1778	98
GUADALUPE	30,900	39,014	45,846	3.3	2.84	23,831	29,841	3.2	54,041	61,583	451	20
HALE	11,975	11,796	11,648	-0.2	2.84	9,142	8,931	-0.3	38,051	43,158	1993	129
HALL	1,548	1,464	1,409	-0.8	2.45	1,014	947	-0.9	26,924	30,519	3041	245
HAMILTON	3,374	3,410	3,453	0.1	2.40	2,323	2,322	0.0	38,021	43,739	1996	130
HANSFORD	2,005	1,986	1,974	-0.1	2.60	1,489	1,461	-0.3	41,685	46,920	1497	75
HARDEMAN	1,943	1,825	1,725	-0.9	2.38	1,319	1,225	-1.0	35,015	40,060	2426	177
HARDIN	17,805	19,649	20,650	1.4	2.64	13,644	14,929	1.2	44,342	50,687	1177	55
HARRIS	1,205,516	1,379,626	1,487,889	1.9	2.81	834,290	944,281	1.7	55,164	65,463	399	16
HARRISON	23,087	24,403	25,332	0.8	2.59	16,952	17,750	0.6	40,422	46,061	1670	91
HARTLEY	1,604	1,588	1,564	-0.1	2.53	1,221	1,198	-0.3	52,996	58,941	501	24
HASKELL	2,569	2,416	2,326	-0.8	2.30	1,775	1,650	-1.0	29,553	33,730	2928	240
HAYS	33,410	46,647	58,000	4.7	2.71	22,135	30,534	4.5	56,282	66,048	356	14
HEMPHILL	1,280	1,303	1,317	0.2	2.44	948	956	0.1	41,728	47,033	1486	74
HENDERSON	28,804	32,194	34,858	1.5	2.51	20,982	23,222	1.4	40,724	47,331	1639	87
HIDALGO	156,824	205,804	244,775	3.8	3.53	132,859	173,396	3.7	30,519	35,078	2884	236
HILL	12,204	13,395	14,126	1.3	2.59	8,731	9,486	1.2	38,116	43,348	1987	127
HOCKLEY	7,994	8,126	8,199	0.2	2.70	6,088	6,134	0.1	37,409	42,320	2080	139
HOOD	16,176	19,599	22,187	2.7	2.48	12,103	14,536	2.6	53,299	60,839	485	23
HOPKINS	12,286	13,038	13,422	0.8	2.55	8,885	9,336	0.7	38,986	44,413	1855	107
HOUSTON	8,259	8,370	8,418	0.2	2.42	5,756	5,767	0.0	34,010	38,778	2548	197
HOWARD	11,389	11,016	10,724	-0.5	2.50	7,946	7,601	-0.6	37,371	43,239	2083	140
HUDSPETH	1,092	1,129	1,162	0.5	3.05	842	863	0.3	25,618	29,423	3080	250
HUNT	28,742	31,154	32,787	1.1	2.62	20,519	22,013	1.0	44,489	51,436	1160	52
HUTCHINSON	9,283	8,804	8,472	-0.7	2.51	6,869	6,452	-0.9	44,401	51,241	1166	53
IRION	694	711	721	0.3	2.50	524	532	0.2	43,899	50,071	1223	58
JACK	3,047	3,194	3,302	0.7	2.52	2,228	2,313	0.5	38,649	43,909	1905	114
JACKSON	5,336	5,347	5,345	0.0	2.64	3,891	3,862	-0.1	42,538	48,667	1394	66
JASPER	13,450	13,758	13,924	0.3	2.54	9,970	10,104	0.2	36,753	41,711	2158	147
JEFF DAVIS	896	1,001	1,083	1.5	2.37	633	700	1.4	39,366	44,108	1806	102
JEFFERSON	92,880	94,218	94,955	0.2	2.53	63,806	63,991	0.0	43,066	50,120	1321	60
JIM HOGG	1,815	1,817	1,798	0.0	2.83	1,360	1,349	-0.1	30,734	34,943	2859	234
JIM WELLS	12,961	13,770	14,217	0.8	2.96	10,102	10,650	0.7	34,376	38,543	2507	187
JOHNSON	43,636	52,257	58,645	2.5	2.85	34,440	40,931	2.4	54,389	61,868	428	18
JONES	6,140	5,959	5,880	-0.4	2.57	4,525	4,351	-0.5	35,909	40,757	2295	161
KARNES	4,454	4,493	4,546	0.1	2.60	3,246	3,242	0.0	32,010	36,640	2763	219
KAUFMAN	24,367	33,026	41,172	4.3	2.87	19,228	25,865	4.2	54,501	62,212	422	17
KENDALL	8,613	11,609	14,435	4.2	2.72	6,694	8,951	4.1	60,587	69,470	249	10
KENEDY	138	138	137	0.0	2.93	111	110	-0.1	30,000	34,282	2910	238
KENT	353	323	306	-1.2	2.28	247	224	-1.3	36,843	41,755	2149	146
KERR	17,813	19,478	20,672	1.2	2.34	12,300	13,303	1.1	42,279	49,607	1419	68
KIMBLE	1,866	1,967	2,020	0.7	2.32	1,286	1,341	0.6	35,634	40,386	2346	167
KING	108	95	90	-1.8	2.75	89	78	-1.8	40,742	45,780	1636	85
KINNEY	1,314	1,302	1,285	-0.1	2.54	941	924	-0.3	35,336	41,342	2395	171
KLEBERG	10,896	10,922	10,906	0.0	2.74	7,684	7,621	-0.1	36,045	41,540	2268	158
KNOX	1,690	1,615	1,574	-0.6	2.41	1,166	1,102	-0.8	30,968	35,458	2834	230
LAMAR	19,077	19,845	20,338	0.5	2.46	13,473	13,870	0.4	38,252	43,625	1968	124
LAMB	5,360	5,333	5,301	-0.1	2.68	3,991	3,934	-0.2	33,265	37,866	2635	209
LAMPASAS	6,554	7,329	7,916	1.6	2.66	4,877	5,406	1.4	42,828	48,972	1348	63
LA SALLE	1,819	1,921	1,998	0.8	2.84	1,352	1,415	0.6	26,019	29,142	3070	248
LAVACA	7,669	7,695	7,687	0.0	2.43	5,389	5,349	-0.1	35,491	40,286	2369	170
LEE	5,663	5,959	6,148	0.7	2.67	4,149	4,323	0.6	42,915	49,053	1341	62
LEON	6,189	6,669	7,015	1.0	2.44	4,510	4,813	0.9	38,241	44,249	1969	125
LIBERTY	23,242	25,659	27,502	1.4	2.82	17,755	19,435	1.3	46,564	53,124	947	36
LIMESTONE	7,906	8,360	8,671	0.8	2.56	5,649	5,913	0.6	35,766	40,643	2320	162
LIPSCOMB	1,205	1,260	1,302	0.6	2.48	846	875	0.5	37,855	43,020	2016	132
LIVE OAK	4,230	4,197	4,188	-0.1	2.49	3,073	3,020	-0.2	39,379	45,531	1800	101
LLANO	7,879	9,079	9,735	2.0	2.12	5,363	6,111	1.8	44,366	53,089	1172	54
LOVING	31	32	32	0.4	2.03	20	20	0.0	50,000	50,739	683	27
LUBBOCK	92,516	99,149	103,335	1.0	2.53	60,090	63,592	0.8	40,736	47,609	1637	86
LYNN	2,354	2,294	2,252	-0.4	2.74	1,778	1,717	-0.5	31,767	35,996	2781	221
MCCULLOCH	3,277	3,241	3,215	-0.2	2.45	2,267	2,218	-0.3	31,308	35,838	2811	222
TEXAS				1.9	2.76			1.8	51,090	60,298		
UNITED STATES				1.2	2.59			1.0	53,154	62,503		

TEXAS

D

INCOME

COUNTY	2007 Per Capita Income	2007 HH Income Base	2007 HOUSEHOLD INCOME DISTRIBUTION (%)					2007 Home Value Base	2007 HOME VALUE DISTRIBUTION (%)					2007 Median Home Value
			Less than $25,000	$25,000 to $49,999	$50,000 to $99,999	$100,000 to $149,999	$150,000 or More		Less than $50,000	$50,000 to $89,999	$90,000 to $174,999	$175,000 to $399,999	$400,000 or More	
FOARD	18,290	645	41.2	32.9	20.3	2.8	2.8	493	61.9	22.9	14.2	0.6	0.4	40,250
FORT BEND	33,097	151,731	9.8	16.3	33.0	21.7	19.2	124,542	5.1	9.8	36.6	40.7	7.8	170,567
FRANKLIN	21,800	4,237	30.4	32.3	25.7	6.9	4.8	3,395	26.3	24.2	30.9	14.8	3.9	89,306
FREESTONE	19,985	7,182	33.2	27.1	30.1	7.1	2.6	5,741	31.3	27.2	29.0	10.8	1.7	77,384
FRIO	13,532	4,977	43.6	31.3	19.4	3.8	1.9	3,519	52.1	26.9	16.3	3.4	1.3	48,090
GAINES	15,791	4,800	33.1	32.3	26.3	5.3	2.9	3,813	43.2	28.5	22.7	4.8	0.7	60,538
GALVESTON	27,355	110,673	22.1	24.1	31.5	14.6	7.8	75,283	13.0	22.3	38.9	22.3	3.6	113,240
GARZA	15,623	1,671	37.6	34.2	20.2	5.7	2.3	1,205	40.0	32.0	21.0	4.1	2.8	58,796
GILLESPIE	25,861	9,932	22.4	31.6	32.9	8.0	5.0	7,843	9.7	13.9	33.9	29.2	13.3	150,877
GLASSCOCK	23,638	474	27.4	29.3	29.5	7.2	6.5	326	22.7	30.4	28.8	15.3	2.8	85,652
GOLIAD	20,935	2,761	31.1	28.9	28.7	8.2	3.1	2,240	28.4	24.5	27.7	14.1	5.3	85,000
GONZALES	17,144	7,148	36.5	30.5	24.7	6.3	2.1	5,089	37.0	24.0	23.7	12.4	2.8	69,306
GRAY	21,293	8,193	30.6	30.5	27.5	8.2	3.2	6,394	48.1	25.2	20.8	5.0	0.9	51,929
GRAYSON	22,850	45,856	25.9	28.3	32.2	9.6	4.0	33,077	20.4	29.3	33.1	15.1	2.1	90,468
GREGG	23,086	44,584	27.9	28.5	29.4	9.5	4.7	29,447	21.0	22.6	37.0	17.4	1.9	100,165
GRIMES	18,820	8,716	31.6	29.0	29.5	6.4	3.5	6,881	29.2	27.5	26.5	14.8	2.0	80,509
GUADALUPE	22,973	39,014	18.2	27.1	37.3	12.8	4.7	30,630	12.4	19.0	38.8	27.2	2.6	126,472
HALE	17,252	11,796	30.7	32.9	27.3	6.4	2.8	7,895	30.9	30.0	29.6	8.9	0.8	75,019
HALL	14,396	1,464	46.4	32.4	17.2	3.5	0.5	1,104	65.8	20.1	12.2	1.6	0.3	35,066
HAMILTON	20,812	3,410	31.9	30.2	27.9	6.6	3.4	2,699	28.4	28.9	24.7	12.9	5.2	79,258
HANSFORD	20,990	1,986	29.0	29.7	31.4	6.1	3.8	1,517	39.2	24.9	27.9	6.9	1.1	62,532
HARDEMAN	20,688	1,825	35.0	31.6	24.4	5.0	3.9	1,359	56.4	25.4	15.6	2.1	0.4	44,913
HARDIN	21,373	19,649	25.0	30.6	30.6	11.0	2.8	16,394	29.4	26.2	31.2	12.2	1.0	81,022
HARRIS	27,751	1,379,613	20.1	25.1	31.2	13.5	10.2	792,075	10.3	21.3	41.1	21.3	6.0	117,580
HARRISON	20,209	24,403	31.1	27.9	30.3	7.9	2.8	19,090	29.5	25.3	32.2	11.7	1.3	82,559
HARTLEY	23,382	1,588	17.8	28.1	37.4	10.1	6.5	1,243	15.3	19.9	39.1	25.2	0.6	119,750
HASKELL	18,547	2,416	43.6	28.8	19.0	6.2	2.4	1,923	53.1	26.6	17.0	3.2	0.1	45,719
HAYS	25,927	46,647	20.6	23.1	34.1	14.0	8.1	31,031	8.9	11.6	32.1	38.1	9.3	168,210
HEMPHILL	21,381	1,303	26.8	32.0	30.5	8.0	2.8	1,023	28.9	30.3	27.7	10.0	3.1	78,636
HENDERSON	22,005	32,194	29.3	30.3	28.3	8.2	4.0	26,080	30.0	25.4	28.7	13.6	2.3	81,368
HIDALGO	12,350	205,804	41.9	29.0	21.1	5.4	2.5	152,058	36.6	31.3	24.6	6.3	1.2	64,885
HILL	18,995	13,395	32.5	29.9	28.1	7.0	2.5	10,244	29.9	28.6	27.5	12.1	1.9	77,542
HOCKLEY	18,458	8,126	30.8	33.7	26.1	6.5	3.0	6,135	37.2	29.7	27.1	5.7	0.3	66,582
HOOD	28,235	19,590	17.5	28.8	35.2	11.6	6.8	16,093	16.8	17.6	33.0	27.9	4.8	121,752
HOPKINS	21,027	13,038	30.4	31.9	27.1	6.9	3.8	9,519	24.2	28.1	33.8	11.3	2.6	85,991
HOUSTON	18,222	8,370	37.4	29.4	25.6	5.1	2.5	6,453	30.7	35.7	23.3	8.6	1.7	69,799
HOWARD	18,707	11,016	34.1	29.8	26.8	6.1	3.1	7,801	45.9	27.8	20.6	5.2	0.5	54,583
HUDSPETH	11,657	1,129	48.9	30.0	16.8	1.9	2.3	916	64.0	23.0	11.5	1.1	0.4	39,059
HUNT	21,532	31,154	26.9	28.0	32.5	9.0	3.7	22,686	30.2	28.3	31.3	9.3	0.9	77,573
HUTCHINSON	21,799	8,804	25.9	29.5	33.0	9.2	2.5	7,014	40.5	29.1	23.1	6.6	0.8	60,734
IRION	25,168	711	27.0	27.6	32.1	6.9	6.5	563	25.0	26.3	32.1	12.8	3.7	88,026
JACK	18,913	3,194	31.6	32.1	28.4	5.4	2.5	2,494	37.1	29.7	22.0	7.3	4.0	66,275
JACKSON	20,312	5,347	28.9	28.0	32.7	7.4	3.0	4,036	27.9	35.0	26.7	8.9	1.5	74,416
JASPER	18,673	13,758	34.8	29.4	27.7	5.7	2.4	11,206	31.6	29.2	29.8	8.6	0.9	73,900
JEFF DAVIS	23,311	1,001	31.6	30.1	26.9	7.2	4.3	716	25.0	17.0	29.6	19.1	9.2	104,798
JEFFERSON	22,428	94,216	29.7	26.5	28.9	10.0	4.8	63,483	29.3	30.4	30.7	8.3	1.3	76,930
JIM HOGG	14,583	1,817	42.6	30.5	20.1	4.7	2.0	1,416	53.0	28.2	16.1	2.7	0.0	47,846
JIM WELLS	15,082	13,770	37.7	29.5	25.4	5.4	2.0	10,620	43.1	29.5	21.2	5.4	0.8	58,249
JOHNSON	22,802	52,257	18.0	27.3	38.0	12.1	4.6	41,754	14.6	28.3	40.0	15.2	1.8	98,898
JONES	17,683	5,958	34.7	31.1	25.7	5.1	3.5	4,770	48.2	25.2	19.8	5.4	1.5	52,574
KARNES	16,421	4,493	38.1	30.6	23.1	5.9	2.4	3,391	45.8	28.2	19.1	6.0	1.0	55,930
KAUFMAN	23,232	33,026	19.5	25.7	36.7	12.5	5.6	26,496	13.5	22.1	39.5	23.3	1.5	112,937
KENDALL	30,393	11,609	17.9	23.3	33.7	14.0	11.1	9,416	9.6	8.6	23.6	38.3	19.8	203,623
KENEDY	16,079	138	36.2	44.2	14.5	1.4	3.6	50	36.0	26.0	22.0	8.0	8.0	75,000
KENT	20,908	323	28.5	37.8	23.5	8.4	1.9	259	56.0	26.6	12.7	4.6	0.0	42,955
KERR	25,163	19,478	27.0	30.9	28.5	8.0	5.5	14,605	17.0	18.7	34.3	23.1	6.9	118,525
KIMBLE	21,350	1,967	34.4	30.5	26.9	5.0	3.2	1,481	31.7	22.4	17.9	16.3	11.6	81,908
KING	13,696	95	35.8	36.8	26.3	1.1	0.0	34	61.8	20.6	8.8	2.9	5.9	29,000
KINNEY	19,112	1,302	36.0	30.6	23.7	5.5	4.1	1,022	43.7	26.4	19.6	8.4	1.9	60,482
KLEBERG	17,553	10,922	36.8	27.1	25.6	7.6	2.9	6,613	35.4	29.7	26.8	7.1	1.0	70,477
KNOX	16,929	1,615	41.0	32.0	20.5	5.0	1.5	1,237	58.6	23.3	14.8	2.3	1.0	41,680
LAMAR	20,656	19,845	33.2	28.7	28.6	6.3	3.2	13,726	26.9	29.6	31.8	10.1	1.5	81,643
LAMB	17,333	5,333	37.0	32.2	22.9	5.4	2.5	4,086	51.2	25.5	18.8	3.9	0.6	48,834
LAMPASAS	20,761	7,329	25.7	31.3	31.8	7.6	3.5	5,534	19.2	25.2	38.2	14.5	2.9	100,313
LA SALLE	12,219	1,921	48.1	31.6	14.9	4.3	1.0	1,447	59.7	19.9	14.9	3.0	2.5	37,204
LAVACA	19,944	7,695	35.6	30.3	25.1	6.1	2.9	6,138	26.4	27.6	29.6	13.7	2.6	84,038
LEE	20,596	5,959	27.4	29.9	30.8	8.6	3.3	4,787	25.7	21.7	32.7	16.9	3.0	95,685
LEON	21,495	6,669	33.2	28.1	26.5	8.7	3.4	5,578	31.5	22.6	30.0	13.6	2.4	81,950
LIBERTY	19,384	25,659	27.2	25.7	35.3	9.1	2.7	20,472	32.4	27.5	30.7	9.0	0.5	74,603
LIMESTONE	18,055	8,360	35.1	28.9	27.6	6.0	2.3	6,360	36.8	29.2	25.6	7.5	0.9	66,779
LIPSCOMB	20,038	1,260	31.0	31.1	28.7	6.0	3.1	992	46.2	25.6	22.7	4.8	0.7	55,758
LIVE OAK	20,326	4,197	30.8	30.0	28.9	6.6	3.6	3,450	30.5	30.4	30.2	7.4	1.4	75,040
LLANO	30,302	9,079	23.5	31.9	29.6	8.3	6.8	7,446	17.6	18.9	30.4	24.0	9.2	123,943
LOVING	27,615	32	31.3	18.8	34.4	15.6	0.0	27	74.1	18.5	0.0	0.0	7.4	14,375
LUBBOCK	22,112	99,142	30.8	28.6	27.9	7.9	4.8	60,461	22.8	29.0	34.6	12.0	1.7	87,597
LYNN	17,125	2,294	39.4	27.6	23.0	6.9	3.1	1,734	46.6	25.8	21.7	5.1	0.8	54,097
MCCULLOCH	16,977	3,241	41.5	31.0	21.9	3.7	1.8	2,395	48.6	21.4	19.1	8.7	2.1	52,273
TEXAS	25,413		22.9	25.9	31.0	12.0	8.1		16.4	21.8	36.0	21.0	4.7	110,551
UNITED STATES	27,916		21.9	25.0	32.3	12.3	8.4		7.9	10.5	27.1	35.6	19.0	192,285

COUNTY	FINANCIAL SERVICES				THE HOME						ENTERTAINMENT						PERSONAL			
					Home Improvements		Furnishings													
	Auto Loan	Home Loan	Invest-ments	Retire-ment Plans	Home Repair	Lawn & Garden	Comput-ers & Hard-ware	Major Appli-ances	TV, Radio, Sound Equip-ment	Furni-ture	Dine out/Carry out	Sports Equip-ment	Fees & Tickets	Toys & Games	Travel	Cable TV	Apparel & Services	Auto Repairs	Health Insur-ance	Pets & Supplies
FOARD	71	50	39	49	57	76	56	67	63	51	61	59	47	65	55	68	51	62	78	71
FORT BEND	153	172	160	172	159	146	151	150	144	161	145	142	159	150	152	139	133	148	137	149
FRANKLIN	88	65	46	63	74	98	68	86	75	64	73	74	59	77	69	80	63	78	93	90
FREESTONE	82	63	47	60	68	88	64	78	71	62	69	67	56	72	64	76	60	72	85	82
FRIO	65	50	31	45	48	60	48	58	55	51	56	51	42	54	47	58	49	57	61	59
GAINES	81	61	39	57	63	79	61	73	67	61	67	66	53	68	59	70	58	70	76	77
GALVESTON	102	98	98	100	94	96	98	96	99	99	99	88	97	100	97	99	89	98	98	98
GARZA	68	51	38	48	52	66	53	62	61	53	60	55	47	60	53	64	52	61	69	63
GILLESPIE	95	79	65	78	89	110	79	97	83	77	82	84	72	84	83	88	71	89	102	100
GLASSCOCK	121	77	33	73	95	136	81	113	90	77	91	101	63	99	80	97	76	100	119	126
GOLIAD	92	64	36	61	74	103	66	87	73	63	73	77	54	77	66	79	62	79	93	95
GONZALES	78	57	36	53	60	78	57	71	65	57	64	63	49	66	57	69	55	67	76	74
GRAY	75	65	70	66	68	77	69	73	75	66	72	63	66	74	70	78	63	71	84	73
GRAYSON	87	77	76	77	78	87	79	83	83	77	82	73	76	83	79	85	72	82	89	85
GREGG	85	78	80	79	77	83	80	81	84	80	83	72	78	83	80	85	74	82	86	83
GRIMES	87	65	43	61	69	89	65	80	72	64	72	70	56	74	64	77	62	75	85	84
GUADALUPE	98	94	83	92	90	95	88	93	90	90	90	84	87	92	88	91	80	91	93	94
HALE	76	66	54	62	63	71	65	71	70	67	69	64	61	69	64	71	61	71	73	70
HALL	57	41	33	40	46	60	45	54	51	41	49	47	39	52	45	55	42	50	63	56
HAMILTON	80	60	48	59	68	88	64	78	71	60	69	67	56	73	65	77	59	72	88	81
HANSFORD	97	63	32	60	75	107	67	90	76	63	76	81	53	82	66	82	63	81	98	99
HARDEMAN	78	57	49	57	63	81	64	73	72	59	69	64	56	73	63	77	59	70	86	76
HARDIN	92	75	58	73	77	92	72	84	78	73	78	75	67	81	72	82	68	80	88	89
HARRIS	111	105	99	107	97	95	111	102	109	110	110	100	107	108	104	106	100	110	99	102
HARRISON	85	67	53	65	69	86	68	78	74	67	73	69	62	76	67	78	64	74	84	82
HARTLEY	114	86	56	84	99	127	85	110	91	84	92	98	74	99	86	96	79	99	113	119
HASKELL	69	50	39	49	56	74	55	66	61	51	59	58	47	63	55	65	50	61	75	69
HAYS	102	97	95	99	93	92	108	97	101	101	102	93	101	101	100	97	92	102	93	98
HEMPHILL	89	64	43	62	74	98	66	84	73	63	72	74	56	77	66	78	62	76	91	91
HENDERSON	85	73	62	70	77	93	71	84	77	71	75	72	67	75	74	81	65	80	91	86
HIDALGO	67	58	45	54	52	57	56	60	61	60	62	54	53	58	55	62	55	62	61	58
HILL	81	62	45	59	67	86	63	76	69	61	68	66	55	71	63	74	59	71	83	80
HOCKLEY	79	65	53	62	64	76	66	73	71	65	70	65	60	71	65	73	61	71	77	74
HOOD	106	96	89	95	98	112	92	104	97	92	96	90	90	96	96	101	84	99	110	106
HOPKINS	85	67	56	66	71	89	70	80	76	67	75	70	63	78	69	80	65	76	88	84
HOUSTON	73	55	42	53	60	79	58	70	65	56	64	60	51	65	58	70	55	66	78	74
HOWARD	73	63	62	63	64	72	65	69	70	65	69	61	62	70	65	73	61	69	76	70
HUDSPETH	57	47	33	43	43	51	45	51	50	48	50	45	41	49	44	51	44	51	52	50
HUNT	87	73	67	73	73	84	77	81	81	74	80	72	71	82	75	83	70	80	86	83
HUTCHINSON	81	73	70	72	75	84	72	78	77	72	76	68	70	78	73	80	67	76	84	80
IRION	112	74	36	70	89	126	77	105	85	73	86	93	61	92	76	92	72	93	111	116
JACK	83	60	41	58	68	90	62	78	69	59	68	68	53	73	62	74	58	71	85	84
JACKSON	90	65	46	63	72	96	68	84	76	65	75	73	58	79	67	82	64	77	93	90
JASPER	81	58	37	55	64	85	59	74	67	58	66	65	51	69	59	72	56	69	81	80
JEFF DAVIS	95	69	40	66	80	108	70	92	76	67	76	80	59	79	71	81	64	83	96	99
JEFFERSON	82	75	82	77	74	78	79	77	83	79	82	68	78	82	78	85	73	80	84	79
JIM HOGG	67	54	35	48	48	57	51	58	59	56	59	51	46	56	50	60	52	59	60	57
JIM WELLS	71	58	43	54	54	64	57	63	63	59	63	57	52	62	56	64	56	64	66	63
JOHNSON	98	92	85	91	89	95	88	92	90	89	90	83	86	93	88	91	80	90	93	94
JONES	78	60	51	59	64	79	64	72	70	60	68	63	57	71	63	75	59	69	82	75
KARNES	74	56	38	52	57	73	56	67	64	56	63	59	49	64	56	68	55	65	73	70
KAUFMAN	101	96	84	94	91	96	90	94	92	93	92	86	89	95	90	93	82	93	94	96
KENDALL	116	122	126	124	126	128	112	121	111	114	110	107	116	112	118	112	99	115	120	122
KENEDY	75	62	42	55	52	60	58	64	67	65	68	56	54	63	57	69	61	68	66	61
KENT	82	56	38	54	65	89	62	77	69	57	68	68	51	72	61	74	57	71	87	82
KERR	89	77	72	76	83	100	78	91	83	76	81	77	73	80	81	87	71	86	98	92
KIMBLE	81	60	41	59	68	91	63	80	69	59	68	69	54	71	64	74	58	73	86	84
KING	68	43	19	41	53	77	46	64	51	44	52	57	35	56	45	55	43	57	67	71
KINNEY	73	63	55	59	64	77	62	72	68	62	67	60	58	64	65	72	58	70	80	71
KLEBERG	73	61	54	60	57	64	67	66	69	65	69	61	61	67	63	69	61	69	67	66
KNOX	67	47	37	46	54	71	52	63	59	48	57	55	44	61	52	64	48	59	73	66
LAMAR	78	64	61	64	67	79	67	73	73	65	71	64	63	73	67	76	62	71	81	76
LAMB	77	56	38	53	59	77	58	71	66	57	65	62	50	67	57	70	56	67	78	74
LAMPASAS	85	73	67	72	74	86	73	80	78	72	77	71	69	79	73	81	67	77	86	83
LA SALLE	54	46	32	41	41	47	44	49	48	47	48	44	40	46	43	48	43	50	49	47
LAVACA	82	59	40	56	66	89	61	77	68	58	67	67	52	71	61	73	57	70	84	82
LEE	91	73	52	69	74	91	72	84	77	71	77	76	64	79	71	80	66	80	87	89
LEON	86	67	47	64	73	93	66	83	72	65	72	72	59	74	67	76	61	77	87	87
LIBERTY	89	73	58	71	72	86	73	81	78	72	78	73	67	80	71	81	68	79	85	85
LIMESTONE	76	57	45	56	62	79	60	71	67	58	66	61	53	68	60	71	57	67	78	74
LIPSCOMB	84	63	38	59	68	86	65	79	67	63	68	73	54	71	62	69	59	75	79	83
LIVE OAK	85	68	51	65	73	93	67	83	73	67	73	71	61	73	69	78	63	77	89	86
LLANO	93	87	85	85	94	110	82	98	88	83	86	82	82	81	91	94	74	94	110	98
LOVING	91	71	46	70	82	108	72	93	75	68	75	81	62	77	74	80	64	83	94	98
LUBBOCK	81	72	72	73	68	71	82	76	81	77	81	70	76	80	76	80	72	70	77	76
LYNN	80	58	33	53	61	80	58	73	65	59	66	65	49	67	57	68	56	69	75	77
MCCULLOCH	65	49	41	49	53	67	54	61	60	51	58	53	47	60	53	64	50	59	69	63
TEXAS	104	95	88	96	90	94	98	96	99	98	99	90	94	99	94	98	89	99	96	97
UNITED STATES	100	100	100	100	100	100	100	100	100	100	100	100	100	100	100	100	100	100	100	100

COUNTY	FIPS Code	CBSA Code	DMA Code	POPULATION			2000-2007 ANNUAL RATE		RACE (%)					
									White		Black		Asian/Pacific	
				2000	2007	2012	% Rate	State Rank	2000	2007	2000	2007	2000	2007
MCLENNAN	309	47380	625	213,517	230,315	241,657	1.1	69	72.2	68.7	15.2	15.8	1.1	1.4
MCMULLEN	311	00000	641	851	868	879	0.3	139	88.4	88.0	1.2	1.2	0.0	0.0
MADISON	313	00000	625	12,940	13,507	13,960	0.6	105	66.8	63.4	22.9	23.8	0.4	0.5
MARION	315	00000	612	10,941	11,144	11,248	0.3	139	72.7	70.1	23.9	25.9	0.2	0.3
MARTIN	317	00000	633	4,746	4,649	4,587	-0.3	202	79.0	78.4	1.6	1.6	0.2	0.2
MASON	319	00000	635	3,738	3,874	3,965	0.5	117	91.6	89.5	0.1	0.2	0.1	0.1
MATAGORDA	321	13060	618	37,957	37,676	37,380	-0.1	178	67.8	64.4	12.7	12.7	2.4	2.8
MAVERICK	323	20580	641	47,297	52,929	55,773	1.6	50	70.9	70.5	0.3	0.3	0.4	0.4
MEDINA	325	41700	641	39,304	43,993	47,301	1.6	50	79.4	76.6	2.2	2.2	0.4	0.4
MENARD	327	00000	661	2,360	2,310	2,274	-0.3	202	87.5	87.1	0.5	0.5	0.4	0.4
MIDLAND	329	33260	633	116,009	122,327	126,569	0.7	94	77.3	74.0	7.0	7.1	1.0	1.1
MILAM	331	00000	625	24,238	25,692	26,522	0.8	87	78.9	76.0	11.0	11.6	0.2	0.3
MILLS	333	00000	625	5,151	5,494	5,761	0.9	82	89.2	86.5	1.3	1.4	0.2	0.2
MITCHELL	335	00000	662	9,698	9,467	9,254	-0.3	202	74.5	72.0	12.8	12.9	0.4	0.5
MONTAGUE	337	00000	627	19,117	19,786	20,275	0.5	117	96.0	94.9	0.2	0.2	0.3	0.4
MONTGOMERY	339	26420	618	293,768	409,876	499,008	4.7	6	88.3	85.9	3.5	3.7	1.1	1.4
MOORE	341	20300	634	20,121	20,094	20,029	0.0	170	63.9	63.0	0.7	0.7	0.9	0.9
MORRIS	343	00000	612	13,048	13,324	13,529	0.3	139	71.7	68.9	24.1	26.0	0.2	0.3
MOTLEY	345	00000	651	1,426	1,359	1,313	-0.7	229	87.4	86.8	3.5	3.7	0.3	0.3
NACOGDOCHES	347	34860	709	59,203	61,984	64,090	0.6	105	75.0	71.9	16.7	17.8	0.8	0.9
NAVARRO	349	18620	623	45,124	49,322	51,942	1.2	65	70.8	67.2	16.8	17.5	0.8	1.0
NEWTON	351	00000	692	15,072	14,509	13,981	-0.5	219	75.8	73.3	20.7	22.4	0.3	0.4
NOLAN	353	45020	662	15,802	15,203	14,814	-0.5	219	78.5	74.6	4.7	4.8	0.3	0.4
NUECES	355	18580	600	313,645	330,810	343,289	0.7	94	72.0	69.5	4.2	4.0	1.2	1.3
OCHILTREE	357	00000	634	9,006	9,379	9,660	0.6	105	86.2	83.4	0.1	0.1	0.4	0.4
OLDHAM	359	00000	634	2,185	2,200	2,177	0.1	159	90.7	90.4	1.9	1.9	0.4	0.4
ORANGE	361	13140	692	84,966	85,812	86,370	0.1	159	88.0	90.0	8.4	6.1	0.8	0.5
PALO PINTO	363	33420	623	27,026	27,670	28,066	0.3	139	88.2	85.6	2.3	2.5	0.6	0.7
PANOLA	365	00000	612	22,756	23,436	23,908	0.4	128	78.8	76.4	17.7	19.2	0.2	0.3
PARKER	367	19100	623	88,495	108,355	123,883	2.8	19	92.6	91.0	1.8	2.0	0.4	0.5
PARMER	369	00000	634	10,016	9,848	9,713	-0.2	190	66.0	61.0	1.0	1.0	0.4	0.4
PECOS	371	00000	633	16,809	16,172	15,744	-0.5	219	75.8	74.0	4.4	4.1	0.5	0.6
POLK	373	00000	618	41,133	46,539	50,717	1.7	47	79.6	77.1	13.2	14.1	0.4	0.5
POTTER	375	11100	634	113,546	122,153	127,538	1.0	75	68.6	64.4	10.0	10.1	2.5	3.0
PRESIDIO	377	00000	633	7,304	8,123	8,567	1.5	54	85.0	84.3	0.3	0.3	0.1	0.1
RAINS	379	00000	623	9,139	11,114	12,461	2.7	20	91.9	90.3	2.9	3.2	0.4	0.5
RANDALL	381	11100	634	104,312	111,067	115,080	0.9	82	90.4	88.2	1.5	1.6	1.1	1.3
REAGAN	383	00000	633	3,326	2,989	2,767	-1.5	253	64.6	59.9	3.0	2.9	0.3	0.3
REAL	385	00000	641	3,047	3,148	3,222	0.5	117	91.4	89.5	0.2	0.2	0.2	0.3
RED RIVER	387	00000	623	14,314	14,115	13,953	-0.2	190	78.0	75.6	17.8	19.3	0.1	0.2
REEVES	389	37780	633	13,137	12,259	11,239	-0.9	238	79.3	78.0	2.1	1.9	0.4	0.4
REFUGIO	391	00000	600	7,828	7,820	7,825	0.0	170	80.2	79.9	6.8	6.8	0.3	0.3
ROBERTS	393	37420	634	887	882	885	-0.1	178	96.5	96.4	0.3	0.3	0.1	0.1
ROBERTSON	395	17780	625	16,000	16,444	16,746	0.4	128	66.2	63.0	24.2	25.2	0.2	0.3
ROCKWALL	397	19100	623	43,080	72,122	103,611	7.4	1	89.2	86.9	3.2	3.5	1.4	1.7
RUNNELS	399	00000	662	11,495	11,321	11,250	-0.2	190	81.4	77.7	1.4	1.4	0.3	0.4
RUSK	401	30980	709	47,372	49,098	50,196	0.5	117	74.9	72.1	19.2	20.5	0.2	0.3
SABINE	403	00000	709	10,469	10,871	11,212	0.5	117	87.8	86.3	9.9	11.0	0.1	0.1
SAN AUGUSTINE	405	00000	709	8,946	9,023	9,006	0.1	159	69.3	68.6	27.9	28.6	0.2	0.2
SAN JACINTO	407	26420	618	22,246	25,356	27,845	1.8	43	83.6	81.6	12.6	13.8	0.4	0.4
SAN PATRICIO	409	18580	600	67,138	71,989	75,149	1.0	75	76.8	74.0	2.8	2.7	0.7	0.8
SAN SABA	411	00000	625	6,186	6,275	6,294	0.2	148	84.5	83.9	2.7	2.8	0.1	0.1
SCHLEICHER	413	00000	661	2,935	2,783	2,676	-0.7	229	76.6	72.7	1.5	1.7	0.2	0.3
SCURRY	415	43660	662	16,361	15,867	15,582	-0.4	211	81.3	78.4	6.1	6.2	0.2	0.3
SHACKELFORD	417	00000	662	3,302	3,446	3,487	0.6	105	94.2	92.6	0.5	0.6	0.0	0.0
SHELBY	419	00000	612	25,224	26,257	27,108	0.6	105	72.6	69.4	19.4	20.7	0.2	0.3
SHERMAN	421	00000	634	3,186	3,293	3,355	0.5	117	82.5	78.6	0.5	0.6	0.0	0.0
SMITH	423	46340	709	174,706	196,814	213,364	1.7	47	72.6	69.5	19.1	20.1	0.7	0.9
SOMERVELL	425	24180	623	6,809	7,914	8,676	2.1	33	92.2	90.2	0.3	0.3	0.3	0.3
STARR	427	40100	636	53,597	62,732	70,233	2.2	30	87.9	87.7	0.1	0.2	0.3	0.3
STEPHENS	429	00000	662	9,674	9,589	9,453	-0.1	178	86.9	86.4	2.9	3.0	0.3	0.3
STERLING	431	00000	661	1,393	1,329	1,285	-0.6	225	85.7	85.0	0.1	0.1	0.1	0.1
STONEWALL	433	00000	662	1,693	1,511	1,431	-1.6	254	88.2	85.5	3.0	3.4	0.4	0.5
SUTTON	435	00000	661	4,077	4,030	4,001	-0.2	190	75.3	74.7	0.2	0.2	0.2	0.2
SWISHER	437	00000	634	8,378	7,875	7,506	-0.9	238	71.7	67.5	5.8	5.8	0.2	0.2
TARRANT	439	19100	623	1,446,219	1,697,075	1,882,392	2.2	30	71.2	67.6	12.8	13.2	3.8	4.5
TAYLOR	441	10180	662	126,555	127,508	128,352	0.1	159	80.6	77.3	6.7	7.1	1.3	1.6
TERRELL	443	00000	633	1,081	1,015	1,009	-0.9	238	88.3	88.0	0.0	0.0	0.6	0.7
TERRY	445	00000	651	12,761	12,201	11,834	-0.6	225	76.6	73.7	5.0	4.9	0.2	0.3
THROCKMORTON	447	00000	662	1,850	1,689	1,616	-1.2	248	92.1	89.9	0.1	0.1	0.1	0.1
TITUS	449	34420	612	28,118	29,666	30,438	0.7	94	70.1	66.0	10.7	10.8	0.5	0.5
TOM GREEN	451	41660	661	104,010	103,951	103,151	0.0	170	79.1	78.5	4.1	4.2	0.9	0.9
TRAVIS	453	12420	635	812,280	960,550	1,063,968	2.3	27	68.2	64.0	9.3	9.3	4.5	5.3
TRINITY	455	00000	618	13,779	14,639	15,251	0.8	87	83.8	81.5	11.9	13.0	0.2	0.3
TYLER	457	00000	692	20,871	21,230	21,482	0.2	148	83.8	81.6	12.0	13.1	0.2	0.3
UPSHUR	459	30980	709	35,291	37,819	39,531	1.0	75	85.7	83.7	10.1	11.1	0.2	0.3
UPTON	461	00000	633	3,404	3,138	3,027	-1.1	245	77.8	74.1	1.6	1.8	0.1	0.1
TEXAS							2.0		71.0	68.4	11.5	11.4	2.8	3.3
UNITED STATES							1.2		75.1	72.7	12.3	12.6	3.8	4.5

COUNTY	% HISPANIC ORIGIN		2007 AGE DISTRIBUTION (%)									MEDIAN AGE	% 2007 Males	% 2007 Females
	2000	2007	0-4	5-9	10-14	15-19	20-24	25-44	45-64	65-84	85+	18+	2007		
MCLENNAN	17.9	22.2	7.4	6.6	6.5	8.8	10.5	25.0	22.7	10.4	2.1	75.3	32.7	48.8	51.2
MCMULLEN	33.1	34.8	4.5	3.9	4.0	7.8	6.1	19.8	34.3	17.3	2.2	82.9	46.8	49.5	50.5
MADISON	15.8	19.6	5.8	5.5	5.1	5.7	10.3	31.8	22.1	11.4	2.3	80.4	34.3	58.7	41.3
MARION	2.4	3.1	5.5	5.4	5.1	5.9	5.4	20.2	31.4	18.5	2.5	80.4	46.6	49.3	50.7
MARTIN	40.6	42.2	9.2	8.5	7.6	7.4	7.6	24.1	22.2	11.5	1.9	69.7	34.5	49.6	50.4
MASON	20.9	26.3	5.5	5.5	4.7	5.8	6.2	19.1	30.3	18.9	3.8	80.6	47.2	47.9	52.1
MATAGORDA	31.3	37.2	7.9	6.4	6.8	7.5	8.9	23.7	26.1	11.1	1.6	74.3	35.7	50.1	49.9
MAVERICK	95.0	96.0	10.4	9.1	9.8	9.1	8.2	24.8	19.3	8.3	0.9	65.1	28.0	48.3	51.7
MEDINA	45.5	52.6	7.6	6.8	7.1	7.1	7.9	26.4	25.0	10.5	1.6	73.9	35.5	51.5	48.5
MENARD	31.7	33.2	5.3	4.5	4.6	6.2	9.4	18.2	30.6	17.8	3.3	81.3	46.1	49.4	50.6
MIDLAND	29.0	35.1	7.8	6.9	7.3	8.2	9.0	23.6	25.5	10.3	1.5	73.1	34.2	48.4	51.6
MILAM	18.6	23.2	7.2	6.2	6.7	6.7	6.7	23.2	26.5	13.8	3.0	75.7	39.5	49.6	50.4
MILLS	13.0	16.8	6.1	5.8	5.7	7.5	6.8	18.5	28.3	16.9	4.4	77.0	44.7	50.4	49.6
MITCHELL	31.0	37.1	5.0	4.0	4.5	7.1	10.5	29.7	25.5	11.1	2.6	83.1	38.7	62.6	37.4
MONTAGUE	5.4	7.1	6.4	5.9	5.2	6.7	6.0	22.0	27.5	17.2	3.2	78.4	43.5	48.4	51.6
MONTGOMERY	12.6	16.2	7.8	7.4	7.6	7.1	6.8	27.1	26.7	8.5	0.9	72.7	35.5	49.5	50.5
MOORE	47.5	49.1	9.7	8.7	8.5	8.0	7.3	27.2	20.7	8.5	1.4	67.9	30.8	50.3	49.7
MORRIS	3.7	4.7	6.1	5.7	5.9	6.5	6.8	22.3	28.1	15.9	2.6	78.4	42.4	48.6	51.4
MOTLEY	12.1	12.9	6.3	6.4	5.4	5.2	5.7	21.0	28.2	18.8	2.9	78.7	44.9	51.7	48.3
NACOGDOCHES	11.2	14.3	6.7	6.2	5.8	9.4	12.9	25.3	21.8	10.1	1.9	77.7	30.5	48.3	51.7
NAVARRO	15.8	19.7	7.5	6.8	6.6	7.7	7.3	26.0	24.0	11.6	2.3	74.8	36.4	49.6	50.4
NEWTON	3.8	4.9	6.8	6.5	6.1	6.2	7.5	25.5	27.0	13.1	1.4	77.1	38.9	51.2	48.8
NOLAN	28.0	34.2	7.2	6.3	6.2	7.6	8.3	22.9	25.8	13.2	2.5	76.0	37.5	48.7	51.3
NUECES	55.8	62.4	8.0	7.2	7.0	6.9	7.9	27.4	24.5	9.7	1.4	73.7	33.7	49.0	51.0
OCHILTREE	31.8	38.4	8.6	8.0	7.3	6.9	6.9	26.7	24.6	9.8	1.4	71.9	34.1	50.1	49.9
OLDHAM	11.0	11.7	6.6	7.0	10.7	11.0	5.3	21.3	26.6	10.2	1.2	67.1	33.7	53.2	46.8
ORANGE	3.6	4.7	7.0	6.4	6.9	6.4	7.0	26.2	26.9	11.8	1.5	75.8	37.9	49.2	50.8
PALO PINTO	13.6	17.4	7.0	6.2	6.1	6.7	6.2	24.0	27.7	13.9	2.3	76.6	40.4	49.6	50.4
PANOLA	3.5	4.6	6.3	6.3	5.9	6.4	6.9	24.0	28.2	13.5	2.4	77.7	40.5	48.4	51.6
PARKER	7.0	9.2	6.5	6.1	6.9	7.4	6.9	26.3	28.6	10.2	1.2	76.0	38.7	50.8	49.2
PARMER	49.2	56.5	9.5	8.3	7.7	7.9	7.7	24.8	21.3	10.5	2.3	69.6	32.5	49.7	50.3
PECOS	61.1	67.3	7.1	6.0	6.6	8.2	11.7	26.1	22.5	10.4	1.5	75.8	32.7	55.3	44.7
POLK	9.4	12.0	6.2	5.8	5.6	5.7	6.9	24.7	26.9	16.2	2.0	79.0	41.4	52.0	48.0
POTTER	28.1	33.8	8.5	7.6	7.1	7.1	7.5	29.0	21.9	9.3	2.0	72.8	32.7	50.7	49.3
PRESIDIO	84.4	87.8	8.4	7.2	9.3	8.7	6.9	24.3	21.8	11.7	1.7	69.3	33.3	48.7	51.3
RAINS	5.5	7.3	5.8	5.5	5.1	5.9	5.9	23.0	30.1	16.8	1.8	79.9	44.1	50.3	49.7
RANDALL	10.3	13.3	7.0	6.6	6.5	7.6	8.1	26.1	25.8	10.9	1.4	75.7	35.9	48.7	51.3
REAGAN	49.5	56.7	8.8	7.6	6.9	8.7	10.9	24.0	23.2	8.7	1.2	70.8	31.7	50.0	50.0
REAL	22.6	28.1	5.1	4.6	5.7	6.5	6.1	19.3	29.9	20.1	2.7	80.4	46.8	49.0	51.0
RED RIVER	4.7	6.1	6.1	5.6	5.9	5.9	5.9	24.3	27.1	15.7	3.4	78.8	42.2	48.2	51.8
REEVES	73.4	78.4	6.6	6.3	6.3	9.9	12.0	24.8	22.0	10.9	1.2	74.9	31.7	57.6	42.4
REFUGIO	44.6	46.3	6.6	5.9	6.3	6.6	7.6	22.9	27.0	14.9	2.2	77.2	40.8	49.5	50.5
ROBERTS	3.2	3.3	5.0	4.9	4.1	7.8	7.0	20.1	34.9	14.7	1.5	81.5	45.7	51.2	48.8
ROBERTSON	14.7	18.4	7.4	6.9	7.4	6.7	6.2	23.1	25.7	14.0	2.6	74.1	38.8	48.0	52.0
ROCKWALL	11.1	14.2	7.6	7.6	8.2	7.2	5.8	27.0	27.9	7.8	1.0	72.0	36.8	50.7	49.3
RUNNELS	29.3	35.7	7.0	6.0	6.3	6.6	8.0	21.8	26.0	14.5	3.7	76.5	40.7	48.4	51.6
RUSK	8.4	10.8	6.5	5.9	5.8	5.9	6.6	26.6	27.2	12.9	2.4	78.0	39.7	51.4	48.6
SABINE	1.8	2.4	5.6	4.9	5.1	5.7	4.9	19.0	29.1	23.0	2.6	80.7	48.5	51.5
SAN AUGUSTINE	3.6	3.8	6.1	5.5	5.9	5.9	5.6	21.9	27.0	18.3	3.9	78.9	44.3	48.0	52.0
SAN JACINTO	4.9	6.3	6.2	5.6	6.0	6.3	6.2	22.3	29.9	16.0	1.5	78.4	43.1	50.1	49.9
SAN PATRICIO	49.4	56.4	8.6	7.5	7.8	7.7	8.1	26.6	22.9	9.7	1.1	71.4	32.6	50.0	50.0
SAN SABA	21.5	22.7	5.7	5.3	6.1	12.2	6.6	18.6	26.9	15.2	3.6	75.5	41.0	52.1	47.9
SCHLEICHER	43.5	50.9	6.8	6.2	5.3	7.4	9.8	20.0	28.4	13.5	2.7	77.0	40.6	49.8	50.2
SCURRY	27.8	33.8	6.5	6.1	5.9	8.1	8.3	24.7	25.4	12.7	2.4	77.4	37.7	52.3	47.7
SHACKELFORD	7.6	10.0	5.6	5.3	6.3	6.8	8.3	21.4	28.2	15.1	2.9	78.1	42.8	48.0	52.0
SHELBY	9.9	12.6	7.4	7.0	6.5	6.4	5.6	26.1	25.1	13.4	2.5	75.2	38.2	48.3	51.7
SHERMAN	27.4	33.8	7.5	6.4	7.9	7.6	5.9	25.6	26.2	10.8	2.0	73.0	37.1	51.0	49.0
SMITH	11.2	14.1	7.2	6.7	6.6	7.0	7.6	25.5	24.9	12.4	2.1	75.5	36.7	48.2	51.8
SOMERVELL	13.4	17.2	6.6	6.2	6.5	7.2	7.8	24.9	27.7	11.0	2.1	76.3	38.6	50.1	49.9
STARR	97.5	98.1	11.3	9.6	9.8	8.4	8.1	27.3	17.5	7.3	0.8	64.2	26.9	48.9	51.1
STEPHENS	14.7	15.5	6.1	4.7	5.8	6.6	10.3	23.4	26.5	14.1	2.6	79.7	39.9	51.8	48.2
STERLING	31.0	32.7	5.8	5.5	5.6	8.4	8.7	23.5	28.0	11.5	3.1	77.4	41.2	49.5	50.5
STONEWALL	11.8	15.2	6.0	5.2	4.7	4.5	8.9	20.2	26.7	18.9	4.8	81.5	45.3	47.2	52.8
SUTTON	51.7	53.4	6.8	6.6	7.1	7.9	7.8	23.4	28.0	10.9	1.4	74.5	37.4	49.8	50.2
SWISHER	35.2	41.9	7.8	6.8	6.2	8.0	8.8	24.1	23.3	12.8	2.1	74.4	34.9	52.5	47.5
TARRANT	19.7	24.2	8.0	7.5	7.3	7.3	7.2	30.3	23.9	7.4	1.1	72.8	33.6	49.5	50.5
TAYLOR	17.6	22.1	7.4	6.3	6.6	8.1	10.4	25.9	22.6	10.8	1.9	75.7	33.2	48.6	51.4
TERRELL	48.6	50.4	6.8	5.4	5.6	7.5	6.8	19.5	29.1	17.5	1.8	77.7	43.6	50.7	49.3
TERRY	44.1	51.1	8.1	6.9	5.6	7.0	8.5	26.1	23.3	12.3	2.3	75.2	35.5	52.5	47.5
THROCKMORTON	9.4	12.2	6.0	5.3	5.6	7.0	6.6	21.8	25.8	18.1	3.7	78.7	43.7	50.2	49.8
TITUS	28.3	34.3	9.1	8.1	7.4	7.5	6.8	28.4	21.0	9.6	2.0	70.9	32.6	49.9	50.1
TOM GREEN	30.7	32.2	7.1	6.2	6.3	8.0	8.9	26.4	23.7	11.3	2.1	76.2	34.5	48.7	51.3
TRAVIS	28.2	33.8	7.3	6.8	6.3	6.9	9.5	34.5	21.9	6.0	0.9	76.1	31.7	51.3	48.7
TRINITY	4.8	6.3	6.1	5.8	5.3	5.8	5.7	20.6	28.3	19.9	2.6	79.1	45.6	48.9	51.1
TYLER	3.8	4.7	6.2	6.0	5.7	5.5	6.5	20.0	28.4	15.7	2.4	78.7	40.4	51.5	48.5
UPSHUR	4.0	5.2	6.9	6.6	6.3	6.6	6.7	24.6	27.6	12.8	1.9	76.3	39.8	49.3	50.7
UPTON	42.6	49.7	6.4	4.3	6.5	7.7	10.1	20.3	28.9	13.5	2.2	77.9	41.0	49.2	50.8
TEXAS	32.0	36.4	8.0	7.4	7.2	7.3	7.8	28.9	23.5	8.6	1.3	73.1	33.4	49.7	50.3
UNITED STATES	12.5	15.0	6.9	6.5	6.8	7.1	7.0	27.6	25.4	10.7	1.9	75.6	36.7	49.2	50.8

COUNTY	HOUSEHOLDS					FAMILIES			MEDIAN HOUSEHOLD INCOME			
	2000	2007	2012	% Annual Rate 2000-2007	2007 Average HH Size	2000	2007	% Annual Rate 2000-2007	2007	2012	2007 National Rank	2007 State Rank
MCLENNAN	78,859	84,190	88,393	0.9	2.62	52,892	55,799	0.7	41,028	47,662	1595	82
MCMULLEN	355	369	378	0.5	2.35	239	246	0.4	38,938	43,684	1860	108
MADISON	3,914	4,125	4,297	0.7	2.58	2,839	2,963	0.6	35,530	40,319	2361	168
MARION	4,610	4,749	4,824	0.4	2.32	3,119	3,176	0.3	32,016	37,484	2759	218
MARTIN	1,624	1,615	1,605	-0.1	2.83	1,257	1,240	-0.2	37,525	41,978	2057	138
MASON	1,607	1,674	1,719	0.6	2.29	1,111	1,146	0.4	37,013	42,273	2125	144
MATAGORDA	13,901	13,949	13,909	0.0	2.67	9,922	9,856	-0.1	39,517	45,149	1780	99
MAVERICK	13,089	14,792	15,657	1.7	3.57	11,231	12,626	1.6	25,870	29,123	3075	249
MEDINA	12,880	14,497	15,657	1.6	2.90	10,136	11,324	1.5	43,131	49,438	1313	59
MENARD	990	975	961	-0.2	2.33	665	647	-0.4	30,532	34,949	2882	235
MIDLAND	42,745	45,514	47,262	0.9	2.65	30,935	32,610	0.7	49,274	57,343	728	29
MILAM	9,199	9,784	10,119	0.9	2.58	6,595	6,942	0.7	40,058	45,696	1719	93
MILLS	2,001	2,130	2,234	0.9	2.44	1,398	1,471	0.7	36,299	41,135	2232	155
MITCHELL	2,837	2,740	2,668	-0.5	2.45	1,996	1,906	-0.6	31,111	35,682	2824	228
MONTAGUE	7,770	8,112	8,343	0.6	2.39	5,484	5,665	0.4	38,373	44,451	1952	123
MONTGOMERY	103,296	142,954	174,100	4.6	2.85	80,175	110,066	4.5	64,671	77,023	172	6
MOORE	6,774	6,740	6,704	-0.1	2.95	5,328	5,260	-0.2	41,912	48,181	1456	71
MORRIS	5,215	5,422	5,550	0.5	2.43	3,747	3,856	0.4	35,219	40,074	2402	172
MOTLEY	606	578	559	-0.7	2.35	435	411	-0.8	32,586	36,639	2696	214
NACOGDOCHES	22,006	23,201	24,062	0.7	2.48	14,039	14,613	0.6	35,118	40,489	2414	174
NAVARRO	16,491	17,855	18,784	1.1	2.67	11,908	12,766	1.0	37,591	42,673	2045	136
NEWTON	5,583	5,474	5,314	-0.3	2.54	4,092	3,975	-0.4	34,268	38,869	2516	189
NOLAN	6,170	6,022	5,904	-0.3	2.44	4,288	4,139	-0.5	32,292	37,383	2734	216
NUECES	110,365	117,816	122,985	0.9	2.75	79,693	84,224	0.8	44,742	52,509	1135	50
OCHILTREE	3,261	3,398	3,499	0.6	2.74	2,487	2,569	0.4	45,550	51,668	1047	45
OLDHAM	735	756	754	0.4	2.55	566	577	0.3	38,671	43,294	1900	113
ORANGE	31,642	32,616	33,068	0.4	2.60	23,798	24,315	0.3	44,864	51,344	1125	49
PALO PINTO	10,594	10,925	11,118	0.4	2.50	7,443	7,593	0.3	38,092	43,949	1992	128
PANOLA	8,821	9,217	9,466	0.6	2.49	6,397	6,619	0.5	38,400	43,784	1951	122
PARKER	31,131	37,759	43,266	2.7	2.79	24,310	29,252	2.6	53,967	60,482	456	21
PARMER	3,322	3,282	3,243	-0.2	2.96	2,616	2,565	-0.3	36,415	40,676	2209	152
PECOS	5,153	5,027	4,927	-0.3	2.79	4,029	3,899	-0.5	34,231	38,865	2524	190
POLK	15,119	17,410	19,153	2.0	2.48	10,920	12,452	1.8	37,602	43,512	2044	135
POTTER	40,760	43,270	45,159	0.8	2.64	27,475	28,822	0.7	36,364	41,794	2218	153
PRESIDIO	2,530	2,839	3,006	1.6	2.83	1,864	2,071	1.5	23,557	26,675	3108	251
RAINS	3,617	4,425	4,972	2.8	2.50	2,682	3,250	2.7	40,461	45,483	1664	90
RANDALL	41,240	44,155	45,900	0.9	2.48	28,777	30,481	0.8	53,750	62,629	465	22
REAGAN	1,107	1,028	965	-1.0	2.87	872	804	-1.1	38,472	43,065	1934	121
REAL	1,245	1,320	1,366	0.8	2.33	869	911	0.7	30,998	35,312	2831	229
RED RIVER	5,827	5,791	5,743	-0.1	2.39	4,065	3,997	-0.2	33,348	37,810	2624	206
REEVES	4,091	3,490	3,168	-2.2	2.86	3,130	2,646	-2.3	27,781	31,986	3012	243
REFUGIO	2,985	3,020	3,042	0.2	2.55	2,175	2,180	0.0	36,495	41,294	2191	150
ROBERTS	362	368	373	0.2	2.40	275	277	0.1	51,429	56,323	585	26
ROBERTSON	6,179	6,421	6,575	0.5	2.52	4,355	4,477	0.4	34,702	39,706	2467	184
ROCKWALL	14,530	24,318	34,935	7.4	2.94	11,977	19,917	7.3	82,280	98,882	43	3
RUNNELS	4,428	4,384	4,363	-0.1	2.52	3,159	3,096	-0.3	33,845	38,252	2569	202
RUSK	17,364	18,118	18,630	0.6	2.55	12,720	13,148	0.5	39,462	44,995	1785	100
SABINE	4,485	4,715	4,885	0.7	2.29	3,156	3,284	0.5	33,637	39,344	2591	204
SAN AUGUSTINE	3,575	3,621	3,636	0.2	2.40	2,521	2,527	0.0	32,898	37,511	2667	212
SAN JACINTO	8,651	9,953	10,975	2.0	2.53	6,399	7,294	1.8	39,359	45,600	1807	103
SAN PATRICIO	22,093	24,186	25,425	1.3	2.93	17,237	18,722	1.1	42,930	49,798	1338	61
SAN SABA	2,289	2,330	2,338	0.2	2.45	1,617	1,629	0.1	36,096	40,796	2257	157
SCHLEICHER	1,115	1,088	1,058	-0.3	2.52	817	790	-0.5	35,183	39,660	2407	173
SCURRY	5,756	5,682	5,626	-0.2	2.50	4,163	4,068	-0.3	38,502	43,664	1927	118
SHACKELFORD	1,300	1,349	1,360	0.5	2.51	941	967	0.4	36,479	41,053	2198	151
SHELBY	9,595	9,964	10,269	0.5	2.60	6,907	7,099	0.4	34,703	39,271	2466	183
SHERMAN	1,124	1,150	1,167	0.3	2.79	865	878	0.2	39,020	43,861	1849	106
SMITH	65,692	72,979	79,223	1.5	2.63	46,901	51,570	1.3	45,672	52,555	1032	44
SOMERVELL	2,438	2,848	3,131	2.2	2.72	1,840	2,131	2.0	46,287	52,064	972	38
STARR	14,410	17,211	19,451	2.5	3.62	12,663	15,058	2.4	19,339	21,800	3138	254
STEPHENS	3,661	3,605	3,557	-0.2	2.45	2,592	2,526	-0.4	36,649	43,004	2175	148
STERLING	513	501	489	-0.3	2.60	386	374	-0.4	41,125	46,105	1585	81
STONEWALL	713	645	615	-1.4	2.28	493	441	-1.5	33,742	38,265	2577	203
SUTTON	1,515	1,520	1,519	0.0	2.63	1,145	1,139	-0.1	41,295	47,046	1554	79
SWISHER	2,925	2,737	2,604	-0.9	2.63	2,154	1,997	-1.0	35,496	40,153	2368	169
TARRANT	533,864	618,197	684,080	2.0	2.71	369,306	422,949	1.9	59,237	69,977	283	11
TAYLOR	47,274	48,646	49,266	0.4	2.49	32,537	33,092	0.2	42,062	49,315	1441	69
TERRELL	443	430	433	-0.4	2.36	295	283	-0.6	29,106	33,013	2955	242
TERRY	4,278	4,145	4,046	-0.4	2.70	3,246	3,117	-0.6	33,388	37,853	2618	205
THROCKMORTON	765	692	659	-1.4	2.41	535	479	-1.5	34,168	38,729	2533	192
TITUS	9,552	9,940	10,136	0.6	2.92	7,150	7,373	0.4	38,609	43,816	1916	115
TOM GREEN	39,503	40,162	40,132	0.2	2.48	26,802	26,928	0.1	40,916	47,480	1611	83
TRAVIS	320,766	379,567	420,219	2.3	2.47	183,832	214,218	2.1	61,287	74,685	230	8
TRINITY	5,723	6,128	6,411	0.9	2.36	4,000	4,237	0.8	33,937	39,737	2556	198
TYLER	7,775	7,988	8,123	0.4	2.46	5,674	5,773	0.2	35,641	40,313	2340	164
UPSHUR	13,290	14,374	15,096	1.1	2.60	10,035	10,758	1.0	39,552	44,502	1771	97
UPTON	1,256	1,200	1,174	-0.6	2.59	934	884	-0.8	34,932	39,832	2439	178
TEXAS				1.9	2.76			1.8	51,090	60,298		
UNITED STATES				1.2	2.59			1.0	53,154	62,503		

COUNTY	2007 Per Capita Income	2007 HH Income Base	2007 HOUSEHOLD INCOME DISTRIBUTION (%)					2007 Home Value Base	2007 HOME VALUE DISTRIBUTION (%)					2007 Median Home Value
			Less than $25,000	$25,000 to $49,999	$50,000 to $99,999	$100,000 to $149,999	$150,000 or More		Less than $50,000	$50,000 to $89,999	$90,000 to $174,999	$175,000 to $399,999	$400,000 or More	
MCLENNAN	21,193	84,190	30.8	28.1	28.5	8.0	4.6	52,367	25.5	28.1	33.0	11.7	1.8	84,388
MCMULLEN	24,136	369	32.2	32.0	23.6	7.0	5.1	302	36.1	29.5	17.5	5.3	11.6	67,742
MADISON	18,297	4,125	32.7	34.8	23.3	5.3	3.9	3,237	32.1	25.7	27.4	11.8	2.9	75,519
MARION	18,878	4,749	41.1	26.5	24.6	5.4	2.3	3,940	44.8	24.6	23.6	6.0	1.0	57,021
MARTIN	18,307	1,615	32.0	33.6	24.0	6.5	3.9	1,224	38.6	23.2	31.1	6.5	0.5	68,308
MASON	23,569	1,674	32.6	30.5	26.4	6.8	3.8	1,358	22.4	27.6	26.7	14.7	8.6	90,000
MATAGORDA	19,358	13,949	31.9	28.5	27.0	9.9	2.7	9,551	28.2	29.7	32.7	8.4	0.9	80,761
MAVERICK	10,307	14,792	48.4	29.4	16.8	3.6	1.8	10,453	34.6	34.6	26.3	4.1	0.4	66,771
MEDINA	18,497	14,497	26.2	31.1	31.4	8.2	3.1	11,721	22.4	23.3	33.2	18.0	3.0	97,372
MENARD	18,499	975	42.1	31.3	18.2	5.7	2.8	742	51.6	22.0	11.7	7.1	7.5	48,500
MIDLAND	26,323	45,514	23.7	26.9	30.3	11.1	8.1	32,215	16.5	22.0	35.3	22.0	4.1	114,612
MILAM	20,038	9,784	30.6	29.6	30.0	7.1	2.8	7,318	30.5	29.2	27.5	10.9	1.9	75,810
MILLS	20,023	2,130	34.6	30.7	24.9	6.0	3.8	1,732	27.8	24.9	27.5	15.8	4.0	85,481
MITCHELL	16,998	2,740	40.6	31.2	21.8	4.3	2.2	2,104	54.6	25.1	16.3	3.6	0.4	45,689
MONTAGUE	21,126	8,112	33.3	30.0	26.9	6.6	3.2	6,474	29.2	29.2	28.8	10.4	2.4	78,370
MONTGOMERY	31,954	142,949	16.0	22.0	32.0	16.9	13.1	113,244	12.2	15.8	34.2	29.2	8.7	138,256
MOORE	17,999	6,740	25.6	33.5	31.3	7.1	2.4	4,844	29.6	31.1	30.9	7.8	0.6	74,506
MORRIS	19,711	5,422	35.1	29.7	26.8	5.7	2.7	4,281	37.7	31.2	25.6	5.1	0.4	63,042
MOTLEY	18,587	578	37.4	33.4	21.5	6.1	1.7	453	57.8	23.8	14.6	3.1	0.7	44,779
NACOGDOCHES	20,091	23,201	38.3	26.3	23.7	7.6	4.0	14,660	27.7	21.1	32.7	16.1	2.4	91,848
NAVARRO	18,780	17,855	34.4	27.7	28.0	6.7	3.2	12,907	29.0	28.5	31.1	9.7	1.7	77,576
NEWTON	16,823	5,474	37.4	32.2	25.1	3.5	1.9	4,648	41.7	29.9	22.7	5.1	0.7	60,671
NOLAN	17,991	6,022	39.8	28.8	24.0	4.6	2.7	4,145	50.8	26.6	17.2	4.8	0.6	49,254
NUECES	21,591	117,808	27.6	26.9	30.9	9.7	4.9	74,690	15.7	28.6	38.6	14.7	2.4	99,038
OCHILTREE	20,224	3,398	26.1	27.4	35.5	7.7	3.3	2,524	35.5	29.0	25.9	8.6	1.1	66,130
OLDHAM	19,374	756	28.6	35.2	28.0	4.6	3.6	513	37.4	25.5	29.0	6.4	1.6	67,821
ORANGE	21,891	32,616	27.4	26.7	31.8	10.5	3.6	25,545	31.0	29.4	30.0	9.1	0.5	74,805
PALO PINTO	19,273	10,925	31.9	30.7	29.3	5.7	2.3	8,037	35.8	29.4	22.5	10.1	2.3	66,468
PANOLA	19,656	9,217	32.2	30.3	27.0	8.2	2.3	7,522	34.9	27.1	27.7	9.2	1.1	70,341
PARKER	24,567	37,759	18.1	27.4	35.2	13.4	5.9	30,875	14.1	20.6	36.2	24.2	4.9	114,401
PARMER	16,590	3,282	31.2	35.2	25.6	4.5	3.5	2,420	34.2	29.5	27.1	7.8	1.4	69,479
PECOS	15,633	5,027	33.7	30.8	28.0	6.1	1.4	3,789	46.5	30.7	17.1	5.1	0.6	53,818
POLK	19,851	17,410	31.4	31.4	27.0	7.3	3.0	14,368	34.2	28.7	26.1	9.6	1.5	70,652
POTTER	18,553	43,270	32.9	31.4	26.4	6.1	3.2	26,757	29.9	35.4	24.4	9.1	1.3	69,147
PRESIDIO	11,565	2,839	52.4	29.1	14.4	3.1	1.0	2,031	54.9	26.7	13.9	3.5	1.0	46,231
RAINS	20,181	4,425	29.7	29.5	30.8	7.7	2.2	3,700	24.6	29.4	32.4	11.1	2.4	84,163
RANDALL	27,483	44,155	18.4	27.8	35.8	12.2	5.8	31,672	9.9	19.8	47.5	20.3	2.5	118,075
REAGAN	16,380	1,028	24.2	39.6	29.1	5.5	1.6	817	38.4	29.7	25.7	5.0	1.1	62,358
REAL	17,563	1,320	40.2	32.2	22.3	4.1	1.3	1,036	29.5	24.4	27.0	12.7	6.3	82,931
RED RIVER	18,570	5,791	36.9	32.4	23.7	4.7	2.3	4,428	47.2	27.1	19.2	4.9	1.6	53,443
REEVES	13,235	3,490	43.9	33.0	18.7	3.3	1.2	2,751	71.4	19.7	7.5	1.3	0.1	34,163
REFUGIO	19,386	3,020	34.2	28.0	28.8	6.3	2.7	2,299	42.6	31.4	19.2	5.7	1.0	57,705
ROBERTS	25,542	368	22.3	25.8	38.3	9.5	4.1	295	25.1	34.6	28.1	10.8	1.4	77,000
ROBERTSON	18,245	6,421	38.4	26.1	26.2	6.8	2.5	4,693	30.8	29.5	27.8	10.1	1.7	74,885
ROCKWALL	37,081	24,318	8.9	16.4	35.3	22.1	17.4	20,398	4.5	7.6	29.3	47.7	10.9	196,436
RUNNELS	16,893	4,384	37.3	32.0	24.9	4.1	1.7	3,432	43.2	27.2	22.5	5.5	1.5	57,614
RUSK	20,392	18,118	30.0	31.0	28.7	7.0	3.3	14,645	28.7	25.4	32.4	11.7	1.7	83,379
SABINE	20,439	4,715	36.0	33.1	23.3	4.5	3.1	4,082	36.8	27.1	27.6	7.3	1.2	65,879
SAN AUGUSTINE	19,133	3,621	38.7	30.4	22.7	5.5	2.7	2,968	41.0	28.1	23.6	6.4	0.8	63,351
SAN JACINTO	20,051	9,953	32.1	28.8	30.0	6.0	3.1	8,746	33.6	26.2	26.7	11.4	2.0	77,482
SAN PATRICIO	19,208	24,186	27.9	28.7	30.4	9.1	3.9	16,946	26.5	26.2	35.9	10.4	0.9	85,202
SAN SABA	19,383	2,330	31.1	35.0	25.3	5.5	3.1	1,797	36.1	25.4	22.6	11.3	4.6	73,527
SCHLEICHER	19,226	1,088	34.3	27.8	28.2	7.6	2.1	836	42.7	21.5	20.6	8.4	6.8	63,061
SCURRY	20,113	5,682	32.3	28.2	29.9	6.2	3.3	4,276	43.0	22.8	27.4	6.4	0.4	59,085
SHACKELFORD	19,446	1,349	32.5	30.7	27.2	7.3	2.2	1,083	41.7	28.2	21.6	6.7	1.8	59,521
SHELBY	18,079	9,964	35.9	31.1	24.2	6.4	2.5	7,916	36.2	27.2	26.0	8.6	2.0	68,688
SHERMAN	19,829	1,150	26.9	36.3	27.2	5.2	4.3	869	31.9	34.8	24.7	7.4	1.3	71,479
SMITH	23,441	72,979	25.8	28.3	30.8	9.7	5.4	51,968	18.1	21.3	37.3	19.8	3.5	106,738
SOMERVELL	21,024	2,848	23.6	29.3	33.3	10.6	3.1	2,186	18.6	18.1	32.1	22.3	9.0	125,315
STARR	8,219	17,211	60.2	24.7	11.3	2.8	1.0	13,862	46.0	31.8	18.3	3.7	0.2	53,690
STEPHENS	19,469	3,605	30.3	34.5	26.5	5.7	3.0	2,650	40.0	29.4	20.3	7.4	2.8	61,858
STERLING	21,570	501	29.1	31.1	28.3	7.8	3.6	388	30.7	33.5	22.7	11.3	1.8	73,810
STONEWALL	19,720	645	37.8	29.8	24.5	5.9	2.0	514	54.5	25.9	14.4	3.1	2.1	46,667
SUTTON	21,327	1,520	30.7	28.6	29.2	7.7	3.8	1,121	36.6	28.8	21.9	7.9	4.9	65,054
SWISHER	17,540	2,737	31.0	35.2	25.3	6.3	2.2	1,968	41.9	27.8	20.9	8.6	0.7	58,071
TARRANT	28,782	618,195	16.7	24.8	34.3	14.8	9.4	388,010	9.6	20.5	42.9	22.5	4.4	119,209
TAYLOR	21,995	48,644	27.0	31.1	30.0	7.8	4.0	30,775	27.5	28.0	31.7	11.3	1.5	82,441
TERRELL	16,808	430	43.7	30.2	18.1	6.5	1.4	334	64.7	21.0	10.2	1.2	3.0	39,444
TERRY	16,670	4,145	38.8	28.9	23.9	5.3	3.1	3,013	42.3	26.5	25.9	4.9	0.4	61,687
THROCKMORTON	20,735	692	34.4	34.2	23.4	4.3	3.6	541	48.2	32.2	15.3	3.0	1.3	51,727
TITUS	18,334	9,940	32.4	29.8	26.5	7.9	3.4	7,329	23.6	30.3	30.7	13.1	2.3	85,648
TOM GREEN	21,787	40,162	28.7	31.3	29.0	7.3	3.6	26,401	17.6	32.2	36.7	11.6	1.9	90,308
TRAVIS	34,409	379,546	16.9	23.2	32.5	14.9	12.4	203,376	4.6	7.6	34.6	38.8	14.4	184,306
TRINITY	19,105	6,128	37.2	31.0	24.4	5.1	2.3	5,004	35.7	30.0	26.5	6.1	1.7	69,744
TYLER	19,016	7,988	35.1	29.6	27.0	5.7	2.0	6,756	30.7	26.8	23.8	8.0	1.7	64,072
UPSHUR	19,502	14,374	30.6	31.2	28.7	7.0	2.5	11,877	27.9	29.5	31.5	9.4	1.8	80,913
UPTON	18,279	1,200	35.8	28.8	27.4	5.8	2.3	921	58.4	28.1	11.5	1.4	0.5	41,842
TEXAS	25,413		22.9	25.9	31.0	12.0	8.1		16.4	21.8	36.0	21.0	4.7	110,551
UNITED STATES	27,916		21.9	25.0	32.3	12.3	8.4		7.9	10.5	27.1	35.6	19.0	192,285

SPENDING POTENTIAL INDICES

COUNTY	FINANCIAL SERVICES				THE HOME						ENTERTAINMENT						PERSONAL			
					Home Improvements		Furnishings													
	Auto Loan	Home Loan	Invest-ments	Retire-ment Plans	Home Repair	Lawn & Garden	Comput-ers & Hard-ware	Major Appli-ances	TV, Radio, Sound Equip-ment	Furni-ture	Dine out/Carry out	Sports Equip-ment	Fees & Tickets	Toys & Games	Travel	Cable TV	Apparel & Services	Auto Repairs	Health Insur-ance	Pets & Supplies
MCLENNAN	81	71	71	73	69	75	79	75	80	76	80	68	74	80	75	81	71	78	79	76
MCMULLEN	100	68	35	64	80	112	69	94	77	67	77	82	56	82	69	83	65	84	100	103
MADISON	87	60	33	57	69	95	62	82	70	59	70	72	51	73	62	76	59	74	88	89
MARION	68	56	47	53	62	77	55	69	61	54	59	58	51	59	59	65	51	64	76	70
MARTIN	90	63	33	58	70	95	63	83	71	63	72	73	52	74	63	76	61	77	88	89
MASON	93	63	37	61	74	103	67	88	75	63	74	78	55	79	67	81	63	80	95	96
MATAGORDA	82	65	52	64	65	78	68	74	72	67	72	67	62	73	66	75	64	74	77	77
MAVERICK	58	49	35	44	42	47	47	50	52	51	53	45	43	49	45	53	47	53	51	48
MEDINA	88	72	54	69	73	87	70	81	75	70	75	72	64	77	70	78	65	77	84	85
MENARD	71	51	36	50	58	77	55	68	62	51	60	59	47	63	55	66	51	62	76	71
MIDLAND	100	96	94	96	91	91	97	94	97	98	97	87	95	96	95	96	88	98	94	94
MILAM	84	65	49	63	69	88	66	79	73	64	72	69	59	76	66	78	62	74	86	83
MILLS	83	58	38	57	68	92	63	80	69	58	68	70	52	73	63	74	58	73	88	85
MITCHELL	71	54	44	53	57	72	58	67	65	56	63	58	51	65	58	69	54	64	75	68
MONTAGUE	81	62	49	60	69	88	65	78	72	61	70	67	57	73	66	77	60	73	88	82
MONTGOMERY	133	134	124	133	126	126	125	127	124	129	124	117	126	127	125	123	112	126	123	128
MOORE	81	71	60	69	69	74	71	76	74	72	74	70	67	75	69	74	66	76	76	75
MORRIS	79	57	43	55	63	83	61	74	69	57	67	64	52	70	61	74	57	68	84	78
MOTLEY	79	50	22	48	62	89	53	74	58	50	60	66	41	65	52	63	50	66	78	82
NACOGDOCHES	77	60	54	61	61	72	73	71	74	66	73	65	63	73	66	74	65	73	74	74
NAVARRO	78	64	58	63	65	78	66	73	72	65	71	64	61	72	65	75	62	71	79	75
NEWTON	75	52	30	49	58	79	52	68	60	51	60	60	44	63	52	66	51	63	75	74
NOLAN	67	53	50	53	55	65	59	63	65	56	63	55	54	65	58	67	54	62	71	64
NUECES	86	82	76	81	75	77	82	81	83	84	84	74	79	82	80	83	75	84	81	80
OCHILTREE	93	70	45	67	74	95	70	86	76	70	77	77	61	80	69	79	66	81	89	91
OLDHAM	92	61	30	59	73	101	64	86	69	61	70	77	51	76	62	74	59	77	89	95
ORANGE	87	76	70	75	77	88	75	82	80	75	79	72	72	82	75	83	69	79	88	85
PALO PINTO	76	59	49	58	64	81	63	73	69	59	67	63	55	70	63	73	58	69	81	76
PANOLA	82	61	43	59	66	86	62	76	69	60	68	67	54	71	62	74	58	71	82	81
PARKER	105	99	90	98	97	105	92	99	95	94	94	89	92	97	94	97	84	96	101	102
PARMER	83	62	36	57	63	80	62	75	68	63	69	68	53	69	60	70	59	72	77	78
PECOS	72	57	41	53	57	69	56	66	63	57	62	59	51	62	56	65	54	64	69	68
POLK	80	64	50	61	69	88	63	78	70	62	69	67	57	69	66	75	59	73	86	82
POTTER	71	63	65	64	60	64	68	66	71	67	71	59	65	70	66	72	63	69	70	66
PRESIDIO	53	42	28	37	38	46	40	46	47	43	47	40	36	44	40	48	41	47	49	45
RAINS	86	61	36	58	70	96	62	82	70	60	69	71	52	73	62	76	59	74	88	88
RANDALL	96	93	99	97	91	91	96	92	95	95	95	84	96	96	94	94	85	94	93	93
REAGAN	78	62	42	59	63	77	61	72	64	61	65	66	54	67	59	66	56	68	72	75
REAL	68	50	32	49	58	77	52	67	56	49	56	58	44	58	53	61	48	60	70	71
RED RIVER	75	53	35	51	59	80	56	70	63	53	62	61	47	65	55	68	53	64	78	75
REEVES	59	50	36	45	44	49	48	53	53	52	54	47	44	51	47	54	48	55	53	50
REFUGIO	80	59	47	58	65	84	63	75	71	60	69	65	55	72	63	76	59	70	84	79
ROBERTS	111	70	30	67	87	125	74	104	82	71	83	93	57	91	73	89	70	92	109	116
ROBERTSON	75	55	42	54	60	78	58	69	66	56	64	60	51	66	58	70	55	66	77	73
ROCKWALL	154	171	165	172	164	155	150	153	145	159	146	142	160	150	154	142	133	148	143	154
RUNNELS	70	50	36	49	55	73	54	65	61	51	60	57	46	62	53	65	51	61	73	69
RUSK	87	65	48	63	72	93	67	81	75	65	73	71	59	77	67	80	63	76	89	87
SABINE	73	60	48	57	66	84	58	74	64	58	63	62	54	62	62	69	54	69	81	76
SAN AUGUSTINE	76	56	40	54	62	82	58	72	65	56	64	62	50	66	58	71	55	67	80	76
SAN JACINTO	83	65	45	62	71	91	64	80	70	63	69	69	57	71	65	75	59	74	85	84
SAN PATRICIO	86	77	65	74	73	79	75	79	79	77	78	72	72	78	74	79	70	80	80	79
SAN SABA	81	58	41	56	66	89	62	78	69	58	67	68	52	71	62	74	57	71	86	82
SCHLEICHER	82	60	35	55	62	82	60	75	67	61	68	66	51	68	59	71	59	71	78	78
SCURRY	82	66	54	63	69	84	67	77	74	66	73	67	61	75	67	78	63	73	84	80
SHACKELFORD	84	58	34	56	68	93	61	80	68	58	67	70	50	71	60	73	57	72	86	86
SHELBY	82	56	33	53	63	87	58	75	66	56	66	66	48	69	57	72	56	68	82	81
SHERMAN	101	64	28	61	79	114	68	95	75	64	76	85	52	83	67	81	64	84	99	105
SMITH	92	82	79	83	82	90	83	87	87	83	86	78	80	87	83	89	76	87	91	89
SOMERVELL	93	78	62	76	77	91	75	84	80	75	79	75	70	82	74	84	69	81	89	88
STARR	47	39	26	34	33	38	37	40	42	41	43	36	34	39	36	43	38	43	42	39
STEPHENS	74	59	57	60	63	75	65	71	71	62	68	61	59	70	65	74	59	69	80	72
STERLING	99	68	35	64	79	111	69	93	77	66	77	82	56	82	69	83	65	83	99	102
STONEWALL	77	52	33	50	61	84	57	73	64	53	63	64	46	67	56	68	53	66	81	78
SUTTON	92	73	49	68	72	86	72	84	78	74	78	76	64	79	70	79	68	82	84	86
SWISHER	76	58	42	54	59	74	60	70	67	61	66	61	52	66	59	70	57	68	76	71
TARRANT	111	107	104	110	99	98	111	103	109	111	109	98	108	110	105	106	99	109	101	103
TAYLOR	80	71	75	73	69	73	78	75	80	75	79	68	75	79	75	80	70	77	79	75
TERRELL	64	48	35	45	49	63	50	59	57	49	56	52	43	57	49	60	48	57	66	60
TERRY	74	56	42	54	59	74	58	68	64	58	64	60	51	66	57	67	55	66	73	71
THROCKMORTON	84	58	39	56	67	91	63	79	71	58	69	70	52	74	62	76	58	73	89	85
TITUS	83	71	60	69	69	79	71	76	76	71	75	68	67	76	69	78	66	75	80	79
TOM GREEN	79	71	70	71	69	74	75	75	77	74	77	67	71	77	73	78	68	77	78	75
TRAVIS	122	112	109	117	104	102	126	111	120	122	122	109	119	121	116	116	111	120	106	112
TRINITY	70	57	46	54	62	78	57	70	63	56	61	59	52	61	60	68	53	66	78	72
TYLER	82	58	36	55	65	88	59	76	67	57	66	66	50	69	59	72	56	70	83	82
UPSHUR	85	64	44	61	69	90	64	79	70	62	70	69	56	73	64	75	60	73	85	85
UPTON	81	57	34	53	63	85	58	75	66	58	66	66	49	68	58	71	56	69	81	80
TEXAS	104	95	88	96	90	94	98	96	99	98	99	90	94	99	94	98	89	99	96	97
UNITED STATES	100	100	100	100	100	100	100	100	100	100	100	100	100	100	100	100	100	100	100	100

COUNTY	FIPS Code	CBSA Code	DMA Code	POPULATION			2000-2007 ANNUAL RATE		RACE (%)					
									White		Black		Asian/Pacific	
				2000	2007	2012	% Rate	State Rank	2000	2007	2000	2007	2000	2007
UVALDE	463	46620	641	25,926	27,119	27,922	0.6	105	75.7	73.3	0.4	0.4	0.5	0.5
VAL VERDE	465	19620	641	44,856	47,982	49,456	0.9	82	76.4	75.0	1.5	1.4	0.6	0.6
VAN ZANDT	467	00000	623	48,140	52,930	55,968	1.3	61	92.0	90.3	2.9	3.2	0.2	0.3
VICTORIA	469	47020	626	84,088	86,391	87,662	0.4	128	74.2	70.9	6.3	6.2	0.8	0.9
WALKER	471	26660	618	61,758	65,154	67,334	0.7	94	69.1	66.6	23.9	24.9	0.8	1.0
WALLER	473	26420	618	32,663	38,548	41,903	2.3	27	57.8	54.6	29.2	29.8	0.4	0.5
WARD	475	00000	633	10,909	10,495	10,242	-0.5	219	79.8	77.3	4.6	4.5	0.3	0.3
WASHINGTON	477	14780	618	30,373	32,237	33,357	0.8	87	74.7	71.7	18.7	19.9	1.2	1.5
WEBB	479	29700	749	193,117	242,664	280,927	3.2	17	82.2	81.8	0.4	0.4	0.5	0.5
WHARTON	481	20900	618	41,188	42,284	43,036	0.4	128	69.0	65.9	15.0	15.0	0.4	0.4
WHEELER	483	00000	634	5,284	4,869	4,710	-1.1	245	87.8	85.1	2.8	3.0	0.6	0.8
WICHITA	485	48660	627	131,664	131,120	130,357	-0.1	178	78.8	75.6	10.2	10.9	1.9	2.4
WILBARGER	487	46900	627	14,676	14,078	13,823	-0.6	225	78.2	74.8	8.9	9.2	0.7	0.8
WILLACY	489	39700	636	20,082	20,901	21,429	0.6	105	70.4	69.4	2.2	1.9	0.1	0.1
WILLIAMSON	491	12420	635	249,967	364,296	467,767	5.3	3	82.4	79.3	5.1	5.4	2.7	3.3
WILSON	493	41700	641	32,408	38,634	43,013	2.5	23	81.2	77.8	1.2	1.2	0.3	0.4
WINKLER	495	00000	633	7,173	6,817	6,601	-0.7	229	74.8	70.9	1.9	1.8	0.2	0.2
WISE	497	19100	623	48,793	58,153	65,476	2.5	23	91.0	88.9	1.2	1.3	0.3	0.3
WOOD	499	00000	709	36,752	42,879	47,792	2.1	33	89.1	87.3	6.1	6.7	0.2	0.3
YOAKUM	501	00000	651	7,322	7,279	7,276	-0.1	178	70.6	69.9	1.4	1.4	0.1	0.1
YOUNG	503	00000	627	17,943	18,033	18,053	0.1	159	91.0	90.6	1.2	1.2	0.3	0.3
ZAPATA	505	00000	749	12,182	14,318	16,040	2.3	27	84.1	83.3	0.4	0.4	0.2	0.2
ZAVALA	507	00000	641	11,600	11,658	11,703	0.1	159	65.1	65.3	0.5	0.5	0.1	0.1
TEXAS							2.0		71.0	68.4	11.5	11.4	2.8	3.3
UNITED STATES							1.2		75.1	72.7	12.3	12.6	3.8	4.5

TEXAS

B

POPULATION COMPOSITION

COUNTY	% HISPANIC ORIGIN		2007 AGE DISTRIBUTION (%)										MEDIAN AGE	% 2007 Males	% 2007 Females
	2000	2007	0-4	5-9	10-14	15-19	20-24	25-44	45-64	65-84	85+	18+	2007		
UVALDE	65.9	72.0	8.9	8.0	7.9	7.9	7.0	24.3	22.5	11.3	2.0	70.4	33.1	49.1	50.9
VAL VERDE	75.5	80.2	9.3	8.1	7.9	8.0	8.4	26.5	20.2	10.3	1.3	69.6	31.5	49.6	50.4
VAN ZANDT	6.6	8.7	6.7	6.2	5.8	6.3	6.7	23.3	27.3	15.4	2.3	77.4	41.5	49.3	50.7
VICTORIA	39.2	46.0	8.0	7.2	7.2	7.1	7.6	25.8	25.0	10.5	1.6	73.4	35.0	48.7	51.3
WALKER	14.1	17.5	5.0	4.4	4.3	10.1	16.1	30.2	20.4	8.3	1.2	83.3	31.3	60.2	39.8
WALLER	19.4	23.7	7.2	6.4	6.2	9.6	10.7	26.5	23.7	8.5	1.1	76.3	31.6	50.0	50.0
WARD	42.0	48.9	7.2	6.1	6.8	9.3	8.4	21.8	26.3	12.5	1.6	73.7	37.3	50.2	49.8
WASHINGTON	8.7	11.1	6.4	5.8	5.5	8.3	7.9	24.1	26.2	12.9	3.0	78.3	38.8	49.1	50.9
WEBB	94.3	95.5	11.2	10.0	9.7	8.1	7.5	29.7	17.0	6.1	0.7	64.1	27.2	48.5	51.5
WHARTON	31.3	37.3	7.6	6.7	6.9	6.8	8.2	25.0	25.3	11.4	2.1	74.7	36.2	49.5	50.5
WHEELER	12.6	16.1	6.5	6.2	5.8	6.0	6.9	20.1	28.5	16.2	3.8	77.9	43.7	48.0	52.0
WICHITA	12.2	15.5	7.1	6.3	6.1	8.5	9.6	26.7	22.8	11.0	1.8	76.7	34.0	51.1	48.9
WILBARGER	20.5	25.5	7.2	6.4	6.3	8.7	7.2	23.3	24.8	13.0	3.0	74.7	37.1	49.6	50.4
WILLACY	85.7	88.7	8.9	7.9	8.2	7.9	8.9	27.3	19.9	9.9	1.2	70.3	29.9	51.6	48.4
WILLIAMSON	17.2	21.5	8.6	8.3	7.7	7.2	6.6	30.9	23.2	6.7	0.9	70.9	33.9	49.7	50.3
WILSON	36.5	43.5	7.1	6.6	7.3	7.0	7.5	25.6	27.1	10.2	1.6	74.6	37.9	49.8	50.2
WINKLER	44.0	51.3	7.7	6.8	6.9	7.6	8.8	23.5	24.7	12.2	1.9	74.0	35.9	49.0	51.0
WISE	10.8	13.9	7.1	6.5	6.5	7.7	7.2	26.7	26.9	10.2	1.3	75.3	37.6	50.2	49.8
WOOD	5.7	7.5	5.5	5.1	5.3	5.7	6.5	21.2	29.2	18.8	2.7	80.9	45.5	49.7	50.3
YOAKUM	45.9	47.6	8.4	7.6	6.8	7.5	9.1	23.6	25.4	10.1	1.4	72.4	35.2	49.0	51.0
YOUNG	10.6	11.3	6.1	5.8	5.4	6.9	7.0	21.5	27.7	16.3	3.3	78.3	42.9	48.3	51.7
ZAPATA	84.8	88.1	10.1	8.7	8.6	7.8	7.1	24.9	20.0	11.2	1.6	67.9	30.3	49.4	50.6
ZAVALA	91.2	91.7	9.6	8.5	8.8	8.8	8.6	25.5	19.9	9.2	1.3	67.9	29.3	49.5	50.5
TEXAS	32.0	36.4	8.0	7.4	7.2	7.3	7.8	28.9	23.5	8.6	1.3	73.1	33.4	49.7	50.3
UNITED STATES	12.5	15.0	6.9	6.5	6.8	7.1	7.0	27.6	25.4	10.7	1.9	75.6	36.7	49.2	50.8

62-B

COUNTY	HOUSEHOLDS					FAMILIES			MEDIAN HOUSEHOLD INCOME			
	2000	2007	2012	% Annual Rate 2000-2007	2007 Average HH Size	2000	2007	% Annual Rate 2000-2007	2007	2012	2007 National Rank	2007 State Rank
UVALDE	8,559	9,045	9,359	0.8	2.93	6,645	6,966	0.7	32,218	36,756	2743	217
VAL VERDE	14,151	15,301	15,858	1.1	3.08	11,323	12,160	1.0	33,863	38,619	2565	201
VAN ZANDT	18,195	20,061	21,240	1.4	2.59	13,657	14,923	1.2	41,875	47,957	1464	72
VICTORIA	30,071	31,331	31,946	0.6	2.71	22,201	22,916	0.4	46,936	53,779	913	34
WALKER	18,303	19,430	20,400	0.8	2.42	11,389	11,929	0.6	38,914	45,063	1863	109
WALLER	10,557	12,602	13,781	2.5	2.80	7,747	9,160	2.3	46,478	53,026	953	37
WARD	3,964	3,901	3,850	-0.2	2.59	2,931	2,858	-0.3	35,640	40,550	2342	165
WASHINGTON	11,322	12,082	12,546	0.9	2.52	7,934	8,376	0.8	44,090	50,609	1195	56
WEBB	50,740	64,434	74,970	3.4	3.72	43,436	54,872	3.3	34,138	39,295	2535	193
WHARTON	14,799	15,272	15,581	0.4	2.72	10,744	10,979	0.3	38,531	43,846	1923	117
WHEELER	2,152	2,002	1,941	-1.0	2.37	1,486	1,367	-1.1	37,109	41,973	2115	143
WICHITA	48,441	49,039	48,998	0.2	2.44	32,902	32,928	0.0	41,852	48,974	1468	73
WILBARGER	5,537	5,404	5,307	-0.3	2.48	3,746	3,612	-0.5	36,300	41,674	2231	154
WILLACY	5,584	5,869	6,045	0.7	3.38	4,586	4,788	0.6	26,146	29,271	3065	247
WILLIAMSON	86,766	124,823	160,309	5.1	2.88	66,991	95,588	5.0	78,899	93,633	58	4
WILSON	11,038	13,327	14,952	2.6	2.85	8,826	10,580	2.5	47,381	52,943	875	32
WINKLER	2,584	2,507	2,451	-0.4	2.66	1,970	1,895	-0.5	36,641	41,769	2177	149
WISE	17,178	20,542	23,178	2.5	2.77	13,465	15,979	2.4	49,837	55,539	689	28
WOOD	14,583	17,219	19,356	2.3	2.40	10,651	12,453	2.2	39,941	46,196	1736	96
YOAKUM	2,469	2,494	2,511	0.1	2.90	2,008	2,014	0.0	37,680	42,160	2036	133
YOUNG	7,167	7,254	7,291	0.2	2.43	5,084	5,090	0.0	37,527	43,273	2055	137
ZAPATA	3,921	4,674	5,272	2.5	3.05	3,164	3,745	2.4	29,709	34,063	2924	239
ZAVALA	3,428	3,537	3,594	0.4	3.19	2,806	2,877	0.3	20,150	22,915	3133	253
TEXAS				1.9	2.76			1.8	51,090	60,298		
UNITED STATES				1.2	2.59			1.0	53,154	62,503		

COUNTY	2007 Per Capita Income	2007 HH Income Base	2007 HOUSEHOLD INCOME DISTRIBUTION (%)					2007 Home Value Base	2007 HOME VALUE DISTRIBUTION (%)					2007 Median Home Value
			Less than $25,000	$25,000 to $49,999	$50,000 to $99,999	$100,000 to $149,999	$150,000 or More		Less than $50,000	$50,000 to $89,999	$90,000 to $174,999	$175,000 to $399,999	$400,000 or More	
UVALDE	15,488	9,045	39.2	29.2	23.1	6.2	2.2	6,649	39.2	29.1	20.6	9.6	1.4	62,960
VAL VERDE	14,700	15,301	38.1	29.7	23.9	6.2	2.1	10,358	31.3	27.9	31.7	8.4	0.7	75,236
VAN ZANDT	20,720	20,061	29.2	29.2	30.8	7.6	3.2	16,389	22.1	25.9	33.7	15.4	2.9	92,968
VICTORIA	22,509	31,331	24.4	28.3	32.2	10.4	4.8	21,691	20.7	26.7	37.5	13.4	1.7	93,684
WALKER	19,410	19,430	32.7	27.4	28.2	8.3	3.5	11,905	25.6	23.8	31.5	17.0	2.1	91,016
WALLER	21,148	12,602	27.6	24.9	30.2	11.8	5.5	9,337	21.9	23.4	29.3	20.6	4.9	101,137
WARD	18,001	3,901	36.2	29.2	25.9	6.5	2.2	3,078	55.7	25.2	16.2	2.7	0.2	45,700
WASHINGTON	22,093	12,082	28.8	26.6	32.0	8.6	4.1	9,051	17.4	17.2	35.4	22.7	7.3	119,607
WEBB	13,226	64,434	37.0	29.6	23.3	6.8	3.4	43,486	16.0	28.2	40.8	13.3	1.8	98,824
WHARTON	19,054	15,272	32.0	28.8	27.7	8.4	3.2	10,794	28.2	29.6	30.8	9.6	1.9	79,361
WHEELER	19,694	2,002	32.0	34.6	25.3	5.5	2.6	1,584	46.3	28.0	20.1	4.2	1.4	54,683
WICHITA	21,692	49,039	26.5	32.0	30.7	7.4	3.4	31,424	26.4	31.9	31.7	8.7	1.3	79,675
WILBARGER	21,110	5,404	32.7	31.2	26.0	5.9	4.1	3,680	37.7	29.6	25.1	6.1	1.5	65,559
WILLACY	10,742	5,869	47.8	30.5	17.1	3.4	1.3	4,551	51.9	31.4	13.8	2.8	0.2	48,538
WILLIAMSON	32,643	124,823	8.7	17.0	39.1	22.2	13.0	94,715	2.6	4.6	33.8	52.8	6.1	190,408
WILSON	21,029	13,327	22.6	29.4	34.2	9.7	4.2	11,395	19.6	23.7	33.5	21.6	1.6	103,604
WINKLER	16,841	2,507	31.3	36.3	26.0	5.1	1.4	2,108	62.6	26.5	9.7	0.9	0.3	40,037
WISE	21,230	20,542	22.4	27.7	36.0	10.3	3.5	16,922	18.2	21.1	34.8	21.6	4.3	108,950
WOOD	22,099	17,219	29.3	31.4	29.2	6.3	3.7	14,162	20.6	25.7	35.6	15.2	2.8	95,767
YOAKUM	18,226	2,494	33.3	30.1	26.1	6.1	4.5	1,972	46.7	30.3	17.7	4.9	0.5	53,143
YOUNG	20,916	7,254	33.2	31.0	25.9	6.2	3.7	5,445	35.2	30.2	24.5	8.8	1.2	65,684
ZAPATA	13,473	4,674	42.2	30.3	21.8	2.9	2.8	3,875	47.0	27.7	21.0	3.7	0.6	53,520
ZAVALA	9,475	3,537	57.9	26.2	12.5	2.3	1.0	2,607	68.2	20.0	10.4	1.2	0.2	34,852
TEXAS	25,413		22.9	25.9	31.0	12.0	8.1		16.4	21.8	36.0	21.0	4.7	110,551
UNITED STATES	27,916		21.9	25.0	32.3	12.3	8.4		7.9	10.5	27.1	35.6	19.0	192,285

COUNTY	FINANCIAL SERVICES				THE HOME						ENTERTAINMENT						PERSONAL			
					Home Improvements		Furnishings													
	Auto Loan	Home Loan	Invest-ments	Retire-ment Plans	Home Repair	Lawn & Garden	Comput-ers & Hard-ware	Major Appli-ances	TV, Radio, Sound Equip-ment	Furni-ture	Dine out/ Carry out	Sports Equip-ment	Fees & Tickets	Toys & Games	Travel	Cable TV	Apparel & Services	Auto Repairs	Health Insur-ance	Pets & Supplies
UVALDE	72	60	43	55	57	67	59	66	63	60	63	60	53	62	58	65	56	66	68	66
VAL VERDE	72	59	43	55	54	62	59	63	64	61	64	57	54	62	56	65	57	65	64	62
VAN ZANDT	89	67	49	65	74	95	68	84	75	66	74	73	60	78	69	80	64	77	91	89
VICTORIA	89	84	80	83	80	84	83	84	85	84	85	76	81	85	82	86	76	85	86	84
WALKER	77	61	60	63	60	68	78	70	76	69	76	66	68	74	70	75	67	75	73	73
WALLER	95	82	69	80	80	91	81	88	85	81	84	80	76	87	80	87	74	87	90	91
WARD	75	60	46	57	61	74	60	69	66	60	66	61	54	67	59	69	57	67	74	71
WASHINGTON	88	72	63	71	76	92	75	84	80	72	79	74	68	81	74	83	68	80	90	88
WEBB	74	69	53	63	60	62	65	67	68	69	69	62	62	66	63	67	62	70	65	64
WHARTON	81	66	58	65	68	82	67	76	73	67	72	67	62	75	67	77	63	73	82	79
WHEELER	79	55	37	53	63	86	59	75	66	55	65	65	49	69	59	72	55	68	84	80
WICHITA	77	70	75	72	69	73	76	73	78	74	77	66	73	78	74	79	69	75	79	74
WILBARGER	80	64	63	64	68	81	70	76	77	67	75	66	64	76	70	81	65	74	87	77
WILLACY	57	46	32	41	41	48	44	50	51	48	51	43	40	48	43	53	45	51	52	48
WILLIAMSON	136	144	131	144	132	126	132	130	127	139	128	123	135	132	131	123	116	130	121	130
WILSON	98	82	62	79	82	97	78	90	83	78	83	80	72	86	77	87	72	85	93	94
WINKLER	70	58	50	56	57	66	59	64	64	59	63	56	55	65	58	67	55	63	69	64
WISE	95	82	64	79	80	93	77	87	81	78	81	78	73	84	77	84	71	84	89	91
WOOD	85	67	52	66	75	96	69	85	74	66	73	73	61	75	71	79	62	78	92	88
YOAKUM	89	67	42	63	70	89	67	82	73	67	73	74	58	76	65	76	63	77	84	86
YOUNG	80	61	55	60	67	84	67	76	74	62	71	66	59	74	66	78	61	72	86	79
ZAPATA	65	54	38	48	50	60	51	59	58	55	58	51	47	54	51	60	51	60	62	58
ZAVALA	48	39	27	35	33	38	37	41	43	41	43	35	34	39	36	43	38	43	42	38
TEXAS	104	95	88	96	90	94	98	96	99	98	99	90	94	99	94	98	89	99	96	97
UNITED STATES	100	100	100	100	100	100	100	100	100	100	100	100	100	100	100	100	100	100	100	100

COUNTY	FIPS Code	CBSA Code	DMA Code	POPULATION			2000-2007 ANNUAL RATE		RACE (%)					
									White		Black		Asian/Pacific	
				2000	2007	2012	% Rate	State Rank	2000	2007	2000	2007	2000	2007
BEAVER	001	00000	770	6,005	6,321	6,506	0.7	22	93.2	92.2	0.3	0.3	0.7	0.8
BOX ELDER	003	14940	770	42,745	47,295	50,781	1.4	14	92.9	91.7	0.2	0.2	1.0	1.2
CACHE	005	30860	770	91,391	105,730	116,120	2.0	10	92.2	91.0	0.4	0.4	2.2	2.5
CARBON	007	39220	770	20,422	19,951	19,737	-0.3	29	91.1	89.7	0.3	0.3	0.4	0.4
DAGGETT	009	00000	770	921	927	974	0.1	25	94.6	94.5	0.7	0.6	0.1	0.1
DAVIS	011	36260	770	238,994	289,931	330,111	2.7	8	92.3	91.2	1.1	1.3	1.8	2.1
DUCHESNE	013	00000	770	14,371	15,858	16,983	1.4	14	90.2	89.5	0.1	0.2	0.3	0.3
EMERY	015	00000	770	10,860	10,723	10,616	-0.2	28	95.6	95.0	0.2	0.2	0.4	0.5
GARFIELD	017	00000	770	4,735	4,825	4,869	0.3	23	95.0	94.8	0.2	0.2	0.4	0.5
GRAND	019	00000	770	8,485	9,029	9,389	0.9	20	92.6	92.1	0.2	0.3	0.3	0.3
IRON	021	16260	770	33,779	41,206	47,228	2.8	7	93.0	92.3	0.4	0.4	1.0	1.2
JUAB	023	39340	770	8,238	9,576	10,602	2.1	9	96.6	96.2	0.1	0.2	0.4	0.5
KANE	025	00000	770	6,046	6,550	6,939	1.1	18	96.0	95.7	0.0	0.0	0.3	0.3
MILLARD	027	00000	770	12,405	13,158	13,639	0.8	21	93.9	93.1	0.1	0.1	0.7	0.8
MORGAN	029	36260	770	7,129	8,801	10,232	2.9	6	98.1	97.9	0.0	0.1	0.2	0.2
PIUTE	031	00000	770	1,435	1,428	1,419	-0.1	26	95.6	95.5	0.1	0.1	0.3	0.3
RICH	033	00000	770	1,961	2,194	2,367	1.6	11	98.2	97.9	0.0	0.0	0.4	0.5
SALT LAKE	035	41620	770	898,387	982,732	1,046,429	1.2	17	86.3	84.5	1.1	1.2	3.8	4.2
SAN JUAN	037	00000	770	14,413	14,254	14,171	-0.2	28	40.8	39.9	0.1	0.1	0.2	0.2
SANPETE	039	00000	770	22,763	24,924	26,325	1.3	16	92.4	91.2	0.3	0.4	0.8	0.9
SEVIER	041	00000	770	18,842	20,098	21,009	0.9	20	95.6	95.2	0.3	0.3	0.4	0.4
SUMMIT	043	41620	770	29,736	37,100	42,304	3.1	5	91.8	90.3	0.2	0.3	1.0	1.2
TOOELE	045	41620	770	40,735	53,600	63,652	3.9	3	89.2	87.7	1.3	1.5	0.8	0.9
UINTAH	047	46860	770	25,224	27,649	29,503	1.3	16	87.7	87.2	0.1	0.1	0.3	0.3
UTAH	049	39340	770	368,536	479,736	582,069	3.7	4	92.4	91.3	0.3	0.3	1.6	1.8
WASATCH	051	25720	770	15,215	20,911	25,803	4.5	2	95.6	95.0	0.2	0.2	0.4	0.4
WASHINGTON	053	41100	770	90,354	133,599	178,120	5.5	1	93.6	92.9	0.2	0.2	0.9	1.0
WAYNE	055	00000	770	2,509	2,522	2,492	0.1	25	97.3	97.3	0.2	0.2	0.2	0.2
WEBER	057	36260	770	196,533	219,570	233,539	1.5	12	87.7	85.7	1.4	1.6	1.4	1.6
UTAH							2.2		89.2	88.0	0.8	0.9	2.3	2.6
UNITED STATES							1.2		75.1	72.7	12.3	12.6	3.8	4.5

COUNTY	% HISPANIC ORIGIN		2007 AGE DISTRIBUTION (%)										MEDIAN AGE	% 2007 Males	% 2007 Females
	2000	2007	0-4	5-9	10-14	15-19	20-24	25-44	45-64	65-84	85+	18+	2007		
BEAVER	5.5	6.6	10.3	8.6	8.1	7.3	6.7	25.0	21.9	10.0	2.1	68.2	31.1	51.7	48.3
BOX ELDER	6.5	7.8	10.4	8.4	8.3	8.1	8.3	25.7	20.3	9.1	1.4	67.9	28.8	50.6	49.4
CACHE	6.3	7.5	10.9	8.5	6.9	9.0	13.7	29.2	15.0	5.5	1.3	69.8	25.4	49.2	50.8
CARBON	10.3	12.1	7.9	7.0	6.5	7.8	8.3	25.0	25.1	10.4	1.9	74.4	33.6	48.7	51.3
DAGGETT	5.1	5.2	7.2	6.6	5.2	3.9	6.8	25.8	30.3	13.7	0.5	78.6	40.3	55.3	44.7
DAVIS	5.4	6.4	10.8	9.3	8.2	7.8	7.9	29.9	18.9	6.3	0.8	66.9	28.0	50.0	50.0
DUCHESNE	3.5	4.1	10.2	8.2	7.5	9.4	9.9	22.6	21.9	9.5	0.9	68.0	28.8	50.8	49.2
EMERY	5.2	6.1	9.4	7.8	7.4	8.0	9.5	23.0	24.3	9.1	1.5	70.3	30.3	50.5	49.5
GARFIELD	2.9	2.9	9.2	8.4	7.2	6.4	7.9	22.4	25.5	11.4	1.6	70.9	34.1	51.3	48.7
GRAND	5.6	6.4	6.9	6.8	5.9	7.3	7.5	24.4	28.8	11.0	1.5	75.8	38.2	48.8	51.2
IRON	4.1	4.8	10.7	8.3	7.0	8.7	12.5	27.9	17.1	6.9	1.0	70.0	26.1	49.6	50.4
JUAB	2.6	3.1	12.5	10.2	9.3	7.5	6.8	26.2	18.5	7.5	1.6	63.1	27.2	49.9	50.1
KANE	2.3	2.7	6.9	6.1	6.4	7.7	8.5	19.7	29.4	13.3	2.1	75.8	40.4	49.8	50.2
MILLARD	7.2	8.4	9.6	7.6	8.4	8.3	10.7	20.8	23.0	9.9	1.8	69.1	29.8	51.3	48.7
MORGAN	1.4	1.7	9.5	8.1	8.0	8.6	9.1	24.0	23.2	8.6	0.9	69.3	29.8	50.7	49.3
PIUTE	4.5	4.6	8.4	7.8	7.8	6.8	4.8	20.2	26.1	15.1	3.0	70.9	40.1	51.6	48.4
RICH	1.8	2.2	8.2	7.0	7.3	8.4	9.4	20.1	27.8	10.1	1.7	72.1	35.1	51.6	48.4
SALT LAKE	11.9	13.8	9.7	8.7	7.4	6.7	7.3	32.6	19.7	6.8	1.1	70.3	29.7	50.4	49.6
SAN JUAN	3.7	4.3	10.6	8.7	9.1	11.1	9.2	23.6	19.5	7.1	1.1	64.6	26.1	50.0	50.0
SANPETE	6.6	8.0	9.8	7.9	7.8	10.8	10.8	23.6	19.2	8.6	1.5	69.7	26.9	50.7	49.3
SEVIER	2.6	3.0	10.0	8.8	7.4	8.0	8.2	23.5	21.9	10.5	1.8	68.8	29.9	49.5	50.5
SUMMIT	8.1	9.7	7.2	7.0	7.7	6.8	7.1	30.0	28.5	5.3	0.4	73.8	34.6	51.7	48.3
TOOELE	10.3	12.1	11.8	10.1	7.8	7.9	7.1	30.6	17.9	5.9	0.8	65.6	27.9	49.3	50.7
UINTAH	3.5	4.1	9.4	7.4	7.6	8.2	10.3	24.5	22.8	8.7	1.1	70.6	29.4	49.9	50.1
UTAH	7.0	8.2	12.4	10.0	7.8	8.5	11.9	30.1	13.7	4.9	0.8	65.6	24.8	49.6	50.4
WASATCH	5.1	6.0	10.0	8.6	8.0	7.5	7.8	28.3	22.0	7.0	0.9	68.9	30.0	50.8	49.2
WASHINGTON	5.2	6.2	10.3	8.4	7.3	7.4	7.6	23.7	19.6	13.5	2.1	69.8	31.0	49.3	50.7
WAYNE	2.0	2.0	9.9	8.6	7.5	6.6	5.6	23.6	25.4	11.0	1.9	69.9	33.8	50.3	49.7
WEBER	12.6	14.8	9.6	8.4	7.3	6.8	7.4	29.9	20.8	8.4	1.4	70.8	29.9	50.2	49.8
UTAH	9.0	10.4	10.4	8.9	7.6	7.5	8.7	30.0	18.7	7.0	1.1	68.9	28.3	50.1	49.9
UNITED STATES	12.5	15.0	6.9	6.5	6.8	7.1	7.0	27.6	25.4	10.7	1.9	75.6	36.7	49.2	50.8

HOUSEHOLDS

COUNTY	HOUSEHOLDS					FAMILIES			MEDIAN HOUSEHOLD INCOME			
	2000	2007	2012	% Annual Rate 2000-2007	2007 Average HH Size	2000	2007	% Annual Rate 2000-2007	2007	2012	2007 National Rank	2007 State Rank
BEAVER	1,982	2,102	2,170	0.8	2.91	1,531	1,589	0.5	41,848	47,388	1471	20
BOX ELDER	13,144	14,730	15,903	1.6	3.18	10,809	11,920	1.4	55,531	64,285	383	8
CACHE	27,543	31,860	35,192	2.0	3.21	21,018	23,786	1.7	50,114	58,015	670	10
CARBON	7,413	7,442	7,450	0.1	2.61	5,379	5,265	-0.3	41,847	47,470	1472	21
DAGGETT	340	354	379	0.6	2.40	240	243	0.2	38,192	43,943	1976	26
DAVIS	71,201	88,201	101,329	3.0	3.25	59,273	72,303	2.8	68,795	82,546	131	2
DUCHESNE	4,559	5,204	5,659	1.8	3.01	3,669	4,114	1.6	37,581	42,159	2047	27
EMERY	3,468	3,547	3,563	0.3	3.00	2,799	2,813	0.1	47,222	52,566	890	12
GARFIELD	1,576	1,625	1,648	0.4	2.89	1,199	1,208	0.1	42,612	48,077	1381	18
GRAND	3,434	3,762	3,963	1.3	2.37	2,170	2,297	0.8	40,684	46,549	1643	24
IRON	10,627	13,105	15,146	2.9	3.07	8,073	9,740	2.6	42,292	49,537	1418	19
JUAB	2,456	2,825	3,112	1.9	3.35	1,983	2,242	1.7	47,145	54,330	895	13
KANE	2,237	2,521	2,712	1.7	2.57	1,629	1,791	1.3	41,699	47,240	1492	22
MILLARD	3,840	4,159	4,350	1.1	3.13	3,093	3,291	0.9	44,234	50,021	1185	15
MORGAN	2,046	2,550	2,975	3.1	3.45	1,782	2,195	2.9	61,227	70,725	233	5
PIUTE	509	511	510	0.1	2.76	390	383	-0.2	35,979	40,878	2280	28
RICH	645	744	814	2.0	2.92	522	592	1.8	48,438	55,114	785	11
SALT LAKE	295,141	324,917	346,258	1.3	2.98	214,102	229,848	1.0	62,443	75,751	203	3
SAN JUAN	4,089	4,147	4,168	0.2	3.38	3,233	3,215	-0.1	34,960	40,391	2435	29
SANPETE	6,547	7,161	7,585	1.2	3.27	5,065	5,427	1.0	40,842	46,809	1621	23
SEVIER	6,081	6,584	6,928	1.1	2.99	4,907	5,218	0.9	43,599	49,298	1262	16
SUMMIT	10,332	12,997	14,863	3.2	2.85	7,502	9,204	2.9	82,398	100,135	42	1
TOOELE	12,677	16,778	19,972	3.9	3.12	10,126	13,155	3.7	59,405	71,133	281	7
UINTAH	8,187	9,259	10,019	1.7	2.96	6,543	7,263	1.5	42,744	48,390	1358	17
UTAH	99,937	131,358	160,127	3.8	3.58	80,738	104,248	3.6	59,577	71,259	276	6
WASATCH	4,743	6,605	8,195	4.7	3.15	3,872	5,303	4.4	62,139	73,561	209	4
WASHINGTON	29,939	45,699	61,738	6.0	2.89	23,429	35,055	5.7	46,344	52,878	964	14
WAYNE	890	924	926	0.5	2.72	669	679	0.2	39,279	44,764	1823	25
WEBER	65,698	74,435	79,317	1.7	2.91	49,549	54,883	1.4	55,397	65,122	388	9
UTAH				2.3	3.11			2.0	58,372	69,104		
UNITED STATES				1.2	2.59			1.0	53,154	62,503		

COUNTY	2007 Per Capita Income	2007 HH Income Base	2007 HOUSEHOLD INCOME DISTRIBUTION (%)					2007 Home Value Base	2007 HOME VALUE DISTRIBUTION (%)					2007 Median Home Value
			Less than $25,000	$25,000 to $49,999	$50,000 to $99,999	$100,000 to $149,999	$150,000 or More		Less than $50,000	$50,000 to $89,999	$90,000 to $174,999	$175,000 to $399,999	$400,000 or More	
BEAVER	17,271	2,102	26.7	33.8	31.7	6.1	1.6	1,685	5.1	5.6	65.1	22.9	1.3	141,143
BOX ELDER	19,860	14,730	15.6	27.3	42.4	11.6	3.1	11,970	2.9	3.0	39.1	51.1	3.8	182,523
CACHE	19,491	31,860	19.9	30.0	35.8	9.7	4.6	20,992	4.2	2.5	49.8	39.8	3.7	165,209
CARBON	19,506	7,442	30.0	28.8	30.2	9.1	1.8	5,829	4.4	13.7	59.7	20.2	1.9	133,555
DAGGETT	20,119	354	28.5	31.6	31.1	7.3	1.4	255	14.5	11.4	55.3	14.9	3.9	113,269
DAVIS	26,164	88,201	9.7	21.8	40.6	18.3	9.6	69,283	2.6	2.5	30.2	56.6	8.1	204,438
DUCHESNE	15,454	5,204	30.9	35.0	27.9	4.3	1.9	4,220	10.0	10.3	61.5	15.6	2.5	132,886
EMERY	17,625	3,547	23.8	29.5	36.9	8.5	1.3	2,946	10.5	10.8	62.5	15.5	0.7	127,829
GARFIELD	16,460	1,625	26.8	33.0	32.9	6.9	0.4	1,308	5.0	10.3	58.9	23.2	2.4	138,830
GRAND	22,154	3,761	30.1	32.3	27.8	6.2	3.5	2,722	11.0	9.4	39.3	34.6	5.6	159,713
IRON	17,380	13,105	25.6	33.7	29.9	7.7	3.1	8,909	4.3	4.6	46.0	41.4	3.7	168,930
JUAB	16,032	2,825	25.2	28.2	36.7	8.1	1.8	2,282	6.9	6.0	44.4	39.0	3.7	164,021
KANE	19,233	2,521	24.6	35.9	32.3	5.7	1.5	1,997	7.0	10.5	53.1	26.0	3.5	145,178
MILLARD	17,018	4,159	24.8	31.7	34.9	6.4	2.1	3,361	5.9	12.7	61.1	19.0	1.3	131,656
MORGAN	22,750	2,550	12.2	25.8	39.3	14.9	7.8	2,269	2.0	1.9	20.3	61.0	14.9	246,062
PIUTE	15,596	511	33.7	34.2	26.6	3.9	1.6	445	6.3	15.5	58.7	17.5	2.0	125,744
RICH	20,923	744	20.2	31.6	36.3	7.5	4.4	629	4.9	14.9	52.3	20.3	7.5	137,500
SALT LAKE	26,645	324,917	14.2	23.1	38.1	15.6	9.0	228,398	1.8	2.0	17.4	64.6	14.2	235,401
SAN JUAN	13,341	4,147	40.0	26.1	27.0	5.0	1.9	3,310	32.7	12.5	36.0	16.9	1.8	100,214
SANPETE	15,390	7,161	27.7	33.7	30.6	6.1	1.9	5,658	4.6	6.0	52.0	34.5	2.9	156,309
SEVIER	17,506	6,584	24.4	34.5	32.2	6.5	2.6	5,454	3.4	6.2	61.0	26.4	3.0	149,360
SUMMIT	44,987	12,997	9.2	18.0	32.3	17.6	22.9	9,970	2.0	0.7	5.5	33.6	58.2	460,837
TOOELE	21,493	16,778	14.2	24.1	44.8	12.8	4.2	13,310	4.7	3.8	27.8	58.5	5.3	196,073
UINTAH	17,518	9,259	27.4	31.3	32.2	6.6	2.4	7,206	8.1	10.5	59.1	20.4	1.9	132,937
UTAH	20,789	131,356	14.7	25.9	37.6	14.3	7.5	90,093	2.0	1.2	18.4	66.0	12.4	232,050
WASATCH	25,833	6,604	11.1	25.6	41.9	12.6	8.8	5,397	4.7	1.8	13.0	49.7	30.8	298,965
WASHINGTON	20,412	45,699	21.7	33.5	32.5	7.9	4.3	34,428	3.8	3.6	17.8	56.9	17.8	246,307
WAYNE	18,017	924	30.3	31.8	29.1	7.1	1.6	732	3.4	8.7	50.5	29.2	8.1	152,644
WEBER	23,535	74,435	17.0	26.3	38.3	12.7	5.7	56,450	3.2	5.0	51.5	36.6	3.7	157,887
UTAH	23,819		15.8	25.4	37.4	13.9	7.5		3.0	3.1	27.4	55.1	11.4	211,217
UNITED STATES	27,916		21.9	25.0	32.3	12.3	8.4		7.9	10.5	27.1	35.6	19.0	192,285

SPENDING POTENTIAL INDICES

COUNTY	FINANCIAL SERVICES				THE HOME						ENTERTAINMENT						PERSONAL			
					Home Improvements		Furnishings													
	Auto Loan	Home Loan	Invest-ments	Retire-ment Plans	Home Repair	Lawn & Garden	Comput-ers & Hard-ware	Major Appli-ances	TV, Radio, Sound Equip-ment	Furni-ture	Dine out/ Carry out	Sports Equip-ment	Fees & Tickets	Toys & Games	Travel	Cable TV	Apparel & Services	Auto Repairs	Health Insur-ance	Pets & Supplies
BEAVER	86	61	38	59	71	96	63	82	68	61	69	72	53	74	63	73	58	74	86	89
BOX ELDER	93	90	87	90	90	96	84	90	86	86	86	80	85	90	86	87	77	87	92	93
CACHE	91	81	78	84	77	80	93	84	88	87	89	80	86	90	85	85	80	88	81	85
CARBON	77	67	65	67	68	77	68	73	73	66	71	64	65	73	68	75	62	70	80	74
DAGGETT	80	62	40	61	72	94	63	82	65	60	65	71	54	67	65	70	56	73	83	85
DAVIS	119	129	125	130	120	111	120	116	115	124	115	109	124	119	119	111	105	117	108	115
DUCHESNE	74	58	47	57	61	76	61	69	65	59	64	61	54	67	59	67	56	66	73	73
EMERY	89	70	49	67	73	92	66	81	72	67	72	72	60	77	66	77	63	75	84	87
GARFIELD	78	61	40	59	68	88	61	77	64	59	64	67	53	66	62	68	55	70	78	81
GRAND	78	68	67	69	69	79	72	76	74	68	72	67	67	74	72	76	63	74	80	77
IRON	80	72	63	73	68	72	76	74	74	74	75	69	71	76	71	73	66	75	72	75
JUAB	81	76	72	75	73	78	71	75	74	73	74	66	71	77	72	75	65	74	78	77
KANE	78	64	49	62	70	87	64	78	67	62	67	68	58	68	66	71	57	72	82	81
MILLARD	88	68	48	66	74	94	68	83	73	66	73	74	60	77	68	77	62	76	87	89
MORGAN	108	123	125	124	123	116	106	112	103	113	104	102	114	109	112	102	95	106	105	113
PIUTE	78	50	21	47	61	88	52	73	58	50	59	65	40	64	51	62	49	65	77	81
RICH	105	74	40	72	88	121	77	103	82	73	83	90	63	87	77	88	70	92	106	111
SALT LAKE	109	114	114	116	107	101	114	106	109	115	110	101	114	110	110	106	100	110	101	106
SAN JUAN	71	60	46	57	56	65	57	64	63	60	63	56	54	62	57	64	55	63	65	64
SANPETE	76	61	57	62	65	78	69	73	71	63	70	65	62	72	66	72	61	71	77	76
SEVIER	82	70	58	69	73	86	68	78	72	67	71	69	64	74	69	75	62	74	82	82
SUMMIT	175	193	188	197	188	173	182	177	169	186	172	173	187	174	183	163	158	177	161	178
TOOELE	97	101	93	100	92	89	94	92	91	97	92	87	95	95	92	89	83	93	87	92
UINTAH	79	69	65	69	68	76	70	73	72	69	72	66	66	74	69	74	63	72	76	76
UTAH	105	106	102	108	98	94	109	99	103	108	104	96	107	105	103	98	94	103	93	100
WASATCH	116	123	119	123	118	114	112	114	109	117	110	105	116	115	113	107	99	111	108	115
WASHINGTON	85	82	81	82	81	87	80	84	81	80	80	75	79	80	82	82	71	83	87	84
WAYNE	84	59	32	57	70	97	61	82	66	58	66	72	50	70	61	71	56	73	85	89
WEBER	95	98	101	99	94	91	95	93	94	97	94	85	97	96	95	93	85	94	92	93
UTAH	105	106	103	107	100	98	105	101	102	105	102	95	104	104	102	99	92	103	97	101
UNITED STATES	100	100	100	100	100	100	100	100	100	100	100	100	100	100	100	100	100	100	100	100

COUNTY	FIPS Code	CBSA Code	DMA Code	POPULATION			2000-2007 ANNUAL RATE		RACE (%)					
									White		Black		Asian/Pacific	
				2000	2007	2012	% Rate	State Rank	2000	2007	2000	2007	2000	2007
ADDISON	001	00000	523	35,974	37,625	38,612	0.6	8	96.9	96.3	0.5	0.7	0.8	1.1
BENNINGTON	003	13540	532	36,994	38,382	39,326	0.5	11	97.7	97.3	0.4	0.5	0.6	0.9
CALEDONIA	005	00000	523	29,702	31,194	32,284	0.7	5	97.5	97.2	0.3	0.4	0.4	0.5
CHITTENDEN	007	15540	523	146,571	153,762	157,809	0.7	5	95.1	94.0	0.9	1.2	2.0	2.8
ESSEX	009	13620	523	6,459	6,701	6,880	0.5	11	96.6	96.3	0.2	0.2	0.3	0.4
FRANKLIN	011	15540	523	45,417	49,538	52,648	1.2	3	96.1	95.7	0.3	0.4	0.3	0.4
GRAND ISLE	013	15540	523	6,901	7,872	8,644	1.8	1	97.4	97.2	0.1	0.2	0.3	0.4
LAMOILLE	015	00000	523	23,233	25,264	26,397	1.2	3	97.3	97.0	0.3	0.4	0.4	0.6
ORANGE	017	30100	523	28,226	29,525	30,386	0.6	8	98.0	97.8	0.2	0.3	0.4	0.5
ORLEANS	019	00000	523	26,277	27,583	28,564	0.7	5	97.2	96.8	0.4	0.5	0.3	0.4
RUTLAND	021	40860	523	63,400	64,432	65,210	0.2	14	98.1	97.8	0.3	0.4	0.4	0.6
WASHINGTON	023	12740	523	58,039	60,460	62,253	0.6	8	97.0	96.6	0.5	0.6	0.6	0.8
WINDHAM	025	00000	506	44,216	45,290	46,104	0.3	13	96.7	96.2	0.5	0.6	0.8	1.2
WINDSOR	027	30100	523	57,418	58,962	59,657	0.4	12	97.7	97.3	0.3	0.4	0.7	0.9
VERMONT							0.6		96.8	96.2	0.5	0.6	0.9	1.2
UNITED STATES							1.2		75.1	72.7	12.3	12.6	3.8	4.5

VERMONT

B

POPULATION COMPOSITION

COUNTY	% HISPANIC ORIGIN		2007 AGE DISTRIBUTION (%)										MEDIAN AGE	% 2007 Males	% 2007 Females
	2000	2007	0-4	5-9	10-14	15-19	20-24	25-44	45-64	65-84	85+	18+	2007		
ADDISON	1.1	1.3	5.5	5.6	6.3	9.2	8.6	23.5	29.8	9.9	1.6	78.2	39.1	49.6	50.4
BENNINGTON	0.9	1.1	5.1	4.9	5.7	7.2	6.6	22.1	31.5	14.3	2.6	80.2	43.9	48.2	51.8
CALEDONIA	0.7	0.8	5.4	5.2	6.0	7.7	7.8	23.5	30.6	11.8	2.1	79.0	41.2	50.0	50.0
CHITTENDEN	1.1	1.2	5.6	5.4	6.2	8.9	10.2	26.7	27.0	8.6	1.5	78.6	36.2	48.8	51.2
ESSEX	0.5	0.6	5.7	5.2	6.2	7.4	6.5	24.1	29.9	13.1	1.8	79.2	41.8	50.4	49.6
FRANKLIN	0.6	0.7	7.0	6.9	7.6	7.2	5.9	26.7	27.8	9.4	1.4	74.3	38.0	49.5	50.5
GRAND ISLE	0.4	0.5	5.4	5.8	5.5	7.2	4.5	23.6	35.1	11.7	1.1	78.5	43.7	50.2	49.8
LAMOILLE	0.8	0.9	5.5	5.3	6.2	7.7	6.3	27.9	29.3	10.2	1.7	78.5	39.2	50.3	49.7
ORANGE	0.6	0.7	5.6	5.8	6.0	7.6	6.6	23.7	31.4	11.7	1.7	78.4	41.6	49.9	50.1
ORLEANS	0.7	0.8	5.6	5.7	5.9	6.6	6.2	24.1	30.7	12.8	2.4	78.5	42.1	49.9	50.1
RUTLAND	0.7	0.8	5.1	5.0	5.5	7.7	6.8	23.6	31.3	12.6	2.5	80.0	42.6	48.9	51.1
WASHINGTON	1.3	1.5	5.2	5.0	5.8	7.6	7.7	24.1	31.2	11.3	2.2	79.7	41.5	49.1	50.9
WINDHAM	1.1	1.3	5.2	4.8	5.9	7.2	7.4	22.7	33.1	11.6	2.2	79.9	43.0	48.9	51.1
WINDSOR	0.8	1.0	4.9	4.6	5.7	7.0	6.4	22.1	33.8	13.1	2.4	80.5	44.6	48.8	51.2
VERMONT	0.9	1.1	5.5	5.3	6.1	7.8	7.7	24.5	30.2	11.0	2.0	78.8	40.5	49.2	50.8
UNITED STATES	12.5	15.0	6.9	6.5	6.8	7.1	7.0	27.6	25.4	10.7	1.9	75.6	36.7	49.2	50.8

COUNTY	HOUSEHOLDS					FAMILIES			MEDIAN HOUSEHOLD INCOME			
	2000	2007	2012	% Annual Rate 2000-2007	2007 Average HH Size	2000	2007	% Annual Rate 2000-2007	2007	2012	2007 National Rank	2007 State Rank
ADDISON	13,068	14,112	14,649	1.1	2.48	9,105	9,577	0.7	53,998	63,547	454	3
BENNINGTON	14,846	15,909	16,490	1.0	2.33	9,914	10,323	0.6	51,433	61,973	584	7
CALEDONIA	11,663	12,649	13,244	1.1	2.39	7,901	8,332	0.7	43,984	51,304	1211	12
CHITTENDEN	56,452	60,779	62,962	1.0	2.41	35,168	36,654	0.6	63,895	77,867	181	1
ESSEX	2,602	2,784	2,889	0.9	2.40	1,807	1,882	0.6	36,638	41,474	2178	14
FRANKLIN	16,765	18,735	20,061	1.5	2.61	12,194	13,305	1.2	52,439	61,204	525	6
GRAND ISLE	2,761	3,248	3,604	2.3	2.42	1,954	2,240	1.9	54,046	62,973	449	2
LAMOILLE	9,221	10,326	10,897	1.6	2.39	5,980	6,498	1.2	51,066	61,483	611	8
ORANGE	10,936	11,849	12,354	1.1	2.44	7,614	8,038	0.8	50,386	59,768	650	9
ORLEANS	10,446	11,437	12,028	1.3	2.35	7,153	7,623	0.9	38,461	44,341	1936	13
RUTLAND	25,678	26,933	27,564	0.7	2.32	16,740	17,040	0.2	47,822	57,465	834	11
WASHINGTON	23,659	25,486	26,567	1.0	2.29	15,053	15,711	0.6	53,595	64,216	471	4
WINDHAM	18,375	19,465	20,059	0.8	2.27	11,456	11,749	0.3	49,144	58,066	738	10
WINDSOR	24,162	25,589	26,168	0.8	2.28	15,724	16,159	0.4	52,995	63,615	502	5
VERMONT				1.0	2.37			0.6	52,729	63,137		
UNITED STATES				1.2	2.59			1.0	53,154	62,503		

COUNTY	2007 Per Capita Income	2007 HH Income Base	2007 HOUSEHOLD INCOME DISTRIBUTION (%)					2007 Home Value Base	2007 HOME VALUE DISTRIBUTION (%)					2007 Median Home Value
			Less than $25,000	$25,000 to $49,999	$50,000 to $99,999	$100,000 to $149,999	$150,000 or More		Less than $50,000	$50,000 to $89,999	$90,000 to $174,999	$175,000 to $399,999	$400,000 or More	
ADDISON	25,789	14,112	19.0	26.2	38.4	10.8	5.6	10,905	3.1	4.1	20.4	57.7	14.7	227,957
BENNINGTON	28,846	15,909	23.0	25.3	34.3	10.4	7.0	11,781	4.9	4.8	21.9	51.7	16.7	219,844
CALEDONIA	22,600	12,649	27.4	28.7	33.3	7.1	3.5	9,489	3.7	7.7	43.6	39.1	5.8	167,445
CHITTENDEN	32,983	60,779	15.0	22.2	36.9	15.7	10.3	41,608	2.4	2.5	11.3	66.5	17.4	261,682
ESSEX	18,514	2,784	34.0	33.0	27.7	4.0	1.2	2,264	5.6	12.6	53.8	25.9	2.1	139,189
FRANKLIN	23,183	18,735	19.9	26.8	40.1	10.1	3.1	14,497	3.4	5.3	30.5	54.6	6.1	190,924
GRAND ISLE	28,870	3,248	18.2	27.1	36.9	11.7	6.2	2,704	3.6	4.3	23.9	47.4	20.7	236,932
LAMOILLE	27,728	10,326	19.8	28.9	34.6	10.1	6.5	7,579	4.6	4.7	24.3	49.0	17.5	219,879
ORANGE	24,537	11,849	20.6	28.9	37.3	9.4	3.8	9,529	4.9	4.8	31.3	50.1	9.0	192,625
ORLEANS	20,756	11,437	31.3	30.9	29.6	5.6	2.6	8,740	5.3	8.5	45.3	34.2	6.7	161,190
RUTLAND	25,339	26,933	24.2	28.1	35.1	8.4	4.3	19,472	3.0	4.0	35.0	49.8	8.2	188,851
WASHINGTON	28,807	25,486	20.2	26.1	36.1	11.6	6.0	18,117	3.1	3.5	28.9	54.2	10.3	204,351
WINDHAM	27,445	19,465	23.2	27.6	33.9	9.9	5.4	13,768	3.5	4.3	23.5	56.5	12.1	218,980
WINDSOR	30,330	25,589	20.0	26.7	35.6	10.4	7.3	18,948	3.4	4.7	27.7	47.1	17.1	214,157
VERMONT	27,894		20.7	26.2	35.8	11.0	6.3		3.4	4.4	26.0	53.4	12.7	213,014
UNITED STATES	27,916		21.9	25.0	32.3	12.3	8.4		7.9	10.5	27.1	35.6	19.0	192,285

COUNTY	FINANCIAL SERVICES				THE HOME						ENTERTAINMENT						PERSONAL			
					Home Improvements		Furnishings													
	Auto Loan	Home Loan	Invest-ments	Retire-ment Plans	Home Repair	Lawn & Garden	Comput-ers & Hard-ware	Major Appli-ances	TV, Radio, Sound Equip-ment	Furni-ture	Dine out/ Carry out	Sports Equip-ment	Fees & Tickets	Toys & Games	Travel	Cable TV	Apparel & Services	Auto Repairs	Health Insur-ance	Pets & Supplies
ADDISON	100	89	79	89	97	111	86	100	89	86	90	89	83	93	89	93	79	93	102	105
BENNINGTON	101	90	88	90	97	111	91	102	94	88	93	89	87	95	94	98	82	96	107	104
CALEDONIA	83	68	63	68	74	90	72	82	76	69	75	72	66	77	72	80	65	78	87	85
CHITTENDEN	109	113	122	117	111	105	118	109	112	115	113	103	118	112	115	110	103	112	105	109
ESSEX	77	54	33	51	60	82	55	70	62	53	61	62	46	65	54	67	52	64	76	76
FRANKLIN	90	83	80	83	87	96	80	89	83	80	83	79	79	87	82	86	73	84	92	92
GRAND ISLE	111	93	71	92	104	127	90	111	93	89	93	97	82	97	93	98	81	101	113	117
LAMOILLE	96	93	96	94	92	95	92	94	93	91	91	84	92	94	93	93	82	92	96	94
ORANGE	93	81	70	80	87	102	78	92	82	78	81	81	75	85	81	86	71	85	95	95
ORLEANS	80	60	45	59	68	88	63	77	68	60	67	68	54	71	63	72	58	71	83	82
RUTLAND	86	77	80	78	82	92	80	86	83	77	82	76	77	84	81	86	72	83	92	88
WASHINGTON	93	91	100	93	93	96	92	93	93	91	92	84	92	93	93	94	82	92	97	94
WINDHAM	92	82	78	83	88	100	85	93	86	82	86	83	80	87	86	89	76	89	96	96
WINDSOR	101	92	90	92	97	110	94	103	95	90	94	90	89	95	95	98	83	98	107	104
VERMONT	97	90	89	91	94	102	92	97	93	89	92	87	88	94	92	94	82	94	100	99
UNITED STATES	100	100	100	100	100	100	100	100	100	100	100	100	100	100	100	100	100	100	100	100

POPULATION CHANGE

COUNTY	FIPS Code	CBSA Code	DMA Code	POPULATION 2000	2007	2012	2000-2007 ANNUAL RATE % Rate	State Rank	White 2000	White 2007	Black 2000	Black 2007	Asian/Pacific 2000	Asian/Pacific 2007
ACCOMACK	001	00000	544	38,305	40,625	42,296	0.8	68	63.4	59.9	31.6	33.2	0.3	0.4
ALBEMARLE	003	16820	584	79,236	95,543	103,807	2.6	19	85.2	81.1	9.7	11.6	2.9	4.1
ALLEGHANY	005	00000	573	17,215	16,997	16,874	-0.2	118	93.0	91.9	5.5	6.1	0.2	0.3
AMELIA	007	40060	556	11,400	12,805	13,891	1.6	31	70.6	67.9	28.1	30.3	0.2	0.2
AMHERST	009	31340	573	31,894	32,678	33,259	0.3	93	77.7	75.2	19.8	21.6	0.4	0.5
APPOMATTOX	011	31340	573	13,705	14,436	14,961	0.7	75	75.9	73.5	22.9	25.0	0.2	0.2
ARLINGTON	013	47900	511	189,453	203,123	213,605	1.0	54	68.9	63.9	9.3	9.1	8.7	10.5
AUGUSTA	015	44420	569	65,615	72,586	77,919	1.4	37	95.0	93.8	3.6	4.0	0.3	0.7
BATH	017	00000	573	5,048	5,016	4,986	-0.1	114	92.3	92.0	6.3	6.5	0.4	0.5
BEDFORD	019	31340	573	60,371	67,695	73,375	1.6	31	92.2	91.0	6.2	6.9	0.4	0.6
BLAND	021	00000	573	6,871	7,179	7,319	0.6	79	94.8	94.0	4.2	4.7	0.1	0.2
BOTETOURT	023	40220	573	30,496	33,443	35,317	1.3	42	94.9	94.0	3.5	3.9	0.5	0.7
BRUNSWICK	025	00000	556	18,419	18,755	18,972	0.2	99	42.0	39.2	56.9	59.4	0.2	0.3
BUCHANAN	027	00000	531	26,978	25,122	23,945	-1.0	133	96.7	96.2	2.6	2.9	0.1	0.2
BUCKINGHAM	029	00000	556	15,623	16,505	17,099	0.8	68	59.1	56.0	39.1	41.6	0.2	0.2
CAMPBELL	031	31340	573	51,078	53,014	54,402	0.5	84	83.2	81.1	14.7	16.1	0.6	0.8
CAROLINE	033	40060	556	22,121	27,128	32,959	2.9	16	62.6	59.5	34.4	36.7	0.4	0.5
CARROLL	035	00000	573	29,245	30,252	30,929	0.5	84	98.0	97.3	0.4	0.5	0.1	0.1
CHARLES CITY	036	40060	556	6,926	7,277	7,501	0.7	75	35.7	32.9	54.9	56.9	0.1	0.1
CHARLOTTE	037	00000	573	12,472	12,931	13,203	0.5	84	65.5	62.7	32.9	35.2	0.2	0.2
CHESTERFIELD	041	40060	556	259,903	304,093	337,430	2.2	23	76.7	73.7	17.8	19.1	2.4	3.2
CLARKE	043	47900	511	12,652	14,424	15,808	1.8	29	91.1	89.7	6.7	7.4	0.5	0.7
CRAIG	045	40220	573	5,091	5,209	5,279	0.3	93	98.9	98.7	0.2	0.2	0.2	0.2
CULPEPER	047	19020	511	34,262	46,343	58,172	4.3	5	78.3	75.6	18.2	19.6	0.7	0.9
CUMBERLAND	049	40060	556	9,017	9,749	10,302	1.1	51	60.4	57.3	37.4	39.8	0.4	0.5
DICKENSON	051	00000	531	16,395	16,399	16,434	0.0	110	99.0	98.9	0.4	0.4	0.1	0.1
DINWIDDIE	053	40060	556	24,533	26,798	28,717	1.2	47	64.6	61.6	33.7	36.1	0.4	0.5
ESSEX	057	00000	556	9,989	10,923	11,640	1.2	47	58.0	54.8	39.0	41.5	0.8	1.1
FAIRFAX	059	47900	511	969,749	1,042,470	1,088,138	1.0	54	69.9	64.6	8.6	8.5	13.1	16.1
FAUQUIER	061	47900	511	55,139	68,277	79,539	3.0	15	88.4	86.6	8.8	9.6	0.6	0.8
FLOYD	063	00000	573	13,874	15,233	16,129	1.3	42	96.7	96.0	2.0	2.2	0.1	0.1
FLUVANNA	065	16820	584	20,047	26,508	31,306	3.9	8	79.4	77.1	18.4	20.1	0.4	0.6
FRANKLIN	067	40220	573	47,286	51,888	54,874	1.3	42	89.0	87.4	9.3	10.3	0.4	0.5
FREDERICK	069	49020	511	59,209	73,453	85,663	3.0	15	95.0	93.8	2.6	2.9	0.7	0.9
GILES	071	13980	573	16,657	17,249	17,655	0.5	84	97.4	96.9	1.6	1.8	0.2	0.3
GLOUCESTER	073	47260	544	34,780	38,383	41,120	1.4	37	86.7	84.7	10.3	11.3	0.7	1.0
GOOCHLAND	075	40060	556	16,863	20,539	23,882	2.8	18	72.7	70.1	25.6	27.8	0.5	0.7
GRAYSON	077	00000	573	17,917	16,745	16,582	-0.9	132	91.7	92.3	6.8	5.3	0.1	0.3
GREENE	079	16820	584	15,244	18,281	20,432	2.5	20	91.0	89.4	6.4	7.1	0.5	0.7
GREENSVILLE	081	00000	556	11,560	11,619	12,038	0.1	105	38.9	38.0	59.7	60.7	0.4	0.4
HALIFAX	083	00000	573	37,355	36,680	36,202	-0.3	121	60.3	57.3	38.0	40.5	0.2	0.3
HANOVER	085	40060	556	86,320	101,278	111,456	2.2	23	88.3	86.6	9.3	10.3	0.8	1.1
HENRICO	087	40060	556	262,300	290,250	308,836	1.4	37	68.9	65.4	24.7	26.2	3.6	4.8
HENRY	089	32300	573	57,930	56,114	54,700	-0.4	125	74.4	71.7	22.7	24.3	0.4	0.6
HIGHLAND	091	00000	573	2,536	2,504	2,476	-0.2	118	99.3	99.2	0.1	0.1	0.1	0.1
ISLE OF WIGHT	093	47260	544	29,728	34,641	38,633	2.1	25	71.1	68.4	27.1	29.3	0.4	0.5
JAMES CITY	095	47260	544	48,102	62,649	75,679	3.7	10	82.0	79.6	14.4	15.6	1.5	2.0
KING AND QUEEN	097	40060	556	6,630	7,033	7,335	0.8	68	61.2	58.2	35.7	38.1	0.3	0.4
KING GEORGE	099	00000	511	16,803	22,198	28,000	3.9	8	77.7	75.1	18.7	20.3	1.1	1.4
KING WILLIAM	101	40060	556	13,146	15,472	17,365	2.3	21	73.8	71.2	22.8	24.7	0.4	0.5
LANCASTER	103	00000	556	11,567	12,146	12,604	0.7	75	69.9	67.2	28.9	31.2	0.4	0.5
LEE	105	00000	531	23,589	25,560	25,842	1.1	51	98.4	98.0	0.4	0.5	0.2	0.3
LOUDOUN	107	47900	511	169,599	290,880	407,801	7.7	1	82.8	79.1	6.9	7.3	5.4	7.0
LOUISA	109	40060	556	25,627	31,410	36,342	2.8	18	76.5	74.1	21.6	23.5	0.3	0.4
LUNENBURG	111	00000	556	13,146	13,422	13,592	0.3	93	59.1	56.0	38.6	41.0	0.3	0.3
MADISON	113	00000	584	12,520	13,921	15,024	1.5	34	86.7	84.9	11.4	12.6	0.5	0.7
MATHEWS	115	47260	544	9,207	9,581	9,824	0.6	79	87.3	85.7	11.3	12.4	0.2	0.3
MECKLENBURG	117	00000	560	32,380	33,445	34,125	0.4	89	59.2	56.2	39.1	41.6	0.3	0.4
MIDDLESEX	119	00000	556	9,932	10,955	11,748	1.4	37	78.5	76.2	20.1	22.0	0.1	0.2
MONTGOMERY	121	13980	573	83,629	89,267	92,787	0.9	61	90.0	87.5	3.7	4.0	4.0	5.4
NELSON	125	16820	573	14,445	15,459	16,158	0.9	61	82.7	80.5	14.9	16.2	0.3	0.4
NEW KENT	127	40060	556	13,462	17,305	20,820	3.5	11	80.3	77.9	16.2	17.7	0.5	0.7
NORTHAMPTON	131	00000	544	13,093	14,074	14,846	1.0	54	53.3	49.9	43.0	45.1	0.2	0.3
NORTHUMBERLAND	133	00000	556	12,259	13,620	14,518	1.5	34	72.2	69.6	26.6	28.8	0.2	0.3
NOTTOWAY	135	00000	556	15,725	16,108	16,442	0.3	93	57.2	53.9	40.6	43.0	0.4	0.6
ORANGE	137	00000	584	25,881	32,276	37,780	3.1	13	84.4	82.4	13.8	15.1	0.4	0.5
PAGE	139	00000	511	23,177	24,413	25,330	0.7	75	96.3	95.4	2.2	2.4	0.3	0.4
PATRICK	141	00000	518	19,407	19,727	19,939	0.2	99	91.7	90.3	6.2	6.8	0.2	0.3
PITTSYLVANIA	143	19260	573	61,745	62,662	63,127	0.2	99	75.0	72.5	23.7	25.7	0.2	0.3
POWHATAN	145	40060	556	22,377	27,942	32,373	3.1	13	81.5	79.4	16.9	18.5	0.2	0.3
PRINCE EDWARD	147	00000	556	19,720	21,081	21,972	0.9	61	62.2	59.1	35.8	38.3	0.6	0.8
PRINCE GEORGE	149	40060	556	33,047	37,600	39,112	1.8	29	60.9	59.1	32.5	32.2	1.9	2.8
PRINCE WILLIAM	153	47900	511	280,813	383,710	470,003	4.4	4	68.9	64.8	18.8	19.2	3.9	5.0
PULASKI	155	13980	573	35,127	34,847	34,494	-0.1	114	92.6	91.3	5.6	6.2	0.4	0.5
RAPPAHANNOCK	157	00000	511	6,983	7,427	7,734	0.9	61	92.6	91.4	5.4	6.0	0.2	0.3
RICHMOND	159	00000	556	8,809	9,390	9,677	0.9	61	64.8	61.8	33.2	35.4	0.4	0.5
ROANOKE	161	40220	573	85,778	91,237	95,258	0.9	61	93.6	92.2	3.4	3.7	1.6	2.2
VIRGINIA							1.5		72.3	69.6	19.6	20.1	3.7	4.7
UNITED STATES							1.2		75.1	72.7	12.3	12.6	3.8	4.5

COUNTY	% HISPANIC ORIGIN		2007 AGE DISTRIBUTION (%)										MEDIAN AGE	% 2007 Males	% 2007 Females
	2000	2007	0-4	5-9	10-14	15-19	20-24	25-44	45-64	65-84	85+	18+	2007		
ACCOMACK	5.4	7.6	6.3	5.7	6.4	5.8	5.8	25.0	28.1	14.7	2.3	78.1	41.7	48.5	51.5
ALBEMARLE	2.6	3.9	5.8	6.0	6.6	7.8	6.9	26.1	27.6	11.4	1.7	77.3	38.6	48.3	51.7
ALLEGHANY	0.5	0.7	5.6	5.4	6.0	5.6	5.5	23.3	29.6	16.3	2.7	79.5	44.1	48.8	51.2
AMELIA	0.8	1.1	6.4	6.4	6.0	6.3	5.5	26.0	28.9	12.6	1.9	77.1	41.2	49.5	50.5
AMHERST	1.0	1.3	5.7	5.7	6.0	8.1	6.3	25.5	27.8	13.2	1.7	78.4	40.4	47.9	52.1
APPOMATTOX	0.5	0.7	6.3	6.1	6.4	5.8	5.6	25.1	28.9	14.0	1.8	77.7	41.4	48.9	51.1
ARLINGTON	18.6	24.5	5.1	5.1	4.6	4.6	5.4	42.0	24.1	7.4	1.6	82.5	35.9	50.8	49.2
AUGUSTA	0.9	1.5	5.6	5.7	6.2	6.4	5.5	26.2	30.3	12.6	1.6	78.8	41.8	50.3	49.7
BATH	0.4	0.4	4.3	4.1	5.5	6.4	4.8	25.5	30.4	16.7	2.0	81.8	44.6	50.6	49.4
BEDFORD	0.7	1.1	5.7	5.8	6.2	6.3	5.0	24.7	32.0	12.8	1.4	78.2	42.8	49.9	50.1
BLAND	0.5	0.7	4.4	4.5	4.6	5.0	5.3	29.5	30.9	13.9	1.9	83.4	42.8	54.9	45.1
BOTETOURT	0.6	0.9	5.5	6.1	5.6	6.0	5.0	23.4	33.5	13.5	1.4	79.0	44.0	50.1	49.9
BRUNSWICK	1.3	1.6	5.0	5.0	4.8	6.5	7.0	29.6	27.0	13.3	1.8	81.8	39.8	53.4	46.6
BUCHANAN	0.5	0.7	4.7	4.7	5.5	4.8	5.8	28.4	31.9	12.8	1.3	82.1	42.5	51.2	48.8
BUCKINGHAM	0.8	1.1	5.1	4.9	5.3	6.9	5.8	30.1	27.7	12.4	1.7	80.2	40.4	55.2	44.8
CAMPBELL	0.8	1.2	5.8	5.6	6.3	6.3	5.2	27.4	28.4	13.4	1.6	78.4	40.7	48.9	51.1
CAROLINE	1.3	1.8	6.5	6.1	6.4	6.1	5.4	27.2	28.8	12.0	1.5	77.2	40.3	49.9	50.1
CARROLL	1.6	2.5	5.6	5.9	5.5	5.4	4.5	27.4	28.8	14.7	2.2	79.7	42.2	49.7	50.3
CHARLES CITY	0.6	0.9	5.4	5.7	5.6	4.7	4.9	25.8	33.6	13.0	1.2	80.4	43.8	49.5	50.5
CHARLOTTE	1.7	2.4	5.8	5.3	6.6	6.2	5.7	24.4	28.7	15.0	2.4	78.7	42.2	48.4	51.6
CHESTERFIELD	2.9	4.2	6.5	6.6	7.4	7.8	6.5	25.7	30.0	8.6	1.0	74.6	38.4	48.7	51.3
CLARKE	1.5	2.2	5.2	5.2	7.3	6.3	5.0	23.5	31.5	13.9	2.2	78.3	43.7	49.8	50.2
CRAIG	0.3	0.5	5.6	5.9	6.0	6.4	4.5	26.0	31.0	13.3	1.4	78.3	42.4	51.2	48.8
CULPEPER	2.5	3.6	6.5	6.2	7.1	6.9	5.9	27.6	27.1	11.0	1.7	75.9	38.7	50.3	49.7
CUMBERLAND	1.7	2.3	6.2	6.0	6.6	6.4	4.8	26.7	28.2	13.3	1.7	77.1	40.9	47.8	52.2
DICKENSON	0.4	0.4	5.4	5.8	4.9	5.0	5.3	26.6	31.4	13.8	1.8	81.0	42.9	49.0	51.0
DINWIDDIE	1.0	1.3	5.7	5.4	6.4	6.5	5.5	27.3	29.7	12.2	1.4	78.4	41.4	49.8	50.2
ESSEX	0.7	0.9	5.1	4.8	6.1	6.3	4.6	25.1	31.1	14.5	2.5	80.1	43.7	47.5	52.5
FAIRFAX	11.0	14.8	6.5	7.5	7.4	6.5	5.1	29.6	28.1	8.3	1.1	74.5	37.6	49.5	50.5
FAUQUIER	2.0	3.0	6.2	6.3	7.0	6.9	5.5	24.9	30.6	11.0	1.5	76.0	41.2	49.5	50.5
FLOYD	1.3	2.0	5.6	5.8	5.6	5.4	4.5	26.4	30.6	14.0	2.3	79.8	42.9	49.8	50.2
FLUVANNA	1.2	1.7	6.2	6.5	6.5	5.8	4.5	27.6	26.7	14.8	1.3	77.0	40.9	46.5	53.5
FRANKLIN	1.2	1.8	5.4	5.5	5.8	6.2	5.1	25.5	31.4	13.5	1.6	79.8	42.8	49.5	50.5
FREDERICK	1.7	2.5	6.6	6.2	7.2	6.8	5.5	28.2	27.9	10.4	1.3	75.7	39.2	50.1	49.9
GILES	0.6	1.0	5.7	5.6	5.5	5.7	4.9	26.2	29.7	14.4	2.4	79.7	42.7	49.4	50.6
GLOUCESTER	1.6	2.4	6.0	5.5	6.7	7.0	5.9	25.6	30.1	11.5	1.6	77.3	41.2	49.3	50.7
GOOCHLAND	0.9	1.2	4.8	5.6	5.7	5.9	4.1	26.0	33.3	13.2	1.3	79.8	43.7	50.3	49.7
GRAYSON	1.5	2.5	5.0	5.0	5.4	5.5	4.7	26.7	29.7	15.8	2.2	81.4	43.4	50.2	49.8
GREENE	1.3	2.0	7.4	7.3	6.9	7.1	4.8	30.4	25.9	9.0	1.2	73.9	37.6	49.7	50.3
GREENSVILLE	0.9	0.9	4.1	4.0	4.3	5.8	6.1	34.4	28.9	11.1	1.3	83.9	40.0	59.9	40.1
HALIFAX	1.2	1.7	5.9	5.7	6.4	5.6	5.3	23.9	29.5	15.2	2.6	78.6	43.0	48.1	51.9
HANOVER	1.0	1.4	6.4	6.7	7.6	7.9	5.5	25.4	29.1	10.1	1.3	74.3	39.9	49.4	50.6
HENRICO	2.3	3.2	6.6	6.5	6.8	6.5	6.0	29.1	26.1	10.3	2.1	76.0	37.7	47.3	52.7
HENRY	3.5	5.0	5.6	5.7	5.4	6.0	5.0	27.6	28.5	14.5	1.7	79.7	41.8	49.1	50.9
HIGHLAND	0.5	0.5	3.8	3.5	4.9	5.8	4.5	19.6	36.3	18.5	3.2	84.3	48.7	50.0	50.0
ISLE OF WIGHT	0.9	1.2	5.7	6.2	6.6	6.7	4.6	25.1	30.8	12.7	1.5	77.2	42.3	49.1	50.9
JAMES CITY	1.7	2.5	5.4	5.3	6.0	6.2	4.9	22.7	30.3	16.9	2.3	79.3	44.7	48.4	51.6
KING AND QUEEN	0.9	1.2	5.3	5.4	5.6	5.8	4.6	25.2	32.1	13.8	2.3	80.2	43.9	48.9	51.1
KING GEORGE	1.8	2.6	7.6	7.3	6.7	6.7	6.8	27.7	26.6	9.3	1.2	74.4	36.8	49.7	50.3
KING WILLIAM	0.9	1.2	6.8	7.0	6.7	6.1	5.1	27.9	28.3	10.7	1.4	75.5	39.5	49.3	50.7
LANCASTER	0.6	0.8	4.3	4.2	4.5	5.0	4.7	16.6	32.4	23.5	4.9	84.0	52.2	46.8	53.2
LEE	0.5	0.8	5.5	5.6	5.0	5.8	5.6	28.6	28.8	13.1	1.9	80.4	40.7	52.1	47.9
LOUDOUN	5.9	8.5	9.8	10.8	9.0	6.1	3.4	33.1	22.2	5.0	0.7	66.4	34.8	49.3	50.7
LOUISA	0.7	1.0	5.9	5.8	6.3	6.0	5.0	26.1	31.0	12.4	1.5	78.3	42.2	49.2	50.8
LUNENBURG	1.8	2.5	4.8	4.9	4.7	6.5	6.0	27.0	29.3	14.7	2.1	81.7	42.4	53.9	46.1
MADISON	0.8	1.1	5.8	6.0	5.9	6.0	5.3	24.4	30.7	13.8	2.1	78.5	42.8	48.4	51.6
MATHEWS	0.8	1.2	4.7	4.6	4.9	4.9	4.5	20.3	35.3	17.8	3.0	82.6	48.5	48.7	51.3
MECKLENBURG	1.2	1.7	5.4	5.3	5.3	5.4	5.3	25.6	29.2	16.2	2.3	80.6	43.4	49.8	50.2
MIDDLESEX	0.6	0.8	3.7	3.5	4.7	5.8	4.5	19.9	35.7	19.4	2.8	84.4	50.1	48.3	51.7
MONTGOMERY	1.6	2.3	4.7	4.5	4.4	12.4	21.2	23.8	19.7	8.1	1.2	83.6	27.1	52.5	47.5
NELSON	2.1	3.1	5.1	5.6	4.6	5.4	5.1	22.4	34.7	15.3	1.9	81.2	46.2	49.3	50.7
NEW KENT	1.3	1.9	5.5	5.4	6.8	6.8	5.1	25.7	33.6	10.1	0.9	78.0	42.2	50.8	49.2
NORTHAMPTON	3.5	4.8	5.6	5.5	5.4	6.5	6.0	20.8	29.9	17.2	3.0	79.4	45.1	47.2	52.8
NORTHUMBERLAND	0.9	1.3	4.4	4.3	4.7	4.7	4.2	17.5	32.8	24.3	3.1	83.8	51.8	47.9	52.1
NOTTOWAY	1.6	2.2	5.8	5.5	5.4	6.4	6.8	26.8	26.5	14.1	2.8	79.3	40.5	51.7	48.3
ORANGE	1.3	1.9	5.9	6.0	5.6	5.6	4.9	24.1	28.7	16.9	2.2	79.0	43.7	48.4	51.6
PAGE	1.1	1.6	5.8	5.5	6.0	5.6	5.4	27.3	28.3	14.0	2.1	79.2	41.5	49.2	50.8
PATRICK	1.9	2.7	5.9	6.0	5.7	5.0	4.9	26.6	28.5	14.9	2.4	79.3	42.2	49.5	50.5
PITTSYLVANIA	1.2	1.8	5.7	5.9	5.6	5.7	5.7	25.9	30.7	13.2	1.7	79.4	42.3	49.2	50.8
POWHATAN	0.8	1.2	5.9	6.0	6.6	6.9	5.4	30.6	29.0	8.7	0.9	77.2	39.2	54.2	45.8
PRINCE EDWARD	0.9	1.3	4.9	4.7	4.9	12.9	13.3	21.3	23.3	12.0	2.6	81.9	33.5	49.1	50.9
PRINCE GEORGE	4.9	6.3	5.6	5.6	5.8	8.8	9.8	32.4	23.5	7.9	0.8	79.2	33.5	56.4	43.6
PRINCE WILLIAM	9.7	13.4	8.5	8.4	8.0	7.0	5.9	31.3	24.7	5.9	0.5	70.7	34.1	49.7	50.3
PULASKI	1.0	1.4	5.3	5.4	5.3	5.3	4.8	27.5	29.9	14.2	2.3	80.8	42.5	49.8	50.2
RAPPAHANNOCK	1.3	1.9	4.8	5.2	5.5	6.1	3.8	21.5	36.7	14.0	1.4	80.4	46.5	50.0	50.0
RICHMOND	2.1	3.0	4.2	3.9	4.2	5.0	7.0	30.4	27.1	14.8	3.3	84.4	42.1	56.5	43.5
ROANOKE	1.0	1.5	5.0	5.2	6.3	6.6	5.5	22.9	31.0	14.9	2.7	79.5	44.0	47.5	52.5
VIRGINIA	4.7	6.4	6.5	6.5	6.6	7.0	6.6	28.5	26.5	10.2	1.5	76.4	37.6	49.2	50.8
UNITED STATES	12.5	15.0	6.9	6.5	6.8	7.1	7.0	27.6	25.4	10.7	1.9	75.6	36.7	49.2	50.8

COUNTY	HOUSEHOLDS					FAMILIES			MEDIAN HOUSEHOLD INCOME			
	2000	2007	2012	% Annual Rate 2000-2007	2007 Average HH Size	2000	2007	% Annual Rate 2000-2007	2007	2012	2007 National Rank	2007 State Rank
ACCOMACK	15,299	16,296	16,996	0.9	2.44	10,387	10,693	0.4	35,830	40,321	2308	108
ALBEMARLE	31,876	37,225	40,970	2.2	2.39	21,069	23,723	1.6	63,654	75,205	186	21
ALLEGHANY	6,990	7,041	7,050	0.1	2.35	5,015	4,900	-0.3	43,093	49,948	1319	70
AMELIA	4,240	4,856	5,314	1.9	2.62	3,177	3,541	1.5	47,576	52,815	857	53
AMHERST	11,941	12,595	12,970	0.7	2.45	8,648	8,857	0.3	45,539	51,627	1048	61
APPOMATTOX	5,322	5,713	5,972	1.0	2.50	4,013	4,197	0.6	43,343	49,068	1299	69
ARLINGTON	86,352	90,726	95,118	0.7	2.19	39,322	39,004	-0.1	81,733	100,224	47	7
AUGUSTA	24,818	27,882	30,170	1.6	2.53	18,903	20,702	1.3	51,831	58,547	559	42
BATH	2,053	2,091	2,101	0.3	2.29	1,452	1,433	-0.2	43,583	50,443	1268	66
BEDFORD	23,838	27,138	29,621	1.8	2.48	18,158	20,149	1.4	52,228	59,196	532	41
BLAND	2,568	2,766	2,865	1.0	2.35	1,907	1,997	0.6	35,529	39,481	2362	112
BOTETOURT	11,700	13,011	13,845	1.5	2.52	9,117	9,899	1.1	59,131	66,577	285	30
BRUNSWICK	6,277	6,577	6,751	0.6	2.41	4,310	4,367	0.2	36,641	40,698	2177	105
BUCHANAN	10,464	10,097	9,738	-0.5	2.36	7,899	7,424	-0.9	26,472	29,356	3055	134
BUCKINGHAM	5,324	5,783	6,085	1.1	2.46	3,760	3,958	0.7	34,980	38,744	2430	115
CAMPBELL	20,639	21,986	22,829	0.9	2.39	14,702	15,185	0.4	45,489	51,494	1053	62
CAROLINE	8,021	10,109	12,451	3.2	2.63	6,009	7,373	2.9	48,096	54,268	808	50
CARROLL	12,186	12,895	13,319	0.8	2.31	8,786	9,023	0.4	35,591	39,499	2352	111
CHARLES CITY	2,670	2,916	3,050	1.2	2.50	1,977	2,100	0.8	50,633	57,182	632	46
CHARLOTTE	4,951	5,270	5,452	0.9	2.40	3,437	3,540	0.4	33,912	37,584	2560	121
CHESTERFIELD	93,772	111,485	124,535	2.4	2.69	72,139	83,672	2.1	74,650	85,894	93	14
CLARKE	4,942	5,850	6,519	2.4	2.41	3,514	4,034	1.9	63,263	74,630	191	22
CRAIG	2,060	2,152	2,202	0.6	2.40	1,507	1,530	0.2	42,750	47,637	1357	71
CULPEPER	12,141	16,930	21,558	4.7	2.64	9,050	12,279	4.3	56,319	65,166	353	34
CUMBERLAND	3,528	3,928	4,207	1.5	2.47	2,488	2,684	1.1	37,567	42,195	2050	97
DICKENSON	6,732	7,001	7,119	0.5	2.32	4,887	4,934	0.1	27,188	30,194	3032	133
DINWIDDIE	9,107	10,284	11,161	1.7	2.52	6,722	7,380	1.3	51,071	57,712	610	45
ESSEX	3,995	4,475	4,822	1.6	2.41	2,741	2,970	1.1	45,825	51,804	1021	58
FAIRFAX	350,714	379,804	397,074	1.1	2.72	250,281	262,880	0.7	104,509	125,688	3	2
FAUQUIER	19,842	25,072	29,477	3.3	2.70	15,140	18,647	2.9	77,946	91,136	66	9
FLOYD	5,791	6,475	6,911	1.6	2.34	4,160	4,513	1.1	37,180	41,321	2105	103
FLUVANNA	7,387	9,979	11,974	4.2	2.54	5,706	7,522	3.9	56,817	64,940	334	32
FRANKLIN	18,963	21,326	22,797	1.6	2.39	13,928	15,224	1.2	45,634	51,105	1037	60
FREDERICK	22,097	27,789	32,670	3.2	2.61	16,718	20,482	2.8	57,134	65,582	325	31
GILES	6,994	7,404	7,653	0.8	2.32	4,890	5,014	0.3	42,675	49,413	1370	73
GLOUCESTER	13,127	14,695	15,845	1.6	2.59	9,883	10,773	1.2	54,566	61,900	419	38
GOOCHLAND	6,158	7,760	9,227	3.2	2.45	4,712	5,790	2.9	68,598	80,215	132	18
GRAYSON	7,259	7,388	7,401	0.2	2.25	5,087	5,013	-0.2	33,427	37,286	2613	123
GREENE	5,574	6,737	7,555	2.6	2.69	4,291	5,061	2.3	55,167	62,627	398	36
GREENSVILLE	3,375	3,727	3,957	1.4	2.42	2,397	2,566	0.9	37,452	41,604	2072	98
HALIFAX	15,018	15,152	15,129	0.1	2.36	10,514	10,274	-0.3	35,000	39,023	2429	114
HANOVER	31,121	36,744	40,582	2.3	2.70	24,463	28,224	2.0	75,227	86,601	87	12
HENRICO	108,121	120,247	128,265	1.5	2.38	69,834	74,783	0.9	62,021	72,655	212	24
HENRY	23,910	23,749	23,418	-0.1	2.34	16,953	16,323	-0.5	38,039	42,855	1995	96
HIGHLAND	1,131	1,149	1,151	0.2	2.18	764	750	-0.3	35,439	39,904	2376	113
ISLE OF WIGHT	11,319	13,457	15,143	2.4	2.56	8,672	10,056	2.1	55,304	62,778	394	35
JAMES CITY	19,003	25,456	31,125	4.1	2.42	13,989	18,217	3.7	69,763	82,107	120	17
KING AND QUEEN	2,673	2,916	3,081	1.2	2.41	1,897	2,007	0.8	42,353	47,826	1411	74
KING GEORGE	6,091	8,189	10,419	4.2	2.67	4,524	5,918	3.8	61,420	71,320	229	26
KING WILLIAM	4,846	5,813	6,580	2.5	2.64	3,786	4,436	2.2	60,809	68,407	248	28
LANCASTER	5,004	5,367	5,621	1.0	2.19	3,412	3,538	0.5	41,434	48,180	1529	77
LEE	9,706	10,155	10,422	0.6	2.33	6,856	6,948	0.2	27,414	31,047	3023	132
LOUDOUN	59,900	102,024	142,916	7.6	2.84	45,020	74,664	7.2	108,082	133,097	2	1
LOUISA	9,945	12,460	14,560	3.2	2.51	7,264	8,843	2.8	47,636	53,469	850	52
LUNENBURG	4,998	5,233	5,371	0.6	2.33	3,385	3,425	0.2	33,354	37,910	2622	125
MADISON	4,739	5,439	5,957	1.9	2.52	3,521	3,931	1.5	47,349	52,926	880	54
MATHEWS	3,932	4,115	4,228	0.6	2.31	2,822	2,865	0.2	52,293	59,177	529	40
MECKLENBURG	12,951	13,668	14,090	0.7	2.33	8,962	9,152	0.3	37,410	42,175	2079	99
MIDDLESEX	4,253	4,797	5,196	1.7	2.23	2,912	3,177	1.2	45,660	51,797	1035	59
MONTGOMERY	30,997	33,283	34,837	1.0	2.40	17,212	17,631	0.3	40,393	46,892	1676	84
NELSON	5,887	6,492	6,880	1.4	2.35	4,147	4,432	0.9	45,162	51,402	1092	63
NEW KENT	4,925	6,475	7,875	3.8	2.61	3,897	5,010	3.5	64,415	74,165	174	20
NORTHAMPTON	5,321	5,826	6,198	1.3	2.35	3,546	3,745	0.8	34,194	38,421	2528	117
NORTHUMBERLAND	5,470	6,180	6,636	1.7	2.20	3,785	4,138	1.2	46,546	52,841	950	56
NOTTOWAY	5,664	5,931	6,105	0.6	2.45	3,888	3,939	0.2	37,360	42,027	2085	100
ORANGE	10,150	12,964	15,379	3.4	2.44	7,471	9,275	3.0	51,759	58,703	563	43
PAGE	9,305	10,079	10,595	1.1	2.39	6,632	6,968	0.7	40,074	45,915	1715	86
PATRICK	8,141	8,460	8,636	0.5	2.30	5,814	5,860	0.1	33,554	37,425	2600	122
PITTSYLVANIA	24,684	25,735	26,245	0.6	2.42	18,218	18,467	0.2	41,172	46,026	1579	80
POWHATAN	7,258	9,372	11,078	3.6	2.70	5,901	7,469	3.3	66,039	76,261	162	19
PRINCE EDWARD	6,561	7,221	7,673	1.3	2.38	4,272	4,527	0.8	38,643	44,846	1906	92
PRINCE GEORGE	10,159	11,255	11,928	1.4	2.70	8,097	8,776	1.1	61,442	71,414	227	25
PRINCE WILLIAM	94,570	131,917	162,726	4.7	2.90	72,737	98,978	4.3	83,660	100,007	36	6
PULASKI	14,643	14,848	14,876	0.2	2.26	10,141	9,949	-0.3	41,842	48,411	1473	76
RAPPAHANNOCK	2,788	3,025	3,180	1.1	2.45	2,004	2,109	0.7	56,758	66,348	338	33
RICHMOND	2,937	3,197	3,366	1.2	2.33	2,000	2,104	0.7	41,190	47,685	1572	79
ROANOKE	34,686	37,346	39,289	1.0	2.38	24,690	25,779	0.6	60,514	70,403	252	29
VIRGINIA				1.6	2.52			1.2	59,797	70,833		
UNITED STATES				1.2	2.59			1.0	53,154	62,503		

COUNTY	2007 Per Capita Income	2007 HH Income Base	2007 HOUSEHOLD INCOME DISTRIBUTION (%)					2007 Home Value Base	2007 HOME VALUE DISTRIBUTION (%)					2007 Median Home Value
			Less than $25,000	$25,000 to $49,999	$50,000 to $99,999	$100,000 to $149,999	$150,000 or More		Less than $50,000	$50,000 to $89,999	$90,000 to $174,999	$175,000 to $399,999	$400,000 or More	
ACCOMACK	19,187	16,296	34.5	31.9	25.6	5.8	2.3	12,310	12.5	13.4	32.9	34.6	6.6	154,775
ALBEMARLE	35,396	37,225	15.2	22.1	34.6	16.5	11.7	24,750	3.7	1.6	9.4	55.6	29.7	309,730
ALLEGHANY	23,132	7,041	27.5	30.3	32.0	7.4	2.9	5,569	9.0	13.9	35.6	38.8	2.7	155,475
AMELIA	22,615	4,856	20.0	32.8	34.2	9.5	3.5	3,993	5.6	8.6	32.2	48.4	5.2	182,637
AMHERST	22,082	12,595	24.6	30.3	34.3	8.1	2.7	9,872	7.8	10.0	50.4	29.0	2.8	149,256
APPOMATTOX	21,549	5,713	26.5	31.1	32.5	7.1	2.9	4,645	11.2	13.9	41.8	29.9	3.2	142,062
ARLINGTON	51,355	90,726	10.2	16.1	33.8	19.7	20.2	39,336	0.1	0.5	4.7	29.1	65.5	500,926
AUGUSTA	24,294	27,882	18.8	28.8	38.5	10.2	3.7	23,193	6.3	4.2	19.1	59.8	10.6	224,953
BATH	26,199	2,091	22.0	34.6	32.1	7.2	4.1	1,679	5.6	9.4	34.3	42.9	7.8	176,855
BEDFORD	26,919	27,138	17.4	29.9	35.5	12.2	5.0	23,441	7.8	6.8	30.7	46.8	7.9	186,945
BLAND	20,367	2,766	31.6	32.9	26.9	6.6	2.0	2,379	13.0	13.7	32.7	37.4	3.2	149,463
BOTETOURT	28,344	13,011	17.2	24.1	38.8	13.9	6.1	11,413	5.1	5.8	28.2	53.0	8.0	202,062
BRUNSWICK	19,002	6,574	34.8	30.5	27.3	5.1	2.3	5,128	11.7	12.3	38.6	32.9	4.4	148,474
BUCHANAN	15,515	10,097	47.4	28.8	18.9	3.9	1.0	8,322	26.8	20.2	34.3	17.6	1.3	99,412
BUCKINGHAM	18,060	5,783	36.0	30.8	25.4	6.6	1.3	4,530	12.7	11.6	34.8	36.3	4.6	156,734
CAMPBELL	22,559	21,986	25.7	29.8	33.9	8.5	2.1	17,060	13.6	10.6	40.5	33.7	1.5	150,265
CAROLINE	22,380	10,109	21.0	31.1	34.7	10.3	2.9	8,298	5.9	4.2	37.2	47.7	5.0	179,599
CARROLL	19,773	12,895	34.9	32.7	26.5	3.9	2.0	10,518	9.8	12.8	41.8	32.3	3.3	145,588
CHARLES CITY	24,068	2,916	23.1	26.2	36.8	11.3	2.6	2,472	6.2	13.0	36.1	37.6	7.1	165,076
CHARLOTTE	18,378	5,270	38.5	30.6	24.7	4.0	2.2	4,111	13.3	12.0	33.5	37.0	4.2	155,481
CHESTERFIELD	33,691	111,485	8.8	19.8	40.4	19.1	11.8	90,248	2.0	1.1	21.8	64.0	11.1	223,985
CLARKE	32,103	5,850	14.0	24.2	37.8	16.5	7.6	4,473	0.9	0.3	8.2	50.3	40.4	352,944
CRAIG	21,246	2,152	25.7	34.4	31.7	5.7	2.5	1,755	9.5	11.2	38.8	35.3	5.3	152,992
CULPEPER	25,715	16,930	18.4	25.0	37.5	13.7	5.4	12,060	3.2	1.7	8.4	67.6	19.2	274,294
CUMBERLAND	18,704	3,928	30.1	32.0	29.8	7.1	0.9	3,046	5.9	11.7	41.9	36.4	4.0	153,852
DICKENSON	15,476	7,001	45.8	33.1	17.5	2.5	1.2	5,726	21.6	22.0	35.9	19.7	0.9	104,306
DINWIDDIE	23,934	10,284	20.1	28.6	38.1	10.0	3.2	8,186	5.4	8.1	39.4	44.2	3.0	170,736
ESSEX	22,526	4,475	25.7	28.7	34.7	8.5	2.4	3,467	6.4	5.6	31.5	47.7	8.8	190,861
FAIRFAX	51,244	379,804	5.7	10.7	30.6	23.3	29.8	270,240	1.0	0.7	2.1	27.7	68.4	507,507
FAUQUIER	37,511	25,072	11.2	17.1	35.9	20.4	15.4	19,341	1.4	0.8	2.1	39.9	55.8	426,491
FLOYD	20,205	6,475	30.5	33.6	29.2	4.9	1.7	5,325	9.2	9.1	32.7	44.0	5.0	172,977
FLUVANNA	26,051	9,979	15.6	25.9	40.6	13.2	4.7	8,502	1.7	3.3	14.4	68.5	12.1	242,596
FRANKLIN	24,608	21,326	25.9	29.3	32.1	8.1	4.5	17,344	9.7	9.8	34.9	36.2	9.5	166,388
FREDERICK	26,381	27,789	14.3	27.3	40.4	12.9	5.1	22,409	4.3	2.9	11.5	66.8	14.5	253,660
GILES	23,107	7,404	27.3	31.2	32.3	6.5	2.7	5,853	11.8	19.6	47.5	18.9	2.3	123,807
GLOUCESTER	24,907	14,695	16.7	27.6	40.6	11.1	4.0	11,989	3.9	3.5	14.3	66.7	11.5	235,806
GOOCHLAND	39,290	7,760	15.1	18.7	34.7	17.2	14.4	6,735	2.2	2.9	16.3	54.1	24.5	257,293
GRAYSON	19,718	7,388	36.7	32.9	24.0	4.6	1.8	6,014	13.1	15.7	36.9	31.3	3.0	141,252
GREENE	23,849	6,737	14.6	28.4	42.1	11.4	3.5	5,515	4.0	3.0	13.5	71.4	8.2	233,476
GREENSVILLE	19,191	3,727	33.2	30.5	28.4	6.1	1.9	2,925	14.4	13.0	39.5	31.2	1.9	147,370
HALIFAX	19,910	15,152	35.9	29.4	26.8	5.9	2.0	11,572	9.5	10.9	38.8	37.3	3.5	156,599
HANOVER	33,149	36,744	9.8	19.2	39.2	21.1	10.6	30,978	2.0	1.0	8.8	70.9	17.3	273,008
HENRICO	34,099	120,247	13.5	25.0	36.9	14.8	9.6	79,268	0.6	1.0	28.6	57.1	12.7	220,142
HENRY	20,883	23,749	30.6	33.0	28.9	5.2	2.2	18,334	10.7	11.1	39.4	35.7	3.1	156,576
HIGHLAND	20,727	1,149	32.5	37.3	24.3	3.6	2.3	961	6.2	4.6	33.7	47.6	7.9	185,019
ISLE OF WIGHT	25,750	13,457	20.7	23.4	37.2	14.2	4.5	10,942	10.6	4.8	16.5	51.6	16.5	241,465
JAMES CITY	39,138	25,455	13.4	19.5	34.9	18.8	13.4	19,676	4.3	1.8	8.0	53.2	32.8	316,168
KING AND QUEEN	21,924	2,916	28.2	30.8	30.3	7.8	2.9	2,407	12.1	6.8	36.6	39.0	5.6	164,727
KING GEORGE	27,913	8,189	12.5	26.3	38.3	16.0	6.9	5,929	5.6	3.4	11.9	64.3	14.8	258,564
KING WILLIAM	26,222	5,813	15.3	24.8	40.9	14.4	4.5	4,955	3.1	2.8	23.2	65.9	5.1	204,849
LANCASTER	29,742	5,367	28.2	29.0	25.3	10.0	7.5	4,462	6.1	8.8	25.8	38.5	20.8	198,583
LEE	16,848	10,155	46.1	29.2	18.3	4.6	1.8	7,595	19.0	17.4	36.8	25.0	1.8	124,673
LOUDOUN	47,752	102,024	4.6	9.8	30.3	27.3	27.9	81,614	0.6	0.3	0.9	25.7	72.6	513,433
LOUISA	23,865	12,460	23.5	29.0	34.6	9.0	3.9	10,174	5.1	4.8	32.2	50.8	7.1	188,615
LUNENBURG	18,643	5,233	39.6	28.8	24.8	5.0	1.9	4,076	10.7	16.6	35.7	34.5	2.5	143,765
MADISON	23,565	5,439	21.1	32.0	34.4	8.8	3.6	4,235	3.4	3.8	20.8	61.2	10.9	229,866
MATHEWS	27,615	4,115	19.2	28.1	38.3	10.2	4.2	3,482	2.4	3.1	19.8	58.9	15.9	231,942
MECKLENBURG	21,280	13,668	32.7	32.3	25.4	6.7	2.9	10,247	10.5	10.2	34.9	38.9	5.5	162,565
MIDDLESEX	27,442	4,797	24.1	30.2	32.4	8.3	5.0	3,990	5.7	5.3	24.9	48.5	15.6	216,486
MONTGOMERY	22,647	33,283	32.1	27.0	28.0	8.4	4.5	18,481	12.4	6.6	32.1	42.1	6.9	173,029
NELSON	27,262	6,492	24.1	30.5	30.5	9.4	5.5	5,269	6.5	7.2	27.2	45.2	13.9	196,979
NEW KENT	29,200	6,475	14.1	22.1	39.4	18.0	6.5	5,743	2.6	3.1	18.2	65.3	10.8	247,811
NORTHAMPTON	21,426	5,826	38.0	29.8	23.1	5.2	3.9	4,039	11.2	11.9	33.0	35.5	8.5	159,945
NORTHUMBERLAND	28,494	6,180	27.7	25.4	32.0	8.0	6.9	5,384	5.7	7.0	28.1	38.0	21.2	210,744
NOTTOWAY	19,344	5,931	35.2	26.5	30.3	5.8	2.2	4,240	9.6	11.2	36.7	39.1	3.5	161,155
ORANGE	26,407	12,964	19.8	28.1	35.9	11.7	4.5	10,089	3.6	2.5	17.9	63.7	12.3	237,835
PAGE	20,536	10,079	29.2	31.9	30.4	6.5	2.1	7,522	5.8	3.9	33.1	52.2	5.0	186,385
PATRICK	19,012	8,460	35.1	34.0	24.8	4.7	1.4	6,804	11.1	10.8	37.3	37.4	3.5	157,626
PITTSYLVANIA	20,595	25,735	28.7	31.1	31.9	6.4	2.0	20,687	17.6	20.3	45.7	15.5	0.9	107,049
POWHATAN	29,855	9,372	11.9	21.7	39.4	17.8	9.2	8,325	1.4	0.8	14.6	69.7	13.6	259,843
PRINCE EDWARD	20,755	7,221	34.7	27.3	28.4	5.9	3.7	4,981	8.7	9.2	26.1	47.9	8.1	188,302
PRINCE GEORGE	25,065	11,255	15.1	23.8	39.3	15.7	6.2	8,264	8.8	2.7	19.7	62.4	6.4	214,082
PRINCE WILLIAM	35,102	131,916	6.6	15.8	37.4	24.9	15.4	95,407	1.3	0.6	1.6	53.0	43.4	378,751
PULASKI	23,309	14,848	29.4	28.6	32.2	7.0	2.7	10,979	11.7	13.8	46.1	26.1	2.3	135,796
RAPPAHANNOCK	31,223	3,025	16.4	24.7	37.0	13.8	8.2	2,270	1.2	1.1	13.8	52.8	31.1	295,189
RICHMOND	21,514	3,197	32.5	26.2	30.0	8.5	2.8	2,478	5.5	6.3	30.9	47.5	9.8	185,791
ROANOKE	31,643	37,346	13.8	25.7	38.1	15.0	7.4	28,877	1.8	2.3	34.9	54.0	7.0	193,036
VIRGINIA	31,988		18.1	23.3	33.3	14.5	10.8		4.3	4.3	19.9	46.6	25.0	249,117
UNITED STATES	27,916		21.9	25.0	32.3	12.3	8.4		7.9	10.5	27.1	35.6	19.0	192,285

SPENDING POTENTIAL INDICES

| COUNTY | FINANCIAL SERVICES | | | | THE HOME | | | | | | ENTERTAINMENT | | | | | | PERSONAL | | | |
| | | | | | Home Improvements | | Furnishings | | | | | | | | | | | | | |
	Auto Loan	Home Loan	Invest-ments	Retire-ment Plans	Home Repair	Lawn & Garden	Comput-ers & Hard-ware	Major Appli-ances	TV, Radio, Sound Equipment	Furni-ture	Dine out/ Carry out	Sports Equip-ment	Fees & Tickets	Toys & Games	Travel	Cable TV	Apparel & Services	Auto Repairs	Health Insur-ance	Pets & Supplies
ACCOMACK	78	57	38	55	64	84	59	74	65	56	65	65	50	67	59	70	55	68	80	79
ALBEMARLE	122	124	124	128	122	120	123	120	119	124	120	112	124	121	122	117	109	121	116	121
ALLEGHANY	81	72	71	71	77	89	71	81	76	70	75	70	69	78	73	80	66	75	87	83
AMELIA	98	79	57	76	84	104	74	91	81	75	81	80	69	85	75	85	70	84	95	97
AMHERST	83	73	69	72	77	88	71	81	76	71	75	71	69	79	73	79	66	76	86	84
APPOMATTOX	90	69	50	66	76	97	67	84	75	66	74	74	60	79	68	80	64	76	90	90
ARLINGTON	145	139	147	150	139	128	168	142	159	160	163	149	162	155	157	153	151	156	136	143
AUGUSTA	92	87	82	86	91	99	81	91	84	83	84	81	81	88	84	86	75	85	92	94
BATH	92	80	69	78	90	108	77	95	83	77	82	81	73	84	82	88	72	86	100	98
BEDFORD	102	95	82	93	97	108	87	99	90	90	90	88	86	94	90	93	80	93	100	103
BLAND	82	61	40	59	70	92	60	78	66	59	66	68	52	70	61	71	57	70	83	84
BOTETOURT	109	102	90	101	108	120	93	108	96	96	96	96	92	101	97	99	86	100	108	113
BRUNSWICK	79	57	35	54	64	86	57	74	65	56	64	65	49	68	57	70	55	67	80	80
BUCHANAN	64	42	21	39	47	67	44	58	52	42	51	52	36	54	43	57	43	53	64	64
BUCKINGHAM	79	54	28	50	61	86	54	73	62	53	62	64	45	65	54	67	52	66	78	80
CAMPBELL	84	72	61	70	74	87	70	80	75	70	74	71	66	77	70	78	65	75	84	83
CAROLINE	94	80	62	77	83	99	75	89	80	76	80	79	71	84	76	84	70	83	93	94
CARROLL	78	56	39	54	62	82	57	71	63	56	63	63	49	67	56	68	54	65	76	77
CHARLES CITY	95	79	64	77	86	106	75	92	82	76	82	80	71	86	78	87	71	84	97	98
CHARLOTTE	77	53	29	50	60	84	54	71	61	52	61	63	45	64	54	67	52	64	77	78
CHESTERFIELD	124	140	142	141	133	124	126	124	122	132	122	115	134	125	129	120	112	124	118	124
CLARKE	111	111	112	112	117	123	104	115	105	105	104	101	106	107	110	107	93	108	116	116
CRAIG	85	67	49	64	73	92	63	79	70	64	70	70	58	75	64	74	61	72	83	85
CULPEPER	91	100	108	101	101	96	95	95	93	96	93	87	99	94	98	92	85	93	93	96
CUMBERLAND	77	59	40	56	63	81	58	72	64	57	64	63	51	66	58	68	55	66	76	76
DICKENSON	64	42	20	39	47	67	43	57	51	42	50	52	35	53	42	56	42	53	63	64
DINWIDDIE	94	82	73	81	87	100	78	90	83	79	83	79	76	88	80	87	73	85	95	94
ESSEX	84	70	57	69	77	94	70	84	74	68	74	73	64	75	72	78	64	78	88	87
FAIRFAX	178	212	219	214	211	183	199	189	185	205	188	182	213	188	202	180	177	188	172	186
FAUQUIER	135	161	166	161	158	142	140	142	133	148	134	132	152	136	147	131	124	137	131	141
FLOYD	80	60	39	57	68	89	58	76	64	58	65	66	51	69	59	69	55	68	80	82
FLUVANNA	96	96	97	95	98	104	88	97	91	90	90	84	90	92	93	94	80	92	101	98
FRANKLIN	96	76	58	74	83	104	75	91	81	74	80	80	68	84	76	86	70	84	96	97
FREDERICK	99	102	97	102	101	102	93	99	93	97	93	90	95	97	96	93	84	95	96	100
GILES	84	66	57	65	73	91	69	81	76	65	74	70	62	77	70	81	64	75	91	84
GLOUCESTER	94	93	89	92	94	99	85	93	87	88	87	83	87	89	89	89	78	89	93	95
GOOCHLAND	143	150	147	151	155	158	133	147	133	139	133	132	139	136	142	135	120	138	143	150
GRAYSON	76	54	35	51	61	82	55	70	61	53	61	62	47	65	54	66	52	64	75	76
GREENE	98	97	83	95	92	95	86	92	86	91	87	84	87	91	87	86	77	89	89	94
GREENSVILLE	84	57	30	53	64	89	58	76	67	56	67	69	48	70	57	74	57	70	83	84
HALIFAX	77	58	44	55	64	83	59	72	66	57	65	64	52	68	59	71	56	67	79	78
HANOVER	122	140	144	141	136	125	125	125	120	131	120	116	134	123	129	117	110	122	118	125
HENRICO	111	114	120	117	109	104	115	107	112	116	113	100	117	113	113	110	103	111	106	108
HENRY	81	61	45	59	66	85	62	75	68	60	68	67	55	72	61	73	58	70	81	80
HIGHLAND	79	54	27	52	65	90	56	76	60	53	61	67	45	65	56	65	51	68	79	83
ISLE OF WIGHT	98	94	89	94	98	105	85	96	89	89	89	85	87	92	90	92	80	90	98	100
JAMES CITY	130	139	147	141	139	139	129	134	128	133	128	119	135	125	136	129	115	132	135	134
KING AND QUEEN	89	65	42	62	74	99	65	85	73	63	72	74	56	76	66	78	62	76	91	91
KING GEORGE	105	108	108	108	105	104	103	104	102	104	102	96	105	104	104	101	92	103	102	105
KING WILLIAM	98	105	105	104	105	104	92	99	93	98	93	88	98	98	97	93	84	94	97	101
LANCASTER	98	87	79	86	97	117	83	102	89	84	88	86	80	86	91	95	76	95	111	104
LEE	66	47	32	45	52	70	49	61	55	47	54	54	41	57	48	60	46	57	68	66
LOUDOUN	184	222	213	225	208	181	193	186	176	207	179	181	208	187	195	167	166	183	163	184
LOUISA	94	79	65	78	85	102	77	92	82	76	81	81	72	85	79	86	71	85	95	96
LUNENBURG	73	52	36	50	58	79	55	69	62	51	61	60	46	64	55	67	51	63	77	73
MADISON	92	82	73	81	89	103	76	90	80	78	80	79	75	86	79	84	71	82	93	95
MATHEWS	104	81	52	79	94	123	82	107	85	78	85	92	70	88	85	91	73	95	108	111
MECKLENBURG	82	62	44	59	69	89	63	78	69	61	69	69	55	71	64	74	59	72	84	83
MIDDLESEX	99	79	55	77	91	117	78	101	82	76	82	87	69	83	82	88	70	91	104	105
MONTGOMERY	80	66	68	69	64	69	87	73	81	75	81	70	76	79	75	78	73	79	73	75
NELSON	102	84	68	82	93	115	81	101	87	81	87	87	75	89	85	93	75	92	106	105
NEW KENT	108	117	120	118	119	117	102	110	102	108	102	99	109	107	109	102	93	104	107	112
NORTHAMPTON	81	61	50	59	67	87	65	77	72	61	70	68	56	72	65	77	60	72	86	82
NORTHUMBERLAND	99	81	62	80	92	117	79	101	84	78	83	86	72	83	84	90	72	92	106	105
NOTTOWAY	76	59	47	58	65	81	61	72	67	59	66	63	55	69	61	72	57	68	79	77
ORANGE	95	90	88	89	95	106	83	95	88	86	87	82	84	88	89	92	77	90	94	97
PAGE	80	63	49	61	68	86	62	75	68	61	68	66	56	72	63	73	58	69	81	80
PATRICK	77	54	32	51	59	81	54	69	61	53	61	61	45	64	53	65	52	63	74	76
PITTSYLVANIA	85	63	42	60	69	90	62	78	69	61	69	69	55	73	62	74	59	71	83	84
POWHATAN	118	129	130	130	129	127	113	121	111	120	112	109	120	117	119	111	101	114	116	122
PRINCE EDWARD	79	63	58	62	68	84	68	77	72	63	71	67	61	72	67	76	61	73	84	80
PRINCE GEORGE	103	104	106	105	102	101	100	100	99	102	100	91	103	103	101	99	90	99	99	101
PRINCE WILLIAM	139	157	152	159	147	132	144	138	135	150	137	132	151	141	144	130	126	138	125	137
PULASKI	80	68	66	68	72	84	71	78	75	67	73	68	66	76	71	78	62	76	88	86
RAPPAHANNOCK	113	108	95	108	117	131	100	118	101	101	101	104	98	103	106	104	90	109	116	121
RICHMOND	84	66	53	65	72	92	69	82	73	65	72	72	61	74	69	77	62	76	88	86
ROANOKE	100	110	126	111	112	108	103	103	103	106	103	92	109	103	109	105	93	103	108	105
VIRGINIA	115	113	112	114	112	114	113	112	112	113	112	104	112	112	112	112	102	113	112	114
UNITED STATES	100	100	100	100	100	100	100	100	100	100	100	100	100	100	100	100	100	100	100	100

COUNTY	FIPS Code	CBSA Code	DMA Code	POPULATION			2000-2007 ANNUAL RATE		RACE (%)					
									White		Black		Asian/Pacific	
				2000	2007	2012	% Rate	State Rank	2000	2007	2000	2007	2000	2007
ROCKBRIDGE	163	00000	573	20,808	22,275	23,115	0.9	61	95.4	94.6	3.0	3.3	0.4	0.6
ROCKINGHAM	165	25500	569	67,725	74,369	79,380	1.3	42	96.6	95.6	1.4	1.5	0.3	0.4
RUSSELL	167	00000	531	30,308	29,415	29,547	-0.4	125	96.1	96.2	3.1	2.3	0.1	0.4
SCOTT	169	28700	531	23,403	23,387	23,347	0.0	110	98.5	98.5	0.6	0.6	0.1	0.1
SHENANDOAH	171	00000	511	35,075	40,980	45,852	2.2	23	95.6	92.5	1.2	3.1	0.4	0.5
SMYTH	173	00000	531	33,081	32,931	32,820	-0.1	114	96.9	96.2	1.9	2.1	0.2	0.3
SOUTHAMPTON	175	00000	544	17,482	18,082	18,631	0.5	84	56.0	52.9	42.9	45.6	0.2	0.2
SPOTSYLVANIA	177	47900	511	90,395	123,790	151,322	4.4	4	82.9	80.3	12.5	13.5	1.4	1.9
STAFFORD	179	47900	511	92,446	127,097	153,052	4.5	2	82.0	79.2	12.1	13.0	1.7	2.3
SURRY	181	47260	544	6,829	7,349	7,677	1.0	54	46.9	43.9	51.6	54.2	0.2	0.2
SUSSEX	183	40060	556	12,504	12,170	11,752	-0.4	125	36.4	33.5	62.1	64.5	0.1	0.2
TAZEWELL	185	14140	559	44,598	44,909	45,214	0.1	105	96.2	95.4	2.3	2.6	0.6	0.8
WARREN	187	47900	511	31,584	36,539	40,428	2.0	27	92.7	91.4	4.8	5.3	0.5	0.6
WASHINGTON	191	28700	531	51,103	53,142	54,608	0.5	84	97.6	97.0	1.3	1.5	0.3	0.4
WESTMORELAND	193	00000	511	16,718	17,689	18,419	0.8	68	65.4	62.2	30.9	32.8	0.4	0.5
WISE	195	00000	531	40,123	42,501	42,633	0.8	68	96.9	94.2	1.8	3.4	0.3	0.8
WYTHE	197	00000	573	27,599	28,519	29,072	0.5	84	95.8	95.0	2.9	3.2	0.4	0.5
YORK	199	47260	544	56,297	64,856	70,142	2.0	27	80.0	76.9	13.4	14.4	3.4	4.5
ALEXANDRIA CITY	510	47900	511	128,283	139,748	146,895	1.2	47	59.8	55.5	22.5	22.3	5.7	7.0
BEDFORD CITY	515	31340	573	6,299	6,170	6,049	-0.3	121	75.3	72.8	22.4	24.3	0.7	0.9
BRISTOL CITY	520	28700	531	17,367	17,307	17,185	0.0	110	92.5	92.3	5.6	5.8	0.4	0.4
BUENA VISTA CITY	530	00000	573	6,349	6,556	6,541	0.4	89	93.6	92.5	4.8	5.3	0.4	0.6
CHARLOTTESVILLE CITY	540	16820	584	45,049	40,683	41,068	-1.4	134	69.6	65.5	22.2	24.8	5.0	5.5
CHESAPEAKE CITY	550	47260	544	199,184	223,419	241,955	1.6	31	66.9	63.6	28.5	30.4	1.9	2.5
COLONIAL HEIGHTS CIT	570	40060	556	16,897	17,525	17,982	0.5	84	89.1	86.9	6.3	6.9	2.8	3.8
COVINGTON CITY	580	00000	573	6,303	6,058	5,858	-0.5	128	84.1	81.9	13.1	14.4	0.7	0.9
DANVILLE CITY	590	19260	573	48,411	45,517	43,733	-0.8	131	53.9	50.7	44.1	46.6	0.6	0.8
EMPORIA CITY	595	00000	556	5,665	5,706	5,625	0.1	105	42.5	41.5	56.2	57.1	0.6	0.6
FAIRFAX CITY	600	47900	511	21,498	22,823	23,778	0.8	68	72.9	67.3	5.1	5.0	12.2	15.0
FALLS CHURCH CITY	610	47900	511	10,377	10,655	10,803	0.4	89	85.0	81.3	3.3	3.4	6.6	8.4
FRANKLIN CITY	620	00000	544	8,346	8,446	8,910	0.2	99	45.7	44.7	52.3	53.3	0.8	0.8
FREDERICKSBURG CITY	630	47900	511	19,279	21,099	22,039	1.3	42	73.2	69.8	20.4	21.7	1.6	2.0
GALAX CITY	640	00000	573	6,837	6,807	6,796	-0.1	114	86.1	85.7	6.3	6.5	0.7	0.7
HAMPTON CITY	650	47260	544	146,437	146,993	147,725	0.1	105	49.5	46.2	44.7	46.4	1.9	2.5
HARRISONBURG CITY	660	25500	569	40,468	44,036	46,337	1.2	47	84.8	77.9	5.9	9.4	3.1	4.3
HOPEWELL CITY	670	40060	556	22,354	22,622	22,874	0.2	99	62.3	59.0	33.5	35.4	0.9	1.1
LEXINGTON CITY	678	00000	573	6,867	6,936	6,993	0.1	105	86.0	85.6	10.4	10.8	1.9	2.0
LYNCHBURG CITY	680	31340	573	65,269	69,146	70,522	0.8	68	66.6	63.5	29.7	31.8	1.3	1.7
MANASSAS CITY	683	47900	511	35,135	37,862	39,098	1.0	54	72.1	67.4	12.9	13.0	3.5	4.4
MANASSAS PARK CITY	685	47900	511	10,290	13,693	16,093	4.0	6	72.8	68.0	11.2	11.3	4.1	5.1
MARTINSVILLE CITY	690	32300	573	15,416	14,621	14,079	-0.7	129	55.4	52.4	42.5	44.9	0.5	0.6
NEWPORT NEWS CITY	700	47260	544	180,150	182,973	185,959	0.2	99	53.5	50.0	39.1	40.5	2.4	3.1
NORFOLK CITY	710	47260	544	234,403	237,072	235,801	0.2	99	48.4	44.9	44.1	45.5	2.9	3.7
NORTON CITY	720	00000	531	3,904	3,760	3,644	-0.5	128	91.6	90.2	6.1	6.8	1.1	1.5
PETERSBURG CITY	730	40060	556	33,740	31,818	30,559	-0.8	131	18.5	16.8	79.0	80.0	0.7	0.9
POQUOSON CITY	735	47260	544	11,566	12,193	12,658	0.7	75	96.3	95.1	0.7	0.8	1.6	2.2
PORTSMOUTH CITY	740	47260	544	100,565	100,676	100,821	0.0	110	45.8	42.7	50.6	52.8	0.8	1.1
RADFORD CITY	750	13980	573	15,859	15,410	15,199	-0.4	125	88.2	86.2	8.1	8.9	1.5	2.0
RICHMOND CITY	760	40060	556	197,790	194,320	190,505	-0.2	118	38.3	35.3	57.2	58.9	1.3	1.7
ROANOKE CITY	770	40220	573	94,911	93,048	91,808	-0.3	121	69.4	66.3	26.7	28.7	1.2	1.6
SALEM CITY	775	40220	573	24,747	25,156	25,342	0.2	99	91.9	90.5	5.9	6.5	1.0	1.4
STAUNTON CITY	790	44420	569	23,853	23,469	23,856	-0.2	118	83.3	81.1	14.0	15.3	0.5	0.6
SUFFOLK CITY	800	47260	544	63,677	84,197	99,641	3.9	8	53.8	50.7	43.5	46.0	0.8	1.0
VIRGINIA BEACH CITY	810	47260	544	425,257	447,850	463,278	0.7	75	71.4	67.6	19.0	19.9	5.0	6.5
WAYNESBORO CITY	820	44420	569	19,520	20,763	21,854	0.9	61	86.5	84.3	10.0	10.8	0.6	0.8
WILLIAMSBURG CITY	830	47260	544	11,998	13,149	13,925	1.3	42	79.5	76.3	13.3	14.3	4.6	6.1
WINCHESTER CITY	840	49020	511	23,585	25,770	27,478	1.2	47	82.1	78.8	10.5	11.1	1.6	2.1
VIRGINIA							1.5		72.3	69.6	19.6	20.1	3.7	4.7
UNITED STATES							1.2		75.1	72.7	12.3	12.6	3.8	4.5

POPULATION COMPOSITION

COUNTY	% HISPANIC ORIGIN		2007 AGE DISTRIBUTION (%)										MEDIAN AGE	% 2007 Males	% 2007 Females
	2000	2007	0-4	5-9	10-14	15-19	20-24	25-44	45-64	65-84	85+	18+	2007		
ROCKBRIDGE	0.6	0.9	5.5	5.4	5.3	5.8	4.6	26.3	30.4	15.2	1.6	80.2	43.1	50.3	49.7
ROCKINGHAM	3.3	4.9	6.2	6.4	6.3	6.7	5.5	26.6	27.8	12.3	2.1	77.4	40.1	49.4	50.6
RUSSELL	0.8	1.0	5.4	5.4	5.3	5.2	6.1	28.1	29.9	13.1	1.6	81.0	41.3	49.8	50.2
SCOTT	0.4	0.4	5.3	5.2	5.3	5.1	4.6	26.2	29.6	16.3	2.5	81.1	43.9	48.6	51.4
SHENANDOAH	3.4	5.0	5.6	5.4	6.0	5.9	5.1	24.5	29.6	15.7	2.4	80.2	43.4	49.0	51.0
SMYTH	0.9	1.3	5.4	5.1	5.9	5.8	5.1	26.9	28.2	15.3	2.3	80.1	42.2	49.0	51.0
SOUTHAMPTON	0.7	0.9	5.3	5.2	5.6	6.5	7.6	25.4	29.0	13.4	1.9	80.1	41.7	52.7	47.3
SPOTSYLVANIA	2.8	4.1	7.7	7.1	7.7	7.5	6.1	28.7	26.2	8.1	1.0	72.9	35.6	49.2	50.8
STAFFORD	3.6	5.2	7.8	7.5	8.5	8.0	6.4	29.5	25.5	6.1	0.7	71.1	34.4	50.0	50.0
SURRY	0.7	1.0	5.8	5.7	6.5	6.9	5.4	23.9	31.5	12.4	1.8	77.8	42.4	48.4	51.6
SUSSEX	0.8	1.1	4.5	4.5	5.1	4.9	8.2	32.1	26.7	12.0	1.9	82.8	39.4	58.2	41.8
TAZEWELL	0.5	0.8	5.1	5.3	5.6	5.1	5.4	25.4	31.5	14.5	2.1	81.0	43.6	48.3	51.7
WARREN	1.6	2.3	6.6	6.3	6.9	7.1	6.0	26.4	27.7	11.3	1.6	75.9	39.8	49.3	50.7
WASHINGTON	0.6	1.0	5.0	5.1	5.4	5.8	5.5	26.3	30.3	14.7	2.0	81.1	42.9	48.8	51.2
WESTMORELAND	3.5	4.9	5.2	4.9	5.6	6.3	5.0	21.3	31.7	17.6	2.5	80.3	46.1	48.0	52.0
WISE	0.7	1.4	5.7	5.6	5.6	6.9	6.9	27.0	28.4	12.1	1.7	80.1	39.0	49.4	50.6
WYTHE	0.6	0.8	5.4	5.5	5.6	5.4	5.1	27.9	28.3	14.3	2.4	80.1	41.6	48.3	51.7
YORK	2.7	3.8	6.5	6.3	7.5	7.5	6.6	25.9	29.1	9.6	1.0	74.9	38.8	48.9	51.1
ALEXANDRIA CITY	14.7	19.6	5.7	5.7	4.6	4.3	5.4	40.2	24.8	7.8	1.6	81.4	36.7	48.7	51.3
BEDFORD CITY	0.9	1.3	5.7	4.6	6.1	6.5	7.4	22.6	25.6	16.8	4.8	79.6	42.7	48.3	51.7
BRISTOL CITY	1.0	1.0	5.3	5.1	5.3	6.7	5.7	24.7	26.4	17.2	3.5	80.6	42.8	45.7	54.3
BUENA VISTA CITY	1.0	1.5	6.0	5.5	5.2	9.2	7.0	24.1	24.7	15.5	2.7	79.4	39.2	46.3	53.7
CHARLOTTESVILLE CITY	2.4	3.3	4.9	4.4	4.6	9.3	20.0	25.5	19.9	9.4	2.0	83.0	29.5	47.0	53.0
CHESAPEAKE CITY	2.0	2.9	7.2	6.7	7.2	7.7	7.2	27.5	26.6	8.9	1.1	74.0	36.5	48.5	51.5
COLONIAL HEIGHTS CIT	1.6	2.4	5.5	4.9	5.7	7.4	5.3	26.0	26.5	15.8	2.8	79.2	41.7	47.1	52.9
COVINGTON CITY	0.6	0.9	6.4	6.2	5.7	5.5	4.9	27.5	25.9	15.0	2.9	78.2	40.9	48.6	51.4
DANVILLE CITY	1.3	1.7	6.0	6.0	5.9	6.6	5.8	23.4	27.3	15.7	3.4	78.2	42.1	46.0	54.0
EMPORIA CITY	1.5	1.5	6.7	5.7	6.5	7.4	6.8	23.6	24.0	15.2	4.1	76.6	40.2	45.6	54.4
FAIRFAX CITY	13.6	18.3	5.8	6.0	5.4	5.1	6.0	32.2	25.6	11.8	2.1	79.7	38.8	48.9	51.1
FALLS CHURCH CITY	8.4	11.9	4.9	4.9	6.0	7.2	8.8	23.8	33.0	9.0	2.4	79.6	41.3	49.0	51.0
FRANKLIN CITY	0.6	0.5	5.4	4.3	6.7	7.2	7.3	22.3	27.6	15.5	3.8	79.1	42.6	44.5	55.5
FREDERICKSBURG CITY	4.9	6.9	5.7	4.4	4.3	11.5	14.4	25.9	20.5	11.1	2.1	82.8	30.3	44.9	55.1
GALAX CITY	11.1	11.4	6.5	6.4	6.0	5.5	5.2	25.6	26.8	14.7	3.3	77.7	40.9	48.3	51.7
HAMPTON CITY	2.8	3.8	6.3	5.7	6.4	8.3	8.4	30.2	23.4	10.0	1.3	77.4	34.7	49.7	50.3
HARRISONBURG CITY	8.8	12.8	5.1	4.5	4.0	11.0	23.8	25.0	16.2	8.6	1.9	83.6	25.9	48.9	51.1
HOPEWELL CITY	2.9	4.0	7.7	6.7	7.4	6.7	6.6	27.5	23.5	11.9	2.0	74.1	35.5	47.1	52.9
LEXINGTON CITY	1.6	1.6	2.8	2.6	2.8	19.7	23.4	14.0	17.6	14.0	3.1	89.3	24.7	55.2	44.8
LYNCHBURG CITY	1.3	1.9	5.7	5.4	5.8	10.1	9.8	24.3	22.8	12.8	3.3	79.3	35.2	46.1	53.9
MANASSAS CITY	15.1	20.5	8.4	7.9	8.5	6.8	6.6	32.3	23.2	5.6	0.7	71.0	32.8	51.0	49.0
MANASSAS PARK CITY	15.0	20.4	10.3	10.6	7.8	6.3	5.3	36.5	18.5	4.3	0.2	67.2	31.7	51.1	48.9
MARTINSVILLE CITY	2.3	3.2	5.7	5.3	5.6	6.6	6.4	23.4	26.7	16.5	3.8	79.3	42.9	45.7	54.3
NEWPORT NEWS CITY	4.2	5.7	7.9	7.0	7.2	7.6	7.9	29.2	22.4	9.3	1.4	73.7	33.3	48.3	51.7
NORFOLK CITY	3.8	5.1	7.0	6.4	6.3	8.6	12.6	29.0	19.9	8.7	1.6	76.6	29.6	51.8	48.2
NORTON CITY	0.9	1.3	5.1	4.5	6.8	5.0	5.3	27.4	29.0	14.4	2.4	80.5	41.0	44.8	55.2
PETERSBURG CITY	1.4	1.7	6.4	5.8	6.7	7.4	6.3	25.6	26.0	13.4	2.4	76.6	38.9	46.0	54.0
POQUOSON CITY	1.1	1.6	4.9	4.5	6.5	8.2	6.6	21.6	32.1	13.6	1.9	78.8	43.6	50.1	49.9
PORTSMOUTH CITY	1.7	2.3	7.1	6.5	6.5	7.6	8.1	26.7	23.5	11.8	2.2	75.6	35.7	48.5	51.5
RADFORD CITY	1.2	1.7	3.5	3.3	3.2	17.3	28.7	18.2	16.1	8.3	1.5	87.7	24.0	45.7	54.3
RICHMOND CITY	2.6	3.4	6.0	5.6	5.9	7.9	8.6	29.4	23.8	10.5	2.3	79.0	35.3	47.1	52.9
ROANOKE CITY	1.5	2.1	6.3	6.1	6.4	6.2	5.6	27.5	26.6	12.3	2.9	77.5	39.2	47.3	52.7
SALEM CITY	0.8	1.2	4.7	4.5	5.4	8.3	7.7	23.8	27.7	15.1	2.6	81.6	41.4	47.3	52.7
STAUNTON CITY	1.1	1.6	5.2	4.7	5.1	7.1	7.1	24.8	27.2	15.5	3.3	81.0	42.0	46.8	53.2
SUFFOLK CITY	1.3	1.7	7.5	7.3	7.3	7.2	5.7	27.7	25.8	10.0	1.5	73.5	37.5	48.1	51.9
VIRGINIA BEACH CITY	4.2	5.8	7.1	6.8	7.2	7.6	7.2	30.9	23.7	8.2	1.1	74.3	34.4	49.6	50.4
WAYNESBORO CITY	3.3	4.8	6.7	5.8	6.3	6.7	5.9	24.9	26.0	14.9	2.7	77.0	40.3	47.3	52.7
WILLIAMSBURG CITY	2.5	3.6	2.8	2.5	2.5	17.7	26.6	17.7	17.7	10.7	1.9	90.4	24.6	45.1	54.9
WINCHESTER CITY	6.5	9.3	6.1	5.3	6.1	6.9	8.0	29.1	24.5	12.0	2.0	79.3	36.6	48.7	51.3
VIRGINIA	4.7	6.4	6.5	6.5	6.6	7.0	6.6	28.5	26.5	10.2	1.5	76.4	37.6	49.2	50.8
UNITED STATES	12.5	15.0	6.9	6.5	6.8	7.1	7.0	27.6	25.4	10.7	1.9	75.6	36.7	49.2	50.8

COUNTY	HOUSEHOLDS					FAMILIES			MEDIAN HOUSEHOLD INCOME			
	2000	2007	2012	% Annual Rate 2000-2007	2007 Average HH Size	2000	2007	% Annual Rate 2000-2007	2007	2012	2007 National Rank	2007 State Rank
ROCKBRIDGE	8,486	9,240	9,650	1.2	2.39	6,072	6,416	0.8	43,992	49,833	1209	64
ROCKINGHAM	25,355	28,483	30,651	1.6	2.55	18,899	20,661	1.2	49,006	54,770	746	49
RUSSELL	11,789	12,210	12,433	0.5	2.37	8,818	8,887	0.1	32,063	36,335	2755	128
SCOTT	9,795	10,087	10,208	0.4	2.28	7,023	7,020	0.0	32,377	36,728	2722	127
SHENANDOAH	14,296	16,953	19,099	2.4	2.39	10,066	11,565	1.9	47,926	54,229	826	51
SMYTH	13,493	13,779	13,890	0.3	2.31	9,601	9,508	-0.1	35,672	40,084	2334	110
SOUTHAMPTON	6,279	6,709	6,997	0.9	2.48	4,505	4,670	0.5	40,472	45,703	1663	83
SPOTSYLVANIA	31,308	43,284	53,240	4.6	2.85	24,635	33,289	4.2	71,298	82,979	115	16
STAFFORD	30,187	41,509	50,136	4.5	3.03	24,493	33,002	4.2	84,204	100,636	32	5
SURRY	2,619	2,852	2,994	1.2	2.58	1,916	2,027	0.8	43,421	48,984	1282	67
SUSSEX	4,126	4,080	3,958	-0.2	2.34	2,808	2,684	-0.6	36,481	40,612	2195	106
TAZEWELL	18,277	18,956	19,360	0.5	2.32	13,228	13,319	0.1	33,041	37,331	2652	126
WARREN	12,087	14,065	15,630	2.1	2.55	8,526	9,617	1.7	52,557	59,642	519	39
WASHINGTON	21,056	22,544	23,469	0.9	2.30	14,949	15,517	0.5	39,646	45,419	1760	89
WESTMORELAND	6,846	7,381	7,749	1.0	2.38	4,687	4,886	0.6	43,381	49,442	1290	68
WISE	16,013	16,621	16,921	0.5	2.36	11,517	11,600	0.1	31,134	35,283	2821	130
WYTHE	11,511	12,230	12,625	0.8	2.30	8,103	8,343	0.4	38,157	42,991	1980	95
YORK	20,000	23,424	25,517	2.2	2.74	15,887	18,201	1.9	74,780	87,683	90	13
ALEXANDRIA CITY	61,889	67,133	70,558	1.1	2.05	27,749	28,389	0.3	72,995	87,610	103	15
BEDFORD CITY	2,519	2,475	2,425	-0.2	2.25	1,593	1,505	-0.8	34,193	39,033	2529	118
BRISTOL CITY	7,678	7,767	7,792	0.2	2.13	4,795	4,661	-0.4	34,568	40,070	2489	116
BUENA VISTA CITY	2,547	2,594	2,614	0.3	2.33	1,749	1,722	-0.2	40,284	46,786	1691	85
CHARLOTTESVILLE CITY	16,851	17,430	17,738	0.5	2.23	7,626	7,452	-0.3	38,182	44,341	1979	94
CHESAPEAKE CITY	69,900	79,475	86,614	1.8	2.76	54,158	60,106	1.4	63,132	74,477	192	23
COLONIAL HEIGHTS CIT	7,027	7,427	7,686	0.8	2.33	4,720	4,818	0.3	55,163	65,419	400	37
COVINGTON CITY	2,835	2,742	2,670	-0.5	2.18	1,742	1,618	-1.0	37,182	43,112	2103	102
DANVILLE CITY	20,607	19,677	19,023	-0.6	2.23	12,931	11,870	-1.2	33,396	38,594	2617	124
EMPORIA CITY	2,226	2,273	2,252	0.3	2.40	1,406	1,380	-0.3	37,301	43,246	2092	101
FAIRFAX CITY	8,035	8,564	8,930	0.9	2.61	5,407	5,566	0.4	86,840	103,455	24	4
FALLS CHURCH CITY	4,471	4,578	4,634	0.3	2.31	2,622	2,569	-0.3	100,352	122,959	7	3
FRANKLIN CITY	3,384	3,519	3,763	0.5	2.32	2,279	2,289	0.1	38,741	45,043	1889	91
FREDERICKSBURG CITY	8,102	9,001	9,562	1.5	2.04	3,925	4,129	0.7	43,890	51,075	1225	65
GALAX CITY	2,950	2,964	2,971	0.1	2.25	1,845	1,781	-0.5	34,168	39,026	2533	120
HAMPTON CITY	53,887	55,329	56,023	0.4	2.44	35,911	35,583	-0.1	50,005	58,269	682	47
HARRISONBURG CITY	13,133	14,369	15,144	1.2	2.58	6,442	6,680	0.5	36,905	42,482	2140	104
HOPEWELL CITY	9,055	9,334	9,499	0.4	2.40	6,073	6,045	-0.1	40,920	47,965	1610	81
LEXINGTON CITY	2,232	2,315	2,365	0.5	2.02	1,080	1,062	-0.2	36,293	42,175	2233	107
LYNCHBURG CITY	25,477	26,301	26,974	0.4	2.30	15,588	15,439	-0.1	39,930	46,363	1737	88
MANASSAS CITY	11,757	12,624	13,026	1.0	2.92	8,437	8,789	0.6	76,420	89,190	77	11
MANASSAS PARK CITY	3,254	4,300	5,037	3.9	3.18	2,558	3,304	3.6	78,219	94,562	64	8
MARTINSVILLE CITY	6,498	6,231	6,024	-0.6	2.24	4,025	3,706	-1.1	34,180	39,489	2531	119
NEWPORT NEWS CITY	69,686	73,139	74,843	0.7	2.46	46,358	46,955	0.2	45,887	52,700	1015	57
NORFOLK CITY	86,210	87,899	88,026	0.3	2.40	51,915	50,744	-0.3	40,061	46,746	1716	87
NORTON CITY	1,730	1,730	1,701	0.0	2.15	1,067	1,023	-0.6	28,514	33,055	2980	131
PETERSBURG CITY	13,799	13,158	12,696	-0.7	2.35	8,508	7,790	-1.2	35,754	40,815	2323	109
POQUOSON CITY	4,166	4,477	4,687	1.0	2.70	3,370	3,549	0.7	77,213	90,006	73	10
PORTSMOUTH CITY	38,170	38,415	38,658	0.1	2.49	25,482	24,750	-0.4	42,155	49,351	1433	75
RADFORD CITY	5,809	5,876	5,864	0.2	2.17	2,644	2,525	-0.6	31,278	36,582	2813	129
RICHMOND CITY	84,549	82,705	81,203	-0.3	2.19	43,649	40,561	-1.0	39,178	46,152	1832	90
ROANOKE CITY	42,003	42,029	41,805	0.0	2.15	24,255	23,200	-0.6	38,329	44,507	1959	93
SALEM CITY	9,954	10,166	10,289	0.3	2.29	6,544	6,441	-0.2	49,265	57,329	729	48
STAUNTON CITY	9,676	10,066	10,326	0.5	2.15	5,766	5,744	-0.1	41,318	48,572	1550	78
SUFFOLK CITY	23,283	31,298	37,325	4.2	2.66	17,730	23,232	3.8	51,197	59,056	601	44
VIRGINIA BEACH CITY	154,455	165,227	172,127	0.9	2.66	110,953	115,173	0.5	60,991	71,019	242	27
WAYNESBORO CITY	8,332	8,996	9,533	1.1	2.28	5,434	5,654	0.5	40,649	47,152	1649	82
WILLIAMSBURG CITY	3,619	4,206	4,597	2.1	2.06	1,787	1,970	1.4	47,061	54,238	905	55
WINCHESTER CITY	10,001	11,053	11,835	1.4	2.27	5,649	5,963	0.7	42,732	50,176	1361	72
VIRGINIA				1.6	2.52			1.2	60,707	70,833		
UNITED STATES				1.2	2.59			1.0	53,154	62,503		

COUNTY	2007 Per Capita Income	2007 HH Income Base	2007 HOUSEHOLD INCOME DISTRIBUTION (%) Less than $25,000	$25,000 to $49,999	$50,000 to $99,999	$100,000 to $149,999	$150,000 or More	2007 Home Value Base	2007 HOME VALUE DISTRIBUTION (%) Less than $50,000	$50,000 to $89,999	$90,000 to $174,999	$175,000 to $399,999	$400,000 or More	2007 Median Home Value
ROCKBRIDGE	22,441	9,240	26.3	32.3	31.9	6.8	2.6	7,213	8.1	8.0	25.7	44.5	13.6	193,097
ROCKINGHAM	23,374	28,483	20.4	30.6	36.4	8.9	3.6	22,415	5.4	3.6	27.8	55.1	8.1	197,414
RUSSELL	17,737	12,210	37.3	33.3	23.1	4.6	1.7	9,885	20.2	15.4	33.9	28.8	1.8	128,729
SCOTT	18,121	10,087	38.9	30.4	25.4	4.3	1.0	7,908	23.0	20.3	39.8	16.0	0.9	101,570
SHENANDOAH	24,793	16,953	21.2	31.5	35.0	8.7	3.6	12,508	3.2	1.5	21.5	64.0	9.9	219,628
SMYTH	20,129	13,779	32.9	33.5	26.7	4.6	2.3	10,282	13.3	14.1	39.7	31.2	1.8	143,770
SOUTHAMPTON	20,419	6,709	31.0	28.1	31.1	7.6	2.2	5,032	8.4	7.7	33.4	46.2	4.3	175,875
SPOTSYLVANIA	29,349	43,284	9.8	20.5	40.6	20.8	8.3	35,638	2.6	1.5	3.8	64.0	28.1	330,684
STAFFORD	32,502	41,509	6.8	15.2	38.2	26.1	13.7	33,523	2.5	1.0	2.3	46.8	47.4	390,310
SURRY	20,277	2,852	27.6	29.3	33.9	7.6	1.6	2,224	12.1	5.9	27.5	47.0	7.6	186,644
SUSSEX	19,633	4,080	32.9	30.7	27.5	6.6	2.3	2,873	12.5	14.6	41.6	30.3	1.0	139,887
TAZEWELL	19,243	18,956	37.0	32.3	23.7	4.6	2.4	14,706	17.9	15.4	36.9	27.1	2.7	129,901
WARREN	24,641	14,065	18.8	28.3	36.4	13.1	3.3	10,481	1.9	0.8	7.6	71.9	17.9	285,433
WASHINGTON	23,227	22,544	29.7	30.8	29.1	7.1	3.3	17,420	13.7	13.9	41.7	27.2	3.5	133,861
WESTMORELAND	23,283	7,381	30.1	26.2	31.6	8.5	3.5	5,853	6.9	4.5	26.7	53.0	8.8	194,814
WISE	18,096	16,621	40.3	30.2	23.3	4.3	1.8	12,594	17.3	17.7	35.5	27.6	1.9	126,700
WYTHE	22,059	12,230	31.7	30.4	29.6	5.1	3.1	9,468	10.5	11.7	37.2	37.3	3.3	152,596
YORK	33,301	23,424	8.5	20.7	36.5	21.5	12.7	17,845	2.0	0.8	7.2	60.2	29.8	318,632
ALEXANDRIA CITY	49,988	67,133	11.3	19.3	35.3	17.4	16.7	27,037	0.3	0.3	6.8	45.5	47.1	384,992
BEDFORD CITY	20,145	2,475	37.8	30.9	23.8	4.1	3.4	1,495	3.5	9.1	58.5	26.8	2.2	151,246
BRISTOL CITY	22,041	7,767	36.0	33.2	22.7	5.1	2.9	5,101	9.2	23.9	49.9	15.8	1.2	115,648
BUENA VISTA CITY	21,087	2,594	28.7	33.2	30.2	5.5	2.4	1,837	6.0	5.8	46.8	40.3	1.1	162,176
CHARLOTTESVILLE CITY	24,663	17,430	33.4	28.0	25.0	8.6	4.9	7,190	1.1	0.6	22.1	61.1	15.2	239,251
CHESAPEAKE CITY	27,011	79,475	14.3	22.7	40.0	16.6	6.5	59,451	2.4	1.0	14.2	68.2	14.2	256,682
COLONIAL HEIGHTS CIT	29,731	7,427	13.7	30.2	37.3	13.4	5.4	5,176	0.8	1.6	43.8	51.5	2.3	182,523
COVINGTON CITY	21,032	2,742	31.7	32.5	30.4	3.9	1.6	1,911	10.7	22.2	48.9	17.4	0.8	116,494
DANVILLE CITY	21,527	19,677	38.3	28.4	24.6	5.5	3.2	11,597	16.0	28.0	42.9	11.8	1.4	97,880
EMPORIA CITY	20,366	2,273	32.9	31.6	26.8	6.1	2.6	1,190	3.0	13.1	44.2	36.2	3.4	152,390
FAIRFAX CITY	43,211	8,564	6.2	13.5	37.3	22.8	20.1	5,910	0.4	0.2	5.1	23.2	71.1	474,153
FALLS CHURCH CITY	58,914	4,578	7.8	10.8	31.2	20.9	29.3	2,790	0.4	0.3	1.7	19.2	78.4	622,074
FRANKLIN CITY	24,226	3,519	34.8	26.1	24.6	9.3	5.3	1,916	0.0	4.5	31.8	54.7	8.9	199,716
FREDERICKSBURG CITY	30,115	9,001	26.7	28.8	28.7	8.6	7.3	3,245	1.4	0.8	8.4	58.1	31.4	314,134
GALAX CITY	22,476	2,964	36.3	28.9	28.3	3.1	3.4	1,984	15.5	12.2	35.7	33.7	2.8	145,856
HAMPTON CITY	24,376	55,329	21.5	28.5	35.2	10.8	4.1	32,673	1.4	1.2	27.0	66.0	4.3	205,494
HARRISONBURG CITY	20,001	14,369	34.3	28.9	25.4	6.8	4.6	5,678	3.8	0.8	20.0	66.5	8.9	223,351
HOPEWELL CITY	20,912	9,332	27.3	31.7	31.9	7.0	2.1	5,301	1.8	6.9	59.2	30.6	1.5	153,907
LEXINGTON CITY	26,024	2,315	37.2	21.9	21.6	11.8	7.3	1,267	1.3	1.0	28.3	49.7	19.7	236,092
LYNCHBURG CITY	23,558	26,301	31.6	28.5	26.7	8.7	4.5	15,476	7.0	13.3	46.2	29.4	4.1	143,501
MANASSAS CITY	31,284	12,624	8.1	18.3	39.9	22.3	11.4	8,804	1.9	0.1	6.3	53.3	38.4	347,262
MANASSAS PARK CITY	27,987	4,300	7.9	16.0	43.6	23.3	9.3	3,376	0.0	0.5	1.7	63.7	34.1	342,241
MARTINSVILLE CITY	21,678	6,231	38.1	27.9	24.8	5.7	3.5	3,775	3.7	14.3	46.1	30.8	5.1	153,294
NEWPORT NEWS CITY	22,670	73,139	25.0	29.4	33.8	8.7	3.1	38,451	3.4	2.1	20.3	69.7	4.6	217,162
NORFOLK CITY	22,129	87,896	29.7	31.1	27.8	7.3	4.1	40,518	1.9	1.7	27.2	59.4	9.8	200,284
NORTON CITY	19,775	1,730	45.7	24.2	22.1	5.7	2.3	970	20.0	10.6	40.8	25.6	3.0	124,016
PETERSBURG CITY	20,326	13,158	34.6	30.2	26.6	6.1	2.5	6,807	5.6	14.3	56.7	22.5	1.0	137,680
POQUOSON CITY	34,185	4,477	9.4	18.4	39.5	19.4	13.3	3,759	4.4	1.2	5.0	61.2	28.2	326,985
PORTSMOUTH CITY	20,963	38,415	27.8	30.8	30.8	7.8	2.7	22,638	0.9	1.9	38.8	55.3	3.0	186,504
RADFORD CITY	21,413	5,876	42.6	22.0	26.6	4.8	4.0	2,624	5.2	4.4	47.4	39.2	3.8	163,869
RICHMOND CITY	26,246	82,705	32.0	28.5	25.9	7.8	5.9	38,370	2.2	8.5	44.3	34.1	10.9	165,060
ROANOKE CITY	23,997	42,029	31.5	31.3	27.3	6.7	3.2	23,805	4.1	14.2	55.5	22.2	4.0	137,252
SALEM CITY	26,498	10,161	20.0	30.7	34.2	9.7	5.4	6,933	5.5	3.7	45.8	39.5	5.5	168,281
STAUNTON CITY	26,179	10,066	28.1	29.3	30.4	7.5	4.6	6,202	0.6	2.8	35.1	57.4	4.1	191,535
SUFFOLK CITY	23,984	31,298	23.4	25.3	34.4	11.4	5.5	22,870	3.8	4.4	18.4	60.2	13.3	237,771
VIRGINIA BEACH CITY	28,719	165,227	12.0	26.1	40.0	14.2	7.6	108,713	1.5	0.4	11.9	68.1	18.1	264,009
WAYNESBORO CITY	23,141	8,996	30.0	28.9	30.9	7.4	2.8	5,553	2.5	2.6	32.8	55.9	6.1	192,492
WILLIAMSBURG CITY	29,249	4,206	25.2	27.7	28.3	9.1	9.7	1,904	2.6	2.1	25.0	36.7	33.6	266,197
WINCHESTER CITY	27,006	11,053	25.3	31.5	29.2	8.4	5.6	5,149	0.9	1.5	13.3	65.8	18.5	244,349
VIRGINIA	31,988		18.1	23.3	33.3	14.5	10.8		4.3	4.3	19.9	46.6	25.0	249,117
UNITED STATES	27,916		21.9	25.0	32.3	12.3	8.4		7.9	10.5	27.1	35.6	19.0	192,285

COUNTY	FINANCIAL SERVICES				THE HOME							ENTERTAINMENT						PERSONAL			
					Home Improvements		Furnishings														
	Auto Loan	Home Loan	Invest-ments	Retire-ment Plans	Home Repair	Lawn & Garden	Comput-ers & Hard-ware	Major Appli-ances	TV, Radio, Sound Equip-ment	Furni-ture		Dine out/ Carry out	Sports Equip-ment	Fees & Tickets	Toys & Games	Travel	Cable TV	Apparel & Services	Auto Repairs	Health Insur-ance	Pets & Supplies
ROCKBRIDGE	86	68	52	67	76	96	68	84	73	67		73	74	62	76	69	78	63	77	88	89
ROCKINGHAM	94	81	70	80	87	101	77	90	81	78		81	80	74	86	79	85	71	83	93	95
RUSSELL	72	51	33	48	56	76	52	66	59	50		58	58	44	62	52	64	50	61	72	71
SCOTT	69	50	35	48	56	74	51	64	58	49		57	56	44	60	52	63	49	59	72	69
SHENANDOAH	91	77	71	77	83	98	78	89	82	75		81	78	73	84	79	86	71	83	94	92
SMYTH	76	58	46	57	63	80	59	71	65	58		65	62	53	68	59	70	56	66	77	75
SOUTHAMPTON	83	65	52	64	72	89	65	78	71	64		70	69	59	75	66	75	61	72	84	83
SPOTSYLVANIA	119	130	119	129	121	115	116	116	112	122		112	109	120	116	117	109	102	114	108	117
STAFFORD	135	156	150	157	146	131	139	135	131	147		132	128	147	137	140	126	122	134	122	135
SURRY	89	65	41	62	75	99	64	84	71	63		71	73	56	75	65	77	61	75	89	91
SUSSEX	82	56	33	53	62	86	59	75	67	56		66	67	48	70	58	73	56	69	83	82
TAZEWELL	73	55	40	53	60	78	56	69	63	54		62	61	49	65	56	68	53	64	76	73
WARREN	87	90	94	89	90	91	86	89	86	87		86	79	87	88	88	87	78	86	89	89
WASHINGTON	85	68	58	66	73	89	69	80	75	67		74	71	63	77	69	79	64	76	87	85
WESTMORELAND	86	70	59	69	78	98	71	86	76	69		75	75	65	76	74	81	65	80	92	90
WISE	72	53	36	50	57	75	54	67	60	52		59	59	47	62	54	64	51	62	72	71
WYTHE	82	64	53	62	69	86	65	77	71	63		70	68	59	73	65	75	61	72	82	81
YORK	123	139	143	142	134	122	129	125	122	134		123	117	136	126	131	119	113	124	117	124
ALEXANDRIA CITY	138	124	129	136	120	115	153	128	145	145		149	131	144	143	139	140	137	143	124	130
BEDFORD CITY	59	57	78	59	58	59	65	60	67	61		65	52	64	64	64	68	58	62	67	59
BRISTOL CITY	65	59	72	60	62	68	64	65	69	60		66	56	62	66	65	72	58	64	76	64
BUENA VISTA CITY	69	65	77	66	67	71	68	69	71	66		69	60	67	71	68	72	61	68	75	69
CHARLOTTESVILLE CITY	74	59	72	65	57	61	89	68	83	74		83	65	77	78	75	79	75	78	70	69
CHESAPEAKE CITY	103	110	111	112	104	98	104	101	102	108		102	94	108	104	104	100	93	102	97	101
COLONIAL HEIGHTS CIT	92	97	113	100	96	94	96	93	96	96		95	83	100	96	98	96	86	94	97	93
COVINGTON CITY	68	55	58	56	57	66	61	63	69	57		65	55	57	68	61	72	56	63	76	64
DANVILLE CITY	68	59	66	60	61	68	64	65	70	62		68	56	62	68	64	74	60	66	75	66
EMPORIA CITY	65	62	79	64	63	66	67	65	71	65		69	55	67	68	67	73	61	66	74	64
FAIRFAX CITY	139	169	174	166	172	147	160	153	152	165		155	147	174	153	165	150	147	152	141	150
FALLS CHURCH CITY	166	198	211	200	202	173	200	184	181	197		185	187	207	177	201	174	173	188	167	181
FRANKLIN CITY	75	73	82	76	72	73	77	73	81	78		80	64	78	78	76	83	73	77	79	74
FREDERICKSBURG CITY	92	74	80	82	69	72	96	80	94	90		95	78	87	92	85	92	86	92	82	82
GALAX CITY	77	62	57	61	66	80	66	73	73	63		71	64	60	74	66	77	62	70	83	76
HAMPTON CITY	83	80	90	84	77	77	86	79	86	85		85	72	85	85	83	85	77	84	82	80
HARRISONBURG CITY	73	57	63	62	54	57	86	66	78	71		79	65	73	76	71	74	71	75	65	67
HOPEWELL CITY	67	64	77	67	64	65	69	65	72	68		71	56	69	72	68	73	64	67	72	65
LEXINGTON CITY	78	70	94	74	72	75	91	78	89	80		88	72	85	82	85	89	79	84	87	78
LYNCHBURG CITY	77	69	82	72	69	73	78	74	82	75		80	65	76	79	76	83	71	77	82	74
MANASSAS CITY	130	134	128	137	123	115	133	123	125	135		127	119	133	129	127	120	116	128	113	123
MANASSAS PARK CITY	122	138	130	137	128	113	128	122	118	133		120	120	132	123	126	112	110	123	108	119
MARTINSVILLE CITY	66	61	76	63	61	64	67	64	72	64		69	55	66	69	67	74	61	66	73	64
NEWPORT NEWS CITY	77	70	76	74	67	67	80	71	79	77		79	67	76	78	75	78	72	77	73	72
NORFOLK CITY	74	66	74	70	63	65	78	69	78	74		78	64	74	77	73	78	71	75	72	70
NORTON CITY	64	50	52	50	53	64	57	61	62	52		60	54	51	60	56	64	51	60	68	63
PETERSBURG CITY	64	56	68	59	55	60	65	61	70	63		69	52	63	66	63	73	62	65	70	62
POQUOSON CITY	124	142	152	144	140	130	127	128	123	133		123	116	137	124	134	122	113	126	123	128
PORTSMOUTH CITY	71	68	78	71	66	67	73	68	75	72		74	60	73	74	71	75	67	72	73	69
RADFORD CITY	65	49	61	54	48	53	81	60	73	63		73	58	67	68	66	69	65	68	63	60
RICHMOND CITY	79	68	80	74	66	70	85	73	86	79		85	67	79	82	78	86	77	81	79	75
ROANOKE CITY	69	65	78	68	64	66	72	67	75	70		73	59	71	73	71	76	66	70	74	67
SALEM CITY	82	85	103	87	86	86	86	85	87	85		85	73	88	86	88	88	76	85	91	84
STAUNTON CITY	75	74	96	76	75	76	81	76	82	77		80	67	80	79	81	84	72	78	85	75
SUFFOLK CITY	90	95	93	95	91	89	86	88	87	91		87	80	90	89	88	86	79	87	86	89
VIRGINIA BEACH CITY	106	108	109	111	102	97	110	102	105	110		106	96	110	107	106	103	97	106	97	102
WAYNESBORO CITY	70	67	83	69	68	69	73	70	76	70		74	61	73	74	73	78	66	71	78	69
WILLIAMSBURG CITY	101	84	97	91	83	91	110	94	106	97		106	87	99	99	101	104	94	103	100	95
WINCHESTER CITY	80	78	90	82	78	75	88	80	87	85		87	75	87	85	85	86	80	85	81	80
VIRGINIA	115	113	112	114	112	114	113	112	112	113		112	104	112	114	112	112	102	113	112	114
UNITED STATES	100	100	100	100	100	100	100	100	100	100		100	100	100	100	100	100	100	100	100	100

WASHINGTON

POPULATION CHANGE

COUNTY	FIPS Code	CBSA Code	DMA Code	POPULATION			2000-2007 ANNUAL RATE		RACE (%)					
									White		Black		Asian/Pacific	
				2000	2007	2012	% Rate	State Rank	2000	2007	2000	2007	2000	2007
ADAMS	001	00000	881	16,428	17,555	18,420	0.9	26	65.0	60.9	0.3	0.3	0.6	0.6
ASOTIN	003	30300	881	20,551	21,237	21,779	0.5	37	95.6	95.0	0.2	0.2	0.5	0.6
BENTON	005	28420	810	142,475	164,259	180,666	2.0	4	86.2	83.9	0.9	1.0	2.3	2.6
CHELAN	007	48300	819	66,616	71,939	75,705	1.1	20	83.6	80.7	0.3	0.3	0.8	0.9
CLALLAM	009	38820	819	64,525	70,908	76,720	1.3	18	89.1	88.0	0.8	0.9	1.3	1.7
CLARK	011	38900	820	345,238	419,406	480,715	2.7	2	88.8	87.2	1.7	1.8	3.6	4.1
COLUMBIA	013	00000	881	4,064	4,120	4,143	0.2	38	93.7	93.7	0.2	0.2	0.5	0.5
COWLITZ	015	31020	820	92,948	99,019	103,540	0.9	26	91.8	90.5	0.5	0.5	1.4	1.7
DOUGLAS	017	48300	819	32,603	36,488	39,566	1.6	14	84.7	81.9	0.3	0.4	0.6	0.7
FERRY	019	00000	881	7,260	7,641	7,921	0.7	32	75.5	74.5	0.2	0.2	0.3	0.4
FRANKLIN	021	28420	810	49,347	71,224	93,452	5.2	1	61.9	58.1	2.5	2.5	1.7	1.8
GARFIELD	023	00000	881	2,397	2,384	2,376	-0.1	39	96.5	96.4	0.0	0.0	0.7	0.7
GRANT	025	34180	881	74,698	82,859	88,993	1.4	17	76.5	73.2	1.0	1.0	0.9	1.0
GRAYS HARBOR	027	10140	819	67,194	71,744	73,608	0.9	26	88.3	87.0	0.3	0.4	1.3	1.5
ISLAND	029	36020	819	71,558	80,567	87,700	1.6	14	87.2	85.4	2.4	2.6	4.6	5.3
JEFFERSON	031	00000	819	25,953	29,621	32,186	1.8	9	92.2	91.0	0.4	0.5	1.3	1.7
KING	033	42660	819	1,737,034	1,859,574	1,943,506	0.9	26	75.7	72.9	5.4	5.7	11.3	12.8
KITSAP	035	14740	819	231,969	245,400	254,519	0.8	30	84.3	82.3	2.9	3.1	5.2	5.9
KITTITAS	037	21260	810	33,362	38,717	41,716	2.1	3	91.8	90.5	0.7	0.8	2.3	2.7
KLICKITAT	039	00000	820	19,161	20,220	20,895	0.7	32	87.6	85.8	0.3	0.3	0.9	1.1
LEWIS	041	16500	819	68,600	74,454	78,755	1.1	20	93.0	91.8	0.4	0.4	0.9	1.0
LINCOLN	043	00000	881	10,184	10,599	10,798	0.6	35	95.6	95.2	0.2	0.2	0.3	0.4
MASON	045	43220	819	49,405	55,726	60,837	1.7	11	88.5	87.2	1.2	1.3	1.5	1.7
OKANOGAN	047	00000	881	39,564	41,225	42,377	0.6	35	75.3	73.0	0.3	0.3	0.5	0.6
PACIFIC	049	00000	819	20,984	21,839	22,376	0.6	35	90.5	89.2	0.2	0.2	2.2	2.5
PEND OREILLE	051	00000	881	11,732	12,599	13,206	1.0	23	93.5	92.9	0.1	0.2	0.8	1.0
PIERCE	053	42660	819	700,820	782,855	842,507	1.5	16	78.4	76.0	7.0	7.4	5.9	6.7
SAN JUAN	055	00000	819	14,077	15,944	17,024	1.7	11	95.0	94.2	0.3	0.3	1.0	1.1
SKAGIT	057	34580	819	102,979	117,229	128,434	1.8	9	86.5	84.3	0.4	0.5	1.7	1.9
SKAMANIA	059	38900	820	9,872	10,959	11,817	1.5	16	92.1	91.1	0.3	0.3	0.7	0.8
SNOHOMISH	061	42660	819	606,024	685,472	745,663	1.7	11	85.6	83.7	1.7	1.8	6.1	7.0
SPOKANE	063	44060	881	417,939	453,859	476,916	1.1	20	91.4	90.3	1.6	1.7	2.0	2.4
STEVENS	065	00000	881	40,066	43,123	45,413	1.0	23	90.0	89.3	0.3	0.3	0.6	0.7
THURSTON	067	36500	819	207,355	237,813	261,954	1.9	6	85.7	83.8	2.4	2.5	4.9	5.6
WAHKIAKUM	069	00000	820	3,824	4,016	4,160	0.7	32	93.5	92.5	0.3	0.3	0.5	0.6
WALLA WALLA	071	47460	810	55,180	58,820	61,597	0.9	26	85.3	82.9	1.7	1.8	1.3	1.5
WHATCOM	073	13380	819	166,814	191,791	210,324	1.9	6	88.4	86.9	0.7	0.8	2.9	3.4
WHITMAN	075	39420	881	40,740	46,854	47,438	1.9	6	88.1	86.2	1.5	1.8	5.8	6.8
YAKIMA	077	49420	810	222,581	236,325	246,020	0.8	30	65.6	61.7	1.0	1.0	1.0	1.1
WASHINGTON							1.4		81.8	79.6	3.2	3.4	5.9	6.6
UNITED STATES							1.2		75.1	72.7	12.3	12.6	3.8	4.5

COUNTY	% HISPANIC ORIGIN		2007 AGE DISTRIBUTION (%)										MEDIAN AGE	% 2007 Males	% 2007 Females
	2000	2007	0-4	5-9	10-14	15-19	20-24	25-44	45-64	65-84	85+	18+	2007		
ADAMS	47.1	53.4	10.0	9.0	9.2	7.3	8.2	26.1	20.4	8.5	1.3	67.3	29.3	51.1	48.9
ASOTIN	2.0	2.5	7.0	6.2	6.2	6.1	7.9	22.6	27.8	13.4	2.8	77.0	40.2	48.2	51.8
BENTON	12.5	15.5	7.7	6.8	7.3	7.6	8.1	24.9	26.9	9.1	1.5	73.4	35.6	49.5	50.5
CHELAN	19.3	23.5	7.2	6.5	6.9	7.2	7.3	24.1	27.3	11.4	2.2	74.9	37.9	49.9	50.1
CLALLAM	3.4	4.3	5.0	4.8	5.4	6.1	6.0	19.2	31.4	18.5	3.5	81.1	47.3	49.5	50.5
CLARK	4.7	6.0	7.8	7.3	7.5	7.1	6.7	27.6	26.2	8.5	1.4	73.0	35.4	49.5	50.5
COLUMBIA	6.3	6.4	5.5	4.9	6.0	6.1	7.5	20.6	30.5	15.9	2.9	79.7	44.4	48.2	51.8
COWLITZ	4.6	5.8	6.8	5.9	6.9	7.1	6.9	25.0	27.6	11.7	2.1	76.1	38.5	49.5	50.5
DOUGLAS	19.7	24.1	7.8	7.2	7.4	7.3	7.4	23.9	26.4	10.9	1.8	73.1	36.7	49.5	50.5
FERRY	2.8	3.5	5.5	5.3	6.4	9.2	5.8	20.0	33.4	13.1	1.2	76.8	43.2	51.7	48.3
FRANKLIN	46.7	52.8	10.4	9.5	8.8	7.8	8.0	27.5	20.5	6.5	1.0	66.3	28.4	52.2	47.8
GARFIELD	2.0	2.0	4.9	3.9	5.7	7.1	9.7	17.9	30.8	16.5	3.4	81.0	45.4	49.2	50.8
GRANT	30.1	35.7	9.3	8.2	7.8	7.8	7.7	26.0	22.4	9.2	1.5	69.9	31.5	51.1	48.9
GRAYS HARBOR	4.8	6.1	6.3	5.8	5.8	6.7	7.5	24.2	29.0	12.8	2.1	78.1	40.4	51.1	48.9
ISLAND	4.0	5.0	6.6	5.8	6.3	6.4	7.6	24.1	28.6	12.8	1.9	77.4	40.2	50.1	49.9
JEFFERSON	2.1	2.7	3.9	4.2	5.2	5.4	4.7	17.6	37.5	18.8	2.7	83.4	50.3	48.8	51.2
KING	5.5	6.8	5.9	5.6	6.3	6.5	6.5	31.2	27.2	8.8	1.8	78.2	37.5	49.9	50.1
KITSAP	4.1	5.2	6.6	6.1	6.9	7.1	8.2	25.7	28.4	9.4	1.7	76.1	37.6	50.6	49.4
KITTITAS	5.0	6.4	4.8	4.2	5.2	11.2	17.0	21.5	24.3	10.0	1.9	82.4	31.2	49.5	50.5
KLICKITAT	7.8	9.8	6.2	6.1	6.2	7.1	6.9	20.9	32.2	12.4	1.9	76.8	42.3	49.9	50.1
LEWIS	5.4	6.9	6.6	6.1	5.9	7.1	7.1	23.2	28.1	13.3	2.5	76.9	40.2	49.6	50.4
LINCOLN	1.9	2.4	5.9	5.6	5.8	6.6	6.8	18.1	31.7	16.5	3.0	78.4	45.7	49.9	50.1
MASON	4.8	6.1	5.5	4.8	5.8	6.5	6.8	22.2	30.4	15.8	2.1	80.1	43.8	51.4	48.6
OKANOGAN	14.4	17.7	6.6	5.8	6.5	7.4	7.8	21.6	29.9	12.7	1.8	76.4	40.4	49.9	50.1
PACIFIC	5.0	6.4	4.6	4.4	4.8	7.0	5.7	18.2	32.5	19.9	2.9	81.8	48.5	49.8	50.2
PEND OREILLE	2.1	2.6	5.5	5.2	6.7	7.8	5.3	19.5	34.7	13.5	1.7	77.3	44.9	50.4	49.6
PIERCE	5.5	6.9	7.2	6.4	6.8	7.5	8.1	27.8	25.6	9.1	1.5	75.3	35.6	49.8	50.2
SAN JUAN	2.4	3.1	3.4	4.1	5.0	5.3	3.5	17.2	42.0	17.1	2.4	84.5	51.0	48.8	51.2
SKAGIT	11.2	14.0	6.7	6.1	6.8	7.1	7.2	24.3	27.6	11.9	2.4	76.2	39.0	49.6	50.4
SKAMANIA	4.0	5.1	6.3	6.7	5.9	7.0	7.0	22.4	32.7	10.7	1.4	76.7	41.6	50.0	50.0
SNOHOMISH	4.7	6.0	7.1	6.8	7.3	7.1	6.8	28.7	26.6	8.2	1.4	74.5	36.4	50.0	50.0
SPOKANE	2.8	3.6	6.5	5.9	6.5	7.7	8.6	25.7	26.5	10.3	2.4	76.8	36.9	49.1	50.9
STEVENS	1.8	2.3	6.1	5.5	6.8	7.3	8.5	19.3	32.5	12.1	1.7	76.8	42.1	49.6	50.4
THURSTON	4.5	5.7	6.2	5.8	6.4	6.6	7.5	26.8	28.7	10.1	1.9	77.7	38.4	48.9	51.1
WAHKIAKUM	2.6	3.3	5.5	5.6	5.4	5.4	6.3	19.7	32.9	16.5	2.8	80.3	46.7	50.0	50.0
WALLA WALLA	15.7	19.4	6.5	5.6	6.0	8.6	10.4	23.5	24.5	11.8	3.1	77.9	36.1	50.3	49.7
WHATCOM	5.2	6.6	6.0	5.6	6.1	7.9	10.4	25.6	26.4	10.1	1.9	78.4	35.7	49.3	50.7
WHITMAN	3.0	3.8	4.4	3.4	3.6	13.5	30.4	20.4	16.4	6.5	1.4	86.1	24.1	48.8	51.2
YAKIMA	35.9	41.8	9.1	8.1	8.0	7.7	7.6	26.2	22.4	9.0	1.8	70.1	31.7	50.1	49.9
WASHINGTON	7.5	9.2	6.7	6.3	6.7	7.1	7.5	27.5	26.8	9.7	1.8	76.2	36.9	49.8	50.2
UNITED STATES	12.5	15.0	6.9	6.5	6.8	7.1	7.0	27.6	25.4	10.7	1.9	75.6	36.7	49.2	50.8

HOUSEHOLDS

COUNTY	HOUSEHOLDS					FAMILIES			MEDIAN HOUSEHOLD INCOME			
	2000	2007	2012	% Annual Rate 2000-2007	2007 Average HH Size	2000	2007	% Annual Rate 2000-2007	2007	2012	2007 National Rank	2007 State Rank
ADAMS	5,229	5,498	5,729	0.7	3.15	4,094	4,259	0.5	42,792	50,246	1354	30
ASOTIN	8,364	8,747	9,009	0.6	2.39	5,650	5,821	0.4	41,699	48,350	1492	33
BENTON	52,866	60,168	66,057	1.8	2.71	38,075	42,775	1.6	60,410	72,035	254	4
CHELAN	25,021	26,582	27,796	0.8	2.66	17,356	18,175	0.6	47,054	55,899	906	20
CLALLAM	27,164	30,622	33,442	1.7	2.26	18,068	20,056	1.5	45,334	53,080	1072	21
CLARK	127,208	153,768	176,080	2.6	2.71	90,958	108,501	2.5	62,139	74,637	209	3
COLUMBIA	1,687	1,731	1,750	0.4	2.34	1,139	1,151	0.1	43,907	51,876	1220	25
COWLITZ	35,850	38,349	40,152	0.9	2.55	25,056	26,438	0.7	49,391	57,670	714	12
DOUGLAS	11,726	13,021	14,068	1.5	2.78	8,871	9,740	1.3	48,506	56,669	781	17
FERRY	2,823	3,059	3,214	1.1	2.43	1,988	2,126	0.9	37,585	43,452	2046	37
FRANKLIN	14,840	20,915	27,343	4.8	3.35	11,603	16,189	4.7	48,931	58,184	752	15
GARFIELD	987	984	981	0.0	2.39	670	658	-0.2	42,056	49,359	1442	32
GRANT	25,204	27,417	29,250	1.2	2.98	18,674	20,071	1.0	44,229	51,782	1187	23
GRAYS HARBOR	26,808	27,965	28,730	0.6	2.47	17,914	18,403	0.4	43,018	50,509	1329	28
ISLAND	27,784	31,434	34,361	1.7	2.52	20,241	22,617	1.5	56,717	66,107	340	8
JEFFERSON	11,645	13,347	14,627	1.9	2.18	7,578	8,547	1.7	47,633	56,555	852	19
KING	710,916	763,895	800,276	1.0	2.37	419,959	442,795	0.7	71,420	86,191	114	1
KITSAP	86,416	93,392	97,384	1.1	2.56	61,344	65,411	0.9	60,027	69,784	270	6
KITTITAS	13,382	15,048	16,334	1.6	2.33	7,787	8,590	1.4	40,832	47,110	1624	34
KLICKITAT	7,473	8,012	8,338	1.0	2.50	5,305	5,611	0.8	42,566	49,572	1387	31
LEWIS	26,306	28,447	30,127	1.1	2.57	18,559	19,801	0.9	44,029	51,196	1205	24
LINCOLN	4,151	4,332	4,418	0.6	2.42	2,914	3,000	0.4	43,746	51,297	1244	26
MASON	18,912	21,582	23,694	1.8	2.48	13,391	15,075	1.6	48,975	57,136	749	14
OKANOGAN	15,027	15,697	16,161	0.6	2.57	10,585	10,907	0.4	36,764	42,556	2155	38
PACIFIC	9,096	9,535	9,831	0.7	2.24	5,886	6,071	0.4	37,955	43,391	2004	36
PEND OREILLE	4,639	5,068	5,347	1.2	2.47	3,260	3,512	1.0	39,730	45,790	1755	35
PIERCE	260,800	292,387	315,820	1.6	2.59	180,199	199,153	1.4	57,619	68,716	315	7
SAN JUAN	6,466	7,443	8,005	2.0	2.13	4,014	4,538	1.7	54,729	64,505	413	9
SKAGIT	38,852	43,951	48,064	1.7	2.62	27,343	30,509	1.5	53,626	63,618	469	10
SKAMANIA	3,755	4,221	4,576	1.6	2.58	2,758	3,062	1.5	48,981	57,538	748	13
SNOHOMISH	224,852	258,423	282,304	1.9	2.61	157,820	178,903	1.7	68,275	80,881	138	2
SPOKANE	163,611	178,200	188,030	1.2	2.44	106,017	113,612	1.0	47,661	56,589	848	18
STEVENS	15,017	16,381	17,352	1.2	2.61	11,018	11,871	1.0	42,942	50,011	1336	29
THURSTON	81,625	93,875	103,750	1.9	2.49	54,951	62,247	1.7	60,065	69,952	268	5
WAHKIAKUM	1,553	1,647	1,713	0.8	2.40	1,109	1,161	0.6	48,817	56,927	759	16
WALLA WALLA	19,647	21,012	22,048	0.9	2.55	13,238	13,945	0.7	45,100	52,926	1101	22
WHATCOM	64,446	75,395	83,168	2.2	2.47	41,094	47,278	2.0	50,235	60,031	661	11
WHITMAN	15,257	15,814	16,156	0.5	2.28	8,057	8,173	0.2	35,798	41,663	2313	39
YAKIMA	73,993	76,944	79,545	0.5	3.01	54,584	56,078	0.4	43,344	50,970	1298	27
WASHINGTON				1.4	2.53			1.2	59,060	70,229		
UNITED STATES				1.2	2.59			1.0	53,154	62,503		

COUNTY	2007 Per Capita Income	2007 HH Income Base	2007 HOUSEHOLD INCOME DISTRIBUTION (%)					2007 Home Value Base	2007 HOME VALUE DISTRIBUTION (%)					2007 Median Home Value
			Less than $25,000	$25,000 to $49,999	$50,000 to $99,999	$100,000 to $149,999	$150,000 or More		Less than $50,000	$50,000 to $89,999	$90,000 to $174,999	$175,000 to $399,999	$400,000 or More	
ADAMS	16,523	5,498	23.9	35.4	33.0	5.5	2.2	3,902	11.1	8.4	42.6	34.7	3.2	157,320
ASOTIN	22,802	8,747	27.7	31.4	29.3	8.1	3.5	6,096	5.3	3.4	23.9	56.1	11.3	211,337
BENTON	27,097	60,168	16.8	24.4	36.2	15.4	7.1	43,005	5.7	6.8	45.5	38.9	3.1	161,051
CHELAN	24,380	26,582	23.7	29.0	31.2	9.7	6.4	18,071	3.3	2.4	16.7	60.9	16.7	244,858
CLALLAM	25,474	30,622	25.6	29.6	32.8	8.1	3.9	23,065	4.6	3.5	19.8	57.4	14.6	228,382
CLARK	28,092	153,768	15.1	23.1	38.8	15.4	7.6	107,857	2.5	1.7	6.4	67.8	21.5	282,913
COLUMBIA	22,962	1,731	28.3	28.2	32.9	7.6	2.9	1,255	3.3	9.5	43.5	38.6	5.2	163,656
COWLITZ	23,765	38,349	24.1	26.5	34.7	10.5	4.2	27,047	3.9	3.5	26.3	57.7	8.5	209,528
DOUGLAS	21,227	13,021	22.7	28.9	34.8	10.3	3.4	9,581	5.8	5.0	19.6	60.4	9.2	223,296
FERRY	19,059	3,059	35.0	29.0	29.1	4.9	2.0	2,322	8.7	9.8	35.0	38.6	7.9	166,277
FRANKLIN	18,864	20,915	25.4	25.6	32.4	11.2	5.4	14,296	6.3	7.7	40.4	32.1	13.6	164,987
GARFIELD	21,557	984	29.3	27.3	33.5	7.7	2.1	750	7.6	17.3	42.1	29.2	3.7	138,859
GRANT	18,649	27,417	25.7	31.6	30.9	8.0	3.8	19,116	6.9	6.6	34.5	45.1	6.9	178,641
GRAYS HARBOR	21,356	27,965	28.6	29.9	30.4	8.2	2.8	20,118	5.6	7.9	35.7	43.4	7.2	176,542
ISLAND	27,759	31,434	16.2	26.6	38.7	12.4	6.0	22,844	2.8	1.4	6.1	60.1	29.6	311,918
JEFFERSON	28,612	13,347	24.5	27.7	32.6	10.1	5.1	10,482	4.0	4.0	13.9	48.9	29.2	277,389
KING	39,393	763,889	14.0	19.8	33.7	18.4	14.1	478,795	1.9	1.2	4.0	39.9	53.0	418,170
KITSAP	28,664	93,392	16.1	24.4	37.7	14.6	7.2	65,507	2.0	1.8	10.0	59.9	26.3	285,980
KITTITAS	23,489	15,048	33.9	24.9	27.9	9.1	4.3	9,220	4.3	1.9	16.6	58.4	18.8	241,145
KLICKITAT	20,869	8,012	29.4	28.6	31.6	8.1	2.3	5,767	3.7	4.9	29.6	47.4	14.4	198,149
LEWIS	21,326	28,447	27.3	29.2	32.6	7.9	3.0	21,047	4.4	4.4	26.1	55.8	9.4	209,098
LINCOLN	22,811	4,332	24.4	33.1	31.1	8.1	3.3	3,423	6.7	11.6	38.6	37.4	5.8	162,283
MASON	23,446	21,582	22.2	28.8	36.2	9.4	3.3	17,461	2.8	4.2	25.2	53.2	14.6	219,051
OKANOGAN	18,538	15,697	34.1	31.9	25.7	5.8	2.4	11,239	6.4	8.3	36.7	38.9	9.7	172,573
PACIFIC	21,746	9,535	32.7	30.5	28.2	6.1	2.5	7,384	4.6	7.3	34.8	45.2	8.0	181,411
PEND OREILLE	20,332	5,068	33.1	28.0	28.9	7.2	2.7	4,026	6.7	7.1	30.9	44.5	11.0	188,228
PIERCE	27,259	292,387	17.4	25.4	37.1	13.3	6.8	194,476	2.9	2.0	9.6	64.6	20.9	281,934
SAN JUAN	40,061	7,443	19.4	26.1	33.5	10.7	10.3	5,686	2.2	0.7	5.2	29.5	62.4	531,079
SKAGIT	26,222	43,951	19.6	26.3	36.0	12.0	6.1	31,820	3.2	2.4	8.0	59.9	26.5	296,067
SKAMANIA	23,509	4,221	22.4	28.8	35.7	9.0	4.1	3,230	5.6	2.4	12.8	59.3	20.0	261,517
SNOHOMISH	31,047	258,423	12.6	21.5	38.1	18.8	9.0	182,235	2.6	2.1	5.2	52.2	37.9	358,130
SPOKANE	24,821	178,199	23.8	28.5	32.8	10.0	4.8	121,401	2.8	2.6	34.0	53.2	7.5	195,210
STEVENS	20,060	16,381	29.5	28.1	32.7	7.2	2.6	13,099	4.4	5.8	29.0	51.3	9.6	195,958
THURSTON	28,767	93,875	16.2	24.5	38.9	14.1	6.3	65,368	3.8	2.8	10.0	64.7	18.6	270,743
WAHKIAKUM	24,895	1,647	19.5	31.8	38.0	7.9	2.8	1,342	3.5	6.3	21.5	52.0	16.7	237,658
WALLA WALLA	21,815	21,012	27.3	27.1	32.6	9.2	3.7	14,257	3.2	4.6	30.6	52.9	8.9	197,385
WHATCOM	26,205	75,395	23.2	26.5	33.8	10.9	5.6	49,950	3.4	2.2	8.3	58.3	27.8	304,450
WHITMAN	20,675	15,805	37.6	25.4	25.1	8.0	3.8	8,046	6.5	6.5	27.4	50.6	9.1	197,267
YAKIMA	19,113	76,944	26.7	29.9	30.4	8.8	4.3	51,833	7.2	7.7	43.4	37.8	3.9	157,072
WASHINGTON	29,955		18.1	24.0	34.9	14.5	8.6		3.1	2.6	13.9	51.3	29.1	260,240
UNITED STATES	27,916		21.9	25.0	32.3	12.3	8.4		7.9	10.5	27.1	35.6	19.0	192,285

COUNTY	FINANCIAL SERVICES				THE HOME						ENTERTAINMENT						PERSONAL			
					Home Improvements		Furnishings													
	Auto Loan	Home Loan	Invest-ments	Retire-ment Plans	Home Repair	Lawn & Garden	Comput-ers & Hard-ware	Major Appli-ances	TV, Radio, Sound Equip-ment	Furni-ture	Dine out/ Carry out	Sports Equip-ment	Fees & Tickets	Toys & Games	Travel	Cable TV	Apparel & Services	Auto Repairs	Health Insur-ance	Pets & Supplies
ADAMS	80	69	53	65	68	76	70	77	72	69	72	63	63	73	68	72	63	76	76	77
ASOTIN	77	69	78	71	72	79	76	77	78	71	76	68	72	77	75	79	67	76	83	77
BENTON	104	104	103	105	100	99	102	100	101	103	101	93	102	102	101	100	91	101	99	101
CHELAN	92	88	90	88	89	95	89	93	90	87	89	83	87	90	90	91	79	91	95	93
CLALLAM	83	77	79	76	82	93	77	86	80	75	78	73	75	76	81	83	68	83	93	86
CLARK	104	110	113	111	105	100	107	103	104	108	104	97	109	105	106	102	95	104	99	103
COLUMBIA	77	71	76	72	76	84	71	78	75	70	73	67	70	76	74	77	65	74	85	79
COWLITZ	85	83	88	84	83	86	82	84	84	83	83	75	83	85	83	85	75	83	87	85
DOUGLAS	88	80	74	79	81	88	79	85	81	79	81	77	76	83	79	82	72	83	86	87
FERRY	76	57	39	56	66	87	59	75	63	56	63	65	51	65	60	68	54	68	79	79
FRANKLIN	89	89	80	86	85	81	88	87	86	88	87	87	86	86	86	83	80	89	81	85
GARFIELD	84	59	45	58	68	90	66	80	74	60	72	70	55	76	65	80	61	74	92	84
GRANT	83	75	68	73	75	81	75	80	77	74	76	73	71	78	74	77	68	79	81	81
GRAYS HARBOR	78	70	69	70	73	83	70	77	74	69	73	67	68	74	72	77	64	74	83	79
ISLAND	106	92	79	93	96	111	95	104	96	92	96	94	89	97	95	98	85	101	105	107
JEFFERSON	90	85	81	84	91	106	81	95	85	82	84	80	80	81	88	89	73	89	101	96
KING	123	131	137	135	129	118	137	125	129	135	131	122	138	128	133	125	121	130	118	124
KITSAP	102	104	109	106	102	99	104	101	101	104	101	93	105	102	103	100	92	102	99	101
KITTITAS	81	66	65	68	69	80	84	79	80	73	81	73	73	79	76	80	71	81	80	81
KLICKITAT	82	66	53	65	72	90	68	81	72	65	71	71	61	73	69	76	61	75	85	84
LEWIS	82	72	69	72	75	86	73	81	76	71	75	71	69	77	74	79	66	77	85	83
LINCOLN	89	69	51	67	79	101	71	88	75	67	75	77	62	78	72	80	64	81	93	93
MASON	88	78	70	77	84	98	76	89	80	76	79	77	73	80	80	84	69	84	94	91
OKANOGAN	75	60	49	59	64	79	63	73	66	60	65	64	56	67	62	69	57	69	77	75
PACIFIC	75	63	54	61	70	86	63	76	67	61	66	65	58	66	66	72	57	71	83	78
PEND OREILLE	80	62	45	61	71	92	65	81	69	61	68	70	56	70	66	73	58	74	85	85
PIERCE	98	99	103	101	96	93	101	96	98	100	99	90	101	99	99	97	89	99	95	96
SAN JUAN	127	114	101	114	125	150	110	132	114	110	114	113	106	110	119	121	99	124	139	135
SKAGIT	97	95	97	96	97	101	94	98	94	94	94	88	94	94	96	96	84	96	99	99
SKAMANIA	93	82	70	81	85	98	81	92	83	79	82	81	76	85	82	85	72	86	92	94
SNOHOMISH	112	118	118	120	113	107	115	110	111	117	111	104	117	113	114	108	102	112	105	111
SPOKANE	83	82	93	85	81	81	87	82	86	84	85	74	86	85	85	85	77	84	85	82
STEVENS	80	68	59	68	73	87	69	79	72	67	71	70	64	73	70	75	62	75	83	82
THURSTON	101	102	103	104	100	99	100	99	98	101	99	91	101	99	100	98	89	99	97	100
WAHKIAKUM	96	75	55	74	85	110	78	97	82	74	81	84	68	83	79	86	69	88	100	101
WALLA WALLA	79	73	80	74	74	79	80	79	80	75	79	71	76	78	78	81	71	79	83	79
WHATCOM	90	87	90	89	86	88	94	89	91	89	91	83	90	90	90	89	82	91	88	90
WHITMAN	73	53	52	57	54	64	81	66	74	65	75	65	66	72	67	71	66	72	67	69
YAKIMA	83	78	75	77	76	78	79	80	80	79	80	74	77	80	78	79	72	81	80	79
WASHINGTON	105	105	108	107	104	102	108	104	105	106	105	97	107	105	106	104	96	106	102	104
UNITED STATES	100	100	100	100	100	100	100	100	100	100	100	100	100	100	100	100	100	100	100	100

COUNTY	FIPS Code	CBSA Code	DMA Code	POPULATION			2000-2007 ANNUAL RATE		RACE (%)					
									White		Black		Asian/Pacific	
				2000	2007	2012	% Rate	State Rank	2000	2007	2000	2007	2000	2007
BARBOUR	001	00000	598	15,557	15,860	16,120	0.3	20	97.4	97.0	0.5	0.5	0.3	0.4
BERKELEY	003	25180	511	75,905	100,503	125,176	3.9	1	92.7	92.2	4.7	4.8	0.5	0.7
BOONE	005	16620	564	25,535	25,574	25,633	0.0	32	98.5	98.5	0.7	0.7	0.1	0.1
BRAXTON	007	00000	564	14,702	14,617	14,517	-0.1	36	98.0	98.0	0.7	0.7	0.2	0.2
BROOKE	009	48260	554	25,447	24,387	23,553	-0.6	49	97.9	97.7	0.8	0.9	0.4	0.5
CABELL	011	26580	564	96,784	93,367	90,750	-0.5	44	93.4	92.8	4.3	4.4	0.8	1.2
CALHOUN	013	00000	564	7,582	7,794	7,914	0.4	16	98.9	98.8	0.1	0.1	0.1	0.2
CLAY	015	16620	564	10,330	10,661	10,840	0.4	16	98.2	98.0	0.1	0.1	0.0	0.0
DODDRIDGE	017	17220	598	7,403	7,518	7,558	0.2	25	98.3	98.1	0.3	0.3	0.1	0.2
FAYETTE	019	36060	559	47,579	47,901	48,079	0.1	29	92.7	92.4	5.6	5.7	0.3	0.5
GILMER	021	00000	598	7,160	8,694	8,568	2.7	3	97.3	97.0	0.9	0.9	0.6	0.8
GRANT	023	00000	511	11,299	11,885	12,263	0.7	11	98.3	98.1	0.7	0.7	0.2	0.2
GREENBRIER	025	00000	559	34,453	35,723	36,542	0.5	13	95.2	94.9	3.0	3.1	0.2	0.3
HAMPSHIRE	027	49020	511	20,203	22,572	24,392	1.5	5	98.0	97.8	0.8	0.8	0.2	0.3
HANCOCK	029	48260	554	32,667	31,130	30,137	-0.7	52	96.4	96.1	2.3	2.3	0.4	0.5
HARDY	031	00000	511	12,669	13,843	14,676	1.2	8	96.9	96.7	1.9	2.0	0.1	0.2
HARRISON	033	17220	598	68,652	68,441	68,376	0.0	32	96.5	96.1	1.6	1.6	0.6	0.9
JACKSON	035	00000	564	28,000	28,695	29,144	0.3	20	98.7	98.5	0.1	0.1	0.2	0.4
JEFFERSON	037	47900	511	42,190	51,495	59,417	2.8	2	91.0	90.4	6.1	6.2	0.6	0.9
KANAWHA	039	16620	564	200,073	191,504	185,595	-0.6	49	90.5	89.8	7.0	7.1	0.9	1.3
LEWIS	041	00000	598	16,919	17,358	17,642	0.4	16	98.6	98.4	0.1	0.1	0.3	0.4
LINCOLN	043	16620	564	22,108	22,377	22,532	0.2	25	99.0	98.9	0.1	0.1	0.1	0.1
LOGAN	045	00000	564	37,710	36,188	35,057	-0.6	49	96.3	96.1	2.6	2.6	0.3	0.5
MCDOWELL	047	00000	559	27,329	25,743	24,717	-0.8	54	87.1	86.7	11.9	12.1	0.1	0.1
MARION	049	21900	598	56,598	55,343	54,417	-0.3	40	95.1	94.7	3.2	3.3	0.4	0.6
MARSHALL	051	48540	554	35,519	34,203	33,135	-0.5	44	98.4	98.2	0.4	0.4	0.3	0.4
MASON	053	38580	564	25,957	25,905	25,838	0.0	32	98.4	98.4	0.5	0.5	0.3	0.3
MERCER	055	14140	559	62,980	60,907	59,541	-0.5	44	92.6	92.1	5.8	5.9	0.5	0.7
MINERAL	057	19060	511	27,078	28,050	28,741	0.5	13	96.2	95.9	2.5	2.6	0.2	0.3
MINGO	059	00000	564	28,253	27,307	26,476	-0.5	44	96.4	96.1	2.3	2.4	0.2	0.3
MONONGALIA	061	34060	508	81,866	86,525	88,902	0.8	10	92.2	90.5	3.4	3.8	2.5	3.6
MONROE	063	00000	559	14,583	13,460	13,644	-1.1	55	92.7	93.3	6.0	5.1	0.2	0.3
MORGAN	065	25180	511	14,943	17,194	18,740	2.0	4	98.3	98.1	0.6	0.6	0.1	0.2
NICHOLAS	067	00000	564	26,562	26,551	26,565	0.0	32	98.8	98.8	0.1	0.1	0.2	0.2
OHIO	069	48540	554	47,427	44,816	43,248	-0.8	54	94.5	94.0	3.6	3.6	0.8	1.2
PENDLETON	071	00000	569	8,196	8,105	8,014	-0.2	38	96.3	96.3	2.1	2.1	0.2	0.2
PLEASANTS	073	37620	597	7,514	7,437	7,383	-0.1	36	98.3	98.3	0.5	0.5	0.2	0.2
POCAHONTAS	075	00000	559	9,131	8,848	8,619	-0.4	41	98.4	98.2	0.8	0.8	0.1	0.2
PRESTON	077	34060	508	29,334	31,984	32,581	1.2	8	98.8	98.7	0.3	0.3	0.2	0.2
PUTNAM	079	16620	564	51,589	55,362	57,907	1.0	9	98.0	97.6	0.6	0.6	0.6	0.9
RALEIGH	081	13220	559	79,220	80,334	81,169	0.2	25	89.6	89.1	8.5	8.6	0.7	1.1
RANDOLPH	083	00000	598	28,262	28,850	29,274	0.3	20	97.7	97.4	1.1	1.1	0.4	0.6
RITCHIE	085	00000	598	10,343	10,624	10,809	0.4	16	98.7	98.5	0.1	0.1	0.1	0.2
ROANE	087	00000	564	15,446	15,619	15,753	0.2	25	98.6	98.3	0.2	0.2	0.2	0.3
SUMMERS	089	00000	559	12,999	14,295	14,228	1.3	6	96.6	95.2	2.2	3.3	0.1	0.3
TAYLOR	091	17220	598	16,089	16,345	16,510	0.2	25	98.1	97.9	0.8	0.9	0.2	0.3
TUCKER	093	00000	598	7,321	6,962	6,704	-0.7	52	98.9	98.7	0.1	0.1	0.1	0.2
TYLER	095	00000	554	9,592	9,380	9,201	-0.3	40	99.4	99.3	0.0	0.0	0.1	0.1
UPSHUR	097	00000	598	23,404	23,728	24,030	0.2	25	98.2	97.9	0.6	0.6	0.3	0.5
WAYNE	099	26580	564	42,903	42,466	41,837	-0.1	36	98.8	98.6	0.1	0.1	0.2	0.3
WEBSTER	101	00000	598	9,719	9,836	9,950	0.2	25	99.2	99.1	0.0	0.0	0.1	0.1
WETZEL	103	00000	554	17,693	16,971	16,484	-0.6	49	98.9	98.7	0.1	0.1	0.3	0.5
WIRT	105	37620	564	5,873	6,040	6,154	0.4	16	98.6	98.4	0.3	0.3	0.1	0.1
WOOD	107	37620	597	87,986	87,499	87,110	-0.1	36	97.3	96.9	1.0	1.0	0.5	0.8
WYOMING	109	00000	559	25,708	24,745	24,053	-0.5	44	98.6	98.5	0.6	0.7	0.1	0.1
WEST VIRGINIA							0.2		95.0	94.6	3.2	3.2	0.5	0.8
UNITED STATES							1.2		75.1	72.7	12.3	12.6	3.8	4.5

POPULATION COMPOSITION

COUNTY	% HISPANIC ORIGIN		2007 AGE DISTRIBUTION (%)										MEDIAN AGE	% 2007 Males	% 2007 Females
	2000	2007	0-4	5-9	10-14	15-19	20-24	25-44	45-64	65-84	85+	18+	2007		
BARBOUR	0.5	0.5	5.5	5.3	5.8	6.6	6.3	25.8	28.8	13.7	2.3	79.7	41.3	49.5	50.5
BERKELEY	1.5	1.7	6.6	6.2	6.7	6.6	5.8	28.7	27.7	10.4	1.2	76.3	38.2	49.7	50.3
BOONE	0.5	0.5	6.1	6.7	5.6	4.9	4.4	26.8	31.8	12.0	1.7	78.4	41.2	49.0	51.0
BRAXTON	0.4	0.4	5.3	5.2	5.5	5.9	5.7	26.7	29.9	13.4	2.3	80.3	42.0	50.9	49.1
BROOKE	0.4	0.4	4.9	4.8	5.2	5.9	6.4	23.9	30.0	16.1	2.8	82.0	44.2	47.9	52.1
CABELL	0.7	0.7	5.3	5.3	5.1	6.5	8.1	26.6	26.2	14.4	2.4	81.4	39.3	47.9	52.1
CALHOUN	0.6	0.6	5.4	5.0	4.8	5.4	6.5	24.1	32.2	14.4	2.3	81.4	44.2	49.8	50.2
CLAY	0.4	0.4	6.2	5.9	6.2	6.2	6.1	26.4	28.9	12.6	1.6	77.9	39.9	49.4	50.6
DODDRIDGE	0.6	0.6	6.1	5.8	5.9	6.6	6.3	24.3	29.4	13.9	1.7	78.0	41.6	50.4	49.6
FAYETTE	0.7	0.7	5.6	5.7	5.3	5.2	6.2	26.2	29.7	13.7	2.4	80.4	41.8	50.1	49.9
GILMER	0.7	0.8	4.2	3.9	3.3	7.6	12.0	32.1	24.0	10.9	1.9	85.5	36.3	59.3	40.7
GRANT	0.5	0.6	6.1	6.7	5.8	5.5	4.4	27.9	28.1	13.6	2.1	78.2	40.7	49.8	50.2
GREENBRIER	0.7	0.7	5.5	5.4	5.5	5.4	5.6	23.7	30.6	15.6	2.6	80.3	44.2	48.7	51.3
HAMPSHIRE	0.6	0.6	6.2	6.3	6.3	6.5	5.4	25.5	28.7	13.4	1.6	77.0	40.9	49.9	50.1
HANCOCK	0.7	0.8	5.2	5.3	5.4	5.2	4.8	25.1	29.8	16.4	2.8	80.9	44.3	48.2	51.8
HARDY	0.7	0.7	6.0	5.8	6.2	5.9	4.6	27.1	29.0	13.5	1.7	78.3	41.5	49.8	50.2
HARRISON	1.0	1.1	5.9	5.6	6.1	5.8	5.9	25.8	28.7	13.6	2.5	78.9	41.5	48.1	51.9
JACKSON	0.3	0.3	6.2	6.0	5.9	6.0	5.3	26.2	27.6	14.9	1.9	78.3	41.0	48.5	51.5
JEFFERSON	1.7	1.9	6.2	6.1	5.9	6.8	6.5	27.4	28.7	11.0	1.4	78.4	39.6	49.3	50.7
KANAWHA	0.6	0.6	5.5	5.6	5.5	5.5	5.1	26.0	29.9	14.5	2.5	80.2	42.7	47.9	52.1
LEWIS	0.5	0.6	5.4	5.0	6.0	5.5	5.0	26.4	29.9	14.4	2.3	80.3	42.7	49.0	51.0
LINCOLN	0.5	0.6	6.1	6.0	5.8	5.1	5.1	28.2	29.4	12.6	1.6	79.0	40.6	49.5	50.5
LOGAN	0.5	0.6	5.6	5.8	5.5	4.7	5.2	26.8	31.6	13.1	1.6	80.3	41.9	48.9	51.1
MCDOWELL	0.5	0.5	5.2	5.1	5.7	5.9	6.2	23.9	32.2	13.5	2.3	80.3	43.4	48.1	51.9
MARION	0.7	0.8	5.2	5.0	5.3	5.5	6.3	26.6	28.3	14.7	3.0	81.5	41.7	47.9	52.1
MARSHALL	0.6	0.7	5.2	5.1	6.0	6.0	5.7	24.8	30.5	14.6	2.3	80.0	43.0	48.9	51.1
MASON	0.5	0.5	5.9	5.6	5.7	5.1	5.5	25.6	29.8	15.0	1.8	79.7	42.5	49.2	50.8
MERCER	0.5	0.5	5.7	5.8	5.2	5.2	5.6	26.1	29.0	14.9	2.5	80.4	42.1	48.2	51.8
MINERAL	0.6	0.6	5.6	5.6	6.0	6.7	5.8	25.5	29.2	13.6	2.0	79.0	41.2	49.1	50.9
MINGO	0.5	0.5	5.9	5.8	5.8	5.5	6.3	26.9	31.1	11.3	1.4	79.2	40.5	48.7	51.3
MONONGALIA	1.0	1.1	4.9	4.5	4.7	8.5	14.8	28.0	23.3	9.6	1.7	83.3	32.6	50.4	49.6
MONROE	0.5	0.5	5.3	5.2	5.2	6.1	5.5	27.3	29.2	14.2	1.9	81.2	41.6	47.9	52.1
MORGAN	0.8	0.9	5.8	5.9	6.0	5.4	4.4	25.1	29.7	16.0	1.7	79.0	43.4	49.0	51.0
NICHOLAS	0.5	0.5	5.4	5.4	5.4	5.8	5.5	25.9	30.5	14.2	2.1	80.3	42.7	49.0	51.0
OHIO	0.5	0.5	5.0	5.0	5.4	7.3	7.0	22.6	28.6	16.0	3.1	80.9	43.1	46.9	53.1
PENDLETON	0.9	0.9	5.3	5.4	5.6	5.9	4.6	25.6	29.7	15.3	2.7	80.1	43.4	50.2	49.8
PLEASANTS	0.4	0.4	5.9	5.7	6.4	5.3	5.8	26.8	29.3	12.8	2.0	78.7	41.1	50.6	49.4
POCAHONTAS	0.4	0.5	5.0	4.9	5.1	5.6	4.3	25.9	30.4	15.2	2.6	81.5	44.5	51.2	48.8
PRESTON	0.6	0.6	5.3	5.3	5.2	5.9	6.2	28.4	29.2	12.7	1.8	80.5	40.7	52.3	47.7
PUTNAM	0.5	0.6	6.4	6.6	6.3	6.0	5.0	27.3	29.8	11.2	1.4	77.0	40.2	49.3	50.7
RALEIGH	0.9	1.0	5.4	5.3	5.4	5.3	5.7	27.0	30.2	13.5	2.1	80.6	41.6	49.6	50.4
RANDOLPH	0.7	0.7	5.2	5.2	5.8	6.3	5.9	27.2	28.7	13.2	2.4	79.9	41.3	50.5	49.5
RITCHIE	0.5	0.5	5.7	5.3	6.1	5.2	5.7	25.3	30.4	14.2	2.1	79.7	42.7	49.2	50.8
ROANE	0.7	0.7	5.9	5.9	5.1	5.4	5.8	26.1	29.9	13.9	2.1	79.8	42.0	49.7	50.3
SUMMERS	0.5	0.6	4.3	4.1	5.0	8.4	7.8	23.2	28.7	15.7	2.9	84.3	42.9	48.5	51.5
TAYLOR	0.6	0.7	5.4	5.3	5.5	6.1	5.8	27.1	29.2	13.3	2.2	80.0	41.5	49.3	50.7
TUCKER	0.2	0.3	5.0	4.6	5.8	5.3	5.1	24.3	30.4	16.8	2.8	81.3	45.0	48.8	51.2
TYLER	0.4	0.5	5.3	5.4	5.5	6.2	5.2	24.4	30.5	15.4	2.2	79.8	43.6	48.8	51.2
UPSHUR	0.6	0.6	5.4	5.0	5.8	7.6	8.2	24.4	28.5	13.0	2.1	80.5	40.2	48.9	51.1
WAYNE	0.5	0.5	5.9	5.8	6.0	5.4	5.3	27.5	28.0	14.3	1.7	78.9	40.5	49.1	50.9
WEBSTER	0.4	0.4	5.2	4.9	5.9	5.6	5.4	24.6	32.1	14.0	2.2	80.5	43.6	49.2	50.8
WETZEL	0.4	0.4	5.7	5.6	5.9	5.9	6.2	23.6	29.3	15.6	2.2	79.3	43.0	49.0	51.0
WIRT	0.3	0.3	6.1	5.2	6.3	6.2	6.0	26.5	28.7	13.5	1.5	78.5	41.3	50.4	49.6
WOOD	0.6	0.6	5.7	5.6	5.9	6.0	5.6	25.9	28.8	14.2	2.4	79.2	41.8	48.3	51.7
WYOMING	0.5	0.6	5.5	5.9	5.0	4.9	5.3	25.4	33.1	13.3	1.5	80.6	43.3	49.3	50.7
WEST VIRGINIA	0.7	0.8	5.6	5.5	5.6	6.0	6.3	26.3	29.0	13.6	2.1	79.9	41.1	49.0	51.0
UNITED STATES	12.5	15.0	6.9	6.5	6.8	7.1	7.0	27.6	25.4	10.7	1.9	75.6	36.7	49.2	50.8

COUNTY	HOUSEHOLDS					FAMILIES			MEDIAN HOUSEHOLD INCOME			
	2000	2007	2012	% Annual Rate 2000-2007	2007 Average HH Size	2000	2007	% Annual Rate 2000-2007	2007	2012	2007 National Rank	2007 State Rank
BARBOUR	6,123	6,427	6,598	0.7	2.40	4,367	4,448	0.3	29,338	33,157	2941	43
BERKELEY	29,569	40,057	50,325	4.3	2.48	20,702	27,196	3.8	46,793	53,108	927	3
BOONE	10,291	10,695	10,877	0.5	2.38	7,464	7,538	0.1	30,077	33,477	2906	41
BRAXTON	5,771	5,916	5,942	0.3	2.38	4,099	4,078	-0.1	28,931	32,706	2965	46
BROOKE	10,396	10,322	10,102	-0.1	2.28	7,156	6,884	-0.5	40,370	47,010	1682	8
CABELL	41,180	40,211	39,330	-0.3	2.23	25,474	23,928	-0.9	35,645	41,223	2336	21
CALHOUN	3,071	3,269	3,366	0.9	2.37	2,202	2,276	0.5	25,670	29,079	3079	51
CLAY	4,020	4,301	4,435	0.9	2.46	2,942	3,061	0.5	26,399	29,517	3057	50
DODDRIDGE	2,845	2,960	2,999	0.5	2.50	2,102	2,130	0.2	31,944	36,037	2769	39
FAYETTE	18,945	19,604	19,902	0.5	2.34	13,121	13,155	0.0	29,975	34,281	2913	42
GILMER	2,768	2,791	2,774	0.1	2.35	1,862	1,817	-0.3	27,146	30,970	3033	48
GRANT	4,591	5,005	5,238	1.2	2.35	3,274	3,465	0.8	33,363	37,367	2621	27
GREENBRIER	14,571	15,517	16,075	0.9	2.25	9,927	10,232	0.4	32,539	37,134	2700	35
HAMPSHIRE	7,955	9,173	10,034	2.0	2.41	5,641	6,311	1.6	37,495	41,960	2064	13
HANCOCK	13,678	13,483	13,224	-0.2	2.28	9,507	9,083	-0.6	42,090	49,109	1436	4
HARDY	5,204	5,851	6,268	1.6	2.35	3,564	3,881	1.2	37,395	42,223	2082	15
HARRISON	27,867	28,447	28,657	0.3	2.37	19,085	18,867	-0.2	37,184	43,230	2102	16
JACKSON	11,061	11,695	12,018	0.8	2.43	8,207	8,449	0.4	39,328	44,560	1816	9
JEFFERSON	16,165	20,414	23,867	3.3	2.47	11,319	13,861	2.8	55,511	64,633	384	1
KANAWHA	86,226	83,845	81,907	-0.4	2.24	55,922	52,461	-0.9	41,994	49,086	1447	5
LEWIS	6,946	7,340	7,542	0.8	2.33	4,805	4,920	0.3	32,943	37,525	2663	31
LINCOLN	8,664	9,134	9,332	0.7	2.44	6,536	6,718	0.4	26,557	29,811	3053	49
LOGAN	14,880	14,929	14,667	0.0	2.39	10,935	10,677	-0.3	29,182	33,122	2952	44
MCDOWELL	11,169	11,037	10,747	-0.2	2.30	7,841	7,513	-0.6	20,013	21,831	3134	55
MARION	23,652	23,740	23,584	0.1	2.27	15,510	15,029	-0.4	35,772	41,306	2319	19
MARSHALL	14,207	14,068	13,773	-0.1	2.37	10,108	9,716	-0.5	38,139	44,370	1985	11
MASON	10,587	10,921	11,032	0.4	2.35	7,571	7,584	0.0	32,700	36,685	2684	33
MERCER	26,509	26,628	26,378	0.1	2.25	17,943	17,440	-0.4	32,320	36,852	2728	36
MINERAL	10,784	11,538	11,968	0.9	2.39	7,708	8,007	0.5	36,944	41,634	2134	17
MINGO	11,303	11,518	11,329	0.3	2.36	8,218	8,142	-0.1	25,000	27,779	3093	53
MONONGALIA	33,446	35,363	36,683	0.8	2.25	18,504	18,695	0.1	35,141	39,999	2412	23
MONROE	5,447	5,745	5,898	0.7	2.33	3,885	3,977	0.3	32,960	37,226	2657	29
MORGAN	6,145	7,275	8,011	2.4	2.34	4,345	4,991	1.9	41,633	47,519	1500	6
NICHOLAS	10,722	11,131	11,300	0.5	2.37	7,761	7,832	0.1	32,275	36,407	2737	37
OHIO	19,733	19,092	18,526	-0.5	2.22	12,147	11,299	-1.0	38,102	44,260	1990	12
PENDLETON	3,350	3,429	3,438	0.3	2.31	2,354	2,337	-0.1	35,750	40,228	2325	20
PLEASANTS	2,887	2,926	2,928	0.2	2.45	2,135	2,108	-0.2	38,439	44,115	1941	10
POCAHONTAS	3,835	3,820	3,759	-0.1	2.24	2,526	2,431	-0.5	31,763	35,954	2782	40
PRESTON	11,544	12,296	12,721	0.9	2.42	8,353	8,646	0.5	33,305	37,390	2629	28
PUTNAM	20,028	22,156	23,439	1.4	2.49	15,291	16,511	1.1	51,749	60,287	565	2
RALEIGH	31,793	33,416	34,275	0.7	2.29	22,103	22,520	0.3	34,623	39,363	2486	24
RANDOLPH	11,072	11,625	11,928	0.7	2.35	7,663	7,793	0.2	33,408	38,093	2616	26
RITCHIE	4,184	4,415	4,534	0.7	2.39	3,001	3,077	0.3	33,622	38,089	2593	25
ROANE	6,161	6,407	6,528	0.5	2.42	4,479	4,527	0.1	29,054	32,994	2956	45
SUMMERS	5,530	5,690	5,742	0.4	2.24	3,756	3,739	-0.1	25,447	29,045	3084	52
TAYLOR	6,320	6,569	6,696	0.5	2.41	4,486	4,524	0.1	32,562	36,576	2697	34
TUCKER	3,052	2,994	2,917	-0.3	2.28	2,121	2,017	-0.7	32,013	36,901	2761	38
TYLER	3,836	3,866	3,835	0.1	2.40	2,833	2,780	-0.3	35,200	39,549	2403	22
UPSHUR	8,972	9,425	9,667	0.7	2.38	6,353	6,475	0.3	32,952	37,154	2660	30
WAYNE	17,239	17,648	17,614	0.3	2.40	12,648	12,599	-0.1	32,765	36,920	2677	32
WEBSTER	4,010	4,242	4,355	0.8	2.30	2,816	2,889	0.4	24,557	26,920	3097	54
WETZEL	7,164	7,097	6,977	-0.1	2.37	5,080	4,885	-0.5	37,439	42,879	2077	14
WIRT	2,284	2,408	2,474	0.7	2.50	1,700	1,747	0.4	36,044	40,020	2270	18
WOOD	36,275	37,143	37,360	0.3	2.32	24,898	24,686	-0.1	41,203	47,722	1570	7
WYOMING	10,454	10,573	10,426	0.2	2.33	7,705	7,584	-0.2	28,080	31,931	2999	47
WEST VIRGINIA				0.6	2.33			0.1	36,308	41,079		
UNITED STATES				1.2	2.59			1.0	53,154	62,503		

INCOME

COUNTY	2007 Per Capita Income	2007 HH Income Base	2007 HOUSEHOLD INCOME DISTRIBUTION (%)					2007 Home Value Base	2007 HOME VALUE DISTRIBUTION (%)					2007 Median Home Value
			Less than $25,000	$25,000 to $49,999	$50,000 to $99,999	$100,000 to $149,999	$150,000 or More		Less than $50,000	$50,000 to $89,999	$90,000 to $174,999	$175,000 to $399,999	$400,000 or More	
BARBOUR	15,407	6,427	43.1	33.2	19.4	3.3	1.0	5,173	25.3	29.3	35.3	9.7	0.4	81,909
BERKELEY	22,621	40,057	22.4	31.3	34.5	9.0	2.8	30,652	14.4	7.1	22.1	48.8	7.5	188,564
BOONE	17,240	10,695	42.8	27.9	23.9	3.9	1.5	8,637	36.9	26.2	30.4	6.1	0.4	70,371
BRAXTON	16,354	5,916	44.2	30.4	19.7	3.8	1.9	4,755	29.1	27.3	32.9	9.4	1.3	80,114
BROOKE	21,962	10,322	28.9	32.4	29.6	6.5	2.6	8,101	23.2	28.9	40.3	7.0	0.6	87,256
CABELL	21,816	40,211	36.9	28.3	24.6	6.5	3.7	27,087	16.9	25.2	42.9	13.4	1.6	99,478
CALHOUN	14,313	3,269	48.8	29.2	18.8	2.9	0.3	2,638	30.9	32.4	31.3	4.5	0.9	71,263
CLAY	14,239	4,301	47.9	30.3	17.8	2.6	1.4	3,477	39.6	28.2	27.3	4.5	0.3	64,022
DODDRIDGE	16,414	2,960	39.3	34.9	21.0	3.5	1.4	2,452	28.1	23.9	39.2	8.5	0.4	86,597
FAYETTE	16,909	19,604	42.8	30.4	21.2	4.1	1.5	15,486	28.0	31.9	32.8	6.7	0.6	75,637
GILMER	13,946	2,791	45.6	29.9	18.6	3.9	2.0	2,089	21.6	26.9	39.8	10.8	0.9	92,148
GRANT	18,591	5,005	36.8	33.8	24.3	3.2	1.9	4,134	20.0	17.9	46.7	13.6	1.8	110,667
GREENBRIER	20,144	15,517	39.2	31.6	22.0	4.2	3.0	12,229	22.3	21.4	39.0	14.7	2.5	101,980
HAMPSHIRE	18,385	9,173	32.3	33.5	29.4	3.2	1.7	7,597	11.1	14.5	35.4	34.8	4.2	146,875
HANCOCK	22,786	13,483	27.5	31.0	32.2	6.5	2.8	10,702	18.3	29.9	44.8	6.4	0.5	91,825
HARDY	19,453	5,851	32.5	34.0	26.4	5.3	1.8	4,812	19.8	20.1	42.6	14.5	3.0	108,584
HARRISON	20,756	28,447	34.0	29.3	27.1	7.0	2.6	21,906	20.1	24.9	39.4	13.9	1.7	98,456
JACKSON	19,520	11,695	32.5	30.5	29.3	5.6	2.1	9,537	17.4	17.1	47.1	16.4	1.9	112,587
JEFFERSON	27,201	20,414	20.8	24.0	35.3	13.6	6.3	15,888	5.4	4.8	13.8	50.0	26.0	271,402
KANAWHA	25,822	83,845	29.3	28.1	28.7	8.9	5.0	61,070	19.7	26.2	39.6	12.4	2.0	95,211
LEWIS	17,407	7,340	39.0	32.2	23.7	3.3	1.7	5,553	22.3	25.7	40.7	10.0	1.3	93,232
LINCOLN	15,295	9,134	47.3	27.3	20.5	3.6	1.3	7,397	33.2	29.3	30.6	6.5	0.3	72,650
LOGAN	17,858	14,929	43.4	27.6	22.0	4.9	2.1	11,772	26.9	25.1	38.9	8.4	0.7	86,727
MCDOWELL	12,697	11,037	59.5	26.8	11.2	1.4	1.2	8,969	67.6	20.0	11.2	1.2	0.0	33,828
MARION	20,498	23,740	36.0	29.5	26.1	5.9	2.6	18,224	19.8	27.2	41.5	10.6	0.8	94,126
MARSHALL	20,798	14,068	33.6	27.8	29.2	6.7	2.6	11,170	21.5	30.9	39.4	7.8	0.4	86,612
MASON	18,230	10,921	39.5	29.9	24.0	4.6	2.0	9,001	26.7	23.9	38.0	10.5	1.0	88,895
MERCER	19,517	26,628	39.5	30.8	22.5	4.9	2.3	20,954	27.8	23.9	37.1	10.0	1.2	87,092
MINERAL	18,995	11,538	33.1	32.7	27.1	5.4	1.7	9,223	11.2	14.2	37.9	33.4	3.3	144,904
MINGO	15,649	11,518	50.0	26.7	18.2	3.4	1.7	9,145	33.0	23.9	35.2	7.7	0.2	78,261
MONONGALIA	21,477	35,363	37.9	25.6	24.6	7.8	4.0	22,454	17.2	11.7	30.6	34.1	6.4	146,834
MONROE	19,548	5,745	37.7	32.1	23.2	4.0	3.0	4,927	22.4	22.8	41.9	11.9	1.0	96,250
MORGAN	22,161	7,275	25.6	34.1	32.1	5.9	2.3	6,152	10.7	12.5	27.4	43.7	5.5	172,798
NICHOLAS	19,021	11,131	38.6	32.4	22.3	4.0	2.6	9,350	31.4	23.6	35.7	8.3	1.1	81,920
OHIO	22,843	19,092	34.3	26.8	28.2	6.8	3.9	13,622	18.5	26.0	39.9	13.4	2.2	97,125
PENDLETON	19,496	3,429	32.5	38.5	23.4	3.0	2.6	2,796	19.6	18.8	45.5	14.0	2.1	108,958
PLEASANTS	19,531	2,926	31.2	33.8	25.8	7.2	1.9	2,404	26.0	21.5	43.8	7.6	1.1	93,468
POCAHONTAS	17,677	3,820	39.4	33.6	21.5	4.4	1.1	3,136	22.3	24.6	37.1	13.8	2.3	93,944
PRESTON	16,445	12,296	38.0	33.1	23.5	3.8	1.6	10,381	19.0	21.6	39.8	18.2	1.4	108,746
PUTNAM	26,103	22,156	21.8	26.3	34.6	12.5	4.9	18,944	16.3	15.8	43.7	21.9	2.3	117,576
RALEIGH	20,367	33,416	37.5	28.9	24.8	6.0	2.8	26,218	23.2	22.7	39.8	12.7	1.6	96,289
RANDOLPH	18,171	11,625	37.0	33.9	22.9	4.6	1.7	9,069	20.4	21.4	43.3	13.7	1.2	102,653
RITCHIE	17,663	4,415	38.7	31.4	24.4	4.1	1.5	3,673	31.2	26.6	31.9	9.0	1.3	77,930
ROANE	16,274	6,407	42.3	32.4	19.1	4.7	1.4	5,220	24.5	27.0	36.5	11.3	0.7	87,727
SUMMERS	14,956	5,690	49.3	29.0	17.8	2.9	1.0	4,598	28.0	26.2	36.6	8.2	1.0	82,717
TAYLOR	17,094	6,569	38.2	32.9	23.0	4.6	1.3	5,342	28.9	22.4	36.5	10.7	1.6	87,669
TUCKER	19,299	2,994	40.4	31.6	22.0	3.2	2.8	2,505	26.1	24.6	36.4	12.3	0.5	88,697
TYLER	18,968	3,866	33.9	33.9	24.7	5.8	1.7	3,286	25.3	22.2	43.5	8.6	0.4	93,705
UPSHUR	17,367	9,425	38.3	31.4	24.5	4.3	1.5	7,430	17.6	21.4	46.6	12.9	1.6	104,055
WAYNE	18,470	17,648	39.0	29.0	25.2	4.8	2.0	14,129	24.4	25.0	41.8	8.2	0.6	90,765
WEBSTER	14,657	4,242	50.6	30.3	16.1	1.7	1.3	3,425	34.7	33.7	27.9	3.3	0.4	65,729
WETZEL	20,721	7,097	34.9	28.1	28.2	6.2	2.6	5,705	24.6	21.3	44.7	9.0	0.3	94,957
WIRT	16,932	2,408	35.3	37.7	21.1	4.2	1.8	2,040	29.3	28.3	36.0	5.9	0.5	78,411
WOOD	23,141	37,143	29.0	30.5	28.8	8.0	3.8	28,158	15.1	27.2	44.3	12.4	1.1	98,890
WYOMING	17,554	10,573	45.8	27.3	20.5	4.2	2.1	8,914	38.6	30.9	26.5	3.7	0.2	62,261
WEST VIRGINIA	20,634		35.2	29.6	26.0	6.3	2.9		21.9	22.6	36.9	16.0	2.6	98,467
UNITED STATES	27,916		21.9	25.0	32.3	12.3	8.4		7.9	10.5	27.1	35.6	19.0	192,285

COUNTY	FINANCIAL SERVICES				THE HOME						ENTERTAINMENT						PERSONAL			
					Home Improvements		Furnishings													
	Auto Loan	Home Loan	Invest-ments	Retire-ment Plans	Home Repair	Lawn & Garden	Comput-ers & Hard-ware	Major Appli-ances	TV, Radio, Sound Equip-ment	Furni-ture	Dine out/ Carry out	Sports Equip-ment	Fees & Tickets	Toys & Games	Travel	Cable TV	Apparel & Services	Auto Repairs	Health Insur-ance	Pets & Supplies
BARBOUR	63	44	30	42	50	68	47	59	53	44	52	52	39	54	46	57	44	54	65	63
BERKELEY	85	77	71	76	76	83	75	80	78	75	78	72	73	80	75	80	69	78	83	83
BOONE	73	47	23	44	54	76	49	66	58	48	58	59	40	61	48	64	49	60	72	73
BRAXTON	68	48	28	45	54	74	49	64	55	47	55	56	41	58	49	60	47	58	70	69
BROOKE	77	63	62	62	68	82	67	75	74	63	71	65	61	73	67	78	62	71	86	77
CABELL	72	60	65	61	63	72	70	69	72	64	71	62	64	70	67	74	62	70	77	71
CALHOUN	58	40	26	38	45	61	42	53	49	40	47	47	35	50	42	53	40	49	60	57
CLAY	62	40	22	38	46	64	43	56	50	41	49	50	35	52	42	54	42	51	61	62
DODDRIDGE	70	49	31	47	56	77	51	66	58	49	57	57	43	60	51	63	48	60	73	71
FAYETTE	65	48	38	46	53	69	51	61	58	48	57	54	44	59	51	63	48	58	70	65
GILMER	63	44	30	43	49	66	49	59	54	45	53	52	41	55	47	58	46	55	64	63
GRANT	76	53	33	51	59	80	54	69	62	53	61	61	46	65	53	66	52	63	75	75
GREENBRIER	74	56	43	54	62	80	59	71	65	55	63	62	51	66	59	69	54	66	79	75
HAMPSHIRE	77	55	36	52	62	83	56	71	62	54	62	62	48	65	55	67	53	65	76	77
HANCOCK	76	69	70	68	74	84	67	76	74	67	72	64	66	74	70	78	63	71	85	77
HARDY	79	56	36	53	62	84	57	73	64	55	63	64	48	67	56	68	54	66	78	79
HARRISON	76	61	58	61	66	80	65	73	71	61	69	64	59	71	65	75	59	70	82	76
JACKSON	76	62	50	60	65	80	61	72	66	60	66	63	56	68	61	70	57	67	78	75
JEFFERSON	95	96	99	97	96	97	93	95	93	94	93	86	95	95	95	94	84	93	95	96
KANAWHA	84	75	78	75	78	88	78	83	83	75	81	73	75	82	79	86	71	81	92	85
LEWIS	67	49	37	47	54	72	52	63	58	49	57	55	44	59	52	63	48	59	71	67
LINCOLN	67	43	21	40	49	70	45	60	53	43	52	54	36	55	44	58	44	55	66	66
LOGAN	71	51	36	49	56	75	54	66	61	51	60	59	46	63	53	66	51	62	74	71
MCDOWELL	50	34	21	32	37	52	36	45	42	34	42	41	30	43	35	46	35	42	51	50
MARION	71	58	56	57	62	74	63	69	68	58	66	60	57	68	62	72	57	66	78	71
MARSHALL	75	63	61	62	68	81	65	73	71	62	69	63	61	72	66	75	60	69	83	75
MASON	70	53	40	51	58	74	54	65	61	52	60	57	48	62	54	65	51	61	73	70
MERCER	69	54	47	53	58	73	57	66	63	54	62	58	51	63	57	67	53	63	74	69
MINERAL	75	56	43	54	61	79	58	70	65	56	64	61	51	67	58	69	55	65	77	74
MINGO	64	42	25	40	47	66	45	58	53	43	52	52	37	54	44	58	44	54	64	64
MONONGALIA	74	59	59	62	59	67	77	68	74	67	74	64	67	73	68	73	66	72	70	70
MONROE	79	55	33	52	63	86	56	73	63	54	63	64	47	66	56	68	53	66	79	79
MORGAN	85	65	51	63	71	91	66	80	73	64	72	70	59	75	66	78	62	74	88	85
NICHOLAS	76	54	35	51	61	83	56	71	63	54	63	62	47	65	56	69	53	65	79	77
OHIO	73	67	75	67	70	77	70	73	75	68	73	63	68	73	71	79	64	72	84	74
PENDLETON	79	56	32	53	63	86	56	73	63	54	63	64	47	66	56	68	53	66	79	80
PLEASANTS	82	59	42	57	66	88	61	76	69	59	68	67	53	72	61	74	58	70	85	81
POCAHONTAS	67	49	32	47	55	74	51	64	56	48	55	56	43	58	51	61	47	59	70	69
PRESTON	70	50	33	48	57	76	51	66	58	50	57	57	44	60	51	62	49	60	72	71
PUTNAM	98	92	83	90	94	103	84	95	89	87	88	84	84	92	87	92	78	90	98	99
RALEIGH	76	59	50	57	64	81	62	72	68	59	67	63	55	69	62	73	58	68	81	76
RANDOLPH	71	55	44	53	60	76	56	67	62	54	61	59	50	63	56	66	53	62	74	71
RITCHIE	71	50	34	48	57	77	53	67	60	50	59	58	45	62	53	65	50	61	74	71
ROANE	67	47	30	45	53	72	49	62	56	47	55	55	41	58	49	60	46	57	69	67
SUMMERS	58	43	32	41	48	63	45	55	50	43	49	48	39	51	45	54	42	51	61	59
TAYLOR	69	51	39	50	55	72	53	64	60	51	58	56	47	61	53	64	50	60	71	67
TUCKER	72	52	41	51	59	77	57	68	64	52	62	60	49	65	57	69	52	64	79	72
TYLER	76	56	39	53	63	84	57	72	64	55	63	63	49	66	57	69	54	66	77	77
UPSHUR	69	52	40	50	58	75	55	66	60	52	59	57	48	62	54	64	51	61	72	70
WAYNE	73	54	41	52	59	76	56	68	63	54	62	60	49	64	56	67	53	63	75	72
WEBSTER	60	39	20	36	44	62	41	53	48	39	48	48	33	50	40	53	40	49	60	59
WETZEL	79	60	48	58	66	84	62	75	70	60	68	65	55	72	63	75	59	70	84	79
WIRT	74	52	28	49	59	82	52	69	58	50	58	60	43	61	51	63	49	62	73	75
WOOD	79	70	72	70	73	83	72	78	77	69	75	68	69	77	73	80	66	75	86	79
WYOMING	70	47	28	45	53	73	50	64	59	48	57	57	41	61	50	64	49	59	72	70
WEST VIRGINIA	76	61	53	59	65	80	64	72	69	61	68	64	58	70	63	75	59	69	80	76
UNITED STATES	100	100	100	100	100	100	100	100	100	100	100	100	100	100	100	100	100	100	100	100

WISCONSIN

POPULATION CHANGE

A

COUNTY	FIPS Code	CBSA Code	DMA Code	POPULATION			2000-2007 ANNUAL RATE		RACE (%)					
									White		Black		Asian/Pacific	
				2000	2007	2012	% Rate	State Rank	2000	2007	2000	2007	2000	2007
ADAMS	001	00000	705	18,643	21,918	23,124	2.3	2	97.6	96.5	0.3	0.8	0.3	0.6
ASHLAND	003	00000	676	16,866	16,687	16,572	-0.1	70	87.1	85.9	0.2	0.3	0.4	0.5
BARRON	005	00000	613	44,963	48,222	50,205	1.0	25	97.7	97.3	0.1	0.2	0.4	0.5
BAYFIELD	007	00000	676	15,013	15,724	15,921	0.6	45	88.5	87.4	0.1	0.2	0.3	0.4
BROWN	009	24580	658	226,778	248,070	263,277	1.2	21	91.1	89.2	1.2	1.4	2.2	3.0
BUFFALO	011	00000	702	13,804	14,281	14,627	0.5	51	98.7	98.4	0.1	0.1	0.3	0.5
BURNETT	013	00000	613	15,674	16,726	17,264	0.9	29	93.2	92.5	0.4	0.4	0.3	0.4
CALUMET	015	11540	658	40,631	45,698	48,437	1.6	6	96.7	95.8	0.3	0.4	1.6	2.2
CHIPPEWA	017	20740	702	55,195	61,915	64,779	1.6	6	97.8	97.3	0.2	0.2	0.9	1.3
CLARK	019	00000	702	33,557	34,827	35,625	0.5	51	98.1	97.6	0.1	0.2	0.3	0.4
COLUMBIA	021	31540	669	52,468	56,952	60,054	1.1	23	97.2	96.6	0.9	1.1	0.4	0.5
CRAWFORD	023	00000	702	17,243	17,464	17,567	0.2	64	97.3	96.7	1.4	1.7	0.3	0.4
DANE	025	31540	669	426,526	475,924	505,908	1.5	9	89.0	86.3	4.0	4.8	3.5	4.7
DODGE	027	13180	617	85,897	89,663	91,817	0.6	45	95.3	94.2	2.5	3.0	0.4	0.5
DOOR	029	00000	658	27,961	29,640	30,771	0.8	35	97.8	97.4	0.2	0.2	0.3	0.4
DOUGLAS	031	20260	676	43,287	44,575	45,522	0.4	56	95.3	94.6	0.6	0.7	0.7	0.9
DUNN	033	32860	613	39,858	43,795	46,300	1.3	18	96.1	95.0	0.3	0.4	2.1	3.0
EAU CLAIRE	035	20740	702	93,142	97,731	100,283	0.7	40	95.0	93.3	0.5	1.0	2.5	3.5
FLORENCE	037	27020	553	5,088	5,061	5,012	-0.1	70	98.2	98.1	0.2	0.2	0.3	0.3
FOND DU LAC	039	22540	658	97,296	101,500	104,440	0.6	45	96.2	95.1	0.9	1.2	0.9	1.2
FOREST	041	00000	705	10,024	10,326	10,544	0.4	56	85.9	84.6	1.2	1.4	0.2	0.3
GRANT	043	38420	669	49,597	50,296	50,463	0.2	64	98.2	97.8	0.5	0.6	0.5	0.7
GREEN	045	33820	669	33,647	36,794	39,194	1.2	21	98.1	97.7	0.3	0.3	0.3	0.4
GREEN LAKE	047	00000	658	19,105	19,279	19,361	0.1	67	97.8	97.3	0.2	0.2	0.3	0.5
IOWA	049	31540	669	22,780	24,774	26,279	1.2	21	98.7	98.4	0.2	0.2	0.4	0.5
IRON	051	00000	676	6,861	7,014	7,116	0.3	61	98.3	98.1	0.1	0.1	0.2	0.2
JACKSON	053	00000	702	19,100	20,442	21,500	0.9	29	89.6	88.2	2.3	2.8	0.2	0.3
JEFFERSON	055	48020	617	74,021	81,885	86,654	1.4	14	96.3	95.2	0.3	0.5	0.5	0.7
JUNEAU	057	00000	669	24,316	27,548	28,675	1.7	4	96.6	96.0	0.3	0.4	0.5	0.6
KENOSHA	059	16980	617	149,577	165,647	177,598	1.4	14	88.4	85.9	5.1	6.1	1.0	1.3
KEWAUNEE	061	24580	658	20,187	21,512	22,505	0.9	29	98.6	98.3	0.2	0.2	0.1	0.2
LA CROSSE	063	29100	702	107,120	111,531	114,568	0.6	45	94.2	92.6	0.9	1.2	3.2	4.4
LAFAYETTE	065	00000	669	16,137	16,740	17,178	0.5	51	99.0	98.8	0.1	0.1	0.3	0.4
LANGLADE	067	00000	705	20,740	21,569	22,141	0.5	51	97.9	97.6	0.1	0.2	0.3	0.4
LINCOLN	069	32980	705	29,641	30,564	31,200	0.4	56	97.8	97.3	0.4	0.5	0.4	0.6
MANITOWOC	071	31820	658	82,887	83,711	84,296	0.1	67	95.9	94.8	0.3	0.3	2.0	2.8
MARATHON	073	48140	705	125,834	133,546	139,154	0.8	35	93.8	91.9	0.3	0.3	4.6	6.2
MARINETTE	075	31940	658	43,384	44,244	44,704	0.3	61	98.1	97.7	0.2	0.3	0.3	0.4
MARQUETTE	077	00000	669	15,832	15,751	16,664	-0.1	70	93.7	93.4	3.4	3.7	0.4	0.6
MENOMINEE	078	00000	658	4,562	4,700	4,792	0.4	56	11.6	10.8	0.1	0.1	0.0	0.0
MILWAUKEE	079	33340	617	940,164	927,424	917,150	-0.2	72	65.6	60.7	24.6	27.8	2.6	3.3
MONROE	081	00000	702	40,899	43,648	45,630	0.9	29	96.5	95.8	0.5	0.6	0.5	0.7
OCONTO	083	24580	658	35,634	39,938	42,699	1.6	6	97.8	97.4	0.1	0.2	0.2	0.3
ONEIDA	085	00000	705	36,776	39,069	40,516	0.8	35	97.7	97.3	0.3	0.4	0.3	0.5
OUTAGAMIE	087	11540	658	160,971	177,636	189,562	1.4	14	93.9	92.4	0.5	0.7	2.3	3.1
OZAUKEE	089	33340	617	82,317	87,617	90,976	0.9	29	96.7	95.7	0.9	1.3	1.1	1.5
PEPIN	091	00000	702	7,213	7,720	7,983	0.9	29	98.9	98.7	0.1	0.1	0.2	0.3
PIERCE	093	33460	613	36,804	41,039	44,187	1.5	9	98.0	97.0	0.2	0.8	0.5	0.6
POLK	095	00000	613	41,319	46,718	50,777	1.7	4	97.6	97.3	0.2	0.2	0.3	0.4
PORTAGE	097	44620	705	67,182	69,823	71,473	0.5	51	95.7	94.5	0.3	0.4	2.3	3.2
PRICE	099	00000	705	15,822	15,870	15,940	0.0	68	98.2	98.2	0.1	0.1	0.3	0.3
RACINE	101	39540	617	188,831	197,998	204,977	0.7	40	83.0	79.7	10.5	12.3	0.8	1.0
RICHLAND	103	00000	669	17,924	18,223	18,347	0.2	64	98.4	98.1	0.2	0.2	0.2	0.3
ROCK	105	27500	669	152,307	161,103	167,788	0.8	35	91.0	89.0	4.6	5.6	0.8	1.1
RUSK	107	00000	702	15,347	15,772	16,091	0.4	56	97.7	97.2	0.5	0.6	0.4	0.5
ST. CROIX	109	33460	613	63,155	82,889	99,115	3.8	1	97.8	97.4	0.3	0.3	0.6	0.9
SAUK	111	12660	669	55,225	61,299	65,585	1.4	14	97.4	96.9	0.3	0.3	0.3	0.4
SAWYER	113	00000	676	16,196	17,918	18,973	1.4	14	81.7	80.3	0.3	0.4	0.3	0.4
SHAWANO	115	00000	658	40,664	42,666	43,923	0.7	40	91.6	90.7	0.2	0.3	0.4	0.5
SHEBOYGAN	117	43100	617	112,646	117,376	120,779	0.6	45	92.7	90.7	1.1	1.3	3.3	4.5
TAYLOR	119	00000	705	19,680	20,051	20,325	0.3	61	98.7	98.5	0.1	0.1	0.2	0.3
TREMPEALEAU	121	00000	702	27,010	28,557	29,718	0.8	35	98.8	98.6	0.1	0.2	0.1	0.2
VERNON	123	00000	702	28,056	29,587	30,697	0.7	40	98.8	98.6	0.1	0.1	0.2	0.3
VILAS	125	00000	705	21,033	22,478	23,227	0.9	29	89.7	88.8	0.2	0.2	0.2	0.3
WALWORTH	127	48580	617	93,759	103,137	111,436	1.3	18	94.5	93.1	0.8	0.9	0.7	0.9
WASHBURN	129	00000	613	16,036	17,464	18,309	1.2	21	97.3	96.9	0.2	0.2	0.2	0.3
WASHINGTON	131	33340	617	117,493	131,089	141,514	1.5	9	97.7	97.1	0.4	0.5	0.6	0.8
WAUKESHA	133	33340	617	360,767	388,343	405,660	1.0	25	95.8	94.6	0.7	0.9	1.5	2.1
WAUPACA	135	00000	658	51,731	53,950	55,028	0.6	45	97.9	97.5	0.2	0.2	0.3	0.4
WAUSHARA	137	00000	658	23,154	25,642	26,720	1.4	14	96.8	95.6	0.3	0.8	0.4	0.5
WINNEBAGO	139	36780	658	156,763	164,189	167,637	0.6	45	94.9	93.6	1.1	1.4	1.9	2.6
WOOD	141	32270	705	75,555	76,947	77,938	0.3	61	96.4	95.5	0.3	0.3	1.6	2.3
WISCONSIN							0.8		88.9	87.3	5.7	6.2	1.7	2.2
UNITED STATES							1.2		75.1	72.7	12.3	12.6	3.8	4.5

COUNTY	% HISPANIC ORIGIN		2007 AGE DISTRIBUTION (%)										MEDIAN AGE	% 2007 Males	% 2007 Females
	2000	2007	0-4	5-9	10-14	15-19	20-24	25-44	45-64	65-84	85+	18+	2007		
ADAMS	1.4	2.0	4.6	4.3	4.7	5.3	5.0	24.1	30.9	19.0	2.1	83.3	46.2	54.0	46.0
ASHLAND	1.1	1.4	6.7	5.9	5.7	8.1	8.9	23.4	26.1	12.2	3.0	77.4	38.1	49.5	50.5
BARRON	1.0	1.3	6.0	5.4	5.8	6.4	7.4	24.5	28.6	13.0	2.8	78.7	41.2	49.7	50.3
BAYFIELD	0.6	0.8	5.3	5.6	5.4	6.6	6.5	19.5	34.6	14.3	2.2	79.6	45.6	50.5	49.5
BROWN	3.8	5.0	7.0	6.3	6.7	7.5	7.9	28.8	25.4	8.8	1.7	75.8	35.6	49.7	50.3
BUFFALO	0.6	0.8	6.2	5.6	5.9	6.5	6.1	24.4	28.8	14.1	2.5	78.2	41.8	50.3	49.7
BURNETT	0.8	1.0	5.1	4.7	5.4	5.9	5.9	19.7	31.9	19.0	2.5	81.1	47.1	50.6	49.4
CALUMET	1.1	1.4	7.3	6.9	7.1	7.0	6.9	27.8	26.7	8.7	1.5	74.4	37.3	50.1	49.9
CHIPPEWA	0.5	0.7	6.4	6.0	6.0	6.7	7.0	25.0	27.7	12.1	3.2	77.5	40.5	49.9	50.1
CLARK	1.2	1.6	8.3	7.6	6.6	6.9	7.5	23.5	25.1	11.8	2.7	73.3	37.1	50.2	49.8
COLUMBIA	1.6	2.1	6.3	5.9	6.2	6.9	7.0	25.5	27.9	11.9	2.4	77.3	40.3	50.6	49.4
CRAWFORD	0.7	1.0	6.2	6.1	6.2	7.5	8.0	22.0	28.7	12.8	2.5	76.7	40.6	51.2	48.8
DANE	3.4	4.3	5.9	5.7	5.8	7.7	11.1	28.9	25.4	7.9	1.5	78.8	34.7	49.5	50.5
DODGE	2.5	3.3	6.2	5.8	5.8	6.7	7.4	27.9	26.4	11.3	2.5	78.3	38.9	52.4	47.6
DOOR	1.0	1.3	4.6	4.3	5.6	6.1	5.9	21.2	33.5	16.0	3.0	81.8	46.4	49.4	50.6
DOUGLAS	0.7	1.0	6.0	5.4	5.8	6.6	8.0	25.6	28.4	11.7	2.5	79.2	40.1	49.3	50.7
DUNN	0.8	1.1	6.0	5.5	5.4	9.4	14.6	24.7	23.7	8.8	1.9	79.3	32.0	50.5	49.5
EAU CLAIRE	0.9	1.3	6.1	5.5	5.6	8.5	12.9	25.3	24.2	9.8	2.2	79.0	33.8	48.7	51.3
FLORENCE	0.5	0.5	4.8	4.8	5.9	6.1	5.0	23.3	31.9	15.3	3.0	80.5	45.1	51.1	48.9
FOND DU LAC	2.0	2.7	6.2	5.7	6.2	7.3	7.5	26.0	27.2	11.4	2.5	77.7	39.0	49.0	51.0
FOREST	1.1	1.3	6.2	5.4	6.1	7.8	6.4	21.9	27.0	16.7	2.6	77.8	42.4	50.1	49.9
GRANT	0.6	0.7	5.5	5.0	5.7	9.0	11.3	23.2	25.1	12.7	2.6	79.8	37.3	51.4	48.6
GREEN	1.0	1.3	6.5	6.3	6.8	6.8	6.4	24.9	28.0	11.5	2.6	75.9	40.2	49.5	50.5
GREEN LAKE	2.1	2.7	6.0	5.6	5.5	5.8	6.8	22.6	30.5	14.0	3.2	79.4	43.5	49.5	50.5
IOWA	0.3	0.4	6.7	6.2	6.6	6.6	6.3	26.3	28.7	10.6	2.0	76.1	40.2	50.0	50.0
IRON	0.7	0.8	4.2	3.6	4.3	5.7	6.5	19.9	32.1	19.3	4.4	84.5	48.1	48.8	51.2
JACKSON	1.9	2.4	5.9	5.6	5.7	6.9	7.1	26.7	27.4	12.3	2.4	78.6	39.8	53.2	46.8
JEFFERSON	4.1	5.3	6.4	6.1	6.0	7.5	7.0	27.4	26.9	10.9	1.9	77.5	38.4	49.8	50.2
JUNEAU	1.4	1.9	6.0	5.4	5.9	6.0	6.5	23.2	27.5	15.5	4.0	79.0	43.0	49.7	50.3
KENOSHA	7.2	9.2	7.1	6.4	7.1	7.8	7.1	28.0	25.3	9.6	1.8	74.9	36.5	49.7	50.3
KEWAUNEE	0.8	1.0	6.4	5.9	6.1	6.5	6.2	26.9	27.7	11.7	2.7	77.6	40.2	50.6	49.4
LA CROSSE	0.9	1.2	6.0	5.6	6.1	8.4	11.7	25.1	24.7	10.2	2.2	78.5	34.9	48.5	51.5
LAFAYETTE	0.6	0.8	6.6	5.9	6.4	6.5	7.0	24.5	27.8	13.1	2.2	76.9	40.7	50.7	49.3
LANGLADE	0.8	1.1	5.8	5.0	5.6	7.1	7.0	22.6	28.1	15.8	3.0	79.2	43.0	50.1	49.9
LINCOLN	0.8	1.1	6.0	5.5	6.2	7.2	6.6	23.9	28.3	13.4	2.8	77.4	41.3	50.3	49.7
MANITOWOC	1.6	2.1	6.2	5.5	6.3	6.8	7.1	25.0	28.3	12.2	2.6	77.9	40.6	49.9	50.1
MARATHON	0.8	1.0	6.7	6.1	6.7	6.8	6.9	26.9	27.1	10.7	2.1	76.3	38.5	50.0	50.0
MARINETTE	0.7	1.0	5.3	4.9	5.5	7.0	7.7	22.0	29.9	14.8	2.9	80.3	43.4	49.5	50.5
MARQUETTE	2.7	3.4	5.4	5.0	4.8	6.6	6.4	23.6	29.4	16.5	2.2	81.0	43.8	51.8	48.2
MENOMINEE	2.7	3.0	10.2	8.6	10.3	9.4	7.5	22.2	21.4	9.9	0.5	64.8	28.3	48.9	51.1
MILWAUKEE	8.8	10.6	7.2	6.5	7.0	7.4	7.9	27.7	23.8	10.2	2.2	75.1	35.0	48.1	51.9
MONROE	1.8	2.4	7.1	6.2	6.7	7.1	7.5	24.8	27.5	11.0	2.1	75.5	38.6	50.6	49.4
OCONTO	0.7	0.9	6.0	5.5	6.2	6.9	6.9	24.5	28.9	12.9	2.1	78.2	41.4	50.4	49.6
ONEIDA	0.7	0.9	4.7	4.5	5.2	6.3	6.3	21.4	32.4	16.8	2.4	81.6	45.9	49.9	50.1
OUTAGAMIE	2.0	2.6	7.2	6.5	7.0	7.5	7.3	28.7	25.4	8.7	1.7	74.7	36.2	50.0	50.0
OZAUKEE	1.3	1.8	5.9	6.2	7.1	7.7	6.5	22.1	30.8	11.8	2.0	76.0	41.6	49.2	50.8
PEPIN	0.3	0.5	6.6	5.3	6.6	5.7	8.4	23.8	27.7	12.7	3.2	77.9	40.1	50.8	49.2
PIERCE	0.8	1.2	5.8	5.6	5.9	9.1	11.9	25.8	25.6	8.6	1.7	78.7	34.3	49.6	50.4
POLK	0.8	1.0	6.1	5.8	6.5	6.6	6.6	24.2	29.1	12.7	2.4	77.4	41.3	50.0	50.0
PORTAGE	1.4	1.9	5.9	5.5	5.9	8.5	11.5	26.0	25.4	9.6	1.7	78.8	34.8	49.9	50.1
PRICE	0.7	0.8	5.0	4.7	5.8	6.5	6.8	21.8	31.3	15.0	3.2	80.5	44.6	50.2	49.8
RACINE	7.9	10.0	7.0	6.6	6.7	7.1	7.2	25.8	26.9	10.7	1.9	75.3	38.0	49.5	50.5
RICHLAND	0.9	1.2	5.9	5.4	5.5	6.9	7.4	23.4	28.5	14.0	2.8	79.1	41.8	49.8	50.2
ROCK	3.9	5.1	6.9	6.3	6.9	7.3	6.8	26.7	26.4	10.8	1.9	75.5	37.7	49.3	50.7
RUSK	0.8	1.0	5.7	5.1	6.2	6.9	7.5	22.1	28.3	14.9	3.2	78.8	42.4	49.8	50.2
ST. CROIX	0.8	1.0	7.0	6.7	7.0	7.0	6.6	28.0	27.7	8.5	1.6	74.8	37.3	50.1	49.9
SAUK	1.7	2.2	6.6	6.2	6.2	7.2	6.6	25.6	27.8	11.4	2.4	76.6	39.4	49.5	50.5
SAWYER	0.9	1.1	5.8	5.5	5.4	6.7	6.5	20.1	31.6	16.0	2.3	79.2	45.0	50.4	49.6
SHAWANO	1.0	1.3	6.6	6.0	6.2	6.7	6.0	25.2	26.9	13.7	2.8	76.8	40.9	50.1	49.9
SHEBOYGAN	3.4	4.4	6.6	6.1	6.3	6.9	7.5	26.2	27.1	10.9	2.4	76.9	38.7	50.0	50.0
TAYLOR	0.6	0.9	6.4	5.7	6.4	7.0	7.0	25.4	27.5	11.8	2.7	77.0	39.9	50.9	49.1
TREMPEALEAU	0.9	1.2	6.4	6.1	6.6	6.2	5.7	25.9	27.7	12.5	2.9	77.0	40.8	50.2	49.8
VERNON	0.7	0.9	7.0	6.1	6.3	6.9	7.2	21.7	28.7	13.3	2.8	76.1	41.3	49.9	50.1
VILAS	0.9	1.1	4.4	4.0	5.0	6.0	5.2	19.2	33.1	20.2	2.9	82.8	48.6	50.0	50.0
WALWORTH	6.5	8.6	6.1	5.7	6.3	7.8	9.7	24.8	26.2	11.2	2.2	77.6	37.7	49.9	50.1
WASHBURN	0.9	1.2	5.3	5.0	5.4	6.5	6.3	20.9	32.5	15.3	2.8	80.0	45.3	50.2	49.8
WASHINGTON	1.3	1.7	6.8	6.7	6.8	6.8	6.0	27.6	27.4	10.0	1.8	75.3	38.9	49.7	50.3
WAUKESHA	2.6	3.5	6.2	6.6	6.9	7.4	5.9	24.5	29.6	11.1	1.9	75.6	40.6	49.1	50.9
WAUPACA	1.4	1.8	6.2	5.9	6.5	6.7	6.5	24.5	27.7	13.1	2.9	77.5	41.0	50.2	49.8
WAUSHARA	3.7	4.8	5.0	4.6	5.6	7.0	5.9	20.8	29.4	17.8	3.9	80.7	45.6	50.4	49.6
WINNEBAGO	2.0	2.6	6.0	5.6	6.1	7.8	9.3	26.9	25.8	10.3	2.2	78.3	37.0	49.9	50.1
WOOD	0.9	1.2	6.4	6.0	6.3	6.7	7.0	25.1	27.5	12.3	2.8	77.1	40.1	49.3	50.7
WISCONSIN	3.6	4.5	6.5	6.1	6.4	7.3	7.9	26.2	26.6	10.8	2.2	76.8	37.9	49.5	50.5
UNITED STATES	12.5	15.0	6.9	6.5	6.8	7.1	7.0	27.6	25.4	10.7	1.9	75.6	36.7	49.2	50.8

COUNTY	HOUSEHOLDS					FAMILIES			MEDIAN HOUSEHOLD INCOME			
	2000	2007	2012	% Annual Rate 2000-2007	2007 Average HH Size	2000	2007	% Annual Rate 2000-2007	2007	2012	2007 National Rank	2007 State Rank
ADAMS	7,900	8,939	9,563	1.7	2.26	5,464	6,039	1.4	41,044	46,998	1592	60
ASHLAND	6,718	6,826	6,837	0.2	2.33	4,281	4,232	-0.2	39,370	45,583	1805	67
BARRON	17,851	19,723	20,743	1.4	2.41	12,349	13,329	1.1	45,154	51,163	1093	43
BAYFIELD	6,207	6,694	6,844	1.0	2.33	4,275	4,503	0.7	40,234	45,563	1696	64
BROWN	87,295	98,484	105,656	1.7	2.44	57,539	63,264	1.3	58,521	67,966	295	11
BUFFALO	5,511	5,895	6,105	0.9	2.40	3,783	3,952	0.6	45,371	51,385	1067	41
BURNETT	6,613	7,269	7,582	1.3	2.26	4,503	4,833	1.0	41,966	48,411	1453	55
CALUMET	14,910	17,382	18,672	2.1	2.61	11,164	12,770	1.9	64,009	75,558	180	5
CHIPPEWA	21,356	24,001	25,444	1.6	2.46	15,006	16,491	1.3	47,542	53,430	859	35
CLARK	12,047	12,698	13,043	0.7	2.69	8,678	8,960	0.4	40,944	45,788	1607	61
COLUMBIA	20,439	22,812	24,304	1.5	2.43	14,160	15,442	1.2	55,489	63,466	385	18
CRAWFORD	6,677	6,960	7,088	0.6	2.40	4,611	4,694	0.2	41,261	46,719	1559	58
DANE	173,484	198,558	213,136	1.9	2.32	100,856	111,857	1.4	62,378	73,343	205	6
DODGE	31,417	34,029	35,332	1.1	2.46	22,313	23,644	0.8	55,180	63,325	397	20
DOOR	11,828	13,027	13,729	1.3	2.25	7,997	8,595	1.0	48,053	55,068	811	34
DOUGLAS	17,808	18,856	19,443	0.8	2.30	11,280	11,618	0.4	43,774	50,550	1240	51
DUNN	14,337	16,295	17,451	1.8	2.50	9,265	10,255	1.4	46,350	52,037	963	38
EAU CLAIRE	35,822	39,107	40,613	1.2	2.37	22,270	23,626	0.8	49,034	56,517	744	31
FLORENCE	2,133	2,208	2,219	0.5	2.25	1,441	1,456	0.1	40,907	45,715	1612	62
FOND DU LAC	36,931	39,656	41,308	1.0	2.45	25,467	26,718	0.7	55,872	64,521	366	16
FOREST	4,043	4,327	4,482	0.9	2.31	2,768	2,893	0.6	38,428	43,572	1943	69
GRANT	18,465	19,253	19,581	0.6	2.42	12,399	12,611	0.2	43,828	50,052	1232	50
GREEN	13,212	14,809	15,904	1.6	2.45	9,215	10,094	1.3	52,705	60,862	512	21
GREEN LAKE	7,703	8,002	8,117	0.5	2.36	5,322	5,402	0.2	47,389	53,307	873	36
IOWA	8,764	9,823	10,531	1.6	2.49	6,210	6,808	1.3	51,882	58,735	556	25
IRON	3,083	3,247	3,333	0.7	2.12	1,960	2,007	0.3	34,695	38,744	2468	71
JACKSON	7,070	7,816	8,316	1.4	2.43	4,835	5,220	1.1	44,783	50,403	1131	45
JEFFERSON	28,205	31,390	33,581	1.5	2.49	19,894	21,652	1.2	57,734	65,558	313	12
JUNEAU	9,696	10,779	11,355	1.5	2.40	6,701	7,277	1.1	42,343	47,771	1412	54
KENOSHA	56,057	62,526	67,386	1.5	2.58	38,451	41,884	1.2	59,529	68,723	278	10
KEWAUNEE	7,623	8,388	8,878	1.3	2.53	5,548	5,980	1.0	51,328	56,922	591	27
LA CROSSE	41,599	44,840	46,529	1.0	2.37	25,599	26,809	0.6	49,135	56,689	740	30
LAFAYETTE	6,211	6,638	6,886	0.9	2.50	4,378	4,576	0.6	43,977	49,129	1213	49
LANGLADE	8,452	9,037	9,375	0.9	2.35	5,819	6,076	0.6	40,840	46,718	1622	63
LINCOLN	11,721	12,481	12,888	0.9	2.38	8,230	8,568	0.6	47,355	53,301	878	37
MANITOWOC	32,721	34,284	34,911	0.6	2.40	22,364	22,882	0.3	52,572	59,654	518	23
MARATHON	47,702	52,616	55,512	1.4	2.50	33,884	36,521	1.1	55,378	63,426	389	19
MARINETTE	17,585	18,579	19,020	0.8	2.30	11,840	12,202	0.4	42,720	48,809	1363	52
MARQUETTE	5,986	6,664	7,123	1.5	2.34	4,167	4,534	1.2	42,679	48,195	1369	53
MENOMINEE	1,345	1,433	1,479	0.9	3.24	1,065	1,118	0.7	34,508	38,555	2497	72
MILWAUKEE	377,729	380,954	379,167	0.1	2.37	225,046	220,155	-0.3	48,169	55,588	801	33
MONROE	15,399	16,882	17,810	1.3	2.53	10,790	11,565	1.0	44,526	50,179	1154	47
OCONTO	13,979	16,147	17,435	2.0	2.46	10,046	11,360	1.7	50,092	56,228	671	28
ONEIDA	15,333	16,762	17,552	1.2	2.28	10,493	11,200	0.9	44,603	50,290	1145	46
OUTAGAMIE	60,530	68,892	74,312	1.8	2.53	42,219	46,964	1.5	61,583	71,733	222	7
OZAUKEE	30,857	33,931	35,699	1.3	2.53	23,014	24,822	1.0	79,982	96,897	52	1
PEPIN	2,759	3,022	3,149	1.3	2.51	1,934	2,071	0.9	44,237	49,303	1184	48
PIERCE	13,015	15,041	16,418	2.0	2.57	9,030	10,196	1.7	60,929	70,411	244	9
POLK	16,254	18,911	20,768	2.1	2.44	11,325	12,880	1.8	49,002	54,589	747	32
PORTAGE	25,040	27,137	28,183	1.1	2.44	16,496	17,422	0.8	52,595	59,791	517	22
PRICE	6,564	6,828	6,947	0.5	2.29	4,416	4,483	0.2	41,700	47,273	1490	56
RACINE	70,819	76,183	79,606	1.0	2.53	49,861	52,459	0.7	61,092	71,049	237	8
RICHLAND	7,118	7,473	7,611	0.7	2.40	4,833	4,955	0.3	41,124	47,169	1586	59
ROCK	58,617	63,311	66,393	1.1	2.49	40,403	42,626	0.7	56,809	65,545	336	15
RUSK	6,095	6,467	6,673	0.8	2.38	4,158	4,306	0.5	37,828	42,794	2021	70
ST. CROIX	23,410	31,724	38,040	4.3	2.58	16,946	22,492	4.0	67,730	79,752	141	4
SAUK	21,644	24,677	26,651	1.8	2.45	14,863	16,551	1.5	52,175	60,391	538	24
SAWYER	6,640	7,546	8,070	1.8	2.33	4,581	5,085	1.5	39,048	44,904	1847	68
SHAWANO	15,815	17,118	17,810	1.1	2.44	11,154	11,806	0.8	45,332	50,973	1073	42
SHEBOYGAN	43,545	46,614	48,453	0.9	2.44	29,936	31,299	0.6	56,836	65,567	333	14
TAYLOR	7,529	7,973	8,202	0.8	2.48	5,343	5,536	0.5	46,089	51,535	991	39
TREMPEALEAU	10,747	11,734	12,352	1.2	2.38	7,239	7,711	0.9	45,500	51,003	1050	40
VERNON	10,825	11,642	12,138	1.0	2.50	7,502	7,883	0.7	39,374	44,001	1802	66
VILAS	9,066	9,947	10,382	1.3	2.23	6,297	6,750	1.0	41,344	47,300	1542	57
WALWORTH	34,522	39,793	43,304	2.0	2.51	23,271	26,178	1.6	57,084	66,172	326	13
WASHBURN	6,604	7,392	7,819	1.6	2.33	4,531	4,951	1.2	39,387	44,108	1797	65
WASHINGTON	43,842	50,785	55,650	2.0	2.56	32,757	37,224	1.8	72,361	84,237	107	3
WAUKESHA	135,229	149,457	158,035	1.4	2.56	100,502	108,939	1.1	79,920	96,603	53	2
WAUPACA	19,863	21,259	21,878	0.9	2.45	13,877	14,519	0.6	49,311	55,510	720	29
WAUSHARA	9,336	10,227	10,763	1.3	2.37	6,583	7,051	1.0	44,807	50,868	1130	44
WINNEBAGO	61,157	66,179	68,247	1.1	2.35	39,547	41,662	0.7	55,834	65,048	369	17
WOOD	30,135	31,893	32,763	0.8	2.37	20,506	21,187	0.5	51,454	59,409	581	26
WISCONSIN				1.2	2.43			0.9	54,628	63,236		
UNITED STATES				1.2	2.59			1.0	53,154	62,503		

COUNTY	2007 Per Capita Income	2007 HH Income Base	2007 HOUSEHOLD INCOME DISTRIBUTION (%)					2007 Home Value Base	2007 HOME VALUE DISTRIBUTION (%)					2007 Median Home Value
			Less than $25,000	$25,000 to $49,999	$50,000 to $99,999	$100,000 to $149,999	$150,000 or More		Less than $50,000	$50,000 to $89,999	$90,000 to $174,999	$175,000 to $399,999	$400,000 or More	
ADAMS	21,764	8,939	26.4	34.3	30.9	6.4	2.1	7,669	10.5	23.2	41.6	22.2	2.5	119,456
ASHLAND	20,097	6,826	30.3	32.8	30.5	4.7	1.8	4,908	15.8	29.2	41.3	12.5	1.1	96,875
BARRON	22,627	19,723	25.8	29.9	33.5	7.5	3.2	15,169	8.9	18.2	46.3	23.6	2.9	125,118
BAYFIELD	20,655	6,694	30.6	31.2	29.7	7.0	1.5	5,587	8.4	15.9	42.8	28.6	4.4	133,976
BROWN	28,524	98,484	16.7	24.9	39.2	13.2	6.0	66,133	2.8	6.0	50.4	37.7	3.1	156,971
BUFFALO	22,824	5,895	24.4	30.6	35.2	7.0	2.8	4,584	7.5	17.7	45.4	24.5	5.0	130,587
BURNETT	22,663	7,269	25.3	34.5	31.1	6.6	2.5	6,179	9.0	17.5	43.0	26.6	3.9	131,236
CALUMET	28,712	17,382	11.1	23.7	44.3	15.0	5.9	14,180	3.6	8.2	53.9	32.0	2.3	146,846
CHIPPEWA	22,668	24,001	22.5	30.4	36.3	8.3	2.6	18,478	7.5	14.2	51.5	24.4	2.4	127,866
CLARK	18,393	12,698	28.3	32.2	31.8	5.6	2.0	10,391	12.1	25.5	42.4	18.1	1.9	109,765
COLUMBIA	26,336	22,812	17.4	26.6	40.0	12.0	4.0	17,377	4.5	4.8	35.6	46.3	6.8	185,222
CRAWFORD	21,267	6,960	28.0	32.0	30.7	6.7	2.6	5,443	15.7	19.5	41.7	20.4	2.8	117,356
DANE	32,736	198,558	15.9	23.0	37.9	15.0	8.2	118,490	1.8	1.1	19.7	67.3	10.1	227,144
DODGE	25,003	34,029	16.2	27.1	42.5	10.7	3.5	25,592	3.5	5.6	43.3	43.0	4.6	170,318
DOOR	26,953	13,027	22.5	29.4	34.4	8.8	4.9	10,485	5.3	7.3	34.8	37.9	14.8	182,387
DOUGLAS	22,775	18,856	26.9	30.6	31.3	9.0	2.2	13,667	11.6	20.0	43.9	22.3	2.2	121,533
DUNN	21,925	16,295	23.9	29.7	34.8	8.7	2.9	11,493	10.6	11.9	42.2	32.5	2.8	143,399
EAU CLAIRE	25,684	39,107	21.0	30.0	34.5	9.8	4.8	26,003	5.8	10.7	51.7	29.6	2.2	138,163
FLORENCE	22,065	2,208	29.0	32.3	31.0	5.8	1.9	1,899	11.2	24.2	38.1	24.2	2.3	122,062
FOND DU LAC	25,926	39,656	18.3	24.4	42.0	11.1	4.3	29,541	5.0	8.4	50.3	33.5	2.8	145,289
FOREST	20,600	4,327	30.7	33.1	28.4	5.5	2.3	3,466	10.9	21.8	44.4	20.5	2.4	117,246
GRANT	21,262	19,253	25.0	32.3	33.2	7.1	2.4	14,181	9.9	18.3	47.3	21.6	2.9	124,165
GREEN	25,853	14,809	18.3	28.0	39.8	9.6	4.2	11,181	3.8	7.6	45.0	38.0	5.6	161,870
GREEN LAKE	24,013	8,002	21.3	31.7	36.9	7.4	2.7	6,303	4.7	12.8	49.2	28.0	5.3	142,842
IOWA	24,429	9,823	19.7	28.0	38.5	10.5	3.4	7,608	5.1	10.7	43.2	33.5	7.5	152,882
IRON	20,801	3,247	33.2	37.1	22.9	5.0	1.8	2,635	20.3	26.8	29.4	20.0	3.5	95,930
JACKSON	21,944	7,816	25.5	31.2	33.3	6.9	3.0	5,978	11.6	20.3	42.7	22.8	2.7	121,924
JEFFERSON	26,766	31,390	15.3	26.5	40.6	13.2	4.5	23,086	5.5	4.1	29.6	53.8	6.9	194,623
JUNEAU	21,383	10,779	25.4	33.5	32.9	5.6	2.7	8,438	11.7	24.7	42.2	18.8	2.7	111,589
KENOSHA	27,055	62,526	17.2	24.3	37.1	15.4	6.0	44,281	3.8	3.5	35.9	51.4	5.4	187,356
KEWAUNEE	23,016	8,388	21.0	27.2	39.8	9.4	2.5	6,937	6.1	14.7	49.8	25.8	3.5	133,723
LA CROSSE	26,009	44,840	22.3	28.5	34.1	9.9	5.2	29,943	8.2	9.5	50.6	29.0	2.7	141,804
LAFAYETTE	20,801	6,638	25.0	31.9	34.6	6.8	1.7	5,232	8.4	17.7	49.5	19.9	4.5	124,169
LANGLADE	21,161	9,037	28.5	31.5	32.1	5.8	2.1	7,208	8.4	27.1	43.5	18.9	2.1	110,027
LINCOLN	22,949	12,481	24.2	28.3	36.7	8.5	2.2	9,878	7.1	14.3	47.7	28.4	2.5	134,965
MANITOWOC	25,679	34,284	18.8	28.2	39.9	9.7	3.4	26,504	4.0	11.8	50.5	30.8	2.9	142,505
MARATHON	26,757	52,616	17.2	26.7	39.4	11.8	4.8	40,531	5.9	11.3	54.4	26.2	2.3	135,403
MARINETTE	22,273	18,579	25.9	32.6	31.6	7.6	2.2	14,929	12.8	25.6	40.9	19.1	1.6	108,814
MARQUETTE	21,809	6,664	25.6	33.9	32.8	5.5	2.3	5,540	7.4	14.6	45.5	29.1	3.5	137,640
MENOMINEE	12,658	1,433	35.1	32.4	27.8	4.3	0.4	1,069	25.6	25.8	31.3	15.4	1.8	87,847
MILWAUKEE	25,680	380,945	24.1	27.6	32.7	10.6	4.9	208,077	3.7	12.6	41.5	38.7	3.4	159,307
MONROE	21,351	16,882	24.5	31.6	33.9	7.3	2.7	12,708	11.0	17.7	46.7	22.2	2.4	124,683
OCONTO	23,882	16,147	21.3	28.6	38.1	9.0	3.0	13,523	9.3	19.6	41.2	27.4	2.5	127,061
ONEIDA	24,949	16,762	24.8	30.8	32.2	8.5	3.7	13,509	5.1	11.2	40.7	35.0	8.1	157,217
OUTAGAMIE	28,621	68,892	13.5	24.1	42.3	14.2	5.8	50,975	2.0	6.8	57.0	31.9	2.2	144,703
OZAUKEE	42,249	33,931	8.6	18.1	35.5	20.8	16.9	26,391	0.3	0.5	8.7	64.9	25.6	283,632
PEPIN	21,040	3,022	25.2	30.7	34.3	7.1	2.6	2,435	6.7	16.6	49.3	24.1	3.4	130,315
PIERCE	26,293	15,041	15.2	24.2	42.5	13.4	4.7	11,185	4.8	5.3	25.4	52.4	12.2	213,865
POLK	23,760	18,911	21.6	29.5	36.5	9.7	2.7	15,378	8.3	11.2	38.8	36.6	5.0	156,761
PORTAGE	25,762	27,137	20.6	26.3	36.9	11.4	4.7	19,605	5.8	9.2	45.1	36.7	3.3	154,467
PRICE	22,154	6,828	28.7	31.1	31.4	6.5	2.3	5,568	12.6	23.8	43.1	18.8	1.6	112,400
RACINE	28,174	76,183	17.1	22.8	39.0	14.9	6.2	54,959	1.9	5.9	45.6	42.2	4.5	168,629
RICHLAND	21,549	7,473	28.0	31.4	32.0	6.0	2.7	5,639	10.3	18.9	44.6	22.7	3.4	124,669
ROCK	26,948	63,311	16.5	26.8	38.3	13.3	5.1	46,081	5.2	12.1	51.9	28.8	1.9	139,218
RUSK	19,367	6,467	31.2	33.0	28.7	5.5	1.5	5,146	15.3	27.5	40.3	15.2	1.7	102,129
ST. CROIX	31,552	31,724	12.0	20.0	39.9	19.1	9.0	24,601	4.1	3.0	15.9	60.5	16.6	248,628
SAUK	25,547	24,677	18.9	28.1	38.8	10.1	4.2	18,440	7.6	7.9	38.7	39.8	6.0	165,326
SAWYER	22,173	7,546	31.9	29.3	29.1	7.0	2.7	5,917	8.4	17.1	37.4	29.7	7.3	139,783
SHAWANO	22,355	17,118	23.7	32.4	32.9	8.3	2.8	13,613	7.2	15.4	47.4	26.6	3.4	133,094
SHEBOYGAN	27,286	46,614	16.0	26.2	41.1	12.0	4.7	33,992	2.6	6.4	52.4	35.5	3.1	148,959
TAYLOR	22,198	7,973	24.1	30.2	35.7	7.2	2.9	6,489	10.7	19.5	46.3	21.6	1.9	121,960
TREMPEALEAU	22,228	11,734	24.7	30.2	35.7	7.0	2.4	8,905	9.0	17.3	47.1	23.8	2.9	127,015
VERNON	19,561	11,642	29.8	32.3	30.1	5.6	2.1	9,322	14.7	18.2	39.8	24.3	3.0	120,328
VILAS	23,429	9,947	27.7	31.8	30.8	6.7	3.0	8,235	4.7	7.8	36.8	38.1	12.5	176,855
WALWORTH	27,421	39,793	17.6	24.6	38.5	13.6	5.7	28,205	2.7	4.1	31.0	51.8	10.5	199,077
WASHBURN	21,346	7,392	28.8	33.8	29.0	6.1	2.2	6,041	9.8	18.9	41.0	25.4	4.9	129,317
WASHINGTON	32,650	50,785	10.0	19.2	43.7	17.7	9.4	39,344	1.6	1.5	13.6	70.5	12.8	246,503
WAUKESHA	39,169	149,457	9.0	16.5	37.8	21.9	14.9	116,381	0.7	0.7	8.3	70.7	19.6	274,845
WAUPACA	23,404	21,259	22.7	28.0	37.0	9.5	2.8	16,617	4.8	12.7	47.8	31.0	3.7	141,874
WAUSHARA	22,559	10,227	24.2	32.8	33.4	7.0	2.7	8,599	6.7	17.8	43.9	27.9	3.7	134,006
WINNEBAGO	27,824	66,179	16.6	27.1	39.6	11.8	4.9	46,055	3.2	11.0	55.1	27.5	3.1	136,748
WOOD	26,364	31,893	20.7	27.6	37.2	10.1	4.4	24,129	5.3	17.5	51.2	24.4	1.5	128,771
WISCONSIN	27,589		19.1	26.0	36.8	12.3	5.8		4.7	9.4	38.9	40.8	6.2	167,000
UNITED STATES	27,916		21.9	25.0	32.3	12.3	8.4		7.9	10.5	27.1	35.6	19.0	192,285

SPENDING POTENTIAL INDICES

COUNTY	FINANCIAL SERVICES				THE HOME						ENTERTAINMENT						PERSONAL			
					Home Improvements		Furnishings													
	Auto Loan	Home Loan	Invest-ments	Retire-ment Plans	Home Repair	Lawn & Garden	Comput-ers & Hard-ware	Major Appli-ances	TV, Radio, Sound Equip-ment	Furni-ture	Dine out/ Carry out	Sports Equip-ment	Fees & Tickets	Toys & Games	Travel	Cable TV	Apparel & Services	Auto Repairs	Health Insur-ance	Pets & Supplies
ADAMS	81	64	47	62	72	93	64	82	70	62	69	70	57	69	67	75	59	75	88	85
ASHLAND	71	58	59	59	61	72	64	68	68	60	66	60	59	68	63	71	58	66	76	69
BARRON	84	69	63	69	74	89	72	82	77	69	75	72	66	79	72	80	65	77	88	85
BAYFIELD	77	62	45	61	69	87	62	77	65	60	65	67	55	68	63	69	56	70	79	81
BROWN	97	98	103	100	94	91	100	94	98	99	98	87	100	99	97	96	89	97	94	95
BUFFALO	88	67	54	66	76	96	71	85	76	67	75	75	62	80	71	81	65	79	92	90
BURNETT	80	66	54	65	74	92	66	81	71	64	69	70	61	70	69	75	60	75	87	83
CALUMET	113	107	96	106	107	115	100	109	102	103	102	98	99	108	101	103	91	104	108	112
CHIPPEWA	86	75	71	75	79	90	75	83	79	74	78	73	72	82	76	81	68	79	88	86
CLARK	83	59	41	57	67	90	63	78	70	59	69	69	53	73	62	75	58	72	87	84
COLUMBIA	91	91	98	92	94	96	90	93	90	89	89	83	90	92	92	91	80	90	94	94
CRAWFORD	86	64	45	62	72	94	66	82	71	63	71	72	57	76	65	79	61	75	87	88
DANE	105	104	109	108	99	96	114	101	107	109	108	97	111	108	107	104	99	106	97	102
DODGE	90	89	93	89	91	95	85	90	87	86	86	79	86	90	88	89	77	86	93	92
DOOR	92	79	71	79	87	103	80	93	83	77	82	81	75	85	82	87	72	87	98	95
DOUGLAS	75	67	73	69	70	77	73	74	75	69	73	65	69	75	72	76	65	73	79	75
DUNN	87	70	61	71	72	85	79	81	79	73	79	74	70	81	74	80	69	80	84	85
EAU CLAIRE	86	80	89	83	81	83	90	84	88	84	87	77	86	88	86	87	78	86	86	85
FLORENCE	82	61	42	59	70	92	64	81	69	60	68	70	54	71	64	74	58	73	86	85
FOND DU LAC	91	89	96	90	91	95	88	91	90	88	89	80	88	92	89	91	79	88	95	92
FOREST	78	59	42	57	67	88	61	77	67	58	65	66	53	67	62	71	56	70	83	81
GRANT	83	64	55	64	70	88	71	80	75	65	74	71	62	77	69	78	64	76	86	84
GREEN	92	80	90	87	91	98	85	92	88	85	87	80	84	91	87	90	77	87	96	94
GREEN LAKE	90	74	60	73	82	100	73	88	79	72	78	77	67	82	75	83	67	81	93	93
IOWA	98	78	62	77	86	106	79	94	83	77	83	83	71	89	79	87	72	87	99	100
IRON	69	53	45	52	59	76	58	68	63	53	61	59	50	63	58	67	52	64	76	70
JACKSON	89	68	53	66	76	98	70	86	76	67	75	75	62	79	70	81	65	79	92	91
JEFFERSON	95	96	101	97	98	99	93	96	93	93	93	86	94	96	95	94	84	93	97	97
JUNEAU	85	65	51	64	71	91	67	81	74	65	72	70	59	76	67	78	62	75	88	86
KENOSHA	95	100	108	102	99	95	97	96	97	99	97	86	100	99	98	97	88	96	96	96
KEWAUNEE	94	74	61	73	83	102	75	90	81	73	80	79	68	85	76	86	69	82	97	95
LA CROSSE	88	82	91	85	82	84	91	85	89	85	88	77	87	89	87	88	79	87	88	86
LAFAYETTE	88	62	42	60	72	96	65	83	72	62	72	73	55	77	65	77	61	75	90	90
LANGLADE	76	63	60	63	69	82	65	74	70	63	69	65	61	71	66	74	60	70	82	77
LINCOLN	82	71	70	72	77	89	73	81	77	71	76	71	69	79	74	80	66	77	87	84
MANITOWOC	88	85	91	85	88	94	83	88	86	83	85	76	83	89	85	88	76	84	93	89
MARATHON	98	93	94	93	94	101	90	96	93	91	92	85	90	96	92	94	82	92	99	98
MARINETTE	78	67	63	67	73	86	67	78	72	66	71	67	64	74	69	76	62	73	84	80
MARQUETTE	81	65	50	63	72	91	65	80	71	63	69	69	59	71	67	75	60	74	86	84
MENOMINEE	64	51	42	52	53	66	53	60	57	53	57	52	48	58	53	60	50	58	64	64
MILWAUKEE	81	78	90	81	76	76	87	79	88	84	87	72	85	86	84	88	80	84	83	80
MONROE	84	71	66	70	74	87	72	80	76	70	75	71	67	79	72	79	65	76	85	83
OCONTO	92	78	66	77	82	98	76	89	81	76	80	78	72	83	78	84	69	83	94	92
ONEIDA	88	73	63	73	81	98	76	89	79	72	78	78	69	80	77	82	67	82	92	92
OUTAGAMIE	102	104	108	105	102	102	100	100	100	102	100	91	102	103	101	100	90	99	101	101
OZAUKEE	140	164	179	167	165	150	150	149	144	156	144	137	162	145	157	142	134	146	142	149
PEPIN	85	65	52	64	73	92	68	82	75	64	73	71	60	78	68	80	63	75	91	86
PIERCE	99	95	93	96	97	101	97	94	95	95	96	90	94	98	95	95	86	96	97	101
POLK	90	77	68	77	83	97	76	88	80	75	79	77	72	83	78	83	69	82	91	91
PORTAGE	92	85	89	87	86	91	91	89	90	87	90	81	87	92	88	90	80	89	91	91
PRICE	81	63	50	62	70	89	66	79	71	62	70	69	58	73	66	76	60	73	86	82
RACINE	95	102	115	104	101	97	99	97	99	101	99	87	104	101	101	99	90	97	99	97
RICHLAND	83	62	53	62	70	89	68	79	72	64	72	70	59	76	66	76	62	74	86	84
ROCK	93	94	103	96	94	95	92	93	94	93	93	82	94	96	95	95	84	92	96	94
RUSK	75	56	44	55	63	82	59	72	65	56	64	63	51	67	59	69	55	67	78	76
ST. CROIX	112	120	122	121	119	114	113	113	110	116	111	105	117	114	115	109	101	111	109	115
SAUK	91	84	85	84	87	95	85	91	87	83	86	80	82	89	86	89	76	88	94	92
SAWYER	82	65	52	64	73	92	68	82	71	64	71	71	60	72	69	75	61	76	86	85
SHAWANO	86	71	62	70	78	94	71	83	76	69	75	73	66	79	72	80	65	77	89	87
SHEBOYGAN	92	93	103	95	95	96	92	93	93	92	93	83	94	96	94	94	84	91	96	94
TAYLOR	90	69	54	67	76	97	71	86	77	68	76	76	63	80	71	81	65	79	92	91
TREMPEALEAU	86	67	53	66	74	93	68	82	74	66	73	72	61	78	68	78	63	76	88	87
VERNON	81	59	43	58	67	88	62	77	69	59	68	68	54	72	62	73	58	71	84	82
VILAS	82	67	50	66	76	97	68	85	71	65	70	73	60	71	70	75	60	77	88	88
WALWORTH	98	96	99	97	96	99	98	97	96	96	96	88	96	98	96	96	86	96	97	98
WASHBURN	80	61	46	60	69	90	64	79	70	60	68	69	56	71	65	75	58	72	86	82
WASHINGTON	111	127	133	127	125	115	116	115	112	120	113	106	123	115	120	111	103	113	110	115
WAUKESHA	132	155	164	156	152	137	140	138	134	147	135	128	151	136	146	132	125	136	131	137
WAUPACA	88	76	73	76	81	93	77	86	81	75	80	75	73	84	78	84	70	81	91	88
WAUSHARA	88	69	52	67	77	98	70	86	75	67	74	75	62	77	71	80	64	79	92	91
WINNEBAGO	92	91	101	94	91	91	94	91	94	93	93	82	94	95	93	93	84	92	93	91
WOOD	89	85	93	86	88	94	84	88	88	84	86	77	85	90	86	90	77	86	94	90
WISCONSIN	95	92	95	93	93	96	94	94	94	93	94	85	92	96	93	95	84	94	97	96
UNITED STATES	100	100	100	100	100	100	100	100	100	100	100	100	100	100	100	100	100	100	100	100

COUNTY	FIPS Code	CBSA Code	DMA Code	POPULATION			2000-2007 ANNUAL RATE		RACE (%)					
									White		Black		Asian/Pacific	
				2000	2007	2012	% Rate	State Rank	2000	2007	2000	2007	2000	2007
ALBANY	001	29660	751	32,014	33,245	33,622	0.5	13	91.3	90.2	1.1	1.2	1.8	2.3
BIG HORN	003	00000	756	11,461	11,521	11,582	0.1	17	94.0	93.9	0.1	0.1	0.3	0.3
CAMPBELL	005	23940	751	33,698	37,981	41,389	1.7	3	96.1	95.6	0.2	0.2	0.4	0.5
CARBON	007	00000	751	15,639	15,595	15,679	0.0	19	90.1	89.9	0.7	0.7	0.7	0.7
CONVERSE	009	00000	767	12,052	12,879	13,517	0.9	8	94.7	94.2	0.1	0.1	0.3	0.4
CROOK	011	00000	764	5,887	6,333	6,688	1.0	7	97.9	97.7	0.1	0.0	0.1	0.1
FREMONT	013	40180	767	35,804	37,236	38,287	0.5	13	76.5	75.1	0.1	0.1	0.3	0.4
GOSHEN	015	00000	759	12,538	12,479	12,464	-0.1	20	93.8	93.7	0.2	0.2	0.3	0.3
HOT SPRINGS	017	00000	767	4,882	4,648	4,486	-0.7	23	96.0	95.6	0.3	0.4	0.2	0.3
JOHNSON	019	00000	751	7,075	7,815	8,396	1.4	5	97.0	96.8	0.1	0.1	0.1	0.2
LARAMIE	021	16940	759	81,607	88,353	93,502	1.1	6	88.9	87.8	2.6	2.7	1.1	1.4
LINCOLN	023	00000	770	14,573	16,721	18,432	1.9	2	97.1	96.8	0.1	0.1	0.3	0.4
NATRONA	025	16220	767	66,533	70,649	73,803	0.8	10	94.2	93.5	0.8	0.8	0.5	0.6
NIOBRARA	027	00000	751	2,407	2,376	2,370	-0.2	21	98.0	98.0	0.1	0.1	0.1	0.1
PARK	029	00000	756	25,786	27,334	28,506	0.8	10	96.5	96.0	0.1	0.1	0.5	0.6
PLATTE	031	00000	751	8,807	8,889	8,927	0.1	17	96.2	96.1	0.2	0.2	0.2	0.2
SHERIDAN	033	43260	764	26,560	28,201	29,410	0.8	10	95.9	95.4	0.2	0.2	0.5	0.7
SUBLETTE	035	00000	770	5,920	6,954	7,722	2.2	1	97.5	97.3	0.2	0.2	0.3	0.4
SWEETWATER	037	40540	770	37,613	38,693	39,584	0.4	15	91.6	90.7	0.7	0.7	0.7	0.9
TETON	039	27220	758	18,251	20,227	21,393	1.4	5	93.6	92.8	0.1	0.2	0.6	0.8
UINTA	041	21740	770	19,742	20,321	20,744	0.4	15	94.3	93.7	0.1	0.1	0.3	0.4
WASHAKIE	043	00000	767	8,289	8,021	7,841	-0.5	22	90.2	89.1	0.1	0.1	0.7	1.0
WESTON	045	00000	764	6,644	6,703	6,758	0.1	17	95.9	95.9	0.1	0.1	0.2	0.2
WYOMING							0.8		92.1	91.4	0.8	0.8	0.6	0.8
UNITED STATES							1.2		75.1	72.7	12.3	12.6	3.8	4.5

POPULATION COMPOSITION

B

COUNTY	% HISPANIC ORIGIN		2007 AGE DISTRIBUTION (%)										MEDIAN AGE	% 2007 Males	% 2007 Females
	2000	2007	0-4	5-9	10-14	15-19	20-24	25-44	45-64	65-84	85+	18+	2007		
ALBANY	7.5	8.4	4.9	3.7	3.9	9.3	22.3	25.5	21.6	7.7	1.1	84.9	27.5	51.7	48.3
BIG HORN	6.2	6.3	7.2	6.5	6.5	6.7	7.7	20.6	27.4	14.6	2.8	75.5	40.3	49.7	50.3
CAMPBELL	3.5	3.9	7.5	6.7	7.3	7.5	8.3	27.2	29.2	5.8	0.6	73.8	33.8	51.4	48.6
CARBON	13.8	14.1	5.8	5.4	5.0	6.0	9.3	23.8	32.1	11.2	1.4	80.1	41.4	53.1	46.9
CONVERSE	5.5	6.1	6.4	6.2	6.9	6.8	8.1	22.3	31.9	10.1	1.3	76.0	39.7	50.0	50.0
CROOK	0.9	1.0	5.6	4.9	6.1	6.6	6.7	22.8	31.5	13.5	2.2	78.7	43.3	50.7	49.3
FREMONT	4.4	4.7	6.7	6.2	6.2	7.2	8.3	22.0	29.4	12.4	1.6	76.7	39.8	49.2	50.8
GOSHEN	8.8	9.0	6.0	5.4	5.3	7.0	7.3	21.5	29.5	15.0	3.0	79.5	42.9	49.8	50.2
HOT SPRINGS	2.4	2.6	4.9	4.7	4.5	6.4	7.7	17.7	32.4	18.4	3.4	81.7	47.3	47.6	52.4
JOHNSON	2.1	2.3	5.0	4.7	5.9	5.9	7.0	18.7	34.9	15.2	2.5	80.6	46.6	49.3	50.7
LARAMIE	10.9	12.1	6.7	6.0	6.6	6.9	7.4	28.0	26.8	9.9	1.7	76.4	36.8	50.3	49.7
LINCOLN	2.2	2.4	7.4	6.6	7.1	7.4	7.4	21.1	29.6	11.2	1.6	74.2	38.3	50.2	49.8
NATRONA	4.9	5.5	6.7	5.9	6.2	7.3	7.9	25.2	28.0	11.2	1.7	77.0	37.7	49.3	50.7
NIOBRARA	1.5	1.5	4.7	4.6	5.1	6.8	7.6	20.3	31.8	16.5	2.6	81.4	45.5	49.2	50.8
PARK	3.7	4.2	5.8	5.5	5.7	7.1	7.4	22.0	31.6	12.6	2.4	79.0	42.4	48.7	51.3
PLATTE	5.3	5.4	5.5	5.0	5.8	6.5	7.7	21.1	31.4	14.7	2.4	79.8	43.9	49.5	50.5
SHERIDAN	2.4	2.7	5.3	5.3	5.8	7.1	6.4	22.1	33.0	12.5	2.5	79.1	43.4	48.9	51.1
SUBLETTE	1.9	2.1	5.8	6.0	5.2	6.6	5.7	23.0	35.0	11.5	1.3	78.8	43.6	50.8	49.2
SWEETWATER	9.4	10.5	7.0	6.4	6.4	7.3	9.3	25.0	30.1	7.4	1.1	76.0	35.3	50.4	49.6
TETON	6.5	7.3	4.9	4.4	4.9	5.4	6.3	36.5	29.2	7.7	0.7	82.5	36.7	53.2	46.8
UINTA	5.3	6.0	8.6	7.3	7.2	8.2	10.2	24.2	27.4	6.1	0.8	71.7	31.6	50.8	49.2
WASHAKIE	11.5	12.8	6.1	5.6	6.2	8.1	8.0	20.8	29.6	13.4	2.4	76.8	41.6	49.7	50.3
WESTON	2.1	2.1	5.7	5.4	4.4	6.1	8.9	21.2	32.2	13.7	2.5	80.9	43.8	51.1	48.9
WYOMING	6.4	7.0	6.4	5.8	6.1	7.2	8.8	24.8	28.9	10.4	1.6	77.6	37.8	50.2	49.8
UNITED STATES	12.5	15.0	6.9	6.5	6.8	7.1	7.0	27.6	25.4	10.7	1.9	75.6	36.7	49.2	50.8

COUNTY	HOUSEHOLDS					FAMILIES			MEDIAN HOUSEHOLD INCOME			
	2000	2007	2012	% Annual Rate 2000-2007	2007 Average HH Size	2000	2007	% Annual Rate 2000-2007	2007	2012	2007 National Rank	2007 State Rank
ALBANY	13,269	14,239	14,563	1.0	2.17	7,001	7,189	0.4	36,080	42,339	2261	22
BIG HORN	4,312	4,408	4,452	0.3	2.56	3,087	3,073	-0.1	39,867	45,691	1742	17
CAMPBELL	12,207	14,228	15,708	2.1	2.65	9,004	10,238	1.8	60,850	69,223	247	2
CARBON	6,129	6,429	6,560	0.7	2.29	4,134	4,207	0.2	43,407	49,475	1283	11
CONVERSE	4,694	5,193	5,525	1.4	2.46	3,410	3,677	1.0	48,109	54,964	807	6
CROOK	2,308	2,595	2,783	1.6	2.40	1,646	1,802	1.3	42,702	48,190	1366	14
FREMONT	13,545	14,537	15,131	1.0	2.50	9,484	9,896	0.6	39,844	45,721	1747	18
GOSHEN	5,061	5,208	5,265	0.4	2.30	3,426	3,423	0.0	39,370	45,318	1805	19
HOT SPRINGS	2,108	2,067	2,015	-0.3	2.18	1,353	1,283	-0.7	37,796	44,281	2026	21
JOHNSON	2,959	3,375	3,671	1.8	2.29	2,005	2,219	1.4	41,963	48,229	1454	15
LARAMIE	31,927	35,577	38,047	1.5	2.39	21,600	23,353	1.1	50,505	60,221	640	5
LINCOLN	5,266	6,322	7,074	2.6	2.63	3,948	4,630	2.2	47,896	53,330	828	7
NATRONA	26,819	28,904	30,428	1.0	2.39	17,747	18,534	0.6	46,820	55,613	924	8
NIOBRARA	1,011	1,017	1,018	0.1	2.24	679	663	-0.3	36,073	41,952	2262	23
PARK	10,312	11,308	11,946	1.3	2.34	7,092	7,552	0.9	43,984	50,611	1211	10
PLATTE	3,625	3,767	3,824	0.5	2.34	2,495	2,518	0.1	41,179	46,832	1576	16
SHERIDAN	11,167	12,201	12,864	1.2	2.25	7,079	7,475	0.8	42,825	49,418	1349	13
SUBLETTE	2,371	2,870	3,222	2.7	2.40	1,707	2,013	2.3	46,316	51,926	968	9
SWEETWATER	14,105	15,043	15,617	0.9	2.53	10,096	10,488	0.5	58,111	67,306	303	3
TETON	7,688	8,705	9,268	1.7	2.31	4,177	4,532	1.1	76,422	96,824	75	1
UINTA	6,823	7,329	7,594	1.0	2.72	5,147	5,403	0.7	53,604	61,604	470	4
WASHAKIE	3,278	3,265	3,224	-0.1	2.40	2,311	2,240	-0.4	42,915	49,420	1341	12
WESTON	2,624	2,754	2,819	0.7	2.32	1,869	1,910	0.3	39,055	45,043	1843	20
WYOMING				1.2	2.41			0.8	47,628	55,650		
UNITED STATES				1.2	2.59			1.0	53,154	62,503		

COUNTY	2007 Per Capita Income	2007 HH Income Base	2007 HOUSEHOLD INCOME DISTRIBUTION (%)					2007 Home Value Base	2007 HOME VALUE DISTRIBUTION (%)					2007 Median Home Value
			Less than $25,000	$25,000 to $49,999	$50,000 to $99,999	$100,000 to $149,999	$150,000 or More		Less than $50,000	$50,000 to $89,999	$90,000 to $174,999	$175,000 to $399,999	$400,000 or More	
ALBANY	22,494	14,239	36.0	26.6	26.9	7.5	3.0	7,648	10.8	4.2	18.4	55.5	11.1	216,592
BIG HORN	18,951	4,408	29.1	33.8	29.0	5.8	2.3	3,386	10.7	16.8	41.6	25.4	5.6	137,275
CAMPBELL	25,692	14,228	15.6	23.3	42.4	14.7	4.1	10,764	11.8	8.1	29.7	43.3	7.1	175,957
CARBON	23,378	6,429	28.2	27.8	33.3	7.9	2.8	4,696	13.8	13.8	44.1	24.4	4.0	135,142
CONVERSE	22,622	5,193	27.0	24.8	36.3	9.7	2.2	3,963	8.2	8.6	43.1	34.2	6.0	158,943
CROOK	21,677	2,595	29.6	27.7	31.2	9.2	2.2	2,118	12.2	10.1	33.8	32.4	11.4	162,828
FREMONT	20,397	14,537	30.1	31.9	28.9	6.3	2.8	10,887	12.4	9.1	34.3	34.3	9.9	163,392
GOSHEN	20,599	5,208	35.1	26.6	30.4	5.6	2.3	3,803	10.7	11.4	43.0	28.7	6.3	146,558
HOT SPRINGS	22,214	2,064	32.5	30.4	26.8	8.4	1.9	1,460	10.1	11.6	45.2	25.5	7.5	151,786
JOHNSON	24,380	3,375	26.1	31.3	32.7	5.4	4.5	2,569	8.5	4.6	26.4	49.2	11.3	207,853
LARAMIE	25,583	35,577	20.3	29.0	35.3	11.1	4.2	25,325	8.6	5.6	42.3	38.8	4.7	165,283
LINCOLN	21,620	6,322	21.0	31.6	35.9	9.0	2.4	5,235	7.1	8.5	32.5	41.1	10.8	179,341
NATRONA	24,534	28,904	24.3	28.8	33.8	9.0	4.1	20,775	9.6	16.7	52.0	19.2	2.5	121,930
NIOBRARA	20,800	1,017	35.1	31.7	23.9	7.0	2.4	762	12.5	17.1	39.0	16.3	15.2	132,500
PARK	23,412	11,308	26.0	31.0	32.2	7.4	3.4	8,346	7.6	4.9	27.8	46.7	12.8	200,555
PLATTE	22,398	3,767	28.7	30.7	30.2	7.2	3.2	2,939	11.9	13.7	35.3	33.2	5.8	152,486
SHERIDAN	25,221	12,201	28.9	28.4	29.6	8.9	4.1	8,686	7.4	5.7	32.5	42.0	12.3	186,183
SUBLETTE	24,506	2,870	23.4	30.7	33.8	7.9	4.1	2,180	6.5	6.3	23.7	44.6	18.9	218,167
SWEETWATER	25,917	15,043	18.7	23.5	39.6	13.9	4.4	11,564	13.4	8.3	27.9	44.8	5.5	175,834
TETON	48,864	8,705	10.1	20.0	36.0	17.0	16.8	4,990	4.1	2.1	3.0	13.6	77.2	685,656
UINTA	21,703	7,329	21.1	24.8	42.4	9.5	2.1	5,621	10.0	7.6	40.6	38.2	3.6	161,205
WASHAKIE	23,417	3,265	28.8	29.1	28.8	8.1	5.2	2,457	7.8	8.6	45.8	31.3	6.5	154,872
WESTON	21,530	2,754	30.0	31.1	28.8	8.1	2.1	2,191	16.2	16.7	40.4	22.0	4.8	123,943
WYOMING	24,724		24.4	27.9	33.9	9.8	4.1		9.9	8.9	36.2	35.6	9.4	164,730
UNITED STATES	27,916		21.9	25.0	32.3	12.3	8.4		7.9	10.5	27.1	35.6	19.0	192,285

COUNTY	FINANCIAL SERVICES				THE HOME						ENTERTAINMENT						PERSONAL			
					Home Improvements		Furnishings													
	Auto Loan	Home Loan	Invest-ments	Retire-ment Plans	Home Repair	Lawn & Garden	Comput-ers & Hard-ware	Major Appli-ances	TV, Radio, Sound Equip-ment	Furni-ture	Dine out/ Carry out	Sports Equip-ment	Fees & Tickets	Toys & Games	Travel	Cable TV	Apparel & Services	Auto Repairs	Health Insur-ance	Pets & Supplies
ALBANY	70	56	60	60	54	59	80	64	73	66	73	62	68	70	68	69	65	71	63	65
BIG HORN	79	59	45	57	67	87	61	76	68	58	67	66	54	71	62	73	57	69	84	80
CAMPBELL	100	99	91	99	92	93	94	94	93	96	93	87	94	96	93	92	84	94	91	96
CARBON	86	69	54	68	72	89	72	82	75	70	75	73	65	78	71	78	65	79	85	86
CONVERSE	87	75	64	74	77	89	73	82	77	72	76	73	69	80	74	80	67	78	86	86
CROOK	88	66	43	64	75	97	66	84	70	64	71	74	57	75	66	75	61	76	87	90
FREMONT	78	66	60	66	70	82	68	76	71	66	70	67	63	72	68	74	61	73	80	79
GOSHEN	75	60	51	59	65	80	63	73	67	60	66	64	56	68	62	70	57	69	78	76
HOT SPRINGS	72	61	61	63	66	77	67	73	68	61	66	63	61	68	67	71	58	70	78	73
JOHNSON	89	70	52	69	80	102	72	90	76	69	75	78	63	77	74	81	64	83	95	94
LARAMIE	86	85	91	87	84	84	86	85	86	85	85	77	86	87	86	86	76	85	86	85
LINCOLN	91	77	59	75	80	96	73	87	78	73	77	77	68	80	74	81	67	81	89	91
NATRONA	82	81	85	82	79	81	81	81	82	81	81	72	81	82	81	83	73	81	84	81
NIOBRARA	77	54	41	53	62	83	60	73	68	55	66	64	50	70	59	73	55	68	84	77
PARK	83	73	69	73	76	88	74	82	77	71	75	72	70	77	75	80	66	78	87	84
PLATTE	86	65	47	63	73	95	66	83	72	64	72	72	58	76	67	77	61	75	89	88
SHERIDAN	82	74	79	75	78	88	78	83	80	74	78	73	74	79	78	82	69	80	88	84
SUBLETTE	95	77	53	75	85	107	76	95	79	74	79	83	67	81	78	84	68	86	96	99
SWEETWATER	96	94	91	94	89	92	90	91	91	91	90	82	90	93	90	91	80	91	93	92
TETON	152	153	150	160	151	142	166	152	153	160	156	155	161	152	159	147	142	160	140	153
UINTA	90	82	73	82	77	82	81	82	82	81	82	76	79	84	79	82	73	83	82	84
WASHAKIE	84	73	71	73	78	90	75	83	80	72	77	72	71	80	76	83	67	79	91	84
WESTON	82	63	47	61	69	88	65	78	71	61	70	68	57	72	65	76	59	73	86	82
WYOMING	88	80	77	80	80	88	82	85	83	80	83	77	78	84	81	84	73	84	80	87
UNITED STATES	100	100	100	100	100	100	100	100	100	100	100	100	100	100	100	100	100	100	100	100

Summary Data Section

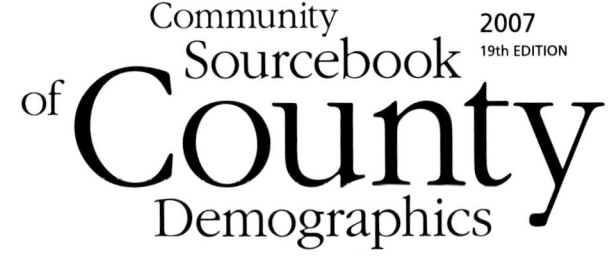

Community
Sourcebook
of
County
Demographics

2007
19th EDITION

State Summary Data

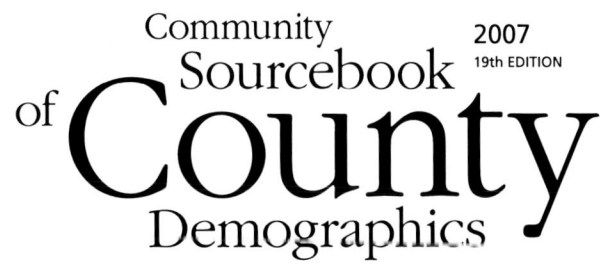

Community
Sourcebook
of **County**
Demographics

2007
19th EDITION

POPULATION CHANGE

STATE AND U.S. TOTALS

A

STATE	STATE FIPS CODE	POPULATION			2000-2007 ANNUAL RATE		RACE (%)					
							White		Black		Asian/Pacific	
		2000	2007	2012	% Rate	National Rank	2000	2007	2000	2007	2000	2007
ALABAMA	01	4,447,100	4,663,715	4,837,102	0.7	35	71.1	69.8	26.0	26.6	0.7	1.0
ALASKA	02	626,932	679,581	717,126	1.1	21	69.3	67.2	3.5	3.2	4.5	4.8
ARIZONA	04	5,130,632	6,363,799	7,443,390	3.0	2	75.5	73.0	3.1	3.2	1.9	2.3
ARKANSAS	05	2,673,400	2,889,091	3,057,156	1.1	21	80.0	78.7	15.7	15.8	0.8	1.1
CALIFORNIA	06	33,871,648	37,483,448	40,011,731	1.4	13	59.5	55.5	6.7	6.3	11.3	12.2
COLORADO	08	4,301,261	4,883,413	5,299,740	1.8	8	82.8	81.1	3.8	3.8	2.3	2.8
CONNECTICUT	09	3,405,565	3,556,875	3,659,841	0.6	39	81.6	78.8	9.1	9.7	2.5	3.5
DELAWARE	10	783,600	880,458	955,571	1.6	10	74.6	71.5	19.2	20.7	2.1	3.1
DISTRICT OF COLUMBIA	11	572,059	591,318	606,595	0.5	43	30.8	33.1	60.0	56.5	2.7	3.1
FLORIDA	12	15,982,378	18,893,813	21,311,920	2.3	4	78.0	75.4	14.6	15.6	1.7	2.2
GEORGIA	13	8,186,453	9,654,958	10,783,656	2.3	4	65.1	62.1	28.7	29.8	2.2	2.7
HAWAII	15	1,211,537	1,299,555	1,364,283	1.0	23	24.3	24.7	1.8	2.2	51.0	49.7
IDAHO	16	1,293,953	1,513,708	1,695,048	2.2	6	91.0	89.9	0.4	0.5	1.0	1.2
ILLINOIS	17	12,419,293	13,122,246	13,678,993	0.8	29	73.5	71.2	15.1	15.3	3.4	4.2
INDIANA	18	6,080,485	6,413,133	6,667,834	0.7	35	87.5	86.0	8.4	8.8	1.0	1.4
IOWA	19	2,926,324	3,030,140	3,110,913	0.5	43	93.9	92.4	2.1	2.4	1.3	2.0
KANSAS	20	2,688,418	2,811,114	2,901,178	0.6	39	86.1	84.2	5.7	5.8	1.8	2.5
KENTUCKY	21	4,041,769	4,258,898	4,416,954	0.7	35	90.1	89.2	7.3	7.5	0.8	1.1
LOUISIANA	22	4,468,976	4,385,281	4,551,245	-0.3	51	63.9	62.2	32.5	33.5	1.3	1.6
MAINE	23	1,274,923	1,352,536	1,404,394	0.8	29	96.9	96.4	0.5	0.6	0.7	1.0
MARYLAND	24	5,296,486	5,727,376	6,023,200	1.1	21	64.0	60.1	27.9	29.6	4.0	5.0
MASSACHUSETTS	25	6,349,097	6,530,311	6,655,942	0.4	46	84.5	81.7	5.4	5.9	3.8	5.0
MICHIGAN	26	9,938,444	10,322,677	10,552,949	0.5	43	80.2	78.6	14.2	14.5	1.8	2.6
MINNESOTA	27	4,919,479	5,360,578	5,685,392	1.2	19	89.4	87.5	3.5	4.1	2.9	3.7
MISSISSIPPI	28	2,844,658	2,969,306	3,072,081	0.6	39	61.4	60.1	36.3	37.0	0.7	0.9
MISSOURI	29	5,595,211	5,911,718	6,153,642	0.8	29	84.9	83.7	11.2	11.7	1.2	1.6
MONTANA	30	902,195	959,171	1,008,407	0.8	29	90.6	89.9	0.3	0.3	0.6	0.7
NEBRASKA	31	1,711,263	1,807,569	1,882,521	0.8	29	89.6	87.5	4.0	4.3	1.3	2.0
NEVADA	32	1,998,257	2,645,277	3,171,711	3.9	1	75.2	72.7	6.8	7.1	4.9	4.9
NEW HAMPSHIRE	33	1,235,786	1,352,812	1,435,390	1.3	16	96.0	95.1	0.7	0.8	1.3	1.9
NEW JERSEY	34	8,414,350	8,891,611	9,222,688	0.8	29	72.6	69.2	13.6	13.9	5.7	7.4
NEW MEXICO	35	1,819,046	1,993,495	2,131,104	1.3	16	66.8	65.4	1.9	2.0	1.1	1.4
NEW YORK	36	18,976,457	19,581,872	19,995,757	0.4	46	67.9	65.5	15.9	16.4	5.6	6.6
NORTH CAROLINA	37	8,049,313	9,068,106	9,873,032	1.7	9	72.1	70.4	21.6	21.5	1.5	2.0
NORTH DAKOTA	38	642,200	657,816	669,945	0.3	49	92.4	91.2	0.6	0.7	0.6	0.9
OHIO	39	11,353,140	11,631,492	11,848,406	0.3	49	85.0	83.5	11.5	12.0	1.2	1.8
OKLAHOMA	40	3,450,654	3,650,017	3,794,622	0.8	29	76.2	73.7	7.6	7.8	1.4	1.9
OREGON	41	3,421,399	3,752,734	4,004,796	1.3	16	86.6	84.4	1.6	1.7	3.2	3.9
PENNSYLVANIA	42	12,281,054	12,642,856	12,909,599	0.4	46	85.4	83.7	10.0	10.5	1.8	2.5
RHODE ISLAND	44	1,048,319	1,085,885	1,105,196	0.5	43	85.0	82.2	4.5	4.9	2.3	3.0
SOUTH CAROLINA	45	4,012,012	4,425,765	4,744,656	1.4	13	67.2	66.1	29.5	29.5	0.9	1.3
SOUTH DAKOTA	46	754,844	805,562	847,028	0.9	24	88.7	87.2	0.6	0.8	0.6	0.9
TENNESSEE	47	5,689,283	6,185,390	6,560,843	1.2	19	80.2	78.9	16.4	16.8	1.0	1.4
TEXAS	48	20,851,820	23,986,432	26,358,319	2.0	7	71.0	68.4	11.5	11.4	2.8	3.3
UTAH	49	2,233,169	2,610,198	2,923,928	2.2	6	89.2	88.0	0.8	0.9	2.3	2.6
VERMONT	50	608,827	636,590	654,774	0.6	39	96.8	96.2	0.5	0.6	0.9	1.2
VIRGINIA	51	7,078,515	7,862,029	8,475,970	1.5	11	72.3	69.6	19.6	20.1	3.7	4.7
WASHINGTON	53	5,894,121	6,516,384	6,975,742	1.4	13	81.8	79.6	3.2	3.4	5.9	6.6
WEST VIRGINIA	54	1,808,344	1,839,521	1,866,215	0.2	50	95.0	94.6	3.2	3.2	0.5	0.8
WISCONSIN	55	5,363,675	5,687,426	5,902,771	0.8	29	88.9	87.3	5.7	6.2	1.7	2.2
WYOMING	56	493,782	523,174	545,102	0.8	29	92.1	91.4	0.8	0.8	0.6	0.8
UNITED STATES					1.2		75.1	72.7	12.3	12.6	3.8	4.5

POPULATION COMPOSITION
STATE AND U.S. TOTALS

B

STATE	% HISPANIC ORIGIN		2007 AGE DISTRIBUTION (%)										MEDIAN AGE	% 2007 Males	% 2007 Females
	2000	2007	0-4	5-9	10-14	15-19	20-24	25-44	45-64	65-84	85+	18+	2007		
ALABAMA	1.7	2.5	6.8	6.5	6.5	6.6	6.7	27.5	26.1	11.5	1.8	76.4	37.5	48.6	51.4
ALASKA	4.1	5.2	7.5	6.6	7.4	8.2	8.6	27.0	27.8	6.4	0.6	73.4	33.9	51.3	48.7
ARIZONA	25.3	29.6	7.7	7.0	6.9	6.9	6.9	27.6	23.3	11.9	1.8	74.3	35.4	49.9	50.1
ARKANSAS	3.2	4.5	7.0	6.5	6.3	6.6	6.9	27.1	25.6	12.1	2.0	76.5	37.5	49.1	50.9
CALIFORNIA	32.4	37.2	7.5	6.9	7.8	7.6	7.3	29.0	23.5	9.0	1.5	73.4	34.2	49.9	50.1
COLORADO	17.1	19.6	6.9	6.8	6.7	7.0	7.0	29.5	26.3	8.5	1.3	75.5	35.8	50.3	49.7
CONNECTICUT	9.4	11.4	6.3	6.5	7.0	7.5	6.2	25.6	27.0	11.4	2.5	75.8	39.3	48.6	51.4
DELAWARE	4.8	6.1	6.5	6.3	6.7	7.1	6.7	27.1	25.9	12.0	1.8	76.6	38.1	48.6	51.4
DISTRICT OF COLUMBIA	7.9	8.8	5.6	5.4	5.9	7.0	7.4	32.2	24.3	10.4	1.9	79.9	35.9	47.2	52.8
FLORIDA	16.8	20.5	6.0	5.6	6.0	6.4	6.4	25.5	26.2	15.2	2.7	78.5	41.0	48.8	51.2
GEORGIA	5.3	6.9	7.3	7.0	6.9	7.0	7.1	30.3	24.6	8.7	1.3	74.8	35.0	49.4	50.6
HAWAII	7.2	8.1	6.5	6.0	6.6	6.6	7.3	27.5	26.3	11.2	1.9	76.9	37.4	50.1	49.9
IDAHO	7.9	9.0	8.0	7.1	7.0	7.5	8.1	26.8	24.7	9.3	1.6	73.6	33.9	50.1	49.9
ILLINOIS	12.3	14.9	7.1	6.9	7.1	7.0	6.8	28.3	24.7	10.2	1.9	74.8	35.9	49.1	50.9
INDIANA	3.5	4.6	7.0	6.7	6.7	7.1	7.2	27.2	25.7	10.6	1.8	75.6	36.6	49.3	50.7
IOWA	2.8	3.7	6.6	6.2	6.4	7.1	7.9	25.5	26.0	11.7	2.6	76.9	37.9	49.3	50.7
KANSAS	7.0	8.9	7.2	6.7	6.6	7.3	8.0	26.2	25.3	10.5	2.2	75.3	36.1	49.6	50.4
KENTUCKY	1.5	2.2	6.6	6.4	6.3	6.4	6.6	28.3	26.5	11.1	1.7	77.0	37.7	49.2	50.8
LOUISIANA	2.4	2.7	7.3	6.8	6.7	7.0	7.7	27.4	25.2	10.3	1.5	75.1	35.5	48.7	51.3
MAINE	0.7	1.0	5.5	5.3	5.9	7.1	6.8	24.9	30.1	12.3	2.2	79.1	41.5	48.9	51.1
MARYLAND	4.3	5.8	6.5	6.5	7.1	7.3	6.4	27.3	26.8	10.4	1.7	75.5	38.0	48.4	51.6
MASSACHUSETTS	6.8	8.4	6.1	6.2	6.7	7.4	6.6	27.6	26.1	10.9	2.3	76.8	38.3	48.4	51.6
MICHIGAN	3.3	3.9	6.7	6.5	7.0	7.2	6.8	26.8	26.5	10.7	1.8	75.6	37.4	49.2	50.8
MINNESOTA	2.9	3.8	6.9	6.5	6.6	7.2	7.4	27.6	25.7	9.9	2.1	75.7	36.8	49.6	50.4
MISSISSIPPI	1.4	1.8	7.4	7.0	6.9	7.0	7.5	27.4	24.6	10.5	1.7	74.8	35.2	48.6	51.4
MISSOURI	2.1	2.6	6.8	6.3	6.5	7.0	7.2	26.7	26.0	11.5	2.1	76.4	37.7	48.8	51.2
MONTANA	2.0	2.4	6.2	5.7	6.1	7.2	8.2	24.0	29.1	11.4	2.1	77.8	39.5	49.9	50.1
NEBRASKA	5.5	7.2	7.1	6.6	6.6	7.2	7.6	26.7	25.3	10.7	2.2	75.6	36.3	49.4	50.6
NEVADA	19.7	23.7	7.3	6.6	6.9	6.6	6.3	29.0	25.3	10.9	1.1	75.3	36.7	50.5	49.5
NEW HAMPSHIRE	1.7	2.1	5.9	5.8	6.7	7.6	6.9	25.4	29.1	10.6	1.9	77.1	39.9	49.3	50.7
NEW JERSEY	13.3	16.1	6.5	6.7	7.2	7.0	5.9	27.4	26.0	11.3	2.1	75.3	38.3	48.7	51.3
NEW MEXICO	42.1	43.7	7.5	6.7	6.9	7.5	7.9	26.3	25.4	10.3	1.5	74.5	35.3	49.2	50.8
NEW YORK	15.1	16.4	6.5	6.2	7.0	7.2	6.7	28.1	25.3	10.9	2.0	76.0	37.2	48.4	51.6
NORTH CAROLINA	4.7	6.2	6.7	6.5	6.4	6.7	6.5	29.2	25.8	10.7	1.6	76.6	37.2	49.3	50.7
NORTH DAKOTA	1.2	1.6	6.4	5.7	6.0	7.7	9.5	25.1	25.6	11.3	2.7	77.8	36.8	50.0	50.0
OHIO	1.9	2.2	6.7	6.4	6.6	7.0	7.0	26.3	26.4	11.5	2.0	76.3	38.0	48.7	51.3
OKLAHOMA	5.2	6.5	7.1	6.4	6.3	6.9	7.9	26.5	25.6	11.4	1.9	76.3	36.6	49.4	50.6
OREGON	8.0	10.5	6.5	6.1	6.3	6.8	7.2	26.7	27.7	10.6	2.0	77.1	37.8	49.7	50.3
PENNSYLVANIA	3.2	3.9	5.9	5.8	6.4	7.2	6.6	25.4	27.2	13.0	2.6	77.9	40.2	48.5	51.5
RHODE ISLAND	8.7	11.2	6.0	5.7	6.5	7.8	7.3	26.3	26.0	11.7	2.6	77.6	38.5	48.3	51.7
SOUTH CAROLINA	2.4	3.2	6.6	6.3	6.4	7.0	6.9	27.7	26.3	11.2	1.6	76.7	37.4	48.9	51.1
SOUTH DAKOTA	1.4	1.8	7.1	6.4	6.5	7.5	8.5	25.1	25.4	11.1	2.4	75.9	36.4	49.7	50.3
TENNESSEE	2.2	3.0	6.6	6.4	6.4	6.5	6.4	28.4	26.4	11.2	1.7	76.8	37.8	49.0	51.0
TEXAS	32.0	36.4	8.0	7.4	7.2	7.3	7.8	28.9	23.5	8.6	1.3	73.1	33.4	49.7	50.3
UTAH	9.0	10.4	10.4	8.9	7.6	7.5	8.7	30.0	18.7	7.0	1.1	68.9	28.3	50.1	49.9
VERMONT	0.9	1.1	5.5	5.3	6.1	7.8	7.7	24.5	30.2	11.0	2.0	78.8	40.5	49.2	50.8
VIRGINIA	4.7	6.4	6.5	6.5	6.6	7.0	6.6	28.5	26.5	10.2	1.5	76.4	37.6	49.2	50.8
WASHINGTON	7.5	9.2	6.7	6.3	6.7	7.1	7.5	27.5	26.8	9.7	1.8	76.2	36.9	49.8	50.2
WEST VIRGINIA	0.7	0.8	5.6	5.5	5.6	6.0	6.3	26.3	29.0	13.6	2.1	79.9	41.1	49.0	51.0
WISCONSIN	3.6	4.5	6.5	6.1	6.4	7.3	7.9	26.2	26.6	10.8	2.2	76.8	37.9	49.5	50.5
WYOMING	6.4	7.0	6.4	5.8	6.1	7.2	8.8	24.8	28.9	10.4	1.6	77.6	37.8	50.2	49.8
UNITED STATES	12.5	15.0	6.9	6.5	6.8	7.1	7.0	27.6	25.4	10.7	1.9	75.6	36.7	49.2	50.8

HOUSEHOLDS
STATE AND U.S. TOTALS

C

STATE	HOUSEHOLDS					FAMILIES			MEDIAN HOUSEHOLD INCOME		
	2000	2007	2012	% Annual Rate 2000-2007	2007 Average HH Size	2000	2007	% Annual Rate 2000-2007	2007	2012	2007 National Rank
ALABAMA	1,737,080	1,858,450	1,943,747	0.9	2.45	1,215,968	1,277,539	0.7	39,727	44,191	47
ALASKA	221,600	242,510	257,103	1.3	2.71	152,337	163,958	1.0	63,746	74,891	5
ARIZONA	1,901,327	2,354,799	2,755,516	3.0	2.65	1,287,367	1,575,121	2.8	53,299	64,719	22
ARKANSAS	1,042,696	1,137,621	1,209,498	1.2	2.47	732,261	776,634	0.8	41,124	48,510	46
CALIFORNIA	11,502,870	12,540,420	13,323,850	1.2	2.92	7,920,049	8,694,399	1.3	60,268	70,268	9
COLORADO	1,658,238	1,880,935	2,037,154	1.8	2.54	1,084,461	1,209,950	1.5	60,976	72,859	8
CONNECTICUT	1,301,670	1,360,574	1,404,376	0.6	2.53	881,170	914,102	0.5	68,430	81,316	2
DELAWARE	298,736	336,020	366,757	1.6	2.55	204,590	224,368	1.3	60,094	69,601	10
DISTRICT OF COLUMBIA	248,338	260,635	269,548	0.7	2.13	114,166	115,517	0.2	50,151	58,997	30
FLORIDA	6,337,929	7,510,601	8,501,036	2.4	2.46	4,210,760	4,910,148	2.1	48,591	56,912	34
GEORGIA	3,006,369	3,554,655	3,973,517	2.3	2.65	2,111,647	2,434,464	2.0	55,102	65,884	18
HAWAII	403,240	441,517	467,348	1.3	2.86	287,068	310,276	1.1	59,776	67,554	12
IDAHO	469,645	558,578	628,244	2.4	2.65	335,588	394,388	2.3	48,501	58,059	35
ILLINOIS	4,591,779	4,844,339	5,044,162	0.7	2.64	3,105,513	3,197,064	0.4	58,985	68,478	14
INDIANA	2,336,306	2,507,578	2,621,920	1.0	2.49	1,602,501	1,660,827	0.5	52,632	61,929	24
IOWA	1,149,276	1,213,728	1,253,509	0.8	2.41	769,684	796,716	0.5	49,331	57,806	32
KANSAS	1,037,891	1,091,910	1,129,364	0.7	2.50	701,547	728,510	0.5	51,343	60,554	27
KENTUCKY	1,590,647	1,717,791	1,797,003	1.1	2.41	1,104,398	1,152,369	0.6	42,861	50,528	44
LOUISIANA	1,656,053	1,645,507	1,720,644	-0.1	2.59	1,156,438	1,131,229	-0.3	37,186	40,783	49
MAINE	518,200	562,502	590,710	1.1	2.34	340,685	362,289	0.9	45,463	52,125	40
MARYLAND	1,980,859	2,143,641	2,260,638	1.1	2.61	1,359,318	1,430,232	0.7	65,627	76,746	4
MASSACHUSETTS	2,443,580	2,526,982	2,584,319	0.5	2.50	1,576,646	1,613,524	0.3	66,046	79,243	3
MICHIGAN	3,785,661	3,990,807	4,107,776	0.7	2.52	2,575,699	2,643,367	0.4	54,480	62,717	20
MINNESOTA	1,895,127	2,096,099	2,232,066	1.4	2.49	1,255,141	1,355,548	1.1	61,307	73,160	7
MISSISSIPPI	1,046,434	1,116,597	1,165,347	0.9	2.57	747,159	780,875	0.6	35,903	39,445	51
MISSOURI	2,194,594	2,341,592	2,447,596	0.9	2.45	1,476,516	1,535,908	0.5	47,568	55,657	37
MONTANA	358,667	384,213	405,956	1.0	2.43	237,407	246,568	0.5	39,634	45,166	48
NEBRASKA	666,184	710,662	743,147	0.9	2.47	443,411	467,332	0.7	49,064	57,487	33
NEVADA	751,165	994,525	1,190,546	3.9	2.63	498,333	651,983	3.8	56,308	65,921	17
NEW HAMPSHIRE	474,606	523,423	558,576	1.4	2.51	323,651	351,688	1.2	62,216	72,795	6
NEW JERSEY	3,064,645	3,232,069	3,356,278	0.7	2.69	2,154,539	2,268,169	0.7	69,831	81,268	1
NEW MEXICO	677,971	763,192	823,599	1.6	2.56	466,515	508,968	1.2	43,379	51,081	43
NEW YORK	7,056,860	7,279,758	7,446,125	0.4	2.61	4,639,387	4,747,142	0.3	56,704	67,544	16
NORTH CAROLINA	3,132,013	3,583,756	3,924,768	1.9	2.45	2,158,869	2,404,772	1.5	49,687	58,375	31
NORTH DAKOTA	257,152	271,093	279,538	0.7	2.33	166,150	167,488	0.1	44,455	52,373	42
OHIO	4,445,773	4,621,957	4,735,863	0.5	2.45	2,993,023	3,023,510	0.1	50,660	58,568	29
OKLAHOMA	1,342,293	1,434,397	1,497,441	0.9	2.46	921,750	966,434	0.7	41,984	48,966	45
OREGON	1,333,723	1,461,068	1,560,770	1.3	2.51	877,671	954,138	1.2	51,735	60,975	25
PENNSYLVANIA	4,777,003	4,965,988	5,094,984	0.5	2.45	3,208,388	3,244,580	0.2	51,375	60,635	26
RHODE ISLAND	408,424	420,492	429,569	0.4	2.48	265,398	267,335	0.1	53,334	62,664	21
SOUTH CAROLINA	1,533,854	1,737,176	1,884,758	1.7	2.47	1,072,822	1,172,497	1.2	46,513	54,235	38
SOUTH DAKOTA	290,245	316,679	335,476	1.2	2.45	194,330	210,558	1.1	45,336	54,010	41
TENNESSEE	2,232,905	2,466,845	2,632,633	1.4	2.45	1,547,835	1,669,106	1.0	46,151	54,180	39
TEXAS	7,393,354	8,462,224	9,291,022	1.9	2.76	5,247,794	5,961,828	1.8	51,090	60,298	28
UTAH	701,281	826,106	926,971	2.3	3.11	535,294	619,270	2.0	58,372	69,104	15
VERMONT	240,634	259,301	269,536	1.0	2.37	157,763	165,131	0.6	52,729	63,137	23
VIRGINIA	2,699,173	3,022,239	3,267,453	1.6	2.52	1,847,796	2,018,669	1.2	59,797	70,833	11
WASHINGTON	2,271,398	2,514,308	2,695,030	1.4	2.53	1,499,127	1,636,830	1.2	59,060	70,229	13
WEST VIRGINIA	736,481	767,587	786,321	0.6	2.33	504,055	509,536	0.1	36,308	41,679	50
WISCONSIN	2,084,544	2,270,252	2,378,939	1.2	2.43	1,386,815	1,475,680	0.9	54,628	63,236	19
WYOMING	193,608	211,341	222,618	1.2	2.41	130,497	138,318	0.8	47,628	55,650	36
UNITED STATES				1.2	2.59			1.0	53,154	62,503	

STATE	2007 Per Capita Income	2007 HH Income Base	2007 HOUSEHOLD INCOME DISTRIBUTION (%)					2007 Home Value Base	2007 HOME VALUE DISTRIBUTION (%)					2007 Median Home Value
			Less than $25,000	$25,000 to $49,999	$50,000 to $99,999	$100,000 to $149,999	$150,000 or More		Less than $50,000	$50,000 to $89,999	$90,000 to $174,999	$175,000 to $399,999	$400,000 or More	
ALABAMA	21,955	1,858,448	32.2	28.3	27.3	8.4	3.9	1,377,002	17.5	21.0	36.4	20.7	4.4	110,498
ALASKA	29,430	242,510	15.5	22.7	34.8	17.1	9.9	161,698	7.5	5.6	19.9	55.6	11.4	227,284
ARIZONA	27,079	2,354,768	20.3	26.3	32.8	12.5	8.0	1,627,508	5.3	4.7	19.5	50.1	20.5	241,092
ARKANSAS	21,735	1,137,620	30.3	29.3	29.3	7.0	4.1	810,182	20.3	25.0	35.7	16.0	3.1	98,558
CALIFORNIA	28,915	12,540,215	19.6	22.1	31.8	14.6	11.8	7,343,605	2.0	1.7	4.1	28.4	63.8	499,578
COLORADO	31,684	1,880,918	16.6	23.3	35.2	14.4	10.6	1,323,243	4.0	3.5	20.1	55.0	17.5	234,884
CONNECTICUT	37,645	1,360,568	16.3	20.0	31.6	17.3	14.8	949,427	1.0	1.5	11.2	54.8	31.5	297,091
DELAWARE	29,822	336,020	17.6	23.2	35.5	14.7	8.9	250,506	5.3	3.5	16.6	58.2	16.4	244,022
DISTRICT OF COLUMBIA	37,402	260,626	26.1	23.8	26.5	11.5	12.0	112,895	0.3	0.4	3.3	42.1	53.9	429,220
FLORIDA	27,311	7,510,552	23.3	28.0	31.3	10.4	7.0	5,467,546	3.9	5.6	21.7	48.5	20.2	231,576
GEORGIA	28,047	3,554,639	21.3	23.7	33.4	12.5	9.2	2,453,085	9.8	12.6	35.8	33.1	8.8	148,827
HAWAII	27,254	441,507	18.6	23.0	33.0	16.3	9.1	260,706	0.7	0.9	2.8	22.9	72.8	603,121
IDAHO	23,464	558,574	22.4	29.2	33.6	9.9	4.9	413,335	6.5	7.0	36.2	41.2	9.1	175,701
ILLINOIS	29,497	4,844,255	19.3	22.8	34.2	14.1	9.6	3,383,663	5.2	7.9	27.4	44.0	15.4	208,761
INDIANA	26,366	2,507,528	20.8	26.3	35.6	11.7	5.6	1,821,254	10.4	20.0	44.7	21.9	3.0	119,366
IOWA	25,252	1,213,728	21.8	28.9	35.0	9.8	4.5	899,228	13.7	20.9	42.4	20.1	2.9	113,209
KANSAS	26,438	1,091,901	20.9	27.6	34.5	10.6	6.4	773,422	16.9	21.4	36.0	22.2	3.5	112,948
KENTUCKY	23,912	1,717,779	29.2	27.7	29.0	9.1	4.9	1,228,616	18.5	19.6	39.0	19.8	3.1	112,948
LOUISIANA	19,796	1,645,459	34.5	28.1	26.2	7.6	3.6	1,131,603	18.1	19.9	36.5	21.5	3.9	109,419
MAINE	24,625	562,498	25.8	28.9	32.3	8.8	4.2	406,482	5.6	8.4	33.1	43.3	9.6	112,331
MARYLAND	33,153	2,143,594	15.6	21.1	34.4	17.0	12.0	1,489,630	1.5	1.8	9.6	50.5	36.6	341,459
MASSACHUSETTS	35,397	2,526,961	18.4	19.5	31.6	17.1	13.3	1,611,145	0.6	0.8	8.0	51.5	39.0	348,621
MICHIGAN	27,982	3,990,766	20.7	25.1	33.5	13.3	7.4	2,977,774	9.3	13.4	39.3	32.1	5.8	145,372
MINNESOTA	31,101	2,096,098	16.5	23.5	36.5	14.2	9.3	1,599,981	5.0	7.2	28.0	48.9	11.0	201,524
MISSISSIPPI	18,800	1,116,595	35.6	29.5	25.6	6.3	3.0	811,065	22.0	26.4	34.0	15.1	2.5	92,555
MISSOURI	25,475	2,341,567	24.2	28.2	31.9	10.2	5.6	1,688,799	11.5	16.8	39.7	26.8	5.2	130,140
MONTANA	20,909	384,203	30.5	31.5	28.6	6.4	3.0	265,625	10.3	9.3	31.2	38.7	10.6	173,301
NEBRASKA	25,004	710,660	21.9	29.0	34.0	10.1	5.0	498,401	14.0	19.3	43.3	20.4	3.0	115,851
NEVADA	27,752	994,510	18.0	25.5	36.4	12.5	7.7	621,933	3.6	2.3	8.4	61.8	24.0	297,001
NEW HAMPSHIRE	31,189	523,423	15.5	23.1	37.5	14.4	9.5	375,635	3.2	3.9	18.7	57.5	16.6	245,115
NEW JERSEY	35,359	3,232,020	16.3	19.2	32.4	16.6	15.6	2,214,791	0.9	1.4	7.2	49.0	41.6	362,535
NEW MEXICO	22,579	763,172	28.7	28.0	29.3	9.0	4.9	535,918	12.5	11.8	31.7	34.9	9.1	159,748
NEW YORK	31,116	7,279,584	22.5	22.2	30.6	13.1	11.7	4,046,282	2.9	4.7	19.9	38.6	33.8	296,301
NORTH CAROLINA	26,409	3,583,753	23.6	26.7	33.2	10.0	6.5	2,530,170	11.3	13.3	38.1	30.6	6.7	139,312
NORTH DAKOTA	23,628	271,089	26.1	29.8	32.3	7.9	3.8	182,190	21.5	19.2	39.8	17.7	1.8	105,753
OHIO	26,868	4,621,936	22.0	27.3	32.9	11.6	6.2	3,330,685	8.1	16.4	45.5	26.3	3.7	129,643
OKLAHOMA	22,509	1,434,389	28.9	29.5	29.2	8.2	4.2	984,176	20.6	25.7	36.9	14.4	2.4	95,826
OREGON	26,912	1,461,067	20.9	27.2	34.2	10.9	6.8	974,567	4.3	3.4	15.0	55.1	22.2	267,166
PENNSYLVANIA	27,602	4,965,964	22.8	25.8	32.4	11.8	7.1	3,576,793	7.0	10.9	34.4	38.2	9.5	169,830
RHODE ISLAND	27,627	420,492	24.0	22.9	33.1	12.2	7.8	253,547	0.7	0.7	4.9	69.8	24.0	301,595
SOUTH CAROLINA	24,375	1,737,163	25.8	27.6	31.7	9.7	5.2	1,280,371	14.4	17.5	37.6	24.2	6.4	123,378
SOUTH DAKOTA	23,161	316,675	25.2	29.7	32.9	8.1	4.1	220,142	20.2	18.5	39.3	19.0	3.0	111,328
TENNESSEE	24,928	2,466,838	26.4	27.4	31.5	9.3	5.4	1,753,150	10.8	17.5	40.9	25.4	5.4	127,358
TEXAS	25,413	8,462,123	22.9	25.9	31.0	12.0	8.1	5,564,188	16.4	21.8	36.0	21.0	4.7	110,551
UTAH	23,819	826,102	15.8	25.4	37.4	13.9	7.5	601,508	3.0	3.1	27.4	55.1	11.4	211,217
VERMONT	27,894	259,301	20.7	26.2	35.8	11.0	6.3	189,401	3.4	4.4	26.0	53.4	12.7	213,014
VIRGINIA	31,988	3,022,224	18.1	23.3	33.3	14.5	10.8	2,086,231	4.3	4.3	19.9	46.6	25.0	249,117
WASHINGTON	29,955	2,514,292	18.1	24.0	34.9	14.5	8.6	1,696,419	3.1	2.6	13.9	51.3	29.1	289,249
WEST VIRGINIA	20,634	767,587	35.2	29.6	26.0	6.3	2.9	593,708	21.9	22.6	36.9	16.0	2.6	98,467
WISCONSIN	27,589	2,270,243	19.1	26.0	36.8	12.3	5.8	1,594,260	4.7	9.4	38.9	40.8	6.2	167,603
WYOMING	24,724	211,338	24.4	27.9	33.9	9.8	4.1	152,365	9.9	8.9	36.2	35.6	9.4	164,730
UNITED STATES	27,916		21.9	25.0	32.3	12.3	8.4		7.9	10.5	27.1	35.6	19.0	192,285

STATE	Auto Loan	Home Loan	Invest-ments	Retire-ment Plans	Home Repair	Lawn & Garden	Comput-ers & Hard-ware	Major Appli-ances	TV, Radio, Sound Equip-ment	Furni-ture	Dine out/ Carry out	Sports Equip-ment	Fees & Tickets	Toys & Games	Travel	Cable TV	Apparel & Services	Auto Repairs	Health Insur-ance	Pets & Supplies
ALABAMA	83	70	62	70	71	83	72	77	76	71	76	69	67	77	71	79	67	76	82	81
ALASKA	114	113	109	115	107	106	114	109	110	113	111	103	112	112	110	108	100	112	105	110
ARIZONA	102	100	98	99	96	98	100	99	99	101	99	91	99	97	99	99	89	102	100	99
ARKANSAS	84	69	61	69	71	85	72	79	77	70	76	70	66	78	71	80	66	77	84	82
CALIFORNIA	111	119	116	117	117	105	123	116	115	120	116	117	121	113	120	110	108	120	106	112
COLORADO	112	113	113	115	110	107	115	110	111	114	112	104	114	112	112	109	101	112	106	110
CONNECTICUT	120	139	155	139	141	127	135	130	132	137	132	121	144	130	139	131	123	130	127	128
DELAWARE	106	108	110	108	108	108	105	106	105	106	105	96	107	105	107	106	95	106	107	107
DISTRICT OF COLUMBIA	101	96	104	102	97	92	117	100	119	113	122	97	115	114	111	120	114	109	103	102
FLORIDA	93	92	96	92	92	95	92	93	93	93	93	84	92	91	94	95	83	95	97	93
GEORGIA	111	102	94	103	98	104	103	103	104	103	104	96	100	106	100	104	93	104	104	106
HAWAII	100	112	112	111	111	99	115	108	105	111	106	108	114	104	113	101	98	111	99	106
IDAHO	93	85	78	85	84	91	86	89	86	84	86	81	82	88	84	87	76	87	90	91
ILLINOIS	105	108	112	109	108	104	109	106	109	109	109	99	110	109	109	108	100	107	106	106
INDIANA	95	89	91	91	89	94	90	92	93	90	92	82	89	95	90	94	82	91	95	93
IOWA	90	81	80	82	83	92	84	88	87	81	85	78	80	88	83	88	76	86	93	90
KANSAS	97	89	88	90	89	95	92	93	93	90	93	84	88	95	90	94	82	93	97	95
KENTUCKY	89	76	68	75	77	89	78	84	82	76	81	75	73	84	77	84	71	82	88	87
LOUISIANA	77	67	62	67	67	75	69	72	73	68	72	65	66	73	68	75	64	72	76	75
MAINE	85	77	75	77	80	90	79	84	81	77	80	75	75	81	79	83	71	82	88	87
MARYLAND	114	125	131	125	124	115	121	117	119	124	120	109	127	119	123	118	110	118	114	117
MASSACHUSETTS	110	128	138	126	131	116	126	120	122	127	124	114	133	120	129	122	116	120	116	118
MICHIGAN	99	98	103	100	98	100	97	98	99	98	98	88	98	100	98	100	89	98	101	99
MINNESOTA	109	109	110	111	109	110	109	108	107	109	108	100	109	109	108	107	97	108	108	110
MISSISSIPPI	77	62	52	62	63	76	64	70	69	63	69	63	59	71	63	72	60	69	75	74
MISSOURI	92	84	84	85	84	91	86	88	88	85	88	79	83	89	85	90	78	87	92	90
MONTANA	76	66	63	66	68	78	70	74	72	67	71	66	65	72	69	74	62	72	78	76
NEBRASKA	92	82	79	83	83	91	85	88	87	84	87	80	81	89	84	88	77	87	92	91
NEVADA	101	100	99	102	96	95	103	98	100	102	100	93	101	100	100	98	91	102	96	98
NEW HAMPSHIRE	108	112	116	114	113	111	110	110	108	110	108	101	112	109	111	107	98	109	108	111
NEW JERSEY	117	139	148	136	142	125	133	129	130	136	132	121	143	128	138	130	124	128	124	126
NEW MEXICO	85	78	74	78	76	81	79	81	81	79	80	74	77	80	78	81	72	81	82	81
NEW YORK	99	107	114	107	111	103	113	107	115	112	117	100	117	111	114	117	110	108	109	107
NORTH CAROLINA	99	87	79	87	87	97	89	93	91	88	91	73	84	93	87	93	81	92	96	96
NORTH DAKOTA	85	70	65	71	72	83	78	80	79	73	79	73	70	81	74	81	69	80	84	83
OHIO	92	90	97	92	91	93	91	91	93	91	92	81	91	93	91	94	83	91	95	92
OKLAHOMA	84	72	69	73	73	82	76	79	79	74	78	71	72	80	74	81	69	78	84	81
OREGON	95	92	93	93	92	95	95	94	94	93	94	87	93	94	94	94	84	95	95	95
PENNSYLVANIA	93	94	102	94	97	99	93	95	96	93	95	84	95	95	95	98	86	93	100	96
RHODE ISLAND	87	97	109	97	98	90	98	93	96	98	97	88	102	95	99	96	90	95	92	92
SOUTH CAROLINA	93	80	72	80	81	92	81	87	85	81	85	78	77	87	80	88	75	86	91	90
SOUTH DAKOTA	87	74	68	74	76	87	79	83	81	75	80	75	72	83	76	83	70	81	87	86
TENNESSEE	93	80	75	81	81	92	83	87	86	81	86	78	78	88	81	88	76	86	91	90
TEXAS	104	95	88	96	90	94	98	96	99	98	99	90	94	99	94	98	89	99	96	97
UTAH	105	106	103	107	100	98	105	101	102	105	102	95	104	104	102	99	92	103	97	101
VERMONT	97	90	89	91	94	102	92	97	93	89	92	87	88	94	92	94	82	94	100	99
VIRGINIA	115	113	112	114	112	114	113	112	112	113	112	104	112	114	112	112	102	113	112	114
WASHINGTON	105	105	108	107	104	102	108	104	105	106	105	97	107	105	106	104	96	106	102	104
WEST VIRGINIA	76	61	53	59	65	80	64	72	69	61	68	64	58	70	63	73	59	69	80	76
WISCONSIN	95	92	95	93	93	96	94	94	94	93	94	85	92	96	93	95	84	94	97	96
WYOMING	88	80	77	80	80	88	82	85	83	80	83	77	78	84	81	84	73	84	88	87
UNITED STATES	100	100	100	100	100	100	100	100	100	100	100	100	100	100	100	100	100	100	100	100

CBSA Summary Data

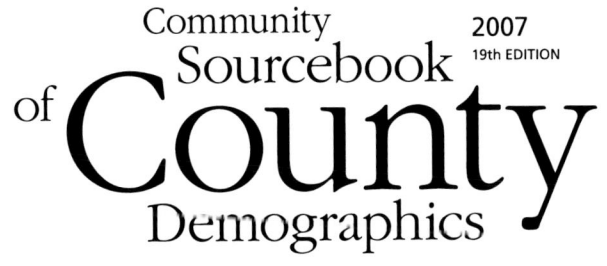

Community
Sourcebook 2007
19th EDITION
of County
Demographics

POPULATION CHANGE

CBSA AND U.S. TOTALS

CBSA	CBSA Code	POPULATION			2000-2007 ANNUAL RATE		RACE (%)					
							White		Black		Asian/Pacific	
		2000	2007	2012	% Rate	National Rank	2000	2007	2000	2007	2000	2007
ABBEVILLE, LA	10020	53,807	56,659	58,905	0.7	444	82.7	78.1	14.2	17.4	1.8	2.9
ABERDEEN, SD	10100	39,827	39,372	39,208	-0.2	841	95.9	94.9	0.3	0.3	0.4	0.7
ABERDEEN, WA	10140	67,194	71,744	73,608	0.9	352	88.3	87.0	0.3	0.4	1.3	1.5
ABILENE, TX	10180	160,245	161,677	162,981	0.1	723	81.5	78.5	6.8	6.8	1.1	1.4
ADA, OK	10220	35,143	35,750	36,229	0.2	679	75.8	73.6	2.1	2.2	0.5	0.6
ADRIAN, MI	10300	98,890	103,377	106,648	0.6	494	92.5	91.2	2.1	2.3	0.5	0.7
AKRON, OH	10420	694,960	707,682	715,326	0.3	633	85.9	84.1	11.0	12.0	1.3	1.9
ALAMOGORDO, NM	10460	62,298	64,998	66,623	0.6	494	73.7	72.2	3.9	4.1	1.3	1.5
ALBANY, GA	10500	157,833	164,709	170,210	0.6	494	49.3	47.1	48.7	50.5	0.6	0.7
ALBANY-LEBANON, OR	10540	103,069	111,474	117,958	1.1	288	93.2	92.1	0.3	0.4	0.9	1.1
ALBANY-SCH.-TROY, NY	10580	825,875	861,146	887,316	0.6	494	89.1	87.3	6.4	7.1	1.9	2.5
ALBEMARLE, NC	10620	58,100	60,470	61,823	0.6	494	84.7	83.2	11.5	11.7	1.8	2.4
ALBERT LEA, MN	10660	32,584	32,194	31,886	-0.2	841	95.2	93.8	0.2	0.3	0.6	0.8
ALBERTVILLE, AL	10700	82,231	88,120	92,643	1.0	318	93.4	91.2	1.5	1.5	0.3	0.4
ALBUQUERQUE, NM	10740	729,649	833,634	918,967	1.9	113	69.7	68.2	2.5	2.6	1.7	2.0
ALEXANDER CITY, AL	10760	53,677	53,654	53,061	0.0	765	71.3	70.6	27.4	28.0	0.2	0.2
ALEXANDRIA, LA	10780	145,035	151,638	155,611	0.6	494	68.9	65.2	28.0	31.1	0.8	1.1
ALEXANDRIA, MN	10820	32,821	37,177	40,280	1.7	140	98.5	98.1	0.2	0.2	0.4	0.6
ALICE, TX	10860	39,326	41,199	42,280	0.6	494	77.9	76.4	0.6	0.6	0.5	0.6
ALLEGAN, MI	10880	105,665	116,417	123,841	1.3	225	93.5	92.2	1.3	1.4	0.6	0.8
ALLENTWN-BETH-EASTON	10900	740,395	808,151	859,071	1.2	255	90.4	88.4	2.8	3.2	1.6	2.2
ALMA, MI	10940	42,285	42,503	42,688	0.1	723	92.0	90.8	3.7	4.1	0.4	0.5
ALPENA, MI	10980	31,314	30,120	29,298	-0.5	911	98.2	97.9	0.2	0.3	0.3	0.5
ALTOONA, PA	11020	129,144	126,760	124,568	-0.3	873	97.6	97.1	1.2	1.4	0.4	0.5
ALTUS, OK	11060	28,439	26,987	25,829	-0.7	926	76.1	72.6	8.0	8.2	1.3	1.7
AMARILLO, TX	11100	226,522	242,048	251,575	0.9	352	79.6	76.4	5.7	5.8	1.8	2.1
AMERICUS, GA	11140	36,966	37,440	37,346	0.2	679	50.0	47.4	47.2	49.7	0.6	0.6
AMES, IA	11180	79,981	85,539	88,147	0.9	352	91.1	88.1	1.8	2.1	5.1	7.7
AMSTERDAM, NY	11220	49,708	49,397	49,264	-0.1	805	94.9	94.0	1.2	1.3	0.5	0.7
ANCHORAGE, AK	11260	319,605	364,248	396,178	1.8	127	75.1	72.7	4.9	4.3	5.4	5.7
ANDERSON, IN	11300	133,358	131,896	131,035	-0.2	841	89.9	88.5	7.9	8.7	0.4	0.6
ANDERSON, SC	11340	165,740	180,513	191,510	1.2	255	81.6	80.5	16.6	17.1	0.4	0.6
ANDREWS, TX	11380	13,004	12,717	12,543	-0.3	873	77.1	73.4	1.6	1.6	0.7	0.8
ANGOLA, IN	11420	33,214	35,377	36,996	0.9	352	97.2	96.5	0.4	0.4	0.4	0.6
ANN ARBOR, MI	11460	322,895	354,947	374,037	1.3	225	77.4	73.7	12.3	13.0	6.3	8.9
ANNISTON-OXFORD, AL	11500	112,249	112,267	112,506	0.0	765	78.9	78.3	18.5	19.0	0.6	0.6
APPLETON, WI	11540	201,602	223,334	237,999	1.4	196	94.4	93.1	0.5	0.6	2.1	2.9
ARCADIA, FL	11580	32,209	34,935	36,965	1.1	288	73.3	68.7	12.7	13.6	0.4	0.5
ARDMORE, OK	11620	54,452	57,012	58,800	0.6	494	78.9	76.7	6.7	7.1	0.6	0.6
ARKADELPHIA, AR	11660	23,546	23,745	24,043	0.1	723	74.3	71.6	22.0	23.8	0.7	0.9
ASHEVILLE, NC	11700	369,171	407,274	434,770	1.4	196	91.5	90.1	5.1	5.5	0.6	0.8
ASHLAND, OH	11740	52,523	54,553	55,706	0.5	545	97.5	97.0	0.8	0.9	0.6	0.9
ASHTABULA, OH	11780	102,728	104,283	105,168	0.2	679	94.1	93.2	3.2	3.5	0.4	0.5
ASTORIA, OR	11820	35,630	37,028	38,069	0.5	545	93.1	91.9	0.5	0.6	1.4	1.7
ATCHISON, KS	11860	16,774	16,708	16,658	-0.1	805	91.6	91.3	5.3	5.5	0.4	0.4
ATHENS, OH	11900	62,223	62,134	62,384	0.0	765	93.5	93.3	2.4	2.5	1.9	2.0
ATHENS, TN	11940	49,015	51,868	53,642	0.8	396	92.7	91.5	4.5	4.9	0.7	1.0
ATHENS, TX	11980	73,277	82,205	88,927	1.6	155	88.5	86.6	6.6	7.2	0.3	0.4
ATHENS-CLARKE CTY,GA	12020	166,079	190,136	204,819	1.9	113	73.5	69.7	20.5	22.5	2.2	2.8
ATLANTA-SNDY SPRINGS	12060	4,247,981	5,322,915	6,166,421	3.2	30	63.5	60.9	28.6	29.2	3.3	3.9
ATLANTIC CITY, NJ	12100	252,552	280,554	302,352	1.5	173	68.4	63.8	17.6	18.5	5.1	6.6
AUBURN, IN	12140	40,285	42,120	43,391	0.6	494	97.8	97.2	0.3	0.3	0.4	0.5
AUBURN, NY	12180	81,963	81,764	81,958	0.0	765	93.3	92.3	4.0	4.5	0.4	0.6
AUBURN-OPELIKA, AL	12220	115,092	130,385	141,287	1.7	140	74.1	71.9	22.7	23.7	1.7	2.3
AUGUSTA-RICHMOND CTY	12260	499,684	541,258	571,794	1.1	288	60.8	58.5	35.1	36.2	1.5	2.0
AUGUSTA-WATERV.,ME	12300	117,114	123,172	127,809	0.7	444	97.5	97.0	0.3	0.4	0.6	0.9
AUSTIN, MN	12380	38,603	39,251	39,686	0.2	679	94.7	93.1	0.6	0.7	1.5	2.0
AUSTIN-ROUND ROCK,TX	12420	1,249,763	1,569,880	1,820,572	3.2	30	72.5	69.2	8.0	7.9	3.6	4.1
BAINBRIDGE, GA	12460	28,240	29,981	31,172	0.8	396	57.1	52.1	39.9	44.0	0.4	0.5
BAKERSFIELD, CA	12540	661,645	796,111	907,690	2.6	57	61.6	56.9	6.0	5.8	3.5	3.9
BALTIMORE-TOWSON, MD	12580	2,552,994	2,699,671	2,798,670	0.8	396	67.3	63.9	27.4	29.3	2.7	3.6
BANGOR, ME	12620	144,919	149,947	153,534	0.5	545	96.6	96.0	0.5	0.6	0.7	1.0
BARABOO, WI	12660	55,225	61,299	65,585	1.4	196	97.4	96.9	0.3	0.3	0.3	0.4
BARNSTABLE TOWN, MA	12700	222,230	230,069	235,166	0.5	545	94.2	93.2	1.8	2.1	0.7	0.9
BARRE, VT	12740	58,039	60,460	62,253	0.6	494	97.0	96.6	0.5	0.6	0.6	0.8
BARTLESVILLE, OK	12780	48,996	49,237	49,267	0.1	723	81.2	78.7	2.5	2.6	0.8	1.0
BASTROP, LA	12820	31,021	30,188	29,171	-0.4	896	55.8	51.4	43.4	47.6	0.2	0.3
BATAVIA, NY	12860	60,370	59,755	59,162	-0.1	805	94.7	93.8	2.1	2.4	0.5	0.7
BATESVILLE, AR	12900	34,233	35,577	36,508	0.5	545	94.9	94.0	2.0	2.3	0.7	0.9
BATON ROUGE, LA	12940	705,973	762,905	808,238	1.1	288	63.0	60.4	34.1	36.1	1.3	1.7
BATTLE CREEK, MI	12980	137,985	139,466	140,147	0.1	723	83.9	81.9	10.9	11.8	1.1	1.6
BAY CITY, MI	13020	110,157	109,920	109,629	0.0	765	94.9	94.0	1.3	1.4	0.5	0.7
BAY CITY, TX	13060	37,957	37,676	37,380	-0.1	805	67.8	64.4	12.7	12.7	2.4	2.8
BEATRICE, NE	13100	22,993	23,631	24,052	0.4	590	97.7	97.3	0.3	0.4	0.3	0.5
BEAUMONT-PT ARTHURTX	13140	385,090	392,820	396,772	0.3	633	68.2	66.4	24.8	25.4	2.1	2.3
BEAVER DAM, WI	13180	85,897	89,663	91,817	0.6	494	95.3	94.2	2.5	3.0	0.4	0.5
BECKLEY, WV	13220	79,220	80,334	81,169	0.2	679	89.6	89.1	8.5	8.6	0.7	1.1
UNITED STATES					1.2		75.1	72.7	12.3	12.6	3.8	4.5

CBSA	% HISPANIC ORIGIN 2000	2007	0-4	5-9	10-14	15-19	20-24	25-44	45-64	65-84	85+	18+	MEDIAN AGE 2007	% 2007 Males	% 2007 Females
ABBEVILLE, LA	1.4	1.7	7.6	6.9	6.7	6.4	6.8	27.3	25.1	11.3	2.0	74.9	36.9	48.7	51.3
ABERDEEN, SD	0.6	0.8	6.5	6.0	5.8	7.0	7.6	25.1	26.0	13.0	3.0	77.9	39.1	48.4	51.6
ABERDEEN, WA	4.8	6.1	6.3	5.8	5.8	6.7	7.5	24.2	29.0	12.8	2.1	78.1	40.4	51.1	48.9
ABILENE, TX	17.2	21.3	7.0	6.0	6.3	8.3	10.4	25.7	23.0	11.3	2.0	76.6	34.2	49.4	50.6
ADA, OK	2.3	2.9	6.6	5.6	6.0	6.9	9.0	25.5	24.7	13.1	2.4	78.1	37.2	48.4	51.6
ADRIAN, MI	7.0	8.6	6.3	6.1	6.6	7.2	6.7	26.3	27.8	11.0	1.9	76.7	38.5	50.0	50.0
AKRON, OH	0.8	1.0	6.4	6.3	6.7	7.1	6.9	26.1	26.8	11.7	2.0	76.6	38.5	48.4	51.6
ALAMOGORDO, NM	32.2	33.8	7.7	6.7	7.1	8.0	8.5	25.8	23.8	11.3	1.2	73.7	34.8	49.9	50.1
ALBANY, GA	1.3	1.6	7.6	7.1	7.0	7.7	7.6	26.9	24.9	9.9	1.5	73.9	34.8	47.7	52.3
ALBANY-LEBANON, OR	4.4	5.9	7.0	6.4	6.4	6.6	6.8	24.9	27.5	11.9	2.4	76.1	38.7	49.4	50.6
ALBANY-SCH.-TROY, NY	2.5	2.9	5.9	5.7	6.4	7.6	7.0	25.8	27.5	11.7	2.4	77.9	39.5	48.7	51.3
ALBEMARLE, NC	2.1	2.8	6.4	6.1	6.5	6.8	5.6	27.9	26.4	12.3	2.0	77.0	39.1	49.9	50.1
ALBERT LEA, MN	6.3	8.5	6.2	5.6	5.5	6.0	7.0	23.2	27.8	15.3	3.5	79.1	42.6	49.3	50.7
ALBERTVILLE, AL	5.7	8.6	6.9	6.6	6.6	5.7	5.6	28.1	25.9	12.8	1.8	76.4	38.7	49.0	51.0
ALBUQUERQUE, NM	41.5	43.1	7.3	6.8	6.7	7.0	7.3	28.2	25.5	9.6	1.6	75.0	35.6	49.1	50.9
ALEXANDER CITY, AL	0.7	0.8	6.3	6.1	6.3	5.7	5.5	25.5	28.6	13.7	2.3	77.9	41.1	48.9	51.1
ALEXANDRIA, LA	1.3	1.5	7.2	6.8	6.8	6.5	7.1	26.7	25.2	11.7	1.8	75.1	37.0	48.5	51.5
ALEXANDRIA, MN	0.6	0.8	5.9	5.2	5.4	6.0	7.7	23.4	28.3	14.7	3.5	80.1	42.3	49.7	50.3
ALICE, TX	75.7	80.5	8.8	8.0	7.4	7.7	8.0	25.1	22.6	10.6	1.6	70.9	32.9	49.0	51.0
ALLEGAN, MI	5.7	7.1	7.5	6.9	7.1	7.2	6.6	26.7	26.8	9.5	1.6	74.2	37.0	50.0	50.0
ALLENTWN-BETH-EASTON	7.3	9.0	5.8	5.7	6.5	7.2	6.3	24.8	28.2	12.8	2.7	77.7	41.0	48.7	51.3
ALMA, MI	4.4	5.5	6.1	5.7	5.9	7.5	8.2	28.3	24.8	11.1	2.4	78.4	36.9	52.2	47.8
ALPENA, MI	0.6	0.7	5.8	5.2	5.3	6.5	7.0	22.7	30.0	14.9	2.6	79.8	43.2	48.9	51.1
ALTOONA, PA	0.5	0.6	5.7	5.4	5.8	6.4	6.3	25.1	28.0	14.4	2.9	79.7	41.7	48.3	51.7
ALTUS, OK	15.6	19.4	8.6	7.4	6.8	7.1	7.9	27.4	22.8	10.0	1.9	73.0	33.4	50.2	49.8
AMARILLO, TX	19.1	23.5	7.7	7.1	6.8	7.3	7.8	27.4	23.9	10.2	1.8	74.3	34.4	49.7	50.3
AMERICUS, GA	2.7	2.7	7.9	7.5	6.9	7.4	7.7	27.0	23.2	9.9	2.4	73.6	33.9	47.5	52.5
AMES, IA	1.5	2.0	5.2	4.6	4.8	10.7	20.6	23.8	20.3	8.0	1.9	82.2	27.5	51.2	48.8
AMSTERDAM, NY	6.9	8.2	6.2	5.5	6.1	6.5	6.4	24.0	27.8	13.8	3.7	78.0	41.7	48.0	52.0
ANCHORAGE, AK	5.1	6.4	7.4	6.7	7.5	7.9	8.1	27.8	27.9	6.3	0.5	73.5	34.3	50.6	49.4
ANDERSON, IN	1.5	2.0	6.4	6.1	6.2	6.5	6.5	26.8	26.3	12.8	2.2	77.5	39.0	49.4	50.6
ANDERSON, SC	1.1	1.5	6.7	6.5	6.4	6.2	5.3	27.2	27.6	12.3	1.8	76.7	39.4	48.7	51.3
ANDREWS, TX	40.0	47.1	8.0	7.0	6.7	8.2	9.2	23.8	24.7	11.1	1.3	73.2	35.0	49.5	50.5
ANGOLA, IN	2.1	2.8	6.8	6.3	6.7	7.1	6.8	27.2	27.0	10.5	1.5	76.3	37.3	50.7	49.3
ANN ARBOR, MI	2.7	3.3	6.1	5.8	5.9	8.5	11.6	29.2	24.4	7.4	1.3	78.7	33.0	50.2	49.8
ANNISTON-OXFORD, AL	1.6	1.6	6.2	6.0	6.1	6.2	6.5	27.0	27.5	12.7	1.8	78.3	39.2	48.1	51.9
APPLETON, WI	1.8	2.3	7.2	6.6	7.1	7.4	7.2	28.5	25.7	8.7	1.6	74.7	36.5	50.1	49.9
ARCADIA, FL	24.9	32.4	6.3	5.4	5.7	6.5	8.1	27.3	22.2	16.4	2.1	78.8	37.4	56.0	44.0
ARDMORE, OK	3.5	4.4	6.8	6.6	6.2	6.3	6.4	24.2	27.3	13.8	2.4	76.4	40.1	48.6	51.4
ARKADELPHIA, AR	2.4	3.2	6.3	5.8	5.1	8.9	11.3	25.8	22.6	12.1	2.2	79.7	33.3	48.6	51.4
ASHEVILLE, NC	3.2	4.2	5.5	5.5	5.6	5.9	5.1	26.1	28.7	15.0	2.6	79.9	42.5	48.5	51.5
ASHLAND, OH	0.6	0.8	6.8	6.4	6.3	7.7	7.7	24.5	26.4	11.9	2.3	76.5	37.7	49.5	50.5
ASHTABULA, OH	2.2	2.7	6.7	6.2	6.5	6.7	6.5	25.1	27.6	12.4	2.3	76.5	39.6	48.8	51.2
ASTORIA, OR	4.5	6.1	5.5	5.3	5.6	7.4	7.5	21.9	31.5	13.0	2.4	79.3	42.6	49.5	50.5
ATCHISON, KS	1.9	2.1	6.9	6.1	6.4	8.6	8.3	23.2	24.5	13.0	3.0	76.1	37.1	48.4	51.6
ATHENS, OH	1.0	1.0	4.9	4.4	4.6	11.9	20.7	23.0	20.7	8.5	1.4	83.4	27.4	49.1	50.9
ATHENS, TN	1.8	2.5	6.4	6.2	6.5	5.8	5.5	27.1	27.6	13.1	1.9	77.5	39.9	48.7	51.3
ATHENS, TX	6.9	9.0	6.5	6.2	5.8	6.2	5.7	22.6	28.4	16.4	2.2	77.8	42.7	49.5	50.5
ATHENS-CLARKE CTY,GA	4.8	6.3	5.9	5.5	5.5	9.3	15.0	27.4	21.9	8.3	1.3	79.6	30.2	49.1	50.9
ATLANTA-SNDY SPRINGS	6.4	8.0	7.4	7.2	7.1	6.9	6.6	32.1	24.5	7.2	1.0	74.2	34.7	49.5	50.5
ATLANTIC CITY, NJ	12.2	15.4	6.4	6.0	7.4	7.4	6.5	25.7	26.6	11.9	2.0	75.6	38.8	48.4	51.6
AUBURN, IN	1.7	2.3	7.7	7.3	7.2	6.8	5.8	27.8	26.4	9.3	1.7	73.5	36.3	50.2	49.8
AUBURN, NY	2.0	2.3	6.1	5.6	6.2	7.0	7.4	26.1	27.4	11.9	2.4	77.9	39.6	50.6	49.4
AUBURN-OPELIKA, AL	1.4	2.1	6.4	5.9	6.0	9.7	16.0	27.1	20.5	7.4	1.0	78.3	28.8	49.5	50.5
AUGUSTA-RICHMOND CTY	2.4	3.1	7.0	6.6	7.0	7.3	7.3	27.3	26.1	9.9	1.4	75.1	36.1	48.7	51.3
AUGUSTA-WATERV.,ME	0.7	1.0	5.5	5.3	5.9	7.3	7.1	24.5	30.2	12.1	2.1	79.0	41.4	48.6	51.4
AUSTIN, MN	4.3	5.8	6.7	5.7	6.2	6.2	7.3	24.4	25.5	14.1	3.9	77.6	40.6	49.5	50.5
AUSTIN-ROUND ROCK,TX	26.2	31.2	7.6	7.1	6.6	7.1	9.1	32.5	22.6	6.5	0.9	74.8	32.3	50.8	49.2
BAINBRIDGE, GA	3.2	4.2	7.8	7.5	6.9	6.7	6.5	26.8	24.8	11.1	2.0	73.7	36.2	48.2	51.8
BAKERSFIELD, CA	38.4	44.6	8.8	7.4	8.4	8.4	8.5	27.7	21.8	7.9	1.2	70.4	30.6	51.3	48.7
BALTIMORE-TOWSON, MD	2.0	2.9	6.3	6.3	7.0	7.4	6.5	26.8	26.9	10.9	1.9	76.0	38.5	48.2	51.8
BANGOR, ME	0.6	0.8	5.3	4.9	5.5	7.8	8.7	25.5	28.8	11.7	1.8	80.2	39.9	49.1	50.9
BARABOO, WI	1.7	2.2	6.6	6.2	6.2	7.2	6.6	25.6	27.8	11.4	2.4	76.6	39.4	49.5	50.5
BARNSTABLE TOWN, MA	1.3	1.8	4.5	4.5	5.4	6.1	5.0	19.6	32.0	19.0	3.8	81.6	47.9	47.4	52.6
BARRE, VT	1.3	1.5	5.2	5.0	5.8	7.6	7.7	24.1	31.2	11.3	2.2	79.7	41.5	49.1	.50.9
BARTLESVILLE, OK	2.6	3.4	6.1	5.6	6.0	6.8	7.6	21.7	27.9	15.5	2.9	78.2	41.8	48.3	51.7
BASTROP, LA	0.7	0.8	7.4	6.8	6.9	6.3	7.1	25.8	25.1	12.4	2.2	75.1	37.0	48.0	52.0
BATAVIA, NY	1.5	1.8	6.3	5.7	6.7	7.0	7.2	25.5	27.3	12.0	2.3	76.9	39.7	49.5	50.5
BATESVILLE, AR	1.5	2.1	6.5	6.7	5.7	6.3	6.9	25.8	27.6	12.5	2.0	77.7	39.6	49.2	50.8
BATON ROUGE, LA	1.6	1.9	7.3	6.8	6.8	7.4	8.6	28.5	24.7	8.7	1.2	75.2	33.9	49.1	50.9
BATTLE CREEK, MI	3.2	3.9	6.5	6.0	6.7	7.4	7.1	25.9	26.6	11.7	2.1	76.3	38.1	48.7	51.3
BAY CITY, MI	3.9	4.9	6.2	5.9	6.3	6.3	6.0	25.6	28.6	12.8	2.4	77.8	40.6	48.8	51.2
BAY CITY, TX	31.3	37.2	7.9	6.4	6.8	7.5	8.9	23.7	26.1	11.1	1.6	74.3	35.7	50.1	49.9
BEATRICE, NE	0.9	1.2	6.3	5.8	5.7	6.4	7.3	23.6	27.1	14.3	3.7	78.5	41.6	48.9	51.1
BEAUMONT-PT ARTHURTX	8.0	10.0	6.9	6.3	6.7	6.6	7.5	27.0	25.7	11.4	1.8	76.1	36.8	49.9	50.1
BEAVER DAM, WI	2.5	3.3	6.2	5.8	5.8	6.7	7.4	27.9	26.4	11.3	2.5	78.3	38.9	52.4	47.6
BECKLEY, WV	0.9	1.0	5.4	5.3	5.4	5.3	5.7	27.0	30.2	13.5	2.1	80.6	41.6	49.6	50.4
UNITED STATES	12.5	15.0	6.9	6.5	6.8	7.1	7.0	27.6	25.4	10.7	1.9	75.6	36.7	49.2	50.8

CBSA	HOUSEHOLDS					FAMILIES			MEDIAN HOUSEHOLD INCOME		
	2000	2007	2012	% Annual Rate 2000-2007	2007 Average HH Size	2000	2007	% Annual Rate 2000-2007	2007	2012	2007 National Rank
ABBEVILLE, LA	19,832	21,306	22,335	1.0	2.62	14,453	15,158	0.7	32,041	34,581	892
ABERDEEN, SD	16,319	16,661	16,757	0.3	2.28	10,533	10,646	0.1	43,693	51,674	488
ABERDEEN, WA	26,808	27,965	28,730	0.6	2.47	17,914	18,403	0.4	43,018	50,509	513
ABILENE, TX	58,475	60,060	60,891	0.4	2.50	40,814	41,450	0.2	41,090	47,821	603
ADA, OK	13,978	14,366	14,602	0.4	2.41	9,426	9,487	0.1	33,674	38,678	868
ADRIAN, MI	35,930	38,363	39,972	0.9	2.57	26,052	27,137	0.6	53,995	60,737	141
AKRON, OH	274,237	282,386	287,170	0.4	2.44	183,802	183,254	0.0	53,023	61,510	162
ALAMOGORDO, NM	22,984	24,497	25,354	0.9	2.58	16,802	17,436	0.5	37,843	43,566	746
ALBANY, GA	57,403	61,074	63,508	0.9	2.60	41,219	42,812	0.5	41,941	49,091	560
ALBANY-LEBANON, OR	39,541	42,852	45,409	1.1	2.58	28,232	30,350	1.0	46,778	54,066	359
ALBANY-SCH.-TROY, NY	330,246	347,149	359,862	0.7	2.39	209,951	219,193	0.6	56,338	66,218	105
ALBEMARLE, NC	22,223	23,362	23,980	0.7	2.50	16,156	16,598	0.4	44,575	50,403	445
ALBERT LEA, MN	13,356	13,448	13,413	0.1	2.35	9,013	8,804	-0.3	46,033	53,526	382
ALBERTVILLE, AL	32,547	34,817	36,632	0.9	2.50	23,527	24,724	0.7	37,822	42,172	749
ALBUQUERQUE, NM	281,052	330,730	367,779	2.3	2.48	186,601	212,708	1.8	49,942	59,257	256
ALEXANDER CITY, AL	21,338	21,953	21,966	0.4	2.39	15,214	15,372	0.1	35,410	39,004	826
ALEXANDRIA, LA	54,193	57,442	59,601	0.8	2.52	38,407	39,690	0.5	32,838	35,804	878
ALEXANDRIA, MN	13,276	15,449	16,930	2.1	2.36	9,030	10,203	1.7	46,681	54,358	362
ALICE, TX	12,961	13,770	14,217	0.8	2.96	10,102	10,650	0.7	34,376	38,543	855
ALLEGAN, MI	38,165	43,145	46,276	1.7	2.65	28,405	31,390	1.4	54,007	60,814	140
ALLENTWN-BETH-EASTON	285,808	314,021	335,333	1.3	2.50	197,081	211,311	1.0	57,873	68,399	84
ALMA, MI	14,501	14,926	15,128	0.4	2.51	10,401	10,442	0.1	44,953	50,682	434
ALPENA, MI	12,818	12,692	12,488	-0.1	2.33	8,694	8,366	-0.5	41,349	46,469	590
ALTOONA, PA	51,518	51,636	51,133	0.0	2.38	34,895	33,945	-0.4	41,586	49,198	580
ALTUS, OK	10,590	10,164	9,749	-0.6	2.58	7,666	7,227	-0.8	38,674	45,144	705
AMARILLO, TX	85,272	90,791	94,489	0.9	2.56	58,749	61,851	0.7	44,658	52,017	443
AMERICUS, GA	13,460	13,678	13,738	0.2	2.59	9,540	9,390	-0.2	37,517	42,786	758
AMES, IA	29,383	32,682	34,020	1.5	2.33	17,056	18,515	1.1	49,757	57,791	262
AMSTERDAM, NY	20,038	20,217	20,293	0.1	2.39	13,111	13,121	0.0	40,386	46,478	638
ANCHORAGE, AK	115,378	132,374	144,354	1.9	2.68	79,188	89,446	1.7	67,604	78,402	21
ANDERSON, IN	53,052	53,117	53,078	0.0	2.38	36,211	34,847	-0.5	48,921	57,028	289
ANDERSON, SC	65,649	72,467	77,416	1.4	2.45	47,276	50,474	0.9	44,921	51,456	437
ANDREWS, TX	4,601	4,602	4,583	0.0	2.75	3,519	3,489	-0.1	40,525	46,242	629
ANGOLA, IN	12,738	13,875	14,623	1.2	2.48	8,911	9,350	0.7	53,215	61,100	156
ANN ARBOR, MI	125,327	139,351	148,001	1.5	2.39	73,690	79,042	1.0	64,207	75,077	34
ANNISTON-OXFORD, AL	45,307	46,768	47,441	0.4	2.35	31,300	31,675	0.2	36,712	40,427	784
APPLETON, WI	75,440	86,274	92,984	1.9	2.55	53,383	59,734	1.6	62,103	72,561	46
ARCADIA, FL	10,746	11,655	12,341	1.1	2.73	7,676	8,188	0.9	36,906	41,824	780
ARDMORE, OK	21,434	22,736	23,556	0.8	2.46	15,198	15,824	0.6	36,430	41,834	795
ARKADELPHIA, AR	8,912	9,172	9,326	0.4	2.36	5,820	5,787	-0.1	35,520	41,227	821
ASHEVILLE, NC	154,290	173,965	187,187	1.7	2.28	103,656	113,738	1.3	45,408	52,259	417
ASHLAND, OH	19,524	20,527	21,120	0.7	2.53	14,015	14,329	0.3	47,433	53,664	336
ASHTABULA, OH	39,397	40,761	41,433	0.5	2.51	27,768	27,900	0.1	43,457	49,852	497
ASTORIA, OR	14,703	15,432	15,952	0.7	2.33	9,450	9,820	0.5	45,804	53,188	392
ATCHISON, KS	6,275	6,319	6,326	0.1	2.48	4,278	4,250	-0.1	41,850	47,830	569
ATHENS, OH	22,501	23,204	23,535	0.4	2.34	12,710	12,555	-0.2	32,991	37,166	877
ATHENS, TN	19,721	21,274	22,178	1.1	2.40	14,318	15,078	0.7	39,473	45,751	674
ATHENS, TX	28,804	32,194	34,858	1.5	2.51	20,982	23,222	1.4	40,724	47,331	625
ATHENS-CLARKE CTY,GA	63,406	73,380	79,442	2.0	2.46	37,877	42,379	1.6	41,806	48,558	571
ATLANTA-SNDY SPRINGS	1,554,154	1,938,092	2,240,089	3.1	2.70	1,078,735	1,316,706	2.8	67,092	80,088	25
ATLANTIC CITY, NJ	95,024	105,219	113,377	1.4	2.60	63,151	69,751	1.4	54,266	62,974	136
AUBURN, IN	15,134	16,219	16,856	1.0	2.57	10,915	11,298	0.5	55,335	63,752	123
AUBURN, NY	30,558	31,163	31,512	0.3	2.48	20,829	21,079	0.2	46,171	53,226	380
AUBURN-OPELIKA, AL	45,702	53,204	58,221	2.1	2.36	27,270	30,941	1.8	35,466	38,932	823
AUGUSTA-RICHMOND CTY	184,801	204,617	217,789	1.4	2.56	132,165	142,646	1.1	47,968	56,989	314
AUGUSTA-WATERV.,ME	47,683	51,608	54,193	1.1	2.32	31,328	33,212	0.8	43,285	49,124	504
AUSTIN, MN	15,582	15,988	16,201	0.4	2.40	10,318	10,260	-0.1	46,286	54,516	377
AUSTIN-ROUND ROCK,TX	471,855	588,948	681,059	3.1	2.60	295,809	368,096	3.1	63,581	77,238	36
BAINBRIDGE, GA	10,380	11,170	11,704	1.0	2.61	7,543	7,877	0.6	35,199	40,420	831
BAKERSFIELD, CA	208,652	246,047	279,857	2.3	3.10	156,401	185,081	2.3	44,072	51,397	461
BALTIMORE-TOWSON, MD	974,071	1,028,554	1,068,940	0.8	2.55	653,781	671,934	0.4	62,208	73,179	43
BANGOR, ME	58,096	62,033	64,405	0.9	2.31	37,813	39,535	0.6	40,964	46,587	614
BARABOO, WI	21,644	24,677	26,651	1.8	2.45	14,863	16,551	1.5	52,175	60,391	191
BARNSTABLE TOWN, MA	94,822	100,125	103,035	0.8	2.24	61,041	63,664	0.6	61,707	75,067	49
BARRE, VT	23,659	25,486	26,567	1.0	2.29	15,053	15,711	0.6	53,595	64,216	147
BARTLESVILLE, OK	20,179	20,590	20,715	0.3	2.36	14,031	14,042	0.0	44,898	51,965	438
BASTROP, LA	11,382	11,406	11,152	0.0	2.56	8,319	8,143	-0.3	28,271	30,734	919
BATAVIA, NY	22,770	22,917	22,864	0.1	2.54	15,823	15,812	0.0	49,708	57,383	263
BATESVILLE, AR	13,467	14,236	14,720	0.8	2.43	9,670	9,939	0.4	39,599	45,937	669
BATON ROUGE, LA	256,637	284,197	303,780	1.4	2.59	179,355	194,704	1.1	42,068	45,852	552
BATTLE CREEK, MI	54,100	55,299	55,873	0.3	2.44	36,249	35,981	-0.1	47,369	54,052	340
BAY CITY, MI	43,930	44,907	45,327	0.3	2.41	30,039	29,900	-0.1	46,925	53,479	352
BAY CITY, TX	13,901	13,949	13,909	0.0	2.67	9,922	9,856	-0.1	39,517	45,149	672
BEATRICE, NE	9,316	9,696	9,915	0.6	2.33	6,208	6,381	0.4	42,048	47,638	554
BEAUMONT-PT ARTHUR,TX	142,327	146,403	148,673	0.4	2.56	101,248	103,235	0.3	43,654	50,454	490
BEAVER DAM, WI	31,417	34,029	35,332	1.1	2.46	22,313	23,644	0.8	55,180	63,325	125
BECKLEY, WV	31,793	33,416	34,275	0.7	2.29	22,103	22,520	0.3	34,623	39,363	847
UNITED STATES				1.2	2.59			1.0	53,154	62,503	

INCOME
CBSA AND U.S. TOTALS

D

CBSA	2007 Per Capita Income	2007 HH Income Base	2007 HOUSEHOLD INCOME DISTRIBUTION (%) Less than $25,000	$25,000 to $49,999	$50,000 to $99,999	$100,000 to $149,999	$150,000 or More	2007 Home Value Base	2007 HOME VALUE DISTRIBUTION (%) Less than $50,000	$50,000 to $89,999	$90,000 to $174,999	$175,000 to $399,999	$400,000 or More	2007 Median Home Value
ABBEVILLE, LA	16,406	21,306	40.6	27.9	24.3	5.5	1.8	16,324	24.8	24.6	34.8	13.8	2.0	91,025
ABERDEEN, SD	23,693	16,661	26.9	29.3	33.8	6.9	3.1	11,535	21.4	22.2	40.1	14.6	1.7	100,899
ABERDEEN, WA	21,356	27,965	28.6	29.9	30.4	8.2	2.8	20,118	5.6	7.9	35.7	43.4	7.2	176,542
ABILENE, TX	21,169	60,057	28.2	31.3	29.4	7.4	3.7	40,002	30.6	27.9	29.8	10.2	1.4	77,935
ADA, OK	18,903	14,366	37.3	30.3	24.9	4.9	2.6	9,661	27.4	27.3	32.7	10.7	1.9	82,189
ADRIAN, MI	24,870	38,363	18.4	27.3	37.8	12.2	4.4	30,305	6.7	10.6	47.0	33.0	2.7	146,209
AKRON, OH	28,316	282,386	20.5	26.4	33.2	13.0	6.9	206,475	5.9	15.8	45.2	29.3	3.8	136,706
ALAMOGORDO, NM	17,757	24,497	30.9	33.7	28.2	5.6	1.6	16,550	14.3	18.6	44.8	19.8	2.5	116,896
ALBANY, GA	21,761	61,074	31.6	25.6	29.4	8.4	4.9	38,910	17.9	27.6	39.0	13.7	1.8	96,356
ALBANY-LEBANON, OR	22,252	42,852	23.6	29.7	34.6	8.6	3.5	30,114	5.0	4.0	19.0	58.6	13.4	228,161
ALBANY-SCH.-TROY, NY	29,747	347,149	19.0	25.3	34.9	12.9	8.0	234,675	2.5	2.0	21.2	67.6	6.7	220,012
ALBEMARLE, NC	21,798	23,362	27.6	28.2	33.8	7.3	3.2	18,088	11.1	16.5	44.8	24.2	3.5	125,729
ALBERT LEA, MN	23,557	13,448	23.3	31.6	34.9	7.4	3.0	10,736	8.0	19.4	45.8	23.1	3.7	128,289
ALBERTVILLE, AL	19,898	34,817	32.5	31.1	26.5	7.1	2.9	26,631	15.3	21.1	39.2	19.3	5.1	113,336
ALBUQUERQUE, NM	26,292	330,726	22.7	27.3	32.7	11.0	6.2	225,979	6.3	5.0	29.0	50.3	9.4	198,084
ALEXANDER CITY, AL	19,992	21,953	35.8	30.3	24.9	6.3	2.8	17,434	23.7	25.4	30.7	15.4	4.8	91,516
ALEXANDRIA, LA	18,426	57,442	38.3	29.6	23.3	5.9	2.9	39,871	23.2	24.5	36.1	14.3	1.9	93,153
ALEXANDRIA, MN	24,394	15,449	25.0	28.3	34.8	8.0	3.9	12,129	5.4	8.2	37.1	42.6	6.6	173,556
ALICE, TX	15,082	13,770	37.7	29.5	25.4	5.4	2.0	10,620	43.1	29.5	21.2	5.4	0.8	58,249
ALLEGAN, MI	24,218	43,145	18.0	27.3	39.2	11.3	4.3	35,973	9.2	8.6	45.5	32.6	4.2	150,545
ALLENTWN-BETH-EASTON	28,884	314,021	19.0	24.0	35.0	14.2	7.8	228,330	2.0	3.2	23.9	58.6	12.4	230,969
ALMA, MI	20,706	14,926	25.1	31.1	32.9	8.5	2.3	11,710	12.3	23.7	46.9	16.0	1.1	108,186
ALPENA, MI	21,712	12,692	29.3	30.1	32.1	6.2	2.3	10,101	8.0	22.3	51.1	16.9	1.7	110,596
ALTOONA, PA	21,665	51,636	28.9	30.0	31.4	7.0	2.7	37,936	13.8	21.9	44.8	17.7	1.8	111,345
ALTUS, OK	19,424	10,164	31.1	30.6	29.2	6.3	2.8	6,161	25.4	30.0	32.6	10.3	1.7	81,745
AMARILLO, TX	22,794	90,791	25.5	29.6	31.2	9.2	4.5	61,241	19.6	27.1	36.6	14.9	1.9	95,352
AMERICUS, GA	19,048	13,678	33.0	30.9	26.2	6.6	3.2	9,088	21.3	31.8	32.9	12.4	1.6	85,650
AMES, IA	25,941	32,682	23.6	26.6	33.0	11.2	5.5	19,775	9.6	8.1	43.7	35.0	3.7	150,921
AMSTERDAM, NY	21,490	20,217	29.9	30.2	30.3	6.5	3.1	14,172	5.5	12.6	45.4	34.0	2.5	151,956
ANCHORAGE, AK	31,654	132,374	13.5	21.8	35.5	17.8	11.4	89,711	5.7	3.9	15.2	62.6	12.5	247,688
ANDERSON, IN	25,280	53,117	21.7	29.3	33.6	11.1	4.3	39,924	14.2	32.7	42.9	9.2	1.0	93,835
ANDERSON, SC	23,011	72,467	26.6	28.9	31.6	9.3	3.6	56,271	16.1	22.3	39.6	19.4	2.6	107,671
ANDREWS, TX	18,938	4,602	28.0	33.9	30.0	5.5	2.6	3,692	42.4	31.0	20.9	5.4	0.3	56,409
ANGOLA, IN	25,466	13,875	17.2	28.5	40.1	10.1	4.1	10,947	11.9	15.5	43.3	23.8	5.4	124,409
ANN ARBOR, MI	34,830	139,351	17.8	21.3	32.0	16.3	12.5	84,790	4.1	4.5	20.0	53.9	17.5	235,557
ANNISTON-OXFORD, AL	20,733	46,768	34.8	30.4	25.3	6.6	2.8	34,638	22.2	25.1	37.6	13.0	2.0	93,342
APPLETON, WI	28,640	86,274	13.0	24.0	42.7	14.4	5.9	65,155	2.4	7.1	56.3	31.9	2.2	145,140
ARCADIA, FL	17,597	11,655	32.1	33.4	26.9	5.0	2.5	8,997	9.2	17.4	38.0	28.5	6.9	138,220
ARDMORE, OK	19,646	22,736	33.8	29.8	27.7	6.3	2.4	16,648	29.0	28.6	29.7	10.9	1.8	78,091
ARKADELPHIA, AR	18,743	9,172	38.3	27.3	25.7	6.4	2.3	6,200	28.1	22.0	34.5	13.4	2.1	89,863
ASHEVILLE, NC	25,419	173,965	25.2	29.9	32.6	7.9	4.4	130,245	11.5	9.4	28.6	39.8	10.6	176,490
ASHLAND, OH	22,356	20,527	21.8	31.1	34.3	9.5	3.3	16,020	7.8	15.3	49.4	24.5	3.0	131,043
ASHTABULA, OH	21,272	40,761	25.7	30.7	32.9	8.0	2.7	31,228	12.1	24.6	45.9	16.1	1.2	108,078
ASTORIA, OR	24,804	15,432	25.5	28.4	34.1	8.0	4.0	10,319	5.0	3.1	14.7	57.5	19.7	252,221
ATCHISON, KS	19,489	6,319	27.0	33.7	31.9	5.7	1.7	4,719	23.9	33.4	32.7	9.5	0.6	79,030
ATHENS, OH	19,202	23,204	39.8	27.4	23.0	6.7	3.2	14,749	23.9	23.4	35.2	15.3	2.2	95,723
ATHENS, TN	20,626	21,274	31.3	30.0	29.3	7.1	2.3	16,296	13.8	21.4	43.3	17.9	3.6	110,127
ATHENS, TX	22,005	32,194	29.3	30.3	28.3	8.2	4.0	26,080	30.0	25.4	28.7	13.6	2.3	81,368
ATHENS-CLARKE CTY,GA	23,669	73,380	31.9	25.3	28.1	8.7	6.0	42,462	12.3	12.4	37.3	30.4	7.5	140,953
ATLANTA-SNDY SPRINGS	33,080	1,938,081	14.5	20.6	36.0	15.9	13.1	1,327,952	3.9	6.0	34.1	43.7	12.2	190,129
ATLANTIC CITY, NJ	26,034	105,219	20.2	25.2	36.0	12.2	6.4	72,400	1.6	1.9	11.4	65.1	19.9	280,182
AUBURN, IN	25,117	16,219	17.2	26.7	40.7	11.8	3.7	13,302	13.0	20.5	46.9	17.7	1.9	110,607
AUBURN, NY	22,395	31,162	23.8	30.5	34.2	8.2	3.3	23,252	4.4	6.6	42.9	42.6	3.6	169,349
AUBURN-OPELIKA, AL	20,587	53,204	39.1	23.3	26.1	8.5	3.1	33,824	21.8	12.3	32.7	26.9	6.3	132,893
AUGUSTA-RICHMOND CTY	24,284	204,617	25.9	25.9	31.8	10.7	5.8	146,257	12.6	18.3	43.2	21.8	4.1	119,897
AUGUSTA-WATERV.,ME	22,765	51,608	27.3	29.7	32.8	7.3	2.9	37,051	5.5	7.9	44.1	38.4	4.2	164,006
AUSTIN, MN	24,499	15,988	23.0	31.1	33.9	8.0	3.9	12,697	6.9	19.1	49.0	21.6	3.4	128,104
AUSTIN-ROUND ROCK,TX	32,358	588,927	15.8	22.2	34.2	16.1	11.7	358,749	5.5	8.3	34.5	40.9	10.8	179,500
BAINBRIDGE, GA	18,479	11,170	36.8	28.3	26.1	5.8	3.1	8,187	21.4	28.1	34.5	13.6	2.4	90,735
BAKERSFIELD, CA	19,039	246,041	28.9	26.5	29.7	10.0	4.9	155,852	3.0	2.7	12.3	64.0	18.1	260,476
BALTIMORE-TOWSON, MD	31,850	1,028,507	17.8	21.8	33.7	16.0	10.7	708,138	1.7	2.0	11.8	55.1	29.4	305,618
BANGOR, ME	22,280	62,030	29.9	29.7	29.6	7.9	3.0	43,633	8.8	13.4	46.8	28.4	2.6	143,960
BARABOO, WI	25,547	24,677	18.9	28.1	38.8	10.1	4.2	18,440	7.6	7.9	38.7	39.8	6.0	165,326
BARNSTABLE TOWN, MA	35,135	100,125	17.0	22.8	35.2	15.2	9.9	79,250	0.3	0.3	1.8	48.0	49.6	398,289
BARRE, VT	28,807	25,486	20.2	26.1	36.1	11.6	6.0	18,117	3.1	3.5	28.9	54.2	10.3	204,351
BARTLESVILLE, OK	26,456	20,590	27.7	27.6	28.9	9.5	6.3	15,271	23.3	26.3	35.5	12.8	2.1	90,467
BASTROP, LA	15,603	11,406	45.4	27.4	21.4	4.1	1.8	8,076	30.4	29.8	29.8	9.2	0.9	73,333
BATAVIA, NY	23,201	22,917	18.8	31.5	37.5	8.9	3.3	17,283	2.7	2.7	40.5	51.9	2.1	180,027
BATESVILLE, AR	20,543	14,236	31.4	31.3	29.7	4.6	3.0	10,839	23.4	30.8	32.7	11.5	1.6	84,478
BATON ROUGE, LA	21,603	284,191	30.2	27.0	29.1	9.4	4.3	196,819	14.0	17.2	38.6	26.1	4.0	125,335
BATTLE CREEK, MI	23,913	55,297	24.6	28.2	33.2	10.2	3.8	40,660	12.0	22.4	42.5	20.9	2.2	113,989
BAY CITY, MI	24,640	44,967	25.1	28.0	31.3	11.6	4.0	35,848	9.9	19.2	49.2	19.8	2.0	116,602
BAY CITY, TX	19,358	13,949	31.9	28.5	27.0	9.9	2.7	9,551	28.2	29.7	32.7	8.4	0.9	80,761
BEATRICE, NE	21,324	9,696	25.9	33.8	32.1	6.1	2.2	7,161	18.4	28.3	37.9	14.5	0.9	94,866
BEAUMONT-PT ARTHURTX	22,170	146,481	28.6	27.1	29.8	10.2	4.3	105,422	29.7	29.5	30.6	9.1	1.1	76,988
BEAVER DAM, WI	25,003	34,029	16.2	27.1	42.5	10.7	3.5	25,592	3.5	5.6	43.3	43.0	4.6	170,318
BECKLEY, WV	20,367	33,416	37.5	28.9	24.8	6.0	2.8	26,218	23.2	22.7	39.8	12.7	1.6	96,289
UNITED STATES	27,916		21.9	25.0	32.3	12.3	8.4		7.9	10.5	27.1	35.6	19.0	192,285

CBSA	FINANCIAL SERVICES				THE HOME						ENTERTAINMENT						PERSONAL			
					Home Improvements		Furnishings													
	Auto Loan	Home Loan	Invest-ments	Retire-ment Plans	Home Repair	Lawn & Garden	Comput-ers & Hard-ware	Major Appli-ances	TV, Radio, Sound Equip-ment	Furni-ture	Dine out/ Carry out	Sports Equip-ment	Fees & Tickets	Toys & Games	Travel	Cable TV	Apparel & Services	Auto Repairs	Health Insur-ance	Pets & Supplies
ABBEVILLE, LA	72	54	38	52	57	74	54	65	60	54	60	58	48	62	54	64	52	62	71	70
ABERDEEN, SD	82	69	70	71	73	83	74	79	77	71	76	70	69	79	73	80	67	77	85	81
ABERDEEN, WA	78	70	69	70	73	83	70	77	74	69	73	67	68	74	72	77	64	74	83	79
ABILENE, TX	80	69	68	70	68	75	75	75	77	72	76	67	70	78	72	79	68	76	79	76
ADA, OK	70	55	54	56	58	70	62	66	66	58	64	58	56	66	60	69	56	65	73	68
ADRIAN, MI	94	90	92	91	93	98	87	93	90	88	89	82	87	93	89	91	79	89	95	95
AKRON, OH	94	97	108	99	96	95	96	94	97	97	96	84	99	98	97	97	87	95	97	95
ALAMOGORDO, NM	70	60	53	60	60	67	62	65	64	61	64	59	58	65	61	66	56	65	68	67
ALBANY, GA	86	73	69	74	72	82	76	79	81	76	80	70	72	81	74	84	71	80	84	82
ALBANY-LEBANON, OR	83	77	76	77	79	85	77	82	79	76	79	73	75	80	78	81	70	80	85	84
ALBANY-SCH.-TROY, NY	95	99	112	101	100	97	100	97	100	100	99	88	102	99	101	100	91	98	99	98
ALBEMARLE, NC	87	72	61	70	77	92	71	82	77	70	76	72	66	80	71	81	66	77	88	87
ALBERT LEA, MN	82	72	70	72	78	88	72	80	77	72	77	70	70	80	74	81	68	77	87	84
ALBERTVILLE, AL	82	63	49	61	67	85	64	75	70	62	69	67	57	73	63	74	60	71	81	80
ALBUQUERQUE, NM	92	90	90	91	86	86	92	89	90	91	90	83	90	90	89	89	82	91	88	88
ALEXANDER CITY, AL	81	58	39	56	64	85	60	75	68	58	67	66	52	70	60	73	57	69	82	80
ALEXANDRIA, LA	72	61	56	61	61	71	61	67	66	61	66	59	59	67	61	69	58	66	72	69
ALEXANDRIA, MN	86	74	72	75	80	93	77	86	81	74	79	76	72	81	78	84	69	82	92	88
ALICE, TX	71	58	43	54	54	64	57	63	63	59	63	57	52	62	56	64	56	64	66	63
ALLEGAN, MI	99	91	80	90	91	100	86	94	88	87	88	84	84	92	87	90	78	90	95	97
ALLENTWN-BETH-EASTON	97	103	116	105	105	102	100	100	101	101	100	89	104	101	103	101	91	99	102	100
ALMA, MI	82	72	70	72	75	86	71	79	76	71	75	69	69	79	72	78	66	75	84	81
ALPENA, MI	77	65	62	65	70	83	67	76	71	65	70	66	63	72	68	74	61	71	81	78
ALTOONA, PA	74	68	73	68	72	78	69	73	73	68	72	63	68	74	70	76	64	71	81	74
ALTUS, OK	76	61	60	63	61	70	70	70	74	65	72	63	64	74	67	75	63	71	76	71
AMARILLO, TX	84	79	81	80	76	78	82	80	83	81	83	72	80	83	80	83	74	82	82	80
AMERICUS, GA	78	61	53	61	63	76	66	71	71	64	71	63	60	72	64	74	62	70	77	75
AMES, IA	89	77	84	81	75	79	99	83	92	86	92	80	88	90	88	89	83	90	84	85
AMSTERDAM, NY	75	64	69	64	68	78	69	74	74	65	72	64	65	73	69	77	63	71	82	75
ANCHORAGE, AK	120	120	117	124	114	110	122	115	117	122	118	110	121	119	118	114	107	119	109	116
ANDERSON, IN	86	82	90	83	84	90	82	85	87	82	85	74	82	88	84	89	75	83	93	86
ANDERSON, SC	88	74	66	74	77	90	74	83	80	74	79	73	70	82	74	83	69	79	88	86
ANDREWS, TX	79	69	62	67	68	77	67	74	73	69	73	65	65	74	68	75	64	73	78	74
ANGOLA, IN	99	85	75	84	89	103	84	94	88	83	88	84	79	92	84	91	77	90	98	99
ANN ARBOR, MI	117	114	121	120	110	106	128	112	120	122	122	109	124	120	120	116	111	119	108	113
ANNISTON-OXFORD, AL	76	62	56	61	64	76	65	71	69	63	68	62	60	70	64	73	60	69	77	74
APPLETON, WI	105	105	106	106	103	104	100	102	101	102	100	92	101	104	101	100	90	100	102	104
ARCADIA, FL	74	62	55	60	66	79	62	73	67	62	66	62	59	66	64	71	57	70	79	74
ARDMORE, OK	76	61	54	60	64	78	63	71	69	61	67	62	58	70	63	73	58	69	79	74
ARKADELPHIA, AR	74	55	46	54	59	74	62	68	66	57	65	62	53	66	59	69	57	66	74	72
ASHEVILLE, NC	88	77	71	76	80	92	77	86	81	76	80	75	73	82	78	85	70	82	91	88
ASHLAND, OH	85	77	76	77	80	90	76	83	80	76	79	73	74	83	77	83	70	79	88	85
ASHTABULA, OH	78	71	72	71	74	82	71	76	75	70	74	66	69	77	72	78	65	73	83	78
ASTORIA, OR	84	76	75	77	79	89	79	84	80	76	80	74	75	80	80	83	70	82	88	86
ATCHISON, KS	74	61	59	61	66	78	65	71	70	62	68	62	60	72	64	73	59	68	79	74
ATHENS, OH	70	54	51	56	54	64	70	64	68	60	68	60	60	67	62	67	60	66	67	66
ATHENS, TN	80	62	51	61	67	83	64	74	70	62	69	65	58	73	63	75	60	70	81	79
ATHENS, TX	85	73	62	70	77	93	71	84	77	71	75	72	67	75	74	81	65	80	91	86
ATHENS-CLARKE CTY,GA	87	71	68	74	70	77	88	79	85	79	86	75	78	84	79	84	76	84	80	82
ATLANTA-SNDY SPRINGS	128	127	122	130	119	116	127	120	124	128	125	114	126	126	123	121	113	124	116	122
ATLANTIC CITY, NJ	88	94	102	95	93	88	95	91	94	95	94	84	98	93	95	94	87	92	90	90
AUBURN, IN	97	88	85	89	91	100	85	94	89	86	88	82	84	94	87	91	78	89	97	97
AUBURN, NY	81	75	78	76	78	85	76	80	78	75	78	71	74	80	77	81	69	78	85	82
AUBURN-OPELIKA, AL	72	58	57	61	55	60	76	64	72	66	72	62	66	70	66	69	64	70	64	66
AUGUSTA-RICHMOND CTY	93	85	81	86	83	89	85	87	88	85	87	78	83	89	84	90	78	87	90	90
AUGUSTA-WATERV.,ME	78	70	72	70	72	81	72	77	75	70	74	68	69	75	72	77	65	75	82	78
AUSTIN, MN	85	78	82	79	82	90	78	84	83	78	82	73	77	84	80	86	72	81	92	86
AUSTIN-ROUND ROCK,TX	122	115	109	119	107	106	123	112	118	121	119	109	118	119	115	114	108	119	107	113
BAINBRIDGE, GA	79	59	46	58	63	80	62	72	69	60	68	64	55	71	61	73	59	69	79	77
BAKERSFIELD, CA	83	81	77	80	77	75	83	81	81	82	81	78	80	81	80	79	74	83	77	79
BALTIMORE-TOWSON, MD	107	117	126	118	115	108	114	109	113	116	113	100	119	112	115	112	104	110	108	109
BANGOR, ME	78	67	66	68	69	78	72	75	74	68	73	67	67	74	70	76	64	74	79	77
BARABOO, WI	91	84	85	84	87	95	85	91	87	83	86	80	82	89	86	89	76	88	94	92
BARNSTABLE TOWN, MA	107	113	118	112	120	125	105	116	107	108	106	101	110	102	115	111	95	111	121	115
BARRE, VT	93	91	100	93	93	96	92	93	93	91	92	84	92	93	93	94	82	92	97	94
BARTLESVILLE, OK	90	83	89	84	85	93	84	88	89	82	86	77	83	88	86	92	76	86	97	89
BASTROP, LA	66	47	36	46	51	66	51	59	58	49	57	52	44	58	49	62	49	57	66	64
BATAVIA, NY	83	81	88	82	84	88	80	84	82	80	81	73	81	84	82	84	73	81	87	85
BATESVILLE, AR	84	63	47	61	68	87	64	77	71	62	70	68	57	74	63	76	60	72	84	83
BATON ROUGE, LA	84	75	71	76	72	79	77	77	80	77	79	70	74	80	75	81	71	79	80	80
BATTLE CREEK, MI	83	78	85	80	79	83	80	81	83	80	82	71	80	85	80	85	74	80	86	82
BAY CITY, MI	81	82	92	82	84	87	79	83	83	80	81	71	82	83	83	85	73	80	89	83
BAY CITY, TX	82	65	52	64	65	78	68	74	72	67	72	67	62	73	66	75	64	74	77	77
BEATRICE, NE	78	62	58	62	68	82	66	75	72	63	70	65	61	74	66	75	61	71	83	78
BEAUMONT-PT ARTHUR,TX	84	75	76	76	75	82	77	79	82	77	80	70	75	82	77	84	72	80	85	81
BEAVER DAM, WI	90	89	93	89	91	95	85	90	87	86	86	79	86	90	88	89	77	86	93	92
BECKLEY, WV	76	59	50	57	64	81	62	72	68	59	67	63	55	69	62	73	58	68	81	76
UNITED STATES	100	100	100	100	100	100	100	100	100	100	100	100	100	100	100	100	100	100	100	100

POPULATION CHANGE
CBSA AND U.S. TOTALS

A

CBSA	CBSA Code	POPULATION			2000-2007 ANNUAL RATE		RACE (%)					
							White		Black		Asian/Pacific	
		2000	2007	2012	% Rate	National Rank	2000	2007	2000	2007	2000	2007
BEDFORD, IN	13260	45,922	45,435	44,979	-0.1	805	97.9	97.5	0.4	0.4	0.3	0.4
BEEVILLE, TX	13300	32,359	32,997	32,671	0.3	633	67.9	65.7	9.9	9.3	0.5	0.6
BELLEFONTAINE, OH	13340	46,005	47,990	49,280	0.6	494	96.1	95.5	1.7	1.9	0.4	0.6
BELLINGHAM, WA	13380	166,814	191,791	210,324	1.9	113	88.4	86.9	0.7	0.8	2.9	3.4
BEMIDJI, MN	13420	39,650	43,575	46,001	1.3	225	76.7	75.7	0.4	0.5	0.6	0.8
BEND, OR	13460	115,367	156,004	194,015	4.3	10	94.8	93.9	0.2	0.2	0.8	1.0
BENNETTSVILLE, SC	13500	28,818	29,275	28,317	0.2	679	44.5	43.0	50.7	51.2	0.2	0.3
BENNINGTON, VT	13540	36,994	38,382	39,326	0.5	545	97.7	97.3	0.4	0.5	0.6	0.9
BERLIN, NH-VT	13620	39,570	40,415	40,807	0.3	633	97.8	97.5	0.1	0.2	0.4	0.5
BIG RAPIDS, MI	13660	40,553	43,403	45,633	0.9	352	92.7	90.6	3.6	4.8	0.9	1.3
BIG SPRING, TX	13700	33,627	33,449	32,563	-0.1	805	80.1	77.3	4.1	4.1	0.6	0.7
BILLINGS, MT	13740	138,904	151,280	160,874	1.2	255	93.1	92.1	0.4	0.5	0.6	0.7
BINGHAMTON, NY	13780	252,320	249,305	246,633	-0.2	841	92.6	91.2	2.7	3.0	2.4	3.0
BIRMINGHAM-HOOVER,AL	13820	1,052,238	1,115,659	1,170,766	0.8	396	69.9	69.1	27.6	27.6	0.8	1.0
BISHOP, CA	13860	17,945	18,426	18,736	0.4	590	80.1	77.2	0.2	0.2	1.0	1.2
BISMARCK, ND	13900	94,719	103,777	110,612	1.3	225	95.2	94.1	0.2	0.3	0.4	0.6
BLACKFOOT, ID	13940	41,735	44,513	46,563	0.9	352	82.4	80.6	0.2	0.2	0.6	0.7
BLACKSBURG-RADFORD	13980	151,272	156,773	160,135	0.5	545	91.2	89.3	4.3	4.7	2.5	3.4
BLOOMINGTON, IN	14020	175,506	185,500	193,263	0.8	396	93.2	91.7	2.1	2.3	2.4	3.4
BLOOMINGTON-NORM.,IL	14060	150,433	166,785	178,759	1.4	196	89.2	87.2	6.2	6.9	2.1	2.7
BLOOMSBURG-BERW.,PA	14100	82,387	84,914	86,367	0.4	590	97.4	96.7	0.9	1.0	0.7	1.0
BLUEFIELD, WV-VA	14140	107,578	105,816	104,755	-0.2	841	94.1	93.5	4.4	4.5	0.5	0.8
BLYTHEVILLE, AR	14180	51,979	48,337	45,798	-1.0	936	64.4	61.6	32.7	35.0	0.4	0.5
BOGALUSA, LA	14220	43,926	45,009	45,854	0.3	633	67.4	63.4	31.5	35.3	0.2	0.2
BOISE CITY-NAMPA, ID	14260	464,840	587,526	686,063	3.3	26	89.8	88.3	0.5	0.6	1.5	1.8
BONHAM, TX	14300	31,242	34,311	36,550	1.3	225	86.6	84.5	8.0	8.7	0.3	0.4
BOONE, IA	14340	26,224	26,892	27,409	0.3	633	98.5	98.1	0.4	0.4	0.2	0.3
BOONE, NC	14380	42,695	45,576	46,157	0.9	352	96.5	93.7	1.6	3.4	0.6	0.8
BORGER, TX	14420	23,857	22,379	21,426	-0.9	932	87.0	84.3	2.4	2.6	0.4	0.5
BOSTON-CAMBRIDGE, MA	14460	4,391,344	4,515,779	4,600,633	0.4	590	83.3	80.4	6.1	6.5	4.6	6.1
BOULDER, CO	14500	269,794	285,787	293,516	0.8	396	88.4	86.6	0.9	0.9	3.1	3.7
BOWLING GREEN, KY	14540	104,166	114,738	122,913	1.3	225	88.3	86.6	7.7	8.0	1.3	1.8
BOZEMAN, MT	14580	67,831	84,457	99,081	3.1	34	96.2	95.6	0.2	0.3	1.0	1.2
BRADFORD, PA	14620	45,936	44,532	43,342	-0.4	896	96.5	95.8	1.9	2.2	0.3	0.5
BRAINERD, MN	14660	82,249	92,661	98,957	1.7	140	94.0	93.6	0.2	0.3	0.3	0.4
BRANSON, MO	14700	68,361	76,418	82,499	1.5	173	96.8	96.3	0.2	0.3	0.3	0.5
BREMERTON-SILV., WA	14740	231,969	245,400	254,519	0.8	396	84.3	82.3	2.9	3.1	5.2	5.9
BRENHAM, TX	14780	30,373	32,237	33,357	0.8	396	74.7	71.7	18.7	19.9	1.2	1.5
BREVARD, NC	14820	29,334	30,960	32,170	0.7	444	93.7	93.0	4.2	4.4	0.4	0.5
BRIDGEPORT-STAMFORD	14860	882,567	918,315	943,125	0.5	545	79.3	76.1	10.0	10.6	3.3	4.7
BRIGHAM CITY, UT	14940	42,745	47,295	50,781	1.4	196	92.9	91.7	0.2	0.2	1.0	1.2
BROOKHAVEN, MS	15020	33,166	34,106	34,673	0.4	590	69.4	67.4	29.7	31.4	0.3	0.4
BROOKINGS, OR	15060	21,137	22,664	23,814	1.0	318	92.9	92.1	0.2	0.2	0.8	1.0
BROOKINGS, SD	15100	28,220	29,853	30,717	0.8	396	96.4	95.2	0.3	0.4	1.4	2.1
BROWNSVILLE, TN	15140	19,797	19,881	19,924	0.1	723	46.7	45.6	51.0	52.2	0.1	0.1
BROWNSVILLE-HARLN,TX	15180	335,227	395,867	440,440	2.3	78	80.3	79.4	0.5	0.5	0.5	0.5
BROWNWOOD, TX	15220	37,674	38,531	39,028	0.3	633	87.4	84.9	4.0	4.3	0.4	0.5
BRUNSWICK, GA	15260	93,044	103,271	110,970	1.4	196	73.3	69.4	24.1	27.3	0.5	0.7
BUCYRUS, OH	15340	46,966	45,792	44,979	-0.3	873	98.0	97.6	0.6	0.7	0.3	0.5
BUFFALO-NIAGFALLS,NY	15380	1,170,111	1,152,143	1,136,469	-0.2	841	83.8	81.7	11.7	12.9	1.3	1.7
BURLEY, ID	15420	41,590	41,195	40,724	-0.1	805	81.5	79.0	0.2	0.3	0.4	0.5
BURLINGTON, IA-IL	15460	50,564	48,857	47,639	-0.5	911	94.5	93.5	3.0	3.4	0.5	0.8
BURLINGTON, NC	15500	130,800	144,506	154,475	1.4	196	75.6	73.5	18.8	18.9	0.9	1.2
BURLINGTON-S BURL,VT	15540	198,889	211,172	219,101	0.8	396	95.4	94.5	0.7	0.9	1.6	2.1
BUTTE-SILVER BOW, MT	15580	34,606	33,148	32,205	-0.6	921	95.4	94.7	0.2	0.2	0.5	0.6
CADILLAC, MI	15620	44,962	48,907	51,525	1.2	255	97.4	96.9	0.2	0.2	0.4	0.6
CALHOUN, GA	15660	44,104	53,264	60,294	2.6	57	89.7	86.2	3.5	4.0	0.6	0.8
CAMBRIDGE, MD	15700	30,674	32,577	34,011	0.8	396	69.4	63.9	28.4	33.3	0.7	0.9
CAMBRIDGE, OH	15740	40,792	41,419	41,801	0.2	679	96.3	95.7	1.5	1.7	0.3	0.5
CAMDEN, AR	15780	34,534	33,281	32,291	-0.5	911	62.2	59.7	36.1	38.5	0.2	0.3
CAMPBELLSVILLE, KY	15820	22,927	23,241	23,460	0.2	679	93.6	93.1	5.1	5.3	0.2	0.3
CANON CITY, CO	15860	46,145	48,890	50,224	0.8	396	89.5	88.8	5.3	5.6	0.6	0.7
CANTON, IL	15900	38,250	38,212	38,221	0.0	765	95.1	94.6	3.6	3.4	0.3	0.7
CANTON-MASSILLON, OH	15940	406,934	411,749	415,391	0.2	679	90.8	89.6	6.7	7.4	0.5	0.8
CAPE CORAL-FT MYERS	15980	440,888	634,375	831,457	5.1	5	87.7	84.7	6.6	7.7	0.8	1.1
CAPE GIRARDEAU-JACKS	16020	90,312	92,638	94,407	0.4	590	89.8	88.4	7.7	8.6	0.7	1.0
CARBONDALE, IL	16060	59,612	58,310	57,934	-0.3	873	80.8	77.4	13.0	14.2	3.1	4.4
CARLSBAD-ARTESIA, NM	16100	51,658	51,269	51,128	-0.1	805	76.3	75.2	1.6	1.7	0.5	0.6
CARSON CITY, NV	16180	52,457	56,641	58,574	1.1	288	85.3	83.4	1.8	1.9	1.9	1.9
CASPER, WY	16220	66,533	70,649	73,803	0.8	396	94.2	93.5	0.8	0.8	0.6	0.6
CEDAR CITY, UT	16260	33,779	41,206	47,228	2.8	46	93.0	92.3	0.4	0.4	1.0	1.2
CEDAR RAPIDS, IA	16300	237,230	253,929	266,224	0.9	352	94.7	93.4	2.2	2.6	1.2	1.8
CEDARTOWN, GA	16340	38,127	42,356	45,093	1.5	173	80.5	76.2	13.3	15.2	0.4	0.5
CELINA, OH	16380	40,924	41,758	42,385	0.3	633	98.4	98.1	0.1	0.1	0.3	0.5
CENTRAL CITY, KY	16420	31,839	31,627	31,343	-0.1	805	94.2	93.7	4.6	4.9	0.1	0.2
CENTRALIA, IL	16460	41,691	40,916	40,412	-0.3	873	94.0	93.0	3.8	4.3	0.6	0.8
CENTRALIA, WA	16500	68,600	74,454	78,755	1.1	288	93.0	91.8	0.4	0.4	0.9	1.0
UNITED STATES					1.2		75.1	72.7	12.3	12.6	3.8	4.5

CBSA	% HISPANIC ORIGIN		2007 AGE DISTRIBUTION (%)									MEDIAN AGE	% 2007 Males	% 2007 Females
	2000	2007	0-4	5-9	10-14	15-19	20-24	25-44	45-64	65-84	85+	18+	2007		
BEDFORD, IN	0.9	1.2	6.4	6.5	6.3	5.7	5.3	26.5	27.7	13.4	2.1	77.3	40.5	49.0	51.0
BEEVILLE, TX	53.9	60.4	6.1	5.5	5.4	6.9	11.1	35.4	19.7	8.6	1.3	79.4	31.5	60.9	39.1
BELLEFONTAINE, OH	0.7	0.9	7.1	6.4	6.9	6.3	6.3	25.6	27.4	12.1	2.0	75.8	39.0	49.3	50.7
BELLINGHAM, WA	5.2	6.6	6.0	5.6	6.1	7.9	10.4	25.6	26.4	10.1	1.9	78.4	35.7	49.3	50.7
BEMIDJI, MN	1.0	1.2	7.4	6.4	6.8	9.0	10.6	24.0	23.9	9.9	1.9	74.6	32.1	49.3	50.7
BEND, OR	3.7	5.1	6.1	5.8	6.3	6.9	6.4	25.0	30.1	11.7	1.7	77.5	40.5	49.5	50.5
BENNETTSVILLE, SC	0.7	0.9	6.3	6.1	6.2	6.3	7.2	30.2	26.3	10.0	1.5	77.6	36.7	52.4	47.6
BENNINGTON, VT	0.9	1.1	5.1	4.9	5.7	7.2	6.6	22.1	31.5	14.3	2.6	80.2	43.9	48.2	51.8
BERLIN, NH-VT	0.6	0.8	5.1	4.8	5.7	6.5	6.3	22.6	31.1	14.7	3.2	80.5	44.3	49.3	50.7
BIG RAPIDS, MI	1.3	1.8	6.1	5.6	5.5	8.5	12.0	23.9	24.1	12.7	1.6	79.2	34.8	51.1	48.9
BIG SPRING, TX	37.5	44.3	6.1	5.2	5.5	6.3	8.9	30.2	23.5	12.3	2.0	79.6	36.7	56.0	44.0
BILLINGS, MT	3.6	4.4	6.5	6.2	6.5	6.8	6.5	25.5	28.6	11.3	2.2	76.7	39.2	49.0	51.0
BINGHAMTON, NY	1.8	2.1	5.8	5.4	6.1	8.0	7.9	23.6	27.2	13.4	2.7	78.7	40.3	48.7	51.3
BIRMINGHAM-HOOVER,AL	1.8	2.6	6.7	6.6	6.5	6.4	6.1	28.5	26.5	11.0	1.8	76.4	37.5	48.4	51.6
BISHOP, CA	12.6	16.0	5.3	5.1	6.0	7.1	6.6	18.9	32.8	15.3	2.8	79.0	45.6	49.0	51.0
BISMARCK, ND	0.7	0.9	6.5	6.0	6.4	7.2	7.7	26.7	26.9	10.6	2.2	77.0	37.6	49.2	50.8
BLACKFOOT, ID	13.3	15.1	9.8	8.1	7.8	7.9	9.0	24.5	22.8	8.8	1.3	69.3	30.1	50.0	50.0
BLACKSBURG-RADFORD	1.3	1.9	4.8	4.7	4.6	10.6	16.5	24.3	22.7	10.1	1.6	83.0	32.1	50.9	49.1
BLOOMINGTON, IN	1.5	2.0	5.5	5.1	5.0	9.6	14.4	26.0	23.0	9.7	1.5	81.1	32.2	49.4	50.6
BLOOMINGTON-NORM.,IL	2.5	3.3	6.5	6.3	6.4	9.3	12.4	27.4	22.4	7.9	1.6	77.1	31.6	48.5	51.5
BLOOMSBURG-BERW.,PA	0.9	1.2	5.0	4.8	5.4	8.4	9.2	23.3	27.5	13.5	2.7	81.0	40.5	47.8	52.2
BLUEFIELD, WV-VA	0.5	0.6	5.4	5.6	5.4	5.2	5.5	25.8	30.1	14.7	2.4	80.7	42.8	48.2	51.8
BLYTHEVILLE, AR	2.2	2.9	8.6	7.7	7.2	6.7	7.2	26.6	23.6	10.4	1.7	72.3	33.8	48.2	51.8
BOGALUSA, LA	0.8	0.8	7.3	7.1	6.6	6.0	6.8	25.5	26.5	12.4	1.9	75.4	37.7	49.0	51.0
BOISE CITY-NAMPA, ID	9.0	10.5	8.4	7.7	7.3	6.8	7.1	29.7	23.7	7.9	1.4	72.5	33.2	50.0	50.0
BONHAM, TX	5.6	7.3	6.2	5.6	5.9	6.2	7.6	26.9	25.7	13.6	2.5	78.9	39.7	53.1	46.9
BOONE, IA	0.8	1.1	6.2	5.8	6.1	6.8	6.5	25.2	27.5	12.6	3.1	77.6	40.2	49.0	51.0
BOONE, NC	1.5	2.1	4.3	4.1	4.5	8.8	13.5	25.8	26.8	10.6	1.5	83.3	36.1	50.2	49.8
BORGER, TX	14.7	18.7	7.1	6.6	6.4	6.7	8.5	22.0	27.7	12.8	2.3	75.9	38.5	49.1	50.9
BOSTON-CAMBRIDGE, MA	6.4	7.8	6.1	6.3	6.7	7.3	6.5	28.8	25.8	10.3	2.1	76.7	37.7	48.5	51.5
BOULDER, CO	10.7	12.7	5.9	6.0	6.0	7.9	9.2	30.3	26.5	7.0	1.2	78.4	34.9	50.5	49.5
BOWLING GREEN, KY	2.4	3.6	6.5	6.0	5.9	7.4	8.6	29.5	24.5	9.9	1.5	78.2	34.4	49.2	50.8
BOZEMAN, MT	1.5	1.9	5.9	5.3	5.2	7.8	12.5	29.5	25.3	7.3	1.2	80.0	31.6	52.1	47.9
BRADFORD, PA	1.1	1.3	5.9	5.5	6.1	6.6	6.5	26.0	27.3	13.5	2.7	78.5	40.3	50.5	49.5
BRAINERD, MN	0.7	1.0	6.0	5.3	6.2	6.5	6.7	22.2	29.1	15.6	2.4	78.6	42.9	49.8	50.2
BRANSON, MO	1.8	2.3	5.9	5.7	5.6	5.8	5.8	23.4	28.9	17.0	1.9	79.6	43.4	48.7	51.3
BREMERTON-SILV., WA	4.1	5.2	6.6	6.1	6.9	7.1	8.2	25.7	28.4	9.4	1.7	76.1	37.6	50.6	49.4
BRENHAM, TX	8.7	11.1	6.4	5.8	5.5	8.3	7.9	24.1	26.2	12.9	3.0	78.3	38.8	49.1	50.9
BREVARD, NC	1.0	1.3	4.9	4.9	4.9	6.3	5.0	21.4	29.9	19.6	3.0	81.7	46.7	48.2	51.8
BRIDGEPORT-STAMFORD	11.9	14.4	6.9	7.7	7.8	7.1	5.2	26.3	26.1	10.8	2.2	73.2	38.5	48.6	51.4
BRIGHAM CITY, UT	6.5	7.8	10.4	8.4	8.3	8.1	8.3	25.7	20.3	9.1	1.4	67.9	28.8	50.6	49.4
BROOKHAVEN, MS	0.7	0.9	7.3	7.1	6.9	5.8	6.4	27.1	25.8	11.6	1.9	75.1	37.0	48.2	51.8
BROOKINGS, OR	3.6	4.8	4.1	3.8	4.5	5.7	5.1	15.9	35.1	22.5	3.2	83.8	51.8	49.2	50.8
BROOKINGS, SD	0.9	1.1	5.7	5.0	4.8	10.8	18.3	24.8	20.3	8.2	2.1	81.5	27.8	50.3	49.7
BROWNSVILLE, TN	2.6	2.6	7.2	6.9	7.9	6.0	5.8	27.1	26.1	10.8	2.1	74.3	36.7	47.2	52.8
BROWNSVILLE-HARLN,TX	84.3	87.7	10.1	8.9	8.5	8.2	7.6	26.7	19.4	9.4	1.2	67.6	29.6	48.2	51.8
BROWNWOOD, TX	15.4	19.5	6.4	5.9	5.9	8.6	7.7	22.8	26.1	13.9	2.6	76.8	39.2	49.7	50.3
BRUNSWICK, GA	2.4	3.2	6.6	6.4	6.5	7.2	6.5	24.8	27.7	12.4	1.9	76.1	39.2	48.6	51.4
BUCYRUS, OH	0.8	0.9	6.8	6.3	6.0	6.4	6.7	25.1	27.1	13.4	2.4	77.2	39.7	48.6	51.4
BUFFALO-NIAGFALLS,NY	2.9	3.4	6.0	5.7	6.5	7.2	6.6	25.0	27.1	13.3	2.7	77.6	40.2	48.0	52.0
BURLEY, ID	22.0	24.8	9.3	7.9	7.8	7.0	8.2	24.1	23.6	10.3	1.8	70.6	32.5	50.3	49.7
BURLINGTON, IA-IL	1.6	2.1	6.5	5.8	6.1	5.8	6.9	24.6	28.0	13.7	2.7	78.2	41.1	48.8	51.2
BURLINGTON, NC	6.8	8.8	6.4	6.3	6.2	7.4	6.1	27.9	25.9	11.9	2.0	77.1	38.2	48.4	51.6
BURLINGTON-S BURL,VT	0.9	1.1	5.9	5.7	6.5	8.4	9.0	26.6	27.5	8.9	1.5	77.6	36.9	49.0	51.0
BUTTE-SILVER BOW, MT	2.7	3.4	5.9	5.4	6.1	6.8	6.7	24.6	28.5	13.1	2.9	78.7	40.9	49.5	50.5
CADILLAC, MI	1.1	1.3	6.7	6.1	6.5	6.7	7.1	24.6	27.7	12.7	1.9	76.5	40.0	49.9	50.1
CALHOUN, GA	7.4	10.5	7.3	7.1	6.6	5.9	5.7	31.5	24.6	10.0	1.2	75.3	36.2	50.0	50.0
CAMBRIDGE, MD	1.3	1.8	5.5	5.2	6.2	6.5	5.7	24.1	29.2	15.2	2.4	78.8	42.9	47.6	52.4
CAMBRIDGE, OH	0.6	0.8	6.9	6.5	6.4	6.5	6.6	24.8	27.4	13.0	2.0	76.2	39.6	48.8	51.2
CAMDEN, AR	0.9	1.0	6.3	5.8	6.3	6.5	6.8	24.0	28.2	13.5	2.5	77.7	40.8	47.9	52.1
CAMPBELLSVILLE, KY	0.8	1.2	6.2	5.8	5.9	6.7	6.7	25.4	27.4	14.1	1.9	78.6	40.7	48.5	51.5
CANON CITY, CO	10.3	12.4	4.9	4.6	4.9	6.2	7.7	29.3	27.6	12.6	2.3	81.7	40.4	56.9	43.1
CANTON, IL	1.2	1.4	5.7	5.4	5.4	6.8	6.9	26.1	26.0	14.4	3.2	80.1	40.5	50.3	49.7
CANTON-MASSILLON, OH	0.9	1.1	6.3	6.1	6.4	6.8	6.1	24.7	28.2	13.1	2.4	77.2	40.5	48.3	51.7
CAPE CORAL-FT MYERS	9.5	13.5	5.4	5.0	5.2	5.3	5.0	20.9	27.5	22.4	3.3	81.2	47.4	48.8	51.2
CAPE GIRARDEAU-JACKS	0.9	1.2	6.1	5.6	6.1	7.3	8.2	26.5	25.8	12.0	2.3	78.3	37.8	49.1	50.9
CARBONDALE, IL	2.4	3.7	5.4	4.8	4.9	8.0	16.9	27.5	21.3	9.3	1.9	81.8	30.1	51.2	48.8
CARLSBAD-ARTESIA, NM	38.8	41.0	7.7	6.9	6.9	6.9	8.3	22.6	26.5	11.9	2.3	74.3	37.1	48.7	51.3
CARSON CITY, NV	14.2	17.4	6.3	5.6	6.3	6.3	7.0	25.6	27.1	13.5	2.4	78.0	40.0	51.3	48.7
CASPER, WY	4.9	5.5	6.7	5.9	6.2	7.3	7.9	25.2	28.0	11.2	1.7	77.0	37.7	49.3	50.7
CEDAR CITY, UT	4.1	4.8	10.7	8.3	7.0	8.7	12.5	27.9	17.1	6.9	1.0	70.0	26.1	49.6	50.4
CEDAR RAPIDS, IA	1.3	1.7	7.0	6.5	6.9	6.6	6.9	27.8	25.5	10.7	2.1	75.8	37.1	50.4	50.4
CEDARTOWN, GA	7.7	10.5	7.4	7.3	6.1	6.3	6.2	28.7	24.4	11.7	1.8	75.3	36.5	50.3	49.7
CELINA, OH	1.1	1.4	7.7	7.1	7.5	7.1	6.9	24.3	25.9	11.4	2.1	73.3	36.8	50.4	49.6
CENTRAL CITY, KY	0.7	1.1	6.1	6.3	5.5	5.8	5.5	27.4	27.7	13.4	2.3	78.7	40.6	50.0	50.0
CENTRALIA, IL	0.9	1.2	6.7	6.2	6.5	6.4	6.5	25.0	28.0	13.2	2.9	76.7	39.9	48.6	51.4
CENTRALIA, WA	5.4	6.9	6.6	6.1	5.9	7.1	7.1	23.2	28.1	13.3	2.5	76.9	40.2	49.6	50.4
UNITED STATES	12.5	15.0	6.9	6.5	6.8	7.1	7.0	27.6	25.4	10.7	1.9	75.6	36.7	49.2	50.8

CBSA	HOUSEHOLDS					FAMILIES			MEDIAN HOUSEHOLD INCOME		
	2000	2007	2012	% Annual Rate 2000-2007	2007 Average HH Size	2000	2007	% Annual Rate 2000-2007	2007	2012	2007 National Rank
BEDFORD, IN	18,535	18,900	18,930	0.3	2.36	13,139	12,925	-0.2	44,875	51,206	439
BEEVILLE, TX	9,061	9,144	9,087	0.1	2.70	6,580	6,574	0.0	34,817	39,346	840
BELLEFONTAINE, OH	17,956	19,079	19,729	0.8	2.48	12,731	13,142	0.4	50,345	57,044	237
BELLINGHAM, WA	64,446	75,395	83,168	2.2	2.47	41,094	47,278	2.0	50,235	60,031	243
BEMIDJI, MN	14,337	16,039	17,105	1.6	2.58	9,752	10,592	1.1	41,599	48,215	579
BEND, OR	45,595	62,836	78,564	4.5	2.46	31,953	43,669	4.4	52,074	61,423	193
BENNETTSVILLE, SC	10,478	10,405	10,168	-0.1	2.50	7,338	7,032	-0.6	32,310	36,898	886
BENNINGTON, VT	14,846	15,909	16,490	1.0	2.33	9,914	10,323	0.6	51,433	61,973	209
BERLIN, NH-VT	16,563	17,180	17,532	0.5	2.29	10,971	11,181	0.3	40,317	45,735	641
BIG RAPIDS, MI	14,915	16,586	17,725	1.5	2.42	9,893	10,676	1.1	40,420	45,295	635
BIG SPRING, TX	11,389	11,016	10,724	-0.5	2.50	7,946	7,601	-0.6	37,371	43,239	762
BILLINGS, MT	56,149	61,745	66,001	1.3	2.40	36,925	39,391	0.9	43,691	50,160	489
BINGHAMTON, NY	100,474	100,920	100,697	0.1	2.36	64,557	64,330	0.0	45,559	52,901	408
BIRMINGHAM-HOOVER,AL	412,376	444,255	468,794	1.0	2.46	287,200	304,632	0.8	45,042	50,540	429
BISHOP, CA	7,703	7,863	8,009	0.3	2.32	4,937	5,066	0.4	42,584	49,094	526
BISMARCK, ND	37,559	42,330	45,727	1.7	2.37	25,129	27,208	1.1	52,334	62,855	187
BLACKFOOT, ID	13,317	14,556	15,356	1.2	3.03	10,713	11,612	1.1	45,034	52,129	430
BLACKSBURG-RADFORD	58,443	61,411	63,230	0.7	2.33	34,887	35,119	0.1	40,370	46,839	639
BLOOMINGTON, IN	68,552	74,312	78,258	1.1	2.30	40,295	41,564	0.4	41,951	48,166	559
BLOOMINGTON-NORM.,IL	56,746	63,145	68,184	1.5	2.45	35,470	38,121	1.0	58,489	67,433	81
BLOOMSBURG-BERW.,PA	32,000	33,411	34,262	0.6	2.39	21,381	21,644	0.2	43,377	50,302	501
BLUEFIELD, WV-VA	44,786	45,584	45,738	0.2	2.28	31,171	30,759	-0.2	32,674	37,095	881
BLYTHEVILLE, AR	19,349	18,263	17,410	-0.8	2.60	13,908	12,766	-1.2	34,539	40,187	849
BOGALUSA, LA	16,467	17,331	17,835	0.7	2.50	11,646	11,947	0.4	26,581	28,746	928
BOISE CITY-NAMPA, ID	170,291	218,578	256,216	3.5	2.63	120,145	152,529	3.3	55,223	66,836	124
BONHAM, TX	11,105	12,228	13,093	1.3	2.52	7,990	8,711	1.2	41,384	47,369	589
BOONE, IA	10,374	10,810	11,052	0.6	2.41	7,135	7,302	0.3	51,311	60,178	212
BOONE, NC	16,540	18,267	18,707	1.4	2.20	9,410	10,021	0.9	40,571	46,240	627
BORGER, TX	9,283	8,804	8,472	-0.7	2.51	6,869	6,452	-0.9	44,401	51,241	451
BOSTON-CAMBRIDGE, MA	1,679,659	1,737,213	1,775,064	0.5	2.52	1,075,725	1,101,544	0.3	73,001	87,853	10
BOULDER, CO	106,542	113,472	116,564	0.9	2.44	63,070	65,209	0.5	71,929	85,147	13
BOWLING GREEN, KY	40,013	45,586	49,354	1.8	2.39	26,888	29,424	1.3	44,079	51,739	460
BOZEMAN, MT	26,323	33,029	39,002	3.2	2.46	16,196	19,641	2.7	46,248	53,745	378
BRADFORD, PA	18,024	17,667	17,294	-0.3	2.36	12,098	11,503	-0.7	41,802	48,917	574
BRAINERD, MN	33,143	38,350	41,321	2.0	2.38	22,913	25,754	1.6	45,765	53,290	395
BRANSON, MO	27,980	31,495	34,072	1.6	2.37	19,896	21,787	1.3	38,821	44,916	694
BREMERTON-SILV., WA	86,416	93,392	97,384	1.1	2.56	61,344	65,411	0.9	60,027	69,784	68
BRENHAM, TX	11,322	12,082	12,546	0.9	2.52	7,934	8,376	0.8	44,090	50,609	459
BREVARD, NC	12,320	13,434	14,140	1.2	2.23	8,666	9,213	0.8	48,589	55,850	295
BRIDGEPORT-STAMFORD	324,232	335,228	344,121	0.5	2.68	228,399	234,506	0.4	84,825	102,263	3
BRIGHAM CITY, UT	13,144	14,730	15,903	1.6	3.18	10,809	11,920	1.4	55,531	64,285	120
BROOKHAVEN, MS	12,538	13,152	13,468	0.7	2.54	9,191	9,439	0.4	31,496	34,332	901
BROOKINGS, OR	9,543	10,395	11,010	1.2	2.15	6,180	6,665	1.0	36,550	41,672	790
BROOKINGS, SD	10,665	11,430	11,903	1.0	2.32	6,219	6,590	0.8	44,948	52,873	435
BROWNSVILLE, TN	7,558	7,781	7,879	0.4	2.52	5,418	5,440	0.1	33,286	38,095	872
BROWNSVILLE-HARLN,TX	97,267	115,756	129,335	2.4	3.38	79,944	94,531	2.3	31,956	36,654	894
BROWNWOOD, TX	14,306	14,716	14,948	0.4	2.47	10,013	10,189	0.2	37,871	43,697	745
BRUNSWICK, GA	36,846	41,106	44,467	1.5	2.47	25,568	27,601	1.1	43,873	50,476	480
BUCYRUS, OH	18,957	18,915	18,752	0.0	2.39	13,173	12,754	-0.4	44,121	50,869	457
BUFFALO-NIAGFALLS,NY	468,719	468,711	465,222	0.0	2.38	301,941	299,375	-0.1	49,020	57,857	285
BURLEY, ID	14,033	14,154	14,061	0.1	2.88	10,849	10,838	0.0	40,217	45,958	646
BURLINGTON, IA-IL	20,635	20,350	19,961	-0.2	2.36	13,912	13,441	-0.5	45,477	52,349	413
BURLINGTON, NC	51,584	57,274	61,387	1.5	2.45	35,526	38,424	1.1	48,368	55,980	298
BURLINGTON-S BURL,VT	75,978	82,762	86,627	1.2	2.45	49,316	52,199	0.8	60,458	72,880	64
BUTTE-SILVER BOW, MT	14,432	13,934	13,584	-0.5	2.30	8,931	8,338	-0.9	36,669	42,149	787
CADILLAC, MI	17,274	19,195	20,381	1.5	2.52	12,432	13,472	1.1	41,896	46,905	563
CALHOUN, GA	16,173	19,642	22,288	2.7	2.69	12,261	14,497	2.3	46,869	52,901	354
CAMBRIDGE, MD	12,706	13,714	14,430	1.1	2.32	8,506	8,861	0.6	40,444	44,832	633
CAMBRIDGE, OH	16,094	16,583	16,821	0.4	2.47	11,234	11,233	0.0	36,278	41,391	799
CAMDEN, AR	13,930	13,692	13,400	-0.2	2.39	9,699	9,251	-0.7	35,902	41,181	812
CAMPBELLSVILLE, KY	9,233	9,611	9,792	0.6	2.35	6,559	6,594	0.1	35,096	40,180	833
CANON CITY, CO	15,232	16,334	16,876	1.0	2.43	10,501	11,009	0.7	41,871	48,288	567
CANTON, IL	14,877	15,000	15,064	0.1	2.38	10,252	10,045	-0.3	40,099	45,135	648
CANTON-MASSILLON, OH	159,442	162,859	165,130	0.3	2.47	110,895	109,907	-0.1	48,167	55,243	305
CAPE CORAL-FT MYERS	188,599	274,210	361,253	5.3	2.29	127,611	182,156	5.0	50,569	59,663	230
CAPE GIRARDEAU-JACKS	35,364	37,015	37,982	0.6	2.39	23,879	24,270	0.2	41,864	48,173	568
CARBONDALE, IL	24,215	24,427	24,422	0.1	2.17	12,653	12,226	-0.5	29,453	33,363	913
CARLSBAD-ARTESIA, NM	19,379	19,802	19,930	0.3	2.55	14,060	13,975	-0.1	38,802	44,732	697
CARSON CITY, NV	20,171	21,773	22,500	1.1	2.45	13,256	14,140	0.9	52,926	62,195	167
CASPER, WY	26,819	28,904	30,428	1.0	2.39	17,747	18,534	0.6	46,820	55,613	356
CEDAR CITY, UT	10,627	13,105	15,146	2.9	3.07	8,073	9,740	2.6	42,292	49,537	539
CEDAR RAPIDS, IA	94,059	103,114	108,997	1.3	2.39	62,689	67,384	1.0	56,768	66,273	99
CEDARTOWN, GA	14,012	15,654	16,698	1.5	2.65	10,338	11,222	1.1	39,637	44,994	666
CELINA, OH	14,756	15,447	15,860	0.6	2.67	11,017	11,254	0.3	52,444	60,604	181
CENTRAL CITY, KY	12,357	12,683	12,723	0.4	2.37	9,056	8,999	-0.1	34,509	39,575	851
CENTRALIA, IL	16,619	16,461	16,321	-0.1	2.43	11,487	11,059	-0.5	42,364	48,558	534
CENTRALIA, WA	26,306	28,447	30,127	1.1	2.57	18,559	19,801	0.9	44,029	51,196	464
UNITED STATES				1.2	2.59			1.0	53,154	62,503	

INCOME
CBSA AND U.S. TOTALS

D

CBSA	2007 Per Capita Income	2007 HH Income Base	2007 HOUSEHOLD INCOME DISTRIBUTION (%)					2007 Home Value Base	2007 HOME VALUE DISTRIBUTION (%)					2007 Median Home Value
			Less than $25,000	$25,000 to $49,999	$50,000 to $99,999	$100,000 to $149,999	$150,000 or More		Less than $50,000	$50,000 to $89,999	$90,000 to $174,999	$175,000 to $399,999	$400,000 or More	
BEDFORD, IN	22,579	18,900	26.1	29.7	33.4	8.7	2.1	15,043	18.0	27.5	40.9	12.7	0.8	96,374
BEEVILLE, TX	15,591	9,144	36.7	29.4	27.4	5.1	1.4	6,185	31.9	36.0	24.4	6.4	1.3	69,375
BELLEFONTAINE, OH	24,251	19,079	21.0	28.6	35.7	11.1	3.6	14,889	10.6	21.5	45.9	19.4	2.6	114,675
BELLINGHAM, WA	26,205	75,395	23.2	26.5	33.8	10.9	5.6	49,950	3.4	2.2	8.3	58.3	27.8	304,450
BEMIDJI, MN	19,905	16,039	29.4	30.0	30.7	7.0	3.0	12,146	15.0	18.5	40.0	23.3	3.2	127,855
BEND, OR	28,214	62,836	18.8	28.9	34.9	10.6	6.8	46,698	2.5	2.6	8.6	48.4	38.0	340,652
BENNETTSVILLE, SC	16,550	10,405	40.2	29.1	24.0	4.9	1.7	7,555	25.8	34.9	33.4	5.4	0.4	78,070
BENNINGTON, VT	28,846	15,909	23.0	25.3	34.3	10.4	7.0	11,781	4.9	4.8	21.9	51.7	16.7	219,844
BERLIN, NH-VT	20,968	17,180	30.2	31.5	31.0	5.4	1.9	12,801	7.4	13.4	51.1	25.3	2.8	137,424
BIG RAPIDS, MI	20,865	16,586	30.3	31.4	28.2	7.0	3.1	12,311	11.5	17.4	44.0	24.5	2.5	122,641
BIG SPRING, TX	18,707	11,016	34.1	29.8	26.8	6.1	3.1	7,801	45.9	27.8	20.6	5.2	0.5	54,583
BILLINGS, MT	23,572	61,745	27.2	29.5	31.4	7.7	4.2	42,921	7.9	7.7	42.9	36.1	5.4	161,340
BINGHAMTON, NY	24,686	100,920	25.9	28.5	31.5	9.2	4.9	70,948	6.4	11.4	53.0	27.3	1.9	143,906
BIRMINGHAM-HOOVER,AL	25,197	444,253	27.6	27.5	28.9	10.2	5.8	328,036	13.4	19.1	33.9	26.7	6.8	125,779
BISHOP, CA	23,844	7,863	31.0	26.1	29.5	9.7	3.8	5,313	14.5	6.6	9.9	35.7	33.3	300,950
BISMARCK, ND	26,446	42,330	21.0	26.4	37.3	10.4	5.0	30,018	16.0	11.2	44.8	25.6	2.4	131,517
BLACKFOOT, ID	18,112	14,556	23.6	32.7	33.0	8.1	2.7	11,712	7.8	9.7	54.7	25.1	2.7	142,216
BLACKSBURG-RADFORD	22,724	61,411	31.9	27.4	29.4	7.5	3.8	37,937	11.6	10.5	39.6	33.7	4.6	152,365
BLOOMINGTON, IN	23,373	74,311	30.2	27.5	29.2	9.1	4.0	47,189	13.5	14.3	43.6	25.2	3.4	127,854
BLOOMINGTON-NORM.,IL	28,789	63,145	19.1	23.0	36.2	13.9	7.8	43,357	7.8	9.8	47.4	32.1	2.9	145,968
BLOOMSBURG-BERW.,PA	22,660	33,411	26.7	30.9	30.6	8.2	3.6	24,403	7.2	7.6	45.0	35.5	4.7	161,901
BLUEFIELD, WV-VA	19,401	45,584	38.4	31.4	23.0	4.8	2.4	35,660	23.7	20.4	37.0	17.0	1.8	99,545
BLYTHEVILLE, AR	17,762	18,263	38.2	28.1	24.5	6.6	2.7	11,082	26.4	34.5	29.6	8.9	0.7	75,965
BOGALUSA, LA	14,777	17,331	47.2	29.0	18.9	3.5	1.4	13,091	28.4	25.6	32.3	11.8	1.9	83,779
BOISE CITY-NAMPA, ID	26,776	218,578	17.8	26.8	36.2	12.4	6.9	160,723	4.7	4.4	27.4	52.9	10.6	202,532
BONHAM, TX	20,027	12,228	30.0	28.7	30.9	7.4	2.9	9,311	26.9	28.6	31.0	12.0	1.5	80,770
BOONE, IA	25,074	10,810	19.9	28.4	39.2	8.6	3.9	8,375	14.8	24.9	40.1	17.9	2.2	105,403
BOONE, NC	22,924	18,267	31.8	28.2	29.0	7.7	3.3	11,686	9.1	8.7	28.8	40.6	12.8	187,373
BORGER, TX	21,799	8,804	25.9	29.5	33.0	9.2	2.5	7,014	40.5	29.1	23.1	6.6	0.8	60,734
BOSTON-CAMBRIDGE, MA	38,631	1,737,203	16.1	17.8	31.7	18.5	16.0	1,094,739	0.8	1.0	5.5	46.4	46.3	383,167
BOULDER, CO	39,633	113,471	14.6	18.9	32.5	17.6	16.4	76,189	4.0	1.0	6.3	52.6	36.2	328,233
BOWLING GREEN, KY	24,161	45,578	28.2	27.1	30.5	9.4	4.8	30,602	14.1	14.3	43.7	24.6	3.3	124,403
BOZEMAN, MT	23,724	33,029	23.3	30.7	32.9	8.8	4.3	20,651	8.4	3.7	11.3	52.6	24.1	266,664
BRADFORD, PA	21,299	17,667	28.2	30.8	31.8	6.7	2.4	13,308	13.3	27.2	44.3	14.0	1.1	105,578
BRAINERD, MN	23,782	38,350	25.5	29.0	33.9	7.9	3.6	31,664	6.5	11.3	34.7	37.4	10.0	168,945
BRANSON, MO	21,448	31,495	27.9	36.2	26.8	6.0	3.1	23,854	14.0	16.1	38.5	26.1	5.3	129,712
BREMERTON-SILV., WA	28,664	93,392	16.1	24.4	37.7	14.6	7.2	65,507	2.0	1.8	10.0	59.9	26.3	285,980
BRENHAM, TX	22,093	12,082	28.8	26.6	32.0	8.6	4.1	9,051	17.4	17.2	35.4	22.7	7.3	119,607
BREVARD, NC	26,218	13,434	24.0	27.4	35.0	9.7	3.9	10,761	11.3	12.2	33.0	35.2	8.4	155,849
BRIDGEPORT-STAMFORD	49,464	335,228	13.0	16.3	27.1	18.9	24.6	240,892	0.9	1.4	5.3	30.6	61.8	492,672
BRIGHAM CITY, UT	19,860	14,730	15.6	27.3	42.4	11.6	3.1	11,970	2.9	3.0	39.1	51.1	3.8	182,523
BROOKHAVEN, MS	16,643	13,152	39.7	30.3	22.2	5.9	1.8	10,235	26.8	30.4	31.0	10.4	1.4	80,739
BROOKINGS, OR	22,748	10,395	32.2	32.9	26.9	4.8	3.2	7,833	12.4	6.1	19.8	43.1	18.6	218,271
BROOKINGS, SD	22,779	11,430	27.2	27.6	33.1	8.6	3.5	6,811	14.9	15.2	43.7	23.8	2.4	127,106
BROWNSVILLE, TN	18,233	7,781	38.6	27.7	26.0	5.5	2.2	5,251	12.9	30.1	41.4	13.9	1.6	98,024
BROWNSVILLE-HARLN,TX	13,293	115,756	39.8	29.1	22.7	5.7	2.7	80,004	35.1	32.0	24.0	7.8	1.1	66,429
BROWNWOOD, TX	19,547	14,716	33.5	28.8	28.7	6.3	2.7	10,844	35.3	30.5	24.6	8.4	1.2	68,137
BRUNSWICK, GA	24,540	41,106	28.1	27.2	29.3	10.0	5.4	29,490	16.5	17.6	28.6	24.1	13.2	128,698
BUCYRUS, OH	22,103	18,915	25.0	31.5	33.3	7.8	2.3	14,231	12.7	29.0	46.3	11.0	1.0	99,428
BUFFALO-NIAGFALLS,NY	26,366	468,688	25.3	25.6	32.6	10.8	5.8	323,680	4.8	11.2	49.0	32.9	2.2	147,161
BURLEY, ID	17,532	14,154	29.6	32.6	29.7	5.5	2.6	10,812	8.9	11.1	57.3	19.3	3.4	133,460
BURLINGTON, IA-IL	23,762	20,350	24.8	30.4	33.8	7.8	3.1	15,620	17.1	29.5	38.6	13.3	1.5	94,834
BURLINGTON, NC	24,308	57,274	23.6	28.0	34.9	9.0	4.6	40,918	15.9	15.3	42.4	23.5	2.9	116,907
BURLINGTON-S BURL,VT	30,531	82,762	16.2	23.4	37.6	14.2	8.5	58,809	2.7	3.3	16.6	62.7	14.7	243,120
BUTTE-SILVER BOW, MT	20,992	13,934	33.7	30.8	27.1	5.6	2.7	9,789	9.6	17.0	43.5	26.1	3.8	132,465
CADILLAC, MI	20,682	19,195	26.3	34.5	29.8	6.8	2.6	15,572	13.7	20.6	43.8	19.3	2.6	112,667
CALHOUN, GA	21,575	19,642	24.8	28.1	35.4	8.2	3.5	14,354	13.0	15.2	46.3	21.3	4.2	120,756
CAMBRIDGE, MD	22,959	13,714	31.0	28.6	29.8	7.3	3.4	9,812	4.9	5.5	24.4	51.5	13.7	209,456
CAMBRIDGE, OH	18,813	16,583	32.5	33.8	26.6	5.2	1.9	12,582	21.0	32.4	34.7	10.7	1.2	86,043
CAMDEN, AR	18,878	13,692	37.6	29.1	26.3	4.7	2.3	10,234	35.5	31.5	26.8	5.3	0.9	66,200
CAMPBELLSVILLE, KY	19,366	9,611	37.5	31.2	23.7	5.2	2.4	7,032	14.9	26.0	46.4	11.0	1.7	98,666
CANON CITY, CO	20,628	16,333	28.1	30.1	32.1	7.6	2.1	12,739	7.4	9.3	46.3	32.8	4.2	147,595
CANTON, IL	21,033	15,000	28.4	32.6	30.1	6.7	2.3	11,709	15.9	27.1	43.6	12.3	1.1	99,982
CANTON-MASSILLON, OH	25,102	162,859	22.5	29.3	33.4	9.8	5.0	123,060	8.4	19.7	48.5	21.2	2.1	120,450
CAPE CORAL-FT MYERS	30,666	274,203	19.6	29.7	33.6	9.5	7.5	215,742	2.8	3.7	17.4	49.3	26.7	266,762
CAPE GIRARDEAU-JACKS	22,548	37,015	28.7	29.9	30.2	7.1	4.0	26,695	16.2	15.8	37.7	26.2	4.1	127,349
CARBONDALE, IL	20,277	24,427	43.4	25.2	22.7	5.8	2.9	13,639	20.6	20.1	38.7	17.8	2.8	107,515
CARLSBAD-ARTESIA, NM	19,663	19,802	33.4	29.0	28.1	6.8	2.7	14,761	13.6	24.4	45.4	14.5	2.2	106,349
CARSON CITY, NV	27,145	21,773	20.0	26.7	36.6	10.6	6.1	14,151	6.8	3.6	9.8	58.6	21.2	282,575
CASPER, WY	24,534	28,904	24.3	28.8	33.8	9.0	4.1	20,775	9.6	16.7	52.0	19.2	2.5	121,930
CEDAR CITY, UT	17,380	13,105	25.0	33.7	29.9	7.7	3.1	8,909	4.3	4.6	46.0	41.4	3.7	168,930
CEDAR RAPIDS, IA	28,421	103,114	16.7	26.1	38.9	12.6	5.8	77,775	9.4	14.8	51.1	22.2	2.5	122,417
CEDARTOWN, GA	18,904	15,654	30.6	31.3	29.4	6.2	2.6	11,330	12.8	24.8	44.7	15.4	2.3	107,424
CELINA, OH	23,189	15,457	18.1	28.7	39.3	10.0	3.9	12,696	8.7	15.4	40.0	24.1	3.0	123,037
CENTRAL CITY, KY	18,862	12,683	37.0	30.2	24.9	5.9	2.1	10,520	32.5	30.1	28.8	7.7	1.0	72,321
CENTRALIA, IL	21,446	16,461	28.5	30.1	32.0	6.9	2.6	12,890	22.0	25.9	39.1	11.8	1.2	92,652
CENTRALIA, WA	21,326	28,447	27.3	29.2	32.6	7.9	3.0	21,047	4.4	4.4	26.1	55.8	9.4	209,098
UNITED STATES	27,916		21.9	25.0	32.3	12.3	8.4		7.9	10.5	27.1	35.6	19.0	192,285

SPENDING POTENTIAL INDICES
CBSA AND U.S. TOTALS

E

CBSA	FINANCIAL SERVICES				THE HOME						ENTERTAINMENT						PERSONAL			
					Home Improvements		Furnishings													
	Auto Loan	Home Loan	Invest-ments	Retire-ment Plans	Home Repair	Lawn & Garden	Comput-ers & Hard-ware	Major Appli-ances	TV, Radio, Sound Equip-ment	Furni-ture	Dine out/ Carry out	Sports Equip-ment	Fees & Tickets	Toys & Games	Travel	Cable TV	Apparel & Services	Auto Repairs	Health Insur-ance	Pets & Supplies
BEDFORD, IN	85	68	59	66	72	89	69	80	76	67	74	70	63	78	69	80	64	75	88	84
BEEVILLE, TX	68	56	47	54	56	67	57	64	62	57	61	56	52	62	56	64	54	62	68	65
BELLEFONTAINE, OH	89	81	80	81	84	94	80	87	84	80	83	77	78	87	82	87	73	84	92	90
BELLINGHAM, WA	90	87	90	89	86	88	94	89	91	89	91	83	90	90	90	89	82	91	88	90
BEMIDJI, MN	78	67	63	68	67	75	72	73	73	69	73	66	67	74	69	74	64	73	76	76
BEND, OR	100	97	93	98	97	102	95	99	95	95	95	90	94	95	96	96	84	98	99	101
BENNETTSVILLE, SC	73	51	33	49	55	75	53	66	62	52	61	59	45	64	52	67	52	62	73	72
BENNINGTON, VT	101	90	88	90	97	111	91	102	94	88	93	89	87	95	94	98	82	96	107	104
BERLIN, NH-VT	75	60	53	59	65	81	63	73	68	60	67	64	57	69	63	72	58	68	80	76
BIG RAPIDS, MI	80	64	54	64	67	81	71	75	73	66	73	68	63	72	68	74	63	74	79	79
BIG SPRING, TX	73	63	62	63	64	72	65	69	70	65	69	61	62	70	65	73	61	69	76	70
BILLINGS, MT	80	76	81	77	76	80	78	79	80	77	79	71	77	79	78	81	70	79	82	80
BINGHAMTON, NY	82	78	87	79	79	84	81	81	83	79	82	72	80	83	81	85	73	81	87	82
BIRMINGHAM-HOOVER,AL	92	84	79	85	83	91	84	87	87	84	87	78	81	88	83	89	77	87	90	90
BISHOP, CA	77	74	79	73	78	85	75	81	76	72	75	71	72	74	77	79	66	78	85	81
BISMARCK, ND	91	87	89	88	85	87	89	88	89	87	88	80	87	90	87	89	79	89	90	89
BLACKFOOT, ID	87	73	60	71	75	88	71	81	76	71	75	72	67	79	71	79	66	77	85	85
BLACKSBURG-RADFORD	79	65	66	67	65	74	80	74	78	71	78	68	71	77	73	77	69	76	77	76
BLOOMINGTON, IN	82	67	67	70	68	76	82	76	80	73	80	71	73	79	74	79	71	78	78	78
BLOOMINGTON-NORM.,IL	101	98	102	102	94	93	106	97	101	102	102	91	102	103	100	99	92	100	95	98
BLOOMSBURG-BERW.,PA	82	71	71	71	75	85	75	79	78	72	77	70	71	80	74	81	68	77	85	82
BLUEFIELD, WV-VA	71	54	44	53	59	75	57	67	63	54	62	59	50	64	57	67	53	63	75	71
BLYTHEVILLE, AR	73	59	50	58	60	72	60	66	66	60	65	59	56	68	59	69	57	65	72	70
BOGALUSA, LA	61	44	32	43	48	63	46	56	53	45	52	49	40	54	46	58	45	53	63	60
BOISE CITY-NAMPA, ID	103	101	96	102	96	96	99	98	97	100	97	91	98	100	97	96	87	98	95	99
BONHAM, TX	84	64	52	63	70	88	67	79	74	64	73	69	59	76	67	79	62	74	87	83
BOONE, IA	87	82	90	84	84	90	83	87	86	81	84	76	82	87	85	87	74	84	92	87
BOONE, NC	81	61	53	62	64	79	78	76	76	67	76	70	65	75	70	76	66	77	78	80
BORGER, TX	81	73	70	72	75	84	72	78	77	72	76	68	70	78	73	80	67	76	84	80
BOSTON-CAMBRIDGE, MA	119	141	150	139	145	125	139	132	134	140	136	127	148	132	142	132	129	132	125	129
BOULDER, CO	131	136	140	141	131	121	146	129	134	141	136	127	144	134	138	128	125	136	120	130
BOWLING GREEN, KY	87	78	74	79	77	84	82	82	83	80	83	75	78	84	79	83	74	83	84	85
BOZEMAN, MT	87	76	75	79	75	80	86	81	83	80	84	76	80	84	80	82	75	84	81	83
BRADFORD, PA	78	66	62	64	70	84	66	76	73	65	71	65	62	74	67	77	62	71	84	79
BRAINERD, MN	86	74	66	74	79	94	76	86	78	73	77	75	70	79	77	81	67	81	90	88
BRANSON, MO	79	65	56	64	71	86	67	78	71	64	70	68	61	70	68	75	60	74	84	81
BREMERTON-SILV., WA	102	104	109	106	102	99	104	101	101	104	101	93	105	102	103	100	92	102	99	101
BRENHAM, TX	88	72	63	71	76	92	75	84	80	72	79	74	68	81	74	83	68	80	90	88
BREVARD, NC	92	76	65	74	83	103	76	91	82	74	81	78	70	81	79	87	70	85	99	95
BRIDGEPORT-STAMFORD	160	198	215	195	205	174	189	181	179	193	182	174	205	176	196	176	173	179	169	176
BRIGHAM CITY, UT	93	90	87	90	90	96	84	90	86	86	86	80	85	90	86	87	77	87	92	93
BROOKHAVEN, MS	69	53	42	51	55	70	54	63	60	53	60	55	48	62	53	64	52	60	69	67
BROOKINGS, OR	72	65	60	63	71	84	63	76	67	63	65	64	61	63	68	71	56	72	82	76
BROOKINGS, SD	84	65	62	68	66	76	85	77	81	73	81	72	73	80	75	80	72	80	78	80
BROWNSVILLE, TN	75	56	44	55	59	76	59	68	66	57	65	60	52	68	57	70	56	65	74	73
BROWNSVILLE-HARLN,TX	69	59	47	55	54	60	58	62	63	61	64	56	54	60	57	64	57	64	63	60
BROWNWOOD, TX	76	61	55	60	65	80	64	73	70	61	68	63	58	70	64	73	59	69	80	75
BRUNSWICK, GA	91	81	75	81	81	91	81	86	85	81	84	77	78	85	81	87	74	85	91	89
BUCYRUS, OH	76	70	75	71	72	79	71	74	75	70	73	64	70	77	72	77	65	72	81	76
BUFFALO-NIAGFALLS,NY	83	86	102	88	87	86	86	85	89	87	88	74	89	88	88	91	80	85	91	85
BURLEY, ID	84	62	43	60	68	87	64	78	70	62	70	69	55	74	63	74	60	73	83	83
BURLINGTON, IA-IL	82	74	75	74	77	87	74	81	79	73	78	70	72	81	75	82	69	77	87	83
BURLINGTON, NC	89	80	78	81	81	88	81	85	84	80	83	76	79	85	81	86	74	83	89	87
BURLINGTON-S BURL,VT	105	106	110	108	106	105	108	105	105	106	105	97	107	106	106	104	95	105	103	106
BUTTE-SILVER BOW, MT	68	63	73	63	65	70	67	68	70	64	68	59	65	69	67	72	60	67	76	68
CADILLAC, MI	82	67	57	66	71	87	67	77	73	66	72	69	62	75	68	76	62	74	84	82
CALHOUN, GA	96	75	56	73	77	96	75	87	81	74	80	78	67	84	73	85	70	82	91	93
CAMBRIDGE, MD	78	70	70	70	73	83	71	77	75	70	74	67	68	75	72	77	65	74	82	79
CAMBRIDGE, OH	72	58	53	57	61	74	61	68	68	59	65	59	56	67	61	69	56	65	75	70
CAMDEN, AR	74	55	42	54	59	76	58	68	65	56	64	59	51	67	57	70	55	64	75	72
CAMPBELLSVILLE, KY	72	57	50	56	62	77	59	69	65	57	64	60	53	66	59	69	55	65	75	72
CANON CITY, CO	75	68	71	69	70	78	70	74	72	67	71	65	67	71	71	74	62	72	80	75
CANTON, IL	76	63	63	63	68	81	67	74	72	64	70	64	62	73	67	76	61	70	83	76
CANTON-MASSILLON, OH	86	86	93	86	88	91	84	87	87	85	86	76	85	88	86	89	77	85	92	88
CAPE CORAL-FT MYERS	95	98	107	96	102	106	93	100	96	96	95	86	96	90	100	99	84	99	108	99
CAPE GIRARDEAU-JACKS	81	70	69	71	72	81	75	77	77	72	77	69	70	78	73	79	68	76	82	80
CARBONDALE, IL	64	49	53	52	49	56	70	58	66	58	66	56	59	64	60	65	59	63	62	60
CARLSBAD-ARTESIA, NM	76	66	60	65	66	75	66	72	71	66	70	63	63	71	66	73	61	70	77	73
CARSON CITY, NV	89	93	100	94	92	90	93	91	91	93	91	83	94	90	94	91	82	92	92	90
CASPER, WY	82	81	85	82	79	81	81	81	82	81	81	72	81	82	81	83	73	81	84	81
CEDAR CITY, UT	80	72	63	73	68	72	76	74	74	74	75	69	71	76	71	73	66	75	72	75
CEDAR RAPIDS, IA	96	95	100	97	95	96	94	95	95	95	95	85	95	97	95	96	85	94	97	96
CEDARTOWN, GA	84	62	48	60	66	85	65	76	72	62	71	67	57	75	63	76	61	71	83	81
CELINA, OH	92	85	82	85	90	99	81	91	85	82	85	80	80	89	83	88	75	85	94	94
CENTRAL CITY, KY	77	56	37	53	62	82	56	71	64	55	63	63	49	67	56	69	54	65	78	77
CENTRALIA, IL	79	67	64	66	70	82	68	75	71	67	73	65	65	76	69	78	64	72	84	77
CENTRALIA, WA	82	72	69	72	75	86	73	81	76	71	75	71	69	77	74	79	66	77	85	83
UNITED STATES	100	100	100	100	100	100	100	100	100	100	100	100	100	100	100	100	100	100	100	100

POPULATION CHANGE
CBSA AND U.S. TOTALS

A

CBSA	CBSA Code	POPULATION			2000-2007 ANNUAL RATE		RACE (%)					
							White		Black		Asian/Pacific	
		2000	2007	2012	% Rate	National Rank	2000	2007	2000	2007	2000	2007
CHAMBERSBURG, PA	16540	129,313	142,664	153,170	1.4	196	95.3	94.4	2.3	2.7	0.6	0.8
CHAMPAIGN-URBANA, IL	16580	210,275	223,394	231,793	0.8	396	81.7	78.4	9.6	10.6	5.6	7.1
CHARLESTON, WV	16620	309,635	305,478	302,507	-0.2	841	93.2	92.9	4.7	4.6	0.7	1.0
CHARLESTON-MATT., IL	16660	64,449	63,242	62,544	-0.3	873	96.0	93.9	1.9	3.0	0.7	1.3
CHARLESTON-N CHARLES	16700	549,033	628,187	691,541	1.9	113	65.1	63.6	30.8	31.0	1.4	1.8
CHARLOTTE-GASTONIA	16740	1,330,448	1,621,635	1,869,178	2.8	46	71.7	69.7	22.2	22.2	2.1	2.7
CHARLOTTESVILLE, VA	16820	174,021	196,474	212,771	1.7	140	80.8	78.1	14.1	15.4	2.7	3.3
CHATTANOOGA, TN-GA	16860	476,531	508,709	531,301	0.9	352	83.1	81.6	13.9	14.6	1.0	1.4
CHESTER, SC	16900	34,068	33,153	32,137	-0.4	896	59.9	58.7	38.7	39.5	0.3	0.4
CHEYENNE, WY	16940	81,607	88,353	93,502	1.1	288	88.9	87.8	2.6	2.7	1.1	1.4
CHICAGO-NAPERVILLE	16980	9,098,316	9,747,870	10,261,963	1.0	318	66.9	64.6	18.6	18.4	4.3	5.1
CHICO, CA	17020	203,171	220,904	233,944	1.2	255	84.5	80.8	1.4	1.5	3.5	4.2
CHILLICOTHE, OH	17060	73,345	75,420	76,678	0.4	590	91.7	90.7	6.2	6.9	0.4	0.6
CINCINNATI-MIDDLET'N	17140	2,009,632	2,118,580	2,209,310	0.7	444	85.5	84.7	11.5	11.5	1.3	1.8
CITY OFTHE DALLES,OR	17180	23,791	24,098	24,289	0.2	679	86.6	84.2	0.3	0.3	1.3	1.6
CLAREMONT, NH	17200	40,458	43,394	45,647	1.0	318	98.0	97.7	0.2	0.3	0.4	0.6
CLARKSBURG, WV	17220	92,144	92,304	92,444	0.0	765	97.0	96.6	1.4	1.4	0.5	0.7
CLARKSDALE, MS	17260	30,622	28,919	27,785	-0.8	929	29.3	27.5	69.2	70.6	0.5	0.7
CLARKSVILLE, TN-KY	17300	232,000	258,226	279,160	1.5	173	74.2	71.8	19.1	19.7	1.7	2.3
CLEARLAKE, CA	17340	58,309	66,564	72,989	1.8	127	86.2	83.5	2.1	2.2	1.0	1.2
CLEVELAND, MS	17380	40,633	40,208	39,946	-0.1	805	33.2	31.8	65.1	66.2	0.5	0.7
CLEVELAND, TN	17420	104,015	111,646	117,478	1.0	318	93.8	92.7	3.4	3.7	0.5	0.7
CLEVELAND-ELYRIA,OH	17460	2,148,143	2,150,129	2,154,978	0.0	765	76.1	74.4	19.3	20.0	1.4	2.1
CLEWISTON, FL	17500	36,210	39,613	42,449	1.2	255	66.1	62.4	14.7	14.7	0.5	0.6
CLINTON, IA	17540	50,149	49,537	49,177	-0.2	841	95.9	95.1	1.9	2.2	0.6	0.9
CLOVIS, NM	17580	45,044	46,740	48,094	0.5	545	72.4	70.8	6.9	7.2	1.9	2.3
COEUR D'ALENE, ID	17660	108,685	137,096	164,992	3.3	26	95.8	95.5	0.2	0.2	0.6	0.7
COFFEYVILLE, KS	17700	36,252	34,564	33,488	-0.7	926	85.8	84.3	6.1	6.5	0.5	0.7
COLDWATER, MI	17740	45,787	47,632	48,382	0.5	545	93.4	91.8	2.6	3.4	0.4	0.6
COLLEGE STA.-BRYANTX	17780	184,885	203,475	212,851	1.3	225	73.7	70.2	12.3	12.7	3.4	4.1
COLORADO SPRINGS, CO	17820	537,484	616,432	675,787	1.9	113	81.7	79.8	6.3	6.6	2.7	3.3
COLUMBIA, MO	17860	145,666	161,111	170,255	1.4	196	85.8	83.2	8.4	9.5	2.8	4.0
COLUMBIA, SC	17900	647,158	719,810	774,704	1.5	173	63.4	62.2	32.9	33.0	1.3	1.7
COLUMBIA, TN	17940	69,498	81,118	90,584	2.2	85	82.4	80.4	14.3	15.2	0.4	0.5
COLUMBUS, GA-AL	17980	281,768	291,341	298,859	0.5	545	54.6	50.6	40.2	42.9	1.4	1.6
COLUMBUS, IN	18020	71,435	74,435	76,658	0.6	494	94.2	92.8	1.8	2.0	1.9	2.7
COLUMBUS, MS	18060	61,586	61,334	61,274	-0.1	805	56.5	54.1	41.6	43.3	0.6	0.8
COLUMBUS, NE	18100	31,662	31,806	31,881	0.1	723	94.3	92.6	0.4	0.4	0.4	0.6
COLUMBUS, OH	18140	1,612,694	1,780,581	1,914,004	1.4	196	82.0	80.1	12.9	13.4	2.3	3.4
CONCORD, NH	18180	136,225	151,780	163,113	1.5	173	97.1	96.5	0.5	0.6	0.9	1.3
CONNERSVILLE, IN	18220	25,588	24,983	24,563	-0.3	873	97.2	96.7	1.7	1.9	0.3	0.4
COOKEVILLE, TN	18260	93,417	101,709	107,886	1.2	255	95.9	94.8	1.2	1.3	0.7	1.0
COOS BAY, OR	18300	62,779	64,076	66,023	0.3	633	92.0	91.1	0.3	0.3	1.1	1.3
CORBIN, KY	18340	35,865	37,845	39,270	0.7	444	98.4	98.1	0.3	0.4	0.2	0.3
CORDELE, GA	18380	21,996	22,353	22,479	0.2	679	54.1	49.0	43.4	47.7	0.7	0.9
CORINTH, MS	18420	34,558	35,497	36,142	0.4	590	87.4	86.1	11.1	11.9	0.3	0.4
CORNELIA, GA	18460	35,902	42,852	48,743	2.5	64	88.9	85.7	4.5	5.2	2.0	2.6
CORNING, NY	18500	98,726	99,898	100,626	0.2	679	96.4	95.7	1.4	1.5	0.9	1.2
CORPUS CHRISTI, TX	18580	403,280	428,222	446,108	0.8	396	73.7	71.1	3.8	3.6	1.2	1.4
CORSICANA, TX	18620	45,124	49,322	51,942	1.2	255	70.8	67.2	16.8	17.5	0.8	1.0
CORTLAND, NY	18660	48,599	48,665	48,574	0.0	765	96.9	96.3	0.9	1.2	0.4	0.5
CORVALLIS, OR	18700	78,153	82,483	85,965	0.7	444	89.2	87.2	0.8	0.9	4.7	5.8
COSHOCTON, OH	18740	36,655	36,535	36,460	0.0	765	97.4	95.7	1.1	2.3	0.3	0.5
CRAWFORDSVILLE, IN	18820	37,629	38,547	39,154	0.3	633	96.8	96.0	0.8	0.9	0.5	0.6
CRESCENT CITY, CA	18860	27,507	29,547	31,053	1.0	318	78.9	76.0	4.3	4.4	2.4	2.9
CROSSVILLE, TN	18900	46,802	52,915	57,709	1.7	140	98.1	97.6	0.1	0.1	0.3	0.4
CROWLEY, LA	18940	58,861	60,192	61,085	0.3	633	80.7	77.8	18.2	20.9	0.2	0.2
CULLMAN, AL	18980	77,483	81,338	84,207	0.7	444	96.8	96.0	1.0	1.0	0.2	0.3
CULPEPER, VA	19020	34,262	46,343	58,172	4.3	10	78.3	75.6	18.2	19.6	0.7	0.9
CUMBERLAND, MD-WV	19060	102,008	102,117	101,966	0.0	765	93.9	92.4	4.6	5.6	0.5	0.6
DALLAS-FT WORTH-ARL	19100	5,161,544	6,118,183	6,888,211	2.4	71	69.2	67.0	13.9	13.3	3.9	4.7
DALTON, GA	19140	120,031	137,765	149,756	1.9	113	85.3	80.8	2.9	3.1	0.7	0.9
DANVILLE, IL	19180	83,919	82,265	81,249	-0.3	873	85.8	83.7	10.6	11.8	0.6	0.8
DANVILLE, KY	19220	51,058	54,247	56,371	0.8	396	91.6	90.9	6.4	6.6	0.4	0.5
DANVILLE, VA	19260	110,156	108,179	106,860	-0.2	841	65.7	63.4	32.6	34.5	0.4	0.5
DAPHNE-FAIRHOPE, AL	19300	140,415	175,513	205,887	3.1	34	87.1	85.9	10.3	11.2	0.4	0.3
DAVENPORT-MOLINE	19340	376,019	380,003	382,897	0.1	723	88.8	86.8	5.7	6.3	1.1	1.7
DAYTON, OH	19380	848,153	848,761	848,461	0.0	765	82.1	80.2	14.4	15.5	1.4	2.0
DECATUR, AL	19460	145,867	150,076	152,977	0.4	590	83.3	81.5	11.7	12.3	0.4	0.6
DECATUR, IL	19500	114,706	111,415	109,039	-0.4	896	83.5	81.3	14.1	15.7	0.6	0.8
DECATUR, IN	19540	33,625	34,027	34,203	0.2	679	97.3	96.5	0.1	0.2	0.2	0.3
DEFIANCE, OH	19580	39,500	39,047	38,720	-0.2	841	92.6	91.4	1.8	1.9	0.4	0.6
DEL RIO, TX	19620	44,856	47,982	49,456	0.9	352	76.4	75.0	1.5	1.4	0.6	0.6
DELTONA-DAYTONA BCH.	19660	443,343	517,851	577,704	2.2	85	86.1	83.1	9.3	10.9	1.0	1.4
DEMING, NM	19700	25,016	26,909	28,272	1.0	318	74.3	73.6	0.9	1.0	0.3	0.4
DENVER-AURORA, CO	19740	2,179,388	2,469,929	2,678,971	1.7	140	79.8	78.0	5.4	5.3	3.0	3.6
DE RIDDER, LA	19760	32,986	34,672	36,319	0.7	444	84.2	81.5	12.9	14.9	0.6	0.9
UNITED STATES					1.2		75.1	72.7	12.3	12.6	3.8	4.5

POPULATION COMPOSITION
CBSA AND U.S. TOTALS

B

CBSA	% HISPANIC ORIGIN		2007 AGE DISTRIBUTION (%)										MEDIAN AGE	% 2007 Males	% 2007 Females
	2000	2007	0-4	5-9	10-14	15-19	20-24	25-44	45-64	65-84	85+	18+	2007		
CHAMBERSBURG, PA	1.8	2.2	6.3	6.1	6.2	6.4	5.4	26.0	27.1	14.0	2.6	77.5	40.7	48.6	51.4
CHAMPAIGN-URBANA, IL	2.6	3.4	5.8	5.5	5.6	10.4	14.4	25.4	22.0	8.9	1.8	79.4	30.8	50.2	49.8
CHARLESTON, WV	0.6	0.6	5.8	5.9	5.7	5.6	5.1	26.5	29.9	13.5	2.1	79.3	41.8	48.4	51.6
CHARLESTON-MATT., IL	1.2	2.1	5.9	5.4	5.3	7.5	13.1	25.2	24.1	11.4	2.3	80.1	34.7	48.9	51.1
CHARLESTON-N CHARLES	2.4	3.1	6.7	6.2	6.4	7.7	7.8	28.8	25.4	9.7	1.3	76.5	35.7	49.1	50.9
CHARLOTTE-GASTONIA	5.1	6.7	7.2	7.0	6.9	6.8	6.1	31.3	25.0	8.5	1.2	74.9	35.8	49.3	50.7
CHARLOTTESVILLE, VA	2.2	3.2	5.8	5.8	6.0	7.6	9.0	26.3	26.3	11.5	1.7	78.4	37.8	48.0	52.0
CHATTANOOGA, TN-GA	1.5	2.0	6.1	6.1	6.2	6.4	5.9	27.7	27.6	12.2	1.9	78.0	39.3	48.5	51.5
CHESTER, SC	0.7	0.9	6.8	6.5	6.8	7.0	6.2	26.9	27.0	11.4	1.5	75.6	38.0	48.7	51.3
CHEYENNE, WY	10.9	12.1	6.7	6.0	6.6	6.9	7.4	28.0	26.8	9.9	1.7	76.4	36.8	50.3	49.7
CHICAGO-NAPERVILLE	16.4	19.6	7.5	7.2	7.5	7.0	6.4	29.2	24.2	9.4	1.7	73.6	35.1	49.0	51.0
CHICO, CA	10.5	13.5	5.8	5.2	6.1	8.1	11.0	22.9	25.9	12.3	2.7	78.6	37.1	49.3	50.7
CHILLICOTHE, OH	0.6	0.7	6.3	5.9	6.0	6.1	6.8	29.0	27.2	11.2	1.7	78.2	38.7	52.2	47.8
CINCINNATI-MIDDLET'N	1.1	1.4	7.1	6.8	6.8	7.2	7.2	27.6	25.5	10.1	1.7	75.1	36.4	48.7	51.3
CITY OFTHE DALLES,OR	9.3	12.4	6.6	6.0	6.0	6.7	7.1	21.5	29.4	14.0	2.6	77.1	41.7	49.4	50.6
CLAREMONT, NH	0.5	0.7	5.5	5.3	6.1	6.8	5.7	24.1	30.8	13.5	2.3	78.8	42.8	49.6	50.4
CLARKSBURG, WV	0.9	0.9	5.8	5.6	6.0	5.9	5.9	25.9	28.9	13.6	2.4	79.0	41.5	48.5	51.5
CLARKSDALE, MS	0.9	1.1	9.4	8.4	7.9	8.0	8.1	23.7	22.6	9.8	2.0	69.4	31.5	46.2	53.8
CLARKSVILLE, TN-KY	4.6	6.3	8.9	7.7	6.8	6.8	8.4	31.9	20.3	8.2	1.1	73.0	31.4	50.7	49.3
CLEARLAKE, CA	11.4	14.5	5.2	4.7	6.2	7.1	5.8	19.8	32.7	15.9	2.6	79.1	45.7	49.7	50.3
CLEVELAND, MS	1.2	2.7	7.8	7.4	7.1	8.6	9.6	26.0	22.6	9.2	1.7	73.2	31.4	47.0	53.0
CLEVELAND, TN	1.9	2.6	6.6	6.4	6.1	6.1	5.7	29.6	26.4	11.7	1.5	77.6	38.1	49.2	50.8
CLEVELAND-ELYRIA,OH	3.4	3.9	6.5	6.4	6.9	6.9	6.0	25.4	27.1	12.4	2.4	76.0	39.5	48.0	52.0
CLEWISTON, FL	39.6	48.3	8.4	7.1	7.5	8.6	9.4	28.9	19.7	9.3	1.0	71.9	30.4	55.0	45.0
CLINTON, IA	1.3	1.7	6.7	6.3	6.1	6.9	6.8	24.5	27.1	12.8	2.8	76.7	40.0	48.9	51.1
CLOVIS, NM	30.4	32.1	9.0	7.1	7.0	7.7	10.1	26.3	21.2	9.8	1.8	72.5	31.6	49.7	50.3
COEUR D'ALENE, ID	2.3	2.6	7.0	6.4	7.0	6.9	6.7	26.2	27.5	10.6	1.7	75.4	37.6	49.5	50.5
COFFEYVILLE, KS	3.1	4.1	6.6	5.6	6.1	6.8	7.8	23.3	26.6	14.0	3.2	77.9	40.4	48.5	51.5
COLDWATER, MI	3.0	3.7	6.6	5.9	6.1	6.6	7.0	28.2	26.3	11.5	1.8	77.6	38.1	51.1	48.9
COLLEGE STA.-BRYANTX	17.3	21.5	6.7	5.5	5.5	10.6	19.7	26.0	17.7	7.0	1.2	78.8	26.0	50.4	49.6
COLORADO SPRINGS, CO	11.0	13.1	7.6	7.0	7.0	7.6	7.6	28.8	25.4	7.8	1.1	73.9	34.6	50.1	49.9
COLUMBIA, MO	1.7	2.1	6.2	5.5	5.8	9.6	13.2	28.3	22.3	7.7	1.5	78.7	30.5	48.5	51.5
COLUMBIA, SC	2.4	3.2	6.5	6.3	6.6	7.6	7.6	28.2	26.2	9.5	1.4	76.5	36.2	48.6	51.4
COLUMBIA, TN	3.3	4.5	6.9	6.7	6.2	7.0	6.0	26.7	28.7	10.3	1.6	75.8	38.3	49.0	51.0
COLUMBUS, GA-AL	4.0	5.0	7.3	6.6	6.9	7.5	8.6	27.7	23.7	10.2	1.5	75.2	34.2	49.5	50.5
COLUMBUS, IN	2.2	3.0	7.2	7.1	6.9	6.6	5.5	26.7	26.8	11.5	1.7	74.7	38.0	49.4	50.6
COLUMBUS, MS	1.1	1.4	7.9	7.3	7.2	7.1	7.5	27.9	23.7	9.7	1.7	73.4	34.2	47.7	52.3
COLUMBUS, NE	6.5	8.8	7.6	7.0	6.8	7.4	7.7	24.5	26.1	10.8	2.1	74.1	36.7	50.0	50.0
COLUMBUS, OH	1.8	2.0	7.2	6.9	6.8	7.0	7.5	29.4	24.8	9.1	1.4	75.3	35.3	49.2	50.8
CONCORD, NH	1.0	1.3	5.7	5.6	6.6	7.8	7.1	24.7	29.8	10.5	2.2	77.5	40.5	49.4	50.6
CONNERSVILLE, IN	0.5	0.7	6.5	6.1	6.6	5.5	6.0	26.4	27.3	13.2	2.4	77.3	39.6	48.8	51.2
COOKEVILLE, TN	2.3	3.3	6.1	5.8	5.7	6.7	8.1	27.3	25.7	12.6	1.8	79.0	37.8	49.7	50.3
COOS BAY, OR	3.4	4.6	4.8	4.6	4.9	6.5	7.0	20.4	32.2	16.7	2.8	81.8	46.1	48.9	51.1
CORBIN, KY	0.7	1.0	6.5	6.2	6.7	7.1	6.9	26.8	26.2	11.7	1.9	76.6	37.7	48.6	51.4
CORDELE, GA	1.7	2.3	8.0	7.2	7.2	6.5	7.0	25.6	25.0	11.5	2.0	73.7	36.1	47.3	52.7
CORINTH, MS	1.3	1.7	6.6	6.6	6.1	5.5	5.4	28.0	26.7	12.9	2.2	77.4	39.1	49.0	51.0
CORNELIA, GA	7.7	10.4	6.3	6.2	5.9	6.7	6.5	27.2	26.7	12.6	1.8	77.9	38.7	51.2	48.8
CORNING, NY	0.8	1.0	6.3	5.8	6.5	6.9	6.9	24.2	28.1	13.0	2.3	77.1	40.6	49.1	50.9
CORPUS CHRISTI, TX	52.7	59.2	8.0	7.2	7.0	7.0	7.9	26.8	24.6	10.2	1.4	73.6	34.2	49.2	50.8
CORSICANA, TX	15.8	19.7	7.5	6.8	6.6	7.7	7.3	26.0	24.0	11.6	2.3	74.8	36.4	49.6	50.4
CORTLAND, NY	1.2	1.3	5.9	5.4	6.1	9.7	10.9	24.1	24.9	11.0	2.0	78.7	35.8	48.6	51.4
CORVALLIS, OR	4.7	6.2	5.1	5.0	5.4	9.0	13.3	26.4	25.5	8.5	1.7	80.4	32.4	50.0	50.0
COSHOCTON, OH	0.6	0.7	6.7	6.3	6.4	6.6	6.7	24.9	27.2	13.2	2.1	76.8	39.6	49.0	51.0
CRAWFORDSVILLE, IN	1.6	2.2	6.8	6.2	7.0	7.3	6.5	25.7	26.1	12.3	2.1	75.9	38.7	50.1	49.9
CRESCENT CITY, CA	13.9	17.4	5.9	4.9	5.8	7.0	8.7	28.1	27.4	10.7	1.6	79.1	37.9	55.0	45.0
CROSSVILLE, TN	1.2	1.8	5.5	5.2	5.4	5.3	4.9	23.2	27.2	21.2	2.1	80.6	45.4	48.4	51.6
CROWLEY, LA	0.9	1.0	8.2	7.7	7.0	7.0	7.1	26.2	24.5	10.6	1.7	72.9	35.3	48.9	51.1
CULLMAN, AL	2.2	3.4	6.6	6.4	6.1	5.8	5.8	27.8	26.4	13.2	1.9	77.4	39.1	49.6	50.4
CULPEPER, VA	2.5	3.6	6.5	6.2	7.1	6.9	5.9	27.6	27.1	11.0	1.7	75.9	38.7	50.3	49.7
CUMBERLAND, MD-WV	0.7	1.0	5.3	5.0	5.3	7.1	7.7	25.5	26.7	14.7	2.7	80.7	40.7	50.0	50.0
DALLAS-FT WORTH-ARL	21.7	25.2	8.1	7.7	7.4	7.1	7.2	30.9	23.5	7.1	1.0	72.6	33.4	49.8	50.2
DALTON, GA	17.0	22.4	8.2	8.0	6.9	6.1	6.0	30.9	23.6	9.2	1.2	73.2	34.7	50.5	49.5
DANVILLE, IL	3.0	3.9	6.8	6.2	6.3	6.1	6.6	25.4	26.5	13.7	2.4	77.0	39.6	49.4	50.6
DANVILLE, KY	1.2	1.7	6.1	5.9	6.5	6.7	7.0	27.3	26.4	12.2	1.8	77.6	38.6	49.4	50.6
DANVILLE, VA	1.2	1.7	5.8	5.9	5.7	6.0	5.7	24.9	29.2	14.3	2.4	78.9	42.2	47.8	52.2
DAPHNE-FAIRHOPE, AL	1.8	2.4	6.3	6.2	6.3	6.3	5.8	25.2	28.3	13.8	1.9	77.4	41.0	49.1	50.9
DAVENPORT-MOLINE	5.6	7.1	6.6	6.2	6.2	7.0	7.0	25.8	27.3	11.6	2.3	77.0	38.6	48.9	51.1
DAYTON, OH	1.2	1.4	6.4	6.0	6.3	7.2	7.7	25.5	26.7	12.2	2.0	77.3	38.3	48.4	51.6
DECATUR, AL	2.8	4.2	6.6	6.4	6.6	6.3	5.9	28.4	26.7	11.4	1.6	76.6	38.6	49.2	50.8
DECATUR, IL	1.0	1.3	6.2	5.9	6.3	7.2	7.3	23.7	27.8	13.2	2.4	77.6	39.9	47.8	52.2
DECATUR, IN	3.3	4.5	8.6	7.6	8.3	7.3	6.6	25.8	23.0	10.3	2.6	71.0	33.9	49.8	50.2
DEFIANCE, OH	7.2	8.6	7.1	6.7	6.2	6.5	7.3	25.2	27.8	11.4	1.8	76.3	37.8	49.6	50.4
DEL RIO, TX	75.5	80.2	9.3	8.1	7.9	8.0	8.4	26.5	20.2	10.3	1.3	69.6	31.5	49.6	50.4
DELTONA-DAYTONA BCH.	6.6	9.4	4.9	4.7	5.2	6.3	6.0	22.3	28.5	18.7	3.4	81.6	45.4	48.5	51.5
DEMING, NM	57.7	60.0	8.5	7.4	7.4	7.1	6.8	21.7	23.1	15.9	2.2	72.2	37.3	48.4	51.6
DENVER-AURORA, CO	18.4	20.8	7.1	7.2	7.1	6.7	6.1	30.6	26.0	8.0	1.2	74.5	35.9	50.1	49.9
DE RIDDER, LA	1.4	1.7	7.2	6.8	7.1	6.6	7.1	26.7	25.8	11.4	1.4	75.0	36.9	50.3	49.7
UNITED STATES	12.5	15.0	6.9	6.5	6.8	7.1	7.0	27.6	25.4	10.7	1.9	75.6	36.7	49.2	50.8

CBSA	HOUSEHOLDS					FAMILIES			MEDIAN HOUSEHOLD INCOME		
	2000	2007	2012	% Annual Rate 2000-2007	2007 Average HH Size	2000	2007	% Annual Rate 2000-2007	2007	2012	2007 National Rank
CHAMBERSBURG, PA	50,633	56,790	61,445	1.6	2.46	36,410	39,781	1.2	50,162	57,579	247
CHAMPAIGN-URBANA, IL	82,711	89,197	93,435	1.0	2.32	47,938	49,691	0.5	47,785	54,938	321
CHARLESTON, WV	129,229	130,131	129,990	0.1	2.32	88,155	86,289	-0.3	40,469	46,941	632
CHARLESTON-MATT., IL	25,411	25,620	25,487	0.1	2.32	15,156	14,743	-0.4	39,745	45,157	660
CHARLESTON-N CHARLES	207,957	244,495	272,401	2.3	2.49	141,405	160,568	1.8	49,793	58,675	260
CHARLOTTE-GASTONIA	510,516	630,744	729,658	3.0	2.52	350,778	422,099	2.6	60,735	71,977	62
CHARLOTTESVILLE, VA	67,575	77,863	85,117	2.0	2.40	42,839	48,190	1.6	54,721	63,411	129
CHATTANOOGA, TN-GA	189,607	205,597	216,284	1.1	2.42	132,261	139,673	0.8	46,754	54,438	360
CHESTER, SC	12,880	12,937	12,694	0.1	2.54	9,343	9,083	-0.4	39,602	45,596	668
CHEYENNE, WY	31,927	35,577	38,047	1.5	2.39	21,600	23,353	1.1	50,505	60,221	232
CHICAGO-NAPERVILLE	3,280,055	3,496,913	3,673,550	0.9	2.74	2,232,273	2,325,851	0.6	64,756	76,559	32
CHICO, CA	79,566	86,802	92,088	1.2	2.47	49,386	54,172	1.3	39,808	45,803	659
CHILLICOTHE, OH	27,136	28,414	29,167	0.6	2.45	19,174	19,503	0.2	45,330	51,515	422
CINCINNATI-MIDDLET'N	779,226	832,650	871,652	0.9	2.49	525,604	548,331	0.6	56,845	67,005	93
CITY OFTHE DALLES,OR	9,401	9,509	9,588	0.2	2.48	6,503	6,519	0.0	44,503	51,690	447
CLAREMONT, NH	16,530	18,131	19,270	1.3	2.36	11,179	12,077	1.1	49,668	56,703	265
CLARKSBURG, WV	37,032	37,976	38,352	0.3	2.38	25,673	25,521	-0.1	35,861	41,196	815
CLARKSDALE, MS	10,553	10,149	9,810	-0.5	2.77	7,479	7,026	-0.9	25,292	27,039	934
CLARKSVILLE, TN-KY	83,332	94,778	103,104	1.8	2.61	61,733	68,451	1.4	45,686	53,541	398
CLEARLAKE, CA	23,974	26,728	29,260	1.5	2.45	15,370	17,221	1.6	35,779	40,785	818
CLEVELAND, MS	13,776	14,094	14,192	0.3	2.70	9,719	9,714	0.0	26,948	29,391	927
CLEVELAND, TN	40,729	44,738	47,509	1.3	2.45	29,410	31,511	1.0	42,637	49,588	524
CLEVELAND-ELYRIA,OH	853,165	865,573	871,904	0.2	2.43	560,570	552,825	-0.2	52,755	61,456	170
CLEWISTON, FL	10,850	11,894	12,741	1.3	3.12	8,141	8,798	1.1	40,217	45,694	646
CLINTON, IA	20,105	20,289	20,285	0.1	2.39	13,676	13,546	-0.1	46,623	53,831	363
CLOVIS, NM	16,766	17,894	18,587	0.9	2.54	11,869	12,302	0.5	35,932	41,517	811
COEUR D'ALENE, ID	41,308	52,210	62,912	3.3	2.60	29,668	37,054	3.1	47,146	54,758	345
COFFEYVILLE, KS	14,903	14,343	13,940	-0.5	2.35	9,954	9,449	-0.7	37,964	43,364	741
COLDWATER, MI	16,349	17,113	17,491	0.6	2.57	11,570	11,801	0.3	46,450	52,438	370
COLLEGE STA.-BRYANTX	67,744	75,948	79,768	1.6	2.51	39,317	43,311	1.3	37,054	43,519	776
COLORADO SPRINGS, CO	200,402	231,549	254,433	2.0	2.59	139,754	157,953	1.7	60,254	72,114	65
COLUMBIA, MO	56,930	64,898	69,182	1.8	2.33	34,024	37,346	1.3	46,509	54,102	367
COLUMBIA, SC	245,347	280,653	306,002	1.9	2.44	167,078	184,037	1.3	51,058	60,239	218
COLUMBIA, TN	26,444	31,293	35,123	2.3	2.55	19,274	22,265	2.0	52,207	61,290	189
COLUMBUS, GA-AL	103,982	109,489	113,184	0.7	2.52	72,623	74,383	0.3	42,361	49,065	535
COLUMBUS, IN	27,936	29,289	30,278	0.7	2.51	20,067	20,317	0.2	54,845	63,956	127
COLUMBUS, MS	22,849	23,234	23,373	0.2	2.56	16,405	16,311	-0.1	36,375	39,864	796
COLUMBUS, NE	12,076	12,340	12,453	0.3	2.55	8,461	8,546	0.1	48,070	54,900	310
COLUMBUS, OH	636,602	710,253	766,482	1.5	2.45	411,591	447,215	1.2	56,053	65,774	111
CONCORD, NH	51,843	57,937	62,615	1.5	2.51	35,473	39,060	1.3	61,465	71,148	53
CONNERSVILLE, IN	10,199	10,211	10,129	0.0	2.40	7,151	6,898	-0.5	47,954	55,524	316
COOKEVILLE, TN	37,441	41,139	43,903	1.3	2.40	25,482	27,182	0.9	35,968	41,372	809
COOS BAY, OR	26,213	27,115	28,137	0.5	2.31	17,448	17,877	0.3	39,477	45,199	673
CORBIN, KY	13,780	14,992	15,738	1.2	2.44	9,888	10,398	0.7	27,781	31,904	923
CORDELE, GA	8,337	8,585	8,693	0.4	2.54	5,872	5,853	0.0	32,336	37,147	885
CORINTH, MS	14,224	14,977	15,404	0.7	2.33	9,921	10,201	0.4	32,745	35,709	880
CORNELIA, GA	13,259	16,160	18,499	2.8	2.55	9,854	11,675	2.4	43,435	49,510	498
CORNING, NY	39,011	39,962	40,502	0.3	2.46	26,212	26,599	0.2	44,013	50,544	466
CORPUS CHRISTI, TX	141,590	152,464	159,891	1.0	2.76	103,327	110,197	0.9	43,978	51,509	468
CORSICANA, TX	16,491	17,855	18,784	1.1	2.67	11,908	12,766	1.0	37,591	42,673	754
CORTLAND, NY	18,210	18,511	18,642	0.2	2.45	11,619	11,708	0.1	42,119	48,404	548
CORVALLIS, OR	30,145	32,556	34,140	1.1	2.39	18,244	19,486	0.9	52,607	61,831	175
COSHOCTON, OH	14,356	14,547	14,604	0.2	2.48	10,168	10,008	-0.2	42,156	48,228	546
CRAWFORDSVILLE, IN	14,595	15,142	15,423	0.5	2.47	10,246	10,241	0.0	50,687	57,967	227
CRESCENT CITY, CA	9,170	9,897	10,486	1.1	2.59	6,293	6,822	1.1	35,622	40,538	820
CROSSVILLE, TN	19,508	22,733	25,120	2.1	2.30	14,518	16,539	1.8	38,763	45,433	700
CROWLEY, LA	21,142	22,055	22,565	0.6	2.68	15,676	15,991	0.3	29,915	32,391	912
CULLMAN, AL	30,706	32,435	33,749	0.8	2.48	22,487	23,352	0.5	37,872	42,192	744
CULPEPER, VA	12,141	16,930	21,558	4.7	2.64	9,050	12,279	4.3	56,319	65,166	107
CUMBERLAND, MD-WV	40,106	40,926	41,188	0.3	2.32	26,604	26,237	-0.2	37,285	42,369	766
DALLAS-FT WORTH-ARL	1,881,056	2,194,690	2,463,904	2.1	2.75	1,301,572	1,509,230	2.1	62,125	75,378	45
DALTON, GA	42,671	48,332	52,349	1.7	2.82	32,410	35,757	1.4	46,563	53,079	364
DANVILLE, IL	33,406	33,112	32,863	-0.1	2.39	22,313	21,441	-0.5	40,780	45,962	623
DANVILLE, KY	19,780	21,690	22,815	1.3	2.37	14,077	14,924	0.8	38,157	44,475	734
DANVILLE, VA	45,291	45,412	45,268	0.0	2.34	31,149	30,337	-0.4	37,590	42,646	755
DAPHNE-FAIRHOPE, AL	55,336	71,166	84,429	3.5	2.43	40,260	50,883	3.3	46,838	51,858	355
DAVENPORT-MOLINE	149,726	152,750	154,609	0.3	2.43	100,280	99,752	-0.1	50,489	59,057	233
DAYTON, OH	338,979	345,833	348,588	0.3	2.38	226,083	223,582	-0.2	51,691	59,190	200
DECATUR, AL	57,140	60,024	61,701	0.7	2.47	41,642	42,984	0.4	41,951	46,333	559
DECATUR, IL	46,561	46,101	45,442	-0.1	2.34	30,960	29,719	-0.6	46,526	52,931	365
DECATUR, IN	11,818	12,236	12,433	0.5	2.74	8,668	8,682	0.0	50,395	58,617	235
DEFIANCE, OH	15,138	15,380	15,427	0.2	2.50	11,016	10,896	-0.2	54,898	63,479	126
DEL RIO, TX	14,151	15,301	15,858	1.1	3.08	11,323	12,160	1.0	33,863	38,619	864
DELTONA-DAYTONA BCH.	184,723	215,195	240,739	2.1	2.34	120,064	137,113	1.8	44,066	51,205	462
DEMING, NM	9,397	10,256	10,798	1.2	2.60	6,592	6,984	0.8	24,841	27,758	935
DENVER-AURORA, CO	852,205	960,612	1,036,868	1.7	2.54	546,907	609,403	1.5	67,517	81,217	22
DE RIDDER, LA	12,104	13,071	13,858	1.1	2.56	9,080	9,593	0.8	36,355	39,973	797
UNITED STATES				1.2	2.59			1.0	53,154	62,503	

INCOME
CBSA AND U.S. TOTALS

D

CBSA	2007 Per Capita Income	2007 HH Income Base	2007 HOUSEHOLD INCOME DISTRIBUTION (%)					2007 Home Value Base	2007 HOME VALUE DISTRIBUTION (%)					2007 Median Home Value
			Less than $25,000	$25,000 to $49,999	$50,000 to $99,999	$100,000 to $149,999	$150,000 or More		Less than $50,000	$50,000 to $89,999	$90,000 to $174,999	$175,000 to $399,999	$400,000 or More	
CHAMBERSBURG, PA	24,460	56,790	20.3	29.5	36.1	10.6	3.5	42,454	5.5	4.2	37.5	48.0	4.9	180,040
CHAMPAIGN-URBANA, IL	25,893	89,194	26.2	25.8	32.9	10.1	5.1	54,902	8.0	13.5	48.4	27.2	2.8	133,754
CHARLESTON, WV	23,979	130,131	31.0	27.8	28.4	8.5	4.3	99,525	22.2	24.6	38.5	13.0	1.7	94,416
CHARLESTON-MATT., IL	22,018	25,620	32.0	28.0	29.7	7.2	3.0	17,366	11.2	19.2	47.2	19.8	2.6	120,141
CHARLESTON-N CHARLES	25,844	244,495	23.6	26.6	32.8	10.9	6.1	167,671	9.1	8.9	30.2	38.0	13.7	180,394
CHARLOTTE-GASTONIA	31,670	630,744	16.5	23.5	36.5	13.5	10.0	434,703	5.7	9.2	36.7	38.7	9.6	170,186
CHARLOTTESVILLE, VA	30,198	77,863	20.0	25.1	33.5	13.3	8.0	51,226	3.3	2.5	14.3	59.1	20.8	264,348
CHATTANOOGA, TN-GA	25,246	205,597	25.5	27.6	32.4	9.1	5.4	146,549	10.7	17.2	45.1	22.2	4.8	122,727
CHESTER, SC	18,868	12,937	31.1	30.6	29.7	7.0	1.5	10,273	20.8	26.5	38.9	12.6	1.2	93,601
CHEYENNE, WY	25,583	35,577	20.3	29.0	35.3	11.1	4.2	25,325	8.6	5.6	42.3	38.8	4.7	165,283
CHICAGO-NAPERVILLE	31,498	3,496,825	16.8	20.5	34.7	16.2	11.8	2,377,403	1.9	2.5	19.7	54.9	21.1	252,751
CHICO, CA	22,080	86,802	32.2	27.5	28.3	8.1	3.9	53,944	4.9	3.4	12.1	56.1	23.5	282,448
CHILLICOTHE, OH	22,201	28,414	25.9	29.5	32.1	9.0	3.5	21,639	17.9	19.4	43.9	17.3	1.4	107,374
CINCINNATI-MIDDLET'N	29,902	832,647	19.2	24.7	33.7	13.8	8.6	585,430	5.3	10.4	46.1	32.7	5.5	149,375
CITY OF THE DALLES,OR	22,022	9,509	26.1	30.0	32.5	8.2	3.2	6,725	5.6	5.4	32.1	48.7	8.3	187,049
CLAREMONT, NH	26,489	18,131	20.8	29.6	36.2	8.8	4.6	13,432	4.6	6.4	39.3	40.9	8.8	174,546
CLARKSBURG, WV	19,754	37,976	35.2	30.4	25.9	6.3	2.3	29,700	22.3	24.4	38.9	12.9	1.6	95,377
CLARKSDALE, MS	14,207	10,149	49.5	25.0	18.6	4.5	2.4	5,855	30.8	34.4	27.2	6.1	1.5	68,595
CLARKSVILLE, TN-KY	21,031	94,777	23.4	31.8	33.5	8.0	3.3	61,003	9.5	16.3	53.3	18.5	2.4	119,692
CLEARLAKE, CA	19,860	26,728	35.8	29.2	25.0	7.3	2.8	19,301	6.1	5.4	15.8	50.2	22.5	250,777
CLEVELAND, MS	14,373	14,094	46.8	28.7	18.4	4.0	2.2	8,686	29.4	32.7	28.0	9.0	1.0	71,881
CLEVELAND, TN	22,452	44,738	28.9	29.1	30.4	7.7	3.8	32,086	10.6	16.3	44.7	24.0	4.4	128,470
CLEVELAND-ELYRIA,OH	28,763	865,565	21.5	25.7	32.7	12.6	7.4	616,477	3.8	12.3	47.5	31.9	4.5	147,596
CLEWISTON, FL	16,419	11,894	30.8	30.7	28.8	7.1	2.6	8,899	10.1	15.0	39.3	30.3	5.3	142,507
CLINTON, IA	22,630	20,289	24.9	28.7	35.8	8.4	2.2	15,166	15.8	25.5	44.2	12.7	1.8	100,946
CLOVIS, NM	18,802	17,894	33.7	32.7	25.4	5.0	3.2	10,755	11.9	25.7	46.8	13.8	1.9	107,390
COEUR D'ALENE, ID	22,694	52,210	22.6	30.7	33.6	9.4	3.7	39,754	6.3	5.6	19.6	53.5	15.0	222,478
COFFEYVILLE, KS	20,120	14,343	32.4	32.2	27.9	5.6	1.8	10,481	35.1	31.7	26.1	6.6	0.6	65,832
COLDWATER, MI	20,992	17,113	22.5	31.7	35.1	8.6	2.1	13,622	10.5	19.5	46.8	20.3	2.9	116,528
COLLEGE STA.-BRYANTX	21,369	75,948	36.9	23.8	25.8	8.5	5.1	39,954	20.3	19.4	35.4	21.5	3.5	110,388
COLORADO SPRINGS, CO	29,346	231,549	14.9	24.6	37.3	14.4	8.8	158,400	3.4	2.0	22.8	59.4	12.4	223,355
COLUMBIA, MO	25,725	64,898	25.2	28.0	30.5	11.3	5.0	39,205	11.6	11.3	40.5	31.2	5.5	142,408
COLUMBIA, SC	26,461	280,643	22.3	26.6	33.3	11.6	6.1	201,310	10.0	15.0	44.6	25.0	5.4	130,900
COLUMBIA, TN	24,749	31,293	22.6	24.8	36.1	11.6	4.9	23,130	7.2	13.1	43.8	31.3	4.7	143,276
COLUMBUS, GA-AL	21,957	109,489	29.2	28.1	30.1	8.2	4.4	67,727	10.4	18.7	45.0	21.9	4.0	119,911
COLUMBUS, IN	26,738	29,289	19.2	25.6	36.2	13.7	5.3	22,028	12.2	10.7	48.7	25.6	2.8	128,100
COLUMBUS, MS	19,116	23,234	35.1	29.3	25.6	6.9	3.1	15,572	16.0	26.6	39.8	15.7	1.9	100,831
COLUMBUS, NE	22,590	12,340	21.4	30.2	36.8	8.5	3.1	9,376	10.5	23.1	49.3	15.5	1.7	107,166
COLUMBUS, OH	29,785	710,250	18.7	25.9	34.0	13.5	8.0	473,804	4.4	11.1	42.8	35.6	6.2	156,003
CONCORD, NH	29,528	57,937	15.0	23.9	39.3	13.9	7.9	41,452	4.7	4.0	21.4	58.2	11.7	219,278
CONNERSVILLE, IN	24,083	10,211	23.5	28.4	35.3	9.3	3.6	7,418	10.2	28.2	46.7	13.6	1.3	103,744
COOKEVILLE, TN	19,747	41,139	34.8	30.6	26.4	5.5	2.7	29,481	13.3	17.4	44.3	20.8	4.2	120,284
COOS BAY, OR	21,678	27,115	32.2	29.8	29.5	5.8	2.9	19,133	7.0	6.3	36.7	42.2	7.8	175,041
CORBIN, KY	16,483	14,992	45.4	29.7	18.4	4.2	2.3	10,989	37.8	27.2	26.8	7.0	1.2	68,271
CORDELE, GA	18,112	8,585	41.6	24.9	23.5	7.3	2.7	5,323	23.8	25.5	34.3	13.5	2.8	91,106
CORINTH, MS	18,366	14,977	39.2	30.5	23.9	4.8	1.7	11,069	24.8	30.5	32.2	10.5	2.0	83,670
CORNELIA, GA	21,553	16,160	27.4	29.4	32.4	7.1	3.7	12,472	11.8	16.0	39.2	27.5	5.5	133,027
CORNING, NY	22,979	39,962	26.7	30.4	31.0	7.7	4.2	30,170	7.9	12.6	41.2	34.5	3.8	155,582
CORPUS CHRISTI, TX	21,279	152,456	27.9	27.3	30.5	9.6	4.7	99,664	18.5	27.5	37.5	14.1	2.4	96,734
CORSICANA, TX	18,780	17,855	34.4	27.7	28.0	6.7	3.2	12,907	29.0	28.5	31.1	9.7	1.7	77,576
CORTLAND, NY	21,221	18,511	28.9	29.5	31.1	7.1	3.3	12,462	4.1	5.7	45.8	41.9	2.6	168,495
CORVALLIS, OR	28,721	32,556	23.2	24.6	31.7	12.8	7.8	19,446	4.2	2.4	9.5	63.7	20.2	270,123
COSHOCTON, OH	20,863	14,547	25.8	33.0	31.3	7.9	2.0	11,399	18.6	24.9	39.5	15.4	1.7	100,571
CRAWFORDSVILLE, IN	23,810	15,142	21.1	28.0	38.5	9.4	3.1	11,294	8.6	19.7	54.0	16.2	1.6	116,264
CRESCENT CITY, CA	18,609	9,897	37.6	26.3	25.7	7.9	2.5	6,399	8.7	4.8	14.2	53.3	18.9	242,755
CROSSVILLE, TN	21,456	22,733	31.2	33.0	26.8	6.1	2.8	18,425	12.9	19.4	38.6	25.0	4.0	119,165
CROWLEY, LA	15,730	22,055	43.1	28.2	22.2	4.2	2.3	15,816	27.1	26.5	33.9	11.1	1.4	84,335
CULLMAN, AL	19,869	32,435	32.1	32.2	26.8	6.0	2.9	25,740	17.3	18.5	38.6	21.1	4.5	117,041
CULPEPER, VA	25,715	16,930	18.4	25.0	37.5	13.7	5.4	12,060	3.2	1.7	8.4	67.6	19.2	274,294
CUMBERLAND, MD-WV	20,086	40,926	33.3	30.7	27.8	6.1	2.0	30,173	7.2	12.4	37.9	38.8	3.8	159,587
DALLAS-FT WORTH-ARL	30,955	2,194,673	15.8	23.5	33.7	15.3	11.7	1,379,390	8.8	17.7	38.9	28.2	6.5	132,585
DALTON, GA	21,499	48,332	23.5	29.5	33.9	8.2	4.9	34,186	15.8	16.7	42.7	20.3	4.6	118,868
DANVILLE, IL	20,914	33,112	28.7	31.2	30.8	7.2	2.1	24,422	23.6	30.8	34.9	10.0	0.6	83,335
DANVILLE, KY	21,271	21,690	33.9	28.5	27.1	7.0	3.4	16,167	18.6	21.7	41.6	15.8	2.2	100,594
DANVILLE, VA	20,987	45,412	32.9	29.9	28.7	6.0	2.5	32,284	17.0	23.1	44.7	14.1	1.1	103,480
DAPHNE-FAIRHOPE, AL	25,474	71,166	23.9	29.8	31.7	9.5	5.2	57,533	11.9	12.0	33.2	32.2	10.7	157,672
DAVENPORT-MOLINE	25,552	152,750	22.1	27.3	34.7	11.1	4.7	112,683	10.0	22.2	46.4	19.3	2.1	113,386
DAYTON, OH	27,744	345,828	21.1	27.1	33.3	12.2	6.3	242,359	5.3	17.9	50.5	23.7	2.6	123,494
DECATUR, AL	21,981	60,024	29.4	28.7	29.6	8.9	3.5	46,131	18.3	25.2	38.4	16.2	1.8	97,992
DECATUR, IL	25,173	46,101	25.5	28.3	32.3	9.8	4.1	33,923	19.6	28.4	39.2	11.5	1.2	92,408
DECATUR, IN	21,655	12,236	19.5	30.0	36.5	10.7	3.4	9,538	9.6	22.7	49.0	17.3	1.4	110,695
DEFIANCE, OH	25,487	15,380	17.2	26.8	39.3	13.3	3.4	12,532	11.1	20.2	50.1	17.4	1.1	113,054
DEL RIO, TX	14,700	15,301	38.1	29.7	23.9	6.2	2.1	10,358	31.3	27.9	31.7	8.4	0.7	75,236
DELTONA-DAYTONA BCH.	24,844	215,195	25.6	30.8	31.0	8.0	4.7	166,602	4.3	4.0	24.7	55.2	11.8	213,747
DEMING, NM	13,888	10,256	50.3	27.1	18.6	2.4	1.6	7,710	21.6	27.1	40.9	9.2	1.3	92,794
DENVER-AURORA, CO	34,982	960,607	13.4	21.4	36.2	16.1	12.9	673,902	2.1	1.7	16.0	62.0	18.2	249,144
DE RIDDER, LA	18,502	13,071	33.9	30.6	26.1	7.1	2.3	10,353	28.2	23.8	33.7	12.7	1.6	86,157
UNITED STATES	27,916		21.9	25.0	32.3	12.3	8.4		7.9	10.5	27.1	35.6	19.0	192,285

SPENDING POTENTIAL INDICES

CBSA AND U.S. TOTALS

E

CBSA	Auto Loan	Home Loan	Invest-ments	Retire-ment Plans	Home Repair	Lawn & Garden	Comput-ers & Hard-ware	Major Appli-ances	TV, Radio, Sound Equip-ment	Furni-ture	Dine out/ Carry out	Sports Equip-ment	Fees & Tickets	Toys & Games	Travel	Cable TV	Apparel & Services	Auto Repairs	Health Insur-ance	Pets & Supplies
	FINANCIAL SERVICES				**THE HOME** Home Improvements		Furnishings				**ENTERTAINMENT**						**PERSONAL**			
CHAMBERSBURG, PA	87	83	85	82	86	93	80	87	84	81	83	76	80	85	83	86	74	83	91	89
CHAMPAIGN-URBANA, IL	87	77	82	81	75	79	91	81	88	84	88	76	85	87	84	86	79	86	83	83
CHARLESTON, WV	85	72	66	70	76	89	73	82	79	71	77	72	68	79	74	83	68	78	89	85
CHARLESTON-MATT., IL	75	63	67	65	65	73	74	71	74	68	73	64	68	74	70	75	65	72	76	73
CHARLESTON-N CHARLES	95	88	84	90	86	90	91	90	91	90	91	83	88	92	88	91	81	91	91	92
CHARLOTTE-GASTONIA	115	112	109	114	107	108	112	109	111	113	112	101	111	114	110	110	101	111	108	111
CHARLOTTESVILLE, VA	104	99	100	101	98	102	105	101	102	102	103	93	101	102	101	101	92	102	101	103
CHATTANOOGA, TN-GA	91	82	80	82	83	91	82	87	86	82	85	77	80	87	82	88	76	85	92	89
CHESTER, SC	80	60	45	59	63	80	61	71	68	60	67	63	54	70	60	72	58	68	77	76
CHEYENNE, WY	86	85	91	87	84	84	85	85	86	85	85	77	86	87	86	86	76	85	86	85
CHICAGO-NAPERVILLE	112	122	127	123	120	110	122	115	119	123	120	110	126	118	121	117	111	118	111	114
CHICO, CA	77	70	71	71	71	77	78	76	76	73	76	69	73	74	75	76	68	77	78	77
CHILLICOTHE, OH	86	74	68	73	75	87	74	81	78	73	78	71	70	81	74	81	68	78	86	84
CINCINNATI-MIDDLET'N	103	104	110	106	101	100	105	101	104	105	104	92	105	105	104	104	94	102	102	102
CITY OFTHE DALLES,OR	78	72	77	72	74	82	74	78	77	72	75	68	72	76	75	79	66	76	84	79
CLAREMONT, NH	92	84	85	84	89	99	83	91	87	82	86	80	81	89	85	90	76	87	96	94
CLARKSBURG, WV	74	59	52	58	64	79	62	71	68	58	66	62	56	68	62	72	57	67	80	74
CLARKSDALE, MS	58	47	48	49	47	55	51	52	58	52	57	45	49	57	50	61	51	54	60	55
CLARKSVILLE, TN-KY	85	72	64	73	69	77	78	77	79	75	79	72	72	81	73	79	70	79	78	79
CLEARLAKE, CA	72	64	58	63	70	82	63	75	66	62	65	64	60	64	67	69	57	70	79	75
CLEVELAND, MS	61	47	42	47	48	59	51	55	57	50	56	48	46	56	50	61	49	55	62	58
CLEVELAND, TN	86	71	62	70	74	88	73	81	77	71	77	72	67	80	72	81	67	77	86	85
CLEVELAND-ELYRIA,OH	92	98	112	100	98	95	96	94	98	98	97	84	101	97	99	99	89	95	98	94
CLEWISTON, FL	78	69	58	67	66	74	68	73	71	69	71	66	64	72	67	72	63	73	74	74
CLINTON, IA	79	70	73	71	73	82	72	77	77	71	76	67	70	79	73	80	66	75	85	79
CLOVIS, NM	70	61	62	62	59	63	67	65	69	65	68	59	63	69	64	69	60	67	68	65
COEUR D'ALENE, ID	88	82	77	82	80	87	80	84	81	80	81	76	78	82	80	82	72	82	85	86
COFFEYVILLE, KS	71	58	57	59	62	73	63	68	69	59	66	59	58	69	63	72	58	66	78	70
COLDWATER, MI	85	73	67	73	78	90	72	82	77	72	76	71	69	81	73	80	67	77	87	85
COLLEGE STA.-BRYANTX	79	62	60	65	59	66	86	71	80	73	81	69	73	78	73	77	72	78	71	73
COLORADO SPRINGS, CO	106	109	111	112	103	99	109	103	105	110	105	97	110	106	107	102	96	106	99	103
COLUMBIA, MO	88	77	79	81	74	77	92	81	88	84	88	77	84	88	83	86	79	86	81	83
COLUMBIA, SC	97	91	86	91	88	92	91	91	92	91	92	83	89	94	89	93	82	92	93	94
COLUMBIA, TN	93	87	86	87	87	93	85	89	88	85	87	80	84	90	86	90	78	87	93	92
COLUMBUS, GA-AL	81	73	75	75	72	77	77	76	80	76	79	68	75	80	75	81	71	78	80	78
COLUMBUS, IN	97	92	94	93	93	98	91	94	94	91	93	84	90	96	92	95	83	92	97	96
COLUMBUS, MS	75	64	60	65	64	73	66	69	70	66	69	61	63	71	65	72	61	69	74	72
COLUMBUS, NE	85	78	78	78	81	90	76	83	80	77	79	73	75	83	78	82	70	80	88	86
COLUMBUS, OH	102	100	105	103	97	96	104	98	102	103	102	91	103	103	101	101	93	101	98	99
CONCORD, NH	102	107	114	109	108	105	105	105	103	105	102	96	107	103	106	102	93	103	103	105
CONNERSVILLE, IN	85	75	78	75	78	88	77	82	83	75	81	72	74	84	78	85	71	80	90	85
COOKEVILLE, TN	77	58	46	57	61	78	64	71	68	59	67	64	55	69	61	71	58	68	76	75
COOS BAY, OR	73	64	64	64	68	79	67	74	70	64	69	64	63	69	69	73	60	71	81	75
CORBIN, KY	67	48	36	47	52	69	52	62	58	49	57	55	44	59	50	62	49	58	68	66
CORDELE, GA	72	55	47	55	57	71	60	66	67	58	65	58	54	67	58	70	57	65	73	69
CORINTH, MS	71	53	41	51	57	73	54	65	61	53	60	57	48	63	54	65	52	61	71	69
CORNELIA, GA	91	71	54	69	76	96	71	85	77	70	77	75	64	80	71	82	66	79	90	91
CORNING, NY	84	74	72	73	78	89	75	82	79	73	78	72	71	80	76	82	69	79	88	85
CORPUS CHRISTI, TX	86	80	73	79	75	79	80	81	82	82	82	74	77	81	78	82	74	83	81	80
CORSICANA, TX	78	64	58	63	65	78	66	73	72	65	71	64	61	72	65	75	62	71	79	75
CORTLAND, NY	75	69	73	70	69	74	74	72	75	71	74	65	71	75	72	75	66	73	76	74
CORVALLIS, OR	96	92	97	96	89	88	105	92	98	98	99	88	100	97	97	95	90	98	90	93
COSHOCTON, OH	79	67	62	67	71	83	67	75	73	67	72	66	64	75	68	76	63	72	82	79
CRAWFORDSVILLE, IN	86	79	82	79	83	91	79	85	83	78	82	74	78	86	80	86	73	81	90	87
CRESCENT CITY, CA	71	62	58	61	66	74	64	71	66	61	65	63	59	65	64	68	57	68	74	73
CROSSVILLE, TN	78	62	52	59	68	87	63	76	69	61	66	66	57	68	65	74	58	72	85	80
CROWLEY, LA	69	52	39	51	54	70	53	62	60	53	59	55	48	62	53	64	51	60	69	67
CULLMAN, AL	81	63	50	61	66	84	63	74	69	62	68	66	57	71	63	73	59	70	80	79
CULPEPER, VA	91	100	108	101	101	96	95	95	93	96	93	87	99	94	98	92	85	93	93	96
CUMBERLAND, MD-WV	69	59	61	58	62	73	63	67	68	59	66	58	59	67	63	71	57	65	76	69
DALLAS-FT WORTH-ARL	122	117	112	120	110	108	121	113	118	121	119	108	118	120	115	115	108	119	110	114
DALTON, GA	97	80	63	78	81	94	80	89	84	80	84	81	74	87	78	87	74	86	91	93
DANVILLE, IL	74	63	65	63	66	76	67	71	73	64	70	62	63	73	67	76	62	69	81	73
DANVILLE, KY	82	64	55	63	69	85	67	77	73	65	72	68	61	75	66	77	62	73	83	81
DANVILLE, VA	77	61	53	60	65	80	63	72	69	62	68	63	58	71	63	74	59	69	80	76
DAPHNE-FAIRHOPE, AL	95	85	75	84	88	100	82	92	85	82	85	82	79	86	84	88	74	88	95	95
DAVENPORT-MOLINE	86	85	94	86	86	88	85	86	88	85	86	75	86	88	86	89	77	85	91	86
DAYTON, OH	91	91	102	93	90	91	92	90	93	92	92	80	94	93	93	94	84	91	94	90
DECATUR, AL	86	71	60	70	73	87	71	79	76	70	75	71	66	79	70	79	66	76	85	84
DECATUR, IL	82	78	87	79	79	84	80	81	84	79	83	71	80	84	81	86	74	81	88	82
DECATUR, IN	90	78	75	78	83	96	78	87	83	77	82	76	75	87	79	87	72	82	94	90
DEFIANCE, OH	96	86	83	86	90	100	84	92	89	84	88	81	82	93	86	92	78	88	98	96
DEL RIO, TX	72	59	40	55	54	62	59	63	64	61	64	57	54	62	56	65	57	65	64	62
DELTONA-DAYTONA BCH.	80	79	88	79	82	87	78	82	81	78	80	71	79	77	82	84	71	81	90	82
DEMING, NM	59	44	32	42	47	61	46	55	51	44	50	48	39	51	45	54	43	52	60	58
DENVER-AURORA, CO	121	120	120	120	121	113	127	119	121	128	123	114	128	122	124	118	113	123	112	118
DE RIDDER, LA	79	61	46	59	64	80	61	72	67	60	66	64	55	70	60	71	57	68	77	77
UNITED STATES	100	100	100	100	100	100	100	100	100	100	100	100	100	100	100	100	100	100	100	100

POPULATION CHANGE
CBSA AND U.S. TOTALS

A

CBSA	CBSA Code	POPULATION 2000	POPULATION 2007	POPULATION 2012	2000-2007 ANNUAL RATE % Rate	2000-2007 ANNUAL RATE National Rank	RACE (%) White 2000	White 2007	Black 2000	Black 2007	Asian/Pacific 2000	Asian/Pacific 2007
DES MNS-W D MNS, IA	19780	481,394	540,397	589,162	1.6	155	90.2	88.0	3.9	4.2	2.2	3.2
DETROIT-WARREN-LIV.	19820	4,452,557	4,561,522	4,621,157	0.3	633	71.4	69.8	22.8	23.0	2.3	3.3
DICKINSON, ND	19860	23,524	23,597	23,671	0.0	765	97.6	97.0	0.2	0.3	0.3	0.4
DILLON, SC	19900	30,722	30,810	30,541	0.0	765	50.4	49.9	45.3	45.9	0.4	0.4
DIXON, IL	19940	36,062	36,020	36,244	0.0	765	92.7	92.2	4.9	5.3	0.6	0.6
DODGE CITY, KS	19980	32,458	34,434	35,910	0.8	396	74.9	70.5	1.6	1.6	2.2	2.6
DOTHAN, AL	20020	130,861	139,830	146,674	0.9	352	74.9	72.9	22.8	24.1	0.5	0.7
DOUGLAS, GA	20060	45,022	48,953	51,459	1.2	255	68.0	62.7	24.8	27.5	0.5	0.7
DOVER, DE	20100	126,697	152,757	177,094	2.6	57	73.5	70.3	20.7	22.4	1.7	2.6
DUBLIN, GA	20140	53,434	57,078	58,749	0.9	352	63.3	58.6	34.9	39.2	0.7	0.9
DUBOIS, PA	20180	83,382	84,517	84,545	0.2	679	97.4	96.9	1.5	1.7	0.3	0.4
DUBUQUE, IA	20220	89,143	92,767	95,199	0.6	494	97.1	96.3	0.9	1.0	0.7	1.0
DULUTH, MN-WI	20260	275,486	278,579	278,753	0.2	679	94.6	93.7	0.8	1.0	0.6	0.9
DUMAS, TX	20300	20,121	20,094	20,029	0.0	765	63.9	63.0	0.7	0.7	0.9	0.9
DUNCAN, OK	20340	43,182	43,740	44,181	0.2	679	88.4	86.8	2.2	2.3	0.3	0.5
DUNN, NC	20380	91,025	108,100	121,923	2.4	71	71.1	69.0	22.5	22.6	0.7	0.9
DURANGO, CO	20420	43,941	50,436	55,038	1.9	113	87.3	86.1	0.3	0.3	0.5	0.6
DURANT, OK	20460	36,534	38,549	40,124	0.7	444	80.0	77.9	1.4	1.5	0.5	0.6
DURHAM, NC	20500	426,493	477,119	510,408	1.6	155	62.7	60.1	28.8	28.7	3.0	3.8
DYERSBURG, TN	20540	37,279	38,315	38,807	0.4	590	85.4	83.9	12.9	13.9	0.4	0.5
EAGLE PASS, TX	20580	47,297	52,929	55,773	1.6	155	70.9	70.5	0.3	0.3	0.4	0.4
E LIVERPOOL-SALEM,OH	20620	112,075	110,904	110,062	-0.1	805	96.4	95.9	2.2	2.5	0.3	0.4
EASTON, MD	20660	33,812	38,575	42,443	1.8	127	82.0	77.8	15.4	18.6	0.9	1.3
EAST STROUDSBURG, PA	20700	138,687	171,850	199,550	3.0	38	88.2	86.2	6.0	6.8	1.1	1.6
EAU CLAIRE, WI	20740	148,337	159,646	165,062	1.0	318	96.0	94.8	0.4	0.7	1.9	2.6
EDWARDS, CO	20780	49,471	58,067	63,977	2.2	85	84.1	82.1	0.3	0.4	0.8	1.0
EFFINGHAM, IL	20820	34,264	34,851	35,209	0.2	679	98.7	98.3	0.2	0.2	0.3	0.4
EL CAMPO, TX	20900	41,188	42,284	43,036	0.4	590	69.0	65.9	15.0	15.0	0.4	0.4
EL CENTRO, CA	20940	142,361	170,210	193,352	2.5	64	49.4	47.1	4.0	3.5	2.1	2.1
EL DORADO, AR	20980	45,629	44,302	42,974	-0.4	896	66.1	63.4	32.0	34.4	0.4	0.5
ELIZABETH CITY, NC	21020	53,150	61,382	68,432	2.0	101	63.0	62.2	34.5	34.6	0.7	1.0
ELIZABETHTOWN, KY	21060	107,547	113,649	118,092	0.8	396	83.6	81.7	10.8	11.1	1.8	2.5
ELK CITY, OK	21120	19,799	19,139	19,776	-0.5	911	87.1	85.3	5.5	5.9	0.4	0.6
ELKHART-GOSHEN, IN	21140	182,791	200,091	213,376	1.3	225	86.4	83.6	5.2	5.7	1.0	1.3
ELKO, NV	21220	46,942	48,630	49,734	0.5	545	82.3	80.3	0.6	0.6	0.8	0.8
ELLENSBURG, WA	21260	33,362	38,717	41,716	2.1	93	91.8	90.5	0.7	0.8	2.3	2.7
ELMIRA, NY	21300	91,070	89,603	88,351	-0.2	841	91.0	89.0	5.8	6.7	0.8	1.1
EL PASO, TX	21340	679,622	751,891	804,703	1.4	196	73.9	73.0	3.1	2.8	1.1	1.1
EMPORIA, KS	21380	38,965	39,442	39,824	0.2	679	84.3	80.8	2.2	2.2	1.9	2.5
ENID, OK	21420	57,813	57,775	57,789	0.0	765	88.7	88.5	3.3	3.3	1.3	1.4
ENTERPRISE-OZARK, AL	21460	92,744	95,643	97,904	0.4	590	75.7	73.5	19.4	20.2	1.1	1.5
ERIE, PA	21500	280,843	283,041	284,981	0.1	723	90.9	89.1	6.1	7.3	0.7	1.0
ESCANABA, MI	21540	38,520	38,863	39,120	0.1	723	95.8	95.4	0.1	0.1	0.3	0.5
ESPANOLA, NM	21580	41,190	42,104	42,637	0.3	633	56.6	56.1	0.3	0.4	0.3	0.3
EUFAULA, AL-GA	21640	31,636	31,503	31,037	-0.1	805	51.3	50.4	46.4	47.3	0.3	0.3
EUGENE-SPRINGF'LD,OR	21660	322,959	342,781	357,477	0.8	396	90.6	89.1	0.8	0.8	2.2	2.7
EUREKA-ARCAT-FORT,CA	21700	126,518	132,810	137,299	0.7	444	84.7	81.8	0.9	0.9	1.8	2.3
EVANSTON, WY	21740	19,742	20,321	20,744	0.4	590	94.3	93.7	0.1	0.1	0.3	0.4
EVANSVILLE, IN-KY	21780	342,815	351,661	358,180	0.4	590	92.3	91.4	5.6	6.1	0.6	0.9
FAIRBANKS, AK	21820	82,840	89,457	94,305	1.1	288	77.8	75.1	5.8	5.4	2.4	2.6
FAIRMONT, MN	21860	21,802	21,421	21,169	-0.2	841	97.2	96.3	0.3	0.3	0.4	0.6
FAIRMONT, WV	21900	56,598	55,343	54,417	-0.3	873	95.1	94.7	3.2	3.3	0.4	0.6
FALLON, NV	21980	23,982	25,517	26,611	0.9	352	84.2	82.8	1.6	1.7	2.9	3.0
FARGO, ND-MN	22020	174,367	194,208	208,938	1.5	173	94.8	93.5	0.7	0.9	1.2	1.8
FARIBAULT-NORTHFIELD	22060	56,665	64,563	69,228	1.8	127	93.6	91.9	1.3	1.6	1.5	2.0
FARMINGTON, MO	22100	55,641	61,770	64,829	1.5	173	96.1	95.5	2.0	2.3	0.3	0.5
FARMINGTON, NM	22140	113,801	125,916	135,300	1.4	196	52.8	49.7	0.4	0.5	0.3	0.4
FAYETTEVILLE, NC	22180	336,609	353,650	367,472	0.7	444	54.1	51.6	35.2	34.9	2.1	2.6
FAYETTEVL-SPRINGDALE	22220	347,045	438,460	517,004	3.3	26	89.7	87.4	1.2	1.3	1.5	1.9
FERGUS FALLS, MN	22260	57,159	58,492	59,365	0.3	633	97.1	96.4	0.3	0.4	0.5	0.7
FERNLEY, NV	22280	34,501	52,742	73,370	6.0	3	88.6	87.0	0.7	0.7	0.7	0.8
FINDLAY, OH	22300	71,295	75,565	78,464	0.8	396	95.1	94.0	1.1	1.2	1.2	1.9
FITZGERALD, GA	22340	27,415	27,639	27,660	0.1	723	66.4	63.4	30.2	32.9	0.3	0.3
FLAGSTAFF, AZ	22380	116,320	128,439	136,437	1.4	196	63.1	61.2	1.0	1.1	0.9	1.0
FLINT, MI	22420	436,141	448,530	457,013	0.4	590	75.3	72.9	20.4	21.9	0.8	1.2
FLORENCE, SC	22500	193,155	200,318	205,489	0.5	545	58.1	56.8	40.2	40.9	0.5	0.7
FLORENCE-MUSCLE SHLS	22520	142,950	143,606	143,904	0.1	723	85.7	84.8	12.5	13.0	0.3	0.4
FOND DU LAC, WI	22540	97,296	101,500	104,440	0.6	494	96.2	95.1	0.9	1.2	0.9	1.2
FOREST CITY, NC	22580	62,899	65,027	66,255	0.5	545	86.8	85.9	11.2	11.6	0.4	0.5
FORREST CITY, AR	22620	29,329	29,743	29,007	0.2	679	48.4	45.8	49.0	51.0	0.6	0.7
FT. COLLINS-LOVELAND	22660	251,494	288,955	308,656	1.9	113	91.4	90.1	0.7	0.7	1.6	2.0
FORT DODGE, IA	22700	40,235	39,493	38,581	-0.3	873	93.4	92.0	3.4	3.8	0.7	1.2
FORT LEONARD WOOD,MO	22780	41,165	44,803	45,616	1.2	255	78.4	75.5	12.0	13.0	2.6	3.6
FT MADISON-KEO,IA-MO	22800	45,468	44,369	43,533	-0.3	873	95.0	94.0	2.4	2.7	0.4	0.7
FORT MORGAN, CO	22820	27,171	28,637	29,626	0.7	444	79.7	76.9	0.3	0.4	0.4	0.4
FORT PAYNE, AL	22840	64,452	68,200	70,797	0.8	396	92.6	90.2	1.7	1.8	0.2	0.3
FORT POLK SOUTH, LA	22860	52,531	51,199	50,316	-0.4	896	73.7	69.6	17.1	19.1	1.9	2.6
UNITED STATES					1.2		75.1	72.7	12.3	12.6	3.8	4.5

POPULATION COMPOSITION
CBSA AND U.S. TOTALS

B

CBSA	% HISPANIC ORIGIN		2007 AGE DISTRIBUTION (%)										MEDIAN AGE	% 2007 Males	% 2007 Females
	2000	2007	0-4	5-9	10-14	15-19	20-24	25-44	45-64	65-84	85+	18+	2007		
DES MNS-W D MNS, IA	4.0	5.3	7.4	7.2	6.8	6.7	6.7	28.6	25.3	9.5	1.8	74.7	36.1	48.9	51.1
DETROIT-WARREN-LIV.	2.9	3.3	6.9	6.9	7.5	6.8	5.5	27.7	26.4	10.4	1.8	74.5	37.6	48.7	51.3
DICKINSON, ND	1.0	1.4	5.9	5.4	6.7	8.5	8.4	22.8	26.8	12.4	3.0	77.3	39.1	49.5	50.5
DILLON, SC	1.8	1.8	7.6	7.1	7.2	7.0	6.7	27.1	25.6	10.3	1.6	73.7	35.6	47.0	53.0
DIXON, IL	3.2	3.3	5.8	5.3	6.0	7.1	7.0	27.0	27.3	12.1	2.5	78.7	40.0	51.0	49.0
DODGE CITY, KS	37.7	45.2	9.7	8.3	7.7	7.3	7.9	28.7	20.0	8.5	1.9	70.0	30.3	51.7	48.3
DOTHAN, AL	1.4	2.0	6.6	6.4	6.2	6.3	6.0	26.4	27.2	12.7	2.2	76.8	39.4	48.1	51.9
DOUGLAS, GA	8.5	11.4	8.3	7.9	7.1	6.6	7.4	30.1	22.6	8.7	1.3	73.0	33.2	50.1	49.9
DOVER, DE	3.2	4.1	7.3	6.6	6.9	7.9	7.1	27.1	24.7	10.8	1.5	74.9	36.1	48.3	51.7
DUBLIN, GA	1.1	1.4	7.0	6.7	6.9	7.9	6.0	25.9	25.5	12.0	2.2	74.2	37.3	49.3	50.7
DUBOIS, PA	0.6	0.7	5.6	5.3	5.7	6.1	6.0	27.1	27.9	13.7	2.6	79.7	41.3	50.8	49.2
DUBUQUE, IA	1.2	1.6	6.7	6.4	6.7	7.2	7.6	24.7	25.7	12.3	2.7	76.3	38.2	48.6	51.4
DULUTH, MN-WI	0.8	1.1	5.4	5.1	5.6	7.3	8.6	23.7	28.6	12.6	3.0	80.2	40.9	49.6	50.4
DUMAS, TX	47.5	49.1	9.7	8.7	8.5	8.0	7.3	27.2	20.7	8.5	1.4	67.9	30.8	50.3	49.7
DUNCAN, OK	4.0	5.1	6.5	6.3	5.6	5.9	6.7	22.7	28.1	15.3	2.9	78.1	42.3	48.6	51.4
DUNN, NC	5.9	7.7	7.7	7.1	7.0	7.0	6.4	31.5	22.9	9.2	1.2	74.2	34.4	49.7	50.3
DURANGO, CO	10.4	12.3	4.9	5.0	6.0	8.0	10.1	25.8	30.1	9.0	1.1	80.2	37.8	51.0	49.0
DURANT, OK	2.6	3.4	6.7	6.0	6.0	6.8	7.5	26.4	25.3	12.9	2.4	77.5	37.3	48.9	51.1
DURHAM, NC	6.5	8.6	6.1	6.0	6.0	7.5	8.0	31.1	24.8	8.9	1.6	78.1	35.3	48.6	51.4
DYERSBURG, TN	1.2	1.6	6.8	6.3	7.1	6.0	6.0	27.9	26.5	11.4	2.0	76.1	38.2	48.3	51.7
EAGLE PASS, TX	95.0	96.0	10.4	9.1	9.8	9.1	8.2	24.8	19.3	8.3	0.9	65.1	28.0	48.3	51.7
E LIVERPOOL-SALEM,OH	1.2	1.4	5.9	5.7	6.0	6.4	6.2	26.1	28.6	12.8	2.2	78.5	40.5	50.0	50.0
EASTON, MD	1.8	2.7	5.0	4.9	5.7	6.0	5.1	21.2	31.2	17.8	3.1	80.5	46.4	47.8	52.2
EAST STROUDSBURG, PA	6.6	8.1	6.0	5.8	7.1	8.0	6.7	24.5	29.0	11.3	1.5	76.3	40.2	49.5	50.5
EAU CLAIRE, WI	0.8	1.1	6.2	5.7	5.8	7.8	10.6	25.1	25.6	10.7	2.6	78.4	36.5	49.1	50.9
EDWARDS, CO	25.3	29.0	7.0	6.1	5.7	5.8	7.0	39.6	23.9	4.5	0.3	77.8	32.8	54.4	45.6
EFFINGHAM, IL	0.7	1.0	7.6	6.8	7.2	7.0	7.1	25.3	25.7	11.2	2.2	74.2	37.2	50.1	49.9
EL CAMPO, TX	31.3	37.3	7.6	6.7	6.9	6.8	8.2	25.0	25.3	11.4	2.1	74.7	36.2	49.5	50.5
EL CENTRO, CA	72.2	77.0	8.2	7.1	7.9	8.8	9.1	28.1	21.0	8.8	1.1	71.3	31.1	52.0	48.0
EL DORADO, AR	1.1	1.5	6.7	6.1	6.4	6.2	6.5	25.5	26.7	13.1	2.8	77.0	39.9	48.4	51.6
ELIZABETH CITY, NC	1.0	1.3	6.0	5.7	5.8	7.5	7.3	25.3	27.4	12.9	2.1	78.3	40.0	48.8	51.2
ELIZABETHTOWN, KY	3.1	4.4	7.2	6.7	6.5	7.3	8.0	28.0	25.2	9.9	1.3	75.5	35.7	50.3	49.7
ELK CITY, OK	5.4	7.0	7.2	6.3	6.1	6.1	7.2	25.6	26.6	12.2	2.7	76.7	38.6	49.1	50.9
ELKHART-GOSHEN, IN	8.9	11.7	8.1	7.6	7.2	7.3	6.2	28.5	24.2	9.3	1.7	72.6	34.6	49.8	50.2
ELKO, NV	19.4	23.4	8.9	7.5	7.6	7.9	8.4	27.9	24.4	6.7	0.7	71.1	31.8	51.5	48.5
ELLENSBURG, WA	5.0	6.4	4.8	4.2	5.2	11.2	17.0	21.5	24.3	10.0	1.9	82.4	31.2	49.5	50.5
ELMIRA, NY	1.8	2.4	6.0	5.7	6.2	7.2	7.6	25.0	27.1	12.9	2.5	78.2	39.7	49.8	50.2
EL PASO, TX	78.2	82.3	9.2	8.1	8.4	7.9	8.3	28.0	20.7	8.4	1.0	69.5	30.3	48.5	51.5
EMPORIA, KS	15.6	20.0	7.1	6.1	6.0	8.2	11.6	25.7	23.6	9.2	2.4	76.9	32.4	49.5	50.5
ENID, OK	4.1	4.2	7.0	6.2	5.9	6.0	6.9	25.9	26.2	13.3	2.6	77.2	39.0	48.8	51.2
ENTERPRISE-OZARK, AL	3.0	4.5	7.1	6.3	6.0	6.3	7.2	27.4	25.7	12.4	1.7	76.9	37.2	49.4	50.6
ERIE, PA	2.2	2.7	6.2	5.8	6.6	7.8	8.2	25.0	26.4	11.7	2.4	77.2	37.8	49.1	50.9
ESCANABA, MI	0.5	0.6	5.7	5.3	5.5	6.3	6.7	23.2	30.4	14.2	2.7	79.6	43.0	49.5	50.5
ESPANOLA, NM	72.9	73.3	7.2	6.4	6.9	7.9	7.2	27.0	26.5	9.7	1.2	74.6	35.6	49.4	50.6
EUFAULA, AL-GA	1.6	1.6	6.4	5.9	6.4	6.5	7.5	28.4	25.6	11.3	1.9	77.3	37.4	52.1	47.9
EUGENE-SPRINGF'LD,OR	4.6	6.2	5.7	5.3	5.8	7.1	9.1	25.4	28.1	11.3	2.2	79.5	38.3	49.2	50.8
EUREKA-ARCAT-FORT,CA	6.5	8.3	5.6	5.1	5.8	7.4	9.2	25.9	28.5	10.5	1.9	79.4	37.5	49.5	50.5
EVANSTON, WY	5.3	6.0	8.6	7.3	7.2	8.2	10.2	24.2	27.4	6.1	0.8	71.7	31.6	50.8	49.2
EVANSVILLE, IN-KY	0.9	1.2	6.4	6.0	6.2	6.7	7.0	26.3	27.3	11.9	2.2	77.5	38.9	48.5	51.5
FAIRBANKS, AK	4.2	5.4	7.9	6.5	6.6	8.3	11.2	29.0	24.7	5.5	0.5	74.2	30.1	51.9	48.1
FAIRMONT, MN	1.9	2.7	5.9	5.1	5.9	6.5	7.8	20.2	29.8	14.7	4.1	79.1	43.9	49.0	51.0
FAIRMONT, WV	0.7	0.8	5.2	5.0	5.3	5.5	6.3	26.6	28.3	14.7	3.0	81.5	41.7	47.9	52.1
FALLON, NV	8.7	10.7	8.4	7.1	6.9	7.3	7.9	25.4	24.9	10.6	1.5	73.2	35.4	49.9	50.1
FARGO, ND-MN	1.9	2.6	6.7	5.9	6.1	8.4	11.1	28.6	23.0	8.4	1.8	77.5	32.0	49.7	50.3
FARIBAULT-NORTHFIELD	5.5	7.4	6.3	6.0	6.4	9.8	11.0	24.5	24.5	9.5	2.1	76.8	34.5	50.5	49.5
FARMINGTON, MO	0.8	1.0	6.1	5.5	5.6	6.2	7.3	28.5	25.5	12.9	2.5	79.2	39.0	51.9	48.1
FARMINGTON, NM	15.0	15.3	8.6	7.3	7.8	8.2	9.2	25.7	23.9	8.4	1.0	71.4	31.3	49.7	50.3
FAYETTEVILLE, NC	6.9	8.8	8.3	7.3	6.8	7.6	9.6	31.2	20.7	7.7	0.8	73.5	31.0	50.8	49.2
FAYETTEVL-SPRINGDALE	8.3	11.1	7.7	7.0	6.5	6.9	7.9	28.8	23.1	10.6	1.5	75.1	34.4	49.9	50.1
FERGUS FALLS, MN	1.7	2.3	5.9	5.2	5.6	6.5	7.5	20.7	29.7	15.4	3.4	79.3	43.9	50.4	49.6
FERNLEY, NV	11.0	13.5	6.7	6.5	6.9	7.4	5.8	24.2	28.5	12.7	1.3	75.1	40.2	50.2	49.8
FINDLAY, OH	3.1	3.7	6.8	6.4	6.7	7.1	6.8	26.3	26.5	11.0	2.4	76.1	37.7	48.6	51.4
FITZGERALD, GA	3.7	3.9	7.3	6.9	6.6	7.7	6.5	26.5	24.7	11.6	2.1	74.1	36.1	48.9	51.1
FLAGSTAFF, AZ	10.9	13.2	7.4	6.5	7.3	8.8	11.2	27.2	23.9	7.0	0.8	74.0	30.3	49.9	50.1
FLINT, MI	2.3	2.8	7.1	6.8	7.6	6.9	6.2	26.7	26.4	10.8	1.5	74.3	37.0	48.2	51.8
FLORENCE, SC	1.1	1.4	6.6	6.4	6.9	6.8	6.3	27.3	27.1	10.9	1.7	76.0	37.7	47.4	52.6
FLORENCE-MUSCLE SHLS	1.1	1.4	6.1	5.9	6.1	6.0	6.0	27.1	27.1	13.6	2.2	78.5	40.0	48.1	51.9
FOND DU LAC, WI	2.0	2.7	6.2	5.7	6.2	7.3	7.5	26.0	27.2	11.4	2.5	77.7	39.0	49.0	51.0
FOREST CITY, NC	1.8	2.3	6.2	6.1	6.7	5.8	5.0	27.5	26.8	13.6	2.3	77.4	40.0	48.8	51.2
FORREST CITY, AR	4.9	6.2	7.7	6.4	6.6	6.3	7.5	30.7	23.6	9.5	1.6	75.3	34.4	54.2	45.8
FT. COLLINS-LOVELAND	8.3	9.9	6.1	5.8	5.9	7.8	8.8	29.0	26.8	8.4	1.3	78.3	34.8	50.0	50.0
FORT DODGE, IA	2.3	3.1	6.5	6.0	5.7	7.6	8.5	23.4	25.5	13.3	3.4	78.3	38.7	49.4	50.6
FORT LEONARD WOOD,MO	5.8	7.1	7.4	6.5	5.8	12.2	14.1	27.3	18.6	7.2	0.9	76.3	27.5	54.1	45.9
FT MADISON-KEO,IA-MO	2.1	2.8	6.2	5.6	6.0	6.5	6.5	24.5	26.5	13.6	2.9	78.6	41.4	49.8	50.2
FORT MORGAN, CO	31.2	35.8	8.9	8.1	7.6	6.7	7.0	26.3	23.4	10.4	2.1	71.2	34.4	50.6	49.4
FORT PAYNE, AL	5.6	8.4	7.1	6.8	6.7	5.3	5.6	29.1	25.8	11.9	1.8	76.2	37.6	49.3	50.7
FORT POLK SOUTH, LA	5.9	6.8	9.6	7.3	6.2	6.6	11.9	30.2	19.1	8.1	0.9	73.4	29.1	52.4	47.6
UNITED STATES	12.5	15.0	6.9	6.5	6.8	7.1	7.0	27.6	25.4	10.7	1.9	75.6	36.7	49.2	50.8

CBSA	HOUSEHOLDS					FAMILIES			MEDIAN HOUSEHOLD INCOME		
	2000	2007	2012	% Annual Rate 2000-2007	2007 Average HH Size	2000	2007	% Annual Rate 2000-2007	2007	2012	2007 National Rank
DES MNS-W D MNS, IA	189,371	216,605	237,126	1.9	2.44	126,155	141,762	1.6	58,824	69,071	76
DETROIT-WARREN-LIV.	1,696,943	1,755,158	1,787,258	0.5	2.57	1,150,002	1,158,409	0.1	61,856	71,889	47
DICKINSON, ND	9,298	9,638	9,802	0.5	2.35	6,130	6,099	-0.1	40,926	48,028	618
DILLON, SC	11,199	11,628	11,685	0.5	2.61	8,065	8,098	0.1	32,767	37,058	879
DIXON, IL	13,253	13,544	13,716	0.3	2.46	9,138	9,075	-0.1	51,073	59,211	217
DODGE CITY, KS	10,852	11,220	11,622	0.5	3.00	7,856	8,028	0.3	47,966	56,447	315
DOTHAN, AL	52,836	57,545	60,928	1.2	2.40	37,298	39,860	0.9	37,159	41,035	772
DOUGLAS, GA	16,071	17,474	18,474	1.2	2.68	11,772	12,428	0.8	35,871	40,554	813
DOVER, DE	47,224	57,574	67,264	2.8	2.59	33,615	39,963	2.4	50,818	59,477	220
DUBLIN, GA	20,213	21,628	22,477	0.9	2.50	14,417	14,944	0.5	37,358	42,507	764
DUBOIS, PA	32,785	33,561	33,889	0.3	2.39	22,926	22,820	-0.1	38,911	44,941	691
DUBUQUE, IA	33,690	36,006	37,442	0.9	2.44	23,111	24,251	0.7	49,138	56,995	284
DULUTH, MN-WI	112,491	116,257	117,389	0.5	2.28	71,060	71,139	0.0	46,459	54,435	369
DUMAS, TX	6,774	6,740	6,704	-0.1	2.95	5,328	5,260	-0.2	41,912	48,181	561
DUNCAN, OK	17,463	17,917	18,177	0.4	2.41	12,591	12,688	0.1	37,442	43,082	760
DUNN, NC	33,800	40,145	45,391	2.4	2.62	24,107	27,947	2.1	43,904	50,785	475
DURANGO, CO	17,342	20,236	22,293	2.2	2.40	10,892	12,372	1.8	49,685	56,936	264
DURANT, OK	14,422	15,401	16,079	0.9	2.45	9,943	10,405	0.6	34,127	39,131	858
DURHAM, NC	168,704	193,849	208,548	1.9	2.35	104,141	116,867	1.6	53,986	63,421	142
DYERSBURG, TN	14,751	15,318	15,565	0.5	2.46	10,459	10,587	0.2	41,436	48,442	587
EAGLE PASS, TX	13,089	14,792	15,657	1.7	3.57	11,231	12,626	1.6	25,870	29,123	932
E LIVERPOOL-SALEM,OH	42,973	42,952	42,861	0.0	2.49	30,688	29,814	-0.4	41,437	47,184	586
EASTON, MD	14,307	16,550	18,319	2.0	2.29	9,630	10,757	1.5	52,946	60,259	166
EAST STROUDSBURG, PA	49,454	61,119	71,022	3.0	2.75	36,459	43,969	2.6	57,768	66,377	86
EAU CLAIRE, WI	57,178	63,108	66,057	1.4	2.40	37,276	40,117	1.0	48,392	55,238	297
EDWARDS, CO	18,125	21,028	23,035	2.1	2.74	10,935	12,308	1.6	78,466	95,499	6
EFFINGHAM, IL	13,001	13,459	13,704	0.5	2.55	9,182	9,250	0.1	48,091	54,564	308
EL CAMPO, TX	14,799	15,272	15,581	0.4	2.72	10,744	10,979	0.3	38,531	43,846	715
EL CENTRO, CA	39,384	47,357	54,076	2.6	3.36	31,465	37,944	2.6	39,060	44,334	685
EL DORADO, AR	17,989	17,700	17,262	-0.2	2.45	12,652	12,088	-0.6	36,944	43,059	777
ELIZABETH CITY, NC	20,214	23,892	26,976	2.3	2.45	14,496	16,760	2.0	38,709	44,336	703
ELIZABETHTOWN, KY	39,772	43,559	45,852	1.3	2.51	29,213	30,986	0.8	46,493	54,003	368
ELK CITY, OK	7,356	7,822	8,136	0.9	2.40	5,002	5,209	0.6	33,796	38,757	867
ELKHART-GOSHEN, IN	66,154	72,969	77,893	1.4	2.70	47,659	50,768	0.9	54,586	63,240	132
ELKO, NV	16,304	16,822	17,166	0.4	2.84	11,933	12,203	0.3	61,096	70,502	57
ELLENSBURG, WA	13,382	15,048	16,334	1.6	2.33	7,787	8,590	1.4	40,832	47,110	621
ELMIRA, NY	35,049	35,104	34,854	0.0	2.40	23,280	23,129	-0.1	45,627	52,682	403
EL PASO, TX	210,022	235,442	253,041	1.6	3.14	166,226	184,953	1.5	38,488	44,472	719
EMPORIA, KS	14,937	15,201	15,372	0.2	2.48	9,459	9,480	0.0	41,052	47,721	606
ENID, OK	23,175	23,365	23,437	0.1	2.40	15,799	15,608	-0.2	40,980	47,408	613
ENTERPRISE-OZARK, AL	36,299	38,535	39,931	0.8	2.42	26,122	27,237	0.6	37,721	41,545	752
ERIE, PA	106,507	107,926	109,152	0.2	2.49	71,039	69,796	-0.2	46,023	53,980	384
ESCANABA, MI	15,836	16,486	16,809	0.6	2.32	10,684	10,804	0.2	41,891	46,494	564
ESPANOLA, NM	15,044	16,083	16,528	0.9	2.59	10,815	11,241	0.5	35,792	41,180	817
EUFAULA, AL-GA	11,456	11,642	11,579	0.2	2.46	8,149	8,121	0.0	29,160	32,121	915
EUGENE-SPRINGF'LD,OR	130,453	139,621	146,278	0.9	2.40	82,180	87,043	0.8	46,448	53,851	371
EUREKA-ARCAT-FORT,CA	51,238	53,804	55,864	0.7	2.39	30,645	32,365	0.8	38,702	44,405	704
EVANSTON, WY	6,823	7,329	7,594	1.0	2.72	5,147	5,403	0.7	53,604	61,604	146
EVANSVILLE, IN-KY	136,768	143,011	146,663	0.6	2.39	92,947	93,740	0.1	48,496	56,329	296
FAIRBANKS, AK	29,777	32,029	33,939	1.0	2.67	20,502	21,650	0.8	61,107	71,681	56
FAIRMONT, MN	9,067	9,100	9,067	0.1	2.30	6,045	5,882	-0.4	43,054	50,073	511
FAIRMONT, WV	23,652	23,740	23,584	0.1	2.27	15,510	15,029	-0.4	35,772	41,306	819
FALLON, NV	8,912	9,509	9,914	0.9	2.65	6,465	6,831	0.8	49,176	55,419	282
FARGO, ND-MN	69,985	80,713	88,109	2.0	2.29	42,172	46,473	1.3	49,909	59,432	257
FARIBAULT-NORTHFIELD	18,888	21,969	23,792	2.1	2.62	13,347	15,105	1.7	61,015	70,131	59
FARMINGTON, MO	20,793	22,842	24,278	1.3	2.44	14,669	15,688	0.9	38,339	43,973	726
FARMINGTON, NM	37,711	43,195	46,981	1.9	2.89	28,930	32,369	1.6	42,426	49,327	531
FAYETTEVILLE, NC	118,731	128,994	135,366	1.2	2.58	86,402	91,872	0.9	47,067	55,240	349
FAYETTEVL-SPRINGDALE	131,939	167,402	197,755	3.3	2.56	92,903	114,505	2.9	46,392	54,988	372
FERGUS FALLS, MN	22,671	23,604	24,101	0.6	2.42	15,768	15,954	0.2	43,583	50,683	492
FERNLEY, NV	13,007	19,945	27,784	6.1	2.62	9,449	14,351	5.9	47,265	52,739	343
FINDLAY, OH	27,898	30,322	31,809	1.2	2.43	19,127	20,151	0.7	53,221	60,547	155
FITZGERALD, GA	10,317	10,475	10,548	0.2	2.55	7,327	7,208	-0.2	34,515	39,511	850
FLAGSTAFF, AZ	40,448	45,500	48,831	1.6	2.75	26,946	29,907	1.4	50,358	60,373	236
FLINT, MI	169,825	177,451	182,064	0.6	2.50	115,956	117,789	0.2	51,660	60,284	201
FLORENCE, SC	72,940	76,871	79,622	0.7	2.54	52,242	53,228	0.3	41,527	47,720	584
FLORENCE-MUSCLE SHLS	58,549	60,173	60,889	0.4	2.35	41,201	41,554	0.1	37,910	41,750	743
FOND DU LAC, WI	36,931	39,656	41,308	1.0	2.45	25,467	26,718	0.7	55,872	64,521	115
FOREST CITY, NC	25,191	26,589	27,305	0.7	2.39	17,938	18,480	0.4	37,456	42,268	759
FORREST CITY, AR	10,043	9,866	9,680	-0.2	2.59	7,227	6,906	-0.6	31,923	36,917	895
FT. COLLINS-LOVELAND	97,164	112,365	120,416	2.0	2.51	63,197	71,257	1.7	61,770	72,705	48
FORT DODGE, IA	15,878	15,716	15,410	-0.1	2.34	10,300	9,987	-0.4	44,475	51,530	448
FORT LEONARD WOOD,MO	13,433	14,174	14,636	0.7	2.61	9,949	10,251	0.4	41,776	48,305	575
FT MADISON-KEO,IA-MO	18,127	17,989	17,767	-0.1	2.36	12,327	11,988	-0.4	43,393	49,729	500
FORT MORGAN, CO	9,539	9,911	10,180	0.5	2.84	6,969	7,101	0.3	42,166	48,267	545
FORT PAYNE, AL	25,113	26,620	27,693	0.8	2.53	18,440	19,213	0.6	35,355	39,243	829
FORT POLK SOUTH, LA	18,260	18,219	18,081	0.0	2.62	13,706	13,381	-0.3	34,835	37,573	839
UNITED STATES				1.2	2.59			1.0	53,154	62,503	

CBSA	2007 Per Capita Income	2007 HH Income Base	2007 HOUSEHOLD INCOME DISTRIBUTION (%) Less than $25,000	$25,000 to $49,999	$50,000 to $99,999	$100,000 to $149,999	$150,000 or More	2007 Home Value Base	2007 HOME VALUE DISTRIBUTION (%) Less than $50,000	$50,000 to $89,999	$90,000 to $174,999	$175,000 to $399,999	$400,000 or More	2007 Median Home Value
DES MNS-W D MNS, IA	30,251	216,605	16.2	25.5	36.9	13.9	7.5	157,612	7.1	13.6	44.7	30.3	4.4	142,046
DETROIT-WARREN-LIV.	31,352	1,755,122	18.4	22.1	33.2	16.2	10.2	,292,690	8.7	12.2	34.1	37.2	7.8	161,717
DICKINSON, ND	20,890	9,638	30.0	30.0	30.7	6.8	2.5	6,859	15.4	20.8	50.9	11.6	1.2	105,913
DILLON, SC	16,507	11,628	39.9	29.1	24.1	5.0	2.0	8,559	30.2	28.6	33.1	7.4	0.6	77,926
DIXON, IL	24,307	13,544	20.2	28.4	37.0	10.5	3.8	10,325	5.9	9.9	54.5	25.8	3.9	141,602
DODGE CITY, KS	19,464	11,220	21.9	30.3	36.1	7.5	4.2	7,484	21.7	27.7	38.8	10.9	0.8	90,854
DOTHAN, AL	21,030	57,545	35.0	28.3	26.3	7.1	3.3	43,037	18.4	25.9	37.1	16.1	2.5	98,793
DOUGLAS, GA	18,009	17,474	34.8	31.1	25.5	5.5	3.1	13,171	36.1	27.2	26.6	8.8	1.3	69,031
DOVER, DE	23,600	57,574	22.1	26.9	36.3	10.4	4.4	41,664	9.3	4.6	21.0	56.8	8.4	209,137
DUBLIN, GA	19,936	21,628	35.1	27.2	27.6	6.8	3.3	15,888	26.0	27.6	33.4	11.4	1.6	84,064
DUBOIS, PA	20,129	33,561	31.4	31.4	28.7	6.3	2.2	26,646	13.3	21.3	44.5	19.3	1.6	116,636
DUBUQUE, IA	24,717	36,006	20.7	30.2	36.2	8.8	4.0	27,142	7.6	13.4	51.3	24.3	3.5	130,655
DULUTH, MN-WI	24,415	116,257	26.1	27.5	33.9	8.9	3.6	88,708	8.1	19.5	45.3	24.2	2.9	129,937
DUMAS, TX	17,999	6,740	25.6	33.5	31.3	7.1	2.4	4,844	29.6	31.1	30.9	7.8	0.6	74,506
DUNCAN, OK	20,542	17,917	32.5	31.8	26.4	6.4	2.9	13,548	26.6	30.0	33.0	9.1	1.2	77,789
DUNN, NC	20,420	40,145	28.6	27.8	33.0	7.4	3.1	28,825	17.3	14.3	43.7	22.0	2.7	121,199
DURANGO, CO	27,775	20,236	23.5	26.7	32.6	10.2	6.9	14,385	9.3	4.2	13.4	48.8	24.2	265,049
DURANT, OK	17,994	15,401	37.2	31.9	24.0	5.0	2.0	10,740	31.0	27.5	31.1	9.4	0.9	75,970
DURHAM, NC	30,722	193,849	21.9	24.3	32.8	11.9	9.1	119,026	6.7	7.6	34.4	41.0	10.3	178,700
DYERSBURG, TN	20,783	15,318	31.2	28.4	30.7	6.7	2.9	10,309	11.4	26.5	44.2	16.1	1.9	105,832
EAGLE PASS, TX	10,307	14,792	48.4	29.4	16.8	3.6	1.8	10,453	34.6	34.6	26.3	4.1	0.4	66,771
E LIVERPOOL-SALEM,OH	20,567	42,952	27.4	32.5	30.4	7.2	2.5	33,625	17.8	27.0	41.4	12.8	1.1	97,308
EASTON, MD	35,271	16,550	21.4	25.3	31.7	11.2	10.4	12,094	0.8	2.1	7.4	50.5	39.3	342,945
EAST STROUDSBURG, PA	25,034	61,119	18.5	24.4	36.1	15.4	5.5	48,280	2.1	2.1	21.1	65.3	9.4	232,813
EAU CLAIRE, WI	24,514	63,108	21.5	30.1	35.2	9.2	3.9	44,481	6.5	12.2	51.6	27.4	2.3	134,333
EDWARDS, CO	38,113	21,028	9.1	18.0	37.1	19.1	16.7	14,006	6.8	5.9	10.5	27.2	49.7	397,977
EFFINGHAM, IL	23,125	13,459	22.9	29.2	36.0	7.9	4.0	10,477	9.2	11.6	46.1	29.0	4.0	140,440
EL CAMPO, TX	19,054	15,272	32.0	28.8	27.7	8.4	3.2	10,794	28.2	29.6	30.8	9.6	1.9	79,361
EL CENTRO, CA	16,091	47,353	33.8	26.5	27.2	8.8	3.7	28,465	8.1	5.1	18.8	61.1	6.9	209,654
EL DORADO, AR	20,539	17,700	34.8	28.9	26.1	6.7	3.5	13,170	33.9	29.0	26.4	8.9	1.7	70,852
ELIZABETH CITY, NC	19,724	23,892	33.2	29.0	28.1	7.3	2.4	17,352	13.8	15.9	45.0	22.3	3.0	120,764
ELIZABETHTOWN, KY	22,527	43,559	22.5	31.4	33.5	9.2	3.4	30,300	12.3	13.7	46.1	23.9	4.0	133,980
ELK CITY, OK	19,179	7,822	36.9	31.9	23.0	5.2	2.9	5,561	36.1	24.7	27.6	10.2	1.3	71,576
ELKHART-GOSHEN, IN	24,934	72,969	17.6	26.9	39.7	10.5	5.4	53,471	10.0	17.2	50.7	19.7	2.5	121,566
ELKO, NV	23,821	16,822	16.8	22.5	43.7	13.0	4.1	12,117	11.2	4.7	18.6	57.4	8.2	224,904
ELLENSBURG, WA	23,489	15,048	33.9	24.9	27.9	9.1	4.3	9,220	4.3	1.9	16.6	58.4	18.8	241,145
ELMIRA, NY	23,585	35,104	25.4	30.0	31.9	8.4	4.3	25,101	11.1	29.3	40.8	17.4	1.4	104,560
EL PASO, TX	16,921	235,442	31.7	29.6	27.2	7.8	3.7	153,782	8.2	22.5	54.0	13.2	2.0	111,776
EMPORIA, KS	20,278	15,201	27.6	31.6	30.9	7.6	2.3	9,702	23.3	25.4	39.3	11.2	0.9	91,972
ENID, OK	21,515	23,365	28.6	32.8	28.8	6.5	3.2	16,481	26.7	30.2	31.4	10.4	1.3	79,965
ENTERPRISE-OZARK, AL	20,022	38,535	33.1	31.2	26.5	6.7	2.4	26,930	19.4	25.6	38.9	13.9	2.2	97,248
ERIE, PA	22,957	107,926	25.4	28.7	32.8	9.1	4.0	75,336	12.3	20.3	45.7	19.6	2.0	114,504
ESCANABA, MI	22,401	16,486	28.9	29.3	31.7	7.7	2.4	13,187	10.5	24.1	45.3	18.1	1.9	108,961
ESPANOLA, NM	18,196	16,083	34.6	29.6	27.1	6.3	2.4	13,090	17.3	13.3	31.9	28.5	8.9	142,302
EUFAULA, AL-GA	16,704	11,642	44.2	26.7	21.3	5.4	2.4	8,787	31.1	28.1	26.9	11.8	2.0	76,282
EUGENE-SPRINGF'LD,OR	25,123	139,620	25.4	28.4	32.5	8.7	5.1	90,410	5.0	3.2	15.0	62.3	14.6	241,143
EUREKA-ARCAT-FORT,CA	21,930	53,804	33.5	28.2	27.5	7.3	3.6	31,877	4.0	2.5	7.8	55.9	29.8	313,241
EVANSTON, WY	21,703	7,329	21.1	24.8	42.4	9.5	2.1	5,621	10.0	7.6	40.6	38.2	3.6	161,205
EVANSVILLE, IN-KY	25,475	143,009	24.0	27.4	33.8	10.2	4.5	104,190	14.9	25.9	40.5	16.8	2.0	102,995
FAIRBANKS, AK	28,249	32,029	15.7	23.7	35.9	15.7	9.0	18,668	5.8	6.0	29.1	54.4	4.7	202,057
FAIRMONT, MN	23,391	9,100	26.4	31.1	33.8	5.8	2.9	7,160	13.1	25.5	40.9	17.3	3.2	110,480
FAIRMONT, WV	20,498	23,740	36.0	29.5	26.1	5.9	2.6	18,224	19.8	27.2	41.5	10.6	0.8	94,126
FALLON, NV	23,220	9,509	20.6	30.2	36.7	8.0	4.5	6,436	8.0	4.6	13.4	63.2	10.9	231,374
FARGO, ND-MN	27,137	80,713	22.1	28.0	34.4	9.9	5.6	48,687	7.1	11.2	49.1	30.2	2.5	142,236
FARIBAULT-NORTHFIELD	25,632	21,969	15.8	23.9	41.2	13.4	5.7	17,429	4.9	3.4	24.6	55.5	11.6	215,095
FARMINGTON, MO	18,997	22,842	32.2	31.8	28.0	6.1	1.9	17,059	16.6	23.9	39.5	17.3	2.5	104,829
FARMINGTON, NM	18,294	43,193	29.9	28.4	30.6	8.0	3.1	32,617	19.8	13.7	34.6	27.9	4.0	132,292
FAYETTEVILLE, NC	21,998	128,994	23.6	30.0	34.2	8.3	3.9	80,971	10.3	15.5	55.8	16.7	1.7	116,855
FAYETTEVL-SPRINGDALE	23,301	167,402	24.5	29.0	33.1	8.0	5.4	114,799	8.6	11.9	43.9	28.4	7.1	145,568
FERGUS FALLS, MN	22,493	23,604	26.2	31.4	32.3	6.8	3.3	19,150	8.4	14.9	42.6	29.7	4.5	142,843
FERNLEY, NV	22,089	19,944	21.8	31.8	36.6	6.1	3.6	15,432	4.4	2.7	20.0	61.2	11.8	233,532
FINDLAY, OH	26,892	30,322	18.1	28.2	36.7	11.9	5.1	22,945	9.1	14.2	47.5	26.3	2.8	129,452
FITZGERALD, GA	18,013	10,475	37.6	27.8	25.3	6.7	2.6	7,472	29.0	32.4	27.8	9.7	1.1	75,829
FLAGSTAFF, AZ	23,497	45,499	23.3	26.3	32.1	12.5	5.8	28,530	13.1	7.4	12.6	40.0	26.9	266,888
FLINT, MI	26,160	177,451	23.3	25.1	33.1	12.6	5.9	130,934	15.5	18.3	40.3	23.6	2.3	119,414
FLORENCE, SC	21,703	76,871	31.0	27.9	28.8	8.1	4.2	58,213	22.8	25.3	35.8	13.8	2.2	92,631
FLORENCE-MUSCLE SHLS	21,493	60,173	33.7	29.1	26.6	7.7	2.9	45,521	13.5	23.8	40.1	19.3	3.3	109,401
FOND DU LAC, WI	25,926	39,656	18.3	24.4	42.0	11.1	4.3	29,541	5.0	8.4	50.3	33.5	2.8	145,289
FOREST CITY, NC	19,932	26,589	33.2	30.6	28.3	5.5	2.4	20,145	17.8	22.4	40.2	16.9	2.6	105,603
FORREST CITY, AR	15,569	9,866	42.1	27.5	24.0	3.9	2.4	6,434	31.0	31.5	28.6	7.6	1.2	75,354
FT. COLLINS-LOVELAND	30,936	112,365	16.6	22.4	36.8	15.1	9.2	79,279	4.6	2.3	14.1	63.5	15.5	237,981
FORT DODGE, IA	23,178	15,716	25.3	31.2	32.5	7.8	3.3	11,497	18.2	29.8	39.2	11.1	1.7	92,383
FORT LEONARD WOOD,MO	17,936	14,172	23.2	37.5	32.1	5.5	1.7	8,562	19.3	20.4	41.5	17.5	1.2	107,405
FT MADISON-KEO,IA-MO	22,391	17,989	26.5	31.4	32.5	6.7	3.0	13,044	24.6	29.9	33.5	10.5	1.4	83,998
FORT MORGAN, CO	18,578	9,911	25.0	34.0	31.8	6.6	2.7	7,089	8.9	8.5	48.6	30.2	3.8	139,457
FORT PAYNE, AL	18,155	26,620	35.4	31.6	26.0	4.9	2.2	21,341	23.5	25.2	35.0	13.3	3.0	91,886
FORT POLK SOUTH, LA	16,223	18,213	32.8	36.6	24.7	4.4	1.5	10,217	29.2	22.8	36.5	9.8	1.7	86,503
UNITED STATES	27,916		21.9	25.0	32.3	12.3	8.4		7.9	10.5	27.1	35.6	19.0	192,285

SPENDING POTENTIAL INDICES
CBSA AND U.S. TOTALS

E

CBSA	Auto Loan	Home Loan	Investments	Retirement Plans	Home Repair	Lawn & Garden	Computers & Hardware	Major Appliances	TV, Radio, Sound Equipment	Furniture	Dine out/ Carry out	Sports Equipment	Fees & Tickets	Toys & Games	Travel	Cable TV	Apparel & Services	Auto Repairs	Health Insurance	Pets & Supplies
	FINANCIAL SERVICES				**THE HOME**						**ENTERTAINMENT**						**PERSONAL**			
DES MNS-W D MNS, IA	104	103	108	106	100	100	104	101	103	104	103	92	104	105	103	102	93	102	101	101
DETROIT-WARREN-LIV.	107	114	126	117	113	108	111	108	111	114	111	97	116	111	113	111	101	109	110	108
DICKINSON, ND	74	63	63	64	65	74	69	71	71	65	70	64	63	71	67	72	61	71	76	74
DILLON, SC	71	52	38	51	55	71	54	64	62	54	61	57	48	63	53	66	53	62	71	69
DIXON, IL	88	83	87	84	86	94	81	87	85	82	84	75	81	89	83	87	74	84	93	89
DODGE CITY, KS	86	79	70	76	76	80	80	83	81	80	81	77	76	82	78	81	73	84	82	82
DOTHAN, AL	80	66	54	65	68	81	65	74	71	65	70	66	61	72	65	74	61	71	79	78
DOUGLAS, GA	81	62	44	60	64	80	62	73	68	62	68	65	55	71	61	72	59	70	77	78
DOVER, DE	90	85	82	85	83	87	84	86	85	84	85	78	83	87	83	86	76	85	87	88
DUBLIN, GA	82	63	48	62	66	83	64	75	71	64	71	67	58	73	63	76	61	72	81	80
DUBOIS, PA	77	61	54	60	67	82	63	73	69	61	68	64	58	70	64	73	58	69	81	77
DUBUQUE, IA	86	84	90	85	86	90	83	86	86	83	85	75	83	87	85	88	76	84	91	88
DULUTH, MN-WI	79	75	83	76	78	82	77	79	80	75	78	69	76	79	78	81	70	78	85	80
DUMAS, TX	81	71	60	69	69	74	71	76	74	72	74	70	67	75	69	74	66	76	76	75
DUNCAN, OK	76	62	56	61	66	81	64	73	71	61	69	64	59	71	65	75	59	70	83	76
DUNN, NC	85	71	59	70	70	81	72	78	75	71	75	70	67	77	70	77	65	76	81	81
DURANGO, CO	99	89	85	91	88	95	96	94	94	91	94	87	90	94	91	93	84	95	94	97
DURANT, OK	69	54	47	54	57	70	59	65	63	55	62	57	52	64	57	66	54	63	71	67
DURHAM, NC	106	96	96	100	94	97	104	99	103	102	104	92	100	104	99	103	94	103	99	101
DYERSBURG, TN	80	65	59	65	67	80	68	74	73	66	72	65	63	75	66	76	63	72	79	78
EAGLE PASS, TX	58	49	35	44	42	47	47	50	52	51	53	45	43	49	45	53	47	53	51	48
E LIVERPOOL-SALEM,OH	78	67	64	66	71	82	68	75	73	66	72	65	64	75	68	76	63	72	82	78
EASTON, MD	112	111	118	111	117	126	109	118	111	109	110	103	109	107	115	114	98	114	124	118
EAST STROUDSBURG, PA	99	101	100	101	102	105	93	99	93	96	93	89	96	96	96	94	84	95	98	101
EAU CLAIRE, WI	86	78	82	80	80	86	84	84	84	80	84	76	80	86	82	85	75	83	87	86
EDWARDS, CO	145	145	136	150	134	126	154	138	143	150	145	141	149	145	145	136	132	146	127	138
EFFINGHAM, IL	88	77	78	78	81	91	79	86	83	77	81	76	75	85	79	85	72	82	91	88
EL CAMPO, TX	81	66	58	65	68	82	67	76	73	67	72	67	62	75	67	77	63	73	82	79
EL CENTRO, CA	78	74	61	69	68	68	72	74	73	74	74	71	69	71	70	71	67	77	70	71
EL DORADO, AR	80	63	54	63	67	82	65	74	72	64	71	65	60	73	65	76	62	71	82	78
ELIZABETH CITY, NC	76	63	55	62	65	78	64	72	69	62	68	63	59	69	64	72	59	69	78	75
ELIZABETHTOWN, KY	88	76	70	77	75	84	78	81	80	77	80	74	74	83	76	81	71	80	83	84
ELK CITY, OK	72	56	49	56	59	73	61	67	67	57	65	59	54	68	60	70	56	65	76	70
ELKHART-GOSHEN, IN	98	91	91	92	92	98	91	95	94	91	93	85	90	97	91	96	83	93	98	97
ELKO, NV	100	100	89	98	92	92	93	94	92	96	92	87	93	95	92	91	82	94	91	95
ELLENSBURG, WA	81	66	65	69	69	80	84	79	80	73	81	73	73	79	76	80	71	81	80	81
ELMIRA, NY	80	75	84	76	78	83	78	79	82	76	80	69	77	81	79	84	72	78	87	80
EL PASO, TX	78	72	64	70	65	66	72	71	74	75	75	67	69	72	70	73	67	75	70	69
EMPORIA, KS	75	62	61	63	64	72	72	71	73	66	72	64	65	73	67	73	63	71	75	73
ENID, OK	76	66	69	68	69	78	70	74	74	68	72	64	67	75	70	77	63	72	81	75
ENTERPRISE-OZARK, AL	76	62	55	62	63	74	65	70	69	63	68	63	60	71	64	71	60	69	75	73
ERIE, PA	81	78	86	79	79	82	79	80	82	79	81	70	79	82	80	84	73	79	85	81
ESCANABA, MI	77	68	66	67	73	84	68	77	73	67	72	67	65	74	70	76	63	73	83	79
ESPANOLA, NM	74	64	52	62	63	71	62	69	65	63	65	62	59	66	62	66	57	67	70	71
EUFAULA, AL-GA	72	51	32	49	54	73	52	65	60	51	59	58	45	62	51	65	51	61	71	70
EUGENE-SPRINGF'LD,OR	84	80	84	82	80	83	86	83	85	82	84	76	83	84	84	84	76	84	84	84
EUREKA-ARCAT-FORT,CA	74	66	69	68	68	73	75	73	74	69	73	67	70	73	72	74	65	74	75	74
EVANSTON, WY	90	82	73	82	77	82	81	82	82	81	82	76	79	84	79	82	73	83	82	84
EVANSVILLE, IN-KY	88	82	85	83	83	88	84	85	87	82	85	76	82	88	83	88	76	85	90	87
FAIRBANKS, AK	107	103	103	107	96	92	111	100	106	108	107	97	108	108	104	102	97	106	95	100
FAIRMONT, MN	84	67	61	66	73	89	71	81	77	67	75	71	64	78	71	81	65	76	90	84
FAIRMONT, WV	71	58	56	57	62	74	63	69	68	58	66	60	57	68	62	72	57	66	78	71
FALLON, NV	91	83	78	84	82	88	84	86	84	83	85	79	81	87	82	85	75	86	86	88
FARGO, ND-MN	91	82	84	86	78	80	93	84	90	88	90	80	87	91	86	88	81	89	84	86
FARIBAULT-NORTHFIELD	98	102	106	103	102	100	97	99	96	99	96	90	100	99	99	96	87	97	97	100
FARMINGTON, MO	74	60	54	59	63	77	63	70	68	60	67	62	57	69	62	71	58	67	77	73
FARMINGTON, NM	80	73	64	71	69	74	71	74	73	72	73	67	68	74	70	74	65	74	75	75
FAYETTEVILLE, NC	86	77	72	78	72	76	81	78	82	80	81	72	77	83	77	81	72	81	79	80
FAYETTEVL-SPRINGDALE	92	79	71	79	79	88	83	86	84	81	84	78	77	85	80	85	74	85	87	88
FERGUS FALLS, MN	85	68	58	68	76	94	72	85	76	68	75	74	64	77	72	79	65	79	90	88
FERNLEY, NV	90	80	68	78	80	92	75	85	79	76	78	76	72	81	77	81	69	81	87	89
FINDLAY, OH	93	90	94	91	92	96	90	92	91	89	90	82	90	94	91	92	81	90	95	94
FITZGERALD, GA	76	56	43	54	60	77	59	69	66	57	65	61	51	68	57	71	56	65	76	74
FLAGSTAFF, AZ	94	86	82	88	82	85	93	88	91	90	91	82	88	90	88	89	82	92	86	89
FLINT, MI	90	90	98	92	88	89	89	88	92	91	91	78	91	92	90	93	82	89	92	89
FLORENCE, SC	87	72	61	71	73	86	72	80	78	73	78	72	68	80	72	82	68	78	85	85
FLORENCE-MUSCLE SHLS	78	64	59	64	68	80	67	74	71	65	70	65	62	72	66	75	62	71	80	77
FOND DU LAC, WI	91	89	96	90	91	95	88	91	90	88	89	80	88	92	89	91	79	88	95	92
FOREST CITY, NC	81	59	42	57	64	83	60	73	67	59	67	65	53	70	59	72	57	68	79	79
FORREST CITY, AR	67	52	45	52	54	66	56	61	62	55	61	54	51	63	54	65	54	60	67	65
FT. COLLINS-LOVELAND	108	109	110	112	105	103	113	106	107	111	108	100	111	108	109	104	98	108	101	106
FORT DODGE, IA	82	70	72	70	73	84	75	79	80	71	78	69	70	81	74	83	68	77	89	81
FORT LEONARD WOOD,MO	78	60	52	61	60	70	70	70	71	64	70	65	62	73	64	71	62	71	72	72
FT MADISON-KEO,IA-MO	81	68	65	68	73	85	70	78	76	68	75	68	66	78	71	80	65	75	87	81
FORT MORGAN, CO	81	68	60	67	70	81	70	77	73	68	73	69	65	75	69	75	64	75	81	79
FORT PAYNE, AL	80	58	37	55	62	82	57	71	64	57	62	64	50	68	56	69	55	66	76	78
FORT POLK SOUTH, LA	69	50	40	51	50	61	61	61	62	55	62	57	52	64	55	62	54	62	62	63
UNITED STATES	100	100	100	100	100	100	100	100	100	100	100	100	100	100	100	100	100	100	100	100

CBSA	CBSA Code	POPULATION			2000-2007 ANNUAL RATE		RACE (%)					
							White		Black		Asian/Pacific	
		2000	2007	2012	% Rate	National Rank	2000	2007	2000	2007	2000	2007
FORT SMITH, AR-OK	22900	273,170	290,825	303,735	0.9	352	82.8	80.3	3.5	3.7	1.8	2.4
FORT VALLEY, GA	22980	23,668	25,803	27,316	1.2	255	51.3	46.4	45.4	49.3	0.4	0.4
FT WALTON BCH-CREST.	23020	170,498	193,913	210,241	1.8	127	83.4	79.9	9.1	10.6	2.6	3.5
FORT WAYNE, IN	23060	390,156	412,381	428,441	0.8	396	85.4	83.2	9.6	10.5	1.3	1.7
FRANKFORT, IN	23140	33,866	33,996	33,996	0.1	723	94.4	92.7	0.3	0.3	0.2	0.3
FRANKFORT, KY	23180	66,798	69,817	71,783	0.6	494	90.4	89.7	7.4	7.5	0.6	0.8
FREDERICKSBURG, TX	23240	20,814	23,921	26,387	1.9	113	92.8	91.0	0.2	0.2	0.2	0.3
FREEPORT, IL	23300	48,979	48,331	47,920	-0.2	841	89.3	87.6	7.7	8.6	0.7	1.0
FREMONT, NE	23340	36,160	36,729	37,194	0.2	679	95.9	94.7	0.4	0.5	0.6	0.9
FREMONT, OH	23380	61,792	61,321	60,990	-0.1	805	92.2	91.0	2.7	2.9	0.3	0.4
FRESNO, CA	23420	799,407	915,824	1,007,851	1.9	113	54.3	49.7	5.3	4.9	8.2	8.9
GADSDEN, AL	23460	103,459	103,475	103,514	0.0	765	82.9	82.4	14.7	15.1	0.5	0.5
GAFFNEY, SC	23500	52,537	53,632	54,176	0.3	633	76.9	75.6	20.6	21.0	0.3	0.4
GAINESVILLE, FL	23540	232,392	261,567	280,896	1.6	155	74.5	70.3	18.5	21.0	3.4	4.4
GAINESVILLE, GA	23580	139,277	176,932	204,351	3.4	22	80.8	75.8	7.3	8.0	1.5	1.9
GAINESVILLE, TX	23620	36,363	39,158	40,678	1.0	318	88.8	86.5	3.1	3.3	0.3	0.4
GALESBURG, IL	23660	74,571	72,225	70,659	-0.4	896	91.3	89.7	5.1	5.7	0.6	0.8
GALLUP, NM	23700	74,798	76,285	77,196	0.3	633	16.4	14.9	0.4	0.4	0.5	0.5
GARDEN CITY, KS	23780	40,523	40,042	39,407	-0.2	841	69.1	64.2	1.3	1.2	2.9	3.5
GARDNERVILLE RNCH,NV	23820	41,259	51,304	59,550	3.1	34	91.9	90.8	0.3	0.3	1.4	1.4
GEORGETOWN, SC	23860	55,797	64,246	70,987	2.0	101	59.7	58.4	38.6	39.3	0.3	0.4
GETTYSBURG, PA	23900	91,292	102,417	110,924	1.6	155	95.4	94.4	1.2	1.4	0.5	0.7
GILLETTE, WY	23940	33,698	37,981	41,389	1.7	140	96.1	95.6	0.2	0.2	0.4	0.5
GLASGOW, KY	23980	48,070	50,233	51,519	0.6	494	94.9	94.3	3.6	3.8	0.4	0.5
GLENS FALLS, NY	24020	124,345	131,695	137,173	0.8	396	96.2	95.6	1.8	2.0	0.4	0.6
GLOVERSVILLE, NY	24100	55,073	56,311	57,310	0.3	633	96.0	95.1	1.8	2.0	0.5	0.9
GOLDSBORO, NC	24140	113,329	116,891	119,812	0.4	590	61.3	59.2	33.0	33.1	1.0	1.3
GRANBURY, TX	24180	47,909	57,244	64,188	2.5	64	94.4	93.0	0.3	0.4	0.3	0.4
GRAND FORKS, ND-MN	24220	97,478	98,971	98,712	0.2	679	93.4	92.2	1.0	1.2	0.8	1.2
GRAND ISLAND, NE	24260	68,305	70,657	72,406	0.5	545	90.8	88.1	0.3	0.4	1.0	1.4
GRAND JUNCTION, CO	24300	116,255	137,377	154,280	2.3	78	92.3	91.2	0.5	0.6	0.6	0.8
GR RAPIDS-WYOMING,MI	24340	740,482	788,817	818,376	0.9	352	85.7	83.6	7.4	7.9	1.6	2.2
GRANTS, NM	24380	25,595	27,815	28,633	1.2	255	39.6	37.5	1.0	1.0	0.4	0.5
GRANTS PASS, OR	24420	75,726	83,038	88,563	1.3	225	93.9	93.0	0.3	0.3	0.7	0.9
GREAT BEND, KS	24460	28,205	27,963	27,819	-0.1	805	93.0	91.3	1.1	1.2	0.2	0.3
GREAT FALLS, MT	24500	80,357	80,456	80,578	0.0	765	90.7	90.3	1.1	1.2	0.9	0.9
GREELEY, CO	24540	180,798	249,299	306,249	4.5	7	81.7	79.2	0.6	0.6	0.9	1.1
GREEN BAY, WI	24580	282,599	309,520	328,481	1.3	225	92.5	90.9	1.0	1.2	1.8	2.5
GREENEVILLE, TN	24620	62,909	67,385	70,602	1.0	318	96.4	95.8	2.1	2.3	0.3	0.4
GREENSBORO-H. PT,NC	24660	643,430	691,871	726,269	1.0	318	71.4	69.4	23.1	23.3	1.8	2.4
GREENSBURG, IN	24700	24,555	25,393	25,953	0.5	545	98.5	98.1	0.0	0.1	0.7	1.0
GREENVILLE, MS	24740	62,977	59,903	57,927	-0.7	926	34.0	32.0	64.6	66.1	0.5	0.7
GREENVILLE, NC	24780	152,772	171,668	186,312	1.6	155	60.8	59.1	34.6	34.8	1.0	1.3
GREENVILLE, OH	24820	53,309	53,277	53,262	0.0	765	98.1	98.0	0.4	0.4	0.3	0.3
GREENVILLE, SC	24860	559,940	608,312	643,555	1.1	288	79.3	77.7	17.0	17.4	1.2	1.7
GREENWOOD, MS	24900	48,716	48,221	47,783	-0.1	805	37.2	35.5	60.8	62.1	0.6	0.8
GREENWOOD, SC	24940	66,271	68,726	70,120	0.5	545	65.6	64.2	31.7	32.2	0.7	1.0
GRENADA, MS	24980	23,263	23,603	23,899	0.2	679	57.9	55.7	40.9	42.9	0.4	0.5
GULFPORT-BILOXI, MS	25060	246,190	230,635	222,965	-0.9	932	76.5	73.3	18.5	20.6	2.2	2.7
GUYMON, OK	25100	20,107	21,157	21,743	0.7	444	76.7	72.5	0.7	0.7	0.7	0.8
HAGERSTOWN-MRTNSBRG	25180	222,771	264,278	302,237	2.4	71	91.3	89.7	6.2	7.2	0.7	0.9
HAMMOND, LA	25220	100,588	117,017	130,337	2.1	93	69.8	63.4	28.4	34.5	0.4	0.3
HANFORD-CORCORAN, CA	25260	129,461	150,408	166,076	2.1	93	53.7	50.3	8.3	7.4	3.3	4.0
HANNIBAL, MO	25300	37,915	38,615	39,082	0.3	633	94.4	93.7	3.7	4.2	0.3	0.4
HARRIMAN, TN	25340	51,910	53,976	55,538	0.5	545	95.2	94.5	2.7	3.0	0.4	0.6
HARRISBURG, IL	25380	26,733	26,491	26,308	-0.1	805	94.1	93.2	4.1	4.6	0.2	0.3
HARRISBURG-CARL., PA	25420	509,074	535,228	554,495	0.7	444	86.2	84.1	9.4	10.4	1.7	2.4
HARRISON, AR	25460	42,556	44,809	46,227	0.7	444	97.6	97.1	0.1	0.1	0.3	0.4
HARRISONBURG, VA	25500	108,193	118,405	125,717	1.3	225	92.2	89.1	3.1	4.5	1.4	1.8
HARTFORD-WHART-EHART	25540	1,148,618	1,203,355	1,240,753	0.6	494	80.7	77.7	9.6	10.2	2.3	3.4
HASTINGS, NE	25580	38,190	39,131	39,608	0.3	633	95.1	93.7	0.6	0.6	1.4	2.0
HATTIESBURG, MS	25620	123,812	133,798	141,520	1.1	288	72.1	70.7	26.0	26.8	0.7	0.9
HAVRE, MT	25660	16,673	16,194	15,915	-0.4	896	79.5	77.3	0.1	0.1	0.4	0.5
HAYS, KS	25700	27,507	27,111	26,776	-0.2	841	96.1	95.1	0.7	0.7	0.8	1.2
HEBER, UT	25720	15,215	20,911	25,803	4.5	7	95.6	95.0	0.2	0.2	0.4	0.4
HELENA, MT	25740	65,765	71,030	75,187	1.1	288	95.3	94.7	0.2	0.2	0.6	0.7
HENDERSON, NC	25780	42,954	43,762	44,102	0.3	633	48.2	46.8	48.3	48.5	0.4	0.5
HEREFORD, TX	25820	18,561	18,629	18,706	0.1	723	72.3	71.8	1.5	1.5	0.4	0.4
HICKRY-MRGNTN-LENOIR	25860	341,851	364,397	378,142	0.9	352	87.5	85.5	6.9	7.0	2.4	3.2
HILO, HI	25900	148,677	178,585	203,810	2.6	57	31.5	31.9	0.5	0.6	38.0	37.1
HILTON HEAD ISL-BEAU	25940	141,615	177,712	205,989	3.2	30	66.5	65.2	28.2	27.6	0.8	1.0
HINESVILLE-FTSTEWART	25980	71,914	75,194	77,262	0.6	494	49.8	44.8	40.2	42.7	2.0	2.4
HOBBS, NM	26020	55,511	56,428	57,162	0.2	679	67.1	65.6	4.4	4.6	0.4	0.5
HOLLAND-GR. HAVEN,MI	26100	238,314	267,058	282,621	1.6	155	91.5	89.5	1.0	1.1	2.1	3.0
HOMOSASSA SPRINGS,FL	26140	118,085	142,431	164,661	2.6	57	95.0	93.8	2.4	2.9	0.8	1.1
HONOLULU, HI	26180	876,156	911,056	934,955	0.5	545	21.3	21.4	2.4	2.9	54.9	54.0
HOOD RIVER, OR	26220	20,411	22,527	23,898	1.4	196	78.9	74.4	0.6	0.7	1.6	1.9
UNITED STATES					1.2		75.1	72.7	12.3	12.6	3.8	4.5

POPULATION COMPOSITION
CBSA AND U.S. TOTALS

B

CBSA	% HISPANIC ORIGIN 2000	% HISPANIC ORIGIN 2007	0-4	5-9	10-14	15-19	20-24	25-44	45-64	65-84	85+	18+	MEDIAN AGE 2007	% 2007 Males	% 2007 Females
FORT SMITH, AR-OK	4.5	6.0	7.4	6.8	6.5	6.5	6.6	27.3	25.7	11.4	1.8	75.3	37.2	49.5	50.5
FORT VALLEY, GA	4.2	5.3	6.6	6.2	6.8	8.0	9.5	27.9	24.0	9.8	1.1	76.4	33.8	48.5	51.5
FT WALTON BCH-CREST.	4.3	6.1	6.5	5.6	5.9	6.4	7.7	27.8	25.8	12.9	1.3	78.2	38.3	50.0	50.0
FORT WAYNE, IN	3.7	4.9	7.5	7.1	7.2	7.0	6.7	27.1	25.9	9.7	1.7	73.9	35.8	49.1	50.9
FRANKFORT, IN	7.3	9.7	7.3	6.6	6.8	6.7	6.5	27.2	24.6	11.8	2.7	75.4	37.2	49.7	50.3
FRANKFORT, KY	1.0	1.5	6.4	6.3	6.3	6.3	5.9	28.8	27.6	10.7	1.6	77.3	38.5	48.8	51.2
FREDERICKSBURG, TX	15.9	20.2	5.3	5.0	5.4	5.4	5.5	18.8	30.2	19.8	4.4	80.9	48.1	47.4	52.6
FREEPORT, IL	1.5	2.0	6.4	5.6	6.3	6.6	7.0	24.4	27.3	13.5	2.8	77.7	40.7	48.3	51.7
FREMONT, NE	3.9	5.3	6.5	5.7	5.9	6.9	7.6	24.7	25.4	13.9	3.4	78.2	39.9	48.4	51.6
FREMONT, OH	7.0	8.3	6.7	6.2	6.4	6.6	6.6	25.5	27.4	12.2	2.3	76.6	39.2	49.3	50.7
FRESNO, CA	44.0	49.7	9.0	7.6	8.5	8.5	8.6	27.5	20.9	8.1	1.4	69.8	30.0	50.1	49.9
GADSDEN, AL	1.7	1.7	6.5	6.3	5.9	5.9	5.6	26.6	27.0	13.8	2.3	77.6	39.8	48.2	51.8
GAFFNEY, SC	2.1	2.9	7.2	7.1	6.7	6.6	5.6	28.9	25.7	10.6	1.6	75.1	37.0	48.9	51.1
GAINESVILLE, FL	5.5	7.7	5.1	4.6	5.1	9.8	16.3	25.5	23.0	9.1	1.5	81.7	30.1	49.1	50.9
GAINESVILLE, GA	19.6	25.4	8.3	8.1	6.7	6.2	6.2	32.2	22.6	8.6	1.1	73.2	33.6	51.1	48.9
GAINESVILLE, TX	10.0	12.9	7.0	6.2	6.4	7.9	6.9	24.1	26.1	13.1	2.2	75.6	38.5	49.7	50.3
GALESBURG, IL	3.2	4.2	5.8	5.5	5.5	7.0	7.8	24.5	26.7	14.0	3.2	79.6	40.5	49.6	50.4
GALLUP, NM	12.4	11.8	9.7	8.0	9.5	10.2	9.3	25.1	20.6	6.7	0.8	66.4	27.4	48.4	51.6
GARDEN CITY, KS	43.3	50.8	10.6	9.2	8.6	8.1	8.1	28.7	19.6	6.1	0.9	66.9	28.5	51.1	48.9
GARDNERVILLE RNCH,NV	7.4	9.2	4.9	5.2	6.2	7.2	5.8	20.4	32.4	16.2	1.6	79.2	45.2	50.1	49.9
GEORGETOWN, SC	1.6	2.2	6.1	6.0	6.2	6.3	5.0	23.7	30.1	14.9	1.7	77.7	42.5	48.0	52.0
GETTYSBURG, PA	3.6	4.5	6.0	5.7	6.6	7.5	6.9	26.0	27.4	11.8	2.1	77.5	39.5	49.1	50.9
GILLETTE, WY	3.5	3.9	7.5	6.7	7.3	7.5	8.3	27.2	29.2	5.8	0.6	73.8	33.8	51.4	48.6
GLASGOW, KY	0.8	1.3	6.6	6.3	6.4	5.6	5.9	26.7	27.1	13.2	2.1	77.3	39.9	48.7	51.3
GLENS FALLS, NY	1.5	1.8	5.5	5.1	6.2	7.3	6.3	25.5	29.3	12.7	2.1	78.7	41.2	50.1	49.9
GLOVERSVILLE, NY	1.6	1.9	5.8	5.2	6.4	7.2	6.6	24.8	28.5	12.7	2.7	77.9	41.1	49.5	50.5
GOLDSBORO, NC	4.9	6.6	7.1	6.5	6.5	6.7	7.0	28.8	24.8	11.2	1.3	75.9	36.3	49.5	50.5
GRANBURY, TX	8.1	10.5	5.9	5.7	5.8	6.2	6.3	22.0	28.9	17.2	2.1	78.8	43.7	49.1	50.9
GRAND FORKS, ND-MN	2.9	3.5	6.4	5.5	5.6	9.4	12.1	26.5	22.5	9.6	2.4	78.5	31.6	50.7	49.3
GRAND ISLAND, NE	11.3	14.7	7.5	6.9	6.9	6.6	6.7	25.6	25.7	11.8	2.4	74.6	37.6	49.7	50.3
GRAND JUNCTION, CO	10.0	12.0	6.3	5.8	6.1	7.2	7.0	23.9	28.1	13.2	2.4	77.6	40.2	49.0	51.0
GR RAPIDS-WYOMING,MI	6.0	7.3	7.6	7.0	7.2	7.5	7.3	28.2	24.6	9.0	1.6	73.8	34.6	49.8	50.2
GRANTS, NM	33.4	33.3	8.0	6.8	7.4	7.5	8.3	27.1	24.1	9.8	1.1	73.2	33.5	50.7	49.3
GRANTS PASS, OR	4.3	5.8	5.4	4.9	5.7	6.6	6.3	20.0	32.3	16.0	2.8	79.9	45.8	48.6	51.4
GREAT BEND, KS	8.3	11.1	6.7	6.2	6.2	7.6	7.3	22.3	26.5	14.0	3.2	76.7	40.4	48.6	51.4
GREAT FALLS, MT	2.4	2.5	6.9	5.9	6.1	7.0	8.2	25.0	26.4	12.2	2.2	76.9	38.0	49.5	50.5
GREELEY, CO	27.1	31.3	8.0	7.5	7.0	7.8	7.6	29.2	23.8	7.9	1.1	73.3	32.8	50.2	49.8
GREEN BAY, WI	3.2	4.2	6.8	6.1	6.6	7.4	7.7	28.1	26.0	9.5	1.8	76.2	36.7	49.9	50.1
GREENEVILLE, TN	1.0	1.5	5.7	5.7	5.9	5.8	5.0	27.9	27.8	14.2	1.9	79.1	41.0	49.1	50.9
GREENSBORO-H. PT,NC	4.3	5.5	6.4	6.3	6.3	6.9	6.1	29.2	26.1	10.8	1.7	77.1	37.5	48.5	51.5
GREENSBURG, IN	0.5	0.7	7.6	7.3	6.4	6.1	5.6	28.2	25.2	11.6	2.0	75.0	37.3	49.7	50.3
GREENVILLE, MS	0.8	1.0	8.7	7.9	8.1	7.1	7.9	25.1	23.7	9.7	1.8	71.0	32.6	47.3	52.7
GREENVILLE, NC	3.7	5.0	6.7	6.1	6.0	8.0	10.6	29.4	23.1	8.8	1.4	77.9	32.6	48.2	51.8
GREENVILLE, OH	0.9	0.9	6.9	6.4	6.6	6.4	6.0	25.7	26.6	12.6	2.8	76.2	39.6	49.1	50.9
GREENVILLE, SC	3.1	4.2	6.6	6.5	6.3	7.2	7.3	28.2	25.7	10.5	1.7	76.8	36.9	49.2	50.8
GREENWOOD, MS	1.6	2.0	7.7	7.2	7.0	7.7	9.0	26.4	23.1	10.1	1.9	73.9	33.0	48.8	51.2
GREENWOOD, SC	2.9	3.8	6.9	6.4	6.7	7.3	6.9	26.9	25.0	11.8	2.0	75.7	36.7	47.3	52.7
GRENADA, MS	0.6	0.8	7.0	6.7	7.0	7.0	5.7	27.1	25.3	12.0	2.2	75.0	37.5	47.2	52.8
GULFPORT-BILOXI, MS	2.4	2.9	7.2	6.6	6.6	7.3	7.5	27.6	25.1	11.0	1.2	75.8	36.0	49.9	50.1
GUYMON, OK	29.9	36.0	8.8	7.8	6.7	7.0	9.0	28.8	21.8	8.8	1.3	72.8	31.6	51.7	48.3
HAGERSTOWN-MRTNSBRG	1.3	1.7	6.3	6.0	6.4	6.4	6.1	28.0	27.1	11.9	1.8	77.3	39.2	50.4	49.6
HAMMOND, LA	1.5	1.8	7.5	6.9	6.8	7.2	8.5	27.4	25.1	9.4	1.3	75.0	33.9	48.5	51.5
HANFORD-CORCORAN, CA	43.6	48.9	8.7	7.0	7.3	7.8	9.9	32.9	18.8	6.5	1.0	72.8	29.8	56.3	43.7
HANNIBAL, MO	0.8	1.0	6.7	6.1	6.4	7.0	7.1	24.4	26.7	12.7	2.8	76.6	39.7	48.1	51.9
HARRIMAN, TN	0.7	1.0	5.8	6.0	5.5	5.5	5.2	25.3	29.6	15.0	2.0	79.3	42.6	48.9	51.1
HARRISBURG, IL	1.0	1.3	6.0	5.6	5.4	7.8	6.0	23.2	27.2	15.5	3.4	78.2	42.2	48.4	51.6
HARRISBURG-CARL., PA	2.7	3.2	5.7	5.5	6.2	7.1	6.7	25.5	28.3	12.6	2.3	78.5	40.4	48.5	51.5
HARRISON, AR	1.1	1.5	6.3	5.8	6.1	5.8	6.2	24.9	27.7	14.8	2.4	78.2	41.5	49.1	50.9
HARRISONBURG, VA	5.4	7.8	5.8	5.7	5.5	8.3	12.3	26.0	23.5	10.9	2.0	79.7	34.5	49.2	50.8
HARTFORD-WHART-EHART	9.4	11.3	6.0	6.1	6.7	7.6	6.7	25.0	27.4	11.8	2.6	76.8	39.8	48.5	51.5
HASTINGS, NE	4.4	5.7	6.5	5.7	6.0	8.0	8.1	24.0	25.8	12.7	3.2	77.7	38.7	49.2	50.8
HATTIESBURG, MS	1.2	1.5	7.5	6.4	6.6	7.2	10.6	28.1	22.7	9.5	1.5	76.0	32.4	47.8	52.2
HAVRE, MT	1.2	1.4	7.6	6.6	6.2	7.8	8.7	24.4	26.6	10.3	2.0	75.2	34.4	50.0	50.0
HAYS, KS	2.4	3.2	5.9	5.0	5.1	9.1	13.1	24.9	22.7	11.5	2.6	80.0	33.3	49.0	51.0
HEBER, UT	5.1	6.0	10.0	8.6	8.0	7.5	7.8	28.3	22.0	7.0	0.9	68.9	30.0	50.8	49.2
HELENA, MT	1.5	1.8	5.9	5.5	6.2	7.5	7.6	23.1	31.9	10.4	1.8	77.7	41.0	49.4	50.6
HENDERSON, NC	4.6	5.8	7.0	6.4	7.7	7.5	6.0	27.2	25.4	11.2	1.6	74.4	36.6	47.9	52.1
HEREFORD, TX	57.4	59.1	9.4	8.7	8.1	8.0	7.3	25.0	20.7	11.0	1.9	68.9	31.2	48.8	51.2
HICKRY-MRGNTN-LENOIR	4.0	5.3	6.4	6.4	6.4	6.3	5.1	29.1	26.9	11.8	1.6	77.2	38.8	50.0	50.0
HILO, HI	9.5	10.5	6.0	5.8	6.9	7.1	6.8	23.1	30.8	11.6	1.8	76.8	40.5	50.1	49.9
HILTON HEAD ISL-BEAU	6.6	8.8	6.7	5.9	5.7	6.7	7.4	24.9	24.4	16.5	1.7	78.2	39.1	50.4	49.6
HINESVILLE-FTSTEWART	8.2	10.4	11.0	8.6	7.3	8.1	12.4	32.6	15.5	4.2	0.4	69.1	26.1	52.3	47.7
HOBBS, NM	39.6	41.7	8.3	7.2	7.0	7.6	8.5	25.9	23.5	10.7	1.4	73.1	33.4	50.1	49.9
HOLLAND-GR. HAVEN,MI	7.0	8.6	7.8	7.2	7.1	8.5	8.3	27.3	23.4	8.7	1.7	73.5	33.2	49.2	50.8
HOMOSASSA SPRINGS,FL	2.7	3.9	3.8	3.4	4.1	5.0	4.4	15.5	30.6	29.0	4.3	85.6	55.3	48.1	51.9
HONOLULU, HI	6.7	7.4	6.6	6.0	6.5	6.4	7.4	28.9	24.7	11.4	2.0	77.1	36.7	50.2	49.8
HOOD RIVER, OR	25.0	31.5	7.5	7.1	6.8	7.2	6.9	26.2	26.7	9.4	2.2	74.0	36.3	49.8	50.2
UNITED STATES	12.5	15.0	6.9	6.5	6.8	7.1	7.0	27.6	25.4	10.7	1.9	75.6	36.7	49.2	50.8

CBSA	HOUSEHOLDS					FAMILIES			MEDIAN HOUSEHOLD INCOME		
	2000	2007	2012	% Annual Rate 2000-2007	2007 Average HH Size	2000	2007	% Annual Rate 2000-2007	2007	2012	2007 National Rank
FORT SMITH, AR-OK	104,506	112,027	117,379	1.0	2.55	75,038	78,549	0.6	39,723	46,406	662
FORT VALLEY, GA	8,436	9,363	10,007	1.4	2.63	6,002	6,455	1.0	41,303	46,949	595
FT WALTON BCH-CREST.	66,269	77,209	84,443	2.1	2.45	46,499	53,266	1.9	51,932	61,156	195
FORT WAYNE, IN	150,858	161,980	169,407	1.0	2.50	102,465	105,743	0.4	54,598	64,027	131
FRANKFORT, IN	12,545	12,708	12,738	0.2	2.60	9,059	8,867	-0.3	50,765	57,981	224
FRANKFORT, KY	27,227	29,198	30,271	1.0	2.32	18,365	19,015	0.5	52,416	61,700	183
FREDERICKSBURG, TX	8,521	9,932	11,043	2.1	2.35	6,081	7,015	2.0	45,897	52,231	390
FREEPORT, IL	19,785	19,735	19,657	0.0	2.41	13,471	13,043	-0.4	49,218	55,822	281
FREMONT, NE	14,433	14,872	15,132	0.4	2.39	9,750	9,923	0.2	45,729	52,204	397
FREMONT, OH	23,717	24,136	24,252	0.2	2.50	16,960	16,772	-0.2	49,790	57,631	261
FRESNO, CA	252,940	284,994	311,891	1.7	3.15	186,736	211,175	1.7	43,147	50,392	507
GADSDEN, AL	41,615	42,598	42,981	0.3	2.38	29,467	29,604	0.1	36,128	39,724	804
GAFFNEY, SC	20,495	21,517	21,974	0.7	2.46	14,614	14,829	0.2	41,173	47,334	601
GAINESVILLE, FL	92,530	106,970	115,941	2.0	2.31	51,534	58,169	1.7	38,276	44,021	728
GAINESVILLE, GA	47,381	58,958	67,705	3.1	2.96	36,021	43,654	2.7	56,358	65,625	104
GAINESVILLE, TX	13,643	14,692	15,276	1.0	2.60	10,004	10,668	0.9	45,447	51,875	415
GALESBURG, IL	29,222	28,593	28,064	-0.3	2.33	19,397	18,400	-0.7	43,515	49,919	495
GALLUP, NM	21,476	22,263	22,700	0.5	3.39	16,679	16,904	0.2	30,574	35,477	906
GARDEN CITY, KS	12,948	12,726	12,484	-0.2	3.10	9,750	9,483	-0.4	49,287	58,165	278
GARDNERVILLE RNCH,NV	16,401	20,714	24,207	3.3	2.47	11,894	14,877	3.1	66,474	77,881	29
GEORGETOWN, SC	21,659	26,103	29,290	2.6	2.44	15,844	18,498	2.2	44,209	51,490	455
GETTYSBURG, PA	33,652	38,081	41,530	1.7	2.59	24,777	27,362	1.4	52,459	60,532	179
GILLETTE, WY	12,207	14,228	15,708	2.1	2.65	9,004	10,238	1.8	60,850	69,223	61
GLASGOW, KY	19,362	20,755	21,472	1.0	2.38	13,822	14,316	0.5	36,845	42,940	782
GLENS FALLS, NY	48,184	52,137	54,940	1.1	2.43	32,866	35,288	1.0	47,445	54,307	334
GLOVERSVILLE, NY	21,884	22,806	23,383	0.6	2.39	14,520	15,012	0.5	41,882	48,184	565
GOLDSBORO, NC	42,612	45,170	46,688	0.8	2.49	30,244	31,282	0.5	42,495	49,206	527
GRANBURY, TX	18,614	22,447	25,318	2.6	2.51	13,943	16,667	2.5	52,482	59,801	178
GRAND FORKS, ND-MN	37,505	38,667	39,010	0.4	2.35	23,668	23,414	-0.1	45,343	53,206	420
GRAND ISLAND, NE	26,111	27,145	27,842	0.5	2.55	18,191	18,690	0.4	45,030	51,470	432
GRAND JUNCTION, CO	45,823	54,334	61,297	2.4	2.47	31,563	36,579	2.1	44,190	50,956	456
GR RAPIDS-WYOMING,MI	272,130	294,583	307,346	1.1	2.61	188,209	198,289	0.7	54,692	62,674	130
GRANTS, NM	8,327	9,039	9,459	1.1	2.83	6,281	6,650	0.8	33,276	37,941	873
GRANTS PASS, OR	31,000	34,220	36,626	1.4	2.40	21,364	23,377	1.2	38,750	44,435	701
GREAT BEND, KS	11,393	11,410	11,408	0.0	2.38	7,530	7,436	-0.2	39,645	45,187	665
GREAT FALLS, MT	32,547	32,860	33,091	0.1	2.38	21,450	21,010	-0.3	40,238	46,233	644
GREELEY, CO	63,197	86,974	106,734	4.5	2.81	45,206	60,934	4.2	53,167	62,656	159
GREEN BAY, WI	108,897	123,019	131,969	1.7	2.45	73,133	80,604	1.4	56,560	65,362	102
GREENEVILLE, TN	25,756	28,066	29,689	1.2	2.34	18,130	19,246	0.8	37,365	43,379	763
GREENSBORO-H. PT,NC	256,315	277,897	292,723	1.1	2.43	173,361	182,741	0.7	51,150	60,064	216
GREENSBURG, IN	9,389	10,036	10,392	0.9	2.50	6,878	7,111	0.5	50,151	58,367	248
GREENVILLE, MS	22,158	21,663	21,171	-0.3	2.73	15,937	15,232	-0.6	29,417	31,774	914
GREENVILLE, NC	59,235	68,708	75,498	2.1	2.39	37,195	41,772	1.6	41,312	47,657	593
GREENVILLE, OH	20,419	20,908	21,110	0.3	2.50	14,898	14,849	0.0	47,475	53,690	332
GREENVILLE, SC	217,152	240,589	256,574	1.4	2.44	149,335	159,380	0.9	49,011	57,192	286
GREENWOOD, MS	17,027	17,254	17,244	0.2	2.61	11,958	11,839	-0.1	26,490	28,855	929
GREENWOOD, SC	25,729	26,847	27,518	0.6	2.47	17,754	17,857	0.1	42,442	48,710	529
GRENADA, MS	8,820	9,232	9,464	0.6	2.50	6,301	6,446	0.3	31,667	34,611	899
GULFPORT-BILOXI, MS	93,182	89,093	86,661	-0.6	2.49	64,055	59,759	-1.0	38,630	40,869	708
GUYMON, OK	7,153	7,411	7,562	0.5	2.80	5,248	5,345	0.3	43,873	50,159	480
HAGERSTOWN-MRTNSBRG	85,440	103,832	119,990	2.7	2.44	59,139	69,637	2.3	47,407	53,423	339
HAMMOND, LA	36,558	43,239	48,599	2.3	2.63	25,768	29,696	2.0	32,052	34,526	891
HANFORD-CORCORAN, CA	34,418	39,738	44,313	2.0	3.23	26,989	31,250	2.0	44,241	50,851	453
HANNIBAL, MO	14,802	15,275	15,534	0.4	2.44	10,307	10,352	0.1	41,068	47,298	605
HARRIMAN, TN	21,200	22,523	23,383	0.8	2.37	15,242	15,797	0.5	41,491	47,885	585
HARRISBURG, IL	10,992	10,966	10,919	0.0	2.31	7,229	6,988	-0.5	33,060	36,658	876
HARRISBURG-CARL., PA	202,380	215,392	224,635	0.9	2.39	134,529	138,902	0.4	55,796	65,626	117
HARRISON, AR	17,351	18,633	19,384	1.0	2.37	12,354	12,894	0.6	36,120	42,067	805
HARRISONBURG, VA	38,488	42,852	45,795	1.5	2.56	25,341	27,341	1.1	45,456	51,426	414
HARTFORD-WHART-EHART	445,870	467,594	484,132	0.7	2.47	297,070	309,156	0.6	66,728	79,334	27
HASTINGS, NE	14,897	15,241	15,443	0.3	2.44	9,950	10,050	0.1	45,499	52,784	411
HATTIESBURG, MS	45,999	50,797	54,172	1.4	2.51	31,359	33,861	1.1	34,796	38,016	841
HAVRE, MT	6,457	6,354	6,282	-0.2	2.49	4,255	4,061	-0.6	36,583	41,369	789
HAYS, KS	11,193	11,250	11,200	0.1	2.30	6,773	6,695	-0.2	42,084	49,597	550
HEBER, UT	4,743	6,605	8,195	4.7	3.15	3,872	5,303	4.4	62,139	73,561	44
HELENA, MT	26,597	29,076	30,956	1.2	2.39	17,804	18,914	0.8	45,247	51,189	424
HENDERSON, NC	16,199	16,825	17,070	0.5	2.55	11,643	11,810	0.2	38,269	43,663	729
HEREFORD, TX	6,180	6,275	6,334	0.2	2.93	4,834	4,870	0.1	35,037	39,735	834
HICKRY-MRGNTN-LENOIR	133,966	144,284	150,437	1.0	2.47	95,585	100,498	0.7	45,977	52,117	385
HILO, HI	52,985	64,744	74,503	2.8	2.71	36,903	44,513	2.6	48,166	54,678	306
HILTON HEAD ISL-BEAU	52,574	68,808	80,915	3.8	2.47	38,152	48,338	3.3	57,388	67,438	90
HINESVILLE-FTSTEWART	22,957	24,284	25,054	0.8	2.91	17,823	18,391	0.4	40,396	46,066	636
HOBBS, NM	19,699	20,629	21,113	0.6	2.64	14,714	15,022	0.3	36,206	41,636	802
HOLLAND-GR. HAVEN,MI	81,002	90,401	99,853	1.9	2.75	61,360	68,707	1.6	64,285	73,214	33
HOMOSASSA SPRINGS,FL	52,634	63,326	73,423	2.6	2.22	36,339	42,962	2.3	40,156	44,950	735
HONOLULU, HI	286,450	303,237	313,155	0.8	2.90	205,672	215,138	0.6	62,824	72,139	39
HOOD RIVER, OR	7,240	7,803	8,338	1.2	2.74	5,175	5,590	1.1	47,588	55,333	327
UNITED STATES				1.2	2.59			1.0	53,154	62,503	

CBSA	2007 Per Capita Income	2007 HH Income Base	2007 HOUSEHOLD INCOME DISTRIBUTION (%)					2007 Home Value Base	2007 HOME VALUE DISTRIBUTION (%)					2007 Median Home Value
			Less than $25,000	$25,000 to $49,999	$50,000 to $99,999	$100,000 to $149,999	$150,000 or More		Less than $50,000	$50,000 to $89,999	$90,000 to $174,999	$175,000 to $399,999	$400,000 or More	
FORT SMITH, AR-OK	20,113	112,027	31.2	30.6	28.5	6.3	3.4	80,552	21.4	31.1	34.9	10.8	1.8	86,962
FORT VALLEY, GA	20,212	9,363	31.6	25.6	29.2	10.1	3.5	6,516	18.4	22.3	41.4	16.6	1.3	102,065
FT WALTON BCH-CREST.	26,635	77,209	17.7	30.0	35.7	11.2	5.4	53,438	3.3	4.7	22.3	55.0	14.7	223,155
FORT WAYNE, IN	26,924	161,980	18.7	26.4	37.1	12.1	5.6	118,977	11.7	24.9	43.8	17.2	2.5	108,206
FRANKFORT, IN	22,282	12,708	22.3	26.8	38.0	10.2	2.8	9,414	7.9	23.0	53.2	14.5	1.4	108,206
FRANKFORT, KY	27,130	29,198	20.7	26.8	35.9	11.8	4.8	20,426	9.1	12.3	51.4	24.8	2.3	109,111
FREDERICKSBURG, TX	25,861	9,932	22.4	31.6	32.9	8.0	5.0	7,843	9.7	13.9	33.9	29.2	13.3	128,808
FREEPORT, IL	24,267	19,735	22.6	28.2	36.0	10.3	2.9	15,123	10.0	13.5	47.1	26.7	2.6	150,877
FREMONT, NE	22,462	14,872	24.1	30.9	35.0	7.2	2.7	10,519	12.8	21.9	48.0	15.9	1.4	135,936
FREMONT, OH	24,568	24,136	19.8	30.5	35.0	10.9	3.9	18,777	7.5	20.1	52.2	18.9	1.3	110,534
														117,411
FRESNO, CA	19,002	284,988	28.7	27.7	29.0	9.2	5.4	165,222	2.3	1.7	9.2	62.4	24.5	280,067
GADSDEN, AL	20,072	42,598	35.3	29.7	25.8	6.5	2.7	32,320	22.8	25.4	34.6	15.1	2.1	93,488
GAFFNEY, SC	20,758	21,517	30.0	29.5	30.6	7.2	2.6	16,229	18.5	23.8	42.0	14.5	1.2	100,565
GAINESVILLE, FL	23,913	106,966	34.3	26.4	25.2	8.9	5.2	63,648	5.5	9.1	30.4	45.1	9.9	187,299
GAINESVILLE, GA	24,324	58,958	18.8	24.4	36.8	12.8	7.3	42,405	8.1	8.1	36.0	36.4	11.4	169,135
GAINESVILLE, TX	21,926	14,692	26.2	28.5	31.9	10.0	3.4	10,846	18.3	25.5	34.0	18.0	4.2	100,702
GALESBURG, IL	22,471	28,593	25.7	31.1	33.2	7.5	2.5	21,257	12.5	25.7	45.5	14.3	2.0	107,188
GALLUP, NM	12,596	22,260	43.3	27.0	22.5	5.0	2.2	16,093	39.6	16.5	28.0	13.5	2.4	71,826
GARDEN CITY, KS	19,688	12,726	19.7	31.0	37.1	7.9	4.3	8,489	18.8	17.4	47.4	15.0	1.3	107,734
GARDNERVILLE RNCH,NV	34,531	20,714	14.0	20.7	40.0	14.4	10.9	15,734	1.7	2.0	4.8	44.9	46.6	386,702
GEORGETOWN, SC	25,758	26,103	28.1	27.0	30.0	8.7	6.2	21,467	19.3	15.8	30.5	23.1	11.3	125,906
GETTYSBURG, PA	23,476	38,081	18.6	28.5	38.9	10.6	3.4	29,521	3.7	3.1	27.3	58.3	7.5	203,490
GILLETTE, WY	25,692	14,228	15.6	23.3	42.4	14.7	4.1	10,764	11.8	8.1	29.7	43.3	7.1	175,957
GLASGOW, KY	20,402	20,755	34.7	29.5	27.2	5.8	2.8	15,474	19.6	26.1	40.1	12.2	1.9	96,223
GLENS FALLS, NY	24,520	52,137	22.1	30.8	33.9	9.2	4.1	38,914	1.8	2.3	18.7	66.7	10.5	225,804
GLOVERSVILLE, NY	21,419	22,806	28.1	31.4	31.1	6.8	2.7	16,990	5.3	13.5	41.6	36.8	2.9	156,615
GOLDSBORO, NC	21,395	45,170	27.4	30.9	31.1	7.2	3.4	30,278	18.6	19.7	45.0	15.1	1.6	106,582
GRANBURY, TX	27,238	22,438	18.3	28.9	35.0	11.5	6.3	18,279	17.0	17.6	32.8	27.2	5.3	122,117
GRAND FORKS, ND-MN	23,204	38,667	24.4	30.2	33.6	7.9	3.8	23,768	11.9	16.9	45.5	24.0	1.8	128,775
GRAND ISLAND, NE	21,365	27,145	25.2	31.0	33.8	6.6	3.3	19,258	12.6	24.2	47.0	14.5	1.7	106,790
GRAND JUNCTION, CO	23,585	54,334	25.2	31.2	31.3	8.2	4.1	40,755	5.1	3.3	26.2	52.8	12.6	211,597
GR RAPIDS-WYOMING,MI	26,161	294,583	18.8	26.4	36.9	11.9	6.1	217,204	6.7	9.6	48.0	31.3	4.5	147,729
GRANTS, NM	14,898	9,030	37.7	32.5	23.6	4.7	1.5	6,937	22.0	24.6	41.2	10.0	2.1	96,457
GRANTS PASS, OR	21,088	34,220	31.7	32.4	26.6	6.2	3.2	24,800	5.5	4.0	23.0	54.8	12.7	219,721
GREAT BEND, KS	20,949	11,410	29.6	32.6	29.7	6.0	2.1	8,396	28.7	31.3	33.1	6.3	0.5	75,335
GREAT FALLS, MT	21,572	32,860	29.6	32.0	29.4	5.7	3.3	21,347	7.4	8.7	41.5	38.0	4.5	163,981
GREELEY, CO	23,852	86,971	21.0	25.2	35.6	12.3	5.9	62,362	5.6	4.3	26.9	50.5	12.6	200,187
GREEN BAY, WI	27,542	123,019	17.6	25.6	39.1	12.4	5.3	86,593	4.0	8.9	48.9	35.2	3.0	149,760
GREENEVILLE, TN	20,214	28,066	32.8	31.9	27.7	5.3	2.3	21,764	16.0	20.4	44.5	16.1	3.1	108,062
GREENSBORO-H. PT,NC	27,576	277,897	21.8	26.9	34.3	10.2	6.9	189,343	9.3	16.2	45.4	25.1	4.0	124,437
GREENSBURG, IN	23,764	10,036	18.9	30.9	37.1	10.4	2.8	7,494	8.4	17.5	52.4	19.5	2.2	117,139
GREENVILLE, MS	15,679	21,663	43.7	28.0	21.1	4.4	2.7	13,028	26.9	35.1	27.9	8.2	1.8	73,923
GREENVILLE, NC	22,576	68,700	32.4	26.2	29.0	8.2	4.2	41,952	16.3	21.6	43.1	16.9	2.1	105,570
GREENVILLE, OH	23,427	20,908	22.2	30.5	34.7	9.0	3.6	16,511	7.3	17.9	50.8	21.4	2.7	123,063
GREENVILLE, SC	26,033	240,589	23.7	27.2	32.4	10.4	6.2	172,987	12.9	17.4	41.7	24.0	4.0	122,146
GREENWOOD, MS	15,347	17,254	47.8	26.4	18.7	4.4	2.6	10,606	25.7	36.0	26.7	10.0	1.5	74,797
GREENWOOD, SC	21,949	26,847	29.3	28.9	30.2	7.8	3.8	19,007	12.7	22.4	42.1	19.8	3.1	114,309
GRENADA, MS	16,703	9,232	39.0	32.0	22.7	4.6	1.7	6,422	19.0	29.8	38.0	11.8	1.4	91,535
GULFPORT-BILOXI, MS	20,101	89,092	31.8	31.2	27.5	6.4	3.2	59,602	12.8	18.6	42.3	22.0	4.3	121,957
GUYMON, OK	19,238	7,411	26.1	31.5	31.8	8.0	2.7	5,007	24.3	27.0	35.9	10.6	2.1	88,370
HAGERSTOWN-MRTNSBRG	23,463	103,832	23.0	29.7	34.7	9.2	3.4	74,889	7.9	4.9	18.0	59.1	10.1	221,418
HAMMOND, LA	16,565	43,239	39.9	28.4	23.9	5.9	2.0	31,360	21.4	17.7	36.0	21.1	3.8	111,119
HANFORD-CORCORAN, CA	18,535	39,724	25.9	30.8	29.8	9.4	4.2	22,884	2.5	2.5	15.3	67.3	12.4	236,578
HANNIBAL, MO	20,610	15,275	29.1	29.9	32.2	6.6	2.2	11,448	18.2	24.2	36.8	18.2	2.6	103,006
HARRIMAN, TN	23,071	22,523	30.3	28.3	29.3	8.4	3.7	17,639	16.5	19.5	39.8	20.4	3.7	113,277
HARRISBURG, IL	18,756	10,966	37.1	31.8	24.2	5.1	1.8	8,557	27.9	27.5	33.4	9.7	1.5	81,430
HARRISBURG-CARL., PA	29,094	215,392	18.1	26.1	36.0	13.0	6.8	151,818	5.5	6.9	39.9	42.6	5.0	171,124
HARRISON, AR	20,051	18,633	34.8	33.4	24.6	4.3	3.0	14,222	16.4	23.9	40.0	17.2	2.6	104,857
HARRISONBURG, VA	22,120	42,852	25.1	30.1	32.7	8.2	3.9	28,093	5.1	3.0	26.2	57.4	8.3	201,109
HARTFORD-WHART-EHART	34,879	467,593	16.7	20.4	32.8	17.4	12.7	324,386	0.9	1.5	14.3	64.4	18.9	263,044
HASTINGS, NE	22,627	15,241	23.6	31.6	34.0	7.6	3.2	10,927	18.0	27.6	40.2	12.9	1.3	96,041
HATTIESBURG, MS	18,981	50,796	36.6	29.9	24.5	5.8	3.2	34,355	20.6	24.6	34.8	16.9	3.1	98,564
HAVRE, MT	18,570	6,353	34.7	30.6	27.3	5.2	2.3	4,106	13.0	14.1	43.1	27.6	2.2	133,817
HAYS, KS	24,316	11,250	28.9	28.4	31.3	7.1	4.3	7,290	13.5	16.4	50.4	18.1	1.6	118,372
HEBER, UT	25,833	6,604	11.1	25.6	41.9	12.6	8.8	5,397	4.7	1.8	13.0	49.7	30.8	298,965
HELENA, MT	23,097	29,076	24.4	30.9	33.5	8.6	2.8	20,951	8.7	5.3	24.3	52.1	9.8	199,865
HENDERSON, NC	19,775	16,825	33.7	30.0	26.9	6.3	3.1	11,404	19.0	20.1	40.4	17.4	3.1	106,522
HEREFORD, TX	15,870	6,275	33.9	34.1	24.6	5.1	2.2	4,344	34.7	32.0	26.0	6.4	1.0	67,031
HICKRY-MRGNTN-LENOIR	22,963	144,284	23.8	30.5	34.4	7.7	3.6	108,916	14.3	18.8	45.8	18.4	2.7	112,582
HILO, HI	23,511	64,744	25.7	25.9	30.6	12.2	5.6	42,870	1.3	1.6	6.5	42.0	48.5	392,597
HILTON HEAD ISL-BEAU	31,981	68,808	18.6	24.7	33.5	12.7	10.5	51,671	9.4	8.7	23.9	30.6	27.5	219,095
HINESVILLE-FTSTEWART	16,813	24,284	26.8	35.2	30.0	5.8	2.2	13,122	17.0	20.0	49.9	12.0	1.1	105,292
HOBBS, NM	17,928	20,629	34.5	30.3	27.0	5.9	2.3	15,008	23.8	29.9	35.6	9.7	1.0	84,716
HOLLAND-GR. HAVEN,MI	27,633	93,491	12.8	22.7	42.1	15.4	7.1	75,934	5.8	4.8	42.4	41.9	5.1	169,924
HOMOSASSA SPRINGS,FL	23,008	63,326	29.2	34.3	27.0	6.7	2.9	55,017	4.4	10.5	33.9	42.8	8.4	178,181
HONOLULU, HI	28,096	303,227	16.9	22.1	33.3	17.5	10.2	173,032	0.6	0.8	2.2	19.0	77.5	654,067
HOOD RIVER, OR	22,113	7,893	20.7	31.9	34.7	7.5	5.2	5,327	6.2	2.0	10.4	55.8	25.6	280,726
UNITED STATES	27,916		21.9	25.0	32.3	12.3	8.4		7.9	10.5	27.1	35.6	19.0	192,285

SPENDING POTENTIAL INDICES
CBSA AND U.S. TOTALS

E

CBSA	FINANCIAL SERVICES				THE HOME						ENTERTAINMENT						PERSONAL			
					Home Improvements		Furnishings													
	Auto Loan	Home Loan	Invest-ments	Retire-ment Plans	Home Repair	Lawn & Garden	Comput-ers & Hard-ware	Major Appli-ances	TV, Radio, Sound Equip-ment	Furni-ture	Dine out/ Carry out	Sports Equip-ment	Fees & Tickets	Toys & Games	Travel	Cable TV	Apparel & Services	Auto Repairs	Health Insur-ance	Pets & Supplies
FORT SMITH, AR-OK	80	65	57	65	68	81	68	75	73	66	72	67	62	75	67	76	63	72	81	78
FORT VALLEY, GA	84	70	60	69	70	82	69	76	76	70	75	67	66	76	69	80	66	75	82	80
FT WALTON BCH-CREST.	93	89	92	91	87	88	93	89	91	91	91	82	91	92	91	91	82	91	90	90
FORT WAYNE, IN	95	93	98	95	91	92	93	92	95	94	94	82	94	97	93	95	84	92	94	93
FRANKFORT, IN	86	78	77	78	81	90	77	83	82	77	81	73	76	85	78	84	72	80	89	86
FRANKFORT, KY	92	85	88	86	86	92	87	89	89	85	88	80	85	90	87	91	79	88	94	91
FREDERICKSBURG, TX	95	79	65	78	89	110	79	97	83	77	82	84	72	84	83	88	71	89	102	100
FREEPORT, IL	84	77	80	78	81	89	78	83	82	77	81	73	76	83	79	84	72	81	89	85
FREMONT, NE	79	71	73	72	73	81	72	76	77	72	75	67	71	78	73	79	67	75	83	78
FREMONT, OH	89	84	88	84	87	94	82	88	86	82	84	76	82	89	84	88	75	84	93	90
FRESNO, CA	83	82	77	81	78	74	85	81	82	84	83	80	82	81	81	79	76	85	76	79
GADSDEN, AL	73	61	57	61	64	76	62	69	68	62	67	61	59	69	63	71	59	67	76	72
GAFFNEY, SC	83	65	51	63	67	83	66	75	72	65	72	67	60	75	65	76	62	72	81	80
GAINESVILLE, FL	81	65	66	69	63	69	87	73	81	75	82	70	76	79	75	79	73	79	74	75
GAINESVILLE, GA	106	101	93	100	97	100	99	101	99	100	99	95	97	101	97	98	89	101	99	102
GAINESVILLE, TX	87	76	72	75	78	88	76	82	81	75	79	72	73	82	76	84	70	80	89	85
GALESBURG, IL	78	68	71	68	72	81	71	76	76	69	74	66	68	77	72	79	65	74	85	78
GALLUP, NM	65	57	46	54	52	58	55	59	60	58	60	53	52	59	54	61	53	60	61	59
GARDEN CITY, KS	89	84	78	83	79	80	86	84	85	85	85	79	82	86	82	83	76	87	83	84
GARDNERVILLE RNCH,NV	113	127	138	128	127	122	115	119	114	120	113	106	123	112	123	114	103	116	118	118
GEORGETOWN, SC	101	80	62	78	87	110	79	97	87	79	86	84	72	87	82	94	75	91	105	102
GETTYSBURG, PA	89	86	86	86	89	95	82	89	84	83	84	79	82	87	84	86	75	84	91	91
GILLETTE, WY	100	99	91	99	92	93	94	94	93	96	93	87	94	95	92	92	84	94	91	96
GLASGOW, KY	79	61	50	59	66	82	63	74	69	61	68	65	56	71	62	73	59	69	80	78
GLENS FALLS, NY	89	80	77	80	85	96	80	89	83	79	82	77	77	85	82	86	73	84	94	91
GLOVERSVILLE, NY	75	67	69	67	70	80	69	74	73	67	71	65	66	73	70	75	63	72	80	76
GOLDSBORO, NC	82	71	65	71	70	78	72	75	76	72	75	68	69	77	71	78	67	75	79	78
GRANBURY, TX	105	94	85	92	95	109	90	101	95	90	93	88	87	94	93	99	82	97	107	104
GRAND FORKS, ND-MN	83	68	71	72	69	76	82	77	82	75	81	72	75	82	76	81	72	80	81	79
GRAND ISLAND, NE	80	72	72	73	74	81	74	78	77	72	76	69	71	78	74	78	67	76	82	80
GRAND JUNCTION, CO	83	79	82	80	79	84	80	82	81	79	80	73	79	80	80	82	71	81	85	82
GR RAPIDS-WYOMING,MI	97	95	96	96	93	94	95	94	95	95	95	86	95	97	94	95	86	95	95	96
GRANTS, NM	67	53	43	52	55	67	55	62	60	54	59	55	50	61	54	63	51	60	67	66
GRANTS PASS, OR	76	64	58	64	70	85	67	77	70	64	69	67	61	69	69	73	59	73	82	79
GREAT BEND, KS	76	62	59	62	66	79	66	73	71	63	70	64	61	72	66	75	60	70	82	75
GREAT FALLS, MT	74	66	73	67	67	73	72	72	74	68	72	64	69	74	71	75	64	72	77	72
GREELEY, CO	97	96	90	95	91	91	94	93	92	94	92	87	93	94	92	90	83	94	90	94
GREEN BAY, WI	97	94	95	95	92	92	95	94	95	94	94	86	93	96	93	94	85	94	94	95
GREENEVILLE, TN	79	59	44	57	64	82	60	73	67	59	66	64	53	70	60	71	57	68	79	78
GREENSBORO-H. PT,NC	99	90	87	91	89	96	92	93	95	92	94	85	89	96	90	96	84	94	96	96
GREENSBURG, IN	89	80	78	80	84	94	79	86	83	79	82	76	77	87	80	85	72	82	91	89
GREENVILLE, MS	63	53	54	55	53	61	56	58	62	56	61	50	54	61	55	65	54	59	65	60
GREENVILLE, NC	84	67	58	69	65	75	78	74	78	73	79	70	69	79	71	78	69	77	76	78
GREENVILLE, OH	88	78	76	78	83	95	77	86	82	77	81	75	75	85	79	85	71	81	92	89
GREENVILLE, SC	97	86	80	87	85	94	88	90	91	87	90	82	84	92	86	92	80	90	94	93
GREENWOOD, MS	63	48	43	49	50	61	53	57	59	52	58	49	48	59	51	63	52	57	64	61
GREENWOOD, SC	83	69	66	70	71	82	74	78	78	71	77	69	69	79	72	81	68	77	83	80
GRENADA, MS	69	51	39	50	53	68	53	62	60	52	59	54	47	61	52	64	51	60	68	66
GULFPORT-BILOXI, MS	75	67	66	68	66	72	69	71	72	68	71	63	67	72	68	73	63	71	74	72
GUYMON, OK	86	69	55	68	71	85	73	80	75	70	75	73	65	78	70	77	65	78	83	84
HAGERSTOWN-MRTNSBRG	83	78	79	79	79	85	78	81	80	78	80	73	77	81	79	82	71	80	85	83
HAMMOND, LA	70	55	46	55	55	67	58	63	62	56	62	57	53	63	56	64	54	62	67	66
HANFORD-CORCORAN, CA	86	80	71	79	75	75	84	81	81	82	82	79	79	83	79	79	74	85	77	80
HANNIBAL, MO	77	65	63	65	68	80	67	74	72	65	70	65	63	74	67	75	61	71	80	76
HARRIMAN, TN	86	70	61	69	74	90	71	81	77	69	76	71	65	79	71	81	66	77	88	85
HARRISBURG, IL	68	52	47	51	56	71	57	65	63	53	61	56	50	63	56	67	52	61	74	67
HARRISBURG-CARL., PA	96	97	106	98	99	100	96	97	98	97	97	86	98	98	98	99	88	96	101	98
HARRISON, AR	76	59	50	58	65	81	62	72	67	59	66	63	55	68	62	71	57	68	78	76
HARRISONBURG, VA	87	73	68	74	75	86	80	82	81	76	81	75	74	83	76	81	71	81	83	85
HARTFORD-WHART-EHART	111	125	140	126	126	115	122	118	120	124	121	108	129	119	125	120	112	118	116	117
HASTINGS, NE	83	73	75	74	77	86	76	81	79	74	78	71	72	81	76	81	68	79	87	84
HATTIESBURG, MS	73	61	56	62	60	68	68	67	69	64	69	61	62	69	64	70	61	68	70	70
HAVRE, MT	68	59	63	60	60	67	64	65	66	61	65	58	60	67	62	68	57	65	70	67
HAYS, KS	80	71	76	74	71	75	83	76	81	76	80	70	77	80	77	80	72	79	79	78
HEBER, UT	116	123	119	123	118	114	112	114	109	117	110	105	116	115	113	107	99	111	108	115
HELENA, MT	81	76	74	77	76	82	76	79	77	75	76	71	74	77	76	77	68	78	80	81
HENDERSON, NC	78	65	58	64	65	76	66	72	72	66	71	64	62	72	65	75	62	71	78	75
HEREFORD, TX	73	61	46	57	58	67	59	66	65	62	65	59	55	64	59	67	58	67	69	66
HICKRY-MRGNTN-LENOIR	92	74	59	72	77	94	74	85	80	73	79	76	67	83	73	83	69	81	90	90
HILO, HI	88	89	88	88	93	96	87	93	86	86	86	84	87	86	90	87	77	89	92	93
HILTON HEAD ISL-BEAU	119	109	104	109	110	122	109	116	112	109	111	103	106	109	111	115	98	115	121	118
HINESVILLE-FTSTEWART	75	61	53	63	55	59	72	65	70	67	71	63	65	72	64	68	63	71	63	66
HOBBS, NM	73	63	54	60	61	68	62	67	67	63	67	60	59	67	62	69	59	67	71	68
HOLLAND-GR. HAVEN,MI	109	115	114	115	110	107	107	107	105	110	105	98	110	108	108	103	95	106	104	107
HOMOSASSA SPRINGS,FL	72	69	69	66	75	88	64	78	69	66	68	64	65	63	72	75	58	75	90	79
HONOLULU, HI	104	117	117	116	115	100	122	112	110	117	112	114	121	109	119	105	104	116	101	108
HOOD RIVER, OR	93	80	71	80	81	92	83	88	84	81	84	81	77	86	81	85	74	87	90	91
UNITED STATES	100	100	100	100	100	100	100	100	100	100	100	100	100	100	100	100	100	100	100	100

POPULATION CHANGE
CBSA AND U.S. TOTALS

CBSA	CBSA Code	POPULATION			2000-2007 ANNUAL RATE		RACE (%)					
							White		Black		Asian/Pacific	
		2000	2007	2012	% Rate	National Rank	2000	2007	2000	2007	2000	2007
HOPE, AR	26260	33,542	35,650	37,318	0.8	396	64.4	61.4	30.6	32.4	0.1	0.2
HOT SPRINGS, AR	26300	88,068	95,740	101,427	1.2	255	88.9	87.4	7.8	8.6	0.5	0.7
HOUGHTON, MI	26340	38,317	39,115	39,758	0.3	633	95.5	94.4	1.1	1.2	1.7	2.5
HOUMA-BAYOU CANE, LA	26380	194,477	207,039	216,553	0.9	352	78.1	74.2	15.4	18.0	0.8	1.1
HOUSTON-BAY-SUGAR,TX	26420	4,715,407	5,620,734	6,265,747	2.5	64	62.8	59.9	16.9	16.5	4.9	5.7
HUDSON, NY	26460	63,094	65,674	67,753	0.6	494	92.1	90.8	4.5	5.0	0.8	1.1
HUMBOLDT, TN	26480	48,152	48,759	49,145	0.2	679	78.7	76.8	19.7	21.2	0.2	0.2
HUNTINGDON, PA	26500	45,586	46,971	47,764	0.4	590	93.3	92.2	5.1	6.0	0.2	0.3
HUNTINGTON, IN	26540	38,075	38,175	38,200	0.0	765	98.2	98.1	0.2	0.2	0.3	0.3
HUNTINGTON-ASHLAND	26580	288,649	284,144	280,329	-0.2	841	95.9	95.5	2.4	2.5	0.4	0.6
HUNTSVILLE, AL	26620	342,376	380,907	410,736	1.5	173	74.3	72.1	21.0	21.9	1.6	2.2
HUNTSVILLE, TX	26660	61,758	65,154	67,334	0.7	444	69.1	66.6	23.9	24.9	0.8	1.0
HURON, SD	26700	17,023	15,827	15,037	-1.0	936	96.9	96.2	0.7	0.9	0.3	0.5
HUTCHINSON, KS	26740	64,790	63,819	63,163	-0.2	841	91.6	90.0	2.9	3.1	0.5	0.7
HUTCHINSON, MN	26780	34,898	37,927	40,255	1.2	255	96.6	95.6	0.2	0.3	0.6	0.8
IDAHO FALLS, ID	26820	101,677	119,399	134,356	2.2	85	92.4	91.3	0.4	0.6	0.8	0.9
INDIANA, PA	26860	89,605	89,830	89,754	0.0	765	96.9	96.1	1.6	1.8	0.8	1.1
INDNPLS-CARMEL, IN	26900	1,525,104	1,701,870	1,845,573	1.5	173	81.8	81.1	14.1	13.9	1.3	1.8
INDIANOLA, MS	26940	34,369	33,407	32,760	-0.4	896	28.9	27.1	69.9	71.2	0.4	0.5
IOWA CITY, IA	26980	131,676	145,916	155,872	1.4	196	91.2	88.5	2.5	2.9	3.6	5.5
IRON MOUNTAIN, MI-WI	27020	32,560	32,907	33,158	0.1	723	98.0	97.6	0.1	0.1	0.4	0.6
ITHACA, NY	27060	96,501	101,681	104,248	0.7	444	85.5	81.7	3.6	5.3	7.2	8.5
JACKSON, MI	27100	158,422	166,133	170,591	0.7	444	88.5	87.1	7.9	8.7	0.6	0.8
JACKSON, MS	27140	497,197	539,724	575,085	1.1	288	53.0	52.4	45.3	45.4	0.7	1.0
JACKSON, TN	27180	107,377	115,153	120,104	1.0	318	68.5	66.2	29.2	30.9	0.6	0.8
JACKSON, WY-ID	27220	24,250	29,268	32,521	2.6	57	93.0	91.9	0.2	0.2	0.5	0.7
JACKSONVILLE, FL	27260	1,122,750	1,359,173	1,557,843	2.7	51	72.9	69.5	21.5	23.5	2.3	3.0
JACKSONVILLE, IL	27300	42,153	41,799	41,599	-0.1	805	93.3	92.1	4.7	5.1	0.4	0.8
JACKSONVILLE, NC	27340	150,355	163,334	167,545	1.1	288	72.1	69.4	18.5	18.4	1.9	2.4
JACKSONVILLE, TX	27380	46,659	49,376	51,041	0.8	396	74.3	71.1	16.0	16.8	0.5	0.6
JAMESTOWN, ND	27420	21,908	21,107	20,527	-0.5	911	97.5	96.9	0.3	0.3	0.4	0.6
JAMESTOWN-DUNKIRK,NY	27460	139,750	137,116	134,796	-0.3	873	94.0	92.9	2.2	2.6	0.4	0.5
JANESVILLE, WI	27500	152,307	161,103	167,788	0.8	396	91.0	89.0	4.6	5.6	0.8	1.1
JASPER, IN	27540	52,511	55,590	57,826	0.8	396	97.9	97.3	0.1	0.1	0.2	0.3
JEFFERSON CITY, MO	27620	140,052	146,925	152,248	0.7	444	90.1	88.6	7.1	7.9	0.7	1.0
JENNINGS, LA	27660	31,435	31,622	31,728	0.1	723	80.6	77.6	17.8	20.4	0.2	0.3
JESUP, GA	27700	26,565	29,336	31,225	1.4	196	76.7	72.8	20.3	23.2	0.5	0.6
JOHNSON CITY, TN	27740	181,607	194,396	202,773	0.9	352	95.3	94.5	2.6	2.8	0.5	0.8
JOHNSTOWN, PA	27780	152,598	147,230	143,255	-0.5	911	95.8	95.0	2.8	3.3	0.4	0.6
JONESBORO, AR	27860	107,762	115,979	122,294	1.0	318	89.7	88.2	7.6	8.4	0.5	0.7
JOPLIN, MO	27900	157,322	168,163	176,225	0.9	352	92.8	91.7	1.2	1.3	0.7	1.0
JUNEAU, AK	27940	30,711	31,592	32,114	0.4	590	74.8	71.1	0.8	0.7	5.1	5.6
KAHULUI-WAILUKU, HI	27980	128,094	146,794	159,119	1.9	113	33.9	34.3	0.4	0.5	41.7	40.9
KALAMAZOO-PORTAGE,MI	28020	314,866	328,873	338,760	0.6	494	85.4	83.3	8.6	9.4	1.5	2.1
KALISPELL, MT	28060	74,471	86,440	98,259	2.1	93	96.3	95.8	0.2	0.2	0.5	0.7
KANKAKEE-BRADLEY, IL	28100	103,833	110,495	115,350	0.9	352	79.9	77.2	15.5	17.0	0.7	0.9
KANSAS CITY, MO-KS	28140	1,836,038	1,997,567	2,119,898	1.2	255	81.3	79.9	12.4	12.5	1.7	2.3
KAPAA, HI	28180	58,463	62,999	66,288	1.0	318	29.5	29.8	0.3	0.4	45.1	44.4
KEARNEY, NE	28260	49,141	52,472	55,011	0.9	352	95.5	94.4	0.5	0.5	0.6	1.0
KEENE, NH	28300	73,825	79,350	83,368	1.0	318	97.8	97.4	0.4	0.4	0.5	0.7
KENDALLVILLE, IN	28340	46,275	48,387	49,611	0.6	494	94.0	92.0	0.4	0.4	0.4	0.8
KENNETT, MO	28380	33,155	32,491	31,999	-0.3	873	88.6	87.1	8.7	9.7	0.3	0.4
KENNEWICK-RICHLAND	28420	191,822	235,483	274,118	2.9	42	80.0	76.1	1.3	1.4	2.2	2.4
KERRVILLE, TX	28500	43,653	47,529	50,217	1.2	255	88.9	86.5	1.8	1.9	0.6	0.7
KETCHIKAN, AK	28540	14,070	13,315	12,773	-0.8	929	74.3	70.9	0.5	0.5	4.4	5.0
KEY WEST-MARATHON,FL	28580	79,589	79,765	78,627	0.0	765	90.7	88.9	4.8	5.4	0.9	1.1
KILL DEVIL HILLS, NC	28620	29,967	36,789	42,277	2.9	42	94.7	93.9	2.7	2.7	0.4	0.6
KILLEEN-TEMPLE-FT HD	28660	330,714	374,779	410,263	1.7	140	65.1	61.3	19.8	20.5	2.7	3.3
KINGSPORT-BRISTOL	28700	298,484	306,404	312,062	0.4	590	96.8	96.3	1.8	2.0	0.3	0.5
KINGSTON, NY	28740	177,749	188,788	196,874	0.8	396	88.9	87.2	5.4	6.0	1.3	1.7
KINGSVILLE, TX	28780	31,963	31,440	31,204	-0.2	841	71.8	69.9	3.7	3.4	1.6	1.7
KINSTON, NC	28820	59,648	58,919	58,112	-0.2	841	56.5	54.9	40.4	40.9	0.4	0.5
KIRKSVILLE, MO	28860	29,147	29,067	28,911	0.0	765	96.2	93.8	1.0	2.7	1.3	1.8
KLAMATH FALLS, OR	28900	63,775	67,237	69,486	0.7	444	87.3	85.7	0.6	0.7	0.9	1.1
KNOXVILLE, TN	28940	616,079	675,798	721,826	1.3	225	90.6	89.3	6.4	6.9	1.1	1.5
KODIAK, AK	28980	13,913	13,843	13,730	-0.1	805	59.7	58.2	1.0	1.0	16.8	17.3
KOKOMO, IN	29020	101,541	101,637	101,618	0.0	765	91.1	89.7	5.5	6.1	0.9	1.3
LACONIA, NH	29060	56,325	63,373	68,788	1.6	155	97.6	97.2	0.3	0.3	0.6	0.8
LA CROSSE, WI-MN	29100	126,838	131,820	135,150	0.5	545	94.8	93.4	0.8	1.0	2.7	3.8
LAFAYETTE, IN	29140	178,541	190,888	199,544	0.9	352	90.3	87.1	2.1	3.0	3.8	5.2
LAFAYETTE, LA	29180	239,086	256,093	268,852	1.0	318	71.9	68.0	25.5	28.6	1.1	1.5
LA FOLLETTE, TN	29220	39,854	41,284	42,067	0.5	545	98.1	97.8	0.3	0.3	0.2	0.3
LA GRANDE, OR	29260	24,530	25,066	25,492	0.3	633	94.3	93.4	0.5	0.6	1.5	1.8
LAGRANGE, GA	29300	58,779	64,554	68,411	1.3	225	65.8	61.1	31.9	35.9	0.6	0.8
LAKE CHARLES, LA	29340	193,568	199,974	205,395	0.5	545	74.6	67.6	22.9	29.4	0.7	1.0
LAKE CITY, FL	29380	56,513	65,939	73,786	2.2	85	79.7	76.1	17.0	19.9	0.7	0.9
LAKE HAVASU-KINGMAN	29420	155,032	202,681	245,965	3.8	14	90.1	88.6	0.5	0.6	0.9	1.1
UNITED STATES					1.2		75.1	72.7	12.3	12.6	3.8	4.5

CBSA	% HISPANIC ORIGIN 2000	2007	2007 AGE DISTRIBUTION (%) 0-4	5-9	10-14	15-19	20-24	25-44	45-64	65-84	85+	18+	MEDIAN AGE 2007	% 2007 Males	% 2007 Females
HOPE, AR	6.3	8.0	7.5	7.2	6.3	6.0	6.2	27.5	25.1	11.8	2.3	75.3	37.2	48.8	51.2
HOT SPRINGS, AR	2.6	3.5	5.6	5.3	5.2	5.6	5.2	22.9	28.7	18.5	3.0	80.6	45.1	48.9	51.1
HOUGHTON, MI	0.7	0.9	5.5	5.1	5.1	9.3	12.9	21.9	24.8	12.3	3.1	80.5	35.5	53.4	46.6
HOUMA-BAYOU CANE, LA	1.5	1.8	7.6	6.8	6.8	6.9	7.4	28.7	24.9	9.7	1.2	74.7	35.5	49.0	51.0
HOUSTON-BAY-SUGAR,TX	28.7	33.4	8.1	7.6	7.6	7.3	7.2	29.5	24.5	7.2	0.9	72.2	33.3	49.8	50.2
HUDSON, NY	2.5	3.0	5.3	4.9	6.3	7.4	5.8	23.0	31.5	13.3	2.6	78.7	43.3	49.9	50.1
HUMBOLDT, TN	1.1	1.5	6.5	6.1	6.4	5.9	5.6	26.6	26.1	14.0	2.8	77.4	40.4	47.8	52.2
HUNTINGDON, PA	1.1	1.4	5.4	5.5	5.0	7.0	7.5	27.5	27.0	13.0	2.1	80.3	39.7	52.9	47.1
HUNTINGTON, IN	1.0	1.0	6.9	6.4	6.4	7.3	6.9	26.3	26.0	11.1	2.7	76.1	37.6	49.1	50.9
HUNTINGTON-ASHLAND	0.7	0.9	5.7	5.6	5.7	5.9	6.5	26.8	27.6	14.3	2.0	79.8	40.4	48.5	51.5
HUNTSVILLE, AL	2.0	3.0	6.8	6.7	6.7	6.9	6.1	28.9	26.0	10.6	1.3	75.8	37.5	49.3	50.7
HUNTSVILLE, TX	14.1	17.5	5.0	4.4	4.3	10.1	16.1	30.2	20.4	8.3	1.2	83.3	31.3	60.2	39.8
HURON, SD	0.9	1.2	6.0	5.3	5.7	6.8	6.5	23.2	28.0	14.7	3.7	78.9	42.4	49.2	50.8
HUTCHINSON, KS	5.7	7.6	6.6	6.3	5.8	6.4	7.7	25.0	26.4	12.8	3.1	77.6	39.3	50.6	49.4
HUTCHINSON, MN	3.6	5.0	7.3	6.8	6.4	7.7	7.0	26.9	24.9	10.5	2.4	74.5	36.8	49.8	50.2
IDAHO FALLS, ID	7.5	8.7	9.1	7.9	7.7	7.9	8.3	25.5	23.6	8.7	1.2	70.2	31.4	49.9	50.1
INDIANA, PA	0.5	0.6	5.0	4.8	5.2	8.3	12.1	22.7	27.0	12.5	2.4	81.7	38.3	48.7	51.3
INDNPLS-CARMEL, IN	2.7	3.4	7.5	7.2	7.1	7.0	6.5	28.9	25.1	9.1	1.5	73.9	35.8	49.0	51.0
INDIANOLA, MS	1.3	1.6	7.6	6.9	7.2	7.9	10.0	30.5	20.8	7.6	1.6	74.1	30.9	53.9	46.1
IOWA CITY, IA	2.5	3.3	5.9	5.5	5.4	9.0	13.9	29.0	22.4	7.3	1.6	79.8	30.6	49.7	50.3
IRON MOUNTAIN, MI-WI	0.6	0.8	5.6	5.2	6.5	6.8	6.5	22.7	30.0	13.6	3.1	78.3	42.9	49.9	50.1
ITHACA, NY	3.1	4.0	4.4	4.1	5.0	10.8	16.9	25.5	23.3	8.3	1.7	82.9	30.9	50.2	49.8
JACKSON, MI	2.2	2.7	6.6	6.2	6.6	7.0	6.4	27.2	27.0	11.0	2.0	76.3	38.5	51.2	48.8
JACKSON, MS	1.0	1.3	7.4	7.2	7.0	7.3	7.3	28.5	24.6	9.3	1.5	74.3	34.7	47.9	52.1
JACKSON, TN	1.6	2.2	6.9	6.6	6.7	7.4	7.1	27.8	25.3	10.3	1.9	75.8	35.9	48.6	51.4
JACKSON, WY-ID	7.8	9.2	6.1	5.7	5.8	5.9	6.5	35.0	27.4	7.0	0.7	78.8	35.3	53.0	47.0
JACKSONVILLE, FL	3.8	5.2	6.9	6.4	6.6	7.2	7.1	27.9	26.6	9.9	1.5	75.8	37.0	48.7	51.3
JACKSONVILLE, IL	1.2	1.7	5.8	5.4	5.8	7.9	8.0	24.9	26.4	13.0	2.8	79.1	39.6	49.3	50.7
JACKSONVILLE, NC	7.2	9.4	8.6	6.5	5.4	9.1	18.1	29.4	16.2	6.2	0.5	76.3	26.0	57.1	42.9
JACKSONVILLE, TX	13.2	16.7	7.3	6.5	6.6	6.6	6.7	26.9	24.7	12.3	2.3	75.8	37.2	50.6	49.4
JAMESTOWN, ND	0.9	1.3	5.4	5.1	5.7	8.1	8.5	22.4	27.9	13.7	3.3	79.6	41.5	49.5	50.5
JAMESTOWN-DUNKIRK,NY	4.2	5.0	5.9	5.4	6.2	7.8	8.6	23.2	27.1	13.0	2.8	78.3	39.8	49.1	50.9
JANESVILLE, WI	3.9	5.1	6.9	6.3	6.9	7.3	6.8	26.7	26.4	10.8	1.9	75.5	37.7	49.3	50.7
JASPER, IN	2.2	3.1	7.0	6.9	6.7	6.4	6.1	26.5	27.0	11.5	2.0	75.5	38.9	49.9	50.1
JEFFERSON CITY, MO	1.3	1.6	6.6	6.2	6.3	7.2	7.6	28.3	25.8	10.1	1.9	77.1	36.9	50.7	49.3
JENNINGS, LA	1.0	1.1	8.0	7.3	7.4	6.6	6.8	25.7	24.9	11.7	1.7	73.3	36.1	48.5	51.5
JESUP, GA	3.8	5.0	6.8	6.2	6.4	6.6	6.7	30.1	25.5	10.4	1.3	76.5	36.8	52.6	47.4
JOHNSON CITY, TN	1.3	1.8	5.7	5.6	5.4	5.9	6.1	28.5	27.5	13.1	2.2	80.0	40.1	49.0	51.0
JOHNSTOWN, PA	0.9	1.1	5.0	4.8	5.3	6.5	6.5	24.1	28.7	15.6	3.4	81.3	43.3	48.9	51.1
JONESBORO, AR	2.0	2.7	7.1	6.4	6.1	6.7	7.3	29.8	24.2	10.6	1.7	76.9	35.1	48.8	51.2
JOPLIN, MO	3.0	3.8	7.4	6.7	6.6	6.7	7.0	26.8	25.4	11.5	2.0	75.5	36.6	48.9	51.1
JUNEAU, AK	3.4	4.3	6.1	5.5	6.8	7.6	7.6	26.2	32.1	7.1	0.9	76.6	38.4	49.7	50.3
KAHULUI-WAILUKU, HI	7.8	8.9	6.5	6.2	6.7	7.0	7.2	25.9	28.9	9.9	1.7	76.2	38.1	49.9	50.1
KALAMAZOO-PORTAGE,MI	3.8	4.7	6.5	6.2	6.4	8.2	9.7	25.4	25.7	10.0	1.8	76.7	35.4	48.7	51.3
KALISPELL, MT	1.4	1.8	5.8	5.7	6.5	6.7	7.2	22.7	32.0	11.6	1.9	77.8	41.7	49.5	50.5
KANKAKEE-BRADLEY, IL	4.8	6.2	7.2	6.5	7.2	7.3	7.0	26.5	25.3	11.0	2.0	74.9	36.3	49.0	51.0
KANSAS CITY, MO-KS	5.1	6.3	7.3	7.0	6.8	6.8	6.5	28.3	25.7	9.7	1.7	74.6	36.6	49.0	51.0
KAPAA, HI	8.2	9.1	6.1	5.7	7.4	7.6	7.1	23.4	29.2	11.4	2.1	75.9	39.5	49.8	50.2
KEARNEY, NE	4.3	5.8	6.7	6.0	6.4	9.1	11.0	25.5	23.5	9.5	2.3	76.5	32.9	49.4	50.6
KEENE, NH	0.7	0.9	5.1	5.0	5.8	8.9	8.7	23.4	28.9	12.0	2.2	79.8	40.3	48.8	51.2
KENDALLVILLE, IN	7.1	9.5	8.2	7.7	7.3	6.8	6.3	28.6	24.7	8.9	1.5	72.8	34.8	50.6	49.4
KENNETT, MO	2.5	3.1	7.4	6.9	6.4	6.1	5.7	25.1	25.6	13.9	2.8	75.5	39.2	47.8	52.2
KENNEWICK-RICHLAND	21.3	26.8	8.5	7.6	7.8	7.7	8.0	25.7	25.0	8.3	1.4	71.3	33.0	50.4	49.6
KERRVILLE, TX	19.1	24.0	5.5	5.0	5.3	6.7	6.8	18.9	27.5	20.3	4.0	79.9	46.2	48.1	51.9
KETCHIKAN, AK	2.6	3.3	6.8	6.2	7.1	7.9	8.2	24.8	29.7	8.4	1.0	75.8	37.7	50.7	49.3
KEY WEST-MARATHON,FL	15.8	21.8	4.2	4.1	4.5	4.8	4.7	25.9	36.6	13.7	1.6	84.4	46.0	53.0	47.0
KILL DEVIL HILLS, NC	2.2	2.9	5.0	5.5	5.5	5.4	4.2	27.2	32.3	13.5	1.3	80.5	43.3	50.5	49.5
KILLEEN-TEMPLE-FT HD	15.7	19.5	8.9	7.6	6.7	7.3	10.0	31.7	19.3	7.2	1.1	72.9	29.8	50.3	49.7
KINGSPORT-BRISTOL	0.7	1.0	5.5	5.6	5.7	5.8	5.1	26.5	29.0	14.8	2.1	79.8	42.2	48.5	51.5
KINGSTON, NY	6.2	7.2	5.4	5.3	6.4	7.6	7.3	25.4	29.0	11.6	2.0	78.6	40.4	49.8	50.2
KINGSVILLE, TX	65.6	71.2	8.1	6.9	6.2	8.1	10.5	28.8	20.5	9.5	1.3	74.7	30.2	50.6	49.4
KINSTON, NC	3.2	4.2	6.5	6.3	6.7	6.3	5.8	25.3	27.5	13.7	1.9	76.5	40.1	47.8	52.2
KIRKSVILLE, MO	1.2	1.4	5.5	4.9	4.8	9.7	15.2	23.8	22.6	11.2	2.4	81.5	32.5	48.1	51.9
KLAMATH FALLS, OR	7.8	10.3	6.4	5.8	6.4	7.4	6.8	23.7	28.9	12.7	2.0	77.0	40.0	50.2	49.8
KNOXVILLE, TN	1.3	1.8	5.9	5.8	5.9	6.5	6.7	27.3	27.6	12.4	1.9	78.8	39.6	48.6	51.4
KODIAK, AK	6.1	6.2	8.9	8.4	7.9	7.2	8.9	27.1	25.5	5.5	0.5	70.1	31.7	52.3	47.7
KOKOMO, IN	1.9	2.5	6.9	6.6	6.4	6.5	6.2	25.9	27.5	12.2	2.0	76.2	38.9	48.7	51.3
LACONIA, NH	0.7	1.0	5.3	5.2	6.3	6.2	5.9	23.9	32.2	12.8	2.2	79.3	43.2	49.3	50.7
LA CROSSE, WI-MN	0.9	1.1	6.0	5.6	6.2	8.3	11.0	24.8	25.4	10.5	2.3	78.2	35.8	48.7	51.3
LAFAYETTE, IN	4.9	6.4	6.1	5.6	5.7	9.7	14.5	27.2	21.2	8.4	1.5	79.4	29.8	51.4	48.6
LAFAYETTE, LA	1.6	1.8	7.6	7.0	6.6	7.1	8.1	28.6	24.7	8.9	1.2	74.7	33.9	48.7	51.3
LA FOLLETTE, TN	0.7	1.0	6.0	5.8	5.9	5.7	5.2	28.1	27.4	14.3	1.9	78.8	40.5	48.6	51.4
LA GRANDE, OR	2.4	3.3	6.0	5.6	5.5	7.7	8.7	23.0	28.9	11.8	2.8	78.7	39.2	48.8	51.2
LAGRANGE, GA	1.7	2.2	7.2	6.9	7.0	7.2	6.7	27.1	25.5	10.2	1.8	74.1	36.0	48.1	51.9
LAKE CHARLES, LA	1.4	1.6	7.4	6.8	6.8	6.8	7.4	27.3	25.4	10.6	1.5	75.0	35.7	48.9	51.1
LAKE CITY, FL	2.7	3.9	6.7	6.2	6.1	6.5	7.4	25.4	26.6	13.3	1.7	77.1	38.8	50.6	49.4
LAKE HAVASU-KINGMAN	11.1	13.6	6.1	5.5	6.1	5.9	5.4	20.2	29.1	19.7	2.0	78.7	45.6	49.8	50.2
UNITED STATES	12.5	15.0	6.9	6.5	6.8	7.1	7.0	27.6	25.4	10.7	1.9	75.6	36.7	49.2	50.8

HOUSEHOLDS
CBSA AND U.S. TOTALS

CBSA	HOUSEHOLDS					FAMILIES			MEDIAN HOUSEHOLD INCOME		
	2000	2007	2012	% Annual Rate 2000-2007	2007 Average HH Size	2000	2007	% Annual Rate 2000-2007	2007	2012	2007 National Rank
HOPE, AR	12,852	13,748	14,440	0.9	2.55	9,101	9,454	0.5	34,412	39,340	854
HOT SPRINGS, AR	37,813	41,021	43,523	1.1	2.29	25,250	26,509	0.7	40,533	47,775	628
HOUGHTON, MI	14,791	15,381	15,736	0.5	2.33	8,748	8,777	0.0	33,908	37,826	863
HOUMA-BAYOU CANE, LA	68,054	73,724	77,783	1.1	2.77	51,705	54,845	0.8	39,216	42,448	682
HOUSTON-BAY-SUGAR,TX	1,656,799	1,956,486	2,173,637	2.3	2.83	1,182,385	1,387,316	2.2	57,613	68,642	89
HUDSON, NY	24,796	26,412	27,510	0.9	2.39	16,580	17,519	0.8	52,040	60,409	194
HUMBOLDT, TN	19,518	20,060	20,332	0.4	2.38	13,578	13,582	0.0	38,340	44,602	725
HUNTINGDON, PA	16,759	17,566	18,059	0.7	2.39	11,798	12,035	0.3	41,008	46,724	610
HUNTINGTON, IN	14,242	14,620	14,749	0.4	2.51	10,280	10,193	-0.1	51,640	60,403	203
HUNTINGTON-ASHLAND	117,697	118,534	118,079	0.1	2.34	81,068	79,181	-0.3	36,544	42,175	791
HUNTSVILLE, AL	134,643	152,194	165,493	1.7	2.44	93,573	103,716	1.4	50,326	56,093	239
HUNTSVILLE, TX	18,303	19,430	20,400	0.8	2.42	11,389	11,929	0.6	38,914	45,063	689
HURON, SD	7,210	6,888	6,604	-0.6	2.23	4,532	4,286	-0.8	37,746	43,665	750
HUTCHINSON, KS	25,498	25,338	25,151	-0.1	2.39	17,309	16,970	-0.3	43,693	50,664	488
HUTCHINSON, MN	13,449	14,945	16,004	1.5	2.51	9,433	10,194	1.1	57,699	66,086	88
IDAHO FALLS, ID	34,654	41,840	47,511	2.6	2.82	26,343	31,493	2.5	52,907	63,508	168
INDIANA, PA	34,123	34,986	35,343	0.3	2.41	22,517	22,371	-0.1	37,525	43,413	757
INDNPLS-CARMEL, IN	594,874	673,421	732,031	1.7	2.48	398,591	439,481	1.4	60,100	71,322	66
INDIANOLA, MS	9,637	9,476	9,290	-0.2	2.97	7,312	7,051	-0.5	28,576	31,084	917
IOWA CITY, IA	52,136	59,863	64,706	1.9	2.29	29,206	32,597	1.5	49,365	57,610	273
IRON MOUNTAIN, MI-WI	13,519	14,039	14,291	0.5	2.30	9,020	9,103	0.1	41,687	46,736	578
ITHACA, NY	36,420	38,381	39,699	0.7	2.31	19,120	19,917	0.6	47,929	56,469	318
JACKSON, MI	58,168	61,604	63,659	0.8	2.52	40,840	42,123	0.4	51,755	59,393	198
JACKSON, MS	180,556	201,027	216,242	1.5	2.59	127,662	139,188	1.2	43,957	48,976	472
JACKSON, TN	41,212	44,745	46,943	1.1	2.47	28,850	30,503	0.8	46,183	53,977	379
JACKSON, WY-ID	9,766	11,933	13,285	2.8	2.44	5,642	6,779	2.6	68,526	84,319	18
JACKSONVILLE, FL	432,627	530,236	610,272	2.8	2.52	297,301	358,985	2.6	53,209	62,873	158
JACKSONVILLE, IL	16,261	16,336	16,334	0.1	2.35	10,813	10,534	-0.4	44,931	50,884	436
JACKSONVILLE, NC	48,122	51,936	54,077	1.1	2.62	36,594	38,700	0.8	43,055	50,537	510
JACKSONVILLE, TX	16,651	17,636	18,238	0.8	2.64	12,098	12,688	0.7	34,844	39,508	838
JAMESTOWN, ND	8,954	8,858	8,706	-0.1	2.20	5,648	5,346	-0.8	42,066	49,043	553
JAMESTOWN-DUNKIRK,NY	54,515	54,527	53,966	0.0	2.40	35,966	35,681	-0.1	41,546	48,144	582
JANESVILLE, WI	58,617	63,311	66,393	1.1	2.49	40,403	42,626	0.7	56,809	65,545	95
JASPER, IN	19,932	21,601	22,654	1.1	2.53	14,425	15,105	0.6	51,197	58,725	215
JEFFERSON CITY, MO	51,637	55,792	58,290	1.1	2.46	35,589	37,393	0.7	50,254	58,044	242
JENNINGS, LA	11,480	11,808	11,956	0.4	2.64	8,525	8,570	0.1	30,889	33,605	903
JESUP, GA	9,324	10,448	11,271	1.6	2.57	6,937	7,559	1.2	39,376	44,253	678
JOHNSON CITY, TN	75,197	81,196	85,442	1.1	2.30	51,039	53,541	0.7	38,184	44,637	733
JOHNSTOWN, PA	60,531	59,743	58,690	-0.2	2.31	40,615	38,878	-0.6	38,634	45,780	707
JONESBORO, AR	42,327	45,940	48,647	1.1	2.46	29,332	30,856	0.7	39,151	46,078	683
JOPLIN, MO	61,552	65,934	69,153	1.0	2.50	42,676	44,460	0.6	40,306	46,447	642
JUNEAU, AK	11,543	12,013	12,263	0.6	2.58	7,638	7,790	0.3	76,437	86,715	7
KAHULUI-WAILUKU, HI	43,507	50,840	55,462	2.2	2.86	29,899	34,482	2.0	58,456	65,953	82
KALAMAZOO-PORTAGE,MI	121,461	130,071	135,122	0.9	2.44	78,263	81,272	0.5	50,021	56,901	252
KALISPELL, MT	29,588	33,560	38,237	1.8	2.54	20,425	22,544	1.4	40,511	45,489	631
KANKAKEE-BRADLEY, IL	38,182	40,924	42,949	1.0	2.59	26,759	27,896	0.6	51,539	59,985	206
KANSAS CITY, MO-KS	717,761	785,712	836,032	1.3	2.50	482,723	517,840	1.0	59,055	69,263	73
KAPAA, HI	20,183	22,598	24,137	1.6	2.76	14,572	16,125	1.4	54,112	61,841	138
KEARNEY, NE	18,573	20,142	21,264	1.1	2.45	12,124	12,956	0.9	45,279	51,502	423
KEENE, NH	28,299	30,735	32,552	1.1	2.44	18,784	20,080	0.9	52,624	61,202	174
KENDALLVILLE, IN	16,696	17,735	18,262	0.8	2.69	12,294	12,637	0.4	52,335	60,122	186
KENNETT, MO	13,411	13,308	13,163	-0.1	2.39	9,166	8,836	-0.5	30,160	34,204	910
KENNEWICK-RICHLAND	67,706	81,083	93,400	2.5	2.87	49,678	58,964	2.4	56,769	66,955	98
KERRVILLE, TX	17,813	19,478	20,672	1.2	2.34	12,300	13,303	1.1	42,279	49,607	540
KETCHIKAN, AK	5,399	5,198	5,025	-0.5	2.51	3,634	3,430	-0.8	63,102	72,845	38
KEY WEST-MARATHON,FL	35,086	35,348	34,872	0.1	2.22	20,387	20,056	-0.2	53,014	62,303	164
KILL DEVIL HILLS, NC	12,690	15,864	18,352	3.1	2.30	8,451	10,270	2.7	53,014	61,631	164
KILLEEN-TEMPLE-FT HD	112,011	129,608	143,327	2.0	2.69	82,630	94,561	1.9	45,672	53,116	400
KINGSPORT-BRISTOL	124,021	131,260	135,219	0.8	2.29	87,501	90,136	0.4	39,671	45,756	664
KINGSTON, NY	67,499	72,188	75,832	0.9	2.45	43,563	46,192	0.8	54,240	63,845	137
KINGSVILLE, TX	11,034	11,060	11,043	0.0	2.74	7,795	7,731	-0.1	35,987	41,437	808
KINSTON, NC	23,862	24,170	24,034	0.2	2.37	16,182	15,952	-0.2	37,974	43,317	740
KIRKSVILLE, MO	11,394	11,495	11,471	0.1	2.28	6,536	6,362	-0.4	33,149	38,271	875
KLAMATH FALLS, OR	25,205	26,224	27,158	0.5	2.51	17,293	17,828	0.4	38,626	44,349	709
KNOXVILLE, TN	253,005	280,815	301,835	1.4	2.35	168,877	182,164	1.1	47,216	55,522	344
KODIAK, AK	4,424	4,433	4,389	0.0	3.08	3,257	3,214	-0.2	68,301	79,948	19
KOKOMO, IN	41,269	41,654	41,875	0.1	2.41	28,322	27,499	-0.4	56,268	65,094	109
LACONIA, NH	22,459	25,823	28,290	1.9	2.41	15,501	17,566	1.7	53,336	61,863	151
LA CROSSE, WI-MN	49,232	52,874	54,752	1.0	2.39	31,007	32,349	0.6	49,500	57,099	268
LAFAYETTE, IN	66,502	73,667	77,869	1.4	2.39	40,638	42,800	0.7	49,887	57,672	258
LAFAYETTE, LA	89,536	97,928	103,722	1.2	2.56	61,822	65,822	0.9	39,919	43,359	654
LA FOLLETTE, TN	16,125	17,248	17,820	0.9	2.36	11,575	12,075	0.6	30,346	34,785	909
LA GRANDE, OR	9,740	10,068	10,298	0.5	2.42	6,514	6,672	0.3	41,987	48,314	556
LAGRANGE, GA	21,920	24,247	25,847	1.4	2.59	15,615	16,734	1.0	43,355	50,047	502
LAKE CHARLES, LA	72,205	76,770	79,698	0.8	2.54	51,737	53,631	0.5	39,224	42,736	681
LAKE CITY, FL	20,925	24,751	28,031	2.3	2.53	14,919	17,359	2.1	36,891	41,820	781
LAKE HAVASU-KINGMAN	62,809	81,817	99,444	3.7	2.46	43,372	55,801	3.5	40,896	48,717	619
UNITED STATES				1.2	2.59			1.0	53,154	62,503	

CBSA	2007 Per Capita Income	2007 HH Income Base	2007 HOUSEHOLD INCOME DISTRIBUTION (%)					2007 Home Value Base	2007 HOME VALUE DISTRIBUTION (%)					2007 Median Home Value
			Less than $25,000	$25,000 to $49,999	$50,000 to $99,999	$100,000 to $149,999	$150,000 or More		Less than $50,000	$50,000 to $89,999	$90,000 to $174,999	$175,000 to $399,999	$400,000 or More	
HOPE, AR	17,099	13,748	37.6	29.6	26.2	4.7	1.9	10,028	34.2	31.5	26.1	7.0	1.2	67,705
HOT SPRINGS, AR	23,151	41,021	30.6	30.5	27.5	7.6	3.8	29,952	15.1	15.9	34.0	27.5	7.5	134,650
HOUGHTON, MI	18,818	15,381	37.0	31.0	24.4	5.6	2.0	11,205	26.2	28.5	31.8	11.6	1.9	82,746
HOUMA-BAYOU CANE, LA	18,525	73,724	32.6	28.9	28.6	6.9	3.0	56,041	18.3	20.9	41.1	17.3	2.4	107,781
HOUSTON-BAY-SUGAR,TX	28,188	1,956,468	19.2	24.1	31.7	14.5	10.6	1,238,245	11.2	19.7	39.3	23.9	5.9	120,986
HUDSON, NY	28,811	26,412	19.9	28.0	34.3	10.4	7.4	19,390	3.1	2.6	15.8	65.6	12.8	238,375
HUMBOLDT, TN	20,117	20,060	31.3	30.8	29.5	6.5	1.9	14,693	16.8	29.1	39.9	12.8	1.4	95,493
HUNTINGDON, PA	20,001	17,566	28.8	31.8	30.9	6.8	1.8	13,685	10.2	15.0	45.0	26.7	3.1	139,563
HUNTINGTON, IN	24,094	14,620	18.6	29.3	39.1	9.6	3.4	11,401	10.8	28.3	44.8	15.0	1.1	103,325
HUNTINGTON-ASHLAND	20,842	118,534	35.3	28.8	26.2	6.6	3.1	88,049	20.1	27.5	40.3	10.9	1.2	92,963
HUNTSVILLE, AL	26,818	152,194	24.0	25.7	30.9	13.7	5.8	111,029	8.2	16.0	43.1	28.1	4.6	133,244
HUNTSVILLE, TX	19,410	19,430	32.7	27.4	28.2	8.3	3.5	11,905	25.6	23.8	31.5	17.0	2.1	91,016
HURON, SD	21,922	6,888	32.4	30.1	29.1	6.0	2.4	4,776	24.0	30.6	35.4	9.0	1.0	84,525
HUTCHINSON, KS	22,989	25,338	24.6	32.3	32.7	6.9	3.4	18,332	20.1	29.0	38.7	11.0	1.3	91,385
HUTCHINSON, MN	26,034	14,945	16.1	26.4	42.1	11.5	3.8	11,866	4.5	5.1	37.1	46.8	6.6	182,210
IDAHO FALLS, ID	23,315	41,840	20.1	26.7	36.3	11.6	5.4	32,524	6.2	9.7	54.0	26.9	3.2	141,560
INDIANA, PA	19,779	34,986	33.7	30.0	26.7	6.9	2.6	25,233	13.7	16.3	42.9	24.2	3.0	134,287
INDNPLS-CARMEL, IN	30,942	673,391	17.2	23.9	35.9	14.2	8.8	469,863	6.7	13.8	44.5	29.9	5.1	143,711
INDIANOLA, MS	13,309	9,476	44.4	28.0	21.5	3.8	2.3	5,909	24.9	40.8	28.2	5.2	0.9	71,944
IOWA CITY, IA	28,701	59,863	24.3	26.3	30.6	11.7	7.1	36,766	10.4	8.0	37.8	37.1	6.7	161,797
IRON MOUNTAIN, MI-WI	22,335	14,039	28.7	31.1	30.6	7.1	2.5	11,438	14.7	30.3	35.9	17.1	2.0	96,418
ITHACA, NY	26,997	38,376	26.2	25.5	31.2	9.2	7.9	21,831	5.1	3.8	31.8	52.2	7.1	193,100
JACKSON, MI	24,513	61,603	21.6	26.6	36.3	11.1	4.4	47,564	10.1	15.4	44.3	27.4	2.8	128,479
JACKSON, MS	22,782	201,027	28.2	28.3	29.3	9.1	5.2	141,295	16.6	24.2	36.9	18.9	3.4	105,411
JACKSON, TN	24,434	44,745	26.4	27.6	31.4	9.4	5.0	31,012	15.3	25.1	42.8	14.5	2.3	102,048
JACKSON, WY-ID	41,065	11,933	11.5	22.1	38.2	14.8	13.3	7,410	6.0	3.2	7.9	25.3	57.5	470,025
JACKSONVILLE, FL	27,861	530,235	20.0	26.6	34.4	11.9	7.1	374,373	3.3	6.5	28.8	47.5	13.8	205,585
JACKSONVILLE, IL	22,841	16,336	25.4	30.5	33.1	8.0	3.0	12,031	11.2	18.4	47.0	20.9	2.4	121,912
JACKSONVILLE, NC	18,845	51,936	24.7	33.5	32.9	6.4	2.4	31,045	8.8	8.2	27.5	47.9	7.6	186,113
JACKSONVILLE, TX	17,557	17,636	34.6	32.5	25.2	5.2	2.6	13,289	32.1	29.2	27.0	10.0	1.6	73,090
JAMESTOWN, ND	22,475	8,858	28.9	29.5	32.6	6.4	2.7	6,057	20.7	23.5	44.3	10.3	1.3	96,546
JAMESTOWN-DUNKIRK,NY	21,743	54,527	27.9	31.4	30.3	7.2	3.1	39,207	6.2	14.5	44.2	32.1	3.1	150,216
JANESVILLE, WI	26,948	63,311	16.5	26.8	38.3	13.3	5.1	46,081	5.2	12.1	51.9	28.8	1.9	139,218
JASPER, IN	24,087	21,601	19.8	28.8	38.4	9.7	3.4	17,248	14.2	22.0	44.0	18.0	1.8	109,863
JEFFERSON CITY, MO	23,915	55,792	21.0	28.7	36.7	9.9	3.7	41,518	10.9	15.3	47.0	23.7	3.0	125,794
JENNINGS, LA	15,557	11,808	41.9	28.8	22.9	4.8	1.6	8,782	23.1	26.7	38.8	10.3	1.1	90,253
JESUP, GA	19,532	10,448	33.0	27.2	29.2	7.5	3.1	8,061	28.8	26.3	30.7	12.2	2.0	81,697
JOHNSON CITY, TN	21,776	81,196	33.1	29.9	27.3	6.4	3.4	58,515	12.2	16.9	43.5	23.4	3.9	125,120
JOHNSTOWN, PA	21,262	59,743	30.9	31.6	28.3	6.4	2.8	44,916	18.4	24.8	40.5	14.6	1.6	100,191
JONESBORO, AR	20,922	45,940	32.6	28.6	28.2	6.9	3.8	30,699	24.8	31.6	32.7	9.3	1.6	82,099
JOPLIN, MO	20,691	65,934	28.8	32.8	29.1	6.4	2.9	47,455	17.8	28.6	39.2	12.5	1.9	94,833
JUNEAU, AK	35,044	12,013	11.1	18.6	35.0	23.2	12.1	8,131	5.3	6.8	11.5	50.8	25.7	292,428
KAHULUI-WAILUKU, HI	27,238	50,840	18.5	23.4	34.3	15.1	8.8	30,541	0.5	0.6	1.5	18.9	78.5	635,826
KALAMAZOO-PORTAGE,MI	26,160	130,071	23.1	26.9	33.1	11.5	5.4	90,708	8.2	12.6	45.9	29.4	3.9	140,737
KALISPELL, MT	20,762	33,560	29.0	33.0	28.4	6.2	3.4	24,668	8.0	4.8	21.3	49.5	16.4	215,934
KANKAKEE-BRADLEY, IL	23,808	40,924	22.3	26.1	36.1	11.0	4.5	29,434	8.0	10.1	47.3	31.9	2.7	145,452
KANSAS CITY, MO-KS	30,026	785,696	17.0	24.8	36.0	13.7	8.5	551,413	7.8	13.3	40.0	33.4	5.6	148,450
KAPAA, HI	25,768	22,598	20.9	24.6	33.3	14.7	6.5	14,263	0.4	0.3	1.6	21.2	76.5	564,428
KEARNEY, NE	21,951	20,142	23.8	31.5	33.9	7.9	3.0	13,720	15.6	17.7	44.7	20.0	1.9	114,621
KEENE, NH	26,480	30,735	18.5	28.5	37.2	10.5	5.3	22,400	4.3	4.3	26.2	55.6	9.6	202,858
KENDALLVILLE, IN	22,596	17,735	17.7	29.5	39.6	10.1	3.0	13,985	10.5	17.9	48.8	20.9	2.0	117,616
KENNETT, MO	16,750	13,308	43.5	28.4	22.4	4.1	1.6	9,103	30.1	33.2	30.3	5.5	0.9	69,670
KENNEWICK-RICHLAND	24,607	81,083	19.0	24.7	35.3	14.3	6.6	57,301	5.8	7.0	44.2	37.2	5.7	161,842
KERRVILLE, TX	25,163	19,478	27.0	30.9	28.5	8.0	5.5	14,605	17.0	18.7	34.3	23.1	6.9	118,525
KETCHIKAN, AK	31,390	5,198	12.6	24.9	37.6	16.9	8.0	3,377	5.8	3.6	16.0	56.4	18.2	260,027
KEY WEST-MARATHON,FL	33,374	35,344	20.9	26.0	32.8	12.0	8.3	23,349	6.1	3.6	5.9	27.5	56.9	454,037
KILL DEVIL HILLS, NC	30,326	15,864	18.2	28.1	36.4	10.8	6.6	12,065	5.9	4.2	30.9	46.1	13.0	198,793
KILLEEN-TEMPLE-FT HD	21,104	129,608	21.3	33.5	33.0	8.4	3.9	76,186	14.4	25.9	45.2	12.7	1.8	101,029
KINGSPORT-BRISTOL	22,722	131,260	31.2	30.1	28.5	6.9	3.3	100,731	15.2	18.8	42.7	20.5	2.8	117,274
KINGSTON, NY	27,280	72,188	20.5	25.4	35.1	12.3	6.7	51,164	1.7	1.7	10.8	70.9	14.9	268,049
KINGSVILLE, TX	17,534	11,060	36.8	27.3	25.4	7.6	2.9	6,663	35.4	29.6	26.7	7.1	1.1	70,497
KINSTON, NC	20,965	24,170	33.8	28.8	28.2	6.2	3.0	16,559	19.4	22.2	41.7	14.8	1.8	103,754
KIRKSVILLE, MO	20,180	11,490	39.2	29.5	22.7	5.2	3.5	7,409	20.3	22.1	35.4	18.6	3.6	105,121
KLAMATH FALLS, OR	20,217	26,224	31.2	30.9	28.9	5.9	3.2	18,433	6.0	10.3	40.7	36.5	6.5	161,137
KNOXVILLE, TN	26,653	280,812	26.0	26.7	31.3	10.1	6.1	199,843	8.8	13.8	43.3	28.2	6.0	138,236
KODIAK, AK	28,236	4,433	12.6	21.7	34.1	19.5	12.2	2,618	4.9	4.0	22.9	53.4	14.7	238,827
KOKOMO, IN	28,009	41,654	19.9	24.2	36.0	14.2	5.7	30,811	11.3	32.9	42.0	12.7	1.1	96,603
LACONIA, NH	28,455	25,823	17.7	28.4	37.1	11.0	5.8	19,644	4.7	4.8	25.3	53.9	11.5	204,013
LA CROSSE, WI-MN	25,785	52,874	21.9	28.6	34.8	9.8	4.9	36,537	8.1	10.6	49.7	28.6	3.0	140,944
LAFAYETTE, IN	25,434	73,661	23.9	26.2	33.5	11.0	5.4	44,852	8.0	17.9	52.3	19.6	2.3	119,439
LAFAYETTE, LA	21,344	97,928	32.4	27.7	27.2	8.5	4.2	66,893	18.3	17.8	36.8	23.5	3.6	116,269
LA FOLLETTE, TN	16,778	17,248	43.1	30.9	20.6	3.8	1.6	12,844	25.2	28.5	35.0	9.8	1.5	84,680
LA GRANDE, OR	21,520	10,068	30.0	29.6	30.1	7.0	3.3	6,924	6.5	7.2	36.0	41.0	9.4	175,739
LAGRANGE, GA	22,358	24,247	29.5	26.6	30.4	8.3	5.2	16,027	11.7	20.6	43.0	20.9	3.9	118,132
LAKE CHARLES, LA	20,692	76,769	32.3	28.5	27.9	7.8	3.5	54,818	20.8	25.3	36.5	15.4	2.0	96,741
LAKE CITY, FL	18,699	24,751	32.7	31.8	27.0	6.3	2.2	19,572	7.7	12.5	35.6	38.3	5.8	161,329
LAKE HAVASU-KINGMAN	21,792	81,817	27.1	33.3	28.6	7.7	3.3	61,222	5.2	9.9	35.7	42.1	7.1	173,408
UNITED STATES	27,916		21.9	25.0	32.3	12.3	8.4		7.9	10.5	27.1	35.6	19.0	192,285

CBSA	Auto Loan	Home Loan	Invest-ments	Retire-ment Plans	Home Repair	Lawn & Garden	Comput-ers & Hard-ware	Major Appli-ances	TV, Radio, Sound Equip-ment	Furni-ture	Dine out/ Carry out	Sports Equip-ment	Fees & Tickets	Toys & Games	Travel	Cable TV	Apparel & Services	Auto Repairs	Health Insur-ance	Pets & Supplies
HOPE, AR	73	52	37	51	57	75	55	67	63	53	61	59	48	65	54	67	53	63	74	72
HOT SPRINGS, AR	79	69	68	67	74	86	70	79	75	69	73	67	66	72	72	79	64	76	87	80
HOUGHTON, MI	67	52	52	52	55	67	63	64	66	55	64	57	55	64	60	68	55	63	73	65
HOUMA-BAYOU CANE, LA	81	67	56	66	68	81	67	75	72	67	71	67	62	74	66	75	62	72	79	79
HOUSTON-BAY-SUGAR,TX	115	110	103	112	103	101	113	107	111	113	112	103	110	111	108	108	101	112	103	107
HUDSON, NY	100	93	91	93	100	111	94	104	96	92	95	91	91	96	97	99	84	98	107	107
HUMBOLDT, TN	77	59	50	58	63	79	62	71	69	60	67	62	55	71	61	73	58	68	79	75
HUNTINGDON, PA	78	63	55	61	69	85	64	75	69	62	68	66	58	72	64	73	59	70	81	79
HUNTINGTON, IN	90	83	84	84	85	93	82	87	86	82	85	76	81	89	83	88	75	84	93	89
HUNTINGTON-ASHLAND	75	61	57	60	65	78	65	72	70	62	69	63	60	70	65	74	60	69	80	74
HUNTSVILLE, AL	96	91	89	92	89	93	90	91	91	91	91	83	89	93	89	92	82	91	93	93
HUNTSVILLE, TX	77	61	60	63	60	68	78	70	76	69	76	66	68	74	70	75	67	75	73	73
HURON, SD	75	60	58	59	66	80	65	73	71	61	69	64	59	71	65	75	59	70	83	76
HUTCHINSON, KS	81	73	74	74	76	84	75	79	78	73	77	69	72	80	75	81	68	77	85	81
HUTCHINSON, MN	92	92	92	92	93	95	90	92	89	90	89	84	90	92	90	90	81	90	91	94
IDAHO FALLS, ID	95	93	93	94	91	93	90	92	90	91	90	83	90	93	90	90	81	91	92	93
INDIANA, PA	74	59	53	59	63	77	67	71	69	61	68	63	59	70	64	71	60	69	77	74
INDNPLS-CARMEL, IN	108	107	110	110	103	102	108	104	107	108	107	95	108	109	106	106	97	106	104	105
INDIANOLA, MS	63	51	47	52	51	61	54	57	60	54	59	50	50	60	53	63	52	58	64	61
IOWA CITY, IA	98	84	83	89	82	86	101	90	96	93	97	86	92	96	92	93	87	96	89	92
IRON MOUNTAIN, MI-WI	77	67	66	67	72	83	68	76	73	66	71	65	65	74	70	76	62	72	84	78
ITHACA, NY	91	80	87	85	79	83	100	86	95	90	95	83	91	92	91	92	86	92	87	88
JACKSON, MI	89	88	94	89	89	92	85	88	88	87	87	78	87	90	88	89	78	86	92	90
JACKSON, MS	88	80	77	82	78	84	81	82	84	82	84	74	79	85	80	85	75	83	85	85
JACKSON, TN	90	80	78	81	79	88	83	85	87	82	86	76	79	87	81	89	76	85	90	88
JACKSON, WY-ID	141	140	129	143	135	132	144	137	135	141	137	137	140	137	139	131	125	142	129	139
JACKSONVILLE, FL	100	97	97	99	93	94	98	95	98	98	98	87	97	98	96	98	88	98	96	96
JACKSONVILLE, IL	81	71	72	71	74	85	73	79	78	71	76	69	70	78	74	80	67	76	86	81
JACKSONVILLE, NC	79	68	61	69	63	68	74	71	74	71	74	67	69	76	69	73	65	74	71	72
JACKSONVILLE, TX	77	59	44	57	62	79	60	71	66	58	65	62	53	68	59	70	56	67	76	75
JAMESTOWN, ND	79	63	61	63	67	80	70	75	74	65	72	67	63	74	68	76	63	73	83	78
JAMESTOWN-DUNKIRK,NY	75	68	70	69	72	80	70	75	74	69	73	65	68	75	71	77	65	73	81	77
JANESVILLE, WI	93	94	103	96	94	95	92	93	94	93	93	82	94	96	94	95	84	92	96	94
JASPER, IN	94	81	75	80	85	98	80	90	85	79	84	79	76	89	81	88	74	85	95	94
JEFFERSON CITY, MO	90	82	78	82	82	89	82	85	84	81	84	77	79	86	81	86	74	84	89	88
JENNINGS, LA	68	50	37	49	54	70	52	62	58	50	57	55	45	60	51	63	49	59	69	67
JESUP, GA	81	67	56	65	69	82	67	76	72	66	71	67	62	73	66	75	62	73	80	79
JOHNSON CITY, TN	79	64	57	63	67	80	68	74	72	64	71	66	61	73	66	75	62	72	80	78
JOHNSTOWN, PA	71	65	70	64	69	78	66	71	72	64	70	61	64	71	68	76	61	69	82	72
JONESBORO, AR	81	66	58	66	67	79	70	74	74	68	73	67	64	75	68	76	64	73	79	78
JOPLIN, MO	79	67	64	67	68	79	69	74	74	67	72	65	65	75	69	76	63	72	80	76
JUNEAU, AK	123	132	136	135	127	118	128	122	123	131	124	115	132	124	128	120	113	125	117	122
KAHULUI-WAILUKU, HI	100	113	112	112	111	99	115	108	104	111	105	110	113	102	113	99	97	111	98	106
KALAMAZOO-PORTAGE,MI	91	85	89	87	85	88	91	88	91	88	91	80	88	92	88	91	81	89	90	90
KALISPELL, MT	79	71	66	71	73	83	71	78	73	70	72	69	68	74	72	75	64	75	80	80
KANKAKEE-BRADLEY, IL	88	86	90	87	85	88	84	85	87	86	86	76	85	88	85	88	77	85	89	87
KANSAS CITY, MO-KS	105	105	110	108	102	101	105	101	105	106	104	93	106	106	104	104	94	103	103	102
KAPAA, HI	89	108	107	103	110	97	100	101	94	101	95	98	105	93	105	92	88	99	93	98
KEARNEY, NE	83	71	67	72	73	81	77	79	77	73	77	72	71	79	74	78	68	78	81	81
KEENE, NH	93	90	93	91	93	98	90	94	91	89	90	84	89	92	91	92	81	91	95	95
KENDALLVILLE, IN	93	82	75	82	85	95	80	89	84	81	84	79	77	88	81	87	74	85	92	92
KENNETT, MO	64	48	39	47	52	66	51	59	58	49	56	52	46	59	51	62	49	57	67	63
KENNEWICK-RICHLAND	100	100	97	100	96	94	98	97	97	99	97	91	98	98	97	95	88	98	94	97
KERRVILLE, TX	89	77	72	76	83	100	78	91	83	76	81	77	73	80	81	87	71	86	98	92
KETCHIKAN, AK	103	114	122	114	113	104	112	108	108	112	108	101	115	109	112	106	100	108	103	107
KEY WEST-MARATHON,FL	108	99	89	99	104	115	101	110	101	99	101	101	97	100	103	103	90	107	110	111
KILL DEVIL HILLS, NC	108	93	74	91	101	122	91	109	94	89	94	95	84	95	94	99	82	101	112	113
KILLEEN-TEMPLE-FT HD	87	75	70	77	70	75	83	78	82	79	82	74	77	84	77	81	73	82	78	79
KINGSPORT-BRISTOL	81	67	60	65	71	85	68	77	74	66	72	68	63	75	68	78	63	73	85	81
KINGSTON, NY	92	95	103	95	98	97	95	96	94	94	94	86	96	94	97	95	85	94	97	96
KINGSVILLE, TX	73	61	54	60	57	64	67	66	69	65	69	61	61	67	63	69	61	69	67	66
KINSTON, NC	78	63	55	62	65	78	65	72	71	64	70	63	60	71	64	75	61	70	79	76
KIRKSVILLE, MO	72	54	52	56	57	70	69	68	69	60	68	62	59	69	63	70	60	68	72	70
KLAMATH FALLS, OR	76	65	62	65	69	78	68	74	71	66	70	65	64	71	68	74	62	72	79	75
KNOXVILLE, TN	92	83	84	84	84	92	87	88	89	84	88	79	83	89	85	90	78	88	92	90
KODIAK, AK	120	119	118	123	114	109	127	117	119	123	121	114	124	122	121	115	110	122	110	117
KOKOMO, IN	96	91	99	93	92	92	92	94	95	91	93	82	91	97	93	97	83	92	100	95
LACONIA, NH	100	95	92	95	100	109	92	102	94	92	93	90	91	95	95	96	83	96	103	104
LA CROSSE, WI-MN	88	82	88	84	82	86	89	86	88	84	88	78	86	89	86	87	78	87	89	87
LAFAYETTE, IN	90	80	82	83	78	83	92	84	89	86	90	79	86	90	85	88	80	88	85	86
LAFAYETTE, LA	82	73	68	73	70	76	75	75	77	74	77	69	72	78	73	78	68	77	77	78
LA FOLLETTE, TN	67	47	33	45	52	70	50	61	56	47	56	54	42	58	49	61	47	57	68	66
LA GRANDE, OR	79	65	61	66	69	81	72	76	73	67	73	68	65	73	70	75	64	74	80	79
LAGRANGE, GA	87	75	71	76	76	85	78	81	83	77	82	72	74	84	76	85	72	81	86	84
LAKE CHARLES, LA	78	70	68	70	69	76	71	73	75	71	74	65	69	75	70	77	65	73	78	75
LAKE CITY, FL	74	62	55	61	62	74	63	69	67	61	66	61	58	67	62	70	57	67	74	72
LAKE HAVASU-KINGMAN	78	71	69	70	75	86	70	80	74	69	72	68	68	71	74	78	63	77	87	80
UNITED STATES	100	100	100	100	100	100	100	100	100	100	100	100	100	100	100	100	100	100	100	100

CBSA	CBSA Code	POPULATION			2000-2007 ANNUAL RATE		RACE (%)					
							White		Black		Asian/Pacific	
		2000	2007	2012	% Rate	National Rank	2000	2007	2000	2007	2000	2007
LAKELAND, FL	29460	483,924	581,653	664,210	2.6	57	79.6	75.5	13.5	15.4	1.0	1.3
LAMESA, TX	29500	14,985	14,300	13,871	-0.6	921	72.5	70.0	8.7	8.3	0.2	0.3
LANCASTER, PA	29540	470,658	503,871	527,947	0.9	352	91.5	89.4	2.8	3.3	1.5	2.1
LANCASTER, SC	29580	61,351	65,179	67,795	0.8	396	71.0	69.7	26.9	27.5	0.3	0.4
LANSING-E LANSING MI	29620	447,728	469,278	483,659	0.7	444	84.4	82.2	8.1	8.6	2.7	3.7
LARAMIE, WY	29660	32,014	33,245	33,622	0.5	545	91.3	90.2	1.1	1.2	1.8	2.3
LAREDO, TX	29700	193,117	242,664	280,927	3.2	30	82.2	81.8	0.4	0.4	0.5	0.5
LAS CRUCES, NM	29740	174,682	202,485	224,870	2.1	93	67.8	67.1	1.6	1.6	0.8	1.0
LAS VEGAS, NM	29780	30,126	29,084	28,404	-0.5	911	56.2	55.8	0.8	0.8	0.6	0.7
LAS VEGAS-PARAD., NV	29820	1,375,765	1,893,507	2,308,978	4.5	7	71.6	69.4	9.1	9.3	5.7	5.6
LAUREL, MS	29860	83,107	86,219	88,491	0.5	545	65.7	63.5	32.1	33.6	0.2	0.3
LAURINBURG, NC	29900	35,998	37,540	37,902	0.6	494	51.5	49.9	37.3	37.7	0.5	0.7
LAWRENCE, KS	29940	99,962	107,920	112,759	1.1	288	86.1	83.9	4.2	4.5	3.2	4.4
LAWRENCEBURG, TN	29980	39,926	41,688	43,026	0.6	494	96.8	96.2	1.5	1.6	0.3	0.4
LAWTON, OK	30020	114,996	115,386	115,017	0.0	765	65.2	62.2	19.0	19.4	2.5	3.3
LEBANON, MO	30060	32,513	35,266	37,341	1.1	288	97.0	96.5	0.4	0.5	0.3	0.5
LEBANON, NH-VT	30100	167,387	177,182	183,784	0.8	396	96.8	96.1	0.4	0.5	1.1	1.7
LEBANON, PA	30140	120,327	129,684	136,703	1.0	318	94.5	93.2	1.3	1.4	0.9	1.3
LEVELLAND, TX	30220	22,716	22,608	22,572	-0.1	805	74.4	70.3	3.7	3.7	0.2	0.2
LEWISBURG, PA	30260	41,624	44,602	45,897	1.0	318	90.1	88.4	6.9	7.8	1.1	1.6
LEWISBURG, TN	30280	26,767	29,683	31,595	1.4	196	89.4	87.9	7.8	8.4	0.3	0.4
LEWISTON, ID-WA	30300	57,961	59,638	60,883	0.4	590	93.0	92.4	0.2	0.3	0.7	0.8
LEWISTON-AUBURN, ME	30340	103,793	109,926	114,593	0.8	396	97.0	96.5	0.7	0.8	0.6	0.8
LEWISTOWN, PA	30380	46,486	46,850	47,104	0.1	723	98.5	98.2	0.5	0.6	0.3	0.4
LEXINGTON, NE	30420	26,508	27,034	27,401	0.3	633	83.7	79.5	0.3	0.3	0.6	0.9
LEXINGTON-FAYETTE,KY	30460	408,326	450,105	480,521	1.4	196	85.3	83.9	10.4	10.5	1.7	2.4
LEXINGTON PARK, MD	30500	86,211	102,578	115,929	2.4	71	81.6	77.2	13.9	16.8	1.9	2.5
LIBERAL, KS	30580	22,510	23,443	24,066	0.6	494	65.4	60.6	3.8	3.5	2.9	3.5
LIMA, OH	30620	108,473	106,239	105,781	-0.3	873	84.9	83.2	12.2	13.4	0.6	0.8
LINCOLN, IL	30660	31,183	30,852	30,580	-0.1	805	91.7	90.4	6.6	7.4	0.6	0.7
LINCOLN, NE	30700	266,787	291,904	310,702	1.2	255	90.6	88.4	2.7	2.8	2.8	4.1
LINCOLNTON, NC	30740	63,780	73,688	80,786	2.0	101	90.2	88.9	6.4	6.6	0.3	0.4
LITTLE ROCK-N L ROCK	30780	610,518	673,404	721,475	1.4	196	75.4	74.0	21.0	21.7	1.0	1.3
LOCK HAVEN, PA	30820	37,914	38,263	38,547	0.1	723	98.3	97.9	0.5	0.6	0.4	0.6
LOGAN, UT-ID	30860	102,720	118,617	130,226	2.0	101	92.5	91.3	0.4	0.4	2.0	2.3
LOGANSPORT, IN	30900	40,930	40,241	39,704	-0.2	841	93.7	92.1	1.3	1.4	0.6	0.8
LONDON, KY	30940	52,715	56,455	59,228	0.9	352	97.7	97.3	0.6	0.7	0.4	0.5
LONGVIEW, TX	30980	194,042	203,587	209,509	0.7	444	75.7	73.0	17.9	19.1	0.5	0.6
LONGVIEW, WA	31020	92,948	99,019	103,540	0.9	352	91.8	90.5	0.5	0.6	1.4	1.7
LOS ALAMOS, NM	31060	18,343	19,680	20,759	1.0	318	90.3	89.0	0.4	0.4	3.8	4.6
LOS ANGELES-L. BEACH	31100	12,365,627	13,192,758	13,672,686	0.9	352	52.4	48.6	7.9	7.3	12.6	13.7
LSVL-JEFF CTY, KY-IN	31140	1,161,975	1,247,196	1,311,392	1.0	318	83.9	83.0	12.9	13.0	1.0	1.4
LUBBOCK, TX	31180	249,700	267,880	277,858	1.0	318	74.0	70.1	7.6	7.7	1.3	1.6
LUFKIN, TX	31260	80,130	83,452	85,732	0.6	494	75.1	71.8	14.7	15.5	0.7	0.8
LUMBERTON, NC	31300	123,339	128,885	131,737	0.6	494	32.8	31.0	25.1	24.5	0.4	0.5
LYNCHBURG, VA	31340	228,616	243,139	252,568	0.9	352	79.4	77.4	18.2	19.5	0.7	1.0
MACOMB, IL	31380	32,913	33,231	32,967	0.1	723	92.9	90.3	3.5	4.8	2.1	2.7
MACON, GA	31420	222,368	233,293	239,737	0.7	444	56.3	52.3	41.4	44.8	0.9	1.1
MADERA, CA	31460	123,109	149,180	172,133	2.7	51	62.2	57.7	4.1	4.0	1.4	1.6
MADISON, IN	31500	31,705	32,671	33,432	0.4	590	96.2	95.5	1.5	1.6	0.6	0.9
MADISON, WI	31540	501,774	557,650	592,241	1.5	173	90.3	87.9	3.5	4.2	3.0	4.1
MADISONVILLE, KY	31580	46,519	46,186	45,958	-0.1	805	92.0	91.3	6.2	6.5	0.4	0.5
MAGNOLIA, AR	31620	25,603	25,322	24,930	-0.2	841	62.1	59.2	36.1	38.6	0.4	0.5
MALONE, NY	31660	51,134	51,592	52,048	0.1	723	84.0	82.4	6.6	7.3	0.4	0.5
MANCHESTER-NASHUA,NH	31700	380,841	414,036	437,419	1.2	255	93.9	92.4	1.3	1.5	2.0	2.9
MANHATTAN, KS	31740	108,999	110,937	112,554	0.2	679	81.4	79.7	9.7	9.7	2.9	3.9
MANITOWOC, WI	31820	82,887	83,711	84,296	0.1	723	95.9	94.8	0.3	0.4	2.0	2.8
MANKATO-N MANKATO,MN	31860	85,712	93,820	99,210	1.3	225	95.4	94.2	1.1	1.3	1.6	2.2
MANSFIELD, OH	31900	128,852	128,920	128,891	0.0	765	88.2	88.0	9.4	9.5	0.5	0.6
MARINETTE, WI-MI	31940	68,710	69,742	70,320	0.2	679	97.4	97.1	0.2	0.2	0.3	0.4
MARION, IN	31980	73,403	70,626	68,431	-0.5	911	89.2	87.7	7.2	8.0	0.6	0.8
MARION, OH	32020	66,217	66,661	66,866	0.1	723	92.1	91.0	5.7	6.3	0.5	0.9
MARION-HERRIN, IL	32060	61,296	64,375	66,587	0.7	444	95.3	94.5	2.5	2.8	0.5	0.7
MARQUETTE, MI	32100	64,634	64,904	64,934	0.1	723	95.1	94.4	1.3	1.4	0.5	0.8
MARSHALL, MN	32140	25,425	25,650	25,934	0.1	723	93.6	91.8	1.5	1.9	1.7	2.3
MARSHALL, MO	32180	23,756	23,320	23,056	-0.3	873	90.0	88.5	5.4	6.0	0.6	0.8
MARSHALL, TX	32220	62,110	64,971	67,027	0.6	494	71.3	68.5	24.0	25.8	0.3	0.4
MARSHALLTOWN, IA	32260	39,311	39,967	40,453	0.2	679	90.4	87.7	0.9	1.0	0.8	1.2
MARSHFLD-WIS RAP, WI	32270	75,555	76,947	77,938	0.3	633	96.4	95.5	0.3	0.3	1.6	2.3
MARTIN, TN	32280	34,895	34,550	34,645	-0.1	805	90.3	88.8	6.9	7.5	1.3	1.9
MARTINSVILLE, VA	32300	73,346	70,735	68,779	-0.5	911	70.4	67.7	26.8	28.6	0.4	0.6
MARYVILLE, MO	32340	21,912	22,060	22,196	0.1	723	96.6	95.8	1.3	1.5	0.9	1.3
MASON CITY, IA	32000	54,356	53,169	52,480	-0.3	873	96.6	95.7	0.7	0.8	0.6	1.0
MAYFIELD, KY	32460	37,028	36,564	36,167	-0.2	841	92.7	91.0	4.4	4.6	0.2	0.3
MAYSVILLE, KY	32500	30,892	30,816	30,763	0.0	765	94.5	94.1	4.0	4.2	0.2	0.3
MCALESTER, OK	32540	43,953	44,675	45,104	0.2	679	77.2	75.0	4.0	4.2	0.3	0.4
MCALLEN-EDIN-PHAR,TX	32580	569,463	732,166	865,301	3.5	18	77.7	70.9	0.5	0.5	0.6	0.6
UNITED STATES					1.2		75.1	72.7	12.3	12.6	3.8	4.5

B

CBSA	% HISPANIC ORIGIN		2007 AGE DISTRIBUTION (%)										MEDIAN AGE	% 2007 Males	% 2007 Females
	2000	2007	0-4	5-9	10-14	15-19	20-24	25-44	45-64	65-84	85+	18+	2007		
LAKELAND, FL	9.5	13.2	6.6	6.2	6.3	6.5	6.0	24.7	25.6	15.7	2.3	76.9	40.4	49.1	50.9
LAMESA, TX	48.2	55.0	6.8	5.9	5.8	6.7	8.7	30.1	22.5	11.2	2.3	77.4	35.8	55.9	44.1
LANCASTER, PA	5.7	7.0	6.9	6.7	7.1	7.3	6.3	25.7	25.9	11.7	2.5	75.1	37.9	49.1	50.9
LANCASTER, SC	1.6	2.2	6.6	6.4	6.8	6.3	6.1	28.6	26.6	11.2	1.5	76.4	38.0	50.2	49.8
LANSING-E LANSING MI	4.7	5.7	6.3	5.9	6.3	8.3	10.4	26.2	26.0	9.0	1.6	77.5	34.8	48.8	51.2
LARAMIE, WY	7.5	8.4	4.9	3.7	3.9	9.3	22.3	25.5	21.6	7.7	1.1	84.9	27.5	51.7	48.3
LAREDO, TX	94.3	95.5	11.2	10.0	9.7	8.1	7.5	29.7	17.0	6.1	0.7	64.1	27.2	48.5	51.5
LAS CRUCES, NM	63.4	65.3	8.1	7.1	7.4	8.7	9.6	26.2	22.0	9.7	1.2	72.7	31.0	49.1	50.9
LAS VEGAS, NM	78.0	79.3	6.9	6.0	6.8	8.6	8.2	25.0	26.5	10.5	1.6	75.7	36.2	49.3	50.7
LAS VEGAS-PARAD., NV	22.0	26.0	7.4	6.7	6.9	6.4	6.1	30.0	24.5	10.8	1.1	75.0	36.3	50.4	49.6
LAUREL, MS	1.7	2.2	7.3	7.0	6.5	6.2	6.3	27.1	25.4	12.3	1.9	75.7	37.1	48.6	51.4
LAURINBURG, NC	1.2	1.5	7.1	6.7	7.2	7.9	7.1	25.6	25.9	10.6	2.0	74.6	36.3	47.3	52.7
LAWRENCE, KS	3.3	4.4	5.6	5.0	5.0	10.2	17.5	28.6	20.1	6.7	1.2	81.0	28.1	49.9	50.1
LAWRENCEBURG, TN	1.0	1.4	7.0	6.6	6.9	6.4	5.7	28.1	24.9	12.5	1.9	75.7	38.0	49.1	50.9
LAWTON, OK	8.4	10.4	8.2	7.1	6.6	8.1	10.1	28.8	21.1	8.8	1.2	74.0	30.8	51.8	48.2
LEBANON, MO	1.2	1.6	7.3	6.7	6.4	6.3	6.7	26.6	25.7	12.3	1.9	75.7	38.2	49.2	50.8
LEBANON, NH-VT	0.9	1.2	5.0	4.9	5.7	8.1	8.3	22.7	30.9	12.1	2.1	80.1	41.6	49.3	50.7
LEBANON, PA	5.0	6.1	6.1	5.9	6.1	6.5	5.8	25.3	27.9	13.5	2.8	78.1	41.1	49.0	51.0
LEVELLAND, TX	37.2	44.2	8.0	6.8	7.0	8.1	9.3	24.6	23.6	10.7	1.8	73.9	33.3	49.3	50.7
LEWISBURG, PA	3.9	4.7	4.7	4.7	4.9	8.3	9.6	29.3	24.5	11.5	2.4	82.2	37.4	56.3	43.7
LEWISBURG, TN	2.9	4.0	6.7	6.2	6.7	5.9	6.2	28.2	28.0	10.5	1.7	76.8	38.4	49.1	50.9
LEWISTON, ID-WA	1.9	2.3	6.5	5.7	6.0	6.3	7.4	24.5	27.3	13.5	2.8	78.2	39.8	48.7	51.3
LEWISTON-AUBURN, ME	1.0	1.3	5.9	5.6	5.9	7.2	7.0	26.4	27.5	12.1	2.5	78.5	40.1	48.7	51.3
LEWISTOWN, PA	0.6	0.7	6.5	6.2	6.2	6.4	5.4	25.8	26.7	14.1	2.6	77.0	40.7	48.8	51.2
LEXINGTON, NE	23.4	29.5	8.5	8.0	7.1	6.6	6.5	25.3	24.7	10.8	2.5	72.5	35.8	50.6	49.4
LEXINGTON-FAYETTE,KY	2.7	3.9	6.5	6.2	6.1	6.9	7.8	31.2	24.9	9.1	1.4	77.7	35.1	49.1	50.9
LEXINGTON PARK, MD	2.0	2.9	7.2	7.0	7.4	7.7	6.7	28.7	25.1	9.0	1.2	73.8	36.1	50.3	49.7
LIBERAL, KS	42.1	49.6	9.9	8.7	7.8	7.7	8.8	28.9	19.7	7.1	1.4	69.2	29.2	51.2	48.8
LIMA, OH	1.4	1.7	6.8	6.3	6.5	7.3	7.4	25.1	26.5	12.0	2.2	76.4	37.9	49.8	50.2
LINCOLN, IL	1.6	2.1	5.5	5.2	5.5	7.4	8.1	28.2	25.4	12.0	2.7	80.3	37.9	50.2	49.8
LINCOLN, NE	3.2	4.3	6.6	6.1	6.0	7.8	9.1	30.1	23.8	8.7	1.7	77.6	33.1	49.9	50.1
LINCOLNTON, NC	5.7	7.3	6.4	6.3	6.8	6.1	5.0	29.6	27.7	10.8	1.4	76.7	39.0	50.0	50.0
LITTLE ROCK-N L ROCK	2.1	2.7	7.0	6.6	6.4	6.8	6.8	28.8	25.8	10.3	1.6	76.0	36.3	48.6	51.3
LOCK HAVEN, PA	0.5	0.7	5.5	5.0	5.4	8.0	9.1	23.5	26.6	14.5	2.6	80.5	40.0	48.7	51.3
LOGAN, UT-ID	6.2	7.4	10.9	8.6	7.1	8.9	13.0	28.7	15.5	5.9	1.4	69.3	25.6	49.3	50.7
LOGANSPORT, IN	7.1	9.4	7.2	6.6	6.0	6.8	6.4	26.6	26.4	11.9	2.2	75.9	38.1	50.5	49.5
LONDON, KY	0.6	0.8	7.2	7.2	6.4	5.6	5.4	29.4	27.0	10.6	1.3	75.9	37.6	49.2	50.8
LONGVIEW, TX	8.0	10.2	7.0	6.4	6.5	6.7	7.3	26.0	26.2	12.0	2.0	76.2	37.6	49.5	50.5
LONGVIEW, WA	4.6	5.8	6.8	5.9	6.9	7.1	6.9	25.0	27.6	11.7	2.1	76.1	38.5	49.5	50.5
LOS ALAMOS, NM	11.7	12.7	5.3	5.8	7.4	6.9	5.2	21.8	33.6	12.2	1.9	77.0	43.5	49.9	50.1
LOS ANGELES-L. BEACH	41.4	46.4	7.7	7.1	8.3	7.7	7.0	30.3	22.2	8.3	1.4	72.3	33.2	49.7	50.3
LSVL-JEFF CTY, KY-IN	1.7	2.4	6.7	6.6	6.6	6.3	6.1	27.8	27.2	10.9	1.7	76.3	38.3	48.7	51.3
LUBBOCK, TX	28.1	33.9	7.4	6.6	6.2	8.0	10.6	28.3	21.9	9.4	1.6	75.9	31.1	49.1	50.9
LUFKIN, TX	14.3	18.1	8.0	7.2	6.7	6.7	7.1	27.5	24.1	10.8	1.8	74.0	35.1	49.2	50.8
LUMBERTON, NC	4.9	6.1	8.1	7.4	7.2	7.1	7.0	28.9	23.9	9.1	1.2	73.2	33.6	49.1	50.9
LYNCHBURG, VA	1.0	1.4	5.7	5.6	6.1	7.6	6.7	25.3	27.7	13.2	2.1	78.6	40.2	48.2	51.8
MACOMB, IL	1.5	2.4	4.5	4.5	4.7	10.0	17.5	22.6	22.1	11.3	2.8	83.0	31.7	49.6	50.4
MACON, GA	1.3	1.6	7.0	6.7	7.0	7.2	6.6	26.6	26.2	10.9	1.8	75.2	37.0	47.4	52.6
MADERA, CA	44.3	50.9	8.1	6.9	8.0	7.5	7.8	27.4	23.3	9.7	1.3	72.3	33.0	48.2	51.8
MADISON, IN	1.0	1.4	6.4	5.9	6.4	7.3	7.4	26.0	27.1	11.7	1.7	77.5	38.5	49.4	50.6
MADISON, WI	3.0	3.9	6.0	5.7	5.8	7.6	10.5	28.5	25.8	8.4	1.6	78.5	35.5	49.7	50.3
MADISONVILLE, KY	0.9	1.4	6.1	6.0	6.1	6.2	5.6	26.3	28.6	12.9	2.4	78.1	40.3	47.9	52.1
MAGNOLIA, AR	1.1	1.4	6.4	5.8	6.1	7.6	8.1	25.6	24.7	13.2	2.6	77.9	37.6	48.2	51.8
MALONE, NY	4.0	4.6	5.2	4.7	6.0	7.0	8.1	29.8	26.4	10.8	1.9	80.0	38.4	55.0	45.0
MANCHESTER-NASHUA,NH	3.2	4.1	6.5	6.4	7.3	7.6	6.3	27.1	27.4	9.6	1.8	75.2	38.3	49.4	50.6
MANHATTAN, KS	5.2	6.7	7.1	5.9	5.2	9.7	17.7	26.4	18.7	7.6	1.6	78.3	27.3	51.8	48.2
MANITOWOC, WI	1.6	2.1	6.2	5.5	6.3	6.8	7.1	25.0	28.3	12.2	2.6	77.9	40.6	49.9	50.1
MANKATO-N MANKATO,MN	1.8	2.4	5.9	5.2	5.2	9.4	13.8	25.9	23.0	9.3	2.2	80.3	31.3	49.9	50.1
MANSFIELD, OH	0.9	1.0	6.4	6.2	6.2	6.7	6.7	25.7	27.0	13.0	2.1	77.2	39.2	50.2	49.8
MARINETTE, WI-MI	0.7	1.0	5.6	5.3	5.5	6.7	7.3	22.4	30.0	14.5	2.8	79.7	43.1	49.7	50.3
MARION, IN	2.4	3.2	6.0	5.5	6.3	7.9	8.6	23.7	26.5	13.3	2.2	78.6	38.9	48.4	51.6
MARION, OH	1.1	1.3	6.2	5.7	6.1	6.9	7.3	27.4	26.7	11.8	2.0	78.1	38.5	51.4	48.6
MARION-HERRIN, IL	1.2	1.7	6.1	5.7	5.7	5.9	6.0	26.5	27.2	14.2	2.8	79.0	40.9	48.5	51.5
MARQUETTE, MI	0.7	1.0	5.1	4.7	5.1	8.2	9.8	24.9	28.3	11.6	2.3	81.6	38.8	50.1	49.9
MARSHALL, MN	4.0	5.4	6.9	6.1	6.2	7.8	10.8	24.1	24.2	10.6	3.2	77.2	35.2	49.2	50.8
MARSHALL, MO	4.4	5.5	6.5	5.9	5.7	7.8	8.3	24.6	25.7	12.6	3.0	77.9	38.2	49.5	50.5
MARSHALL, TX	5.3	6.9	6.7	6.3	6.4	7.4	8.1	24.8	27.3	11.2	1.8	76.5	37.9	48.8	51.2
MARSHALLTOWN, IA	9.0	11.8	6.7	5.9	6.5	6.2	7.4	24.0	27.4	13.3	2.7	77.2	40.0	50.1	49.9
MARSHFLD-WIS RAP, WI	0.9	1.2	6.4	6.0	6.3	6.7	7.0	25.1	27.5	12.3	2.8	77.1	40.1	49.3	50.7
MARTIN, TN	1.2	1.6	6.2	5.7	5.6	7.2	9.6	26.9	24.5	12.1	2.2	79.5	36.4	49.0	51.0
MARTINSVILLE, VA	3.2	4.6	5.6	5.6	5.4	6.1	5.3	26.8	28.1	14.9	2.2	79.6	42.0	48.4	51.6
MARYVILLE, MO	0.7	0.9	4.8	4.5	4.8	11.0	17.7	21.8	21.4	11.1	2.9	82.7	31.0	50.1	49.9
MASON CITY, IA	2.6	3.4	6.0	5.7	6.1	6.5	7.0	24.0	27.7	13.7	3.1	78.3	41.2	48.6	51.4
MAYFIELD, KY	2.4	3.6	6.8	6.7	6.1	6.0	5.8	26.5	26.6	12.9	2.6	76.7	39.7	49.2	50.8
MAYSVILLE, KY	0.7	1.0	6.4	6.1	6.2	6.0	5.7	27.6	27.7	12.3	2.0	77.6	39.6	49.3	50.7
MCALESTER, OK	2.1	2.7	5.7	5.3	5.8	5.9	7.2	24.9	27.8	14.9	2.6	79.6	41.7	50.9	49.1
MCALLEN-EDIN-PHAR,TX	88.3	90.9	10.8	9.6	9.1	8.2	7.6	28.2	17.6	8.0	1.0	65.6	28.0	48.7	51.3
UNITED STATES	12.5	15.0	6.9	6.5	6.8	7.1	7.0	27.6	25.4	10.7	1.9	75.6	36.7	49.2	50.8

CBSA	HOUSEHOLDS					FAMILIES			MEDIAN HOUSEHOLD INCOME		
	2000	2007	2012	% Annual Rate 2000-2007	2007 Average HH Size	2000	2007	% Annual Rate 2000-2007	2007	2012	2007 National Rank
LAKELAND, FL	187,233	227,336	260,744	2.7	2.50	132,305	157,978	2.5	43,899	50,379	476
LAMESA, TX	4,726	4,542	4,408	-0.5	2.65	3,503	3,335	-0.7	34,039	38,504	860
LANCASTER, PA	172,560	187,870	198,135	1.2	2.61	124,129	131,668	0.8	57,258	66,128	91
LANCASTER, SC	23,178	25,436	26,821	1.3	2.48	16,840	17,890	0.8	42,703	48,984	520
LANSING-E LANSING MI	172,413	183,299	190,436	0.8	2.45	109,994	113,913	0.5	54,364	62,485	135
LARAMIE, WY	13,269	14,239	14,563	1.0	2.17	7,001	7,189	0.4	36,080	42,339	807
LAREDO, TX	50,740	64,434	74,970	3.4	3.72	43,436	54,872	3.3	34,138	39,295	857
LAS CRUCES, NM	59,556	71,122	79,720	2.5	2.77	42,912	49,833	2.1	36,916	43,236	779
LAS VEGAS, NM	11,134	11,255	11,141	0.1	2.47	7,533	7,374	-0.3	32,535	37,550	883
LAS VEGAS-PARAD., NV	512,253	704,837	857,673	4.5	2.66	339,693	461,939	4.3	56,432	66,146	103
LAUREL, MS	30,983	32,830	33,967	0.8	2.57	22,511	23,340	0.5	31,767	34,716	896
LAURINBURG, NC	13,399	13,951	14,238	0.6	2.55	9,673	9,837	0.2	38,153	43,616	736
LAWRENCE, KS	38,486	42,851	45,196	1.5	2.32	21,159	23,117	1.2	47,778	55,724	322
LAWRENCEBURG, TN	15,480	16,396	17,013	0.8	2.52	11,369	11,761	0.5	36,931	42,677	778
LAWTON, OK	39,808	41,264	41,433	0.5	2.57	28,858	29,393	0.3	42,354	49,019	537
LEBANON, MO	12,760	13,994	14,874	1.3	2.49	9,190	9,823	0.9	36,085	41,247	806
LEBANON, NH-VT	66,696	72,118	75,570	1.1	2.34	43,604	46,064	0.8	52,392	62,305	185
LEBANON, PA	46,551	50,862	54,018	1.2	2.46	32,761	34,825	0.8	50,703	58,303	225
LEVELLAND, TX	7,994	8,126	8,199	0.2	2.70	6,088	6,134	0.1	37,409	42,320	761
LEWISBURG, PA	13,178	14,167	14,832	1.0	2.45	9,205	9,623	0.6	49,988	57,091	254
LEWISBURG, TN	10,307	11,511	12,274	1.5	2.55	7,475	8,148	1.2	47,990	55,573	313
LEWISTON, ID-WA	23,650	24,659	25,273	0.6	2.38	15,801	16,240	0.4	44,873	52,924	440
LEWISTON-AUBURN, ME	42,028	45,205	47,584	1.0	2.35	27,183	28,619	0.7	42,855	49,152	515
LEWISTOWN, PA	18,413	18,827	19,048	0.3	2.45	12,905	12,834	-0.1	39,683	45,787	663
LEXINGTON, NE	9,687	9,673	9,734	0.0	2.74	6,930	6,843	-0.2	43,868	50,074	481
LEXINGTON-FAYETTE,KY	163,854	185,002	199,135	1.7	2.34	104,239	113,311	1.2	52,758	62,969	169
LEXINGTON PARK, MD	30,642	37,495	42,972	2.8	2.65	22,306	26,512	2.4	66,622	76,737	28
LIBERAL, KS	7,419	7,575	7,720	0.3	3.04	5,503	5,557	0.1	47,412	55,903	338
LIMA, OH	40,646	41,130	41,296	0.2	2.47	28,213	27,690	-0.3	45,412	51,616	416
LINCOLN, IL	11,113	11,063	10,998	-0.1	2.40	7,583	7,328	-0.5	48,863	56,555	290
LINCOLN, NE	105,200	116,960	125,374	1.5	2.38	64,917	71,102	1.3	53,002	62,228	165
LINCOLNTON, NC	24,041	28,120	30,960	2.2	2.59	18,181	20,831	1.9	49,819	55,718	259
LITTLE ROCK-N L ROCK	241,094	268,482	289,285	1.5	2.45	165,360	179,463	1.1	50,091	59,517	249
LOCK HAVEN, PA	14,773	15,218	15,460	0.4	2.37	9,934	9,927	0.0	38,456	44,398	721
LOGAN, UT-ID	31,019	35,866	39,589	2.0	3.21	23,891	27,074	1.7	49,299	56,967	275
LOGANSPORT, IN	15,715	15,667	15,492	0.0	2.50	10,928	10,492	-0.6	48,815	56,947	291
LONDON, KY	20,353	22,603	24,058	1.5	2.47	15,364	16,563	1.0	33,348	38,386	871
LONGVIEW, TX	73,341	77,076	79,543	0.7	2.55	52,432	54,561	0.6	41,310	47,467	594
LONGVIEW, WA	35,850	38,349	40,152	0.9	2.55	25,056	26,438	0.7	49,391	57,670	270
LOS ALAMOS, NM	7,497	8,239	8,749	1.3	2.38	5,341	5,701	0.9	101,199	118,770	1
LOS ANGELES-L. BEACH	4,069,061	4,248,911	4,377,587	0.6	3.05	2,804,894	2,942,160	0.7	59,118	69,300	72
LSVL-JEFF CTY, KY-IN	462,041	504,403	533,681	1.2	2.43	313,225	330,803	0.8	52,396	61,941	184
LUBBOCK, TX	95,028	101,586	105,716	0.9	2.53	61,956	65,384	0.7	40,519	47,315	630
LUFKIN, TX	28,685	30,175	31,111	0.7	2.68	21,263	22,161	0.6	41,131	47,371	602
LUMBERTON, NC	43,677	46,147	47,466	0.8	2.71	32,015	33,068	0.4	34,692	39,909	844
LYNCHBURG, VA	89,736	96,208	100,791	1.0	2.40	62,702	65,332	0.6	45,654	51,997	402
MACOMB, IL	12,360	12,501	12,452	0.2	2.25	7,096	6,902	-0.4	37,544	41,794	756
MACON, GA	84,338	89,006	91,878	0.7	2.54	58,816	60,356	0.4	45,537	52,726	409
MADERA, CA	36,155	43,353	50,046	2.5	3.24	28,610	34,406	2.6	43,883	49,949	478
MADISON, IN	12,148	12,899	13,330	0.8	2.40	8,435	8,623	0.3	47,629	55,378	325
MADISON, WI	202,687	231,193	247,971	1.8	2.34	121,226	134,107	1.4	61,216	71,253	55
MADISONVILLE, KY	18,820	19,217	19,315	0.3	2.36	13,400	13,215	-0.2	38,364	44,861	724
MAGNOLIA, AR	9,981	10,016	9,927	0.0	2.41	6,746	6,555	-0.4	34,490	40,095	852
MALONE, NY	17,931	18,546	18,907	0.5	2.41	11,805	12,108	0.4	38,802	44,373	697
MANCHESTER-NASHUA,NH	144,455	156,368	165,451	1.1	2.60	98,855	105,429	0.9	68,835	81,086	17
MANHATTAN, KS	39,366	40,879	41,877	0.5	2.46	24,771	25,159	0.2	42,084	48,891	550
MANITOWOC, WI	32,721	34,284	34,911	0.6	2.40	22,364	22,882	0.3	52,572	59,654	177
MANKATO-N MANKATO,MN	31,704	35,692	38,262	1.6	2.44	19,930	21,674	1.2	51,798	61,100	197
MANSFIELD, OH	49,534	51,047	51,500	0.4	2.40	34,297	34,285	0.0	45,793	52,693	393
MARINETTE, WI-MI	28,114	29,490	30,109	0.7	2.30	18,846	19,251	0.3	41,549	47,077	581
MARION, IN	28,319	27,876	27,224	-0.2	2.36	19,578	18,547	-0.7	45,611	52,871	406
MARION, OH	24,578	25,098	25,375	0.3	2.46	17,252	17,107	-0.1	47,088	54,030	348
MARION-HERRIN, IL	25,358	26,989	28,103	0.9	2.32	16,969	17,516	0.4	38,615	43,537	710
MARQUETTE, MI	25,767	26,899	27,306	0.6	2.26	16,480	16,662	0.2	42,984	48,431	514
MARSHALL, MN	9,715	10,017	10,194	0.4	2.45	6,331	6,320	0.0	48,210	55,587	302
MARSHALL, MO	9,015	8,881	8,782	-0.2	2.44	6,017	5,750	-0.6	40,985	47,374	612
MARSHALL, TX	23,087	24,403	25,332	0.8	2.59	16,952	17,750	0.6	40,422	46,061	634
MARSHALLTOWN, IA	15,338	15,726	15,933	0.3	2.46	10,456	10,523	0.1	47,682	55,465	323
MARSHFLD-WIS RAP, WI	30,135	31,893	32,763	0.8	2.37	20,506	21,187	0.5	51,454	59,409	208
MARTIN, TN	13,599	13,905	14,036	0.3	2.34	9,125	9,063	-0.1	36,215	41,395	801
MARTINSVILLE, VA	30,408	29,980	29,442	-0.2	2.32	20,978	20,029	-0.6	37,220	42,154	769
MARYVILLE, MO	8,138	8,411	8,561	0.5	2.28	4,818	4,799	-0.1	38,892	44,620	693
MASON CITY, IA	22,652	22,591	22,397	0.0	2.29	14,662	14,323	-0.3	45,561	53,342	407
MAYFIELD, KY	14,041	14,862	14,743	0.0	2.41	10,562	10,215	-0.5	38,317	44,861	727
MAYSVILLE, KY	12,269	12,606	12,721	0.4	2.40	8,747	8,687	-0.1	31,961	30,014	803
MCALESTER, OK	17,157	17,611	17,857	0.4	2.37	11,944	12,022	0.1	34,930	40,076	836
MCALLEN-EDIN-PHAR,TX	150,024	205,804	244,775	3.8	3.53	132,859	173,396	3.7	30,519	35,078	907
UNITED STATES				1.2	2.59			1.0	53,154	62,503	

CBSA	2007 Per Capita Income	2007 HH Income Base	2007 HOUSEHOLD INCOME DISTRIBUTION (%)					2007 Home Value Base	2007 HOME VALUE DISTRIBUTION (%)					2007 Median Home Value
			Less than $25,000	$25,000 to $49,999	$50,000 to $99,999	$100,000 to $149,999	$150,000 or More		Less than $50,000	$50,000 to $89,999	$90,000 to $174,999	$175,000 to $399,999	$400,000 or More	
LAKELAND, FL	22,923	227,336	25.6	30.8	30.9	8.5	4.1	172,462	7.1	11.7	36.3	39.0	5.9	163,037
LAMESA, TX	18,278	4,542	35.3	32.8	22.8	4.9	4.2	3,402	43.9	29.2	20.1	6.5	0.3	57,647
LANCASTER, PA	26,610	187,870	16.2	26.1	39.1	12.7	5.9	134,471	3.2	2.7	32.2	54.6	7.3	201,884
LANCASTER, SC	20,772	25,436	27.2	30.5	32.1	7.8	2.3	19,491	13.8	21.8	43.9	18.8	1.8	111,443
LANSING-E LANSING MI	27,426	183,298	20.3	25.5	35.1	13.0	6.1	125,648	6.3	10.1	44.2	35.6	3.9	151,558
LARAMIE, WY	22,494	14,239	36.0	26.6	26.9	7.5	3.0	7,648	10.8	4.2	18.4	55.5	11.1	216,592
LAREDO, TX	13,226	64,434	37.0	29.6	23.3	6.8	3.4	43,486	16.0	28.2	40.8	13.3	1.8	98,824
LAS CRUCES, NM	17,975	71,121	35.3	27.9	26.1	7.7	3.1	48,233	17.9	15.6	39.4	23.1	4.0	122,015
LAS VEGAS, NM	17,546	11,255	38.9	29.4	24.7	5.0	2.0	8,231	17.8	14.5	38.4	25.0	4.4	133,893
LAS VEGAS-PARAD., NV	27,543	704,831	17.8	25.6	36.1	12.7	7.9	429,462	2.8	1.9	6.6	64.9	23.9	302,825
LAUREL, MS	16,902	32,830	38.2	33.2	21.6	4.6	2.2	25,865	31.0	30.9	27.5	9.0	1.7	73,541
LAURINBURG, NC	19,876	13,951	34.7	25.2	29.7	6.9	3.5	9,840	18.9	26.1	38.5	14.9	1.5	96,005
LAWRENCE, KS	26,697	42,851	25.2	27.0	31.9	9.6	6.3	23,071	7.2	6.3	43.1	37.6	5.7	163,767
LAWRENCEBURG, TN	19,426	16,396	32.8	32.7	27.2	4.7	2.6	12,776	14.4	23.2	45.5	15.3	1.7	106,367
LAWTON, OK	19,747	41,264	28.5	30.4	31.0	7.4	2.7	25,004	7.2	15.3	47.0	27.3	3.2	138,393
LEBANON, MO	19,328	13,994	32.9	33.0	25.6	5.8	2.6	10,419	20.0	20.3	38.5	17.6	3.6	107,597
LEBANON, NH-VT	28,465	72,118	20.1	27.0	36.2	10.0	6.7	52,893	4.1	5.2	28.9	47.5	14.4	203,213
LEBANON, PA	25,023	50,862	19.7	29.5	35.4	11.2	4.2	37,361	4.6	7.8	43.3	40.0	4.3	165,752
LEVELLAND, TX	18,458	8,126	30.8	33.7	26.1	6.5	3.0	6,135	37.2	29.7	27.1	5.7	0.3	66,582
LEWISBURG, PA	22,949	14,167	23.2	26.8	34.6	10.7	4.7	10,504	4.6	4.4	37.1	46.3	7.6	182,500
LEWISBURG, TN	22,149	11,511	25.0	26.8	35.6	9.7	2.9	8,555	9.0	17.1	49.5	20.2	4.3	125,600
LEWISTON, ID-WA	23,698	24,659	25.6	29.7	32.5	8.8	3.3	17,316	5.7	3.9	25.2	55.9	9.4	210,648
LEWISTON-AUBURN, ME	22,583	45,205	27.5	30.1	31.7	7.7	2.9	29,195	5.8	6.9	45.5	38.7	3.1	164,790
LEWISTOWN, PA	19,583	18,827	30.8	32.2	29.3	5.7	2.0	14,080	7.7	15.0	49.3	25.5	2.5	140,314
LEXINGTON, NE	19,622	9,673	25.3	31.9	33.6	5.9	3.4	7,048	19.6	33.6	36.5	9.2	1.1	86,367
LEXINGTON-FAYETTE,KY	29,928	185,002	21.6	25.9	32.1	12.4	8.0	113,094	5.5	9.1	46.2	32.8	6.5	149,617
LEXINGTON PARK, MD	29,163	37,495	13.1	21.1	40.1	18.1	7.6	27,470	2.4	0.9	3.9	56.6	36.1	354,282
LIBERAL, KS	18,980	7,575	22.1	30.5	35.2	8.3	3.9	4,984	24.3	27.3	36.1	11.0	1.3	88,137
LIMA, OH	22,613	41,130	25.5	29.4	32.2	9.2	3.7	30,724	13.4	25.5	43.0	16.4	1.7	107,190
LINCOLN, IL	23,049	11,063	22.2	28.9	36.5	9.4	3.0	8,179	8.4	14.4	55.9	19.6	1.6	128,785
LINCOLN, NE	27,462	116,958	19.3	27.3	36.1	11.4	5.9	75,111	4.1	9.7	54.1	28.7	3.3	139,784
LINCOLNTON, NC	23,106	28,120	21.1	29.1	36.7	9.0	4.0	22,386	11.6	14.0	41.2	27.5	5.7	134,440
LITTLE ROCK-N L ROCK	26,170	268,482	22.8	27.1	34.3	9.7	6.1	184,510	14.3	23.2	39.5	19.6	3.4	110,364
LOCK HAVEN, PA	20,169	15,218	32.3	31.9	27.1	6.2	2.5	11,164	10.1	12.0	49.7	25.7	2.6	146,502
LOGAN, UT-ID	19,262	35,866	19.9	30.8	35.5	9.4	4.4	24,274	4.2	3.6	51.8	37.1	3.4	160,108
LOGANSPORT, IN	23,563	15,667	20.3	30.8	34.4	10.9	3.6	11,685	13.7	33.4	41.8	10.2	0.9	93,494
LONDON, KY	18,159	22,603	38.0	32.2	22.0	5.2	2.5	17,558	26.4	24.1	35.7	12.2	1.5	89,066
LONGVIEW, TX	21,771	77,076	28.9	29.6	29.1	8.4	3.9	55,969	24.5	24.8	34.6	14.2	1.8	91,118
LONGVIEW, WA	23,765	38,349	24.1	26.5	34.7	10.5	4.2	27,047	3.9	3.5	26.3	57.7	8.5	209,528
LOS ALAMOS, NM	48,744	8,239	7.2	10.5	31.4	27.0	23.9	6,515	3.9	1.7	8.6	43.0	42.8	366,102
LOS ANGELES-L. BEACH	27,830	4,248,815	20.6	22.2	30.8	14.5	12.0	2,224,300	1.3	1.4	2.3	17.1	77.8	620,934
LSVL-JEFF CTY, KY-IN	28,227	504,399	21.2	26.3	33.4	12.2	6.9	356,556	7.0	13.9	46.4	28.0	4.7	135,318
LUBBOCK, TX	21,985	101,579	31.1	28.6	27.7	7.9	4.7	62,195	23.6	29.0	34.1	11.7	1.6	86,459
LUFKIN, TX	19,599	30,175	29.3	30.2	30.0	7.4	3.1	22,234	27.5	30.1	31.5	9.6	1.3	80,440
LUMBERTON, NC	16,507	46,147	37.7	28.7	26.1	5.4	2.1	34,052	28.2	26.8	35.6	8.3	1.1	82,168
LYNCHBURG, VA	23,872	96,208	25.2	29.7	32.1	9.3	3.7	71,989	9.1	10.0	40.3	36.0	4.4	157,464
MACOMB, IL	20,456	12,501	35.2	28.4	27.4	6.5	2.4	8,154	17.3	23.9	40.2	16.4	2.1	103,500
MACON, GA	23,570	89,006	28.8	24.8	31.2	10.1	5.2	60,104	16.2	24.4	39.7	16.9	2.8	103,753
MADERA, CA	18,101	43,353	28.6	27.9	30.5	8.3	4.6	29,145	1.5	1.6	6.7	58.2	32.0	323,278
MADISON, IN	23,042	12,899	22.9	29.5	35.0	10.1	2.6	9,742	12.4	21.4	46.9	17.1	2.2	111,463
MADISON, WI	31,754	231,193	16.2	23.5	38.2	14.5	7.6	143,475	2.3	2.0	22.9	63.2	9.6	220,419
MADISONVILLE, KY	21,606	19,217	31.7	31.3	27.7	5.9	3.4	14,465	30.9	30.7	29.5	8.0	1.0	72,928
MAGNOLIA, AR	19,595	10,016	37.1	27.2	26.2	6.4	3.1	7,306	34.3	27.3	25.6	11.9	0.8	70,085
MALONE, NY	19,503	18,546	30.7	31.4	29.9	5.9	2.1	13,562	7.7	14.7	40.2	34.4	3.0	153,136
MANCHESTER-NASHUA,NH	33,184	156,368	13.6	20.4	37.5	16.7	11.8	105,164	1.4	2.1	12.0	67.3	17.2	267,164
MANHATTAN, KS	21,553	40,879	28.0	30.2	30.0	8.1	3.7	22,686	14.8	18.6	46.1	18.5	2.0	114,434
MANITOWOC, WI	25,679	34,284	18.8	28.2	39.9	9.7	3.4	26,504	4.0	11.8	50.5	30.8	2.9	142,505
MANKATO-N MANKATO,MN	25,439	35,692	19.2	28.8	37.3	9.8	4.8	25,414	7.6	7.1	36.9	42.5	5.9	172,340
MANSFIELD, OH	23,727	51,047	24.5	29.7	32.4	9.4	4.0	37,910	11.5	21.6	47.4	18.2	1.3	111,998
MARINETTE, WI-MI	21,632	29,490	27.6	32.5	31.3	6.7	2.0	23,647	15.2	26.0	41.0	16.3	1.4	103,335
MARION, IN	23,454	27,876	26.0	28.6	32.3	9.8	3.3	20,718	17.4	34.0	39.4	8.5	0.7	88,439
MARION, OH	22,604	25,098	22.5	30.3	35.3	9.0	2.9	18,923	11.3	28.7	44.5	14.0	1.5	102,547
MARION-HERRIN, IL	21,734	26,989	32.5	29.1	28.7	6.6	3.0	20,360	17.4	24.0	39.4	16.7	2.5	105,642
MARQUETTE, MI	23,147	26,899	27.6	29.6	32.5	7.4	2.9	18,956	12.5	23.5	47.8	14.7	1.5	107,893
MARSHALL, MN	22,885	10,017	23.8	28.3	36.6	8.2	3.1	7,052	9.6	14.6	45.1	28.0	2.7	141,628
MARSHALL, MO	20,561	8,881	28.6	32.4	29.7	6.3	3.0	6,305	22.1	24.7	35.6	15.2	2.4	95,276
MARSHALL, TX	20,209	24,403	31.1	27.9	30.3	7.9	2.8	19,090	29.5	25.3	32.2	11.7	1.3	82,559
MARSHALLTOWN, IA	23,126	15,726	22.2	30.3	35.0	9.1	3.4	11,851	15.5	27.7	42.0	13.8	1.0	98,486
MARSHFLD-WIS RAP, WI	26,364	31,893	20.7	27.6	37.2	10.1	4.4	24,129	5.3	17.5	51.2	24.4	1.5	128,771
MARTIN, TN	19,495	13,905	35.0	29.3	28.9	4.8	2.0	9,779	18.0	26.3	41.3	12.9	1.5	97,400
MARTINSVILLE, VA	21,047	29,980	32.2	32.0	28.1	5.3	2.5	22,109	9.5	11.7	40.5	34.9	3.5	155,985
MARYVILLE, MO	20,141	8,411	31.5	30.7	29.8	5.4	2.6	5,489	20.7	18.9	35.0	22.6	2.8	111,010
MASON CITY, IA	24,348	22,591	25.2	29.5	34.5	7.2	3.6	16,805	12.5	26.1	43.3	15.5	2.5	102,960
MAYFIELD, KY	20,680	14,862	34.9	27.4	27.7	7.0	3.0	11,599	24.3	27.7	36.4	10.8	0.9	87,058
MAYSVILLE, KY	18,585	12,606	39.2	30.0	23.0	5.4	2.4	9,376	31.5	26.1	30.4	10.4	1.5	76,975
MCALESTER, OK	18,852	17,611	37.0	30.2	25.3	5.3	2.2	13,373	30.8	30.6	27.8	9.4	1.4	73,341
MCALLEN-EDIN-PHAR,TX	12,350	205,804	41.9	29.0	21.1	5.4	2.5	152,058	36.6	31.3	24.6	6.3	1.2	64,885
UNITED STATES	27,916		21.9	25.0	32.3	12.3	8.4		7.9	10.5	27.1	35.6	19.0	192,285

CBSA	Auto Loan	Home Loan	Invest-ments	Retire-ment Plans	Home Repair	Lawn & Garden	Comput-ers & Hard-ware	Major Appli-ances	TV, Radio, Sound Equip-ment	Furni-ture	Dine out/ Carry out	Sports Equip-ment	Fees & Tickets	Toys & Games	Travel	Cable TV	Apparel & Services	Auto Repairs	Health Insur-ance	Pets & Supplies
LAKELAND, FL	84	77	76	76	78	87	77	83	80	76	79	72	75	78	79	83	69	81	89	83
LAMESA, TX	80	65	51	60	66	80	64	75	72	65	71	64	59	71	64	75	62	72	81	76
LANCASTER, PA	97	98	103	99	99	100	96	98	96	96	96	88	97	98	97	97	87	96	99	99
LANCASTER, SC	85	67	53	65	70	86	67	77	73	66	73	68	61	76	66	78	63	74	83	82
LANSING-E LANSING MI	94	92	100	95	91	91	97	92	96	95	96	84	96	97	95	95	86	94	93	93
LARAMIE, WY	70	56	60	60	54	59	80	64	73	66	73	62	68	70	68	69	65	71	63	65
LAREDO, TX	74	69	53	63	60	62	65	67	68	65	69	62	62	66	63	67	62	70	65	64
LAS CRUCES, NM	74	66	61	65	62	66	69	68	71	68	70	62	65	69	66	70	63	70	69	68
LAS VEGAS, NM	66	57	52	55	56	63	59	62	62	57	61	55	54	61	58	63	53	62	65	63
LAS VEGAS-PARAD., NV	102	100	99	102	96	94	103	98	100	103	101	94	102	100	100	98	92	102	96	98
LAUREL, MS	73	53	37	51	57	76	55	67	62	53	61	59	47	64	54	67	52	63	73	72
LAURINBURG, NC	80	66	59	66	67	78	68	73	73	67	72	65	63	73	67	76	63	72	79	77
LAWRENCE, KS	89	77	84	82	73	75	100	82	93	88	93	79	90	91	88	88	83	90	81	83
LAWRENCEBURG, TN	83	61	43	58	65	86	62	75	69	60	68	66	54	73	60	74	59	70	81	81
LAWTON, OK	76	67	67	69	64	68	73	70	74	71	74	64	69	75	69	74	66	72	73	71
LEBANON, MO	78	60	49	59	63	79	62	71	68	61	67	63	56	70	61	72	58	68	78	76
LEBANON, NH-VT	99	89	86	90	95	106	93	100	94	89	93	89	88	94	93	96	82	96	103	102
LEBANON, PA	89	84	88	85	88	95	83	89	87	83	86	77	83	89	85	89	77	85	94	91
LEVELLAND, TX	79	65	53	62	64	76	66	73	71	65	70	65	60	71	65	73	61	71	77	74
LEWISBURG, PA	92	85	85	85	90	99	83	91	87	83	86	80	82	89	85	90	77	87	96	94
LEWISBURG, TN	88	75	66	74	77	89	74	82	79	74	78	72	70	82	74	83	69	78	87	85
LEWISTON, ID-WA	80	72	80	74	74	81	78	79	80	74	78	70	75	79	77	82	69	78	85	80
LEWISTON-AUBURN, ME	76	70	77	72	72	77	73	75	76	72	75	66	72	76	73	77	66	74	79	76
LEWISTOWN, PA	75	61	54	60	66	80	62	72	68	60	67	63	57	70	62	71	58	67	79	75
LEXINGTON, NE	88	68	51	66	74	92	70	83	75	68	74	75	61	78	69	78	64	78	87	88
LEXINGTON-FAYETTE,KY	101	95	99	99	91	92	102	95	100	99	100	89	99	101	97	99	90	99	96	96
LEXINGTON PARK, MD	108	115	114	116	112	107	109	108	105	112	106	101	112	108	110	103	97	107	102	108
LIBERAL, KS	85	77	70	76	73	75	80	79	80	79	81	76	76	81	77	79	72	82	78	78
LIMA, OH	79	75	83	77	78	82	76	78	80	76	78	68	76	81	78	82	70	77	85	79
LINCOLN, IL	83	76	81	76	81	89	77	83	81	75	80	71	75	83	79	85	70	79	91	84
LINCOLN, NE	92	89	96	93	86	85	96	89	94	93	93	82	94	94	92	92	84	92	89	89
LINCOLNTON, NC	98	80	62	78	83	100	77	90	83	77	82	80	71	86	77	87	72	85	94	96
LITTLE ROCK-N L ROCK	95	86	84	88	84	91	89	89	91	88	90	81	86	92	87	92	80	90	92	92
LOCK HAVEN, PA	73	61	60	60	65	78	64	71	69	61	68	62	60	70	64	73	59	68	78	73
LOGAN, UT-ID	91	80	76	82	77	82	91	84	87	85	88	80	83	89	83	85	78	87	82	86
LOGANSPORT, IN	88	77	79	78	80	91	79	85	84	77	82	74	76	87	80	87	73	82	92	87
LONDON, KY	76	56	39	54	60	78	57	69	63	55	62	61	50	66	56	67	54	64	74	74
LONGVIEW, TX	86	72	65	72	74	87	74	81	79	73	78	72	69	80	73	82	68	79	87	84
LONGVIEW, WA	85	83	88	84	83	86	82	84	84	83	83	75	83	85	83	85	75	83	87	85
LOS ALAMOS, NM	145	182	196	182	184	160	162	160	152	169	153	150	178	153	171	149	144	156	148	158
LOS ANGELES-L. BEACH	108	117	113	115	116	99	125	115	115	120	118	122	123	113	120	109	110	121	102	109
LSVL-JEFF CTY, KY-IN	97	94	100	96	93	96	95	94	96	95	95	84	95	97	95	97	86	94	97	95
LUBBOCK, TX	81	71	71	73	68	72	81	75	81	77	80	70	75	79	76	80	72	79	77	76
LUFKIN, TX	82	69	60	68	69	79	70	76	74	69	74	68	66	76	69	77	65	74	80	78
LUMBERTON, NC	72	57	44	55	58	71	58	66	64	57	63	59	53	65	57	67	55	64	70	70
LYNCHBURG, VA	87	77	74	77	79	89	77	83	81	76	80	74	74	82	77	84	71	80	88	86
MACOMB, IL	70	53	55	55	57	67	71	66	70	60	69	61	60	68	64	70	60	68	71	68
MACON, GA	88	79	78	81	79	86	81	83	85	82	85	73	79	85	80	87	76	84	87	85
MADERA, CA	84	78	70	76	79	82	80	84	79	79	80	80	76	79	79	79	72	83	81	83
MADISON, IN	85	73	72	73	75	86	76	81	80	73	78	71	71	81	76	83	68	79	88	83
MADISON, WI	104	101	105	105	98	97	110	100	105	106	105	95	107	105	104	102	96	104	97	101
MADISONVILLE, KY	81	64	56	64	68	82	67	75	73	65	71	66	61	75	66	77	62	72	83	79
MAGNOLIA, AR	77	59	49	58	63	79	62	71	69	60	68	63	56	70	61	73	59	68	79	76
MALONE, NY	76	60	51	59	66	81	64	74	68	61	67	65	57	69	64	71	58	70	79	77
MANCHESTER-NASHUA,NH	113	126	135	128	123	113	122	116	118	124	119	109	127	119	123	115	110	118	111	116
MANHATTAN, KS	79	63	64	67	62	68	83	73	79	76	79	69	73	79	73	77	70	77	73	74
MANITOWOC, WI	88	85	91	85	88	94	83	88	86	83	85	76	83	89	85	88	76	84	93	89
MANKATO-N MANKATO,MN	91	84	86	86	84	88	92	87	90	87	90	81	87	91	88	89	80	89	88	89
MANSFIELD, OH	81	78	84	79	80	85	78	81	81	78	80	70	78	82	79	83	72	79	86	82
MARINETTE, WI-MI	77	64	59	63	70	83	65	75	70	63	69	65	61	72	66	74	60	71	82	78
MARION, IN	83	75	79	76	77	85	76	80	81	75	79	69	74	83	77	84	70	78	88	82
MARION, OH	81	76	82	77	78	83	76	79	81	76	79	69	76	82	78	83	70	78	86	80
MARION-HERRIN, IL	76	63	63	64	66	77	68	73	73	64	71	64	63	73	68	76	61	71	81	74
MARQUETTE, MI	76	68	73	69	69	76	75	74	76	70	75	66	71	75	73	77	66	74	79	75
MARSHALL, MN	86	71	66	72	75	86	78	82	80	74	80	74	71	82	75	82	70	80	86	85
MARSHALL, MO	78	63	62	64	67	79	69	74	74	65	72	65	63	75	68	77	62	72	83	76
MARSHALL, TX	85	67	53	65	69	86	68	78	74	67	73	69	62	76	67	78	64	74	84	82
MARSHALLTOWN, IA	82	76	80	76	78	85	77	80	81	76	80	70	76	83	78	83	71	79	87	82
MARSHFLD-WIS RAP, WI	89	85	93	86	88	94	84	88	88	84	86	77	85	90	86	90	77	86	94	90
MARTIN, TN	76	56	45	55	60	76	62	69	66	58	66	62	53	68	59	69	57	66	75	74
MARTINSVILLE, VA	78	61	51	60	65	81	63	73	69	61	68	64	57	71	62	73	59	69	79	77
MARYVILLE, MO	73	55	51	56	58	70	70	68	70	61	70	63	59	69	63	70	61	69	72	71
MASON CITY, IA	81	72	76	73	76	85	76	80	79	73	78	70	73	80	76	82	69	78	87	82
MAYFIELD, KY	81	61	50	60	66	84	65	76	71	62	70	67	57	73	64	75	60	71	83	80
MAYSVILLE, KY	75	54	39	52	59	78	57	69	63	54	62	61	49	66	56	67	53	64	76	74
MCALESTER, OK	70	56	52	55	61	75	60	68	65	56	63	59	54	64	60	69	54	65	76	70
MCALLEN-EDIN-PHAR,TX	67	58	45	54	52	57	56	60	61	60	62	54	53	58	55	62	55	62	61	58
UNITED STATES	100	100	100	100	100	100	100	100	100	100	100	100	100	100	100	100	100	100	100	100

POPULATION CHANGE
CBSA AND U.S. TOTALS

CBSA	CBSA Code	POPULATION			2000-2007 ANNUAL RATE		RACE (%)					
							White		Black		Asian/Pacific	
		2000	2007	2012	% Rate	National Rank	2000	2007	2000	2007	2000	2007
MCCOMB, MS	32620	52,539	53,883	54,810	0.3	633	52.6	50.3	46.3	48.2	0.3	0.4
MCMINNVILLE, TN	32660	38,276	39,926	41,034	0.6	494	91.7	89.5	3.2	3.4	0.5	0.6
MCPHERSON, KS	32700	29,554	30,656	31,464	0.5	545	96.5	95.9	0.8	0.9	0.4	0.5
MEADVILLE, PA	32740	90,366	90,956	90,540	0.1	723	97.0	96.4	1.6	1.9	0.3	0.4
MEDFORD, OR	32780	181,269	204,464	220,869	1.7	140	91.6	90.1	0.4	0.4	1.1	1.3
MEMPHIS, TN-MS-AR	32820	1,205,204	1,307,699	1,383,939	1.1	288	52.9	51.6	43.5	43.9	1.4	1.8
MENOMONIE, WI	32860	39,858	43,795	46,300	1.3	225	96.1	95.0	0.3	0.4	2.1	3.0
MERCED, CA	32900	210,554	256,700	294,260	2.8	46	56.2	51.5	3.8	3.6	7.0	7.6
MERIDIAN, MS	32940	106,569	106,535	106,096	0.0	765	58.8	56.7	39.6	41.2	0.4	0.6
MERRILL, WI	32980	29,641	30,564	31,200	0.4	590	97.8	97.3	0.4	0.5	0.4	0.6
MEXICO, MO	33020	25,853	25,525	25,088	-0.2	841	91.1	89.9	7.2	8.1	0.4	0.5
MIAMI, OK	33060	33,194	34,013	34,446	0.3	633	74.1	71.6	0.6	0.6	0.4	0.6
MIAMI-FORT LAUDER.FL	33100	5,007,564	5,607,038	6,018,619	1.6	155	72.1	70.6	18.9	19.1	1.8	2.1
MICHIGAN C-LA PORTE	33140	110,106	112,068	113,572	0.2	679	86.3	84.3	10.1	11.1	0.5	0.9
MIDDLESBOROUGH, KY	33180	30,060	29,530	29,183	-0.2	841	96.0	95.5	2.4	2.5	0.4	0.6
MIDLAND, MI	33220	82,874	85,240	86,837	0.4	590	95.5	94.4	1.0	1.2	1.5	2.2
MIDLAND, TX	33260	116,009	122,327	126,569	0.7	444	77.3	74.0	7.0	7.1	1.0	1.1
MILLEDGEVILLF, GA	33300	54,776	57,332	58,988	0.6	494	48.2	43.9	49.7	53.4	0.8	1.1
MILWAUKEE-WAUKESHA	33340	1,500,741	1,534,473	1,555,300	0.3	633	77.1	74.4	15.7	17.1	2.1	2.7
MINDEN, LA	33380	41,831	41,775	41,785	0.0	765	65.5	63.0	32.8	35.3	0.2	0.2
MINERAL WELLS, TX	33420	27,026	27,670	28,066	0.3	633	88.2	85.6	2.3	2.5	0.6	0.7
MINNEAPOLIS-ST. PAUL	33460	2,968,806	3,313,789	3,578,139	1.5	173	86.1	83.9	5.3	6.0	4.2	5.1
MINOT, ND	33500	67,392	65,877	65,102	-0.3	873	93.2	91.7	2.0	2.2	0.8	1.2
MISSOULA, MT	33540	95,802	104,711	111,447	1.2	255	94.0	93.2	0.3	0.3	1.1	1.4
MITCHELL, SD	33580	21,880	22,909	23,686	0.6	494	96.7	95.9	0.2	0.3	0.4	0.6
MOBERLY, MO	33620	24,663	24,866	25,079	0.1	723	90.6	89.3	7.0	7.9	0.4	0.6
MOBILE, AL	33660	399,843	409,542	416,382	0.3	633	63.1	59.6	33.4	36.1	1.4	1.9
MODESTO, CA	33700	446,997	529,038	584,888	2.4	71	69.3	64.4	2.6	2.5	4.6	5.2
MONROE, LA	33740	170,053	174,297	177,917	0.3	633	65.2	61.0	32.9	36.6	0.6	0.9
MONROE, MI	33780	145,945	156,822	163,765	1.0	318	95.4	94.6	1.9	2.1	0.5	0.7
MONROE, WI	33820	33,647	36,794	39,194	1.2	255	98.1	97.7	0.3	0.3	0.3	0.4
MONTGOMERY, AL	33860	346,528	363,598	377,112	0.7	444	57.3	56.3	40.3	40.6	0.8	1.1
MONTROSE, CO	33940	33,432	39,952	44,908	2.5	64	90.0	88.5	0.3	0.3	0.5	0.6
MOREHEAD CITY, NC	33980	59,383	64,704	68,637	1.2	255	90.3	89.3	7.0	7.2	0.6	0.8
MORGAN CITY, LA	34020	53,500	52,369	51,143	-0.3	873	62.8	58.3	31.8	35.1	1.7	2.3
MORGANTOWN, WV	34060	111,200	118,509	121,483	0.9	352	94.0	92.7	2.6	2.9	1.9	2.7
MORRISTOWN, TN	34100	123,081	134,174	142,344	1.2	255	93.8	92.6	2.8	3.0	0.4	0.6
MOSCOW, ID	34140	34,935	36,632	37,622	0.7	444	93.9	93.2	0.6	0.7	2.2	2.6
MOSES LAKE, WA	34180	74,698	82,859	88,993	1.4	196	76.5	73.2	1.0	1.0	0.9	1.0
MOULTRIE, GA	34220	42,053	44,175	45,624	0.7	444	67.8	62.2	23.5	25.8	0.3	0.4
MOUNTAIN HOME, AR	34260	38,386	41,349	43,427	1.0	318	97.8	97.4	0.1	0.1	0.4	0.5
MOUNTAIN HOME, ID	34300	29,130	30,270	30,992	0.5	545	85.4	83.5	3.2	3.9	1.9	2.2
MOUNT AIRY, NC	34340	71,219	73,922	75,735	0.5	545	90.4	88.3	4.2	4.2	0.6	0.8
MOUNT PLEASANT, MI	34380	63,351	70,671	74,284	1.5	173	91.5	90.2	1.9	2.1	1.4	2.1
MOUNT PLEASANT, TX	34420	28,118	29,666	30,438	0.7	444	70.1	66.0	10.7	10.8	0.5	0.5
MOUNT STERLING, KY	34460	40,195	43,488	45,832	1.1	288	96.0	95.5	2.7	2.8	0.1	0.1
MOUNT VERNON, IL	34500	48,666	48,993	49,269	0.1	723	91.4	90.0	6.6	7.4	0.4	0.5
MOUNT VERNON, OH	34540	54,500	60,216	64,113	1.4	196	97.7	96.5	0.7	1.5	0.4	0.5
MOUNT VERNON-ANAC,WA	34580	102,979	117,229	128,434	1.8	127	86.5	84.3	0.4	0.5	1.7	1.9
MUNCIE, IN	34620	118,769	117,432	115,386	-0.2	841	90.7	89.4	6.7	7.5	0.7	1.0
MURRAY, KY	34660	34,177	35,186	35,897	0.4	590	93.5	92.4	3.6	3.7	1.4	2.0
MUSCATINE, IA	34700	53,905	55,751	57,194	0.5	545	91.4	88.9	0.6	0.7	0.7	1.0
MUSKGN-NORTON SHORES	34740	170,200	177,180	181,580	0.6	494	81.3	79.3	14.2	15.4	0.4	0.6
MUSKOGEE, OK	34780	69,451	72,111	73,916	0.5	545	63.7	61.1	13.2	13.7	0.6	0.8
MYRTLE BEACH-CONWAY	34820	196,629	243,477	288,859	3.0	38	81.0	79.6	15.5	15.8	0.8	1.1
NACOGDOCHES, TX	34860	59,203	61,984	64,090	0.6	494	75.0	71.9	16.7	17.8	0.8	0.9
NAPA, CA	34900	124,279	137,087	145,262	1.4	196	80.0	75.2	1.3	1.7	3.2	3.8
NAPLES-MARCO ISL, FL	34940	251,377	337,239	405,519	4.1	11	86.1	82.7	4.5	5.1	0.7	0.9
NASHVILLE-DAVIDSONTN	34980	1,311,789	1,507,461	1,667,065	1.9	113	80.4	79.1	14.8	14.9	1.6	2.1
NATCHEZ, MS-LA	35020	54,587	52,182	50,572	-0.6	921	51.5	48.6	47.2	49.8	0.3	0.3
NATCHITOCHES, LA	35060	39,080	39,993	41,140	0.3	633	57.9	53.4	38.4	42.2	0.5	0.6
NEW BERN, NC	35100	114,751	118,577	121,853	0.5	545	69.5	67.9	26.0	26.3	0.9	1.2
NEWBERRY, SC	35140	36,108	37,411	38,147	0.5	545	64.0	62.7	33.1	33.5	0.4	0.5
NEW CASTLE, IN	35220	48,508	47,216	46,063	-0.4	896	98.0	97.6	0.9	1.0	0.2	0.3
NEW CASTLE, PA	35260	94,643	92,154	90,363	-0.4	896	95.0	94.1	3.6	4.2	0.3	0.4
NEW HAVEN-MILFORD,CT	35300	824,008	852,576	870,874	0.5	545	79.4	76.3	11.3	12.1	2.4	3.4
NEW IBERIA, LA	35340	73,266	75,691	77,506	0.5	545	65.1	60.6	30.8	34.1	2.0	2.7
NEW ORLEANS-METAIRIE	35380	1,316,510	1,084,072	1,134,222	-2.6	939	57.4	60.2	37.4	33.3	2.2	2.9
NEW PHILADELPHIA, OH	35420	90,914	92,808	94,040	0.3	633	97.9	97.1	0.7	1.2	0.3	0.5
NEWPORT, TN	35460	33,565	35,508	36,920	0.8	396	96.2	95.6	2.0	2.2	0.2	0.2
NEWTON, IA	35500	37,213	37,379	37,444	0.1	723	97.6	97.0	0.8	0.9	0.5	0.7
NEW ULM, MN	35580	26,911	26,699	26,201	-0.1	805	97.8	96.3	0.1	0.8	0.4	0.6
NEW YORK-NO N.J.-LI	35620	18,323,002	19,113,887	19,660,235	0.6	494	61.6	58.7	18.2	18.3	7.5	9.0
NILES-BENTON HBOR,MI	35660	162,453	164,065	165,329	0.1	723	79.7	77.5	15.9	17.2	1.2	1.7
NOGALES, AZ	35700	38,381	46,628	53,595	2.7	51	76.0	75.1	0.4	0.4	0.6	0.6
NORFOLK, NE	35740	49,538	49,976	49,962	0.1	723	93.2	91.5	0.7	0.8	0.4	0.5
NORTH PLATTE, NE	35820	35,939	37,368	38,420	0.5	545	94.8	93.4	0.5	0.6	0.4	0.6
UNITED STATES					1.2		75.1	72.7	12.3	12.6	3.8	4.5

87-A

POPULATION COMPOSITION
CBSA AND U.S. TOTALS

B

CBSA	% HISPANIC ORIGIN		2007 AGE DISTRIBUTION (%)										MEDIAN AGE	% 2007 Males	% 2007 Females
	2000	2007	0-4	5-9	10-14	15-19	20-24	25-44	45-64	65-84	85+	18+	2007		
MCCOMB, MS	0.8	0.9	7.3	6.9	7.0	6.1	7.2	25.0	26.3	12.3	2.1	75.4	37.6	47.7	52.3
MCMINNVILLE, TN	4.9	6.9	6.7	6.5	6.1	5.9	5.7	28.8	26.3	12.3	1.8	77.2	38.4	49.6	50.4
MCPHERSON, KS	1.9	2.7	6.2	5.4	5.8	8.3	9.1	21.9	26.7	12.9	3.6	78.0	39.8	49.0	51.0
MEADVILLE, PA	0.6	0.7	6.0	5.7	6.3	7.5	7.0	24.3	27.8	13.0	2.5	78.0	40.2	48.9	51.1
MEDFORD, OR	6.7	9.0	6.1	5.6	6.3	6.9	6.5	23.8	29.8	12.5	2.5	77.8	41.0	48.8	51.2
MEMPHIS, TN-MS-AR	2.4	3.1	7.5	7.1	7.5	7.3	6.8	28.1	25.2	9.1	1.4	73.5	35.0	48.3	51.7
MENOMONIE, WI	0.8	1.1	6.0	5.5	5.4	9.4	14.6	24.7	23.7	8.8	1.9	79.3	32.0	50.5	49.5
MERCED, CA	45.3	51.2	9.5	7.7	8.8	8.9	9.0	27.0	20.0	8.0	1.2	68.4	28.9	50.2	49.8
MERIDIAN, MS	1.0	1.3	7.1	6.6	6.8	6.9	6.9	26.4	24.9	11.9	2.5	75.6	36.8	48.0	52.0
MERRILL, WI	0.8	1.1	6.0	5.5	6.2	7.2	6.6	23.9	28.3	13.4	2.8	77.4	41.3	50.3	49.7
MEXICO, MO	0.7	0.9	6.6	6.0	6.1	6.1	6.4	27.3	25.4	13.0	3.1	77.5	39.3	45.5	54.5
MIAMI, OK	3.2	4.1	6.8	6.3	6.4	7.6	6.9	23.8	25.5	14.3	2.5	76.4	38.9	48.9	51.1
MIAMI-FORT LAUDER.FL	34.0	39.6	6.3	6.1	6.5	6.6	6.1	27.1	24.8	13.4	3.1	77.1	39.5	48.3	51.7
MICHIGAN C-LA PORTE	3.1	4.1	6.5	6.1	6.3	6.3	7.0	27.0	27.2	11.8	1.9	77.5	38.7	50.9	49.1
MIDDLESBOROUGH, KY	0.6	1.0	6.2	6.1	5.7	6.2	6.0	27.6	28.0	12.5	1.8	78.2	39.8	48.2	51.8
MIDLAND, MI	1.6	1.9	6.4	6.0	7.3	7.5	7.1	25.4	27.5	11.0	1.9	75.9	38.8	49.1	50.9
MIDLAND, TX	29.0	35.1	7.8	6.9	7.3	8.2	9.0	23.6	25.5	10.3	1.5	73.1	34.2	48.4	51.6
MILLEDGEVILLE, GA	1.2	1.5	5.3	4.9	5.5	7.8	9.0	30.6	25.0	10.6	1.5	80.4	36.2	54.0	46.0
MILWAUKEE-WAUKESHA	6.3	7.5	6.8	6.5	6.9	7.4	7.1	26.6	26.0	10.5	2.1	75.3	37.1	48.5	51.5
MINDEN, LA	0.9	0.9	6.8	6.4	5.8	6.6	6.5	25.0	26.5	14.0	2.4	77.0	40.1	48.3	51.7
MINERAL WELLS, TX	13.6	17.4	7.0	6.2	6.1	6.7	6.2	24.0	27.7	13.9	2.3	76.6	40.4	49.6	50.4
MINNEAPOLIS-ST. PAUL	3.3	4.2	7.2	7.0	7.1	7.1	6.6	29.9	25.1	8.3	1.6	74.4	35.7	49.4	50.6
MINOT, ND	1.7	2.4	7.3	6.3	5.9	7.1	9.4	27.0	23.4	11.1	2.6	76.7	34.4	50.0	50.0
MISSOULA, MT	1.6	2.0	5.7	5.1	5.5	7.5	11.2	28.4	26.3	8.6	1.6	80.0	34.0	49.9	50.1
MITCHELL, SD	0.6	0.8	7.0	6.2	6.6	7.6	8.2	25.2	24.2	12.1	3.0	76.1	36.5	49.2	50.8
MOBERLY, MO	1.1	1.4	6.6	5.9	6.1	6.1	7.2	28.1	25.6	12.0	2.4	77.8	38.2	51.9	48.1
MOBILE, AL	1.2	1.6	7.5	6.9	7.1	7.0	6.8	27.0	25.3	10.7	1.6	74.3	35.7	48.0	52.0
MODESTO, CA	31.7	37.6	8.5	7.3	8.1	8.3	7.9	27.8	22.3	8.4	1.5	71.0	31.6	49.3	50.7
MONROE, LA	1.3	1.5	7.5	7.0	6.9	7.3	7.4	27.5	23.7	11.1	1.7	74.5	34.4	47.6	52.4
MONROE, MI	2.1	2.7	6.6	6.4	7.0	7.4	6.3	26.4	28.0	10.4	1.5	75.3	38.3	49.7	50.3
MONROE, WI	1.0	1.3	6.5	6.3	6.8	6.8	6.4	24.9	28.0	11.5	2.6	75.9	40.2	49.5	50.5
MONTGOMERY, AL	1.2	1.7	6.9	6.6	6.8	7.4	7.4	28.1	24.9	10.3	1.6	75.5	35.6	48.5	51.5
MONTROSE, CO	14.9	17.6	6.9	6.4	6.7	6.1	7.1	22.1	29.3	13.2	2.3	76.0	40.8	49.3	50.7
MOREHEAD CITY, NC	1.7	2.2	4.9	4.9	5.1	5.4	4.8	24.0	32.7	16.2	1.9	81.7	45.4	49.3	50.7
MORGAN CITY, LA	2.2	2.4	7.8	7.1	7.5	7.0	7.1	26.3	25.3	10.6	1.3	73.2	36.0	48.9	51.1
MORGANTOWN, WV	0.9	1.0	5.0	4.7	4.9	7.8	12.5	28.1	24.9	10.4	1.7	82.6	35.0	50.9	49.1
MORRISTOWN, TN	3.3	4.6	6.4	6.3	6.1	5.7	5.7	28.7	26.8	12.8	1.5	77.9	39.1	49.8	50.2
MOSCOW, ID	2.1	2.4	5.4	4.5	4.9	11.2	16.8	25.8	21.8	7.7	1.8	82.0	28.7	51.9	48.1
MOSES LAKE, WA	30.1	35.7	9.3	8.2	7.8	7.8	7.7	26.0	22.4	9.2	1.5	69.9	31.5	51.1	48.9
MOULTRIE, GA	10.8	14.5	7.9	7.6	6.6	6.5	7.0	28.8	23.2	10.5	1.8	74.1	34.7	50.1	49.9
MOUNTAIN HOME, AR	1.0	1.4	4.5	4.2	4.8	5.0	5.3	19.1	30.7	22.7	3.7	83.4	50.4	48.4	51.6
MOUNTAIN HOME, ID	12.0	13.5	8.7	7.1	5.7	6.7	12.3	33.7	17.7	7.0	1.0	74.8	29.7	54.7	45.3
MOUNT AIRY, NC	6.5	8.7	6.3	6.3	6.4	5.8	5.0	28.1	26.5	13.4	2.2	77.4	39.8	49.4	50.6
MOUNT PLEASANT, MI	2.2	2.7	5.3	4.6	4.9	13.2	19.8	22.3	20.3	8.2	1.3	81.9	26.5	47.9	52.1
MOUNT PLEASANT, TX	28.3	34.3	9.1	8.1	7.4	7.5	6.8	28.4	21.0	9.6	2.0	70.9	32.6	49.9	50.1
MOUNT STERLING, KY	1.0	1.5	6.8	6.7	6.3	5.9	5.3	28.5	27.2	11.5	1.8	76.6	38.5	49.4	50.6
MOUNT VERNON, IL	1.2	1.6	6.0	5.6	6.1	6.4	6.4	26.4	27.2	13.1	2.7	78.5	39.9	50.8	49.2
MOUNT VERNON, OH	0.7	0.8	6.3	5.9	6.6	8.0	8.3	23.5	26.9	12.4	2.0	77.7	38.6	49.0	51.0
MOUNT VERNON-ANAC,WA	11.2	14.0	6.7	6.1	6.8	7.1	7.2	24.3	27.6	11.9	2.4	76.2	39.0	49.6	50.4
MUNCIE, IN	1.1	1.5	5.8	5.4	5.5	9.1	12.2	24.0	23.9	12.1	2.1	79.8	34.9	48.2	51.8
MURRAY, KY	1.4	2.0	5.0	4.7	4.5	8.2	13.1	24.6	24.3	13.2	2.4	83.0	36.4	48.4	51.6
MUSCATINE, IA	12.1	15.6	7.3	6.8	7.0	6.6	6.6	27.0	26.2	10.5	2.1	74.9	37.2	49.7	50.3
MUSKGN-NORTON SHORES	3.5	4.3	7.0	6.4	7.0	7.1	6.8	26.6	26.2	10.8	2.0	75.1	37.1	49.6	50.4
MUSKOGEE, OK	2.7	3.3	7.2	6.6	6.4	6.3	7.1	25.5	25.8	12.5	2.5	76.1	37.8	48.6	51.4
MYRTLE BEACH-CONWAY	2.6	3.5	5.9	5.4	5.6	5.7	5.7	28.8	26.6	15.0	1.3	79.8	40.3	49.1	50.9
NACOGDOCHES, TX	11.2	14.3	6.7	6.2	5.8	9.4	12.9	25.3	21.8	10.1	1.9	77.7	30.5	48.3	51.7
NAPA, CA	23.7	29.4	5.9	5.9	6.8	6.9	6.6	25.1	27.6	12.4	2.9	77.2	39.8	50.3	49.7
NAPLES-MARCO ISL, FL	19.6	26.6	5.4	5.1	5.2	4.8	4.8	21.7	26.8	23.2	3.0	81.3	47.3	49.7	50.3
NASHVILLE-DAVIDSONTN	3.1	4.2	6.9	6.7	6.5	6.8	7.0	30.0	25.7	9.2	1.4	76.2	36.2	49.2	50.8
NATCHEZ, MS-LA	1.0	1.2	7.1	6.5	6.6	6.4	7.1	23.0	27.6	13.5	2.1	75.9	39.8	47.5	52.5
NATCHITOCHES, LA	1.4	1.6	7.5	6.8	6.0	9.4	10.6	25.2	22.7	10.1	1.8	76.0	31.2	47.9	52.1
NEW BERN, NC	3.6	4.6	6.8	5.9	6.0	6.2	8.2	25.4	26.1	13.8	1.7	78.0	38.4	50.2	49.8
NEWBERRY, SC	4.2	5.6	6.6	6.4	5.9	6.6	6.5	27.0	27.1	11.7	2.2	77.5	39.0	48.9	51.1
NEW CASTLE, IN	0.8	1.1	6.3	6.1	6.2	6.1	5.6	26.2	27.5	13.8	2.3	77.6	40.8	48.5	51.5
NEW CASTLE, PA	0.6	0.7	5.6	5.5	6.0	6.7	6.3	23.0	28.2	15.4	3.4	79.0	42.6	47.9	52.1
NEW HAVEN-MILFORD,CT	10.1	12.3	6.2	6.2	6.8	7.7	6.6	25.7	26.4	11.5	2.8	76.3	38.9	48.2	51.8
NEW IBERIA, LA	1.5	1.7	8.3	7.8	7.1	7.2	6.8	27.0	24.4	9.8	1.6	72.4	34.7	48.3	51.7
NEW ORLEANS-METAIRIE	4.4	5.4	6.9	6.6	6.8	6.9	7.2	27.4	26.6	10.2	1.5	75.6	36.7	48.2	51.8
NEW PHILADELPHIA, OH	0.7	0.9	6.7	6.5	6.2	6.3	6.2	25.6	27.7	12.4	2.3	76.8	39.6	49.2	50.8
NEWPORT, TN	1.1	1.5	6.0	5.9	5.8	5.4	5.2	27.9	29.1	13.2	1.5	79.1	40.8	48.8	51.2
NEWTON, IA	1.0	1.3	6.3	5.9	6.6	6.2	6.3	25.7	26.9	13.4	2.7	77.2	40.4	50.7	49.3
NEW ULM, MN	2.0	3.0	5.8	5.3	5.8	8.3	8.3	23.0	27.2	13.1	3.3	78.6	40.4	49.7	50.3
NEW YORK-NO N.J.-LI	19.5	21.5	6.7	6.6	7.3	6.9	6.0	29.1	24.8	10.7	1.9	75.2	37.0	48.2	51.8
NILES-BENTON HBOR,MI	3.0	3.7	6.6	6.0	6.7	7.1	7.2	24.0	27.7	12.3	2.2	76.4	39.5	48.7	51.3
NOGALES, AZ	80.8	84.2	9.1	8.6	9.0	8.2	6.1	25.3	22.7	9.5	1.1	68.0	31.9	48.2	51.8
NORFOLK, NE	6.6	8.7	7.2	6.3	6.5	7.5	8.4	24.8	25.2	11.1	2.8	75.8	36.7	50.0	50.0
NORTH PLATTE, NE	5.3	7.1	6.8	6.0	6.5	6.5	7.9	23.4	28.1	12.3	2.4	76.0	39.3	49.4	50.6
UNITED STATES	12.5	15.0	6.9	6.5	6.8	7.1	7.0	27.6	25.4	10.7	1.9	75.6	36.7	49.2	50.8

HOUSEHOLDS
CBSA AND U.S. TOTALS

CBSA	HOUSEHOLDS					FAMILIES			MEDIAN HOUSEHOLD INCOME		
	2000	2007	2012	% Annual Rate 2000-2007	2007 Average HH Size	2000	2007	% Annual Rate 2000-2007	2007	2012	2007 National Rank
MCCOMB, MS	20,063	21,076	21,658	0.7	2.51	14,380	14,768	0.4	27,924	30,434	921
MCMINNVILLE, TN	15,181	16,136	16,710	0.8	2.43	10,821	11,210	0.5	38,407	44,786	723
MCPHERSON, KS	11,205	11,723	12,072	0.6	2.48	7,968	8,235	0.5	51,229	59,734	214
MEADVILLE, PA	34,678	35,540	35,635	0.3	2.45	23,871	23,763	-0.1	41,186	47,172	599
MEDFORD, OR	71,532	81,008	87,723	1.7	2.48	48,423	54,343	1.6	45,911	53,299	388
MEMPHIS, TN-MS-AR	448,473	494,283	525,942	1.4	2.60	312,343	337,012	1.1	50,260	58,859	241
MENOMONIE, WI	14,337	16,295	17,451	1.8	2.50	9,265	10,255	1.4	46,350	52,037	373
MERCED, CA	63,815	76,744	87,783	2.6	3.29	49,760	60,025	2.6	44,062	51,339	463
MERIDIAN, MS	40,877	41,743	41,937	0.3	2.45	28,380	28,295	0.0	32,660	35,327	882
MERRILL, WI	11,721	12,481	12,888	0.9	2.38	8,230	8,568	0.6	47,355	53,301	341
MEXICO, MO	9,844	9,738	9,607	-0.1	2.39	6,758	6,498	-0.5	39,343	44,504	679
MIAMI, OK	12,984	13,202	13,340	0.2	2.49	9,121	9,102	0.0	33,573	38,466	870
MIAMI-FORT LAUDER.FL	1,905,394	2,112,825	2,262,946	1.4	2.61	1,263,668	1,374,415	1.2	50,983	60,758	219
MICHIGAN C-LA PORTE	41,050	42,637	43,555	0.5	2.48	28,597	28,605	0.0	51,588	60,402	204
MIDDLESBOROUGH, KY	12,004	12,307	12,337	0.3	2.34	8,522	8,437	-0.1	23,621	27,001	937
MIDLAND, MI	31,769	33,680	34,631	0.8	2.49	22,691	23,452	0.5	54,780	62,426	128
MIDLAND, TX	42,745	45,514	47,262	0.9	2.65	30,935	32,610	0.7	49,274	57,343	279
MILLEDGEVILLE, GA	17,995	19,366	20,256	1.0	2.47	12,154	12,616	0.5	39,848	45,900	656
MILWAUKEE-WAUKESHA	587,657	615,127	628,551	0.6	2.44	381,319	391,140	0.4	58,998	69,422	75
MINDEN, LA	16,501	16,833	16,984	0.3	2.43	11,559	11,486	-0.1	31,042	33,390	902
MINERAL WELLS, TX	10,594	10,925	11,118	0.4	2.50	7,443	7,593	0.3	38,092	43,949	737
MINNEAPOLIS-ST. PAUL	1,136,615	1,284,424	1,389,675	1.7	2.53	744,303	825,243	1.4	71,394	86,198	14
MINOT, ND	26,652	26,806	26,762	0.1	2.37	17,820	17,224	-0.5	42,006	49,851	555
MISSOULA, MT	38,439	42,476	45,485	1.4	2.38	23,145	24,689	0.9	41,804	48,103	572
MITCHELL, SD	8,700	9,246	9,596	0.8	2.40	5,621	5,929	0.7	43,526	52,124	493
MOBERLY, MO	9,199	9,455	9,597	0.4	2.40	6,234	6,223	0.0	38,480	44,205	720
MOBILE, AL	150,179	154,868	158,178	0.4	2.59	106,745	108,066	0.2	38,640	42,480	706
MODESTO, CA	145,146	168,543	185,166	2.1	3.09	109,517	127,613	2.1	49,943	58,444	255
MONROE, LA	64,073	66,657	68,532	0.5	2.54	44,731	45,324	0.2	35,413	38,517	825
MONROE, MI	53,772	59,505	62,846	1.4	2.61	39,933	43,187	1.1	61,591	69,577	51
MONROE, WI	13,212	14,809	15,904	1.6	2.45	9,215	10,094	1.3	52,705	60,862	171
MONTGOMERY, AL	129,717	139,102	145,649	1.0	2.48	90,290	95,459	0.8	43,167	47,795	506
MONTROSE, CO	13,043	15,706	17,720	2.6	2.51	9,311	10,981	2.3	42,207	47,422	544
MOREHEAD CITY, NC	25,204	28,101	30,114	1.5	2.26	17,376	18,872	1.1	48,161	55,647	307
MORGAN CITY, LA	19,317	19,482	19,267	0.1	2.66	14,090	13,874	-0.2	31,556	34,442	900
MORGANTOWN, WV	44,990	47,659	49,404	0.8	2.29	26,857	27,341	0.2	34,643	39,247	845
MORRISTOWN, TN	48,636	54,068	57,808	1.5	2.43	35,374	38,409	1.1	39,985	46,150	650
MOSCOW, ID	13,059	13,910	14,426	0.9	2.33	7,764	8,129	0.6	42,726	51,235	519
MOSES LAKE, WA	25,204	27,417	29,250	1.2	2.98	18,674	20,071	1.0	44,229	51,782	454
MOULTRIE, GA	15,495	16,433	17,056	0.8	2.61	11,066	11,371	0.4	33,993	38,574	861
MOUNTAIN HOME, AR	17,052	18,621	19,677	1.2	2.18	11,792	12,490	0.8	37,274	44,645	767
MOUNTAIN HOME, ID	9,092	9,672	9,983	0.9	2.71	6,848	7,209	0.7	43,808	51,083	484
MOUNT AIRY, NC	28,408	29,508	30,290	0.5	2.46	20,484	20,783	0.2	40,319	45,348	640
MOUNT PLEASANT, MI	22,425	25,800	27,604	2.0	2.48	13,014	14,427	1.4	40,959	45,941	615
MOUNT PLEASANT, TX	9,552	9,940	10,136	0.6	2.92	7,150	7,373	0.4	38,609	43,816	713
MOUNT STERLING, KY	15,884	17,753	18,945	1.5	2.41	11,529	12,465	1.1	35,420	40,927	824
MOUNT VERNON, IL	18,836	19,144	19,329	0.2	2.42	12,995	12,833	-0.2	38,742	43,416	702
MOUNT VERNON, OH	19,975	22,350	23,936	1.6	2.53	14,364	15,634	1.2	47,550	53,884	330
MOUNT VERNON-ANAC,WA	38,852	43,951	48,064	1.7	2.62	27,343	30,509	1.5	53,626	63,618	145
MUNCIE, IN	47,131	47,270	46,769	0.0	2.31	29,686	28,447	-0.6	43,604	50,723	491
MURRAY, KY	13,862	14,671	15,122	0.8	2.19	8,594	8,691	0.2	37,925	45,000	742
MUSCATINE, IA	20,366	21,410	22,073	0.7	2.56	14,609	15,100	0.5	51,549	61,037	205
MUSKGN-NORTON SHORES	63,330	66,890	68,963	0.8	2.56	44,298	45,553	0.4	46,321	52,661	375
MUSKOGEE, OK	26,458	27,805	28,689	0.7	2.47	18,463	19,028	0.4	35,347	40,648	830
MYRTLE BEACH-CONWAY	81,800	105,211	126,543	3.5	2.29	54,515	67,396	3.0	45,374	52,622	418
NACOGDOCHES, TX	22,006	23,201	24,062	0.7	2.48	14,039	14,613	0.6	35,118	40,489	832
NAPA, CA	45,402	49,884	52,768	1.3	2.64	30,694	33,878	1.4	65,907	77,532	30
NAPLES-MARCO ISL, FL	102,973	137,076	165,065	4.0	2.43	71,264	93,209	3.8	61,221	72,378	54
NASHVILLE-DAVIDSONTN	510,222	594,722	660,258	2.1	2.47	344,257	394,179	1.9	55,986	67,103	113
NATCHEZ, MS-LA	21,198	20,847	20,430	-0.2	2.45	14,836	14,235	-0.6	27,377	29,800	925
NATCHITOCHES, LA	14,263	15,164	15,780	0.8	2.50	9,503	9,812	0.4	28,611	31,030	916
NEW BERN, NC	43,821	47,160	49,072	1.0	2.40	31,716	33,338	0.7	43,826	50,570	483
NEWBERRY, SC	14,026	14,947	15,400	0.9	2.43	9,809	10,088	0.4	40,790	46,901	622
NEW CASTLE, IN	19,486	19,387	19,048	-0.1	2.40	13,975	13,423	-0.6	47,603	55,317	326
NEW CASTLE, PA	37,091	36,521	36,006	-0.2	2.44	25,886	24,779	-0.6	41,979	49,757	557
NEW HAVEN-MILFORD,CT	319,040	330,851	338,989	0.5	2.49	210,687	216,763	0.4	61,558	72,642	52
NEW IBERIA, LA	25,381	26,455	27,249	0.6	2.80	19,165	19,552	0.3	34,551	37,691	848
NEW ORLEANS-METAIRIE	498,587	407,112	427,135	-2.8	2.61	335,595	273,833	-2.8	42,453	46,463	528
NEW PHILADELPHIA, OH	35,653	36,488	37,084	0.3	2.51	25,315	25,173	-0.1	43,108	49,292	508
NEWPORT, TN	13,762	14,967	15,746	1.2	2.35	9,720	10,300	0.8	30,630	35,191	905
NEWTON, IA	14,689	15,033	15,163	0.3	2.37	10,265	10,321	0.1	51,298	60,053	213
NEW ULM, MN	10,598	10,705	10,585	0.1	2.38	7,164	7,026	-0.3	49,460	57,417	269
NEW YORK-NO N.J.-LI	6,676,963	6,919,927	7,114,197	0.5	2.70	4,494,086	4,630,044	0.4	65,073	78,148	31
NILES-BENTON HBOR,MI	63,569	65,467	66,511	0.4	2.44	43,336	43,383	0.0	46,790	53,296	358
NOGALES, AZ	11,809	14,511	16,775	2.9	3.20	9,511	11,595	2.8	37,187	43,336	771
NORFOLK, NE	18,712	19,081	19,144	0.3	2.54	12,821	12,924	0.1	42,617	48,412	525
NORTH PLATTE, NE	14,594	15,497	16,073	0.8	2.37	9,832	10,311	0.7	44,350	50,763	452
UNITED STATES				1.2	2.59			1.0	53,154	62,503	

CBSA	2007 Per Capita Income	2007 HH Income Base	2007 HOUSEHOLD INCOME DISTRIBUTION (%)					2007 Home Value Base	2007 HOME VALUE DISTRIBUTION (%)					2007 Median Home Value
			Less than $25,000	$25,000 to $49,999	$50,000 to $99,999	$100,000 to $149,999	$150,000 or More		Less than $50,000	$50,000 to $89,999	$90,000 to $174,999	$175,000 to $399,999	$400,000 or More	
MCCOMB, MS	16,290	21,076	45.3	29.3	19.3	3.8	2.3	16,258	29.5	31.3	27.0	10.0	2.3	74,013
MCMINNVILLE, TN	19,919	16,136	33.4	28.6	29.6	5.8	2.6	11,882	12.2	24.3	43.8	17.2	2.5	107,369
MCPHERSON, KS	24,033	11,723	19.2	29.0	39.6	8.8	3.4	8,842	10.8	20.4	49.8	17.7	1.3	117,337
MEADVILLE, PA	21,319	35,540	28.1	31.6	30.0	7.4	3.0	27,024	11.1	15.2	44.7	26.0	2.9	137,201
MEDFORD, OR	24,807	81,008	24.7	29.6	31.5	8.8	5.4	55,831	6.6	3.9	10.7	53.6	25.2	276,904
MEMPHIS, TN-MS-AR	25,755	494,282	24.1	25.6	32.6	11.0	6.7	332,946	9.3	25.3	38.1	23.1	4.2	113,727
MENOMONIE, WI	21,925	16,295	23.9	29.7	34.8	8.7	2.9	11,493	10.6	11.9	42.2	32.5	2.8	143,399
MERCED, CA	17,606	76,744	26.9	29.1	31.1	8.7	4.2	46,308	2.2	1.5	4.3	58.7	33.4	340,095
MERIDIAN, MS	17,860	41,743	39.8	28.8	23.9	5.2	2.3	30,091	26.4	30.5	31.0	10.4	1.8	79,885
MERRILL, WI	22,949	12,481	24.2	28.3	36.7	8.5	2.2	9,878	7.1	14.3	47.7	28.4	2.5	134,965
MEXICO, MO	20,128	9,738	29.0	32.5	29.5	6.8	2.2	7,363	18.8	24.5	37.4	17.0	2.3	100,489
MIAMI, OK	17,323	13,202	35.8	34.0	24.6	3.6	2.0	9,745	31.6	30.2	28.0	8.9	1.3	71,716
MIAMI-FORT LAUDER.FL	28,264	2,112,806	23.7	25.3	30.4	11.4	9.2	1,449,392	2.2	3.4	12.8	49.4	32.1	298,129
MICHIGAN C-LA PORTE	24,340	42,637	21.0	27.3	36.7	11.4	3.6	32,395	6.9	13.7	50.6	26.0	2.8	130,340
MIDDLESBOROUGH, KY	14,853	12,307	52.1	27.7	16.2	2.6	1.4	8,461	43.7	28.8	21.9	5.1	0.5	58,146
MIDLAND, MI	29,929	33,680	20.4	25.8	31.6	13.0	9.2	26,602	8.5	15.0	45.6	26.9	4.0	129,500
MIDLAND, TX	26,323	45,514	23.7	26.9	30.3	11.1	8.1	32,215	16.5	22.0	35.3	22.0	4.1	114,612
MILLEDGEVILLE, GA	21,005	19,366	31.8	28.0	28.0	7.4	4.7	13,317	22.1	24.1	35.9	15.2	2.8	95,820
MILWAUKEE-WAUKESHA	30,635	615,118	18.4	23.7	35.0	14.5	8.4	390,193	2.4	7.1	26.6	53.2	10.7	209,602
MINDEN, LA	17,646	16,833	40.6	30.9	21.7	4.8	2.1	12,408	27.7	28.8	31.6	10.2	1.7	79,829
MINERAL WELLS, TX	19,273	10,925	31.9	30.7	29.3	5.7	2.3	8,037	35.8	29.4	22.5	10.1	2.3	66,468
MINNEAPOLIS-ST. PAUL	35,445	1,284,424	12.2	20.2	37.2	17.9	12.6	958,962	2.3	2.1	18.2	61.9	15.5	242,442
MINOT, ND	21,971	26,806	26.1	32.6	31.1	7.1	3.1	17,648	20.5	19.1	43.3	15.7	1.4	105,936
MISSOULA, MT	22,318	42,476	29.2	29.4	30.4	7.6	3.4	26,336	9.3	4.7	12.7	58.1	15.1	239,902
MITCHELL, SD	23,045	9,246	27.1	29.8	31.9	7.5	3.8	6,086	17.6	24.9	40.5	15.3	1.8	101,822
MOBERLY, MO	19,354	9,455	30.4	32.5	29.2	6.0	1.9	6,957	28.5	28.1	29.1	12.1	2.1	77,737
MOBILE, AL	19,972	154,868	33.4	28.3	27.3	7.6	3.3	109,106	13.0	21.8	43.3	18.4	3.6	112,926
MODESTO, CA	20,789	168,542	23.8	26.2	33.6	10.9	5.5	107,002	2.7	1.7	3.1	52.5	40.0	366,373
MONROE, LA	19,497	66,657	36.0	28.6	24.9	7.3	3.2	43,928	23.8	23.8	35.4	14.9	2.1	94,107
MONROE, MI	27,860	59,504	16.8	22.6	37.9	16.4	6.2	48,494	7.9	7.2	37.1	43.1	4.6	170,209
MONROE, WI	25,853	14,809	18.3	28.0	39.8	9.6	4.2	11,181	3.8	7.6	45.0	38.0	5.6	161,870
MONTGOMERY, AL	22,694	139,102	28.3	28.4	29.3	9.7	4.3	100,037	14.1	21.3	39.8	20.7	4.0	113,649
MONTROSE, CO	20,730	15,706	27.4	31.3	31.6	7.4	2.3	12,161	10.7	7.4	33.5	39.6	8.7	170,670
MOREHEAD CITY, NC	26,857	28,101	25.1	26.8	34.0	9.3	4.9	21,864	12.6	11.1	32.1	33.5	10.6	154,280
MORGAN CITY, LA	15,621	19,482	41.2	28.4	23.7	5.3	1.4	14,259	26.1	19.9	40.2	12.0	1.8	98,181
MORGANTOWN, WV	20,119	47,659	37.9	27.6	24.3	6.8	3.4	32,835	17.8	14.8	33.5	29.1	4.8	133,143
MOSCOW, ID	22,974	13,910	29.7	27.2	30.3	9.4	3.5	8,391	13.6	6.3	25.6	46.8	7.7	188,269
MOSES LAKE, WA	18,649	27,417	25.7	31.6	30.9	8.0	3.8	19,116	6.9	6.6	34.5	45.1	6.9	178,641
MOULTRIE, GA	17,609	16,433	37.5	28.8	26.0	5.0	2.7	11,188	28.1	27.3	31.4	11.0	2.2	81,179
MOUNTAIN HOME, AR	22,063	18,621	30.9	35.5	25.5	5.0	3.1	15,052	13.3	18.8	43.5	21.8	2.6	118,200
MOUNTAIN HOME, ID	18,823	9,672	22.4	37.2	31.5	7.1	1.8	5,799	10.0	9.3	45.8	32.7	2.2	151,759
MOUNT AIRY, NC	21,018	29,508	30.6	31.6	28.4	6.2	3.2	22,809	16.2	18.0	41.2	21.7	2.9	116,323
MOUNT PLEASANT, MI	20,758	25,800	30.2	29.8	28.7	8.1	3.2	16,478	10.1	14.8	49.1	23.5	2.5	125,323
MOUNT PLEASANT, TX	18,334	9,940	32.4	29.8	26.5	7.9	3.4	7,329	23.6	30.3	30.7	13.1	2.3	85,648
MOUNT STERLING, KY	19,584	17,753	35.5	30.4	25.3	6.1	2.7	13,506	25.7	23.6	35.5	13.6	1.6	90,942
MOUNT VERNON, IL	20,276	19,144	31.3	30.9	28.9	6.4	2.4	14,863	23.1	21.1	39.1	15.1	1.6	98,661
MOUNT VERNON, OH	22,593	22,350	23.1	29.5	34.4	9.1	3.9	17,460	6.7	15.9	50.6	24.2	2.5	125,591
MOUNT VERNON-ANAC,WA	26,222	43,951	19.6	26.3	36.0	12.0	6.1	31,820	3.2	2.4	8.0	59.9	26.5	296,067
MUNCIE, IN	24,052	47,270	28.6	27.5	30.1	9.7	4.2	32,172	17.3	33.3	39.2	9.2	1.0	89,346
MURRAY, KY	22,162	14,671	31.7	32.0	25.4	7.5	3.4	10,078	18.7	19.3	42.4	17.3	2.4	106,383
MUSCATINE, IA	24,018	21,410	20.0	28.1	37.0	11.1	3.8	16,612	15.5	21.0	42.8	18.6	2.1	109,079
MUSKGN-NORTON SHORES	21,945	66,890	25.5	28.8	34.0	8.5	3.2	52,230	12.8	19.9	48.3	17.0	2.0	113,158
MUSKOGEE, OK	19,081	27,805	36.1	29.8	25.8	5.4	2.9	19,378	26.4	29.8	33.5	9.2	1.2	81,674
MYRTLE BEACH-CONWAY	25,516	105,211	22.9	32.1	32.4	8.1	4.5	78,189	10.1	9.9	28.9	41.5	9.7	178,232
NACOGDOCHES, TX	20,091	23,201	38.3	26.3	23.7	7.6	4.0	14,660	27.7	21.1	32.7	16.1	2.4	91,848
NAPA, CA	34,057	49,875	14.3	22.8	33.3	16.9	12.8	33,206	2.8	3.1	4.3	16.2	73.6	583,018
NAPLES-MARCO ISL, FL	38,689	137,076	15.0	24.9	32.3	14.2	13.6	106,893	1.7	1.7	5.3	36.6	54.7	434,526
NASHVILLE-DAVIDSONTN	29,370	594,720	19.3	24.7	35.8	12.4	7.8	406,923	4.6	7.4	38.9	39.1	10.0	172,910
NATCHEZ, MS-LA	16,666	20,847	46.1	28.7	18.8	4.0	2.4	15,020	25.6	31.9	30.8	9.4	2.2	79,273
NATCHITOCHES, LA	16,357	15,164	44.9	28.6	19.2	4.8	2.5	9,674	26.3	20.7	36.0	14.5	2.5	94,948
NEW BERN, NC	22,796	47,160	27.2	29.0	32.5	7.7	3.6	33,516	14.7	15.4	41.6	24.0	4.3	122,689
NEWBERRY, SC	20,539	14,947	30.4	29.8	29.1	7.9	2.7	11,660	19.3	23.6	36.4	17.8	2.9	102,737
NEW CASTLE, IN	24,316	19,387	23.3	29.3	33.7	10.2	3.5	15,081	10.8	24.3	48.5	14.8	1.6	109,608
NEW CASTLE, PA	21,755	36,521	29.5	29.1	30.3	7.7	3.4	28,338	10.7	17.7	41.0	27.3	3.2	137,723
NEW HAVEN-MILFORD,CT	32,277	330,850	19.2	21.9	32.0	15.9	11.0	219,317	0.9	1.5	12.1	61.1	24.5	283,854
NEW IBERIA, LA	16,400	26,450	38.2	28.3	25.1	5.9	2.6	19,268	21.8	22.3	38.9	15.0	2.1	100,462
NEW ORLEANS-METAIRIE	22,515	407,090	29.3	27.8	28.3	9.7	5.0	262,714	6.9	12.9	37.5	34.4	8.3	155,719
NEW PHILADELPHIA, OH	21,262	36,488	24.4	34.3	31.4	7.0	2.8	28,280	12.2	20.7	46.9	18.6	1.6	113,180
NEWPORT, TN	17,274	14,967	42.6	30.8	21.2	3.6	1.8	11,442	25.0	22.8	38.4	12.0	1.9	92,846
NEWTON, IA	24,616	15,033	19.9	28.4	39.4	9.2	3.2	11,663	8.9	18.5	50.0	20.9	1.8	116,571
NEW ULM, MN	24,868	10,705	21.4	29.2	37.5	8.3	3.6	8,715	8.0	13.6	45.6	29.3	3.4	147,382
NEW YORK-NO N.J.-LI	34,906	6,919,751	20.1	19.1	29.8	15.2	15.7	3,699,474	1.1	1.0	4.0	38.1	55.8	433,590
NILES-BENTON HBOR,MI	24,818	65,407	26.4	26.0	31.7	10.2	4.9	47,864	9.0	12.9	43.4	28.9	5.8	140,536
NOGALES, AZ	17,309	14,511	34.1	27.9	25.5	7.6	4.9	10,069	7.2	4.4	22.1	51.1	15.1	209,393
NORFOLK, NE	20,303	19,081	26.2	31.7	32.4	7.6	2.2	13,789	16.1	26.2	42.7	13.7	1.3	99,537
NORTH PLATTE, NE	23,043	15,497	26.4	29.8	32.3	8.4	3.1	11,183	17.4	24.7	41.6	14.3	1.9	100,925
UNITED STATES	27,916		21.9	25.0	32.3	12.3	8.4		7.9	10.5	27.1	35.6	19.0	192,285

CBSA	Auto Loan	Home Loan	Invest-ments	Retire-ment Plans	Home Repair	Lawn & Garden	Comput-ers & Hard-ware	Major Appli-ances	TV, Radio, Sound Equip-ment	Furni-ture	Dine out/ Carry out	Sports Equip-ment	Fees & Tickets	Toys & Games	Travel	Cable TV	Apparel & Services	Auto Repairs	Health Insur-ance	Pets & Supplies
	FINANCIAL SERVICES				THE HOME						ENTERTAINMENT						PERSONAL			
MCCOMB, MS	68	49	34	47	53	69	51	62	59	50	58	55	45	60	50	63	50	59	68	67
MCMINNVILLE, TN	78	60	49	59	64	79	63	72	68	61	68	64	56	71	61	72	59	69	77	76
MCPHERSON, KS	90	79	80	80	82	93	81	87	85	79	83	76	78	87	82	88	73	84	94	89
MEADVILLE, PA	82	67	61	66	73	88	69	79	74	67	73	69	64	76	69	78	64	74	85	82
MEDFORD, OR	87	82	83	83	85	91	84	88	85	82	84	79	82	84	85	86	75	86	90	89
MEMPHIS, TN-MS-AR	96	90	91	93	87	90	92	90	94	93	94	82	91	95	90	95	85	93	93	92
MENOMONIE, WI	87	70	61	71	72	85	79	81	79	73	79	74	70	81	74	80	69	80	84	85
MERCED, CA	81	81	72	77	77	73	81	81	78	81	79	80	78	79	78	76	72	83	74	78
MERIDIAN, MS	70	54	46	54	56	69	57	64	64	56	63	57	52	64	56	67	55	63	70	68
MERRILL, WI	82	71	70	72	77	89	73	81	77	71	76	71	69	79	74	80	66	77	87	84
MEXICO, MO	78	60	54	60	66	82	65	74	72	61	69	65	58	73	64	76	60	70	84	77
MIAMI, OK	67	53	48	52	57	70	57	64	63	54	61	55	51	63	56	66	53	61	72	66
MIAMI-FORT LAUDER.FL	98	101	108	101	100	96	103	99	102	104	102	93	104	99	103	102	93	103	101	98
MICHIGAN C-LA PORTE	87	84	90	85	85	90	83	86	86	83	85	75	83	88	85	88	76	84	91	87
MIDDLESBOROUGH, KY	59	40	26	39	44	60	43	53	50	41	49	48	36	51	42	54	42	50	60	58
MIDLAND, MI	107	106	107	106	106	110	101	105	103	103	102	95	102	105	103	104	92	103	107	107
MIDLAND, TX	100	96	94	96	91	91	97	94	97	98	97	87	95	96	95	96	88	98	94	94
MILLEDGEVILLE, GA	83	69	63	69	69	80	74	77	79	72	78	69	69	78	72	81	69	77	82	80
MILWAUKEE-WAUKESHA	99	103	115	106	101	97	106	99	105	106	105	91	108	104	105	104	96	102	101	100
MINDEN, LA	68	53	44	52	56	70	55	63	61	54	60	55	50	62	54	65	52	61	70	67
MINERAL WELLS, TX	76	59	49	58	64	81	63	73	69	59	67	63	55	70	63	73	58	69	81	76
MINNEAPOLIS-ST. PAUL	121	131	137	133	126	117	128	121	123	130	124	114	132	125	127	120	114	123	116	121
MINOT, ND	78	65	65	67	66	74	74	74	75	69	75	67	68	76	71	76	66	75	78	75
MISSOULA, MT	76	69	72	71	68	71	79	73	76	73	76	68	73	75	74	75	68	75	73	74
MITCHELL, SD	83	69	72	71	73	83	77	80	80	72	78	71	71	81	75	82	68	79	86	82
MOBERLY, MO	72	60	60	60	63	73	64	68	68	61	67	60	59	69	63	71	58	66	76	70
MOBILE, AL	77	68	67	69	67	74	70	71	74	70	73	63	67	74	69	76	65	72	76	74
MODESTO, CA	89	92	87	89	88	84	90	89	87	90	88	86	89	87	89	85	80	90	84	87
MONROE, LA	75	63	60	64	63	72	67	69	71	66	70	62	63	71	65	73	62	70	74	72
MONROE, MI	99	107	114	107	107	104	98	101	99	102	99	91	104	101	103	99	90	99	101	102
MONROE, WI	92	87	90	87	91	98	85	92	88	85	87	80	84	91	87	90	77	87	96	94
MONTGOMERY, AL	85	77	74	78	76	82	78	79	81	78	80	71	76	81	77	82	71	80	83	82
MONTROSE, CO	81	67	57	66	71	86	69	79	72	66	71	69	63	73	69	75	62	74	83	82
MOREHEAD CITY, NC	94	80	69	79	86	103	79	93	84	78	83	81	74	84	82	88	72	88	99	96
MORGAN CITY, LA	66	52	42	51	53	66	53	60	59	53	58	53	48	60	52	63	51	58	66	64
MORGANTOWN, WV	74	57	52	58	59	70	70	68	70	62	70	63	61	69	64	70	61	69	71	71
MORRISTOWN, TN	83	65	51	63	69	85	66	77	72	64	71	68	59	75	65	76	62	72	82	82
MOSCOW, ID	79	64	65	67	64	70	85	73	80	73	80	70	74	78	74	77	71	78	73	75
MOSES LAKE, WA	83	75	68	73	75	81	75	80	77	74	76	73	71	78	74	77	68	79	81	81
MOULTRIE, GA	75	57	46	56	60	75	59	68	65	58	65	60	53	67	58	69	56	65	74	72
MOUNTAIN HOME, AR	72	63	58	60	68	82	62	75	67	61	66	62	59	64	66	72	56	71	83	75
MOUNTAIN HOME, ID	79	67	60	68	64	70	73	71	73	69	73	66	67	75	68	72	64	73	72	73
MOUNT AIRY, NC	85	65	52	63	69	88	67	78	73	64	72	69	59	75	66	77	62	74	85	83
MOUNT PLEASANT, MI	78	62	60	64	61	70	81	71	77	70	77	68	70	76	71	75	69	76	72	74
MOUNT PLEASANT, TX	83	71	60	69	69	79	71	76	73	71	75	68	67	76	69	78	66	75	80	79
MOUNT STERLING, KY	78	60	44	57	64	81	60	72	66	59	66	64	53	69	59	70	57	67	77	77
MOUNT VERNON, IL	78	62	53	61	66	82	64	74	70	62	69	64	58	71	64	74	59	70	81	77
MOUNT VERNON, OH	86	79	81	79	82	91	78	84	81	77	80	74	76	83	79	84	71	81	89	87
MOUNT VERNON-ANAC,WA	97	95	97	96	97	101	94	98	94	94	94	88	94	94	96	96	84	96	99	99
MUNCIE, IN	80	72	79	74	72	77	81	77	83	76	82	68	77	82	78	83	73	79	83	78
MURRAY, KY	78	59	54	60	63	77	72	73	73	64	72	66	62	72	66	74	63	72	77	76
MUSCATINE, IA	90	84	86	85	86	92	82	87	86	83	85	77	82	89	84	88	75	85	92	89
MUSKGN-NORTON SHORES	81	77	79	78	77	83	76	79	79	77	78	69	76	81	77	81	70	78	83	81
MUSKOGEE, OK	71	60	60	60	62	72	63	68	69	61	67	59	60	68	63	71	59	66	75	70
MYRTLE BEACH-CONWAY	88	77	72	77	77	87	79	84	81	78	81	74	75	80	79	84	71	83	88	86
NACOGDOCHES, TX	77	60	54	61	61	72	73	71	74	66	73	65	63	73	66	74	65	73	74	74
NAPA, CA	115	135	138	131	138	124	129	129	121	129	122	124	134	118	133	119	113	127	120	124
NAPLES-MARCO ISL, FL	127	132	142	130	137	125	124	136	127	128	126	117	129	117	136	132	112	134	146	133
NASHVILLE-DAVIDSONTN	105	100	99	102	97	99	102	100	102	102	102	92	100	104	99	102	92	101	100	102
NATCHEZ, MS-LA	64	50	44	50	52	65	52	59	59	52	58	51	48	59	52	63	50	58	66	62
NATCHITOCHES, LA	66	48	39	48	50	64	55	60	60	51	59	54	47	60	52	62	51	59	65	64
NEW BERN, NC	86	72	64	72	74	87	74	81	78	72	77	72	69	78	73	81	68	79	86	84
NEWBERRY, SC	82	62	47	61	67	85	65	76	71	63	70	68	57	74	64	75	61	72	82	81
NEW CASTLE, IN	86	77	79	77	81	91	77	84	83	77	81	72	76	85	79	86	71	80	91	86
NEW CASTLE, PA	76	71	76	70	75	84	70	77	75	70	74	66	70	75	73	79	65	73	85	78
NEW HAVEN-MILFORD,CT	101	115	129	115	116	105	114	109	112	115	112	101	120	110	116	111	105	110	107	107
NEW IBERIA, LA	72	59	52	58	60	71	60	66	65	59	64	58	56	66	59	68	56	64	71	70
NEW ORLEANS-METAIRIE	82	80	84	82	78	79	82	79	83	82	82	72	81	82	81	83	74	81	81	80
NEW PHILADELPHIA, OH	80	71	69	70	74	84	70	77	75	70	74	68	68	77	71	78	65	74	83	80
NEWPORT, TN	69	49	33	47	54	72	51	63	57	49	57	55	43	60	50	62	48	58	69	68
NEWTON, IA	87	80	82	80	84	92	79	86	83	78	82	75	78	86	81	85	72	82	91	88
NEW ULM, MN	89	82	82	82	86	95	79	87	83	80	82	76	78	86	82	86	73	83	93	90
NEW YORK-NO N.J.-LI	108	127	134	125	132	114	132	122	132	132	135	117	140	127	134	134	129	124	120	120
NILES-BENTON HBOR,MI	87	81	85	82	83	89	82	85	86	82	84	75	81	87	83	88	75	84	91	87
NOGALES, AZ	83	78	64	74	71	75	73	78	76	77	76	71	71	74	73	76	68	79	77	76
NORFOLK, NE	80	67	61	67	70	81	69	75	74	67	72	67	65	75	68	75	63	73	80	79
NORTH PLATTE, NE	82	72	71	72	75	84	73	79	77	72	76	70	70	79	73	79	67	76	84	81
UNITED STATES	100	100	100	100	100	100	100	100	100	100	100	100	100	100	100	100	100	100	100	100

POPULATION CHANGE
CBSA AND U.S. TOTALS

A

CBSA	CBSA Code	POPULATION 2000	2007	2012	2000-2007 ANNUAL RATE % Rate	National Rank	RACE (%) White 2000	White 2007	Black 2000	Black 2007	Asian/Pacific 2000	Asian/Pacific 2007
NORTH VERNON, IN	35860	27,554	28,684	29,416	0.6	494	97.5	97.0	0.7	0.8	0.3	0.4
NORTH WILKESBORO, NC	35900	65,632	69,182	71,759	0.7	444	93.0	91.8	4.2	4.3	0.4	0.5
NORWALK, OH	35940	59,487	60,889	61,936	0.3	633	96.0	95.3	1.0	1.1	0.3	0.4
NORWICH-N LONDON, CT	35980	259,088	271,317	279,062	0.6	494	87.0	84.4	5.3	5.9	2.0	3.0
OAK HARBOR, WA	36020	71,558	80,567	87,700	1.6	155	87.2	85.4	2.4	2.6	4.6	5.3
OAK HILL, WV	36060	47,579	47,901	48,079	0.1	723	92.7	92.4	5.6	5.7	0.3	0.5
OCALA, FL	36100	258,916	328,656	389,684	3.3	26	84.2	81.0	11.5	13.5	0.7	1.0
OCEAN CITY, NJ	36140	102,326	105,752	108,398	0.5	545	91.6	89.9	5.1	5.7	0.7	1.0
OCEAN PINES, MD	36180	46,543	51,713	54,551	1.5	173	81.2	77.0	16.7	20.1	0.6	0.8
ODESSA, TX	36220	121,123	126,294	128,880	0.6	494	73.7	70.2	4.6	4.5	0.7	0.8
OGDEN-CLEARFIELD, UT	36260	442,656	518,302	573,882	2.2	85	90.3	89.0	1.2	1.4	1.6	1.9
OGDENSBURG-MASS., NY	36300	111,931	112,878	113,515	0.1	723	94.5	93.5	2.4	2.8	0.7	1.0
OIL CITY, PA	36340	57,565	56,728	56,205	-0.2	841	97.6	97.2	1.1	1.3	0.2	0.4
OKEECHOBEE, FL	36380	35,910	39,610	42,262	1.4	196	79.3	74.4	7.9	8.8	0.7	0.9
OKLAHOMA CITY, OK	36420	1,095,421	1,198,114	1,276,640	1.2	255	76.2	73.6	10.5	10.6	2.5	3.4
OLEAN, NY	36460	83,955	83,121	82,485	-0.1	805	94.6	93.5	1.1	1.5	0.5	0.6
OLYMPIA, WA	36500	207,355	237,813	261,954	1.9	113	85.7	83.8	2.4	2.5	4.9	5.6
OMAHA-COUNCIL BLUFFS	36540	767,054	842,715	902,199	1.3	225	86.1	84.1	7.8	8.1	1.5	2.2
ONEONTA, NY	36580	61,676	65,081	65,936	0.7	444	95.8	94.0	1.7	2.6	0.7	1.0
ONTARIO, OR-ID	36620	52,193	54,745	56,474	0.7	444	81.5	81.2	0.8	0.8	1.6	1.6
OPELOUSAS-EUNICE, LA	36660	87,700	91,014	93,378	0.5	545	56.5	52.1	42.1	46.3	0.2	0.3
ORANGEBURG, SC	36700	91,582	93,514	92,455	0.3	633	37.2	36.1	60.9	61.5	0.4	0.6
ORLANDO, FL	36740	1,644,561	2,098,102	2,490,290	3.4	22	75.0	71.2	13.9	14.9	2.8	3.4
OSHKOSH-NEENAH, WI	36780	156,763	164,189	167,637	0.6	494	94.9	93.6	1.1	1.4	1.9	2.6
OSKALOOSA, IA	36820	22,335	22,411	22,463	0.0	765	97.2	97.2	0.6	0.6	0.9	0.9
OTTAWA-STREATOR, IL	36860	153,098	156,525	159,157	0.3	633	95.5	94.4	1.2	1.4	0.5	0.7
OTTUMWA, IA	36900	36,051	36,371	36,704	0.1	723	96.3	95.3	0.9	1.1	0.7	1.0
OWATONNA, MN	36940	33,680	37,113	39,722	1.3	225	95.2	93.8	1.1	1.3	0.9	1.2
OWENSBORO, KY	36980	109,875	112,941	114,469	0.4	590	94.5	93.8	3.7	3.9	0.4	0.6
OWOSSO, MI	37020	71,687	74,431	76,408	0.5	545	97.4	96.9	0.2	0.2	0.3	0.4
OXFORD, MS	37060	38,744	43,019	46,261	1.5	173	71.9	69.5	25.0	26.4	1.7	2.4
OXNARD-TH OAKS-VENT.	37100	753,197	827,163	874,025	1.3	225	69.9	65.0	1.9	2.0	5.6	6.3
PADUCAH, KY-IL	37140	98,765	97,571	96,793	-0.2	841	89.5	88.7	8.3	8.7	0.4	0.6
PAHRUMP, NV	37220	32,485	42,728	52,061	3.9	13	89.6	88.3	1.2	1.3	1.1	1.1
PALATKA, FL	37260	70,423	76,969	82,104	1.2	255	77.9	73.7	17.0	19.6	0.5	0.6
PALESTINE, TX	37300	55,109	56,842	57,977	0.4	590	66.4	62.8	23.5	24.6	0.5	0.5
PALM BAY-MELB-TITUS	37340	476,230	557,320	623,285	2.2	85	86.8	84.0	8.4	9.9	1.6	2.1
PALM COAST, FL	37380	49,832	100,050	171,946	10.1	1	87.3	84.6	8.8	10.4	1.2	1.6
PAMPA, TX	37420	23,631	21,923	20,832	-1.0	936	82.7	79.6	5.6	6.0	0.4	0.5
PANAMA CITY-L HAVEN	37460	148,217	170,892	188,982	2.0	101	84.2	80.9	10.6	12.6	1.8	2.5
PARAGOULD, AR	37500	37,331	40,331	42,539	1.1	288	97.4	97.0	0.1	0.1	0.2	0.3
PARIS, TN	37540	31,115	32,134	32,685	0.4	590	89.2	88.0	9.0	9.7	0.3	0.4
PARIS, TX	37580	48,499	50,020	50,995	0.4	590	82.5	80.4	13.5	14.7	0.4	0.5
PARKERSBURG-MARIETTA	37620	164,624	163,283	162,159	-0.1	805	97.4	97.0	0.9	1.0	0.5	0.7
PARSONS, KS	37660	22,835	22,423	22,189	-0.3	873	89.3	88.1	4.7	5.0	0.3	0.5
PASCAGOULA, MS	37700	150,564	160,177	166,832	0.9	352	77.1	75.2	19.3	20.3	1.4	2.0
PAYSON, AZ	37740	51,335	53,308	54,618	0.5	545	77.8	75.9	0.4	0.4	0.5	0.6
PECOS, TX	37780	13,137	12,259	11,239	-0.9	932	79.3	78.0	2.1	1.9	0.4	0.4
PELLA, IA	37800	32,052	33,874	35,003	0.8	396	97.5	96.6	0.4	0.5	1.1	1.6
PENDLETON-HERMIS.,OR	37820	81,543	87,058	89,598	0.9	352	81.2	77.5	0.7	0.8	0.9	1.0
PENSACOLA-FERRY PASS	37860	412,153	462,147	504,251	1.6	155	77.6	74.6	16.5	18.2	2.1	2.7
PEORIA, IL	37900	366,899	375,672	382,227	0.3	633	88.5	87.1	8.4	9.2	1.1	1.4
PERU, IN	37940	36,082	35,092	34,271	-0.4	896	93.7	92.8	3.0	3.4	0.3	0.5
PHILADELPHIA-CAMDEN	37980	5,687,147	5,930,083	6,106,974	0.6	494	72.6	70.1	19.9	20.6	3.3	4.4
PHOENIX LK-CEDAR R.	38020	54,501	59,730	61,173	1.3	225	89.4	87.1	2.1	2.2	0.9	1.1
PHOENIX-MESA-SCOT,AZ	38060	3,251,876	4,163,757	4,974,097	3.5	18	77.0	74.0	3.7	3.8	2.2	2.6
PICAYUNE, MS	38100	48,621	54,522	58,319	1.6	155	85.6	84.1	12.2	13.0	0.3	0.4
PIERRE, SD	38180	19,253	19,932	20,280	0.5	545	89.5	87.4	0.2	0.2	0.4	0.6
PIERRE PART, LA	38200	23,388	23,850	24,184	0.3	633	67.2	63.1	31.5	35.2	0.3	0.3
PINE BLUFF, AR	38220	107,341	106,202	104,377	-0.1	805	53.6	51.1	44.4	46.6	0.6	0.7
PITTSBURG, KS	38260	38,242	38,542	38,774	0.1	723	93.3	92.1	1.8	2.0	1.2	1.7
PITTSBURGH, PA	38300	2,431,087	2,404,190	2,382,392	-0.2	841	89.8	88.2	7.9	8.8	1.1	1.5
PITTSFIELD, MA	38340	134,953	134,073	133,550	-0.1	805	95.0	93.9	2.0	2.3	1.0	1.4
PLAINVIEW, TX	38380	36,602	35,925	35,421	-0.3	873	66.8	62.9	5.8	5.6	0.3	0.4
PLATTEVILLE, WI	38420	49,597	50,296	50,463	0.2	679	98.2	97.8	0.5	0.6	0.5	0.7
PLATTSBURGH, NY	38460	79,894	84,129	87,517	0.7	444	93.3	92.3	3.6	4.0	0.7	0.9
PLYMOUTH, IN	38500	45,128	47,032	48,448	0.6	494	95.5	94.3	0.3	0.3	0.3	0.5
POCATELLO, ID	38540	83,103	86,819	89,532	0.6	494	90.6	89.8	0.5	0.7	1.1	1.3
POINT PLEASANT,WV-OH	38580	57,026	56,711	56,514	-0.1	805	96.7	96.3	1.7	1.9	0.3	0.4
PONCA CITY, OK	38620	48,080	47,299	46,524	-0.2	841	84.2	82.1	1.8	1.9	0.6	0.7
PONTIAC, IL	38700	39,678	39,517	39,657	-0.1	805	92.3	91.0	5.2	5.8	0.3	0.4
POPLAR BLUFF, MO	38740	40,867	40,921	40,977	0.0	765	92.2	91.8	5.2	5.6	0.4	0.5
PORTALES, NM	38780	18,018	18,408	18,540	0.3	633	74.1	72.6	1.7	1.8	0.7	0.8
PORT ANGELES, WA	38820	64,525	70,908	76,720	1.3	225	89.1	88.0	0.0	0.9	1.3	1.7
PORTLAND-BIDDEFORD	38860	487,568	529,286	555,704	1.1	288	96.5	95.8	0.8	1.0	1.1	1.6
PORTLAND-VANCOUVER	38900	1,927,881	2,102,068	2,345,078	1.6	155	84.6	82.2	2.7	2.7	4.9	5.8
PT ST LUCIE-FT PIERC	38940	319,426	422,461	520,962	3.9	13	83.4	79.5	11.4	13.7	0.9	1.2
UNITED STATES					1.2		75.1	72.7	12.3	12.6	3.8	4.5

CBSA	% HISPANIC ORIGIN		2007 AGE DISTRIBUTION (%)										MEDIAN AGE	% 2007 Males	% 2007 Females
	2000	2007	0-4	5-9	10-14	15-19	20-24	25-44	45-64	65-84	85+	18+	2007		
NORTH VERNON, IN	0.7	0.9	7.6	6.9	7.7	6.4	5.7	28.6	25.9	10.1	1.2	73.8	36.7	49.8	50.2
NORTH WILKESBORO, NC	3.4	4.6	6.1	6.4	5.9	5.2	4.8	28.5	28.2	13.0	1.8	78.3	40.6	49.7	50.3
NORWALK, OH	3.6	4.3	7.6	7.0	7.1	7.1	6.3	26.8	25.8	10.5	1.7	74.0	36.4	49.2	50.8
NORWICH-N LONDON, CT	5.1	6.4	6.1	6.0	6.6	7.6	6.9	25.9	27.4	11.5	2.2	77.0	39.3	49.4	50.6
OAK HARBOR, WA	4.0	5.0	6.6	5.8	6.3	6.4	7.6	24.1	28.6	12.8	1.9	77.4	40.2	50.1	49.9
OAK HILL, WV	0.7	0.7	5.6	5.7	5.3	5.2	6.2	26.2	29.7	13.7	2.4	80.4	41.8	50.1	49.9
OCALA, FL	6.0	8.6	5.2	4.7	5.1	5.8	5.6	20.2	27.0	23.2	3.1	81.4	47.3	48.2	51.8
OCEAN CITY, NJ	3.3	4.5	5.1	4.7	5.9	6.5	5.5	21.4	29.5	18.0	3.4	80.2	45.5	48.2	51.8
OCEAN PINES, MD	1.3	1.9	4.7	4.6	5.2	5.4	4.5	22.8	30.3	20.0	2.4	82.1	46.7	48.9	51.1
ODESSA, TX	42.4	49.3	8.4	7.1	7.4	7.8	9.3	25.8	23.2	9.7	1.3	72.5	31.9	49.0	51.0
OGDEN-CLEARFIELD, UT	8.6	9.9	10.3	8.9	7.8	7.4	7.7	29.8	19.8	7.2	1.1	68.6	28.8	50.1	49.9
OGDENSBURG-MASS., NY	1.8	2.2	5.5	5.2	5.9	9.0	10.1	24.8	26.2	11.5	1.8	79.5	37.3	51.0	49.0
OIL CITY, PA	0.5	0.6	5.8	5.4	5.7	7.1	6.2	23.1	29.9	14.5	2.3	78.6	42.6	49.0	51.0
OKEECHOBEE, FL	18.6	25.2	6.7	5.9	6.1	7.2	7.3	26.6	23.9	14.6	1.7	77.0	37.5	53.9	46.1
OKLAHOMA CITY, OK	6.7	8.3	7.1	6.5	6.3	6.9	8.1	28.1	25.4	10.0	1.5	76.2	35.2	49.2	50.8
OLEAN, NY	0.9	1.3	6.2	6.0	6.3	8.3	7.6	23.5	27.6	12.4	2.2	76.9	39.3	49.2	50.8
OLYMPIA, WA	4.5	5.7	6.2	5.8	6.4	6.6	7.5	26.8	28.7	10.1	1.9	77.7	38.4	48.9	51.1
OMAHA-COUNCIL BLUFFS	5.2	6.9	7.5	7.2	7.1	7.0	6.8	28.7	24.9	9.3	1.6	74.0	35.3	49.2	50.8
ONEONTA, NY	1.9	2.5	4.8	4.8	5.8	9.3	10.4	21.8	28.2	12.5	2.4	80.2	39.8	48.8	51.2
ONTARIO, OR-ID	20.2	20.7	8.1	7.1	7.1	7.0	8.0	26.1	23.6	10.9	2.1	73.6	34.5	52.0	48.0
OPELOUSAS-EUNICE, LA	0.9	1.0	8.3	7.6	6.8	6.7	7.3	25.3	24.6	11.6	1.8	73.1	35.9	48.0	52.0
ORANGEBURG, SC	1.0	1.2	6.5	6.2	6.4	8.1	8.5	25.0	25.4	11.9	2.0	77.1	36.8	46.8	53.2
ORLANDO, FL	16.5	22.1	6.6	6.1	6.6	6.9	7.0	29.1	25.1	11.0	1.6	76.7	36.9	49.2	50.8
OSHKOSH-NEENAH, WI	2.0	2.6	6.0	5.6	6.1	7.8	9.3	26.9	25.8	10.3	2.2	78.3	37.0	49.9	50.1
OSKALOOSA, IA	0.9	0.9	6.8	6.1	6.3	6.7	7.6	25.0	25.9	12.9	2.8	76.9	38.9	50.0	50.0
OTTAWA-STREATOR, IL	5.0	6.6	6.5	6.0	6.2	6.4	6.9	25.1	26.7	13.3	2.9	77.3	40.3	49.5	50.5
OTTUMWA, IA	2.2	3.0	6.1	5.7	6.0	6.8	6.4	24.7	27.4	13.9	3.0	78.4	40.7	48.9	51.1
OWATONNA, MN	3.8	5.1	7.1	6.3	6.6	7.6	7.2	26.3	25.5	11.0	2.4	75.2	37.6	49.5	50.5
OWENSBORO, KY	0.9	1.3	6.9	6.6	6.3	6.5	6.6	26.4	26.6	12.0	2.0	76.3	38.3	48.5	51.5
OWOSSO, MI	1.8	2.3	6.8	6.5	7.0	6.7	6.0	26.7	27.8	10.9	1.6	75.6	38.7	49.4	50.6
OXFORD, MS	1.1	1.4	5.6	4.9	4.6	9.9	17.3	28.0	19.4	8.8	1.6	82.1	28.4	49.6	50.4
OXNARD-TH OAKS-VENT.	33.4	39.5	7.4	7.3	8.4	7.6	6.5	27.2	25.1	8.8	1.6	72.2	35.1	49.9	50.1
PADUCAH, KY-IL	1.0	1.3	6.0	5.9	6.2	5.6	5.5	25.8	28.8	13.6	2.6	78.6	41.7	48.2	51.8
PAHRUMP, NV	8.4	10.3	5.8	5.2	5.9	6.8	5.7	18.5	31.3	19.2	1.3	78.7	46.2	51.2	48.8
PALATKA, FL	5.9	8.3	6.4	5.7	6.1	6.3	6.0	22.2	28.6	16.7	1.9	78.0	42.8	49.6	50.4
PALESTINE, TX	12.2	15.3	5.7	5.4	4.8	5.3	8.1	36.1	23.0	9.8	1.8	80.9	36.2	60.8	39.2
PALM BAY-MELB-TITUS	4.6	6.6	5.3	4.9	5.8	6.3	6.0	22.2	28.2	18.4	2.9	80.2	44.7	48.7	51.3
PALM COAST, FL	5.1	7.3	4.4	4.3	4.5	4.9	4.2	17.8	30.3	26.9	2.7	83.6	52.1	47.7	52.3
PAMPA, TX	12.6	16.0	6.1	5.4	6.1	6.4	8.2	24.4	25.5	14.9	3.1	78.8	40.2	51.7	48.3
PANAMA CITY-L HAVEN	2.4	3.5	6.1	5.6	6.1	6.0	6.2	27.6	27.7	13.0	1.5	78.5	40.2	49.6	50.4
PARAGOULD, AR	1.2	1.6	6.9	6.7	6.6	6.1	5.7	29.0	25.2	12.1	1.8	76.1	37.7	49.3	50.7
PARIS, TN	1.0	1.4	5.7	5.6	5.4	5.5	5.1	24.8	29.1	16.1	2.6	79.9	43.4	49.1	50.9
PARIS, TX	3.3	4.3	7.4	6.7	6.3	6.7	6.4	25.6	25.3	13.0	2.8	75.8	38.4	47.9	52.1
PARKERSBURG-MARIETTA	0.5	0.6	5.8	5.6	6.0	6.1	6.0	25.3	28.9	13.9	2.3	79.0	41.6	48.6	51.4
PARSONS, KS	3.1	4.1	6.6	5.7	6.0	7.3	8.5	23.7	26.1	12.6	3.4	77.5	39.7	49.4	50.6
PASCAGOULA, MS	2.1	2.4	7.4	6.8	7.2	6.8	6.7	28.1	25.3	10.4	1.1	74.4	36.0	49.6	50.4
PAYSON, AZ	16.6	20.1	6.2	5.7	6.1	6.7	6.0	18.9	29.6	18.4	2.5	77.8	45.3	49.2	50.8
PECOS, TX	73.4	78.4	6.6	6.3	6.3	9.9	12.0	24.8	22.0	10.9	1.2	74.9	31.7	57.6	42.4
PELLA, IA	0.8	1.1	6.3	6.1	6.4	8.5	8.0	23.6	25.6	12.7	2.8	78.0	38.4	50.0	50.0
PENDLETON-HERMIS.,OR	17.2	22.4	7.8	7.0	7.1	6.4	8.1	26.6	25.0	10.1	1.8	74.1	34.8	51.5	48.5
PENSACOLA-FERRY PASS	2.6	3.8	6.4	5.9	6.0	7.5	7.5	27.2	25.9	11.9	1.6	77.8	37.7	49.7	50.3
PEORIA, IL	1.5	2.0	6.6	6.2	6.5	6.7	6.7	25.5	27.0	12.4	2.5	76.8	38.9	48.7	51.3
PERU, IN	1.3	1.8	6.5	5.9	6.6	6.7	6.0	27.3	27.1	11.5	1.7	77.0	38.6	50.8	49.2
PHILADELPHIA-CAMDEN	5.0	5.9	6.4	6.4	7.0	7.4	6.5	26.7	26.0	11.4	2.2	75.8	38.1	48.2	51.8
PHOENIX LK-CEDAR R.	8.2	10.6	4.2	4.1	4.7	5.6	7.7	23.2	31.7	16.2	2.5	83.8	45.3	54.3	45.7
PHOENIX-MESA-SCOT,AZ	25.1	29.8	8.1	7.4	7.1	6.6	6.6	29.5	22.1	10.9	1.7	73.4	34.4	50.1	49.9
PICAYUNE, MS	1.4	1.9	7.2	7.0	6.7	6.5	6.2	26.2	26.4	12.3	1.4	75.3	37.9	48.8	51.2
PIERRE, SD	1.1	1.4	6.5	6.2	7.2	7.0	8.1	23.0	28.3	11.0	2.6	75.5	39.5	48.4	51.6
PIERRE PART, LA	1.2	1.3	7.3	6.7	7.2	6.5	6.8	28.0	26.5	9.7	1.4	74.9	36.5	48.6	51.4
PINE BLUFF, AR	1.1	1.5	6.9	6.5	6.3	6.8	7.8	27.7	24.9	11.1	2.0	76.6	36.4	50.8	49.2
PITTSBURG, KS	2.4	3.2	6.7	5.5	5.3	7.6	11.6	24.7	23.3	11.9	3.3	79.1	34.7	49.0	51.0
PITTSBURGH, PA	0.7	0.9	5.5	5.4	5.9	6.6	6.1	24.4	28.6	14.6	3.0	79.4	42.4	48.0	52.0
PITTSFIELD, MA	1.7	2.2	5.1	4.9	5.9	7.7	7.2	22.3	29.0	14.6	3.4	79.9	43.0	47.9	52.1
PLAINVIEW, TX	47.9	54.9	8.9	7.7	7.5	8.2	8.5	25.6	20.8	10.7	2.0	71.5	32.0	50.7	49.3
PLATTEVILLE, WI	0.6	0.7	5.5	5.0	5.7	9.0	11.3	23.2	25.1	12.7	2.6	79.8	37.3	51.4	.48.6
PLATTSBURGH, NY	2.5	2.9	5.3	5.2	6.1	7.8	8.9	28.3	25.6	11.1	1.6	79.3	37.5	51.3	48.7
PLYMOUTH, IN	5.9	7.9	7.5	7.1	7.0	6.6	6.4	26.7	26.0	10.7	1.9	74.2	37.0	50.2	49.8
POCATELLO, ID	6.2	6.8	8.5	7.2	6.8	7.5	9.4	27.8	22.7	8.6	1.4	73.4	30.5	49.6	50.4
POINT PLEASANT,WV-OH	0.5	0.6	6.2	5.9	6.1	5.9	6.3	25.7	28.5	13.6	1.8	78.4	40.8	49.1	50.9
PONCA CITY, OK	4.3	5.4	7.3	6.3	6.4	6.7	7.6	22.9	26.2	13.7	2.8	76.0	39.3	48.8	51.2
PONTIAC, IL	2.7	3.5	6.4	5.7	6.1	6.7	7.5	26.4	26.3	12.0	2.8	77.8	38.7	49.5	50.5
POPLAR BLUFF, MO	1.0	1.0	6.6	6.1	5.8	6.0	6.2	25.5	27.0	14.5	2.3	77.9	40.4	48.1	51.9
PORTALES, NM	33.3	35.3	7.8	6.6	7.2	9.3	10.3	26.3	20.8	9.9	1.7	74.2	29.8	49.1	50.9
PORT ANGELES, WA	3.4	4.3	5.0	4.8	5.4	6.1	6.0	19.2	31.4	18.5	3.5	81.1	47.3	49.5	50.5
PORTLAND-BIDDEFORD	0.9	1.2	5.7	5.5	6.2	7.3	6.6	25.6	29.5	11.5	2.2	78.2	40.8	48.7	51.3
PORTLAND-VANCOUVER	7.4	9.7	7.0	6.7	6.7	6.7	6.6	29.2	26.8	8.6	1.7	75.6	36.2	49.7	50.3
PT ST LUCIE-FT PIERC	7.9	11.2	5.2	4.9	5.7	6.0	5.1	20.6	27.4	21.5	3.6	80.5	46.6	48.7	51.3
UNITED STATES	12.5	15.0	6.9	6.5	6.8	7.1	7.0	27.6	25.4	10.7	1.9	75.6	36.7	49.2	50.8

CBSA	HOUSEHOLDS					FAMILIES			MEDIAN HOUSEHOLD INCOME		
	2000	2007	2012	% Annual Rate 2000-2007	2007 Average HH Size	2000	2007	% Annual Rate 2000-2007	2007	2012	2007 National Rank
NORTH VERNON, IN	10,134	10,768	11,117	0.8	2.61	7,604	7,830	0.4	47,453	54,093	333
NORTH WILKESBORO, NC	26,650	28,424	29,683	0.9	2.40	19,311	20,123	0.6	40,943	46,032	617
NORWALK, OH	22,307	23,306	23,897	0.6	2.59	16,225	16,495	0.2	49,666	56,921	266
NORWICH-N LONDON, CT	99,835	106,266	110,320	0.9	2.43	67,193	70,975	0.8	63,477	75,445	37
OAK HARBOR, WA	27,784	31,434	34,361	1.7	2.52	20,241	22,617	1.5	56,717	66,107	100
OAK HILL, WV	18,945	19,604	19,902	0.5	2.34	13,121	13,155	0.0	29,975	34,281	911
OCALA, FL	106,755	137,142	164,005	3.5	2.34	74,637	94,251	3.3	39,452	45,435	676
OCEAN CITY, NJ	42,148	44,465	45,904	0.7	2.32	27,372	28,806	0.7	52,423	61,946	182
OCEAN PINES, MD	19,694	22,339	23,773	1.8	2.28	13,278	14,545	1.3	48,710	54,450	292
ODESSA, TX	43,846	45,823	46,904	0.6	2.71	31,716	32,821	0.5	38,767	45,368	699
OGDEN-CLEARFIELD, UT	138,945	165,186	183,621	2.4	3.10	110,604	129,381	2.2	62,562	75,500	42
OGDENSBURG-MASS., NY	40,506	41,181	41,742	0.2	2.47	26,939	27,163	0.1	39,948	46,034	652
OIL CITY, PA	22,747	22,836	22,808	0.1	2.40	15,926	15,544	-0.3	41,028	47,878	608
OKEECHOBEE, FL	12,593	13,979	15,030	1.5	2.66	9,022	9,852	1.2	36,780	41,670	783
OKLAHOMA CITY, OK	429,743	476,486	510,676	1.4	2.44	287,885	313,210	1.2	46,316	54,276	376
OLEAN, NY	32,023	32,450	32,502	0.2	2.46	21,662	21,780	0.1	40,997	46,650	611
OLYMPIA, WA	81,625	93,875	103,750	1.9	2.49	54,951	62,247	1.7	60,065	69,952	67
OMAHA-COUNCIL BLUFFS	294,502	326,838	351,543	1.4	2.53	197,581	217,130	1.3	56,804	66,880	96
ONEONTA, NY	23,291	24,879	25,435	0.9	2.39	15,120	16,017	0.8	41,257	47,215	598
ONTARIO, OR-ID	17,592	18,355	18,920	0.6	2.79	12,922	13,383	0.5	38,611	44,259	711
OPELOUSAS-EUNICE, LA	32,328	34,077	35,301	0.7	2.63	23,205	23,864	0.4	25,586	27,462	933
ORANGEBURG, SC	34,118	35,529	35,617	0.6	2.48	23,876	23,997	0.1	36,265	41,231	800
ORLANDO, FL	625,248	801,055	951,653	3.5	2.58	425,052	536,109	3.3	52,194	61,092	190
OSHKOSH-NEENAH, WI	61,157	66,179	68,247	1.1	2.35	39,547	41,662	0.7	55,834	65,048	116
OSKALOOSA, IA	8,880	9,044	9,111	0.3	2.41	6,147	6,148	0.0	45,756	52,784	396
OTTAWA-STREATOR, IL	60,014	62,067	63,357	0.5	2.47	41,479	41,685	0.1	50,265	58,245	240
OTTUMWA, IA	14,784	15,146	15,342	0.3	2.34	9,797	9,840	0.1	39,879	46,088	655
OWATONNA, MN	12,846	14,349	15,453	1.5	2.54	9,077	9,868	1.2	57,807	66,379	85
OWENSBORO, KY	43,232	45,988	47,103	0.9	2.40	30,145	30,921	0.4	45,618	53,131	405
OWOSSO, MI	26,896	28,657	29,715	0.9	2.57	19,862	20,676	0.6	50,208	56,596	245
OXFORD, MS	14,373	16,502	18,063	1.9	2.31	8,318	9,239	1.5	31,669	33,848	898
OXNARD-TH OAKS-VENT.	243,234	263,529	277,874	1.1	3.09	182,959	198,910	1.2	76,319	90,005	8
PADUCAH, KY-IL	41,388	41,779	41,740	0.1	2.29	28,083	27,326	-0.4	41,070	47,794	604
PAHRUMP, NV	13,309	17,754	21,766	4.1	2.39	9,068	11,961	3.9	44,702	51,740	442
PALATKA, FL	27,839	30,238	32,299	1.1	2.50	19,464	20,785	0.9	33,812	38,257	866
PALESTINE, TX	15,678	16,491	17,029	0.7	2.55	11,343	11,818	0.6	38,497	43,832	718
PALM BAY-MELB-TITUS	198,195	233,013	261,850	2.3	2.35	132,480	152,836	2.0	50,329	59,311	238
PALM COAST, FL	21,294	43,360	75,121	10.3	2.29	15,683	31,459	10.1	49,298	56,977	276
PAMPA, TX	9,155	8,561	8,148	-0.9	2.36	6,327	5,852	-1.1	39,742	46,300	661
PANAMA CITY-L HAVEN	59,597	70,576	78,859	2.4	2.37	40,480	47,065	2.1	44,008	50,490	467
PARAGOULD, AR	14,750	16,093	17,048	1.2	2.47	10,703	11,364	0.8	38,423	44,736	722
PARIS, TN	13,019	13,649	13,962	0.7	2.32	9,006	9,188	0.3	36,705	42,490	785
PARIS, TX	19,077	19,845	20,338	0.5	2.46	13,473	13,870	0.4	38,252	43,625	731
PARKERSBURG-MARIETTA	66,583	67,750	67,926	0.2	2.36	46,416	45,801	-0.2	40,771	46,896	624
PARSONS, KS	9,194	9,120	9,057	-0.1	2.36	6,118	5,987	-0.3	37,646	42,960	753
PASCAGOULA, MS	54,418	58,941	61,848	1.1	2.68	41,032	43,576	0.8	42,421	45,316	532
PAYSON, AZ	20,140	21,065	21,663	0.6	2.49	14,090	14,560	0.5	39,955	47,181	651
PECOS, TX	4,091	3,490	3,168	-2.2	2.86	3,130	2,646	-2.3	27,781	31,986	923
PELLA, IA	12,017	12,861	13,374	0.9	2.47	8,527	8,972	0.7	52,080	60,934	192
PENDLETON-HERMIS.,OR	28,971	30,398	31,212	0.7	2.72	20,766	21,619	0.6	45,227	52,025	425
PENSACOLA-FERRY PASS	154,842	176,134	193,464	1.8	2.48	107,484	120,664	1.6	45,932	53,387	387
PEORIA, IL	143,607	149,526	153,100	0.6	2.43	98,282	99,541	0.2	53,210	61,614	157
PERU, IN	13,716	13,726	13,542	0.0	2.45	9,803	9,468	-0.5	48,191	54,839	304
PHILADELPHIA-CAMDEN	2,134,404	2,235,538	2,310,444	0.6	2.57	1,440,062	1,478,085	0.4	62,790	75,624	40
PHOENIX LK-CEDAR R.	21,004	22,272	22,965	0.8	2.36	14,249	15,178	0.9	47,096	54,003	346
PHOENIX-MESA-SCOT,AZ	1,194,250	1,517,006	1,808,834	3.4	2.70	808,321	1,014,463	3.2	59,039	71,801	74
PICAYUNE, MS	18,078	20,806	22,474	2.0	2.58	13,583	15,327	1.7	35,016	37,944	835
PIERRE, SD	7,623	8,072	8,297	0.8	2.36	5,085	5,338	0.7	52,650	62,220	173
PIERRE PART, LA	8,239	8,678	8,924	0.7	2.73	6,312	6,512	0.4	34,861	38,054	837
PINE BLUFF, AR	38,093	38,588	38,209	0.2	2.51	27,152	26,750	-0.2	38,811	45,198	695
PITTSBURG, KS	15,504	15,652	15,750	0.1	2.35	9,436	9,372	-0.1	36,137	41,468	803
PITTSBURGH, PA	995,505	999,101	996,243	0.1	2.34	651,964	634,861	-0.4	48,056	56,854	311
PITTSFIELD, MA	56,006	56,373	56,598	0.1	2.27	35,110	34,889	-0.1	49,287	57,957	278
PLAINVIEW, TX	11,975	11,796	11,648	-0.2	2.84	9,142	8,931	-0.3	38,051	43,158	738
PLATTEVILLE, WI	18,465	19,253	19,581	0.6	2.42	12,399	12,611	0.2	43,828	50,052	482
PLATTSBURGH, NY	29,423	31,857	33,625	1.1	2.42	19,261	20,680	1.0	45,904	52,609	389
PLYMOUTH, IN	16,519	17,540	18,156	0.8	2.65	12,188	12,523	0.4	52,456	61,259	180
POCATELLO, ID	29,752	31,868	33,121	1.0	2.65	21,181	22,406	0.8	46,981	56,866	351
POINT PLEASANT,WV-OH	22,647	23,188	23,361	0.3	2.40	16,163	16,075	-0.1	34,762	39,266	843
PONCA CITY, OK	19,157	19,001	18,715	-0.1	2.43	13,136	12,772	-0.4	37,727	43,468	751
PONTIAC, IL	14,374	14,618	14,745	0.2	2.48	9,948	9,833	-0.2	50,575	57,172	229
POPLAR BLUFF, MO	16,718	17,034	17,175	0.3	2.35	11,313	11,192	-0.1	33,602	38,932	869
PORTALES, NM	6,639	6,789	6,845	0.3	2.57	4,544	4,502	-0.1	32,082	36,704	890
PORT ANGELES, WA	27,164	30,022	33,442	1.7	2.26	18,068	20,056	1.5	45,334	53,080	421
PORTLAND-BIDDEFORD	196,669	216,803	229,748	1.4	2.38	128,154	138,419	1.1	54,004	62,767	139
PORTLAND-VANCOUVER	745,531	830,829	899,164	1.5	2.56	485,098	537,075	1.4	60,579	71,707	63
PT ST LUCIE-FT PIERC	132,221	174,480	215,300	3.9	2.38	90,452	117,740	3.7	48,195	55,949	303
UNITED STATES				1.2	2.59			1.0	53,154	62,503	

INCOME
CBSA AND U.S. TOTALS

D

CBSA	2007 Per Capita Income	2007 HH Income Base	2007 HOUSEHOLD INCOME DISTRIBUTION (%)					2007 Home Value Base	2007 HOME VALUE DISTRIBUTION (%)					2007 Median Home Value
			Less than $25,000	$25,000 to $49,999	$50,000 to $99,999	$100,000 to $149,999	$150,000 or More		Less than $50,000	$50,000 to $89,999	$90,000 to $174,999	$175,000 to $399,999	$400,000 or More	
NORTH VERNON, IN	21,190	10,768	21.2	32.6	35.6	8.0	2.5	8,602	18.7	23.1	45.9	10.7	1.7	101,825
NORTH WILKESBORO, NC	21,389	28,424	30.2	31.2	29.8	5.8	3.1	22,454	16.9	16.3	40.2	23.0	3.6	118,827
NORWALK, OH	22,605	23,306	19.9	30.4	37.6	9.2	2.9	17,482	9.9	13.7	51.3	23.1	2.0	124,914
NORWICH-N LONDON, CT	32,251	106,262	15.8	22.5	35.9	16.1	9.7	74,227	2.0	1.6	9.8	64.1	22.5	279,094
OAK HARBOR, WA	27,759	31,434	16.2	26.6	38.7	12.4	6.0	22,844	2.8	1.4	6.1	60.1	29.6	311,918
OAK HILL, WV	16,909	19,604	42.8	30.4	21.2	4.1	1.5	15,486	28.0	31.9	32.8	6.7	0.6	75,637
OCALA, FL	22,112	137,142	29.6	33.2	27.3	6.6	3.3	112,057	6.1	9.7	30.5	44.6	9.1	184,543
OCEAN CITY, NJ	31,409	44,465	21.8	25.7	31.6	12.6	8.3	34,081	1.0	1.1	8.2	50.7	38.9	344,537
OCEAN PINES, MD	27,647	22,339	22.3	29.0	33.9	9.4	5.4	16,996	1.9	3.6	14.4	57.5	22.6	259,705
ODESSA, TX	18,833	45,823	31.1	31.4	27.7	6.6	3.2	31,960	32.6	32.2	27.1	7.4	0.7	70,421
OGDEN-CLEARFIELD, UT	24,992	165,186	13.0	23.9	39.5	15.8	7.8	128,002	2.9	3.6	39.4	47.9	6.3	183,019
OGDENSBURG-MASS., NY	19,794	41,176	30.8	30.6	29.6	6.5	2.6	30,126	8.4	16.2	40.3	32.8	2.3	147,186
OIL CITY, PA	20,870	22,836	30.0	30.3	30.4	6.8	2.6	17,539	14.8	24.7	43.4	15.5	1.6	109,023
OKEECHOBEE, FL	18,371	13,979	31.3	33.3	26.8	6.0	2.6	10,821	6.7	11.8	38.5	36.7	6.3	162,341
OKLAHOMA CITY, OK	24,798	476,478	24.7	28.9	31.3	9.9	5.1	311,920	12.9	24.5	41.9	18.0	2.7	110,227
OLEAN, NY	20,309	32,450	28.1	33.0	30.1	6.6	2.1	24,885	8.3	15.1	41.3	33.1	2.2	148,346
OLYMPIA, WA	28,767	93,875	16.2	24.5	38.9	14.1	6.3	65,368	3.8	2.8	10.0	64.7	18.6	270,743
OMAHA-COUNCIL BLUFFS	28,096	326,838	17.4	25.9	36.6	13.2	6.9	227,522	7.4	15.2	46.8	26.4	4.2	135,634
ONEONTA, NY	21,975	24,879	28.1	31.3	30.1	6.8	3.6	18,737	5.8	7.1	37.0	44.7	5.3	175,064
ONTARIO, OR-ID	17,958	18,355	30.6	32.8	28.6	5.2	2.8	12,966	6.7	9.4	45.2	33.2	5.5	157,611
OPELOUSAS-EUNICE, LA	13,805	34,077	49.1	26.9	18.8	3.8	1.4	23,858	26.4	28.2	32.6	11.5	1.3	82,816
ORANGEBURG, SC	19,108	35,529	36.8	27.4	26.4	6.6	2.8	27,286	23.1	25.3	37.7	12.1	1.8	92,279
ORLANDO, FL	26,973	801,055	19.3	28.1	33.6	12.0	6.9	554,692	3.5	3.9	17.6	58.0	17.1	238,309
OSHKOSH-NEENAH, WI	27,824	66,179	16.6	27.1	39.6	11.8	4.9	46,055	3.2	11.0	55.1	27.5	3.1	136,748
OSKALOOSA, IA	22,427	9,044	24.3	31.1	35.1	6.7	2.8	6,619	17.1	27.1	39.8	14.1	2.0	96,573
OTTAWA-STREATOR, IL	24,188	62,067	22.5	27.2	36.5	10.3	3.5	48,203	5.8	12.9	48.4	29.8	3.1	143,116
OTTUMWA, IA	20,952	15,146	29.4	33.5	28.8	5.7	2.5	11,686	30.4	30.7	28.3	9.1	1.4	71,639
OWATONNA, MN	26,093	14,349	15.3	26.3	42.5	11.3	4.6	11,661	3.2	4.7	38.8	47.8	5.6	181,397
OWENSBORO, KY	23,680	45,988	27.0	27.6	32.5	9.2	3.7	33,464	16.3	29.9	39.2	13.4	1.2	94,440
OWOSSO, MI	23,866	28,657	20.6	29.1	35.8	10.9	3.6	23,164	7.3	10.9	52.5	27.0	2.4	137,027
OXFORD, MS	18,837	16,502	41.4	25.4	25.3	5.1	2.8	9,954	20.2	20.1	31.4	23.1	5.2	109,774
OXNARD-TH OAKS-VENT.	32,144	263,527	12.6	18.1	34.0	19.3	16.0	181,195	1.4	1.6	2.8	13.0	81.1	630,182
PADUCAH, KY-IL	23,863	41,779	30.6	28.1	28.7	8.8	3.8	30,820	21.7	23.4	35.5	17.1	2.3	97,679
PAHRUMP, NV	22,791	17,754	26.3	29.9	31.9	8.7	3.1	13,794	6.3	3.9	21.7	60.3	7.8	216,409
PALATKA, FL	18,848	30,238	36.4	31.0	24.2	5.6	2.8	24,688	8.5	17.6	39.4	29.4	5.1	135,719
PALESTINE, TX	18,054	16,491	31.7	30.9	28.4	6.1	2.9	12,408	27.5	30.4	29.2	10.9	1.9	79,280
PALM BAY-MELB-TITUS	27,380	233,013	21.0	28.7	33.7	11.0	5.7	179,022	3.1	3.3	22.6	54.2	16.9	226,720
PALM COAST, FL	27,795	43,360	19.7	31.1	34.7	9.4	5.1	37,137	1.9	1.8	10.2	60.2	25.9	292,772
PAMPA, TX	21,464	8,561	30.3	30.3	28.0	8.3	3.2	6,689	47.1	25.6	21.1	5.2	0.9	53,009
PANAMA CITY-L HAVEN	23,809	70,576	26.6	29.6	31.4	8.5	3.9	50,419	5.7	8.7	29.3	45.8	10.4	189,059
PARAGOULD, AR	19,884	16,093	32.0	31.7	28.7	4.6	2.9	11,794	16.7	30.8	37.2	13.8	1.6	93,632
PARIS, TN	19,730	13,649	33.1	32.7	27.1	5.4	1.7	10,654	17.1	25.0	38.7	16.4	2.7	100,246
PARIS, TX	20,656	19,845	33.2	28.7	28.6	6.3	3.2	13,726	26.9	29.6	31.8	10.1	1.5	81,643
PARKERSBURG-MARIETTA	22,520	67,750	28.9	31.0	28.8	8.0	3.3	52,435	16.8	26.4	42.8	12.8	1.2	98,695
PARSONS, KS	19,326	9,120	31.2	33.8	28.5	5.1	1.4	6,776	40.6	28.6	23.8	6.1	0.9	61,142
PASCAGOULA, MS	19,839	58,941	27.8	30.9	30.9	7.5	3.0	44,953	9.3	13.4	39.7	32.2	5.4	145,463
PAYSON, AZ	21,443	21,065	31.3	29.2	28.9	6.9	3.6	16,715	12.7	9.9	24.6	40.2	12.7	185,006
PECOS, TX	13,235	3,490	43.9	33.0	18.7	3.3	1.2	2,751	71.4	19.7	7.5	1.3	0.1	34,163
PELLA, IA	23,730	12,861	20.6	26.7	39.2	10.5	3.0	9,964	13.0	18.5	42.9	22.8	2.9	121,273
PENDLETON-HERMIS.,OR	20,216	30,398	24.7	30.7	33.8	7.8	3.0	20,831	9.2	6.8	35.6	41.8	6.5	171,923
PENSACOLA-FERRY PASS	23,812	176,134	24.6	29.6	31.8	9.4	4.6	130,191	6.0	11.4	36.8	39.3	6.6	165,893
PEORIA, IL	26,793	149,526	20.8	25.9	35.9	11.8	5.5	111,802	8.5	18.3	48.3	22.6	2.3	123,437
PERU, IN	22,782	13,725	22.9	29.2	36.4	8.9	2.5	10,561	19.5	30.8	38.6	10.1	1.1	89,699
PHILADELPHIA-CAMDEN	32,067	2,235,518	18.7	21.3	32.9	15.7	11.4	1,594,072	3.3	5.3	18.5	53.7	19.3	250,621
PHOENIX LK-CEDAR R.	25,181	22,272	24.8	28.6	32.8	9.0	4.8	16,199	4.0	2.3	5.1	51.5	37.1	351,432
PHOENIX-MESA-SCOT,AZ	29,049	1,516,977	16.9	24.8	34.6	14.1	9.6	1,047,003	3.7	3.1	15.2	53.5	24.5	269,845
PICAYUNE, MS	17,939	20,806	35.4	31.4	25.4	5.5	2.4	16,640	20.6	25.2	35.3	16.4	2.5	96,920
PIERRE, SD	27,076	8,072	19.5	27.1	39.2	9.5	4.8	5,610	15.0	15.3	44.9	23.5	1.3	128,872
PIERRE PART, LA	16,668	8,678	38.0	27.1	27.1	5.9	1.9	7,212	31.1	19.6	32.8	14.9	1.5	88,479
PINE BLUFF, AR	19,204	38,588	33.5	28.3	27.4	7.8	3.0	27,259	23.6	30.5	34.3	10.1	1.5	84,466
PITTSBURG, KS	20,181	15,652	34.5	29.6	27.6	5.5	2.8	10,343	29.7	29.8	29.1	10.3	1.0	74,815
PITTSBURGH, PA	27,465	999,107	25.1	26.6	31.4	10.7	6.2	720,416	10.9	17.8	43.9	23.8	3.7	126,544
PITTSFIELD, MA	28,348	56,373	24.9	25.8	31.9	11.1	6.4	38,815	2.1	2.7	30.1	51.4	13.7	208,627
PLAINVIEW, TX	17,252	11,796	30.7	32.9	27.3	6.4	2.8	7,895	30.9	30.0	29.6	8.9	0.8	75,019
PLATTEVILLE, WI	21,262	19,253	25.0	32.3	33.2	7.1	2.4	14,181	9.9	18.3	47.3	21.6	2.9	124,165
PLATTSBURGH, NY	22,565	31,857	27.3	27.4	33.2	8.8	3.3	22,742	6.2	7.5	31.7	50.4	4.1	181,768
PLYMOUTH, IN	23,579	17,540	18.5	28.0	38.8	10.8	3.9	13,654	7.8	18.8	51.8	18.8	2.7	117,894
POCATELLO, ID	22,505	31,868	25.3	27.7	32.5	10.0	4.6	23,050	8.1	11.4	57.6	21.2	1.7	130,367
POINT PLEASANT,WV-OH	18,793	23,188	37.2	30.4	24.4	6.0	2.0	18,497	26.1	24.5	37.3	11.0	1.1	89,150
PONCA CITY, OK	20,957	19,001	32.0	30.6	27.1	6.8	3.5	13,650	29.4	30.1	30.0	9.3	1.2	75,625
PONTIAC, IL	23,304	14,618	21.5	27.7	37.4	10.2	3.2	11,155	9.7	13.2	50.8	24.4	1.9	133,503
POPLAR BLUFF, MO	19,891	17,034	38.0	31.0	23.0	4.9	3.1	12,083	24.3	26.7	34.0	12.1	2.9	88,065
PORTALES, NM	17,201	6,789	41.2	27.6	24.0	4.8	2.5	4,275	17.5	27.7	40.7	12.8	1.3	97,677
PORT ANGELES, WA	25,474	30,622	25.6	29.6	32.8	8.1	3.9	23,065	4.6	3.5	19.8	57.4	14.6	228,382
PORTLAND-BIDDEFORD	28,847	216,803	19.4	26.1	36.3	11.7	6.5	152,150	2.7	3.0	17.5	60.4	16.4	242,409
PORTLAND-VANCOUVER	30,298	830,829	16.0	24.0	36.7	14.1	9.2	544,275	2.8	1.9	7.0	60.2	28.1	304,693
PT ST LUCIE-FT PIERC	28,234	174,489	22.1	29.7	32.0	9.4	6.8	140,726	4.0	4.3	19.2	51.7	20.8	238,013
UNITED STATES	27,916		21.9	25.0	32.3	12.3	8.4		7.9	10.5	27.1	35.6	19.0	192,285

SPENDING POTENTIAL INDICES
CBSA AND U.S. TOTALS

CBSA	FINANCIAL SERVICES				THE HOME						ENTERTAINMENT						PERSONAL			
					Home Improvements		Furnishings													
	Auto Loan	Home Loan	Invest-ments	Retire-ment Plans	Home Repair	Lawn & Garden	Comput-ers & Hard-ware	Major Appli-ances	TV, Radio, Sound Equip-ment	Furni-ture	Dine out/ Carry out	Sports Equip-ment	Fees & Tickets	Toys & Games	Travel	Cable TV	Apparel & Services	Auto Repairs	Health Insur-ance	Pets & Supplies
NORTH VERNON, IN	88	74	63	73	76	89	72	82	78	73	77	72	68	81	72	81	67	78	86	85
NORTH WILKESBORO, NC	87	65	46	62	71	91	64	79	71	64	71	70	57	76	64	76	61	73	85	86
NORWALK, OH	85	78	80	79	81	89	78	83	82	78	81	73	77	84	79	84	72	80	88	86
NORWICH-N LONDON, CT	104	114	130	116	114	107	112	108	110	113	110	99	117	110	114	109	101	109	107	108
OAK HARBOR, WA	106	92	79	93	96	111	95	104	96	92	96	94	89	97	95	98	85	101	105	107
OAK HILL, WV	65	48	38	46	53	69	51	61	58	48	57	54	44	59	51	63	48	58	70	65
OCALA, FL	75	70	68	67	74	85	67	78	71	68	70	65	66	68	72	75	61	75	86	78
OCEAN CITY, NJ	97	103	118	103	107	109	98	103	100	100	99	89	103	96	105	104	89	101	111	102
OCEAN PINES, MD	91	83	83	83	89	103	83	94	87	82	86	81	80	84	87	91	75	90	101	95
ODESSA, TX	75	68	63	67	63	67	70	69	72	70	72	63	67	72	68	72	64	72	71	69
OGDEN-CLEARFIELD, UT	108	115	114	115	108	102	109	105	106	111	106	98	111	108	108	103	96	106	101	105
OGDENSBURG-MASS., NY	76	62	57	62	67	80	67	74	70	63	69	65	61	71	66	73	60	71	79	77
OIL CITY, PA	77	64	59	63	69	83	66	75	72	64	70	65	61	73	66	76	61	71	83	77
OKEECHOBEE, FL	74	67	59	64	68	77	65	73	68	65	67	64	62	66	67	70	58	71	77	73
OKLAHOMA CITY, OK	88	81	83	83	78	82	86	82	84	84	86	75	83	87	83	86	77	85	85	84
OLEAN, NY	77	65	60	64	69	81	66	74	71	64	70	65	62	72	66	74	61	70	80	77
OLYMPIA, WA	101	102	103	104	100	99	100	99	98	101	99	91	101	99	100	98	89	99	97	100
OMAHA-COUNCIL BLUFFS	100	98	103	101	95	95	100	96	100	100	99	88	99	101	98	99	89	98	98	97
ONEONTA, NY	83	67	59	67	73	88	73	81	75	68	75	72	65	76	72	78	65	77	85	84
ONTARIO, OR-ID	80	62	49	61	67	82	65	75	70	63	69	68	58	72	64	73	60	72	80	79
OPELOUSAS-EUNICE, LA	58	43	34	43	45	58	46	52	52	45	51	46	41	53	45	56	45	51	59	56
ORANGEBURG, SC	78	60	47	58	63	79	62	72	69	61	68	64	56	70	61	73	59	69	78	77
ORLANDO, FL	98	96	95	98	92	92	98	94	96	98	97	88	96	96	96	95	87	98	94	95
OSHKOSH-NEENAH, WI	92	91	101	94	91	91	94	91	94	93	93	82	94	95	93	93	84	92	93	91
OSKALOOSA, IA	83	67	65	68	73	87	73	80	77	69	76	71	66	79	72	80	66	77	88	83
OTTAWA-STREATOR, IL	85	82	88	82	85	90	80	85	84	80	82	74	80	85	82	86	73	82	91	86
OTTUMWA, IA	72	63	65	63	66	75	65	70	71	63	69	61	63	71	66	74	60	68	79	72
OWATONNA, MN	93	95	98	95	95	95	91	93	91	92	91	84	93	94	92	91	82	91	94	94
OWENSBORO, KY	83	76	77	76	78	85	76	81	80	76	79	71	75	82	77	83	70	79	86	83
OWOSSO, MI	90	86	86	86	88	94	81	88	84	83	84	77	82	88	84	86	75	84	91	90
OXFORD, MS	69	52	50	55	52	60	70	62	67	60	67	59	60	66	61	66	59	66	63	64
OXNARD-TH OAKS-VENT.	126	151	150	146	150	128	143	139	132	144	133	139	148	131	145	126	125	139	124	133
PADUCAH, KY-IL	83	70	67	70	73	86	73	79	78	70	76	70	68	78	73	81	67	77	87	82
PAHRUMP, NV	80	72	69	70	76	88	71	82	75	70	73	69	69	71	75	79	63	79	90	82
PALATKA, FL	73	60	52	57	64	79	61	72	66	59	65	62	55	64	62	70	56	68	79	74
PALESTINE, TX	78	63	55	62	66	80	65	74	71	64	70	64	60	71	65	74	61	71	80	77
PALM BAY-MELB-TITUS	86	90	103	90	91	92	87	89	89	89	88	77	91	86	92	91	79	89	95	88
PALM COAST, FL	92	88	87	87	94	108	81	96	86	84	85	80	82	81	90	91	74	91	104	96
PAMPA, TX	76	65	69	66	69	79	69	74	75	66	73	64	66	75	70	79	63	72	85	75
PANAMA CITY-L HAVEN	82	75	74	76	75	82	78	80	79	76	78	71	75	79	77	80	69	79	83	81
PARAGOULD, AR	81	61	49	60	65	82	63	74	70	61	69	65	57	73	62	74	59	70	81	78
PARIS, TN	74	56	45	55	62	79	58	70	65	56	64	61	52	66	59	69	55	66	77	74
PARIS, TX	78	64	61	64	67	79	67	73	73	65	71	64	63	73	67	76	62	71	81	76
PARKERSBURG-MARIETTA	80	69	68	69	73	84	71	78	76	69	74	68	67	76	72	79	65	74	85	80
PARSONS, KS	69	56	57	57	59	70	61	65	67	58	65	57	57	67	61	70	56	64	75	67
PASCAGOULA, MS	80	73	68	73	72	79	70	75	74	72	74	67	69	76	71	76	65	74	79	78
PAYSON, AZ	80	69	63	68	74	89	69	81	74	68	73	69	65	71	72	78	63	77	88	81
PECOS, TX	59	50	36	45	44	49	48	53	53	52	54	47	44	51	47	54	48	55	53	50
PELLA, IA	88	80	83	81	84	92	80	87	84	79	82	76	78	86	82	87	73	83	93	88
PENDLETON-HERMIS.,OR	83	73	67	72	74	82	75	79	77	73	76	71	70	79	74	79	67	78	82	82
PENSACOLA-FERRY PASS	87	82	83	83	81	86	81	83	84	81	83	74	80	84	82	85	74	83	87	85
PEORIA, IL	90	90	100	92	91	94	89	90	92	90	91	79	91	93	91	93	81	89	96	91
PERU, IN	88	73	65	72	77	92	74	83	80	73	79	73	69	83	74	83	69	79	90	87
PHILADELPHIA-CAMDEN	106	121	131	119	121	111	115	112	115	118	115	101	123	113	118	115	107	111	111	111
PHOENIX LK-CEDAR R.	88	81	79	81	88	100	80	92	83	79	82	79	78	80	85	87	72	87	97	93
PHOENIX-MESA-SCOT,AZ	110	111	109	111	106	104	110	107	108	112	108	100	110	107	109	106	98	111	105	106
PICAYUNE, MS	76	60	46	58	64	79	59	71	65	58	64	62	54	67	59	69	56	66	76	75
PIERRE, SD	97	90	86	90	89	96	88	92	90	88	90	83	86	91	88	92	80	91	95	95
PIERRE PART, LA	78	57	36	54	61	80	56	70	64	56	63	63	49	67	55	68	54	65	75	76
PINE BLUFF, AR	79	64	56	64	66	79	65	72	72	65	71	63	61	73	65	76	62	71	79	77
PITTSBURG, KS	71	57	58	58	59	69	67	67	70	61	68	60	60	69	63	71	59	67	73	69
PITTSBURGH, PA	88	87	99	88	90	93	87	89	91	87	90	78	89	90	90	94	80	88	97	90
PITTSFIELD, MA	86	89	105	91	92	92	89	90	91	89	90	79	92	89	93	93	81	89	95	90
PLAINVIEW, TX	76	66	54	62	63	71	65	71	70	67	69	64	61	69	64	71	61	71	73	70
PLATTEVILLE, WI	83	64	55	64	70	88	71	80	75	65	74	71	62	77	69	78	64	76	86	84
PLATTSBURGH, NY	82	75	75	75	76	83	76	79	78	75	78	71	74	79	76	80	69	78	82	81
PLYMOUTH, IN	92	84	85	85	89	98	82	90	87	83	86	79	81	91	84	90	76	86	96	93
POCATELLO, ID	86	80	82	81	78	81	85	82	84	81	83	75	81	85	82	83	74	83	83	83
POINT PLEASANT,WV-OH	73	54	44	54	61	77	57	68	64	56	63	60	51	65	57	68	54	64	75	73
PONCA CITY, OK	76	64	65	65	67	78	68	73	74	65	71	64	64	74	68	77	62	71	82	75
PONTIAC, IL	90	76	74	77	81	94	78	87	83	76	82	76	74	86	79	86	71	83	94	90
POPLAR BLUFF, MO	73	59	54	59	61	73	62	68	67	60	66	59	57	68	61	70	57	66	75	70
PORTALES, NM	68	53	47	53	53	63	62	63	64	57	63	57	54	64	57	64	55	64	66	64
PORT ANGELES, WA	83	77	79	78	82	90	77	86	80	75	78	73	75	76	81	83	68	83	93	86
PORTLAND-BIDDEFORD	95	96	101	98	98	98	96	97	95	96	95	88	97	95	97	95	86	96	97	98
PORTLAND-VANCOUVER	105	109	114	112	106	101	111	105	107	110	107	99	112	107	109	105	98	107	101	105
PT ST LUCIE-FT PIERC	90	95	106	94	90	102	80	90	92	92	91	82	93	87	97	95	81	94	104	95
UNITED STATES	100	100	100	100	100	100	100	100	100	100	100	100	100	100	100	100	100	100	100	100

POPULATION CHANGE
CBSA AND U.S. TOTALS

A

CBSA	CBSA Code	POPULATION 2000	POPULATION 2007	POPULATION 2012	2000-2007 ANNUAL RATE % Rate	2000-2007 ANNUAL RATE National Rank	RACE (%) White 2000	White 2007	Black 2000	Black 2007	Asian/Pacific 2000	Asian/Pacific 2007
PORTSMOUTH, OH	39020	79,195	76,854	75,510	-0.4	896	94.9	94.2	2.7	3.0	0.3	0.4
POTTSVILLE, PA	39060	150,336	149,951	149,176	0.0	765	96.6	95.8	2.1	2.4	0.4	0.7
POUGHKEEPSIE-NEWBRG	39100	621,517	684,296	725,959	1.3	225	83.7	81.5	8.6	9.4	2.0	2.5
PRESCOTT, AZ	39140	167,517	218,514	264,859	3.7	16	91.9	90.5	0.4	0.4	0.6	0.7
PRICE, UT	39220	20,422	19,951	19,737	-0.3	873	91.1	89.7	0.3	0.3	0.4	0.4
PRINEVILLE, OR	39260	19,182	22,842	25,820	2.4	71	93.0	91.4	0.0	0.1	0.5	0.6
PROVIDENCE-NEW BEDFD	39300	1,582,997	1,639,860	1,670,379	0.5	545	87.0	84.6	3.6	4.1	2.0	2.6
PROVO-OREM, UT	39340	376,774	489,312	592,671	3.7	16	92.5	91.4	0.3	0.3	1.6	1.8
PUEBLO, CO	39380	141,472	154,712	163,229	1.2	255	79.5	77.5	1.9	1.9	0.7	0.8
PULLMAN, WA	39420	40,740	46,854	47,438	1.9	113	88.1	86.2	1.5	1.8	5.8	6.8
PUNTA GORDA, FL	39460	141,627	167,237	184,721	2.3	78	92.6	90.7	4.4	5.3	0.9	1.2
QUINCY, IL-MO	39500	78,771	78,326	77,823	-0.1	805	95.2	94.4	3.0	3.4	0.4	0.5
RACINE, WI	39540	188,831	197,998	204,977	0.7	444	83.0	79.7	10.5	12.3	0.8	1.0
RALEIGH-CARY, NC	39580	797,071	1,023,620	1,222,174	3.5	18	72.9	70.5	19.7	19.7	2.8	3.6
RAPID CITY, SD	39660	112,818	123,759	131,863	1.3	225	88.0	85.5	1.0	1.2	0.9	1.3
RAYMONDVILLE, TX	39700	20,082	20,901	21,429	0.6	494	70.4	69.4	2.2	1.9	0.1	0.1
READING, PA	39740	373,638	406,222	430,127	1.2	255	88.2	85.9	3.7	4.1	1.0	1.5
RED BLUFF, CA	39780	56,039	63,673	69,817	1.8	127	84.8	81.3	0.6	0.6	0.9	1.1
REDDING, CA	39820	163,256	183,901	198,963	1.7	140	89.3	86.9	0.8	0.8	2.0	2.5
RED WING, MN	39860	44,127	47,578	50,131	1.0	318	96.6	95.8	0.6	0.8	0.6	0.8
RENO-SPARKS, NV	39900	342,885	425,289	493,027	3.0	38	80.5	78.4	2.1	2.2	4.7	4.7
REXBURG, ID	39940	39,286	50,200	61,247	3.4	22	94.3	93.7	0.2	0.3	0.7	0.8
RICHMOND, IN	39980	71,097	70,123	69,503	-0.2	841	92.0	90.8	5.1	5.7	0.5	0.8
RICHMOND, VA	40060	1,096,957	1,215,134	1,301,993	1.4	196	64.9	63.2	30.4	30.7	1.9	2.6
RICHMOND-BEREA, KY	40080	87,454	96,811	104,105	1.4	196	94.1	93.3	3.6	3.9	0.6	0.9
RIO GRANDE CITY, TX	40100	53,597	62,732	70,233	2.2	85	87.9	87.7	0.1	0.2	0.3	0.3
RIVERSIDE-SAN BERN.	40140	3,254,821	4,152,464	4,889,267	3.4	22	62.1	58.0	7.7	7.3	4.5	5.0
RIVERTON, WY	40180	35,804	37,236	38,287	0.5	545	76.5	75.1	0.1	0.1	0.3	0.4
ROANOKE, VA	40220	288,309	299,981	307,878	0.5	545	85.0	83.5	12.2	12.8	1.1	1.4
ROANOKE RAPIDS, NC	40260	79,456	79,000	78,687	-0.1	805	41.6	40.4	54.5	55.1	0.4	0.6
ROCHELLE, IL	40300	51,032	55,369	58,629	1.1	288	95.3	94.1	0.4	0.5	0.5	0.6
ROCHESTER, MN	40340	163,618	187,300	202,744	1.9	113	92.0	89.8	2.1	2.6	3.4	4.5
ROCHESTER, NY	40380	1,037,831	1,054,376	1,065,234	0.2	679	83.3	81.2	10.7	11.7	1.9	2.5
ROCKFORD, IL	40420	320,204	350,085	374,912	1.2	255	83.5	80.9	9.3	9.9	1.6	2.0
ROCKINGHAM, NC	40460	46,564	47,685	48,261	0.3	633	64.8	63.3	30.5	31.0	0.7	0.9
ROCKLAND, ME	40500	39,618	42,289	43,904	0.9	352	98.3	98.0	0.2	0.3	0.4	0.5
ROCK SPRINGS, WY	40540	37,613	38,693	39,584	0.4	590	91.6	90.7	0.7	0.7	0.7	0.9
ROCKY MOUNT, NC	40580	143,026	148,738	152,192	0.5	545	53.4	52.5	43.1	42.8	0.4	0.6
ROLLA, MO	40620	39,825	42,118	43,422	0.8	396	93.2	91.7	1.5	1.7	2.4	3.5
ROME, GA	40660	90,565	96,522	100,003	0.9	352	81.3	77.4	13.3	15.3	1.0	1.3
ROSEBURG, OR	40700	100,399	105,822	109,884	0.7	444	93.9	93.1	0.2	0.2	0.7	0.9
ROSWELL, NM	40740	61,382	61,924	62,073	0.1	723	72.0	70.7	2.0	2.1	0.6	0.7
RUIDOSO, NM	40760	19,411	21,318	22,754	1.3	225	83.6	82.5	0.4	0.4	0.3	0.4
RUSSELLVILLE, AR	40780	75,608	80,878	84,157	0.9	352	91.7	90.0	2.3	2.5	0.7	0.9
RUSTON, LA	40820	57,906	59,353	60,511	0.3	633	61.0	58.5	36.7	38.6	1.0	1.4
RUTLAND, VT	40860	63,400	64,432	65,210	0.2	679	98.1	97.8	0.3	0.4	0.4	0.6
SACRAMENTO-ARDEN,CA	40900	1,796,857	2,141,388	2,389,579	2.4	71	70.0	66.0	7.1	6.9	9.5	10.9
SAFFORD, AZ	40940	42,036	42,342	42,496	0.1	723	68.5	65.8	1.6	1.6	0.5	0.6
SAGINAW-SAG TOWNSHIP	40980	210,039	208,714	206,568	-0.1	805	75.3	72.9	18.6	19.9	0.8	1.1
ST. CLOUD, MN	41060	167,392	190,175	207,703	1.8	127	96.0	95.1	0.8	0.9	1.5	2.0
ST. GEORGE, UT	41100	90,354	133,599	178,120	5.5	4	93.6	92.9	0.2	0.2	0.9	1.0
ST. JOSEPH, MO-KS	41140	122,336	123,954	124,474	0.2	679	93.3	92.0	4.1	4.8	0.4	0.6
ST. LOUIS, MO-IL	41180	2,698,687	2,833,676	2,945,082	0.7	444	78.9	77.6	17.7	18.3	1.4	1.9
ST. MARYS, GA	41220	43,664	49,246	54,932	1.8	127	75.0	70.8	20.1	22.9	1.1	1.4
ST. MARYS, PA	41260	35,112	33,700	32,606	-0.6	921	99.0	98.7	0.1	0.2	0.4	0.6
SALEM, OR	41420	347,214	383,801	409,338	1.4	196	83.0	79.6	0.8	0.9	2.0	2.3
SALINA, KS	41460	59,760	61,339	62,465	0.4	590	90.0	88.0	2.8	3.0	1.6	2.1
SALINAS, CA	41500	401,762	425,924	437,469	0.8	396	55.9	51.8	3.7	3.4	6.5	7.1
SALISBURY, MD	41540	109,391	121,658	131,004	1.5	173	68.9	63.5	27.3	31.5	1.5	2.0
SALISBURY, NC	41580	130,340	136,558	140,092	0.6	494	80.0	78.3	15.8	16.0	0.9	1.2
SALT LAKE CITY, UT	41620	968,858	1,073,432	1,152,385	1.4	196	86.6	84.8	1.0	1.2	3.6	3.9
SAN ANGELO, TX	41660	105,781	105,729	104,936	0.0	765	79.3	78.7	4.1	4.1	0.9	0.9
SAN ANTONIO, TX	41700	1,711,703	1,985,996	2,200,073	2.1	93	71.4	69.2	6.2	5.9	1.5	1.6
SAN DIEGO-CARLSBAD	41740	2,813,833	3,064,142	3,192,305	1.2	255	66.5	61.8	5.7	5.6	9.4	10.7
SANDUSKY, OH	41780	79,551	79,773	79,947	0.0	765	88.6	87.2	8.6	9.5	0.4	0.6
SANFORD, NC	41820	49,040	56,213	62,122	1.9	113	70.0	66.9	20.5	20.1	0.7	0.9
SAN FRANCISCO-OAKLND	41860	4,123,740	4,316,905	4,437,731	0.6	494	56.7	52.1	9.6	9.3	19.8	22.2
SAN JOSE-SUNNYVALE	41940	1,735,819	1,829,059	1,896,048	0.7	444	54.2	48.9	2.8	2.6	25.2	27.9
SAN LUIS OBISPO-PASO	42020	246,681	267,623	280,261	1.1	288	84.6	80.4	2.0	1.9	2.8	3.4
SANTA BARBARA-GOLETA	42060	399,347	422,299	438,575	0.8	396	72.7	68.1	2.3	2.4	4.3	4.8
SANTA CRUZ-WATSONVIL	42100	255,602	264,678	270,870	0.5	545	75.1	70.2	1.0	1.0	3.6	4.2
SANTA FE, NM	42140	129,292	144,001	154,484	1.5	173	73.5	72.5	0.6	0.7	0.9	1.1
SANTA ROSA-PETALUMA	42220	458,614	483,728	495,810	0.7	444	81.6	77.5	1.4	1.5	3.3	3.9
SARASOTA-BRADENTON	42260	589,959	716,099	822,743	2.7	51	89.8	87.4	6.0	7.0	0.9	1.2
SAULT STE. MARIE, MI	42300	38,543	39,841	40,876	0.5	545	75.9	74.4	5.5	6.0	0.5	0.8
SAVANNAH, GA	42340	293,000	333,533	365,715	1.8	127	61.2	57.8	34.9	37.4	1.5	1.9
SAYRE, PA	42380	62,761	63,798	64,552	0.2	679	97.9	97.5	0.4	0.5	0.5	0.7
UNITED STATES					1.2		75.1	72.7	12.3	12.6	3.8	4.5

POPULATION COMPOSITION
CBSA AND U.S. TOTALS

B

CBSA	% HISPANIC ORIGIN		2007 AGE DISTRIBUTION (%)										MEDIAN AGE	% 2007 Males	% 2007 Females
	2000	2007	0-4	5-9	10-14	15-19	20-24	25-44	45-64	65-84	85+	18+	2007		
PORTSMOUTH, OH	0.6	0.7	6.5	6.2	5.8	6.2	6.5	27.4	25.9	13.4	2.1	77.8	38.5	49.2	50.8
POTTSVILLE, PA	1.1	1.5	5.0	4.7	5.4	6.0	6.0	26.1	28.1	15.5	3.3	81.5	42.8	50.2	49.8
POUGHKEEPSIE-NEWBRG	9.3	10.8	6.9	6.6	7.5	8.3	7.1	25.6	26.4	9.9	1.7	74.2	37.2	50.0	50.0
PRESCOTT, AZ	9.8	12.1	5.1	4.8	5.2	6.0	5.8	19.2	31.3	19.9	2.8	81.3	47.8	49.0	51.0
PRICE, UT	10.3	12.1	7.9	7.0	6.5	7.8	8.3	25.0	25.1	10.4	1.9	74.4	33.6	48.7	51.3
PRINEVILLE, OR	5.6	7.6	6.5	5.8	6.4	7.3	5.6	22.7	30.1	14.0	1.7	77.0	41.5	49.8	50.2
PROVIDENCE-NEW BEDFD	7.0	9.0	6.1	5.9	6.6	7.7	7.0	26.6	26.1	11.5	2.6	77.2	38.5	48.3	51.7
PROVO-OREM, UT	6.9	8.1	12.4	10.0	7.8	8.5	11.8	30.0	13.8	5.0	0.8	65.5	24.8	49.6	50.4
PUEBLO, CO	38.0	42.8	6.9	6.4	6.7	6.7	6.9	26.0	25.8	12.3	2.2	76.0	37.6	49.0	51.0
PULLMAN, WA	3.0	3.8	4.4	3.4	3.6	13.5	30.4	20.4	16.4	6.5	1.4	86.1	24.1	48.8	51.2
PUNTA GORDA, FL	3.3	4.8	3.6	3.4	3.9	4.3	3.8	15.4	29.3	31.2	5.1	86.4	56.9	47.5	52.5
QUINCY, IL-MO	0.8	1.1	6.6	5.9	6.2	7.0	7.4	24.3	25.6	13.7	3.3	77.4	39.7	48.5	51.5
RACINE, WI	7.9	10.0	7.0	6.6	6.7	7.1	7.2	25.8	26.9	10.7	1.9	75.3	38.0	49.5	50.5
RALEIGH-CARY, NC	5.7	7.4	7.3	7.2	7.0	6.8	6.5	32.8	24.4	7.0	1.0	74.6	35.0	49.7	50.3
RAPID CITY, SD	2.5	3.1	7.3	6.4	6.1	7.4	8.6	26.0	26.4	10.1	1.6	75.9	35.6	49.7	50.3
RAYMONDVILLE, TX	85.7	88.7	8.9	7.9	8.2	7.9	8.9	27.3	19.9	9.9	1.2	70.3	29.9	51.6	48.4
READING, PA	9.7	11.8	6.2	5.8	6.7	7.4	6.3	25.8	26.9	12.4	2.5	77.2	39.8	49.1	50.9
RED BLUFF, CA	15.8	20.0	6.7	5.5	6.7	7.3	8.3	22.5	27.4	13.5	2.1	76.4	40.0	49.5	50.5
REDDING, CA	5.5	7.1	6.1	5.3	6.4	7.6	8.1	21.8	29.6	13.0	2.2	77.6	41.1	48.9	51.1
RED WING, MN	1.1	1.5	6.4	6.0	6.2	6.9	7.8	24.0	28.2	11.7	2.8	77.0	40.4	49.7	50.3
RENO-SPARKS, NV	16.5	19.9	6.9	6.6	6.6	7.0	6.7	28.2	26.9	9.8	1.3	75.8	36.9	50.3	49.7
REXBURG, ID	5.9	6.5	7.8	6.6	6.8	19.1	18.0	17.5	16.5	6.6	1.1	73.6	22.7	49.0	51.0
RICHMOND, IN	1.4	1.8	6.3	5.9	5.9	7.0	7.1	25.6	26.4	13.3	2.3	77.8	39.5	48.3	51.7
RICHMOND, VA	2.2	3.1	6.3	6.2	6.7	7.2	6.5	27.6	27.5	10.3	1.6	76.5	38.3	48.6	51.4
RICHMOND-BEREA, KY	0.9	1.3	6.4	5.9	5.8	7.7	8.8	31.4	23.4	9.3	1.3	78.5	33.6	49.0	51.0
RIO GRANDE CITY, TX	97.5	98.1	11.3	9.6	9.8	8.4	8.1	27.3	17.5	7.3	0.8	64.2	26.9	48.9	51.1
RIVERSIDE-SAN BERN.	37.8	43.8	8.4	7.3	8.5	8.4	7.7	26.9	22.2	9.3	1.4	70.6	32.2	49.8	50.2
RIVERTON, WY	4.4	4.7	6.7	6.2	6.2	7.2	8.3	22.0	29.4	12.4	1.6	76.7	39.8	49.2	50.8
ROANOKE, VA	1.1	1.6	5.5	5.6	6.1	6.5	5.6	25.0	29.7	13.7	2.4	79.0	42.2	48.1	51.9
ROANOKE RAPIDS, NC	0.9	1.2	6.3	5.7	6.7	6.7	6.3	24.9	27.9	13.5	2.1	77.1	40.5	48.2	51.8
ROCHELLE, IL	6.0	7.9	6.6	6.1	7.2	7.2	7.1	24.7	27.7	11.4	2.1	75.6	39.1	49.7	50.3
ROCHESTER, MN	2.4	3.2	7.2	6.8	6.7	7.1	7.1	27.2	26.1	9.8	1.9	74.8	37.0	49.4	50.6
ROCHESTER, NY	4.5	5.2	6.2	6.0	6.8	8.0	7.5	25.3	27.0	10.9	2.3	76.6	38.3	48.7	51.3
ROCKFORD, IL	7.6	10.0	7.2	6.8	7.0	7.1	6.4	27.0	26.2	10.5	1.8	74.6	37.3	49.2	50.8
ROCKINGHAM, NC	2.8	3.6	6.8	6.5	6.8	7.2	6.7	26.7	25.3	12.2	1.8	76.0	37.3	49.8	50.2
ROCKLAND, ME	0.6	0.8	5.2	5.0	5.3	6.1	6.1	23.5	32.4	13.5	2.8	80.5	44.1	49.3	50.7
ROCK SPRINGS, WY	9.4	10.5	7.0	6.4	6.4	7.3	9.3	25.0	30.1	7.4	1.1	76.0	35.3	50.4	49.6
ROCKY MOUNT, NC	3.1	4.2	6.5	6.4	7.0	6.8	6.0	27.0	27.3	11.4	1.8	76.2	38.5	47.9	52.1
ROLLA, MO	1.2	1.5	5.8	5.4	5.6	8.5	9.4	25.5	25.4	12.3	2.1	79.1	36.6	50.9	49.1
ROME, GA	5.5	7.5	6.6	6.3	6.3	7.1	6.8	27.5	25.0	12.4	2.1	77.0	37.4	48.7	51.3
ROSEBURG, OR	3.3	4.4	5.7	5.3	5.6	6.5	6.6	21.8	30.8	15.4	2.4	79.4	43.8	49.2	50.8
ROSWELL, NM	43.8	46.1	7.5	6.6	7.0	7.8	8.1	24.0	24.2	12.4	2.4	74.2	35.7	49.4	50.6
RUIDOSO, NM	25.6	27.4	5.2	4.7	5.5	6.5	5.7	19.4	33.8	17.6	1.6	80.7	46.8	48.7	51.3
RUSSELLVILLE, AR	5.0	6.6	6.9	6.2	6.4	7.4	7.1	28.1	24.7	11.3	2.1	76.8	36.5	49.6	50.4
RUSTON, LA	1.0	1.1	6.5	5.8	5.4	9.2	13.1	24.7	22.4	10.9	2.1	78.9	31.8	48.9	51.1
RUTLAND, VT	0.7	0.8	5.1	5.0	5.5	7.7	6.8	23.6	31.3	12.6	2.5	80.0	42.6	48.9	51.1
SACRAMENTO-ARDEN,CA	15.5	18.6	7.2	6.8	7.5	7.5	7.3	27.7	25.0	9.5	1.6	74.1	35.5	49.1	50.9
SAFFORD, AZ	30.3	35.0	8.5	7.6	7.6	8.3	8.5	26.5	21.2	10.3	1.5	71.6	31.7	52.8	47.2
SAGINAW-SAG TOWNSHIP	6.7	8.1	6.7	6.4	7.0	7.0	6.6	25.5	26.7	11.7	2.3	75.7	38.0	48.2	51.8
ST. CLOUD, MN	1.3	1.8	7.0	6.4	6.2	8.2	10.8	27.9	23.0	8.9	1.7	76.2	32.8	50.2	49.8
ST. GEORGE, UT	5.2	6.2	10.3	8.4	7.3	7.4	7.6	23.7	19.6	13.5	2.1	69.8	31.0	49.3	50.7
ST. JOSEPH, MO-KS	2.0	2.5	6.4	5.8	6.0	7.3	7.5	27.5	25.1	11.8	2.5	77.9	37.8	50.5	49.5
ST. LOUIS, MO-IL	1.5	1.8	6.7	6.4	6.9	7.1	6.7	26.9	26.3	11.0	2.0	75.7	37.8	48.4	51.6
ST. MARYS, GA	3.6	4.8	9.2	7.4	7.5	8.1	8.2	33.4	20.4	5.2	0.5	70.8	30.1	50.7	49.3
ST. MARYS, PA	0.4	0.5	5.9	5.7	5.8	6.3	6.0	25.3	27.7	14.5	2.7	78.5	41.7	49.8	50.2
SALEM, OR	15.6	20.1	7.4	6.7	6.8	7.4	7.8	26.4	24.7	10.4	2.3	74.8	35.0	50.0	50.0
SALINA, KS	5.5	7.4	6.9	6.3	6.6	7.1	7.6	25.3	26.1	11.8	2.3	76.0	37.9	49.7	50.3
SALINAS, CA	46.8	52.8	8.1	7.1	8.0	7.8	8.0	29.8	21.9	8.0	1.4	73.2	31.9	51.8	48.2
SALISBURY, MD	2.0	2.8	5.9	5.7	5.9	7.9	8.3	26.2	26.6	11.6	1.8	78.6	38.0	49.0	51.0
SALISBURY, NC	4.1	5.4	6.7	6.4	6.4	6.6	6.0	28.3	26.0	11.5	2.1	76.6	38.2	49.6	50.4
SALT LAKE CITY, UT	11.7	13.6	9.7	8.7	7.4	6.8	7.3	32.4	19.9	6.7	1.1	70.2	29.7	50.4	49.6
SAN ANGELO, TX	30.6	32.1	7.1	6.2	6.3	8.0	8.9	26.3	23.8	11.3	2.1	76.3	34.7	48.8	51.2
SAN ANTONIO, TX	50.4	56.3	7.8	7.2	7.1	7.4	7.6	28.0	24.0	9.3	1.4	73.4	34.1	48.9	51.1
SAN DIEGO-CARLSBAD	26.7	31.7	7.1	6.6	7.1	7.4	7.7	29.8	23.2	9.2	1.7	75.0	34.2	50.4	49.6
SANDUSKY, OH	2.1	2.5	6.0	5.7	6.3	6.5	6.4	23.4	29.1	14.4	2.4	78.0	42.0	48.9	51.1
SANFORD, NC	11.7	15.3	7.0	6.5	6.4	6.4	6.4	27.9	26.3	11.5	1.6	76.3	37.9	49.6	50.4
SAN FRANCISCO-OAKLND	17.8	21.0	6.1	6.0	6.6	6.3	6.1	31.0	26.3	9.8	1.8	77.4	37.6	49.6	50.4
SAN JOSE-SUNNYVALE	24.7	28.4	7.1	6.9	7.2	6.7	6.4	31.9	24.0	8.5	1.3	74.9	35.5	50.7	49.3
SAN LUIS OBISPO-PASO	16.3	20.5	5.0	4.9	5.8	8.6	10.2	23.3	27.7	12.2	2.3	80.2	39.0	50.8	49.2
SANTA BARBARA-GOLETA	34.2	40.6	6.7	6.0	7.0	7.9	9.1	27.5	23.0	10.6	2.2	76.1	34.3	50.3	49.7
SANTA CRUZ-WATSONVIL	26.8	32.4	6.0	5.7	6.4	7.9	8.0	28.7	27.6	8.0	1.7	77.8	35.8	50.0	50.0
SANTA FE, NM	49.0	51.2	6.0	5.8	5.9	6.8	7.1	26.1	30.6	10.3	1.4	78.2	39.8	48.9	51.1
SANTA ROSA-PETALUMA	17.3	21.6	5.9	5.7	6.8	7.0	6.9	26.2	28.8	10.4	2.3	77.4	39.0	49.3	50.7
SARASOTA-BRADENTON	6.6	9.4	4.7	4.0	4.0	5.2	4.6	19.6	28.1	23.7	4.7	82.6	49.7	47.8	52.2
SAULT STE. MARIE, MI	1.6	1.9	5.5	5.0	4.9	7.9	9.5	23.4	25.6	10.9	1.7	81.3	36.9	54.6	45.4
SAVANNAH, GA	2.2	2.8	7.0	6.4	6.7	7.1	7.6	28.1	25.0	10.5	1.6	75.9	35.7	48.8	51.2
SAYRE, PA	0.6	0.8	6.2	5.9	6.3	6.6	6.2	24.1	28.5	13.7	2.4	77.4	41.3	49.1	50.9
UNITED STATES	12.5	15.0	6.9	6.5	6.8	7.1	7.0	27.6	25.4	10.7	1.9	75.6	36.7	49.2	50.8

CBSA	HOUSEHOLDS					FAMILIES			MEDIAN HOUSEHOLD INCOME		
	2000	2007	2012	% Annual Rate 2000-2007	2007 Average HH Size	2000	2007	% Annual Rate 2000-2007	2007	2012	2007 National Rank
PORTSMOUTH, OH	30,871	30,778	30,506	0.0	2.39	21,372	20,670	-0.5	33,923	38,261	862
POTTSVILLE, PA	60,530	61,497	61,672	0.2	2.31	40,116	39,494	-0.2	41,907	49,686	562
POUGHKEEPSIE-NEWBRG	214,324	234,944	249,870	1.3	2.78	153,658	167,360	1.2	67,933	80,910	20
PRESCOTT, AZ	70,171	91,430	111,185	3.7	2.35	46,754	60,104	3.5	45,976	54,894	386
PRICE, UT	7,413	7,442	7,450	0.1	2.61	5,379	5,265	-0.3	41,847	47,470	570
PRINEVILLE, OR	7,354	8,737	9,878	2.4	2.58	5,425	6,400	2.3	43,282	50,000	505
PROVIDENCE-NEW BEDFD	613,835	635,001	649,452	0.5	2.49	406,008	412,579	0.2	53,979	63,408	143
PROVO-OREM, UT	102,393	134,183	163,239	3.8	3.58	82,721	106,490	3.5	59,194	70,774	71
PUEBLO, CO	54,579	59,956	63,444	1.3	2.51	37,332	40,084	1.0	41,283	48,218	597
PULLMAN, WA	15,257	15,814	16,156	0.5	2.28	8,057	8,173	0.2	35,798	41,663	816
PUNTA GORDA, FL	63,864	75,891	84,219	2.4	2.17	44,123	51,516	2.2	45,033	52,291	431
QUINCY, IL-MO	30,816	31,000	30,921	0.1	2.41	20,713	20,216	-0.3	41,537	47,448	583
RACINE, WI	70,819	76,183	79,606	1.0	2.53	49,861	52,459	0.7	61,092	71,049	58
RALEIGH-CARY, NC	306,478	394,879	472,223	3.6	2.54	205,332	257,151	3.2	66,885	79,545	26
RAPID CITY, SD	43,446	49,151	53,022	1.7	2.45	29,971	33,625	1.6	47,574	56,845	329
RAYMONDVILLE, TX	5,584	5,869	6,045	0.7	3.38	4,586	4,788	0.6	26,146	29,271	930
READING, PA	141,570	153,215	162,509	1.1	2.56	98,463	103,595	0.7	56,332	65,591	106
RED BLUFF, CA	21,013	23,830	26,134	1.8	2.63	14,897	16,963	1.8	37,835	42,978	747
REDDING, CA	63,426	70,970	77,020	1.6	2.54	44,002	49,447	1.6	41,802	48,076	574
RED WING, MN	16,983	18,620	19,749	1.3	2.49	11,900	12,685	0.9	59,218	68,080	70
RENO-SPARKS, NV	133,546	165,338	191,292	3.0	2.54	84,721	103,566	2.8	58,775	69,249	77
REXBURG, ID	11,014	14,490	17,792	3.9	3.36	7,884	10,161	3.6	40,595	46,274	626
RICHMOND, IN	28,469	28,272	28,143	-0.1	2.40	19,308	18,422	-0.6	43,926	51,002	474
RICHMOND, VA	425,100	473,324	508,936	1.5	2.48	288,121	313,986	1.2	58,635	68,583	80
RICHMOND-BEREA, KY	33,696	38,160	41,552	1.7	2.39	22,981	25,019	1.2	38,780	45,368	698
RIO GRANDE CITY, TX	14,410	17,211	19,451	2.5	3.62	12,663	15,058	2.4	19,339	21,800	939
RIVERSIDE-SAN BERN.	1,034,812	1,292,151	1,515,987	3.1	3.15	776,713	971,983	3.1	53,548	62,739	149
RIVERTON, WY	13,545	14,537	15,131	1.0	2.50	9,484	9,896	0.6	39,844	45,721	657
ROANOKE, VA	119,366	126,030	130,227	0.8	2.31	80,041	82,073	0.3	48,630	55,965	294
ROANOKE RAPIDS, NC	30,813	31,541	31,783	0.3	2.42	21,254	21,194	0.0	32,235	36,653	888
ROCHELLE, IL	19,278	21,056	22,361	1.2	2.60	14,168	15,099	0.9	56,044	64,418	112
ROCHESTER, MN	62,504	72,832	79,372	2.1	2.52	43,039	48,713	1.7	63,879	76,192	35
ROCHESTER, NY	397,303	408,101	414,546	0.4	2.48	262,084	267,147	0.3	56,314	65,890	108
ROCKFORD, IL	122,577	133,324	142,560	1.2	2.58	84,926	90,043	0.8	55,891	64,670	114
ROCKINGHAM, NC	17,873	18,556	18,910	0.5	2.46	12,574	12,733	0.2	34,788	39,478	842
ROCKLAND, ME	16,608	18,068	18,977	1.2	2.25	10,728	11,425	0.9	45,120	52,099	426
ROCK SPRINGS, WY	14,105	15,043	15,617	0.9	2.53	10,096	10,488	0.5	58,111	67,306	83
ROCKY MOUNT, NC	54,036	57,089	58,801	0.8	2.54	38,743	39,962	0.4	42,691	49,005	521
ROLLA, MO	15,683	16,901	17,561	1.0	2.35	10,235	10,687	0.6	36,466	42,314	793
ROME, GA	34,028	36,334	37,719	0.9	2.54	24,214	25,051	0.5	43,951	51,303	473
ROSEBURG, OR	39,821	42,528	44,464	0.9	2.45	28,218	29,889	0.8	40,879	46,974	620
ROSWELL, NM	22,561	23,066	23,273	0.3	2.60	16,077	15,970	-0.1	34,444	39,176	853
RUIDOSO, NM	8,202	9,328	10,079	1.8	2.26	5,631	6,207	1.4	41,313	47,522	592
RUSSELLVILLE, AR	28,623	30,566	31,929	0.9	2.55	20,814	21,629	0.5	39,435	45,931	677
RUSTON, LA	21,321	22,441	23,150	0.7	2.40	13,986	14,277	0.3	30,436	32,940	908
RUTLAND, VT	25,678	26,933	27,564	0.7	2.32	16,740	17,040	0.2	47,822	57,465	320
SACRAMENTO-ARDEN,CA	665,298	789,006	880,156	2.4	2.67	445,835	532,526	2.5	58,766	69,352	78
SAFFORD, AZ	13,233	13,451	13,560	0.2	2.90	9,880	9,947	0.1	40,134	46,253	647
SAGINAW-SAG TOWNSHIP	80,430	80,729	80,429	0.1	2.51	55,790	54,494	-0.3	46,913	53,507	353
ST. CLOUD, MN	60,669	71,210	78,914	2.2	2.56	40,647	46,265	1.8	53,283	62,044	152
ST. GEORGE, UT	29,939	45,699	61,738	6.0	2.89	23,429	35,055	5.7	46,344	52,878	374
ST. JOSEPH, MO-KS	46,531	47,459	47,883	0.3	2.42	31,220	30,957	-0.1	43,397	50,051	499
ST. LOUIS, MO-IL	1,048,279	1,110,486	1,158,645	0.8	2.50	708,467	734,120	0.5	55,742	65,108	118
ST. MARYS, GA	14,705	17,255	19,195	2.2	2.82	11,375	13,017	1.9	51,880	60,687	196
ST. MARYS, PA	14,124	13,889	13,582	-0.2	2.39	9,748	9,311	-0.6	47,419	54,712	337
SALEM, OR	124,699	136,137	144,966	1.2	2.71	86,588	93,725	1.1	50,778	59,897	222
SALINA, KS	23,866	24,623	25,111	0.4	2.42	15,928	16,209	0.2	47,093	54,606	347
SALINAS, CA	121,236	128,182	131,279	0.8	3.14	87,931	93,329	0.8	60,932	71,515	60
SALISBURY, MD	40,579	46,010	49,994	1.7	2.46	27,225	29,809	1.3	43,972	49,471	469
SALISBURY, NC	49,940	52,875	54,357	0.8	2.49	35,495	36,678	0.5	45,881	52,254	391
SALT LAKE CITY, UT	318,150	354,692	381,093	1.5	2.98	231,730	252,207	1.2	62,754	76,077	41
SAN ANGELO, TX	40,197	40,873	40,853	0.2	2.48	27,326	27,460	0.1	40,949	47,514	616
SAN ANTONIO, TX	601,265	696,474	773,436	2.0	2.79	432,161	496,171	1.9	49,359	57,053	274
SAN DIEGO-CARLSBAD	994,677	1,075,598	1,119,523	1.1	2.75	663,170	720,463	1.1	59,771	70,352	69
SANDUSKY, OH	31,727	32,774	33,241	0.4	2.38	21,750	21,774	0.0	52,277	60,543	188
SANFORD, NC	18,466	21,228	23,478	1.9	2.61	13,361	15,007	1.6	48,307	54,918	300
SAN FRANCISCO-OAKLND	1,551,948	1,612,512	1,650,843	0.5	2.63	958,443	1,002,406	0.6	79,153	95,205	5
SAN JOSE-SUNNYVALE	581,748	610,859	631,123	0.7	2.95	408,454	430,720	0.7	93,422	112,300	2
SAN LUIS OBISPO-PASO	92,739	103,357	109,080	1.5	2.44	58,654	65,711	1.6	53,233	62,361	154
SANTA BARBARA-GOLETA	136,622	145,125	150,803	0.8	2.79	89,555	95,580	0.9	58,748	68,781	79
SANTA CRUZ-WATSONVIL	91,139	95,467	97,707	0.6	2.68	57,132	60,163	0.7	69,128	81,292	15
SANTA FE, NM	52,482	57,945	62,402	1.4	2.43	32,787	34,861	0.8	54,453	64,838	134
SANTA ROSA-PETALUMA	172,403	181,921	186,475	0.7	2.59	112,397	119,183	0.8	67,499	79,410	23
SARASOTA-BRADENTON	262,397	319,721	368,303	2.8	2.20	168,254	200,948	2.5	51,324	60,591	211
SAULT STE. MARIE, MI	13,474	14,432	15,030	1.0	2.35	8,962	9,316	0.5	41,699	47,577	577
SAVANNAH, GA	111,105	127,382	140,437	1.9	2.53	76,431	85,438	1.5	50,476	60,028	234
SAYRE, PA	24,453	25,387	25,929	0.5	2.47	17,308	17,483	0.1	42,680	49,308	522
UNITED STATES				1.2	2.59			1.0	53,154	62,503	

CBSA	2007 Per Capita Income	2007 HH Income Base	2007 HOUSEHOLD INCOME DISTRIBUTION (%)					2007 Home Value Base	2007 HOME VALUE DISTRIBUTION (%)					2007 Median Home Value
			Less than $25,000	$25,000 to $49,999	$50,000 to $99,999	$100,000 to $149,999	$150,000 or More		Less than $50,000	$50,000 to $89,999	$90,000 to $174,999	$175,000 to $399,999	$400,000 or More	
PORTSMOUTH, OH	19,055	30,778	37.5	29.9	24.2	5.9	2.4	22,473	25.4	33.3	30.9	9.5	0.8	78,398
POTTSVILLE, PA	22,340	61,497	28.6	30.2	31.6	6.5	3.0	47,997	11.8	22.4	38.6	24.7	2.6	125,451
POUGHKEEPSIE-NEWBRG	29,995	234,939	15.1	20.5	35.0	17.7	11.7	166,451	1.3	1.2	5.5	70.2	21.8	315,260
PRESCOTT, AZ	26,284	91,430	24.6	30.5	30.3	9.3	5.3	68,208	4.2	4.6	19.5	47.9	23.8	247,495
PRICE, UT	19,506	7,442	30.0	28.8	30.2	9.1	1.8	5,829	4.4	13.7	59.7	20.2	1.9	133,555
PRINEVILLE, OR	20,509	8,737	26.7	30.7	34.2	6.2	2.3	6,659	7.0	5.3	29.0	46.1	12.5	190,297
PROVIDENCE-NEW BEDFD	27,587	635,001	23.9	22.6	32.8	13.2	7.6	390,353	0.6	0.7	4.8	68.1	25.7	314,422
PROVO-OREM, UT	20,696	134,181	14.9	26.0	37.6	14.2	7.4	92,375	2.1	1.3	19.0	65.4	12.2	230,538
PUEBLO, CO	21,656	59,952	29.8	28.8	29.7	8.0	3.7	43,740	6.4	13.6	53.1	24.6	2.3	129,571
PULLMAN, WA	20,675	15,805	37.6	25.4	25.1	8.0	3.8	8,046	6.5	6.5	27.4	50.6	9.1	197,267
PUNTA GORDA, FL	27,401	75,891	23.4	32.1	31.9	8.3	4.3	64,567	1.5	4.4	28.6	50.8	14.7	216,084
QUINCY, IL-MO	21,860	31,000	27.8	31.5	31.1	6.3	3.3	23,555	14.1	18.5	44.3	20.4	2.7	118,900
RACINE, WI	28,174	76,183	17.1	22.8	39.0	14.9	6.2	54,959	1.9	5.9	45.6	42.2	4.5	168,629
RALEIGH-CARY, NC	33,794	394,876	14.6	21.3	35.6	15.4	13.0	272,669	7.1	5.7	29.9	46.7	10.5	193,070
RAPID CITY, SD	24,639	49,151	21.0	31.4	34.2	8.9	4.5	33,435	13.9	11.7	43.0	26.6	4.8	134,648
RAYMONDVILLE, TX	10,742	5,869	47.8	30.5	17.1	3.4	1.3	4,551	51.9	31.4	13.8	2.8	0.2	48,538
READING, PA	26,756	153,215	19.2	24.9	36.3	13.5	6.2	114,150	4.0	8.3	32.6	48.9	6.2	186,788
RED BLUFF, CA	19,290	23,830	32.6	30.5	27.5	6.4	3.0	16,400	4.5	3.9	15.6	59.4	16.6	238,249
REDDING, CA	22,036	70,970	30.1	28.1	29.1	8.7	4.0	47,807	5.1	2.6	8.2	61.6	22.5	287,414
RED WING, MN	28,410	18,620	17.1	23.7	40.3	12.6	6.3	14,943	5.3	4.5	30.2	49.5	10.4	200,901
RENO-SPARKS, NV	30,430	165,338	17.3	24.2	36.6	13.0	8.9	101,407	4.4	2.2	8.1	55.1	30.3	322,408
REXBURG, ID	15,316	14,486	28.5	33.4	29.6	5.8	2.7	9,829	9.9	9.4	40.0	35.5	5.2	159,671
RICHMOND, IN	22,511	28,272	26.9	29.2	32.9	8.0	3.0	19,752	12.7	26.2	46.5	13.4	1.2	105,076
RICHMOND, VA	30,263	473,322	17.4	24.6	35.5	14.2	8.3	331,619	2.5	3.2	27.9	55.5	10.9	211,182
RICHMOND-BEREA, KY	20,695	38,160	32.5	29.5	27.7	7.5	2.8	24,534	20.9	20.2	38.8	19.0	1.2	104,500
RIO GRANDE CITY, TX	8,219	17,211	60.2	24.7	11.3	2.8	1.0	13,862	46.0	31.8	18.3	3.7	0.2	53,690
RIVERSIDE-SAN BERN.	21,933	1,292,124	21.8	24.8	33.7	12.7	6.9	876,801	3.6	2.3	6.2	44.7	43.2	367,349
RIVERTON, WY	20,397	14,537	30.1	31.9	28.9	6.3	2.8	10,887	12.4	9.1	34.3	34.3	9.9	163,392
ROANOKE, VA	27,074	126,025	22.8	28.6	33.1	10.4	5.1	90,127	4.8	7.6	40.4	40.5	6.7	170,257
ROANOKE RAPIDS, NC	17,864	31,541	41.1	27.2	24.1	5.4	2.1	22,486	23.6	27.4	36.7	10.3	1.9	88,461
ROCHELLE, IL	25,795	21,056	18.1	25.5	38.2	12.9	5.2	16,177	4.2	5.1	43.1	42.8	4.8	171,118
ROCHESTER, MN	32,026	72,832	14.3	23.0	38.7	14.3	9.8	57,439	5.5	7.4	45.4	36.4	5.3	158,144
ROCHESTER, NY	28,684	408,097	19.8	24.5	34.4	13.4	7.9	288,120	4.4	10.7	48.1	33.7	3.1	151,159
ROCKFORD, IL	26,850	133,324	19.4	24.8	36.2	13.6	6.0	97,705	5.2	12.0	53.3	27.2	2.4	138,284
ROCKINGHAM, NC	18,173	18,556	37.1	29.4	26.2	5.2	2.1	13,557	24.7	29.4	36.4	8.7	1.0	84,423
ROCKLAND, ME	25,360	18,068	24.8	30.8	31.9	7.9	4.6	13,491	2.7	4.8	29.9	46.4	16.2	205,493
ROCK SPRINGS, WY	25,917	15,043	18.7	23.5	39.6	13.9	4.4	11,564	13.4	8.3	27.9	44.8	5.5	175,834
ROCKY MOUNT, NC	21,473	57,089	30.1	27.7	30.3	8.0	3.9	38,935	20.9	23.8	40.3	12.8	2.1	97,204
ROLLA, MO	20,361	16,901	34.3	30.1	26.6	6.0	3.0	11,459	17.1	19.5	40.4	20.3	2.7	111,595
ROME, GA	22,251	36,334	27.4	28.0	32.0	8.2	4.3	24,734	11.2	22.5	43.1	19.2	4.0	113,788
ROSEBURG, OR	20,895	42,528	28.3	32.3	30.6	6.1	2.7	31,470	6.5	5.7	34.4	44.3	9.1	182,253
ROSWELL, NM	18,220	23,066	36.1	30.5	24.7	6.0	2.6	16,464	17.8	28.1	37.6	14.1	2.4	96,883
RUIDOSO, NM	24,760	9,328	29.8	29.1	28.2	8.9	4.0	7,262	10.0	13.2	37.7	29.4	9.8	148,563
RUSSELLVILLE, AR	19,606	30,566	31.5	30.5	28.2	6.7	3.1	22,408	18.6	28.2	37.8	13.3	2.1	94,671
RUSTON, LA	17,432	22,438	42.4	26.4	23.8	5.1	2.3	14,313	23.4	22.2	34.9	16.5	3.1	98,019
RUTLAND, VT	25,339	26,933	24.2	28.1	35.1	8.4	4.3	19,472	3.0	4.0	35.0	49.8	8.2	188,851
SACRAMENTO-ARDEN,CA	28,863	789,004	18.7	23.2	34.3	14.3	9.5	498,034	2.3	1.2	3.7	46.2	46.5	385,642
SAFFORD, AZ	16,771	13,451	31.5	29.5	30.9	6.2	2.0	9,319	8.9	14.7	38.3	34.4	3.8	150,169
SAGINAW-SAG TOWNSHIP	23,977	80,729	25.4	27.7	30.7	11.9	4.3	60,077	16.4	19.8	43.3	19.1	1.4	111,223
ST. CLOUD, MN	25,220	71,209	19.0	27.2	38.1	10.4	5.2	52,670	4.9	6.9	42.5	41.0	4.7	168,143
ST. GEORGE, UT	20,412	45,699	21.7	33.5	32.5	7.9	4.3	34,428	3.8	3.6	17.8	56.9	17.8	246,307
ST. JOSEPH, MO-KS	21,869	47,459	27.4	29.9	32.2	7.3	3.2	34,097	17.3	24.7	40.1	16.1	1.9	100,937
ST. LOUIS, MO-IL	28,844	1,110,478	19.8	24.9	34.7	13.0	7.6	818,542	6.9	13.7	39.1	33.1	7.2	148,988
ST. MARYS, GA	21,228	17,255	19.9	27.3	39.7	9.5	3.6	11,050	14.0	16.0	48.5	18.8	2.9	118,255
ST. MARYS, PA	23,265	13,889	23.7	29.1	36.1	9.1	2.1	11,093	6.3	14.4	48.0	28.8	2.4	149,278
SALEM, OR	23,146	136,137	20.3	28.8	35.9	10.2	4.8	90,223	4.3	3.8	22.9	57.5	11.4	217,078
SALINA, KS	23,782	24,623	21.8	31.5	35.7	7.3	3.7	17,692	10.9	23.3	44.6	19.4	1.8	113,612
SALINAS, CA	25,661	128,179	16.5	23.7	34.5	14.8	10.5	71,841	1.7	1.2	1.9	13.6	81.6	731,032
SALISBURY, MD	22,939	46,010	27.4	28.8	31.0	8.8	4.1	31,578	6.4	10.5	45.8	32.9	4.4	151,736
SALISBURY, NC	22,214	52,875	25.3	29.1	33.8	8.7	3.1	39,446	11.5	14.7	46.0	24.3	3.4	127,726
SALT LAKE CITY, UT	27,021	354,692	14.0	22.9	38.2	15.6	9.3	251,678	2.0	2.0	17.4	63.0	15.5	236,525
SAN ANGELO, TX	21,844	40,873	28.7	31.2	29.1	7.3	3.7	26,964	17.8	32.0	36.6	11.6	1.9	90,258
SAN ANTONIO, TX	23,176	696,459	23.3	27.2	32.7	10.7	6.1	463,353	13.1	25.2	37.2	20.3	4.3	109,611
SAN DIEGO-CARLSBAD	29,468	1,075,585	18.1	23.8	32.7	15.1	10.3	610,427	2.3	1.9	2.9	25.1	67.8	503,538
SANDUSKY, OH	27,369	32,774	19.8	27.8	35.3	11.8	5.4	24,555	6.2	12.3	44.2	32.8	4.5	147,458
SANFORD, NC	23,471	21,228	24.4	27.3	32.7	11.3	4.3	15,470	11.4	13.5	43.0	28.5	3.6	135,625
SAN FRANCISCO-OAKLND	42,085	1,612,502	14.0	16.4	31.5	18.3	19.7	916,035	0.9	1.3	1.9	13.6	82.3	750,208
SAN JOSE-SUNNYVALE	44,247	610,859	9.8	12.9	30.5	20.7	26.1	374,163	0.8	1.6	3.5	6.7	87.4	854,949
SAN LUIS OBISPO-PASO	28,635	103,354	22.2	24.8	33.2	12.0	7.8	64,965	2.0	2.0	4.4	27.2	64.4	493,665
SANTA BARBARA-GOLETA	29,256	145,122	18.7	23.4	33.2	13.7	11.0	83,386	1.7	1.8	3.4	26.6	66.4	630,561
SANTA CRUZ-WATSONVIL	35,450	95,467	15.8	20.3	31.2	17.0	15.7	58,301	1.0	1.5	3.9	12.8	80.8	772,167
SANTA FE, NM	30,522	57,944	20.2	25.8	32.3	12.9	8.9	39,915	7.6	5.0	10.5	42.5	34.3	308,299
SANTA ROSA-PETALUMA	33,537	181,921	14.5	21.0	35.1	18.0	11.4	119,173	2.4	2.1	3.2	17.8	74.4	572,266
SARASOTA-BRADENTON	32,476	319,721	20.3	28.2	33.3	10.4	7.8	252,237	4.2	4.5	16.3	50.9	24.1	249,493
SAULT STE. MARIE, MI	19,920	14,432	30.0	29.7	31.8	6.4	2.0	10,780	14.1	22.9	44.9	16.4	1.7	108,103
SAVANNAH, GA	26,677	127,382	24.6	24.8	32.4	10.9	7.3	84,072	7.2	10.6	35.7	35.1	11.4	166,211
SAYRE, PA	21,764	25,387	26.3	32.4	30.0	7.3	3.2	19,050	9.0	12.2	47.5	26.3	4.0	142,846
UNITED STATES	27,916		21.9	25.0	32.3	12.3	8.4		7.9	10.5	27.1	35.6	19.0	192,285

SPENDING POTENTIAL INDICES
CBSA AND U.S. TOTALS

CBSA	FINANCIAL SERVICES				THE HOME						ENTERTAINMENT						PERSONAL			
					Home Improvements		Furnishings													
	Auto Loan	Home Loan	Invest-ments	Retire-ment Plans	Home Repair	Lawn & Garden	Comput-ers & Hard-ware	Major Appli-ances	TV, Radio, Sound Equip-ment	Furni-ture	Dine out/ Carry out	Sports Equip-ment	Fees & Tickets	Toys & Games	Travel	Cable TV	Apparel & Services	Auto Repairs	Health Insur-ance	Pets & Supplies
PORTSMOUTH, OH	71	57	52	57	61	74	60	67	65	58	64	59	55	66	60	69	56	65	74	70
POTTSVILLE, PA	76	68	73	67	72	81	69	75	75	67	73	65	67	75	71	79	64	72	85	76
POUGHKEEPSIE-NEWBRG	108	126	134	123	126	113	118	116	115	121	116	108	126	115	122	114	108	114	111	114
PRESCOTT, AZ	89	83	83	82	87	99	81	92	85	81	84	78	80	81	87	89	73	89	99	92
PRICE, UT	77	67	65	67	68	77	68	73	73	66	71	64	65	73	68	75	62	70	80	74
PRINEVILLE, OR	83	67	56	66	73	90	69	81	74	67	73	70	63	75	70	78	63	76	87	84
PROVIDENCE-NEW BEDFD	87	98	109	97	99	90	98	94	96	98	97	87	102	95	99	96	90	94	92	92
PROVO-OREM, UT	105	106	101	108	98	94	109	99	102	107	103	95	106	104	102	98	93	103	93	100
PUEBLO, CO	76	73	80	74	73	76	74	75	77	74	75	66	74	76	75	78	67	75	80	75
PULLMAN, WA	73	53	52	57	54	64	81	66	74	65	75	65	66	72	67	71	66	72	67	69
PUNTA GORDA, FL	80	81	92	78	89	99	76	88	81	78	79	72	79	73	86	87	69	85	101	87
QUINCY, IL-MO	78	70	69	70	73	81	71	76	75	70	74	66	69	77	71	78	65	73	82	78
RACINE, WI	95	102	115	104	101	97	99	97	99	101	99	87	104	101	101	99	90	97	99	97
RALEIGH-CARY, NC	125	124	115	126	116	115	122	118	119	124	119	112	121	122	118	116	108	120	113	119
RAPID CITY, SD	89	81	81	82	79	85	85	85	86	82	85	77	81	86	83	86	75	85	87	86
RAYMONDVILLE, TX	57	46	32	41	41	48	44	50	51	48	51	43	40	48	43	53	45	51	52	48
READING, PA	95	97	106	98	99	99	94	96	96	96	95	85	97	97	97	98	86	94	100	97
RED BLUFF, CA	76	64	56	63	69	81	67	76	70	65	69	67	62	69	67	72	61	73	78	78
REDDING, CA	80	74	75	74	77	83	77	80	78	74	77	72	74	77	77	79	68	79	83	81
RED WING, MN	102	99	101	100	102	106	97	102	98	97	97	91	97	100	99	100	87	99	104	104
RENO-SPARKS, NV	106	106	109	109	101	97	111	103	106	109	107	98	109	106	107	103	97	107	99	103
REXBURG, ID	79	60	50	61	61	73	76	71	73	66	74	67	64	74	67	72	65	73	72	75
RICHMOND, IN	78	70	77	71	72	79	74	76	78	72	76	66	72	79	74	80	67	75	83	77
RICHMOND, VA	106	106	109	108	103	103	105	103	105	106	105	94	106	106	105	104	95	104	103	104
RICHMOND-BEREA, KY	79	63	54	63	63	75	69	72	72	66	72	66	62	73	65	74	63	72	75	76
RIO GRANDE CITY, TX	47	39	26	34	33	38	37	40	42	41	43	36	34	39	36	43	38	43	42	39
RIVERSIDE-SAN BERN.	95	99	94	96	95	91	97	96	94	97	94	92	96	93	96	91	86	98	91	93
RIVERTON, WY	78	66	60	66	70	82	68	76	71	66	70	67	63	72	68	74	61	73	80	79
ROANOKE, VA	88	85	91	86	87	92	85	88	88	85	87	77	85	88	87	90	78	87	93	90
ROANOKE RAPIDS, NC	72	52	36	50	56	74	54	66	63	53	61	58	47	63	54	67	52	62	74	71
ROCHELLE, IL	96	93	95	93	96	101	90	96	92	90	92	86	90	95	92	94	82	92	99	98
ROCHESTER, MN	114	116	118	118	113	112	113	112	111	115	111	103	114	114	113	110	101	112	110	113
ROCHESTER, NY	98	99	110	101	99	99	99	97	101	100	100	87	101	101	100	101	91	98	101	98
ROCKFORD, IL	96	96	104	98	94	94	96	94	97	97	96	84	97	98	96	97	87	95	97	94
ROCKINGHAM, NC	73	56	44	54	59	74	57	66	65	56	63	59	52	66	57	69	55	64	73	71
ROCKLAND, ME	89	75	66	75	81	98	77	89	80	74	79	78	71	81	78	84	69	83	93	92
ROCK SPRINGS, WY	96	94	91	94	89	92	90	91	91	91	90	82	90	93	90	91	80	91	93	92
ROCKY MOUNT, NC	85	71	62	71	73	86	71	79	77	72	76	70	67	79	71	80	67	77	84	83
ROLLA, MO	72	61	61	61	64	74	67	70	69	62	68	62	61	69	65	71	59	68	76	72
ROME, GA	85	74	72	75	76	85	77	81	81	75	80	72	73	81	76	84	70	80	87	83
ROSEBURG, OR	78	66	60	65	71	84	67	77	71	65	70	67	63	71	69	75	61	73	83	79
ROSWELL, NM	71	62	59	61	63	71	62	68	67	62	66	59	60	67	63	70	58	66	74	68
RUIDOSO, NM	91	71	50	70	80	103	72	90	76	69	76	78	63	78	74	81	65	82	93	94
RUSSELLVILLE, AR	80	64	55	64	67	81	74	72	72	65	71	67	61	74	66	74	62	72	79	79
RUSTON, LA	65	50	48	52	51	61	60	59	62	55	62	54	53	62	56	64	54	61	64	62
RUTLAND, VT	86	77	80	78	82	92	80	86	83	77	82	76	77	84	81	86	72	83	92	88
SACRAMENTO-ARDEN,CA	103	110	111	110	107	99	110	104	105	110	106	100	111	105	108	102	97	107	99	103
SAFFORD, AZ	76	66	56	64	64	74	64	70	68	64	67	62	61	69	64	70	59	69	74	72
SAGINAW-SAG TOWNSHIP	84	82	90	83	82	86	81	83	85	82	84	72	83	85	83	87	76	82	89	84
ST. CLOUD, MN	94	88	89	90	87	91	92	90	91	90	91	83	89	93	89	90	82	91	91	92
ST. GEORGE, UT	85	82	81	82	81	87	80	84	81	80	80	75	79	80	82	82	71	83	87	84
ST. JOSEPH, MO-KS	79	70	73	71	72	80	73	76	78	71	76	67	70	78	73	80	67	75	83	78
ST. LOUIS, MO-IL	100	101	108	103	99	100	99	98	101	101	100	88	101	101	100	101	91	99	101	99
ST. MARYS, GA	93	86	71	85	80	84	83	85	82	84	83	79	80	86	80	82	73	84	82	87
ST. MARYS, PA	83	74	74	73	80	91	72	82	78	72	76	70	71	80	75	82	67	76	89	84
SALEM, OR	88	85	88	86	84	85	89	87	87	87	87	80	87	87	87	87	79	88	87	87
SALINA, KS	83	77	82	79	78	82	79	80	82	78	80	71	78	83	79	83	72	80	85	81
SALINAS, CA	106	114	110	111	113	99	119	112	109	115	111	118	116	108	115	104	104	117	100	107
SALISBURY, MD	83	75	76	76	77	84	78	80	80	76	79	72	75	81	77	82	71	80	84	83
SALISBURY, NC	87	73	66	73	75	87	74	81	79	73	78	71	70	81	73	82	68	78	86	84
SALT LAKE CITY, UT	111	117	116	118	109	103	115	108	110	116	111	103	116	112	112	107	101	111	103	108
SAN ANGELO, TX	80	71	70	71	69	75	75	75	78	74	77	68	71	77	73	78	69	77	79	76
SAN ANTONIO, TX	95	89	83	89	83	86	89	88	90	91	91	81	87	90	87	90	82	91	88	88
SAN DIEGO-CARLSBAD	107	112	113	113	111	100	119	109	111	116	113	110	117	110	115	107	105	115	102	107
SANDUSKY, OH	89	92	103	93	94	94	88	90	91	90	90	79	92	92	92	92	81	88	95	91
SANFORD, NC	90	83	81	83	82	89	82	86	86	83	85	76	81	87	82	88	76	85	90	87
SAN FRANCISCO-OAKLND	138	157	161	158	158	136	163	149	149	159	152	154	165	146	161	143	143	155	135	146
SAN JOSE-SUNNYVALE	165	191	190	191	190	161	195	180	173	190	177	189	195	171	192	163	165	187	157	174
SAN LUIS OBISPO-PASO	95	96	100	96	97	96	102	98	97	97	98	93	99	95	100	96	88	100	97	98
SANTA BARBARA-GOLETA	106	114	116	113	115	103	122	112	111	116	113	114	120	109	118	107	105	117	103	109
SANTA CRUZ-WATSONVIL	121	138	140	138	138	119	144	133	128	137	130	138	142	124	140	120	121	138	117	128
SANTA FE, NM	102	106	106	106	104	100	105	102	102	105	102	98	105	101	105	100	93	105	100	103
SANTA ROSA-PETALUMA	114	128	130	126	128	117	125	122	117	124	118	118	127	115	126	114	109	123	115	120
SARASOTA-BRADENTON	96	100	112	98	104	109	95	102	98	97	97	87	99	91	103	102	86	101	112	101
SAULT STE. MARIE, MI	73	64	64	65	66	75	67	71	69	65	68	62	64	70	67	71	60	69	75	73
SAVANNAH, GA	98	92	91	94	88	93	94	92	96	96	95	84	92	96	92	96	86	95	95	94
SAYRE, PA	85	69	60	68	76	92	69	82	75	68	74	71	64	78	71	79	64	76	88	86
UNITED STATES	100	100	100	100	100	100	100	100	100	100	100	100	100	100	100	100	100	100	100	100

CBSA	CBSA Code	POPULATION			2000-2007 ANNUAL RATE		RACE (%)					
							White		Black		Asian/Pacific	
		2000	2007	2012	% Rate	National Rank	2000	2007	2000	2007	2000	2007
SCOTTSBLUFF, NE	42420	37,770	37,505	37,382	-0.1	805	87.8	84.8	0.3	0.3	0.6	0.8
SCOTTSBORO, AL	42460	53,926	54,579	54,858	0.2	679	91.9	90.7	3.7	4.0	0.3	0.4
SCOTTSBURG, IN	42500	22,960	23,775	24,283	0.5	545	98.6	98.3	0.0	0.1	0.2	0.3
SCRANTON-WILKES-BARR	42540	560,625	556,812	553,310	-0.1	805	96.7	96.0	1.5	1.7	0.6	0.9
SEAFORD, DE	42580	156,638	191,685	219,226	2.8	46	80.3	77.7	14.9	16.3	0.8	1.2
SEARCY, AR	42620	67,165	73,938	78,969	1.3	225	93.5	92.0	3.6	4.5	0.3	0.5
SEATTLE-TACOMA-BELLE	42660	3,043,878	3,327,901	3,531,676	1.2	255	78.3	75.8	5.0	5.3	9.0	10.2
SEBASTN-VERO BCH, FL	42680	112,947	141,440	166,391	3.2	30	87.4	84.6	8.2	9.6	0.8	1.0
SEBRING, FL	42700	87,366	100,654	111,339	2.0	101	83.5	79.9	9.3	10.6	1.1	1.4
SEDALIA, MO	42740	39,403	40,094	40,576	0.2	679	92.1	90.7	3.0	3.4	0.4	0.6
SELINSGROVE, PA	42780	37,546	38,602	39,379	0.4	590	97.9	97.5	0.8	0.9	0.4	0.6
SELMA, AL	42820	46,365	43,469	41,574	-0.9	932	35.6	33.7	63.3	64.9	0.4	0.5
SENECA, SC	42860	66,215	72,013	76,280	1.2	255	89.1	88.0	8.4	8.6	0.4	0.5
SENECA FALLS, NY	42900	33,342	35,034	35,313	0.7	444	95.0	94.1	2.3	2.5	0.7	0.9
SEVIERVILLE, TN	42940	71,170	84,552	95,383	2.4	71	97.3	96.6	0.6	0.6	0.6	0.8
SEYMOUR, IN	42980	41,335	42,309	42,906	0.3	633	96.1	95.1	0.5	0.6	0.8	1.2
SHAWNEE, OK	43060	65,521	69,495	72,159	0.8	396	79.9	77.8	2.9	3.0	0.7	1.0
SHEBOYGAN, WI	43100	112,646	117,376	120,779	0.6	494	92.7	90.7	1.1	1.3	3.3	4.5
SHELBY, NC	43140	96,287	99,965	102,293	0.5	545	76.8	75.6	20.9	21.4	0.7	0.9
SHELBYVILLE, TN	43180	37,586	44,354	49,972	2.3	78	86.8	84.9	8.5	9.0	0.5	0.7
SHELTON, WA	43220	49,405	55,726	60,837	1.7	140	88.5	87.2	1.2	1.3	1.5	1.7
SHERIDAN, WY	43260	26,560	28,201	29,410	0.8	396	95.9	95.4	0.2	0.2	0.5	0.7
SHERMAN-DENISON, TX	43300	110,595	120,067	126,941	1.1	288	87.2	85.1	5.9	6.4	0.6	0.8
SHREVEPORT-BOSSIER	43340	375,965	393,854	407,381	0.6	494	58.8	54.9	38.2	41.4	0.8	1.2
SIDNEY, OH	43380	47,910	49,114	49,973	0.3	633	96.0	95.1	1.5	1.7	1.0	1.5
SIERRA VISTA-DOUGLAS	43420	117,755	132,044	143,117	1.6	155	76.7	74.1	4.5	4.6	1.9	2.2
SIKESTON, MO	43460	40,422	41,156	41,679	0.2	679	87.7	86.1	10.5	11.7	0.2	0.3
SILVER CITY, NM	43500	31,002	30,883	30,777	-0.1	805	75.7	74.8	0.5	0.6	0.3	0.4
SILVERTHORNE, CO	43540	23,548	25,715	27,082	1.2	255	91.8	90.6	0.7	0.7	0.9	1.2
SIOUX CITY, IA-NE-SD	43580	143,053	144,361	145,332	0.1	723	87.4	84.5	1.6	1.7	2.4	3.4
SIOUX FALLS, SD	43620	187,093	221,466	251,265	2.4	71	94.1	92.7	1.3	1.5	0.9	1.4
SNYDER, TX	43660	16,361	15,867	15,582	-0.4	896	81.3	78.4	6.1	6.2	0.2	0.3
SOMERSET, KY	43700	56,217	59,274	61,390	0.7	444	97.5	97.0	1.1	1.1	0.4	0.6
SOMERSET, PA	43740	80,023	79,989	79,276	0.0	765	97.4	97.2	1.6	1.7	0.2	0.3
SOUTH BEND-MISHAWAKA	43780	316,663	321,671	324,200	0.2	679	83.5	81.0	10.6	11.6	1.3	1.7
SOU. PINES-PINEHURST	43860	74,769	84,923	92,724	1.8	127	80.2	78.6	15.5	15.8	0.5	0.7
SPARTANBURG, SC	43900	253,791	275,235	291,145	1.1	288	75.1	73.4	20.8	21.1	1.5	2.0
SPEARFISH, SD	43940	21,802	23,572	24,901	1.1	288	95.8	94.8	0.2	0.3	0.4	0.6
SPENCER, IA	43980	17,372	17,069	16,877	-0.2	841	98.1	97.5	0.2	0.2	0.8	1.3
SPIRIT LAKE, IA	44020	16,424	17,069	17,559	0.5	545	98.9	98.7	0.2	0.2	0.2	0.3
SPOKANE, WA	44060	417,939	453,859	476,916	1.1	288	91.4	90.3	1.6	1.7	2.0	2.4
SPRINGFIELD, IL	44100	201,437	208,074	212,835	0.4	590	88.1	86.3	9.1	10.2	1.1	1.4
SPRINGFIELD, MA	44140	680,014	693,880	703,171	0.3	633	83.5	80.2	6.0	6.7	1.8	2.4
SPRINGFIELD, MO	44180	368,374	413,710	450,942	1.6	155	94.8	93.9	1.6	1.8	0.9	1.2
SPRINGFIELD, OH	44220	144,742	141,426	139,720	-0.3	873	88.1	86.6	8.9	9.9	0.5	0.8
STARKVILLE, MS	44260	42,902	44,023	44,774	0.4	590	58.7	56.0	37.4	38.8	2.6	3.5
STATE COLLEGE, PA	44300	135,758	145,418	150,743	1.0	318	91.4	89.1	2.6	3.0	4.0	5.7
STATESBORO, GA	44340	55,983	65,115	71,854	2.1	93	68.7	64.2	28.8	32.5	0.9	1.1
STATESVILLE-M'VILLE	44380	122,660	149,877	171,561	2.8	46	82.2	80.5	13.7	13.9	1.3	1.7
STAUNTON-WAYNESBORO	44420	108,988	116,818	123,629	1.0	318	90.9	89.6	7.0	7.5	0.4	0.7
STEPHENVILLE, TX	44500	33,001	34,968	36,151	0.8	396	89.7	87.2	0.8	0.9	0.4	0.5
STERLING, CO	44540	20,504	20,736	20,732	0.2	679	91.7	89.9	2.0	2.0	0.5	0.6
STERLING, IL	44580	60,653	60,175	59,848	-0.1	805	92.8	91.0	1.0	1.1	0.4	0.5
STEVENS POINT, WI	44620	67,182	69,823	71,473	0.5	545	95.7	94.5	0.3	0.4	2.3	3.2
STILLWATER, OK	44660	68,190	73,622	76,714	1.1	288	84.3	81.8	3.6	3.8	3.0	4.2
STOCKTON, CA	44700	563,598	694,530	799,025	2.9	42	58.1	53.1	6.7	6.4	11.8	13.1
STORM LAKE, IA	44740	20,411	20,442	20,514	0.0	765	88.0	88.0	0.4	0.4	4.3	4.3
STURGIS, MI	44780	62,422	64,176	65,489	0.4	590	93.5	92.4	2.6	2.8	0.6	0.9
SULPHUR SPRINGS, TX	44860	31,960	33,737	34,657	0.7	444	85.1	82.7	8.0	8.6	0.3	0.4
SUMMERVILLE, GA	44900	25,470	26,703	27,383	0.7	444	86.7	84.0	11.2	13.2	0.1	0.2
SUMTER, SC	44940	104,646	107,718	109,972	0.4	590	50.1	48.7	46.7	47.2	1.0	1.3
SUNBURY, PA	44980	94,556	93,303	92,363	-0.2	841	97.1	96.5	1.5	1.8	0.2	0.3
SUSANVILLE, CA	45000	33,828	36,102	36,848	0.9	352	80.8	75.7	8.8	8.4	1.2	1.8
SWEETWATER, TX	45020	15,802	15,203	14,814	-0.5	911	78.5	74.6	4.7	4.8	0.3	0.4
SYRACUSE, NY	45060	650,154	653,964	655,701	0.1	723	88.4	86.7	6.9	7.5	1.6	2.1
TAHLEQUAH, OK	45140	42,521	46,332	48,980	1.2	255	56.4	53.9	1.2	1.2	0.3	0.4
TALLADEGA-SYLAC., AL	45180	80,321	80,671	81,086	0.1	723	67.0	65.0	31.5	33.1	0.2	0.4
TALLAHASSEE, FL	45220	320,304	362,802	392,796	1.7	140	63.6	59.5	32.2	35.3	1.5	2.0
TALLULAH, LA	45260	13,728	12,561	12,149	-1.2	938	37.9	33.9	60.3	64.1	0.2	0.2
TAMPA-ST PETE-CLEAR	45300	2,395,997	2,765,528	3,076,858	2.0	101	82.9	79.8	10.2	11.4	1.9	2.5
TAOS, NM	45340	29,979	31,750	32,630	0.8	396	63.8	62.7	0.4	0.4	0.5	0.6
TAYLORVILLE, IL	45380	35,372	35,283	35,215	0.0	765	96.3	96.1	2.1	2.3	0.4	0.4
TERRE HAUTE, IN	45460	170,943	170,998	170,625	0.0	765	93.1	92.1	4.4	4.8	1.0	1.2
TEXARKANA, TX-AR	45500	129,749	136,750	141,575	0.7	444	73.5	71.0	23.0	25.1	0.4	0.6
THE VILLAGES, FL	45540	53,345	86,433	121,740	6.9	2	82.6	79.3	13.8	16.0	0.5	0.6
THOMASTON, GA	45580	27,597	28,409	28,928	0.4	590	70.6	66.3	27.9	31.8	0.4	0.5
THOMASVILLE, GA	45620	42,737	46,229	48,668	1.1	288	59.0	54.1	30.9	43.2	0.5	0.6
UNITED STATES					1.2		75.1	72.7	12.3	12.6	3.8	4.5

POPULATION COMPOSITION
CBSA AND U.S. TOTALS

B

CBSA	% HISPANIC ORIGIN		2007 AGE DISTRIBUTION (%)										MEDIAN AGE	% 2007 Males	% 2007 Females
	2000	2007	0-4	5-9	10-14	15-19	20-24	25-44	45-64	65-84	85+	18+	2007	2007	2007
SCOTTSBLUFF, NE	16.9	21.7	6.7	6.0	6.4	6.6	7.7	23.1	27.2	13.4	2.9	76.9	39.9	48.0	52.0
SCOTTSBORO, AL	1.1	1.7	6.3	6.4	6.3	5.7	5.4	27.9	27.4	13.0	1.6	77.4	39.4	49.2	50.8
SCOTTSBURG, IN	1.0	1.3	7.5	7.4	6.1	6.4	6.0	29.5	25.6	10.3	1.2	75.2	36.7	49.8	50.2
SCRANTON-WILKES-BARR	1.2	1.5	5.2	4.9	5.6	6.6	6.2	24.8	27.8	15.4	3.5	80.6	42.7	48.3	51.7
SEAFORD, DE	4.4	5.8	5.8	5.5	5.7	5.5	5.2	23.4	29.1	17.7	2.2	79.6	44.3	49.0	51.0
SEARCY, AR	1.9	2.6	6.6	6.1	6.2	7.6	8.2	27.1	24.5	11.7	2.0	77.4	36.7	48.9	51.1
SEATTLE-TACOMA-BELLE	5.3	6.7	6.4	6.2	6.6	6.9	6.9	29.9	26.7	8.8	1.6	76.7	36.9	49.9	50.1
SEBASTN-VERO BCH, FL	6.5	9.4	4.9	4.6	5.1	5.4	5.3	19.3	27.5	23.2	4.7	82.2	48.7	48.3	51.7
SEBRING, FL	12.1	16.8	5.1	4.5	4.8	5.2	5.3	18.1	25.9	26.5	4.6	82.4	50.7	48.9	51.1
SEDALIA, MO	3.9	4.8	7.5	6.7	6.2	6.5	6.8	26.9	25.0	12.2	2.3	75.7	37.5	48.9	51.1
SELINSGROVE, PA	1.0	1.2	5.8	5.6	5.8	8.3	7.8	25.2	26.9	12.6	2.0	78.7	39.2	49.2	50.8
SELMA, AL	0.6	0.7	7.8	7.2	7.0	6.8	7.5	24.3	25.6	12.0	2.0	74.1	36.4	45.8	54.2
SENECA, SC	2.4	3.2	6.0	6.0	5.9	5.4	4.7	26.3	28.1	15.7	1.7	78.7	41.7	49.5	50.5
SENECA FALLS, NY	2.0	2.3	5.5	4.9	6.2	6.8	7.6	25.7	28.0	12.9	2.5	79.1	40.2	50.8	49.2
SEVIERVILLE, TN	1.2	1.8	5.9	5.9	5.9	5.6	4.9	28.4	29.3	12.6	1.4	78.8	40.8	49.2	50.8
SEYMOUR, IN	2.7	3.6	7.3	6.9	6.8	5.8	5.7	29.1	25.6	11.0	1.9	75.4	37.2	50.0	50.0
SHAWNEE, OK	2.4	3.0	7.0	6.3	6.3	7.2	7.8	26.2	25.2	12.1	1.9	76.6	36.8	48.8	51.2
SHEBOYGAN, WI	3.4	4.4	6.6	6.1	6.3	6.9	7.5	26.2	27.1	10.9	2.4	76.9	38.7	50.0	50.0
SHELBY, NC	1.5	1.9	6.6	6.5	6.9	6.8	5.4	27.6	26.4	11.8	1.9	75.9	38.5	48.6	51.4
SHELBYVILLE, TN	7.5	10.3	7.7	7.2	6.5	5.7	5.5	30.2	24.8	10.8	1.6	75.0	36.2	49.9	50.1
SHELTON, WA	4.8	6.1	5.5	4.8	5.8	6.5	6.8	22.2	30.4	15.8	2.1	80.1	43.8	51.4	48.6
SHERIDAN, WY	2.4	2.7	5.3	5.3	5.8	7.1	6.4	22.1	33.0	12.5	2.5	79.1	43.4	48.9	51.1
SHERMAN-DENISON, TX	6.8	8.8	6.7	5.8	6.3	6.9	7.5	25.0	27.0	12.5	2.3	77.3	39.1	48.7	51.3
SHREVEPORT-BOSSIER	1.9	2.2	7.2	6.8	6.6	7.1	7.3	26.5	25.2	11.2	1.9	75.1	36.1	48.1	51.9
SIDNEY, OH	0.8	1.0	7.7	7.5	7.5	6.6	6.1	27.1	25.5	9.9	2.0	73.1	36.5	49.9	50.1
SIERRA VISTA-DOUGLAS	30.7	35.8	6.8	6.0	6.1	7.5	8.0	22.4	26.7	14.8	1.7	76.8	39.4	50.1	49.9
SIKESTON, MO	1.1	1.4	7.2	6.5	7.0	6.8	6.4	26.5	25.9	11.7	2.0	75.1	37.7	48.4	51.6
SILVER CITY, NM	48.8	51.1	7.1	6.6	5.9	6.7	7.0	22.1	27.9	14.5	2.2	76.3	40.3	48.7	51.3
SILVERTHORNE, CO	9.8	11.7	5.0	4.0	3.8	4.5	8.7	46.6	22.7	4.5	0.1	84.6	32.1	58.5	41.5
SIOUX CITY, IA-NE-SD	10.2	12.9	7.8	7.0	7.3	7.0	7.2	26.8	24.4	10.3	2.1	73.8	35.1	49.4	50.6
SIOUX FALLS, SD	1.8	2.3	7.5	6.9	6.8	7.0	7.4	29.1	24.6	8.8	1.9	75.4	35.0	49.7	50.3
SNYDER, TX	27.8	33.8	6.5	6.1	5.9	8.1	8.3	24.7	25.4	12.7	2.4	77.4	37.7	52.3	47.7
SOMERSET, KY	0.8	1.2	5.9	5.9	5.9	5.9	5.5	27.3	27.7	14.0	1.8	78.6	40.9	49.0	51.0
SOMERSET, PA	0.7	0.7	5.4	5.1	5.4	6.1	6.0	25.6	28.5	14.8	3.0	80.5	42.4	50.0	50.0
SOUTH BEND-MISHAWAKA	4.4	5.7	6.9	6.5	6.6	7.8	7.9	25.6	25.5	11.1	2.1	75.9	36.6	49.0	51.0
SOU. PINES-PINEHURST	4.0	5.3	5.6	5.4	5.7	5.8	5.0	22.8	26.6	19.6	3.5	79.7	44.8	48.1	51.9
SPARTANBURG, SC	2.8	3.8	6.6	6.5	6.6	6.6	5.8	28.4	26.6	11.2	1.7	76.6	38.1	49.0	51.0
SPEARFISH, SD	1.8	2.4	5.1	4.6	5.6	9.3	8.8	24.7	28.1	11.2	2.6	80.0	38.5	49.1	50.9
SPENCER, IA	1.1	1.5	6.3	5.9	6.2	6.1	6.3	25.3	28.2	12.9	3.0	78.0	40.7	48.5	51.5
SPIRIT LAKE, IA	0.7	0.9	5.2	5.3	5.2	5.8	5.4	22.0	31.2	16.5	3.4	80.7	45.8	48.9	51.1
SPOKANE, WA	2.8	3.6	6.5	5.9	6.5	7.7	8.6	25.7	26.5	10.3	2.4	76.8	36.9	49.1	50.9
SPRINGFIELD, IL	1.0	1.4	6.3	6.2	6.7	6.5	6.5	26.4	27.9	11.3	2.2	76.8	39.4	48.1	51.9
SPRINGFIELD, MA	11.2	13.9	5.9	5.6	6.4	8.5	8.4	24.6	26.8	11.2	2.5	77.7	38.3	47.9	52.1
SPRINGFIELD, MO	1.6	2.0	6.7	6.3	6.1	7.2	8.3	27.4	25.1	11.0	2.0	77.2	36.3	48.9	51.1
SPRINGFIELD, OH	1.2	1.4	6.5	6.2	6.3	6.9	7.1	24.3	26.9	13.3	2.4	77.0	39.5	48.1	51.9
STARKVILLE, MS	1.1	1.4	6.3	5.2	5.0	9.7	20.6	25.2	19.1	7.7	1.1	80.4	26.7	50.4	49.6
STATE COLLEGE, PA	1.7	2.0	4.6	4.3	4.7	10.2	19.4	25.3	20.9	9.2	1.5	83.5	29.3	51.5	48.5
STATESBORO, GA	1.9	2.5	6.0	5.1	5.4	12.7	16.6	25.0	19.8	8.2	1.3	80.2	27.5	48.9	51.1
STATESVILLE-M'VILLE	3.4	4.5	6.9	6.7	7.2	6.4	4.9	28.8	26.6	11.0	1.5	75.2	38.4	49.5	50.5
STAUNTON-WAYNESBORO	1.4	2.1	5.7	5.5	6.0	6.6	5.9	25.7	29.0	13.6	2.1	78.9	41.6	49.0	51.0
STEPHENVILLE, TX	15.0	19.2	6.7	6.0	5.9	8.7	9.7	27.8	22.4	10.4	2.4	77.7	32.4	49.8	50.2
STERLING, CO	11.9	14.6	6.9	6.3	6.2	7.4	8.1	25.9	25.1	11.9	2.3	76.9	36.7	51.3	48.7
STERLING, IL	8.8	11.5	6.6	6.1	6.1	6.5	6.9	24.6	27.2	13.4	2.7	77.5	40.2	49.1	50.9
STEVENS POINT, WI	1.4	1.9	5.9	5.5	5.9	8.5	11.5	26.0	25.4	9.6	1.7	78.8	34.8	49.9	50.1
STILLWATER, OK	2.1	2.7	5.5	4.6	4.5	9.7	18.9	26.3	19.9	8.6	1.9	82.4	28.4	51.1	48.9
STOCKTON, CA	30.5	35.4	8.4	7.5	8.3	8.4	7.9	27.0	22.5	8.5	1.5	70.8	32.2	50.0	50.0
STORM LAKE, IA	12.5	12.7	6.1	6.0	6.6	8.0	8.9	23.7	25.3	12.3	3.1	77.2	37.8	50.3	49.7
STURGIS, MI	4.0	4.9	7.5	6.8	6.6	6.6	6.7	26.9	25.9	11.2	1.9	74.9	37.2	49.5	50.5
SULPHUR SPRINGS, TX	9.3	12.0	6.9	6.3	6.3	6.4	6.9	26.0	26.4	12.5	2.4	76.7	38.5	49.3	50.7
SUMMERVILLE, GA	2.1	2.9	6.7	6.9	5.6	5.4	6.6	29.2	25.3	12.4	1.9	77.7	37.8	51.8	48.2
SUMTER, SC	1.8	2.4	7.6	7.0	6.8	7.2	8.0	27.2	24.4	10.3	1.6	74.4	35.1	48.7	51.3
SUNBURY, PA	1.1	1.4	5.2	4.9	5.1	6.4	6.5	24.9	28.2	15.6	3.2	80.7	42.9	49.6	50.4
SUSANVILLE, CA	13.8	18.9	5.0	4.5	5.5	7.2	10.3	33.5	24.7	7.9	1.2	81.0	35.4	61.7	38.3
SWEETWATER, TX	28.0	34.2	7.2	6.3	6.2	7.6	8.3	22.9	25.8	13.2	2.5	76.0	37.5	48.7	51.3
SYRACUSE, NY	2.1	2.4	6.4	6.0	6.8	8.2	7.9	24.9	26.4	11.2	2.1	76.4	37.9	48.4	51.6
TAHLEQUAH, OK	4.1	5.1	7.2	6.3	6.3	8.3	9.9	25.5	23.7	11.2	1.7	76.1	33.4	49.2	50.8
TALLADEGA-SYLAC., AL	1.0	1.4	6.5	6.3	6.3	6.3	6.4	27.5	27.0	11.9	1.7	77.6	38.4	49.4	50.6
TALLAHASSEE, FL	3.7	5.0	5.8	5.4	5.6	8.7	13.1	26.9	24.8	8.3	1.3	79.6	32.8	48.4	51.6
TALLULAH, LA	2.1	2.3	8.9	8.0	7.6	9.1	8.5	24.4	22.2	9.6	1.8	69.5	30.9	50.0	50.0
TAMPA-ST PETE-CLEAR	10.4	14.5	5.8	5.6	5.9	6.1	6.0	24.9	27.0	15.5	3.1	79.0	42.1	48.3	51.7
TAOS, NM	57.9	59.6	5.5	5.5	5.7	6.3	5.9	24.6	33.0	11.9	1.5	79.2	42.8	49.4	50.6
TAYLORVILLE, IL	1.0	1.0	6.2	5.7	6.2	6.4	6.1	25.6	26.9	13.7	3.2	77.9	40.8	50.4	49.6
TERRE HAUTE, IN	1.0	1.3	6.2	5.8	5.8	6.9	8.4	26.8	25.9	11.9	2.3	78.7	37.6	50.3	49.7
TEXARKANA, TX-AR	3.6	4.6	6.9	6.4	6.3	6.1	7.1	27.9	25.9	11.2	2.1	76.7	37.3	48.1	51.9
THE VILLAGES, FL	6.3	8.9	3.9	3.6	3.9	4.0	4.7	20.7	26.1	30.9	2.3	86.2	53.1	52.6	47.4
THOMASTON, GA	1.2	1.5	6.6	6.2	6.7	6.7	5.6	27.3	25.9	12.6	2.4	76.5	39.1	48.1	51.9
THOMASVILLE, GA	1.7	2.2	7.0	6.4	6.7	7.0	7.1	25.6	26.4	11.6	2.2	75.5	38.3	47.3	52.7
UNITED STATES	12.5	15.0	6.9	6.5	6.8	7.1	7.0	27.6	25.4	10.7	1.9	75.6	36.7	49.2	50.8

CBSA	HOUSEHOLDS					FAMILIES			MEDIAN HOUSEHOLD INCOME		
	2000	2007	2012	% Annual Rate 2000-2007	2007 Average HH Size	2000	2007	% Annual Rate 2000-2007	2007	2012	2007 National Rank
SCOTTSBLUFF, NE	15,198	15,328	15,370	0.1	2.40	10,408	10,372	0.0	39,618	45,599	667
SCOTTSBORO, AL	21,615	22,510	22,892	0.6	2.40	15,830	16,207	0.3	37,339	41,615	765
SCOTTSBURG, IN	8,832	9,422	9,733	0.9	2.50	6,495	6,703	0.4	42,075	47,577	551
SCRANTON-WILKES-BARR	227,667	230,139	230,623	0.1	2.32	147,766	144,617	-0.3	43,971	51,961	470
SEAFORD, DE	62,577	77,504	89,265	3.0	2.43	43,869	52,956	2.6	50,067	59,690	250
SEARCY, AR	25,148	28,153	30,325	1.6	2.50	18,412	20,072	1.2	40,394	46,765	637
SEATTLE-TACOMA-BELLE	1,196,568	1,314,705	1,398,400	1.3	2.47	757,978	820,851	1.1	67,187	80,720	24
SEBASTN-VERO BCH, FL	49,137	62,728	74,447	3.4	2.22	32,708	40,969	3.2	49,144	57,838	283
SEBRING, FL	37,471	42,620	47,075	1.8	2.33	25,794	28,827	1.5	36,597	42,015	788
SEDALIA, MO	15,568	15,941	16,155	0.3	2.47	10,568	10,507	-0.1	39,334	45,737	680
SELINSGROVE, PA	13,654	14,322	14,740	0.7	2.54	9,979	10,209	0.3	43,884	50,164	477
SELMA, AL	17,841	17,263	16,723	-0.5	2.49	12,494	11,858	-0.7	25,906	28,467	931
SENECA, SC	27,283	30,277	32,380	1.4	2.36	19,589	21,023	1.0	45,347	52,532	419
SENECA FALLS, NY	12,630	12,988	13,205	0.4	2.47	8,632	8,811	0.3	46,107	53,267	381
SEVIERVILLE, TN	28,467	34,231	38,865	2.6	2.45	20,836	24,468	2.2	43,033	50,126	512
SEYMOUR, IN	16,052	16,869	17,264	0.7	2.48	11,573	11,748	0.2	48,965	55,613	288
SHAWNEE, OK	24,540	26,165	27,296	0.9	2.53	17,730	18,565	0.6	38,906	44,875	692
SHEBOYGAN, WI	43,545	46,614	48,453	0.9	2.44	29,936	31,299	0.6	56,836	65,567	94
SHELBY, NC	37,046	38,911	40,011	0.7	2.50	27,001	27,721	0.4	42,642	48,186	523
SHELBYVILLE, TN	13,905	16,345	18,373	2.3	2.68	10,350	11,893	1.9	45,622	52,737	404
SHELTON, WA	18,912	21,582	23,694	1.8	2.48	13,391	15,075	1.6	48,975	57,136	287
SHERIDAN, WY	11,167	12,201	12,864	1.2	2.25	7,079	7,475	0.8	42,825	49,418	517
SHERMAN-DENISON, TX	42,849	45,857	48,448	0.9	2.55	30,191	31,973	0.8	45,778	52,565	394
SHREVEPORT-BOSSIER	144,293	153,471	159,848	0.9	2.51	98,576	102,189	0.5	37,212	40,725	770
SIDNEY, OH	17,636	18,527	19,041	0.7	2.62	13,083	13,398	0.3	54,501	62,998	133
SIERRA VISTA-DOUGLAS	43,893	50,455	55,326	1.9	2.50	30,786	34,968	1.8	42,210	50,246	543
SIKESTON, MO	15,626	16,171	16,480	0.5	2.51	11,223	11,317	0.1	38,527	44,317	716
SILVER CITY, NM	12,146	12,694	12,835	0.6	2.38	8,511	8,629	0.2	35,381	40,692	827
SILVERTHORNE, CO	9,120	9,988	10,519	1.3	2.48	4,768	5,047	0.8	73,095	86,485	9
SIOUX CITY, IA-NE-SD	53,586	54,546	55,001	0.2	2.58	36,747	36,831	0.0	49,380	58,497	272
SIOUX FALLS, SD	72,492	87,553	99,833	2.6	2.46	48,279	58,081	2.6	56,239	68,418	110
SNYDER, TX	5,756	5,682	5,626	-0.2	2.50	4,163	4,068	-0.3	38,502	43,664	717
SOMERSET, KY	22,719	24,719	25,908	1.2	2.35	16,339	17,189	0.7	34,097	39,142	859
SOMERSET, PA	31,222	31,786	31,845	0.2	2.38	22,044	21,839	-0.1	38,259	44,240	730
SOUTH BEND-MISHAWAKA	120,419	124,421	126,056	0.5	2.47	81,100	80,646	-0.1	50,765	59,738	224
SOU. PINES-PINEHURST	30,713	35,023	38,390	1.8	2.37	21,950	24,437	1.5	51,658	60,100	202
SPARTANBURG, SC	97,735	107,643	114,718	1.3	2.49	69,299	73,725	0.9	46,792	54,405	357
SPEARFISH, SD	8,881	9,946	10,668	1.6	2.25	5,560	6,163	1.4	41,009	48,397	609
SPENCER, IA	7,259	7,311	7,284	0.1	2.30	4,774	4,715	-0.2	43,773	50,398	485
SPIRIT LAKE, IA	7,103	7,532	7,802	0.8	2.23	4,760	4,950	0.5	47,351	53,901	342
SPOKANE, WA	163,611	178,200	188,030	1.2	2.44	106,017	113,612	1.0	47,661	56,589	324
SPRINGFIELD, IL	83,595	87,077	89,478	0.6	2.35	53,448	53,861	0.1	53,504	62,096	150
SPRINGFIELD, MA	260,745	269,420	274,700	0.5	2.45	168,007	171,414	0.3	51,712	60,636	199
SPRINGFIELD, MO	145,304	166,542	182,727	1.9	2.39	97,447	108,937	1.5	42,231	49,297	542
SPRINGFIELD, OH	56,648	56,216	55,866	-0.1	2.46	39,383	37,915	-0.5	49,382	56,862	271
STARKVILLE, MS	15,945	17,193	17,726	1.0	2.34	9,265	9,668	0.6	27,725	29,586	924
STATE COLLEGE, PA	49,323	53,581	56,183	1.1	2.41	28,501	29,778	0.6	45,494	53,697	412
STATESBORO, GA	20,743	24,502	27,403	2.3	2.49	12,341	13,942	1.7	36,690	42,642	786
STATESVILLE-M'VILLE	47,360	58,487	67,222	3.0	2.53	34,658	41,842	2.6	52,663	61,292	172
STAUNTON-WAYNESBORO	42,826	46,944	50,029	1.3	2.40	30,103	32,100	0.9	48,071	54,523	309
STEPHENVILLE, TX	12,568	13,142	13,579	0.6	2.50	8,108	8,372	0.4	37,110	42,177	774
STERLING, CO	7,551	7,623	7,623	0.1	2.46	5,064	4,997	-0.2	39,927	45,315	653
STERLING, IL	23,684	23,825	23,838	0.1	2.47	16,759	16,408	-0.3	50,539	58,355	231
STEVENS POINT, WI	25,040	27,137	28,183	1.1	2.44	16,496	17,422	0.8	52,595	59,791	176
STILLWATER, OK	26,680	28,124	29,489	0.7	2.32	15,316	15,711	0.4	35,868	41,730	814
STOCKTON, CA	181,629	220,637	253,321	2.7	3.07	134,708	164,239	2.8	51,408	60,397	210
STORM LAKE, IA	7,499	7,529	7,550	0.1	2.53	5,125	5,051	-0.2	43,069	49,576	509
STURGIS, MI	23,381	24,455	25,097	0.6	2.58	16,603	16,921	0.3	47,846	53,732	319
SULPHUR SPRINGS, TX	12,286	13,038	13,422	0.8	2.55	8,885	9,336	0.7	38,986	44,413	687
SUMMERVILLE, GA	9,577	10,256	10,617	0.9	2.44	6,836	7,094	0.5	37,112	42,171	773
SUMTER, SC	37,728	40,175	41,608	0.9	2.60	27,611	28,482	0.4	41,185	47,251	600
SUNBURY, PA	38,835	39,067	39,001	0.1	2.29	25,589	24,941	-0.4	39,535	46,192	670
SUSANVILLE, CA	9,625	10,209	10,547	0.8	2.56	6,777	7,218	0.9	44,511	51,148	446
SWEETWATER, TX	6,170	6,022	5,904	-0.3	2.44	4,288	4,139	-0.5	32,292	37,383	887
SYRACUSE, NY	252,043	258,788	261,609	0.4	2.44	164,130	167,156	0.3	50,233	58,797	244
TAHLEQUAH, OK	16,175	17,816	18,976	1.3	2.49	11,077	11,955	1.1	33,170	38,149	874
TALLADEGA-SYLAC., AL	30,674	31,477	31,981	0.4	2.45	21,911	22,069	0.1	36,458	40,173	794
TALLAHASSEE, FL	125,533	146,015	160,023	2.1	2.35	75,278	85,688	1.8	44,750	51,647	441
TALLULAH, LA	4,469	4,303	4,184	-0.5	2.69	3,140	2,946	-0.9	23,223	25,074	938
TAMPA-ST PETE-CLEAR	1,009,316	1,158,693	1,286,704	1.9	2.34	637,653	721,176	1.7	47,027	54,866	350
TAOS, NM	12,675	14,167	14,776	1.5	2.22	7,755	8,341	1.0	32,420	37,010	884
TAYLORVILLE, IL	13,921	14,054	14,099	0.1	2.38	9,477	9,290	-0.3	43,700	49,597	486
TERRE HAUTE, IN	65,795	66,870	67,022	0.2	2.38	43,781	42,734	-0.3	42,357	48,987	536
TEXARKANA, TX-AR	48,695	52,401	54,832	1.0	2.46	34,506	36,563	0.8	40,026	46,512	649
THE VILLAGES, FL	20,779	35,168	51,841	7.5	2.20	15,035	25,048	7.3	00,000	43,852	713
THOMASTON, GA	10,722	11,156	11,420	0.5	2.50	7,690	7,757	0.1	38,050	43,338	739
THOMASVILLE, GA	16,309	17,920	10,044	1.0	2.50	11,466	12,195	0.9	37,828	42,943	748
UNITED STATES				1.2	2.59			1.0	53,154	62,503	

CBSA	2007 Per Capita Income	2007 HH Income Base	2007 HOUSEHOLD INCOME DISTRIBUTION (%)					2007 Home Value Base	2007 HOME VALUE DISTRIBUTION (%)					2007 Median Home Value
			Less than $25,000	$25,000 to $49,999	$50,000 to $99,999	$100,000 to $149,999	$150,000 or More		Less than $50,000	$50,000 to $89,999	$90,000 to $174,999	$175,000 to $399,999	$400,000 or More	
SCOTTSBLUFF, NE	21,446	15,328	29.8	32.3	27.5	7.4	3.0	10,602	18.2	29.6	38.4	12.6	1.2	92,745
SCOTTSBORO, AL	19,545	22,510	33.0	31.3	27.5	6.2	1.9	17,861	24.2	24.8	34.3	14.4	2.3	91,633
SCOTTSBURG, IN	20,508	9,422	28.1	32.1	30.1	7.5	2.2	7,220	18.2	29.8	41.2	10.2	0.6	92,802
SCRANTON-WILKES-BARR	24,274	230,139	28.4	27.8	30.4	9.1	4.3	162,370	5.6	12.6	49.3	29.4	3.1	143,067
SEAFORD, DE	26,088	77,504	22.4	27.5	35.4	9.1	5.6	63,729	9.2	6.3	21.4	47.7	15.4	210,761
SEARCY, AR	20,083	28,152	31.1	30.2	29.7	6.0	3.0	21,031	23.5	24.8	35.6	13.6	2.5	93,021
SEATTLE-TACOMA-BELLE	34,819	1,314,699	14.5	21.4	35.3	17.3	11.5	855,506	2.3	1.6	5.5	48.1	42.5	365,552
SEBASTN-VERO BCH, FL	33,987	62,728	22.3	28.5	30.7	9.7	8.8	50,075	4.7	5.7	24.3	45.3	20.0	219,148
SEBRING, FL	20,941	42,620	32.3	34.3	24.5	6.0	2.9	34,718	7.7	13.0	37.8	35.8	5.7	157,622
SEDALIA, MO	20,090	15,941	27.8	35.0	29.3	5.6	2.4	11,793	15.6	25.1	40.7	16.3	2.4	103,065
SELINSGROVE, PA	21,326	14,322	24.8	32.9	32.3	6.8	3.2	11,047	5.3	6.5	45.5	38.2	4.6	165,939
SELMA, AL	15,895	17,263	48.8	24.0	20.6	4.8	1.9	11,675	29.1	24.8	33.2	11.1	1.8	81,140
SENECA, SC	24,373	30,277	25.8	29.4	32.0	8.6	4.2	24,174	16.7	17.2	35.9	22.7	7.4	121,058
SENECA FALLS, NY	22,466	12,988	23.2	31.1	32.6	10.0	3.1	9,894	4.5	8.7	40.5	42.8	3.5	169,088
SEVIERVILLE, TN	22,012	34,231	25.8	32.4	32.0	6.7	3.0	25,618	13.0	11.8	37.5	32.3	5.5	145,478
SEYMOUR, IN	23,430	16,869	21.1	30.0	37.6	8.1	3.2	12,759	16.2	19.1	47.8	15.1	1.8	110,469
SHAWNEE, OK	19,755	26,165	31.1	31.1	28.6	6.3	3.0	18,957	23.3	32.2	34.2	9.5	0.8	80,997
SHEBOYGAN, WI	27,286	46,614	16.0	26.2	41.1	12.0	4.7	33,992	2.6	6.4	52.4	35.5	3.1	148,959
SHELBY, NC	21,410	38,911	28.9	29.0	32.1	6.9	3.2	28,906	15.2	17.2	45.5	19.5	2.7	116,000
SHELBYVILLE, TN	20,469	16,345	26.2	29.1	34.0	8.0	2.7	12,209	9.9	19.1	47.9	18.8	4.2	116,778
SHELTON, WA	23,446	21,582	22.2	28.8	36.2	9.4	3.3	17,461	2.8	4.2	25.2	53.2	14.6	219,051
SHERIDAN, WY	25,221	12,201	28.9	28.4	29.6	8.9	4.1	8,686	7.4	5.7	32.5	42.0	12.3	186,183
SHERMAN-DENISON, TX	22,850	45,856	25.9	28.3	32.2	9.6	4.0	33,077	20.4	29.3	33.1	15.1	2.1	90,468
SHREVEPORT-BOSSIER	20,637	153,466	34.1	28.6	26.3	7.3	3.7	100,561	20.0	23.6	37.0	16.8	2.5	101,137
SIDNEY, OH	25,185	18,527	17.2	27.4	37.7	13.1	4.6	14,301	6.9	12.3	52.2	26.1	2.5	130,526
SIERRA VISTA-DOUGLAS	21,441	50,455	29.3	28.8	30.1	8.5	3.2	34,618	6.8	10.7	33.6	41.3	7.6	172,547
SIKESTON, MO	19,360	16,171	32.2	29.9	29.0	6.8	2.1	11,527	21.4	25.8	35.7	15.1	1.9	94,961
SILVER CITY, NM	19,226	12,694	35.2	31.3	26.3	4.8	2.4	9,502	12.9	13.9	41.4	26.7	5.2	137,029
SILVERTHORNE, CO	37,753	9,988	9.4	19.8	38.2	19.1	13.6	6,184	3.6	1.4	8.9	35.4	50.7	405,022
SIOUX CITY, IA-NE-SD	23,672	54,546	21.7	28.8	35.5	9.7	4.2	38,991	17.6	29.2	39.1	12.6	1.6	93,468
SIOUX FALLS, SD	27,969	87,553	16.2	26.9	38.9	11.6	6.3	60,602	8.7	12.8	48.2	26.9	3.4	137,106
SNYDER, TX	20,113	5,682	32.3	28.2	29.9	6.2	3.3	4,276	43.0	22.8	27.4	6.4	0.4	59,085
SOMERSET, KY	19,228	24,719	37.1	31.9	23.5	5.0	2.6	18,922	24.9	25.3	36.2	12.1	1.6	89,834
SOMERSET, PA	19,660	31,784	31.3	33.0	28.7	5.1	1.9	24,933	13.0	17.8	44.6	21.7	2.9	126,635
SOUTH BEND-MISHAWAKA	25,345	124,421	21.7	27.4	34.8	11.0	5.1	92,130	8.3	24.4	45.5	19.3	2.5	113,999
SOU. PINES-PINEHURST	28,989	35,023	21.5	26.7	34.8	9.5	7.5	27,796	12.6	11.5	29.5	35.3	11.0	160,056
SPARTANBURG, SC	23,727	107,640	25.1	27.9	32.9	9.5	4.6	79,373	15.1	23.0	42.7	16.7	2.4	106,742
SPEARFISH, SD	23,433	9,946	30.1	30.7	29.4	5.9	3.9	6,584	18.7	18.5	36.8	21.9	4.2	118,758
SPENCER, IA	23,784	7,311	25.5	32.6	32.3	6.3	3.3	5,221	14.4	23.9	44.2	14.7	2.9	104,992
SPIRIT LAKE, IA	27,084	7,532	21.0	31.9	34.3	8.0	4.8	5,996	10.7	15.2	39.1	27.1	8.0	132,754
SPOKANE, WA	24,821	178,199	23.8	28.5	32.8	10.0	4.8	121,401	2.8	2.6	34.0	53.2	7.5	195,210
SPRINGFIELD, IL	28,788	87,077	20.1	26.2	35.7	11.8	6.2	63,260	10.7	20.9	45.5	20.6	2.2	116,412
SPRINGFIELD, MA	26,407	269,410	24.0	24.4	32.7	12.7	6.3	175,238	0.9	1.7	23.1	63.9	10.4	224,947
SPRINGFIELD, MO	23,384	166,539	26.6	31.9	29.5	7.6	4.3	116,079	9.4	15.6	47.4	23.9	3.7	126,820
SPRINGFIELD, OH	24,688	56,216	22.1	28.4	34.2	10.9	4.4	41,724	10.6	25.1	48.0	15.2	1.1	108,417
STARKVILLE, MS	17,354	17,193	45.9	25.2	20.0	6.5	2.4	9,513	23.7	21.3	33.0	18.6	3.4	100,138
STATE COLLEGE, PA	23,833	53,576	27.5	26.7	30.5	10.1	5.3	32,660	7.5	5.8	36.0	43.5	7.2	176,988
STATESBORO, GA	20,456	24,502	35.7	26.8	25.6	7.8	4.1	14,509	19.2	16.7	38.2	22.1	3.7	115,037
STATESVILLE-M'VILLE	26,399	58,487	20.2	26.7	36.7	10.3	6.0	44,762	7.8	9.7	38.7	33.5	10.4	155,742
STAUNTON-WAYNESBORO	24,468	46,944	22.9	28.9	35.3	9.1	3.7	34,948	4.7	3.7	24.1	58.8	8.7	211,117
STEPHENVILLE, TX	20,143	13,142	32.9	31.6	24.0	8.0	3.4	8,567	23.9	24.2	33.2	15.2	3.6	93,615
STERLING, CO	20,982	7,623	31.2	28.5	30.8	6.4	3.1	5,549	9.9	17.0	41.3	28.8	2.9	127,399
STERLING, IL	24,108	23,825	20.6	28.7	38.5	8.6	3.6	18,226	4.3	15.3	56.2	22.5	1.7	129,943
STEVENS POINT, WI	25,762	27,137	20.6	26.3	36.9	11.4	4.7	19,605	5.8	9.2	45.1	36.7	3.3	154,467
STILLWATER, OK	20,559	28,124	37.3	27.1	24.4	7.5	3.7	15,797	22.2	20.8	36.3	18.2	2.5	103,569
STOCKTON, CA	21,635	220,637	24.2	24.5	32.7	12.3	6.3	137,040	2.4	1.5	5.2	47.7	43.1	369,842
STORM LAKE, IA	20,462	7,529	24.9	33.9	31.9	6.1	3.1	5,487	20.6	28.0	36.4	12.2	2.8	91,796
STURGIS, MI	22,056	24,455	23.3	29.3	35.9	8.2	3.3	18,993	8.8	18.7	51.2	19.0	2.4	118,417
SULPHUR SPRINGS, TX	21,027	13,038	30.4	31.9	27.1	6.9	3.8	9,519	24.2	28.1	33.8	11.3	2.6	85,991
SUMMERVILLE, GA	18,209	10,256	33.0	31.3	29.3	4.9	1.5	7,823	24.1	28.7	34.0	11.4	1.9	85,883
SUMTER, SC	19,986	40,175	30.5	29.4	29.7	7.2	3.2	28,644	18.2	24.4	40.9	14.8	1.6	100,734
SUNBURY, PA	21,068	39,067	31.2	30.9	29.8	6.0	2.0	28,839	14.1	17.2	39.9	26.1	2.8	136,857
SUSANVILLE, CA	20,873	10,209	28.5	26.9	32.8	8.9	2.9	7,145	5.4	4.3	14.1	57.2	19.1	249,152
SWEETWATER, TX	17,991	6,022	39.8	28.8	24.0	4.6	2.7	4,145	50.8	26.6	17.2	4.8	0.6	49,254
SYRACUSE, NY	26,521	258,788	23.3	26.5	32.9	11.1	6.2	180,604	4.4	9.9	51.2	32.0	2.5	147,584
TAHLEQUAH, OK	17,412	17,816	38.5	30.4	24.2	5.0	1.9	11,929	21.5	27.8	36.6	12.3	1.8	90,997
TALLADEGA-SYLAC., AL	18,818	31,477	36.5	29.5	25.3	6.5	2.2	24,438	25.0	24.4	33.1	14.8	2.6	90,999
TALLAHASSEE, FL	25,504	146,013	28.5	26.1	29.5	10.1	5.8	95,244	5.9	10.2	30.9	44.1	9.0	182,183
TALLULAH, LA	12,003	4,303	52.7	30.1	14.0	2.4	0.8	2,628	34.9	26.8	28.9	8.2	1.1	71,046
TAMPA-ST PETE-CLEAR	27,461	1,158,682	23.6	29.4	30.8	9.9	6.2	849,349	5.0	6.1	27.5	48.3	13.1	203,722
TAOS, NM	21,230	14,167	40.3	29.3	22.2	5.0	3.2	10,768	13.8	9.4	22.7	35.2	18.9	190,793
TAYLORVILLE, IL	21,995	14,054	25.9	31.4	33.0	7.2	2.5	10,963	12.8	26.1	45.8	14.1	1.2	105,622
TERRE HAUTE, IN	22,082	66,869	28.8	29.2	31.0	7.5	3.4	48,719	19.5	31.5	37.3	10.7	1.0	88,701
TEXARKANA, TX-AR	21,386	52,461	32.7	27.1	28.9	7.7	3.6	37,474	27.1	29.0	33.0	9.3	1.5	80,934
THE VILLAGES, FL	21,564	35,168	29.7	35.2	26.6	6.2	2.4	30,832	6.3	10.1	24.6	45.4	13.5	205,497
THOMASTON, GA	20,143	11,156	32.6	29.7	28.0	6.8	2.9	7,910	16.1	30.7	39.3	12.5	1.5	93,756
THOMASVILLE, GA	20,156	17,920	34.3	27.5	28.0	6.8	3.5	12,747	20.4	25.4	34.7	16.3	3.2	97,232
UNITED STATES	27,916		21.9	25.0	32.3	12.3	8.4		7.9	10.5	27.1	35.6	19.0	192,285

SPENDING POTENTIAL INDICES
CBSA AND U.S. TOTALS

CBSA	FINANCIAL SERVICES				THE HOME						ENTERTAINMENT						PERSONAL			
					Home Improvements		Furnishings													
	Auto Loan	Home Loan	Invest-ments	Retire-ment Plans	Home Repair	Lawn & Garden	Comput-ers & Hard-ware	Major Appli-ances	TV, Radio, Sound Equip-ment	Furni-ture	Dine out/ Carry out	Sports Equip-ment	Fees & Tickets	Toys & Games	Travel	Cable TV	Apparel & Services	Auto Repairs	Health Insur-ance	Pets & Supplies
SCOTTSBLUFF, NE	75	66	68	66	69	77	70	73	74	67	72	64	66	74	69	76	64	72	80	75
SCOTTSBORO, AL	80	58	41	56	63	83	59	72	66	58	65	64	51	69	58	70	56	67	78	78
SCOTTSBURG, IN	81	65	57	65	66	79	67	74	73	66	72	65	62	75	66	76	63	72	80	77
SCRANTON-WILKES-BARR	78	76	88	76	80	84	77	80	81	75	79	69	77	80	79	84	70	78	89	80
SEAFORD, DE	96	85	77	83	90	106	82	96	87	82	86	83	79	86	86	92	75	91	102	98
SEARCY, AR	84	65	51	63	68	85	66	77	72	65	72	69	60	74	65	76	62	73	82	82
SEATTLE-TACOMA-BELLE	116	122	126	124	118	110	124	116	119	124	120	111	125	119	122	116	110	119	111	116
SEBASTN-VERO BCH, FL	104	106	114	103	111	119	98	109	103	102	102	92	102	97	108	108	90	107	120	108
SEBRING, FL	69	64	65	61	69	81	62	73	67	63	66	60	61	61	68	72	57	71	83	73
SEDALIA, MO	75	63	62	64	65	75	66	71	71	65	70	62	63	73	66	74	61	69	78	72
SELINSGROVE, PA	85	72	65	71	78	91	72	82	77	71	76	72	68	80	73	80	67	77	88	86
SELMA, AL	61	48	43	48	49	60	50	56	57	51	56	48	47	57	50	60	49	55	62	59
SENECA, SC	95	74	56	71	79	100	73	88	80	72	79	78	66	82	74	85	68	82	95	94
SENECA FALLS, NY	83	75	76	75	79	89	76	83	80	74	78	72	73	81	78	83	69	79	89	85
SEVIERVILLE, TN	84	72	62	71	75	88	71	81	74	70	74	71	67	76	72	77	64	76	84	84
SEYMOUR, IN	90	78	71	78	81	92	76	85	81	77	80	74	73	85	77	83	70	81	89	88
SHAWNEE, OK	78	65	59	65	67	79	67	74	72	65	71	65	62	73	67	75	62	71	80	76
SHEBOYGAN, WI	92	93	103	95	95	96	92	93	93	92	93	83	94	96	94	94	84	91	96	94
SHELBY, NC	87	69	56	68	73	90	69	80	76	68	75	71	63	79	69	80	65	76	87	85
SHELBYVILLE, TN	87	71	60	70	74	88	71	80	77	71	76	71	66	81	71	81	67	77	86	85
SHELTON, WA	88	78	70	77	84	98	76	89	80	76	79	77	73	80	80	84	69	84	94	91
SHERIDAN, WY	82	74	79	75	78	88	78	83	79	74	78	73	74	79	78	82	69	80	88	84
SHERMAN-DENISON, TX	87	77	76	77	78	87	79	83	83	77	82	73	76	83	79	85	72	82	89	85
SHREVEPORT-BOSSIER	75	67	68	69	66	72	70	70	74	70	73	63	68	74	69	76	65	72	75	72
SIDNEY, OH	95	92	95	93	95	101	88	94	91	89	90	82	89	95	91	93	80	90	98	96
SIERRA VISTA-DOUGLAS	80	71	67	70	71	80	73	78	76	71	75	69	69	74	73	78	66	77	82	78
SIKESTON, MO	74	62	58	62	64	75	64	70	69	63	68	61	60	70	63	72	60	68	75	73
SILVER CITY, NM	70	60	54	59	62	72	60	68	64	59	63	59	57	64	61	67	55	65	72	69
SILVERTHORNE, CO	138	118	110	130	107	108	140	119	134	136	137	119	130	137	125	129	124	133	113	123
SIOUX CITY, IA-NE-SD	89	81	83	82	82	88	84	86	87	82	86	76	81	89	83	88	76	85	91	87
SIOUX FALLS, SD	100	95	96	97	92	94	97	95	97	97	96	88	95	99	95	96	86	97	96	97
SNYDER, TX	82	66	54	63	69	84	67	77	74	66	73	67	61	75	67	78	63	73	84	80
SOMERSET, KY	74	56	45	54	60	77	58	69	64	56	63	61	51	66	57	68	54	65	76	73
SOMERSET, PA	75	59	52	58	65	81	61	72	67	59	66	63	56	69	62	71	57	67	80	75
SOUTH BEND-MISHAWAKA	89	86	93	88	87	89	87	87	89	87	88	77	87	91	87	90	79	87	92	88
SOU. PINES-PINEHURST	103	94	90	93	96	110	90	101	96	91	95	87	89	93	94	100	83	97	109	103
SPARTANBURG, SC	92	78	70	78	80	92	79	86	84	78	83	76	75	86	78	87	73	83	91	90
SPEARFISH, SD	80	67	64	68	70	81	74	78	76	70	75	69	68	76	72	78	66	77	82	80
SPENCER, IA	84	68	64	68	74	88	73	81	77	69	76	72	66	80	72	80	66	78	88	85
SPIRIT LAKE, IA	93	78	69	77	84	102	79	92	84	76	83	80	73	84	81	88	72	87	99	95
SPOKANE, WA	83	82	93	85	81	81	87	82	86	84	85	74	86	85	85	85	77	84	85	82
SPRINGFIELD, IL	93	93	102	96	92	92	94	92	95	94	94	82	94	95	94	95	84	93	95	92
SPRINGFIELD, MA	85	90	104	92	91	86	92	88	92	92	91	80	95	90	93	91	84	89	89	87
SPRINGFIELD, MO	83	74	73	75	73	80	79	79	80	76	79	72	74	81	76	81	70	79	82	81
SPRINGFIELD, OH	83	84	96	85	85	86	82	83	86	83	84	72	85	86	85	87	76	82	89	83
STARKVILLE, MS	62	45	44	48	45	53	66	55	63	54	63	54	54	61	56	61	55	60	57	58
STATE COLLEGE, PA	85	75	78	78	76	81	90	81	86	81	87	76	83	85	83	84	78	84	82	83
STATESBORO, GA	78	61	56	63	60	69	77	70	75	68	75	66	67	74	68	74	66	74	72	73
STATESVILLE-M'VILLE	101	93	86	93	93	101	90	96	92	91	92	86	88	95	90	94	82	93	98	99
STAUNTON-WAYNESBORO	84	80	86	81	83	88	80	84	82	79	81	74	79	83	81	84	73	81	88	85
STEPHENVILLE, TX	79	63	57	63	65	77	71	74	73	66	72	67	63	74	67	74	63	73	77	77
STERLING, CO	80	66	63	66	70	82	70	77	73	67	72	68	64	75	69	76	63	74	82	79
STERLING, IL	85	80	86	81	84	90	79	84	84	80	82	73	80	86	82	86	73	81	91	86
STEVENS POINT, WI	92	85	89	87	86	91	91	89	90	87	90	81	87	92	88	90	80	89	91	91
STILLWATER, OK	72	58	59	61	57	64	76	66	73	66	73	62	66	71	67	71	64	70	69	68
STOCKTON, CA	90	95	91	93	92	86	93	92	90	94	91	88	93	90	92	88	83	93	86	90
STORM LAKE, IA	85	66	56	66	71	88	69	79	75	66	73	70	62	78	69	78	63	75	87	84
STURGIS, MI	87	74	69	74	79	92	75	84	80	74	79	73	71	83	75	83	69	79	89	87
SULPHUR SPRINGS, TX	85	67	56	66	71	89	70	80	76	67	75	70	63	78	69	80	65	76	88	84
SUMMERVILLE, GA	78	55	35	52	59	80	56	70	64	54	63	62	48	67	55	68	54	65	76	76
SUMTER, SC	81	68	59	68	68	79	69	75	74	69	73	67	65	76	68	76	65	74	79	78
SUNBURY, PA	71	62	65	62	65	75	65	69	70	62	68	61	62	70	65	73	60	67	78	71
SUSANVILLE, CA	80	76	71	75	77	82	73	79	74	73	74	70	72	75	74	76	66	76	80	80
SWEETWATER, TX	67	53	50	53	55	65	59	64	63	56	63	55	54	65	58	67	54	62	71	64
SYRACUSE, NY	90	88	97	90	88	90	89	89	92	89	91	79	90	91	90	93	82	89	93	90
TAHLEQUAH, OK	67	53	48	53	55	67	60	63	62	56	62	57	53	62	57	64	54	62	67	66
TALLADEGA-SYLAC., AL	75	59	47	57	62	78	59	69	66	59	65	61	54	68	59	71	57	66	76	74
TALLAHASSEE, FL	88	77	76	80	75	79	90	82	87	83	87	77	83	86	82	85	78	86	81	84
TALLULAH, LA	50	36	31	36	37	49	41	45	48	40	46	39	36	47	40	51	40	45	52	48
TAMPA-ST PETE-CLEAR	89	88	94	88	88	91	88	89	90	88	89	79	88	87	90	91	79	90	95	89
TAOS, NM	76	59	44	58	65	84	61	74	65	58	64	65	53	66	61	69	55	69	78	74
TAYLORVILLE, IL	79	67	67	67	72	84	69	77	75	67	73	67	66	76	71	79	64	73	86	79
TERRE HAUTE, IN	80	68	69	69	71	81	73	76	77	70	75	67	68	78	72	80	66	75	84	79
TEXARKANA, TX-AR	82	68	63	68	69	81	71	76	76	69	75	67	66	77	70	80	66	75	83	79
THE VILLAGES, FL	71	65	63	60	73	88	60	76	66	62	65	61	60	61	68	72	55	72	87	77
THOMASTON, GA	81	63	52	61	66	82	65	74	72	63	71	65	59	74	64	77	61	71	82	78
THOMASVILLE, GA	79	66	57	65	67	78	66	73	71	66	71	64	62	72	66	75	62	71	78	76
UNITED STATES	100	100	100	100	100	100	100	100	100	100	100	100	100	100	100	100	100	100	100	100

POPULATION CHANGE
CBSA AND U.S. TOTALS

A

CBSA	CBSA Code	POPULATION			2000-2007 ANNUAL RATE		RACE (%)					
							White		Black		Asian/Pacific	
		2000	2007	2012	% Rate	National Rank	2000	2007	2000	2007	2000	2007
THOMASVILLE-LEXING,NC	45640	147,246	159,144	167,235	1.1	288	87.1	85.6	9.1	9.3	0.8	1.1
TIFFIN, OH	45660	58,683	57,830	57,246	-0.2	841	95.0	94.2	1.8	2.0	0.4	0.6
TIFTON, GA	45700	38,407	40,831	42,633	0.8	396	65.3	60.1	28.0	30.9	1.0	1.2
TOCCOA, GA	45740	25,435	25,575	25,275	0.1	723	85.7	83.0	12.0	14.1	0.7	0.9
TOLEDO, OH	45780	659,188	667,360	672,433	0.2	679	83.0	81.1	12.0	12.9	1.1	1.6
TOPEKA, KS	45820	224,551	233,278	239,439	0.5	545	85.9	84.2	6.9	7.2	0.8	1.1
TORRINGTON, CT	45860	182,193	193,083	201,037	0.8	396	95.8	94.7	1.1	1.2	1.2	1.8
TRAVERSE CITY, MI	45900	131,342	147,902	158,779	1.7	140	96.1	95.6	0.3	0.4	0.4	0.6
TRENTON-EWING, NJ	45940	350,761	371,660	385,426	0.8	396	68.5	64.0	19.8	21.2	5.0	6.6
TROY, AL	45980	29,605	30,062	30,617	0.2	679	60.8	58.6	36.6	38.2	0.4	0.5
TRUCKEE-GR VALLEY,CA	46020	92,033	102,193	109,532	1.5	173	93.4	91.5	0.3	0.3	0.9	1.1
TUCSON, AZ	46060	843,746	976,521	1,082,822	2.0	101	75.1	72.1	3.0	3.1	2.2	2.5
TULLAHOMA, TN	46100	93,024	100,876	106,160	1.1	288	93.1	91.9	4.3	4.7	0.6	0.8
TULSA, OK	46140	859,532	919,698	962,698	0.9	352	75.8	73.3	8.7	8.9	1.2	1.6
TUPELO, MS	46180	125,251	131,496	135,728	0.7	444	79.4	77.7	19.0	20.1	0.4	0.5
TUSCALOOSA, AL	46220	192,034	202,146	209,282	0.7	444	63.0	61.1	34.6	35.8	0.8	1.1
TUSKEGEE, AL	46260	24,105	23,084	22,355	-0.6	921	14.0	13.0	84.6	85.3	0.4	0.5
TWIN FALLS, ID	46300	82,626	92,968	101,194	1.6	155	91.3	90.1	0.2	0.2	0.7	0.9
TYLER, TX	46340	174,706	196,814	213,364	1.7	140	72.6	69.5	19.1	20.1	0.7	0.9
UKIAH, CA	46380	86,265	90,385	93,152	0.6	494	80.8	77.0	0.6	0.7	1.3	1.6
UNION, SC	46420	29,881	29,135	28,517	-0.3	873	67.8	66.7	31.0	31.9	0.2	0.3
UNION CITY, TN-KY	46460	40,202	39,354	38,627	-0.3	873	85.6	84.5	12.4	13.0	0.2	0.3
URBANA, OH	46500	38,890	39,934	40,350	0.4	590	95.7	95.1	2.3	2.6	0.3	0.4
UTICA-ROME, NY	46540	299,896	299,124	299,162	0.0	765	91.8	90.4	4.6	5.1	1.0	1.4
UVALDE, TX	46620	25,926	27,119	27,922	0.6	494	75.7	73.3	0.4	0.4	0.5	0.5
VALDOSTA, GA	46660	119,560	131,160	140,250	1.3	225	62.4	57.6	33.4	37.0	1.0	1.3
VALLEJO-FAIRFIELD,CA	46700	394,542	426,952	442,616	1.1	288	56.4	51.7	14.9	14.6	13.5	15.4
VALLEY, AL	46740	36,583	35,245	34,316	-0.5	911	60.9	58.9	38.1	39.9	0.2	0.2
VAN WERT, OH	46780	29,659	28,970	28,517	-0.3	873	97.4	97.0	0.7	0.8	0.2	0.3
VERMILLION, SD	46820	13,537	13,243	12,927	-0.3	873	92.8	90.7	1.0	1.2	2.0	3.0
VERNAL, UT	46860	25,224	27,649	29,503	1.3	225	87.7	87.2	0.1	0.1	0.3	0.3
VERNON, TX	46900	14,676	14,078	13,823	-0.6	921	78.2	74.8	8.9	9.2	0.7	0.8
VICKSBURG, MS	46980	49,644	49,269	49,059	-0.1	805	55.0	52.7	43.2	45.0	0.6	0.9
VICTORIA, TX	47020	111,663	114,304	115,754	0.3	633	75.4	72.2	5.5	5.5	1.2	1.4
VIDALIA, GA	47080	34,337	36,619	38,265	0.9	352	69.3	64.3	24.9	27.8	0.4	0.5
VINCENNES, IN	47180	39,256	37,871	37,044	-0.5	911	96.4	95.7	1.9	2.1	0.6	0.8
VINELAND-M'VILLE, NJ	47220	146,438	154,911	160,663	0.8	396	65.9	62.7	20.2	20.0	1.0	1.7
VIRGINIA BCH-NORFOLK	47260	1,576,370	1,691,070	1,776,655	1.0	318	62.4	59.6	31.0	32.0	2.8	3.6
VISALIA-PORTERVILLE	47300	368,021	431,643	484,123	2.2	85	58.1	53.2	1.6	1.6	3.4	3.7
WABASH, IN	47340	34,960	33,858	32,870	-0.4	896	97.4	96.9	0.4	0.5	0.4	0.6
WACO, TX	47380	213,517	230,315	241,657	1.1	288	72.2	68.7	15.2	15.8	1.1	1.4
WAHPETON, ND-MN	47420	25,136	24,527	24,209	-0.3	873	97.1	96.4	0.3	0.3	0.2	0.4
WALLA WALLA, WA	47460	55,180	58,820	61,597	0.9	352	85.3	82.9	1.7	1.8	1.3	1.5
WALTERBORO, SC	47500	38,264	40,272	41,407	0.7	444	55.5	54.2	42.2	42.9	0.3	0.4
WAPAKONETA, OH	47540	46,611	47,298	47,782	0.2	679	98.1	97.7	0.2	0.3	0.4	0.7
WARNER ROBINS, GA	47580	110,765	135,930	154,482	2.9	42	70.6	66.1	24.8	28.0	1.7	2.1
WARREN, PA	47620	43,863	42,239	41,106	-0.5	911	98.7	98.4	0.2	0.2	0.3	0.4
WARRENSBURG, MO	47660	48,258	51,650	53,893	0.9	352	90.1	88.4	4.3	4.8	1.6	2.2
WARSAW, IN	47700	74,057	78,293	81,246	0.8	396	94.6	93.0	0.6	0.7	0.6	0.8
WASHINGTON, IN	47780	29,820	30,223	30,520	0.2	679	97.5	96.9	0.4	0.5	0.3	0.4
WASHINGTON, NC	47820	44,958	47,055	48,574	0.6	494	68.4	67.1	29.0	29.5	0.2	0.3
WASHINGTON, OH	47860	28,433	29,272	29,902	0.4	590	95.6	94.9	2.1	2.3	0.5	0.7
WASHINGTON-ARLINGTON	47900	4,796,183	5,451,302	5,954,314	1.8	127	59.4	56.7	26.5	26.0	6.9	8.3
WATERLOO-CEDAR FALLS	47940	163,706	165,016	166,607	0.1	723	90.6	89.1	6.3	7.0	0.9	1.4
WATERTOWN, SD	47980	31,437	32,296	32,938	0.4	590	97.1	96.3	0.1	0.2	0.3	0.4
WATERTOWN-FT ATK. WI	48020	74,021	81,885	86,654	1.4	196	96.3	95.2	0.3	0.5	0.5	0.7
WATERTOWN-FT DRUM NY	48060	111,738	117,433	121,521	0.7	444	88.7	87.0	5.8	6.5	1.1	1.3
WAUCHULA, FL	48100	26,938	28,677	29,349	0.9	352	70.7	65.5	8.3	8.6	0.4	0.4
WAUSAU, WI	48140	125,834	133,546	139,154	0.8	396	93.8	91.9	0.3	0.3	4.6	6.2
WAYCROSS, GA	48180	51,119	51,866	53,274	0.2	679	74.9	71.6	22.8	25.3	0.4	0.5
WEIRTON-STEUB.,WV-OH	48260	132,008	125,951	121,448	-0.6	921	94.5	93.4	3.9	4.7	0.4	0.6
WENATCHEE, WA	48300	99,219	108,427	115,271	1.2	255	84.0	81.1	0.3	0.3	0.7	0.8
WEST HELENA, AR	48340	26,445	24,645	23,516	-1.0	936	39.2	36.5	59.0	61.5	0.3	0.4
WEST PLAINS, MO	48460	37,238	38,957	40,184	0.6	494	96.4	95.9	0.3	0.3	0.4	0.6
WEST POINT, MS	48500	21,979	21,431	21,018	-0.3	873	42.8	40.7	56.3	58.2	0.2	0.2
WHEELING, WV-OH	48540	153,172	148,041	144,548	-0.5	911	95.6	95.1	2.9	3.1	0.5	0.7
WHITEWATER, WI	48580	93,759	103,137	111,436	1.3	225	94.5	93.1	0.8	0.9	0.7	0.9
WICHITA, KS	48620	571,166	599,959	620,390	0.7	444	82.4	79.7	7.5	7.8	2.8	3.7
WICHITA FALLS, TX	48660	151,524	151,668	151,372	0.0	765	80.9	78.2	8.9	9.4	1.7	2.1
WILLIAMSPORT, PA	48700	120,044	119,726	119,979	0.0	765	93.9	92.4	4.3	5.4	0.4	0.6
WILLIMANTIC, CT	48740	109,091	118,229	124,990	1.1	288	91.3	89.4	1.9	2.0	0.9	1.3
WILLISTON, ND	48780	19,761	19,294	19,000	-0.3	873	92.9	91.6	0.1	0.1	0.2	0.3
WILLMAR, MN	48820	41,203	42,170	42,840	0.3	633	93.6	91.7	0.5	0.6	0.4	0.6
WILMINGTON, NC	48900	274,532	339,906	400,087	3.0	38	79.5	78.2	17.3	17.6	0.6	0.8
WILMINGTON, OH	48940	40,543	42,997	44,709	0.8	396	96.0	95.3	2.2	2.4	0.4	0.6
WILSON, NC	48980	73,814	78,746	81,964	0.9	352	55.8	54.0	39.3	39.4	0.4	0.6
WINCHESTER, VA-WV	49020	102,997	121,795	137,533	2.3	78	92.6	91.4	4.1	4.3	0.8	1.1
UNITED STATES					1.2		75.1	72.7	12.3	12.6	3.8	4.5

POPULATION COMPOSITION
CBSA AND U.S. TOTALS

CBSA	% HISPANIC ORIGIN		2007 AGE DISTRIBUTION (%)										MEDIAN AGE	% 2007 Males	% 2007 Females
	2000	2007	0-4	5-9	10-14	15-19	20-24	25-44	45-64	65-84	85+	18+	2007		
THOMASVILLE-LEXING,NC	3.2	4.3	6.5	6.4	6.5	5.9	5.1	28.9	27.6	11.6	1.6	77.0	39.5	49.2	50.8
TIFFIN, OH	3.4	4.0	6.4	6.0	6.5	7.4	7.4	25.6	27.3	11.6	2.0	77.0	38.0	49.8	50.2
TIFTON, GA	7.7	10.2	7.9	7.2	6.8	7.2	7.5	27.3	24.1	10.5	1.6	74.3	34.3	48.9	51.1
TOCCOA, GA	1.0	1.3	6.2	6.0	6.1	6.8	6.6	25.6	26.7	13.7	2.4	78.2	39.4	48.4	51.6
TOLEDO, OH	4.3	5.1	6.6	6.2	6.7	7.7	7.8	26.0	26.1	10.9	2.1	76.4	36.7	48.5	51.5
TOPEKA, KS	5.9	7.7	6.7	6.4	6.3	6.7	6.9	25.1	27.6	12.0	2.2	76.5	39.2	48.9	51.1
TORRINGTON, CT	2.1	2.7	5.6	5.8	6.8	7.2	5.1	23.5	31.2	12.2	2.6	77.2	42.6	49.0	51.0
TRAVERSE CITY, MI	1.7	2.1	6.0	5.7	6.2	6.6	6.3	24.3	30.2	12.6	2.1	78.0	41.4	49.2	50.8
TRENTON-EWING, NJ	9.7	12.4	6.2	6.4	7.1	7.7	6.7	27.3	26.1	10.5	2.0	76.1	37.6	48.8	51.2
TROY, AL	1.2	1.7	6.9	6.3	6.0	7.6	9.2	27.4	23.8	10.9	1.9	77.2	33.7	47.4	52.6
TRUCKEE-GR VALLEY,CA	5.7	7.4	4.5	4.9	6.3	6.6	5.5	20.3	34.4	14.9	2.5	80.1	46.1	49.7	50.3
TUCSON, AZ	29.3	34.3	6.7	6.0	6.4	7.2	7.6	26.2	25.1	12.7	2.1	76.9	37.0	48.9	51.1
TULLAHOMA, TN	1.8	2.6	6.4	6.2	6.1	6.4	6.6	26.0	26.8	13.5	1.9	77.6	39.8	49.0	51.0
TULSA, OK	4.6	5.8	7.2	6.7	6.8	6.9	7.5	26.7	25.9	10.6	1.7	75.2	36.4	49.0	51.0
TUPELO, MS	1.3	1.7	7.3	7.0	7.1	6.8	6.2	28.2	24.7	10.8	1.8	74.6	36.5	48.6	51.4
TUSCALOOSA, AL	1.2	1.8	6.8	6.5	6.4	7.4	9.3	27.4	24.4	10.3	1.6	76.6	34.2	48.2	51.8
TUSKEGEE, AL	0.7	0.8	6.4	6.4	6.7	10.3	10.4	22.0	23.7	12.0	2.2	76.5	33.4	46.2	53.8
TWIN FALLS, ID	11.1	12.6	8.1	7.0	6.8	6.7	8.0	25.9	24.4	10.7	2.3	74.0	34.6	49.6	50.4
TYLER, TX	11.2	14.1	7.2	6.7	6.6	7.0	7.6	25.5	24.9	12.4	2.1	75.5	36.7	48.2	51.8
UKIAH, CA	16.5	20.7	6.0	5.5	6.2	6.9	7.4	23.0	31.6	11.5	2.0	78.1	41.0	49.8	50.2
UNION, SC	0.7	0.9	6.4	6.5	6.5	5.7	5.0	26.8	27.4	13.6	2.1	77.1	40.4	47.4	52.6
UNION CITY, TN-KY	1.7	2.4	6.5	6.5	6.1	5.4	5.8	26.5	27.6	13.3	2.4	77.5	39.9	48.5	51.5
URBANA, OH	0.7	0.8	6.7	6.3	6.8	6.6	6.6	25.8	28.2	11.2	1.9	76.3	39.0	49.3	50.7
UTICA-ROME, NY	2.7	3.2	5.7	5.3	6.3	7.4	7.4	24.6	26.8	13.4	3.0	78.8	40.3	49.2	50.8
UVALDE, TX	65.9	72.0	8.9	8.0	7.9	7.9	7.0	24.3	22.5	11.3	2.0	70.4	33.1	49.1	50.9
VALDOSTA, GA	3.2	4.2	7.3	6.7	6.5	7.6	9.5	30.1	22.0	8.9	1.3	75.4	32.1	49.9	50.1
VALLEJO-FAIRFIELD,CA	17.6	21.0	7.3	6.8	7.7	7.5	7.6	28.1	25.3	8.5	1.3	73.6	34.8	50.2	49.8
VALLEY, AL	0.8	1.0	6.9	6.5	6.6	5.6	5.9	26.7	26.4	12.9	2.6	76.6	38.9	47.8	52.2
VAN WERT, OH	1.6	1.9	6.7	6.0	6.9	6.6	6.4	25.5	27.1	12.5	2.3	76.4	39.1	49.5	50.5
VERMILLION, SD	0.9	1.1	5.4	4.6	4.4	12.3	22.4	22.7	18.1	8.2	2.0	82.6	25.5	48.6	51.4
VERNAL, UT	3.5	4.1	9.4	7.4	7.6	8.2	10.3	24.5	22.8	8.7	1.1	70.6	29.4	49.9	50.1
VERNON, TX	20.5	25.5	7.2	6.4	6.3	8.7	7.2	23.3	24.8	13.0	3.0	74.7	37.1	49.6	50.4
VICKSBURG, MS	1.0	1.3	7.7	7.0	7.4	6.6	7.0	25.6	26.7	10.1	1.8	73.8	36.0	47.1	52.9
VICTORIA, TX	39.3	46.0	7.9	7.1	7.2	6.9	7.3	25.5	25.4	11.1	1.6	73.6	35.9	49.2	50.8
VIDALIA, GA	7.5	10.0	7.8	7.2	6.5	7.2	7.9	26.9	24.0	10.7	1.7	74.3	34.9	49.2	50.8
VINCENNES, IN	0.8	1.1	6.0	5.5	5.5	8.6	9.2	23.7	26.2	12.8	2.6	79.3	38.6	49.8	50.2
VINELAND-M'VILLE, NJ	19.0	23.6	6.4	5.6	6.7	7.4	7.7	28.6	24.5	11.0	2.0	77.1	36.5	50.5	49.5
VIRGINIA BCH-NORFOLK	3.1	4.2	6.9	6.5	6.8	7.8	8.0	28.5	24.4	9.7	1.4	75.4	35.2	49.4	50.6
VISALIA-PORTERVILLE	50.8	57.3	9.5	8.0	8.7	8.3	8.5	27.1	20.5	8.1	1.3	68.7	29.3	50.1	49.9
WABASH, IN	1.2	1.6	6.1	5.7	5.9	7.6	7.3	25.3	26.5	12.7	2.8	78.1	39.0	48.8	51.2
WACO, TX	17.9	22.2	7.4	6.6	6.5	8.8	10.5	25.0	22.7	10.4	2.1	75.3	32.7	48.8	51.2
WAHPETON, ND-MN	0.9	1.3	6.5	5.9	5.8	9.2	9.2	22.9	25.9	11.6	3.0	77.4	38.0	51.3	48.7
WALLA WALLA, WA	15.7	19.4	6.5	5.6	6.0	8.6	10.4	23.5	24.5	11.8	3.1	77.9	36.1	50.3	49.7
WALTERBORO, SC	1.4	1.9	7.0	6.8	6.9	6.7	6.6	24.9	27.5	12.0	1.6	75.2	38.5	48.2	51.8
WAPAKONETA, OH	0.7	0.8	7.1	6.5	7.0	6.8	6.9	25.4	26.7	11.2	2.5	75.3	38.3	49.3	50.7
WARNER ROBINS, GA	3.0	3.9	7.4	6.4	7.2	7.7	8.4	28.3	24.9	8.5	1.0	74.3	34.5	49.1	50.9
WARREN, PA	0.3	0.4	5.7	5.6	5.8	6.5	6.4	22.9	30.0	14.5	2.5	78.8	42.9	49.2	50.8
WARRENSBURG, MO	2.9	3.6	6.9	5.9	6.1	9.4	14.3	26.6	21.0	8.4	1.4	77.4	29.4	50.6	49.4
WARSAW, IN	5.0	6.7	7.6	7.3	6.9	6.6	6.1	27.2	26.0	10.6	1.8	74.2	36.6	50.2	49.8
WASHINGTON, IN	2.1	2.8	7.9	7.2	7.1	6.7	6.6	25.3	24.7	12.0	2.4	73.6	36.6	49.7	50.3
WASHINGTON, NC	3.2	4.2	6.0	5.8	5.9	5.7	5.2	24.5	30.4	14.4	2.1	78.8	42.6	48.2	51.8
WASHINGTON, OH	1.2	1.5	6.7	6.3	6.4	6.2	6.1	26.4	27.2	12.6	2.0	76.6	39.2	49.3	50.7
WASHINGTON-ARLINGTON	9.0	11.6	6.8	7.1	7.2	6.9	5.9	30.2	26.1	8.5	1.3	74.7	36.6	48.7	51.3
WATERLOO-CEDAR FALLS	1.6	2.1	6.1	5.6	6.1	7.6	10.0	24.3	25.5	12.0	2.7	78.5	36.8	48.4	51.6
WATERTOWN, SD	1.0	1.3	7.6	6.4	6.3	6.2	8.1	25.7	25.3	11.5	2.8	75.8	37.1	49.7	50.3
WATERTOWN-FT ATK. WI	4.1	5.3	6.4	6.1	6.0	7.5	7.0	27.4	26.9	10.9	1.9	77.5	38.4	49.8	50.2
WATERTOWN-FT DRUM NY	4.2	4.9	7.5	6.1	6.5	7.0	10.1	28.5	23.0	9.5	1.7	75.9	33.7	51.9	48.1
WAUCHULA, FL	35.7	44.8	8.2	7.5	6.5	6.4	7.4	30.5	20.7	11.5	1.4	74.2	33.3	54.9	45.1
WAUSAU, WI	0.8	1.0	6.7	6.1	6.7	6.8	6.9	26.9	27.1	10.7	2.1	76.3	38.5	50.0	50.0
WAYCROSS, GA	2.0	2.8	6.8	6.5	6.4	6.6	6.3	26.8	26.1	12.3	2.1	76.3	38.2	49.3	50.7
WEIRTON-STEUB.,WV-OH	0.6	0.7	5.1	5.1	5.3	5.7	6.0	23.9	29.8	16.3	2.9	81.3	44.2	48.3	51.7
WENATCHEE, WA	19.4	23.7	7.4	6.8	7.1	7.3	7.3	24.0	27.0	11.2	2.0	74.3	37.5	49.8	50.2
WEST HELENA, AR	1.4	1.8	9.2	7.7	7.9	7.4	7.5	22.3	23.7	12.3	2.0	70.6	33.7	46.0	54.0
WEST PLAINS, MO	1.2	1.5	7.0	6.3	6.0	6.5	7.1	23.8	26.0	14.7	2.6	76.7	40.1	48.6	51.4
WEST POINT, MS	0.9	1.1	7.8	7.4	7.5	6.7	7.1	26.0	25.2	10.5	1.8	73.4	34.5	47.8	52.2
WHEELING, WV-OH	0.5	0.5	5.1	5.0	5.5	6.3	6.5	24.0	29.5	15.1	3.0	80.8	43.2	48.6	51.4
WHITEWATER, WI	6.5	8.6	6.1	5.7	6.3	7.8	9.7	24.8	26.2	11.2	2.2	77.6	37.7	49.9	50.1
WICHITA, KS	7.2	9.5	7.8	7.2	7.2	7.1	7.1	26.9	25.3	9.6	1.8	73.5	35.2	49.5	50.5
WICHITA FALLS, TX	11.2	14.1	7.0	6.3	6.1	8.2	9.2	26.3	23.7	11.3	1.8	76.7	35.1	50.8	49.2
WILLIAMSPORT, PA	0.7	0.9	5.6	5.2	5.9	7.5	7.6	24.9	27.5	13.3	2.5	79.3	40.3	49.0	51.0
WILLIMANTIC, CT	7.1	8.9	6.1	5.8	6.7	7.8	7.1	26.8	27.3	10.3	2.2	77.2	38.7	49.5	50.5
WILLISTON, ND	0.9	1.3	6.2	5.1	5.6	6.9	11.1	19.7	29.3	12.9	3.1	78.8	41.1	48.8	51.2
WILLMAR, MN	8.0	10.8	6.8	5.8	6.4	6.7	8.4	24.5	27.3	11.4	2.7	77.0	38.1	49.7	50.3
WILMINGTON, NC	2.5	3.2	5.5	5.5	5.5	6.0	9.1	27.0	28.7	14.1	1.6	80.2	41.1	48.9	51.1
WILMINGTON, OH	0.7	0.8	7.2	6.6	6.4	7.3	7.2	26.7	26.3	10.5	1.7	76.0	37.0	49.3	50.7
WILSON, NC	6.0	7.9	6.7	6.7	6.7	6.4	6.0	26.6	27.1	12.1	1.6	76.2	38.4	48.2	51.8
WINCHESTER, VA-WV	2.6	3.6	6.4	6.0	6.8	6.8	6.0	27.0	27.3	11.3	1.5	76.7	39.0	49.8	50.2
UNITED STATES	12.5	15.0	6.9	6.5	6.8	7.1	7.0	27.6	25.4	10.7	1.9	75.6	36.7	49.2	50.8

CBSA	HOUSEHOLDS					FAMILIES			MEDIAN HOUSEHOLD INCOME		
	2000	2007	2012	% Annual Rate 2000-2007	2007 Average HH Size	2000	2007	% Annual Rate 2000-2007	2007	2012	2007 National Rank
THOMASVILLE-LEXING,NC	58,156	63,215	66,670	1.2	2.49	42,535	45,197	0.8	46,714	52,797	361
TIFFIN, OH	22,292	22,510	22,515	0.1	2.49	15,741	15,439	-0.3	46,028	52,149	383
TIFTON, GA	13,919	15,039	15,822	1.1	2.61	10,105	10,591	0.7	40,286	45,944	643
TOCCOA, GA	9,951	10,135	10,062	0.3	2.43	7,070	6,974	-0.2	35,933	41,168	810
TOLEDO, OH	259,973	266,561	270,587	0.3	2.43	169,451	168,035	-0.1	49,240	56,609	280
TOPEKA, KS	89,600	94,780	97,800	0.8	2.40	60,080	62,721	0.6	50,783	58,549	221
TORRINGTON, CT	71,551	76,102	79,519	0.9	2.50	49,598	52,372	0.8	72,253	85,842	11
TRAVERSE CITY, MI	51,760	59,662	64,796	2.0	2.42	36,171	40,578	1.6	50,631	57,811	228
TRENTON-EWING, NJ	125,807	133,327	138,697	0.8	2.63	86,288	91,233	0.8	72,155	83,763	12
TROY, AL	11,933	12,529	12,888	0.7	2.32	7,646	7,847	0.4	28,360	31,157	918
TRUCKEE-GR VALLEY,CA	36,894	41,181	44,255	1.5	2.46	25,930	29,065	1.6	56,575	65,674	101
TUCSON, AZ	332,350	386,116	429,352	2.1	2.47	212,092	242,839	1.9	48,329	57,567	299
TULLAHOMA, TN	36,099	39,883	42,340	1.4	2.46	26,436	28,526	1.1	44,015	50,938	465
TULSA, OK	337,215	362,106	379,271	1.0	2.50	230,791	243,614	0.7	47,544	56,042	331
TUPELO, MS	48,070	50,719	52,553	0.7	2.54	34,874	36,014	0.4	39,518	43,113	671
TUSCALOOSA, AL	74,863	81,010	84,883	1.1	2.38	48,946	51,768	0.8	37,255	41,034	768
TUSKEGEE, AL	8,950	8,787	8,601	-0.3	2.35	5,543	5,311	-0.6	24,314	26,212	936
TWIN FALLS, ID	30,151	34,386	37,561	1.8	2.66	21,773	24,526	1.7	43,503	50,932	496
TYLER, TX	65,692	72,979	79,223	1.5	2.63	46,901	51,570	1.3	45,672	52,555	400
UKIAH, CA	33,266	34,984	36,149	0.7	2.52	21,864	23,106	0.8	43,967	50,571	471
UNION, SC	12,087	12,217	12,129	0.1	2.35	8,495	8,288	-0.3	39,052	45,095	686
UNION CITY, TN-KY	16,419	16,392	16,206	0.0	2.35	11,519	11,192	-0.4	38,911	45,487	691
URBANA, OH	14,952	15,647	15,946	0.6	2.50	10,868	11,068	0.3	53,163	61,239	160
UTICA-ROME, NY	116,230	118,445	119,460	0.3	2.39	76,271	77,089	0.1	44,112	51,024	458
UVALDE, TX	8,559	9,045	9,359	0.8	2.93	6,645	6,966	0.7	32,218	36,756	889
VALDOSTA, GA	42,666	48,263	52,241	1.7	2.56	29,482	32,221	1.2	38,583	44,360	714
VALLEJO-FAIRFIELD,CA	130,403	140,259	145,300	1.0	2.93	97,375	105,109	1.1	68,894	80,596	16
VALLEY, AL	14,522	14,382	14,159	-0.1	2.41	10,197	9,909	-0.4	34,278	37,550	856
VAN WERT, OH	11,587	11,600	11,532	0.0	2.46	8,358	8,139	-0.4	47,995	55,210	312
VERMILLION, SD	4,874	4,833	4,728	-0.1	2.27	2,720	2,664	-0.3	34,640	41,104	846
VERNAL, UT	8,187	9,259	10,019	1.7	2.96	6,543	7,263	1.5	42,744	48,390	518
VERNON, TX	5,537	5,404	5,307	-0.3	2.48	3,746	3,612	-0.5	36,300	41,674	798
VICKSBURG, MS	18,756	19,012	19,076	0.2	2.56	13,220	13,092	-0.1	39,833	43,435	658
VICTORIA, TX	40,157	41,611	42,327	0.5	2.70	29,748	30,539	0.4	45,530	52,313	410
VIDALIA, GA	12,796	13,866	14,605	1.1	2.55	8,888	9,314	0.6	33,853	38,467	865
VINCENNES, IN	15,552	15,384	15,137	-0.1	2.31	10,136	9,604	-0.7	38,977	44,636	688
VINELAND-M'VILLE, NJ	49,143	51,587	53,694	0.7	2.75	35,185	36,853	0.6	47,946	55,440	317
VIRGINIA BCH-NORFOLK	580,278	633,170	670,138	1.2	2.57	406,036	431,366	0.8	53,656	62,441	144
VISALIA-PORTERVILLE	110,385	125,594	139,995	1.8	3.39	87,061	99,390	1.8	41,879	48,099	566
WABASH, IN	13,215	13,117	12,833	-0.1	2.43	9,393	8,992	-0.6	50,053	58,166	251
WACO, TX	78,859	84,190	88,393	0.9	2.62	52,892	55,799	0.7	41,028	47,662	608
WAHPETON, ND-MN	9,637	9,678	9,632	0.1	2.40	6,354	6,142	-0.5	46,511	54,195	366
WALLA WALLA, WA	19,647	21,012	22,048	0.9	2.55	13,238	13,945	0.7	45,100	52,926	428
WALTERBORO, SC	14,470	15,786	16,468	1.2	2.53	10,494	11,079	0.8	36,485	41,896	792
WAPAKONETA, OH	17,376	18,054	18,415	0.5	2.56	12,776	12,929	0.2	53,250	61,833	153
WARNER ROBINS, GA	40,911	50,948	58,338	3.1	2.61	30,221	36,567	2.7	55,427	64,957	121
WARREN, PA	17,696	17,357	17,018	-0.3	2.37	12,122	11,544	-0.7	44,601	51,362	444
WARRENSBURG, MO	17,410	18,797	19,712	1.1	2.56	11,814	12,387	0.7	43,525	50,325	494
WARSAW, IN	27,283	29,852	31,237	1.2	2.58	19,997	21,161	0.8	53,160	60,998	161
WASHINGTON, IN	10,894	11,179	11,311	0.4	2.66	7,823	7,749	-0.1	41,747	47,224	576
WASHINGTON, NC	18,319	19,742	20,625	1.0	2.35	12,954	13,618	0.7	38,231	43,663	732
WASHINGTON, OH	11,054	11,643	12,005	0.7	2.46	7,841	8,025	0.3	45,011	51,914	433
WASHINGTON-ARLINGTON	1,800,263	2,043,838	2,231,518	1.8	2.62	1,186,517	1,318,073	1.5	80,082	94,806	4
WATERLOO-CEDAR FALLS	63,527	65,908	66,967	0.5	2.39	41,871	42,615	0.2	47,444	55,003	335
WATERTOWN, SD	12,405	13,003	13,338	0.7	2.44	8,324	8,649	0.5	45,663	53,648	401
WATERTOWN-FT ATK. WI	28,205	31,390	33,581	1.5	2.49	19,894	21,652	1.2	57,734	65,558	87
WATERTOWN-FT DRUM NY	40,068	42,891	44,896	0.9	2.54	28,142	29,912	0.8	42,332	48,608	538
WAUCHULA, FL	8,166	8,470	8,636	0.5	3.10	6,253	6,400	0.3	35,499	39,558	822
WAUSAU, WI	47,702	52,616	55,512	1.4	2.50	33,849	36,521	1.1	55,378	63,426	122
WAYCROSS, GA	19,433	20,481	21,211	0.7	2.46	13,738	14,050	0.3	35,369	40,240	828
WEIRTON-STEUB.,WV-OH	54,491	53,805	52,513	-0.2	2.28	37,259	35,640	-0.6	39,068	44,983	684
WENATCHEE, WA	36,747	39,603	41,864	1.0	2.70	26,227	27,915	0.9	47,582	56,194	328
WEST HELENA, AR	9,711	9,174	8,804	-0.8	2.65	6,767	6,203	-1.2	27,339	31,650	926
WEST PLAINS, MO	14,762	15,624	16,183	0.8	2.44	10,611	10,947	0.4	30,855	35,149	904
WEST POINT, MS	8,152	8,227	8,167	0.1	2.56	5,888	5,813	-0.2	31,673	34,511	897
WHEELING, WV-OH	62,249	61,403	60,405	-0.2	2.30	41,518	39,636	-0.6	37,082	42,656	775
WHITEWATER, WI	34,522	39,793	43,304	2.0	2.51	23,271	26,178	1.6	57,084	66,172	92
WICHITA, KS	220,440	232,328	240,564	0.7	2.54	149,841	155,854	0.5	53,562	62,898	148
WICHITA FALLS, TX	56,109	57,041	57,217	0.2	2.46	38,600	38,818	0.1	42,139	49,149	547
WILLIAMSPORT, PA	47,003	48,427	49,003	0.4	2.37	31,703	31,691	0.0	42,441	49,650	530
WILLIMANTIC, CT	41,142	44,533	47,295	1.1	2.56	28,223	30,330	1.0	55,549	64,599	119
WILLISTON, ND	8,095	8,185	8,175	0.2	2.30	5,261	5,099	-0.4	39,459	46,541	675
WILLMAR, MN	15,936	16,648	17,048	0.6	2.48	10,972	11,137	0.2	50,005	59,000	253
WILMINGTON, NC	114,675	146,812	175,172	3.5	2.27	75,339	94,143	3.1	48,274	56,321	301
WILMINGTON, OH	15,416	16,658	17,448	1.1	2.52	11,075	11,635	0.7	49,568	55,959	267
WILSON, NC	28,613	30,694	32,049	1.0	2.51	19,782	20,672	0.6	41,326	47,159	591
WINCHESTER, VA-WV	40,053	48,015	54,539	2.5	2.49	28,008	32,756	2.2	50,207	57,642	246
UNITED STATES				1.2	2.59			1.0	53,154	62,503	

CBSA	2007 Per Capita Income	2007 HH Income Base	2007 HOUSEHOLD INCOME DISTRIBUTION (%)					2007 Home Value Base	2007 HOME VALUE DISTRIBUTION (%)					2007 Median Home Value
			Less than $25,000	$25,000 to $49,999	$50,000 to $99,999	$100,000 to $149,999	$150,000 or More		Less than $50,000	$50,000 to $89,999	$90,000 to $174,999	$175,000 to $399,999	$400,000 or More	
THOMASVILLE-LEXING,NC	22,684	63,215	24.7	28.4	35.5	8.4	3.0	47,731	12.7	13.7	42.9	27.7	3.0	132,297
TIFFIN, OH	21,789	22,510	22.4	32.4	35.1	7.8	2.4	17,468	11.8	26.2	45.4	15.4	1.1	106,481
TIFTON, GA	21,151	15,039	31.9	27.2	28.1	8.7	4.1	10,233	25.0	21.4	33.6	16.5	3.5	96,558
TOCCOA, GA	19,737	10,135	33.3	32.3	25.6	5.9	2.8	7,462	15.3	24.6	41.6	15.6	2.8	105,903
TOLEDO, OH	26,105	266,560	23.6	27.0	32.3	11.4	5.6	189,089	12.4	18.7	42.6	23.3	3.0	119,364
TOPEKA, KS	25,711	94,780	20.4	28.6	36.6	10.2	4.1	68,641	13.6	24.2	43.5	17.2	1.5	109,207
TORRINGTON, CT	36,903	76,102	13.3	19.6	34.3	19.2	13.6	59,173	0.4	1.2	12.1	58.9	27.3	288,111
TRAVERSE CITY, MI	26,875	59,662	18.6	30.6	35.9	9.5	5.4	48,400	5.8	8.3	39.4	36.2	10.2	167,561
TRENTON-EWING, NJ	37,002	133,326	16.2	18.3	31.9	17.3	16.2	92,919	0.6	2.2	16.1	50.2	30.9	300,676
TROY, AL	17,652	12,529	44.9	28.4	20.1	4.1	2.5	8,615	28.7	24.7	28.9	14.8	2.9	83,337
TRUCKEE-GR VALLEY,CA	30,660	41,181	18.5	25.3	34.7	13.3	8.2	31,580	1.8	1.4	3.4	27.3	66.1	488,984
TUCSON, AZ	26,496	386,116	23.8	28.0	30.7	11.1	6.4	252,359	5.8	5.6	25.1	49.1	14.4	207,213
TULLAHOMA, TN	22,253	39,883	28.3	28.1	32.2	7.7	3.6	30,364	13.2	19.2	43.1	20.3	4.2	116,083
TULSA, OK	25,180	362,106	24.2	28.2	31.8	10.0	5.7	245,708	16.1	23.5	41.1	16.4	2.9	104,922
TUPELO, MS	20,168	50,719	30.6	31.5	28.5	6.2	3.2	37,510	18.3	26.5	38.6	14.2	2.4	96,973
TUSCALOOSA, AL	21,397	81,010	35.4	26.4	26.7	8.0	3.5	54,470	17.5	14.7	35.7	27.5	4.6	129,535
TUSKEGEE, AL	16,001	8,787	50.9	26.4	16.9	3.9	2.0	6,018	21.0	27.6	39.9	10.1	1.4	91,963
TWIN FALLS, ID	20,745	34,386	26.0	32.7	30.8	7.1	3.4	24,322	6.6	7.8	47.8	32.2	5.6	154,776
TYLER, TX	23,441	72,979	25.8	28.3	30.8	9.7	5.4	51,968	18.1	21.3	37.3	19.8	3.5	106,738
UKIAH, CA	23,534	34,984	27.8	28.7	29.9	9.1	4.6	21,739	5.3	2.9	6.2	36.6	49.0	394,983
UNION, SC	20,202	12,217	31.6	31.5	29.1	5.9	1.9	9,511	25.8	26.1	37.9	9.1	1.2	87,060
UNION CITY, TN-KY	21,314	16,392	32.5	29.4	28.9	6.3	3.0	11,711	19.1	30.8	36.5	11.9	1.7	90,228
URBANA, OH	24,649	15,647	19.2	27.4	38.5	11.3	3.6	12,286	9.0	15.2	50.4	23.1	2.4	126,329
UTICA-ROME, NY	23,029	118,445	27.2	28.8	32.0	8.0	3.9	83,949	7.4	14.2	49.9	26.8	1.7	140,158
UVALDE, TX	15,488	9,045	39.2	29.2	23.1	6.2	2.2	6,649	39.2	29.1	20.6	9.6	1.4	62,960
VALDOSTA, GA	20,145	48,258	32.9	27.4	29.1	6.8	3.8	31,457	15.0	17.8	35.7	26.7	4.7	128,102
VALLEJO-FAIRFIELD,CA	28,330	140,259	13.8	20.1	36.9	18.7	10.5	93,399	1.7	1.0	2.9	35.0	59.4	442,473
VALLEY, AL	18,096	14,382	38.2	30.3	25.4	4.3	1.7	11,079	21.7	31.8	35.0	9.7	1.7	84,122
VAN WERT, OH	23,451	11,600	18.3	33.8	36.2	9.1	2.5	9,669	13.8	29.7	43.7	11.8	1.0	98,661
VERMILLION, SD	19,848	4,833	37.4	25.2	27.7	6.4	3.3	2,679	20.9	17.3	41.0	18.1	2.7	108,106
VERNAL, UT	17,518	9,259	27.4	31.3	32.2	6.6	2.4	7,206	8.1	10.5	59.1	20.4	1.9	132,937
VERNON, TX	21,110	5,404	32.7	31.2	26.0	5.9	4.1	3,680	37.7	29.6	25.1	6.1	1.5	65,559
VICKSBURG, MS	20,619	19,012	31.9	28.9	26.9	8.9	3.4	13,024	23.6	22.2	35.6	16.4	2.2	96,997
VICTORIA, TX	21,959	41,611	25.6	28.4	31.7	9.9	4.4	29,533	23.2	27.4	35.1	12.6	1.7	89,067
VIDALIA, GA	18,015	13,866	38.5	26.9	25.7	6.4	2.4	9,627	32.1	24.6	31.3	10.5	1.4	77,089
VINCENNES, IN	20,949	15,384	33.5	27.7	29.5	6.7	2.7	10,767	22.4	34.5	31.0	10.6	1.6	80,559
VINELAND-M'VILLE, NJ	21,637	51,587	25.8	26.0	33.3	10.2	4.7	36,424	3.4	5.5	32.8	54.1	4.2	189,055
VIRGINIA BCH-NORFOLK	26,184	633,166	19.2	26.7	35.8	12.3	6.0	405,137	2.6	1.7	17.7	63.8	14.2	238,312
VISALIA-PORTERVILLE	16,859	125,589	30.0	28.5	28.4	8.6	4.5	78,934	3.0	2.3	14.1	66.2	14.4	235,633
WABASH, IN	23,642	13,117	20.1	29.8	37.5	9.8	2.7	10,078	12.2	28.0	44.4	14.3	1.1	102,667
WACO, TX	21,193	84,190	30.8	28.1	28.5	8.0	4.6	52,367	25.5	28.1	33.0	11.7	1.8	84,388
WAHPETON, ND-MN	21,828	9,676	24.7	29.4	36.0	7.3	2.5	7,127	20.4	22.6	40.6	15.3	1.1	101,755
WALLA WALLA, WA	21,815	21,012	27.3	27.1	32.6	9.2	3.7	14,257	3.2	4.6	30.6	52.9	8.9	197,385
WALTERBORO, SC	18,628	15,786	35.4	28.5	28.2	5.3	2.6	12,805	20.6	25.6	36.1	13.9	3.8	95,967
WAPAKONETA, OH	25,467	18,054	17.0	28.8	37.1	12.6	4.5	14,518	6.8	22.7	49.6	19.0	1.9	116,158
WARNER ROBINS, GA	25,119	50,948	17.7	26.7	37.9	12.3	5.4	35,444	8.8	21.9	50.4	17.6	1.3	113,720
WARREN, PA	22,814	17,357	25.0	31.3	33.1	7.9	2.7	13,647	10.5	20.9	47.9	19.0	1.7	122,162
WARRENSBURG, MO	20,607	18,797	26.4	30.5	32.2	8.0	3.0	11,937	11.8	15.2	41.6	27.9	3.5	135,481
WARSAW, IN	24,984	29,852	18.0	27.7	39.5	10.2	4.7	23,828	13.6	17.5	44.9	20.8	3.2	118,424
WASHINGTON, IN	19,896	11,179	28.5	30.3	31.8	6.4	2.9	8,841	17.3	30.5	39.4	11.7	1.2	93,359
WASHINGTON, NC	21,263	19,742	34.3	27.8	27.2	7.7	3.1	15,017	19.3	22.1	36.4	17.8	4.4	104,713
WASHINGTON, PA	22,647	11,643	23.2	32.1	34.3	6.7	3.7	8,186	7.0	19.4	54.2	17.0	2.4	116,914
WASHINGTON-ARLINGTON	40,751	2,043,828	11.0	16.9	33.4	20.3	18.4	1,340,631	0.9	0.6	2.9	40.2	55.4	430,688
WATERLOO-CEDAR FALLS	24,580	65,908	22.9	29.8	33.8	9.2	4.3	48,104	12.5	22.1	43.6	19.3	2.4	112,813
WATERTOWN, SD	22,834	13,003	24.9	30.0	34.4	6.7	3.9	9,527	15.2	21.4	43.4	18.0	2.0	111,723
WATERTOWN-FT ATK. WI	26,766	31,390	15.3	26.5	40.6	13.2	4.5	23,086	5.5	4.1	29.6	53.8	6.9	194,623
WATERTOWN-FT DRUM NY	20,124	42,891	27.9	31.6	31.0	6.7	2.7	26,979	5.7	10.6	42.1	38.1	3.5	160,871
WAUCHULA, FL	15,706	8,470	33.5	33.1	25.2	5.5	2.7	6,459	9.3	18.6	38.9	27.9	5.3	133,992
WAUSAU, WI	26,757	52,616	17.2	26.7	39.4	11.8	4.8	40,531	5.9	11.3	54.4	26.2	2.3	135,403
WAYCROSS, GA	18,313	20,481	36.5	29.8	26.1	5.6	2.0	15,262	30.8	29.0	29.5	9.3	1.5	78,201
WEIRTON-STEUB.,WV-OH	21,600	53,805	30.9	30.9	29.3	6.5	2.4	41,834	21.8	31.3	39.1	7.2	0.7	86,088
WENATCHEE, WA	23,319	39,603	23.3	29.0	32.4	9.9	5.4	27,652	4.2	3.3	17.7	60.7	14.1	236,530
WEST HELENA, AR	15,534	9,174	47.5	27.2	19.2	3.9	2.4	5,379	38.6	30.5	23.9	6.2	0.8	64,560
WEST PLAINS, MO	17,052	15,624	40.5	33.4	20.6	3.4	1.9	11,756	19.2	22.8	39.2	15.7	3.1	102,034
WEST POINT, MS	17,405	8,227	40.4	28.1	23.4	5.7	2.5	6,037	19.8	35.5	33.6	9.4	1.7	84,704
WHEELING, WV-OH	21,072	61,403	34.5	28.8	27.6	6.4	2.8	46,633	20.1	29.4	38.0	11.1	1.4	90,775
WHITEWATER, WI	27,421	39,793	17.6	24.6	38.5	13.6	5.7	28,205	2.7	4.1	31.0	51.8	10.5	199,077
WICHITA, KS	25,905	232,328	19.2	26.9	37.2	11.3	5.4	162,184	14.7	28.7	40.4	14.5	1.7	99,761
WICHITA FALLS, TX	21,686	57,041	26.3	31.8	30.9	7.5	3.4	38,073	27.4	31.1	31.4	8.9	1.3	78,880
WILLIAMSPORT, PA	22,430	48,427	27.0	32.1	29.9	7.6	3.4	34,044	6.7	11.3	52.8	26.5	2.6	140,763
WILLIMANTIC, CT	26,298	44,533	19.9	24.8	35.7	14.2	5.4	31,432	2.1	1.7	19.9	68.1	8.2	222,498
WILLISTON, ND	22,202	8,185	29.8	32.4	28.2	6.6	2.9	5,887	25.5	29.6	37.5	7.0	0.3	82,998
WILLMAR, MN	25,061	16,648	20.6	29.4	35.8	9.7	4.5	12,800	5.7	8.1	46.8	33.0	6.4	157,083
WILMINGTON, NC	27,757	140,012	24.8	26.9	32.9	9.6	5.9	107,641	7.3	6.6	23.0	46.5	16.6	211,126
WILMINGTON, OH	23,383	16,658	20.9	29.5	36.0	10.6	3.0	12,036	7.8	14.7	51.4	23.3	2.8	126,608
WILSON, NC	21,427	30,694	32.2	26.8	29.8	7.3	3.9	19,378	12.0	16.3	48.4	20.6	2.7	119,799
WINCHESTER, VA-WV	25,031	40,015	20.3	29.4	35.7	10.0	4.6	35,155	5.3	5.2	17.0	59.7	12.9	232,026
UNITED STATES	27,916		21.9	25.0	32.3	12.3	8.4		7.9	10.5	27.1	35.6	19.0	192,285

SPENDING POTENTIAL INDICES
CBSA AND U.S. TOTALS

CBSA	FINANCIAL SERVICES				THE HOME						ENTERTAINMENT						PERSONAL			
					Home Improvements		Furnishings													
	Auto Loan	Home Loan	Invest-ments	Retire-ment Plans	Home Repair	Lawn & Garden	Comput-ers & Hard-ware	Major Appli-ances	TV, Radio, Sound Equip-ment	Furni-ture	Dine out/ Carry out	Sports Equip-ment	Fees & Tickets	Toys & Games	Travel	Cable TV	Apparel & Services	Auto Repairs	Health Insur-ance	Pets & Supplies
THOMASVILLE-LEXING,NC	88	75	67	75	78	90	74	82	79	74	78	73	70	82	74	82	69	78	87	86
TIFFIN, OH	81	72	73	73	76	85	72	79	77	72	75	68	71	80	74	79	67	75	85	81
TIFTON, GA	84	71	66	71	70	80	75	77	80	74	79	69	70	80	73	82	70	78	82	81
TOCCOA, GA	78	59	49	58	64	81	62	73	69	59	67	64	55	71	62	73	58	69	80	77
TOLEDO, OH	88	86	95	88	86	88	89	86	90	88	89	77	89	90	88	91	80	87	91	87
TOPEKA, KS	88	84	87	85	85	89	84	87	87	84	86	77	84	88	85	88	77	86	91	88
TORRINGTON, CT	117	139	156	139	142	129	129	129	125	132	124	117	138	124	135	124	115	125	125	127
TRAVERSE CITY, MI	98	91	84	91	93	103	88	96	89	88	89	86	86	90	90	92	79	93	98	98
TRENTON-EWING, NJ	124	144	158	144	146	130	139	133	136	142	137	124	149	135	143	136	128	133	130	132
TROY, AL	65	50	41	50	51	62	55	59	59	53	59	53	49	60	52	62	52	59	63	62
TRUCKEE-GR VALLEY,CA	105	106	106	106	111	118	102	111	101	102	101	99	102	99	107	104	90	107	112	111
TUCSON, AZ	92	89	91	89	86	87	92	89	91	91	91	82	90	89	91	91	82	92	91	89
TULLAHOMA, TN	88	71	60	69	75	91	71	82	78	70	77	73	66	80	71	82	67	78	89	87
TULSA, OK	91	84	84	86	82	87	87	86	89	86	88	78	84	90	85	89	79	87	90	88
TUPELO, MS	84	66	52	65	69	85	67	76	72	66	72	68	61	75	65	76	63	73	81	82
TUSCALOOSA, AL	78	65	61	66	64	73	72	71	74	68	74	65	66	74	68	75	65	73	75	74
TUSKEGEE, AL	60	45	41	46	46	58	50	54	57	49	55	47	45	56	48	60	49	54	61	58
TWIN FALLS, ID	82	72	70	73	74	83	74	79	77	72	76	70	70	79	74	79	67	77	83	81
TYLER, TX	92	82	79	83	82	90	83	87	87	83	86	78	80	87	83	89	76	87	91	89
UKIAH, CA	86	79	75	79	82	91	81	87	82	78	81	78	77	81	81	83	72	84	88	88
UNION, SC	81	57	39	55	62	83	59	72	68	58	67	64	51	70	58	73	57	68	81	79
UNION CITY, TN-KY	81	62	52	61	66	83	65	74	72	63	71	65	58	74	64	76	61	71	83	79
URBANA, OH	92	84	83	85	88	97	82	90	85	82	85	79	81	90	84	88	75	85	93	93
UTICA-ROME, NY	77	74	83	74	77	82	75	78	79	74	77	67	75	78	77	81	69	76	85	79
UVALDE, TX	72	60	43	55	57	67	59	66	63	60	63	60	53	62	58	65	56	66	68	66
VALDOSTA, GA	79	67	60	67	64	72	72	72	74	70	74	66	67	75	68	75	66	74	74	74
VALLEJO-FAIRFIELD,CA	109	124	124	122	121	108	119	114	113	120	114	110	123	114	119	110	106	115	106	112
VALLEY, AL	73	53	39	51	56	74	55	66	63	53	62	58	48	65	54	67	53	62	73	70
VAN WERT, OH	87	78	75	77	82	93	75	84	80	76	79	73	74	84	77	83	70	79	90	88
VERMILLION, SD	72	52	52	55	53	63	78	65	73	63	73	63	63	71	65	71	64	71	68	68
VERNAL, UT	79	69	65	69	68	76	70	73	72	69	72	66	66	74	69	74	63	72	76	76
VERNON, TX	80	64	63	64	68	81	70	76	77	67	75	66	64	76	70	81	65	74	87	77
VICKSBURG, MS	79	69	67	70	68	76	71	73	75	70	74	65	68	75	70	78	66	74	78	76
VICTORIA, TX	90	80	72	79	79	87	79	84	83	80	83	76	76	84	79	84	73	83	87	86
VIDALIA, GA	71	59	52	58	59	70	61	66	66	60	65	59	56	67	60	68	57	65	71	69
VINCENNES, IN	73	60	62	61	63	74	68	70	71	63	69	62	62	71	66	74	61	69	78	72
VINELAND-M'VILLE, NJ	82	81	89	81	82	84	82	83	85	82	84	73	83	85	83	86	76	82	86	83
VIRGINIA BCH-NORFOLK	94	93	96	96	89	88	95	90	94	95	94	84	95	95	93	93	86	94	90	91
VISALIA-PORTERVILLE	81	79	71	76	75	74	79	79	78	79	78	77	76	78	77	76	71	81	75	77
WABASH, IN	89	76	74	76	80	93	77	85	83	76	82	74	73	86	78	87	71	81	94	88
WACO, TX	81	71	71	73	69	75	79	75	80	76	80	68	74	80	75	81	71	78	79	76
WAHPETON, ND-MN	86	65	52	66	71	88	72	81	75	68	75	73	62	79	69	77	65	78	85	86
WALLA WALLA, WA	79	73	80	74	74	79	80	79	80	75	79	71	76	78	78	81	71	79	83	79
WALTERBORO, SC	77	60	44	57	62	78	60	71	67	59	66	63	54	68	60	70	57	68	76	76
WAPAKONETA, OH	93	93	100	94	96	100	87	93	90	90	89	81	90	94	91	92	80	89	98	95
WARNER ROBINS, GA	96	94	90	95	87	87	92	89	91	94	91	82	91	94	90	90	82	91	88	90
WARREN, PA	84	67	65	69	76	90	70	81	76	69	75	70	66	79	72	80	66	76	88	85
WARRENSBURG, MO	81	66	62	68	65	73	79	73	77	72	78	69	71	79	72	76	69	76	74	76
WARSAW, IN	100	87	79	86	90	103	85	95	89	85	89	84	81	93	86	93	78	90	99	99
WASHINGTON, IN	83	66	60	66	72	87	69	79	75	67	74	69	63	77	69	79	64	74	86	83
WASHINGTON, NC	79	64	53	62	68	83	64	75	70	63	69	66	59	71	65	74	60	71	81	79
WASHINGTON, OH	84	73	72	73	77	87	74	81	79	73	77	70	71	82	75	82	68	77	88	83
WASHINGTON-ARLINGTON	139	154	158	157	152	136	153	142	146	155	148	137	159	147	152	143	138	145	134	142
WATERLOO-CEDAR FALLS	84	79	87	80	80	85	82	82	85	80	83	73	81	85	82	86	74	82	88	83
WATERTOWN, SD	84	72	70	72	76	87	75	82	78	73	77	72	70	80	75	81	68	79	87	85
WATERTOWN-FT ATK. WI	95	96	101	97	98	99	93	96	93	93	93	86	94	96	95	94	84	93	97	97
WATERTOWN-FT DRUM NY	77	65	63	66	65	74	72	73	73	68	73	66	67	74	69	74	64	73	76	74
WAUCHULA, FL	82	61	40	57	64	84	61	75	68	60	68	66	53	70	60	73	58	70	81	80
WAUSAU, WI	98	93	94	93	94	101	90	96	93	91	92	85	90	96	92	94	82	92	99	98
WAYCROSS, GA	73	56	45	55	59	74	58	67	64	57	63	59	52	66	57	68	55	64	74	71
WEIRTON-STEUB.,WV-OH	73	63	64	62	68	79	64	72	71	63	69	62	62	71	66	75	60	68	82	74
WENATCHEE, WA	91	85	84	85	87	93	86	90	87	84	86	81	83	87	86	88	77	88	92	91
WEST HELENA, AR	63	48	44	49	49	62	52	57	61	52	59	49	48	59	51	65	52	58	66	60
WEST PLAINS, MO	68	51	41	50	55	70	54	63	59	51	58	55	47	61	53	63	50	60	70	67
WEST POINT, MS	73	54	42	53	57	73	57	65	64	56	63	57	51	66	55	68	55	63	72	70
WHEELING, WV-OH	72	62	64	62	67	77	65	71	71	62	69	61	62	70	66	75	60	68	81	73
WHITEWATER, WI	98	96	99	97	96	99	98	97	96	96	96	88	96	98	97	96	86	96	97	98
WICHITA, KS	93	90	94	92	88	89	91	89	93	91	92	81	90	94	90	93	82	90	92	90
WICHITA FALLS, TX	79	70	71	71	70	77	75	75	78	73	77	67	72	78	73	79	68	76	81	77
WILLIAMSPORT, PA	77	71	75	72	74	81	72	76	76	71	75	66	71	77	73	78	66	74	82	77
WILLIMANTIC, CT	88	97	111	98	98	92	94	93	94	96	93	84	99	94	97	94	86	92	92	92
WILLISTON, ND	78	63	60	63	66	78	70	74	74	65	72	67	63	75	68	76	63	73	81	76
WILLMAR, MN	92	81	79	82	85	95	85	90	85	82	86	81	80	89	84	89	76	88	94	93
WILMINGTON, NC	93	85	82	86	86	95	86	91	88	85	87	81	83	87	87	89	77	89	94	93
WILMINGTON, OH	88	80	80	81	82	89	80	85	82	79	82	75	78	85	80	84	72	82	88	87
WILSON, NC	82	68	63	69	70	82	71	76	77	70	76	68	67	77	70	80	67	75	83	80
WINCHESTER, VA-WV	91	87	82	87	88	93	84	90	86	85	86	82	83	88	85	87	77	87	90	92
UNITED STATES	100	100	100	100	100	100	100	100	100	100	100	100	100	100	100	100	100	100	100	100

CBSA	CBSA Code	POPULATION			2000-2007 ANNUAL RATE		RACE (%)					
							White		Black		Asian/Pacific	
		2000	2007	2012	% Rate	National Rank	2000	2007	2000	2007	2000	2007
WINFIELD, KS	49060	36,291	35,590	34,802	-0.3	873	90.1	88.5	2.7	2.9	1.5	2.1
WINONA, MN	49100	49,985	51,163	51,739	0.3	633	95.8	94.6	0.8	1.0	1.9	2.6
WINSTON-SALEM, NC	49180	421,961	464,838	496,798	1.3	225	75.0	73.1	19.9	20.1	0.8	1.1
WOODWARD, OK	49260	18,486	19,304	19,645	0.6	494	92.2	90.7	1.1	1.2	0.5	0.7
WOOSTER, OH	49300	111,564	116,057	119,030	0.5	545	96.5	95.8	1.6	1.7	0.7	1.0
WORCESTER, MA	49340	750,963	806,147	848,423	1.0	318	89.6	87.1	2.7	3.1	2.7	3.7
WORTHINGTON, MN	49380	20,832	20,695	20,587	-0.1	805	86.5	82.8	1.1	1.3	4.1	5.2
YAKIMA, WA	49420	222,581	236,325	246,020	0.8	396	65.6	61.7	1.0	1.0	1.0	1.1
YANKTON, SD	49460	21,652	22,061	22,064	0.3	633	95.1	93.9	1.2	1.5	0.4	0.7
YAZOO CITY, MS	49540	28,149	29,683	29,588	0.7	444	44.7	43.3	54.0	55.1	0.4	0.5
YORK-HANOVER, PA	49620	381,751	422,449	453,855	1.4	196	92.8	91.3	3.7	4.2	0.9	1.3
YOUNGSTOWN-WARREN	49660	602,964	590,887	578,397	-0.3	873	86.9	85.5	10.8	11.8	0.5	0.7
YUBA CITY, CA	49700	139,149	166,165	189,720	2.5	64	68.9	63.5	2.5	2.5	9.8	11.5
YUMA, AZ	49740	160,026	193,572	223,870	2.7	51	68.3	65.3	2.2	2.2	1.1	1.2
ZANESVILLE, OH	49780	84,585	85,989	87,051	0.2	679	93.9	93.1	4.0	4.5	0.3	0.4
UNITED STATES					1.2		75.1	72.7	12.3	12.6	3.8	4.5

POPULATION COMPOSITION
CBSA AND U.S. TOTALS

B

CBSA	% HISPANIC ORIGIN		2007 AGE DISTRIBUTION (%)										MEDIAN AGE	% 2007 Males	% 2007 Females
	2000	2007	0-4	5-9	10-14	15-19	20-24	25-44	45-64	65-84	85+	18+	2007		
WINFIELD, KS	3.6	4.8	6.8	5.9	6.4	7.5	8.0	24.1	25.8	12.6	2.9	76.8	38.5	49.1	50.9
WINONA, MN	1.4	1.9	5.7	5.2	5.3	9.8	13.2	23.9	23.8	10.5	2.6	80.1	33.3	48.6	51.4
WINSTON-SALEM, NC	5.7	7.4	6.4	6.5	6.6	6.6	5.7	28.1	26.6	11.7	1.8	76.6	38.6	48.5	51.5
WOODWARD, OK	4.8	6.3	6.9	6.3	5.3	6.6	8.1	25.4	26.7	12.2	2.4	77.6	38.6	50.6	49.4
WOOSTER, OH	0.8	0.9	7.1	6.8	6.9	7.6	7.1	25.4	26.4	10.9	1.8	74.9	36.9	49.6	50.4
WORCESTER, MA	6.8	8.7	6.5	6.5	7.2	7.7	6.5	26.4	26.5	10.4	2.3	75.3	38.3	49.0	51.0
WORTHINGTON, MN	11.2	14.6	7.4	6.8	6.3	6.0	7.4	24.2	25.9	12.8	3.3	75.8	38.7	50.3	49.7
YAKIMA, WA	35.9	41.8	9.1	8.1	8.0	7.7	7.6	26.2	22.4	9.0	1.8	70.1	31.7	50.1	49.9
YANKTON, SD	1.8	2.4	6.5	5.9	6.7	6.7	7.3	26.1	27.0	11.1	2.7	77.0	38.5	51.2	48.8
YAZOO CITY, MS	4.4	5.6	7.5	6.7	6.9	6.2	6.8	30.6	24.0	9.7	1.7	75.1	34.9	54.0	46.0
YORK-HANOVER, PA	3.0	3.7	6.0	5.8	6.6	6.9	6.1	26.0	28.5	11.9	2.1	77.4	40.5	49.3	50.7
YOUNGSTOWN-WARREN	1.7	2.0	5.9	5.7	6.1	6.5	6.2	24.3	27.9	14.4	3.0	78.4	41.5	48.6	51.4
YUBA CITY, CA	20.1	24.3	8.0	6.9	7.8	7.8	7.9	26.4	23.3	10.3	1.5	72.4	33.6	49.9	50.1
YUMA, AZ	50.5	56.3	8.4	7.3	7.4	7.5	7.6	24.1	20.5	15.5	1.6	72.4	34.7	50.1	49.9
ZANESVILLE, OH	0.5	0.6	6.9	6.2	6.7	7.0	7.0	25.8	26.0	12.3	2.2	76.3	38.2	48.2	51.8
UNITED STATES	12.5	15.0	6.9	6.5	6.8	7.1	7.0	27.6	25.4	10.7	1.9	75.6	36.7	49.2	50.8

HOUSEHOLDS

CBSA	HOUSEHOLDS					FAMILIES			MEDIAN HOUSEHOLD INCOME		
	2000	2007	2012	% Annual Rate 2000-2007	2007 Average HH Size	2000	2007	% Annual Rate 2000-2007	2007	2012	2007 National Rank
WINFIELD, KS	14,039	13,883	13,605	-0.2	2.43	9,616	9,381	-0.3	42,240	48,288	541
WINONA, MN	18,744	19,414	19,822	0.5	2.42	11,704	11,711	0.0	48,683	57,389	293
WINSTON-SALEM, NC	169,685	190,066	204,056	1.6	2.39	115,582	126,014	1.2	51,518	60,322	207
WOODWARD, OK	7,141	7,448	7,640	0.6	2.43	5,078	5,196	0.3	41,384	47,415	589
WOOSTER, OH	40,445	42,992	44,423	0.8	2.62	29,488	30,507	0.5	50,700	58,221	226
WORCESTER, MA	283,927	303,106	320,146	0.9	2.58	192,423	203,148	0.8	61,627	72,804	50
WORTHINGTON, MN	7,939	7,912	7,865	0.0	2.57	5,520	5,346	-0.4	45,109	52,477	427
YAKIMA, WA	73,993	76,944	79,545	0.5	3.01	54,584	56,078	0.4	43,344	50,970	503
YANKTON, SD	8,187	8,394	8,449	0.3	2.38	5,407	5,494	0.2	44,412	51,824	450
YAZOO CITY, MS	9,178	9,264	9,264	0.1	2.77	6,644	6,558	-0.2	28,222	30,813	920
YORK-HANOVER, PA	148,219	165,835	179,207	1.6	2.50	105,486	114,902	1.2	56,775	65,367	97
YOUNGSTOWN-WARREN	238,319	236,802	233,804	-0.1	2.39	162,900	156,950	-0.5	44,458	51,067	449
YUBA CITY, CA	47,568	56,125	63,878	2.3	2.91	34,747	41,155	2.4	42,417	48,835	533
YUMA, AZ	53,848	67,516	78,696	3.2	2.79	41,664	51,767	3.0	41,287	49,020	596
ZANESVILLE, OH	32,518	33,228	33,766	0.3	2.51	22,873	22,693	-0.1	42,832	49,027	516
UNITED STATES				1.2	2.59			1.0	53,154	62,503	

CBSA	2007 Per Capita Income	2007 HH Income Base	2007 HOUSEHOLD INCOME DISTRIBUTION (%)					2007 Home Value Base	2007 HOME VALUE DISTRIBUTION (%)					2007 Median Home Value
			Less than $25,000	$25,000 to $49,999	$50,000 to $99,999	$100,000 to $149,999	$150,000 or More		Less than $50,000	$50,000 to $89,999	$90,000 to $174,999	$175,000 to $399,999	$400,000 or More	
WINFIELD, KS	21,223	13,883	28.9	29.1	32.6	6.7	2.8	10,081	27.3	32.2	31.4	8.3	0.8	77,263
WINONA, MN	23,772	19,414	23.1	28.2	35.6	9.2	4.0	14,102	6.3	7.1	42.6	38.4	5.5	164,325
WINSTON-SALEM, NC	28,286	190,066	21.8	26.6	34.0	10.6	7.0	134,869	10.4	14.0	44.4	27.0	4.2	131,843
WOODWARD, OK	20,711	7,448	28.7	32.5	28.9	7.5	2.5	5,385	24.7	30.1	36.5	7.6	1.0	84,043
WOOSTER, OH	23,228	42,992	19.0	30.1	36.7	10.2	3.9	32,710	9.4	9.4	49.6	28.6	2.9	140,742
WORCESTER, MA	30,413	303,105	19.9	21.1	32.2	16.7	10.2	200,822	0.6	0.9	12.8	66.2	19.6	264,757
WORTHINGTON, MN	21,413	7,912	25.2	29.9	34.5	7.0	3.4	6,060	14.2	25.2	39.9	18.1	2.5	110,938
YAKIMA, WA	19,113	76,944	26.7	29.9	30.4	8.8	4.3	51,833	7.2	7.7	43.4	37.8	3.9	157,072
YANKTON, SD	22,204	8,394	25.1	31.5	33.5	6.2	3.6	5,932	15.3	20.7	45.1	16.3	2.7	110,537
YAZOO CITY, MS	13,906	9,264	45.5	27.8	20.4	4.4	1.8	6,382	32.1	31.6	27.8	8.1	0.4	71,102
YORK-HANOVER, PA	27,112	165,835	16.6	26.5	39.4	12.2	5.3	126,928	4.1	3.7	31.3	54.2	6.7	197,227
YOUNGSTOWN-WARREN	23,568	236,801	26.3	29.5	31.0	9.4	3.7	180,150	15.9	25.4	42.3	15.2	1.3	102,548
YUBA CITY, CA	19,363	56,125	28.7	29.0	29.4	8.9	3.9	33,710	3.7	2.2	6.7	59.8	27.6	302,686
YUMA, AZ	19,930	67,515	27.8	31.8	28.6	8.0	3.9	49,296	10.8	8.9	38.1	37.1	5.1	159,628
ZANESVILLE, OH	21,714	33,228	27.0	30.9	31.6	7.1	3.4	25,225	15.6	23.6	43.5	15.9	1.4	106,459
UNITED STATES	27,916		21.9	25.0	32.3	12.3	8.4		7.9	10.5	27.1	35.6	19.0	192,285

SPENDING POTENTIAL INDICES
CBSA AND U.S. TOTALS

CBSA	FINANCIAL SERVICES				THE HOME						ENTERTAINMENT						PERSONAL			
					Home Improvements		Furnishings													
	Auto Loan	Home Loan	Invest- ments	Retire- ment Plans	Home Repair	Lawn & Garden	Comput- ers & Hard- ware	Major Appli- ances	TV, Radio, Sound Equip- ment	Furni- ture	Dine out/ Carry out	Sports Equip- ment	Fees & Tickets	Toys & Games	Travel	Cable TV	Apparel & Services	Auto Repairs	Health Insur- ance	Pets & Supplies
WINFIELD, KS	80	66	63	66	70	83	69	76	75	66	73	66	64	76	69	78	63	73	85	79
WINONA, MN	84	78	84	80	79	83	83	82	84	80	83	73	81	84	82	84	74	82	86	83
WINSTON-SALEM, NC	99	91	89	92	91	97	93	94	95	92	95	86	90	96	92	96	85	94	97	97
WOODWARD, OK	83	64	51	63	68	84	67	77	73	64	72	68	60	76	66	77	62	73	85	81
WOOSTER, OH	90	83	82	83	87	94	82	88	85	82	84	79	80	88	83	87	75	85	92	91
WORCESTER, MA	100	115	128	114	115	104	111	107	108	112	109	99	117	108	114	107	101	107	104	106
WORTHINGTON, MN	84	70	64	69	76	90	72	82	77	70	76	72	67	79	72	80	66	78	88	85
YAKIMA, WA	83	78	75	77	76	78	79	80	80	79	80	74	77	80	78	79	72	81	80	79
YANKTON, SD	84	72	69	73	74	84	75	80	78	73	77	71	70	79	74	80	67	78	84	83
YAZOO CITY, MS	65	48	38	48	50	65	51	58	58	50	57	51	45	58	50	62	50	57	65	63
YORK-HANOVER, PA	95	95	101	96	97	99	92	95	94	93	93	84	94	96	94	95	84	93	98	97
YOUNGSTOWN-WARREN	80	77	85	77	79	84	76	79	81	76	79	68	77	81	78	83	71	78	87	80
YUBA CITY, CA	80	76	71	75	75	77	79	79	77	77	78	74	75	78	76	77	70	80	77	78
YUMA, AZ	80	75	71	71	74	80	74	79	77	76	77	70	72	73	75	79	68	80	83	77
ZANESVILLE, OH	82	71	71	72	74	84	73	78	78	72	76	69	70	79	73	81	67	76	85	81
UNITED STATES	100	100	100	100	100	100	100	100	100	100	100	100	100	100	100	100	100	100	100	100

DMA Summary Data

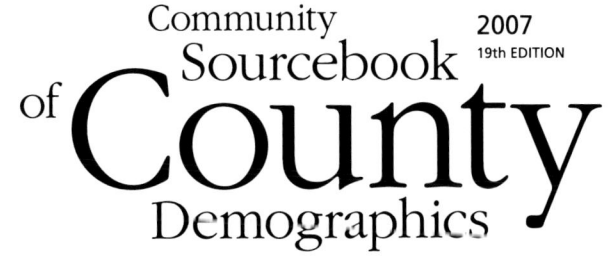

Community
Sourcebook
of County
Demographics
2007
19th EDITION

| DMA | DMA Code | POPULATION | | | 2000-2007 ANNUAL RATE | | RACE (%) | | | | | |
| | | | | | | | White | | Black | | Asian/Pacific | |
		2000	2007	2012	% Rate	National Rank	2000	2007	2000	2007	2000	2007
ABILENE-SWEETWATER	662	310,016	309,455	309,573	0.0	189	83.0	80.2	5.5	5.6	0.7	0.9
ALBANY, GA	525	404,488	422,167	434,745	0.6	130	58.4	54.8	37.6	40.0	0.5	0.6
ALBANY-SCHENEC.-TROY	532	1,343,616	1,393,093	1,430,308	0.5	143	91.3	89.8	4.8	5.4	1.5	1.9
ALBUQUERQUE-SANTA FE	790	1,686,548	1,841,965	1,963,155	1.2	62	65.0	63.8	1.7	1.8	1.1	1.3
ALEXANDRIA, LA	644	239,047	245,624	249,635	0.4	153	69.9	66.0	25.9	28.9	0.9	1.3
ALPENA	583	43,033	42,061	41,486	-0.3	206	98.2	97.9	0.2	0.2	0.3	0.4
AMARILLO	634	511,269	523,769	531,489	0.3	162	78.3	75.6	4.4	4.6	1.2	1.4
ANCHORAGE, AK	743	369,296	415,843	448,990	1.7	37	76.6	74.0	4.3	3.8	4.8	5.2
ATLANTA	524	5,149,717	6,385,943	7,346,756	3.0	10	66.6	63.7	26.0	26.8	2.9	3.5
AUGUSTA, GA	520	638,671	679,715	709,693	0.9	92	58.4	56.2	37.9	39.1	1.2	1.6
AUSTIN	635	1,371,385	1,709,650	1,973,770	3.1	8	73.9	70.6	7.5	7.6	3.3	3.8
BAKERSFIELD	800	590,316	713,454	816,184	2.6	14	59.7	55.5	6.1	5.7	3.5	3.8
BALTIMORE	512	2,721,726	2,894,264	3,013,285	0.9	92	68.6	65.3	26.3	28.1	2.6	3.4
BANGOR	537	335,054	349,394	359,259	0.6	130	96.9	96.4	0.3	0.4	0.5	0.7
BATON ROUGE	716	806,772	863,541	908,162	0.9	92	62.6	59.9	34.5	36.6	1.3	1.7
BEAUMONT-PORT ARTHUR	692	456,637	464,391	468,247	0.2	171	70.0	68.0	23.5	24.3	1.8	2.0
BEND, OR	821	115,367	156,004	194,015	4.3	3	94.8	93.9	0.2	0.2	0.8	1.0
BILLINGS	756	251,620	265,806	276,868	0.8	103	90.4	89.6	0.3	0.4	0.5	0.6
BILOXI-GULFPORT	746	353,787	356,834	357,836	0.1	180	75.1	72.3	20.3	22.0	2.1	2.6
BINGHAMTON	502	351,776	350,258	349,886	-0.1	197	93.9	92.8	2.2	2.5	1.8	2.3
BIRMINGHAM	630	1,763,729	1,842,387	1,908,726	0.6	130	72.8	71.7	24.9	25.3	0.7	0.9
BLUEFLD-BECKLEY-OAK.	559	358,580	356,865	355,806	-0.1	197	93.0	92.5	5.5	5.6	0.4	0.6
BOISE	757	568,258	697,184	800,284	2.9	11	88.9	87.6	0.7	0.8	1.5	1.7
BOSTON	506	6,080,476	6,332,080	6,510,187	0.6	130	85.9	83.4	4.9	5.3	3.9	5.1
BOWLING GREEN	736	182,691	197,537	208,409	1.1	70	91.1	89.8	6.0	6.3	0.8	1.2
BUFFALO	514	1,655,724	1,632,975	1,612,919	-0.2	203	86.9	85.1	9.0	9.9	1.1	1.4
BURLINGTON-PLATTSBGH	523	819,697	861,076	889,623	0.7	115	95.5	94.8	1.3	1.5	0.9	1.2
BUTTE-BOZEMAN, MT	754	145,136	161,030	175,564	1.4	48	95.8	95.3	0.2	0.2	0.7	0.9
CASPER-RIVERTON	767	127,560	133,433	137,934	0.6	130	89.1	88.3	0.5	0.5	0.4	0.5
C. RAPIDS-W'LOO-DUB.	637	829,684	867,565	895,511	0.6	130	94.3	93.0	2.4	2.8	1.2	1.9
CHAMPN.-S'FIELD-DEC.	648	950,854	965,144	974,578	0.2	171	88.8	86.8	7.4	8.3	1.7	2.3
CHARLESTON, SC	519	680,311	770,951	841,178	1.7	37	62.3	61.1	34.0	34.1	1.2	1.6
CHARLESTON-HUNTINGTN	564	1,177,650	1,170,101	1,162,643	-0.1	197	96.0	95.7	2.4	2.4	0.4	0.6
CHARLOTTE	517	2,412,463	2,787,595	3,090,689	2.0	28	76.4	74.3	18.5	18.8	1.7	2.3
CHARLOTTESVILLE	584	197,977	227,212	249,417	1.9	32	81.5	78.9	13.8	15.1	2.4	2.9
CHATTANOOGA	575	840,075	907,449	954,718	1.1	70	86.7	84.9	9.2	9.6	0.8	1.1
CHEYEN-SCTSBLF-STERL	759	132,571	138,998	144,018	0.7	115	89.1	87.6	1.7	1.8	0.9	1.1
CHICAGO	602	9,274,187	9,919,359	10,430,290	0.9	92	67.2	64.9	18.5	18.3	4.2	5.0
CHICO-REDDING	868	471,390	520,469	557,112	1.4	48	85.7	82.4	1.0	1.1	2.5	3.1
CINCINNATI	515	2,190,930	2,309,876	2,407,171	0.7	115	86.4	85.6	10.7	10.7	1.2	1.7
CLARKSBURG-WESTON	598	267,427	269,559	269,958	0.1	180	97.1	96.8	1.4	1.4	0.4	0.6
CLEVELAND	510	3,914,599	3,948,206	3,973,527	0.1	180	82.4	81.0	13.9	14.5	1.1	1.7
COLORADO SPR.-PUEBLO	752	789,639	884,673	953,989	1.6	41	81.9	80.0	5.1	5.4	2.0	2.5
COLUMBIA, SC	546	932,115	1,013,588	1,071,889	1.2	62	58.1	57.1	38.6	38.5	1.1	1.5
COLUMBIA-JEFF. CITY	604	425,254	452,779	470,827	0.9	92	89.9	88.2	6.6	7.4	1.3	1.9
COLUMBUS, GA	522	536,148	559,541	576,130	0.6	130	58.0	55.2	38.1	39.9	1.2	1.5
COLUMBUS, OH	535	2,158,681	2,338,675	2,480,138	1.1	70	85.4	83.6	10.2	10.9	1.9	2.7
COLUMBUS-TUPELO-W.PT	673	488,226	498,164	504,803	0.3	162	68.7	67.2	29.6	30.6	0.5	0.6
CORPUS CHRISTI	600	553,442	579,692	597,530	0.6	130	74.2	71.9	3.8	3.6	1.1	1.2
DALLAS-FT.WORTH	623	5,761,057	6,766,745	7,569,755	2.2	23	70.8	68.5	13.3	12.9	3.5	4.3
DAVENPORT-R.ISL-MOL.	682	780,959	782,615	784,037	0.0	189	91.6	89.9	3.8	4.2	0.9	1.2
DAYTON	542	1,337,641	1,339,681	1,340,716	0.0	189	86.4	84.9	10.6	11.4	1.0	1.5
DENVER	751	3,450,751	3,905,104	4,226,713	1.7	37	83.0	81.4	3.6	3.6	2.4	2.9
DES MOINES-AMES	679	1,016,958	1,079,411	1,128,998	0.8	103	93.2	91.3	2.3	2.6	1.7	2.6
DETROIT	505	4,965,944	5,118,983	5,205,266	0.4	153	72.7	71.1	21.3	21.5	2.5	3.6
DOTHAN	606	235,959	247,692	256,653	0.7	115	73.9	71.8	22.8	24.0	0.7	1.0
DULUTH-SUPERIOR	676	422,365	429,037	430,939	0.2	171	93.7	92.8	0.7	0.8	0.5	0.7
EL PASO	765	860,623	960,567	1,035,704	1.5	44	72.7	71.8	2.7	2.5	1.0	1.1
ELMIRA	565	250,393	251,348	251,708	0.1	180	94.7	93.7	2.9	3.3	0.7	1.0
ERIE	516	415,072	416,236	416,627	0.0	189	93.0	91.6	4.5	5.4	0.6	0.8
EUGENE	801	564,290	595,162	619,349	0.7	115	91.2	89.8	0.6	0.7	2.2	2.7
EUREKA	802	154,025	162,357	168,352	0.7	115	83.7	80.8	1.5	1.6	1.9	2.4
EVANSVILLE	649	713,832	729,160	739,396	0.3	162	93.9	93.1	4.3	4.6	0.4	0.6
FAIRBANKS	745	82,840	89,457	94,305	1.1	70	77.8	75.1	5.8	5.4	2.4	2.6
FARGO-VALLEY CITY	724	585,206	605,246	618,992	0.5	143	94.3	93.3	0.5	0.6	0.7	1.0
FLINT-SAGINAW-B.CITY	513	1,203,155	1,229,634	1,244,936	0.3	162	84.6	82.9	11.2	12.0	0.8	1.1
FRESNO-VISALIA	866	1,647,682	1,922,435	2,144,297	2.2	23	56.3	51.8	4.4	4.1	6.0	6.5
FT. MYERS-NAPLES	571	912,887	1,224,464	1,512,444	4.1	4	86.5	83.7	6.3	7.1	0.8	1.1
FT.SMITH-FAY-SPRNGDL	670	654,797	766,473	860,120	2.2	23	87.2	85.2	2.2	2.2	1.6	2.1
FT. WAYNE	509	688,348	715,336	734,235	0.5	143	90.4	88.7	5.6	6.2	0.9	1.2
GAINESVILLE	592	280,669	317,664	343,060	1.7	37	76.6	72.7	17.1	19.4	2.8	3.7
GLENDIVE	798	10,258	9,717	9,393	-0.7	209	97.5	97.2	0.2	0.3	0.1	0.2
GRAND JCT.-MONTROSE	773	156,281	184,720	207,099	2.3	20	91.9	90.7	0.4	0.5	0.6	0.7
G.RAPIDS-K'ZOO-B.CRK	563	1,903,860	2,024,372	2,098,499	0.9	92	87.1	85.2	6.8	7.3	1.3	1.9
GREAT FALLS	755	170,048	168,023	166,753	-0.2	203	84.1	82.9	0.6	0.6	0.5	0.6
GREEN BAY-APPLETON	658	1,057,034	1,127,873	1,173,768	0.9	92	94.4	93.1	0.7	0.8	1.5	2.0
GR'NSBORO-H.PT-W.SLM	518	1,560,695	1,686,700	1,777,460	1.1	70	76.2	74.2	18.7	18.0	1.2	1.6
UNITED STATES					1.2		75.1	72.7	12.3	12.6	3.8	4.5

POPULATION COMPOSITION
DMA AND U.S. TOTALS

DMA	% HISPANIC ORIGIN		2007 AGE DISTRIBUTION (%)										MEDIAN AGE		
	2000	2007	0-4	5-9	10-14	15-19	20-24	25-44	45-64	65-84	85+	18+	2007	% 2007 Males	% 2007 Females
ABILENE-SWEETWATER	18.4	22.7	6.7	5.8	6.0	7.9	9.3	24.2	24.6	12.9	2.5	77.2	37.1	49.8	50.2
ALBANY, GA	4.1	5.4	7.7	7.3	6.9	7.2	7.2	27.7	24.2	10.3	1.6	74.0	34.8	48.8	51.2
ALBANY-SCHENEC.-TROY	2.5	2.9	5.7	5.5	6.3	7.5	6.9	24.9	28.3	12.4	2.6	78.4	40.6	48.9	51.1
ALBUQUERQUE-SANTA FE	37.7	39.1	7.4	6.7	6.9	7.5	7.7	26.2	25.9	10.2	1.5	74.6	35.7	49.3	50.7
ALEXANDRIA, LA	2.3	2.5	7.7	6.9	6.7	6.5	8.1	27.6	23.9	10.9	1.7	74.9	35.0	49.5	50.5
ALPENA	0.6	0.8	5.3	4.9	5.2	5.9	6.5	21.2	30.8	17.4	2.7	80.9	45.6	49.5	50.5
AMARILLO	25.1	28.8	7.8	7.0	6.9	7.4	8.0	26.1	23.8	11.0	2.0	74.0	34.7	50.1	49.9
ANCHORAGE, AK	4.7	6.0	7.3	6.6	7.4	7.9	8.1	27.1	28.6	6.5	0.6	73.8	34.9	50.7	49.3
ATLANTA	6.4	8.2	7.3	7.1	6.9	6.9	6.7	31.5	24.6	7.9	1.1	74.6	34.9	49.5	50.5
AUGUSTA, GA	2.2	2.9	6.9	6.6	6.9	7.2	7.2	27.1	26.3	10.4	1.5	75.4	36.6	48.8	51.2
AUSTIN	25.1	30.1	7.4	7.0	6.5	7.1	8.8	31.5	23.1	7.4	1.1	75.2	33.1	50.7	49.3
BAKERSFIELD	41.1	47.0	8.9	7.5	8.5	8.4	8.5	27.8	21.4	7.8	1.2	70.0	30.3	51.2	48.8
BALTIMORE	2.0	2.9	6.3	6.3	6.9	7.4	6.5	26.7	27.0	11.0	1.9	76.0	38.6	48.3	51.7
BANGOR	0.6	0.8	5.3	5.0	5.6	7.1	7.3	24.7	30.6	12.5	2.0	80.0	41.7	49.2	50.8
BATON ROUGE	1.6	1.8	7.3	6.8	6.8	7.3	8.4	28.2	24.8	9.0	1.3	75.1	34.3	49.1	50.9
BEAUMONT-PORT ARTHUR	7.3	9.2	6.9	6.3	6.6	6.5	7.4	26.8	25.7	11.8	1.9	76.2	37.2	50.0	50.0
BEND, OR	3.7	5.1	6.1	5.8	6.3	6.9	6.4	25.0	30.1	11.7	1.7	77.5	40.5	49.5	50.5
BILLINGS	3.2	3.8	6.5	6.1	6.4	6.9	6.8	23.9	29.4	11.7	2.3	76.7	40.1	49.2	50.8
BILOXI-GULFPORT	2.3	2.8	7.3	6.7	6.9	7.1	7.3	28.1	24.8	10.4	1.2	75.0	35.5	49.8	50.2
BINGHAMTON	1.7	2.0	5.8	5.3	6.1	7.8	7.5	23.4	27.8	13.6	2.7	78.7	40.9	48.9	51.1
BIRMINGHAM	1.6	2.3	6.6	6.5	6.4	6.4	6.4	28.0	26.4	11.5	1.8	76.8	37.7	48.5	51.5
BLUEFLD-BECKLEY-OAK.	0.6	0.7	5.4	5.4	5.4	5.4	5.8	25.7	30.4	14.2	2.3	80.7	42.6	49.0	51.0
BOISE	10.1	11.4	8.3	7.5	7.2	6.8	7.3	29.3	23.7	8.3	1.5	72.9	33.4	50.4	49.6
BOSTON	5.8	7.1	6.1	6.2	6.7	7.4	6.5	27.8	26.5	10.7	2.2	76.7	38.4	48.7	51.3
BOWLING GREEN	1.8	2.6	6.6	6.2	6.1	6.7	7.5	28.6	25.5	11.1	1.7	77.7	36.6	49.2	50.8
BUFFALO	2.8	3.2	6.0	5.7	6.4	7.5	7.1	24.8	27.0	13.0	2.6	77.7	39.8	48.6	51.4
BURLINGTON-PLATTSBGH	1.3	1.5	5.4	5.2	6.0	7.9	8.0	25.3	29.1	11.1	1.9	79.1	39.9	49.9	50.1
BUTTE-BOZEMAN, MT	1.9	2.3	5.6	5.2	5.4	7.6	9.9	26.4	27.9	10.0	1.8	79.7	36.7	51.6	48.4
CASPER-RIVERTON	5.1	5.6	6.5	5.9	6.2	7.2	8.0	23.5	29.0	11.8	1.7	77.0	39.1	49.3	50.7
C. RAPIDS-W'LOO-DUB.	1.5	2.0	6.5	6.0	6.3	7.3	8.8	25.9	25.4	11.2	2.5	77.4	36.8	49.3	50.7
CHAMPN.-S'FIELD-DEC.	1.8	2.4	6.2	5.9	6.1	7.6	8.9	25.4	25.8	11.7	2.3	77.9	37.3	49.2	50.8
CHARLESTON, SC	2.2	2.9	6.7	6.2	6.4	7.4	7.4	28.0	26.0	10.4	1.4	76.5	36.4	49.0	51.0
CHARLESTON-HUNTINGTN	0.6	0.7	5.9	5.9	5.8	5.7	5.9	27.0	28.7	13.2	1.9	79.0	40.6	48.9	51.1
CHARLOTTE	4.3	5.7	6.9	6.7	6.7	6.7	6.0	30.1	25.7	9.8	1.4	75.7	36.9	49.5	50.5
CHARLOTTESVILLE	2.0	2.9	5.8	5.9	6.1	7.4	8.4	26.1	26.3	12.2	1.8	78.3	38.4	48.0	52.0
CHATTANOOGA	3.7	5.2	6.5	6.4	6.2	6.2	5.8	28.3	26.6	11.9	1.7	77.2	38.5	49.0	51.0
CHEYEN-SCTSBLF-STERL	12.4	14.4	6.7	5.9	6.5	6.8	7.4	26.1	27.2	11.4	2.1	76.9	38.1	49.6	50.4
CHICAGO	16.2	19.3	7.4	7.2	7.5	6.9	6.4	29.1	24.2	9.5	1.7	73.7	35.2	49.1	50.9
CHICO-REDDING	10.3	13.1	6.1	5.4	6.3	7.8	9.3	22.4	27.6	12.8	2.3	77.7	39.3	49.3	50.7
CINCINNATI	1.1	1.4	7.1	6.8	6.8	7.2	7.1	27.5	25.6	10.3	1.7	75.2	36.5	48.8	51.2
CLARKSBURG-WESTON	0.7	0.7	5.4	5.2	5.7	6.0	6.3	26.2	28.8	13.8	2.5	80.2	41.5	49.1	50.9
CLEVELAND	2.3	2.7	6.5	6.4	6.8	6.9	6.3	25.4	27.1	12.3	2.3	76.2	39.2	48.4	51.6
COLORADO SPR.-PUEBLO	17.5	19.8	7.2	6.7	6.8	7.3	7.5	28.0	25.8	9.3	1.5	75.1	35.9	50.5	49.5
COLUMBIA, SC	2.2	2.9	6.6	6.3	6.5	7.5	7.7	27.6	26.1	10.1	1.5	76.4	36.4	48.5	51.5
COLUMBIA-JEFF. CITY	1.3	1.6	6.4	5.9	6.0	7.7	9.4	27.3	24.8	10.5	2.0	77.9	35.6	49.6	50.4
COLUMBUS, GA	2.8	3.5	7.0	6.4	6.6	7.8	9.8	27.3	23.5	9.9	1.6	76.1	33.7	49.3	50.7
COLUMBUS, OH	1.5	1.7	7.0	6.6	6.6	7.1	7.8	28.5	25.1	9.7	1.5	75.9	35.8	49.3	50.7
COLUMBUS-TUPELO-W.PT	1.2	1.6	7.2	6.8	6.7	6.8	7.8	27.1	24.5	11.2	1.9	75.5	35.9	48.6	51.4
CORPUS CHRISTI	56.5	62.4	7.9	7.1	6.9	7.1	8.2	27.1	24.0	10.3	1.5	74.0	33.9	50.1	49.9
DALLAS-FT.WORTH	20.4	24.0	7.9	7.5	7.2	7.1	7.2	30.4	23.7	7.8	1.1	73.1	33.9	49.9	50.1
DAVENPORT-R.ISL-MOL.	5.0	6.5	6.5	6.1	6.2	6.7	7.0	25.2	27.3	12.5	2.6	77.4	39.5	49.2	50.8
DAYTON	1.1	1.3	6.6	6.2	6.4	7.1	7.3	25.4	26.7	12.2	2.1	76.8	38.5	48.6	51.4
DENVER	16.9	19.4	6.9	6.8	6.7	7.0	7.0	29.9	26.3	8.2	1.3	75.6	35.7	50.4	49.6
DES MOINES-AMES	3.0	4.0	6.8	6.4	6.3	7.1	8.1	25.9	25.6	11.4	2.5	76.7	37.3	49.3	50.7
DETROIT	2.8	3.3	6.8	6.8	7.4	7.0	6.0	27.8	26.3	10.2	1.8	74.8	37.3	48.9	51.1
DOTHAN	2.0	2.9	6.8	6.4	6.2	6.3	6.5	26.6	26.5	12.6	2.0	76.7	38.5	48.6	51.4
DULUTH-SUPERIOR	0.8	1.0	5.4	5.1	5.5	7.1	8.1	22.8	29.5	13.5	3.0	80.2	42.1	49.8	50.2
EL PASO	75.2	78.7	9.0	7.9	8.2	8.1	8.6	27.6	21.0	8.7	1.0	70.2	30.4	48.6	51.4
ELMIRA	1.1	1.5	6.0	5.6	6.2	7.1	7.4	24.2	27.8	13.1	2.4	78.0	40.4	49.4	50.6
ERIE	1.6	2.1	6.1	5.7	6.5	7.6	7.8	24.6	27.8	12.3	2.4	77.5	38.9	49.1	50.9
EUGENE	4.2	5.7	5.5	5.2	5.6	7.2	9.0	24.4	28.7	12.3	2.2	79.9	39.4	49.3	50.7
EUREKA	7.8	10.0	5.7	5.1	5.8	7.3	9.1	26.3	28.3	10.5	1.9	79.3	37.6	50.5	49.5
EVANSVILLE	1.0	1.4	6.5	6.2	6.2	6.5	6.6	26.3	27.3	12.3	2.2	77.4	39.3	48.9	51.1
FAIRBANKS	4.2	5.4	7.9	6.5	6.6	8.3	11.2	29.0	24.7	5.5	0.5	74.2	30.1	51.9	48.1
FARGO-VALLEY CITY	1.8	2.3	6.4	5.7	5.9	7.9	9.6	24.7	25.7	11.6	2.7	78.0	37.1	50.1	49.9
FLINT-SAGINAW-B.CITY	3.1	3.8	6.5	6.2	6.8	7.2	7.2	25.5	26.9	11.8	1.9	76.3	38.2	48.8	51.2
FRESNO-VISALIA	45.3	51.3	9.0	7.6	8.4	8.4	8.7	27.7	20.8	8.1	1.3	69.9	30.0	50.5	49.5
FT. MYERS-NAPLES	13.1	17.6	5.3	4.9	5.2	5.2	5.0	20.9	27.1	23.2	3.3	81.5	47.8	49.3	50.7
FT.SMITH-FAY-SPRNGDL	6.4	8.7	7.5	6.9	6.4	6.7	7.3	28.1	24.3	11.1	1.7	75.3	35.7	49.7	50.3
FT. WAYNE	3.3	4.3	7.4	7.0	7.1	7.0	6.6	26.9	25.9	10.2	1.9	74.3	36.3	49.4	50.6
GAINESVILLE	5.2	7.2	5.3	4.7	5.2	9.1	14.5	25.0	24.2	10.4	1.5	81.3	32.7	49.3	50.7
GLENDIVE	0.9	1.0	5.1	4.5	5.1	7.1	8.1	20.2	32.1	14.9	3.0	81.5	45.0	49.8	50.2
GRAND JCT.-MONTROSE	10.9	13.1	6.3	5.8	6.2	6.9	7.0	24.3	28.4	12.8	2.3	77.5	40.1	49.3	50.7
G.RAPIDS-K'ZOO-B.CRK	5.1	6.3	7.2	6.7	6.9	7.6	7.7	27.1	25.2	9.7	1.7	74.7	35.5	49.6	50.4
GREAT FALLS	1.7	1.8	7.0	6.0	6.3	7.2	8.5	23.1	27.2	12.4	2.4	76.4	38.9	49.6	50.4
GREEN BAY-APPLETON	2.1	2.8	6.5	5.9	6.4	7.2	7.5	26.5	26.9	10.9	2.2	77.0	38.5	49.8	50.2
GR'NSBORO-H.PT-W.SLM	4.9	6.4	6.4	6.4	6.4	6.6	5.8	28.6	26.6	11.6	1.8	77.1	38.5	48.8	51.2
UNITED STATES	12.5	15.0	6.9	6.5	6.8	7.1	7.0	27.6	25.4	10.7	1.9	75.6	36.7	49.2	50.8

DMA	HOUSEHOLDS					FAMILIES			MEDIAN HOUSEHOLD INCOME		
	2000	2007	2012	% Annual Rate 2000-2007	2007 Average HH Size	2000	2007	% Annual Rate 2000-2007	2007	2012	2007 National Rank
ABILENE-SWEETWATER	115,665	116,778	117,308	0.1	2.47	80,824	80,709	0.0	37,886	43,838	181
ALBANY, GA	147,145	155,904	161,621	0.8	2.61	106,004	109,225	0.4	37,376	42,920	185
ALBANY-SCHENEC.-TROY	536,618	563,142	582,306	0.7	2.38	345,683	359,863	0.6	52,372	61,592	55
ALBUQUERQUE-SANTA FE	629,495	706,448	760,762	1.6	2.56	431,200	468,934	1.2	44,133	51,945	119
ALEXANDRIA, LA	87,189	91,296	93,852	0.6	2.54	62,697	64,031	0.3	32,127	34,957	205
ALPENA	17,950	18,051	18,010	0.1	2.29	12,262	11,991	-0.3	40,364	45,428	164
AMARILLO	189,787	194,907	198,185	0.4	2.58	134,529	136,151	0.2	40,836	47,199	155
ANCHORAGE, AK	133,816	151,972	164,629	1.8	2.66	91,904	102,716	1.5	65,895	76,783	5
ATLANTA	1,891,713	2,338,648	2,686,331	3.0	2.68	1,318,222	1,593,311	2.6	62,639	75,206	12
AUGUSTA, GA	236,890	258,149	271,703	1.2	2.54	168,955	179,240	0.8	44,231	52,126	116
AUSTIN	520,683	645,087	742,647	3.0	2.58	330,611	407,741	2.9	61,756	75,141	15
BAKERSFIELD	182,226	216,862	247,628	2.4	3.16	137,519	164,434	2.5	43,255	50,638	131
BALTIMORE	1,038,364	1,103,341	1,151,865	0.8	2.55	699,993	724,141	0.5	61,626	72,080	16
BANGOR	136,578	146,970	153,251	1.0	2.31	90,383	95,290	0.7	39,126	44,751	174
BATON ROUGE	293,042	321,619	341,429	1.3	2.59	206,145	221,633	1.0	40,699	44,363	157
BEAUMONT-PORT ARTHUR	169,135	173,703	176,034	0.4	2.55	120,984	123,087	0.2	42,202	48,699	140
BEND, OR	45,595	62,836	78,564	4.5	2.46	31,953	43,669	4.4	52,074	61,423	57
BILLINGS	100,046	107,230	112,454	1.0	2.42	67,042	69,735	0.5	41,337	47,218	148
BILOXI-GULFPORT	130,703	134,400	135,581	0.4	2.58	93,265	94,021	0.1	40,583	43,072	159
BINGHAMTON	139,670	141,486	142,634	0.2	2.37	90,838	91,314	0.1	43,948	50,653	123
BIRMINGHAM	694,090	739,231	771,436	0.9	2.43	483,476	506,047	0.6	40,937	45,696	153
BLUEFLD-BECKLEY-OAK.	146,530	150,986	152,562	0.4	2.29	102,035	101,910	0.0	30,921	35,289	208
BOISE	205,762	256,666	296,164	3.1	2.64	146,221	180,247	2.9	52,552	63,534	54
BOSTON	2,333,959	2,441,598	2,518,406	0.6	2.51	1,515,155	1,568,456	0.5	69,067	82,653	4
BOWLING GREEN	71,203	79,261	84,396	1.5	2.40	49,230	52,736	1.0	40,071	46,855	168
BUFFALO	651,334	652,700	648,862	0.0	2.41	426,230	423,310	-0.1	47,079	54,996	91
BURLINGTON-PLATTSBGH	317,923	343,088	358,352	1.1	2.39	208,736	220,139	0.7	51,026	60,689	64
BUTTE-BOZEMAN, MT	57,559	64,224	70,261	1.5	2.40	36,409	39,286	1.1	41,817	48,462	141
CASPER-RIVERTON	50,444	53,966	56,323	0.9	2.42	34,305	35,630	0.5	44,356	51,796	115
C. RAPIDS-W'LOO-DUB.	324,069	348,043	362,493	1.0	2.39	213,461	224,189	0.7	49,979	58,316	68
CHAMPN.-S'FIELD-DEC.	378,004	388,830	395,049	0.4	2.37	243,675	242,235	-0.1	47,248	54,071	88
CHARLESTON, SC	257,800	300,561	332,146	2.1	2.49	177,793	200,213	1.7	47,540	55,866	85
CHARLESTON-HUNTINGTN	475,170	484,900	486,890	0.3	2.36	334,926	332,057	-0.1	34,720	39,488	198
CHARLOTTE	929,063	1,088,639	1,212,219	2.2	2.50	649,692	741,140	1.8	53,132	62,769	47
CHARLOTTESVILLE	76,577	89,774	99,573	2.2	2.41	49,684	56,964	1.9	54,368	62,647	40
CHATTANOOGA	328,544	359,576	380,538	1.3	2.47	234,508	250,227	0.9	44,199	51,149	118
CHEYEN-SCTSBLF-STERL	52,480	56,411	58,985	1.0	2.38	35,640	37,355	0.7	46,069	54,006	99
CHICAGO	3,346,647	3,563,061	3,738,897	0.9	2.73	2,279,018	2,370,588	0.5	64,308	75,978	9
CHICO-REDDING	182,548	201,211	215,759	1.4	2.53	121,194	134,298	1.4	39,888	45,665	169
CINCINNATI	848,599	907,339	949,459	0.9	2.49	575,890	600,897	0.6	55,441	65,191	36
CLARKSBURG-WESTON	107,811	110,975	112,251	0.4	2.35	74,171	73,986	0.0	33,881	38,611	201
CLEVELAND	1,536,768	1,570,928	1,589,699	0.3	2.46	1,033,315	1,026,167	-0.1	51,268	59,384	62
COLORADO SPR.-PUEBLO	294,799	332,729	359,799	1.7	2.56	204,220	225,500	1.4	53,632	64,100	43
COLUMBIA, SC	349,917	391,811	420,034	1.6	2.47	241,888	260,949	1.1	47,124	55,061	90
COLUMBIA-JEFF. CITY	162,439	177,365	185,906	1.2	2.40	106,916	112,926	0.8	44,929	51,653	108
COLUMBUS, GA	202,115	215,542	224,043	0.9	2.47	136,811	141,591	0.5	38,219	43,291	178
COLUMBUS, OH	842,893	925,012	986,000	1.3	2.45	554,657	591,841	0.9	52,181	60,956	56
COLUMBUS-TUPELO-W.PT	186,472	194,454	198,631	0.6	2.50	132,558	135,078	0.3	34,128	37,155	199
CORPUS CHRISTI	190,737	202,495	210,225	0.8	2.76	139,760	146,977	0.7	41,395	48,237	145
DALLAS-FT.WORTH	2,105,016	2,437,789	2,720,230	2.0	2.73	1,462,780	1,682,651	2.0	59,840	71,801	19
DAVENPORT-R.ISL-MOL.	309,636	314,366	316,570	0.2	2.42	210,346	208,414	-0.1	48,717	56,361	80
DAYTON	527,191	537,993	542,698	0.3	2.42	360,147	356,559	-0.1	51,074	58,532	63
DENVER	1,340,120	1,512,943	1,631,948	1.7	2.54	863,113	959,769	1.5	63,038	75,743	11
DES MOINES-AMES	400,943	433,124	455,012	1.1	2.40	266,541	282,523	0.8	51,419	60,906	60
DETROIT	1,892,913	1,971,698	2,016,169	0.6	2.55	1,275,794	1,293,083	0.2	61,792	71,689	14
DOTHAN	93,830	100,829	105,596	1.0	2.41	66,714	70,322	0.7	37,114	40,999	188
DULUTH-SUPERIOR	173,389	180,094	182,648	0.5	2.28	111,664	112,555	0.1	44,562	51,839	113
EL PASO	271,722	308,687	335,228	1.8	3.05	210,777	236,396	1.6	38,067	44,083	179
ELMIRA	97,419	99,357	100,221	0.3	2.43	65,872	66,448	0.1	43,703	50,278	125
ERIE	158,881	160,823	161,805	0.2	2.47	107,032	105,103	-0.3	44,779	52,240	111
EUGENE	226,632	241,820	253,019	0.9	2.40	146,090	154,295	0.8	45,253	52,414	104
EUREKA	60,408	63,701	66,350	0.7	2.42	36,938	39,187	0.8	38,258	43,833	177
EVANSVILLE	282,331	295,077	301,628	0.6	2.40	196,431	198,299	0.1	45,340	52,426	103
FAIRBANKS	29,777	32,029	33,939	1.0	2.67	20,502	21,650	0.8	61,107	71,681	18
FARGO-VALLEY CITY	232,621	246,893	255,392	0.8	2.34	150,019	152,835	0.3	45,202	52,883	105
FLINT-SAGINAW-B.CITY	463,667	483,651	494,027	0.6	2.48	320,254	324,817	0.2	47,749	54,457	83
FRESNO-VISALIA	504,326	577,845	641,996	1.9	3.22	383,646	441,308	2.0	43,072	50,000	133
FT. MYERS-NAPLES	380,884	514,779	639,794	4.2	2.34	261,579	346,730	4.0	51,354	60,746	61
FT.SMITH-FAY-SPRNGDL	250,086	294,162	330,791	2.3	2.55	177,735	203,328	1.9	43,050	50,868	134
FT. WAYNE	262,466	277,914	287,317	0.8	2.53	182,993	186,634	0.3	52,887	61,854	51
GAINESVILLE	111,602	129,395	141,022	2.1	2.32	64,868	73,582	1.8	36,955	42,074	189
GLENDIVE	4,162	4,023	3,924	-0.5	2.29	2,832	2,659	-0.9	35,744	39,574	197
GRAND JCT.-MONTROSE	61,881	73,497	82,760	2.4	2.46	42,298	49,132	2.1	44,475	51,037	114
G RAPIDS-K'ZOO-B.CRK	702,435	760,089	793,051	1.1	2.58	488,398	515,101	0.7	52,569	60,504	53
GREAT FALLS	66,587	66,237	66,007	-0.1	2.47	44,981	43,465	-0.5	37,169	42,042	187
GREEN BAY-APPLETON	409,150	449,968	473,304	1.3	2.43	278,738	299,342	1.0	54,314	62,686	41
GR'NSBORO-H.PT-W.SLM	622,050	679,513	719,020	1.2	2.43	429,370	456,612	0.9	48,861	56,536	77
UNITED STATES				1.2	2.59			1.0	53,154	62,503	

INCOME
DMA AND U.S. TOTALS

D

DMA	2007 Per Capita Income	2007 HH Income Base	2007 HOUSEHOLD INCOME DISTRIBUTION (%)					2007 Home Value Base	2007 HOME VALUE DISTRIBUTION (%)					2007 Median Home Value
			Less than $25,000	$25,000 to $49,999	$50,000 to $99,999	$100,000 to $149,999	$150,000 or More		Less than $50,000	$50,000 to $89,999	$90,000 to $174,999	$175,000 to $399,999	$400,000 or More	
ABILENE-SWEETWATER	20,039	116,775	32.0	30.9	27.4	6.4	3.2	82,650	37.9	27.5	25.1	8.1	1.3	66,570
ALBANY, GA	19,584	155,904	34.8	27.6	26.9	7.0	3.7	106,194	25.2	27.5	33.5	12.1	1.9	86,102
ALBANY-SCHENEC.-TROY	28,182	563,142	21.1	26.6	34.0	11.5	6.9	391,484	2.7	3.2	23.5	62.6	8.0	213,614
ALBUQUERQUE-SANTA FE	23,000	706,429	28.1	27.9	29.7	9.2	5.1	501,293	12.4	10.7	29.9	36.8	10.2	167,140
ALEXANDRIA, LA	17,247	91,290	38.9	30.6	22.9	5.1	2.4	61,613	24.9	24.7	36.1	12.5	1.7	90,524
ALPENA	21,730	18,051	29.6	31.9	30.3	5.9	2.3	14,906	8.4	21.3	49.1	18.5	2.6	112,846
AMARILLO	20,685	194,907	28.9	30.7	29.2	7.6	3.6	135,080	26.3	27.5	33.1	11.5	1.6	84,059
ANCHORAGE, AK	31,047	151,972	14.4	22.2	35.2	17.5	10.7	104,779	6.0	4.3	17.1	60.9	11.7	239,439
ATLANTA	31,315	2,338,637	16.8	21.8	35.2	14.6	11.6	1,614,755	5.5	7.8	34.8	40.6	11.3	180,156
AUGUSTA, GA	22,945	258,149	29.1	26.1	30.1	9.6	5.1	186,909	16.5	20.7	40.1	19.2	3.6	111,184
AUSTIN	31,704	645,066	16.7	22.8	34.0	15.5	11.1	403,649	6.7	9.5	34.2	39.0	10.6	174,004
BAKERSFIELD	18,633	216,860	29.5	26.7	29.1	9.8	4.9	137,696	2.5	2.1	10.6	65.3	19.4	267,678
BALTIMORE	31,545	1,103,294	17.9	22.1	33.8	15.7	10.4	764,206	1.8	2.1	11.8	55.6	28.8	302,121
BANGOR	21,531	146,967	31.1	30.7	28.5	7.1	2.6	110,094	8.4	13.5	42.9	29.9	5.3	147,664
BATON ROUGE	20,922	321,613	31.6	27.2	28.4	8.8	4.0	226,100	16.2	17.8	38.0	24.2	3.8	120,326
BEAUMONT-PORT ARTHUR	21,589	173,701	29.6	27.6	29.4	9.4	4.0	128,032	30.8	29.4	29.9	8.8	1.1	75,559
BEND, OR	28,214	62,836	18.8	28.9	34.9	10.6	6.8	46,698	2.5	2.6	8.6	48.4	38.0	340,652
BILLINGS	21,870	107,230	29.1	30.6	30.1	6.8	3.4	75,591	10.2	9.6	39.3	33.5	7.4	158,136
BILOXI-GULFPORT	19,998	134,399	29.8	31.1	29.1	6.9	3.1	93,700	10.4	15.9	41.8	27.0	5.0	133,849
BINGHAMTON	23,704	141,486	26.6	29.7	30.9	8.6	4.3	102,472	7.0	11.5	48.3	30.8	2.5	148,511
BIRMINGHAM	23,131	739,229	30.8	28.4	27.6	8.7	4.6	548,697	17.0	20.1	34.4	23.1	5.3	114,928
BLUEFLD-BECKLEY-OAK.	18,531	150,986	41.3	30.1	21.8	4.5	2.2	120,137	28.5	23.7	34.8	11.7	1.4	86,058
BOISE	25,536	256,666	19.3	27.9	35.1	11.5	6.2	187,397	5.1	5.0	29.7	50.2	10.0	195,906
BOSTON	36,553	2,441,587	16.5	19.1	32.6	17.6	14.2	1,584,806	1.0	1.2	7.7	50.8	39.2	347,963
BOWLING GREEN	22,118	79,253	31.5	28.5	28.7	7.6	3.8	56,260	18.1	20.4	40.7	18.3	2.5	107,908
BUFFALO	24,858	652,677	25.5	27.3	32.5	9.8	4.9	462,134	5.7	12.4	47.1	32.6	2.2	147,210
BURLINGTON-PLATTSBGH	26,593	343,088	21.8	27.0	35.3	10.2	5.7	250,155	4.0	5.6	29.2	50.2	10.9	197,678
BUTTE-BOZEMAN, MT	22,033	64,224	28.1	30.9	30.3	7.2	3.4	43,057	8.9	8.9	25.4	41.1	15.7	197,785
CASPER-RIVERTON	23,047	53,963	26.7	29.3	32.2	8.3	3.5	39,542	10.1	13.1	45.6	25.8	5.3	137,140
C. RAPIDS-W'LOO-DUB.	25,703	348,043	21.4	28.7	35.2	10.0	4.7	255,506	11.6	17.4	45.5	22.3	3.3	121,021
CHAMPN.-S'FIELD-DEC.	24,831	388,827	24.7	28.1	33.5	9.4	4.3	277,172	12.5	20.6	45.2	19.7	2.1	115,567
CHARLESTON, SC	24,987	300,561	25.6	26.7	31.8	10.1	5.8	213,447	12.1	11.6	30.6	33.5	12.2	162,602
CHARLESTON-HUNTINGTN	19,980	484,900	37.2	28.8	25.0	6.2	2.8	373,719	26.3	26.6	35.6	10.2	1.2	85,712
CHARLOTTE	27,796	1,088,639	20.6	26.0	35.0	11.1	7.3	781,430	9.3	12.8	39.3	31.4	7.2	143,150
CHARLOTTESVILLE	29,453	89,774	19.7	25.6	34.1	13.1	7.4	60,281	3.1	2.2	14.2	61.3	19.3	261,489
CHATTANOOGA	23,342	359,576	27.3	28.6	31.4	8.2	4.6	261,126	12.8	18.0	43.6	21.2	4.3	119,439
CHEYEN-SCTSBLF-STERL	24,005	56,411	24.3	29.8	32.6	9.6	3.7	39,942	11.6	12.6	41.2	30.7	4.0	145,927
CHICAGO	31,319	3,562,973	17.0	20.7	34.7	16.0	11.6	2,429,755	2.0	2.8	20.5	54.0	20.7	249,187
CHICO-REDDING	21,373	201,211	31.7	28.4	28.2	8.0	3.7	131,671	4.9	3.2	11.7	58.5	21.7	272,152
CINCINNATI	29,186	907,336	19.8	25.2	33.6	13.3	8.1	641,983	6.0	11.4	45.9	31.4	5.3	146,119
CLARKSBURG-WESTON	18,653	110,975	37.6	31.0	24.3	5.1	2.1	86,841	22.3	25.3	39.7	11.5	1.2	93,490
CLEVELAND	27,278	1,570,920	21.6	27.1	33.1	11.8	6.5	1,143,831	5.8	14.6	47.1	28.7	3.8	137,950
COLORADO SPR.-PUEBLO	26,791	332,724	19.9	26.1	34.8	12.2	7.1	233,252	5.0	6.0	31.3	48.2	9.5	194,195
COLUMBIA, SC	24,419	391,801	25.6	27.2	31.7	10.3	5.2	285,335	13.4	17.9	42.7	21.7	4.3	120,674
COLUMBIA-JEFF. CITY	23,156	177,365	25.6	29.8	31.9	9.0	3.7	124,890	14.3	16.8	40.9	24.2	3.7	123,375
COLUMBUS, GA	20,619	215,542	34.2	27.1	27.6	7.6	3.6	140,577	18.1	20.3	37.9	19.8	3.9	110,058
COLUMBUS, OH	27,680	925,009	20.8	27.0	33.3	12.1	6.8	634,919	7.4	14.4	42.7	30.4	5.1	139,730
COLUMBUS-TUPELO-W.PT	18,045	194,454	37.2	30.5	24.7	5.3	2.3	143,232	23.5	29.8	33.4	11.5	1.8	85,656
CORPUS CHRISTI	19,925	202,487	30.5	27.6	29.2	8.6	4.1	135,843	24.5	28.2	33.5	11.9	2.0	85,853
DALLAS-FT.WORTH	29,981	2,437,763	17.2	24.1	33.2	14.5	10.9	1,564,778	10.9	18.7	37.9	26.4	6.1	125,255
DAVENPORT-R.ISL-MOL.	24,454	314,366	22.8	28.5	35.2	9.7	3.9	236,316	11.0	21.8	46.0	18.8	2.3	113,735
DAYTON	26,442	537,988	21.1	27.7	34.1	11.6	5.5	389,036	6.9	19.0	49.9	21.9	2.3	120,565
DENVER	32,904	1,512,931	15.8	22.4	35.4	15.0	11.4	1,060,865	4.1	3.5	17.6	55.9	18.9	241,792
DES MOINES-AMES	26,677	433,124	20.5	27.9	35.4	10.9	5.4	317,742	13.1	19.1	41.6	23.0	3.2	119,826
DETROIT	31,390	1,971,661	18.4	22.1	33.2	16.1	10.2	1,440,547	8.4	11.6	33.5	38.2	8.2	165,547
DOTHAN	20,480	100,829	34.7	29.3	26.1	6.9	2.9	73,455	19.5	26.0	37.3	14.8	2.3	96,831
DULUTH-SUPERIOR	23,651	180,094	27.2	28.5	33.0	8.2	3.2	140,326	10.4	20.0	42.9	23.5	3.3	126,632
EL PASO	17,116	308,686	32.6	29.2	26.9	7.7	3.5	203,646	10.9	20.9	50.2	15.5	2.5	113,017
ELMIRA	22,555	99,357	26.7	30.9	31.1	7.6	3.8	74,114	9.5	18.4	41.4	27.9	2.8	136,714
ERIE	22,584	160,823	25.9	29.6	32.2	8.6	3.6	116,007	11.8	19.2	45.7	21.0	2.2	119,549
EUGENE	24,499	241,819	26.3	28.7	31.7	8.5	4.8	160,509	5.4	3.9	20.7	56.5	13.4	225,954
EUREKA	21,325	63,701	34.1	27.9	27.2	7.4	3.4	38,276	4.8	2.9	8.9	55.4	28.0	303,145
EVANSVILLE	23,675	295,075	26.3	28.5	32.6	8.9	3.7	222,242	18.8	27.1	38.4	14.1	1.6	95,680
FAIRBANKS	28,249	32,029	15.7	23.7	35.9	15.7	9.0	18,668	5.8	6.0	29.1	54.4	4.7	202,057
FARGO-VALLEY CITY	23,650	246,889	25.4	29.9	33.1	7.8	3.8	171,900	15.7	18.2	42.5	21.4	2.3	119,518
FLINT-SAGINAW-B.CITY	24,536	483,651	24.6	27.7	31.9	11.1	4.7	370,001	13.0	18.3	44.4	22.1	2.2	118,619
FRESNO-VISALIA	18,268	577,820	28.6	28.3	29.3	9.0	4.9	347,784	2.4	1.8	9.8	62.6	23.4	276,588
FT. MYERS-NAPLES	31,496	514,772	19.6	28.9	32.7	10.4	8.4	408,476	2.7	3.9	17.1	45.2	31.0	280,747
FT.SMITH-FAY-SPRNGDL	21,862	294,162	27.7	29.7	31.0	7.2	4.4	206,872	14.7	20.7	39.6	20.3	4.7	116,376
FT. WAYNE	25,449	277,914	18.7	27.9	37.6	11.2	4.6	211,416	12.1	24.6	44.4	16.8	2.2	107,855
GAINESVILLE	22,873	129,391	35.0	27.4	24.7	8.2	4.7	82,853	6.6	11.2	32.0	41.2	8.9	175,383
GLENDIVE	18,621	4,023	36.6	31.5	25.4	5.1	1.5	2,996	18.9	23.4	43.3	12.7	1.7	101,389
GRAND JCT.-MONTROSE	23,876	73,497	25.3	30.7	31.5	8.4	4.1	54,816	6.3	4.2	27.2	49.3	13.1	204,742
G.RAPIDS-K'ZOO-B.CRK	25,157	760,087	20.3	26.9	36.2	11.4	5.2	574,201	8.3	12.2	46.5	29.2	3.8	141,018
GREAT FALLS	19,287	66,228	32.9	32.0	27.2	5.2	2.6	44,450	11.3	13.2	42.6	28.4	4.3	144,237
GREEN BAY-APPLETON	26,506	449,968	18.3	26.8	39.0	11.4	4.6	334,181	4.8	11.0	50.2	30.8	3.2	142,279
GR'NSBORO-H.PT-W.SLM	26,115	679,513	23.5	27.6	33.6	9.5	5.8	484,466	11.4	15.4	44.0	25.4	3.8	125,517
UNITED STATES	27,916		21.9	25.0	32.3	12.3	8.4		7.9	10.5	27.1	35.6	19.0	192,285

SPENDING POTENTIAL INDICES
DMA AND U.S. TOTALS

DMA	FINANCIAL SERVICES				THE HOME						ENTERTAINMENT						PERSONAL			
					Home Improvements		Furnishings													
	Auto Loan	Home Loan	Invest-ments	Retire-ment Plans	Home Repair	Lawn & Garden	Comput-ers & Hard-ware	Major Appli-ances	TV, Radio, Sound Equip-ment	Furni-ture	Dine out/ Carry out	Sports Equip-ment	Fees & Tickets	Toys & Games	Travel	Cable TV	Apparel & Services	Auto Repairs	Health Insur-ance	Pets & Supplies
ABILENE-SWEETWATER	77	63	58	63	65	76	68	72	72	65	71	64	62	73	66	75	62	71	79	74
ALBANY, GA	81	65	55	64	66	79	67	74	73	66	72	66	62	74	66	76	63	72	79	78
ALBANY-SCHENEC.-TROY	93	92	100	93	95	97	93	94	94	92	94	84	94	94	95	96	84	93	98	95
ALBUQUERQUE-SANTA FE	86	80	75	79	78	83	81	83	82	80	82	75	78	82	80	82	73	83	84	83
ALEXANDRIA, LA	70	55	48	55	56	68	58	64	63	57	62	57	54	64	57	66	55	63	68	67
ALPENA	76	64	58	63	70	85	65	76	69	63	68	65	60	69	67	73	59	71	82	78
AMARILLO	81	69	64	69	70	78	73	76	76	71	76	68	68	77	71	78	67	76	80	78
ANCHORAGE, AK	118	117	113	120	112	110	118	113	114	118	115	107	117	116	114	111	104	116	108	115
ATLANTA	122	117	111	120	112	113	118	115	116	119	117	108	116	119	114	115	106	117	112	117
AUGUSTA, GA	90	78	70	78	78	88	78	84	83	78	82	75	74	84	77	86	73	83	88	87
AUSTIN	119	112	105	115	105	107	119	111	115	117	116	106	113	116	112	112	105	116	108	112
BAKERSFIELD	82	81	76	79	77	75	82	80	80	82	81	78	80	80	80	78	73	83	77	78
BALTIMORE	106	116	124	116	114	108	113	109	111	115	112	100	118	111	114	111	103	110	108	109
BANGOR	78	64	55	63	68	83	66	75	70	63	69	66	60	71	66	73	60	71	80	79
BATON ROUGE	82	72	66	73	70	78	74	76	77	74	77	69	71	78	72	79	68	77	79	79
BEAUMONT-PORT ARTHUR	84	72	69	73	73	83	74	79	79	74	78	69	70	80	73	82	69	78	85	82
BEND, OR	100	97	93	98	97	102	95	99	95	95	95	90	94	95	96	96	84	98	99	101
BILLINGS	79	69	68	70	72	81	72	77	75	70	74	68	68	75	72	77	65	75	81	79
BILOXI-GULFPORT	77	70	68	70	68	74	70	72	73	70	72	65	68	74	70	75	64	72	76	74
BINGHAMTON	82	74	77	74	77	86	77	81	80	74	79	71	74	80	77	83	70	79	87	83
BIRMINGHAM	86	74	67	74	75	86	75	81	80	75	79	72	71	81	74	82	70	79	85	84
BLUEFLD-BECKLEY-OAK.	70	52	40	50	57	74	55	66	61	52	60	58	48	62	55	66	51	62	74	70
BOISE	100	95	88	96	91	95	94	95	93	94	93	88	92	96	92	93	83	95	93	96
BOSTON	115	133	142	132	136	121	131	125	126	132	128	119	138	125	134	125	120	125	120	124
BOWLING GREEN	84	69	60	69	71	84	72	78	76	70	75	70	66	78	70	78	66	76	82	82
BUFFALO	82	81	92	82	83	86	82	83	85	82	84	72	83	85	84	87	75	82	89	84
BURLINGTON-PLATTSBGH	94	86	84	87	90	99	88	94	89	86	89	84	85	90	88	91	79	91	97	96
BUTTE-BOZEMAN, MT	79	69	68	70	71	79	75	76	76	71	75	69	70	76	73	77	66	76	79	78
CASPER-RIVERTON	82	75	74	75	76	83	76	80	78	74	77	71	73	79	76	80	68	78	83	81
C. RAPIDS-W'LOO-DUB.	91	82	82	83	84	92	86	88	88	83	87	79	82	89	84	89	77	87	92	90
CHAMPN.-S'FIELD-DEC.	86	77	81	79	79	85	82	83	84	79	83	74	79	85	81	86	74	82	88	84
CHARLESTON, SC	94	84	77	84	83	91	86	89	88	85	88	81	82	89	84	89	78	88	91	91
CHARLESTON-HUNTINGTN	76	59	48	57	63	79	61	71	67	59	66	63	55	69	61	72	57	68	78	76
CHARLOTTE	106	95	86	95	94	103	95	99	98	95	97	90	91	100	93	99	87	98	101	102
CHARLOTTESVILLE	102	98	99	100	98	102	101	100	100	99	100	91	99	100	99	100	90	100	100	101
CHATTANOOGA	89	76	68	75	78	90	76	84	81	76	80	75	72	83	76	84	71	81	89	88
CHEYEN-SCTSBLF-STERL	83	77	80	78	78	82	79	81	81	78	80	72	77	81	79	82	71	80	84	82
CHICAGO	112	121	126	122	119	109	121	114	118	122	119	109	124	118	120	116	110	117	111	113
CHICO-REDDING	77	70	69	70	72	80	75	77	75	71	75	70	70	74	74	76	66	77	80	78
CINCINNATI	102	101	106	103	99	100	102	100	102	102	101	91	102	103	101	102	92	100	101	101
CLARKSBURG-WESTON	71	54	46	53	59	75	58	67	64	54	62	59	51	64	57	68	53	63	75	71
CLEVELAND	91	93	104	95	94	94	92	92	94	93	93	81	94	94	94	95	84	91	96	92
COLORADO SPR.-PUEBLO	97	96	98	98	93	93	97	94	96	96	95	87	96	96	96	95	86	96	94	95
COLUMBIA, SC	93	82	75	82	81	90	83	87	86	83	86	79	79	88	82	88	76	86	90	90
COLUMBIA-JEFF. CITY	85	73	69	74	74	83	79	80	80	75	80	73	73	81	76	82	70	80	84	83
COLUMBUS, GA	78	64	60	66	64	73	72	71	74	68	73	65	66	74	68	75	65	73	75	74
COLUMBUS, OH	97	92	94	95	91	94	96	93	96	95	96	85	94	97	93	96	86	95	95	95
COLUMBUS-TUPELO-W.PT	75	56	42	54	59	76	59	68	65	57	64	60	52	67	57	68	55	65	73	73
CORPUS CHRISTI	83	74	66	72	70	76	75	77	78	76	78	70	71	77	73	78	69	79	78	77
DALLAS-FT.WORTH	119	112	106	114	106	107	115	111	114	115	115	105	112	115	111	112	104	115	108	111
DAVENPORT-R.ISL-MOL.	85	79	84	80	82	89	80	84	84	79	82	73	79	85	81	86	73	82	90	85
DAYTON	89	88	90	97	89	91	88	88	90	88	89	78	89	91	89	92	80	88	93	89
DENVER	116	117	116	119	113	110	119	113	115	119	116	108	118	116	116	112	105	116	109	114
DES MOINES-AMES	95	86	86	87	87	94	89	91	91	87	90	82	86	93	88	92	80	90	96	93
DETROIT	108	114	124	116	112	108	111	108	111	114	111	97	115	111	113	111	101	109	109	108
DOTHAN	78	64	53	63	66	79	65	73	70	64	69	65	60	71	64	73	60	70	78	76
DULUTH-SUPERIOR	79	71	74	72	75	84	74	79	77	71	76	69	71	77	75	79	67	76	85	80
EL PASO	77	71	63	68	64	66	71	71	73	73	74	65	68	72	69	73	66	74	70	69
ELMIRA	82	72	71	71	76	87	73	80	78	72	77	70	70	79	74	81	68	77	87	83
ERIE	81	75	78	75	77	85	76	80	80	75	79	70	74	81	77	82	70	78	86	82
EUGENE	84	77	79	78	78	84	83	82	82	79	82	75	79	82	81	83	73	83	85	84
EUREKA	73	66	67	67	68	74	73	73	73	68	72	66	68	72	71	73	64	73	75	74
EVANSVILLE	86	75	72	75	78	88	76	82	81	75	80	73	73	83	76	84	70	80	88	85
FAIRBANKS	107	103	103	107	96	92	111	100	106	108	107	97	108	108	104	102	97	106	95	100
FARGO-VALLEY CITY	86	70	64	71	73	86	78	81	80	73	79	74	70	81	74	81	69	80	86	85
FLINT-SAGINAW-B.CITY	87	82	85	83	84	90	82	86	86	82	85	75	82	86	83	88	76	84	90	87
FRESNO-VISALIA	83	80	74	79	77	75	83	81	80	82	81	79	79	80	79	78	74	83	76	79
FT. MYERS-NAPLES	101	103	111	100	107	114	97	107	101	100	99	91	100	94	106	105	88	105	116	105
FT.SMITH-FAY-SPRNGDL	87	73	64	72	74	86	76	81	79	74	78	73	70	81	74	81	69	79	85	84
FT. WAYNE	94	87	88	89	88	94	87	90	90	87	89	80	86	93	87	92	80	89	94	93
GAINESVILLE	79	63	62	66	63	71	81	73	78	71	78	68	71	76	72	76	69	77	74	75
GLENDIVE	69	53	44	52	69	74	57	66	61	53	60	58	50	62	56	65	51	63	74	69
GRAND JCT.-MONTROSE	85	79	78	79	80	87	80	84	82	79	81	75	78	81	81	83	72	82	87	85
G.RAPIDS-K'ZOO-B.CRK	94	90	90	91	89	93	90	91	91	90	91	82	89	90	89	92	81	90	93	93
GREAT FALLS	72	59	58	60	63	74	65	69	68	61	67	61	59	69	63	70	58	68	76	72
GREEN BAY-APPLETON	94	89	90	90	90	96	89	92	90	90	90	82	87	93	89	92	80	90	95	94
GR'NSBORO-H.PT-W.SLM	96	84	79	85	85	95	86	90	89	85	89	81	82	91	85	91	79	89	94	94
UNITED STATES	100	100	100	100	100	100	100	100	100	100	100	100	100	100	100	100	100	100	100	100

POPULATION CHANGE
DMA AND U.S. TOTALS

DMA	DMA Code	POPULATION			2000-2007 ANNUAL RATE		RACE (%)					
							White		Black		Asian/Pacific	
		2000	2007	2012	% Rate	National Rank	2000	2007	2000	2007	2000	2007
GREENVL.-N.BERN-WAS.	545	699,994	745,340	774,116	0.9	92	65.9	64.1	28.6	28.5	0.9	1.2
GRNVL-SPR'BG-ASH-AND	567	1,949,003	2,104,315	2,214,341	1.1	70	82.3	80.9	14.2	14.5	0.8	1.1
GREENWOOD-GREENVILLE	647	238,978	232,667	228,422	-0.4	207	37.0	35.2	61.4	62.8	0.5	0.6
HARLIN-W'LCO-B'VL-MC	636	978,369	1,211,666	1,397,403	3.0	10	79.0	78.2	0.5	0.5	0.6	0.6
HARRISBG-LAN-LEB-YRK	566	1,771,722	1,907,260	2,009,117	1.0	79	91.2	89.6	4.6	5.1	1.2	1.7
HARRISONBURG, VA	569	225,377	243,328	257,360	1.1	70	91.7	89.5	4.9	5.8	0.9	1.2
HARTFORD & NEW HAVEN	533	2,522,998	2,638,560	2,716,716	0.6	130	82.5	79.7	8.8	9.4	2.2	3.1
HATTIESBURG-LAUREL	710	273,137	288,031	299,269	0.7	115	68.2	66.5	30.0	31.2	0.4	0.6
HELENA	766	60,101	64,458	67,740	1.0	79	95.3	94.7	0.2	0.2	0.5	0.7
HONOLULU	744	1,211,537	1,299,555	1,364,283	1.0	79	24.3	24.7	1.8	2.2	51.0	49.7
HOUSTON	618	5,020,575	5,941,314	6,597,125	2.3	20	63.4	60.5	16.8	16.5	4.7	5.4
HUNTSVILLE-DECATUR	691	894,365	949,612	991,033	0.8	103	82.8	80.7	12.8	13.6	0.8	1.1
IDAHO FLS.-POCATELLO	758	313,424	353,621	387,493	1.7	37	91.1	90.2	0.4	0.4	0.8	0.9
INDIANAPOLIS	527	2,582,135	2,763,418	2,909,189	0.9	92	86.5	85.3	9.8	10.1	1.1	1.6
JACKSON, MS	718	880,706	927,381	963,796	0.7	115	51.7	50.7	46.6	47.1	0.5	0.7
JACKSON, TN	639	236,104	246,692	253,261	0.6	130	78.2	76.2	19.9	21.4	0.4	0.5
JACKSONVILLE,BRUNSWK	561	1,476,478	1,750,264	1,978,057	2.4	17	73.7	70.2	21.2	23.5	1.9	2.5
JOHNSTOWN-ALTOONA	574	763,493	766,924	765,357	0.1	180	96.1	95.1	1.9	2.2	1.0	1.4
JONESBORO	734	216,934	229,896	239,650	0.8	103	94.3	93.3	3.2	3.7	0.3	0.4
JOPLIN-PITTSBURG	603	389,755	400,745	408,652	0.4	153	91.6	90.4	1.3	1.4	0.6	0.8
JUNEAU, AK	747	30,711	31,592	32,114	0.4	153	74.8	71.1	0.8	0.7	5.1	5.6
KANSAS CITY	616	2,200,456	2,372,965	2,502,179	1.0	79	83.1	81.6	10.8	11.0	1.6	2.2
KNOXVILLE	557	1,195,921	1,302,380	1,382,860	1.2	62	93.3	92.3	4.1	4.4	0.7	1.0
LA CROSSE-EAU CLAIRE	702	527,389	554,927	571,389	0.7	115	96.1	95.1	0.6	0.8	1.5	2.0
LAFAYETTE, IN	582	166,795	179,033	187,521	1.0	79	89.8	86.6	2.3	3.1	4.0	5.5
LAFAYETTE, LA	642	579,589	607,536	628,245	0.7	115	71.0	67.0	26.7	29.9	0.9	1.3
LAKE CHARLES, LA	643	251,994	260,279	267,707	0.4	153	75.6	69.5	21.8	27.3	0.6	1.0
LANSING	551	652,677	683,846	703,176	0.6	130	86.3	84.4	7.5	8.1	2.0	2.8
LAREDO	749	205,299	256,982	296,967	3.1	8	82.3	81.9	0.4	0.4	0.4	0.4
LAS VEGAS	839	1,412,415	1,940,577	2,365,505	4.5	2	72.1	69.8	8.9	9.1	5.6	5.5
LEXINGTON	541	1,155,252	1,233,727	1,289,587	0.9	92	92.1	91.1	5.3	5.6	0.8	1.2
LIMA	558	143,199	141,426	141,306	-0.2	203	87.7	86.3	9.3	10.1	0.5	0.7
LINCOLN-HAST'GS-KRNY	722	690,546	715,746	734,594	0.5	143	93.5	91.7	1.2	1.4	1.4	2.2
LITTLE ROCK-PINE BLF	693	1,326,007	1,412,828	1,475,962	0.9	92	77.8	76.4	18.9	19.5	0.7	0.9
LOS ANGELES	803	16,140,635	17,823,791	18,984,580	1.4	48	55.0	51.3	7.7	7.1	10.8	11.6
LOUISVILLE	529	1,556,798	1,656,015	1,730,040	0.9	92	86.1	85.1	10.8	11.0	1.0	1.3
LUBBOCK	651	408,555	424,255	432,103	0.5	143	73.6	70.0	6.4	6.5	0.9	1.1
MACON	503	595,835	642,840	672,881	1.1	70	58.8	54.9	38.5	41.6	0.9	1.1
MADISON	669	866,759	945,404	996,135	1.2	62	92.2	90.3	3.0	3.6	2.0	2.7
MANKATO	737	129,765	135,304	138,747	0.6	130	95.5	94.1	0.7	1.0	1.2	1.6
MARQUETTE	553	222,498	223,712	224,624	0.1	180	94.6	94.0	1.2	1.3	0.6	0.9
MEDFORD-KLAMATH FLS.	813	393,630	431,086	457,878	1.3	55	90.9	89.4	0.5	0.5	1.0	1.2
MEMPHIS	640	1,719,358	1,824,783	1,902,134	0.8	103	56.5	54.9	40.4	41.1	1.1	1.4
MERIDIAN	711	187,811	189,018	189,483	0.1	180	57.6	55.6	38.4	39.7	0.3	0.4
MIAMI-FT. LAUDERDALE	528	3,955,969	4,355,477	4,611,782	1.3	55	70.5	69.4	20.1	20.0	1.8	2.1
MILWAUKEE	617	2,205,472	2,290,179	2,348,561	0.5	143	81.3	78.9	12.1	13.2	1.8	2.3
MINNEAPOLIS-ST. PAUL	613	4,128,556	4,567,409	4,896,640	1.4	48	88.7	86.8	4.0	4.5	3.2	4.0
MINOT-BISMK.-DICK'SN	687	347,381	349,579	352,709	0.1	180	88.4	87.1	0.5	0.6	0.4	0.6
MISSOULA	762	249,791	277,983	302,072	1.5	44	92.6	91.9	0.2	0.2	0.7	0.9
MOBILE-PENSACOLA	686	1,259,025	1,376,606	1,471,401	1.2	62	73.1	70.8	22.2	23.4	1.5	2.0
MONROE-EL DORADO	628	486,046	484,476	483,258	0.0	189	63.9	60.4	34.3	37.4	0.5	0.6
MONTEREY-SALINAS	828	710,598	748,484	769,249	0.7	115	63.5	59.0	2.5	2.4	5.1	5.7
MONTGOMERY	698	620,070	631,654	641,127	0.3	162	55.3	54.3	42.8	43.2	0.6	0.7
MYRTLE BEACH-FLORENC	570	644,127	705,197	757,282	1.3	55	58.0	57.9	31.2	30.5	0.6	0.8
NASHVILLE	659	2,253,210	2,524,944	2,741,870	1.6	41	83.4	81.9	12.3	12.6	1.2	1.7
NEW ORLEANS	622	1,768,305	1,563,259	1,639,172	-1.7	210	62.1	63.7	33.0	30.4	1.8	2.2
NEW YORK	501	20,181,238	21,097,587	21,729,726	0.6	130	63.5	60.8	17.3	17.5	7.0	8.4
NORFOLK-P'MTH-N.NEWS	544	1,806,442	1,943,381	2,046,579	1.0	79	62.1	59.6	31.8	32.7	2.5	3.2
NORTH PLATTE	740	36,668	38,003	39,001	0.5	143	94.9	93.5	0.5	0.6	0.4	0.6
ODESSA-MIDLAND	633	373,208	382,442	386,659	0.3	162	76.6	73.5	4.7	4.7	0.7	0.8
OKLAHOMA CITY	650	1,620,574	1,732,679	1,816,800	0.9	92	78.5	76.0	8.1	8.3	2.0	2.7
OMAHA	652	988,275	1,062,511	1,120,800	1.0	79	88.2	86.2	6.1	6.5	1.2	1.8
ORLANDO-D.BEACH-MEL.	534	2,926,227	3,688,412	4,374,739	3.2	6	79.8	76.2	12.0	13.4	2.1	2.6
OTTUMWA-KIRKSVILLE	631	130,916	131,057	131,136	0.0	189	96.6	95.6	0.9	1.3	0.8	1.1
PADUC-CG-HARR-MTVERN	632	953,659	957,693	961,886	0.1	180	90.8	89.6	6.8	7.4	0.6	0.8
PALM SPRINGS	804	322,284	449,677	561,640	4.7	1	67.7	63.2	2.1	2.1	2.2	2.4
PANAMA CITY	656	319,537	369,965	409,370	2.0	28	82.2	79.1	13.3	15.2	1.1	1.4
PARKERSBURG, WV	597	158,751	157,243	156,005	-0.1	197	97.4	97.0	0.9	1.0	0.5	0.7
PEORIA-BLOOMINGTON	675	617,384	642,412	661,167	0.5	143	89.7	88.2	7.1	7.7	1.2	1.6
PHILADELPHIA	504	7,532,764	7,933,461	8,231,898	0.7	115	74.2	71.5	17.7	18.4	3.1	4.2
PHOENIX	753	3,913,906	4,956,240	5,879,745	3.3	5	76.9	74.2	3.2	3.3	2.0	2.3
PITTSBURGH	508	2,901,329	2,880,558	2,860,151	-0.1	197	90.8	89.3	6.9	7.8	1.0	1.5
PORTLAND, OR	820	2,743,072	3,044,555	3,274,430	1.4	48	85.4	83.0	2.0	2.1	3.8	4.6
PORTLAND-AUBURN	500	942,708	1,011,962	1,057,643	1.0	79	97.1	96.5	0.6	0.7	0.8	1.1
PRESQUE ISLE	552	73,938	73,496	73,449	-0.1	197	96.8	96.3	0.4	0.5	0.5	0.7
PROVIDENCE-N.BEDFORD	521	1,582,997	1,639,860	1,670,379	0.5	143	87.0	84.6	3.6	4.1	2.0	2.6
QUINCY-HAN'BL-KEOKUK	717	272,719	271,490	269,953	-0.1	197	95.1	94.1	2.9	3.4	0.5	0.7
UNITED STATES					1.2		75.1	72.7	12.3	12.6	3.8	4.5

POPULATION COMPOSITION
DMA AND U.S. TOTALS

B

DMA	% HISPANIC ORIGIN		2007 AGE DISTRIBUTION (%)										MEDIAN AGE	% 2007 Males	% 2007 Females
	2000	2007	0-4	5-9	10-14	15-19	20-24	25-44	45-64	65-84	85+	18+	2007		
GREENVL.-N.BERN-WAS.	4.8	6.4	6.9	6.1	5.9	7.1	9.9	27.2	24.3	11.0	1.5	77.7	34.6	50.7	49.3
GRNVL-SPR'BG-ASH-AND	2.5	3.4	6.2	6.2	6.1	6.5	6.0	27.1	27.2	12.7	2.0	77.8	39.5	48.8	51.2
GREENWOOD-GREENVILLE	1.2	1.7	7.8	7.2	7.4	7.5	8.4	26.5	23.3	9.9	1.9	73.1	33.1	48.6	51.4
HARLIN-W'LCO-B'VL-MC	87.4	90.2	10.6	9.3	8.9	8.2	7.6	27.7	18.2	8.4	1.1	66.2	28.5	48.6	51.4
HARRISBG-LAN-LEB-YRK	3.6	4.4	6.2	6.0	6.5	7.0	6.3	25.8	27.5	12.4	2.3	77.1	39.9	48.9	51.1
HARRISONBURG, VA	3.3	4.9	5.8	5.6	5.7	7.4	9.0	25.8	26.3	12.3	2.1	79.3	38.5	49.2	50.8
HARTFORD & NEW HAVEN	8.5	10.4	6.1	6.1	6.7	7.6	6.6	25.3	27.4	11.6	2.6	76.7	39.6	48.6	51.4
HATTIESBURG-LAUREL	1.2	1.6	7.5	6.8	6.8	6.7	8.4	27.4	24.0	10.8	1.7	75.3	34.6	48.2	51.8
HELENA	1.5	1.8	6.0	5.5	6.1	7.3	7.7	23.4	31.2	10.8	1.9	77.8	40.8	49.3	50.7
HONOLULU	7.2	8.1	6.5	6.0	6.6	6.6	7.3	27.5	26.3	11.2	1.9	76.9	37.4	50.1	49.9
HOUSTON	28.2	32.8	8.0	7.5	7.5	7.3	7.3	29.3	24.5	7.5	0.9	72.5	33.4	49.9	50.1
HUNTSVILLE-DECATUR	2.7	4.0	6.7	6.5	6.5	6.3	5.9	28.3	26.4	11.8	1.6	76.6	38.4	49.1	50.9
IDAHO FLS.-POCATELLO	7.6	8.5	8.4	7.3	7.1	9.2	9.8	25.3	23.1	8.5	1.3	72.5	30.4	50.0	50.0
INDIANAPOLIS	2.4	3.1	7.1	6.8	6.7	7.1	7.2	27.7	25.3	10.2	1.7	75.3	36.3	49.1	50.9
JACKSON, MS	1.2	1.6	7.5	7.1	7.0	7.0	7.2	27.5	24.9	10.1	1.7	74.4	35.2	48.1	51.9
JACKSON, TN	1.3	1.8	6.6	6.3	6.5	6.6	6.3	27.3	26.1	12.2	2.2	76.9	38.4	48.5	51.5
JACKSONVILLE,BRUNSWK	3.7	5.1	6.9	6.4	6.6	7.1	7.1	27.7	26.5	10.4	1.5	75.9	37.2	49.2	50.8
JOHNSTOWN-ALTOONA	0.8	1.0	5.3	5.1	5.4	7.1	8.8	25.4	26.8	13.6	2.6	80.7	39.9	50.0	50.0
JONESBORO	1.4	1.9	6.6	6.2	6.0	6.3	6.4	27.6	25.3	13.4	2.2	77.7	38.4	49.0	51.0
JOPLIN-PITTSBURG	2.9	3.7	7.1	6.4	6.4	7.0	7.5	25.4	25.5	12.3	2.5	76.2	37.6	49.0	51.0
JUNEAU, AK	3.4	4.3	6.1	5.5	6.8	7.6	7.6	26.2	32.1	7.1	0.9	76.6	38.4	49.7	50.3
KANSAS CITY	4.7	5.8	7.2	6.8	6.6	7.1	7.3	27.9	25.4	9.9	1.8	75.3	36.3	49.0	51.0
KNOXVILLE	1.3	1.9	6.0	5.9	5.9	6.2	6.1	27.5	27.7	12.9	1.8	78.6	39.9	49.0	51.0
LA CROSSE-EAU CLAIRE	1.0	1.3	6.3	5.8	6.0	7.7	9.6	24.5	26.1	11.3	2.5	77.7	37.5	49.5	50.5
LAFAYETTE, IN	4.9	6.4	6.0	5.5	5.6	10.0	15.1	27.2	20.8	8.3	1.5	79.7	29.4	51.5	48.5
LAFAYETTE, LA	1.3	1.5	7.9	7.3	6.8	6.9	7.5	27.3	24.6	10.1	1.5	73.8	34.9	48.6	51.4
LAKE CHARLES, LA	1.7	1.9	7.3	6.7	6.8	6.7	7.4	27.7	25.2	10.7	1.5	75.2	35.9	49.8	50.2
LANSING	3.9	4.7	6.4	6.0	6.4	7.9	9.1	26.4	26.4	9.7	1.7	77.2	36.0	49.4	50.6
LAREDO	93.7	95.1	11.2	10.0	9.6	8.1	7.4	29.4	17.2	6.4	0.8	64.3	27.4	48.5	51.5
LAS VEGAS	21.6	25.6	7.4	6.7	6.9	6.4	6.1	29.7	24.7	11.0	1.1	75.1	36.4	50.4	49.6
LEXINGTON	1.5	2.2	6.4	6.2	6.2	6.5	6.9	29.6	26.0	10.5	1.6	77.6	36.9	49.3	50.7
LIMA	2.1	2.6	7.0	6.6	6.7	7.2	7.1	25.3	26.3	11.7	2.2	75.6	37.6	49.8	50.2
LINCOLN-HAST'GS-KRNY	4.3	5.7	6.6	6.1	6.1	7.4	8.2	25.9	25.5	11.5	2.7	77.2	37.0	49.7	50.3
LITTLE ROCK-PINE BLF	2.1	2.8	6.7	6.3	6.2	6.7	6.8	27.1	26.2	12.1	2.0	77.0	38.0	48.9	51.1
LOS ANGELES	40.0	45.2	7.9	7.2	8.4	7.9	7.1	29.5	22.4	8.3	1.4	71.9	33.0	49.7	50.3
LOUISVILLE	1.7	2.4	6.8	6.6	6.6	6.4	6.2	27.8	27.0	11.0	1.7	76.3	38.2	49.0	51.0
LUBBOCK	33.8	39.5	7.7	6.8	6.4	7.9	9.8	27.2	22.2	10.2	1.8	74.9	32.3	49.8	50.2
MACON	1.8	2.4	6.9	6.4	6.7	7.3	7.3	27.8	25.5	10.4	1.6	75.8	36.4	49.3	50.7
MADISON	2.7	3.6	6.2	5.8	6.1	7.5	9.2	27.1	26.3	9.9	1.9	77.9	36.9	49.7	50.3
MANKATO	3.0	4.0	6.1	5.4	5.5	8.2	11.0	24.6	25.1	11.3	2.8	79.3	35.7	49.7	50.3
MARQUETTE	0.7	0.9	5.3	4.9	5.4	7.3	8.7	23.2	28.9	13.5	2.8	80.6	41.4	50.8	49.2
MEDFORD-KLAMATH FLS.	6.3	8.4	5.8	5.3	6.0	6.9	6.5	22.0	30.9	14.1	2.5	78.7	43.0	49.1	50.9
MEMPHIS	2.2	2.8	7.4	7.0	7.3	7.2	7.0	27.9	25.0	9.7	1.5	74.0	35.2	48.5	51.5
MERIDIAN	1.0	1.3	7.3	6.9	6.8	6.8	6.8	26.1	25.0	11.9	2.3	75.1	36.7	47.9	52.1
MIAMI-FT. LAUDERDALE	39.8	46.1	6.5	6.2	6.7	6.8	6.4	28.3	24.7	11.8	2.6	76.5	38.1	48.5	51.5
MILWAUKEE	6.1	7.5	6.8	6.4	6.8	7.3	7.3	26.6	26.1	10.6	2.1	75.6	37.4	49.0	51.0
MINNEAPOLIS-ST. PAUL	3.0	3.8	7.0	6.7	6.8	7.2	7.2	28.4	25.5	9.4	1.9	75.2	36.4	49.6	50.4
MINOT-BISMK.-DICK'SN	1.0	1.3	6.6	5.8	6.4	7.3	8.5	23.3	27.0	12.4	2.8	76.9	39.2	49.6	50.4
MISSOULA	1.7	2.0	5.8	5.4	5.9	7.2	8.6	24.1	29.9	11.1	1.9	78.6	39.7	49.7	50.3
MOBILE-PENSACOLA	2.1	3.0	6.8	6.3	6.4	6.9	7.1	27.0	26.0	11.9	1.6	76.5	37.6	49.2	50.8
MONROE-EL DORADO	1.3	1.5	7.2	6.7	6.6	7.1	7.9	26.3	24.5	11.7	2.0	75.7	35.8	48.6	51.4
MONTEREY-SALINAS	39.7	45.7	7.4	6.7	7.5	7.8	7.9	29.3	23.9	7.9	1.5	74.4	33.2	51.1	48.9
MONTGOMERY	1.0	1.4	6.9	6.5	6.7	7.2	7.4	26.7	25.4	11.3	1.9	75.9	36.6	48.1	51.9
MYRTLE BEACH-FLORENC	2.3	3.0	6.7	6.3	6.5	6.5	6.3	28.1	26.2	11.9	1.5	76.7	37.6	48.5	51.5
NASHVILLE	3.0	4.1	7.0	6.7	6.4	6.6	6.8	29.4	25.5	10.1	1.5	76.2	36.5	49.5	50.5
NEW ORLEANS	3.7	4.3	7.1	6.6	6.8	6.9	7.2	27.4	26.3	10.3	1.4	75.4	36.5	48.4	51.6
NEW YORK	18.6	20.6	6.7	6.7	7.3	7.0	6.0	28.8	25.0	10.7	2.0	75.1	37.1	48.3	51.7
NORFOLK-P'MTH-N.NEWS	3.0	4.0	6.8	6.3	6.7	7.6	7.8	28.0	25.0	10.2	1.5	75.9	36.0	49.3	50.7
NORTH PLATTE	5.2	7.0	6.8	6.0	6.5	6.5	7.9	23.3	28.3	12.3	2.4	76.8	39.4	49.5	50.5
ODESSA-MIDLAND	40.4	46.5	7.7	6.7	7.0	7.9	9.2	25.0	24.3	10.6	1.5	73.8	33.9	50.1	49.9
OKLAHOMA CITY	5.9	7.3	7.0	6.3	6.1	6.9	8.5	27.1	25.4	10.8	1.9	76.8	35.9	49.4	50.6
OMAHA	5.1	6.7	7.3	6.9	6.9	7.0	6.9	27.6	25.3	10.2	2.0	74.7	36.3	49.3	50.7
ORLANDO-D.BEACH-MEL.	11.8	16.1	5.9	5.5	6.0	6.5	6.5	25.8	26.4	15.2	2.2	78.7	40.8	49.0	51.0
OTTUMWA-KIRKSVILLE	1.8	2.2	6.2	5.8	5.7	7.2	8.4	23.6	27.1	13.2	3.0	78.7	39.8	49.1	50.9
PADUC-CG-HARR-MTVERN	1.3	1.7	6.1	5.7	5.8	6.4	7.3	26.1	26.6	13.4	2.5	78.8	39.7	49.3	50.7
PALM SPRINGS	46.1	52.5	7.7	6.4	7.1	6.7	6.5	23.1	22.9	17.1	2.5	74.6	38.7	50.0	50.0
PANAMA CITY	2.5	3.6	5.9	5.4	5.7	5.8	6.1	27.6	28.0	13.7	1.7	79.5	40.8	51.2	48.8
PARKERSBURG, WV	0.5	0.6	5.8	5.6	6.0	6.1	6.0	25.3	28.9	14.0	2.3	79.0	41.7	48.6	51.4
PEORIA-BLOOMINGTON	1.8	2.4	6.5	6.1	6.4	7.3	8.2	26.0	25.7	11.4	2.3	77.2	37.1	48.8	51.2
PHILADELPHIA	6.3	7.6	6.3	6.3	7.0	7.4	6.5	26.4	26.2	11.6	2.3	76.1	38.4	48.3	51.7
PHOENIX	23.0	27.3	7.8	7.2	7.0	6.7	6.7	28.2	23.0	11.7	1.7	74.0	35.2	50.1	49.9
PITTSBURGH	0.7	0.9	5.4	5.4	5.9	6.7	6.6	24.5	28.4	14.3	2.9	79.6	41.9	48.2	51.8
PORTLAND, OR	8.2	10.7	6.6	6.5	6.7	6.8	6.9	27.0	27.0	9.5	1.8	75.8	36.7	49.7	50.3
PORTLAND-AUBURN	0.8	1.1	5.5	5.3	6.0	7.1	6.6	24.8	30.1	12.2	2.3	78.9	41.6	48.8	51.2
PRESQUE ISLE	0.6	0.8	5.0	4.9	5.4	6.8	6.7	23.2	30.5	15.0	2.5	80.7	43.6	48.9	51.1
PROVIDENCE-N.BEDFORD	7.0	9.0	6.1	5.9	6.6	7.7	7.0	26.6	26.1	11.5	2.6	77.2	38.5	48.3	51.7
QUINCY-HAN'BL-KEOKUK	1.1	1.5	6.1	5.6	5.9	7.0	8.2	24.3	26.3	13.4	3.1	78.5	39.8	49.4	50.6
UNITED STATES	12.5	15.0	6.9	6.5	6.8	7.1	7.0	27.6	25.4	10.7	1.9	75.6	36.7	49.2	50.8

DMA	HOUSEHOLDS					FAMILIES			MEDIAN HOUSEHOLD INCOME		
	2000	2007	2012	% Annual Rate 2000-2007	2007 Average HH Size	2000	2007	% Annual Rate 2000-2007	2007	2012	2007 National Rank
GREENVL.-N.BERN-WAS.	263,682	286,969	301,684	1.2	2.44	184,102	194,973	0.8	40,959	47,163	152
GRNVL-SPR'BG-ASH-AND	776,056	854,420	906,601	1.3	2.39	540,005	575,406	0.9	44,899	51,671	109
GREENWOOD-GREENVILLE	81,886	81,846	81,140	0.0	2.69	58,697	57,332	-0.3	28,190	30,780	210
HARLIN-W'LCO-B'VL-MC	274,085	344,640	399,606	3.2	3.48	230,052	287,773	3.1	30,319	34,811	209
HARRISBG-LAN-LEB-YRK	680,992	742,822	787,542	1.2	2.49	477,464	507,022	0.8	54,597	63,278	39
HARRISONBURG, VA	84,664	93,225	99,262	1.3	2.47	57,798	61,778	0.9	46,166	52,346	98
HARTFORD & NEW HAVEN	977,438	1,025,046	1,060,255	0.7	2.48	652,771	679,596	0.6	64,478	76,838	7
HATTIESBURG-LAUREL	101,301	109,244	114,490	1.0	2.55	71,890	75,796	0.7	32,374	35,424	204
HELENA	24,602	26,737	28,283	1.2	2.36	16,228	17,106	0.7	44,089	49,998	122
HONOLULU	403,240	441,517	467,348	1.3	2.86	287,068	310,276	1.1	59,776	67,554	20
HOUSTON	1,764,138	2,070,185	2,291,959	2.2	2.82	1,257,793	1,466,345	2.1	56,424	67,134	26
HUNTSVILLE-DECATUR	354,369	382,081	401,575	1.0	2.44	252,250	266,763	0.8	42,721	47,623	138
IDAHO FLS.-POCATELLO	107,537	124,023	136,452	2.0	2.80	78,215	89,032	1.8	48,775	58,234	78
INDIANAPOLIS	1,009,977	1,097,642	1,160,062	1.2	2.45	679,254	714,809	0.7	54,654	64,828	38
JACKSON, MS	320,864	345,167	361,944	1.0	2.59	228,531	240,558	0.7	37,329	41,391	186
JACKSON, TN	93,241	98,793	102,053	0.8	2.42	65,715	67,824	0.4	41,421	48,093	144
JACKSONVILLE,BRUNSWK	563,379	676,143	768,276	2.5	2.53	390,652	460,783	2.3	50,368	59,584	66
JOHNSTOWN-ALTOONA	296,870	303,299	305,358	0.3	2.38	199,505	197,485	-0.1	40,871	47,651	154
JONESBORO	86,908	92,877	97,187	0.9	2.42	60,886	63,166	0.5	36,016	41,971	194
JOPLIN-PITTSBURG	153,603	158,244	161,417	0.4	2.46	104,941	105,810	0.1	37,649	43,229	184
JUNEAU, AK	11,543	12,013	12,263	0.6	2.58	7,638	7,790	0.3	76,442	86,715	2
KANSAS CITY	859,420	933,777	987,532	1.2	2.48	573,122	609,588	0.9	55,479	65,437	35
KNOXVILLE	484,301	536,663	574,631	1.4	2.37	336,799	363,380	1.1	40,805	47,597	156
LA CROSSE-EAU CLAIRE	202,284	218,512	227,305	1.1	2.43	133,517	140,539	0.7	46,316	52,800	95
LAFAYETTE, IN	62,003	69,078	73,208	1.5	2.38	37,375	39,589	0.8	49,558	57,439	71
LAFAYETTE, LA	212,435	226,964	236,786	0.9	2.62	151,997	158,304	0.6	33,550	36,638	203
LAKE CHARLES, LA	92,411	98,295	102,245	0.9	2.55	66,744	69,267	0.5	37,991	41,491	180
LANSING	247,916	263,380	272,902	0.8	2.48	163,378	169,071	0.5	53,056	61,077	49
LAREDO	54,661	69,108	80,242	3.3	3.67	46,600	58,617	3.2	33,794	38,867	202
LAS VEGAS	527,102	724,239	881,156	4.5	2.65	349,772	474,969	4.3	56,052	65,725	30
LEXINGTON	454,836	500,245	528,538	1.3	2.38	312,869	331,821	0.8	39,377	46,372	173
LIMA	52,846	53,869	54,321	0.3	2.53	37,516	37,179	-0.1	47,745	54,172	84
LINCOLN-HAST'GS-KRNY	272,627	285,570	294,329	0.6	2.41	178,925	184,485	0.4	45,417	52,272	102
LITTLE ROCK-PINE BLF	521,156	561,650	590,407	1.0	2.44	363,288	380,804	0.7	42,862	50,537	135
LOS ANGELES	5,262,826	5,680,293	6,012,991	1.1	3.08	3,710,377	4,031,179	1.2	58,797	68,734	22
LOUISVILLE	613,261	665,451	700,337	1.1	2.44	422,452	443,454	0.7	49,656	58,265	69
LUBBOCK	149,146	155,083	158,698	0.5	2.61	103,130	105,748	0.3	38,548	44,748	176
MACON	218,206	237,721	250,869	1.2	2.55	154,464	163,520	0.8	43,629	50,825	126
MADISON	343,636	384,797	409,475	1.6	2.38	218,185	237,331	1.2	56,456	65,367	25
MANKATO	50,620	53,929	55,830	0.9	2.39	32,582	33,522	0.4	48,945	57,556	74
MARQUETTE	89,861	93,007	94,435	0.5	2.28	58,079	58,273	0.0	39,719	44,218	170
MEDFORD-KLAMATH FLS.	158,920	174,691	186,185	1.3	2.43	107,643	117,436	1.2	41,346	47,779	147
MEMPHIS	639,984	690,579	724,586	1.1	2.57	447,225	471,518	0.7	44,693	52,050	112
MERIDIAN	71,863	74,169	75,087	0.4	2.47	50,368	50,852	0.1	31,325	33,983	207
MIAMI-FT. LAUDERDALE	1,466,305	1,597,300	1,684,140	1.2	2.68	980,283	1,048,702	0.9	49,135	58,351	73
MILWAUKEE	852,222	905,662	936,213	0.8	2.46	565,045	588,256	0.6	58,775	68,571	23
MINNEAPOLIS-ST. PAUL	1,579,158	1,773,772	1,909,052	1.6	2.51	1,048,518	1,152,305	1.3	63,903	76,750	10
MINOT-BISMK.-DICK'SN	136,919	141,607	144,448	0.5	2.40	92,863	92,484	-0.1	41,364	48,886	146
MISSOULA	99,565	110,884	121,005	1.5	2.45	65,719	71,074	1.1	38,921	43,903	175
MOBILE-PENSACOLA	477,529	531,629	573,132	1.5	2.50	337,684	369,878	1.3	43,578	49,496	127
MONROE-EL DORADO	180,470	183,825	184,979	0.3	2.51	127,228	126,165	-0.1	31,662	34,832	206
MONTEREY-SALINAS	228,260	240,627	246,722	0.7	2.97	157,956	167,310	0.8	64,473	76,098	8
MONTGOMERY	236,574	246,997	253,208	0.6	2.45	163,766	168,188	0.4	36,627	40,684	192
MYRTLE BEACH-FLORENC	246,794	277,777	303,303	1.6	2.48	173,359	188,034	1.1	40,545	47,056	160
NASHVILLE	872,774	992,751	1,082,899	1.8	2.48	606,112	674,380	1.5	49,599	58,728	70
NEW ORLEANS	661,633	583,193	614,300	-1.7	2.63	455,669	400,688	-1.8	40,204	43,736	165
NEW YORK	7,349,339	7,636,001	7,862,598	0.5	2.70	4,965,515	5,128,899	0.4	65,703	78,855	6
NORFOLK-P'MTH-N.NEWS	670,590	733,982	779,101	1.3	2.55	468,829	499,557	0.9	51,680	60,016	59
NORTH PLATTE	14,919	15,798	16,352	0.8	2.36	10,048	10,509	0.6	44,111	50,500	120
ODESSA-MIDLAND	133,631	137,614	139,878	0.4	2.67	97,113	98,949	0.3	40,398	47,009	163
OKLAHOMA CITY	633,460	684,953	722,133	1.1	2.44	426,475	452,156	0.8	43,083	50,404	132
OMAHA	382,029	414,669	439,156	1.1	2.50	257,445	276,338	1.0	53,230	62,992	46
ORLANDO-D.BEACH-MEL.	1,156,994	1,464,933	1,745,209	3.3	2.47	782,951	976,816	3.1	48,881	56,808	76
OTTUMWA-KIRKSVILLE	52,771	53,443	53,644	0.2	2.35	34,226	33,807	-0.2	36,783	42,010	191
PADUC-CG-HARR-MTVERN	382,580	391,260	395,512	0.3	2.34	258,250	255,936	-0.1	36,586	41,728	193
PALM SPRINGS	118,410	161,346	198,695	4.4	2.76	78,008	107,587	4.5	47,458	54,752	86
PANAMA CITY	123,334	146,818	164,791	2.4	2.37	84,695	98,923	2.2	39,422	45,067	172
PARKERSBURG, WV	64,299	65,342	65,452	0.2	2.35	44,716	44,054	-0.2	41,056	47,302	151
PEORIA-BLOOMINGTON	238,408	251,227	260,101	0.7	2.44	160,264	163,781	0.3	53,066	61,423	48
PHILADELPHIA	2,827,544	2,989,033	3,112,519	0.8	2.57	1,914,026	1,984,672	0.5	61,298	73,053	17
PHOENIX	1,443,692	1,819,667	2,158,224	3.2	2.68	981,284	1,221,435	3.1	55,753	67,764	34
PITTSBURGH	1,179,044	1,187,322	1,186,781	0.1	2.34	774,157	756,130	-0.3	46,212	54,444	96
PORTLAND, OR	1,054,750	1,163,925	1,250,210	1.4	2.57	699,206	765,698	1.3	56,167	66,278	29
PORTLAND-AUBURN	383,578	419,421	442,801	1.2	2.35	251,342	269,371	1.0	48,756	56,072	79
PRESQUE ISLE	30,356	31,270	31,707	0.4	2.28	20,436	20,642	0.1	34,124	38,411	200
PROVIDENCE-N.BEDFORD	613,835	635,001	649,452	0.5	2.49	406,008	412,579	0.2	53,979	63,408	42
QUINCY-HAN'BL-KEOKUK	106,547	107,215	107,071	0.1	2.39	71,473	69,903	-0.3	40,480	45,890	162
UNITED STATES				1.2	2.59			1.0	53,154	62,503	

DMA	2007 Per Capita Income	2007 HH Income Base	2007 HOUSEHOLD INCOME DISTRIBUTION (%)					2007 Home Value Base	2007 HOME VALUE DISTRIBUTION (%)					2007 Median Home Value
			Less than $25,000	$25,000 to $49,999	$50,000 to $99,999	$100,000 to $149,999	$150,000 or More		Less than $50,000	$50,000 to $89,999	$90,000 to $174,999	$175,000 to $399,999	$400,000 or More	
GREENVL.-N.BERN-WAS.	21,221	286,969	30.5	28.9	30.0	7.2	3.4	195,568	16.3	17.8	37.9	23.7	4.3	117,591
GRNVL-SPR'BG-ASH-AND	23,969	854,417	26.5	28.9	31.6	8.5	4.4	640,236	14.2	17.9	38.0	24.7	5.2	122,025
GREENWOOD-GREENVILLE	15,000	81,846	45.2	28.3	20.1	4.1	2.4	52,104	28.3	34.2	27.5	8.7	1.3	73,585
HARLIN-W'LCO-B'VL-MC	12,416	344,640	42.2	28.8	21.1	5.4	2.5	250,075	37.0	31.6	23.9	6.5	1.1	64,277
HARRISBG-LAN-LEB-YRK	26,723	742,822	18.0	27.1	37.4	12.0	5.5	543,835	4.5	5.0	35.6	48.9	6.0	185,295
HARRISONBURG, VA	23,160	93,225	24.3	29.8	33.7	8.5	3.8	65,837	5.5	4.1	25.9	56.3	8.3	201,997
HARTFORD & NEW HAVEN	33,532	1,025,340	17.3	21.2	33.1	16.8	11.6	708,535	1.0	1.5	13.2	63.1	21.2	270,688
HATTIESBURG-LAUREL	17,570	109,243	38.7	31.1	22.5	5.0	2.7	81,435	27.6	27.9	30.4	12.0	2.1	81,387
HELENA	23,061	26,737	24.7	31.9	32.5	8.2	2.7	18,929	8.9	5.3	25.3	51.8	8.7	195,628
HONOLULU	27,254	441,507	18.6	23.0	33.0	16.3	9.1	260,706	0.7	0.9	2.8	22.9	72.8	603,121
HOUSTON	27,737	2,070,167	19.8	24.3	31.5	14.1	10.2	1,321,546	12.3	20.2	38.7	23.2	5.6	118,712
HUNTSVILLE-DECATUR	23,089	382,081	29.2	28.2	28.8	9.9	4.0	288,279	14.2	21.0	40.0	21.2	3.6	113,580
IDAHO FLS.-POCATELLO	22,541	124,019	22.9	28.4	33.7	10.0	5.0	91,842	7.5	9.8	49.4	25.7	7.5	143,728
INDIANAPOLIS	28,391	1,097,610	19.9	25.5	35.0	12.7	6.9	777,464	9.4	18.7	44.3	23.8	3.8	124,174
JACKSON, MS	19,961	345,167	34.5	28.4	25.9	7.3	3.9	250,268	22.8	27.1	33.0	14.4	2.6	90,095
JACKSON, TN	22,068	98,793	30.3	29.4	29.2	7.6	3.5	72,633	18.3	26.5	39.6	13.7	1.9	96,800
JACKSONVILLE,BRUNSWK	26,207	676,142	22.3	27.3	33.2	10.9	6.3	483,959	5.8	9.0	30.3	42.7	12.2	188,795
JOHNSTOWN-ALTOONA	21,394	303,292	29.4	30.9	29.8	7.0	2.9	224,613	12.6	18.1	42.9	23.5	2.9	127,427
JONESBORO	19,714	92,877	34.8	31.2	25.5	5.4	3.1	67,381	24.3	31.9	32.0	10.3	1.5	82,074
JOPLIN-PITTSBURG	19,467	158,244	31.7	32.8	27.8	5.3	2.4	115,487	26.1	28.9	33.0	10.5	1.5	81,763
JUNEAU, AK	35,044	12,013	11.1	18.6	35.0	23.2	12.1	8,131	5.3	6.8	11.5	50.8	25.7	292,428
KANSAS CITY	28,729	933,761	18.9	25.8	34.9	12.6	7.7	650,318	9.5	14.2	39.6	31.5	5.2	143,138
KNOXVILLE	22,979	536,660	31.1	28.6	28.3	7.7	4.3	396,984	15.3	17.5	40.0	22.7	4.5	119,606
LA CROSSE-EAU CLAIRE	23,298	218,512	23.8	30.1	34.2	8.3	3.6	160,032	9.0	14.6	47.2	26.3	2.9	133,153
LAFAYETTE, IN	25,527	69,072	24.2	26.2	33.1	11.0	5.5	41,198	7.9	17.4	52.5	19.7	2.5	120,610
LAFAYETTE, LA	17,806	226,959	39.1	27.6	24.2	6.3	2.9	160,127	22.3	22.6	35.7	17.0	2.4	98,777
LAKE CHARLES, LA	19,897	98,294	33.4	28.7	27.2	7.5	3.2	71,538	22.4	25.2	36.0	14.6	1.8	93,916
LANSING	26,321	263,378	20.8	26.1	35.4	12.2	5.5	188,098	7.6	12.0	44.2	32.6	3.5	143,759
LAREDO	13,240	69,108	37.3	29.6	23.2	6.6	3.3	47,361	18.5	28.2	39.2	12.5	1.7	95,163
LAS VEGAS	27,422	724,233	18.0	25.7	36.0	12.6	7.7	444,523	2.9	1.9	7.1	64.7	23.4	299,325
LEXINGTON	22,785	500,245	32.5	27.9	26.7	8.3	4.5	347,203	21.3	18.8	37.8	19.1	3.1	106,722
LIMA	22,924	53,869	23.6	28.6	34.1	9.9	3.7	41,660	12.5	23.2	44.9	17.9	1.5	111,214
LINCOLN-HAST'GS-KRNY	23,435	285,568	24.1	30.9	32.9	8.1	3.9	200,489	17.6	20.2	42.2	17.7	2.3	108,242
LITTLE ROCK-PINE BLF	22,828	561,649	29.0	28.6	30.2	7.7	4.5	402,295	20.4	25.1	35.6	16.0	3.0	98,045
LOS ANGELES	26,693	5,680,164	20.4	22.5	31.6	14.4	11.1	3,199,000	1.9	1.6	3.4	23.9	69.3	539,443
LOUISVILLE	26,492	665,447	22.9	27.5	32.8	11.0	5.9	477,981	9.8	16.1	45.4	24.7	4.1	126,199
LUBBOCK	20,264	155,076	32.2	29.8	26.7	7.2	4.1	101,705	30.8	28.7	29.9	9.4	1.2	76,310
MACON	22,073	237,721	29.3	26.3	30.8	9.2	4.5	167,377	19.6	24.9	38.8	14.7	2.0	98,107
MADISON	28,886	384,797	17.7	25.7	37.6	12.8	6.2	258,207	4.4	7.1	33.6	48.1	6.8	186,206
MANKATO	24,924	53,929	21.4	29.7	36.3	8.4	4.2	40,088	9.5	13.7	39.9	32.4	4.5	151,554
MARQUETTE	21,527	93,007	30.7	30.6	29.7	6.6	2.3	71,386	17.3	26.4	39.9	14.6	1.8	98,321
MEDFORD-KLAMATH FLS.	22,778	174,691	29.1	30.4	29.0	7.2	4.2	122,694	6.5	5.2	19.7	50.0	18.6	234,797
MEMPHIS	23,346	690,578	28.6	26.5	30.2	9.2	5.5	467,304	14.2	26.9	36.1	19.4	3.4	103,331
MERIDIAN	17,274	74,169	41.3	28.7	23.1	4.8	2.1	56,143	29.5	30.1	29.3	9.3	1.8	76,554
MIAMI-FT. LAUDERDALE	26,065	1,597,278	25.4	25.4	30.0	11.0	8.3	1,049,649	2.0	3.1	11.6	50.5	32.7	303,800
MILWAUKEE	29,488	905,653	17.9	24.1	36.4	14.2	7.4	600,308	2.6	6.4	31.5	50.6	8.9	196,338
MINNEAPOLIS-ST. PAUL	32,199	1,773,771	15.0	22.6	36.9	15.4	10.1	1,347,313	4.0	5.1	24.3	54.0	12.6	218,932
MINOT-BISMK.-DICK'SN	21,752	141,607	28.8	30.3	30.5	7.3	3.2	102,228	25.1	20.4	38.5	14.3	1.6	97,395
MISSOULA	20,845	110,883	30.9	31.9	27.7	6.3	3.2	77,022	8.6	5.4	19.2	50.3	16.6	225,883
MOBILE-PENSACOLA	22,644	531,629	27.6	29.1	30.3	8.8	4.2	393,112	11.2	15.0	35.5	31.4	6.9	143,847
MONROE-EL DORADO	17,517	183,822	40.7	28.5	22.7	5.6	2.5	128,527	29.5	25.9	31.2	11.7	1.7	80,900
MONTEREY-SALINAS	29,215	240,624	16.0	22.1	33.2	16.0	12.8	141,995	1.4	1.3	2.7	13.4	81.2	728,063
MONTGOMERY	20,359	246,997	35.6	28.0	25.5	7.6	3.4	180,708	20.8	23.6	35.5	16.7	3.4	99,389
MYRTLE BEACH-FLORENC	21,319	277,777	30.4	29.6	29.2	7.2	3.7	206,547	19.3	20.3	33.1	22.7	4.6	110,133
NASHVILLE	25,868	992,748	23.5	26.9	33.6	10.2	5.8	699,193	8.7	12.8	41.1	30.3	7.0	144,039
NEW ORLEANS	21,031	583,171	31.4	28.2	27.6	8.6	4.2	396,917	11.5	15.7	37.6	28.8	6.4	136,690
NEW YORK	35,264	7,635,820	19.7	19.1	29.9	15.4	15.9	4,212,426	1.1	1.0	4.4	39.7	53.8	423,076
NORFOLK-P'MTH-N.NEWS	25,542	733,978	21.0	27.1	34.7	11.6	5.6	479,510	4.4	3.8	20.6	58.3	12.9	225,745
NORTH PLATTE	22,976	15,798	26.7	29.9	32.2	8.3	3.0	11,412	18.1	24.6	41.1	14.2	1.9	100,090
ODESSA-MIDLAND	20,696	137,614	30.0	29.9	27.8	7.8	4.5	98,859	32.8	27.1	26.9	11.3	1.9	74,306
OKLAHOMA CITY	23,213	684,945	27.6	29.6	29.7	8.8	4.4	459,324	18.9	25.7	37.9	15.2	2.2	98,971
OMAHA	26,670	414,669	19.3	27.3	35.7	11.8	5.9	293,483	10.2	17.8	45.1	23.2	3.6	124,341
ORLANDO-D.BEACH-MEL.	26,198	1,464,933	21.7	29.4	32.5	10.5	5.9	1,080,342	3.8	4.5	20.8	55.2	15.6	227,973
OTTUMWA-KIRKSVILLE	20,186	53,438	33.0	32.7	26.3	5.4	2.7	39,532	27.1	26.3	32.3	12.2	2.1	83,495
PADUC-CG-HARR-MTVERN	20,411	391,260	34.6	29.8	26.7	6.2	2.7	288,111	22.4	24.7	36.1	14.8	2.0	94,521
PALM SPRINGS	25,248	161,346	24.6	27.8	29.5	9.9	8.2	106,765	5.1	2.9	8.3	42.1	41.7	351,971
PANAMA CITY	21,638	146,818	31.0	30.5	28.1	7.1	3.3	112,703	7.9	12.2	30.4	38.9	10.6	173,758
PARKERSBURG, WV	22,735	65,342	28.6	30.8	29.1	8.1	3.4	50,395	16.3	26.3	43.1	13.0	1.2	99,478
PEORIA-BLOOMINGTON	26,601	251,227	21.0	25.8	35.7	11.8	5.7	185,207	9.1	16.6	47.9	24.1	2.3	127,229
PHILADELPHIA	31,242	2,989,012	18.9	21.9	33.3	15.2	10.7	2,132,812	3.1	4.9	19.6	54.0	18.3	245,279
PHOENIX	27,916	1,819,637	18.7	25.7	33.7	13.2	8.7	1,268,938	4.6	4.0	17.2	51.4	22.9	256,682
PITTSBURGH	26,282	1,187,322	26.4	27.0	30.8	10.1	5.7	859,298	11.3	17.7	43.1	24.2	3.7	127,426
PORTLAND, OR	28,119	1,163,925	18.1	25.6	35.9	12.6	7.7	773,696	3.4	2.6	12.0	58.4	23.5	280,002
PORTLAND-AUBURN	26,177	419,420	23.0	28.2	34.2	9.6	5.0	300,459	4.1	5.4	28.3	49.9	12.2	201,947
PRESQUE ISLE	18,808	31,270	36.7	31.8	25.6	4.3	1.6	22,964	11.4	22.0	49.2	16.4	1.0	114,701
PROVIDLNCL-N.BEDFORD	27,587	635,001	23.9	22.6	32.8	13.2	7.6	390,353	0.6	0.7	4.8	68.1	25.7	314,422
QUINCY-HAN'BL-KEOKUK	20,875	107,215	29.4	31.2	30.9	5.9	2.6	81,042	19.2	23.8	39.0	15.8	2.2	100,803
UNITED STATES	27,916		21.9	25.0	32.3	12.3	8.4		7.9	10.5	27.1	35.6	19.0	192,285

DMA	FINANCIAL SERVICES				THE HOME						ENTERTAINMENT						PERSONAL			
					Home Improvements		Furnishings													
	Auto Loan	Home Loan	Invest-ments	Retire-ment Plans	Home Repair	Lawn & Garden	Comput-ers & Hard-ware	Major Appli-ances	TV, Radio, Sound Equip-ment	Furni-ture	Dine out/ Carry out	Sports Equip-ment	Fees & Tickets	Toys & Games	Travel	Cable TV	Apparel & Services	Auto Repairs	Health Insur-ance	Pets & Supplies
GREENVL.-N.BERN-WAS.	83	67	55	66	67	80	71	76	74	68	74	69	64	76	68	77	65	75	80	80
GRNVL-SPR'BG-ASH-AND	90	75	66	75	78	92	76	85	81	75	80	75	71	83	76	84	70	82	90	88
GREENWOOD-GREENVILLE	63	49	44	50	50	62	53	57	59	52	58	50	48	59	52	63	51	57	64	61
HARLIN-W'LCO-B'VL-MC	67	58	44	53	51	57	56	59	61	59	61	53	52	58	54	61	54	62	61	57
HARRISBG-LAN-LEB-YRK	94	93	98	94	95	98	91	94	93	92	92	84	92	95	93	95	83	92	97	96
HARRISONBURG, VA	85	76	75	76	78	87	79	82	81	77	80	74	75	82	78	82	71	80	86	85
HARTFORD & NEW HAVEN	107	120	135	121	121	111	118	113	116	119	116	104	124	114	121	115	107	114	112	112
HATTIESBURG-LAUREL	73	56	43	55	58	72	59	66	65	57	64	60	53	66	57	68	56	65	71	71
HELENA	80	74	72	75	75	80	75	78	76	74	75	70	73	76	75	77	67	77	80	79
HONOLULU	100	112	112	111	111	99	115	108	105	111	106	108	114	104	113	101	98	111	99	106
HOUSTON	113	108	100	109	101	101	110	106	109	111	110	101	107	109	106	107	99	110	103	106
HUNTSVILLE-DECATUR	88	74	65	74	76	89	75	82	79	74	79	74	70	81	74	82	69	79	86	86
IDAHO FLS.-POCATELLO	94	85	79	86	84	92	88	89	88	85	88	82	83	90	85	88	78	89	90	92
INDIANAPOLIS	100	95	98	97	94	97	97	96	98	96	98	87	96	100	96	99	88	97	99	98
JACKSON, MS	81	67	58	67	68	79	69	74	74	69	74	67	65	75	68	77	65	74	79	78
JACKSON, TN	85	68	59	68	71	85	71	78	76	69	75	70	65	78	69	80	66	76	85	83
JACKSONVILLE,BRUNSWK	97	91	88	92	88	92	91	91	93	92	92	83	90	93	90	93	83	93	93	93
JOHNSTOWN-ALTOONA	77	66	65	66	70	81	69	75	74	67	72	66	65	74	69	77	64	72	82	77
JONESBORO	77	60	50	59	63	78	63	71	68	61	67	63	57	70	62	72	58	68	78	75
JOPLIN-PITTSBURG	75	60	55	60	63	76	64	70	69	61	67	62	58	70	63	72	59	68	77	73
JUNEAU, AK	123	132	136	135	127	118	128	122	123	131	124	115	132	124	128	120	113	125	117	122
KANSAS CITY	101	98	101	100	96	97	100	97	100	100	100	89	99	101	98	100	90	99	100	99
KNOXVILLE	85	70	62	70	73	87	73	80	77	71	76	72	67	78	72	80	67	77	86	84
LA CROSSE-EAU CLAIRE	86	74	71	74	77	88	78	83	81	75	80	74	73	82	77	83	70	81	88	86
LAFAYETTE, IN	90	79	83	83	78	81	93	84	90	86	90	79	86	90	86	88	81	88	85	85
LAFAYETTE, LA	73	59	50	59	60	72	61	67	66	61	66	60	57	67	60	69	58	66	72	71
LAKE CHARLES, LA	78	67	62	67	67	76	68	72	73	67	72	64	65	73	67	75	63	72	77	75
LANSING	93	90	96	92	90	91	93	91	93	91	92	82	92	94	91	93	83	91	92	92
LAREDO	74	68	52	62	59	62	64	67	68	68	68	61	61	65	62	67	61	70	65	64
LAS VEGAS	101	99	98	101	95	94	102	98	100	102	100	93	101	99	99	98	91	101	96	98
LEXINGTON	86	70	60	69	72	85	73	79	78	71	77	72	67	79	71	80	67	78	84	84
LIMA	84	79	82	79	82	89	78	83	82	78	81	72	78	84	80	85	72	80	89	85
LINCOLN-HAST'GS-KRNY	87	73	67	74	76	88	78	83	80	75	80	75	72	82	76	82	70	81	87	86
LITTLE ROCK-PINE BLF	87	73	64	72	74	87	75	81	79	73	79	73	70	80	74	82	69	80	87	85
LOS ANGELES	106	115	111	113	113	99	120	112	111	117	113	116	118	110	116	106	106	117	100	107
LOUISVILLE	94	88	88	89	88	94	88	91	91	88	90	81	87	92	88	92	80	90	94	93
LUBBOCK	80	68	62	67	66	74	74	74	76	71	76	68	68	76	70	77	67	76	77	75
MACON	88	75	66	74	75	86	76	81	81	76	80	73	71	82	74	84	71	80	86	85
MADISON	99	93	95	96	93	97	98	96	97	96	97	88	95	98	96	96	87	97	97	98
MANKATO	89	78	78	80	81	89	84	86	85	80	85	77	79	87	82	86	75	85	90	88
MARQUETTE	74	62	61	62	66	78	67	73	71	63	69	64	62	71	67	74	60	70	80	74
MEDFORD-KLAMATH FLS.	81	72	69	72	76	87	74	82	76	72	76	72	70	75	75	79	66	79	85	83
MEMPHIS	90	79	75	81	78	86	82	83	86	82	85	75	78	86	80	88	76	84	87	87
MERIDIAN	70	52	39	51	55	71	55	64	61	53	61	57	48	63	54	65	53	61	70	68
MIAMI-FT. LAUDERDALE	93	95	99	95	92	88	98	93	97	98	98	89	98	94	97	96	89	98	93	92
MILWAUKEE	98	101	112	104	100	97	102	98	102	103	102	89	104	102	102	102	93	100	99	99
MINNEAPOLIS-ST. PAUL	113	115	117	114	114	113	114	113	112	114	112	104	115	114	114	111	102	112	111	114
MINOT-BISMK.-DICK'SN	81	66	60	67	69	82	71	77	74	68	74	69	65	76	69	77	64	75	82	80
MISSOULA	76	67	63	67	69	78	71	75	72	67	71	67	66	72	70	73	63	74	77	77
MOBILE-PENSACOLA	85	76	73	76	76	84	77	80	80	76	79	72	74	81	76	82	70	80	85	83
MONROE-EL DORADO	70	54	45	54	56	70	58	64	64	56	63	57	52	64	56	67	55	63	70	68
MONTEREY-SALINAS	113	126	123	123	124	108	129	122	117	125	119	127	127	115	126	111	111	126	108	116
MONTGOMERY	78	65	56	64	66	77	66	72	72	66	71	64	62	72	65	75	62	71	77	76
MYRTLE BEACH-FLORENC	83	68	58	68	70	82	70	77	75	69	74	69	65	75	69	78	65	75	82	81
NASHVILLE	98	86	79	86	85	94	88	91	90	87	90	83	84	93	86	92	80	90	94	94
NEW ORLEANS	80	74	72	75	73	79	75	77	78	75	77	69	73	78	74	79	69	77	80	79
NEW YORK	110	130	136	127	135	117	133	124	133	134	136	119	142	128	136	134	130	125	121	122
NORFOLK-P'MTH-N.NEWS	93	88	89	91	87	89	91	89	91	91	91	82	90	92	89	91	82	91	90	91
NORTH PLATTE	81	71	70	72	74	84	73	79	77	71	75	69	69	79	73	79	66	76	84	81
ODESSA-MIDLAND	83	74	67	73	71	77	75	77	78	76	78	70	72	78	74	79	70	79	80	78
OKLAHOMA CITY	84	74	73	75	74	81	79	79	81	76	80	72	75	82	77	82	71	80	84	81
OMAHA	97	91	92	93	90	95	92	93	94	92	93	84	91	96	91	94	83	93	96	95
ORLANDO-D.BEACH-MEL.	91	89	89	89	88	92	89	90	90	89	89	81	89	88	90	91	80	91	93	90
OTTUMWA-KIRKSVILLE	75	58	52	58	63	78	64	71	68	60	67	63	57	70	63	71	58	68	78	75
PADUC-CG-HARR-MTVERN	75	59	52	59	63	77	64	71	69	60	68	63	58	70	63	72	59	68	78	74
PALM SPRINGS	95	94	96	91	95	99	94	98	95	94	95	90	93	89	97	97	85	100	103	95
PANAMA CITY	80	67	58	67	71	84	68	77	72	67	72	68	63	73	69	75	62	74	82	81
PARKERSBURG, WV	80	70	70	69	74	84	72	78	76	69	75	68	68	77	72	80	65	75	86	80
PEORIA-BLOOMINGTON	92	89	95	91	90	93	90	91	92	89	91	81	90	93	91	93	82	90	95	92
PHILADELPHIA	104	117	127	116	117	109	112	109	112	115	112	99	119	111	115	112	104	109	110	109
PHOENIX	106	105	102	104	101	102	104	103	103	105	103	96	103	101	103	102	93	106	103	103
PITTSBURGH	86	83	91	83	86	91	84	87	88	83	86	76	84	87	86	90	77	85	94	88
PORTLAND, OR	100	100	103	102	99	98	102	99	100	101	99	92	101	100	100	100	91	100	98	100
PORTLAND-AUBURN	89	83	84	84	87	94	84	89	86	83	85	80	82	86	85	88	76	87	92	91
PRESQUE ISLE	67	52	47	52	57	72	57	65	62	53	60	57	50	62	56	65	52	61	72	68
PROVIDENCE-N.BEDFORD	87	98	109	97	99	90	98	94	96	98	97	87	102	95	99	96	90	94	92	92
QUINCY-HAN'BL-KEOKUK	78	63	57	63	68	81	67	74	72	64	70	65	61	73	66	75	61	71	81	77
UNITED STATES	100	100	100	100	100	100	100	100	100	100	100	100	100	100	100	100	100	100	100	100

DMA	DMA Code	POPULATION			2000-2007 ANNUAL RATE		RACE (%)					
							White		Black		Asian/Pacific	
		2000	2007	2012	% Rate	National Rank	2000	2007	2000	2007	2000	2007
RALEIGH-DURHAM	560	2,366,511	2,723,187	3,013,620	2.0	28	64.0	62.4	28.6	27.9	1.9	2.6
RAPID CITY	764	233,927	250,330	262,288	0.9	92	84.8	83.2	0.6	0.7	0.6	0.8
RENO	811	611,650	736,026	841,486	2.6	14	82.5	80.3	2.1	2.1	3.4	3.5
RICHMOND-PETERSBURG	556	1,249,371	1,375,364	1,467,900	1.3	55	64.2	62.4	31.5	32.0	1.7	2.3
ROANOKE-LYNCHBURG	573	1,083,440	1,114,954	1,135,453	0.4	153	82.0	80.4	15.3	16.1	0.9	1.2
ROCH.-MAS.CTY-AUSTIN	611	350,202	371,901	386,151	0.8	103	94.5	92.7	1.2	1.6	1.9	2.8
ROCHESTER, NY	538	1,018,281	1,036,256	1,047,734	0.2	171	83.5	81.3	10.6	11.6	2.0	2.5
ROCKFORD	610	456,277	489,805	517,705	1.0	79	86.1	83.9	7.8	8.4	1.3	1.6
SACRAM-STOCKTN-MODES	862	3,425,623	4,062,850	4,526,915	2.4	17	68.8	64.4	6.2	6.1	8.6	9.8
SALISBURY	576	343,246	397,633	438,792	2.0	28	75.8	72.2	20.3	22.9	1.0	1.4
SALT LAKE CITY	770	2,389,005	2,774,294	3,094,190	2.1	25	89.3	88.1	0.8	0.9	2.2	2.4
SAN ANGELO	661	141,148	140,564	139,419	-0.1	197	80.4	79.5	3.3	3.3	0.7	0.7
SAN ANTONIO	641	2,007,065	2,296,958	2,520,080	1.9	32	72.2	70.0	5.8	5.5	1.3	1.5
SAN DIEGO	825	2,813,833	3,064,142	3,192,305	1.2	62	66.5	61.8	5.7	5.6	9.4	10.7
S.FRAN-OAKLND-S.JOSE	807	6,680,641	7,020,085	7,236,657	0.7	115	58.4	53.7	7.2	7.0	19.6	21.8
S.BARB.-S.MARIA-SLO	855	646,028	689,922	718,836	0.9	92	77.3	72.9	2.2	2.2	3.7	4.3
SAVANNAH	507	753,604	853,416	930,181	1.7	37	62.9	59.7	32.4	34.3	1.1	1.3
SEATTLE-TACOMA	819	4,234,510	4,649,364	4,951,384	1.3	55	80.8	78.5	4.0	4.2	7.4	8.3
SHERMAN,TX-ADA,OK	657	307,340	324,366	336,756	0.7	115	80.8	78.8	4.7	5.0	0.5	0.6
SHREVEPORT	612	980,780	1,015,445	1,040,789	0.5	143	65.4	62.2	29.9	32.3	0.5	0.7
SIOUX CITY	624	417,944	418,019	417,984	0.0	189	92.3	90.7	0.8	0.9	1.2	1.7
SIOUX FLS.(MITCHELL)	725	623,069	655,986	684,434	0.7	115	91.5	90.2	0.6	0.8	0.7	1.0
SOUTH BEND-ELKHART	588	873,823	907,966	932,445	0.5	143	86.4	84.3	8.0	8.6	1.0	1.3
SPOKANE	881	990,552	1,085,055	1,153,814	1.3	55	90.1	89.0	0.9	1.0	1.5	1.7
SPRINGFIELD, MO	619	942,604	1,028,401	1,091,880	1.2	62	95.1	94.3	1.3	1.4	0.6	0.9
SPRINGFIELD-HOLYOKE	543	680,014	693,880	703,171	0.3	162	83.5	80.2	6.0	6.7	1.8	2.4
ST. JOSEPH, MO	638	122,336	123,954	124,474	0.2	171	93.3	92.0	4.1	4.8	0.4	0.6
ST. LOUIS	609	3,058,385	3,203,353	3,320,783	0.6	130	80.8	79.5	16.0	16.6	1.3	1.8
SYRACUSE	555	1,018,554	1,028,734	1,033,551	0.1	180	89.8	88.0	5.5	6.2	1.9	2.4
TALLAHASSEE-THOMASVL	530	650,312	720,298	769,720	1.4	48	64.4	60.0	31.8	35.1	1.1	1.4
TAMPA-ST.PETE,S'SOTA	539	3,702,269	4,335,042	4,869,160	2.2	23	83.9	80.8	9.7	10.9	1.6	2.0
TERRE HAUTE	581	379,964	379,115	377,545	0.0	189	95.4	94.7	2.6	2.9	0.6	0.8
TOLEDO	547	1,080,654	1,097,206	1,108,126	0.2	171	87.4	85.8	8.0	8.5	0.9	1.3
TOPEKA	605	442,433	451,732	458,692	0.3	162	86.3	84.6	6.2	6.4	1.3	1.8
TRAVERSE CITY-CAD'LC	540	597,222	642,539	672,566	1.0	79	94.2	93.5	1.2	1.4	0.4	0.6
TRI-CITIES, TN-VA	531	772,555	799,547	816,015	0.5	143	96.5	95.9	2.0	2.2	0.3	0.5
TUCSON(SIERRA VISTA)	789	999,882	1,155,193	1,279,534	2.0	28	75.3	72.5	3.1	3.2	2.1	2.4
TULSA	671	1,280,821	1,353,504	1,404,543	0.8	103	74.1	71.6	7.3	7.5	0.9	1.3
TWIN FALLS	760	161,406	176,628	187,907	1.3	55	88.2	86.9	0.2	0.3	0.6	0.7
TYLER-LONGVIEW, TX	709	655,099	704,366	739,628	1.0	79	75.3	72.5	17.1	18.1	0.6	0.7
UTICA	526	253,577	256,579	257,341	0.2	171	91.7	90.2	4.7	5.3	1.1	1.5
VICTORIA	626	84,088	86,391	87,662	0.4	153	74.2	70.9	6.3	6.2	0.8	0.9
WACO-TEMPLE-BRYAN	625	833,593	917,124	976,023	1.3	55	69.9	66.3	16.5	17.1	2.2	2.6
WASHINGTON, DC	511	5,481,417	6,241,973	6,838,152	1.8	33	63.2	60.7	24.1	23.8	6.2	7.4
WATERTOWN	549	250,613	257,708	262,727	0.4	153	92.3	91.0	3.7	4.2	0.8	1.1
WAUSAU-RHINELANDER	705	440,930	462,161	475,582	0.7	115	95.5	94.4	0.3	0.4	2.1	2.8
W.PALM BCH-FT.PIERCE	548	1,599,467	1,934,837	2,215,079	2.7	12	80.5	77.0	12.8	14.5	1.4	1.8
WHEELING-STEUBENVLLE	554	357,559	345,798	337,236	-0.5	208	95.5	94.9	3.1	3.5	0.4	0.5
WICHITA FALLS-LAWTON	627	423,391	421,761	419,634	-0.1	197	78.3	75.8	9.8	10.2	1.5	1.9
WICHITA-HUTCHINSON	678	1,169,481	1,192,835	1,209,090	0.3	162	86.1	83.6	4.4	4.7	1.8	2.5
WILKES BARRE- SCRAN.	577	1,481,798	1,525,656	1,559,035	0.4	153	95.8	94.7	2.2	2.6	0.6	0.9
WILMINGTON, NC	550	361,559	428,737	489,866	2.4	17	75.1	74.3	21.2	21.0	0.5	0.7
YAKIMA-PAS-RICH-KENN	810	584,488	656,403	713,049	1.6	41	75.9	72.5	1.1	1.2	1.5	1.7
YOUNGSTOWN	536	715,039	701,791	688,459	-0.3	206	88.4	87.1	9.4	10.3	0.4	0.6
YUMA,AZ-EL CENTRO,CA	771	302,387	363,782	417,222	2.6	14	59.4	56.8	3.0	2.8	1.5	1.6
ZANESVILLE	596	84,585	85,989	87,051	0.2	171	93.9	93.1	4.0	4.5	0.3	0.4
UNITED STATES					1.2		75.1	72.7	12.3	12.6	3.8	4.5

DMA	% HISPANIC ORIGIN		2007 AGE DISTRIBUTION (%)									MEDIAN AGE	% 2007 Males	% 2007 Females
	2000	2007	0-4	5-9	10-14	15-19	20-24	25-44	45-64	65-84	85+	18+	2007		
RALEIGH-DURHAM	5.8	7.6	7.0	6.7	6.7	6.9	7.0	30.7	24.5	9.1	1.3	75.6	35.4	49.5	50.5
RAPID CITY	2.3	2.9	6.9	6.1	6.4	7.8	8.2	24.0	27.6	11.1	2.0	76.0	37.5	49.7	50.3
RENO	15.2	18.4	6.6	6.2	6.5	7.1	6.9	27.3	27.5	10.6	1.3	76.4	37.8	51.2	48.8
RICHMOND-PETERSBURG	2.1	2.9	6.1	6.0	6.5	7.2	6.5	27.3	27.7	10.9	1.7	77.1	38.8	49.0	51.0
ROANOKE-LYNCHBURG	1.3	1.9	5.5	5.5	5.7	7.1	7.4	25.1	28.0	13.5	2.2	79.7	40.6	48.8	51.2
ROCH.-MAS.CTY-AUSTIN	2.7	3.7	6.8	6.3	6.4	6.7	7.0	25.2	26.6	12.1	2.8	76.4	39.2	49.3	50.7
ROCHESTER, NY	4.4	5.1	6.2	6.0	6.9	8.0	7.4	25.2	27.1	11.0	2.3	76.5	38.4	48.6	51.4
ROCKFORD	6.4	8.5	7.0	6.5	6.9	7.0	6.6	26.5	26.6	11.0	2.0	75.3	38.0	49.3	50.7
SACRAM-STOCKTN-MODES	20.0	24.0	7.4	6.8	7.6	7.7	7.5	27.1	24.7	9.6	1.6	73.5	35.0	49.6	50.4
SALISBURY	2.9	4.0	5.6	5.4	5.8	6.3	6.1	24.2	28.5	15.9	2.1	79.6	42.6	48.9	51.1
SALT LAKE CITY	9.1	10.4	10.3	8.8	7.5	7.5	8.7	29.7	19.2	7.1	1.1	69.2	28.5	50.1	49.9
SAN ANGELO	31.6	33.7	6.8	6.1	6.1	7.8	8.7	25.4	24.7	12.1	2.3	76.7	36.3	49.2	50.8
SAN ANTONIO	51.4	57.1	7.8	7.2	7.1	7.4	7.6	27.5	23.9	9.7	1.5	73.4	34.3	49.1	50.9
SAN DIEGO	26.7	31.7	7.1	6.6	7.1	7.4	7.7	29.8	23.2	9.2	1.7	75.0	34.2	50.4	49.6
S.FRAN-OAKLND-S.JOSE	19.3	22.7	6.3	6.2	6.8	6.5	6.3	30.5	26.1	9.6	1.8	76.8	37.2	49.9	50.1
S.BARB.-S.MARIA-SLO	27.4	32.8	6.0	5.6	6.6	8.1	9.6	25.9	24.8	11.2	2.2	77.8	35.9	50.5	49.5
SAVANNAH	4.3	5.6	7.2	6.5	6.4	7.5	8.5	27.6	23.7	11.1	1.5	76.0	34.6	49.9	50.1
SEATTLE-TACOMA	5.6	7.0	6.4	6.1	6.5	6.9	7.2	28.3	27.2	9.6	1.8	77.0	37.5	49.9	50.1
SHERMAN,TX-ADA,OK	4.3	5.6	6.7	6.0	6.1	6.6	7.2	24.9	26.6	13.4	2.4	77.4	39.4	49.0	51.0
SHREVEPORT	3.8	4.7	7.1	6.6	6.5	6.9	7.2	26.1	25.6	11.9	2.1	75.8	37.2	48.7	51.3
SIOUX CITY	5.6	7.1	7.0	6.3	6.6	7.3	7.8	24.1	25.6	12.3	2.9	75.9	37.8	49.4	50.6
SIOUX FLS.(MITCHELL)	1.5	1.9	7.0	6.3	6.4	7.3	8.3	25.1	25.2	11.6	2.8	76.3	37.0	49.6	50.4
SOUTH BEND-ELKHART	5.0	6.6	7.3	6.9	6.9	7.3	7.0	26.3	25.6	10.9	2.0	74.7	36.5	49.4	50.6
SPOKANE	5.8	6.9	6.5	5.9	6.4	7.8	9.1	24.3	27.0	10.9	2.1	76.9	37.0	49.7	50.3
SPRINGFIELD, MO	2.0	2.5	6.4	6.0	5.9	6.7	7.3	24.8	26.8	14.0	2.2	78.1	39.9	49.3	50.7
SPRINGFIELD-HOLYOKE	11.2	13.9	5.9	5.6	6.4	8.5	8.4	24.6	26.8	11.2	2.5	77.7	38.3	47.9	52.1
ST. JOSEPH, MO	2.0	2.5	6.4	5.8	6.0	7.3	7.5	27.5	25.1	11.8	2.5	77.9	37.8	50.5	49.5
ST. LOUIS	1.4	1.8	6.7	6.3	6.8	7.0	6.7	26.8	26.3	11.3	2.1	76.0	38.0	48.6	51.4
SYRACUSE	2.1	2.5	6.0	5.7	6.5	8.4	8.9	25.0	26.2	11.2	2.1	77.6	37.6	49.0	51.0
TALLAHASSEE-THOMASVL	3.6	4.8	6.4	6.0	6.0	7.8	10.4	27.5	24.7	9.8	1.5	77.9	34.5	49.2	50.8
TAMPA-ST.PETE,S'SOTA	9.6	13.4	5.7	5.4	5.7	6.0	5.7	23.6	27.1	17.6	3.4	79.6	43.6	48.4	51.6
TERRE HAUTE	1.0	1.3	6.3	5.8	5.9	6.8	7.5	25.9	26.4	12.8	2.5	78.3	39.1	49.8	50.2
TOLEDO	4.6	5.5	6.6	6.2	6.6	7.4	7.4	26.0	26.5	11.1	2.1	76.4	37.4	48.9	51.1
TOPEKA	5.8	7.6	6.8	6.1	5.9	7.6	10.0	24.9	25.0	11.1	2.4	77.2	35.8	49.7	50.3
TRAVERSE CITY-CAD'LC	1.4	1.7	5.9	5.5	5.9	6.7	6.9	23.4	29.4	14.3	2.0	78.7	41.9	50.2	49.8
TRI-CITIES, TN-VA	0.9	1.2	5.6	5.5	5.6	5.8	5.5	27.5	28.7	13.8	2.0	80.0	41.3	49.1	50.9
TUCSON(SIERRA VISTA)	31.5	36.5	6.8	6.1	6.4	7.3	7.6	25.7	25.2	12.8	2.0	76.5	37.0	49.0	51.0
TULSA	3.9	4.9	7.1	6.5	6.6	6.8	7.4	25.9	26.1	11.7	1.9	75.8	37.4	49.1	50.9
TWIN FALLS	14.4	16.1	8.1	7.1	7.0	6.8	7.6	25.7	25.3	10.5	2.0	73.7	35.1	50.2	49.8
TYLER-LONGVIEW, TX	10.1	12.8	7.0	6.4	6.4	6.9	7.6	25.6	25.3	12.7	2.1	76.4	37.4	49.2	50.8
UTICA	2.8	3.3	5.5	5.2	6.1	7.6	8.0	24.0	27.1	13.5	3.1	79.3	40.5	48.9	51.1
VICTORIA	39.2	46.0	8.0	7.2	7.2	7.1	7.6	25.8	25.0	10.5	1.6	73.4	35.0	48.7	51.3
WACO-TEMPLE-BRYAN	16.5	20.5	7.7	6.7	6.3	8.4	12.0	27.9	20.6	8.8	1.6	75.3	30.1	50.0	50.0
WASHINGTON, DC	8.0	10.4	6.7	7.0	7.1	6.9	5.9	29.9	26.2	8.9	1.4	75.1	36.9	48.9	51.1
WATERTOWN	2.7	3.3	6.5	5.7	6.2	7.9	9.7	26.6	24.9	10.6	1.8	77.6	35.8	51.3	48.7
WAUSAU-RHINELANDER	0.9	1.2	6.0	5.5	6.1	6.9	7.4	24.8	28.1	12.9	2.4	78.3	40.7	50.1	49.9
W.PALM BCH-FT.PIERCE	11.3	15.4	5.4	5.3	5.7	5.9	5.1	22.2	26.4	19.5	4.3	79.9	45.2	48.3	51.7
WHEELING-STEUBENVLLE	0.5	0.6	5.2	5.1	5.5	6.0	6.3	24.2	29.5	15.4	2.8	80.8	43.3	48.9	51.1
WICHITA FALLS-LAWTON	10.0	12.4	7.3	6.5	6.2	7.6	8.6	25.9	23.9	11.8	2.1	76.0	35.5	50.4	49.6
WICHITA-HUTCHINSON	9.2	11.6	7.4	6.8	6.8	7.2	7.5	25.5	25.4	11.1	2.4	74.7	36.5	49.7	50.3
WILKES BARRE- SCRAN.	1.7	2.2	5.4	5.1	5.8	7.0	6.7	24.8	28.1	14.3	2.9	79.9	41.8	49.2	50.8
WILMINGTON, NC	2.5	3.3	5.8	5.7	5.7	5.9	6.1	26.9	28.5	13.8	1.6	79.5	40.8	48.9	51.1
YAKIMA-PAS-RICH-KENN	24.8	29.7	8.2	7.3	7.5	7.8	8.6	25.6	24.0	9.2	1.8	72.5	32.9	50.3	49.7
YOUNGSTOWN	1.6	1.9	5.9	5.7	6.1	6.5	6.2	24.6	28.0	14.1	2.9	78.4	41.3	48.8	51.2
YUMA,AZ-EL CENTRO,CA	60.7	66.0	8.3	7.2	7.6	8.1	8.3	25.9	20.7	12.4	1.4	71.9	32.9	51.0	49.0
ZANESVILLE	0.5	0.6	6.9	6.2	6.7	7.0	7.0	25.8	26.0	12.3	2.2	76.3	38.2	48.2	51.8
UNITED STATES	12.5	15.0	6.9	6.5	6.8	7.1	7.0	27.6	25.4	10.7	1.9	75.6	36.7	49.2	50.8

DMA	HOUSEHOLDS					FAMILIES			MEDIAN HOUSEHOLD INCOME		
	2000	2007	2012	% Annual Rate 2000-2007	2007 Average HH Size	2000	2007	% Annual Rate 2000-2007	2007	2012	2007 National Rank
RALEIGH-DURHAM	900,060	1,051,971	1,169,658	2.2	2.50	613,687	697,987	1.8	53,020	62,966	50
RAPID CITY	89,647	98,821	104,778	1.4	2.46	61,194	66,614	1.2	42,736	50,207	137
RENO	233,207	281,495	322,317	2.6	2.54	152,888	182,663	2.5	55,918	65,429	32
RICHMOND-PETERSBURG	481,184	534,085	572,771	1.4	2.47	326,389	354,075	1.1	56,030	65,508	31
ROANOKE-LYNCHBURG	437,639	457,845	470,112	0.6	2.34	295,617	299,707	0.2	42,584	49,127	139
ROCH.-MAS.CTY-AUSTIN	138,685	149,475	155,858	1.0	2.43	93,775	98,538	0.7	52,798	62,657	52
ROCHESTER, NY	390,969	401,960	408,580	0.4	2.48	257,529	262,755	0.3	56,329	65,922	28
ROCKFORD	174,893	187,659	198,294	1.0	2.56	121,703	127,260	0.6	54,667	63,276	37
SACRAM-STOCKTN-MODES	1,209,341	1,423,245	1,583,810	2.3	2.79	850,381	1,005,959	2.3	55,777	65,439	33
SALISBURY	135,556	159,567	177,462	2.3	2.41	92,878	106,171	1.9	47,179	54,250	89
SALT LAKE CITY	756,597	885,729	989,373	2.2	3.08	575,962	662,390	1.9	57,999	68,505	24
SAN ANGELO	53,599	54,265	54,185	0.2	2.47	36,832	36,858	0.0	39,468	45,483	171
SAN ANTONIO	700,646	802,197	882,853	1.9	2.79	507,356	575,588	1.8	46,616	54,449	94
SAN DIEGO	994,677	1,075,598	1,119,523	1.1	2.75	663,170	720,463	1.1	59,771	70,352	21
S.FRAN-OAKLND-S.JOSE	2,443,817	2,552,689	2,622,293	0.6	2.70	1,570,534	1,650,304	0.7	79,726	95,891	1
S.BARB.-S.MARIA-SLO	229,361	248,482	259,883	1.1	2.64	148,209	161,291	1.2	56,401	65,982	27
SAVANNAH	276,419	319,120	351,365	2.0	2.55	194,243	217,629	1.6	45,467	53,224	101
SEATTLE-TACOMA	1,658,835	1,831,296	1,955,447	1.4	2.48	1,074,588	1,169,319	1.2	62,615	75,368	13
SHERMAN,TX-ADA,OK	120,407	127,425	132,585	0.8	2.48	84,190	87,683	0.6	36,897	42,446	190
SHREVEPORT	374,069	393,426	405,963	0.7	2.51	261,842	269,507	0.4	35,771	39,954	196
SIOUX CITY	159,468	161,584	162,142	0.2	2.50	109,613	109,369	0.0	45,117	51,969	107
SIOUX FLS.(MITCHELL)	241,887	259,576	272,381	1.0	2.43	161,177	171,354	0.8	45,670	54,348	100
SOUTH BEND-ELKHART	327,161	345,482	356,339	0.8	2.56	229,102	234,021	0.3	50,885	59,059	65
SPOKANE	381,422	417,902	445,834	1.3	2.49	256,252	277,053	1.1	44,227	51,857	117
SPRINGFIELD, MO	376,594	415,809	444,035	1.4	2.39	262,067	281,615	1.0	37,817	43,958	183
SPRINGFIELD-HOLYOKE	260,745	269,420	274,700	0.5	2.45	168,007	171,414	0.3	51,712	60,636	58
ST. JOSEPH, MO	46,531	47,459	47,883	0.3	2.42	31,220	30,957	-0.1	43,397	50,051	129
ST. LOUIS	1,185,539	1,253,124	1,304,594	0.8	2.49	804,053	830,728	0.5	53,421	62,572	45
SYRACUSE	390,536	401,433	406,729	0.4	2.43	252,207	256,932	0.3	48,932	56,978	75
TALLAHASSEE-THOMASVL	245,825	278,808	301,523	1.8	2.44	160,548	177,191	1.4	40,157	45,965	166
TAMPA-ST.PETE,S'SOTA	1,557,217	1,820,166	2,044,885	2.2	2.34	1,006,598	1,158,291	2.0	46,660	54,290	93
TERRE HAUTE	147,923	149,676	149,799	0.2	2.40	100,502	98,012	-0.3	41,247	47,183	149
TOLEDO	419,870	433,563	441,559	0.4	2.46	283,248	283,578	0.0	50,146	57,307	67
TOPEKA	171,873	178,286	182,042	0.5	2.42	113,483	115,926	0.3	46,119	53,186	97
TRAVERSE CITY-CAD'LC	235,923	260,430	275,555	1.4	2.39	163,702	175,890	1.0	43,274	49,116	130
TRI-CITIES, TN-VA	316,698	334,965	345,767	0.8	2.31	223,198	229,394	0.4	35,783	41,130	195
TUCSON(SIERRA VISTA)	388,052	451,082	501,453	2.1	2.50	252,389	289,402	1.9	47,365	56,190	87
TULSA	501,712	533,383	554,506	0.8	2.48	346,491	361,955	0.6	43,478	50,702	128
TWIN FALLS	58,457	65,020	69,522	1.5	2.68	42,232	46,260	1.3	44,804	52,466	110
TYLER-LONGVIEW, TX	245,367	263,918	277,990	1.0	2.57	174,708	186,060	0.9	40,672	46,945	158
UTICA	98,846	101,722	102,833	0.4	2.37	63,514	64,845	0.3	41,556	48,166	143
VICTORIA	30,071	31,331	31,946	0.6	2.71	22,201	22,916	0.4	46,936	53,779	92
WACO-TEMPLE-BRYAN	296,608	329,435	352,264	1.5	2.61	201,857	221,622	1.3	41,786	48,916	142
WASHINGTON, DC	2,063,426	2,353,673	2,580,784	1.8	2.60	1,370,472	1,528,629	1.5	75,379	87,734	3
WATERTOWN	90,614	94,530	97,331	0.6	2.51	62,388	64,638	0.5	41,166	47,206	150
WAUSAU-RHINELANDER	173,485	187,940	195,849	1.1	2.40	119,681	126,675	0.8	49,382	55,918	72
W.PALM BCH-FT.PIERCE	668,126	802,069	918,455	2.6	2.37	435,954	514,330	2.3	53,516	62,877	44
WHEELING-STEUBENVLLE	144,705	143,649	141,423	-0.1	2.31	98,936	95,213	-0.5	37,863	43,461	182
WICHITA FALLS-LAWTON	157,874	160,117	160,103	0.2	2.48	111,222	111,216	0.0	40,083	46,389	167
WICHITA-HUTCHINSON	451,366	462,003	468,756	0.3	2.51	308,131	311,308	0.1	48,246	56,169	81
WILKES BARRE- SCRAN.	582,787	608,536	625,438	0.6	2.40	392,329	398,409	0.2	44,102	51,653	121
WILMINGTON, NC	148,880	182,694	211,857	2.9	2.30	99,322	118,667	2.5	45,160	52,667	106
YAKIMA-PAS-RICH-KENN	203,699	224,485	242,539	1.3	2.83	146,053	159,196	1.2	48,092	56,752	82
YOUNGSTOWN	281,292	279,754	276,665	-0.1	2.41	193,588	186,764	-0.5	43,905	50,480	124
YUMA,AZ-EL CENTRO,CA	93,232	114,873	132,772	2.9	3.02	73,129	89,711	2.9	40,535	47,339	161
ZANESVILLE	32,518	33,228	33,766	0.3	2.51	22,873	22,693	-0.1	42,832	49,027	136
UNITED STATES				1.2	2.59			1.0	53,154	62,503	

DMA	2007 Per Capita Income	2007 HH Income Base	2007 HOUSEHOLD INCOME DISTRIBUTION (%)					2007 Home Value Base	2007 HOME VALUE DISTRIBUTION (%)					2007 Median Home Value
			Less than $25,000	$25,000 to $49,999	$50,000 to $99,999	$100,000 to $149,999	$150,000 or More		Less than $50,000	$50,000 to $89,999	$90,000 to $174,999	$175,000 to $399,999	$400,000 or More	
RALEIGH-DURHAM	27,843	1,051,968	21.9	25.1	33.3	11.4	8.3	709,900	10.7	11.3	37.2	33.7	7.1	146,730
RAPID CITY	22,271	98,820	26.9	30.9	30.8	7.7	3.6	68,606	18.9	14.2	36.7	24.3	5.8	126,498
RENO	28,529	281,486	18.4	25.5	36.9	11.7	7.6	181,813	4.8	2.9	10.1	53.8	28.4	304,029
RICHMOND-PETERSBURG	29,276	534,080	19.1	25.1	34.7	13.4	7.8	378,470	3.2	4.1	28.4	53.5	10.7	205,765
ROANOKE-LYNCHBURG	23,610	457,840	28.1	29.6	30.6	8.0	3.7	331,523	9.2	11.1	39.6	35.2	4.9	155,716
ROCH.-MAS.CTY-AUSTIN	27,598	149,475	19.6	27.4	36.3	10.4	6.2	116,972	9.1	16.2	44.3	26.3	4.1	133,178
ROCHESTER, NY	28,804	401,956	19.8	24.4	34.3	13.5	8.0	283,473	4.0	10.0	47.9	34.7	3.4	153,893
ROCKFORD	26,289	187,659	19.6	25.5	36.4	13.0	5.5	139,330	5.6	11.2	51.5	28.9	2.8	141,599
SACRAM-STOCKTN-MODES	26,060	1,423,241	20.5	24.0	34.0	13.5	8.1	914,202	2.4	1.4	4.1	46.5	45.6	382,098
SALISBURY	25,071	159,567	24.6	28.2	33.4	8.9	4.9	122,115	7.1	6.9	27.0	45.5	13.4	199,257
SALT LAKE CITY	23,766	885,725	16.1	25.5	37.5	13.7	7.2	647,351	3.4	3.4	27.8	54.3	11.1	208,746
SAN ANGELO	21,221	54,265	30.5	30.9	28.2	6.9	3.5	37,062	24.0	30.2	32.2	11.0	2.7	83,431
SAN ANTONIO	22,242	802,182	25.3	27.6	31.5	10.0	5.6	541,143	16.1	25.3	35.6	18.9	4.0	104,157
SAN DIEGO	29,468	1,075,585	18.1	23.8	32.7	15.1	10.3	610,427	2.3	1.9	2.9	25.1	67.8	503,538
S.FRAN-OAKLND-S.JOSE	41,278	2,552,670	13.5	16.4	31.5	18.6	20.0	1,506,251	1.2	1.6	2.7	13.5	81.0	736,818
S.BARB.-S.MARIA-SLO	29,015	248,476	20.1	24.0	33.2	13.0	9.7	148,351	1.9	1.9	3.9	26.9	65.5	543,686
SAVANNAH	24,310	319,120	27.3	26.6	30.4	9.4	6.2	219,537	15.2	15.3	32.5	25.5	11.6	134,702
SEATTLE-TACOMA	32,437	1,831,290	16.2	22.9	35.4	15.7	9.8	1,223,890	2.6	2.0	8.1	51.1	36.2	332,546
SHERMAN,TX-ADA,OK	19,802	127,424	34.0	29.8	26.9	6.6	2.8	92,120	27.6	29.2	30.3	11.1	1.7	79,593
SHREVEPORT	19,510	393,421	35.8	28.8	25.7	6.6	3.1	279,878	27.2	26.3	32.4	12.2	1.8	84,382
SIOUX CITY	22,204	161,584	24.1	31.3	33.6	7.7	3.3	120,330	18.1	27.1	39.0	13.6	2.2	95,888
SIOUX FLS.(MITCHELL)	23,202	259,573	25.1	29.6	33.4	8.0	4.0	184,216	19.5	20.5	39.9	17.8	2.4	108,450
SOUTH BEND-ELKHART	24,555	345,482	21.3	27.6	35.9	10.4	4.8	259,585	9.6	19.6	46.5	21.2	3.2	120,061
SPOKANE	22,444	417,892	26.6	29.7	31.3	8.6	3.8	295,346	5.6	5.4	32.2	48.0	8.8	189,844
SPRINGFIELD, MO	20,945	415,804	31.0	33.4	26.4	5.9	3.2	308,407	14.7	19.1	41.3	21.2	3.8	116,630
SPRINGFIELD-HOLYOKE	26,407	269,410	24.0	24.4	32.7	12.7	6.3	175,238	0.9	1.7	23.1	63.9	10.4	224,947
ST. JOSEPH, MO	21,869	47,459	27.4	29.9	32.2	7.3	3.2	34,097	17.3	24.7	40.1	16.1	1.9	100,937
ST. LOUIS	27,809	1,253,114	21.1	25.6	34.1	12.2	7.0	929,207	8.2	14.9	39.2	31.1	6.6	143,253
SYRACUSE	25,611	401,427	23.8	27.2	33.0	10.2	5.7	279,118	4.7	9.2	48.4	34.9	2.9	154,412
TALLAHASSEE-THOMASVL	22,218	278,800	31.9	27.2	28.3	8.1	4.5	191,887	11.2	16.0	32.8	33.3	6.6	147,123
TAMPA-ST.PETE,S'SOTA	27,305	1,820,155	23.7	29.7	31.0	9.6	6.0	1,370,242	5.2	6.9	27.1	47.0	13.8	203,630
TERRE HAUTE	21,330	149,675	29.6	29.7	30.8	7.1	2.8	113,611	20.2	29.9	37.2	11.4	1.2	89,873
TOLEDO	25,463	433,562	21.9	28.0	34.1	11.1	4.9	320,072	11.2	18.4	45.1	22.9	2.5	120,015
TOPEKA	23,417	178,286	24.1	30.0	33.5	8.8	3.6	122,541	17.9	24.0	41.3	15.4	1.4	102,614
TRAVERSE CITY-CAD'LC	22,881	260,430	26.0	32.4	30.7	7.4	3.4	210,867	10.3	16.6	42.3	25.2	5.7	129,061
TRI-CITIES, TN-VA	20,643	334,965	35.1	30.3	26.0	5.8	2.8	254,917	17.5	18.7	40.3	20.8	2.7	115,109
TUCSON(SIERRA VISTA)	25,547	451,082	24.7	28.1	30.5	10.7	6.0	297,046	5.9	6.2	26.0	48.3	13.6	202,057
TULSA	23,364	533,383	27.8	29.0	29.8	8.6	4.8	372,696	20.2	25.2	37.6	14.4	2.6	96,861
TWIN FALLS	22,419	65,020	25.1	31.4	31.0	7.7	4.9	47,104	6.8	8.2	44.3	28.0	12.7	157,712
TYLER-LONGVIEW, TX	21,336	263,918	30.0	29.5	28.5	8.0	4.1	192,748	24.3	25.2	33.6	14.6	2.3	90,795
UTICA	22,264	101,722	29.4	29.5	30.1	7.3	3.7	71,611	7.2	13.4	46.0	30.8	2.6	147,023
VICTORIA	22,509	31,331	24.4	28.3	32.2	10.4	4.8	21,691	20.7	26.7	37.5	13.4	1.7	93,684
WACO-TEMPLE-BRYAN	20,953	329,435	28.8	29.5	29.4	8.1	4.2	199,122	21.5	25.4	37.1	13.8	2.2	94,503
WASHINGTON, DC	38,643	2,353,663	12.6	18.5	33.5	18.9	16.5	1,568,297	1.7	1.3	5.5	42.2	49.3	396,620
WATERTOWN	19,838	94,525	29.2	31.2	30.5	6.5	2.5	65,416	7.0	13.5	41.7	35.0	2.8	153,776
WAUSAU-RHINELANDER	24,983	187,940	22.0	28.6	36.0	9.6	3.9	146,287	6.7	14.5	47.7	27.7	3.4	136,116
W.PALM BCH-FT.PIERCE	33,635	802,068	20.0	26.6	31.6	11.4	10.3	624,714	3.4	4.5	17.4	46.8	27.9	261,962
WHEELING-STEUBENVLLE	20,940	143,649	32.7	30.3	28.3	6.2	2.5	111,697	21.7	29.9	38.3	9.2	1.0	87,877
WICHITA FALLS-LAWTON	20,540	160,117	29.9	31.1	29.0	6.9	3.0	108,150	25.3	26.6	33.5	12.8	1.8	86,889
WICHITA-HUTCHINSON	23,795	462,003	22.3	29.4	34.9	9.1	4.3	330,740	20.0	27.8	38.2	12.7	1.4	93,462
WILKES BARRE- SCRAN.	23,115	608,536	27.1	29.2	31.2	8.7	3.7	450,416	6.9	11.6	42.9	34.4	4.2	154,832
WILMINGTON, NC	25,765	182,694	27.8	27.0	31.4	8.6	5.2	135,582	10.5	10.5	26.1	39.5	13.4	183,545
YAKIMA-PAS-RICH-KENN	21,730	224,485	24.2	27.5	32.6	10.7	4.9	153,442	6.4	6.7	39.8	40.8	6.3	169,068
YOUNGSTOWN	23,094	279,753	26.5	30.0	30.9	9.1	3.5	213,775	16.2	25.7	42.2	14.8	1.2	101,737
YUMA,AZ-EL CENTRO,CA	18,134	114,868	30.2	29.6	28.0	8.3	3.8	77,761	9.8	7.5	31.0	45.8	5.8	178,233
ZANESVILLE	21,714	33,228	27.0	30.9	31.6	7.1	3.4	25,225	15.6	23.6	43.5	15.9	1.4	106,459
UNITED STATES	27,916		21.9	25.0	32.3	12.3	8.4		7.9	10.5	27.1	35.6	19.0	192,285

DMA	FINANCIAL SERVICES				THE HOME							ENTERTAINMENT						PERSONAL			
					Home Improvements		Furnishings														
	Auto Loan	Home Loan	Invest-ments	Retire-ment Plans	Home Repair	Lawn & Garden	Comput-ers & Hard-ware	Major Appli-ances	TV, Radio, Sound Equip-ment	Furni-ture	Dine out/ Carry out	Sports Equip-ment	Fees & Tickets	Toys & Games	Travel	Cable TV	Apparel & Services	Auto Repairs	Health Insur-ance	Pets & Supplies
RALEIGH-DURHAM	105	96	88	97	93	99	97	98	98	97	98	90	94	100	94	99	88	99	99	100
RAPID CITY	83	71	66	72	73	84	75	80	78	72	77	72	70	79	74	79	67	78	84	82
RENO	101	101	101	102	98	97	102	99	99	101	100	93	101	100	100	98	90	101	97	99
RICHMOND-PETERSBURG	104	101	101	103	100	103	100	101	101	101	101	92	100	102	100	102	91	101	102	103
ROANOKE-LYNCHBURG	84	72	68	71	75	87	74	80	78	72	77	71	70	79	74	81	68	78	86	83
ROCH.-MAS.CTY-AUSTIN	99	91	90	92	93	101	91	96	94	90	93	86	89	96	92	96	83	94	101	99
ROCHESTER, NY	98	99	110	101	99	99	100	98	101	100	100	88	101	101	100	102	91	98	101	99
ROCKFORD	94	93	99	94	92	94	92	93	94	93	93	83	93	96	93	95	84	92	96	94
SACRAM-STOCKTN-MODES	99	104	102	103	101	97	103	100	99	103	100	95	103	99	102	97	91	102	96	99
SALISBURY	90	81	77	80	85	97	80	89	84	80	83	78	77	83	83	88	73	86	95	92
SALT LAKE CITY	104	105	101	105	99	98	104	100	101	104	101	94	103	102	101	99	91	102	97	101
SAN ANGELO	80	68	62	67	68	77	72	75	75	70	75	67	66	75	70	77	66	75	80	76
SAN ANTONIO	92	85	77	84	80	84	85	86	87	87	87	78	82	87	83	87	78	88	86	86
SAN DIEGO	107	112	113	113	111	100	119	109	111	116	113	110	117	110	115	107	105	115	102	107
S.FRAN-OAKLND-S.JOSE	140	160	162	160	161	139	164	152	150	160	153	156	166	147	163	143	143	157	138	149
S.BARB.-S.MARIA-SLO	101	106	109	106	107	100	113	107	106	108	107	105	111	103	111	103	98	110	101	104
SAVANNAH	95	82	75	83	81	92	86	89	89	84	88	80	81	89	84	90	78	89	92	92
SEATTLE-TACOMA	110	113	116	115	111	107	115	110	111	114	112	104	115	111	113	109	102	112	107	110
SHERMAN,TX-ADA,OK	76	62	56	61	65	78	65	72	70	62	69	63	59	71	65	73	60	70	79	75
SHREVEPORT	76	62	54	61	64	76	64	71	70	63	69	63	59	71	63	73	60	69	77	74
SIOUX CITY	86	71	65	71	75	89	74	83	79	71	78	73	68	81	74	82	68	79	89	86
SIOUX FLS.(MITCHELL)	87	73	66	73	76	88	78	83	81	74	80	75	71	83	76	83	70	81	88	87
SOUTH BEND-ELKHART	92	85	86	86	87	94	85	89	88	85	88	79	83	91	85	90	78	87	94	92
SPOKANE	82	74	73	75	75	82	78	80	79	75	78	72	74	79	77	80	69	79	83	81
SPRINGFIELD, MO	78	64	56	64	67	81	67	75	71	65	70	66	62	72	67	74	61	72	80	78
SPRINGFIELD-HOLYOKE	85	90	104	92	91	86	92	88	92	92	91	80	95	90	93	91	84	89	89	87
ST. JOSEPH, MO	79	70	73	71	72	80	73	76	78	71	76	67	70	78	73	80	67	75	83	78
ST. LOUIS	98	96	101	97	96	98	95	96	97	96	96	86	96	98	96	98	87	96	100	97
SYRACUSE	88	84	92	86	85	88	88	87	89	86	88	77	87	89	87	90	79	87	91	88
TALLAHASSEE-THOMASVL	84	69	61	70	69	79	77	77	78	73	78	71	70	78	72	79	69	78	80	81
TAMPA-ST.PETE,S'SOTA	88	87	93	87	88	94	86	90	89	87	87	79	87	85	90	91	78	90	97	90
TERRE HAUTE	79	65	62	65	69	82	69	76	74	66	72	67	64	75	68	77	63	73	83	79
TOLEDO	89	85	90	87	86	90	86	87	88	86	87	77	86	90	86	90	78	86	92	89
TOPEKA	84	73	73	75	75	83	80	80	81	76	80	73	75	82	77	82	71	80	85	83
TRAVERSE CITY-CAD'LC	85	72	63	71	77	92	72	84	76	71	75	73	67	77	74	80	66	79	88	86
TRI-CITIES, TN-VA	77	60	49	58	64	81	62	72	68	60	67	64	55	69	61	72	58	68	79	77
TUCSON(SIERRA VISTA)	90	86	87	87	84	86	89	88	89	88	89	80	87	87	88	89	80	90	89	87
TULSA	87	76	73	77	77	85	79	82	82	77	81	73	75	83	78	84	72	81	87	84
TWIN FALLS	92	79	69	78	82	94	80	88	83	78	83	79	75	86	79	85	72	85	92	92
TYLER-LONGVIEW, TX	85	71	62	70	73	86	73	80	78	72	77	71	68	78	72	81	68	78	86	83
UTICA	75	69	75	70	73	80	72	76	76	70	74	66	70	75	73	78	66	74	82	77
VICTORIA	89	84	80	83	80	84	83	84	85	84	85	76	81	85	82	86	76	85	86	84
WACO-TEMPLE-BRYAN	83	69	64	71	67	74	80	76	80	75	80	70	73	80	74	79	71	79	78	77
WASHINGTON, DC	133	144	147	146	143	132	143	136	138	145	139	129	147	139	142	135	129	137	129	136
WATERTOWN	77	63	59	64	66	78	69	73	71	65	71	66	63	72	67	73	62	72	78	76
WAUSAU-RHINELANDER	90	80	77	80	84	96	81	89	84	79	83	78	77	86	82	86	73	85	93	91
W.PALM BCH-FT.PIERCE	106	113	126	112	116	117	107	112	109	111	108	98	113	103	115	112	97	112	119	110
WHEELING-STEUBENVLLE	74	62	60	61	67	80	64	72	70	62	68	62	60	70	65	74	59	68	82	74
WICHITA FALLS-LAWTON	77	65	63	66	66	76	70	73	74	67	73	65	65	75	69	76	64	73	79	75
WICHITA-HUTCHINSON	89	79	76	80	80	89	81	85	85	80	84	70	78	86	81	86	74	84	90	87
WILKES BARRE- SCRAN.	81	74	78	74	78	87	75	80	79	73	78	70	73	79	77	82	69	77	88	82
WILMINGTON, NC	90	79	70	78	81	93	79	87	83	78	82	77	75	83	80	85	72	84	91	90
YAKIMA-PAS-RICH-KENN	89	84	82	83	82	85	86	86	86	84	86	80	83	86	84	85	77	87	86	86
YOUNGSTOWN	79	75	82	76	78	84	75	79	79	75	78	68	75	80	77	82	69	77	86	80
YUMA,AZ-EL CENTRO,CA	79	75	67	70	71	75	73	77	75	75	75	70	71	72	73	75	67	79	78	75
ZANESVILLE	82	71	71	72	74	84	73	78	78	72	76	69	70	79	73	81	67	76	85	81
UNITED STATES	100	100	100	100	100	100	100	100	100	100	100	100	100	100	100	100	100	100	100	100

Business Data by County

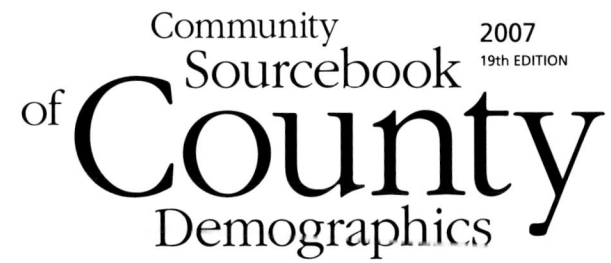

Community
Sourcebook
of
County
Demographics

2007
19th EDITION

COUNTY	2007 Total Firms	2007 Total Employees	TOP INDUSTRY RANKED on 2007 EMPLOYMENT	COUNTY	2007 Total Firms	2007 Total Employees	TOP INDUSTRY RANKED on 2007 EMPLOYMENT
AUTAUGA, AL	1417	10984	FOOD SVCS & DRINKING PLACES	LAKE AND PENINSULA, AK	187	738	FOOD MANUFACTURING
BALDWIN, AL	8676	64993	FOOD SVCS & DRINKING PLACES	MATANUSKA-SUSITNA, AK	4112	22768	EDUCATIONAL SERVICES
BARBOUR, AL	1071	10169	FABRICATED METAL PRODUCT MFG	NOME, AK	556	3443	EDUCATIONAL SERVICES
BIBB, AL	534	4238	EDUCATIONAL SERVICES	NORTH SLOPE, AK	370	3954	EXEC.; LEGIS.; & OTHER SUPPORT
BLOUNT, AL	1589	9571	EDUCATIONAL SERVICES	NORTHWEST ARCTIC, AK	340	3062	RELIG.; GRANT; CIVIC; PROF ORG
BULLOCK, AL	355	3235	FOOD MANUFACTURING	PR OF WALES-OUT KTCH, AK	373	2037	EDUCATIONAL SERVICES
BUTLER, AL	288	2633	PAPER MANUFACTURING	SITKA CITY/BOROUGH, AK	679	5164	HOSPITALS
CALHOUN, AL	4256	45508	FOOD SVCS & DRINKING PLACES	SKAGWAY-HOONAH-ANGOON, AK	408	2610	EDUCATIONAL SERVICES
CHAMBERS, AL	1071	10554	TEXTILE MILLS	SOUTHEAST FAIRBANKS, AK	449	2106	NAT'L SECURITY & INT'L AFFAIRS
CHEROKEE, AL	852	5688	MOTOR VEHICLE & PARTS DEALERS	VALDEZ-CORDOVA, AK	915	5969	MERCH. WHOLESALERS;NONDUR. GDS
CHILTON, AL	1224	8714	EDUCATIONAL SERVICES	WADE HAMPTON, AK	336	1909	EDUCATIONAL SERVICES
CHOCTAW, AL	596	5079	PAPER MANUFACTURING	WRANGELL-PETERSBURG, AK	524	3307	FOOD MANUFACTURING
CLARKE, AL	1108	9397	EDUCATIONAL SERVICES	YAKUTAT CITY/BOROUGH, AK	70	326	RELIG.; GRANT; CIVIC; PROF ORG
CLAY, AL	454	4649	FURNITURE & RELATED PROD. MFG	YUKON-KOYUKUK, AK	499	1760	EXEC.; LEGIS.; & OTHER SUPPORT
CLEBURNE, AL	382	2880	MERCH. WHOLESALERS;NONDUR. GDS	APACHE, AZ	1518	16471	EDUCATIONAL SERVICES
COFFEE, AL	1740	13928	EDUCATIONAL SERVICES	COCHISE, AZ	4131	42148	TRANSPORTATION EQUIPMENT MFG
COLBERT, AL	2253	19942	FOOD SVCS & DRINKING PLACES	COCONINO, AZ	5489	63120	EDUCATIONAL SERVICES
CONECUH, AL	466	3921	TRUCK TRANSPORTATION	GILA, AZ	2242	18693	PRIMARY METAL MANUFACTURING
COOSA, AL	208	1530	FURNITURE & RELATED PROD. MFG	GRAHAM, AZ	843	9845	REPAIR AND MAINTENANCE
COVINGTON, AL	1503	13678	FURN. & HOME FURNISHGS STORES	GREENLEE, AZ	234	3689	MINING (EXCEPT OIL AND GAS)
CRENSHAW, AL	269	2001	FOOD MANUFACTURING	LA PAZ, AZ	1057	7099	ACCOMMODATION
CULLMAN, AL	2906	29454	EDUCATIONAL SERVICES	MARICOPA, AZ	108300	1456301	FOOD SVCS & DRINKING PLACES
DALE, AL	1814	19566	SUPPORT ACT. FOR TRANSPORT.	MOHAVE, AZ	8312	55289	EDUCATIONAL SERVICES
DALLAS, AL	1690	17212	EDUCATIONAL SERVICES	NAVAJO, AZ	3515	34317	EDUCATIONAL SERVICES
DEKALB, AL	2243	23911	APPAREL MANUFACTURING	PIMA, AZ	30741	356654	EDUCATIONAL SERVICES
ELMORE, AL	2077	15468	EDUCATIONAL SERVICES	PINAL, AZ	4799	47662	EXEC.; LEGIS.; & OTHER SUPPORT
ESCAMBIA, AL	1486	12997	EDUCATIONAL SERVICES	SANTA CRUZ, AZ	1748	15474	FOOD AND BEVERAGE STORES
ETOWAH, AL	3706	38092	EDUCATIONAL SERVICES	YAVAPAI, AZ	8991	70967	EDUCATIONAL SERVICES
FAYETTE, AL	187	1385	APPAREL MANUFACTURING	YUMA, AZ	4381	63546	NAT'L SECURITY & INT'L AFFAIRS
FRANKLIN, AL	1054	8969	REAL ESTATE	ARKANSAS, AR	997	8696	MERCH. WHOLESALERS;DURABLE GDS
GENEVA, AL	950	5703	FABRICATED METAL PRODUCT MFG	ASHLEY, AR	939	7752	EDUCATIONAL SERVICES
GREENE, AL	295	2188	AMUSEMENT; GAMBLING;& RECREAT.	BAXTER, AR	2252	15791	MERCH. WHOLESALERS;DURABLE GDS
HALE, AL	467	4815	HOSPITALS	BENTON, AR	7222	81183	GENERAL MERCHANDISE STORES
HENRY, AL	633	4422	TEXTILE PRODUCT MILLS	BOONE, AR	2121	14699	EDUCATIONAL SERVICES
HOUSTON, AL	5370	52939	HOSPITALS	BRADLEY, AR	529	4153	WOOD PRODUCT MANUFACTURING
JACKSON, AL	1652	14645	TEXTILE PRODUCT MILLS	CALHOUN, AR	207	1048	CHEMICAL MANUFACTURING
JEFFERSON, AL	26502	360888	EDUCATIONAL SERVICES	CARROLL, AR	1568	11525	FOOD MANUFACTURING
LAMAR, AL	227	2601	TRANSPORTATION EQUIPMENT MFG	CHICOT, AR	601	3735	EDUCATIONAL SERVICES
LAUDERDALE, AL	3429	29655	FOOD SVCS & DRINKING PLACES	CLARK, AR	881	9078	EDUCATIONAL SERVICES
LAWRENCE, AL	855	5140	EDUCATIONAL SERVICES	CLAY, AR	604	4815	FURNITURE & RELATED PROD. MFG
LEE, AL	3706	53093	EDUCATIONAL SERVICES	CLEBURNE, AR	1195	8130	EDUCATIONAL SERVICES
LIMESTONE, AL	2032	22044	COMPUTER & ELECTRONIC PROD MFG	CLEVELAND, AR	262	1384	EDUCATIONAL SERVICES
LOWNDES, AL	341	2094	EDUCATIONAL SERVICES	COLUMBIA, AR	1133	9695	EDUCATIONAL SERVICES
MACON, AL	627	6769	EDUCATIONAL SERVICES	CONWAY, AR	790	6487	EDUCATIONAL SERVICES
MADISON, AL	12591	148637	PROF.; SCIENTIFIC; & TECH SVCS	CRAIGHEAD, AR	3768	43184	EDUCATIONAL SERVICES
MARENGO, AL	950	8659	WOOD PRODUCT MANUFACTURING	CRAWFORD, AR	1819	15935	FOOD MANUFACTURING
MARION, AL	1017	10393	MERCH. WHOLESALERS;DURABLE GDS	CRITTENDEN, AR	1680	18160	TRUCK TRANSPORTATION
MARSHALL, AL	3540	36580	FOOD MANUFACTURING	CROSS, AR	751	4467	EDUCATIONAL SERVICES
MOBILE, AL	15103	169454	HOSPITALS	DALLAS, AR	447	3335	BLDG MATL & GARDEN EQPMT DLRS
MONROE, AL	933	8382	PAPER MANUFACTURING	DESHA, AR	715	4954	MERCH. WHOLESALERS;NONDUR. GDS
MONTGOMERY, AL	9539	124622	EXEC.; LEGIS.; & OTHER SUPPORT	DREW, AR	748	6077	EDUCATIONAL SERVICES
MORGAN, AL	4324	47592	FOOD SVCS & DRINKING PLACES	FAULKNER, AR	3352	31343	FOOD SVCS & DRINKING PLACES
PERRY, AL	335	2758	FOOD MANUFACTURING	FRANKLIN, AR	582	4742	MERCH. WHOLESALERS;NONDUR. GDS
PICKENS, AL	587	4230	EDUCATIONAL SERVICES	FULTON, AR	411	2134	EDUCATIONAL SERVICES
PIKE, AL	1188	12312	PRIMARY METAL MANUFACTURING	GARLAND, AR	4560	38381	FOOD SVCS & DRINKING PLACES
RANDOLPH, AL	818	4895	EDUCATIONAL SERVICES	GRANT, AR	507	3575	FABRICATED METAL PRODUCT MFG
RUSSELL, AL	1665	14222	MERCH. WHOLESALERS;DURABLE GDS	GREENE, AR	1279	16005	TRANSPORTATION EQUIPMENT MFG
ST. CLAIR, AL	1369	11283	MERCH. WHOLESALERS;DURABLE GDS	HEMPSTEAD, AR	929	7850	EDUCATIONAL SERVICES
SHELBY, AL	5896	62306	FOOD SVCS & DRINKING PLACES	HOT SPRING, AR	923	7972	EDUCATIONAL SERVICES
SUMTER, AL	485	3762	EDUCATIONAL SERVICES	HOWARD, AR	660	8054	FOOD MANUFACTURING
TALLADEGA, AL	2298	24854	EDUCATIONAL SERVICES	INDEPENDENCE, AR	1539	14980	FOOD MANUFACTURING
TALLAPOOSA, AL	1471	16455	MISCELLANEOUS MANUFACTURING	IZARD, AR	586	3254	EDUCATIONAL SERVICES
TUSCALOOSA, AL	5726	82432	EDUCATIONAL SERVICES	JACKSON, AR	704	5058	EDUCATIONAL SERVICES
WALKER, AL	2287	17529	EDUCATIONAL SERVICES	JEFFERSON, AR	2782	30434	EDUCATIONAL SERVICES
WASHINGTON, AL	509	4532	CHEMICAL MANUFACTURING	JOHNSON, AR	925	9106	FOOD MANUFACTURING
WILCOX, AL	461	3807	PAPER MANUFACTURING	LAFAYETTE, AR	345	1946	EDUCATIONAL SERVICES
WINSTON, AL	825	9408	FURNITURE & RELATED PROD. MFG	LAWRENCE, AR	688	4887	EDUCATIONAL SERVICES
ALEUTIANS EAST, AK	162	2264	FOOD MANUFACTURING	LEE, AR	337	2139	JUSTICE; PUBIC ORDER/SAFETY
ALEUTIANS WEST, AK	304	7549	FOOD MANUFACTURING	LINCOLN, AR	333	2867	JUSTICE; PUBIC ORDER/SAFETY
ANCHORAGE, AK	15977	163352	EXEC.; LEGIS.; & OTHER SUPPORT	LITTLE RIVER, AR	541	3948	PAPER MANUFACTURING
BETHEL, AK	937	5094	EDUCATIONAL SERVICES	LOGAN, AR	771	6437	FOOD MANUFACTURING
BRISTOL BAY, AK	233	2457	FOOD MANUFACTURING	LONOKE, AR	1578	11917	EDUCATIONAL SERVICES
DENALI, AK	207	3320	ACCOMMODATION	MADISON, AR	476	3310	FOOD MANUFACTURING
DILLINGHAM, AK	383	2417	EDUCATIONAL SERVICES	MARION, AR	963	5834	MISCELLANEOUS STORE RETAILERS
FAIRBANKS NORTH STAR, AK	5203	40931	EXEC.; LEGIS.; & OTHER SUPPORT	MILLER, AR	1610	14217	PLASTICS & RUBBER PRODUCTS MFG
HAINES, AK	267	1156	FOOD SVCS & DRINKING PLACES	MISSISSIPPI, AR	1798	18945	EDUCATIONAL SERVICES
JUNEAU CITY/BOROUGH, AK	2064	19434	EXEC.; LEGIS.; & OTHER SUPPORT	MONROE, AR	505	2743	EDUCATIONAL SERVICES
KENAI PENINSULA, AK	4347	22490	EDUCATIONAL SERVICES	MONTGOMERY, AR	357	2071	ACCOMMODATION
KETCHIKAN GATEWAY, AK	1104	8558	FOOD MANUFACTURING	NEVADA, AR	329	2321	PETROLEUM & COAL PRODUCTS MFG
KODIAK ISLAND, AK	857	7044	FOOD MANUFACTURING	NEWTON, AR	362	1608	EDUCATIONAL SERVICES

COUNTY	2007 Total Firms	2007 Total Employees	TOP INDUSTRY RANKED on 2007 EMPLOYMENT	COUNTY	2007 Total Firms	2007 Total Employees	TOP INDUSTRY RANKED on 2007 EMPLOYMENT
OUACHITA, AR	1168	9680	COMPUTER & ELECTRONIC PROD MFG	YOLO, CA	6459	86644	AMBULATORY HEALTH CARE SVCS
PERRY, AR	289	1343	EDUCATIONAL SERVICES	YUBA, CA	1869	17341	EDUCATIONAL SERVICES
PHILLIPS, AR	957	6243	EDUCATIONAL SERVICES	ADAMS, CO	11661	140132	EDUCATIONAL SERVICES
PIKE, AR	554	3216	EDUCATIONAL SERVICES	ALAMOSA, CO	1028	7541	EDUCATIONAL SERVICES
POINSETT, AR	1016	6599	EDUCATIONAL SERVICES	ARAPAHOE, CO	21936	239774	PROF.; SCIENTIFIC; & TECH SVCS
POLK, AR	932	7186	EDUCATIONAL SERVICES	ARCHULETA, CO	1569	4741	ACCOMMODATION
POPE, AR	2562	24278	EDUCATIONAL SERVICES	BACA, CO	301	6322	CROP PRODUCTION
PRAIRIE, AR	318	1663	EDUCATIONAL SERVICES	BENT, CO	234	1918	HOSPITALS
PULASKI, AR	17656	259135	PROF.; SCIENTIFIC; & TECH SVCS	BOULDER, CO	14665	150676	PROF.; SCIENTIFIC; & TECH SVCS
RANDOLPH, AR	560	4827	EDUCATIONAL SERVICES	BROOMFIELD, CO	2039	26862	TELECOMMUNICATIONS
ST. FRANCIS, AR	1116	8466	EDUCATIONAL SERVICES	CHAFFEE, CO	1424	7177	FOOD SVCS & DRINKING PLACES
SALINE, AR	2585	20908	FOOD SVCS & DRINKING PLACES	CHEYENNE, CO	170	738	EDUCATIONAL SERVICES
SCOTT, AR	390	3240	FOOD MANUFACTURING	CLEAR CREEK, CO	541	3772	ACCOMMODATION
SEARCY, AR	370	1746	EDUCATIONAL SERVICES	CONEJOS, CO	304	1174	EDUCATIONAL SERVICES
SEBASTIAN, AR	5416	71428	MERCH. WHOLESALERS;NONDUR. GDS	COSTILLA, CO	218	788	EDUCATIONAL SERVICES
SEVIER, AR	660	5955	MERCH. WHOLESALERS;NONDUR. GDS	CROWLEY, CO	149	1167	JUSTICE; PUBIC ORDER/SAFETY
SHARP, AR	931	4575	EDUCATIONAL SERVICES	CUSTER, CO	338	1136	EDUCATIONAL SERVICES
STONE, AR	728	4028	FOOD SVCS & DRINKING PLACES	DELTA, CO	1777	9881	HOSPITALS
UNION, AR	2257	21217	EDUCATIONAL SERVICES	DENVER, CO	30036	379867	PROF.; SCIENTIFIC; & TECH SVCS
VAN BUREN, AR	722	4525	NURSING & RESID. CARE FACILIT.	DOLORES, CO	154	487	EXEC.; LEGIS.; & OTHER SUPPORT
WASHINGTON, AR	7762	90124	FOOD MANUFACTURING	DOUGLAS, CO	7815	91000	COMPUTER & ELECTRONIC PROD MFG
WHITE, AR	2563	22036	EDUCATIONAL SERVICES	EAGLE, CO	3981	33852	FOOD SVCS & DRINKING PLACES
WOODRUFF, AR	303	1982	AMBULATORY HEALTH CARE SVCS	ELBERT, CO	808	3473	EDUCATIONAL SERVICES
YELL, AR	770	5407	FOOD MANUFACTURING	EL PASO, CO	21736	272578	EDUCATIONAL SERVICES
ALAMEDA, CA	63825	615095	PROF.; SCIENTIFIC; & TECH SVCS	FREMONT, CO	1796	13314	JUSTICE; PUBIC ORDER/SAFETY
ALPINE, CA	109	1309	ACCOMMODATION	GARFIELD, CO	4047	24658	SPECIAL TRADE CONTRACTORS
AMADOR, CA	2092	13582	ACCOMMODATION	GILPIN, CO	219	5193	AMUSEMENT; GAMBLING;& RECREAT.
BUTTE, CA	10391	80521	EDUCATIONAL SERVICES	GRAND, CO	1502	9501	ACCOMMODATION
CALAVERAS, CA	2192	11109	EDUCATIONAL SERVICES	GUNNISON, CO	1227	9096	ACCOMMODATION
COLUSA, CA	915	6985	TRUCK TRANSPORTATION	HINSDALE, CO	137	412	ACCOMMODATION
CONTRA COSTA, CA	39140	313296	EDUCATIONAL SERVICES	HUERFANO, CO	440	2455	NURSING & RESID. CARE FACILIT.
DEL NORTE, CA	1042	7342	EDUCATIONAL SERVICES	JACKSON, CO	143	535	EDUCATIONAL SERVICES
EL DORADO, CA	8500	59694	INSURANCE CARRIERS & RELATED	JEFFERSON, CO	20434	200082	PROF.; SCIENTIFIC; & TECH SVCS
FRESNO, CA	31635	291939	EDUCATIONAL SERVICES	KIOWA, CO	144	562	EDUCATIONAL SERVICES
GLENN, CA	1136	8320	EDUCATIONAL SERVICES	KIT CARSON, CO	525	2830	EDUCATIONAL SERVICES
HUMBOLDT, CA	6624	48155	EDUCATIONAL SERVICES	LAKE, CO	400	1833	EDUCATIONAL SERVICES
IMPERIAL, CA	4906	49955	EDUCATIONAL SERVICES	LA PLATA, CO	4504	30278	ACCOMMODATION
INYO, CA	1126	8800	EXEC.; LEGIS.; & OTHER SUPPORT	LARIMER, CO	13407	127654	EDUCATIONAL SERVICES
KERN, CA	22214	251072	NAT'L SECURITY & INT'L AFFAIRS	LAS ANIMAS, CO	835	5568	EDUCATIONAL SERVICES
KINGS, CA	3065	45308	NAT'L SECURITY & INT'L AFFAIRS	LINCOLN, CO	350	2048	JUSTICE; PUBIC ORDER/SAFETY
LAKE, CA	3215	18257	EDUCATIONAL SERVICES	LOGAN, CO	1120	7734	JUSTICE; PUBIC ORDER/SAFETY
LASSEN, CA	1232	7775	EDUCATIONAL SERVICES	MESA, CO	6371	61962	AMBULATORY HEALTH CARE SVCS
LOS ANGELES, CA	405093	3638463	EDUCATIONAL SERVICES	MINERAL, CO	137	412	ACCOMMODATION
MADERA, CA	4206	38591	EDUCATIONAL SERVICES	MOFFAT, CO	703	4608	UTILITIES
MARIN, CA	19693	108166	PROF.; SCIENTIFIC; & TECH SVCS	MONTEZUMA, CO	1645	12488	BROADCASTING
MARIPOSA, CA	916	4582	ACCOMMODATION	MONTROSE, CO	2309	14956	FOOD AND BEVERAGE STORES
MENDOCINO, CA	5619	35018	EDUCATIONAL SERVICES	MORGAN, CO	1312	11133	FOOD MANUFACTURING
MERCED, CA	6071	64533	EDUCATIONAL SERVICES	OTERO, CO	1086	7156	EDUCATIONAL SERVICES
MODOC, CA	581	3303	EXEC.; LEGIS.; & OTHER SUPPORT	OURAY, CO	464	1772	ACCOMMODATION
MONO, CA	1086	9961	ACCOMMODATION	PARK, CO	801	3123	ACCOMMODATION
MONTEREY, CA	17272	148015	EDUCATIONAL SERVICES	PHILLIPS, CO	352	1776	EDUCATIONAL SERVICES
NAPA, CA	8045	68379	ACCOMMODATION	PITKIN, CO	2741	19184	FOOD SVCS & DRINKING PLACES
NEVADA, CA	7228	38312	ACCOMMODATION	PROWERS, CO	871	5697	TRANSPORTATION EQUIPMENT MFG
ORANGE, CA	144053	1343259	PROF.; SCIENTIFIC; & TECH SVCS	PUEBLO, CO	5893	60084	HOSPITALS
PLACER, CA	15364	137814	FOOD SVCS & DRINKING PLACES	RIO BLANCO, CO	436	3197	MINING (EXCEPT OIL AND GAS)
PLUMAS, CA	1573	8792	EXEC.; LEGIS.; & OTHER SUPPORT	RIO GRANDE, CO	732	4533	EXEC.; LEGIS.; & OTHER SUPPORT
RIVERSIDE, CA	58116	556016	EDUCATIONAL SERVICES	ROUTT, CO	1888	16533	ACCOMMODATION
SACRAMENTO, CA	52693	534636	PROF.; SCIENTIFIC; & TECH SVCS	SAGUACHE, CO	399	1769	EDUCATIONAL SERVICES
SAN BENITO, CA	2007	15980	MERCH. WHOLESALERS;NONDUR. GDS	SAN JUAN, CO	149	424	FOOD SVCS & DRINKING PLACES
SAN BERNARDINO, CA	62177	583361	EDUCATIONAL SERVICES	SAN MIGUEL, CO	1000	5447	ACCOMMODATION
SAN DIEGO, CA	125591	1264381	PROF.; SCIENTIFIC; & TECH SVCS	SEDGWICK, CO	176	994	FOOD MANUFACTURING
SAN FRANCISCO, CA	48776	554893	PROF.; SCIENTIFIC; & TECH SVCS	SUMMIT, CO	2504	23747	ACCOMMODATION
SAN JOAQUIN, CA	19328	203055	EDUCATIONAL SERVICES	TELLER, CO	977	7306	AMUSEMENT; GAMBLING;& RECREAT.
SAN LUIS OBISPO, CA	15830	105397	FOOD SVCS & DRINKING PLACES	WASHINGTON, CO	277	1302	EDUCATIONAL SERVICES
SAN MATEO, CA	32175	303476	PROF.; SCIENTIFIC; & TECH SVCS	WELD, CO	8410	78692	EDUCATIONAL SERVICES
SANTA BARBARA, CA	18451	171285	EDUCATIONAL SERVICES	YUMA, CO	751	3639	EDUCATIONAL SERVICES
SANTA CLARA, CA	69286	812054	COMPUTER & ELECTRONIC PROD MFG	FAIRFIELD, CT	48649	404016	PROF.; SCIENTIFIC; & TECH SVCS
SANTA CRUZ, CA	13678	106330	EDUCATIONAL SERVICES	HARTFORD, CT	41789	486071	INSURANCE CARRIERS & RELATED
SHASTA, CA	9760	65440	EDUCATIONAL SERVICES	LITCHFIELD, CT	9889	68704	EDUCATIONAL SERVICES
SIERRA, CA	217	924	JUSTICE; PUBIC ORDER/SAFETY	MIDDLESEX, CT	8678	69072	EDUCATIONAL SERVICES
SISKIYOU, CA	2818	15700	EDUCATIONAL SERVICES	NEW HAVEN, CT	36598	361559	EDUCATIONAL SERVICES
SOLANO, CA	14954	121307	FOOD SVCS & DRINKING PLACES	NEW LONDON, CT	11604	108633	ACCOMMODATION
SONOMA, CA	24556	186353	EDUCATIONAL SERVICES	TOLLAND, CT	4878	41044	EDUCATIONAL SERVICES
STANISLAUS, CA	17492	168460	EDUCATIONAL SERVICES	WINDHAM, CT	4323	46824	EDUCATIONAL SERVICES
SUTTER, CA	3279	29117	EDUCATIONAL SERVICES	KENT, DE	5688	60670	NAT'L SECURITY & INT'L AFFAIRS
TEHAMA, CA	2316	19196	MERCH. WHOLESALERS;DURABLE GDS	NEW CASTLE, DE	21416	248878	PROF.; SCIENTIFIC; & TECH SVCS
TRINITY, CA	673	3917	EDUCATIONAL SERVICES	SUSSEX, DE	8911	73597	FOOD SVCS & DRINKING PLACES
TULARE, CA	12255	128676	MERCH. WHOLESALERS;NONDUR. GDS	DISTRICT OF COLUMBIA, DC	38495	572737	PROF.; SCIENTIFIC; & TECH SVCS
TUOLUMNE, CA	2931	21157	JUSTICE; PUBIC ORDER/SAFETY	ALACHUA, FL	9611	131294	EDUCATIONAL SERVICES
VENTURA, CA	32733	304016	PROF.; SCIENTIFIC; & TECH SVCS	BAKER, FL	724	7524	HOSPITALS

COUNTY	2007 Total Firms	2007 Total Employees	TOP INDUSTRY RANKED on 2007 EMPLOYMENT	COUNTY	2007 Total Firms	2007 Total Employees	TOP INDUSTRY RANKED on 2007 EMPLOYMENT
BAY, FL	7901	76352	FOOD SVCS & DRINKING PLACES	BULLOCH, GA	2623	19430	FOOD SVCS & DRINKING PLACES
BRADFORD, FL	987	7823	JUSTICE; PUBIC ORDER/SAFETY	BURKE, GA	747	6352	PROF.; SCIENTIFIC; & TECH SVCS
BREVARD, FL	22083	196505	FOOD SVCS & DRINKING PLACES	BUTTS, GA	681	5471	EXEC.; LEGIS.; & OTHER SUPPORT
BROWARD, FL	81702	722385	PROF.; SCIENTIFIC; & TECH SVCS	CALHOUN, GA	218	1411	APPAREL MANUFACTURING
CALHOUN, FL	540	3999	JUSTICE; PUBIC ORDER/SAFETY	CAMDEN, GA	1851	21697	NAT'L SECURITY & INT'L AFFAIRS
CHARLOTTE, FL	6671	50617	AMBULATORY HEALTH CARE SVCS	CANDLER, GA	413	2873	FOOD SVCS & DRINKING PLACES
CITRUS, FL	6148	34606	FOOD SVCS & DRINKING PLACES	CARROLL, GA	3999	34414	MERCH. WHOLESALERS;DURABLE GDS
CLAY, FL	5443	44539	FOOD SVCS & DRINKING PLACES	CATOOSA, GA	1765	16316	HOSPITALS
COLLIER, FL	19427	134470	FOOD SVCS & DRINKING PLACES	CHARLTON, GA	352	2124	EDUCATIONAL SERVICES
COLUMBIA, FL	2390	22117	HOSPITALS	CHATHAM, GA	11519	128674	FOOD SVCS & DRINKING PLACES
DESOTO, FL	1021	9504	HOSPITALS	CHATTAHOOCHEE, GA	240	35291	NAT'L SECURITY & INT'L AFFAIRS
DIXIE, FL	388	2837	JUSTICE; PUBIC ORDER/SAFETY	CHATTOOGA, GA	669	6303	EDUCATIONAL SERVICES
DUVAL, FL	32950	412169	HOSPITALS	CHEROKEE, GA	7098	44400	EDUCATIONAL SERVICES
ESCAMBIA, FL	11980	159475	NAT'L SECURITY & INT'L AFFAIRS	CLARKE, GA	4554	67085	EDUCATIONAL SERVICES
FLAGLER, FL	2780	20468	FOOD SVCS & DRINKING PLACES	CLAY, GA	120	848	CONSTRUCTION OF BUILDINGS
FRANKLIN, FL	912	3755	REAL ESTATE	CLAYTON, GA	8534	79120	FOOD SVCS & DRINKING PLACES
GADSDEN, FL	1323	17094	HOSPITALS	CLINCH, GA	242	2457	FABRICATED METAL PRODUCT MFG
GILCHRIST, FL	403	2634	EDUCATIONAL SERVICES	COBB, GA	29084	270371	PROF.; SCIENTIFIC; & TECH SVCS
GLADES, FL	254	1573	ADMINISTRATIVE & SUPPORT SVCS	COFFEE, GA	1511	14951	MERCH. WHOLESALERS;NONDUR. GDS
GULF, FL	888	5119	JUSTICE; PUBIC ORDER/SAFETY	COLQUITT, GA	1527	15784	APPAREL MANUFACTURING
HAMILTON, FL	395	3817	CHEMICAL MANUFACTURING	COLUMBIA, GA	3856	27854	EDUCATIONAL SERVICES
HARDEE, FL	851	6764	EDUCATIONAL SERVICES	COOK, GA	592	4309	FOOD SVCS & DRINKING PLACES
HENDRY, FL	1377	12747	SUPPORT ACTIVITIES: AGR./FOR.	COWETA, GA	3486	28755	FOOD SVCS & DRINKING PLACES
HERNANDO, FL	5480	40319	GENERAL MERCHANDISE STORES	CRAWFORD, GA	259	1271	EDUCATIONAL SERVICES
HIGHLANDS, FL	4297	29259	FOOD SVCS & DRINKING PLACES	CRISP, GA	953	9415	HOSPITALS
HILLSBOROUGH, FL	44345	502176	PROF.; SCIENTIFIC; & TECH SVCS	DADE, GA	520	4612	MOTOR VEHICLE & PARTS DEALERS
HOLMES, FL	554	3441	JUSTICE; PUBIC ORDER/SAFETY	DAWSON, GA	1054	5646	FOOD SVCS & DRINKING PLACES
INDIAN RIVER, FL	7826	52309	FOOD SVCS & DRINKING PLACES	DECATUR, GA	1161	10945	PAPER MANUFACTURING
JACKSON, FL	1897	14448	EDUCATIONAL SERVICES	DEKALB, GA	27885	313867	EDUCATIONAL SERVICES
JEFFERSON, FL	633	3076	JUSTICE; PUBIC ORDER/SAFETY	DODGE, GA	654	5419	EDUCATIONAL SERVICES
LAFAYETTE, FL	192	1914	JUSTICE; PUBIC ORDER/SAFETY	DOOLY, GA	518	3808	FOOD MANUFACTURING
LAKE, FL	13364	86331	FOOD SVCS & DRINKING PLACES	DOUGHERTY, GA	4211	52253	EDUCATIONAL SERVICES
LEE, FL	27455	227874	SPECIAL TRADE CONTRACTORS	DOUGLAS, GA	4308	33969	FOOD SVCS & DRINKING PLACES
LEON, FL	11481	140048	EXEC.; LEGIS.; & OTHER SUPPORT	EARLY, GA	568	3683	PAPER MANUFACTURING
LEVY, FL	1527	8870	EDUCATIONAL SERVICES	ECHOLS, GA	51	472	FOOD AND BEVERAGE STORES
LIBERTY, FL	279	2853	MERCH. WHOLESALERS;DURABLE GDS	EFFINGHAM, GA	1231	9441	TEXTILE MILLS
MADISON, FL	756	5287	EDUCATIONAL SERVICES	ELBERT, GA	918	8202	FOOD AND BEVERAGE STORES
MANATEE, FL	12196	101312	FOOD SVCS & DRINKING PLACES	EMANUEL, GA	866	7768	MERCH. WHOLESALERS;NONDUR. GDS
MARION, FL	13273	111218	FOOD SVCS & DRINKING PLACES	EVANS, GA	408	4083	FOOD MANUFACTURING
MARTIN, FL	8785	59739	FOOD SVCS & DRINKING PLACES	FANNIN, GA	1321	6332	EDUCATIONAL SERVICES
MIAMI-DADE, FL	103164	927576	PROF.; SCIENTIFIC; & TECH SVCS	FAYETTE, GA	4904	39843	COMPUTER & ELECTRONIC PROD MFG
MONROE, FL	6112	45416	ACCOMMODATION	FLOYD, GA	3270	39794	HOSPITALS
NASSAU, FL	2823	19478	FOOD SVCS & DRINKING PLACES	FORSYTH, GA	6324	52103	EDUCATIONAL SERVICES
OKALOOSA, FL	8778	79922	FOOD SVCS & DRINKING PLACES	FRANKLIN, GA	906	8076	TEXTILE MILLS
OKEECHOBEE, FL	1704	11773	JUSTICE; PUBIC ORDER/SAFETY	FULTON, GA	51788	634231	PROF.; SCIENTIFIC; & TECH SVCS
ORANGE, FL	52087	630260	ACCOMMODATION	GILMER, GA	1783	9582	FOOD MANUFACTURING
OSCEOLA, FL	9829	75521	ACCOMMODATION	GLASCOCK, GA	93	348	SOCIAL ASSISTANCE
PALM BEACH, FL	66818	536745	FOOD SVCS & DRINKING PLACES	GLYNN, GA	4292	43886	JUSTICE; PUBIC ORDER/SAFETY
PASCO, FL	14560	101644	EDUCATIONAL SERVICES	GORDON, GA	1916	20799	TEXTILE PRODUCT MILLS
PINELLAS, FL	38105	413796	FOOD SVCS & DRINKING PLACES	GRADY, GA	848	7275	BLDG MATL & GARDEN EQPMT DLRS
POLK, FL	17820	194503	EDUCATIONAL SERVICES	GREENE, GA	671	5085	ACCOMMODATION
PUTNAM, FL	2456	18931	BLDG MATL & GARDEN EQPMT DLRS	GWINNETT, GA	30271	303620	MERCH. WHOLESALERS;DURABLE GDS
ST. JOHNS, FL	7283	57603	FOOD SVCS & DRINKING PLACES	HABERSHAM, GA	1761	14589	EDUCATIONAL SERVICES
ST. LUCIE, FL	10176	72953	EXEC.; LEGIS.; & OTHER SUPPORT	HALL, GA	6813	65666	FOOD MANUFACTURING
SANTA ROSA, FL	4989	33223	FOOD SVCS & DRINKING PLACES	HANCOCK, GA	241	1246	EDUCATIONAL SERVICES
SARASOTA, FL	22106	162952	AMBULATORY HEALTH CARE SVCS	HARALSON, GA	994	7473	ADMINISTRATIVE & SUPPORT SVCS
SEMINOLE, FL	20535	165462	FOOD SVCS & DRINKING PLACES	HARRIS, GA	737	5695	FOOD MANUFACTURING
SUMTER, FL	1840	15866	JUSTICE; PUBIC ORDER/SAFETY	HART, GA	943	6781	APPAREL MANUFACTURING
SUWANNEE, FL	1273	10709	FOOD MANUFACTURING	HEARD, GA	233	1548	EDUCATIONAL SERVICES
TAYLOR, FL	869	7451	PAPER MANUFACTURING	HENRY, GA	5618	38643	FOOD SVCS & DRINKING PLACES
UNION, FL	266	6118	JUSTICE; PUBIC ORDER/SAFETY	HOUSTON, GA	4063	58809	NAT'L SECURITY & INT'L AFFAIRS
VOLUSIA, FL	21533	177005	FOOD SVCS & DRINKING PLACES	IRWIN, GA	250	2270	EDUCATIONAL SERVICES
WAKULLA, FL	881	5474	JUSTICE; PUBIC ORDER/SAFETY	JACKSON, GA	1819	17310	FOOD MANUFACTURING
WALTON, FL	2948	22348	FOOD SVCS & DRINKING PLACES	JASPER, GA	353	2686	EDUCATIONAL SERVICES
WASHINGTON, FL	771	6402	REPAIR AND MAINTENANCE	JEFF DAVIS, GA	489	4622	TEXTILE MILLS
APPLING, GA	698	5340	AMBULATORY HEALTH CARE SVCS	JEFFERSON, GA	692	5315	EDUCATIONAL SERVICES
ATKINSON, GA	249	1910	MISCELLANEOUS STORE RETAILERS	JENKINS, GA	269	2906	WOOD PRODUCT MANUFACTURING
BACON, GA	523	3941	TEXTILE MILLS	JOHNSON, GA	258	1591	RELIG.; GRANT; CIVIC; PROF ORG
BAKER, GA	64	404	EXEC.; LEGIS.; & OTHER SUPPORT	JONES, GA	639	3360	EDUCATIONAL SERVICES
BALDWIN, GA	1599	16852	JUSTICE; PUBIC ORDER/SAFETY	LAMAR, GA	499	3523	EDUCATIONAL SERVICES
BANKS, GA	564	4645	FOOD SVCS & DRINKING PLACES	LANIER, GA	195	1267	EDUCATIONAL SERVICES
BARROW, GA	1816	16579	EDUCATIONAL SERVICES	LAURENS, GA	2043	20569	EDUCATIONAL SERVICES
BARTOW, GA	3727	30529	EDUCATIONAL SERVICES	LEE, GA	677	6018	EDUCATIONAL SERVICES
BEN HILL, GA	716	8689	TRANSPORTATION EQUIPMENT MFG	LIBERTY, GA	1659	35251	NAT'L SECURITY & INT'L AFFAIRS
BERRIEN, GA	537	4243	TEXTILE MILLS	LINCOLN, GA	287	1400	EDUCATIONAL SERVICES
BIBB, GA	7824	82398	EDUCATIONAL SERVICES	LONG, GA	155	704	EDUCATIONAL SERVICES
BLECKLEY, GA	363	3609	ELECT'L EQPMT; APP; & COMP MFG	LOWNDES, GA	4447	45738	FOOD SVCS & DRINKING PLACES
BRANTLEY, GA	443	2460	EDUCATIONAL SERVICES	LUMPKIN, GA	1108	6098	EDUCATIONAL SERVICES
BROOKS, GA	397	3094	EDUCATIONAL SERVICES	MCDUFFIE, GA	864	8104	MOTOR VEHICLE & PARTS DEALERS
BRYAN, GA	1066	6076	EDUCATIONAL SERVICES	MCINTOSH, GA	531	2604	EDUCATIONAL SERVICES

BUSINESS DATA

COUNTY	2007 Total Firms	2007 Total Employees	TOP INDUSTRY RANKED on 2007 EMPLOYMENT	COUNTY	2007 Total Firms	2007 Total Employees	TOP INDUSTRY RANKED on 2007 EMPLOYMENT
MACON, GA	450	3335	FOOD MANUFACTURING	BUTTE, ID	164	647	AMBULATORY HEALTH CARE SVCS
MADISON, GA	637	4038	EDUCATIONAL SERVICES	CAMAS, ID	63	273	REPAIR AND MAINTENANCE
MARION, GA	178	2659	MERCH. WHOLESALERS;NONDUR. GDS	CANYON, ID	5173	51885	EDUCATIONAL SERVICES
MERIWETHER, GA	732	5023	EDUCATIONAL SERVICES	CARIBOU, ID	346	2761	CHEMICAL MANUFACTURING
MILLER, GA	250	1448	HOSPITALS	CASSIA, ID	1127	9461	MERCH. WHOLESALERS;NONDUR. GDS
MITCHELL, GA	617	9000	FOOD MANUFACTURING	CLARK, ID	75	625	FOOD MANUFACTURING
MONROE, GA	884	5725	EDUCATIONAL SERVICES	CLEARWATER, ID	468	2955	JUSTICE; PUBIC ORDER/SAFETY
MONTGOMERY, GA	229	1669	EDUCATIONAL SERVICES	CUSTER, ID	444	1716	ACCOMMODATION
MORGAN, GA	793	5925	FOOD SVCS & DRINKING PLACES	ELMORE, ID	825	11099	NAT'L SECURITY & INT'L AFFAIRS
MURRAY, GA	933	10263	TEXTILE PRODUCT MILLS	FRANKLIN, ID	361	2581	EDUCATIONAL SERVICES
MUSCOGEE, GA	7264	92533	HOSPITALS	FREMONT, ID	689	4103	EDUCATIONAL SERVICES
NEWTON, GA	2773	23344	EDUCATIONAL SERVICES	GEM, ID	566	3322	EDUCATIONAL SERVICES
OCONEE, GA	1164	9230	EDUCATIONAL SERVICES	GOODING, ID	618	4323	ANIMAL PRODUCTION
OGLETHORPE, GA	298	1509	EDUCATIONAL SERVICES	IDAHO, ID	806	4358	EDUCATIONAL SERVICES
PAULDING, GA	2791	16545	EDUCATIONAL SERVICES	JEFFERSON, ID	694	5420	MERCH. WHOLESALERS;NONDUR. GDS
PEACH, GA	931	8243	TRANSPORTATION EQUIPMENT MFG	JEROME, ID	800	7593	FOOD AND BEVERAGE STORES
PICKENS, GA	1404	8213	FOOD SVCS & DRINKING PLACES	KOOTENAI, ID	6571	51965	FOOD SVCS & DRINKING PLACES
PIERCE, GA	571	3751	EDUCATIONAL SERVICES	LATAH, ID	1357	10410	FOOD SVCS & DRINKING PLACES
PIKE, GA	412	2081	EDUCATIONAL SERVICES	LEMHI, ID	540	2763	SUPPORT ACTIVITIES: AGR./FOR.
POLK, GA	1174	9809	FOOD MANUFACTURING	LEWIS, ID	308	1586	EDUCATIONAL SERVICES
PULASKI, GA	397	2960	JUSTICE; PUBIC ORDER/SAFETY	LINCOLN, ID	166	1409	HEAVY & CIVIL ENG. CONSTRUCT'N
PUTNAM, GA	815	6806	WOOD PRODUCT MANUFACTURING	MADISON, ID	1015	9413	PROF.; SCIENTIFIC; & TECH SVCS
QUITMAN, GA	84	441	EDUCATIONAL SERVICES	MINIDOKA, ID	896	6639	FOOD MANUFACTURING
RABUN, GA	903	6475	ACCOMMODATION	NEZ PERCE, ID	1797	18786	EDUCATIONAL SERVICES
RANDOLPH, GA	345	1961	EDUCATIONAL SERVICES	ONEIDA, ID	184	928	HOSPITALS
RICHMOND, GA	8599	95432	EDUCATIONAL SERVICES	OWYHEE, ID	359	2193	EDUCATIONAL SERVICES
ROCKDALE, GA	3522	34225	FOOD SVCS & DRINKING PLACES	PAYETTE, ID	844	5232	WOOD PRODUCT MANUFACTURING
SCHLEY, GA	135	1321	WOOD PRODUCT MANUFACTURING	POWER, ID	361	2830	FOOD MANUFACTURING
SCREVEN, GA	648	4130	TEXTILE MILLS	SHOSHONE, ID	665	4637	ACCOMMODATION
SEMINOLE, GA	392	2738	EDUCATIONAL SERVICES	TETON, ID	561	2252	SPECIAL TRADE CONTRACTORS
SPALDING, GA	2223	20308	EDUCATIONAL SERVICES	TWIN FALLS, ID	3573	34634	HOSPITALS
STEPHENS, GA	995	10181	TEXTILE MILLS	VALLEY, ID	983	4472	SUPPORT ACTIVITIES: AGR./FOR.
STEWART, GA	190	881	EDUCATIONAL SERVICES	WASHINGTON, ID	444	2771	FOOD AND BEVERAGE STORES
SUMTER, GA	1410	13978	EDUCATIONAL SERVICES	ADAMS, IL	3084	31211	EDUCATIONAL SERVICES
TALBOT, GA	136	895	ADMIN. HUMAN RESOURCE PROGRAMS	ALEXANDER, IL	360	2219	EDUCATIONAL SERVICES
TALIAFERRO, GA	75	358	EDUCATIONAL SERVICES	BOND, IL	560	4224	EXEC.; LEGIS.; & OTHER SUPPORT
TATTNALL, GA	627	6600	CROP PRODUCTION	BOONE, IL	1382	15201	TRANSPORTATION EQUIPMENT MFG
TAYLOR, GA	317	2077	EXEC.; LEGIS.; & OTHER SUPPORT	BROWN, IL	221	3349	MERCH. WHOLESALERS;NONDUR. GDS
TELFAIR, GA	466	4177	MACHINERY MANUFACTURING	BUREAU, IL	1484	12346	EDUCATIONAL SERVICES
TERRELL, GA	409	2525	EDUCATIONAL SERVICES	CALHOUN, IL	213	1009	FOOD SVCS & DRINKING PLACES
THOMAS, GA	2134	24261	HOSPITALS	CARROLL, IL	910	6373	NAT'L SECURITY & INT'L AFFAIRS
TIFT, GA	1873	21719	GENERAL MERCHANDISE STORES	CASS, IL	587	5744	FOOD MANUFACTURING
TOOMBS, GA	1283	11908	EDUCATIONAL SERVICES	CHAMPAIGN, IL	6743	111078	EDUCATIONAL SERVICES
TOWNS, GA	708	3447	ACCOMMODATION	CHRISTIAN, IL	1391	10972	EDUCATIONAL SERVICES
TREUTLEN, GA	206	1126	EDUCATIONAL SERVICES	CLARK, IL	707	5048	COMPUTER & ELECTRONIC PROD MFG
TROUP, GA	2491	31649	EDUCATIONAL SERVICES	CLAY, IL	661	4497	EDUCATIONAL SERVICES
TURNER, GA	360	3402	ADMINISTRATIVE & SUPPORT SVCS	CLINTON, IL	1298	12096	JUSTICE; PUBIC ORDER/SAFETY
TWIGGS, GA	246	1896	NONMETALLIC MINERAL PROD. MFG	COLES, IL	2153	32187	EDUCATIONAL SERVICES
UNION, GA	1199	5834	EDUCATIONAL SERVICES	COOK, IL	195114	2275185	PROF.; SCIENTIFIC; & TECH SVCS
UPSON, GA	907	9594	MERCH. WHOLESALERS;DURABLE GDS	CRAWFORD, IL	769	7042	EDUCATIONAL SERVICES
WALKER, GA	1846	16176	TEXTILE MILLS	CUMBERLAND, IL	377	2193	EDUCATIONAL SERVICES
WALTON, GA	2509	17021	EDUCATIONAL SERVICES	DEKALB, IL	3398	32948	EDUCATIONAL SERVICES
WARE, GA	1590	16800	WOOD PRODUCT MANUFACTURING	DE WITT, IL	697	5294	UTILITIES
WARREN, GA	221	1330	MERCH. WHOLESALERS;DURABLE GDS	DOUGLAS, IL	955	6707	FOOD SVCS & DRINKING PLACES
WASHINGTON, GA	739	8819	MINING (EXCEPT OIL AND GAS)	DUPAGE, IL	44391	529813	PROF.; SCIENTIFIC; & TECH SVCS
WAYNE, GA	958	8536	MERCH. WHOLESALERS;DURABLE GDS	EDGAR, IL	821	7471	BLDG MATL & GARDEN EQPMT DLRS
WEBSTER, GA	63	369	BLDG MATL & GARDEN EQPMT DLRS	EDWARDS, IL	290	2313	TRANSPORTATION EQUIPMENT MFG
WHEELER, GA	182	1258	JUSTICE; PUBIC ORDER/SAFETY	EFFINGHAM, IL	1961	21292	FOOD SVCS & DRINKING PLACES
WHITE, GA	1314	7446	ACCOMMODATION	FAYETTE, IL	803	7632	EDUCATIONAL SERVICES
WHITFIELD, GA	4296	49045	TEXTILE PRODUCT MILLS	FORD, IL	702	5233	NURSING & RESID. CARE FACILIT.
WILCOX, GA	203	1285	JUSTICE; PUBIC ORDER/SAFETY	FRANKLIN, IL	1522	10486	EDUCATIONAL SERVICES
WILKES, GA	452	3157	AMBULATORY HEALTH CARE SVCS	FULTON, IL	1312	8911	EDUCATIONAL SERVICES
WILKINSON, GA	367	4009	MINING (EXCEPT OIL AND GAS)	GALLATIN, IL	249	1551	MERCH. WHOLESALERS;NONDUR. GDS
WORTH, GA	493	3290	EDUCATIONAL SERVICES	GREENE, IL	509	2762	EDUCATIONAL SERVICES
HAWAII, HI	8694	63756	ACCOMMODATION	GRUNDY, IL	1952	15025	EDUCATIONAL SERVICES
HONOLULU, HI	32102	372617	FOOD SVCS & DRINKING PLACES	HAMILTON, IL	347	1694	HOSPITALS
KALAWAO, HI	6	54	EXEC.; LEGIS.; & OTHER SUPPORT	HANCOCK, IL	897	5960	ELECT'L EQPMT; APP; & COMP MFG
KAUAI, HI	3685	30750	ACCOMMODATION	HARDIN, IL	186	1041	EXEC.; LEGIS.; & OTHER SUPPORT
MAUI, HI	7908	74773	ACCOMMODATION	HENDERSON, IL	289	1561	EDUCATIONAL SERVICES
ADA, ID	16157	198308	PROF.; SCIENTIFIC; & TECH SVCS	HENRY, IL	2218	17113	EDUCATIONAL SERVICES
ADAMS, ID	237	1051	SUPPORT ACTIVITIES: AGR./FOR.	IROQUOIS, IL	1493	9582	EDUCATIONAL SERVICES
BANNOCK, ID	3176	31753	EDUCATIONAL SERVICES	JACKSON, IL	2353	32450	EDUCATIONAL SERVICES
BEAR LAKE, ID	259	1488	HOSPITALS	JASPER, IL	406	2546	EDUCATIONAL SERVICES
BENEWAH, ID	416	3131	MERCH. WHOLESALERS;NONDUR. GDS	JEFFERSON, IL	1781	19712	MOTOR VEHICLE & PARTS DEALERS
BINGHAM, ID	1337	12967	FOOD MANUFACTURING	JERSEY, IL	767	5641	FOOD SVCS & DRINKING PLACES
BLAINE, ID	1970	12541	ACCOMMODATION	JO DAVIESS, IL	1379	10244	ACCOMMODATION
BOISE, ID	303	1345	EDUCATIONAL SERVICES	JOHNSON, IL	432	3252	JUSTICE; PUBIC ORDER/SAFETY
BONNER, ID	2272	14300	ACCOMMODATION	KANE, IL	15941	180743	EDUCATIONAL SERVICES
BONNEVILLE, ID	4311	41941	AMBULATORY HEALTH CARE SVCS	KANKAKEE, IL	4286	46996	EDUCATIONAL SERVICES
BOUNDARY, ID	525	3584	MERCH. WHOLESALERS;NONDUR. GDS	KENDALL, IL	2296	16990	EDUCATIONAL SERVICES

COUNTY	2007 Total Firms	2007 Total Employees	TOP INDUSTRY RANKED on 2007 EMPLOYMENT	COUNTY	2007 Total Firms	2007 Total Employees	TOP INDUSTRY RANKED on 2007 EMPLOYMENT
KNOX, IL	2083	22608	MISCELLANEOUS MANUFACTURING	GIBSON, IN	1322	14838	TRANSPORTATION EQUIPMENT MFG
LAKE, IL	26185	318488	EDUCATIONAL SERVICES	GRANT, IN	2409	27734	EDUCATIONAL SERVICES
LA SALLE, IL	4818	47016	EDUCATIONAL SERVICES	GREENE, IN	1065	7045	EDUCATIONAL SERVICES
LAWRENCE, IL	533	5190	INSURANCE CARRIERS & RELATED	HAMILTON, IN	9005	102227	INSURANCE CARRIERS & RELATED
LEE, IL	1381	13820	HOSPITALS	HANCOCK, IN	1896	18322	FOOD SVCS & DRINKING PLACES
LIVINGSTON, IL	1596	15161	PRINT'G & RELATED SUPP'T ACT'S	HARRISON, IN	1075	9006	EDUCATIONAL SERVICES
LOGAN, IL	1177	9663	EDUCATIONAL SERVICES	HENDRICKS, IN	3633	37611	FOOD SVCS & DRINKING PLACES
MCDONOUGH, IL	1278	12877	UNCLASSIFIED ESTABLISHMENTS	HENRY, IN	1550	14575	TRANSPORTATION EQUIPMENT MFG
MCHENRY, IL	11799	106414	HOSPITALS	HOWARD, IN	2940	39334	COMPUTER & ELECTRONIC PROD MFG
MCLEAN, IL	5482	89423	INSURANCE CARRIERS & RELATED	HUNTINGTON, IN	1276	14329	COMPUTER & ELECTRONIC PROD MFG
MACON, IL	4405	53166	AMBULATORY HEALTH CARE SVCS	JACKSON, IN	1623	21657	TRANSPORTATION EQUIPMENT MFG
MACOUPIN, IL	1826	14036	EDUCATIONAL SERVICES	JASPER, IN	1252	9305	FOOD SVCS & DRINKING PLACES
MADISON, IL	9049	92069	EDUCATIONAL SERVICES	JAY, IN	726	6649	FOOD SVCS & DRINKING PLACES
MARION, IL	1759	15941	EDUCATIONAL SERVICES	JEFFERSON, IN	1325	15072	TRANSPORTATION EQUIPMENT MFG
MARSHALL, IL	500	4342	FOOD MANUFACTURING	JENNINGS, IN	859	8455	BLDG MATL & GARDEN EQPMT DLRS
MASON, IL	621	3767	EDUCATIONAL SERVICES	JOHNSON, IN	4556	41948	FOOD SVCS & DRINKING PLACES
MASSAC, IL	561	5427	AMUSEMENT; GAMBLING;& RECREAT.	KNOX, IN	1523	17249	EDUCATIONAL SERVICES
MENARD, IL	445	2536	EDUCATIONAL SERVICES	KOSCIUSKO, IN	3217	36908	MISCELLANEOUS MANUFACTURING
MERCER, IL	670	3381	EDUCATIONAL SERVICES	LAGRANGE, IN	1133	11782	TRANSPORTATION EQUIPMENT MFG
MONROE, IL	1216	8436	FOOD SVCS & DRINKING PLACES	LAKE, IN	15426	183009	FOOD SVCS & DRINKING PLACES
MONTGOMERY, IL	1341	10955	FOOD SVCS & DRINKING PLACES	LAPORTE, IN	3924	46955	FOOD SVCS & DRINKING PLACES
MORGAN, IL	1476	17775	EDUCATIONAL SERVICES	LAWRENCE, IN	1550	15497	MERCH. WHOLESALERS;DURABLE GDS
MOULTRIE, IL	628	4844	FURNITURE & RELATED PROD. MFG	MADISON, IN	4016	44674	FOOD SVCS & DRINKING PLACES
OGLE, IL	1982	17288	EDUCATIONAL SERVICES	MARION, IN	34644	506614	EDUCATIONAL SERVICES
PEORIA, IL	7519	99421	HOSPITALS	MARSHALL, IN	1789	20051	EDUCATIONAL SERVICES
PERRY, IL	732	6804	JUSTICE; PUBIC ORDER/SAFETY	MARTIN, IN	485	8787	NAT'L SECURITY & INT'L AFFAIRS
PIATT, IL	649	3697	EDUCATIONAL SERVICES	MIAMI, IN	1046	10045	MERCH. WHOLESALERS;DURABLE GDS
PIKE, IL	735	4648	EDUCATIONAL SERVICES	MONROE, IN	4506	55217	FOOD SVCS & DRINKING PLACES
POPE, IL	155	982	SOCIAL ASSISTANCE	MONTGOMERY, IN	1429	15849	PRINT'G & RELATED SUPP'T ACT'S
PULASKI, IL	278	2283	EDUCATIONAL SERVICES	MORGAN, IN	1985	16661	FOOD SVCS & DRINKING PLACES
PUTNAM, IL	234	1609	SPECIAL TRADE CONTRACTORS	NEWTON, IN	531	3658	PLASTICS & RUBBER PRODUCTS MFG
RANDOLPH, IL	1288	11818	JUSTICE; PUBIC ORDER/SAFETY	NOBLE, IN	1473	19817	TRANSPORTATION EQUIPMENT MFG
RICHLAND, IL	780	6404	MERCH. WHOLESALERS;DURABLE GDS	OHIO, IN	219	783	EDUCATIONAL SERVICES
ROCK ISLAND, IL	6383	77461	MACHINERY MANUFACTURING	ORANGE, IN	780	6851	FURNITURE & RELATED PROD. MFG
ST. CLAIR, IL	8454	90386	FOOD SVCS & DRINKING PLACES	OWEN, IN	568	5485	MISCELLANEOUS MANUFACTURING
SALINE, IL	1067	8615	EDUCATIONAL SERVICES	PARKE, IN	559	4177	EDUCATIONAL SERVICES
SANGAMON, IL	8515	110561	EXEC.; LEGIS.; & OTHER SUPPORT	PERRY, IN	686	6554	EDUCATIONAL SERVICES
SCHUYLER, IL	287	1998	CONSTRUCTION OF BUILDINGS	PIKE, IN	377	3221	UTILITIES
SCOTT, IL	192	1435	HEAVY & CIVIL ENG. CONSTRUCT'N	PORTER, IN	5884	53209	SPECIAL TRADE CONTRACTORS
SHELBY, IL	868	8145	PROF.; SCIENTIFIC; & TECH SVCS	POSEY, IN	816	8702	PLASTICS & RUBBER PRODUCTS MFG
STARK, IL	279	1695	EDUCATIONAL SERVICES	PULASKI, IN	504	4683	EDUCATIONAL SERVICES
STEPHENSON, IL	2148	20777	MISCELLANEOUS MANUFACTURING	PUTNAM, IN	1242	11958	EDUCATIONAL SERVICES
TAZEWELL, IL	4498	49609	EDUCATIONAL SERVICES	RANDOLPH, IN	878	8569	EDUCATIONAL SERVICES
UNION, IL	695	5312	EDUCATIONAL SERVICES	RIPLEY, IN	1232	11928	MISCELLANEOUS MANUFACTURING
VERMILION, IL	3395	33321	EDUCATIONAL SERVICES	RUSH, IN	677	5341	EDUCATIONAL SERVICES
WABASH, IL	547	3763	EDUCATIONAL SERVICES	ST. JOSEPH, IN	8893	133465	EDUCATIONAL SERVICES
WARREN, IL	752	6143	FOOD MANUFACTURING	SCOTT, IN	881	7218	FOOD SVCS & DRINKING PLACES
WASHINGTON, IL	671	4498	TRANSPORTATION EQUIPMENT MFG	SHELBY, IN	1470	19084	NONMETALLIC MINERAL PROD. MFG
WAYNE, IL	690	4522	TRANSPORTATION EQUIPMENT MFG	SPENCER, IN	671	8680	AMUSEMENT; GAMBLING;& RECREAT.
WHITE, IL	754	4990	EDUCATIONAL SERVICES	STARKE, IN	617	4871	EDUCATIONAL SERVICES
WHITESIDE, IL	2286	22140	EDUCATIONAL SERVICES	STEUBEN, IN	1559	14510	FABRICATED METAL PRODUCT MFG
WILL, IL	19588	176732	EDUCATIONAL SERVICES	SULLIVAN, IN	586	4115	EDUCATIONAL SERVICES
WILLIAMSON, IL	2665	23936	FOOD SVCS & DRINKING PLACES	SWITZERLAND, IN	305	2618	AMUSEMENT; GAMBLING;& RECREAT.
WINNEBAGO, IL	11388	143036	AMBULATORY HEALTH CARE SVCS	TIPPECANOE, IN	4603	69090	FOOD SVCS & DRINKING PLACES
WOODFORD, IL	1259	11604	EDUCATIONAL SERVICES	TIPTON, IN	629	4985	EDUCATIONAL SERVICES
ADAMS, IL	1144	14466	TRANSPORTATION EQUIPMENT MFG	UNION, IN	260	1497	MISCELLANEOUS MANUFACTURING
ALLEN, IN	11615	178547	FOOD SVCS & DRINKING PLACES	VANDERBURGH, IN	7184	112998	FOOD SVCS & DRINKING PLACES
BARTHOLOMEW, IN	2664	36482	FABRICATED METAL PRODUCT MFG	VERMILLION, IN	544	6342	PROF.; SCIENTIFIC; & TECH SVCS
BENTON, IN	361	2075	EDUCATIONAL SERVICES	VIGO, IN	3588	56527	AMBULATORY HEALTH CARE SVCS
BLACKFORD, IN	439	3987	PAPER MANUFACTURING	WABASH, IN	1252	13748	EDUCATIONAL SERVICES
BOONE, IN	2056	15756	FOOD SVCS & DRINKING PLACES	WARREN, IN	251	1781	FABRICATED METAL PRODUCT MFG
BROWN, IN	633	3742	ACCOMMODATION	WARRICK, IN	1593	14963	MERCH. WHOLESALERS;DURABLE GDS
CARROLL, IN	668	5598	FOOD AND BEVERAGE STORES	WASHINGTON, IN	918	7639	MISCELLANEOUS MANUFACTURING
CASS, IN	1246	17090	FOOD MANUFACTURING	WAYNE, IN	2822	32705	EDUCATIONAL SERVICES
CLARK, IN	3470	40001	FOOD SVCS & DRINKING PLACES	WELLS, IN	945	11254	CHEMICAL MANUFACTURING
CLAY, IN	887	8134	TRANSPORTATION EQUIPMENT MFG	WHITE, IN	1115	9740	ACCOMMODATION
CLINTON, IN	1103	13795	MERCH. WHOLESALERS;NONDUR. GDS	WHITLEY, IN	1216	11962	TRANSPORTATION EQUIPMENT MFG
CRAWFORD, IN	322	1882	EDUCATIONAL SERVICES	ADAIR, IA	390	3003	NONMETALLIC MINERAL PROD. MFG
DAVIESS, IN	1182	9750	EDUCATIONAL SERVICES	ADAMS, IA	247	1268	EDUCATIONAL SERVICES
DEARBORN, IN	1735	19308	AMUSEMENT; GAMBLING;& RECREAT.	ALLAMAKEE, IA	817	6065	MERCH. WHOLESALERS;NONDUR. GDS
DECATUR, IN	994	12549	TRANSPORTATION EQUIPMENT MFG	APPANOOSE, IA	659	5040	PLASTICS & RUBBER PRODUCTS MFG
DEKALB, IN	1427	21208	FABRICATED METAL PRODUCT MFG	AUDUBON, IA	392	2306	EDUCATIONAL SERVICES
DELAWARE, IN	3674	50402	EDUCATIONAL SERVICES	BENTON, IA	1110	5982	EDUCATIONAL SERVICES
DUBOIS, IN	1944	28956	FURNITURE & RELATED PROD. MFG	BLACK HAWK, IA	4983	74140	RELIG.; GRANT; CIVIC; PROF ORG
ELKHART, IN	7084	122028	TRANSPORTATION EQUIPMENT MFG	BOONE, IA	931	8774	RELIG.; GRANT; CIVIC; PROF ORG
FAYETTE, IN	875	11050	TRANSPORTATION EQUIPMENT MFG	BREMER, IA	1068	11402	HOSPITALS
FLOYD, IN	2491	28874	EDUCATIONAL SERVICES	BUCHANAN, IA	966	6767	EDUCATIONAL SERVICES
FOUNTAIN, IN	622	6328	TRANSPORTATION EQUIPMENT MFG	BUENA VISTA, IA	929	10211	FOOD MANUFACTURING
FRANKLIN, IN	681	4938	EDUCATIONAL SERVICES	BUTLER, IA	740	4045	EDUCATIONAL SERVICES
FULTON, IN	868	7630	FABRICATED METAL PRODUCT MFG	CALHOUN, IA	505	3402	EDUCATIONAL SERVICES

COUNTY	2007 Total Firms	2007 Total Employ-ees	TOP INDUSTRY RANKED on 2007 EMPLOYMENT	COUNTY	2007 Total Firms	2007 Total Employ-ees	TOP INDUSTRY RANKED on 2007 EMPLOYMENT
CARROLL, IA	1294	12169	EDUCATIONAL SERVICES	WEBSTER, IA	2155	18416	FOOD SVCS & DRINKING PLACES
CASS, IA	842	6517	EDUCATIONAL SERVICES	WINNEBAGO, IA	702	5221	EDUCATIONAL SERVICES
CEDAR, IA	882	5020	EDUCATIONAL SERVICES	WINNESHIEK, IA	986	9320	EDUCATIONAL SERVICES
CERRO GORDO, IA	2549	27759	HOSPITALS	WOODBURY, IA	4161	52884	EDUCATIONAL SERVICES
CHEROKEE, IA	671	5515	FOOD MANUFACTURING	WORTH, IA	381	2236	EDUCATIONAL SERVICES
CHICKASAW, IA	634	4306	EDUCATIONAL SERVICES	WRIGHT, IA	712	6017	FABRICATED METAL PRODUCT MFG
CLARKE, IA	423	3463	AMUSEMENT; GAMBLING;& RECREAT.	ALLEN, KS	702	5539	EDUCATIONAL SERVICES
CLAY, IA	1084	9361	EDUCATIONAL SERVICES	ANDERSON, KS	414	2133	EDUCATIONAL SERVICES
CLAYTON, IA	994	6734	FOOD SVCS & DRINKING PLACES	ATCHISON, KS	683	6575	EDUCATIONAL SERVICES
CLINTON, IA	1999	22338	EDUCATIONAL SERVICES	BARBER, KS	439	1943	EDUCATIONAL SERVICES
CRAWFORD, IA	846	7933	FOOD MANUFACTURING	BARTON, KS	1633	13467	EDUCATIONAL SERVICES
DALLAS, IA	1688	22696	INSURANCE CARRIERS & RELATED	BOURBON, KS	763	6780	EDUCATIONAL SERVICES
DAVIS, IA	407	2224	HOSPITALS	BROWN, KS	650	4334	EDUCATIONAL SERVICES
DECATUR, IA	346	2569	EDUCATIONAL SERVICES	BUTLER, KS	2310	18430	EDUCATIONAL SERVICES
DELAWARE, IA	727	6078	EDUCATIONAL SERVICES	CHASE, KS	167	780	EDUCATIONAL SERVICES
DES MOINES, IA	1771	25231	AMBULATORY HEALTH CARE SVCS	CHAUTAUQUA, KS	218	1100	EDUCATIONAL SERVICES
DICKINSON, IA	1148	9767	FOOD SVCS & DRINKING PLACES	CHEROKEE, KS	957	6894	EDUCATIONAL SERVICES
DUBUQUE, IA	4106	58986	AMBULATORY HEALTH CARE SVCS	CHEYENNE, KS	220	973	EDUCATIONAL SERVICES
EMMET, IA	536	4494	EDUCATIONAL SERVICES	CLARK, KS	182	742	EDUCATIONAL SERVICES
FAYETTE, IA	1000	7199	EDUCATIONAL SERVICES	CLAY, KS	470	3273	EDUCATIONAL SERVICES
FLOYD, IA	774	6900	MERCH. WHOLESALERS;DURABLE GDS	CLOUD, KS	588	4054	EDUCATIONAL SERVICES
FRANKLIN, IA	512	3833	MACHINERY MANUFACTURING	COFFEY, KS	479	2996	HOSPITALS
FREMONT, IA	377	2493	EDUCATIONAL SERVICES	COMANCHE, KS	174	720	EDUCATIONAL SERVICES
GREENE, IA	597	3402	EDUCATIONAL SERVICES	COWLEY, KS	1572	15362	EDUCATIONAL SERVICES
GRUNDY, IA	567	4266	EDUCATIONAL SERVICES	CRAWFORD, KS	2087	18201	EDUCATIONAL SERVICES
GUTHRIE, IA	654	3414	EDUCATIONAL SERVICES	DECATUR, KS	231	1060	NURSING & RESID. CARE FACILIT.
HAMILTON, IA	764	8779	ELECT'L EQPMT; APP; & COMP MFG	DICKINSON, KS	946	6761	NURSING & RESID. CARE FACILIT.
HANCOCK, IA	617	7730	TRANSPORTATION EQUIPMENT MFG	DONIPHAN, KS	370	2608	EDUCATIONAL SERVICES
HARDIN, IA	992	6927	EDUCATIONAL SERVICES	DOUGLAS, KS	4015	47036	EDUCATIONAL SERVICES
HARRISON, IA	723	4390	EDUCATIONAL SERVICES	EDWARDS, KS	205	1004	FABRICATED METAL PRODUCT MFG
HENRY, IA	926	10815	MERCH. WHOLESALERS;DURABLE GDS	ELK, KS	172	665	EDUCATIONAL SERVICES
HOWARD, IA	462	5354	TRANSPORTATION EQUIPMENT MFG	ELLIS, KS	1604	16042	EDUCATIONAL SERVICES
HUMBOLDT, IA	513	3766	MACHINERY MANUFACTURING	ELLSWORTH, KS	360	2923	EDUCATIONAL SERVICES
IDA, IA	393	3565	MERCH. WHOLESALERS;DURABLE GDS	FINNEY, KS	1650	18832	FOOD MANUFACTURING
IOWA, IA	894	10653	ELECT'L EQPMT; APP; & COMP MFG	FORD, KS	1381	19159	FOOD MANUFACTURING
JACKSON, IA	1020	6993	EDUCATIONAL SERVICES	FRANKLIN, KS	1004	9024	MERCH. WHOLESALERS;DURABLE GDS
JASPER, IA	1352	14340	ELECT'L EQPMT; APP; & COMP MFG	GEARY, KS	1106	24400	NAT'L SECURITY & INT'L AFFAIRS
JEFFERSON, IA	955	7993	EDUCATIONAL SERVICES	GOVE, KS	271	1444	EDUCATIONAL SERVICES
JOHNSON, IA	4372	81283	EDUCATIONAL SERVICES	GRAHAM, KS	252	985	HOSPITALS
JONES, IA	889	6802	EDUCATIONAL SERVICES	GRANT, KS	519	3734	EDUCATIONAL SERVICES
KEOKUK, IA	496	2429	EDUCATIONAL SERVICES	GRAY, KS	396	2312	EDUCATIONAL SERVICES
KOSSUTH, IA	977	6817	EDUCATIONAL SERVICES	GREELEY, KS	150	689	HOSPITALS
LEE, IA	1530	18493	FOOD AND BEVERAGE STORES	GREENWOOD, KS	409	1909	EDUCATIONAL SERVICES
LINN, IA	7785	107930	EDUCATIONAL SERVICES	HAMILTON, KS	234	1389	ANIMAL PRODUCTION
LOUISA, IA	432	5148	FOOD MANUFACTURING	HARPER, KS	474	2579	EDUCATIONAL SERVICES
LUCAS, IA	395	4559	FOOD MANUFACTURING	HARVEY, KS	1548	14793	EDUCATIONAL SERVICES
LYON, IA	637	3877	EDUCATIONAL SERVICES	HASKELL, KS	275	1656	ANIMAL PRODUCTION
MADISON, IA	576	3806	EDUCATIONAL SERVICES	HODGEMAN, KS	125	554	HOSPITALS
MAHASKA, IA	952	7945	EDUCATIONAL SERVICES	JACKSON, KS	568	4372	AMUSEMENT; GAMBLING;& RECREAT.
MARION, IA	1269	16165	WOOD PRODUCT MANUFACTURING	JEFFERSON, KS	688	3747	EDUCATIONAL SERVICES
MARSHALL, IA	1497	20961	HOSPITALS	JEWELL, KS	190	918	EDUCATIONAL SERVICES
MILLS, IA	540	4145	SOCIAL ASSISTANCE	JOHNSON, KS	20701	270484	PROF.; SCIENTIFIC; & TECH SVCS
MITCHELL, IA	537	3785	EDUCATIONAL SERVICES	KEARNY, KS	246	1220	EDUCATIONAL SERVICES
MONONA, IA	555	3414	EDUCATIONAL SERVICES	KINGMAN, KS	459	2795	EDUCATIONAL SERVICES
MONROE, IA	357	2317	FABRICATED METAL PRODUCT MFG	KIOWA, KS	241	1194	EDUCATIONAL SERVICES
MONTGOMERY, IA	586	5310	NONSTORE RETAILERS	LABETTE, KS	1017	9898	EDUCATIONAL SERVICES
MUSCATINE, IA	1565	21582	FOOD MANUFACTURING	LANE, KS	183	838	EDUCATIONAL SERVICES
O'BRIEN, IA	895	6593	EDUCATIONAL SERVICES	LEAVENWORTH, KS	2078	27919	CONSTRUCTION OF BUILDINGS
OSCEOLA, IA	325	2577	PAPER MANUFACTURING	LINCOLN, KS	225	945	EDUCATIONAL SERVICES
PAGE, IA	768	6554	FABRICATED METAL PRODUCT MFG	LINN, KS	618	2519	EDUCATIONAL SERVICES
PALO ALTO, IA	602	4399	EDUCATIONAL SERVICES	LOGAN, KS	253	1662	EDUCATIONAL SERVICES
PLYMOUTH, IA	1085	8524	FOOD SVCS & DRINKING PLACES	LYON, KS	1457	17017	FOOD MANUFACTURING
POCAHONTAS, IA	431	2624	EDUCATIONAL SERVICES	MCPHERSON, KS	1428	13673	EDUCATIONAL SERVICES
POLK, IA	17089	260647	INSURANCE CARRIERS & RELATED	MARION, KS	613	4305	EDUCATIONAL SERVICES
POTTAWATTAMIE, IA	3124	39116	AMUSEMENT; GAMBLING;& RECREAT.	MARSHALL, KS	615	4714	FABRICATED METAL PRODUCT MFG
POWESHIEK, IA	882	9366	EDUCATIONAL SERVICES	MEADE, KS	275	1396	EDUCATIONAL SERVICES
RINGGOLD, IA	276	1412	EDUCATIONAL SERVICES	MIAMI, KS	1271	9177	EDUCATIONAL SERVICES
SAC, IA	718	3698	EDUCATIONAL SERVICES	MITCHELL, KS	453	3437	EDUCATIONAL SERVICES
SCOTT, IA	7252	91528	FOOD SVCS & DRINKING PLACES	MONTGOMERY, KS	1812	17394	EDUCATIONAL SERVICES
SHELBY, IA	790	5414	EDUCATIONAL SERVICES	MORRIS, KS	360	1780	FOOD SVCS & DRINKING PLACES
SIOUX, IA	1704	16777	FABRICATED METAL PRODUCT MFG	MORTON, KS	271	1443	HOSPITALS
STORY, IA	2964	42367	EDUCATIONAL SERVICES	NEMAHA, KS	593	4857	EDUCATIONAL SERVICES
TAMA, IA	781	4790	EDUCATIONAL SERVICES	NEOSHO, KS	892	8287	EDUCATIONAL SERVICES
TAYLOR, IA	368	2222	EDUCATIONAL SERVICES	NESS, KS	322	1473	HOSPITALS
UNION, IA	615	6323	MACHINERY MANUFACTURING	NORTON, KS	341	2652	RELIG.; GRANT; CIVIC; PROF ORG
VAN BUREN, IA	425	2290	ELECT'L EQPMT; APP; & COMP MFG	OSAGE, KS	647	3575	EDUCATIONAL SERVICES
WAPELLO, IA	1365	18863	FOOD MANUFACTURING	OSBORNE, KS	316	1699	EDUCATIONAL SERVICES
WARREN, IA	1186	9425	EDUCATIONAL SERVICES	OTTAWA, KS	308	1543	EDUCATIONAL SERVICES
WASHINGTON, IA	1072	7723	EDUCATIONAL SERVICES	PAWNEE, KS	329	3273	HOSPITALS
WAYNE, IA	324	2096	EDUCATIONAL SERVICES	PHILLIPS, KS	394	2397	EDUCATIONAL SERVICES

COUNTY	2007 Total Firms	2007 Total Employees	TOP INDUSTRY RANKED on 2007 EMPLOYMENT	COUNTY	2007 Total Firms	2007 Total Employees	TOP INDUSTRY RANKED on 2007 EMPLOYMENT
POTTAWATOMIE, KS	982	8383	EDUCATIONAL SERVICES	HART, KY	556	4039	PLASTICS & RUBBER PRODUCTS MFG
PRATT, KS	671	4669	HOSPITALS	HENDERSON, KY	1627	20775	PROF.; SCIENTIFIC; & TECH SVCS
RAWLINS, KS	193	759	EDUCATIONAL SERVICES	HENRY, KY	459	2951	EDUCATIONAL SERVICES
RENO, KS	2630	29986	EDUCATIONAL SERVICES	HICKMAN, KY	151	1040	EDUCATIONAL SERVICES
REPUBLIC, KS	349	1810	NURSING & RESID. CARE FACILIT.	HOPKINS, KY	1750	19530	EDUCATIONAL SERVICES
RICE, KS	534	3433	EDUCATIONAL SERVICES	JACKSON, KY	413	3192	EDUCATIONAL SERVICES
RILEY, KS	1964	23324	EDUCATIONAL SERVICES	JEFFERSON, KY	29180	405111	HOSPITALS
ROOKS, KS	394	2230	EDUCATIONAL SERVICES	JESSAMINE, KY	1398	14147	EDUCATIONAL SERVICES
RUSH, KS	247	1157	MERCH. WHOLESALERS;DURABLE GDS	JOHNSON, KY	822	7823	GENERAL MERCHANDISE STORES
RUSSELL, KS	505	2625	FOOD SVCS & DRINKING PLACES	KENTON, KY	4237	59121	HOSPITALS
SALINE, KS	2511	31061	EDUCATIONAL SERVICES	KNOTT, KY	514	3975	MINING (EXCEPT OIL AND GAS)
SCOTT, KS	357	2187	ANIMAL PRODUCTION	KNOX, KY	862	6741	EDUCATIONAL SERVICES
SEDGWICK, KS	19900	244226	TRANSPORTATION EQUIPMENT MFG	LARUE, KY	383	2477	PERSONAL AND LAUNDRY SERVICES
SEWARD, KS	1096	8387	EDUCATIONAL SERVICES	LAUREL, KY	2110	19945	FOOD SVCS & DRINKING PLACES
SHAWNEE, KS	7115	99684	EXEC.; LEGIS.; & OTHER SUPPORT	LAWRENCE, KY	527	3088	EDUCATIONAL SERVICES
SHERIDAN, KS	182	858	HOSPITALS	LEE, KY	226	1914	SOCIAL ASSISTANCE
SHERMAN, KS	369	2567	GENERAL MERCHANDISE STORES	LESLIE, KY	430	2432	MINING (EXCEPT OIL AND GAS)
SMITH, KS	277	1453	TRANSPORTATION EQUIPMENT MFG	LETCHER, KY	768	6821	MINING (EXCEPT OIL AND GAS)
STAFFORD, KS	315	1227	EDUCATIONAL SERVICES	LEWIS, KY	291	2082	EDUCATIONAL SERVICES
STANTON, KS	195	758	ANIMAL PRODUCTION	LINCOLN, KY	579	4461	EDUCATIONAL SERVICES
STEVENS, KS	388	2072	EDUCATIONAL SERVICES	LIVINGSTON, KY	311	2243	MINING (EXCEPT OIL AND GAS)
SUMNER, KS	1198	6858	EDUCATIONAL SERVICES	LOGAN, KY	931	8164	PRIMARY METAL MANUFACTURING
THOMAS, KS	521	3305	EDUCATIONAL SERVICES	LYON, KY	297	2007	JUSTICE; PUBIC ORDER/SAFETY
TREGO, KS	245	1141	HOSPITALS	MCCRACKEN, KY	3208	37786	HOSPITALS
WABAUNSEE, KS	280	1303	FOOD AND BEVERAGE STORES	MCCREARY, KY	467	3406	EDUCATIONAL SERVICES
WALLACE, KS	165	542	EDUCATIONAL SERVICES	MCLEAN, KY	291	1583	EDUCATIONAL SERVICES
WASHINGTON, KS	396	2096	EDUCATIONAL SERVICES	MADISON, KY	2604	28290	EDUCATIONAL SERVICES
WICHITA, KS	187	995	ANIMAL PRODUCTION	MAGOFFIN, KY	459	2707	EDUCATIONAL SERVICES
WILSON, KS	531	4261	TRANSPORTATION EQUIPMENT MFG	MARION, KY	531	7251	FABRICATED METAL PRODUCT MFG
WOODSON, KS	193	851	EDUCATIONAL SERVICES	MARSHALL, KY	1040	9461	FOOD SVCS & DRINKING PLACES
WYANDOTTE, KS	5152	73683	HOSPITALS	MARTIN, KY	329	4051	MINING (EXCEPT OIL AND GAS)
ADAIR, KY	662	4414	EDUCATIONAL SERVICES	MASON, KY	794	9400	MACHINERY MANUFACTURING
ALLEN, KY	537	4177	GENERAL MERCHANDISE STORES	MEADE, KY	736	3408	EDUCATIONAL SERVICES
ANDERSON, KY	578	4536	MERCH. WHOLESALERS;DURABLE GDS	MENIFEE, KY	187	1101	EDUCATIONAL SERVICES
BALLARD, KY	389	2218	PAPER MANUFACTURING	MERCER, KY	663	7400	TRANSPORTATION EQUIPMENT MFG
BARREN, KY	1755	17167	AMBULATORY HEALTH CARE SVCS	METCALFE, KY	202	1724	COMPUTER & ELECTRONIC PROD MFG
BATH, KY	302	2038	EDUCATIONAL SERVICES	MONROE, KY	380	3196	EDUCATIONAL SERVICES
BELL, KY	1018	9815	EDUCATIONAL SERVICES	MONTGOMERY, KY	911	9682	PLASTICS & RUBBER PRODUCTS MFG
BOONE, KY	3633	67074	SUPPORT ACT. FOR TRANSPORT.	MORGAN, KY	394	2991	JUSTICE; PUBIC ORDER/SAFETY
BOURBON, KY	684	6465	EDUCATIONAL SERVICES	MUHLENBERG, KY	942	8972	EDUCATIONAL SERVICES
BOYD, KY	2378	28667	AMBULATORY HEALTH CARE SVCS	NELSON, KY	1415	13518	EDUCATIONAL SERVICES
BOYLE, KY	1284	14622	HOSPITALS	NICHOLAS, KY	173	1050	HOSPITALS
BRACKEN, KY	237	1229	PLASTICS & RUBBER PRODUCTS MFG	OHIO, KY	627	6498	CROP PRODUCTION
BREATHITT, KY	402	3228	EDUCATIONAL SERVICES	OLDHAM, KY	1563	12862	JUSTICE; PUBIC ORDER/SAFETY
BRECKINRIDGE, KY	636	3278	EDUCATIONAL SERVICES	OWEN, KY	219	1699	EDUCATIONAL SERVICES
BULLITT, KY	1740	15067	EDUCATIONAL SERVICES	OWSLEY, KY	159	937	EDUCATIONAL SERVICES
BUTLER, KY	323	2330	EDUCATIONAL SERVICES	PENDLETON, KY	317	2417	EDUCATIONAL SERVICES
CALDWELL, KY	475	4225	FOOD MANUFACTURING	PERRY, KY	1167	13383	EDUCATIONAL SERVICES
CALLOWAY, KY	1337	15185	EDUCATIONAL SERVICES	PIKE, KY	2208	23303	MINING (EXCEPT OIL AND GAS)
CAMPBELL, KY	2357	28661	EDUCATIONAL SERVICES	POWELL, KY	378	2552	EDUCATIONAL SERVICES
CARLISLE, KY	92	250	JUSTICE; PUBIC ORDER/SAFETY	PULASKI, KY	2446	24698	EDUCATIONAL SERVICES
CARROLL, KY	445	6229	PRIMARY METAL MANUFACTURING	ROBERTSON, KY	65	208	NURSING & RESID. CARE FACILIT.
CARTER, KY	855	6542	EDUCATIONAL SERVICES	ROCKCASTLE, KY	473	3853	EDUCATIONAL SERVICES
CASEY, KY	443	3297	WOOD PRODUCT MANUFACTURING	ROWAN, KY	839	8133	HOSPITALS
CHRISTIAN, KY	2149	48713	EXEC.; LEGIS.; & OTHER SUPPORT	RUSSELL, KY	901	6242	APPAREL MANUFACTURING
CLARK, KY	1171	15108	UTILITIES	SCOTT, KY	1246	12022	EDUCATIONAL SERVICES
CLAY, KY	633	4055	EDUCATIONAL SERVICES	SHELBY, KY	1302	13067	MERCH. WHOLESALERS;NONDUR. GDS
CLINTON, KY	371	3686	FOOD MANUFACTURING	SIMPSON, KY	610	8899	PROF.; SCIENTIFIC; & TECH SVCS
CRITTENDEN, KY	275	2536	HOSPITALS	SPENCER, KY	300	1449	EDUCATIONAL SERVICES
CUMBERLAND, KY	266	1942	EDUCATIONAL SERVICES	TAYLOR, KY	1000	9928	BLDG MATL & GARDEN EQPMT DLRS
DAVIESS, KY	3246	41740	FOOD SVCS & DRINKING PLACES	TODD, KY	344	2396	APPAREL MANUFACTURING
EDMONSON, KY	255	1655	EDUCATIONAL SERVICES	TRIGG, KY	414	3562	TRANSPORTATION EQUIPMENT MFG
ELLIOTT, KY	153	748	EDUCATIONAL SERVICES	TRIMBLE, KY	168	1088	EDUCATIONAL SERVICES
ESTILL, KY	384	2410	EDUCATIONAL SERVICES	UNION, KY	461	3896	TRANSPORTATION EQUIPMENT MFG
FAYETTE, KY	11535	173627	EDUCATIONAL SERVICES	WARREN, KY	3866	49920	FOOD SVCS & DRINKING PLACES
FLEMING, KY	421	3301	EDUCATIONAL SERVICES	WASHINGTON, KY	338	2999	EDUCATIONAL SERVICES
FLOYD, KY	1557	12090	EDUCATIONAL SERVICES	WAYNE, KY	578	5958	EDUCATIONAL SERVICES
FRANKLIN, KY	2291	44981	EXEC.; LEGIS.; & OTHER SUPPORT	WEBSTER, KY	392	2726	EDUCATIONAL SERVICES
FULTON, KY	333	2862	AMBULATORY HEALTH CARE SVCS	WHITLEY, KY	1414	12840	EDUCATIONAL SERVICES
GALLATIN, KY	202	1592	TRANSPORTATION EQUIPMENT MFG	WOLFE, KY	258	1462	EDUCATIONAL SERVICES
GARRARD, KY	402	2244	EDUCATIONAL SERVICES	WOODFORD, KY	1086	9388	PRINT'G & RELATED SUPP'T ACT'S
GRANT, KY	597	5733	BLDG MATL & GARDEN EQPMT DLRS	ACADIA, LA	1805	14392	EDUCATIONAL SERVICES
GRAVES, KY	1174	12076	MERCH. WHOLESALERS;DURABLE GDS	ALLEN, LA	791	4950	EDUCATIONAL SERVICES
GRAYSON, KY	791	7827	EDUCATIONAL SERVICES	ASCENSION, LA	2991	29260	EDUCATIONAL SERVICES
GREEN, KY	124	724	HOSPITALS	ASSUMPTION, LA	543	7802	SUPPORT ACTIVITIES FOR MINING
GREENUP, KY	1117	15263	AMBULATORY HEALTH CARE SVCS	AVOYELLES, LA	1288	11853	AMUSEMENT; GAMBLING;& RECREAT.
HANCOCK, KY	210	3369	PRIMARY METAL MANUFACTURING	BEAUREGARD, LA	1030	8723	FOOD MANUFACTURING
HARDIN, KY	3536	36868	FOOD SVCS & DRINKING PLACES	BIENVILLE, LA	523	4003	FOOD MANUFACTURING
HARLAN, KY	979	9944	MINING (EXCEPT OIL AND GAS)	BOSSIER, LA	3393	54002	NAT'L SECURITY & INT'L AFFAIRS
HARRISON, KY	552	5041	CHEMICAL MANUFACTURING	CADDO, LA	10006	126796	EDUCATIONAL SERVICES

COUNTY	2007 Total Firms	2007 Total Employees	TOP INDUSTRY RANKED on 2007 EMPLOYMENT	COUNTY	2007 Total Firms	2007 Total Employees	TOP INDUSTRY RANKED on 2007 EMPLOYMENT
CALCASIEU, LA	6874	87275	EDUCATIONAL SERVICES	FREDERICK, MD	8383	101405	PROF.; SCIENTIFIC; & TECH SVCS
CALDWELL, LA	359	2280	EDUCATIONAL SERVICES	GARRETT, MD	1600	12304	FOOD SVCS & DRINKING PLACES
CAMERON, LA	280	1726	JUSTICE; PUBIC ORDER/SAFETY	HARFORD, MD	8235	77122	CHEMICAL MANUFACTURING
CATAHOULA, LA	388	2335	EDUCATIONAL SERVICES	HOWARD, MD	10841	118178	PROF.; SCIENTIFIC; & TECH SVCS
CLAIBORNE, LA	546	4109	JUSTICE; PUBIC ORDER/SAFETY	KENT, MD	1269	9289	EDUCATIONAL SERVICES
CONCORDIA, LA	723	5571	JUSTICE; PUBIC ORDER/SAFETY	MONTGOMERY, MD	38289	468315	EXEC.; LEGIS.; & OTHER SUPPORT
DE SOTO, LA	786	5921	EDUCATIONAL SERVICES	PRINCE GEORGE'S, MD	26116	321826	EDUCATIONAL SERVICES
EAST BATON ROUGE, LA	21423	228592	PROF.; SCIENTIFIC; & TECH SVCS	QUEEN ANNE'S, MD	2240	13019	FOOD SVCS & DRINKING PLACES
EAST CARROLL, LA	319	2177	JUSTICE; PUBIC ORDER/SAFETY	ST. MARY'S, MD	2809	29767	PROF.; SCIENTIFIC; & TECH SVCS
EAST FELICIANA, LA	568	4702	HOSPITALS	SOMERSET, MD	770	6284	MERCH. WHOLESALERS;NONDUR. GDS
EVANGELINE, LA	1069	7569	HOSPITALS	TALBOT, MD	2483	21858	AMBULATORY HEALTH CARE SVCS
FRANKLIN, LA	791	6119	EDUCATIONAL SERVICES	WASHINGTON, MD	5295	70597	ISPS; WEB SEARCH PORTALS
GRANT, LA	389	2707	EDUCATIONAL SERVICES	WICOMICO, MD	4223	42519	PROF.; SCIENTIFIC; & TECH SVCS
IBERIA, LA	2631	32161	EDUCATIONAL SERVICES	WORCESTER, MD	3709	32015	FOOD SVCS & DRINKING PLACES
IBERVILLE, LA	983	10775	CHEMICAL MANUFACTURING	BALTIMORE CITY, MD	22295	284089	HOSPITALS
JACKSON, LA	522	3180	EDUCATIONAL SERVICES	BARNSTABLE, MA	16538	101471	FOOD SVCS & DRINKING PLACES
JEFFERSON, LA	19949	214951	HOSPITALS	BERKSHIRE, MA	6976	63736	EDUCATIONAL SERVICES
JEFFERSON DAVIS, LA	1044	8217	EDUCATIONAL SERVICES	BRISTOL, MA	20093	216824	FOOD SVCS & DRINKING PLACES
LAFAYETTE, LA	10136	121640	SPECIAL TRADE CONTRACTORS	DUKES, MA	2244	9605	FOOD SVCS & DRINKING PLACES
LAFOURCHE, LA	3133	29387	EDUCATIONAL SERVICES	ESSEX, MA	31754	314704	EDUCATIONAL SERVICES
LA SALLE, LA	655	3934	HOSPITALS	FRANKLIN, MA	3354	27883	EDUCATIONAL SERVICES
LINCOLN, LA	1624	18201	EDUCATIONAL SERVICES	HAMPDEN, MA	16071	204952	EDUCATIONAL SERVICES
LIVINGSTON, LA	2924	17034	EDUCATIONAL SERVICES	HAMPSHIRE, MA	6478	63224	EDUCATIONAL SERVICES
MADISON, LA	478	3579	EDUCATIONAL SERVICES	MIDDLESEX, MA	66228	757858	EDUCATIONAL SERVICES
MOREHOUSE, LA	1030	8337	PAPER MANUFACTURING	NANTUCKET, MA	1377	7393	FOOD SVCS & DRINKING PLACES
NATCHITOCHES, LA	1615	12934	EDUCATIONAL SERVICES	NORFOLK, MA	29989	296745	EDUCATIONAL SERVICES
ORLEANS, LA	14311	196054	EDUCATIONAL SERVICES	PLYMOUTH, MA	20233	173508	EDUCATIONAL SERVICES
OUACHITA, LA	6517	72739	EDUCATIONAL SERVICES	SUFFOLK, MA	34525	511954	PROF.; SCIENTIFIC; & TECH SVCS
PLAQUEMINES, LA	935	12626	SUPPORT ACT. FOR TRANSPORT.	WORCESTER, MA	31499	331513	EDUCATIONAL SERVICES
POINTE COUPEE, LA	721	5396	PROF.; SCIENTIFIC; & TECH SVCS	ALCONA, MI	516	2225	EDUCATIONAL SERVICES
RAPIDES, LA	5662	61016	HOSPITALS	ALGER, MI	591	3521	JUSTICE; PUBIC ORDER/SAFETY
RED RIVER, LA	337	2315	HOSPITALS	ALLEGAN, MI	4066	51409	MERCH. WHOLESALERS;DURABLE GDS
RICHLAND, LA	809	5380	EDUCATIONAL SERVICES	ALPENA, MI	1511	12562	HOSPITALS
SABINE, LA	823	6626	EDUCATIONAL SERVICES	ANTRIM, MI	1374	7929	ACCOMMODATION
ST. BERNARD, LA	694	7736	EDUCATIONAL SERVICES	ARENAC, MI	686	5501	FOOD SVCS & DRINKING PLACES
ST. CHARLES, LA	1482	19474	MERCH. WHOLESALERS;NONDUR. GDS	BARAGA, MI	457	4027	EDUCATIONAL SERVICES
ST. HELENA, LA	228	1791	EDUCATIONAL SERVICES	BARRY, MI	1690	12065	EDUCATIONAL SERVICES
ST. JAMES, LA	611	8207	CHEMICAL MANUFACTURING	BAY, MI	4296	41607	FOOD SVCS & DRINKING PLACES
ST. JOHN THE BAPTIST, LA	1349	13610	EDUCATIONAL SERVICES	BENZIE, MI	971	5059	ACCOMMODATION
ST. LANDRY, LA	2851	23198	EDUCATIONAL SERVICES	BERRIEN, MI	7045	73490	EDUCATIONAL SERVICES
ST. MARTIN, LA	1390	12899	EDUCATIONAL SERVICES	BRANCH, MI	1638	14512	EDUCATIONAL SERVICES
ST. MARY, LA	2322	24397	SUPPORT ACT. FOR TRANSPORT.	CALHOUN, MI	4933	61366	TRANSPORTATION EQUIPMENT MFG
ST. TAMMANY, LA	10628	69519	AMBULATORY HEALTH CARE SVCS	CASS, MI	1566	12669	EDUCATIONAL SERVICES
TANGIPAHOA, LA	4155	38657	HOSPITALS	CHARLEVOIX, MI	1559	11476	EDUCATIONAL SERVICES
TENSAS, LA	267	1509	EDUCATIONAL SERVICES	CHEBOYGAN, MI	1505	9334	FOOD SVCS & DRINKING PLACES
TERREBONNE, LA	4618	48947	SPECIAL TRADE CONTRACTORS	CHIPPEWA, MI	1726	15681	ACCOMMODATION
UNION, LA	715	5902	FOOD MANUFACTURING	CLARE, MI	1098	7875	EDUCATIONAL SERVICES
VERMILION, LA	1698	13726	EDUCATIONAL SERVICES	CLINTON, MI	2152	17519	SPECIAL TRADE CONTRACTORS
VERNON, LA	1451	12119	EDUCATIONAL SERVICES	CRAWFORD, MI	623	6054	AMBULATORY HEALTH CARE SVCS
WASHINGTON, LA	1456	12004	PAPER MANUFACTURING	DELTA, MI	1712	15627	PAPER MANUFACTURING
WEBSTER, LA	1564	13290	EDUCATIONAL SERVICES	DICKINSON, MI	1523	15352	HOSPITALS
WEST BATON ROUGE, LA	963	9364	FABRICATED METAL PRODUCT MFG	EATON, MI	3739	40295	FOOD SVCS & DRINKING PLACES
WEST CARROLL, LA	433	3327	EDUCATIONAL SERVICES	EMMET, MI	2451	21555	ACCOMMODATION
WEST FELICIANA, LA	395	5725	JUSTICE; PUBIC ORDER/SAFETY	GENESEE, MI	14737	140057	FOOD SVCS & DRINKING PLACES
WINN, LA	529	4723	WOOD PRODUCT MANUFACTURING	GLADWIN, MI	858	5984	FOOD SVCS & DRINKING PLACES
ANDROSCOGGIN, ME	3989	49026	EDUCATIONAL SERVICES	GOGEBIC, MI	853	7151	ACCOMMODATION
AROOSTOOK, ME	3236	31126	EDUCATIONAL SERVICES	GRAND TRAVERSE, MI	6192	53766	FOOD SVCS & DRINKING PLACES
CUMBERLAND, ME	16920	173588	EDUCATIONAL SERVICES	GRATIOT, MI	1522	12947	EDUCATIONAL SERVICES
FRANKLIN, ME	1390	11291	PAPER MANUFACTURING	HILLSDALE, MI	1654	14082	EDUCATIONAL SERVICES
HANCOCK, ME	3470	26228	FOOD SVCS & DRINKING PLACES	HOUGHTON, MI	1561	14599	EDUCATIONAL SERVICES
KENNEBEC, ME	5434	67830	HOSPITALS	HURON, MI	1664	13944	FOOD SVCS & DRINKING PLACES
KNOX, ME	2779	17478	AMBULATORY HEALTH CARE SVCS	INGHAM, MI	11470	177152	EDUCATIONAL SERVICES
LINCOLN, ME	2180	13187	FOOD SVCS & DRINKING PLACES	IONIA, MI	1812	16306	EDUCATIONAL SERVICES
OXFORD, ME	2363	21221	ACCOMMODATION	IOSCO, MI	1435	9867	FOOD SVCS & DRINKING PLACES
PENOBSCOT, ME	6305	73304	HOSPITALS	IRON, MI	710	4471	ACCOMMODATION
PISCATAQUIS, ME	759	6733	EDUCATIONAL SERVICES	ISABELLA, MI	2229	28259	ACCOMMODATION
SAGADAHOC, ME	1420	10706	EDUCATIONAL SERVICES	JACKSON, MI	5598	58590	EDUCATIONAL SERVICES
SOMERSET, ME	2071	19849	EDUCATIONAL SERVICES	KALAMAZOO, MI	9441	134369	EDUCATIONAL SERVICES
WALDO, ME	1785	10069	EDUCATIONAL SERVICES	KALKASKA, MI	722	4985	SPECIAL TRADE CONTRACTORS
WASHINGTON, ME	1538	12527	EDUCATIONAL SERVICES	KENT, MI	24744	354453	MERCH. WHOLESALERS;DURABLE GDS
YORK, ME	9141	67063	FOOD SVCS & DRINKING PLACES	KEWEENAW, MI	99	439	ACCOMMODATION
ALLEGANY, MD	2763	30510	EDUCATIONAL SERVICES	LAKE, MI	399	2032	AMBULATORY HEALTH CARE SVCS
ANNE ARUNDEL, MD	19129	203682	FOOD SVCS & DRINKING PLACES	LAPEER, MI	3565	26353	EDUCATIONAL SERVICES
BALTIMORE, MD	29751	352367	EDUCATIONAL SERVICES	LEELANAU, MI	1559	7088	FOOD SVCS & DRINKING PLACES
CALVERT, MD	2986	21905	EDUCATIONAL SERVICES	LENAWEE, MI	3559	40915	GENERAL MERCHANDISE STORES
CAROLINE, MD	1147	9862	EDUCATIONAL SERVICES	LIVINGSTON, MI	6817	52146	FOOD SVCS & DRINKING PLACES
CARROLL, MD	6284	53865	FOOD SVCS & DRINKING PLACES	LUCE, MI	358	2939	JUSTICE; PUBIC ORDER/SAFETY
CECIL, MD	3259	28818	EDUCATIONAL SERVICES	MACKINAC, MI	928	6637	ACCOMMODATION
CHARLES, MD	4222	41793	EDUCATIONAL SERVICES	MACOMB, MI	27702	326767	TRANSPORTATION EQUIPMENT MFG
DORCHESTER, MD	1394	14248	FOOD MANUFACTURING	MANISTEE, MI	1246	9559	EDUCATIONAL SERVICES

COUNTY	2007 Total Firms	2007 Total Employees	TOP INDUSTRY RANKED on 2007 EMPLOYMENT	COUNTY	2007 Total Firms	2007 Total Employees	TOP INDUSTRY RANKED on 2007 EMPLOYMENT
MARQUETTE, MI	2876	27769	EDUCATIONAL SERVICES	MORRISON, MN	1279	11777	TRANSPORTATION EQUIPMENT MFG
MASON, MI	1324	11159	EDUCATIONAL SERVICES	MOWER, MN	1545	16792	MERCH. WHOLESALERS;NONDUR. GDS
MECOSTA, MI	1390	11495	EDUCATIONAL SERVICES	MURRAY, MN	481	3240	EDUCATIONAL SERVICES
MENOMINEE, MI	941	8229	EDUCATIONAL SERVICES	NICOLLET, MN	940	12630	PRINT'G & RELATED SUPP'T ACT'S
MIDLAND, MI	3031	33924	EDUCATIONAL SERVICES	NOBLES, MN	1049	10816	FOOD MANUFACTURING
MISSAUKEE, MI	668	3090	EDUCATIONAL SERVICES	NORMAN, MN	457	2637	NURSING & RESID. CARE FACILIT.
MONROE, MI	4665	43581	EDUCATIONAL SERVICES	OLMSTED, MN	4732	68541	HOSPITALS
MONTCALM, MI	2219	17005	EDUCATIONAL SERVICES	OTTER TAIL, MN	3338	24276	EDUCATIONAL SERVICES
MONTMORENCY, MI	493	2937	EDUCATIONAL SERVICES	PENNINGTON, MN	625	9381	ELECTRONICS & APPLIANCE STORES
MUSKEGON, MI	6496	64781	EDUCATIONAL SERVICES	PINE, MN	984	9207	AMUSEMENT; GAMBLING;& RECREAT.
NEWAYGO, MI	1629	12811	EDUCATIONAL SERVICES	PIPESTONE, MN	565	4440	EDUCATIONAL SERVICES
OAKLAND, MI	63457	688539	PROF.; SCIENTIFIC; & TECH SVCS	POLK, MN	1557	13963	FOOD MANUFACTURING
OCEANA, MI	1123	8615	MERCH. WHOLESALERS;NONDUR. GDS	POPE, MN	609	4265	EDUCATIONAL SERVICES
OGEMAW, MI	1060	7403	EDUCATIONAL SERVICES	RAMSEY, MN	20711	306933	EDUCATIONAL SERVICES
ONTONAGON, MI	472	2367	EDUCATIONAL SERVICES	RED LAKE, MN	253	1455	EDUCATIONAL SERVICES
OSCEOLA, MI	886	6402	EDUCATIONAL SERVICES	REDWOOD, MN	899	8013	CREDIT INTERMEDIATION & RELATD
OSCODA, MI	417	2692	ACCOMMODATION	RENVILLE, MN	861	6685	FOOD MANUFACTURING
OTSEGO, MI	1404	12918	EDUCATIONAL SERVICES	RICE, MN	2203	23436	EDUCATIONAL SERVICES
OTTAWA, MI	10263	106616	EDUCATIONAL SERVICES	ROCK, MN	422	3462	HOSPITALS
PRESQUE ISLE, MI	653	3585	EDUCATIONAL SERVICES	ROSEAU, MN	735	7802	TRANSPORTATION EQUIPMENT MFG
ROSCOMMON, MI	1224	7334	EDUCATIONAL SERVICES	ST. LOUIS, MN	9561	114185	HOSPITALS
SAGINAW, MI	8357	103877	HOSPITALS	SCOTT, MN	3604	49464	FOOD SVCS & DRINKING PLACES
ST. CLAIR, MI	5944	51844	EDUCATIONAL SERVICES	SHERBURNE, MN	2451	23345	EDUCATIONAL SERVICES
ST. JOSEPH, MI	2507	25764	EDUCATIONAL SERVICES	SIBLEY, MN	621	4593	FOOD MANUFACTURING
SANILAC, MI	1848	12797	EDUCATIONAL SERVICES	STEARNS, MN	6140	75198	EDUCATIONAL SERVICES
SCHOOLCRAFT, MI	448	3253	EXEC.; LEGIS.; & OTHER SUPPORT	STEELE, MN	1547	18659	INSURANCE CARRIERS & RELATED
SHIAWASSEE, MI	2442	19644	EDUCATIONAL SERVICES	STEVENS, MN	615	5062	EDUCATIONAL SERVICES
TUSCOLA, MI	1820	16219	EDUCATIONAL SERVICES	SWIFT, MN	593	4490	JUSTICE; PUBIC ORDER/SAFETY
VAN BUREN, MI	2847	24254	EDUCATIONAL SERVICES	TODD, MN	926	6375	FOOD MANUFACTURING
WASHTENAW, MI	14291	214220	EDUCATIONAL SERVICES	TRAVERSE, MN	267	1352	EDUCATIONAL SERVICES
WAYNE, MI	59862	746608	EDUCATIONAL SERVICES	WABASHA, MN	935	8145	EDUCATIONAL SERVICES
WEXFORD, MI	1570	16080	PLASTICS & RUBBER PRODUCTS MFG	WADENA, MN	748	6822	HOSPITALS
AITKIN, MN	795	4897	EDUCATIONAL SERVICES	WASECA, MN	782	9175	PRINT'G & RELATED SUPP'T ACT'S
ANOKA, MN	9427	116476	PROF.; SCIENTIFIC; & TECH SVCS	WASHINGTON, MN	7180	75996	FOOD SVCS & DRINKING PLACES
BECKER, MN	1628	13638	EDUCATIONAL SERVICES	WATONWAN, MN	562	5133	FOOD MANUFACTURING
BELTRAMI, MN	1995	18539	EDUCATIONAL SERVICES	WILKIN, MN	293	2063	NURSING & RESID. CARE FACILIT.
BENTON, MN	1259	16680	BLDG MATL & GARDEN EQPMT DLRS	WINONA, MN	1957	24657	EDUCATIONAL SERVICES
BIG STONE, MN	353	2310	EDUCATIONAL SERVICES	WRIGHT, MN	4072	37343	EDUCATIONAL SERVICES
BLUE EARTH, MN	2869	37913	EDUCATIONAL SERVICES	YELLOW MEDICINE, MN	561	4261	EDUCATIONAL SERVICES
BROWN, MN	1461	16269	MISCELLANEOUS MANUFACTURING	ADAMS, MS	1545	12872	EDUCATIONAL SERVICES
CARLTON, MN	1412	13050	EDUCATIONAL SERVICES	ALCORN, MS	1378	14667	PRINT'G & RELATED SUPP'T ACT'S
CARVER, MN	2793	35298	EDUCATIONAL SERVICES	AMITE, MS	342	2186	EDUCATIONAL SERVICES
CASS, MN	1891	10138	AMUSEMENT; GAMBLING;& RECREAT.	ATTALA, MS	679	5449	EDUCATIONAL SERVICES
CHIPPEWA, MN	687	6404	EDUCATIONAL SERVICES	BENTON, MS	175	1200	MERCH. WHOLESALERS;DURABLE GDS
CHISAGO, MN	1689	16682	EDUCATIONAL SERVICES	BOLIVAR, MS	1321	12084	EDUCATIONAL SERVICES
CLAY, MN	1891	17643	EDUCATIONAL SERVICES	CALHOUN, MS	605	4092	FURNITURE & RELATED PROD. MFG
CLEARWATER, MN	448	2804	TRANSPORTATION EQUIPMENT MFG	CARROLL, MS	208	876	EDUCATIONAL SERVICES
COOK, MN	518	3634	ACCOMMODATION	CHICKASAW, MS	718	8362	FURNITURE & RELATED PROD. MFG
COTTONWOOD, MN	576	5319	MACHINERY MANUFACTURING	CHOCTAW, MS	263	2108	EDUCATIONAL SERVICES
CROW WING, MN	4027	33461	FOOD SVCS & DRINKING PLACES	CLAIBORNE, MS	325	3159	MERCH. WHOLESALERS;NONDUR. GDS
DAKOTA, MN	13141	159961	FOOD SVCS & DRINKING PLACES	CLARKE, MS	467	3675	EDUCATIONAL SERVICES
DODGE, MN	680	4764	EDUCATIONAL SERVICES	CLAY, MS	722	7778	FOOD MANUFACTURING
DOUGLAS, MN	2210	18838	EDUCATIONAL SERVICES	COAHOMA, MS	1069	11332	EDUCATIONAL SERVICES
FARIBAULT, MN	976	6360	EDUCATIONAL SERVICES	COPIAH, MS	834	8619	EDUCATIONAL SERVICES
FILLMORE, MN	1140	6749	NURSING & RESID. CARE FACILIT.	COVINGTON, MS	550	5237	FOOD MANUFACTURING
FREEBORN, MN	1480	14116	AMBULATORY HEALTH CARE SVCS	DESOTO, MS	4175	38846	FOOD SVCS & DRINKING PLACES
GOODHUE, MN	2046	20444	EDUCATIONAL SERVICES	FORREST, MS	3292	39261	EDUCATIONAL SERVICES
GRANT, MN	511	2505	EDUCATIONAL SERVICES	FRANKLIN, MS	272	1800	EDUCATIONAL SERVICES
HENNEPIN, MN	53210	796283	PROF.; SCIENTIFIC; & TECH SVCS	GEORGE, MS	653	4341	HOSPITALS
HOUSTON, MN	968	5810	EDUCATIONAL SERVICES	GREENE, MS	304	1430	EDUCATIONAL SERVICES
HUBBARD, MN	1107	7171	AMBULATORY HEALTH CARE SVCS	GRENADA, MS	1103	11926	MISCELLANEOUS MANUFACTURING
ISANTI, MN	1128	9946	EDUCATIONAL SERVICES	HANCOCK, MS	1188	9086	NAT'L SECURITY & INT'L AFFAIRS
ITASCA, MN	2058	17038	HOSPITALS	HARRISON, MS	7066	82490	RELIG.; GRANT; CIVIC; PROF ORG
JACKSON, MN	481	3585	EDUCATIONAL SERVICES	HINDS, MS	11453	154062	AMBULATORY HEALTH CARE SVCS
KANABEC, MN	524	4333	EDUCATIONAL SERVICES	HOLMES, MS	619	4476	EDUCATIONAL SERVICES
KANDIYOHI, MN	2050	25109	FOOD AND BEVERAGE STORES	HUMPHREYS, MS	374	2660	FOOD MANUFACTURING
KITTSON, MN	372	2008	AMBULATORY HEALTH CARE SVCS	ISSAQUENA, MS	33	145	JUSTICE; PUBIC ORDER/SAFETY
KOOCHICHING, MN	677	5786	PAPER MANUFACTURING	ITAWAMBA, MS	752	5328	EDUCATIONAL SERVICES
LAC QUI PARLE, MN	437	2751	EDUCATIONAL SERVICES	JACKSON, MS	4023	45454	TRANSPORTATION EQUIPMENT MFG
LAKE, MN	587	4641	FOOD SVCS & DRINKING PLACES	JASPER, MS	485	4433	FOOD MANUFACTURING
LAKE OF THE WOODS, MN	326	1858	ACCOMMODATION	JEFFERSON, MS	205	2263	EDUCATIONAL SERVICES
LE SUEUR, MN	1038	8795	FOOD MANUFACTURING	JEFFERSON DAVIS, MS	350	2065	EDUCATIONAL SERVICES
LINCOLN, MN	394	2027	HOSPITALS	JONES, MS	2315	31779	FOOD MANUFACTURING
LYON, MN	1318	13861	EDUCATIONAL SERVICES	KEMPER, MS	263	1433	EDUCATIONAL SERVICES
MCLEOD, MN	1612	20278	COMPUTER & ELECTRONIC PROD MFG	LAFAYETTE, MS	1633	16529	ELECT'L EQPMT; APP; & COMP MFG
MAHNOMEN, MN	289	1765	EDUCATIONAL SERVICES	LAMAR, MS	1588	15292	FOOD SVCS & DRINKING PLACES
MARSHALL, MN	537	3084	EDUCATIONAL SERVICES	LAUDERDALE, MS	3391	39276	HOSPITALS
MARTIN, MN	1109	10236	AMBULATORY HEALTH CARE SVCS	LAWRENCE, MS	409	3031	PAPER MANUFACTURING
MEEKER, MN	929	7658	EDUCATIONAL SERVICES	LEAKE, MS	583	6545	FOOD MANUFACTURING
MILLE LACS, MN	1103	11393	ACCOMMODATION	LEE, MS	3721	47053	FURNITURE & RELATED PROD. MFG

110

COUNTY	2007 Total Firms	2007 Total Employees	TOP INDUSTRY RANKED on 2007 EMPLOYMENT	COUNTY	2007 Total Firms	2007 Total Employees	TOP INDUSTRY RANKED on 2007 EMPLOYMENT
LEFLORE, MS	1491	16428	EDUCATIONAL SERVICES	GRUNDY, MO	489	3924	FOOD MANUFACTURING
LINCOLN, MS	1203	10886	EDUCATIONAL SERVICES	HARRISON, MO	548	2952	EDUCATIONAL SERVICES
LOWNDES, MS	2644	29309	EDUCATIONAL SERVICES	HENRY, MO	1144	8066	HOSPITALS
MADISON, MS	3800	40369	WHOLESALE ELEC. MRKTS & AGENTS	HICKORY, MO	311	1472	EDUCATIONAL SERVICES
MARION, MS	942	8652	EDUCATIONAL SERVICES	HOLT, MO	352	1842	EDUCATIONAL SERVICES
MARSHALL, MS	1043	6558	EDUCATIONAL SERVICES	HOWARD, MO	410	2398	EDUCATIONAL SERVICES
MONROE, MS	1231	11012	CHEMICAL MANUFACTURING	HOWELL, MO	1976	16385	HOSPITALS
MONTGOMERY, MS	445	2885	EDUCATIONAL SERVICES	IRON, MO	501	3508	MINING (EXCEPT OIL AND GAS)
NESHOBA, MS	858	10647	EXEC.; LEGIS.; & OTHER SUPPORT	JACKSON, MO	25234	360905	PROF.; SCIENTIFIC; & TECH SVCS
NEWTON, MS	664	7240	FURNITURE & RELATED PROD. MFG	JASPER, MO	5546	54651	RELIG.; GRANT; CIVIC; PROF ORG
NOXUBEE, MS	404	3249	FOOD MANUFACTURING	JEFFERSON, MO	5795	49001	EDUCATIONAL SERVICES
OKTIBBEHA, MS	1577	25799	EDUCATIONAL SERVICES	JOHNSON, MO	1744	24739	NAT'L SECURITY & INT'L AFFAIRS
PANOLA, MS	1245	10781	MERCH. WHOLESALERS;DURABLE GDS	KNOX, MO	232	1238	EDUCATIONAL SERVICES
PEARL RIVER, MS	1524	10077	EDUCATIONAL SERVICES	LACLEDE, MO	1676	13654	MERCH. WHOLESALERS;DURABLE GDS
PERRY, MS	320	3004	WOOD PRODUCT MANUFACTURING	LAFAYETTE, MO	1590	9678	EDUCATIONAL SERVICES
PIKE, MS	1653	14788	FOOD MANUFACTURING	LAWRENCE, MO	1308	9876	EDUCATIONAL SERVICES
PONTOTOC, MS	792	15357	FURNITURE & RELATED PROD. MFG	LEWIS, MO	419	2694	EDUCATIONAL SERVICES
PRENTISS, MS	821	8134	EDUCATIONAL SERVICES	LINCOLN, MO	1603	11167	EDUCATIONAL SERVICES
QUITMAN, MS	274	1697	EDUCATIONAL SERVICES	LINN, MO	663	4122	EDUCATIONAL SERVICES
RANKIN, MS	4829	54195	HOSPITALS	LIVINGSTON, MO	727	6332	FOOD SVCS & DRINKING PLACES
SCOTT, MS	878	12071	FOOD MANUFACTURING	MCDONALD, MO	877	6783	FOOD MANUFACTURING
SHARKEY, MS	231	1450	EDUCATIONAL SERVICES	MACON, MO	703	4879	EDUCATIONAL SERVICES
SIMPSON, MS	842	7346	HOSPITALS	MADISON, MO	499	3434	EDUCATIONAL SERVICES
SMITH, MS	334	2531	EDUCATIONAL SERVICES	MARIES, MO	271	1511	EDUCATIONAL SERVICES
STONE, MS	516	4141	EDUCATIONAL SERVICES	MARION, MO	1360	13096	EDUCATIONAL SERVICES
SUNFLOWER, MS	958	10448	JUSTICE; PUBIC ORDER/SAFETY	MERCER, MO	200	815	EDUCATIONAL SERVICES
TALLAHATCHIE, MS	395	2820	EDUCATIONAL SERVICES	MILLER, MO	1369	8639	EDUCATIONAL SERVICES
TATE, MS	770	6912	EDUCATIONAL SERVICES	MISSISSIPPI, MO	518	3603	EDUCATIONAL SERVICES
TIPPAH, MS	734	7249	FURNITURE & RELATED PROD. MFG	MONITEAU, MO	627	4046	EDUCATIONAL SERVICES
TISHOMINGO, MS	683	6579	FURNITURE & RELATED PROD. MFG	MONROE, MO	407	3397	PRIMARY METAL MANUFACTURING
TUNICA, MS	499	13219	AMUSEMENT; GAMBLING;& RECREAT.	MONTGOMERY, MO	614	3545	EDUCATIONAL SERVICES
UNION, MS	777	9879	FURNITURE & RELATED PROD. MFG	MORGAN, MO	935	5059	EDUCATIONAL SERVICES
WALTHALL, MS	405	2422	EDUCATIONAL SERVICES	NEW MADRID, MO	731	7506	PRIMARY METAL MANUFACTURING
WARREN, MS	1862	24420	EXEC.; LEGIS.; & OTHER SUPPORT	NEWTON, MO	2359	26944	HOSPITALS
WASHINGTON, MS	2334	21705	HOSPITALS	NODAWAY, MO	970	8939	EDUCATIONAL SERVICES
WAYNE, MS	675	5741	EDUCATIONAL SERVICES	OREGON, MO	423	2439	EDUCATIONAL SERVICES
WEBSTER, MS	341	2359	EDUCATIONAL SERVICES	OSAGE, MO	478	3284	WOOD PRODUCT MANUFACTURING
WILKINSON, MS	307	1858	EDUCATIONAL SERVICES	OZARK, MO	388	1958	EDUCATIONAL SERVICES
WINSTON, MS	611	6417	MERCH. WHOLESALERS;DURABLE GDS	PEMISCOT, MO	746	6912	EDUCATIONAL SERVICES
YALOBUSHA, MS	466	2940	TRANSPORTATION EQUIPMENT MFG	PERRY, MO	713	8993	FOOD MANUFACTURING
YAZOO, MS	795	5954	EDUCATIONAL SERVICES	PETTIS, MO	1686	18164	EDUCATIONAL SERVICES
ADAIR, MO	1018	10466	EDUCATIONAL SERVICES	PHELPS, MO	1884	19668	EDUCATIONAL SERVICES
ANDREW, MO	450	2523	EDUCATIONAL SERVICES	PIKE, MO	762	5991	EDUCATIONAL SERVICES
ATCHISON, MO	440	2076	EDUCATIONAL SERVICES	PLATTE, MO	2937	35634	FOOD SVCS & DRINKING PLACES
AUDRAIN, MO	1020	8849	EDUCATIONAL SERVICES	POLK, MO	1287	11634	AMBULATORY HEALTH CARE SVCS
BARRY, MO	1024	13300	FOOD MANUFACTURING	PULASKI, MO	1499	11871	EDUCATIONAL SERVICES
BARTON, MO	589	4243	FURNITURE & RELATED PROD. MFG	PUTNAM, MO	264	1359	MERCH. WHOLESALERS;NONDUR. GDS
BATES, MO	737	4077	EDUCATIONAL SERVICES	RALLS, MO	362	4269	FOOD MANUFACTURING
BENTON, MO	915	4438	EDUCATIONAL SERVICES	RANDOLPH, MO	1024	10396	EDUCATIONAL SERVICES
BOLLINGER, MO	350	2027	EDUCATIONAL SERVICES	RAY, MO	620	4568	EDUCATIONAL SERVICES
BOONE, MO	6649	85684	EDUCATIONAL SERVICES	REYNOLDS, MO	291	2344	EDUCATIONAL SERVICES
BUCHANAN, MO	3388	43813	NURSING & RESID. CARE FACILIT.	RIPLEY, MO	533	3417	HEALTH & PERSONAL CARE STORES
BUTLER, MO	1901	19069	HOSPITALS	ST. CHARLES, MO	11137	108955	FOOD SVCS & DRINKING PLACES
CALDWELL, MO	336	1582	EDUCATIONAL SERVICES	ST. CLAIR, MO	390	2319	SOCIAL ASSISTANCE
CALLAWAY, MO	1336	11178	EDUCATIONAL SERVICES	STE. GENEVIEVE, MO	671	6639	HOSPITALS
CAMDEN, MO	2811	20610	FOOD SVCS & DRINKING PLACES	ST. FRANCOIS, MO	2309	24269	JUSTICE; PUBIC ORDER/SAFETY
CAPE GIRARDEAU, MO	3460	39733	AMBULATORY HEALTH CARE SVCS	ST. LOUIS, MO	42572	554974	EDUCATIONAL SERVICES
CARROLL, MO	453	2705	EDUCATIONAL SERVICES	SALINE, MO	1019	9676	SOCIAL ASSISTANCE
CARTER, MO	303	1619	EDUCATIONAL SERVICES	SCHUYLER, MO	186	847	EDUCATIONAL SERVICES
CASS, MO	3014	20926	EDUCATIONAL SERVICES	SCOTLAND, MO	295	1652	EDUCATIONAL SERVICES
CEDAR, MO	666	4003	EDUCATIONAL SERVICES	SCOTT, MO	1746	16689	EDUCATIONAL SERVICES
CHARITON, MO	425	1963	EDUCATIONAL SERVICES	SHANNON, MO	320	1656	EDUCATIONAL SERVICES
CHRISTIAN, MO	2715	15724	EDUCATIONAL SERVICES	SHELBY, MO	337	2074	EDUCATIONAL SERVICES
CLARK, MO	316	1410	EDUCATIONAL SERVICES	STODDARD, MO	1358	10227	EDUCATIONAL SERVICES
CLAY, MO	6694	89206	FOOD SVCS & DRINKING PLACES	STONE, MO	1675	8021	FOOD SVCS & DRINKING PLACES
CLINTON, MO	761	5307	JUSTICE; PUBIC ORDER/SAFETY	SULLIVAN, MO	313	2555	FOOD MANUFACTURING
COLE, MO	3909	55707	EXEC.; LEGIS.; & OTHER SUPPORT	TANEY, MO	4424	34493	ACCOMMODATION
COOPER, MO	766	7307	AMUSEMENT; GAMBLING;& RECREAT.	TEXAS, MO	976	6237	EDUCATIONAL SERVICES
CRAWFORD, MO	932	6590	EDUCATIONAL SERVICES	VERNON, MO	883	6488	EDUCATIONAL SERVICES
DADE, MO	318	1955	FOOD MANUFACTURING	WARREN, MO	1138	7317	FABRICATED METAL PRODUCT MFG
DALLAS, MO	543	3309	MERCH. WHOLESALERS;NONDUR. GDS	WASHINGTON, MO	677	4580	EDUCATIONAL SERVICES
DAVIESS, MO	434	1935	EDUCATIONAL SERVICES	WAYNE, MO	524	3057	EDUCATIONAL SERVICES
DEKALB, MO	395	2613	GENERAL MERCHANDISE STORES	WEBSTER, MO	1247	6968	EDUCATIONAL SERVICES
DENT, MO	597	5093	EDUCATIONAL SERVICES	WORTH, MO	165	925	EDUCATIONAL SERVICES
DOUGLAS, MO	439	2514	MACHINERY MANUFACTURING	WRIGHT, MO	780	4423	EDUCATIONAL SERVICES
DUNKLIN, MO	1468	10278	EDUCATIONAL SERVICES	ST. LOUIS CITY, MO	13042	217893	EDUCATIONAL SERVICES
FRANKLIN, MO	4045	37148	EDUCATIONAL SERVICES	BEAVERHEAD, MT	633	3230	EDUCATIONAL SERVICES
GASCONADE, MO	868	6002	EDUCATIONAL SERVICES	BIG HORN, MT	452	4142	EDUCATIONAL SERVICES
GENTRY, MO	394	2554	EDUCATIONAL SERVICES	BLAINE, MT	394	2260	EDUCATIONAL SERVICES
GREENE, MO	13087	166905	HOSPITALS	BROADWATER, MT	213	1171	WOOD PRODUCT MANUFACTURING

COUNTY	2007 Total Firms	2007 Total Employ-ees	TOP INDUSTRY RANKED on 2007 EMPLOYMENT	COUNTY	2007 Total Firms	2007 Total Employ-ees	TOP INDUSTRY RANKED on 2007 EMPLOYMENT
CARBON, MT	609	2749	FOOD SVCS & DRINKING PLACES	DUNDY, NE	182	718	EDUCATIONAL SERVICES
CARTER, MT	91	319	EDUCATIONAL SERVICES	FILLMORE, NE	387	2443	EDUCATIONAL SERVICES
CASCADE, MT	4062	37279	AMBULATORY HEALTH CARE SVCS	FRANKLIN, NE	182	865	EDUCATIONAL SERVICES
CHOUTEAU, MT	412	1454	EDUCATIONAL SERVICES	FRONTIER, NE	186	950	AIR TRANSPORTATION
CUSTER, MT	662	4682	AMBULATORY HEALTH CARE SVCS	FURNAS, NE	403	2331	EDUCATIONAL SERVICES
DANIELS, MT	158	702	TELECOMMUNICATIONS	GAGE, NE	1161	9327	EXEC.; LEGIS.; & OTHER SUPPORT
DAWSON, MT	490	3891	EDUCATIONAL SERVICES	GARDEN, NE	135	578	HOSPITALS
DEER LODGE, MT	401	3092	HOSPITALS	GARFIELD, NE	183	957	NURSING & RESID. CARE FACILIT.
FALLON, MT	218	1283	SPECIAL TRADE CONTRACTORS	GOSPER, NE	100	407	NURSING & RESID. CARE FACILIT.
FERGUS, MT	729	4169	EDUCATIONAL SERVICES	GRANT, NE	120	332	ANIMAL PRODUCTION
FLATHEAD, MT	6200	40720	FOOD SVCS & DRINKING PLACES	GREELEY, NE	171	764	EDUCATIONAL SERVICES
GALLATIN, MT	5570	39867	FOOD SVCS & DRINKING PLACES	HALL, NE	2467	31611	FOOD MANUFACTURING
GARFIELD, MT	102	397	EXEC.; LEGIS.; & OTHER SUPPORT	HAMILTON, NE	589	3910	EDUCATIONAL SERVICES
GLACIER, MT	742	7399	EXEC.; LEGIS.; & OTHER SUPPORT	HARLAN, NE	208	923	EXEC.; LEGIS.; & OTHER SUPPORT
GOLDEN VALLEY, MT	44	176	ANIMAL PRODUCTION	HAYES, NE	39	180	EDUCATIONAL SERVICES
GRANITE, MT	148	638	FOOD SVCS & DRINKING PLACES	HITCHCOCK, NE	180	829	EDUCATIONAL SERVICES
HILL, MT	930	8215	EXEC.; LEGIS.; & OTHER SUPPORT	HOLT, NE	756	4033	EDUCATIONAL SERVICES
JEFFERSON, MT	404	2425	EXEC.; LEGIS.; & OTHER SUPPORT	HOOKER, NE	87	390	AMUSEMENT; GAMBLING;& RECREAT.
JUDITH BASIN, MT	118	406	EDUCATIONAL SERVICES	HOWARD, NE	228	1253	EDUCATIONAL SERVICES
LAKE, MT	1597	10555	EXEC.; LEGIS.; & OTHER SUPPORT	JEFFERSON, NE	467	3186	EDUCATIONAL SERVICES
LEWIS AND CLARK, MT	3376	37106	ADMIN. HUMAN RESOURCE PROGRAMS	JOHNSON, NE	229	1476	MERCH. WHOLESALERS;NONDUR. GDS
LIBERTY, MT	200	817	CROP PRODUCTION	KEARNEY, NE	328	2352	EDUCATIONAL SERVICES
LINCOLN, MT	1135	5857	SUPPORT ACTIVITIES: AGR./FOR.	KEITH, NE	607	3822	FOOD SVCS & DRINKING PLACES
MCCONE, MT	127	780	EDUCATIONAL SERVICES	KEYA PAHA, NE	69	119	EDUCATIONAL SERVICES
MADISON, MT	645	2442	RELIG.; GRANT; CIVIC; PROF ORG	KIMBALL, NE	262	1662	COMPUTER & ELECTRONIC PROD MFG
MEAGHER, MT	131	609	ANIMAL PRODUCTION	KNOX, NE	573	3227	EDUCATIONAL SERVICES
MINERAL, MT	206	1254	EDUCATIONAL SERVICES	LANCASTER, NE	10535	168604	EDUCATIONAL SERVICES
MISSOULA, MT	5543	52881	FOOD SVCS & DRINKING PLACES	LINCOLN, NE	1741	14133	FOOD SVCS & DRINKING PLACES
MUSSELSHELL, MT	251	1148	EDUCATIONAL SERVICES	LOGAN, NE	47	158	EDUCATIONAL SERVICES
PARK, MT	1104	5995	ACCOMMODATION	LOUP, NE	33	116	EDUCATIONAL SERVICES
PETROLEUM, MT	39	102	EDUCATIONAL SERVICES	MCPHERSON, NE	28	69	EDUCATIONAL SERVICES
PHILLIPS, MT	333	1514	EDUCATIONAL SERVICES	MADISON, NE	1828	25081	FOOD MANUFACTURING
PONDERA, MT	441	2240	EDUCATIONAL SERVICES	MERRICK, NE	373	2092	EDUCATIONAL SERVICES
POWDER RIVER, MT	135	490	EDUCATIONAL SERVICES	MORRILL, NE	270	1582	EDUCATIONAL SERVICES
POWELL, MT	309	2915	JUSTICE; PUBIC ORDER/SAFETY	NANCE, NE	199	938	EDUCATIONAL SERVICES
PRAIRIE, MT	90	256	NURSING & RESID. CARE FACILIT.	NEMAHA, NE	346	3359	CHEMICAL MANUFACTURING
RAVALLI, MT	1951	11210	EDUCATIONAL SERVICES	NUCKOLLS, NE	299	1620	EDUCATIONAL SERVICES
RICHLAND, MT	597	4742	FOOD MANUFACTURING	OTOE, NE	739	6301	MERCH. WHOLESALERS;DURABLE GDS
ROOSEVELT, MT	560	3866	EDUCATIONAL SERVICES	PAWNEE, NE	136	629	EDUCATIONAL SERVICES
ROSEBUD, MT	455	3965	EDUCATIONAL SERVICES	PERKINS, NE	238	1188	NURSING & RESID. CARE FACILIT.
SANDERS, MT	625	3137	EDUCATIONAL SERVICES	PHELPS, NE	539	4963	MISCELLANEOUS MANUFACTURING
SHERIDAN, MT	310	1338	HOSPITALS	PIERCE, NE	393	2194	EDUCATIONAL SERVICES
SILVER BOW, MT	1625	14852	HOSPITALS	PLATTE, NE	1743	20311	EDUCATIONAL SERVICES
STILLWATER, MT	448	3374	MINING (EXCEPT OIL AND GAS)	POLK, NE	281	1475	EDUCATIONAL SERVICES
SWEET GRASS, MT	324	1952	MINING (EXCEPT OIL AND GAS)	RED WILLOW, NE	709	5401	EDUCATIONAL SERVICES
TETON, MT	483	2071	EDUCATIONAL SERVICES	RICHARDSON, NE	513	2976	EDUCATIONAL SERVICES
TOOLE, MT	478	2294	EDUCATIONAL SERVICES	ROCK, NE	160	571	EDUCATIONAL SERVICES
TREASURE, MT	59	216	ANIMAL PRODUCTION	SALINE, NE	537	6861	FOOD MANUFACTURING
VALLEY, MT	550	2758	EDUCATIONAL SERVICES	SARPY, NE	3675	47134	EDUCATIONAL SERVICES
WHEATLAND, MT	124	594	EDUCATIONAL SERVICES	SAUNDERS, NE	842	5700	EDUCATIONAL SERVICES
WIBAUX, MT	71	256	EDUCATIONAL SERVICES	SCOTTS BLUFF, NE	1965	18167	EDUCATIONAL SERVICES
YELLOWSTONE, MT	7700	72735	AMBULATORY HEALTH CARE SVCS	SEWARD, NE	611	5837	EDUCATIONAL SERVICES
ADAMS, NE	1504	15823	EDUCATIONAL SERVICES	SHERIDAN, NE	343	1776	EDUCATIONAL SERVICES
ANTELOPE, NE	458	2277	EDUCATIONAL SERVICES	SHERMAN, NE	162	937	PROF.; SCIENTIFIC; & TECH SVCS
ARTHUR, NE	40	72	ANIMAL PRODUCTION	SIOUX, NE	47	116	EDUCATIONAL SERVICES
BANNER, NE	24	116	EDUCATIONAL SERVICES	STANTON, NE	183	911	EDUCATIONAL SERVICES
BLAINE, NE	45	105	EDUCATIONAL SERVICES	THAYER, NE	411	2406	MACHINERY MANUFACTURING
BOONE, NE	380	2702	EDUCATIONAL SERVICES	THOMAS, NE	88	337	EDUCATIONAL SERVICES
BOX BUTTE, NE	526	3923	EDUCATIONAL SERVICES	THURSTON, NE	288	3312	EXEC.; LEGIS.; & OTHER SUPPORT
BOYD, NE	187	810	EDUCATIONAL SERVICES	VALLEY, NE	317	1873	EXEC.; LEGIS.; & OTHER SUPPORT
BROWN, NE	250	1473	EDUCATIONAL SERVICES	WASHINGTON, NE	843	7245	MOTOR VEHICLE & PARTS DEALERS
BUFFALO, NE	2164	25281	HOSPITALS	WAYNE, NE	418	4240	EDUCATIONAL SERVICES
BURT, NE	379	1977	EDUCATIONAL SERVICES	WEBSTER, NE	241	1182	EDUCATIONAL SERVICES
BUTLER, NE	355	2258	EDUCATIONAL SERVICES	WHEELER, NE	60	345	MERCH. WHOLESALERS;NONDUR. GDS
CASS, NE	890	5516	EDUCATIONAL SERVICES	YORK, NE	767	8634	TRUCK TRANSPORTATION
CEDAR, NE	556	2688	EDUCATIONAL SERVICES	CHURCHILL, NV	1036	7669	EDUCATIONAL SERVICES
CHASE, NE	307	1703	EDUCATIONAL SERVICES	CLARK, NV	71575	860052	ACCOMMODATION
CHERRY, NE	415	2262	FOOD SVCS & DRINKING PLACES	DOUGLAS, NV	2798	30471	AMUSEMENT; GAMBLING;& RECREAT.
CHEYENNE, NE	600	5207	SPORTG GDS;HOBBY;BOOK; & MUSIC	ELKO, NV	2007	21476	AMUSEMENT; GAMBLING;& RECREAT.
CLAY, NE	359	2164	EDUCATIONAL SERVICES	ESMERALDA, NV	72	482	JUSTICE; PUBIC ORDER/SAFETY
COLFAX, NE	416	4797	FOOD MANUFACTURING	EUREKA, NV	106	913	MINING (EXCEPT OIL AND GAS)
CUMING, NE	586	3907	FOOD MANUFACTURING	HUMBOLDT, NV	651	7354	MINING (EXCEPT OIL AND GAS)
CUSTER, NE	690	3918	EDUCATIONAL SERVICES	LANDER, NV	255	1559	EDUCATIONAL SERVICES
DAKOTA, NE	693	6136	EDUCATIONAL SERVICES	LINCOLN, NV	247	1266	EDUCATIONAL SERVICES
DAWES, NE	511	3578	EDUCATIONAL SERVICES	LYON, NV	1415	10407	EDUCATIONAL SERVICES
DAWSON, NE	1199	12763	FOOD MANUFACTURING	MINERAL, NV	213	1928	PROF.; SCIENTIFIC; & TECH SVCS
DEUEL, NE	136	713	EDUCATIONAL SERVICES	NYE, NV	1354	8404	EDUCATIONAL SERVICES
DIXON, NE	278	2004	MISCELLANEOUS MANUFACTURING	PERSHING, NV	204	2503	SECURITIES;COMMODITY CONTRACTS
DODGE, NE	1535	16983	MERCH. WHOLESALERS;NONDUR. GDS	STOREY, NV	199	1405	PROF.; SCIENTIFIC; & TECH SVCS
DOUGLAS, NE	19798	324857	EDUCATIONAL SERVICES	WASHOE, NV	16849	196107	ACCOMMODATION

COUNTY	2007 Total Firms	2007 Total Employees	TOP INDUSTRY RANKED on 2007 EMPLOYMENT	COUNTY	2007 Total Firms	2007 Total Employees	TOP INDUSTRY RANKED on 2007 EMPLOYMENT
WHITE PINE, NV	425	3488	JUSTICE; PUBIC ORDER/SAFETY	ERIE, NY	31320	426110	EDUCATIONAL SERVICES
CARSON CITY, NV	3425	34010	EXEC.; LEGIS.; & OTHER SUPPORT	ESSEX, NY	2301	16656	ACCOMMODATION
BELKNAP, NH	3574	28123	FOOD SVCS & DRINKING PLACES	FRANKLIN, NY	2118	20368	EDUCATIONAL SERVICES
CARROLL, NH	3269	23031	ACCOMMODATION	FULTON, NY	2223	19194	EDUCATIONAL SERVICES
CHESHIRE, NH	3357	35373	EDUCATIONAL SERVICES	GENESEE, NY	2102	25122	AMUSEMENT; GAMBLING;& RECREAT.
COOS, NH	1707	14059	ACCOMMODATION	GREENE, NY	2213	15763	EDUCATIONAL SERVICES
GRAFTON, NH	4950	62131	AMBULATORY HEALTH CARE SVCS	HAMILTON, NY	570	2587	ACCOMMODATION
HILLSBOROUGH, NH	18561	180238	EDUCATIONAL SERVICES	HERKIMER, NY	2229	19392	EDUCATIONAL SERVICES
MERRIMACK, NH	7451	79310	EDUCATIONAL SERVICES	JEFFERSON, NY	4268	39943	EDUCATIONAL SERVICES
ROCKINGHAM, NH	15410	135459	EDUCATIONAL SERVICES	KINGS, NY	63615	461950	EDUCATIONAL SERVICES
STRAFFORD, NH	4665	40980	EDUCATIONAL SERVICES	LEWIS, NY	1053	7597	EDUCATIONAL SERVICES
SULLIVAN, NH	1914	15174	EDUCATIONAL SERVICES	LIVINGSTON, NY	2299	19141	EDUCATIONAL SERVICES
ATLANTIC, NJ	13264	152271	ACCOMMODATION	MADISON, NY	2498	24237	EDUCATIONAL SERVICES
BERGEN, NJ	48293	408087	PROF.; SCIENTIFIC; & TECH SVCS	MONROE, NY	26356	334099	EDUCATIONAL SERVICES
BURLINGTON, NJ	16834	191798	EDUCATIONAL SERVICES	MONTGOMERY, NY	1788	18842	EDUCATIONAL SERVICES
CAMDEN, NJ	20722	205696	EDUCATIONAL SERVICES	NASSAU, NY	62773	539282	EDUCATIONAL SERVICES
CAPE MAY, NJ	7682	52281	FOOD SVCS & DRINKING PLACES	NEW YORK, NY	155030	1707252	PROF.; SCIENTIFIC; & TECH SVCS
CUMBERLAND, NJ	5735	57294	EDUCATIONAL SERVICES	NIAGARA, NY	7075	74832	EDUCATIONAL SERVICES
ESSEX, NJ	34005	346016	EDUCATIONAL SERVICES	ONEIDA, NY	8352	110240	EDUCATIONAL SERVICES
GLOUCESTER, NJ	9577	95783	EDUCATIONAL SERVICES	ONONDAGA, NY	20535	272725	EDUCATIONAL SERVICES
HUDSON, NJ	20477	196205	EDUCATIONAL SERVICES	ONTARIO, NY	4909	52130	EDUCATIONAL SERVICES
HUNTERDON, NJ	7427	57486	EDUCATIONAL SERVICES	ORANGE, NY	15562	122953	EDUCATIONAL SERVICES
MERCER, NJ	15528	230421	PROF.; SCIENTIFIC; & TECH SVCS	ORLEANS, NY	1174	11032	EDUCATIONAL SERVICES
MIDDLESEX, NJ	28101	333543	PROF.; SCIENTIFIC; & TECH SVCS	OSWEGO, NY	4078	34820	EDUCATIONAL SERVICES
MONMOUTH, NJ	28623	252113	EDUCATIONAL SERVICES	OTSEGO, NY	2478	25249	EDUCATIONAL SERVICES
MORRIS, NJ	27984	280488	PROF.; SCIENTIFIC; & TECH SVCS	PUTNAM, NY	3879	26118	EDUCATIONAL SERVICES
OCEAN, NJ	20152	158856	EDUCATIONAL SERVICES	QUEENS, NY	61282	449974	EDUCATIONAL SERVICES
PASSAIC, NJ	19125	174457	EDUCATIONAL SERVICES	RENSSELAER, NY	5164	50211	EDUCATIONAL SERVICES
SALEM, NJ	2627	23272	EDUCATIONAL SERVICES	RICHMOND, NY	12065	96511	EDUCATIONAL SERVICES
SOMERSET, NJ	14661	165996	PROF.; SCIENTIFIC; & TECH SVCS	ROCKLAND, NY	13203	108230	EDUCATIONAL SERVICES
SUSSEX, NJ	7320	45158	EDUCATIONAL SERVICES	ST. LAWRENCE, NY	3718	40185	EDUCATIONAL SERVICES
UNION, NJ	23877	234779	PROF.; SCIENTIFIC; & TECH SVCS	SARATOGA, NY	7568	71476	EDUCATIONAL SERVICES
WARREN, NJ	5081	37401	EDUCATIONAL SERVICES	SCHENECTADY, NY	5077	70431	PROF.; SCIENTIFIC; & TECH SVCS
BERNALILLO, NM	26690	304790	EDUCATIONAL SERVICES	SCHOHARIE, NY	1243	9282	EDUCATIONAL SERVICES
CATRON, NM	254	824	EDUCATIONAL SERVICES	SCHUYLER, NY	751	5469	EDUCATIONAL SERVICES
CHAVES, NM	2268	21132	EDUCATIONAL SERVICES	SENECA, NY	1275	13012	MACHINERY MANUFACTURING
CIBOLA, NM	789	8539	EDUCATIONAL SERVICES	STEUBEN, NY	3476	36422	EDUCATIONAL SERVICES
COLFAX, NM	973	6538	SOCIAL ASSISTANCE	SUFFOLK, NY	69222	553314	EDUCATIONAL SERVICES
CURRY, NM	1916	16280	EDUCATIONAL SERVICES	SULLIVAN, NY	3922	28812	ACCOMMODATION
DE BACA, NM	147	565	EDUCATIONAL SERVICES	TIOGA, NY	1644	16014	COMPUTER & ELECTRONIC PROD MFG
DONA ANA, NM	4846	56950	EDUCATIONAL SERVICES	TOMPKINS, NY	3546	39132	EDUCATIONAL SERVICES
EDDY, NM	2043	18886	EDUCATIONAL SERVICES	ULSTER, NY	8360	66467	EDUCATIONAL SERVICES
GRANT, NM	1260	9257	EDUCATIONAL SERVICES	WARREN, NY	3728	39899	ACCOMMODATION
GUADALUPE, NM	341	2105	FOOD SVCS & DRINKING PLACES	WASHINGTON, NY	1883	16318	EDUCATIONAL SERVICES
HARDING, NM	89	215	EDUCATIONAL SERVICES	WAYNE, NY	3352	32664	EDUCATIONAL SERVICES
HIDALGO, NM	285	1577	EDUCATIONAL SERVICES	WESTCHESTER, NY	39735	377322	EDUCATIONAL SERVICES
LEA, NM	2584	25182	SPECIAL TRADE CONTRACTORS	WYOMING, NY	1301	13562	JUSTICE; PUBIC ORDER/SAFETY
LINCOLN, NM	1602	8756	EDUCATIONAL SERVICES	YATES, NY	1042	7761	AMBULATORY HEALTH CARE SVCS
LOS ALAMOS, NM	700	14346	EDUCATIONAL SERVICES	ALAMANCE, NC	5008	56712	FOOD SVCS & DRINKING PLACES
LUNA, NM	753	7165	FOOD MANUFACTURING	ALEXANDER, NC	959	9904	FURNITURE & RELATED PROD. MFG
MCKINLEY, NM	1914	22703	EDUCATIONAL SERVICES	ALLEGHANY, NC	576	3998	RELIG.; GRANT; CIVIC; PROF ORG
MORA, NM	186	1048	EDUCATIONAL SERVICES	ANSON, NC	960	7802	EDUCATIONAL SERVICES
OTERO, NM	1999	17520	EDUCATIONAL SERVICES	ASHE, NC	1288	8820	FOOD SVCS & DRINKING PLACES
QUAY, NM	639	3513	FOOD SVCS & DRINKING PLACES	AVERY, NC	1002	9483	ACCOMMODATION
RIO ARRIBA, NM	1388	12501	EDUCATIONAL SERVICES	BEAUFORT, NC	2070	17653	EDUCATIONAL SERVICES
ROOSEVELT, NM	699	5204	EDUCATIONAL SERVICES	BERTIE, NC	676	6694	FOOD MANUFACTURING
SANDOVAL, NM	2777	25191	COMPUTER & ELECTRONIC PROD MFG	BLADEN, NC	1281	12518	ADMINISTRATIVE & SUPPORT SVCS
SAN JUAN, NM	4467	48498	EDUCATIONAL SERVICES	BRUNSWICK, NC	4112	29503	FOOD SVCS & DRINKING PLACES
SAN MIGUEL, NM	1070	9378	EDUCATIONAL SERVICES	BUNCOMBE, NC	11678	106452	AMBULATORY HEALTH CARE SVCS
SANTA FE, NM	9089	80438	EXEC.; LEGIS.; & OTHER SUPPORT	BURKE, NC	2776	37400	HOSPITALS
SIERRA, NM	612	3726	HOSPITALS	CABARRUS, NC	5333	59680	FOOD SVCS & DRINKING PLACES
SOCORRO, NM	555	5263	RELIG.; GRANT; CIVIC; PROF ORG	CALDWELL, NC	2345	28227	EDUCATIONAL SERVICES
TAOS, NM	2139	13186	ACCOMMODATION	CAMDEN, NC	218	1114	EDUCATIONAL SERVICES
TORRANCE, NM	478	2949	EDUCATIONAL SERVICES	CARTERET, NC	3729	25131	FOOD SVCS & DRINKING PLACES
UNION, NM	322	1354	EDUCATIONAL SERVICES	CASWELL, NC	612	3635	EDUCATIONAL SERVICES
VALENCIA, NM	1766	13052	EDUCATIONAL SERVICES	CATAWBA, NC	6484	89962	FURNITURE & RELATED PROD. MFG
ALBANY, NY	14473	243256	EDUCATIONAL SERVICES	CHATHAM, NC	1871	15268	EDUCATIONAL SERVICES
ALLEGANY, NY	1592	21198	SOCIAL ASSISTANCE	CHEROKEE, NC	1336	9221	HOSPITALS
BRONX, NY	30418	264114	HOSPITALS	CHOWAN, NC	655	7974	REPAIR AND MAINTENANCE
BROOME, NY	7996	95976	EDUCATIONAL SERVICES	CLAY, NC	491	2183	FOOD SVCS & DRINKING PLACES
CATTARAUGUS, NY	2834	33498	EDUCATIONAL SERVICES	CLEVELAND, NC	3260	34060	EDUCATIONAL SERVICES
CAYUGA, NY	2801	26299	EDUCATIONAL SERVICES	COLUMBUS, NC	2152	19206	EXEC.; LEGIS.; & OTHER SUPPORT
CHAUTAUQUA, NY	5943	61476	EDUCATIONAL SERVICES	CRAVEN, NC	4079	35578	FOOD SVCS & DRINKING PLACES
CHEMUNG, NY	3252	37589	EDUCATIONAL SERVICES	CUMBERLAND, NC	10509	99671	EDUCATIONAL SERVICES
CHENANGO, NY	2099	17877	EDUCATIONAL SERVICES	CURRITUCK, NC	1203	5704	FOOD SVCS & DRINKING PLACES
CLINTON, NY	3480	36103	AMBULATORY HEALTH CARE SVCS	DARE, NC	3326	19720	FOOD SVCS & DRINKING PLACES
COLUMBIA, NY	3639	22852	EDUCATIONAL SERVICES	DAVIDSON, NC	5586	49370	EDUCATIONAL SERVICES
CORTLAND, NY	1743	23332	EDUCATIONAL SERVICES	DAVIE, NC	1559	12553	EDUCATIONAL SERVICES
DELAWARE, NY	2606	20399	EDUCATIONAL SERVICES	DUPLIN, NC	1990	18806	FOOD AND BEVERAGE STORES
DUTCHESS, NY	12017	113304	EDUCATIONAL SERVICES	DURHAM, NC	9609	126062	EDUCATIONAL SERVICES

COUNTY	2007 Total Firms	2007 Total Employees	TOP INDUSTRY RANKED on 2007 EMPLOYMENT	COUNTY	2007 Total Firms	2007 Total Employees	TOP INDUSTRY RANKED on 2007 EMPLOYMENT
EDGECOMBE, NC	1895	23190	MERCH. WHOLESALERS;NONDUR. GDS	DUNN, ND	195	1004	COMPUTER & ELECTRONIC PROD MFG
FORSYTH, NC	13195	173726	AMBULATORY HEALTH CARE SVCS	EDDY, ND	176	747	NURSING & RESID. CARE FACILIT.
FRANKLIN, NC	1443	11603	EDUCATIONAL SERVICES	EMMONS, ND	251	1295	EDUCATIONAL SERVICES
GASTON, NC	6648	71497	FOOD SVCS & DRINKING PLACES	FOSTER, ND	299	1998	FOOD MANUFACTURING
GATES, NC	266	1500	EDUCATIONAL SERVICES	GOLDEN VALLEY, ND	192	748	EDUCATIONAL SERVICES
GRAHAM, NC	343	2648	FURNITURE & RELATED PROD. MFG	GRAND FORKS, ND	2651	41962	EDUCATIONAL SERVICES
GRANVILLE, NC	1467	20464	HOSPITALS	GRANT, ND	194	730	RELIG.; GRANT; CIVIC; PROF ORG
GREENE, NC	489	3198	EDUCATIONAL SERVICES	GRIGGS, ND	280	1055	HOSPITALS
GUILFORD, NC	22992	262337	FOOD SVCS & DRINKING PLACES	HETTINGER, ND	188	917	EDUCATIONAL SERVICES
HALIFAX, NC	2060	18177	EDUCATIONAL SERVICES	KIDDER, ND	178	768	EDUCATIONAL SERVICES
HARNETT, NC	2767	24347	EDUCATIONAL SERVICES	LAMOURE, ND	322	1729	EDUCATIONAL SERVICES
HAYWOOD, NC	2452	21339	SOCIAL ASSISTANCE	LOGAN, ND	138	536	RELIG.; GRANT; CIVIC; PROF ORG
HENDERSON, NC	4223	38529	FOOD SVCS & DRINKING PLACES	MCHENRY, ND	306	1354	EDUCATIONAL SERVICES
HERTFORD, NC	930	8871	EDUCATIONAL SERVICES	MCINTOSH, ND	242	1478	EDUCATIONAL SERVICES
HOKE, NC	749	7211	MERCH. WHOLESALERS;NONDUR. GDS	MCKENZIE, ND	344	1678	EDUCATIONAL SERVICES
HYDE, NC	331	2248	MERCH. WHOLESALERS;NONDUR. GDS	MCLEAN, ND	590	4403	UTILITIES
IREDELL, NC	5922	63064	FOOD SVCS & DRINKING PLACES	MERCER, ND	545	4693	OIL AND GAS EXTRACTION
JACKSON, NC	1540	12206	EDUCATIONAL SERVICES	MORTON, ND	1161	9277	EDUCATIONAL SERVICES
JOHNSTON, NC	4779	41064	FOOD SVCS & DRINKING PLACES	MOUNTRAIL, ND	513	3598	EXEC.; LEGIS.; & OTHER SUPPORT
JONES, NC	354	1837	AMBULATORY HEALTH CARE SVCS	NELSON, ND	281	1164	EDUCATIONAL SERVICES
LEE, NC	2298	25371	AMBULATORY HEALTH CARE SVCS	OLIVER, ND	92	631	UTILITIES
LENOIR, NC	2356	26267	EXEC.; LEGIS.; & OTHER SUPPORT	PEMBINA, ND	658	4388	TRANSPORTATION EQUIPMENT MFG
LINCOLN, NC	2394	21861	FABRICATED METAL PRODUCT MFG	PIERCE, ND	251	1731	HOSPITALS
MCDOWELL, NC	1325	17172	CHEMICAL MANUFACTURING	RAMSEY, ND	748	5786	EDUCATIONAL SERVICES
MACON, NC	1908	13402	AMBULATORY HEALTH CARE SVCS	RANSOM, ND	299	2264	MISCELLANEOUS MANUFACTURING
MADISON, NC	591	4340	ELECT'L EQPMT; APP; & COMP MFG	RENVILLE, ND	186	921	EDUCATIONAL SERVICES
MARTIN, NC	976	7632	EDUCATIONAL SERVICES	RICHLAND, ND	817	8256	EDUCATIONAL SERVICES
MECKLENBURG, NC	41775	446921	PROF.; SCIENTIFIC; & TECH SVCS	ROLETTE, ND	427	6582	EXEC.; LEGIS.; & OTHER SUPPORT
MITCHELL, NC	678	6033	FURN. & HOME FURNISHGS STORES	SARGENT, ND	264	2326	MACHINERY MANUFACTURING
MONTGOMERY, NC	1014	11408	EDUCATIONAL SERVICES	SHERIDAN, ND	125	417	CONSTRUCTION OF BUILDINGS
MOORE, NC	3957	39250	HOSPITALS	SIOUX, ND	156	1907	EXEC.; LEGIS.; & OTHER SUPPORT
NASH, NC	3530	38202	AMBULATORY HEALTH CARE SVCS	SLOPE, ND	43	113	SPECIAL TRADE CONTRACTORS
NEW HANOVER, NC	9920	102221	FOOD SVCS & DRINKING PLACES	STARK, ND	1409	12453	EDUCATIONAL SERVICES
NORTHAMPTON, NC	590	4577	EDUCATIONAL SERVICES	STEELE, ND	147	687	EDUCATIONAL SERVICES
ONSLOW, NC	4430	40222	FOOD SVCS & DRINKING PLACES	STUTSMAN, ND	1230	10897	HOSPITALS
ORANGE, NC	4888	63812	EDUCATIONAL SERVICES	TOWNER, ND	183	905	NURSING & RESID. CARE FACILIT.
PAMLICO, NC	566	3421	EDUCATIONAL SERVICES	TRAILL, ND	474	3040	EDUCATIONAL SERVICES
PASQUOTANK, NC	1763	16964	NAT'L SECURITY & INT'L AFFAIRS	WALSH, ND	786	5556	MISCELLANEOUS MANUFACTURING
PENDER, NC	1497	9467	EDUCATIONAL SERVICES	WARD, ND	2726	29312	EDUCATIONAL SERVICES
PERQUIMANS, NC	422	2436	EDUCATIONAL SERVICES	WELLS, ND	361	1776	HOSPITALS
PERSON, NC	1383	11111	TEXTILE MILLS	WILLIAMS, ND	1442	12192	SUPPORT ACTIVITIES FOR MINING
PITT, NC	5939	74637	EDUCATIONAL SERVICES	ADAMS, OH	901	6507	EDUCATIONAL SERVICES
POLK, NC	945	5427	NURSING & RESID. CARE FACILIT.	ALLEN, OH	4230	60764	HOSPITALS
RANDOLPH, NC	5403	52133	FURNITURE & RELATED PROD. MFG	ASHLAND, OH	1721	19775	EDUCATIONAL SERVICES
RICHMOND, NC	1642	15090	EDUCATIONAL SERVICES	ASHTABULA, OH	4111	40224	MERCH. WHOLESALERS;DURABLE GDS
ROBESON, NC	3650	44598	EDUCATIONAL SERVICES	ATHENS, OH	1946	19983	EDUCATIONAL SERVICES
ROCKINGHAM, NC	3386	30763	TEXTILE MILLS	AUGLAIZE, OH	1775	19992	COMPUTER & ELECTRONIC PROD MFG
ROWAN, NC	4047	48157	MISCELLANEOUS MANUFACTURING	BELMONT, OH	2672	24728	FOOD SVCS & DRINKING PLACES
RUTHERFORD, NC	2458	24846	FABRICATED METAL PRODUCT MFG	BROWN, OH	1162	9321	EDUCATIONAL SERVICES
SAMPSON, NC	2377	25131	RELIG.; GRANT; CIVIC; PROF ORG	BUTLER, OH	10634	132673	FOOD SVCS & DRINKING PLACES
SCOTLAND, NC	1151	14578	TEXTILE MILLS	CARROLL, OH	908	7514	FABRICATED METAL PRODUCT MFG
STANLY, NC	2324	26764	MERCH. WHOLESALERS;DURABLE GDS	CHAMPAIGN, OH	1302	12285	MOTOR VEHICLE & PARTS DEALERS
STOKES, NC	1185	8887	EDUCATIONAL SERVICES	CLARK, OH	4314	58401	FOOD SVCS & DRINKING PLACES
SURRY, NC	3122	31095	APPAREL MANUFACTURING	CLERMONT, OH	5511	59867	FOOD SVCS & DRINKING PLACES
SWAIN, NC	842	9917	AMUSEMENT; GAMBLING;& RECREAT.	CLINTON, OH	1459	26098	AIR TRANSPORTATION
TRANSYLVANIA, NC	1553	11462	ACCOMMODATION	COLUMBIANA, OH	3863	35701	EDUCATIONAL SERVICES
TYRRELL, NC	177	1163	CROP PRODUCTION	COSHOCTON, OH	1228	13161	FOOD SVCS & DRINKING PLACES
UNION, NC	5218	49916	SPECIAL TRADE CONTRACTORS	CRAWFORD, OH	1665	15911	FABRICATED METAL PRODUCT MFG
VANCE, NC	1621	15031	EDUCATIONAL SERVICES	CUYAHOGA, OH	51593	752135	HOSPITALS
WAKE, NC	34172	395897	EDUCATIONAL SERVICES	DARKE, OH	1889	19028	EDUCATIONAL SERVICES
WARREN, NC	514	3792	EDUCATIONAL SERVICES	DEFIANCE, OH	1538	17971	PRIMARY METAL MANUFACTURING
WASHINGTON, NC	539	4428	PAPER MANUFACTURING	DELAWARE, OH	5311	52786	FOOD SVCS & DRINKING PLACES
WATAUGA, NC	2531	24301	RELIG.; GRANT; CIVIC; PROF ORG	ERIE, OH	3373	43534	AMUSEMENT; GAMBLING;& RECREAT.
WAYNE, NC	4055	42142	EDUCATIONAL SERVICES	FAIRFIELD, OH	4250	39064	EDUCATIONAL SERVICES
WILKES, NC	2683	22306	EDUCATIONAL SERVICES	FAYETTE, OH	1125	10195	PLASTICS & RUBBER PRODUCTS MFG
WILSON, NC	2769	36208	EDUCATIONAL SERVICES	FRANKLIN, OH	46495	673132	EDUCATIONAL SERVICES
YADKIN, NC	1309	11484	TEXTILE MILLS	FULTON, OH	1565	21161	FURNITURE & RELATED PROD. MFG
YANCEY, NC	617	4706	FOOD SVCS & DRINKING PLACES	GALLIA, OH	967	11599	HOSPITALS
ADAMS, ND	192	993	HOSPITALS	GEAUGA, OH	4267	37562	FURNITURE & RELATED PROD. MFG
BARNES, ND	718	5592	EDUCATIONAL SERVICES	GREENE, OH	4943	54819	EDUCATIONAL SERVICES
BENSON, ND	274	2527	EDUCATIONAL SERVICES	GUERNSEY, OH	1537	15279	AMBULATORY HEALTH CARE SVCS
BILLINGS, ND	110	547	MISCELLANEOUS STORE RETAILERS	HAMILTON, OH	31946	505848	PROF.; SCIENTIFIC; & TECH SVCS
BOTTINEAU, ND	516	2359	EDUCATIONAL SERVICES	HANCOCK, OH	2970	42033	FOOD SVCS & DRINKING PLACES
BOWMAN, ND	267	1673	NURSING & RESID. CARE FACILIT.	HARDIN, OH	981	9935	EDUCATIONAL SERVICES
BURKE, ND	228	850	EDUCATIONAL SERVICES	HARRISON, OH	565	4004	MERCH. WHOLESALERS;DURABLE GDS
BURLEIGH, ND	4181	53753	AMBULATORY HEALTH CARE SVCS	HENRY, OH	1027	11609	FOOD MANUFACTURING
CASS, ND	6401	100736	EDUCATIONAL SERVICES	HIGHLAND, OH	1315	12621	EDUCATIONAL SERVICES
CAVALIER, ND	339	1799	CONSTRUCTION OF BUILDINGS	HOCKING, OH	995	7012	FOOD SVCS & DRINKING PLACES
DICKEY, ND	404	2267	EDUCATIONAL SERVICES	HOLMES, OH	1384	15025	BLDG MATL & GARDEN EQPMT DLRS
DIVIDE, ND	188	840	NURSING & RESID. CARE FACILIT.	HURON, OH	1973	26268	MERCH. WHOLESALERS;NONDUR. GDS

COUNTY	2007 Total Firms	2007 Total Employees	TOP INDUSTRY RANKED on 2007 EMPLOYMENT	COUNTY	2007 Total Firms	2007 Total Employees	TOP INDUSTRY RANKED on 2007 EMPLOYMENT
JACKSON, OH	1197	11238	MERCH. WHOLESALERS;NONDUR. GDS	HUGHES, OK	508	3471	EDUCATIONAL SERVICES
JEFFERSON, OH	2597	26133	PRIMARY METAL MANUFACTURING	JACKSON, OK	1082	13571	NAT'L SECURITY & INT'L AFFAIRS
KNOX, OH	1967	18925	EDUCATIONAL SERVICES	JEFFERSON, OK	337	1459	EDUCATIONAL SERVICES
LAKE, OH	9983	102408	FOOD SVCS & DRINKING PLACES	JOHNSTON, OK	412	3406	TRANSPORTATION EQUIPMENT MFG
LAWRENCE, OH	1557	13406	EDUCATIONAL SERVICES	KAY, OK	2288	21280	PETROLEUM & COAL PRODUCTS MFG
LICKING, OH	5699	53296	EDUCATIONAL SERVICES	KINGFISHER, OK	843	6583	SPECIAL TRADE CONTRACTORS
LOGAN, OH	1674	16922	MERCH. WHOLESALERS;DURABLE GDS	KIOWA, OK	507	2736	EDUCATIONAL SERVICES
LORAIN, OH	9378	106069	EDUCATIONAL SERVICES	LATIMER, OK	468	4435	EDUCATIONAL SERVICES
LUCAS, OH	16437	218155	FOOD SVCS & DRINKING PLACES	LE FLORE, OK	1540	11981	EDUCATIONAL SERVICES
MADISON, OH	1249	13075	JUSTICE; PUBIC ORDER/SAFETY	LINCOLN, OK	1158	7778	EDUCATIONAL SERVICES
MAHONING, OH	9855	106906	AMBULATORY HEALTH CARE SVCS	LOGAN, OK	1195	7289	EDUCATIONAL SERVICES
MARION, OH	2437	28811	ELECT'L EQPMT; APP; & COMP MFG	LOVE, OK	321	3108	AMUSEMENT; GAMBLING;& RECREAT.
MEDINA, OH	5791	63820	BLDG MATL & GARDEN EQPMT DLRS	MCCLAIN, OK	1369	7908	EDUCATIONAL SERVICES
MEIGS, OH	636	4325	EDUCATIONAL SERVICES	MCCURTAIN, OK	1486	11875	EDUCATIONAL SERVICES
MERCER, OH	1534	15149	FOOD SVCS & DRINKING PLACES	MCINTOSH, OK	869	4395	FOOD SVCS & DRINKING PLACES
MIAMI, OH	3880	49646	HOSPITALS	MAJOR, OK	447	2413	SPECIAL TRADE CONTRACTORS
MONROE, OH	523	4209	PRIMARY METAL MANUFACTURING	MARSHALL, OK	645	5253	TRANSPORTATION EQUIPMENT MFG
MONTGOMERY, OH	20124	277517	FOOD SVCS & DRINKING PLACES	MAYES, OK	1620	13724	EDUCATIONAL SERVICES
MORGAN, OH	426	2983	EDUCATIONAL SERVICES	MURRAY, OK	703	4549	EDUCATIONAL SERVICES
MORROW, OH	839	6160	TRANSPORTATION EQUIPMENT MFG	MUSKOGEE, OK	2937	27468	EDUCATIONAL SERVICES
MUSKINGUM, OH	3142	35860	FOOD SVCS & DRINKING PLACES	NOBLE, OK	439	4180	FABRICATED METAL PRODUCT MFG
NOBLE, OH	369	3056	PRIMARY METAL MANUFACTURING	NOWATA, OK	343	2801	EDUCATIONAL SERVICES
OTTAWA, OH	2003	16112	FOOD SVCS & DRINKING PLACES	OKFUSKEE, OK	406	2813	EDUCATIONAL SERVICES
PAULDING, OH	696	6731	EDUCATIONAL SERVICES	OKLAHOMA, OK	32327	420023	FOOD SVCS & DRINKING PLACES
PERRY, OH	949	6946	EDUCATIONAL SERVICES	OKMULGEE, OK	1435	11058	EDUCATIONAL SERVICES
PICKAWAY, OH	1629	16619	MUSEUMS; HIST. SITES;& SIMILAR	OSAGE, OK	1219	7255	EDUCATIONAL SERVICES
PIKE, OH	906	11826	WOOD PRODUCT MANUFACTURING	OTTAWA, OK	1528	12209	EDUCATIONAL SERVICES
PORTAGE, OH	4841	57348	EDUCATIONAL SERVICES	PAWNEE, OK	578	3196	EDUCATIONAL SERVICES
PREBLE, OH	1229	12410	EDUCATIONAL SERVICES	PAYNE, OK	2985	31436	EDUCATIONAL SERVICES
PUTNAM, OH	1306	11639	EDUCATIONAL SERVICES	PITTSBURG, OK	1865	18908	ADMINISTRATIVE & SUPPORT SVCS
RICHLAND, OH	5197	58973	FOOD SVCS & DRINKING PLACES	PONTOTOC, OK	1642	14863	EDUCATIONAL SERVICES
ROSS, OH	2322	28694	EDUCATIONAL SERVICES	POTTAWATOMIE, OK	2400	21733	EDUCATIONAL SERVICES
SANDUSKY, OH	2166	24148	EDUCATIONAL SERVICES	PUSHMATAHA, OK	542	2973	EDUCATIONAL SERVICES
SCIOTO, OH	2602	24153	EDUCATIONAL SERVICES	ROGER MILLS, OK	244	1161	EDUCATIONAL SERVICES
SENECA, OH	1948	20286	EDUCATIONAL SERVICES	ROGERS, OK	2517	24206	EDUCATIONAL SERVICES
SHELBY, OH	1795	32435	MACHINERY MANUFACTURING	SEMINOLE, OK	1017	7936	EDUCATIONAL SERVICES
STARK, OH	14365	172496	FOOD SVCS & DRINKING PLACES	SEQUOYAH, OK	1293	10309	EDUCATIONAL SERVICES
SUMMIT, OH	23813	271738	FOOD SVCS & DRINKING PLACES	STEPHENS, OK	1907	15710	EDUCATIONAL SERVICES
TRUMBULL, OH	7803	92872	HOSPITALS	TEXAS, OK	1334	7369	EDUCATIONAL SERVICES
TUSCARAWAS, OH	3609	36055	FOOD SVCS & DRINKING PLACES	TILLMAN, OK	411	2095	EDUCATIONAL SERVICES
UNION, OH	1604	27838	TRANSPORTATION EQUIPMENT MFG	TULSA, OK	27788	319046	AMBULATORY HEALTH CARE SVCS
VAN WERT, OH	1042	12033	FABRICATED METAL PRODUCT MFG	WAGONER, OK	1435	8500	EDUCATIONAL SERVICES
VINTON, OH	335	2658	EDUCATIONAL SERVICES	WASHINGTON, OK	2128	18073	EDUCATIONAL SERVICES
WARREN, OH	5619	73484	FOOD SVCS & DRINKING PLACES	WASHITA, OK	527	2789	EDUCATIONAL SERVICES
WASHINGTON, OH	2532	25228	EDUCATIONAL SERVICES	WOODS, OK	601	3633	EDUCATIONAL SERVICES
WAYNE, OH	4070	45092	EDUCATIONAL SERVICES	WOODWARD, OK	1186	9737	SUPPORT ACTIVITIES FOR MINING
WILLIAMS, OH	1540	18628	PLASTICS & RUBBER PRODUCTS MFG	BAKER, OR	926	5557	FOOD SVCS & DRINKING PLACES
WOOD, OH	4186	57000	FOOD SVCS & DRINKING PLACES	BENTON, OR	3091	42352	EDUCATIONAL SERVICES
WYANDOT, OH	892	10893	MERCH. WHOLESALERS;DURABLE GDS	CLACKAMAS, OR	14596	140812	FOOD SVCS & DRINKING PLACES
ADAIR, OK	584	5594	EDUCATIONAL SERVICES	CLATSOP, OR	2398	17284	FOOD SVCS & DRINKING PLACES
ALFALFA, OK	358	1644	EDUCATIONAL SERVICES	COLUMBIA, OR	1709	10889	EDUCATIONAL SERVICES
ATOKA, OK	500	3971	EDUCATIONAL SERVICES	COOS, OR	2909	21563	EDUCATIONAL SERVICES
BEAVER, OK	374	1487	EDUCATIONAL SERVICES	CROOK, OR	794	6362	WOOD PRODUCT MANUFACTURING
BECKHAM, OK	1208	8292	SPECIAL TRADE CONTRACTORS	CURRY, OR	1426	6889	FOOD SVCS & DRINKING PLACES
BLAINE, OK	652	3576	EDUCATIONAL SERVICES	DESCHUTES, OR	8998	68206	AMBULATORY HEALTH CARE SVCS
BRYAN, OK	1827	14257	EDUCATIONAL SERVICES	DOUGLAS, OR	4448	38926	WOOD PRODUCT MANUFACTURING
CADDO, OK	1347	8050	EDUCATIONAL SERVICES	GILLIAM, OR	172	710	SUPPORT ACT. FOR TRANSPORT.
CANADIAN, OK	2969	33476	SPECIAL TRADE CONTRACTORS	GRANT, OR	347	2590	WOOD PRODUCT MANUFACTURING
CARTER, OK	2522	20469	PLASTICS & RUBBER PRODUCTS MFG	HARNEY, OR	292	2030	EDUCATIONAL SERVICES
CHEROKEE, OK	1534	13568	EDUCATIONAL SERVICES	HOOD RIVER, OR	1430	10781	ACCOMMODATION
CHOCTAW, OK	654	5465	EDUCATIONAL SERVICES	JACKSON, OR	9502	80317	FOOD SVCS & DRINKING PLACES
CIMARRON, OK	276	840	EDUCATIONAL SERVICES	JEFFERSON, OR	709	6048	WOOD PRODUCT MANUFACTURING
CLEVELAND, OK	7134	75260	EDUCATIONAL SERVICES	JOSEPHINE, OR	4000	24012	FOOD SVCS & DRINKING PLACES
COAL, OK	229	1425	EDUCATIONAL SERVICES	KLAMATH, OR	2717	23445	EDUCATIONAL SERVICES
COMANCHE, OK	4086	40692	EDUCATIONAL SERVICES	LAKE, OR	470	2263	EDUCATIONAL SERVICES
COTTON, OK	254	1180	EDUCATIONAL SERVICES	LANE, OR	13855	142945	EDUCATIONAL SERVICES
CRAIG, OK	819	6256	NURSING & RESID. CARE FACILIT.	LINCOLN, OR	3314	20028	FOOD SVCS & DRINKING PLACES
CREEK, OK	2348	19810	EDUCATIONAL SERVICES	LINN, OR	4241	38393	EDUCATIONAL SERVICES
CUSTER, OK	1400	10658	EDUCATIONAL SERVICES	MALHEUR, OR	1323	12107	FOOD MANUFACTURING
DELAWARE, OK	1568	8665	EDUCATIONAL SERVICES	MARION, OR	11246	126029	EDUCATIONAL SERVICES
DEWEY, OK	400	1618	EDUCATIONAL SERVICES	MORROW, OR	401	3526	FOOD MANUFACTURING
ELLIS, OK	286	1143	EDUCATIONAL SERVICES	MULTNOMAH, OR	34778	438808	EDUCATIONAL SERVICES
GARFIELD, OK	2748	22843	HOSPITALS	POLK, OR	1774	16226	EDUCATIONAL SERVICES
GARVIN, OK	1257	9573	EDUCATIONAL SERVICES	SHERMAN, OR	145	490	FOOD AND BEVERAGE STORES
GRADY, OK	1668	14963	EDUCATIONAL SERVICES	TILLAMOOK, OR	1656	8001	FOOD MANUFACTURING
GRANT, OK	302	1326	EDUCATIONAL SERVICES	UMATILLA, OR	2753	29029	EDUCATIONAL SERVICES
GREER, OK	281	1542	JUSTICE; PUBIC ORDER/SAFETY	UNION, OR	1188	9658	EDUCATIONAL SERVICES
HARMON, OK	165	924	EDUCATIONAL SERVICES	WALLOWA, OR	512	2363	EXEC.; LEGIS.; & OTHER SUPPORT
HARPER, OK	287	1330	EDUCATIONAL SERVICES	WASCO, OR	1325	9159	EDUCATIONAL SERVICES
HASKELL, OK	518	3486	AMBULATORY HEALTH CARE SVCS	WASHINGTON, OR	18175	204546	COMPUTER & ELECTRONIC PROD MFG

COUNTY	2007 Total Firms	2007 Total Employees	TOP INDUSTRY RANKED on 2007 EMPLOYMENT	COUNTY	2007 Total Firms	2007 Total Employees	TOP INDUSTRY RANKED on 2007 EMPLOYMENT
WHEELER, OR	130	296	EDUCATIONAL SERVICES	BEAUFORT, SC	8200	63450	FOOD SVCS & DRINKING PLACES
YAMHILL, OR	3447	29856	EDUCATIONAL SERVICES	BERKELEY, SC	4303	41087	EDUCATIONAL SERVICES
ADAMS, PA	3843	34972	FOOD MANUFACTURING	CALHOUN, SC	394	2865	EDUCATIONAL SERVICES
ALLEGHENY, PA	50342	643332	HOSPITALS	CHARLESTON, SC	18432	187855	AMBULATORY HEALTH CARE SVCS
ARMSTRONG, PA	2509	21660	PRIMARY METAL MANUFACTURING	CHEROKEE, SC	1640	17419	MERCH. WHOLESALERS;NONDUR. GDS
BEAVER, PA	5816	51336	EDUCATIONAL SERVICES	CHESTER, SC	1277	13120	APPAREL MANUFACTURING
BEDFORD, PA	2131	15132	FOOD SVCS & DRINKING PLACES	CHESTERFIELD, SC	1725	15081	FABRICATED METAL PRODUCT MFG
BERKS, PA	14245	163428	EDUCATIONAL SERVICES	CLARENDON, SC	1267	8829	EDUCATIONAL SERVICES
BLAIR, PA	5306	62209	AMBULATORY HEALTH CARE SVCS	COLLETON, SC	1715	11350	EDUCATIONAL SERVICES
BRADFORD, PA	2716	23332	AMBULATORY HEALTH CARE SVCS	DARLINGTON, SC	2113	22019	PAPER MANUFACTURING
BUCKS, PA	27847	250149	PROF.; SCIENTIFIC; & TECH SVCS	DILLON, SC	995	8807	EDUCATIONAL SERVICES
BUTLER, PA	7658	77453	EDUCATIONAL SERVICES	DORCHESTER, SC	3522	30382	FOOD SVCS & DRINKING PLACES
CAMBRIA, PA	5264	61402	EDUCATIONAL SERVICES	EDGEFIELD, SC	685	6386	EDUCATIONAL SERVICES
CAMERON, PA	291	2010	PRIMARY METAL MANUFACTURING	FAIRFIELD, SC	704	6090	EDUCATIONAL SERVICES
CARBON, PA	2290	18674	HOSPITALS	FLORENCE, SC	5329	59410	FOOD SVCS & DRINKING PLACES
CENTRE, PA	4940	79541	EDUCATIONAL SERVICES	GEORGETOWN, SC	3394	24373	FOOD SVCS & DRINKING PLACES
CHESTER, PA	20057	211849	PROF.; SCIENTIFIC; & TECH SVCS	GREENVILLE, SC	19295	212525	PROF.; SCIENTIFIC; & TECH SVCS
CLARION, PA	1805	16842	EDUCATIONAL SERVICES	GREENWOOD, SC	2577	30807	EDUCATIONAL SERVICES
CLEARFIELD, PA	3169	33270	HOSPITALS	HAMPTON, SC	923	6000	EDUCATIONAL SERVICES
CLINTON, PA	1408	11997	PAPER MANUFACTURING	HORRY, SC	13906	116855	FOOD SVCS & DRINKING PLACES
COLUMBIA, PA	2541	21771	EDUCATIONAL SERVICES	JASPER, SC	1103	7345	EDUCATIONAL SERVICES
CRAWFORD, PA	3770	33987	EDUCATIONAL SERVICES	KERSHAW, SC	1963	16449	EDUCATIONAL SERVICES
CUMBERLAND, PA	9502	117066	PROF.; SCIENTIFIC; & TECH SVCS	LANCASTER, SC	2255	19581	EDUCATIONAL SERVICES
DAUPHIN, PA	12199	186059	HOSPITALS	LAURENS, SC	1769	19321	EDUCATIONAL SERVICES
DELAWARE, PA	19839	194621	EDUCATIONAL SERVICES	LEE, SC	495	4192	JUSTICE; PUBIC ORDER/SAFETY
ELK, PA	1558	17743	CHEMICAL MANUFACTURING	LEXINGTON, SC	8736	94477	FOOD SVCS & DRINKING PLACES
ERIE, PA	9970	131983	EDUCATIONAL SERVICES	MCCORMICK, SC	357	2159	JUSTICE; PUBIC ORDER/SAFETY
FAYETTE, PA	4949	41544	FOOD SVCS & DRINKING PLACES	MARION, SC	1174	10921	EXEC.; LEGIS.; & OTHER SUPPORT
FOREST, PA	297	1498	EDUCATIONAL SERVICES	MARLBORO, SC	843	8395	TEXTILE MILLS
FRANKLIN, PA	5569	54418	EDUCATIONAL SERVICES	NEWBERRY, SC	1301	13383	MERCH. WHOLESALERS;NONDUR. GDS
FULTON, PA	587	5043	MACHINERY MANUFACTURING	OCONEE, SC	2396	21160	EDUCATIONAL SERVICES
GREENE, PA	1483	12054	MINING (EXCEPT OIL AND GAS)	ORANGEBURG, SC	3363	32864	EDUCATIONAL SERVICES
HUNTINGDON, PA	1627	12371	JUSTICE; PUBIC ORDER/SAFETY	PICKENS, SC	3211	28515	FOOD SVCS & DRINKING PLACES
INDIANA, PA	3266	31392	EDUCATIONAL SERVICES	RICHLAND, SC	13575	193699	EDUCATIONAL SERVICES
JEFFERSON, PA	2030	15557	FABRICATED METAL PRODUCT MFG	SALUDA, SC	478	5154	FOOD MANUFACTURING
JUNIATA, PA	895	7456	FOOD MANUFACTURING	SPARTANBURG, SC	10227	124696	EDUCATIONAL SERVICES
LACKAWANNA, PA	8963	104365	FOOD SVCS & DRINKING PLACES	SUMTER, SC	3603	37388	EDUCATIONAL SERVICES
LANCASTER, PA	19153	226615	EDUCATIONAL SERVICES	UNION, SC	948	8876	FABRICATED METAL PRODUCT MFG
LAWRENCE, PA	3727	35907	AMBULATORY HEALTH CARE SVCS	WILLIAMSBURG, SC	1148	9185	EDUCATIONAL SERVICES
LEBANON, PA	4357	44649	HOSPITALS	YORK, SC	7285	64965	EDUCATIONAL SERVICES
LEHIGH, PA	13369	154342	AMBULATORY HEALTH CARE SVCS	AURORA, SD	186	737	EDUCATIONAL SERVICES
LUZERNE, PA	13546	144080	HOSPITALS	BEADLE, SD	808	7230	FOOD SVCS & DRINKING PLACES
LYCOMING, PA	4724	51998	EDUCATIONAL SERVICES	BENNETT, SD	108	665	EDUCATIONAL SERVICES
MCKEAN, PA	1845	17142	EDUCATIONAL SERVICES	BON HOMME, SD	339	2110	EDUCATIONAL SERVICES
MERCER, PA	4751	52668	EDUCATIONAL SERVICES	BROOKINGS, SD	1294	16448	EDUCATIONAL SERVICES
MIFFLIN, PA	1679	17778	PRIMARY METAL MANUFACTURING	BROWN, SD	1838	19723	FOOD SVCS & DRINKING PLACES
MONROE, PA	6843	52793	RELIG.; GRANT; CIVIC; PROF ORG	BRULE, SD	382	2637	EDUCATIONAL SERVICES
MONTGOMERY, PA	40242	433876	PROF.; SCIENTIFIC; & TECH SVCS	BUFFALO, SD	86	529	EXEC.; LEGIS.; & OTHER SUPPORT
MONTOUR, PA	677	13996	HOSPITALS	BUTTE, SD	367	2608	EDUCATIONAL SERVICES
NORTHAMPTON, PA	11057	91457	EDUCATIONAL SERVICES	CAMPBELL, SD	116	418	MERCH. WHOLESALERS;NONDUR. GDS
NORTHUMBERLAND, PA	3337	28644	EDUCATIONAL SERVICES	CHARLES MIX, SD	491	4010	EDUCATIONAL SERVICES
PERRY, PA	1592	7985	EDUCATIONAL SERVICES	CLARK, SD	214	1086	EDUCATIONAL SERVICES
PHILADELPHIA, PA	47619	590859	PROF.; SCIENTIFIC; & TECH SVCS	CLAY, SD	472	4891	EDUCATIONAL SERVICES
PIKE, PA	1544	10976	ACCOMMODATION	CODINGTON, SD	1360	15455	AMBULATORY HEALTH CARE SVCS
POTTER, PA	916	5463	HOSPITALS	CORSON, SD	192	961	EDUCATIONAL SERVICES
SCHUYLKILL, PA	5500	50702	EDUCATIONAL SERVICES	CUSTER, SD	399	3162	MISCELLANEOUS STORE RETAILERS
SNYDER, PA	1591	14564	FURNITURE & RELATED PROD. MFG	DAVISON, SD	999	12500	FOOD SVCS & DRINKING PLACES
SOMERSET, PA	3111	29562	EDUCATIONAL SERVICES	DAY, SD	371	2401	EDUCATIONAL SERVICES
SULLIVAN, PA	406	1703	EDUCATIONAL SERVICES	DEUEL, SD	266	1634	EDUCATIONAL SERVICES
SUSQUEHANNA, PA	1790	8638	EDUCATIONAL SERVICES	DEWEY, SD	365	3350	EXEC.; LEGIS.; & OTHER SUPPORT
TIOGA, PA	1919	14864	EDUCATIONAL SERVICES	DOUGLAS, SD	237	1174	NURSING & RESID. CARE FACILIT.
UNION, PA	1740	17403	AMBULATORY HEALTH CARE SVCS	EDMUNDS, SD	233	1473	EDUCATIONAL SERVICES
VENANGO, PA	2321	20522	MACHINERY MANUFACTURING	FALL RIVER, SD	408	2297	HOSPITALS
WARREN, PA	1721	16855	FABRICATED METAL PRODUCT MFG	FAULK, SD	150	677	EDUCATIONAL SERVICES
WASHINGTON, PA	7878	72660	FOOD SVCS & DRINKING PLACES	GRANT, SD	394	3672	MERCH. WHOLESALERS;DURABLE GDS
WAYNE, PA	2662	21774	ACCOMMODATION	GREGORY, SD	324	1538	EDUCATIONAL SERVICES
WESTMORELAND, PA	14155	138604	FOOD SVCS & DRINKING PLACES	HAAKON, SD	144	784	NURSING & RESID. CARE FACILIT.
WYOMING, PA	1433	10603	MERCH. WHOLESALERS;NONDUR. GDS	HAMLIN, SD	252	1479	EDUCATIONAL SERVICES
YORK, PA	14635	163320	AMBULATORY HEALTH CARE SVCS	HAND, SD	211	1191	EDUCATIONAL SERVICES
BRISTOL, RI	1820	14448	EDUCATIONAL SERVICES	HANSON, SD	131	746	EDUCATIONAL SERVICES
KENT, RI	6995	74284	FOOD SVCS & DRINKING PLACES	HARDING, SD	107	404	EDUCATIONAL SERVICES
NEWPORT, RI	4701	36563	FOOD SVCS & DRINKING PLACES	HUGHES, SD	1110	12617	EXEC.; LEGIS.; & OTHER SUPPORT
PROVIDENCE, RI	24065	278925	HOSPITALS	HUTCHINSON, SD	382	2787	NURSING & RESID. CARE FACILIT.
WASHINGTON, RI	6002	47255	EDUCATIONAL SERVICES	HYDE, SD	114	897	EDUCATIONAL SERVICES
ABBEVILLE, SC	752	7267	APPAREL MANUFACTURING	JACKSON, SD	145	1053	EDUCATIONAL SERVICES
AIKEN, SC	4944	54327	UTILITIES	JERAULD, SD	142	1360	MERCH. WHOLESALERS;NONDUR. GDS
ALLENDALE, SC	399	3703	EDUCATIONAL SERVICES	JONES, SD	102	484	EDUCATIONAL SERVICES
ANDERSON, SC	5865	68509	HOSPITALS	KINGSBURY, SD	277	1008	EDUCATIONAL SERVICES
BAMBERG, SC	561	4382	EDUCATIONAL SERVICES	LAKE, SD	490	4741	EDUCATIONAL SERVICES
BARNWELL, SC	863	8399	MACHINERY MANUFACTURING	LAWRENCE, SD	989	10585	ACCOMMODATION

BUSINESS DATA

COUNTY	2007 Total Firms	2007 Total Employees	TOP INDUSTRY RANKED on 2007 EMPLOYMENT	COUNTY	2007 Total Firms	2007 Total Employees	TOP INDUSTRY RANKED on 2007 EMPLOYMENT
LINCOLN, SD	1117	9447	FOOD SVCS & DRINKING PLACES	MCNAIRY, TN	911	8049	PLASTICS & RUBBER PRODUCTS MFG
LYMAN, SD	246	1850	FOOD SVCS & DRINKING PLACES	MACON, TN	718	4839	EDUCATIONAL SERVICES
MCCOOK, SD	286	1602	RELIG.; GRANT; CIVIC; PROF ORG	MADISON, TN	4198	66473	AMBULATORY HEALTH CARE SVCS
MCPHERSON, SD	153	861	EDUCATIONAL SERVICES	MARION, TN	960	6966	FOOD SVCS & DRINKING PLACES
MARSHALL, SD	248	1435	TRANSPORTATION EQUIPMENT MFG	MARSHALL, TN	929	9028	TRANSPORTATION EQUIPMENT MFG
MEADE, SD	759	10079	NAT'L SECURITY & INT'L AFFAIRS	MAURY, TN	2624	33471	TRANSPORTATION EQUIPMENT MFG
MELLETTE, SD	91	541	EDUCATIONAL SERVICES	MEIGS, TN	235	2030	FURN. & HOME FURNISHGS STORES
MINER, SD	157	761	EDUCATIONAL SERVICES	MONROE, TN	1457	12214	MOTOR VEHICLE & PARTS DEALERS
MINNEHAHA, SD	7526	116293	HOSPITALS	MONTGOMERY, TN	3866	43403	FOOD SVCS & DRINKING PLACES
MOODY, SD	223	2134	AMUSEMENT; GAMBLING;& RECREAT.	MOORE, TN	146	1466	BEVERAGE & TOBACCO PRODUCT MFG
PENNINGTON, SD	4453	53839	HOSPITALS	MORGAN, TN	508	2971	EDUCATIONAL SERVICES
PERKINS, SD	251	1213	MISCELLANEOUS MANUFACTURING	OBION, TN	1215	13174	PLASTICS & RUBBER PRODUCTS MFG
POTTER, SD	218	1159	HOSPITALS	OVERTON, TN	748	5503	MERCH. WHOLESALERS;DURABLE GDS
ROBERTS, SD	460	2972	EDUCATIONAL SERVICES	PERRY, TN	257	2273	TRANSPORTATION EQUIPMENT MFG
SANBORN, SD	145	934	REPAIR AND MAINTENANCE	PICKETT, TN	212	1244	TRANSPORTATION EQUIPMENT MFG
SHANNON, SD	279	3489	EDUCATIONAL SERVICES	POLK, TN	567	3215	MOTOR VEHICLE & PARTS DEALERS
SPINK, SD	353	2617	EXEC.; LEGIS.; & OTHER SUPPORT	PUTNAM, TN	3027	35707	AMBULATORY HEALTH CARE SVCS
STANLEY, SD	188	1569	EDUCATIONAL SERVICES	RHEA, TN	964	10648	FURN. & HOME FURNISHGS STORES
SULLY, SD	96	509	EDUCATIONAL SERVICES	ROANE, TN	1580	12946	EDUCATIONAL SERVICES
TODD, SD	251	3676	EDUCATIONAL SERVICES	ROBERTSON, TN	1936	19054	ELECT'L EQPMT; APP; & COMP MFG
TRIPP, SD	356	2560	HOSPITALS	RUTHERFORD, TN	7263	78016	FOOD SVCS & DRINKING PLACES
TURNER, SD	435	2133	NURSING & RESID. CARE FACILIT.	SCOTT, TN	899	6127	WOOD PRODUCT MANUFACTURING
UNION, SD	622	6952	FOOD MANUFACTURING	SEQUATCHIE, TN	495	3481	MACHINERY MANUFACTURING
WALWORTH, SD	411	2681	EDUCATIONAL SERVICES	SEVIER, TN	4352	38913	FOOD SVCS & DRINKING PLACES
YANKTON, SD	1093	14564	ADMIN. HUMAN RESOURCE PROGRAMS	SHELBY, TN	34665	444710	HOSPITALS
ZIEBACH, SD	63	340	EDUCATIONAL SERVICES	SMITH, TN	613	5452	PRIMARY METAL MANUFACTURING
ANDERSON, TN	2872	45233	PROF.; SCIENTIFIC; & TECH SVCS	STEWART, TN	366	2626	UTILITIES
BEDFORD, TN	1363	13220	MISCELLANEOUS STORE RETAILERS	SULLIVAN, TN	5741	73635	PAPER MANUFACTURING
BENTON, TN	571	4307	GENERAL MERCHANDISE STORES	SUMNER, TN	4463	39243	EDUCATIONAL SERVICES
BLEDSOE, TN	446	2615	JUSTICE; PUBIC ORDER/SAFETY	TIPTON, TN	1440	10152	EDUCATIONAL SERVICES
BLOUNT, TN	3764	47451	FOOD SVCS & DRINKING PLACES	TROUSDALE, TN	241	1615	FABRICATED METAL PRODUCT MFG
BRADLEY, TN	3221	39939	FOOD SVCS & DRINKING PLACES	UNICOI, TN	548	5361	CHEMICAL MANUFACTURING
CAMPBELL, TN	1232	10785	NURSING & RESID. CARE FACILIT.	UNION, TN	419	2632	EDUCATIONAL SERVICES
CANNON, TN	439	2207	EDUCATIONAL SERVICES	VAN BUREN, TN	141	6809	FOOD AND BEVERAGE STORES
CARROLL, TN	1054	9480	HEAVY & CIVIL ENG. CONSTRUCT'N	WARREN, TN	2063	14207	FABRICATED METAL PRODUCT MFG
CARTER, TN	1521	11956	EDUCATIONAL SERVICES	WASHINGTON, TN	4933	60908	HOSPITALS
CHEATHAM, TN	958	8842	ELECT'L EQPMT; APP; & COMP MFG	WAYNE, TN	544	4880	JUSTICE; PUBIC ORDER/SAFETY
CHESTER, TN	522	3162	EDUCATIONAL SERVICES	WEAKLEY, TN	1061	9989	EDUCATIONAL SERVICES
CLAIBORNE, TN	763	8630	FURNITURE & RELATED PROD. MFG	WHITE, TN	911	7071	MERCH. WHOLESALERS;DURABLE GDS
CLAY, TN	306	1774	EDUCATIONAL SERVICES	WILLIAMSON, TN	7200	68987	PROF.; SCIENTIFIC; & TECH SVCS
COCKE, TN	995	9799	FOOD SVCS & DRINKING PLACES	WILSON, TN	3058	31585	COMPUTER & ELECTRONIC PROD MFG
COFFEE, TN	2039	24862	EXEC.; LEGIS.; & OTHER SUPPORT	ANDERSON, TX	1963	17932	JUSTICE; PUBIC ORDER/SAFETY
CROCKETT, TN	518	3419	FOOD MANUFACTURING	ANDREWS, TX	561	4872	SPECIAL TRADE CONTRACTORS
CUMBERLAND, TN	1913	16874	FOOD SVCS & DRINKING PLACES	ANGELINA, TX	3238	34062	EDUCATIONAL SERVICES
DAVIDSON, TN	31479	376208	HOSPITALS	ARANSAS, TX	1267	5443	FOOD SVCS & DRINKING PLACES
DECATUR, TN	485	3170	NURSING & RESID. CARE FACILIT.	ARCHER, TX	343	1973	EDUCATIONAL SERVICES
DEKALB, TN	728	6502	TRANSPORTATION EQUIPMENT MFG	ARMSTRONG, TX	100	392	EDUCATIONAL SERVICES
DICKSON, TN	1568	15759	FOOD SVCS & DRINKING PLACES	ATASCOSA, TX	1241	8579	EDUCATIONAL SERVICES
DYER, TN	1455	16389	FOOD SVCS & DRINKING PLACES	AUSTIN, TX	1239	8344	EDUCATIONAL SERVICES
FAYETTE, TN	1033	6654	EDUCATIONAL SERVICES	BAILEY, TX	381	2697	EDUCATIONAL SERVICES
FENTRESS, TN	748	4498	EDUCATIONAL SERVICES	BANDERA, TX	928	3227	EDUCATIONAL SERVICES
FRANKLIN, TN	1344	17093	TRANSPORTATION EQUIPMENT MFG	BASTROP, TX	2090	12949	EDUCATIONAL SERVICES
GIBSON, TN	1804	17157	EDUCATIONAL SERVICES	BAYLOR, TX	249	1475	AMBULATORY HEALTH CARE SVCS
GILES, TN	1008	8981	FABRICATED METAL PRODUCT MFG	BEE, TX	944	9119	EXEC.; LEGIS.; & OTHER SUPPORT
GRAINGER, TN	515	3312	EDUCATIONAL SERVICES	BELL, TX	8089	101264	HOSPITALS
GREENE, TN	2274	25751	EXEC.; LEGIS.; & OTHER SUPPORT	BEXAR, TX	57020	622411	EDUCATIONAL SERVICES
GRUNDY, TN	626	2352	EDUCATIONAL SERVICES	BLANCO, TX	564	2880	UTILITIES
HAMBLEN, TN	2195	29254	TRANSPORTATION EQUIPMENT MFG	BORDEN, TX	28	188	EDUCATIONAL SERVICES
HAMILTON, TN	14407	174857	FOOD SVCS & DRINKING PLACES	BOSQUE, TX	806	4533	EDUCATIONAL SERVICES
HANCOCK, TN	172	1276	EDUCATIONAL SERVICES	BOWIE, TX	4155	38485	EDUCATIONAL SERVICES
HARDEMAN, TN	862	7666	MACHINERY MANUFACTURING	BRAZORIA, TX	8445	80799	CHEMICAL MANUFACTURING
HARDIN, TN	1047	8383	HOSPITALS	BRAZOS, TX	5171	67529	PUBLISHING INDUSTRIES
HAWKINS, TN	1278	14523	TRANSPORTATION EQUIPMENT MFG	BREWSTER, TX	737	4347	EDUCATIONAL SERVICES
HAYWOOD, TN	649	5772	PLASTICS & RUBBER PRODUCTS MFG	BRISCOE, TX	108	340	EDUCATIONAL SERVICES
HENDERSON, TN	953	9915	TRANSPORTATION EQUIPMENT MFG	BROOKS, TX	376	2129	EDUCATIONAL SERVICES
HENRY, TN	1234	12028	PLASTICS & RUBBER PRODUCTS MFG	BROWN, TX	1519	15611	EDUCATIONAL SERVICES
HICKMAN, TN	601	3687	EDUCATIONAL SERVICES	BURLESON, TX	589	3620	EDUCATIONAL SERVICES
HOUSTON, TN	305	1737	SOCIAL ASSISTANCE	BURNET, TX	2448	13698	ACCOMMODATION
HUMPHREYS, TN	699	7620	CONSTRUCTION OF BUILDINGS	CALDWELL, TX	1177	8076	EDUCATIONAL SERVICES
JACKSON, TN	369	2376	MERCH. WHOLESALERS;DURABLE GDS	CALHOUN, TX	873	9159	CHEMICAL MANUFACTURING
JEFFERSON, TN	1253	11982	EDUCATIONAL SERVICES	CALLAHAN, TX	549	2156	EDUCATIONAL SERVICES
JOHNSON, TN	589	4588	JUSTICE; PUBIC ORDER/SAFETY	CAMERON, TX	10760	120432	EDUCATIONAL SERVICES
KNOX, TN	18492	214178	HOSPITALS	CAMP, TX	460	3153	AMBULATORY HEALTH CARE SVCS
LAKE, TN	235	1799	JUSTICE; PUBIC ORDER/SAFETY	CARSON, TX	291	1330	EDUCATIONAL SERVICES
LAUDERDALE, TN	690	6769	FABRICATED METAL PRODUCT MFG	CASS, TX	1309	9190	PAPER MANUFACTURING
LAWRENCE, TN	1430	13100	MACHINERY MANUFACTURING	CASTRO, TX	370	2198	EDUCATIONAL SERVICES
LEWIS, TN	407	2454	EDUCATIONAL SERVICES	CHAMBERS, TX	1072	7773	EDUCATIONAL SERVICES
LINCOLN, TN	1036	9306	ELECTRONICS & APPLIANCE STORES	CHEROKEE, TX	1585	15502	EDUCATIONAL SERVICES
LOUDON, TN	1513	13797	FOOD SVCS & DRINKING PLACES	CHILDRESS, TX	362	2068	ADMIN. OF ECONOMIC PROGRAMS
MCMINN, TN	1752	19872	TRANSPORTATION EQUIPMENT MFG	CLAY, TX	298	1594	EDUCATIONAL SERVICES

COUNTY	2007 Total Firms	2007 Total Employees	TOP INDUSTRY RANKED on 2007 EMPLOYMENT	COUNTY	2007 Total Firms	2007 Total Employees	TOP INDUSTRY RANKED on 2007 EMPLOYMENT
COCHRAN, TX	144	944	EDUCATIONAL SERVICES	JACKSON, TX	580	5375	MERCH. WHOLESALERS;NONDUR. GDS
COKE, TX	160	908	EDUCATIONAL SERVICES	JASPER, TX	1572	11700	EDUCATIONAL SERVICES
COLEMAN, TX	530	2373	EDUCATIONAL SERVICES	JEFF DAVIS, TX	162	1682	EDUCATIONAL SERVICES
COLLIN, TX	25604	249836	PROF.; SCIENTIFIC; & TECH SVCS	JEFFERSON, TX	10870	118627	EDUCATIONAL SERVICES
COLLINGSWORTH, TX	187	1102	EDUCATIONAL SERVICES	JIM HOGG, TX	250	1411	FOOD AND BEVERAGE STORES
COLORADO, TX	1069	6674	EDUCATIONAL SERVICES	JIM WELLS, TX	1552	16157	SPECIAL TRADE CONTRACTORS
COMAL, TX	4434	37500	FOOD SVCS & DRINKING PLACES	JOHNSON, TX	4842	33583	EDUCATIONAL SERVICES
COMANCHE, TX	680	3660	EDUCATIONAL SERVICES	JONES, TX	644	4018	EDUCATIONAL SERVICES
CONCHO, TX	156	976	JUSTICE; PUBIC ORDER/SAFETY	KARNES, TX	563	3760	EDUCATIONAL SERVICES
COOKE, TX	1680	14664	EDUCATIONAL SERVICES	KAUFMAN, TX	3657	25488	EDUCATIONAL SERVICES
CORYELL, TX	1500	11095	EDUCATIONAL SERVICES	KENDALL, TX	1616	10585	INSURANCE CARRIERS & RELATED
COTTLE, TX	110	449	EDUCATIONAL SERVICES	KENEDY, TX	17	127	ANIMAL PRODUCTION
CRANE, TX	192	1494	SPECIAL TRADE CONTRACTORS	KENT, TX	69	221	NURSING & RESID. CARE FACILIT.
CROCKETT, TX	266	1369	SPECIAL TRADE CONTRACTORS	KERR, TX	3087	19438	HOSPITALS
CROSBY, TX	287	1573	EDUCATIONAL SERVICES	KIMBLE, TX	286	1414	EDUCATIONAL SERVICES
CULBERSON, TX	199	1022	ACCOMMODATION	KING, TX	23	102	ANIMAL PRODUCTION
DALLAM, TX	668	3579	CROP PRODUCTION	KINNEY, TX	120	531	UTILITIES
DALLAS, TX	107383	1196751	PROF.; SCIENTIFIC; & TECH SVCS	KLEBERG, TX	1174	8897	EDUCATIONAL SERVICES
DAWSON, TX	568	4254	JUSTICE; PUBIC ORDER/SAFETY	KNOX, TX	262	1149	EDUCATIONAL SERVICES
DEAF SMITH, TX	804	6632	EDUCATIONAL SERVICES	LAMAR, TX	2267	19977	HOSPITALS
DELTA, TX	204	862	EDUCATIONAL SERVICES	LAMB, TX	579	5194	EDUCATIONAL SERVICES
DENTON, TX	15472	146845	EDUCATIONAL SERVICES	LAMPASAS, TX	711	4102	EDUCATIONAL SERVICES
DEWITT, TX	840	6258	EDUCATIONAL SERVICES	LA SALLE, TX	326	1461	JUSTICE; PUBIC ORDER/SAFETY
DICKENS, TX	187	710	EDUCATIONAL SERVICES	LAVACA, TX	821	7797	EDUCATIONAL SERVICES
DIMMIT, TX	357	3158	EDUCATIONAL SERVICES	LEE, TX	703	5557	EDUCATIONAL SERVICES
DONLEY, TX	203	908	EDUCATIONAL SERVICES	LEON, TX	827	5631	EDUCATIONAL SERVICES
DUVAL, TX	369	3354	EDUCATIONAL SERVICES	LIBERTY, TX	2167	15907	EDUCATIONAL SERVICES
EASTLAND, TX	1001	6958	SPECIAL TRADE CONTRACTORS	LIMESTONE, TX	982	7671	EDUCATIONAL SERVICES
ECTOR, TX	5564	49876	MERCH. WHOLESALERS;DURABLE GDS	LIPSCOMB, TX	202	940	EDUCATIONAL SERVICES
EDWARDS, TX	167	569	EDUCATIONAL SERVICES	LIVE OAK, TX	478	2344	PETROLEUM & COAL PRODUCTS MFG
ELLIS, TX	4597	40171	EDUCATIONAL SERVICES	LLANO, TX	943	3838	FOOD SVCS & DRINKING PLACES
EL PASO, TX	20034	249697	EDUCATIONAL SERVICES	LOVING, TX	18	22	EXEC.; LEGIS.; & OTHER SUPPORT
ERATH, TX	1560	13020	EDUCATIONAL SERVICES	LUBBOCK, TX	10816	126283	EDUCATIONAL SERVICES
FALLS, TX	520	3732	JUSTICE; PUBIC ORDER/SAFETY	LYNN, TX	250	1514	EDUCATIONAL SERVICES
FANNIN, TX	1096	7741	EDUCATIONAL SERVICES	MCCULLOCH, TX	466	3029	TRANSPORTATION EQUIPMENT MFG
FAYETTE, TX	1365	8478	EDUCATIONAL SERVICES	MCLENNAN, TX	8934	101469	EDUCATIONAL SERVICES
FISHER, TX	167	1386	EDUCATIONAL SERVICES	MCMULLEN, TX	75	260	EDUCATIONAL SERVICES
FLOYD, TX	300	1995	EDUCATIONAL SERVICES	MADISON, TX	439	4223	JUSTICE; PUBIC ORDER/SAFETY
FOARD, TX	114	500	EDUCATIONAL SERVICES	MARION, TX	402	1872	FOOD SVCS & DRINKING PLACES
FORT BEND, TX	11721	123589	EDUCATIONAL SERVICES	MARTIN, TX	176	1270	EDUCATIONAL SERVICES
FRANKLIN, TX	357	3131	MERCH. WHOLESALERS;DURABLE GDS	MASON, TX	320	987	EDUCATIONAL SERVICES
FREESTONE, TX	880	5710	EDUCATIONAL SERVICES	MATAGORDA, TX	1520	9273	EDUCATIONAL SERVICES
FRIO, TX	547	3575	EDUCATIONAL SERVICES	MAVERICK, TX	1453	12190	EDUCATIONAL SERVICES
GAINES, TX	606	3975	EDUCATIONAL SERVICES	MEDINA, TX	1309	7695	EDUCATIONAL SERVICES
GALVESTON, TX	9881	85804	FOOD SVCS & DRINKING PLACES	MENARD, TX	148	526	EDUCATIONAL SERVICES
GARZA, TX	275	1390	SOCIAL ASSISTANCE	MIDLAND, TX	7207	60181	HOSPITALS
GILLESPIE, TX	1709	8908	FOOD SVCS & DRINKING PLACES	MILAM, TX	914	6877	MERCH. WHOLESALERS;DURABLE GDS
GLASSCOCK, TX	56	345	EDUCATIONAL SERVICES	MILLS, TX	271	1320	EDUCATIONAL SERVICES
GOLIAD, TX	290	1371	EDUCATIONAL SERVICES	MITCHELL, TX	307	2553	EXEC.; LEGIS.; & OTHER SUPPORT
GONZALES, TX	819	6477	MERCH. WHOLESALERS;NONDUR. GDS	MONTAGUE, TX	985	4751	EDUCATIONAL SERVICES
GRAY, TX	1147	8458	EDUCATIONAL SERVICES	MONTGOMERY, TX	12833	115891	EDUCATIONAL SERVICES
GRAYSON, TX	5426	44037	EDUCATIONAL SERVICES	MOORE, TX	852	12125	FOOD MANUFACTURING
GREGG, TX	6668	69014	SPECIAL TRADE CONTRACTORS	MORRIS, TX	469	4077	PRIMARY METAL MANUFACTURING
GRIMES, TX	844	10897	PERFORM'G ARTS; SPEC. SPORTS	MOTLEY, TX	108	312	EDUCATIONAL SERVICES
GUADALUPE, TX	2938	28928	EDUCATIONAL SERVICES	NACOGDOCHES, TX	2394	24598	FOOD MANUFACTURING
HALE, TX	1481	15491	FOOD AND BEVERAGE STORES	NAVARRO, TX	2113	16075	EDUCATIONAL SERVICES
HALL, TX	205	867	EDUCATIONAL SERVICES	NEWTON, TX	350	1992	EDUCATIONAL SERVICES
HAMILTON, TX	509	2725	EDUCATIONAL SERVICES	NOLAN, TX	773	5832	EDUCATIONAL SERVICES
HANSFORD, TX	320	2114	EDUCATIONAL SERVICES	NUECES, TX	13196	142611	EDUCATIONAL SERVICES
HARDEMAN, TX	261	1241	NONMETALLIC MINERAL PROD. MFG	OCHILTREE, TX	577	4082	SPECIAL TRADE CONTRACTORS
HARDIN, TX	1700	9485	EDUCATIONAL SERVICES	OLDHAM, TX	155	1470	ANIMAL PRODUCTION
HARRIS, TX	168324	1661889	PROF.; SCIENTIFIC; & TECH SVCS	ORANGE, TX	3207	24574	EDUCATIONAL SERVICES
HARRISON, TX	2350	20877	EDUCATIONAL SERVICES	PALO PINTO, TX	1270	8526	EDUCATIONAL SERVICES
HARTLEY, TX	164	897	EDUCATIONAL SERVICES	PANOLA, TX	936	8131	SPECIAL TRADE CONTRACTORS
HASKELL, TX	342	1580	EDUCATIONAL SERVICES	PARKER, TX	3838	25095	EDUCATIONAL SERVICES
HAYS, TX	4699	35677	FOOD SVCS & DRINKING PLACES	PARMER, TX	378	4432	FOOD MANUFACTURING
HEMPHILL, TX	294	1550	SPECIAL TRADE CONTRACTORS	PECOS, TX	757	5913	SUPPORT ACTIVITIES FOR MINING
HENDERSON, TX	3329	16592	EDUCATIONAL SERVICES	POLK, TX	1606	13112	EXEC.; LEGIS.; & OTHER SUPPORT
HIDALGO, TX	18591	192081	EDUCATIONAL SERVICES	POTTER, TX	7312	81671	FOOD SVCS & DRINKING PLACES
HILL, TX	1458	8988	EDUCATIONAL SERVICES	PRESIDIO, TX	385	2041	EDUCATIONAL SERVICES
HOCKLEY, TX	836	7720	EDUCATIONAL SERVICES	RAINS, TX	397	1587	EDUCATIONAL SERVICES
HOOD, TX	2172	11618	FOOD SVCS & DRINKING PLACES	RANDALL, TX	3460	27939	EDUCATIONAL SERVICES
HOPKINS, TX	1446	12250	MERCH. WHOLESALERS;NONDUR. GDS	REAGAN, TX	181	1437	SPECIAL TRADE CONTRACTORS
HOUSTON, TX	880	6433	EDUCATIONAL SERVICES	REAL, TX	300	937	EDUCATIONAL SERVICES
HOWARD, TX	1221	11525	HOSPITALS	RED RIVER, TX	476	3137	EDUCATIONAL SERVICES
HUDSPETH, TX	193	779	EDUCATIONAL SERVICES	REEVES, TX	572	4339	CROP PRODUCTION
HUNT, TX	3190	26714	TRANSPORTATION EQUIPMENT MFG	REFUGIO, TX	388	2180	CROP PRODUCTION
HUTCHINSON, TX	977	8914	PETROLEUM & COAL PRODUCTS MFG	ROBERTS, TX	56	223	EDUCATIONAL SERVICES
IRION, TX	85	389	EDUCATIONAL SERVICES	ROBERTSON, TX	675	3696	EDUCATIONAL SERVICES
JACK, TX	404	2031	EDUCATIONAL SERVICES	ROCKWALL, TX	2456	17815	EDUCATIONAL SERVICES

COUNTY	2007 Total Firms	2007 Total Employees	TOP INDUSTRY RANKED on 2007 EMPLOYMENT	COUNTY	2007 Total Firms	2007 Total Employees	TOP INDUSTRY RANKED on 2007 EMPLOYMENT
RUNNELS, TX	536	3072	EDUCATIONAL SERVICES	WASATCH, UT	850	5766	EDUCATIONAL SERVICES
RUSK, TX	1531	12839	EDUCATIONAL SERVICES	WASHINGTON, UT	4613	44369	HOSPITALS
SABINE, TX	430	2843	ACCOMMODATION	WAYNE, UT	178	1221	EDUCATIONAL SERVICES
SAN AUGUSTINE, TX	307	2075	EDUCATIONAL SERVICES	WEBER, UT	6491	87191	EDUCATIONAL SERVICES
SAN JACINTO, TX	492	2209	EDUCATIONAL SERVICES	ADDISON, VT	1704	12778	EDUCATIONAL SERVICES
SAN PATRICIO, TX	2179	16839	EDUCATIONAL SERVICES	BENNINGTON, VT	2257	18580	EDUCATIONAL SERVICES
SAN SABA, TX	429	1982	EDUCATIONAL SERVICES	CALEDONIA, VT	1585	12188	EDUCATIONAL SERVICES
SCHLEICHER, TX	144	803	SPECIAL TRADE CONTRACTORS	CHITTENDEN, VT	7686	94720	AMBULATORY HEALTH CARE SVCS
SCURRY, TX	778	6433	SPECIAL TRADE CONTRACTORS	ESSEX, VT	235	1541	FURNITURE & RELATED PROD. MFG
SHACKELFORD, TX	202	970	EDUCATIONAL SERVICES	FRANKLIN, VT	1701	13930	EDUCATIONAL SERVICES
SHELBY, TX	1009	7627	FOOD MANUFACTURING	GRAND ISLE, VT	299	1331	ACCOMMODATION
SHERMAN, TX	177	790	ANIMAL PRODUCTION	LAMOILLE, VT	1392	11986	ACCOMMODATION
SMITH, TX	10086	103584	HOSPITALS	ORANGE, VT	1121	8164	EDUCATIONAL SERVICES
SOMERVELL, TX	386	2690	EDUCATIONAL SERVICES	ORLEANS, VT	1349	10111	EDUCATIONAL SERVICES
STARR, TX	1151	8310	EDUCATIONAL SERVICES	RUTLAND, VT	3463	30459	ACCOMMODATION
STEPHENS, TX	602	3117	EDUCATIONAL SERVICES	WASHINGTON, VT	3656	34415	EDUCATIONAL SERVICES
STERLING, TX	81	344	EDUCATIONAL SERVICES	WINDHAM, VT	2835	25152	ACCOMMODATION
STONEWALL, TX	129	575	EDUCATIONAL SERVICES	WINDSOR, VT	3479	24972	ACCOMMODATION
SUTTON, TX	318	2118	SPECIAL TRADE CONTRACTORS	ACCOMACK, VA	1629	14035	FOOD MANUFACTURING
SWISHER, TX	345	2619	EDUCATIONAL SERVICES	ALBEMARLE, VA	3555	52930	EDUCATIONAL SERVICES
TARRANT, TX	63210	651491	FOOD SVCS & DRINKING PLACES	ALLEGHANY, VA	300	2827	APPAREL MANUFACTURING
TAYLOR, TX	5879	56615	EDUCATIONAL SERVICES	AMELIA, VA	431	2495	EDUCATIONAL SERVICES
TERRELL, TX	113	334	EDUCATIONAL SERVICES	AMHERST, VA	961	8871	EDUCATIONAL SERVICES
TERRY, TX	487	3527	EDUCATIONAL SERVICES	APPOMATTOX, VA	436	3570	FURNITURE & RELATED PROD. MFG
THROCKMORTON, TX	109	430	EDUCATIONAL SERVICES	ARLINGTON, VA	7380	88037	PROF.; SCIENTIFIC; & TECH SVCS
TITUS, TX	1296	18207	FOOD MANUFACTURING	AUGUSTA, VA	1317	21576	MERCH. WHOLESALERS;DURABLE GDS
TOM GREEN, TX	4209	39100	EDUCATIONAL SERVICES	BATH, VA	313	2954	ACCOMMODATION
TRAVIS, TX	44313	503822	PROF.; SCIENTIFIC; & TECH SVCS	BEDFORD, VA	1624	10983	EDUCATIONAL SERVICES
TRINITY, TX	481	2696	EDUCATIONAL SERVICES	BLAND, VA	180	2101	MERCH. WHOLESALERS;NONDUR. GDS
TYLER, TX	625	3842	EDUCATIONAL SERVICES	BOTETOURT, VA	936	7191	EDUCATIONAL SERVICES
UPSHUR, TX	1144	7528	EDUCATIONAL SERVICES	BRUNSWICK, VA	504	4009	EDUCATIONAL SERVICES
UPTON, TX	219	1411	EDUCATIONAL SERVICES	BUCHANAN, VA	886	7478	MINING (EXCEPT OIL AND GAS)
UVALDE, TX	1174	9761	EDUCATIONAL SERVICES	BUCKINGHAM, VA	403	2770	JUSTICE; PUBIC ORDER/SAFETY
VAL VERDE, TX	1567	14694	NAT'L SECURITY & INT'L AFFAIRS	CAMPBELL, VA	1204	9589	TEXTILE MILLS
VAN ZANDT, TX	1848	11186	EDUCATIONAL SERVICES	CAROLINE, VA	731	5228	FOOD SVCS & DRINKING PLACES
VICTORIA, TX	3675	37183	EDUCATIONAL SERVICES	CARROLL, VA	705	7758	RELIG.; GRANT; CIVIC; PROF ORG
WALKER, TX	1825	23935	EXEC.; LEGIS.; & OTHER SUPPORT	CHARLES CITY, VA	191	1292	EDUCATIONAL SERVICES
WALLER, TX	1196	10808	EDUCATIONAL SERVICES	CHARLOTTE, VA	482	3118	EDUCATIONAL SERVICES
WARD, TX	497	3354	EDUCATIONAL SERVICES	CHESTERFIELD, VA	9060	110051	FOOD SVCS & DRINKING PLACES
WASHINGTON, TX	1553	14304	EDUCATIONAL SERVICES	CLARKE, VA	585	3865	PRINT'G & RELATED SUPP'T ACT'S
WEBB, TX	7950	75345	EDUCATIONAL SERVICES	CRAIG, VA	137	546	EDUCATIONAL SERVICES
WHARTON, TX	1839	13544	EDUCATIONAL SERVICES	CULPEPER, VA	1784	13869	EDUCATIONAL SERVICES
WHEELER, TX	357	1785	EDUCATIONAL SERVICES	CUMBERLAND, VA	158	919	EDUCATIONAL SERVICES
WICHITA, TX	5776	55306	HOSPITALS	DICKENSON, VA	456	2899	EDUCATIONAL SERVICES
WILBARGER, TX	644	5720	HOSPITALS	DINWIDDIE, VA	341	2177	EDUCATIONAL SERVICES
WILLACY, TX	436	3319	EDUCATIONAL SERVICES	ESSEX, VA	550	4349	FOOD SVCS & DRINKING PLACES
WILLIAMSON, TX	11734	116831	COMPUTER & ELECTRONIC PROD MFG	FAIRFAX, VA	34045	389369	PROF.; SCIENTIFIC; & TECH SVCS
WILSON, TX	887	5322	EDUCATIONAL SERVICES	FAUQUIER, VA	2886	18876	EDUCATIONAL SERVICES
WINKLER, TX	326	1982	SPECIAL TRADE CONTRACTORS	FLOYD, VA	512	2365	EDUCATIONAL SERVICES
WISE, TX	2137	16851	SPECIAL TRADE CONTRACTORS	FLUVANNA, VA	653	3508	EDUCATIONAL SERVICES
WOOD, TX	1954	10483	EDUCATIONAL SERVICES	FRANKLIN, VA	1577	11440	WOOD PRODUCT MANUFACTURING
YOAKUM, TX	421	2750	SPECIAL TRADE CONTRACTORS	FREDERICK, VA	2027	22584	FOOD SVCS & DRINKING PLACES
YOUNG, TX	1140	7160	MERCH. WHOLESALERS;NONDUR. GDS	GILES, VA	663	5075	PAPER MANUFACTURING
ZAPATA, TX	459	3957	EDUCATIONAL SERVICES	GLOUCESTER, VA	1337	9768	EDUCATIONAL SERVICES
ZAVALA, TX	294	2634	EDUCATIONAL SERVICES	GOOCHLAND, VA	560	4747	MERCH. WHOLESALERS;DURABLE GDS
BEAVER, UT	291	2380	ANIMAL PRODUCTION	GRAYSON, VA	338	2277	EDUCATIONAL SERVICES
BOX ELDER, UT	1373	16743	TRANSPORTATION EQUIPMENT MFG	GREENE, VA	571	3193	EDUCATIONAL SERVICES
CACHE, UT	3029	42867	EDUCATIONAL SERVICES	GREENSVILLE, VA	23	289	WOOD PRODUCT MANUFACTURING
CARBON, UT	932	9345	EDUCATIONAL SERVICES	HALIFAX, VA	1556	12463	EDUCATIONAL SERVICES
DAGGETT, UT	58	350	JUSTICE; PUBIC ORDER/SAFETY	HANOVER, VA	3909	48213	AMUSEMENT; GAMBLING;& RECREAT.
DAVIS, UT	7416	78008	EDUCATIONAL SERVICES	HENRICO, VA	11101	151562	FOOD SVCS & DRINKING PLACES
DUCHESNE, UT	806	6626	SPECIAL TRADE CONTRACTORS	HENRY, VA	1293	10578	FURNITURE & RELATED PROD. MFG
EMERY, UT	493	4194	MINING (EXCEPT OIL AND GAS)	HIGHLAND, VA	193	721	EDUCATIONAL SERVICES
GARFIELD, UT	366	3259	ACCOMMODATION	ISLE OF WIGHT, VA	1126	11103	FOOD AND BEVERAGE STORES
GRAND, UT	853	4362	ACCOMMODATION	JAMES CITY, VA	1147	12005	HOSPITALS
IRON, UT	1593	14938	EDUCATIONAL SERVICES	KING AND QUEEN, VA	185	922	EDUCATIONAL SERVICES
JUAB, UT	345	3080	FOOD SVCS & DRINKING PLACES	KING GEORGE, VA	718	5417	PROF.; SCIENTIFIC; & TECH SVCS
KANE, UT	391	2917	REPAIR AND MAINTENANCE	KING WILLIAM, VA	570	3612	EDUCATIONAL SERVICES
MILLARD, UT	570	4169	UTILITIES	LANCASTER, VA	819	5033	HOSPITALS
MORGAN, UT	255	1578	EDUCATIONAL SERVICES	LEE, VA	606	5116	EDUCATIONAL SERVICES
PIUTE, UT	68	289	EDUCATIONAL SERVICES	LOUDOUN, VA	9299	85527	EDUCATIONAL SERVICES
RICH, UT	170	977	ACCOMMODATION	LOUISA, VA	818	4860	EDUCATIONAL SERVICES
SALT LAKE, UT	38395	491861	PROF.; SCIENTIFIC; & TECH SVCS	LUNENBURG, VA	380	2002	MERCH. WHOLESALERS;DURABLE GDS
SAN JUAN, UT	548	4233	EDUCATIONAL SERVICES	MADISON, VA	470	2973	FURN. & HOME FURNISHGS STORES
SANPETE, UT	867	7468	EDUCATIONAL SERVICES	MATHEWS, VA	371	1769	EDUCATIONAL SERVICES
SEVIER, UT	829	7704	EDUCATIONAL SERVICES	MECKLENBURG, VA	1504	11806	EDUCATIONAL SERVICES
SUMMIT, UT	2354	21018	ACCOMMODATION	MIDDLESEX, VA	639	3560	EDUCATIONAL SERVICES
TOOELE, UT	1155	10439	EDUCATIONAL SERVICES	MONTGOMERY, VA	2935	36801	EDUCATIONAL SERVICES
UINTAH, UT	1205	10477	SPECIAL TRADE CONTRACTORS	NELSON, VA	683	3603	ACCOMMODATION
UTAH, UT	12244	148402	EDUCATIONAL SERVICES	NEW KENT, VA	490	2863	EDUCATIONAL SERVICES

COUNTY	2007 Total Firms	2007 Total Employees	TOP INDUSTRY RANKED on 2007 EMPLOYMENT	COUNTY	2007 Total Firms	2007 Total Employees	TOP INDUSTRY RANKED on 2007 EMPLOYMENT
NORTHAMPTON, VA	760	7450	MERCH. WHOLESALERS;NONDUR. GDS	DOUGLAS, WA	955	8182	EDUCATIONAL SERVICES
NORTHUMBERLAND, VA	545	2676	EDUCATIONAL SERVICES	FERRY, WA	320	1596	EXEC.; LEGIS.; & OTHER SUPPORT
NOTTOWAY, VA	647	4997	JUSTICE; PUBIC ORDER/SAFETY	FRANKLIN, WA	1824	21829	FOOD MANUFACTURING
ORANGE, VA	1328	8320	PLASTICS & RUBBER PRODUCTS MFG	GARFIELD, WA	125	765	MERCH. WHOLESALERS;NONDUR. GDS
PAGE, VA	971	6757	EDUCATIONAL SERVICES	GRANT, WA	3096	34863	ADMINISTRATIVE & SUPPORT SVCS
PATRICK, VA	717	5191	TEXTILE MILLS	GRAYS HARBOR, WA	2846	23083	EDUCATIONAL SERVICES
PITTSYLVANIA, VA	1177	11219	TEXTILE MILLS	ISLAND, WA	3210	27973	NAT'L SECURITY & INT'L AFFAIRS
POWHATAN, VA	764	4529	EDUCATIONAL SERVICES	JEFFERSON, WA	1790	8588	FOOD SVCS & DRINKING PLACES
PRINCE EDWARD, VA	966	8280	EDUCATIONAL SERVICES	KING, WA	88782	974967	EDUCATIONAL SERVICES
PRINCE GEORGE, VA	434	5033	FOOD AND BEVERAGE STORES	KITSAP, WA	9542	65704	EDUCATIONAL SERVICES
PRINCE WILLIAM, VA	6026	59853	EDUCATIONAL SERVICES	KITTITAS, WA	1857	12237	FOOD SVCS & DRINKING PLACES
PULASKI, VA	901	12551	TRANSPORTATION EQUIPMENT MFG	KLICKITAT, WA	971	5928	EDUCATIONAL SERVICES
RAPPAHANNOCK, VA	410	1279	EDUCATIONAL SERVICES	LEWIS, WA	3142	26068	EDUCATIONAL SERVICES
RICHMOND, VA	413	2938	JUSTICE; PUBIC ORDER/SAFETY	LINCOLN, WA	599	3150	EDUCATIONAL SERVICES
ROANOKE, VA	3241	33001	EDUCATIONAL SERVICES	MASON, WA	1953	13086	EDUCATIONAL SERVICES
ROCKBRIDGE, VA	346	4706	TEXTILE MILLS	OKANOGAN, WA	1961	16494	MERCH. WHOLESALERS;NONDUR. GDS
ROCKINGHAM, VA	1576	20060	FOOD MANUFACTURING	PACIFIC, WA	1241	6688	EDUCATIONAL SERVICES
RUSSELL, VA	837	6160	AMBULATORY HEALTH CARE SVCS	PEND OREILLE, WA	423	2959	EDUCATIONAL SERVICES
SCOTT, VA	699	4580	EDUCATIONAL SERVICES	PIERCE, WA	24632	269135	HOSPITALS
SHENANDOAH, VA	1896	16262	FOOD MANUFACTURING	SAN JUAN, WA	1665	6204	ACCOMMODATION
SMYTH, VA	1069	13649	HOSPITALS	SKAGIT, WA	4973	47175	FOOD SVCS & DRINKING PLACES
SOUTHAMPTON, VA	394	2866	JUSTICE; PUBIC ORDER/SAFETY	SKAMANIA, WA	434	2369	ACCOMMODATION
SPOTSYLVANIA, VA	818	5588	EDUCATIONAL SERVICES	SNOHOMISH, WA	21054	196028	EDUCATIONAL SERVICES
STAFFORD, VA	2820	23263	EDUCATIONAL SERVICES	SPOKANE, WA	18007	191311	EDUCATIONAL SERVICES
SURRY, VA	211	1786	UTILITIES	STEVENS, WA	1504	10291	EDUCATIONAL SERVICES
SUSSEX, VA	466	5319	JUSTICE; PUBIC ORDER/SAFETY	THURSTON, WA	9976	92445	EXEC.; LEGIS.; & OTHER SUPPORT
TAZEWELL, VA	1958	16013	GENERAL MERCHANDISE STORES	WAHKIAKUM, WA	232	935	JUSTICE; PUBIC ORDER/SAFETY
WARREN, VA	1484	11784	EDUCATIONAL SERVICES	WALLA WALLA, WA	2062	23637	EDUCATIONAL SERVICES
WASHINGTON, VA	1800	14719	EDUCATIONAL SERVICES	WHATCOM, WA	8468	75411	EDUCATIONAL SERVICES
WESTMORELAND, VA	686	3552	EDUCATIONAL SERVICES	WHITMAN, WA	1392	16044	EDUCATIONAL SERVICES
WISE, VA	1360	10685	EDUCATIONAL SERVICES	YAKIMA, WA	7472	86746	MERCH. WHOLESALERS;NONDUR. GDS
WYTHE, VA	1261	11657	FOOD SVCS & DRINKING PLACES	BARBOUR, WV	409	2953	EDUCATIONAL SERVICES
YORK, VA	1482	11448	EDUCATIONAL SERVICES	BERKELEY, WV	2477	27284	HOSPITALS
ALEXANDRIA CITY, VA	7563	84470	PROF.; SCIENTIFIC; & TECH SVCS	BOONE, WV	683	7628	MINING (EXCEPT OIL AND GAS)
BEDFORD CITY, VA	855	7164	FOOD SVCS & DRINKING PLACES	BRAXTON, WV	466	4371	MINING (EXCEPT OIL AND GAS)
BRISTOL CITY, VA	1248	16206	FOOD SVCS & DRINKING PLACES	BROOKE, WV	718	9120	PRIMARY METAL MANUFACTURING
BUENA VISTA CITY, VA	295	3072	TRANSPORTATION EQUIPMENT MFG	CABELL, WV	3748	49903	HOSPITALS
CHARLOTTESVILLE CITY, VA	4212	46091	HOSPITALS	CALHOUN, WV	197	1253	HOSPITALS
CHESAPEAKE CITY, VA	7691	83038	SPECIAL TRADE CONTRACTORS	CLAY, WV	242	1974	MINING (EXCEPT OIL AND GAS)
COLONIAL HEIGHTS CITY, V	1094	11991	GENERAL MERCHANDISE STORES	DODDRIDGE, WV	141	721	EDUCATIONAL SERVICES
COVINGTON CITY, VA	648	7993	PAPER MANUFACTURING	FAYETTE, WV	1419	12023	EDUCATIONAL SERVICES
DANVILLE CITY, VA	2488	31445	TEXTILE MILLS	GILMER, WV	218	1771	EDUCATIONAL SERVICES
EMPORIA CITY, VA	575	5513	BLDG MATL & GARDEN EQPMT DLRS	GRANT, WV	404	2933	HOSPITALS
FAIRFAX CITY, VA	5150	65336	PROF.; SCIENTIFIC; & TECH SVCS	GREENBRIER, WV	1455	11401	ACCOMMODATION
FALLS CHURCH CITY, VA	1239	9372	FURN. & HOME FURNISHGS STORES	HAMPSHIRE, WV	647	5293	ACCOMMODATION
FRANKLIN CITY, VA	690	6881	PAPER MANUFACTURING	HANCOCK, WV	1070	12043	AMUSEMENT; GAMBLING;& RECREAT.
FREDERICKSBURG CITY, VA	5499	48900	FOOD SVCS & DRINKING PLACES	HARDY, WV	519	5957	FOOD MANUFACTURING
GALAX CITY, VA	710	8542	FURNITURE & RELATED PROD. MFG	HARRISON, WV	2953	31445	JUSTICE; PUBIC ORDER/SAFETY
HAMPTON CITY, VA	3804	53668	SPACE RESEARCH AND TECHNOLOGY	JACKSON, WV	841	8048	PRIMARY METAL MANUFACTURING
HARRISONBURG CITY, VA	2638	40138	PROF.; SCIENTIFIC; & TECH SVCS	JEFFERSON, WV	1555	16144	EDUCATIONAL SERVICES
HOPEWELL CITY, VA	813	8900	CHEMICAL MANUFACTURING	KANAWHA, WV	8545	111460	HOSPITALS
LEXINGTON CITY, VA	876	8871	EDUCATIONAL SERVICES	LEWIS, WV	587	5616	HOSPITALS
LYNCHBURG CITY, VA	4322	61022	HOSPITALS	LINCOLN, WV	408	2491	EDUCATIONAL SERVICES
MANASSAS CITY, VA	3434	46378	SPECIAL TRADE CONTRACTORS	LOGAN, WV	1297	10887	MINING (EXCEPT OIL AND GAS)
MANASSAS PARK CITY, VA	1038	8680	EDUCATIONAL SERVICES	MCDOWELL, WV	748	4681	EDUCATIONAL SERVICES
MARTINSVILLE CITY, VA	1982	19915	FURNITURE & RELATED PROD. MFG	MARION, WV	2207	19712	EDUCATIONAL SERVICES
NEWPORT NEWS CITY, VA	6321	87892	TRANSPORTATION EQUIPMENT MFG	MARSHALL, WV	768	7770	NONSTORE RETAILERS
NORFOLK CITY, VA	10313	119124	EDUCATIONAL SERVICES	MASON, WV	747	5822	HOSPITALS
NORTON CITY, VA	427	5233	HOSPITALS	MERCER, WV	3221	26214	HOSPITALS
PETERSBURG CITY, VA	1813	19038	EDUCATIONAL SERVICES	MINERAL, WV	854	6442	EDUCATIONAL SERVICES
POQUOSON CITY, VA	284	1719	EDUCATIONAL SERVICES	MINGO, WV	845	7063	MINING (EXCEPT OIL AND GAS)
PORTSMOUTH CITY, VA	3372	39930	HOSPITALS	MONONGALIA, WV	3613	45478	AMBULATORY HEALTH CARE SVCS
RADFORD CITY, VA	769	8447	EDUCATIONAL SERVICES	MONROE, WV	368	1798	EDUCATIONAL SERVICES
RICHMOND CITY, VA	9767	148820	EDUCATIONAL SERVICES	MORGAN, WV	462	2943	EDUCATIONAL SERVICES
ROANOKE CITY, VA	5038	67661	PROF.; SCIENTIFIC; & TECH SVCS	NICHOLAS, WV	921	7919	GENERAL MERCHANDISE STORES
SALEM CITY, VA	1769	28245	HOSPITALS	OHIO, WV	2150	29446	HOSPITALS
STAUNTON CITY, VA	1579	15947	EDUCATIONAL SERVICES	PENDLETON, WV	243	1558	NAT'L SECURITY & INT'L AFFAIRS
SUFFOLK CITY, VA	2291	26103	EXEC.; LEGIS.; & OTHER SUPPORT	PLEASANTS, WV	226	2003	CHEMICAL MANUFACTURING
VIRGINIA BEACH CITY, VA	17428	173313	FOOD SVCS & DRINKING PLACES	POCAHONTAS, WV	388	5253	ACCOMMODATION
WAYNESBORO CITY, VA	1156	10985	PAPER MANUFACTURING	PRESTON, WV	918	6071	EDUCATIONAL SERVICES
WILLIAMSBURG CITY, VA	2417	39819	EDUCATIONAL SERVICES	PUTNAM, WV	1612	15084	MERCH. WHOLESALERS;DURABLE GDS
WINCHESTER CITY, VA	2310	26032	HOSPITALS	RALEIGH, WV	3120	28134	FOOD SVCS & DRINKING PLACES
ADAMS, WA	761	6731	FOOD MANUFACTURING	RANDOLPH, WV	1073	11355	HOSPITALS
ASOTIN, WA	685	5700	AMBULATORY HEALTH CARE SVCS	RITCHIE, WV	355	2148	EDUCATIONAL SERVICES
BENTON, WA	4959	60428	PROF.; SCIENTIFIC; & TECH SVCS	ROANE, WV	305	3104	HOSPITALS
CHELAN, WA	3440	37122	MERCH. WHOLESALERS;NONDUR. GDS	SUMMERS, WV	359	2320	FOOD SVCS & DRINKING PLACES
CLALLAM, WA	3317	25052	EDUCATIONAL SERVICES	TAYLOR, WV	396	3115	EDUCATIONAL SERVICES
CLARK, WA	12627	115729	EDUCATIONAL SERVICES	TUCKER, WV	323	2934	AMUSEMENT; GAMBLING;& RECREAT.
COLUMBIA, WA	229	1086	EXEC.; LEGIS.; & OTHER SUPPORT	TYLER, WV	241	2394	CHEMICAL MANUFACTURING
COWLITZ, WA	3585	37019	EDUCATIONAL SERVICES	UPSHUR, WV	814	7708	EDUCATIONAL SERVICES

COUNTY	2007 Total Firms	2007 Total Employees	TOP INDUSTRY RANKED on 2007 EMPLOYMENT	COUNTY	2007 Total Firms	2007 Total Employees	TOP INDUSTRY RANKED on 2007 EMPLOYMENT
WAYNE, WV	837	9241	EDUCATIONAL SERVICES	CAMPBELL, WY	2032	25591	MINING (EXCEPT OIL AND GAS)
WEBSTER, WV	245	2044	WOOD PRODUCT MANUFACTURING	CARBON, WY	1106	7237	TRUCK TRANSPORTATION
WETZEL, WV	665	6178	MERCH. WHOLESALERS;NONDUR. GDS	CONVERSE, WY	650	4621	EDUCATIONAL SERVICES
WIRT, WV	127	714	EDUCATIONAL SERVICES	CROOK, WY	353	2015	WOOD PRODUCT MANUFACTURING
WOOD, WV	3552	37761	FOOD SVCS & DRINKING PLACES	FREMONT, WY	2260	16422	EDUCATIONAL SERVICES
WYOMING, WV	705	3894	EDUCATIONAL SERVICES	GOSHEN, WY	611	4209	EDUCATIONAL SERVICES
ADAMS, WI	690	4016	FOOD SVCS & DRINKING PLACES	HOT SPRINGS, WY	408	2138	EDUCATIONAL SERVICES
ASHLAND, WI	997	8651	EDUCATIONAL SERVICES	JOHNSON, WY	561	2932	ACCOMMODATION
BARRON, WI	2256	24730	FOOD AND BEVERAGE STORES	LARAMIE, WY	3665	43864	PROF.; SCIENTIFIC; & TECH SVCS
BAYFIELD, WI	1099	5008	ACCOMMODATION	LINCOLN, WY	1164	6014	EDUCATIONAL SERVICES
BROWN, WI	9864	151327	FOOD SVCS & DRINKING PLACES	NATRONA, WY	4224	34334	FOOD SVCS & DRINKING PLACES
BUFFALO, WI	662	4303	EDUCATIONAL SERVICES	NIOBRARA, WY	182	749	EDUCATIONAL SERVICES
BURNETT, WI	897	6382	EXEC.; LEGIS.; & OTHER SUPPORT	PARK, WY	2052	13621	ACCOMMODATION
CALUMET, WI	1400	15667	MACHINERY MANUFACTURING	PLATTE, WY	494	3380	UTILITIES
CHIPPEWA, WI	2570	26236	EDUCATIONAL SERVICES	SHERIDAN, WY	1772	12501	EDUCATIONAL SERVICES
CLARK, WI	1276	10745	EDUCATIONAL SERVICES	SUBLETTE, WY	721	3804	SPECIAL TRADE CONTRACTORS
COLUMBIA, WI	2548	25530	EDUCATIONAL SERVICES	SWEETWATER, WY	2150	22095	SPECIAL TRADE CONTRACTORS
CRAWFORD, WI	878	7829	PROF.; SCIENTIFIC; & TECH SVCS	TETON, WY	2380	18427	ACCOMMODATION
DANE, WI	21678	324045	PROF.; SCIENTIFIC; & TECH SVCS	UINTA, WY	1049	8939	EDUCATIONAL SERVICES
DODGE, WI	3024	36939	FABRICATED METAL PRODUCT MFG	WASHAKIE, WY	670	3980	EDUCATIONAL SERVICES
DOOR, WI	2360	16581	FOOD SVCS & DRINKING PLACES	WESTON, WY	374	1904	EDUCATIONAL SERVICES
DOUGLAS, WI	2372	19803	EDUCATIONAL SERVICES				
DUNN, WI	1504	16947	EDUCATIONAL SERVICES				
EAU CLAIRE, WI	3903	51716	AMBULATORY HEALTH CARE SVCS				
FLORENCE, WI	249	1558	EDUCATIONAL SERVICES				
FOND DU LAC, WI	3931	51253	FOOD SVCS & DRINKING PLACES				
FOREST, WI	582	3812	AMUSEMENT; GAMBLING;& RECREAT.				
GRANT, WI	2208	24124	FOOD SVCS & DRINKING PLACES				
GREEN, WI	1713	15839	NONSTORE RETAILERS				
GREEN LAKE, WI	985	7862	HOSPITALS				
IOWA, WI	1005	11431	CLOTHING & CLOTH'G ACC. STORES				
IRON, WI	434	2437	FOOD SVCS & DRINKING PLACES				
JACKSON, WI	799	6308	EXEC.; LEGIS.; & OTHER SUPPORT				
JEFFERSON, WI	3540	37979	FOOD SVCS & DRINKING PLACES				
JUNEAU, WI	1061	9768	MACHINERY MANUFACTURING				
KENOSHA, WI	4996	63856	EDUCATIONAL SERVICES				
KEWAUNEE, WI	823	6533	EDUCATIONAL SERVICES				
LA CROSSE, WI	4439	70794	EDUCATIONAL SERVICES				
LAFAYETTE, WI	716	4025	EDUCATIONAL SERVICES				
LANGLADE, WI	961	8045	FOOD SVCS & DRINKING PLACES				
LINCOLN, WI	1236	12054	EDUCATIONAL SERVICES				
MANITOWOC, WI	3111	37413	EDUCATIONAL SERVICES				
MARATHON, WI	4904	81093	HOSPITALS				
MARINETTE, WI	2079	18680	EDUCATIONAL SERVICES				
MARQUETTE, WI	691	4745	FOOD MANUFACTURING				
MENOMINEE, WI	136	2863	EXEC.; LEGIS.; & OTHER SUPPORT				
MILWAUKEE, WI	32182	472584	EDUCATIONAL SERVICES				
MONROE, WI	1893	19423	HOSPITALS				
OCONTO, WI	1447	10383	EDUCATIONAL SERVICES				
ONEIDA, WI	2690	19725	AMBULATORY HEALTH CARE SVCS				
OUTAGAMIE, WI	7831	95171	FOOD SVCS & DRINKING PLACES				
OZAUKEE, WI	4119	44062	MERCH. WHOLESALERS;DURABLE GDS				
PEPIN, WI	396	2383	FOOD SVCS & DRINKING PLACES				
PIERCE, WI	1432	10469	EDUCATIONAL SERVICES				
POLK, WI	2008	15712	EDUCATIONAL SERVICES				
PORTAGE, WI	2839	38934	INSURANCE CARRIERS & RELATED				
PRICE, WI	903	7850	PAPER MANUFACTURING				
RACINE, WI	6910	78732	EDUCATIONAL SERVICES				
RICHLAND, WI	832	6778	ELECT'L EQPMT; APP; & COMP MFG				
ROCK, WI	5855	76317	RELIG.; GRANT; CIVIC; PROF ORG				
RUSK, WI	725	6567	EDUCATIONAL SERVICES				
ST. CROIX, WI	3247	27320	FOOD SVCS & DRINKING PLACES				
SAUK, WI	2851	42258	AMUSEMENT; GAMBLING;& RECREAT.				
SAWYER, WI	1214	7569	ACCOMMODATION				
SHAWANO, WI	1841	14255	FOOD SVCS & DRINKING PLACES				
SHEBOYGAN, WI	4193	63965	FABRICATED METAL PRODUCT MFG				
TAYLOR, WI	859	7936	FABRICATED METAL PRODUCT MFG				
TREMPEALEAU, WI	1180	12919	FURNITURE & RELATED PROD. MFG				
VERNON, WI	1406	9091	EDUCATIONAL SERVICES				
VILAS, WI	1829	8777	ACCOMMODATION				
WALWORTH, WI	4561	41350	EDUCATIONAL SERVICES				
WASHBURN, WI	1035	6838	EDUCATIONAL SERVICES				
WASHINGTON, WI	4698	56637	FOOD SVCS & DRINKING PLACES				
WAUKESHA, WI	17517	230263	PROF.; SCIENTIFIC; & TECH SVCS				
WAUPACA, WI	2437	22128	FOOD SVCS & DRINKING PLACES				
WAUSHARA, WI	1085	6879	FOOD SVCS & DRINKING PLACES				
WINNEBAGO, WI	6175	93406	AMBULATORY HEALTH CARE SVCS				
WOOD, WI	3419	39603	AMBULATORY HEALTH CARE SVCS				
ALBANY, WY	1471	17599	EDUCATIONAL SERVICES				
BIG HORN, WY	718	4775	EDUCATIONAL SERVICES				

Appendixes

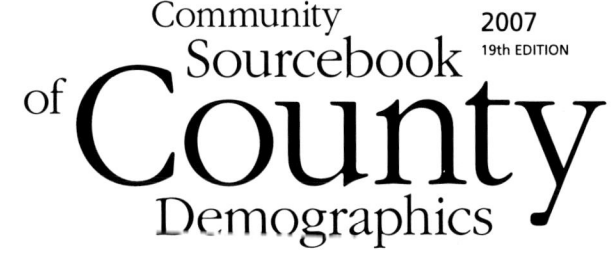

Community
Sourcebook
of
County
Demographics
2007
19th EDITION

Appendix I:
State Codes

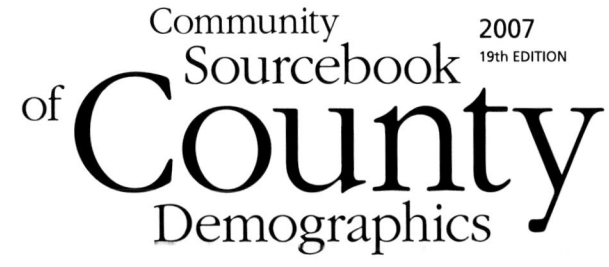

Community
Sourcebook 2007
19th EDITION
of County
Demographics

State Codes

State Name	State Code	State Name	State Code
Alabama	01	Montana	30
Alaska	02	Nebraska	31
Arizona	04	Nevada	32
Arkansas	05	New Hampshire	33
California	06	New Jersey	34
Colorado	08	New Mexico	35
Connecticut	09	New York	36
Delaware	10	North Carolina	37
District of Columbia	11	North Dakota	38
Florida	12	Ohio	39
Georgia	13	Oklahoma	40
Hawaii	15	Oregon	41
Idaho	16	Pennsylvania	42
Illinois	17	Rhode Island	44
Indiana	18	South Carolina	45
Iowa	19	South Dakota	46
Kansas	20	Tennessee	47
Kentucky	21	Texas	48
Louisiana	22	Utah	49
Maine	23	Vermont	50
Maryland	24	Virginia	51
Massachusetts	25	Washington	53
Michigan	26	West Virginia	54
Minnesota	27	Wisconsin	55
Mississippi	28	Wyoming	56
Missouri	29		

Appendix II:
CBSA Codes

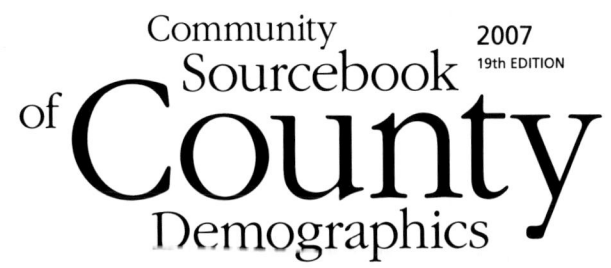

CBSA CODES

CBSA Name	CBSA Code	CBSA Name	CBSA Code
Abbeville, LA Micro	10020	Astoria, OR Micro	11820
Aberdeen, SD Micro	10100	Atchison, KS Micro	11860
Aberdeen, WA Micro	10140	Athens, OH Micro	11900
Abilene, TX Metro	10180	Athens, TN Micro	11940
Ada, OK Micro	10220	Athens, TX Micro	11980
Adrian, MI Micro	10300	Athens-Clarke County, GA Metro	12020
Akron, OH Metro	10420	Atlanta-Sandy Springs-Marietta, GA Metro	12060
Alamogordo, NM Micro	10460	Atlantic City, NJ Metro	12100
Albany, GA Metro	10500	Auburn, IN Micro	12140
Albany-Lebanon, OR Micro	10540	Auburn, NY Micro	12180
Albany-Schenectady-Troy, NY Metro	10580	Auburn-Opelika, AL Metro	12220
Albemarle, NC Micro	10620	Augusta-Richmond County, GA-SC Metro	12260
Albert Lea, MN Micro	10660	Augusta-Waterville, ME Micro	12300
Albertville, AL Micro	10700	Austin, MN Micro	12380
Albuquerque, NM Metro	10740	Austin-Round Rock, TX Metro	12420
Alexander City, AL Micro	10760	Bainbridge, GA Micro	12460
Alexandria, LA Metro	10780	Bakersfield, CA Metro	12540
Alexandria, MN Micro	10820	Baltimore-Towson, MD Metro	12580
Alice, TX Micro	10860	Bangor, ME Metro	12620
Allegan, MI Micro	10880	Baraboo, WI Micro	12660
Allentown-Bethlehem-Easton, PA-NJ Metro	10900	Barnstable Town, MA Metro	12700
Alma, MI Micro	10940	Barre, VT Micro	12740
Alpena, MI Micro	10980	Bartlesville, OK Micro	12780
Altoona, PA Metro	11020	Bastrop, LA Micro	12820
Altus, OK Micro	11060	Batavia, NY Micro	12860
Amarillo, TX Metro	11100	Batesville, AR Micro	12900
Americus, GA Micro	11140	Baton Rouge, LA Metro	12940
Ames, IA Metro	11180	Battle Creek, MI Metro	12980
Amsterdam, NY Micro	11220	Bay City, MI Metro	13020
Anchorage, AK Metro	11260	Bay City, TX Micro	13060
Anderson, IN Metro	11300	Beatrice, NE Micro	13100
Anderson, SC Metro	11340	Beaumont-Port Arthur, TX Metro	13140
Andrews, TX Micro	11380	Beaver Dam, WI Micro	13180
Angola, IN Micro	11420	Beckley, WV Micro	13220
Ann Arbor, MI Metro	11460	Bedford, IN Micro	13260
Anniston-Oxford, AL Metro	11500	Beeville, TX Micro	13300
Appleton, WI Metro	11540	Bellefontaine, OH Micro	13340
Arcadia, FL Micro	11580	Bellingham, WA Metro	13380
Ardmore, OK Micro	11620	Bemidji, MN Micro	13420
Arkadelphia, AR Micro	11660	Bend, OR Metro	13460
Asheville, NC Metro	11700	Bennettsville, SC Micro	13500
Ashland, OH Micro	11740	Bonnington, VT Micro	13540
Ashtabula, OH Micro	11780	Berlin, NH-VT Micro	13620

CBSA CODES

CBSA Name	CBSA Code	CBSA Name	CBSA Code
Big Rapids, MI Micro	13660	Burlington, NC Metro	15500
Big Spring, TX Micro	13700	Burlington-South Burlington, VT Metro	15540
Billings, MT Metro	13740	Butte-Silver Bow, MT Micro	15580
Binghamton, NY Metro	13780	Cadillac, MI Micro	15620
Birmingham-Hoover, AL Metro	13820	Calhoun, GA Micro	15660
Bishop, CA Micro	13860	Cambridge, MD Micro	15700
Bismarck, ND Metro	13900	Cambridge, OH Micro	15740
Blackfoot, ID Micro	13940	Camden, AR Micro	15780
Blacksburg-Christiansburg-Radford, VA Metro	13980	Campbellsville, KY Micro	15820
Bloomington, IN Metro	14020	Canon City, CO Micro	15860
Bloomington-Normal, IL Metro	14060	Canton, IL Micro	15900
Bloomsburg-Berwick, PA Micro	14100	Canton-Massillon, OH Metro	15940
Bluefield, WV-VA Micro	14140	Cape Coral-Fort Myers, FL Metro	15980
Blytheville, AR Micro	14180	Cape Girardeau-Jackson, MO-IL Micro	16020
Bogalusa, LA Micro	14220	Carbondale, IL Micro	16060
Boise City-Nampa, ID Metro	14260	Carlsbad-Artesia, NM Micro	16100
Bonham, TX Micro	14300	Carson City, NV Metro	16180
Boone, IA Micro	14340	Casper, WY Metro	16220
Boone, NC Micro	14380	Cedar City, UT Micro	16260
Borger, TX Micro	14420	Cedar Rapids, IA Metro	16300
Boston-Cambridge-Quincy, MA-NH Metro	14460	Cedartown, GA Micro	16340
Boulder, CO Metro	14500	Celina, OH Micro	16380
Bowling Green, KY Metro	14540	Central City, KY Micro	16420
Bozeman, MT Micro	14580	Centralia, IL Micro	16460
Bradford, PA Micro	14620	Centralia, WA Micro	16500
Brainerd, MN Micro	14660	Chambersburg, PA Micro	16540
Branson, MO Micro	14700	Champaign-Urbana, IL Metro	16580
Bremerton-Silverdale, WA Metro	14740	Charleston, WV Metro	16620
Brenham, TX Micro	14780	Charleston-Mattoon, IL Micro	16660
Brevard, NC Micro	14820	Charleston-North Charleston, SC Metro	16700
Bridgeport-Stamford-Norwalk, CT Metro	14860	Charlotte-Gastonia-Concord, NC-SC Metro	16740
Brigham City, UT Micro	14940	Charlottesville, VA Metro	16820
Brookhaven, MS Micro	15020	Chattanooga, TN-GA Metro	16860
Brookings, OR Micro	15060	Chester, SC Micro	16900
Brookings, SD Micro	15100	Cheyenne, WY Metro	16940
Brownsville, TN Micro	15140	Chicago-Naperville-Joliet, IL-IN-WI Metro	16980
Brownsville-Harlingen, TX Metro	15180	Chico, CA Metro	17020
Brownwood, TX Micro	15220	Chillicothe, OH Micro	17060
Brunswick, GA Metro	15260	Cincinnati-Middletown, OH-KY-IN Metro	17140
Bucyrus, OH Micro	15340	City of The Dalles, OR Micro	17180
Buffalo-Niagara Falls, NY Metro	15380	Claremont, NH Micro	17200
Burley, ID Micro	15420		
Burlington, IA-IL Micro	15460		

CBSA CODES

CBSA Name	CBSA Code	CBSA Name	CBSA Code
Clarksburg, WV Micro	17220	Dallas-Fort Worth-Arlington, TX Metro	19100
Clarksdale, MS Micro	17260	Dalton, GA Metro	19140
Clarksville, TN-KY Metro	17300	Danville, IL Metro	19180
Clearlake, CA Micro	17340	Danville, KY Micro	19220
Cleveland, MS Micro	17380	Danville, VA Metro	19260
Cleveland, TN Metro	17420	Daphne-Fairhope-Foley, AL Micro	19300
Cleveland-Elyria-Mentor, OH Metro	17460	Davenport-Moline-Rock Island, IA-IL Metro	19340
Clewiston, FL Micro	17500	Dayton, OH Metro	19380
Clinton, IA Micro	17540	De Ridder, LA Micro	19760
Clovis, NM Micro	17580	Decatur, AL Metro	19460
Coeur d'Alene, ID Metro	17660	Decatur, IL Metro	19500
Coffeyville, KS Micro	17700	Decatur, IN Micro	19540
Coldwater, MI Micro	17740	Defiance, OH Micro	19580
College Station-Bryan, TX Metro	17780	Del Rio, TX Micro	19620
Colorado Springs, CO Metro	17820	Deltona-Daytona Beach-Ormond Beach, FL Metro	19660
Columbia, MO Metro	17860	Deming, NM Micro	19700
Columbia, SC Metro	17900	Denver-Aurora, CO Metro	19740
Columbia, TN Micro	17940	Des Moines–West Des Moines, IA Metro	19780
Columbus, GA-AL Metro	17980	Detroit-Warren-Livonia, MI Metro	19820
Columbus, IN Metro	18020	Dickinson, ND Micro	19860
Columbus, MS Micro	18060	Dillon, SC Micro	19900
Columbus, NE Micro	18100	Dixon, IL Micro	19940
Columbus, OH Metro	18140	Dodge City, KS Micro	19980
Concord, NH Micro	18180	Dothan, AL Metro	20020
Connersville, IN Micro	18220	Douglas, GA Micro	20060
Cookeville, TN Micro	18260	Dover, DE Metro	20100
Coos Bay, OR Micro	18300	Dublin, GA Micro	20140
Corbin, KY Micro	18340	DuBois, PA Micro	20180
Cordele, GA Micro	18380	Dubuque, IA Metro	20220
Corinth, MS Micro	18420	Duluth, MN-WI Metro	20260
Cornelia, GA Micro	18460	Dumas, TX Micro	20300
Corning, NY Micro	18500	Duncan, OK Micro	20340
Corpus Christi, TX Metro	18580	Dunn, NC Micro	20380
Corsicana, TX Micro	18620	Durango, CO Micro	20420
Cortland, NY Micro	18660	Durant, OK Micro	20460
Corvallis, OR Metro	18700	Durham, NC Metro	20500
Coshocton, OH Micro	18740	Dyersburg, TN Micro	20540
Crawfordsville, IN Micro	18820	Eagle Pass, TX Micro	20580
Crescent City, CA Micro	18860	East Liverpool-Salem, OH Micro	20620
Crossville, TN Micro	18900	East Stroudsburg, PA Micro	20700
Crowley, LA Micro	18940	Easton, MD Micro	20660
Cullman, AL Micro	18980		
Culpeper, VA Micro	19020		
Cumberland, MD-WV Metro	19060		

CBSA CODES

CBSA Name	CBSA Code	CBSA Name	CBSA Code
Eau Claire, WI Metro	20740	Fond du Lac, WI Metro	22540
Edwards, CO Micro	20780	Forest City, NC Micro	22580
Effingham, IL Micro	20820	Forrest City, AR Micro	22620
El Campo, TX Micro	20900	Fort Collins-Loveland, CO Metro	22660
El Centro, CA Metro	20940	Fort Dodge, IA Micro	22700
El Dorado, AR Micro	20980	Fort Leonard Wood, MO Micro	22780
El Paso, TX Metro	21340	Fort Madison - Keokuk, IA-MO Micro	22800
Elizabeth City, NC Micro	21020	Fort Morgan, CO Micro	22820
Elizabethtown, KY Metro	21060	Fort Payne, AL Micro	22840
Elk City, OK Micro	21120	Fort Polk South, LA Micro	22860
Elkhart-Goshen, IN Metro	21140	Fort Smith, AR-OK Metro	22900
Elko, NV Micro	21220	Fort Valley, GA Micro	22980
Ellensburg, WA Micro	21260	Fort Walton Beach-Crestview-Destin, FL Metro	23020
Elmira, NY Metro	21300	Fort Wayne, IN Metro	23060
Emporia, KS Micro	21380	Frankfort, IN Micro	23140
Enid, OK Micro	21420	Frankfort, KY Micro	23180
Enterprise-Ozark, AL Micro	21460	Fredericksburg, TX Micro	23240
Erie, PA Metro	21500	Freeport, IL Micro	23300
Escanaba, MI Micro	21540	Fremont, NE Micro	23340
Espanola, NM Micro	21580	Fremont, OH Micro	23380
Eufaula, AL-GA Micro	21640	Fresno, CA Metro	23420
Eugene-Springfield, OR Metro	21660	Gadsden, AL Metro	23460
Eureka-Arcata-Fortuna, CA Micro	21700	Gaffney, SC Micro	23500
Evanston, WY Micro	21740	Gainesville, FL Metro	23540
Evansville, IN-KY Metro	21780	Gainesville, GA Metro	23580
Fairbanks, AK Metro	21820	Gainesville, TX Micro	23620
Fairmont, MN Micro	21860	Galesburg, IL Micro	23660
Fairmont, WV Micro	21900	Gallup, NM Micro	23700
Fallon, NV Micro	21980	Garden City, KS Micro	23780
Fargo, ND-MN Metro	22020	Gardnerville Ranchos, NV Micro	23820
Faribault-Northfield, MN Micro	22060	Georgetown, SC Micro	23860
Farmington, MO Micro	22100	Gettysburg, PA Micro	23900
Farmington, NM Metro	22140	Gillette, WY Micro	23940
Fayetteville, NC Metro	22180	Glasgow, KY Micro	23980
Fayetteville-Springdale-Rogers, AR-MO Metro	22220	Glens Falls, NY Metro	24020
Fergus Falls, MN Micro	22260	Gloversville, NY Micro	24100
Fernley, NV Micro	22280	Goldsboro, NC Metro	24140
Findlay, OH Micro	22300	Granbury, TX Micro	24180
Fitzgerald, GA Micro	22340	Grand Forks, ND-MN Metro	24220
Flagstaff, AZ Metro	22380	Grand Island, NE Micro	24260
Flint, MI Metro	22420	Grand Junction, CO Metro	24300
Florence, SC Metro	22500	Grand Rapids-Wyoming, MI Metro	24340
Florence-Muscle Shoals, AL Metro	22520	Grants Pass, OR Micro	24420

CBSA CODES

CBSA Name	CBSA Code	CBSA Name	CBSA Code
Grants, NM Micro	24380	Homosassa Springs, FL Micro	26140
Great Bend, KS Micro	24460	Honolulu, HI Metro	26180
Great Falls, MT Metro	24500	Hood River, OR Micro	26220
Greeley, CO Metro	24540	Hope, AR Micro	26260
Green Bay, WI Metro	24580	Hot Springs, AR Metro	26300
Greeneville, TN Micro	24620	Houghton, MI Micro	26340
Greensboro-High Point, NC Metro	24660	Houma-Bayou Cane-Thibodaux, LA Metro	26380
Greensburg, IN Micro	24700	Houston-Sugar Land-Baytown, TX Metro	26420
Greenville, MS Micro	24740	Hudson, NY Micro	26460
Greenville, NC Metro	24780	Humboldt, TN Micro	26480
Greenville, OH Micro	24820	Huntingdon, PA Micro	26500
Greenville-Mauldin-Easley, SC Metro	24860	Huntington, IN Micro	26540
Greenwood, MS Micro	24900	Huntington-Ashland, WV-KY-OH Metro	26580
Greenwood, SC Micro	24940	Huntsville, AL Metro	26620
Grenada, MS Micro	24980	Huntsville, TX Micro	26660
Gulfport-Biloxi, MS Metro	25060	Huron, SD Micro	26700
Guymon, OK Micro	25100	Hutchinson, KS Micro	26740
Hagerstown-Martinsburg, MD-WV Metro	25180	Hutchinson, MN Micro	26780
Hammond, LA Micro	25220	Idaho Falls, ID Metro	26820
Hanford-Corcoran, CA Metro	25260	Indiana, PA Micro	26860
Hannibal, MO Micro	25300	Indianapolis-Carmel, IN Metro	26900
Harriman, TN Micro	25340	Indianola, MS Micro	26940
Harrisburg, IL Micro	25380	Iowa City, IA Metro	26980
Harrisburg-Carlisle, PA Metro	25420	Iron Mountain, MI-WI Micro	27020
Harrison, AR Micro	25460	Ithaca, NY Metro	27060
Harrisonburg, VA Metro	25500	Jackson, MI Metro	27100
Hartford-West Hartford-East Hartford, CT Metro	25540	Jackson, MS Metro	27140
Hastings, NE Micro	25580	Jackson, TN Metro	27180
Hattiesburg, MS Metro	25620	Jackson, WY-ID Micro	27220
Havre, MT Micro	25660	Jacksonville, FL Metro	27260
Hays, KS Micro	25700	Jacksonville, IL Micro	27300
Heber, UT Micro	25720	Jacksonville, NC Metro	27340
Helena, MT Micro	25740	Jacksonville, TX Micro	27380
Henderson, NC Micro	25780	Jamestown, ND Micro	27420
Hereford, TX Micro	25820	Jamestown-Dunkirk-Fredonia, NY Micro	27460
Hickory-Lenoir-Morganton, NC Metro	25860	Janesville, WI Metro	27500
Hilo, HI Micro	25900	Jasper, IN Micro	27540
Hilton Head Island-Beaufort, SC Micro	25940	Jefferson City, MO Metro	27620
Hinesville-Fort Stewart, GA Metro	25980	Jennings, LA Micro	27660
Hobbs, NM Micro	26020	Jesup, GA Micro	27700
Holland-Grand Haven, MI Metro	26100	Johnson City, TN Metro	27740
		Johnstown, PA Metro	27780

CBSA CODES

CBSA Name	CBSA Code	CBSA Name	CBSA Code
Jonesboro, AR Metro	27860	Lansing-East Lansing, MI Metro	29620
Joplin, MO Metro	27900	Laramie, WY Micro	29660
Juneau, AK Micro	27940	Laredo, TX Metro	29700
Kahului-Wailuku, HI Micro	27980	Las Cruces, NM Metro	29740
Kalamazoo-Portage, MI Metro	28020	Las Vegas, NM Micro	29780
Kalispell, MT Micro	28060	Las Vegas-Paradise, NV Metro	29820
Kankakee-Bradley, IL Metro	28100	Laurel, MS Micro	29860
Kansas City, MO-KS Metro	28140	Laurinburg, NC Micro	29900
Kapaa, HI Micro	28180	Lawrence, KS Metro	29940
Kearney, NE Micro	28260	Lawrenceburg, TN Micro	29980
Keene, NH Micro	28300	Lawton, OK Metro	30020
Kendallville, IN Micro	28340	Lebanon, MO Micro	30060
Kennett, MO Micro	28380	Lebanon, NH-VT Micro	30100
Kennewick-Richland-Pasco, WA Metro	28420	Lebanon, PA Metro	30140
Kerrville, TX Micro	28500	Levelland, TX Micro	30220
Ketchikan, AK Micro	28540	Lewisburg, PA Micro	30260
Key West, FL Micro	28580	Lewisburg, TN Micro	30280
Kill Devil Hills, NC Micro	28620	Lewiston, ID-WA Metro	30300
Killeen-Temple-Fort Hood, TX Metro	28660	Lewiston-Auburn, ME Metro	30340
Kingsport-Bristol-Bristol, TN-VA Metro	28700	Lewistown, PA Micro	30380
Kingston, NY Metro	28740	Lexington Park, MD Micro	30500
Kingsville, TX Micro	28780	Lexington, NE Micro	30420
Kinston, NC Micro	28820	Lexington-Fayette, KY Metro	30460
Kirksville, MO Micro	28860	Liberal, KS Micro	30580
Klamath Falls, OR Micro	28900	Lima, OH Metro	30620
Knoxville, TN Metro	28940	Lincoln, IL Micro	30660
Kodiak, AK Micro	28980	Lincoln, NE Metro	30700
Kokomo, IN Metro	29020	Lincolnton, NC Micro	30740
La Crosse, WI-MN Metro	29100	Little Rock-North Little Rock-Conway, AR Metro	30780
La Follette, TN Micro	29220	Lock Haven, PA Micro	30820
La Grande, OR Micro	29260	Logan, UT-ID Metro	30860
Laconia, NH Micro	29060	Logansport, IN Micro	30900
Lafayette, IN Metro	29140	London, KY Micro	30940
Lafayette, LA Metro	29180	Longview, TX Metro	30980
LaGrange, GA Micro	29300	Longview, WA Metro	31020
Lake Charles, LA Metro	29340	Los Alamos, NM Micro	31060
Lake City, FL Micro	29380	Los Angeles-Long Beach-Santa Ana, CA Metro	31100
Lake Havasu City-Kingman, AZ Metro	29420	Louisville-Jefferson County, KY-IN Metro	31140
Lakeland, FL Metro	29460	Lubbock, TX Metro	31180
Lamesa, TX Micro	29500	Lufkin, TX Micro	31260
Lancaster, PA Metro	29540	Lumberton, NC Micro	31300
Lancaster, SC Micro	29580	Lynchburg, VA Metro	31340
		Macomb, IL Micro	31380

135

CBSA CODES

CBSA Name	CBSA Code	CBSA Name	CBSA Code
Macon, GA Metro	31420	Miami-Fort Lauderdale-Pompano Beach, FL Metro	33100
Madera, CA Metro	31460	Michigan City-La Porte, IN Metro	33140
Madison, IN Micro	31500	Middlesborough, KY Micro	33180
Madison, WI Metro	31540	Midland, MI Micro	33220
Madisonville, KY Micro	31580	Midland, TX Metro	33260
Magnolia, AR Micro	31620	Milledgeville, GA Micro	33300
Malone, NY Micro	31660	Milwaukee-Waukesha-West Allis, WI Metro	33340
Manchester-Nashua, NH Metro	31700	Minden, LA Micro	33380
Manhattan, KS Micro	31740	Mineral Wells, TX Micro	33420
Manitowoc, WI Micro	31820	Minneapolis-St. Paul-Bloomington, MN-WI Metro	33460
Mankato-North Mankato, MN Micro	31860	Minot, ND Micro	33500
Mansfield, OH Metro	31900	Missoula, MT Metro	33540
Marinette, WI-MI Micro	31940	Mitchell, SD Micro	33580
Marion, IN Micro	31980	Moberly, MO Micro	33620
Marion, OH Micro	32020	Mobile, AL Metro	33660
Marion-Herrin, IL Micro	32060	Modesto, CA Metro	33700
Marquette, MI Micro	32100	Monroe, LA Metro	33740
Marshall, MN Micro	32140	Monroe, MI Metro	33780
Marshall, MO Micro	32180	Monroe, WI Micro	33820
Marshall, TX Micro	32220	Montgomery, AL Metro	33860
Marshalltown, IA Micro	32260	Montrose, CO Micro	33940
Marshfield - Wisconsin Rapids, WI Micro	32270	Morehead City, NC Micro	33980
Martin, TN Micro	32280	Morgan City, LA Micro	34020
Martinsville, VA Micro	32300	Morgantown, WV Metro	34060
Maryville, MO Micro	32340	Morristown, TN Metro	34100
Mason City, IA Micro	32380	Moscow, ID Micro	34140
Mayfield, KY Micro	32460	Moses Lake, WA Micro	34180
Maysville, KY Micro	32500	Moultrie, GA Micro	34220
McAlester, OK Micro	32540	Mount Airy, NC Micro	34340
McAllen-Edinburg-Mission, TX Metro	32580	Mount Pleasant, MI Micro	34380
McComb, MS Micro	32620	Mount Pleasant, TX Micro	34420
McMinnville, TN Micro	32660	Mount Sterling, KY Micro	34460
McPherson, KS Micro	32700	Mount Vernon, IL Micro	34500
Meadville, PA Micro	32740	Mount Vernon, OH Micro	34540
Medford, OR Metro	32780	Mount Vernon-Anacortes, WA Metro	34580
Memphis, TN-MS-AR Metro	32820	Mountain Home, AR Micro	34260
Menomonie, WI Micro	32860	Mountain Home, ID Micro	34300
Merced, CA Metro	32900	Muncie, IN Metro	34620
Meridian, MS Micro	32940	Murray, KY Micro	34660
Merrill, WI Micro	32980	Muscatine, IA Micro	34700
Mexico, MO Micro	33020	Muskegon-Norton Shores, MI Metro	34740
Miami, OK Micro	33060		

CBSA CODES

CBSA Name	CBSA Code	CBSA Name	CBSA Code
Muskogee, OK Micro	34780	Olympia, WA Metro	36500
Myrtle Beach-Conway-North Myrtle Beach, SC Metro	34820	Omaha-Council Bluffs, NE-IA Metro	36540
Nacogdoches, TX Micro	34860	Oneonta, NY Micro	36580
Napa, CA Metro	34900	Ontario, OR-ID Micro	36620
Naples-Marco Island, FL Metro	34940	Opelousas-Eunice, LA Micro	36660
Nashville-Davidson--Murfreesboro—Franklin, TN Metro	34980	Orangeburg, SC Micro	36700
Natchez, MS-LA Micro	35020	Orlando-Kissimmee, FL Metro	36740
Natchitoches, LA Micro	35060	Oshkosh-Neenah, WI Metro	36780
New Bern, NC Micro	35100	Oskaloosa, IA Micro	36820
New Castle, IN Micro	35220	Ottawa-Streator, IL Micro	36860
New Castle, PA Micro	35260	Ottumwa, IA Micro	36900
New Haven-Milford, CT Metro	35300	Owatonna, MN Micro	36940
New Iberia, LA Micro	35340	Owensboro, KY Metro	36980
New Orleans-Metairie-Kenner, LA Metro	35380	Owosso, MI Micro	37020
New Philadelphia-Dover, OH Micro	35420	Oxford, MS Micro	37060
New Ulm, MN Micro	35580	Oxnard-Thousand Oaks-Ventura, CA Metro	37100
New York-Northern New Jersey-Long Island, NY-NJ-PA Metro	35620	Paducah, KY-IL Micro	37140
Newberry, SC Micro	35140	Pahrump, NV Micro	37220
Newport, TN Micro	35460	Palatka, FL Micro	37260
Newton, IA Micro	35500	Palestine, TX Micro	37300
Niles-Benton Harbor, MI Metro	35660	Palm Bay-Melbourne-Titusville, FL Metro	37340
Nogales, AZ Micro	35700	Palm Coast, FL Metro	37380
Norfolk, NE Micro	35740	Pampa, TX Micro	37420
North Platte, NE Micro	35820	Panama City-Lynn Haven, FL Metro	37460
North Vernon, IN Micro	35860	Paragould, AR Micro	37500
North Wilkesboro, NC Micro	35900	Paris, TN Micro	37540
Norwalk, OH Micro	35940	Paris, TX Micro	37580
Norwich-New London, CT Metro	35980	Parkersburg-Marietta-Vienna, WV-OH Metro	37620
Oak Harbor, WA Micro	36020	Parsons, KS Micro	37660
Oak Hill, WV Micro	36060	Pascagoula, MS Metro	37700
Ocala, FL Metro	36100	Payson, AZ Micro	37740
Ocean City, NJ Metro	36140	Pecos, TX Micro	37780
Ocean Pines, MD Micro	36180	Pella, IA Micro	37800
Odessa, TX Metro	36220	Pendleton-Hermiston, OR Micro	37820
Ogden-Clearfield, UT Metro	36260	Pensacola-Ferry Pass-Brent, FL Metro	37860
Ogdensburg-Massena, NY Micro	36300	Peoria, IL Metro	37900
Oil City, PA Micro	36340	Peru, IN Micro	37940
Okeechobee, FL Micro	36380	Philadelphia-Camden-Wilmington, PA-NJ-DE-MD Metro	37980
Oklahoma City, OK Metro	36420	Phoenix Lake-Cedar Ridge, CA Micro	38020
Olean, NY Micro	36460		

CBSA CODES

CBSA Name	CBSA Code	CBSA Name	CBSA Code
Phoenix-Mesa-Scottsdale, AZ Metro	38060	Redding, CA Metro	39820
Picayune, MS Micro	38100	Reno-Sparks, NV Metro	39900
Pierre Part, LA Micro	38200	Rexburg, ID Micro	39940
Pierre, SD Micro	38180	Richmond, IN Micro	39980
Pine Bluff, AR Metro	38220	Richmond, VA Metro	40060
Pittsburg, KS Micro	38260	Richmond-Berea, KY Micro	40080
Pittsburgh, PA Metro	38300	Rio Grande City-Roma, TX Micro	40100
Pittsfield, MA Metro	38340	Riverside-San Bernardino-Ontario, CA Metro	40140
Plainview, TX Micro	38380	Riverton, WY Micro	40180
Platteville, WI Micro	38420	Roanoke Rapids, NC Micro	40260
Plattsburgh, NY Micro	38460	Roanoke, VA Metro	40220
Plymouth, IN Micro	38500	Rochelle, IL Micro	40300
Pocatello, ID Metro	38540	Rochester, MN Metro	40340
Point Pleasant, WV-OH Micro	38580	Rochester, NY Metro	40380
Ponca City, OK Micro	38620	Rock Springs, WY Micro	40540
Pontiac, IL Micro	38700	Rockford, IL Metro	40420
Poplar Bluff, MO Micro	38740	Rockingham, NC Micro	40460
Port Angeles, WA Micro	38820	Rockland, ME Micro	40500
Port St. Lucie, FL Metro	38940	Rocky Mount, NC Metro	40580
Portales, NM Micro	38780	Rolla, MO Micro	40620
Portland-South Portland-Biddeford, ME Metro	38860	Rome, GA Metro	40660
Portland-Vancouver-Beaverton, OR-WA Metro	38900	Roseburg, OR Micro	40700
		Roswell, NM Micro	40740
Portsmouth, OH Micro	39020	Ruidoso, NM Micro	40760
Pottsville, PA Micro	39060	Russellville, AR Micro	40780
Poughkeepsie-Newburgh-Middletown, NY Metro	39100	Ruston, LA Micro	40820
		Rutland, VT Micro	40860
Prescott, AZ Metro	39140	Sacramento--Arden-Arcade--Roseville, CA Metro	40900
Price, UT Micro	39220	Safford, AZ Micro	40940
Prineville, OR Micro	39260	Saginaw-Saginaw Township North, MI Metro	40980
Providence-New Bedford-Fall River, RI-MA Metro	39300	Salem, OR Metro	41420
Provo-Orem, UT Metro	39340	Salina, KS Micro	41460
Pueblo, CO Metro	39380	Salinas, CA Metro	41500
Pullman, WA Micro	39420	Salisbury, MD Metro	41540
Punta Gorda, FL Metro	39460	Salisbury, NC Micro	41580
Quincy, IL-MO Micro	39500	Salt Lake City, UT Metro	41620
Racine, WI Metro	39540	San Angelo, TX Metro	41660
Raleigh-Cary, NC Metro	39580	San Antonio, TX Metro	41700
Rapid City, SD Metro	39660	San Diego-Carlsbad-San Marcos, CA Metro	41740
Raymondville, TX Micro	39700	San Francisco-Oakland-Fremont, CA Metro	41860
Reading, PA Metro	39740	San Jose-Sunnyvale-Santa Clara, CA Metro	41940
Red Bluff, CA Micro	39780		
Red Wing, MN Micro	39860		

CBSA CODES

CBSA Name	CBSA Code	CBSA Name	CBSA Code
San Luis Obispo-Paso Robles, CA Metro	42020	Silverthorne, CO Micro	43540
Sandusky, OH Metro	41780	Sioux City, IA-NE-SD Metro	43580
Sanford, NC Micro	41820	Sioux Falls, SD Metro	43620
Santa Barbara-Santa Maria-Goleta, CA Metro	42060	Snyder, TX Micro	43660
Santa Cruz-Watsonville, CA Metro	42100	Somerset, KY Micro	43700
Santa Fe, NM Metro	42140	Somerset, PA Micro	43740
Santa Rosa-Petaluma, CA Metro	42220	South Bend-Mishawaka, IN-MI Metro	43780
Sarasota-Bradenton-Venice, FL Metro	42260	Southern Pines-Pinehurst, NC Micro	43860
Sault Ste. Marie, MI Micro	42300	Spartanburg, SC Metro	43900
Savannah, GA Metro	42340	Spearfish, SD Micro	43940
Sayre, PA Micro	42380	Spencer, IA Micro	43980
Scottsbluff, NE Micro	42420	Spirit Lake, IA Micro	44020
Scottsboro, AL Micro	42460	Spokane, WA Metro	44060
Scottsburg, IN Micro	42500	Springfield, IL Metro	44100
Scranton--Wilkes-Barre, PA Metro	42540	Springfield, MA Metro	44140
Seaford, DE Micro	42580	Springfield, MO Metro	44180
Searcy, AR Micro	42620	Springfield, OH Metro	44220
Seattle-Tacoma-Bellevue, WA Metro	42660	St. Cloud, MN Metro	41060
Sebastian - Vero Beach, FL Metro	42680	St. George, UT Metro	41100
Sebring, FL Micro	42700	St. Joseph, MO-KS Metro	41140
Sedalia, MO Micro	42740	St. Louis, MO-IL Metro	41180
Selinsgrove, PA Micro	42780	St. Marys, GA Micro	41220
Selma, AL Micro	42820	St. Marys, PA Micro	41260
Seneca Falls, NY Micro	42900	Starkville, MS Micro	44260
Seneca, SC Micro	42860	State College, PA Metro	44300
Sevierville, TN Micro	42940	Statesboro, GA Micro	44340
Seymour, IN Micro	42980	Statesville-Mooresville, NC Micro	44380
Shawnee, OK Micro	43060	Staunton-Waynesboro, VA Micro	44420
Sheboygan, WI Metro	43100	Stephenville, TX Micro	44500
Shelby, NC Micro	43140	Sterling, CO Micro	44540
Shelbyville, TN Micro	43180	Sterling, IL Micro	44580
Shelton, WA Micro	43220	Stevens Point, WI Micro	44620
Sheridan, WY Micro	43260	Stillwater, OK Micro	44660
Sherman-Denison, TX Metro	43300	Stockton, CA Metro	44700
Shreveport-Bossier City, LA Metro	43340	Storm Lake, IA Micro	44740
Sidney, OH Micro	43380	Sturgis, MI Micro	44780
Sierra Vista-Douglas, AZ Micro	43420	Sulphur Springs, TX Micro	44860
Sikeston, MO Micro	43460	Summerville, GA Micro	44900
Silver City, NM Micro	43500	Sumter, SC Metro	44940
		Sunbury, PA Micro	44980
		Susanville, CA Micro	45000
		Sweetwater, TX Micro	45020
		Syracuse, NY Metro	45060

CBSA CODES

CBSA Name	CBSA Code	CBSA Name	CBSA Code
Tahlequah, OK Micro	45140	Vernon, TX Micro	46900
Talladega-Sylacauga, AL Micro	45180	Vicksburg, MS Micro	46980
Tallahassee, FL Metro	45220	Victoria, TX Metro	47020
Tallulah, LA Micro	45260	Vidalia, GA Micro	47080
Tampa-St. Petersburg-Clearwater, FL Metro	45300	Vincennes, IN Micro	47180
Taos, NM Micro	45340	Vineland-Millville-Bridgeton, NJ Metro	47220
Taylorville, IL Micro	45380	Virginia Beach-Norfolk-Newport News, VA-NC Metro	47260
Terre Haute, IN Metro	45460	Visalia-Porterville, CA Metro	47300
Texarkana, TX-Texarkana, AR Metro	45500	Wabash, IN Micro	47340
The Villages, FL Micro	45540	Waco, TX Metro	47380
Thomaston, GA Micro	45580	Wahpeton, ND-MN Micro	47420
Thomasville, GA Micro	45620	Walla Walla, WA Micro	47460
Thomasville-Lexington, NC Micro	45640	Walterboro, SC Micro	47500
Tiffin, OH Micro	45660	Wapakoneta, OH Micro	47540
Tifton, GA Micro	45700	Warner Robins, GA Metro	47580
Toccoa, GA Micro	45740	Warren, PA Micro	47620
Toledo, OH Metro	45780	Warrensburg, MO Micro	47660
Topeka, KS Metro	45820	Warsaw, IN Micro	47700
Torrington, CT Micro	45860	Washington, IN Micro	47780
Traverse City, MI Micro	45900	Washington, NC Micro	47820
Trenton-Ewing, NJ Metro	45940	Washington, OH Micro	47860
Troy, AL Micro	45980	Washington-Arlington-Alexandria, DC-VA-MD-WV Metro	47900
Truckee-Grass Valley, CA Micro	46020	Waterloo-Cedar Falls, IA Metro	47940
Tucson, AZ Metro	46060	Watertown, SD Micro	47980
Tullahoma, TN Micro	46100	Watertown-Fort Atkinson, WI Micro	48020
Tulsa, OK Metro	46140	Watertown-Fort Drum, NY Micro	48060
Tupelo, MS Micro	46180	Wauchula, FL Micro	48100
Tuscaloosa, AL Metro	46220	Wausau, WI Metro	48140
Tuskegee, AL Micro	46260	Waycross, GA Micro	48180
Twin Falls, ID Micro	46300	Weirton-Steubenville, WV-OH Metro	48260
Tyler, TX Metro	46340	Wenatchee, WA Metro	48300
Ukiah, CA Micro	46380	West Helena, AR Micro	48340
Union City, TN-KY Micro	46460	West Plains, MO Micro	48460
Union, SC Micro	46420	West Point, MS Micro	48500
Urbana, OH Micro	46500	Wheeling, WV-OH Metro	48540
Utica-Rome, NY Metro	46540	Whitewater, WI Micro	48580
Uvalde, TX Micro	46620	Wichita Falls, TX Metro	48660
Valdosta, GA Metro	46660	Wichita, KS Metro	48620
Vallejo-Fairfield, CA Metro	46700	Williamsport, PA Metro	48700
Valley, AL Micro	46740	Willimantic, CT Micro	48740
Van Wert, OH Micro	46780	Williston, ND Micro	48780
Vermillion, SD Micro	46820		
Vernal, UT Micro	46860		

CBSA CODES

CBSA Name	CBSA Code	CBSA Name	CBSA Code
Willmar, MN Micro	48820	Worthington, MN Micro	49380
Wilmington, NC Metro	48900	Yakima, WA Metro	49420
Wilmington, OH Micro	48940	Yankton, SD Micro	49460
Wilson, NC Micro	48980	Yazoo City, MS Micro	49540
Winchester, VA-WV Metro	49020	York-Hanover, PA Metro	49620
Winfield, KS Micro	49060	Youngstown-Warren-Boardman, OH-PA Metro	49660
Winona, MN Micro	49100	Yuba City, CA Metro	49700
Winston-Salem, NC Metro	49180	Yuma, AZ Metro	49740
Woodward, OK Micro	49260	Zanesville, OH Micro	49780
Wooster, OH Micro	49300		
Worcester, MA Metro	49340		

Appendix III:
CBSA Definitions

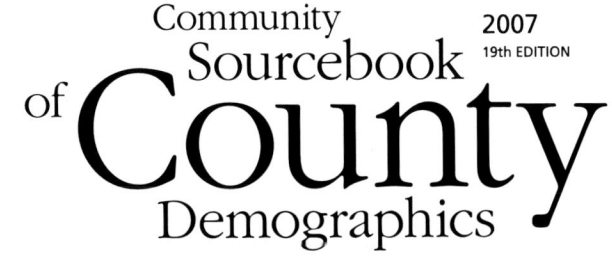

Community
Sourcebook
of County
Demographics

2007
19th EDITION

CBSA DEFINITIONS

CBSA (CBSA Code) County		FIPS Codes	
Abbeville, LA Micro (10020)			
Vermilion	LA	22	113
Aberdeen, SD Micro (10100)			
Brown	SD	46	013
Edmunds			045
Aberdeen, WA Micro (10140)			
Grays Harbor	WA	53	027
Abilene, TX Metro (10180)			
Callahan	TX	48	059
Jones			253
Taylor			441
Ada, OK Micro (10220)			
Pontotoc	OK	40	123
Adrian, MI Micro (10300)			
Lenawee	MI	26	091
Akron, OH Metro (10420)			
Portage	OH	39	133
Summit			153
Alamogordo, NM Micro (10460)			
Otero	NM	35	035
Albany, GA Metro (10500)			
Baker	GA	13	007
Dougherty			095
Lee			177
Terrell			273
Worth			321
Albany-Lebanon, OR Micro (10540)			
Linn	OR	41	043
Albany-Schenectady-Troy, NY Metro (10580)			
Albany	NY	36	001
Rensselaer			083
Saratoga			091
Schenectady			093
Schoharie			095
Albemarle, NC Micro (10620)			
Stanly	NC	37	167
Albert Lea, MN Micro (10660)			
Freeborn	MN	27	047
Albertville, AL Micro (10700)			
Marshall	AL	01	095
Albuquerque, NM Metro (10740)			
Bernalillo	NM	35	001
Sandoval			043
Torrance			057
Valencia			061

CBSA (CBSA Code) County		FIPS Codes	
Alexander City, AL Micro (10760)			
Coosa	AL	01	037
Tallapoosa			123
Alexandria, LA Metro (10780)			
Grant	LA	22	043
Rapides			079
Alexandria, MN Micro (10820)			
Douglas	MN	27	041
Alice, TX Micro (10860)			
Jim Wells	TX	48	249
Allegan, MI Micro (10880)			
Allegan	MI	26	005
Allentown-Bethlehem-Easton, PA-NJ Metro (10900)			
Warren	NJ	34	041
Carbon	PA	42	025
Lehigh			077
Northampton			095
Alma, MI Micro (10940)			
Gratiot	MI	26	057
Alpena, MI Micro (10980)			
Alpena	MI	26	007
Altoona, PA Metro (11020)			
Blair	PA	42	013
Altus, OK Micro (11060)			
Jackson	OK	40	065
Amarillo, TX Metro (11100)			
Armstrong	TX	48	011
Carson			065
Potter			375
Randall			381
Americus, GA Micro (11140)			
Schley	GA	13	249
Sumter			261
Ames, IA Metro (11180)			
Story	IA	19	169
Amsterdam, NY Micro (11220)			
Montgomery	NY	36	057
Anchorage, AK Metro (11260)			
Anchorage Municipality	AK	02	020
Matanuska-Susitna			170
Anderson, IN Metro (11300)			
Madison	IN	18	095
Anderson, SC Metro (11340)			
Anderson	SC	45	007

CBSA DEFINITIONS

CBSA (CBSA Code) County		FIPS Codes	
Andrews, TX Micro (11380)			
Andrews	TX	48	003
Angola, IN Micro (11420)			
Steuben	IN	18	151
Ann Arbor, MI Metro (11460)			
Washtenaw	MI	26	161
Anniston-Oxford, AL Metro (11500)			
Calhoun	AL	01	015
Appleton, WI Metro (11540)			
Calumet	WI	55	015
Outagamie			087
Arcadia, FL Micro (11580)			
DeSoto	FL	12	027
Ardmore, OK Micro (11620)			
Carter	OK	40	019
Love			085
Arkadelphia, AR Micro (11660)			
Clark	AR	05	019
Asheville, NC Metro (11700)			
Buncombe	NC	37	021
Haywood			087
Henderson			089
Madison			115
Ashland, OH Micro (11740)			
Ashland	OH	39	005
Ashtabula, OH Micro (11780)			
Ashtabula	OH	39	007
Astoria, OR Micro (11820)			
Clatsop	OR	41	007
Atchison, KS Micro (11860)			
Atchison	KS	20	005
Athens, OH Micro (11900)			
Athens	OH	39	009
Athens, TN Micro (11940)			
McMinn	TN	47	107
Athens, TX Micro (11980)			
Henderson	TX	48	213
Athens-Clarke County, GA Metro (12020)			
Clarke	GA	13	059
Madison			195
Oconee			219
Oglethorpe			221

CBSA (CBSA Code) County		FIPS Codes	
Atlanta-Sandy Springs-Marietta, GA Metro (12060)			
Barrow	GA	13	013
Bartow			015
Butts			035
Carroll			045
Cherokee			057
Clayton			063
Cobb			067
Coweta			077
Dawson			085
DeKalb			089
Douglas			097
Fayette			113
Forsyth			117
Fulton			121
Gwinnett			135
Haralson			143
Heard			149
Henry			151
Jasper			159
Lamar			171
Meriwether			199
Newton			217
Paulding			223
Pickens			227
Pike			231
Rockdale			247
Spalding			255
Walton			297
Atlantic City, NJ Metro (12100)			
Atlantic	NJ	34	001
Auburn, IN Micro (12140)			
DeKalb	IN	18	033
Auburn, NY Micro (12180)			
Cayuga	NY	36	011
Auburn-Opelika, AL Metro (12220)			
Lee	AL	01	081
Augusta-Richmond County, GA-SC Metro (12260)			
Burke	GA	13	033
Columbia			073
McDuffie			189
Richmond			245
Aiken	SC	45	003
Edgefield			037
Augusta-Waterville, ME Micro (12300)			
Kennebec	ME	23	011
Austin, MN Micro (12380)			
Mower	MN	27	099

145

CBSA DEFINITIONS

CBSA (CBSA Code) County — FIPS Codes

Austin-Round Rock, TX Metro (12420)

County	State		FIPS
Bastrop	TX	48	021
Caldwell			055
Hays			209
Travis			453
Williamson			491

Bainbridge, GA Micro (12460)

County	State		FIPS
Decatur	GA	13	087

Bakersfield, CA Metro (12540)

County	State		FIPS
Kern	CA	06	029

Baltimore-Towson, MD Metro (12580)

County	State		FIPS
Anne Arundel	MD	24	003
Baltimore			005
Carroll			013
Harford			025
Howard			027
Queen Anne's			035
Baltimore city			510

Bangor, ME Metro (12620)

County	State		FIPS
Penobscot	ME	23	019

Baraboo, WI Micro (12660)

County	State		FIPS
Sauk	WI	55	111

Barnstable Town, MA Metro (12700)

County	State		FIPS
Barnstable	MA	25	001

Barre, VT Micro (12740)

County	State		FIPS
Washington	VT	50	023

Bartlesville, OK Micro (12780)

County	State		FIPS
Washington	OK	40	147

Bastrop, LA Micro (12820)

County	State		FIPS
Morehouse	LA	22	067

Batavia, NY Micro (12860)

County	State		FIPS
Genesee	NY	36	037

Batesville, AR Micro (12900)

County	State		FIPS
Independence	AR	05	063

Baton Rouge, LA Metro (12940)

County	State		FIPS
Ascension	LA	22	005
East Baton Rouge			033
East Feliciana			037
Iberville			047
Livingston			063
Pointe Coupee			077
St. Helena			091
West Baton Rouge			121
West Feliciana			125

Battle Creek, MI Metro (12980)

County	State		FIPS
Calhoun	MI	26	025

Bay City, MI Metro (13020)

County	State		FIPS
Bay	MI	26	017

Bay City, TX Micro (13060)

County	State		FIPS
Matagorda	TX	48	321

Beatrice, NE Micro (13100)

County	State		FIPS
Gage	NE	31	067

Beaumont-Port Arthur, TX Metro (13140)

County	State		FIPS
Hardin	TX	48	199
Jefferson			245
Orange			361

Beaver Dam, WI Micro (13180)

County	State		FIPS
Dodge	WI	55	027

Beckley, WV Micro (13220)

County	State		FIPS
Raleigh	WV	54	081

Bedford, IN Micro (13260)

County	State		FIPS
Lawrence	IN	18	093

Beeville, TX Micro (13300)

County	State		FIPS
Bee	TX	48	025

Bellefontaine, OH Micro (13340)

County	State		FIPS
Logan	OH	39	091

Bellingham, WA Metro (13380)

County	State		FIPS
Whatcom	WA	53	073

Bemidji, MN Micro (13420)

County	State		FIPS
Beltrami	MN	27	007

Bend, OR Metro (13460)

County	State		FIPS
Deschutes	OR	41	017

Bennettsville, SC Micro (13500)

County	State		FIPS
Marlboro	SC	45	069

Bennington, VT Micro (13540)

County	State		FIPS
Bennington	VT	50	003

Berlin, NH-VT Micro (13620)

County	State		FIPS
Coos	NH	33	007
Essex	VT	50	009

Big Rapids, MI Micro (13660)

County	State		FIPS
Mecosta	MI	26	107

Big Spring, TX Micro (13700)

County	State		FIPS
Howard	TX	48	227

Billings, MT Metro (13740)

County	State		FIPS
Carbon	MT	30	009
Yellowstone			111

Binghamton, NY Metro (13780)

County	State		FIPS
Broome	NY	36	007
Tioga			107

CBSA DEFINITIONS

CBSA (CBSA Code) County			FIPS Codes
Birmingham-Hoover, AL Metro (13820)			
Bibb	AL	01	007
Blount			009
Chilton			021
Jefferson			073
St. Clair			115
Shelby			117
Walker			127
Bishop, CA Micro (13860)			
Inyo	CA	06	027
Bismarck, ND Metro (13900)			
Burleigh	ND	38	015
Morton			059
Blackfoot, ID Micro (13940)			
Bingham	ID	16	011
Blacksburg-Christiansburg-Radford, VA Metro (13980)			
Giles	VA	51	071
Montgomery			121
Pulaski			155
Radford city			750
Bloomington, IN Metro (14020)			
Greene	IN	18	055
Monroe			105
Owen			119
Bloomington-Normal, IL Metro (14060)			
McLean	IL	17	113
Bloomsburg-Berwick, PA Micro (14100)			
Columbia	PA	42	037
Montour			093
Bluefield, WV-VA Micro (14140)			
Tazewell	VA	51	185
Mercer	WV	54	055
Blytheville, AR Micro (14180)			
Mississippi	AR	05	093
Bogalusa, LA Micro (14220)			
Washington	LA	22	117
Boise City-Nampa, ID Metro (14260)			
Ada	ID	16	001
Boise			015
Canyon			027
Gem			045
Owyhee			073
Bonham, TX Micro (14300)			
Fannin	TX	48	147
Boone, IA Micro (14340)			
Boone	IA	19	015

CBSA (CBSA Code) County			FIPS Codes
Boone, NC Micro (14380)			
Watauga	NC	37	189
Borger, TX Micro (14420)			
Hutchinson	TX	48	233
Boston-Cambridge-Quincy, MA-NH Metro (14460)			
Essex	MA	25	009
Middlesex			017
Norfolk			021
Plymouth			023
Suffolk			025
Rockingham	NH	33	015
Strafford			017
Boulder, CO Metro (14500)			
Boulder	CO	08	013
Bowling Green, KY Metro (14540)			
Edmonson	KY	21	061
Warren			227
Bozeman, MT Micro (14580)			
Gallatin	MT	30	031
Bradford, PA Micro (14620)			
McKean	PA	42	083
Brainerd, MN Micro (14660)			
Cass	MN	27	021
Crow Wing			035
Branson, MO Micro (14700)			
Stone	MO	29	209
Taney			213
Bremerton-Silverdale, WA Metro (14740)			
Kitsap	WA	53	035
Brenham, TX Micro (14780)			
Washington	TX	48	477
Brevard, NC Micro (14820)			
Transylvania	NC	37	175
Bridgeport-Stamford-Norwalk, CT Metro (14860)			
Fairfield	CT	09	001
Brigham City, UT Micro (14940)			
Box Elder	UT	49	003
Brookhaven, MS Micro (15020)			
Lincoln	MS	28	085
Brookings, OR Micro (15060)			
Curry	OR	41	015
Brookings, SD Micro (15100)			
Brookings	SD	46	011
Brownsville, TN Micro (15140)			
Haywood	TN	47	075

CBSA DEFINITIONS

CBSA (CBSA Code) County		FIPS Codes	

Brownsville-Harlingen, TX Metro (15180)
| Cameron | TX | 48 | 061 |

Brownwood, TX Micro (15220)
| Brown | TX | 48 | 049 |

Brunswick, GA Metro (15260)
Brantley	GA	13	025
Glynn			127
McIntosh			191

Bucyrus, OH Micro (15340)
| Crawford | OH | 39 | 033 |

Buffalo-Niagara Falls, NY Metro (15380)
| Erie | NY | 36 | 029 |
| Niagara | | | 063 |

Burley, ID Micro (15420)
| Cassia | ID | 16 | 031 |
| Minidoka | | | 067 |

Burlington, IA-IL Micro (15460)
| Henderson | IL | 17 | 071 |
| Des Moines | IA | 19 | 057 |

Burlington, NC Metro (15500)
| Alamance | NC | 37 | 001 |

Burlington-South Burlington, VT Metro (15540)
Chittenden	VT	50	007
Franklin			011
Grand Isle			013

Butte-Silver Bow, MT Micro (15580)
| Silver Bow | MT | 30 | 093 |

Cadillac, MI Micro (15620)
| Missaukee | MI | 26 | 113 |
| Wexford | | | 165 |

Calhoun, GA Micro (15660)
| Gordon | GA | 13 | 129 |

Cambridge, MD Micro (15700)
| Dorchester | MD | 24 | 019 |

Cambridge, OH Micro (15740)
| Guernsey | OH | 39 | 059 |

Camden, AR Micro (15780)
| Calhoun | AR | 05 | 013 |
| Ouachita | | | 103 |

Campbellsville, KY Micro (15820)
| Taylor | KY | 21 | 217 |

Canon City, CO Micro (15860)
| Fremont | CO | 08 | 043 |

Canton, IL Micro (15900)
| Fulton | IL | 17 | 057 |

Canton-Massillon, OH Metro (15940)
| Carroll | OH | 39 | 019 |
| Stark | | | 151 |

Cape Coral-Fort Myers, FL Metro (15980)
| Lee | FL | 12 | 071 |

Cape Girardeau-Jackson, MO-IL Micro (16020)
Alexander	IL	17	003
Bollinger	MO	29	017
Cape Girardeau			031

Carbondale, IL Micro (16060)
| Jackson | IL | 17 | 077 |

Carlsbad-Artesia, NM Micro (16100)
| Eddy | NM | 35 | 015 |

Carson City, NV Metro (16180)
| Carson City | NV | 32 | 510 |

Casper, WY Metro (16220)
| Natrona | WY | 56 | 025 |

Cedar City, UT Micro (16260)
| Iron | UT | 49 | 021 |

Cedar Rapids, IA Metro (16300)
Benton	IA	19	011
Jones			105
Linn			113

Cedartown, GA Micro (16340)
| Polk | GA | 13 | 233 |

Celina, OH Micro (16380)
| Mercer | OH | 39 | 107 |

Central City, KY Micro (16420)
| Muhlenberg | KY | 21 | 177 |

Centralia, IL Micro (16460)
| Marion | IL | 17 | 121 |

Centralia, WA Micro (16500)
| Lewis | WA | 53 | 041 |

Chambersburg, PA Micro (16540)
| Franklin | PA | 42 | 055 |

Champaign-Urbana, IL Metro (16580)
Champaign	IL	17	019
Ford			053
Piatt			147

Charleston, WV Metro (16620)
Boone	WV	54	005
Clay			015
Kanawha			039
Lincoln			043
Putnam			079

CBSA DEFINITIONS

CBSA (CBSA Code) County		FIPS Codes	

Charleston-Mattoon, IL Micro (16660)

Coles	IL	17	029
Cumberland			035

Charleston-North Charleston, SC Metro (16700)

Berkeley	SC	45	015
Charleston			019
Dorchester			035

Charlotte-Gastonia-Concord, NC-SC Metro (16740)

Anson	NC	37	007
Cabarrus			025
Gaston			071
Mecklenburg			119
Union			179
York	SC	45	091

Charlottesville, VA Metro (16820)

Albemarle	VA	51	003
Fluvanna			065
Greene			079
Nelson			125
Charlottesville city			540

Chattanooga, TN-GA Metro (16860)

Catoosa	GA	13	047
Dade			083
Walker			295
Hamilton	TN	47	065
Marion			115
Sequatchie			153

Chester, SC Micro (16900)

Chester	SC	45	023

Cheyenne, WY Metro (16940)

Laramie	WY	56	021

Chicago-Naperville-Joliet, IL-IN-WI Metro (16980)

Cook	IL	17	031
DeKalb			037
DuPage			043
Grundy			063
Kane			089
Kendall			093
Lake			097
McHenry			111
Will			197
Jasper	IN	18	073
Lake			089
Newton			111
Porter			127
Kenosha	WI	55	059

Chico, CA Metro (17020)

Butte	CA	06	007

Chillicothe, OH Micro (17060)

Ross	OH	39	141

Cincinnati-Middletown, OH-KY-IN Metro (17140)

Dearborn	IN	18	029
Franklin			047
Ohio			115
Boone	KY	21	015
Bracken			023
Campbell			037
Gallatin			077
Grant			081
Kenton			117
Pendleton			191
Brown	OH	39	015
Butler			017
Clermont			025
Hamilton			061
Warren			165

City of The Dalles, OR Micro (17180)

Wasco	OR	41	065

Claremont, NH Micro (17200)

Sullivan	NH	33	019

Clarksburg, WV Micro (17220)

Doddridge	WV	54	017
Harrison			033
Taylor			091

Clarksdale, MS Micro (17260)

Coahoma	MS	28	027

Clarksville, TN-KY Metro (17300)

Christian	KY	21	047
Trigg			221
Montgomery	TN	47	125
Stewart			161

Clearlake, CA Micro (17340)

Lake	CA	06	033

Cleveland, MS Micro (17380)

Bolivar	MS	28	011

Cleveland, TN Metro (17420)

Bradley	TN	47	011
Polk			139

Cleveland-Elyria-Mentor, OH Metro (17460)

Cuyahoga	OH	39	035
Geauga			055
Lake			085
Lorain			093
Medina			103

Clewiston, FL Micro (17500)

Hendry	FL	12	051

CBSA DEFINITIONS

CBSA (CBSA Code) County   FIPS Codes

Clinton, IA Micro (17540)

Clinton	IA	19	045

Clovis, NM Micro (17580)

Curry	NM	35	009

Coeur d'Alene, ID Metro (17660)

Kootenai	ID	16	055

Coffeyville, KS Micro (17700)

Montgomery	KS	20	125

Coldwater, MI Micro (17740)

Branch	MI	26	023

College Station-Bryan, TX Metro (17780)

Brazos	TX	48	041
Burleson			051
Robertson			395

Colorado Springs, CO Metro (17820)

El Paso	CO	08	041
Teller			119

Columbia, MO Metro (17860)

Boone	MO	29	019
Howard			089

Columbia, SC Metro (17900)

Calhoun	SC	45	017
Fairfield			039
Kershaw			055
Lexington			063
Richland			079
Saluda			081

Columbia, TN Micro (17940)

Maury	TN	47	119

Columbus, GA-AL Metro (17980)

Russell	AL	01	113
Chattahoochee	GA	13	053
Harris			145
Marion			197
Muscogee			215

Columbus, IN Metro (18020)

Bartholomew	IN	18	005

Columbus, MS Micro (18060)

Lowndes	MS	28	087

Columbus, NE Micro (18100)

Platte	NE	31	141

Columbus, OH Metro (18140)

Delaware	OH	39	041
Fairfield			045
Franklin			049
Licking			089

Columbus, OH Metro (18140) (continued)

Madison			097
Morrow			117
Pickaway			129
Union			159

Concord, NH Micro (18180)

Merrimack	NH	33	013

Connersville, IN Micro (18220)

Fayette	IN	18	041

Cookeville, TN Micro (18260)

Jackson	TN	47	087
Overton			133
Putnam			141

Coos Bay, OR Micro (18300)

Coos	OR	41	011

Corbin, KY Micro (18340)

Whitley	KY	21	235

Cordele, GA Micro (18380)

Crisp	GA	13	081

Corinth, MS Micro (18420)

Alcorn	MS	28	003

Cornelia, GA Micro (18460)

Habersham	GA	13	137

Corning, NY Micro (18500)

Steuben	NY	36	101

Corpus Christi, TX Metro (18580)

Aransas	TX	48	007
Nueces			355
San Patricio			409

Corsicana, TX Micro (18620)

Navarro	TX	48	349

Cortland, NY Micro (18660)

Cortland	NY	36	023

Corvallis, OR Metro (18700)

Benton	OR	41	003

Coshocton, OH Micro (18740)

Coshocton	OH	39	031

Crawfordsville, IN Micro (18820)

Montgomery	IN	18	107

Crescent City, CA Micro (18860)

Del Norte	CA	06	015

Crossville, TN Micro (18900)

Cumberland	TN	47	035

CBSA DEFINITIONS

CBSA (CBSA Code) County		FIPS Codes	
Crowley, LA Micro (18940)			
Acadia	LA	22	001
Cullman, AL Micro (18980)			
Cullman	AL	01	043
Culpeper, VA Micro (19020)			
Culpeper	VA	51	047
Cumberland, MD-WV Metro (19060)			
Allegany	MD	24	001
Mineral	WV	54	057
Dallas-Fort Worth-Arlington, TX Metro (19100)			
Collin	TX	48	085
Dallas			113
Delta			119
Denton			121
Ellis			139
Hunt			231
Johnson			251
Kaufman			257
Parker			367
Rockwall			397
Tarrant			439
Wise			497
Dalton, GA Metro (19140)			
Murray	GA	13	213
Whitfield			313
Danville, IL Metro (19180)			
Vermilion	IL	17	183
Danville, KY Micro (19220)			
Boyle	KY	21	021
Lincoln			137
Danville, VA Metro (19260)			
Pittsylvania	VA	51	143
Danville city			590
Daphne-Fairhope-Foley, AL Micro (19300)			
Baldwin	AL	01	003
Davenport-Moline-Rock Island, IA-IL Metro (19340)			
Henry	IL	17	073
Mercer			131
Rock Island			161
Scott	IA	19	163
Dayton, OH Metro (19380)			
Greene	OH	39	057
Miami			109
Montgomery			113
Preble			135
De Ridder, LA Micro (19760)			
Beauregard	LA	22	011

CBSA (CBSA Code) County		FIPS Codes	
Decatur, AL Metro (19460)			
Lawrence	AL	01	079
Morgan			103
Decatur, IL Metro (19500)			
Macon	IL	17	115
Decatur, IN Micro (19540)			
Adams	IN	18	001
Defiance, OH Micro (19580)			
Defiance	OH	39	039
Del Rio, TX Micro (19620)			
Val Verde	TX	48	465
Deltona-Daytona Beach-Ormond Beach, FL Metro (19660)			
Volusia	FL	12	127
Deming, NM Micro (19700)			
Luna	NM	35	029
Denver-Aurora, CO Metro (19740)			
Adams	CO	08	001
Arapahoe			005
Broomfield			014
Clear Creek			019
Denver			031
Douglas			035
Elbert			039
Gilpin			047
Jefferson			059
Park			093
Des Moines-West Des Moines, IA Metro (19780)			
Dallas	IA	19	049
Guthrie			077
Madison			121
Polk			153
Warren			181
Detroit-Warren-Livonia, MI Metro (19820)			
Lapeer	MI	26	087
Livingston			093
Macomb			099
Oakland			125
St. Clair			147
Wayne			163
Dickinson, ND Micro (19860)			
Billings	ND	38	007
Stark			089
Dillon, SC Micro (19900)			
Dillon	SC	45	033
Dixon, IL Micro (19940)			
Lee	IL	17	103

CBSA DEFINITIONS

CBSA DEFINITIONS

CBSA (CBSA Code) County		FIPS Codes	
Erie, PA Metro (21500)			
Erie	PA	42	049
Escanaba, MI Micro (21540)			
Delta	MI	26	041
Espanola, NM Micro (21580)			
Rio Arriba	NM	35	039
Eufaula, AL-GA Micro (21640)			
Barbour	AL	01	005
Quitman	GA	13	239
Eugene-Springfield, OR Metro (21660)			
Lane	OR	41	039
Eureka-Arcata-Fortuna, CA Micro (21700)			
Humboldt	CA	06	023
Evanston, WY Micro (21740)			
Uinta	WY	56	041
Evansville, IN-KY Metro (21780)			
Gibson	IN	18	051
Posey			129
Vanderburgh			163
Warrick			173
Henderson	KY	21	101
Webster			233
Fairbanks, AK Metro (21820)			
Fairbanks North Star	AK	02	090
Fairmont, MN Micro (21860)			
Martin	MN	27	091
Fairmont, WV Micro (21900)			
Marion	WV	54	049
Fallon, NV Micro (21980)			
Churchill	NV	32	001
Fargo, ND-MN Metro (22020)			
Clay	MN	27	027
Cass	ND	38	017
Faribault-Northfield, MN Micro (22060)			
Rice	MN	27	131
Farmington, MO Micro (22100)			
St. Francois	MO	29	187
Farmington, NM Metro (22140)			
San Juan	NM	35	045
Fayetteville, NC Metro (22180)			
Cumberland	NC	37	051
Hoke			093

CBSA (CBSA Code) County		FIPS Codes	
Fayetteville-Springdale-Rogers, AR-MO Metro (22220)			
Benton	AR	05	007
Madison			087
Washington			143
McDonald	MO	29	119
Fergus Falls, MN Micro (22260)			
Otter Tail	MN	27	111
Fernley, NV Micro (22280)			
Lyon	NV	32	019
Findlay, OH Micro (22300)			
Hancock	OH	39	063
Fitzgerald, GA Micro (22340)			
Ben Hill	GA	13	017
Irwin			155
Flagstaff, AZ Metro (22380)			
Coconino	AZ	04	005
Flint, MI Metro (22420)			
Genesee	MI	26	049
Florence, SC Metro (22500)			
Darlington	SC	45	031
Florence			041
Florence-Muscle Shoals, AL Metro (22520)			
Colbert	AL	01	033
Lauderdale			077
Fond du Lac, WI Metro (22540)			
Fond du Lac	WI	55	039
Forest City, NC Micro (22580)			
Rutherford	NC	37	161
Forrest City, AR Micro (22620)			
St. Francis	AR	05	123
Fort Collins-Loveland, CO Metro (22660)			
Larimer	CO	08	069
Fort Dodge, IA Micro (22700)			
Webster	IA	19	187
Fort Leonard Wood, MO Micro (22780)			
Pulaski	MO	29	169
Fort Madison - Keokuk, IA-MO Micro (22800)			
Lee	IA	19	111
Clark	MO	29	045
Fort Morgan, CO Micro (22820)			
Morgan	CO	08	087

CBSA DEFINITIONS

CBSA (CBSA Code) County		FIPS Codes	
Fort Payne, AL Micro (22840)			
DeKalb	AL	01	049
Fort Polk South, LA Micro (22860)			
Vernon	LA	22	115
Fort Smith, AR-OK Metro (22900)			
Crawford	AR	05	033
Franklin			047
Sebastian			131
Le Flore	OK	40	079
Sequoyah			135
Fort Valley, GA Micro (22980)			
Peach	GA	13	225
Fort Walton Beach-Crestview-Destin, FL Metro (23020)			
Okaloosa	FL	12	091
Fort Wayne, IN Metro (23060)			
Allen	IN	18	003
Wells			179
Whitley			183
Frankfort, IN Micro (23140)			
Clinton	IN	18	023
Frankfort, KY Micro (23180)			
Anderson	KY	21	005
Franklin			073
Fredericksburg, TX Micro (23240)			
Gillespie	TX	48	171
Freeport, IL Micro (23300)			
Stephenson	IL	17	177
Fremont, NE Micro (23340)			
Dodge	NE	31	053
Fremont, OH Micro (23380)			
Sandusky	OH	39	143
Fresno, CA Metro (23420)			
Fresno	CA	06	019
Gadsden, AL Metro (23460)			
Etowah	AL	01	055
Gaffney, SC Micro (23500)			
Cherokee	SC	45	021
Gainesville, FL Metro (23540)			
Alachua	FL	12	001
Gilchrist			041
Gainesville, GA Metro (23580)			
Hall	GA	13	139
Gainesville, TX Micro (23620)			
Cooke	TX	48	097

CBSA (CBSA Code) County		FIPS Codes	
Galesburg, IL Micro (23660)			
Knox	IL	17	095
Warren			187
Gallup, NM Micro (23700)			
McKinley	NM	35	031
Garden City, KS Micro (23780)			
Finney	KS	20	055
Gardnerville Ranchos, NV Micro (23820)			
Douglas	NV	32	005
Georgetown, SC Micro (23860)			
Georgetown	SC	45	043
Gettysburg, PA Micro (23900)			
Adams	PA	42	001
Gillette, WY Micro (23940)			
Campbell	WY	56	005
Glasgow, KY Micro (23980)			
Barren	KY	21	009
Metcalfe			169
Glens Falls, NY Metro (24020)			
Warren	NY	36	113
Washington			115
Gloversville, NY Micro (24100)			
Fulton	NY	36	035
Goldsboro, NC Metro (24140)			
Wayne	NC	37	191
Granbury, TX Micro (24180)			
Hood	TX	48	221
Somervell			425
Grand Forks, ND-MN Metro (24220)			
Polk	MN	27	119
Grand Forks	ND	38	035
Grand Island, NE Micro (24260)			
Hall	NE	31	079
Howard			093
Merrick			121
Grand Junction, CO Metro (24300)			
Mesa	CO	08	077
Grand Rapids-Wyoming, MI Metro (24340)			
Barry	MI	26	015
Ionia			067
Kent			081
Newaygo			123
Grants Pass, OR Micro (24420)			
Josephine	OR	41	033

CBSA DEFINITIONS

CBSA (CBSA Code) County			FIPS Codes
Grants, NM Micro (24380)			
Cibola	NM	35	006
Great Bend, KS Micro (24460)			
Barton	KS	20	009
Great Falls, MT Metro (24500)			
Cascade	MT	30	013
Greeley, CO Metro (24540)			
Weld	CO	08	123
Green Bay, WI Metro (24580)			
Brown	WI	55	009
Kewaunee			061
Oconto			083
Greeneville, TN Micro (24620)			
Greene	TN	47	059
Greensboro-High Point, NC Metro (24660)			
Guilford	NC	37	081
Randolph			151
Rockingham			157
Greensburg, IN Micro (24700)			
Decatur	IN	18	031
Greenville, MS Micro (24740)			
Washington	MS	28	151
Greenville, NC Metro (24780)			
Greene	NC	37	079
Pitt			147
Greenville, OH Micro (24820)			
Darke	OH	39	037
Greenville-Mauldin-Easley, SC Metro (24860)			
Greenville	SC	45	045
Laurens			059
Pickens			077
Greenwood, MS Micro (24900)			
Carroll	MS	28	015
Leflore			083
Greenwood, SC Micro (24940)			
Greenwood	SC	45	047
Grenada, MS Micro (24980)			
Grenada	MS	28	043
Gulfport-Biloxi, MS Metro (25060)			
Hancock	MS	28	045
Harrison			047
Stone			131
Guymon, OK Micro (25100)			
Texas	OK	40	139

CBSA (CBSA Code) County			FIPS Codes
Hagerstown-Martinsburg, MD-WV Metro (25180)			
Washington	MD	24	043
Berkeley	WV	54	003
Morgan			065
Hammond, LA Micro (25220)			
Tangipahoa	LA	22	105
Hanford-Corcoran, CA Metro (25260)			
Kings	CA	06	031
Hannibal, MO Micro (25300)			
Marion	MO	29	127
Ralls			173
Harriman, TN Micro (25340)			
Roane	TN	47	145
Harrisburg, IL Micro (25380)			
Saline	IL	17	165
Harrisburg-Carlisle, PA Metro (25420)			
Cumberland	PA	42	041
Dauphin			043
Perry			099
Harrison, AR Micro (25460)			
Boone	AR	05	009
Newton			101
Harrisonburg, VA Metro (25500)			
Rockingham	VA	51	165
Harrisonburg city			660
Hartford-West Hartford-East Hartford, CT Metro (25540)			
Hartford	CT	09	003
Middlesex			007
Tolland			013
Hastings, NE Micro (25580)			
Adams	NE	31	001
Clay			035
Hattiesburg, MS Metro (25620)			
Forrest	MS	28	035
Lamar			073
Perry			111
Havre, MT Micro (25660)			
Hill	MT	30	041
Hays, KS Micro (25700)			
Ellis	KS	20	051
Heber, UT Micro (25720)			
Wasatch	UT	49	051
Helena, MT Micro (25740)			
Jefferson	MT	30	043
Lewis and Clark			049

155

CBSA DEFINITIONS

CBSA (CBSA Code) County — FIPS Codes

CBSA (CBSA Code) County			FIPS Codes
Henderson, NC Micro (25780)			
Vance	NC	37	181
Hereford, TX Micro (25820)			
Deaf Smith	TX	48	117
Hickory-Lenoir-Morganton, NC Metro (25860)			
Alexander	NC	37	003
Burke			023
Caldwell			027
Catawba			035
Hilo, HI Micro (25900)			
Hawaii	HI	15	001
Hilton Head Island-Beaufort, SC Micro (25940)			
Beaufort	SC	45	013
Jasper			053
Hinesville-Fort Stewart, GA Metro (25980)			
Liberty	GA	13	179
Long			183
Hobbs, NM Micro (26020)			
Lea	NM	35	025
Holland-Grand Haven, MI Metro (26100)			
Ottawa	MI	26	139
Homosassa Springs, FL Micro (26140)			
Citrus	FL	12	017
Honolulu, HI Metro (26180)			
Honolulu	HI	15	003
Hood River, OR Micro (26220)			
Hood River	OR	41	027
Hope, AR Micro (26260)			
Hempstead	AR	05	057
Nevada			099
Hot Springs, AR Metro (26300)			
Garland	AR	05	051
Houghton, MI Micro (26340)			
Houghton	MI	26	061
Keweenaw			083
Houma-Bayou Cane-Thibodaux, LA Metro (26380)			
Lafourche	LA	22	057
Terrebonne			109
Houston-Sugar Land-Baytown, TX Metro (26420)			
Austin	TX	48	015
Brazoria			039
Chambers			071
Fort Bend			157
Galveston			107
Harris			201
Liberty			291

CBSA (CBSA Code) County			FIPS Codes
Houston-Sugar Land-Baytown, TX Metro (26420) (continued)			
Montgomery			339
San Jacinto			407
Waller			473
Hudson, NY Micro (26460)			
Columbia	NY	36	021
Humboldt, TN Micro (26480)			
Gibson	TN	47	053
Huntingdon, PA Micro (26500)			
Huntingdon	PA	42	061
Huntington, IN Micro (26540)			
Huntington	IN	18	069
Huntington-Ashland, WV-KY-OH Metro (26580)			
Boyd	KY	21	019
Greenup			089
Lawrence	OH	39	087
Cabell	WV	54	011
Wayne			099
Huntsville, AL Metro (26620)			
Limestone	AL	01	083
Madison			089
Huntsville, TX Micro (26660)			
Walker	TX	48	471
Huron, SD Micro (26700)			
Beadle	SD	46	005
Hutchinson, KS Micro (26740)			
Reno	KS	20	155
Hutchinson, MN Micro (26780)			
McLeod	MN	27	085
Idaho Falls, ID Metro (26820)			
Bonneville	ID	16	019
Jefferson			051
Indiana, PA Micro (26860)			
Indiana	PA	42	063
Indianapolis-Carmel, IN Metro (26900)			
Boone	IN	18	011
Brown			013
Hamilton			057
Hancock			059
Hendricks			063
Johnson			081
Marion			097
Morgan			109
Putnam			133
Shelby			145

CBSA DEFINITIONS

<table>
<tr><td colspan="4">CBSA (CBSA Code)
County</td><td colspan="2">FIPS
Codes</td></tr>
</table>

CBSA (CBSA Code) County			FIPS Codes	
Indianola, MS Micro (26940)				
Sunflower	MS	28	133	
Iowa City, IA Metro (26980)				
Johnson	IA	19	103	
Washington			183	
Iron Mountain, MI-WI Micro (27020)				
Dickinson	MI	26	043	
Florence	WI	55	037	
Ithaca, NY Metro (27060)				
Tompkins	NY	36	109	
Jackson, MI Metro (27100)				
Jackson	MI	26	075	
Jackson, MS Metro (27140)				
Copiah	MS	28	029	
Hinds			049	
Madison			089	
Rankin			121	
Simpson			127	
Jackson, TN Metro (27180)				
Chester	TN	47	023	
Madison			113	
Jackson, WY-ID Micro (27220)				
Teton	ID	16	081	
Teton	WY	56	039	
Jacksonville, FL Metro (27260)				
Baker	FL	12	003	
Clay			019	
Duval			031	
Nassau			089	
St. Johns			109	
Jacksonville, IL Micro (27300)				
Morgan	IL	17	137	
Scott			171	
Jacksonville, NC Metro (27340)				
Onslow	NC	37	133	
Jacksonville, TX Micro (27380)				
Cherokee	TX	48	073	
Jamestown, ND Micro (27420)				
Stutsman	ND	38	093	
Jamestown-Dunkirk-Fredonia, NY Micro (27460)				
Chautauqua	NY	36	013	
Janesville, WI Metro (27500)				
Rock	WI	55	105	
Jasper, IN Micro (27540)				
Dubois	IN	18	037	
Pike			125	

CBSA (CBSA Code) County			FIPS Codes	
Jefferson City, MO Metro (27620)				
Callaway	MO	29	027	
Cole			051	
Moniteau			135	
Osage			151	
Jennings, LA Micro (27660)				
Jefferson Davis	LA	22	053	
Jesup, GA Micro (27700)				
Wayne	GA	13	305	
Johnson City, TN Metro (27740)				
Carter	TN	47	019	
Unicoi			171	
Washington			179	
Johnstown, PA Metro (27780)				
Cambria	PA	42	021	
Jonesboro, AR Metro (27860)				
Craighead	AR	05	031	
Poinsett			111	
Joplin, MO Metro (27900)				
Jasper	MO	29	097	
Newton			145	
Juneau, AK Micro (27940)				
Juneau City and Borough	AK	02	110	
Kahului-Wailuku, HI Micro (27980)				
Maui	HI	15	009	
Kalamazoo-Portage, MI Metro (28020)				
Kalamazoo	MI	26	077	
Van Buren			159	
Kalispell, MT Micro (28060)				
Flathead	MT	30	029	
Kankakee-Bradley, IL Metro (28100)				
Kankakee	IL	17	091	
Kansas City, MO-KS Metro (28140)				
Franklin	KS	20	059	
Johnson			091	
Leavenworth			103	
Linn			107	
Miami			121	
Wyandotte			209	
Bates	MO	29	013	
Caldwell			025	
Cass			037	
Clay			047	
Clinton			049	
Jackson			095	
Lafayette			107	
Platte			165	
Ray			177	

CBSA DEFINITIONS

CBSA (CBSA Code) County		FIPS Codes	
Kapaa, HI Micro (28180)			
Kauai	HI	15	007
Kearney, NE Micro (28260)			
Buffalo	NE	31	019
Kearney			099
Keene, NH Micro (28300)			
Cheshire	NH	33	005
Kendallville, IN Micro (28340)			
Noble	IN	18	113
Kennett, MO Micro (28380)			
Dunklin	MO	29	069
Kennewick-Richland-Pasco, WA Metro (28420)			
Benton	WA	53	005
Franklin			021
Kerrville, TX Micro (28500)			
Kerr	TX	48	265
Ketchikan, AK Micro (28540)			
Ketchikan Gateway	AK	02	130
Key West, FL Micro (28580)			
Monroe	FL	12	087
Kill Devil Hills, NC Micro (28620)			
Dare	NC	37	055
Killeen-Temple-Fort Hood, TX Metro (28660)			
Bell	TX	48	027
Coryell			099
Lampasas			281
Kingsport-Bristol-Bristol, TN-VA Metro (28700)			
Hawkins	TN	47	073
Sullivan			163
Scott	VA	51	169
Washington			191
Bristol city			520
Kingston, NY Metro (28740)			
Ulster	NY	36	111
Kingsville, TX Micro (28780)			
Kenedy	TX	48	261
Kleberg			273
Kinston, NC Micro (28820)			
Lenoir	NC	37	107
Kirksville, MO Micro (28860)			
Adair	MO	29	001
Schuyler			197
Klamath Falls, OR Micro (28900)			
Klamath	OR	41	035

CBSA (CBSA Code) County		FIPS Codes	
Knoxville, TN Metro (28940)			
Anderson	TN	47	001
Blount			009
Knox			093
Loudon			105
Union			173
Kodiak, AK Micro (28980)			
Kodiak Island	AK	02	150
Kokomo, IN Metro (29020)			
Howard	IN	18	067
Tipton			159
La Crosse, WI-MN Metro (29100)			
Houston	MN	27	055
La Crosse	WI	55	063
La Follette, TN Micro (29220)			
Campbell	TN	47	013
La Grande, OR Micro (29260)			
Union	OR	41	061
Laconia, NH Micro (29060)			
Belknap	NH	33	001
Lafayette, IN Metro (29140)			
Benton	IN	18	007
Carroll			015
Tippecanoe			157
Lafayette, LA Metro (29180)			
Lafayette	LA	22	055
St. Martin			099
LaGrange, GA Micro (29300)			
Troup	GA	13	285
Lake Charles, LA Metro (29340)			
Calcasieu	LA	22	019
Cameron			023
Lake City, FL Micro (29380)			
Columbia	FL	12	023
Lake Havasu City-Kingman, AZ Metro (29420)			
Mohave	AZ	04	015
Lakeland, FL Metro (29460)			
Polk	FL	12	105
Lamesa, TX Micro (29500)			
Dawson	TX	48	115
Lancaster, PA Metro (29540)			
Lancaster	PA	42	071
Lancaster, SC Micro (29580)			
Lancaster	SC	45	057

CBSA DEFINITIONS

CBSA (CBSA Code) County — FIPS Codes

Lansing-East Lansing, MI Metro (29620)
County	State		
Clinton	MI	26	037
Eaton			045
Ingham			065

Laramie, WY Micro (29660)
County	State		
Albany	WY	56	001

Laredo, TX Metro (29700)
County	State		
Webb	TX	48	479

Las Cruces, NM Metro (29740)
County	State		
Dona Ana	NM	35	013

Las Vegas, NM Micro (29780)
County	State		
San Miguel	NM	35	047

Las Vegas-Paradise, NV Metro (29820)
County	State		
Clark	NV	32	003

Laurel, MS Micro (29860)
County	State		
Jasper	MS	28	061
Jones			067

Laurinburg, NC Micro (29900)
County	State		
Scotland	NC	37	165

Lawrence, KS Metro (29940)
County	State		
Douglas	KS	20	045

Lawrenceburg, TN Micro (29980)
County	State		
Lawrence	TN	47	099

Lawton, OK Metro (30020)
County	State		
Comanche	OK	40	031

Lebanon, MO Micro (30060)
County	State		
Laclede	MO	29	105

Lebanon, NH-VT Micro (30100)
County	State		
Grafton	NH	33	009
Orange	VT	50	017
Windsor			027

Lebanon, PA Metro (30140)
County	State		
Lebanon	PA	42	075

Levelland, TX Micro (30220)
County	State		
Hockley	TX	48	219

Lewisburg, PA Micro (30260)
County	State		
Union	PA	42	119

Lewisburg, TN Micro (30280)
County	State		
Marshall	TN	47	117

Lewiston, ID-WA Metro (30300)
County	State		
Nez Perce	ID	16	069
Asotin	WA	53	003

Lewiston-Auburn, ME Metro (30340)
County	State		
Androscoggin	ME	23	001

Lewistown, PA Micro (30380)
County	State		
Mifflin	PA	42	087

Lexington Park, MD Micro (30500)
County	State		
St. Mary's	MD	24	037

Lexington, NE Micro (30420)
County	State		
Dawson	NE	31	047
Gosper			073

Lexington-Fayette, KY Metro (30460)
County	State		
Bourbon	KY	21	017
Clark			049
Fayette			067
Jessamine			113
Scott			209
Woodford			239

Liberal, KS Micro (30580)
County	State		
Seward	KS	20	175

Lima, OH Metro (30620)
County	State		
Allen	OH	39	003

Lincoln, IL Micro (30660)
County	State		
Logan	IL	17	107

Lincoln, NE Metro (30700)
County	State		
Lancaster	NE	31	109
Seward			159

Lincolnton, NC Micro (30740)
County	State		
Lincoln	NC	37	109

Little Rock-North Little Rock-Conway, AR Metro (30780)
County	State		
Faulkner	AR	05	045
Grant			053
Lonoke			085
Perry			105
Pulaski			119
Saline			125

Lock Haven, PA Micro (30820)
County	State		
Clinton	PA	42	035

Logan, UT-ID Metro (30860)
County	State		
Franklin	ID	16	041
Cache	UT	49	005

Logansport, IN Micro (30900)
County	State		
Cass	IN	18	017

London, KY Micro (30940)
County	State		
Laurel	KY	21	125

Longview, TX Metro (30980)
County	State		
Gregg	TX	48	183
Rusk			401
Upshur			459

CBSA DEFINITIONS

CBSA (CBSA Code) County		FIPS Codes	
Longview, WA Metro (31020)			
Cowlitz	WA	53	015
Los Alamos, NM Micro (31060)			
Los Alamos	NM	35	028
Los Angeles-Long Beach-Santa Ana, CA Metro (31100)			
Los Angeles	CA	06	037
Orange			059
Louisville-Jefferson County, KY-IN Metro (31140)			
Clark	IN	18	019
Floyd			043
Harrison			061
Washington			175
Bullitt	KY	21	029
Henry			103
Jefferson			111
Meade			163
Nelson			179
Oldham			185
Shelby			211
Spencer			215
Trimble			223
Lubbock, TX Metro (31180)			
Crosby	TX	48	107
Lubbock			303
Lufkin, TX Micro (31260)			
Angelina	TX	48	005
Lumberton, NC Micro (31300)			
Robeson	NC	37	155
Lynchburg, VA Metro (31340)			
Amherst	VA	51	009
Appomattox			011
Bedford			019
Campbell			031
Bedford city			515
Lynchburg city			680
Macomb, IL Micro (31380)			
McDonough	IL	17	109
Macon, GA Metro (31420)			
Bibb	GA	13	021
Crawford			079
Jones			169
Monroe			207
Twiggs			289
Madera, CA Metro (31460)			
Madera	CA	06	039
Madison, IN Micro (31500)			
Jefferson	IN	18	077

CBSA (CBSA Code) County		FIPS Codes	
Madison, WI Metro (31540)			
Columbia	WI	55	021
Dane			025
Iowa			049
Madisonville, KY Micro (31580)			
Hopkins	KY	21	107
Magnolia, AR Micro (31620)			
Columbia	AR	05	027
Malone, NY Micro (31660)			
Franklin	NY	36	033
Manchester-Nashua, NH Metro (31700)			
Hillsborough	NH	33	011
Manhattan, KS Micro (31740)			
Geary	KS	20	061
Pottawatomie			149
Riley			161
Manitowoc, WI Micro (31820)			
Manitowoc	WI	55	071
Mankato-North Mankato, MN Micro (31860)			
Blue Earth	MN	27	013
Nicollet			103
Mansfield, OH Metro (31900)			
Richland	OH	39	139
Marinette, WI-MI Micro (31940)			
Menominee	MI	26	109
Marinette	WI	55	075
Marion, IN Micro (31980)			
Grant	IN	18	053
Marion, OH Micro (32020)			
Marion	OH	39	101
Marion-Herrin, IL Micro (32060)			
Williamson	IL	17	199
Marquette, MI Micro (32100)			
Marquette	MI	26	103
Marshall, MN Micro (32140)			
Lyon	MN	27	083
Marshall, MO Micro (32180)			
Saline	MO	29	195
Marshall, TX Micro (32220)			
Harrison	TX	48	203
Marshalltown, IA Micro (32260)			
Marshall	IA	19	127
Marshfield - Wisconsin Rapids, WI Micro (32270)			
Wood	WI	55	141

CBSA DEFINITIONS

CBSA (CBSA Code) County		FIPS Codes	

Martin, TN Micro (32280)
Weakley	TN	47	183

Martinsville, VA Micro (32300)
Henry	VA	51	089
Martinsville city			690

Maryville, MO Micro (32340)
Nodaway	MO	29	147

Mason City, IA Micro (32380)
Cerro Gordo	IA	19	033
Worth			195

Mayfield, KY Micro (32460)
Graves	KY	21	083

Maysville, KY Micro (32500)
Lewis	KY	21	135
Mason			161

McAlester, OK Micro (32540)
Pittsburg	OK	40	121

McAllen-Edinburg-Mission, TX Metro (32580)
Hidalgo	TX	48	215

McComb, MS Micro (32620)
Amite	MS	28	005
Pike			113

McMinnville, TN Micro (32660)
Warren	TN	47	177

McPherson, KS Micro (32700)
McPherson	KS	20	113

Meadville, PA Micro (32740)
Crawford	PA	42	039

Medford, OR Metro (32780)
Jackson	OR	41	029

Memphis, TN-MS-AR Metro (32820)
Crittenden	AR	05	035
DeSoto	MS	28	033
Marshall			093
Tate			137
Tunica			143
Fayette	TN	47	047
Shelby			157
Tipton			167

Menomonie, WI Micro (32860)
Dunn	WI	55	033

Merced, CA Metro (32900)
Merced	CA	06	047

Meridian, MS Micro (32940)
Clarke	MS	28	023
Kemper			069
Lauderdale			075

Merrill, WI Micro (32980)
Lincoln	WI	55	069

Mexico, MO Micro (33020)
Audrain	MO	29	007

Miami, OK Micro (33060)
Ottawa	OK	40	115

Miami-Fort Lauderdale-Pompano Beach, FL Metro (33100)
Broward	FL	12	011
Miami-Dade			086
Palm Beach			099

Michigan City-La Porte, IN Metro (33140)
LaPorte	IN	18	091

Middlesborough, KY Micro (33180)
Bell	KY	21	013

Midland, MI Micro (33220)
Midland	MI	26	111

Midland, TX Metro (33260)
Midland	TX	48	329

Milledgeville, GA Micro (33300)
Baldwin	GA	13	009
Hancock			141

Milwaukee-Waukesha-West Allis, WI Metro (33340)
Milwaukee	WI	55	079
Ozaukee			089
Washington			131
Waukesha			133

Minden, LA Micro (33380)
Webster	LA	22	119

Mineral Wells, TX Micro (33420)
Palo Pinto	TX	48	363

Minneapolis-St. Paul-Bloomington, MN-WI Metro (33460)
Anoka	MN	27	003
Carver			019
Chisago			025
Dakota			037
Hennepin			053
Isanti			059
Ramsey			123
Scott			139
Sherburne			141

CBSA DEFINITIONS

CBSA (CBSA Code) County		FIPS Codes	
Minneapolis-St. Paul-Bloomington, MN-WI Metro (33460) (continued)			
Washington	MN	27	163
Wright			171
Pierce	WI	55	093
St. Croix			109
Minot, ND Micro (33500)			
McHenry	ND	38	049
Renville			075
Ward			101
Missoula, MT Metro (33540)			
Missoula	MT	30	063
Mitchell, SD Micro (33580)			
Davison	SD	46	035
Hanson			061
Moberly, MO Micro (33620)			
Randolph	MO	29	175
Mobile, AL Metro (33660)			
Mobile	AL	01	097
Modesto, CA Metro (33700)			
Stanislaus	CA	06	099
Monroe, LA Metro (33740)			
Ouachita	LA	22	073
Union			111
Monroe, MI Metro (33780)			
Monroe	MI	26	115
Monroe, WI Micro (33820)			
Green	WI	55	045
Montgomery, AL Metro (33860)			
Autauga	AL	01	001
Elmore			051
Lowndes			085
Montgomery			101
Montrose, CO Micro (33940)			
Montrose	CO	08	085
Morehead City, NC Micro (33980)			
Carteret	NC	37	031
Morgan City, LA Micro (34020)			
St. Mary	LA	22	101
Morgantown, WV Metro (34060)			
Monongalia	WV	54	061
Preston			077
Morristown, TN Metro (34100)			
Grainger	TN	47	057
Hamblen			063
Jefferson			089

CBSA (CBSA Code) County		FIPS Codes	
Moscow, ID Micro (34140)			
Latah	ID	16	057
Moses Lake, WA Micro (34180)			
Grant	WA	53	025
Moultrie, GA Micro (34220)			
Colquitt	GA	13	071
Mount Airy, NC Micro (34340)			
Surry	NC	37	171
Mount Pleasant, MI Micro (34380)			
Isabella	MI	26	073
Mount Pleasant, TX Micro (34420)			
Titus	TX	48	449
Mount Sterling, KY Micro (34460)			
Bath	KY	21	011
Menifee			165
Montgomery			173
Mount Vernon, IL Micro (34500)			
Hamilton	IL	17	065
Jefferson			081
Mount Vernon, OH Micro (34540)			
Knox	OH	39	083
Mount Vernon-Anacortes, WA Metro (34580)			
Skagit	WA	53	057
Mountain Home, AR Micro (34260)			
Baxter	AR	05	005
Mountain Home, ID Micro (34300)			
Elmore	ID	16	039
Muncie, IN Metro (34620)			
Delaware	IN	18	035
Murray, KY Micro (34660)			
Calloway	KY	21	035
Muscatine, IA Micro (34700)			
Louisa	IA	19	115
Muscatine			139
Muskegon-Norton Shores, MI Metro (34740)			
Muskegon	MI	26	121
Muskogee, OK Micro (34780)			
Muskogee	OK	40	101
Myrtle Beach-Conway-North Myrtle Beach, SC Metro (34820)			
Horry	SC	45	051
Nacogdoches, TX Micro (34860)			
Nacogdoches	TX	48	347

CBSA DEFINITIONS

Napa, CA Metro (34900)

Napa	CA	06	055

Naples-Marco Island, FL Metro (34940)

Collier	FL	12	021

Nashville-Davidson--Murfreesboro--Franklin, TN Metro (34980)

Cannon	TN	47	015
Cheatham			021
Davidson			037
Dickson			043
Hickman			081
Macon			111
Robertson			147
Rutherford			149
Smith			159
Sumner			165
Trousdale			169
Williamson			187
Wilson			189

Natchez, MS-LA Micro (35020)

Concordia	LA	22	029
Adams	MS	28	001

Natchitoches, LA Micro (35060)

Natchitoches	LA	22	069

New Bern, NC Micro (35100)

Craven	NC	37	049
Jones			103
Pamlico			137

New Castle, IN Micro (35220)

Henry	IN	18	065

New Castle, PA Micro (35260)

Lawrence	PA	42	073

New Haven-Milford, CT Metro (35300)

New Haven	CT	09	009

New Iberia, LA Micro (35340)

Iberia	LA	22	045

New Orleans-Metairie-Kenner, LA Metro (35380)

Jefferson	LA	22	051
Orleans			071
Plaquemines			075
St. Bernard			087
St. Charles			089
St. John the Baptist			095
St. Tammany			103

New Philadelphia-Dover, OH Micro (35420)

Tuscarawas	OH	39	157

New Ulm, MN Micro (35580)

Brown	MN	27	015

New York-Northern New Jersey-Long Island, NY-NJ-PA Metro (35620)

Bergen	NJ	34	003
Essex			013
Hudson			017
Hunterdon			019
Middlesex			023
Monmouth			025
Morris			027
Ocean			029
Passaic			031
Somerset			035
Sussex	NJ	34	037
Union			039
Bronx	NY	36	005
Kings			047
Nassau			059
New York			061
Putnam			079
Queens			081
Richmond			085
Rockland			087
Suffolk			103
Westchester			119
Pike	PA	42	103

Newberry, SC Micro (35140)

Newberry	SC	45	071

Newport, TN Micro (35460)

Cocke	TN	47	029

Newton, IA Micro (35500)

Jasper	IA	19	099

Niles-Benton Harbor, MI Metro (35660)

Berrien	MI	26	021

Nogales, AZ Micro (35700)

Santa Cruz	AZ	04	023

Norfolk, NE Micro (35740)

Madison	NE	31	119
Pierce			139
Stanton			167

North Platte, NE Micro (35820)

Lincoln	NE	31	111
Logan			113
McPherson			117

North Vernon, IN Micro (35860)

Jennings	IN	18	079

North Wilkesboro, NC Micro (35900)

Wilkes	NC	37	193

Norwalk, OH Micro (35940)

Huron	OH	39	077

CBSA DEFINITIONS

CBSA (CBSA Code) County		FIPS Codes	
Norwich-New London, CT Metro (35980)			
New London	CT	09	011
Oak Harbor, WA Micro (36020)			
Island	WA	53	029
Oak Hill, WV Micro (36060)			
Fayette	WV	54	019
Ocala, FL Metro (36100)			
Marion	FL	12	083
Ocean City, NJ Metro (36140)			
Cape May	NJ	34	009
Ocean Pines, MD Micro (36180)			
Worcester	MD	24	047
Odessa, TX Metro (36220)			
Ector	TX	48	135
Ogden-Clearfield, UT Metro (36260)			
Davis	UT	49	011
Morgan			029
Weber			057
Ogdensburg-Massena, NY Micro (36300)			
St. Lawrence	NY	36	089
Oil City, PA Micro (36340)			
Venango	PA	42	121
Okeechobee, FL Micro (36380)			
Okeechobee	FL	12	093
Oklahoma City, OK Metro (36420)			
Canadian	OK	40	017
Cleveland			027
Grady			051
Lincoln			081
Logan			083
McClain			087
Oklahoma			109
Olean, NY Micro (36460)			
Cattaraugus	NY	36	009
Olympia, WA Metro (36500)			
Thurston	WA	53	067
Omaha-Council Bluffs, NE-IA Metro (36540)			
Harrison	IA	19	085
Mills			129
Pottawattamie			155
Cass	NE	31	025
Douglas			055
Sarpy			153
Saunders			155
Washington			177

CBSA (CBSA Code) County		FIPS Codes	
Oneonta, NY Micro (36580)			
Otsego	NY	36	077
Ontario, OR-ID Micro (36620)			
Payette	ID	16	075
Malheur	OR	41	045
Opelousas-Eunice, LA Micro (36660)			
St. Landry	LA	22	097
Orangeburg, SC Micro (36700)			
Orangeburg	SC	45	075
Orlando-Kissimmee, FL Metro (36740)			
Lake	FL	12	069
Orange			095
Osceola			097
Seminole			117
Oshkosh-Neenah, WI Metro (36780)			
Winnebago	WI	55	139
Oskaloosa, IA Micro (36820)			
Mahaska	IA	19	123
Ottawa-Streator, IL Micro (36860)			
Bureau	IL	17	011
La Salle			099
Putnam			155
Ottumwa, IA Micro (36900)			
Wapello	IA	19	179
Owatonna, MN Micro (36940)			
Steele	MN	27	147
Owensboro, KY Metro (36980)			
Daviess	KY	21	059
Hancock			091
McLean			149
Owosso, MI Micro (37020)			
Shiawassee	MI	26	155
Oxford, MS Micro (37060)			
Lafayette	MS	28	071
Oxnard-Thousand Oaks-Ventura, CA Metro (37100)			
Ventura	CA	06	111
Paducah, KY-IL Micro (37140)			
Massac	IL	17	127
Ballard	KY	21	007
Livingston			139
McCracken			145
Pahrump, NV Micro (37220)			
Nye	NV	32	023

CBSA DEFINITIONS

<table>
<thead>
<tr><th>CBSA (CBSA Code)
County</th><th colspan="3">FIPS
Codes</th></tr>
</thead>
<tbody>
<tr><td colspan="4">Palatka, FL Micro (37260)</td></tr>
<tr><td>Putnam</td><td>FL</td><td>12</td><td>107</td></tr>
<tr><td colspan="4">Palestine, TX Micro (37300)</td></tr>
<tr><td>Anderson</td><td>TX</td><td>48</td><td>001</td></tr>
<tr><td colspan="4">Palm Bay-Melbourne-Titusville, FL Metro (37340)</td></tr>
<tr><td>Brevard</td><td>FL</td><td>12</td><td>009</td></tr>
<tr><td colspan="4">Palm Coast, FL Metro (37380)</td></tr>
<tr><td>Flagler</td><td>FL</td><td>12</td><td>035</td></tr>
<tr><td colspan="4">Pampa, TX Micro (37420)</td></tr>
<tr><td>Gray</td><td>TX</td><td>48</td><td>179</td></tr>
<tr><td>Roberts</td><td></td><td></td><td>393</td></tr>
<tr><td colspan="4">Panama City-Lynn Haven, FL Metro (37460)</td></tr>
<tr><td>Bay</td><td>FL</td><td>12</td><td>005</td></tr>
<tr><td colspan="4">Paragould, AR Micro (37500)</td></tr>
<tr><td>Greene</td><td>AR</td><td>05</td><td>055</td></tr>
<tr><td colspan="4">Paris, TN Micro (37540)</td></tr>
<tr><td>Henry</td><td>TN</td><td>47</td><td>079</td></tr>
<tr><td colspan="4">Paris, TX Micro (37580)</td></tr>
<tr><td>Lamar</td><td>TX</td><td>48</td><td>277</td></tr>
<tr><td colspan="4">Parkersburg-Marietta-Vienna, WV-OH Metro (37620)</td></tr>
<tr><td>Washington</td><td>OH</td><td>39</td><td>167</td></tr>
<tr><td>Pleasants</td><td>WV</td><td>54</td><td>073</td></tr>
<tr><td>Wirt</td><td></td><td></td><td>105</td></tr>
<tr><td>Wood</td><td></td><td></td><td>107</td></tr>
<tr><td colspan="4">Parsons, KS Micro (37660)</td></tr>
<tr><td>Labette</td><td>KS</td><td>20</td><td>099</td></tr>
<tr><td colspan="4">Pascagoula, MS Metro (37700)</td></tr>
<tr><td>George</td><td>MS</td><td>28</td><td>039</td></tr>
<tr><td>Jackson</td><td></td><td></td><td>059</td></tr>
<tr><td colspan="4">Payson, AZ Micro (37740)</td></tr>
<tr><td>Gila</td><td>AZ</td><td>04</td><td>007</td></tr>
<tr><td colspan="4">Pecos, TX Micro (37780)</td></tr>
<tr><td>Reeves</td><td>TX</td><td>48</td><td>389</td></tr>
<tr><td colspan="4">Pella, IA Micro (37800)</td></tr>
<tr><td>Marion</td><td>IA</td><td>19</td><td>125</td></tr>
<tr><td colspan="4">Pendleton-Hermiston, OR Micro (37820)</td></tr>
<tr><td>Morrow</td><td>OR</td><td>41</td><td>049</td></tr>
<tr><td>Umatilla</td><td></td><td></td><td>059</td></tr>
<tr><td colspan="4">Pensacola-Ferry Pass-Brent, FL Metro (37860)</td></tr>
<tr><td>Escambia</td><td>FL</td><td>12</td><td>033</td></tr>
<tr><td>Santa Rosa</td><td></td><td></td><td>113</td></tr>
</tbody>
</table>

<table>
<thead>
<tr><th>CBSA (CBSA Code)
County</th><th colspan="3">FIPS
Codes</th></tr>
</thead>
<tbody>
<tr><td colspan="4">Peoria, IL Metro (37900)</td></tr>
<tr><td>Marshall</td><td>IL</td><td>17</td><td>123</td></tr>
<tr><td>Peoria</td><td></td><td></td><td>143</td></tr>
<tr><td>Stark</td><td></td><td></td><td>175</td></tr>
<tr><td>Tazewell</td><td></td><td></td><td>179</td></tr>
<tr><td>Woodford</td><td></td><td></td><td>203</td></tr>
<tr><td colspan="4">Peru, IN Micro (37940)</td></tr>
<tr><td>Miami</td><td>IN</td><td>18</td><td>103</td></tr>
<tr><td colspan="4">Philadelphia-Camden-Wilmington, PA-NJ-DE-MD Metro (37980)</td></tr>
<tr><td>New Castle</td><td>DE</td><td>10</td><td>003</td></tr>
<tr><td>Cecil</td><td>MD</td><td>24</td><td>015</td></tr>
<tr><td>Burlington</td><td>NJ</td><td>34</td><td>005</td></tr>
<tr><td>Camden</td><td></td><td></td><td>007</td></tr>
<tr><td>Gloucester</td><td></td><td></td><td>015</td></tr>
<tr><td>Salem</td><td></td><td></td><td>033</td></tr>
<tr><td>Bucks</td><td>PA</td><td>42</td><td>017</td></tr>
<tr><td>Chester</td><td></td><td></td><td>029</td></tr>
<tr><td>Delaware</td><td></td><td></td><td>045</td></tr>
<tr><td>Montgomery</td><td></td><td></td><td>091</td></tr>
<tr><td>Philadelphia</td><td></td><td></td><td>101</td></tr>
<tr><td colspan="4">Phoenix Lake-Cedar Ridge, CA Micro (38020)</td></tr>
<tr><td>Tuolumne</td><td>CA</td><td>06</td><td>109</td></tr>
<tr><td colspan="4">Phoenix-Mesa-Scottsdale, AZ Metro (38060)</td></tr>
<tr><td>Maricopa</td><td>AZ</td><td>04</td><td>013</td></tr>
<tr><td>Pinal</td><td></td><td></td><td>021</td></tr>
<tr><td colspan="4">Picayune, MS Micro (38100)</td></tr>
<tr><td>Pearl River</td><td>MS</td><td>28</td><td>109</td></tr>
<tr><td colspan="4">Pierre Part, LA Micro (38200)</td></tr>
<tr><td>Assumption</td><td>LA</td><td>22</td><td>007</td></tr>
<tr><td colspan="4">Pierre, SD Micro (38180)</td></tr>
<tr><td>Hughes</td><td>SD</td><td>46</td><td>065</td></tr>
<tr><td>Stanley</td><td></td><td></td><td>117</td></tr>
<tr><td colspan="4">Pine Bluff, AR Metro (38220)</td></tr>
<tr><td>Cleveland</td><td>AR</td><td>05</td><td>025</td></tr>
<tr><td>Jefferson</td><td></td><td></td><td>069</td></tr>
<tr><td>Lincoln</td><td></td><td></td><td>079</td></tr>
<tr><td colspan="4">Pittsburg, KS Micro (38260)</td></tr>
<tr><td>Crawford</td><td>KS</td><td>20</td><td>037</td></tr>
<tr><td colspan="4">Pittsburgh, PA Metro (38300)</td></tr>
<tr><td>Allegheny</td><td>PA</td><td>42</td><td>003</td></tr>
<tr><td>Armstrong</td><td></td><td></td><td>005</td></tr>
<tr><td>Beaver</td><td></td><td></td><td>007</td></tr>
<tr><td>Butler</td><td></td><td></td><td>019</td></tr>
<tr><td>Fayette</td><td></td><td></td><td>051</td></tr>
<tr><td>Washington</td><td></td><td></td><td>125</td></tr>
<tr><td>Westmoreland</td><td></td><td></td><td>129</td></tr>
</tbody>
</table>

CBSA DEFINITIONS

CBSA (CBSA Code) County		FIPS Codes	

CBSA (CBSA Code) County		FIPS Codes	
Pittsfield, MA Metro (38340)			
Berkshire	MA	25	003
Plainview, TX Micro (38380)			
Hale	TX	48	189
Platteville, WI Micro (38420)			
Grant	WI	55	043
Plattsburgh, NY Micro (38460)			
Clinton	NY	36	019
Plymouth, IN Micro (38500)			
Marshall	IN	18	099
Pocatello, ID Metro (38540)			
Bannock	ID	16	005
Power			077
Point Pleasant, WV-OH Micro (38580)			
Gallia	OH	39	053
Mason	WV	54	053
Ponca City, OK Micro (38620)			
Kay	OK	40	071
Pontiac, IL Micro (38700)			
Livingston	IL	17	105
Poplar Bluff, MO Micro (38740)			
Butler	MO	29	023
Port Angeles, WA Micro (38820)			
Clallam	WA	53	009
Port St. Lucie, FL Metro (38940)			
Martin	FL	12	085
St. Lucie			111
Portales, NM Micro (38780)			
Roosevelt	NM	35	041
Portland-South Portland-Biddeford, ME Metro (38860)			
Cumberland	ME	23	005
Sagadahoc			023
York			031
Portland-Vancouver-Beaverton, OR-WA Metro (38900)			
Clackamas	OR	41	005
Columbia			009
Multnomah			051
Washington			067
Yamhill			071
Clark	WA	53	011
Skamania			059
Portsmouth, OH Micro (39020)			
Scioto	OH	39	145

CBSA (CBSA Code) County		FIPS Codes	
Pottsville, PA Micro (39060)			
Schuylkill	PA	42	107
Poughkeepsie-Newburgh-Middletown, NY Metro (39100)			
Dutchess	NY	36	027
Orange			071
Prescott, AZ Metro (39140)			
Yavapai	AZ	04	025
Price, UT Micro (39220)			
Carbon	UT	49	007
Prineville, OR Micro (39260)			
Crook	OR	41	013
Providence-New Bedford-Fall River, RI-MA Metro (39300)			
Bristol	MA	25	005
Bristol	RI	44	001
Kent			003
Newport			005
Providence			007
Washington			009
Provo-Orem, UT Metro (39340)			
Juab	UT	49	023
Utah			049
Pueblo, CO Metro (39380)			
Pueblo	CO	08	101
Pullman, WA Micro (39420)			
Whitman	WA	53	075
Punta Gorda, FL Metro (39460)			
Charlotte	FL	12	015
Quincy, IL-MO Micro (39500)			
Adams	IL	17	001
Lewis	MO	29	111
Racine, WI Metro (39540)			
Racine	WI	55	101
Raleigh-Cary, NC Metro (39580)			
Franklin	NC	37	069
Johnston			101
Wake			183
Rapid City, SD Metro (39660)			
Meade	SD	46	093
Pennington			103
Raymondville, TX Micro (39700)			
Willacy	TX	48	489
Reading, PA Metro (39740)			
Berks	PA	42	011

CBSA DEFINITIONS

CBSA (CBSA Code) County		FIPS Codes	
Red Bluff, CA Micro (39780)			
Tehama	CA	06	103
Red Wing, MN Micro (39860)			
Goodhue	MN	27	049
Redding, CA Metro (39820)			
Shasta	CA	06	089
Reno-Sparks, NV Metro (39900)			
Storey	NV	32	029
Washoe			031
Rexburg, ID Micro (39940)			
Fremont	ID	16	043
Madison			065
Richmond, IN Micro (39980)			
Wayne	IN	18	177
Richmond, VA Metro (40060)			
Amelia	VA	51	007
Caroline			033
Charles City			036
Chesterfield			041
Cumberland			049
Dinwiddie			053
Goochland			075
Hanover			085
Henrico			087
King and Queen			097
King William			101
Louisa			109
New Kent			127
Powhatan			145
Prince George			149
Sussex			183
Colonial Heights city			570
Hopewell city			670
Petersburg city			730
Richmond city			760
Richmond-Berea, KY Micro (40080)			
Madison	KY	21	151
Rockcastle			203
Rio Grande City-Roma, TX Micro (40100)			
Starr	TX	48	427
Riverside-San Bernardino-Ontario, CA Metro (40140)			
Riverside	CA	06	065
San Bernardino			071
Riverton, WY Micro (40180)			
Fremont	WY	56	013

CBSA (CBSA Code) County		FIPS Codes	
Roanoke Rapids, NC Micro (40260)			
Halifax	NC	37	083
Northampton			131
Roanoke, VA Metro (40220)			
Botetourt	VA	51	023
Craig			045
Franklin			067
Roanoke			161
Roanoke city			770
Salem city			775
Rochelle, IL Micro (40300)			
Ogle	IL	17	141
Rochester, MN Metro (40340)			
Dodge	MN	27	039
Olmsted			109
Wabasha			157
Rochester, NY Metro (40380)			
Livingston	NY	36	051
Monroe			055
Ontario			069
Orleans			073
Wayne			117
Rock Springs, WY Micro (40540)			
Sweetwater	WY	56	037
Rockford, IL Metro (40420)			
Boone	IL	17	007
Winnebago			201
Rockingham, NC Micro (40460)			
Richmond	NC	37	153
Rockland, ME Micro (40500)			
Knox	ME	23	013
Rocky Mount, NC Metro (40580)			
Edgecombe	NC	37	065
Nash			127
Rolla, MO Micro (40620)			
Phelps	MO	29	161
Rome, GA Metro (40660)			
Floyd	GA	13	115
Roseburg, OR Micro (40700)			
Douglas	OR	41	019
Roswell, NM Micro (40740)			
Chaves	NM	35	005
Ruidoso, NM Micro (40760)			
Lincoln	NM	35	027

CBSA DEFINITIONS

<table>
<tr><td colspan="4">CBSA (CBSA Code)
County</td><td>FIPS
Codes</td></tr>
</table>

Russellville, AR Micro (40780)

Pope	AR	05	115
Yell			149

Ruston, LA Micro (40820)

Jackson	LA	22	049
Lincoln			061

Rutland, VT Micro (40860)

Rutland	VT	50	021

Sacramento--Arden-Arcade--Roseville, CA Metro (40900)

El Dorado	CA	06	017
Placer			061
Sacramento			067
Yolo			113

Safford, AZ Micro (40940)

Graham	AZ	04	009
Greenlee			011

Saginaw-Saginaw Township North, MI Metro (40980)

Saginaw	MI	26	145

Salem, OR Metro (41420)

Marion	OR	41	047
Polk			053

Salina, KS Micro (41460)

Ottawa	KS	20	143
Saline			169

Salinas, CA Metro (41500)

Monterey	CA	06	053

Salisbury, MD Metro (41540)

Somerset	MD	24	039
Wicomico			045

Salisbury, NC Micro (41580)

Rowan	NC	37	159

Salt Lake City, UT Metro (41620)

Salt Lake	UT	49	035
Summit			043
Tooele			045

San Angelo, TX Metro (41660)

Irion	TX	48	235
Tom Green			451

San Antonio, TX Metro (41700)

Atascosa	TX	48	013
Bandera			019
Bexar			029
Comal			091
Guadalupe			187
Kendall			259

San Antonio, TX Metro (41700) (continued)

Medina	TX	48	325
Wilson			493

San Diego-Carlsbad-San Marcos, CA Metro (41740)

San Diego	CA	06	073

San Francisco-Oakland-Fremont, CA Metro (41860)

Alameda	CA	06	001
Contra Costa			013
Marin			041
San Francisco			075
San Mateo			081

San Jose-Sunnyvale-Santa Clara, CA Metro (41940)

San Benito	CA	06	069
Santa Clara			085

San Luis Obispo-Paso Robles, CA Metro (42020)

San Luis Obispo	CA	06	079

Sandusky, OH Metro (41780)

Erie	OH	39	043

Sanford, NC Micro (41820)

Lee	NC	37	105

Santa Barbara-Santa Maria-Goleta, CA Metro (42060)

Santa Barbara	CA	06	083

Santa Cruz-Watsonville, CA Metro (42100)

Santa Cruz	CA	06	087

Santa Fe, NM Metro (42140)

Santa Fe	NM	35	049

Santa Rosa-Petaluma, CA Metro (42220)

Sonoma	CA	06	097

Sarasota-Bradenton-Venice, FL Metro (42260)

Manatee	FL	12	081
Sarasota			115

Sault Ste. Marie, MI Micro (42300)

Chippewa	MI	26	033

Savannah, GA Metro (42340)

Bryan	GA	13	029
Chatham			051
Effingham			103

Sayre, PA Micro (42380)

Bradford	PA	42	015

Scottsbluff, NE Micro (42420)

Banner	NE	31	007
Scotts Bluff			157

CBSA DEFINITIONS

CBSA (CBSA Code) County — FIPS Codes

Scottsboro, AL Micro (42460)

County	State		
Jackson	AL	01	071

Scottsburg, IN Micro (42500)

Scott	IN	18	143

Scranton--Wilkes-Barre, PA Metro (42540)

Lackawanna	PA	42	069
Luzerne			079
Wyoming			131

Seaford, DE Micro (42580)

Sussex	DE	10	005

Searcy, AR Micro (42620)

White	AR	05	145

Seattle-Tacoma-Bellevue, WA Metro (42660)

King	WA	53	033
Pierce			053
Snohomish			061

Sebastian - Vero Beach, FL Metro (42680)

Indian River	FL	12	061

Sebring, FL Micro (42700)

Highlands	FL	12	055

Sedalia, MO Micro (42740)

Pettis	MO	29	159

Selinsgrove, PA Micro (42780)

Snyder	PA	42	109

Selma, AL Micro (42820)

Dallas	AL	01	047

Seneca Falls, NY Micro (42900)

Seneca	NY	36	099

Seneca, SC Micro (42860)

Oconee	SC	45	073

Sevierville, TN Micro (42940)

Sevier	TN	47	155

Seymour, IN Micro (42980)

Jackson	IN	18	071

Shawnee, OK Micro (43060)

Pottawatomie	OK	40	125

Sheboygan, WI Metro (43100)

Sheboygan	WI	55	117

Shelby, NC Micro (43140)

Cleveland	NC	37	045

Shelbyville, TN Micro (43180)

Bedford	TN	47	003

Shelton, WA Micro (43220)

Mason	WA	53	045

Sheridan, WY Micro (43260)

Sheridan	WY	56	033

Sherman-Denison, TX Metro (43300)

Grayson	TX	48	181

Shreveport-Bossier City, LA Metro (43340)

Bossier	LA	22	015
Caddo			017
De Soto			031

Sidney, OH Micro (43380)

Shelby	OH	39	149

Sierra Vista-Douglas, AZ Micro (43420)

Cochise	AZ	04	003

Sikeston, MO Micro (43460)

Scott	MO	29	201

Silver City, NM Micro (43500)

Grant	NM	35	017

Silverthorne, CO Micro (43540)

Summit	CO	08	117

Sioux City, IA-NE-SD Metro (43580)

Woodbury	IA	19	193
Dakota	NE	31	043
Dixon			051
Union	SD	46	127

Sioux Falls, SD Metro (43620)

Lincoln	SD	46	083
McCook			087
Minnehaha			099
Turner			125

Snyder, TX Micro (43660)

Scurry	TX	48	415

Somerset, KY Micro (43700)

Pulaski	KY	21	199

Somerset, PA Micro (43740)

Somerset	PA	42	111

South Bend-Mishawaka, IN-MI Metro (43780)

St. Joseph	IN	18	141
Cass	MI	26	027

Southern Pines-Pinehurst, NC Micro (43860)

Moore	NC	37	125

Spartanburg, SC Metro (43900)

Spartanburg	SC	45	083

Spearfish, SD Micro (43940)

Lawrence	SD	46	081

CBSA DEFINITIONS

CBSA (CBSA Code) County		FIPS Codes	
Spencer, IA Micro (43980)			
Clay	IA	19	041
Spirit Lake, IA Micro (44020)			
Dickinson	IA	19	059
Spokane, WA Metro (44060)			
Spokane	WA	53	063
Springfield, IL Metro (44100)			
Menard	IL	17	129
Sangamon			167
Springfield, MA Metro (44140)			
Franklin	MA	25	011
Hampden			013
Hampshire			015
Springfield, MO Metro (44180)			
Christian	MO	29	043
Dallas			059
Greene			077
Polk			167
Webster			225
Springfield, OH Metro (44220)			
Clark	OH	39	023
St. Cloud, MN Metro (41060)			
Benton	MN	27	009
Stearns			145
St. George, UT Metro (41100)			
Washington	UT	49	053
St. Joseph, MO-KS Metro (41140)			
Doniphan	KS	20	043
Andrew	MO	29	003
Buchanan			021
DeKalb			063
St. Louis, MO-IL Metro (41180)			
Bond	IL	17	005
Calhoun			013
Clinton			027
Jersey			083
Macoupin			117
Madison			119
Monroe			133
St. Clair			163
Franklin	MO	29	071
Jefferson			099
Lincoln			113
St. Charles			183
St. Louis			189
Warren			219
Washington			221
St. Louis city			510

CBSA (CBSA Code) County		FIPS Codes	
St. Marys, GA Micro (41220)			
Camden	GA	13	039
St. Marys, PA Micro (41260)			
Elk	PA	42	047
Starkville, MS Micro (44260)			
Oktibbeha	MS	28	105
State College, PA Metro (44300)			
Centre	PA	42	027
Statesboro, GA Micro (44340)			
Bulloch	GA	13	031
Statesville-Mooresville, NC Micro (44380)			
Iredell	NC	37	097
Staunton-Waynesboro, VA Micro (44420)			
Augusta	VA	51	015
Staunton city			790
Waynesboro city			820
Stephenville, TX Micro (44500)			
Erath	TX	48	143
Sterling, CO Micro (44540)			
Logan	CO	08	075
Sterling, IL Micro (44580)			
Whiteside	IL	17	195
Stevens Point, WI Micro (44620)			
Portage	WI	55	097
Stillwater, OK Micro (44660)			
Payne	OK	40	119
Stockton, CA Metro (44700)			
San Joaquin	CA	06	077
Storm Lake, IA Micro (44740)			
Buena Vista	IA	19	021
Sturgis, MI Micro (44780)			
St. Joseph	MI	26	149
Sulphur Springs, TX Micro (44860)			
Hopkins	TX	48	223
Summerville, GA Micro (44900)			
Chattooga	GA	13	055
Sumter, SC Metro (44940)			
Sumter	SC	45	085
Sunbury, PA Micro (44980)			
Northumberland	PA	42	097
Susanville, CA Micro (45000)			
Lassen	CA	06	035

CBSA DEFINITIONS

CBSA (CBSA Code) County		FIPS Codes	
Sweetwater, TX Micro (45020)			
Nolan	TX	48	353
Syracuse, NY Metro (45060)			
Madison	NY	36	053
Onondaga			067
Oswego			075
Tahlequah, OK Micro (45140)			
Cherokee	OK	40	021
Talladega-Sylacauga, AL Micro (45180)			
Talladega	AL	01	121
Tallahassee, FL Metro (45220)			
Gadsden	FL	12	039
Jefferson			065
Leon			073
Wakulla			129
Tallulah, LA Micro (45260)			
Madison	LA	22	065
Tampa-St. Petersburg-Clearwater, FL Metro (45300)			
Hernando	FL	12	053
Hillsborough			057
Pasco			101
Pinellas			103
Taos, NM Micro (45340)			
Taos	NM	35	055
Taylorville, IL Micro (45380)			
Christian	IL	17	021
Terre Haute, IN Metro (45460)			
Clay	IN	18	021
Sullivan			153
Vermillion			165
Vigo			167
Texarkana, TX-Texarkana, AR Metro (45500)			
Miller	AR	05	091
Bowie	TX	48	037
The Villages, FL Micro (45540)			
Sumter	FL	12	119
Thomaston, GA Micro (45580)			
Upson	GA	13	293
Thomasville, GA Micro (45620)			
Thomas	GA	13	275
Thomasville-Lexington, NC Micro (45640)			
Davidson	NC	37	057
Tiffin, OH Micro (45660)			
Seneca	OH	39	147

CBSA (CBSA Code) County		FIPS Codes	
Tifton, GA Micro (45700)			
Tift	GA	13	277
Toccoa, GA Micro (45740)			
Stephens	GA	13	257
Toledo, OH Metro (45780)			
Fulton	OH	39	051
Lucas			095
Ottawa			123
Wood			173
Topeka, KS Metro (45820)			
Jackson	KS	20	085
Jefferson			087
Osage			139
Shawnee			177
Wabaunsee			197
Torrington, CT Micro (45860)			
Litchfield	CT	09	005
Traverse City, MI Micro (45900)			
Benzie	MI	26	019
Grand Traverse			055
Kalkaska			079
Leelanau			089
Trenton-Ewing, NJ Metro (45940)			
Mercer	NJ	34	021
Troy, AL Micro (45980)			
Pike	AL	01	109
Truckee-Grass Valley, CA Micro (46020)			
Nevada	CA	06	057
Tucson, AZ Metro (46060)			
Pima	AZ	04	019
Tullahoma, TN Micro (46100)			
Coffee	TN	47	031
Franklin			051
Moore			127
Tulsa, OK Metro (46140)			
Creek	OK	40	037
Okmulgee			111
Osage			113
Pawnee			117
Rogers			131
Tulsa			143
Wagoner			145
Tupelo, MS Micro (46180)			
Itawamba	MS	28	057
Lee			081
Pontotoc			115

CBSA DEFINITIONS

CBSA (CBSA Code) County		FIPS Codes	
Tuscaloosa, AL Metro (46220)			
Greene	AL	01	063
Hale			065
Tuscaloosa			125
Tuskegee, AL Micro (46260)			
Macon	AL	01	087
Twin Falls, ID Micro (46300)			
Jerome	ID	16	053
Twin Falls			083
Tyler, TX Metro (46340)			
Smith	TX	48	423
Ukiah, CA Micro (46380)			
Mendocino	CA	06	045
Union City, TN-KY Micro (46460)			
Fulton	KY	21	075
Obion	TN	47	131
Union, SC Micro (46420)			
Union	SC	45	087
Urbana, OH Micro (46500)			
Champaign	OH	39	021
Utica-Rome, NY Metro (46540)			
Herkimer	NY	36	043
Oneida			065
Uvalde, TX Micro (46620)			
Uvalde	TX	48	463
Valdosta, GA Metro (46660)			
Brooks	GA	13	027
Echols			101
Lanier			173
Lowndes			185
Vallejo-Fairfield, CA Metro (46700)			
Solano	CA	06	095
Valley, AL Micro (46740)			
Chambers	AL	01	017
Van Wert, OH Micro (46780)			
Van Wert	OH	39	161
Vermillion, SD Micro (46820)			
Clay	SD	46	027
Vernal, UT Micro (46860)			
Uintah	UT	49	047
Vernon, TX Micro (46900)			
Wilbarger	TX	48	487
Vicksburg, MS Micro (46980)			
Warren	MS	28	149

CBSA (CBSA Code) County		FIPS Codes	
Victoria, TX Metro (47020)			
Calhoun	TX	48	057
Goliad			175
Victoria			469
Vidalia, GA Micro (47080)			
Montgomery	GA	13	209
Toombs			279
Vincennes, IN Micro (47180)			
Knox	IN	18	083
Vineland-Millville-Bridgeton, NJ Metro (47220)			
Cumberland	NJ	34	011
Virginia Beach-Norfolk-Newport News, VA-NC Metro (47260)			
Currituck	NC	37	053
Gloucester	VA	51	073
Isle of Wight			093
James City			095
Mathews			115
Surry			181
York			199
Chesapeake city			550
Hampton city			650
Newport News city			700
Norfolk city			710
Poquoson city			735
Portsmouth city			740
Suffolk city			800
Virginia Beach city			810
Williamsburg city			830
Visalia-Porterville, CA Metro (47300)			
Tulare	CA	06	107
Wabash, IN Micro (47340)			
Wabash	IN	18	169
Waco, TX Metro (47380)			
McLennan	TX	48	309
Wahpeton, ND-MN Micro (47420)			
Wilkin	MN	27	167
Richland	ND	38	077
Walla Walla, WA Micro (47460)			
Walla Walla	WA	53	071
Walterboro, SC Micro (47500)			
Colleton	SC	45	029
Wapakoneta, OH Micro (47540)			
Auglaize	OH	39	011
Warner Robins, GA Metro (47580)			
Houston	GA	13	153

CBSA DEFINITIONS

CBSA (CBSA Code) County		FIPS Codes	
Warren, PA Micro (47620)			
Warren	PA	42	123
Warrensburg, MO Micro (47660)			
Johnson	MO	29	101
Warsaw, IN Micro (47700)			
Kosciusko	IN	18	085
Washington, IN Micro (47780)			
Daviess	IN	18	027
Washington, NC Micro (47820)			
Beaufort	NC	37	013
Washington, OH Micro (47860)			
Fayette	OH	39	047
Washington-Arlington-Alexandria, DC-VA-MD-WV Metro (47900)			
District of Columbia	DC	11	001
Calvert	MD	24	009
Charles			017
Frederick			021
Montgomery			031
Prince George's			033
Arlington	VA	51	013
Clarke			043
Fairfax			059
Fauquier			061
Loudoun			107
Prince William			153
Spotsylvania			177
Stafford			179
Warren			187
Alexandria city			510
Fairfax city			600
Falls Church city			610
Fredericksburg city			630
Manassas city			683
Manassas Park city			685
Jefferson	WV	54	037
Waterloo-Cedar Falls, IA Metro (47940)			
Black Hawk	IA	19	013
Bremer			017
Grundy			075
Watertown, SD Micro (47980)			
Codington	SD	46	029
Hamlin			057
Watertown-Fort Atkinson, WI Micro (48020)			
Jefferson	WI	55	055
Watertown-Fort Drum, NY Micro (48060)			
Jefferson	NY	36	045

CBSA (CBSA Code) County		FIPS Codes	
Wauchula, FL Micro (48100)			
Hardee	FL	12	049
Wausau, WI Metro (48140)			
Marathon	WI	55	073
Waycross, GA Micro (48180)			
Pierce	GA	13	229
Ware			299
Weirton-Steubenville, WV-OH Metro (48260)			
Jefferson	OH	39	081
Brooke	WV	54	009
Hancock			029
Wenatchee, WA Metro (48300)			
Chelan	WA	53	007
Douglas			017
West Helena, AR Micro (48340)			
Phillips	AR	05	107
West Plains, MO Micro (48460)			
Howell	MO	29	091
West Point, MS Micro (48500)			
Clay	MS	28	025
Wheeling, WV-OH Metro (48540)			
Belmont	OH	39	013
Marshall	WV	54	051
Ohio			069
Whitewater, WI Micro (48580)			
Walworth	WI	55	127
Wichita Falls, TX Metro (48660)			
Archer	TX	48	009
Clay			077
Wichita			485
Wichita, KS Metro (48620)			
Butler	KS	20	015
Harvey			079
Sedgwick			173
Sumner			191
Williamsport, PA Metro (48700)			
Lycoming	PA	42	081
Willimantic, CT Micro (48740)			
Windham	CT	09	015
Williston, ND Micro (48780)			
Williams	ND	38	105
Willmar, MN Micro (48820)			
Kandiyohi	MN	27	067

CBSA DEFINITIONS

Appendix IV:
DMA Codes

Community
Sourcebook 2007
19th EDITION
of County
Demographics

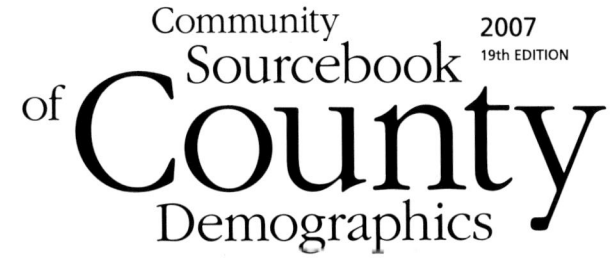

DMA CODES
Alphabetical List

DMA Name	DMA Code	DMA Name	DMA Code
Abilene-Sweetwater TX	662	Columbia SC	546
Albany GA	525	Columbia-Jefferson City MO	604
Albany-Schenectady-Troy NY	532	Columbus GA	522
Albuquerque-Santa Fe NM	790	Columbus OH	535
Alexandria LA	644	Columbus-Tupelo-West Point MS	673
Alpena MI	583	Corpus Christi TX	600
Amarillo TX	634	Dallas-Ft. Worth TX	623
Anchorage AK	743	Davenport IA-Rock Island-Moline, IL	682
Atlanta GA	524	Dayton OH	542
Augusta GA	520	Denver CO	751
Austin TX	635	Des Moines-Ames IA	679
Bakersfield CA	800	Detroit MI	505
Baltimore MD	512	Dothan AL	606
Bangor ME	537	Duluth MN-Superior, WI	676
Baton Rouge LA	716	El Paso TX (Las Cruces, NM)	765
Beaumont-Port Arthur TX	692	Elmira (Corning) NY	565
Bend OR	821	Erie PA	516
Billings MT	756	Eugene OR	801
Biloxi-Gulfport MS	746	Eureka CA	802
Binghamton NY	502	Evansville IN	649
Birmingham (Anniston & Tuscaloosa) AL	630	Fairbanks AK	745
Bluefield-Beckley-Oak Hill WV	559	Fargo-Valley City ND	724
Boise ID	757	Flint-Saginaw-Bay City MI	513
Boston MA (Manchester, NH)	506	Fresno-Visalia CA	866
Bowling Green KY	736	Ft. Myers-Naples FL	571
Buffalo NY	514	Ft. Smith-Fayetteville-Springdale-Rogers AR	670
Burlington VT-Plattsburgh, NY	523	Ft. Wayne IN	509
Butte-Bozeman MT	754	Gainesville FL	592
Casper-Riverton WY	767	Glendive MT	798
Cedar Rapids-Waterloo-Iowa City & Dubuque IA	637	Grand Junction-Montrose CO	773
Champaign & Springfield-Decatur IL	648	Grand Rapids-Kalamazoo-Battle Creek MI	563
Charleston SC	519	Great Falls MT	755
Charleston-Huntington WV	564	Green Bay-Appleton WI	658
Charlotte NC	517	Greensboro-High Point-Winston Salem NC	518
Charlottesville VA	584	Greenville-New Bern-Washington NC	545
Chattanooga TN	575	Greenville-Spartanburg SC-Asheville, NC-Anderson, SC	567
Cheyenne WY-Scottsbluff, NE	759	Greenwood-Greenville MS	647
Chicago IL	602	Harlingen-Weslaco-Brownsville-Mcallen TX	636
Chico-Redding CA	868	Harrisburg-Lancaster-Lebanon-York PA	566
Cincinnati OH	515	Harrisonburg VA	569
Clarksburg-Weston WV	598	Hartford & New Haven CT	533
Cleveland-Akron (Canton) OH	510		
Colorado Springs-Pueblo CO	752		

DMA CODES
Alphabetical List

DMA Name	DMA Code	DMA Name	DMA Code
Hattiesburg-Laurel MS	710	Monroe LA-El Dorado, AR	628
Helena MT	766	Monterey-Salinas CA	828
Honolulu HI	744	Montgomery-Selma, AL	698
Houston TX	618	Myrtle Beach-Florence SC	570
Huntsville-Decatur (Florence) AL	691	Nashville TN	659
Idaho Falls-Pocatello ID	758	New Orleans LA	622
Indianapolis IN	527	New York NY	501
Jackson MS	718	Norfolk-Portsmouth-Newport News VA	544
Jackson TN	639	North Platte NE	740
Jacksonville FL	561	Odessa-Midland TX	633
Johnstown-Altoona PA	574	Oklahoma City OK	650
Jonesboro AR	734	Omaha NE	652
Joplin MO-Pittsburg, KS	603	Orlando-Daytona Beach-Melbourne FL	534
Juneau AK	747	Ottumwa IA-Kirksville, MO	631
Kansas City MO	616	Paducah KY-Cape Girardeau, MO-Harrisburg, IL	632
Knoxville TN	557	Palm Springs CA	804
La Crosse-Eau Claire WI	702	Panama City FL	656
Lafayette IN	582	Parkersburg WV	597
Lafayette LA	642	Peoria-Bloomington IL	675
Lake Charles LA	643	Philadelphia PA	504
Lansing MI	551	Phoenix (Prescott) AZ	753
Laredo TX	749	Pittsburgh PA	508
Las Vegas NV	839	Portland OR	820
Lexington KY	541	Portland-Auburn ME	500
Lima OH	558	Presque Isle ME	552
Lincoln & Hastings-Kearney NE	722	Providence RI-New Bedford, MA	521
Little Rock-Pine Bluff AR	693	Quincy IL-Hannibal, MO-Keokuk, IA	717
Los Angeles CA	803	Raleigh-Durham (Fayetteville) NC	560
Louisville KY	529	Rapid City SD	764
Lubbock TX	651	Reno NV	811
Macon GA	503	Richmond-Petersburg VA	556
Madison WI	669	Roanoke-Lynchburg VA	573
Mankato MN	737	Rochester NY	538
Marquette MI	553	Rochester MN-Mason City,IA-Austin,MN	611
Medford-Klamath Falls OR	813	Rockford IL	610
Memphis TN	640	Sacramento-Stockton-Modesto CA	862
Meridian MS	711	Salisbury MD	576
Miami-Ft. Lauderdale FL	528	Salt Lake City UT	770
Milwaukee WI	617	San Angelo TX	661
Minneapolis-St. Paul MN	613	San Antonio TX	641
Minot-Bismarck-Dickinson (Williston), ND	687	San Diego CA	825
Missoula MT	762	San Francisco-Oakland-San Jose CA	807
Mobile AL-Pensacola (Ft. Walton Beach), FL	686	Santa Barbara-Santa Maria-San Luis Obispo CA	855

DMA CODES
Alphabetical List

DMA Name	DMA Code	DMA Name	DMA Code
Savannah GA	507	Tulsa OK	671
Seattle-Tacoma WA	819	Twin Falls ID	760
Sherman TX-Ada, OK	657	Tyler-Longview (Lufkin & Nacogdoches) TX	709
Shreveport LA	612	Utica NY	526
Sioux City IA	624	Victoria TX	626
Sioux Falls (Mitchell) SD	725	Waco-Temple-Bryan TX	625
South Bend-Elkhart IN	588	Washington DC (Hagerstown MD)	511
Spokane WA	881	Watertown NY	549
Springfield MO	619	Wausau-Rhinelander WI	705
Springfield-Holyoke MA	543	West Palm Beach-Fort Pierce FL	548
St. Joseph MO	638	Wheeling WV-Steubenville, OH	554
St. Louis MO	609	Wichita Falls TX & Lawton, OK	627
Syracuse NY	555	Wichita-Hutchinson KS Plus	678
Tallahassee FL-Thomasville, GA	530	Wilkes Barre-Scranton PA	577
Tampa-St. Petersburg (Sarasota) FL	539	Wilmington NC	550
Terre Haute IN	581	Yakima-Pasco-Richland-Kennewick WA	810
Toledo OH	547	Youngstown OH	536
Topeka KS	605	Yuma AZ-El Centro, CA	771
Traverse City-Cadillac MI	540	Zanesville OH	596
Tri-Cities TN-VA	531		
Tucson (Sierra Vista) AZ	789		

DMA CODES
Numerical List

DMA Name	DMA Code	DMA Name	DMA Code
Portland-Auburn ME	500	Norfolk-Portsmouth-Newport News VA	544
New York NY	501	Greenville-New Bern-Washington NC	545
Binghamton NY	502	Columbia SC	546
Macon GA	503	Toledo OH	547
Philadelphia PA	504	West Palm Beach-Fort Pierce FL	548
Detroit MI	505	Watertown NY	549
Boston MA (Manchester, NH)	506	Wilmington NC	550
Savannah GA	507	Lansing MI	551
Pittsburgh PA	508	Presque Isle ME	552
Ft. Wayne IN	509	Marquette MI	553
Cleveland-Akron (Canton) OH	510	Wheeling WV-Steubenville, OH	554
Washington DC (Hagerstown MD)	511	Syracuse NY	555
Baltimore MD	512	Richmond-Petersburg VA	556
Flint-Saginaw-Bay City MI	513	Knoxville TN	557
Buffalo NY	514	Lima OH	558
Cincinnati OH	515	Bluefield-Beckley-Oak Hill WV	559
Erie PA	516	Raleigh-Durham (Fayetteville) NC	560
Charlotte NC	517	Jacksonville FL	561
Greensboro-High Point-Winston Salem NC	518	Grand Rapids-Kalamazoo-Battle Creek MI	563
Charleston SC	519	Charleston-Huntington WV	564
Augusta GA	520	Elmira (Corning) NY	565
Providence RI-New Bedford, MA	521	Harrisburg-Lancaster-Lebanon-York PA	566
Columbus GA	522	Greenville-Spartanburg SC-Asheville, NC-Anderson, SC	567
Burlington VT-Plattsburgh, NY	523	Harrisonburg VA	569
Atlanta GA	524	Myrtle Beach-Florence SC	570
Albany GA	525	Ft. Myers-Naples FL	571
Utica NY	526	Roanoke-Lynchburg VA	573
Indianapolis IN	527	Johnstown-Altoona PA	574
Miami-Ft. Lauderdale FL	528	Chattanooga TN	575
Louisville KY	529	Salisbury MD	576
Tallahassee FL-Thomasville, GA	530	Wilkes Barre-Scranton PA	577
Tri-Cities TN-VA	531	Terre Haute IN	581
Albany-Schenectady-Troy NY	532	Lafayette IN	582
Hartford & New Haven CT	533	Alpena MI	583
Orlando-Daytona Beach-Melbourne FL	534	Charlottesville VA	584
Columbus OH	535	South Bend-Elkhart IN	588
Youngstown OH	536	Gainesville FL	592
Bangor ME	537	Zanesville OH	596
Rochester NY	538	Parkersburg WV	597
Tampa-St. Petersburg (Sarasota) FL	539	Clarksburg-Weston WV	598
Traverse City-Cadillac MI	540	Corpus Christi TX	600
Lexington KY	541	Chicago IL	602
Dayton OH	542	Joplin MO-Pittsburg, KS	603
Springfield-Holyoke MA	543		

DMA CODES
Numerical List

DMA Name	DMA Code	DMA Name	DMA Code
Columbia-Jefferson City MO	604	Sherman TX-Ada, OK	657
Topeka KS	605	Green Bay-Appleton WI	658
Dothan AL	606	Nashville TN	659
St. Louis MO	609	San Angelo TX	661
Rockford IL	610	Abilene-Sweetwater TX	662
Rochester MN-Mason City,IA-Austin,MN	611	Madison WI	669
Shreveport LA	612	Ft. Smith-Fayetteville-Springdale-Rogers AR	670
Minneapolis-St. Paul MN	613	Tulsa OK	671
Kansas City MO	616	Columbus-Tupelo-West Point MS	673
Milwaukee WI	617	Peoria-Bloomington IL	675
Houston TX	618	Duluth MN-Superior, WI	676
Springfield MO	619	Wichita-Hutchinson KS Plus	678
New Orleans LA	622	Des Moines-Ames IA	679
Dallas-Ft. Worth TX	623	Davenport IA-Rock Island-Moline, IL	682
Sioux City IA	624	Mobile AL-Pensacola (Ft. Walton Beach), FL	686
Waco-Temple-Bryan TX	625	Minot-Bismarck-Dickinson (Williston), ND	687
Victoria TX	626	Huntsville-Decatur (Florence) AL	691
Wichita Falls TX & Lawton, OK	627	Beaumont-Port Arthur TX	692
Monroe LA-El Dorado, AR	628	Little Rock-Pine Bluff AR	693
Birmingham (Anniston & Tuscaloosa) AL	630	Montgomery-Selma, AL	698
Ottumwa IA-Kirksville, MO	631	La Crosse-Eau Claire WI	702
Paducah KY-Cape Girardeau, MO-Harrisburg, IL	632	Wausau-Rhinelander WI	705
Odessa-Midland TX	633	Tyler-Longview (Lufkin & Nacogdoches) TX	709
Amarillo TX	634	Hattiesburg-Laurel MS	710
Austin TX	635	Meridian MS	711
Harlingen-Weslaco-Brownsville-Mcallen TX	636	Baton Rouge LA	716
Cedar Rapids-Waterloo-Iowa City & Dubuque IA	637	Quincy IL-Hannibal, MO-Keokuk, IA	717
St. Joseph MO	638	Jackson MS	718
Jackson TN	639	Lincoln & Hastings-Kearney NE	722
Memphis TN	640	Fargo-Valley City ND	724
San Antonio TX	641	Sioux Falls (Mitchell) SD	725
Lafayette LA	642	Jonesboro AR	734
Lake Charles LA	643	Bowling Green KY	736
Alexandria LA	644	Mankato MN	737
Greenwood-Greenville MS	647	North Platte NE	740
Champaign & Springfield-Decatur IL	648	Anchorage AK	743
Evansville IN	649	Honolulu HI	744
Oklahoma City OK	650	Fairbanks AK	745
Lubbock TX	651	Biloxi-Gulfport MS	746
Omaha NE	652	Juneau AK	747
Panama City FL	656	Laredo TX	749
		Denver CO	751
		Colorado Springs-Pueblo CO	752

DMA CODES
Numerical List

DMA Name	DMA Code	DMA Name	DMA Code
Phoenix (Prescott) AZ	753	Eugene OR	801
Butte-Bozeman MT	754	Eureka CA	802
Great Falls MT	755	Los Angeles CA	803
Billings MT	756	Palm Springs CA	804
Boise ID	757	San Francisco-Oakland-San Jose CA	807
Idaho Falls-Pocatello ID	758	Yakima-Pasco-Richland-Kennewick WA	810
Cheyenne WY-Scottsbluff, NE	759	Reno NV	811
Twin Falls ID	760	Medford-Klamath Falls OR	813
Missoula MT	762	Seattle-Tacoma WA	819
Rapid City SD	764	Portland OR	820
El Paso TX (Las Cruces, NM)	765	Bend OR	821
Helena MT	766	San Diego CA	825
Casper-Riverton WY	767	Monterey-Salinas CA	828
Salt Lake City UT	770	Las Vegas NV	839
Yuma AZ-El Centro, CA	771	Santa Barbara-Santa Maria-San Luis Obispo CA	855
Grand Junction-Montrose CO	773	Sacramento-Stockton-Modesto CA	862
Tucson (Sierra Vista) AZ	789	Fresno-Visalia CA	866
Albuquerque-Santa Fe NM	790	Chico-Redding CA	868
Glendive MT	798	Spokane WA	881
Bakersfield CA	800		

Appendix V:
DMA Definitions

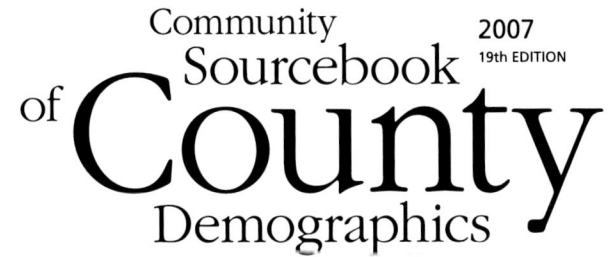

Community
Sourcebook
2007
19th EDITION
of County
Demographics

DMA DEFINITIONS

DMA (DMA Code) County			FIPS Codes		DMA (DMA Code) County			FIPS Codes
Abilene-Sweetwater TX (662)					**Albuquerque-Santa Fe NM (790)** (continued)			
Brown	TX	48	049		Montezuma			083
Callahan			059		Bernalillo	NM	35	001
Coleman			083		Catron			003
Eastland			133		Chaves			005
Fisher			151		Cibola			006
Haskell			207		Colfax			007
Jones			253		De Baca			011
Knox			275		Eddy			015
Mitchell			335		Grant			017
Nolan			353		Guadalupe			019
Runnels			399		Harding			021
Scurry			415		Hidalgo			023
Shackelford			417		Lea (part)			025
Stephens			429		Lincoln			027
Stonewall			433		Los Alamos			028
Taylor			441		Luna			029
Throckmorton			447		McKinley			031
					Mora			033
Albany GA (525)					Otero			035
Atkinson	GA	13	003		Rio Arriba			039
Baker			007		Sandoval			043
Ben Hill			017		San Juan			045
Berrien			019		San Miguel			047
Calhoun			037		Santa Fe			049
Coffee			069		Sierra			051
Colquitt			071		Socorro			053
Cook			075		Taos			055
Crisp			081		Torrance			057
Dougherty			095		Valencia			061
Irwin			155					
Lee			177		**Alexandria LA (644)**			
Mitchell			205		Avoyelles	LA	22	009
Terrell			273		Grant			043
Tift			277		Rapides			079
Turner			287		Vernon			115
Worth			321					
					Alpena MI (583)			
Albany-Schenectady-Troy NY (532)					Alcona	MI	26	001
Berkshire	MA	25	003		Alpena			007
Albany	NY	36	001					
Columbia			021		**Amarillo TX (634)**			
Fulton			035		Curry	NM	35	009
Greene			039		Quay			037
Hamilton			041		Roosevelt			041
Montgomery			057		Union			059
Rensselaer			083		Beaver	OK	40	007
Saratoga			091		Cimarron			025
Schenectady			093		Texas			139
Schoharie			095		Armstrong	TX	48	011
Warren			113		Briscoe			045
Washington			115		Carson			065
Bennington	VT	50	003		Castro			069
					Childress			075
Albuquerque-Santa Fe NM (790)					Collingsworth			087
Apache (part)	AZ	04	001		Cottle			101
La Plata	CO	08	067		Dallam			111

DMA DEFINITIONS

DMA (DMA Code) County			FIPS Codes
Amarillo TX (634) (continued)			
Deaf Smith			117
Donley			129
Gray			179
Hall			191
Hansford			195
Hartley			205
Hemphill			211
Hutchinson			233
Lipscomb			295
Moore			341
Ochiltree			357
Oldham			359
Parmer			369
Potter			375
Randall			381
Roberts			393
Sherman			421
Swisher			437
Wheeler			483
Anchorage AK (743)			
Anchorage Municipality 020	AK	02	
Kenai Peninsula			122
Matanuska-Susitna			170
Atlanta GA (524)			
Cleburne	AL	01	029
Randolph			111
Banks	GA	13	011
Barrow			013
Bartow			015
Butts			035
Carroll			045
Chattooga			055
Cherokee			057
Clarke			059
Clayton			063
Cobb			067
Coweta			077
Dawson			085
DeKalb			089
Douglas			097
Fannin			111
Fayette			113
Floyd			115
Forsyth			117
Fulton			121
Gilmer			123
Gordon			129
Greene			133
Gwinnett			135
Habersham			137
Hall			139
Haralson			143
Heard			149
Henry			151

DMA (DMA Code) County			FIPS Codes
Atlanta GA (524) (continued)			
Jackson			157
Jasper			159
Lamar			171
Lumpkin			187
Madison			195
Meriwether			199
Morgan			211
Newton			217
Oconee			219
Oglethorpe			221
Paulding			223
Pickens			227
Pike			231
Polk			233
Putnam			237
Rabun			241
Rockdale			247
Spalding			255
Towns			281
Troup			285
Union			291
Upson			293
Walton			297
White			311
Clay	NC	37	043
Augusta GA (520)			
Burke	GA	13	033
Columbia			073
Emanuel			107
Glascock			125
Jefferson			163
Jenkins			165
Lincoln			181
McDuffie			189
Richmond			245
Taliaferro			265
Warren			301
Wilkes			317
Aiken	SC	45	003
Allendale			005
Bamberg			009
Barnwell			011
Edgefield			037
McCormick			065
Austin TX (635)			
Bastrop	TX	48	021
Blanco			031
Burnet			053
Caldwell			055
Fayette			149
Gillespie			171
Hays			209
Lee			287
Llano			299

DMA DEFINITIONS

DMA (DMA Code) County			FIPS Codes	DMA (DMA Code) County			FIPS Codes
Austin TX (635) (continued)				**Billings MT (756)** (continued)			
Mason			319	Carbon			009
Travis			453	Custer			017
Williamson			491	Garfield			033
				Golden Valley			037
Bakersfield CA (800)				Meagher			059
Kern (part)	CA	06	029	Musselshell			065
				Park			067
Baltimore MD (512)				Petroleum			069
Anne Arundel	MD	24	003	Powder River			075
Baltimore			005	Rosebud			087
Caroline			011	Stillwater			095
Carroll			013	Sweet Grass			097
Cecil			015	Treasure			103
Harford			025	Wheatland			107
Howard			027	Yellowstone			111
Kent			029	Big Horn	WY	56	003
Queen Anne's			035	Park			029
Talbot			041				
Baltimore city			510	**Biloxi-Gulfport MS (746)**			
				George	MS	28	039
Bangor ME (537)				Harrison			047
Hancock	ME	23	009	Jackson			059
Penobscot			019	Stone			131
Piscataquis			021				
Somerset			025	**Binghamton NY (502)**			
Waldo			027	Broome	NY	36	007
Washington			029	Chenango			017
				Delaware			025
Baton Rouge LA (716)				Tioga			107
Ascension	LA	22	005				
Assumption			007	**Birmingham (Anniston & Tuscaloosa) AL (630)**			
East Baton Rouge			033	Bibb	AL	01	007
East Feliciana			037	Blount			009
Iberville			047	Calhoun			015
Livingston			063	Cherokee			019
Pointe Coupee			077	Chilton			021
St. Helena			091	Clay			027
St. Mary			101	Coosa			037
West Baton Rouge			121	Cullman			043
West Feliciana			125	Etowah			055
Amite	MS	28	005	Fayette			057
Wilkinson			157	Greene			063
				Hale			065
Beaumont-Port Arthur TX (692)				Jefferson			073
Hardin	TX	48	199	Marion			093
Jasper			241	Pickens			107
Jefferson			245	St. Clair			115
Newton			351	Shelby			117
Orange			361	Talladega			121
Tyler			457	Tuscaloosa			125
				Walker			127
Bend OR (821)				Winston			133
Deschutes	OR	41	017				
				Bluefield-Beckley-Oak Hill WV (559)			
Billings MT (756)				Tazewell	VA	51	185
Big Horn	MT	30	003	Fayette	WV	54	019

DMA DEFINITIONS

DMA (DMA Code) County			FIPS Codes
Bluefield-Beckley-Oak Hill WV (559)			
(continued)			
Greenbrier			025
McDowell			047
Mercer			055
Monroe			063
Pocahontas			075
Raleigh			081
Summers			089
Wyoming			109
Boise ID (757)			
Ada	ID	16	001
Adams			003
Boise			015
Camas			025
Canyon			027
Elmore			039
Gem			045
Owyhee			073
Payette			075
Valley			085
Washington			087
Malheur	OR	41	045
Boston MA (Manchester, NH) (506)			
Barnstable	MA	25	001
Dukes			007
Essex			009
Middlesex			017
Nantucket			019
Norfolk			021
Plymouth			023
Suffolk			025
Worcester			027
Belknap	NH	33	001
Cheshire			005
Hillsborough			011
Merrimack			013
Rockingham			015
Strafford			017
Windham	VT	50	025
Bowling Green KY (736)			
Barren	KY	21	009
Butler			031
Edmonson			061
Hart			099
Metcalfe			169
Warren			227
Buffalo NY (514)			
Allegany	NY	36	003
Cattaraugus			009
Chautauqua			013
Erie			029
Genesee			037
Niagara			063

DMA (DMA Code) County			FIPS Codes
Buffalo NY (514) (continued)			
Orleans			073
Wyoming			121
McKean	PA	42	083
Potter			105
Burlington VT-Plattsburgh, NY (523)			
Grafton	NH	33	009
Sullivan			019
Clinton	NY	36	019
Essex			031
Franklin			033
Addison	VT	50	001
Caledonia			005
Chittenden			007
Essex			009
Franklin			011
Grand Isle			013
Lamoille			015
Orange			017
Orleans			019
Rutland			021
Washington			023
Windsor			027
Butte-Bozeman MT (754)			
Beaverhead	MT	30	001
Deer Lodge			023
Gallatin			031
Jefferson			043
Madison			057
Powell			077
Silver Bow			093
Casper-Riverton WY (767)			
Converse	WY	56	009
Fremont			013
Hot Springs			017
Natrona			025
Washakie			043
Cedar Rapids-Waterloo-Iowa City & Dubuque IA (637)			
Allamakee	IA	19	005
Benton			011
Black Hawk			013
Bremer			017
Buchanan			019
Butler			023
Cedar			031
Chickasaw			037
Clayton			043
Delaware			055
Dubuque			061
Fayette			065
Grundy			075
Iowa			095

DMA DEFINITIONS

DMA (DMA Code) County			FIPS Codes

Cedar Rapids-Waterloo-Iowa City & Dubuque IA (637) (continued)

Johnson			103
Jones			105
Keokuk			107
Linn			113
Tama			171
Washington			183
Winneshiek			191

Champaign & Springfield-Decatur IL (648)

Cass	IL	17	017
Champaign			019
Christian			021
Coles			029
Cumberland			035
De Witt			039
Douglas			041
Edgar			045
Effingham			049
Ford			053
Iroquois			075
Logan			107
Macon			115
Menard			129
Morgan			137
Moultrie			139
Piatt			147
Sangamon			167
Shelby			173
Vermilion			183

Charleston SC (519)

Berkeley	SC	45	015
Charleston			019
Colleton			029
Dorchester			035
Georgetown			043
Williamsburg			089

Charleston-Huntington WV (564)

Boyd	KY	21	019
Carter			043
Elliott			063
Floyd			071
Greenup			089
Johnson			115
Lawrence			127
Lewis			135
Martin			159
Pike			195
Gallia	OH	39	053
Jackson			079
Lawrence			087
Meigs			105
Scioto			145
Vinton			163

Charleston-Huntington WV (564) (continued)

Boone	WV	54	005
Braxton			007
Cabell			011
Calhoun			013
Clay			015
Jackson			035
Kanawha			039
Lincoln			043
Logan			045
Mason			053
Mingo			059
Nicholas			067
Putnam			079
Roane			087
Wayne			099
Wirt			105

Charlotte NC (517)

Alexander	NC	37	003
Anson			007
Ashe			009
Avery			011
Burke			023
Cabarrus			025
Caldwell			027
Catawba			035
Cleveland			045
Gaston			071
Iredell			097
Lincoln			109
Mecklenburg			119
Richmond			153
Rowan			159
Stanly			167
Union			179
Watauga			189
Chester	SC	45	023
Chesterfield			025
Lancaster			057
York			091

Charlottesville VA (584)

Albemarle	VA	51	003
Fluvanna			065
Greene			079
Madison			113
Orange			137
Charlottesville city			540

Chattanooga TN (575)

Catoosa	GA	13	047
Dade			083
Murray			213
Walker			295
Whitfield			313
Cherokee	NC	37	039

DMA DEFINITIONS

DMA (DMA Code) County			FIPS Codes		DMA (DMA Code) County			FIPS Codes
Chattanooga TN (575) (continued)					**Cincinnati OH (515)** (continued)			
Bledsoe	TN	47	007		Mason			161
Bradley			011		Owen			187
Grundy			061		Pendleton			191
Hamilton			065		Robertson			201
McMinn			107		Adams	OH	39	001
Marion			115		Brown			015
Meigs			121		Butler			017
Polk			139		Clermont			025
Rhea			143		Clinton			027
Sequatchie			153		Hamilton			061
					Highland			071
Cheyenne WY-Scottsbluff NE (759)					Warren			165
Scotts Bluff	NE	31	157					
Sioux			165		**Clarksburg-Weston WV (598)**			
Goshen	WY	56	015		Barbour	WV	54	001
Laramie			021		Doddridge			017
					Gilmer			021
Chicago IL (602)					Harrison			033
Cook	IL	17	031		Lewis			041
DeKalb			037		Marion			049
DuPage			043		Randolph			083
Grundy			063		Ritchie			085
Kane			089		Taylor			091
Kankakee			091		Tucker			093
Kendall			093		Upshur			097
Lake			097		Webster			101
La Salle			099					
McHenry			111		**Cleveland-Akron (Canton) OH (510)**			
Will			197		Ashland	OH	39	005
Jasper	IN	18	073		Ashtabula			007
Lake			089		Carroll			019
LaPorte			091		Cuyahoga			035
Newton			111		Erie			043
Porter			127		Geauga			055
					Holmes			075
Chico-Redding CA (868)					Huron			077
Butte	CA	06	007		Lake			085
Glenn			021		Lorain			093
Modoc			049		Medina			103
Shasta			089		Portage			133
Tehama			103		Richland			139
Trinity			105		Stark			151
					Summit			153
Cincinnati OH (515)					Tuscarawas			157
Dearborn	IN	18	029		Wayne			169
Franklin			047					
Ohio			115		**Colorado Springs-Pueblo CO (752)**			
Ripley			137		Baca	CO	08	009
Switzerland			155		Bent			011
Union			161		Crowley			025
Boone	KY	21	015		Custer			027
Bracken			023		El Paso			041
Campbell			037		Fremont			043
Gallatin			077		Huerfano			055
Grant			081		Kiowa			061
Kenton			117		Las Animas			071

DMA DEFINITIONS

DMA (DMA Code) County			FIPS Codes
Colorado Springs-Pueblo CO (752)			
(continued)			
Otero			089
Pueblo			101
Teller			119
Columbia SC (546)			
Calhoun	SC	45	017
Clarendon			027
Fairfield			039
Kershaw			055
Lee			061
Lexington			063
Newberry			071
Orangeburg			075
Richland			079
Saluda			081
Sumter			085
Columbia-Jefferson City MO (604)			
Audrain	MO	29	007
Boone			019
Callaway			027
Chariton			041
Cole			051
Cooper			053
Howard			089
Maries			125
Miller			131
Moniteau			135
Montgomery			139
Morgan			141
Osage			151
Randolph			175
Columbus GA (522)			
Barbour	AL	01	005
Chambers			017
Lee			081
Russell			113
Chattahoochee	GA	13	053
Clay			061
Harris			145
Marion			197
Muscogee			215
Quitman			239
Randolph			243
Schley			249
Stewart			259
Sumter			261
Talbot			263
Taylor			269
Webster			307
Columbus OH (535)			
Athens	OH	39	009
Coshocton			031
Crawford			033

DMA (DMA Code) County			FIPS Codes
Columbus OH (535) (continued)			
Delaware			041
Fairfield			045
Fayette			047
Franklin			049
Guernsey			059
Hardin			065
Hocking			073
Knox			083
Licking			089
Madison			097
Marion			101
Morgan			115
Morrow			117
Perry			127
Pickaway			129
Pike			131
Ross			141
Union			159
Columbus-Tupelo-West Point MS (673)			
Lamar	AL	01	075
Calhoun	MS	28	013
Chickasaw			017
Choctaw			019
Clay			025
Itawamba			057
Lee			081
Lowndes			087
Monroe			095
Montgomery			097
Noxubee			103
Oktibbeha			105
Pontotoc			115
Prentiss			117
Tishomingo			141
Union			145
Webster			155
Winston			159
Yalobusha			161
Corpus Christi TX (600)			
Aransas	TX	48	007
Bee			025
Brooks			047
Duval			131
Jim Hogg			247
Jim Wells			249
Kenedy			261
Kleberg			273
Live Oak			297
Nueces			355
Refugio			391
San Patricio			409
Dallas-Ft. Worth TX (623)			
Anderson	TX	48	001

DMA DEFINITIONS

DMA (DMA Code) County			FIPS Codes
Dallas-Ft. Worth TX (623) (continued)			
Bosque			035
Collin			085
Comanche			093
Cooke			097
Dallas			113
Delta			119
Denton			121
Ellis			139
Erath			143
Fannin			147
Freestone			161
Hamilton			193
Henderson			213
Hill			217
Hood			221
Hopkins			223
Hunt			231
Jack			237
Johnson			251
Kaufman			257
Lamar			277
Navarro			349
Palo Pinto			363
Parker			367
Rains			379
Red River			387
Rockwall			397
Somervell			425
Tarrant			439
Van Zandt			467
Wise			497
Davenport IA-Rock Island-Moline, IL (682)			
Bureau	IL	17	011
Carroll			015
Henderson			071
Henry			073
Jo Daviess			085
Knox			095
Mercer			131
Rock Island			161
Warren			187
Whiteside			195
Clinton	IA	19	045
Des Moines			057
Henry			087
Jackson			097
Louisa			115
Muscatine			139
Scott			163
Dayton OH (542)			
Wayne	IN	18	177
Auglaize	OH	39	011
Champaign			021
Clark			023

DMA (DMA Code) County			FIPS Codes
Dayton OH (542) (continued)			
Darke			037
Greene			057
Logan			091
Mercer			107
Miami			109
Montgomery			113
Preble			135
Shelby			149
Denver CO (751)			
Adams	CO	08	001
Alamosa			003
Arapahoe			005
Archuleta			007
Boulder			013
Broomfield			014
Chaffee			015
Cheyenne			017
Clear Creek			019
Conejos			021
Costilla			023
Delta			029
Denver			031
Dolores			033
Douglas			035
Eagle			037
Elbert			039
Garfield			045
Gilpin			047
Grand			049
Gunnison			051
Hinsdale			053
Jackson			057
Jefferson			059
Kit Carson			063
Lake			065
Larimer			069
Lincoln			073
Logan			075
Mineral			079
Moffat			081
Morgan			087
Ouray			091
Park			093
Phillips			095
Pitkin			097
Prowers			099
Rio Blanco			103
Rio Grande			105
Routt			107
Saguache			109
San Juan			111
Sedgwick			115
Summit			117
Washington			121
Weld			123

DMA DEFINITIONS

DMA (DMA Code) County			FIPS Codes
Denver CO (751) (continued)			
Yuma			125
Arthur	NE	31	005
Banner			007
Box Butte			013
Cherry			031
Cheyenne			033
Dawes			045
Deuel			049
Garden			069
Grant			075
Hooker			091
Keith			101
Kimball			105
Sheridan			161
Albany	WY	56	001
Campbell			005
Carbon			007
Johnson			019
Niobrara			027
Platte			031
Des Moines-Ames IA (679)			
Adair	IA	19	001
Adams			003
Appanoose			007
Audubon			009
Boone			015
Calhoun			025
Carroll			027
Clarke			039
Dallas			049
Decatur			053
Franklin			069
Greene			073
Guthrie			077
Hamilton			079
Hardin			083
Humboldt			091
Jasper			099
Kossuth			109
Lucas			117
Madison			121
Mahaska			123
Marion			125
Marshall			127
Monroe			135
Pocahontas			151
Polk			153
Poweshiek			157
Ringgold			159
Story			169
Taylor			173
Union			175
Warren			181
Wayne			185
Webster			187

DMA (DMA Code) County			FIPS Codes
Des Moines-Ames IA (679) (continued)			
Wright			197
Detroit MI (505)			
Lapeer	MI	26	087
Livingston			093
Macomb			099
Monroe			115
Oakland			125
St. Clair			147
Sanilac			151
Washtenaw			161
Wayne			163
Dothan AL (606)			
Coffee	AL	01	031
Dale			045
Geneva			061
Henry			067
Houston			069
Early	GA	13	099
Duluth MN-Superior, WI (676)			
Gogebic	MI	26	053
Carlton	MN	27	017
Cook			031
Itasca			061
Koochiching			071
Lake			075
St. Louis			137
Ashland	WI	55	003
Bayfield			007
Douglas			031
Iron			051
Sawyer			113
El Paso TX (Las Cruces, NM) (765)			
Dona Ana	NM	35	013
Culberson	TX	48	109
El Paso			141
Hudspeth			229
Elmira (Corning) NY (565)			
Chemung	NY	36	015
Schuyler			097
Steuben			101
Tioga	PA	42	117
Erie PA (516)			
Crawford	PA	42	039
Erie			049
Warren			123
Eugene OR (801)			
Benton	OR	41	003
Coos			011
Douglas			019

DMA DEFINITIONS

DMA (DMA Code) County			FIPS Codes
Eugene OR (801) (continued)			
Lane			039
Eureka CA (802)			
Del Norte	CA	06	015
Humboldt			023
Evansville IN (649)			
Edwards	IL	17	047
Wabash			185
Wayne			191
White			193
Dubois	IN	18	037
Gibson			051
Perry			123
Pike			125
Posey			129
Spencer			147
Vanderburgh			163
Warrick			173
Daviess	KY	21	059
Hancock			091
Henderson			101
Hopkins			107
McLean			149
Muhlenberg			177
Ohio			183
Union			225
Webster			233
Fairbanks AK (745)			
Fairbanks North Star	AK	02	090
Fargo-Valley City ND (724)			
Becker	MN	27	005
Clay			027
Clearwater			029
Kittson			069
Lake of the Woods			077
Mahnomen			087
Marshall			089
Norman			107
Otter Tail			111
Pennington			113
Polk			119
Red Lake			125
Roseau			135
Wilkin			167
Barnes	ND	38	003
Benson			005
Cass			017
Cavalier			019
Dickey			021
Eddy			027
Foster			031
Grand Forks			035
Griggs			039

DMA (DMA Code) County			FIPS Codes
Fargo-Valley City ND (724) (continued)			
LaMoure			045
Nelson			063
Pembina			067
Ramsey			071
Ransom			073
Richland			077
Sargent			081
Steele			091
Stutsman			093
Towner			095
Traill			097
Walsh			099
Flint-Saginaw-Bay City MI (513)			
Arenac	MI	26	011
Bay			017
Genesee			049
Gladwin			051
Gratiot			057
Huron			063
Iosco			069
Isabella			073
Midland			111
Ogemaw			129
Saginaw			145
Shiawassee			155
Tuscola			157
Fresno-Visalia CA (866)			
Fresno	CA	06	019
Kings			031
Madera			039
Mariposa			043
Merced			047
Tulare			107
Ft. Myers-Naples FL (571)			
Charlotte	FL	12	015
Collier			021
DeSoto			027
Glades			043
Hendry			051
Lee			071
Ft. Smith-Fayetteville-Springdale-Rogers AR (670)			
Benton	AR	05	007
Crawford			033
Franklin			047
Johnson			071
Logan			083
Madison			087
Scott			127
Sebastian			131
Washington			143
Le Flore	OK	40	079

DMA DEFINITIONS

DMA (DMA Code) County			FIPS Codes	DMA (DMA Code) County			FIPS Codes
Ft. Smith-Fayetteville-Springdale-Rogers AR				**Great Falls MT (755)** (continued)			
(670) (continued)				Judith Basin			045
Sequoyah			135	Liberty			051
				Phillips			071
Ft. Wayne IN (509)				Pondera			073
Adams	IN	18	001	Teton			099
Allen			003	Toole			101
DeKalb			033	Valley			105
Huntington			069				
Jay			075	**Green Bay-Appleton WI (658)**			
Noble			113	Menominee	MI	26	109
Steuben			151	Brown	WI	55	009
Wabash			169	Calumet			015
Wells			179	Door			029
Whitley			183	Fond du Lac			039
Paulding	OH	39	125	Green Lake			047
Van Wert			161	Kewaunee			061
				Manitowoc			071
Gainesville FL (592)				Marinette			075
Alachua	FL	12	001	Menominee			078
Dixie			029	Oconto			083
Gilchrist			041	Outagamie			087
Levy			075	Shawano			115
				Waupaca			135
Glendive MT (798)				Waushara			137
Dawson	MT	30	021	Winnebago			139
Prairie			079				
				Greensboro-High Point-Winston Salem NC			
Grand Junction-Montrose CO (773)				**(518)**			
Mesa	CO	08	077	Alamance	NC	37	001
Montrose			085	Alleghany			005
San Miguel			113	Caswell			033
				Davidson			057
Grand Rapids-Kalamazoo-Battle Creek MI				Davie			059
(563)				Forsyth			067
Allegan	MI	26	005	Guilford			081
Barry			015	Montgomery			123
Branch			023	Randolph			151
Calhoun			025	Rockingham			157
Ionia			067	Stokes			169
Kalamazoo			077	Surry			171
Kent			081	Wilkes			193
Montcalm			117	Yadkin			197
Muskegon			121	Patrick	VA	51	141
Newaygo			123				
Oceana			127	**Greenville-New Bern-Washington NC (545)**			
Ottawa			139	Beaufort	NC	37	013
St. Joseph			149	Bertie			015
Van Buren			159	Carteret			031
				Craven			049
Great Falls MT (755)				Duplin			061
Blaine	MT	30	005	Greene			079
Cascade			013	Hyde			095
Chouteau			015	Jones			103
Fergus			027	Lenoir			107
Glacier			035	Martin			117
Hill			041	Onslow			133

DMA DEFINITIONS

DMA (DMA Code) County			FIPS Codes
Greenville-New Bern-Washington NC (545)			
(continued)			
Pamlico			137
Pitt			147
Tyrrell			177
Washington			187
Greenville-Spartanburg SC-Asheville,			
NC-Anderson, SC (567)			
Elbert	GA	13	105
Franklin			119
Hart			147
Stephens			257
Buncombe	NC	37	021
Graham			075
Haywood			087
Henderson			089
Jackson			099
McDowell			111
Macon			113
Madison			115
Mitchell			121
Polk			149
Rutherford			161
Swain			173
Transylvania			175
Yancey			199
Abbeville	SC	45	001
Anderson			007
Cherokee			021
Greenville			045
Greenwood			047
Laurens			059
Oconee			073
Pickens			077
Spartanburg			083
Union			087
Greenwood-Greenville MS (647)			
Chicot	AR	05	017
Bolivar	MS	28	011
Carroll			015
Grenada			043
Leflore			083
Sunflower			133
Tallahatchie			135
Washington			151
Harlingen-Weslaco-Brownsville-Mcallen TX			
(636)			
Cameron	TX	48	061
Hidalgo			215
Starr			427
Willacy			489
Harrisburg-Lancaster-Lebanon-York PA (566)			
Adams	PA	42	001

DMA (DMA Code) County			FIPS Codes
Harrisburg-Lancaster-Lebanon-York PA (566)			
(continued)			
Cumberland			041
Dauphin			043
Franklin			055
Juniata			067
Lancaster			071
Lebanon			075
Mifflin			087
Perry			099
York			133
Harrisonburg VA (569)			
Augusta	VA	51	015
Rockingham			165
Harrisonburg city			660
Staunton city			790
Waynesboro city			820
Pendleton	WV	54	071
Hartford & New Haven CT (533)			
Hartford	CT	09	003
Litchfield			005
Middlesex			007
New Haven			009
New London			011
Tolland			013
Windham			015
Hattiesburg-Laurel MS (710)			
Covington	MS	28	031
Forrest			035
Jasper			061
Jones			067
Lamar			073
Marion			091
Perry			111
Wayne			153
Helena MT (766)			
Broadwater	MT	30	007
Lewis and Clark			049
Honolulu HI (744)			
Hawaii	HI	15	001
Honolulu			003
Kalawao			005
Kauai			007
Maui			009
Houston TX (618)			
Austin	TX	48	015
Brazoria			039
Calhoun			057
Chambers			071
Colorado			089
Fort Bend			157

DMA DEFINITIONS

DMA (DMA Code) County			FIPS Codes
Houston TX (618) (continued)			
Galveston			167
Grimes			185
Harris			201
Jackson			239
Liberty			291
Matagorda			321
Montgomery			339
Polk			373
San Jacinto			407
Trinity			455
Walker			471
Waller			473
Washington			477
Wharton			481
Huntsville-Decatur (Florence) AL (691)			
Colbert	AL	01	033
DeKalb			049
Franklin			059
Jackson			071
Lauderdale			077
Lawrence			079
Limestone			083
Madison			089
Marshall			095
Morgan			103
Lincoln	TN	47	103
Idaho Falls-Pocatello ID (758)			
Bannock	ID	16	005
Bingham			011
Bonneville			019
Butte			023
Caribou			029
Clark			033
Custer			037
Fremont			043
Jefferson			051
Lemhi			059
Madison			065
Power			077
Teton			081
Teton	WY	56	039
Indianapolis IN (527)			
Bartholomew	IN	18	005
Blackford			009
Boone			011
Brown			013
Carroll			015
Cass			017
Clinton			023
Decatur			031
Delaware			035
Fayette			041
Fountain			045

DMA (DMA Code) County			FIPS Codes
Indianapolis IN (527) (continued)			
Grant			053
Hamilton			057
Hancock			059
Hendricks			063
Henry			065
Howard			067
Johnson			081
Lawrence			093
Madison			095
Marion			097
Miami			103
Monroe			105
Montgomery			107
Morgan			109
Owen			119
Putnam			133
Randolph			135
Rush			139
Shelby			145
Tipton			159
White			181
Jackson MS (718)			
Adams	MS	28	001
Attala			007
Claiborne			021
Copiah			029
Franklin			037
Hinds			049
Holmes			051
Humphreys			053
Issaquena			055
Jefferson			063
Jefferson Davis			065
Lawrence			077
Leake			079
Lincoln			085
Madison			089
Pike			113
Rankin			121
Scott			123
Sharkey			125
Simpson			127
Smith			129
Walthall			147
Warren			149
Yazoo			163
Jackson TN (639)			
Carroll	TN	47	017
Chester			023
Gibson			053
Hardin			071
Henderson			077
Madison			113

DMA DEFINITIONS

DMA (DMA Code) County		FIPS Codes		DMA (DMA Code) County		FIPS Codes	

Jacksonville FL (561)

Baker	FL	12	003
Bradford			007
Clay			019
Columbia			023
Duval			031
Nassau			089
Putnam			107
St. Johns			109
Union			125
Brantley	GA	13	025
Camden			039
Charlton			049
Glynn			127
Pierce			229
Ware			299

Johnstown-Altoona PA (574)

Bedford	PA	42	009
Blair			013
Cambria			021
Cameron			023
Centre			027
Clearfield			033
Elk			047
Huntingdon			061
Jefferson			065
Somerset			111

Jonesboro AR (734)

Clay	AR	05	021
Craighead			031
Greene			055
Izard			065
Lawrence			075
Randolph			121
Sharp			135
Ripley	MO	29	181

Joplin MO-Pittsburg, KS (603)

Allen	KS	20	001
Bourbon			011
Cherokee			021
Crawford			037
Labette			099
Neosho			133
Wilson			205
Woodson			207
Barton	MO	29	011
Jasper			097
McDonald			119
Newton			145
Vernon			217
Ottawa	OK	40	115

Juneau AK (747)

Juneau City & Borough	AK	02	110

Kansas City MO (616)

Anderson	KS	20	003
Atchison			005
Douglas			045
Franklin			059
Johnson			091
Leavenworth			103
Linn			107
Miami			121
Wyandotte			209
Bates	MO	29	013
Caldwell			025
Carroll			033
Cass			037
Clay			047
Clinton			049
Daviess			061
Gentry			075
Grundy			079
Harrison			081
Henry			083
Holt			087
Jackson			095
Johnson			101
Lafayette			107
Linn			115
Livingston			117
Mercer			129
Nodaway			147
Pettis			159
Platte			165
Ray			177
Saline			195
Worth			227

Knoxville TN (557)

Bell	KY	21	013
Harlan			095
McCreary			147
Anderson	TN	47	001
Blount			009
Campbell			013
Claiborne			025
Cocke			029
Cumberland			035
Fentress			049
Grainger			057
Hamblen			063
Hancock			067
Jefferson			089
Knox			093
Loudon			105
Monroe			123
Morgan			129
Roane			145
Scott			151
Sevier			155

DMA DEFINITIONS

DMA (DMA Code) County			FIPS Codes
Knoxville TN (557) (continued)			
Union			173
La Crosse-Eau Claire WI (702)			
Houston	MN	27	055
Winona			169
Buffalo	WI	55	011
Chippewa			017
Clark			019
Crawford			023
Eau Claire			035
Jackson			053
La Crosse			063
Monroe			081
Pepin			091
Rusk			107
Trempealeau			121
Vernon			123
Lafayette IN (582)			
Benton	IN	18	007
Tippecanoe			157
Warren			171
Lafayette LA (642)			
Acadia	LA	22	001
Evangeline			039
Iberia			045
Jefferson Davis			053
Lafayette			055
St. Landry			097
St. Martin			099
Vermilion			113
Lake Charles LA (643)			
Allen	LA	22	003
Beauregard			011
Calcasieu			019
Cameron			023
Lansing MI (551)			
Clinton	MI	26	037
Eaton			045
Hillsdale			059
Ingham			065
Jackson			075
Laredo TX (749)			
Webb	TX	48	479
Zapata			505
Las Vegas NV (839)			
Clark	NV	32	003
Lincoln			017
Nye			023

DMA (DMA Code) County			FIPS Codes
Lexington KY (541)			
Anderson	KY	21	005
Bath			011
Bourbon			017
Boyle			021
Breathitt			025
Casey			045
Clark			049
Clay			051
Estill			065
Fayette			067
Fleming			069
Franklin			073
Garrard			079
Harrison			097
Jackson			109
Jessamine			113
Knott			119
Knox			121
Laurel			125
Lee			129
Lincoln			137
Madison			151
Magoffin			153
Menifee			165
Mercer			167
Montgomery			173
Morgan			175
Nicholas			181
Owsley			189
Perry			193
Powell			197
Pulaski			199
Rockcastle			203
Rowan			205
Russell			207
Scott			209
Wayne			231
Whitley			235
Wolfe			237
Woodford			239
Lima OH (558)			
Allen	OH	39	003
Putnam			137
Lincoln & Hastings-Kearney NE (722)			
Jewell	KS	20	089
Phillips			147
Republic			157
Smith			183
Adams	NE	31	001
Antelope			003
Blaine			009
Boone			011
Boyd			015
Brown			017

DMA DEFINITIONS

DMA (DMA Code) County	FIPS Codes

Lincoln & Hastings-Kearney NE (722)
(continued)

County	FIPS Codes
Buffalo	019
Butler	023
Chase	029
Clay	035
Custer	041
Dawson	047
Fillmore	059
Franklin	061
Frontier	063
Furnas	065
Gage	067
Garfield	071
Gosper	073
Greeley	077
Hall	079
Hamilton	081
Harlan	083
Hayes	085
Hitchcock	087
Holt	089
Howard	093
Jefferson	095
Kearney	099
Keya Paha	103
Lancaster	109
Loup	115
Merrick	121
Nance	125
Nuckolls	129
Pawnee	133
Perkins	135
Phelps	137
Polk	143
Red Willow	145
Rock	149
Saline	151
Seward	159
Sherman	163
Thayer	169
Valley	175
Webster	181
Wheeler	183
York	185

Little Rock-Pine Bluff AR (693)

County			FIPS Codes
Arkansas	AR	05	001
Bradley			011
Calhoun			013
Clark			019
Cleburne			023
Cleveland			025
Conway			029
Dallas			039
Desha			041
Drew			043

Little Rock-Pine Bluff AR (693) (continued)

County	FIPS Codes
Faulkner	045
Garland	051
Grant	053
Hot Spring	059
Independence	063
Jackson	067
Jefferson	069
Lincoln	079
Lonoke	085
Monroe	095
Montgomery	097
Nevada	099
Ouachita	103
Perry	105
Pike	109
Polk	113
Pope	115
Prairie	117
Pulaski	119
Saline	125
Searcy	129
Stone	137
Van Buren	141
White	145
Woodruff	147
Yell	149

Los Angeles CA (803)

County			FIPS Codes
Inyo	CA	06	027
Kern (part)			029
Los Angeles			037
Orange			059
Riverside (part)			065
San Bernardino			071
Ventura			111

Louisville KY (529)

County			FIPS Codes
Clark	IN	18	019
Crawford			025
Floyd			043
Harrison			061
Jackson			071
Jefferson			077
Jennings			079
Orange			117
Scott			143
Washington			175
Adair	KY	21	001
Breckinridge			027
Bullitt			029
Carroll			041
Grayson			085
Green			087
Hardin			093
Henry			103
Jefferson			111

DMA DEFINITIONS

DMA (DMA Code) County			FIPS Codes	DMA (DMA Code) County			FIPS Codes
Louisville KY (529) (continued)				**Madison WI (669)**			
Larue			123	Columbia	WI	55	021
Marion			155	Dane			025
Meade			163	Grant			043
Nelson			179	Green			045
Oldham			185	Iowa			049
Shelby			211	Juneau			057
Spencer			215	Lafayette			065
Taylor			217	Marquette			077
Trimble			223	Richland			103
Washington			229	Rock			105
				Sauk			111
Lubbock TX (651)							
Bailey	TX	48	017	**Mankato MN (737)**			
Borden			033	Blue Earth	MN	27	013
Cochran			079	Brown			015
Crosby			107	Martin			091
Dawson			115	Nicollet (part)			103
Dickens			125	Watonwan			165
Floyd			153				
Gaines			165	**Marquette MI (553)**			
Garza			169	Alger	MI	26	003
Hale			189	Baraga			013
Hockley			219	Delta			041
Kent			263	Dickinson			043
Lamb			279	Houghton			061
Lubbock			303	Iron			071
Lynn			305	Keweenaw			083
Motley			345	Marquette			103
Terry			445	Ontonagon			131
Yoakum			501	Schoolcraft			153
				Florence	WI	55	037
Macon GA (503)							
Baldwin	GA	13	009	**Medford-Klamath Falls OR (813)**			
Bibb			021	Siskiyou	CA	06	093
Bleckley			023	Curry	OR	41	015
Crawford			079	Jackson			029
Dodge			091	Josephine			033
Dooly			093	Klamath			035
Hancock			141	Lake			037
Houston			153				
Johnson			167	**Memphis TN (640)**			
Jones			169	Crittenden	AR	05	035
Laurens			175	Cross			037
Macon			193	Lee			077
Monroe			207	Mississippi			093
Peach			225	Phillips			107
Pulaski			235	Poinsett			111
Telfair			271	St. Francis			123
Treutlen			283	Alcorn	MS	28	003
Twiggs			289	Benton			009
Washington			303	Coahoma			027
Wheeler			309	DeSoto			033
Wilcox			315	Lafayette			071
Wilkinson			319	Marshall			093
				Panola			107
				Quitman			119

DMA DEFINITIONS

DMA (DMA Code) County			FIPS Codes
Memphis TN (640) (continued)			
Tate			137
Tippah			139
Tunica			143
Pemiscot	MO	29	155
Crockett	TN	47	033
Dyer			045
Fayette			047
Hardeman			069
Haywood			075
Lauderdale			097
McNairy			109
Shelby			157
Tipton			167
Meridian MS (711)			
Choctaw	AL	01	023
Sumter			119
Clarke	MS	28	023
Kemper			069
Lauderdale			075
Neshoba			099
Newton			101
Miami-Ft. Lauderdale FL (528)			
Broward	FL	12	011
Miami-Dade			086
Monroe			087
Milwaukee WI (617)			
Dodge	WI	55	027
Jefferson			055
Kenosha			059
Milwaukee			079
Ozaukee			089
Racine			101
Sheboygan			117
Walworth			127
Washington			131
Waukesha			133
Minneapolis-St. Paul MN (613)			
Aitkin	MN	27	001
Anoka			003
Beltrami			007
Benton			009
Big Stone			011
Carver			019
Cass			021
Chippewa			023
Chisago			025
Cottonwood			033
Crow Wing			035
Dakota			037
Douglas			041
Faribault			043
Goodhue			049

DMA (DMA Code) County			FIPS Codes
Minneapolis-St. Paul MN (613) (continued)			
Grant			051
Hennepin			053
Hubbard			057
Isanti			059
Jackson			063
Kanabec			065
Kandiyohi			067
Lac qui Parle			073
Le Sueur			079
Lyon			083
McLeod			085
Meeker			093
Mille Lacs			095
Morrison			097
Nicollet (part)			103
Pine			115
Pope			121
Ramsey			123
Redwood			127
Renville			129
Rice			131
Scott			139
Sherburne			141
Sibley			143
Stearns			145
Steele			147
Stevens			149
Swift			151
Todd			153
Traverse			155
Wabasha			157
Wadena			159
Waseca			161
Washington			163
Wright			171
Yellow Medicine			173
Barron	WI	55	005
Burnett			013
Dunn			033
Pierce			093
Polk			095
St. Croix			109
Washburn			129
Minot-Bismarck-Dickinson (Williston), ND (687)			
Daniels	MT	30	019
Fallon			025
McCone			055
Richland			083
Roosevelt			085
Sheridan			091
Wibaux			109
Adams	ND	38	001
Billings			007
Bottineau			009
Bowman			011

DMA DEFINITIONS

DMA (DMA Code) County			FIPS Codes
Minot-Bismarck-Dickinson (Williston), ND (687)			
(continued)			
Burke			013
Burleigh			015
Divide			023
Dunn			025
Emmons			029
Golden Valley			033
Grant			037
Hettinger			041
Kidder			043
Logan			047
McHenry			049
McIntosh			051
McKenzie			053
McLean			055
Mercer			057
Morton			059
Mountrail			061
Oliver			065
Pierce			069
Renville			075
Rolette			079
Sheridan			083
Sioux			085
Slope			087
Stark			089
Ward			101
Wells			103
Williams			105
Campbell	SD	46	021
Corson			031
Missoula MT (762)			
Flathead	MT	30	029
Granite			039
Lake			047
Mineral			061
Missoula			063
Ravalli			081
Sanders			089
Mobile AL-Pensacola (Ft. Walton Beach), FL (686)			
Baldwin	AL	01	003
Clarke			025
Conecuh			035
Escambia			053
Mobile			097
Monroe			099
Washington			129
Escambia	FL	12	033
Okaloosa			091
Santa Rosa			113
Greene	MS	28	041

DMA (DMA Code) County			FIPS Codes
Monroe LA-El Dorado, AR (628)			
Ashley	AR	05	003
Union			139
Caldwell	LA	22	021
Catahoula			025
Concordia			029
East Carroll			035
Franklin			041
Jackson			049
La Salle			059
Lincoln			061
Madison			065
Morehouse			067
Ouachita			073
Richland			083
Tensas			107
Union			111
West Carroll			123
Winn			127
Monterey-Salinas CA (828)			
Monterey	CA	06	053
San Benito			069
Santa Cruz			087
Montgomery-Selma, AL (698)			
Autauga	AL	01	001
Bullock			011
Butler			013
Covington			039
Crenshaw			041
Dallas			047
Elmore			051
Lowndes			085
Macon			087
Marengo			091
Montgomery			101
Perry			105
Pike			109
Tallapoosa			123
Wilcox			131
Myrtle Beach-Florence SC (570)			
Robeson	NC	37	155
Scotland			165
Darlington	SC	45	031
Dillon			033
Florence			041
Horry			051
Marion			067
Marlboro			069
Nashville TN (659)			
Allen	KY	21	003
Christian			047

DMA DEFINITIONS

DMA (DMA Code) County			FIPS Codes
Nashville TN (659) (continued)			
Clinton			053
Cumberland			057
Logan			141
Monroe			171
Simpson			213
Todd			219
Trigg			221
Bedford	TN	47	003
Benton			005
Cannon			015
Cheatham			021
Clay			027
Coffee			031
Davidson			037
Decatur			039
DeKalb			041
Dickson			043
Franklin			051
Giles			055
Henry			079
Hickman			081
Houston			083
Humphreys			085
Jackson			087
Lawrence			099
Lewis			101
Macon			111
Marshall			117
Maury			119
Montgomery			125
Moore			127
Overton			133
Perry			135
Pickett			137
Putnam			141
Robertson			147
Rutherford			149
Smith			159
Stewart			161
Sumner			165
Trousdale			169
Van Buren			175
Warren			177
Wayne			181
White			185
Williamson			187
Wilson			189
New Orleans LA (622)			
Jefferson	LA	22	051
Lafourche			057
Orleans			071
Plaquemines			075
St. Bernard			087
St. Charles			089
St. James			093

DMA (DMA Code) County			FIPS Codes
New Orleans LA (622) (continued)			
St. John the Baptist			095
St. Tammany			103
Tangipahoa			105
Terrebonne			109
Washington			117
Hancock	MS	28	045
Pearl River			109
New York NY (501)			
Fairfield	CT	09	001
Bergen	NJ	34	003
Essex			013
Hudson			017
Hunterdon			019
Middlesex			023
Monmouth			025
Morris			027
Ocean			029
Passaic			031
Somerset			035
Sussex			037
Union			039
Warren			041
Bronx	NY	36	005
Dutchess			027
Kings			047
Nassau			059
New York			061
Orange			071
Putnam			079
Queens			081
Richmond			085
Rockland			087
Suffolk			103
Sullivan			105
Ulster			111
Westchester			119
Pike	PA	42	103
Norfolk-Portsmouth-Newport News VA (544)			
Camden	NC	37	029
Chowan			041
Currituck			053
Dare			055
Gates			073
Hertford			091
Northampton			131
Pasquotank			139
Perquimans			143
Accomack	VA	51	001
Gloucester			073
Isle of Wight			093
James City			095
Mathews			115
Northampton			131
Southampton			175

DMA DEFINITIONS

DMA (DMA Code) County			FIPS Codes	DMA (DMA Code) County			FIPS Codes
Norfolk-Portsmouth-Newport News VA (544)				**Oklahoma City OK (650)** (continued)			
(continued)				Harmon			057
Surry			181	Harper			059
York			199	Hughes			063
Chesapeake city			550	Kay			071
Franklin city			620	Kingfisher			073
Hampton city			650	Kiowa			075
Newport News city			700	Lincoln			081
Norfolk city			710	Logan			083
Poquoson city			735	McClain			087
Portsmouth city			740	Major			093
Suffolk city			800	Murray			099
Virginia Beach city			810	Noble			103
Williamsburg city			830	Oklahoma			109
				Payne			119
North Platte NE (740)				Pottawatomie			125
Lincoln	NE	31	111	Roger Mills			129
Logan			113	Seminole			133
McPherson			117	Washita			149
Thomas			171	Woods			151
				Woodward			153
Odessa-Midland TX (633)							
Lea (part)	NM	35	025	**Omaha NE (652)**			
Andrews	TX	48	003	Cass	IA	19	029
Brewster			043	Crawford			047
Crane			103	Fremont			071
Ector			135	Harrison			085
Glasscock			173	Mills			129
Howard			227	Montgomery			137
Jeff Davis			243	Page			145
Loving			301	Pottawattamie			155
Martin			317	Shelby			165
Midland			329	Atchison	MO	29	005
Pecos			371	Burt	NE	31	021
Presidio			377	Cass			025
Reagan			383	Colfax			037
Reeves			389	Cuming			039
Terrell			443	Dodge			053
Upton			461	Douglas			055
Ward			475	Johnson			097
Winkler			495	Nemaha			127
				Otoe			131
Oklahoma City OK (650)				Platte			141
Alfalfa	OK	40	003	Richardson			147
Beckham			009	Sarpy			153
Blaine			011	Saunders			155
Caddo			015	Washington			177
Canadian			017				
Cleveland			027	**Orlando-Daytona Beach-Melbourne FL (534)**			
Custer			039	Brevard	FL	12	009
Dewey			043	Flagler			035
Ellis			045	Lake			069
Garfield			047	Marion			083
Garvin			049	Orange			095
Grady			051	Osceola			097
Grant			053	Seminole			117
Greer			055	Sumter			119

DMA DEFINITIONS

DMA (DMA Code) County			FIPS Codes
Orlando-Daytona Beach-Melbourne FL (534)			
(continued)			
Volusia			127
Ottumwa IA-Kirksville, MO (631)			
Davis	IA	19	051
Jefferson			101
Van Buren			177
Wapello			179
Adair	MO	29	001
Macon			121
Putnam			171
Schuyler			197
Scotland			199
Sullivan			211
Paducah KY-Cape Girardeau, MO-Harrisburg, IL (632)			
Alexander	IL	17	003
Franklin			055
Gallatin			059
Hamilton			065
Hardin			069
Jackson			077
Jefferson			081
Johnson			087
Massac			127
Perry			145
Pope			151
Pulaski			153
Saline			165
Union			181
Williamson			199
Ballard	KY	21	007
Caldwell			033
Calloway			035
Carlisle			039
Crittenden			055
Fulton			075
Graves			083
Hickman			105
Livingston			139
Lyon			143
McCracken			145
Marshall			157
Bollinger	MO	29	017
Butler			023
Cape Girardeau			031
Carter			035
Dunklin			069
Madison			123
Mississippi			133
New Madrid			143
Perry			157
Scott			201
Stoddard			207
Wayne			223

DMA (DMA Code) County			FIPS Codes
Paducah KY-Cape Girardeau, MO-Harrisburg, IL (632) (continued)			
Lake	TN	47	095
Obion			131
Weakley			183
Palm Springs CA (804)			
Riverside (part)	CA	06	065
Panama City FL (656)			
Bay	FL	12	005
Calhoun			013
Franklin			037
Gulf			045
Holmes			059
Jackson			063
Liberty			077
Walton			131
Washington			133
Parkersburg WV (597)			
Washington	OH	39	167
Pleasants	WV	54	073
Wood			107
Peoria-Bloomington IL (675)			
Fulton	IL	17	057
Livingston			105
McLean			113
Marshall			123
Mason			125
Peoria			143
Putnam			155
Stark			175
Tazewell			179
Woodford			203
Philadelphia PA (504)			
Kent	DE	10	001
New Castle			003
Atlantic	NJ	34	001
Burlington			005
Camden			007
Cape May			009
Cumberland			011
Gloucester			015
Mercer			021
Salem			033
Berks	PA	42	011
Bucks			017
Chester			029
Delaware			045
Lehigh			077
Montgomery			091
Northampton			095
Philadelphia			101

DMA DEFINITIONS

DMA (DMA Code) County			FIPS Codes
Phoenix (Prescott) AZ (753)			
Apache (part)	AZ	04	001
Coconino			005
Gila			007
Graham			009
Greenlee			011
La Paz			012
Maricopa			013
Mohave			015
Navajo			017
Pinal			021
Yavapai			025
Pittsburgh PA (508)			
Garrett	MD	24	023
Allegheny	PA	42	003
Armstrong			005
Beaver			007
Butler			019
Clarion			031
Fayette			051
Forest			053
Greene			059
Indiana			063
Lawrence			073
Venango			121
Washington			125
Westmoreland			129
Monongalia	WV	54	061
Preston			077
Portland OR (820)			
Baker	OR	41	001
Clackamas			005
Clatsop			007
Columbia			009
Crook			013
Gilliam			021
Grant			023
Harney			025
Hood River			027
Jefferson			031
Lincoln			041
Linn			043
Marion			047
Multnomah			051
Polk			053
Sherman			055
Tillamook			057
Union			061
Wasco			065
Washington			067
Wheeler			069
Yamhill			071
Clark	WA	53	011
Cowlitz			015
Klickitat			039

DMA (DMA Code) County			FIPS Codes
Portland OR (820) (continued)			
Skamania			059
Wahkiakum			069
Portland-Auburn ME (500)			
Androscoggin	ME	23	001
Cumberland			005
Franklin			007
Kennebec			011
Knox			013
Lincoln			015
Oxford			017
Sagadahoc			023
York			031
Carroll	NH	33	003
Coos			007
Presque Isle ME (552)			
Aroostook	ME	23	003
Providence RI-New Bedford, MA (521)			
Bristol	MA	25	005
Bristol	RI	44	001
Kent			003
Newport			005
Providence			007
Washington			009
Quincy IL-Hannibal, MO-Keokuk, IA (717)			
Lee	IA	19	111
Adams	IL	17	001
Brown			009
Hancock			067
McDonough			109
Pike			149
Schuyler			169
Scott			171
Clark	MO	29	045
Knox			103
Lewis			111
Marion			127
Monroe			137
Ralls			173
Shelby			205
Raleigh-Durham (Fayetteville) NC (560)			
Chatham	NC	37	037
Cumberland			051
Durham			063
Edgecombe			065
Franklin			069
Granville			077
Halifax			083
Harnett			085
Hoke			093
Johnston			101
Lee			105

DMA DEFINITIONS

DMA (DMA Code) County			FIPS Codes	DMA (DMA Code) County			FIPS Codes
Raleigh-Durham (Fayetteville) NC (560)				**Richmond-Petersburg VA (556)** (continued)			
(continued)				Charles City			036
Moore			125	Chesterfield			041
Nash			127	Cumberland			049
Orange			135	Dinwiddie			053
Person			145	Essex			057
Sampson			163	Goochland			075
Vance			181	Greensville			081
Wake			183	Hanover			085
Warren			185	Henrico			087
Wayne			191	King and Queen			097
Wilson			195	King William			101
Mecklenburg	VA	51	117	Lancaster			103
				Louisa			109
Rapid City SD (764)				Lunenburg			111
Carter	MT	30	011	Middlesex			119
Morrill	NE	31	123	New Kent			127
Bennett	SD	46	007	Northumberland			133
Butte			019	Nottoway			135
Custer			033	Powhatan			145
Fall River			047	Prince Edward			147
Haakon			055	Prince George			149
Harding			063	Richmond			159
Jackson			071	Sussex			183
Jones			075	Colonial Heights city			570
Lawrence			081	Emporia city			595
Meade			093	Hopewell city			670
Pennington			103	Petersburg city			730
Perkins			105	Richmond city			760
Shannon			113				
Ziebach			137	**Roanoke-Lynchburg VA (573)**			
Crook	WY	56	011	Alleghany	VA	51	005
Sheridan			033	Amherst			009
Weston			045	Appomattox			011
				Bath			017
Reno NV (811)				Bedford			019
Alpine	CA	06	003	Bland			021
El Dorado (part)			017	Botetourt			023
Lassen			035	Campbell			031
Mono			051	Carroll			035
Churchill	NV	32	001	Charlotte			037
Douglas			005	Craig			045
Esmeralda			009	Floyd			063
Humboldt			013	Franklin			067
Lander			015	Giles			071
Lyon			019	Grayson			077
Mineral			021	Halifax			083
Pershing			027	Henry			089
Storey			029	Highland			091
Washoe			031	Montgomery			121
Carson City			510	Nelson			125
				Pittsylvania			143
Richmond-Petersburg VA (556)				Pulaski			155
Amelia	VA	51	007	Roanoke			161
Brunswick			025	Rockbridge			163
Buckingham			029	Wythe			197
Caroline			033	Bedford city			515

DMA DEFINITIONS

DMA (DMA Code) County			FIPS Codes	DMA (DMA Code) County			FIPS Codes
Roanoke-Lynchburg VA (573) (continued)				**Salisbury MD (576)**			
Buena Vista city			530	Sussex	DE	10	005
Covington city			580	Dorchester	MD	24	019
Danville city			590	Somerset			039
Galax city			640	Wicomico			045
Lexington city			678	Worcester			047
Lynchburg city			680				
Martinsville city			690	**Salt Lake City UT (770)**			
Radford city			750	Bear Lake	ID	16	007
Roanoke city			770	Franklin			041
Salem city			775	Oneida			071
				Elko	NV	32	007
Rochester NY (538)				Eureka			011
Livingston	NY	36	051	White Pine			033
Monroe			055	Beaver	UT	49	001
Ontario			069	Box Elder			003
Wayne			117	Cache			005
Yates			123	Carbon			007
				Daggett			009
Rochester MN-Mason City, IA-Austin, MN (611)				Davis			011
Cerro Gordo	IA	19	033	Duchesne			013
Floyd			067	Emery			015
Hancock			081	Garfield			017
Howard			089	Grand			019
Mitchell			131	Iron			021
Winnebago			189	Juab			023
Worth			195	Kane			025
Dodge	MN	27	039	Millard			027
Fillmore			045	Morgan			029
Freeborn			047	Piute			031
Mower			099	Rich			033
Olmsted			109	Salt Lake			035
				San Juan			037
Rockford IL (610)				Sanpete			039
Boone	IL	17	007	Sevier			041
Lee			103	Summit			043
Ogle			141	Tooele			045
Stephenson			177	Uintah			047
Winnebago			201	Utah			049
				Wasatch			051
Sacramento-Stockton-Modesto CA (862)				Washington			053
Amador	CA	06	005	Wayne			055
Calaveras			009	Weber			057
Colusa			011	Lincoln	WY	56	023
El Dorado (part)			017	Sublette			035
Nevada			057	Sweetwater			037
Placer			061	Uinta			041
Plumas			063				
Sacramento			067	**San Angelo TX (661)**			
San Joaquin			077	Coke	TX	48	081
Sierra			091	Concho			095
Solano (part)			095	Crockett			105
Stanislaus			099	Irion			235
Sutter			101	Kimble			267
Tuolumne			109	McCulloch			307
Yolo			113	Menard			327
Yuba			116	Schleicher			413

DMA DEFINITIONS

DMA (DMA Code) County			FIPS Codes
San Angelo TX (661) (continued)			
Sterling			431
Sutton			435
Tom Green			451
San Antonio TX (641)			
Atascosa	TX	48	013
Bandera			019
Bexar			029
Comal			091
DeWitt			123
Dimmit			127
Edwards			137
Frio			163
Goliad			175
Gonzales			177
Guadalupe			187
Karnes			255
Kendall			259
Kerr			265
Kinney			271
La Salle			283
Lavaca			285
McMullen			311
Maverick			323
Medina			325
Real			385
Uvalde			463
Val Verde			465
Wilson			493
Zavala			507
San Diego CA (825)			
San Diego	CA	06	073
San Francisco-Oakland-San Jose CA (807)			
Alameda	CA	06	001
Contra Costa			013
Lake			033
Marin			041
Mendocino			045
Napa			055
San Francisco			075
San Mateo			081
Santa Clara			085
Solano (part)			095
Sonoma			097
Santa Barbara-Santa Maria-San Luis Obispo CA (855)			
San Luis Obispo	CA	06	079
Santa Barbara			083
Savannah GA (507)			
Appling	GA	13	001
Bacon			005
Bryan			029

DMA (DMA Code) County			FIPS Codes
Savannah GA (507) (continued)			
Bulloch			031
Candler			043
Chatham			051
Effingham			103
Evans			109
Jeff Davis			161
Liberty			179
Long			183
McIntosh			191
Montgomery			209
Screven			251
Tattnall			267
Toombs			279
Wayne			305
Beaufort	SC	45	013
Hampton			049
Jasper			053
Seattle-Tacoma WA (819)			
Chelan	WA	53	007
Clallam			009
Douglas			017
Grays Harbor			027
Island			029
Jefferson			031
King			033
Kitsap			035
Lewis			041
Mason			045
Pacific			049
Pierce			053
San Juan			055
Skagit			057
Snohomish			061
Thurston			067
Whatcom			073
Sherman TX-Ada, OK (657)			
Atoka	OK	40	005
Bryan			013
Carter			019
Choctaw			023
Coal			029
Johnston			069
Love			085
Marshall			095
Pontotoc			123
Pushmataha			127
Grayson	TX	48	181
Shreveport LA (612)			
Columbia	AR	05	027
Hempstead			057
Howard			061
Lafayette			073
Little River			081

DMA DEFINITIONS

DMA (DMA Code) County			FIPS Codes	DMA (DMA Code) County			FIPS Codes
Shreveport LA (612) (continued)				**Sioux Falls (Mitchell) SD (725)** (continued)			
Miller			091	Bon Homme			009
Sevier			133	Brookings			011
Bienville	LA	22	013	Brown			013
Bossier			015	Brule			015
Caddo			017	Buffalo			017
Claiborne			027	Charles Mix			023
De Soto			031	Clark			025
Natchitoches			069	Clay			027
Red River			081	Codington			029
Sabine			085	Davison			035
Webster			119	Day			037
McCurtain	OK	40	089	Deuel			039
Bowie	TX	48	037	Dewey			041
Cass			067	Douglas			043
Harrison			203	Edmunds			045
Marion			315	Faulk			049
Morris			343	Grant			051
Panola			365	Gregory			053
Shelby			419	Hamlin			057
Titus			449	Hand			059
				Hanson			061
Sioux City IA (624)				Hughes			065
Buena Vista	IA	19	021	Hutchinson			067
Cherokee			035	Hyde			069
Clay			041	Jerauld			073
Dickinson			059	Kingsbury			077
Emmet			063	Lake			079
Ida			093	Lincoln			083
Monona			133	Lyman			085
O'Brien			141	McCook			087
Palo Alto			147	McPherson			089
Plymouth			149	Marshall			091
Sac			161	Mellette			095
Sioux			167	Miner			097
Woodbury			193	Minnehaha			099
Cedar	NE	31	027	Moody			101
Dakota			043	Potter			107
Dixon			051	Roberts			109
Knox			107	Sanborn			111
Madison			119	Spink			115
Pierce			139	Stanley			117
Stanton			167	Sully			119
Thurston			173	Todd			121
Wayne			179	Tripp			123
Union	SD	46	127	Turner			125
				Walworth			129
Sioux Falls (Mitchell) SD (725)				Yankton			135
Lyon	IA	19	119				
Osceola			143	**South Bend-Elkhart IN (588)**			
Lincoln	MN	27	081	Elkhart	IN	18	039
Murray			101	Fulton			049
Nobles			105	Kosciusko			085
Pipestone			117	LaGrange			087
Rock			133	Marshall			099
Aurora	SD	46	003	Pulaski			131
Beadle			005	St. Joseph			141

DMA DEFINITIONS

DMA (DMA Code) County	FIPS Codes		

South Bend-Elkhart IN (588) (continued)

County			FIPS
Starke			149
Berrien	MI	26	021
Cass			027

Spokane WA (881)

County			FIPS
Benewah	ID	16	009
Bonner			017
Boundary			021
Clearwater			035
Idaho			049
Kootenai			055
Latah			057
Lewis			061
Nez Perce			069
Shoshone			079
Lincoln	MT	30	053
Wallowa	OR	41	063
Adams	WA	53	001
Asotin			003
Columbia			013
Ferry			019
Garfield			023
Grant			025
Lincoln			043
Okanogan			047
Pend Oreille			051
Spokane			063
Stevens			065
Whitman			075

Springfield MO (619)

County			FIPS
Baxter	AR	05	005
Boone			009
Carroll			015
Fulton			049
Marion			089
Newton			101
Barry	MO	29	009
Benton			015
Camden			029
Cedar			039
Christian			043
Dade			057
Dallas			059
Dent			065
Douglas			067
Greene			077
Hickory			085
Howell			091
Laclede			105
Lawrence			109
Oregon			149
Ozark			153
Polk			167
Pulaski			169
St. Clair			185

Springfield MO (619) (continued)

County			FIPS
Shannon			203
Stone			209
Taney			213
Texas			215
Webster			225
Wright			229

Springfield-Holyoke MA (543)

County			FIPS
Franklin	MA	25	011
Hampden			013
Hampshire			015

St. Joseph MO (638)

County			FIPS
Doniphan	KS	20	043
Andrew	MO	29	003
Buchanan			021
DeKalb			063

St. Louis MO (609)

County			FIPS
Bond	IL	17	005
Calhoun			013
Clay			025
Clinton			027
Fayette			051
Greene			061
Jersey			083
Macoupin			117
Madison			119
Marion			121
Monroe			133
Montgomery			135
Randolph			157
St. Clair			163
Washington			189
Crawford	MO	29	055
Franklin			071
Gasconade			073
Iron			093
Jefferson			099
Lincoln			113
Phelps			161
Pike			163
Reynolds			179
St. Charles			183
Ste. Genevieve			186
St. Francois			187
St. Louis			189
Warren			219
Washington			221
St. Louis city			510

Syracuse NY (555)

County			FIPS
Cayuga	NY	36	011
Cortland			023
Madison			053
Oneida (part)			065

DMA DEFINITIONS

DMA (DMA Code) County			FIPS Codes

Syracuse NY (555) (continued)

County			
Onondaga			067
Oswego			075
Seneca			099
Tompkins			109

Tallahassee FL-Thomasville, GA (530)

County	State		FIPS
Gadsden	FL	12	039
Hamilton			047
Jefferson			065
Lafayette			067
Leon			073
Madison			079
Suwannee			121
Taylor			123
Wakulla			129
Brooks	GA	13	027
Clinch			065
Decatur			087
Echols			101
Grady			131
Lanier			173
Lowndes			185
Miller			201
Seminole			253
Thomas			275

Tampa-St.Petersburg (Sarasota) FL (539)

County	State		FIPS
Citrus	FL	12	017
Hardee			049
Hernando			053
Highlands			055
Hillsborough			057
Manatee			081
Pasco			101
Pinellas			103
Polk			105
Sarasota			115

Terre Haute IN (581)

County	State		FIPS
Clark	IL	17	023
Crawford			033
Jasper			079
Lawrence			101
Richland			159
Clay	IN	18	021
Daviess			027
Greene			055
Knox			083
Martin			101
Parke			121
Sullivan			153
Vermillion			165
Vigo			167

Toledo OH (547)

County	State		FIPS
Lenawee	MI	26	091

Toledo OH (547) (continued)

County	State		FIPS
Defiance	OH	39	039
Fulton			051
Hancock			063
Henry			069
Lucas			095
Ottawa			123
Sandusky			143
Seneca			147
Williams			171
Wood			173
Wyandot			175

Topeka KS (605)

County	State		FIPS
Brown	KS	20	013
Clay			027
Cloud			029
Coffey			031
Geary			061
Jackson			085
Jefferson			087
Lyon			111
Marshall			117
Morris			127
Nemaha			131
Osage			139
Pottawatomie			149
Riley			161
Shawnee			177
Wabaunsee			197
Washington			201

Traverse City-Cadillac MI (540)

County	State		FIPS
Antrim	MI	26	009
Benzie			019
Charlevoix			029
Cheboygan			031
Chippewa			033
Clare			035
Crawford			039
Emmet			047
Grand Traverse			055
Kalkaska			079
Lake			085
Leelanau			089
Luce			095
Mackinac			097
Manistee			101
Mason			105
Mecosta			107
Missaukee			113
Montmorency			119
Osceola			133
Oscoda			135
Otsego			137
Presque Isle			141
Roscommon			143

DMA DEFINITIONS

DMA (DMA Code) County			FIPS Codes
Traverse City-Cadillac MI (540) (continued)			
Wexford			165
Tri-Cities TN-VA (531)			
Leslie	KY	21	131
Letcher			133
Carter	TN	47	019
Greene			059
Hawkins			073
Johnson			091
Sullivan			163
Unicoi			171
Washington			179
Buchanan	VA	51	027
Dickenson			051
Lee			105
Russell			167
Scott			169
Smyth			173
Washington			191
Wise			195
Bristol city			520
Norton city			720
Tucson (Sierra Vista) AZ (789)			
Cochise	AZ	04	003
Pima			019
Santa Cruz			023
Tulsa OK (671)			
Chautauqua	KS	20	019
Montgomery			125
Adair	OK	40	001
Cherokee			021
Craig			035
Creek			037
Delaware			041
Haskell			061
Latimer			077
McIntosh			091
Mayes			097
Muskogee			101
Nowata			105
Okfuskee			107
Okmulgee			111
Osage			113
Pawnee			117
Pittsburg			121
Rogers			131
Tulsa			143
Wagoner			145
Washington			147
Twin Falls ID (760)			
Blaine	ID	16	013
Cassia			031
Gooding			047

DMA (DMA Code) County			FIPS Codes
Twin Falls ID (760) (continued)			
Jerome			053
Lincoln			063
Minidoka			067
Twin Falls			083
Tyler-Longview (Lufkin & Nacogdoches) TX (709)			
Angelina	TX	48	005
Camp			063
Cherokee			073
Franklin			159
Gregg			183
Houston			225
Nacogdoches			347
Rusk			401
Sabine			403
San Augustine			405
Smith			423
Upshur			459
Wood			499
Utica NY (526)			
Herkimer	NY	36	043
Oneida (part)			065
Otsego			077
Victoria TX (626)			
Victoria	TX	48	469
Waco-Temple-Bryan TX (625)			
Bell	TX	48	027
Brazos			041
Burleson			051
Coryell			099
Falls			145
Lampasas			281
Leon			289
Limestone			293
McLennan			309
Madison			313
Milam			331
Mills			333
Robertson			395
San Saba			411
Washington DC (Hagerstown MD) (511)			
District of Columbia	DC	11	001
Allegany	MD	24	001
Calvert			009
Charles			017
Frederick			021
Montgomery			031
Prince George's			033
St. Mary's			037
Washington			043
Fulton	PA	42	057

DMA DEFINITIONS

DMA (DMA Code) County			FIPS Codes

Washington DC (Hagerstown MD) (511)
(continued)

Arlington	VA	51	013
Clarke			043
Culpeper			047
Fairfax			059
Fauquier			061
Frederick			069
King George			099
Loudoun			107
Page			139
Prince William			153
Rappahannock			157
Shenandoah			171
Spotsylvania			177
Stafford			179
Warren			187
Westmoreland			193
Alexandria city			510
Fairfax city			600
Falls Church city			610
Fredericksburg city			630
Manassas city			683
Manassas Park city			685
Winchester city			840
Berkeley	WV	54	003
Grant			023
Hampshire			027
Hardy			031
Jefferson			037
Mineral			057
Morgan			065

Watertown NY (549)

Jefferson	NY	36	045
Lewis			049
St. Lawrence			089

Wausau-Rhinelander WI (705)

Adams	WI	55	001
Forest			041
Langlade			067
Lincoln			069
Marathon			073
Oneida			085
Portage			097
Price			099
Taylor			119
Vilas			125
Wood			141

West Palm Beach-Fort Pierce FL (548)

Indian River	FL	12	061
Martin			085
Okeechobee			093
Palm Beach			099
St. Lucie			111

Wheeling WV-Steubenville, OH (554)

Belmont	OH	39	013
Harrison			067
Jefferson			081
Monroe			111
Noble			121
Brooke	WV	54	009
Hancock			029
Marshall			051
Ohio			069
Tyler			095
Wetzel			103

Wichita Falls TX & Lawton, OK (627)

Comanche	OK	40	031
Cotton			033
Jackson			065
Jefferson			067
Stephens			137
Tillman			141
Archer	TX	48	009
Baylor			023
Clay			077
Foard			155
Hardeman			197
King			269
Montague			337
Wichita			485
Wilbarger			487
Young			503

Wichita-Hutchinson KS Plus (678)

Barber	KS	20	007
Barton			009
Butler			015
Chase			017
Cheyenne			023
Clark			025
Comanche			033
Cowley			035
Decatur			039
Dickinson			041
Edwards			047
Elk			049
Ellis			051
Ellsworth			053
Finney			055
Ford			057
Gove			063
Graham			065
Grant			067
Gray			069
Greeley			071
Greenwood			073
Hamilton			075
Harper			077
Harvey			079

DMA DEFINITIONS

DMA (DMA Code) County	FIPS Codes
Wichita-Hutchinson KS Plus (678) (continued)	
Haskell	081
Hodgeman	083
Kearny	093
Kingman	095
Kiowa	097
Lane	101
Lincoln	105
Logan	109
McPherson	113
Marion	115
Meade	119
Mitchell	123
Morton	129
Ness	135
Norton	137
Osborne	141
Ottawa	143
Pawnee	145
Pratt	151
Rawlins	153
Reno	155
Rice	159
Rooks	163
Rush	165
Russell	167
Saline	169
Scott	171
Sedgwick	173
Seward	175
Sheridan	179
Sherman	181
Stafford	185
Stanton	187
Stevens	189
Sumner	191
Thomas	193
Trego	195
Wallace	199
Wichita	203
Dundy NE 31	057

DMA (DMA Code) County	FIPS Codes
Wilkes Barre-Scranton PA (577)	
Bradford PA 42	015
Carbon	025
Clinton	035
Columbia	037
Lackawanna	069
Luzerne	079
Lycoming	081
Monroe	089
Montour	093
Northumberland	097
Schuylkill	107
Snyder	109
Sullivan	113
Susquehanna	115

DMA (DMA Code) County	FIPS Codes
Wilkes Barre-Scranton PA (577) (continued)	
Union	119
Wayne	127
Wyoming	131
Wilmington NC (550)	
Bladen NC 37	017
Brunswick	019
Columbus	047
New Hanover	129
Pender	141
Yakima-Pasco-Richland-Kennewick WA (810)	
Morrow OR 41	049
Umatilla	059
Benton WA 53	005
Franklin	021
Kittitas	037
Walla Walla	071
Yakima	077
Youngstown OH (536)	
Columbiana OH 39	029
Mahoning	099
Trumbull	155
Mercer PA 42	085
Yuma AZ-El Centro, CA (771)	
Yuma AZ 04	027
Imperial CA 06	025
Zanesville OH (596)	
Muskingum OH 39	119

Appendix VI:
NAICS Code Definitions

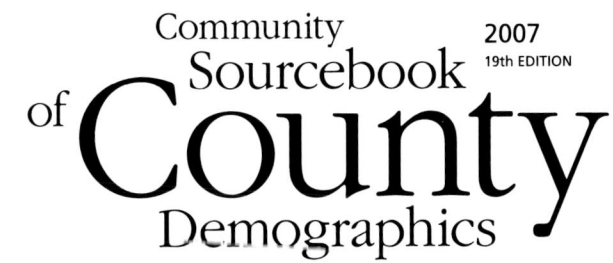

Community
Sourcebook
of County
Demographics

2007
19th EDITION

APPENDIX VI
NAICS Codes

111	Crop Production
112	Animal Production
113	Forestry and Logging
114	Fishing, Hunting and Trapping
115	Support Activities for Agriculture and Forestry
211	Oil and Gas Extraction
212	Mining (except Oil and Gas)
213	Support Activities for Mining
221	Utilities
236	Construction of Buildings
237	Heavy and Civil Engineering Construction
238	Specialty Trade Contractors
311	Food Manufacturing
312	Beverage and Tobacco Product Manufacturing
313	Textile Mills
314	Textile Product Mills
315	Apparel Manufacturing
316	Leather and Allied Product Manufacturing
321	Wood Product Manufacturing
322	Paper Manufacturing
323	Printing and Related Support Activities
324	Petroleum and Coal Products Manufacturing
325	Chemical Manufacturing
326	Plastics and Rubber Products Manufacturing
327	Nonmetallic Mineral Product Manufacturing
331	Primary Metal Manufacturing
332	Fabricated Metal Product Manufacturing
333	Machinery Manufacturing
334	Computer and Electronic Product Manufacturing
335	Electrical Equipment, Appliance, and Component Manufacturing
336	Transportation Equipment Manufacturing
337	Furniture and Related Product Manufacturing
339	Miscellaneous Manufacturing
423	Merchant Wholesalers, Durable Goods
424	Merchant Wholesalers, Nondurable Goods
425	Wholesale Electronic Markets and Agents and Brokers
441	Motor Vehicle and Parts Dealers
442	Furniture and Home Furnishings Stores
443	Electronics and Appliance Stores
444	Building Material and Garden Equipment and Supplies Dealers
445	Food and Beverage Stores
446	Health and Personal Care Stores
447	Gasoline Stations
448	Clothing and Clothing Accessories Stores
451	Sporting Goods, Hobby, Book, and Music Stores
452	General Merchandise Stores
453	Miscellaneous Store Retailers
454	Nonstore Retailers
481	Air Transportation
482	Rail Transportation
483	Water Transportation
484	Truck Transportation
485	Transit and Ground Passenger Transportation
486	Pipeline Transportation
487	Scenic and Sightseeing Transportation
488	Support Activities for Transportation
491	Postal Service
492	Couriers and Messengers
493	Warehousing and Storage
511	Publishing Industries (except Internet)
512	Motion Picture and Sound Recording Industries
515	Broadcasting (except Internet)
516	Internet Publishing and Broadcasting
517	Telecommunications
518	Internet Service Providers, Web Search Portals, and Data Processing Services
519	Other Information Services
521	Monetary Authorities - Central Bank
522	Credit Intermediation and Related Activities
523	Securities/Commodity Contracts/Othr Fin. Inv./Related Activities
524	Insurance Carriers and Related Activities
525	Funds, Trusts, and Other Financial Vehicles
531	Real Estate
532	Rental and Leasing Services
533	Lessors of Nonfinancial Intangible Assets (except Copyrighted Works)
541	Professional, Scientific, and Technical Services
551	Management of Companies and Enterprises
561	Administrative and Support Services
562	Waste Management and Remediation Services
611	Educational Services
621	Ambulatory Health Care Services
622	Hospitals
623	Nursing and Residential Care Facilities
624	Social Assistance
711	Performing Arts, Spectator Sports, and Related Industries
712	Museums, Historical Sites, and Similar Institutions
713	Amusement, Gambling, and Recreation Industries
721	Accommodation
722	Food Services and Drinking Places
811	Repair and Maintenance
812	Personal and Laundry Services
813	Religious, Grantmaking, Civic, Professional, and Similar Organizations
814	Private Households
921	Executive, Legislative, and Other General Government Support
922	Justice, Public Order, and Safety Activities
923	Administration of Human Resource Programs
924	Administration of Environmental Quality Programs
925	Administration of Housing Programs, Urban Planning, & Community Dev.
926	Administration of Economic Programs
927	Space Research and Technology
928	National Security and International Affairs
999	Unclassified Establishments

County Maps

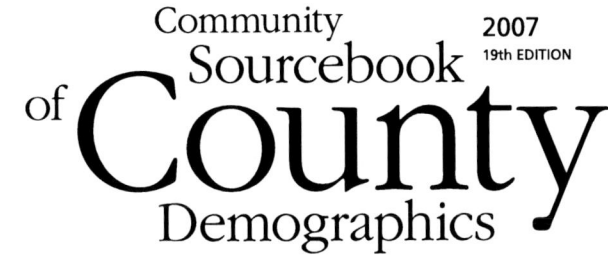

Community
Sourcebook
of County
Demographics

2007
19th EDITION

Alabama

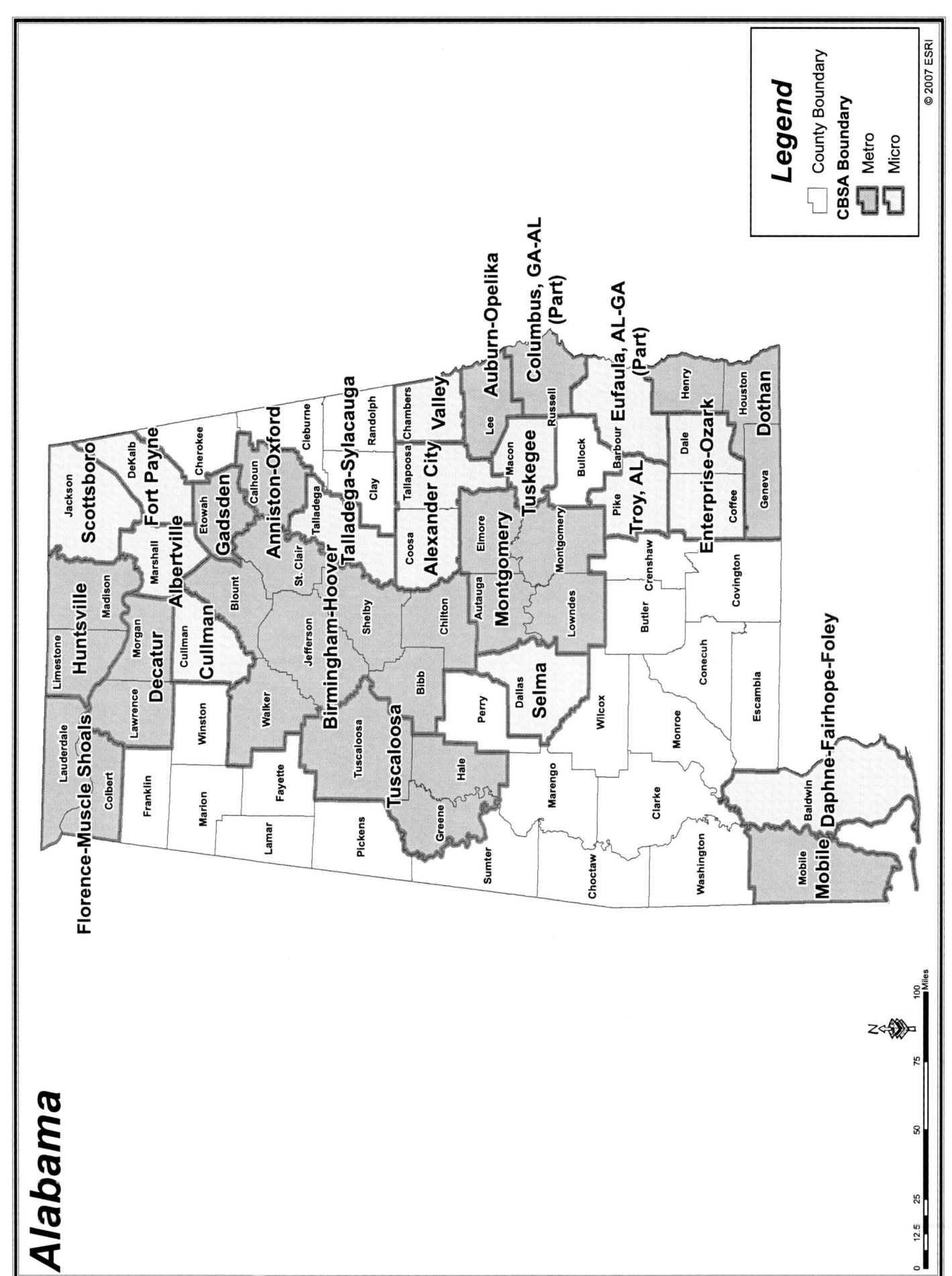

Alaska

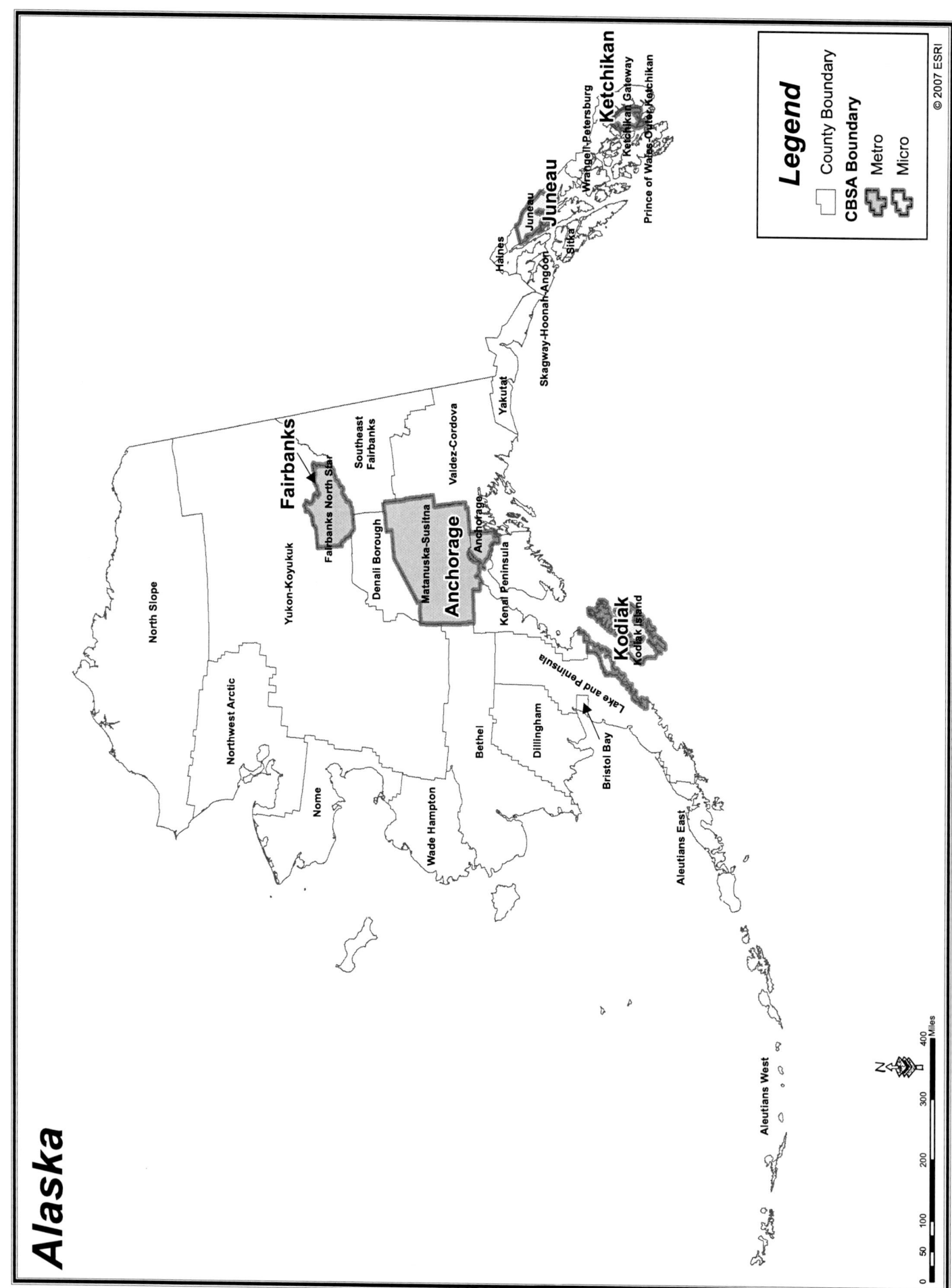

Ketchikan

Juneau

Haines

Sitka

Skagway-Hoonah-Angoon

Wrangell-Petersburg

Ketchikan Gateway

Prince of Wales-Outer Ketchikan

Yakutat

Southeast Fairbanks

Valdez-Cordova

Fairbanks

Fairbanks North Star

North Slope

Yukon-Koyukuk

Denali Borough

Matanuska-Susitna

Anchorage

Kenai Peninsula

Northwest Arctic

Kodiak

Kodiak Island

Nome

Wade Hampton

Bethel

Dillingham

Lake and Peninsula

Bristol Bay

Aleutians East

Aleutians West

N

0   50 100   200   300   400
                                    Miles

Legend

County Boundary

CBSA Boundary

Metro

Micro

Arizona

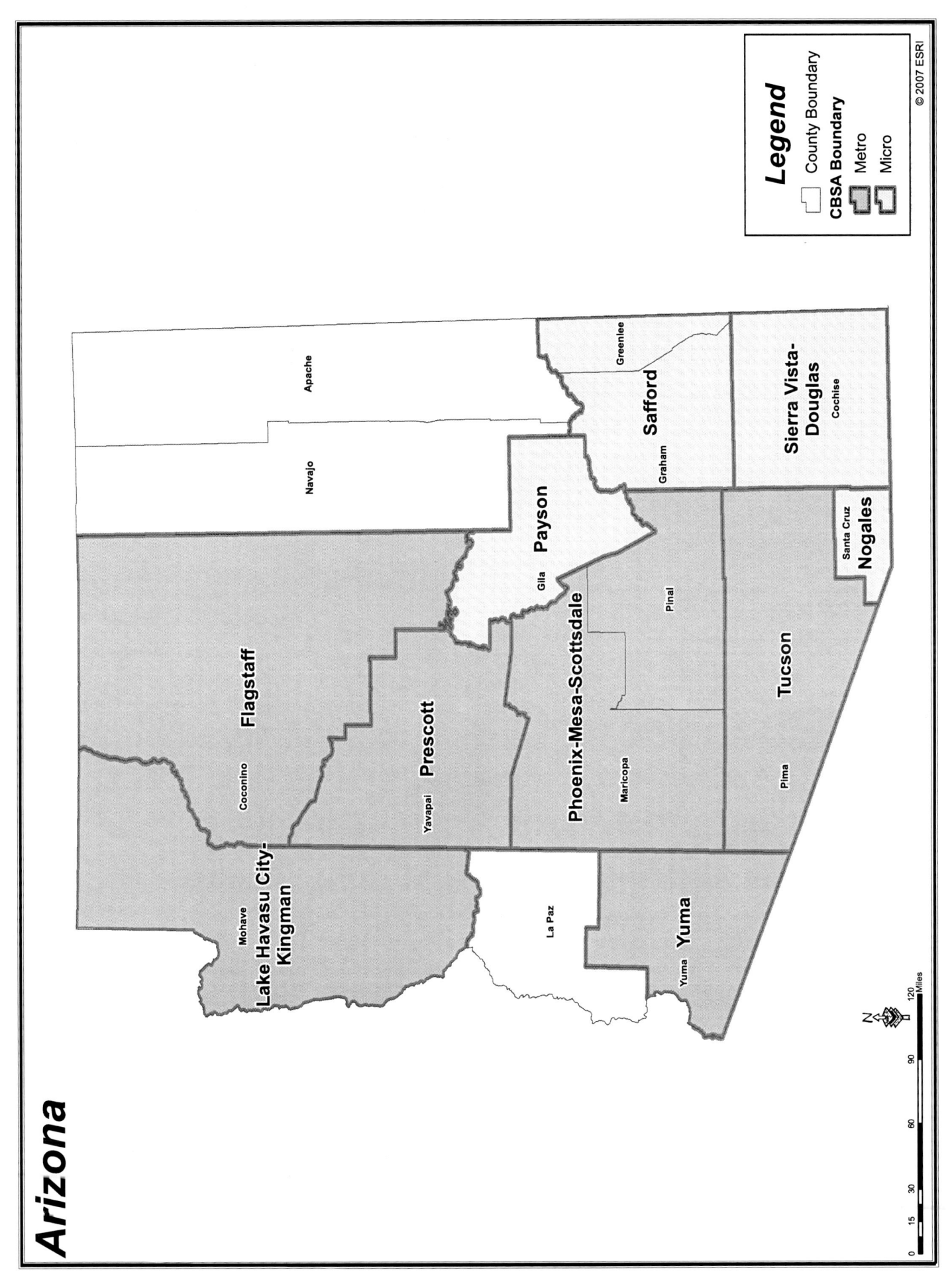

Legend

County Boundary

CBSA Boundary

Metro

Micro

226

Arkansas

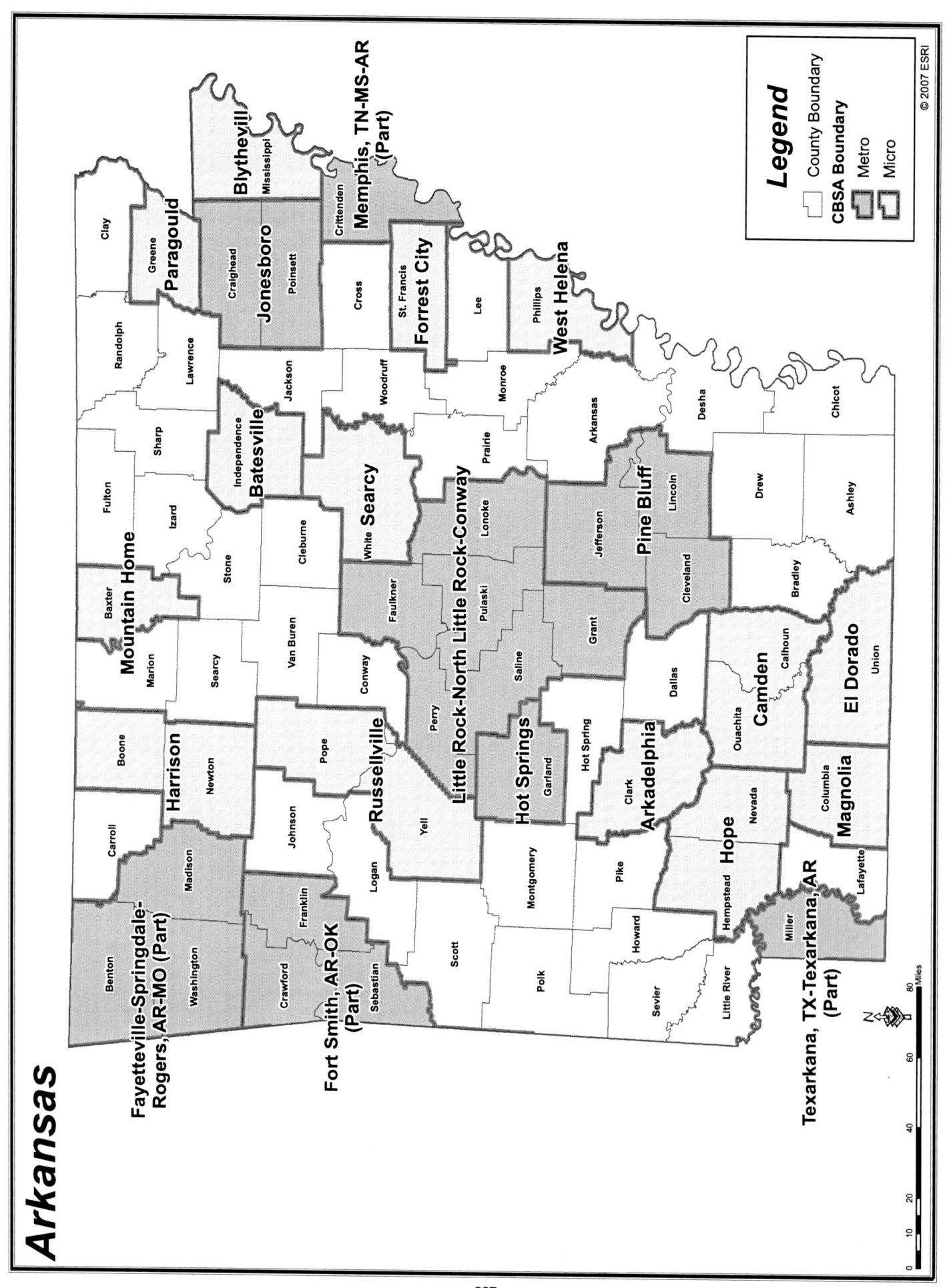

Northern California

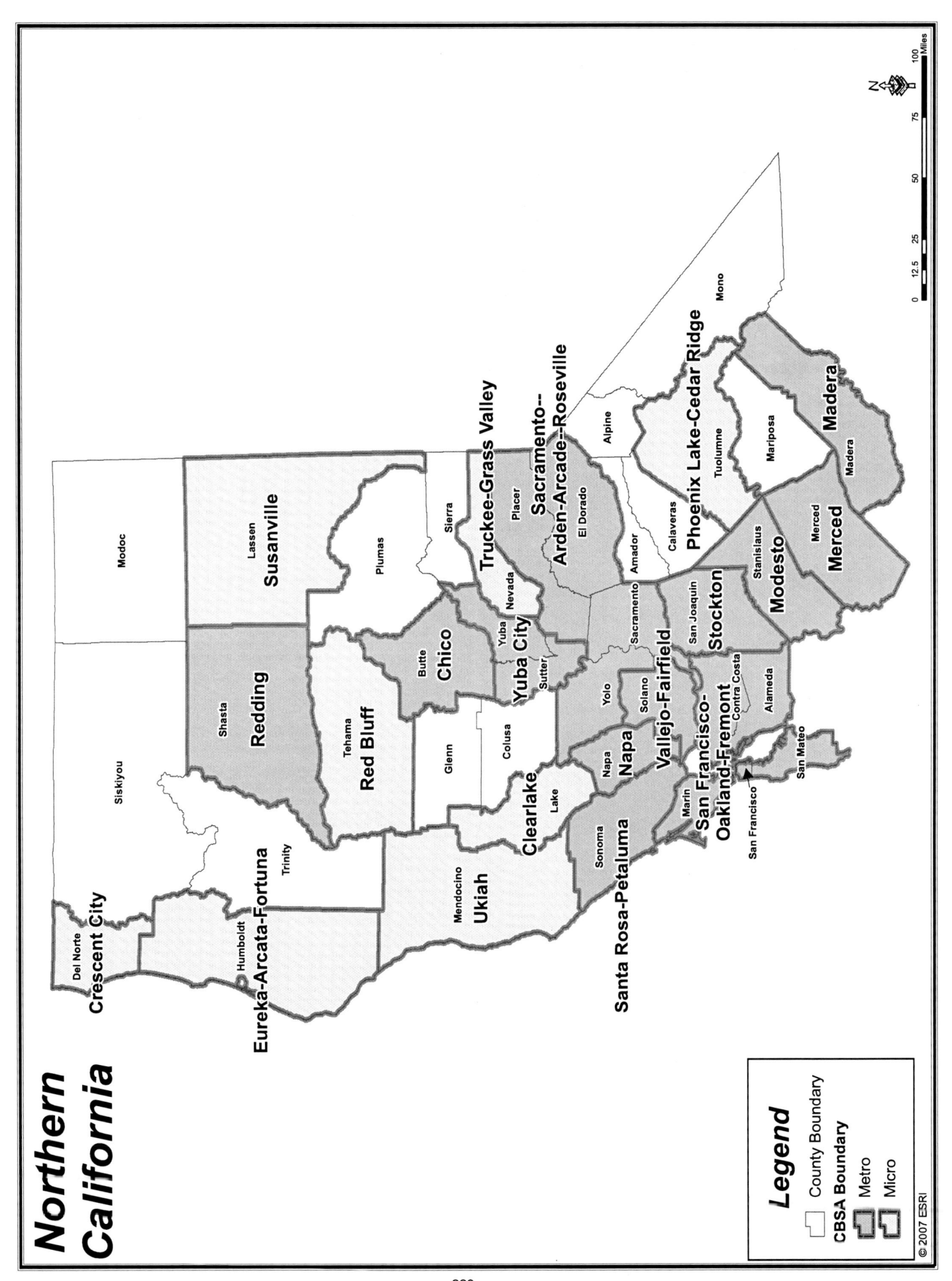

Legend

County Boundary

CBSA Boundary

Metro

Micro

© 2007 ESRI

Crescent City

Del Norte

Eureka-Arcata-Fortuna

Humboldt

Trinity

Siskiyou

Modoc

Lassen
Susanville

Redding

Shasta

Plumas

Sierra

Red Bluff

Tehama

Chico

Butte

Glenn

Colusa

Mendocino

Ukiah

Lake

Clearlake

Sonoma

Santa Rosa-Petaluma

Napa

Napa

Marin

Yolo

Solano

Vallejo-Fairfield

San Francisco-
Oakland-Fremont

San Francisco

San Mateo

Alameda

Contra Costa

Yuba City

Yuba

Sutter

Nevada

Placer

Truckee-Grass Valley

Sacramento

El Dorado

Alpine

Sacramento--
Arden-Arcade--Roseville

Amador

Calaveras

Phoenix Lake-Cedar Ridge

Tuolumne

Mariposa

San Joaquin

Stockton

Stanislaus

Modesto

Merced

Merced

Madera

Madera

Mono

N

0   12.5   25   50   75   100
Miles

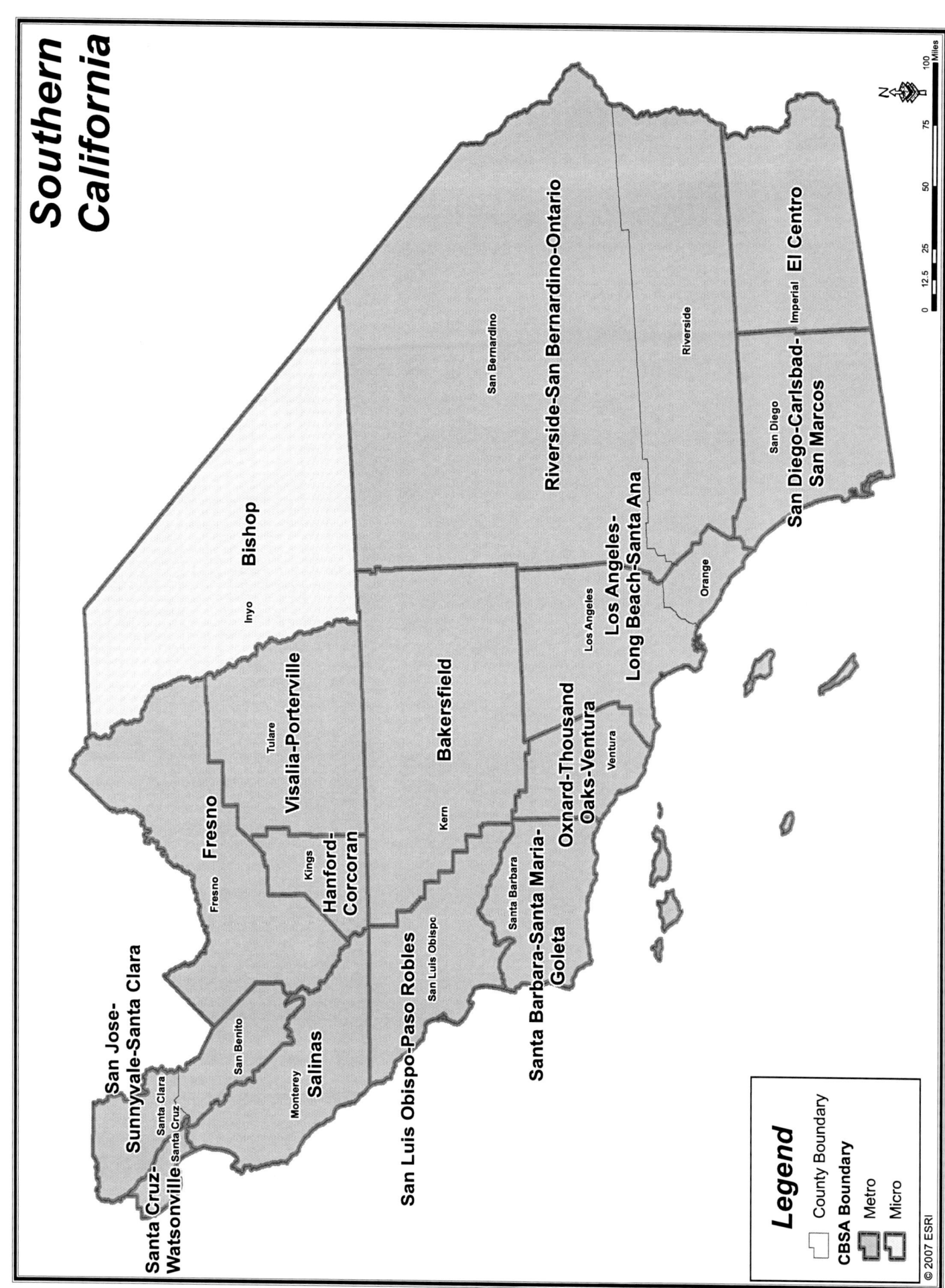

Southern California

Legend
County Boundary
CBSA Boundary
Metro
Micro

© 2007 ESRI

N

0 12.5 25   50   75   100
Miles

San Jose-
Sunnyvale-Santa Clara

Santa Cruz-
Watsonville

Santa Clara

Santa Cruz

San Benito

Monterey

Salinas

Fresno

Fresno

Kings

Hanford-
Corcoran

Visalia-Porterville

Tulare

Bishop

Inyo

Bakersfield

Kern

San Luis Obispo-Paso Robles

San Luis Obispo

Santa Barbara-Santa Maria-
Goleta

Santa Barbara

Oxnard-Thousand
Oaks-Ventura

Ventura

San Bernardino

Riverside-San Bernardino-Ontario

Riverside

Los Angeles-
Long Beach-Santa Ana

Los Angeles

Orange

San Diego-Carlsbad-
San Marcos

San Diego

Imperial   El Centro

229

Colorado

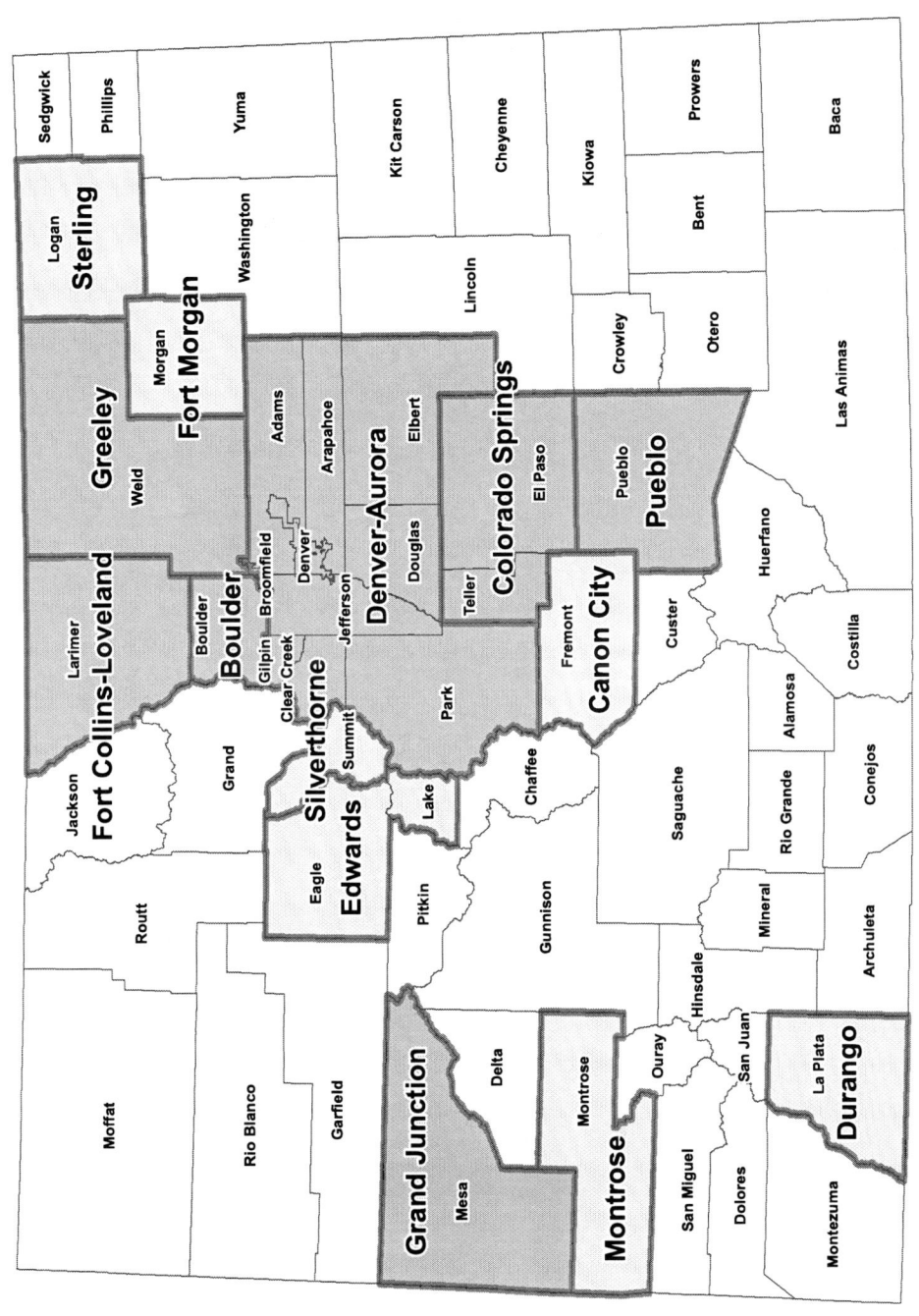

Connecticut

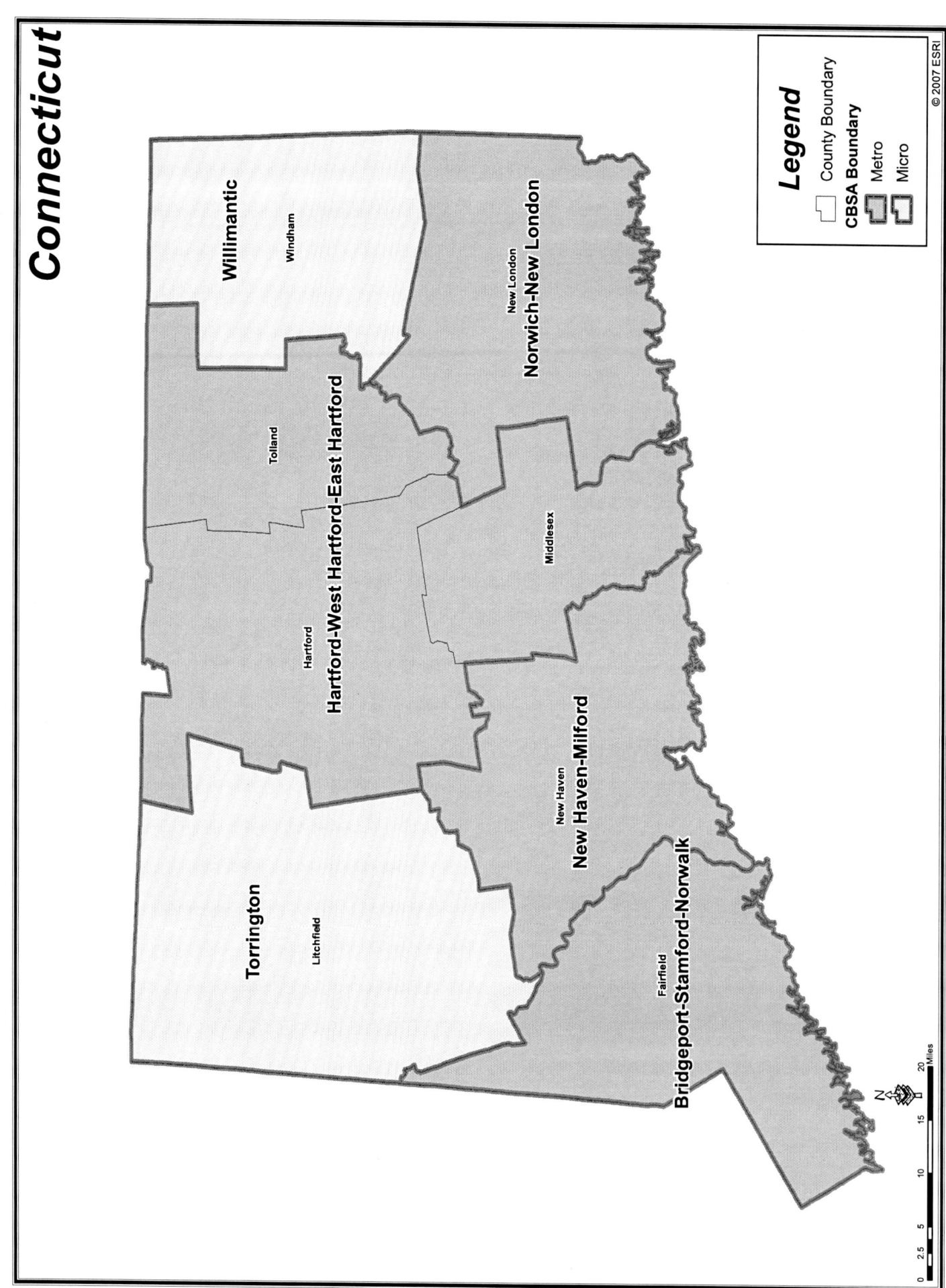

Willimantic

Windham

Norwich-New London

New London

Tolland

Hartford-West Hartford-East Hartford

Hartford

Middlesex

New Haven-Milford

New Haven

Torrington

Litchfield

Fairfield

Bridgeport-Stamford-Norwalk

Legend

County Boundary

CBSA Boundary

Metro

Micro

© 2007 ESRI

N

0 2.5 5   10   15   20
Miles

Delaware

Philadelphia-Camden-
Wilmington, PA-NJ-DE-MD
(Part)

New Castle

Dover

Kent

Seaford

Sussex

Legend

County Boundary

CBSA Boundary

Metro

Micro

N

0 3   6   12   18   24
Miles

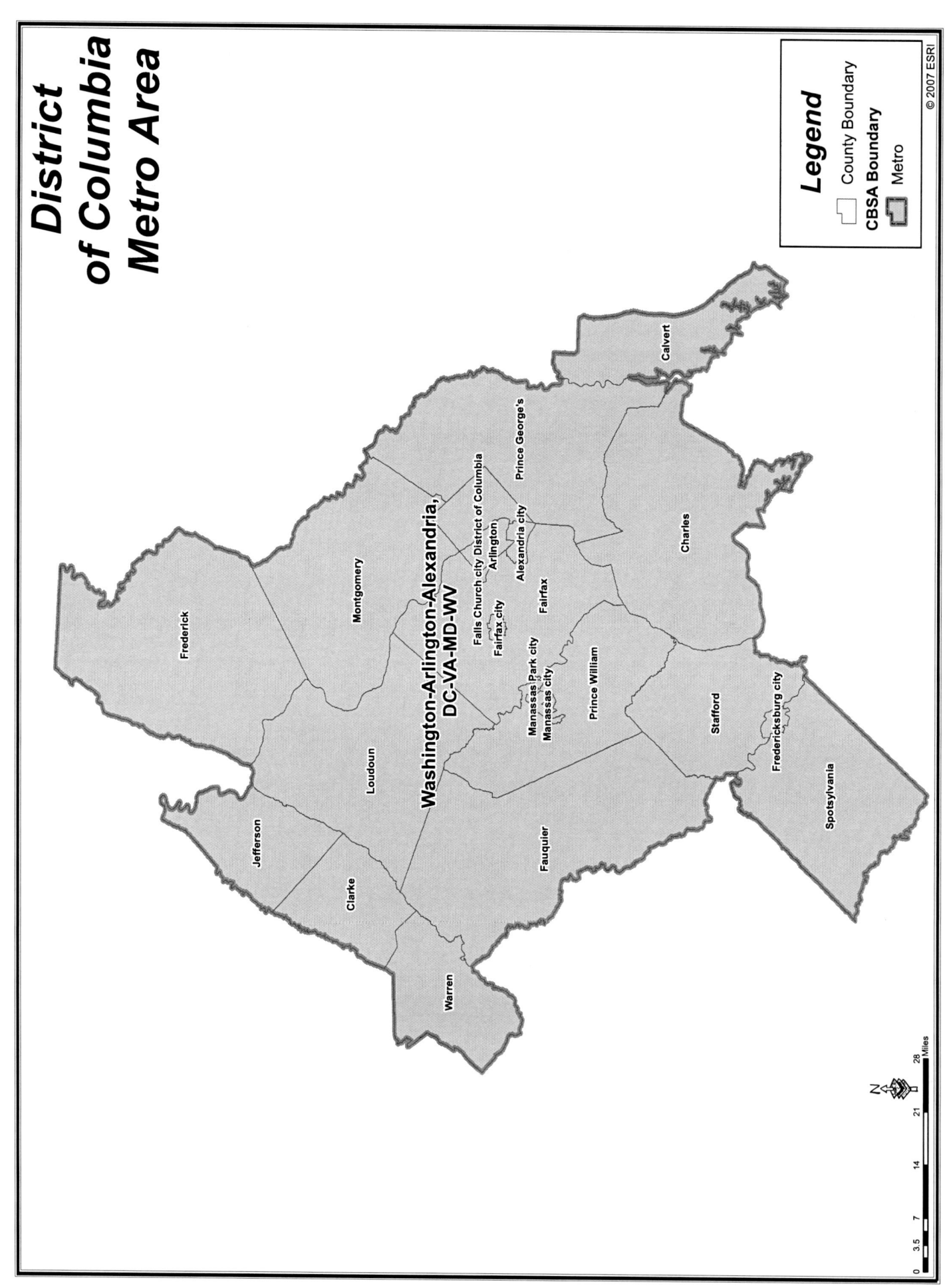

District
of Columbia
Metro Area

Washington-Arlington-Alexandria,
DC-VA-MD-WV

District of Columbia
Prince George's
Calvert
Charles
Falls Church city
Arlington
Alexandria city
Fairfax city
Fairfax
Montgomery
Manassas Park city
Manassas city
Prince William
Frederick
Stafford
Fredericksburg city
Loudoun
Spotsylvania
Fauquier
Jefferson
Clarke
Warren

Legend

County Boundary
CBSA Boundary
Metro

N

0 3.5 7   14   21   28
                              Miles

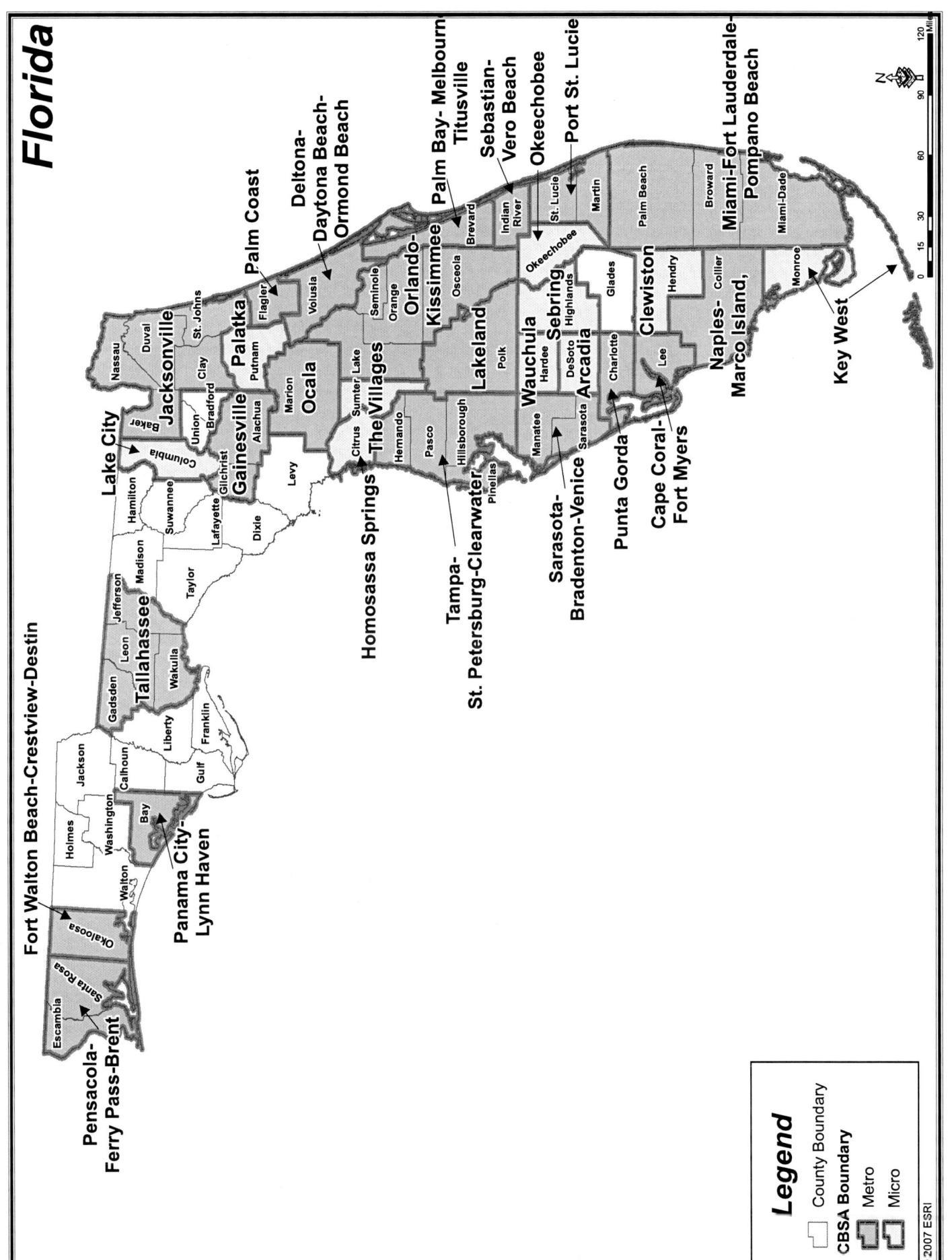

Florida

Legend

County Boundary

CBSA Boundary

Metro

Micro

© 2007 ESRI

Fort Walton Beach-Crestview-Destin

Pensacola-Ferry Pass-Brent

Panama City-Lynn Haven

Tallahassee

Lake City

Jacksonville

Gainesville

Palatka

Palm Coast

Deltona-Daytona Beach-Ormond Beach

Ocala

The Villages

Homosassa Springs

Orlando-Kissimmee

Palm Bay- Melbourne-Titusville

Sebastian-Vero Beach

Okeechobee

Port St. Lucie

Lakeland

Wauchula

Sebring

Arcadia

Tampa-St. Petersburg-Clearwater

Sarasota-Bradenton-Venice

Punta Gorda

Cape Coral-Fort Myers

Naples-Marco Island,

Clewiston

Miami-Fort Lauderdale-Pompano Beach

Key West

Escambia

Santa Rosa

Okaloosa

Walton

Holmes

Washington

Bay

Jackson

Calhoun

Liberty

Gulf

Franklin

Gadsden

Leon

Wakulla

Jefferson

Madison

Taylor

Hamilton

Suwannee

Lafayette

Dixie

Columbia

Baker

Nassau

Duval

Union

Bradford

Clay

St. Johns

Flagler

Putnam

Alachua

Gilchrist

Levy

Marion

Volusia

Lake

Sumter

Citrus

Hernando

Seminole

Orange

Osceola

Brevard

Indian River

St. Lucie

Martin

Palm Beach

Okeechobee

Glades

Highlands

Hardee

DeSoto

Polk

Hillsborough

Pasco

Pinellas

Manatee

Sarasota

Charlotte

Lee

Hendry

Collier

Broward

Miami-Dade

Monroe

N

0 15 30 60 90 120 Miles

Georgia

Chattanooga, TN-GA (Part)

Summerville

Athens-Clarke County

Augusta-Richmond County, GA-SC (Part)

Columbus, GA-AL (Part)

Eufaula, AL-GA (Part)

Thomasville

Legend

	County Boundary
	CBSA Boundary
	Metro
	Micro

© 2007 ESRI

N

0 10 20 40 60 80
Miles

235

Hawaii

Kapaa

Kauai

Kauai

Honolulu

Honolulu

Maui

Kalawao

Maui

Maui

Kahului-Wailuku

Hilo

Hawaii

N

0 10 20 40 60 80
Miles

Idaho

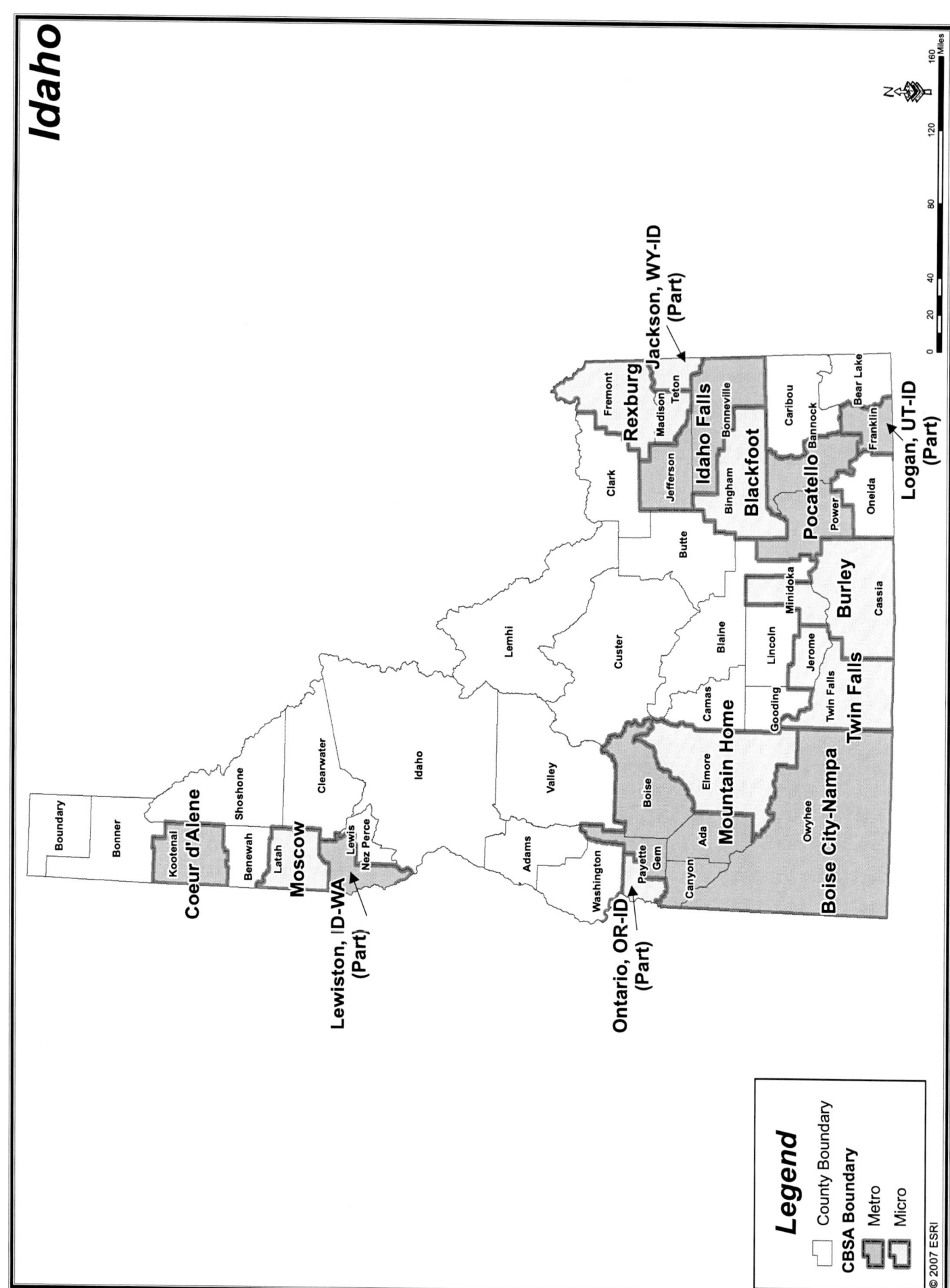

Legend

County Boundary

CBSA Boundary
Metro
Micro

© 2007 ESRI

Coeur d'Alene

Moscow

Lewiston, ID-WA (Part)

Ontario, OR-ID (Part)

Mountain Home

Boise City-Nampa

Twin Falls

Burley

Pocatello

Logan, UT-ID (Part)

Blackfoot

Idaho Falls

Rexburg

Jackson, WY-ID (Part)

Boundary

Bonner

Kootenal

Benewah

Shoshone

Latah

Lewis

Nez Perce

Clearwater

Idaho

Adams

Washington

Payette

Gem

Canyon

Ada

Owyhee

Boise

Elmore

Valley

Custer

Lemhi

Clark

Butte

Camas

Gooding

Twin Falls

Lincoln

Blaine

Jerome

Minidoka

Cassia

Jefferson

Fremont

Madison

Teton

Bingham

Bonneville

Caribou

Bannock

Power

Oneida

Franklin

Bear Lake

0 20 40 80 120 160
Miles

Illinois

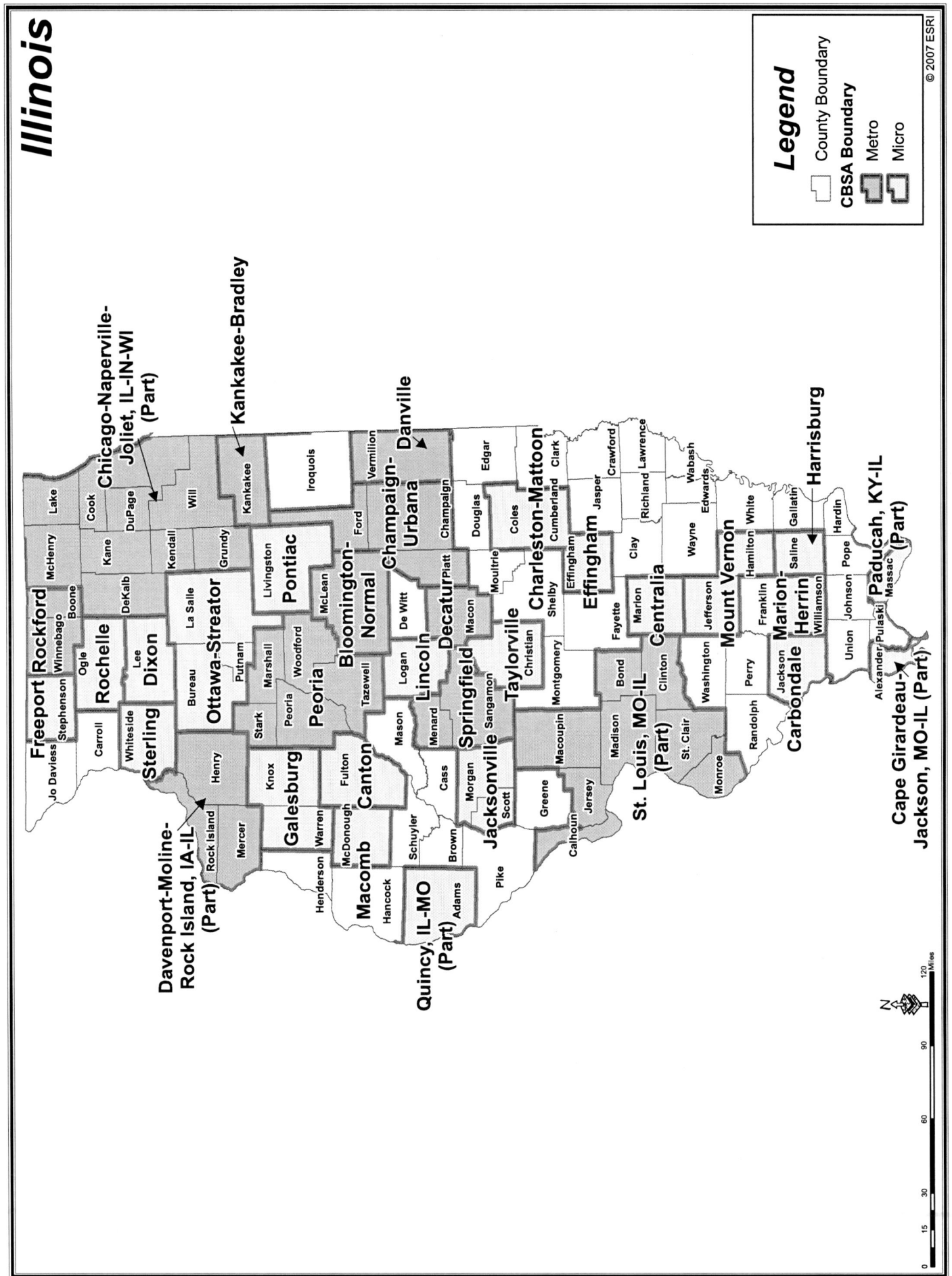

Freeport
Rockford
Rochelle
Sterling Dixon

Davenport-Moline-
Rock Island, IA-IL
(Part)

Galesburg

Macomb

Quincy, IL-MO
(Part)

Chicago-Naperville-
Joliet, IL-IN-WI
(Part)

Kankakee-Bradley

Ottawa-Streator

Pontiac

Bloomington-
Normal

Peoria

Canton

Jacksonville

Lincoln

Decatur

Champaign-
Urbana

Danville

Springfield

Taylorville

Charleston-Mattoon

Effingham

Centralia

Mount Vernon

Marion-
Herrin
Carbondale

Harrisburg

Paducah, KY-IL
(Part)

Cape Girardeau-
Jackson, MO-IL (Part)

St. Louis, MO-IL
(Part)

Jo Daviess
Stephenson
Winnebago
Boone
McHenry
Lake
Carroll
Ogle
DeKalb
Kane
Cook
DuPage
Whiteside
Lee
Kendall
Will
Grundy
Rock Island
Henry
Bureau
La Salle
Livingston
Mercer
Putnam
Marshall
Woodford
McLean
Ford
Iroquois
Stark
Knox
Peoria
Tazewell
Kankakee
Warren
Henderson
Fulton
Mason
De Witt
Champaign
Vermilion
McDonough
Schuyler
Cass
Menard
Logan
Piatt
Douglas
Edgar
Hancock
Brown
Morgan
Sangamon
Christian
Moultrie
Coles
Clark
Adams
Pike
Scott
Greene
Macoupin
Montgomery
Shelby
Cumberland
Jasper
Crawford
Calhoun
Jersey
Madison
Bond
Fayette
Effingham
Clay
Richland
Lawrence
Monroe
St. Clair
Clinton
Marion
Wayne
Edwards
Wabash
Randolph
Washington
Jefferson
Perry
Franklin
Hamilton
White
Jackson
Williamson
Saline
Gallatin
Union
Johnson
Pope
Hardin
Alexander
Pulaski
Massac

Legend

County Boundary

CBSA Boundary

Metro

Micro

© 2007 ESRI

N

0 15 30   60   90   120
                              Miles

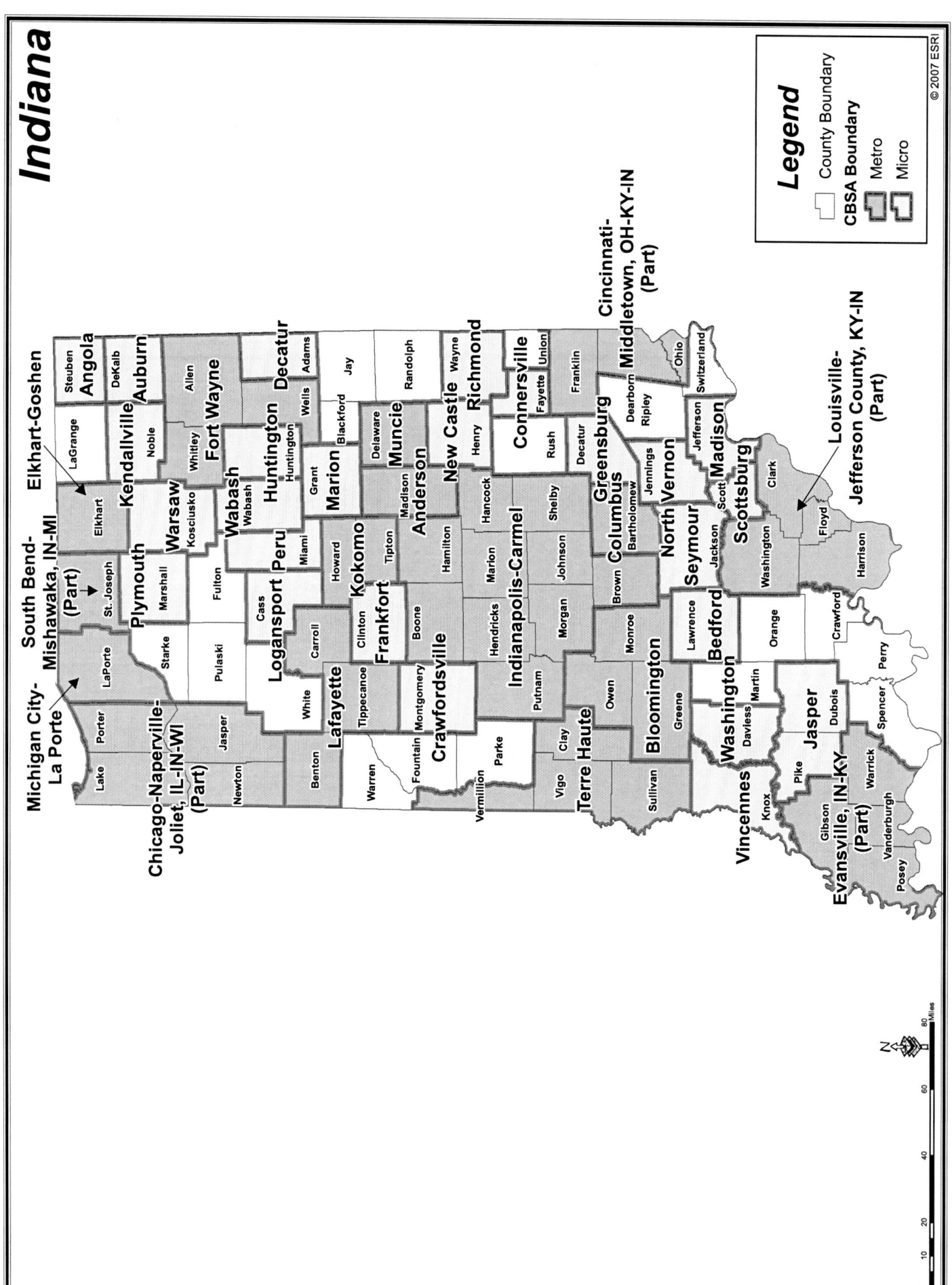

Indiana

© 2007 ESRI

Legend

County Boundary

CBSA Boundary

Metro   Micro

Iowa

Sioux City, IA-NE-SD (Part)

Spirit Lake

Spencer

Storm Lake

Omaha-Council Bluffs, NE-IA (Part)

Fort Dodge

Mason City

Waterloo-Cedar Falls

Boone

Ames

Des Moines-West Des Moines

Marshalltown

Newton

Pella

Oskaloosa

Ottumwa

Cedar Rapids

Iowa City

Muscatine

Dubuque

Clinton

Davenport-Moline-Rock Island, IA-IL (Part)

Burlington, IA-IL (Part)

Fort Madison-Keokuk, IA-MO (Part)

Lyon, Osceola, Dickinson, Emmet, Winnebago, Worth, Mitchell, Howard, Winneshiek, Allamakee

Sioux, O'Brien, Clay, Palo Alto, Hancock, Cerro Gordo, Floyd, Chickasaw, Fayette, Clayton

Plymouth, Cherokee, Buena Vista, Pocahontas, Humboldt, Wright, Franklin, Butler, Bremer, Delaware, Dubuque

Woodbury, Ida, Sac, Calhoun, Webster, Hamilton, Hardin, Grundy, Black Hawk, Buchanan

Monona, Crawford, Carroll, Greene, Boone, Story, Marshall, Tama, Benton, Linn, Jones, Jackson

Harrison, Shelby, Audubon, Guthrie, Dallas, Polk, Jasper, Poweshiek, Iowa, Johnson, Cedar, Clinton, Scott

Pottawattamie, Cass, Adair, Madison, Warren, Marion, Mahaska, Keokuk, Washington, Muscatine, Louisa

Mills, Montgomery, Adams, Union, Clarke, Lucas, Monroe, Wapello, Jefferson, Henry, Des Moines

Fremont, Page, Taylor, Ringgold, Decatur, Wayne, Appanoose, Davis, Van Buren, Lee

Legend

County Boundary

CBSA Boundary

Metro

Micro

Miles
0 10 20 40 60 80

N

Kansas

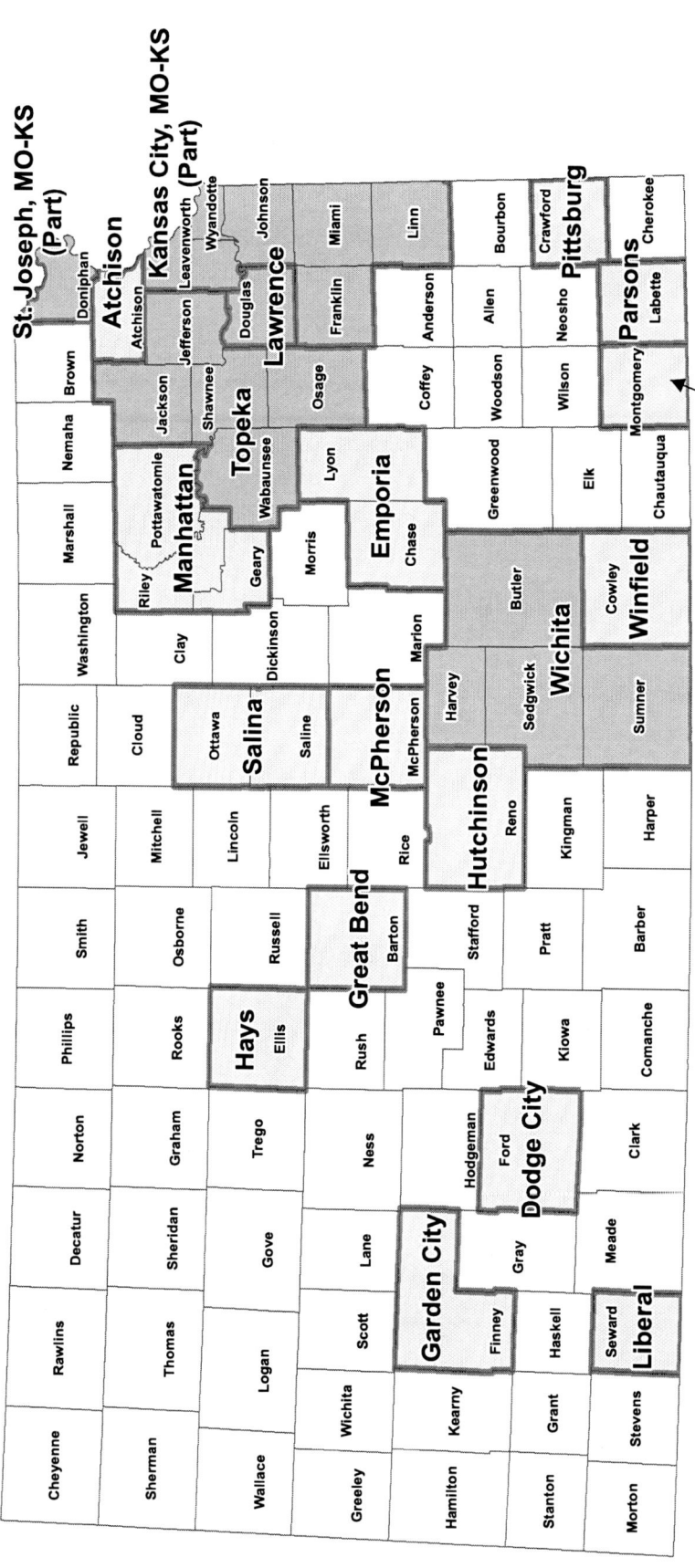

Legend

County Boundary

CBSA Boundary

Metro

Micro

© 2007 ESRI

St. Joseph, MO-KS (Part)

Kansas City, MO-KS (Part)

Atchison

Lawrence

Topeka

Manhattan

Emporia

Pittsburg

Parsons

Coffeyville

Winfield

Wichita

Salina

McPherson

Hutchinson

Great Bend

Hays

Dodge City

Garden City

Liberal

Cheyenne
Rawlins
Decatur
Norton
Phillips
Smith
Jewell
Republic
Washington
Marshall
Nemaha
Brown
Doniphan

Sherman
Thomas
Sheridan
Graham
Rooks
Osborne
Mitchell
Cloud
Clay
Riley
Pottawatomie
Jackson
Jefferson
Leavenworth
Wyandotte

Wallace
Logan
Gove
Trego
Ellis
Russell
Lincoln
Ottawa
Saline
Dickinson
Geary
Wabaunsee
Shawnee
Douglas
Johnson

Greeley
Wichita
Scott
Lane
Ness
Rush
Barton
Ellsworth
Rice
McPherson
Marion
Morris
Lyon
Osage
Franklin
Miami

Hamilton
Kearny
Finney
Hodgeman
Pawnee
Stafford
Reno
Harvey
Chase
Coffey
Anderson
Linn

Stanton
Grant
Haskell
Gray
Ford
Edwards
Pratt
Kingman
Sedgwick
Butler
Greenwood
Woodson
Allen
Bourbon
Crawford

Morton
Stevens
Seward
Meade
Clark
Comanche
Kiowa
Barber
Harper
Sumner
Cowley
Elk
Wilson
Neosho
Cherokee

Chautauqua
Montgomery
Labette

N

0   12.5   25   50   75   100
Miles

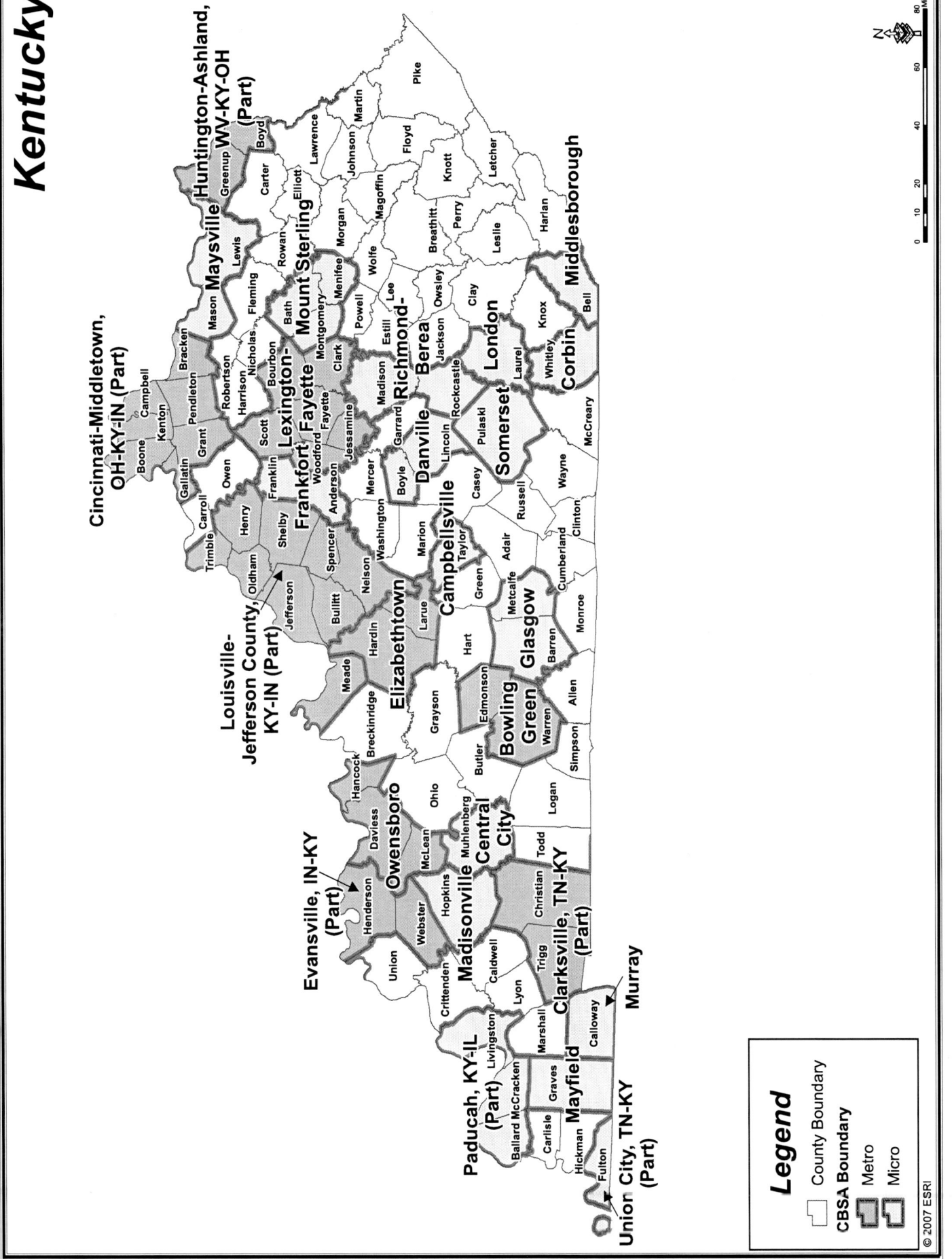

Kentucky

Legend

County Boundary

CBSA Boundary

Metro

Micro

---

0 10 20 40 60 80 Miles

N

Louisiana

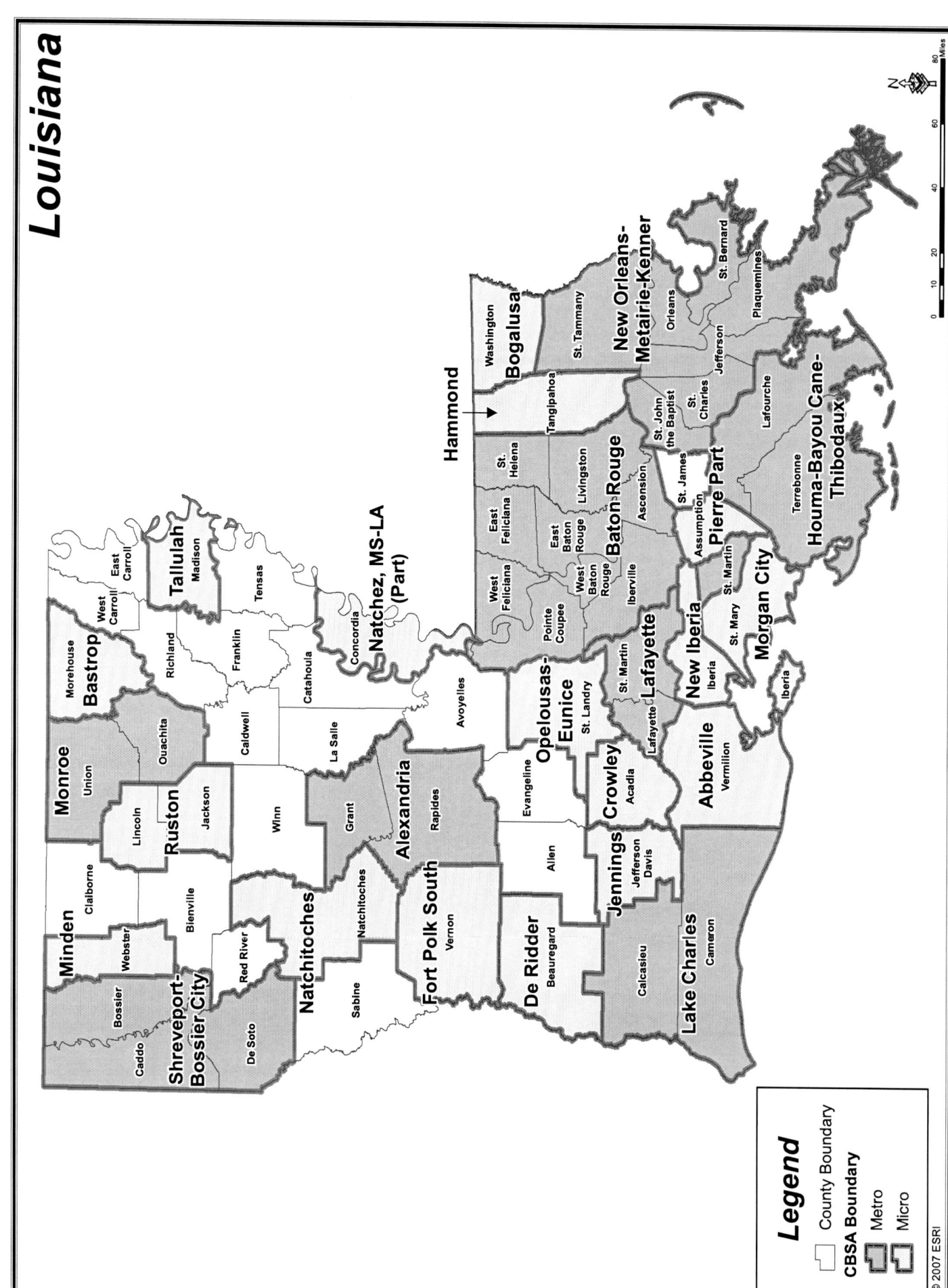

Legend

County Boundary

CBSA Boundary

Metro

Micro

© 2007 ESRI

243

Maine

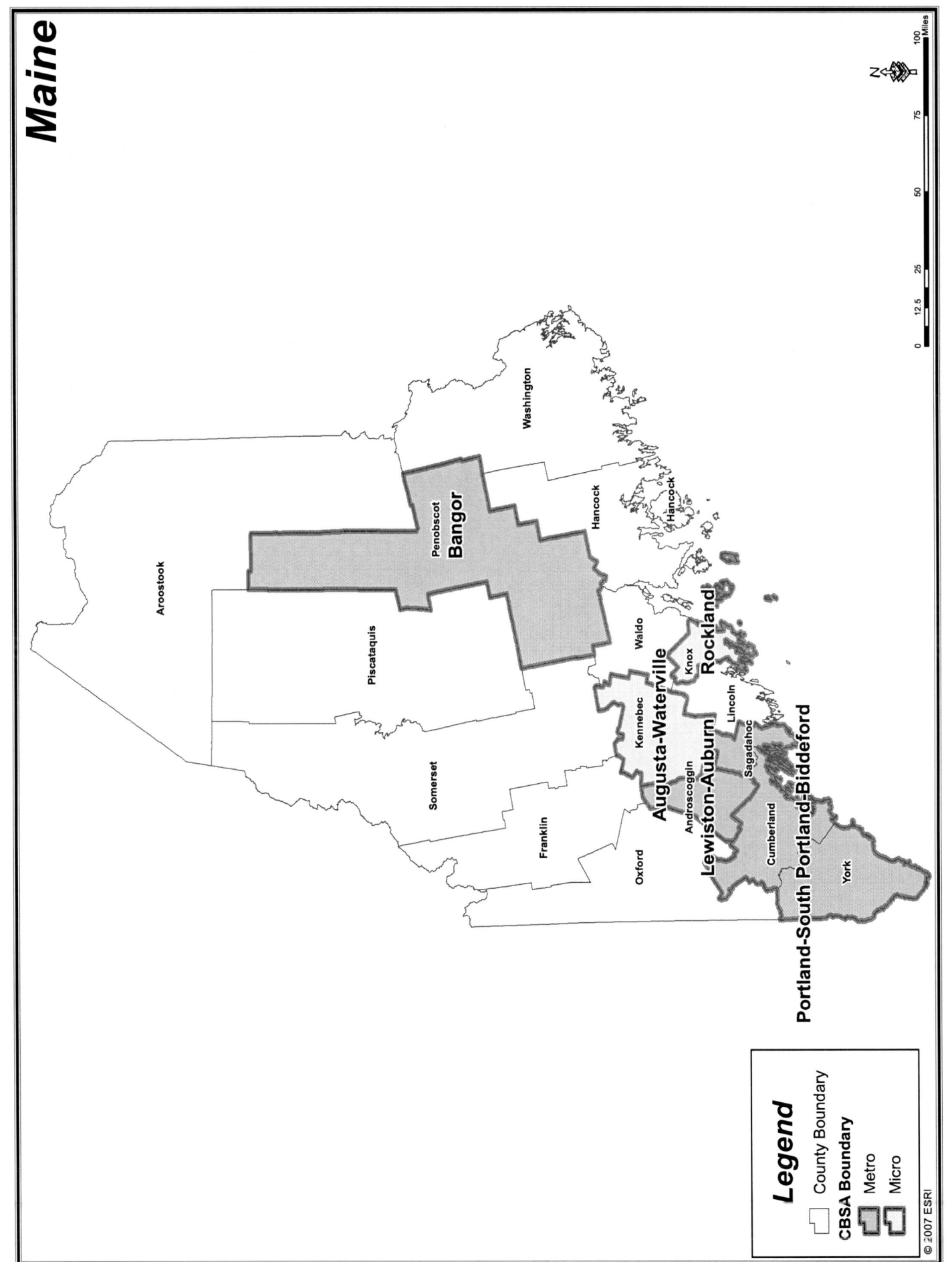

Legend

County Boundary

CBSA Boundary

Metro

Micro

© 2007 ESRI

0   12.5   25   50   75   100
Miles

N

Aroostook

Piscataquis

Penobscot
Bangor

Washington

Hancock

Hancock

Somerset

Franklin

Oxford

Kennebec

Androscoggin

Waldo

Knox

Rockland

Lincoln

Sagadahoc

Augusta-Waterville

Lewiston-Auburn

Cumberland

Portland-South Portland-Biddeford

York

Maryland

Philadelphia-Camden-Wilmington, PA-NJ-DE-MD (Part)

Baltimore-Towson

Washington-Arlington-Alexandria, DC-VA-MD-WV (Part)

Hagerstown-Martinsburg, MD-WV (Part)

Cumberland, MD-WV (Part)

Easton

Cambridge

Salisbury

Ocean Pines

Lexington Park, MD

Garrett

Allegany

Washington

Frederick

Carroll

Baltimore

Baltimore city

Howard

Montgomery

Harford

Cecil

Kent

Queen Anne's

Anne Arundel

Queen Anne's

Prince George's

Charles

St. Mary's

Calvert

Caroline

Talbot

Dorchester

Wicomico

Somerset

Worcester

N

0 5 10   20   30   40
Miles

Legend

County Boundary

CBSA Boundary

Metro

Micro

© 2007 ESRI

245

Massachusetts

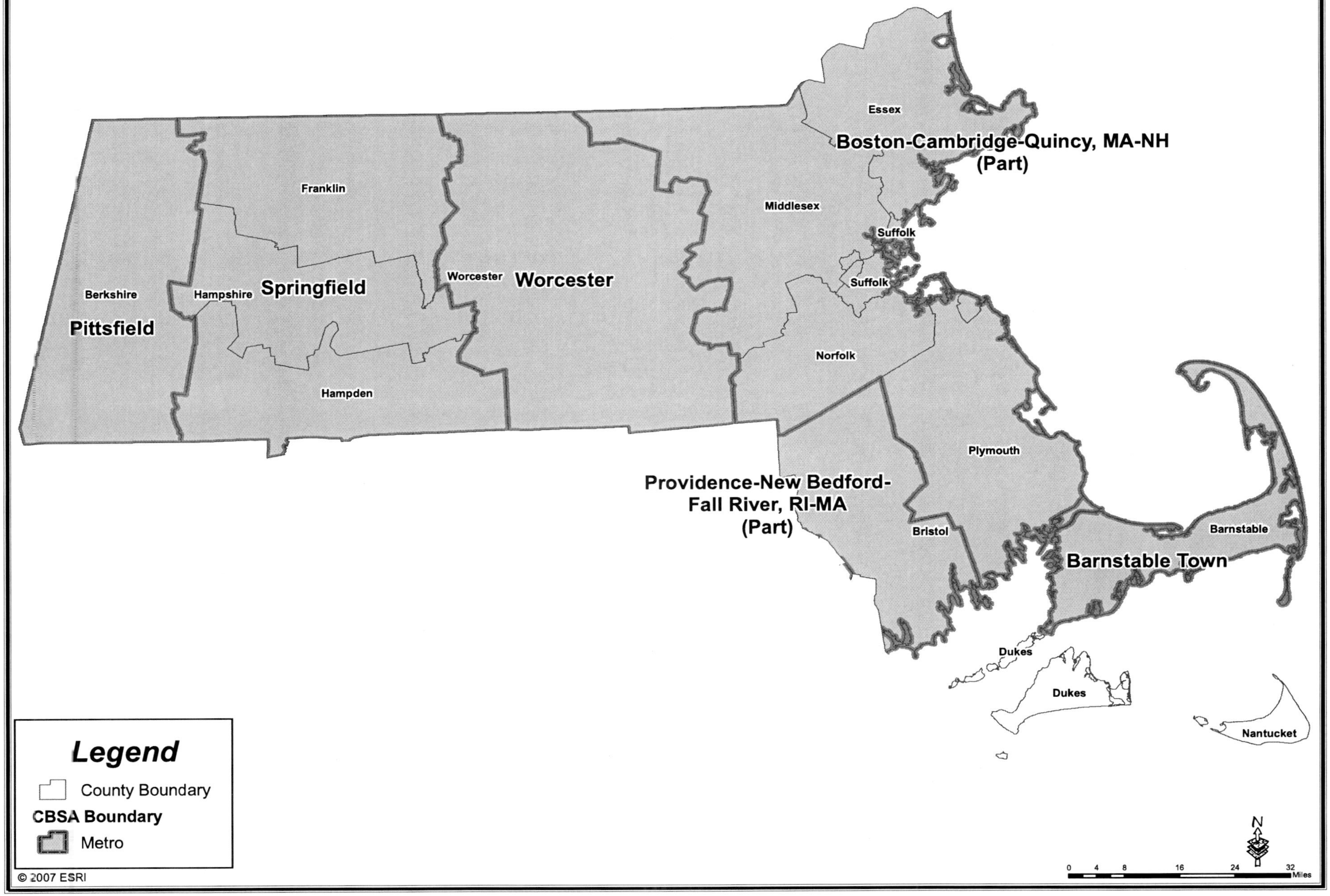

Barnstable

Nantucket

Boston-Cambridge-Quincy, MA-NH
(Part)

Barnstable Town

Dukes

Dukes

Plymouth

Essex

Suffolk

Suffolk

Bristol

Middlesex

Norfolk

Providence-New Bedford-
Fall River, RI-MA
(Part)

Worcester

Worcester

Franklin

Springfield

Hampden

Hampshire

Berkshire

Pittsfield

Legend

☐ County Boundary

CBSA Boundary

▢ Metro

N

0 4 8 16 24 32
Miles

Michigan

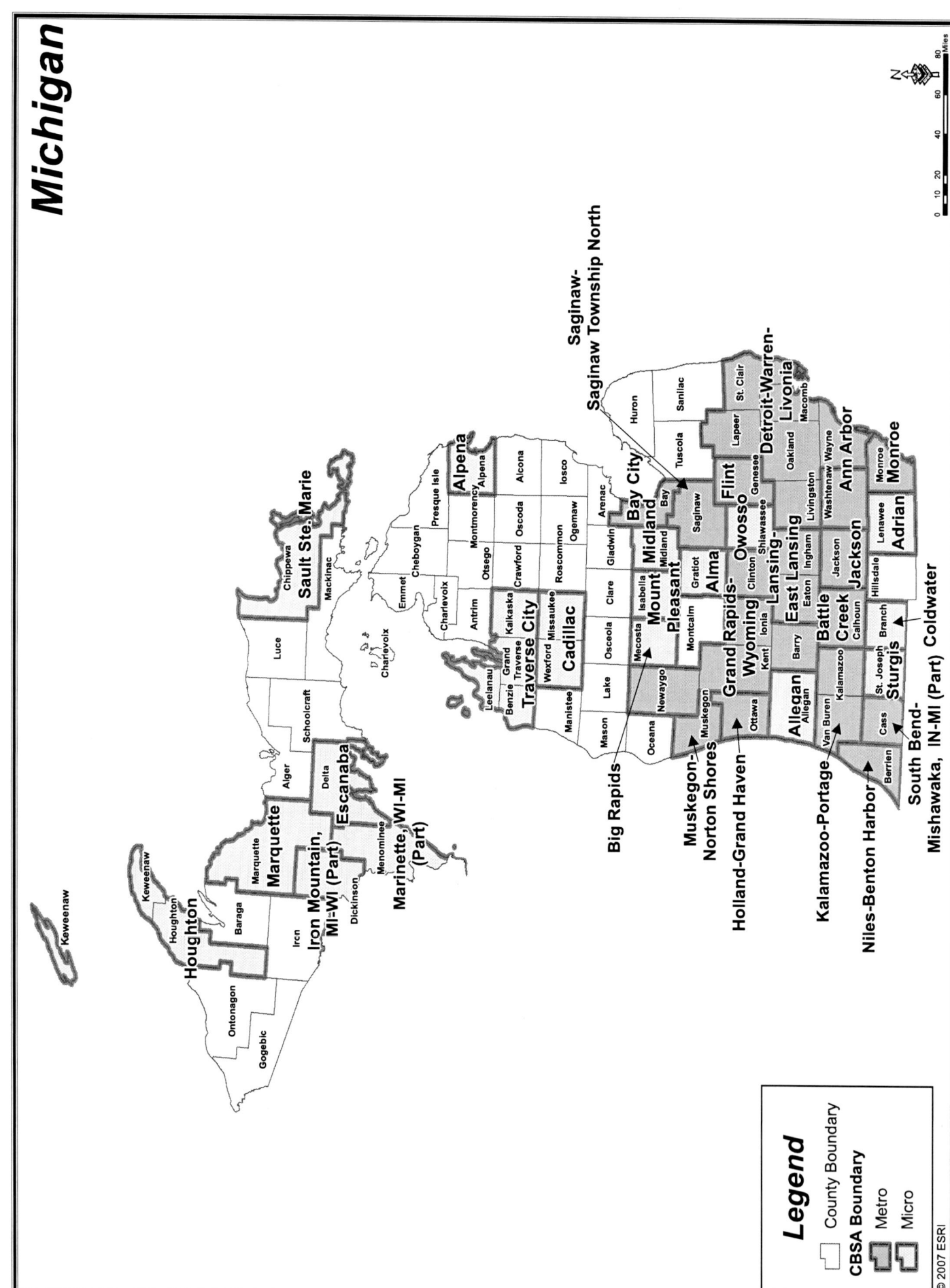

Legend

County Boundary

CBSA Boundary

Metro

Micro

© 2007 ESRI

247

Minnesota

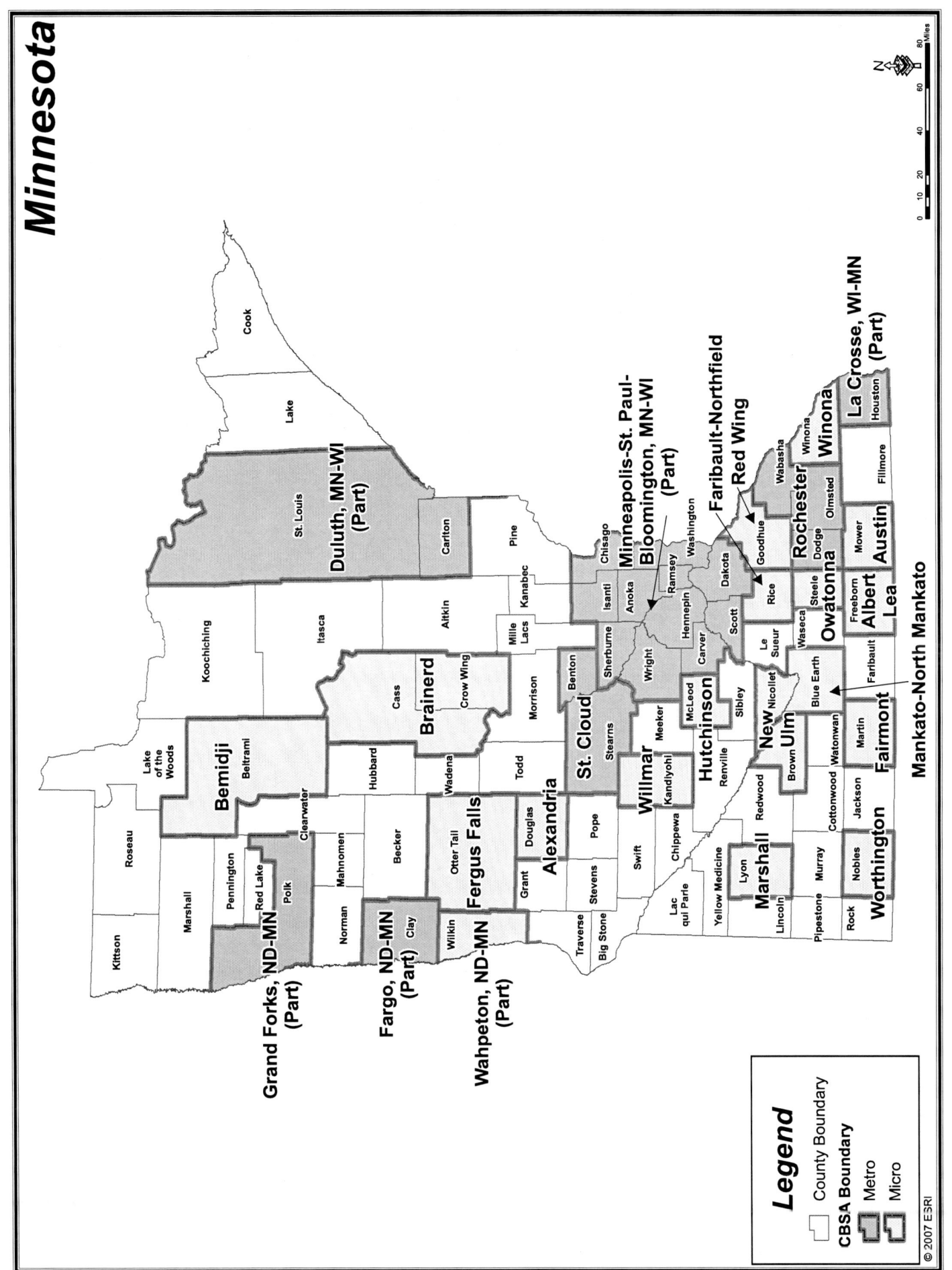

Legend

County Boundary

CBSA Boundary

Metro

Micro

© 2007 ESRI

248

Mississippi

Legend

County Boundary

CBSA Boundary

Metro

Micro

© 2007 ESRI

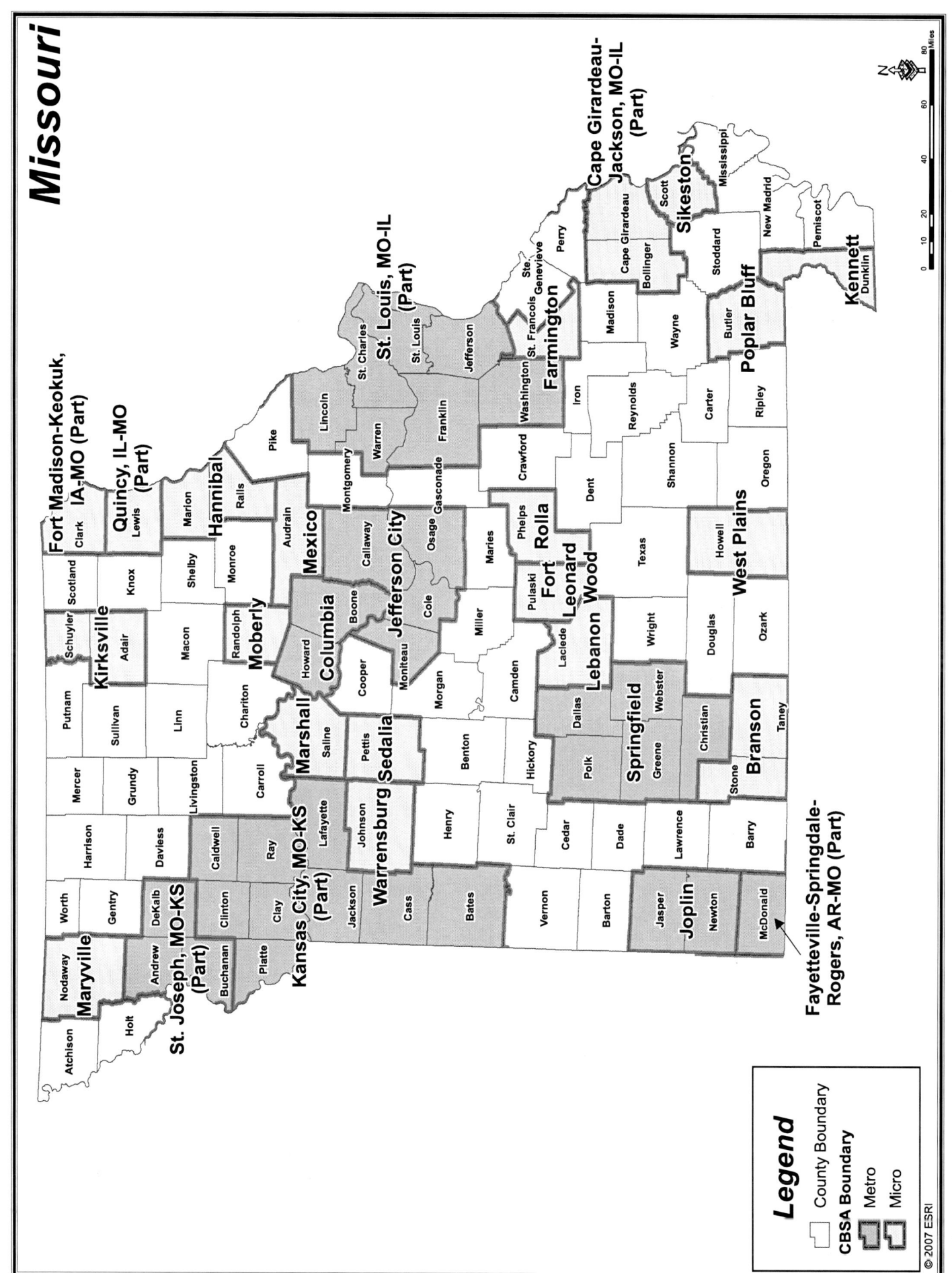

Missouri

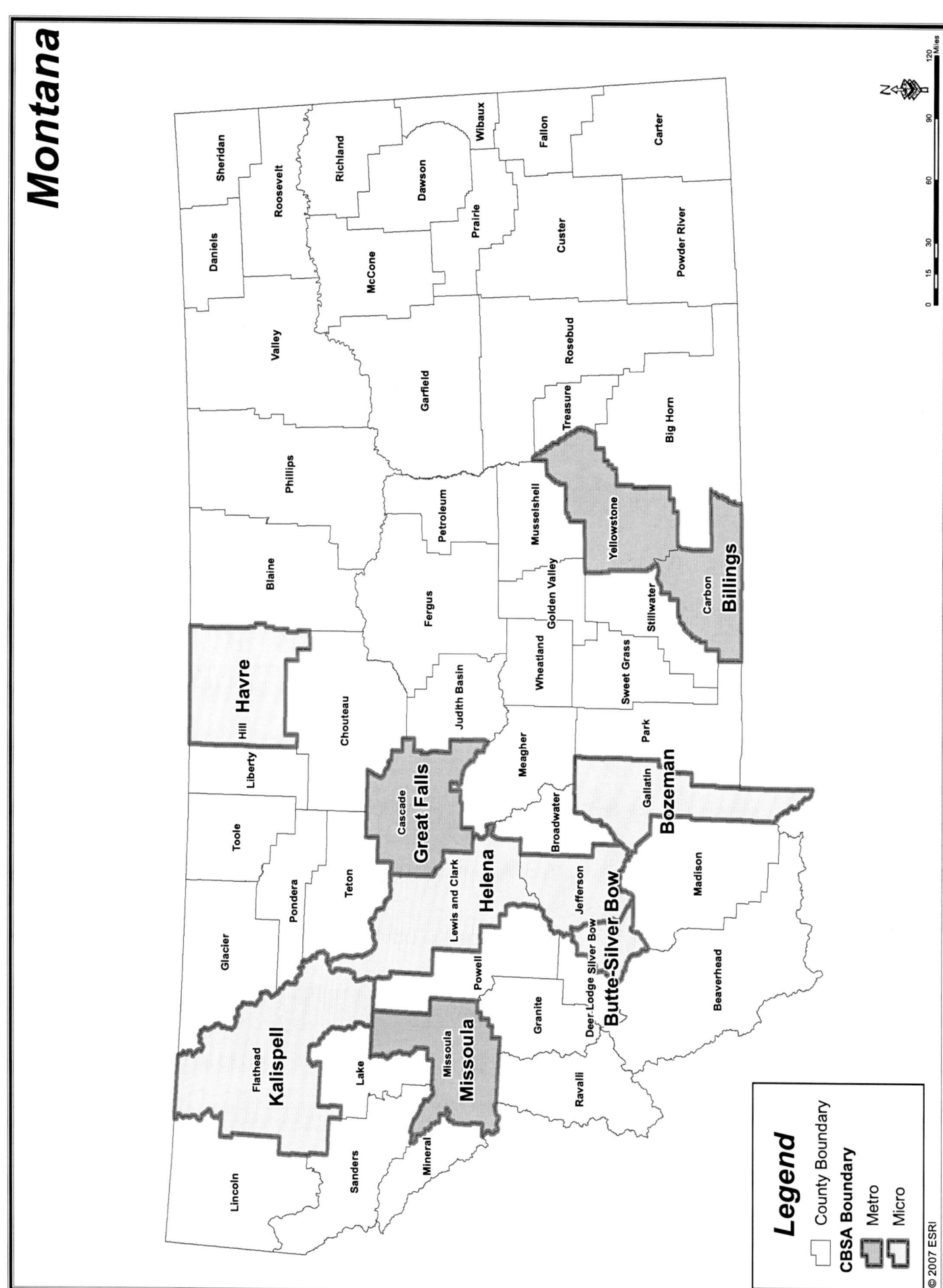

Montana

251

Nebraska

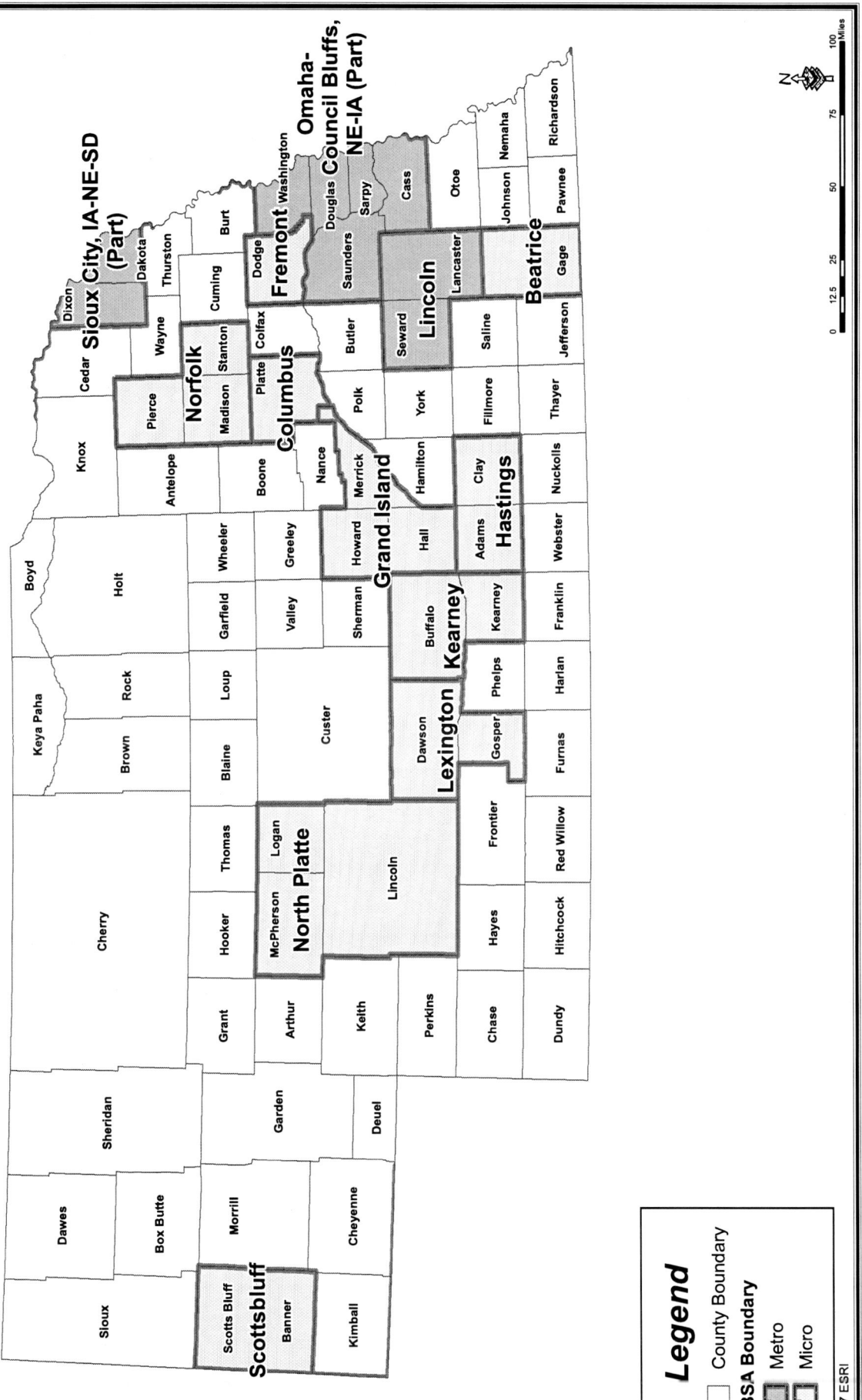

Legend

County Boundary

CBSA Boundary

Metro

Micro

© 2007 ESRI

252

Nevada

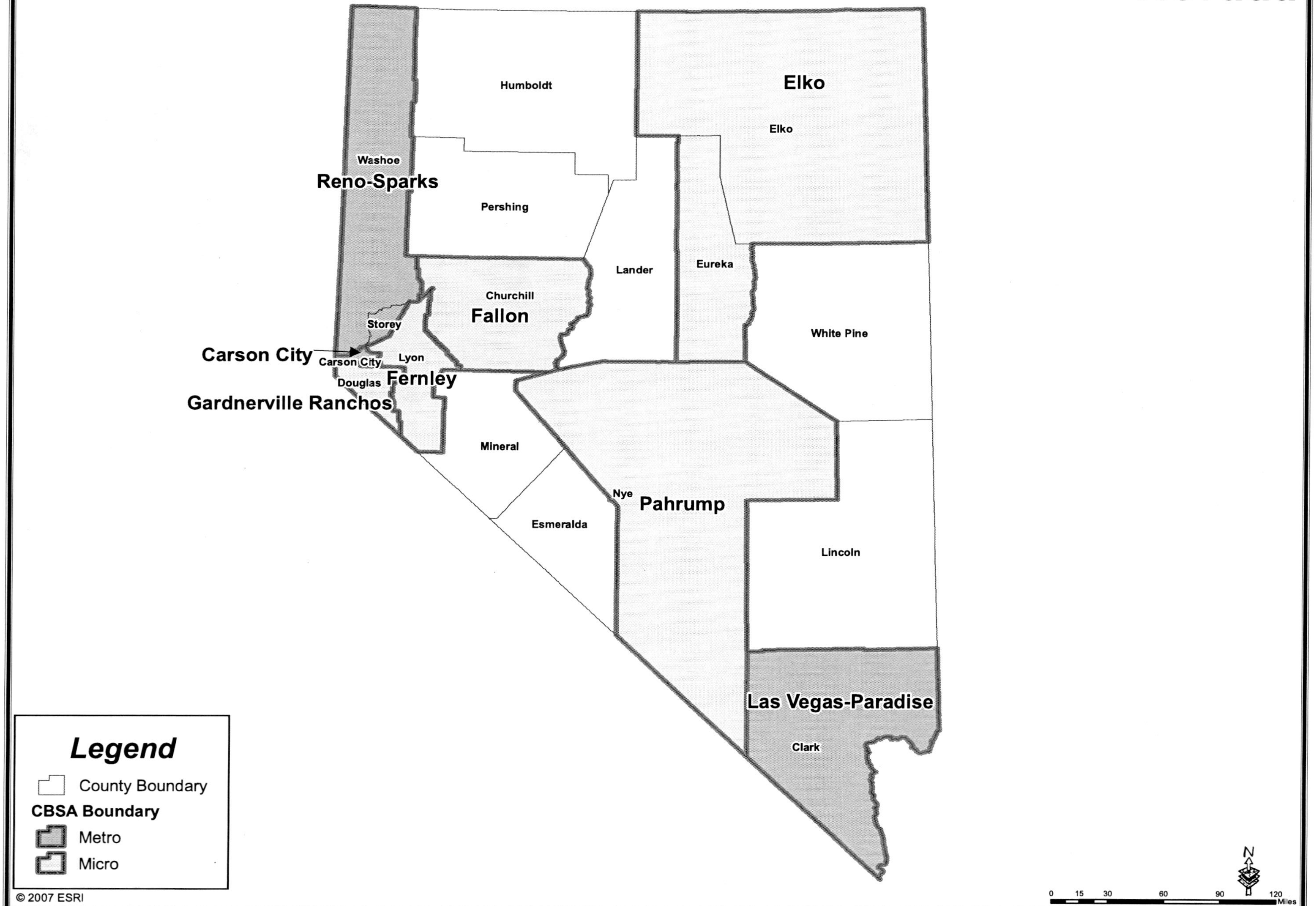

Elko
Elko

White Pine

Humboldt

Pershing

Lander

Eureka

Lincoln

Churchill
Fallon

Nye
Pahrump

Esmeralda

Mineral

Washoe
Reno-Sparks

Storey

Lyon

Fernley

Douglas

Carson City

Clark
Las Vegas-Paradise

Carson City

Gardnerville Ranchos

Legend

County Boundary

CBSA Boundary

Metro

Micro

© 2007 ESRI

N

0 15 30 60 90 120
Miles

New Hampshire

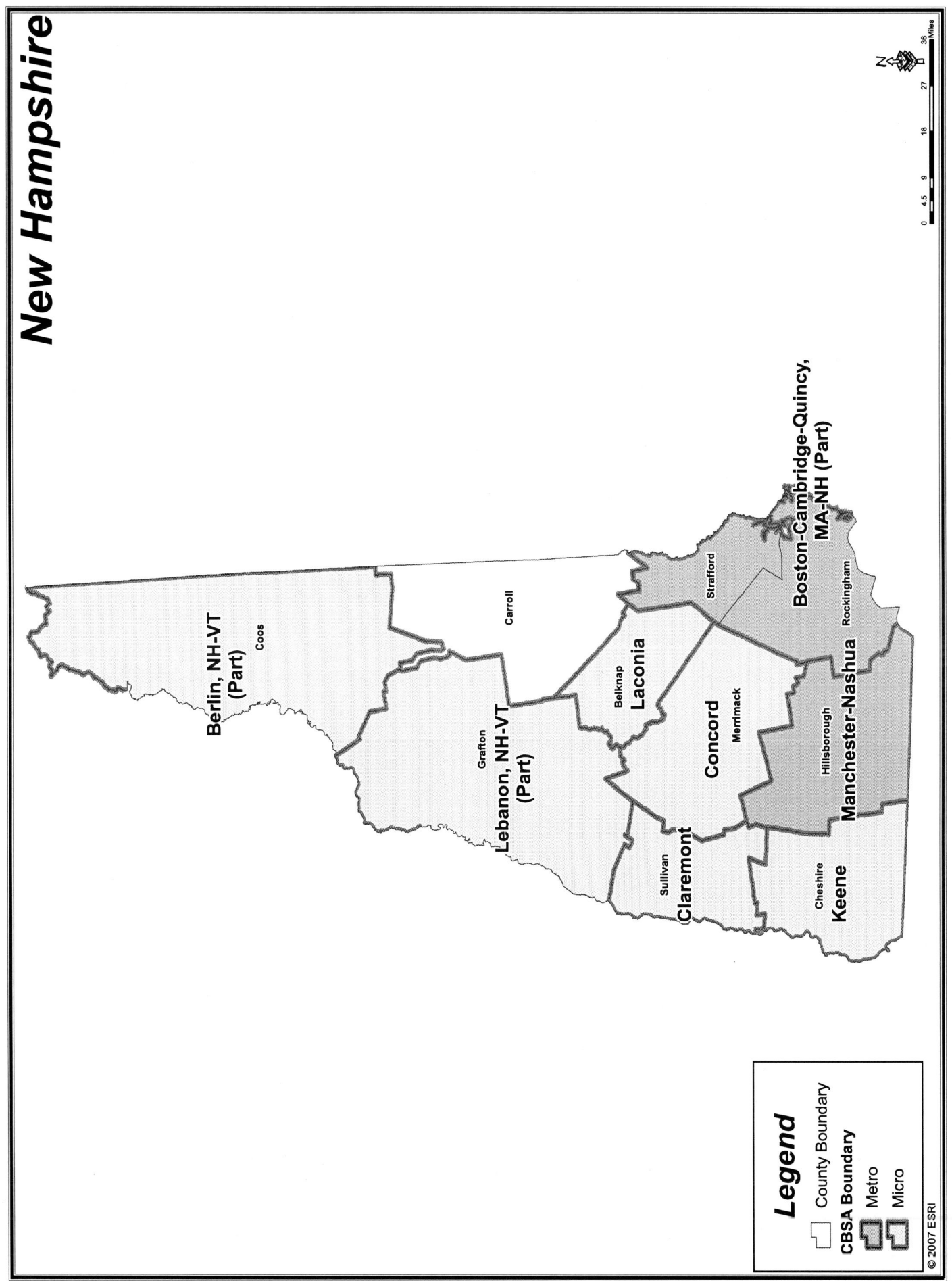

Berlin, NH-VT (Part)

Coos

Lebanon, NH-VT (Part)

Grafton

Carroll

Belknap

Laconia

Strafford

Boston-Cambridge-Quincy, MA-NH (Part)

Rockingham

Concord

Merrimack

Sullivan

Claremont

Hillsborough

Manchester-Nashua

Cheshire

Keene

N

0 4.5 9   18   27   36
Miles

Legend

County Boundary

CBSA Boundary

Metro

Micro

© 2007 ESRI

New Jersey

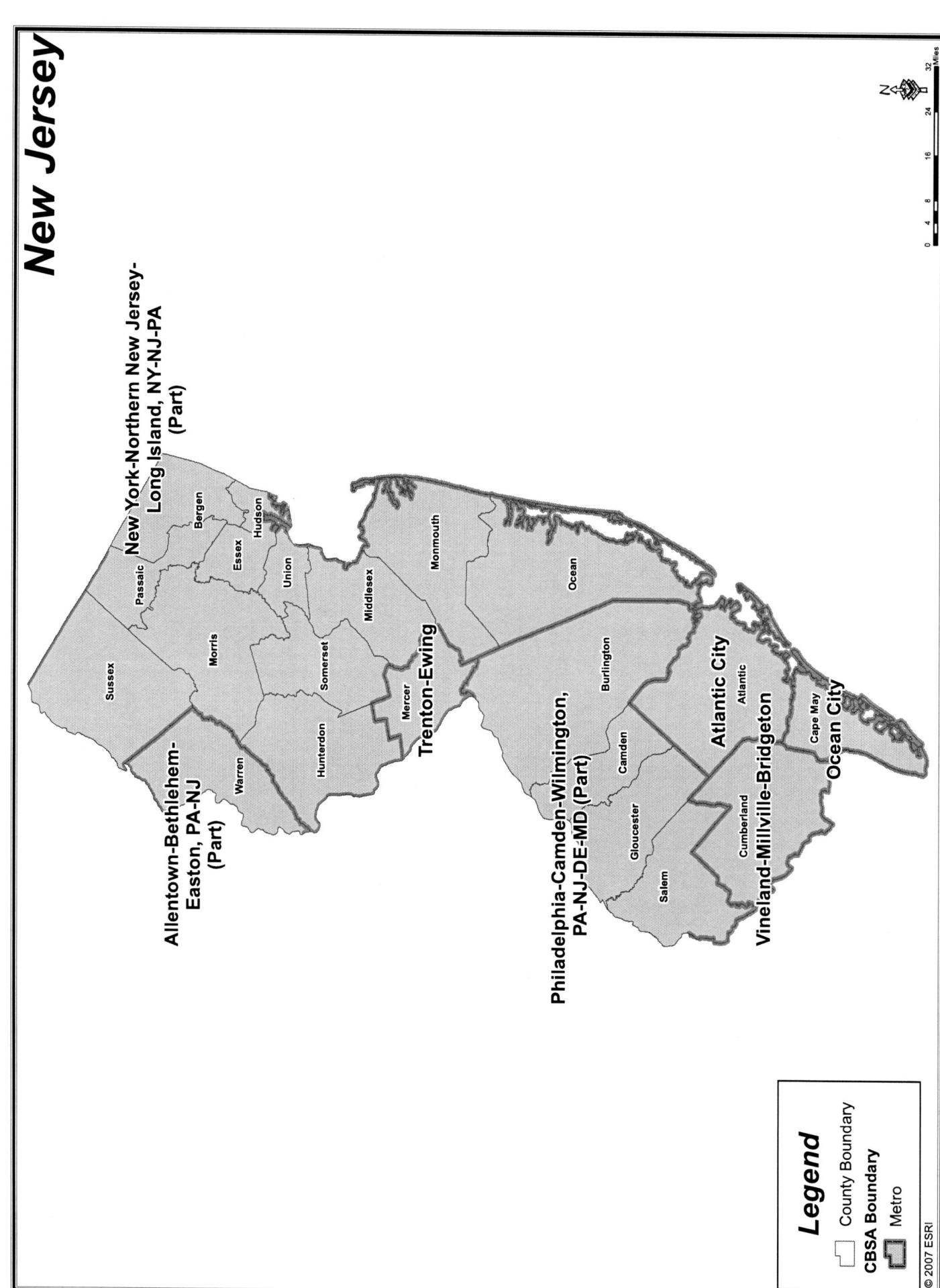

Legend

County Boundary

CBSA Boundary

Metro

New York-Northern New Jersey-Long Island, NY-NJ-PA (Part)

Allentown-Bethlehem-Easton, PA-NJ (Part)

Trenton-Ewing

Philadelphia-Camden-Wilmington, PA-NJ-DE-MD (Part)

Atlantic City

Vineland-Millville-Bridgeton

Ocean City

Sussex

Passaic

Bergen

Hudson

Essex

Union

Morris

Middlesex

Monmouth

Warren

Somerset

Hunterdon

Mercer

Ocean

Burlington

Camden

Atlantic

Gloucester

Cumberland

Salem

Cape May

0 4 8 16 24 32 Miles

N

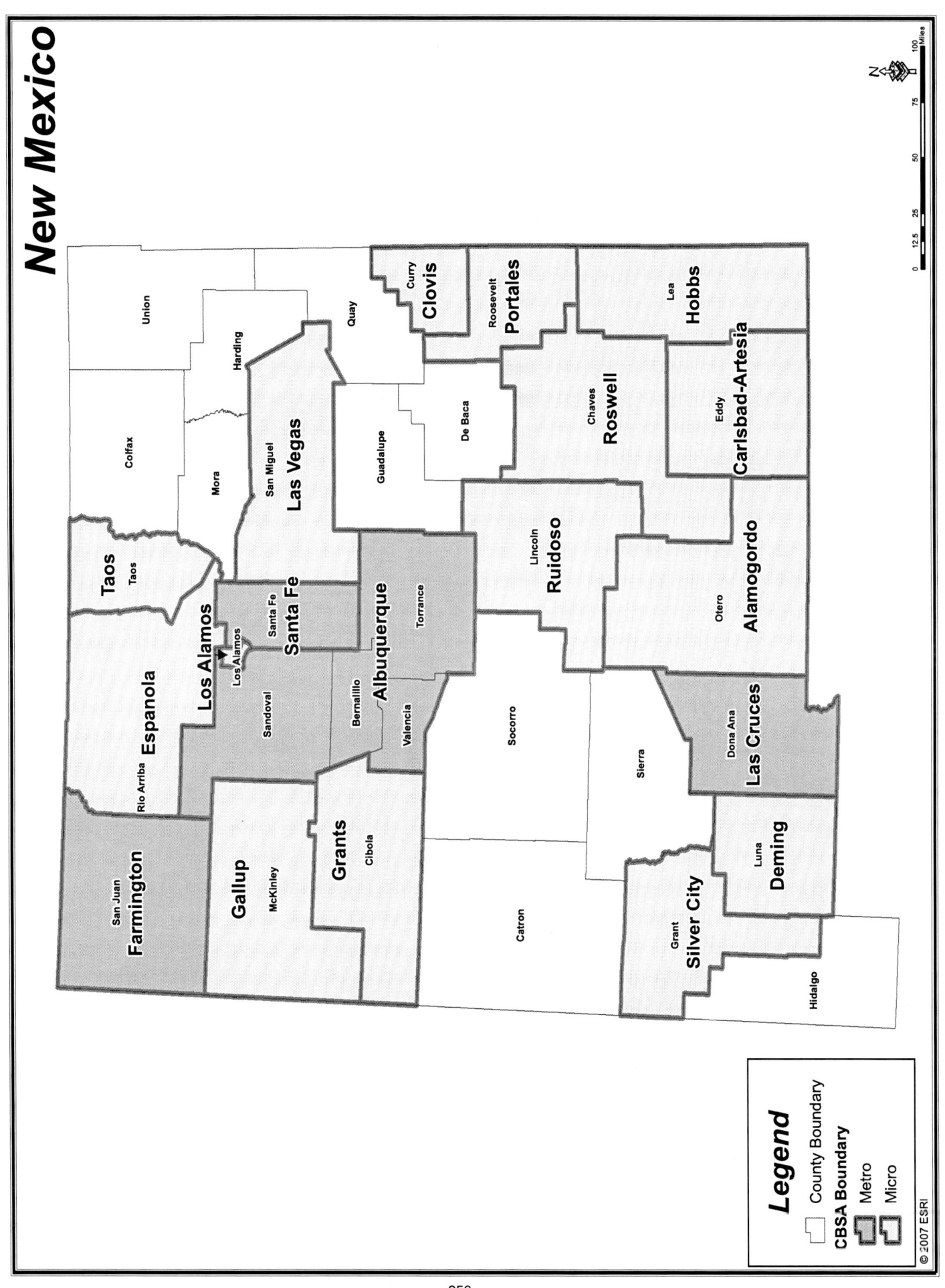

New Mexico

Union

Colfax

Harding

Mora

San Miguel
Las Vegas

Quay

Curry
Clovis

Roosevelt
Portales

Guadalupe

De Baca

Chaves
Roswell

Lea
Hobbs

Eddy
Carlsbad-Artesia

Taos
Taos

Rio Arriba
Espanola

San Juan
Farmington

Los Alamos
Los Alamos

Santa Fe
Santa Fe

Sandoval

Bernalillo
Albuquerque

Valencia

Torrance

Lincoln
Ruidoso

Otero
Alamogordo

McKinley
Gallup

Cibola
Grants

Catron

Socorro

Sierra

Dona Ana
Las Cruces

Grant
Silver City

Luna
Deming

Hidalgo

N

0   12.5   25   50   75   100
Miles

Legend

County Boundary

CBSA Boundary

Metro

Micro

© 2007 ESRI

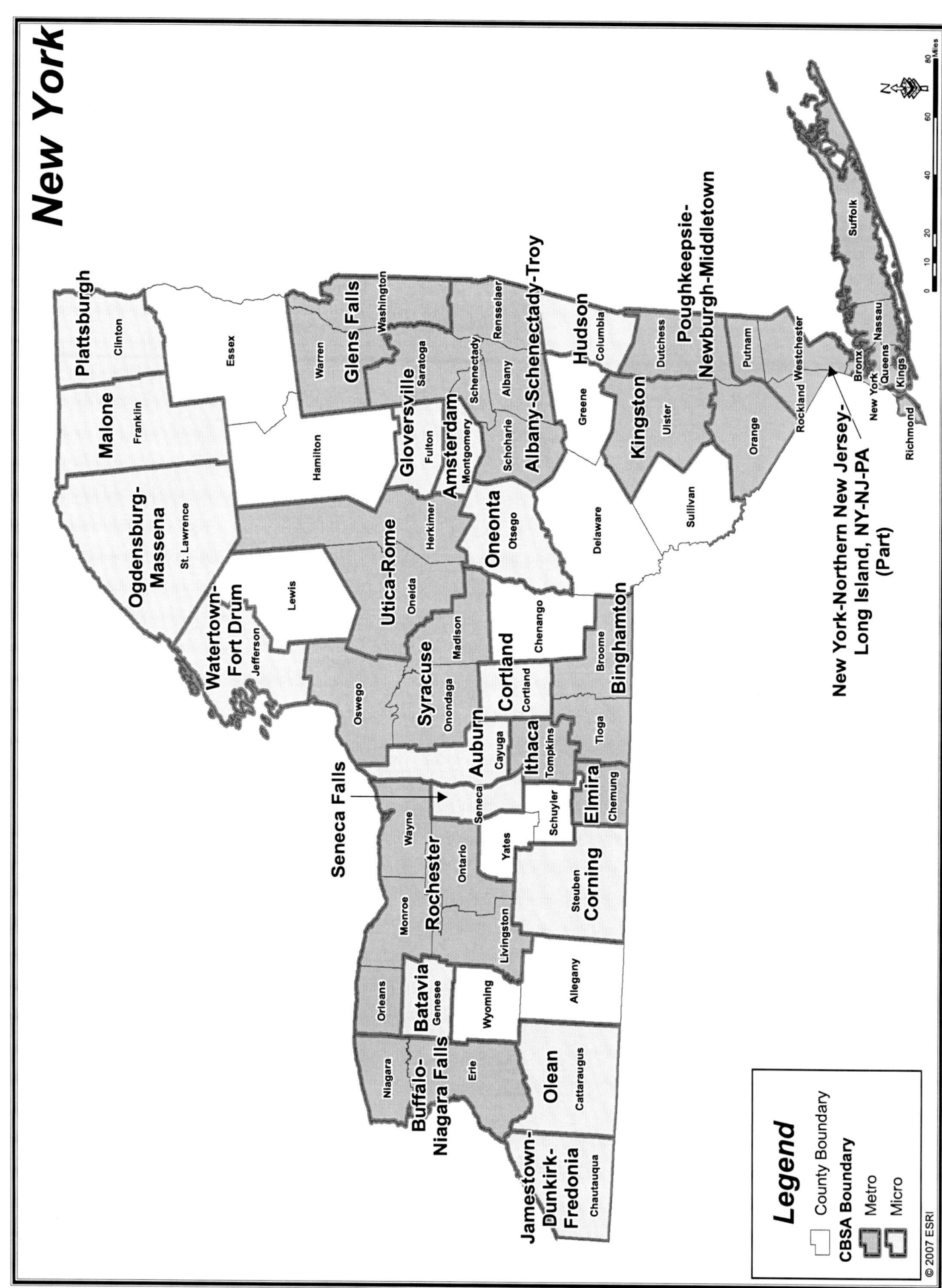

New York

Glens Falls
Washington
Warren
Plattsburgh
Clinton
Malone
Franklin
Essex
Gloversville
Saratoga
Schenectady
Rensselaer
Albany-Schenectady-Troy
Hudson
Columbia
Poughkeepsie-
Newburgh-Middletown
Amsterdam
Fulton
Montgomery
Albany
Schoharie
Greene
Dutchess
Putnam
Ogdensburg-
Massena
St. Lawrence
Hamilton
Utica-Rome
Herkimer
Oneonta
Otsego
Delaware
Ulster
Orange
Rockland
Westchester
Bronx
Nassau
New York
Queens
Kings
Richmond
Suffolk
Kingston
Sullivan
New York-Northern New Jersey-
Long Island, NY-NJ-PA
(Part)
Watertown-
Fort Drum
Jefferson
Lewis
Oneida
Madison
Syracuse
Onondaga
Cortland
Chenango
Binghamton
Broome
Oswego
Seneca Falls
Wayne
Ontario
Seneca
Yates
Auburn
Cayuga
Ithaca
Tompkins
Schuyler
Tioga
Elmira
Chemung
Corning
Steuben
Rochester
Monroe
Livingston
Orleans
Batavia
Genesee
Wyoming
Allegany
Niagara
Buffalo-
Niagara Falls
Erie
Olean
Cattaraugus
Jamestown-
Dunkirk-
Fredonia
Chautauqua

Legend
County Boundary
CBSA Boundary
Metro
Micro

N

0 10 20 40 60 80 Miles

© 2007 ESRI

257

North Carolina

Virginia Beach-Norfolk-
Newport News,
VA-NC (Part)

Hickory-Lenoir-Morganton

Mount Airy

Winston-Salem

Greensboro-High Point

Kill Devil Hills

Morehead City

Jacksonville

Wilmington

Roanoke
Rapids

Rocky Mount

Greenville

New Bern

Kinston

Henderson

Durham

Raleigh-Cary

Dunn

Sanford

Fayetteville

Lumberton

Laurinburg

Boone

North
Wilkesboro

Salisbury

Charlotte-Gastonia-
Concord, NC-SC
(Part)

Shelby

Forest
City

Asheville

Brevard

Counties

Currituck, Camden, Perquimans, Pasquotank, Chowan, Gates, Hertford, Bertie, Washington, Tyrrell, Dare, Hyde, Northampton, Halifax, Nash, Edgecombe, Martin, Beaufort, Pamlico, Craven, Jones, Onslow, Pender, New Hanover, Brunswick, Carteret

Warren, Vance, Franklin, Granville, Wilson, Pitt, Greene, Wayne, Lenoir, Duplin, Sampson, Bladen, Columbus

Caswell, Person, Orange, Durham, Alamance, Chatham, Lee, Harnett, Johnston, Cumberland, Hoke, Robeson, Scotland, Moore, Richmond, Anson, Stanly, Montgomery, Randolph, Guilford, Rockingham

Stokes, Surry, Alleghany, Ashe, Watauga, Wilkes, Yadkin, Forsyth, Davidson, Davie, Iredell, Alexander, Caldwell, Burke, McDowell, Avery, Mitchell, Yancey, Madison, Buncombe, Henderson, Transylvania, Jackson, Macon, Swain, Graham, Cherokee, Clay, Rutherford, Polk, Cleveland, Gaston, Lincoln, Catawba, Mecklenburg, Cabarrus, Rowan, Union

Legend

County Boundary

CBSA Boundary

Metro

Micro

© 2007 ESRI

CSBA Boundary

1. Lincolnton
2. Statesville-Mooresville
3. Thomasville-Lexington
4. Albemarle
5. Burlington
6. Southern Pines-Pinehurst
7. Rockingham
8. Goldsboro
9. Wilson
10. Washington
11. Elizabeth City

N

0 15 30   60   90   120
Miles

North Dakota

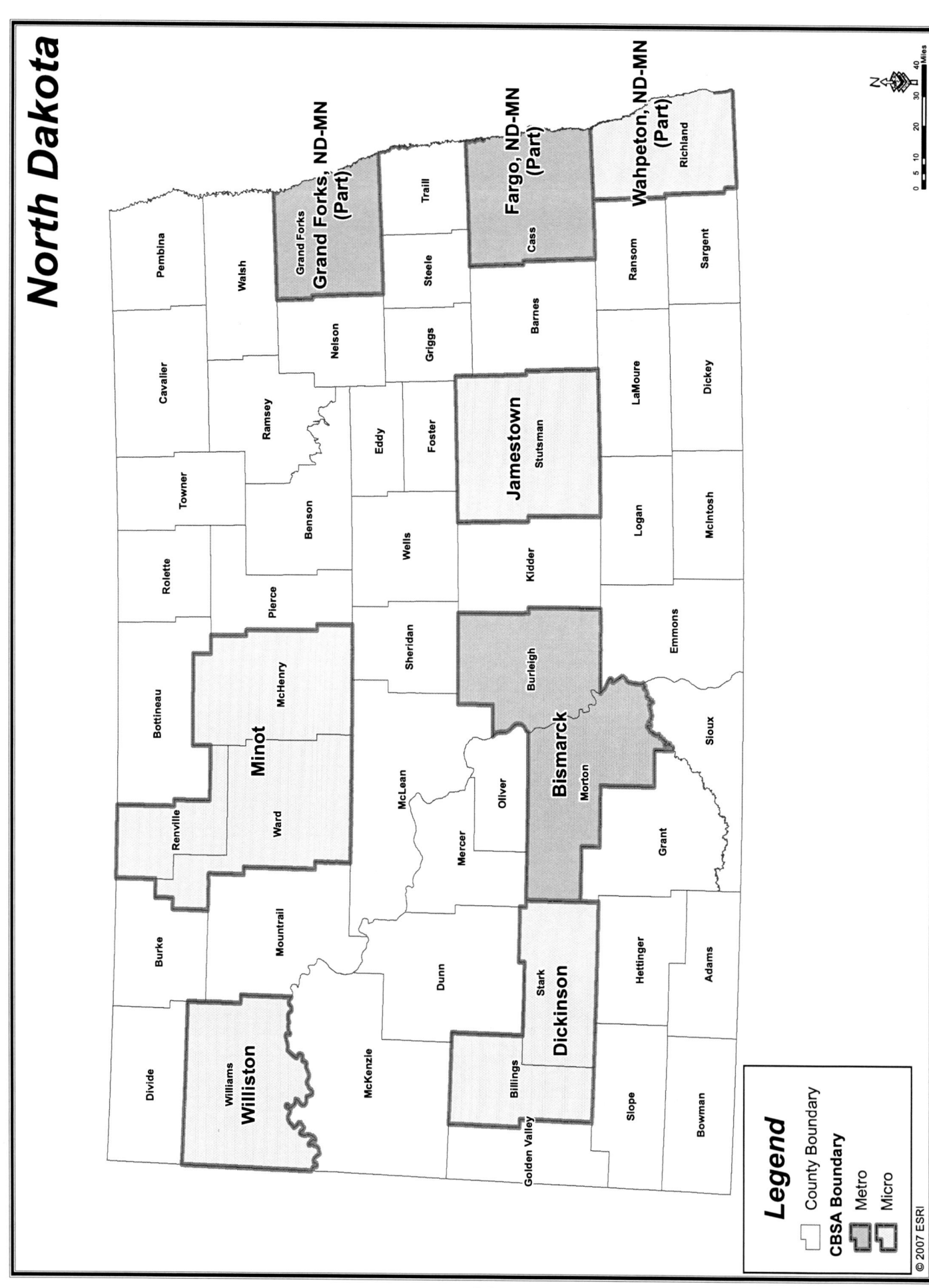

Ohio

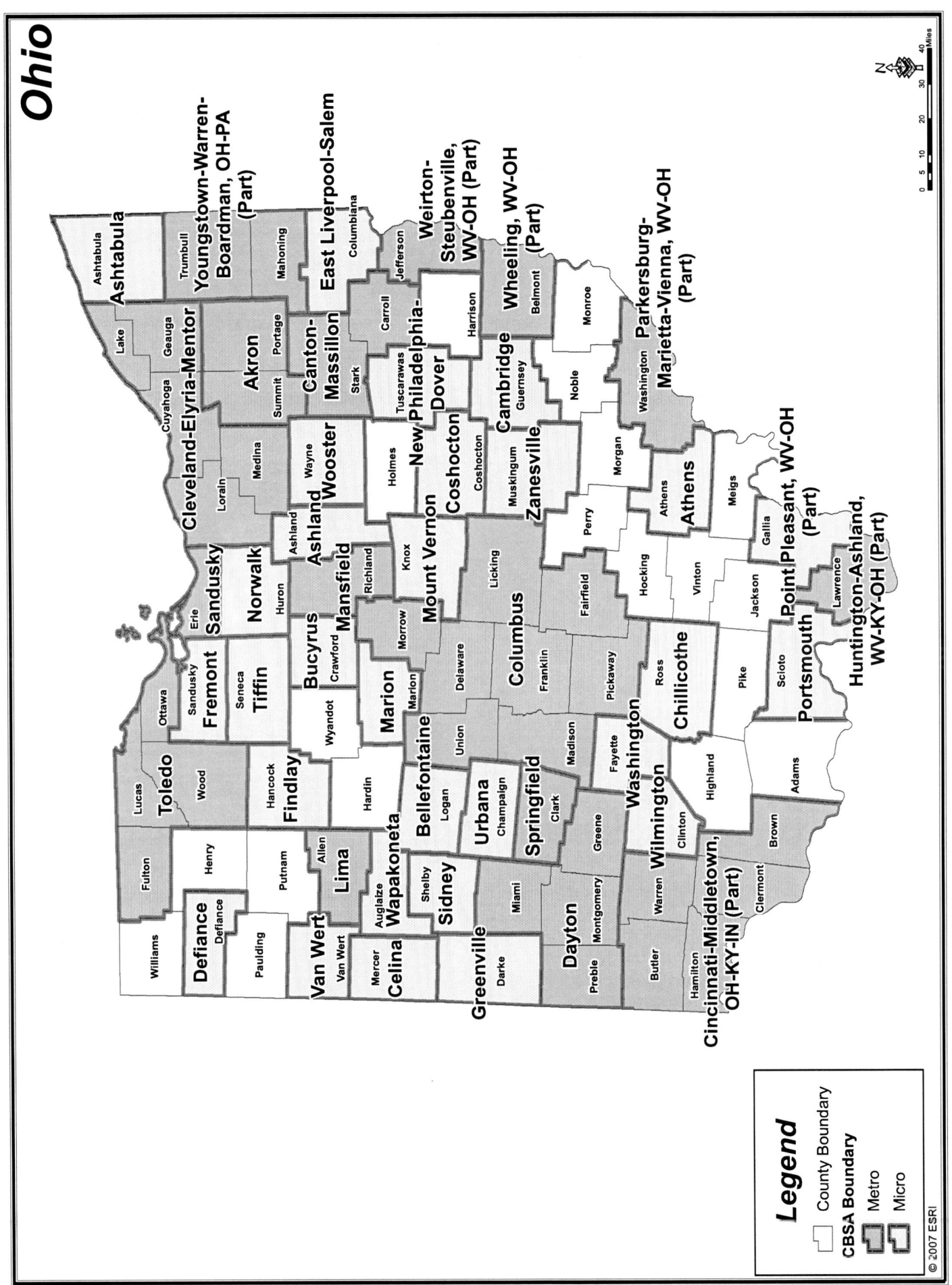

Legend

County Boundary

CBSA Boundary

Metro

Micro

© 2007 ESRI

Oklahoma

Legend

County Boundary

CBSA Boundary

Metro

Micro

© 2007 ESRI

261

Oregon

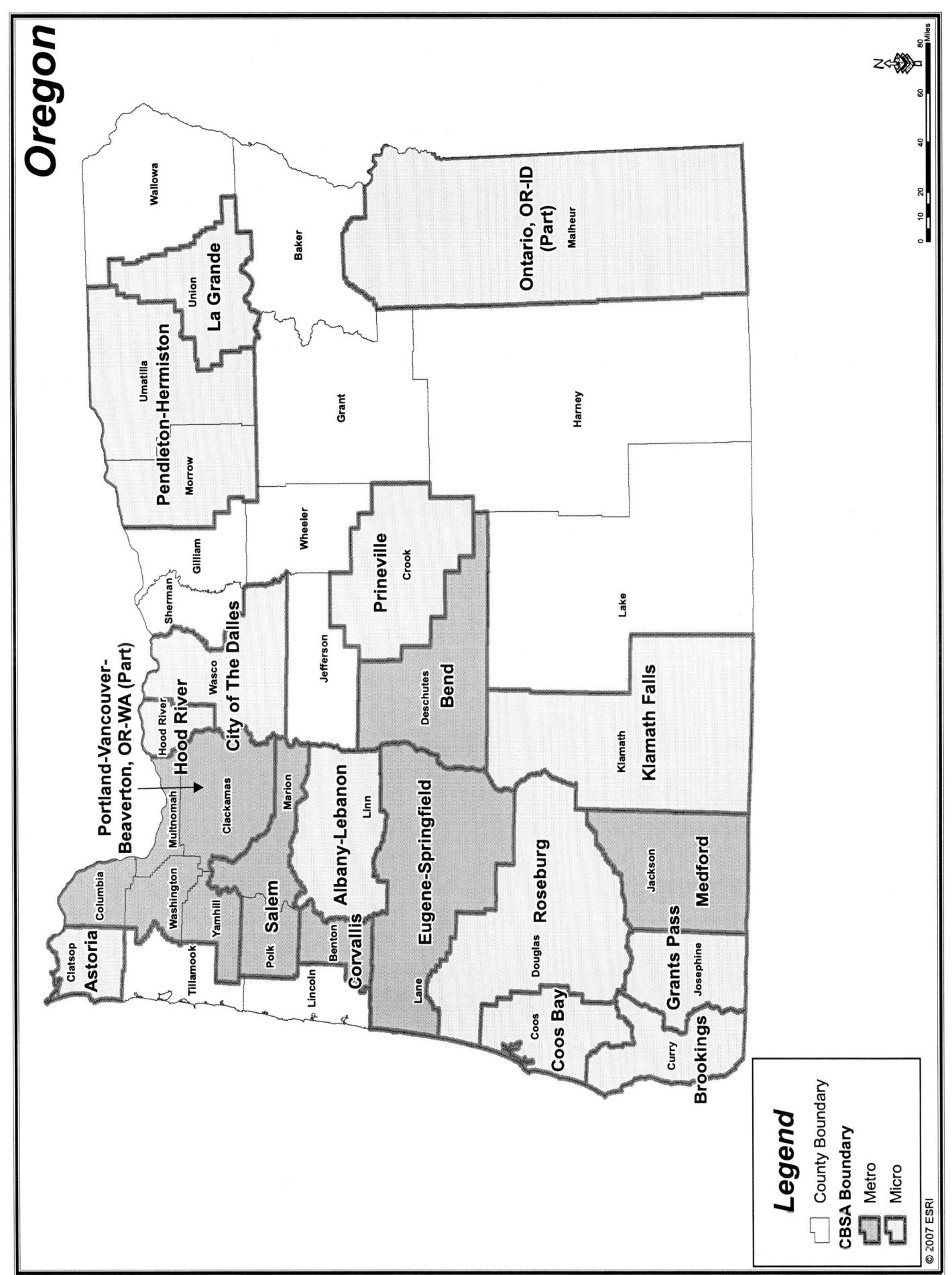

Wallowa

Union

La Grande

Pendleton-Hermiston

Umatilla

Morrow

Baker

Ontario, OR-ID (Part)

Malheur

Grant

Harney

Gilliam

Wheeler

Prineville

Crook

Sherman

Wasco

City of The Dalles

Lake

Jefferson

Bend

Deschutes

Hood River

Hood River

Portland-Vancouver-Beaverton, OR-WA (Part)

Multnomah

Clackamas

Marion

Albany-Lebanon

Linn

Klamath Falls

Klamath

Columbia

Astoria

Clatsop

Washington

Yamhill

Salem

Polk

Benton

Corvallis

Lincoln

Eugene-Springfield

Lane

Roseburg

Douglas

Jackson

Medford

Grants Pass

Josephine

Tillamook

Coos

Coos Bay

Curry

Brookings

Legend

County Boundary

CBSA Boundary

Metro

Micro

© 2007 ESRI

N

0 10 20   40   60   80
Miles

262

Pennsylvania

Legend

County Boundary

CBSA Boundary

Metro

Micro

New York-Northern New Jersey-Long Island, NY-NJ-PA (Part)

East Stroudsburg

Allentown-Bethlehem-Easton, PA-NJ (Part)

Philadelphia-Camden-Wilmington, PA-NJ-DE-MD (Part)

Scranton--Wilkes-Barre

Bloomsburg-Berwick

Sunbury

Pottsville

Reading

Lebanon

Lancaster

York-Hanover

Gettysburg

Sayre

Williamsport

Lewisburg

Selinsgrove

Harrisburg-Carlisle

Chambersburg

Lock Haven

State College

Lewistown

Huntingdon

Altoona

Johnstown

DuBois

St. Marys

Bradford

Warren

Meadville

Oil City

New Castle

Youngstown-Warren-Boardman, OH-PA (Part)

Erie

Pittsburgh

Indiana

Somerset

Counties

Wayne, Pike, Susquehanna, Wyoming, Lackawanna, Luzerne, Monroe, Carbon, Northampton, Lehigh, Bucks, Montgomery, Philadelphia, Delaware, Chester, Berks, Schuylkill, Columbia, Montour, Northumberland, Snyder, Union, Lycoming, Bradford, Sullivan, Tioga, Potter, Cameron, Clinton, Centre, Clearfield, Elk, McKean, Jefferson, Forest, Clarion, Venango, Crawford, Erie, Mercer, Lawrence, Butler, Beaver, Allegheny, Washington, Greene, Fayette, Westmoreland, Armstrong, Indiana, Cambria, Somerset, Bedford, Blair, Huntingdon, Fulton, Franklin, Adams, York, Cumberland, Perry, Juniata, Mifflin, Dauphin, Lebanon, Lancaster

0 10 20 40 60 80 Miles

N

© 2007 ESRI

263

Rhode Islands

Legend

County Boundary

CBSA Boundary

Metro

264

South Carolina

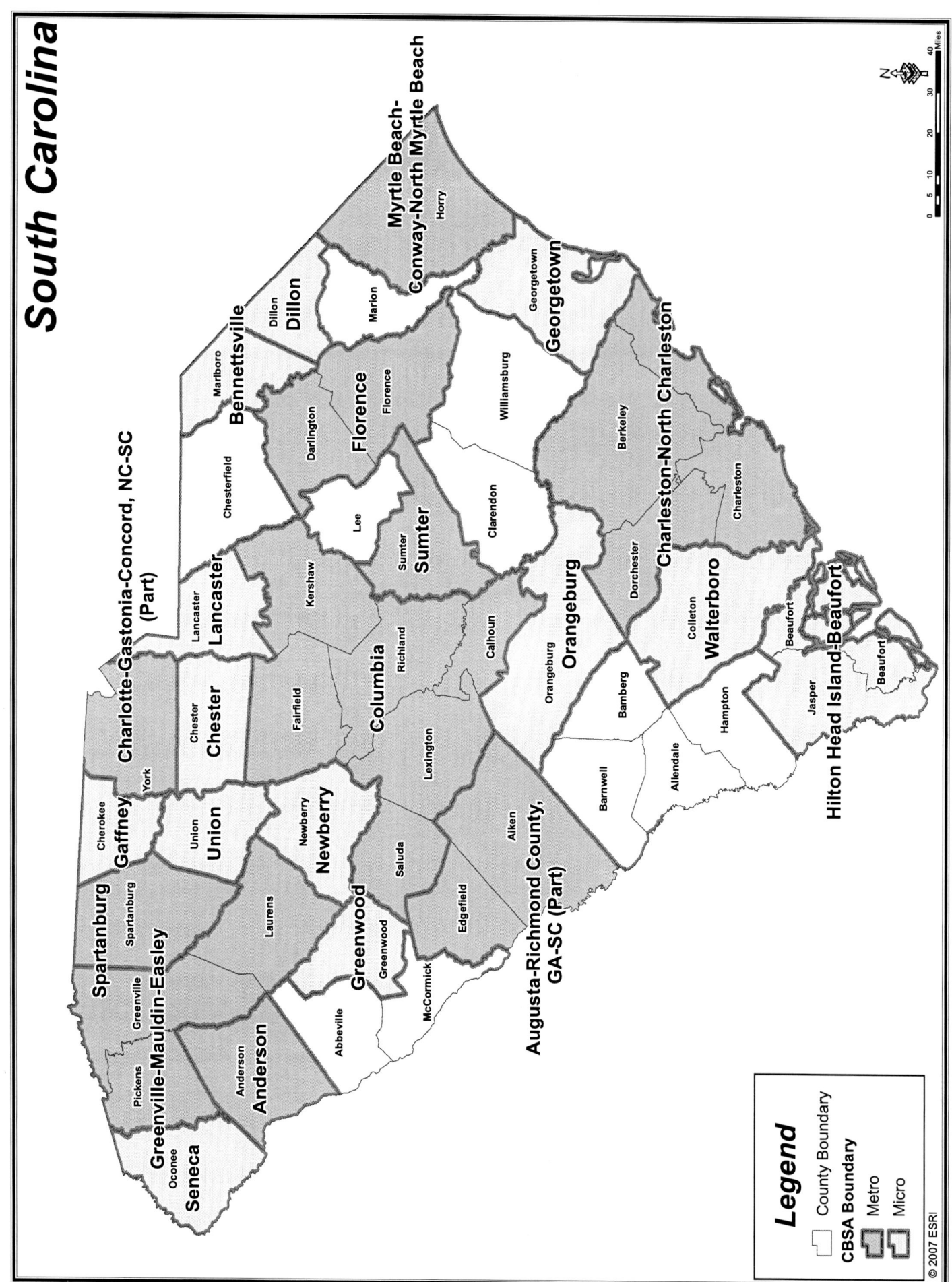

© 2007 ESRI

Legend

☐ County Boundary

CBSA Boundary

Metro

Micro

South Dakota

Sioux City, IA-NE-SD (Part)

Legend

County Boundary

CBSA Boundary

Metro

Micro

© 2007 ESRI

266

Tennessee

Kingsport-Bristol-Bristol, TN-VA (Part)

Union City, TN-KY (Part)

Clarksville, TN-KY (Part)

Nashville-Davidson-Murfreesboro-Franklin

Chattanooga, TN-GA (Part)

Lewisburg

Memphis, TN-MS-AR (Part)

Johnson City

Greeneville

Morristown

Newport

Sevierville

La Follette

Knoxville

Harriman

Athens

Cleveland

Crossville

Cookeville

McMinnville

Tullahoma

Shelbyville

Columbia

Lawrenceburg

Paris

Martin

Humboldt

Jackson

Brownsville

Dyersburg

Counties: Johnson, Sullivan, Washington, Carter, Unicoi, Hawkins, Hamblen, Greene, Cocke, Hancock, Claiborne, Grainger, Jefferson, Sevier, Union, Knox, Blount, Campbell, Anderson, Loudon, Monroe, Scott, Morgan, Roane, Meigs, McMinn, Polk, Fentress, Cumberland, Rhea, Bradley, Pickett, Overton, Putnam, White, Van Buren, Bledsoe, Sequatchie, Hamilton, Clay, Jackson, DeKalb, Warren, Grundy, Marion, Macon, Smith, Cannon, Coffee, Trousdale, Wilson, Rutherford, Franklin, Sumner, Moore, Robertson, Davidson, Williamson, Bedford, Marshall, Lincoln, Cheatham, Maury, Moore, Montgomery, Dickson, Hickman, Lewis, Giles, Stewart, Houston, Humphreys, Perry, Lawrence, Wayne, Benton, Decatur, Hardin, Henry, Carroll, Henderson, McNairy, Weakley, Madison, Chester, Gibson, Hardeman, Obion, Crockett, Haywood, Fayette, Lake, Dyer, Lauderdale, Tipton, Shelby

Legend

County Boundary

CBSA Boundary

Metro

Micro

© 2007 ESRI

N

0 12.5 25 50 75 100
Miles

267

Texas

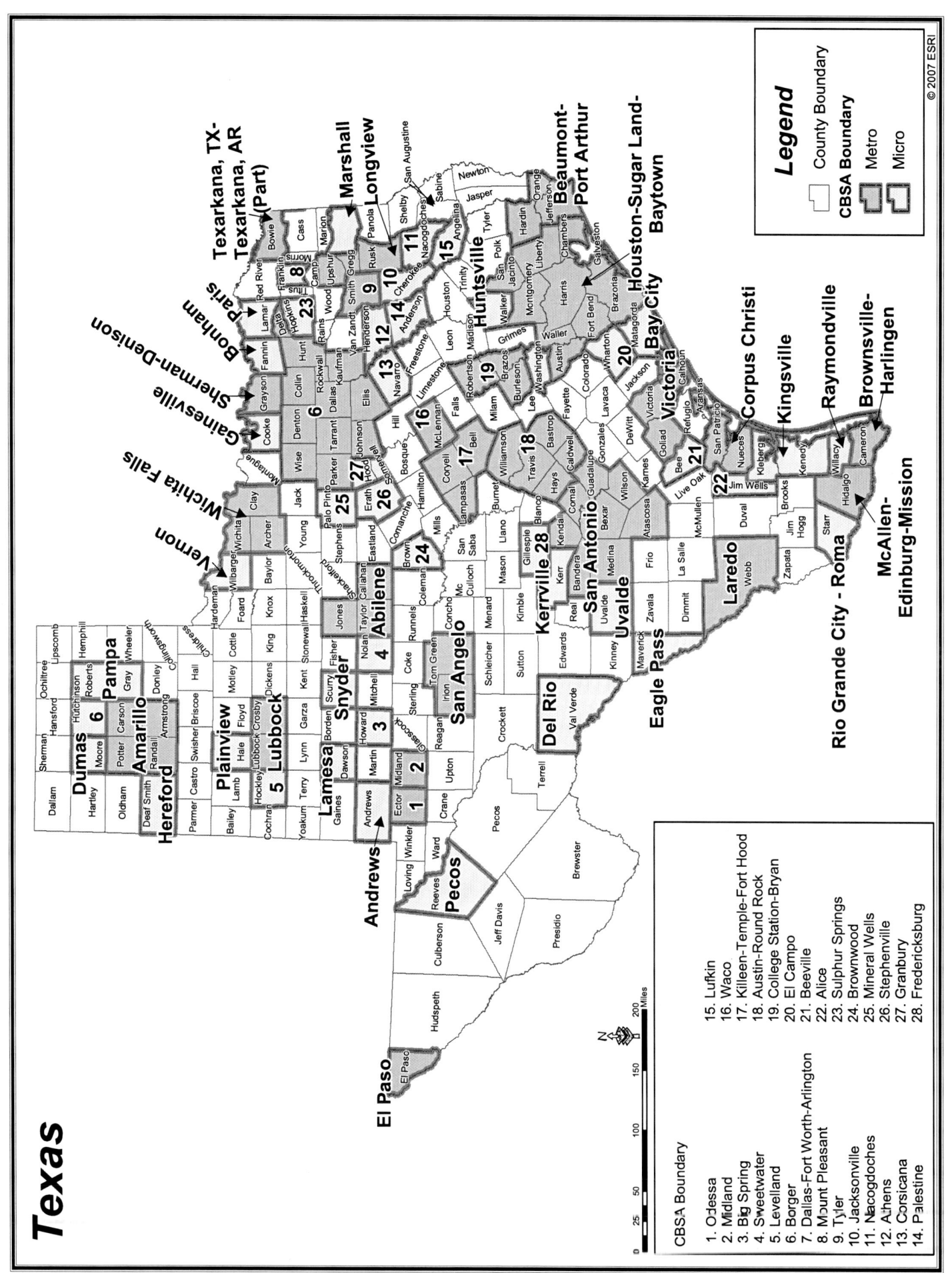

Utah

Logan, UT-ID (Part)

Rich

Cache

Box Elder **Brigham City**

Weber

Morgan

Davis

Ogden-Clearfield

Summit

Daggett

Uintah **Vernal**

Duchesne

Carbon **Price**

Heber

Wasatch

Salt Lake

Salt Lake City

Tooele

Utah

Provo-Orem

Juab

Sanpete

Sevier

Piute

Millard

Beaver

Emery

Grand

San Juan

Wayne

Garfield

Kane

Iron **Cedar City**

Washington **St. George**

N

0 10 20   40   60   80
Miles

Legend

County Boundary

CBSA Boundary

Metro

Micro

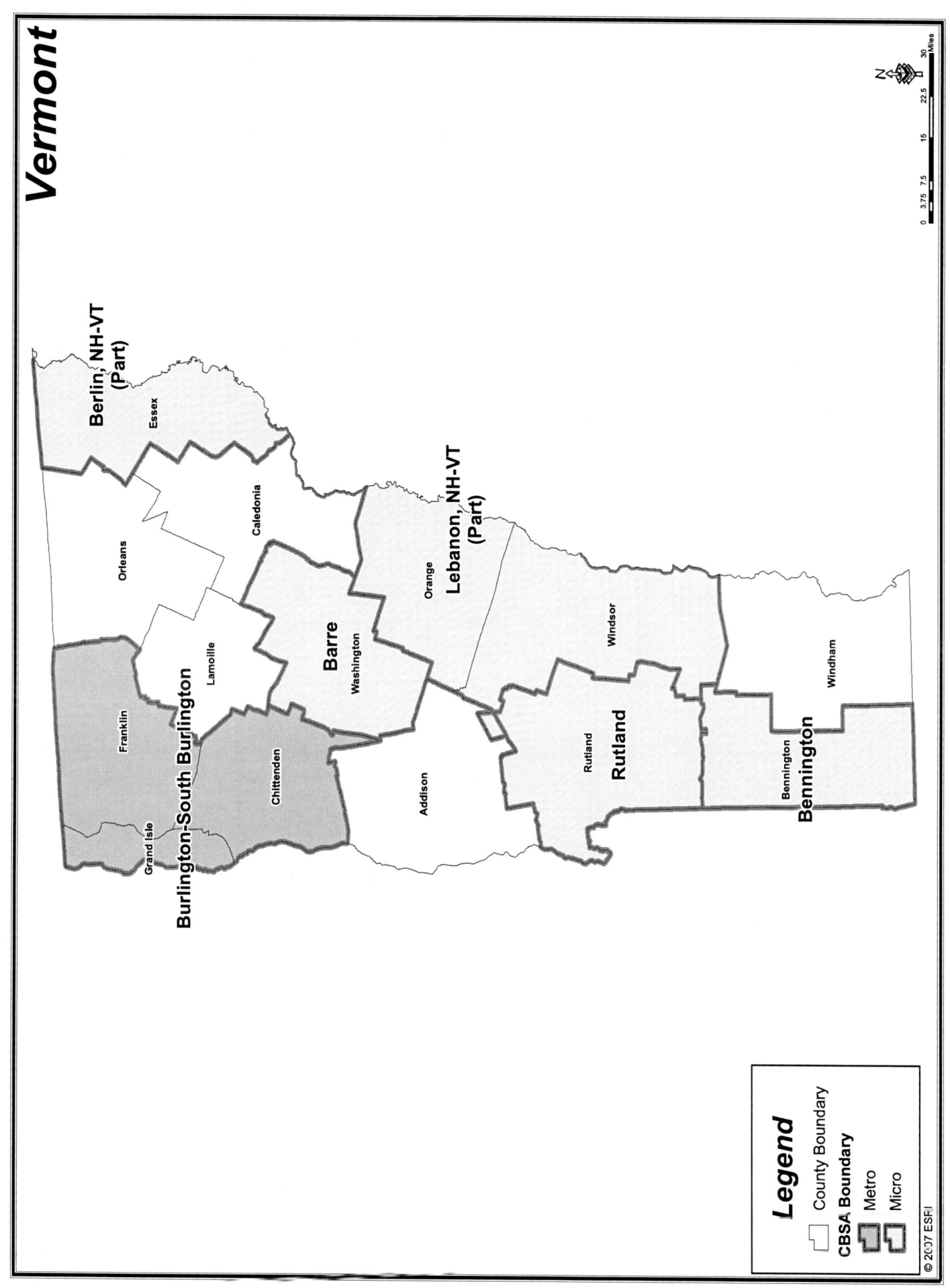

Vermont

Berlin, NH-VT
(Part)

Essex

Caledonia

Orleans

Lebanon, NH-VT
(Part)

Orange

Barre

Lamoille

Washington

Windsor

Franklin

Burlington-South Burlington

Chittenden

Addison

Rutland
Rutland

Windham

Grand Isle

Bennington
Bennington

N

0 3.75 7.5   15   22.5   30
                                  Miles

Legend

County Boundary

CBSA Boundary

Metro

Micro

© 2007 ESRI

Virginia

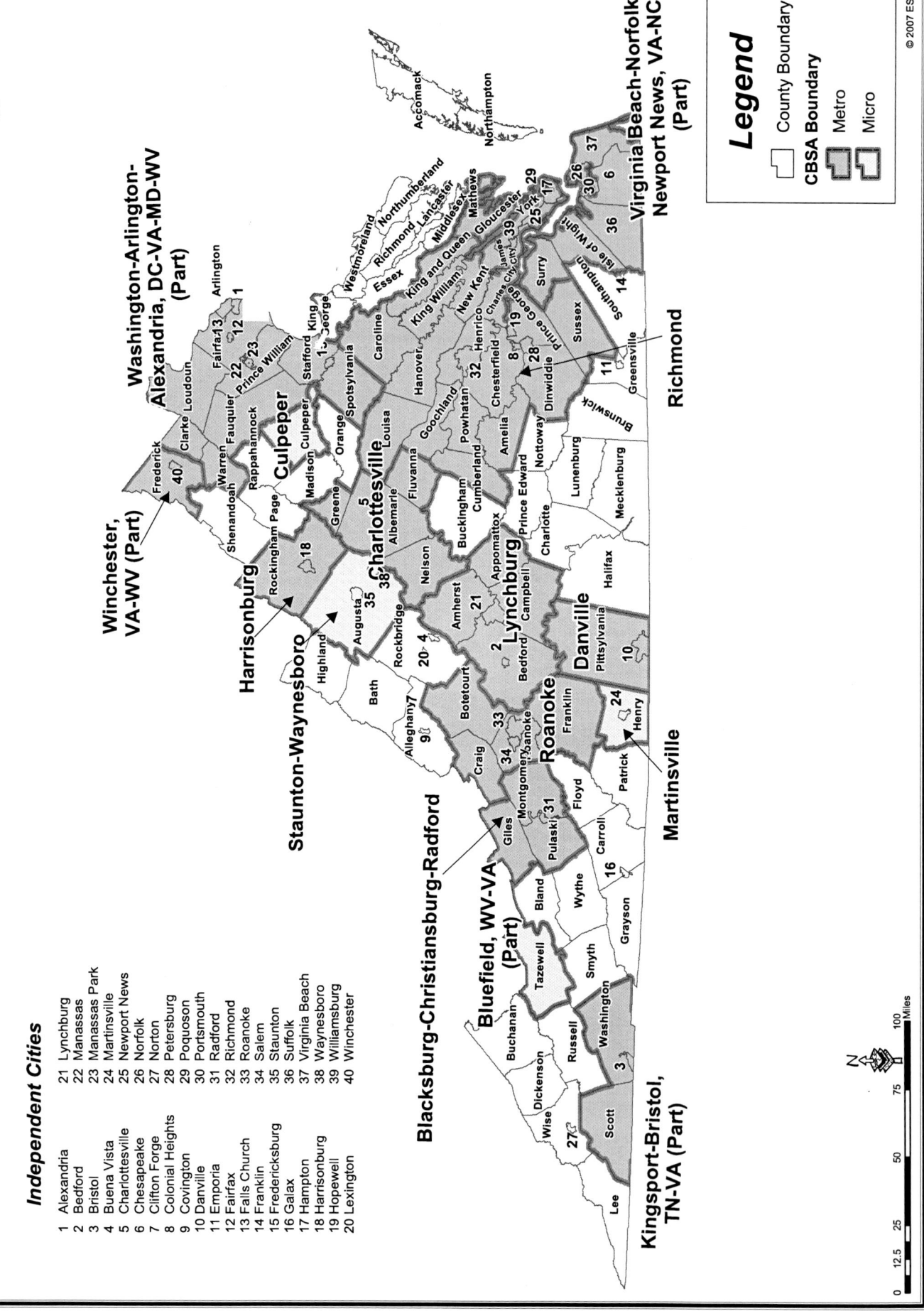

Independent Cities

1 Alexandria	21 Lynchburg
2 Bedford	22 Manassas
3 Bristol	23 Manassas Park
4 Buena Vista	24 Martinsville
5 Charlottesville	25 Newport News
6 Chesapeake	26 Norfolk
7 Clifton Forge	27 Norton
8 Colonial Heights	28 Petersburg
9 Covington	29 Poquoson
10 Danville	30 Portsmouth
11 Emporia	31 Radford
12 Fairfax	32 Richmond
13 Falls Church	33 Roanoke
14 Franklin	34 Salem
15 Fredericksburg	35 Staunton
16 Galax	36 Suffolk
17 Hampton	37 Virginia Beach
18 Harrisonburg	38 Waynesboro
19 Hopewell	39 Williamsburg
20 Lexington	40 Winchester

Legend

County Boundary

CBSA Boundary
Metro
Micro

© 2007 ESRI

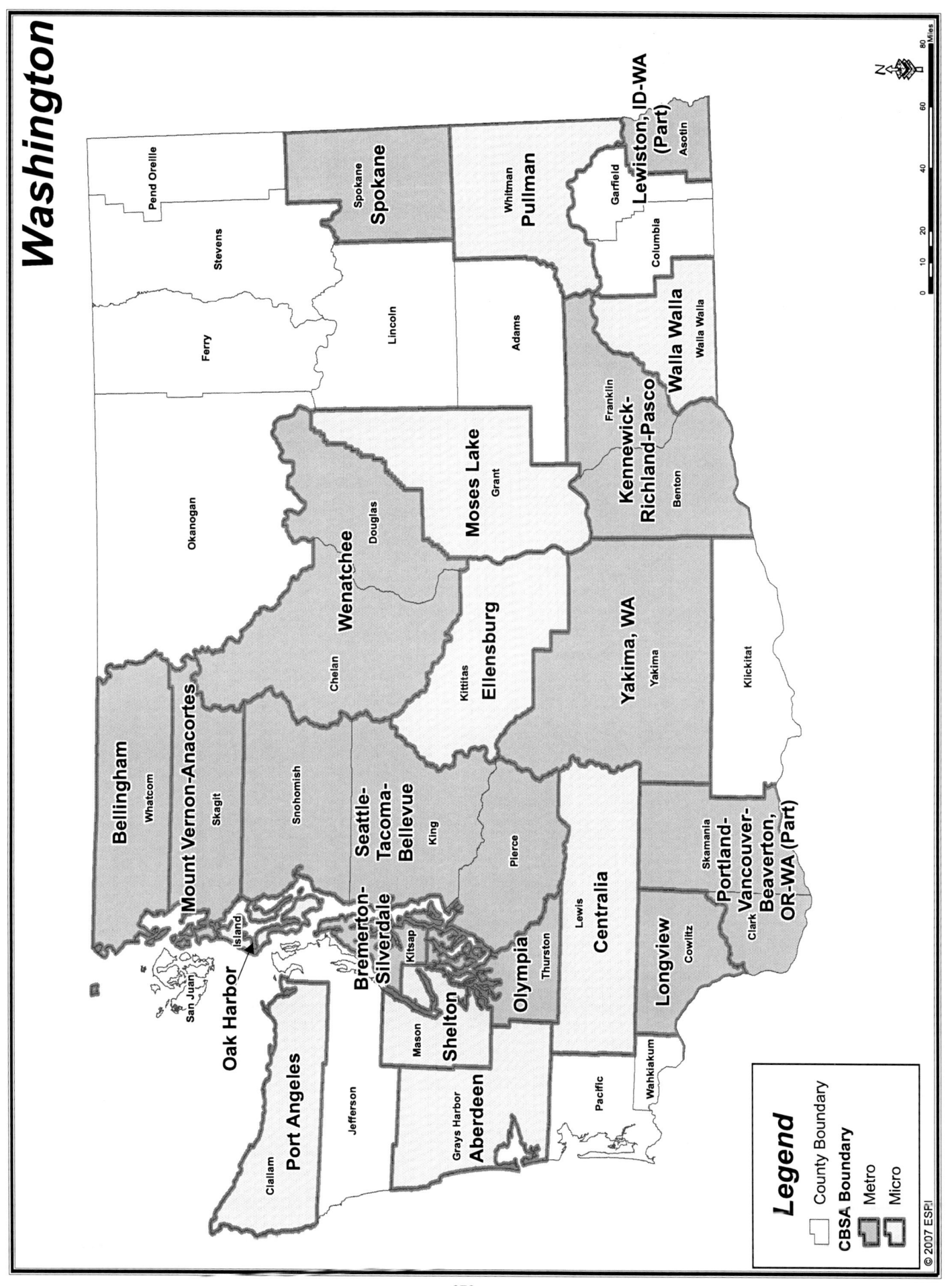

Washington

Legend

County Boundary

CBSA Boundary

Metro

Micro

© 2007 ESRI

272

West Virginia

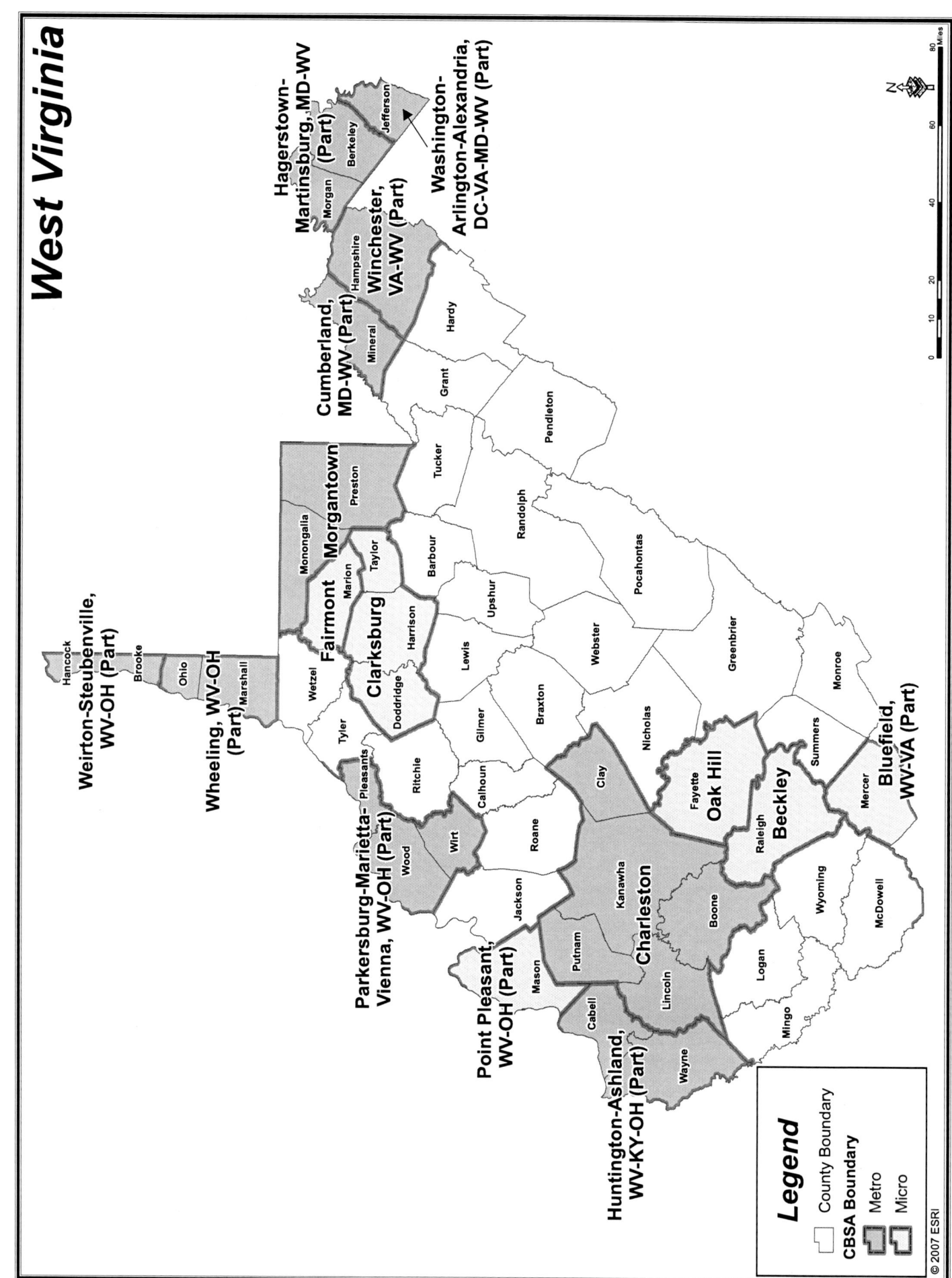

Wisconsin

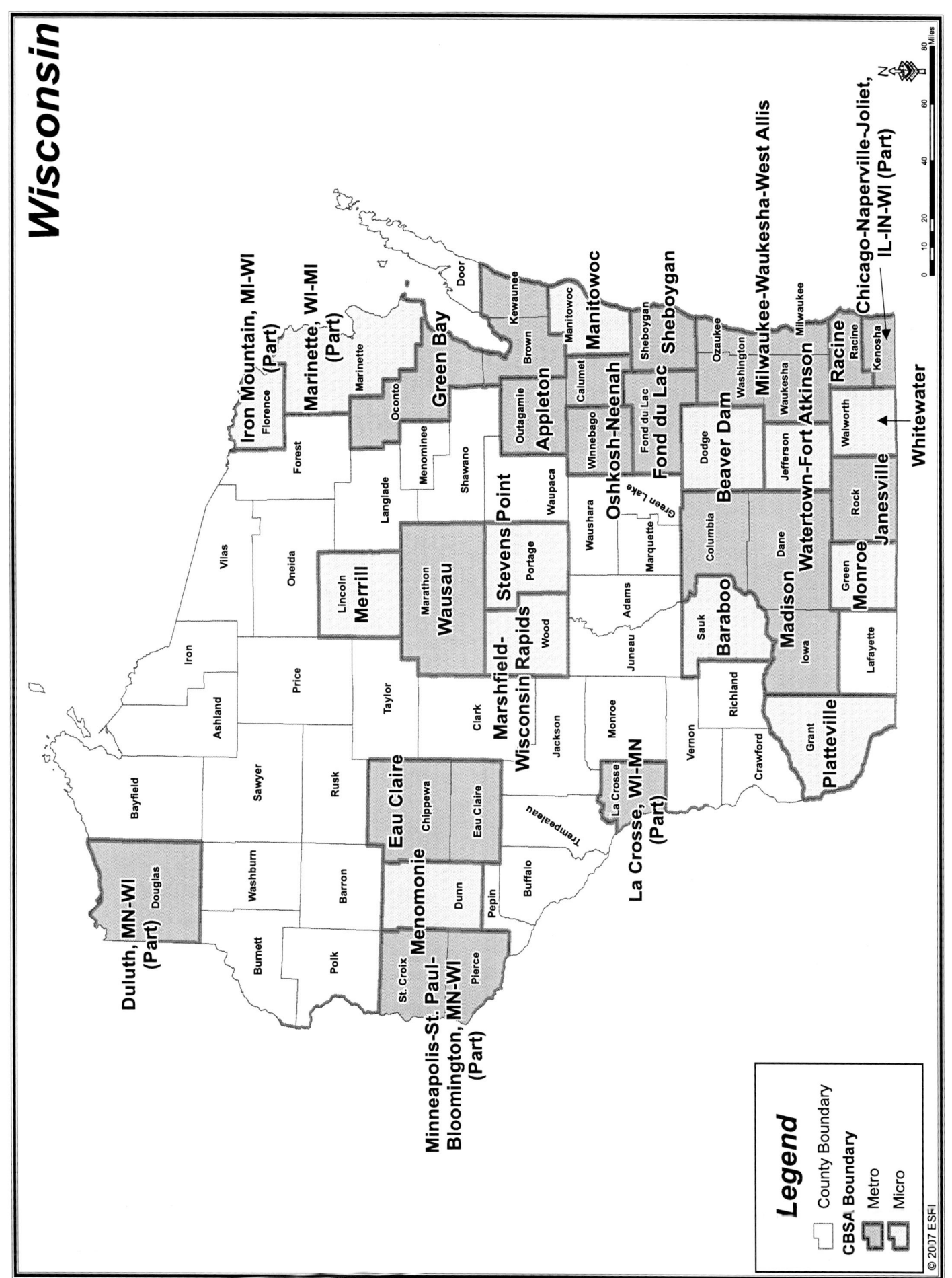

Wyoming

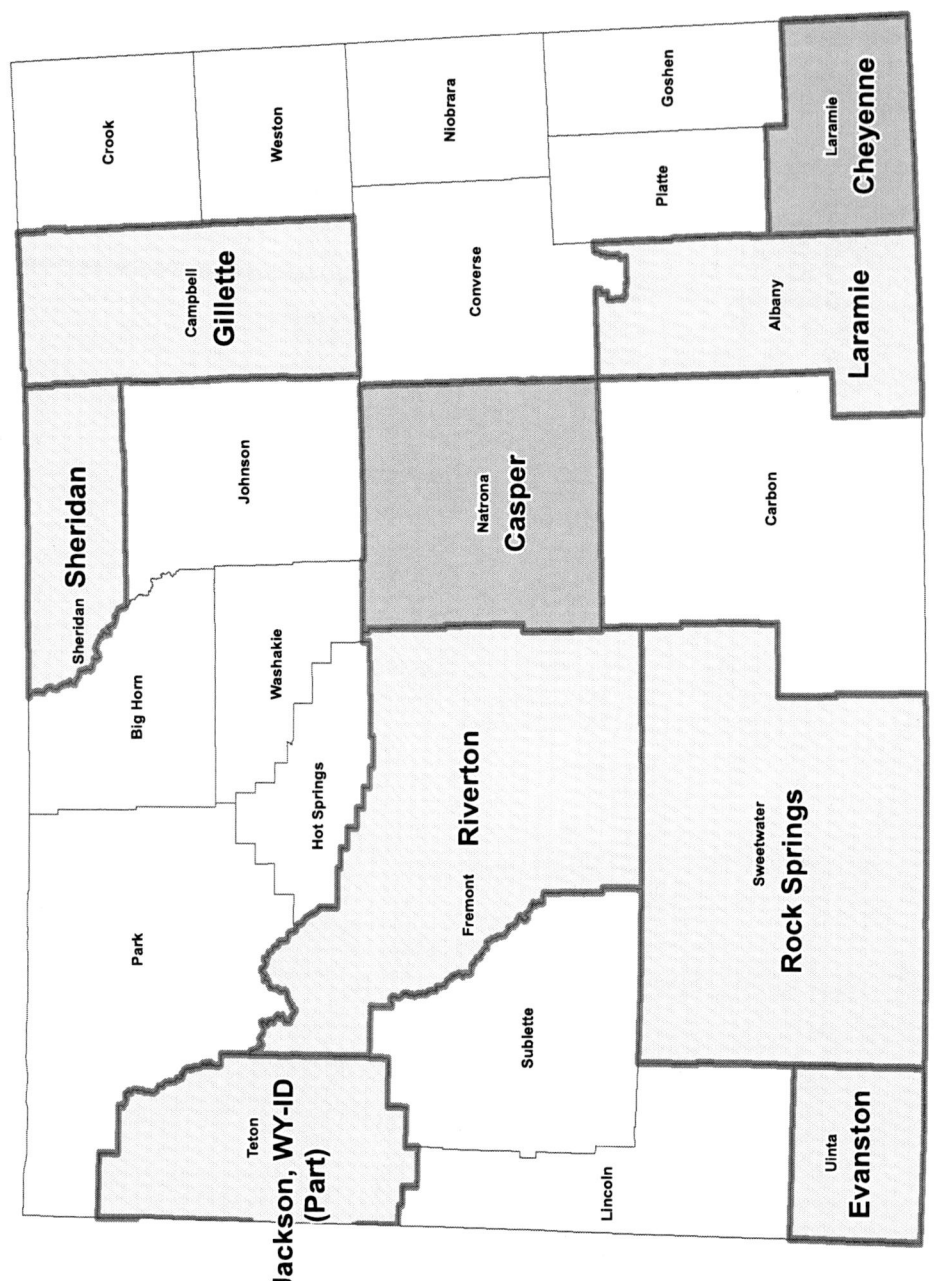

Crook
Weston
Niobrara
Goshen
Campbell
Gillette
Converse
Platte
Laramie
Cheyenne
Sheridan
Sheridan
Johnson
Natrona
Casper
Albany
Laramie
Big Horn
Washakie
Carbon
Park
Hot Springs
Riverton
Fremont
Sweetwater
Rock Springs
Teton
Jackson, WY-ID (Part)
Sublette
Lincoln
Uinta
Evanston

N

0   12.5   25   50   75   100
Miles

Legend

☐ County Boundary

CBSA Boundary

◼ Metro

▢ Micro

© 2007 ESRI

275